Guide to U.S. Elections

Congressional Quarterly's
Guide to U.S. Elections

FOURTH EDITION • VOLUME I

EDITORS

JOHN L. MOORE

JON P. PREIMESBERGER

DAVID R. TARR

CQ PRESS

A Division of Congressional Quarterly Inc.
Washington, D.C.

CQ Press
A Division of Congressional Quarterly Inc.
1255 22nd Street, N.W., Suite 400
Washington, D.C. 20037
(202) 822-1475; (800) 638-1710

www.cqpress.com

Copyright © 2001 Congressional Quarterly Inc.

Cover design: Kachergis Book Design, Pittsboro, North Carolina

Printed in the United States of America

05 04 03 02 01   5 4 3 2 1

∞ The paper used in this publication meets the minimum requirements of the American National Standard for Information Science—Permanence of Paper for Printed Library Materials, ANSI Z39.48-1984.

Illustration credits and acknowledgments appear on page 1609, Vol. II, which constitutes a continuation of the copyright page.

LIBRARY OF CONGRESS CATALOGING-IN-PUBLICATION DATA
Congressional Quarterly's guide to U.S. elections.—4th ed.
   p.   cm.
   Rev. ed. of: Congressional Quarterly's guide to U.S. elections. 3rd ed. © 1994.
   Includes bibliographical references and index.
   ISBN 1-56802-601-3 (v. 1: alk. paper)
   ISBN 1-56802-602-1 (v. 2: alk. paper)
   ISBN 1-56802-603-x (set: alk. paper)
   1. Elections—United States—History—Statistics. 2. Political conventions—United States—History. 3. Political parties—United States—History. I. Congressional Quarterly, Inc. II. Congressional Quarterly's guide to U.S. elections.
JK1967.C662   2001
324.973—dc21   2001037955

Summary Table of Contents

VOLUME I

PART I Elections in America   1

PART II Political Parties   41

PART III Presidential Elections   207

   Indexes, *following page 782*

VOLUME II

PART IV Congressional Elections   783

PART V Gubernatorial Elections   1375

   Reference Materials   1543

   Selected Bibliography   1601

   Indexes, *following page 1610*

Contents

VOLUME I

Tables, Figures, and Boxes   XIII
Editors' Note   XV
Introduction   XIX

PART I   Elections in America   1

CHAPTER 1   The Evolution of American Elections   3
Challenging the Two Parties   3
The Basic Layout   5
Republicans Start Fast   5
Democrats Take Charge   6
Postwar Politics: Kennedy and Nixon   8
Split-Level Realignment   8
The Era of Closeness   10
A Tale of Two Nations   11
Historic Milestones in U.S. Elections   14

CHAPTER 2   Elections: An Expanding Franchise   21
Broadening the Franchise   21
The Black Vote: A Long, Painful Struggle   24
Women's Vote: A Victory in Stages   31
The Eighteen-Year-Old Vote   33
Voter Registration   33
Removing Obstacles to Voting   35

PART II   Political Parties   41

CHAPTER 3   Political Party Development   43
Political Issues and the Emergence of Parties   43
Presidents, Parties, and Policies, 1800–1860   43
Parties in U.S. Politics since 1860   45
Party Systems   48
Internal Party Politics   48
Third Parties   48

CHAPTER 4   Historical Profiles of
American Political Parties   51
American Independent Party and American Party   51
Anti-Federalists   51
Anti-Masonic Party   51
Breckinridge (Southern) Democrats   52
Citizens Party   53
Communist Party   53
Conservative Party   54

Constitutional Union Party   54
Democratic Party   54
Democratic-Republican Party   61
Dixicrats (States' Rights Party)   61
Federalists   62
Free Soil Party   63
Green Party   63
Greenback Party   63
Know Nothing (American) Party   64
Liberal Party   65
Liberal Republican Party   65
Libertarian Party   65
Liberty Party   66
National Democratic Party   66
National Republican Party   67
National Unity Party (Independent John B. Anderson)   67
Natural Law Party   68
New Alliance Party   68
Peace and Freedom Party   68
People's Party   69
Populist (People's) Party   69
Progressive (Bull Moose) Party   69
Progressive Party (La Follette)   70
Progressive Party (Wallace)   71
Progressive Labor Party   71
Prohibition Party   71
Reform Party (Independent Ross Perot)   72
Republican Party   73
Socialist Party   78
Socialist Labor Party   79
Socialist Workers Party   79
Union Party   79
U.S. Labor Party (Independent Lyndon LaRouche)   80
U.S. Taxpayers Party and Constitution Party   80
Whig Party   80
Workers World Party   81

CHAPTER 5   Campaign Finance   83

Controversy Surrounds Financing System   83
Candidates' Contributions and Expenditures   87
Campaign Finance Issues and Proposals   100
Financing Campaigns: Historical Development   108
Major Reform Laws Enacted in the 1970s   112
Congressional Stalemates on Campaign Reform Proposals   121

CHAPTER 6   The Historical Significance of Southern Primaries   129

Runoff Primaries   129
Preferential Primaries   130
County Unit System: Georgia   131
Special Elections   131
Racial Discrimination   132

CHAPTER 7 Politics and Issues, 1945–2000   133

    Post–World War II Years   136
    The Vietnam War Years   163
    Years of Uneasy Peace   176
    The Post–Cold War Era   192
    A Partisan Era   196

PART III Presidential Elections   207

CHAPTER 8 Introduction   209

    Who Runs for President   209
    The Exploratory Stage   210
    The Primary and Caucus Schedule   210
    The Presidential Nomination   212
    General Election Campaign   213
    Electoral College   220
    Term of Office   220
    Roads to the White House   220

CHAPTER 9 Chronology of Presidential Elections   225

    The Emergence of the Electoral Process   225
    The Age of Jackson   233
    The Idea of a Party System   236
    Slavery Divides the Nation   239
    Postwar Radicalism   245
    The Age of Republicanism   248
    The Age of Reform   252
    The "Return to Normalcy" and the Roaring Twenties   258
    The New Deal Coalition   263
    The Breakup of Consensus   278
    The New Conservative Discourse   284
    Democrats Regain the White House   289
    2000 Cliffhanger: GOP Retakes the Presidency   295

CHAPTER 10 Presidential Primaries   305

    "Front-Loaded" Process   305
    An Evolutionary Process   307
    Current Arrangement   308
    Legacy of the Progressive Era   309
    Regional Primaries and Super Tuesday   314

CHAPTER 11 Presidential Primary Returns, 1910–2000   319

CHAPTER 12 Nominating Conventions   411

    Convention Sites   411
    Delegate Selection   411
    Controversial Rules   421
    Convention Officers   421
    Party Platforms   421
    Filling Vacancies   425
    Communications and the Media   425

CHAPTER 13   Political Party Nominees, 1831–2000   429

CHAPTER 14   Convention Chronology, 1831–2000   441

CHAPTER 15   Key Convention Ballots   573

CHAPTER 16   Popular Vote Returns for President   643
   Presidential Popular Vote Returns: Minor Candidates and Parties, 1824–2000   689

CHAPTER 17   The Electoral College   701
   Constitutional Background   701
   Methods of Choosing Electors   703
   Historical Anomalies   705
   Election by Congress   707
   Counting the Electoral Vote   710
   Reform Proposals   713
   Presidential Disability   714

CHAPTER 18   Electoral Votes for President, 1789–2000   717
   Electoral Votes for Vice President, 1804–2000   772

CHAPTER 19   Biographical Directory of Presidential and Vice-Presidential Candidates   775

INDEXES, *following page 782*
   Presidential Candidates Index   I-1
   General Subject Index   I-3

VOLUME II

PART IV   Congressional Elections   783

CHAPTER 20   Introduction   785
   Characteristics of Members   786
   Women in Congress   787
   Blacks in Congress   790
   Hispanics in Congress   792
   Turnover in Membership   793
   Shifts between Chambers   796

CHAPTER 21   House Elections   799
   The People's Branch   799
   Special Elections   803
   Disputed House Elections   803
   Party Control Shifts   804

CHAPTER 22 Reapportionment and Redistricting 807

Early History of Reapportionment 808
Reapportionment: The Number of Seats 809
Redistricting: Drawing the Lines 815

CHAPTER 23 House Returns, 1824–2000 827

CHAPTER 24 Senate Elections 1229

Election by State Legislatures 1229
Changing Election Procedures 1229
Demands for Popular Election 1230
Senate's Three Classes 1231
Sessions and Terms 1231
The Modern Senate 1233

CHAPTER 25 U.S. Senators, 1789–2001 1235

CHAPTER 26 Senate General Election Returns, 1913–2000 1267

CHAPTER 27 Senate Primary Election Returns, 1920–2000 1305

PART V Gubernatorial Elections 1375

CHAPTER 28 Introduction 1377

Length of Terms 1377
Elections in Nonpresidential Years 1378
Method of Election 1378
Number of Terms 1379
Majority Vote Requirement 1380

CHAPTER 29 Governors of the States, 1776–2001 1383

CHAPTER 30 Gubernatorial General Election Returns, 1776–2000 1415

CHAPTER 31 Gubernatorial Primary Election Returns, 1919–2000 1479

REFERENCE MATERIALS 1543

Constitutional Provisions and Amendments on Elections 1545
Population of the United States and Puerto Rico, 1790–2000 1548
Changing Methods of Electing Presidential Electors, 1788–1836 1550
Presidential Nominating Campaign Lengths, 1968–2000 1552
Victorious Party in Presidential Races, 1860–2000 1554
Distribution of House Seats and Electoral Votes 1556
Bush v. Gore: Excerpts from the 2000 Supreme Court Decision on the Florida Recount 1557
Election Results, Congress and the Presidency, 1860–2000 1569
The Partisan Landscape, 2000: Presidential Voting by Congressional District 1572
Results of House Elections, 1928–2000 1574
Sessions of U.S. Congress, 1789–2000 1578
Speakers of the House of Representatives, 1789–2001 1588

House Floor Leaders, 1899–2001   1590
Senate Floor Leaders, 1911–2001   1592
Election-Related Web Sites   1594
Political Party Abbreviations   1596
Selected Bibliography   1601

Illustration Credits and Acknowledgments   1609

INDEXES, *following page 1610*

House Candidates Index   I-1
Senate General Election Candidates Index   I-113
Senate Primary Candidates Index   I-120
Gubernatorial General Election Candidates Index   I-129
Gubernatorial Primary Candidates Index   I-143
General Index   I-153

Tables, Figures, and Boxes

TABLES

1-1 Growing Franchise in the United States, 1930–2000   4
2-1 The Nation's Voters 1980–1998   23
5-1 Contribution Limits   95
6-1 Preference and Runoff Primaries   131
8-1 U.S. Presidents and Vice Presidents   211
8-2 Voter Turnout in 2000 Elections   217
8-3 "Minority" Presidents   223
10-1 Votes Cast and Delegates Selected in Presidential Primaries, 1912–2000   307
20-1 Age Structure of Congress, 1949–2001   786
20-2 Women in Congress, 1947–2001   787
20-3 Blacks in Congress, 1947–2001   790
20-4 Hispanics in Congress, 1947–2001   793
20-5 Longest Service in Congress   795
22-1 Congressional Apportionment, 1789–2000   810
22-2 State Population Totals, House Seat Changes after the 2000 Census   816
28-1 Party Lineup of Governors   1378
28-2 Length of Governor Terms   1379
28-3 Limitations on Governor Terms   1380

FIGURES

2-1 Voter Turnout, 1789-2000   22
2-2 Partisan Identification, 1952-2000   37
3-1 American Political Parties, 1789-2000   47
5-1 National Party Soft Money Receipts   98
5-2 Congressional Campaign Spending by Election Year   101
5-3 Incumbent Advantage in Reelection   103
22-1 2000 Reapportionment: Gainers and Losers   814

BOXES

Part I: Elections in America

Electoral Anomalies   12
Constitutional Provisions for House and Senate Elections   30
Voting Machine   36

Part II: Political Parties

Campaign Finance Glossary   85
Federal Election Commission   118
Campaign Finance Overhaul Legislation   124
Actions of the "Do-Nothing" Eightieth Congress   141
Members of Congress Who Became President   155
Governors Who Became President   176
Term Limits   194

Part III: Presidential Elections

What They Did Before They Became President   214
In Wake of 2000 Election "News Disaster," Pressure Mounts of Voting, Coverage Reform   218
President of the Confederacy   244
Countdown in Florida   298
Types of Primaries and Procedures   306
Selection by Caucus Method   310
Choosing a Running Mate   312
Presidents' Reelection Chances   313
VPs Who Have Become President   314
Growth of Presidential Primaries: More and More, Earlier and Earlier   316
Sites of Major Party Conventions, 1832–2000   412
Republican and Democratic Convention Delegates, 1932–2000   413
Democratic Conventions, 1832–2000   414
Chief Officers and Keynote Speakers at Democratic National Conventions, 1832–2000   415
Republican Conventions, 1856–2000   416
Chief Officers and Keynote Speakers at Republican National Conventions, 1856–2000   417
Political Party Organization and Rules   418
Changes in Democrats' Nominating Rules   419
GOP Primary Rules   420
Democrats' Two-Thirds Rule   421
Notable Credential Fights   422
Major Platform Fights   423
Third Parties Usually Fade Rapidly   424
Chief Officers at Other National Party Conventions, 1831–1892   425
National Party Chairs, 1848–2000   426
Highlights of National Party Conventions, 1831–2000   428
Splitting of States' Electoral Votes: Fractionalism and "Faithless Electors"   702
Electoral College Chronology   706
Presidential Election by House   708
Law for Counting Electoral Votes in Congress   712

Part IV: Congressional Elections

Limiting Terms   794
Congressional Characteristics and Public Opinion   800
Constitutional Provisions   809
Origins of the Gerrymander   817
Gerrymandering: The Shape of the House   819
How Should the Census Count the Population?   820
Senate Appointments and Special Elections   1232

Part V: Gubernatorial Elections

Removal of a Governor from Office   1381

Editors' Note

The fourth edition of *Congressional Quarterly's Guide to U.S. Elections* has been revised and expanded in many ways to provide readers a logical and more comprehensive explanation of the fundamental act of self-government: voting.

The most noticeable improvement is the change to two volumes, making the *Guide* easier to handle and allowing more than one reader to use it simultaneously. At more than 1,800 pages, the *Guide* is nearly 15 percent longer than the third edition published in 1994. Partly, this is the result of new data from the several elections held since then, as well as additional historical information that has become available from recent scholarly research. The added length also comes from new and reorganized chapters that give increased attention to the historical development of American elections, and particularly the period from the 1930s when President Franklin D. Roosevelt built a new electoral coalition that lasted until nearly the end of the twentieth century.

Equally important is the reorganization of this more heavily illustrated edition into five distinct parts that give the reader an overview of American elections and political parties, followed by details of presidential, congressional, and gubernatorial elections. Throughout the *Guide*, the editors have retained all of the features and content of earlier editions, including the multiple ways of accessing information through cross-reference page flags and several indexes. This edition continues the emphasis on explaining the origins and development of U.S. elections at the federal and state levels. This historical background provides a framework to better understand the seemingly overwhelming array of election returns that are the central feature of the *Guide*.

Part I: Elections in America. This section, new to the *Guide*, gives readers context for the detailed material that follows. The introductory chapter discusses American election history with a particular emphasis on the last seventy years of the twentieth century. This chapter outlines the broad history of elections from the founding of the nation to the essentially deadlocked division that occurred with the 2000 elections. The second chapter in Part I discusses the long—and often slow—expansion of the franchise in America from a highly restricted right to vote in the earliest days to the universal voting privilege that exists today. This part also includes a thumbnail list of election milestones over the past two hundred years.

Part II: Political Parties. This material has been greatly expanded from earlier editions to help readers better understand the history and dynamics of parties in American politics and elections. The first chapter provides a history of the evolution of parties, supplemented in the next chapter by brief profiles of all major and most minor parties, most of which no longer exist.

Entirely new to the *Guide* is the Part II chapter on campaign finance. The overriding importance—and influence—of campaign spending and contributions became the single most controversial aspect of U.S. elections at the end of the twentieth century. Part II also contains a chapter explaining the historical significance of southern primaries, along with a useful review of politics and issues from 1945 through 2000 that is designed to help readers better understand the context in which the elections of this period were held.

Part III: Presidential Elections. This part describes all U.S. presidential races, including a detailed elections chronology, nominating convention highlights and platforms, electoral college results (with accompanying maps), and popular vote returns for both primaries and general elections.

Part IV: Congressional Elections. Here the reader will find detailed election returns for the House and Senate. The election data are supported by chapters explaining the history and evolution of voting for members of the legislative branch of government. Part IV also includes a chapter on the history of reapportionment and redistricting, the decennial process that realigns representation in the House after every census.

Part V: Gubernatorial Elections. This part follows the pattern of the previous sections with a detailed listing of general and primary returns for the election of governors, supported by a chapter discussing gubernatorial history.

FINDING INFORMATION

A reader can locate information in a number of ways. The table of contents offers an overall view of the book's scope and allows quick access to major sections. Primary divisional headings help to direct a reader quickly to the information being sought. A separate table of contents lists tables, figures, and boxes.

For more specific direction to information, the reader can turn to one of the six candidate indexes: presidential; gubernatorial general; gubernatorial primary; Senate general; Senate primary; and House. Each candidate index lists the years of candidacy for each candidate. Instructions for use of the candidate indexes appear on the first page of each index.

The general index provides page references for all sections of the *Guide*, except the popular returns, which are indexed in the special candidate indexes. The general index can be used independently as a source of information separate from the candidate indexes.

ICPSR AND OTHER ELECTION DATA

The bulk of election returns used in the *Guide to U.S. Elections* for presidential, gubernatorial, Senate, House, and south-

ICPSR Historical Election Returns File

The election returns obtained from the Inter-University Consortium for Political and Social Research for the *Guide to U.S. Elections* represent constituency-level totals for candidates appearing in elections for the offices of president from 1924 to 1916, for governor and U.S. representative from 1824 to 1973, and for U.S. senator from 1913 to 1973. Congressional Quarterly obtained returns for the elections from 1974 through 2000 chiefly from its own research and publications.

The 1824 starting point for the ICPSR Historical Election Returns File was based on consideration of factors such as the pronounced trend by that time toward popular election of the presidential electors, as well as the availability, accessibility, and quality of returns for presidential, gubernatorial, and House elections.

Collection of the Data

The original data collection effort, begun in 1962, was supported by the Social Science Research Council and the National Science Foundation. The continuing addition of contemporary election returns is supported by the annual membership fee of more than 300 colleges and universities affiliated with the consortium.

As is the case with any enterprise of the magnitude represented by this data collection, many individuals contributed to its development and growth. Those who provided the initial impetus for the project included Lee Benson, Allan G. Bogue, Dewey Grantham Jr., Samuel P. Hays, Morton P. Keller, V. O. Key, Richard P. McCormick, Phillip Mason, Warren E. Miller, Thomas J. Pressly, William H. Riker, and Charles G. Sellers Jr. The ad hoc Committee to Collect the Basic Quantitative Data for American Political History of the American Historical Association obtained the assistance of more than one hundred archivists, historians, and political scientists in the collection of the data.

Through the efforts of Warren E. Miller, the executive director of the consortium, financial support was obtained for completion of the data collection, conversion to electronic form, and the extensive processing that followed. The data collection and processing effort was successively directed by Walter Dean Burnham, Howard W. Allen, and Jerome M. Clubb at the Survey Research Center, and more recently the Center for Political Studies, in the Institute for Social Research, the University of Michigan.

The initial data collection was conducted by scholars in the various states who volunteered their time and effort in locating little-known publications, searching state and local archives for unpublished data, exploring newspaper files, and evaluating the accuracy and reliability of these sources. In as many cases as possible, multiple sources were consulted. While general preference was given to official sources, these scholars were charged with the task of evaluating all available resources in terms of their quality and completeness. While the complete source annotations for the collection are too extensive to publish here, information on the sources for returns from specific elections can be obtained from the ICPSR.

The result of this initial effort, and subsequent work by the ICPSR staff, was the recovery of returns for more than 90 percent of all the elections for president, governor, senator, and representative in the period covering 1824 to 1973. This estimate was based on a review of the periodicity of elections by state and office, indicating where elections apparently occurred but no returns could be located. Such hypotheses were confirmed by reference to state manuals and histories or *Biographical Directory of the American Congress, 1774–1996* (Washington, D.C.: CQ Staff Directories, 1997), which indicates the changes in the membership of state delegations.

Format of the Election Returns File

In the ICPSR data format, an election is defined as a set of returns by party or candidate for a specified office in a specified state at a specified time. As a result, the collection through 1973 included returns for more than 25,000 individual elections and records the names of almost 115,000 candidates.

The ICPSR data also preserves the original party designations appearing on each original source. Consequently, almost 1,700 unique partisan labels appear in the collection, most of which, of course, represent short-lived or localized minor parties and the combinations and permutations of multiparty support received by individual candidates. In the ICPSR data collection, separate vote totals are recorded for candidates who appeared more than once on a ballot with different and distinct party designations. In short, the data appear in the collection virtually as they appeared in the original sources, with no combination of either candidate or party totals.

A comprehensive series of error-checking procedures was carried out on these data, and errors discovered through them were corrected. The ICPSR maintains returns for these elections at the county level in separate and larger electronic files. Using these data, it was possible to ascertain that the individual candidate returns summed to the total number of votes cast in the country. Subsequently, county returns were summed as a check against the state or congressional district level returns, both by candidate and in terms of the total number of votes cast. All discrepancies encountered in this process were resolved where possible, and appropriate corrections to the electronic files were made. No further systematic error checks are planned, although errors discovered through the use of the data are corrected as they are reported to the ICPSR.

Requests for Electronic Data. Requests for electronic data from the Historical Election Returns File should be addressed to Executive Director, Inter-University Consortium for Political and Social Research, Box 1248, Ann Arbor, MI 48106-1248. Or visit the ICPSR Web site: *www.icpsr.umich.edu*

ern primary races was supplied by the Inter-University Consortium for Political and Social Research (ICPSR) at the University of Michigan. Except where noted, returns through 1972 came from the ISPSR. *(See box, ICPSR Historical Election Returns File, p. xvi; details on the presentation of these returns in this book, pp. 643, 827, 1267, and 1415.)*

CQ Press is grateful to the ICPSR staff for its assistance and advice in supplementing this information since the first edition in 1975. We thank especially Richard C. Rockwell, executive director, and Erik W. Austin, director of archival development.

Major sources used to update or supplement the ICPSR data are identified at the beginning of each section. The primary sources include the biennial *America Votes* series, compiled by Richard M. Scammon, Alice V. McGillivray, and Rhodes Cook, and *American State Governors 1776–1976*, Vol. 1, by Joseph E. Kallenbach and Jessamine S. Kallenbach. Additional valuable assistance in adding and correcting data and supplying missing full names was provided by elections scholar Michael Dubin and Prof. Kenneth C. Martis, author and editor of *The Historical Atlas of United States Congressional Districts, 1789–1983.*

CONTRIBUTORS

Any reference book of more than 1,800 pages is the work of many individuals, and this edition of the *Guide* is no exception. Principal contributors to the fourth edition were Rhodes Cook, Michael Dubin, Paul Finkelman, John L. Moore, and Patricia Ann O'Connor, all of whom also prepared material for one or more earlier editions. Other contributors to earlier editions include Bob Benenson, Phil Duncan, Ronald D. Elving, Alan Ehrenhalt, Charles C. Euchner, Warden Moxley, Matt Pinkus, Jon P. Preimesberger, Robert H. Resnick, and Elizabeth Wehr.

The editors are grateful to Prof. Richard Rose, internationally known elections expert, for his thoughtful introduction to this work. Professor Rose is the author of many books and studies on elections, including the recently published *International Encyclopedia of Elections* (CQ Press).

This edition of the *Guide* was under the direction of David R. Tarr, CQ Press executive editor for reference publishing; Jon P. Preimesberger, CQ Press senior editor; and John L. Moore, former CQ Press staff member who served as editor of the third edition. Also making major contributions to this edition were

Acknowledgments

CQ Press expresses appreciation to the following copyright owners for permission to use material from their books in the *Guide to U.S. Elections*, fourth edition:

• Brookings Institution, Washington, D.C.: *Convention Decisions and Voting Records*, by Richard C. Bain and Judith H. Parris. Copyright 1973.

• James W. Davis: *Presidential Primaries: Road to the White House*, Greenwood Press, Westport, Conn., and London, England, reprint. Copyright 1967, 1980.

• Joseph E. Kallenbach and Jessamine S. Kallenbach: *American State Governors, 1776–1976*, vol. 1, Oceana Publications, Dobbs Ferry, N.Y. Copyright 1977.

• Svend Petersen: *A Statistical History of the American Presidential Elections, With Supplementary Tables Covering 1968–1980*, Greenwood Press, Westport, Conn., and London, England, reprint. Copyright 1963, 1968, 1981

For illustration credits and acknowledgments, see page 1609 in Volume II.

the general indexer, Jan Danis; compositors, Jessica Forman and Paul Pressau; proofreaders, Robert Tewksbury and Sue Nedrow; and production editors, Jeanne Hickman and Belinda Josey.

Inevitably in a reference work of this size and complexity, errors and omissions occur. We are grateful to the diligent readers who have noted possible errors in earlier editions and have supplied additional details where existing information was missing or incomplete. In all cases, editors have attempted to verify new details brought to our attention and have made revisions where possible. CQ Press again invites comments and suggestions from scholars and other users of the *Guide to U.S. Elections.*

CQ Press Editors
July 2001

American Elections: A Surprising Mixture of Old and New

RICHARD ROSE, UNIVERSITY OF STRATHCLYDE, GLASGOW

Two words can headline the results of an election—X wins—but two volumes are needed to tell the full story of what happens when the American people decide who will govern. Two volumes are necessary because elections in America have spread over three centuries, and federalism ensures that election results come in the plural. The vote for the presidency is not the only vote that Americans cast: more than 450 federal offices are contested on the first Tuesday after the first Monday in November, and elections for governorships push the total even higher.

The outcome of the Bush-Gore election shows us that although the American electoral system is very old, it can still surprise. The novelty in 2000 was not in the uncertainty before the votes were counted, as in pollsters' cautioning that the result was too close to forecast and that those voters who were undecided on election day morning would be decisive. The novelty came the day after the election, when supporters of Republican George W. Bush and Democrat Al Gore disagreed about who had won. Entry to the White House was left hanging by a few chads on a small proportion of Florida paper ballots, and lawyers rushed to present conflicting answers to the seemingly simple question: What is a valid vote? A succession of court cases revealed that judges disagreed, too. It took five weeks after votes were initially cast and counted before the U.S. Supreme Court, in a 5–4 ruling, in effect, decided the election in Bush's favor.

This splendid reference work reminds us that much that is surprising about American elections is not new. The outcome of the 1876 presidential election was not decided until two days before the inauguration of Rutherford B. Hayes on March 4, 1877. The critical decision that prevented Hayes's opponent, Samuel Tilden, from being sworn in as president was not taken by millions of voters or by judges but by an 8–7 vote of a highly partisan congressional commission.

Nor was the 2000 election the only election in which the candidate winning the most votes failed to win the White House. The election of president is decided by counting votes in the electoral college. In 1888 Benjamin Harrison became president with almost 1 percent of the popular vote less than incumbent Grover Cleveland but with 16 percent more of the electoral college vote. A distinctive feature of the Bush-Gore contest in 2000 was that the two candidates were close in both popular and electoral college votes. Gore won the popular vote by a plurality of 537,179 votes, or only 0.5 percent more than Bush. Bush won the electoral college vote by a slim 271–266 margin.

Rhetorically, every winner of the White House would like to claim that he or she is president of all the people in the nation.

But this assertion is literally a denial of democracy, for it implies that everyone votes for the same person. The logic of free competitive elections is that the winner should have the most votes, but not all the votes. Moreover, a plurality can be secured without winning half the votes, and the presence of third-party candidates makes this possible. Since 1824, the winner of the presidential race has failed to secure as much as half the vote in eighteen presidential elections. George W. Bush is not alone in entering the White House with less than half the vote; the same outcome occurred in the elections of Bill Clinton (twice), Richard Nixon, John F. Kennedy, Harry S. Truman, and Abraham Lincoln. Nor could Al Gore claim to be the choice of the majority of the American people—his 48.4 percent of the popular vote fell short of winning a bare majority.

Two centuries ago, the United States pioneered putting decisions about who governs to the popular vote. Thanks to a "third wave" of democratization, free competitive elections can now be found around the world. Sham elections without competition, as in the Soviet Union in the 1960s and 1970s, or elections without the majority of adults being able to vote, as in South Africa in the 1980s, have been replaced around the world by competitive ones. Democratization was unthinkable in many nations two decades ago. Today, more than eighty countries both respect political and civil liberties and hold competitive elections. However, most countries have not adopted the American approach of electing a president and Congress to share power but instead have a European system of parliamentary government. Whereas the average American voter receives a lengthy ballot listing dozens of federal, state, and local offices to be filled by election, a British voter casts a ballot for only one office, a candidate for the post of member of Parliament for the local constituency. The choice of prime minister depends on which party wins the most seats in Parliament.

A majority of democratic countries have rejected the American electoral system of rewarding individual offices in favor of a system of proportional representation in which a party's seats in the legislature are allocated in proportion to a party's share of the popular vote. Had this system been in effect in the United States in 1992, Ross Perot's followers might have claimed about one-fifth of the seats in Congress and held the balance of power there during Bill Clinton's first years in office.

Most democratic countries have also not shown the apathy that characterizes an increasing portion of the American electorate. As the *Guide* documents, in the nineteenth century as many as four-fifths of those eligible actually cast their votes. But participation in presidential elections fell in the twentieth century from 73.8 percent in 1900 to below 50 percent in 1996. Notwithstanding changes in the laws to make electoral registration easier, barely half of the eligible citizenry cast a presidential vote in 2000. Turnout in American elections lags about 25 percent below turnout in established democracies elsewhere.

This fourth edition of the *Guide to U.S. Elections* is welcome, for it goes well beyond updating the previous edition with election results from 1994 to 2000. At a time when the significance of political parties is being questioned by single-issue pressure groups, the expanded discussion of the development of American political parties emphasizes the strong institutional roots of partisanship in the American political system. The growing importance of money in American elections—and disputes about how much ought to be spent and who ought to be allowed to give money—is covered in a new chapter on campaign finance.

With more materials to include, the *Guide* has been divided into two convenient volumes so that readers need not be weight lifters. The two-volume format also facilitates simultaneous use by double the number of library users. New features have built on decades of authoritative work on American elections by CQ Press staff and their associates. The fourth edition makes good use of CQ Press's expertise in presenting complex information clearly in both prose and tables, and the large-page size of this reference book increases flexibility in presentation.

The first part of the *Guide* on the history of American elections is valuable in showing how the constitutional framework of elections has survived more than two hundred years by a process of adaptation. It also shows that while America has the oldest continuous history of competitive elections, elections were far from democratic during more than half of its history. Initially, the right to vote was restricted to adult white males with property, and some states followed the English practice of not allowing citizens of Roman Catholic or Jewish faith to vote. In the nineteenth century, the right to vote was granted to a large majority of white males. Between the Civil War and World War I, some states allowed African Americans and women the vote, but the right to vote was not guaranteed women until the ratification of the Nineteenth Amendment in 1920. There was no federal guarantee of the right to vote for African Americans until after passage of the Voting Rights Act of 1965. Even today the principal method used to register voters, a necessary step in casting a ballot, is based on English practices of two centuries ago that were abandoned in Britain in 1918.

The second part of the *Guide* clarifies what is obscured by the statement "America has a two-party system." In the early days of the Republic, elections were not fought by parties, and the term "party" was a term of abuse. In the 1820s electoral competition between two parties emerged. In 1848 the presidency was even contested by three parties, while in the pre–Civil War election of 1860 the electoral college votes were divided among four parties. The long U.S. history of two-party competition has been repeatedly disrupted by the entry of one or more third parties, such as the Progressive Party of Theodore Roosevelt in 1912, George Wallace's American Independent Party in 1968, and Ross Perot's Independent supporters in 1992. Third parties have not won the White House or many seats in Congress, but their

presence has at times determined which of the two leading parties won and forced changes in the majority parties' positions. In addition to providing a detailed analysis of party politics and issues, the *Guide* devotes special attention to the role of primaries in the era of one-party competition in the American South.

Presidential elections have changed greatly since the unanimous election of George Washington in 1789, and this process is fully documented in Part III. From the launch of party politics until the mid-twentieth century, national conventions of party workers decided the Democratic and Republican candidates; full facts and figures are given for each convention. In the past half-century, presidential primaries have determined each party's nominee before the convention meets. Because primaries are held at different times and by different rules in different states, the *Guide* offers an indispensable and up-to-date source of information about the changing practice of primaries and how they work today.

How voters cast their presidential ballots is only the starting point in deciding how the White House is won and lost. The next step is tallying the popular vote within each of the fifty states to select the presidential electors for each state. It is the vote of the state's electors in the electoral college that determines who will be inaugurated as president. The *Guide* documents how this process is intended to work. It also documents what happens when things do not work smoothly, as happened in the 2000 contest and in the election of 1876.

In an era of nationwide television and nationwide personalities, far less attention is given to congressional elections than to the White House race, but the outcome of elections for the House and Senate is critical in determining what a president can and cannot do. The fourth part of the *Guide* documents the results of elections for the House since 1824 and of elections for the Senate since 1913, when senators were first popularly elected.

Part IV shows how the increase in split-ticket voting (an individual voting for candidates of different parties for president and for Congress) has led to an era of divided government, with different parties in control of the White House and Congress. Divided government is alternatively praised, because it requires partisans to moderate their views to achieve a cross-party coalition to enact legislation, or attacked, because it makes it more difficult for the president, the only official accountable to the nation as a whole, to carry through a program.

From a grassroots perspective, the character of individual members of Congress has become somewhat more important than the party to which they belong. Incumbents try to win support by convincing people to think of themselves as "their" member of Congress and thus insulate themselves against a national downturn in the party's fortunes. Part IV shows the extent to which this strategy is successful.

In the U.S. system of government, the governors of the fifty states are closer to their voters than is the president of the United States. Part V documents the outcome of gubernatorial elections from the beginning of the nation in 1776 to the present. Altogether, Parts III, IV, and V make it possible for readers from Alabama to Wyoming to trace how their states voted in presidential, congressional, and state elections for as long as their states have been part of the nation.

Given the number of offices up for election in a four-year period and the number of elections since 1789, any reference book on elections must be a big book. The two-volume format of this *Guide* is a convenience, for it is large enough to offer readers a "one-stop" service, bringing together results that would otherwise be scattered across many library shelves or many libraries. Most of this information is currently unavailable on Web sites, because American elections are more than two hundred years older than the Internet, and the Internet best covers events during its short history. The *Guide*'s comprehensive general index makes it easy to find information quickly, and a format mixing prose, tables, and boxed highlights invites hours of browsing for insights into American politics past and present.

Guide to U.S. Elections

PART I

Elections in America

1. The Evolution of American Elections   3

2. Elections: An Expanding Franchise   21

CHAPTER 1

The Evolution of American Elections

AMERICAN POLITICAL HISTORY has been a story of eras—and eras within eras. Throughout it all, there have never been more than two major parties at one time occupying center stage. At first, there were the Federalists and the Democratic-Republicans; through the mid-1800s, the Democrats and the Whigs; and since the Civil War, the Democrats and the Republicans.

External events have played a major role in which party held the upper hand. The successful prosecution of the Civil War propelled the Republicans into dominance for nearly three-quarters of a century. The Great Depression helped move the Democrats into hegemony for the generation that followed. The turmoil of the 1960s—from racial rioting in many of the nation's cities to the controversial war in Vietnam—left a political landscape that neither party has been able to control. Interludes have occurred within each era, where the partisan balance has temporarily shifted. Usually such shifts have been an aberration, with a return to the previous norm after an interval of two, four, or eight years.

During this history of U.S. elections, the American electorate has steadily grown and become more diverse. Barely 365,000 voters cast ballots in the election of 1824, the first in which there is record of a nationwide popular vote for president. Less than 5 million voters participated in 1860, when Abraham Lincoln became the nation's first Republican president, beginning an era of GOP hegemony that lasted almost one-third of the way through the twentieth century. Nearly 40 million voters took part in the Depression-era election of 1932, which conclusively shifted the balance of power to the Democrats, led by Franklin D. Roosevelt, for the next generation.

More than 105 million voters cast ballots in the election of 2000, which—in its historic closeness—confirmed a nation at the dawn of the twenty-first century almost evenly divided between the two major parties. When all the ballots had been counted, Republican George W. Bush had won a bare majority of electoral votes, even though he was the first presidential winner in more than a century to lose the popular vote. As for the other end of Pennsylvania Avenue: Voting for the Senate resulted in an unusual 50–50 tie, while Republicans maintained a tenuous majority in the House of Representatives.

In 2000 there were roughly 205 million Americans of voting age, almost 160 million of whom had taken the critical first step of registering to vote. Of those who participated in the 2000 election, exit polls showed that almost 20 percent were from minority groups—principally blacks, Hispanics, and Asians. A quarter of the voters were Catholic. Fewer than half were white Protestants. Slightly more women than men cast ballots.

That diversity was a far cry from the early years of the Republic, when the franchise was largely limited to a comparative handful of white male landowners. Women were not given the right to vote until 1920; large numbers of blacks across the South were denied the ballot until the 1960s; and it was not until 1971—in the midst of the Vietnam War—that the voting age was lowered nationally from twenty-one to eighteen.

The steady expansion of the voting pool has been accompanied by demographic changes that have dramatically altered the complexion of the electorate. In its formative years the Republic was a rural, agrarian society. It became increasingly urban in the decades of industrialization and immigration that followed the Civil War. As the nation became more mobile over the course of the twentieth century, the population began to move out from central cities into sprawling, fast-growing suburbs.

Gradually, the suburbs have assumed the balance of power in American politics. Tending to have a more mobile, more affluent, and less politically rooted citizenry than the cities or small-town America, the suburbs have been bastions of political independence. Since the end of World War II, they have often been the decisive voting bloc in state and national elections. In the 2000 election Bush won in forty-five of the fifty fastest-growing, mostly suburban counties. Democrat Al Gore, the popular vote winner nationally, won in only five of those counties.

With the rise of the suburbs, and independent voting in general, voters have been increasingly willing to split their ticket between candidates of different parties. The result has been long periods of divided government—primarily a Republican president and a Democratic Congress, but in the waning years of the twentieth century, a Democratic president and a Republican Congress. Additionally, it has not been unusual for Congress itself to be divided, with one party controlling the Senate and the other party the House of Representatives.

Challenging the Two Parties

Through it all, third parties have remained part of the supporting cast, though assuming an increasingly critical role in influencing election outcomes in recent years. No president since 1988 has been elected with a majority of the popular vote, and neither party since 1994 has won a majority of the nationwide vote cast for the House of Representatives.

Throughout American history, third parties have served as a "miner's canary"—warning the two major parties of areas of disaffection within the body politic—on the slavery question prior to the Civil War, on trade and currency issues in the late nineteenth century, on government and corporate reform in

Table 1-1
Growing Franchise in the United States, 1930–2000

Year	Estimated Population of Voting Age	Vote Cast for Presidential Electors		Vote Cast for U.S. Representatives	
		Number	*Percent*	*Number*	*Percent*
1930	73,623,000	—	—	24,777,000	33.7
1932	75,768,000	39,758,759	52.5	37,657,000	49.7
1934	77,997,000	—	—	32,256,000	41.4
1936	80,174,000	45,654,763	56.9	42,886,000	53.5
1938	82,354,000	—	—	36,236,000	44.0
1940	84,728,000	49,900,418	58.9	46,951,000	55.4
1942	86,465,000	—	—	28,074,000	32.5
1944	85,654,000	47,976,670	56.0	45,103,000	52.7
1946	92,659,000	—	—	34,398,000	37.1
1948	95,573,000	48,793,826	51.1	45,933,000	48.1
1950	98,134,000	—	—	40,342,000	41.1
1952	99,929,000	61,550,918	61.6	57,571,000	57.6
1954	102,075,000	—	—	42,580,000	41.7
1956	104,515,000	62,026,908	59.3	58,426,000	55.9
1958	106,447,000	—	—	45,818,000	43.0
1960	109,672,000	68,838,219	62.8	64,133,000	58.5
1962	112,952,000	—	—	51,267,000	45.4
1964	114,090,000	70,644,592	61.9	65,895,000	57.8
1966	116,638,000	—	—	52,908,000	45.4
1968	120,285,000	73,211,875	60.9	66,288,000	55.1
1970	124,498,000	—	—	54,173,000	43.5
1972	140,777,000	77,718,554	55.2	71,430,000	50.7
1974	146,338,000	—	—	52,495,000	35.9
1976	152,308,000	81,555,889	53.5	74,422,000	48.9
1978	158,369,000	—	—	55,332,000	34.9
1980	163,945,000	86,515,221	52.8	77,995,000	47.6
1982	169,643,000	—	—	64,514,000	38.0
1984	173,995,000	92,652,842	53.3	83,231,000	47.8
1986	177,922,000	—	—	59,619,000	33.5
1988	181,956,000	91,594,809	50.3	81,786,000	44.9
1990	185,812,000	—	—	61,513,000	33.1
1992	189,524,000	104,425,014	55.1	96,239,000	50.8
1994	193,650,000	—	—	69,770,000	36.0
1996	196,511,000	96,277,223	49.0	92,272,000	47.0
1998	200,515,000	—	—	65,896,772	32.9
2000	205,814,000	105,396,627	51.2	97,226,268	47.2

Source: Bureau of the Census, *Statistical Abstract of the United States 1996* (Washington, D.C.: U.S. Government Printing Office, 1996); Federal Election Commission, *Federal Elections 96* (Washington, D.C.: Federal Election Commission, 1997); Rhodes Cook, *America Votes 23* (Washington, D.C.: Congressional Quarterly, 1999); Rhodes Cook, *America Votes 23* (Washington, D.C.: Congressional Quarterly, 1999);

both the early and late twentieth century, and the issues of states' rights and racial politics at midcentury. Traditionally, however, third parties have had neither the money nor the numbers of supporters to effectively compete. The boldest of the lot have rallied around a well-known "celebrity" as their national standard-bearer—such as former presidents Martin Van Buren (the Free Soil nominee in 1848) and Theodore Roosevelt (the Progressive Party nominee in 1912). Roosevelt finished second in the election of 1912, and his Progressives won several seats in Congress. This minor success has been about as good as it gets for third parties. Those parties that could reach even 5 percent of the presidential vote have been few and far between.

That changed a bit, though, in the volatile political atmosphere of the late twentieth century. Former Alabama Gov. George C. Wallace mounted a third-party campaign in 1968 that polled 13.5 percent of the nationwide popular vote, carried five southern states, and served as an important bridge in the transformation of the South from a cornerstone of the Democratic Party to the prime building block of the Republican Party. Twelve years later Republican Rep. John B. Anderson of Illinois drew 7 percent of the vote running as an Independent. In 1992 Texas billionaire H. Ross Perot won 19 percent, also as an Independent, and four years later took 8 percent as the nominee of his newly created Reform Party.

Collectively, third parties polled in double digits percentage-wise in the two presidential elections of the 1990s for the first time in back-to-back elections since the eve of the Civil War. Perot's showing in 1992 was the best for a third-party candidate since Roosevelt drew 27 percent of the vote in 1912.

Recent voter willingness to consider options beyond the two major parties has not been limited to the presidency. Over the course of the 1990s, independents or third-party candidates won governorships in Alaska, Connecticut, Maine, and Minnesota. And in the spring of 2001 James M. Jeffords of Vermont tipped the Senate balance to the Democrats by changing his party affiliation from Republican to Independent.

The Basic Layout

The American electoral process has remained essentially the same since the Republic was launched in 1789. The president serves a term of four years and from the beginning has been formally elected by a majority vote of the electoral college. Each state's electoral vote is equal to its total of senators and House members. If no candidate wins an electoral vote majority, the choice is made by the House of Representatives. That has happened twice, in 1800 and 1824. On three other occasions—1876, 1888, and 2000—the winner of the electoral vote has lost the popular vote.

Senators are elected to six-year terms, with two per state. One-third of the Senate is up for election every two years. Senators were first elected by their state legislatures, but since 1913 they have been elected by direct popular vote.

Members of the House of Representatives serve two-year terms and represent districts within states, the number allotted to each state determined after each decennial census. From the beginning of the Republic, House members have been elected by popular vote.

More than two-thirds of the governors are elected in midterm elections, not in the presidential election year. Five states elect their governor in off-years, either the year after or the year before a presidential election.

Meanwhile, the length of terms for governors and their method of selection are a matter for each state to decide. In the nation's formative years, terms were of one, two, or even three years, with some states electing their governors by popular vote and others leaving that power in the hands of the state legislature. Over time, though, terms grew longer and election by direct popular vote became universal. In 1900 nearly half the states had four-year gubernatorial terms. In 2000 all but two states—New Hampshire and Vermont—did.

Members of Congress can serve as many terms as they wish. Presidents, though, have been limited to two terms since 1951, and most states currently impose a limit of two consecutive terms on their governors.

Over the course of the nation's history, there have been three periods of great electoral reform. The first, in the 1820s and 1830s, saw several steps taken toward direct democracy—an expansion of the vote among white males as property and taxpaying qualifications began to be relaxed; the institution of popular balloting on a nationwide basis for presidential electors; and the advent of party conventions to nominate presidential candidates. Before conventions, the selection of a party's standard-bearer had been made in most cases by a caucus of the party's members in Congress.

The second great period of electoral reform came in the early 1900s, with the institution of direct election of senators, the creation of the first presidential primaries to give voters an advisory role in the nominating process, and the extension of the vote to women.

The third period of electoral reform came in the 1960s and 1970s. The voting age was lowered across the country from twenty-one to eighteen; the vote was extended to millions of blacks across the South; the number of presidential primaries increased, to the point they replaced conventions as the determining step in the nominating process; public financing of presidential campaigns was launched; and "one person, one vote" became the law of the land in drawing congressional districts.

As the size of the electorate has grown over the decades, voter participation—as a percentage of the voting-age population—has tended to decline. In the late 1800s, for instance, around 80 percent of eligible voters often cast ballots in presidential elections. With the waves of foreign immigration around the turn of the century, followed by the expansion of the vote to women, turnout rates plunged to roughly 50 percent in the early 1920s. They moved upward into the 60 percent range in the 1960s, only to begin falling downward again with the lowering of the voting age in the early 1970s. By the end of the twentieth century, the national turnout rate hovered around 50 percent for presidential elections and 35 percent for midterm elections, when the number of ballots cast is always much lower.

Still, there are some basic constants about voter turnout. The proportion of those voting tends to increase with age, income, and education, and whites tend to vote at a higher rate than minorities. Ultimately, however, whether turnout is viewed as high or low can depend on the way it is measured. For instance, the 105 million Americans who cast ballots in the presidential election of 2000 represented a bare majority of the nation's voting-age population but were nearly two-thirds of those who were actually registered to vote.

Republicans Start Fast

The first period of electoral reform took place under the long shadow of Andrew Jackson, a Democrat with both a large and a small "d." At first, the Democrats' prime competition came from the ill-starred Whig Party, whose only two presidential victories (in 1840 and 1848) were followed by the death in office of the winner.

The Whigs dissolved in the political turmoil that preceded the Civil War, with the newly formed Republican Party filling the void. Rooted solely in the North and with opposition to the expansion of slavery into the territories as their primary cause, the Republicans made headway quickly, winning control of the House of Representatives in 1858, just four years after the party came into existence.

President Abraham Lincoln discusses battlefield strategy with his Union generals. From the 1860s to 1930, the Republican Party dominated national politics.

With regional fissures within the more broadly based Democratic Party turning into a chasm, Republicans captured the presidency and both houses of Congress in 1860. Democrats broke apart that year, with the northern and southern wings of the party each fielding a presidential ticket. The split enabled the GOP standard-bearer, Abraham Lincoln, to win the White House with less than 40 percent of the popular vote, the lowest winning percentage for any presidential candidate with the exception of the election of 1824.

Republicans were to dominate the political scene for the next seventy-two years—controlling the White House for fifty-six of those years, the Senate for sixty and the House for fifty. In the traumatic years in the wake of the Civil War, Republicans "waved the bloody shirt," and offered the nation a succession of former officers in the Union Army as their presidential standard-bearers, beginning in 1868 with Ulysses S. Grant. As wartime memories faded, the GOP was able to tie together a winning coalition of urban and rural voters above the Mason-Dixon line, while the South remained solidly Democratic.

Democratic problems were compounded by their convention nominating rules. While Republicans nominated their presidential candidate by simple majority vote, Democrats until 1936 required a two-thirds majority. The result, on occasion, was a long, exhausting convention that ultimately nominated a colorless compromise candidate.

During the period from 1860 to 1932, the Republicans had only one convention that took more than twenty ballots to choose a nominee, the Democrats had five, culminating with the party's 1924 conclave, which took 103 ballots to pick the little-known John W. Davis. Altogether, during this Republican era, GOP presidential candidates won a majority of the popular vote ten times, the Democrats only once and that in 1876, when Samuel J. Tilden lost by one electoral vote to Rutherford B. Hayes.

This era saw only two Democrats advance to the White

House: Grover Cleveland, who won two nonconsecutive terms in the late nineteenth century, and Woodrow Wilson, who capitalized on the bitter split within Republican ranks in 1912 between President William Howard Taft and former president Theodore Roosevelt to win with a modest 42 percent of the popular vote.

Republicans rebounded strongly from the eight-year "Wilson aberration," dominating both ends of Pennsylvania Avenue in the 1920s. At the beginning of 1929, the party was near its zenith. Herbert Hoover had been elected president the previous November with 58 percent of the vote—the second-highest winning percentage up to that time in the nation's history—and Republicans held roughly 60 percent of the seats in both the Senate and House.

Yet in the entrails of the 1928 election returns were early signs of changes to come in the party coalitions. In nominating Alfred E. Smith, the first Roman Catholic to head a major-party presidential ticket, Democrats temporarily lost much of their base in the South but made inroads among the burgeoning number of urban ethnic voters in the North, which proved lasting.

Smith was the first Democratic presidential candidate in the 1920s to win a state outside the South, carrying Massachusetts and Rhode Island. At the same time, voters in the nation's most populous state, New York, elected Democrat Franklin D. Roosevelt as governor to succeed Smith.

With the stock market crash in October 1929 and the onset of the Great Depression, more dramatic changes in the political landscape came quickly. In the midterm election of 1930, Democrats won control of the House and pulled virtually even with the Republicans in the Senate.

Democrats Take Charge

In 1932 Democrats completed their breakthrough, easily capturing the White House and both houses of Congress. Roosevelt

Two political campaign buttons of the 1930s promote Franklin D. Roosevelt and the Democratic Party as the remedy to the Great Depression. From the 1930s to the 1990s the Democrats were the congressional power.

led the Democratic sweep, besting Hoover in all but six northeastern states, and his long coattails helped Democrats emerge with more than 70 percent of the seats in the House and more than 60 percent in the Senate.

Just as important were the next two elections. They affirmed that 1932 was not a one-time, anti-Republican vote, but the start of a new political era in which the Democrats would dominate. Historically, the party occupying the White House has lost congressional seats in midterm elections, but in 1934 Democrats added to their hefty majorities in both the Senate and the House. In 1936 they gained even more seats, as FDR swept to a landslide reelection victory.

Roosevelt carried all but two states, Maine and Vermont, winning 60.8 percent of the popular vote (second only to Lyndon B. Johnson's 61.1 percent in 1964) and registering a 523-to-8 victory in the electoral vote, the most lopsided margin in the nation's history. Meanwhile, the Democrats emerged from the 1936 election with 333 seats in the House and 75 seats in the Senate, the most that either party has held in either chamber. At the state level, the Democratic success was equally broad, as their total of governorships soared to thirty-eight, compared with just seven for the Republicans (with the other three going to third parties or independents).

Put another way, the Republicans—who had dominated American politics since the Civil War—were about as close to extinction as any major party has been. They staggered away from the election of 1936 with just 20 percent of the seats in the House of Representatives, 18 percent of those in the Senate, 15 percent of the nation's governorships, and just 2 percent of the electoral vote for president.

Over the next decade, the Republicans would steadily gain ground and the Democrats lose it. The Democrats remained the nation's majority party for the next generation, however, because they were able to maintain the cornerstone of their new coalition, the South and the cities. The South, in particular, had a strong voice in the party's congressional leadership. Alben W. Barkley of Kentucky and Lyndon Johnson of Texas held the post of Senate majority leader for much of the 1940s and 1950s, while

Sam Rayburn of Texas served as House speaker through much of the same period.

To be sure, Democratic dominance during this period was not monolithic. Republicans won both houses of Congress in the midterm election of 1946 and again in 1952, when Republican Dwight D. Eisenhower won the first of his two terms as president. Congressional Republicans were also able to frustrate more than one Democratic president during this period by joining with conservative Democrats, mainly from the South, to form a "conservative coalition" that prevailed on a number of issues.

Still, the Democrats' hegemony from 1932 to 1968 was about as solid as it had been for the Republicans during the previous era; it was just half as long. The Democrats held the White House for twenty-eight of the thirty-six years, and both the Senate and the House for thirty-two of them.

Unlike the previous GOP era, though, when Republicans were arguably strongest near its close, Democrats were most dominant at the beginning of their era—when Republicans were clearly identified as the "party of the Depression" and Democrats were associated with the activist, optimistic government of FDR's New Deal.

From 1940 through 1956, the Democratic share of the presidential vote declined each election. But it was the end of World War II, or maybe more precisely, the death of Roosevelt in April 1945, that marked a transition from a strongly Democratic era to a more tenuous one.

Through the post-Depression years of the 1930s and the war effort in the early 1940s, FDR defined American politics. With his death, and the end of World War II several months later, the political playing field changed. The electorate began to grow more mobile, suburbs began to sprout, and voters began to show an increasing independence from the political machines and their interest group allies that held sway in the past. Neither party had a leader to loom over the political landscape as FDR did through his four presidential election victories.

The dominant mood that swept both sides of the Atlantic in the wake of World War II was a desire for change. In the British parliamentary elections of 1945, the Conservative government of Winston Churchill was thrown out of office. The following year, the Democrats lost both houses of Congress. It was also widely assumed that in 1948 the Democrats would lose the presidency as well. Roosevelt's successor, Harry S. Truman, had trouble persuading voters, many in his party, that he was up to the job. The broad Democratic coalition that FDR patched together—from conservative white southerners on one hand, to urban ethnics, union members, and minority voters on the other—showed signs of coming apart.

Both the liberal and conservative wings of the Democratic Party fielded tickets of their own in 1948. On Truman's left was former vice president Henry A. Wallace (number two during FDR's third term), who led the Progressive Party. On Truman's right, South Carolina governor J. Strom Thurmond headed the States' Rights Party, informally called the Dixiecrats.

The rest is legend. Trailing Republican Thomas E. Dewey in the polls throughout much of the year and looking hopelessly beaten, Truman ran a spirited fall campaign that produced one of the greatest upsets in American political history. Truman carried twenty-eight states, rolling over the New York governor in every region except the Northeast, while the Thurmond and Wallace challenges were held in check. Thurmond carried four southern states, but Truman won the rest of the region. Wallace ended up carrying no states.

However, the Democrats' euphoria with Truman's comeback victory and the election of a Democratic Congress masked the fact that Truman had won with less than a majority of the popular vote—a perceptibly poorer showing than FDR in any of his four presidential election victories. The 1948 election was conducted against a backdrop of voter apathy; turnout was just 51 percent of the voting-age population, the lowest for any presidential election since the 1920s.

Four years later, Republican Eisenhower won the White House and helped the GOP win both houses of Congress as well. But it soon became apparent that Ike's was a personal, not a party, victory. In 1954 Democrats regained Congress, and two years later they added seats to their congressional majorities, even as Eisenhower was coasting to a landslide reelection victory.

Postwar Politics: Kennedy and Nixon

It was not Eisenhower—who had led the Allied troops during World War II—who defined American politics in the immediate postwar period, but two junior officers in the Navy, John F. Kennedy and Richard M. Nixon. They proved to be among the most ambitious and successful politicians of their generation.

Both won House seats in 1946: Democrat Kennedy in the Boston area; Republican Nixon in the fast-growing suburbs of southern California. Both won Senate seats in the early 1950s. Although Nixon was elected vice president in 1952, Kennedy also vaulted onto the national stage in 1956 with a nearly successful bid for the Democratic vice-presidential nomination.

The two faced each other in the presidential election of 1960 in a race that was close from beginning to end. Throughout, it had a special drama to it, particularly surrounding Kennedy. As vice president, Nixon had the air of a semi-incumbent and ran unopposed for the Republican nomination. Kennedy did not have that luxury, and as a Catholic, felt he had to demonstrate his electability in the scattered array of presidential primaries. He succeeded, culminating with a legendary victory over Sen. Hubert H. Humphrey of Minnesota in heavily Protestant West Virginia, which put Kennedy within range of the nomination.

Voter interest in the race, already high, was heightened that fall by a series of televised debates—the first ever between presidential nominees. On election day, 63 percent of the voting-age population turned out, the highest percentage in any presidential contest since World War I. The result was one of the closest presidential elections ever, with Kennedy winning by barely 100,000 votes out of nearly 70 million cast.

Critical to Kennedy's victory was the Democrats' urban base. His winning margin in New York City (New York), Philadelphia (Pennsylvania), Baltimore (Maryland), Detroit (Michigan), Chicago (Illinois), and St. Louis (Missouri), was larger than his victory margin in the state each was in. Like Truman twelve years earlier, Kennedy was able to win a large portion of the South.

The political environment of the 1960s, though, was buffeted by trauma and tragedy, starting with Kennedy's assassination in November 1963. The event created a sympathy vote of sorts for Kennedy's successor, Lyndon Johnson, who led a Democratic landslide the following year almost equal in scope to the party's titanic win in 1936. Johnson defeated Republican Sen. Barry M. Goldwater of Arizona with a record 61.1 percent of the popular vote, and the Democrats emerged with 295 seats in the House and 68 in the Senate, their highest totals since the 1930s.

The Democratic landslide of 1964 was not nearly so total or its effects so lasting as the one in 1936. Moderate Republicans—such as New York's Nelson A. Rockefeller, Pennsylvania's William W. Scranton, Michigan's George W. Romney, and Ohio's James A. Rhodes—still held a number of big-state governorships. While sweeping the Deep South, from Louisiana to South Carolina, Goldwater established a beachhead among conservative white southerners that Republican presidential candidates have exploited to this day.

Instead of reviving the Democratic era, the election of 1964 proved to be the era's "last hurrah." Against the backdrop of an increasingly unpopular war in Southeast Asia and racial rioting in many of the nation's cities, Johnson launched a series of liberal "Great Society" programs that quickly proved controversial. In 1966 Republicans gained forty-seven seats in the House and three in the Senate. Two years later, they won the presidency.

Split-Level Realignment

The election of 1968 proved to be one of those rare realigning elections, like 1860 and 1932, that define American politics for a generation to come. However, instead of producing a top-down realignment felt at all levels of government, the 1968 election brought about a split-level realignment, with Republicans dominating presidential contests for the next two decades, but Democrats retaining the upper hand in Congress and the states.

John F. Kennedy used the relatively new medium of television to defeat Richard Nixon in the 1960 presidential election.

The political environment in 1968 was highly volatile. Not only was there war abroad and racial rioting at home, but violence impacted the presidential campaign as well. Civil rights leader Martin Luther King Jr. was assassinated in April 1968. Sen. Robert F. Kennedy of New York, a brother of the late president and a leading candidate for the Democratic presidential nomination, was killed two months later after winning the California primary.

That August, Vice President Humphrey was nominated by the Democratic convention in Chicago, as thousands of rioters took to the streets to oppose both the war and the lack of openness in the party's nominating process. Humphrey had not competed that spring in a single primary state, but, backed by the party establishment, he was nominated on the first ballot. Down in the polls and with the Democrats divided, Humphrey rallied in the fall but still fell roughly 500,000 votes short of Republican Richard Nixon, with nearly ten million votes going to third-party candidate George Wallace. Nixon and Wallace emphasized law and order, though, with Wallace also touting states' rights.

Nixon won only 43 percent of the popular vote yet carried thirty-two states. The focus of political transition was in the South, where Nixon won seven states, Wallace carried five, and Humphrey, just one (LBJ's home state of Texas). It was by far the fewest number of southern states that any Democratic presidential nominee had carried since the Civil War.

For the rest of the century, the South was to be the cornerstone of the Republican presidential coalition. Through the 1970s and 1980s, the GOP also dominated presidential voting in the burgeoning suburbs and much of rural America, which helped give the party five victories in a twenty-year span. The lone Democratic winner in this period was Jimmy Carter, who in the wake of the Watergate scandal that forced Nixon's resignation from office in 1974, won by a margin of only 2 percentage points two years later.

The rest of the time Republican presidential candidates won by huge margins. Nixon in 1972, Ronald Reagan in 1980 and 1984, and George Bush in 1988 each carried at least forty states, with Nixon and Reagan sweeping forty-nine in their landslide reelection victories. So dominant had the GOP become at the presidential level that by the late 1980s there was talk of a Republican "lock" on the electoral college.

In the wake of the GOP's presidential victory in 1968, many political observers assumed that it would not be long before the party dominated at other levels as well. Population trends seemingly were in their favor—with the ongoing movement from the cities to the suburbs, and from the Frost Belt to the Sun Belt. The Democratic behemoths of the New Deal days—industrial states from Massachusetts to Illinois—were rapidly losing both voters and congressional seats to Republican-trending states in the booming Sun Belt from Florida to California.

Yet Democrats continued to control Congress as well as most of the nation's statehouses. With an assist from Reagan's coattails, Republicans would win the Senate in 1980 for a six-year span, but would not take both houses of Congress until 1994, by which time Democrat Bill Clinton would be in the White House. Democrats also held a majority of the nation's governorships for virtually the entire period from 1968 to 1994.

In previous eras a party's congressional strength often ebbed and flowed with the fortunes of its presidential candidates. After 1968, however, the link between the two was conspicuously weaker. Presidential coattails shortened almost to the point of nonexistence, and congressional politics entered what might be considered a "dead ball" era.

Big partisan swings in Congress became fewer and farther between. From 1932 until 1968, for instance, there were seven elections in which there was a swing of at least forty House seats from one party to the other. Since 1968 there have been only two such elections—the post-Watergate contest of 1974, in which the

Democrats added to their already hefty majorities, and 1994, when the GOP gained control of the House for the first time in forty years.

Altogether, from 1968 to the end of the century, one party controlled both ends of Pennsylvania Avenue for just six of the thirty-two years—the four years of the Carter administration in the late 1970s, and the first two years of the Clinton administration in the early 1990s. For fourteen years, there was a Republican president and a Democratic Congress; for six years, a Democratic president and a Republican Congress. The other six years, there was a Republican president and Senate, but a Democratic House.

"Divided government" became the catchword to describe the unique new political arrangement. It was due, in part, to changes in the country—namely, an increasingly independent electorate that was willing to split their tickets.

It was also due, in part, to changes in the system—with incumbents increasingly able to raise huge sums of money independent of declining party organizations, money that was often plowed into expensive media advertising campaigns that deterred significant competition.

In part, some say, it was due to attitudinal differences between the parties, with the Democrats' more positive attitude toward government enabling the party to find more attractive candidates than the GOP. In part, it was also due to simple bad luck that befell each party. Republican efforts to complete a top-down realignment were first stalled in the mid-1970s by the Watergate crisis and then, in the early 1980s after Reagan's election, by a devastating recession.

Meanwhile, Democrats were hindered by a series of divisive presidential nominating contests in the 1970s and 1980s that left their nominees in a weakened condition, with Democratic congressional candidates keeping their distance from the national ticket. The infighting in Democratic primary campaigns was a product of dramatic changes in their presidential nominating process. After the tumultuous convention in Chicago in 1968, party rules were rewritten to shift control from a cadre of Democratic leaders and elected officials to grassroots voters.

The result was a dramatic growth in presidential primaries, first spread across the calendar from midwinter to late spring, then increasingly concentrated in February and March. Growing from a total of just fifteen in 1968 to more than forty in 1996, the primaries quickly became the preeminent part of the presidential nominating process for both parties.

No candidate since Humphrey has been nominated without first competing in the primaries, and no candidate since Democrat George McGovern in 1972 has been nominated without winning the most primary votes. In the process, the party's summertime convention has been reduced to little more than a giant, made-for-TV pep rally for the party faithful.

Still, the number of voters casting ballots in the presidential primaries has rarely been more than one-third of those participating in the fall election. Through the 1970s and 1980s, the basic tendency was for the Democrats to nominate candidates on the left side of the political spectrum, Republicans on the right. Goldwater had set the tone for the rightward movement of the GOP with a campaign that stressed limited government and strident anticommunism. The conservative movement, however, did not come to full flower until the election of Reagan in 1980.

It was a rare example of presidential coattails in the era of divided government. With Reagan soundly defeating President Carter by 10 percentage points, Republicans picked up a dozen Senate seats to win control of the upper chamber and approached parity in the governorships. The GOP remained a minority in the House, but with the addition of thirty-three House seats they were able to rejuvenate the "conservative coalition"— the decades-old alliance of Republicans and conservative Democrats on Capitol Hill—to give Reagan a number of legislative victories.

One of Reagan's basic themes was the return of power to the states, and during his administration it was popular for many politicians, Republicans in particular, to aim for seats in state legislatures and governorships, rather than to seek a seat in Congress.

The Era of Closeness

For nearly a quarter century after 1968, the basic norm had been a Republican president and a Democratic Congress. In the early 1990s, however, the political equation reversed.

Since Kennedy, every Democrat that had won the presidency has been from the South. In 1992 Democrats captured the White House with an all-southern ticket led by Arkansas Gov. Bill Clinton. With Sen. Al Gore of Tennessee as Clinton's running-mate, the Democratic ticket consciously positioned itself near the political center.

Meanwhile, President Bush was bedeviled on several fronts. His success a year earlier in the Persian Gulf War—where the United States led a coalition of twenty-eight nations in turning back an Iraqi invasion of neighboring Kuwait—was overshadowed by the widespread perception of recession in 1992. Conservative Republicans were restive, upset by a tax hike in the middle of his administration. Texas billionaire H. Ross Perot also mounted a well-financed independent candidacy that aimed much of its fire at Bush and the Republicans.

Clinton won with just 43 percent of the popular vote, but still scored the most sweeping Democratic presidential victory since 1964. He carried thirty-two states, making deep inroads into the suburbs and even rural America. In addition, Democratic majorities in both the Senate and the House accompanied him to Washington.

Yet there were signs in the 1992 vote that the long era of Democratic dominance on Capitol Hill was waning. In the congressional primaries that spring and summer, a postwar record nineteen incumbents were beaten, fourteen of them Democrats. That fall, Democrats lost ten more House seats.

The first two years of the Clinton administration, culminating with an ill-starred attempt to overhaul the national health care system, left the Democrats even more vulnerable. Republicans in 1994 took advantage of that vulnerability with their promises for government reform capsulized in a document

"MINE! MINE! ALL MINE!"

thump

thump

©1994

© 1994 by Herblock

called the "Contract with America." Republicans gained fifty-two seats in the House and eight in the Senate, to win both houses of Congress for the first time since 1952. The GOP posted gains in all parts of the country in 1994, gaining six House seats in Washington state alone, where one of the Democratic casualties was House Speaker Thomas S. Foley. In addition, the number of Republican governors jumped to thirty, the party's highest total in a quarter century.

Yet it was the South, already the cornerstone of the Republican presidential coalition, that was the centerpiece of the party's landslide in 1994. The combination of anti-Clinton sentiment, a plethora of Democratic retirements, and favorable congressional redistricting that eliminated a number of racially marginal Democratic districts finally enabled the Republicans to capture dozens of districts across the South that had been voting Republican for president for decades.

Just as it had been for the Democrats, the South quickly became the GOP's prime building block, both at the presidential and congressional levels. It has not only provided Republicans since 1994 with more congressional seats than any other region, but also many of their leading voices on Capitol Hill—first, Newt Gingrich of Georgia (House speaker from 1995 through 1998), then Trent Lott of Mississippi (Senate majority leader from 1996 until June 2001). In 2000 the South was crucial to the election of Republican Gov. George W. Bush of Texas as presi-

dent. He swept all 163 of the region's electoral votes, 60 percent of his nationwide total.

Yet since 1994 neither party has been able to expand their beachheads into dominance of the political process. The new Republican majority in Congress, led by Gingrich, was widely seen as overplaying its hand, and it has steadily lost seats in every election since 1994. President Clinton, after winning an easy reelection victory in 1996, was impeached in 1998 for lying about his relationship to a White House intern, a personal embarrassment that also discomfited his Democratic allies.

As a result, American politics has grown closer and closer at all levels, culminating in the election of 2000, which became an instant classic because of its almost-impossible-to-resolve closeness. For the first time since 1888, there were different winners in the electoral vote (Republican George W. Bush) and the popular vote (Democrat Al Gore). Bush's margin of five in the electoral vote was the closest since 1876; Gore's margin of barely 500,000 votes in the popular vote was the closest since 1968.

The closeness of the election led to a historic intervention by the U.S. Supreme Court, which by a 5–4 margin halted the recount in Florida, where the national electoral college outcome hung in the balance. The Court's ruling that the manual recount violated voters' civil rights left an uncertain legacy for the U.S. electoral process. *(See "The 2000 Cliffhanger," p. 295; and excerpts from* Bush v. Gore, *p. 1557 in Reference Materials, Vol. II.)*

The 50–50 Senate tie that resulted from the 2000 election was the first partisan tie in the upper chamber since the election of 1880. The postelection breakdown in the House of 221 Republicans, 212 Democrats, and 2 independents was the closest disparity between the two parties in the lower chamber since 1952.

Exit polls showed some of the same partisan divisions within the electorate that had existed for decades. Men favored Bush, women favored Gore (the fabled "gender gap"); whites preferred Bush, nonwhites backed Gore; the more affluent voted strongly for Bush, the less affluent heavily favored Gore; rural and small-town America went for Bush, urban America for Gore.

Several other groups that had broken sharply for one party or the other over much of the previous generation were "swing voters" in the election of 2000. Suburban voters and independents, both Republican-leaning groups in presidential voting in the 1970s and 1980s, split almost evenly between Bush and Gore in 2000. So did Catholics, a cornerstone of the Democratic coalition from 1932 to 1968.

A Tale of Two Nations

Geographically, the vote in 2000 divided the nation into two distinct sectors—a Republican-oriented "L-shaped" sector that included the South, the Plains, and the Mountain states plus Alaska; and a Democratic-oriented bicoastal, industrial heartland sector that was composed of the Northeast, the industrial Midwest, and the Pacific Coast states plus Hawaii.

The Republican "L" was much more rural and geographically expansive, though it did include the heart of the fast-growing Sun Belt. The Democratic bicoastal-industrial sector was more urban and generally slower growing.

Electoral Anomalies

The American political system sometimes produces a result that deviates from what normally would be expected. One such anomaly is the phenomenon of *minority* presidents—the eighteen presidents elected through 2000 without receiving a majority of the Popular Vote. (*See Table 8-3, p. 223.*)

Four of those candidates actually lost the popular vote to their opponents and still won the presidency: John Quincy Adams in 1824, Rutherford B. Hayes in 1876, Benjamin Harrison in 1888, and George W. Bush in 2000.

In Adams's case, the election was thrown to the House of Representatives after he and three other candidates failed to gain the required majority of electoral college votes. Under the Twelfth Amendment, the House had to choose from among the three highest vote-getters. It chose Adams, who had run second to Andrew Jackson in both popular and electoral votes. The third contender, Treasury Secretary William H. Crawford, was paralyzed from a recent stroke. Speaker Henry Clay, who ran fourth and was therefore out of the running, helped swing the House vote to Adams.

Only one other presidential election was decided by the House. That was in 1800 when Thomas Jefferson and his intended vice president, Aaron Burr, tied in the electoral vote before the Twelfth Amendment required separate voting for president and vice president. The House chose Jefferson on the thirty-sixth ballot to succeed John Adams, father of John Quincy Adams, and Burr became vice president.

In 1876 Democrat Samuel J. Tilden outpolled Republican Hayes, but his electoral vote total was one short of a majority, with the votes of three southern states in dispute. To resolve the crisis Congress set up a special fifteen-member commission, which decided the disputed votes in Hayes's favor, giving him a bare majority victory of 185 votes to Tilden's 184. Under a compromise that broke the impasse, Hayes agreed to remove federal troops from the South after he took office, ending the Reconstruction era that had bitterly divided the nation. Southern whites gained domination of Congress, and Republican industrial interests solidified a hold on presidential politics that lasted until Franklin D. Roosevelt was elected in 1932.

Electoral Vote Effect

All other instances of a president's being elected with less than a majority of the popular vote (including Harrison in 1888 and Bush in 2000) were attributable to the electoral college system, which tends to exaggerate narrow victories and permit a minority president to claim something of a mandate to enact the administration's legislative agenda.

In 1888 Republican Harrison trailed Democratic president Grover Cleveland in the popular vote, 48.6 percent to 47.8 percent, with other candidates sharing the 3.6 percent remainder. But by winning New York and other populous states of the North and West, Harrison took 58.1 percent of the electoral vote, a clear majority. Four years later the ousted Cleveland defeated Harrison to become the only president to serve two nonconsecutive terms.

In the election of 2000, Vice President Al Gore, the Democratic candidate, outpolled Republican George W. Bush by approximately 540,000 votes out of more than 105 million cast nationwide. The popular vote count was bitterly contested in Florida for a month following the election. Bush prevailed in Florida and in twenty-nine other states, winning 271 electoral votes; Gore carried twenty states and the District of Columbia, for 267 electoral votes. (Gore was officially credited with 266 electoral votes because a so-called faithless elector in the District of Columbia withheld her vote from Gore to protest the District's lack of voting representation in Congress.)

With his 49.2 percent popular vote reelection victory in 1996, Bill Clinton became only the third president in history to win two terms with less than half of the vote each time. (He won in 1992 with 43.0 percent.) The other two were Cleveland, 1884 and 1892, and Woodrow Wilson, in 1912 and 1916.

An electoral vote anomaly of another sort arose in 1872 when famed newspaper editor Horace Greeley, the Democratic/Liberal Republican presidential candidate, died after losing the election to Ulysses S. Grant. Electors from the six states he won divided their votes among other candidates. Three of the electors voted for Greeley anyway, but Congress did not recognize their votes.

In another unusual circumstance, Vice President James S. Sherman died shortly before the 1912 election that he and President William Howard Taft lost to Woodrow Wilson and Thomas R.

This alignment had been in the making in presidential elections for several decades. From 1968 through 1988, Republicans often won the White House by dominating the "L" so conclusively that they were free to roam at will for votes in the Democrats' domain. In the 1990s Clinton, however, reversed the equation, showing such strong appeal in the bicoastal-industrial midlands that he was free to make forays into the "L," ultimately making the Republican base look like a piece of Swiss cheese.

For many years, the disparity between the two sectors was merely a phenomenon of presidential elections, because Democrats dominated congressional voting across the country. That changed, though, in 1994 when the Republican tidal wave that swept the GOP into control on Capitol Hill came rolling out of the "L." In 1996 Republicans won the presidential and congressional voting within the "L" (albeit the former quite narrowly), while Democrats held the edge in presidential and congressional voting outside the "L" (with the advantage quite large in balloting for the White House).

It was the 2000 election, however, that marked a full coming of age for this "tale of two nations." The "L" was decisively Republican; the rest of the country decisively Democratic. Bush swept all but one state in the "L" (narrowly losing New Mexico).

Marshall. It was too late for Sherman's name to be changed on the ballots in every state, so his electoral votes went to his replacement, Nicholas Murray Butler.

Oddities in Congressional Elections

Congressional elections have produced a number of anomalies, particularly in the South, where slavery, the Civil War, Reconstruction, and racial antagonisms created special problems in the electoral process. The counting of slaves for the apportionment of House seats posed an especially difficult problem.

Under a compromise adopted in the Constitution (Article I, section 2) every five slaves would be counted as three persons. After the Civil War and the emancipation of slaves, the Fourteenth Amendment required that blacks be fully counted for apportionment purposes. On this basis, several southern states tried to claim additional representation on readmission to the Union. Tennessee, for example, elected an extra U.S. representative in 1868, claiming that adding the full slave population entitled the state to nine instead of eight House members. Virginia and South Carolina followed suit. But the House refused to seat the additional representatives, requiring the states to wait for the regular reapportionment after the 1870 census for any changes in their representation.

A formula in the Fourteenth Amendment, designed to coerce southern states to accept black voting participation by reducing House seats wherever voting rights were abridged, never was implemented because of its complexity. Instead, the Republican-controlled House unseated Democrats from districts in former Confederate states where abuses of the right to vote were charged. Between 1881 and 1897, the House unseated eighteen Democrats on this basis.

Another anomaly, of a different sort, arose from the 1930 midterm election, when the beginning of the Great Depression threatened to end the Republicans' seventeen-year domination of the House. On election night in November it appeared that the Republicans had nevertheless retained the House by a narrow margin. The tally showed 218 Republicans elected, against 216 Democrats and one independent. But in those days, before the Twentieth Amendment moved up the convening date, thirteen months elapsed between the election and the convening of the new Congress. During that interval, an unusually large number of deaths (fourteen) occurred among the newly elected representatives.

In special elections to fill the vacancies, several had no effect on the political balance because the same party retained the seat. But in three cases Republicans who died were replaced by Democrats, tipping the balance to the Democrats' favor in time for them to organize the new Congress in December 1931. A fourth Republican vacancy went to the Democrats in early 1932.

When the Seventy-second Congress convened on December 7, 1931, House Democrats held the edge, 219 to 215, with one independent. As the majority, they were able to elect as Speaker John Nance Garner of Texas. In 1932 Garner was elected as Franklin D. Roosevelt's first vice president.

Even without the special election gains, control of the House likely would have passed to the Democrats in 1931. Immediately after the 1930 general election, a group of Farm Belt Republicans announced that they would withhold their votes from veteran Speaker Nicholas Longworth of Ohio and allow the Democrats to organize the House, which they did. The vote for Garner as Speaker was 218 to 207, a margin greater than the three seats the Democrats gained during the preceding thirteen months.

The 1972 House election oddity resulted from the preelection disappearance of two House Democrats, Majority Leader Hale Boggs of Louisiana and Nick Begich of Alaska, during an Alaskan airplane trip. Despite their absence, both were reelected. Boggs's wife, Lindy, was elected to succeed him after he was declared legally dead in 1973. Begich was declared legally dead after the 1972 election, and a special election to replace him was held in 1973.

Similarly, a dead man was elected to the U.S. Senate for the first time in 2000. Running for a Senate seat, Democratic governor Mel Carnahan of Missouri was killed in a airplane crash three weeks before the November election. As it was too late for officials to remove his name from the ballot, Carnahan polled 50.5 percent of the vote to defeat Republican incumbent John Ashcroft. Although some in his party thought Ashcroft could make a strong case in challenging the result, Ashcroft did not. Democrat Roger B. Wilson, who succeeded to the office of Missouri governor, appointed Carnahan's widow, Jean, to the seat until a special election could be held in 2002. Alongside this Senate oddity was another unique occurrence in 2000: Hillary Rodham Clinton became the first first lady to win elective office when she captured a New York Senate seat.

Gore won nineteen of twenty-four states in the bicoastal-industrial midlands. Bush enjoyed a huge 218-to-5 electoral-vote lead in the Republican sector of the country. Gore posted a 261-to-53 advantage in the Democratic sector (with the one "faithless" Democratic elector from the District of Columbia). Bush won the South, Plains states, and Mountain West by a margin of 5.3 million in the popular vote. Gore won the Northeast, industrial Midwest, and Pacific West by more than 5.8 million votes.

Republicans won forty-four more House seats within the "L" than the Democrats. Democrats won thirty-five more House seats than the Republicans in the rest of the country. Republi-

cans finished the election holding eighteen more Senate seats than the Democrats inside the "L." Elsewhere, Democrats held eighteen more Senate seats than the Republicans, including that of First Lady Hillary Rodham Clinton, who in 2000 handily won an open Senate seat in New York. In short, add the two sectors together, and there was roughly a dead heat in balloting up and down the ticket.

Ironically, Republicans ended up controlling both ends of Pennsylvania Avenue for the first time since 1952, even though the Democrats in 2000 had won more votes for president, the Senate, and in contested races for the House of Representatives.

George Washington set many precedents during his two terms, often consciously so. Here, he delivers his inaugural address, in April 1789.

The political landscape, however, is always changing, and one era—sometimes swiftly, sometimes slowly—is always evolving into another. In the spring of 2001, the short-lived era of Republican dominance ended abruptly when Vermont's Senator Jeffords changed his party affiliation from Republican to Independent, giving control of the Senate to the Democrats.

Historic Milestones in U.S. Elections

The following chronology lists the historic events in more than 210 years of U.S. elections.

1787

The "Great Compromise" at the Constitutional Convention in Philadelphia pacifies the smaller states by giving each state two senators and a House delegation based on population, assuring even the smallest state at least three votes in Congress (and in the electoral college). Senators are to be elected by the state legislatures (changed in 1913 to popular vote election by the Seventeenth Amendment) for six-year terms. Representatives are to be popularly elected to two-year terms.

1789

George Washington wins the first U.S. presidential election on February 4. The election is tantamount to unanimous as Washington receives the maximum possible number of electoral votes, sixty-nine. John Adams, second with thirty-four votes, wins the vice presidency. Washington is inaugurated on April 30 in New York City.

1800

Thomas Jefferson and Aaron Burr tie in electoral votes for the presidency. The election devolves to the House of Representatives, which elects Jefferson. The unforeseen possibility of a tie

vote leads to adoption of the Twelfth Amendment to the Constitution (1804), requiring separate electoral college voting for president and vice president.

1807

Jefferson formalizes Washington's two-term precedent for presidents. Jefferson sets forth his reasons in a December 10 letter to the Vermont state legislature, which had asked him to run for a third term. Seven other states sent similar letters.

1824

"King Caucus" dies, ending the decades-long system of presidential candidate selection by congressional party caucuses. State legislatures nominate four candidates representing different factions of the Democratic-Republican Party. Andrew Jackson of Tennessee wins the popular vote but falls short of the required electoral vote majority, throwing the election to the House for the second time in U.S. history. The House elects John Quincy Adams of Massachusetts, who placed second in both the electoral and popular vote. Jackson's loss leads to his election in 1828 and formation of the present-day Democratic Party.

1831

The first national party conventions are held in Baltimore. The Anti-Masons nominate William Wirt in September and the National Republicans nominate Henry Clay in December. Both lose to President Andrew Jackson in 1832.

1832

The Democrats hold their first national convention, also in Baltimore, and adopt a two-thirds rule for presidential nomination. Jackson is nominated for reelection by the required two-thirds majority vote.

1837

For the first and only time, the Senate decides a vice-presidential election as the Constitution provides. Democrat Martin Van Buren's running mate, Richard M. Johnson, falls one vote short of the required majority because Virginia electors object to his moral character. The Senate nevertheless votes along party lines (33–16) to elect Johnson.

1840

Van Buren and Johnson become the first sitting president and vice president defeated for reelection. They lose to Whigs William Henry Harrison and John Tyler. Harrison dies April 4, 1841, after just one month in office, and Tyler establishes the precedent for the vice president's becoming president rather than just the "acting president."

1844

The Democrats nominate the first "dark horse" presidential candidate, James K. Polk, who wins the election.

1854

Antislavery sympathizers opposed to the expansion of slavery into the western territories gather at Ripon, Wisconsin, and form the Republican Party. With the Whigs torn over the slavery issue, the Republicans soon emerge as the Democrats' counterpart in the nation's two-party system.

1856

Democrat Franklin Pierce becomes the only elected president denied renomination by his own party. He had alienated fellow Northerners by signing legislation that made the Kansas territory a bloody battleground over the slavery issue. James Buchanan wins the nomination and the presidency.

1860

The new Republican Party elects its first president, Abraham Lincoln, and the divided nation advances toward Civil War. The election is the last in which at least one state (South Carolina) has no popular voting for president. (South Carolina allows popular voting after the war, when it and other former Confederate states resume participation in presidential elections.)

1865

Abraham Lincoln is assassinated six weeks after beginning his second term. He dies on April 15 after being shot the night before by John Wilkes Booth. Vice President Andrew Johnson succeeds to the presidency and immediately comes in conflict with the radical northern Republicans who plan harsh postwar treatment of the rebel states. The Radical Republicans gain control of Congress in the 1866 midterm elections and later impeach Johnson, who narrowly escapes conviction.

1870

The Fifteenth Amendment, enfranchising newly freed slaves, is ratified on February 3. The first blacks are elected to Congress: Republican Hiram R. Revels of Mississippi serves in the Senate from 1870 to 1871. Mississippi Republican Blanche K. Bruce is elected to the Senate in 1874 and is the first black member to serve a full term in that chamber.

1874

The donkey and elephant emerge as symbols of the Democratic and Republican parties after drawings by Thomas Nast. They are important as guides to illiterate and semiliterate voters and are a boon to editorial cartoonists.

1876

A special commission decides a contested presidential election for the first and only time. Democrat Samuel J. Tilden wins the popular vote against Republican Rutherford B. Hayes, but the electoral vote outcome hangs on a single vote, with votes of three southern states in dispute. Congress appoints a commission that reaches a compromise on March 2, 1877, and awards the vote to Hayes, 185–184, in return for his pledge to remove federal troops from the South.

Romualdo Pacheco, California Republican, is the first Hispanic elected to Congress.

1881

On July 2, near the beginning of his term, President James A. Garfield is shot by Charles J. Guiteau in Washington, D.C. The bullet lodges near Garfield's spine and he dies on September 19. He is succeeded by Vice President Chester A. Arthur, who fails to win the Republican nomination in 1884.

1887

Congress enacts the Electoral Count Act, which charges states with resolving future electoral vote disputes similar to the one that followed the Tilden-Hayes contest in 1876.

1888

Benjamin Harrison becomes the third president elected without winning the popular vote. He defeats incumbent Democrat Grover Cleveland with 233 electoral votes to Cleveland's 168.

1892

A mechanical voting machine built by Jacob H. Myers is used for the first time at Lockport, New York. Inventor Thomas A. Edison had received his first patent for a similar machine twenty-three years earlier.

1901

The first presidential primary law is passed in Florida. The primary gets its biggest impetus when the 1904 Republican convention refuses seating to backers of Wisconsin governor Robert M. La Follette, leader of the GOP's Progressive wing. In 1905 La Follette successfully promotes legislation in his state that provides for primary election of delegates to national party conventions.

Six months after his inauguration, President William McKinley is shot in Buffalo, New York, by Leon Czolgosz, an anarchist disturbed by social injustice. The president dies a week later, on September 14, and is succeeded by Vice President Theodore Roosevelt. In 1904 Roosevelt is elected to a full four-year term.

1912

Former president Theodore Roosevelt deserts the Republican Party to run on his own Progressive "Bull Moose" ticket. He attains the highest third-party vote in history, but the GOP split helps to elect Democrat Woodrow Wilson.

1913

Popular election of senators becomes the norm when the Seventeenth Amendment is ratified, replacing election by state legislatures. Some states instituted popular election of senators before it became mandatory, beginning with the 1914 midterm elections.

1916

The first woman, Jeannette Rankin, Montana Republican, is elected to the U.S. House, four years before the Nineteenth Amendment ensures women's suffrage in all states. During her two terms (1917–1919 and 1941–1943) Rankin becomes the only member of Congress to vote against both World Wars.

1918

Socialist Party leader Eugene V. Debs is sentenced to ten years in prison for his antiwar statements. He nevertheless receives almost a million votes in 1920, his last election. President Warren G. Harding frees him in 1921.

1920

The Nineteenth Amendment, giving full voting rights to women, is ratified on August 26. Some states allowed women to vote as early as 1890 (Wyoming).

1923

Harding dies in office August 2. Calvin Coolidge becomes president.

1924

The first women governors are elected: Miriam "Ma" Ferguson in Texas and Nellie Tayloe Ross in Wyoming. Both succeed their husbands.

1928

The first Roman Catholic, New York governor Alfred E. Smith, is nominated for president on a major party ticket (Democratic). The urbanite Smith favors repeal of Prohibition, opposes the Ku Klux Klan, and is an unabashed liberal—all considered "alien traits" by much of the still rural, dry United States. He loses to Republican Herbert C. Hoover.

1932

In Chicago, Democrat Franklin D. Roosevelt becomes the first major party candidate to accept the presidential nomina-

The first woman to serve in Congress, Jeannette Rankin entered Congress in 1917, four years before ratification of the Nineteenth Amendment guaranteeing women the right to vote.

tion in person. He promises a "new deal" for the American people. The Democrats win control of the White House and Congress as the nation battles the Great Depression, the worst in U.S. history. Roosevelt's first three and a half months in office produce an unprecedented flood of economic legislation and establish the "hundred-day" yardstick for measuring the initial success of future presidents.

1934

The second session of the Seventy-third Congress meets for the first time on January 3 in accordance with the Twentieth Amendment (the so-called Lame Duck Amendment) to the Constitution. The amendment, ratified in 1933, also fixes January 20 as the beginning of each four-year presidential term, effective in 1937.

1936

At their convention, Democrats abolish the two-thirds majority rule for presidential or vice-presidential nomination, which previously resulted in protracted balloting. The South objects because the rule gives the region virtual veto power over any nominee. To make up for the loss, the South is given more votes at later conventions.

1940

President Roosevelt breaks the traditional two-term limit for presidents when he is elected for a third term. His popular margin of victory narrows from four years earlier, however, in part because some voters object to his disregard of the unwritten "no-third-term" rule.

The Republicans hold the first televised national convention, in Philadelphia.

1944

The Supreme Court in *Smith v. Allwright* outlaws so-called white primaries. Previously, political parties as "private" organizations, particularly in the South, were permitted to exclude blacks from membership and participation.

1945

Roosevelt dies in office April 12 and is succeeded by Harry S. Truman.

1948

President Truman fools the pollsters and defeats his Republican challenger, Thomas E. Dewey. The upset produces a historic photo of Truman gleefully holding up the erroneous *Chicago Daily Tribune* banner headline, "Dewey Defeats Truman."

1951

The Twenty-second Amendment, setting a two-term limit for presidents, is ratified February 27. The law excludes Truman, who became president in 1945 on Roosevelt's death and was elected in his own right in 1948, but Truman declines to seek another full term in 1952.

1952

In danger of being dumped as Dwight D. Eisenhower's running mate for ethical lapses, Richard Nixon saves himself with an emotional address to the nation September 23. It becomes known as the "Checkers speech" because Nixon refers to a little gift dog he refuses to give up.

1954

Strom Thurmond of South Carolina becomes the only senator ever elected by write-in vote.

1958

Hiram L. Fong, Hawaii Republican, is elected senator, making him the first Asian American member of Congress.

1960

The first debate between presidential candidates, Democrat John F. Kennedy and Republican Richard Nixon, is televised in Chicago, Illinois, on September 26. The 1960 general election is the first in which television is the dominant national news medium. With a narrow victory over Nixon, Kennedy becomes the first Catholic president.

1961

Ratification of the Twenty-third Amendment on March 29 gives District of Columbia residents the right to vote in presidential elections.

1962

The Supreme Court in *Baker v. Carr* permits federal court suits to require reapportionment and redistricting of state legislative districts that violate the principle of one person, one vote. The Court later extends the requirement to congressional districts.

1963

Gray v. Sanders, the first major one-person, one-vote Supreme Court decision, is handed down on March 18. The Court rules that Georgia's "county unit" system of electing officers to state posts violates the equal protection guarantee of the Fourteenth Amendment by giving more weight to the votes of persons in rural counties than in urban counties.

President Kennedy is assassinated by Lee Harvey Oswald in Dallas, Texas, on November 22. He is succeeded by Vice President Lyndon B. Johnson, a former Senate majority leader who wins approval of much of Kennedy's "New Frontier" legislative program.

1964

The Twenty-fourth Amendment is ratified on February 4, abolishing the poll tax as a requisite to voting in primary or general elections for president and other federal officials. The controversial tax had often been a bar to voting, especially among poor blacks.

The *Wesberry v. Sanders* decision is handed down by the Supreme Court on February 17, extending the one-person, one-vote doctrine to congressional districts. The Court rules that substantial disparity in a state's district populations results in unequal representation in the U.S. House. Congressional districts should be as nearly equal in population "as is practicable."

1964

Lyndon Johnson scores the largest popular vote landslide in history, taking 61.1 percent of the vote to Barry Goldwater's 38.5 percent. LBJ's margin surpasses Franklin Roosevelt's 60.8–36.5 victory over Alfred M. Landon in 1936.

1964-1965

Congress passes the Civil Rights Act of 1964, which prohibits discrimination in employment, public accommodations, and federally funded programs. Passage helps pave the way for the Voting Rights Act of 1965, which provides protections for African Americans wishing to vote.

1967

The Twenty-fifth Amendment, ratified February 10, sets procedure in case of presidential disability or vacancy in the office of vice president.

1968

Urban riots break out in response to the April 4 assassination of civil rights leader Martin Luther King Jr. in Memphis.

Widespread opposition to the Vietnam War prompts President Johnson to decline renomination. Robert F. Kennedy, a leading candidate for the nomination, is assassinated in Los Angeles by Sirhan Sirhan on June 6. Riotous protests against the candidacy of Johnson's handpicked successor, Hubert H. Humphrey, mar the Democratic convention at Chicago and the party split helps to elect Republican Richard Nixon. At their convention the Democrats drop the controversial unit rule allowing convention delegations to vote as a whole despite minority objections. (The Republican Party never used the unit rule.)

In 1968 congressional elections, New York Democrat Shirley Chisholm becomes the first black woman elected to the U.S. House.

1969

Powell v. McCormack, the landmark Supreme Court decision handed down on June 16, prohibits the House of Representatives from adding to the constitutional qualifications for House membership. The Court rules that the House lacked the authority to exclude a duly elected representative who met the constitutional qualifications of age, residence, and citizenship. The decision reinstates Adam Clayton Powell, New York Democrat, who was excluded for misconduct and misuse of public funds.

1971

The Twenty-sixth Amendment lowers the voting age to eighteen nationally. Ratification takes only 107 days, less than half the time required for any other constitutional amendment. It is spurred by an unusually large number of young people in the population, together with the Vietnam War, where eighteen-year-olds can be conscripted into the army.

Congress passes the Federal Election Campaign Act of 1971, which creates the Federal Election Commission, limits spending for political advertising by candidates for federal office, and requires full disclosure of campaign contributions and expenditures. Major amendments are enacted in 1974 and 1976. The spending limits are later (in 1976) found unconstitutional except for presidential candidates who accept public financing of their campaigns.

1972

Alabama governor George C. Wallace is shot May 15 at a Laurel, Maryland, shopping center while campaigning for the Democratic presidential nomination. Partially paralyzed, he withdraws as a candidate.

President Richard Nixon easily wins the election that culminates in the first presidential resignation. A preelection burglary at the Democratic National Committee headquarters in Washington's Watergate Hotel is traced to Republican operatives. Investigation discloses Nixon's active role in the subsequent attempted coverup.

The Democrats adopt McGovern-Fraser Commission proposals opening the party to more participation by women and minorities. The commission's guidelines are designed to counteract rules and practices that inhibited access to the states' delegate-selection process or diluted the influence of those who had access.

1973

Vice President Spiro T. Agnew resigns on October 10 as part of a plea bargain with federal prosecutors. Agnew faced trial on corruption charges from his years as governor of Maryland. In the first use of the Twenty-fifth Amendment (1967) to fill a vacancy in the vice presidency, President Nixon nominates Gerald R. Ford, who wins confirmation by Congress.

1974

Facing near-certain impeachment in the Watergate scandal, President Nixon resigns August 9 and is succeeded by Vice President Ford. Ford is the first president to take office without being elected by the electoral college as vice president or president.

1976

In *Buckley v. Valeo,* the Supreme Court sanctions public financing of presidential elections but bars spending limits for candidates who reject federal funding.

The first debate of vice-presidential candidates, Democrat Walter F. Mondale and Republican Robert Dole, is televised October 15 in Houston, Texas.

1981

The Iranian hostage crisis that plagued the presidency of Jimmy Carter ends January 20 when the Americans held hostage for 444 days are freed as Ronald Reagan becomes president. Reagan is wounded in an assassination attempt March 30 outside a Washington hotel.

1984

Democratic presidential nominee Mondale chooses Geraldine Ferraro of New York as his running mate. Ferraro, a three-term House member, becomes the first woman nominated on a major party presidential ticket.

1988

Republican George Bush defeats Democrat Michael S. Dukakis to become the first sitting vice president since Martin Van Buren (in 1836) to win the presidency.

1989

Virginia elects the first African American governor, L. Douglas Wilder, Democrat.

1990

Kansas elects Gov. Joan Finney, Democrat, making it the first state to have a woman governor, senator (Nancy Landon Kassebaum, Republican), and House member (Jan Meyers, Republican) at the same time.

1992

Bush, also like Van Buren, is defeated after a single term in office. Texas billionaire Ross Perot mounts the strongest-ever individual presidential campaign and receives 18.9 percent of the popular vote as an independent. Perot's candidacy splits the GOP vote. Democrat Bill Clinton is elected despite Gennifer Flowers's claim that she had been Clinton's mistress in his early years as governor of Arkansas.

Carol Moseley-Braun of Illinois wins election as the first black woman U.S. senator. California becomes the first state to have two woman senators, Barbara Boxer and Dianne Feinstein.

In the 1990s candidates began using the Internet as another means of connecting to the voters. One survey at the end of the decade found that some 8.5 million voters found Internet information influenced their vote.

1994

In a midterm setback to the Democratic administration of President Clinton, the Republican Party wins control of both chambers of Congress for the first time in forty years. The House GOP strategy engineered by Newt Gingrich of Georgia centers on his proposed "Contract with America." The House elects Gingrich as Speaker.

1995

Ruling in an Arkansas case, *U.S. Term Limits Inc. v. Thornton,* the Supreme Court on May 22 strikes down state attempts to impose term limits on House and Senate members. Only a constitutional amendment can change the qualifications for service in Congress, the Court rules.

1996

President Clinton is the first Democrat elected to a second full term since Franklin Roosevelt in 1936. Newt Gingrich of Georgia is the first Republican reelected as Speaker of the House in sixty-eight years.

The election results are subtly historic. Only 10 years out of 140 has the country had a Democratic president and Republican Congress. The election also clearly establishes the South as the GOP's new bastion. With the Plains and Rocky Mountain states, half the country is strongly Republican. The other half, made up of the Northeast, Midwest, and Pacific Coast states, is strongly Democratic. In 1996 some states, notably Oregon, conduct the first experiments with elections by mail, other than those associated with absentee voting.

Washington state elects the first Asian governor, Democrat Gary Locke, a Chinese American.

1998

The nation is stunned in January by revelation of a sex scandal that threatens the Clinton presidency. Clinton is accused of having an affair in 1995–1997 with Monica S. Lewinsky, then a twenty-one-year-old White House intern. Clinton at first denies the allegations, both to the news media and under oath in court depositions, then later admits to having sexual relations with Lewinsky. After receiving independent counsel Kenneth W. Starr's report to Congress the House impeaches Clinton December 19 on charges of perjury and obstruction of justice.

1999

Voting February 12 largely along party lines, the Senate acquits Clinton on both impeachment charges. With a two-thirds majority (67 votes) needed for conviction, neither article receives even a simple majority (51 votes). The historic Senate trial, with Chief Justice William H. Rehnquist presiding, includes excerpts from Monica Lewinsky's videotaped deposition as a witness.

2000

For the first time, the Supreme Court in effect settles a disputed presidential election. Voting 5–4 in *Bush v. Gore,* the

Court ends Al Gore's thirty-six-day challenge to George W. Bush's narrow popular vote victory in Florida. The Court rules that to continue the hand count of punch-card ballots without uniform standards would deny Bush equal protection of the laws. The action gives Bush 271 electoral votes, one more than needed to win. It also gives the country its second father-son presidential pair, matching John Adams in 1796 and his son John Quincy Adams in 1824. Bush's father, George H. W. Bush, was elected president in 1988.

The 2000 election is the fourth in which the popular vote winner loses the election. Gore receives 48.38 percent of the popular vote to Bush's 47.87 percent.

Gore's running mate, Joseph I. Lieberman of Connecticut, is the first Jew to run on a major party ticket.

Hillary Rodham Clinton wins a New York Senate seat, becoming the first presidential wife elected to public office.

2001

The Senate, evenly split between the two major parties at 50–50, enters into a historic power-sharing arrangement. Although it remains under GOP control by virtue of Vice President Richard Cheney's role of breaking tie votes as presiding Senate officer, the Democrats gain equal seats on committees, equal funding, and other powers previously given only to the party in majority. The rare arrangement is short-lived, however, as Sen. James Jeffords of Vermont, a moderate, bolts the Republican Party to become an Independent in June 2001, giving control of the Senate to the Democrats for the first time since 1994.

CHAPTER 2

Elections: An Expanding Franchise

EW ELEMENTS OF THE AMERICAN POLITICAL SYSTEM have changed so markedly over the years as has the electorate. Since the early days of the nation, when the voting privilege was limited to the upper economic classes, one voting barrier after another has fallen to pressures for wider suffrage. First, men who did not own property, then women, then African Americans, and finally young people obtained the franchise. By the early 1970s virtually every adult citizen eighteen and older had won the right to vote.

But by the elections of 2000 only about half of those eligible to vote were exercising that right in high-profile presidential elections and barely one-third of those eligible were bothering to vote in midterm congressional elections. The comparatively low turnout led some observers to speculate that people stayed away from the polls because they were disillusioned with the political process. Others said concern about low turnout was overblown.

Broadening the Franchise

During the nation's first decades, all thirteen of the original states restricted voting to adult male property holders and taxpayers. The framers of the Constitution apparently were content to continue this time-honored practice. The Constitutional Convention adopted without dissent the recommendation of its Committee of Detail that qualifications for the electors of the House of Representatives "shall be the same . . . as those of the electors in the several states of the most numerous branch of their own legislatures."[1]

Under this provision fewer than half of the adult white men in the United States were eligible to vote in federal elections. With most women and indentured servants disqualified, fewer than one of every four white adults could cast a ballot. Slaves also were ineligible to vote, although freed slaves could vote in some states if they met whatever other qualifications the state placed on its voters.

Those practices actually represented a liberalization of restrictions on voting that had prevailed at one time in the colonial period. Roman Catholics had been disenfranchised in almost every colony; Jews in most colonies; Quakers and Baptists in some. Not until 1842 did Rhode Island permit Jews to vote.

Voting for president and U.S. senators was even more constricted. The Founding Fathers who wrote the Constitution were wary of direct election by the masses. As a result, they provided for indirect election of the president by what would later be known as the electoral college. Electors in the states would vote for president but the method of selecting the electors was left to the states. In the early elections most electors were chosen by state legislatures, but after the first three elections (1789, 1792,

and 1796) popular vote increasingly became the preferred method. By 1824 only six of the twenty-four states still used legislative appointment. Senators were chosen by state legislatures for a much longer time, until 1913 when a constitutional amendment required their selection by popular vote also.

For half a century before the Civil War, the electorate was steadily broadened. The new western settlements supplied a stimulus for allowing all men to vote, and Jacksonian democracy—named for President Andrew Jackson who became associated with enlarging the franchise—encouraged its acceptance. Gradually, seven states that had limited voting strictly to men who owned property substituted a taxpaying qualification, and by the middle of the century most states had removed even that requirement.

The Fourteenth Amendment, ratified in 1868, made everyone born or naturalized in the United States a citizen and directed Congress to reduce the number of representatives from any state that disenfranchised adult male citizens for any reason other than commission of a crime. Although no such reduction was ever made, that amendment—together with the Fifteenth Amendment, which said that the right to vote could not be denied on the basis of "race, color, or previous condition of servitude"—legally opened the polling booths to black men.

Former slaves did vote in the years immediately following the Civil War, but by the turn of the century, most southern states had in place laws and election practices that effectively barred blacks from voting. Not until passage of the Voting Rights Act of 1965 would the promise held out by the Fifteenth Amendment begin to be fulfilled.

Women fought for nearly ninety years to win their right to vote; success came with ratification of the Nineteenth Amendment in 1920. Residents of the District of Columbia were given the right to vote in presidential elections with ratification of the Twenty-third Amendment in 1961. And in 1970 Congress authorized residents of the nation's capital to elect a nonvoting delegate to the House of Representatives.

In 1971 the Twenty-sixth Amendment lowered the voting age to eighteen for federal, state, and local elections. A Supreme Court ruling in 1972 effectively required states to reduce the time citizens had to be a resident to be eligible to vote; no state now requires more than a thirty-day residency. By the end of the century, only insanity, a felony conviction, or failure to meet a residency requirement barred voting-age citizens from going to the polls.

TURNOUT TRENDS

Most significant liberalizations of election law have resulted in a sharp increase in voting. From 1824 to 1856, a period of

Figure 2-1 Voter Turnout, 1789–2000

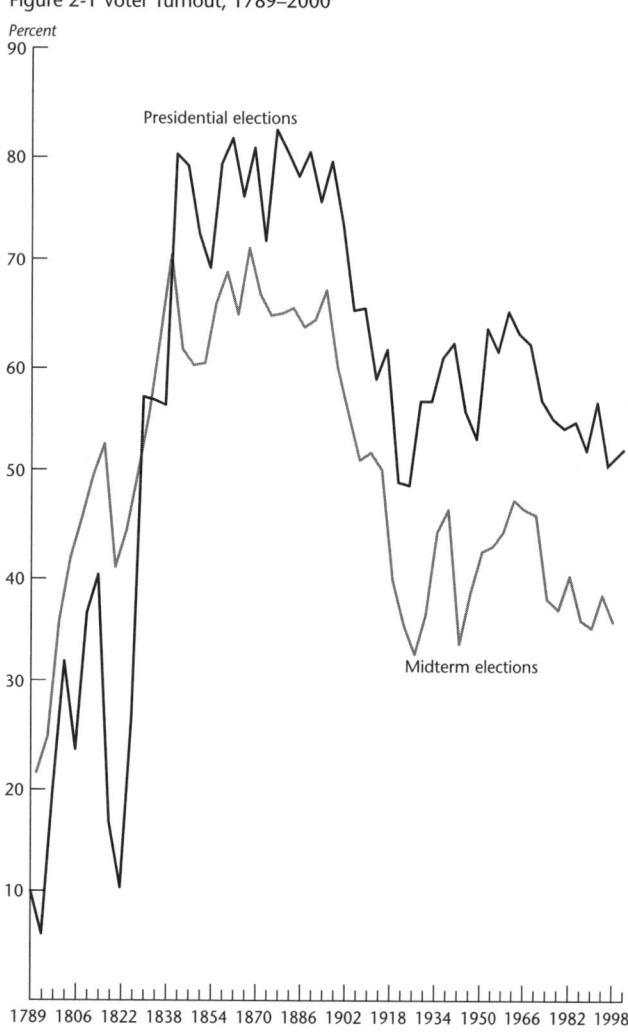

Source: Harold W. Stanley and Richard G. Niemi, *Vital Statistics on American Politics,* 8th ed. (Washington, D.C.: CQ Press, 2001).

gradual relaxation in the states' property and taxpaying qualifications for voting, voter participation in presidential elections increased from 3.8 percent to 16.7 percent of the population. In 1920, when the Nineteenth Amendment gave women the franchise, it rose to 25.1 percent.

Between 1932 and 1976 both the voting-age population and the number of voters in presidential elections roughly doubled. Except for the 1948 presidential election, when barely half the people of voting age went to the polls, the turnout in the postwar years through 1968 was approximately 60 percent, according to Census Bureau surveys. This relatively high figure was attributed to a high sense of civic duty that permeated American society in the immediate postwar years, a population more rooted than it was to be later in the century, and to new civil rights laws encouraging blacks to vote.

Despite larger numbers of people voting, the rate of voter participation slumped after 1968. In that year's presidential election, 61 percent of the voting-age population went to the polls. Through successive stages, that mark fell to 51.2 percent in 2000,

up slightly from the 1996 election where it fell below 50 percent, the lowest level of voter turnout since 1924.

The number of registered voters nationwide at any given time is impossible to calculate. States have different registration deadlines; people who move may be registered in more than one state at the same time, or temporarily may not be recorded in any state; and some states do not require preregistration before voting, while others do not require towns and municipalities to keep registration records.

The famous postwar baby boom, together with a lower voting age, had produced by the early 1970s a disproportionate number of young voters—voters who are the least likely to vote. In the 1972 presidential election, the first in which eighteen-year-olds could vote nationwide, some eleven million young voters entered the electorate. But the actual number of voting participants was only 4.4 million greater than in 1968, resulting in a five-point drop in the ratio of eligible to actual voters.

Voting participation continued on a general downward course throughout the rest of the century even as the baby boomers grew older. There were a few upticks in turnout in both the 1980s and 1990s, most notably in the election of 1992—when the excitement of the nation's first baby-boom ticket (Democrats Bill Clinton and Al Gore), a well-financed independent candidate (H. Ross Perot), and the widespread perception of recession—pushed the turnout above 100 million for the first time in the nation's history. The turnout again waned throughout the 1990s, with the presidential election of 1996 and the midterm congressional contests of 1998 posting the lowest turnout rates for elections of their type since the end of World War II. However, the 2000 presidential elections—the most closely contested in the nation's history—drew 105.4 million voters.

Many reasons for the declining turnouts have been offered. Mark Mellman, a Democratic campaign consultant, has been among those who said they have detected public cynicism about the political process. "There's a sense that the political system is out of their control on the one hand and not responsive on the other," Mellman has said. Campaigns that once thrived at the grassroots level—with storefront political headquarters manned by volunteers and stocked with buttons and stickers—were being waged through the more impersonal medium of television.

But another school of thought has contended that low turnout might be overrated as an indicator of voter apathy and cynicism. As expressed by Richard Scammon, former director of the U.S. Bureau of the Census: "Peace and prosperity can generally operate to keep the vote down. . . . In a sense, a low voter turnout is consent. A pool of disinterest may be valuable for a democracy."[2]

One question frequently asked is that if everyone voted would the results be different. In a paper that they wrote in 1998, two University of California political scientists, Benjamin Highton and Raymond E. Wolfinger, answered: probably not. "The two most common demographic features of nonvoters are their residential mobility and youth, two characteristics that do not suggest political distinctiveness," they wrote. "To be sure, the

Table 2-1
The Nation's Voters, 1980–1998
(Percentages of voting-age Americans who said they had voted)

	Presidential election years						Congressional election years				
	1980	1984	1988	1992	1996		1982	1986	1990	1994	1998
Race/ethnicity											
White	61	61	59	64	56		50	47	47	47	43
Black	51	56	52	54	51		43	43	39	37	40
Hispanic	30	33	29	29	27		25	24	21	20	20
Gender											
Male	59	59	56	60	53		49	46	45	45	41
Female	59	61	58	58	56		48	46	45	45	42
Region											
Northeast	59	60	57	61	55		50	44	45	46	41
Midwest	66	66	63	67	59		55	50	49	49	47
South	56	57	55	59	52		42	43	42	41	39
West	57	59	56	59	52		51	48	45	47	42
Age											
18–20	36	37	33	39	31		20	19	18	17	14
21–24	43	44	38	46	33		28	24	22	22	19
25–44	59	58	54	58	49		45	41	41	39	35
45–64	69	70	68	70	64		62	59	56	57	54
65 and older	65	68	69	70	67		60	61	60	61	60
Employment											
Employed	62	62	58	64	55		50	46	45	45	41
Unemployed	41	44	39	46	37		34	31	28	28	28
Not in labor force	57	59	57	59	54		49	48	47	45	44
Education											
8 years or less	43	43	37	35	30		36	33	28	23	24
1–3 years high school	46	44	41	41	34		38	34	31	27	25
4 years high school	59	59	55	58	49		47	44	42	40	37
1–3 years college	67	68	65	69	61		53	50	50	49	46
4 or more years college	80	79	78	81	73		67	63	63	63	57
Total	59	60	57	61	54		49	46	45	45	42

Source: U.S. Bureau of the Census, Current Population Reports on voting and registration in general elections, 1980–1998.

poor, less educated, and minorities are overrepresented among nonvoters. But the young and the transient are even more numerous. . . . What our findings have demonstrated is that the "party of nonvoters" is truly heterogeneous. Taken as a whole, nonvoters appear well represented by those who vote."[3]

Nonetheless, studies by the Census Bureau have shown marked differences in participation among various classes of voters. Older voters tend to vote at a higher rate than younger voters. Well-educated voters tend to vote at a higher rate than those less educated. Whites tend to vote at a higher rate than blacks and Hispanics. *(See Table 2-1, this page.)*

GROWTH OF INDEPENDENTS

Although more people identify themselves as Democrats than Republicans, there has been a steady rise over the last half century in voters who do not identify with either party. A Washington Post–ABC News poll released in April 2001 found that 34 percent of the American voters considered themselves Democrats, 26 percent Republicans, and 40 percent independents.[4]

Other polls show the independent strain strongest among white, young, northern, and rural voters.

Yet when it comes to the act of voter registration, most voters still sign up with one of the two major parties, at least that is the case in the twenty-seven states (and the District of Columbia) where there is such a choice to be made. According to a compilation by the political newsletter *Ballot Access News* in late 2000, Democrats had the registration advantage in thirteen states plus the District of Columbia (a total that included the four most populous states where voters can register by party—California, Florida, New York, and Pennsylvania). Republicans led in seven states (all in the Plains or Rocky Mountain region), and independents had the edge in seven states, five of them in the Northeast (Connecticut, Maine, Massachusetts, New Hampshire, and New Jersey). Overall, Democrats led in registration with 43.8 percent of the total. Republicans had 32.8 percent and independents and miscellaneous categories accounted for 21.6 percent. None of the operating third parties in 2000 had more than 0.4 percent.

The Black Vote: A Long, Painful Struggle

In no period of U.S. history were all African Americans excluded from the polls. At the time of the Constitutional Convention free blacks had the right of suffrage in all the original states except Georgia, South Carolina, and Virginia. Their right to vote stemmed from the fact that the first black people were brought to America not as slaves but as indentured servants, who could expect freedom after a fixed number of years' service to a master. By 1800, however, the majority of black people were held in slavery. As it grew, so did disenfranchisement. At the outbreak of the Civil War, black Americans were disfranchised, solely on the basis of their race, in all except six of the thirty-three states.

President Abraham Lincoln's Emancipation Proclamation of 1863 freed the slaves but did not accord them voting rights. To ease the impact of change on the South, Lincoln preferred to move cautiously in expanding the black electorate. After the Civil War several Southern states promptly enacted "Black Codes" barring the newly liberated slaves from voting or holding office. Radical Republicans in Congress responded by passing the Reconstruction Act of 1867, which established provisional military governments in the Southern states. The return of civilian control was conditioned on their ratification of the Fourteenth Amendment, which buttressed individual liberty with "due process" and "equal protection" under the law. The amendment's second section threatened to reduce any state's representation in Congress for denying the vote to any male citizen twenty-one years of age or older.

The Reconstruction Act further stated that a secessionist state could not be readmitted to the Union unless it extended the franchise to all adult males, white and black. Congress followed in February 1869 by submitting the Fifteenth Amendment, prohibiting racial discrimination in voting, to the states. It was ratified twelve months later.

The Radical Republican majority in Congress feared that unless blacks were allowed to vote, Democrats and ex-rebels would quickly regain control of the national government. In the presidential election of 1868, in fact, Gen. Ulysses S. Grant defeated his Democratic opponent, Horatio Seymour, by fewer than 305,000 votes; the new black vote probably decided the election.

Former slaves obtained important positions in the governments formed under the Reconstruction Act of 1867. P. B. S. Pinchback served briefly as acting governor of Louisiana; Mississippi, South Carolina, and Louisiana had black lieutenant governors. Between 1870 and 1900, southern states sent twenty-two African Americans to Congress—two of them, Hiram R. Revels and Blanche Kelso Bruce represented Mississippi as senators. Bruce served a full six-year term (1875–1881) and was a presiding officer of the Republican National Convention of 1880.

The white South did not yield gracefully to this turn of events. Gunnar Myrdal noted in his landmark study of black people in America, *An American Dilemma*, that: "The Fourteenth and Fifteenth Amendments were . . . looked upon as the supreme foolishness of the North and, worse still, as an expression of ill-will of the Yankees toward the defeated South. The

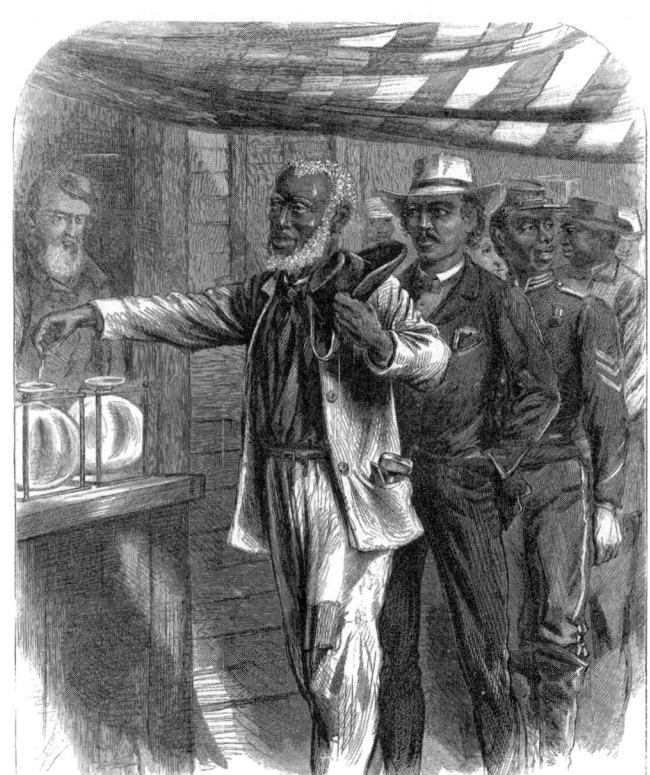

Blacks, including a Union soldier, are depicted casting their first ballots in an image published November 16, 1867. In fact, it would take another hundred years to secure voting rights for African Americans.

Negro franchise became the symbol of the humiliation of the South."[5]

AFTER RECONSTRUCTION

Congress in 1870 passed an enforcement act to protect black voting rights in the South, but the Supreme Court in 1876 ruled that Congress had exceeded its authority. In the case of *United States v. Reese*, the Court held that the Fifteenth Amendment did not give anyone the right to vote; it simply guaranteed the right to be free from racial discrimination in exercising that right. The extension of the right to vote itself, the Court said, was up to the states, not the federal government. Therefore, the Court said, Congress had overreached its power to enforce the Fifteenth Amendment when it enacted the 1870 law that penalized state officials who denied African Americans the right to vote, or refused to count their votes, or obstructed them from voting.

At the same time, the North clearly was growing weary of the crusade for betterment of the condition of blacks. When the federal troops were withdrawn in April 1877, the remaining Radical Reconstruction governments in the South quickly disintegrated. Some of the newly enfranchised citizens continued to vote, but by 1900, according to historian Paul Lewinson in his book *Race, Class and Party,* "all factions united in a white man's party once more, to put the Negro finally beyond the pale of political activity."[6]

Mississippi led the way in prohibiting black political activity. A new state constitution drawn up in 1890 required prospective voters to pay a poll tax of two dollars and to demonstrate their ability to read any section of the state constitution or to interpret it when read to them.

Literacy Tests for Voters

In Mississippi and other southern states that adopted voter literacy tests, care was taken not to disfranchise illiterate whites. Five states exempted white voters from literacy and other requirements by "grandfather clauses"—regulations allowing prospective voters, if not otherwise qualified, to register if they were descended from persons who had voted, or served in the state's military forces, before 1867. Other provisions allowed illiterates to register if they owned a certain amount of property or could show themselves to be of good moral character—requirements easily twisted to exclude only blacks.

At one time or another, twenty-one states imposed literacy requirements as a condition for voting. The first to do so, Connecticut in 1855 and Massachusetts in 1857, sought to disqualify a flood of European immigrants. Between 1890 and 1910, Mississippi, South Carolina, Louisiana, North Carolina, Alabama, Virginia, Georgia, and Oklahoma adopted literacy tests—primarily to restrict the black vote.

Nineteen of the twenty-one states demanded that voters be able to read English, and all but four of them (New York, Washington, Alaska, and Hawaii) required the reading of some legal document or passage from the state or federal Constitution. Either in lieu of or in addition to the reading requirements, fourteen states required an ability to write.

As applied in the South, literacy tests and other voting restrictions virtually disenfranchised black citizens. Outside the South the New York test was by far the most stringent, although there were seldom any complaints that it was applied in a discriminatory way. Despite pressures by civil libertarians, Congress declined for years to void literacy tests on grounds that to do so would violate a state's right to impose its own voting requirements.

Reports of extreme voter discrimination in the South gradually moved Congress to search for remedial legislation. In 1965 it passed a sweeping Voting Rights Act that suspended literacy tests in seven southern states and parts of another. Five years later Congress expanded the law to bar all voter-literacy tests.

Poll-Tax Barrier to Voting

The first poll taxes in America were substitutes for property ownership and were intended to enlarge the voting franchise. But only a few states retained them at the time of the Civil War. They were afterward revived for a far different purpose—to restrict the franchise—in all eleven states of the old Confederacy: Florida (1889), Mississippi and Tennessee (1890), Arkansas (1892), South Carolina (1895), Louisiana (1898), North Carolina (1900), Alabama (1901), Virginia and Texas (1902), and Georgia (1908).

The ostensible purpose was to "cleanse" elections of mass abuses, but the records of constitutional conventions held in five southern states during the period revealed statements praising the poll tax as a measure to bar blacks and poor whites from the polls. Some historians have asserted that the main intent of

these measures was to limit the popular base of a so-called agrarian revolt inspired by the Populist Party against the existing political structure.[7]

After the Populist era many states voluntarily dropped use of the poll tax, including six southern states—North Carolina (1920), Louisiana (1934), Florida (1937), Georgia (1945), South Carolina (1951), and Tennessee (1953). Proposals to abolish the poll tax were introduced in every Congress from 1939 to 1962. By 1960 only four states still required its payment by voters. In August 1962, the House approved a constitutional amendment—already accepted by the Senate—that outlawed poll taxes in federal elections, and that amendment, the Twenty-fourth, was ratified in January 1964. In 1966 the Supreme Court held that the poll tax was an unconstitutional requirement for voting in state and local elections as well. "Voter qualifications have no relation to wealth nor to paying or not paying this or any other tax. Wealth, like race, creed, or color, is not germane to one's ability to participate intelligently in the electoral process," Justice William O. Douglas wrote for the majority in *Harper v. Virginia Board of Elections*.

White Primaries

Even more than literacy tests or poll taxes, perhaps the most effective disfranchisement of southern blacks was their exclusion from the Democratic Party's primary elections. In the solidly Democratic South of the post-Reconstruction era, winning the party's nomination virtually assured election. Being excluded from voting in the primary was equivalent to being excluded from voting altogether.

Not until 1941 did the Supreme Court make clear that Congress had the power to regulate primary, as well as general, elections. Indeed, in a 1921 decision involving campaign spending, *Newberry v. United States*, the Court seemed to say that Congress lacked power to regulate primary elections. This doubt about the reach of federal power encouraged the eleven states that had composed the Confederacy to begin systematic exclusion of black voters from the primary. The Democratic Party was often organized on a statewide or county basis as a private club or association that could freely exclude blacks.

The effort of Texas to use the white primary to shut blacks out of the political process came before the Supreme Court in five cases, brought over a span of twenty-five years. In 1923 the Texas Legislature passed a law forbidding blacks to vote in the state Democratic primary. Dr. L. A. Nixon, a black resident of El Paso, challenged the law, arguing that it clearly violated the Fourteenth and Fifteenth Amendments. In the case of *Nixon v. Herndon*, decided in 1927, the Supreme Court agreed with Nixon's Fourteenth Amendment claim.

After the 1927 *Herndon* decision, the Texas Legislature authorized the executive committees of state political parties to establish their own qualifications for voting in the primary. Dr. Nixon again sued, challenging the law as racially discriminatory. Attorneys for the state argued that the Fourteenth Amendment's equal protection clause did not apply because the party, not state officials, set up the allegedly discriminatory standards.

With Benjamin N. Cardozo writing for a five-justice majority, the Court held in 1932 that the executive committee of the

Democratic Party acted as a delegate of the state in setting voter qualifications and that its action was equivalent to state action and was thus within the scope of the equal protection guarantee, which it violated (*Nixon v. Condon*).

The Texas Democratic Party responded by acting without state authorization to put itself off-limits to black voters. Confronted with this situation, the Court in 1935 retreated to its *Newberry* reasoning and ruled, in *Grovey v. Townsend,* that in this instance the party had acted not as a creature of the state but as a voluntary association of individuals. As such, its actions—even in controlling access to the vote—were not restricted by the Constitution.

In 1941 the Court switched signals again, discarding the *Newberry* doctrine in the case of *United States v. Classic. Classic* was not a racial discrimination case but instead concerned a man convicted of falsifying election returns. His conviction was based on a federal law that made it a crime "to injure, oppress, threaten, or intimidate any citizen in the free exercise or enjoyment of any right or privilege secured to him by the Constitution." He challenged his conviction, arguing that the right to vote in a primary election was not a right secured by the Constitution.

But the Court upheld the conviction, ruling that the primary was an integral part of the election process. The authority of Congress under Article I, Section 4, to regulate elections included the authority to regulate primary elections, wrote Justice Stone, "when, as in this case, they are a step in the exercise by the people of their choice of representatives in Congress."

Three years later, in 1944, the Court overturned *Grovey* and held the all-white primary unconstitutional. This case, *Smith v. Allwright,* arose out of the refusal of S. S. Allwright, a county election official, to permit Lonnie E. Smith, a black man, to vote in the 1940 Texas Democratic primary. Smith sued, saying Allwright had deprived him of his civil rights. Smith was represented by two attorneys for the National Association for the Advancement of Colored People (NAACP), William H. Hastie and Thurgood Marshall. Both were later made judges, with Marshall becoming the first African American justice on the Supreme Court.

The relentless effort of Texas Democrats to maintain the white primary at last came to an end in 1953 with another Supreme Court decision. In one Texas county an all-white Democratic organization conducted all-white primary elections under the name of Jaybird Club, a self-declared private club. In *Terry v. Adams* the Court declared this a ploy in violation of the Fifteenth Amendment.

Physical and Psychic Coercion

Throughout this period legal devices to curtail black political activity were buttressed by physical and economic intimidation. As Myrdal wrote: "Physical coercion is not so often practiced against the Negro, but the mere fact that it can be used with impunity . . . creates a psychic coercion that exists nearly everywhere in the South. . . . [I]t is no wonder that the great majority of Negroes in the South make no attempt to vote and—if they make attempts which are rebuffed—seldom demand their full rights under the federal Constitution."[8]

Blacks who summoned up the courage to try to register oftentimes encountered delays and verbal harassment sufficient to send them away. If applicants persisted, registrars were likely to ignore them, tell them that there were no more registration forms, or direct them to another place of registration, which, if it existed, was usually closed. Southern registrars also displayed a tendency to lose registration forms filled out by black applicants.

More subtle practices limited black political participation in the North as well. With the exception of Chicago, white-controlled city machines excluded black people from any significant role in politics for the first half of the twentieth century. During that time, Congress did virtually nothing to encourage black voting.

CIVIL RIGHTS LEGISLATION

Not until the 1950s, when the civil rights movement began to gather force, did Congress, at the urging of the executive branch, begin to reassert federal power to ensure the right of black citizens to vote. Its first action was passage of the Civil Rights Act of 1957, which was intended to enforce the voting guarantee set out in the Fifteenth Amendment.

The 1957 act authorized the attorney general to bring lawsuits to halt public and private interference with the right of black people to vote, and expanded federal jurisdiction over such suits. The law also created the Civil Rights Commission to investigate and publicly disclose problems of racial discrimination, including voting problems. The investigatory procedures of the commission and the authorization of the federal lawsuits were upheld by the Supreme Court in 1960, in *United States v. Raines.*

Responding to reports that progress in securing voting rights for blacks still was slow even under the provisions of the 1957 act, Congress in 1960 passed a measure that permitted the U.S. attorney general to sue a state for deprivation of voting rights even if the individuals named initially as defendants—usually voting registrars—had left office. This provision remedied a situation that had arisen in a suit brought by the United States against Alabama voting officials. In addition, Title VI of the 1960 law authorized the appointment of special federal "voting referees" to oversee voter registration in counties where a federal court detected a pattern of voter discrimination.

The Civil Rights Act of 1964 mandated state adoption of standard procedures and requirements for all persons seeking to register to vote. The law also required local officials to justify rejecting an applicant who had completed the sixth grade or had equivalent evidence of intellectual competence. Other provisions of the 1964 law expedited the movement of voting rights cases to the Supreme Court.

In two cases brought under the 1964 act, *United States v. Louisiana* and *United States v. Mississippi,* the Supreme Court in 1965 sanctioned the government's efforts to break the pattern of case-by-case litigation of voting rights violations. The Court upheld federal power to challenge a state's entire constitutional legal framework for voter registration and conduct of elections.

Voting rights was one of many reforms sought by civil rights supporters, including Martin Luther King Jr., (front row, second from left), who marched in Washington in August 1963. Prodded by the civil rights movement, Congress began to reassert federal power to ensure the right of black citizens to vote.

The Voting Rights Act

But progress still was slow. In Dallas County, Alabama, three new federal laws and four years of litigation had produced the registration of only 383 black voters out of a potential pool of fifteen thousand. On March 8, 1965, the Rev. Martin Luther King Jr., led a "Walk for Freedom" to dramatize the need for additional efforts in behalf of registering African American voters in Selma, the county seat, and elsewhere in the South. The violence of the reaction of local white law enforcement officers and white bystanders to the peaceful demonstration drew nationwide attention to the dimensions of the problem.

A week later, President Lyndon B. Johnson addressed a joint session of Congress to ask for passage of a new voting rights measure to close legal loopholes that enabled local officials to stall black voter registration. Johnson explained that "no law that we now have on the books . . . can ensure the right to vote when local officials are determined to deny it." Later that month, NAACP official Roy Wilkins appeared before a Senate committee on behalf of the Leadership Conference on Civil Rights to urge Congress to "transform this retail litigation method of registration into a wholesale administration proce-

dure registering all who seek to exercise their democratic birthright." Within five months Congress had approved the sweeping Voting Rights Act of 1965.

The law suspended literacy tests and provided for the appointment of federal supervisors of voter registration in all states and counties where literacy tests or similar qualifying devices were in effect on November 1, 1964, and where fewer than 50 percent of the voting-age residents had registered to vote or voted in the 1964 presidential election.

The law established criminal penalties for persons found guilty of interfering with the voting rights of others. State or county governments in areas of low voter registration were required to obtain federal approval of any new voting laws, standards, practices, or procedures before implementing them. A state or county covered by the act could escape from the law's provisions if it could persuade a three-judge federal court in the District of Columbia that no racial discrimination in registration or voting had occurred in the previous five years.

The act placed federal registration machinery in six southern states (Alabama, Georgia, Mississippi, South Carolina, Louisiana, and Virginia), Alaska, twenty-eight counties in North

Carolina, three counties in Arizona, and one in Idaho.

Passage of the voting rights act heralded a significant increase in the number of blacks registered to vote. Within four years, almost a million blacks had registered to vote under its provisions. The Civil Rights Commission reported in 1968 that registration of blacks had climbed to more than 50 percent of the black voting-age population in every southern state. Before the act, black registration had exceeded 50 percent in only three, Florida, Tennessee, and Texas. The most dramatic increase occurred in Mississippi, where black registration rose from 6.7 percent to 59.8 percent of the voting-age population.[9]

Voting Law Extended

In renewing the act in 1970 for an additional five years, its supporters turned back the efforts of southern senators to dilute key provisions. State and local governments were forbidden to use literacy tests or other voter-qualifying devices, and the triggering formula was altered to apply to any state or county that used a literacy test for voting and where less than 50 percent of the voting-age residents were registered on November 1, 1968, or had voted in the 1968 general election.

Under the 1970 law, the preclearance requirement applied to those areas affected by the 1965 law and ten more: three Alaska districts; Apache County, Arizona; Imperial County, California; Elmore County, Idaho; the Bronx, Kings (Brooklyn), and New York (Manhattan) counties, New York; and Wheeler County, Oregon.

By the time the act was due for its second extension in 1975, an estimated two million African Americans had been added to the voting rolls in the South, more than doubling the previous total. The number of blacks holding elective office also increased. The Joint Center for Political Studies reported that the number of black elected officials in the seven southern states covered by the Voting Rights Act had gone up from fewer than one hundred in 1964 to 963 in just ten years. The total included one member of the House of Representatives, thirty-six state legislators, and 927 county and municipal officials.

The Voting Rights Act was renewed for seven years and substantially expanded in 1975. The triggering formula was amended to bring under coverage of the law any state or county that was using a literacy test in 1972 and where less than 50 percent of the residents eligible to vote had registered as of November 1, 1972. Two additional provisions gave greater protection to certain language minorities, defined as persons of Hispanic heritage, Native Americans, Asian Americans, and Alaskan natives.

The federal preclearance provisions were expanded to apply to any jurisdiction where:

• The Census Bureau determined that more than 5 percent of the voting-age citizens were of a single language minority.

• Election materials had been printed only in English for the 1972 presidential election.

• Fewer than 50 percent of the voting-age citizens had registered for or voted in the 1972 presidential election.

These amendments significantly expanded coverage of the act, bringing in all of Alaska, Texas, and Arizona, and selected counties in several other states, including California and Florida. In addition, provisions were added requiring certain parts of the country to provide bilingual voting materials.

Congress approved a third extension of the act on June 23, 1982, two months before the law was due to expire. The 1982 legislation represented a major victory for a coalition of civil rights groups that included black, Hispanic, labor, religious, and civic organizations. Many of them had criticized President Ronald Reagan's administration for its hesitation and reservations about earlier versions and certain features of the measure.

However, the bill received widespread bipartisan support and strong backing from members of both chambers, including southerners. More than twice as many southern Democrats in both the Senate and House voted for passage in 1982 than in 1965 when the law was first approved. The steady upward trend in southern support for the act reflected changing social and political mores, and a great increase in black voting in the South.

The 1982 law had four main elements. First, it extended for twenty-five years provisions that required nine states and portions of thirteen others to obtain Justice Department approval for any changes in their election laws and procedures. Second, starting in 1984, a jurisdiction could be released from the restrictions by showing a clean voting rights record for the previous ten years. Third, it overturned a 1980 Supreme Court ruling that "intent to discriminate" must be shown to prove a violation. Fourth, it extended the bilingual election provisions through 1992.

The requirement for Justice Department approval of election-law changes figured prominently in redistricting being carried out in the affected states on the basis of the 1990 census. While that proved to be a matter of considerable controversy, there is little doubt that the Voting Rights Act has had a positive effect on the numbers of blacks winning elective office. Nationwide in January 1999, according to a compilation by the Joint Center for Political Studies, the number of black elected officials included thirty-nine members of Congress, 583 state legislators, 450 mayors, and 3,980 other municipal officials; more than 880 judges or magistrates; and nearly sixty police chiefs, sheriffs, and local marshals. (These totals were from the fifty states, the District of Columbia, and the Virgin Islands.)

JUDICIAL SUPPORT

Not surprisingly, the unprecedented assertion of federal power over electoral and voting matters embodied in the Voting Rights Act was immediately challenged as exceeding the constitutional authority of Congress and encroaching on states' rights. But in 1966, in direct contrast to its post–Civil War rulings, the Supreme Court firmly backed the power of Congress to pass such a law. In that case, *South Carolina v. Katzenbach,* the state argued that Congress had exceeded its authority in suspending South Carolina voting standards, permitting the use of federal election examiners, and adopting a "triggering" formula that affected some states but not others. At the Court's invitation, Alabama, Georgia, Louisiana, Mississippi, and Virginia filed briefs in support of South Carolina's challenge. Twenty other states filed briefs in support of the law.

Strong Court Backing

The Supreme Court rejected all constitutional challenges to the act. "Congress," wrote Chief Justice Earl Warren for the decision's 8–1 majority, "has full remedial powers [under the Fifteenth Amendment] to effectuate the constitutional prohibition against racial discrimination in voting." The federal approval requirement for new voting rules in the states covered by the act, Warren observed, "may have been an uncommon exercise of congressional power, as South Carolina contends, but the Court has recognized that exceptional conditions can justify legislative measures not otherwise appropriate."

Also in 1966, in *Katzenbach v. Morgan,* the Court upheld the portion of the Voting Rights Act that permitted persons educated in accredited "American-flag" schools to vote even if they were unable to read and write English. The provision was aimed at enfranchising Puerto Ricans educated in such schools, living in the United States, but unable to demonstrate literacy in English.

Although the basic constitutionality of the Voting Rights Act was now settled, a steady stream of voting rights cases came to the Court in the late 1960s and the 1970s, testing the scope and application of the law. But the Court continued to back and broadly interpret the act. In the 1969 case of *Gaston County v. United States,* for example, the Court refused to let a North Carolina county reinstate a literacy test.

Some Exceptions Allowed

In 1975, however, the Court held in *Richmond v. United States* that a federally approved annexation plan did not violate the Voting Rights Act—even if it reduced the percentage of black voters in the city's population—so long as there were legitimate reasons for the annexation. Despite its willingness to affirm the sweeping provisions of the 1965 law, the Court refused to interpret it as forbidding all use of racial criteria in legislative redistricting or as requiring that blacks be given proportional representation on elected bodies.

In a 1976 decision, *Beer v. United States,* the Court upheld a city's reapportionment of the districts from which city council members were chosen. The change resulted in an increase in the number of black council members, but not in a proportional representation of black voters among the council members. The Court held that the Voting Rights Act was satisfied so long as such changes did not reduce the voting strength of racial minorities.

The next year, in *United Jewish Organizations of Williamsburgh v. Cary,* the Court upheld New York's 1974 redistricting law, which purposely redrew certain districts to give them non-white majorities. The county (Kings) affected in the case was one of three in New York that had been brought under the coverage of the Voting Rights Act by the 1970 amendments to that law. The Hasidic Jewish community of the Williamsburgh sec-

tion of Brooklyn objected that the new boundaries divided their voting strength between two districts. The objectors argued that such use of racial criteria in the redistricting deprived them of the equal protection guaranteed by the Fourteenth Amendment and diluted their voting strength in violation of the Fifteenth Amendment.

The Constitution did not prevent all use of racial criteria in districting and apportionment, wrote Justice Byron R. White for the seven-member Supreme Court majority in that case. Nor, he continued, did it "prevent a State subject to the Voting Rights Act from deliberately creating or preserving black majorities in particular districts in order to ensure that its reapportionment plan complies with [the act]. . . ."

"There is no doubt," White continued, that the state, in drawing new district lines, "deliberately used race in a purposeful manner. But its plan represented no racial slur or stigma with respect to whites or any other race, and we discern no discrimination violative of the Fourteenth Amendment nor any abridgment of the right to vote on account of race within the meaning of the Fifteenth Amendment."

In the 1980 case of *Mobile v. Bolden,* the Court for the first time narrowed the reach of the Voting Rights Act. Justice Potter Stewart wrote on behalf of a 6–3 majority that the fact that no black person had ever been elected city commissioner in Mobile, Alabama, under the city's challenged system of at-large elections was not enough to prove the system was in violation of the Voting Rights Act and the Constitution. "The Fifteenth Amendment does not entail the right to have Negro candidates elected," Stewart wrote, but only guaranteed that blacks would be able to "register and vote without hindrance."

Mobile Decision Overturned

The decision set off a reaction in Congress that resulted in specific language being written into the 1982 extension of the Voting Rights Act declaring that a voting practice or law that had the effect of discriminating was in violation of the federal law, whatever the local intent might have been. In 1986 the Court applied the new test to *Thornburg v. Gingles,* ruling that six of North Carolina's multimember legislative districts impermissibly diluted the strength of black votes in the state. The fact that very few black candidates had been elected from those districts was enough to prove that the system was in violation of the law, the Court held.

In 1991 the Supreme Court relied on the 1982 revisions of the Voting Rights Act to rule that the act applied to the election of judges.

Court Decisions in the 1990s

Entering the 1990s, blacks and Hispanics were still underrepresented in Congress. To remedy this situation, the Justice Department sought to use the "preclearance" provision of the Voting Rights Act to encourage states with histories of minority voting rights violations to create so-called majority-minority districts—districts where black or Hispanic populations were in the majority.

Constitutional Provisions for House and Senate Elections

Article I, Section 2

The House of Representatives shall be composed of Members chosen every second Year by the People of the several States, and the Electors in each State shall have the Qualifications requisite for Electors of the most numerous Branch of the State Legislature.

No Person shall be a Representative who shall not have attained to the age of twenty five Years, and been seven Years a Citizen of the United States, and who shall not, when elected, be an Inhabitant of that State in which he shall be chosen.

Representatives and direct Taxes shall be apportioned among the several States which may be included within this Union, according to their respective Numbers, which shall be determined By adding to the whole Number of free Persons, including those bound to Service for a Term of Years, and excluding Indians not taxed, three fifths of all other Persons. The actual Enumeration shall be made within three Years after the first Meeting of the Congress of the United States, and within every subsequent Term of ten Years, in such Manner as they shall by Law direct. The Number of Representatives shall not exceed one for every thirty Thousand, but each State shall have at Least one Representative; and until such enumeration shall be made, the State of New Hampshire shall be entitled to chuse three, Massachusetts eight, Rhode-Island and Providence Plantations one, Connecticut five, New York six, New Jersey four, Pennsylvania eight, Delaware one, Maryland six, Virginia ten, North Carolina five, South Carolina five, and Georgia three.

When vacancies happen in the Representation from any State, the Executive Authority thereof shall issue Writs of Election to fill such Vacancies.

Article I, Section 3

The Senate of the United States shall be composed of two Senators from each State, chosen by the Legislature thereof, for six Years; and each Senator shall have one Vote.

Immediately after they shall be assembled in Consequence of the first Election, they shall be divided as equally as may be into three Classes. The Seats of the Senators of the first Class shall be vacated at the Expiration of the second Year, of the second class at the Expiration of the fourth Year, and of the third class at the Expiration of the sixth Year, so that one third may be chosen every second Year; and if Vacancies happen by Resignation, or otherwise, during the Recess of the Legislature of any State, the Executive thereof may make temporary Appointments until the next Meeting of the Legislature, which shall then fill such Vacancies.

No Person shall be a Senator who shall not have attained the Age of thirty Years, and been nine Years a Citizen of the United States, and who shall not, when elected, be an Inhabitant of that State for which he shall be chosen.

Article I, Section 4

The Times, Places and Manner of holding Elections for Senators and Representatives, shall be prescribed in each State by the Legis-

---

With newly drawn majority-minority districts, the 1992 election produced a large increase in the total of black and Hispanic House members. The number of blacks jumped from twenty-six to thirty-nine; the number of Hispanics from eleven to seventeen. But some of the districts were sharply criticized as a form of racial gerrymandering because of their irregular shapes, and the Supreme Court in 1993 demonstrated that these districts would come under tough legal scrutiny.

At issue in 1993 was a district that wound its way in a snake-like fashion through central North Carolina, picking up black neighborhoods in four metropolitan areas. The district, drawn at the urging of the Justice Department, was challenged by a group of white voters who alleged that North Carolina had set up "a racially discriminatory voting process" and deprived them of the right to vote in "a color-blind" election. Their suit was dismissed by a federal district court but reinstated by the Supreme Court in a 5–4 decision, *Shaw v. Reno* (1993).

In her opinion for the court, Justice Sandra Day O'Connor acknowledged that racial considerations could not be excluded from the redistricting process. But she said that in "some exceptional cases" a plan could be "so highly irregular that, on its face, it rationally cannot be understood as anything other than an effort to segregate voters on the basis of race." To justify such a plan, O'Connor said, the government must show that it is narrowly tailored to serve a compelling government interest.[10]

The decision in *Shaw v. Reno* returned the case to a lower court for further hearings. Meanwhile, challenges to racially drawn redistricting plans were proceeding in other states, which the Supreme Court used to refine its position on racial redistricting. In 1995 the Court struck down a Georgia plan that had created three black-majority districts, including one that stretched from the Atlanta suburbs across half the state to the coastal city of Savannah. The 5–4 vote in *Miller v. Johnson* was the same as in the North Carolina case, but the Court made clear that challenges were not limited to plans with irregularly shaped districts.

Writing for the majority, Justice Anthony M. Kennedy argued that government should not treat citizens as members of a racial class, and he said that the Georgia map could not be justified on the grounds that it was necessary to comply with the Voting Rights Act because the Justice Department had incorrectly interpreted the law to require the maximum number of majority-black districts be created. Redistricting plans were subject to challenge, Kennedy said, if race was "the predominant factor motivating the legislature's decision to place a significant number of voters within or without a particular district."

The decision was widely criticized. President Bill Clinton called the ruling "a setback in the struggle to ensure that all Americans participate fully in the electoral process." But the crit-

lature thereof; but the Congress may at any time by Law make or alter such Regulations, except as to the Places of chusing Senators.

The Congress shall assemble at least once in every Year, and such Meeting shall be on the first Monday in December, unless they shall by Law appoint a different day.

Article I, Section 5

Each House shall be the Judge of the Elections, Returns and Qualifications of its own Members, and a Majority of each shall constitute a Quorum to do Business; but a smaller Number may adjourn from day to day, and may be authorized to compel the Attendance of absent Members in such Manner, and under such Penalties as each House may provide.

Amendment XIV

(Ratified July 28, 1868)

Section 2. Representatives shall be apportioned among the several States according to their respective numbers, counting the whole number of persons in each State, excluding Indians not taxed. But when the right to vote at any election for the choice of electors for President and Vice President of the United States, Representatives in Congress, the Executive and Judicial officers of a State, or the members of the Legislature thereof, is denied to any of the male inhabitants of such State, being twenty-one years of age, and citizens of the United States, or in any way abridged, except for participation in rebellion, or other crime, the basis of representation therein shall be reduced in the proportion which the number of such male citizens shall bear to the whole number of male citizens twenty-one years of age in such State.

Amendment XVII

(Ratified May 31, 1913)

The Senate of the United States shall be composed of two Senators from each State, elected by the people thereof, for six years; and each Senator shall have one vote. The electors in each State shall have the qualifications requisite for electors of the most numerous branch of the State legislatures.

When vacancies happen in the representation of any State in the Senate, the executive authority of such State shall issue writs of election to fill such vacancies: *Provided,* That the legislature of any State may empower the executive thereof to make temporary appointments until the people fill the vacancies by election as the legislature may direct.

This amendment shall not be so construed as to affect the election or term of any Senator chosen before it becomes valid as part of the Constitution.

Amendment XX

(Ratified January 23, 1933)

Section 1. The terms of the President and Vice President shall end at noon on the 20th day of January, and the terms of Senators and Representatives at noon on the 3d day of January, of the years in which such terms would have ended if this article had not been ratified; and the terms of their successors shall then begin.

Section 2. The Congress shall assemble at least once in every year, and such meeting shall begin at noon on the 3d day of January, unless they shall by law appoint a different day.

---

icism did not sway the Court's majority. In 1996 the same five-justice majority in *Shaw v. Hunt* rejected the serpentine North Carolina district that it had scrutinized in 1993, arguing that the state had neglected traditional districting criteria, such as compactness, while overemphasizing the importance of race. The Court in *Bush v. Vera* also found that Texas had improperly used racial considerations in the drawing of three congressional districts. District maps in parts of Florida, Louisiana, New York, and Virginia were also successfully challenged on the basis of race.

Civil rights groups complained that the rulings would make it more difficult for minorities to be elected to Congress. But their warnings were tempered by the election results. In the 2000 elections, a record number of blacks, seventy, ran for Congress on major party tickets, according to the Joint Center for Political and Economic Studies. However, the number elected to the 107th Congress, thirty-nine (thirty-seven members and two delegates), was the same number as in the 106th Congress.

Women's Vote: A Victory in Stages

The drive for women's suffrage, which began in the late 1830s, was closely related in the beginning to the movement for abolition of slavery. Women, because of their extensive legal disadvantages under the common law, often compared their lot to that of slaves and thus directed the bulk of their political activi-

ty against proposals for extending slavery. Women were disfranchised at every level of government. Only in New Jersey did they have a theoretical right to vote. That right had been included inadvertently in the state constitutions of 1776 and 1797, but the state legislature repealed the provision at the outset of the nineteenth century when some women actually attempted to vote.

Early victories for the women's suffrage movement came mostly in connection with school elections. Kentucky in 1838 gave the right to vote in such elections to widows and unmarried women with property that was subject to taxation for school purposes. Kansas in 1861 gave women the vote on all school questions, and by 1880 Michigan, Utah, Minnesota, Colorado, New Hampshire, and Massachusetts had followed suit.

The Woman's Rights Convention at Seneca Falls, New York, in July 1848 is generally cited as the beginning of the women's suffrage movement in the United States. But the Declaration of Principles which Elizabeth Cady Stanton read at that meeting and which thereafter became a sacred text for the movement, was a much broader and more revolutionary document than a simple claim for the franchise.

STEPS TOWARD THE VOTE

Direct-action tactics first were applied by suffragists shortly after the Civil War, when Susan B. Anthony urged women to go to the polls and claim the right to vote under terms of the newly

PRESIDENT WILSON IS DECEIVING THE WORLD
WHEN HE APPEARS AS THE PROPHET OF DEMOCRACY
PRESIDENT WILSON HAS OPPOSED THOSE WHO
DEMAND DEMOCRACY FOR THIS COUNTRY
E IS RESPONSIBLE FOR THE DISFRANCHISEMENT
OF MILLIONS OF AMERICANS
WE IN AMERICA KNOW THIS
THE WORLD WILL FIND HIM OUT.

Supporters of the Nineteenth Amendment—giving women the right to vote—picket the White House in 1916. The Nineteenth Amendment was ratified in 1920.

adopted Fourteenth Amendment. In the national elections of 1872, Anthony voted in her home city of Rochester, New York; she subsequently was tried and convicted of the crime of "voting without having a lawful right to vote." For almost a quarter of a century, Anthony and her followers pressed Congress for a constitutional amendment granting women's suffrage. On January 25, 1887, the Senate finally considered the proposal but rejected it by a 16–34 vote.

The suffrage forces had more success in some western states. As a territory, Wyoming extended full suffrage to women in 1869 and retained it upon becoming a state in 1890. Colorado, Utah, and Idaho granted women voting rights before the turn of the century. But after that the advocates of suffrage for women encountered stronger opposition, and it was not until the height of the Progressive movement that other states, mostly in the West, gave women full voting rights. Washington granted equal suffrage in 1910, California in 1911, Arizona, Kansas, and Oregon in 1912, Montana and Nevada in 1914, and New York in 1917.

Opponents argued that women were the "weaker sex," that their temperament was unsuited to make the kinds of decisions necessary in casting a ballot and that suffrage might alter the relationship between the sexes. In the two decades preceding women's enfranchisement, extravagant claims were made by extremists on both sides. Radical feminists often insisted that women voters would be able to cleanse American politics of its corruption and usher in some ill-defined, utopian golden age. Antifranchise forces were as far-reaching in their claims. During World War I, Henry A. Wise Wood, president of the Aero Club of America, told the House Committee on Woman Suffrage that giving women the vote would mean "the dilution with the qualities of the cow of the qualities of the bull upon which all the herd's safety must depend." And the January 1917 issue of *Remonstrance,* an antisuffrage journal, cautioned that women's

suffrage would lead to the nationalization of women, free love, and communism.[11]

CONSTITUTIONAL AMENDMENT

On the eve of World War I, the advocates of militant tactics took the lead in a national campaign for women's rights. In the congressional elections of 1914, they set out to defeat all Democratic candidates in the nine states (which had increased to eleven by election day) where women had the right to vote. They held the majority Democrats in Congress responsible for not submitting a constitutional amendment to the states for their approval of women's voting rights. Only twenty of the forty-three challenged candidates were elected. However, this showing of electoral strength did not move President Woodrow Wilson to take up their cause.

Wilson's opposition to a constitutional amendment prompted a series of stormy demonstrations by the suffragettes around the White House and other sites in Washington after the United States had entered World War I. The demonstrators insisted that it was unconscionable for this country to be denying its own female citizens a right to participate in government while at the same time it was fighting a war on the premise of "making the world safe for democracy."

At the direction of the administration, thousands of the women demonstrators were arrested and brought to trial. Some were beaten by hostile crowds—often made up of soldiers and sailors who viewed the demonstrations as unpatriotic. At their trials, many of the women stood mute or made speeches advocating suffrage and attacking President Wilson for his refusal to endorse the constitutional amendment.

The jailing of many of these women caused a severe housing problem for District of Columbia penal authorities and created a wave of sympathy for the suffragettes. Public support for their position was heightened by the prisoners' claims that they had been treated inhumanely and had been subjected to unsanitary conditions in prison. To protest these conditions, some of the prisoners went on a hunger strike, and the authorities resorted to forced feeding, an action that aroused even greater public sympathy.

President Wilson capitulated, announcing on January 9, 1918, his support for the proposed suffrage amendment. The House of Representatives approved it the next day by a 274–136 vote, one vote more than the necessary two-thirds majority. But the Senate fell short of the two-thirds majority in October 1918 and again in February 1919. However, when the Congress elected in November 1918 met for the first time on May 19, 1919, it took little more than two weeks to gain the required majorities in both chambers.

On August 18, 1920, Tennessee became the thirty-sixth state to approve the amendment, enough for ratification. On August 26, Secretary of State Bainbridge Colby signed a proclamation formally adding the Nineteenth Amendment to the Constitution. It stated simply that "The right of citizens of the United States to vote shall not be denied or abridged by the United States or by any state on account of sex."

In the 1920 presidential election, the first in which women could vote, it was estimated that only about 30 percent of those who were eligible actually voted. Analyses of the 1924 election indicated that scarcely one-third of all eligible women voted while more than two-thirds of the eligible men had done so. The women's electoral performance came as a bitter blow to the suffragists. In more recent national elections, however, surveys by the Census Bureau have found that voting participation by women is about the same as that of men.

By the end of the twentieth century, women's representation in Congress, though, was well below half. The 107th Congress began in 2001 with seventy-two women members—thirteen in the Senate and fifty-nine in the House—representing 13.5 percent of the seats in Congress. The United States ranked forty-fifth among 178 legislatures in female representation, according to the Inter-Parliamentary Union. Sweden ranked first—43 percent of the seats in its single-house legislature were held by women.

The Eighteen-Year-Old Vote

Twenty-one was the minimum voting age in every state until 1943, when Georgia lowered it to eighteen—the age at which young men were being drafted to fight in World War II. The slogan, "Old enough to fight, old enough to vote," had a certain logic and public appeal. But no other state followed Georgia's lead until after the war. In 1946 South Carolina Democrats authorized eighteen-year-olds to vote in party primaries, but later withdrew that privilege. In 1955 Kentucky voters lowered the voting age to eighteen. Alaska and Hawaii, upon entering the Union in 1959, adopted minimum voting ages of nineteen and twenty, respectively.

Meanwhile, in 1954, President Dwight D. Eisenhower had proposed a constitutional amendment granting eighteen-year-olds the right to vote nationwide, but the proposal was rejected by the Senate. Eventually Congress was persuaded—perhaps by the demographics of America's fast-expanding youth population, which during the 1960s had begun to capture the nation's attention; perhaps by the separate hopes of Republicans and Democrats to win new voters, perhaps by the Vietnam War in which the young were called on to fight again. In the Voting Rights Act of 1970, Congress added a provision to lower the voting age to eighteen in all federal, state, and local elections, effective January 1, 1971.

On signing the bill into law, President Richard Nixon restated his belief that the provision was unconstitutional because Congress had no power to extend suffrage by statute, and directed Attorney General John N. Mitchell to ask for a swift court test of the law's validity. The Supreme Court, ruling in *Oregon v. Mitchell* only weeks before the law was due to take effect, sustained its application to federal elections but held it unconstitutional in regard to state and local elections.

After the Court ruled, Congress wasted little time in approving and sending to the states a proposed Twenty-sixth Amendment to the Constitution, stating: "The right of citizens of the United States, who are eighteen years of age or older, to vote shall not be denied or abridged by the United States or by any State on account of age. The Congress shall have power to enforce this article by appropriate legislation." The proposal received final congressional approval March 23, 1971, and was ratified by the necessary three-fourths of the states by July 1, record time for a constitutional amendment.

More than twenty-five million Americans became eligible to vote for the first time in the 1972 presidential election. It was the biggest influx of potential voters since women won the right to vote in 1920. But the younger age group has never fulfilled its potential power at the polls; in election after election, younger voters had the lowest turnout rate of any age category. In the 2000 elections, 17 percent of eligible voters between the ages of eighteen and twenty-nine went to the polls.

Voter Registration

To guard against abuses of the American electoral system, states employ a number of devices designed to restrict voting within their jurisdictions to persons legally entitled to do so. Chief among these protections is the voter registration process. The need for such a system is a reflection of America's growth in population and diversity. According to the Federal Election Commission (FEC), there were 141.9 million registered voters in 1998, or about 71 percent of the voting age population.

When the United States was primarily a rural nation, its scattered communities were small and most people knew each other. Voting was a relatively simple matter: a voter simply had to show up at the polls, be recognized by the election judges, and cast his ballot. If he were challenged, he could either sign or mark an affidavit that swore to his qualifications or produce other voters who were recognized from the area to attest to his standing. (At that time, women's suffrage had not come into existence, so all voters were men.)

But toward the end of the nineteenth century, the country had ceased to be rural in nature. The growth of cities and their

A senior citizen registers to vote. In the late 1990s about 71 percent of the U.S. voting age population was registered to vote.

concentrations of people made the simple system of voter recognition and approval, while still workable in some places, impractical and highly susceptible to fraudulent voting practices.

In the urban areas, practices such as "repeating" (casting ballots at multiple polling places), and "voting the graveyard" (using the names of dead people to cast ballots), became commonplace. As the franchise grew, sheer numbers of voters outweighed the ability of election judges to know who was eligible to vote and who was not. States began to turn to systems of registering voters, and, by the beginning of the twentieth century, all the states had a type of registration in place and working. When women gained the right to vote, more names were added to the burgeoning rolls.

REGISTRATION FORMS
AND PROCEDURES

Registration forms common in most states are simple and straightforward. An applicant is asked to check off whether the registration is a new one or represents a change of address or name. The applicant then fills in his or her name, address, date of birth, mailing address (if different from residence), a home telephone (optional), and information about the person's previous voter registration, including the county name, if it is in a different voting area.

The potential voter is also asked to "swear or affirm" that he or she is a U.S. citizen, that the address provided is correct, that he or she will be eighteen years of age on or before the next elec-

tion, and is not on parole, probation, or serving a sentence for any indictable offense under federal or state law. This affidavit form also asks if the signer understands that making a false or fraudulent registration may subject him or her to a fine and/or imprisonment.

Once the form is completed, signed, and received by election officials, the new voter is registered on the election rolls of the appropriate voting precinct. The registration office may then, if the voter is reregistering at a new address, inform the voter's previous voting district that his or her name should be removed from those rolls.

The closing date for registration before an election varies from state to state. Some allow registration up to election day, but on average registration must take place twenty-eight days prior to the election.

Most states register voters according to party affiliation, largely to prevent "party raiding" by limiting closed primary and caucus elections to party members. Usually the state requires changes in party registration to be made well in advance of the primary or caucus date. Several states, however, hold open primaries not restricted to party members.

Voter registration lists are a public record and copies are available to candidates and others, usually for a fee. Some states, however, have passed legislation creating secret voting lists to protect women from abusive partners. Such laws allow the abuse victims to be put on the secret list and vote by mail if they receive a court restraining or "no contact" order against the partner trying to locate them. Civil libertarians have opposed the laws, however, arguing that voter registrations are "the quintessential public record" and should be kept that way.

FRAUD PROTECTION

The overriding purpose of the registration systems, whatever their particularities, is to ensure that votes are cast only by eligible voters. To thwart the election day schemes of the unscrupulous, all the systems provided a register, prepared in advance, of all voters in a given district eligible to vote in that election. This roster, while not a complete protection against election fraud or corrupt election judges, offers some assurance that, in almost every situation, eligibility questions have been answered and that a voter duly listed on the rolls can vote when he or she reaches the polls. With passage of the Voting Rights Act of 1965, virtually all bars to voting eligibility disappeared.

The states employ a variety of registration systems, but all follow one of two basic approaches. The first is the *periodic* system, in which the existing voting rolls are cast aside at certain stipulated periods and new lists are drawn up, requiring voters to reregister. The second is the *permanent* system, under which the same list of voters is used indefinitely, with legally specified types of updates regarding additions and deletions of voters' names. Because the permanent system offers states some savings in time and money, and also because it appears to be more immune to fraudulent practices, it is the preferred choice.

In the United States, the burden of registering to vote rests primarily with the individual voter. Except in North Dakota, which has no formal registration system, registration is a prerequisite to voting, and the citizen of voting age must take the initiative of getting on the rolls. This policy is in contrast to that in most other Western democracies, where registration is virtually automatic. American voters as a rule must go to a designated office to register or to obtain a registration form that can be mailed in.

MOTOR-VOTER:
MAKING REGISTRATION EASIER

In most Western nations government agencies sign up voters, but the United States places the burden for qualifying for electoral participation on the citizen. Signed into law by President Bill Clinton on May 20, 1993, motor-voter required states to provide all eligible citizens the opportunity to register when they applied for or renewed a driver's license. It also required states to allow mail-in registration and to provide voter registration forms at agencies that supplied public assistance, such as welfare checks or help for the disabled. Compliance with the federally mandated program was required by 1995. Costs were to be borne by the states.

Partly as a result of the legislation, a record number of new voters, some ten million, signed up in the first three years following implementation of the act. The Federal Election Commission reported that motor-voter registration accounted for a quarter of voter registration applications in the 1997–1998 election period. However, the 140 million registered voters in 1998, or 70.8 percent of the voting-age population, was a drop from

1996 when it reached the highest level since 1960, when national registration figures first became available.

Congressional Republicans had opposed the legislation on political grounds, namely that it would allow citizens of traditionally Democratic constituencies—the urban poor and minorities, among others—easier access to the voting booth. Opponents also argued that easier registration could lead to election fraud. But the motor-voter law had neither the negative results that critics feared nor the positive impact that supporters hoped. One year after the law was enacted, Republicans won control of both houses of Congress, which they retained through the 2000 elections. In spite of the increased number of registered voters, election turnout continued to decline slightly in the late 1990s, although there was a small increase in the elections of 2000.

The Motor Voter Act is also credited with helping to keep the voting rolls up to date. Voters who fail to respond to election board mailings can be placed on an inactive list and removed from the rolls if they do not vote during a specified period. The requirements for keeping accurate and current voting lists indirectly affect political candidates as well. The registration indicates whether a candidate meets the residency requirements for the office being sought, and there have been numerous instances of candidates being kept off the ballot for being registered in the wrong area.

Removing Obstacles to Voting

In the late twentieth century the federal government and the states experimented with various other measures designed to increase citizen participation in the electoral process. The Voting Rights Act of 1970 helped pave the way in removing residency restrictions on new voters. Other measures to increase voter turnout came at the state level, with a number of states experimenting with new voting methods, such as election-day voter registration, easier absentee balloting, and mail-in ballots.

REDUCING RESIDENCY REQUIREMENTS

Every state at some time has imposed a minimum period of residence in the state (and some of them a shorter period of residence in a county or voting district) as a qualification for voting. The rationale for this practice has been that individuals cannot vote intelligently, at least on state and local affairs, until they have lived in an area for a given period of time. Until the 1970s most of the states required one year's residence for voting. At one time or another, Alabama, Louisiana, Mississippi, Rhode Island, and South Carolina required residency of as much as two years.

In 1970 thirty-three states imposed residency requirements of one year, fifteen required six months, and two (New York and Pennsylvania) three months. As another condition for voting in 1970, every state except New Hampshire required voters to have lived in the same county or voting district for a stipulated period of time. The most stringent of these requirements were in Maryland and Texas, where six months was required in the county and voting district.

Voting Machine

The mechanical voting machine made its debut more than a century ago. Today half of American voters in three-fourths of the states cast their ballots on such machines or their electronic successors.

Although Thomas A. Edison invented the voting machine and received his first patent for it in 1869, it was twenty-three years later that a similar machine was first used, at a Lockport, New York, town meeting on April 15, 1892. The creator was Jacob H. Myers, a Rochester safemaker, who built the machine to "protect mechanically the voter from rascaldom, and make the process of casting the ballot perfectly plain, simple and secret."

Unlike the Edison device, which was meant for recording and counting votes in Congress, Myers's machine was intended for public use. As Myers continued to develop his machine, his company expanded to become the Automatic Voting Machine Co. of Jamestown, New York. Its AVM machines are still in use throughout the United States, along with mechanical voting machines built by other companies.

In the 1980s manufacturers introduced electronic voting machines that used computer technology to make the recording, tallying, and delivery of voting results faster and more accurate. Among the new systems was the AVC Advantage made by the AVM successor company, Sequoia Pacific Voting Equipment Inc.

Electronic systems were soon replacing older voting technologies. In Florida, for example, only eight counties in 1998 were using mechanical voting machines, and only one was using manually tabulated paper ballots. The remaining fifty-eight counties were using electronic systems certified by the state Division of Elections. In all, eleven voting systems were certified in Florida, including Sequoia's AVC Advantage.

Although the makers insisted that the electronic machines kept ballots secret and secure, conservative critics were openly skeptical of that claim. In Clark County, Nevada, Republican con-gressional candidate Pat MacMillan filed a federal lawsuit to disqualify the Sequoia Pacific DRE (direct recording electronic) machines used by the county. MacMillan said the machines did not meet Federal Election Commission (FEC) standards and that they allowed the "fixing" of elections. Sequoia, however, said that its machines were FEC certified and that "no system has been more publicly and thoroughly examined and tested than the AVC Advantage."

The FEC sets standards for voting systems but does not certify them. Instead, it recommends use of systems tested and certified by the National Association of State Election Directors (NASED). Sequoia Pacific said its AVC Advantage was certified after testing by one of NASED's independent test authorities and had been approved for use by twenty states.

Sequoia Pacific literature said Clark County had 1,800 machines in 802 precincts "accommodating early voting and utilizing a complete networked Windows-based election management system." Early voting permits a single machine to accept votes from up to two thousand precincts. Several states have early voting laws that allow ballots to be cast before Election Day by mail or at designated polling places.

One complaint of the critics was that unlike older technologies the electronic machines did not leave a "paper trail" to verify results in case of a contested election, recount, or suspected election fraud, a charge that the manufacturers deny. Sequoia, for example, said that its machine "stores an electronic randomized record of all votes cast" and that this "Audit Trail can be printed on demand."

Nevertheless, suspicion of the electronic, networked direct recording devices could be found on the Internet Web sites of several organizations. One group called Voting Integrity Project Inc. (VIP) said it was exploring "the potential for a national institute of electronic voting" to certify the machines and programs in use throughout the country.

Federal voting rights legislation in 1970 permitted voting in presidential elections after thirty days of residence. This provision, upheld by the Supreme Court, extended the franchise to about five million people who might otherwise have been disqualified from voting in the 1972 presidential election. Soon thereafter the Court decided (*Dunn v. Blumstein*) that a state cannot constitutionally restrict the franchise to persons who have lived in the state at least one year and in the county at least three months. The 6–1 opinion, rendered March 21, 1972, caused all the states to change their residency requirements. By 2000, twenty-four states and the District of Columbia had no minimum residency requirement; no other state imposed more than a thirty-day residence requirement.[12]

ELECTION-DAY REGISTRATION

In the late 1970s President Jimmy Carter proposed federal legislation to allow voters to register at the polls on election day, but it was not enacted. Several states, though, have adopted election-day registration on their own, including Minnesota. In 1998, when Reform Party candidate Jesse Ventura closed fast to win the Minnesota governorship, more than 330,000 citizens registered to vote on election day (which represented 16 percent of the ballots cast).

ABSENTEE VOTING

Absentee voting began during the Civil War when Union soldiers were caught up in the political struggle and, with Abraham Lincoln's encouragement, wanted to participate in the elections back home. Since then the absentee ballot has become a widely used staple of American elections, especially in today's busy world, when voters may not have the time or capability to travel to the polls on a given day. Even polling officials, who cannot leave their posts during voting hours, must use absentee ballots if they are assigned to a polling station in another district.

Figure 2-2 Partisan Identification, 1952–2000

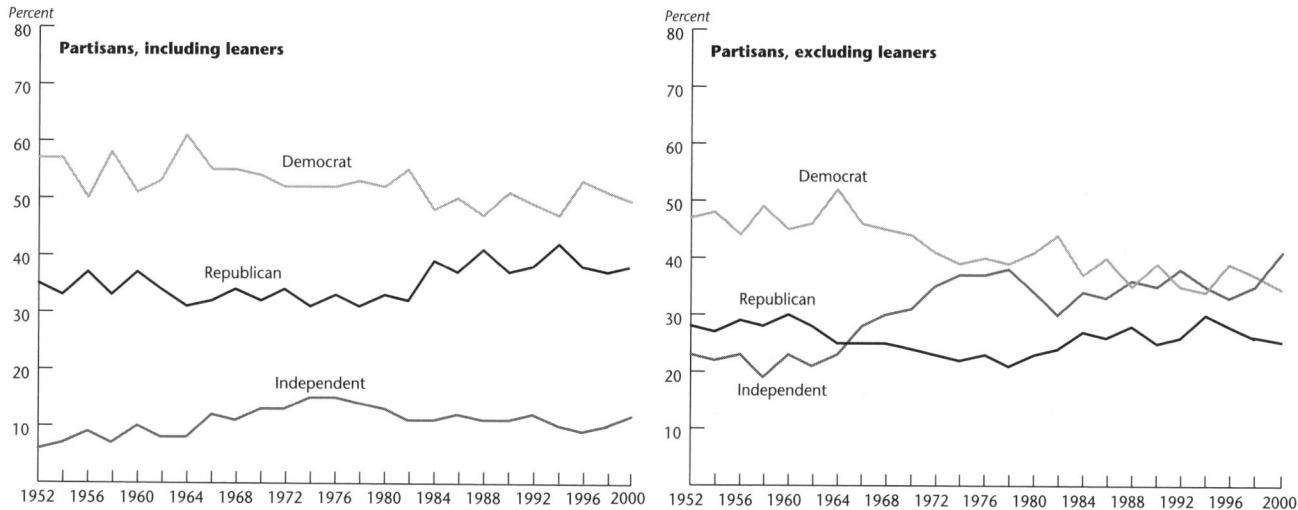

Note: "Leaners" are independents who consider themselves closer to one party.
Source: Harold W. Stanley and Richard G. Niemi, *Vital Statistics on American Politics*, 8th ed. (Washington, D.C.: CQ Press, 2001). Calculated by the authors from National Election Studies codebooks and data sets.

About half the states now have an "early voting" option, including "no-fault" absentee voting open to all voters with no need to plead sickness, disability, or any other reason for wanting to vote before election day. And the number of early voters has grown so significantly that candidates are increasingly adapting their campaign strategies to them. In Florida in the elections of 2000, for example, the Republican Party mailed applications for absentee ballots to about two million registered party members. The Democrats also used this strategy, mailing roughly 150,000. In 2000 about 15 percent of voters nationwide cast absentee ballots; in California the figure was 25 percent.

To receive an absentee ballot, the voter must apply for a ballot that must be returned within a designated period set by law. For the vote to be certified and counted, the voter must carefully follow the canvassing board's instructions, because in a recount a flawed ballot will be challenged and might be thrown out. Absentee votes have decided many a contested election. Much of the litigation that occurred in Florida in the presidential election of 2000 revolved around absentee ballots that lacked the proper postmarks and requests for absentee ballots that lacked a voter identification number.

Absentee Fraud

Because absentee ballots are assumed to be ripe for fraud, election workers devote considerable time to ensuring that they are legitimate. When the ballot is received, a worker usually checks the name on the envelope to verify that the person is a qualified absentee voter and that the signatures match. The worker also must verify that the person has not already voted.

In many states the ballot may then be entered into a computer that counts it, but by law the ballot cannot actually be tabulated until after the polls close on election day. In contrast, the ballots marked in a voting booth are presumed to be authentic and are counted at the polling place or a central election station

when the polls close. Mechanical or computerized voting machines provide an immediate tally at each polling place.

Because many absentee voters mail or drop off their ballots at the last minute, election workers already may be swamped with regular returns when the last batches of time-consuming absentee ballots come in. The absentee ballots are usually set aside, sometimes by law, to be dealt with the day after the election—or as long as it takes to verify that they are not fraudulent. If the election is close, it may be days, weeks, or even months before the winner is known.

During the 2000 elections, the absentee count in California took several days because of the sheer volume (more than two million absentee ballots). Moreover, the counties had twenty-eight days from the date of the election to forward absentee ballots to the state capital. In other states, including Florida, the process also took more than a week because election workers had to wait for all ballots postmarked on election day to arrive. In Washington State, for example, officials count qualified absentee ballots received as many as fifteen days after the election, provided the ballot was postmarked on or before election day. California and Oregon count only ballots received before the polls close at 8:00 p.m. on election day.

Overseas and Military Absentee Voting

In 1976 President Gerald R. Ford signed the Overseas Citizens Voting Rights Act (OCVRA) establishing uniform absentee voting procedures for American citizens who lived overseas. OCVRA gives Americans living abroad the right to vote by absentee ballot. Before going overseas they must have voted in the state where they last lived. Most states limit this group to absentee balloting in federal, not state, elections. Both major political parties currently have overseas organizations of absentee voters, Democrats Abroad and Republicans Abroad.

In 1978 Congress approved legislation that prevented states

Sen. Ron Wyden of Oregon, second from left, reenacts his swearing-in by Vice President Al Gore at the U.S. Capitol February 6, 1996. To Wyden's left is Sen. Mark Hatfield and to his right is Wyden's wife, Carrie. Wyden was the first senator elected by mail.

from using evidence that an American living overseas voted in a state or federal election as proof of residency for tax purposes. Sponsors said many Americans living abroad did not vote because they feared they might have to pay additional taxes.

Men and women in military service make up one of the biggest blocs of absentee voters. Their right to vote, as well as that of other Americans living abroad, is protected by the Federal Voting Assistance Act of 1955 (FVAA) and OCVRA. FVAA applies to military and merchant marine personnel temporarily stationed outside the United States, as well as to their spouses and dependents.

Under both FVAA and OCVRA, application for an absentee ballot is made on federal postcard application, a postage-free U.S. government form that also serves as a voter registration form. Most states accept the postcard as a registration or waive their own registration requirement when the postcard is submitted. A few send out their own registration form along with the absentee ballot.

In the 1996 election cycle, the Federal Voting Assistance Program (FVAP) implemented a program—in cooperation with state and county election bodies—that allowed military personnel to register by fax and in some cases vote by fax as well. Enactment of the 1975 OCVRA significantly changed the meaning of the term—voting residence—for U.S. citizens living outside the country. Under the act, their state of residence became the last one they voted in, even if they had no home there and no intention to return there.

Previously, under the Constitution, states determined eligibility for voting, usually defining residence as the place where the voter or a candidate actually lived. In some cases this restriction forced candidates to maintain residences or voting addresses in the district or precinct they represented, even though they lived elsewhere. Gradually, over the years after OCVRA, the Supreme Court struck down the strictest residency requirements, giving more weight to the national right to vote and holding, in effect, that the voter or candidate is the one who decides what to call home for voting purposes.

VOTING BY MAIL

Given the success of absentee voting and the dependability of the postal service, various groups have advocated vote-by-mail plans to encourage wider participation in the electoral process, which in the United States has been characterized by a voter turnout much lower than in many other industrialized countries. Proponents argue that the benefits of voting by mail—including convenience, speed, and lower costs—outweigh the disadvantages, including the possible abuse of the system, and the lost sociability that comes with gathering at the polls.

In 1995 and 1996 the vote-by-mail concept was put to the test in two states, Nevada and Oregon. In Nevada the 1996 Republican presidential primary was held entirely by mail-in vote. Oregon in 1995 conducted the largest test, using mail-in votes for a special election to fill a vacant Senate seat. The winner was Democrat Ron Wyden, the first senator elected by mail. Both the Senate primaries in 1995 and the general election in early 1996 were conducted by mail. Oregon officials were pleased with the turnout—about 57 percent of the eligible 1.8 million voters. More than three-quarters of those Oregonians polled said they preferred voting by mail over going to the polling places. Women and older voters were strongest in favor of mail voting.

Oregon subsequently became the first state to decide to hold all elections by mail, approving a ballot measure in 1998 requiring vote by mail in biennial primary and general elections. The measure eliminated polling places, but it did not affect existing law allowing absentee ballots or voting at local election offices. Oregon conducted all of its 2000 balloting by mail. The rate of voter participation in Oregon in 2000 was reported to be in the neighborhood of 80 percent, which is significantly higher than the national average.

A potential for abuse of the vote-by-mail system surfaced in Oregon when candidates were able to obtain from election officials the names of voters who had not yet returned their ballots. Critics said this information left voters open to undue solicitation or even harassment by candidates.

An argument against use of the mails to provide a longer voting period is that it could invite fraud, and indeed there have been instances where the number of votes cast in an election, including absentee ballots, exceeded the number of people living in the community. Another problem with mail-in votes is that duplicate or undelivered ballots could be cast by the wrong persons. But the chances of this particular fraud's being successful are reduced by the standard requirement that the voter's signature be on the envelope.

Mail elections are estimated to cost one-third to one-half less than conventional elections. The U.S. Postal Service in promotional advertising has estimated that the cost of postal voting can be as much as $1 million lower, because there are no polling personnel to pay, no space to rent, no polling equipment to transport and set up.

Although mail voting may be cheaper than a regular election, absentee voting in conjunction with a voting-booth election is more expensive per vote than the polling place balloting. Election officials estimate that absentee ballots require three to four times more labor to process.

Postal voting is part of a larger trend since the 1980s toward easier voting. A few states such as Colorado, Texas, and Tennessee have experimented with opening voting-style booths before election day in stores or other public places. Most states, however, have simply made absentee ballots available to all, creating a hybrid system that proponents of postal mail decry as the worst of both worlds, combining the labor-intensive costs of absentee voting with the equipment and location costs of voting booth elections.

More than twenty states have early voting options, with polling stations open as much as twenty-one days before the election. Citizens can use them to vote early without giving a reason, and their votes are counted on election day like regular ballots, causing no delays. Because of their growing numbers, early voters are being courted by candidates as never before. In 1998 California Democrat Lois Capps urged supporters to take advantage of the state's liberal absentee voting law. The 18,000 early absentee votes she received helped her to win a difficult race for reelection to the U.S. House.

VOTING BY INTERNET

Voting by telephone or the Internet has been suggested as another way to make election day more convenient. Computerized voting machines can report their totals through modems, and with passwords and other security precautions they could receive the voters' choice just as easily.

In 1996 the Reform Party sent 1.3 million primary ballots to Reform Party members across the country in conducting their one-week-long "national primary." Party members could choose to vote via mail, phone, or electronic mail. Ross Perot won his party's nomination via these methods.

Between 1996 and 2000 the Defense Department began to develop an Internet-based system for military voters. By the elections of 2000, the Federal Voting Assistance Program had in place a demonstration project that allowed a small sample of test voters from all five armed services to cast their ballots over the Internet. The goal was to prove that the concept met the basic goals of an Internet-based voting system: secrecy of the ballot, security of the ballot from tampering, and consistency with all requirements of a paper ballot, including a (digital) signature.

After the controversial presidential election of 2000, which revealed an array of problems with old-fashioned voting machinery, Congress and voting organizations began to look more closely at Internet voting in the drive to modernize voting systems. As with the military test program of 2000, once Internet ballot security and secrecy can be guaranteed, Internet voting may become widespread in the near future.

Notes

1. Max Farrand, ed., *The Records of the Federal Convention of 1787* (New Haven, Conn.: Yale University Press, 1966), vol. 2, 178.

2. Mellman and Scammon are quoted in *President Bush, The Challenge Ahead* (Washington, D.C.: Congressional Quarterly, 1989), 3.

3. Benjamin Highton and Raymond E. Wolfinger, "The Political Implications of Higher Turnout" (paper presented at the 1998 annual meeting of the American Political Science Association), Boston, September 1998, 10.

4. Claudia Deane, "With the GOP Takeover, There Should Be a Voter Shift Between the Parties. Right?" *Washington Post,* April 29, 2001, A13.

5. Gunnar Myrdal, *An American Dilemma: The Negro Problem and Modern Democracy* (New York: Harper and Row, 1944), 445.

6. Paul Lewinson, *Race, Class and Party: A History of Negro Suffrage and White Politics in the South* (New York: Oxford University Press, 1932), 194.

7. Frederic D. Ogden, *The Poll Tax in the South* (University: University of Alabama Press, 1958), 2–4.

8. Myrdal, *An American Dilemma,* 485.

9. U.S. Commission on Civil Rights, *Voter Participation* (May 1968), 223. See also U.S. Commission on Civil Rights, *The Voting Rights Act: Ten Years Later* (January 1975), 60.

10. Joan Biskupic and Elder Witt, *Guide to the U.S. Supreme Court* (Washington, D.C.: Congressional Quarterly, 1997), 529.

11. Mary Costello, "Women Voters," *Editorial Research Reports* (Washington, D.C.: Congressional Quarterly, 1972), 776.

12. Information from annual editions of *The Book of the States* (Washington, D.C.: The Council of State Governments).

PART II

Political Parties

3. Political Party Development   43

4. Historical Profiles of American
   Political Parties   51

5. Campaign Finance   83

6. The Historical Significance of
   Southern Primaries   129

7. Politics and Issues, 1945-2000   133

CHAPTER 3

Political Party Development

POLITICAL PARTIES are organizations that seek to gain control of government to further their social, economic, or ideological goals. The United States has usually had a two-party system, dominated since 1860 by the Democratic and Republican Parties. Yet more than eighty political parties have formed since the 1790s, and "third parties" have occasionally had a decisive impact on presidential elections. For example, in 1912 the "Bull Moose Party" of former president Theodore Roosevelt siphoned enough Republican votes from the incumbent, William Howard Taft, to enable the Democrat, Woodrow Wilson, to win the election.

The United States did not start out with a two-party system—or any parties at all. Initially there were no formal parties, and in the early 1820s the nation had in effect only one party. The Founders did not anticipate parties-which they derisively called factions-and this central aspect of American politics was unplanned and had no formal constitutional or legal status. Indeed, having seen the ill effects of overzealous parties in monarchical England and (beginning in 1789) revolutionary France, the Founders hoped to avoid similar pitfalls in the fledgling nation. Thus, in Federalist 10 James Madison bragged that one of the Constitution's great virtues was that it would head off "the mischiefs of faction." In 1789 Thomas Jefferson declared: "If I could not go to heaven but with a party, I would not go there at all." Similarly, in his farewell address in 1796 George Washington warned that, in elective popular governments, the dangers of excess in the "spirit of party" demanded "a uniform vigilance to prevent its bursting into a flame."

By the time Washington issued his warning, he was the titular head of the Federalist Party, which faded after 1800 and, except for some local officeholders, was dead by 1821. Meanwhile, since 1794 Madison and Jefferson had been the leaders of another party, variously called the Democratic-Republicans, the Jeffersonian Democrats, and the Jeffersonian Republicans, but today understood as the kernel of what became the modern Demo-cratic Party.

Political Issues
and the Emergence of Parties

The debate over ratification of the Constitution led to the organization of factions but not parties. Future Democratic-Republicans and Federalists, like Madison and Alexander Hamilton, worked together for ratification, just as future Democratic-Republicans and Federalists, like James Monroe and Samuel Chase, worked against ratification of the Constitution.

Ratification brought about a new national government, where parties were unknown. Presidential electors unanimously elected Washington as the first president, and nearly half of them supported Adams, who was easily elected vice president. Washington's cabinet included future leaders of the nation's first two parties: the future Federalist leader Alexander Hamilton and the future leader of the Democratic-Republicans, Thomas Jefferson.

By the end of Washington's administration two parties were fully engaged in politics. The parties differed over the nature of public policy and the interpretation of the Constitution. The Federalists, led by Hamilton, John Adams, and John Jay, favored a national government vigorously involved in economic development. Key to the Federalist program was the establishment of a national bank, federal funding at face value of all state and national bonds issued during the Revolution, and a flexible interpretation of the Constitution. The Federalists also wanted to strengthen diplomatic and commercial ties with England.

Jefferson's followers, called Democratic-Republicans at this time, opposed funding the war debts at par because many of the original bond holders had sold their bonds at depreciated values to speculators. Their hostility to commerce and business also led them to oppose the establishment of a national bank. Unsuccessful on these issues, the Democratic-Republicans were nonetheless able to thwart Hamilton's plan to use high tariffs to stimulate commerce and manufacturing in the new country. Jefferson and his followers wanted a strict interpretation of the Constitution, favored states' rights over national power, and in foreign policy supported France in its wars with England.

On issues involving race, slavery, and foreign policy, the parties also differed. The Federalists favored giving full diplomatic recognition to Haiti, a black republic in the Caribbean, and refused to seek the return of slaves who had escaped with the British at the end of the Revolution. Jefferson, by contrast, unsuccessfully demanded the return of the slaves but was successful as president in blocking any diplomatic ties to Haiti.

Presidents, Parties,
and Policies, 1800–1860

By the time of Jefferson's election in 1800, ending twelve years of Federalist control, the party concept was entrenched in U.S. politics. Despite his previous denunciation of parties, Jefferson justified his own party leadership as a necessary opposition to the "Monocrats of our country." Jefferson's election by the House, after a tie electoral vote between him and Aaron Burr, led to adoption of the Twelfth Amendment to the Constitution in 1804. That amendment, which required electors to

Political parties emerged in part from differences over policy in President George Washington's cabinet. Left to right: President Washington, Secretary of War Henry Knox, Secretary of the Treasury Alexander Hamilton, Secretary of State Thomas Jefferson, and Attorney General Edmund Randolph.

vote separately for president and vice president, further buried the likelihood of "partyless" U.S. elections.

Federalists nearly won the presidency in 1800 and 1812, but the party quickly withered after the War of 1812, when many party leaders opposed the war and flirted with secession, most notably at the Hartford Convention of 1814–1815. Federalists made a brief comeback in 1819–1820 during the debates over allowing slavery in Missouri on its admission to the Union, but the party was effectively dead by the end of 1820, when James Monroe ran unopposed for reelection.

A system with only one party was less stable than a system with two or more parties. In 1824 four candidates competed for the presidency, with no one getting a majority of the popular or the electoral vote. The House of Representatives chose John Quincy Adams, who ran second in both categories. Andrew Jackson, who had led in popular and electoral votes, immediately began his campaign for the presidency, and he won in 1828. In 1832 the Anti-Masonic Party made its brief appearance, winning seven electoral votes, while Jackson was easily reelected. Jackson inherited the mantle of Jefferson and his party, while his political and personal opponents, such as Daniel Webster, Henry Clay, and John Quincy Adams, migrated in the 1830s to the newly formed Whig Party. In 1836 four Whigs, representing different regions of the country, competed for the presidency against Jackson's heir, Martin Van Buren.

The Whigs won the presidency in 1840 and 1848; Democrats won in 1836, 1844, 1852, and 1856. The Whigs favored a national bank, federal support for internal improvements, national bankruptcy laws, protective tariffs, and a relatively humane policy toward American Indians. The Democrats disagreed with all these positions. Whigs opposed territorial acquisition, especially by force, whereas Democrats annexed Texas and eventually pushed the United States into a war with Mexico to gain new territory in the Southwest, advocating that it was the "manifest destiny" of the United States to control the continent. The Jacksonian Democrats pushed for universal adult white male suffrage throughout the country, but at the same time worked to take the vote away from free blacks and to strengthen slavery at the national and local level. Jackson's presidency is most remembered for his veto of the rechartering of the Second Bank of the United States, his successful opposition to internal improvements, and his policy of Indian removal, which pushed almost all Native Americans in the east into the Indian Territory (present-day Oklahoma). On an important issue that seemed to transcend party politics, Jackson vigorously opposed extreme states' rights ideology when South Carolina attempted to nullify a federal tariff. However, following the nullification crisis, the Democrats became increasingly solicitous of states' rights and southern demands for protections for slavery. Jackson and his fellow Democrats also accepted the South Carolinians' critique of the tariff, even as they rejected the Carolinians' response, nullification.

The nation had two major parties in the 1840s, but third parties influenced some elections. In 1844 the antislavery Liberty Party won enough votes in New York to cost the Whigs the state and the presidential election, assuming all the Liberty voters would have supported the Whigs. The Whig candidate, Henry Clay, opposed expansion and was more moderate on slavery than his opponent, but it seems unlikely that the committed abolitionists who voted for the Liberty Party would otherwise

Illustration of the Republican nomination convention of 1860 that chose Abraham Lincoln for president.

have voted for the slave-owning Clay as the lesser of two evils. In 1848, however, the Free Soil candidate, former president Martin Van Buren, won more than 290,000 votes, many of which would have otherwise gone to the Democratic candidate, Lewis Cass of Michigan. As a result, the Whig candidate, Gen. Zachary Taylor, won the election. Equally significant, Free Soilers won state and local races, and in Ohio they held the balance of power in the state legislature and were able to elect an antislavery Democrat, Salmon P. Chase, to the U.S. Senate.

Yet the victorious Whigs of 1848 managed to carry only four states in 1852, and the party disappeared two years later. The 1856 election saw two new parties emerge: the Know Nothing (American) Party and the Republican Party.

The Know Nothing, or American, Party was a single-issue party, opposed to immigration in general and Catholic immigration in particular. The Know Nothings won a number of governorships and dominated a few state legislatures, including Massachusetts, in this period. In 1856 the Speaker of the House of Representatives, Nathaniel Banks, was a Know Nothing.

The Republican Party adopted many Whig policies but opposed the extension of slavery into the western territories. Many Republican leaders were former Whigs, including Abraham Lincoln and his secretary of state, William H. Seward. Others came from the antislavery wing of the Democratic Party, among them Lincoln's vice president, Hannibal Hamlin, and secretary of the Treasury, Salmon P. Chase. By 1858 many Know Nothings had also joined this party. In 1856 the Republican candidate, John C. Fremont, and the Know Nothing candidate, Millard Fillmore, together won about 400,000 more popular votes than James Buchanan, but Buchanan had the plurality of popular votes

and, more important, carried nineteen states to win the election. Buchanan was the first "sectional" president since 1824, as fourteen of the states he carried were in the South. This election underscored that the Democrats had become the party of slavery and the South.

The proslavery southerners who controlled the Democratic Party insisted on fidelity to their program to expand slavery into the territories. This arrangement unraveled in 1860, as the Democrats split into two parties-regular Democrats nominating Stephen A. Douglas of Illinois and southern Democrats nominating John C. Breckinridge of Kentucky. The Republican candidate, Abraham Lincoln, carried every northern state. Moderates in the North and the South supported the Constitutional Union Party, which hoped to hold the Union together by not discussing any of the key issues. The two Democratic parties and the Constitutional Unionists combined for more popular votes than Lincoln (who was not even on the ballot in many southern states), but Lincoln carried eighteen states and easily won a majority of the electoral college.

Parties in U.S. Politics since 1860

Lincoln's victory set the stage for Republican dominance in national politics for the next half-century. During this period the Republicans stood at various times for preservation of the Union, homestead laws to facilitate western settlement, federal support for a transcontinental railroad, protective tariffs, abolition of slavery, guarantees of African Americans' civil rights, and the suppression of Mormon polygamists in the West. Democrats favored lower tariffs; opposed emancipation and civil

Franklin D. Roosevelt's presidential victory in 1932 ushered in an era of Democratic control of the federal government.

rights; and championed white immigrants (but not immigrants from Asia), labor unions, and (at the end of the century) small farmers in the South and West. In international affairs, the late-nineteenth-century Republicans favored expansion, ultimately leading to war with Spain and the acquisition of an overseas empire, while Democrats opposed these trends, with Grover Cleveland (the only Democratic president in this period) refusing to annex Hawaii.

From 1868 to 1908 various third parties-including the Liberal Republican, Greenback, Prohibitionist, Equal Rights, Anti-Monopoly, Workers, Socialist Labor, Socialist, United Christian, and Populist Parties-ran candidates. With the exception of the Populists in 1892, however, none ever won any electoral votes. Some of these parties did, however, elect candidates to state and local office and to Congress. James B. Weaver, for example, ran successfully for Congress on the Greenback ticket in 1878, 1884, and 1886; ran for president on the Greenback ticket in 1880; and ran for president on the Populist ticket in 1892.

In 1912 a third party determined the outcome of the presidential race. The Republicans split as former president Theodore Roosevelt tried, and failed, to gain renomination after a term out of the White House. Roosevelt thought that his successor, William Howard Taft, had abandoned the progressive goals of the party. Running on the Progressive ("Bull Moose") ticket, Roosevelt carried six states and won about half a million more popular votes than Taft. Together they outpolled Wilson, but Wilson carried forty states and won the election. The Socialist candidate, Eugene V. Debs, won nearly a million votes in the 1912 election, and, although he carried no states, Socialists won various local elections and sent some party members to Congress. Victor Berger of Milwaukee, for example, served in Congress as a Socialist from 1911 to 1913 and from 1923 to 1929. He was also elected in 1918, but in that year Congress refused to allow him to take his seat because of his opposition to World War I.

Between the 1910s and the 1940s, Democrats became increasingly internationalist, while Republicans opposed American entrance into the League of Nations after World War I and were isolationist in the 1930s as the world moved toward a second

world war. Democratic support came from labor, white southerners, and most northern urban immigrant groups. By the 1930s, blacks began to leave the Republican Party, forced out by "lily white" Republicans in the South and welcomed into the emerging New Deal coalition. The Republicans by this time had become the party of conservative business interests, white Protestants (outside the South), small town and rural northerners, and owners of small businesses.

Various third parties ran presidential candidates in the 1920s and 1930s, but only Robert M. La Follette, running as the Progressive Party candidate in 1924, won any electoral votes. In 1948, though, southern "Dixiecrats," who abandoned the Democratic Party to protest President Harry S. Truman's support for civil rights and racial equality, took four Deep South states. Some other Democrats supported former vice president Henry A. Wallace, running on the Progressive ticket that year. Despite these defections, Truman won. At the state and local level, third parties were sometimes successful, and various candidates running on socialist, communist, or various other tickets sporadically held office. For example, Wisconsin elected Progressives Robert M. La Follette Jr. to the Senate in 1934 and 1940 and Merlin Hull to the House from 1934 to 1944. Benjamin J. Davis, running as a Communist, served on the New York City Council as the "Communist Councilman from Harlem," while Vito Marcantonio, who had served one term in Congress as a Republican (1935–1937), served six terms in Congress (1939–1951) running on the ticket of the American Labor Party, which had Communist Party support. Independents also had some success; Henry F. Reams of Ohio, for example, served two full terms in the House (1951–1955).

By the 1960s, Republicans and Democrats had swapped places on the issue of African Americans' civil rights since a hundred years earlier. In 1964 large numbers of white southerners left the Democratic Party over President Lyndon Johnson's support for civil rights. Since then the Democratic constituency has generally comprised urban, northern, and far western liberals; Catholics and Jews; African Americans, Hispanics, Asian-Americans, and ethnic minorities; blue-collar workers; and the underprivileged. Republicans are viewed as conservatives, southerners, white Protestants, and the affluent.

Third parties continued to run presidential candidates, and in some places candidates for Congress and state and local offices. In the 1960s John Lindsay, a former Republican congressman, was elected mayor of New York City on the Liberal Party line, and in 1970 James L. Buckley won a U.S. Senate seat from New York, running on the Conservative Party line. But third-party candidates have also been spoilers, as in 1980 when incumbent Republican senator Jacob Javits of New York lost his party's nomination and ran as a Liberal Party candidate, dividing the votes of moderates, liberals, and Democrats and thus allowing for the election of conservative Republican Alfonse D'Amato.

George C. Wallace, running in 1968 as the presidential candidate of the segregationist American Independent Party, captured five states in the South. Most of his supporters voted Republican in subsequent elections. In 1980 former U.S. represen-

Figure 3-1   American Political Parties 1789–2000

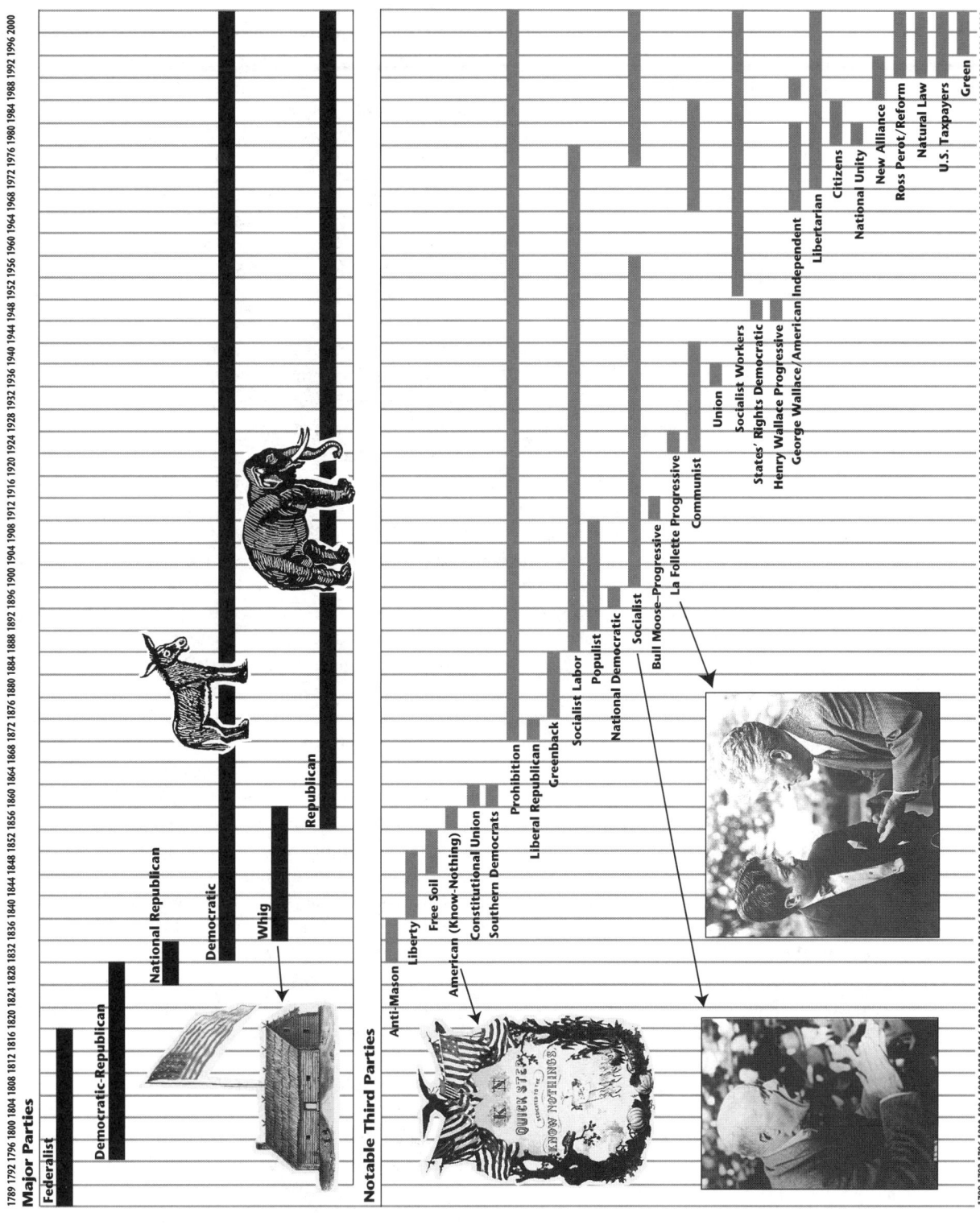

Note: Throughout U.S. history there have been more than 1,500 political parties. For this chart Congressional Quarterly editors have selected those parties that achieved national significance during presidential election years. The spaces between the rules on this chart indicate the election year only. For example, the Constitutional Union Party and the Southern Democrats were in existence for the 1860 election only and were gone by 1864. Similarly, the Green Party first fielded a presidential candidate in 1996.

tative John Anderson ran on the National Unity Party ticket and carried more than 5 million popular votes, but he did not affect the election of Ronald Reagan. In 1992 H. Ross Perot ran as an independent and won almost 20 million votes, and he may have cost the incumbent, George Herbert Walker Bush, a few states. Perot influenced policy in the 1990s by highlighting the importance of the national debt and thus nudging a change in policy that brought balanced budgets and a declining debt by the end of the decade. When he ran again in 1996, however, he had no effect on the election. In 2000 Ralph Nader, running on the Green Party ticket, won enough votes in several states to give their electoral college votes to Gov. George W. Bush instead of Vice President Al Gore.

Party Systems

Historians and political scientists often use the concept "party systems" to refer to eras that more or less hang together in terms of major party alignment. The first, from 1789 to approximately 1824, marked the emergence of a two-party system and lasted from Washington's presidency through the end of the "Virginia Dynasty." The second, from 1828 through 1854, marked the years from Jackson's elections through the demise of the Whig Party. The third, from 1856 through 1896, marked the emergence of the Republican Party and its rise to dominance. The 1896 election marked a transition to a period that featured the Progressive era and persisted through World War I and the 1920s. The election of Franklin D. Roosevelt in 1932 marked another great electoral realignment, although the Democrats occasionally lost the presidency or one or both chambers of Congress in the years that followed.

In the sixty-eight-year period from 1933 through 2001, Democrats held the White House for forty years. The exceptions were the eight Eisenhower years (1953–1961), the eight Nixon-Ford years (1969–1977), and the twelve Reagan-Bush years (1981–1993). In Congress, Democratic dominance was even more striking. Democrats controlled the House for all but four years (1947–1949 and 1953–1955) from 1933 until the Republican takeover of both chambers in 1995. Democratic control of the Senate was less consistent, with four periods of Republican majorities totaling sixteen years between 1933 and 2001. During this period third-party candidates became increasingly insignificant, although by 2001 one "socialist" and one "independent" served in the House, and one "independent" served in the Senate.

Internal Party Politics

Although all presidents since 1852 have been either Democrats or Republicans, their parties have sometimes borrowed ideas from third parties that quickly faded from the U.S. political scene. For example, the Democrats under Andrew Jackson in 1832 followed the example of the Anti-Masons in holding a national convention to nominate their presidential candidate. Previously, party caucuses in Congress, called King Caucus, chose their nominees in secret meetings. The 1824 election of John Quincy Adams, nominated by the Massachusetts legislature,

spelled the end of King Caucus. The House decided the election when none of the four candidates, all Democratic-Republicans, failed to win the required electoral vote majority. The 1828 election, won by Jackson, marked a transition to the as-yet-unborn convention system.

National nominating conventions have remained a staple of the political party system, but they have been more show than substance in the age of primaries and television. With the presumptive nominee known well in advance, the convention nomination is a formality, although the convention still has the important duty of writing a party platform.

The Democratic convention of 1952, which chose Adlai Stevenson to oppose Republican Dwight D. Eisenhower, was the most recent to require more than one ballot to select a nominee. Multiple ballots were common earlier, particularly at Democratic conventions because of the party's rule requiring a two-thirds majority for nomination. Democrats dropped the rule, never used by Republicans, in 1936.

The primary system was a creation of the Progressive era of the early twentieth century. Progressive governor Robert M. La Follette of Wisconsin pushed through a state primary law in 1905, but few other states followed suit until after 1968. Primary elections and caucuses became the de facto presidential nominating mechanisms after the tumultuous 1968 Democratic convention, won by Hubert H. Humphrey without entering any primaries. As the Democrats strengthened their primary rules in the 1970s and 1980s, primaries proliferated in both parties, and they came earlier and earlier in the election year. In 1996 more than forty states held presidential primaries, most of them before April. In 2000 Al Gore and George W. Bush had locked up their nominations early in the primary season.

Federal and state campaign finance reforms enacted since the 1970s have both helped and hindered political parties. Beginning in 1976 presidential candidates became eligible for public financing of their campaigns, which reduced their reliance on money from party coffers. However, the legislation allowed "soft money," contributions given directly to the parties, ostensibly for party building but often diverted to indirect support for the party's candidate. The reform legislation also permitted interest groups and candidates to form political action committees (PACs) to raise and spend money for campaigns. This further reduced candidates' dependence on the political parties, with the result that more and more campaigns are candidate-centered rather than party-centered.

Third Parties

Although the United States has always had a two-party system, third parties have frequently played a vital role in the political order. No third-party candidate has ever been elected to the presidency, but many have been elected to other federal, state, and local offices. The votes third parties have garnered have also been a crucial factor in the outcome of elections. Moreover, the issues spotlighted by minor parties have often ended up being co-opted into the platforms of the major parties.

William Wirt.

NINETEENTH-CENTURY THIRD PARTIES

As the original party system of Hamiltonian Federalists and Jeffersonian Democratic-Republicans broke down, and the National Republican Party developed and transformed itself into the Whig Party, there also arose the Anti-Masonic Party, which ran William Wirt for president in 1832, gaining almost 8 percent of the popular vote. Nonetheless, they achieved some state and local offices, particularly in New York State, where the party originated.

In 1844 the Liberty Party, which opposed slavery, won 2.3 percent of the popular vote, and it may have affected the outcome of the election. In 1848, however, the less radical Free Soil Party, which was dedicated to stopping the spread of slavery in the territories, played the role of spoiler. Running former president Martin Van Buren, the party won enough votes, mostly from Democrats, to enable the Whig candidate, Zachary Taylor, to defeat the Democrat, Lewis Cass. It ran John P. Hale for president in 1852, obtaining 5 percent of the popular vote. The demise of the Free Soil Party was caused primarily by the rise of the Republican Party, which took up its stance in opposition to slavery in the territories.

In the 1850s the American Party, otherwise known as the Know Nothing Party, reaped large votes in Pennsylvania and New York and even briefly gained control over the Massachusetts government. The party's main goals were excluding Catholics from public office, enacting restrictive immigration laws, and establishing literacy tests for voting.

Parties such as the Greenback Party (1874–1884) and the Prohibition Party, which started in 1869 and has continued ever since, never attracted many votes on the national level, but their success rested in convincing one of the major parties to take up their cause. Eventually the Republican Party embraced Prohibition, while the Democratic Party espoused the expansion of the money supply, albeit with the free coinage of silver rather than by printing greenbacks.

The Populist (or People's) Party, which represented the interests of farmers and labor, arose in the South and West in the 1880s. Because it spoke for a perennial debtor class, the party tended to favor the free coinage of silver and backed free trade and the regulation of the railroads. The Populist platform would eventually be adopted by the Democratic Party under its 1896 presidential candidate, William Jennings Bryan.

THIRD PARTIES IN THE TWENTIETH CENTURY

The Socialist Party came to prominence in the Progressive era, with members winning state and local offices and serving in Congress. In 1904 it ran Eugene V. Debs for president, winning 3 percent of the vote against the Republican incumbent Theodore Roosevelt and Alton B. Parker, the Democrat. Debs would run again in 1908, 1912, and 1920, and in this last election (campaigning from a federal penitentiary, where he was imprisoned for opposition to World War I) he tallied 915,490 votes (3.4 percent). Later, Norman Thomas would serve as the Socialist Party standard bearer in several elections, with his largest vote in 1932 when he won 884,649 votes (2.2 percent). Before World War I, socialist Victor Berger served as mayor of Milwaukee, and he served as a member of the House of Representatives from 1911 to 1913 and from 1923 to 1929.

Although they lack the long-term ideological impact of the third parties described above, some minor parties have served as vehicles for the candidacies of certain individuals. The Progressive (or Bull Moose) Party became a vehicle for Theodore Roosevelt's attempt to recapture the White House in 1912, running against Democrat Woodrow Wilson and Republican William Howard Taft. In that race, all three candidates were Progressives to an extent. When Taft's people prevented Roosevelt delegates from some states from being seated at the Republican convention, Roosevelt bolted the party and ran as a Progressive. The result was a split of the Republican vote and a victory for Wilson.

In 1924 the Progressive Party ran Robert M. La Follette for president, capturing 16.6 percent of the vote. In 1948, using the Progressive Party label, Henry A. Wallace, Franklin D. Roosevelt's former vice president and secretary of agriculture, scored 2.4 percent of the vote in a four-way race that saw Harry Truman reelected. Wallace ran to the left of Truman on both domestic and foreign affairs, where he pushed for greater cooperation with the Soviet Union. The 1948 election also saw the emergence of another third party, the States' Rights, or Dixiecrat, Party. The Dixiecrats ran J. Strom Thurmond, the governor of South Carolina, for president, opposing the Democratic Party's adoption of a civil rights plank in its 1948 platform. Thurmond won 2.4 percent of the vote.

In the close 1968 presidential race between Richard M. Nixon and Hubert H. Humphrey, George C. Wallace, the governor of Alabama, captured 13.5 percent of the popular vote and forty-six electoral votes. He ran on the American Independent ticket, pushing a conservative and somewhat racist agenda. In 1980 John B. Anderson ran on an independent line against Ronald Reagan and Jimmy Carter and received 6.6 percent of the popular vote but no electoral votes. In 1992 H. Ross Perot ran for president as an Independent, receiving 18.9 percent of the vote but no electoral votes. In 1996 he ran again under the Reform Party banner. This party has run candidates for state and local office across the country, and in 1998 Jesse Ventura was elected governor of Minnesota on the Reform Party line. In 2000 the Reform Party seemed destined for oblivion as it split down the middle over the contested nomination of Patrick J. Buchanan for president.

Today the Libertarian Party and the Green Party offer fairly consistent ideologies through their third-party movements. Because they are primarily ideologically based, however, they are the more likely to be absorbed eventually by a major party that has co-opted their ideas and raided their constituencies.

CHAPTER 4

Historical Profiles of American Political Parties

Aᴸᴛʜᴏᴜɢʜ ᴘᴏʟɪᴛɪᴄᴀʟ ᴘᴀʀᴛɪᴇs are not directly mentioned in the U.S. Constitution, they emerged in short order to become and remain an integral part of the American system of elected government. Today, as well as when they appeared in the 1790s, they satisfy an important need for U.S. democracy: bringing people with the same beliefs together to govern at the local and national levels. At nearly every moment in the nation's history there have been two major political parties in operation. Since the 1860s, the Democratic and Republican Parties have been dominant.

Third parties also have had an important role in history: providing the forum for radical ideas, not accepted by the ruling parties of the day, to take root. Ideas such as the abolition of slavery, women's suffrage, minimum wages, and Social Security were first long advocated by third parties before they were finally adopted by the major parties and accepted by the nation as a whole. This chapter examines the origins, development, and important policy ideas of all major parties and noteworthy third parties in U.S. history.

American Independent Party (1968–) and American Party (1972–)

Both the American Party and the American Independent Party descended from the American Independent Party that served as the vehicle for George C. Wallace's third-party presidential candidacy in 1968.

Wallace, governor of Alabama (1963–1967; 1971–1979), burst onto the national scene in 1964 as a Democratic presidential candidate opposed to the 1964 Civil Rights Act. Entering three northern primaries—Wisconsin, Indiana, and Maryland—he surprised political observers by winning between 30 percent and 43 percent of the popular vote in the three states. His unexpectedly strong showing brought the term "white backlash" into the political vocabulary as a description of the racial undertone of the Wallace vote.

In 1968 Wallace broke with the Democrats and embarked on his second presidential campaign as a third-party candidate under the American Independent Party label. His candidacy capitalized on the bitter reactions of millions of voters, especially whites and blue-collar workers, to the civil rights activism, urban riots, antiwar demonstrations, and heavy federal spending on Johnson administration "Great Society" programs that marked the mid-1960s. With the help of his Alabama advisers and volunteer groups, Wallace was able to get his party on the ballot in all fifty states.

The former governor did not hold a convention for his party, but in October he announced his vice-presidential running

mate (retired air force general Curtis LeMay) and released a platform. In the November election the Wallace-LeMay ticket received 9,906,473 votes (13.5 percent of the popular vote), carried five southern states, and won forty-six electoral votes. The party's showing was the best by a third party since 1924, when Robert M. La Follette collected 16.6 percent of the vote on the Progressive Party ticket.

After his defeat in that election, Wallace returned to the Democratic Party, competing in Democratic presidential primaries in 1972 and 1976. Wallace's American Independent Party began to break into factions after the 1968 election but in 1972 united behind John G. Schmitz, a Republican U.S. representative from southern California (1970–1973), as its presidential nominee. Thomas J. Anderson, a farm magazine and syndicated news features publisher from Tennessee, was the party's vice-presidential candidate. In many states, the party shortened its name to American Party. In the November election, the Schmitz-Anderson ticket won 1,099,482 votes (1.4 percent of the popular vote) but failed to win any electoral votes. The ticket ran best in the West, taking 9 percent of the vote in Idaho, 7 percent in Alaska, and 6 percent in Utah.

In December 1972 a bitter fight occurred for the chairmanship of the American Independent Party between Anderson and William K. Shearer, the California chairman of the party. Anderson defeated Shearer, retaining control of the party but renaming it the American Party. Shearer, over the following four years, expanded his California-based group into a new national party. He had kept the name American Independent Party in California and made that the name of the new nationwide group.

By 1976 there were two distinct entities: the American Party headed by Anderson and the American Independent Party headed by Shearer.

The 1976 American Party convention was held in Salt Lake City, Utah, in June. Anderson was nominated for president and Rufus Shackleford of Florida for vice president.

The party's nomination of Anderson followed its failure to enlist a prominent conservative to lead the ticket. Both Gov. Meldrim Thomson Jr. of New Hampshire and Sen. Jesse Helms of North Carolina were approached, but both decided to remain in the Republican Party. With well-known conservatives declining the party's overtures, the convention turned to Anderson. He easily won the nomination on the first ballot by defeating six party workers.

Anderson's campaign stressed the "permanent principles" of the party, augmented by the 1976 platform. These principles included opposition to foreign aid, U.S. withdrawal from the United Nations, and an end to trade with or recognition of communist nations. The platform included planks opposing abortion, gun control, the Equal Rights Amendment, and government-sponsored health care and welfare programs. In general, the party favored limits on federal power and was against budget deficits except in wartime.

The American Party was on the ballot in eighteen states, including eight states where the American Independent Party was also. In seven of those eight states, Anderson ran ahead of the American Independent Party ticket. Anderson's strength was spread fairly evenly across the country. His best showings were in Utah (2.5 percent of the vote) and Montana (1.8 percent). Anderson's total of 160,773 popular votes (0.2 percent) placed him almost 10,000 votes behind the American Independent Party candidate nationally.

The American Independent Party convention met in Chicago in August 1976 and chose former Georgia governor Lester Maddox (1967–1971), a Democrat, as its presidential nominee and former Madison, Wisconsin, mayor William Dyke, a Republican, as its vice-presidential candidate. Maddox won a first-ballot nomination over Dallas columnist Robert Morris and former representative John R. Rarick, a Democrat of Louisiana (1967–1975).

At the convention, a group of nationally prominent conservatives made a bid to take over the party and use it as a vehicle to build a new conservative coalition. Richard Viguerie, a fundraiser for Wallace and a nationally known direct mail expert, was the leader of the group. He was joined at the convention by two leading conservatives—William Rusher, publisher of the *National Review,* and Howard Phillips, the former head of the Office of Economic Opportunity (1973) and leader of the Conservative Caucus, an activist conservative group. Viguerie, Phillips, and Rusher all argued that the American Independent Party should be overhauled, changed from a fringe group to a philosophical home for believers in free enterprise and traditional moral values. They also hoped they could attract Sen. Helms, Gov. Thomson, or Rep. Philip M. Crane, R-Ill. When none of these men agreed to run on the American Independent Party ticket, Viguerie and his allies found themselves unable to promote Morris, a lesser-known substitute, successfully.

Many American Independent Party members favored Maddox because they saw him as a colorful personality, one capable of drawing media attention and perhaps of picking up the 5 percent of the national vote needed to qualify the party for federal funding. Maddox never came close to that goal, however, achieving only 0.2 percent of the national vote (170,531). It was 51,098 votes in California, where American Party nominee Anderson was not on the ballot, that enabled Maddox to run slightly ahead of Anderson nationally.

Despite the power struggle between Anderson and Shearer, there was little difference between their two party platforms. Like the American Party, the American Independent Party opposed abortion, gun control, forced busing, foreign aid, and membership in the United Nations.

By 1980 neither party was much of a force in American politics. Both retained the same basic platforms, but each was on the ballot in only a handful of states. The American Independent Party's nominee, former Democratic representative Rarick, ran in only eight states. Economist Percy L. Greaves Jr., the American Party candidate, was listed in just seven.

The American Independent Party did not field a presidential candidate in 1984, while the American Party placed Delmar Dennis, a book publisher from Pigeon Forge, Tennessee, on the ballot in six states.

Dennis also ran under the American Party banner in 1988 and, with his running mate, Earl Jeppson, received 3,475 votes. The American Independent Party fared better with their candidates, presidential nominee James C. Griffin and vice-presidential nominee Charles J. Morsa, receiving 27,818 votes.

By 1992 fortunes for both parties had dwindled. American Party presidential nominee Robert J. Smith and running mate Doris Feimer were on the ballot only in Utah, where they received 292 votes. In 1996 the American Party ticket of Diane Beall Templin and Gary Van Horn made the ballot in two states, Colorado and Utah, and collected a total of 1,847 votes. The American Independent Party did not appear on any presidential ballots in the 1990s.

Anti-Federalists (1789–1796)

Never a formal party, the Anti-Federalists were a loosely organized group opposed to ratification of the Constitution. With the ratification of the Constitution in 1788, the Anti-Federalists served as the opposition to the Federalists in the early years of Congress.

Anti-Federalists were primarily rural, agrarian men from inland regions who favored individual freedom and states' rights, which they felt would be jeopardized by the new Constitution. After ratification, the efforts of the Anti-Federalists led to adoption of the first ten amendments, the Bill of Rights, which spelled out the major limitations on federal power.

As the opposition faction in Congress during the formative years of the Republic, the Anti-Federalists basically held to a strict interpretation of the Constitution, particularly in regard to the various economic proposals of Treasury Secretary Alexander Hamilton to centralize more power in the federal government.

Although never the majority faction in Congress, the Anti-Federalists were a forerunner of Thomas Jefferson's Democratic-Republican Party, which came into existence in the 1790s and dominated American politics for the first quarter of the nineteenth century.

Anti-Masonic Party (1828–1836)

Born in the mid-1820s in upstate New York, the Anti-Masonic Party focused the strong, antielitist mood of the period on a conspicuous symbol of privilege, the Masons. The Masons were a secret fraternal organization with membership drawn largely from the upper class. Conversely, the appeal of the Anti-Masonic movement was to the common man—poor farmers and laborers especially—who resented the secrecy and privilege of the Masons.

The spark that created the party came in 1826, when William Morgan, a dissident Mason from Batavia, New York, allegedly on the verge of exposing the inner workings of the order, mysteriously disappeared and never was seen again. Refusal of Masonic leaders to cooperate in the inconclusive investigation of Morgan's disappearance led to suspicions that Masons had kidnapped and murdered him and were suppressing the inquiry.

From 1828 through 1831, the new Anti-Masonic Party spread through New England and the Middle Atlantic states, in many places establishing itself as the primary opposition to the Democrats. In addition to its appeal to the working classes, particularly in northern rural areas, and its opposition to Masonry, the Anti-Masons displayed a fervor against immorality, as seen not only in secret societies but also in slavery, intemperance, and urban life.

In September 1831 the party held the first national nominating convention in American history. One hundred and sixteen delegates from thirteen states gathered in Baltimore, Maryland, and nominated former Attorney General William Wirt of Maryland for the presidency. In the 1832 elections, Wirt received only 100,715 votes (7.8 percent of the popular vote) and carried just one state, Vermont, but it was the first third party in U.S. politics to win any electoral college votes. The Anti-Masons did reasonably well at other levels, winning the Vermont governorship several years and competing in close elections in a few other states. In the U.S. House they had fifteen members in the Twenty-second Congress (1831–1833) and twenty-four in the Twenty-third Congress (1833–1835).

But the decline of Masonry, especially in New York, where the number of lodges dropped from 507 in 1826 to 48 six years later, robbed the Anti-Masons of an emotional issue and hastened their decline. The 1832 election was the high point for the Anti-Masons as a national party. In the 1836 campaign the party endorsed Whig candidate William Henry Harrison. Subsequently, the bulk of the Anti-Masonic constituency moved into the Whig Party. In 1836 the major parties also held their own conventions and wrote their own platforms. Despite its short life, the Anti-Masons were one of the most important American third parties, contributing to the openness of the system and establishing party platforms and conventions as part of modern political practices.

Breckinridge (Southern) Democrats (1860)

Agitation over the slavery issue, building for a generation, reached a climax in 1860 and produced a sectional split in the Democratic Party. Throughout the mid-nineteenth century the Democrats had remained unified by supporting the various pieces of compromise legislation that both protected slavery in the southern states and endorsed the policy of popular sovereignty in the territories. But in 1860 southern Democrats wanted the Democratic convention (meeting in Charleston, S.C.) to insert a plank specifically protecting slavery in the territories. When their plank was defeated, delegates from most of the southern states walked out.

The northern wing of the party, after recessing for six weeks, reconvened in Baltimore, where Illinois senator Stephen A.

John C. Breckinridge

Douglas of Illinois was nominated as its presidential candidate. Most of the southern delegates, plus those from California and Oregon, nominated their own ticket in a rump convention held after Douglas's selection. John C. Breckinridge (1821–1875) of Kentucky, the incumbent vice president under President James Buchanan, accepted the southern wing's nomination. Joseph Lane, a states' rights advocate from Oregon, was selected as his running mate. After the formation of the two sectional tickets, two separate Democratic national committees operated in Washington, D.C., to oversee their campaigns.

The platforms of the Douglas and Breckinridge Democrats agreed that the Fugitive Slave Law must be enforced, but the Breckinridge Democrats also insisted on a federal slave code for the territories and on the right of slaveholders to take their slave property into the western territories, decisions that the Douglas platform said it would leave to the Supreme Court and that the Republican Party and its candidate, Abraham Lincoln, absolutely opposed. The four-way election also included John Bell of the Constitutional Union Party.

The Breckinridge ticket placed third in popular votes behind Lincoln and Douglas, receiving 848,019 votes (18.1 percent of the popular vote) and winning eleven of the fifteen slave states, and second in electoral votes with seventy-two. Although the combined Douglas-Breckinridge vote comprised a plurality of the ballots cast, the split in Democratic ranks was a boon to the campaign of the Republican candidate, Abraham Lincoln, who won with less than 40 percent of the vote. Lincoln's victory in the electoral college, however, did not depend on a divided opposition, for he took an absolute majority in enough northern states to win regardless. Breckinridge's support came mostly from the South, although it did not necessarily reflect the degree of proslavery sentiment in the region, since some voters who later supported secession voted for Douglas or Bell, and many of Breckinridge's supporters were traditional Democrats who did not see themselves as voting on secession. Indeed, Breckinridge saw himself as the only candidate who could prevent secession, since if he won, the South would happily remain in the Union.

Lincoln's election led to secession by seven Deep South states, and four more joined the Confederacy soon after his inauguration. Before Lincoln's inauguration, Vice President Breckinridge worked with other Democrats in Washington to fashion a compromise that might prevent a civil war. On the main point of contention, however, slavery in the territories, Lincoln would not budge, so no settlement could be reached. Breckinridge, while still vice president, had been elected to the U.S. Senate, his term to begin when his vice presidency ended. As a senator in 1861 he defended the right of southern states to secede and opposed Lincoln's efforts to raise an army.

By late 1861 Union and Confederate forces alike had entered Kentucky, and Breckinridge offered his services to the Confederacy. He resigned from the Senate before it expelled him for his pro-Confederate behavior. He served as a major general in the Confederate army and then as Confederate secretary of war. During the war the Southern Democrats provided much of the leadership for the Confederate government, including its president, Jefferson Davis.

When the war ended with the Confederacy's defeat and slavery's abolition, the particular issues that had animated Breckinridge's presidential bid in 1860 no longer mattered. The Southern Democrats made no attempt to continue as a separate sectional entity and rejoined the national Democratic Party.

Citizens Party (1979–1984)

Organized in 1979 as a coalition of dissident liberals and populists, the first Citizens Party convention chose author and environmental scientist Barry Commoner as its 1980 presidential candidate and La Donna Harris, wife of former Democratic senator Fred R. Harris of Oklahoma, as his running mate. The Citizens Party ticket ran on the central theme that major decisions in America were made to benefit corporations and not the average citizen. The party proposed public control of energy industries and multinational corporations; a halt to the use of nuclear power; a sharp cut in military spending; and price controls on food, fuel, housing, and health care.

Commoner ran in all of the large electoral vote states except Florida and Texas. He made his biggest push in California, Illinois, Michigan, New York, and Pennsylvania, where party leaders believed they could tap a "sophisticated working-class population" and appeal to political activists who had been involved in the environmental and antinuclear movements that sprang up in the late 1970s.

The Commoner-Harris ticket was on the ballot in twenty-nine states and the District of Columbia in 1980. Party leaders

asserted that it was the largest number of ballot positions attained by any third party in its first campaign. In addition to its presidential ticket, the Citizens Party also fielded twenty-two candidates for other offices, including two for the U.S. Senate and seven for the House. The Citizens Party won 234,294 votes in the 1980 presidential election, or 0.3 percent of the vote.

As its 1984 presidential nominee, the Citizens Party chose outspoken feminist Sonia Johnson of Virginia. Johnson first attracted national attention in 1979, when the Mormon Church excommunicated her for supporting the Equal Rights Amendment (ERA). In 1982 she staged a thirty-seven-day hunger strike in an unsuccessful effort to pressure the Illinois legislature to approve the ERA. The Citizens Party selected party activist Richard J. Walton of Rhode Island to accompany Johnson on the ticket. Winning 72,200 votes in 1984, the ticket garnered 0.1 percent of the vote. That was the last year that the Citizens Party fielded a national ticket.

Communist Party (1919–)

In 1919, shortly after the Russian Revolution, Soviet communists encouraged American left-wing groups to withdraw from the Socialist Party and to form a communist party in the United States. The party arose at that time as part of the social and economic turmoil that followed World War I and the Bolshevik Revolution in Russia. Two major organizations emerged from the American Socialist Party: the larger Communist Party of America and the Communist Labor Party. But both were aggressively prosecuted by the U.S. government in the period around 1920, causing a drop in their already small membership and forcing them underground.

By the mid-1920s, the Communist Party of the USA was formed to implant the revolutionary aims of the Soviet Union in America. William Z. Foster, a labor organizer, was the party's first presidential candidate, in 1924. National tickets were run every four years through 1940 and from 1968 through 1984, but the party's peak year at the polls was 1932, when Foster received 103,253 votes (0.3 percent of the popular vote).

The Communists have a distinctive place in American political history as the only party to have had international ties. In 1929 a party split brought the formal creation of the Communist Party of the United States, with acknowledged status as a part of the worldwide communist movement (the Communist International).

The Communist International terminated during World War II, and in 1944 the party's leader in America, Earl Browder, dissolved the party and committed the movement to operate within the two-party system. In the 1944 campaign the Communists endorsed President Franklin D. Roosevelt, who repudiated their support.

However, with the breakup of the U.S.–Soviet alliance after World War II, the Communists reconstituted themselves as a political party. They supported Henry Wallace's Progressive Party candidacy in 1948 but were limited in the cold war period of the 1950s by restrictive federal and state legislation that virtually outlawed the party.

With the gradual easing of restrictive measures, the Communist Party resumed electoral activities in the late 1960s. In a policy statement written in 1966, the party described itself as "a revolutionary party whose aim is the fundamental transformation of society."

The party's success at the polls, however, continued to be minimal. Its presidential candidates in 1968, 1972, 1976, 1980, and 1984—the last year that they appeared on the ballot—each received less than one-tenth of 1 percent of the vote.

Conservative Party (1962–)

In 1962 the New York State Conservative Party began to take shape under the direction of J. Daniel Mahoney, a New York attorney, and his brother-in-law, Kieran O'Doherty. They were motivated primarily by the belief that real political alternatives were no longer being offered to the state electorate. They saw the three dominant parties in the state—the Liberal Party, the Democratic Party, and the Republican Party under Gov. Nelson A. Rockefeller and Sen. Jacob K. Javits—as offering a generally liberal agenda.

Although political commentators predicted the early demise of the party—particularly in the aftermath of Barry Goldwater's overwhelming defeat in the 1964 presidential elections—the party continued to grow both in membership and in candidate endorsements. In 1965 the nationally known columnist and intellectual William F. Buckley ran for mayor of New York City, generating national publicity for the party. One year later, the Conservative candidate for governor, Professor Paul Adams, outpolled Liberal Party candidate Franklin D. Roosevelt Jr., obtaining Row C of the ballot for the party. A party's position on the ballot is determined by the number of votes cast for its candidate for governor. Appearing in Row C is significant because the higher the row, the more notice voters are likely to take of the party's candidates. In 1970 James Buckley was elected to the U.S. Senate on Row C alone, and from the mid-1970s onward no statewide Republican candidate gained office without Conservative Party cross-endorsement.

Although the Conservative Party suffered some setbacks, such as the loss of Row C to the Independence (Reform) Party in 1996 and the siphoning off of some supporters to the Right to Life Party, it remains a major force in New York State politics. The Conservative Party has opposed abortion since it became a political issue; nonetheless, the party has occasionally backed prochoice candidates whose conservative credentials were otherwise satisfactory. The Right to Life Party never backs candidates who support abortion.

Even though some members of the Conservative Party are Protestant fundamentalists, the plurality of its membership and much of its leadership are traditionalist Roman Catholics. In a very real sense, the rise of the party has mirrored the rise of the conservative movement in America—from Goldwater's capture of the 1964 Republican nomination to Ronald Reagan's electoral triumphs in 1980 and 1984. In addition, the party has successfully fought the image of extremism while generally remaining true to its core principles—tax limitation, education reform, and tough anticrime policies.

Constitutional Union Party (1860)

The short-lived Constitutional Union Party was formed in 1859 to promote national conciliation in the face of rampant sectionalism, which included southern threats of secession. The party appealed to conservative remnants of the American (Know Nothing) and Whig parties, who viewed preservation of the Union as their primary goal.

The Constitutional Union Party held its first and only national convention in Baltimore in May 1860. For president the party nominated John Bell of Tennessee, a former senator and Speaker of the House of Representatives, who previously had been both a Democrat and a Whig. The convention adopted a short platform, which intentionally avoided controversial subjects, most notably the divisive slavery issue. Instead, the platform simply urged support for "the Constitution, the Union and the Laws."

In the fall election, Bell received 590,901 votes (12.6 percent of the popular vote) and won Kentucky, Tennessee, and Virginia. However, the Bell ticket finished last in the four-way presidential race and, together with the sectional split in the Democratic Party, was a prominent factor in the victory of Republican Abraham Lincoln.

In the months after the 1860 election the Constitutional Union Party continued to urge national conciliation, but with the outbreak of the Civil War the party disappeared.

Democratic Party (1828–)

The Democratic Party is the oldest political organization in the United States. Indeed, a history of the party is in some ways a political history of the nation. In the first few years of the Republic, political parties did not exist, although factions tied to issues and the personal ambitions of political leaders influenced elections and policies. The Democratic Party traces its roots to this factionalism, beginning with opposition to the Federalist policies of Alexander Hamilton in the first administration of George Washington.

ORIGINS OF THE DEMOCRATIC PARTY

Opposition to Federalist policies, organized by U.S. Rep. James Madison and Secretary of State Thomas Jefferson, first coalesced around Hamilton's proposal for a national bank, which Congress passed and Washington signed, over the strenuous objections of Jefferson and Madison. The two Virginians were more successful in preventing the adoption of Hamilton's larger plan for federal support for the development of American industry. The Federalists, led by Hamilton and John Adams, favored a strong central government and a flexible interpretation of the Constitution. Key to their program was a national bank, which would facilitate economic growth and strengthen national and international commerce.

Jefferson's Democratic-Republicans advocated "strict construction" of the Constitution and opposed a national bank. Moreover, they favored friendly relations with France, while the Federalists sought to forge friendly diplomatic and commercial

Andrew Jackson

relations with England. Both parties had supporters throughout the country, but the Democratic-Republicans were strongest in the South and among slaveowners, and the Federalists were strongest in New England and among men with commercial and manufacturing interests. From the 1790s until the late 1820s various terms—Democratic-Republicans, Jeffersonian Republicans, Jeffersonian Democrats, and National Republicans—were applied to the people and leaders who, opposed to the Federalists, gradually became known as Democrats.

The Democratic-Republicans grew stronger as the Federalists began to fade during the presidency of John Adams. A new alliance of agrarian southerners and urban northerners helped Jefferson defeat Adams in 1800 and win reelection in 1804. After Jefferson the presidency went to his friends and allies, James Madison (1809–1817) and James Monroe (1817–1825). By 1820 the Federalist Party had all but disappeared, and James Monroe won reelection with no opposition.

Indicative of the change in the party of Jefferson was its attitude toward the Bank of the United States. In 1791 Jefferson and Madison had vigorously opposed the creation of this bank, arguing that establishment of such a bank was unconstitutional. We might date the development of the Democratic Party from that debate over the bank. In 1811 the bank's twenty-year charter expired, and the Democrats who controlled Congress and the presidency did not renew it. By 1816, however, Madison supported the creation of a new bank and renounced his former public

policy and constitutional opposition to it. Congress, controlled by Democrats, passed the bill.

The inherent instability of one-party politics became clear in 1824, as four candidates—Andrew Jackson, John Quincy Adams, William Crawford, and Henry Clay, all claiming to represent the Jeffersonian tradition—ran for president. No candidate received a majority of popular or electoral votes, and the House of Representatives chose John Quincy Adams, although Andrew Jackson had received more popular votes and more electoral votes. After 1824 the old Jeffersonian party unraveled. Adams had broken with the Federalist Party during the War of 1812 and had served as Monroe's secretary of state, but he was never a true "Jeffersonian." By the end of his administration in 1829 he and supporters like Henry Clay emerged as members of a faction that eventually became the Whig Party.

THE JACKSON LEGACY

War of 1812 hero Andrew Jackson defeated John Quincy Adams in 1828 and became the first president to represent the "Democratic Party." The party has maintained that name ever since, although it was often divided over issues such as slavery, economic policy, and national unity in the nineteenth century and foreign policy, civil rights, and economic policy in the twentieth.

Jackson, nominated in 1828 by the Tennessee legislature, led the Democrats into adopting a nominating convention as the method for choosing the party's future standard-bearers. The Democrats held their first national convention at Baltimore, Maryland, in 1832, eight months after the Anti-Masons held the first such convention, also in Baltimore. The 1832 Democratic convention adopted two rules that lasted more than a century. The two-thirds rule, requiring a two-thirds majority for nomination, led to numerous floor fights over the choosing of a Democratic presidential candidate. The unit rule allowed convention delegations to override minority objections within the delegation and to vote as a whole for one candidate or position.

From Jackson's election in 1828 through the end of James Buchanan's term in 1861, the Democrats dominated national politics. In this period the Democrats opposed any national bank, high tariffs, internal improvements, and even a uniform bankruptcy law. High points of Jackson's presidency included his veto of bills to support internal improvements and to extend the charter of the Second Bank of the United States. Jackson and other Democrats in this period vigorously supported territorial expansion through Indian removal, the annexation of Texas, and ultimately the Mexican-American War. Their support for territorial gains followed Jefferson's expansionist policies that led to the peaceful acquisition of Louisiana from France in 1803. Most Democrats, and almost all party leaders, supported the demands of the South between 1828 and 1861 on issues involving slavery. Meanwhile, Jackson's opponents—led by Henry Clay, Daniel Webster, and William Henry Harrison—formed the Whig Party. The Whigs—who favored higher tariffs, a national bank, federally funded internal improvements, and a weak presidency—provided the main opposition to the Democrats until the emergence of the Republican Party in 1854.

Jackson's election ushered in an era known as "Jacksonian Democracy," which stressed political equality—for white men. Jacksonians throughout the country made war on black voters, taking away their voting rights in Pennsylvania, New Jersey, Tennessee, and North Carolina and opposing their voting rights elsewhere. Jackson himself led the movement to force Native Americans out of the states east of the Mississippi River.

Jefferson, already considered the "father" of the Democratic Party, had been the first president to remove officeholders and replace them with his supporters. Jackson renewed this policy through the "spoils system," a term that stemmed from the phrase "to the victors go the spoils." As the party in power during most of the period from 1829 to 1861, the Democrats controlled the growing bureaucracy and rewarded many supporters with patronage jobs.

Jackson's legacy was a Democratic Party that endured into the twenty-first century. Dominating national politics during the first half of the nineteenth century, the Democrats lost the presidential election only twice (in 1840 and 1848) between 1800 and 1856. From Jackson's inauguration in 1829 until the year 2001, the Democrats controlled the House of Representatives for fifty-five two-year sessions and the Senate for forty-six sessions; the Whigs or Republicans controlled the House for thirty-two sessions and the Senate for forty-one sessions.

Despite their long-term success, the Democrats barely survived their severest test, over slavery and secession. In 1846 northern Democrats supported the Wilmot Proviso, introduced in the House by Pennsylvania Democrat David Wilmot. The proviso would have prohibited slavery in any territory acquired during the Mexican-American War. Southern Democrats uniformly opposed the proviso. In 1848 many antislavery Democrats from New York, Pennsylvania, and New England voted for former president Martin Van Buren, who was running on the Free Soil Party ticket. These defections led to the election of the Whig candidate, Zachary Taylor. The Democrats regained the presidency in 1852, but slavery soon splintered the party. In 1856 Democrat Franklin Pierce became the first elected president denied renomination by his own party. He had alienated fellow northerners by signing legislation that allowed slavery into Kansas Territory, which in turn led it to become a battleground between pro- and antislavery forces. Another northerner, James Buchanan, won the nomination but also became a one-term president. By 1860 many northern Democrats, among them Sens. Salmon P. Chase of Ohio and Hannibal Hamlin of Maine, had joined the new Republican Party.

At the 1860 convention in Charleston, South Carolina, northern and southern Democrats were divided over how much support to give slavery in the territories. Northerners, backing Stephen A. Douglas of Illinois, favored opening all territories to slavery under a system of popular sovereignty, in which settlers would decide for themselves whether to permit slavery. Most of the southerners bolted after the defeat of platform planks endorsing a federal slave code for the territories and guaranteeing the right of slaveowners to carry their human property into all federal territories. The northern delegates nominated Douglas for president. The southern Democrats nominated John C. Breckinridge of Kentucky for president. Even had the Democrats remained united, it is doubtful they could have prevented the Republican candidate, Abraham Lincoln, from winning an electoral majority, as he swept every free state but New Jersey, which he split with Douglas. The split in the Democratic Party presaged the more important split in the nation, which occurred with the secession of eleven southern states in 1860–1861.

DECLINE AND RESURGENCE

During the Civil War, northern Democrats remained divided. War Democrats generally supported the war effort and Lincoln's initial goal of bringing the South back into the Union, although they objected to Lincoln's emancipation policies and after 1863 were far less enthusiastic about the war or its goals. Throughout the war, by contrast, the Copperhead faction opposed the war effort and sought peace negotiations with the Confederacy.

Democrats came back together after the Civil War, but both their commitment to white supremacy and their image of disloyalty continued. During Reconstruction, Democrats opposed civil rights laws and the Fourteenth and Fifteenth Amendments, which were designed to establish blacks' citizenship, recognize blacks' civil rights, and guarantee blacks' voting rights. As late as the 1880s, the Democrats were termed the party of "rum, romanism, and rebellion," because of the party's opposition to temperance laws, its support among Irish Catholics, and the fact that much of its support came from former Confederates.

In 1876 the Democratic governor of New York, Samuel J. Tilden, won the popular vote against Republican Rutherford B. Hayes, but Tilden lost the election when a congressional compromise awarded Hayes all the disputed electoral votes of three southern states. Election fraud, intimidation, and outright violence by white southern Democrats prevented thousands of blacks from voting. Had the election been run fairly, it is likely that Hayes would have won outright. As part of the compromise that brought Hayes to the White House, the new president promised to remove federal troops from the South, effectively ending Reconstruction. Their removal led to a gradual disfranchisement of blacks in the South, which soon became solidly Democratic and would remain largely so until the presidential election of 1964. Despite a virtual lock on all southern electoral votes, the Democrats captured the presidency only twice between 1860 and 1912; Grover Cleveland won in 1884 and 1892.

By the late nineteenth century the Democratic Party's policies had changed somewhat from the antebellum period. Still a "white man's party," it was hostile to African Americans' civil rights and to Chinese immigration. With slavery ended, however, the party had dropped its aggressive expansionism of the earlier period. Cleveland refused to annex Hawaii, and some Democrats opposed the Spanish-American War in 1898. Democrats remained hostile to high tariffs, but they split on the issue of an expansive monetary policy; western Democrats favored the free coinage of silver, and eastern Democrats, among them Cleveland, opposed it. Most southern whites gave their allegiance to the Democrats, but in the North by the 1890s, and especially following the 1893 depression, economic and cultural

THE MODERN BALAAM AND HIS ASS.

In the first appearance of the Democratic donkey, this unfavorable 1837 political cartoon shows Martin Van Buren walking behind his predecessor, Andrew Jackson, who rides the donkey.

issues outweighed memories of Civil War enmity in voter choices between the two major parties.

The GOP continued to dominate presidential politics for twelve years into the twentieth century. In 1912 the Republicans split when former president Theodore Roosevelt failed in his attempt to gain his party's nomination over the incumbent, William Howard Taft. Roosevelt ran anyway, on the Progressive—or Bull Moose—ticket, winning six states and 4.1 million votes. Roosevelt came in second, and Taft a distant third, but Taft and Roosevelt combined for 1.3 million more popular votes than the Democrat, Woodrow Wilson. Had the Republicans been united, their candidate—either Roosevelt or Taft—would have won. But divided they enabled Wilson to carry forty states and the election, ending the Democrats' long presidential drought. Wilson demonstrated the Democrats' hostility to civil rights and racial equality, as he ordered the segregation of all federal facilities in Washington, D.C. He was a progressive reformer on many issues, however, and brought such innovations as the Federal Reserve System, in contrast to historic Democratic hostility to federal government intervention in the economy.

Wilson also led the Democrats away from their historic position on foreign policy. Before the Civil War, the Democrats, in part spurred by the demands of the South for more territory for slavery, had pursued an aggressive policy of land acquisition, ultimately leading to war with Mexico. Pre–Civil War Democrats had had little interest in international affairs be-

yond the Western Hemisphere, however. In 1917, by contrast, Wilson successfully asked Congress for a declaration of war, and he continued his internationalist policies after the end of World War I, as he vainly attempted to bring the United States into the League of Nations. For the next half- century the Democratic Party stood for intervention and international responsibility, while the Republicans retreated into a large measure of diplomatic isolationism.

After World War I the Republicans took back the White House in 1920, kept it in 1924, and won again with Herbert Hoover's 1928 victory over Democrat Alfred E. Smith, the first Roman Catholic presidential nominee. After the stock market crashed in 1929, however, the Great Depression paved the way for a new Democratic dominance in the White House and an even longer one in Congress.

NEW DEAL TO GREAT SOCIETY

The election of Franklin D. Roosevelt in 1932 made a dramatic and lasting change in American politics. Democrats sang "Happy Days Are Here Again" as they became the majority party and rallied behind FDR's bold New Deal programs. Democrats, long the party of states' rights and localism, became identified with national initiatives on economic and social issues. During the New Deal, rural electrification brought light and heat to much of the nation; a range of programs helped the poor and the unemployed; the nation's labor policy went through a sea change with the Wagner Labor Relations Act; and massive public works programs, such as the Tennessee Valley Authority, not only created jobs but constructed public buildings, roads, and dams. Once a party opposed to regulation, the Democrats helped create the regulatory state. Social programs, most notably Social Security, set the stage for the modern industrial state that provides a social safety net for citizens.

At Roosevelt's urging, the 1936 Democratic convention abolished the controversial two-thirds rule, which in effect had long given the South a veto in choosing the national party ticket. Southern delegates agreed to a compromise, basing the size of future delegations on a state's Democratic voting strength instead of population size.

During the Roosevelt years and after, for the first time in its history, the Democratic Party welcomed black support and even supported some civil rights legislation, and President Roosevelt and his successor, Harry S. Truman, issued executive orders to combat some types of racial segregation and other discrimination. The "New Deal coalition"—northern blacks, southern whites, farmers, labor unionists, intellectuals, and ethnic urban voters—kept Roosevelt and Truman in office for twenty consecutive years, ending in 1953.

As Europe moved toward war in the 1930s and then fought in World War II, Roosevelt pushed an international agenda, building on Wilson's legacy. Here Roosevelt had the support of southern Democrats, who opposed some of his domestic agenda. Opposition came from Republican isolationists, but, unlike Wilson, FDR was able to bring the nation along with him, and thus the United States took the lead in establishing the United Nations (UN). Truman continued this internationalist policy, first with the Marshall Plan to help Europe recover from World War II and then with the development of NATO and other international defense pacts. In 1950 Truman pushed for UN intervention when North Korea attacked South Korea, and soon the United States was heavily involved in another war in Asia.

In domestic politics, Truman pushed an activist agenda that he called the "Fair Deal" and called for expanded enforcement of African Americans' civil rights. Running for another term in 1948, he confronted schisms within his party from two quarters: the South and the left. Displeased with Truman's civil rights plank, conservative southerners bolted the Democratic Party in 1948 and ran J. Strom Thurmond of South Carolina as the States' Rights Democratic (Dixiecrats) nominee. Under the Progressive Party banner, Henry A. Wallace also challenged Truman. Thurmond won four states; Wallace took none. Despite the split, Truman defeated Republican Thomas E. Dewey.

After Truman left office in 1953, a Republican, Dwight D. Eisenhower, served the next two terms, but then the Democrats took back the White House in 1960, as John F. Kennedy, the first Roman Catholic president, narrowly defeated Eisenhower's vice president, Richard Nixon. Kennedy's slogan, "New Frontier," mirrored traditional Democratic slogans, such as Wilson's "New Freedom," FDR's "New Deal," and Truman's "Fair Deal." Kennedy continued the Democratic agenda of internationalism, with the Peace Corps and aid to the pro-Western regime in South Vietnam, and of federal support for domestic improvements, with a massive tax cut and federal programs in housing.

Kennedy made tentative moves toward an expanded role for the national government in civil rights, but he moved cautiously because of the power of southern whites within his party.

After Kennedy's assassination in 1963, President Lyndon B. Johnson completed much of Kennedy's "New Frontier" agenda and called for additional programs in pursuit of the "Great Society," including a civil rights program that was termed by some a "Second Reconstruction." Applying all the skills he had learned as Senate majority leader, Johnson pushed through the Civil Rights Act of 1964. Johnson's support for civil rights ended the "solid South" as a Democratic stronghold. In 1964 Johnson won in a landslide. Carrying all but five states, he took 61.1 percent of the popular vote, the largest popular victory of any presidential election in U.S. history. The Deep South, however, supported Republican Barry Goldwater, who had opposed the Civil Rights Act of 1964 and had flirted with the ultraright John Birch Society and segregationist White Citizens' Councils. Johnson's mandate enabled him to win passage of the Voting Rights Act of 1965, further solidifying Democratic support among African Americans while further undermining Democratic power among white southerners.

Johnson expanded U.S. involvement in an increasingly unpopular war in Vietnam, thereby splitting the party and prompting his decision against running for reelection in 1968. Two antiwar candidates, Sen. Robert F. Kennedy of New York, brother of the slain president, and Sen. Eugene McCarthy of Minnesota, dueled for the nomination in primaries across the nation. But Kennedy was assassinated the night he won the California primary, and McCarthy was outmaneuvered by party insiders. The Democratic convention that year, held in Chicago, was marred by police violence against antiwar demonstrators. Vice President Hubert H. Humphrey, nominated without entering any primaries, also faced competition in November from the American Independent candidacy of George C. Wallace, former Democratic governor of Alabama. All these divisive factors contributed to Humphrey's narrow defeat by Republican Richard Nixon.

THE DEMOCRATIC PARTY SINCE 1968

Still chafing from the dissension and bossism at the 1968 convention and the subsequent loss to Nixon, the Democrats in the 1970s drastically reformed their delegate-selection and nominating rules, encouraging minority representation, dividing delegations equally between men and women, and awarding delegates to candidates in proportion to their primary votes. The party's 1972 candidate, George S. McGovern, led many of the reforms, most of which took effect in 1980. The changes enhanced the role of primaries in the nominating process, leading to more primaries and fewer state caucuses.

The 1972 election was the last privately financed presidential election. Nixon raised $61.4 million versus McGovern's $21.2 million. McGovern, running as a peace candidate with a commitment to massive domestic spending, lost to Nixon in a landslide. The election-related Watergate scandal, however, drove Nixon from office two years later and brought Vice President Gerald R. Ford to the presidency. Evidence from the Watergate

President Bill Clinton vetoes a budget bill in 1995.

investigation showed that Nixon's operatives had used "dirty tricks" in the Democratic primaries to sabotage the candidacy of Edmond S. Muskie, who might have been a more formidable candidate than McGovern.

Skillful use of the primaries, as well as Ford's unpopular full pardon of President Nixon for his criminal activities in the Watergate cover-up, helped the relatively unknown Jimmy Carter of Georgia defeat incumbent Ford in 1976. Carter's primary strategy also served him in 1980, staving off a renomination challenge from Sen. Edward M. Kennedy, brother of the late president. But Carter's inability to curb inflation or obtain the release of American hostages held in Iran for 444 days doomed him to a one-term presidency and to defeat at the hands of Republican Ronald Reagan.

Although the popular Reagan handily won reelection in 1984, his vice president and successor, George Herbert Walker Bush, fell victim in 1992 to Bill Clinton of Arkansas, as Democrats returned to the White House after twelve Republican years. As a presidential candidate Clinton addressed economic worries. His advisers reminded campaign workers, "It's the economy, stupid," and the strategy worked. He was the first Democrat to win without taking Texas and, with Al Gore of Tennessee as his running mate, the first president elected on an all-South ticket since 1828.

Clinton won as a moderate, declaring that "the era of big government is over." Behind him was a modified New Deal coalition that included "Reagan Democrats," union members, women, African Americans, Hispanics, Jews, a majority of Roman Catholics, public sector employees, and intellectuals. In one of his first acts he instituted a "don't ask, don't tell" policy toward homosexuals in the military. Although Clinton's convention call for a "new covenant with the American people" never caught on as a slogan, and although he and Hillary Rodham Clinton failed in an abortive attempt to reform the nation's health system, peace and an improved economy soon had the Democratic administration basking in high approval ratings in public opinion polls. Nevertheless, the voters in 1994 broke the Democratic lock on Congress, turning both chambers over to Republican control.

Two years later the electorate opted to continue a divided government, giving Clinton another four-year term in 1996 while leaving Congress in GOP hands. Although he was the first Democrat elected to a second full term since Franklin Roosevelt, Clinton again won with less than a majority of the popular vote. For the moment, Clinton's victories eased doubts that the Democrats' once-solid South had become a Republican bastion. Of the eleven states of the Old Confederacy, the Clinton-Gore ticket won four in 1992 and four in 1996. Unfortunately for the Democrats that success did not hold up four years later.

Democrats made history on various fronts from 1960 through the end of the century. In 1960 the party ran the nation's first successful Catholic presidential candidate, John F. Kennedy. In 1968 New York voters elected Democrat Shirley Chisholm as the first black woman member of the U.S. House, and in 1992 another Democrat, Carol Moseley-Braun of Illinois, became the first black woman U.S. senator. When former vice president Walter F. Mondale chose Geraldine A. Ferraro as his running mate against Reagan in 1984, she became the first woman in U.S. history to run on a major-party ticket. In 1989 L. Douglas Wilder of Virginia became the first African American to be elected state governor. In 2000 the Democratic nominee for president, Vice President Al Gore, chose Sen. Joseph Lieberman of Connecticut as his running mate. This was the first time a Jew was on a national ticket. Also in 2000, Hillary Rodham Clinton became the first presidential wife to seek a major elective office, a U.S. Senate seat from New York, which she won.

Nevertheless, the 2000 elections were a major disappointment for Democrats. Gore lost a disputed election to Republican George W. Bush, son of the former president. Moreover, the Republicans retained control of both houses of Congress, although by the narrowest of margins. Still, it gave the GOP full control of the federal government for the first time since 1953 and sent the Democrats to the sidelines as loyal opposition but with little leverage to block the GOP program much less advance their own. However, by June 2001 the Democrats regained control of the Senate when Republican moderate Jim Jeffords became an Independent.

The 2000 presidential elections reasserted trends many noted in recent years. As political analyst Rhodes Cook put it: "Exit polls showed men favored Bush, women favored Gore; whites preferred Bush, non-whites preferred Gore; the more affluent voted strongly for Bush, the less affluent heavily favored Gore; rural and small town America went for Bush, urban America for Gore." In the South, the Republicans reasserted primacy, showing that this region was not the center of the party. Bush won the entire South—the eleven states of the Old Confederacy plus Kentucky and Oklahoma. Bush even won Gore's home state of Tennessee and Clinton's home state of Arkansas. The Democrats' strength was on the west and east coasts, north of Virginia, and into the industrial heartland. The GOP dominated everywhere else—a giant "L"-shaped area from the South through the Plains states and Southwest and into the Mountain states.

Democratic-Republican Party (1792–1828)

The Democratic-Republican Party developed in the early 1790s as the organized opposition to the incumbent Federalists and successor to the Anti-Federalists, who were a loose alliance of elements initially opposed to the ratification of the Constitution and subsequently to the policies of the George Washington administration, which were designed to centralize power in the federal government.

Thomas Jefferson was the leader of the new party, whose members as early as 1792 referred to themselves as Republicans. This remained their primary name throughout the party's history, although in some states they became known as Democratic-Republicans, the label used frequently by historians to avoid confusing Jefferson's party with the later Republican Party, which began in 1854. Party members were called Jeffersonian Republicans as well.

The Democratic-Republicans favored states' rights, a literal interpretation of the Constitution, and expanded democracy through extension of suffrage and popular control of the government. The party was dominated by rural, agrarian interests,

intent on maintaining their dominance over the growing commercial and industrial interests of the Northeast. The principal strength of the party came from states in the South and Middle Atlantic.

The Democratic-Republicans first gained control of the federal government in 1800, when Jefferson was elected president and the party won majorities in both houses of Congress. For the next twenty-four years the party controlled both the White House and Congress, the last eight years virtually without opposition. For all but four years during this twenty-four-year period, there was a Virginia–New York alliance controlling the executive branch, with all three presidents from Virginia—Jefferson, James Madison, and James Monroe—and three of the four vice presidents from New York. Lacking an opposition party, the Democratic-Republicans in the 1820s became increasingly divided. In 1824, when four party leaders ran for president, John Quincy Adams won the election in the House of Representatives, although Andrew Jackson had received more popular votes.

The deep factionalism evident in the 1824 election doomed the Democratic-Republican Party. The two-party system revived shortly thereafter with the emergence of the National Republican Party, an outgrowth of the Adams faction, and the Democratic-Republican Party, the political organization of the Jackson faction. After 1830 the Jacksonians adopted the name Democratic Party.

Dixiecrats (States' Rights Party) (1948)

The States' Rights Democratic Party was a conservative southern faction that bolted from the Democrats in 1948. The immediate reason for the new party, popularly known as the Dixiecrats, was dissatisfaction with President Harry Truman's civil rights program. But the Dixiecrat effort to maintain a segregated way of life was also an attempt to demonstrate the political power of the twentieth-century southern Democrats and to reestablish their importance in the Democratic Party.

The Mississippi Democratic Party's state executive committee met in Jackson in May 1948 to lay the groundwork for the Dixiecrat secession. The meeting called for a bolt by southern delegates if the Democratic National Convention endorsed Truman's civil rights program. When the convention did approve a strong civil rights plank, the entire Mississippi delegation and half the Alabama delegation left the convention. Gov. Fielding L. Wright of Mississippi invited all anti-Truman delegates to meet in Birmingham three days after the close of the Democratic convention to select a states' rights ticket.

Most southern Democrats with something at stake—national prominence, seniority in Congress, patronage privileges—shunned the new Dixiecrat Party. The party's leaders came from the ranks of southern governors and other state and local officials. The Birmingham convention chose two governors to lead the party: J. Strom Thurmond of South Carolina for president and Wright of Mississippi for vice president.

Other than the presidential ticket, the Dixiecrats did not run candidates for any office. Rather than try to develop an independent party organization, the Dixiecrats, whenever possible, used existing Democratic Party apparatus.

The party was on the ballot in only one state outside the South and in the November election received only 1,157,326 votes (2.4 percent of the popular vote). The Thurmond ticket carried four Deep South states where it ran under the Democratic Party label, but it failed in its basic objective to prevent the reelection of President Truman.

After the election the party ceased to exist almost as abruptly as it had begun, with most of its members returning to the Democratic Party. In a statement upon reentering the Democratic fold, Thurmond characterized the Dixiecrat episode as "a fight within our family." (While serving in the U.S. Senate sixteen years later, Thurmond switched to the Republican Party.)

Federalists (1792–1816)

Two related groups in late-eighteenth-century American politics called themselves Federalists. First were the proponents of ratifying the Constitution as framed in 1787, chief among them Alexander Hamilton and James Madison. They won. Next was the group that dominated national politics in the 1790s, as Americans began to form political parties.

The two groups were not identical. Madison, successful in promoting adoption of the new Constitution, led a political opposition that emerged in 1792. He, along with fellow Virginian Thomas Jefferson, argued for strict construction, or a narrow interpretation, of the powers of the new national government and organized a rival political party, the Democratic- (or Jeffersonian) Republicans, which came to power with Jefferson's election in 1800.

The Federalist Party, led by Hamilton as President George Washington's secretary of the Treasury, dominated national politics during the administrations of Washington and John Adams. The Federalists wanted to make the national government stronger by assuming state debts, chartering a national bank, and supporting manufacturing interests. In foreign affairs, they pursued policies that would protect commercial and political harmony with Britain, goals that led to ratification of Jay's Treaty in 1795. Under the treaty, Britain withdrew the last of its troops from American outposts and the United States agreed to honor debts owed to British merchants.

Though committed to a republican form of government, Federalists believed society to be properly hierarchical. Federalists such as William Cooper of New York and Henry Knox of Massachusetts professed that politics was an arena best left to the "natural aristocracy" of wealthy and talented men. Consequently, Federalists generally sought to limit suffrage, tighten naturaliza-tion policy, and silence antiadministration opinions. Recent examinations of the Federalists have disclosed a softer side to their conservatism, showing that, as self-proclaimed protectors of society, they sometimes sought to protect the basic rights of minorities. They tended to be more sympathetic than their Jeffersonian opponents to the plight of Native Americans and African Americans and less resistant to the inclusion of women in political processes.

Alexander Hamilton

Federalists drew their support primarily from the Northeast, where their procommercial and promanufacturing policies attracted merchants and businessmen. Although they had some southern strongholds in parts of Virginia and the Carolinas (especially Charleston), Federalists had considerably less success in attracting the support of western farmers and southern planters who opposed their elitism, antislavery bias, and promanufacturing economic policies.

Several factors contributed to the demise of the Federalist Party. Its passage of the highly unpopular Alien and Sedition Acts of 1798 served as a rallying cry for Jeffersonian Republicans. A more important factor may have been the Federalists' sharp division in the 1800 elections over Adams's foreign policies. Second-generation Federalists continued to mobilize regional support, mainly in New England, and, after Jefferson's unpopular embargo forbidding exports (1807–1809), they made something of a national comeback in the 1808 and 1812 elections. Many Federalists opposed the War of 1812, however, and in 1814 the Hartford Convention, a meeting of arch-Federalists, considered secession from the union, thereby permanently tainting the Federalist name and ending the party's legitimacy at the national level. Federalists continued to play a limited, though sometimes important, role in state and local politics into the 1820s, challenging for key offices in several states.

Federalist leadership during the nation's critical early years contributed greatly to preserving the American experiment. In large part they were responsible for laying the foundation for a national economy (later carried forward by the National Republicans and then the Whigs), a national foreign policy agenda, and creating a strong national judicial system. The last of these was perhaps the Federalists' most enduring legacy as John Marshall used his position as chief justice (1801–1835) to incorporate Federalist principles into constitutional law.

Free Soil Party (1848–1852)

Born as a result of opposition to the extension of slavery into the newly acquired southwest territories, the Free Soil Party was launched formally at a convention in Buffalo, New York, in August 1848. The Free Soilers were composed of antislavery elements from the Democratic and Whig parties as well as remnants of the Liberty Party. Representatives from all the northern states and three border states attended the Buffalo convention, where the slogan "Free Soil, Free Speech, Free Labor and Free Men" was adopted. This slogan expressed the antislavery sentiment of the Free Soilers as well as the desire for cheap western land.

Former Democratic president Martin Van Buren (1837–1841) was selected by the convention as the party's presidential candidate and Charles Francis Adams, the son of President John Quincy Adams (1825–1829), was chosen as his running mate.

In the 1848 election the Free Soil ticket received 291,501 votes (10.1 percent of the popular vote) but was unable to carry a single state. The party did better at the congressional level, winning nine House seats and holding the balance of power in the organization of the closely divided new Congress.

The 1848 election marked the peak of the party's influence. With the passage of compromise legislation on slavery in 1850, the Free Soilers lost their basic issue and began a rapid decline. The party ran its second and last national ticket in 1852, headed by John Hale, who received 155,210 votes (4.9 percent of the popular vote). As in 1848, the Free Soil national ticket failed to carry a single state.

Although the party went out of existence shortly thereafter, its program and constituency were absorbed by the Republican Party, whose birth and growth dramatically paralleled the resurgence of the slavery issue in the mid-1850s.

Green Party (1996–)

With famed consumer activist Ralph Nader heading its ticket, the Green Party made an impressive debut in U.S. presidential politics in 1996. Nader received 685,040 votes (0.7 percent of the popular vote) to finish fourth, albeit a distant fourth, behind the Reform Party's Ross Perot. Four years later, he made an even more impressive showing, winning 2.9 million votes (2.7 percent of the total vote), and finished third, well ahead of other third party candidates in the race. His showing probably tipped the outcome to the Republican Party in one or two states.

Nader received votes in every state except three (South Dakota, North Carolina, and Oklahoma), a significant increase from four years earlier when he was on the ballot in twenty-two states. As before, he ran best in western states but also drew a strong following in a few northeastern states. His running mate was Winona LaDuke of the White Earth reservation in Min-

nesota. A Harvard graduate, LaDuke was active as an advocate and writer on human rights and Native American environmental causes.

Although new to the United States, the Green Party was part of a decentralized worldwide movement for peace, social justice, and the environment. Until the collapse of international communism and the fall of the Berlin Wall, the Greens were best known for their political inroads in Germany. But the party lost ground after opposing reunification and it only recently has returned to the German parliament.

Unlike four years earlier, Nader and LaDuke in 2000 ran an aggressive and active campaign. He took his populist, anticorporate campaign to a variety of venues, ranging from TV studios to union meetings, in a bid to put together what he described as a "blue-green" coalition of disaffected voters. Nationwide polls in the summer of 2000 showed Nader drawing roughly 5 percent of the vote, and even more than that in several battleground states, including California. In the end, however, he received far fewer votes nationwide than expected. Nader was on the ballot in a number of closely contested states but most were won by the Democratic nominee, Al Gore, who was seen by analysts as the candidate most likely to be hurt by Nader's presence in the contest. Of these states, none was more important than Florida. In that state, Nader took more than 97,400 votes in a contest decided by a few hundred in favor of Republican George W. Bush. That win put Bush over the top in electoral votes and gave the White House back to the Republicans. Some political observers thought that had Nader not been on the ticket, Gore would have won Florida and the White House.

Greenback Party (1874–1884)

The National Independent or Greenback-Labor Party, commonly known as the Greenback Party, was launched in Indianapolis in November 1874 at a meeting organized by the Indiana Grange. The party grew out of the Panic of 1873, a post–Civil War economic depression, which hit farmers and industrial workers particularly hard. Currency was the basic issue of the new party, which opposed a return to the gold standard and favored retention of the inflationary paper money (known as greenbacks), first introduced as an emergency measure during the Civil War.

In the 1876 presidential election the party ran Peter Cooper, a New York philanthropist, and drafted a platform that focused entirely on the currency issue. Cooper received 75,973 votes (0.9 percent of the popular vote), mainly from agrarian voters. Aided by the continuing depression, a Greenback national convention in 1878 effected the merger of the party with various labor reform groups and adopted a platform that addressed labor and currency issues. Showing voting strength in the industrial East as well as in the agrarian South and Midwest, the Greenbacks polled more than one million votes in the 1878 congressional elections and won fourteen seats in the U.S. House of Representatives. This marked the high point of the party's strength.

Returning prosperity, the prospect of fusion with one of the major parties, and a split between the party's agrarian and labor leadership served to undermine the Greenback Party. In the 1880 election the party elected only eight representatives and its presidential candidate, Rep. James B. Weaver of Iowa, received 305,997 votes (3.3 percent of the popular vote), far less than party leaders expected.

The party slipped further four years later, when the Greenbacks' candidate for president, former Massachusetts governor Benjamin F. Butler, received 175,096 votes (1.7 percent of the popular vote). With the demise of the Greenbacks, most of the party's constituency moved into the Populist Party, the agrarian reform movement that swept the South and Midwest in the 1890s.

Know Nothing (American) Party (1856)

The Know Nothing Party of the 1850s was the most formidable nativist political organization in American history; for two years in mid-decade it was the nation's second-largest party. Nativism involved the fear of aliens and opposition to an internal minority believed to be un-American. Members of the American Party would be called Know Nothings because when asked about their organization they were instructed to say, "I know nothing." For them, fear and hatred of Catholics, particularly "papist conspirators," created this need for secrecy.

The Know Nothings emerged from one of the many nativist secret societies proliferating in the pre–Civil War period. The migration of millions of Catholics from Ireland and Germany stimulated an intense antialien activism in the United States. Key leaders of the Order of the Star Spangled Banner saw their group as a useful instrument for shaping a new political party in 1853. Like nativists of earlier decades, leaders of the Know Nothing Party accused Catholics of undermining the public school system and of being responsible for a host of social problems accompanying the influx of so many poverty-stricken newcomers into the great port cities.

The party emerged at a critical moment in American political history. The slavery controversy was ripping apart the Whig Party, and the Democratic Party was suffering fissures in different states and sections. Out of this turmoil came a flood of members to the new nativist movement. For many people, a party organized around nativist themes—one that advanced "American" interests and stood for stability and union—offered a way out of the conflict between northerner and southerner, abolitionist and slaveholder. A common crusade against foreigners, they thought, could cement broken institutions and warring people.

The political divisions of the day meant that Know Nothing membership varied from section to section. In New York, where the party was born and had its strongest support, the leadership was composed of conservative Whig refugees, men who opposed free soil and antislavery elements in their former party. These included James Barker and Daniel Ullmann, the party candidate in the New York gubernatorial race in 1855. In New England the antislavery wing of the former Whig Party, "Conscience Whigs," played the key role. Leaders in Massachusetts included Henry Wilson, president of the state senate who was a

An 1854 political cartoon depicting the Know Nothing Party.

U.S. senator in 1855, and Henry J. Gardner, elected state governor in the Know Nothing landslide that year. Also swelling the party rolls in New England were abolitionists from the other major party, anti–Nebraska Act Democrats.

In the West, where Know Nothings struggled to find support, nativists sought fusion with "Free Soil" activists in Indiana and Illinois, but in Wisconsin two factions (the Sams and the Jonathans) shared antialien attitudes yet split over slavery.

In the South, which contained a small immigrant population, nativism appealed to those who viewed "aliens" in the Northeast and West as threatening to the southern way of life because it was assumed that newcomers would be opposed to slavery. The nativist party in the South represented an escape from the divisive struggle that threatened civil strife, but it had only limited impact.

Despite its political success in 1854 and 1855, the national Know Nothing Party could not survive the antislavery controversy. At the party gathering in Philadelphia in June 1855, a proslavery resolution led to wild debate and a massive defection led by Massachusetts nativists but including representatives from many states. Further divisions in the party, including personal rivalries between New York leaders Barker and Ullmann, created more problems.

In 1856 the party nominated former president Millard Fillmore as its presidential candidate. But Fillmore—who had joined a Know Nothing lodge as a political maneuver and had never been a real nativist—failed at the polls, trailing in a three-way race with only 22 percent of the popular vote and taking only Maryland's eight electoral college votes. The Know Nothings did not recover, losing members rapidly in subsequent months. In 1857 the party held its last national council.

Liberal Party (1944–)

New York State's Liberal Party was founded in 1944 by anti-communist trade unionists and other politically liberal individuals who left communist-dominated political parties. The party in 2000 described itself as providing an "alternative to a state Democratic Party dominated by local party machines rife with corruption and a Republican Party controlled by special interests." Many of the state's labor and educational leaders were instrumental in creating the party, which calls itself the nation's "longest existing third party."

The Liberal Party has played a major role in several elections. It provided crucial support for Franklin D. Roosevelt in 1944 and John F. Kennedy in 1960. Some political historians believe Roosevelt and Kennedy owed their national victories to the Liberal Party vote that carried New York State for them. John Lindsay, nominally a Republican, won reelection in New York City's 1969 mayoral race as the Liberal Party candidate. In 2000 Democrat Hillary Rodham Clinton won the Liberal line in her campaign for the U.S. Senate.

The party proclaims to nominate candidates on the basis of "merit, independence, and progressive viewpoints." Many of the state's most prominent liberal politicians have sought and won the party's nomination for New York City mayor, governor, and U.S. senator, regardless of their major party affiliation. When the party has not run candidates of its own, it has usually been supportive of Democrats. Sometimes, however, the party's role has been that of a spoiler, particularly in close races, where its support represents the balance of power. In modern Senate races, for example, political analysts say Liberal Party endorsement of moderate or liberal candidates has sometimes drawn enough votes from Democratic candidates to throw the election to conservative Republicans.

The party is active in pushing its political agenda, which is pro-choice, pro-universal health care, and pro-public education (it has aggressively opposed school voucher programs, for example). Its successful Supreme Court suit for congressional reapportionment contributed to the 1968 election of Shirley Chisholm of New York, the first African American congresswoman.

Through the latter part of the twentieth century, the Liberal Party served as a counterweight in Empire State politics to New York's Conservative Party. In 1966, for instance, each party's gubernatorial candidate drew over a half million votes. The Liberal nominee was Franklin D. Roosevelt Jr.

Both parties have lost ground at the polls since then, the Liberals a bit more than the Conservatives. In 1998, for instance, the Liberal Party's gubernatorial nominee drew fewer than 80,000 votes, while the Conservative Party line provided Republican incumbent George E. Pataki with nearly 350,000 votes.

Liberal Republican Party (1872)

A faction of the Republican Party, dissatisfied with President Ulysses S. Grant's first term in office, withdrew from the party in 1872 to form a new party. Composed of party reformers, as well as anti-Grant politicians and newspaper editors, the new party focused on the corruption of the Grant administration and the need for civil service reform and for an end to the Reconstruction policy in the South.

The call for the Liberal Republican national convention came from the state party in Missouri, the birthplace of the reform movement. The convention, meeting in Cincinnati, Ohio, in May 1872, nominated Horace Greeley, editor of the *New York Tribune,* for president and Missouri governor B. Gratz Brown as his running mate. Greeley, the choice of anti-Grant politicians but suspect among reformers, was not popular among many Democrats either, who recalled his longtime criticism of the Democratic Party.

With the hope of victory in the fall election, however, the Democratic National Convention, meeting in July, endorsed the Liberal Republican ticket and platform. The coalition was an unsuccessful one, as many Democrats refused to vote for Greeley. He received 2,834,761 votes (43.8 percent of the popular vote) but carried only six states and lost to Grant by more than 750,000 votes out of nearly 6.5 million cast. Greeley died shortly after the election.

Underfinanced, poorly organized, and dependent on the Democrats for their success, the Liberal Republicans went out of existence after the 1872 election.

Libertarian Party (1971–)

In the brief period of four years, 1972 to 1976, the Libertarian Party leaped from a fledgling organization on the presidential ballot in only two states to the nation's largest third party. In the presidential election of 2000, although the party's candidate ran fifth in the race and won fewer popular votes than four years earlier, the Libertarians still claimed to be the third largest party in the nation.

Formed in Colorado in 1971, the party nominated John Hospers of California for president in 1972. On the ballot only in Colorado and Washington, Hospers garnered 3,673 votes (including write-in votes from other states). But he received a measure of national attention when a Republican presidential elector from Virginia, Roger MacBride, cast his electoral vote for the Libertarian presidential nominee.

MacBride's action made him a hero in Libertarian circles, and the party chose him as its 1976 standard-bearer at its August 1975 convention in New York City. MacBride had served in the Vermont legislature in the 1960s and was defeated for the Republican gubernatorial nomination in that state in 1964. In the 1970s he settled on a farm near Charlottesville, Virginia, and devoted himself to writing and party affairs. He was cocreator of the television show *Little House on the Prairie.*

Making a major effort in 1976, the Libertarians got on the ballot in thirty-two states, more than Eugene J. McCarthy—who ran independent of any political party—or any other third-party candidate. The reward was a vote of 173,011, more than for any other minor party candidate but far below McCarthy's total and only 0.2 percent of the national vote. MacBride's strength was centered in the West; he received 5.5 percent of the vote in Alaska and 1.0 percent or more in Arizona, Hawaii, and Idaho. He also ran well ahead of his national average in California (0.7 percent) and Nevada (0.8 percent). His running mate was David P. Bergland, a California lawyer.

In 1980 the Libertarian Party appeared on the ballot in all fifty states and the District of Columbia for the first time. The party also fielded about 550 candidates for other offices, a number that dwarfed other third-party efforts. The party nominees, Edward E. Clark of California for president and David Koch of New York for vice president, garnered 921,299 votes or 1.1 percent of the vote nationwide. As in previous elections, the major support for the Libertarians came from western states.

Of all minor-party presidential candidates running in 1984, the Libertarians appeared on the greatest number of ballots: thirty-eight states and the District of Columbia. David Bergland, who had run in 1976 for the second slot, was the party's presidential candidate, and Jim Lewis, a Connecticut business executive, his running mate. In 1988 the Libertarian presidential and vice-presidential nominees—Ron Paul and Andre V. Marrou, respectively—were on the ballot in all fifty-one jurisdictions save four and received 432,179 votes.

In 1992 Nevada real estate broker Marrou was the presidential nominee with running mate Nancy Lord, a lawyer from Georgia. The pair was on the ballot in all states and the District of Columbia and had a campaign budget of $1 million. Marrou received 291,627 votes in a fourth-place finish behind Ross Perot, who stole most of the third-party candidates' thunder that year. The Libertarians maintained their strong base in the West, especially in California, Nevada, and Hawaii, where they also ran candidates in 1992 for most House seats.

In 1996 the Libertarians regained voting strength but nevertheless dropped to fifth place in the presidential race behind Ralph Nader of the newly formed Green Party. The Libertarian candidate, financial analyst Harry Browne of Tennessee, and running mate Jo Anne Jorgensen of South Carolina drew 485,798 votes or 0.50 percent of the total. It was the party's best showing since 1980.

The story in the 2000 presidential race was similar but not as favorable. The party won votes in forty-nine states, but its candidates, again Browne and running mate Art Olivier of California, won just 386,024 votes, or 0.37 percent of all votes, down 20 percent from four years earlier.

Individual responsibility and minimal government interference are the hallmarks of the Libertarian philosophy. The party has favored repeal of laws against so-called victimless crimes—such as pornography, drug use, and homosexual activity—the abolition of all federal police agencies, and the elimination of all government subsidies to private enterprise. In foreign and military affairs, the Libertarians have advocated the removal of U.S. troops from abroad, a cut in the defense budget, and the emergence of the United States as a "giant Switzerland," with no in-ternational treaty obligations. Libertarians also have favored repeal of legislation that they believe hinders individual or corporate action. They have opposed gun control, civil rights laws, price controls on oil and gas, labor protection laws, federal welfare and poverty programs, forced busing, compulsory education, Social Security, national medical care, and federal land-use restrictions.

Liberty Party (1839–1848)

Born in 1839, the Liberty Party was the product of a split in the antislavery movement between a faction led by William Lloyd Garrison that favored action outside the political process and a second led by James G. Birney that proposed action within the political system through the establishment of an independent antislavery party. The Birney faction launched the Liberty Party in November 1839. The following April a national convention with delegates from six states nominated Birney for the presidency.

Although the Liberty Party was the first political party to take an antislavery position, and the only one at the time to do so, most abolitionist voters in the 1840 election supported the Democratic or Whig presidential candidates. Birney received only 6,797 votes (0.3 percent of the popular vote).

Aided by the controversy over the annexation of slaveholding Texas, the Liberty Party's popularity increased in 1844. Birney, again the party's presidential nominee, received 62,103 votes (2.3 percent of the popular vote) but again, as in 1840, carried no states. The peak strength of the party was reached two years later in 1846, when in various state elections Liberty Party candidates received 74,017 votes.

In October 1847 the party nominated New Hampshire senator John P. Hale for the presidency, but his candidacy was withdrawn the following year when the Liberty Party joined the broader-based Free Soil Party.

National Democratic Party (1896)

A conservative faction in favor of the gold standard, the National Democrats bolted from the Democratic Party after the 1896 convention adopted a prosilver platform and nominated William Jennings Bryan for president. With the nation in the midst of a depression and the Populists in the agrarian Midwest and South demanding monetary reform, currency was the dominant issue of the 1896 campaign. This produced a brief realignment in American politics.

The Republican Party was controlled by leaders who favored maintenance of the gold standard, a noninflationary currency. Agrarian midwestern and southern Democrats, reflecting a populist philosophy, gained control of the Democratic Party in 1896 and committed it to the free coinage of silver, an inflationary currency demanded by rural elements threatened by debts. The Democrats attracted prosilver bolters from the Republican Party, but gold standard Democrats, opposed to the Republicans' protectionist position on the tariff issue, established an independent party.

William Jennings Bryan

Meeting in Indianapolis in September 1896, the National Democrats adopted a platform favoring maintenance of the gold standard and selected a ticket headed by seventy-nine-year-old Illinois senator John M. Palmer.

Democratic president Grover Cleveland and leading members of his administration, repudiated by the convention that chose Bryan, supported the National Democrats. During the campaign the National Democrats encouraged conservative Democrats to vote either for the National Democratic ticket or for the Republican candidate, William McKinley. The Palmer ticket received 133,435 votes (1.0 percent of the popular vote), and McKinley defeated Bryan.

In the 1890s returning prosperity and the Spanish-American War overshadowed the currency issue, and the intense Democratic Party factionalism that produced the National Democratic Party ended.

National Republican Party (1828–1832)

The Democratic-Republican Party splintered after the 1824 election into two factions. The group led by Andrew Jackson retained the name Democratic-Republicans, which eventually was shortened to Democrats; the other faction, headed by President John Quincy Adams, assumed the name National Republicans. Reflecting the belief of President Adams in the establishment of a national policy by the federal government, the new party supported a protective tariff, the Bank of the United States, federal administration of public lands, and national programs of internal improvements. But Adams's belief in a strong national government contrasted with the period's prevailing mood of populism and states' rights.

The Adams forces controlled Congress for two years, 1825 to 1827, but as party structures formalized the National Republicans became a minority in Congress and suffered a decisive loss in the 1828 presidential election. Running for reelection, Adams was beaten by Jackson. Adams received 43.6 percent of the popular vote and carried eight states, none in the South. Henry Clay, the party's candidate against Jackson four years later, had even less success. He received only 37.4 percent of the popular vote and carried just six states, none of which, again, were in the South.

Poorly organized, with dwindling support and a heritage of defeat, the National Republicans went out of existence after the 1832 election, but their members provided the base for a new anti-Jackson party, the Whigs, which came into being in 1834.

National Unity Party (Independent John B. Anderson) (1980–1988)

Republican representative John B. Anderson of Illinois formed the National Unity Campaign as the vehicle for his independent presidential campaign in 1980. Anderson began his quest for the presidency by trying to win the Republican Party nomination. But as a liberal in a party coming under conservative control, he won no primaries and could claim only fifty-seven convention delegates by April 1980. Anderson withdrew from the Republican race and declared his independent candidacy.

Anderson focused his campaign on the need to establish a viable third party as an alternative to domination of the political scene by the Republican and Democratic parties. The National Unity Campaign platform touted the Anderson program as a "new public philosophy"—more innovative than that of the Democrats, who "cling to the policies of the New Deal," and more enlightened than that of the Republicans, who talk "incessantly about freedom, but hardly ever about justice." Generally, the group took positions that were fiscally conservative and socially liberal. Anderson and his running mate, former Democratic governor Patrick J. Lucey of Wisconsin, tried to appeal to Republican and Democratic voters disenchanted with their parties and to the growing bloc of voters who classified themselves as independents.

The National Unity Campaign ticket was on the ballot in all fifty states in 1980, although Anderson had to wage costly legal battles in some states to ensure that result. In the end, the party won 6.6 percent of the presidential vote, well over the 5 percent necessary to qualify for retroactive federal campaign funding.

In April 1984 Anderson announced that he would not seek the presidency in that year. He said that instead he would focus his energies on building the National Unity Party, which he established officially in December 1983. He planned to concentrate initially on running candidates at the local level. In August Anderson endorsed Walter F. Mondale, the Democratic nominee for president, and his running mate, Geraldine A. Ferraro.

The National Unity Party did not run a presidential candidate in the 1988 race and by 1992 was no longer a political party.

Natural Law Party (1992–)

The Natural Law Party, which in its second presidential campaign in 1996 won 113,668 votes nationwide, experienced a large decline in voter support in 2000. Its presidential candidate, John Hagelin of Fairfield, Iowa, received 83,520 votes, down almost 27 percent from four years earlier. In 1992 Hagelin won a total of 39,179 votes. Among third parties, Hagelin's vote was seventh highest in 2000.

Hagelin was on the ballot in thirty-eight states in 2000. Because the Natural Law Party fulfilled the necessary requirements, it was assured automatic ballot access in ten states in the next presidential election in 2004. Hagelin not only was the Natural Law nominee again in 2000, but he challenged Patrick J. Buchanan for the Reform Party nomination. Losing that nomination, Hagelin and his Reform Party supporters set up a splinter Reform Party that later joined in coalition with the Natural Law Party.

Hagelin, a Harvard-trained quantum physicist, was born in Pittsburgh in 1954 and grew up in Connecticut. He became associated with Maharishi International University in Iowa in 1983. His running mate was fellow Maharishi scientist Mike Tompkins, a Harvard graduate and specialist in crime prevention programs.

The Natural Law Party has described itself as "the fastest growing grassroots party," standing for the environment, educa-tion, economic growth, job creation, and lower taxes. Despite its title, the party seemed to have little connection with the philosophic concept of natural law, which holds that some rules of society—such as the prohibition against murder—are so basic and inherent that they must be obeyed whether or not they are legislated.

Hagelin and the party have advocated prevention-oriented government and meditative, tension-relieving programs "designed to bring national life into harmony with natural law."

New Alliance Party (1988–1992)

The New Alliance Party formed in the late 1980s to promote a combination of minority interests. Self-described as "black-led, multiracial, pro-gay and pro-socialist," the party aggressively filed lawsuits to attain ballot access. In 1988 presidential candidate Lenora B. Fulani, a New York psychologist, drew 217,219 votes nationwide for a fourth-place finish. Her best showing was in the District of Columbia, where she received more than 1 percent of the vote.

In 1992, with the party qualifying for $1.8 million in federal matching funds, Fulani ran again, this time with California teacher Maria Munoz as a running mate. Fulani campaigned for equal employment for all. "I believe that a job at a union wage is the right of all Americans," she said. The New Alliance ticket appeared on the ballot in thirty-nine states and the District of Columbia and received 73,714 votes, slightly less than 0.1 percent nationwide.

Peace and Freedom Party (1967–)

Although founded in Michigan, the radical Peace and Freedom Party has been active largely in California—the only state where it appeared on the ballot in 1996.

From the outset, the party worked with the California Black Panther Party to oppose U.S. involvement in the Vietnam War and espouse black nationalism and other so-called New Left causes. The first Peace and Freedom nominee for president, in 1968, was Black Panther leader Eldridge Cleaver. Running with various vice-presidential candidates, Cleaver received 36,563 votes.

Cleaver's autobiographical, antiracist polemic, *Soul on Ice*, was published in 1968. After the election Cleaver, a paroled convict awaiting trial for murder, went into exile. On his return years later, he became a born-again Christian.

Before the 1968 election, black activist-comedian Dick Gregory broke with the Peace and Freedom Party and set up the similarly named Freedom and Peace Party with himself as the presidential nominee. He received 47,133 votes.

After 1968 no Peace and Freedom candidate attracted significant numbers of presidential votes until 1980, when Maureen Smith and Elizabeth Barron received 18,116. In 1972, however, noted pacifist and pediatrician Benjamin Spock, the People's Party nominee, ran under the Peace and Freedom banner in California. He received 55,167 votes there and 23,589 votes in other states.

In 1974 the California Peace and Freedom Party declared itself to be socialist. In recent elections its presidential ticket has received at least 10,000 votes: 1988, Herbert Lewin and Vikki Murdock, 10,370; 1992, Ron Daniels and Asiba Tupahache, 27,961; and 1996, Marsha Feinland and Kate McClatchy, 25,332. In 2000 the party ran no presidential candidates.

People's Party (1971–)

Delegates from activist and peace groups established the People's Party at a November 1971 convention held in Dallas, Texas. The initial cochairmen were pediatrician Benjamin Spock and author Gore Vidal.

The People's Party first ran a presidential candidate in 1972. They chose Dr. Spock for president and black activist Julius Hobson of Washington, D.C., for vice president. Despite hopes for widespread backing from the poor and social activists, the ticket received only 78,756 votes, 0.1 percent of the national total. A total of 55,167 of those votes came from California alone.

At its convention, held in St. Louis, Missouri, August 31, 1975, the People's Party chose black civil rights activist Margaret Wright of California for president and Maggie Kuhn of Pennsylvania, a leader in the Gray Panthers movement for rights for the elderly, for vice president. Kuhn, however, declined the nomination and was replaced on the ticket by Spock.

The party platform focused on cutting the defense budget, closing tax loopholes, and making that money available for social programs. Other planks included redistribution of land and wealth, unconditional amnesty for war objectors, and free health care. In her campaign, Wright stressed the necessity for active participation by citizens in the governmental process, so that institutions and programs could be run from the grass roots up rather than from the top down.

As in 1972, the party's main backing came in California, where it was supported by the state Peace and Freedom Party. Wright's total national vote in 1976 was 49,024, and 85.1 percent (41,731 votes) of those votes came from California. The party has not fielded presidential candidates since 1976.

Populist (People's) Party (1891–1908)

The Populist (or People's) Party, a third party founded in May 1891 in Cincinnati, Ohio, grew out of a period of agrarian revolt and remained politically active until 1908.

Following the Civil War, farmers battled falling commodity prices, high railroad rates, and heavy mortgage debt. The Patrons of Husbandry (the Grange), organized in 1867 by Oliver Kelley, began as a group intent on improving educational and social opportunities for farm men and women but soon adopted economic and political initiatives such as the cooperative movement of the 1870s. The inability of the Grange to give farmers an effective political voice led many Grangers, in the 1880s, to join the Farmers' Alliance, a precursor to the Populist Party. More aggressive and politically oriented, the Farmers' Alliance considered all agricultural problems as economic and pursued remedies such as political education and cooperative marketing, particularly in the South, as a means to break the grip of the furnishing merchants, who extended credit through crop liens.

Women, while active members, held far fewer offices in the Farmers' Alliance than those in the Grange. Existing racial prejudices led to the separate creation of a Colored Farmers' National Alliance in 1888.

In June 1890 Kansas farmers founded the People's Party based on the Southern Alliance platform, which included government ownership of railroads, free and unlimited coinage of silver, and a subtreasury (a system by which farmers could turn over a staple crop to a government warehouse and receive a loan for 80 percent of its value at 2 percent interest per month). As a national third party in 1891, the Populists also sought a farmer-laborer political coalition that championed the belief, expressed by Minnesota Populist Ignatius Donnelly, that the "public good is paramount to private interests."

For a time, the party attempted to bridge the racial gulf and recruited black farmers as well as white. Populism in the South, however, became mired in the volatility of race, epitomized by Georgia's Tom Watson and South Carolina's Benjamin Tillman. Although not immune to the negative racial and ethnic overtones of the period, the Populist Party was nevertheless more concerned with achieving economic reforms, a humane industrial society, and a just polity than it was with attacking cultural issues. The party's greatest support came from white land-owning cotton farmers in the South and wheat farmers in the West.

The Populists rallied behind a policy of monetary inflation in the expectation that it would increase the amount of currency in circulation, boost commodity prices, and ease farmers' indebtedness. In 1892, when the People's Party nominated James B. Weaver of Iowa as its presidential candidate, its demands included a graduated income tax, antitrust regulations, public ownership of railroads, and unlimited coinage of silver and gold at a ratio of sixteen to one. Democrat Grover Cleveland was elected to a second term, with Weaver carrying only four states in the West. In 1896 the Populists nominated William Jennings Bryan, a free-silver candidate from Nebraska who was also the Democratic nominee, but the Republicans won with William McKinley.

Having lost on the silver issue and having lost their identity through a "fusion" with the Democrats, the Populists declined in strength and influence, particularly as new discoveries of gold eased the monetary crisis and agricultural conditions improved. Although the People's Party receded, some of the reforms it had championed, including a graduated income tax, were instituted during the Progressive era. The Populists' main significance lay in their visionary use of politics to turn a spotlight on the conditions facing farm families and thereby seek more democratic reform measures.

Progressive (Bull Moose) Party (1912)

A split in Republican ranks, spurred by the bitter personal and ideological dispute between President William Howard Taft (1909–1913) and former president Theodore Roosevelt

(1901–1909), resulted in the withdrawal of the Roosevelt forces from the Republican Party after the June 1912 convention and the creation of the Progressive Party two months later. The new party was known popularly as the Bull Moose Party, a name resulting from Roosevelt's assertion early in the campaign that he felt as fit as a bull moose. While the Taft-Roosevelt split was the immediate reason for the new party, the Bull Moosers were an outgrowth of the Progressive movement that was a powerful force in both major parties in the early years of the twentieth century.

Although in 1908 Roosevelt had handpicked Taft as his successor, his disillusionment with Taft's conservative philosophy came quickly, and with the support of progressive Republicans Roosevelt challenged the incumbent for the 1912 Republican presidential nomination. Roosevelt outpolled Taft in the presidential primary states. Taft nevertheless won the nomination with nearly solid support in the South and among party conservatives, providing the narrow majority of delegates that enabled him to win the bulk of the key credentials challenges.

Although few Republican politicians followed Roosevelt in his bolt, the new party demonstrated a popular base at its convention in Chicago in August 1912. Thousands of delegates, basically middle- and upper-class reformers from small towns and cities, attended the convention that launched the party and nominated Roosevelt for president and California governor Hiram Johnson as his running mate. Roosevelt appeared in person to deliver his "Confession of Faith," a speech detailing his nationalistic philosophy and progressive reform ideas. The Bull Moose platform reflected key tenets of the Progressive movement, calling for more extensive government antitrust action and for labor, social, government, and electoral reform.

Roosevelt was wounded in an assassination attempt while campaigning in Milwaukee, Wisconsin, in October, but he finished the campaign. In the general election Roosevelt received more than 4 million votes (27.4 percent of the popular vote) and carried six states. His percentage of the vote was the highest ever received by a third-party candidate in American history, but his candidacy split the Republican vote and enabled the Democrats' nominee, Woodrow Wilson, to win the election. The Progressive Party had minimal success at the state and local levels, winning thirteen House seats but electing no senators or governors.

Roosevelt declined the Progressive nomination in 1916 and endorsed the Republican candidate, Charles Evans Hughes. With the defection of its leader, the decline of the Progressive movement, and the lack of an effective party organization, the Bull Moose Party ceased to exist.

Progressive Party (La Follette) (1924)

Like the Bull Moose Party of Theodore Roosevelt, the Progressive Party that emerged in the mid-1920s was a reform effort led by a Republican. Wisconsin senator Robert M. La Follette led the new Progressive Party, a separate entity from the Bull Moosers, which, unlike the middle- and upper-class Roosevelt party of the previous decade, had its greatest appeal among farmers and organized labor.

Theodore Roosevelt

The La Follette Progressive Party grew out of the Conference for Progressive Political Action (CPPA), a coalition of railway union leaders and a remnant of the Bull Moose effort that was formed in 1922. The Socialist Party joined the coalition the following year. Throughout 1923 the Socialists and labor unions argued over whether their coalition should form a third party, with the Socialists in favor and the labor unions against it. It was finally decided to run an independent presidential candidate, La Follette, in the 1924 election but not to field candidates at the state and local levels. La Follette was given the power to choose his running mate and selected Montana senator Burton K. Wheeler, a Democrat.

Opposition to corporate monopolies was the major issue of the La Follette campaign, although the party advocated various other reforms, particularly aimed at farmers and workers, which were proposed earlier by either the Populists or Bull Moosers. But the Progressive Party itself was a major issue in the 1924 campaign, as the Republicans attacked the alleged radicalism of the party.

Although La Follette had its endorsement, the American Federation of Labor (AFL) provided minimal support. The basic strength of the Progressives, like that of the Populists in the 1890s, derived from agrarian voters west of the Mississippi River. La Follette received 4,832,532 votes (16.6 percent of the popular vote) but carried just one state, his native Wisconsin. When La Follette died in 1925, the party collapsed as a national force. It was revived by La Follette's sons on a statewide level in Wisconsin in the mid-1930s.

Progressive Party (Wallace) (1948)

Henry A. Wallace's Progressive Party resulted from the dissatisfaction of liberal elements in the Democratic Party with the leadership of President Harry S. Truman, particularly in the realm of foreign policy. The Progressive Party was one of two bolting groups from the Democratic Party in 1948; conservative southern elements withdrew to form the States' Rights Party.

Henry Wallace, the founder of the Progressive Party, was secretary of agriculture, vice president, and finally secretary of commerce under President Franklin Roosevelt. He carried the reputation of one of the most liberal idealists in the Roosevelt administration. Fired from the Truman cabinet in 1946 after breaking with administration policy and publicly advocating peaceful coexistence with the Soviet Union, Wallace began to consider the idea of a liberal third-party candidacy. Supported by the American Labor Party, the Progressive Citizens of America, and other progressive organizations in California and Illinois, Wallace announced his third-party candidacy in December 1947.

The Progressive Party was launched formally the following July at a convention in Philadelphia, which ratified the selection of Wallace for president and Sen. Glen H. Taylor, D-Idaho, as his running mate. The party adopted a platform that emphasized foreign policy—opposing the cold war anticommunism of the Truman administration and specifically urging abandonment of the Truman Doctrine and the Marshall Plan. These measures were designed to contain the spread of communism and bolster noncommunist nations. On domestic issues the Progressives stressed humanitarian concerns and equal rights for both sexes and all races.

Minority groups—women, youth, African Americans, Jews, Hispanic Americans—were active in the new party, but the openness of the Progressives brought Wallace a damaging endorsement from the Communist Party. Believing the two parties could work together, Wallace accepted the endorsement while characterizing his philosophy as "progressive capitalism."

In 1948 the Progressives appeared on the presidential ballot in forty-five states, but the Communist endorsement helped keep the party on the defensive the entire campaign. In the November election Wallace received only 1,157,326 votes (2.4 percent of the national popular vote), with nearly half of the votes from the state of New York. Not only were the Progressives unable to carry a single state, but in spite of their defection from the Democratic Party, President Truman won reelection. The Progressives had poor results in the congressional races, failing to elect one representative or senator.

The Progressive Party's opposition to the Korean War in 1950 drove many moderate elements out of the party, including Henry Wallace. The party ran a national ticket in 1952 but received only 140,023 votes nationwide or 0.2 percent of the national popular vote. The party crumbled completely after the election.

Progressive Labor Party (1960–)

The Progressive Labor Party (PLP) emerged out of the Communist Party USA in the early 1960s. It was the first Maoist party in the United States, following the revolutionary philosophies of Joseph Stalin and Mao Zedong and adhering to Mao's dictum that "power emanates from the barrel of a gun." The PLP envisions Stalin's dictatorship as the ideal state and opposes democracy, elections, capitalism, religion, and freedom in any form.

The PLP took over the Students for a Democratic Society (SDS) in 1969, prompting the non–Progressive Labor people to walk out of SDS and leaving the organization as a shell of its former self. The SDS was an activist—its critics said radical—student organization that started in Michigan and drew many supporters on campuses nationwide, particularly during the Vietnam War years.

The PLP contends that experiments with socialism and communism failed in the former Soviet Union and in today's People's Republic of China, where, it says, capitalism has triumphed. The PLP's doctrine, proclaimed on its Web site, envisions the party leading an "armed struggle by masses of workers, soldiers, students and others, to destroy the dictatorship of the capitalist class and set up a dictatorship of the working class."

The PLP publishes a newspaper, *Challenge,* and a magazine, *Communist,* as well as leaflets on such topics as "The Imperialist War in the Mideast," "Smash Racist Police Terror," and "Fascism Grows in the Auto Industry." In strict adherence to its policy of "armed struggle," the party disavows electoral politics and has run almost no candidates for office during its history.

Prohibition Party (1869–)

Prohibition and temperance movements sought to legislate an end to consumption of intoxicating beverages. Colonial and early national Americans preferred alcohol to impure water or milk and more expensive coffee or tea. By 1825 those over fifteen years of age drank an average of seven gallons of pure alcohol per year, diluted in cider, beer, wine, and distilled liquor; white males typically consumed substantially more, women much less, and black slaves very little. Physicians, Protestant ministers, and temperance advocates concerned about damage to health, morals, and industrial production urged voluntary abstinence from drinking. After achieving remarkable success, the temperance movement sought legal banishment of liquor. During the 1850s a dozen states—led by Maine in 1851—adopted alcohol bans.

After the Civil War, temperance crusaders created effective political pressure groups: the Prohibition Party in 1869, the Woman's Christian Temperance Union in 1874, and the Anti-Saloon League of America in 1895. Their campaigns won numerous statewide prohibition and local option laws, the latter giving individual communities the right to outlaw the sale of alcohol. In 1913 Congress banned shipment of liquor into any state that chose to bar it. Dissatisfied by uneven and sometimes short-lived state and local successes, goaded by rivalries between the Anti-Saloon League and competing temperance groups, and inspired by adoption of the first federal constitutional amendments in more than forty years (the income tax and direct Senate election amendments of 1913), reformers began calling for a total, permanent, nationwide solution to the liquor problem: a prohibition amendment to the Constitution.

Advocates against Pro-
hibition present peti-
tions to Congress.

National prohibition gathered support from evangelical Protestant denominations, feminists, nativists opposed to the recent flood of immigrants who drank, progressive social and political reformers, and industrial employers. Employing the unusual political tactic of pledging electoral support or punishment solely on the basis of a candidate's stand on the single issue of alcohol, proponents of Prohibition were able to get more and more supporters elected to Congress. U.S. entry into World War I against Germany added a final argument of patriotism, because the army needed the grain for bread and the troops needed to be sober to perform effectively. The Eighteenth (or Prohibition) Amendment was adopted with bipartisan backing in January 1919 and went into effect one year later; it operated with mixed success for fourteen years.

The Republicans, who were responsible for enforcement as the party in power throughout the 1920s, continued to defend Prohibition even as the Democrats' support was waning, especially in the urban North, as first Al Smith and later Franklin D. Roosevelt aligned with the repeal campaign. Differences regarding Prohibition were among the most clear-cut partisan divisions in the 1932 elections and helped account for the shift in the national political balance during the depths of the Great Depression. National Prohibition, widely viewed as a mistake, was repealed by the Twenty-first Amendment, which was ratified in December 1933.

The party remained after the repeal of Prohibition, however, becoming the longest running third party in American history in the twentieth century. The party has run a national ticket in every presidential election since 1872, but its candidates have never carried a single state. After the 1976 election, the Prohibi-

tion Party changed its name to the National Statesman Party, and its 1980 candidate registered using that party name. The 1984 candidate, Earl F. Dodge of Colorado, emphasized that his party—on the ballots once again as Prohibitionists—no longer focused on a single issue: the party backed religious liberty and an antiabortion amendment. Dodge ran again in 1988, 1992, 1996, and 2000. In 2000 the party could only muster 208 votes nationwide.

Reform Party (Independent Ross Perot) (1992–)

The Reform Party emerged almost full grown from Texas billionaire Ross Perot's independent self-financed presidential candidacy of 1992. That year Perot drew the highest vote share of any independent or third-party candidate in eighty years. Relying heavily on his wealth and on grass-roots volunteer efforts to get his name on the ballot in all fifty states and the District of Columbia, Perot received 19,741,657 votes or 18.9 percent of the nationwide vote. He did not win any sizable constituency or receive any electoral votes, but he drew a respectable 10 percent to 30 percent in popular voting across the nation.

Perot, who announced the possibility of his candidacy in February 1992, ran his early unofficial campaign mainly on one issue—eliminating the federal deficit. He had the luxury of funding his entire campaign, which included buying huge amounts of television time. Drawing on the disenchantment of voters, Perot and his folksy, no-nonsense approach to government reform struck a populist chord. But he also demonstrated his quirkiness by bizarrely withdrawing from the presidential race in mid-July and then reversing himself and reentering in October. He chose as his running mate retired admiral James B. Stockdale, who as a navy flier had been a prisoner during much of the Vietnam War.

United We Stand America (UWSA), formed from the ashes of Perot's candidacy, did not bill itself as an official political party. Promoting itself instead as a nonpartisan educational organization, UWSA called for a balanced budget, government reform, and health care reform. The group's leaders did not endorse candidates or offer them financial assistance.

In 1993 Perot, rather than UWSA, commanded considerable attention on Capitol Hill, from marshaling grass-roots support on congressional reform to unsuccessfully opposing the North American Free Trade Agreement (NAFTA). Democrats and Republicans were unable to co-opt his following as they had those of major third-party movements in the past. Perot continued to use his supporters' anger with government and the political process to sustain himself as an independent political force. In the fall of 1995 Perot created a full-fledged political party, the Reform Party, and ran as its nominee in a campaign financed with federal funds.

The Reform Party effort of 1996 qualified for federal funding and went along with the limitations that acceptance of the money entailed. By garnering more than 5 percent of the 1992 presidential vote, Perot's party qualified in 1996 for some $30 million, less than half the amount he spent from his own pocket four years earlier.

Perot was challenged for the Reform Party nomination by Richard D. Lamm, a former Democratic governor of Colorado who had shown a willingness to risk voter displeasure. Lamm had called, for example, for deep cuts in Medicare, the popular health care program for the elderly.

Perot defeated Lamm in an unusual two-stage procedure, with a preliminary vote after nominating speeches at a convention in Long Beach, California, followed by a mail and electronic vote with the winner announced a week later in Valley Forge, Pennsylvania. Ballots had been sent to 1.3 million voters who were registered party members or signers of its ballot access petitions. Less than 50,000 votes, though, were actually cast, with Perot a winner by a margin of nearly 2-to-1.

Perot again was on the general election ballot in all states. He chose as his running mate Pat Choate, a native Texan and economist who had coached Perot in his unsuccessful fight against NAFTA. The Reform Party also had congressional candidates in ten states.

Locked out of the presidential debates, Perot spent much of his campaign money on television "infomercials" espousing the party's principles. Besides a balanced budget these included higher ethical standards for the White House and Congress, campaign and election reforms, a new tax system, and lobbying restrictions.

Even with the restricted budget, Perot again placed third in the national election after the two major party candidates. However, his 8,085,402 votes, 8.4 percent of the total, came to less than half of his 1992 achievement of 18.9 percent, a third-party figure surpassed in the twentieth century only by former president Theodore Roosevelt and his Bull Moose candidacy of 1912. Perot had his best showing in Maine, where he received 14.2 percent of the vote. He won no electoral votes.

In 1998 the Reform Party scored a high-profile victory when former professional wrestler Jesse Ventura was elected governor of Minnesota running on the party label. Ventura's victory helped give the Reform Party the look of a growth stock, and several well-known personalities publicly considered running for the party's presidential nomination in 2000, including former Connecticut governor Lowell P. Weicker Jr. and financier Donald Trump. Ultimately, they did not run, although Patrick J. Buchanan did, bolting the Republican Party in October 1999.

Highly public party infighting followed, with Perot loyalists arrayed against Buchanan supporters. The latter claimed they offered the party energy and new blood; the former contended Buchanan was intent on a hostile takeover designed to give the Reform Party a socially conservative face.

Calling the party "dysfunctional," Ventura announced in February 2000 that he was leaving to become an independent. In June Perot publicly distanced himself from his creation by declining to run against Buchanan in the party's mail-in primary in July. But John Hagelin, the candidate of the Natural Law Party in 1992 and 1996, did enter.

The Reform Party's convention in Long Beach, California, in August, disintegrated into two competing conclaves: one favorable to Buchanan, the other, dominated by Perot loyalists, favorable to Hagelin. After Buchanan wrested control of the party and nomination, the Hagelin forces set up a splinter Reform Party. Hagelin chose Nat Goldhaber of California for the vice-presidential spot on his ticket. In September the splinter group joined in coalition with the Natural Law Party, Hagelin's old party.

Nevertheless, Buchanan retained control of the base party's apparatus, and a federal court awarded him full use of the $12.6 million in federal funds that Perot's 1996 showing had qualified the party's 2000 nominee to receive. Buchanan chose for his running mate Ezola Foster, a California teacher. The bipartisan Commission on Presidential Debates, however, denied Buchanan participation in the three presidential debates held in October. Buchanan support in the polls was under the 15 percent required to enter the debates.

The actual 2000 election results were a major disappointment to Reform Party supporters. Although commentators thought Buchanan's message would attract many social conservatives, the party garnered only 448,868 votes, just 0.43 percent of the total presidential vote. Some commentators, however, noted that Buchanan was on the ballot in four competitive states that were won by Democratic candidate Al Gore. They argued that the Reform vote in those states may have drawn off enough support from Republican George W. Bush to swing the states' thirty electoral votes into the Democratic column.

Republican Party (1854–)

The Republican Party, founded in 1854, dominated national politics from 1860 to the New Deal era and again from 1968 to

Abraham Lincoln

the present. The party emerged in 1854–1856 out of a political frenzy, in all northern states, revolving around the expansion of slavery into the western territories. The new party was so named because "republicanism" was the core value of American politics, and it seemed to be mortally threatened by the expanding "slave power." The enemy was not so much the institution of slavery or the mistreatment of the slaves. Rather, it was the political-economic system that controlled the South, exerted disproportionate control over the national government, and threatened to seize power in the new territories.

ORIGINS THROUGH RECONSTRUCTION

The party came into being in reaction to federal legislation allowing the new settlers of Kansas Territory to decide for themselves whether to adopt slavery or to continue the Compromise of 1820, which explicitly forbade slavery there. The new party lost on this issue, but in addition to bringing in most northern Whigs, it gained support from "Free Soil" northern Democrats who opposed the expansion of slavery. Only a handful of abolitionists joined. The Republicans adopted most of the modernization programs of the Whigs, favoring banks, tariffs, and internal improvements and adding, as well, a demand for a homestead law that would provide free farms to western settlers. In state after state, the Republicans outmaneuvered rival parties (the old Whigs, the Prohibitionists, and the Know Nothings), absorbing most of their supporters without accepting their doctrines.

The 1856 campaign, with strong pietistic, Protestant overtones, was a crusade for "Free Soil, Free Labor, Free Men, and Fremont!" John C. Fremont was defeated by a sharp countercru-

sade that warned against fanaticism and the imminent risk of civil war. By the late 1850s the new party dominated every northern state. It controlled enough electoral votes to win, despite its almost complete lack of support below the Mason-Dixon line. Leaders such as William H. Seward of New York and Salmon P. Chase of Ohio were passed over as presidential candidates in 1860 because they were too radical in their rhetoric and their states were safely in the Republican column. Abraham Lincoln was more moderate, and had more of an appeal in the closely divided western states of Illinois and Indiana. With only 40 percent of the popular vote, Lincoln swept the North and easily carried the electoral college. Interpreting the Republican victory as a signal of intense, permanent Yankee hostility, seven states of the Deep South seceded and formed their own confederation.

The Republicans had not expected secession and were baffled by it. The Lincoln administration, stiffened by the unionist pleas of conservative northern Democrats, rejected both the suggestion of abolitionists that the slaveholders be allowed to depart in peace and the insistence of Confederates that they had a right to revolution and self-governance.

Lincoln proved brilliantly successful in uniting all the factions of his party to fight for the Union. Most northern Democrats were likewise supportive until the fall of 1862, when Lincoln added the abolition of slavery as a war goal. All the state Republican parties accepted the antislavery goal except Kentucky. In Congress the party passed major legislation to promote rapid modernization, including measures for a national banking system, high tariffs, homestead laws, and aid to education and agriculture. How to deal with the ex- Confederates was a major issue; by 1864 radical Republicans controlled Congress and demanded more aggressive action against slavery and more vengeance toward the Confederates. Lincoln held them off, but just barely. His successor, Andrew Johnson, proved eager to reunite the nation, allowing the radicals to seize control of Congress, the party, and the army and nearly convict Johnson on a close impeachment vote.

Ulysses S. Grant was elected president in 1868 with strong support from radicals and the new Republican regimes in the South. He in turn vigorously supported radical Reconstruction programs in the South, the Fourteenth Amendment, and equal civil and voting rights for the freedmen. Most of all, he was the hero of the war veterans, who gave him strong support. The party had become so large that factionalism was inevitable; it was hastened by Grant's tolerance of high levels of corruption. The Liberal Republicans split off in 1872 on the grounds that it was time to declare the war finished and bring the troops home from the occupied southern states.

LATE NINETEENTH CENTURY

The depression of 1873 energized the Democrats. They won control of the House and formed "Redeemer" coalitions that recaptured control of each southern state, often using threats and violence. The Compromise of 1877 resolved the disputed election of 1876 by giving the White House to the Republicans and all of the southern states to the Democrats. The GOP, as it was

THE THIRD-TERM PANIC.
"An Ass, having put on the Lion's skin, roamed about in the Forest, and amused himself by frightening all the foolish Animals he met with in his wanderings."—SHAKSPEARE OR BACON.

The Republican ele-
phant made its first ap-
pearance in a Thomas
Nast illustration for
Harper's Weekly on
November 7, 1874.

now nicknamed, split into "Stalwart" and "Half-Breed" factions. In 1884, "Mugwump" reformers split off and helped elect Democrat Grover Cleveland.

In the North the Republican Party proved most attractive to men with an ambitious vision of a richer, more modern, and more complex society and economy. The leading modernizers were well-educated men from business, finance, and the professions. Commercial farmers, skilled mechanics, and office clerks largely supported the GOP, while unskilled workers and traditional farmers were solidly Democratic. The moral dimension of the party attracted pietistic Protestants, especially Methodists, Congregationalists, Presbyterians, Scandinavian Lutherans, and Quakers. By contrast, the high church or "liturgical" denominations (Roman Catholics, Mormons, German Lutherans, and Episcopalians) were offended by Republican crusaders who wanted to impose their own moral standards, especially through prohibition and control over public schools.

Millions of immigrants entered the political system after 1850 and usually started voting only a few years after arrival. The Catholics (Irish, German, and Dutch) became Democrats, but the Republicans won majorities among the Protestant British, German, Dutch, and Scandinavian newcomers and among German Jews. After 1890 new, much poorer ethnic groups arrived in large numbers—especially Italians, Poles, and Yiddish-speaking Jews. For the most part they did not become politically active until the 1920s. After 1876 southern voting was quite distinct from the rest of America—with very few white Republicans, apart from pockets of GOP strength in the Appalachian and Ozark Mountain districts. The party remained popular among

black southerners, even as disenfranchisement minimized their political role. (They were allowed to select delegates to the Republican national convention.)

In the 1888 election, for the first time since 1872, the Republicans gained control of the White House and both houses of Congress. New procedural rules in the House gave the Republican leaders (especially Speaker Thomas Reed) the ability to pass major legislation. New spending bills, such as one that provided generous pensions to Civil War veterans, coupled with the new McKinley tariff, made the GOP the target of charges of "paternalism." Democrats ridiculed the "Billion Dollar Congress," to which Reed shot back, "It's a billion dollar country!"

At the grass roots, militant pietists overcame the advice of more tolerant professionals to endorse statewide prohibition. In the Midwest, reformers declared war on the large German community, trying to shut down their parochial schools as well as their saloons. The Republicans, relying too much on the old-stock coalition that had always dominated the party's voting base, were badly defeated in the 1890 off-year election and the 1892 presidential contest, won by Cleveland. Alarmed professionals thereupon reasserted control over the local organizations, leading to a sort of "bossism" that (after 1900) fueled the outrage of progressives. Meanwhile, a severe economic depression struck both rural and urban America in 1893—on Cleveland's watch. The depression, combined with violent nationwide coal and railway strikes and snarling factionalism inside the Democratic Party, led to a sweeping victory for the GOP in 1894.

The party seemed invincible in 1896, until the Democrats unexpectedly selected William Jennings Bryan as their presidential candidate. Bryan's hugely popular crusade against the gold standard, financiers, railroads, and industrialists—indeed, against the cities—created a crisis for Republican candidate William McKinley and his campaign manager, Marc Hanna. Because of civil service reforms, parties could no longer finance themselves internally. Hanna solved that problem by directly obtaining $3.5 million from large corporations threatened by Bryan. Over the next century, campaign finance would be hotly debated. McKinley promised prosperity for everyone and every group, with no governmental attacks on property or ethnic groups. The business community, factory workers, white-collar workers, and commercial farmers responded enthusiastically, becoming major components of the new Republican majority. As voter turnout soared to the 95 percent level throughout much of the North, Germans and other ethnic groups grew alarmed by Bryan's moralism and voted Republican.

EARLY TWENTIETH CENTURY

Rejuvenated by their triumphs in 1894 and 1896 and by the glamour of a highly popular short war in 1898, against Spain over Cuba, the Philippines, and other Spanish possessions, the Republicans rolled to victory after victory. However, the party had again grown too large, and factionalism increasingly tore it apart.

The break within the party came in 1912 over the issue of progressivism. President William Howard Taft favored conservative reform controlled by the courts; former president Theodore Roosevelt went to the grass roots, attacking Taft, bosses, courts, big business, and the "malefactors of great wealth." Defeated at the convention, Roosevelt bolted and formed a third party. The vast majority of progressive politicians refused to follow Roosevelt's rash action, for it allowed the conservatives to seize control of the GOP; they kept it for the next thirty years. Roosevelt's quixotic crusade also allowed Democrat Woodrow Wilson to gain the White House with only 40 percent of the vote. But after Wilson's fragile coalition collapsed in 1920, the GOP won three consecutive presidential contests.

Herbert Hoover, elected in 1928, represented the quintessence of the modernizing engineer, bringing efficiency to government and the economy. His poor skills at negotiating with politicians hardly seemed to matter when the economy boomed in the 1920s and Democrats were in disarray. However, when the Great Depression hit in the 1930s, his political ineptitude compounded the party's weaknesses. For the next four decades, whenever Democrats were at a loss for words, they could always ridicule Hoover.

NEW DEAL AND DEMOCRATIC DOMINANCE

The Great Depression sidelined the GOP for decades. The old conservative formulas for prosperity had lost their magic. The Democrats, by contrast, built up majorities that depended on labor unions, big city machines, federal relief funds, and the mobilization of Catholics, Jews, and African Americans. However, middle-class hostility to new taxes, and fears about a repeat of the First World War, eventually led to a Republican rebound. Franklin Roosevelt's immense popularity gave him four consec-

utive victories, but by 1938 the GOP was doing quite well in off-year elections when FDR's magic was not at work.

In 1948 taxes were high, federal relief had ended, and big-city machines were collapsing, but union strength helped Harry S. Truman reassemble FDR's coalition for one last hurrah. The year 1948 proved to be the high-water mark of class polarization in American politics; afterward, the differences narrowed between the middle class and the working class.

The issues of Korea, communism, and corruption gave World War II hero Dwight D. Eisenhower a victory in 1952 for Republicans, along with narrow control of Congress. However, the GOP remained a minority party and was factionalized, with a northeastern liberal element basically favorable to the New Deal welfare state and the policy of containing communist expansion, versus midwestern conservatives who bitterly opposed New Deal taxes, regulation, labor unions, and internationalism. Both factions used the issue of anticommunism and attacked the Democrats for harboring spies and allowing communist gains in China and Korea. New York governors Thomas E. Dewey and Nelson Rockefeller led the liberal wing, while Sens. Robert Taft of Ohio and Barry Goldwater of Arizona spoke for the conservatives. Eisenhower represented internationalism in foreign policy, and he sidetracked the isolationism represented by Taft and Hoover.

Richard Nixon, who was Eisenhower's vice president, was aligned with the eastern liberal GOP. Nominated in 1960 to succeed Eisenhower, he lost because the Democrats had a larger base of loyal supporters, especially among Catholics who turned out to support their candidate, John F. Kennedy. The defeat of yet another candidate sponsored by the eastern "establishment" opened the way for Goldwater's 1964 crusade against the New Deal and then-president Lyndon Johnson's Great Society programs. Goldwater permanently knocked out the eastern liberals, but in turn his crushing defeat as the GOP presidential candidate in 1964 retired many old-line conservatives. Goldwater in 1964 and independent George Wallace in 1968 took southern whites and many northern Catholics away from their Democratic roots, while at the same time the Democratic commitment to civil rights won over nine-tenths of all African American voters.

REPUBLICAN REVIVAL

President Johnson, who was Kennedy's vice president and succeeded him on Kennedy's assassination in 1963, won an overwhelming victory in 1964 and brought with him a large Democratic majority in Congress that enacted sweeping social programs that Johnson called the Great Society. However, support for these programs collapsed in the mid-1960s in the face of violence and protest over racial anger as the civil rights movement gained steam, the Vietnam War, generational conflicts, the perception of increased crime, burning inner cities growing in part from the assassination of important civil rights leaders, and charges that the federal government was badly out of control.

Nixon seized the moment and ran again, winning narrowly in 1968. As president he largely ignored his party—his 1972 reelection campaign was practically nonpartisan but wildly suc-

President Ronald Reagan meets with Republican members of Congress in front of the White House in 1984.

cessful as he buried his Democratic opponent. But Nixon was not to serve out his second term. The Watergate scandal, which revealed White House and presidential involvement in criminal activities, forced him to resign from office in the face of certain congressional impeachment and removal from office. Nixon's self-destruction wreaked havoc in the 1974 election, in which Democrats swept to a massive victory in off-year contests, and set the stage for the Carter interregnum.

Georgia governor Jimmy Carter won the White House for the Democrats in 1976 but his presidency crashed even before it expired in 1981. Foreign affairs were unusually salient, as public opinion saw failure in policy toward the Soviet Union, Middle Eastern nations that forced an energy crises by withholding oil supplies, and Iranian revolutionaries that held Americans hostage for months. "Stagflation" in the economy meant a combination of high unemployment and high inflation. Most of all there was a sense of drift or, worse, of malaise. The country craved leadership.

Ronald Reagan answered that need. A former movie actor and Republican governor of California, Reagan had been a supporter of Goldwater and an articulate spokesman for the conservative views that the 1964 presidential candidate set in motion. Reagan led a political revolution in 1980, capitalizing on grievances and mobilizing an entirely new voting bloc, the religious right. Southern Baptists and other fundamentalists and evangelicals had been voting Democratic since the New Deal. Suddenly they began to react strongly against a perceived national tolerance of immorality (especially regarding abortion and homosexuality), rising crime, and America's apparent rejection of traditional family values. Reagan had vision and leadership qualities that many in the traditional political establish-

ment did not initially understand. Reagan oversaw a massive military buildup, very large tax cuts, and—inadvertently—a massive increase in the national debt.

By 1984 inflation had declined significantly, unemployment had eased, profits were soaring, some changes had been made in the Social Security system, and Reagan carried forty-nine states in winning reelection. Most astonishing of all was Reagan's aggressive pursuit of cold war policy, followed closely by the collapse of the Soviet Union and the end of international communism in most nations. The best issue for the Democrats was the soaring national debt—long a conservative theme. For the first time since 1932, the GOP pulled abreast of the Democrats in terms of party identification on the part of voters. A greater number of higher-income people were voting Republican, which was not offset by the lower-income groups that had always been the mainstay of the Democratic Party. By the 1980s a gender gap was apparent, with men and housewives more Republican while single, divorced, and professional women tended to be Democratic. Groups that were part of the religious right helped deliver to the GOP the votes of their membership. Those gains were largely offset by the Democratic increases among holders of college and postgraduate degrees for the party's positions regarding multiculturalism and a tolerance of homosexuality and abortion.

George Herbert Walker Bush rode to the White House in 1988 on Reagan's popularity and could himself claim important victories in the cold war and in the Middle East, where the Persian Gulf War liberated Kuwait in 1991 after an invasion by neighboring Iraq. But Bush—so knowledgeable on international affairs—seemed unconcerned about taxes, deficits, and other domestic issues that bothered Americans far more. Most importantly, Bush was ambushed by the remnants of a nasty recession in 1990–1991 just as he was running for reelection in 1992, allowing Arkansas governor Bill Clinton to take back the White House for the Democrats.

The 1990s was a decade of travail for the Republican Party. It lost the 1992 and 1996 presidential elections to Clinton, the first time the GOP had lost successive White House elections since 1960 and 1964. Clinton proved a popular if controversial president, raising the specter that the generally Republican trend of recent decades had finally been broken. However, the GOP roared back in 1994, gaining control of Congress—both the House and Senate—for the first time since 1952 as well as control of governors' mansions in nearly all the major states. This remarkable achievement was engineered in important part by a back-bencher Republican representative from Georgia, Newt Gingrich. As a result, he became House Speaker but then proceeded to all but self-destruct through an aggressive and ultimately futile combat with Clinton over programs and policies.

The rancorous leadership of Gingrich soured politics in Washington, and he was unable to deliver on most of his conservative program that he called the "Contract with America." The Republican condition worsened when the party attempted to impeach and remove Clinton from office over a scandal that had its roots in a messy affair between Clinton and a young female intern in the White House that Clinton at first denied. The public, appalled at the scandal, never showed enthusiasm for removing Clinton and the Senate refused to convict the president after the House—in highly partisan proceedings—approved impeachment. This event, the Gingrich overreaching, and other missteps by Republicans gradually whittled down the Republican's control of Congress in elections after 1994.

Nevertheless, in the 2000 elections the Republican Party achieved a dream long thought impossible. In a contested election, former president Bush's son, George W. Bush, defeated Democrat Al Gore, a victory—although one of the most narrow in history—that revived the GOP dominance of national level politics that began with Richard Nixon in 1968. Equally important, the GOP retained control of Congress, giving it complete control of the federal government for the first time since 1953. To be sure, their margin in the House was further eroded and the margin in the Senate evaporated entirely with an exact tie of fifty Democrats and fifty Republicans, with the GOP retaining control since the new vice president could break a tie vote. However, with the defection of moderate senator Jim Jeffords of Vermont to the independent ranks in June 2001, the Senate reverted to Democratic control.

Socialist Party (1901–)

The inception of the Socialist Party marked a unique, brief era of leftist organizational unity. Founded in 1901 by New York attorney Morris Hillquit and railroad worker and labor leader Eugene Debs, the Socialist Party brought together the Social Democratic Party; Social Laborites; Christian Socialists; a wing of the Socialist Labor Party; and followers of Henry George, Edward Bellamy, and assorted populist sympathizers. Rapid

growth and early success continued through the 1912 presidential election, when Debs earned 6 percent of the votes cast and some twelve hundred Socialist Party candidates won state and local elections, including seventy-nine mayoral races.

Despite the party's continued strong showing in the 1916 and 1920 elections, World War I took a toll on the Socialist Party. Although party members were already persecuted for their opposition to the war, the Sedition Act of 1918 resulted in additional arrests and prevented the Socialist Party from using the mail to communicate with branches beyond its East Coast and Midwest bases. While many, including Debs, were being sent to prison for either their pacifist views or Sedition Act violations, the 1917 Bolshevik Revolution in Russia led by Vladimir Lenin further hastened the party's demise.

By 1919, Leninist sympathizers threatened the Socialist Party leadership. A schism ensued, resulting in the expulsion of radical party elements and the invalidation of the national executive committee elections. Thereafter, the Socialist Party and the Communist Party became two distinct organizations with decidedly different agendas. By breaking with its labor roots, the Socialist Party lost its legitimacy as an agent of radical social action. Debs's death in 1926 signaled the end of the worker-oriented party and the start of a more urban-middle-class-centered party under Norman Thomas's leadership. The Socialist Party, which had 9,500 members in 1929, experienced a revival between 1929 and 1934: membership increased during the Great Depression to almost 17,000 in 1932, when Thomas polled almost 900,000 votes in the presidential race, and to 20,000 in 1934.

Many new members were young militants who increasingly disagreed with the party's old guard. Until Hillquit died in 1933, the old guard held their own, but they lost their grip thereafter. At the 1934 party convention in Detroit, the young militant wing, joined by Thomas and the Milwaukee mayor, Daniel W. Hoan, passed a new Socialist Party declaration of principles that the old guard believed encouraged too forcefully the nonelectoral seizure of power and sympathized too greatly with Soviet Russia. The old guard formally broke away in 1936 and formed the Social Democratic Federation (SDF). Party membership fell to 12,000 in 1936 and shrank to 6,500 the following year. More important, Thomas garnered only 187,000 votes during the 1936 presidential election and less than 100,000 in 1940.

From 1933 to 1940 the Socialist Party experienced further internal strains by criticizing President Franklin D. Roosevelt and the New Deal. Party members viewed New Deal programs as more sympathetic to corporate interests than to organized labor's concerns. Remaining party members split over wartime policy, with Thomas leading a pacifist faction; the party lost any influence it had as it was effectively co-opted by Roosevelt. Only in the cities of Bridgeport, Connecticut, and Milwaukee, Wisconsin, did the old Socialist Party maintain a real presence. However, Thomas continued to run as the Socialist presidential candidate through the 1948 election.

In the post–World War II era, all radicalism was suspect. Although the Socialists made inroads into the Congress of Industrial Organizations and helped organize Detroit autoworkers and southern sharecroppers, the party disintegrated as an organization. The party continued to field a presidential candidate until the 1960 election, when it failed to run a candidate. Radicals shifted their emphasis from organized labor to civil rights and, later, worked against the war in Vietnam.

In the early 1960s the Democratic Socialist Organizing Committee (DSOC), the New American Movement (NAM), and the Students for a Democratic Society (SDS) became the main organizational vehicles for the New Left. The SDS faded after Martin Luther King's assassination in 1968 and the Paris Peace Accords in 1973. Meanwhile NAM devoted its energies to feminism, gay rights, and local community organizing into the early 1980s.

The DSOC continued to operate in the old socialist manner as the left wing of the New Deal coalition—not as a separate political party as much as a socialist force within the Democratic Party and the labor movement. The DSOC was successful in attracting activists such as machinist union leader William Winpisinger, feminist Gloria Steinem, and gay rights activist Harry Britt. Bernard Sanders, member of Congress from Vermont who was elected in 1991, was the first self-avowed socialist elected to Congress in decades and perhaps the best known since Victor Berger served in the House of Representatives during the 1920s.

NAM and DSOC completed a formal merger in 1983 and emerged as the Democratic Socialists of America (DSA). The DSA brought together for the first time since World War I the disparate segments of leftist opinion, including the SDF and former socialists and communists. Although the American left was in disarray in the late 1960s and the administrations of Richard M. Nixon, Ronald Reagan, George Bush, and Bill Clinton were by and large conservative, a kind of socialist revival occurred at the end of the twentieth century. Although membership remained low, Socialist Party influences such as government-supported health care, minimum wage, and human rights were more apparent in the national political debate than at any time since the 1960s. In addition, more than one socialist faction has fielded a candidate in every presidential election since 1976.

Socialist Labor Party (1874–)

The Socialist Labor Party, the first national socialist party in the United States, ranks second only to the Prohibitionists among third parties in longevity. Formed in 1874 by elements of the Socialist International in New York, it was first known as the Social Democratic Workingmen's Party. In 1877 the group adopted the name Socialist Labor Party. Throughout the 1880s the party worked in concert with other left-wing third parties, including the Greenbacks.

The Socialist Labor Party ran national tickets in every presidential election from 1892 through 1976. The party collected its highest proportion of the national vote in 1896, when its candidate received 36,356 votes (0.3 percent of the popular vote).

Led by the autocratic Daniel DeLeon (1852–1914), a former Columbia University law lecturer, the Socialist Labor Party became increasingly militant and made its best showing in local races in 1898. But DeLeon's insistence on rigid party discipline and his opposition to the organized labor movement created a feeling of alienation among many members. Moderate elements bolted from the party, eventually joining the Socialist Party of Eugene V. Debs, which formed in 1901.

The Socialist Labor Party continued as a small, tightly organized far-left group bound to DeLeon's uncompromising belief in revolution. As late as 1976 the party advocated direct worker action to take over control of production and claimed 5,000 members nationwide.

Socialist Workers Party (1938–)

The Socialist Workers Party was formed in 1938 by followers of the Russian revolutionary Leon Trotsky. Originally a faction within the U.S. Communist Party, the Trotskyites were expelled in 1936 on instructions from Soviet leader Joseph Stalin. A brief Trotskyite coalition with the Socialist Party ended in 1938 when the dissidents decided to organize independently as the Socialist Workers Party. Through its youth arm, the Young Socialist Alliance, the Socialist Workers Party was active in the anti–Vietnam War movement and contributed activists to civil rights protests.

Since 1948 the party has run a presidential candidate, but its entries have never received more than 0.1 percent of the popular vote. In 1992 presidential candidate James Warren was on the ballot in thirteen states and the District of Columbia and drew 23,096 votes nationwide. The party's 2000 candidate, James E. Harris Jr. of Georgia, received 7,378 votes.

Union Party (1936)

Advocating more radical economic measures in light of the Great Depression, several early supporters of President Franklin D. Roosevelt broke with him and ran their own ticket in 1936 under the Union Party label. Largely an outgrowth of the Rev. Charles E. Coughlin's National Union for Social Justice, the new party also had the support of Dr. Francis E. Townsend, leader of a movement for government-supported old-age pensions, and Gerald L. K. Smith, self-appointed heir of Louisiana senator Huey P. Long's share-the-wealth program.

Father Coughlin was the keystone of the Union Party and was instrumental in choosing its presidential ticket in June 1936—Rep. William Lemke, R-N.D., for president and Thomas O'Brien, a Massachusetts railroad union lawyer, for vice president. The new party did not hold a convention. The party's platform reportedly was written by Coughlin, Lemke, and O'Brien and was similar to the program espoused by Coughlin's National Union. Among the features of the Union Party platform were proposals for banking and currency reform, a guaranteed income for workers, restrictions on wealth, and an isolationist foreign policy.

Lacking organization and finances during the campaign, the party further suffered from the increasingly violent and often anti-Semitic tone of the oratory of both Coughlin and Smith.

The Union Party failed miserably in its primary goal of defeating Roosevelt. Roosevelt won a landslide victory and the Lemke ticket received only 892,267 votes (2 percent of the popular vote). The party standard-bearers were unable to carry a single state, and the Union Party's candidates for the House and Senate all were defeated. The party continued on a local level until it was finally dissolved in 1939.

U.S. Labor Party (Independent Lyndon LaRouche) (1973–)

Formed in 1973 as the political arm of the National Caucus of Labor Committees (NCLC), the U.S. Labor Party made its debut in national politics in 1976. The NCLC, a Marxist group, was organized in 1968 by splinters of the radical movements of the 1960s. New Yorker Lyndon LaRouche, the party's chairman and a self-taught economist who worked in the management and computer fields, became its 1976 presidential nominee and Wayne Evans, a Detroit steelworker, his running mate.

The party directed much of its fire at the Rockefeller family. It charged that banks controlled by the Rockefellers were strangling the U.S. and world economies. In an apocalyptic vein, the party predicted a world monetary collapse by election day and the destruction of the country by thermonuclear war by the summer of 1977.

LaRouche's party developed a reputation for harassment because of its shouted interruptions and demonstrations against its political foes, including the Communist Party and the United Auto Workers. It accused some left-wing organizations and individuals, such as linguist Noam Chomsky and Marcus Raskin and his Institute for Policy Studies, of conspiring with the Rockefellers and the Central Intelligence Agency.

During the 1976 campaign, LaRouche was more critical of challenger Jimmy Carter than President Gerald R. Ford. He depicted Ford as a well-meaning man out of his depth in the presidency, but Carter as a pawn of nuclear war advocates and a disgracefully unqualified presidential candidate. LaRouche captured only 40,043 votes, less than 0.1 percent of the national vote. He was on the ballot in twenty-three states and the District of Columbia.

Although the U.S. Labor Party did not run a presidential candidate in the 1980 election, LaRouche ran a strident campaign—as a Democrat. By this time, LaRouche's politics had shifted to the right, and his speeches were fraught with warnings of conspiracy.

He continued his crusade in 1984 but as an "independent Democrat," dismissing Democratic presidential nominee Walter F. Mondale as an "agent of Soviet influence." LaRouche received 78,807 votes, or 0.1 percent of the vote, in the fall election.

In 1988 LaRouche again attempted to run as a Democrat but, failing the nomination, garnered 25,562 votes under the banner of the National Economic Recovery Party. On December 16, 1988, LaRouche and six of his associates were convicted on forty-seven counts of mail fraud and conspiracy to commit mail fraud. LaRouche was sentenced to fifteen years in prison.

In 1992 the unflagging LaRouche ran again for president from his jail cell. As a convicted felon, he no longer had the right to vote himself. LaRouche ran as an independent although his name appeared on several state ballots under various party names, including Economic Recovery. His supporters, experi-

enced in winning ballot access, placed him on the ballot in seventeen states and the District of Columbia. He received 26,333 votes nationwide.

In 1996 LaRouche's name disappeared from the general election ballot, although he continued to be a quadrennial entry in the Democratic primaries. LaRouche ran in the party's primaries in every election from 1980 through 2000, with his best showing in 1996 when President Bill Clinton had no major opposition for renomination. That year, LaRouche drew nearly 600,000 Democratic primary votes (5.4 percent of the party's total primary ballots). In 2000 LaRouche received only 3,743 votes in the Democratic primaries.

U.S. Taxpayers Party and Constitution Party (1992–)

Making its second appearance in a presidential election, the U.S. Taxpayers Party was on the ballot in thirty-nine states in 1996. Its nominee, Howard Phillips of Virginia, drew 184,658 votes or more than four times his 1992 total of 43,434. Of the eighteen minor parties receiving at least 750 votes in 1996, the Taxpayers Party received the fourth highest total. In 2000 Phillips—running under the banner of several party labels—was on the ballot in 41 states. He won 98,004 votes, the sixth highest total of all presidential candidates in 2000.

Phillips, longtime chairman of the Conservative Caucus, founded the party to counter what he perceived to be a left-of-center movement by the Republican Party under George Herbert Walker Bush. Failing to recruit rightist icons such as Pat Buchanan, Oliver North, or Jesse Helms to be the party's nominee, Phillips ran himself as its standard-bearer. In addition to taxes the party opposed welfare, abortion, and affirmative action.

Phillips was nominated to run for president again in 2000, by which time the U.S. Taxpayers had changed its name to the Constitution Party, to more broadly reflect its conservative agenda. Phillips, though, was willing to step aside at several stages of the campaign when the prospect of the party nominating a more prominent politician was possible. First, it was New Hampshire senator Robert C. Smith, a short-lived independent who returned to the Republican Party on the eve of the third party's convention in September 1999. Second, was Republican presidential contender Alan Keyes, who indicated in the spring of 2000 that he might bolt to the Constitution Party if the GOP weakened the antiabortion plank in the party's platform. It did not, and Keyes stayed in the Republican Party.

Whig Party (1834–1856)

Whigs were nineteenth-century modernizers who saw President Andrew Jackson (1829–1837) as a dangerous man with a reactionary opposition to the forces of social, economic, and moral change. As Jackson purged his opponents, vetoed internal improvements, and killed the Bank of the United States, alarmed local elites fought back.

The Whigs, led by Henry Clay, celebrated Clay's vision of the "American System." They demanded government support for a more modern, market-oriented economy, in which skill, expertise, and bank credit would count for more than physical strength or land ownership. They also sought to promote industrialization through high tariffs, a business-oriented money supply based on a national bank, and a vigorous program of government-funded "internal improvements," especially expansion of the road and canal systems. To modernize the inner American, the Whigs helped create public schools, private colleges, charities, and cultural institutions.

The Democrats, by contrast, harkened to the Jeffersonian ideal of an equalitarian agricultural society, insisting that traditional farm life bred republican simplicity, whereas modernization threatened to create a politically powerful caste of rich aristocrats who might subvert democracy. In general, the Democrats enacted their policies at the national level; the Whigs succeeded in passing modernization projects in most states.

Although the Whigs won votes in every socioeconomic class, including the poorest, they appealed especially to more prosperous Americans. The Democrats likewise won support up and down the scale, but they often sharpened their appeals to the lower half by ridiculing the aristocratic pretensions of the Whigs. Most bankers, storekeepers, factory owners, master mechanics, clerks, and professionals favored the Whigs. Moreover, commercially oriented farmers in the North voted Whig, as did most large-scale planters in the South.

In general, the commercial and manufacturing towns and cities were heavily Whig, save for Democratic wards filled with recent Irish Catholic and German immigrants. Waves of Protestant religious revivals in the 1830s injected a moralistic element into the Whig ranks. Nonreligious individuals who found themselves the targets of moral reform, such as calls for prohibition, denounced the Whigs as Puritans and sought refuge in the Democratic Party. Rejecting the automatic party loyalty that was the hallmark of the tight Democratic Party organization, the Whigs suffered from factionalism. Yet the party's superb network of newspapers provided an internal information system.

Whigs clashed with Democrats throughout what historians term the "Second American Party System." When they controlled the Senate, Whigs passed a censure motion in 1834 denouncing Jackson's arrogant assumption of executive power in the face of the true will of the people as represented by Congress. Backing Henry Clay in 1832 and a medley of candidates in 1836, the opposition finally coalesced in 1840 behind a popular general, William Henry Harrison, and proved that the national Whig Party could win. Moreover, in the 1840s Whigs won 49 percent of gubernatorial elections, with strong bases in the manufacturing Northeast and in the border states. Yet the party revealed limited staying power. Whigs were ready to enact their programs in 1841, but Harrison died and was succeeded by John Tyler, an old-line Democrat who never believed in Whiggery and was, in fact, disowned by the party while he was president. Factionalism ruined the party's program and helped defeat Henry Clay, the Whig presidential candidate, in 1844. In 1848 opportunity beckoned as the Democrats split. By ignoring Clay and nominating a famous war hero, Gen. Zachary Taylor, the Whigs papered over their deepening splits on slavery, and they won. The trend, however, was for the Democratic vote to grow faster and for the Whigs to lose more and more marginal states

Henry Clay

and districts. After the close 1844 contest, the Democratic advantage widened and the Whigs could win the White House only if the Democrats split.

The Whigs were unable to deal with the slavery issue after 1850. Almost all of their southern leaders owned slaves. The northeastern Whigs, led by Daniel Webster, represented businessmen who loved the national flag and a national market but cared little about slavery one way or another. Many Whig voters in the North, however, felt slavery was incompatible with a free labor–free market economy, and no one discovered a compromise that would keep the party united. Furthermore, the burgeoning economy made full-time careers in business or law much more attractive than politics for ambitious young Whigs. For example, the party leader in Illinois, Abraham Lincoln, simply abandoned politics for several years after 1849. When new issues of nativism, prohibition, and antislavery burst on the scene in the mid-1850s, no one looked to the fast-disintegrating Whig Party for answers. In the North most ex-Whigs joined the new Republican Party, and in the South they flocked to a new, short-lived "American" (Know Nothing) Party. During the Lincoln administration (1861–1865), ex-Whigs enacted much of the "American System"; in the long run, America adopted Whiggish economic policies coupled with a Democratic strong presidency.

Workers World Party (1959–)

With the Hungarian citizen revolt and other developments in eastern Europe providing some impetus, the Workers World Party in 1959 split off from the Socialist Workers Party. The party theoretically supports worker uprisings in all parts of the world. Yet it backed the communist governments that put down rebellions in Hungary during the 1950s, Czechoslovakia in the 1960s, and Poland in the 1980s. Workers World is an activist revolutionary group that, until 1980, concentrated its efforts on specific issues, such as the antiwar and civil rights demonstrations during the 1960s and 1970s. The party has an active youth organization, Youth Against War and Fascism.

In 1980 party leaders saw an opportunity, created by the weakness of the U.S. economy and the related high unemployment, to interest voters in its revolutionary ideas. That year it placed Deirdre Griswold, the editor of the party's newspaper and one of its founding members, on the presidential ballot in ten states. Together with her running mate Larry Holmes, a twenty-seven-year-old black activist, Griswold received 13,300 votes. In 1984 Holmes ran as the presidential candidate, getting on the ballot in eight states and receiving 15,329 votes. In 1988 Holmes ran with Gloria La Riva, and they garnered 7,846 votes. La Riva ran as the presidential candidate in 1992 and was on the ballot only in New Mexico, where she received 181 votes.

The Workers World Party dramatically improved its electoral fortunes in 1996. Its candidate, Monica Moorehead of New Jersey, was on the ballot in twelve states and received 29,082 votes. But in 2000 Moorehead won only 4,795 votes in three states.

CHAPTER 5

Campaign Finance

CAMPAIGN FINANCE changed dramatically over the past century, going from its early freewheeling days to a heavily regulated system. Campaigns now must disclose where their money comes from and how it is spent. Contributors must adhere to specific limits on how much they can give to federal candidates. Detailed campaign reports are available for public scrutiny, even on the Internet. Most presidential candidates limit their spending in return for public funds. Campaigns have to hire lawyers and bookkeepers just to comply with federal laws.

The changes have, indeed, been striking. Yet the similarities have been striking as well. Demands for reform at the beginning of the twentieth century sounded much the same as those voiced at the end. Reformers still were calling for curbs on the ability of special interests and wealthy individuals to dominate the flow of campaign money and for disclosure of the sources and uses of money moving outside federal disclosure requirements.

The debate over the campaign finance system took place against a backdrop of ever spiraling costs. Early estimates of the cost of the 2000 presidential and congressional elections ranged from $2.4 billion to upwards of $3 billion.[1]

Controversy Surrounds Financing System

Critics of the campaign financing system became increasingly vocal in the closing decades of the twentieth century and the beginning of the next century. But reaching a consensus on what was wrong with the system—or even whether there was something wrong—let alone what would make it right seemed almost impossible at times.

Some expressed dismay at skyrocketing campaign costs, but others said the costs were small when compared with a major corporation's advertising budget or what Americans spent on cosmetics or gambling.[2]

Some deplored the influx of unlimited and basically unregulated "soft" money from corporations, labor unions, and individuals to the political parties, but others welcomed the resulting resurgence of parties as major players in electoral politics.

Some wanted to regulate advertising they said crossed the line between advocating issues to advocating particular candidates, but others defended the ads as important tools in educating voters.

Some condemned the role special interests, particularly political action committees (PACs), played in American politics, but others defended this role as a manifestation of democracy's pluralism.

Some called for limits on congressional campaign spending, but others charged that limits would only further entrench incumbents and put challengers at a disadvantage.

Some saw public money as the way to eliminate outside influences in politics, but others scoffed at the use of taxpayer money, even in times of budget surpluses.

Some criticized independent expenditures for or against candidates, but others saw such spending as part of their First Amendment right to free speech.

Beyond specific policy disagreements was the less tangible love-hate relationship some politicians had with the system. A presidential candidate might call for a ban on soft money, while at the same time benefiting from an elaborate advertising campaign paid for with party soft money. Members of Congress were being asked to vote to change a system that returned the vast majority of them to the halls of Congress election after election. As Sen. Robert C. Byrd, D-W.Va., once explained: "We are afraid to let go of the slick ads and the high-priced consultants, afraid to let go of the PAC money and the polls, unsure that we want to change the rules of the game that we all understand and know so well."[3]

UNCERTAINTIES IN CHANGE

Reformers faced the enormous task of proposing legislation that would bridge the differences between Democrats and Republicans, representatives and senators, incumbents and challengers. Politicians were apprehensive of the unknowns that surrounded change—how each party would adapt to it and whether it might give the opposing party an advantage.

Their caution was well-founded. It was difficult to calculate all the ramifications of the many reform proposals on the table at any one time. As political scientist Frank J. Sorauf described it: "Available money seeks an outlet, and if some outlets are narrowed or closed off, money flows with increased pressure to the outlets still open. It is the law that systems of campaign finance share with hydraulic systems."[4]

There had been ample examples of changes with unanticipated results. Congressional attempts to curtail the influence of the wealthy "fat cat" donors in the wake of the 1970s Watergate scandal resulted in more stringent limits on individual contributions than on political committees. This made contributions through PACs much more attractive to some givers and in turn became a significant factor in the rise of PACs.

Section 527 of the tax code—written in the wake of the Watergate scandal to set tax rules for political groups—contained a loophole allowing a new breed of political organizations to avoid disclosing their campaign spending, until Congress changed the law in 2000.

The dramatic growth of soft money was another example of a development no one had anticipated. Soft money was the unlimited, largely unregulated money contributed primarily to political parties for activities and expenses not directly related to specific federal elections. It was called "soft" to distinguish it from the "hard money" that was used for federal election campaigns and regulated by the Federal Election Campaign Act (FECA)—money that was "hard" to raise because of the FECA's limits and restrictions. Although corporations and labor unions had been prohibited from participating directly in federal elections for a good part of the twentieth century and individuals were subject to an aggregate contribution limit beginning in the 1970s, soft money opened a whole new outlet for contributing to the parties or spending on nonfederal activities.

In the 1970s the Federal Election Commission (FEC), the independent agency charged with overseeing compliance with the federal election laws, relaxed some of the rules covering the separation of federal campaign funds from state and local parties' nonfederal money. The FEC allowed the state and local parties for the first time to use nonfederal soft money to pay for a portion of their administrative expenses, as well as voter drives and generic party activities, even if they had an indirect effect on federal campaigns. Congress then passed legislation to encourage greater participation of these parties in presidential election campaigns, allowing them to spend unlimited amounts of hard money on things like voter drives and campaign materials.

The combination of these actions by the FEC and Congress triggered the surge in soft money. Once the national parties determined that they, too, could use soft money for certain expenses, they began raising millions of dollars for their nonfederal accounts. Soon the money was being spent not only for get-out-the-vote drives but for major advertising campaigns said to promote party issues, not candidates. Being able to use soft money for certain party expenses had the added advantage of freeing up more hard dollars for direct aid to federal candidates, further fueling the upward spiral of campaign spending.

Uncertainty over the effect of rewriting campaign finance law permeated the 2001 debate on reform legislation. Both parties had become quite proficient at raising soft money. Which would have the advantage if soft money were curtailed or eliminated? Which would benefit if some of the contribution limits on hard money were raised as a tradeoff for a soft money ban? If the parties no longer had access to soft money, would special interests and labor have an increased advantage? Much was at stake, and the political ramifications of each provision and each amendment were carefully weighed as Capitol Hill once again contemplated changing the system.

There were, however, some things about campaign finance that many people did agree on. Many acknowledged that the parties' enthusiasm for soft money in the 1996 election campaign helped produce the most significant campaign finance scandal since Watergate. And most were aware of the public's dim view of the campaign finance system.

1996 SCANDAL

Public attention was riveted on the flaws of the campaign finance system by actions taken during the 1996 presidential election campaign. At the root of the scandal were allegations that foreign money—particularly Chinese—had made it into the campaign in violation of federal law and that the parties' pursuit and use of soft money may have crossed the line into illegal activity.

Much of the focus was on the Democrats. As the scandal unfolded, it was revealed that the Democratic National Committee (DNC) had accepted nearly $3 million in illegal or suspect contributions, money the DNC said it would return. The fund-raising tactics of President Bill Clinton and Vice President Al Gore were also central to the scandal. The news media provided accounts of the Clintons entertaining large donors at private White House coffees and inviting some contributors for overnight stays in the Lincoln bedroom or to go along on government foreign trade missions, and of Gore making fund-raising calls from his office and attending a controversial fund-raiser at a Buddhist temple in California.

The Republican-led Congress launched investigations in both chambers, which seemed to do little more than embarrass the Democrats for their fund-raising excesses. Senate Governmental Affairs Committee investigators in 1997 came up with no proof of allegations that the Chinese government had conspired to influence U.S. elections through large campaign contributions or that the White House had knowingly accepted illegal foreign contributions or that the Clinton administration ever changed policy in exchange for campaign contributions. And along the way, Democrats managed to reveal that a Republican National Committee (RNC) think tank, the National Policy Forum, had also accepted foreign money that may have been passed on to the RNC. A parallel campaign finance investigation was conducted by the House Government Reform and Oversight Committee.

Various requests were made for the appointment of an independent counsel to look into alleged Democratic fund-raising abuses. Attorney General Janet Reno was urged to do so by such high-ranking officials as FBI Director Louis J. Freeh and the head of the Justice Department's Campaign Financing Task Force, Charles G. LaBella. But Reno concluded that the allegations did not meet the standard for such an appointment.

Reno declined to get into the area of soft money because it did not fall under the provisions of the FECA. The attorney general looked at fund-raising phone calls made by Clinton from the White House and Gore from his office but determined that they were to solicit soft money and therefore did not violate the ban on soliciting hard money contributions on federal property. Moreover, according to Reno, Clinton's calls were from the White House residence, which was not covered by the solicitation ban.

The attorney general also examined the question of whether the Clinton-Gore campaign committees had been illegally involved in the political issue ad campaign financed by the DNC. A preliminary investigation by FEC auditors had concluded that both the DNC and the RNC had coordinated millions of dollars worth of issue ads with their respective presidential candidates' campaign committees, making the ads an in-kind contribution in violation of federal spending limits for presidential candidates who accept public funding. But Reno found no criminal intent to violate the law by Clinton or Gore, based on the fact

Campaign Finance Glossary

Following is a glossary of some commonly used terms in the campaign finance field. It was drawn from documents produced by the Federal Election Commission, Center for Responsive Politics, Congressional Research Service of the Library of Congress, and Congressional Quarterly. The definitions reflect the laws and regulations in force as of June 2001.

Bundling. The practice of aggregating separate contributions from various individuals for delivery to a candidate, thereby generating clout for the individual or organization that collects and delivers the contributions. The bundler could focus on employees of a particular business, members of a particular profession, or activists committed to a particular policy. Because the bundler merely forwarded batches of checks made out by individuals to a candidate, the contributions did not count against the bundler's own contribution limits.

Hard Money. Money raised and spent for federal election campaigns under the limitations and prohibitions of the Federal Election Campaign Act (FECA).

Independent Expenditures. Money spent for such things as broadcast advertisements or direct mail that expressly advocated the election or defeat of a federal candidate. Such spending was deemed "independent" so long as the individual or group making the expenditure did not coordinate, cooperate, or consult in any way with the candidate's campaign.

These expenditures were regulated by federal election laws. Thus, while individuals or groups could spend unlimited amounts of money on independent campaign efforts, they had to report these expenditures to the Federal Election Commission (FEC) once they reached a certain level. In addition, the entity sponsoring the independent advertising campaign had to identify itself in its ads and note that the ad was not authorized by the candidate's committee.

Issue Advocacy Advertising. Advertisements advocating a particular position on an issue. Such advertising often implicitly supported the candidates of one political party by advocating the same position they held on an issue. But because the focus was on an issue—such as congressional term limits or family values—none of the campaign laws in force in June 2001 applied. As long as individuals or groups avoided expressly urging people to vote for or against a specific candidate, they could raise and spend unlimited amounts of money. There were no disclosure or reporting requirements in campaign finance law for issue ads, unless the group was a federal PAC or party committee. However, proposals to restrict issue ads were under consideration in Congress. *(See box, Campaign Finance Overhaul Legislation, p. 124.)*

Political Action Committee (PAC). Organizations created to raise and spend money for candidates for federal office. They were typically begun by corporations, industries, trade associations, labor unions, ideology groups, or others with shared policy interests.

A "leadership PAC" was such a committee run by one or more congressional leaders, or other members who aspired to leadership positions. When members outside the leadership structure started creating PACs, the term "politician's PAC" also came into use. Contributions to this type of PAC were considered separate from contributions to the campaign committee of the individual member who sponsored the PAC. A contributor who had given the maximum amount allowed to the House Speaker's campaign committee, for example, still could give to the Speaker's leadership PAC. These PACs were subject to the same constraints as other PACs.

Soft Money. Money raised and spent outside the limitations and prohibitions of the Federal Election Campaign Act and, therefore, not to be used for activities directly related to federal election campaigns. This money was raised primarily by the national, state, and local Republican and Democratic parties initially for grassroots and party-building activities and later for issue ads. The parties could use the funds for get-out-the-vote efforts, administrative costs, generic party advertising, and to help state and local candidates. (Activities that benefited both federal and state and local candidates had to be funded in part by hard money.) As of June 2001, there was no limit on the amount of money that a donor (an individual, corporation, labor union, or PAC) could give to a party's soft money account, but the party had to disclose the source of contributions in excess of $200. However, legislation to ban the national parties from accepting or using soft money and restrict its use by state and local parties was under consideration in Congress. *(See box, Campaign Finance Overhaul Legislation, p. 124.)*

that they had been advised by counsel that the advertising campaign complied with the law. (The FEC subsequently rejected the auditors' recommendations that the campaigns of Clinton and Republican candidate Bob Dole be required to repay millions in public funding.)

Another request for an outside investigation of Gore came in the midst of his 2000 presidential race. Robert Conrad, who had taken over as head of the Campaign Financing Task Force, urged Reno to appoint a special counsel to investigate whether Gore had told the truth when questioned by the task force about the White House coffees and the luncheon at the Buddhist tem-

ple. During the interview, Gore insisted that he had not known the event at the Buddhist temple was a fund-raiser. A key figure at that event was later convicted of campaign finance law violations growing out of a scheme to tap the temple, among other sources, for money to illegally reimburse "straw" donors listed as contributors on reports filed with the Federal Election Commission. Attorney General Reno concluded that the transcript of the Gore interview did not reflect false statements or perjury but rather misunderstandings over what was being asked.

While rejecting calls for independent counsels, Reno emphasized that the Justice Department's task force was conducting an ongoing investigation into allegations of wrongdoing in the 1996 election cycle. As of early 2001, the task force had brought charges against two corporations and twenty-six people, most of whom were Democratic contributors or fund-raisers. The various charges included making illegal foreign or corporate contributions and channeling donations through conduit or "straw" contributors who were later reimbursed. The two corporations and twenty-one individuals had either pled guilty or been convicted, one person had been acquitted, and four others were fugitives. One plea bargain agreement included a record $8.6 million in fines.

DISSATISFACTION WITH SYSTEM

The 1996 scandal did little to shore up public confidence in the system. Although campaign finance was not high on their list of priorities Washington should attend to, people still registered a deep disdain for the system.

A 1997 public opinion survey found that a majority (57 percent) of Americans were dissatisfied with the state of the political system, and the role of money was one of the main sources of that discontent. About two-thirds of those polled cited as major problems the excessive influence of political contributions on elections and government policy, as well as the conflict of interest created when elected officials solicited or took contributions while making policy decisions. Majorities also said that elected officials spent too much time fund-raising and that the high cost of campaigns discouraged good people from running for office.

Similarly, a Gallup poll in January 2001 found that 56 percent of Americans were dissatisfied with the country's campaign finance laws and another poll in March 2001 showed that Americans, by a margin of 76 percent to 19 percent, favored new laws limiting contributions by individuals or groups to the political parties.[5]

But fundamental changes in the campaign finance system never come easily. Reform advocate Fred Wertheimer, while serving as Common Cause president, summed it up: "There are no fights like campaign finance fights because they are battles about the essence of politics and power."[6]

REFORM EFFORTS

Campaign finance reformers over the years have sought to curb campaign spending by limiting and regulating campaign expenditures and donations made to candidates as well as by informing voters of the amounts and sources of the donations, and the amounts, purposes, and recipients of the expenditures. Disclosure was intended to reveal which candidates, if any, were unduly indebted to interest groups, in time to forewarn the voters.

Congress has argued the issues of campaign finance since the first law regulating campaigns was enacted during the administration of Theodore Roosevelt in 1907. Major new laws in the twentieth century, however, came only after the scandals of Teapot Dome in the 1920s and Watergate in the 1970s.

In 1925 the Teapot Dome scandal yielded the Federal Corrupt Practices Act, an extensive statute governing the conduct of federal campaigns. That act codified earlier laws limiting campaign expenditures, but the limits were so unrealistically low and the law so riddled with loopholes that it was ineffectual.

Watergate, though, changed all that. The June 1972 break-in at Democratic national headquarters in Washington's Watergate office building touched off a scandal that became the 1970s' code word for governmental corruption. Although the scandal had many aspects, money in politics was at its roots. Included in Watergate's catalog of misdeeds were specific violations of campaign spending laws, violations of other criminal laws facilitated by the availability of virtually unlimited campaign contributions, and still other instances where campaign funds were used in a manner that strongly suggested influence peddling.

Congress had begun to move on campaign finance even before Watergate. Less than six months before the break-in, Congress had adopted two pieces of legislation containing some of the ground rules under which elections were still being conducted in mid-2001. First, Congress approved legislation allowing a one-dollar tax checkoff to finance presidential campaigns. (The amount was increased to three dollars by 1993 legislation.) Congress also passed the Federal Election Campaign Act (FECA), requiring comprehensive disclosure of campaign contributions and expenditures by candidates for federal office and placing a limit on the amount of money candidates could spend on media advertising. (The media spending limits were repealed in 1974.) The 1971 FECA ultimately had a limited impact on controlling campaign spending.

But Watergate focused public attention on campaign spending at all levels of government and produced a mood in Congress that even the most reluctant legislators found difficult to resist. In the aftermath came the most significant overhaul in campaign finance legislation in the nation's history. Major legislation enacted in 1974 (the House had passed its version on the day Richard Nixon announced he would resign the presidency) and 1976, coming on the heels of the 1971 legislation, radically altered the system of financing federal elections.

The FECA Amendments of 1974 set limits on contributions and expenditures for congressional and presidential elections, established the FEC, and created the framework for providing presidential candidates with public financing.

Before the sweeping 1974 act received its first real test, it was extensively pruned by the Supreme Court. The Court in its 1976 decision in *Buckley v. Valeo* upheld the FECA's disclosure requirements, contribution limitations, and public financing of presidential elections. But it struck down spending limits for congressional and presidential races, including restraints on the use of a candidate's personal assets, except for presidential candidates who accepted public financing. It also struck down limits on independent expenditures, which were expenditures made in support of or opposition to a candidate but without the knowledge or cooperation of the candidate.

The justices weighed First Amendment rights against the 1974 act's underlying purpose: prevention of the abuses that surfaced during Watergate. In the case of contributions, the Court concluded that First Amendment considerations were outweighed because "the quantity of communication by the con-

tributor does not increase perceptibly with the size of his contribution." But it found limiting expenditures to be a "substantial"
restraint on free speech that could preclude "significant use of
the most effective modes of communication."

Many subsequent congressional efforts to change the campaign finance system were driven by the desire to find a way to
limit congressional campaign spending without violating the
mandates of the Court decision. With the ceilings on expenditures removed, campaign costs grew apace and candidates became increasingly dependent on raising money in what was
then the easiest and most cost-effective way—from PACs.

In striking down restraints on independent expenditures, the
Supreme Court opened the door for individuals and PACs to
spend millions of dollars independently. Such spenders were
generally derided by candidates and party leaders as unwelcome
"loose cannons" in the political process. Sharply negative ads
underwritten by nonconnected, or ideological, PACs earned the
enmity of both parties.

In 1979 Congress amended the FECA, in part to encourage
more grassroots and political party activity in federal campaigns. Included in the package of amendments was the section
allowing state and local parties to underwrite voter drives in behalf of presidential tickets without regard to financial limits.

Throughout the late 1970s reformers sought to extend public
financing to congressional races, but their efforts failed. A bill to
limit the role of PACs was passed by the House in 1979 but
blocked by the threat of a filibuster in the Senate.

After the 1970s Congress proved less amenable to further major changes in campaign financing. Proposals were debated, but
it would be a decade before either chamber passed a major campaign finance bill. And once again it would be scandals that provided the impetus.

In 1989 allegations of ethical violations and questionable financial dealings involving Speaker Jim Wright, D-Texas, intensified pressures on House Democrats to act on campaign finance
legislation. Wright, facing charges that would eventually lead to
his resignation from Congress, embraced campaign finance reform and created a bipartisan task force to develop a reform
plan.

Further pressure for change came the following year in the
form of the Keating Five scandal, so named for five senators suspected of doing favors for a wealthy campaign contributor,
Charles H. Keating Jr. At the heart of the scandal was $1.5 mil-
lion in contributions made or solicited by Keating, the powerful
owner of a savings and loan and real estate empire, for the campaigns or other political causes of the five senators. More than
half of the money—$850,000—was paid out of corporate funds
to nonprofit voter registration organizations with which one of
the senators, Alan Cranston, D-Calif., was affiliated. Keating also
employed a technique called "bundling," through which he
raised many individual contributions from family members, associates, and employees of his companies and handed the contributions over in a lump sum designed to impress the recipient
politicians. Televised hearings and news stories revealing Keating's use of his fund-raising skills to assemble clout in Washington proved far more effective at raising questions about the rela-

tionship between elected officials and major contributors than
the flood of statistics about PACs that were issued by good government groups.

Both chambers passed bills in 1990, over GOP objections, but
action came late in the session and the bills died when Congress
adjourned and went home for the elections.

The House and Senate again passed bills in 1991. There were
vast differences between the two versions and compromise
seemed unlikely. But this time scandals at the House bank and
post office sent Democratic leaders on a reform mission and
reignited the campaign finance issue. Conferees reconciled differences in 1992 by letting each chamber live by its own rules.
But President George Bush objected to that approach, along
with the bill's spending limits and public funding provisions,
and vetoed the bill.

Reformers' hopes were high, when Clinton came into the
White House vowing to overhaul the system. Both chambers approved radically different bills in 1993, but the Democrats did
not work out a compromise until late the next year. At that
point Senate Democrats were unable to shut off a GOP-led filibuster. Some questioned the Democrats' sincerity in pursuing
campaign reform and wondered if they had purposely waited
until it was too late in the session to overcome Republican opposition.

Many expected that the scandal surrounding the 1996 election would renew fervor for reform. And it did, but not enough
to lead to enactment of a new law. The House passed a bill in
1998, but the Senate bill was again blocked by a GOP filibuster.
The same thing happened in the next Congress.

After more than twenty years, a new campaign finance-related law was finally enacted in 2000. The statute required a group
of political organizations, named "527s" for a section of the tax
code, to disclose their heretofore secret finances. It was a small
but highly controversial corner of campaign finance.

The issue of campaign finance reform gained momentum in
the 2000 election. Reform advocate Sen. John McCain of Arizona made it the centerpiece of his campaign for the Republican
presidential nomination. Although he failed to win his party's
nomination, he promised to continue to battle on the Senate
floor for changes in the campaign finance system, in particular
for a ban on soft money, which he argued had led to the "corruption" of American politics. Prospects for legislation in the
Senate increased dramatically in 2001, when it became apparent
that there were finally enough votes to break the perennial filibuster against campaign finance legislation. The Senate passed a
bill in early April 2001 and sent it on to the House. *(See box,
Campaign Finance Overhaul Legislation, p. 124.)*

Candidates' Contributions
and Expenditures

The modern election is a complex financial affair. Fund-raisers, accountants, lawyers, and a variety of consultants play crucial roles in today's campaigns. Decisions on how to raise money and how to marshal a campaign's resources can be key to
electoral success.

Sen. John McCain of Arizona (left) and Sen. Russell Feingold of Wisconsin (center) discuss their campaign finance bill in March 2001.

Money and services pour in from a vast array of sources—not all of them controlled by the candidate—including individuals, PACs, party committees, candidates themselves and their families, and independent organizations running their own campaigns to influence the outcome. And for those running for president, public funding is usually a major element. Money flows out for rent, computers, salaries, polls, consulting fees, printing, postage, and radio, television, and newspaper advertising.

Much of the money that at one time moved in the shadows of campaigns is now a matter of public record, thanks to the stringent disclosure provisions of the FECA. All candidates for federal office, once they cross a certain threshold, periodically must submit to the FEC itemized accounts of contributions and expenditures in excess of $200 and debts and obligations owed to or by the candidate or committee. These detailed reports, which are made public by the FEC, provide a window on the modern political campaign.

CONTRIBUTIONS TO
PRESIDENTIAL CANDIDATES

FEC figures for the 2000 presidential election indicated that a field of eighteen candidates reported receipts in the prenomination campaign totaling nearly $343 million through July 31, 2000. Individual donors constituted the single most important source of money for primary candidates, followed by public funding payouts from the federal Treasury. Other sources included contributions by PACs and the political parties and loans either from the candidates themselves or others.

For the 2000 general election campaign, the two major party candidates each received $67.56 million in public funding. In return, they agreed to limit themselves for the most part to that amount and not accept outside money. The Reform Party ticket received $12.6 million but was allowed to supplement those public funds with private contributions up to the same spend-

ing limit as the major party candidates. Other candidates relied on private funding for their campaigns.

There are several exceptions to the no-outside-money rule. Publicly funded candidates may accept private contributions to a special account maintained exclusively to pay for expenses related to complying with federal campaign finance law. This is known as a general election legal and accounting compliance (GELAC) fund. In addition, publicly funded candidates may spend up to $50,000 of their own money. Also, political parties are permitted to spend a specific amount of money on behalf of their candidates. *(See "Political Parties," p. 92.)*

There were, of course, millions of additional dollars being spent to influence the outcome of presidential primaries and elections. Soft money contributions to national party committees and other entities, although barred from direct use on federal campaigns, had an enormous impact on federal races, especially in funding the purchase of issue advocacy ads. Labor unions, corporations, and other organizations also spent big money on things like issue ads and get-out-the-vote efforts that impacted on the candidate of their choice. Individuals, PACs, and political parties could make independent expenditures for or against a particular candidate as well. *(See "Soft Money," p. 104; "Issue Advocacy Ads," p. 105; "Independent Expenditures," p. 106.)*

Public Funding

Presidential elections have been financed in part by public funds since 1976, with the inauguration of a voluntary system of matching funds for primary election candidates and full funding for presidential nominees who agree to spending limits. It was hoped that the program would reduce the influence of wealthy donors, relieve candidates of some fund-raising burdens, and level the playing field plan so qualified candidates would not be shut out by the spiraling costs of campaigns.

Background. Concern over the financing of elections was not a modern phenomenon. Wealthy donors had begun playing a role in politics long before the Civil War. Industrialism only expanded their influence. Entrepreneurs who donated money to Ulysses Grant in the 1868 election included Jay Cooke, Cornelius Vanderbilt, A. T. Stewart, Henry Hilton, and John Astor. "Never before was a candidate placed under such great obligation to men of wealth as was Grant," wrote one historian.[7]

Concern over the influence of big business and big donors grew in the wake of revelations by "muckraking" journalists and agitation by Progressive Party reformers. Corporations, banks, railroads, and other businesses had become major sources of political money, with many corporations reportedly making donations to the national parties of $50,000 or more.[8]

The role of campaign professionals also triggered alarm among reformers. Marc Hanna, an Ohio mining magnate and a key strategist for William McKinley in the elections of 1896 and 1900, raised money for the Republican Party through a systematic assessment of banks and corporations in amounts that were said to represent their share in the nation's prosperity. He used the money to make McKinley financially solvent, to influence possible delegates, and to pay for the kind of mass propaganda campaign that would change the face of national politics forever. As if to validate the notoriety that surrounded him, Hanna was said to have commented: "There are only two important things in politics. The first is money, and I can't remember the second."[9]

McKinley's successor, Theodore Roosevelt, accepted large gifts in his 1904 campaign, arguing that "the wrong lies not in receiving the contribution" but in exercising improper pressure or making promises to get it.[10]

Not all agreed. Legislation to use public funds to finance presidential elections was first introduced in 1904 by Rep. William Bourke Cockran, a Democrat from New York. Cockran believed that "it might be possible for the government of the United States to do away with any excuse for soliciting large subscriptions of money" by using public funds to finance elections. In his December 1907 annual message, Roosevelt joined those calling for the "very radical measure" of public funding of party organizations. But no action was taken.

Congress did approve legislation in 1907 to ban bank and corporate gifts to federal candidates and in the ensuing decades placed other restrictions and requirements on the campaign finance system. *(See "Corporate Contribution Ban," p. 109.)*

But it would be more than a half century before public funding was enacted, and approval did not come easily.

Program Established. Beginning in the mid-1950s, presidential public funding bills were introduced regularly in Congress. Support grew and in 1966 Congress approved a plan to set up a fund to provide money to presidential general election campaigns through payments to their political parties. The program was to be financed by allowing taxpayers to check a box on their income tax forms if they wished to designate $1 of the tax payment ($2 for a joint return) to go to the fund. However, the following year—before the program ever went into effect—Congress suspended it, pending the adoption of guidelines for distributing the money. Congress never adopted the guidelines.

After a bitter partisan struggle, Congress in 1971 again enacted public funding legislation. The Revenue Act of 1971 created the Presidential Election Campaign Fund for federal financing of presidential general election campaigns through direct payments to qualifying presidential candidates who agreed to limit their spending to the amount of the federal subsidy. The fund was to be financed by a voluntary $1 tax checkoff ($2 if a joint return) on federal tax returns.

Democrats, whose party was deeply in debt and traditionally received less campaign financing than the Republican Party, sponsored and defended the public funding proposal. They argued that such a financing plan would remove politics from the influence of large contributors. Republicans decried the move as a brazen political act and, with the help of a veto threat from President Richard Nixon, succeeded in winning approval for postponing implementation of the fund until after the 1972 presidential election.

Comprehensive campaign finance legislation enacted in 1974 extended public funding to presidential primaries and nominating conventions.

The constitutionality of the 1974 statute was quickly challenged in the courts by a diverse group of plaintiffs who claimed, among other things, that its contribution and spending limits curbed freedom of expression. In the landmark 1976 *Buckley v. Valeo* decision, the Supreme Court found key parts of the statute to be unconstitutional, including most of its expenditure limits. However, the Court upheld public financing and its spending limits because, unlike the others, these restrictions were voluntary—candidates were free to reject public funding and the limits that came with it. *(See* Buckley v. Valeo, p. 117.)

The presidential election funding system set up by the 1971 and 1974 acts has remained basically the same, with only a few changes over the years. Congress in 1993 tripled the tax checkoff to $3 ($6 for a joint return).

How It Works. To be eligible to receive public funds, presidential candidates and party convention committees must meet certain requirements.[11] Once the Federal Election Commission determines that these have been met, it certifies the amount of money the U.S. Treasury should pay out of the Presidential Election Campaign Fund.

There are three main components of the program:

• Primary matching funds. Partial payments are made to eligible presidential primary candidates through a matching program. The federal government will match up to $250 of the total contribution by an individual to a candidate. (Individuals may contribute up to $1,000 to a candidate, but only the first $250 can be matched.) Party and PAC contributions are not eligible for matching.

To participate in the matching program, a candidate first must raise over $100,000, of which more than $5,000 must be raised in each of twenty states. Because only $250 of each contribution counts toward this threshold, there would have to be more than twenty individual donors in each of those states. A candidate must agree to a total national spending limit of $10 million plus a cost-of-living adjustment (COLA), as well as state-by-state limits ($200,000 plus COLA, or sixteen cents times the state's voting age population, whichever is greater). A candidate also must agree to limit personal spending on the campaign to $50,000. (Some expenses are exempt from the spending limits.)

Primary candidates can lose their eligibility for matching funds if they fail to receive 10 percent of the vote in two consecutive primaries. However, they are permitted to notify the FEC that they would like to exclude certain primaries from the 10 percent requirement and thus maintain their eligibility.

Candidates who are no longer actively campaigning may continue to request matching funds to wind down their campaigns and pay off campaign debts.

In the 2000 presidential race, candidates who accepted public funding were allowed to spend $40,536,000 on their prenomination efforts. Eligible candidates could receive up to half of that in public funding. State spending limits ranged from $675,600 in smaller states to a high of more than $13 million in California.

By November 2000 the FEC had certified a total of nearly $61 million in matching funds to ten presidential primary candidates in the 2000 election campaign. This included $29.3 million to three Democrats, $25.7 million to four Republicans, and $5.7 million to three minor party candidates.

• Nominating conventions. Major political parties are entitled to receive $4 million, plus COLA, for their national presidential nominating conventions. (The subsidy base originally was $2 million, but it was raised to $3 million in 1979 and $4 million in 1984.) A qualified minor party may receive funding based on its nominee's share of the popular vote in the previous presidential election.

The two major political parties each received $13.5 million and the Reform Party, $2.5 million, for their 2000 presidential nominating conventions. This marked the first time a third party received public funds for its convention.

Party convention committees in theory could not spend more than the amount to which their parties were entitled. However, the FEC has permitted additional spending from a variety of sources. Host state and city governments and local groups such as businesses and labor unions have been permitted to provide certain supplemental services. For example, a host city could provide additional public transportation to and from the convention site, or a business could sell or rent equipment to the convention committee at a discount. Contributions could also be accepted for a special account used to pay legal and accounting expenses incurred in complying with the campaign finance law. In addition, local officials and businesspeople could establish "host committees" ostensibly to promote their city and its commerce during the convention. Although these committees had to report their receipts and expenditures to the FEC, there were no restrictions on who could contribute to these committees or how much they could give. The host committee for the GOP national convention reported expenditures of more than $51 million in calendar year 2000, while the Democratic convention's two host committees reported spending nearly $39.8 million.

• General election funding. Major party nominees who are eligible for public funding in the general election receive a grant of $20 million, plus COLA. In the 2000 race, this amounted to $67.56 million each.

To receive public funds, the nominees must agree to limit their spending to that amount and may not accept private contributions to their campaign. Certain legal and accounting expenses related to complying with the campaign finance law are exempt from these requirements. Also, candidates may contribute up to $50,000 of their own money without having it count against the expenditure limit.

Minor party candidates and new party candidates may be eligible for partial funding in the general election. A minor party candidate is the nominee of a party whose candidate received between 5 and 25 percent of the total popular vote in the last presidential election. The amount the minor party candidate receives is based on the party's performance in that preceding election. A new party candidate—the nominee of neither a major nor a minor party—may become eligible for public funds after the current election if he or she receives at least 5 percent of the popular vote. Minor and new party candidates who accept public funds are subject to the same expenditure limit and other requirements as major party candidates, although because they do not receive as much as the major party candidates, they may supplement their partial public funds with private contributions.

Participation. More than $1 billion in public funding had been given out through the 2000 presidential election. From 1976 through 1996, a total of nearly $885 million[12] in public funding was distributed: $253.1 million to seventy-four primary candidates, $92.5 million for twelve major party nominating conventions, and $539.5 million to twelve major party nominees and two independent or third-party candidates.[13] Preliminary figures for the 2000 presidential race would add some $238 million to the overall total: $61.1 million for ten primary candidates, $29.5 million for the nominating conventions of the two major parties and one minor party, and $147.7 million to two major party nominees and one minor party nominee.

Since the program began, most presidential candidates have accepted public funding. Among those who did not accept public funding for their primary campaigns were Republicans John Connally in 1980, Steve Forbes in 1996 and 2000, and George W. Bush in 2000. Bush was the first candidate to win a major party nomination after refusing public funding for the primary campaign. Independent candidate H. Ross Perot did not take public funding for his 1992 general election campaign, but accepted it when he ran again in 1996 as the Reform Party nominee.

Despite the near-unanimous participation in the program, Joseph Cantor of the Congressional Research Service noted that most of the candidates actually opposed public financing and had checked "no" to the voluntary contribution to the fund on their own income tax forms. "Their participation resulted from the obvious advantages in easier access to funds and, in a larger sense, to a general acceptance of the public funding system in the political community and the media," Cantor wrote.[14]

Judging by the number of taxpayers who mark "yes" to the tax checkoff, the general public has not been too fond of the program either, even though the contribution adds nothing to their tax obligation. From 1976 to 1996, the percentage of taxpayers participating in the program ranged from a high of 28.7 percent in the 1980 tax year to a low of 12.4 percent in the 1996 tax year.[15]

Pros and Cons. People have strong opinions on public funding. "Supporters see it as a democratic, egalitarian system, offering the best chance to reduce corrosive effects of money on the political process and renew public confidence in it," Cantor wrote. On the other hand, "[o]pponents see it as a waste of tax money, which artificially skews the results and forces taxpayers to fund candidates whom they oppose."[16]

An FEC report cited three problems the public funding program was supposed to correct:

  • "The disproportionate influence (or the appearance of influence) of wealthy contributors;
  • "The demands of fundraising that prevented some candidates from adequately presenting their views to the public; and
  • "The increasing cost of Presidential campaigns that effectively disqualified candidates who did not have access to large sums of money."[17]

An examination of public funding's affect on these three problems produces a mixed scoresheet.

In an attempt to put an end to the dominant role of wealthy donors—the so-called fat cats—the public funding program for primary campaigns was designed specifically to encourage candidates to seek out numerous small contributions from individual donors. And in the general election campaign, if a candidate accepted public funding, no outside contributions were permitted.

But campaigns found ways to circumvent these seemingly stringent rules. Through the use of soft-money donations to national party committees, big donors continued to be major players in presidential politics. By the 2000 presidential election campaign, it was becoming commonplace for corporations, labor unions, and wealthy individuals to make donations of $100,000 or more to party soft-money accounts. According to FEC figures, soft-money donations to national party committees amounted to $495.1 million in the 1999–2000 election cycle, up from $262.1 million in 1996 and $86.1 million in 1992.

Whether candidates had been relieved of the burdens of fund-raising was debatable. While major party candidates no longer had to spend time raising money for their general election campaigns, they instead began to devote time and energy to raising funds for their parties' soft-money accounts. As for primary races, some critics said that candidates had to work harder now to find numerous small individual donors to meet the requirements of the matching program.

The program's plan to level the playing field through a combination of public funding and expenditure limits had mixed results. Supporters argued that public funding had helped candidates compete, pointing to the fact that in the elections from 1976 to 1996, challengers, who historically had been underfunded, defeated three incumbent presidents.[18] Yet, outside money, in the form of soft money and independent expenditures, could still skew the results of publicly funded campaigns. And, of course, since the program was voluntary there was no assurance that all candidates would be playing by the same rules. Republi-

can candidates in the race for their party's 2000 nomination found themselves competing against a front-runner who declined public funding. Elizabeth Dole dropped out of the race in October 1999—months before the first primary—after concluding she would never be financially competitive with George W. Bush. "The bottom line is money," Dole said as she announced her withdrawal. At the time, she reportedly had $861,000 in cash on hand, while Bush had $37.7 million.[19]

One critic in a discussion of the 1996 election wrote:

Presidential campaigns continue to push the limits of the law, finding new and creative means of gathering additional resources for their campaigns. They continue to adapt their own patterns of spending to conform to new forms of finance, especially the growth of soft money and the rise of issue advocacy advertising. Consequently, they continue to undermine the objectives of the current regulations, which have essentially been rendered meaningless as a result of continued abuse.[20]

Individual Contributions

Political campaigns for the White House and Congress have traditionally been financed by the contributions of individual donors. The biggest difference today is that many more contributors are now involved in the process. The pre-Watergate contributors of unlimited amounts of money to federal candidates were largely replaced by smaller donors, who either gave directly to a candidate or contributed through a political party committee or PAC. The big donors, of course, did not disappear. After coming up against statutory limits on direct contributions to federal campaigns, they found other outlets, such as soft money contributions to the parties.

Under the limits in place in mid-2001, an individual could give a primary candidate up to $1,000 during the entire primary season, no matter how many presidential primaries the candidate entered. An individual could give another $1,000 to a candidate during the general election campaign, if the candidate was permitted to accept private funds. (Congress in 2001 was considering raising the individual limits as part of its effort to rewrite campaign finance law.)

As noted above, contributions by individuals are especially important during the presidential primary season because these are the only donations eligible for federal matching. The idea behind matching only $250 of an individual donation and requiring candidates to meet a $100,000 threshold was to make them demonstrate broad-based support.

Eighteen presidential campaigns in 2000 reported, as of July 31, 2000, that more than two-thirds of their total receipts had come from individual contributions directly to their campaigns—$233.6 million of a nearly $343 million total. Individual donors were also the dominant source of campaign money for most of the primary candidates who did not receive public funding. George W. Bush, for example, reported receipts of $94.5 million through July 2000, with $91.3 million coming from individual donors.

In the 1996 primary campaign, a little more than half of the total campaign receipts reported by seventeen candidates came from direct contributions by individuals—$128.5 million of a $248.3 million total.

Political Parties

As would be expected, political party committees maintain, at least officially, a neutral stance during the presidential primary season as members fight it out for the party's nomination. Little more than $14,000 in party contributions was reported in the 1996 primary campaign, illustrating how negligible party contributions are at that point of the election cycle.

Conventions. However, the parties have a highly visible role in the general election campaign. They hold national conventions where their presidential and vice-presidential candidates are formally nominated. The parties work hard to impress the American people with their presidential ticket and national platform and to invigorate party regulars to go out and campaign for a victory in November.

But there is other work to be done. The political parties also use the conventions to entertain campaign contributors—the more the donors have given, the more lavish and exclusive the occasion. The guests are warmly rewarded for their past generosity, and then asked for more. As former GOP chair Frank J. Fahrenkopf Jr., put it: "You've got most of your die-hard supporters in one place. . . . It's a very, very critical source of money for both parties."[21]

But the political parties have to compete with lobbyists and other interests who are doing their own elaborate entertaining to curry favor with powerful politicians. "Nominating conventions are less and less about nominating, and more and more about networking and partying," said Jim Owen, a spokesman for the Edison Electric Institute, a trade association that joined with other energy-related trade associations to sponsor tributes to powerful members of Congress at both the Republican and Democratic 2000 conventions.[22]

Coordinated Expenditures. During the general election campaign, national party committees are permitted to make "coordinated expenditures" to support their nominee. The parties make the actual expenditures for goods and services rather than giving the money to the candidate's campaign, but they may consult with the campaign on how the money should be spent. This money is used for everything from consultants and media costs to lodging and car rentals.

The total amount that parties can spend is determined by a formula: 2 cents multiplied by the national voting age population and adjusted for the cost of living. In the 2000 campaign, this amounted to nearly $13.7 million for each party. This money does not count against a publicly funded candidate's spending limit, but the parties must report expenditures to the FEC. The Democratic National Committee reported spending $12.6 million on behalf of its 2000 presidential ticket, and the Republican National Committee reported coordinated expenditures of $13.5 million.

A legal challenge to any type of restriction on what political parties could spend to help specific candidates (presidential or congressional) was halted by the Supreme Court in June 2001. The Court by a narrow 5–4 vote in *Federal Election Commission v. Colorado Republican Federal Campaign Committee* upheld strict limits on what political parties could spend in coordination with candidates. *(See "Coordinated Expenditures," p. 106.)*

Independent Expenditures. A new avenue for parties was opened in 1996 when the Supreme Court threw out restrictions on independent expenditures by political parties *(Colorado Republican Federal Campaign Committee v. Federal Election Commission).* The ruling meant that the parties could spend unlimited amounts on such things as advertising that called for the election—or defeat—of specific candidates, as long as they did not coordinate those expenditures with the campaigns of their candidates.

But the parties showed little interest in taking advantage of the ruling in the 1996 presidential campaign—the only party independent expenditures for or against presidential candidates were made by state and local committees and they amounted to less than $18,000. The national party committees reported no independent expenditures for or against presidential candidates in the 2000 race, and state and local committees reported spending less than $21,000.

Soft Money. The national parties' growing use of so-called soft money—essentially unregulated money raised from sources and in amounts barred under federal election law—had an enormous affect on presidential campaigns. Although this money could not by law be used for federal candidates, when it was channeled into such grassroots activities as voter registration, education, and turnout, or bought generic party advertising, party candidates at all levels benefited. The money also could be used to pay a portion of the overhead expenses of party committees, thus freeing up federal money for other uses. Moreover, soft money became an increasingly significant source for funding issue advocacy advertising—those ads that promoted the party's positions but did not "expressly advocate" the election or defeat of candidates.

The Citizens' Research Foundation's study of the 1996 election found that $48.2 million of a total $149.7 million in Republican soft money spending and $54.1 million of a total of $121.8 million in Democratic soft money expenditures benefited their respective presidential tickets.[23]

Candidate's Own Money

Those candidates who accept public funding must also accept a $50,000 limit on how much of their own money they can contribute to the campaign. But for those who do not take public funds the sky's the limit, as H. Ross Perot and Malcolm S. "Steve" Forbes demonstrated in recent elections.

Perot, who made his fortune in the computer industry, spent more than $63 million of it in pursuit of the presidency in 1992. In the end, he won nearly nineteen percent of the popular vote, the third best showing for a third-party candidate in U.S. history. If he had raised the required amount of money from individuals and spent only $50,000 of his own money, Perot would have been eligible for public funding retroactively. Obviously, he did not. However, when he ran again in 1996—this time as the Reform Party candidate—he received more than $29 million in public funds.[24]

Publishing magnate Forbes unsuccessfully sought the Republican nomination in 1996 and again in 2000. In 1996 Forbes loaned his campaign nearly $38 million. During the 2000 prenomination campaign, he forgave most of that debt and gave his 2000 race nearly $39 million.

Political Action Committees

Labor unions, corporations, and incorporated trade and membership organizations are prohibited by law from using their general treasury funds to make contributions or expenditures in federal elections. They, therefore, participate indirectly in the electoral process through what are called "separate segregated funds." These funds, along with the political committees of other organizations (such as ideological and issue groups) that raise money for candidates, are known as political action committees. Most PACs are permitted to contribute $5,000 per candidate per election, with no overall limit. They also may give $15,000 per year to a national party committee.

But PACs spend little of their money on presidential candidates, preferring instead to focus on congressional races whose outcome could have direct impact on their legislative interests on Capitol Hill. Indeed, PACs are "mostly invisible" in presidential primary politics, according to academics Wesley Joe and Clyde Wilcox. The two cited a study of the 1996 campaign that found that "no presidential candidate raised as much as 4 percent of their total receipts from PACs."[25]

It was much the same story in the 2000 primary contests. By July 31, 2000, only one candidate reported receiving more than four percent, and that was Republican senator Orrin G. Hatch of Utah, with not quite 7 percent from PACs. Hatch's position as chairman of the Senate Judiciary Committee may have inspired some of those contributions.

FEC figures showed that PACs contributed just $2.5 million to presidential candidates in the 2000 race. They reported another $5.9 million in independent expenditures for or against presidential candidates.

In addition to creating PACs, companies, trade associations, and labor unions are allowed to promote specific candidates in mailings and phone calls that reach only their employees or members, not the general public. FEC regulations permit unlimited spending on such communication efforts, but, as of spring 2000, labor unions had made the most effective use of the strategy. Vice President Gore's presidential campaign, for example, benefited from $174,493 in communications by unions during the 2000 primary season, according to FEC records. The FEC at that time listed a total of 241 communications accounts, of which all but sixty-six were affiliated with labor unions. (Some of these had been active for years, while others focused on only a single race.) Business groups, however, were vowing to catch up, if not in the 2000 race, then in the near future.[26]

Companies, trade associations, and labor unions, of course, were participating indirectly through soft money contributions to the nonfederal accounts of the national parties and through the purchase of issue ads.

PRESIDENTIAL CANDIDATES' EXPENDITURES

In the 2000 prenomination campaign, eighteen contenders reported spending a total of more than $326 million through

Advocates of overhauling campaign finance laws in the late 1990s and early 2000s included House Republican Christopher Shays of Connecticut, left, and Democrat Martin T. Meehan of Massachusetts, right.

July 31, 2000. The two major party nominees—Gore and Bush—reported spending a combined total of $131.6 million. Gore reported expenditures of $42.5 million, while Bush reported about $89 million. The reason for the wide gap was that Gore had accepted federal matching funds in the primary campaign and its $40.536 million spending limit for the primary campaign (Gore's $42.5 million included some expenditures that were exempt from the limit), while Bush declined public funds and, therefore, could spend as much as he could raise under the FECA.

In the 2000 general election, both Bush and Gore accepted public funding and agreed to abide by the $67.56 million spending limit, as did Reform Party candidate Pat Buchanan. Each party could spend an additional $13.68 million in conjunction with its presidential ticket. Democrats reported coordinated expenditures of $12.6 million and Republicans, $13.5 million.

But these numbers would represent only a portion of what was actually spent in the 2000 battle for the White House once everything was tallied up. Many millions more poured into the campaign in the form of soft money, issue advocacy, generic advertising, and independent expenditures.

The 1996 presidential race illustrated that the hard dollars and public funding reported by campaigns to the FEC are just part of the picture. Campaign finance scholar Herbert E. Alexander, who has been studying the financing of presidential races since 1960, calculated the cost of the 1996 presidential election at $700 million.[27] About a third of that came from public funds.

Seventeen candidates reported expenditures of about $240 million in the 1996 prenomination race. But Alexander estimated the cost at $282.5 million, after adding in about $31 million for party soft-money advertising, along with spending for compliance costs, communications costs, and independent expenditures.

Each party received $12.3 million in 1996 for their national conventions. However, Alexander put the actual cost of the conventions at $31 million for the Republicans and $34 million for the Democrats, after adding in spending by the convention cities' municipal host committees, tourist bureaus, and corporate and labor sponsors.

FEC records indicated that the Clinton, Dole, and Perot tickets received just over $150 million in public funds for their general election campaigns. But Alexander estimated the real cost at twice that, after adding in, among other things, $18.4 million for party coordinated expenditures, $13.6 million for GELAC (compliance) costs, $68 million for party soft money use and issue advertising, $25 million for nonpartisan organizations' voter drives, and $20 million for spending by labor, corporations, and associations.

On top of all that, Alexander estimated miscellaneous out-of-pocket expenditures at all levels at about $52 million, for the grand total of $700 million.

Planes, Polls, Pizza

In their study of the 1996 prenomination campaign, Joe and Wilcox noted the various challenges candidates face in seeking their party's presidential nomination. Contenders must make important decisions on issues, strategy, and tactics, but—"above all"—they must raise enough money to get their message across:

Money does not buy victory, but without it a candidate cannot get on the plane and fly to the next stop, cannot answer his or her opponents charges with a television advertisement, cannot commission a poll, or even pay for pizza to feed campaign workers.[28]

The authors pointed out that the money chase had become particularly important in recent campaigns because of the increasingly compressed nomination period.

Beyond paying for planes and pizza, there was a certain image that came with successful fund-raising. According to Joe and Wilcox, journalists devoted much air time and newspaper space to candidates' fund-raising prowess in the 1996 campaign. "Indeed, articles as early as October 1995 began to discount candidates who had done less well than expected in the fund-raising race—nearly five months before the first caucus or primary was held. . . ."[29]

Some factors are beyond a candidate's control.

For instance, Clinton was virtually unopposed for the Democratic nomination in 1996, but Dole had to battle a number of primary opponents for his party's nomination. Clinton had the luxury of spending his primary money to advance his general election campaign, while Dole had to focus on the next round of primaries. At the same time, Clinton's campaign was bolstered by DNC issue ads paid for with the enormous amounts of soft money that the White House had begun raising in 1995. It was only after Dole secured the GOP nomination that the RNC began running its own issue ads to benefit its candidate—and just in time, too, since Dole was nearly out of money.

Candidates can also be put at serious disadvantage when an opponent decides to spend millions of a personal fortune in pursuit of a presidential nomination—as Forbes did in 1996 and 2000. Similarly, a candidate who declines public funding, as Bush did in 2000, has some distinct advantages over an opponent who accepts public funding and the fund-raising requirements and spending limits that go with it.

Media Expenditures

Presidential candidates must get out their message as quickly, as widely, as efficiently as possible. Today there is only one sure way of doing that: through television advertising. As a result, media expenditures have come to dominate the budgets of modern presidential campaigns.

Clinton and Dole, for example, each spent more than 60 percent of their general election budgets on electronic advertising, most of it on television, according to an analysis by the Campaign Study Group (CSG) for the *Washington Post*.[30] Clinton spent $46.1 million, nearly 63 percent of his total expenditures, and Dole, $46.9 million, or about 61 percent. The campaigns spent an average of about 19 percent on overhead costs, such as salaries, travel, telephones, computers, and rent; 15 percent on campaign events and material; about 2 percent on fund-raising; and about 1 percent on polling.

In a discussion of the CSG study, campaign finance expert Anthony Corrado pointed out that Clinton and Dole had spent significantly less on media in their primary campaigns: $13.1 million (about 32 percent) by Clinton and $7.2 million (about 18 percent) by Dole. Their media budgets increased substantially in the general election campaign because they no longer had fund-raising expenses to worry about and party soft money was paying for voter mobilization programs.[31]

With so much more money available in the general election campaign, the Clinton and Dole campaigns "pursued the most sophisticated advertising strategies yet seen in a national election," according to Corrado. "New technologies allowed the candidates to target markets and messages more precisely than ever before, and dramatically expanded the speed with which they could respond to an opponent's message or change their media buys."[32] A campaign could have a response ad on the air within a day or two, sometimes even the same day.

Moreover, it could monitor ads in many more media markets than just the national ones, which allowed a campaign to tailor its response ad to a particular local audience and save money on the less expensive local media buys. "As the experience of 1996 indicates, the future may be found in highly localized media buying, digital transmissions, day-by-day media strategies, and the Internet," Corrado concluded.[33]

CONTRIBUTIONS TO CONGRESSIONAL CANDIDATES

FEC figures indicated that congressional candidates in the 2000 general election raised a total of more than $1 billion during the 1999–2000 election cycle. House and Senate incumbents together raised nearly $492.5 million; challengers raised about $227 million. An additional $327.8 million was raised by candidates for open seats.

When broken down by chamber, the figures showed that Senate candidates raised a total of nearly $437 million, with incumbents attracting $130.6 million, challengers $99.7 million, and open-seat candidates $206.7 million.

House candidates took in a total of more than $610 million. The incumbents' share was $361.9 million, while challengers raised $127.4 million and open-seat candidates $121.1 million.

Table 5-1
Contribution Limits (as of June 2001)

Donors	Recipients					Special limits
	Candidate committee	PAC[1]	Local party committee[2]	State party committee[2]	National party committee[3]	
Individual[4]	$1,000 per election[5]	$5,000 per year	$5,000 per year combined limit		$20,000 per year	$25,000 per year overall limit[6]
Local party committee[2]	$5,000 per election[5] combined limit	$5,000 per year combined limit	unlimited transfers to other party committees			
State party committee[2] (multicandidate)[7]			unlimited transfers to other party committees			
National party committee[3] (multicandidate)[7]	$5,000 per election[5]	$5,000 per year	unlimited transfers to other party committees			$17,500 to Senate candidate per campaign[8]
PAC[1] (multicandidate)[7]	$5,000 per election[5]	$5,000 per year	$5,000 per year combined limit		$15,000 per year	
PAC[1] (not multicandidate)[7]	$1,000 per election[5]	$5,000 per year	$5,000 per year combined limit		$20,000 per year	

1. These limits apply to separate segregated funds and nonconnected PACs. Affiliated PACs share the same set of limits on contributions received and made.

2. A state party committee shares its limits with local party committees in that state unless a local committee's independence can be demonstrated.

3. A party's national committee, Senate campaign committee, and House campaign committee are each considered national party committees and each have separate limits except for contributions to Senate candidates. See Special Limits column.

4. The Senate passed legislation in April 2001 that would raise the limits on contributions by individuals to candidates and to national party committees, as well as their overall annual limit. *(See box, Campaign Finance Overhaul Legislation, p. 124.)*

5. Each of the following is considered a separate election with a separate limit: primary election, caucus or convention with authority to nominate, general election, and special election.

6. A contribution to a party committee or a PAC counts against the annual limit for the year in which the contribution is made. A contribution to a candidate counts against the limit for the year of the election for which the contribution is made.

7. A multicandidate committee is a political committee that has been registered for at least six months, has received contributions from more than fifty contributors and, with the exception of a state party committee, has made contributions to at least five federal candidates.

8. This limit is shared by the national committee and the Senate campaign committee.

Source: Federal Election Commission.

Much of this money came from two principal sources: individual contributions and PACs. Lesser amounts came from the candidates themselves, usually in the form of loans, and from the political parties.

Individual Contributions

As of June 2001, individuals were limited to contributions of $1,000 per candidate per election (a primary election, general election, and special election were considered separate elections with separate limits), $20,000 a year to a national party committee, and $5,000 a year to a PAC, with an overall limit of $25,000 per calendar year. (However, Congress was considering increasing contribution limits for individuals as part of the 2001 effort to overhaul campaign finance law.) *(See Table 5-1, this page; box, Campaign Finance Overhaul Legislation, p. 124.)*

Direct contributions by individuals to House and Senate campaigns in the 1999–2000 election cycle amounted to $567.7 million, or about 54 percent of their total receipts. When broken down by chamber, individual contributions accounted for nearly 58 percent ($252.1 million) of Senate candidates' receipts and nearly 52 percent ($315.6 million) of House candidates' receipts.

FEC figures for all House and Senate candidates in 1999–2000 indicated that the gifts came in all sizes. Nearly 30 percent were for less than $200 and 44 percent were for $750 or more.

Individual donors' reasons for giving are varied, as political scientist Paul Herrnson pointed out in a study of House races. They may give simply because they want to see a change in Congress. They may want access to influential incumbent members or they may like hobnobbing with political elites. They may want to support those with whom they share a common ethnic, racial, or religious bond.[34]

Although rarely used by individuals in congressional elections, an "independent expenditure" is another avenue for affecting elections. This is an expenditure for communications advocating the election or defeat of a candidate that is made without the knowledge or cooperation of the candidate or the candidate's campaign organization. Congress had placed a limit on such expenditures in the 1974 FECA amendments but it, along with most other limits, was thrown out by the Supreme Court in 1976 as a violation of First Amendment rights. PACs and political parties have used independent expenditures more than individual donors have, but a $1.1 million expenditure in 1984 by businessperson Michael Goland urging the defeat of Sen. Charles Percy, R-Ill.—reportedly because of his Middle East stance—highlighted the potential of such spending when Percy lost. Independent expenditures must be reported to the FEC when they exceed $250 per year.

Political Action Committees

PACs have been around for some time. The Congress of Industrial Organizations (CIO) founded the first modern PAC in 1943 when labor unions were barred from contributing directly. But their significance increased dramatically in the 1970s and 1980s. The number of registered PACs was 608 at the end of 1974, when the FEC first began its PAC count. It reached a high of 4,268 at the end of 1988 but had dropped to 3,907 by the end of 2000. Registration, however, does not necessarily imply that the PAC actually made contributions during an election cycle. More than half of the decline since 1988 was the result of the FEC's removal of inactive groups from its PAC list in 1997.

Direct Contributions. The more telling statistics on PAC growth are those on PAC giving. In the 1979–1980 election cycle, PACs contributed $55 million to congressional candidates; in the 1989–1990 election cycle, they reported contributions of nearly $150 million. And by 1999–2000 the total had reached more than $245 million, constituting almost 32 percent of House candidates' receipts but less than 12 percent of contributions to Senate candidates.

Why the explosive growth in PAC numbers and dollars? The answer can be found in part in the reform legislation of the 1970s. In 1971 Congress sanctioned the use of regular corporate and union funds to pay the overhead costs of PACs. Legislation in 1974 placed more stringent limits on individual contributions than on those of PACs. Most PACs, in fact, could give five times more than an individual contributor to a candidate—$5,000 versus $1,000. That same year Congress also lifted restrictions on the formation of PACs by government contractors.

PACs also tended to fill a void left by weakened political parties in the 1970s. "As citizen loyalties to political parties waned, as the party organizations weakened, and as the parties lost control of campaigns to the media and candidates, interest groups became the political organization of choice for many Americans concerned about specific (and even narrow) interests and issues," explained political scientist Frank J. Sorauf.[35]

Further impetus for growth came in 1975 when the FEC ruled that the Sun Oil Co. could establish a PAC and solicit contributions to SunPAC from stockholders and employees; the ruling eliminated the last barrier that had prevented corporations from forming PACs. FEC figures show that the number of corporate PACs jumped from 139 at the time of the SunPAC ruling in November 1975 to 433 by the end of 1976. PACs also reaped benefits from the Supreme Court's 1976 decision striking down restrictions on independent spending. *(See "1976 Amendments," p. 120.)*

Reaction to the rapid growth of PAC numbers and influence varied dramatically. Some saw it as a manifestation of democracy at work in a pluralist society, while others perceived it as a threat by special interests to the integrity of the electoral system and governmental process. *(See "PAC Phenomenon," p. 103.)*

But certain facts about PACs have been beyond dispute. For one thing, PACs have been overwhelmingly oriented toward incumbents. FEC figures showed that of the $245.4 million that congressional candidates in the 1999–2000 election cycle reported receiving from PACs, $184 million went to incumbents, while only about $27 million went to challengers and about $34.3 million to open-seat candidates.

While some critics contended that PACs were out to buy votes with their contributions, many observers believed that their aim was to buy access to members in positions to help—or hinder—their cause. An example of this could be seen in the jump in contributions business PACs made to Democratic incumbents in the House during the 1980s. This increase was attributed to the persuasive powers of California Rep. Tony Coelho, chairman of the Democratic Congressional Campaign Committee in the early 1980s, who was said to have convinced traditionally conservative PACs of the logic of having access to a sitting member of the House instead of wasting money on a challenger who was likely to lose.

Thus, pragmatism won out over ideology, as corporate PAC contributions to Democrats edged up to more than 50 percent. But with the Republican takeover of Congress in the mid-1990s, corporate PACs were able to return to old loyalties. "Their ideological brethren had taken control of Congress. At the same time, the newly powerful House Republicans launched an aggressive campaign to cajole the PACs into making up for their past indiscretions by cutting off the Democrats and giving as much money as possible to Republicans," wrote Larry Makinson of the Center for Responsive Politics, a nonpartisan research organization.[36]

In 1999–2000, corporate PACs gave more than twice as much to the Republicans as to the Democrats in both chambers—nearly $57 million to the GOP and about $27 million to the Democrats. Labor PACs, however, showed none of the corporate PACs' pragmatism. They were in the Democratic camp when the Democrats controlled Congress and they were in the Democratic camp when the GOP was in control. Of the $50.2 million labor PACs gave to congressional candidates in that same period, about $46 million went to Democrats.

Independent Expenditures. In addition to direct contributions to candidates, PACs also can make independent expenditures. According to a Library of Congress report, PACs made independent expenditures of $14.7 million for or against congressional candidates in the 2000 races. The amount was small when compared to overall PAC spending but the potential for larger expenditures did exist because there were no statutory limits on them. One often-cited example of the potency of carefully targeted independent expenditures occurred in 1980 when the National Conservative Political Action Committee (NCPAC) spent more than $1 million against six liberal Senate incumbents, four of whom were defeated. But independent spending did not become a major PAC tactic because, as Sorauf pointed out, these expenditures can earn more enmity than gratitude from candidates and do not produce the close political relationship with candidates that PACs are seeking.[37]

Leadership PACs. Although PACs are usually associated with interest groups outside Congress, a small but influential group of PACs called "leadership PACs"—also known as "personal PACs," "member PACs," or "politicians' PACs"—exists within Congress. These are separate PACs formed by members of Congress or other political leaders independent of their own campaign committees. They often are the PACs of presidential hopefuls, congressional leaders, or would-be leaders. "In almost all cases—and this is central to their role as brokers—sponsoring individuals are raising and giving money at least in part to support their own political careers, positions, or goals," Sorauf wrote.[38]

Leadership PACs offer several other advantages, according to former FEC Commissioner Trevor Potter. If they qualify as multicandidate committees, the PACs can accept $5,000 from individual donors. Since these PACs are considered to be separate from a candidate's campaign committee, the candidate can accept contributions from the same source twice—once for the campaign committee and once for the leadership PAC. These PACs also are increasingly being used as a source of funding for a member's travel or other political expenses.[39]

By the late 1990s, several dozen leadership PACs had set up soft money nonfederal accounts to assist state candidates and to cover certain operating expenses.

Assistance from Political Parties

Political parties traditionally have provided direct assistance to candidates in two ways: through contributions and through payments to vendors in a candidate's behalf. The latter, known as "coordinated expenditures," fund any number of campaign services such as polling, research, direct mailings, advertising, or buying TV time.

Party committees also persuade others to contribute. Convincing PACs, individuals, and incumbent House and Senate members to support a party's most competitive challengers and open-seat candidates has been one of the major tasks of the congressional campaign committees.[40] These congressional, or Hill, committees are the Democratic Senatorial Campaign Committee, National Republican Senatorial Committee, Democratic Congressional Campaign Committee, and the National Republican Congressional Committee.

Parties have found other ways to aid candidates, creating a great deal of controversy along the way. This type of assistance includes everything from get-out-the vote drives to so-called issue ads that stop just short of asking for a vote to independent expenditures in support of a party's candidates.

Direct Contributions, Coordinated Expenditures. National committees, which include the party's national committee as well as the House and Senate campaign committees, were each permitted to make contributions of $5,000 per candidate per election. That amounted to a total of $20,000 in combined party money for candidates' primary and general election races for the House, but for Senate candidates there was a $17,500 limit. State and local party committees could give a combined total of $5,000 per election.

Parties were also permitted to make coordinated expenditures

to benefit their House and Senate candidates. These expenditures were made only in general elections, and the amount the parties could spend on behalf of a candidate was set by formula. For House candidates in states with more than one member, the national party expenditure limit was set at $10,000, adjusted for inflation, which translated into a $33,780 limit in 2000. For House candidates in states with only one congressional district, the national parties could spend up to the limit for Senate candidates in those states, which in 2000 was $67,560. For Senate candidates, the party could spend the greater of either $20,000, adjusted for inflation—$67,560 in 2000—or two cents for every person of voting age in that state, again adjusted for inflation. According to this formula, coordinated expenditures for Senate candidates in 2000 ranged from the base figure of $67,560 in the less populous states to a high of $1,636,438 in California.

State party committees also were allowed to make coordinated expenditures in the same amounts as the national party. State parties, however, often did not have that kind of money, so the national party was permitted to use its money to make the expenditures on behalf of the state, in effect doubling its expenditure limit for a particular state or district.

A legal challenge to any limits on a political party's expenditures on behalf of its candidates was heard by the Supreme Court in early 2001. In June 2001 the Court by a narrow 5–4 vote ruled that strict limits on what political parties could spend in coordination with candidates were constitutional. *(See "Coordinated Expenditures," p. 106.)*

The Republican Party has proven itself over the years to be the more successful fund-raiser of the two parties. GOP fundraising prowess certainly could be expected when it was the majority party in Congress, but Herrnson found that some of their advantage was more permanent, including a superior direct-mail fund-raising list and a wealthier constituency.[41]

In the 1999–2000 election cycle, national, state, and local Republican Party committees reported federal (hard dollar) receipts of $465.8 million and expenditures of $427 million. Of this, they contributed $2.3 million directly to congressional candidates and made coordinated expenditures of $15.2 million. Democrats raised a total of $275.2 million in hard dollars and spent $265.8 million. They contributed about $1.3 million to congressional candidates and spent almost $8.5 million in their behalf. The bulk of the hard dollars the political parties raise goes for party-building, electoral, and fund-raising activities.

While direct contributions and expenditures by the parties constitute a comparatively small percentage of the overall receipts of candidates, parties help candidates in other ways.

Soft Money. Although legislation to change the system was being considered by Congress, parties as of mid-2001 could raise unlimited amounts of so-called soft money—essentially unregulated money—from unions, corporations, trade associations, and individuals. Although this money was barred from federal races, spending for carefully targeted voter drives at the state and local levels or for potent issue ads could have a decisive effect on federal races. Plus, any party expenses that could be paid for with soft money freed up more hard dollars for the congressional campaigns.

Figure 5-1   National Party Soft Money Receipts

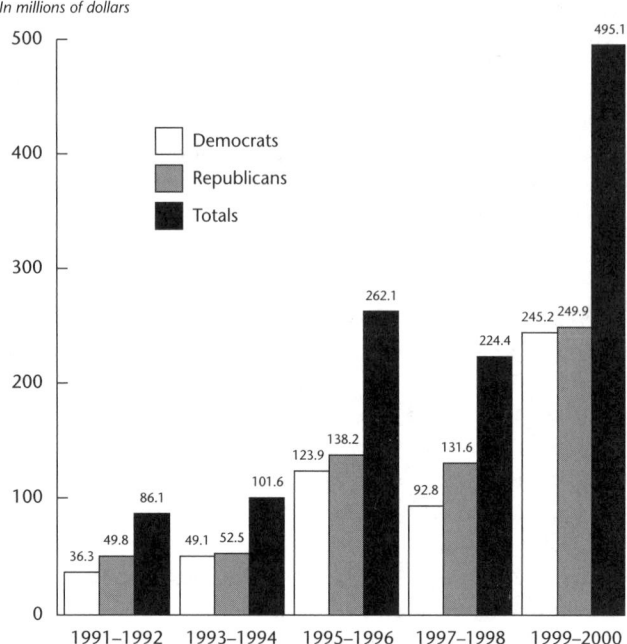

In millions of dollars

Source: Federal Election Commission.

During the 1999–2000 election cycle, Republican national party committees raised $249.9 million in soft money, an 81 percent increase over 1995–1996, the last presidential cycle. Democrats collected $245.2 million, a 98 percent increase. Soft money represented 35 percent of the Republican Party's fund-raising and 47 percent of the Democratic Party's. *(See Figure 5-1, p. 98.)*

Independent Expenditures. After the Supreme Court ruled in 1996 that political parties could make independent expenditures on behalf of their candidates, the Republican Party jumped right in, making $10 million in independent expenditures in the 1996 election campaign. Democrats spent $1.5 million. GOP independent expenditures dropped off significantly in the 1998 midterm election campaign—less than $264,000 was reported. Democrats again spent $1.5 million. In the 2000 congressional elections, Republicans reported spending $1.6 million and Democrats, $2.3 million.

Other Assistance. Political parties like to act as conduits, passing contributions through their committees to candidates. Thanks to sophisticated computers and mass mailings, a party can target those who might be interested in a race and encourage them to contribute. Through a practice called "earmarking," a contributor can direct money to a candidate or committee through an intermediary, such as the party. The money counts against the donor's contribution limit for the recipient candidate. If the party directs or controls who the recipient will be, it will count against the party limit as well. The party must report to the FEC any earmarked contributions it receives and forwards.

Candidate's Own Money

Another source of money for congressional campaigns is the candidate's own bank account. Candidates can reach as deeply

into their own pockets as they want because there are no limits on how much they may contribute or loan to their own campaigns. Deep personal pockets are not only welcomed by the parties but are sometimes even expected. Political scientists David Magleby and Candice Nelson wrote in 1990 that the political parties may expect challengers and open-seat candidates to give or loan their campaigns $25,000 or more in House races and even more for Senate campaigns.[42]

Candidates usually opt to loan the money to their campaigns in the hope that, if they win, they may be able to get some of it back from fund-raising after the election.

In 1974 Congress attempted to set limits on how much House and Senate candidates could contribute to their own campaigns, but before the limits could take effect they were ruled unconstitutional by the Supreme Court in the 1976 *Buckley* decision. The Court ruled that "the candidate, no less than any other person, has a First Amendment right to engage in the discussion of public issues and vigorously and tirelessly to advocate his own election."

In keeping with the law's intent to clean up campaign finance activities, the justices also wrote that "the use of personal funds reduces the candidate's dependence on outside contributions and thereby counteracts the coercive pressure and attendant risks of abuse to which the act's contribution limitations are directed."

Most political observers agreed that the Court had given wealthy contenders a tremendous advantage. Simply having access to money and a willingness to pour a lot of it into a campaign does not guarantee victory in November—or even in a primary. But wealthy candidates can afford expensive, professional consultants and plan their strategy with greater assurance than candidates without a personal fortune.

And money enables the wealthy, but unknown, candidate to make the first splash in a crowded field of relatively obscure contenders for an open seat in Congress. While dozens of potential candidates may jockey for position, the one who can begin a campaign with an early television blitz is likely to start several lengths ahead.

Television stations require campaigns to pay their bills before any material is aired. For this reason, candidates who have the ability to loan or contribute a sizable sum can purchase expensive television advertising whenever they want. Those who are less well-off financially are forced to wait until the money comes in before beginning their media buy.

As the campaign progresses, especially after the primary, the advantage of personal wealth diminishes. Candidates without a personal fortune then have greater access to other sources of money, particularly from party coffers; the field is smaller, making it easier for voters to draw clear distinctions between the candidates; and more free publicity is available as the general election draws nearer. There are many cases where a rich candidate was able to clear out the primary field but then lost in the general election.

While candidates' ability to bankroll a large portion of their own campaigns has many advantages, it also has several clear disadvantages. The most obvious and frequently encountered is that it opens self-financed candidates to charges that they are trying to "buy" the election. Sometimes the opposition levels the charge; often the media raise it.

Another disadvantage is that outside money is harder to raise. Potential contributors often assume the rich candidates do not need their money. In some cases that may be true. But from a political standpoint, a healthy list of contributors can give a campaign more credibility by indicating that the candidate, besides having a fat war chest, has a broad base of support.

FEC figures for the 1999–2000 election cycle showed that congressional candidates loaned themselves $150.9 million—$89 million in the Senate and $61.9 million in the House. Candidates contributed $25 million to their campaigns—nearly $18.7 million in the Senate and $6.3 million in the House.

The largest user of personal money in the 2000 elections was Democrat Jon S. Corzine of New Jersey, a Wall Street businessperson who loaned his successful Senate campaign $60.2 million. Corzine's generosity to his campaign easily surpassed the previous record set by Michael Huffington, a first-term Republican House member who spent $28.3 million of his own money—$16.3 million in contributions and $12 million in loans—in his 1994 campaign to unseat Democratic Sen. Dianne Feinstein of California. Huffington lost the race by a margin of only 2 percent.

As part of the 2001 effort to rewrite campaign finance laws, Congress was considering raising the federal limits on contributions from individuals and PACs to a candidate who faced a self-financed opponent. *(See box, Campaign Finance Overhaul Legislation, p. 124.)*

CONGRESSIONAL CANDIDATES' EXPENDITURES

Congressional candidates spent about $1 billion in the 1999–2000 election cycle, about $265 million more than during the 1997–1998 election cycle. House and Senate incumbents together spent a total of $457.2 million, while challengers spent nearly $225 million and open-seat candidates, $324.8 million. Incumbents reported a more than $138 million cash surplus—proof that they had plenty of firepower to summon had they felt the need. Their opponents reported less than $4 million on hand.

Figures for Senate candidates showed total expenditures of $434.7 million. Incumbents spent $130.2 million; challengers, $99.3 million; and open-seat candidates, $205.1 million. House candidates spent $572.3 million, with incumbents spending nearly $327 million; challengers, $125.6 million; and open-seat candidates, $119.7 million.

How money is spent varies from one campaign to another. The needs of a House candidate are different from those of a Senate candidate. The needs of a challenger are different from those of an incumbent. A Senate candidate in a large state runs a different campaign than a candidate in a small state. Representatives of urban, suburban, and rural congressional districts run vastly different campaigns. Costs skyrocket in hotly contested races and are negligible in races with little or no opposition.

But some generalizations may be made. Campaigns have to pay for staff and rent. They hire consultants, media experts, and polling firms. They send out computerized mailings. They buy postage, buttons, bumper stickers, billboards, newspaper ads, radio spots, and television time—lots of television time.

Television Costs

Television advertising plays a significant role in campaigns. For many candidates, being on or off the air can determine the outcome of the election. "The hard fact of life for a candidate is that if you are not on TV, you are not truly in the race," Sen. Ernest F. Hollings, D-S.C., told a congressional committee in 1990.[43]

And it is costly. "You simply transfer money from contributors to television stations," summed up Sen. Bill Bradley, D-N.J., in 1991.[44]

The Congressional Research Service (CRS), in a 1997 report on proposals to give candidates free or reduced-rate television time, found electronic media advertising to be the single largest category of aggregate Senate and House campaign expenditures. (This category included radio and TV airtime, production costs, and consultant fees.) Studies of the 1990, 1992, and 1994 elections cited by CRS found these costs consumed about 27 percent of campaign budgets in House races and about 40–45 percent in Senate races. The percentages went up for more competitive races and in Senate races in larger states, as well as for challengers and open seat contenders.[45]

Although television has been an important tool in House campaigns, it has not been consistently so. For example, Sara Fritz and Dwight Morris in a *Los Angeles Times* study found that in the 1990 campaign more than a quarter of House incumbents reported spending no money on broadcast advertising.[46] In urban centers such as Los Angeles, New York, and Chicago, it was not seen as cost effective. An assistant to Rep. Howard L. Berman, D-Calif., who represented the San Fernando Valley suburbs of Los Angeles, explained:

You spend thousands for one thirty-second spot on one TV station, in a city where cable is rampant and there are a zillion channels. There are sixteen to seventeen congressional districts in L.A., so the vast majority of those who see it are not your constituents and can't vote for you anyway.[47]

In rural areas and in the Southwest, however, costs can be dramatically lower. Herrnson noted that in 1998 a thirty-second prime-time ad would have cost $35,000 in a New York City congressional district but only $1,200 in Texas's eleventh district.[48]

Other Costs

Congressional candidates face a variety of other costs in their pursuit of a seat in the House or Senate. As with media costs, there are many variables. Incumbents, challengers, and open-seat candidates will allocate funds differently, depending on the competitiveness of the race, the size of their constituency, and, of course, their resources.

In a study of the 1992 races, Dwight Morris and Murielle E. Gamache found that House incumbents on average spent about 25 percent of their money on overhead, which included everything from rent, office furniture, telephones and computers to salaries, taxes, travel and food. About 15 percent was spent on fund-raising (events, direct mail, and telemarketing); 4 percent on polling; 27 percent on electronic and other advertising; 20 percent on other campaign activity (voter contact mail, actual campaigning, and food, gifts, etc., for staff and volunteers); 5 percent on donations (to other candidates, political parties, and civic organizations); and 4 percent on miscellaneous gifts and expenses. Senate incumbents reported about 25 percent on overhead, 21 percent on fund-raising, 3 percent on polling, 41 percent on advertising, 8 percent on other campaign activities, 1 percent on donations, and 2 percent on miscellaneous items.[49]

Record Spending

Another CRS study found that average Senate campaign costs went from $595,000 to $3.3 million between 1976 and 1996. This represented a 459 percent increase. When adjusted for inflation, the average rose by 102 percent and actually declined in five elections.

The CRS study also gave statistics on just the winning candidates. For Senate winners, average spending rose from $609,000 to $3.8 million during the twenty-year period. And, according to another CRS report, by 2000 an average winning Senate race cost $7 million.[50]

Until 2000 the most expensive Senate race on record had been the 1994 California race between Feinstein and Huffington. Together they spent about $44.4 million. But that record was shattered in 2000 by the New York Senate race. First Lady Hillary Rodham Clinton, the Democratic candidate, and her Republican opponent, Rep. Rick A. Lazio, together spent about $70.5 million. (The total included money Lazio spent on his House campaign before he began his run for the Senate.) New York Mayor Rudolph W. Giuliani, who Lazio replaced as the GOP candidate, reported spending $20.8 million before dropping out of the Senate race.[51]

The CRS study found average spending by House candidates rose from $73,000 in 1976 to $493,000 in 1996, a 575 percent increase. When adjusted for inflation the average rose by 143 percent and declined three out of ten times. The average House winner spent $680,000 in 1996, a 682 percent rise from the $87,000 in 1976. By 2000, that average had risen to $816,000.[52]

The most expensive House race on record through 2000 was the race in California's Twenty-seventh district that year. Incumbent Republican Rep. James E. Rogan spent nearly $6.9 million, while his Democratic opponent Adam Schiff spent nearly $4.4 million. Rogan was among just a handful of incumbents who lost their seats. Prior to 2000 the most costly House contest had been waged in 1998 between Newt Gingrich, the Republican Speaker of the House, and his Democratic challenger, Gary Pelphrey, who spent a combined $7.6 million. Of that total, Pelphrey spent $11,232 and Gingrich spent the rest![53] But apparently much of Gingrich's money was not spent to defeat Pelphrey. A study by the Center for Responsive Politics of the first fifteen months of the election cycle found that Gingrich had spent $3.7 million by that point, even though he did not yet have a registered opponent and that the "bulk of Gingrich's expenditures supported a direct-mail fund-raising operation, a costly technique used primarily to develop a wider base, especially useful for candidates contemplating a presidential run."[54]

Moreover, Gingrich used a sizable portion of his campaign funds to assist other candidates and committees. For example, his reports to the FEC indicated a "transfer of excess funds" in the amount of $500,000 to the National Republican Campaign Committee in October 1998 and of $100,000 to his personal PAC in November 1998.

Campaign Finance Issues and Proposals

Debates on campaign finance proposals after the 1970s highlighted the vastly different views people held on the system and on what, if anything, needed fixing. Democrats and Republicans took opposing views on issue after issue, with many votes in Congress routinely dividing along partisan lines. Some proposals were favored by one chamber but not the other or by Congress but not the White House.

Despite the lack of consensus, there were some issues that repeatedly surfaced.

CONTROVERSIES

For many, there were certain basic problems in the campaign finance system. One was the high cost of running for office. That in turn led to another problem: the incessant search for contributions to pay the bills, a problem that had both personal and institutional ramifications.

The relentless search for money would then spawn other controversies. For a time, PACs were seen by many reformers as the villains. Others saw the fund-raising advantage of incumbents as a nearly insurmountable obstacle for congressional challengers.

But by the 1990s new campaign finance controversies had erupted and the targets for reform changed. Soft money contributions and issue advocacy ads were seen by many as major loopholes in the system. Also troubling to many reformers were independent expenditures, especially by the political parties, and the practice of an intermediary pulling together, or "bundling," political contributions to a candidate from a number of donors. Secrecy surrounding the political activities of some unregulated groups galvanized new reform efforts in 2000.

Campaigns' High Costs

"Politics has got so expensive that it takes lots of money to even get beat with," humorist Will Rogers remarked in 1931.[55] If it was true then, it is much more so today.

And for some that cost is too high. These people see "[t]he high cost of elections and the perception that they are 'bought and sold' . . . as contributing to public cynicism about the political process," observed CRS analyst Joseph E. Cantor. Others have raised concerns that the cost of running for office has given wealthy candidates the advantage over others of more modest means and that it may have fueled reliance on more sophisticated—often negative—media advertising. But on the other side of the issue, Cantor pointed out, are those who say that the expenditures are not too high—maybe not even high enough—when compared to overall government spending or commercial advertising. For example, "the nation's two leading commercial advertisers, Proctor and Gamble and General Motors, spent more in promoting their products in 1996 ($5 billion) than was spent on all U.S. elections."[56]

Herbert Alexander estimated the total for all U.S. campaign spending in 1996 at $4.2 billion. The price tag for federal campaigns was $2.8 billion, $500 million more than in 1992.

Several factors have contributed to the spiraling costs of campaigns. The most obvious cause has been inflation. As the costs of other goods and services in the economy have inflated, so too have those of campaigns.

But even when inflation is accounted for, the cost of campaigns has increased dramatically in recent decades. A key reason has been the rise in the cost of fund-raising and of educating the electorate.

Since the 1960s, campaigns have undergone tremendous change. Most have been transformed from the volunteers-stuffing-envelopes-and-canvassing-voters type of campaign to highly technical, mechanized campaigns that are likely to use computerized mass mailings and Internet web sites to solicit contributions and thirty-second TV ads to get their message across to voters. Candidates hire political consultants to direct their campaigns and polling companies to tell them how they are doing. All of the high-tech trappings of modern campaigns cost money—big money.

Population growth affects campaigns—as the electorate expands so too does the cost of reaching voters. With the U.S. population going from 203,302,031 in 1970 to 281,421,906 in 2000, the population of a congressional district, on average, went from 467,000 to 647,000.

House candidates' campaign costs are also affected by the demographics of districts. Candidates in urban, suburban, or rural districts run very different campaigns with very different price tags. TV ads may not be cost-effective in an urban district, but they may be the only way a rural candidate can reach far-flung constituents.

The proliferation of media outlets has increased the cost as well. People are listening to or watching many more stations than they used to, so to reach them, campaigns have to spread their ads around.

The level of competition in a campaign also affects spending. A crowded field of candidates seeking their party's presidential nomination will generate greater spending than uncontested races. The same is true for congressional candidates. Costs stay down if an incumbent has little or no opposition, but they rise sharply if an electoral threat appears. This is also true of contests for open congressional seats, which frequently are the most competitive races. In open-seat races, explained political scientist Gary Jacobson, "neither candidate enjoys the benefits of incumbency, both parties normally field strong candidates, and the election is usually close." Senate races also tend to attract money, according to Jacobson, because incumbent senators are often perceived as vulnerable, most of their challengers are well-known public figures, and elections to the 100-member Senate have a greater political impact than do those to the 435-member House.[57]

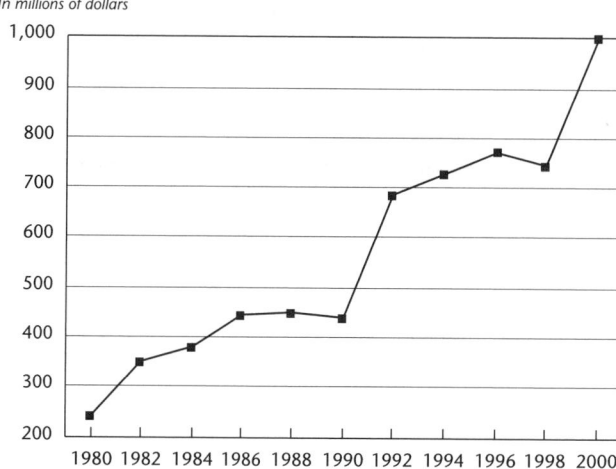

Figure 5-2 Congressional Campaign Spending by Election Year

In millions of dollars

Source: Federal Election Commission.

Some observers believe that so much money is raised in campaigns because so much money is available. But candidates have reasons to raise as much money as they can. One of these is "deterrence." Front-runners and incumbents want to use their campaign "war chests" to scare off potential opponents. And if deterrence does not work, they want to be ready for any surprises their opponents may come up with.

Incumbents also feel more secure with sizable reserves in the bank. Bill Clinton felt vulnerable in the wake of the GOP takeover of Congress after the 1994 election. To ensure that he would not be a one-term president, the Democratic Party raised record amounts of soft money to use on issue ads. Similarly, congressional incumbents like the security of deep reserves. They want to be ready in case a millionaire opponent decides to run against them. They want to be able to counter negative issue ads or independent expenditures. House members may anticipate a tough challenge because of an upcoming redistricting. Others stockpile money in case they decide to run for higher office, such as a House member running for the Senate or a senator running for the presidency.

Quest for Money

By many accounts, one of the most onerous tasks a politician faces is fund-raising.

The public funding system was aimed in part at relieving presidential candidates of this burden. However, candidates still must raise a certain amount in order to qualify for matching funds during the presidential primaries. Moreover, even though presidential campaigns are publicly funded, the candidates still play a major role in their parties' fund-raising activities.

In congressional races, fund-raising "takes a toll of the time, energy, and attention of legislators," according to Sorauf. "It is a task that tires even the most enthusiastic fund-raisers, and it depresses those incumbents who find it distasteful."[58]

Facing reelection contests every two years, members of the House are essentially campaigning and fund-raising all the

"WHEN—IT'S OVER! TOMORROW WE START RAISING MONEY FOR THE NEXT ELECTION"

time. One election campaign runs into the next. And even in the Senate, where the six-year term was once considered a luxury, members are beginning their campaigns earlier and earlier. Races with multimillion dollar price tags require increased attention to fund-raising.

For some that price is too high. When Democratic Sen. Frank R. Lautenberg of New Jersey announced that he would not seek a fourth term in the Senate in 2000, he said that a powerful factor in his decision was "the searing reality" that he would have had to spend half of every day between his mid-February 1999 announcement and the November 2000 election fund-raising. He explained:

To run an effective campaign, I would have to ask literally thousands of people for money. I would have had to raise $125,000 a week, or $25,000 every working day. That's about $3,000 an hour—more than lots of people earn in a month—distracted from the job I was hired to do.[59]

And more than a few find the task demeaning as well. At one Democratic Party training session, candidates were offered the following advice: "Learn how to beg, and do it in a way that leaves you some dignity."[60] That may be easier said than done, as Sen. Tom Daschle, D-S.D., found during his successful 1986 campaign to unseat an incumbent senator: "You're with people you have nothing in common with. You have a cosmetic conversation. You paint the best face you can on their issues and feel uncomfortable through the whole thing. You sheepishly accept their check and leave feeling not very good."[61]

At least he left with the check, which is more than can be said for many challengers. Attempting to unseat a sitting member of Congress is an enormously difficult task for a number of reasons, not the least of which is the obstacle of having to bankroll a campaign. Rep. David E. Price, D-N.C., a political scientist who ran successfully against an incumbent in 1986, said that he had undertaken few ventures as difficult and discouraging as raising money for his primary campaign. He held small fund-raisers, sent mail appeals to party activists, and approached potential large contributors, with mixed success. He and his wife contacted people on their old Christmas card lists, as well as professional colleagues and family members. They took out a second mortgage on their home. Price won the primary but still found fund-raising for the general election a continuing struggle. He later reflected on his campaign:

I will . . . never forget how difficult it was to raise the first dollars. I understand quite well why many potentially strong challengers and potentially able representatives simply cannot or will not do what it takes to establish financial "viability" and why so many who do reach that point can do so only on the basis of personal wealth. The modus operandi of most large contributors, PACs, and even party committees often makes their calculations of an incumbent's "safety" a self-fulfilling prophecy.[62]

The difficulties that surround fund-raising have institutional, as well as personal, consequences. For one thing, the time members of Congress spend raising money is time away from the business of legislating. Sen. Robert Byrd, D-W.Va., said that one of his biggest problems when he served as Senate majority leader was accommodating the senators' need for time away from the floor to raise money for their campaigns. "They have to go raise the money and they don't want any roll-call votes," Byrd lamented. "Now how can a majority leader run the Senate under such circumstances?" To Byrd the culprit was clear: "Mad, seemingly limitless escalation of campaign costs."[63] Byrd ended up revamping the Senate's work schedule in 1988 to give members time off to campaign and attend fund-raisers.

As Rep. Price indicated, there is another institutional consequence: the high cost of elections discourages people from running for Congress. "Potential challengers or candidates for open seats realize that unless they can raise a lot of money, they have little chance of winning," wrote Magleby and Nelson. As a result, party committees have found "it is increasingly hard to convince people to run, given the low probability of success and the high investment of time and money necessary to even hope to be competitive."[64]

Incumbent Advantage

Incumbency offers some distinct advantages, as sitting presidents and members of Congress routinely demonstrate.

As the incumbent president in the 1996 election, Clinton had no real opposition during the primary season and therefore could devote money for his primary campaign to efforts that would help him win in the November general election. GOP nominee Dole, on the other hand, exhausted his primary campaign budget winning his party's nomination. In the 2000 race, when there was no incumbent, both the Democratic and Republican front-runners faced surprisingly strong competition during the primary season and had to spend accordingly. Incumbency provides no assurances of a victory in the general election campaign for the White House, as the defeats of Presidents Gerald R. Ford, Jimmy Carter, and George Bush proved in the last few decades of the twentieth century.

The same is not true when it comes to running for reelection to Congress. Voters in 2000 returned congressional incumbents to Washington en masse, as they pretty much had been doing for years. Of the 403 House incumbents who sought reelection in 2000, 395 won—a 98 percent reelection rate. The last time the reelection rate in the House had dipped below 90 percent was in 1992 and the time before that was in 1974. On the Senate side the reelection rates have been much more erratic. In the 2000 election, twenty-three of twenty-nine incumbents seeking reelection won, which put the reelection rate at 79 percent. *(See Figure 5-3, this page.)*

This very decided advantage of congressional incumbents at the polls has produced much study and speculation. According to Roger H. Davidson and Walter J. Oleszek, political scientists have launched "a veritable cottage industry" to answer the question of why incumbents are so formidable.[65]

Several reasons can be cited. Incumbents have name recognition. They have a public record to run on, which can be especially helpful if they can demonstrate they have voted to protect the interests of their constituents and have brought home federal grants and projects. Incumbents are highly visible because of easy and regular access to the media.

A real plus for incumbents is that they continue to receive their salary throughout the campaign. Many challengers are not so lucky. Candidates are not permitted to pay themselves a salary from their campaign account. The prospect of doing without a salary while campaigning full-time for a year or more probably has deterred many a potential candidate from running.

Moreover, incumbents enjoy a number of perquisites, the most important being large staffs on Capitol Hill and in state or district offices ready to respond to the needs and inquiries of constituents. Thanks to the franking privilege, most letters and newsletters to constituents can be mailed free of charge, although there are restrictions aimed at curtailing blatant use of the privilege for political purposes or just before an election. Members also benefit from allowances for phone calls and for travel back to their home district or state.

Incumbents also enjoy a distinct advantage in raising money for their reelection campaigns. FEC figures showed that House incumbents had a fund-raising advantage over challengers of almost three to one in 1999–2000. Incumbents raised $361.9 million, compared with $127.4 million raised by challengers. And incumbents clearly had more to spend—altogether, they reported $118 million in cash on hand at the end of the election year.

The advantage of incumbents in the Senate was not nearly as great. Senate incumbents raised $130.6 million, while challengers raised about $99.7 million. Incumbents finished the campaign year with a combined reserve of just over $20 million.

Both individual donors and PACs favored incumbents over challengers in the 2000 campaigns. About 47 percent of all indi-

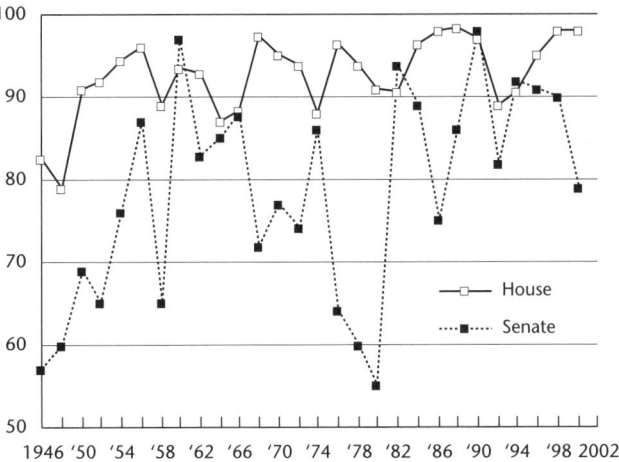

Figure 5-3   Incumbent Advantage in Reelection, 1946–2000

Winning percentages of those seeking reelection

Sources: Norman J. Ornstein, Thomas E. Mann, and Michael J. Malbin, *Vital Statistics on Congress,* 1997–1998 (Washington, D.C.: Congressional Quarterly, 1988), 61, 62; *CQ Weekly.*

vidual contributions went to incumbents and only 22 percent to challengers. The rest went to open-seat races. The percentage was much higher for PAC contributions—about 75 percent went to incumbents. When just the receipts of incumbents and challengers are counted—and not those of open-seat candidates—the incumbent advantage is even more pronounced: nearly 68 percent of individual contributions and 87 percent of PAC contributions went to incumbents.

Over the years the implications of the tilt toward incumbents have preoccupied members, reformers, and observers of Congress alike. Some warned of a trend toward a "permanent Congress" with little turnover, and they deplored PACs "buying" access to members of Congress. But others dismissed the notion and framed these contributions in a more positive light—contributors wanted to go with a winner, and most incumbents were seen as sure bets.

Fears of incumbents' advantage were allayed in the 1990s when an anti-incumbent sentiment, redistricting, and the 1995 GOP takeover of both houses of Congress for the first time in forty years ushered in a new generation of lawmakers. Indeed, the turnover was so great that by the start of 2001 almost two-thirds of the House—65 percent—had first been elected in 1992 or later. On the Senate side, forty-five senators had been in that chamber for six years or less, a figure not matched since 1981.

PAC Phenomenon

The rapid growth in the 1970s and 1980s of PAC money and influence in the electoral process generated a great deal of controversy. Defenders of PACs insisted they were an outgrowth of a democratic society. "PACs are both natural and inevitable in a free, pluralist democracy," political scientist Larry J. Sabato wrote. "In fact, the vibrancy and health of a democracy depend in good part on the flourishing of interest groups and associations among its citizenry." [66]

But critics branded PACs as a source of tainted money because their giving often was tied to specific legislation, to a leadership position, to membership on a certain committee, or to the mere fact of incumbency. Wertheimer voiced Common Cause's view before the Senate Rules Committee in 1989: "It is increasingly clear that PAC participation represents a threat to the public trust in the integrity of our electoral and congressional decision-making processes."[67]

One member of Congress who renounced PAC contributions said he thought PACs symbolized why voters had become alienated from politics. "People feel like it's big money, big business, big labor, the lobbyists who are represented, that little by little the playing field has been tilted," Romano L. Mazzoli, D-Ky., stated in 1990.[68]

However, a fellow Democrat in the House held the opposite view. In an opinion piece in the *Washington Post* in 1994, John Lewis, D-Ga., argued that PACs "give working people and people with little means the ability to participate in the political process." He went on: "Many of these people who contribute through a 'checkoff,' or small deduction from their paycheck each week, would effectively be denied participation in the process if it weren't for their union or company PAC."[69]

PACs became a dominant issue in campaign finance debates. But the question of what to do, if anything, about them was a particularly divisive one between the parties and the chambers. Democrats were more dependent on PAC contributions than were Republicans, and House members relied on them more than senators. Those who wanted to curb PAC influence put forward proposals ranging from banning them completely to limiting how much PACs could give or candidates could receive from PACs.

But the urgency to do something about PACs diminished, as their numbers leveled off and other controversies began to overshadow them. "The PAC issue has been greatly supplanted by more fundamental issues of election regulation, with observers finding new appreciation for the limited, disclosed nature of PAC funds," wrote Cantor.[70]

Bundling of Contributions

Bundling refers to an intermediary pulling together contributions to a certain candidate from a number of individual donors and passing those checks on in a "bundle" to the candidate. (The checks could also be sent separately, but it still would be obvious who had instigated the flow.) The intermediary earns the gratitude of the candidate without having the money count against its own contribution limits. Bundling can be done by an individual, PAC, or political party committee.

For bundling to be legal, however, the original donors must retain control over designation of the eventual recipient. The entity that bundles the checks does not have to report its role to the FEC.

Critics argue that, because there are no limits on the overall amount a conduit group may collect and pass on to a candidate, bundling essentially allows the group to circumvent election law. But bundlers say they are simply matching donors with like-minded candidates.

The Council for a Livable World, a nuclear arms control lobbying group, first bundled checks in 1962, sending contributions to an obscure Democratic Senate candidate from South Dakota named George McGovern. But it was EMILY's List, which backed Democratic women candidates who favored abortion rights, that perfected the practice. In addition to its regular PAC contributions, EMILY's List required its members to contribute a minimum of $100 to at least two candidates endorsed by the group.

EMILY's List was something of an exception. In most cases, according to Sorauf, bundlers and the interests they represented were not publicly known. In a discussion of PAC bundling, Sorauf wrote: "Virtually all the important information that PACs must and do disclose to the FEC is lost if organized giving is simply bundled instead."[71]

Soft Money

Campaign finance laws adopted at various points in the twentieth century barred corporations and unions from contributing to federal campaigns, and set an annual ceiling of $25,000 on an individual's aggregate contributions to federal candidates and the national party committees. The laws, however, did not prevent these entities from giving "soft" money—unlimited and largely unregulated contributions to political party committees for activities ostensibly unrelated to federal candidates. It was called "soft" to distinguish it from the tightly regulated "hard" dollars (money that was "hard" to raise within the limitations) that could go straight to parties, PACs, and candidates for direct use in federal campaigns.

Soft money donations skyrocketed in the 1990s, as did the controversy surrounding them. For some, soft money represented a return to the Watergate era when fat cat contributors won special access with six-figure donations. But party officials lauded the contributions, saying they kept party organizations relevant and strong.

Ironically, soft money was an outgrowth of the tough post-Watergate reforms that sought to clamp down on flagrant campaign finance abuses. The 1974 Federal Election Campaign Act (FECA) set limits on contributions and introduced some public financing of presidential elections. But the new law was so strict that candidates, party committees, and even academics joined in protest following the 1976 election cycle, arguing that the new rules were stifling volunteer and grassroots party activity. For example, bumper stickers, lawn signs, and the like were considered in-kind contributions to the candidates. Also, public financing of presidential campaigns had brought with it restrictions on spending and tight limits on additional fund-raising by parties and campaign committees. The campaigns opted to spend their resources on advertising rather than local party activities. Party leaders complained that the new law had almost completely eliminated state and local party organizations from presidential campaigns.

Responding to those complaints, the FEC issued a controversial ruling in 1978 allowing a state party to use money that was not permitted under federal campaign finance law—in this case, corporate and labor contributions—to pay for a portion of

CH. 5 CAMPAIGN FINANCE 105

grassroots and generic party activities, even if they indirectly aided federal candidates. Previously, the FEC had allowed the use of nonfederal money to pay a portion of a party's overhead and administrative costs but had barred the use of such money to pay for any portion of get-out-the-vote or voter registration activities because of their indirect effect on federal races.

FEC Commissioner Thomas E. Harris issued a sharp dissent to the agency's 1978 ruling, arguing that it would allow the use of corporate and union money to pay most of the costs of voter drives because there usually were more state and local elections than federal races in a state. "His point was not lost on party leaders, who quickly began to adapt their financial strategies to take advantage of the new opportunities inherent in the FEC's decision," political scientist Anthony Corrado observed. Because the national parties also were involved in state and local election activities, it was assumed that they too could use money not permitted under the FECA for certain expenses as long as they kept this nonfederal money in a separate account.[72]

And then in 1979 Congress approved amendments to the FECA allowing state and local parties to spend as much as they wanted on campaign materials for volunteer activities to promote any federal candidate. Such items included buttons, bumper stickers, handbills, brochures, posters, and yard signs. Also, those party organizations were allowed to conduct, without financial limit, certain kinds of voter registration and get-out-the-vote drives on behalf of presidential tickets.

The 1978 FEC ruling and the 1979 amendments gave rise to the soft money phenomenon. The FEC had sanctioned the use of both federal and nonfederal money for election activities as long as it was kept in separate accounts and the 1979 law allowed state parties to spend unlimited amounts of hard dollars for activities that would aid their entire slate of candidates, including federal candidates. With traditional funding sources restricted by the FECA contribution limits, there was a strong incentive for parties to find other sources of money so they could take advantage of the new avenues opened to them.

Republicans were faster to seize on soft money's possibilities in the 1980 presidential campaign, but Democrats quickly caught up and resisted early calls to abolish the practice. The rapid growth of soft money led Common Cause to sue the FEC to force it to tighten its regulations. In a partial victory, a federal judge ordered the agency to amend its rules; one of the effects of the new rules was to make national party soft money reportable. Previously disclosures of soft money had been largely voluntary; however, at the beginning of 1991, regulations went into effect requiring that the money be reported to the FEC and the reports be made available to the public.

In the 1992 election cycle, the first in which soft money had to be reported, the national party committees reported soft money receipts of $86 million—$49.8 million went to the Republicans and $36.3 million to the Democrats. By the 1996 cycle, the parties were aggressively seeking soft money and managed to raise $262 million—$138.2 million went to the GOP and $123.9 million to the Democrats. Moreover, they had found an important new use for it: television issue advocacy advertising. "To a certain extent, there was only so much money you could

spend on get-out-the-vote," explained Corrado. "But once you started moving to advertising, the demand for soft money rose dramatically."[73]

The parties' pursuit of soft money played a key role in the scandal that erupted in the 1996 presidential election. It was the most significant campaign finance scandal since Watergate. (See "1996 Scandal," p. 84.)

Despite the scandal and resulting embarrassment, the parties' appetite for soft money continued unabated. In fact, soft money, which previously had been largely a phenomenon of presidential politics, became a major factor in congressional politics as well. One study found the growth in party soft money activity, including party issue advocacy, to be "the most important money and politics development in the 1998 congressional elections."[74]

Democratic Party committees—the national committee and congressional campaign committees—raised $92.8 million in the 1997–1998 election cycle compared with $49.1 million in the last midterm election in 1994, while Republicans raised $131.6 million compared with $52.5 million in 1994. And the numbers jumped again in the 1999–2000 election cycle when the Democrats' national party committees had soft money receipts of $245.2 million and the Republicans, $249.9 million.

The booming soft money business on Capitol Hill had some wondering why, if soft money was to be used for generic party-building activities and for state and local elections, were the congressional campaign committees raising it? Most of the committees claimed they were taking on broader party functions and giving to state and local candidates. Soft money also became an attractive option for congressional fund-raisers who believed that the two national committees were so focused on presidential contests that they had neglected voter turnout in competitive House and Senate races. But a big reason for their aggressive pursuit of soft money was the purchase of issue ads. And they were quite successful—it was hard to say no to congressional leaders.[75]

Issue Advocacy Ads

Issue advocacy advertising is a type of communication that is supposed to promote certain ideas or issues, as opposed to express advocacy ads that call for the election or defeat of particular candidates. The line between the two types of advertising, however, can be rather thin at times and nearly impossible to discern. In a study of issue ads by the University of Pennsylvania's Annenberg Public Policy Center, the center's director, Kathleen Hall Jamieson, called the distinction between issue advocacy and express advocacy "a fiction."[76]

Issue ads may be broadcast on TV or radio, conveyed by telephone, or printed in fliers or mailers. They usually point out a particular candidate's position on a given issue, painting either a dark or glowing picture of the candidate based on that one position, be it abortion or term limits or environmental protection or whatever. But, most importantly, the ads stop just short of specifically asking for a vote for or against a candidate.

The Supreme Court in its 1976 Buckley decision ruled that limits on campaign contributions applied only to "communications that in express terms advocate the election or defeat of a clearly identified candidate for federal office." A footnote in the ruling defined express terms to include such phrases as "vote for," "elect," or "support." As a result, many took the position that if issue ads did not include such terms, they were not subject to any reporting requirements or spending limits.

The use of issue ads by the parties and outside groups grew dramatically in the 1990s, although there were no exact numbers available since soft money expenditures for issue ads did not have to be disclosed. The Annenberg Public Policy Center estimated that more than $509 million was spent on issue ads in the 1999–2000 election cycle, as compared to between $250 million and $341 million in the 1997–1998 election cycle and between $135 million and $150 million in the 1995–1996 election cycle.

Soft money was used for the first time in a big way to pay for issue ads in the 1996 election. Federal regulations barred the national parties from using soft money for more than 40 percent of the costs of such ads, while limits on state parties varied depending on the ratio of federal to nonfederal candidates. Interest groups and individuals, however, had no restrictions on how much unregulated money they could spend on the ads.

The potency of issue advocacy was vividly illustrated in the 1996 election cycle, when the AFL-CIO spent $35 million on an issue ad campaign—$25 million on paid media and the rest on direct mail and related organizing activities. The ads, which focused on such issues as Medicare, minimum wage, education, and pensions, ran heavily in vulnerable Republican districts. A coalition of business groups, formed to counter labor's effort, spent $5 million on issue ads.

Republicans learned in the 1998 campaign that negative issue ads can sometimes backfire. In the final week of the campaign, the National Republican Congressional Committee (NRCC) began running three ads addressing President Bill Clinton's affair with White House intern Monica Lewinsky. Many analysts thought the ads, which had the approval of Speaker Gingrich, were a mistake and that the GOP should have kept their focus on basic issues that affect voters' everyday lives, such as education and jobs. The ad campaign contributed to the ill will in the House that ultimately caused Gingrich to step down as Speaker.

Opponents of issue ads said they were nothing more than thinly veiled pitches for or against individual candidates and represented a giant loophole in campaign spending laws. They also complained that the public had no way of knowing who paid for the ad. For example, according to the Annenberg Center's study, the top spender on issue ads in the 2000 election cycle was an organization called Citizens for Better Medicare, which spent an estimated $65 million. Most people were not aware of the fact that the group was funded primarily by the pharmaceutical industry.

But supporters argued that issue ads educated the public and helped create a better-informed electorate. They insisted that any limits on issue advocacy would impede their constitutional right to free speech.

Independent Expenditures

The Supreme Court in the *Buckley* decision ruled that the 1974 FECA's $1,000 ceiling on independent expenditures was a clear violation of the First Amendment right of free expression. Independent expenditures are defined as communications that expressly advocate the election or defeat of a candidate but are made without consultation or coordination with any candidate or any candidate's committee or agent.

Although there no longer is a limit on the amount that can be spent, independent expenditures are subject to FECA disclosure requirements and must be paid for with funds that are legally permitted in a federal election campaign. In other words, an independent expenditure could not be financed by labor or most corporate money (certain small, ideologically based nonprofit corporations are exempt), nor by a contribution from a foreign national.

Independent expenditures have been controversial for several reasons. Some question whether such expenditures are truly independent. Others criticize the clout it gives a wealthy individual or an organization to influence the outcome of an election. Still others point out that candidates themselves sometimes resent this outside interference even when the communication favors their campaigns. (*See "Individual Contributions," p. 91; "Political Action Committees," p. 93.*)

The debate over independent expenditures intensified when the Supreme Court in 1996 ruled that limits on independent expenditures by political parties were unconstitutional. In the *Colorado Republican Federal Campaign Committee v. Federal Election Commission* decision, the Court held that state and national parties were free to make unlimited expenditures in a congressional campaign as long as the party and the candidate were not working together. The Court thus rejected the prevailing assumption that a party was uniquely connected to its candidates—especially given the coordinated expenditures it made on behalf of its candidates—and could not act independently of them.

Coordinated Expenditures

In its 1996 Colorado decision—sometimes referred to as "Colorado I"—the Supreme Court left undecided the question of whether limits on coordinated party expenditures were unconstitutional as well. The issue was remanded to the district court for further consideration.

In 1999 the district court ruled that the FECA's limits on coordinated expenditures were a violation of the First Amendment rights of political parties. The decision, in what was now known as *Federal Election Commission v. Colorado Republican Federal Campaign Committee*, or "Colorado II," was upheld by the U.S. Court of Appeals for the Tenth Circuit in May 2000.

The FEC decided to appeal the ruling to the Supreme Court. Concerned that the parties might start spending over the limits without waiting for the high court to act, the FEC warned that the decision applied only to the states within the jurisdiction of the Tenth Circuit. Furthermore, the FEC said that if the appeals court decision was reversed by the Supreme Court, the commission could take action against anyone who violated the limits, whether they were within the Tenth Circuit's jurisdiction or not.

In June 2001 the Supreme Court ruled on "Colorado II," reversing the lower courts and upholding strict limits on what political parties could spend in coordination with candidates. The Court, in the narrow 5–4 vote, rejected the claim of the Colorado Republicans that such restrictions violated First Amendment rights. The Court said lifting the limits on coordinated expenditures could allow parties to serve as conduits for wealthy donors seeking to evade contribution limits and exert improper influence. "Despite years of enforcement of challenged limits," the majority opinion read, "substantial evidence demonstrates how candidates, donors, and parties test the limits of the current law, and it shows beyond serious doubt how contribution limits would be eroded if inducement to circumvent them were enhanced by declaring parties' coordinated spending wide open."

"Section 527" Groups

Controversy erupted in 2000 over so-called Section 527 groups, prompting Congress to move quickly to close what many saw as an egregious loophole in the campaign disclosure law.

These organizations—named after Section 527 of the tax code—were political groups formed to influence elections. Section 527 was written in 1975 after the Watergate scandal to set tax rules for political groups. Originally, they were expected to report their fund-raising and spending to the FEC. But as long as the groups did not contribute or expressly advocate the election or defeat of a specific candidate, they were not required to report anything. They could run ads attacking or praising a candidate; they could distribute voter guides condemning the political philosophy of candidates; and they could engage in other political activities that fell under the broad title of "issue advocacy." Individuals, corporations, unions, even foreign governments, could donate unlimited amounts of money to them, none of which had to be disclosed.

Because there were no public registration laws for such groups, their numbers and influence were incalculable. The Center for Responsive Politics and Common Cause identified more than a dozen Section 527 groups. They ranged ideologically from the far left to the far right. Several were affiliated with prominent special interest groups, such as the Christian Coalition, the League of Conservation Voters, and the Sierra Club. Some were closely affiliated with GOP congressional leaders. Others were independent.

Special attention was focused on this type of group when two backers of Texas Gov. George W. Bush formed a Section 527 group called Republicans for Clean Air, which ran about $2.5 million worth of television ads before the March 2000 presidential primaries attacking Bush's challenger, Sen. John McCain, R-Ariz., for his environmental record.

Legislation requiring Section 527 groups to disclose their expenditures and donors was enacted into law in 2000 with overwhelming bipartisan support.

ONGOING DEBATE

The law enacted in 2000 to require Section 527 groups to disclose their finances was lauded on Capitol Hill and in the White House, not only for its content but for the bipartisanship with which it was passed. But for reform advocates it was just a beginning.

"This bill will not solve what is wrong with our campaign finance system. It will not do away with the millions of soft-money dollars that are polluting our elections," said McCain, a leading advocate of reform in the Senate.[77] But McCain and others were hopeful that the action would translate into momentum for broader reform.

Opponents of reform dismissed the significance of the bill, yet recognized a vote for campaign finance reform would play to voters in an election year. "I do not think this is a spear worth falling on . . . four months in advance of an election," said Mitch McConnell of Kentucky, chair of the National Republican Senatorial Committee and a bitter foe of McCain's campaign finance reform crusade.[78] McConnell opposed the bill but did not filibuster it as he had done in past campaign finance debates.

Congress had revisited campaign finance issues regularly since the mid-1980s. Each party had tried to capitalize on its strengths and curb those of the other party, resulting in stalemate after stalemate.

In the early debates the Democrats contended that the system operated like an arms race—that congressional candidates engaged in a never-ending quest for a financial edge. Hence, most Democrats insisted that any new law had to limit campaign spending. They advocated partial public funding of candidates who promised to abide by spending limits, which they said would allow challengers to spend on a level equal to incumbents.

But most Republicans strenuously opposed taxpayer financing of congressional campaigns, which they likened to welfare for politicians. Many Republicans also argued that spending limits locked in incumbent advantages. They said challengers needed the option to outspend incumbents to make themselves equally visible to voters. They also saw the problem as one of tainted sources of money. Instead of capping spending, they proposed curbing specific sources, such as PACs and large out-of-state contributions. And they wanted to encourage political parties to spend even more money in behalf of their candidates.

Further complicating matters was the fact that incumbent factions in each party savored the easy flow of money from Washington fund-raisers. House Democrats in particular found it difficult to think of parting with PAC dollars. Some accused the Senate of posturing in their attempts to ban PACs, knowing full well that House members, who received a much higher portion of their contributions from PACs than did senators, would vote to preserve PACs or that the Supreme Court ultimately would declare the ban unconstitutional.

Proposals to limit but not ban PACs generated another type of controversy. Although PACs could give $10,000 to a candidate in an election cycle ($5,000 for the primary and $5,000 for the general), most gave far less. However, labor PACs often gave Democrats in close races the full $10,000 permitted—money they did not want to lose.

Democrats also objected to Republican proposals to let political parties give more to, or spend more in behalf of, their candidates than existing law allowed, primarily because the GOP was better at raising money.

The debate went on in Congress after Congress. Rep. Bob Franks, R-N.J., described it as "an intricate game of ping-pong. . . . One chamber would pass a law, knowing the other would not. It was playing politics."[79] Legislation was passed, rejected, filibustered, never made it to conference, or vetoed.

In the mid-1990s the explosive growth of soft money and issue advocacy advertising added a new urgency to the campaign finance debate. Congress's preoccupation with PACs, spending limits, and public funding gave way to efforts to curtail the new types of campaign spending. But partisan divisions existed on these issues as well. Republicans, for example, complained that clamping down on soft money without inhibiting labor's independent spending on behalf of Democrats would amount to unilateral disarmament by the GOP.

The issue of campaign finance reform gained prominence during the 2000 presidential campaign, as Senator McCain touted it in one campaign speech after another. Although McCain failed in his quest for the GOP presidential nomination, he returned to the Senate invigorated by the enthusiasm his crusade had generated on the campaign trail. New-found support for the cause in the Senate translated into enough votes to ward off a filibuster and to secure passage of a major campaign finance bill in April 2001. But efforts to pass a campaign finance legislation in the House stalled in July 2001, amid sharply partisan differences over competing proposals. *(See box, Campaign Finance Overhaul Legislation, p. 124.)*

And so the heated debate over the financing of elections continued, as it had throughout the history of American politics.

Financing Campaigns: Historical Development

In early American politics the source of money to finance a political campaign was never a question. Politics was a gentleman's pursuit and the gentleman paid. But, as political scientist Robert Mutch pointed out, the expenses were small and campaigns in the modern sense were few. "Candidates were supposed to attract support by virtue of their reputations, not by actually mingling with voters," Mutch wrote.[80] Candidates' expenses might have included the costs of printing and distributing campaign literature or perhaps providing food and drink for the voters on election day.

George Washington, for example, during his campaign for the House of Burgesses in Virginia in 1757, dispensed twenty-eight gallons of rum, fifty gallons of rum punch, thirty-four gallons of wine, forty-six gallons of beer, and two gallons of cider royal! "Even in those days this was considered a large campaign expenditure," writer George Thayer observed, "because there were only 391 voters in his district, for an average outlay of more than a quart and a half per person."[81]

But by the early nineteenth century money had begun to play an increasingly significant role. Politics no longer was the exclusive domain of the wealthy merchant or the gentleman farmer. The professional politician had emerged. Lacking personal wealth, the new breed was dependent on others for campaign support and on salaries for their livelihood. And with the expansion of the electorate in the 1820s, as more and more states switched to a system of selecting presidential electors by popular vote, the need for campaign money grew. Candidates found that reaching an expanded pool of voters required mass propaganda and that, in turn, required money.

Modern political parties also had begun to emerge, and with them came the spoils system. When a new president came in, government jobs were transferred to his supporters. It was not long before the new appointees were having to pay for the privilege of a government job, with the political parties exacting percentages from the salaries of federal employees.

The first known cases of assessments on government workers were levied by the Democratic Party on U.S. customs employees in New York City during the 1830s. But attempts to legislate against the practice went nowhere because, as Mutch noted, "few politicians were willing to eliminate such a valuable source of party funds, and the system of assessments continued to grow."[82]

The first provision of federal law relating to campaign finance was incorporated into an act of March 2, 1867, making naval appropriations for fiscal 1868. The act's final section read:

And be it further enacted, That no officer or employee of the government shall require or request any workingman in any navy yard to contribute or pay any money for political purposes, nor shall any workingman be removed or discharged for political opinion; and any officer or employee of the government who shall offend against the provisions of this section shall be dismissed from the service of the United States.

Reports circulated the following year that at least 75 percent of the money raised by the Republican Congressional Committee came from federal officeholders. Continued agitation on this and other aspects of the spoils system in federal employment—tragically highlighted by the assassination in 1881 of President James A. Garfield by a disappointed office seeker—led to adoption of the 1883 Civil Service Reform Act. The act, also known as the Pendleton Act, authorized the establishment of personnel rules, one of which stated, "That no person in the public service is for that reason under any obligation to contribute to any political fund . . . and that he will not be removed or otherwise prejudiced for refusing to do so." The law made it a crime for any federal employee to solicit campaign funds from another federal employee.

But shrewd campaign managers found money elsewhere. Business money had become increasingly important in the post–Civil War period and was dominant by the close of the century. In the legendary 1896 campaign between Republican William McKinley and Democrat-Populist William Jennings Bryan, McKinley's successful effort was managed by Marcus A. (Marc) Hanna, a wealthy Ohio financier and industrialist who turned the art of political fund-raising into a system for assessing campaign contributions from banks and corporations.

As these political contributions grew, so too did public concern over the role of corporate money in politics. "The concern among the electorates of the industrialized nineteenth century was that their elected representatives might not be the real policymakers, that government might still be controlled by those who provided campaign funds," Mutch wrote.[83] In the late 1800s several states enacted campaign finance laws, some requiring disclosure of information on the sources and uses of campaign contributions and others actually prohibiting corporate contributions. The push was on for action on the national level.

Links between money and politics were a target for editorial cartoonists even before Thomas Nast drew this in 1871.

EARLY LEGISLATION

Reacting to the increasingly lavish corporate involvement in political campaigns, the hearty band of reformers known as the "muckrakers" pressed for the nation's first extensive campaign finance legislation. During the first decade of the twentieth century, they worked to expose big business's influence on government through unrestrained spending on behalf of favored candidates.

Corporate Contribution Ban

Revelations during congressional hearings that several corporations had secretly financed Theodore Roosevelt's 1904 presidential campaign provided impetus for change. The establishment of the National Publicity Law Organization, headed by former Rep. Perry Belmont, D-N.Y., focused further attention on the issue.

President Roosevelt, in his annual message to Congress, proposed on December 5, 1905, that "all contributions by corporations to any political committee or for any political purpose should be forbidden by law." Roosevelt repeated the proposal the following December, suggesting that it be the first item of congressional business.

Congress in 1907 passed the first federal campaign finance law, the Tillman Act, which made it unlawful for a corporation or a national bank to make "a money contribution in connection with any election" of candidates for federal office. Although Roosevelt is generally regarded as having initiated the series of actions leading to the 1907 law, Mutch points out that the bill passed by Congress had actually been written and introduced five years earlier.[84]

Also in 1907, Roosevelt gave his support to a drive for public funding of party organizations, but nothing came of the effort. (See "Public Funding," p. 88.)

Disclosure Mandated

Three years later the first Federal Corrupt Practices Act (also known as the Publicity Act of 1910) was passed, establishing disclosure requirements for U.S. House candidates. Specifically, the law required every political committee "which shall in two or more states influence the result or attempt to influence the result of an election at which Representatives in Congress are to be elected" to file with the clerk of the House of Representatives, within thirty days after the election, the name and address of each contributor of $100 or more, the name and address of each recipient of $10 or more from the committee, and the total amounts that the committee received and disbursed. Individuals who engaged in similar activities outside the framework of committees also were required to submit such reports.

The following year legislation was passed extending the filing requirements to committees influencing Senate elections and requiring candidates for House and Senate seats to file financial reports. (Popular election of senators, instead of election by state legislatures, was mandated by the Seventeenth Amendment, approved by Congress in 1912 and ratified in 1913.) Both pre- and postelection reports were required. The most important innovation of the 1911 act was the limit that was placed on the amount candidates could spend campaigning for nomination and election: candidates for the Senate, no more than $10,000 or the maximum amount permitted in their states, whichever was less; for the House, no more than $5,000 or the maximum amount permitted in their states, whichever was less.

1925 Corrupt Practices Act

No further changes in federal campaign law were made for more than a decade. But then the system was overhauled with passage of the Federal Corrupt Practices Act of 1925, which served as the basic campaign finance law until the early 1970s.

The Teapot Dome scandal gave Congress the push it needed to pass reform legislation. During a congressional investigation of alleged improprieties in the Harding administration's leasing of naval oil reserves to private operators, it had been discovered that an official of the company that had leased the Teapot Dome reserve in Wyoming had not only bribed the official in charge of the leasing but had also contributed generously to the Republican Party to help retire the party's 1920 campaign debt. The contribution had been made in a nonelection year and therefore did not have to be reported under existing law—a loophole that was closed by the 1925 act's requirement that contributions of $100 or more be reported, whether made in an election year or not.

The 1925 act regulated campaign spending and disclosure of receipts and expenditures by House and Senate candidates, as well as disclosure by national political committees and their subsidiaries and by other committees seeking to influence elections in more than one state. The 1925 act limited its restrictions to general election campaigns because the Supreme Court in 1921 had ruled that Congress did not have jurisdiction over primaries. *(See "Restrictions on Primaries," p. 110.)*

The act revised the amounts that candidates could legally spend. Unless a state law prescribed a smaller amount, the act set the ceilings at $10,000 for a Senate candidate and $2,500 for a House candidate; or an amount equal to three cents for each vote cast in the last preceding election for the office sought, but not more than $25,000 for the Senate and $5,000 for the House.

The 1925 act incorporated the existing prohibition against campaign contributions by corporations and national banks, the ban on solicitation of political contributions from federal employees by candidates or other federal employees, and the requirement that reports on campaign finances be filed. It prohibited giving or offering money to anyone in exchange for his or her vote. In amending the provisions of the 1907 act on contributions, the new law substituted for the word "money" the phrase "a gift, subscription, loan, advance, or deposit of money, or anything of value."

The Corrupt Practices Act, however, was riddled with loopholes and contained no provisions for enforcement. It did not mandate publication of the reports or review of the reports for errors and omissions. It did not require reports of contributions and expenditures in either presidential or congressional primary campaigns, nor in connection with a party's presidential nomination. It did not require reports by political committees so long as they confined their activities to a single state and were not actual subsidiaries of a national political committee. Frequently, congressional candidates reported they had received and spent nothing on their campaigns, maintaining that the campaign committees established to elect them to office had been working without their "knowledge and consent."

Candidates were able to evade the spending limitations by channeling most of their campaign expenditures through separate committees that were not required to report federally, thus making the federal ceilings, from a practical standpoint, meaningless.

No candidate for the House or the Senate ever was prosecuted under the 1925 act, although it was widely known that most candidates spent more than the act allowed and did not report all they spent. Only two persons elected to Congress—Republicans William S. Vare of Pennsylvania and Frank L. Smith of Illinois, both elected to the Senate in 1926—ever were excluded from office for spending in excess of the act's limits.

The 1925 act's requirement that political committees seeking to influence the election of presidential electors in two or more states file contribution and spending reports was challenged in the courts as an unconstitutional infringement on states' rights. The Supreme Court in 1934, in *Burroughs and Cannon v. United States,* upheld the act's applicability to the election of presidential electors and implicitly sanctioned federal regulation of campaign financing in congressional elections.

On the topic of disclosure, the Court stated: "Congress reached the conclusion that public disclosure of political contributions, together with the names of contributors and other details, would tend to prevent the corrupt use of money to affect elections. The verity of this conclusion reasonably cannot be denied."

Hatch Act and Labor Restrictions

During the period between the early efforts to regulate spending and the broad reforms of the 1970s, some laws related to campaign financing were enacted, although they had less direct effects than the corrupt practices laws.

A 1939 law, commonly called the Hatch Act but also known as the Clean Politics Act, barred federal employees from active participation in national politics and prohibited collection of political contributions from persons receiving relief funds provided by the federal government.

A 1940 amendment to the Hatch Act made several significant additions to campaign finance law. It placed a ceiling of $3 million in a calendar year on expenditures by a political committee operating in two or more states. (In practice, however, the parties easily evaded this stipulation.) The 1940 amendment forbade federal contractors, whether individuals or companies, to contribute to any political committee or candidate. It also asserted Congress's right to regulate primary elections for the nomination of candidates for federal office and made it unlawful for anyone to contribute more than $5,000 to a federal candidate or political committee in a single year. But Congress opened a big loophole when it specifically exempted from this limitation "contributions made to or by a state or local committee."

Three years later Congress passed the War Labor Disputes Act (Smith-Connally Act), temporarily extending the 1907 prohibition on political contributions by national banks and corporations to include labor unions. This prohibition was made permanent by the Labor-Management Relations Act of 1947 (Taft-Hartley Act).

Restrictions on Primaries

Legislative and judicial decisions in the first half of the twentieth century repeatedly redefined the relationship of campaign finance laws to primary elections. The 1911 act limiting campaign expenditures in congressional elections covered primaries as well as general elections. In 1921, however, the Supreme Court in the case of *Newberry v. United States* struck down the law's application to primaries on the ground that the power the Constitution gave Congress to regulate the "manner of holding elections" did not extend to party primaries and conventions. The Corrupt Practices Act of 1925 exempted primaries from its coverage.

The Hatch Act amendments of 1940 made primaries again subject to federal restrictions on campaign contributions despite the *Newberry* decision. This legislation was upheld in 1941, when the Supreme Court in *United States v. Classic* reversed its *Newberry* decision by ruling that Congress had the power to regulate primary elections when the primary was an integral part of the process of selecting candidates for federal office. The *Classic* decision was reaffirmed by the Court in 1944 in *Smith v. Allwright.* When the Taft-Hartley Act was adopted in 1947, its prohibition of political contributions by corporations, national banks, and labor organizations was phrased to cover primaries as well as general elections.

LOOPHOLES ABOUND

Even with the revisions of the 1930s and 1940s, the campaign system was filled with loopholes. In a 1967 message to Congress proposing election reforms, President Lyndon B. Johnson said of the Corrupt Practices and Hatch acts: "Inadequate in their scope when enacted, they are now obsolete. More loophole than law, they invite evasion and circumvention."

Contributors' Loopholes

The Corrupt Practices Act required the treasurer of a political committee active in two or more states to report at specified times the name and address of every donor of $100 or more to a campaign. To evade such recording, a donor could give less than $100 to each of numerous committees supporting the candidate of his choice. A Senate subcommittee in 1956 checked the contributions of sums between $50 and $99.99 to one committee. It found that of ninety-seven contributions in that range, eighty-eight were over $99, including fifty-seven that were exactly $99.99.

Technically, an individual could not contribute more than $5,000 to any national committee or federal candidate. However, he or she could contribute unlimited funds to state, county, and local groups that passed along the money in the organization's name.

Members of the same family could legally contribute up to $5,000 each. A wealthy donor wanting to give more than $5,000 to a candidate or a political committee could privately subsidize gifts by relatives.

Both parties relied on big contributors. Well-known contributors to the Republicans included the Mellons, Rockefellers, and Whitneys. Among the Democrats' donors were the Laskers, Kennedys, and Harrimans. Large contributions also came from foreigners.

Corporations. Corporations could skirt the prohibition of contributions to a political campaign by giving bonuses or salary increases to executives in the expectation that as individuals they would make corresponding political contributions to candidates favored by the corporation.

Political campaign managers learned to watch for contribution checks drawn directly on corporate funds and to return them to avoid direct violation of the law. Often this money made its way back to the political managers in some other form.

Corporations were allowed to place advertisements in political journals, even though there was no apparent benefit to the corporations from the ads, and they could lend billboards, office furniture, equipment, mailing lists, and airplanes to candidates or political committees. If a loan of this kind was deemed a violation of the letter of the law, the corporation could rent these items to a candidate or committee, instead of lending them, and then write off the rental fee as uncollectible.

Unions. Labor unions could contribute to a candidate or political committee funds collected from members apart from dues. Money could be taken directly from union treasuries and used for technically "nonpartisan" purposes, such as promoting voter registration, encouraging members to vote, or publishing the voting records of members of Congress or state legislators.

Organized labor's registration and get-out-the-vote drives overwhelmingly supported Democratic candidates, being keyed to areas where regular Democratic efforts were considered deficient or where an overwhelming Democratic vote was traditionally necessary to overcome a Republican plurality in some other section of the district, state, or country.

Public service activities, such as union newspapers or radio programs, could be financed directly from regular union treasuries. As with corporate newspapers and radio programs, a sharply partisan viewpoint could be, and often was, expressed.

Candidates' Loopholes

Federal or state limitations on the amount of money a candidate might knowingly receive or spend were easily evaded. A loophole in the law enabled numerous candidates to report that they received and spent not one cent on their campaigns because any financial activity was conducted without their "knowledge or consent." In 1964 four senators reported that their campaign books showed zero receipts and zero expenditures—Vance Hartke, D-Ind.; Roman L. Hruska, R-Neb.; Edmund S. Muskie, D-Maine; and John C. Stennis, D-Miss.

Four years later, when Sen. George McGovern, D-S.D., reported no receipts or expenditures, one of his staff explained that they were careful to make sure that McGovern never saw the campaign receipts. Two senators elected in 1968—William B. Saxbe, R-Ohio, and Richard S. Schweiker, R-Pa.—reported general election expenditures of $769,614 and $664,614, respectively, to their state authorities, while reporting expenditures of only $20,962 and $5,736, respectively, to the secretary of the Senate.

Another measure of the recorded figures' incompleteness was the contrast between the reported total political spending in 1960—$28.3 million—and the $175 million spending estimate by political experts. In 1962, $18.4 million was reported spent in congressional races, but Congressional Quarterly estimated the actual total at almost $100 million.

The credibility gap fostered by the "knowledge or consent" loophole was widened further because the Federal Corrupt Practices Act applied only to political committees operating in two or more states. If a committee operated in one state only and was not a subdivision of a national committee, the law did not apply. If a committee operated in the District of Columbia only, receiving funds there and mailing checks to candidates in a single state, the law did not cover it.

Limits on the expenditures that a political committee might make were evaded by establishing more than one committee and apportioning receipts and expenditures among them, so that no one committee exceeded the limit. Because the law limited spending by a political committee operating in two or more states to $3 million annually, the major parties formed committees under various names, each of which was free to spend up to $3 million.

Although the Corrupt Practices Act provided criminal penalties for false reporting or failure to report, successive administrations ignored them, even though news reporters repeatedly uncovered violations. Eisenhower administration Attorney General Herbert Brownell stated in 1954 the Justice Department's position that the initiative in such cases rested with the secretary of the Senate and the clerk of the House, and that policy was continued.

Secretaries of the Senate and clerks of the House for many years winked at violations of the filing requirements. The situation changed in 1967 when former Rep. W. Pat Jennings, D-Va., became House clerk. He began sending lists of violations to the Justice Department for prosecution, but the department refused to act.

Attempts at Reform

Attempts to rewrite the 1925 act were made regularly during the late 1950s and the 1960s but with little success.

In April 1962 the President's Commission on Campaign Costs issued a report recommending proposals to encourage greater citizen participation in financing presidential campaigns. The commission had been named in October 1961 by President John F. Kennedy. Alexander Heard, dean of the University of North Carolina Graduate School, was the chairman and Herbert Alexander, director of the Citizens' Research Foundation, was the executive director. Among the commission's recommendations were that:

• Tax credits or deductions be given for certain levels of individuals' political contributions.

• The existing limits on expenditures of interstate political committees and individual contributions to those committees be repealed, leaving no limit.

• All candidates for president and vice president and committees spending at least $2,500 a year be required to report expenditures made in both primary and general election campaigns.

• A Registry of Election Finance be established to help enforce political financing regulations.

• The government pay the transition costs of a president-elect during the period between election and inauguration.

In May 1962 President Kennedy submitted to Congress five draft bills encompassing proposals identical or similar to the commission's. But the only bill reported was one to finance transition costs, and it died on the House floor.

Tax Checkoff Attempt. Congress did not act again in the area of campaign finance until the mid-1960s, when it passed a tax checkoff plan to provide government subsidies to presidential election campaigns. An act approved in 1966 authorized any individual paying federal income tax to direct that one dollar of the tax due in any year be paid into a Presidential Election Campaign Fund. The fund, to be set up in the U.S. Treasury, was to disburse its receipts proportionately among political parties whose presidential candidates had received five million or more votes in the preceding presidential election. Congress, however, failed to adopt the required guidelines for distribution of the funds, so the 1966 act was in effect voided in 1967.

Skyrocketing Costs. But the mood in Washington was beginning to change. In addition to growing irritation with the tooth-

lessness of the disclosure laws, uneasiness was increasing over campaign costs.

Rising campaign costs were evident soon after World War II ended. Heard wrote in 1960:

Radio and television broadcasting eat up millions. Thousands go to pay for rent, electricity, telephone, telegraph, auto hire, airplanes, airplane tickets, registration drives, hillbilly bands, public relations counsel, the Social Security tax on payrolls. Money pays for writers and for printing what they write, for advertising in many blatant forms, and for the boodle in many subtle guises. All these expenditures are interlarded with outlays for the hire of donkeys and elephants, for comic books, poll taxes and sample ballots, for gifts to the United Negro College Fund and the Police Relief Association, for a $5.25 traffic ticket in Maryland and $66.30 worth of "convention liquor" in St. Louis.[85]

Radio and television ads came to occupy a greater and greater portion of campaign budgets, as broadcasting emerged as the dominant political medium in the 1960s. "Overall, political broadcasting increased from 17.3 percent of the estimated total of all political spending ($200 million) in 1964 to 19.6 percent (of $300 million) in 1968, ensuring its position as the largest single cost in political campaigns," according to Herbert Alexander.[86]

Congressional incumbents came to see limits as necessary to prevent media costs from draining campaign treasuries and making candidates increasingly dependent on wealthy contributors and powerful lobbying groups. And many Democrats saw a limit on TV outlays as a way to overcome what they viewed as the Republicans' lopsided advantage in raising money.

In addition, incumbents of both parties feared that without limits rich challengers could use TV "blitzes" to overpower them, a concern that had been fanned in 1970 by the high-cost campaigns of two relative unknowns—Rep. Richard L. Ottinger of New York and Ohio parking-lot magnate Howard M. Metzenbaum—who succeeded in winning Democratic primary races for the U.S. Senate, although they lost in the general election.

Against this backdrop of skyrocketing campaign costs, the administration of Richard Nixon tightened enforcement of the Federal Corrupt Practices Act, successfully pressing charges in 1969 against corporations (mostly in California) that had contributed money in 1968.

Major Reform Laws
Enacted in the 1970s

By the 1970s all sides acknowledged the need for new campaign finance legislation. Within a five-year period—between 1971 and 1976—Congress passed four major laws that changed the way political campaigns for national office were financed and conducted. Stunned by the campaign abuses that came to light during the Watergate scandal, state governments and the courts also moved to alter the methods of campaign financing.

1971 REFORM LAWS

In 1971 Congress passed two separate pieces of legislation: the Federal Election Campaign Act (FECA) of 1971, which for the first time set a ceiling on the amount federal candidates could spend on media advertising and required full disclosure of campaign contributions and expenditures; and the Revenue Act of 1971, which included a tax checkoff section to allow taxpayers to contribute to a general public campaign fund for eligible presidential candidates.

FECA: Limits and Disclosure

The 1971 act was the first major piece of campaign finance legislation passed since 1925. It combined two sharply different approaches to reform. One section clamped limits on how much a federal candidate could spend on all forms of communications media. The second part provided, for the first time, for relatively complete and timely public reports by candidates on who was financing their campaigns and how much they were spending. Meaningful disclosure would reduce the likelihood of corruption and unfair advantage, it was theorized.

Media Limits. The bill went into effect April 7, 1972, sixty days after President Nixon signed it. The heart of the new law was the section placing ceilings on media costs, which was applicable separately to the primary campaign and to the general election. For a House candidate, the limit was set at $50,000 or ten cents for each voting-age person in the congressional district, whichever was greater. For a Senate candidate, the limit was $50,000 or ten cents for each voting-age person in the state.

The ceiling, which was to rise automatically with the cost of living, applied to spending for television, radio, newspaper, magazine, billboard, and automated telephone advertising. The centerpiece of this section was the restriction that no more than 60 percent of the overall media total could go for radio and television advertising. In practice, this meant in the 1972 elections that a candidate for the House could spend no more than $52,150 for *all* media outlays in the primary campaign and no more than $52,150 in the general election campaign. (The cost-of-living factor had raised these figures from the initial $50,000.) In each case, only $31,290 of the overall media total could go for radio and television.

Because of population differences between states, the figures for Senate races ranged from an overall media limit of $52,150 in thinly populated states such as Alaska and Montana (of which only $31,290 could be for radio and TV) to as much as $1.4 million in California (of which about $840,000 could be for radio and TV).

Presidential limits also were computed on the basis of ten cents per voting-age person. For each presidential candidate, the overall media limit was $14.3 million, of which less than $8.6 million could be used for radio and TV.

Disclosure Requirements. The 1971 FECA required that any candidate or political committee in a federal campaign file quarterly spending and receipts reports that itemized receipts or expenditures of $100 or more by listing the name, address, occupation, and place of business of the contributor or recipient. During election years, added reports were required to be filed fifteen and five days before an election, and any contribution of $5,000 or more had to be reported within forty-eight hours if received after the last preelection report.

Closing numerous loopholes in previous law, the statute applied the reporting requirements to primaries, conventions, and runoffs as well as to the general election. Any political committee had to report, even if it operated in only one state, provided it spent or received in excess of $1,000 a year. This meant, in effect, that the loophole of avoiding reports by having separate campaign fund groups in each state was eliminated for presidential candidates and that members of Congress with campaign fund groups operating only in their home states would henceforth have to report their receipts and expenditures.

The reports were to be filed with the House clerk for House candidates, secretary of the Senate for Senate candidates, and General Accounting Office (GAO) for presidential candidates. These would be made available for public inspection within forty-eight hours of being received and would be periodically published; reports also were required to be filed with the secretary of state of each state and made available for public inspection by the end of the day on which they were received.

On the theory that disclosure alone would eliminate corruption, all the ineffective spending and contribution limits were repealed, except provisions barring contributions directly from corporate funds and directly from union funds raised from dues money. (However, *voluntary* funds raised from union members and administered by a union unit were permitted.)

Proponents of reform, cognizant of the partisan considerations that could have threatened any revision of campaign laws, worked to avoid writing a law that would favor any political party or candidate. Republicans, aware of the relatively healthy financial condition of their party in 1971, were eager to protect their coffers; Democrats did not want to jeopardize their large contributions from organized labor.

The reform movement also included various groups outside Congress, such as the National Committee for an Effective Congress, the chief pressure group; Common Cause; labor unions; and some media organizations.

Income Tax Checkoff

The Revenue Act of 1971 containing the income tax checkoff cleared Congress on December 9, 1971, after a bitter partisan debate dominated by the approaching 1972 presidential election. President Nixon reluctantly signed the bill but forced a change in the effective date of the fund from the 1972 election to 1976 as the price of his acquiescence.

The plan gave each taxpayer the option beginning in 1973 of designating one dollar of his or her annual federal income tax payment for a general campaign fund to be divided among eligible presidential candidates. Those filing joint returns could designate two dollars.

Democrats, whose party was $9 million in debt following the 1968 presidential election, said the voluntary tax checkoff was needed to free presidential candidates from obligations to their wealthy campaign contributors. Republicans, whose party treasury was well stocked, charged that the plan was a device to rescue the Democratic Party from financial difficulty.

THE WATERGATE ELECTION

Both 1971 laws were campaign finance milestones, but they left intact the existing system of private financing for the 1972 presidential campaign. While the FECA drew high marks for improving campaign disclosure and received some credit for reducing media costs, its successes were overshadowed by the massive misuse of campaign funds that characterized Watergate, one of the nation's worst political scandals.

The predominant theory at the time of passage was that merely by writing a good, tight campaign finance law emphasizing disclosure, Congress could reduce excessive contributions from any one source to any one candidate. Candidates, according to this theory, would want to avoid the appearance of being dominated by a few large donors. Good disclosure would allow the public to identify the political activities of special interest groups and take necessary corrective action at the polls.

But it did not work that way. Huge individual and corporate donations were near the center of the Watergate scandal as largely unreported private contributions financed the activities of the 1972 Nixon reelection campaign. Of the $63 million collected by the Nixon camp, nearly $20 million was in contributions from 153 donors giving $50,000 or more. More than $11 million was raised during the month before the FECA disclosure rules took effect on April 7, 1972, including $2.3 million on April 5 and $3 million on April 6.[87]

The Finance Committee for the Reelection of the President kept its pre–April 7 lists confidential until a Common Cause lawsuit sought disclosure under provisions of the old Federal Corrupt Practices Act and forced them into the open in 1973. Such reticence was partly explained by the existence of questionable contributions to the Nixon campaign: $200,000 in financier Robert Vesco's attaché case; a $100,000 secret donation from millionaire industrialist Howard Hughes, which Nixon confidant Bebe Rebozo purportedly kept locked in a safe deposit box; and $2 million pledged to Nixon by the dairy industry.

Illegal corporate gifts also motivated secrecy. In a report issued in July 1974, the Senate Select Committee on Presidential Campaign Activities (known as the Senate Watergate Committee) charged that "during the 1972 presidential campaign, it appears that at least thirteen corporations made contributions totaling over $780,000 in corporate funds. . . . Of these, twelve gave approximately $749,000 to the president's reelection campaign, which constituted the bulk of the illegal corporate contributions."

The primary sources of such corporate money, according to the Senate committee, were "foreign subsidiaries." Other sources included corporate reserves and expense accounts. The committee added that "although the bulk of the contributions preceded April 7, 1972, there was no disclosure of any of the contributions until July 6, 1973—or fifteen months after almost all of them were made."

Presidential lawyer Herbert Kalmbach, who headed the corporate gifts campaign, in June 1974 was sentenced to six to eighteen months in jail and fined $10,000 after pleading guilty to illegal campaign operations. Kalmbach collected more than $10 million from U.S. corporations, the bulk of it prior to April 7, 1972. According to staff reports of the Senate Watergate Committee, Kalmbach and other fund-raisers sought donations on an industry-by-industry basis, by using an influential corporate executive to raise money among other executives in his industry.

The leading individual giver in the 1972 campaign was Chicago insurance executive W. Clement Stone, chairman of the Combined Insurance Co. of America. In the April 7–December 31, 1972, reporting period monitored by the GAO, Stone was listed as giving $73,054 to reelect Nixon. But even before the revelations forced by Common Cause, Stone had admitted to pre-April giving of $2 million. The second highest giver was Richard Scaife, heir to the Mellon banking and oil fortune, who contributed $1 million to Nixon's reelection before April 7.

John Gardner, then the head of Common Cause, said in April 1973:

Watergate is not primarily a story of political espionage, nor even of White House intrigue. It is a particularly malodorous chapter in the annals of campaign financing. The money paid to the Watergate conspirators before the break-in—and the money passed to them later—was money from campaign gifts.[88]

Gardner's charge was dramatically confirmed by President Nixon's August 5, 1974, release of a June 23, 1972, tape recording of conversations between himself and his chief of staff, H. R. Haldeman. The tape revealed that Nixon was told at that time of the use of campaign funds in the June 17, 1972, Watergate break-in and agreed to help cover up that fact. Nixon's resignation August 9, 1974, followed the August 5 disclosure.

Disclosure Provisions

The campaign disclosure provisions of the 1971 FECA proved extremely useful, enabling scholars and the relevant committees of Congress to get a clear picture for the first time of patterns of contributions and spending. Emerging from the reports were data on enormous contributions by the milk industry, on corporate contributions, on formerly concealed large contributions by individuals, and on "laundered money"—information that played a key role in uncovering misconduct in the Watergate scandal.

Although thousands of reports were late or faulty, overall compliance with the disclosure law probably was fairly good. Nevertheless, a great many problems remained. The reports, especially those made in the last few days before the election, were extremely difficult for a reporter or a rival political camp to collate and decipher. Multiple contributions by a wealthy individual made to one candidate through a system of dummy organizations with cryptic names were difficult to track rapidly. Investigating an industry-wide campaign of financial support to a candidate or a group of candidates proved to be an extremely tedious task.

State finance committees and other committees—with titles such as Democrats for Nixon or Writers for McGovern—were created to prevent big contributors from being inhibited by

President Richard Nixon announces his resignation in August 1974. Revelations about campaign finance abuses tied to the Watergate scandal, which had brought about Nixon's downfall, spurred the most significant overhaul of campaign finance laws in the nation's history.

high gift taxes. An individual could give up to $3,000, tax-free, to an independent campaign committee. Records showed that the Nixon campaign benefited from 220 of these finance committees. McGovern had 785 such committees, according to his national campaign treasurer, Marian Pearlman, "created for Stewart Mott." General Motors heir Mott, who donated about $400,000 to McGovern, even declared himself a campaign committee.

The Internal Revenue Service interpreted campaign committees as being independent if one out of three officers was different from officers for other committees, if the candidates supported by the committees were different, or if the committees' purposes were different. As a result, campaign finance committees proliferated in 1972, and contributors were hardly deterred from giving large sums to one candidate.

More important, the crucial element in effectiveness of the law was enforcement. The Justice Department was given sole power to prosecute violations, despite its forty-six-year record of somnolence in enforcing previous regulations. It was traditionally understood that Justice Department bureaucrats feared to undertake vigorous enforcement lest they endanger the party in power and be fired.

The question became: Would the department make a powerful, massive effort not only to round up serious violators but to require that reports be on time and complete? Without such action from the department, the practice of filing sloppy, incomplete, or even misleading reports, and filing them late, would clearly vitiate much of the effect of the law and render it null in practice.

Although thousands of violations—some serious but most technical (late or incomplete)—were referred to the Justice Department in 1972 and 1973 by the House, Senate, and GAO, only a handful of prosecutions resulted. During the 1972 campaign

the department had only one full-time attorney supervising enforcement of the act, according to reports.

Another provision in the law requiring periodic reporting of contributions and expenditures further impeded enforcement. According to many members of Congress, the frequent filing of these reports during primary and general election campaigns by all political committees of candidates created monumental bookkeeping chores for the candidates. Correspondingly, the mammoth number of reports filed with the House clerk, the Senate secretary, and the comptroller general made closer scrutiny practically impossible.

To remedy the latter problem, Common Cause, at a cost of more than $250,000 and thousands of hours from volunteer workers, organized teams of people in 1972 to collect and collate information on reports, which it then distributed to the press in time for use before election day.

Fred Wertheimer, who at that time was the legislative director of Common Cause, said the aim was to make the law work and to give it a good start. But it was clear that depending on private organizations alone probably would be inadequate. Unless some permanent way were found, perhaps at government expense, to speed up collation and distribution of the materials—particularly late in the campaign—the objectives of disclosure would be undermined.

Media Expenditures

The 1972 election was more expensive than any that preceded it. About $425 million was spent in all races, with the Senate Watergate Committee estimating that the presidential race cost about $100 million, more than double the $44.2 million spent in the 1968 presidential election. During the 1972 campaign, presidential and Senate outlays for radio and television campaign advertising dropped sharply compared with 1968 and 1970, but

With congressional leaders looking on, President Gerald R. Ford signs the Federal Election Campaign Act Amendments of 1974.

whether this decline resulted from the FECA's media advertising limits was unclear.

In the presidential race, part of the drop was due to the strength of the incumbent, who had loads of free airtime available to him when he chose to address the nation in "nonpolitical" speeches as president, instead of seeking paid time as merely a candidate.

The drop in Senate spending was less easily explained, but many senators said one factor was the realization that electronic media, while enormously effective, did not provide the quantum leap in campaigning techniques that had been expected. The notion that television could "do it all," which was virtually an article of faith in the late 1960s and in 1970, had begun to fade, and more resources were put into other forms of advertising and into traditional organizational and legwork efforts. Broadcast spending totals also were reduced by the requirement in the 1971 law that TV stations charge politicians the lowest unit rate for any time slot.

Also, many senators learned in 1972 that TV station coverage was not well designed for campaign purposes in many areas. In some large states, such as Kentucky, it was impossible to cover the whole state with stations broadcasting only within that state. To cover border areas, it was necessary to buy time on stations located in other states, only a portion of whose viewers were in Kentucky. To send a message to one corner of the state a candidate had to pay for coverage outside the state as well, a wasteful and costly practice.

The same was true in some large central metropolitan areas located between two or three states. For northern New Jersey, a candidate had to pay rates for New York too, since many of the stations in that area broadcast simultaneously to New York City, Connecticut, and northern New Jersey.

Some senators found it cheaper under these conditions to use other ways of reaching the voters. Federal Communications Commission reports showed that while a handful of senators went slightly over their campaign limits, the TV limits as a whole were observed. Because of the TV "targeting" problems, many in Congress began to argue that a flat spending limit for TV was too inflexible. They said an overall spending limit for all campaign costs—similar to that repealed in 1971, but with real scope and enforcement teeth—would be better. Such a proposal, they argued, would still limit any massive use of TV because a candidate would not be able to exceed his total campaign spending limit. But it would allow greater flexibility as to which portion of overall costs went to TV and which to other items.

The media limits were repealed in 1974.

1974 REFORM LAW

Almost two and a half years after it passed the FECA of 1971, Congress, reacting to presidential campaign abuses and public opinion favoring reform, enacted another landmark campaign reform bill that substantially overhauled the existing system of financing election campaigns. Technically, the 1974 law was a set of amendments to the 1971 legislation, but in fact it was the most comprehensive campaign finance bill Congress had ever passed.

The new measure, which President Gerald R. Ford signed into law October 15, repealed some provisions of the 1971 law, expanded others, and broke new ground in such areas as public financing and contribution and expenditure limitations.

The Federal Election Campaign Act Amendments of 1974:

• Established a Federal Election Commission consisting of six voting members—two appointed by the president and four designated by congressional leaders—as well as two nonvoting members, the clerk of the House and secretary of the Senate. All six voting members had to be confirmed by both the House and Senate.

• Instituted numerous contribution limitations, including: for individuals, a limit of $1,000 per candidate per primary, runoff, or general election, not to exceed $25,000 to all federal candidates annually; for political committees, a limit of $5,000 per candidate per election, with no aggregate limit; for presidential and vice-presidential candidates and their families, a limit of $50,000 to their own campaigns. A limit of $1,000 was established for independent expenditures on behalf of a candidate. Cash contributions of more than $100 were prohibited, as were foreign contributions in any amount.

• Set limits on spending by federal candidates and the national parties, including: a total of $10 million per candidate for all presidential primaries, $20 million per candidate in the presidential general election, and $2 million for each major political party's nominating convention and lesser amounts for minor parties' conventions; $100,000 or eight cents per voting-age person in their state, whichever was greater, for Senate primary candidates and $150,000 or twelve cents per voting-age person, whichever was greater, for Senate general election candidates; $70,000 for House primary candidates and $70,000 for House general election candidates. National party spending was limited to $10,000 per candidate in House general elections; $20,000 or two cents per the voting-age population in the state, whichever was greater, for each candidate in Senate general elections; and two cents for every voting-age person in presidential general elections. (The party expenditures were above the candidates' individual spending limits.) Senate spending limits were applied to House candidates who represented a whole state. The act exempted certain expenditures from the limits and provided that the limits would increase with inflation. The act repealed the media spending limits adopted in 1971.

• Extended public funding for presidential campaigns to include not only general election campaigns but also prenomination campaigns and national nominating conventions. Eligible candidates seeking a presidential nomination would receive public funds matching their privately raised money within prescribed limits. Eligible candidates in a general election would each receive $20 million U.S. Treasury grants (to be adjusted for inflation) to finance their campaigns. Eligible political parties would receive grants of $2 million (to be adjusted for inflation) to conduct their nominating conventions. The amendments stipulated that if the level of money in the tax checkoff fund established by the 1971 Revenue Act was insufficient to finance all three stages of the electoral process, the funds would be disbursed for the general election, the conventions, and the primaries, in that order.

• Created a number of disclosure and reporting procedures, including: establishment by each candidate of one central campaign committee through which all contributions and expenditures on behalf of that candidate would be reported; reporting names and addresses, as well as occupation and place of business, of those contributing more than $100; filing of full reports of contributions and expenditures with the FEC ten days before and thirty days after each election, and within ten days of the close of each quarter. Presidential candidates were not required, however, to file more than twelve reports in any one year.

The final bill did not contain Senate-passed provisions for partial public financing of congressional campaigns. Senate conferees dropped the fight for some form of public financing for House and Senate races in return for higher spending limits

Sen. James L. Buckley, C-N.Y., was the lead plaintiff in the lawsuit that prompted the Supreme Court to overturn some of the ground rules of campaign finance in 1976.

for congressional campaigns and a stronger independent election commission to enforce the law.

BUCKLEY V. VALEO

As soon as the 1974 law took effect, it was challenged in court by a diverse array of plaintiffs, including Sen. James L. Buckley, C-N.Y.; former Sen. Eugene J. McCarthy, D-Minn.; the New York Civil Liberties Union; and *Human Events,* a conservative publication. They filed suit on January 2, 1975.

Their basic arguments were that the law's new limits on campaign contributions and expenditures curbed the freedom of contributors and candidates to express themselves in the political marketplace and that the public financing provisions discriminated against minor parties and lesser-known candidates in favor of the major parties and better-known candidates.

The U.S. Court of Appeals for the District of Columbia on August 14, 1975, upheld all of the law's major provisions, thus setting the stage for Supreme Court action. The Supreme Court handed down its ruling, *Buckley v. Valeo,* on January 30, 1976, in an unsigned 137-page opinion. In five separate, signed opinions, several justices concurred with and dissented from separate issues in the case.

In its decision, the Court upheld the provisions that:

• Set limits on how much individuals and political committees could contribute to candidates.

Federal Election Commission

Given all the controversy that has surrounded the campaign finance system, it is no surprise that the agency established to monitor that system has been steeped in controversy as well. Critics charge that the Federal Election Commission (FEC) has been weak and ineffective in its enforcement of federal campaign finance law. And many also say that is exactly what Congress had in mind when it created the agency.

FEC Mandate

The Federal Election Commission (FEC) was created by Congress in 1974 to administer and enforce the Federal Election Campaign Act (FECA) of 1971 and its amendments. The FEC's duties include receiving and making public the campaign finance reports mandated by the FECA. These reports are available for examination at the FEC, as well as at the FEC Web site: *http://www.fec.gov.*

FEC staff members review the reports for omissions and may request additional information. If the FEC finds an apparent law violation, it has the authority to seek a conciliation agreement, sometimes with a fine. If a conciliation agreement cannot be reached, the FEC may sue for enforcement in U.S. District Court. The commission may refer possible criminal violations to the Justice Department for prosecution.

The FEC also administers the Presidential Election Campaign Fund, which makes possible the public funding of presidential primaries, national party conventions, and presidential general elections.

FEC Members

The 1974 amendments established the FEC as a six-member commission, with the clerk of the House and secretary of the Senate serving as nonvoting ex officio members. No more than three of the six commissioners were to be from the same political party.

The 1974 law stipulated that four of the six members would be selected by Congress, a provision the Supreme Court soon found, among others, to be unconstitutional. In its 1976 *Buckley v. Valeo* decision, the Court declared the method violated the separation-of-

powers and appointments clauses of the Constitution because the four commissioners were appointed by congressional officials but exercised executive powers.

Amendments passed in 1976 reconstituted the FEC as a six-member commission appointed by the president and confirmed by the Senate. However, Congress in effect continued to control four of the appointments by providing the White House with a list of acceptable nominees for these slots.

The makeup of the FEC was again called into question when the D.C. Circuit Court of Appeals in 1993 ruled that the commission had violated the constitutional separation of powers by including the two nonvoting congressional staff members in its deliberations. The FEC reconstituted itself without the clerk of the House and the secretary of the Senate but asked the Supreme Court to review the decision. The Court in 1994 rejected the appeal on technical grounds, ruling that the agency lacked authority to appeal the matter to the Supreme Court *(Federal Election Commission v. NRA Political Victory Fund).* The Court held that the FECA gave only the solicitor general the authority to make such appeals. As a result, there are no ex officio members of the commission.

In other action affecting the makeup of the commission, Congress in 1997 limited, beginning in 1998, future nominees for FEC commissioner slots to one six-year term. An attempt to place term limits on the FEC's general counsel and staff director failed in 1998.

Agency Critics

The FEC has not lacked its critics. Some have objected to actions taken by the agency, but for many others the problem has been its inaction.

"The system is not designed to function but rather to protect an environment in which abuses can flourish," wrote Charles G. LaBella of the Justice Department and James DeSarno of the FBI in an interim report on the 1996 campaign finance scandal. "Say what you will, but the FEC is not an effective enforcement mechanism."[1]

In a front-page article entitled "The Little Agency That Can't," the *Washington Post* in 1997 detailed the complaints against the

• Provided for the public financing of presidential primary and general election campaigns.

• Required the disclosure of campaign contributions of more than $100 and campaign expenditures of more than $100.

But the Court overturned other features of the law, ruling that the campaign spending limits were unconstitutional violations of the First Amendment guarantee of free expression. For presidential candidates who accepted federal matching funds, however, the ceiling on the expenditures remained intact. The Court also struck down the method for selecting members of the FEC.

Spending Limits Overturned

The Court stated: "A restriction on the amount of money a person or group can spend on political communication during a campaign necessarily reduces the quantity of expression by restricting the number of issues discussed, the depth of their exploration and the size of the audience reached. This is because virtually every means of communicating ideas in today's mass society requires the expenditure of money."

Only Justice Byron R. White dissented on this point; he would have upheld the limitations. Rejecting the argument that money is speech, White wrote that there are "many expensive campaign activities that are not themselves communicative or remotely related to speech."

FEC. "Once hailed as the two-fisted enforcer that would protect the body politic from future Watergate scandals and the corrupting scourge of unregulated campaign cash, the commission has proved to be weak, slow-footed and largely ineffectual."[2]

Many critics have placed much of the blame for FEC shortcomings on Congress. In 1997 Thomas E. Mann, then-director of Governmental Studies at the Brookings Institution, wrote that ". . . Congress had no interest in an independent, powerful FEC. It designed the agency carefully to ensure that it would operate on a tight leash held firmly by its master."

For starters, Mann pointed out, Congress gave itself the authority to appoint four of the six commissioners and supply two of its officers as ex officio members. The requirement that no more than three commissioners could be from the same party resulted in a three Democrat–three Republican commission, making it nearly impossible to take serious action against either party. Congress subsequently required an affirmative vote of four members for the commission to issue regulations and advisory opinions and initiate civil actions and investigations. In addition, the FEC was given no authority to impose sanctions and had to depend instead on the federal court and the Justice Department to pursue violators. Congress even had veto power over FEC rules and regulations until the Supreme Court declared all legislative vetoes unconstitutional in 1983.

Moreover, according to Mann, Congress took other steps "to ensure that delay and timidity would become the watchwords of the agency." These included denying the FEC the multiyear budgeting authority enjoyed by other independent agencies, skeptically reviewing FEC requests for budget increases despite the agency's expanding workload, banning random audits of candidates, insisting on time-consuming procedures, and keeping up "a barrage of criticism that weakened the FEC's legitimacy and reinforced the contempt with which political operatives came to view the Commission."[3]

The *Post* article also placed blame on Congress for creating an agency that "no individual could control—or lead" and that "guaranteed partisan gridlock and timidity in challenging the political status quo." The article criticized the federal courts as well for having "repeatedly gutted the agency's enforcement efforts" and a succession of presidents for having "appointed pliant commissioners who rarely displayed get-tough independence."

1996 Scandal

Critics of the FEC were particularly vocal in the wake of the 1996 campaign finance scandal because of the agency's inaction in the face of numerous allegations of campaign funding irregularities. The FEC indirectly exposed some of the 1996 irregularities through its required disclosure reports but did little more as the Senate and House launched investigations and the Justice Department pursued possible criminal violations.

At the center of the controversy was the frenzied raising of millions of dollars in unregulated soft money by the political parties. The parties insisted the money went for party-building activities, but others argued that much of it was used to support the candidacies of President Bill Clinton and Republican challenger Bob Dole, even though each received $61.8 million in public funding and was limited by law to spending only that amount. An FEC staff audit charged that both presidential campaigns had illegally coordinated with the Democratic and Republican national committees to spend millions of dollars on issue ads that benefited their candidacies, which amounted to spending in excess of the federal grants. FEC commissioners, however, unanimously rejected the staff recommendations that the campaigns be required to return that excess money to the federal Treasury. *(See "1996 Scandal," p. 84.)*

Supporters of campaign finance overhaul attacked the commissioners' decision. "This is an agency that is supposed to protect the public interest, and instead it's protecting the two parties who have joined hands to run roughshod over the law," said Donald Simon, executive vice president of Common Cause, a government watchdog group.

1. Charles G. LaBella and James DeSarno, "Interim Report for Janet Reno, Attorney General, and Louis J. Freeh, Director, Federal Bureau of Investigation," July 16, 1998, 86.

2. Benjamin Weiser and Bill McAllister, "The Little Agency That Can't: Election-Law Enforcer Is Weak by Design, Paralyzed by Division," *Washington Post*, February 12, 1997, A1, 16–17.

3. Thomas E. Mann, "The Federal Election Commission: Implementing and Enforcing Federal Campaign Finance Law," in *Campaign Finance Reform: A Sourcebook* ed. Anthony Corrado et al. (Washington, D.C.: Brookings Institution, 1997), 277–278.

Although the Court acknowledged that contribution and spending limits had First Amendment implications, it distinguished between the two by saying that the act's "expenditure ceilings impose significantly more severe restrictions on protected freedom of political expression and association than do its limitations on financial contributions."

The Court removed all the limits imposed on political spending and, by so doing, weakened the effect of the contribution ceilings. The law had placed spending limits on House, Senate, and presidential campaigns and on party nominating conventions. To plug a loophole in the contribution limits, the bill also had placed a $1,000 annual limit on how much an individual could spend independently on behalf of a candidate.

The independent expenditure ceiling, the opinion said, was a clear violation of the First Amendment. The Court wrote:

While the . . . ceiling thus fails to serve any substantial governmental interest in stemming the reality or appearance of corruption in the electoral process, it heavily burdens core First Amendment expression. . . . Advocacy of the election or defeat of candidates for federal office is no less entitled to protection under the First Amendment than the discussion of political policy generally or advocacy of the passage or defeat of legislation.

The Court also struck down the limits on how much of their own money candidates could spend on their campaigns. The law had set a $25,000 limit on House candidates, $35,000 on Senate candidates, and $50,000 on presidential candidates. "The candidate, no less than any other person, has a First Amendment right to engage in the discussion of public issues and vigorously and tirelessly to advocate his own election and the election of other candidates," the opinion said.

The ruling made it possible for a wealthy candidate to finance his own campaign and thus to avoid the limits on how much others could give him. The Court wrote that "the use of personal funds reduces the candidate's dependence on outside contributions and thereby counteracts the coercive pressures and attendant risks of abuse to which the act's contribution limitations are directed."

Justice Thurgood Marshall rejected the Court's reasoning in striking down the limit on how much candidates may spend on their campaigns. "It would appear to follow," he said, "that the candidate with a substantial personal fortune at his disposal is off to a significant 'head start.'" Moreover, he added, keeping the limitations on contributions but not on spending "put[s] a premium on a candidate's personal wealth."

FEC Makeup Faulted

The Court held unanimously that the FEC was unconstitutional. The Court said the method for appointing commissioners violated the Constitution's separation-of-powers and appointments clauses because some members were named by congressional officials but exercised executive powers. The justices refused to accept the argument that the commission, because it oversaw congressional as well as presidential elections, could have congressionally appointed members. The Court wrote:

We see no reason to believe that the authority of Congress over federal election practices is of such a wholly different nature from the other grants of authority to Congress that it may be employed in such a manner as to offend well established constitutional restrictions stemming from the separation of powers.

According to the decision, the commission could exercise only those powers Congress was allowed to delegate to congressional committees—investigating and information gathering. The Court ruled that only if the commission's members were appointed by the president, as required under the Constitution's appointments clause, could the commission carry out the administrative and enforcement responsibilities the law originally gave it.

The last action put Congress on the spot, because the justices stayed their ruling for thirty days, until February 29, 1976, to give the House and Senate time to "reconstitute the commission by law or adopt other valid enforcement mechanisms." As it developed, Congress took much longer than thirty days to act, and instead of merely reconstituting the commission, it passed a whole new campaign finance law.

1976 AMENDMENTS

The Court decision forced Congress to return to campaign finance legislation once again. The 1976 election campaign was already under way, but the Court said that the FEC could not continue to disburse public funds to presidential candidates so long as some commission members were congressional appointees.

President Ford had wanted only a simple reconstitution of the commission, but Congress insisted on going much further. The new law, arrived at after much maneuvering and arguing between Democrats and Republicans, closed old loopholes and opened new ones, depending on the point of view of the observer.

In its basic provision, the law signed by the president May 11, 1976, reconstituted the FEC as a six-member panel appointed by the president and confirmed by the Senate. Commission members were not allowed to engage in outside business activities. The commission was given exclusive authority to prosecute civil violations of the campaign finance law and was vested with jurisdiction over violations formerly covered only in the criminal code, thus strengthening its enforcement power. But the bill also required an affirmative vote of four members for the commission to issue regulations and advisory opinions and initiate civil actions and investigations. The commission was limited to issuing advisory opinions only for specific fact situations. And Congress was given the power to disapprove proposed regulations.

A major controversy that delayed enactment stemmed from organized labor's insistence that corporate fund-raising activity through PACs be curtailed. Labor was angered by the FEC's SunPAC decision in November 1975 that encouraged the growth of corporate PACs. *(See "Direct Contributions," p. 96.)*

In the wake of Watergate many corporations had been skittish about what they were permitted to do. Not until the FEC released its landmark ruling in the case involving the Sun Oil Co.'s political action committee, SunPAC, did many businesses feel comfortable in establishing PACs. The FEC decision was in response to Sun Oil's request to use general funds to create, administer, and solicit voluntary contributions to its political action committee. Besides approving the request, the decision allowed business PACs to solicit all employees and stockholders for contributions. Labor PACs had been restricted to soliciting only their members.

Eventually a compromise was reached between the Democrats, who did not hesitate to use their overwhelming numerical strength to make changes that would have severely restricted the ability of business to raise political money, and the Republicans, who lacked the strength to fend off the antibusiness amendments but had the votes to sustain a filibuster and a veto.

Labor won some but not all of its goals. The final law permitted company committees to seek contributions only from stockholders and executive and administrative personnel and their families. It continued to restrict union PACs to soliciting contributions from union members and their families. Twice a year, however, union and corporate PACs were permitted to seek campaign contributions, by mail only, from all employees. Contributions would have to remain anonymous and would be received by an independent third party that would keep records but pass the money on to the PACs.

The final bill contained another provision prompted by the Supreme Court decision. Besides finding the FEC's makeup unconstitutional, the Court had thrown out the 1974 law's limitations on independent political expenditures as a clear violation of the First Amendment. To plug the potential loophole, Congress required political committees and individuals making independent political expenditures of more than $100 to swear that the expenditures were not made in collusion with the candidate.

The 1976 legislation also set some new contribution limits: An individual could give no more than $5,000 a year to a PAC and $20,000 to the national committee of a political party (the 1974 law set a $1,000 per election limit on individual contributions to a candidate and an aggregate contribution limit for individuals of $25,000 a year; no specific limits, except the aggregate limit, had applied to contributions to political committees). A PAC could give no more than $15,000 a year to the national committee of a political party (the 1974 law set only a limit of $5,000 per election per candidate). The Democratic and Republican senatorial campaign committees could give up to $17,500 a year to a candidate (the 1974 law had set a $5,000 per election limit).

HILL PUBLIC FUNDING DEFEATED

Following the 1976 election, the spotlight in campaign finance quickly focused on extending public financing to House and Senate races. Prospects for passage seemed far better than they had been in 1974, the last time the proposal had been considered. At that time, leading officials, from the White House on down, had been either opposed or seemingly indifferent to its passage.

But in 1977 Jimmy Carter, a strong advocate of public funding, was in the White House. Key congressional leaders favored the proposal. And the Democrats had an overwhelming advantage in the House, far larger than during the 93rd Congress (1973–1975), when the House rejected congressional public financing after it had been approved by the Senate.

Despite the high hopes of public financing supporters, legislation to extend the concept to congressional races was blocked in 1977 by a filibuster in the Senate and opposition in the House Administration Committee. Renewed attempts to push the legislation in 1978 and 1979 also went nowhere.

1979 FECA AMENDMENTS

In a rare demonstration of harmony on a campaign finance measure, Congress in late 1979 passed legislation to eliminate much of the red tape created by the FECA and to encourage political party activity. Agreement was not difficult because the drafters concentrated on solving FECA's noncontroversial problems.

The amendments, signed into law January 8, 1980, reduced FECA's paperwork requirements in several ways. First, the act decreased the maximum number of reports a federal candidate would have to file with the FEC during a two-year election cycle from twenty-four to nine. For Senate candidates, the number of reports mandated over the six-year election cycle was reduced from twenty-eight to seventeen. Second, candidates who raised or spent less than $5,000 in their campaigns would not have to file reports at all. In 1978 about seventy House candidates, including five winners, fell below the $5,000 threshold. Previously, all candidates were required to report their finances regardless of the amount. Also, candidates would have to report in less detail. The legislation raised the threshold for itemizing both contributions and expenditures to $200 from $100. The threshold for reporting independent expenditures was also increased, from $100 to $250.

In 1976 political party leaders had complained that the FECA almost completely precluded state and local party organizations from helping with the presidential campaign. Because they had only limited federal funds to spend, both the Democratic and Republican presidential campaigns focused on media advertising. At the same time, they cut back expenditures on items such as buttons and bumper stickers that traditionally were used in promoting grassroots activity.

In response to the complaints, the 1979 bill permitted state and local party groups to purchase, without limit, campaign materials for volunteer activities to promote any federal candidate. Those items included buttons, bumper stickers, handbills, brochures, posters, and yard signs. Also, those party organizations were allowed to conduct, without financial limit, certain kinds of voter registration and get-out-the-vote drives on behalf of presidential tickets.

The incidental mention of a presidential candidate on the campaign literature of local candidates was no longer counted as a campaign contribution. Previously, such references had been counted, which created paperwork problems in reporting those costs to the FEC. Local party groups would be required to report their finances only if annual spending for volunteer activities exceeded $5,000 or if costs for nonvolunteer projects were more than $1,000. Before, such groups had to file campaign reports if total spending exceeded $1,000 a year.

Volunteer political activity by individuals was encouraged by raising to $1,000, from $500, the amount of money a person could spend in providing his or her home, food, or personal travel on behalf of a candidate without reporting it to the FEC as a contribution. If the volunteer activity was on behalf of a political party, the person could spend up to $2,000 before the amount was treated as a contribution.

The 1979 act also prohibited members from converting leftover campaign funds to personal use. However, those in Congress at the time of the law's enactment were exempted. Because Senate rules flatly prohibited personal use of such funds by former members as well as incumbents, the bill's exemption was of benefit only to sitting House members. The loophole became a target for reformers and caused resentment among senators and younger House members who could not take advantage of it. In 1989 Congress moved to close it by including a provision in an ethics-and-pay law that forced the grandfathered House members to either leave Congress before the beginning of the 103rd Congress in 1993 or lose their right to take the money. The funds that could be converted were frozen at no more than what they had on hand when the 1989 ethics law was enacted.

Congressional Stalemates on Campaign Reform Proposals

The campaign finance debate changed dramatically over the next two decades as new issues came to the forefront. But the outcome was always the same: no major legislation was enacted. Reform fell victim to differences between the parties and the chambers over what was wrong with the system and how it should be remedied.

Congress did pass legislation in 2000 to close a small, albeit controversial, loophole in campaign finance law.

PAC ISSUE DEBATE

PACs came to the forefront of the campaign finance debate in the 1980s. The rise in the number of PACs and their influence in political campaigns put lawmakers on the defensive against a public perception that special interest groups had undue influence on politicians.

The House in 1979 passed a bill to reduce PAC contributions, but the bill died in the Senate the following year under the threat of a filibuster. Although the bill applied only to House races, opponents in the Senate feared that its passage could renew interest in public financing or could lead to PAC spending ceilings in Senate races.

Several years passed before the issue was debated again. This time, in 1986, the Senate went on record twice in favor of strict new controls on PACs. The Senate first adopted an amendment offered by the Democrats that would have set caps on what a candidate could take from PACs overall and singly and also would have closed loopholes on PAC giving that generally favored Republicans. The Senate then adopted a Republican counterproposal to prohibit PAC contributions to national party organizations, which Democrats relied on more heavily than the GOP. But the legislation got caught in partisan maneuvering over who should get the credit—or blame—for reforming campaign finance guidelines, and which party would suffer the most under the proposed restrictions. A final vote was never taken.

COMPREHENSIVE REFORM ATTEMPT

In the next Congress, the Senate debated the most comprehensive campaign finance bill to come before Congress since 1974. But the legislation ultimately was shelved after a record-setting eight cloture votes in 1987–1988 failed to cut off a Republican filibuster.

The cornerstone of the Senate Democrats' bill was a proposal for campaign spending limits, which backers saw as the key to curbing skyrocketing election costs. But such limits were bitterly opposed by Republicans, who thought a spending cap would institutionalize the Democrats' majority in Congress. Another key element that many Republicans abhorred was a provision for public financing for Senate candidates who agreed to abide by the spending limits. Most Republicans said it represented a government intrusion into what generally had been a private realm. Republicans also criticized the bill's aggregate limit on what Senate candidates could accept from PACs on the ground that the provision would favor the well-organized, well-funded PACs that could donate early in an election cycle, freezing out other PACs that wanted to donate later.

The protracted debate over the bill was marked by extraordinary partisanship and elaborate parliamentary maneuvering. Majority Leader Robert Byrd attempted to break the GOP fili-

buster by keeping the Senate in session around the clock. During one of two all-night sessions, Republicans responded in kind, by repeatedly moving for quorum calls and then boycotting the floor. That forced Democrats to keep enough members present to maintain the quorum needed for the Senate to remain in session. Byrd then resorted to a little-known power of the Senate, last used in 1942, to have absent members arrested and brought to the floor. This led to the spectacle of Oregon Republican Bob Packwood being arrested and physically carried onto the Senate floor in the wee hours of February 24, 1988.

A truce was eventually reached, the final unsuccessful cloture vote taken, and the bill was pulled from the floor. A later attempt to adopt a constitutional amendment to overcome the *Buckley v. Valeo* decision forbidding mandatory campaign spending limits suffered a similar fate, as it would in later Congresses.

REPEATED IMPASSES IN 1990S

The movement in the next Congress (1989–1991) to rewrite campaign finance laws ended where it began, mired in disagreement. The House and Senate passed separate bills—both generally backed by Democrats and strongly opposed by Republicans—containing voluntary spending limits and reducing the influence of PACs. But the two chambers' proposals differed substantially. The Senate would have dismantled PACs, while the House would have set limits on their contributions. The bills also were wide apart on the issue of soft money. The Senate proposal would have taken a big step toward imposing federal rules on state election activities; the House plan limited itself primarily to abuses that cropped up in the 1988 presidential campaigns. Facing these broad differences late in the session, as well as a threat from President George Bush to veto any bill with campaign spending limits, conferees on the two bills never met.

Bush in 1989 had proposed what he called a "sweeping system of reform" that sought to eliminate most PACs, enhance the role of political parties, and grind down the electoral advantages enjoyed by incumbents (including one of the major weapons in an incumbent's arsenal, the frank, by banning "unsolicited mass mailings" from congressional offices). Democrats had assailed the Bush plan as baldly partisan. Even within the GOP, there was no consensus on major items such as curbing the frank and eliminating certain PACs.

With campaign finance overhaul presumed dead for the year, lawmakers attempted to peel off the one part of the effort that every politician could agree on: getting broadcasters to lower advertising rates for candidates. But neither chamber acted on the proposal because the effort encountered opposition not only from broadcasters but also from Common Cause, which said the legislation would provide a major benefit to incumbents without dealing with the fundamental problems in the campaign finance system.

Scandals in the next Congress (1991–1993) heightened pressure on both chambers to enact some type of reform measure. The Senate was rocked by the Keating Five savings and loan investigation of 1990–1991, which Common Cause characterized as "the smoking gun" that proved the corruption of the election

Protesters from the National Campaign Finance Reform Coalition wave signs and shout slogans intent on convincing President George Bush not to veto campaign finance legislation in 1992. Bush vetoed the bill and campaign finance reform was dead for the remainder of the decade.

finance system. On the House side, scandals at the House bank and post office reignited the campaign finance issue in 1992, as House Democratic leaders grasped for reform measures large and small.

Both chambers passed bills in 1991 to limit spending and subsidize campaigns with public dollars. The bills, however, were vastly different and finding common ground seemed unlikely. But with the impetus of the ethics scandals, conferees came up with a compromise bill, in part by letting each chamber live by its own rules on public financing. The Senate backed off from its ban on PACs and the House went along with the Senate's more restrictive language on soft money. But in the end what they produced was a Democratic bill and, without bipartisan support, it was doomed. President Bush—objecting to its spending limits, public funding, and creation of separate systems for House and Senate campaigns—vetoed the bill. The Senate fell nine votes short of overriding Bush's veto. In the wake of the legislation's failure in 1992, both Democrats and Republicans aggressively argued that the other side stymied their efforts at reform.

Given the strong backing from Democrats in the previous Congress and incoming President Bill Clinton's vow to overhaul the system, the 103rd Congress (1993–1995) opened with high expectations for enactment of a new campaign finance law. Both chambers did pass bills in 1993, but again they were radically different. The Senate bill banned PACs, while the House bill set an aggregate cap on PAC contributions to a campaign. Both measures contained spending limits but offered vastly different incentives to encourage candidates to comply. House and Senate Democrats worked out a compromise, but the bill died

late in the 1994 session when a GOP-led filibuster blocked the Senate from sending its bill to conference.

Failure to enact the bill in 1994 was a major defeat for Clinton and Democratic congressional leaders. Democrats, however, had set the stage for defeat by waiting until the eleventh hour to come up with a compromise version. Indeed, the long history of the legislation was rich with evidence that many Democrats in both chambers shared GOP objections to establishing a system that would provide congressional candidates with federal subsidies. Other Democrats, particularly in the House, were deeply, if privately, opposed to an overhaul of the system that had protected their seats and majority status for years. In the end, it was the inability of Democrats to iron out their internal differences that delayed the bill so long that it became vulnerable to procedural snags. Some supporters of the legislation blamed Clinton, who had campaigned on the issue but exerted litle pressure on Congress to pass reform in 1994.

The Republican takeover in the next Congress (1995–1997) made little difference in campaign finance legislation. Despite promises to overhaul the system, Republicans had no more success than their Democratic predecessors. The most memorable development on campaign finance in 1995 turned out to be the least important: a much-publicized handshake by President Clinton and House Speaker Newt Gingrich on agreement to create a commission to explore changes in the system. Nothing came of it.

With their new majority status in Congress helping to fill GOP election coffers, many Republicans found themselves loath to change the system. Although rank-and-file members managed to force the leadership to allow floor debates on the issue,

Campaign Finance Overhaul Legislation

Senate

The Senate passed campaign finance legislation early in 2001, but similar legislation in the House had stalled at midyear and faced an uncertain future.

Given its history of death-by-filibuster, a proposal to overhaul the Federal Election Campaign Act seemed an unlikely candidate to be the first major bill passed by the Senate in the 107th Congress (2001–2003). But it was.

Much had happened since the last time the Senate had considered campaign finance legislation in 1999. Sen. John McCain of Arizona, a key proponent of changing the campaign finance system, had made the issue the hallmark of his campaign for the 2000 Republican presidential nomination. Although he failed to win the nomination, McCain—and the issue itself—seemed to have been energized by the enthusiastic response of his supporters. Democratic wins at the polls in the November 2000 election realigned the Senate to be more favorably disposed to the tenets of overhaul legislation. And when a sturdy foe of the bill, Republican Thad Cochran of Mississippi, changed his mind and endorsed it, supporters claimed they had enough votes to ward off yet another filibuster.

McCain and Democratic sponsor Russell D. Feingold of Wisconsin got the freewheeling debate they had long sought and in early April 2001 the Senate passed an amended McCain-Feingold bill by a comfortable margin of 59–41.

The Senate-passed measure banned the national political parties from accepting or spending soft-money contributions and barred state and local parties from spending soft money on federal election activities. The bill blocked labor unions, corporations, and, after a floor amendment, many nonprofit groups from using soft money for issue ads that targeted a federal candidate within sixty days of a general election and thirty days of a primary election. The bill was amended on the floor to allow individuals to contribute $2,000 per election to a candidate (instead of the $1,000 permitted since 1974) and $25,000 per year to national political parties (up from $20,000), with an overall limit of $37,500 per year (up from $25,000). The new limits were to be indexed to rise with inflation.

Senators adopted an amendment to protect themselves from wealthy challengers by raising contribution limits for candidates facing self-financed opponents. The Senate also approved an amendment to ensure that candidates and political parties obtained broadcast advertising at the lowest rate all year, thus avoiding any sharp increases near election day. Among other successful amendments were ones to strengthen disclosure.

McCain-Feingold supporters fended off several divisive proposals. In prior years, Republicans had pushed the issue of "paycheck protection" which involved requiring unions to get written permission before using dues or fees for campaign-related activities. The unions—and their Democratic supporters in Congress—had vigorously resisted such a requirement. During the Senate debate, the GOP put forward a proposal favored by President George W. Bush that would have required both unions and corporations to obtain members' or shareholders' consent before using general funds revenues for political activities. The amendment, which also would have mandated sweeping disclosures of virtually any political activity, was defeated.

The most serious challenge to the bill was an amendment to add a "nonseverability clause," which said that if any portion of the law was found unconstitutional, the entire law would fail. Because several provisions in the McCain-Feingold bill were certain to be challenged in the courts as unconstitutional, the amendment could have ultimately doomed the legislation. It, too, was rejected.

Senate passage of the McCain-Feingold bill marked the first time in eight years that the chamber had approved a broad campaign finance package. Its supporters, while jubilant at the bill's success, were well aware that a number of obstacles lay ahead in the House, a possible conference committee, the White House, and eventually the courts.

House

Efforts to take up campaign finance legislation in the House were abruptly halted in July 2001, when a resolution containing the rules for the debate went down to defeat. The vote reflected the deep division in the House over competing campaign finance bills.

Connecticut Republican Christopher Shays and Massachusetts Democrat Martin T. Meehan had proposed a bill that closely resembled the McCain-Feingold bill. Like the Senate-passed bill, the Shays-Meehan proposal barred the national parties from accepting or spending soft money. It also went along with the Senate provision to permit larger hard-dollar contributions by individuals to Senate candidates but did not raise the limits on individual contributions to House candidates.

Another proposal was offered by Ohio Republican Bob Ney, chairman of the House Administration Committee, and Maryland Democrat Albert R. Wynn, chairman of the Congressional Black Caucus's campaign finance task force. Instead of an outright ban on soft money, the Ney-Wynn bill capped a contributor's soft money donations to any national political party committee at $75,000 per year. It kept the existing limits on hard money contributions by individuals.

Shays and Meehan had agreed to make changes in their bill to attract more support and wanted to offer the revisions as a single amendment when the bill reached the floor. But the Republican leadership proposed instead a rule that would have required fourteen separate votes on the amendments. The Shays-Meehan camp balked at the prospect of separate votes that could unravel their already fragile base of support and rebound to the benefit of the Ney-Wynn proposal.

The House erupted in charges and countercharges. Unable to agree on a compromise, the House rejected the original rule on July 12 by a sharply partisan vote—208 Democrats, 19 Republicans, and one Independent voted against it, while 201 Republicans, one Democrat, and one Independent supported it.

What would happen next for campaign finance reform was uncertain in the immediate aftermath of the vote.

they failed to pass legislation in either chamber. A bipartisan effort to revise campaign finance laws was stopped once again by a filibuster in the Senate. The bill called for voluntary spending limits in return for certain incentives and would have banned PAC and soft money contributions. In the House, a GOP bill that would have set new contribution limits for individuals and PACs was defeated, in part because of an unrelated provision that would have required labor unions to get signed agreements from workers before using their dues for political contributions. A House Democratic alternative was defeated as well.

SOFT MONEY, ISSUE ADS DEBATE

Advocates of a campaign finance overhaul failed again in the 105th Congress (1997–1999). They had hoped revelations of campaign abuses in the 1996 election would outrage the public sufficiently to put pressure on Congress to move legislation, but Republican leaders focused instead on investigations into Democratic fund-raising activities. The House passed a sweeping measure after its backers surmounted attempts by the GOP leadership to block its consideration on the House floor. The leaders relented in the face of a growing number of signatures on a discharge petition to bring the bill to the floor without committee action, a procedural move that would have cost the leadership control of the floor and allowed backers to debate a variety of campaign finance bills on their own terms. A Senate bill succumbed once again to a filibuster.

But what was interesting this time around was how much the focus of the campaign finance debate had changed. PAC contributions, spending limits, and public funding were no longer the dominant themes. In fact, the House-passed bill included no provisions in those areas. And on the Senate side, sponsors of campaign finance legislation dropped those provisions in an attempt to broaden GOP support for their bill. The House and Senate bills focused instead on soft money and issue advocacy advertising, reflecting the dramatic growth of both in the 1990s and the enormous controversy surrounding them. The bills would have banned national parties from receiving or spending soft money and would have prohibited state and local parties from using soft money for federal election activity. They also would have redefined express advocacy so that more of what was then classified as issue advocacy advertising would be regulated.

In the next Congress (1999–2001), the House passed a bill that was substantively the same as the legislation it had approved in 1998. Senate sponsors put aside—at least for the time being—their proposal to more closely regulate issue ads and opted instead for a narrow bill that focused on banning soft money. They hoped this move would neutralize GOP opponents' argument that the bill was a violation of free speech rights at least enough to pick up the votes to overcome a filibuster. But the new strategy, like the old ones, failed.

"SECTION 527" LOOPHOLE CLOSED

Months after he had dropped out of a presidential campaign built on a call for an overhaul of campaign finance laws, Sen. John McCain led a successful effort to win passage of legislation to require full disclosure of contributors and spending by a growing number of secret political groups. McCain had been targeted during the primary campaign by one of the groups, called "527s" after the section of the tax code that governed their existence. *(See "Section 527" Groups, p. 107.)*

The new law, passed overwhelmingly by both chambers, required any Section 527 group that raised at least $25,000 annually to report to the IRS each donor of $200 or more and any spending of more than $500. The IRS and the groups were required to make the reports public.

McCain and others hoped that their victory—a precision attack on a single area of the law—would pressure colleagues to support their broader goal of a complete ban on soft money. In an August 2000 television interview, McCain vowed to tie up the Senate the next year until campaign finance reform was passed. "We will have blood all over the floor of the Senate until we accede to the demands now, not the wishes, the demands of the American people to be represented in Washington again," McCain insisted.[89]

Efforts by McCain and his Democratic counterpart on the issue, Russell D. Feingold of Wisconsin, were energized in the 107th Congress (2001–2003), thanks to Democratic gains in the Senate in the 2000 election and the conversion of conservative Republican Sen. Thad Cochran of Mississippi to their cause. Cochran's support was touted as providing the sixtieth vote needed to shut down the perennial filibuster against campaign finance-related legislation. This new-found support allowed the Senate to pass major campaign finance legislation in early 2001. *(See box, Campaign Finance Overhaul Legislation, p. 124.)*

Notes

1. Estimate of $2.4–$2.5 billion: Joseph E. Cantor, "Campaign Finance in the 2000 Federal Elections: Overview and Estimates of the Flow of Money," Library of Congress, Congressional Research Service, Report No. RL30884, March 16, 2001. Estimates in $3 billion range: Center for Responsive Politics and Common Cause (November 2000).

Unless otherwise noted, the figures in this chapter on campaign receipts and expenditures were from the Federal Election Commission (FEC). Figures on congressional campaign finance include money that moved in all congressional races, including those of primary losers. Most figures came from "FEC Reports on Congressional Financial Activity for 2000," a May 15, 2001, FEC press release, and "FEC Reports Increase in Party Fundraising for 2000," a May 15, 2001, FEC press release. Figures on presidential campaign finance came from FEC press releases and "Receipts of 1999–2000 Presidential Campaigns Through July 31, 2000," which was available on the FEC Web site http://www.fec.gov.

2. Herbert E. Alexander, "Spending in the 1996 Elections," in *Financing the 1996 Election*, ed. John C. Green (Armonk, N.Y.: M.E. Sharpe, 1999), 12.

3. Quoted in Chuck Alston, "Image Problems Propel Congress Back to Campaign Finance Bills," *Congressional Quarterly Weekly Report*, February 2, 1991, 281.

4. Frank J. Sorauf, *Money in American Elections* (Glenview, Ill.: Scott, Foresman, 1988), 73–74.

5. 1997 poll: Center for Responsive Politics and Princeton Survey Research Associates, "Money and Politics: A National Survey of the Public's Views on How Money Impacts Our Political System" (Washington, D.C.: Center for Responsive Politics, April–May 1997). 2001 polls: The Gallup Organization, "Widespread Public Support for Campaign Finance Reform" (Princeton, N.J.: The Gallup Organization, March 20, 2001).

6. Quoted in Larry J. Sabato, *PAC Power: Inside the World of Political Action Committees* (New York: Norton, 1984), 171.

7. Jasper B. Shannon, *Money and Politics,* (New York: Random House, 1959), 25.

8. Anthony Corrado, "Money and Politics: A History of Federal Campaign Finance Law," in *Campaign Finance Reform: A Sourcebook,* ed. Anthony Corrado et al. (Washington, D.C.: Brookings Institution, 1997), 27.

9. Quoted in Charles Lewis and the Center for Public Integrity, *The Buying of the President 2000,* (New York: Avon Books, 2000), ix.

10. Shannon, *Money and Politics,* 37.

11. General information in this section came primarily from two Federal Election Commission publications: *Public Funding of Presidential Elections* (August 1996) and *The Presidential Public Funding Program* (April 1993). Specifics on the 2000 presidential race came from a series of FEC press releases, including "FEC Announces 2000 Presidential Spending Limits," March 1, 2000; "FEC Approves Matching Funds for 2000 Presidential Candidates," May 31, 2000; "Republican and Democratic Parties to Receive Additional Funds for Party Nominating Conventions," March 28, 2000; "Reform Party to Receive Additional Funds for Nominating Convention," May 25, 2000. Charts with the receipts and disbursements of the 1999–2000 presidential campaigns through July 31, 2000, were available on the FEC Web site: http://www.fec.gov.

12. The total cost to the Presidential Election Campaign Fund was actually higher—$890.5 million—because any repayments that convention and general election committees are required to make after an FEC audit do not return to the Fund. (Repayments by primary candidates' committees do go back into the fund.)

13. Joseph E. Cantor, "The Presidential Election Campaign Fund and Tax Checkoff: Background and Current Issues," Rept. No. RS20133, Library of Congress, Congressional Research Service, March 26, 1999, 3; Federal Election Commission, *Annual Report 1998,* 87.

14. Ibid.

15. Alexander, "Spending in the 1996 Elections," in *Financing the 1996 Election,* 31.

16. Cantor, "The Presidential Election Campaign Fund and Tax Checkoff: Background and Current Issues," 3.

17. Federal Election Commission, *The Presidential Public Funding Program,* 28.

18. Cantor, "The Presidential Election Campaign Fund and Tax Checkoff: Background and Current Issues," 4.

19. Ruth Marcus, "Analysis: Dollars Dictate Early Exits," *Washington Post,* October 21, 1999, 1.

20. Anthony Corrado "Financing the 1996 Presidential General Election," in *Financing the 1996 Election,* 92–93.

21. Allen, Mike. "For Party Faithful, 'Packages' and Perks," *Washington Post,* June 20, 2000, A6.

22. Ibid., A1, A6.

23. Alexander, "Spending in the 1996 Elections," in *Financing the 1996 Election,* 22, 24.

24. A postelection audit required a $1.7 million repayment, so Perot's net public funding amounted to about $27 million.

25. Wesley Joe and Clyde Wilcox, "Financing the 1996 Presidential Nominations," in *Financing the 1996 Election,* 42.

26. Derek Willis, "Rx for Business: Grass Roots," *CQ Weekly,* May 27, 2000, 1253–1254.

27. Alexander, "Spending in the 1996 Elections," in *Financing the 1996 Election,* 16–22.

28. Joe and Wilcox, "Financing the 1996 Presidential Nominations," in *Financing the 1996 Election,* 37–38.

29. Ibid., 48.

30. Ira Chinoy, "In Presidential Race, TV Ads Were Biggest '96 Cost By Far," *Washington Post,* March 31, 1997, A19.

31. Corrado, "Financing the 1996 Presidential General Election," in *Financing the 1996 Election,* 86–87.

32. Ibid., 87.

33. Ibid., 92.

34. Paul S. Herrnson, "Money and Motives: Spending in House Elections," in *Congress Reconsidered,* 6th ed., ed. Lawrence C. Dodd and Bruce I. Oppenheimer (Washington, D.C.: CQ Press, 1997), 114.

35. Frank J. Sorauf, "Political Action Committees," in *Campaign Finance Reform: A Sourcebook,* 123.

36. Larry Makinson, "The Big Picture: Money Follows Power Shift on Capitol Hill" (Washington, D.C.: Center for Responsive Politics, 1997), 10.

37. Cantor, "Campaign Finance in the 2000 Federal Elections," 9; Sorauf, "Political Action Committees," 126.

38. Sorauf, *Money in American Elections,* 174.

39. Trevor Potter, "Where Are We Now? The Current State of Campaign Finance Law," in *Campaign Finance Reform: A Sourcebook,* 7.

40. Herrnson, "Money and Motives," in *Congress Reconsidered,* 107–108.

41. Ibid., 105.

42. David B. Magleby and Candice J. Nelson, *The Money Chase: Congressional Campaign Finance Reform* (Washington, D.C.: Brookings Institution, 1990), 58.

43. Senate Committee on the Judiciary, Subcommittee on the Constitution, "Hearing on Campaign Finance Reform," 100th Cong., 2nd sess., February 28, 1990, 7.

44. Quoted in Chuck Alston, "Forcing Down Cost of TV Ads Appeals to Both Parties," *Congressional Quarterly Weekly Report,* March 16, 1991, 647.

45. Joseph E. Cantor, Denis Steven Rutkus, and Kevin B. Greely, "Free and Reduced-Rate Television Time for Political Candidates," Rept. No. 97-680 GOV, Library of Congress, Congressional Research Service, July 7, 1997, iii, 3–4.

46. Sara Fritz and Dwight Morris, *Gold-Plated Politics: Running for Congress in the 1990s* (Washington, D.C.: CQ Press, 1992), 128.

47. Quoted in Alston, "Forcing Down Cost of TV Ads Appeals to Both Parties," 648.

48. Herrnson, *Congressional Elections: Campaigning at Home and in Washington,* 3d ed. (Washington, D.C.: CQ Press, 2000), 205.

49. Dwight Morris and Murielle E. Gamache, *Handbook of Campaign Spending: Money in the 1992 Congressional Races* (Washington D.C.: Congressional Quarterly, 1994), 8–12.

50. Joseph E. Cantor, "Congressional Campaign Spending: 1976–1996," Rept. No. 97-793 GOV, Library of Congress, Congressional Research Service, August 19, 1997, 3–4; Cantor, "Campaign Financing," Report No. IB87020, Library of Congress, Congressional Research Service, March 30, 2001, 2.

51. 1994 figures: Common Cause News, April 8, 1999. 2000 figures: Federal Election Commission.

52. Cantor, "Congressional Campaign Spending: 1976–1996," 3–4; Cantor, "Campaign Financing," 2.

53. 2000 figures: Federal Election Commission. 1998 figures: Common Cause News, April 8, 1999.

54. Sheila Krumholz, "Tracking the Cash: Candidate Fund-Raising in the 1998 Elections" (Washington, D.C.: Center for Responsive Politics, 1998).

55. Quoted in Larry J. Sabato, *Paying for Elections: The Campaign Finance Thicket* (New York: Twentieth Century Fund/Priority Press, 1989), 11.

56. Joseph E. Cantor, "Campaign Financing," Rept. No. IB87020, Library of Congress, Congressional Research Service, March 30, 2001, 2.

57. Gary C. Jacobson, "Money in the 1980 and 1982 Congressional Elections," in *Money and Politics in the United States: Financing Elections in the 1980s,* ed. Michael J. Malbin (Washington, D.C.: American Enterprise Institute, 1984), 58.

58. Sorauf, *Money in American Elections,* 333.

59. Helen Dewar, "Lautenberg to Retire from Senate in 2000," *Washington Post,* February 18, 1999, A3.

60. Diane Granat, "Parties' Schools for Politicians Grooming Troops for Elections," *Congressional Quarterly Weekly Report,* May 5, 1984, 1036.

61. Quoted in Andy Plattner, "The High Cost of Holding—and Keeping—Public Office," *U.S. News & World Report,* June 22, 1987, 30.

62. David E. Price, "The House of Representatives: A Report from the Field," in *Congress Reconsidered,* 4th ed., ed. Lawrence C. Dodd and Bruce I. Oppenheimer (Washington, D.C.: CQ Press, 1989), 417–418.

63. Senate Committee on Rules and Administration, *Hearings on Senate Campaign Finance Proposals,* 100th Cong., 1st sess., March 5 and 18, April 22 and 23, 1987, 7–8.

64. Magleby and Nelson, *The Money Chase,* 44.

65. Roger H. Davidson and Walter J. Oleszek, *Congress and Its Members,* 7th ed. (Washington, D.C.: CQ Press, 2000), 68.

66. Sabato, *Paying for Elections,* 4.

67. Senate Committee on Rules and Administration, Hearings on Campaign Finance Reform, 101st Cong., 1st sess., Fred Wertheimer testimony, April 20, 1989, committee handout, 30.

68. Quoted in Chuck Alston, "A Political Money Tree Waits for Incumbents in Need," *Congressional Quarterly Weekly Report,* June 30, 1990, 2026.

69. John Lewis, "In Defense of PACs," *Washington Post,* July 1, 1994, A25.

70. Cantor, "Campaign Financing," 2.

71. Sorauf, "Political Action Committees," in *Campaign Finance Reform: A Sourcebook,* 128.

72. Anthony Corrado, "Party Soft Money," in *Campaign Finance Reform: A Sourcebook,* 172.

73. Quoted in Alan Greenblatt, "Soft Money: The Root of All Evil or a Party-Building Necessity?" *Congressional Quarterly Weekly Report,* September 6, 1997, 2065.

74. David B. Magleby and Marianne Holt, ed., "Outside Money: Soft Money & Issue Ads in Competitive 1998 Congressional Elections" (Provo, Utah: Brigham Young University, 1999), 12.

75. Jackie Koszczuk, " 'Soft Money' Speaks Loudly on Capitol Hill This Season," *CQ Weekly,* June 27, 1998, 1738.

76. Lorie Slass et al., "Issue Advertising in the 1999–2000 Election Cycle," (Philadelphia: University of Pennsylvania, Annenberg Public Policy Center, 2001), 2.

77. Andrew Taylor, " '527' Measure Sent to Clinton As Anaylsts Play Down Significance," *CQ Weekly,* July 1, 2000, 1587.

78. Ibid.

79. Quoted in Rebecca Carr, "Campaign Finance: Lingering Doubts," *Congressional Quarterly Weekly Report,* February 8, 1997, 353.

80. Robert E. Mutch, *Campaigns, Congress, and Courts: The Making of Federal Campaign Finance Law* (New York: Praeger, 1988), xv.

81. George Thayer, *Who Shakes the Money Tree? American Campaign Financing Practices from 1789 to the Present* (New York: Simon and Schuster, 1973), 25.

82. Mutch, *Campaigns, Congress, and Courts,* xvi.

83. Ibid., xvii.

84. Ibid., 4.

85. Alexander Heard, *The Costs of Democracy* (Chapel Hill: University of North Carolina Press, 1960), 388.

86. Herbert E. Alexander, *Financing the 1968 Election* (Lexington, Mass.: D.C. Heath, 1971), 93.

87. Herbert E. Alexander, *Financing the 1972 Election* (Lexington, Mass.: D.C. Heath, 1976), 7.

88. *Facts on File,* April 29–May 5, 1973, 357.

89. Jim Lehrer interview with Sen. John McCain, R-Ariz., on "The NewsHour with Jim Lehrer," Public Broadcasting Service, August 1, 2000.

CHAPTER 6

The Historical Significance
of Southern Primaries

Because of the overwhelming dominance of the Democratic Party in the South during the first half of the twentieth century, the party's primaries became, in effect, the region's significant elections. The eleven states that constitute the South—all members of the Civil War Confederacy—are Alabama, Arkansas, Florida, Georgia, Louisiana, Mississippi, North Carolina, South Carolina, Tennessee, Texas, and Virginia.

In his classic study *Southern Politics in State and Nation,* V. O. Key Jr. concluded, "In fact, the Democratic primary is no nominating method at all. The primary is the election. . . ." That was in 1949, shortly before Republicans began seriously challenging Democrats for hegemony in the region.

But Key's observation holds true for the twentieth century up through the time of his study and for much of the period since, depending on the particular state and election involved. Of the 132 elections to the Senate held in the eleven former Confederate states in the period 1919–1948, the Democratic nominee won 131 times. The only exception was a special election in Arkansas in 1937 when the Democratic nominee lost to an independent Democrat.

The southern shift to the Republican Party began on the presidential level in 1964, when Barry Goldwater's criticisms of civil rights laws found a wide audience. In 1972 Republican presidential nominee Richard Nixon carried all eleven states of the Old South with at least 65 percent of the vote. In 1984 and 1988 Ronald Reagan and George Bush did almost as well, carrying every southern state with at least 58 percent (Reagan) or 54 percent (Bush) of the vote. Although the Democrats regained the White House in 1992 and 1996, the party's all-southern ticket of Bill Clinton of Arkansas and Al Gore of Tennessee carried only four southern states in both elections. In 1992 Clinton and Gore won Arkansas, Georgia, Louisiana, and Tennessee. In 1996 the ticket lost Georgia but picked up Florida—the first time the state had gone Democratic since 1976. In the close 2000 presidential race, Republican George W. Bush won every southern state, including Tennessee, the home state of his Democratic opponent Gore.

From the 1960s to the 1990s, the growth of the Republican Party in southern congressional delegations was steady but slower than on the presidential level. The first popularly elected Republican U.S. senator from the South, John G. Tower of Texas, won a special election in 1961. Thereafter, Republicans won their first Senate seats in South Carolina (1966), Tennessee (1966), Florida (1968), North Carolina and Virginia (1972), Mississippi (1978), Alabama and Georgia (1980), and Arkansas (1996). By 2001 Louisiana was the only southern state not to ever popularly elect a Republican senator.

Thirty years of political realignment in the South culminated in the 1994 congressional elections when the Republican Party won majority status in the South. Not since Reconstruction had the GOP held a majority of the region's seats in the House or in the Senate. The historic election also ushered in Republican control of Congress with southern GOP leadership: in 1995 Newt Gingrich of Georgia was elected Speaker of the House and in 1996 Trent Lott of Mississippi was elected Senate majority leader. (Gingrich stepped down as Speaker in 1999 after a poor showing by the Republicans in the 1998 midterm elections, and Lott lost majority control of the Senate in 2001 when Republican Jim Jeffords became an independent.) By 2001, however, GOP congressional gains in the South had solidified. In the eleven southern states, the Republicans outnumbered the Democrats thirteen to nine in Senate seats and seventy-one to fifty-four in U.S. House seats.

By 2001 Republican dominance in the South looked secure for the foreseeable future. The dramatic population influx in the 1980s and 1990s had reshaped the southern political landscape to the Republicans' advantage. Old-time Democratic voters were overwhelmed in many parts of the South by more independent or GOP-oriented newcomers. Younger voters found the region's historical Democratic roots irrelevant to their concerns. The GOP also aggressively fielded candidates where it once gave the Democrats a free ride. For their part, these candidates emphasized traditional values, an emphasis that resonated among the regions' white voters, who constituted a majority of the electorate in every southern state. Although most of the Senate contests in the South were competitive in the 1990s, one sign of the swing to Republican power in the region came in 1990 when Republican senator Thad Cochran of Mississippi faced no Democratic opposition in the general election.

Runoff Primaries

The South along with the rest of the nation instituted primaries during the first two decades of the twentieth century. By 1920 all eleven southern states were choosing their Democratic senatorial nominees through the primary process.

But because the primaries were, for all practical purposes, the deciding election, many legislators began to doubt the effectiveness of a system that frequently allowed a candidate in a multicandidate race to win a plurality of the popular vote—and thus the Democratic nomination that ensured election—even though he received only a small percentage of the total primary vote.

So, most southern states adopted the runoff primary—a second election following the first primary, usually by two to four weeks—that matched only the top two contenders from the first primary. The runoff system was adopted in Alabama in 1931, Arkansas in 1939, Florida in 1929, Georgia in 1917 (with the county unit system (see "County Unit System: Georgia," p. 131), Louisiana in 1922, Mississippi in 1902, North Carolina in 1915, South Carolina in 1915, and Texas in 1918. (Arkansas had adopted the runoff in 1933, abandoned it in 1935, then reinstituted it in 1939.) Virginia adopted the runoff in 1969 but repealed it in 1971.

After 1969 Tennessee remained the only southern state to nominate by plurality. In that state's 1976 Senate race, James Sasser won the Democratic nomination with only 44.2 percent of the vote in a field of five candidates. Sasser went on to win his first election to the Senate in November.

Runoffs are not always obligatory. In most states, if the second-place finisher in the primary does not want a runoff, the first-place candidate is then the winner without a runoff. In the Virginia Democratic primary of 1970, for example, front-runner George C. Rawlings missed winning a majority of the vote in the first primary, winding up with 45.7 percent. However, Clive L. DuVal who placed a close second with 45.1 percent, declined a runoff. No runoff was held and Rawlings automatically became the Democratic nominee. (Rawlings lost the general election to former Democratic senator Harry F. Byrd Jr., who ran as an independent.)

Jesse L. Jackson, contender for the 1984 Democratic presidential nomination, mounted an attack against the runoff feature in the spring of that year. Jackson hoped to persuade the ten other southern states to join Tennessee in avoiding the runoff.

Jackson argued that runoffs injured black candidates' chances of victory because in the second election whites, who comprised the majority of registered voters, usually voted on the basis of race.

Jackson carried his plea to the Democratic National Convention, which defeated his move to abolish runoffs, 2,500.8 to 1,253.2. Supporters argued that runoffs prevented the election of fringe candidates when more qualified candidates split the vote in hotly contested primaries. In addition, conservative southerners opposed having a national convention decide their state's election procedures.

Preferential Primaries

Three southern states—Alabama, Florida, and Louisiana—tried to avoid the effort and expense of runoff elections by experimenting with a preferential system of primary voting. All three later switched to the runoff system—Alabama after the election of 1930, Florida after the election of 1928, and Louisiana (whose system was similar to Alabama's) after the election of 1920. Louisiana modified its system yet again in 1975, this time to a two-step process: an initial nonpartisan primary followed by a general election runoff between the two top finishers.

Under the preferential system voters, instead of simply marking an X opposite one candidate's name, write the digits 1 or 2, beside the names of two candidates. This indicates the "preference" order voters give each of the candidates, the number one indicating their first choice, the number two their second choice. To determine the winner, without a runoff, second-choice votes are added to the first-choice votes and the candidate with the highest combined total wins.

ALABAMA

Under the Alabama system, each voter expressed a first and second choice. if no candidate received a majority of the first choices, all but the two leaders were eliminated. All second choices expressed for the two leaders were then added to their first-choice totals, the candidate with the highest combined total winning.

In the Democratic primary for U.S. senator on May 13, 1920, for a special four-year term to fill a vacancy, the candidates were J. Thomas Heflin and three persons whose first names are not available: White, O'Neal, and Rushton. Heflin, with 49,554 first-choice votes, led the field but received only 37.9 percent of the total. White ran second with 34,854 first-choice votes, or 26.6 percent; O'Neal had 33,174 first-choice votes, or 25.4 percent, and Rushton was last with 13,232 first-choice votes, or 10.1 percent. Thus, in many southern states a runoff would have been necessary. But instead of a runoff all second-choice votes cast for the two leaders—Heflin and White—were added to their first-choice ballots. A total of 11,062 second-choice votes were cast for Heflin by voters whose first choice had gone to one of the other three candidates. Added to his first-choice vote of 49,554, this gave Heflin a grand total of 60,016 votes. White received 12,699 second-choice votes—more than Heflin—but the second-choice votes were not enough to raise his grand total above Heflin's. White thus wound up with a grand total of 47,553 votes, and Heflin was the winner.

FLORIDA

The Florida system of preference voting differed somewhat from the Alabama system. In Florida, as in Alabama, each voter expressed a first and second choice. Also as in Alabama, if no candidate received a majority of first choices, all candidates but the two highest first-choice candidates were eliminated. To determine the winner, the second choices expressed for the two highest *on the ballots of eliminated candidates only* were added to the first-choice totals. (In Alabama, the second choices for the two leaders expressed on ballots for *all* candidates, including the two leaders, were added to the first-choice totals.)

The preference system, however, did not prove useful. Apparently it was too confusing for voters, most of whom did not bother to cast second-choice votes. In the Alabama election discussed above, for example, there were 130,814 first-choice votes, but only 34,768 second-choice votes.

LOUISIANA

Not satisfied with either the partisan runoff or the preferential primary, Louisiana adopted a law in 1975 that allowed its voters to participate in an initial open primary followed by a runoff general election between the two top finishers. In the primary, all candidates of all parties were to be on the ballot, but party designations were optional and at the individual candi-

Table 6-1
Preference and Runoff Primaries

State	Preferential primary	Runoff primary adopted
Alabama	Until 1931	1931
Arkansas	—	1939[1]
Florida	Until 1929	1929
Georgia	—	1917[2]
Louisiana[3]	Until 1922	1922
Mississippi	—	1902
North Carolina	—	1915
South Carolina	—	1915
Tennessee[4]	—	—
Texas	—	1918
Virginia[5]	—	—

1. Arkansas adopted the runoff in 1933, abandoned it in 1935, and reinstituted it in 1939.

2. Runoff held under county unit system.

3. Louisiana used the runoff "for a time prior to 1916," according to political scientist V. O. Key Jr.; in 1975 Louisiana adopted an initial *nonpartisan* primary followed by a general election runoff.

4. Tennessee has never used the preferential or runoff primary. Candidates are nominated by winning a plurality.

5. Virginia adopted the runoff primary in 1969 and repealed it in 1971.

Sources: Alexander Heard and Donald S. Strong, *Southern Primaries and Elections,* Reprint 1950 (Salem, N.H.: Ayers, 1970); V. O. Key Jr., *Southern Politics in State and Nation* (New York: Knopf, 1949); and Virginia secretary of state.

date's discretion. A candidate receiving more than 50 percent of the primary vote would be unopposed in the general election. If no candidate received more than 50 percent of the vote, the two candidates receiving the greatest number of votes—regardless of party—would oppose each other in the runoff general election.

Thus, in 1978, when the first Senate seat was chosen under this new system, two candidates, both Democrats, entered the initial open primary. There were no Republicans, independent or minor party candidates. J. Bennett Johnston received 59.4 percent of the vote, and he was elected senator. (Louisiana in 1978 dispensed with the runoff general election if the primary winner received more than 50 percent of the vote.) If Johnston had placed first with less than 50 percent of the vote, the runoff general election would have been between him and the second-place finisher, even though the other candidate was also a Democrat.

County Unit System: Georgia

Another variant of the primary system was Georgia's county unit system. Each county in the state was apportioned a certain number of unit votes. The candidate who received the largest number of popular votes in the county was awarded all the county's unit votes, even if he won only a plurality and not a majority. A candidate had to have a majority of the state's county unit votes to win the primary; otherwise a runoff became necessary. The runoff also was held on the basis of the county unit system.

For example, as of 1946, there were 410 county unit votes. The eight most populous counties had six unit votes each, the next thirty most populous counties had four each, and the re-

maining 121 counties had two each. The system was weighted toward rural and sparsely populated areas, because every county, no matter how small, had at least two unit votes.

The county unit system sometimes produced winners who received less than a majority of popular votes. Although no senators were ever elected through the county unit system without also attaining a majority of the popular vote, political scientist Key found that in two of sixteen gubernatorial races between 1915 and 1948 the winner of a majority of county units received less than a majority of the popular votes. In a third case, that of 1946, the winner of the county unit vote, Eugene Talmadge, actually received fewer popular votes than his chief opponent, James V. Carmichael.

The county unit system fell before the Supreme Court's "one-person, one-vote" doctrine. In the 1963 case, *Gray v. Sanders,* the court declared the Georgia county unit system unconstitutional because of the disparity in representation between the urban and rural areas.

Special Elections

As in other states, special elections in the South are held to fill vacancies for Senate seats when they occur. However, vacancies sometimes happen at times inconvenient for going through the lengthy runoff primary process prior to the special election. Either the filing deadline for the primaries has passed, or the vacancy occurs in a year when there is no regular primary scheduled. In such cases, the Democratic state committee sometimes selects the party nominee without holding a primary.

This process has led to unexpected results. In Arkansas in 1937, for example, a special election was held on Oct. 19 for the five years remaining in the term of Democratic senator Joseph T. Robinson, who had died in office. The Democratic state committee chose Gov. Carl E. Bailey as the party's official nominee. But Rep. John E. Miller of the 2nd District promptly jumped into the race as an independent Democrat, complaining that Democratic voters had not been given a choice of who their nominee should be. The result was a Miller victory, with 60.5 percent of the vote.

In an even more sensational case, this time in a regular election, the Democratic Party leadership in South Carolina found its wishes thwarted in 1954 when it nominated Edgar A. Brown following the death of Sen. Burnet R. Maybank, who had won renomination in the June Democratic primary. Former governor Strom Thurmond, feeling aggrieved that he had been deprived of a chance for the Senate nomination, entered the November election as a write-in candidate. With the backing of the outgoing governor, James F. Byrnes, Thurmond won the race overwhelmingly, 143,444 to 83,525—making him the only senator ever elected on a write-in vote.

To avoid the pitfalls sometimes encountered when candidates are chosen without a primary, Texas adopted a unique method of holding special elections for U.S. House and Senate seats. All candidates, no matter which party they belong to, compete in a free-for-all first election. If no one receives a majority, a second election is held between the top two candidates, regardless of party. Thus, the second election could occur between two Democrats, between two Republicans, or between a Democrat and a Republican or even between third-party candidates. The system was used in the 1961 special Senate contest to fill the vacancy caused when Democratic senator Lyndon B. Johnson resigned to become vice president. In the first contest, there were seventy-three candidates competing, with Republican John G. Tower and Democrat William Blakley finishing first and second. The second election resulted in a Tower victory, 448,217 to 437,874. The same system prevails for Texas' special U.S. House elections.

Racial Discrimination

Closely connected with the history of southern Democratic primaries is the issue of race. In many southern states, African Americans were long barred from participation in the Democratic primary, either on a statewide basis or in various counties. To exclude blacks from the primaries, the Democratic Party was designated as a private association or club. The practice was defended as constitutional because the Fifteenth Amendment, ratified in 1870, prohibited only *states,* not private associations, from denying the right to vote to persons on account of race or color. However, in 1944 the Supreme Court, in the case of *Smith v. Allwright,* declared the white primary unconstitutional, holding that it was an integral part of the election machinery for choosing state and federal officials.

POLL TAX

Another device used in limiting both black and white voters was the poll tax, which required the payment of a fee before voting. The amount of the poll tax ranged from one to two dollars, but in Alabama, Mississippi, Virginia, and Georgia before 1945 the tax was cumulative. Thus, a new voter in Georgia could face up to $47 in fees. Various regulations as to the time and manner of payment of the tax also substantially reduced the number of voters. In Mississippi, for example, a person wanting to vote in the Democratic primary (usually held in August) had to pay the poll tax on or before the first day of the two preceding Februarys—long before most voters had even begun to think about the election.

The poll tax was barred in federal elections by ratification of the Twenty-fourth Amendment in January 1964. The amendment simply stated that the "right of citizens of the United States to vote in any primary or other election . . . shall not be denied or abridged by the United States or any other State by reason of failure to pay any poll tax or other tax."

LITERACY TESTS

The literacy test was another method used to limit the southern franchise to whites. Voters were required to read and/or write correctly—usually a section of the state or federal Constitution. Sometimes, voters who could not pass the test could have the materials read to them, to see if they could "understand" or "interpret" it correctly. This provision allowed local voting officials, inevitably whites, to judge whether voters passed the tests; it usually resulted in whites passing and blacks failing.

However, in his study of southern politics, Key concluded that informal pressures—including economic reprisals and other sanctions—were more important in limiting the black franchise than were the official suffrage limitations.

By the 1970s most formal bars to voting in the South, and many informal ones, had been lifted, either by constitutional amendment, federal laws, state action, or protest movements.

CHAPTER 7

Politics and Issues, 1945–2000

WHAT AN EXTRAORDINARY fifty-six years it was. For much of the period the United States and the Soviet Union were locked in a cold war. Then suddenly the war was over, the Soviet Union collapsed, and the Berlin Wall came tumbling down.

Economic boom times mingled with recessions, and by the end billion-dollar budget deficits had turned into billion-dollar surpluses that were projected to total in the trillions.

Until a Republican revolution in the 1990s proved otherwise, Democrats for much of the time appeared to be the permanent majority in Congress, even while Republicans increasingly dominated in the race for the presidency as the twentieth century wound down.

Civil rights battles tore at the conscience of the nation, and barriers to equal rights and opportunity gave way.

A vast legislative program called the Great Society built on Depression-era New Deal programs and the federal social safety net held tight—until the federal government ended its sixty-one-year-old promise of welfare and turned it over to the states.

Technology advances ushered in the age of television, space exploration, computers, and astounding medical advances. Human beings walked on the moon and everyday people ventured onto the Internet's information highway.

The nation was battered by a divisive war. It mourned the loss of a young president and other leaders cut down by assassins' bullets. It weathered scandals that led to the resignation of one president and the impeachment of another. And it survived a presidential election that showed the country almost evenly divided politically and in the end was decided by the Supreme Court.

Changes seemed to come at breathtaking speed. It was, indeed, an extraordinary period in American history.

POLITICS OF CONSENSUS

When the leaders of the world war II generation stepped aside for a new generation in the closing decade of the twentieth century, they turned over a very different country from the one they inherited a half century earlier. A country once seemingly bound together by a politics of national consensus, particularly in foreign policy, was torn by an increasingly wide ideological chasm in social, economic, and political ideas that spawned a politics of division.

The United States had emerged from World War II in general agreement over its domestic and foreign policy goals. Much of the American public accepted the New Deal's expansion of the role of government into a quasi-welfare state, which they expected to provide a safety net. Coming out of World War II with vivid memories of the Great Depression of the 1930s, most Americans wanted a government that would protect them from social and economic misfortune. Even the Republican administration of war hero Dwight D. Eisenhower in the 1950s and most of the dominant liberal wing of the GOP largely accepted the basic welfare state tenets inherited from the New Deal.

On the international front, there was consensus as well. The country understood that the United States was now a global power and could not retreat into the isolationism that characterized the 1930s and earlier decades. As the first atomic power and leader of the community of free nations, the United States found itself at the forefront of the struggle to contain world communism. It constructed a complex series of global alliances, was the architect of the economic revival of postwar Europe, and entered the Korean War to maintain its position in Asia. In the context of the cold war struggle between democratic nations, led by the United States, and the Communist bloc, led by the Soviet Union, the overall direction of U.S. policies went unquestioned for several decades.

While this consensus was real, and in foreign policy all but unavoidable in light of the cold war, it camouflaged a festering unhappiness and discontent among a significant number of very conservative Republicans, and some sympathetic Democrats, who never fully bought into the GOP liberal wing's embrace of New Deal heritage. This previously latent force emerged dramatically in 1964 in a challenge by conservative GOP presidential candidate Barry Goldwater. The American voters overwhelmingly rejected the challenge at the time but that election turned out to be the harbinger of a fundamental shift in the political fortunes—and the ideological underpinnings—of the major political parties and country's political direction. Strains in the bipartisan consensus were not far off, as the country headed into a turbulent thirty-five-year period.

TOLL ON NATIONAL UNITY

After his landslide victory over Goldwater in 1964, President Lyndon B. Johnson moved to greatly expand the nation's social safety net through a comprehensive domestic program, known as the Great Society, to fight poverty, ignorance, disease, and other social problems. In time, some of the more controversial programs were ended and rising crime rates and urban riots in the 1960s made many people less sympathetic to the needs of the poor. However, the core of the Great Society in areas such as health care, education, and civil rights endured.

But the national consensus on U.S. policy abroad started to fall apart, even in the face of a continued agreement about the cold war struggle between the two superpowers. The root of the disintegrating consensus was in the Southeast Asian country of Vietnam, where a civil war between the communist North and the noncommunist South broke out in the aftermath of the end of colonialism following World War II. Politically in the United States, the war was projected on the superpower struggle and South Vietnam was seen as a possible "domino" that could fall to Communist expansion. Consequently, the United States was drawn into the conflict—first with economic help and military aid and later with troops—that turned the war into one of the most painful and divisive experiences in American history. Despite the deployment of hundreds of thousands of troops and the use of modern air power from the mid-1960s into the early 1970s, the U.S. military could not break the will of the Communists to continue fighting to take over South Vietnam. Disagreement over the morality and necessity of the war divided the American people and led to angry social protest and debate. For the first time since the end of World War II, serious questions were raised about the U.S. role as a global policeman. The Vietnam War had produced the first real cracks in the foreign policy consensus.

The assassinations in the 1960s of President John F. Kennedy, civil rights leader Martin Luther King Jr., and New York Sen. Robert F. Kennedy, the president's brother, added to the nation's turmoil.

And then, in the early 1970s, came Watergate, perhaps the greatest political scandal in U.S. history. Revelations of White House involvement in a burglary and other political sabotage, as well as cover-up efforts, severely damaged the American public's confidence in government and led to the conviction of many top government officials and the resignation of President Richard M. Nixon under the threat of imminent impeachment. It was the first resignation of a president in U.S. history.

Vietnam and Watergate together exacted a heavy toll on national unity and the authority of government. To these were added huge economic dislocations during the 1970s resulting from rampant double-digit inflation, an economic recession and an oil embargo—imposed by Arab oil-producing nations displeased with the West's pro-Israeli stance—that sent prices even higher and created seemingly endless lines at the gas station. The long cascade of bad news from the 1960s onward was capped in the late 1970s when Iranian revolutionaries seized the American embassy in Tehran and held fifty-two Americans hostage for 444 days, making the United States look foolish and impotent.

BIG GOVERNMENT OUT OF STYLE

By the 1980s, many Americans were becoming increasingly disenchanted with "big government." Ronald Reagan—who in 1964 gave a notable televised campaign speech for Barry Goldwater that established his credentials as an articulate spokesperson for the conservative wing of the party—successfully campaigned for the White House with a message that included a promise to get the federal government "off the backs of the people." Reagan's view that government was not the solution to the problem, but rather the problem itself, seemed to strike a sympathetic chord with many Americans.

It was a sentiment that would expand through the 1980s and have significant ramifications in the 1990s. In his successful bid for the White House in 1992, Democrat Bill Clinton stressed the need to reinvent government to make it more efficient. Public weariness with big government—and the high taxes it took to run it—was seen as a decisive factor in the GOP takeover of both chambers of Congress for the first time in forty years. The Democrats, long seen as the creator and protector of popular domestic programs, lost control of Congress in the 1994 elections.

The GOP majority worked with the Democratic White House to implement another of Clinton's campaign promises to "end welfare as we know it." Their effort brought an end to the federal welfare guarantee that dated back six decades to the New Deal and instead shifted responsibility to the states.

FOREIGN POLICY QUANDARY

Historic changes were sweeping the international arena as well. The demise of Soviet communism produced the most profound changes in the global landscape in half a century. A series of tumultuous events in 1991 culminated in the breakup of the Soviet Union, sweeping away the superpower rivalry that had shaped U.S. foreign policy since the end of World War II.

The new era brought the promise of reduced tensions and dramatic cuts in national security expenditures. Yet it soon became clear that the post–cold war era would be no less prone to violence and instability than its predecessor. No longer facing the clearly defined military threat the Soviet Union had posed, the United States found itself increasingly involved in United Nations and NATO operations as regional conflicts proliferated.

But there was no consensus on the direction of U.S. foreign policy because there was no agreement on the national interests of the United States in the post–cold war world.

PARTISAN DIVIDE

The 1990s proved to be one of the most partisan periods in American history. The underpinnings of this partisanship had been developing for many years, rooted both in the politics of the era and changing public attitudes. An important factor was the exceptionally long Democratic dominance in Congress and the corresponding Republican frustrations at perceived mistreatment. Another was the emerging conservative hold on the Republican Party that more starkly than in previous decades contrasted the new GOP to the still largely liberal Democratic Party that favored activist government. A third was the increasing disappearance of the middle in both parties as Republican moderates, often identified with eastern New England Republicanism, left office in retirement or defeat and conservative southern Democrats switched parties, retired, or were defeated in the increasingly Republican South. This left both parties more solidly in the control of their wings farthest from the center and eager to do battle with the other. The public's distaste for this conflict combined with its increasing distrust in government—identified by many observers as starting with Vietnam and Watergate—and the expansion of divisive social issues such as abortion, religious influence in politics, and parental authority also contributed.

The intense partisan rancor of the 1990s culminated in the impeachment of a president. Here on January 7, 1999, the one hundred members of the Senate take an oath of impartiality at the start of the trial of President Bill Clinton, who ultimately was acquitted.

In Congress, the mantra of "to get along, go along" that had prevailed for decades gave way to a new adversarial approach, largely developed by back-bench Republicans who concluded they would never get more than dismissive attention from Democrats without a direct frontal attack. This was the battle plan developed by Rep. Newt Gingrich of Georgia and like-minded colleagues. The tone was set over a period of years but was brought center stage in 1989 when Democratic Speaker Jim Wright of Texas became the first House Speaker in history to be forced by scandal to resign in the middle of his term. The move against Wright was led by Gingrich, who would go on to spearhead the GOP takeover of the House in 1995 and become Speaker. Clinton's 1992 defeat of an incumbent Republican president, George Bush, added to the tension between the parties.

Intense party-line voting and heightened incivility at a time of divided government and narrow majorities in Congress proved to be a perfect recipe for gridlock in the 1990s. Just how far things had deteriorated was illustrated by budget battles that resulted in partial shutdowns of the federal government. The animosity was palpable, as each side waited for the other to blink.

The political divide in Washington got appreciably wider when the House GOP launched an investigation that led to the impeachment of President Clinton on charges of perjury and obstruction of justice for his attempts to cover up an affair with a White House intern. The articles of impeachment were adopted on near-party-line votes. The Senate fulfilled its constitutional duty to try the case—against the better judgment of many members—but did not come close to convicting and removing Clinton from office. The tone of the Senate trial was much less rancorous and partisan than that of the House proceedings and

Clinton was acquitted with the support of every Senate Democrat and some Republicans.

The political dynamics of the president's impeachment—only the second in U.S. history—were complex. The impeachment was a testament to the power of the social conservatives who dominated the House Republican Caucus and leadership, as well as its electoral base. It was an illustration of the bitter partisan split that had all but paralyzed the House, as well as a sign of deep cultural division over standards of personal behavior for public officials. It also showed—and may have added to—the erosion of the political middle ground that had hamstrung moderates from both parties.

Public disapproval of the impeachment inquiry was thought to have contributed to GOP losses in the 1998 elections. House Speaker Gingrich resigned in the election aftermath.

The bitter partisanship in Washington and divisions among the American people continued in the 2000 elections. The closely-fought races narrowed the GOP margin in the House and split the Senate right down the middle, 50–50. The presidential race hung in the balance for five weeks, while Democrat Al Gore, who had won the national popular vote, battled Republican George W. Bush for the electoral votes of Florida, which would put one of them over the top in the electoral college. Bush had a slim lead, but the Gore camp was certain that would disappear with vote recounts. A decision by a sharply divided Supreme Court ended the Democratic push for more recounts and secured the White House for Bush.

Some political observers thought the 2000 elections, with no presidential incumbent, would answer questions about the direction voters wanted the nation to take. But a new politics of national consensus did not appear imminent in the wake of the evenly divided electorate, the debacle in Florida that left the true winner in the voting uncertain, and charges that a politicized Supreme Court had essentially given the White House to the Republicans. The one certainty was that major challenges loomed ahead. Decisions would have to be made on what to do with the record surpluses the booming economy of the 1990s had started churning out and indeed whether they would continue as economic conditions began to look more fragile in early 2001. There were social and education programs to deal with and energy and environmental questions to resolve. Military, economic, and political trouble spots abroad were not expected to go away either. Congress, the White House, and the two political parties had much to work on as the twenty-first century began.

Following is a narrative chronology of the political and legislative events of the years from the end of World War II until the end of the twentieth century, putting in perspective the national and state elections that took place during that period.

Post–World War II Years

By the end of World War II the American people had come to two fundamental decisions that would have a deep influence on the political life of the nation in the postwar years from 1945 through the mid-1960s. In domestic affairs, Americans in general had concluded that the social and economic reforms of the New Deal years ought to be preserved and that government had a legitimate role in protecting the individual against economic disaster. On the international front, isolationism clearly was rejected in favor of acceptance of a role of active leadership for the United States in world affairs.

These two decisions paved the way for a politics of national consensus in the postwar years. The ideological conflicts of the 1930s were softened, and it was possible for the two major political parties to argue more about means and less about basic national aims.

The main issue usually was which party could best provide for the needs of the people in a steadily expanding economy and at the same time provide firm, reliable leadership for the United States and the free world in a protracted cold war with the Communist bloc. Implicit in both parties' appeals were two basic elements: an acceptance of government's role in the social welfare field and close industry-government ties at home, coupled with a desire to avoid nuclear confrontation with the Soviet Union abroad. When, in 1964, one of the two major national parties sought to deny this postwar consensus in both its domestic and foreign aspects, it encountered the most sweeping electoral repudiation in a quarter-century.

By and large the Democratic Party was more successful than the Republican in presenting itself as the party better able to carry out the national consensus in the postwar years. Three Democrats were elected to the presidency—Harry S. Truman, John F. Kennedy, and Lyndon B. Johnson—while only one Republican, Dwight D. Eisenhower, was successful, and then largely because of his status as a hero of World War II. Of the ten Congresses elected in the postwar period, eight had Democratic and only two had Republican majorities. Except for brief periods in 1947–1948 and 1951–1954, the Democrats held a majority of the state governorships. Democrats maintained regular majorities in most state legislatures. Even the eight-year incumbency of a Republican president failed to strengthen the Republican Party appreciably.

The frequent Democratic victories, however, did not reflect the depth of loyalty to the Democratic Party that had existed in the 1930s, when the fresh recollection of the Great Depression maintained an unwavering Democratic mandate. In fact, the political movements of the postwar period demonstrated a rapidly changing and ambiguous electoral mandate: Republicans scored major victories in 1946 and 1952, but the Democrats achieved significant and far-reaching success in 1948, 1958, and 1964.

Even in the years of party sweeps, voters showed an increasing tendency to vote for the candidate rather than the party. The trend toward split tickets was especially evident in 1956, when Eisenhower was reelected by a landslide but the Democrats held Congress, and in 1964, when numerous Republican candidates eked out narrow victories despite the massive national vote for Johnson. Part of the trend toward split tickets could be attributed to an increasingly well educated electorate. But it also seemed to reflect a willingness among the voters to support superior candidates of either party—candidates who represented, in large part, the domestic and foreign policy consensus of the postwar era.

In the early 1960s a new awareness emerged on the issue of civil rights. Civil rights for African Americans had divided northern and southern Democrats in Congress for decades and had even caused a rump southern Dixiecrat Party in the 1948 presidential election. But pressures for equal rights for blacks continued to increase and reached a climax with a series of nationwide demonstrations in 1963. Many white Americans, with church and union groups at the fore, joined the fight for legislative action for equal rights. The result was the comprehensive, bipartisanly sponsored Civil Rights Act of 1964.

Throughout the postwar period Congress was slower to reflect the national consensus on major issues than was the president or the judicial branch of the government. As a rule it was the executive branch that proposed major new programs in fields such as education, welfare, and domestic aid—programs that Congress accepted slowly if at all. And it was the Supreme Court that, with its 1954 decision outlawing segregation in the public schools, sparked the movement toward bringing blacks into the mainstream of American life. Other decisions of the Court on constitutional rights, ranging from legislative apportionment to the rights of witnesses and the accused, far outstripped anything Congress was willing to consider.

When Congress did assume a more central role—helping, for instance, to formulate and develop foreign aid programs from the mid-1940s on, pushing aggressively for broader domestic programs while Eisenhower was in the White House, or remolding and expanding the scope of the 1964 Civil Rights Act—its actions stood out as exceptions to the pattern of executive or judicial initiative.

Congress's conservatism and its reticence in initiating programs were based in large part on the committee seniority system and restrictive legislative rules. Committee chairs often were southern Democrats or midwestern Republicans, representing the most rigidly held districts and states. The congressional representatives least able to build up seniority, and thus the least likely to head committees, were those from the politically volatile suburbs and city fringe areas where the major new population movements—and many major problems—of the postwar era occurred.

During this period the House, intended by the Framers of the Constitution to be the chamber closest to the people, actually was the more conservative body, blocking a substantial amount of legislation approved by the Senate. The Senate, especially after the liberal Democratic sweep of 1958, became markedly liberal in its orientation. A principal explanation for the Senate's position was that metropolitan centers, with their pressing demands, had sprung up in virtually every state, prompting senators to be responsive to their needs.

The postwar era might be remembered as one in which both American parties became truly national. Democrats extended their power and influence into midwestern and northern New England territory that had been unwaveringly Republican in the past. Republicans made significant new breakthroughs in the growing industrial South and in their best years won the votes of millions of Americans who had never voted Republican before.

The 1964 election, at the end of the era, left the Democratic Party in control of most of the power centers, from the presidency to the state legislatures. But many Republicans, noting the somber outcome of an election in which their party had moved far to the right and by implication had repudiated the national stance on most matters, began to work to return the party to a central course. The 1964 election, by underlining the strength of the American consensus on vital issues of domestic economy, civil rights, and foreign policy, had demonstrated anew the broad opportunities for a party willing to offer solutions to national needs.

1945–1947:
THE SEVENTY-NINTH CONGRESS

The death of a president who had led his country through twelve years of economic and military crisis, the end of the greatest war in history, and the inauguration of the atomic age all took place in the two-year interval between Franklin D. Roosevelt's election to a fourth term in 1944 and the 1946 midterm congressional elections.

The president died April 12, 1945, of a cerebral hemorrhage. Two weeks later, on April 25, delegates from Allied powers gathered in San Francisco to write the United Nations charter. (The U.S. Senate ratified the charter July 28, a contrast to the unwillingness of the Senate in 1919 to join the League of Nations.) On April 28 Italian partisans captured and butchered dictator Benito Mussolini. Adolph Hitler was reported to have committed suicide April 29 in his ruined Berlin chancery while Soviet troops poured into the city. Germany surrendered unconditionally on May 7.

In the Pacific, American airplanes administered the coup de grace to the tottering Japanese empire by dropping the first atomic bomb on Hiroshima August 6, 1945; another was used

on Nagasaki August 9. World War II ended with the unconditional surrender of Japan on August 14.

In 1944, running on the theme that the nation shouldn't "change horses in the middle of the stream," President Roosevelt had won an unprecedented fourth term with a national vote plurality of 3,594,993 (of 47,976,670 cast) and a total of 432 (of 531) electoral votes. Reversing Democratic losses in the 1942 midterm elections, Congress went heavily Democratic. After the 1944 election, fifty-seven Democrats and thirty-eight Republicans were in the Senate, and the House was balanced 243–190 in favor of the Democrats. Less than three months later Roosevelt was dead.

Roosevelt's successor, Harry S. Truman, took office April 12. He faced a perplexing task as he sought to hold together the coalition of big-city machines, organized labor, conservative southern Democrats, farmers, minority groups, ethnic and religious blocs, and intellectual liberals, which FDR had brought together for his successive electoral victories.

Pent-up tensions erupted with the end of World War II. The country was hit by a wave of strikes that climaxed in a May 1946 nationwide rail strike, which President Truman tried to break with a proposal to draft strikers into the army, thus incurring deep resentment in the ranks of organized labor. On the right wing, southern Democrats continued to abandon the administration on almost every item of domestic legislation as they had since 1938. Conservative forces in Congress pressed for a relaxation of wartime price controls far more rapidly than Truman thought advisable.

Despite its failure to reach agreement on such basic issues as labor-management relations, a national housing program, federal aid to schools, and national health insurance, the Seventy-ninth Congress produced some notable legislation, including the Atomic Energy Act of 1946, which transferred control over all aspects of atomic energy development from the War Department to a civilian Atomic Energy Commission.

The Employment Act of 1946, considerably weaker than the "Full Employment" bill first proposed—which bordered on a government guarantee of jobs for all—nevertheless broke new ground in fixing responsibility for national economic policies. The Hospital Survey and Construction Act of 1946 authorized a program of matching federal grants to state and local health bodies for hospital construction. The Legislative Reorganization Act of 1946 cut the number of standing committees in the House and the Senate, provided for preparation of an annual legislative budget to complement the president's budget, and raised the salaries of senators and representatives from $10,000 to $12,500, plus a $2,500 tax-free expense account. Included in the law, as a separate title, was the Federal Regulation of Lobbying Act, requiring lobbyists to register and report their lobbying expenses.

Congress also authorized a fifty-year loan of $3.75 billion to Great Britain, intended to assist the British in removing trade and currency exchange restrictions hampering postwar programs for economic reconstruction and trade liberalization.

1946 Midterm Elections

The 1946 congressional election campaign was marked by two events disadvantageous to the administration. First,

President Truman on September 20, 1946, dismissed Secretary of Commerce Henry A. Wallace, former vice president (1941–1945) and only original New Dealer still remaining in the cabinet and a spokesperson of labor and progressive groups. The dismissal followed a speech Wallace gave—which Wallace had read to Truman in advance—criticizing the allegedly anti-Soviet tone of the foreign policy of Secretary of State James F. Byrnes. The incident encouraged Republicans to pin the "red" label on all candidates for whom Wallace subsequently spoke during the campaign.

A second bad break for the administration came in a seven-week national meat shortage just before the election. Truman was forced to issue an order, October 14, ending all meat price controls. His action drew sharp criticism from organized labor and a charge by the Republican national chairman, Rep. B. Carroll Reece of Tennessee, that he was taking action "after the horse has gone to the butcher shop." The mood of the country was clearly in favor of an early end to all remaining wartime controls. The pent-up frustrations of wartime were directly appealed to in the Republican slogans: "Had enough?" and "It's time for a change." Reece promised that a Republican Congress would restore "orderly, capable, and honest government in Washington and replace controls, confusion, corruption, and communism."

Symptomatic of the tone of the times—pictured by contemporary observers as a desire to return to "normalcy"—were two election-morning newspaper headlines. One read, "Gay Crowd Hails Return of National Horse Show." A second read, "Crackers, Sugar Back in Stores."

The Democratic congressional campaign was lackadaisical. Democratic national chairman Robert E. Hannegan did warn the country that a GOP victory would be a "surrender to the will of a few who want only large profits for themselves." But Truman failed to hit the campaign trail and offered scarcely any comment on the important races and issues.

The Democrats appeared to depend in large measure on frequent radio broadcasts of the late president Roosevelt's campaign addresses recorded in earlier years. The most publicized activity for Democratic candidates was carried out by the political action committee of the CIO (Congress of Industrial Organizations), headed by the controversial Sidney Hillman.

Results of the 1946 Elections

The 1946 campaign proved to be the most successful for the Republicans since the 1920s—and the best year they would have for many years to come. Across the nation Republicans swept Senate, House, and gubernatorial contests. The Republicans increased their Senate membership from thirty-eight to fifty-one seats, while the Democrats slipped from fifty-seven to forty-five seats.

Among the new Republican senators were John W. Bricker of Ohio, Irving M. Ives of New York, William E. Jenner of Indiana, William F. Knowland of California (who had been appointed to the Senate in 1945), George W. Malone of Nevada, Arthur V. Watkins of Utah, and John J. Williams of Delaware. The Progressive candidate, Robert La Follette Jr. of Wisconsin, lost to

Republican Joseph R. McCarthy. With the exception of Ives, all represented their party's most conservative wing.

The House Republican delegation rose from 190 seats to 246 seats, while the Democratic delegation dropped from 243 to 188; this was the lowest figure since the 1928 elections. The ratio among the nation's governorships changed from 26–22 in favor of the Democrats to 25–23 in favor of the Republicans.

Important Republican gubernatorial victories included the reelection of Thomas E. Dewey of New York and Earl Warren of California and the elections of Robert F. Bradford of Massachusetts, Alfred E. Driscoll of New Jersey, James H. Duff of Pennsylvania, Thomas J. Herbert of Ohio, Kim Sigler of Michigan, and L. W. Youngdahl of Minnesota. The only Democrats to win in generally two-party states were William L. Knous of Colorado, William P. Lane Jr. of Maryland, and Lester C. Hunt of Wyoming.

1947–1949: THE EIGHTIETH CONGRESS

In 1947 and 1948 the nation proceeded to shake off most of the remaining wartime economic controls and to enjoy an economic boom marred somewhat by substantial inflation and the beginnings of the first postwar recession in late 1948. Americans began to realize that the postwar period would be one of continuing international tensions rather than a return to "normalcy."

The foreign scene was darkened by increasing Soviet intransigence at the United Nations; by the civil war in Greece and Communist pressures on Turkey, which led to the announcement of the Truman Doctrine in 1947; by the ouster of noncommunists from the Hungarian government in May 1947; by the Communist coup d'état in Czechoslovakia in February 1948; and by the beginning of the Soviet blockade of Berlin in April 1948. Faced with the responsibility of formulating new solutions for the new problems of the postwar era, the Republican-controlled Eightieth Congress wrote some basic laws that governed domestic and foreign policy for many years to come.

On May 15, 1947, Congress approved the Greek-Turkish aid program requested by President Truman (the Truman Doctrine). The concept of massive economic aid to European countries to assist them in their postwar recovery, suggested by Secretary of State George C. Marshall, received final congressional approval in passage of the European Recovery Program (Marshall Plan) April 2, 1948. International tensions paved the way for congressional approval of a peacetime draft law June 19, 1948.

The legislation that placed the most strain on bipartisan foreign policy was extension of the Reciprocal Trade Agreements Act. Congress in 1948 turned down presidential requests for a three-year extension, granting only a single year's extension in a limited form.

During its first session, the Eightieth Congress approved legislation for unifying the armed forces under a single Department of Defense with separate army, navy, and air force departments under the secretary of defense, and for forming the Central Intelligence Agency.

In domestic affairs, the Democratic president and Republican Congress generally were at loggerheads. Presidential recommendations to extend New Deal social welfare concepts were largely ignored by Congress. The most significant single piece of domestic legislation approved by the Congress was the Taft-Hartley Labor-Management Relations Act, passed over President Truman's veto June 23, 1947. The bill outlawed the closed shop, jurisdictional strikes, and secondary boycotts, and was bitterly opposed by organized labor. Its chief provisions were to remain on the statute books throughout the postwar period.

The Eightieth Congress completed two significant actions concerning the office of president: it passed a bill, approved by Truman on July 18, 1947, making the Speaker of the House and the president pro tempore of the Senate the next two in line of succession to the presidency after the vice president, ahead of the secretary of state and other cabinet members. In a slap at President Roosevelt's four terms, it sent to the states a constitutional amendment limiting the tenure of future presidents to two terms. The Twenty-second Amendment became law in February 1951. The communist issue monopolized national attention in the summer of 1948, as Elizabeth Bentley and Whittaker Chambers, self-confessed former Communist Party members, spread before the House Un-American Activities Committee charges that numerous high administration officials during the 1930s and war years had been members of communist spy rings. Chambers's August 3 testimony that former State Department aide Alger Hiss had been a communist spy became the most celebrated case of all. It was highly dramatized on nationwide television on August 25, when Hiss and Chambers confronted each other at a hearing of the committee.

The 1948 Campaigns

Truman's underdog victory in the 1948 presidential election set the pattern of rapid and startling reversals in domestic political trends during the postwar years. His victory was accompanied by a Democratic congressional and gubernatorial sweep that reversed, in overwhelming measure, the Republican triumph of 1946.

The year 1947 had appeared to be a favorable one for Truman. The Marshall Plan, his "get-tough-with-Russia" policy, his advocacy of government action to curb rising prices, and his willingness to deal firmly with labor leader John L. Lewis had all increased the president's popularity in sharp contrast to its nadir at the time of the 1946 elections. In November 1947 elections the Democrats were especially successful, electing a governor in Kentucky and winning other important races.

By the late spring of 1948, however, Truman's popularity had plummeted to such depths that leaders of his own party cast about for another nominee to head the Democratic ticket. Several developments contributed to the sharp dip in presidential popularity. Reacting in part to Henry A. Wallace's December 1947 announcement that he was forming a third party, Truman included in his 1948 State of the Union address requests for new social welfare legislation plus a call for a straight $40 tax cut for each individual in the nation. Even some liberal Democrats accused the president of having made a "political harangue" in the most partisan spirit.

In February the president's advocacy of a far-sweeping civil rights program, based on recommendations of his civil rights

In his 1948 whistle-stop campaign Harry S. Truman traveled more than 31,700 miles across the country and delivered 356 speeches to win a surprising reelection.

commission, created a predictably bitter reaction in the southern wing of his party. The stage was set for the States' Rights ticket, putting four parties in the upcoming presidential campaign. Truman's reelection in the face of open revolts on the left wing (Wallaceites) and the right wing (Dixiecrats) seemed almost impossible.

Fearing defeat for the party in the November elections, an unusual coalition of Democrats began to press in late spring for General Dwight D. Eisenhower's nomination by the Democratic National Convention. The coalition included states' rights southerners, big-city bosses from the North, and party liberals. In statements on June 5 and 9, however, Eisenhower made clear his refusal to consider seeking or accepting the nomination. Neither Eisenhower's political philosophy nor his party were known; it was not until 1952 that he identified himself as a Republican.

A brief effort to draft Supreme Court Justice William O. Douglas also collapsed. No further obstacle remained to Truman's renomination when the Democrats assembled gloomily in Philadelphia July 12 for their thirtieth national convention.

Truman was nominated on the first ballot on July 15, receiving 947 ½ votes to 263 for Sen. Richard Russell of Georgia. Senate Democratic leader Alben W. Barkley of Kentucky, who had roused the delegates with a fiery keynote speech July 12, was later nominated for vice president.

Truman's acceptance speech created a sensation. Lashing into the Republicans as "the party of special interests," he called for repeal of the Taft-Hartley Act, criticized Congress for its failure to control prices, or pass a housing bill, and said that the tax reduction measure approved was a "Republican rich-man's tax bill." He then announced it was his duty to call Congress back into session on July 26 to act on anti-inflation legislation, housing, aid to education, a national health program, civil rights, an increase in the minimum wage from 40 cents to 75 cents hourly, extension of Social Security, public power and cheaper electricity projects, and a new "adequate" displaced-persons bill.

The closing day of the Democratic convention was marked by a walkout of delegations from Mississippi and Alabama, when the convention, at the instigation of Minneapolis mayor Hubert H. Humphrey and other party liberals, adopted a tough substitute civil rights plank. Following an impassioned speech by Humphrey in behalf of the stronger plank, the convention approved it by a 651 ½ to 582 ½ vote, substituting it for a noncontroversial plank recommended by the Resolutions (Platform) Committee.

Rebellious southerners from thirteen states convened in Birmingham, Alabama, on July 17 as the States' Rights Party and nominated Gov. J. Strom Thurmond, D-S.C., for president and Gov. Fielding L. Wright, D-Miss., for vice president. They urged southern Democratic parties to substitute Thurmond and Wright for Truman and Barkley as the Democratic candidates on the ballot. The convention adopted a platform terming the national Democratic civil rights plank "this infamous and iniquitous program" that would mean a "police state in a totalitarian, centralized, bureaucratic government." The platform stated, "We stand for the segregation of the races and the integrity of each race."

Another group met in Philadelphia in July. Calling itself the Progressive Party, it nominated Henry A. Wallace for president and Sen. Glen H. Taylor, D-Idaho, for vice president. Party leaders denied that the party was communist-dominated, though most observers considered it heavily influenced by the extreme left. In his acceptance speech, Wallace blamed Truman for the Berlin crisis. He said there had been a "great betrayal" following President Roosevelt's death in which the administration inaugurated its "get tough" policy, thus "slamming the door" on peace talks with the Soviet Union. The Progressive platform called for a program of U.S. disarmament, a conciliatory policy toward the Soviet Union, an end to segregation, nationalization of key industries, repeal of Taft-Hartley, high farm price supports, and the Townsend plan, giving a $100 monthly pension to everyone at the age of sixty.

Scenting victory, Republicans engaged in a lively contest for their party's presidential nomination. The three chief candidates were New York governor Thomas E. Dewey, former Minnesota governor Harold E. Stassen, and Sen. Robert A. Taft of Ohio. Taft enjoyed the support of most of the more conservative party regulars.

As the primaries developed during the spring, it first appeared that Stassen might be on his way to the nomination. After losing to Dewey in New Hampshire, he won an overwhelming victory in Wisconsin over Dewey and native son Gen. Douglas MacArthur, who had been considered the strong favorite. Stassen won nineteen delegates to eight for MacArthur and none for Dewey. In the Nebraska primary Stassen again won against Dewey, Taft, and several other candidates whose names were placed on the ballot.

Observers began to predict Stassen's nomination, but he then made what later appeared to be a serious error. He entered the May 4 Ohio primary, bluntly antagonizing the Taft wing of the party. (He won only nine of the twenty-three contested delegate spots, the rest going to Taft.) In Oregon, where Stassen had been an early favorite, he lost to Dewey in the May 21 primary (117,554

votes to 107,946), after a radio debate between the two men in which Stassen endorsed and Dewey opposed outlawing the Communist Party. Observers believe the debate and primary returns effectively finished Stassen's chances.

When the Twenty-fourth Republican National Convention opened in Philadelphia June 21, the Dewey victory already seemed probable. Taft was handicapped because many conservatives considered his stands for federal aid to education and housing too liberal, while many party professionals feared his coauthorship of the Taft-Hartley Act might harm the party among union voters. California governor Earl Warren and Michigan senator Arthur Vandenberg both had hopes that a convention deadlock might turn the delegates toward them, but neither ambition was justified. Dewey began with the solid bloc of New York State and enjoyed substantial support in delegations from every part of the country.

In first ballot voting June 24, with 547 needed to win, Dewey received 434 votes to 224 for Taft and 157 for Stassen. Favorite-son candidates shared the rest. On the second ballot Dewey's total rose to 515 against 274 for Taft and 149 for Stassen. Following this, the other candidates quickly fell behind Dewey. His nomination on the third roll call was merely a formality.

During the following night Dewey conferred with influential party leaders and decided on Governor Warren as his running mate. The party adopted a platform backing a "bipartisan" foreign policy; foreign aid to anticommunist countries; "full" recognition of Israel; housing, anti-inflation, and civil rights legislation; and promised a fight against communists inside and outside government.

The Truman and Dewey campaigns became historic examples. The Truman effort showed how a determined candidate can win by going to the people, even with the odds against him; the Dewey performance was an example of how a supposedly sure candidate can lose by waging a lackluster campaign of overconfidence.

Truman undertook a 31,700-mile "barnstorming" whistle-stop tour by train, appearing before an estimated six million persons. At each opportunity the president would deliver one of his "give-'em-hell" attacks on the Republicans. The "do-nothing Republican Eightieth Congress" was Mr. Truman's chief target: "When I called them back into session, what did they do? Nothing. Nothing. That Congress never did anything the whole time it was in session." If the Republicans win, "they'll tear you apart." The Republicans are "predatory animals who don't care if you people are thrown into a depression. . . . They like runaway prices."

Toward the end of the campaign Truman began a special appeal to minority racial and religious groups, calling for strong civil rights legislation and condemning Republican leaders for passing the Displaced Persons Act, which he said discriminated against Catholics and Jews.

Dewey's campaign was characterized by his aloofness and cool manner, his skirting of issues and his diffuse, repetitious calls for "national unity." Dewey called the Eightieth Congress "one of the best," but he failed to come to the defense of its individual programs even when they were under direct attack from Truman. Assured by the pollsters, campaign strategists, advertising consultants, and reporters that he had the election well in hand, Dewey refrained from direct or forceful answers to any of the Truman attacks. Even more than Dewey, vice-presidential candidate Warren disdained to enter the partisan fray.

The Dewey program was particularly vague on farm legislation, which was a new field to him as a New York governor. "There are some people who would like to inject politics into the necessities of food raising in our country. I don't believe in that," Dewey said. He expressed a general support for price supports, not indicating whether they should be at parity or close to it or on a flexible or rigid scale. Meanwhile, farm prices were taking a nosedive that was concerning farmers across the Midwest. Also, storage capacity in grain elevators was short, adding to rural dissatisfaction.

Both the Progressive and Dixiecrat movements, meanwhile, were faltering. Wallace became increasingly identified with the communists and few "liberal" leaders joined his cause. His campaign crowds dwindled to a fraction of their size earlier in the year.

The Dixiecrat ticket failed to make substantial headway as most southern governors and senators—including some who had been most vociferous in denouncing Truman's civil rights proposals—chose the route of party regularity and backed the president. Only four southern Democratic parties—those in Alabama, Louisiana, Mississippi, and South Carolina—followed through on the plea of the Birmingham convention to put Thurmond and Wright on the ballot as the regular Democratic nominees. They went on the ballot as States' Rights Party candidates in ten other states: Arkansas, California, Florida, Georgia, Kentucky, North Carolina, North Dakota, Tennessee, Texas, and Virginia.

With the first election eve returns from the northeastern states, Truman took a lead that he never lost despite the closeness of the election. As the night wore on, state after state considered "safe Republican" moved into the Truman column. Dewey carried Pennsylvania, New Jersey, Indiana, Maryland, Michigan, and New York (the last three evidently because of usual Democratic voters defecting to Wallace). But the president carried Massachusetts, won the border states, took all but four southern states (Alabama, Louisiana, Mississippi, and South Carolina) that were in the Dixiecrat column and carried the farm belt. Finally California fell in his column. When Ohio conclusively went for Truman at 11 o'clock Wednesday morning, November 3, Dewey conceded.

The election returns seemed to indicate that the Democratic New Deal philosophy was so generally accepted by the electorate that the president's warnings of a return to "Republican" depression days remained a telling point. On a less philosophical level many observers felt the Truman "Mr. Average" approach, compared to Dewey's "Olympian airs," drew a large sympathy vote from the average people in the street for the conceded "underdog."

Results of the 1948 Elections

With the Truman victory the Democrats took control of Congress with commanding majorities in both the Senate and the House. The Democrats picked up nine Senate seats to make

Actions of the "Do-Nothing" Eightieth Congress

The Eightieth Congress (1947–1949), characterized by a hard-campaigning President Harry Truman as the "do-nothing Republican Eightieth Congress," actually produced a great deal of legislation, some of which Truman wanted, some over his serious objections. A partial list of Eightieth Congress actions:

- Truman doctrine of aid to Greece and Turkey.
- Marshall Plan for aid to Europe.
- Peace treaties approved with Italy, Hungary, Bulgaria, and Romania.
- Inter-American Treaty of Mutual Assistance approved.
- Vandenberg Resolution favoring collective and regional mutual assistance pacts.
- Unification of armed forces under Department of Defense; creation of Central Intelligence Agency.
- $65 million building loan for UN headquarters.
- Peacetime draft law.
- Passage of Taft-Hartley Act, over veto.
- Presidential succession change.
- Constitutional amendment to limit presidential tenure to two terms.
- Hope-Aiken flexible price support bill.
- Newsboys excluded from Social Security system, over veto.
- A tax-reduction bill, over veto.
- Liberalized housing credit terms.
- Extended rent control.

the new balance 54–42 in their favor. Among the new Democratic senators were Lyndon B. Johnson (Texas), Paul H. Douglas (Illinois), Hubert H. Humphrey (Minnesota), Estes Kefauver (Tennessee), Robert S. Kerr (Oklahoma), and Clinton P. Anderson (New Mexico). Republican Margaret Chase Smith was elected senator from Maine. And in House elections Democrats made a net gain of seventy-five seats; the new total was 263 Democrats and 171 Republicans.

The Democrats also ran strong in gubernatorial contests, winning twenty of the thirty-two seats up for election and reversing the Republican trend of the immediate past years. The new totals were thirty Democratic and eighteen Republican governorships. Among the new Democratic governors were Chester Bowles (Connecticut), Adlai E. Stevenson (Illinois), and G. Mennen Williams (Michigan).

1949–1951:
THE EIGHTY-FIRST CONGRESS

The international situation in the years 1949 and 1950 was marked by stabilization and cooling of tensions in Europe, in sharp contrast to renewed Communist conquest and the threat of nuclear war in Asia. In April 1949 the North Atlantic Treaty was signed by the United States, Canada, and ten European nations, agreeing that "an armed attack against any one or more of them in Europe and North America shall be considered an attack against all." A direct reaction to Communist power moves, which included the 1948 takeover of Czechoslovakia, the treaty of the North Atlantic Treaty Organization (NATO) laid down a policy of containment of Soviet expansionist ambitions that helped to preserve a territorial status quo on the European continent for years to come. On September 30, 1949, the Soviets lifted a blockade of Berlin, which had been in effect since April 1, 1948.

In Asia, however, the Western position was disintegrating rapidly. On January 22, 1949, the Chinese Communists took Beijing. On April 23 they crossed the Yangtze and captured Nanjing. On August 6 Secretary of State Dean Acheson blamed Generalissimo Chiang Kai-shek's "reactionary" clique for the Communist victory and gave notice that no further aid would be given Chiang's government. On December 7, 1949, the Nationalist Chinese government fled to Formosa.

The takeover of mainland China by a hostile Communist power did not shake the Western world, however, as much as the surprise attack of Communist North Korean troops on South Korea June 25, 1950. The UN Security Council immediately ordered a cease-fire. Two days later President Truman ordered U.S. forces under Gen. Douglas MacArthur to repel the North Koreans. This became a UN "peace action" but was largely an American venture. U.S. involvement in Korea led to a near-wartime mobilization of the U.S. economy. It also led to President Truman's dispute with General MacArthur over the proposed bombing of Manchuria, which in turn led to MacArthur's dismissal in April 1951. As the war dragged on for two years with heavy U.S. casualties, it became a source of great frustration for the American people.

In other important developments, the Soviet Union in September 1949 exploded its first atomic bomb, ending the U.S. atomic monopoly; India was proclaimed independent in January 1950; Alger Hiss was found guilty of perjury on January 21, 1950; and Truman, in January 1950, authorized the Atomic Energy Commission to produce the hydrogen bomb.

In his inaugural address January 20, 1949, President Truman included a "Point IV" proposal of American foreign policy for "a bold new program for making the benefits of our scientific advances and industrial progress available for the improvement and growth of underdeveloped areas." Over the succeeding years, foreign aid assistance for capital investment to build up the economies of fledgling nations of Africa, Asia, and Latin America became a cornerstone of U.S. foreign policy.

When the heavily Democratic Eighty-first Congress assembled in Washington January 3, 1949, liberals had high hopes that it would enact a new body of social welfare legislation such as that proposed by Truman in the 1948 campaign. The first signs for the Truman program seemed bright as the House on January 3 adopted a new rule to break the power of its Rules Committee to bottle up legislation indefinitely. The "twenty-one-day rule" provided that, if the Rules Committee failed to act on a bill after twenty-one legislative days, the chair of the legislative committee that originally approved it could ask the House to vote on whether to consider the measure or not, with a majority vote

required to bring the bill to the floor. The rule was dropped by the House when the Eighty-second Congress organized in 1951.

On January 5 Truman appeared before Congress to urge a sweeping new Fair Deal program of social reform. But Congress in general proved to be a disappointment to the liberal camp on domestic issues. Approval was given to a long-range housing bill providing for expanded federal programs in slum clearance, public housing, and farm improvement programs, which Truman signed into law July 15, 1949, "with deep satisfaction." The administration also scored an important victory in passage of the Social Security Expansion Act of 1950 and a limited victory in a 1949 minimum wage increase. But otherwise the Fair Deal program hit formidable obstacles.

Legislation to continue the Marshall Plan, military assistance to friendly foreign nations, and a two-year extension of the Trade Agreements Act cleared Congress with some bipartisan support. The Senate on July 21, 1949, approved the North Atlantic Treaty by a 2–1 margin. In domestic affairs important steps toward streamlining the executive branch of the government were made in the Government Reorganization Act of 1949.

An explosive new issue, meanwhile, had developed on the domestic scene. In a February 11, 1950, speech in Wheeling, West Virginia, Sen. Joseph R. McCarthy, R-Wis., charged that there were fifty-seven communists working in the State Department, a charge promptly denied by the department. Until his formal censure by the Senate in 1954, McCarthy and his freewheeling accusations of communist sympathies among high- and low-placed government officials absorbed much of the public attention. The phenomenon of McCarthyism had a major effect on the psychological climate of the early 1950s.

The 1950 Midterm Elections

The liberal Democratic trend apparent in Truman's surprise 1948 victory was sharply reversed in the 1950 elections as Republicans exploited the issues of inflation, Korea, communism, and corruption, to make strong comebacks in congressional and gubernatorial elections.

Truman, delivering his only major speech of the campaign November 4, 1950, sought to bolster the Democratic effort with charges similar to those he leveled against the Republicans in 1948: that they were captives of "special interests," that they would undo the country's progress toward peace and prosperity if they gained control of the national government. Truman said the Republicans were "isolationists" and that "any farmer who votes for the Republican Party ought to have his head examined."

The Republican campaign assumed a far more aggressive tone than it had in 1948. Sen. Robert A. Taft, R-Ohio, said the administration was responsible for high prices, high taxes, the loss of China to the Communists, and the Korean conflict. (Republicans pointed frequently to a January 12, 1950, speech by Secretary of State Dean Acheson before the National Press Club in which Acheson described the U.S. defensive line in the Far East in such a way as to exclude Korea.)

Typical of other Republican attacks was a November 4 reply to Truman by Harold Stassen, charging that the "blinded, blundering, bewildering" Far East policy of the "spy-riddled" Truman administration was directly to blame for American casualties in Korea.

McCarthy's charges of communism in high places in the government played an important part in the campaign. Whether or not the voters believed all of McCarthy's charges, many seemed to accept the thesis that there was something drastically wrong with U.S. foreign policy and that Acheson was a likely villain.

In Maryland, the prominent veteran Democratic senator Millard E. Tydings was defeated by John Marshall Butler, an obscure Republican, after a campaign in which Tydings was accused of having "whitewashed" the State Department as head of a Senate committee investigating McCarthy's charges of communism in the department. Butler was later accused of countenancing distribution of a campaign leaflet with a doctored photograph showing Tydings with U.S. Communist leader Earl Browder.

In California, Republican representative Richard M. Nixon ran for the Senate against Rep. Helen Gahagan Douglas, a prominent liberal Democrat. Nixon's charges that Douglas voted frequently with New York representative Vito Marcantonio, a member of the American Labor Party, whose voting record was often depicted as procommunist, established the image of Nixon as a ruthless campaigner, an image that would harm him in future races.

Another Senate contest with communism as the chief issue took place in North Carolina, where Willis Smith defeated incumbent Frank P. Graham in a June 24 Democratic primary runoff. Smith charged that Graham was badly tainted with socialism because of his alleged "associations with communism."

Among major issues stressed by the Republicans was Truman's program for compulsory health insurance for all, termed "socialized medicine" by doctors who fought it both in the primaries and in the general elections. The issue was thought to have contributed to the defeat of several Democratic senators, including Claude Pepper of Florida and Graham of North Carolina in primaries and Elbert D. Thomas of Utah and Glen H. Taylor of Idaho in the general election. But in each one of these cases and in the California Senate race the "soft-on-communism" issue, at its peak in 1950, played a more important role.

Results of the 1950 Elections

The two most closely watched Senate battles were in Ohio, where Republican senator Robert Taft was the target of an all-out attempt by organized labor to defeat him because of his coauthorship of the Taft-Hartley Act, and in Illinois, where Senate majority leader Scott W. Lucas was challenged by former Republican representative Everett McKinley Dirksen, who campaigned as a conservative near-isolationist. The election returns showed Taft the winner in Ohio by a gigantic 431,184 vote margin (57.5 percent), while Dirksen upset Lucas with 294,354 votes to spare (53.9 percent). Both Taft and Dirksen would later serve as their party's Senate leader.

Assessment of the election returns showed that, while the Democrats retained nominal control of Congress (the Senate by two votes, the House by thirty-five), the Truman–Fair Deal influence on Congress had been virtually nullified. Outside the conservative southern states, the Democrats elected only 126 House members to 196 for the Republicans.

On the Senate side, the Republicans won eighteen and the Democrats nine of the nonsouthern contests. In addition to Dirksen and Nixon, new senators included George A. Smathers, D-Fla.; A. S. Mike Monroney, D-Okla.; and James H. Duff, R-Pa., who was one of the prime movers for the nomination of Eisenhower in 1952.

1951–1953:
THE EIGHTY-SECOND CONGRESS

The Korean conflict continued to dominate American life in 1951 and 1952 and led directly to the defeat of the Democrats in the 1952 elections. On April 11, 1951, President Truman removed General of the Army Douglas MacArthur from his command of UN and U.S. forces in the Far East. MacArthur had wanted to pursue Chinese Communist forces across the Yalu River to their sanctuary in Manchuria in order to destroy the air depots and lines of supply being used to sustain their war effort in Korea. On March 25 MacArthur had threatened Communist China with air and naval attack. These steps, running contrary to the Truman administration policy under Secretary of State Dean Acheson, led to MacArthur's removal. Negotiations for a truce along the thirty-eighth parallel began July 10, 1951, but the fighting continued for another two years.

In other international developments, the Japanese peace treaty was signed in San Francisco on September 8, 1951. War between Germany and the United States was formally ended October 19. On May 26, 1952, a peace contract between Germany and the Western allies was signed. In November 1952 the first hydrogen bomb was exploded by the United States.

A major domestic controversy developed in 1952 when Truman on April 8 ordered seizure of the nation's steel mills to avert a strike by 600,000 CIO steel workers. On June 2, however, the Supreme Court ruled the seizure illegal. The workers struck from June 3 to July 25.

The Eighty-second Congress accomplished very little outside the realm of foreign and military affairs. None of the Fair Deal proposals expounded by the president and the Democratic leadership in 1948 and 1950—national health insurance, aid to education, and increased public health benefits—was enacted into law.

In 1951 the nation's interest was captured by the televised crime hearings of a Senate subcommittee chaired by Sen. Estes Kefauver, D-Tenn. The hearings exposed nationwide criminal organizations that reaped huge illegal profits, influencing local politicians and buying protection.

The 1952 Campaigns

President Truman ended any speculation about his third-term ambitions by announcing March 29 that he would not be a candidate for reelection. The field of possible Democratic nominees included Senator Kefauver; Gov. Adlai E. Stevenson, D-Ill.; W. Averell Harriman of New York; Vice President Alben W.

Barkley of Kentucky; Sen. Robert S. Kerr, D-Okla.; and Sen. Richard B. Russell, D-Ga. Stevenson was Truman's personal choice for the nomination and was offered presidential support as early as January. Truman was willing to back Barkley after Stevenson's repeated disavowals of interest in the nomination; however, influential labor leaders vetoed Barkley's nomination, forcing him to withdraw on the eve of the convention.

Stevenson consistently professed his disinterest in the nomination and only submitted to a draft movement in his behalf while the 1952 Democratic convention, which convened in Chicago July 21, was in progress. The support for Stevenson, already strong, began to snowball with the July 24 announcement of Thomas J. Gavin, President Truman's alternate as a delegate from Missouri, that he would vote for Stevenson on Truman's instructions. Stevenson ran second to Kefauver in both the first and second ballots.

Only on the third ballot, not completed until 12:25 a.m. on July 26, did Stevenson move close to nomination as Harriman withdrew in his favor. A unanimous nomination by acclamation was then moved and carried. Following a conference with President Truman, Stevenson chose Sen. John J. Sparkman, D-Ala., a backer of the national Democratic Party on most issues except civil rights, as his running mate. The convention then confirmed his choice by acclamation.

The contest for the Republican presidential nomination, despite other entries in the field, was fought out between the supporters of two relatively clearly defined groups within the party: Sen. Robert A. Taft of Ohio represented the conservative midwestern and southern wing of the party, and Gen. Dwight D. Eisenhower became the candidate of the "internationalist" wing of the party centered on the East and West coasts. Other announcements of candidacy were made by California governor Earl Warren and by Harold E. Stassen.

Eisenhower in early 1952 was on duty in Paris as commanding general of the new North Atlantic Treaty Organization. The major political question as 1952 began was whether he would permit his name to be put forth for the Republican nomination. Previously he had always rejected talk of his running for president, and he had declined to make his political affiliations known. The mystery ended on January 7 when Sen. Henry Cabot Lodge Jr., R-Mass., announced that he was entering Eisenhower's name in the March 11 New Hampshire primary after having received assurances from the general that he was a Republican. In a January 8 statement from Paris, Eisenhower confirmed his Republican loyalties and said he would run for president if he received a "clear-cut call to political duty." Eisenhower said, however, that he would not actively seek the nomination. Despite his refusal to campaign, Eisenhower ran strongly in most of the primaries where his name was entered.

When the Twenty-fifth Republican National Convention opened in Chicago on July 7, the delegate issue was the hottest—and one of the first—items of business. In a preliminary test the convention voted 658–548 against allowing delegates with disputed seats to vote on other delegate contests until their own credentials were accepted. This resolution, which had been endorsed by twenty-five of the nation's Republican gover-

nors, prevented disputed Taft delegates from the South from voting for each other's seating. The victory of the Eisenhower forces on this issue foreshadowed the general's eventual nomination.

Korea, foreign affairs, corruption in government, internal communism, and the domestic economy were the major issues of the 1952 campaign. Of these, only the domestic economy—booming through the stimulation of the Korean War—proved to be in any way a plus for the Democrats. The other issues aided the Republican campaign.

The most dramatic episode of the campaign opened September 18 with an article in the *New York Post,* charging that GOP vice-presidential nominee Richard M. Nixon had been the beneficiary of an allegedly secret fund financed by California businesses. For a week, controversy raged with many demands that Nixon resign from the ticket so that the corruption issue against the Democrats would not be diluted.

Eisenhower declined to take a firm stand on Nixon's continuance on the ticket. Finally, Nixon on September 23 went on nationwide television for a melodramatic defense of the moral rectitude of the fund and to make a complete accounting of his own relatively limited personal assets. In this speech Nixon referred to his wife's "respectable Republican cloth coat" and a gift dog, Checkers—"regardless of what they say about it, we're going to keep it."

Response to Nixon's speech overwhelmingly favored keeping him on the ticket. Eisenhower immediately issued a statement lauding Nixon for his bravery in a "tough situation." At a September 24 meeting between the two men in Wheeling, West Virginia, Eisenhower announced that Nixon had completely "vindicated himself."

Results of the 1952 Elections

In contrast to 1948, when the pollsters and commentators had all foreseen a sweeping Dewey victory, there was a marked reluctance to make a firm prediction on the outcome of the 1952 campaign. But when the returns started to roll in election eve, it was clear that Eisenhower had won by a landslide and that his victory had probably never been in doubt.

Only nine of the forty-eight states went for Stevenson, and they were in the South or border areas (West Virginia, Kentucky, Alabama, Arkansas, Georgia, Louisiana, Mississippi, North Carolina, and South Carolina). Every state across the East, Midwest, and West went for Eisenhower. And the tide rolled on into many parts of the South, with the Eisenhower-Nixon ticket carrying Texas, Oklahoma, Florida, Virginia, and Tennessee.

The electoral vote count was 442 for Eisenhower, eighty-nine for Stevenson. In popular votes Eisenhower won a 6,621,242-vote plurality. He polled 33,936,234 votes, the highest number of votes ever received by a presidential candidate. But in defeat Stevenson won 27,314,992 votes, the highest number ever received by a losing candidate.

Seeking explanations for the Eisenhower landslide, observers found a multitude of reasons. The doubts, fears, and frustrations stemming from the stalemated Korean War, the Hiss case and the communist spy trials, revelations of corruption in the federal government, rising prices, and high taxes—all contributed to a strong desire for a change in executive leadership. Stevenson's divorce and wit were thought to be unpopular with many voters. Sparkman's identification with the white supremacy views of the Alabama Democratic Party harmed the ticket among black voters.

The lack of enthusiasm for the Republican congressional leadership, the memory of the Depression, and fear of reversal of social-economic gains of the Democratic years might have nullified these Republican advantages, however, if the Republicans had not found in Eisenhower an ideal candidate to allay such fears. A national hero, a man whose leadership had already been proven in World War II and in laying the groundwork for the North Atlantic Alliance, Eisenhower also had the invaluable asset of a personality that charmed voters and the image of being "above politics." Few could seriously believe that "Ike" would scuttle the New Deal reforms.

The uniquely personal aspect of Eisenhower's victory was underlined by the narrow margins with which Republicans moved into control of Congress, despite the presidential landslide. Republicans made a net gain of twenty-two House seats to a new total of 221, only three more than the 218 needed to give them control. The Democratic House total slipped from 235 to 213. In Senate elections the Republicans made a net gain of only one seat, just enough to give them a one-seat edge in the new Senate. The new Senate totals were forty-eight Republicans, forty-seven Democrats, and one Independent (Wayne Morse of Oregon, formerly a Republican).

In what proved to be a significant Senate race, thirty-five-year-old Democratic representative John F. Kennedy defeated Republican Henry Cabot Lodge Jr., a top leader in the Eisenhower drive for the GOP presidential nomination, by a 70,737-vote margin in Massachusetts. Other newly elected senators included Barry Goldwater, R-Ariz.; Stuart Symington, D-Mo.; Mike Mansfield, D-Mont.; Henry M. Jackson, D-Wash.; and Albert Gore, D-Tenn.

On the gubernatorial level, Republicans solidified the national lead they had achieved in 1950 by winning five new seats. The winners were Christian A. Herter, R-Mass.; William G. Stratton, R-Ill.; J. Caleb Boggs, R-Del.; George N. Craig, R-Ind.; and Hugo Aronson, R-Mont. The new governorship totals were thirty Republicans and eighteen Democrats.

1953–1955:
THE EIGHTY-THIRD CONGRESS

Many Americans had hoped that Eisenhower's election to the presidency would usher in an era of domestic tranquillity and international stability. In some respects these wishes were fulfilled. There was a more harmonious relationship between the president and Congress than at any time since World War II. A Korean armistice was finally signed July 27, 1953, with prisoner repatriation following shortly thereafter.

Republicans claimed that President Eisenhower's action in instructing the U.S. Seventh Fleet to stop shielding Communist China from any possible Nationalist Chinese attacks, combined with information relayed to the Chinese that the United States

would resort to full-scale war in Korea if the Communists refused to come to peace terms, were decisive factors in persuading the Communists to come to terms. Democrats replied that the terms of the armistice were no better than those the Truman administration had previously rejected.

Even with a return to relative stability in Korea, however, the international situation remained in flux on other fronts. Soviet Premier Joseph Stalin died March 5, setting off a contest for succession in the Soviet Union. On July 7, 1953, an uprising that broke out in Communist-held East Germany was quelled when the Communists called in Soviet troops and tanks, which mowed down civilians revolting in the streets of East Berlin. The United States did not intervene, drawing into question the wisdom of the "liberation" policy spelled out by Republican campaigners in 1952.

On August 20, 1953, the Soviet Union announced the successful testing of its first hydrogen bomb. President Eisenhower went before the United Nations on December 8 to urge the major powers to cooperate in developing the peaceful uses of atomic energy. The United States on January 21, 1954, launched the *Nautilus,* the first atomic-powered submarine.

The curtain began to go down on France's colonial empire as the nation admitted defeat in its seven-and-a-half-year war against Communist infiltration in Indo-China and submitted to a partition of Vietnam at the spring 1953 Geneva conference on Far Eastern affairs; France subsequently withdrew forces from Vietnam, Cambodia, and Laos. Threatened Communist inroads in Central America were reversed, however, by U.S.-supported anticommunist forces, which invaded Guatemala and overthrew the communist-oriented government of President Jacobo Arbenz Guzman in June 1954.

The Eighty-third Congress produced few innovations in domestic or foreign policy, but neither did it reverse New Deal social reforms. During the first session (1953), foreign aid and military appropriations were pared, the controversial Reconstruction Finance Corp. was abolished, legislation was passed giving the states title to the oil-rich coastal lands previously claimed by the federal government, and Congress permitted the president to carry out a governmental reorganization creating a new Department of Health, Education, and Welfare, which it had denied President Truman in 1949 and 1950.

Sen. Joseph R. McCarthy and his unrestrained accusations of communist influence throughout the government remained a domestic issue. Taking over the chair of the Senate Government Operations Committee in 1953, McCarthy conducted hearings and investigated the State Department, Voice of America, Department of the Army, and other agencies. An opinion-stifling "climate of fear" in many government agencies was said to be one of the results of his probes. The Army-McCarthy hearings, televised in the spring of 1954, were the climax of McCarthy's career and led finally to his censure by the Senate on December 2, 1954. McCarthy's influence waned steadily thereafter. He died May 2, 1957.

The Supreme Court on May 17, 1954, handed down a unanimous decision declaring racial segregation in the public schools to be unconstitutional. The opinion, written by Chief Justice

Sen. Joseph R. McCarthy was Congress's most notorious anticommunist investigator of the post–World War II period. McCarthy's abuse of committee power led to his censure by the Senate in 1954 and reform in congressional committee procedures.

Earl Warren (whom Eisenhower had appointed on the death of Chief Justice Fred M. Vinson in 1953), began a major movement toward racial desegregation across the nation. It inspired bitter hostility in the southern states.

A potential Democratic comeback with the nation's voters was presaged by special elections held during 1953. The traditional Republican hold on New Jersey was broken by the election of Democrat Robert B. Meyner to the governorship. Special elections in the New Jersey Sixth and Wisconsin Ninth Districts resulted in the election of two Democrats, Harrison A. Williams Jr. in New Jersey and Lester Johnson in Wisconsin. They were the first members of their party ever to win in either of those districts.

The 1954 Midterm Elections

The Republican success under Eisenhower in winning both houses of Congress in 1952 was not repeated in 1954. Democrats made significant comebacks, recapturing control of both House and Senate and reversing the Republican gubernatorial trend of recent years. But the swing back to the Democrats, while it indicated that the Republican Party was probably much weaker than its popular president, was by no means strong enough to spell a major change in the nation's mood. Although it was in the majority, much of the Democratic Party strength was concentrated in the conservative South.

President Eisenhower appealed to the voters to return a Republican Congress and he campaigned harder and longer than any other president had ever done in a midterm election. He claimed that Congress had enacted fifty-four of sixty-four legislative proposals he had submitted and that this "batting average of .830" was "pretty good in any league." (Congressional

Quarterly figures showed Congress had approved 150 of 232 specific Eisenhower requests for a batting average of .647.)

In an October 8 televised address he warned that a Democratic congressional victory would start "a cold war of partisan politics between the Congress and the Executive Branch," which would block "the great work" his administration had "begun so well." Congressional Democratic leaders Sam Rayburn and Lyndon B. Johnson, both of Texas, replied in a joint telegram to the president that "there will be no cold war conducted against you by the Democrats" and complained that the president had made an "unjust attack on the many Democrats who have done so much to cooperate with your Administration and to defend your program against attacks by members of your own party."

In a last-minute effort to bolster the Republican vote in critical states, Eisenhower made an unprecedented one-day, 1,521-mile flying trip on October 29, 1954, to address crowds in Cleveland, Detroit, Louisville, and Wilmington, Delaware. In these speeches he implied that Democratic administrations had been able to boast of full employment and prosperity only during war. Following the campaign some observers speculated that Eisenhower may have kept many women's votes by reminding them that the Republicans had put an end to the "futile casualties" in Korea. There was general agreement that his campaign activities averted a still stronger Democratic trend, especially in congressional elections.

Vice President Nixon played a controversial role in the campaign, charging that the Democrats were unfit to govern because of their record on the communist issue.

On the issue of mounting unemployment in several areas of the country, Democrats charged Republicans with a "callous" attitude toward the problem, while Republicans replied that they had provided jobs without war. Public power was also an issue, with Democrats accusing Republicans of "give-aways" to private interests, while Republicans replied that Democratic public power policy had tended toward socialism and government monopoly.

Results of the 1954 Elections

Democrats moved into control of the Senate by a 48–47–1 margin as compared with the 49–46–1 Republican edge before the election. Among the new senators were Richard L. Neuberger, D-Ore., former vice president Alben W. Barkley, D-Ky., and Clifford P. Case, R-N.J.

In the House the new lineup was 232 Democrats and 203 Republicans, a net Democratic gain of nineteen seats over the previous Congress, which had had 221 Republicans and 213 Democrats.

The Democratic congressional majorities grew throughout the remainder of the Eisenhower years. Sam Rayburn, D-Texas, again became Speaker of the House, and Lyndon B. Johnson, D-Texas, Senate majority leader—posts they held through the rest of the decade.

Republicans fared even worse in the governorship races. Including the Democratic victory of Edmund S. Muskie in the September 13 Maine election, the Democrats ousted Republicans from eight state governments, and the Republicans failed to take a single Democratic seat. The gubernatorial balance shifted from 29–19 in favor of the Republicans to 27–21 in favor of the Democrats. In the New York governorship election to succeed retiring three-term governor Thomas E. Dewey, a Republican, Democrat Averell Harriman won a narrow 11,125-vote plurality over Republican senator Irving M. Ives. Other Democratic gubernatorial winners included Abraham Ribicoff in Connecticut, Orville Freeman in Minnesota, and George M. Leader in Pennsylvania.

1955–1957:
THE EIGHTY-FOURTH CONGRESS

Cooperation between a middle-of-the-road president and a middle-of-the-road Congress, tension in the Formosa Strait, growing pressures in Africa and Asia for independence from colonial rule, the Geneva "summit" conference, presidential illnesses, "de-Stalinization" in the Soviet empire, revolt in Poland and Hungary, war over the Suez Canal—these events were highlights of the last half of President Eisenhower's first term in office.

Divided responsibility for government brought unexpectedly harmonious sessions of Congress, with nothing resembling the "cold war of partisan politics" predicted in 1954 by Eisenhower if the Democrats were to take control of Congress. Administration measures fared almost as well as they had during the Republican Eighty-third Congress, again with substantial aid from Democrats.

Especially in foreign affairs the Democratic leadership cooperated substantially with the president. Early in 1955 Congress approved the resolution Eisenhower had requested to give him authority to employ U.S. armed forces to defend Formosa. Prompted by Communist Chinese bombardment of the offshore islands of Quemoy and Matsu, the resolution also gave the president authority to defend, in addition to Formosa, "related positions and territories now in friendly hands," an evident reference to Quemoy and Matsu. Senate moves to delete this authority were overwhelmingly rejected.

The Senate approved, by almost unanimous votes, the Southeast Asia Collective Defense Treaty (which created the Southeast Asia Treaty Organization—SEATO), plus protocols ending the occupation of Germany, restoring sovereignty to West Germany, and permitting West German rearmament and NATO membership. The peace treaty with Austria, creating an independent, neutral state, was signed in Vienna on May 15 and was approved by the Senate June 7, 1955. The controversial constitutional amendment offered by Sen. John W. Bricker, R-Ohio, to trim the president's treaty-making powers was reported out of the Senate Foreign Relations Committee in 1956, but it was not brought up for Senate debate because of the president's firm opposition. In 1955 the Reciprocal Trade Agreements Act was extended for three years, the longest single extension since 1945. Foreign aid appropriations came fairly close to matching presidential requests.

Domestic enactments by the politically divided government were less impressive. The two most important measures approved by Congress appeared to be the multibillion dollar fed-

eral highway program, providing for a 41,000-mile interstate superhighway program as part of the most extensive public works project in the nation's history, and the Agricultural Act of 1956, which included the soil bank program that supporters hoped would limit farm surpluses and raise farmers' incomes. Congress also voted an increase in the minimum wage to $1 an hour (as opposed to the ninety-cent figure recommended by the administration).

On the international scene the first conference of Asian-African countries met April 18–27, 1955, in Bandung, Indonesia. Delegates endorsed an end to colonialism, called for national independence, and demanded UN membership for all states that qualified under the UN charter (including Communist China). In the following month the Warsaw Treaty, counterpart to NATO for the Communist satellites of Eastern Europe, was ratified.

At the Twentieth Congress of the Soviet Communist Party in Moscow, February 14–25, 1956, Nikita Khrushchev proclaimed a new party line, which included destruction of Joseph Stalin as a national idol. The rush to "de-Stalinize" however, loosed forces in the Communist world that the Soviet Union was able to control only by bloody repressions of the June 28, 1956, workers revolt in Poznan, Poland, and the revolt of Hungarians in October and November of 1956.

Reacting adversely to Egyptian president Gamal Abdel Nasser's acceptance of Soviet-bloc arms and economic agreements with the Communist world, the United States on July 19, 1956, informed Egypt that it was withdrawing its offer to aid in construction of the Aswan Dam on the Nile River. Britain on July 20 announced it was also withdrawing from the project. On July 26 Egypt seized the British-held Suez Canal and denounced the Western powers. Prolonged negotiations during the summer and fall failed to persuade Egypt to modify its decision on nationalizing the canal, and on October 29 Israel launched an invasion of Egypt. The move was coordinated with the British and French governments, which attacked Egypt on October 31. The Suez Canal was blocked by sunken and scuttled ships. The Soviet Union stepped into the controversy, threatening atomic war if Britain and France refused to retreat. The United Nations, led by the United States, condemned the French, British, and Israeli moves. A UN cease-fire ended the fighting November 7, and a UN international peace force moved in to enforce the peace, the terms of which allowed Egypt to regain control of the canal and forced Israeli withdrawal.

The question of President Eisenhower's health hung over the nation for a year before the November 1956 election. On September 24, 1955, the sixty-four-year-old president was stricken by a heart attack, which totally incapacitated him for a period of days and necessitated his hospitalization for almost two months. Republican leaders, who had confidently expected Eisenhower to seek (and easily win) reelection in 1956, suddenly faced the possibility that he might not be available. As the president gradually improved, party leaders, particularly GOP national chairman Leonard W. Hall, repeatedly urged him to run again despite his illness. After thorough physical examinations, Eisenhower on February 29, 1956, announced that he was convinced that his health would permit him to carry the "burdens of the Presidency" under a reduced work schedule and that he would seek reelection.

On June 8 the president was again hospitalized, this time with ileitis. He underwent successful surgery on June 9 and was once more hospitalized for several weeks. Again the possibility arose that he might not seek reelection. But on July 10 Eisenhower made it clear he would go ahead with his campaign for reelection.

Without the question of presidential illness, there would probably have been little doubt, at any time, that Ike could achieve reelection. The presidential illness, however, added an element of uncertainty to the entire campaign and made the Democratic nomination appear far more "worth having" than might otherwise have been the case.

The 1956 Campaigns

A familiar cast stepped forward to seek the Democratic presidential nomination: Adlai E. Stevenson, the 1952 nominee; Tennessee senator Estes Kefauver, the popular primary choice of 1952; and New York governor Averell Harriman. Senate majority leader Lyndon B. Johnson of Texas was supported for the nomination by several southern leaders, but he had little backing outside the South.

Early in the spring it appeared that Kefauver might again sweep the primaries. After winning the New Hampshire Democratic primary without opposition on March 13, he went on to pick up 56 percent of the vote in the March 20 Minnesota primary against Stevenson. The decisive contest came on June 5 in California, where both men had waged vigorous campaigns. The results: Stevenson, 1,139,964; Kefauver, 680,722. The Kefauver campaign limped along for a few more weeks. On July 26 Kefauver announced his withdrawal in favor of Stevenson.

When the Democratic National Convention met in Chicago on August 13, Stevenson and Harriman were the only two serious candidates for the nomination. Harriman's candidacy, discounted by most observers, received a boost when former president Truman on August 11 endorsed him. But in the vital contest for actual delegate votes, Stevenson, with Kefauver's support, was too far ahead to be stopped. On the first ballot on August 16 Stevenson was nominated with 905 ½ votes to 210 for Harriman, 80 for Johnson, and the remainder scattered.

Historically, the most significant event at the 1956 convention was the cliff-hanging decision about the Democratic vice-presidential nominee. Following his nomination, Stevenson made a brief appearance before the convention to tell the delegates he had decided "to depart from the precedents of the past." He said "the selection of the vice-presidential nominee should be made through the free processes of this convention."

After a stiff two-ballot contest, Kefauver, on August 17, narrowly won the vice-presidential nomination over Massachusetts senator John F. Kennedy. With 686 ½ votes required for nomination, Kennedy's total moved as high as 648 at one point during the second ballot. But a series of vote switches gave the nomination to Kefauver, who had 755 ½ votes against 589 for Kennedy and 27 ½ scattered. Other unsuccessful aspirants for the vice-presidential nomination, all of whom received substantial first-ballot votes, were Sen. Hubert H. Humphrey of Minnesota, Sen. Albert Gore of Tennessee, and New York mayor Robert F. Wagner.

The vice-presidential fight marked Kennedy's entry into presidential politics. The good showing that Kennedy had made, particularly in southern delegations, convinced his backers that despite his Roman Catholic faith Kennedy could be elected president.

The convention on August 16 adopted a platform including a compromise civil rights plank. It termed Supreme Court rulings "the law of the land" but made no specific pledge to apply the Court's decisions and denounced the use of force to implement them. A move by a northern liberal group led by Gov. G. Mennen Williams of Michigan, Sen. Paul H. Douglas of Illinois, and Sen. Herbert H. Lehman of New York to insert a pledge to "carry out" the Court's decisions, was defeated by voice vote on the convention floor.

On the Republican side from February 29, when Eisenhower announced he would seek a second term, there was no visible opposition to his renomination. Senate minority leader William F. Knowland, R-Calif., had previously announced his "provisional" candidacy, if Eisenhower were not to run, but he quickly withdrew it. The president swept all the primaries where his name was entered.

With the GOP presidential nomination a foregone conclusion, interest centered on the Republican vice-presidential nomination. Eisenhower declined to make an early clear-cut endorsement of Richard M. Nixon for renomination as vice president and was reported to have suggested to Nixon that he consider a cabinet assignment or another government post, if Nixon planned to seek the GOP presidential nomination at a later date.

Presidential disarmament adviser Harold E. Stassen on July 25 attempted to spark a "stop Nixon" movement, claiming that Nixon's presence on the ticket might cost Eisenhower as much as 6 percent of the vote in the fall and endanger Republican congressional campaigns. No major Republican leaders came forward to support Stassen and the stop-Nixon move quickly faded. At Eisenhower's request Stassen actually ended by making a seconding speech for Nixon at the convention, which met in San Francisco August 20–23.

The convention adopted without dissent a platform pledging a "continuation of peace, prosperity and progress." Threatened opposition to the civil rights plank evaporated after the Resolutions Committee modified an earlier and "stronger" version and proposed a plank acceptable to both northern and southern delegates.

The attack on Egypt and uprisings in Hungary and Poland dominated the news during the last weeks of the 1956 campaign, eclipsing domestic issues and changing the emphasis in international policy debates.

Early in the campaign Eisenhower boasted that his administration had offered, "in all levels of government," an "honest" regime of "good judgment," "tolerance," and "conciliation." The voters were asked to reelect him in order to keep the country "going down the straight road of prosperity and peace." Vice President Nixon, answering Democratic criticisms of Eisenhower administration foreign policy, said the families of "157,000 Americans who were killed, wounded or missing in Korea" could testify "whether we have peace today." Nixon said "the great majority of the American people have enjoyed the best four years of their lives under the Eisenhower Administration."

Stevenson's first approach was to challenge the effectiveness of Eisenhower's executive leadership, putting forth his own gospel of "the New America" under a Democratic Party that "can build as we have to build." He criticized the administration for failing to pass school aid legislation and other vitally needed domestic programs. He said the administration had "pilloried innocent men and women under the pretense of conducting loyalty and security investigations."

The tone of the campaign began to change as debate mounted over Stevenson's proposals to end the draft and stop U.S. testing of hydrogen bombs. The Stevenson proposal to end the draft drew the reply from Eisenhower that he saw "no chance of ending the draft and carrying out the responsibilities for the security of the country."

The debate was disturbed, however, by the beginning of the Hungarian uprising on October 23 and the Israeli attack on Egypt on October 29. Whatever the merits of the Stevenson proposals, they appeared to be badly timed in view of the international situation. Eisenhower again stressed that "we need our military draft for the safety of our nation" and that the country must have the "most advanced military weapons." With war threatening both in the Mideast and in Eastern Europe, the general public reaction seemed to be that it was a bad time to change leaders, especially considering the president's military background.

Results of the 1956 Elections

President Eisenhower was reelected with the largest popular vote in history and a plurality second only to that of Franklin D. Roosevelt in 1936. Eisenhower came out with 35,590,472 votes (457 electoral votes) and Stevenson with 26,022,752 (73 electoral votes). Eisenhower's plurality was 9,567,720 votes.

In the North the president carried or ran unusually well in many urban areas formerly considered safe Democratic areas. More blacks voted Republican than in any election since pre–New Deal days. The only states where Eisenhower pluralities dropped from 1952 were several farm states where Secretary of Agriculture Ezra Taft Benson and administration agricultural policies were highly unpopular.

The presidential election did not have the necessary coattail effect to give Republicans control of Congress. Although the returns indicated Ike's tremendous popularity with voters, the outcome for other offices made it clear that most citizens still identified their interests with those of the Democratic Party. For the first time since 1848 the winning presidential candidate was unable to carry at least one house of Congress for his party.

The Democrats amazingly maintained their 49–47 lead in the Senate, taking Republican seats in Colorado, Idaho, Ohio,

and Pennsylvania to make up for their losses in New York, West Virginia, and Kentucky. Democratic senator Wayne Morse, the man whom the Republicans had wanted most to defeat, won over former secretary of the interior Douglas McKay. Newly elected senators included Thruston B. Morton, R-Ky.; Joseph S. Clark, D-Pa.; Jacob K. Javits, R-N.Y.; Frank Church, D-Idaho; and Frank J. Lausche, D-Ohio.

In the House the Democrats added to the twenty-nine-seat margin they had achieved in 1954, bringing their ranks to 234 as against 201 Republicans.

The Democrats made a net gain of one new governorship for a new 28–20 balance in their favor. Important Democratic gubernatorial victories included two in normally Republican farm states: Herschel C. Loveless in Iowa and George Docking in Kansas. Other Democrats winning previously held Republican governorships were Foster Furcolo in Massachusetts and Robert D. Holmes in Oregon. Republicans winning Democratic gubernatorial seats were C. William O'Neill in Ohio, Cecil Underwood in West Virginia, and Edwin L. Mechem in New Mexico.

1957–1959: THE EIGHTY-FIFTH CONGRESS

The first two years of Eisenhower's second term in office were marked by two major events, one domestic and one foreign, in the fall of 1957.

On September 4 a controversy over admission of black students to the previously all-white Central High School in Little Rock, Arkansas, reached a showdown as the National Guard, ordered out by Gov. Orval Faubus, prevented the black students from entering the school. A federal court on September 21 ordered removal of the National Guard. But when the black students reentered the school two days later, they were ordered to leave by local authorities because of fear of mob violence. Eisenhower then ordered federal troops sent into Little Rock to enforce the court's order, and the school began operation on an integrated basis.

The spectacle of angry, racist crowds in the face of fixed bayonets rioting to prevent black children from entering the school shocked the world. The scene was offset in part by the use of federal troops to enforce the constitutional rights of U.S. citizens. Throughout the South, however, the reaction was one of bitterness toward Eisenhower for using troops to enforce a deeply resented Supreme Court decision.

The second major event in the fall of 1957 was the Soviet Union's successful launching, on October 4, of the first manufactured satellite, Sputnik I, into an orbit around the world. Congress and the nation responded with anger, frustration, and alarm, directed chiefly at the Eisenhower administration because it had not pressed the U.S. effort to beat the Soviets into outer space and because it showed, at least initially, little concern about the Soviet achievement. More profound concern developed about the quality of U.S. education, especially in scientific fields. The first successful U.S. satellite, Explorer I, was launched by the Army from Cape Canaveral, Florida, on January 31, 1958.

President Dwight Eisenhower (third from right) confers with leaders of Congress. During Eisenhower's two terms there was generally a harmonious relationship between the White House and Congress.

Other major international events in 1957 and 1958 included:

• On March 25, 1957, the Common Market (European Economic Community) and Euratom (European Atomic Energy Community) treaties were signed in Rome by France, Belgium, the Netherlands, Luxembourg, Italy, and West Germany. These treaties were significant steps toward the U.S.-supported goal of a united Europe.

• Vice President and Mrs. Nixon narrowly escaped injury from Communist-inspired riots while on a goodwill tour in Caracas, Venezuela, on May 13, 1957.

• Great Britain exploded its first hydrogen bomb, May 15, 1957.

• Former premier Georgii M. Malenkov, former foreign minister V. M. Molotov, and L. M. Kaganovich were purged by the Soviet Presidium under Nikita Khrushchev's leadership, July 3–4, 1957, for alleged pro-Stalinist activities. On March 27, 1958, Chairman Khrushchev completed solidification of power by succeeding Nikolai A. Bulganin as premier.

• Charles de Gaulle became head of the French government on June 1, 1958, averting threatened civil war.

• At the request of the Lebanese government, U.S. Marines were dispatched to Lebanon on July 15, 1958, to forestall a threatened effort by Egyptian president Gamal Abdel Nasser's United Arab Republic and the Soviet Union to overthrow Lebanon's pro-Western regime. U.S. troops withdrew in August after calm was restored.

• In the fall of 1958 the United States and the Soviet Union began a three-and-one-half-year unpoliced moratorium on nuclear weapons tests.

Major domestic events included the development of the most serious postwar recession, in mid-1957 and lasting through 1958; a stroke suffered by President Eisenhower November 25, 1957, from which he was pronounced "completely recovered" on

March 1, 1958; and the resignation of Sherman Adams, assistant to the president. Adams's resignation in September 1958 followed revelations before a House subcommittee that he had interceded with various federal agencies in behalf of his friend, Boston industrialist Bernard Goldfine, and that he had received gifts from Goldfine. The Goldfine-Adams episode hurt the Eisenhower administration on the corruption-in-government issue and was one of several elements contributing to the Democratic sweep in the 1958 congressional and gubernatorial elections.

The Eighty-fifth Congress established a record of moderate productivity, all its chief enactments bearing the "middle-of-the-road" stamp that was the natural result of compromise between a "mildly conservative" president and the "mildly liberal" congressional leadership of House Speaker Sam Rayburn and Senate majority leader Lyndon B. Johnson, both of Texas.

The mounting recession pushed the federal budget increasingly into the red, with a $2.8 billion deficit in fiscal 1958 and a $12.4 billion deficit for the fiscal 1959 budget, approved in mid-1958.

In foreign policy the Senate in 1957 approved the International Atomic Energy treaty (stemming from President Eisenhower's Atoms for Peace program). During its first session, Congress approved the Mideast Resolution (Eisenhower Doctrine), in response to the president's request for advance authority to use U.S. troops to protect free Middle East nations from "overt armed aggression" by "power hungry Communists." During the second session, Congress acceded readily to the president's request for authority to extend financial aid and technical assistance to the newly formed European Atomic Energy Community.

A military reorganization bill was approved by Congress in 1958. This bill eliminated the "separately administered" provision for army, navy, and air force written into the 1947 National

Security Act and made it clear that the three military departments were to operate under the direction and control of the secretary of defense. Legislation passed in July 1958 established a civilian-controlled National Aeronautics and Space Administration (NASA). Both houses organized permanent standing committees on space matters.

The major domestic bill passed in 1957 was the Civil Rights Act. The bill created the executive Commission on Civil Rights and empowered the attorney general to seek injunctions when individuals are denied the right to vote. With strengthening amendments in succeeding years, this legislation gave more and more black citizens the power of the ballot, viewed by the bill's advocates as the foundation of most other civil liberties.

The most notable accomplishment of Congress's 1958 session was passage and signature by the president of the Alaska statehood bill, culminating decades of pressure to admit the territory to the Union.

Other important actions of the second session included emergency housing and highway construction legislation to help stem the recession; passage of the National Defense Education Act of 1958, including $295 million for loans to needy college students; the Transportation Act of 1958, designed to revive the failing railroads; and passage of a low-support farm bill with few controls generally in line with administration proposals.

Under the leadership of Democratic national chairman Paul M. Butler, a policy-making Democratic Advisory Committee was organized in November 1956 and became the chief voice for the militantly liberal Democratic point of view. It made sharp partisan attacks on the Eisenhower administration. Democratic congressional leaders Rayburn and Johnson had been asked to join but instead actively opposed it, expressing a preference for policy formulation through regular Democratic congressional leadership channels. Many of the committee's statements reflected severe criticism of the Democratic congressional leadership for alleged lack of sufficiently aggressive opposition to the Eisenhower administration. (The committee was eventually abolished in March 1961 after the Democratic takeover of the White House. The new Democratic National Chairman, John M. Bailey, said the committee had "served a function" only when the party was out of power.)

The 1958 Midterm Elections

The swing of the political pendulum against the Republicans and in favor of the Democrats was apparent as early as mid-1957. It ended November 25, 1958, with a clean Democratic sweep in Alaska's first election as a state. The over-all national result was the most thorough Democratic victory since the Roosevelt landslide year of 1936.

In August 1957 Democrat William Proxmire easily won the Wisconsin Senate seat of the late Republican senator Joseph R. McCarthy, who had died May 2 of the same year. In the November 1957 off-year elections the Democrats reelected New Jersey Democratic governor Robert B. Meyner by a plurality of nearly 200,000 votes, also scoring important victories in Virginia and New York. In the September 8, 1958, Maine elections the Democrats swept that normally Republican state, electing a Democratic governor, a Democratic senator, and two Democratic representatives.

The Republicans began the 1958 campaign with a number of handicaps. The Adams-Goldfine incident had been a source of profound embarrassment for the Eisenhower administration, only partly relieved by Adams's resignation in September. Although recovery from the 1957–1958 recession was already under way, the recession had served to weaken seriously voter confidence in the Eisenhower prosperity formula. Another crisis in the Formosa Strait, with renewed Communist China shelling of Quemoy and Matsu, reminded voters that the administration had yet to find a solution for the China problem. Sputnik had weakened voter confidence in the Eisenhower administration's defense and space programs.

In many states the Republicans backed ballot initiative proposals for right-to-work laws that were bitterly opposed by organized labor. This inspired labor to work particularly hard to get its members out to vote: against right-to-work and for Democrats. A major portion of the blame for Republican debacles in states such as Ohio and California was attributed to GOP right-to-work stands. Still another incident harming the Republicans was deep southern resentment against Eisenhower's ordering of paratroops into Little Rock in 1957. This effectively curtailed Republican efforts for new inroads in the South.

In the campaign the Democrats charged that the Republicans had callously allowed the country to slip into a serious recession, showing little regard for the interests of the unemployed. Adlai Stevenson on October 18 said that the crises over Quemoy, desegregation, education, and recession "could have been avoided if we had an administration which thought in advance instead of waiting placidly on the fairways until the mortal danger is upon us and then angrily calling out the Marines." "The tragedy of the Eisenhower Administration," Stevenson said, "is that its only weapons seem to be platitudes or paratroops."

Alarmed by the apparent Democratic inroads, the Republicans held an October 6 White House strategy session that produced a manifesto declaring that if a new Democratic Congress were elected, "we are certain to go down the left lane which leads inseparably to socialism." In Baltimore, on October 31, Eisenhower used such terms as "political free spenders," "gloomdoggler," and "extremist" to describe his Democratic opponents.

House Speaker Rayburn on November 1 predicted that a new Democratic-controlled Congress would not fight the president despite "desperation" oratory in which Rayburn said Eisenhower went "pretty far in accusing us of being radicals and left-wingers." Rayburn said that "in the past about 85 percent of the time Eisenhower's programs were just an extension of Democratic principles. . . . We're not going to hate Eisenhower bad enough for us to change our principles."

Much of the hard campaigning for Republican candidates throughout the country was done by Vice President Nixon. On October 21 Nixon said that the Democratic Party was split between "essentially moderate" Democratic leaders in Congress and the group "which presently controls the Democratic National Committee, which is radical in its approach to economic problems (and) bitterly partisan in its criticism of the Eisenhower foreign policy."

As the campaign progressed, the Republicans came under increasingly heavy Democratic fire for being antilabor. Eisenhower and Nixon refused to endorse the right-to-work laws, but the president called for legislation to let workers "free themselves of their corrupt labor bosses who have betrayed their trust."

In reply to the potent Democratic "missile gap" issue of allegedly slow U.S. progress in rockets and missiles, Eisenhower repeatedly declared that no more than $1 million had been spent on development of long-range missiles in any year before he became president, but that "the so-called missile gap is being rapidly filled."

Results of the 1958 Elections

As election returns poured in during the evening of November 4, it was clear that the Democratic tide had engulfed Republicans in virtually every area of the nation. Including the November 25 Alaska election, the results showed a new Senate of sixty-four Democrats and thirty-four Republicans, a Democratic gain of fifteen seats and a Republican loss of thirteen from the 49–47 Democratic edge in 1956. Democrats gained seats in California (where Republicans were embroiled in internecine fights and the right-to-work issue), Connecticut, Indiana, Maine, Michigan, Minnesota, Nevada, New Jersey, Ohio, Utah, West Virginia (two seats), and Wyoming, and took the two new seats from Alaska, which became a state January 3, 1959.

The new Democratic senators included Eugene J. McCarthy of Minnesota, Thomas J. Dodd of Connecticut, Clair Engle of California, and Harrison A. Williams Jr. of New Jersey. New Republicans elected to the Senate were Kenneth B. Keating of New York and Hugh Scott of Pennsylvania.

In the House there were 282 Democrats, forty-eight more than the previous Congress's total and the highest figure since the 1936 elections. Republicans slipped from 201 to 154 seats. Republican House losses were heaviest in the Midwest, where twenty-three seats were lost (many in the traditional Republican heartland), and in the East, where twenty were lost. Only two incumbent Democratic House members were defeated: Rep. Coya Knutson of Minnesota, evidently as a result of her marital difficulties, and Rep. Brooks Hays of Arkansas, a moderate on racial issues defeated on a write-in vote by Dale Alford, a Democratic archsegregationist in Arkansas's Fifth (Little Rock) District.

In gubernatorial races there was a net switch of five governorships, plus the new Alaska governorship, to the Democrats for a new total of thirty-five Democratic and fourteen Republican governors. Important Democratic gubernatorial victories included Edmund G. Brown in California (over Senate minority leader William F. Knowland); Michael V. DiSalle, Ohio; Ralph G. Brooks, Nebraska; Ralph Herseth, South Dakota; Gaylord A. Nelson, Wisconsin; and J. Millard Tawes, Maryland. Democrats also reelected Gov. Abraham A. Ribicoff in Connecticut by a record majority and reelected Democratic governor George Docking in traditionally Republican Kansas.

The brightest spot in the entire picture for the Republicans was Nelson A. Rockefeller's New York victory over incumbent governor Averell Harriman by a 573,034-vote margin. Republicans also won the Oregon governorship with Mark Hatfield and the Rhode Island governorship with Christopher Del Sesto.

1959–1961:
THE EIGHTY-SIXTH CONGRESS

Relations between the United States and the Soviet Union dominated the international news, running the gamut from cordial to extremely bitter during 1959–1960.

In November 1958 Soviet premier Nikita S. Khrushchev had demanded an end to the four-power occupation of Berlin and threatened to turn control of Allied supply lines to West Berlin over to East Germany, asking that Berlin be made into a demilitarized "free city." The Soviet Union set May 27, 1959, as the deadline for the end of the occupation of Berlin. An international crisis, threatening atomic war, appeared to develop over the ensuing months. But when the Big Four foreign ministers sat down for consultations in Paris the following May, the Soviet deadline had been lifted and no changes in the Berlin status quo evolved.

Meanwhile, President Eisenhower had lost his key foreign policy adviser when Secretary of State John Foster Dulles was stricken by cancer early in 1959. Dulles resigned by April 15 and died on May 24. Under Secretary Christian A. Herter, former Massachusetts representative and governor, succeeded Dulles.

A period of moderation in U.S.-Soviet relations followed. Vice President Richard Nixon on July 22 left for a thirteen-day tour of the Soviet Union. Nixon received a friendly reception by Russian crowds. In September, at Eisenhower's invitation, Khrushchev visited the United States for consultations with the president and a transcontinental tour. But the 1959 "spirit of Camp David" failed to result in a lasting thaw in the cold war.

In May 1960, just before a scheduled Big Four summit conference in Paris, the Soviet Union announced that an American plane had been shot down over its territory. The United States at first said no violation of Soviet air space had been intended. After Khrushchev revealed that the pilot of the U-2 reconnaissance plane had confessed to being on an intelligence-gathering flight for the U.S. Central Intelligence Agency, Secretary of State Herter admitted that the United States had engaged in "extensive aerial surveillance of the USSR." President Eisenhower took full responsibility for the flights, terming them a "distasteful but vital necessity."

When the Big Four met May 16, Khrushchev denounced the "spy flight" and demanded a U.S. apology and punishment of responsible officials before the summit conference could continue. He withdrew an already-accepted invitation to Eisenhower to visit the Soviet Union in June 1960. Eisenhower said the flights had been discontinued and would not begin again, but he refused to accept Khrushchev's ultimatum. The conference collapsed, and leaders withdrew to their capitals amid mutual recriminations.

The incident weakened the confidence of many voters in the Republicans' skill in handling foreign affairs. Some observers later speculated that if there had been no U-2 incident, and if the summit conference and the Eisenhower trip to the Soviet

Union had proceeded as planned, the country might have been in no mood to replace the Republican hold on the White House in the November elections.

Other important international developments in 1959 and 1960 included the following:

• Fidel Castro assumed power in Cuba after collapse of the Batista dictatorship on January 1, 1959. Communist influence and control over the Castro revolution became increasingly evident in the succeeding years.

• A revolt by the Tibetan people against Chinese Communist rule was crushed in March 1959.

• Eisenhower made goodwill visits to Europe, Asia, and Africa in December 1959, to Latin America in February-March 1960, and to the Far East in early summer 1960. Leftist riots in Japan protesting the new U.S.-Japanese treaty of mutual security and cooperation forced Eisenhower to cancel plans to include that country in his Far Eastern Tour.

• The French tested their first nuclear device in the Sahara, February 13, 1960.

• The Belgian Congo gained independence, becoming the Republic of the Congo on June 30, 1960; soon thereafter the country was plunged into civil war, resulting in UN intervention in July 1960.

On the domestic front heavy Democratic majorities in the Eighty-sixth Congress failed to produce the kind of prolabor, liberal legislation for which many observers had seen a mandate in the 1958 election returns. The two major accomplishments of Congress—Hawaiian statehood and a labor reform law—were in fact just as much administration as Democratic bills.

Statehood for Hawaii, signed into law March 18, 1959, after fifty-nine years of territorial status for the one-time island kingdom, added a fiftieth state to the Union on August 21, 1959. The new state elected the nation's first two representatives of Chinese and Japanese ancestry: Sen. Hiram L. Fong, a Republican, and Rep. Daniel K. Inouye, a Democrat.

In the waning days of the 1959 session, Congress passed a "strong" labor regulation law (the Landrum-Griffin bill), which contained major Taft-Hartley Act amendments favored by business and opposed by organized labor. The continuing exposure of union corruption and labor-management collusion by the Senate Select Committee on Improper Activities in the Labor or Management Field had produced a deluge of letters, telegrams, and editorials calling for action.

The relatively mild Kennedy bill for labor regulation was passed by the Senate April 25. The House, on August 13, by a 229–201 roll call, approved a tougher measure, the Landrum-Griffin bill, which incorporated important Taft-Hartley reforms sought by President Eisenhower. The vote was a major victory for Eisenhower and the House Republican leadership under the newly chosen minority leader, Charles A. Halleck, R-Ind. It was a defeat for House Speaker Sam Rayburn, who preferred a milder measure. Most of Landrum-Griffin was incorporated in the conference committee compromise.

Determined to prevent adoption of expensive domestic programs suggested by liberal Democrats, Eisenhower sought to dramatize the issue of "spending" in his press conferences and other public utterances. Grassroots response was so positive that he was able to galvanize the Republican minority and invigorate the Republican-southern Democratic coalition, preventing passage of most liberal measures and rallying sufficient strength to sustain his vetoes of all but a handful of those that did pass. Thus Democratic proposals for a wide program of aid for school construction and teachers' salaries, for a massive area redevelopment program, for an increased minimum wage, and for medical care for the aged under Social Security all came to naught.

During 1960, however, the liberals found a new issue on which to base their call for increased social welfare legislation: the need for a rapid rate of growth in the national economy. The issue of economic growth developed too late to assist in passage of liberal measures in the Eighty-sixth Congress, but it provided campaign fodder for Democratic nominee John F. Kennedy in the 1960 presidential campaign.

The failure of many important domestic bills to clear Congress was largely attributed to the continuing party division between the executive and legislative branches and the approaching presidential elections. In 1959, for instance, the Senate took time out for a long and bitter debate that ended in rejection of the president's nomination of Lewis L. Strauss to be secretary of commerce. In 1960 a $750 million pay raise for federal employees was passed over the president's veto. Scenting victory in the upcoming elections, Democrats refused to pass a bill creating thirty-five badly needed new federal judgeships.

After long debate over the "missile gap" and the general adequacy of the nation's defense effort, Congress passed the president's defense budget with few overall changes in 1959 but in 1960 added $600 million more than Eisenhower had requested. The missile gap became a major issue in the 1960 presidential campaign, only to recede as an apparent mirage early in 1961.

During the postconvention session of Congress that began August 8, 1960, Democratic presidential candidate John F. Kennedy, a Massachusetts senator, and his running mate, Senate majority leader Lyndon B. Johnson, failed in their efforts to complete action on major Democratic legislation planks. The Senate approved the Kennedy minimum wage bill, but the measure died when House conferees refused to budge from their own truncated version. Medical care for the aged under the Social Security system—a second "must" bill—was rejected by the Senate, and a school construction bill expired when the House Rules Committee refused to send it to conference. As Congress adjourned September 1 and the campaign began in earnest, Republicans made the most of their opponents' plight.

The 1960 Campaigns

The Twenty-second Amendment to the Constitution, placing a two-term limitation on the presidency, meant that Eisenhower was ineligible to seek reelection in 1960. Adlai E. Stevenson's record of two defeats for the presidency appeared to preclude him from being the choice as the Democrats' candidate, barring a convention deadlock. Thus both parties were faced with the prospect of coming up with new nominees in 1960. For the Republicans the choice appeared relatively easy since Vice President Richard Nixon had been in the public eye for eight full years. Nixon had been an extremely active vice president, he was a tireless campaigner for GOP candidates, and he had strong support in Republican organizations throughout the country. For the Democrats the choice was more difficult because no members of the party had clearly established themselves as leaders of presidential stature.

In a departure from the American tendency to select governors for presidential nominees, all four chief contenders for the Democratic nomination were senators. In order of their announcements they were Hubert H. Humphrey of Minnesota, John F. Kennedy of Massachusetts, Stuart Symington of Missouri, and Majority Leader Lyndon B. Johnson of Texas. Of these four, only Kennedy and Humphrey chose to campaign in the primaries. In the end the primaries were the decisive factor in Kennedy's victory.

Symington dismissed primary contests as useless and Johnson maintained that he could not carry out his Senate duties properly and simultaneously run in numerous individual primaries. (Congressional Quarterly 1960 Senate Voting Participation scores showed an average of 80 percent for all Democrats. Kennedy scored 35 percent, Humphrey 49 percent; both campaigned extensively during the session. Symington scored 58 percent, and Johnson, 95 percent.)

The issue of Kennedy's religion dominated much of the preconvention and general-election debate and speculation about his chances. Not since 1928, when the Democrats nominated Alfred E. Smith of New York for the presidency, had a Roman Catholic headed a national ticket. Smith had been resoundingly defeated, with many normally Democratic but heavily Protestant states going against him, although considerations other than religion, perhaps equally important, ran against Smith. In the intervening years Roman Catholics had become a far larger segment of the population than before (16 percent in 1928; 22.8 percent by 1960, with especially large concentrations in the urban areas in the biggest states). The consensus was that the nation had become far more tolerant in its religious outlook.

The spring primaries produced a string of unbroken victories for Kennedy. Unopposed, he piled up an impressive 43,372 vote total in the early-bird New Hampshire primary March 8. In May Humphrey withdrew after the West Virginia primary, leaving Symington and Johnson as opponents for Kennedy. Just before the convention it appeared that Stevenson might reenter the race.

At the Democratic National Convention, which opened in Los Angeles on July 11, Kennedy won on the first ballot. After conferring with Democratic leaders, he announced that Lyndon B. Johnson would be his running mate. Most observers were surprised that Johnson, powerful Senate majority leader and almost ten years Kennedy's senior, would accept the nomination. Most party liberals expressed consternation at Kennedy's selection. Later it became evident that Johnson's presence on the ticket was probably an essential element in holding most of the South behind Kennedy and achieving Democratic victory in one of the closest presidential elections in U.S. history.

Without any significant opposition, Nixon breezed through the primaries and at the Republican National Convention was nominated July 27, receiving 1,321 votes to ten for Barry Goldwater. He selected UN ambassador and former Massachusetts senator Henry Cabot Lodge Jr. as his running mate.

By election day, November 8, Kennedy had covered 75,000 miles and visited forty-six states, while Nixon had traveled more than 60,000 miles and appeared in all fifty states. Speaking as often as a dozen times a day, both candidates were seen and heard by millions of voters, in person as well as on radio and television, in what may have been the most talkative as well as the most expensive campaign on record at the time.

The central issue, Kennedy asserted time and again, was the need for strong presidential leadership to reverse the nation's declining prestige abroad and lagging economy at home. Arguing that the position of the United States relative to that of the Soviets had deteriorated under the Eisenhower administration, he called for a stepped-up defense effort and an enlarged federal role in a wide variety of fields at home and abroad "to get America moving again."

In an unprecedented series of face-to-face encounters, candidates Kennedy and Nixon appeared on four nationally televised, hour-long programs during which they were questioned by panels of journalists and permitted to rebut each other's answers. The time was provided free of charge by the networks when Congress suspended the equal time provision of the Communications Act for the duration of the 1960 campaign. The audiences for the four debates were estimated by the Arbitron rating service at 70 to 75 million, 61 million, 65 million, and 64 million, respectively.

Republicans generally were dismayed by Nixon's appearance on the first debate, blaming it on poor lighting and their candidate's unaggressive stance, but they found little fault with the remaining three programs. Democrats regarded all the debates as highly successful on grounds that they served to demolish the GOP theme of Kennedy's "immaturity" and to project his personality to millions of undecided voters, many of whom were disturbed by his Catholic faith.

Results of the 1960 Elections

On election day 68,838,219 Americans—the largest number up to that time—cast ballots for president. Kennedy emerged the victor with a solid majority in the electoral college. But his popular-vote plurality over Nixon was only 118,574 votes, the smallest vote margin thus far in the twentieth century. In eleven states—eight won by Kennedy, three by Nixon—a shift of less than 1 percent of the vote would have switched the state's electoral votes.

The Kennedy-Johnson ticket carried twenty-three states with 303 electoral votes. They put together a coalition of eastern states (including New York, Pennsylvania, and New Jersey), central industrial states (Illinois, Michigan, and Minnesota) and several of the traditionally Democratic southern states (including Johnson's own Texas) that was sufficient to win, despite loss of almost the entire West and farm belt and several southern states.

Members of Congress Who Became President

From James Madison to George Bush, twenty-four presidents have served previously in the House of Representatives, or the Senate, or both.

Following is a list of these presidents and the chambers in which they served. Three other presidents—George Washington, John Adams, and Thomas Jefferson—had served in the Continental Congress, as had James Madison and James Monroe.

James A. Garfield was elected to the Senate in January 1880 for a term beginning March 4, 1881, but declined to accept in December 1880 because he had been elected president. John Quincy Adams served in the House for seventeen years after his term as president, and Andrew Johnson returned to the Senate five months before he died.

House Only	Senate Only
James Madison	James Monroe
James K. Polk	John Quincy Adams
Millard Fillmore	Martin Van Buren
Abraham Lincoln	Benjamin Harrison
Rutherford B. Hayes	Warren G. Harding
James A. Garfield	Harry S. Truman
William McKinley	
Gerald R. Ford	
George Bush	

Both Chambers

Andrew Jackson	Andrew Johnson
William Henry Harrison	John F. Kennedy
John Tyler	Lyndon B. Johnson
Franklin Pierce	Richard Nixon
James Buchanan	

Sources: Biographical Directory of the American Congress, 1774–1996. Washington, D.C.: CQ Staff Directories, 1996; *American Political Leaders 1789–2000.* Washington, D.C.: CQ Press, 2000.

Democrats maintained their heavy majorities in Congress and among the nation's governors in 1960, but Republicans were able to make some important gains, especially in the House of Representatives. Republican gains, taking place in the face of a victory for Democratic candidate Kennedy, appeared due in part to the return of normally Republican seats to the GOP to offset the serious losses suffered by Republicans in the 1958 Democratic sweep.

The continued heavy Democratic congressional majority, especially in the Senate, made it appear unlikely that Republicans would be able to regain control of Congress at any time during President-elect Kennedy's first term in the White House.

The Republicans made a gain of two Senate seats, replacing Democrats in Delaware and Wyoming. Despite advance predictions of possible trouble for Republican Senate incumbents in Massachusetts and New Jersey, both were able to withstand the Kennedy tide in those states. Democrats held their seats in Minnesota, Missouri, Michigan, and Montana, where Republican challengers ran energetic campaigns. The new Senate balance was sixty-four Democrats and thirty-six Republicans.

The Republican Senate gain was reduced when Senator-elect Keith Thomson, R-Wyo., died on December 9 and was replaced by Democrat J. J. Hickey. But the Senate balance returned to 64–36 in May 1961, when Republican John Tower won the Texas Senate seat vacated by Lyndon B. Johnson, the new vice president.

In House elections Republicans made a net gain of twenty seats. The new House had 263 Democrats and 174 Republicans, as compared to a 283–154 balance in the previous Congress.

In contrast to most presidential elections, the victory of the national Democratic ticket did not appear to play an important part in most congressional contests. If Kennedy coattails existed at all, they were probably evident in New York State, which he carried by a wide margin and where three incumbent GOP representatives were defeated; in Connecticut, where Democrats held two close seats; and in New Jersey, where one Republican seat went Democratic. All other Democratic House gains appeared to be the result of special local conditions.

The most important Republican congressional gains came in the Midwest, where Nixon ran a strong race. Widespread and deep-seated anti-Catholic sentiment, combined with a marked cooling off of the farm issue, which hurt midwestern Republicans so badly in 1958, appeared to form the basis of much of the increased Republican midwestern strength in both presidential and local races.

Many Republican gains, which came through midwestern farm states but also in Connecticut, Maine, Ohio, Vermont, Oregon, and Pennsylvania, seemed to mark the return to the GOP fold of traditionally Republican congressional districts, which had gone Democratic in 1958 in a temporary protest against Republican policies.

In gubernatorial races the Democrats captured seven seats from the Republicans, and the Republicans captured six from the Democrats. The new lineup was thirty-four Democrats to sixteen Republicans, a net gain of one for the Democrats. Among the governors elected were Democrats Otto Kerner of Illinois, Matthew E. Welsh of Indiana, John B. Swainson of Michigan, and Frank B. Morrison of Nebraska. Republican governors elected included John A. Volpe of Massachusetts, Elmer L. Andersen of Minnesota, Norman A. Erbe of Iowa, and John Anderson Jr. of Kansas.

1961–1963:
THE EIGHTY-SEVENTH CONGRESS

Hopes were high, both in America and abroad, when John F. Kennedy took office as president January 20, 1961. In his inaugural address Kennedy called on Americans and all free people "to bear the burden of a long twilight struggle . . . against the common enemies of man: tyranny, poverty, disease and war itself." Kennedy urged Americans: "Ask not what your country can do for you—ask what you can do for your country."

John F. Kennedy delivers perhaps the most memorable and eloquent of inaugural addresses January 20, 1961.

Some of this idealism was translated into specific programs and action during the next two years. A Peace Corps was established, sending young Americans to underdeveloped nations, to provide trained personnel for development projects. Fulfilling another campaign promise, Kennedy got congressional approval of a U.S. Arms Control and Disarmament Agency. On March 14, 1961, the president announced an Alliance for Progress with the countries of Latin America, under which the United States would step up aid to the other Americas but expect to see political and social reforms to guarantee true democracy and promote stability and progress in those countries.

In the domestic field, several items of "liberal" legislation that had failed passage because of a stalemate between President Eisenhower and a Democratic Congress were enacted into law. Chief among these were a hike in the minimum wage to $1.25, a subsidy program for economically distressed areas in the United States, widening of Social Security benefits, a $4.88 billion omnibus housing bill, stepped-up federal aid to localities to battle water pollution, and a vastly increased public works program.

The first two years of Kennedy's term, however, contained disappointments, both foreign and domestic. In January 1961 the administration had high hopes of a period of relaxed tensions with the Soviet world. Congratulating Kennedy on his election, Soviet premier Nikita S. Khrushchev had expressed the "hope that while you are at this post the relations between our countries will again follow the line along which they were developing in Franklin Roosevelt's time." Khrushchev made specific mention of chances for early conclusion of a nuclear test ban treaty and a German peace treaty. During the first week of Kennedy's presidency, the Soviet government freed two U.S. Air Force RB-47 pilots who had been held in the Soviet Union since their plane was downed off Soviet shores in July 1960. But the optimism of January 1961 seemed more like overconfidence by

late 1961 as the tide of events continued to run almost consistently against the nation's foreign policy objectives.

On April 17, 1961, 1,200 Cuban refugees—recruited, trained, and supplied by the U.S. Central Intelligence Agency—landed ninety miles south of Havana; their announced goal was to overthrow the Communist-oriented regime of Fidel Castro. Within three days the invasion had been crushed, inflicting a disastrous blow to American prestige and to that of the new president.

Kennedy met with Khrushchev June 3–4, 1961, in Vienna. At this summit conference Khrushchev made clear his determination to sign a peace treaty with the East German Communist regime, a move long interpreted in the West as part of the effort to force the Western powers out of West Berlin. The Vienna confrontation convinced Kennedy that it was time to muster public support in behalf of a "firm stand" in Berlin. In a July 25 televised report to the nation, he called for an immediate buildup of U.S. and NATO forces along with an extra $3.5 billion in U.S. defense funds. Congress promptly granted his requests.

Khrushchev's reply was to threaten Soviet mobilization and to boast that the Soviets could build a hundred-megaton nuclear warhead. Much more damaging to the West, however, was the Communists' unexpected action on August 13 in sealing off the border between East and West Berlin. The wall virtually stopped the large flow of refugees from East to West that had bled the Communist regime of much of its most valuable personnel during the postwar years.

Adding immeasurably to the tension over Berlin was the Soviet announcement on August 30, 1961, that it would break the three-year voluntary moratorium on testing of nuclear weapons because of the "ever increasing aggressiveness of the policy of the NATO military bloc." The Soviet test series began September 1 and concluded in November 1961. Their tests completed, the Soviets returned to the test ban negotiations in Geneva on November 28. The United States, however, refused to reimpose an uncontrolled moratorium on itself and, between April 25 and November 4, 1962, carried out a series of tests underground and in the atmosphere.

Two southeast Asian nations, Laos and Vietnam, were thorny problems for the new administration. Fearful that a Communist takeover of Laos would make the Western position in Vietnam untenable, the administration supported establishment of a "neutral" government in Laos, in the hope that the tiny kingdom could serve as a buffer. In Vietnam increased Communist guerrilla activity forced increased commitment of U.S. military "advisers," who soon found themselves in the thick of military engagements.

Cuba, however, remained the chief foreign policy problem of the administration. The Castro regime became increasingly identified as a Soviet satellite and was expelled from the Organization of American States. During the summer of 1962, Soviet arms began to pour into Cuba. On October 22 President Kennedy told the American people in a radio-television address that U.S. aerial surveillance of the Soviet military buildup in Cuba had produced "unmistakable evidence" that "a series of offensive missile sites is now in preparation on that imprisoned island. The purpose of these bases can be none other than to provide a nuclear strike capacity against the Western Hemisphere."

As countermeasures the president announced "a strict quarantine on all offensive military equipment under shipment to Cuba" and said that U.S. ships would begin checking incoming shipments to the island. He called on the Soviet leader to withdraw his offensive weapons from Cuba.

For several days the Soviets continued preparation of their missile sites, and the world wondered whether it might be plunged into war. On October 27 Khrushchev, apparently unwilling to take the ultimate risk, sent a note to Kennedy in which he agreed to remove the offensive weapons systems from Cuba under UN observation and supervision in return for removal of the U.S. quarantine and agreement not to launch an invasion of the islands.

In succeeding weeks the removal of the bases took place at a relatively rapid rate. Castro, however, blocked UN inspection, and the United States never formalized its agreement not to invade Cuba. Thousands of Soviet troops and technical personnel remained on the island, along with a heavy array of "defensive" weapons.

Kennedy's chief domestic problem during his first two years in office was the lagging condition of the U.S. economy. The new administration made clear its commitment to a general monetary and fiscal policy aimed at the inducement of economic growth, even at the price of heavy federal budget deficits. Federal expenditures rose from $81.5 billion in fiscal 1961 to $87.8 billion in fiscal 1962 and $94.3 billion in estimated figures for fiscal 1963. The federal deficit rose from $3.8 billion in 1961 to $6.4 billion in 1962 and dropped slightly to $6.2 billion for fiscal 1963.

Aided in part by the sharply increased federal expenditures under Kennedy, the 1960 recession tapered off by mid-1961. But the basic underlying problems remained.

Although President Kennedy had himself served in the House for six years and in the Senate for eight, relations between his administration and Congress were far from ideal. The change in Democratic leadership in both houses, some congressional apprehension about use of political power by the new administration, and a continuing "conservative coalition" between Republicans and southern Democrats all tended to slow down if not wreck parts of the Kennedy program.

Most apparent and serious was the shift in leadership. The elevation of Lyndon B. Johnson to the vice presidency removed one of the strongest majority leaders in the history of the Senate. He was succeeded by Sen. Mike Mansfield, D-Mont., a mild-mannered man who lacked Johnson's drive.

On November 16, 1961, House Speaker Sam Rayburn, D-Texas, died of cancer. Rayburn had been a member of the House for almost forty-nine years and had served as Speaker for seventeen years (twice interrupted by brief periods of Republican majorities). Any successor would have faced difficulties in filling the shoes of "Mr. Sam," a man who understood the House and, until his later years, could draw together the disparate elements of his party with remarkable success. John W. McCormack of Massachusetts, elevated from the majority leadership to be Speaker, faced the unenviable task of succeeding Rayburn. His first year in office was considered a qualified success.

The Eighty-seventh Congress ended on an acrimonious note. A year-long feud between the House and Senate on procedural issues regarding appropriation bills was symptomatic of a broader rift between the two chambers that had been growing for several years. The dispute held up several fund bills for months (well beyond July 1, the start of the new fiscal year) and helped prolong the 1962 session to October 13. Not since the Korean War year of 1951 had a session lasted until so late in the autumn.

During the ensuing months increasing discussion was heard of the need to modernize and streamline congressional procedures.

The 1962 Midterm Elections

The Kennedy administration entered the 1962 campaign determined to reinforce the narrow margin by which the president had been elected in 1960 and to prevent serious losses in Democratic congressional strength. The off-year elections of 1961 had produced mixed results. In a May 1961 special election in Texas the Democrats had lost the Senate seat vacated by Vice President Johnson to Republican John Tower. Not since Reconstruction days had Texas sent a Republican to the Senate.

But in the November 1961 elections, Democrat Richard J. Hughes, aided by a personal appearance on his behalf by President Kennedy, won the New Jersey governorship against no less an opponent than Republican James P. Mitchell, secretary of labor in the Eisenhower administration.

Mayor Robert F. Wagner, a political ally of the president, easily won reelection in New York City. The administration felt confident that with sufficient presidential campaigning, the party could fare well in the 1962 elections.

Kennedy set the tone for the 1962 battle in a July 23 press conference. Declaring that the congressional Republicans were almost wholly negative on domestic social legislation, he said that he would go all-out to defeat them in the fall campaign. Kennedy said a Democratic gain of one or two Senate seats and five or ten House seats would make it possible to enact controversial administration bills in such fields as Medicare, public works, mass transit, and urban affairs. He said the 1962 elections would give the American people a "clear" choice: to "anchor down" by voting Republican or to "sail" by voting Democratic.

In midsummer the president began to make flying campaign trips to various states every weekend and some weekdays. Until halted by the Cuban crisis October 20, the president's campaigning promised to be the most vigorous of any U.S. president in a midterm election. In every appearance he went down the line for all Democratic candidates. The president was accorded a warm personal reception in most cities, confirming the high degree of personal popularity with the people that had been recorded in Gallup polls. Whether his plea to elect "more Democrats" was making a serious impression remained in doubt, however.

By October public uneasiness over the Communist arms buildup in Cuba was growing. Republicans made a central campaign issue of Cuba, and most observers thought the GOP would make some gains. But the president's October 22 announcement of a naval quarantine of Cuba and his ultimatum to Khrushchev blunted the Republican arguments and rallied the country behind him.

The Republicans began the 1962 campaign in hopes they could win important congressional and gubernatorial gains and thereby increase their effectiveness as an opposition party in Washington and prepare for a possible presidential comeback. They counted on the traditional pattern of midterm gains for the party out of power to help them in the congressional elections.

The party, however, was suffering from image problems. The congressional wing of the GOP, headed by Senate minority leader Everett Dirksen, R-Ill., and House minority leader Charles Halleck, R-Ind., had dominated the news of Republican activity in Washington since Eisenhower's retirement. Deprived of the expertise of the executive branch, Hill Republicans came up with few legislative initiatives and had few counterproposals to the stream of legislative requests that flowed from the White House. The only serious competition to Dirksen and Halleck for the Republican spotlight was Sen. Barry Goldwater of Arizona, whose outspoken conservatism made him the favorite of the right wing throughout the country. Moderate and liberal Republicans received scant attention. Eisenhower had retired; Nixon was embroiled in California politics; New York governor Nelson A. Rockefeller was busy preparing for his own reelection campaign in New York and wrestling with possible adverse effects of his divorce announced late in 1961.

The Republicans waged the 1962 campaign with familiar issues: the need for fiscal responsibility in government, calls for a balanced budget, and warnings of the dangers of encroaching federal (especially executive) power. But the GOP lacked any single strong issue, such as the demand for an end to wartime controls in 1946 or alleged Democratic responsibility for the

Korean War in 1950, with which to rout the Democrats. For a while they hoped Cuba would be that issue, but the president's firm action in late October effectively deprived them of it. In the end improved Republican organizations, especially in the big cities, helped the party to some victories. But the only region of the country in which they made any significant congressional gains was the South, where they jumped from nine to fourteen seats.

Results of the 1962 Elections

The Democratic Party confirmed its heavy majorities in both houses of Congress and among the states' governors. Democrats avoided "normal" midterm losses of the party in power by gaining four Senate seats and suffering only a nominal loss in the House. Not since 1934 had the presidential party fared so well in a midterm election. Democrats said that, in contrast to the familiar patterns of major midterm losses by the presidential party, the 1962 results constituted a real vote of confidence in the administration.

Republicans replied that they saw "no endorsement of the New Frontier and its policies." They pointed out that President Kennedy had not carried Democrats into office with him in 1960, actually losing twenty House seats that year, so that there were fewer vulnerable seats for the GOP to pick off in 1962. The Republicans argued that the national House vote for the GOP had actually risen to 47.7 percent, 4.0 points higher than 1958 and 2.7 points higher than 1960. Privately, however, Republicans expressed deep disappointment that they had not been able to register important gains, especially in the House.

Congressional reapportionment after the 1960 census had caused major shifts in the distribution of seats in the House. The eastern states lost a net of seven seats; the South, one; and the Midwest, four. The western states were the beneficiaries, picking up ten new seats; eight of them went to California.

Democrats controlled the California legislature, which redistricted in 1961. As a result they gained eight seats from California in the 1962 elections. A similar Republican gerrymander in New York State misfired, and Republican gains in other areas barely balanced the Democratic bonus from California.

Republicans were especially disappointed by their net loss of four Senate seats. The new Senate was so heavily Democratic that the Republicans had no real hope of regaining control until 1968 or later.

Despite a heavy turnover in the governorship elections (Democrats took seven from the Republicans and lost a like number), the gubernatorial party balance remained 34–16 in favor of the Democrats. The Republicans, however, did seize control of several important state governorships including those of Pennsylvania, Ohio, and Michigan.

The most devastating defeat of the year was suffered by former vice president Richard M. Nixon, who was soundly defeated for governor of California only two years after barely missing election to the presidency. Other political veterans retired by the voters included longtime senators Homer E. Capehart, R-Ind. and Alexander Wiley, R-Wis.; Rep. Walter H. Judd, R-Minn.; and Gov. Michael V. DiSalle, D-Ohio.

The potential national leaders elected in 1962 included Republican representative William W. Scranton, elected governor of Pennsylvania by a 486,651-vote majority; former auto maker George W. Romney, a Republican who ended fourteen years of Democratic control of the Michigan governorship; youthful Democratic state representative Birch Bayh, who toppled Homer Earl Capehart in the Indiana Senate race; Edward M. "Ted" Kennedy, youngest brother of the president, who was elected U.S. senator from Massachusetts; and Robert Taft Jr., a Republican who was elected representative at large from Ohio.

Among the new senators elected in 1962 was Democrat Abraham A. Ribicoff, former governor of Connecticut and first secretary of Health, Education, and Welfare in the Kennedy administration. Hawaiian voters sent Rep. Daniel K. Inouye, a Democrat, to the Senate. He was the first U.S. senator of Japanese ancestry. The new governorship roster included James A. Rhodes, R-Ohio; John A. Love, R-Colo.; Karl Rolvaag, D-Minn.; John B. Connally, D-Texas; and John A. Burns, D-Hawaii.

Among the "miracle men" of 1962 were Philip H. Hoff, who became the first Democratic governor of Vermont in more than a century, and Henry L. Bellmon, who became Oklahoma's first Republican governor since the state joined the Union.

Incumbents who won impressive victories included Sen. Jacob K. Javits, R-N.Y., reelected by a plurality of almost one million; Republican Senate whip Thomas H. Kuchel, R-Calif., reelected by a quarter-million vote margin despite the 296,758-vote triumph of Democratic governor Edmund G. "Pat" Brown over Nixon in the same state's balloting; Sen. Thruston B. Morton, former national chairman of the Republican Party, reelected against powerful Democratic opposition in Kentucky; and New York governor Nelson A. Rockefeller, whose plurality was down slightly from its 1958 level but still big enough to make him appear the top contender for the 1964 Republican presidential nomination.

Across the nation, voters showed a continuing tendency to disregard traditional party lines in choosing people for high office. The success of Democrats in the traditional Republican states of northern New England and breakthroughs for the Republicans in the South—including a near miss in the Alabama Senate race—attested to the possible development of significant new voting patterns.

1963–1965:
THE EIGHTY-EIGHTH CONGRESS

The years 1963–1964 were good years for most Americans as the nation enjoyed continued economic prosperity and international affairs remained relatively tranquil. These same years, however, witnessed the assassination of a president, the launching of the most profound equal rights drive since the Civil War, and seizure of control of one of the major American political parties by a right-wing faction.

John F. Kennedy was shot on November 22, 1963, as his motorcade moved through cheering crowds in downtown Dallas. Approximately one-half hour later the president was pronounced dead. A special presidential commission, headed by Chief Justice Earl Warren, reported September 27, 1964, that Lee

Lyndon Johnson takes the presidential oath aboard Air Force One enroute to Washington after John F. Kennedy's assassination.

Harvey Oswald, "acting alone and without advice or assistance," had shot the president. The report said Jack Ruby was on his own in killing Oswald and that neither was part of "any conspiracy, domestic or foreign," to kill President Kennedy. The report called for an overhauling and modernization of the Secret Service, the group entrusted with physical protection of the president, and of FBI procedures.

At 1:39 p.m., November 22, Vice President Lyndon B. Johnson took the oath of office as the thirty-sixth president aboard the presidential jet plane just before its departure from Dallas to Washington. The next few days witnessed President Kennedy's funeral; the confluence in Washington of heads of state, dignitaries, and emissaries from governments all over the world to pay their respects to the dead president; and the resolute grasp of the reins of power by Lyndon Johnson.

The new president's political roots reached into the liberalism of the New Deal on the one hand and into the conservatism of political life in his native Texas on the other. His wealth of experience in American political life, especially in Congress, served him well as he moved into the presidency. He quickly embraced the salient features of President Kennedy's program, especially the tax cut bill and civil rights legislation; moved to win the confidence of the liberal community by a well-publicized "war on poverty" in America; and won the confidence of the business community and many conservatives by ordering strict economies in federal spending. Johnson's foes accused him of political sleight-of-hand in being both liberal and conservative at the same time, but opinion polls—and the 1964 elections—indicated the American people approved wholeheartedly.

The issue of civil rights produced a profound domestic crisis for the United States in 1963 and 1964. Discontented with the pace of their advances in all spheres of life, black Americans pressed for full rights in every field from voting to employment, from education to housing.

President Kennedy, in February 1963, had sent his first civil rights legislative program to Congress—one characterized by liberals of both parties as "thin." On April 3 mass demonstrations for equal rights began in Birmingham, Alabama. Dramatized by the use of children in the demonstrations and the use of dogs and hoses by the police against the blacks, events in Birmingham sparked a determined nationwide series of protests. By the end of 1963 demonstrations had taken place in more than 800 cities and towns, climaxed by a gigantic but orderly "March on Washington for Jobs and Freedom" in which more than 200,000 persons participated on August 28.

The demonstrations began primarily with black protesters, but millions of white Americans—most noticeably church groups and college students—took interest in the lot of black Americans. At the same time, however, many northern whites showed their hostility to the civil rights drive because it appeared to threaten de facto segregation in housing, employment, and education. Capitalizing on white northern fears, Alabama's segregationist governor, George C. Wallace, entered spring 1964 Democratic presidential primaries in Wisconsin, Indiana, and Maryland and won 33.8, 29.8, and 42.8 percent of the vote in the respective races. But when the new Republican national leadership sought to cultivate the "white backlash" vote in the 1964 presidential campaign, the effort proved singularly unsuccessful outside a few Deep South states.

In early June 1963 congressional Republicans and liberal Democrats began to press for strong civil rights legislation, and on June 11 President Kennedy told the nation: "We cannot say to 10 percent of the population that . . . the only way they are going to get their rights is to go into the streets and demonstrate." A week later he submitted a new and broadened civil rights program to combat discrimination in public accommodations, schools, jobs, and voting, which he urged Congress to enact.

For a while it appeared the bill might go aground, but in November the House Judiciary Committee reported a bipartisan civil rights measure, the fruit of conferences between administration leaders and Republican congressional civil rights advocates. Working under cloture, the Senate passed the bill June 19, 1964, by a 73–27 vote. The House passed the amended bill July 2, and President Johnson signed it into law a few hours later. Among other things the bill expanded federal power to protect voting rights; guaranteed access to all public accommodations and public facilities for all races, with federal power to back up the pledge; gave the federal government power to sue for school desegregation; outlawed denial of equal job opportunities in businesses or unions with twenty-five or more workers; and authorized the federal government to intervene in any court suit alleging denial of equal protection of the laws. It was the most sweeping civil rights measure in American history.

Determined to prevent economic stagnation and give the country's economy a major boost forward, President Kennedy in January 1963 proposed a $10.3 billion personal and corporate income tax cut to take effect July 1, 1963. After protracted hearings in the House and Senate, the final version, reducing taxes $11.5 billion annually, was signed into law by President Johnson February 26, 1964.

In the meantime the economy, which the tax bill had been designed to help, was doing surprisingly well on its own. The 1963 gross national product reached $585 billion, and the Council of Economic Advisers predicted a $623 billion level in 1964. With the exception of unemployment, which remained above 5 percent of the work force, most economic indicators continued a gradual upward rise during 1963 and 1964. In October 1964, 71.2 million Americans were employed. Despite the rise in the economy, only a few economists saw any serious threat of inflation.

In his State of the Union message January 8, 1964, Johnson called for an "unconditional" declaration of "war on poverty in America." The poverty program constituted the chief innovation in the president's legislative proposals. Submitting his specific program to Congress March 16, he called for a fiscal 1965 outlay of $962.5 million to fight poverty. When Congress finished action on his request in August, it had authorized $947.5 million, only $15 million less than the draft proposal, with approval of almost all the president's requests. As enacted, the bill authorized ten separate programs under the supervision of the Office of Economic Opportunity, created by the bill. Major sections authorized a Job Corps to provide youths with work experience and training in conservation camps and in residential training centers, a work-training program to employ youths locally, a community action program under which the government would assist a variety of local efforts to combat poverty, an adult education program, and a "domestic peace corps" program.

The years 1963 and 1964 witnessed a steady relaxation in the tensions of the cold war, perhaps the closest approximation to an East-West detente since 1945. At the beginning of 1963, U.S.-Soviet relations were at a standoff, produced by Russian withdrawal of missiles from Cuba in October 1962. By mid-1963 a Soviet-Chinese rift had deepened, and a lessening of U.S.-Soviet tensions was evident.

In a speech on June 10, 1963, Kennedy announced that the United States, the Soviet Union, and Great Britain would begin talks on a partial test ban, apart from the seventeen-nation Geneva talks that had dragged on intermittently without much hope since 1958. Then, before many realized that progress was at last to be made, a limited treaty was initialed in Moscow July 25. The Senate consented to ratification September 24.

A moderately optimistic tone pervaded U.S.-Soviet relations in 1964. On April 20 both the United States and the Soviet Union announced they were going to cut back their production of nuclear materials for weapons use. The growing tensions between China and the Soviet Union caused the Soviets to turn their attention more and more inward. On October 16 the Western world was shocked to hear that Nikita S. Khrushchev had been ousted from his duties as premier and also as first secretary of the Soviet Communist Party. He was replaced as premier by Aleksei N. Kosygin and as party secretary by Leonid Brezhnev, possibly presaging a prolonged struggle for power within the Soviet hierarchy. The new Soviet leaders quickly made it clear they would follow Khrushchev's policy of "peaceful coexistence" with the West.

The Kennedy-Johnson administration's Alliance for Progress suffered as democratically elected regimes were deposed in

Ecuador, Guatemala, Honduras, the Dominican Republic, and Bolivia. The Johnson administration faced its first major foreign policy crisis in January 1964 when large-scale violence broke out in Central America as Panamanians protested the 1903 treaty under which the United States administered the Panama Canal and Americans enjoyed special privileges in the Canal Zone. The United States was encouraged, however, when President Joao Goulart of Brazil, accused of conducting a leftist and chaotic administration, was deposed in a bloodless coup on April 1, 1964.

Apparently upset by Vietnam government moves against Buddhists, suicidal burnings by Buddhist monks, corruption within the government, and inadequate military success against the Communist Viet Cong, the State Department in 1963 gradually curtailed aid to the Vietnamese regime of President Ngo Dinh Diem. On November 1 a military coup ended the Diem regime. The State Department denied participation in the coup, but unofficially it admitted that it might have encouraged the "proper climate" for such a revolt. The new ruling junta in Vietnam was itself overturned by a coup in January 1964, starting a series of bewildering governmental shifts that lasted through 1964 as the military situation continued to deteriorate.

The off-year elections of November 1963 provided no definite clue to possible trends for 1964. Democrats maintained control of the Kentucky and Mississippi governorships and the Philadelphia mayoralty in the top three races, but the GOP vote was up sharply in all three areas.

Top Republican takeovers of the year were scored in New Jersey, where the Assembly reverted to GOP hands to give the Republicans majorities in both houses, and in Indiana, where the GOP elected twenty-five new mayors. The Republicans also scored gains in Virginia and Mississippi legislative elections. Democratic Representative John F. Shelley won election as mayor of San Francisco, ending fifty-five years of GOP control in technically nonpartisan elections. Suburban New York also showed some Democratic gains.

The 1964 Campaigns

From the beginning of 1964 it was apparent that President Johnson was the strong favorite to win a full four-year White House term in his own right. As the Democrats gathered in Atlantic City for their convention on August 24, Johnson kept silent about his final decision for a running mate. In a move unprecedented in American politics, he appeared before the Democratic National Convention just before his own nomination the same evening to announce to the delegates that Sen. Hubert H. Humphrey of Minnesota was his choice for the vice-presidential slot.

The most fascinating story of the 1964 presidential campaign, however, lay in the opposition party. Throughout the postwar years, the Republican Party, despite its conservative inclinations, had generally embraced the wide consensus of U.S. politics: agreement on basic social welfare responsibilities of the government together with a firm but not bellicose policy toward the Communist world. But in 1964 the Republican Party turned abruptly from the moderate course. For president it

nominated a militantly conservative two-term Arizona senator, Barry Goldwater, known for his hostile views toward the power of the federal government and his apparent willingness to risk nuclear confrontation with the Soviets to advance the Western cause. The course set by Goldwater brought the Republican Party its most devastating defeat in more than a quarter-century. Republican ranks in Congress and the state legislatures were greatly reduced. Even worse, national confidence in the party was so badly shaken that it seemed it might take years to recoup.

Early in 1964, however, only one Republican of national stature was willing to speak out on the possible dangers of Goldwater and his philosophy for the Republican Party. That man was New York governor Nelson A. Rockefeller, who had entered the race for the GOP nomination November 7, 1963. Rockefeller symbolized the eastern progressive wing of the Republican Party that had dominated Republican National Conventions since 1940. The other leaders of the Republican Party's moderate wing—governors William W. Scranton of Pennsylvania and George W. Romney of Michigan, Ambassador Henry Cabot Lodge Jr., and former vice president Richard M. Nixon—all were thought to harbor some presidential ambitions, but none was willing to take the plunge in the presidential primaries or to risk an open challenge to the Goldwater wing of the party.

The "National Draft Goldwater Committee," which organized formally in the spring of 1963, aimed both at nominating Goldwater and at remaking the entire Republican Party into a vehicle for militant conservatism. Their aim appeared to be the reforming of two U.S. political parties along straight liberal versus conservative lines. By the autumn of 1963 the years of Goldwater stewardship within the ranks of the Republican Party had begun to bear fruit. Goldwater supporters held important positions in the Republican Party apparatus. Rep. William E. Miller, R-N.Y., who would later become Goldwater's vice-presidential running mate, was the Republican national chairman.

The Republican National Convention, meeting in San Francisco July 13–16, turned sharply to the right, rejecting the party's moderate tone of the postwar years and substituting instead an unabashed conservatism in domestic affairs and all-out nationalism in foreign policy.

Goldwater's controversial stands and his failure to advance meaningful alternative solutions to national problems relieved Johnson of having to spell out in any substantial detail what his plans for the "great society" were. For the most part Johnson confined himself to calls for national unity and remarks aimed at broadening the breach between Goldwater and the bulk of moderate and liberal Republicans. Johnson was so successful in preempting the vital "middle ground" of American politics that a Democratic victory was assured long before election day.

Results of the 1964 Elections

In the November 3 elections President Johnson led the Democratic Party to its greatest national victory since 1936. Not only did Johnson win a four-year White House term in his own right, amassing the largest vote of any presidential candidate in history, but his broad coattails helped the Democrats score major gains in the House of Representatives and increase their already heavy majority in the Senate.

The Johnson-Humphrey ticket ran 15,951,378 votes ahead of the Goldwater-Miller ticket, easily exceeding the record national popular vote plurality of 11,073,102 by which Franklin D. Roosevelt defeated Alfred M. Landon in 1936. The final, official vote for Johnson-Humphrey was 43,129,566; for Goldwater-Miller, 27,178,188.

Johnson won forty-four states and the District of Columbia (which voted for the first time for president, under the terms of the Twenty-third Amendment to the Constitution). His electoral vote total was 486. Goldwater won six states with a total of fifty-two electoral votes. The Democratic presidential victory began in New England and the East, where Johnson carried every state and chalked up a better than 2–1 majority.

The Democratic sweep continued through the Republican midwestern heartland, where every state also cast its electoral vote for Johnson. The president was the winner in every mountain and Pacific state except Arizona, Goldwater's home state. California, which had boosted Goldwater to the Republican nomination in the June primary, went for Johnson by over a million votes.

Only an unusual degree of ticket splitting saved the Republican Party from almost total annihilation in races for congressional and state posts. As it was, the Republicans were reduced to their lowest congressional levels since Depression days. In elections to the House, the Republicans suffered a net loss of thirty-eight seats. The new House balance was 295 Democrats and 140 Republicans, the lowest GOP membership figure since the 1936 elections. Among the more serious Republican House losses were seven seats in New York, five in Iowa, and four each in New Jersey, Michigan, Ohio, and Washington. Many of the northern Republican representatives defeated were among their party's most conservative, representing formerly "safe Republican" seats. For example, fifty-four Republican House members had backed Goldwater's nomination drive in June by signing a statement saying his nomination would "result in substantial increases in Republican membership in both houses of Congress." Of these, seventeen were defeated, another three retired but saw their districts go Democratic, and all but six saw their winning percentages dwindle. Of the twenty-one northern Republicans who had voted with Goldwater against the 1964 Civil Rights Act, eleven were defeated. Republicans who disassociated themselves from Goldwater and his policies were generally more successful. The most spectacular Republican House victory of the year was scored by Rep. John V. Lindsay of New York, who refused to endorse Goldwater but won a 71.5 percent victory in his district, while Johnson was carrying it by more than 2–1.

The only area of significant Republican House gains was the deep South, where Goldwater coattails helped the party elect five new representatives in Alabama and one each in Georgia and Mississippi. They were the first Republican House members from these states since Reconstruction. But at the same time three conservative GOP southern House members—two in Texas, one in Kentucky—were going down to defeat.

One result of the election was to erode the power base of the "conservative coalition" between Republicans and southern Democrats. Not only would there be less conservative representation in the House, but the relative strength of northern liberals in the Democratic House Caucus would be increased substantially.

The Senate elections resulted in a net Democratic gain of two seats, making the new balance sixty-eight Democrats and thirty-two Republicans. Not since the elections of 1940 had the Democrats held such a heavy majority. But the major story was not the new Democratic Senate gains of 1964 but the fact that the members of the liberal Democratic class of 1958 were all reelected to office. The Democrats' gain of thirteen formerly Republican seats in 1958 had effected a basic realignment of power within the Senate, giving it a much more liberal orientation than the House. The Republicans had long looked forward to 1964 as the year when they would win back many of the class of 1958 seats.

The Democrats actually won three GOP Senate seats in 1964: Kenneth Keating's seat in New York, taken by Robert F. Kennedy (thus making Kennedy a potential future contender for the Democratic presidential nomination); J. Glenn Beall's seat in Maryland, won by Democrat Joseph D. Tydings; and the New Mexico seat of interim senator Edwin L. Mechem, won by Rep. Joseph M. Montoya. The sole GOP gain was in California, where George Murphy scored an upset victory over interim senator Pierre Salinger, former presidential press secretary.

A major blow to the GOP was the defeat in Ohio of Robert Taft Jr., who was challenging Democratic senator Stephen M. Young. Before the election Taft had been looked to as a major future leader of his party. But the Goldwater "drag"—Johnson won Ohio by 1,027,466 votes—was too much for Taft to overcome.

In gubernatorial elections, the Republicans scored gains in Washington, Wisconsin, and Massachusetts, and lost seats they had held in Arizona and Utah. The result was a net gain of one for the GOP. But the already heavy Democratic majority was not weakened significantly. The new lineup was thirty-three Democrats and seventeen Republicans.

Without Goldwater at the head of the ticket the Republicans might have scored much better. Their most disappointing defeat came in Illinois, where Charles H. Percy, who had been regarded as a possible future presidential candidate, went down to defeat in the Democratic landslide.

The most spectacular GOP governorship win was scored by Michigan governor George R. Romney, seeking reelection. He withstood a Johnson landslide of more than 2–1 to win reelection. The outcome established Romney, who had refused to endorse Goldwater's candidacy, as a powerful future leader of his party.

Among the new governors elected were Samuel P. Goddard, D-Ariz.; Roger D. Branigin, D-Ind.; Daniel J. Evans, R-Wash.; and Warren P. Knowles, R-Wis.

Democratic governors who won substantial reelection victories despite the Republican complexion of their states included Frank B. Morrison of Nebraska, Harold E. Hughes of Iowa, John W. King of New Hampshire, and Philip H. Hoff of Vermont. But in normally Democratic Rhode Island, Republican governor

John H. Chaffee won reelection with 61.3 percent of the vote, while Goldwater received only 19.1 percent of the state's vote.

The Vietnam War Years

The years of the 1960s and 1970s were some of the most turbulent in the nation's history. The seeds of the great upheavals ahead were already sprouting even before President Kennedy's death in November 1963. The country's role in the Vietnam War was inching upward. Black Americans were becoming ever more insistent in demanding an end to all forms of racial discrimination. A huge generation of teenagers, born in the post–World War II baby boom, were reaching college age and were preparing to challenge authority on a scale unprecedented in American history. And there were growing indications of conservative political strength, especially within the Republican Party.

In the late 1960s the nation experienced a series of cataclysmic changes that, while they did not appear to endanger the basic economic health of the nation, did jeopardize the postwar politics of consensus and promise as yet unpredictable changes in the social and political climate of American life. Only when the nation found itself entangled in a seemingly endless and unwinnable war in Vietnam in the mid-1960s did the first major cracks appear in the general national consensus behind U.S. foreign policy.

For the first time serious doubts were raised about the role of the nation as a global policeman, and there were indications that a period of limited isolationism might come in the wake of any Vietnam settlement.

Through the 1964 election the United States had enjoyed remarkably stable two-party politics in the postwar years. No major ideological gulfs existed between the parties, and although the Democrats were more frequently victorious at the polls than the Republicans (an apparent legacy of Franklin Roosevelt's New Deal), few Americans were deeply concerned when the party in power changed in Washington or the state capitals. Indeed, two-party politics infused virtually every region of the country for the first time in its history. And as the parties became more competitive, personal allegiances shifted more frequently and ticket splitting became an American electoral pastime.

When Barry Goldwater was repudiated at the polls in 1964, the post-New Deal consensus seemed to have been reaffirmed. Indeed, the year 1965 saw the last major burst of legislative accomplishments and national optimism that the country was to witness for some time. With the large Democratic majorities created by the Johnson landslide, Congress enacted federal aid to education, a national health insurance program, and a voting rights act.

But the Johnson administration's fortunes soon changed. The decision to commit massive American ground forces to Vietnam resulted in increased opposition at home to American participation in the war. The war further stimulated student unrest on the campuses resulting in siege conditions at some universities. Blacks burst forth in anger and destroyed large sections of American cities. And the Rev. Martin Luther King Jr. and Sen. Robert F. Kennedy were assassinated in 1968.

The Democratic Party coalition broke open under these strains in 1968, with the challenge to President Johnson's renomination and the Independent candidacy of Alabama governor George C. Wallace. The result was that Republican Richard Nixon was elected to the presidency.

At the end of the 1960s both parties were clearly in transition. The Democrats, in order to hold their solid base among low-income voters and minorities, would be obliged to remain strong advocates of wide-ranging social reform. But that very course could possibly seal their eventual downfall in the South, even if an increased black vote in that region compensated for some of that loss. And while organized labor had turned out a strong Democratic vote in 1968, its leaders were having increasing difficulty in convincing workers that they should remain unswervingly loyal to the Democratic Party.

The Republicans, even in winning the presidential election of 1968, received only 43 percent of the national vote and had to recognize that in their major base of support—the predominantly white, middle-class rural areas and small cities—they faced a diminishing asset in overall population terms. It was clear that the Republicans' growing strength in the burgeoning white suburban areas of America would hold solidly only as long as the party maintained domestic prosperity and found a way to calm inner-city tensions.

During his first term President Nixon too had to deal with antiwar demonstrations. But his policy of gradual withdrawal of American troops, climaxing with the peace settlement of January 1973, finally removed the war from the top of the American political agenda.

At the same time, with the passage of the baby-boom generation out of college and into the labor market, the nation's campuses became more peaceful. And the movement of many African Americans onto the voter rolls, into public office, and into more jobs and better housing seemed to relieve some of the racial tension.

But at the very moment when things began looking better, the nation was hit by a fresh series of calamities. Throughout 1973 and 1974 the Watergate scandal implicated several top public officials, including the president himself, in illegal activities. The immediate result was the first presidential resignation in U.S. history, but the deeper ramifications could be found in the weakening of the confidence of the people in their government and leaders.

While the revelations were continuing, the United States was hit with an energy crisis when the Arab states cut off the flow of oil during the October 1973 war in the Middle East. Even when the flow was resumed, the price had been jacked up more than 300 percent, and this increase, combined with other trends in the economy, produced some of the worst inflation in the nation's history. Buffeted by these forces, seemingly beyond their control, many Americans wondered about the future of their country and the stability of their economic and political system.

President Gerald Ford, with his low-key personality and image of personal integrity, helped calm the country after these misfortunes. But he was not seen by many as a strong leader and was almost defeated for the presidential nomination of his own party in the 1976 primaries.

1965–1967:
THE EIGHTY-NINE CONGRESS

Buoyed by the largest party majorities enjoyed by any president in three decades, Lyndon Johnson led the Eighty-ninth Congress in an amazingly productive 1965 session. The scope of the legislation was even more impressive than the number of major new laws. In the course of the year, Congress approved programs that had long been on the agenda of the Democratic Party—in the case of medical care for the aged under Social Security, for as long as twenty years. Other long-standing objectives were met by enactment of aid to primary and secondary schools, college scholarships, and immigration reform.

The pace of the 1965 session was so breathless as to cause a major revision of the image, widely prevalent in preceding years, of Congress as structurally incapable of swift decision. The change was because of three primary elements not always present in past years: the decisive Democratic majorities elected in 1964, the personal leadership of President Johnson, and the shaping of legislation to obtain maximum political support in Congress.

The expanded Democratic pluralities were most significant in the House, where the Democrats had not only scored a thirty-eight-seat net gain over the Republicans in the 1964 elections but had also traded a number of conservative Democratic votes in the South for liberal Democratic votes in the North. The new liberal strength in the House showed itself most dramatically in passage of the aid to education and medical care (Medicare) bills. The Senate had passed similar measures in previous years only to see them blocked by the hitherto powerful coalition of Republicans and conservative southern Democrats in the House. But the "conservative coalition," where it did appear in House roll call votes, was victorious only 25 percent of the time in 1965, compared with 67 percent in 1962 and 1964 and 74 percent in 1961, the first year of President Kennedy's term.

The president gained maximum political effect from his efforts to build a broad consensus of support. An excise tax cut, designed to keep the economy growing steadily, appealed to business and consumer interests alike. Lack of strong opposition from business circles made it easier for Democrats to mount the Great Society program of greatly increased civil benefits and tended to smother Republican protests that Congress was merely rubber stamping ill-conceived administration proposals.

The Voting Rights Act of 1965, the most comprehensive legislation to ensure the right to vote in ninety years, was prompted by the brutal suppression of demonstrations in Selma, Ala., and other parts of the South. The bill went beyond the milder courtroom remedies of earlier civil rights acts. In the wake of this legislation, an additional 500,000 southern blacks were registered by the time of the 1966 elections.

Other legislation included a housing bill authorizing $7.8 billion to fund new and existing housing programs through 1969 and a bill establishing a cabinet-level Department of Housing and Urban Development.

The year 1965 was punctuated by major crises in Vietnam. Faced with the threat of success by the Viet Cong Communist insurgents in South Vietnam, President Johnson initiated large-scale bombing raids in North Vietnam, which was giving major aid to the Viet Cong. When this tactic failed to turn the unfavorable course of the war, he ordered a vast increase—from about 20,000 to eventually more than 140,000—in American troop strength in the South and an aggressive prosecution of the land war. Both steps required new outlays for personnel and materiel. Despite highly vocal criticism of his Vietnam policy by a small band of senators, Congress overwhelmingly approved Johnson's special request for funds.

The Vietnam budget pressures soon had serious effects on the domestic economy. As 1966 began, the U.S. economy was already strained to its noninflationary limit. After fifty-nine months of stable economic growth, it was near full employment. Plant capacity was in full use. Any sizable increase in demand under these conditions would be bound to result in inflation. This is precisely what occurred as the defense budget shot upward, without any significant offsetting measures to cut back on other purchasing power. The cost-of-living index jumped from 111.0 percent in January to 113.8 percent in August. The president early in the year asked and received congressional approval of a $5.9 billion bill to accelerate certain types of tax payments and reimpose 1965 excise tax levies, but the measure was hardly adequate to counter the Vietnam spending boom. Almost every leading economist in the nation called for a general tax increase, but President Johnson refused.

With the public increasingly concerned with inflation and the Vietnam War, congressional Republicans found new Democratic allies in the effort to curb the Great Society—not only its spending programs but almost any measure providing social reform. Despite strong persuasive efforts by the president, the administration was rebuffed on many major bills.

An important reason for the defeat of the administration's new civil rights proposals was a wave of summertime riots in black "ghetto" areas of the large cities. In August 1965 a six-day disturbance had erupted in Los Angeles's 95 percent black Watts area, with about 7,000 youths participating in rioting, looting, and arson. The National Guard finally restored order, but only after thirty-four deaths. In the summer of 1966 other riots followed in the black areas of several other American cities. The 1966 riots were attributed not only to decades of frustration among urban blacks in education, housing, and employment fields but to the growth of a new philosophy of "black power," expounded by extremist civil rights groups such as the Congress of Racial Equality (CORE) and the Student Nonviolent Coordinating Committee (SNCC).

In the House, Rep. John William McCormack of Massachusetts continued as Speaker. Sen. Mike Mansfield of Montana remained as Senate majority leader, with Sen. Everett Dirksen of Illinois his Republican counterpart. House minority leader Charles Halleck of Indiana was defeated for reelection to his leadership post by Rep. Gerald R. Ford of Michigan, just before the formal opening of the Eighty-ninth Congress. Ford's election as minority leader was a continuation of the revolt of

Soldiers of the U.S. 9th Division march past a flooded shell crater through an abandoned rice paddy during the Vietnam War. The war was a divisive issue in politics for more than a decade.

younger House Republicans that had begun with Ford's election as House GOP Conference chairman two years before. As in 1963 the leadership struggle seemed to be based less on ideological differences than on the question of which representative could give the most forceful leadership to the depleted Republican House ranks.

The 1964 elections had left the Republicans at such a low point that some resurgence seemed inevitable. In 1965 it began in a spectacular way as Republican-Liberal John V. Lindsay won election as mayor in heavily Democratic New York City. Lindsay's victory, combined with the victories of liberally inclined Republican candidates for district attorney in Philadelphia and mayor in Louisville, Kentucky, signaled a potential Republican resurgence on the left in the very areas where Goldwater had been weakest—in the major cities and especially among blacks and other minority groups.

In New Jersey, however, the Republican gubernatorial candidate took a conservative tack similar to that of the 1964 Goldwater campaign and found himself defeated by Democratic governor Richard J. Hughes by a record 363,572-vote margin. Democrats also held the Virginia governorship and legislature and easily maintained control of the mayors' offices in major cities such as New Haven, St. Louis, Pittsburgh, and Detroit. In Cleveland a black state legislator running as an Independent came within 2,143 votes of upsetting the incumbent Democratic mayor. In the smaller cities some of the most interesting contests took place on June 8 in Hattiesburg and Columbus, Mississippi, where the first Republicans of the twentieth century—all staunch conservatives—were elected mayors.

The 1966 Midterm Elections

From the beginning of the 1966 campaign, the Democrats realized that they faced formidable odds if they hoped to maintain their overwhelming margins of control in Congress and in the state governorships and legislatures. Yet at the end of 1965 it looked as if the minority Republicans might be held to minimal gains. The first session of the Eighty-ninth Congress had passed laws with benefits for almost every segment of the population. President Johnson still enjoyed the wide "consensus" support he had enjoyed in 1964, from every group from organized labor to big business and minorities. And the economy was booming on virtually every front.

By the beginning of the 1966 campaign, however, it was apparent that the odds had shifted significantly to the benefit of the Republicans. Behind the change was the escalation of the Vietnam War, with its heavy toll both in American lives and dollars. The conflict in Vietnam, because of its limited nature, increased frustrations across the country and began to undermine public support of the administration in power.

The war effort generated inflationary pressures that were being felt throughout the country by mid-1966. The Republicans were able to argue with some effectiveness that the Johnson administration should be cutting down, rather than increasing, national expenditures for a wide variety of Great Society programs. Moreover, those very social welfare programs that had looked so politically attractive at the end of 1965 were beginning to encounter serious administrative difficulties, with wide gaps between the administration's promises to improve educational standards, end conditions of poverty, and ensure racial peace, and its ability to deliver on those promises.

President Johnson's own popularity plummeted during the year; wide splits appeared in the Democratic Party in many important states; and at the same time several attractive Republican candidates appeared to lead the GOP in critical states—in sharp contrast to the unpopularity of Goldwater, the party's 1964 standard bearer.

Early in 1965 the Democrats had launched an ambitious Operation Support from within the Democratic National Committee, designed to reelect a large portion of the seventy-one fresh-man Democratic representatives who came into office in the 1964 Democratic sweep—thirty-eight of them from formerly Republican districts. But while Operation Support functioned smoothly in 1965, it tended to fall off in 1966 as the national committee obeyed presidential orders to cut back on its activities in order to pay off a heavy debt left from the 1964 campaign.

The Republican congressional effort, on the other hand, was bolstered by a massive fund-raising campaign that made it possible to funnel thousands of dollars into every doubtful congressional district in the country. Reports just before the elections showed national-level gifts of $1.6 million to GOP congressional candidates from their party headquarters, compared with only $250,000 from national-level Democratic committees.

The primary season indicated some significant shifts in the political landscape. In California, long a bastion of liberal Republicanism, actor Ronald Reagan, an outspoken conservative, won a sweeping gubernatorial primary victory over more liberal opposition. In the Virginia primary two aging House members of traditional conservative southern Democracy were defeated by younger men of more moderate persuasion. In Florida the mayor of Miami, Robert King High, won the Democratic gubernatorial primary with liberal support over the more conservative incumbent governor. Staunch segregationist candidates, on the other hand, won Democratic gubernatorial primaries in the Deep South: Jim Johnson in Arkansas, Lester Maddox in Georgia, and Lurleen Wallace, wife of outgoing governor George C. Wallace (who was ineligible to succeed himself), in Alabama.

As the campaign gathered steam in the fall, the Republicans concentrated their fire increasingly on the issues of inflation, Vietnam, crime, and the alleged credibility gap between what President Johnson and his administration said they were doing and their actual performance.

Results of the 1966 Elections

The Republican Party reasserted itself as a major force in American politics by capturing eight new governorships, three new seats in the Senate, and forty-seven additional House seats in the November 8 elections. In a striking comeback from its devastating defeat of 1964, the GOP elected enough new governors to give it control of twenty-five of the fifty states with a substantial majority of the nation's population. The Senate and House gains left the party still short of a majority but in a position of new power and relevance on the national scene.

A new vigor shown by Republican candidates across the country marked a return to more competitive two-party politics and the possibility that the 1968 presidential election could be closely contested. The vast majority of successful Republican candidates, both for congressional and state offices, appeared to have rejected the ultraconservative ideology espoused by former senator Barry Goldwater. But the winning Republicans did represent a somewhat more conservative philosophy than that of the president and his administration, reflecting a national movement to the right, which many observers felt was reflected in the slowdown on major domestic reforms in the closing ses-

sion of the Eighty-ninth Congress. The 1966 elections appeared to lay the groundwork for a strong moderate Republican challenge to Johnson in 1968.

The party control among the state governorships shifted from 33–17 in favor of the Democrats to 25–25, the greatest Republican strength since the early 1950s. The Republicans gained California and held New York, Pennsylvania, Ohio, and Michigan to give them control of five of the nation's seven largest states. In addition to California, the Republicans added Alaska, Arizona, Arkansas, Florida, Maryland, Minnesota, Nebraska, Nevada, and New Mexico to the list of governorships under their control. Among the new Republican governors were Winthrop Rockefeller of Arkansas; Claude R. Kirk Jr. (in traditionally Democratic Florida); and Spiro T. Agnew of Maryland, a political moderate who defeated George P. Mahoney, the narrow victor in a three-way Democratic primary who had pitched his campaign to the "white backlash" vote. (In general, "backlash" candidates were unsuccessful in the elections.) Republican gubernatorial candidate Howard Callaway won a plurality of the votes in the one-time impregnable Democratic stronghold of Georgia. But Callaway failed to poll an absolute majority, and under the Georgia constitution, the election was thrown into the state legislature, which chose the Democratic runner-up, Lester Maddox.

The Republicans' most spectacular gain was in the House, where they picked up fifty-two seats and lost only five to the Democrats. The new party lineup in the House would be 248 Democrats and 187 Republicans. The Republican total in the thirteen southern states rose to twenty-eight seats, compared with only fourteen in 1962. In Senate elections Republicans gained seats in Illinois, Oregon, and Tennessee, giving them thirty-six seats to the Democrats' sixty-four. Democrats failed to take any Senate seats from the Republicans.

In the state legislatures the Republicans scored net gains of 156 senate seats and 401 seats in the lower houses, reflecting not only the strong party trend running in the Republicans' favor but the fact that reapportionment, by adding seats in suburban areas, was helping them as much as it helped the Democrats, if not more.

1967–1969: THE NINETIETH CONGRESS

The United States in 1967–1968 underwent two of the most trying years in its history as a rising wave of rioting and looting swept over its largely black central cities, the Vietnam War continued to build in human and dollar costs, inflationary pressures mounted, and two major national leaders were assassinated. President Johnson, recognizing the inability of his administration to command continued strong popular support, announced in March 1968 that he would not seek reelection to a second full term in the White House.

The Vietnam War became increasingly troublesome. It often overshadowed civil rights and city problems, distorted the U.S. economy, and loomed over U.S. foreign policy. Its cost soared to more than $2 billion a month. Reflecting the expense of the war, the federal budget by fiscal 1969 was at a record $186 billion, with $80 billion of that for defense.

Hopes for a political settlement in Vietnam were buoyed on October 31, when President Johnson announced he was ordering a complete halt to all American bombing of the North. Though not officially confirmed, it was believed that the bombing halt was undertaken with tacit agreement that it would last only so long as the North Vietnamese did not use it to their military advantage. A new and complicated round of negotiations then began in Paris on the means and protocol for substantive peace negotiations.

The patterns of violence in American life reasserted themselves when two prominent Americans became victims of assassins' bullets. The first was the Rev. Martin Luther King Jr., who was shot and killed April 4, 1968, in Memphis, Tenn. Following his death, rioting, looting, and burning broke out in black districts in more than one hundred cities. On June 5 another apostle of social progress and reconciliation between the races was struck down. Leaving the Los Angeles hotel ballroom in which he had made his California presidential primary victory statement, Sen. Robert F. Kennedy was shot in the head and died twenty-five hours later.

The 1968 Campaigns

Few presidential election years in the history of the nation brought as many surprising developments as 1968. Just a year before the election, it appeared likely that the two candidates might be President Johnson for the Democrats and Michigan's governor George W. Romney for the Republicans. But by late winter 1968 both Johnson and Romney were out of the picture, and each of the major parties was plunged into spirited fights for their presidential nominations. During 1968 continued racial tensions in the nation led to fears that Alabama's former governor George C. Wallace, running as the candidate of his own American Independent Party, might win a major share of the national vote or at least cause deadlock in the electoral college.

For the Democrats the year of surprises began November 30, 1967, when Minnesota's Eugene McCarthy announced that he would enter four 1968 presidential primaries to demonstrate opposition to the Johnson policies. McCarthy's candidacy struck an immediate chord of response, especially among younger Americans who shared his fervent distaste for the war in Vietnam. Most political observers discounted the seriousness of McCarthy's candidacy, but in the March 12 presidential primary in New Hampshire, McCarthy scored an amazing "moral" victory by gathering 42 percent of the vote against the president's 49 percent.

The McCarthy vote in New Hampshire then triggered another major surprise: the entry of Robert Kennedy into the Democratic presidential race, announced March 16. And on March 31 President Johnson stunned the nation by announcing, at the end of a lengthy radio and television address on Vietnam policy, that he would not seek reelection in 1968.

After Johnson withdrew, the race for the Democratic nomination turned into a three-way affair: McCarthy, Kennedy, and Vice President Hubert Humphrey, who entered the fray in April. On June 4, in the conclusive California primary,

Kennedy emerged the narrow victor over McCarthy, only to be assassinated as he left the hotel ballroom where he had claimed victory.

The death of Kennedy, who had shared McCarthy's Vietnam views while taking a far more aggressive stance on urban and minority problems, was followed by an eerie moratorium in Democratic politics as the shaken party factions sought to decide on their next move. But within weeks Humphrey emerged as the odds-on favorite for the nomination.

While violence flared in the city streets and thousands of police and guards imposed security precautions unprecedented in the annals of American presidential conventions, the Thirty-fifth Democratic National Convention met August 26–29 in Chicago to nominate Hubert H. Humphrey of Minnesota for the presidency and to endorse the controversial Vietnam policies of the Johnson-Humphrey administration. Humphrey's selection as running mate was Maine's Sen. Edmund S. Muskie. In the campaign that followed, Muskie's calm-voiced appeals for understanding between the groups in American society would prove an asset for the Democratic ticket.

In a minority were the antiwar factions that rallied around the candidacies of McCarthy and George McGovern. The McCarthy forces mounted a series of challenges to the Humphrey faction, on credentials, rules, the platform, and the nomination itself. An unprecedented number of credentials were challenged. McCarthy, McGovern, and other liberal factions won their greatest breakthrough on convention rules, obtaining abolition of a mandatory unit rule for the 1968 convention and at every level of party activity leading up to and including the 1972 convention. Many Humphrey-pledged delegates also backed the move. For the first time in recent party history, the functioning of party machinery at every level had been questioned. Humphrey won his party's nomination, but he would lead a bitterly divided party into the autumn campaign.

In the Republican Party, George Romney had established himself as the early leader in the race for the nomination, but his liberalism was distasteful to many orthodox Republicans. He was followed into the GOP race by Richard Nixon, who made his long-anticipated candidacy formal on February 1. The two front-runners entered the New Hampshire presidential primary, but it soon became apparent to Romney that he faced a likely loss, and on February 28 he surprised the nation by withdrawing from the contest. Nixon won an overwhelming victory in the March 12 New Hampshire GOP primary. Moderate and liberal Republicans hoped that New York's Gov. Nelson A. Rockefeller would step into the void created by Romney's withdrawal, but Rockefeller declared on March 21 that he would not run because "the majority of (Republican) leaders want the candidacy of Richard Nixon."

Without significant opposition Nixon swept the Wisconsin, Indiana, Nebraska, Oregon, and South Dakota primaries, shedding most of the "loser" image he had acquired from his 1960 defeat for president and 1962 defeat for governor of California. Rockefeller reversed his ground once again by entering the race on April 30, but even in the primaries where write-ins were permitted, the vote for him was generally low.

The Republican National Convention, meeting in Miami Beach August 5–8, wrote a moderately progressive party platform and then chose candidates for president and vice president who, at the moment of their selection, seemed to be taking increasingly restrictive attitudes on the sensitive national issues of law, order, and civil rights.

Nixon won nomination for the presidency on the first ballot, bearing out the predictions of his campaign organization. For vice president, at Nixon's suggestion, the Republicans selected Spiro T. Agnew, governor of Maryland since his election in 1966. The selection of Agnew, one of the major surprises of the year, was announced by Nixon the morning after his own nomination, and in the wake of almost-solid all-night conferences with Republican leaders, chiefly those of a conservative bent. Liberal Republicans were outraged at Agnew's designation.

Nixon seemed to represent the middle ground of the Republican Party of 1968, substantially to the right of Governor Rockefeller and well to the center of the road compared to the conservative Ronald Reagan. The Republican platform of 1968, adopted by the Convention August 6 without a floor fight or any amendments, was generally moderate in tone and contained a preamble calling for a major national effort to rebuild urban and rural slums and attack the root causes of poverty, including racism.

To conduct his second campaign for the presidency, Nixon assembled a massive—and doubtless the best financed—campaign organization in U.S. history. Nixon was intent on avoiding the mistakes of his 1960 campaign, when a frenetic campaign pace resulted in exhaustion and snap decisions.

A central theme of Nixon's campaign was an appeal to a group he called the "forgotten Americans," whom Nixon defined as "the nonshouters," those who "work in America's factories, run America's business, serve in Government, provide most of the soldiers who died to keep us free." By suggesting that his administration would look chiefly to the interest of this group, Nixon was able to make a strong bid for the support of white suburban and small-town America, the traditional heartland of GOP strength in the nation.

Humphrey's bid for the presidency got off to a depressing start in September 1968 with sparse crowds, disordered schedules, and vicious heckling by left-wing, antiwar elements virtually everywhere he sought to speak. Humphrey's first task was to establish some measure of independence from the vastly unpopular Johnson administration. A significant step to win some of the antiwar Democrats to his side came in a September 30 televised address from Salt Lake City, when he said he would stop the bombing of North Vietnam "as an acceptable risk for peace." When President Johnson actually took that step on October 31, Humphrey could hardly restrain his glee. The combination of his own softened stand and the presidential position won him, at least at the last moment, the support of many of the Democrats who had been most disaffected at Chicago.

Humphrey endorsed virtually all the social advances of the Kennedy-Johnson years but called for a substantial broadening of domestic efforts to solve the problems of cities and minorities. He charged that Nixon's economic policies would bring America

"back to McKinley," with recessions and unemployment like those the country experienced during the Eisenhower years.

George Wallace had announced on February 8, 1968, that he would run for president as a third-party candidate under the banner of the American Independent Party. His campaign had a narrower goal: to win the balance of power in electoral college voting, thus depriving either major party of the clear electoral majority required for election. Wallace made it clear that he would then expect one of the major party candidates to make concessions in return for sufficient support from the Wallace supporters to win election. Wallace indicated he expected the election to be resolved in the electoral college and not go to the House of Representatives for resolution. At the end of the campaign, it was revealed that he had obtained affidavits from all his electors in which they promised to vote for Wallace "or whomsoever he may direct" in the electoral college.

Results of the 1968 Elections

In one of the closest elections of the century Richard Nixon on November 5 was elected president. In percentage terms, Nixon had 43.4 percent of the popular vote, the lowest winning percentage for a presidential candidate since 1912, when Woodrow Wilson won by 41.9 percent. Humphrey's percentage was 42.7; Wallace's was 13.5.

For the Republican Party, Nixon's victory had special significance. He was the first successful GOP presidential contender since the 1920s who was closely identified with the party organization. The victories of Dwight D. Eisenhower in the 1950s, followed by Nixon's defeat in 1960, had raised the possibility that the Republicans might lack the broad appeal ever to win a presidential victory unless their candidate possessed special nonparty appeal.

The Democrats had feared that the election would bring a final dissolution of the grand Democratic coalition that had controlled the federal government in most elections since the 1930s. The election returns did show the South deserting the Democratic Party in presidential voting, the Deep South to Wallace, the border South to Nixon. But the other elements of the Democratic coalition held together remarkably well, helping the party to win the electoral votes of several major states and to return a high proportion of its congressional incumbents.

Preelection surveys of Wallace voters had indicated that if they had been obliged to choose between Nixon and Humphrey, about twice as many would have preferred Nixon as Humphrey. If Wallace had not been on the ballot, Nixon would very possibly have carried some of the five Deep South states that went for Wallace, possibly building up a stronger national vote lead in the process. But it was difficult to tell from the election returns whether Wallace had hurt Nixon or Humphrey more in the nonsouthern states.

Another bright spot for the Republicans was on the governorship level, where the GOP added five seats for a new total of thirty-one. But the Democrats retained control of both houses of the Congress.

In the Senate, Republicans gained five new seats, for a total of forty-two, the largest number they had held since 1956. The gain was a major accomplishment for the GOP. It was the biggest gain since 1950, when the Republicans also won five new seats. The breakdown for the new Senate was fifty-eight Democrats and forty-two Republicans. In the Ninetieth Congress, there had been sixty-three Democrats and thirty-seven Republicans. Republicans actually won seven seats previously held by Democrats, but since Democrats won two seats previously held by Republicans, the net gain for the Republicans was five. No incumbent Republican standing for reelection was defeated, while four incumbent Democrats lost their bids for additional terms.

The makeup of the new Senate was expected to result in a shift, although not a dramatic one, to the right. While liberal strength remained the same as in the Ninetieth Congress, strength among moderate senators dropped and strength among conservative senators rose correspondingly.

The seven Republicans who captured Senate seats previously held by Democrats included Barry Goldwater, former senator from Arizona and unsuccessful Republican presidential candidate in 1964. Goldwater, whose previous service gave him seniority over the other Republican freshmen, replaced retiring Carl Hayden, president pro tempore of the Senate.

Three Republican representatives also won Senate seats previously held by Democrats. They were Edward J. Gurney of Florida, Charles McC. Mathias Jr. of Maryland, and Richard S. Schweiker of Pennsylvania. Other Republicans winning seats previously held by Democrats were Henry L. Bellmon of Oklahoma and William B. Saxbe of Ohio. The other two freshman Republicans were Marlow W. Cook of Kentucky and Rep. Robert Dole of Kansas. The two Democrats who won seats previously held by Republicans were Alan Cranston of California and Iowa governor Harold E. Hughes.

In the House the party breakdown when the Ninety-first Congress convened was 243 Democrats and 192 Republicans. In all Republicans took nine seats from the Democrats and lost five of their own for a four-seat net gain. Republicans had scored a net gain of forty-seven seats in the 1966 elections and had won a special election to fill a Democratic vacancy earlier in 1968. The Republicans had lost thirty-eight seats in the 1964 elections.

Of the 435 representatives elected in November, 396 were incumbents (223 Democrats and 173 Republicans), and only thirty-nine (twenty Democrats and nineteen Republicans) were newcomers. The new winners included two former representatives, one a Democrat and the other a Republican.

The new Congress would have the smallest crop of freshman members in years. Between 1940 and 1948 an average of ninety-six newcomers were elected to each new House. The average dropped to sixty-eight between 1950 and 1958 but rose to seventy-two between 1960 and 1966. In 1964 there were ninety-one newcomers elected and in 1966, seventy-three.

In gubernatorial races the Republican Party, winning thirteen of the year's twenty-one races and capturing seven seats held by Democrats, increased its control of the nation's statehouses from twenty-six to thirty-one. Even after the selection of a Democrat to succeed Vice President-elect Agnew, the GOP would boast thirty governors, equaling its holdings after the Eisenhower sweep of 1952, when there were two fewer states.

In light of the extremely close presidential race and the continuing, though narrowed, control of Congress by the Democrats, the Republican margin of ten governorships gave the party its most broad-based mandate for leadership. The GOP scored a net gain of three seats each in the East and the Midwest and lost one in the West. There were no party changes in the South.

Nixon's coattails had a less decisive effect than did Eisenhower's four national elections earlier. Nixon did carry six of the seven states in which Republicans took governorships formerly held by Democrats (including two incumbents). But it was far from clear who helped whom in several of those races. In Montana an easy Nixon win failed to save Gov. Tim M. Babcock, an early Nixon backer. In Rhode Island, the only other race in which a Republican incumbent was beaten, Gov. John H. Chaffee's advocacy of a state income tax appeared to be the major factor in his defeat.

Battling for seats vacated by Democratic incumbents, Republicans won in Indiana, Iowa, West Virginia, New Hampshire, and Vermont. State matters, primarily fiscal, were the main issues in all five states. The Democrats suffered particularly through the voluntary retirement of their popular governors in normally Republican Iowa, New Hampshire, and Vermont. Except for Montana and Rhode Island, the Democrats picked up no seats formerly held by Republicans.

Republicans scored minimal gains in the contests for state legislature seats around the country. As a result of the elections, they would control twenty legislatures, the same number controlled by the Democrats. (The other ten were split in control or nonpartisan.) The GOP rose in strength from 41.8 to 43.4 percent of the seats in all senate chambers around the country but held static at just over 42 percent of all seats in lower houses.

1969–1971:
THE NINETY-FIRST CONGRESS

The Ninety-first Congress, which adjourned on January 2, 1971, compiled a substantial record of domestic accomplishments despite drawn-out disputes with President Nixon over foreign policy and spending.

The Senate made the first substantial attempt since World War II to challenge the president's authority on foreign policy and military involvement. Although the House generally agreed to uphold President Nixon's requests to finance new weapons systems and to send money and troops into Vietnam, the Senate engaged in numerous long debates on those issues.

It was in domestic legislation, however, that Congress compiled its most substantial record of accomplishment. This legislation included major air and water pollution control measures, a $25-billion education authorization, and a bill extending the 1965 Voting Rights Act and allowing eighteen-year-olds to vote in national elections. In the final days of the 1970 session, Congress completed action on a bill extending the food stamp program that, for the first time, provided free food stamps for the poorest families.

Congress and the administration worked to establish new federal agencies. Foremost among these was the government-owned postal corporation to replace the Post Office Department. Congress also agreed to the president's reorganization plans to set up an independent Environmental Protection Agency and a National Atmospheric and Oceanic Administration in the Commerce Department.

Problems concerning the economy dominated Nixon's first two years in office, and Congress attempted periodically to deal with these problems. In 1969 it enacted a major overhaul of the tax code. It sliced funds from military, foreign aid, and space requests and added money to numerous domestic programs, notably education, health, training, and pollution control. Congress enacted a federal spending ceiling for fiscal 1971, as it had for fiscal years 1969 and 1970.

Congress engaged in debates over the Vietnam War in attempts to limit deployment of troops and reduce spending. The Senate voted twice to repeal the 1964 Tonkin Gulf resolution, and the House eventually went along.

The 1970 Midterm Elections

Despite the unprecedented off-year campaign efforts of President Nixon and Vice President Agnew, most observers felt the Republicans suffered a net loss in the elections of November 3, 1970. In their drive to improve the Republican position in Congress and in state capitals, the president campaigned for candidates in twenty-three states during the weeks preceding the election, and the vice president visited twenty-nine states.

Although the effect of a presidential appearance for a candidate was unclear, Nixon and Agnew could point to victories in several states where they campaigned: Senate victories in Maryland, Connecticut, Ohio, and Tennessee, for example, and gubernatorial victories in Connecticut, Tennessee, California, Arizona, Iowa, Vermont, and Wyoming. Administration efforts failed to pay off in other states on the Republican target list. Democratic candidates were elected to the Senate in Utah, New Mexico, Wyoming, Nevada, North Dakota, and Indiana, despite the high-level administration campaigning. And Nixon or Agnew visits failed to persuade voters to elect Republican senators in California, Texas, Illinois, or Florida.

The most spectacular third party victory of the year was that of James L. Buckley of New York, a Conservative Party candidate who was elected to the Senate with a minority of the votes. Buckley's election was made possible by a division of the votes for the Republican-Liberal incumbent, Charles E. Goodell, and the Democratic candidate, Rep. Richard L. Ottinger.

Another third party success belonged to Sen. Harry F. Byrd Jr. of Virginia. In March 1970 the veteran Democrat announced that he would not run as a Democrat because of a party "loyalty oath" that he claimed would force him to commit himself to the Democratic presidential candidate in 1972. Byrd ran as an Independent, easily defeating the Democratic and Republican candidates.

A second incumbent Democratic senator who ran as an Independent was Thomas J. Dodd of Connecticut. Dodd had been censured by the Senate in 1967 for diverting funds from testimonial events and campaign contributions to his personal use. He was regarded as unlikely to win the Senate nomination in a Democratic primary. His Independent candidacy divided the Democratic vote and helped elect a Republican, Rep. Lowell P. Weicker Jr., to his seat.

Results of the 1970 Elections

Republicans registered a net gain of two Senate seats in the November 3 elections, leaving Democrats with a majority of fifty-five to forty-five in the Ninety-second Congress. Of the thirty-five Senate seats being contested, eleven were won by Republicans, twenty-two by Democrats, one by a Conservative Party candidate, and one by an Independent. Democrats had held twenty-five of the seats and Republicans, ten. Republicans who captured Democratic seats were Rep. Weicker, Rep. J. Glenn Beall Jr. of Maryland, Rep. Robert Taft Jr. of Ohio, and Rep. W. E. Brock III of Tennessee.

In Minnesota, Hubert H. Humphrey won back a seat in the Senate, where he had served from 1949 to 1964, when he became vice president. He defeated Republican representative Clark MacGregor for the seat of retiring Democrat Eugene J. McCarthy. In Texas, former Democratic representative Lloyd M. Bentsen defeated Rep. George Bush for the seat held by Ralph W. Yarborough, a Democrat defeated in the May 2 primary.

The Democratic Party showed renewed strength in the Great Plains and the West Coast in the 1970 elections as it gained nine House seats to open up a 255–180 margin for the Ninety-second Congress. Republicans claimed success in limiting Democratic gains to less than the thirty-eight-seat average pickup recorded by the nonpresidential party in off-year elections during this century. Democrats said their gains were significant because President Nixon's 1968 victory carried in few of the marginal candidates, who are normally easy prey to the party out of power in off-year contests.

Registering the most impressive net gain in statehouses by any party since 1938, Democrats in 1970 took thirteen governorships from Republican control, while losing only two, in Tennessee and Connecticut. The balance of state power shifted dramatically from eighteen Democratic and thirty-two Republican governors before the election to twenty-nine Democratic and twenty-one Republican governors.

State-level gains were doubly significant in 1970. Democratic control of a majority of the states furnished vital power bases for the 1972 presidential elections. Democrats won Ohio and Pennsylvania and held Texas, thus controlling three of the most populous states. Democrats also wrested from Republican control Alaska, Florida, Arkansas, and Oklahoma and the western and midwestern states of Idaho, Minnesota, Nebraska, Nevada, New Mexico, South Dakota, and Wisconsin. Republicans continued to hold New York, California, Michigan, and Illinois.

Republicans went into the 1970 elections holding fifty-one of the ninety-nine state legislative bodies (Nebraska has a unicameral legislature). This figure included the two nominally nonpartisan legislatures of Minnesota and Nebraska, which were controlled by conservative, Republican-oriented majorities. Democrats held the other forty-eight chambers. Following the 1970 elections, Democrats gained control of eight new legislative bodies, giving them control of fifty-six.

1971–1973:
THE NINETY-SECOND CONGRESS

The years 1971–1973 saw some of the boldest and most dramatic presidential initiatives in years. In the summer of 1971 President Nixon imposed wage and price controls on the economy, announced that he would visit Communist China, and planned a summit meeting with Soviet leaders. His visits to China and the Soviet Union in 1972 gave Nixon a strong boost in his campaign for reelection.

Dissent over the Vietnam War, which seemed on the rise in the spring of 1971, had waned by midyear following troop withdrawal announcements by Nixon. At year's end 45,000 additional troops were scheduled for withdrawal, practically bringing to an end the offensive combat involvement of U.S. ground forces. By late 1972 it appeared that a settlement of the Vietnam War, or at least a cease-fire and return of U.S. prisoners, was imminent. Presidential aide Henry Kissinger and North Vietnamese officials had hammered out a nine-point agreement, but the Saigon government balked, and the elusive peace had to await a final agreement in January 1973.

In October 1972 Congress gave President Nixon a major legislative victory: passage of a general revenue-sharing measure. The bill was the only one of the president's "six great goals" to pass during the Ninety-second Congress. In 1972 Congress also approved the Equal Rights Amendment, forty-nine years after it was introduced. The amendment was sent to the states for ratification March 22 after the Senate passed it 84–8.

On June 17, 1972, five men were arrested in the Democratic national headquarters at the Watergate building in Washington, D.C. This incident was the beginning of a process that was to continue over the next two years and destroy a presidency. The break-in was immediately tagged the "Watergate caper" by the press. But by the time the election arrived it had become the "Watergate affair," and it was being examined seriously. In the months following the celebrated break-in, allegations of a widespread network of political espionage and sabotage engineered by the Republicans were carried in the news media. Charges of involvement were leveled by the Democrats and the press against persons in high positions in the White House and the Committee for the Reelection of the President.

Seven men were indicted on criminal charges, three civil suits were filed, and one man was found guilty in a Florida court on a minor charge related to Watergate. Two congressional committees initiated staff investigations of the allegations. And Watergate repeatedly surfaced in the presidential campaign, with Democratic nominee George McGovern and his campaign pursuing the charges and President Nixon and his staff denouncing them. Investigators and reporters began to backtrack: meetings, phone calls, financial transactions, and other related events were traced back months before the incident.

The 1972 Campaigns

President Nixon was in a strong position to seek another term as the 1972 presidential election year opened. His wage and price control system had curbed the inflationary spiral, while increased federal spending cut into the unemployment rate. His scheduled trips to Beijing and Moscow promised widespread publicity and a focus on the "peace" half of a peace and prosperity theme. And although he had alienated small groups of Republicans on the left and right wings of his party, Nixon could count on being renominated without much trouble.

The Democrats, meanwhile, headed toward a bruising battle for the nomination that would rip their party apart. Although Maine senator Edmund S. Muskie looked like a strong possibility for the nomination in late 1971, his centrist liberal political stance was not enough to hold the party together. His candidacy soon collapsed in the rush of primary voters toward the left or right wings of the party. Still angry over the Vietnam War, left-wing party activists gathered behind Sen. George McGovern of South Dakota. On the right, Alabama governor George C. Wallace gathered voters angry with busing and the rapid pace of social change in general.

Other well-known candidates who entered the fray for the Democratic presidential nomination were Sen. Henry M. Jackson of Washington and Sen. Hubert H. Humphrey of Minnesota. Several other hopefuls failed to gain any significant momentum; among them were former senator Eugene J. McCarthy of Minnesota and Rep. Shirley Chisholm of New York. Chisholm was the first black to run in a series of presidential primaries.

McGovern began his upward climb to the nomination by a stronger than expected showing in the New Hampshire primary. Although Muskie won the popular vote there, he was labeled a loser because he received far fewer votes than expected. From there it was downhill for Muskie, and after he ran fourth in the Pennsylvania primary on April 25, he ceased active campaigning. McGovern, meanwhile, ran first in Wisconsin on April 4, then won Massachusetts, Nebraska, Oregon, and beat Humphrey in a June 6 showdown in California. From there on he was practically assured of the nomination, although there was a last-minute effort at the convention to stop him.

McGovern's highly vocal and long-standing opposition to the Vietnam War caused many political analysts to look on him as a one-issue candidate. But his major problem was one of recognition. Public opinion polls indicated that he had only 2 percent support from the voters in the field of prospective Democratic nominees. By mid-March, after two months of extensive campaigning, McGovern had gained only 3 percentage points in the polls.

Beyond any doubt the reform commission that McGovern had headed after the disastrous Democratic convention of 1968 had changed the face of the Democratic Party. And beyond any doubt the changes favored McGovern's candidacy by expanding the party's base and bringing more women, minorities, and youths into the process.

At the convention, McGovern's winning of the nomination was never really in doubt, even before the balloting began, and he moved steadily toward his goal. The Democrats chose Sen. Thomas F. Eagleton of Missouri as their nominee for vice president. But on July 25 Eagleton disclosed that he had voluntarily hospitalized himself three times between 1960 and 1966 for "nervous exhaustion and fatigue." Since 1966, said the candidate, he had "experienced good, solid, sound health." But Eagleton's statement, culminating an investigation by reporters of his past difficulties under stress, started a sequence of developments that included increasing pressure for Eagleton to withdraw from the ticket. After a meeting with McGovern on July 31, Eagleton withdrew from the ticket.

His presidential campaign sidetracked, McGovern announced August 5 that his choice to replace Eagleton was R. Sargent Shriver, former director of the Peace Corps and the Office of Economic Opportunity and U.S. ambassador to France. In a display of unity and anti-Nixon oratory, the newly enlarged Democratic National Committee at an August 8 meeting in Washington nominated Shriver with 2,936 of the 3,013 votes cast.

In the Republican camp the renomination of President Nixon did not go completely unchallenged. He had opposition from both the left and the right. Assailing the president from the left was California representative Paul N. McCloskey Jr., who based his campaign on opposition to administration policies and its deception of the news media. McCloskey withdrew six days after the New Hampshire primary because of insufficient funds, but his name remained on the ballot in twelve other states as a symbolic protest. Nixon's opponent on the right was Ohio representative John M. Ashbrook, who attacked the president for what he called his failure to live up to 1968 promises in fiscal matters, foreign affairs, and defense posture. Ashbrook's name was on the ballot in eleven state presidential primaries.

The Republican National Convention was a gigantic television spectacular from start to finish. The main business of the convention, the nomination of President Nixon and Vice President Agnew to a second term, was a preordained ritual.

Nixon did little campaigning for his second term. Because of his strong lead in the polls and lack of speech making, the president also was in the enviable position of making few, if any, concrete campaign pledges to the electorate. He enunciated the major themes of the campaign in his acceptance speech before the Republican convention, emphasizing the divisions in the Democratic Party and urging dissatisfied Democrats to downplay traditional party loyalty.

From almost every standpoint the Democratic campaign contrasted sharply with that of the Republicans. McGovern and his running mate were on the road incessantly from Labor Day until election day. McGovern tried in vain to draw Nixon into debate. His initial tax and welfare reform proposals attracted widespread criticism and helped alienate several traditional sources of Democratic strength, such as ethnic groups and blue-collar workers. When he substituted Shriver for Eagleton, he was attacked for poor judgment and vacillation. His chief issue, administration conduct of the Vietnam War, lost whatever remaining effect it might have had when an administration-negotiated peace appeared to be in sight during the last days of the campaign.

Rather than moving into the offensive against the administration, McGovern was kept on the defensive throughout the campaign, constantly forced to explain earlier positions and rebut Republican charges. The break-in at Democratic headquarters at Watergate in June and ensuing disclosures of the alleged involvement of administration officials in espionage and sabotage directed against the Democrats were potentially damaging, but the revelations failed to excite the voters enough to head off the Nixon sweep.

Results of the 1972 Elections

Nixon swept back into the White House on November 7 with a devastating landslide victory over McGovern. He carried a record of forty-nine states for a total of 520 electoral votes. Only Massachusetts and the District of Columbia, with a meager seventeen electoral votes between them, went for McGovern.

The Nixon landslide was the first Republican sweep since Reconstruction of the once solid Democratic South. By runaway margins Nixon took all eleven states of the old Confederacy, plus all the border states.

Americans engaged in massive ticket splitting in the 1972 election. Nixon's landslide victory was not reflected in significant Republican gains in Congress or in governorships. Despite the avalanche of votes for Nixon, the Democrats scored a net gain of two seats in the Senate, thereby increasing their majority to 57–43 in the Ninety-third Congress. Of the thirty-three seats contested, the Democrats won sixteen and the Republicans won seventeen. Nineteen of those seats had been controlled by the Republicans in the Ninety-second Congress, fourteen by the Democrats.

The most significant, and surprising, element of the Democratic gain was the upset of four seemingly well-entrenched Republican incumbents: Gordon Allott of Colorado, J. Caleb Boggs of Delaware, Jack Miller of Iowa, and Margaret Chase Smith of Maine. If it had not been for Republican gains in three southern states (North Carolina, Oklahoma, and Virginia), the Democratic majority in the Senate would have been much larger.

Half of the eight new Democrats were considered significantly more liberal than the incumbent Republicans they upset. In this category were Floyd K. Haskell, who beat Allott in Colorado; Joseph R. Biden Jr., who defeated Boggs in Delaware; Dick Clark, who retired Miller in Iowa; and Rep. William D. Hathaway, who upset Smith in Maine. A fifth Democrat, Rep. James Abourezk, defeated Republican Robert W. Hirsch in South Dakota to take the seat of retiring Republican incumbent Karl E. Mundt. Abourezk was considered far more liberal than the conservative Mundt.

Two more Democrats were conservatives who replaced conservatives. Sam Nunn of Georgia and J. Bennett Johnston of Louisiana defeated Republican opponents to fill the seats of Democratic incumbents David H. Gambrell of Georgia and the late Allen J. Ellender of Louisiana. The remaining Democrat, Walter "Dee" Huddleston, defied the southern election trend by winning his race against Republican Louie B. Nunn in Kentucky for the seat of retiring Republican John Sherman Cooper. Both the incumbent and his successor were moderates.

Final returns showed that Republicans gained thirteen House seats in the 1972 elections, far short of the number they needed to win control of the House. The thirteen-seat pickup was slightly more than the four House seats gained when President Nixon first was elected in 1968, but it was far less than the winning party usually has gained in a presidential landslide. A close look at the House figures showed that the president not only lacked coattails but appeared to have little if any perceptible effect on House races.

The only semblance of coattail effects in the election was in the South, where the Republicans took seven House seats out of Democratic hands. For several states the election of Republican representatives meant drastic breaks with tradition.

The 1972 election was the first to take place after the reapportionment and redistricting that followed the 1970 census. More than a dozen entirely new districts were created, and others had major changes in their boundary lines. Most of these changes tended to favor the Republicans, because many new districts were placed in fast-growing Republican suburbs and because legislatures in several key states drew the lines to partisan Republican advantage.

Redistricting also played a significant part in the defeat of House incumbents. Thirteen incumbents, eight Democrats and five Republicans, were defeated. For nine of these incumbents, seven of them Democrats, redistricting was the dominant factor in their defeat. Three lost because redistricting forced them to run against other incumbents.

The House of Representatives in the Ninety-third Congress looked quite a bit different from its predecessor, but the reasons were mainly because of redistricting and retirement, not election defeats. The new count was 243 Democrats and 192 Republicans.

Chalking up a net gain of one, the Democrats in 1972 retained the wide margin of statehouse control they won in 1970, holding thirty-one governorships to the Republicans' nineteen. (Democrats had gained the Kentucky governorship in the 1971 off-year elections.) Of the eighteen seats up for election in 1972, Democrats won eleven and Republicans won seven. Despite upsets in several states, the net result was only a minimal change in party power.

Republicans lost governorships in Delaware, Illinois, and Vermont, while ousting Democrats in Missouri and North Carolina. Close races in New Hampshire, North Carolina, Washington, and West Virginia were won by Republicans, who also upset a favored Democratic candidate in Indiana. As expected, Republicans won gubernatorial contests in Iowa and Missouri.

Incumbent or favored Republicans were upset by Democrats in Illinois, North Dakota, Rhode Island, and Vermont, while Democratic incumbents were reelected in Arkansas, Kansas, South Dakota, and Utah. In Montana and Texas, Democrats were elected to succeed retiring Democratic governors. As expected, the Democratic challenger unseated Delaware's Republican incumbent by capitalizing on the issue of taxes.

In West Virginia's gubernatorial race, which drew national attention, Republican governor Arch A. Moore Jr. put together his general popularity and campaigning ability with Nixon's strong showing in the state—and the obvious incongruity of a millionaire populist candidate running in one of the nation's poorest states—to defeat Democratic challenger John D. "Jay" Rockefeller IV, the secretary of state.

1973–1975:
THE NINETY-THIRD CONGRESS

The legislative activities of the Ninety-third Congress were overshadowed by one of the nation's greatest political crises: Watergate. Watergate dominated the news from the beginning of the second Nixon administration in January 1973 until the president's resignation on August 9, 1974. The year 1973 opened with the trial of the seven Watergate burglars beginning January 8. Five of the seven defendants pleaded guilty a few days after the trial opened, while the remaining two stood trial and were found guilty by the end of the month. Sentencing was March 23.

From mid-May until early August 1973, American television screens were filled with politicians and former government officials testifying before the Senate Select Committee on Presidential Campaign Activities—the Watergate committee. Most important of all information produced by the hearings was the revelation that tape recordings had been made of many presidential conversations in the White House during the period in which the break-in occurred and the cover-up began. The tapes contained evidence that ultimately led to Nixon's resignation.

Immediately after the existence of the tapes was made public on July 16, a struggle for the recordings began. The legal battle would last a year, from July 23, 1973, to July 24, 1974, when the Supreme Court ruled that Nixon had to turn over the tapes to U.S. District Judge John J. Sirica for use as evidence in the Watergate cover-up trial.

In the midst of the tapes battle, Spiro Agnew, on October 10, 1973, became the second vice president in American history to resign. Under investigation for multiple charges of alleged conspiracy, extortion, and bribery, Agnew agreed to resign and avoided imprisonment by pleading nolo contendere to charges of income tax evasion.

Two days after Agnew's resignation, President Nixon nominated House Minority Leader Gerald R. Ford of Michigan as his successor. Ford became the fortieth vice president of the United States on December 6, 1973.

While Americans were reeling from these events, they were overtaken by an energy crisis, as a result of the Arab oil embargo, and some of the worst inflation to hit the economy in peacetime history.

But even as public attention focused on the presidency and the economic problems of the country, Congress was passing landmark legislation representing an attempt to change the balance of power between the presidency and Congress. Among measures enacted were limits on a president's right to impound money, the establishment of a more thorough method for Congress to consider the federal budget, and restrictions on the president's war-making powers.

Investigation of Watergate continued. After two months of closed congressional hearings beginning May 9, 1974, and a series of televised debates beginning July 24, the House Judiciary Committee voted to recommend three articles of impeachment.

On August 5 Nixon released three previously undisclosed transcripts. The conversations showed clearly Nixon's participation in the cover-up. In a written statement the president acknowledged that he had withheld the contents of the tapes despite the fact that they contradicted his previous declarations that he had not known of or participated in the cover-up. These admissions destroyed almost all of Nixon's remaining support in Congress. On August 8 Nixon announced his resignation, to be effective at noon the next day, and Vice President Ford became the nation's thirty-eighth president.

A month after assuming office, Ford pardoned Nixon "for all offenses against the United States which he, Richard Nixon, has committed or may have committed" during his years as president.

Ford was succeeded in the vice presidency by Nelson A. Rockefeller, who became vice president December 19, 1974, after the House confirmed his nomination by President Ford, 287–128. The Senate had given its approval December 10, 90–7. Thus the nation for the first time had both a president and a vice president chosen under the Twenty-fifth Amendment to the Constitution rather than by a national election.

Reacting to presidential campaign abuses, Congress in 1974 enacted a landmark campaign reform bill that radically overhauled the existing system of financing election campaigns. The new measure cleared Congress October 10, 1974, and was signed into law five days later by President Ford. It established the first spending limits ever for candidates in presidential primary and general elections and in primary campaigns for the House and Senate.

Although the Arab nations had lifted their oil embargo, they and other oil producing states refused to lower the posted price for oil. The energy situation became intertwined with the grave economic problems President Ford inherited on taking office. Within months, he and Congress were trying to get together on an economic-energy package that reflected the inseparability of the two crises. The continuing high oil prices played havoc with the international monetary system and contributed heavily to the deepening worldwide recession.

The 1974 Midterm Elections

Republicans paid the bill in November 1974 for two years of scandal and economic decline, losing heavily in congressional and gubernatorial elections throughout the country and slipping deeper into a minority status. Democrats gained forty-three seats in the House, three seats in the Senate, and four new governorships.

As soon as the November 5 election returns were in, Republicans began looking for comfort in the fact that parties holding the White House normally lose heavily in midterm elections. But it was a small comfort. Democrats went into the 1974 election with nearly 60 percent of the seats in the Senate and House. For the most part, the Democratic gains in the House were not marginal seats won by Republicans in a previous presidential sweep but solid Republican districts.

If there was one region that disappointed Republicans the most, it was the South. Shortly before the election the South was thought to be the one Republican bright spot. Losses were expected to be lightest in that area, and there was a good chance for the party to gain half a dozen House seats. As it turned out,

Sen. Sam J. Ervin, D-N.C. (center) leads the televised hearings of the Senate Watergate Committee that exposed a web of political scandals in the Nixon administration, leading to the president's resignation in 1974.

Republicans lost ten House seats in the South and won only two Democratic ones.

The Midwest proved even more disastrous for Republicans. Before the election the Midwest had been the only region of the country in which Republicans held a majority of the House seats. But with a net Democratic gain of fourteen seats there, that was no longer true.

A look at the demographics of the election yielded another interesting conclusion: Republicans suffered badly in the suburbs, where much of the so-called emerging Republican majority was supposed to lie. The striking fact about these suburban districts was that they were not marginal. In many cases the suburban districts that went Democratic contained thousands of former Democrats who left their party behind as they became prosperous enough to move outside the city limits. The new suburban middle class had been hard hit by recession and inflation, and Republicans may have paid the price.

Perhaps more important, however, was the prevalence in the suburbs of independent and ticket-splitting voters. Surveys had consistently shown a clear majority of independent voters favoring Democratic congressional candidates in 1974, and the switch in the independent vote probably was concentrated in the suburbs.

The heavy turnover decreed by the election—eleven new senators, ninety-two new representatives, forty incumbent representatives defeated—broke one of the most consistent political patterns of previous years. The tendency since World War II had been for incumbents to seek reelection as long as they were physically able to serve and for nearly all of them to win.

In 1974 that changed. Thanks to the combination of retirement and defeat, there were more first-termers elected to the Ninety-fourth House than to any other since 1949. More than one-third of the new House was elected either in 1972 or 1974.

Results of the 1974 Elections

The Democrats scored a net gain of three Senate seats in the November 5 elections. A fourth gain came later in New Hampshire, where the state ballot law commission had at first declared Republican Louis C. Wyman the winner by two votes. But the Senate refused to seat Wyman, eventually declaring a vacancy that Democrat John Durkin filled after winning a special election in September 1975. In addition, the Democrats had gained a seat in Ohio by appointment early in 1974, which they held in the November balloting.

Two incumbents, both Republicans, were defeated in the election. Marlow W. Cook of Kentucky lost by a substantial margin to Democratic governor Wendell H. Ford. In Colorado, Republican Peter H. Dominick was swamped by Democrat Gary W. Hart.

Democrats also captured two seats from which incumbent Republicans were retiring. In a major upset in Vermont, Patrick J. Leahy beat Rep. Richard W. Mallary in a close race and became the first Democratic senator in the state's history. Leahy replaced retiring George D. Aiken, the Senate's senior Republican.

The Republicans' only Senate gain was in Nevada, where former governor Paul Laxalt was the winner by 624 votes.

In other races for vacant seats, there were no shifts in party lineup. Democratic representative John C. Culver won the seat of retiring Harold E. Hughes in Iowa. In North Carolina former state attorney general Robert B. Morgan easily held the seat of Sam J. Ervin Jr. Two Democrats who defeated incumbents in primaries, former astronaut John H. Glenn of Ohio and Gov. Dale Bumpers of Arkansas, won landslide victories over weak Republican opposition.

Republicans, while losing Aiken's seat, held onto the Utah Senate seat of Wallace F. Bennett, who retired. Salt Lake City mayor Jake Garn won easily over Democratic representative Wayne Owens.

The Democratic gain was kept modest because the Republicans managed to hold their vulnerable Utah seat and to reelect three incumbents who had been in serious trouble: Senators Robert Dole of Kansas, Henry L. Bellmon of Oklahoma, and Milton R. Young of North Dakota.

Three Democratic incumbents in difficult races won reelection. They were Birch Bayh of Indiana, George McGovern of South Dakota, and Mike Gravel of Alaska. Other incumbents in both parties won easily.

In the House, Democrats gained forty-three seats, pushing their number just above the two-thirds mark. They had already made a net gain of five seats in special elections and a party switch, raising their total in the last days of the Ninety-third Congress to 248. Thus, after the elections, they had won 291 seats.

The Democratic trend was as broad as it was deep. It took away four Republican seats in New Jersey and four in California. It took five in Indiana, five in New York, three in Illinois, and two in Michigan. In nearly all cases the change to a new member of the House appeared to mean at least a slight shift to the left. There were a few new conservative Democratic representatives in the new House, such as John Birch Society member Lawrence

P. McDonald of Georgia, but they were exceptions. For the most part liberal Democrats who retired were replaced by persons of similar persuasion, and conservative Republicans were replaced by Democrats who ran against them from the left.

The Republican group in the House was also expected to shift slightly toward liberalism even as it shrank by forty-three members. Nearly every House Republican beaten November 5 was counted among the conservatives; the liberal and moderate Republicans generally had little trouble winning reelection. The only serious casualty among the Republican moderates was John Dellenback of Oregon. Moderates such as John B. Anderson of Illinois and Paul N. McCloskey Jr. of California won without serious contest.

Election night was not pleasant for Republicans who remained loyal to President Nixon in the days just before his resignation. Four Republicans who supported Nixon during the House Judiciary Committee's impeachment inquiry were beaten decisively. They were David W. Dennis of Indiana, Wiley Mayne of Iowa, and Joseph J. Maraziti and Charles W. Sandman Jr. of New Jersey. Harold V. Froehlich of Wisconsin, who supported two articles of impeachment against Nixon but opposed the third, also was defeated. All the Republicans on the Judiciary Committee who consistently voted to impeach Nixon were reelected, as were several Nixon defenders.

Democrats increased their firm hold on the nation's governorships from thirty-two to thirty-six. Of the thirty-five seats up for election, Democrats won twenty-seven, Republicans won seven, and an Independent was elected in Maine. The new lineup of governorships was thirty-six Democrats, thirteen Republicans, and one Independent. Not since the 1930s had the Democrats—or any party—held as many as thirty-six of the nation's governorships.

Republicans lost governorships in three of the nation's ten largest states—New York, California, and Massachusetts. They suffered three losses in the mountain states—Wyoming, Colorado, and Arizona. Besides these states Republicans also lost control of governorships in Oregon, Connecticut, and Tennessee, for a total loss of nine.

The Democrats also suffered some gubernatorial reverses, despite their overall net gain. In Alaska, Ohio, Kansas, and South Carolina, Republicans picked up state capitols held by Democrats, leaving the Republicans with a net loss of five. Democrats also lost Maine to an Independent.

Perhaps the two greatest upsets in the gubernatorial races occurred in Maine and Ohio. In Maine voters rejected both major political parties, choosing instead James B. Longley, who ran as an Independent. Longley was the first Independent to be elected governor of any state since 1930. In Ohio, Democratic governor John J. Gilligan lost to former Republican governor James A. Rhodes.

Minority groups fared well in gubernatorial contests. Both Arizona and New Mexico elected Spanish-surnamed governors, Arizona for the first time in history and New Mexico for the first time in fifty-six years. In Hawaii Democrat George R. Ariyoshi became the first Japanese-American to hold the governorship of any state.

There were fifteen other newcomers, for a total of nineteen new governors. Among them were Edmund G. "Jerry" Brown Jr., D-Calif.; Ella T. Grasso, D-Conn.; Michael S. Dukakis, D-Mass.; David L. Boren, D-Okla.; James B. Edwards, R-S.C.; and Jay Hammond, R-Alaska.

Years of Uneasy Peace

By the time Jimmy Carter took the oath as president in January 1977, America's confidence had been shaken by almost a decade and a half of violence and scandal. The country had in effect lost its first war; had gone through a series of political assassinations and its first case of presidential resignation; had been besieged by urban, campus, and racial violence; and had experienced the strains of an energy crisis and rampant inflation. In large part Carter's victory stemmed from the weariness of the voters with the normal political leadership of the country and their search for a new start. But however great the hopes, President Carter soon became embroiled in national problems and Washington politics. Critics charged him with inflexibility and lack of leadership. His energy bill was stalled and dismantled in Congress. And inflation resumed its seemingly inexorable rise. By mid-1979 few were optimistic that the nation's energy shortages and economic ills would be resolved any time soon. The debate over solutions continued to preoccupy the nation and its leaders.

The Democrats saw a reversal of fortunes in the 1980 election when conservative Ronald Reagan swept Carter from office. Reagan was the first GOP president since Dwight D. Eisenhower to have his party in a majority position in either chamber. The election gave conservatives a chance to control or influence national policy in the executive and legislative branches of government.

In line with his conservative ideology, President Reagan instigated huge tax cuts, which were largely credited with moving the country from recession to prosperity. The president came into office speaking in a traditional Republican manner, calling for a balanced budget. But he presided over the biggest deficits in American history, transforming the United States from the world's biggest creditor nation to the world's biggest debtor nation. During his tenure, the national debt increased nearly threefold, from $931 billion to $2.69 trillion.

The Reagan foreign policy took many turns, gradually toning down an early ideological bent and a tendency to exert military muscle—such as in the 1983 invasion of Grenada and the 1986 bombing of Libya. But the focus always was on the Soviet Union. Over the years the United States had grown accustomed to dealing with a Soviet Union that was predictable. Kremlin leaders came and went, but the fundamental Soviet policies remained the same, and Washington did not have to be particularly creative in responding to them. Gorbachev, who came to power in March 1985, during the early stage of Reagan's second term, upset many of the underlying assumptions about Soviet behavior.

At the outset President Reagan vested much of his energy in

Governors Who Became President

When George W. Bush was elected president in 2000, he continued the trend in recent years of governors advancing to the White House. Between 1976 and 2000, two sitting governors and two former governors won six of the seven presidential elections. The one exception was George Bush, father of George W. Bush. Over the course of U.S. history, seventeen presidents have served previously as state governors.

Following is a list of these presidents and the states in which they served as governor. Thomas Jefferson's term of governor of Virginia was during the Revolutionary War. Two other presidents served as governors of territories: Andrew Jackson was the territorial governor of Florida and William Henry Harrison was the territorial governor of Indiana.

President	State
Thomas Jefferson	Virginia
James Monroe	Virginia
Martin Van Buren	New York
John Tyler	Virginia
James K. Polk	Tennessee
Andrew Johnson	Tennessee
Rutherford B. Hayes	Ohio
Grover Cleveland	New York
William McKinley	Ohio
Theodore Roosevelt	New York
Woodrow Wilson	New Jersey
Calvin Coolidge	Massachusetts
Franklin D. Roosevelt	New York
Jimmy Carter	Georgia
Ronald Reagan	California
Bill Clinton	Arkansas
George W. Bush	Texas

Source: American Political Leaders 1789–2000. Washington, D.C.: CQ Press, 2000.

strengthening the armed forces. He left the presidency as an apostle of superpower disarmament, welcoming U.S.-Soviet summitry that he had once disdained and discarding his earlier belief that the Soviet Union was an "evil empire." Reagan had vowed never to deal with terrorists, but he suffered the humiliation of a White House scandal that involved the secret sale of arms to Iran in an attempt to release American hostages in Lebanon—and the illegal siphoning of some of the sale proceeds to Central American guerrilla fighters.

President Reagan's final year in office was one of warming relations between Washington and Moscow. He took his unique brand of politicking to Moscow May 29–June 2, 1988, for an upbeat summit meeting at which he and Gorbachev exchanged documents ratifying an arms control treaty they had signed the previous December in Washington. It was the first arms treaty ratified by the two countries since 1972 and the first to ban an entire class of nuclear weapons—ground-launched intermediate-range nuclear-force missiles.

Perhaps Reagan's ultimate accolade from the nation's voters was their elevation of his vice president and preferred successor, George Bush, to the Oval Office. In winning the party's nomination and then the presidency in 1988, Bush portrayed himself as the rightful heir to the Reagan legacy.

1975-1977:
THE NINETY-FOURTH CONGRESS

The years 1975–1976 gave America a significant respite from the high political temperature of the previous several years. With Richard Nixon out of office and the Vietnam War over, the two great issues that had convulsed the country for so long were gone. But even as the country was cooling off, it found itself stalemated on the prime issues facing it. Congress and the president failed to agree on a workable energy program. A strategic arms limitation treaty with the Soviet Union was put off. And while inflation lessened, unemployment jumped to alarming heights.

As the Ninety-fourth Congress opened, there were clear differences over what steps to take to cure the continuing economic ills of inflation and recession. The Democrats were calling for a massive tax cut, emergency jobs for the unemployed, housing construction subsidies, an end to certain tax shelters, and other proposals aimed at closing tax loopholes.

Ford, who in late 1974 had called for a tax increase to combat inflation, in March 1975 reluctantly agreed to a tax cut package drafted by the Democrats that was retroactive to January 1. He and his advisers insisted that it was just as important to fight inflation as to reduce taxes. For this reason, he vetoed as too inflationary the Democrats' bill to create more than one million jobs; the veto was sustained by Congress even though the national unemployment rate was climbing to its high of 9.2 percent in May. Ford subsequently made an about-face and agreed to a compromise version that had a lower price tag but contained many of the same jobs programs.

No subject consumed more time during the first session of the Ninety-fourth Congress than energy legislation. But despite the amount of time expended in debate and hearings on energy issues, the legislation enacted fell far short of setting a national energy policy. Congress and the White House were deadlocked on fundamental energy questions, with Ford unable to sell his programs and the Democratic majority unable to draft viable alternatives. After a temporary compromise allowed extension of energy controls until mid-December, a more lasting resolution was attained under which controls would continue until early 1979.

In 1976 Congress generally agreed with the administration's request for increased defense spending. Impressed by evidence of a Soviet military buildup, Congress gave the Defense Department virtually all Ford had requested and accepted the principle that defense spending must continue to grow beyond the amount needed to cover inflation.

The 1976 Campaigns

Both parties witnessed an intense struggle for the presidential nominations in 1976, with President Ford barely surviving an effort by former California governor Ronald Reagan to deny him the Republican nomination and the Democrats selecting an obscure former governor of Georgia, Jimmy Carter.

Because of the scandals of the Nixon regime and the perceived weakness of the Ford administration, Carter was heavily favored to take the presidency at the beginning of the fall campaign. But the race gradually narrowed, until on election day Carter won by only 2.1 percentage points.

Carter's nomination represented a repudiation of the political establishment by Democratic primary voters. Such well-known names as Sen. Henry M. Jackson of Washington, Gov. George C. Wallace of Alabama, 1972 vice-presidential nominee Sargent Shriver, and Rep. Morris K. Udall of Arizona, all fell before the little-known Georgian who espoused an anti-Washington rhetoric combined with an appeal to the old virtues. Tired of political corruption and what they perceived as too much government interference in their lives, voters responded positively to Carter's appeal, despite his lack of experience in the federal government.

On December 2, 1974, Carter announced his candidacy for the 1976 presidential nomination. His speech before the National Press Club included most of the themes of his campaign: restoration of public trust in government; reforms to make government more open and more efficient; a comprehensive energy policy; thorough tax reform; "a simplified, fair, and compassionate welfare program"; and a comprehensive national health program.

Carter won the New Hampshire primary February 24 with 28.4 percent in a field of nine candidates, including write-ins. In Massachusetts on March 2, Carter ran behind Jackson, Udall, and Wallace but picked up sixteen delegates. The same day he won Vermont's advisory primary with more than 42 percent against three other candidates. His next major test came March 9 in Florida, where he had vowed to defeat Wallace. When all the votes were counted, Carter had beaten Wallace 34.5 to 30.5 percent. Jackson was third with 23.9. Most observers felt that if Jackson had stayed out of the race Carter's victory over Wallace would have been much stronger.

Carter ended the longest primary season ever with 38.8 percent of all votes cast. Of the twenty-seven presidential preference primaries, Carter finished first in seventeen and second in eight. On the way to the nomination, he eliminated a dozen candidates who entered the campaign and showed enough strength to block his greatest potential rival, Sen. Hubert H. Humphrey.

Jimmy Carter brought the Democratic Party's diverse elements together in July at its national convention. The four-day convention in New York City was the party's most harmonious in twelve years and a stark contrast to the bitter and divisive conventions of 1968 and 1972.

Balloting for president was merely a formality. Besides Carter, three other names were placed in nomination: Udall,

California governor Jerry Brown, and antiabortion crusader Ellen McCormack. The proceedings, however, turned into a love-feast as Udall before the balloting and Brown afterwards appeared at the convention to declare their support for Carter. On the presidential roll call, Carter received 2,238 of the convention's 3,008 votes, topping the needed majority a little more than halfway through the balloting with the vote from Ohio. The following morning Carter announced that his choice for vice president was Minnesota senator Walter F. Mondale.

Gerald Ford ran his campaign on his two-year performance record as president. The plan was to cultivate the image of an America healed of its divisive internal wounds, involved in a promising economic recovery, and at peace both at home and abroad. In doing this Ford had many of the incumbent's powers of policy making, media access, and patronage. All of these were to be used against Ronald Reagan, who announced his candidacy November 20, 1975.

Ford began early to capitalize on his position, spending considerable time in the fall of 1975 traveling across the country. Knowing that Reagan would have to make bold stands on key issues, Ford hoped to remain presidential in his own low-key manner.

At first the plan seemed to work. Ford won New Hampshire by about 1,500 votes. In Florida, where he was once thought far behind, the president was helped by older voters' fears that Reagan would alter the Social Security system. Ford scored a convincing victory. Following a big win in Illinois March 16, Ford strategists hoped to build a party consensus that would force Reagan to withdraw and support the president's nomination before the campaign moved into Reagan's Sun Belt strongholds. As they had done privately before the campaign had begun, Ford's supporters began publicly urging Reagan to pull out of the race in the name of party unity. It was at that point that the plan, as scheduled, began to bog down.

Reagan scored a series of important victories in the South and Southwest. By mid-May the Ford candidacy had fallen behind in the convention delegate count. Ford survived with a large victory in his home state of Michigan on May 18, breaking Reagan's momentum. Added to that victory were stepped-up efforts to cash in on Ford's incumbency with a flurry of patronage in key primary states and more effective usage of Ford's access to the press. The two candidates split the six May 25 primaries evenly, with Ford taking Kentucky, Tennessee, and Oregon. The border state wins were interpreted as a success for Ford, showing he could compete with Reagan for conservative votes.

The president finally regained the edge in the delegate count in late May by persuading his technically uncommitted supporters in New York and Pennsylvania to declare for him. Ford ended the primary season with an easy win in New Jersey and a hefty margin in Ohio. Reagan kept close with a landslide victory in California, ensuring that the nomination would turn on the status of the uncommitted delegates to the convention.

The Republican delegates arrived in Kansas City for their convention in August more evenly split than they had been since 1952. Both President Ford, breaking with tradition, and Ronald Reagan arrived in town three days before the balloting to continue their pursuit of delegates.

On the presidential roll call, Reagan, bolstered by the votes in California and some Deep South states, took a healthy lead. But Ford's strength in the big northeastern states—New York, New Jersey, Pennsylvania, Connecticut, Ohio—and others such as Minnesota and Illinois pushed Ford ahead. There was a pause as the Virginia delegation was individually polled. And then West Virginia put the president over the top.

The final vote was 1,187 for Ford, 1,070 for Reagan, one vote from the New York delegation for Commerce Secretary Elliot L. Richardson, and one abstention. On a voice vote the convention made the nomination unanimous.

Ford the next day selected Sen. Robert Dole of Kansas as his running mate after Reagan ruled out his acceptance of the second spot. Dole was seen as an effective gut fighter against the Carter forces who would allow Ford to keep his campaign style presidential.

Ford's basic campaign strategy was to portray himself as an experienced leader, a calm and reasonable man who had restored openness and respect to the presidency. Carter's strategy was to attack Ford as an inept leader who lacked the imagination and instincts to move the country forward.

Also campaigning was Eugene J. McCarthy, who ran as an Independent, unaffiliated with any party. The McCarthy campaign was aimed at people who had been frequent nonvoters in the past, a group making up nearly half the potential electorate. The Democrats, however, saw the McCarthy voter as a liberal Democrat who would choose Carter over Ford in a two-way race.

Results of the 1976 Elections

On November 2 Jimmy Carter swept the South, took a majority in the East, and did well enough in the Midwest to struggle home with a victory. But it was not easy. Carter's win in Ohio by 11,000 votes still left him with the smallest electoral college margin since Woodrow Wilson won reelection in 1916. Without Ohio's twenty-five electoral votes, Carter's total would have dropped to 272, giving him the smallest edge in a hundred years.

In several states McCarthy's Independent candidacy appeared to have tipped the balance to Ford, although in the national popular vote count McCarthy made little impact, receiving less than 1 percent of the total.

Carter won by welding together varying proportions of Roosevelt's New Deal coalition: the South, the industrial Northeast, organized labor, minorities, and the liberal community. Carter won majorities in each of these regions and voting groups and made a better than usual showing for a Democratic candidate in the rural Midwest.

Ford made his best showing in the West, winning 53 percent of the popular vote and carrying all but one state, Hawaii. Neither Ford nor Carter ran well in the region during the primaries, but the president benefited from traditional Republican strength and the absence of an intensive Carter effort in the region to score a series of one-sided victories.

An unusual number of new people were elected to the Senate in 1976, but it changed little in ideology and none at all in party lineup. Voters turned nine incumbent senators out of office, more than in any year since 1958. But they took care to treat both parties about the same way, and when the Ninety-fifth Congress convened in January, there were sixty-two Senate Democrats and thirty-eight Republicans, just as there were in the Senate that had left in October.

It was an extraordinarily large freshman class—eighteen, including the replacement for Vice President-elect Mondale. Ten of the first-termers were Democrats; eight were Republicans. The large-scale rejection of incumbents had not been expected. The nine who lost represented more than one-third of all the incumbents seeking reelection. By some stroke of challengers' luck, virtually every senator who found himself in a difficult race lost.

Three Democratic senators in the "class of 1958"—Vance Hartke of Indiana, Gale W. McGee of Wyoming, and Frank E. Moss of Utah—lost decisively. The other four were easy winners. They were Robert C. Byrd of West Virginia, Harrison A. Williams Jr. of New Jersey, Howard W. Cannon of Nevada, and Edmund S. Muskie of Maine.

But the group of senators that did worst in 1976 was the Republican "class of 1970," who had won their first terms six years earlier with Nixon administration help. All six senators ran for second terms in 1976, and four were beaten: J. Glenn Beall Jr. of Maryland, Bill Brock of Tennessee, James L. Buckley of New York (elected as a Conservative), and Robert Taft Jr. of Ohio.

The classes of 1958 and 1970 thus accounted for seven of the nine incumbent defeats on November 2. The other two beaten incumbents were Democrats John V. Tunney of California and Joseph M. Montoya of New Mexico.

The ten new Democrats were Dennis DeConcini of Arizona, Spark M. Matsunaga of Hawaii, John Melcher of Montana, Howard M. Metzenbaum of Ohio, Daniel Patrick Moynihan of New York, Donald W. Riegle Jr. of Michigan, Paul S. Sarbanes of Maryland, Jim Sasser of Tennessee, Edward Zorinsky of Nebraska, and Wendell R. Anderson, appointed from Minnesota.

The eight new Republicans were John H. Chafee of Rhode Island, John C. Danforth of Missouri, Orrin G. Hatch of Utah, S. I. "Sam" Hayakawa of California, John Heinz of Pennsylvania, Richard G. Lugar of Indiana, Harrison "Jack" Schmitt of New Mexico, and Malcolm Wallop of Wyoming.

In the House the Democratic freshmen taught the Republicans a lesson in the power of incumbency, winning reelection almost unanimously to ensure a Democratic majority by the same 2–1 margin the party held in the Ninety-fourth Congress. Democrats won 292 House seats, and the Republicans, 143.

The Democratic freshmen used the perquisites of office with consummate skill to build political strength and resist close identification with the rest of Congress and the federal bureaucracy. The nationwide Republican effort to brand them as big-spending radicals flopped and left the House GOP in the same minority status as before the elections.

Only thirteen House incumbents—eight Democrats and five Republicans—lost their seats. This was far below the number retired by the voters in 1974, when thirty-six Republicans and four Democrats were defeated in the Watergate landslide that raised the Democrats to overwhelming dominance in the chamber.

The majority of the open Democratic seats were safe, while most of the Republican ones were up for grabs, and many were won by the Democrats. The GOP held onto only nine of its seventeen seats while winning three held by Democrats, for a net loss of five in this open category.

In gubernatorial races the Democrats gained one more governorship, defeating Republican candidates in nine states out of the fourteen. The new lineup was thirty-seven Democrats, twelve Republicans, and one Independent, James B. Longley of Maine. Most of the races for governor ended as expected. Voters reelected five incumbents, defeated two others, and elected nine new governors.

The one real upset was in Missouri, where Democrat Joseph P. Teasdale defeated Republican governor Christopher S. "Kit" Bond by 13,000 votes. Bond, Missouri's first GOP governor since World War II, was expected to win a second term.

Four states—Montana, North Dakota, Utah, and Washington—chose Ford over Carter but elected Democratic governors. Delaware voted for Carter but elected a Republican as governor.

1977–1979:
THE NINETY-FIFTH CONGRESS

With a new and unknown president taking office in January 1977, Congress and the nation waited expectantly to see how Carter would tackle the intractable problems of energy and the economy. In addition, the new president would have to work out a constructive relationship with a Congress that had asserted its power after a long period of presidential dominance. It was also a Congress that had selected new Democratic leadership on both sides of the Capitol, caused by the retirement of Senate Majority Leader Mike Mansfield, D-Mont., and House Speaker Carl Albert, D-Okla.

In foreign affairs the country was at peace, but the administration had to plunge into the labyrinths of relations with the Soviet Union and China and wrestle with attempts to achieve peace in the Middle East.

Carter did not hesitate to get to work on these difficult problems, early proposing an economic stimulus package and an energy program. It soon became clear, however, that major roadblocks stood in the way of enacting significant legislation, especially in the energy area.

The lack of consensus on crucial issues, both in Congress and among the public, was one problem. Another was the continued rivalry between the legislative and executive branches, with congressional leaders accusing the new administration of ineptness and lack of leadership and the executive pointing to Congress's inherent inability to lead.

The partial deadlock reflected the malaise of a country that seemed to be ending its era of predominance in the world and continued economic expansion at home. How the country would cope with the new era remained unclear at the close of 1978.

The House installed Thomas P. "Tip" O'Neill Jr., D-Mass., as Speaker. In a sharp contest for House majority leader, moderate representative Jim Wright of Texas won out. In the Senate, Democratic whip Robert C. Byrd of West Virginia was chosen unanimously as the new majority leader. Republicans also had a

President Jimmy Carter, center, grasps hands with Egyptian president Anwar Sadat and Israeli prime minister Menachem Begin at the signing of the Camp David peace accords on March 26, 1979.

leadership contest for Senate minority leader, with Sen. Howard H. Baker Jr., R-Tenn., the victor.

In January 1978 President Carter presented Congress with his major tax cut and reform program. After working on taxes most of the year, Congress gave final approval October 15 to an $18.7 billion tax cut for 1979 that included a substantial reduction in the tax on capital gains. The bill provided individual income tax reductions that were designed to offset Social Security and inflation-induced tax increases for 1979. In addition, it provided about 4.3 million taxpayers—mostly in the middle- and upper-income ranges—with generous capital gains tax reductions. For businesses, the bill included a reduction in corporate income tax rates and expanded investment tax credits.

In April 1977 Carter introduced his energy policy. For most of 1978 the measure was bogged down in the conference committee trying to resolve differences over the natural gas pricing section. Finally, on October 15, 1978, Congress cleared the bill and sent it to the president.

In the summer of 1977 a political scandal hit the Carter administration that damaged the president's popularity. Questions were raised in the press about the propriety of a number of transactions that Bert Lance, Carter's director of the Office of Management and Budget, had engaged in during his banking career. The Lance matter preoccupied the White House until Lance's resignation in September 1977.

The Carter administration in 1977 laid the groundwork for two treaties with Panama, which were ratified by the Senate in April 1978. One would turn over the Panama Canal to Panama by the year 2000; the second guaranteed the United States' right to defend the canal after that date.

Carter's greatest foreign policy triumph came in September 1978 when he met at Camp David with Egyptian president Anwar Sadat and Israeli prime minister Menachem Begin to hammer out the outlines of a Middle East peace. The success of that effort gave Carter a major boost in prestige and in the polls. And it laid the groundwork for a possible solution to the thirty-year-old Middle East conflict.

President Carter had one more big foreign policy surprise for 1978. In a joint communiqué issued December 15, the United States and the People's Republic of China announced that they would formally recognize each other January 1, 1979, and would exchange ambassadors and establish embassies March 1. This announcement ended another long-standing dispute: the thirty-eight-year refusal of the United States to recognize the Communists as the rulers of China.

The 1978 Midterm Elections

Republicans in the 1978 midterm campaign were curiously unable to capitalize on their own carefully developed issues in what ought to have been their kind of year. Without a Republican president to have to defend, GOP congressional candidates were free to run against every branch of the federal government, an approach that brought them enormous gains the last time they tried it, in 1966. Besides, the rise of tax resentment gave them a drum to beat, and they pounded on it in virtually every contested congressional district in the country.

Humiliated by their failure to gain any House or Senate seats at all in 1976, Republicans redesigned their strategy for the 1978 campaign. In the House they abandoned their attempts to defeat many of the Democrats first elected in 1974, switching to place their emphasis on older incumbents weak in constituent service and name identification. In both the House and Senate they involved themselves in primaries to see that promising candidates won.

But Republican leaders made one other decision that did not work as well as they had hoped: they chose to base congressional campaigns throughout the country on a plan, proposed by Rep. Jack F. Kemp of New York and Sen. William V. Roth Jr. of Delaware, to cut federal income taxes by one-third. It was difficult to find a Republican nominee in any contested state or district who did not talk about Kemp-Roth.

The Republican approach allowed Democratic opponents to seize the popular side of the issue by charging that a Kemp-Roth tax cut was inflationary. Democrats insisted that spending cuts were the proper course, co-opting normal Republican rhetoric.

Results of the 1978 Elections

The 1978 elections produced a Republican gain of three seats in the Senate, along with the second largest freshman Senate class in the history of popular elections. The new Senate lineup for the Ninety-sixth Congress was fifty-nine Democrats and forty-one Republicans. The Democratic total included Harry F. Byrd Jr. of Virginia, elected as an Independent. While the GOP increase was not overwhelming, it was slightly greater than what GOP officials themselves expected a year before.

The GOP newcomers included Nancy Landon Kassebaum of Kansas, the first woman elected to the Senate without being preceded in Congress by her husband, and Thad Cochran, the first Republican senator elected in Mississippi since 1875. The only black in the Senate during the Ninety-fifth Congress, Edward W. Brooke of Massachusetts, was defeated.

The large freshman classes of 1976 and 1978 differed markedly from their counterparts of the previous generation. The new freshman classes represented no distinct national trends. The 1976 class of eighteen was composed of eight Republicans and ten Democrats, and the 1978 newcomers included eleven Republicans and nine Democrats. The large Senate turnover in the 1970s meant that nearly half the members—forty-eight—were in their first terms as of January 1979.

The most notable conservative gains in the Senate occurred in Iowa, where Republican Roger Jepsen unseated incumbent Dick Clark, and in New Hampshire, where incumbent Democrat Thomas J. McIntyre lost to Gordon Humphrey.

The Democratic class of 1972 turned out to be somewhat more vulnerable than the Republican group. Democrats lost Clark, William D. Hathaway of Maine, and Floyd K. Haskell of Colorado. In addition to their defeats, the seat of retiring Democratic senator James Abourezk of South Dakota was captured by the Republicans.

Freshmen Democrats included Howell Heflin and Donald Stewart (both of Alabama), David Pryor (Arkansas), Paul E. Tsongas (Massachusetts), Carl Levin (Michigan), Max Baucus (Montana), J. James Exon (Nebraska), Bill Bradley (New Jersey), and David L. Boren (Oklahoma). Republican newcomers were William L. Armstrong (Colorado), William S. Cohen (Maine), Rudy Boschwitz and David Durenberger (Minnesota), Larry Pressler (South Dakota), John Warner (Virginia), and Alan K. Simpson (Wyoming).

In the House, Republicans made modest inroads on the lopsided Democratic majority, making a net gain of eleven seats. But Democrats remained in firm control, winning 277 seats to 158 for the GOP. With a record fifty-eight open seats in the House, Republicans hoped to make their biggest gains in the thirty-nine open districts held by Democrats. But that strategy brought only a net gain of two, as Republicans captured eight Democratic-held open seats but lost six of their nineteen vacant seats to the Democrats.

Campaigning against incumbents, usually a harder task, proved surprisingly successful for the GOP, as fourteen Democratic House members were defeated, compared to five Republicans. It was the largest number of Democratic defeats since 1966, when thirty-nine House Democrats, many of them brought in during the 1964 presidential landslide, lost their jobs.

In gubernatorial politics Republicans moved a step closer to respectability, increasing the number of statehouses under their control from twelve to eighteen. William Clements's upset election in Texas, Richard L. Thornburgh's come-from-behind triumph in Pennsylvania, and James A. Rhodes's narrow survival in Ohio guaranteed that the GOP would enter the 1980 election year with governors in five of the ten "megastates." That news diluted the Republican disappointment at failing to oust Democratic governor Hugh L. Carey in New York or even to come close against incumbent Democrat Jerry Brown in California.

1979–1981:
THE NINETY-SIXTH CONGRESS

The first session of the Ninety-sixth Congress passed into history as a contradiction. Members came to Washington in 1979 spurred by a nationwide antigovernment mood. Legisla-

tors, even some of the more liberal ones, talked bravely of the need to limit federal spending. Contrary to the rhetoric, which continued throughout the year, that session of Congress voted for massive new spending efforts and laid the groundwork for significant new federal involvement in the lives of American businesses and citizens.

The most massive expansion of the federal role was in the package of energy legislation, which was the focus of congressional debate most of the year. It called for spending billions of dollars on synthetic fuels development and imposing a major federal presence in the energy industry. It also was a year when advocates of more defense spending finally recouped from the travails of the Vietnam era and won a pledge of extra billions for the military from a president who initially opposed such increases.

Support for the energy package was grounded in troubled U.S. relations with oil-exporting nations and a continuing upward spiral in the cost of imported oil. Those trends were exacerbated by the crumbling of relations between the United States and Iran after militant Iranians seized the U.S. Embassy in Tehran and held fifty-three Americans hostage for the return of that nation's deposed shah, Mohammed Reza Pahlavi.

Advocates of higher defense spending, using the Iranian hostage situation as an example, argued more vigorously than ever before that America's strength and influence in the world were declining and that U.S. military strength was falling far behind that of the Soviet Union.

But if Congress acted with determination on energy and some other issues, it acted virtually not at all on the economic troubles of the nation. Faced with double-digit inflation and the threatened onset of a recession, Congress—much like the president—did not seem to know what to do. It appeared both were marking time until 1980 to decide whether federal action would help or worsen America's economic problems.

Congress showed little interest in social, consumer, and environmental legislation. The realization was growing that the federal budget was not open-ended and that government spending decisions required some distasteful choices. Nevertheless, members approved Carter's request to create a separate Department of Education.

In 1980, facing an aggressive and unified Republican Party and worried by its own reputation for big spending, the Democratic-controlled Congress began the election year concentrating on trimming programs in order to balance the federal budget. A recession combined with spiraling inflation soon dashed the Democrats' balanced-budget hopes. But these new economic woes also did nothing to encourage the Democrats to resume pushing for some of their favorite programs. In addition, because of escalating campaign pressures, Democratic leaders delayed until after the election consideration of the budget and a number of other key bills.

By year's end, however, the Democrats found their scheme had backfired. Instead of rewarding them for their restraint, the elections had deprived them of their control of the White House and Senate and put them in a substantially weaker position in the House in 1981.

The 1980 *Campaigns*

President Carter won enough delegates in his party's primaries and caucuses to win the Democratic presidential nomination. But he faced significant opposition at the convention from Sen. Edward M. Kennedy of Massachusetts. Carter led Kennedy throughout the primary season, but as the convention neared, the momentum seemed to be with Kennedy. Although Carter continued to win more caucus delegates, Kennedy won five of the last eight primaries, which kept him in contention.

At the same time, the president's position in the popularity polls dropped, and Carter found himself in the midst of an embarrassing controversy over his brother Billy's connection with the Libyan government.

Alarmed by Carter's apparently diminishing reelection prospects, several party leaders grew concerned that a Carter defeat in November would drag down dozens of state and local candidates across the country. They called for an "open convention" that could nominate a compromise candidate. And they teamed up with Senator Kennedy to urge defeat of a proposed convention rule that would bind all delegates to vote on the first ballot for the candidate under whose banner they were elected.

When the convention opened, Carter could count 1,981.1 delegates pledged to him—315 more than he needed for the nomination. Kennedy had 1,225.8 delegates, and the only chance he had to gain the nomination was to defeat the rule. There were 122.1 uncommitted delegates and two for other candidates.

In the days before the convention opening Kennedy strategists claimed that there were continuing defections from the Carter camp. On Sunday they said they were within fifty to a hundred votes of the majority needed to overturn the rule binding the delegates. But the Kennedy predictions and hopes proved to be exaggerated. The final tally on the rule showed 1,936.418 delegates favoring the binding rule and 1,390.580 opposing it. Passage of the rule ensured Carter's renomination. Shortly after the vote, Kennedy ended his nine-month challenge to the president by announcing that his name would not be placed in nomination on August 13.

But Kennedy did not withdraw from the platform debate. The bitterly contested party platform pitted Carter against Kennedy and a coalition of special interest groups. The final document was filled with so many concessions to the Kennedy forces that it won only a halfhearted endorsement from the president.

Kennedy capped his platform victories with an August 12 appearance before the delegates in which he presented a stunning speech to a tumultuous ovation. His speech created a sense of enormous energy within the hall and left the feeling that a significant political event had occurred.

By the following day Carter began to reassert control over the convention. In a statement issued just hours after the platform debate ended, the president refused to accept—as diplomatically as possible—many of the platform revisions. In his carefully worded statement, Carter did not flatly reject any of Kennedy's amendments, but he did not embrace them either. Carter concluded his statement with the unity refrain that had become the hallmark of every White House comment on the

platform since the drafting process began: "The differences within our party on this platform are small in comparison with the differences between the Republican and Democratic party platforms."

Carter won his party's presidential nomination on the first ballot, and his vice president, Walter F. Mondale, easily won renomination. Kennedy pledged his support and even made a brief appearance at the podium with Carter and Mondale as the convention drew to a close. But it was uncertain whether the appeals for unity had succeeded.

On the Republican side Ronald Reagan had carefully cultivated an image as the presumed GOP front-runner for 1980 from the day Gerald Ford was defeated by Carter in 1976. During the primaries Reagan lost only four of the state preference primaries he entered. In states that chose their delegates in caucuses, Reagan was even more impressive, winning just under 400 of the 478 delegates picked by caucuses. But it was in the early primaries that Reagan was able to pare the field from a half-dozen major candidates to just two.

In South Carolina on March 8 Reagan knocked former Texas governor John B. Connally out of the race. Ten days later he deflated John B. Anderson's surging campaign with a victory in the representative's home state of Illinois. A similar result two weeks later in Wisconsin forced Anderson out of the GOP contest and into an unsuccessful Independent bid for the White House.

After four quick defeats Senate minority leader Howard H. Baker Jr. of Tennessee dropped out. Neither Rep. Philip M. Crane of Illinois nor Sen. Robert Dole of Kansas had ever caught the voters' attention. And on March 15 former president Gerald Ford put to rest growing speculation that he might jump into the race in an effort to stop Reagan. By April the GOP contest was reduced to former Texas representative George Bush's frantic efforts to catch Reagan in a few major states. It was too little, too late.

Having outdistanced all the competition, Reagan easily won his party's 1980 nomination at the Republican National Convention in Detroit. Reagan won on the first ballot, receiving 1,939 of the 1,994 delegate votes. His nomination was then made unanimous.

The unusual flap over the selection of the vice-presidential nominee provided the only suspense at the convention. Rumors circulated that Ford was being tapped for the second spot. Ford himself had encouraged that speculation, although he declined to spell out his conditions. It became clear he wanted responsibilities that would have made him, in effect, co-president with Reagan. Late on July 16 the Reagan-Ford arrangement fell apart, and the two men agreed that it would be better for Ford to campaign for the GOP ticket than to be a member of it. The speculation prompted Reagan to make an unusual visit to the convention hall at 12:15 a.m. on July 17 to announce his choice of George Bush as his running mate.

The American hostage crisis was injected into the campaign in the eleventh hour when Iranian leaders miscalculated that Carter would accept their demands in return for release of the hostages before election day. Although Carter tried to keep the negotiations—which reached a peak during the weekend before

November 4—out of the campaign, the publicity given them so close to the election worked against the president.

But what hurt Carter the most, in the opinion of many analysts, was his inability to improve the state of the economy. Throughout the fall campaign, Reagan blamed Carter for almost tripling the inflation rate he had inherited from the Ford administration. During 1980 the rate averaged about 13 percent.

Results of the 1980 Elections

No one publicly forecast the rout that developed election night. Reagan's triumph was nationwide. In most of the states that were expected to be close or to go for Carter, Reagan won, frequently by comfortable margins. In states Reagan was expected to carry, he won overwhelmingly.

Reagan easily carried every region of the country, including the keystones of Carter's victory four years before—the industrial Northeast and the president's native South.

Reagan carried forty-four states in all, for a total of 489 electoral votes. Carter, the first Democratic incumbent president denied reelection since 1888, won only six states and the District of Columbia for a total of forty-nine electoral votes.

The Republican victory did not stop with the presidency. The GOP won control of the Senate for the first time in a quarter-century. Although the Democrats retained their majority in the House, the national shift to the political right combined with a variety of scandals, complacency by some incumbents, and unusually strong Reagan coattails cost the Democrats a net loss of thirty-three seats in the House. That made the Republicans twenty-six seats shy of controlling the House, although conservative Democrats were expected to give the GOP an ideological edge on many issues.

The twelve Senate seats won by Republicans represented the largest net gain in the Senate for any party since 1958, when the Democrats took control over fifteen new seats. The new lineup was fifty-three Republicans and forty-seven Democrats. The 1980 GOP Senate victory was the first since 1952 and ended the longest one-party dominance of the Senate in American history.

In addition to their increases the Republicans held on to the ten seats that were up in 1980. That included holding three open seats in Pennsylvania, Oklahoma, and North Dakota and the New York seat of Republican senator Jacob K. Javits, who was defeated for renomination in the primary but ran for reelection on the Liberal Party ticket.

Democrats had twenty-four seats up in 1980 and lost half of them. Not only would the Senate be more Republican; it would be noticeably more conservative. Several pillars of Democratic liberalism went down to defeat, including George McGovern of South Dakota, Warren G. Magnuson of Washington, and John C. Culver of Iowa.

To replace the Democrats, Republicans elected a freshman Senate class made up largely of dedicated conservatives. Representatives Charles E. Grassley of Iowa, Steven D. Symms of Idaho, James Abdnor of South Dakota, and Robert W. Kasten Jr. of Wisconsin had compiled distinctively conservative records in the House. John P. East of North Carolina, an expert in conserv-

ative political thought, was expected to carry out his beliefs in the Senate.

But there was a contingent of Republican moderates that could leaven some of the conservative impulses. Warren Rudman of New Hampshire, Arlen Specter of Pennsylvania, and Slade Gorton of Washington all were from the moderate wing of their party.

Among the losing Democrats were four of the six prime targets of the National Conservative Political Action Committee, which prepared hard-hitting ads attacking the records of liberal senators. The targeted senators were Birch Bayh of Indiana, Culver of Iowa, McGovern of South Dakota, Thomas F. Eagleton of Missouri, Frank Church of Idaho, and Alan Cranston of California. Bayh, Culver, McGovern, and Church went down to defeat.

In the House the lineup going into the election was 273 Democrats to 159 Republicans. There also were three vacancies that had been held by Democrats. After the November vote, the new lineup was 243 Democrats to 192 Republicans. The Democratic total included one Independent.

The Republican net gain of thirty-three seats was the largest increase for the GOP since 1966. Most of the GOP gains came at the expense of incumbents. In all, thirty-one of the 392 incumbents running for reelection were turned out. Of those, twenty-seven were Democrats who lost to Republicans. Only three incumbent Republicans were defeated.

There were seventy-four new faces in the new House, three fewer than in 1978. Republican freshmen had the edge with fifty-two seats, compared to twenty-two for the Democrats. Four new women—all Republicans—were elected, bringing the total number of women in the House to nineteen. There were four black freshmen, for a total of seventeen black voting members. All were Democrats.

Republicans increased their hold on governorships by four states, bringing their nationwide total to twenty-three. Democrats still maintained a lead, with twenty-seven governors' chairs. The Republican additions came in states west of the Mississippi River: Arkansas, Missouri, North Dakota, and Washington.

The Republican gain continued the party's gradual comeback on the gubernatorial level. After 1968, when the party won thirty-one governorships compared with the Democrats' nineteen, GOP gubernatorial fortunes slid to a low of twelve in 1977. The party began to make gains again in 1978, boosting its total by six. In 1979 the GOP added another governor in Louisiana.

Despite the party's success in gubernatorial races, Republicans advanced only negligibly in state legislatures, which were to redraw political boundaries in post-1980 census redistricting.

1981–1983:
THE NINETY-SEVENTH CONGRESS

Dominated by Republicans for the first time in two and a half decades and guided by a forceful and popular president, Congress took bold steps in 1981 toward reducing the federal government's scope. Following the wishes of President Reagan, the Ninety-seventh Congress slashed government spending, cut taxes for individuals and business, and slimmed down federal regulatory activities.

The 1980 elections not only swept a conservative Republican into the White House but also floated the GOP into its first Senate majority since January 1955. The change in control meant that committee leadership shifted to the Republicans and that the Democrats were relegated to minority leadership. The new Senate majority leader was Howard H. Baker Jr. of Tennessee.

In the House the Democrats, under the leadership of Tip O'Neill of Massachusetts, were still in the majority, though by a slimmer margin (243–192) than they enjoyed in the previous Congress. And the conservative leanings of many of their numbers made the Democratic leadership's grasp on House proceedings tentative at times.

When Reagan entered office in January 1981, he laid out what appeared to some to be contradictory goals for his presidency. To revitalize the economy and strengthen the nation, he would cut federal spending yet increase spending for defense, reduce taxes yet balance the budget. Many traditional Republicans in Congress were uneasy with this "supply-side" economic approach. But the GOP leaders in both houses proved to be effective and loyal lieutenants for their president.

Congress enacted $35.2 billion in fiscal 1982 program reductions, cut nearly $4 billion more from appropriations, approved a cut in individual and business taxes totaling $749 billion over a five-year period, and added about $18 billion to the fiscal 1982 defense budget drafted by President Carter the year before. But the federal deficit for the year appeared to be heading over the $100 billion mark, and the economy was in recession. In the process of getting his program enacted, Reagan exhausted his winning coalition, stretched congressional procedures out of shape, and bruised sensitive legislative egos.

Almost all the sweeping budget cuts Congress approved were made in one package, the budget "reconciliation" bill. The use of the reconciliation method in such a massive way was criticized by some members as an abuse of the budget process. The budget bill touched on virtually every federal activity except defense. Included in it were a multitude of changes in existing law, including provisions to tighten eligibility for public assistance, cut funds for subsidized housing programs, reduce school lunch subsidies, and cut Medicaid payments to the states.

In September, when Reagan proposed a second package of $13 billion in further spending cuts and $3 billion in unspecified revenue increases for 1982, the president's coalition began to crumble. Even members who had worked hard for Reagan's first round of cuts had no stomach for a second in a single year. Moderate House Republicans threatened to desert him unless he shielded their pet programs. Conservative Democrats threatened to bail out over the growing deficit, and the Reagan team was split over the question of tax increases.

The president maintained symbolic pressure on Congress to make additional spending cuts, even bringing the government to a halt for a day in late November by vetoing a temporary funding resolution. But Congress was unwilling to make the cuts he demanded. The appropriations process ground to a halt, and the government limped through the end of the year on a series of temporary funding resolutions.

On defense, Congress granted Reagan's request for significant spending increases. The $200 billion fiscal 1982 defense appropriation was the largest peacetime appropriations bill ever approved.

Congress grew increasingly independent of the White House in 1982. The legislators adhered to President Reagan's general course of restraining domestic programs while increasing military spending, but they rejected many of the president's specific proposals. They substantially rewrote Reagan's fiscal 1983 budget and persuaded the president to support a large tax increase only a year after passing his three-year tax cut plan.

While modifying or rejecting many of Reagan's requests, Congress did not originate much of its own legislation in 1982. Faced with soaring federal deficits, members spent a lot of their time defending existing programs from budget cuts rather than trying to create new ones.

The 1982 Midterm Elections

The 1982 midterm elections produced major change in the House but left the Senate comparatively untouched. A combination of redistricting and recession produced a huge crop of eighty-one House freshmen, fifty-seven of them Democrats. In the previous thirty years only three other elections had brought in that many new Democrats.

Redistricting played a major role in 1982. This was the election in which reapportionment, the rise of the Sun Belt, and the decline of the Frost Belt were supposed to catch up with the Democrats, setting in motion a decade of conservative and Republican advance of power in the House. But it did not work out that way.

The Sun Belt proved the Republicans' greatest disappointment. The nationwide shift in population away from the industrial North gave southern and western states seventeen new districts, and the GOP at one time hoped to take at least a dozen of them. But Democratic legislative cartography and unfriendly federal court action got in the way, and in the end Democrats won ten of the seventeen.

Results of the 1982 Elections

The only thing remarkable about the 1982 Senate results was the sheer absence of change. Not only did the party ratio remain the same—fifty-four Republicans and forty-six Democrats—but ninety-five of the one hundred senators were incumbents. The class of five newcomers was the smallest in the sixty-eight-year history of popular Senate elections.

That stability was itself a dramatic reversal of recent election trends. During the previous decade a Senate seat had been one of the most difficult offices in U.S. politics to hold. While reelection rates for House incumbents regularly had run above 85 percent, senators struggled against well-financed challengers and effective special interest groups.

The Senate outcome was neither the "ratifying" election that Republicans had hoped for after their landslide of 1980 nor the "correcting" election that Democrats had wanted. But there were favorable results for both parties. Republicans kept their beachhead on Capitol Hill, ensuring that Reagan would be the first Republican president since Herbert Hoover to have a GOP Senate majority throughout his four-year term.

Democrats broke even in an election that could have relegated them to minority status in the Senate for a long time. Of the thirty-three seats that were contested in 1982, the Democrats were defending nineteen. They ended up winning 60.6 percent of the races.

In the House, Democrats scored a twenty-six-seat gain, as voters expressed antipathy toward President Reagan's economic program but stopped short of repudiating it altogether. The outcome revealed an unusual degree of voter frustration with a party only two years into national power.

Democrats won 269 seats to 166 seats for the GOP, giving the Democrats a 103-seat advantage. Going into the election, Democrats held 241 seats and Republicans 192, with vacancies in two districts formerly occupied by Democrats. Twenty-six Republican incumbents and three sitting Democrats were beaten, nearly a mirror image of the 1980 election, in which the GOP lost three incumbents and unseated twenty-eight Democratic members.

Hurt by losses in the economically distressed Midwest, Republicans saw their hold on the nation's governorships dwindle to sixteen in the November 2 elections. The Democrats controlled statehouses in thirty-four states. The GOP's net loss of seven statehouses—the party dropped nine and picked up two—ended a comeback in the party's gubernatorial fortunes. Republicans had been posting gains since 1977, when they hit a low point of twelve governors' chairs.

Of the Republican governors' seats that switched to the Democrats, five were in the Midwest, where the recession had been most acute, hitting both manufacturing and farming. Michigan, Minnesota, Nebraska, Ohio, and Wisconsin opted for Democrats. Republican incumbents were retiring in all these states except Nebraska, where Gov. Charles Thone was turned out.

Republicans also encountered a setback in their progress in the South. They held four of the region's thirteen governorships in 1982; in 1983 they had just two. Only Tennessee's Lamar Alexander won reelection.

In addition, Democrats took over GOP governors' seats in Alaska and Nevada. Republicans assumed power in California, where George Deukmejian edged out Democrat Tom Bradley, and in New Hampshire, where GOP challenger John H. Sununu unseated Democratic incumbent Hugh Gallen. Each party had six open seats at stake. Democrats held all theirs except for California. Republicans managed to retain only Iowa.

Democrats also turned the tables on the GOP in state legislative elections, regaining most of the chambers taken by the Republicans in the previous two elections and ending a six-year decline in the number of legislatures under Democratic control.

1983–1985:
THE NINETY-EIGHTH CONGRESS

Congress and President Reagan generally kept to their own turf in 1983, each going about business with little involvement from the other side. Unlike the first two years of the Reagan administration, when the president essentially wrote the economic script, Congress conducted its 1983 debate on deficits without

President Ronald Reagan and Soviet leader Mikhail Gorbachev confer in Washington. Relations between the two superpowers improved over the course of Reagan and Gorbachev's four summit meetings.

Reagan's overt participation. And while Congress tried to assert itself on foreign policy, Reagan consistently called the global shots.

There were important bipartisan agreements in 1983 on Social Security, jobs legislation, the War Powers Resolution, and fiscal 1984 appropriations bills. But these were rare commodities in a year in which political motivations ranked above policy considerations.

The prime example of this dilemma was the way Congress and Reagan reacted to massive federal deficits. No matter how many experts said soaring deficits hurt the economy, few people were willing to take the politically risky steps needed to cure the problem. Reagan made a calculated decision to stay out of the deficit debate, thereby ducking any responsibility for tax increases his advisers viewed as a 1984 election liability. Antideficit rhetoric was a constant refrain among legislators, but Congress took little decisive action on the issue.

Standing behind Reagan, House Speaker O'Neill in September helped push through a measure allowing the president to keep U.S. troops in Lebanon for up to eighteen months. In backing Reagan on Lebanon, Congress for the first time invoked major parts of the 1973 War Powers Resolution. On October 23, 241 U.S. Marines, sailors, and soldiers and fifty-eight French paratroopers were killed by a terrorist truck bomb in Beirut. Subsequent efforts to revise or revoke the measure keeping troops in Lebanon failed in both houses. Under congressional pressure, Reagan announced in February 1984 that he had ordered the troop withdrawal.

Congress reluctantly continued to back Reagan's policy in Nicaragua. The House twice voted to force Reagan to stop backing rightist forces that were fighting to overthrow that country's leftist government. When the Senate refused to go along, a compromise was reached limiting aid to the rebels and requiring Reagan to seek explicit approval from Congress for additional aid.

Reagan won widespread approval in both chambers for the October 25 invasion of the Caribbean island of Grenada. The president said the invasion was necessary to protect some one thousand Americans, mostly medical students, from civil strife that erupted following the murder of Marxist prime minister Maurice Bishop.

Reagan was victorious in most of his defense fights with Congress. He won the go-ahead for production of the MX missile, although the House came within a handful of votes of killing funding for the project.

On domestic issues Reagan met many disappointments on Capitol Hill in 1984. The president could not persuade Congress to approve his social agenda, which featured constitutional amendments to ban abortion and allow school prayer. Nor did Congress adopt his plan to give tuition tax credits to parents who sent their children to private schools, or his enterprise zone system to provide tax relief to businesses that created jobs in depressed areas.

One of the biggest problems remained the massive federal deficit. Although Congress took actions designed to reduce the deficit by $149 billion over three years, the tax increases and spending cuts were viewed as a mere "down payment" on a larger remedy. While legislators spent much of 1984 talking about the evils of the swelling federal deficit, they took only a first step toward a cure. Instead, many members figured they would deal with the problem in 1985, after the November elections.

The 1984 Campaigns

The focus in the early months of the presidential election was not on Reagan but on the Democratic candidates seeking their party's nomination. Sen. Alan Cranston of California was the first to toss his hat in the ring formally, announcing his candidacy February 2, 1983. But Walter Mondale had informally started his campaign shortly after he and President Jimmy Carter lost to Reagan and George Bush in 1980.

Mondale was never particularly popular with the voters. His public personality and speaking style were bland, his traditional "New Deal" Democratic message seemed stale and, to many, ineffective, and his identification as a candidate of the special interests led voters to look closely and often approvingly at Mondale's competitors.

Before the primaries began, Mondale's main opponent seemed to be John Glenn, senator from Ohio and former astronaut. But the first delegate selection event of the season, the Iowa precinct caucuses of February 20, was disastrous for Glenn as well as for two other conservative Democrats in the race, South Carolina senator Ernest F. Hollings and former Florida governor Reubin Askew. Together these three drew less than 10 percent of the vote. In New Hampshire a week later the results for Glenn, Hollings, and Askew were just as discouraging. Hollings and Askew withdrew from the race.

Other challenges came from Colorado senator Gary Hart and from George McGovern, the former South Dakota senator whose losing 1972 presidential campaign Hart had managed. Glenn and McGovern withdrew from the race after Super Tuesday, leaving in contention Mondale, Hart, and the Rev. Jesse Jackson, the first black to pursue seriously the presidential nomination of any major political party.

Hart's momentum was blunted almost as quickly as it began. In the week after Super Tuesday, he ran behind Mondale in six of seven delegate selection events. Then Mondale got a much-needed boost by winning the New York and Pennsylvania primaries. His chance to eliminate Hart evaporated when Hart won Ohio and Indiana. Mondale continued to lead in the number of delegates committed to him, and with his win in New Jersey June 5 he had enough delegates to win the nomination. But his campaign ended on the same lackluster note that had characterized most of the last four months; the same day Mondale claimed the nomination, Hart won three other primaries including California's.

Despite the difficult, sometimes bitter, primary season campaign, Democrats mustered a display of party unity at their convention in San Francisco and made a historic vice-presidential choice. The Democratic National Convention picked Mondale to be the party standard bearer against President Reagan. As in much of his drive for the nomination, Mondale was almost overshadowed again, this time by the attention generated by his selection of New York representative Geraldine A. Ferraro to be his running mate. Ferraro was the first woman ever chosen for the national ticket by a major party.

President Reagan enjoyed the smoothest road to renomination that any presidential candidate could have. Brimming with confidence that President Reagan and Vice President Bush would be "the winning team" in November, a jubilant Republican Party held its convention in Dallas August 20–23. With the ticket's renomination certain beforehand, the convention was more a celebration for GOP activists than a business meeting. Criticisms from the party's shrinking band of moderates, worried by the strongly conservative tone of the platform, did little to dispel the optimistic mood of delegates, who looked forward with confidence to Reagan's easy reelection victory.

Highlights of the fall campaign were the two presidential debates. The first, held October 7, was focused on domestic issues. Mondale made a strong showing, which lessened his negative image. Equally important was the perception that Reagan turned in a poor performance; the seventy-three-year-old president seemed tired and disorganized, leading journalists and Democrats to suggest that age was catching up with Reagan.

The second debate, on October 21, focusing on foreign affairs, was a draw in the opinion of most analysts. The debate was not a significant boost to Mondale's campaign, and it allowed Reagan to ease concerns about his age and competence raised by his performance during the first debate. The vice-presidential candidates also held a nationally televised debate, on October 11. Most analysts viewed it as a draw or gave a slight edge to Bush.

Almost every thrust Mondale made was effectively parried by his Republican opponents. Mondale's efforts to draw attention to the massive budget deficits run up during Reagan's first term by promising a tax increase did not stand a chance against Reagan's promise not to raise taxes. Similarly, Mondale's attempts to paint Reagan as a man who favored the rich over the poor, the majority over the minority, did not overcome charges that Mondale was a tool of the special interests.

In the end perhaps no Democrat could have defeated Ronald Reagan in 1984. For one thing most voters thought they were better off than they had been four years earlier. (Reagan first asked that question during his 1980 run against Carter and Mondale.) Perhaps more important, voters seemed to respond to Reagan's upbeat attitude and his promise of continued peace and prosperity.

Results of the 1984 Elections

There was never much doubt that Ronald Reagan, one of the most popular presidents in American history, would win reelection in 1984. And it would be hard to imagine a vote more decisive than the balloting that gave him his victory. Winning all but one state, he drew 59 percent of the popular vote, and he won a record 525 electoral votes.

Despite the size of Reagan's victory, its meaning remained unclear. The vote clearly exposed the Democrats' limited appeal in presidential elections. On the other hand, Democrats held their own in other elections. In the Senate, rather than gaining as most presidents do, Reagan lost two seats, reducing the Republican majority to 53–47. In the House of Representatives the president's party gained fourteen seats, far short of the historical average for landslides. The GOP gained one governor for a line-up of sixteen Republicans and thirty-four Democrats. Only in the state legislatures did the Republican Party make gains that could be considered significant.

Neither the Republicans nor the Democrats came away with quite what they wanted from the 1984 struggle for control of the Senate. Democrats had hoped to regain the majority they lost in 1980, when Republicans took control of the Senate for the first time since the 1954 elections. Republicans hoped that President Reagan's march to reelection would bring about a modest reprise of 1980, making the GOP hold on the Senate more secure.

But in this election Reagan was no trailblazer. Democrats retained thirteen of the fourteen seats they were defending, and a trio of Democratic House members captured Republican seats: Illinois representative Paul Simon edged out Sen. Charles H. Percy; Iowa representative Tom Harkin defeated Sen. Roger W. Jepsen; and Tennessee representative Albert Gore Jr. took the seat being vacated by Senate majority leader Howard H. Baker Jr. Countering the good news for the Democrats was an unexpected outcome in Kentucky: the defeat of Sen. Walter "Dee" Huddleston at the hands of Mitch McConnell.

Thus Democrats won a net gain of two Senate seats, shifting the party ratio to fifty-three Republicans and forty-seven Democrats. That standing was an improvement over the preelection ratio of 55–45 but a comedown from the Democrats' 1983 prediction that the party could recapture Senate control by picking up a number of Republican seats Democrats regarded as shaky.

As it turned out, Democrats failed to win most of the GOP seats in the "at risk" category. The biggest Democratic disappointment came in North Carolina, where GOP incumbent Jesse Helms narrowly won his bitter battle with Democratic governor James B. Hunt Jr. It was the most expensive Senate contest up to that time, with the campaigns spending a total of about $22 million.

In four other key states where Democrats had hoped to pull upsets, Republicans prevailed easily: Mississippi senator Thad Cochran won against former governor William Winter; Sen. Gordon J. Humphrey won a second term in New Hampshire; Texas representative Phil Gramm, who switched parties in 1983, replaced retiring GOP senator John Tower; and Sen. Rudy Boschwitz took 58 percent of the vote in Minnesota, encountering no problems with Mondale's coattails because the Democratic presidential nominee barely carried his home state.

For the second time in a little over a decade, Republicans watched with disappointment as their presidential standard bearer swept triumphantly across the nation followed by a threadbare retinue of new U.S. House members. The November 6 elections revealed considerable hesitation nationwide over an all-out endorsement of Republican policies, as voters in district after district stopped short of backing GOP challengers who campaigned on their loyalty to Ronald Reagan. After several closely contested battles were decided, Republicans had gained fourteen seats, falling well short of making up the twenty-six seats they lost in the 1982 midterm elections. One seat, still undecided at year's end, eventually remained Democratic.

Not counting the undecided seat, Democrats retained control of the House with 252 members to the GOP's 182. Going into the election, Democrats held 266 seats and Republicans 167, with vacancies in a New Jersey district previously held by a Republican and in a Kentucky district held by a Democrat. Those seats stayed in their respective parties' hands and were filled for the remainder of the term in special elections. As a result of the election there were forty-three House freshmen in 1985, a small class, due mostly to the relatively low number of open seats in 1984.

The gubernatorial elections did little to dent the Democratic Party's 2–1 advantage in governorships. Republicans notched victories in North Carolina, Rhode Island, Utah, and West Virginia, where the statehouses were left vacant by departing Democratic incumbents. But the Democrats captured three seats, toppling Republican incumbents in North Dakota and Washington and picking up the seat left open by retiring GOP governor Richard A. Snelling in Vermont.

Republicans thus scored a net gain of one seat, boosting the total governorships under their control from fifteen to sixteen and reducing the number of states in the Democratic column from thirty-five to thirty-four. The GOP's showing represented an improvement over 1982, when the party suffered a net loss of seven seats. Republicans still remained a long way, however, from capturing a majority of governorships, a feat they had last accomplished in 1969.

1985–1987:
THE NINETY-NINTH CONGRESS

The Ninety-ninth Congress compiled an extraordinary record. It revised the tax code more dramatically than at any time since World War II, rewrote immigration law, approved the most far-reaching environmental bills since the 1970s, boosted student aid, reversed President Reagan's policy toward South Africa, and joined him in openly seeking to overthrow Nicaragua's leftist government.

Congress seized the legislative initiative from the White House in 1985 and dominated the Capitol Hill agenda to a degree unmatched since President Reagan took office in 1981. Although Reagan was able to rescue his top domestic priority—tax-overhaul legislation—with a last-minute personal lobbying campaign, the close call was a testament to the altered relationship between the White House and Capitol Hill.

On other issues ranging from deficit reduction to federal farm spending, from South Africa sanctions to Middle East arms sales, Congress called the shots, in stark contrast to the opening year of Reagan's first term.

Lawmakers made a historic year-end decision: passage of the Gramm-Rudman-Hollings legislation, which mandated paring of the federal deficit over the next five years until the budget was balanced in fiscal 1991. Although Congress embraced the budget reduction plan—offered by Republican senators Phil Gramm of Texas and Warren B. Rudman of New Hampshire and Democratic senator Ernest F. Hollings of South Carolina—as the best hope for future deficit control, many who shaped the measure were skeptical about its chances for working.

Deficit reduction had been the top priority of Senate majority leader Robert "Bob" Dole, R-Kan., when the Ninety-ninth Congress opened, but the expected deficit bequeathed to the next Congress remained about $180 billion.

In the two most important elections of 1985, moderation seemed to be the winning theme. Democrats retained the governorship in Virginia with Gerald L. Baliles, who mimicked the moderate philosophy of outgoing Democratic governor Charles S. Robb. Similarly, New Jersey Republican governor Thomas H. Kean thrived at the polls by positioning himself as more moderate than his party's national image. Because neither of the gubernatorial elections produced a partisan shift, the nationwide party lineup of governors remained at thirty-four Democrats and sixteen Republicans—unchanged from 1984.

The 1986 Midterm Elections

The 1986 Senate campaigns deserve special notice for what they said about the state of electioneering in the latter half of the 1980s. Most spectacularly they laid to rest a theory that took hold in 1980—that the GOP's superior financial resources give it an infallible ability to win close contests. The notion gained widespread currency in 1982, when the GOP's high-tech campaign techniques and last-minute infusions of money saved several endangered Republican candidates. That year the GOP won five of the six contests in which the winner took 52 percent or less of the vote.

But in 1986 nine of the eleven races won by 52 percent or less went to Democrats. That achievement came in spite of daunting obstacles: the National Republican Senatorial Committee's nearly 8–1 funding advantage over its Democratic counterpart, a $10 million nationwide GOP get-out-the-vote effort, and an army of consultants, pollsters, media advisers, and GOP field staff at the disposal of Republican candidates.

The difference lay in what each side did with the resources at its disposal. In many contests Democrats latched onto issues—of substance and of personality—that by election day were helping them frame the terms of the debate. Even more important, while the GOP was spending much of its money on television advertising and on a technology-driven voter mobilization effort, Democrats built on their strength at the grass roots. They developed extensive local organizations and, especially in the South, reawakened old party apparatuses and alliances.

In a year when there were so many close contests, the Republicans' lack of organizational depth hurt them, particularly in states where Democrats latched onto local issues that seemed more compelling to voters than national Republican pleas to keep the Senate in GOP hands.

The most striking examples of the Democrats' ability to outcampaign their opponents came in the South. All Democrats there used a variation on a single theme: that they were homegrown state patriots, while their opponents were national Republicans with little interest in local affairs. And all used their state's traditional Democratic base to surmount better-financed Republican efforts.

Results of the 1986 Elections

Democrats on November 4, 1986, regained control of the Senate, which they had lost to the GOP in 1980. Six Republicans who won their seats that year were defeated in their bids for reelection, as Democrats captured nine GOP seats and lost only one of their own to take a 55–45 Senate majority. The results also gave Democrats the largest class of freshman senators since 1958. Of the thirteen new senators, eleven were Democrats.

The party's most significant set of victories came in the South, where Democrats won six of seven Senate contests. Their gains elsewhere were scattered across the map. Farm unrest in the Midwest cost two GOP members of the class of 1980 their seats. In Washington State, controversy over the possible locating of a high-level nuclear waste site in Hanford helped Brock Adams unseat Republican Slade Gorton.

The Democrats' other gains came in Maryland, where Rep. Barbara A. Mikulski easily won the seat of retiring GOP Sen. Charles McC. Mathias Jr., and in Nevada, where Rep. Harry Reid defeated former representative Jim Santini for the right to succeed retiring GOP senator Paul Laxalt.

The sole Republican pickup was in Missouri. There, former governor Christopher S. "Kit" Bond won the seat held by retiring Democratic veteran Thomas F. Eagleton.

Not every potentially close Senate election broke the Democrats' way. In Oklahoma and Pennsylvania, Democratic representatives James R. Jones and Bob Edgar tried to turn local economic troubles to their advantage. Neither, however, could arouse the core Democratic constituency in the western half of their states. GOP Sens. Don Nickles of Oklahoma and Arlen Specter of Pennsylvania both won handily. And in Idaho, Democratic governor John V. Evans lost to conservative Republican Sen. Steven D. Symms.

In North Carolina, Democrat Terry Sanford won with a campaign that stressed his long-standing ties to the state and painted incumbent James T. Broyhill as a captive of the Washington establishment. In Alabama, Rep. Richard C. Shelby waged a successful campaign against Republican senator Jeremiah Denton, whom he accused of being more interested in his personal agenda of "family" and social issues than in helping Alabama's economy.

Democratic representative John B. Breaux overcame an early lead by GOP representative W. Henson Moore to hold on to the Louisiana seat of retiring Democratic senator Russell B. Long. Breaux hammered away at Moore as a representative of GOP policies that were hurting Louisiana's farmers and its oil and gas industry.

In Georgia, Rep. Wyche Fowler ran an almost picture-perfect campaign against Republican incumbent Mack Mattingly. Fowler carried just under two-thirds of the state's 159 counties.

Florida's Democratic governor Bob Graham, a popular moderate, put Paula Hawkins on the defensive by portraying the first-term senator as a lightweight with a narrow focus. Hawkins won only 45 percent of the vote, the worst showing of any Senate incumbent.

Superior organization proved to be the key element in Democratic representative Timothy E. Wirth's victory over GOP representative Ken Kramer for the Senate seat left vacant by retiring Colorado Democrat Gary Hart. In California, where media ads played a crucial role, Democratic senator Alan Cranston ran a masterful campaign that kept Rep. Ed Zschau's legislative record in the spotlight for much of the campaign and prevented the Republicans from focusing on Cranston's performance.

House Republicans lost only five seats in 1986, giving the Democrats a 258–177 edge for the One Hundredth Congress. It was an extraordinarily good election for incumbents of both parties. The five Republican incumbents who went down to defeat were Mike Strang of Colorado; Webb Franklin of Mississippi; Fred J. Eckert of New York; and Bill Cobey and Bill Hendon, both of North Carolina. The Democrats suffered only one incumbent casualty: Robert A. Young of Missouri. The number of incumbents defeated was the lowest in postwar history.

The freshman House class of 1986 included twenty-three Republicans and twenty-seven Democrats. That was larger than the forty-three-member freshman class of 1984 but much smaller than the seventy-four-member GOP-dominated class of 1980 and the Democrat-heavy, eighty-member contingent elected in 1982.

The Republican Party made a strong showing in gubernatorial contests in 1986, winning a net gain of eight governorships. The Democrats, who entered the election holding thirty-four of the fifty governorships, saw their advantage drop to 26–24. The GOP count was the largest since 1970, when the party last held a majority of the governorships.

Republicans unseated Democratic incumbents in Texas and Wisconsin and won nine open seats that had been held by Democrats, including upset wins in Alabama and Arizona and a solid victory in Florida. Those victories were offset by the loss of three open Republican seats: in Oregon, Pennsylvania, and Tennessee.

The base of the Republican success was a small core of popular incumbents: California's George Deukmejian, Rhode Island's Edward DiPrete, and New Hampshire's John H. Sununu. The farm crisis that helped oust at least two Republican senators did not hurt most of the party's gubernatorial nominees. Iowa incumbent Terry E. Branstad won, as did three GOP candidates for open seats: Mike Hayden in Kansas, Kay A. Orr in Nebraska, and George S. Michelson in South Dakota. Republicans also picked up the governorship in Maine.

Democratic ineptness aided the Republicans in several states, particularly in Alabama, where Guy Hunt became the state's first Republican governor since Reconstruction. In Illinois, incumbent GOP governor James R. Thompson was considered vulnerable to a challenge from Adlai E. Stevenson III, until two associates of Lyndon H. LaRouche Jr. won Democratic primaries for state office, causing Stevenson to renounce his own nomination and run as an Independent. A three-way race in Arizona helped elect conservative Republican Evan Mecham to succeed Democratic governor Bruce Babbitt in Arizona.

Despite the GOP's poor showing in Senate elections in the South, the party made its greatest gubernatorial gains in that region. In addition to picking up Texas and Alabama, the GOP elected Tampa mayor Bob Martinez in Florida, former governor and senator Henry L. Bellmon in Oklahoma, and Carroll A. Campbell Jr. in South Carolina.

Democrats claimed three of the four seats being given up by Republican incumbents. Their largest catch was Pennsylvania, where Bob Casey defeated Lt. Gov. William W. Scranton III.

Republicans, however, were disappointed in their efforts to capture state legislatures. Nationwide, Democrats improved their lead in the number of legislative seats they controlled by 179 and won control of the legislatures in twenty-eight states, two more than they dominated before the election. Republicans controlled both chambers in ten legislatures, down from eleven before the election. Legislative control was split between the two parties in eleven states. (Nebraska has a nonpartisan, unicameral legislature.)

1987–1989:
THE ONE HUNDREDTH CONGRESS

The One Hundredth Congress, by its number, had a historic resonance. It convened in the year that the United States was celebrating the bicentennial of its Constitution and the government of checks and balances created by that Constitution.

Fittingly enough, members commemorated the separation of powers that lay at the heart of the Constitution by challenging the president over the Iran-contra affair and by checking his attempt to reshape the judiciary through the appointment of a controversial justice to a pivotal Supreme Court vacancy. The budget deficit engendered partisan wrangling within Congress and between Congress and the president for much of 1987. After the October 19, 1987, stock market crash, however, Congress and Reagan reached accord on a two-year deficit-reduction package.

For the first time since 1981 Democrats were in control of both chambers. Senate Democrats returned to power with a 55–45 margin; Robert C. Byrd of West Virginia was restored to his former position as majority leader. House Democrats, who increased their already formidable edge to 258–177, named Majority Leader Jim Wright of Texas to succeed Speaker O'Neill, who had retired in 1986. Wright was unopposed.

Two issues consumed as much if not more congressional attention than the perennial budget battles. The Iran-contra affair rarely left the front pages from February 1987, when a White House commission said the president had all but lost control of his national security apparatus, to November, when the Senate and House select committees investigating the scandal published their report. Continual revelations about the White House plan to sell arms to Iran in exchange for U.S. hostages in the Middle East and the subsequent diversion of some of the arms sale profits to "contra" guerrillas fighting the leftist government of Nicaragua severely damaged Reagan's public standing.

Almost as soon as the Iran-contra hearings concluded, Reagan's nomination to fill a Supreme Court vacancy created an equally clamorous controversy. Reagan nominated Robert H. Bork, a federal appeals court judge who had gained notoriety when, as solicitor general in 1973, he fired Watergate special prosecutor Archibald Cox. After a bitter fight, Bork was rejected. Reagan's second nominee, Douglas H. Ginsburg, was forced to withdraw his nomination after he admitted that he had smoked marijuana when he was a law student and law professor. Reagan's third nominee, Anthony M. Kennedy, was confirmed unanimously in February 1988.

Despite these divisive battles and other flare-ups between the Republican White House and the Democratic Congress, the two sides managed to reconcile their differences on a number of major issues, including measures to bail out the Farm Credit System and the Federal Savings and Loan Insurance Corporation. For all its productivity, however, the One Hundredth Congress left for its successor a pile of unfinished business, with the deficit-ridden federal budget teetering at the top.

The 1988 Campaigns

Vice President George Bush's nomination for the presidency was never in any real jeopardy. His candidacy, though, generated little enthusiasm, which encouraged several Republicans to enter the race. Two contenders, former Delaware governor Pierre S. du Pont IV and former secretary of state Alexander M. Haig Jr., left the race early.

The Iowa caucuses gave the Bush forces a momentary scare when their candidate came in third behind Sen. Bob Dole of Kansas and television evangelist Pat Robertson. A week later Bush trounced Dole in New Hampshire and then went on to sweep sixteen states on Super Tuesday, shutting Dole out of the March 8 events altogether. New York representative Jack F. Kemp, who had hoped to win the backing of the party's conservative wing, did not fare well in the early primaries and decided to leave the race after Super Tuesday.

Bush confirmed his standing with Republican voters on March 15, decisively winning Illinois. Dole left the race two weeks later. On April 26 Bush won enough Pennsylvania delegates to clinch the Republican nomination.

On the Democratic side eight candidates entered the contest: former Arizona governor Bruce Babbitt; Sen. Joseph R. Biden Jr. of Delaware; Gov. Michael Dukakis of Massachusetts; Rep. Richard A. Gephardt of Missouri; Sen. Albert Gore Jr. of Tennessee; former senator Gary Hart of Colorado; civil rights leader Jesse Jackson; and Sen. Paul Simon of Illinois. Dukakis did not emerge as the clear front-runner until well into the primary schedule.

By mid-March Jackson had accumulated more primary votes than any other Democrat and only four fewer delegates than Dukakis. Then came Wisconsin, where Dukakis beat Jackson by more than 200,000 votes. Dukakis followed his Wisconsin victory with a decisive win in New York. Dukakis went on to win all the remaining primaries except in the District of Columbia, which Jackson took. Even then, Dukakis was not assured of enough delegates until the last round of voting on June 7.

After years of internal warfare the Democrats staged a remarkable show of unity at their convention in Atlanta. The prospects for party peace were not at all guaranteed as the party gathered for its July 18–21 conclave. In the weeks before the convention Dukakis had two main tasks: to select a running mate and to find a way to involve Jackson in the fall campaign.

Jackson seemed to have scaled back his implicit demands that the vice-presidential nomination be offered to him. At the same time Dukakis seemed to find ways to demonstrate his respect for Jackson without pandering to him. Both men appeared close to accommodation on platforms and rules issues. Then, on July 12, Dukakis announced that he had chosen Texas senator Lloyd Bentsen to be his running mate. The decision angered Jackson supporters, who noted that Bentsen was both southern and conservative and who believed that Jackson and his message had been slighted. But Dukakis, Bentsen, and Jackson subsequently held a meeting and smoothed things over.

Jackson's willingness to compromise on the platform contributed greatly to the bonhomie of Atlanta, signaling a victory of pragmatism over idealism. As a result the rest of the convention was tension-free, providing the backdrop for a Hollywood-style finale. Jackson himself kicked off the unity collaboration in an electrifying speech that unfurled his famous call for social justice and offered strong words of praise for Dukakis.

With the conclusion of Jackson's speech, his virtual domination of the convention gave way to the business at hand. On July 20 Democratic delegates nominated Dukakis, who won 2,876.25 votes to Jackson's 1,218.5. Jackson conceded by telephone, and the convention then ratified Dukakis's nomination by acclamation.

Running behind Michael Dukakis in the public opinion polls, George Bush came to the Republican National Convention in New Orleans in August with one main task: to convince delegates and the viewing public that he was not the "wimp" pictured by political cartoonists. His choice of Sen. Dan Quayle of Indiana as his running mate, however, heightened many of the doubts he had sought to dispel.

To maintain some suspense, Bush had not been expected to name his choice for vice president until the last day of the convention. But at a welcoming ceremony on August 16, he announced his selection. Concern about Quayle's youth and government inexperience quickly surfaced. A major controversy erupted when reporters questioned Quayle about whether he had used family influence to get into the Indiana National Guard in 1969 to avoid service in the Vietnam War.

While controversy swirled around Quayle's selection, the convention business proceeded as if nothing unusual were happening. With no fights over the platform or party rules (both were approved without debate), the Republicans could concentrate on positioning themselves for the fall campaign.

Although Democrats began the fall campaign with high hopes for November, the campaign turned out to be a downhill slide for Dukakis. Dukakis left the Democratic convention as much as seventeen points ahead of Bush in some polls. That lead evaporated under a withering Republican attack that began at the GOP convention. Despite continuing reservations among voters about the Quayle nomination, Bush surged ahead in the polls at the end of August. He maintained that advantage throughout the fall, emphasizing at every opportunity that Dukakis was a liberal out of step with the mainstream. Many scorned Bush for his tactics, but few argued with their effectiveness.

Bush's ability to keep Dukakis on the defensive was reflected in the public opinion polls. A week before the election, they gave Bush as much as a twelve-point lead.

Results of the 1988 Elections

George Bush was elected the nation's forty-first president on November 8, winning 54 percent of the popular vote. Bush's victory confirmed that, absent economic crisis or White House scandal, the burden of proof was on the Democrats to convince voters that their party could be trusted with the executive branch of the federal government.

Bush was the first candidate since John F. Kennedy to win the White House while his party lost seats in the House. And unlike Kennedy's, Bush's victory margin was substantial in a number of states. His inability to carry others into office may have been partly due to his message, which was essentially a call to "stay the course."

In reviewing the results of the 1988 Senate elections, both parties had cause for rue and relief. But it was the Republicans who felt the keener disappointment. Democrats won nineteen of the thirty-three races, maintaining the 55–45 majority they had seized in the 1986 elections. They successfully defended fifteen of their eighteen seats and took over Republican seats in Connecticut, Virginia, Nebraska, and Nevada.

GOP Senate leader Bob Dole conceded on election night that reclaiming the Senate had not been realistic in 1988. And the party could be pleased at capturing three historically Democratic seats as well as holding eleven of its own fifteen. Of the four the GOP lost, the only surprise came in Connecticut, where incumbent Lowell P. Weicker Jr. was edged out by Joseph I. Lieberman.

The GOP had all but conceded the other three seats to the Democrats a year before the election. In Virginia former governor Charles S. Robb succeeded Republican Paul S. Trible Jr., who retired after a single term. David K. Karnes of Nebraska lost to former Democratic governor Robert Kerrey, and Chic Hecht of Nevada lost to sitting Democratic governor Richard H. Bryan.

The only Democratic incumbent the Republicans defeated was John Melcher of Montana. Conrad Burns became the state's

first Republican senator elected in forty-two years. The other two new Republican seats in the Senate were won by House minority whip Trent Lott of Mississippi and Rep. Connie Mack of Florida. The latest emblems of the GOP's new day in the Old South, they replaced retiring Democrats John C. Stennis and Lawton Chiles.

An important measure of a party's performance in any election year is its score in contests where no incumbent is running. In this category the GOP won four of six. The party held on to retiring Robert T. Stafford's seat in Vermont, where at-large representative James M. Jeffords had no trouble moving in. And former GOP senator Slade Gorton, whom the voters had turned out two years before, was elected to succeed retiring Republican senator Daniel J. Evans. Mack and Lott picked up the other two open seats.

The two Democrats winning open seats were Robb and Herbert Kohl of Wisconsin. Kohl succeeded Democrat William Proxmire, who retired.

In the House of Representatives election day was cause for celebration for more than 98 percent of the members seeking reelection. Only six of 408 incumbents on the ballot lost, four Republicans and two Democrats. The Democrats picked up a net of two seats, putting the partisan lineup in the House at 260 Democrats and 175 Republicans.

The most prominent member to fall was Fernand J. St Germain of Rhode Island, who was soundly rejected after being dogged by questions about his ethical conduct. And in Georgia the Democrats had little trouble knocking off Republican representative Pat Swindall, who was under indictment for allegedly lying to a grand jury about a money-laundering scheme.

Democratic representative Bill Chappell Jr. lost his Florida district after being battered by public questions about his links to a defense-procurement scandal. Democratic representative Roy Dyson of Maryland, also plagued by unfavorable stories about his links to the procurement scandal and his conduct in office, narrowly eked out a victory over a challenger he was expected to trounce.

Many victories in 1988 depended on more than political skills, personality, and partisan appeal. The powers of incumbency—free mailing, press attention, and fund-raising advantages—played a significant role in the election.

If the advantage of incumbency helped to explain why Republicans were having trouble reducing the Democratic advantages in the House, it did little to explain why they made no headway in the battle for open seats. In all, only three of the twenty-seven open seats changed partisan hands, with the Democrats winning two formerly GOP seats and the Republicans winning one seat held by the Democrats.

The 1988 results were unlikely to encourage challengers mulling the 1990 election. The 98 percent reelection rate from 1986 may well have played a role in discouraging competition in 1988, one of the quietest election years in recent memory.

There were twelve gubernatorial races on November 8. Of the nine governors seeking reelection, eight won, all by stressing their managerial skill. The only incumbent to fail, West Virginia Republican Arch A. Moore Jr., was ousted because voters had lost confidence in his ability to steer the state's struggling economy toward better times. Democrat Gaston Caperton defeated Moore.

Two other GOP governors were as embattled as Moore—Edward DiPrete in Rhode Island and Norman H. Bangerter in Utah—but both eked out victories over stiff Democratic competition.

Those narrow GOP victories deflated the Democrats' high expectations of gubernatorial gains in 1988. Democrats were defending only four seats, compared with the GOP's eight. In addition, the three Democratic incumbents seeking reelection seemed solid, while Republicans looked to be struggling in at least four states. But on November 8 the Democrats scored a net gain of just one governorship, bringing to twenty-eight their number of chief executives. The GOP held twenty-two governorships.

While Democrats may have been disappointed in the results of the gubernatorial elections, Republicans suffered a setback in their efforts to take control of Democratic-held state legislatures in time to influence the next redistricting. The November 8 elections left the GOP controlling both houses in only eight states, down from nine going into the election. The Democrats retained control of twenty-eight and thirteen other state legislatures were split. (Nebraska's unicameral legislature did not organize along partisan lines.)

The Post–Cold War Era

When the history of the early 1990s is written, the signal event will surely be the collapse of Soviet communism and the dissolution of the Union of Soviet Socialist Republics. The world watched as, one by one, the countries of the Warsaw Pact broke away from the Soviet Union to turn toward democracy and market economies and then as the Soviet Union itself broke apart. Seemingly overnight, the superpower rivalry that had dominated U.S. defense and foreign policy for nearly half a century was over.

For many Americans, however, these astounding events were overshadowed by economic recession. Faced with slow economic growth and high levels of unemployment, more and more people began to fear that they and their children would never be able to realize the American dream of a continually improving standard of living.

Those fears were to make Republican George Bush a one-term president. Bush, entering the White House on the popularity of his predecessor, Ronald Reagan, saw his public approval ratings soar to record heights after the successful U.S.-led military action against Iraq in 1991. But Bush was never able to persuade voters that he had a credible plan for rejuvenating the economy or addressing other domestic problems, including a failing health insurance system and the huge budget deficits caused in part by the Reagan-Bush economic policies.

The Democratic-controlled Congress gave the president little quarter, although the two did cooperate to enact a far-reaching rewrite of the Clean Air Act. Other major achievements of the 101st and 102nd Congresses included measures to make public

White House and congressional negotiators stand by as President George Bush announces a budget package drafted in the 1990 summit meeting. The negotiators' grim faces point to the plan's subsequent defeat.

and work places accessible to Americans with disabilities and to restructure the thrift industry. But severe image problems overshadowed these achievements. More often than not, the Democratic Congress clashed with the Republican White House, with legislative gridlock the result. This perceived ineptitude combined with numerous scandals to drive congressional approval ratings to record lows.

The military victory in Iraq was the crowning moment of George Bush's presidency. But the euphoria was fleeting. Almost as soon as the war had ended, Democrats succeeded in turning the nation's attention to the economy's miserable performance.

When Bush assumed office, the economy was still in what would become the longest peacetime expansion to that time. Unemployment stood at 5.3 percent, and the inflation rate was 4.2 percent. But the expansion slowed during the first quarter of 1989, and the economy slid into recession.

The single action that may have dealt the biggest blow to Bush's political fortunes occurred in 1990 when Bush broke his 1988 campaign promise not to raise taxes. Concerned that a hemorrhaging deficit could severely damage the economy and his own reelection chances in 1992, Bush sought the help of Democrats to work out a bipartisan package deal that was expected to reduce the deficit by $500 billion over the next five years.

1989–1991: THE 101ST CONGRESS

Despite the momentous events that rocked the world and nation in 1989–1991, Congress's focus was on internal politics. Congress was consigned to a role that was, if not peripheral, at most reactive. Moreover, the 1988 elections had not given either the new Republican president, George Bush, or the Democratic-controlled Congress any clear mandate, and neither party had a compelling agenda of its own.

For much of the two years, congressional attention was focused inward, on events surrounding the resignations of House Speaker Jim Wright, D-Texas—the first time in history a Speaker had quit midterm—and House Majority Whip Tony Coelho,

D-Calif. Questions about their personal ethics forced both men out of office. Thomas S. Foley of Washington was elected to succeed Wright as Speaker.

Ethics problems also surfaced for five senators who had intervened with federal regulators in behalf of an ailing savings and loan institution. The senators became known as the Keating Five, after the thrift's owner, Charles H. Keating Jr.

In the Senate, Democrat George J. Mitchell of Maine was serving his first years as majority leader, where he cautiously proceeded to impose order on the legislative schedule and to find consensus among Democrats. Most senators said Mitchell lived up to his promise to have an open, consultative leadership style. Relations with Republicans were easier than they had been under his predecessor, Robert C. Byrd, D-W.Va.

The 101st Congress had some impressive accomplishments, including a plan to reduce the deficit, a massive overhaul of the Clean Air Act, a child-care assistance bill, a rights bill for the disabled, and broad revisions of immigration laws and federal housing and farm programs. These achievements were overshadowed in the minds of many people, however, by Congress's unfinished agenda—notably its inability to pass campaign finance legislation—and the drone of ethics inquiries, partisan caviling, and congressional irresolution. An ugly and public battle over the budget in 1990 provided one of the low points. Rank-and-file House members humiliated the congressional leadership when they rejected a package agreed to by the leaders and the White House.

The 1990 Midterm Elections

War and recession hovered ominously over the 1990 campaign, but neither figured prominently in its outcome. Instead, the election campaigns looked more like a series of hard-fought city council contests, shaped largely by personalities, local issues, and a pronounced absence of clear-cut national themes.

In reaching a compromise on the federal budget just weeks before the election, President Bush and Congress's Democratic leadership prevented the election from becoming a referendum on economic policy. Divisive issues such as taxes and abortion played out inconsistently across party and state lines. Even the growing prospects for war with Iraq failed to stir a wide-ranging debate over U.S. policy in the Persian Gulf.

Results of the 1990 Elections

While frustrated voters talked about "throwing the bums out," on November 6 they returned incumbents to Washington en masse. Only one of the thirty-two Senate incumbents seeking reelection lost, while only fifteen of the 406 House members who ran in the general election were defeated.

Altogether, the Republicans lost one Senate seat and eight House seats, weakening the administration's hand. Bush had come to depend upon a strategy of governing by veto in dealing with the heavily Democratic Congress. (As it turned out, a Bush veto was not overridden until the final days of the 102nd Congress.)

Colorado in 1990 became the first state to impose term limits on federal officeholders. (California, Colorado, and Oklahoma voters also adopted ballot initiatives capping the service of state legislators.) But the broad anti-incumbent sentiment expressed toward Congress in preelection polls did not materialize at the ballot box. (See box, Term limits, p. 194.)

Only one Senate incumbent, Republican Rudy Boschwitz of Minnesota, was defeated. In the House, 96 percent of the incumbents seeking reelection were returned. Total turnover, including retirements, amounted to just 10 percent.

Despite winning more House seats (267) in 1990 than in any other election since the recession-year contest of 1982, the Democrats' share of the total, nationwide congressional vote was their lowest for any midterm election since 1966. In 1990 Democratic candidates drew just 52.9 percent of all House votes. By comparison, when Democrats captured 269 seats in 1982, their share of the nationwide congressional vote was 55.2 percent, more than 2 percentage points higher than in 1990.

The statehouses proved to be the real workshop of democracy in 1990. Anti-incumbent sentiment overtook sitting Republican governors in four states and Democratic governors in two. Eight other statehouses also changed hands, with four going to Republicans, three to Democrats, and one (Alaska) to the Alaska Independence Party. All told, fourteen governorships switched from one party to another and more incumbent governors were toppled than in any other year since 1970.

Six of twenty-three gubernatorial incumbents who sought reelection lost their jobs. Two of the losses—Democrats James J. Blanchard of Michigan and Rudy Perpich of Minnesota—came as surprises.

In Connecticut, former GOP senator Lowell P. Weicker Jr. won the seat vacated by Democrat William A. O'Neill. Weicker, a maverick liberal Republican who lost a 1988 Senate reelection bid, chose to run on his own ticket instead of competing for the GOP nomination.

Alaska voters were similarly unfettered by convention, electing former Republican governor Walter J. Hickel. Hickel had thrown the race into disarray by jumping in on the Alaska Independence Party ticket only six weeks before the election. Republicans had nominated state senator Arliss Sturgulewski, but some were uncomfortable with her abortion rights stance, and even her running mate abandoned the ticket to run with Hickel.

Significant changes occurred in the off-years as well. In Virginia in 1989, the state that billed itself as the "cradle of the Confederacy," Democratic Lt. Gov. L. Douglas Wilder had become the nation's first elected black governor, succeeding another Democrat. In addition, the Democrats had won the New Jersey statehouse from the Republicans in the only other governorship up that year. The GOP picked up Arizona's governorship in February 1991, when Republican candidate Fife Symington won a runoff election. And it gained another statehouse in March 1991 when Louisiana Gov. Buddy Roemer, elected as a Democrat in 1987, switched parties. That left the lineup at twenty-seven Democrats, twenty-one Republicans, and two independents.

1991–1993: THE 102ND CONGRESS

Hobbled by partisanship and purse strings, the 102nd Congress produced one of the shortest lists of legislative accomplish-

Term Limits

The president of the United States, the governors of most states, and an increasing number of state legislators are limited to a fixed number of terms in office. But efforts in the 1990s to limit the tenure of members of Congress proved unsuccessful. The Supreme Court found state attempts to limit congressional terms to be unconstitutional and a congressional push to adopt a constitutional amendment limiting terms failed to attract the requisite number of votes. The departure of scores of senior lawmakers through retirement and electoral defeat tempered the movement as well.

Background

The issue of term limits has been around since the nation's beginning. The original states' suspicion of a strong executive caused several to limit their governors' tenure. The Articles of Confederation had limited the terms of delegates to the Continental Congress. An early draft of the Constitution also included a tenure limitation for members of what was to become the House of Representatives, but the provision was dropped without dissent or debate. Alexander Hamilton also persuaded the delegates to the Constitutional Convention not to require rotation for the presidency. Anti-Federalists complained about the lack of a rotation provision in their unsuccessful effort to prevent ratification of the Constitution.

Despite the lack of mandatory limits, voluntary retirement from federal office was common through the nineteenth century. George Washington unintentionally established a precedent by stepping down from the presidency after completing his second four-year term. The two-term tradition held until Franklin D. Roosevelt won a third term in 1940 and a fourth in 1944. After Roosevelt's death in 1945, Republicans began advocating a constitutional amendment to limit the president to two four-year terms. The Twenty-second Amendment setting the mandatory limits was approved by Congress in 1947 and ratified by the required number of states in 1951.

A proposal to include in the Twenty-second Amendment a limit on congressional terms failed miserably. The issue surfaced from time to time over the years, but it did not gain in importance until late in the century. Popular resentment against Congress as an institution had been building for some time. Members were increasingly viewed as being primarily responsive to large donors whose contributions, combined with the other built-in advantages of incumbency, seemed to be making incumbents impossible to remove in an election. Republicans took up the issue in the 1980s, in part out of frustration with the Democrats' dominance of Congress since the 1950s.

The case for limits was helped along by a series of nagging scandals in the 1980s. The decade began with "Abscam," the exposure of bribe-taking by several members of Congress that resulted in the first expulsion of a member since the Civil War. The trend continued with the resignation of the Speaker of the House in 1989 under an ethics cloud and ended with the exposure of routine overdrafts by more than a hundred representatives at the House's bank for members.

Term Limits Momentum

The terms limits movement exploded onto the national political scene in the early 1990s, with supporters winning ballot initiatives or gaining terms limit laws in twenty-three states within five years.

Supporters argued that mandatory retirement requirements were necessary to bring new people and viewpoints into Congress, to reduce the constant pressure to get reelected, and to control federal spending, which they said resulted from career politicians getting too close to special interest groups seeking federal funds. Opponents countered that term limits would strip Congress of experienced legislators, diminish the political power of less-populated states that were helped by their members gaining seniority, and would merely speed up, not solve, the problem of legislators getting too friendly with special interest groups. Depriving citizens of the right to vote for an incumbent would be undemocratic, opponents added.

In 1994 Republicans made term limits an integral part of their "Contract with America," a platform of ten promises that helped them take control of the House after forty years of Democratic rule. But opponents of term limits pointed to the GOP takeover as proof that voters could express their dissatisfaction at the ballot box and that Congress did not need institutionalized term limits.

Movement Stalls

The Supreme Court weighed in on the issue in a 1995 case challenging an Arkansas term limits law. In a 5–4 decision in *U.S. Term Limits Inc. v. Thornton*, the Court held that the states had no power to change the qualifications for serving in Congress. Those qualifications are minimum age (twenty-five for the House and thirty for the Senate); minimum length of citizenship (seven years for the House and nine years for the Senate); and residence in the state choosing its representation in Congress. The ruling did not affect laws limiting the terms of state officeholders.

The decision left supporters of congressional term limits only one solution: a constitutional amendment. But the outlook was not promising given the fact that just two months before the *Thornton* decision a proposed constitutional amendment had failed in the House for lack of the two-thirds majority needed to pass it.

An attempt in the Senate in 1996 to call up a term limits amendment for a vote was blocked by a filibuster. In 1997 another attempt in the House again failed to attract the number of votes needed for passage.

ments in recent memory. Congress and the president enacted some notable measures, including the first overhaul of energy regulations in a decade, new regulation of the cable television industry, and aid to the former Soviet republics. But the number of achievements paled in comparison with the number of bills that were considered but never enacted.

The 102nd Congress had hardly begun when its signal event arrived on Capitol Hill. After three days of somber but passionate debate, Congress on January 12, 1991, gave President Bush authorization to use force if needed to oust Iraqi invading forces from Kuwait. The vote was the closest Congress had come to declaring war since December 8, 1941. Indeed, many considered the Persian Gulf resolution to be the functional equivalent of a declaration of war.

Less than two months later, a triumphant Bush ascended the dais in the House of Representatives to tell the assembled Congress—and the nation—"Aggression is defeated; the war is over."

The end of the shooting war abroad, however, marked the beginning of a shouting war at home, as lawmakers turned their attention from the victory overseas to the sagging economy and other domestic concerns. But the budget deal that the White House and Congress wrote in 1990, combined with partisan politics in 1991, made significant progress on domestic issues nearly impossible. The Republican president used his veto, real and threatened, to stall Democratic measures he did not like, such as civil rights and extended unemployment benefits legislation. Compromises were forged only after Bush's standing in the public opinion polls began to fall.

Once the war was successfully concluded, Operation Desert Storm receded from preeminence on the national agenda with startling speed. By late August, in what was likely to be a far more momentous development, the Soviet Union was falling apart.

While the war debate was Congress's finest hour in 1991, considerable competition existed for its low point. Two leading contenders were the confirmation hearings of Clarence Thomas to be an associate justice of the Supreme Court and the revelation that House members routinely wrote checks on the House bank without having the funds to cover them.

Thomas, a federal court of appeals judge, had been named to succeed Justice Thurgood Marshall, who was retiring. Thomas's conservative credentials had already made his confirmation as the second black to sit on the Court a subject of great controversy, but the hearings turned into a national soap opera in October after law school professor Anita F. Hill alleged that Thomas had sexually harassed her, and lurid details poured out of the hearing room. Thomas was confirmed, but the Senate's handling of the situation left women outraged and led many senators to call the confirmation process flawed.

The two-year Keating Five investigation also came to a conclusion in 1991. The Senate Ethics Committee reprimanded Alan Cranston, D-Calif., and it criticized in writing the four other senators—Democrats Dennis DeConcini of Arizona, John Glenn of Ohio, and Donald W. Riegle Jr. of Michigan, and Republican John McCain of Arizona—for their poor judgment in

acting in behalf of Charles Keating, who owned a savings and loan that went bankrupt at a $2 billion cost to federal taxpayers.

Perhaps nothing symbolized the gridlock in Washington so much as the debate over urban aid in the wake of the Los Angeles riots in April 1992—the worst incident of domestic violence in twenty years. Congress and President Bush could not agree either on the amount and kind of aid or on how that aid should be funded. Democrats had to settle for $500 million in aid, a third of what they had proposed.

Congress's internal strife complicated matters. Along with the members' bank overdrafts problem, House leaders had to deal with a scandal at the House Post Office involving allegations that legislators had converted public funds into cash and that patronage employees sold drugs at the federal facility. Several employees pleaded guilty to various charges and a federal grand jury subpoenaed expense account records of three House members, including Ways and Means Chair Dan Rostenkowski of Illinois.

The 1992 Campaigns

A year before the 1992 presidential campaign began, President Bush seemed poised for one of the smoothest reelections in White House history. After he led the nation to victory in the brief Persian Gulf War, the president's popularity soared. Yet when he formally launched his candidacy in Washington on February 12, 1992, Bush faced the prospect of spirited competition not only in the fall from the Democrats but also in the Republican primaries.

In the intervening eleven months, the economy had gone into what even the president called a "free fall." So, too, had Bush's popularity. The president had dropped from a peak of 89 percent approval in the Gallup Poll in March 1991 to 44 percent in February 1992. Not much that the White House did before or during the campaign helped revitalize either the economy or the president's political standing.

On the Democratic side, the nomination of Arkansas Gov. Bill Clinton seemed the most likely outcome as the campaign got under way. His campaign was well positioned on all major fronts—organization, message development, fund raising, and endorsements. Clinton's early primary wins put him far ahead of the other Democratic contenders, but continuing doubts about Clinton's character raised questions about the governor's electability.

In addition to Clinton, just four other Democrats actively sought the nomination as the primary season began: former Massachusetts senator Paul E. Tsongas, former California governor Edmund G. "Jerry" Brown Jr., and senators Tom Harkin of Iowa and Bob Kerrey of Nebraska. None of the four had much following beyond their own regions, and all of them were long shots for the nomination. Brown, however, ran an innovative campaign, placing a $100 limit on contributions, which could be pledged by dialing a toll-free 800 number.

On the eve of the New Hampshire primary in February, renewed controversies surfaced about Clinton's draft status during the Vietnam War and allegations of marital infidelity. Calls went out for new candidates to enter the race. Some prominent

Democrats considered but then dropped the idea because the nominating system seriously handicapped any late entry into the race.

As a result, voters in most states did not have a wide choice. In only five primaries could Democrats choose from a full field of active candidates. Clinton, Brown, and Tsongas were the only candidates in another ten primaries. As Harkin, Kerrey, and then Tsongas dropped out, Clinton's main competition in the last two dozen primaries came from Brown.

Although he lost in New Hampshire, Clinton became the first Democrat to win primary victories in each of the ten largest states. He scored more primary victories (thirty-two) than any other Democratic candidate ever had. And his nearly 10.5 million primary votes were more than any previous candidate, Democrat or Republican, had ever won in the history of the presidential primaries.

Bush's nomination for a second term was never in jeopardy, despite his sagging popularity. His only real challenge came from the party's conservative wing, which had been suspicious of Bush since at least 1980 when he ran for the nomination against Ronald Reagan, the conservatives' hero. Seizing what he saw as an opportunity, conservative commentator Patrick J. Buchanan, a former speechwriter for President Richard Nixon and one-time communications director for the Reagan White House, entered the race.

Although he collected fewer than one hundred delegates, Buchanan found some support in his attacks on Bush. Bush won every primary, but he wound up with less than three-fourths of the Republican primary ballots, a far lower share than the last three elected Republican presidents (Reagan, Nixon, and Dwight D. Eisenhower) had received on their road to reelection.

Former Louisiana state representative David Duke also ran a limited campaign for the presidency. But the former Ku Klux Klan member won little support among Republicans and ended his campaign on April 22.

After the conventions, Bush continued to try to focus voter attention on Clinton's character. But Clinton began the final phase of the campaign as the front-runner, and nothing Bush did ever dislodged the Democrat from that position. By the time of the presidential debates in mid-October, the political community had reached virtually unanimous agreement that without a major news development or a Clinton misstep Bush was likely to lose his bid for a second term.

Results of the 1992 Elections

A plurality of American voters listened to Democratic presidential candidate Clinton's call for change in 1992 and turned President Bush out of office after only one term. Clinton carried thirty-two states and the District of Columbia, won 370 of 538 electoral votes, and outscored Bush by 5 percentage points—43 percent to 38 percent.

Clinton's was the most sweeping triumph for any Democrat since President Lyndon B. Johnson in 1964 and the best showing for any Democratic challenger since Franklin D. Roosevelt ousted Republican Herbert Hoover from the White House in 1932. In placing Clinton, 46, and his running mate, Sen. Al Gore of

Tennessee, 44, at the head of the government, Americans for the first time elected a president and vice president both born after World War II.

The widespread desire for a change in government also benefited independent candidate H. Ross Perot, a Texas billionaire who spoke bluntly of the need to reduce the federal budget deficit. Perot won 19 percent of the popular vote, the largest vote total for an independent candidate in presidential election history and the biggest vote share since 1912, when Theodore Roosevelt ran under the Progressive Party banner.

Change also reached Congress, where voters added record numbers of women, African Americans, and Hispanics. The new Senate would be the most diverse up to that time, with the addition of four women, including Carol Moseley-Braun, the first black woman ever elected to the body. More than one-fourth of the House members in 1993 would be freshmen, a result of retirements and redistricting as well as voter rejection of incumbents.

Overall, however, the partisan lineup in Congress was virtually the same, with the Democrats firmly in control of both chambers. The lineup in the Senate remained at fifty-seven Democrats and forty-three Republicans. At the beginning of the 103rd Congress, the House had 258 Democrats, 176 Republicans, and one independent. The Republicans had gained ten seats.

Anti-incumbency and "Year of the Woman" themes may have worked well in some Senate and House elections, but they had little effect in the twelve gubernatorial races in 1992. Voters seemed more concerned about economics and ethics. The four incumbent governors running for reelection—all Democrats—were returned to office. And a former Democratic governor won back his job after an eight-year absence. The three women running for governor in Montana, New Hampshire, and Rhode Island all lost. Women held the governorships in Kansas, Oregon, and Texas.

Altogether, Democrats won three seats formerly held by Republicans, while the GOP picked up one seat held by a Democrat, for a net gain of two seats for the Democrats. That gave the Democrats a total of thirty governorships; the Republicans held eighteen. Two governors were independents.

Voters in fourteen states in 1992 approved limits on the number of terms their representatives and senators in Congress could serve.

A Partisan Era

Enormous political change took place in the remaining years of the twentieth century and the beginning of the twenty-first. Political upheaval became almost commonplace. As power shifted between the two parties and political divisions in Washington and among the American people widened, long-held assumptions no longer seemed to fit.

For decades, voters more often than not had sent a Republican to the White House but chosen Democrats to represent them on Capitol Hill. The Democrats took control of the House in the elections of 1954 and held on to it for forty years. The party controlled the Senate as well for all but six of those years.

Republicans won six of the nine presidential elections in that same period.

One theory put forward to explain the split voting was that during the nearly half-century cold war the American people felt more comfortable with Republicans in the White House handling defense and foreign policy. At the same time they liked having the Democrats in charge of domestic programs and constituent services. But this arrangement was no longer so compelling once the cold war ended and taxpayer disenchantment with big government began to mount.

And that's when the political pendulum started to swing. Voters turned Republican President George Bush out of office in the 1992 election. Bush, who had long experience in foreign affairs and had soared in popularity after presiding over the U.S. victory in the Persian Gulf War, fell on the sword of domestic pocketbook issues and lost his reelection bid to a former war protester, Arkansas governor Bill Clinton.

Capitol Hill was also on the brink of historic change as voter dissatisfaction mounted. People resented paying taxes to a federal government they increasingly perceived as wasteful, overreaching, and inefficient. Democrats proved unable to meet the challenge with much creativity or effectiveness, as could be seen in their failed attempts to overhaul the health care system.

Almost from its beginning in 1993, the 103rd Congress was afflicted with a creeping case of paralysis. By the final days of the 1994 session, an end-of-era atmosphere had settled over the Capitol, especially in the House of Representatives.

The mood was fitting. In the 1994 midterm elections, voters flocked to GOP congressional candidates in record numbers, while at the same time the Democrats had difficulty motivating their core constituents. As a result, the Republicans won in a landslide, recapturing the House and Senate and promising to enact the conservative "Contract with America" legislative proposals on which they had run.

At first, the GOP and its contract agenda seemed unstoppable, especially in the House. Roused from decades-old routines by the new Republican majority, Congress became an institution more active, more partisan, and more willing to defy a president than ever before in the post–World War II period. But in the end the conservatives' confrontational style backfired and voters started to blame the GOP for gridlock in Washington. The Republicans lost control of the debate and their message just as the White House and the once passive congressional Democrats found new self-assurance and grew more confident about attacking GOP priorities. Realizing that they were taking a beating in the public opinion polls, the Republicans softened their rhetoric and abandoned their hard-charging tactics to ensure GOP majority control in the next Congress.

They succeeded in holding on to Congress in the 1996 elections but the White House was Clinton's. Although he had looked like a one-term president after the 1994 elections, Clinton instead became the first Democratic president since Franklin D. Roosevelt to be reelected. The result was the continuation of the historically unusual political arrangement in Washington of a Democratic president and a Republican Congress. But it was even more unusual to have that arrangement

ratified by the voters in a presidential election. Never before had voters reelected a Democratic president and simultaneously entrusted both chambers of Congress to the GOP.

Just how deep the divisions were in Washington became all too apparent in the next few years. House Republicans in 1998 launched an inquiry into a White House sex scandal that culminated in the impeachment of Clinton on charges that included lying to a federal grand jury about his affair with a White House intern. It was only the second presidential impeachment in U.S. history.

The GOP had gone ahead with the impeachment proceedings despite heavy losses in the 1998 midterm elections that many interpreted as voter disapproval of the impeachment inquiry. Many in the party instead had placed the blame for the election losses on House Speaker Newt Gingrich of Georgia, who in the aftermath gave up his leadership position and resigned his House seat. Although Clinton was acquitted in the Senate, his impeachment ordeal left a deep reservoir of acrimony and bitterness in Washington.

It was hard to imagine that anything could surpass the tumult of 1998. But then came the 2000 election. The GOP retained control of Congress but not by much. The Republican margin of control in the House was cut once again and the Senate ended up in a 50–50 tie for the first time in more than a century.

But it was the presidential election that provided the real drama and proof of the deep political divisions in the country. Democrat Al Gore won the nationwide popular vote by more than a half million votes, but the vote in the electoral college remained uncertain for five weeks after the election as the two parties fought over the electoral votes of Florida, which would put one of them over the top. Republican George W. Bush had a razor-thin edge in Florida's popular vote, but the Democrats, charging that there had been problems with voting machines, demanded manual recounts. The battle was fought in county, state, and federal courthouses. In the end, a decision by a very divided U.S. Supreme Court halted the Democrats' push for further recounts and allowed the Florida votes, and thus the election, to go to Bush. His victory meant that a Republican vice president would have the tie-breaking vote in the Senate, thus assuring continued GOP control of that chamber.

1993–1995: THE 103RD CONGRESS

The Democrats had won the presidency and retained Congress in 1992 with a promise of moderate, constructive change. Clinton ran as a "New Democrat" who would have government do fewer things but do them better. Clinton said he would restrain "big nanny" government and reduce the federal budget deficit—an issue forced to the top of the national agenda in part by the independent candidacy of billionaire H. Ross Perot (who received 19 percent of the popular vote). At the same time, the Clinton who campaigned in 1992 was brilliant in addressing the concerns of middle-class voters. He promised to get serious about public finances, but partly as a way to guarantee the financial future of such programs as health care, old-age pensions, and education.

This broad mix of somewhat contradictory expectations went largely unmet. Congress waited for President Clinton to send a reform program with specific measures for it to pass. But when the new president—distracted, unfocused, and inexperienced—had difficulty getting his program started, Congress failed to take the initiative in major areas until it was too late to build a record to defend in the 1994 elections.

When the 103rd adjourned in the fall of 1994, *The Washington Post* called it the worst Congress in living memory, and *The Baltimore Sun* called it simply "dysfunctional."

Clinton was distracted in the early going by symbolic issues of importance to certain Democratic constituencies: such as the acknowledgment of gays in the military and the promotion of more women to the highest ranks of government. Clinton also sacrificed much of his time and energy to foreign crises in Somalia and Haiti, which were of little interest to most Americans.

These issues did little to build momentum for Clinton's legislative program. On the gay issue, he buckled under to opposition from Congress and the military establishment. He succeeded in finding a woman to be attorney general, but only after two highly publicized and embarrassing misfires.

And while he sent ideas to Congress on many issues, there was no effective follow-up. His cheerful ebullience and inability to get things done caused the influential British journal *The Economist,* to describe him in a cover story as "Mister Fizz" (and later to withdraw its 1992 endorsement in favor of his 1996 opponent).

Eventually, the Clinton administration and the Democratic leadership in Congress did agree to go to the voters in 1994 with accomplishments in three key areas—health care, crime, and reducing the deficit. The goal was to lend plausibility to the idea that the Democrats could still deliver on the issues they had raised—and voters had responded to—in 1992.

The 103rd Congress managed to pass a deficit-reduction package in 1993, but without attracting a single Republican vote in either chamber. That left the majority open to the GOP's charge that the bill was more surely a tax-and-spend package than a reduction in the deficit or in unnecessary spending. During the 1994 and 1996 campaigns, Republicans would call the deficit reduction package "the largest peacetime tax increase in American history." The same could have been said of the last two tax increases enacted by Presidents Bush and Ronald Reagan in 1990 and 1982, respectively, which in constant dollars (adjusted for inflation) were even larger. But the charge stuck, in part because neither Clinton nor congressional Democrats did much to convince the nation that higher taxes were necessary. They argued that only the wealthiest Americans were really paying higher income taxes under the 1993 law, but Republicans replied by noting that the gasoline tax had been raised for everyone.

The Omnibus Crime Bill of 1994 was another disappointment in political terms. The Democratic leadership tried to cobble together three bills in one: a tough anticrime bill to please conservatives; a gun-control bill to please liberals; and a facilities construction and jobs creation bill to please voters in the communities affected. When the Republicans attacked the bill as bloated with pork and violative of Second Amendment rights, the House Democratic leaders had trouble keeping their troops in line (the Congressional Black Caucus defected, in part to protest the bill's provisions expanding use of the death penalty). The majority party could not muster the votes to bring the bill to the floor for official consideration in August 1994, a rare and humiliating event.

The leadership had to go humbly to the Republicans, led by then Minority Whip Newt Gingrich, R-Ga., and rewrite parts of the bill to get the votes for floor consideration. Some observers considered this a watershed in the forty-year history of Democratic control, and it took place less than three months before the midterm elections.

But an even greater debacle overtook the Democratic leadership in both chambers in their effort to enact an overhaul of the nation's health care system. Clinton placed First Lady Hillary Rodham Clinton at the head of a special panel on the issue. Her panel held hearings that were closed to the public before presenting a complex and unwieldy bill to Congress, where various individuals, committees, and factions were already working on their versions. In the end, no bill had enough support to emerge from the pivotal House committee, and an eleventh-hour effort to fashion a viable bill in the Senate collapsed in the face of Republican opposition.

These major failures more than offset the 103rd Congress's legislative successes, which included enactment of the "Brady Bill" to require a waiting period for handgun purchases and ratification of the North American Free Trade Agreement (NAFTA)—and NAFTA was passed mostly with Republican votes.

The 1994 Midterm Elections

If the congressional Democrats ended the 103rd Congress in disarray, the House Republicans were on the march. A younger and more combative generation, led by Gingrich, completed their takeover of the party in the House when Minority Leader Robert Michel of Illinois announced he would retire. Gingrich and his cohorts then drew up a ten-plank "Contract with America" that was signed by virtually every Republican running for the House in the fall of 1994—incumbents and challengers alike. It promised a more responsive institution in which issues would be debated in the light of day, and brought to an up-or-down vote. On substantive matters, the Republicans continued to promise lower taxes; a balanced budget; smaller, less intrusive government; and the promotion of morality, ethics, and "family values" in society and government.

Gingrich accused the Democrats of breaking faith with the American people by promising a "New Democrat" administration but governing as free-spending and arrogant "Old Democrats" out of touch with the people. He predicted that the Republicans would regain the House after four decades of Democratic rule.

Although that seemed a bold prediction, there had been signs that the voters were pulling back from the Democrats almost as soon as they had installed them in power. In December 1992, within weeks of Clinton's election, a special run-off election in Georgia brought the defeat of an incumbent Democrat,

Sen. Wyche Fowler. The run-off had been forced by the state's majority-vote requirement, which was repealed in time to elect another Democrat to the state's other Senate seat by a plurality in 1996. In June, Kay Bailey Hutchison gained another Senate seat for the GOP in a special election to replace Sen. Lloyd Bentsen of Texas, who had resigned to become secretary of the Treasury. In November 1993 Republicans won both of the gubernatorial elections held (Christine Todd Whitman in New Jersey and George F. Allen in Virginia) and claimed the mayor's office in New York City as well.

But neither Gingrich's brash self-confidence, nor the election results leading up to November 1994, quite prepared Washington for what happened.

Results of the 1994 Elections

The nation's verdict on the first two years of the Clinton administration—and on the 103rd Congress—could not have been clearer: the Republicans made a net gain of fifty-two House seats—their biggest gain since 1946—and seized control of that chamber for the first time in forty years. They stormed into the majority in the Senate for the first time in eight years with a net gain of eight seats.

Six prominent national Democratic leaders were among the thirty-four incumbent representatives, two incumbent senators, and four incumbent governors defeated for reelection. Thomas S. Foley of Washington was the first Speaker of the House to be unseated since the political turmoil leading into the Civil War. Rep. Dan Rostenkowski of Illinois, chair of Ways and Means and an architect of the tax overhaul of 1986 and the budget agreements of 1990 and 1993, and Rep. Jack Brooks of Texas, chair of the House Judiciary Committee and an author of the Omnibus Crime Bill, both lost. (At the time of his defeat, Rostenkowski was under federal indictment on embezzlement, fraud, and cover-up charges.) Sen. Jim Sasser of Tennessee, chair of the Senate Budget Committee and another author of the 1990 and 1993 budget agreements, was defeated by a Republican doctor, Bill Frist. Had Sasser won, he was expected to be elected the new Democratic leader of the Senate.

Governors Mario Cuomo of New York and Ann Richards of Texas, traditional liberals who had made stirring speeches to Democratic national conventions in 1984 and 1988 respectively, were also defeated. Their loss put GOP governors at the helm in all but one (Florida) of the nation's largest states. Republicans also unseated incumbent Democratic governors in Alabama and New Mexico and gained open gubernatorial offices in Connecticut, Idaho, Kansas, Oklahoma, Pennsylvania, Rhode Island, Tennessee, and Wyoming. They lost open seats in Alaska and Maine (to an Independent), leaving themselves with a 30–19 lead in governors—their first such advantage since 1970. And they made substantial gains in state legislatures.

For the first time since 1920, not a single incumbent Republican representative, senator, or governor was defeated for reelection. The Senate got its first freshman class with no Democrats since the Constitution was amended in 1913 to provide for popular election of senators. Democrats gained just four open seats in the House and the open governorship of Alaska.

The new Republicans in the Senate were Jon Kyl of Arizona, Olympia J. Snowe of Maine, Spencer Abraham of Michigan, Rod Grams of Minnesota, John Ashcroft of Missouri, Mike DeWine of Ohio, James Inhofe of Oklahoma, Rick Santorum of Pennsylvania, Bill Frist and Fred Thompson of Tennessee, and Craig Thomas of Wyoming.

Several incumbent Democrats won closely contested Senate races: Dianne Feinstein was reelected in California, Edward Kennedy in Massachusetts, Frank Lautenberg in New Jersey, Jeff Bingaman in New Mexico, and Charles S. Robb in Virginia. The Democrats also won close governorship races in Florida and Georgia. Otherwise the GOP victory was their most complete since the 1920 landslide that followed World War I.

1995–1997: THE 104TH CONGRESS

The Republicans seemed to misread the nation almost as soon as the election celebrations were over. Just as the Democrats had spoiled their post–1992 opportunity to become the dominant party of the post–cold war era, the GOP set itself up for a backlash in the 1996 elections that would give Clinton a second term and bring the Democrats back to life, if not to the majority, in the House.

But before the Republicans overreached themselves, and alienated the American voter by their combative style and uncompromising assault on government, they did succeed in restoring the House of Representatives as a functioning, open, and responsive institution of government.

Elected Speaker without opposition in his party, Gingrich held his Republican majority to the "Contract with America" that virtually all had signed. And in the first one hundred days of the 104th Congress, the GOP kept its promise of reform. The House voted on all elements of the Contract, passing all but the congressional term limit (which needed two-thirds to amend the Constitution).

Among other things, the Contract items required Congress to appropriate money to pay for federally mandated programs and required that workplace regulations that Congress long ago imposed on private businesses also apply to Congress itself (including employee safety and equal employment opportunities). The Contract also gave the president a line-item veto with which to strike out "pork-barrel" spending. The House also passed a balanced-budget amendment to the Constitution, which failed the two-thirds majority test in the Senate by one vote.

Moreover, the new Republican majority streamlined the House, eliminating committees and sharply reducing staff and budget. It passed rules requiring open debate and public voting on issues. Sensing the public mood, the Democrats went along with most of these reforms. But the more important political question was to what ends these procedural reforms would be used. It was on these substantive issues that the GOP may have misinterpreted its mandate.

Speaker Gingrich, like President Clinton two years earlier, wanted to do everything he heard his voters calling for and do it right away. He called the GOP victory "a revolution."

The centerpiece of his revolution was a proposed budget he said would cut taxes and move toward a balanced budget while protecting Social Security and Medicare. The voters did not believe him, and the Democrats worked as hard to demonize the Republican budget as the GOP had worked to defeat health care and other initiatives in the 103rd Congress. There were warning signs of voter unease as early as the summer of 1995, but the new House Republicans were determined to push for their agenda.

Their aggressiveness on the budget issue gave President Clinton a major opportunity to revive his fortunes. Gingrich and other Republican leaders were convinced Clinton would not dare veto their budget and appear to be blocking tax cuts and a balanced budget on the eve of his reelection campaign.

But Clinton did veto their budget, gambling that the public had turned suspicious of the GOP leadership. In the showdown that followed, the federal government went through two partial shutdowns in late 1995 and 1996. To the horror of congressional Republicans, polls showed the public siding with Clinton and blaming the shutdowns on Congress. It was the media-savvy president who appeared reasonable and interested in serious negotiations. The Republicans lost much of their momentum, good will, and sense of direction. They did not accomplish as much as they might have, and in 1998 they found themselves maneuvered into enacting a largely Democratic agenda that included raising the minimum wage.

Their strongly ideological approach to sensitive issues such as immigration, English-only language requirements, and affirmative action cost them votes among Hispanic and Asian Americans while gaining few votes within their base. Similarly, they energized opposition by threatening to repeal a popular ban on semi-automatic assault weapons and by attacking popular restrictions on mining and logging on public lands.

Still the 104th Congress was able, with bipartisan support, to enact the most comprehensive social welfare legislation in sixty years. The 1996 welfare reform act ended the federal guarantee of a handout and attempted to move welfare recipients back into the job market. Congress also passed legislation extending a worker's right to retain current health insurance coverage after leaving a job.

The 1996 Campaigns

Starting in mid-1995, Clinton began a recovery as remarkable as Bush's decline four years earlier. The 1994 election freed Clinton to ignore the Democratic left—except on such symbolic issues as race relations, equal opportunities for women, and improved educational opportunities. He moved quickly to the command positions at the center, promising to protect the American people from the "radical right."

Objections from the Democratic left were muted—even when Clinton signed the welfare reform bill—and Clinton ran unopposed for renomination in 1996. He was the first incumbent Democratic president to have a clear path to renomination since Franklin Roosevelt in the wartime election of 1944.

In the meantime, the Republicans were unable to rally behind a single champion who could unify the party, present a cogent alternative to Clinton, and plausibly propose to govern the country.

The Republicans, dominated by Main Street economic conservatives, rallied behind Sen. Bob Dole of Kansas, the majority leader in the Senate. Dole was next in line in the GOP hierarchy, and he had many powerful friends. But he was also the choice of the establishment for want of a better candidate. Some supply-side Reagan Republicans, preaching tax cuts as the key to economic growth and a balanced budget, supported Sen. Phil Gramm of Texas. Others preferred Malcolm S. "Steve" Forbes, a political neophyte who was heir to a publishing fortune and willing to spend freely.

Most of the social conservatives and economic nationalists were led once again by Pat Buchanan, who had made a long-shot run for the nomination in 1992. After some rough early going (he lost in New Hampshire), Dole pulled ahead and clinched the Republican nomination by the end of March. But he fell behind Clinton in the polls early in 1996, and was never able to convince voters that he had a unifying view that would help him control his party and govern the country. Moreover, the quintessential "man of the Senate" did not appear to enjoy campaigning. Clinton, whose ebullient optimism and love of people were genuine, again proved himself a superb campaigner regardless of his limited success on the substantive issues.

Results of the 1996 Elections

On November 5, Bill Clinton became the first Democrat since Franklin Roosevelt to win more than one presidential election. The results were strikingly similar to the voting of 1992. Only five states voted differently from four years earlier: Florida and Arizona switched to Clinton, in part because Hispanics moved toward the Democrats and in part because older voters were distrustful of the GOP on Social Security and Medicare. Georgia, Montana, and Colorado switched to the GOP. Clinton won with 49 percent of the vote to Dole's 41 percent. It was an improvement on the 43 percent Clinton had taken in 1992, but it fell shy of a majority. Perot, campaigning under the Reform Party banner, garnered less than half of the 19 percent he had won four years earlier as an independent. Clinton enjoyed a huge 16 percent margin among women voters and even larger majorities among single women and among blacks and Hispanics of both sexes.

Unlike 1992, Clinton claimed no broad mandate for reform. The total vote cast was eight million less than in 1992; and the percentage of eligible voters who turned out at the polls (49 percent) was the lowest since 1924.

Remarkably, the voters chose at the same time to return a Republican Congress, in a distant echo of the results of 1956 and 1848. Considering the presidential result, the congressional results were strikingly similar to 1994. The Republicans had a net loss of only nine seats in the House, and a net gain of two in the Senate, for a 227–207 edge in the House (with one Independent), and a 55–45 margin in the Senate.

The nine new Republican senators were Jeff Sessions of Alabama, Tim Hutchinson of Arkansas, Wayne Allard of Colorado, Sam Brownback and Pat Roberts of Kansas, Susan Collins of Maine, Chuck Hagel of Nebraska, Gordon Smith of Oregon, and Mike Enzi of Wyoming. New Democratic senators were Max

Cleland of Georgia, Richard J. Durbin of Illinois, Mary L. Landrieu of Louisiana, Robert G. Torricelli of New Jersey, Jack Reed of Rhode Island, and Tim Johnson of South Dakota.

Unlike the bloodbath of 1994, only three Democratic House incumbents were defeated in 1996, along with eighteen Republicans. Only one incumbent senator (Larry Pressler, R-S.D.) and no incumbent governor was defeated. Democratic House gains in the Northeast and the West Coast were partly offset by GOP gains in the Mountain West, and by further Republican gains in the South.

Since the 1994 election, the GOP had gained the governorship of Louisiana in late 1995, and West Virginia in 1996, while losing New Hampshire. Clinton's successor as governor of Arkansas resigned after conviction of a felony and was succeeded by a Republican lieutenant governor, leaving the nation with thirty-two Republican governors, seventeen Democrats, and one Independent (in Maine). The new governor of West Virginia, Cecil Underwood, had been the youngest in the nation when he was first elected in 1956. After winning a second term, forty years later, he was now the oldest at seventy-two.

1997–1999: THE 105TH CONGRESS

The 105th Congress started off fairly low-keyed. The partisan confrontation and inflexibility of the preceding Congress seemed to give way to a spirit of moderation and compromise characteristic of earlier times. Together the two parties began to compile a modest record of legislative accomplishments.

But by the end of the Congress things were anything but low-keyed, bipartisan, or moderate. The 105th Congress went into the history books, when, for only the second time ever, the House voted to impeach a president.

At the outset of the Congress, members of both parties agreed that the November 1996 elections had sent a message that encouraged cautious legislating. Republican leaders worked through the committee system to build majority coalitions—many of them bipartisan—to pass bills. Lawmakers looked more often for common ground with their adversaries rather than sticking to ideological purity. And the profile of controversial leaders such as House Speaker Newt Gingrich, R-Ga., receded into the background.

This more traditional style of legislation won Republicans what the bravado of the last Congress had not. The most notable example was a landmark, bipartisan agreement to balance the budget by 2002 while providing the biggest tax cut since the Reagan administration. GOP leaders also got all thirteen regular appropriations bills enacted, abandoning the take-it-or-leave-it strategy that had triggered two government shutdowns and hurt Republicans during their first two years in power. When the GOP did attempt to force President Clinton to accept several controversial policy riders attached to a must-pass disaster relief bill, their ill-conceived plan backfired—Clinton vetoed the bill and the Republicans were forced to retreat.

Both parties had to contend with infighting. The debacle over the disaster relief bill accelerated a revolt against Gingrich that had been brewing secretly for months. Ultimately the coup was unsuccessful, but it illuminated growing discontent with his

As congressional leaders and White House officials watch, President Bill Clinton signs the balanced budget agreement of 1997—one of the few issues Republicans and Democrats could agree on.

leadership and forced Gingrich to assume a more traditional role as Speaker by becoming more involved in the day-to-day operations of the House. Gingrich had been only narrowly reelected Speaker at the beginning of the Congress and just weeks later, because of ethics infractions, had become the first Speaker in history to be formally reprimanded by the House.

On the Democratic side, Clinton suffered his biggest defeat in the first session when House Democrats refused to support the renewal of "fast-track" authority, which guaranteed expedited votes, with no amendments allowed, on trade agreements the president submitted to Congress.

And, despite their cooperation on certain issues, fighting between the parties still went on outside the legislative arena. GOP hearings into campaign finance excesses in the 1996 election made for some embarrassing moments for the Democrats—and a few for the Republicans as well.

But this battle paled in comparison to the partisan warfare that broke out in the second session. Revelations about a Clinton sex scandal emerged early in the session, casting a shadow over the 105th Congress until its final hours when the House voted to impeach the president.

Clinton's impeachment arose out of the findings of an independent counsel, Kenneth W. Starr, who had been appointed in 1994 to investigate a tangled web of political and financial relationships involving an Arkansas land investment—known as Whitewater—by the Clintons in the 1970s and 1980s. Over the years Starr's investigation widened and in January 1998 the independent counsel began looking into allegations that Clinton had had an extramarital affair with White House intern Monica S. Lewinsky, lied about it under oath, and urged her to lie about it under oath. Clinton had denied having a sexual relationship with Lewinsky in a civil deposition in a sexual harassment lawsuit brought against him by former Arkansas state employee Paula Corbin Jones. Lewinsky had signed an affidavit in that case, also denying a sexual relationship with Clinton.

When the allegations became public just days after Clinton's testimony in the Jones case, the president quickly and vehemently denied all charges. But in August, during testimony before the Starr grand jury videotaped at the White House, Clinton admitted having had a relationship with Lewinsky that was "not appropriate" and that he had "misled" the public about it. He insisted that his testimony in the Jones case had been "legally accurate" because of the definition the lawyers used for "sexual relations."

In September, Starr reported the findings of his investigation to Congress, leveling eleven specific charges of wrongdoing against Clinton. After the House voted to release Starr's report, lurid details of the affair were quickly and widely disseminated in the media and over the Internet. Polls indicated that though the public was embarrassed and shocked, people were loath to drag it out further in public proceedings.

But in October the House authorized an impeachment inquiry and on December 11 and 12, the House Judiciary Committee voted along strict party lines to recommend four articles of impeachment. On December 19, despite public opposition and with the concurrence of only a handful of Democrats, the full House adopted, by a vote of 228–206, an article accusing the president of perjury in his August 1998 testimony before the Starr grand jury, and, by a vote of 221–212, a second article accusing the president of obstruction of justice. The House rejected, by a vote of 205–229, an article accusing him of perjury in his deposition in the Jones case, and, by a vote of 148–285, an article alleging abuse of power. Before the vote, Democrats staged a brief protest by walking out of the House chamber en masse. They were upset because the Republican majority would not allow a floor vote on an alternative presidential censure resolution.

Because many Republican leaders believed that voter support for Clinton would eventually wane as the scandal unfolded and that the GOP would reap the benefits at election time, they did not push a legislative agenda in the second session as strongly as in previous years. Although some consequential measures cleared in 1998, none approached the magnitude of the 1997 budget agreement.

The 1998 Midterm Elections

The 1998 election year opened in January with the disclosure of Clinton's affair with Lewinsky. It closed with Congress preparing to hold impeachment hearings. The impending inquiry into Clinton's behavior undoubtedly was the biggest cloud hanging over the congressional elections. But no one was certain of the outcome.

Democrats hoped they could turn the scandal against Republicans, attacking the impeachment hearings as a partisan witch hunt. Republicans generally refrained from making the scandal a major issue in the elections, choosing to ride the tide rather than make waves. They feared a voter backlash if they overplayed their hand.

Party leaders said the scandal's greatest impact would be on voter turnout. Both parties realized their fates hinged on motivating their voter base.

Results of the 1998 Elections

With the economy healthy and the nation at peace, Clinton's popularity remained high through the midterm elections despite the scandal. In an apparent backlash against impeachment, voters sent five more Democrats to the House, handing Republicans the slimmest majority in the House since 1955. The embarrassing setback prompted Gingrich to resign as Speaker and leave the House. It also reinforced the Republican majority's resolve to impeach Clinton.

In the final analysis, the election brought little turnover in either the House or Senate. The incoming House would contain 223 Republicans, 211 Democrats, and one Independent. In the Senate, the breakdown remained the same at fifty-five Republicans and forty-five Democrats. As usual, incumbents were the overwhelming favorites. All but seven of the 401 House members seeking reelection won. Just three of the thirty-four senators up in 1998 were defeated—Alfonse M. D'Amato, R-N.Y., Lauch Faircloth, R-N.C., and Carol Moseley-Braun, D-Ill.

Despite these status quo results, Gingrich initially touted the election as the "first time in seventy years that Republicans kept control of the House for a third term." Democrats gloated that it was the first time since 1934 that the party controlling the White House gained seats in an off-year election—and the first time since James Monroe in 1822 that the president's party picked up House seats in his sixth year in office.

Democrats defied history and conventional wisdom in putting back together much of their old New Deal coalition. Outreach efforts by the party and its allies to encourage blacks, Hispanics, union members, gays, women, and Jews to get out and vote succeeded in the low-turnout midterm environment. The party even restored some of its luster in the eyes of white men in certain races by nominating conservative or centrist candidates.

Republicans were left arguing whether appeals to their conservative base had been too weak, or had been so strong as to drive away potential voters. GOP base turnout had been taken almost as a given, with conservatives expected to cast votes in anger over Clinton's behavior. Instead, many conservatives had grown dispirited as they saw Clinton appearing to survive yet another scandal. They also were angry at congressional Republicans for a less-than-frugal end-of-session budget deal.

Gingrich had strengthened his hand in 1998, after surviving the previous year's overthrow attempt. But ill will and nagging doubts about his ability to lead Republicans in the majority returned in the wake of the unwieldy budget deal and a failed, last-ditch attempt by GOP leaders to improve their electoral standing by running television commercials that focused on Clinton's affair with Lewinsky. Gingrich's decision to resign came three days after the November 3 election and just hours after he drew a challenge from a candidate who appeared to have the stature and connections to beat him—Appropriations Committee Chair Robert L. Livingston, R-La. House Republicans endorsed Livingston to succeed Gingrich, but shortly before the House voted to impeach Clinton the Speaker-designate announced that he would resign from Congress in response to a sex scandal of his own. Republicans quickly turned to Dennis Hastert of Illinois to be the next Speaker.

Senate Republicans fared far better at the polls than their House counterparts, managing to retain their comfortable ten-seat edge. But just a few months earlier, Republicans had dared to dream of sixty seats, enough to overcome a partisan filibuster. Instead, they preserved the numerical status quo, prompting some rumbles of discontent.

Overall, eight new senators were elected—four Republicans and four Democrats. The Republicans were: Michael D. Crapo of Idaho, Peter Fitzgerald of Illinois, Jim Bunning of Kentucky, and George V. Voinovich of Ohio. Democrats included Blanche Lincoln of Arkansas, Evan Bayh of Indiana, Charles E. Schumer of New York, and John Edwards of North Carolina.

Republicans managed to hold on to the lion's share of the nation's governorships, with sixteen incumbents reelected and two defeated, and seven freshmen elected. Democrats had six incumbents reelected, none defeated, and five freshmen elected. This translated into a net loss of one governorship for the GOP, taking the party down to thirty-one. Democrats, who had controlled thirty-one governorships when Clinton entered the White House in 1993, remained well behind at seventeen. The remaining two governorships were won by independents—one incumbent and one freshman.

Republicans watched the Bush brothers, George W. and Jeb, coast to victories in Texas (reelection for George W.) and Florida (first term for Jeb). Sons of former President George Bush, they would be the first brothers to simultaneously preside over two states since Nelson and Winthrop Rockefeller held sway over New York and Arkansas in the late 1960s. And with control of two of the biggest prizes in electoral votes, the Bush brothers were assured a decidedly prominent place on the political landscape—although no one could have anticipated just how prominent.

But the GOP lost the biggest prize—California—when Democrat Gray Davis, California's lieutenant governor, soundly defeated his Republican opponent. California was expected to gain as many as five congressional seats after the 2000 census. With Democrats also controlling the California legislature, the party had high hopes of drawing congressional lines to maximize its strength.

The Minnesota race provided one of the biggest surprises of the 1998 state elections when Reform Party candidate Jesse "The Body" Ventura, a former professional wrestler, was elected governor.

1999–2001: THE 106TH CONGRESS

The 106th Congress would have been seen as historic for its timing alone, spanning the end of one millennium and the beginning of another. But it was what went on between the opening and closing gavels that made it another Congress for the history books.

At the beginning, the Senate, for only the second time ever, conducted a trial of impeachment charges against a president. Although President Clinton was acquitted and Congress attempted to go about its business, partisan warfare was never far from the surface. Two years of feuding and open distrust left the 106th Congress unable to complete its business on time. The two sides agreed to call a truce and return for a lame-duck session after the 2000 election. The idea was to let the voters decide which party, and which philosophy, they preferred to see lead. But the message the American voters sent could not have been murkier.

The outcome of the presidential race hung in the balance for five weeks after election day, as the Democratic candidate, Vice President Al Gore, and his Republican opponent, Texas governor George W. Bush, fought over Florida's electoral votes. And, although the Republicans managed to retain control of Congress, they saw their already thin margin narrowed even more. For many, the end of partisan strife was not in sight. Even the Clinton era was not going to end, thanks to the election of Hillary Rodham Clinton as a U.S. senator from New York—a first for a first lady.

The Senate impeachment trial had opened on January 7, 1999—just one day after the 106th Congress convened—amid pomp, solemnity, and pledges to avoid the acrimony that had permeated the House impeachment proceedings. At the outset few believed that the Senate would muster the two-thirds supermajority needed to convict and remove Clinton from office, especially with the president's popularity high and the public seemingly weary of the scandal. Acquittal seemed all but certain when only fifty-six senators voted to keep the case alive in a January 27 vote.

The Senate deliberated behind closed doors for three days before rendering its verdict of acquittal on February 12, when Supreme Court Chief Justice William H. Rehnquist posed the final question of the trial: "Senators, how say you? Is the respondent, William Jefferson Clinton, guilty or not guilty?" By that point the only real suspense centered on whether either article would garner a simple majority of Senate support. That would have provided a legally meaningless but symbolically important victory for the Republicans who pushed the House to impeach Clinton. But the House prosecutors, who had chafed under limitations imposed by senators during the trial, failed to achieve even that modest goal.

Article I, alleging Clinton committed perjury before a federal grand jury, steadily lost support as the trial progressed and was defeated, 45–55. Ten Republicans joined with all forty-five Democrats in rejecting the charge. Article II, which alleged a scheme by the president to obstruct justice, was regarded by most senators as the far stronger count. But it was defeated on a vote of 50–50. Five Republicans, all of them moderates from the Northeast, joined unanimous Democrats in rejecting the charge.

"We all have our opinion of the president," said Rep. Lindsey Graham, R-S.C., one of the House prosecutors. "But under our system, impeachment is hard. It was meant to be hard. And it's over."

Technically, it was over, but the fallout would be felt for some time. Nonelection years are often when Congress gets its best work done, but chances for a productive 1999 legislative season were undermined by the bitter partisanship left over from impeachment. Clinton used his veto to stop any GOP-backed legislation he opposed. Republicans returned the favor by stalling Democratic legislation. The Senate majority dealt Clinton a stinging defeat by rejecting a treaty to expand restrictions on nuclear testing.

The 106th Congress was sidetracked by other events besides impeachment. Just six weeks after Clinton's acquittal, NATO launched an aerial bombing campaign against Serbia to halt the Serbs' drive to "ethnically cleanse" in Kosovo. That overshadowed Washington's domestic policy debate and submerged the agendas of both parties. And shootings in April at a high school in Littleton, Colorado, shocked the nation and prompted renewed debate on gun control.

By the end of the first session, the list of work left in progress outstripped the session's accomplishments. Democrats made their familiar "do-nothing-Congress" complaint, and indeed there were weeks when the House considered little substantive legislation and the Senate slogged through long lists of amendments. One major accomplishment was enactment of a law allowing banks, securities firms, and insurance companies to compete on one another's traditional turf.

Things did not improve in the second session. Presidential politics were partly to blame, but there were other factors as well. House and Senate Republicans could not agree on how to proceed on politically difficult measures such as broader federal regulation of managed health care plans, which died in a House-Senate conference. While House Republicans pushed legislation they knew could pass with their razor-thin majority, Senate Republicans were less eager to engage in the procedural wrangling necessary to move their priorities. Senate Democrats mastered the art of the filibuster and used it well, slowing the Senate to a crawl when they disagreed with the GOP leadership.

Perhaps the year's most impressive accomplishment was passage of legislation to give China permanent normal trade status. Other successes included legislation to restore Florida's Everglades and the first change, albeit a narrow one, in federal campaign finance law in two decades.

Republicans and Democrats both wanted to add a prescription drug benefit to Medicare but disagreed on the best way to accomplish it. Both chambers passed bills to increase the minimum wage but were unable to iron out their differences. Republicans got two important pieces of their tax strategy—repeal of the estate tax and the so-called marriage tax penalty—through both chambers but failed to override Clinton vetoes. Both sides did agree on a bill to allow more senior citizens to earn as much as they wanted without losing Social Security benefits.

As the scheduled adjournment neared, Republicans decided to reverse the pattern of earlier years when they basically gave in to Clinton's spending demands. The two sides fought bitterly over the final appropriations measures and a lame duck session became inevitable. After the presidential contest was finally settled in Bush's favor, an emboldened GOP leadership insisted on more concessions from Clinton than he had made in the past.

The 2000 Campaigns

The impeachment of President Clinton left Democratic candidates in 2000 in a difficult position: How could they capitalize on the Clinton administration's stellar economic performance while distancing themselves from the scandals that tainted his presidency? No one had a tougher time wrestling with this dilemma than Vice President Al Gore.

Gore's position as the presumptive Democratic party nominee for president initially looked as if it would go unchallenged, as prominent Democrats declined to run. Among them were House Minority Leader Richard A. Gephardt of Missouri, civil

rights activist and two-time presidential hopeful Jesse Jackson, and Sens. Bob Kerrey of Nebraska, John Kerry of Massachusetts, and Paul Wellstone of Minnesota. But then Bill Bradley, a former New York Knicks basketball star and former three-term senator from New Jersey, jumped into the contest.

Both Gore and Bradley were considered centrist "New Democrats" because of their free-market and free-trade credentials and their views on foreign policy. Bradley hoped that weariness with the scandals of the Clinton presidency would attract support. He was especially critical of the Clinton-Gore campaign's fund-raising in the 1996 presidential race and campaigned on a platform of reforming the campaign finance system. But he failed to excite the Democratic faithful and, despite a strong showing in New Hampshire—garnering nearly 46 percent of the vote compared to Gore's nearly 50 percent—did not win a single primary. Bradley dropped out of the race March 9, just two days after the "Super Tuesday" primaries in eleven states.

The GOP presidential nomination race began with a crowded field. Early dropouts included former cabinet secretary Elizabeth Dole, former vice president Dan Quayle, Ohio Rep. John R. Kasich, former Tennessee governor Lamar Alexander, and conservative commentator Patrick J. Buchanan, who switched to the Reform Party. Those still in the race at the beginning of 2000 were Bush, Arizona Sen. John McCain, Utah Sen. Orrin G. Hatch, publisher Steve Forbes, and former Reagan administration officials Gary Bauer and Alan Keyes. Of the six, only Bush, McCain, and Forbes were said to be in contention. Forbes, after spending more than $38 million of his own fortune, dropped out shortly after finishing third in the February 8 Delaware primary.

Bush, son of President George Bush and the presumed front-runner for the Republican nomination, faced an aggressive challenge from McCain. The Arizona senator had a solidly conservative record but still won support from independents and Democrats, who were attracted by his anti-establishment message, compelling personal story as a prisoner of war during the Vietnam conflict, and platform that called for reforming the campaign finance system and fighting pork-barrel government spending. McCain's eighteen-point win in New Hampshire stunned the Bush campaign. The Texas governor bounced back in South Carolina, but McCain regained footing with victories in Michigan and his home state of Arizona. Next Bush won the Virginia and Washington primaries. McCain's crusade came to an end on Super Tuesday, when Bush defeated him in seven of the eleven contests, including those in California, New York, Ohio, and Missouri.

The presidential primary season continued into June, but, with their respective nominations sown up by early March, Gore and Bush quickly focused on their general election campaigns. Both men, mindful of perceived weaknesses in their candidacies, made shrewd choices for running mates. Bush, seen by some critics as lacking the experience and even the intellect needed for the Oval Office, chose Dick Cheney, who had served as a U.S. representative from Wyoming, White House chief of staff under President Gerald R. Ford, and secretary of defense under Bush's father. Cheney's selection had the desired affect of reassuring potential supporters. Gore needed to deflect public dissatisfaction with Clinton's behavior and with his own role in the 1996 campaign finance scandal. To do this, he turned to Joseph I. Lieberman, a Connecticut senator who had won praise for publicly condemning Clinton for the Lewinsky scandal, sharply criticizing the White House for the 1996 fund-raising scandal, and attacking Hollywood for placing profits over moral values. Lieberman was the first Jew ever to run on a national ticket.

The Reform Party, which won nearly 19 percent of the vote in 1992 and 8 percent in 1996, all but self-destructed in 2000. Its presidential ticket was eligible to receive $12.6 million in public funding available for the 2000 campaign because of the party's performance in the last presidential election. When Patrick Buchanan left the Republican Party and sought the Reform Party nomination, his candidacy split the party and turned its convention into a shouting match between rival factions. In the end, Buchanan got the nomination of one of the factions and ultimately the federal money.

Consumer advocate Ralph Nader emerged as the nominee of the Green Party. Not much attention was paid to Nader until it dawned on Democrats that if Nader took votes away from Gore in closely contested states, Bush could win their electoral votes. The Gore campaign tried in the closing days of the race to win over Nader supporters, but nearly three million cast their votes for Nader.

Bush and Gore waged a close and costly battle for the White House. The two fought over everything from the pocketbook issues of taxes and gasoline prices to their competing visions for education, the health care system, Social Security, and Medicare. Bush, hoping to capitalize on the Clinton scandals, promised to restore dignity and respect to the presidency. Gore tried to distance himself from Clinton's troubles by emphasizing that he was his own man, while still taking some credit for the prosperity the nation enjoyed during the Clinton era.

The polls showed Gore and Bush moving up and down in the polls during the campaign, but as the election approached they were basically running neck and neck. The election was expected to go down to the wire, but no one could have anticipated the tumult that lay ahead.

Results of the 2000 Elections

Gore and Bush had appeared to be locked in a virtual dead heat—and rightfully so. American voters were almost evenly divided over their choice for the next president, as evidenced by the near-tie vote cast for president on November 7. The deep political divide in the country was reflected in the congressional races as well, resulting after several recounts in a 50–50 split in the Senate and another razor thin edge for the GOP in the House. Not since the Eighty-third Congress (1953–1955) had the margins been nearly this close in both chambers. The last time the Senate had been evenly split was in the Forty-seventh Congress (1881–1883).

Gore clearly led Bush in the popular vote nationwide. But in the electoral college things were anything but clear. Florida emerged as the make-or-break state—whoever won Florida's twenty-five electoral votes would win the White House. Election night gave a vivid preview of the chaos that was to come: the television networks first declared Gore the winner in Florida, then Bush, and finally said it was too close to call. Gore at one point called Bush to concede the election but retracted his concession about an hour later.

In the days that followed, Bush at first was said to have won by almost 1,800 votes, but an automatic recount triggered by that slim margin cut the difference to just over 300 out of nearly six million votes cast. Bush's attempts to claim victory set off a firestorm. Absentee ballots were still arriving and Gore forces requested hand counts in several heavily Democratic counties. Both sides traded accusations and lawsuits were filed in local, state, and federal court. Manual recounts led to a debate over whether examiners could properly discern the intent of voters who had not punched their ballots all the way through and whether such votes should count.

The atmosphere was bitterly partisan. For starters, the election hinged on the outcome in a state where Bush's brother, Jeb, was governor, although he did initially recuse himself. The secretary of state who under state law had the discretion to certify the results was a Republican who had campaigned for Bush in New Hampshire during the primary race. All the judges on the Florida Supreme Court had been appointed by Democratic governors (one with the concurrence of a Republican governor). Vote counts by Democratic election boards were closely watched by official GOP observers who could challenge their actions. Both sides brought out their party elders and held dueling press conferences. Demonstrators held noisy protests. The Republican-controlled Florida legislature threatened to intervene and choose its own slate of electors if things were not resolved by the time the winning electors were to meet in the state capital to cast their votes. Members of the U.S. Congress championed their party's candidates. In the midst of all the confusion, GOP vice-presidential candidate Cheney suffered a mild heart attack and was sidelined for several days.

The Bush campaign failed to get a federal court in Atlanta to stop the recounts. After the Florida Supreme Court permitted the manual recounts to continue and set a new deadline for certification of the results, the Bush campaign claimed that the state court had overstepped its bounds and appealed to the U.S. Supreme Court. When the court-set deadline of November 26 arrived, the recounts had not been completed, but Bush was certified the winner by 537 votes. Democrats contested the certified results in court and pushed for completion of the recounts.

After hearing arguments on Bush's appeal of the state court decision, the U.S. Supreme Court on December 1 vacated that decision and sent the case back to the Florida Supreme Court for clarification. On December 8, the Florida Supreme Court, by a 4–3 vote, ordered manual recounts of thousands of disputed ballots and added votes discovered in recounts to Gore's total. The Bush campaign appealed the decision and the next day the U.S. Supreme Court ruled 5–4 to halt the recounts and set a date for arguments in the case.

On December 12, the U.S. Supreme Court ruled that Florida's hand counting of votes violated the Constitution because it did not treat all votes equally. The Court's holding that the recount

Election officials and volunteers in West Palm Beach, Florida, scrutinize imperfectly punched ballots in the 2000 presidential election. The disputed Florida vote put the nation on hold for five weeks before the U.S. Supreme Court stopped the state's recount, effectively giving the election to George W. Bush.

violated the Constitution was 7–2, but a narrow 5–4 majority on the Court also found that it was too late to improve the hand counting and stopped any further action in Florida. That decision cemented the vote total certified on November 26, which had Bush ahead. *(See Bush v. Gore, p. 1557 in Vol. II.)*

Although Gore said he disagreed with the Court's finding, he acknowledged the finality of the decision and the authority of the Court by formally conceding the election to Bush on December 13. Bush would be the first president since Benjamin Harrison in 1888 to win the electoral college vote but lose the popular vote. *(See "The Partisan Landscape, 2000: Presidential Voting by Congressional District," p. 1572 in Vol. II.)*

Although overshadowed by the presidential election, the congressional elections provided drama as well.

Republicans went into the 2000 election with a 54–46 edge in the Senate but came out locked in a 50–50 tie with the Democrats. The party breakdown had remained uncertain for some time after the election. A close race in Washington state between Republican incumbent Slade Gorton and Democratic former representative Maria Cantwell went to Cantwell after a recount. But it was not until the presidential contest was settled that the final Senate breakdown was known. Lieberman, Gore's running mate, had not only run on the Democratic Party's national ticket but had also sought reelection to his Senate seat. If Lieberman had become vice president, the Republican governor of Connecticut very likely would have appointed a Republican as Lieberman's successor. Lieberman's return to the Senate resulted in the first tie in more than a century.

The Democrats lost one incumbent senator—Charles S. Robb of Virginia—and the open seat of retiring Democrat Richard H. Bryan in Nevada.

Four GOP Senate incumbents were defeated in addition to Gorton—Spencer Abraham of Michigan, John Ashcroft of Missouri, Rod Grams of Minnesota, and William V. Roth Jr. of Delaware. Of these, the most stunning upset came in the Missouri contest, where the late Gov. Mel Carnahan—who died in a plane crash four weeks before the election—won by nearly 50,000 votes, or 50 percent to Ashcroft's 48 percent. Interim Gov. Roger Wilson had promised to appoint Carnahan's widow, Jean, to the seat for two years. Ashcroft declined to challenge the results. Republicans also lost the sole open GOP-held seat of retiring Sen. Connie Mack.

New York's historic Senate race between Democratic first lady Hillary Rodham Clinton and Republican Rep. Rick A. Lazio was the biggest political story through much of the election year, until overtaken by Missouri's bizarre race and the closeness of the presidential contest. Clinton became the first first lady ever elected to public office when she prevailed over Lazio to take the seat left open by retiring Democratic Sen. Daniel Patrick Moynihan.

On the House side, Republicans knew right after the election that they had retained control. But here again it was more than five weeks before they knew by what margin. After the completion of several recounts, the final breakdown was 221 Republicans, 211 Democrats, two independents, and one vacancy, which was expected to be filled by a Democrat. A 221–212 split would mean a two-vote gain for the Democrats.

With congressional districts due to be redrawn with the 2000 Census data, there was heightened interest in state elections. After the November 7 elections, the GOP held twenty-nine governorships, while Democrats held nineteen, with independents in Maine and Minnesota. Of the eleven gubernatorial races in 2000, the Democrats won eight and the GOP, three. The only Democratic gain—and the only seat where party control changed—came in West Virginia, where Democratic Rep. Bob Wise defeated Republican Gov. Cecil H. Underwood. The elections also resulted in the election of five female governors, a record number.

As a result of the election, Republicans controlled eighteen state legislatures and Democrats, sixteen. In fifteen states, control was divided. Nebraska's unicameral legislature was nonpartisan.

Eight Democratic governors led Democrat-controlled legislatures, and thirteen Republicans governed GOP-controlled legislatures. In most instances, if a party controlled both the legislature and governorship, it could dictate the redistricting process.

PART III

Presidential Elections

8. Introduction — 209

9. Chronology of Presidential Elections — 225

10. Presidential Primaries — 305

11. Presidential Primary Returns, 1912–2000 — 319

12. Nominating Conventions — 411

13. Political Party Nominees — 429

14. Convention Chronology, 1831–2000 — 441

15. Key Convention Ballots — 573

16. Popular Vote for President, 1824–2000 — 643

17. The Electoral College — 701

18. Electoral Votes for President, 1789–2000 — 717

19. Biographical Directory of Presidential and Vice-Presidential Candidates — 775

CHAPTER 8

Introduction

THE U.S. SYSTEM OF SELECTING a president and vice president through indirect means is perhaps more complicated than it needs to be. But it has worked with few major repairs for more than two hundred years, generally satisfying the citizenry and meeting the nation's changing needs.

The election happens every four years and permits the peaceful transfer of power or continuation of the status quo for four more years, no matter how bitter or divisive the campaign that preceded it. Indeed, the American electoral system differs from those of other nations and, for all its flaws, is the envy of many other countries. From time to time, however, pressure mounts for abolishing the electoral college system in favor of the direct popular election process used in other major democracies. After each such wave of protest, the demands for reform have gradually faded and the electoral college has survived into the twenty-first century.

Nevertheless, significant changes have taken place within the system. As the nation and the electorate have grown and technology has evolved, presidential elections have become more expensive, costing an estimated $1.2 billion in 2000. Because of the high costs, money and its abuses account for the biggest continuing blemish on the system, despite the myriad campaign finance reforms enacted since the 1970s to avoid corruption and lessen the influence of special interests.

On the more positive side, presidential nominations have become more open and representative of the voters at large. Party bosses no longer dictate the choice of nominees. Instead, the nominations are won through a hard-fought series of primary elections and party caucuses, where rank-and-file party members have an opportunity to express their preference. Once forums for determining who would head the presidential ticket, national party conventions today perform different functions, including ratification of the nominations won in the primaries.

As televised spectaculars, the conventions remain important to the parties' public relations efforts during the intense weeks before the November election. Although ratings have dropped in recent years, millions of people still watch the conventions on television and major political parties try to capture and hold as much of that audience as possible. With expert advice they have streamlined the proceedings to showcase their nominees in prime time as the countdown begins to election day. In these final campaign stages, today's nominees usually keep intact the organizations they built to help them survive the primaries. These increasingly professional organizations are made up of the candidate, his or her family, a running mate, polling and political consultants, fundraisers, media consultants, issues advisers, schedulers, advance persons, and others. Campaign strategies must be carefully managed if the candidate is to move successfully through the primary season, the nominating conventions, and the general election campaign.

Who Runs for President

Candidates for president or vice president must meet the same few constitutional requirements. They must be at least thirty-five years old and natural-born citizens who have "been fourteen Years a Resident within the United States."

Another requirement, one that affects very few people, is that the candidate must *not* have been elected president twice before. The Twenty-second Amendment, ratified in 1951, limits presidents to two four-year terms. A vice president who succeeds to the presidency and serves more than two years may be elected president only once. Franklin D. Roosevelt, whose breaking of the two-term tradition prompted the term limitation, is the only president who served more than eight years. He died in 1945 while in his fourth term.

More than half (twenty-five) of the nation's presidents have been lawyers. (A nonlawyer, George W. Bush is the forty-third president but only the forty-second person to hold the office; Grover Cleveland is counted twice because he served two separate terms.) Twenty-four presidents served in Congress. Fourteen have been vice presidents. Nineteen presidents have been territorial or state governors, including Bush, the governor of Texas 1995–2001. Most presidents have served in the military and three were career generals: Zachary Taylor, Ulysses S. Grant, and Dwight D. Eisenhower. *(See "Roads to the White House," p. 220.)*

Even for well-known public figures, the decision to seek the presidency is a difficult one. The prospective candidates must make complicated calculations about financial and time requirements. They must sort out the tangle of party and state rules and the makeup of the electorate in each state. And they must assess their own ability to attract endorsements, recruit a competent staff, and develop an "image" suitable for media presentation. They must also consider the effect a campaign will have on their families, the psychological demands of the office, and possible revelations about their personal lives that might hinder a campaign.

An example of family considerations arose in 1996 from the popularity of retired general Colin L. Powell, the first African American to head the Joint Chiefs of Staff. Although polls that year showed Powell would have been a strong contender for the Republican presidential nomination, he declined to seek it, saying he had promised his wife he would stay out of politics. Also

George W. Bush wades into a crowd of supporters while campaigning for president. Bush's dominance in Republican fund-raising helped him wrap up the party's nomination by early March 2000.

in 1996, the man who won the GOP nomination, Robert J. Dole, worried that the press would disclose an affair he had while married to his first wife. In his televised debates with President Bill Clinton, who had faced a similar scandal in 1992, Dole did not raise the character issue, reportedly fearing it would open himself to the same criticism. Although Dole's affair was disclosed before the election, it received scant attention and was not a major factor in Dole's defeat.

The Exploratory Stage

The first stage in a presidential campaign is the exploratory stage, when the candidates "test the waters" for a try at the nation's highest office. Before announcing, candidates routinely establish a political action committee (PAC) to raise money and an exploratory committee to help assess the candidate's chances of challenging the competition. The exploratory advisers identify likely opponents, consider funding prospects and other preliminary factors, and, if conditions appear favorable, the committee may form the nucleus of the candidate's campaign organization.

Since 1976, when Jimmy Carter won the presidency after a two-year campaign, candidates have tended to announce their intentions well ahead of the election, in part to have time to build a strong public profile and in part because early fund raising can be crucial to a campaign. In 2000, with Clinton barred from seeking a third term, the looming White House vacancy drew a large field of Republican candidates. Among the first to form an exploratory committee in 1999 was Elizabeth Dole, wife of the 1996 GOP nominee. She decided against running, citing the difficulty of competing against George W. Bush's fund-raising powerhouse. Several other prominent Republicans challenged Bush, including Arizona senator John McCain, who won the primaries in New Hampshire and six other states. But he, like the other contenders, eventually ceded the nomination to Bush.

Dole's decision to pull out of the race one year before the election illustrates a characteristic of U.S. presidential elections: they are endurance contests. From start to finish they are much longer, for example, than the few months typically devoted to parliamentary elections in Great Britain. By Labor Day, a good two months before the November election, many American voters are tired of listening to the candidates and have already made up their minds who they are going to vote for.

The Primary and Caucus Schedule

If a candidate decides to seek a major party nomination, the next step is to enter the primaries and caucuses where Democratic and Republican Party members select delegates to their national conventions. The states and the parties have a wide variety of rules for ballot access qualifications and allocation of delegates. Candidates must follow legal requirements to qualify for state contests, and they also have to adapt their campaign strategies to each state's particular circumstances.

The filing process can be daunting. In 1988 Colorado representative Patricia Schroeder cited the complexity of state rules as a major factor in her decision not to seek the Democratic presidential nomination. Independent H. Ross Perot made it a condition of his 1992 candidacy that his supporters obtain enough signatures to get his name on the ballot in all fifty states. They succeeded.

Traditionally, the New Hampshire primary and the Iowa caucus are the first delegate-selection events, a head start that gives the two states extraordinary influence over the selection process. (For forty years beginning in 1952, no president was elected without first winning the New Hampshire primary. Clinton broke that precedent in 1992 and Bush did likewise in 2000.) Critics have complained that the system is unrepresentative because both states are predominantly rural, with largely white, Anglo-Saxon, Protestant populations. But no serious efforts have been made to change the pattern.

Democratic Party rules prevent other states from scheduling their primaries earlier than the New Hampshire and Iowa events. Republican caucuses are permitted earlier in Alaska, Hawaii, Louisiana, and Guam. For other states and territories, the primary and caucus period begins in late February or early

Table 8-1
U.S. Presidents and Vice Presidents

President and political party	Born	Died	Age at Inauguration	Native of	Elected from	Term of service	Vice president
George Washington (F)	1732	1799	57	Va.	Va.	April 30, 1789–March 4, 1793	John Adams
George Washington (F)			61			March 4, 1793–March 4, 1797	John Adams
John Adams (F)	1735	1826	61	Mass.	Mass.	March 4, 1797–March 4, 1801	Thomas Jefferson
Thomas Jefferson (DR)	1743	1826	57	Va.	Va.	March 4, 1801–March 4, 1805	Aaron Burr
Thomas Jefferson (DR)			61			March 4, 1805–March 4, 1809	George Clinton
James Madison (DR)	1751	1836	57	Va.	Va.	March 4, 1809–March 4, 1813	George Clinton
James Madison (DR)			61			March 4, 1813–March 4, 1817	Elbridge Gerry
James Monroe (DR)	1758	1831	58	Va.	Va.	March 4, 1817–March 4, 1821	Daniel D. Tompkins
James Monroe (DR)			62			March 4, 1821–March 4, 1825	Daniel D. Tompkins
John Q. Adams (DR)	1767	1848	57	Mass.	Mass.	March 4, 1825–March 4, 1829	John C. Calhoun
Andrew Jackson (D)	1767	1845	61	S.C.	Tenn.	March 4, 1829–March 4, 1833	John C. Calhoun
Andrew Jackson (D)			65			March 4, 1833–March 4, 1837	Martin Van Buren
Martin Van Buren (D)	1782	1862	54	N.Y.	N.Y.	March 4, 1837–March 4, 1841	Richard M. Johnson
W. H. Harrison (W)	1773	1841	68	Va.	Ohio	March 4, 1841–April 4, 1841	John Tyler
John Tyler (W)	1790	1862	51	Va.	Va.	April 6, 1841–March 4, 1845	
James K. Polk (D)	1795	1849	49	N.C.	Tenn.	March 4, 1845–March 4, 1849	George M. Dallas
Zachary Taylor (W)	1784	1850	64	Va.	La.	March 4, 1849–July 9, 1850	Millard Fillmore
Millard Fillmore (W)	1800	1874	50	N.Y.	N.Y.	July 10, 1850–March 4, 1853	
Franklin Pierce (D)	1804	1869	48	N.H.	N.H.	March 4, 1853–March 4, 1857	William R. King
James Buchanan (D)	1791	1868	65	Pa.	Pa.	March 4, 1857–March 4, 1861	John C. Breckinridge
Abraham Lincoln (R)	1809	1865	52	Ky.	Ill.	March 4, 1861–March 4, 1865	Hannibal Hamlin
Abraham Lincoln (R)			56			March 4, 1865–April 15, 1865	Andrew Johnson
Andrew Johnson (R)	1808	1875	56	N.C.	Tenn.	April 15, 1865–March 4, 1869	
Ulysses S. Grant (R)	1822	1885	46	Ohio	Ill.	March 4, 1869–March 4, 1873	Schuyler Colfax
Ulysses S. Grant (R)			50			March 4, 1873–March 4, 1877	Henry Wilson
Rutherford B. Hayes (R)	1822	1893	54	Ohio	Ohio	March 4, 1877–March 4, 1881	William A. Wheeler
James A. Garfield (R)	1831	1881	49	Ohio	Ohio	March 4, 1881–Sept. 19, 1881	Chester A. Arthur
Chester A. Arthur (R)	1830	1886	50	Vt.	N.Y.	Sept. 20, 1881–March 4, 1885	
Grover Cleveland (D)	1837	1908	47	N.J.	N.Y.	March 4, 1885–March 4, 1889	Thomas A. Hendricks
Benjamin Harrison (R)	1833	1901	55	Ohio	Ind.	March 4, 1889–March 4, 1893	Levi P. Morton
Grover Cleveland (D)	1837	1908	55	N.J.	N.Y.	March 4, 1893–March 4, 1897	Adlai E. Stevenson
William McKinley (R)	1843	1901	54	Ohio	Ohio	March 4, 1897–March 4, 1901	Garret A. Hobart
William McKinley (R)			58			March 4, 1901–Sept. 14, 1901	Theodore Roosevelt
Theodore Roosevelt (R)	1858	1919	42	N.Y.	N.Y.	Sept. 14, 1901–March 4, 1905	
Theodore Roosevelt (R)			46			March 4, 1905–March 4, 1909	Charles W. Fairbanks
William H. Taft (R)	1857	1930	51	Ohio	Ohio	March 4, 1909–March 4, 1913	James S. Sherman
Woodrow Wilson (D)	1856	1924	56	Va.	N.J.	March 4, 1913–March 4, 1917	Thomas R. Marshall
Woodrow Wilson (D)			60			March 4, 1917–March 4, 1921	Thomas R. Marshall
Warren G. Harding (R)	1865	1923	55	Ohio	Ohio	March 4, 1921–Aug. 2, 1923	Calvin Coolidge
Calvin Coolidge (R)	1872	1933	51	Vt.	Mass.	Aug. 3, 1923–March 4, 1925	
Calvin Coolidge (R)			52			March 4, 1925–March 4, 1929	Charles G. Dawes
Herbert Hoover (R)	1874	1964	54	Iowa	Calif.	March 4, 1929–March 4, 1933	Charles Curtis
Franklin D. Roosevelt (D)	1882	1945	51	N.Y.	N.Y.	March 4, 1933–Jan. 20, 1937	John N. Garner
Franklin D. Roosevelt (D)			55			Jan. 20, 1937–Jan. 20, 1941	John N. Garner
Franklin D. Roosevelt (D)			59			Jan. 20, 1941–Jan. 20, 1945	Henry A. Wallace
Franklin D. Roosevelt (D)			63			Jan. 20, 1945–April 12, 1945	Harry S. Truman
Harry S. Truman (D)	1884	1972	60	Mo.	Mo.	April 12, 1945–Jan. 20, 1949	
Harry S. Truman (D)			64			Jan. 20, 1949–Jan. 20, 1953	Alben W. Barkley
Dwight D. Eisenhower (R)	1890	1969	62	Texas	N.Y.	Jan. 20, 1953–Jan. 20, 1957	Richard Nixon
Dwight D. Eisenhower (R)			66		Pa.	Jan. 20, 1957–Jan. 20, 1961	Richard Nixon
John F. Kennedy (D)	1917	1963	43	Mass.	Mass.	Jan. 20, 1961–Nov. 22, 1963	Lyndon B. Johnson
Lyndon B. Johnson (D)	1908	1973	55	Texas	Texas	Nov. 22, 1963–Jan. 20, 1965	
Lyndon B. Johnson (D)			56			Jan. 20, 1965–Jan. 20, 1969	Hubert H. Humphrey
Richard Nixon (R)	1913	1994	56	Calif.	N.Y.	Jan. 20, 1969–Jan. 20, 1973	Spiro T. Agnew
Richard Nixon (R)			60		Calif.	Jan. 20, 1973–Aug. 9, 1974	Spiro T. Agnew
							Gerald R. Ford
Gerald R. Ford (R)	1913		61	Neb.	Mich.	Aug. 9, 1974–Jan. 20, 1977	Nelson A. Rockefeller
Jimmy Carter (D)	1924		52	Ga.	Ga.	Jan. 20, 1977–Jan. 20, 1981	Walter F. Mondale
Ronald Reagan (R)	1911		69	Ill.	Calif.	Jan. 20, 1981–Jan. 20, 1985	George Bush
Ronald Reagan (R)			73			Jan. 20, 1985–Jan. 20, 1989	George Bush
George Bush (R)	1924		64	Mass.	Texas	Jan. 20, 1989–Jan. 20, 1993	Dan Quayle
Bill Clinton (D)	1946		46	Ark.	Ark.	Jan. 20, 1993–Jan. 20, 1997	Albert Gore Jr.
Bill Clinton (D)			50			Jan. 20, 1997–Jan. 20, 2001	Albert Gore Jr.
George W. Bush (R)	1946		54	Conn.	Texas	Jan. 20, 2001–	Richard Cheney

Note: D—Democrat; DR—Democratic-Republican; F—Federalist; R—Republican; W—Whig.

March and ends in early June. The early primaries have grown in importance. Especially when the campaign does not have an obvious front-runner, the early contests single out a possible leader. After several early tests, the field of candidates shrinks. In 2000 both Republican Bush and Democrat Al Gore had secured their party's nomination by mid-March, a feat made possible by the "front loading" of primaries earlier and earlier in presidential election years.

In 2000 sixteen states held presidential primaries on Super Tuesday, March 7. Although Bush defeated McCain in most of the primaries after New Hampshire, McCain nevertheless received more than 5 million votes in the 2000 primaries—the most ever amassed by a GOP candidate who did not win the nomination. On the Democratic side, Vice President Gore's closest competitor for the nomination was former senator Bill Bradley of New Jersey, who won no primaries.

The cost of presidential campaigns is offset by grants from the federal income tax checkoff fund. Candidates who accept the grants must abide by limits on campaign spending. In the primary stage, public financing is available to candidates who raise $5,000 in matchable contributions in each of twenty states. PAC contributions are not matchable. In 2000 Bush won the Republican nomination without public funds for his primary campaign. Democrat Al Gore, however, qualified for $15.5 million in primary matching funds.

In a typical election year where, unlike 2000, the fight for delegates continues after the early primaries, the goal of the remaining candidates is to attract media attention by winning or performing better than expected in the rest of the contests. Candidates who fall behind typically withdraw. The number of delegates at stake, particularly in states that award delegates on the basis of proportional representation, begins to be important. All Democratic primaries use proportional representation. Republican primaries in some states award delegates by the winner-take-all method.

The Presidential Nomination

The primary season culminates in the two national party conventions, usually held in late July or August. At these conventions, where guests and reporters outnumber the thousands of delegates, the presidential and vice-presidential nominees are formally selected and a party platform, setting out the party's goals for the next four years, is approved. In recent elections, the convention also has become an important occasion for showcasing party unity after the sometimes divisive primary battles.

The first national convention was held in 1831, and for more than a century afterward state party leaders had the ultimate say in deciding who the presidential nominee would be. As direct primaries took hold in the twentieth century, this influence began to wane. Then in the 1970s and 1980s, the Democrats initiated a series of presidential selection reforms that opened the nominating process. The reforms were expected to result in more open conventions, but instead they led to even more primaries. (See box, "Changes in Democratic Nominating Rules," p. 419.)

Victory in the primaries, however, does not mean the primary leader faces no opposition at the convention. Other candidates may stay in the race because they hope to benefit if the leader falters, or they may use the bloc of delegates committed to them to bargain for specific planks in the platform or to influence the selection of the vice-presidential nominee.

Before the widespread use of primaries, the conventions were more competitive and frenetic than they are today. All the candidates still in the race had substantial campaign operations at the conventions. Campaign managers and strategists kept in close contact with state delegations. Candidates deployed floor leaders and "whips" to direct voting on the convention floor and to deal with any problems that arose among state delegations. In addition, "floaters" wandered the crowded floor in search of any signs of trouble. Floor leaders, whips, and floaters often wore specially colored clothing or caps so that they could be spotted easily on the convention floor.

This spectacle, however, became a rarity. It has been decades since either major party took more than one ballot to nominate a president. But in 1996 Reform Party founder Perot faced opposition from former Colorado governor Richard D. Lamm. In a two-step procedure the party nominated Perot at the second of two conventions. In 2000 the Reform Party split into two factions that fought over the party's share of federal campaign funds. The faction headed by conservative commentator Patrick Buchanan won the money but failed to achieve the 5 percent vote needed to qualify for public funding in 2004.

The Republican and Democratic parties received $13.5 million each for their 2000 nominating conventions. The Reform Party qualified for $2.5 million.

At party conventions, nominating speeches mark the beginning of the formal selection process. These remarks are usually followed by a series of short seconding speeches, and all of the speeches are accompanied by floor demonstrations staged by delegates supporting the candidate. For many years a good deal of convention time was taken up by the nomination of favorite sons, candidates nominated by their own state's delegation. Such nominations were seldom taken seriously, and since 1972 both parties have instituted rules that have effectively stopped them.

In recent years, the balloting for the presidential nominee has been anticlimactic. More attention focuses on whom the presidential nominee will select as a running mate. Even then, much of the suspense has been removed because the leading presidential candidates may have named their running mates before the convention begins.

With the young, politically moderate, all-southern ticket of Clinton and Gore in 1992 an obvious exception, the choice of the vice-presidential candidate often has been motivated by an effort to balance the ticket geographically. For years, a balanced ticket was one that boasted an easterner and a midwesterner. More recently, the balance has shifted so that the split is more often between a northerner and a southerner. Some examples: Democrats John F. Kennedy of Massachusetts and Lyndon B. Johnson of Texas in 1960, Johnson and Hubert H. Humphrey of Minnesota in 1964, Jimmy Carter of Georgia and Walter F. Mon-

In 1960 Vice President Richard Nixon speaks during the first televised presidential debate while his opponent, Sen. John F. Kennedy, takes notes. Since 1976 televised debates have become a regular part of each presidential campaign.

dale of Minnesota in 1976; and Republicans Barry Goldwater of Arizona and William Miller of New York in 1964, and Bush of Texas and Richard Cheney of Wyoming in 2000.

Ideology also plays a part in the balance. A liberal presidential candidate may be paired with a more conservative running mate to attract a broader base of votes. Or the choice of the vice-presidential candidate may be used to appease party factions who are unhappy with the presidential candidate. Further, governors generally choose running mates with Washington credentials, such as senators. With the increasing number of vice presidents who go on to be president, more attention is given to the abilities of the person who is chosen, and more prominent figures are willing to accept the nomination.

The method for nominating the vice-presidential candidate mirrors the procedure for presidential nominations. The climax of the convention then occurs with the two nominees' acceptance speeches and their first appearance together, with their families, on the podium.

General Election Campaign

The traditional opening of the presidential election campaign is Labor Day, just two months before the general election on the first Tuesday after the first Monday in November. In recent years, however, candidates have been unwilling to wait until Labor Day to capitalize on their postconvention bounce in the polls. After the 1992 Democratic convention, for example, Clinton and Gore and their wives boarded buses for campaign swings through Pennsylvania and other must-win states. Their opponent, President George Bush, went from the GOP convention to Florida, which was recovering from the devastation of Hurricane Andrew. Bush won Florida's twenty-five electoral votes.

The campaign organization for the general election is usually an extension of the nomination organization, and it is separate

from the national and state party organizations. Nominees normally have the prerogative of naming their party's national committee chair to help coordinate the campaign.

The national campaign committee, usually based in Washington, D.C., receives its funding from the Federal Election Commission (FEC). In exchange for federal funding, the campaign must agree not to spend more than it receives from the FEC. From 1975, when federal funding of elections began, to 2000 all major party nominees accepted the government funds for their general election campaigns. In 2000 the Bush and Gore organizations each received $67.6 million for their fall campaigns. Neither campaign, however, lived within that income. Both parties also received so-called hard money, regulated contributions given directly to candidates: $447 million for the Republicans and $270 million for the Democrats. Each party's national committee also raised about $243 million in unlimited "soft money" for party activities that indirectly supported their nominees' campaigns.

A president running for reelection has inherent advantages that may tilt the balance in the incumbent's favor. The incumbent already has the stature of the presidency and is able to influence media coverage by using official presidential actions and "pork-barrel politics" to appeal to specific constituencies. The president also benefits from the public's reluctance to reject a tested national leader for an unknown quantity.

In times of economic or foreign policy difficulties, however, the president's prominence can have negative effects on the campaign. Jimmy Carter's bid for a second term was plagued by both a sagging economy and Iran's continued holding of U.S. citizens as hostages. In 1992, after achieving record-high approval ratings for success in the Gulf War, George Bush saw his reelection hopes dashed by an economic recession, which he was slow to acknowledge and which the Democrats used to advantage with their emphasis on "it's the economy, stupid."

What They Did Before They Became President

This list gives the terms of office for each president and the public jobs each held before becoming president.

George Washington. 1759–1774, Virginia House of Burgesses; 1774–1775, delegate to Continental Congress; 1775–1783, commanding general of Continental Army; 1787, president, Constitutional Convention; 1789–1797, president.

John Adams. 1771, Massachusetts colonial legislature; 1774–1778, Continental Congress; 1778, minister to France; 1779, delegate to Massachusetts constitutional convention; 1780–1782, minister to the Netherlands; 1785–1788, minister to Great Britain; 1789–1797, vice president; 1797–1801, president.

Thomas Jefferson. 1769–1774, Virginia House of Burgesses; 1775, delegate to Continental Congress; 1775, delegate to Virginia convention; 1776, delegate to Continental Congress; 1776–1779, Virginia House of Delegates; 1779–1781, governor of Virginia; 1784–1789, envoy and minister to France; 1789–1793, secretary of state; 1797–1801, vice president; 1801–1809, president.

James Madison. 1774, Colonial Committee of Safety; 1776, delegate to Virginia convention; 1776–1777, Virginia House of Delegates; 1777, Virginia State Council; 1778, Virginia Executive Council; 1779–1783, Continental Congress; 1784–1786, Virginia House of Delegates; 1786–1788, Continental Congress; 1787, delegate to Constitutional Convention; 1789–1797, U.S. House (Va.); 1801–1809, secretary of state; 1809–1817, president.

James Monroe. 1780, Virginia House of Delegates; 1781–1783, governor's council; 1783–1786, Continental Congress; 1786, Virginia House of Delegates; 1787, delegate to Constitutional Convention; 1790–1794, U.S. Senate (Va.); 1794–1796, minister to France; 1799–1803, governor of Virginia; 1803, minister to England and France; 1804, minister to Spain; 1810, Virginia House of Delegates; 1811, governor of Virginia; 1811–1817, secretary of state; 1814–1815, secretary of war; 1817–1825, president.

John Quincy Adams. 1794–1796, minister to Netherlands; 1796–1797, minister to Portugal; 1797–1801, minister to Prussia; 1802, Massachusetts Senate; 1803–1808, U.S. Senate (Mass.); 1809–1814, minister to Russia; 1815–1817, minister to Great Britain; 1817–1825, secretary of state; 1825–1829, president.

Andrew Jackson. 1788, solicitor for western North Carolina; 1796, delegate to Tennessee constitutional convention; 1796–1797, U.S. House (Tenn.); 1797–98, U.S. Senate (Tenn.); 1798–1804, Tennessee Supreme Court; 1807, Tennessee Senate; 1812, commander, U.S. militia; 1814, general U.S. Army; 1821, governor of Florida; 1823–1825, U.S. Senate (Tenn.); 1829–1837, president.

Martin Van Buren. 1813–1820, New York Senate; 1815–1819, New York attorney general; 1821–1828, U.S. Senate; 1829, governor of New York; 1829–1831, secretary of state; 1831, minister to Great Britain; 1833–1837, vice president; 1837–1841, president.

William Henry Harrison. 1798–1799, secretary of Northwest Territory; 1799–1800, U.S. House (territorial delegate); 1801–1813, territorial governor of Indiana; 1812–1814, general, U.S. Army; 1816–1819, U.S. House (Ohio); 1819–1821, Ohio Senate; 1825–1828, U.S. Senate; 1828, minister to Colombia; 1841, president.

John Tyler. 1811–1816, Virginia House of Delegates; 1816, Virginia State Council; 1817–1821, U.S. House (Va.); 1823–1825, Virginia House of Delegates; 1825–1827, governor of Virginia; 1827–1836, U.S. Senate (Va.); 1838–1839, Virginia House of Delegates; 1841, vice president; 1841–1845, president.

James Knox Polk. 1821–1823, chief clerk, Tennessee Senate; 1823–1825, Tennessee House; 1825–1839, U.S. House (Tenn.); 1839–1841, governor of Tennessee; 1845–1849, president.

Zachary Taylor. 1808–1849, U.S. Army; 1849–1850, president.

Millard Fillmore. 1828–1831, New York Assembly; 1833–1835, U.S. House (N.Y.); 1837–1843, U.S. House (N.Y.); 1848–1849, New York controller; 1849–1850, vice president; 1850–1853, president.

Franklin Pierce. 1829–1833, New Hampshire House; 1833–1837, U.S. House (N.H.); 1837–1842, U.S. Senate (N.H.); 1850, delegate to New Hampshire constitutional convention; 1853–1857, president.

James Buchanan. 1814–1815, Pennsylvania House; 1821–1831, U.S. House (Pa.); 1832–1833, minister to Russia; 1834–1845, U.S. Senate (Pa.); 1845–1849, secretary of state; 1853–1856, minister to Great Britain; 1857–1861, president.

Abraham Lincoln. 1833, postmaster, New Salem, Illinois; 1835–1840, Illinois General Assembly; 1847–1849, U.S. House (Ill.); 1861–1865, president.

Andrew Johnson. 1828–1829, alderman, Greeneville, Tenn.; 1830–1833, mayor, Greeneville, Tenn.; 1835–1837, Tennessee House; 1839–1841, Tennessee House; 1841, Tennessee Senate; 1843–1853, U.S. House (Tenn.); 1853–1857, governor of Tennessee; 1857–1862, U.S. Senate (Tenn.); 1862–1865, military governor of Tennessee; 1865, vice president; 1865–1869, president.

Ulysses S. Grant. 1843–1854, U.S. Army; 1861–1865, general, U.S. Army; 1867–1868, secretary of war; 1869–1877, president.

Rutherford B. Hayes. 1857–1859, Cincinnati city solicitor; 1865–1867, U.S. House (Ohio); 1868–1872, governor of Ohio; 1876–1877, governor of Ohio; 1877–1881, president.

James A. Garfield. 1859, Ohio Senate; 1863–1880, U.S. House (Ohio); 1881, president.

Chester A. Arthur. 1871–1878, collector for Port of New York; 1881, vice president; 1881–1885, president.

Grover Cleveland. 1863–1865, assistant district attorney of Erie County, N.Y.; 1871–1873, sheriff of Erie County, N.Y.; 1882, mayor of Buffalo, N.Y.; 1883–1885, governor of New York; 1885–1889, president; 1893–1897, president.

Benjamin Harrison. 1864–1868, reporter of decisions, Indiana Supreme Court; 1879, member, Mississippi River Commission; 1881–1887, U.S. Senate (Ind.); 1889–1893, president.

William McKinley. 1869–1871, prosecutor, Stark County, Ohio; 1877–1883, U.S. House (Ohio); 1885–1891, U.S. House (Ohio); 1892–1896, governor of Ohio; 1897–1901, president.

Theodore Roosevelt. 1882–1884, New York State Assembly; 1889–1895, U.S. Civil Service Commission; 1895, president of New York City board of police commissioners; 1897, assistant secretary of the Navy; 1898, U.S. Army; 1899–1901, governor of New York; 1901, vice president; 1901–1909, president.

William Howard Taft. 1881–1882, assistant prosecutor, Cincinnati; 1887, assistant city solicitor, Cincinnati; 1887–1890, Cincinnati Superior Court; 1890–1892, U.S. solicitor general; 1892–1900, U.S. Circuit Court; 1900–1901, president of Philippines Commission; 1901–1904, governor general, Philippine Islands; 1904–1908, secretary of war; 1907, provisional governor of Cuba; 1909–1913, president.

Woodrow Wilson. 1911–1913, governor of New Jersey; 1913–1921, president.

Warren G. Harding. 1895, auditor of Marion County, Ohio; 1899–1903, Ohio Senate; 1904–1905, lieutenant governor of Ohio; 1915–1921, U.S. Senate (Ohio); 1921–1923, president.

Calvin Coolidge. 1899, city council of Northampton, Mass.; 1900–1901, city solicitor of Northampton, Mass.; 1903–1904, clerk of the courts, Hampshire County, Mass.; 1907–1908, Massachusetts House; 1910–1911, mayor of Northampton, Mass.; 1912–1915, Massachusetts Senate; 1916–1918, lieutenant governor of Massachusetts; 1919–1920, governor of Massachusetts; 1921–1923, vice president; 1923–1929, president.

Herbert Hoover. 1914–1915, chairman of American Committee in London; 1915–1918, chairman, Commission for the Relief of Belgium; 1917–1919, U.S. food administrator; 1919, chairman, Supreme Economic Conference in Paris; 1920, chairman, European Relief Council; 1921–1928, secretary of commerce; 1929–1933, president.

Franklin D. Roosevelt. 1911–1913, New York Senate; 1913–1920, assistant secretary of the Navy; 1929–1933, governor of New York; 1933–1945, president.

Harry S. Truman. 1926–1934, administrative judge, court of Jackson County, Missouri; 1935–1945, U.S. Senate (Mo.); 1945, vice president; 1945–1953, president.

Dwight D. Eisenhower. 1915–1948, U.S. Army; 1950–1952, commander of NATO forces in Europe; 1953–1961, president.

John F. Kennedy. 1947–1953, U.S. House (Mass.); 1953–1961, U.S. Senate (Mass.); 1961–1963, president.

Lyndon B. Johnson. 1935–1937, Texas director of National Youth Administration; 1937–1948, U.S. House (Texas); 1949–1961, U.S. Senate (Texas); 1961–1963, vice president; 1963–1969, president.

Richard M. Nixon. 1947–1951, U.S. House (Calif.); 1951–1953, U.S. Senate (Calif.); 1953–1961, vice president; 1969–1974, president.

Gerald R. Ford. 1949–1973, U.S. House (Mich.); 1973–1974, vice president; 1974–1977, president.

Jimmy Carter. 1955–1962, chairman, Sumter County (Ga.) Board of Education; 1963–1967, Georgia Senate; 1971–1975, governor of Georgia; 1977–1981, president.

Ronald Reagan. 1967–1975, governor of California; 1981–1989, president.

George Bush. 1967–1971, U.S. House (Texas); 1971–1973, ambassador to the United Nations; 1974–1975, chief of U.S. Liaison Office, Beijing, People's Republic of China; 1976–1977, director of Central Intelligence Agency; 1981–1989, vice president; 1989–1993, president.

Bill Clinton. 1977–1979, attorney general of Arkansas; 1979–1981, governor of Arkansas; 1983–1993, governor of Arkansas; 1993–2001 president.

George W. Bush. 1995–2000, governor of Texas; 2001– president.

In 2000, with the economy booming and the Treasury overflowing with surpluses, the younger George W. Bush capitalized on the Clinton administration's successes by campaigning on a platform of tax cuts and more money for popular programs such as education and national defense. Gore, by contrast, soft-pedaled his close association with Clinton, whose second term was tainted by his impeachment for lying under oath about his sexual relationship with White House intern Monica S. Lewinsky. Some strategists felt that Gore missed out by not taking advantage of Clinton's continued popularity and failing to claim his share of the credit for turning the economy around during the eight-year Clinton-Gore administration.

DEBATES

Now almost taken for granted, debates between presidential and vice-presidential candidates are a relatively recent phenomenon. Until the second half of the twentieth century, White House nominees did not debate. Richard Nixon and John F. Kennedy began the debate tradition on September 26, 1960, with the first of four televised meetings. When Abraham Lincoln and Stephen Douglas held their famed debates in 1858 they were Senate candidates; they did not debate as presidential candidates two years later.

There were no debates from 1960 until 1976, when President Gerald R. Ford, running behind in the polls, agreed to debate the Democratic nominee, former Georgia governor Jimmy Carter. The relatively unknown Carter gained stature in the exchange when Ford made a gaffe by saying he did not believe East European nations were under Soviet Union control. Since 1976, all major party nominees have debated on live television. Independent candidate Perot was included in the presidential debates in 1992, but he was excluded as the Reform Party nominee in 1996.

Unlike formal, academic debates, the presidential confrontations have been loosely structured, at first with a panel of journalists or audience members asking the questions. Beginning in 1992 debate sponsors began having a journalist moderator question the candidates, with the audience sometimes allowed to participate. Throughout, there have been no judges to award points and therefore no way to determine who "won" or "lost" except by public opinion polling. Media commentators make immediate assessments of winners and losers, however, and their judgments undoubtedly influence the public's opinion about which candidate "won" the debate.

With one exception, vice-presidential nominees have debated since 1976 when Ford's running mate Robert Dole faced Democrat Walter F. Mondale. There was no debate in 1980 between Vice President Mondale and the Republican nominee, George Bush. The nominees in 2000, Republican Richard Cheney and Democrat Joseph I. Lieberman, debated once.

Early in the presidential debate era, the television networks or the League of Women Voters sponsored the debates. Since 1988 they have been sponsored by the bipartisan Commission on Presidential Debates.

THE POPULAR VOTE

The United States' winner-take-all electoral college system gives presidential and vice-presidential nominees an incentive to campaign where the votes are. Because in most states the leading vote-getter wins all that state's electoral votes, the system encourages nominees to win as many populous states as possible. Nominees generally spend most of their time in closely contested states, and just enough time in "likely win" states to ensure victory. Appearances in unfavorable states are usually symbolic efforts to show that the candidate is not conceding anything.

In the electoral college, states have votes equal to their representation in Congress: two for the senators and at least one for the representatives, for a total of 538 votes. (The District of Columbia has the three votes it would have if it were a state.) Two states, Maine and Nebraska, permit splitting their electoral votes between the statewide winner and the winner in each of the congressional districts (two in Maine, three in Nebraska) but as of 2000 no such split had occurred. *(See "Electoral College," p. 220; and Chapter 17, The Electoral College.)*

Four times in U.S. history—most recently in 2000—the winner of the presidential popular vote has lost the electoral college vote. In these and other close presidential races, a shift of a few hundred votes within one or two states could have changed the result of the election. In the most notable example, George W. Bush won Florida's twenty-five electoral votes by a scant 537 votes out of more than six million popular votes cast. After the Supreme Court halted Gore's requested manual recount, those 537 votes gave Bush the bare electoral vote majority he needed to win.

The disputed Florida election brought renewed calls for abolition or reform of the electoral college system. But it also spurred demands for modernization of methods of casting, recording, and reporting of the popular vote throughout the United States. The election brought to light that 37 percent of all U.S. registered voters were still being required to use outmoded punch-card voting systems similar to those blamed for much of the difficulty in Florida. *(See box, "In Wake of 2000 "News Disaster," Pressure Mounts for Voting, Coverage Reforms," p. 218.)*

Previously, little attention had been paid nationally to voting systems. Each state or locality was free to purchase whatever type of system it wanted or could afford, although the Federal Election Commission set standards for such equipment and recommended purchase of systems that met those standards.

Campaign finance reform and efforts to make registration easier and increase voter participation received higher priority from most groups in the final decades of the twentieth century. The National Voter Registration Act of 1993, the so-called motor-voter act, which enabled people to obtain registration forms when they picked up drivers' licenses, was an example of laws that helped put millions more people on the voting rolls. Yet the changes did not necessarily translate into higher turnouts at the polls. *(See "Broadening the Franchise," p. 21.)*

Actions to expand the electorate took place at both the state and federal levels. Voting qualifications varied widely because

Table 8-2
Voter Turnout in 2000 Elections

State	2000 voting age population	November 2000 registration	Percentage voting age registered	Presidential vote	Presidential Vote as Percent of Voting age population	Presidential Vote as Percent of Registered voters
Alabama	3,333,000	2,528,963	75.9%	1,666,272	50.0%	65.9%
Alaska	430,000	473,648	110.2%	285,560	66.4%	60.3%
Arizona	3,625,000	2,654,700	73.2%	1,532,016	42.3%	57.7%
Arkansas	1,929,000	1,555,809	80.7%	921,781	47.8%	59.2%
California	24,873,000	15,707,307	63.2%	10,965,856	44.1%	69.8%
Colorado	3,067,000	2,858,239	93.2%	1,741,368	56.8%	60.9%
Connecticut	2,499,000	2,031,626	81.3%	1,459,525	58.4%	71.8%
Delaware	582,000	503,672	86.5%	327,622	56.3%	65.0%
Florida	11,774,000	8,752,717	74.3%	5,963,110	50.6%	68.1%
Georgia	5,893,000	4,648,205	78.9%	2,596,645	44.1%	55.9%
Hawaii	909,000	637,349	70.1%	367,951	40.5%	57.7%
Idaho	921,000	728,085	79.1%	501,621	54.5%	68.9%
Illinois	8,983,000	7,117,449	79.2%	4,742,123	52.8%	66.6%
Indiana	4,448,000	4,000,809	89.9%	2,199,302	49.4%	55.0%
Iowa	2,165,000	1,969,199	91.0%	1,315,563	60.8%	66.8%
Kansas	1,983,000	1,623,623	81.9%	1,072,218	54.1%	66.0%
Kentucky	2,993,000	2,556,815	85.4%	1,544,187	51.6%	60.4%
Louisiana	3,255,000	2,782,929	85.5%	1,765,656	54.2%	63.4%
Maine	968,000	947,189	97.9%	651,817	67.3%	68.8%
Maryland	3,925,000	2,715,366	69.2%	2,020,480	51.5%	74.4%
Massachusetts	4,749,000	4,000,218	84.2%	2,702,984	56.9%	67.6%
Michigan	7,358,000	6,861,342	93.3%	4,232,711	56.6%	60.7%
Minnesota	3,547,000	2,801,077	79.0%	2,438,685	68.8%	87.1%
Mississippi	2,047,000			994,184	48.6%	
Missouri	4,105,000	3,676,664	89.6%	2,359,892	57.5%	64.2%
Montana	668,000	698,260	104.5%	410,997	61.5%	58.9%
Nebraska	1,234,000	1,085,272	87.9%	697,019	56.5%	64.2%
Nevada	1,390,000	878,970	63.2%	608,970	43.8%	69.3%
New Hampshire	911,000	856,519	94.0%	569,081	62.5%	66.4%
New Jersey	6,245,000	4,710,768	75.4%	3,187,226	51.0%	67.7%
New Mexico	1,263,000	928,931	73.5%	598,605	47.4%	64.4%
New York	13,805,000	11,262,816	81.6%	6,821,999	49.4%	60.6%
North Carolina	5,797,000	5,186,094	89.5%	2,911,262	50.2%	56.1%
North Dakota	477,000			288,256	60.4%	
Ohio	8,433,000	7,537,822	89.4%	4,701,998	55.8%	62.4%
Oklahoma	2,531,000	2,233,602	88.2%	1,234,229	48.8%	55.3%
Oregon	2,530,000	1,950,902	77.1%	1,533,968	60.6%	78.6%
Pennsylvania	9,155,000	7,781,997	85.0%	4,913,119	53.7%	63.1%
Rhode Island	753,000	655,107	87.0%	409,047	54.3%	62.4%
South Carolina	2,977,000	2,266,200	76.1%	1,382,717	46.4%	61.0%
South Dakota	542,000	520,881	96.1%	316,269	58.4%	60.7%
Tennessee	4,221,000	3,400,487	80.6%	2,076,181	49.2%	61.1%
Texas	14,850,000	12,365,235	83.3%	6,407,637	43.1%	51.8%
Utah	1,465,000	1,120,129	76.5%	770,754	52.6%	68.8%
Vermont	460,000	427,354	92.9%	294,308	64.0%	68.9%
Virginia	5,263,000	4,071,471	77.4%	2,739,447	52.1%	67.3%
Washington	4,368,000	3,335,714	76.4%	2,487,433	56.9%	74.6%
West Virginia	1,416,000	1,067,822	75.4%	648,124	45.8%	60.7%
Wisconsin	3,930,000			2,598,607	66.1%	
Wyoming	358,000	220,012	61.5%	218,351	61.0%	99.2%
Dist. of Col.	411,000	354,410		201,894	49.1%	57.0%
Total	205,814,000	159,049,775	77.3%	105,396,627	51.2%	66.3%

Note: Wisconsin and North Dakota do not maintain registration systems. Figures for Mississippi were unavailable. Excluding these states, the percentage of voting age population that was registered was 79.8 percent. The presidential vote as a percent of voting age population was 50.9 and as a percent of registered voters was 63.8.

Sources: Registration figures are from the Committee for the Study of the American Electorate; voting age population figures are from the U.S. Census Bureau.

In Wake of 2000 Election "News Disaster," Pressure Mounts for Voting, Coverage Reforms

The bitterly contested 2000 presidential election exposed serious flaws in how Americans cast their ballots and how the news media project and report the results. In the aftermath of the thirty-six-day Florida countdown, there was broad agreement that both systems needed overhauling.

In Congress, state legislatures, and network television boardrooms, proposals for change abounded. And if the reform fervor continued, it was likely that some improvements would be in place for the 2004 election and perhaps earlier.

Voting Systems

• **Punch Cards.** Among all the proposals, the one that seemed to command the widest agreement was phasing out the obsolescent punch cards widely used in Florida and in much of the nation. The technology, introduced in the 1960s, features the infamous *chad*, the tiny bit of paper that the voter punches out with a stylus to indicate his or her candidate choice. Failure to dislodge the chad fully (leaving it "hanging" or "dimpled") can lead to the vote's not being counted by the electronic reader.

The lack of standards for discerning the voter's intent by visual inspection of punch-card ballots was at the heart of Florida's recount problem and the U.S. Supreme Court's action in *Bush v. Gore*, which halted the spectacle of election officials holding ballots up to the light, looking for dented or incompletely detached chads. Florida counties using punch cards reported about 4 percent of six million ballots cast (240,000 ballots) were void, four times the rate of counties using optical scanning systems.

Two basically similar punch-card systems, the Votomatic and the Datavote, were still in widespread use in 2000. According to the Federal Election Commission (FEC), 37 percent of registered voters used punch-card systems, including 3.8 million in Los Angeles County, the largest U.S. voting jurisdiction.

• **Optical Scans.** The next most common voting system was the increasingly popular marksense or optical scanning device being used by 25 percent of voters. In marksense systems, the voter uses a marker to fill in an incomplete arrow or other empty block to indicate candidate choice on a ballot card. The card is then fed into a device that "reads" the card and tabulates the votes.

An advantage of optical scan over punch cards is that the cards leave a "paper trail" that can be inspected in a manual recount. Ballots spoiled by overvotes or marks outside the designated areas are rejected by the machine and deposited by precinct officials in a locked receptacle. The voter is then given a new ballot, which the machine reads and stores if the new card is properly filled out. In case of a manual recount, the voted ballot cards can be tabulated with little or no guesswork as to the voter's intent.

• **Mechanical Lever Machines.** Other than paper ballots, lever machines are the oldest type of voting system. One invented by Jacob H. Myers, a safemaker, was first officially used at Lockport, New York, in 1892, twenty-three years after Thomas A. Edison patented a similar machine. By the 1930s voting machines were being used in almost all major U.S. cities.

The machine booths typically featured a large lever that closed a privacy curtain as the voter entered. The voter pressed small levers to indicate candidate choices, or a larger lever to vote a straight party ticket. The lever that closed the curtain also opened it and returned the levers to their unvoted position and rotated counters to record the vote. When the polls closed the machines were sealed to prevent tampering in case of a recount.

At the end of the twentieth century, 21 percent of voters were still using mechanical voting machines. But they were no longer being made and computer-based systems were rapidly taking their place.

• **Paper Ballots.** Before voting machines came into widespread use, most states adopted a type of government-printed ballot introduced in Australia in 1876. It gave voters more privacy by sparing them the need to ask for a party-printed ballot. In the age of computers, 2 percent of U.S. voters still were using paper ballots, primarily in small communities. Absentee voting was also largely by paper ballot. And one state, Oregon, began conducting all elections by mail.

• **Direct Recording Electronic.** Called DRE for short, these are the newest voting systems. They display choices that the voter enters by touch-screen, button, or rotation device. A keyboard may be provided for write-in votes. The voter's choices are directly recorded in electronic memory and added to the totals for each candidate. Usage of DREs in 2000 was certain to surpass the 1996 figure of 8 percent of registered voters.

• **Mixed.** The remaining 7 percent of registered voters, according to the FEC, were in jurisdictions using combinations of old and new voting technologies.

Polls taken after the 2000 election showed broad public support for a stronger federal role in election administration. Many voters indicated they were unaware that states set most of the voting rules, even for presidential and congressional elections. A *Washington Post*-ABC News poll showed most Americans favored moving toward a national voting system, including a standard ballot design, a uniform poll-closing time, and consistent rules for manual recounts.

Many reform bills proposed funding for studies or modernization of equipment. Florida officials estimated it would cost $25 million to replace punch-card systems in twenty-four counties. In states where election officials were elected, as in Florida, reformers called for switching to bipartisan or nonpartisan appointed boards.

Although computer voting raised privacy and security concerns, prospects were bright for increased use of Internet voting systems. Arizona pioneered in this area in its 2000 Democratic primary, which gave voters a choice of using paper ballots, computer terminals, or mail-in ballots. The innovation produced a record turnout.

Three technology giants—Unisys, Dell Computer, and Microsoft—announced that they were teaming up to produce an integrated voting, registration, and reporting system. Other election equipment makers were optimistic that the 2000 election difficulties had improved the market for their products.

Media Projections

The news media's success in calling election results minutes after the polls close is based on exit polling, a relatively new technique. Through 2000, exit polls had been widely used in only five presidential elections. Until the system went spectacularly wrong in Florida in 2000, it had been remarkably accurate. But it took only that one embarrassment to force the media to reexamine themselves and promise changes to ensure the Florida mistake would not be repeated.

The reporting debacle began at 7:47 p.m. on November 7, 2000, when the networks called Al Gore the winner in Florida. About two hours later, they began retracting the call for Gore. At 2:16 a.m., some networks projected George W. Bush as the winner, which they later retracted as too close to call. *(See "The 2000 Cliffhanger: GOP Retakes the Presidency," p. 295.)*

Most of the projections were based on data from Voter News Service (VNS), a consortium formed by the Associated Press and the ABC, CBS, CNN, Fox, and NBC networks. Until 2000 VNS had only one other major error—in 1996 when for a time it projected a Democrat as the upset winner of a U.S. Senate seat in New Hampshire.

Warren Mitofsky, a former Census Bureau statistician hired by CBS, is credited with developing exit polling in the 1960s. By interviewing many thousands of citizens just after they have voted, pollsters can accurately predict election results without waiting for the official vote count. They also can gain some insight into why the voters acted as they did, along with indications of how the vote divided along lines of age, sex, race, religion, and income.

Before the formation of VNS, Jimmy Carter's decision to concede to Ronald Reagan in the 1980 presidential race at about 10:00 p.m. Eastern time on election day, while polls were still open in California, aroused controversy about exit polls and the networks' decisions to "declare" winners early. Some felt that this practice discouraged voters who had not yet cast their ballots because they thought their votes could not make a difference.

Some states subsequently tried to ban exit polls by creating so-called no-First-Amendment-zones near voting places, making it difficult if not impossible for poll-takers to identify and interview people who had just voted. But the courts ruled that First Amendment free speech and free press rights cannot be excluded from selected areas.

Congress considered similar legislation, but none was passed. In 1985 the broadcast networks pledged to Congress that they would not release exit poll results until the polls closed.

As in the 1980 case, the premature, erroneous call for Gore in Florida drew criticism because it came while people were still voting in the state's mostly Republican western panhandle, in the central time zone. Some potential voters said they stayed home after hearing Gore had "won."

What caused the wrong call? VNS managers said it was "a combination of many factors," including an unexpected increase in absentee ballots and possible underestimation of the black and Cuban votes. The later, also wrong, call for Bush was based on incorrect data from Volusia County and underestimating Palm Beach County's outstanding votes, the report said.

VNS founder Mitofsky, an election night analyst for CBS and CNN, said later he probably would have made the same call for Gore again. "Every bit of information we had was clearly pointing to a Gore call." That information was based on actual vote totals, he said, so exit polls were "not the source of the problem."

In early 2001 ABC, CBS, and NBC promised not to declare winners in any state in the future until all of its polls are closed. Members of Congress were skeptical, saying they had heard the same thing in 1985.

Fox News indicated it might not use VNS again and was exploring other polling options. CBS and NBC said they were reviewing VNS's performance. All the networks said they would make changes in their coverage, including more explanations of exit polling and how races are called.

At a congressional hearing on what columnist Ben Wattenberg called the "news disaster," he and other witnesses criticized the networks' "get it first" mentality. Wattenberg, coauthor of a CNN report on its coverage, said the networks "were competing with themselves to play beat-the-clock in a way that was ultimately truly senseless."

In an op-ed article entitled "Why Exit Polls Face Extinction," *Washington Post* polling director Richard Morin wrote that "exit polling, at least as we know it, is all but dead." He predicted that Congress would kill it because "irresponsible news organizations and self-aggrandizing" Internet journalists disregarded the networks' pledge to withhold exit poll results until the polls are closed.

Calling exit polls "the single best window we have on voting behavior," Morin mourned their possible demise. "Common sense and pleas for restraint," he said, "are no match for the anarchy of the 'Net in league with the arrogance of the media."

the U.S. Constitution (Article I, Section 2) permits the states to set their own voting standards. Early in the nation's history, the states dropped their property qualifications for voting, but some retained literacy tests as late as 1970.

On the federal level the Constitution has been amended five times to circumvent state qualifications denying the franchise to certain categories of people. The Fourteenth Amendment, ratified in 1868, directed Congress to reduce the number of representatives from any state that disfranchised adult male citizens for any reason other than commission of a crime. However, no such reduction was ever made. The Fifteenth Amendment, ratified in 1870, prohibited denial of the right to vote "on account of race, color or previous condition of servitude," and the Nineteenth Amendment in 1920 prohibited denial of that right "on account of sex." The Twenty-fourth Amendment, which came into effect in 1964, barred denial of the right to vote in any federal election "by reason of failure to pay any poll tax or other tax." Finally, in 1971 the Twenty-sixth Amendment lowered the voting age to eighteen in federal, state, and local elections.

Congress in the 1950s and 1960s enacted a series of statutes to enforce the Fifteenth Amendment's guarantee against racial discrimination in voting. A law passed in 1970 nullified state residence requirements of longer than thirty days for voting in presidential elections, suspended literacy tests for a five-year period (the suspension was made permanent in 1975), and lowered the minimum voting age to eighteen years from twenty-one, the requirement then in effect in most states. A 1970 Supreme Court ruling upheld the voting-age change for federal elections but invalidated it for state and local elections. In the same decision the Court upheld the provision on residence requirements and sustained the suspension of literacy tests with respect to both state and local elections. The Twenty-sixth Amendment was ratified six months after the Court's decision.

The right to vote in presidential elections was extended to citizens of the District of Columbia by the Twenty-third Amendment, ratified in 1961. District residents had been disfranchised from national elections except for a brief period in the 1870s when they elected a nonvoting delegate to the House of Representatives. In 1970 Congress took another step toward full suffrage for District residents by again authorizing the election of a nonvoting delegate to the House.

Through the various state or federal reforms, virtually all citizens aged eighteen or over were eligible to vote at the beginning of the twenty-first century. By 2001, following the decennial census, the U.S. Census Bureau estimated the nation's voting age population at 205.8 million. But a relatively low 105.4 million voted in the November 7, 2000, presidential election, for a turnout rate of 51.2 percent.

Because the United States does not register voters nationally, reliable figures on the number of registered voters were not available until motor-voter required states to report the numbers to the FEC. In 1996 the states reported a total of 146.2 million registered voters. Using that figure, only about 71.0 percent of voting age citizens were registered in 2000, and the turnout among registered voters was about 72.1 percent in the November election that year.

Electoral College

Even after the winner has declared victory and the loser has conceded defeat, at least two more steps must be taken before a president-elect is officially declared. The first occurs on the first Monday after the second Wednesday in December. On that day electors meet in their respective state capitals to cast their votes for president.

Each state has as many electors as it has members of Congress. Typically, slates of electors are pledged before the popular election to each of the presidential nominees. The presidential nominee who wins the state wins that state's electors. Although the Constitution does not require electors to remain faithful to their pledge of support for a particular candidate, many states have laws to that effect. Such laws, however, are generally regarded as unenforceable and likely unconstitutional. There have been several instances in which "faithless electors" did not vote for their party's nominee.

The second step occurs when the electors' ballots are opened and counted before a joint session of Congress in early January. The candidate who wins a majority of the vote is declared the president-elect and is inaugurated three weeks later on January 20. The counting of electoral votes by a joint session of Congress is normally a routine affair. But in 2001 a number of Democratic House members attempted unsuccessfully to have Florida's controversial twenty-five electoral votes for Bush thrown out.

In the rare event that no presidential candidate receives a majority of the electoral college vote, the election is thrown into the House of Representatives. If no vice-presidential candidate receives a majority of the electoral college vote, the Senate is called upon to make the selection.

Term of Office

A president's term begins with inauguration at noon on January 20 following the November election. Until the Twentieth Amendment was ratified in 1933, presidents were not inaugurated until March 4, leaving a four-month hiatus between the election and the inauguration. The briefer interval established by the so-called lame-duck amendment shortened the period in which the nation had, in effect, two presidents—the outgoing president and an incoming president-elect. Yet the amendment allowed time for an orderly transition between the old and the new administrations.

The Twentieth Amendment took effect in 1933 after President Franklin Roosevelt and Vice President John Nance Garner had been sworn in. In 1937, at the beginning of their second terms, they became the first president and vice president inaugurated on January 20.

Roads to the White House

The earliest tradition concerning the path to the presidency developed around the secretary of state, who was considered the preeminent cabinet officer and therefore the most important person in the executive branch after the president. Thomas

Jefferson was Washington's first secretary of state. Although he left the cabinet early in Washington's second term, he went on to become leader of the newly formed Democratic-Republican Party and its candidate for president in 1796, 1800, and 1804. Losing to Adams in 1796, Jefferson came back to win four years later.

In turn, James Madison, Jefferson's secretary of state for two terms, won the presidency in 1808. Madison had been a close ally of Jefferson's in the political struggles of the 1790s and served throughout Jefferson's two presidential terms as secretary of state (1801–1809). During his first term as president, Madison appointed fellow Virginian James Monroe as his secretary of state. And following in what was rapidly becoming a tradition, Monroe went on to the presidency in 1816, serving two terms (1817–1825).

Throughout Monroe's terms, the secretary of state was John Quincy Adams, son of former president John Adams. At the end of Monroe's second term, five major candidates entered the race to succeed him. Three were cabinet officers, including Adams. None of the candidates managed to acquire a majority in the electoral college, so the House of Representatives then chose Secretary of State Adams.

Adams was the last secretary of state to go directly from his cabinet post to the White House. After him, only two secretaries of state made it to the White House at all—Van Buren, who was secretary of state from 1829 to 1831 and president from 1837 to 1841, and James Buchanan, who served as secretary of state under President James K. Polk (1845–1849) and as president from 1857 to 1861.

Two other institutions died at approximately the same time as the cabinet tradition—the Virginia dynasty and "King Caucus," a derogatory term referring to the congressional party caucuses that met throughout the early 1800s to designate presidential nominees.

After the four Virginians who occupied the presidency during the first thirty-six years of the Republic—Washington, Jefferson, Madison, and Monroe—there have been no elected presidents who were born in and made their careers in Virginia. John Tyler was born there but succeeded to the presidency from the vice presidency in 1841 and was not renominated. Three other presidents were born in Virginia but made their careers elsewhere—William Henry Harrison, Zachary Taylor, and Woodrow Wilson.

During its heyday, the Washington-centered mentality of King Caucus had virtually guaranteed that cabinet officers should be among those most often nominated by the party in power. But the caucus came under attack as being undemocratic and unrepresentative and ceased to function as a presidential nominating mechanism after 1824. It was eventually replaced by the national party conventions, bodies that are not connected with Congress and that, as of the 2000 presidential election, had never met in the national capital.

MILITARY MEN

The next cycle of American politics, from the presidency of Jackson (1829–1837) to the Civil War, saw a variety of back-

Andrew Jackson (above) gained his initial fame as hero of the Battle of New Orleans. From George Washington in the late 1700s to Dwight Eisenhower in the 1950s, Americans have occasionally elevated military officers to the presidency.

grounds qualify candidates for the presidency. One of the most prevalent was the military. Jackson, who ran in 1824 (unsuccessfully), 1828, and 1832, was a general in the War of 1812, gaining near-heroic stature by his defeat of the British at the Battle of New Orleans in January 1815. Like most military officers who rose to the presidency, however, Jackson was only a part-time military man. As a politician, he had served in the U.S. House during Washington's presidency and in the Senate during John Adams's administration, as well as later under Monroe and John Quincy Adams. Only presidents Taylor, Ulysses S. Grant, and Dwight Eisenhower were career military officers.

Other candidates during this era who were or had been military officers included William Harrison, a Whig candidate in 1836 and 1840; Taylor, the Whig candidate in 1848; Winfield Scott, the 1852 Whig candidate; Franklin Pierce, the Democratic nominee in 1852; and John C. Fremont in 1856, the Republican Party's first presidential candidate. From 1824 through 1856, all but one presidential election (1844) featured a major candidate with a military background.

Like Jackson, Harrison had a mixed military and political career. A member of a distinguished Virginia family, he was the son of a signer of the Declaration of Independence. Harrison served in Congress during the John Adams administration and again under Madison, Monroe, and John Quincy Adams. In between, he battled the Indians and the British during the War of 1812.

Taylor and Scott led victorious armies in the Mexican War. Pierce also had a command in the Mexican War, although he had been primarily a politician, with service in both the House and the Senate during the 1830s and 1840s. Fremont was famous as an explorer as well as for a dashing military campaign through California during the Mexican War. Later, he was a U.S. senator from the young state of California (1850–1851).

The smoldering political conflicts of the 1840s and 1850s probably contributed to the naming of military men for the presidency. Generals usually had escaped involvement in national politics and had avoided taking stands on the issues that divided the country—slavery, expansion, the currency, and the tariff. In 1840, for example, the Whigs adopted no platform or statement of principle; they simply nominated Harrison and assumed that his personal popularity plus the resentments against Van Buren's administration would suffice for Whig victory. They were correct.

Later on, the nature of the Civil War almost automatically led at least one of the parties to choose a military officer as presidential standard-bearer every four years. To have been on the "right" side during the war—fighting to save the Union and destroy slavery—was a major political asset in the North and Midwest, where tens of thousands of war veterans were effectively organized in the Grand Army of the Republic (GAR). The GAR became part of the backbone of the Republican Party during the last third of the nineteenth century.

Consequently, it became customary for Republicans to have a Civil War officer at the head of their ticket. Except for James G. Blaine in 1884, every Republican presidential nominee from 1868 to 1900 had served as an officer in the Union Army during the Civil War. Blaine, who had spent the war years as a Maine state legislator and a member of the U.S. House, lost the election to Grover Cleveland.

Of all the late nineteenth century Republican nominees, however, only Grant, who was elected president in 1868 and 1872, was a professional military man. The others—Rutherford B. Hayes in 1876, James A. Garfield in 1880, Benjamin Harrison in 1888 and 1892, and William McKinley in 1896 and 1900—were civilians who volunteered for Civil War service. Two of them—Hayes and Garfield—were elected to the House while serving in the army. At the time of their presidential nominations. Hayes was governor of Ohio, Garfield was minority leader of the U.S. House and a senator-elect, Harrison was a former senator from Indiana, and McKinley was a former governor of Ohio.

The Democrats, who had been split over the war, had few prominent military veterans to choose from. Only twice between 1860 and 1900 did the Democrats pick a Civil War officer as their nominee. In 1864, during the war, the Democrats nominated Gen. George B. McClellan, the Union military commander who had fallen out with President Abraham Lincoln. And in 1880 Gen. Winfield Scott Hancock of Pennsylvania was the Democrats' choice.

NEW YORK AND INDIANA

From the Civil War to the midtwentieth century, several governors or former governors of New York were Democratic standard bearers. The 1868 nominee was Horatio Seymour, who had been governor there in 1853–1855 and again in 1863–1865. In 1876 the Democrats chose Samuel J. Tilden, New York's reform governor who was battling Tammany Hall. And in 1884 Cleveland, another New York reform governor, captured the Democratic nomination. He went on to become the first Democrat to win the White House in twenty-eight years. Cleveland was again the Democratic nominee in 1888 and 1892.

Besides being the most populous state, New York was a swing state in presidential politics. During the period from Reconstruction through the turn of the century, most southern states voted Democratic, although the Republicans usually carried Pennsylvania, the Midwest, and New England. A New Yorker appeared as the nominee for president or vice president of at least one of the major parties in every election from 1868 through 1892.

This general tradition was maintained through the candidacy of Thomas E. Dewey, Republican governor of New York, in 1948. Only twice between 1868 and 1948 was there no New Yorker on the national ticket of at least one of the major parties—for president or vice president. Once, in 1944, both major party presidential nominees, Democrat Franklin D. Roosevelt and Republican Dewey, were from New York.

From 1952 to 1996, however, no New Yorkers were nominated by a major party for president and only three for vice president. The latter three were Rep. William E. Miller, R, in 1964; Rep. Geraldine A. Ferraro, D, in 1984; and Rep Jack Kemp, R, in 1996. Eisenhower in 1952 and Nixon in 1968 were technically residents of New York but were generally identified with other states. President Gerald R. Ford's vice president, Nelson Rockefeller, was a former governor of New York, but he was appointed to the vice presidency. He was not asked to be on the ticket when Ford ran in 1976.

Another major swing state in the years from the Civil War through World War I was Indiana. In most elections during this period a prominent Indianan found his way onto one of the major party's national tickets. In the thirteen presidential elections between 1868 and 1916, an Indianan appeared ten times on at least one of the major parties' national tickets. However, from 1916 to 2000 only two Indianans, Wendell Willkie in 1940 and Dan Quayle in 1988 and 1992, were major party nominees.

GOVERNORS

From 1900 to 1956 Democrats tended to favor governors for the presidential nomination, whether from New York or elsewhere. Democratic governors who received their party's presidential nomination included Wilson of New Jersey in 1912, James M. Cox of Ohio in 1920, Alfred E. Smith of New York in 1928, Franklin D. Roosevelt of New York in 1932, and Adlai E. Stevenson of Illinois in 1952.

During the same period, Republican presidential nominees had a wide variety of backgrounds. There were two cabinet officers (Secretary of War William Howard Taft in 1908 and Secretary of Commerce Herbert Hoover in 1928), a Supreme Court justice (Charles Evans Hughes in 1916), a U.S. senator (Warren G. Harding in 1920), two governors (Alfred M. Landon of

Table 8-3
"Minority" Presidents

Under the U.S. electoral system, there have been eighteen presidential elections (decided by either the electoral college itself or by the House of Representatives) where the victor did not receive a majority of the popular votes cast in the election. Four of these presidents—John Quincy Adams in 1824, Rutherford B. Hayes in 1876, Benjamin Harrison in 1888, and George W. Bush in 2000—actually trailed their opponents in the popular vote.

The following table shows the percentage of the popular vote received by candidates in the eighteen elections in which a "minority" president (designated by boldface type) was elected:

Year Elected	Candidate	Percentage of Popular Vote	Candidate	Percentage of Popular Vote	Candidate	Percentage of Popular Vote	Candidate	Percentage of Popular Vote
1824	Jackson	41.34	**Adams**	30.92	Clay	12.99	Crawford	11.17
1844	**Polk**	49.54	Clay	48.08	Birney	2.30		
1848	**Taylor**	47.28	Cass	42.49	Van Buren	10.12		
1856	**Buchanan**	45.28	Fremont	33.11	Fillmore	21.53		
1860	**Lincoln**	39.82	Douglas	29.46	Breckenridge	18.09	Bell	12.61
1876	Tilden	50.97	**Hayes**	47.95	Cooper	.97		
1880	**Garfield**	48.27	Hancock	48.25	Weaver	3.32	Others	.15
1884	**Cleveland**	48.50	Blaine	48.25	Butler	1.74	St. John	1.47
1888	Cleveland	48.62	**Harrison**	47.82	Fisk	2.19	Streeter	1.29
1892	**Cleveland**	46.05	Harrison	42.96	Weaver	8.50	Others	2.25
1912	**Wilson**	41.84	T. Roosevelt	27.39	Taft	23.18	Debs	5.99
1916	**Wilson**	49.24	Hughes	46.11	Benson	3.18	Others	1.46
1948	**Truman**	49.52	Dewey	45.12	Thurmond	2.40	Wallace	2.38
1960	**Kennedy**	49.72	Nixon	49.55	Others	.72		
1968	**Nixon**	43.42	Humphrey	42.72	Wallace	13.53	Others	.33
1992	**Clinton**	43.01	G. Bush	37.45	Perot	18.91	Others	.64
1996	**Clinton**	49.24	Dole	40.71	Perot	8.40	Others	1.65
2000	Gore	48.38	**G. W. Bush**	47.87	Nader	2.74	Others	1.01

Kansas in 1936 and Dewey of New York in 1944 and 1948), a private lawyer (Willkie in 1940), and a general (Eisenhower in 1952 and 1956). Calvin Coolidge of Massachusetts, the 1924 nominee, and Theodore Roosevelt of New York, the 1904 nominee, who succeeded to the presidency from the vice presidency, had been governors of their respective states.

Curiously, the two world wars did not produce a plethora of military candidates. The only general besides Eisenhower who made a strong bid for a presidential nomination was Gen. Leonard Wood, who had commands in the Spanish-American War and World War I. Wood led on five ballots at the 1920 Republican National Convention before losing out on the tenth ballot to Harding. Otherwise only a few military men were even mentioned for the presidency in the twentieth century—most notably Gen. Douglas MacArthur in the 1940s and 1950s (he got little support at GOP conventions) and Gen. Colin Powell in the 1990s. Powell the former chairman of the armed forces joint chiefs of staff during the 1991 Persian Gulf War, received a lot of national attention in 1995 before he announced he would not seek the 1996 Republican nomination.

SENATORS AND FORMER VICE PRESIDENTS

An abrupt change took place in 1960 with the nomination of John F. Kennedy, a senator, and Nixon, a former senator and sitting vice president. It was only the second time in the twentieth century that an incumbent U.S. senator was nominated for the presidency. The first time was in 1920 when the Republicans nominated Harding from Ohio. In the nineteenth century the phenomenon also had been rare, with National-Republican Henry Clay in 1832, Democrat Lewis Cass in 1848, and Democrat Stephen A. Douglas in 1860 the only incumbent senators nominated for president by official party conventions. Republican James A. Garfield was a senator-elect at the time of his election in 1880. Beginning with Kennedy's ascension from the Senate to the White House in 1960, senators dominated presidential campaigns until 1976. During those sixteen years every major party nominee was a senator or former senator.

The nomination of Nixon, like the nomination of Kennedy, was also a sign of things to come. It was the first time since 1860 and only the third time in the history of party nominating conventions that an incumbent vice president was chosen for the presidency. Beginning in 1960 the vice presidency, like the Senate, became a presidential training ground. Vice President Hubert H. Humphrey was chosen by the Democrats for president in 1968. That same year the Republicans renominated Nixon, who went on to win the presidency eight years after being vice president.

Vice President Spiro T. Agnew was the leading contender for the 1976 Republican presidential nomination before his resignation in October 1973. In 1984 former vice president Walter F. Mondale, who had served under Jimmy Carter, emerged as the

Democratic choice for the presidential nomination. When George Bush won the presidency in 1988, after filling the second spot under Reagan for eight years, it marked the first time a sitting vice president had been elected president since Van Buren in 1836. Democratic vice president Al Gore tried to duplicate Bush's success in 2000. He won the popular vote but lost in the electoral college to Bush's son, George W. Bush.

Even defeated vice presidential nominees have been considered for the nomination—witness Henry Cabot Lodge Jr. of Massachusetts in 1964, Edmund S. Muskie of Maine in 1972, Sargent Shriver of Maryland in 1976, and Bob Dole of Kansas in 1980, 1988, and 1996, when he was the GOP nominee.

GOVERNORS AGAIN

The field of candidates for the 1980 presidential nomination continued a trend that first appeared in the 1976 campaign—the reemergence of governors as leading contenders in the nomination sweepstakes. Although there was no shortage of senators in the 1976 campaign, it was the governors who attracted the most attention. Former California governor Reagan came close to depriving incumbent Ford of the Republican presidential nomination. The Democratic nominee and eventual winner, former Georgia governor Carter, faced a dramatic last-minute challenge from the governor of California at the time, Jerry Brown. Reagan (successfully), Carter, and Brown were candidates again in 1980; Reagan was again successful in 1984.

In 1988 and 1992 the field of Democratic presidential candidates contained a near equal mix of governors and senators, but two Democratic governors established momentum early in the primaries. In 1988 Massachusetts governor Michael S. Dukakis won enough delegates by June to take the Democratic nomination, but he lost to Vice President Bush in the November general election. In 1992 Arkansas governor Clinton secured the nomination by early April and went on to defeat the incumbent Bush. Bush's son George, the Texas governor, continued the trend in 2000 by locking up the GOP nomination in March and going on to defeat the incumbent vice president, Gore.

CHAPTER 9

Chronology of Presidential Elections

IN THE EARLY YEARS of the Republic, the American people and their leaders were ambivalent about the concept of democracy. On the one hand, Americans searched for ways to prevent the kind of tyranny they had experienced at the hand of elite rulers such as King George. On the other hand, political elites feared the instability that might result from mass participation in politics. This ambivalence was evident in the compromise for presidential selection worked out at the Constitutional Convention in 1787 and in the halting steps the nation took toward party competition.

The presidential selection process has changed significantly since George Washington was elected to his first term in 1789. The electoral college is still the center of the system, but all of the related institutions and processes are dramatically different, in part because the constitutional provisions for presidential selection are so vague.

The major features of the electoral system have developed over time as a process of trial and error. The Constitution contains no provisions for organizing political parties, nominating candidates, or campaigning for office. The Framers assumed, incorrectly, that the selection process would be a reasoned one that would transcend petty partisanship. The original provision for balloting by the electoral college was flawed and had to be superseded by the Twelfth Amendment in 1804.

Until the eighteenth century, competitive elections were rare. The nation's first legislative body, the Virginia House of Burgesses, had largely single-candidate elections until the 1700s, and later, even when the elections for state legislatures attracted more than one candidate, there was little active campaigning. It was only with the decline of homogeneous communities and the end of elite control over politics that election contests began to occur.

The very concept of the political party—a way to organize electoral coalitions—was viewed with distrust by the nation's earliest leaders. As George Washington described the dangers of parties in a letter: "A fire not to be quenched; it demands a uniform vigilance to prevent its bursting into a flame, lest instead of warming it should consume."[1] Only after the experience of factional debate in Congress, where bitter strife developed over issues such as banking, tariffs, and slavery, did the idea of parties seem necessary and capable of control.

The Emergence of the Electoral Process

The method of choosing presidential and vice-presidential candidates has moved through four distinct phases, according to political scientist Richard P. McCormick.[2] The first phase was a period marked by uncertain and hazardous rules that lasted until the Twelfth Amendment was ratified in 1804. The second phase, continuing through 1820, saw the decline of the Federalists as a national force and the dominance of the Democratic-Republicans. This phase is associated with "King Caucus"—the nomination of candidates by congressional caucuses. In the third phase, King Caucus was replaced by factional politics and unsettled rules for selecting candidates. The fourth phase—still in effect today—evolved between 1832 and 1844. It is characterized by a two-party system that nominates candidates by national conventions. In recent years, however, the conventions have been rendered obsolete by mass politics, which takes the form of mass media presentations of candidates to the public and mass participation of party members in primary elections.

WASHINGTON'S FIRST ELECTION: 1789

Establishment of the rules for democratic decision making in the United States occurred inauspiciously. The states completed their separate ratifications of the Constitution in July 1788—nearly nine months after the close of the Constitutional Convention in Philadelphia. The Continental Congress then decided that New York City would serve as the seat of government. There, on September 13, 1788, Congress passed a resolution requiring the states to appoint electors on the first Wednesday in January, the electors to assemble and vote in their respective states on the first Wednesday in February, and the new government to convene on the first Wednesday in March.

Under the Constitution, the method of choosing electors was left up to the individual state legislatures. *(See "Methods of Choosing Electors," p. 703.)* The requirement that all electors be chosen on the same day proved to be troublesome for the states. Some did not have time to call elections. In New York, for example, where electors were to have been chosen by the legislature, dissension between the two houses led to a stalemate and prevented the state from participating in the election.

No formal nomination of candidates took place in 1788. Nevertheless, it had been widely anticipated since the Constitutional Convention the previous year that George Washington of Virginia, the reluctant hero of the Revolutionary War, would be president. The only real question was who would be the vice president. Leaders of the Federalists, a group organized in the fall of 1787 to achieve ratification of the Constitution, ultimately decided to support John Adams of Massachusetts.

The inherent flaws of the electoral system became evident quickly. Under the Constitution, each elector was to cast two votes for president. The two votes had to be for different persons, and the two candidates could not both receive votes from a

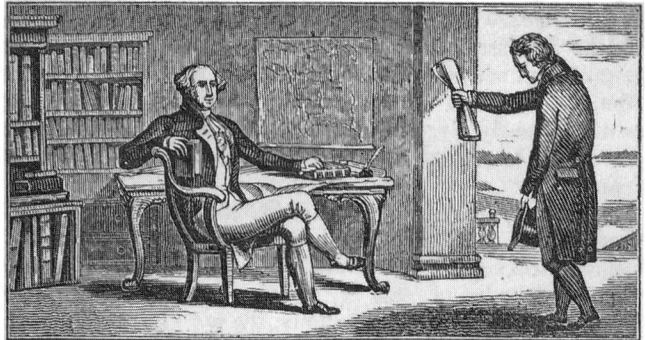

After riding his horse for a full week, Charles Thomson, secretary of the Continental Congress, arrived at Mt. Vernon on April 14, 1789, with the official news of George Washington's election as the first president of the United States.

common home state. The individual receiving the votes of a majority of the electors was to be named president, and the person receiving the second highest total was to be named vice president. Because no distinction was made between balloting for president and vice president, it was possible for more than one candidate to receive an equal number of votes, thereby throwing the election into the House of Representatives. It also was possible that a candidate for vice president—through fluke or machination—actually could end up with the most votes and become president.

The Federalist leader Alexander Hamilton recognized the danger, and his personal animosity toward Adams aggravated his concern. In response, he plotted to siphon away votes from Adams. In a letter to James Wilson of Pennsylvania, Hamilton wrote: "Everybody is aware of that defect in the constitution which renders it possible that the man intended for vice president may in fact turn up president." To prevent such a crisis, Hamilton recommended that several votes that would otherwise have gone to Adams be thrown away on other candidates: "I have proposed to friends in Connecticut to throw away 2 [votes], to others in New Jersey to throw away an equal number and I submit to you whether it would not be well to lose three or four in Pennsylvania."[3]

Hamilton's efforts were successful. Washington was unanimously elected president with sixty-nine electoral votes. Adams, however, won the vice presidency with only thirty-four electoral votes. Just two states—New Hampshire and his own Massachusetts—voted solidly for him. Because in other states Federalist leaders withheld support from Adams and sometimes worked against him, he did not receive *any* votes from Delaware, Georgia, Maryland, and South Carolina, and he received only one vote from New Jersey. The remaining votes were spread among ten other candidates, including John Jay, John Hancock, Robert Harrison, John Rutledge, and George Clinton.

Although the new government was supposed to open its doors on March 4, 1789, not enough members of Congress had arrived in New York City by that date to achieve a quorum. When the Senate finally convened on April 6 and counted the electoral votes, a messenger was dispatched on horseback to deliver the news to President-elect Washington at his home in Mount Vernon, Virginia. He received the news on April 14.

Washington then set out for New York where he was sworn in on April 30.

Before the end of Washington's first term as president, political divisions developed that would lead to a party system. James Madison emerged as the de facto opposition leader in Congress. Seventeen members of the House of Representatives regularly sided with Madison, and a bloc of fifteen supported the administration. The other dozen or so members of the House switched back and forth between the administration's and Madison's faction.[4]

The election of 1789 demonstrated the potential for partisanship and intrigue in presidential contests. It also revealed the weaknesses of the existing election calendar (which had made it difficult for New York to participate in the election) and reminded participants of the danger of the constitutional "defect" in the selection process that made it possible for the person intended to be vice president to become president.

WASHINGTON'S REELECTION: 1792

George Washington remained first in the hearts of his countrymen when his first term as president drew to a close in 1792. But the facade of national unity was showing signs of crumbling as bitter oppositional factions began to develop. From this arose a system of electoral competition.

Washington won a second unanimous term as president in 1792, but the election did produce competition for vice president. An overtly partisan contest broke out when the Democratic-Republicans, as one faction was now known, decided to challenge the Federalist John Adams. Some of Adams's approving statements about the British angered populists, who campaigned behind the scenes against him. Adams managed to win, but not before bitter partisan identities had developed in response to the nation's only unanimous administration.

The election was different from the 1789 one in another way as well. The election calendar was changed and made more flexible by an act of Congress that allowed states to choose electors within a thirty-four-day span before the first Wednesday in December when the electors met to vote. The new law remained in effect until 1845.

Thomas Jefferson, the leader of the Democratic-Republicans, chose not to run for vice president in 1792, in part because he came from the same state as President Washington. Because electors could vote for only one candidate from their own state, Jefferson was tacitly precluded from receiving the large electoral vote of Virginia. Besides, a "balanced ticket" required regional diversity. Instead, Democratic-Republican leaders from New York, Pennsylvania, Virginia, and South Carolina chose New York governor George Clinton as their candidate at a meeting in Philadelphia in October 1792. The endorsement of Clinton was a milestone in the evolution of the presidential nominating process and a step away from the Framers' original understanding of the selection process.

Both Washington and Adams were reelected, but Clinton scored well in the electoral college. Adams received 77 electoral votes to Clinton's 50 (with four votes going to Jefferson and one to Sen. Aaron Burr of New York), and Washington was reelected president by a unanimous electoral vote of 132.

The political tensions brought out by the Adams-Clinton contest became even tauter as policy controversies arose. Thomas Jefferson resigned as secretary of state in 1793 in protest over Secretary of the Treasury Alexander Hamilton's growing influence in foreign affairs. Jefferson complained: "In place of that noble love of liberty and Republican government which carried us triumphantly through the war, an Anglican, Monarchical, and Aristocratical party has sprung up, whose avowed subject is to draw over us the substance as they have already done the forms of the British government." Even Washington was subject to attacks. A Pennsylvania politician wondered aloud if Washington had not "become the tyrant instead of the saviour of his country."[5]

News of the French Revolution's period of terror divided the nation's political leaders. Federalists recoiled in horror with the news of a democratic revolution gone awry, while democrats such as Thomas Jefferson expressed sympathy for France's struggle. The U.S. government's use of troops to suppress the Whiskey Rebellion of 1794, approval of the Jay Treaty of 1794, and maneuvering between the warring French and British also polarized the young nation into factions. State-level Democratic-Republican societies formed during this period in opposition to the Federalists.

THE FIRST SUCCESSION: 1796

George Washington decided not to run for president again in 1796, even though the Constitution did not bar a third term and public sentiment supported it. With Washington out of the race, the United States witnessed its first partisan contest for president. Washington's Farewell Address, published in the summer of 1796, was "a signal, like dropping a hat, for the party racers to start."[6]

On the Democratic-Republican side, Thomas Jefferson faced no opposition as the presidential candidate; a consensus of party leaders selected him to run in 1796. But a caucus of Democratic-Republican senators was unable to agree on a running mate, producing a tie vote for Sen. Aaron Burr of New York and Sen. Pierce Butler of South Carolina that ended with a walkout by Butler's supporters. As a result, there was no formal Democratic-Republican candidate to run with Jefferson.

The Federalists, by contrast, held what historian Roy F. Nichols has described as a "quasi caucus" of the party's members of Congress in Philadelphia in May 1796.[7] The gathering chose Vice President Adams and Minister to Great Britain Thomas Pinckney of South Carolina as the Federalist presidential and vice-presidential candidates. The choice of Adams was not surprising because he was Washington's vice president. Nevertheless, Adams was unpopular in the South, and he continued to be disliked by Hamilton. As a result, Hamilton tried to use the "defect" in the Constitution to make Pinckney president instead of Adams. He urged northern electors to give equal support to Adams and Pinckney in the hopes that the South would not vote for Adams and that Pinckney would therefore win the most votes.

Had the northern electors followed Hamilton's advice, Pinckney might have won the presidency. Instead, eighteen votes were thrown to other Federalists (thereby preventing a

Thomas Pinckney, the Federalist choice for vice president, was not elected in 1796, although Federalist presidential candidate John Adams won the election. Democratic-Republican Thomas Jefferson won the vice presidency. The Twelfth Amendment (1804) precluded future split-ticket administrations.

Pinckney claim to the presidency), giving Adams the presidency with seventy-one electoral votes. Pinckney—with fifty-nine votes—was not even able to win the vice presidency. Jefferson—the candidate of the opposing Democratic-Republican ticket—came in second with sixty-eight votes and became Adams's vice president. Although the results again played up the defects in the constitutional procedure for electing presidents, Federalists and Democratic-Republicans did not seem unduly concerned that the president and vice president were of opposing parties. Both sides felt that they had prevented the opposition from gaining total victory.

For the first and last time, a foreign figure played an active and public role in the election. French Ambassador Pierre Adet promoted Jefferson's campaign in appearances and in written statements. Whether the Adet effort helped or hurt Jefferson is uncertain. The effort aroused supporters of France but angered others who favored Great Britain or resented outside interference.

JEFFERSON'S REVENGE: 1800

The election of 1800 was the first in which both parties used congressional caucuses to nominate candidates for their tickets. Such caucuses were an important innovation in the presidential selection process because they formalized partisan alignments in Congress and demonstrated the emergence of organized political parties.

President Adams was hated bitterly by farmers, populists, and states' rights advocates. In one of the nation's first professionally run smear campaigns, Adams was denounced as a "hideous hermaphroditical character which has neither the force and firmness of a man, nor the gentleness and sensibility of a woman."[8]

Federalist members of Congress met in the Senate chamber in Philadelphia on May 3, 1800, to choose their candidates. As in previous presidential election years, Federalists were divided in their support of Adams, yet they felt they had to nominate him because he was the incumbent president. Their ambivalence toward Adams was revealed, however, when they nominated both Adams and Maj. Gen. Charles Cotesworth Pinckney of South Carolina without giving preference to one or the other for president. Pinckney was the elder brother of the Federalist vice-presidential candidate in 1796.

The choice of Pinckney was made at Hamilton's insistence. Once again Hamilton was plotting to use the constitutional defect against Adams. In 1796 South Carolina had voted for an all-southern ticket—Jefferson and Thomas Pinckney—even though the two were of opposing parties. Hamilton hoped that South Carolina would vote the same way in 1800, and that all other Federalist electors could be persuaded to vote for Adams and Charles Pinckney. That would give Pinckney more votes than Adams, thus making him president.

Although the deliberations of the Federalist caucus were secret, the existence of the meeting was not. It was described by the local Democratic-Republican paper, the Philadelphia *Aurora*, as a "Jacobinical conclave." Further denunciations by the paper's editor, Benjamin F. Bache, earned him a personal rebuke from the U.S. Senate.

The Democratic-Republicans once again chose Jefferson as the presidential candidate by consensus. On May 11 a caucus of Democratic-Republican members of Congress met at Marache's boarding house in Philadelphia to choose a running mate. Their unanimous choice was Aaron Burr.

Although there was no such thing as a formal party platform in 1800, Jefferson wrote fairly detailed statements of principle in letters to various correspondents. Among other things, the Democratic-Republicans believed in states' rights, a small national government, and a relatively weak executive. They opposed standing armies in peacetime, a large naval force, and alliances with other countries. And they denounced the Alien and Sedition Acts, which had been passed by the Federalists in 1798, ostensibly to protect the nation from subversives given the threat of war with France.

The election in 1800 witnessed other signs of formal public campaigning. Tickets listing the names of Democratic-Republican electors were printed and distributed in a number of states, including New York, Massachusetts, Pennsylvania, and Delaware. Speeches in behalf of the candidates increased markedly. Partisan newspapers also helped to spread the party positions—the number of newspapers in the United States had grown dramatically in the last decade of the century, from 91 to 234.[9] Despite attempts by the Federalist Party to muzzle the opposition press with the passage of the Sedition Act of 1798, partisan newspapers on both sides actively defamed the opposition. Ultimately, the Sedition Act worked against the Federalists by turning the Democratic-Republicans into public champions of a free press.

Increased partisan activity spurred voter participation. Because electors still were chosen indirectly in twelve of the sixteen states, voters often expressed themselves through state legislative elections as a means of influencing future presidential elections.[10] The seeds were being sown for a new phase in the development of the presidential election process.

A harbinger of Democratic-Republican success came in May when the New York state party won state legislative elections. Burr managed the campaign in the state, building a machine with ward and precinct organizations. Burr's efforts showed the importance of large-scale mobilization—a lesson that would not be lost on the party in future years.

When the electors voted in December, the constitutional defect did not work as Hamilton had hoped. Instead of resulting in a Pinckney victory, the defect produced an unexpected tie vote between the two Democratic-Republican candidates, Jefferson and Burr—each of whom had seventy-three electoral votes. Adams came in third with sixty-five, and Pinckney followed with sixty-four. In accord with the Constitution, the election was thrown into the Federalist-controlled House of Representatives.

Some Federalists felt that Burr was the lesser of the two evils and plotted to elect him president instead of Jefferson, even though Jefferson was clearly the presidential candidate. Hamilton helped to squelch the idea. After thirty-six ballots, Jefferson carried a majority in the House of Representatives. The crisis—which could have fatally wounded the nation by calling into question the legitimacy of the new president—was over. Jefferson was elected president and Burr vice president.

The near disaster brought about by the constitutional defect led to the passage of the Twelfth Amendment to the Constitution in September 1804. It called for electors to vote for president and vice president on separate ballots, thereby clarifying who was the presidential candidate and eliminating the possibility of a tie between the principal candidate and the running mate.

JEFFERSON'S REELECTION: 1804

By the 1804 election, President Thomas Jefferson had grudgingly accepted the emergence of a party system. Indeed, the president wrote that year: "The party division in this country is certainly not among its pleasant features. To a certain degree it will always exist."[11]

Jefferson's record—lower taxes, a reduced national debt, repeal of the Alien and Sedition Acts, and purchase of the Louisiana Territory from France—assured him of a second term. Particularly important was Jefferson's willingness to expand the nation's reach and power with the Louisiana Purchase, which compromised his philosophical preference for a small republic. The opposition's case against Jefferson was personal. But

LOOK ON THIS PICTURE,   AND ON THIS.

This 1807 anti-Jefferson cartoon compares Washington and Jefferson in contrasting images of good and evil.

the voters were not convinced of the need to make a change.

The 1804 election was the first one held after the Twelfth Amendment went into effect, requiring electors to cast separate votes for president and vice president. Therefore as of that election parties always specifically designated their presidential and vice-presidential candidates.

The Democratic-Republicans retained the caucus system of nomination in 1804, as they did for the next two decades, and for the first time they publicly reported their deliberations. When the party caucus met on February 25, 1804, it attracted 108 of the party's senators and representatives.

President Jefferson was renominated by acclamation, but Vice President Burr, who had fallen out with his party, was not considered for a second term. On the first nominating roll call publicly reported in U.S. political history, New York governor George Clinton was chosen by the caucus to run for vice president. He received sixty-seven votes and easily defeated Sen. John Breckinridge of Kentucky, who collected twenty votes. To "avoid unpleasant discussions" no names were placed in nomination and the vote was conducted by secret ballot.

Before adjourning, the caucus appointed a thirteen-member committee to conduct the campaign and promote the success of Democratic-Republican candidates. A forerunner of party national committees, the new campaign group included members of both the House and Senate, but with no two persons from the same state. Because the Twelfth Amendment had not yet been passed when the caucus met, the committee was designed to "manage" the vote of Democratic-Republican electors to make

sure that the events of 1800 were not repeated. In fact, that precaution was not necessary because the Twelfth Amendment was ratified in September—well before the electors voted.

By 1804 the Federalist Party had deteriorated badly. The new era of dominance by the Virginia-led Democratic-Republicans had begun. The Federalists did not even hold a congressional caucus to elect their nominees. Instead, Federalist leaders informally chose Charles Cotesworth Pinckney for president and Rufus King of New York for vice president. How the Federalists formulated this ticket is not clear. There is no record in 1804 of any formal meeting to nominate Federalist candidates.

The Federalists then mounted a disorganized and dispirited national campaign. Despite concerted efforts to win at least the votes of New England, the Federalists failed miserably. Pinckney received only 14 electoral votes—those of Connecticut and Delaware, plus 2 from Maryland. Jefferson, the Democratic-Republican candidate, was the overwhelming victor with 162 electoral votes.

MADISON'S 1808 VICTORY

Following George Washington's precedent, Thomas Jefferson refused to seek a third term of office. The nation was bitterly divided over Jefferson's policy toward France and Britain. In an attempt to stay out of their war, Jefferson had supported a trade embargo so that neither country would seize American ships. But the embargo only undermined American business interests. Under attack, Jefferson decided to return to his beloved home of Monticello near Charlottesville, Virginia.

Despite the unpopularity of the administration's European policy, Jefferson's secretary of state and chosen successor, James Madison, won the presidency in 1808. Jefferson's retirement provided a serious test to the authority of the Democratic-Republican congressional caucus to select presidential candidates. The caucus met on January 23, 1808, after, for the first time, a formal call was issued. Sen. Stephen R. Bradley of Vermont, chairman of the 1804 caucus, issued the call to all 146 Democratic-Republicans in Congress and several Federalists sympathetic to the Democratic-Republican cause. A few party leaders questioned Bradley's authority to call the caucus, but various reports indicate that between eighty-nine and ninety-four members of Congress attended.

As in 1804, the balloting took place without names being formally placed in nomination. Madison easily won the presidential nomination with eighty-three votes. Despite earlier support for future Secretary of State James Monroe among Democratic-Republicans in Virginia, and Vice President Clinton's desire to be president, each won only three votes at the caucus. But the caucus overwhelmingly renominated Clinton as vice president, giving him seventy-nine votes; runner-up John Langdon of New Hampshire collected five votes.

The Democratic-Republican caucus also repeated its practice of appointing a committee to conduct the campaign. Membership was expanded from thirteen to fifteen House and Senate members, and it was formally called the "committee of correspondence and arrangement." The committee was authorized to fill vacancies on the national ticket, should any occur. Before the caucus adjourned, it passed a resolution defending the caucus system as "the most practicable mode of consulting and respecting the interest and wishes of all." Later caucuses adopted similar resolutions throughout the history of the system.

Still, the Democratic-Republicans suffered divisions. Forty percent of the Democratic-Republican members of Congress had refused to attend the nominating caucus. Monroe refused to withdraw from the presidential race even after his defeat in the caucus. And Clinton, although he was nominated for vice president, was angry at not being nominated for president—so much so that he publicly denounced the caucus, as did Monroe's supporters. Pro-Clinton newspapers in New York launched harsh attacks on Madison and even suggested a Clinton-Monroe ticket. Some Clinton supporters went so far as to hope that Federalists would nominate Clinton for president later in the year. But such a thought was unpalatable to the Federalists, who ultimately nominated Charles Cotesworth Pinckney.

The Federalists chose their ticket at a secret meeting of party leaders in New York City in August 1808. Initially, the meeting was called by the Federalist members of the Massachusetts legislature. Twenty-five to thirty party leaders from seven states, all north of the Potomac River except South Carolina, attended the national meeting. Despite the suggestion from Massachusetts representatives that Clinton be nominated, the gathering decided to run the same ticket they had chosen in 1804: Pinckney and King.

The Federalists did not actively publicize their ticket. The party itself was divided and devoid of leadership. Indeed, many

Virginia Federalists formally endorsed Monroe, even though he was a Democratic-Republican. Others preferred to align themselves with Clinton.

In the end, Madison achieved a wide margin of victory with 122 electoral votes; Pinckney came in second with 47 votes. Monroe received no electoral votes. For the sake of future party unity, Democratic-Republicans had retained Clinton as their vice-presidential nominee even though he had tried to subvert Madison's candidacy. Clinton won, receiving 113 electoral votes for vice president. He even received 6 electoral votes from New York for president.

MADISON'S REELECTION: 1812

The winds of war were sweeping through presidential politics when James Madison sought a second term in 1812. In response to constant agitation by "war hawks," the president asked Congress on June 1 for a declaration of war against Great Britain. Madison, benefiting from the public's willingness to rally in times of national emergency, swept to a second term. The Federalists did not field a candidate but supported a dissident from Madison's party.

The possibility of war had long hung over the United States. Great Britain had taken American ships captive for years—boarding the vessels, taking cargo, and intimidating seamen. Anti-British political forces also charged that the British had encouraged American Indians in their attacks against settlers in the North and West.

The Democratic-Republican Party held its quadrennial nominating caucus on May 18, 1812. Only eighty-three of the 178 Democratic-Republicans in Congress participated. The New England and New York delegations in particular were poorly represented. Many of the New Yorkers supported the candidacy of their state's lieutenant governor, DeWitt Clinton (George Clinton's nephew), who also was maneuvering for the Federalist nomination. New England was noticeably upset with Madison's foreign policy, which was leading to war with England. Others did not attend the caucus because they opposed the system in principle.

Madison won a near-unanimous renomination in the caucus, receiving eighty-two votes. John Langdon of New Hampshire got the vice-presidential nomination by a wide margin, collecting sixty-four votes to sixteen for Gov. Elbridge Gerry of Massachusetts. But Langdon declined the nomination, citing his age (seventy) as the reason. The Democratic-Republicans held a second caucus on June 8 to select another vice-presidential candidate. Gerry was the clear winner with seventy-four votes, and he responded with a formal letter of acceptance. Ten members of Congress who had not been present at the first caucus also took the opportunity to endorse Madison's presidential candidacy.

Democratic-Republicans from New York were unwilling to accept the choice of Madison. They held their own caucus, composed of nearly all party members from the New York state legislature, where they unanimously nominated Clinton, who responded with a written "Address" that was a precursor to party platforms. Clinton won the endorsement of the Federalists as well.

As they had four years earlier, the Federalists convened a three-day secret meeting in New York City. The September meeting was more than twice the size of the 1808 gathering, with seventy representatives from eleven states attending. Delegates were sent to the conference by Federalist general committees, with all but nine of the delegates coming from the New England and Middle Atlantic states.

Debate centered on whether to run a separate Federalist ticket or to endorse Clinton. After much debate, they decided to endorse Clinton, and they nominated Jared Ingersoll of Pennsylvania for vice president. Originally, the caucus's decision was meant to be kept a secret, but leaks eventually were reported by Democratic-Republican newspapers.

The presidential election of 1812 was the first wartime contest for power in the United States. The Federalists, calling Madison a dupe of French emperor Napoleon Bonaparte, aligned themselves with the cause of peace and unimpeded commerce. In some northern states the Federalists even adopted the Peace Party label.

Despite all the opposition to President Madison, he beat Clinton by an electoral vote count of 128–89. The vote reflected the growing split between southern agricultural states, which supported Madison, and northern commercial states, which supported Clinton. Indeed, the common bond that held the Clinton coalition together was a hatred of Virginia—the kingmaker of the Democratic-Republican Party.

The 1812 race was the last real campaign by the Federalists. Disgraced by their obstructionist tactics during the war, isolated by their talk of succession from the Union, and unable to coordinate a national campaign, the Federalists faded from a system increasingly marked by permanent party competition.

MONROE'S 1816 VICTORY

James Monroe, President Madison's old foe who had left the Democratic-Republican Party in 1808, seemed like an unlikely presidential candidate for the party in 1816. But not only did James Monroe return to the Democratic-Republican fold, he also won the White House without any opposition.

The inconclusive War of 1812 colored American politics for years. The United States and Great Britain fought to a stalemate, and then both sides offered conditions for ending the war that the other would not accept. The British, for example, demanded control over the Great Lakes and Mississippi River for commerce, as well as the creation of an Indian state in the Northwest. In the end, both parties simply accepted the end of hostilities. An American representative said the treaty was "a truce rather than a peace."[12] Inconclusive or not, the war sparked a generation of nationalism. Rufus King revived the Federalist Party in 1816 with his race for the governorship of New York. But he lost the race and afterward found the job of maintaining the party a "fruitless struggle." Efforts were made to convene another secret meeting in Philadelphia to nominate candidates for president and vice president, yet the party held no such meeting. With the Federalists not running candidates, nomination by the Democratic-Republican caucus was tantamount to election.

Despite his opposition to Madison in 1808, Monroe had been accepted back into the Democratic-Republican fold in the years that followed. In 1811 Madison had named him secretary of state; by 1816 he was Madison's heir apparent. But many states were increasingly jealous of the Virginia dynasty that had held a grip on the presidency since 1804. Democratic-Republicans in such states opposed Monroe (himself a Virginian) and favored Secretary of War William H. Crawford of Georgia.

A Democratic-Republican caucus met in the House chamber on March 12, 1816, but only fifty-eight members of Congress—mostly Crawford supporters—attended. With the expectation of better attendance, a second caucus was held on March 16. It drew 119 of the 141 Democratic-Republicans in Congress. There, Monroe narrowly defeated Crawford by a vote of 65–54. Forty of Crawford's votes came from five states: Georgia, Kentucky, New Jersey, New York, and North Carolina. The vice-presidential nomination went to New York governor Daniel D. Tompkins, who easily outdistanced Pennsylvania governor Simon Snyder, 85–30.

The nominations of Monroe and Tompkins revived a Virginia-New York alliance that extended back to the late eighteenth century. With the lone exception of 1812, every Democratic-Republican ticket from 1800 to 1820 was composed of a presidential candidate from Virginia and a vice-presidential candidate from New York.

With the Federalist Party still in disarray, the Democratic-Republican ticket won easily. Monroe received 183 electoral votes. The three states—Connecticut, Delaware, and Massachusetts—that had chosen Federalist electors cast their 34 electoral votes for Rufus King.

Although the collapse of the Federalists ensured Democratic-Republican rule, it also increased intraparty friction and spurred further attacks on the caucus system. Twenty-two Democratic-Republican members of Congress had not attended the second party caucus, and at least fifteen were known to be opposed to the system. Mass meetings around the country protested the caucus system.[13] Opponents asserted that the writers of the Constitution did not envision the caucus, that presidential nominating should not be a function of Congress, and that the caucus system encouraged candidates to curry the favor of Congress.

MONROE'S 1820 REELECTION

The 1820 election took place during the "Era of Good Feeling," a phrase coined by a Boston publication, the *Columbian Centinel,* to describe a brief period of virtual one-party rule in the United States. But that phrase glosses over serious sectional divisions that were growing during Monroe's presidency. The divisions, however, did not prevent Monroe from winning another term.

Sectional strife was on the brink of eruption during Monroe's first term over the admission of Missouri as a new state. Tensions between northern and southern states had simmered for years. The emotional core of the struggle was slavery. Therefore whichever region controlled Congress might decide whether slavery was extended into new territories—and the shape of the nation's economy and culture—for years to come.

In the Senate, there was a tenuous balance between the two regions—eleven free states and eleven slave states—but the admission of Missouri threatened that balance. The two sides finally agreed to a compromise in which both Missouri and Maine would apply for statehood at the same time, Maine as a free state and Missouri as a slave state. Monroe remained neutral in the debate leading up to the compromise. Despite a financial panic in 1819, he retained overwhelming popular support, bolstered by peace and a wave of nationalistic feeling that overshadowed any partisan divisions.

While the United States struggled over the slavery issue, President Monroe embarked on a bold new foreign policy. Still smarting over the British presence in North America that had resulted in the War of 1812, the president declared that the United States would view any European attempts to colonize the Western Hemisphere as acts of hostility. The Monroe Doctrine claimed the hemisphere as the preserve of the United States. It was the boldest venture yet of the nation into foreign policy and permanently defined America's role in world affairs.

Although several rival Democratic-Republican candidates aspired to win the presidency when Monroe retired in 1824, none wanted to challenge his reelection in 1820. A nominating caucus was called for early March, but fewer than fifty of the Democratic-Republican Party's 191 members of Congress showed up. The caucus voted unanimously to make no nominations and passed a resolution explaining that it was inexpedient to do so because so few of the party's members were in attendance. Although Monroe and Tompkins were not formally renominated, electoral slates were filed in their behalf.

Because the Federalist Party was finally dead, Monroe ran virtually unopposed. Even John Adams, the last Federalist president, voted for Monroe as an elector from Massachusetts. Only one elector, a Democratic-Republican from New Hampshire, cast a vote against Monroe, supporting instead John Quincy Adams, son of the former president.

LAST OF THE OLD ORDER: 1824

The 1824 election, in an odd way, represented everything that the Framers of the Constitution had hoped to see. Without a permanent party system, a number of candidates vied for the presidency. Unable to win an electoral majority, the top three finishers saw their names submitted to the House of Representatives for a final decision. The candidate representative of elite interests and sensibilities and who had House ties won.

But if the 1824 election of John Quincy Adams represented something old, it also represented something new. The popular winner and House loser, Andrew Jackson, protested loudly that the election had been stolen from the people. In fact, soon he would mobilize the Democratic Party around a populist rallying cry. American politics would never be the same.

In 1824, as in 1820, only one working party existed in the United States: the Democratic-Republican. But that party had an abundance of candidates competing for the presidency: Secretary of State John Quincy Adams of Massachusetts, Sen. Andrew Jackson of Tennessee, Secretary of War John C. Calhoun of South Carolina, House Speaker Henry Clay of Kentucky, and

Secretary of the Treasury William H. Crawford. The number of candidates, coupled with the growing democratization of the U.S. political system, led to the demise of King Caucus in 1824.

Early on, Crawford was the leading candidate. He had strong southern support and appeared likely to win the support of New York's Democratic-Republicans. Because it was assumed that he would win a caucus if one were held, Crawford's opponents joined the growing list of caucus opponents. But Crawford's apparent invincibility suddenly ended in September 1823 when he suffered a paralytic stroke. Nearly blind and unable even to sign his name, he was incapacitated and stayed in seclusion for months.

In early February 1824, eleven Democratic-Republican members of Congress issued a call for a caucus to be held in the middle of the month. Their call was countered by twenty-four other members of Congress from fifteen states who deemed it "inexpedient under existing circumstances" to hold a caucus. They claimed that 181 members of Congress were resolved not to attend if a caucus were held.

The caucus convened in mid-February, but only sixty-six members of Congress showed up. Three-quarters of those attending came from just four states—Georgia, New York, North Carolina, and Virginia. Despite his illness, Crawford won the caucus nomination with sixty-four votes. Albert Gallatin of Pennsylvania was selected for vice president with fifty-seven votes. The caucus adopted a resolution defending its actions as "the best means of collecting and concentrating the feelings and wishes of the people of the Union upon this important subject." The caucus also appointed a committee to write an address to the people. As written, the text of the address viewed with alarm the "dismemberment" of the Democratic-Republican Party.

In fact, the action of the caucus just aggravated splits in the party. Because so few members of Congress attended the caucus—almost all of them Crawford supporters—opponents could argue that the choice was not even representative of the Democratic-Republicans serving in Congress. Crawford was roundly criticized as being an illegitimate candidate. His opponents derided King Caucus, and his physical condition made it even easier for them to reject his nomination. As it stood, other candidates simply refused to follow the caucus's decision. Never again were candidates chosen by the caucus system.

With the caucus devoid of power and the party lacking unity or leadership, there was no chance of rallying behind a single ticket. In addition, many political issues proved to be divisive. Western expansion and protective tariffs, for example, benefited some parts of the country but hurt others. Thus the various candidates came to represent sectional interests.

The candidates themselves recognized that such a crowded field was dangerous. The election would be thrown into the House of Representatives if no candidate received a majority. The candidates therefore made efforts to join forces. Adams tried to lure Jackson as his running mate. Adams was a short, stocky, aloof, well-educated New Englander who came from a family of Federalists, while Jackson was a tall, thin, hot-tempered war hero with little formal education who came to epitomize a new brand of populist democracy. In trying to recruit

This 1836 cartoon depicts Jackson attacking the Bank of the United States with his veto stick. Vice President Van Buren, center, helps to kill the monster, whose heads represent Nicholas Biddle, president of the bank, and directors of the state branches.

Jackson onto their team, Adams supporters envisaged a ticket of "the writer and the fighter." Jackson would have nothing of it.

In the meantime, Crawford dropped Gallatin as his vice-presidential running mate. His supporters then tried to persuade Clay to drop his quest for the presidency and join the Crawford team. They hinted that Crawford's physical condition was such that he would probably not finish out a term of office if elected (in fact, he lived ten more years). But Clay was not swayed. Calhoun then dropped his race for the presidency and joined efforts with Jackson.

Four candidates remained in the field and each collected electoral votes. None, however, received a majority. Jackson received the most with ninety-nine, followed by Adams with eighty-four, Crawford with forty-one, and Clay with thirty-seven. Therefore the election was thrown into the House of Representatives.

In accordance with the Twelfth Amendment, the names of the top three candidates—Jackson, Adams, and Crawford—were placed before the House. Clay, who had come in fourth and was Speaker of the House, would play a major role in tipping the balance in favor of one of the candidates.

In contrast to Jackson, Adams actively lobbied for support, and Washington rocked with rumors of corruption. Clay informed Adams in January that he would support Adams in the House election—a major blow to Jackson. Shortly thereafter, a letter in a Philadelphia newspaper alleged that Adams had offered Clay the post of secretary of state in return for his support. Adams went on to win the House election narrowly by carrying thirteen out of twenty-four state delegations. Jackson came in second with seven, and Crawford third with the remaining four.

Consequently, the candidate who won the most electoral votes and the most popular votes did not win the presidency.

Jackson was furious at what he considered to be unfair bargaining between Adams and Clay. He felt that the will of the people had been thwarted, and he seethed when President Adams proceeded to name Clay secretary of state as rumor had indicated he would. In this way, the events of 1824 kindled the flame of popular democracy. The stage was set for a rematch between Adams and Jackson in 1828.

The Age of Jackson

Andrew Jackson was in many ways the perfect man to usher in an age of popular politics, although his rhetoric was more populist than his style of governing. The textbook version of U.S. history depicts Jackson as a coarse man of the frontier, a war hero, a battler of banks and moneyed interests, and a leader of the unschooled and exploited men who built a mass party on patronage and charismatic leadership. Jackson was the first politician to break the Virginia dynasty that had governed the country since the Revolution. After his bitter defeat in the 1824 election, Jackson fought back and grabbed the reins of government in the turbulent election of 1828. These two elections signaled the passing of elite politics and the rise of popular politics. In 1828 Jackson roused the people to turn Adams and his aristocratic clique out of office.

But the Jacksonian folklore has serious flaws. Jackson traveled in elite business circles, for example, and one of his greatest contributions as president was the creation of a more rationally organized bureaucracy.[14] Still, the textbook depiction of Jackson suffices to show some trends in U.S. politics, including the development of a stable mass party system, sectionalism, urbanization, and shifts in the debate about U.S. expansionism.

While President Adams was struggling with warring factions in Washington, an opposition force was gathering strength, and, in fact, was able to deal the president a number of humiliating defeats. Adams's desire for a national program of roads and canals, education, and research in the arts and sciences antagonized even the most nationalistic groups in the country. U.S. participation in a conference of countries from the Western Hemisphere and the imposition of a tariff (a tax on imported goods designed either to raise revenues or to protect domestic industries from foreign competition) also were divisive issues. But even though Adams was under constant personal attack, the opposition was divided on the same issues. The opposition was united, however, behind "Old Hickory."[15]

Jackson, hero of the Battle of New Orleans in the War of 1812, had a strong appeal to the common man even though he traveled in the circles of southern gentlemen. People who met with Jackson talked of his unerring "intuition" about people and politics. Jackson's decision to push for reforms of the punishment of debtors was an important gesture to small businessmen and workers who were held to a kind of indentured servitude to their creditors. Sen. Martin Van Buren of New York, Jackson's strongest supporter in the Northeast, said the people "were his blood relations—the only blood relations he had."[16]

THE 1828 ELECTION

Jackson and his running mate, John C. Calhoun, easily beat Adams in their 1828 rematch; Jackson won 178 electoral votes, and Adams won 83. (Calhoun also had been vice president under John Quincy Adams.) Of the popular vote, Jackson received 643,000 votes (56.0 percent) to Adams's 501,000 (43.6 percent). Sectional splits showed in the vote distribution. Adams held all but 1 of New England's electoral votes, all of Delaware's and New Jersey's, 16 of New York's 36 votes, and 6 of Maryland's 11 votes. Jackson took all the rest—the South and the West. The election, then, was decided by the newly enfranchised voters in the burgeoning regions of the country. The U.S. electorate, however, was expanding not only in the West but also in the original states. Between 1824 and 1856 voter participation grew from 3.8 percent to 16.7 percent of the total population.[17]

Jackson had only begun to exert electoral influence with his revenge victory over Adams. The expanded pool of politically involved citizens that had brought Jackson victory also brought him demands for patronage jobs with the federal government. Van Buren, a master machine politician from New York State, tutored the beleaguered new president in dealing with the office seekers. Jackson replaced fewer than one-fifth of the government's employees, which he defended as a perfectly reasonable "rotation in office" that would keep the ranks of the bureaucracy fresh. But the effect of his system was greater. Appointees of previous administrations were able to retain their jobs only when they expressed loyalty to Jackson and his party. Far more important than any government turnover, Jackson's spoils system inaugurated an age in which mass party loyalty was a paramount concern in politics.

The increased importance of loyalty, to the president and to the party, became clear with Jackson's dispute with Vice President Calhoun and the subsequent purging of the cabinet. A growing feud between Jackson and Calhoun came to a head when a personal letter in which Calhoun criticized Jackson's conduct of the Seminole Indian campaign and the 1818 invasion of Florida became public. In a letter to Calhoun during the cabinet crisis, Jackson wrote: "Et tu, Brute." A purge of Calhoun men in the cabinet followed the incident. Secretary of State Van Buren enabled the president to make the purge when he and Secretary of War John Eaton, both Jackson allies, resigned their posts; the president then called on the whole cabinet to quit.

The central element of the Jacksonian program was expansion. Much like twentieth-century politicians who would talk about economic growth as the key to opportunity, Jackson maintained that movement West "enlarg[ed] the area of freedom."[18] The administration fought to decentralize the management of expansion. Jackson railed against the "corrupt bargain" between the government and banks, joint-stock companies, and monopolies, which, he said, were squeezing out the average person seeking opportunity.

Indeed, Jackson opposed the Bank of the United States and promoted state banks because of his desire to free finance capital from central control. In his first term, the president carried on a long-running battle with Nicholas Biddle, the head of the Bank of the United States, and with Congress over the status of the bank. Alexander Hamilton had created the bank to manage the nation's monetary policy and investment, but Jackson opposed it as a tool of the eastern financial establishment. Jackson may have failed to close the bank, but he did manage to strip it of much of its basic authority and functions by placing its deposits in a number of regional institutions.

Jackson's presidency was activist from the beginning. His administration negotiated treaties with France, the Ottoman Empire, Russia, and Mexico. Jackson himself established a distinctive interpretation of federalism when he vetoed a number of public improvements bills as unconstitutional infringements of local affairs. He also called for a tariff that would yield revenues for dispersal to the states for their own public projects—an early form of "revenue sharing." And Jackson signed the Indian Removal Act of 1830, which provided for settlement of the territory west of the Mississippi River. Late in his first term, Jackson's strong stand defeated the South Carolina legislature's claim that it could "nullify," or declare "null and void," federal tariff legislation that the state disliked.

JACKSON'S 1832 REELECTION

There was never any doubt that Jackson would be renominated in 1832; in fact, several state legislatures endorsed him before the convention. Jackson's political strength was further underscored with the introduction of a quintessentially party-oriented institution: the national party convention. Jacksonians from New Hampshire proposed the Democratic convention of

1832, and the president and his advisers jumped at the opportunity. The only previous national convention had been held by the Anti-Masonic Party in 1831. Conventions had been the principal means of selecting candidates for local offices since the early part of the century. Especially when compared with the caucus system that preceded it, the convention system was a democratic leap forward.

The convention system enabled the parties to gather partisans from all geographic areas, and it welded them together as a cohesive unit that ultimately was accountable to the electorate, if only in a plebiscitary way. Voters had the opportunity to give approval or disapproval to a party program with one vote. Historian Eugene H. Roseboom has written: "It was representative in character; it divorced nominations from congressional control and added to the independence of the executive; it permitted an authoritative formulation of a party program; and it concentrated the party's strength behind a single ticket, the product of compromise of personal rivalries and group or sectional interests."[19]

Given Jackson's popularity in 1832, the purpose of the convention was to rally behind the president and select a new vice-presidential candidate. Van Buren got the nomination, despite lingering resistance from Calhoun supporters and various "favorite sons" (prominent state and local leaders of state party organizations).

As in 1828, Jackson's political opposition was fragmented. The Whigs—the opposition party that had developed from grassroots protests in the North and West against Jackson's tariff and development policies—held their national convention in Baltimore in December 1831 and unanimously nominated Henry Clay of Kentucky for president. Eighteen states used a variety of selection procedures to determine who would be their convention delegates. The party's platform sharply criticized the Jackson administration's patronage practices, relations with Great Britain, and ill-tempered congressional relations, as well as Supreme Court decisions.

In the election, the incumbent easily dispatched the opposition. "The news from the voting states blows over us like a great cold storm," wrote Rufus Choate, a prominent lawyer, to a friend.[20] Despite last-minute maneuvering to unite the opposition to Jackson and a well-financed campaign by the Bank of the United States, the president won 219 electoral votes to Clay's 49, Independent John Floyd's 11, and Anti-Mason William Wirt's 7. Jackson won all but seven states. Clay won Kentucky, Massachusetts, Rhode Island, Connecticut, and Delaware, plus five electors from Maryland. Jackson won 702,000 popular votes to Clay's 484,000 and Wirt's 101,000.[21]

Jackson, who finally left the political stage in 1837, changed the face of U.S. politics. Even if his pretensions to being an everyman were overstated, he did open up the system to mass participation, and he forced politicians to listen to popular demands. He developed the notion of a strong party organization. He fought, and eventually defeated, the national bank by withdrawing its funds and placing them in state banks. He strongly opposed two forces that could have torn the nation apart—the

nullification principle of state sovereignty and the Supreme Court's bid for broader discretion over political issues (that is, to review legislation and state actions)—by simply proclaiming the law to be "unauthorized by the Constitution" and "therefore null and void."

VAN BUREN'S 1836 WIN

Many historians consider the election of 1836 to be the most important event in the development of the party system. Van Buren, a Democratic follower of Jackson and a theorist on the role of political parties in a democratic system, easily won the election against an uncoordinated Whig Party. The defeat eventually persuaded Whig leaders of the need for a permanent organization for political competition. The emergence of two permanent parties extinguished the American suspicion of the morality of a party system based on unabashed competition for the levers of power.

Van Buren, who had allied with Jackson during the cabinet controversies and promoted his philosophy of parties and patronage, received the Democratic nomination in 1836 at a convention packed with Jackson administration appointees. The vice-presidential nomination of Richard M. Johnson of Kentucky, whose earlier relationship with a mulatto woman caused controversy, damaged the ticket in the South, but the Democrats won anyway.

The Whigs' campaign strategy was to run several favorite sons to prevent any candidate from getting a majority of the electoral votes, thereby throwing the election into the House of Representatives. As one Whig put it: "The disease [Democratic rule] is to be treated as a local disorder—apply local remedies."[22] The Whig expectation was that one of two favorite sons—Gen. William Henry Harrison of Ohio or Hugh Lawson White of Tennessee—would be selected by the House after the electoral college vote proved inconclusive.

Van Buren, however, had Jackson's machine and his personal backing and was able to overcome the Whigs' local strategy. Thus in this race, the last for the White House before presidential elections became dominated by two national parties, Van Buren took 170 electoral votes—22 more than he needed for election. Of the Whig candidates, Harrison received 73 electoral votes; White, 26; and Daniel Webster of Massachusetts, 14. Willie Mangum, an Independent Democrat from North Carolina, received 11 electoral votes from the South Carolina legislature, which was hostile to White because of his role in nullification politics. Van Buren won 764,000 popular votes (50.8 percent); Harrison, 551,000 (36.6 percent); White, 146,000 (9.7 percent); and Webster, 41,000 (2.7 percent). For the only time in history, the Senate selected the vice president, Richard Johnson, who had fallen one vote shy of election by the electoral college. In the Senate, Johnson defeated Francis Granger by a 33–16 vote.

Van Buren was besieged with problems practically from the minute he took the oath of office in March 1837. About midway through his term, the economy crashed after years of feverish business growth, overspeculation in land and business, huge private debt accumulation, and unregulated financial and trade practices. Van Buren's approach to the economic crisis alternated between stubborn refusal to fix a mess that he had not created and action that was guaranteed to antagonize key interest groups.

When Van Buren moved to create an independent treasury to insulate the federal government from state financial institutions, he was opposed by conservative Democrats who were supporters of the state financial institutions that Jackson had promoted in his legendary national bank battles. When Van Buren was not hit from the right, he was hit from the left. The nascent labor movement called for protection of jobs and wages and made protests against monopoly and privilege.

The Idea of a Party System

Whatever problems Van Buren had in governing, he should receive credit at least for helping to establish the principle of party government in the United States. That principle, much derided in the early days of the nation's history, now enjoys widespread allegiance.

Van Buren's arguments for a party system—contained in his book, *An Inquiry into the Origin and Course of Political Parties in the United States*—were similar to the economic principle of Adam Smith, which had held that the pursuit of selfish ends redounded to the good of the entire community. American leaders from George Washington through John Quincy Adams had believed that self-interested factions endangered the functioning and virtue of the Republic. These leaders also had warned against the dangers of democracy, which they often called "mob rule." In the worst possible scenario, permanent parties with strong ideological stances appealed to the mass public for support, undermining the ability of national leaders to guide public virtue.[23]

The basic tension that Van Buren had to resolve was the system's need for stability and responsible leadership and the parties' imperative to gain office. How could a party's selfish desire to run the government and award patronage and contracts to political allies benefit the whole system?

Van Buren argued that the absence of parties—that is, collections of people from disparate backgrounds—resulted in a system of personal politics that fueled demagogy, perpetual campaigns, and a lack of accountability. Personal presidential politics was more polarizing than the politics of consensus or of coalition building. Presidents should be able to do their job without constant carping from outsiders who fancied themselves prospective presidents. Mass parties with certain partisan principles would enable presidents to get the backing they needed to do their work.

Moreover, the existence of two parties would enable the nation to move beyond its many cleavages—that is, toward the general interest and away from simple clashes of particular interests. Competition among parties, like competition among economic enterprises, would bring about a situation in which disparate demands would be promoted by a party. The key was to achieve a balance of competing forces. Summarizing Van Buren, political scientist James W. Ceaser has written:

Established parties . . . may stand 'over' the raw electoral cleavages, possessing some leeway or discretion about which potential issues and

electoral divisions will be emphasized and which will be suppressed or kept at the fringes. This discretion is exercised according to the interests of the organizations and the judgement of their leaders. But it is important to keep in mind that the degree of this discretion is limited. . . . Their discretion is always threatened or held in check by the possibility that they might be displaced by a new party having as its goal the advancement of a certain policy. . . . When a sufficiently powerful and enduring issue exists, an impartial reading of American party history suggests that the party system in the end will have to respond to it, regardless of how the established parties initially react.[24]

The Age of Jackson brought a fundamental shift from republican to democratic values as the nation's territory and activities expanded. Republicanism was the product of a variety of strains of thought—from the Romans Cicero and Tacitus and the Greek Polybius to the Frenchman Charles Montesquieu—that stressed the need for a balancing of interests to produce public virtue. Republicans worried about excess in any single form of governance, particularly "mob rule." For them, *democracy* was a term of derision. That is why the Constitution contained many buffers against this and other forms of excess.

Republicanism declined in many stages. A greater stress on the individual's role in society, embodied in the work of Adam Smith and David Hume, restricted the kinds of issues open to public deliberation. At the same time, the pace of economic change undermined established patterns. As the nation demanded large-scale projects (such as canals and railways), and as rival factions looked to the mobilization of larger and larger parts of the electorate to augment their strength, democratic rhetoric gained respectability. Mass party participation became a vehicle for pursuing civic virtue and balance, and the notion of a constant opposition party gained strength. If the democratic process had enough constitutional "checks," political thinkers now reasoned, the harmful "mob" aspects of democracy could be tempered. The development of the Jacksonian party as a way of arbitrating interests was the final stage in republican decline and democratic ascendance.

Political scientist Russell Hanson has noted that the new democratic ethos sprang from one of the same goals as the old republican ethos: development of a public spirit by rising above particular restraints. "Support for popular sovereignty became the lowest common denominator for a Democratic Party composed of interests seeking liberation from a variety of sectionally specific restraints on the 'will of the people.'"[25]

A two-party system persisted as the nation drifted toward civil war, but it was not a simple two-party system. The Democrats and Whigs competed for the presidency and other political offices until 1856, when the Republican Party fielded its first national ticket and made the Whigs obsolete. But the parties were so unstable that their many elements were constantly forming and breaking up coalitions—and threatening to bolt from the system itself. Moreover, a series of third parties entered the national electoral arena for short periods, applying or relieving pressures on the two major parties.[26]

Only by examining the parties and their various factions and struggles can one understand the presidential contests in the two decades before the Civil War, and the way that the Civil War revealed the basic fault lines of U.S. politics.

THE WHIGS' 1840 VICTORY

The Whigs developed to fill the role of their British name-sake, which had been to mount a republican opposition to the royal ruling power. When the rise of Andrew Jackson and his supposedly imperial presidency threatened the "balance" of the United States, the Whigs rose to restore that balance. The Whigs saw Jackson's Democrats as a faction of the most dangerous variety—a majority faction that had the ability to trample liberties in its mad scramble for spoils.

The key to Whiggery was the notion of balanced development. The Whigs opposed the war with Mexico and other expansionist programs because they feared the perils of overextending the nation's abilities and getting entangled with foreign powers. They favored internal improvements, but only as a way of maintaining balance and staving off the corruption of the Jackson era. The protective tariff was central to the Whigs' program of internal development and protection from outsiders. According to Hanson,

even in America, which was uniquely blessed by an abundance of natural resources and a citizenry of hardy stock, there was need for informed guidance and direction of progress. For the Whigs, government was the primary agent of this progress. Government represented a strong and positive force to be used in calling forth a richer society from the unsettled possibilities of America. In the economic realm this meant that government was responsible for providing the essential conditions for a sound economy, namely, a reliable currency, ample credit, and the impetus for internal improvements. And in the social realm, the government was responsible for promoting virtue in its citizenry through education and exhortation.[27]

The Whigs' desire for balance and compromise was intended to give the party a national rather than a sectional identity. Moreover, their tendency to nominate widely popular military heroes helped to create at least the illusion of a party of national dimensions. A series of Senate battles with President Jackson, especially the tariff battles of 1833, which resulted in an unsatisfying compromise, gave impetus to grassroots organizations in the North and West and to southern Democratic opponents. In fact, the Whigs developed first in the South where voters were dissatisfied with Jackson's selection of Van Buren as his running mate. There, loose coalitions elected candidates in the 1834 and 1835 state and congressional elections. Westerners also organized to oppose the Democratic Party, which was headed by a New Yorker.

The first serious Whig presidential contest was a loss, but an encouraging one. In 1836 the Whig tickets headed by Harrison and others had shown surprising appeal in the loss to the Democrat Van Buren. The Whigs had won Jackson's home state of Tennessee and neighboring Georgia, as well as three border slave states, and were strong competitors elsewhere. Harrison had carried the old Northwest (now the Midwest) and had come close in northern states such as Pennsylvania.

Because of the rise of the antislavery "conscience Whigs," the Whigs eventually moved to a completely different base of support—the North rather than the South and West—but their early organizing at least broke the Democratic stranglehold on the latter two regions. The Whigs nominated Harrison in 1840 after a nomination struggle with Henry Clay. A Clay supporter,

John Tyler of Virginia, was the vice-presidential nominee. This time, the popular if politically inexperienced hero of the War of 1812 won his ticket to the White House. Harrison defeated the incumbent Van Buren in an electoral vote landslide, receiving 234 of the 294 electoral votes—all the states except Alabama, Arkansas, Illinois, Missouri, New Hampshire, South Carolina, and Virginia. For the popular vote, Harrison won 1.3 million (52.9 percent) to Van Buren's 1.1 million (46.8 percent).

According to political scientist Richard P. McCormick,

The campaign of 1840 brought the American party system at last to fruition. In every region of the country, and indeed in every state, politics was conducted within the framework of a two-party system, and in all but a handful of states the parties were so closely balanced as to be competitive. In broad terms, it was the contest for the presidency that shaped this party system and defined its essential purpose.[28]

Harrison's campaign was as vague as his government experience was unimpressive. The image of Harrison as a sort of frontier everyman—which received its popular expression when a Baltimore newspaper mocked him as a sedentary man who would sit in a log cabin and drink cider rather than perform great deeds of leadership—was the theme of numerous parades and mass meetings. On issues from banking and currency to slavery, Harrison spoke in generalities. Harrison's strategist acknowledged that he advised the candidate to "say not a single word about his principles or creed. Let him say nothing—promise nothing."[29]

As it happened, Harrison did not have an opportunity to do much as president besides discipline the aggressive Clay. Clay had assumed that he and the rest of the congressional leadership would play the leading role in the government, but Harrison quickly dispelled that notion in a note rebuking him. But one month after his inauguration, the sixty-eight-year-old Harrison developed pneumonia and died. On April 6, 1841, the burdens of the presidency fell on Vice President John Tyler.

The rift between the White House and Congress widened under Tyler. Clay acted as if he were prime minister during a special session of Congress, pushing through a legislative program that included a recharter of the long-controversial Bank of the United States, higher import taxes, and distribution of proceeds from land sales to the states. Tyler, a lifetime states' rights advocate, vetoed two bills for a national bank, and the Whigs in Congress and his cabinet began a bitter feud with the president. In 1842 Clay left the Senate to promote his presidential aspirations, and everyone in the cabinet except Secretary of State Daniel Webster quit. Tyler was all alone, but he did manage to defeat the Whig program in his four years as president.

POLK'S DARK-HORSE VICTORY IN 1844

The Democrats were transformed into a well-organized party by Andrew Jackson and Martin Van Buren between 1828 and 1836. But, like the Whigs, the Democratic Party became vulnerable because of the irreconcilable differences among many of its parts.

From the beginning, the Democratic Party had contained contradictory elements. According to political scientist James L.

Sundquist: "The party had been formed originally as an alliance between Southern planters and New Yorkers and had always spanned both regions. Northern men of abolitionist sympathies were accustomed to sitting with slaveholders in presidential cabinets and collaborating with them in the halls of Congress."[30] But northern Democrats went so far as to organize antiabolitionist rallies in their cities and towns, and newspapers and churches also defended slavery.

The deepest Democratic divisions—which eventually would lead to the failure not only of the party but also of the nation—were the regional differences based on slavery. But other, more complex divisions also affected the operation of the Democratic Party. When the party was able to reconcile or even delay action on the divisive issues, it won. When the divisions burst into the open, the party was in trouble.

James K. Polk of Tennessee, the first "dark-horse" candidate in history, defeated the Whig Henry Clay in 1844 by supporting an expansionist program and winning the support of the solid South. One of the key issues in the campaign was whether Texas should be admitted to the Union and, if so, whether it should be slave or free. President Van Buren in 1840 had opposed annexation—opposition that may have cost him the presidency—and the Democrats and Whigs hedged on the issue for the next eight years. In 1844 Polk endorsed the annexation of Texas as a slave state; that was enough for him to lock up the South.

During the 1844 nominating convention, the Democrats finessed the sectional dangers of the Texas issue by combining it with a call for occupying Oregon and eventually bringing that state into the Union. The Democrats also appealed to Pennsylvania and the rest of the Northeast by supporting a high tariff. Both parties spoke out against the growing foreign elements in the cities, but the Whigs were more effective because of the Democrats' swelling immigrant ranks.

In the election, the Democrat Polk defeated the Whig Clay, winning 1.34 million votes (49.5 percent) to Clay's 1.30 million (48.1 percent) and 170 electoral votes to Clay's 105. Clay received his strongest support from five northeastern states and five border slave states. Of the expansionist Northwest, only Ohio fell in the Clay column.

The Liberty Party—an abolitionist party formed out of more than two hundred antislavery societies in time for the 1840 election—may have been the deciding factor in the 1844 race. Although the party received only 2.3 percent of the popular vote and no electoral votes, it was strong enough in New York to prevent the Whigs from winning that state's crucial thirty-six electoral votes. Those votes went to the Democrat Polk rather than to the Whig Clay.

The depth of the Democrats' divisions were agonizingly evident even when the party won elections and started to pass out spoils and make policy. Like Harrison, the Whig who had won the presidency four years before, President Polk faced the antagonisms of party factions when he began making appointments after his 1844 win. Westerners were angry when they were shut out of the cabinet and Polk vetoed a rivers and harbors bill. Supporters of both Van Buren and John Calhoun were angry that their faction did not win more prominent positions. Northeast-

erners were upset at tariff cuts. The New York split between the reformist "Barnburners" and the party-regular "Hunkers"—who disagreed on every issue, including banks, currency, internal improvements, and political reforms—also disrupted the administration.

Creating still more dissension was the war with Mexico (1846–1848), fought because of the dispute over the Texas border and the possible annexation of California. Northerners resented the country's fighting Mexico over a slave state.

WHIG SUCCESS UNDER TAYLOR IN 1848

In 1848 the Whigs recaptured the White House behind another military hero, Gen. Zachary Taylor, who was vague on most political issues. Hailing from Louisiana, where he was a slave owner, Taylor defeated the irrepressible Clay and Gen. Winfield Scott for the nomination on the fourth convention ballot. His running mate was New Yorker Millard Fillmore. Clay mounted an impressive public campaign that drew large crowds, but the Whigs had lost too many times with Clay.

The Whigs were so determined to avoid sectional and other splits that they not only nominated the popular Taylor but also eschewed writing a platform. Despite such extreme measures to maintain unity, the convention was disturbed by squabbles between pro- and antislavery forces on the question of the Wilmot Proviso, which would ban slavery in any territory the United States obtained from Mexico.

At the Democratic national convention, Sen. Lewis Cass of Michigan defeated Sen. James Buchanan of Pennsylvania and Supreme Court Justice Levi Woodbury for the presidential nomination, and Gen. William Butler was picked as his running mate. (The Democratic incumbent Polk had declared upon entering office that he would not seek a second term.) But the convention experienced splits between two New York factions: the Barnburners, who were part of the antislavery movement, and the more conservative Hunkers, who had ties to southerners. The Barnburners finally defected from the party to become part of the Free Soil Party.

The Democrats behind Cass praised the administration of the beleaguered Polk, defended the war with Mexico, congratulated the French Republic that emerged from the wave of revolution in Europe, and did everything it could to avoid the nasty slavery issue. The nomination of Cass—a "doughface," or northerner with southern principles—was expected to appeal to both sides of the simmering issue.

But Taylor defeated Cass, winning 1.4 million popular votes (47.3 percent) to Cass's 1.2 million (42.5 percent). New York Democrat Martin Van Buren, the former president, running on the Free Soil ticket, won 291,500 votes (10 percent) but no electoral votes. Taylor received 163 electoral votes to Cass's 127, with a strong showing in the North. Taylor won Connecticut, Massachusetts, New Jersey, New York, Pennsylvania, Rhode Island, and Vermont in the North; Delaware, Kentucky, Maryland, North Carolina, and Tennessee in the border states; and Florida, Georgia, and Louisiana in the Deep South. This combination was enough to beat Cass's coalition of seven slave states, six northwestern states, and two New England states.

On July 10, 1850, Fillmore succeeded to the presidency when Taylor died suddenly. After consuming too many refreshments at a Fourth of July celebration, Taylor had developed cramps and then a fatal illness, probably typhoid fever.

Despite this turn of events, Fillmore was unable to secure the party nomination two years later, in 1852, although he had an early lead in convention polling. Gen. Winfield Scott won the nomination, and the Whigs entered into permanent decline.

Slavery Divides the Nation

Try as they might by selecting military heroes as candidates and taking vague stances on issues, the Whigs could not delay facing the nation's disagreements forever. When divisive issues erupted, the party suffered.

The tariff issue and their mildly probusiness stance gave the Whigs strength in the North. But, like the Democrats, they also needed to attract support in the South—a goal they sought by trying to keep the slavery question out of their rhetoric. The Whigs could count on being competitive in the border slave states but not in the rest of Dixie. In 1844 Clay had won only the northern rim of slave states (Delaware, Kentucky, Maryland, North Carolina, and Tennessee).

The abolitionist movement, which may be dated to the founding of William Lloyd Garrison's newspaper, the *Liberator*, in 1831, posed problems for the Whigs that eventually proved fatal. The antislavery belt developed in the Whigs' strongest territory—New England—and westward into the modern-day Midwest. Abolitionism was largely an upper- or middle-class and religious cause. But it also became a partisan issue: the Whigs, the party out of power for years, needed an issue with which to confront the Democrats, and slavery was a useful one, even if the Whigs' antislavery stance in the North contradicted their accommodating stance in the South.

As Sundquist has noted, both the Whig and Democratic Parties in the pre–Civil War era attempted to ignore the slavery issue, but the Whigs had less room to maneuver. The Democrats' agrarian and populist position gave them the solid South as a foundation, and they could make a variety of antiabolitionist appeals to the rest of the electorate. Democrats could argue that their support for slavery in the South was compatible with their many "moderate" positions. The appeal of Senators Stephen A. Douglas of Illinois and Buchanan rested on such a coalition-building strategy. The Whigs, however, included vociferous opponents of slavery who could not be reconciled easily with "moderate" positions. Abolitionism had upper-class and religious roots that were difficult to use as a foundation. The support the Whigs were able to retain in the South was based on their positions on local issues. In sum, the Whigs did not have the same potential to build a national party organization as the Democrats.

Because both parties contained slavery sympathizers and opponents, neither was willing to take a principled stand against the institution, particularly where it already existed. This was not the case, however, for issues such as westward expansion, banking questions, public improvements, the tariff, and foreign relations, where their differences were more evident. But third parties such as the Liberty and Free Soil Parties had no such hesitations about pressing the slavery issue. In fact, sectional cleavages were so strong that in 1836 Congress passed a "gag rule" that forbade the reading of antislavery statements in Congress. Such attempts to silence abolitionist fervor were in vain, however, because politics was entering an age of mass communication and organization. The slavery issue would become irrepressible.

The slavery issue split the Whigs badly with the controversy over the admission of Texas to the Union in 1845. A splinter group of young party members calling themselves the "Conscience Whigs" argued for a straightforward statement of principle against slavery. An opposition group, "Cotton Whigs," wanted to defuse the slavery issue by ignoring moral arguments and simply calling for a halt to annexation. The party split became complete with Clay's Compromise of 1850, which admitted California as a free state, ended slave trade in the District of Columbia, and admitted Texas but reduced its size by splitting off the New Mexico territory. After agitation from Conscience Whigs and General Scott's nomination in 1852, the party was irreparably rent by the slavery issue.

The 1852 Whig convention platform contained several statements supporting states' rights and the principles behind Clay's compromise[31]—concessions made by northern Whigs to win southern support for their presidential favorite, General Scott. But when no Whigs voted for the Kansas-Nebraska Act in 1854, which permitted new states to determine individually the slavery question, the Whigs' remaining ties to Dixie were severed.

The Whigs' strength in the Northwest was almost nonexistent. Only Ohio, in 1844, went for the Whigs even once over the course of the 1844, 1848, and 1852 presidential elections. Previously strong ties between the "lake region" and the South deteriorated as immigrants and others moved from the Northeast to the Northwest and, after the completion of railroad links, the two regions developed strong economic ties.

The Whigs' last gasp came in 1852, when Scott was demolished by Democrat Franklin Pierce, who won all thirty-one states except two in New England (Massachusetts and Vermont) and two border states (Kentucky and Tennessee). In 1856 the Whigs split their votes among Democrat Buchanan, former Whig Millard Fillmore, and Republican John C. Fremont. At that time, not all Whigs were ready yet to join the nascent Republican Party because of the extremism of some of the party's abolitionists. But the majority of Whigs folded into the Republicans in 1860 when Republican presidential candidate Abraham Lincoln avoided a white "backlash" by insisting that he supported slavery where it existed and opposed its spread only because of how it would affect the economic fortunes of poor northern whites.

The Democrats suffered a North-South cleavage that Abraham Lincoln exploited in the 1860 election against Stephen Douglas. Southern Democrats were intent on protecting slavery, and control of Congress was necessary to their strategy. They believed that extension of slavery to the new states joining the Union was needed to maintain their congressional strength. In short, the extension of slavery was the issue that most divided the Democratic Party.

Northern Democrats were willing to allow Dixie to maintain its peculiar institution but were scared about their electoral prospects if slavery should expand. At first they rallied to Douglas's doctrine of "popular sovereignty" (under which the people of new states could decide whether to adopt slavery), but they became nervous when Lincoln hammered away at his argument that any unchecked slavery threatened the freedom of whites as well as blacks. Lincoln argued that Democrats such as Douglas wanted to make slavery a national, rather than an individual state, institution.

Lincoln planted seeds of doubt about partial solutions to the slavery extension question by asserting that slavery could extend to whites if it were nationalized: "If free negroes should be made *things,* how long, think you, before they will begin to make *things* out of poor white men?"[32] Lincoln also maintained that the extension of slavery into new territories would close off those areas for whites seeking upward mobility: "The whole nation is interested that the best use be made of these Territories. We want them for homes of free white people. This they cannot be, to any considerable extent, if slavery shall be planted within them."[33]

Following Lincoln's lead, the growing movement against the extension of slavery was based on a concern for the upward mobility of labor. Rather than stressing the common interests of blacks and poor, northern, white laborers, the antiextension movement played up the competition between the two groups. Horace Greeley's vision of the frontier as "the great regulator of the relations of Labor and Capital, the safety valve of our industrial and social engine" left little room for the extension of slavery into the new territories.[34]

DEMOCRAT PIERCE'S VICTORY: 1852

Clay's congressional compromise on slavery in the territories, known as the Compromise of 1850, turned out to be the major reason for the Democrats' 1852 victory. The compromise addressed the slavery question in all of the new U.S. territories by making concessions to both sides of the struggle. For the North, California would be admitted as a free state, and the slave trade (but not slavery itself) would be abolished in the District of Columbia. For the South, fugitive slave laws would be strengthened, and the New Mexico territory would be divided into two states where the voters, exercising popular sovereignty, would decide the slave issue.

The compromise was designed to settle the issue of slavery in new territories once and for all. But the slavery issue could not be contained by region; it had an increasingly important "spillover" effect. Because of concerns about the congressional balance of power and the difficulties of enforcing slavery provisions such as the fugitive slave law in states that opposed slavery, it was impossible to isolate the slavery question into particular regions as Clay intended.

President Taylor had stalled action on the compromise for months and even suggested that California and New Mexico might become independent nations. But his successor, Millard Fillmore, had thrown his support behind the compromise. The Whigs were divided on the proposal.

General Scott won the Whig nomination in 1852 after platform concessions to the party's southern delegation. Scott's appeal was always limited to the North, while Fillmore appealed to the South and Daniel Webster appealed to New England. Scott won on the fifty-third ballot.

Gov. Franklin Pierce of New Hampshire, a dark horse candidate who gained fame with his Mexican War record, won the Democratic nomination in 1852. His vice-presidential running mate was Sen. William Rufus de Vane King of Alabama. The party held together a coalition of groups with contradictory positions on the slavery issue and regional affairs. The convention, meeting in Baltimore, pledged to "abide by, and adhere to" Clay's compromise and to do what it could to smother the slavery issue.

Attempts to inject issues of economics and foreign affairs into the election failed, and the campaign degenerated into squabbles over personalities. Pierce easily won with 1.6 million popular votes (50.8 percent) to Scott's 1.4 million (43.9 percent). Pierce carried twenty-seven states and 254 electoral votes to Scott's four states and 42 electoral votes.

THE DEMOCRATS' BRUISING 1856 VICTORY

By 1856 the North-South split had eliminated the Whigs as a national party and fatally damaged the Democrats' chances for winning national elections in the decades ahead.

Congress opened the slavery issue by passing the Kansas-Nebraska Act of 1854. The act declared "null and void" the Missouri Compromise of 1820, which had prohibited slavery in new territories north of the 36"30' parallel except in Missouri. The 1854 legislation created two territories (Kansas and Nebraska) from the original Nebraska territory and left the slavery issue to be determined by popular sovereignty there and in the Utah and New Mexico territories.

The Kansas-Nebraska Act was a vehicle to spur the development of the West. Such development was part of a long-standing American approach to creating opportunity and freedom via growth. Sen. Stephen Douglas of Illinois—the promoter of the law and the main advocate of popular sovereignty—held that the law was necessary if the country was to be bound together by rail and telegraph lines and was to drive Great Britain from the continent. The latter goal was based on the widely held suspicion that Britain was exploiting the slavery issue to distract American politics and stunt American growth.

Whatever the economic motives for unification, the Kansas-Nebraska Act was bitterly divisive. Northern state legislatures passed resolutions denouncing the law. The development of sectional parties continued.

A flood of new settlers into Kansas, and the violence that accompanied balloting over whether Kansas was to be a free or a slave state, further inflamed passions. Neighboring Missourians took part in the controversy, arguing that their status as slave owners would be undermined if Kansas voted to be free. Especially in view of the Supreme Court's infamous 1857 *Dred Scott* decision, which denied Congress the power to ban slavery in the territories and barred blacks from citizenship, and the Lincoln-

Douglas debates in Illinois in 1858, the slavery question was becoming decisive in American politics.

The Democrats won the White House in 1856 when the party endorsed the Kansas-Nebraska Act and nominated the pro-South James Buchanan as its presidential candidate. John Breckinridge of Kentucky, who later served as a Confederate general, was Buchanan's running mate. The Democrats, who were becoming mainly a southern party, benefited from close wins in Buchanan's home state of Pennsylvania and in New Jersey, and in western states such as Illinois, Indiana, and California. But the only strong region for the Democrats was the South. Buchanan won all the slave states except Maryland. Overall, Buchanan won 1.8 million popular votes (45.3 percent) to Fremont's 1.3 million (33.1 percent). The electoral college gave Buchanan a 174–114 victory.

The nativist American Party—or the "Know-Nothings," as they were called—nominated former Whig president Millard Fillmore, but the party was never able to move beyond an urban strength based on parochial resistance to immigration and Catholicism. Fillmore won only the state of Maryland; overall, he got 873,000 popular votes (21.5 percent) and 8 electoral votes.

Col. John Charles Fremont was named the Republicans' first presidential candidate. Former Whig senator William Dayton of New Jersey received the vice-presidential nomination. After an 1854 meeting in Ripon, Wisconsin, where a new national party was first proposed, the Republican Party developed quickly. The Republicans had developed a strong grassroots organization in the Northwest after the Kansas-Nebraska Act passed in 1854 and attracted disgruntled abolitionists, Whigs, Know-Nothings, Northern Democrats, and members of the Liberty and Free Soil Parties who were troubled by the possible extension of slavery. Uncertainty about how the extension of slavery would affect laborers who sought opportunity in the territories also helped to unite the new coalition.

The first Republican nominating convention met in Philadelphia in 1856 with delegates from all of the free states, four border states, three territories, and the District of Columbia. The party's opposition to slavery was far from unanimous, but its willingness to address rather than suppress the issue enabled it to redefine the political dialogue. Besides strong antislavery statements, the party platform contained proposals for several internal improvements advantageous to the North. The party did not offer anything to the solidly Democratic South. To win a national election, it would have to sweep the North.

THE FATEFUL ELECTION OF 1860

In 1860 the Democratic split was complete when the party's southern elements supported Vice President Breckinridge and northerners backed Stephen Douglas. The Buchanan administration earlier had waged war on Douglas by ousting his allies from the federal bureaucracy for opposing the administration's prosouthern stance on the Kansas issue.

When the time came for the 1860 presidential campaign, the Democrats were hopelessly split over slavery. The biggest sticking point was the *Dred Scott* decision, which, by decreeing that Congress had no power to prohibit slavery in a territory, was just what southerners favoring popular sovereignty wanted. Yet it also created uncertainty about any legislature's authority over slavery. If Congress could not regulate slavery, could state legislatures? The Republicans were able to use the decision as a rallying point for popular control of government; the Democrats were in the uncustomary position of defending the Supreme Court, which since Thomas Jefferson they had pictured as elitist. Douglas, the eventual Democratic nominee and architect of the platform, insisted on state resolution of the slavery issue. Jefferson Davis of Mississippi, who later became president of the Confederate States of America, fought in Congress for the right of Congress to promote and protect slavery in new territories.

Eventually, the Davis Democrats held their own convention and nominated Vice President Breckinridge for the presidency. Although the Davis Democrats insisted that they were the backbone of the party and had been strong enough to elect Buchanan four years before, the party divided would not be able to win a national election.

And that was the outcome; Democratic Party splits enabled Lincoln to win the 1860 election, resulting in the secession of seven Southern states from the Union even before his inauguration. (The remaining four states forming the Confederacy seceded after the fall of Fort Sumter, on April 13, 1861.)

Because the regional splits that had been tearing the nation apart for decades reached their peak in 1860, none of the four major candidates who were seeking the presidency could compete seriously throughout the nation. The winner was likely to be a candidate from the North, the region with the most electoral votes—that is, either former U.S. representative Abraham Lincoln of Illinois, a Republican, or Stephen Douglas, a Democrat, who defeated Lincoln for the Illinois Senate seat in 1858. Moderate Constitutional Union nominee John Bell of Tennessee and Democrat John Breckinridge of Kentucky were the candidates competing in the South.

The Republicans succeeded in 1860 because they were able to pull together a variety of potentially warring factions. But above all else the Republicans stood against the extension of slavery into new territories. By accepting slavery where it already existed but warning against the spread of the system, the Republicans divided the Democrats and picked up support from a diverse array of otherwise contentious factions—abolitionists, moderate abolitionists, and whites who feared for their position in the economy. Moreover, the *Dred Scott* decision enabled the Republicans to rail publicly against the high court in the tradition of Jefferson and Jackson. While opposing the Democratic doctrine of popular sovereignty, the Republicans picked up some states' rights sympathizers by having a middle-ground slavery stance.

At a frenzied Republican convention in Chicago, which blocked several radical candidates, Lincoln emerged as the consensus compromise choice. The fact that Lincoln was known widely throughout Illinois had improved his chances at the Chicago convention.

Douglas, Lincoln's principal rival, managed several moderate platform victories at the Democratic convention in Charleston, South Carolina, defeating resolutions that called for acceptance

Stephen Douglas, at five feet and four inches, was the 1860 Democratic candidate for president.

of the *Dred Scott* decision and protection of slavery in the territories. But Douglas's success prompted delegates from ten southern states to bolt the convention. After disputes over quorum rules and fifty-seven ballots, the Democrats were unable to muster the necessary two-thirds majority for Douglas. The convention therefore adjourned, reassembled in Baltimore, and faced disputes about the seating of delegates that caused further defections from the South. With southern radicals effectively eliminated from the convention, Douglas swept to a unanimous nomination victory.

The Democratic defectors named Vice President Breckinridge to run for president in the South. The Constitutional Union Party, which developed as a futile attempt to repair the nation's geographic divisions, nominated Bell to oppose Breckinridge. These two candidates were doomed from the start, however, because the South's electoral vote total was significantly below that of the North.

Thanks to the wide-ranging Republican coalition—one that eluded the Whigs in their last years of existence—Lincoln was able to count on strength in the areas that Fremont had won in 1856: New England and the upper Northwest, as well as New York and Ohio. Lincoln's political ties to Illinois, where he practiced law and began his public career, would help in Illinois and Indiana, and his background as a former Whig was a plus in the Ohio valley. The coal and iron regions of Pennsylvania and Ohio were attracted to the party's high-tariff policy. Urban immigrants, particularly Germans, were attracted by the Republican support of homestead (frontier settlement) legislation and the Lincoln campaign's "Vote Yourself a Farm" appeal.[35] The vice-presidential selection of Hannibal Hamlin of Maine, a former Democrat, broadened the coalition beyond partisan lines. Lincoln's oft-stated desire not to challenge slavery where it then existed was an appeal to border states.

Lincoln won easily with a total of 180 electoral votes to Breckinridge's 72, Bell's 39, and Douglas's 12. Lincoln's closest competitor in the popular vote was Douglas. Lincoln had 1.9 million northern popular votes (40.0 percent); Douglas had 1.4 million (29.5 percent) spread out geographically. The two other principal candidates received much less support, which was concentrated in the South: Breckinridge won 848,000 popular votes (18.1 percent); Bell, 591,000 (12.6 percent).

Because some southerners had vowed to secede from the Union if Lincoln won the election, in the period before Lincoln's inauguration congressional committees sought to put together a compromise that would save the nation from civil war. They failed, however, because of Lincoln's refusal to abandon his policy of containing slavery. He rejected proposals for popular sovereignty or a slave-free geographic division of western states, and he would not comment on proposals for constitutional amendments or popular referenda on the issue.

After Lincoln was elected, South Carolina, Louisiana, Mississippi, Alabama, Georgia, Texas, and Florida seceded from the Union and on February 7, 1861, adopted a constitution forming the Confederate States of America. After a protracted standoff between Union soldiers who held Fort Sumter and the Confederate soldiers who controlled South Carolina, the Confederates fired on the fort. Virginia, Arkansas, North Carolina, and Tennessee then joined the Confederacy, and the Civil War was under way.

THE CIVIL WAR ELECTION: 1864

The Union's military difficulties in 1861 and 1862 created resentment against and impatience with President Lincoln. The splits that developed in the Republican Party seemed to imperil his chances for renomination and reelection.

From the very beginning of his administration, Lincoln suffered because of the difficulty he had finding a general who could successfully prosecute the war. Repeated military setbacks and stalemates—such as the Battles of Fredericksburg and Chancellorsville, Confederate general Robert E. Lee's escape after the battle of Antietam (Sharpsburg), and heavy casualties in the drive to Richmond—hurt the Republicans. Publicized conflicts with Union generals such as George McClellan caused further damage. In addition to the military problems, the president's announcement in September 1862 of the emancipation of slaves in rebellious states (the Emancipation Proclamation) created legal and political controversy.

In the 1862 midterm elections, the Republicans experienced widespread losses in congressional and state elections. Among the more bitter defeats for Lincoln was Democrat John Stuart's victory in the president's old congressional district in Illinois. By the time of the presidential election, Stuart, a former law partner of the president, was an ardent political foe.

The military frustrations gave rise to deep divisions within Lincoln's own cabinet. Treasury Secretary Salmon P. Chase was a constant critic of Lincoln's capacity to serve as commander in chief, and the Philadelphia banker Jay Gould briefly led a movement for Chase's nomination for president in 1864. Chase withdrew only after the Lincoln forces dealt him a severe blow at the party caucus in his home state of Ohio. Other radicals met in Cleveland in May 1864 and named John Fremont to run against Lincoln in the fall. Fremont withdrew only after a series of Union military victories strengthened Lincoln's political standing.

The president manipulated the Republican convention in Baltimore brilliantly, ensuring not only his renomination but also the selection of pro-Union governor Andrew Johnson of Union-occupied Tennessee—a lifelong Democrat—as the vice-presidential candidate. Lincoln professed indifference about a possible running mate. "Wish not to interfere about V.P. Cannot interfere about platform," he said in a letter. "Convention must judge for itself."[36] Nevertheless, he maneuvered to build support for Johnson. Johnson's selection was in accord with the desire of the party, which also called itself the Union Party as a way to attract Democrats and to develop nationwide unity. Yet Lincoln's reelection drive was so uncertain that he obliged his cabinet in August 1864 to sign a statement pledging an orderly transition of power if he lost. The statement read: "This morning, as for some days past, it seems exceedingly probable that this Administration will not be reelected. Then it will be my duty to so cooperate with the President-elect, as to save the Union between the election and the inauguration; as he will have secured his elec-

Republican presidential candidate Abraham Lincoln stood tall at six feet and four inches.

President of the Confederacy

In 1861, two weeks before Abraham Lincoln was inaugurated in Washington, D.C., as the sixteenth president of the United States, another president was inaugurated in Montgomery, Alabama. On February 18, 1861, Jefferson Davis became the first and only president of the Confederate States of America.

Davis was born in Christian (now Todd) County, Kentucky, on June 3, 1808. He was the youngest of the ten children of Samuel and Jane Davis, who moved

Jefferson Davis

their family to a small Mississippi plantation when Jefferson was a boy. He attended private schools and Transylvania University in Lexington, Kentucky, before his oldest brother, Joseph, secured his appointment to West Point in 1824.

After graduating from the academy, Davis was stationed in Wisconsin under Col. Zachary Taylor. There he saw action in the Black Hawk War during the early 1830s and fell in love with Taylor's daughter, Sarah Knox. In 1835 he left the army, married Sarah, and settled on a one-thousand-acre plantation in Mississippi, which was given to him by his brother Joseph. Tragically, Sarah died from malaria three months after the wedding, and for several years Davis devoted himself to developing his land and wealth.

In 1845 Davis married Varina Howell, a member of the Mississippi aristocracy, and was elected to the U.S. House of Representatives. He served in Washington less than a year before the Mexican War began, and he gave up his seat to accept a commission as a colonel. He became a national hero when his company made a

stand at the Battle of Buena Vista that was said to have saved Gen. Zachary Taylor's army from defeat.

In 1847 he left the army and was elected to the Senate. He served there until 1851, when he ran unsuccessfully for governor of Mississippi. He returned to Washington in 1853 after being appointed secretary of war by President Franklin Pierce. Davis was credited with strengthening the armed forces during his time in office. He also was influential in bringing about the Gadsden Purchase from Mexico in 1853, which added southern areas of present-day Arizona and New Mexico to the United States.

In 1857 Davis was reelected to the Senate. Although he became a leading spokesperson for the South, he did not advocate secession until 1860 when it had become inevitable. Davis hoped to be appointed commanding general of the South's army, but instead he was chosen as president by a convention of the seceding states.

Davis believed his first priority as president was to preserve Southern independence. He tried to secure French and British assistance for the Confederacy, but he was largely unsuccessful. Like Lincoln he helped develop military strategy and on occasion interfered with the plans of his generals. In managing the war effort, Davis was hampered by his paradoxical position. The South could fight most effectively as a unified nation run by the central government in Richmond, but the Southern states had succeeded in part to preserve their rights as independent states. Davis took actions, including the suspension of *habeas corpus* and the establishment of conscription, that were regarded as despotic by many Southerners.

When the Union's victory appeared imminent in early 1865, Davis fled south from Richmond and was captured by federal troops. He was indicted for treason and imprisoned for two years, but he never stood trial. He lived in Canada and Europe for several years before retiring to Mississippi. There he wrote his *Rise and Fall of the Confederate Government*, which was published in 1881. He died in New Orleans on December 6, 1889.

---

tion on such ground that he cannot possibly save it afterwards."[37]

The man for whom Lincoln anticipated arranging a wartime transition was Democratic nominee George McClellan, whom Lincoln had fired as general in January 1863. McClellan had won the Democratic nomination with the strong backing of "peace Democrats" such as Clement L. Vallandigham of Ohio, who was arrested by Union general Ambrose E. Burnside after making a series of antiwar speeches. (Vallandigham later took up exile in Canada.) McClellan's running mate was Rep. George Pendleton of Ohio, who after the war would sponsor landmark civil service reform legislation.

Although popular with his soldiers, General McClellan had not won a single major battle of the war despite many infusions

of extra troops. Yet he blamed Lincoln for the losses. Indeed, he was a vocal critic of the administration. McClellan's presidential campaign was built around a call for a cease-fire and a convention to restore the Union. He and his fellow peace Democrats also criticized the administration's violation of civil liberties and other unconstitutional actions.

Lincoln's fortunes improved in the two months before the election. When Gen. William Tecumseh Sherman took Atlanta after a scorched-earth march through the South, the Confederacy was left badly divided geographically. The military victory cut off the Gulf states from the Confederate capital of Richmond. Gen. Philip Sheridan had had important successes in the Shenandoah Valley, and Gen. Ulysses S. Grant had fared well in Virginia.

Not only did the Democrats face a Republican Party reconstituted for the war election as the Union Party and united by recent military victories, but McClellan also had a difficult time developing consistent campaign themes. He was at various times conciliatory toward the Confederacy and solicitous of the soldiers who fought for the Union. The balancing problem was underscored by the inclusion of both war and peace songs in the *McClellan Campaign Songster*, a piece of campaign literature.[38] McClellan also had a difficult time selling his message to Northern industrialists who were profiting from munitions procurement.

Not until the arrival of election results from three state elections on October 11 were Lincoln and the Unionists confident that they would win the national election in November. Republican victories in Indiana, Ohio, and Pennsylvania were the first concrete indications that Lincoln's fortunes had turned around.

Lincoln overwhelmed McClellan by winning all of the loyal states except Delaware, Kentucky, and New Jersey for a 212–21 electoral vote victory. Lincoln garnered 2.2 million popular votes (55.0 percent) to McClellan's 1.8 million (45.0 percent). The electoral votes of Louisiana and Tennessee, the first Confederate states to return to the Union, were not accepted by Congress.

Postwar Radicalism

The end of the Civil War left the nation almost as divided as it had been in the antebellum years. Concerns about punishment of the rebel states, the status of the freedmen, and economic development replaced slavery as the principal sources of disagreement.

The nation undoubtedly would have experienced bitter splits no matter who had served as chief executive, but the assassination of President Lincoln on April 14, 1865, shortly after the Confederate surrender, created a crisis of leadership. Lincoln's vice president, Andrew Johnson, ascended to the presidency and quickly came into conflict with the radical Northern Republicans who controlled Congress. Johnson, a Democrat from Tennessee, was stubborn, which only aggravated the troubles that were inevitable anyway because of his party and regional background.

Johnson intended to continue Lincoln's plans for the reconstruction of the North and South "with malice toward none"; he chafed at the notion of the South as a conquered territory. A states' rights politician, Johnson attempted to put together a coalition of moderates from all parts of the country that would bring about a quick reconciliation between his administration and Congress.

But Congress was intent on establishing political institutions that would respect the rights of former slaves and promote economic growth and vowed to use military occupation to destroy the South's old political elite.[39] Thus Johnson and Congress fought over bills that would extend the life of the Freedmen's Bureau (an agency established to help blacks make the transition from slavery to citizenship) and guarantee the franchise and equal protection to blacks, with the result that Johnson ve-

The 1872 Republican campaign called voters' attention to the humble backgrounds of presidential candidate Ulysses S. Grant and his running mate, Henry Wilson.

toed both bills. Johnson also opposed the Fourteenth Amendment, which guaranteed equal protection, as well as the stipulation that Confederate states approve the amendment as a condition of their readmission to the Union.

When the Radical Republicans took over Congress in the 1866 midterm elections, the war with Johnson began in earnest. In March 1867 Congress established limited military rule in recalcitrant Southern states and in May passed the Tenure of Office Act limiting the president's right to dismiss his appointees. Johnson contemptuously disregarded the tenure act and fired Edwin Stanton, his secretary of war. For this action Johnson was impeached by the House and tried by the Senate. When the Senate voted in May 1868, he avoided the two-thirds total needed for conviction by a single vote (35–19).

THE GRANT VICTORIES: 1868 AND 1872

Ulysses S. Grant was more than a concerned citizen during the dispute between Johnson and Congress. Despite its portrayal in many history books as a clear instance of congressional abuse of power, the affair was more complicated. All of the players in the drama negotiated their way with care, and almost none of them escaped without major scars. Grant was a central figure, and his style of maneuvering was dictated by his ambition to succeed Johnson as president.

Radical Republicans in Congress achieved a lasting victory when they secured passage of the Civil Rights Act of 1866 over President Johnson's veto, but they were increasingly disturbed by reports that the statute was not being enforced. A congressional investigation of violence against blacks in Memphis concluded that the Freedmen's Bureau could not enforce civil rights without help. Radicals began to look to Secretary of War Stanton to enforce the law that the president clearly disliked and repeatedly subverted. When Stanton indicated that he would carry out the law in the Confederacy as Congress intended, Johnson began to think about replacing him. At this point Congress passed the Tenure of Office Act over Johnson's veto in May 1867, reasoning that its constitutional "advise and consent" powers over appointments could be extended to removal as well. Johnson, however, decided to test the law's constitutionality.

In replacing Stanton, Johnson's concern—and indeed the concern of all involved—was who could assume the secretary of war post with minimal threat to Johnson's own position. Johnson first considered General Sherman but decided to appoint Grant on a temporary basis. Originally a Democrat and supporter of moderate policies toward the South, Grant worried about appearing too close to the unpopular president. As a result, after vaguely assuring Johnson that he would accept a temporary appointment, Grant hedged. He increasingly expressed support for the notion that appointees should interpret and obey laws according to congressional intent. Eventually Grant told the president in a letter that he could not accept the appointment.

After the drama of Johnson's impeachment in 1868, Grant was in a good position to seek the White House. He had avoided allying himself with controversy during both Johnson's search for a replacement for Stanton and the ensuing impeachment battle. In fact, he and Chief Justice Salmon Chase were the only ones not tainted by the affair. Grant even managed to maintain his public posture of disinterested duty. Thus during one of the nation's ugliest political episodes, Grant looked clean. He was ready for a presidential campaign.

As Johnson endured his Senate impeachment trial in March, Grant won his first electoral victory. A New Hampshire congressional campaign, which normally would favor the Democrat, became an early Grant referendum when Republican candidate Donald Sickles told voters that a vote for a Republican was a vote for Grant; Sickles won. Just before the Republican convention in May, a Soldiers and Sailors Convention "nominated" Grant. Yet he avoided an excessively military image when he vowed to reduce the size of the standing army. Grant was on his way.

Grant won the presidential nomination without opposition. The real battle at the 1868 Republican convention was for the vice-presidential nomination. Schuyler Colfax of Indiana, the Speaker of the House, won on the sixth ballot; eleven candidates received votes on the initial roll call.

The Democrats had a difficult time finding a nominee. Johnson sought the Democratic nomination, but his appeal was to the South. (Because many Southern states were still outside the Union, Northern politicians were selecting the nominee.) Chief Justice Chase, highly regarded for his fairness during Johnson's Senate trial, was a possibility, but his strong stand for black suffrage was a barrier. Sen. Thomas A. Hendricks of Indiana was strong in the East, and George Pendleton of Ohio, the party's vice-presidential candidate four years earlier, was strong in the West. Gen. Winfield Scott Hancock of Pennsylvania presented the opportunity of running one military hero against another.

After twenty-three bitter ballots in a sweltering New York City, Horatio Seymour, the national party chair and popular war governor of New York, accepted the Democratic nomination against his will. Gen. Francis P. Blair Jr. of Missouri was the vice-presidential nominee. The party platform called for the rapid reentry of Confederate states to the Union, state authority over suffrage questions, and the "Ohio Idea," which promised an inflationary money supply that would help the indebted South.

Both sides were well financed in the election, but the Republicans had the edge. The Republican Party's probusiness positions on the tariff, railroad grants, and the currency attracted millions of dollars. Newspapers and magazines tended to be pro-Republican because of their urban business orientations.

Grant, who ran his campaign from his home in Galena, Illinois, was vague about issues ranging from the currency to voting rights. Appearances in Colorado with fellow generals Sherman and Sheridan were taken to be endorsements. Everything seemed to go Grant's way. Even the traditional campaign gossip about the sexual activities of candidates did not hurt him. Charges that Grant was excessively problack—"I am Captain Grant of the Black Marines, the stupidest man that was ever seen" were the lyrics of one ditty[40]—helped him with the recently enfranchised citizens. Without the black vote, Grant probably would have lost the popular vote and perhaps the electoral vote. Results from October state elections that favored the Republicans created a brief movement for Seymour and Blair to quit the contest so that the Democrats could name a new ticket. Instead Seymour took the October results as an incentive to get to the campaign stump. Seymour was a good speaker, but nothing he could do could help the Democrats.

Grant defeated Seymour by 3.0 million (52.7 percent) to 2.7 million votes (47.3 percent). The electoral vote tally was 214 for Grant and 80 for Seymour. Finally, Grant won all but eight of the thirty-four states taking part in the election. He benefited from Radical Republican reconstructionist sentiment in the North and newly enfranchised blacks in the South.

With Grant's ascension to the presidency in 1869, the Republican Party entered a new era—what the German sociologist Max Weber would have called a shift from "charismatic" to "rational" institutional authority. In other words, the party shifted its devotion from a great moral cause to its own survival as an organization. It had begun as a coalition of activists fervently opposed to the expansion of slavery (many opposed slavery itself) and to the rebellion of Southern states from the Union.

The Republicans' 1868 victory under Grant was the first not dominated wholly by crisis conditions.

The Republicans had a strong base of support: eastern bankers, manufacturers, railroads, and land speculators. With the old Confederacy under the control of military governments and with blacks given the franchise, the Republicans had strength in the South. The West was restive, however, because of depressed farm prices, high taxes, and debt. The industrial-agrarian split between North and South before the Civil War would be resumed as an East-West split in the years after the war.

The Republican leadership itself was changing. Age was claiming a number of the early Republican leaders, such as Thaddeus Stevens, William Seward, Benjamin Wade, Charles Sumner, James Grimes, Edwin Stanton, and Salmon Chase. New party leaders included Senators Roscoe Conkling of New York, Oliver Morton of Indiana, Simon Cameron of Pennsylvania, and Zachariah Chandler of Michigan, and Representatives Benjamin Butler of Massachusetts, John Logan of Illinois, James Garfield of Ohio, and James G. Blaine of Maine.

As for the new Grant administration, it was undistinguished. The new president's inaugural address—spoken without the traditional company of the outgoing president because Grant had neglected to respond to Johnson's polite letters—was decent but uninspiring. Grant vowed that "all laws will be faithfully executed, whether they meet my approval or not," that debtors would not be tolerated, and that blacks should get the vote throughout the country and Indians should be offered "civilization and ultimate citizenship."[41] With a few important exceptions, cabinet positions went to old Grant cronies.

In 1869 the nation experienced a financial panic when financiers Jay Gould and Jim Fisk attempted to corner the world's gold market. Their scheme led to "Black Friday," September 24, 1869. Gould and Fisk had met with President Grant and had urged him not to sell government gold, therefore keeping the price of gold high. At the last minute, however, Grant decided to reject their advice and dumped $4 million worth of gold on the market. That dumping caused a severe drop in gold prices, breaking up the Gould-Fisk conspiracy but also causing tremendous losses for thousands of speculators. It was the worst disaster on Wall Street up to that time. Although it did not cause a depression, the South and West were hard hit by the financial retrenchment program that followed. Tariff rates remained high on most manufactured goods, despite tentative efforts to reform the system.

The spoils system was in full swing during the Grant years. Grant himself was not involved in the scramble for booty, but his family and aides were often shameless in their greed. When Grant learned that liberal Republicans were planning an independent presidential campaign against him in 1872, he took the edge off the spoils issue by creating the Civil Service Reform Commission, but his neglect of the commission made it ineffective.

Before the 1872 election, the *New York Sun* exposed the Crédit Mobilier scandal. The newspaper reported that the firm's board of directors had many of the same members as the Union Pacif-ic Railroad Company, which hired it to build a transcontinental route, and that Crédit Mobilier had paid its board exorbitant profits. To avoid a public investigation, Crédit Mobilier offered stock to Vice President Colfax and Representative (later president) James Garfield. Colfax lost his place on the Republican ticket for his role in the scandal; Sen. Henry Wilson of New Hampshire took his position as the vice-presidential candidate in 1872.

Liberal Republicans, unhappy with protective tariffs, spoils, and the uneven administration of the Southern states, bolted the party in 1872. The group was interested in policies such as civil service and free trade that would promote individual virtue in a laissez-faire economic system. The reformers thought they had a chance to win. The German-born senator Carl Schurz of Missouri wrote to a friend that "the administration with its train of offices and officemongers [is] the great incubus pressing upon the party. . . . The superstition that Grant is the necessary man is rapidly giving way. The spell is broken, and we have only to push through the breach."[42]

Candidates for the nomination from this group of Republicans included former ambassador to Great Britain Charles Francis Adams, son of President John Quincy Adams and grandson of President John Adams; Supreme Court Justice David Davis; Chief Justice Salmon Chase; Sen. Lyman Trumbull of Illinois; and Horace Greeley, editor of the *New York Tribune*. Greeley won the nomination on the sixth ballot and ran as a Democrat and Liberal Republican. The Democrats were so weak that they did not field a candidate of their own. They endorsed the Greeley ticket. (Charles O'Conor of New York was nominated by a group of "Noncoalition Democrats" for president. He did not accept the nomination.)

Since his early days as a newspaper reporter, when he described President Van Buren as an effeminate failure, Greeley had won fame as a pungent social critic. He was a crusading, abolitionist editor and a dedicated reformer, but his rumpled appearance and unpolished speaking style made him appear "unpresidential." Greeley was unable to parlay an amalgam of promises to various interest groups—blacks, soldiers, immigrants, and laborers—into a victory over Grant. Groups that Greeley actively courted found him wanting for a variety of reasons, and even though Greeley advocated the tariff favored by the North, he could not cut into Grant's northeastern strength. One Republican cartoon that revealed Greeley's difficult task showed a fence on which sat a laborer, skeptical because of Greeley's stand against strikes, and a black, concerned because of Greeley's advocacy of amnesty for Confederates. Sitting on the sidelines was a German, upset with Greeley's prohibitionist stance: "Oh! Yaw! You would take my Lager away, den you must get widout me along!"[43]

Even though he went on the stump and delivered a series of impressive speeches, Greeley never had a chance. Republican gubernatorial victories in North Carolina in August and in Pennsylvania, Ohio, and Indiana in October were clear harbingers that the Republican Party would do well in November. Grant took the entire North and the newly admitted South with 3.6 million popular votes (55.6 percent). Greeley won three border states, as well as Tennessee, Texas, and Georgia, with 2.8 million popular votes (43.9 percent). Less than a month after the election, Greeley died. Of the electoral votes, which were cast after Greeley's death, Grant received 286; the Democrats' 63 electoral votes were scattered among various candidates, and 17 Democratic electoral votes were not cast.

THE COMPROMISE OF 1876

The pattern of Republican, northern, and business domination of presidential politics was institutionalized in the 1876 election. Republican Rutherford B. Hayes, the three-time governor of Ohio, lost the popular vote and had a questionable hold on the electoral college vote, but he managed to beat Democrat Samuel J. Tilden for the presidency when the election was settled by a special commission created by Congress. (Hayes won 4.0 million votes to Tilden's 4.3 million—48.0 and 51.0 percent of the popular vote, respectively.) Perhaps the most controversial election outcome in history, some feared it would set off a second civil war.

The problem arose when the vote tallies in Florida, South Carolina, and Louisiana were called into question. Violence had accompanied the voting in all three states, but President Grant had not sent in federal troops to ensure fair balloting. On those states hung the electoral outcome. There was good reason to be suspicious of any vote count in those and other southern states. While the Republicans had controlled the balloting places and mounted vigorous drives to get blacks to the polls, the Democrats had used physical intimidation and bribery to keep blacks away. The bitterness between northern interests and southern whites was apparent in the violence that often took place at polls.

When state election board recounts and investigations did not settle the question of the vote tallies, Congress took up the matter. An electoral commission made up of five senators (three majority-party Republicans, two minority Democrats), five representatives (three majority-party Democrats, two minority Republicans), and five Supreme Court justices (two from each party, one independent) assembled to hear complaints about the disputed states. At the last minute the independent justice disqualified himself, and his place was taken by a Republican who was accepted by Democrats because they considered him to be the most independent of the Republican justices. Weeks of bargaining followed, during which the Republican vote totals of the disputed states were confirmed and the southern Democrats extracted promises of financial aid and political independence from the federal government.

When the validity of the Florida vote count for Hayes was challenged, the commission responded that it did not have the capacity to judge the actual conduct of the balloting, only the validity of the certificates presented to Congress. That decision gave the state to Hayes. Challenges to the vote counts of Louisiana, South Carolina, and Oregon were dismissed in a similar way, so Hayes was awarded the presidency by a single electoral vote, 185 to 184.

The compromise not only settled the partisan dispute between Hayes and Tilden, but also established a rigid alignment of political interests that would dominate U.S. politics for the next half-century. Although Democrats won occasional victories, the Republican, eastern, conservative, business-oriented establishment held sway over the system until Franklin Roosevelt's election in 1932.

The institutional form of the regional splits created by the compromise remained much longer. Historian C. Vann Woodward has argued that secret wheeling and dealing among congressional and party leaders institutionally divided the political system by party, region, economic interest, and governmental branches. Northern Republican industrial interests were given control of the presidential election process, and southern Democratic agricultural interests were given autonomy over their regional politics, which led to domination of Congress.[44] This alignment was not completely dislodged until the passage of important civil rights legislation in the 1960s.

To reward southern Democrats for throwing the 1876 election to the Republican Hayes, northern politicians agreed to pull federal troops out of the South and to allow southern whites to take over the system. Within months southern states were erecting a powerful edifice of racial discrimination that would last until the 1960s. Former South Carolina governor Daniel H. Chamberlain, a Republican, later summed up the deal:

What is the president's Southern policy? [I]t consists in the abandonment of Southern Republicans and especially the colored race, to the control and rule not only of the Democratic Party, but of that class of the South which regarded slavery as a Divine Institution, which waged four years of destructive war for its perpetuation, which steadily opposed citizenship and suffrage for the negro—in a word, a class whose traditions, principles, and history are opposed to every step and feature of what Republicans call our national progress since 1860.[45]

The Age of Republicanism

From 1860 to 1908, the Republicans won eleven elections; the Democrats won only two. Only Grover Cleveland could put together a Democratic win, and he was as conservative on most issues as the Republicans of the period. Presidential election winners after the Great Compromise were Hayes (1876), James Garfield (1880), Cleveland (1884), Benjamin Harrison (1888), Cleveland (1892), William McKinley (1896 and 1900), Theodore Roosevelt (1904), and William Howard Taft (1908).

The political aspirants of the day were required to adhere to the creed of high tariffs, laissez-faire economics, and tight money. Tight money policies—the restricted issuance of currency, which favored bankers and other established interests but hurt debtors and those seeking more rapid expansion of some kinds of investment and spending—provided rare openings for effective Democratic resistance to Republican hegemony. Resistance did develop, however, when the scramble for tariff protections created obvious inequities among businesses and hardships for the consumer. Yet populist uprisings, such as Democrat William Jennings Bryan's 1896 campaign, faltered because of strong mobilization by the Republicans and divisions within the Democratic ranks. Bryan failed to bring a likely Democratic con-

The fiery oratory of 1884 Republican candidate James G. Blaine captured the imagination of the political establishment, but it was not enough to win him the election over Democrat Grover Cleveland.

stituency—the worker—into the fold. Eastern business owners were able to portray their interest in industrial growth as a common concern with labor and Bryan's western agrarian alliance as a danger to that growth.

Although the Republican Party dominated presidential politics, the parties were well balanced in Congress and in state governments until the class and sectional cleavages of the 1890s. The Senate was split evenly in 1881, 37–37, and two years later the Republicans had a 38–36 edge. The Democrats had made gains in northern congressional races, and Republicans were making smaller gains in the South. The House tended to provide a majority for whichever party held the White House.

GARFIELD CARRIES THE REPUBLICAN BANNER: 1880

Hayes honored his pledge to serve only one term, setting off a scramble for both parties' nominations in 1880. When the early momentum for a third term for Grant faltered, the Republican contest became a battle between Grant, Sen. James G. Blaine of Maine, and Treasury Secretary John Sherman of Ohio. Grant was able to muster a first-ballot plurality but could not attract new supporters as the balloting proceeded. A stalemate between Blaine and Sherman ensued.

Rep. James Garfield of Ohio, a former preacher who was impressive in his oratory and organization for Sherman, was the compromise choice for the nomination. He selected as his running mate Chester A. Arthur, the collector of the Port of New York, an important patronage job.

The Democrats named Gen. Winfield Hancock of Pennsylvania and former Indiana representative William English to head their ticket. The Democratic platform advocated the gold standard, a low tariff designed to raise revenue, civil service reform, restrictions on Chinese immigration, and a belated criticism of the 1876 deal that gave the presidency to Hayes. Except for the tariff and 1876 questions, the Democrats' platform was close to the Republicans' statement of principles.

The regional breakdown of support, with most of the North and West falling in Garfield's camp and the South lining up behind Hancock, gave the presidency to Garfield. The popular vote was close—4.45 million (48.27 percent) to 4.44 million (48.25 percent)—but Garfield won a 214–155 electoral vote victory.

The festering issue of patronage and civil service came to a head shortly after Garfield's inauguration. On July 2, 1881, Charles Guiteau, a man later described as a "disappointed office-seeker," shot Garfield while he was en route to Williams College to deliver a commencement address. Garfield died in September, and Arthur became president.

The outstanding feature of Arthur's presidency was the easy passage of the Pendleton Act—legislation that set up a commission to regulate the provision of federal jobs and the behavior of civil servants. The number of federal workers removed from the patronage system was at first small, but successive presidents widened the coverage of nonpartisan workers so that today less than 1 percent of all federal workers are appointed by the president.[46]

The tariff question also emerged as crucial during the Arthur presidency. The Tariff Act of 1883 "gave little or no relief to the consumer and took care of every important industrial interest."[47] The Democrats opposed the bill and later worked for the gradual lowering of rates, but they failed. The tariff would be a major issue in later elections.

DEMOCRAT CLEVELAND WINS: 1884

Arthur wanted the Republican nomination in 1884, and his record as stand-in for the assassinated Garfield arguably should have earned him the nod—even though no successor president during the nineteenth century had been nominated by his party.

Not only was he an important player in civil service reform and the tariff issue, but he initiated modernization of the navy and vetoed the Chinese Exclusion Act of 1882, which prohibited Chinese laborers from entering the United States for ten years. His veto of the $19 million rivers and harbors bill was a model of fiscal probity.

James Blaine of Maine—secretary of state in Arthur's own administration—stood in Arthur's way. After months of public appeals by old-line Republicans interested in stronger leadership and more generous patronage from their party, Blaine quit his administration position and opposed Arthur for the nomination.

Blaine was the most charismatic figure of the period. A former teacher, editor, state legislator, and member of Congress, Blaine's fiery oratory captured the imagination of the political establishment. He had made a national name for himself when he opposed an 1876 congressional resolution expressing forgiveness to Civil War rebels including the Confederate president, Jefferson Davis. Col. Robert G. Ingersoll, a rising political figure in the Republican Party, said of Blaine: "Like an armed warrior, like a plumed knight, James G. Blaine marched down the halls of the American Congress and threw his shining lance full and fair against the brazen forehead of every traitor to his country."[48] The sobriquet "Plumed Knight" caught on.

The Republican convention in Chicago praised Arthur's administration and fudged the tariff issue. The tariff that passed in 1883 was the product of the efforts of swarms of lobbyists for private interests. The Republican platform promised better protection for raw wool interests, angered by their treatment in 1883, and a generally protective stance for domestic industry. The platform also called for an international currency conference, railway regulation, a national agency for labor affairs, and further improvements in the navy.

At a frenzied convention, Blaine took the lead over Arthur on the first ballot. Old-line party leaders quickly united behind Blaine, while Arthur was unable to consolidate the support of reform Republicans still skeptical of his leadership abilities from his days as a patronage politician and collector of the Port of New York. Blaine won the nomination on the fourth ballot. Gen. John Logan of Illinois received the vice-presidential nomination.

The Democrats nominated Grover Cleveland after skirmishes with Sen. Thomas F. Bayard Jr. of Delaware and Sen. Thomas A. Hendricks of Indiana. Hendricks, whose liberal expansionist currency stance would balance the more conservative stance of Cleveland, was named the vice-presidential candidate. The Democratic platform vaguely promised reform of the tariff laws to make them fairer and, even more vaguely, promised a more honest and efficient administration.

Cleveland was a former teacher, lawyer, assistant district attorney, and reform mayor of Buffalo who had won the governorship of New York only two years before. Members of both parties consistently underestimated Cleveland's intellect and resolve. As governor, he had made enemies through his vetoes of low public transit fares and aid to sectarian schools. He also had defied Tammany Hall, the Democratic Party organization that dominated New York politics, especially in New York City.

Cleveland's nomination signaled a triumph for the "educational politics" characteristic of urban progressivism. (Progressives took a patriarchal view of politics in which elites assumed an obligation to better their social underlings through education and various social services.) In a move away from the highly partisan and vitriolic campaigns of the post–Civil War era, Cleveland and other disciples of former New York governor Samuel Tilden promoted their program through a "literary bureau" that distributed pamphlets describing the party's policy positions. Campaign themes were developed at the national level and disseminated via the mails and meetings with the many professional and community organizations. The educational style was adopted by Republican candidate Benjamin Harrison in 1888.[49]

In contrast, Blaine's campaign was one of the dirtiest in U.S. history. He first attempted to spark sectional antagonisms with his "bloody shirt" warnings that the South was trying to reassert its rebel ways through Cleveland. Blaine also tried to rouse the fears of business with claims that Cleveland would institute free trade policies damaging to domestic industries. But that appeal failed because the Democratic platform's plank on the tariff laws specifically supported protection of those interests. Finally, Blaine tried to make a scandal of Cleveland's admission that he had fathered a child out of wedlock years before. Cleveland was charged, among other things, of kidnapping and immuring both the mother and child to cover up the story.

The campaign eventually turned on Cleveland's victory in New York, which resulted from a number of blunders by Blaine. One blunder had occurred years before, when Blaine mocked New York party boss Roscoe Conkling: "The contempt of that large-minded gentleman is so wilted, his haughty disdain, his grandiloquent swell, his majestic, supereminent, overpowering, turkey-gobbler strut, has been so crushing to myself that I know it was an act of the greatest temerity to venture upon a controversy with him."[50] Conkling was so peeved by the turkey image that he spent his whole career battling Blaine, including the presidential campaign of 1884. Blaine's own running mate, Logan, sympathized with Conkling in the dispute.

The other Blaine faux pas occurred a week before the election when a Protestant minister praised Blaine and proclaimed, "We are Republicans, and do not propose to leave our party and identify ourselves with the party whose antecedents have been rum, Romanism, and rebellion." Blaine did not divorce himself from the remark, which angered New York Democrats—and ethnic voters everywhere—and cost him many votes. Later the same day Blaine attended a formal dinner with a number of wealthy persons that became known as "the millionaires dinner." That event belied Blaine's claim to speak for ordinary people.

Of Irish background, Blaine appealed to Irish immigrants in New York for their votes. But Cleveland countered Blaine's Irish tactic by obtaining the last-minute endorsement of the powerful Tammany leader Edward Kelly. On the Saturday before the election, he attended a parade in New York City that attracted forty thousand people chanting: "Blaine, Blaine, James G. Blaine, the Monumental Liar from the State of Maine!" With the help of an economic downturn and the "Mugwumps"—independents and liberal Republicans offended by Blaine—Cleveland won the presidency.

The race, however, was close. Cleveland received 4.9 million votes (48.5 percent) to Blaine's 4.8 million (48.3 percent). He won the solid South, Indiana, Connecticut, New Jersey, and, most important, New York (although by only 1,047 out of 1.13 million votes cast). Still, the election controversy did not end with the balloting. The *New York Tribune* reported that Blaine had won the race, fueling fears about an election deadlock similar to the Hayes-Tilden contest of 1876. But Cleveland received 219 electoral votes to Blaine's 182, making the Democrat the clear winner.

Cleveland's first two years in the White House were productive. His inaugural address and cabinet selections elicited wide praise. And his style of leadership—examined closely in the newspapers—appeared refreshingly unassuming. The Cleveland agenda included issues such as tariff reform (cutting rates on the "necessaries of life"), modernization of the navy, civil service, expansion, and land law reform. The president oversaw passage of the Presidential Succession Act and the Electoral Count Act, changes in currency policy, and labor controversies.

Just as he had done during his terms as mayor of Buffalo and governor of New York, Cleveland icily refused to compromise his values. This steadfastness proved to be a problem, however, for *President* Cleveland. Thousands of Democratic Party workers went to Washington seeking jobs in the new administration only to be disappointed. "Ah, I suppose you mean that I should appoint two horse thieves a day instead of one," Cleveland said in response to one party leader.[51] In vetoing pension bills, Cleveland called their sponsors "blood-suckers," "coffee-boilers," "pension leeches," and "bums."[52] The president appeared just as aloof to labor when a record number of strikes and disturbances swept the nation in 1886; the federal troops that Cleveland sent to the Haymarket riot in Chicago killed thirty people.

When Cleveland did bend to political realities, his timing was off. After standing firm against patronage when party enthusiasm for reform was at its height, Cleveland disappointed reformers when he allowed lieutenants such as First Assistant Postmaster Adlai E. Stevenson to distribute favors.

The biggest controversy of the Cleveland administration involved tariffs. Concerned about federal budget surpluses that threatened to stall economic activity, Cleveland prodded the House of Representatives to pass tariff reductions. The Senate responded with a protective (high) tariff measure.

THE 1888 REPUBLICAN RECOVERY

The tariff issue propelled the two parties into the 1888 election. At their national convention the Democrats nominated Cleveland by acclamation and chose seventy-five-year-old judge Allen G. Thurman of Ohio for the vice presidency. The Democrats tried to soften their low-tariff image by promising that open trade would open world markets to domestic industries. Lower tariffs were said to be necessary for avoiding disastrous federal budget surpluses, preventing the development of monopolies, and ensuring consumers reasonable prices for basic goods.

Captioned "Another Voice for Cleveland," this 1884 cartoon played on Cleveland's admission that he had fathered an illegitimate son.

As for the Republicans, a politics-weary James Blaine sent word from Florence and Paris that he would not be a candidate in 1888, leaving the race open to some lesser political lights, including Sen. John Sherman of Ohio, Gov. Russell Alger of Michigan, Sen. William Allison of Iowa, and Sen. Benjamin Harrison of Indiana. At the Republican national convention Sherman led the early balloting but quickly lost ground to Alger and Harrison. After extensive backroom maneuvering, including a last-minute plea by party members to Blaine to accept the nomination, Harrison, who had the backing of state party bosses, won on the ninth ballot. Levi Morton, a banker, got the vice-presidential nomination.

Harrison, a senator from Indiana, was a former Civil War brigadier and the grandson of President William Henry Harrison. Characterized by a scandal-free if colorless demeanor, Harrison was a good speaker, but he often appeared aloof. One historian wrote: "Those who talked with him were met with a frigid look from two expressionless steel grey eyes; and their remarks were sometimes answered in a few chill monosyllables devoid of the slightest note of interest."[53] Harrison pledged a modernized navy, civil service reforms, and the traditional Republican policies to protect trusts and restrict U.S. markets.

The election turned, as in 1884, on New York and Indiana—both states with extensive evidence of voter intimidation and manipulation of vote counts. Harrison won the two states narrowly—New York by only 14,373 votes out of the 1.3 million cast—and captured the White House. Except for Connecticut and New Jersey, Harrison swept the North and West. Cleveland won the South. Overall, Harrison won 5.4 million popular votes (47.8 percent) and 233 electoral votes; Cleveland won 5.5 million popular votes (48.6 percent) and 168 electoral votes.

Cleveland left the White House with an unusual amount of good will among the public because of his honest tariff campaign. His popularity increased during the next four years as the economy hit slumps and as the former president, while practicing law, delivered speeches calling for a more egalitarian brand of politics. Cleveland would be back in 1892 for vindication.

With a majority in Congress and a president in the White House—the first time the party had accomplished such a feat in a dozen years—the Republicans went about their business briskly after the election. Postmaster General John Wanamaker dispensed patronage with zeal. President Harrison signed into law the McKinley Tariff Act and the Sherman Silver Purchase Act. The former raised duties on manufactured goods to their highest level ever but also included provisions for negotiating with other countries to bring the rates down. The silver act loosened the money supply, which stimulated economic activity but angered creditors and bankers (money, when it is more readily available, is worth less).

CLEVELAND'S COMEBACK: 1892

The 1890 midterm elections brought huge Democratic gains. Voters all over the country—but especially in the depressed farm belt—rebelled against the inflation that high tariffs brought. The Republicans held on to the Senate, but the new House of Representatives had 235 Democrats, 88 Republicans, and 9 Farmers' Alliance members. The brief experiment with party government ended with two years of stalemate.

President Harrison evoked widespread discontent in 1892 for both his demeanor and his policies, but no Republican could mount an effective challenge. Through their strong party government, Republicans had cast their lot with Harrison and had few places to turn for an alternative. Political wizard Mark Hanna, a wealthy coal magnate who had become a powerful behind-the-scenes Republican strategist, promoted Ohio governor William McKinley, and Secretary of State James Blaine became an alternative when he abruptly quit the administration just before the Republican convention. But Harrison received a first-ballot nomination. Former minister to France Whitelaw Reid of New York got the vice-presidential nomination.

In the battle for the Democratic nomination, Cleveland enjoyed widespread backing among rank-and-file voters, but party leaders were suspicious. New York governor David B. Hill got a head start when he called a "snap" state convention and won the delegation. An "anti-snapper" convention from New York sent a rival delegation to the national party convention. Democrats across the country rebelled at Hall's move and rapidly switched their support to Cleveland.

Another problem for Cleveland was the rising sentiment in agrarian states for free and unlimited coinage of silver—a way of boosting sagging farm prices by inducing inflation in the overall economy. Cleveland always had opposed this solution. The former president's consistent, principled stance on the issue not only added to his reputation for integrity but also kept business- and finance-dominated northeastern states in the Democratic camp. Cleveland defeated Hall for the nomination on the

Grover Cleveland is welcomed back on board the "Ship of State" in this 1893 cartoon. Having served as president from 1885 to 1889, he lost the 1888 election but regained the White House in the 1892 contest. Cleveland remains the only president to serve two nonconsecutive terms.

first ballot and selected his former first assistant postmaster Adlai Stevenson of Illinois as his running mate.

The fall campaign was uneventful. Historian Eugene Roseboom wrote: "Honest bearded Benjamin Harrison confronting honest mustached Grover Cleveland in a tariff debate was a repeat performance that did not inspire parades with torches or the chanting of campaign ditties. . . . Democrats, out of power, could assail Republican tariff policy without clarifying their own position."[54]

Cleveland won easily. He received 5.6 million popular votes (46.1 percent) to Harrison's 5.2 million (43.0 percent) and 277 electoral votes to Harrison's 145. Populist general James B. Weaver, advocating expansion of currency and limits on interest rates, won 1.0 million popular votes (8.5 percent) and 22 electoral votes.

The Age of Reform

Throughout the period dominated by Republican conservatism—from Grant's election in 1868 to William McKinley's 1896 win—movements for the reform of political and economic institutions gathered strength at all levels of the American political system. The so-called populists and progressives did not overturn the system, as their rhetoric sometimes suggested, but over time they made major changes in the operation and discourse of U.S. politics.

Depending on the time and place, people who called themselves "populists" and "progressives" promoted such contradictory notions as strict morals and free spirits, tight money and loose money, redistribution to the masses and control of the economy by elites, federal intervention and local control of politics, the opening and closing of electoral participation, technological progress and a return to a long-gone pastoral ideal, individualism and community action, ethnic celebration and immigration barriers, scientific investigation and religion, and internationalism and isolationism.

Reformism was the response to the pressures of national expansion, urban development, and growth. Both major parties had adopted probusiness, laissez-faire policies in the latter part of the nineteenth century; indeed, the parties seemed to exist mainly to ensure the terrain was suitable for economic expansion. But the lack of any program to deal with the undesired consequences of explosive growth led to an accumulation of problems that demanded attention. The most obvious problems evolved on the opposite ends of the rural-urban continuum: on the farms and in the cities.

The farm problem developed as the United States became a major economic power in the world. Agriculture expanded on a vast scale to feed the booming cities and, with international trade, to bring foreign capital to the United States. By 1880, the value of U.S. wheat and flour exports nearly equaled that of cotton exports.[55] As agriculture became part of the international market, farmers became dependent not only on the vagaries of the weather but also on the fluctuations of currency in the larger economy.

In the thirty years after the Civil War, prices for farm staples fell steadily. A debt that could have been paid by producing one thousand bushels of grain immediately after the war required three thousand bushels in 1895. The more farmers produced to meet their obligations, the more prices fell to exacerbate their problems. A solution to the problem required confronting a wide array of issues, including tight money, bankers who charged 20 percent interest for loans, monopolies among farm equipment producers, high tariffs, railroad price gouging, shipping inflation, warehouse monopolies, and land speculation. Throughout the farm belt, particularly in the West, tens of thousands of farmers developed an "intense class consciousness."[56]

All these issues received attention from a variety of third parties and independent organizations, but the two major parties usually were inattentive. The Granger Movement of the 1870s, for example, took hold in several farm states and elected new legislatures and high state officials. The Greenback Party attempted to merge a labor-farmer alliance with a doctrine of silver use for public debts. Later, the Farmers' Alliance politicized the same issues. In 1892 the Populist Party had won 8.5 percent of the vote on a platform calling for free coinage of silver.

Another site of growing reformist strength was the city. The dominance of machines of both parties in the cities established an electoral system based on patronage but stubbornly opposed to any coherent program for addressing urban ills such as

poverty, poor housing, unsanitary conditions, transportation, education, and unfair workplace practices. Electoral fraud spurred mostly middle-class reformers to devise new electoral and city government machinery, while social problems incited some insurgent class politics.[57] The labor movement developed strength during this period.[58]

Other parts of the progressive agenda developed with a greater understanding of the nationalization of the economic and political systems. The wider sphere of economic activities created calls for regulation of corporations, railroads, and banks, as well as attention to health and environmental concerns and product safety.

Until the ascendance of William Jennings Bryan, the Democratic presidential nominee in 1896, 1900, and 1908, the reformers had been unable to capture a major party. Partly because political activism was based at the state and local level, neither national party had adopted the reformers' widely variegated program as its own. But the depression of 1888 caused the populist forces to pull together more than they had during previous economic downturns, probably because of the accumulated effects of inaction. The earlier panic of 1873 had created a sectional rather than a party split, with the Democrats eventually adopting a more conservative stance on the debate over whether the currency should be expanded to spur economic activity and redistribute social burdens.[59]

The Republican presidential candidates in the post–Civil War years steadfastly opposed the class-oriented proposals of the progressive movement, especially the loose-money demands. The only Democrat to win the presidency since the Civil War was Cleveland, a stubborn advocate of hard money and other conservative economic policies, in 1884 and 1892. President Cleveland vetoed dozens of private pension bills, only grudgingly accepted railroad regulation, and did not address domestic problems in any comprehensive way. Cleveland's public statements on the currency question were especially strong. He called the use of silver "a dangerous and reckless experiment" that was "unpatriotic."[60] On the question of labor, Cleveland was just as conservative: he called out federal troops to put down the Pullman strike of 1894 and regularly preached about the evils of disorder that the labor movement seemed to foster.

Despite the complexity of the agriculture issue, the most concerted populist action concentrated on the currency question. The drive to overturn the prevailing conventional economic thought by moving from a gold (tight) to a gold and silver (loose) money standard captured the imagination of the entire farm belt stretching from the Southeast to the prairie and silver-producing states of the West. The silver standard was a very simple answer to the problem of farm prices: "If money was scarce, the farmer reasoned, then the logical thing was to increase the money supply."[61]

REPUBLICANS AND MCKINLEY TRIUMPH: 1896 AND 1900

Gold runs on banks, manipulation of the gold crisis by J. P. Morgan and other leading financiers, procorporation Supreme Court decisions, and antilabor actions all stirred up resentment in the South and West. The silver sentiment escalated. The Democratic convention in 1896 called for the issuance of silver and rejected a resolution praising President Cleveland.[62] The movement for a silver currency found an eloquent advocate in Bryan, a member of the House of Representatives from Nebraska, who defeated Richard P. Bland of Missouri for the 1896 Democratic presidential nomination on the strength of his fiery "Cross of Gold" speech.

The speech was one of the most emotional and successful in U.S. history. Bryan attacked eastern financiers and businessmen who exploited farmers. Using a theme to which his fall campaign would return, Bryan sought to expand the traditional Democratic conception of the independent working man to include farmers and factory workers.[63] In his speech's fortissimo, Bryan declared: "You shall not press down upon the brow of labor this crown of thorns, you shall not crucify mankind upon a cross of gold."[64]

In 1896 the Republicans nominated Ohio governor William McKinley after brilliant maneuvering by his manager, Mark Hanna. Hanna's chief strengths were fund raising and his mastery over state party organizations.

McKinley had little difficulty defeating Bryan. McKinley outspent the prairie populist by as much as ten-to-one, and he attracted the disaffected progold wing of the Democratic Party.[65] The Grand Old Party (or GOP as it was by then called) platform called for retention of the gold standard unless international negotiations could produce a bimetallic (silver and gold) currency system. The platform also called for restored tariff protections and an aggressive foreign policy in the Western Hemisphere.

Bryan's campaign was a political hurricane. He spent just $650,000, most of it donated by silver interests, compared with the millions McKinley spent. But Bryan traveled eighteen thousand miles and gave some six hundred speeches, and his campaign staffers put out an impressive quantity of literature. Several million copies of *Coin's Financial School*, a prosilver pamphlet, were distributed during the fall of 1896. Other silverites also maintained busy speaking schedules in the fall.

Bryan's appeal to industrial workers to join his coalition of independent businessmen failed, largely because they depended for their livelihoods on the very eastern interests that Bryan attacked. McKinley won not only the East but also the small cities and towns in Bryan's southern and western belt of support. Bryan was unable to win rural areas in the East. McKinley won the popular vote 7.1 million (51.0 percent) to 6.5 million (46.7 percent) and the electoral vote 271–176.

The effect of the 1896 presidential election was lasting. James Sundquist wrote: "For 20 years the two-party system had been based on dead issues of the past. It had offered the voters no means of expressing a choice on the crucial issues of domestic policy around which the country had been polarizing. . . . Then suddenly, with the nomination of Bryan in 1896, the party system took on meaning once again."[66]

The new Republican coalition included residents of cities, where capital and labor were both reasonably content with the economic growth that the GOP tariff policy promoted; farmers in the East and Midwest, who had strong ties to the "party of Lincoln" and who had come to favor high tariffs; Catholic, German Lutheran, and other liturgical Christian denominations; and some border states. Sundquist noted: "It was the persistence of the Civil War attachments that made the realignment of the North so largely a one-way movement—pro-Republican."[67]

After 1896, the competitive party balance that had prevailed for years gave way to lopsided party strength according to region—Democrats in the South, Republicans in the North. Strong opposition parties disappeared in all regions of the country, vesting political power in the hands of those already part of the system.

As political scientist E. E. Schattschneider has observed:

The 1896 party cleavage resulted from the tremendous reaction of conservatives in both major parties to the Populist movement. . . . [S]outhern conservatives reacted so strongly that they were willing to revive the tensions and animosities of the Civil War and the Reconstruction in order to set up a one-party sectional southern political monopoly in which nearly all Negroes and many poor whites were disenfranchised. One of the most important consequences of the creation of the Solid South was that it severed permanently the connection between the western and the southern wings of the Populist movement.[68]

Conservative Republicans won the White House in all but two (1912 and 1916) of the nine elections from 1896 to 1928. During this period the country experienced economic prosperity that blunted the possible activism of workers and the previous activism of farmers. With good harvests and rising commodity prices, the agrarian revolt fizzled. The development of new ore extraction methods and discovery of new gold deposits made calls for silver to expand the currency supply superfluous. The Spanish-American War in 1898, which McKinley reluctantly entered and the burgeoning mass media publicized, created a patriotic fervor.

McKinley's reelection in 1900 was even stronger than his 1896 election. He won 7.2 million popular votes (51.7 percent) to Bryan's 6.4 million (45.5 percent), and 292 electoral votes to Bryan's 155. McKinley swept to victory with all states except the South and the silver states of the West (Colorado, Montana, Idaho, and Nevada).

THE RISE OF THEODORE ROOSEVELT: 1904

Because Vice President Garret A. Hobart died in office in 1899, the Republicans selected New York's progressive governor, Theodore Roosevelt, to share the ticket with McKinley in the 1900 election. Roosevelt, an independent-minded environmentalist and trust-buster, was promoted for vice president by New York GOP boss Thomas Platt, who wanted to rid the state of him and his progressive politics. Roosevelt was reluctant to take the job: "I am a comparatively young man yet and I like to work. . . . It would not entertain me to preside in the Senate."[69] He accepted, however, when a convention movement and McKinley prevailed on him.

When McKinley was assassinated in 1901 and Roosevelt became president, presidential politics came under the influence of a variant of the progressive movement. As Gabriel Kolko and other historians have demonstrated, Roosevelt's administration

The Democrats selected sober-visaged judge Alton B. Parker to run against the outgoing Theodore Roosevelt in the 1904 election. Roosevelt won by a wide margin.

was friendly to many of the GOP's traditional conservative allies. But Roosevelt's rhetoric and his legacy of regulation and conservation had strong progressive or reformist elements.[70]

Roosevelt's leadership of the progressives was an example of generational politics. (As each generation assumes control over political and social structures, it stamps those institutions with its distinctive style and ethos.) The new president grew up in an era in which economic expansion was straining the nation's fabric, causing political figures to seek idealistic but pragmatic solutions to a wide variety of problems. The previous generation had grown up in a simpler age when "politics were devoid of substance, built around appeals to tradition and old loyalties and aimed at patronage."[71]

Roosevelt steered his party toward conservation of natural resources, enforcement of antitrust laws, promotion of the concerns of labor, and railroad regulation. The government's suit to dissolve the Northern Securities Company under the Sherman Anti-Trust Act and Roosevelt's intervention in the anthracite coal miners' strike, both in 1902, established the tenor for an activist presidency. T R (the first president identified by his initials) also used his office as a "bully pulpit" to promote his progressive ideology.

Roosevelt had no trouble winning the nomination for election as president in his own right in 1904. The Republican convention, arranged in advance at the White House, unanimously voted for Roosevelt and his platform of trust-busting, tariffs, labor relations, and activist foreign policy. Sen. Charles W. Fairbanks of Indiana was the GOP vice-presidential nominee.

To oppose the rambunctious Roosevelt, the Democrats selected a sober-visaged judge. Alton Parker, the chief justice of the New York State Court of Appeals, received the backing of the Democratic Party's conservative establishment when former president Cleveland turned down entreaties to make a fourth presidential run. Parker was opposed by William Randolph Hearst, a member of Congress and newspaper magnate. Bryan forced the party to adopt a liberal platform, as a balance to the conservative judge.

The Roosevelt victory was a landslide. He won 7.6 million votes (56.4 percent) to Parker's 5.1 million (37.6 percent) and carried all but the southern states. Roosevelt won 336 electoral votes to Parker's 140. Both houses of Congress were overwhelmingly Republican. President Roosevelt pledged not to seek a second term of his own because he had served most of McKinley's second term. He occupied himself with his progressive agenda and groomed his secretary of war, William Howard Taft, as his successor.

ROOSEVELT PICKS TAFT: 1908

Roosevelt appeared to be genuinely dismayed by talk in 1907 of a possible third term, so he made public shows of his support for Taft. Because he also was able to line up state delegations for Taft, the nomination was never in doubt. Taft, through Roosevelt, was particularly strong among Republicans in the South. Attempts to restrict southern representation and pass a more liberal party platform were defeated.

Taft had impressive governmental experience. Before joining Roosevelt's cabinet, he had been a Cincinnati judge, U.S. solicitor general, federal circuit judge, head of the U.S. Commission on the Philippines, and the first civil governor of the Philippines.

Roosevelt's only problem in pushing Taft at the convention was avoiding a stampede in his own favor. Despite a highly disciplined convention, the galleries demonstrated wildly for Roosevelt. But Taft—a newcomer to electoral politics—easily won the nomination on the first ballot. He had 702 votes to the runner-up Philander C. Knox's 68. Rep. James S. Sherman of New York was selected as his running mate.

The Democrats nominated William Jennings Bryan for the third time. The electoral disaster that befell Judge Parker in 1904 was said to be evidence that the party needed an aggressive challenger to the Republicans rather than another conservative candidate. The Democrats were bereft of new talent, especially in competitive states in the East and Midwest, and turned to Bryan despite his disastrous campaign record and the warnings of former president Cleveland.

Taft campaigned on the Roosevelt record. Bryan called for government ownership of railroads and other liberal measures—such as a lower tariff, campaign finance reform, a graduated income tax, labor reforms, and greater enforcement of antitrust and other business regulations.

With Roosevelt and Taft promoting much of the progressive agenda, Bryan's message was no longer distinctive, and Taft won easily. He gathered 7.7 million popular votes (51.6 percent) to Bryan's 6.4 million (43.1 percent), and 321 electoral votes to Bryan's 162. The North, most of the West, and the border states went into the Republican column.

WILSON AND THE DIVIDED REPUBLICANS: 1912 AND 1916

Taft was not, by temperament, an ideal executive. His lifelong ambition had been to serve on the Supreme Court, and his disciplined legal mind and collegial nature eventually would enable him to become one of the high court's most able chief justices. (He was appointed to the Court by President Warren G. Harding in 1921.) But Taft foundered in the presidency. He carried out Roosevelt's program of business regulation and conservation, yet Roosevelt responded not with gratitude but with a series of nasty statements and plans for a campaign against Taft.

The tariff issue proved to be Taft's early trouble spot. Taft was committed to reducing tariffs, but he was less cautious than Roosevelt, who had fudged the divisive issue. As a result, Taft quickly became embroiled in a fight with Congress, which wanted to raise tariffs. The Senate remolded House legislation to push up various duties, and Taft publicly promoted the legislation after he managed to secure new corporate taxes and tariff reductions for raw materials. Overall, then, Taft proved ineffective and indecisive on the tariff issue and, as a consequence, began losing his party.

The Glavis-Ballinger affair further muddied the image of the administration. The scandal broke when the chief forester of the Interior Department, Gifford Pinchot, charged that Secretary Richard A. Ballinger had betrayed the cause of conservation and had even engaged in corrupt practices regarding minerals and water power. Pinchot also charged that Ballinger had wrongly fired another Interior official, Louis Glavis, for trying to expose the scandal. Pinchot took his complaints directly to Taft, but Taft sided with Ballinger and urged Pinchot to drop the matter. After an indignant Pinchot went public with the issue, Taft fired him, fueling suspicion of a cover-up at Interior. The incident was a major embarrassment to Taft because of the priority that conservation had received under Roosevelt and because of the inevitable complaints that Taft was betraying his mentor on the issue.[72]

Divisions within the Republican Party eventually created rival Taft and Roosevelt factions. Tariffs, Arizona's new state constitution (which included a provision for recall of the governor which Taft opposed), treaties, and antitrust issues split the former president and the sitting president. In many ways, the dispute was over personalities. Taft carried out Roosevelt's program but lacked his fervor and decisiveness. In a still conservative age, progressives felt they needed more aggressive leadership than the judicially tempered Taft would ever give them.

Roosevelt spent more than a year of Taft's term hunting in Africa, but he was an active speaker and campaigner when he returned to the United States. He gave a detailed accounting of his philosophy of government in a 1912 speech in Columbus, Ohio, calling for binding votes on public issues, recall of elected officials, and curbs on judicial power. When a dump-Taft movement decided in 1911 that Wisconsin senator Robert La Follette had no chance to defeat the president for the GOP nomination, party discontents turned to the energetic and still young (fifty-two years) Roosevelt.

Roosevelt made an all-out effort for the Republican nomination, entering twelve primaries and winning all but three. More specifically, Roosevelt won 278 delegates in states with primaries to Taft's 48 and La Follette's 36. In today's system, Roosevelt probably would have marched to a first-ballot nomination. (Today, more delegates are allocated by popular votes than by the party organizations, which then dominated the process.) Three crucial Republican states—Pennsylvania, Illinois, and Ohio— went for Roosevelt. He clearly, then, had great popular appeal and vote-getting ability—perhaps more than ever.

But Taft won the nomination. The president controlled the party machinery, and most of the convention's delegates were sent by the state machines. Roosevelt challenged the credentials of Taft delegates at the Chicago convention, and the nomination's outcome turned on battles over almost one-fourth of the delegates. The fight went to the floor of the convention, but Taft's smooth operation defeated Roosevelt. Roosevelt appeared at the convention to buoy his forces and cry foul.

After the defeat, Roosevelt urged his supporters to continue their fight, which motivated some bolting progressive delegates to organize a convention in August to mount a third-party effort. The bolters formed the Progressive Party. When Roosevelt remarked to a reporter during the GOP convention, "I'm feeling like a bull moose," his vigorous campaign had a symbol.

With the Republicans divided, the Democrats saw their first opportunity to win the presidency since Cleveland in 1892. As the 1912 Democratic convention in Baltimore neared, several national candidates and favorite sons were vying for the nomination. The front-runner was House Speaker James Beauchamp "Champ" Clark of Missouri, a party regular who had party organization support and years of experience to recommend him.

Gov. Woodrow Wilson of New Jersey—who held a doctorate in political science and who had moved into politics after a distinguished career as professor and president at Princeton University—was another strong candidate. Wilson's virtues were the opposite of Clark's. He did not have an extensive political record for opponents to attack, and he was supported enthusiastically because of his dynamic presence and reformist rhetoric. Although the New Jersey machine had brought Wilson into politics, he quickly asserted his independence and became something of a crusader.

As a newcomer to national politics, Wilson both refreshed and alienated Democratic crowds in speeches before the convention. He came out strongly for the "radical" platform of referendum, initiative, and recall, prompting a newspaper to report: "The boldness, the directness, the incisiveness, the fearlessness, and the force of the `Virginian-Jerseyan's' words crashed at times through the throng like a series of thunderbolt jolts."[73] But Wilson's embrace of the progressive agenda and attacks on business alienated many southerners; even the delegates from Wilson's home state of Virginia opposed him at the convention.

Other Democratic candidates were the conservative representative Oscar Underwood of Alabama, author of a historic tariff act; another conservative, Gov. Judson Harmon of Ohio; and four favorite-son governors. Clark appeared to have won the nomination when a Tammany bloc of delegates moved to support him after he won a tenth-ballot majority. The requirement for a two-thirds majority, however, gave other candidates time to maneuver. Wilson almost dropped out of the race, but Bryan's late transfer of his support from Clark to Wilson created a bandwagon effect for Wilson. On the forty-sixth ballot, Wilson accumulated the necessary two-thirds of delegates for the nomination. Gov. Thomas Marshall of Indiana, one of the favorite-son candidates, was picked to be the vice-presidential nominee because Underwood, Wilson's choice, would not accept it.

The Democratic platform was progressive. It called for tariff reduction, utility regulation, banking reforms, legislation to curb monopolies, a national income tax, direct election of senators, campaign finance reforms, and a national presidential primary. Theodore Roosevelt actually praised Wilson as "an able man" in the early fall and said he might not have started a third-party effort if he had known Wilson would be the Democrats' candidate. But Wilson and Roosevelt eventually criticized each other's approach to government, especially after Wilson expressed reservations about government activism.[74]

Wilson easily won the election, receiving 435 electoral votes to Roosevelt's 88 and Taft's 8. The Republican split obviously helped Wilson; if Roosevelt and Taft had combined their totals of 4.1 million votes (27.4 percent) and 3.5 million votes (23.2 percent), they would have topped Wilson's 6.3 million (41.8 percent). Yet even though Wilson was a minority president, there was a clear Democratic trend since the Democrats had taken over the House and replaced several Republican governors in the 1910 midterm elections. It was the worst showing ever for an incumbent president—third place with only two states.

Whatever the strength of Wilson's "mandate," he acted as though he had won by a landslide. His first term was one of the most productive in U.S. history. With the Democrats in control of Congress, and with a shrewd political adviser in Col. Edward M. House, Wilson adopted a reform agenda that had been percolating at various levels of government for years. He broke precedent by delivering his first State of the Union message to Congress in person. At the center of the message was a call for reductions in tariff rates. After a bitter fight that raged for a month, Wilson went public with a demand that members of Congress reveal their property holdings. The revelations, in response to public pressure, showed close links between their holdings and the kinds of tariff protections on the books. Congress soon was shamed into passing tariff cuts of 15 percent. Some one hundred items were placed on a free-trade list for the first time.

Woodrow Wilson traveled widely in the 1912 election campaign. His dynamic presence and reformist rhetoric appealed to the crowds who came to hear.

Wilson also addressed other areas successfully: taxes (institution of a graduated income tax in 1913, which replaced reliance on tariffs and various excise and user taxes); banking regulation (the Glass-Owen Act of 1913, which created the Federal Reserve system); antitrust legislation (the Clayton Anti-Trust Act of 1914, creation of the Federal Trade Commission in 1914); labor relations (Section 6 of the Sherman Anti-Trust Act, which exempted unions from antitrust strictures); agriculture (the Smith-Lever Act of 1914, the Federal Farm Loan Act of 1916); conservation (creation of the National Park Service in 1916); and the judiciary (the appointment of Louis Brandeis to the Supreme Court).

Despite his strong leadership—highlighted by his stirring oratory—Wilson still faced the prospect in 1916 of a tough reelection. He had won the presidency in 1912 with only 41.8 percent of the popular vote, and the escalating war in Europe was beginning to disturb the American process of steady economic growth.

Public opinion on the Great War was volatile, largely because more than a third of the U.S. population was either foreign born or the offspring of foreign-born parents. Some eleven million Americans surveyed in the 1910 census were of direct German or Austrian descent, and another five million were from Ireland. Many other immigrants were Russian, Italian, Hungarian, British, and French. Wilson sought to diffuse feelings for the immigrants' native lands when he denounced "hyphenism"—the tendency of many citizens to identify themselves with appellations that linked their ethnic origins and American status—but politicians at lower levels tailored their campaigns to specific nationality voting blocs.[75]

Wilson and Vice President Marshall won renomination without any opposition. The most significant event of the Democratic convention was the passage of the platform, which indicated the party's main campaign theme. By calling for national universal suffrage, Wilson helped himself in the eleven western states where women already had won the vote. The platform praised "the splendid diplomatic victories of our great president, who has preserved the vital interests of our government and its citizens, and kept us out of war." The latter phrase would be repeated endlessly during the fall.[76]

The Republicans gave the presidential nomination to Supreme Court Justice Charles Evans Hughes. Hughes was silent in the months before the convention, but a number of party leaders lined up enough delegates for him to win a third-ballot nomination. Other potential candidates in 1916 included former president Roosevelt, former senator Elihu Root of New York, former vice president Fairbanks, and Senators John Weeks, Albert Cummins, and Lawrence Sherman. Fairbanks won the vice-presidential nomination.

Prosperity and reformism limited the campaign themes available to the Republicans. The GOP railed against Wilson's foreign policy as "shifty expedients" and "phrasemaking" that put the United States in danger of entering the war. Hughes turned out to be a bad campaigner, but he bridged the gap between conservative and progressive Republicans that had cost the party the 1912 election. Wilson was occupied with Congress throughout the summer of 1916, but he emerged to give a series of speeches in the fall. Democratic strategists, meanwhile, conceived and executed a masterful strategy to return Wilson to the White House. The Democrats concentrated all their resources on "swing states" and ignored states they thought Wilson was sure to lose. Illinois, for example, was ignored since it was a certain Republican state. Bryan, Wilson's secretary of state, toured the West.

Wilson won one of the closest elections in history. California, an uncertain state, ensured Wilson's victory when, because of the urban vote, it went the president's way late in the campaign. The margin of victory was 3,420 votes in that state. The president defeated Hughes by a margin of 9.1 million (49.2 percent) to 8.5 million popular votes (46.1 percent). The electoral college gave Wilson 277 votes and Hughes 254.

Even though Wilson's campaign in 1916 was based on his determination to stay out of the Great War, the United States was in the war by 1917. Wilson's conduct of the war won him the status of war hero, but his diplomatic efforts after the war failed. Wilson was the architect of the Treaty of Versailles, which created a League of Nations to prevent future wars. But Wilson was unable to induce the Senate to approve the treaty, and he left office in 1921 a broken and dispirited man.

The "Return to Normalcy" and the Roaring Twenties

After the tumult of Woodrow Wilson's domestic reforms, the First World War, and the divisive battle over the Versailles treaty, the time was ripe for a period of conservatism and Republican government. Deep resentment had developed toward Wilson and the Democratic Party, and the Democrats themselves were divided over many issues, including economic regulation, Prohibition, and race relations.

Blessed with good luck, substantial financial backing, and a strong trend toward split-ticket voting, beginning in the 1920s the Republicans were able to resume their dominance over national politics with three successful presidential campaigns: Warren G. Harding in 1920, Calvin Coolidge in 1924, and Herbert C. Hoover in 1928.

The 1920s are usually pictured as a time of steady, unexciting politics. The conservatives dominated the federal government, and occupying the White House were men who spoke of "normalcy" and a noninterventionist brand of politics in both domestic and foreign affairs. One of the symbols of the age was President Coolidge's program of tax cuts, which reduced the rates on the wealthy. The wartime Revenue Act of 1918 had driven tax rates to the highest point in U.S. history—77 percent in the highest brackets. In 1921, 1923, and 1926, Secretary of the Treasury Andrew Mellon presented to Congress proposals to cut taxes, the most controversial being the reduction in the maximum surtax from 77 to 25 percent. Congress eventually cut the surtax to 40 percent in 1924 and 20 percent in 1926.[77]

But the sober men who filled the presidency in the twenties met challenges from progressives of both parties in Congress and in the state governments. On a wide range of issues—including relief of the poor, subsidies for the depressed farm sector, regulation of utilities, immigration, race relations, states' rights, tax cuts, and Prohibition—the conservative presidents encountered strong challenges. They frequently responded by vetoing legislation, but such an expedient would not prevent the pressures for a more activist government from developing.

HARDING AND "NORMALCY": 1920

Sen. Warren Harding, a product of the GOP machine of Ohio, emerged from a crowded and largely unknown pack to win the Republican nomination in 1920 at a convention dominated by economic interests such as oil, railroads, and steel. The early candidates were Gen. Leonard Wood, an old Roosevelt ally; Gov. Frank Lowden of Illinois, who married into the Pullman family and therefore had ample financing for a campaign; and Sen. Hiram Johnson of California, whose progressive and isolationist stances put him in good stead with voters in many states. A dozen favorite sons hoped that a deadlocked convention might bring the nomination their way. All of the candidates were on hand in Chicago to maneuver for the nomination.

While Wood, Johnson, and Lowden performed reasonably well in the primaries, Harding won only his home state of Ohio and did not arouse much popular enthusiasm. But under the direction of a shrewd campaign manager, Harry Daugherty, Hard-

Democratic presidential candidate James M. Cox of Ohio, left, and vice-presidential candidate Franklin D. Roosevelt (one year before he was stricken with polio), campaign in the 1920 election. They lost to Republican presidential candidate Warren G. Harding and his running mate, Gov. Calvin Coolidge of Massachusetts.

ing gained the support of the party's bosses and won the nomination on the tenth ballot after a brief interview with them in the "smoke-filled room" that was synonymous with boss control. Gov. Calvin Coolidge of Massachusetts, a favorite-son contender for president, became Harding's vice-presidential candidate.

The Democrats selected Gov. James Cox, also from Ohio, after lengthy platform battles and balloting for the nomination. Early ballots put former Treasury secretary William G. McAdoo and Attorney General Mitchell Palmer in the lead, but Cox gained steadily and had the nomination by the forty-fourth roll call. Franklin D. Roosevelt of New York, the assistant secretary of the navy, was rapidly selected to be Cox's running mate.

The image of Woodrow Wilson hung over the convention and would hang over the fall campaign. The Democratic platform praised Wilson's conduct of the war and his domestic reform program. But the results in the November election indicated deep unease over the Democratic administration.

Harding amassed 16.1 million popular votes (60.3 percent) to Cox's 9.1 million (34.2 percent), and 404 electoral votes to Cox's 127. Harding carried the North and West including Oklahoma and all of the southern and border states except Tennessee and Kentucky.

Harding's landslide victory was termed "election by disgust" by political analysts. The wartime sacrifices demanded under Wilson were widely perceived as the cause of Harding's victory rather than a desire for the ideology or policy proposals that Harding was offering. The *New York Post* editorialized: "We are in the backwash from the mighty spiritual and physical effort to which America girded herself when she won the war for the Al-

lies. . . . The war has not been repudiated, though the administration that fought it has been overwhelmed. We are now in the chill that comes with the doctor's bills."[78]

The electorate's ability to shift allegiances from the Republicans to the Democrats and back again—from one period to the next, and from one level of government to the next—suggested a dissolution of partisan alignments. The addition of women to the electorate after passage of the Nineteenth Amendment in 1920 and the increasing independence among all voters induced uncertainty. National exhaustion from the war and the lack of sharp ideological differences between the candidates produced apathy. The electorate's instability was suggested by the divisions within both parties on high-profile issues such as Prohibition, the League of Nations, agricultural policies, and other social and economic matters—among them, technical assistance and trust busting. The appearance of numerous "blocs" in both parties represented "little if anything more than a transitory alignment upon a particular vote or issue."[79]

The shifts in control of congressional and state offices also indicated electoral instability. The Democrats had had comfortable control of Congress under Wilson, but in 1920 the Republicans gained a majority of 301 to 131 in the House and 59 to 37 in the Senate. Impressive liberal gains in congressional and state elections in the midterm election of 1922 appeared to be a slap at the Harding administration. The high turnover of votes also indicated unstable party affiliations: the 14.2 percentage point increase in the Republican vote between the 1916 and 1920 presidential elections was the largest since the Civil War, another time of turmoil.[80]

President Harding died on August 2, 1923, of a heart attack, just as revelations of kickbacks and favoritism in the administration began to surface and several members of the administration quit and two committed suicide. The investigation into the so-called Teapot Dome scandal—so named after the site of naval oil reserves that were transferred to private hands in exchange for bribes—would last five years. The Democrats hoped to make the scandal a major issue in the 1924 election, but Democratic complicity in the wrongdoing and the personal integrity of Harding's successor, Calvin Coolidge, defused the issue.

COOLIDGE CLEANS UP: 1924

President Coolidge fired Attorney General Harry M. Daugherty and other members of Harding's clique and projected an image of puritan cleanliness. Coolidge—a taciturn man who had slowly climbed the political ladder in Massachusetts from city council member to city solicitor, mayor, state legislator, lieutenant governor, and governor before he became vice president—expounded a deeply individualistic Yankee philosophy that helped to separate him from the corrupt men in the Harding White House.

Except for appointing as attorney general Harlan Fiske Stone, former dean of the Columbia University School of Law, Coolidge allowed others to finish cleaning up the mess left behind by Harding. The new president was concerned about unnecessarily alienating himself from party leaders.

By the time Coolidge sought the presidency in his own right in 1924, the economy had rebounded. One of the most conservative presidents ever, Coolidge's platform called for additional tax cuts but said nothing substantive about increasingly salient agriculture and labor issues. Coolidge also pushed an isolationist foreign policy plank. He won the nomination on the first ballot.

While the Republicans were able to "Keep Cool with Coolidge," the Democrats spent sixteen days in a seemingly endless attempt to pick a nominee in New York's sweltering Madison Square Garden. A fight developed because the party was badly split between its northeastern urban bloc and its more conservative southern and western rural bloc. New York governor Alfred E. Smith and former Treasury secretary William McAdoo of California were the key combatants at the convention until the delegates were freed from the instructions of party bosses on the one-hundredth ballot.

Suspicions between the two regional blocs were intense. A platform plank denouncing the Ku Klux Klan created the most controversy. Northerners wanted an explicit repudiation of the society that preached hatred of blacks, Catholics, and Jews; in the end, southerners would settle only for a vaguely worded rebuke. (The Klan had infiltrated the party in many rural areas.) Another divisive issue was Prohibition, with northerners attacking the initiative and southerners supporting it. These sectional splits would cripple the Democrats in the 1924 and 1928 elections.

After the delegates were freed from instructions, a stampede developed for John W. Davis of West Virginia, a lawyer with Wall Street connections. The ticket was balanced with the vice-

"Keep Cool with Coolidge" was the Republican incumbent's 1924 campaign slogan, used on posters, banners, buttons, and decorative stamps such as this one from Wisconsin.

presidential selection of Charles W. Bryan of Nebraska, the younger brother of three-time presidential candidate William Jennings Bryan.

The Progressive candidacy of Robert La Follette complicated the calculations of voters, particularly those on the liberal end of the political spectrum. Because the Democrats had a nearly impenetrable hold on the South, La Follette was not given a reasonable chance of winning. But the conservatism of both Coolidge and Davis meant that La Follette was the only liberal in the race. Still, many liberals voted for Davis or even Coolidge because of the fear of an inconclusive election that would have to be resolved in the House of Representatives.

Coolidge won the election easily, with the Democrats polling their smallest percentage ever. Coolidge won 54.1 percent of the vote, Davis won 28.8 percent, and La Follette won 16.6 percent. Coolidge attracted 15.7 million popular votes and 382 electoral votes; Davis 8.4 million and 136; and La Follette 4.8 million and 13.

On August 2, 1927, when Coolidge announced his decision not to seek reelection by passing out a brief note to reporters and then refusing further comment, the Republicans began jockeying for the nomination for the 1928 election.

THE HOOVER SUCCESSION: 1928

Secretary of Commerce Herbert Hoover was the obvious choice to replace Coolidge at the head of the GOP ticket. A native of Iowa who learned mining engineering at Stanford University, Hoover was immensely popular with most of the party. Hoover's administration of Belgian relief and food distribution programs during World War I had earned him the status of statesman and humanitarian.

Hoover began working for the nomination soon after Coolidge dropped out, spending $400,000 in the nominating phase of the election. He won the nomination on the first ballot over Governors Frank Lowden of Illinois and Charles Curtis of Kansas. Curtis was named Hoover's running mate.

Hoover was religious in his zeal for what he called "the American system" of free enterprise and individualism. He did not see any inconsistency in having the government vigorously support businesses with tax breaks, tariffs, public provision of infrastructures, and police protection, while at the same time denying relief to people in need. Hoover appeared to be less rigid than Coolidge, however. He proposed creation of a special farm board and said he would consider legislation to protect labor unions from abuses in the use of court injunctions.

Al Smith, the Tammany-schooled governor of New York, was the Democratic nominee. Smith had the support of all the party's northern states, and he won a first-ballot nomination. Sen. Joseph T. Robinson of Arkansas was the vice-presidential candidate.

Smith's candidacy polarized the electorate, particularly the South. He was the first Catholic to be nominated for president by a major party, and he endured religious slurs throughout the fall. Moreover, he favored repeal of Prohibition, still a divisive issue, and he was an urbanite, a problem for a nation that had nurtured a rural ideal since Thomas Jefferson. Because he also was a machine politician, he presented a problem for anyone outside (and many people inside) the nation's great cities. He also was a strong opponent of the Klan, which put him in trouble in the South. Finally, he was an unabashed liberal who proposed public works, farm relief programs, stronger protection of workers, and regulation of banking and industry.

During the fall campaign, Hoover acted like the incumbent and Smith barnstormed the country, trying in vain to pick up support in the South and West. The 1928 campaign was the first with extensive radio coverage, and Hoover generally fared better than Smith on the airwaves. Hoover, the small-town boy who made good, represented fulfillment of the American Dream; Smith, the inner-city boy who made good, also embodied that ideal, but he had too many ethnic traits for much of the nation to realize it.

The November election produced another Republican landslide. Hoover carried forty states with 21.4 million popular votes (58.2 percent) and 444 electoral votes, while Smith carried only eight states with 15.0 million popular votes (40.8 percent) and 87 electoral votes. As disastrous as the election appeared to be for the Democrats, it put them in position to build a wide-ranging coalition in future years.

Smith carried only six southern states, but the defection of the others was temporary. More important to the Democrats' long-range fortunes was the movement of cities into the Democratic column, probably for the rest of the century. Immigrants in cities were expanding their vision from local politics to the national stage for the first time. In all, Smith diverted 122 northern counties from the GOP to the Democratic Party. Catholics, whose turnout previously had been low, turned out in record numbers. Smith also seemed to pick up some of the Progressive farm vote that La Follette had tapped before; in Wisconsin, for example, the Democratic vote jumped from 68,000 to 450,000 from 1924 to 1928. Finally, Smith's candidacy put the Democrats solidly in the "wet" column, just as the national temper began to resent Prohibition.

President Hoover impressed political observers with his managerial skills and "coordinating mind." With passage of the Agricultural Marketing Act in June 1929, the administration appeared to address the most pressing economic problem for the business-minded president. He met some legislative setbacks, but, overall, the Great Engineer appeared to be in good political condition as the nation looked back over his record when Congress began its recess in the summer of 1929.

The national economic and social fiesta that had begun at the close of World War I came to an abrupt end on October 29, 1929. After climbing to dizzying new heights for months, the stock market crashed. First described by economists and politicians as a temporary interruption of the good times, the crash quickly led to a wave of business and bank failures, mortgage foreclosures, wage cuts, layoffs, and a crisis of political leadership. By the end of Hoover's term in 1933, more than twelve million workers had lost their jobs; the unemployment rate was approximately 25 percent. An October 1931 advertisement for 6,000 jobs in the Soviet Union brought 100,000 American applications.[81]

President Hoover, who had celebrated his inauguration with a prediction that poverty and hunger were near an end, did not know how to cope with the crisis. In a special session that Hoover called, Congress created the Federal Farm Board to coordinate marketing of agricultural products, but Hoover steadfastly opposed further moves, especially subsidies. In 1930 Hoover signed the Smoot-Hawley Tariff Act to protect manufacturers, but, true to the predictions of economists and bankers, the tariff only aggravated economic conditions by hurting foreign trade.

Hoover later approved agricultural relief and public works programs and established the Reconstruction Finance Corporation. The president refused to approve direct relief to the unemployed and businesses, but he did approve some loans and aid to specific sectors of the economy.

Despite his earnest and tireless efforts, Hoover became a figure of widespread enmity. The low point of his distinguished career came when World War I veterans petitioned for early receipt of their service bonuses, which, by contract, were not to be paid until 1945. They set up camp in Washington, singing old war songs and carrying placards that bore their pleas. The "Bonus Army" numbered twenty thousand at its height. When Hoover feared a protracted protest, he ordered federal troops to take over buildings where some veterans were camping. In two skirmishes, two veterans were killed. The president then sent in Gen. Douglas MacArthur with tanks, infantry, and cavalry soldiers. (MacArthur's junior officers included Dwight D. Eisenhower and George Patton.) After successfully removing the veterans, the military forces overran nearby veterans' camps in a rain of fire and tear gas. Thousands of veterans and their families fled the burning district.

The administration's tough stance against a defeated, ragtag band of former war heroes shocked and embittered the nation. The barricaded White House and administration statements about "insurrectionists" symbolized a dangerous gulf between the government and the people.

Partly because of the economic crisis he did not create, but also because of his dour and unimaginative demeanor, Hoover probably never had a chance to win reelection. The 1930

In 1932 World War I veterans, seeking early receipt of their service bonuses, staged a protest by setting up camps near the Capitol. President Herbert C. Hoover ordered federal troops, headed by Gen. Douglas MacArthur, to disperse the veterans with tear gas.

midterm elections indicated a loss of confidence in the administration. The House went Democratic, 219 to 214, and the Senate came within a seat of going Democratic as well.

Those election results did not convey the bitterness and despair that the depression would aggravate before the next presidential campaign. Hoover was mercilessly ridiculed in newspapers and in Democratic speeches. The Democratic Party coordinated a comprehensive anti-Hoover campaign that made the president politically impotent.

THE ELECTION OF 1932

Franklin D. Roosevelt, fifth cousin to Theodore Roosevelt, was the perfect candidate to oppose Hoover. The New York governor had been an activist in state politics, first opposing the state's Tammany machine and then pioneering many relief and reconstruction programs that Hoover refused to expand to the national scale. Roosevelt had been the party's vice-presidential candidate twelve years earlier, and he had served in the federal government as assistant secretary of the navy.

Perhaps more important than any of his political accomplishments were FDR's image of strength and optimism and his deft handling of hot issues and disparate members of the potential Democratic coalition. Although he was a polio victim, Roosevelt often smiled—a devastating contrast to Hoover. (Gutzon Borglum, the sculptor, wrote: "If you put a rose in Hoover's hand, it would wilt."[82]) Roosevelt was able to campaign for the presidency without putting forth a comprehensive program: the simple promise of a change in leadership was enough.

Some observers found the man from Hyde Park wanting. Journalist Walter Lippmann, for example, complained that Roosevelt was "a pleasant man who, without any important qualifications for the office, would like very much to be president."[83] But those detractors and a large field of Democratic candidates were not able to keep Roosevelt from his "rendezvous with destiny."[84]

The Democratic field included the 1928 Democratic standard-bearer, Al Smith; John Nance Garner, the Speaker of the House; Gov. Albert Ritchie of Maryland; Gov. George White of Ohio; Gov. Harry Byrd of Virginia; and former Sen. James Reed of Missouri. Most considered Smith more of a "stalking horse" for the anti-FDR forces than a serious candidate in his own right. Garner had impressive backing from the newspaper magnate William Randolph Hearst and former Democratic candidate William McAdoo.

The many favorite sons in the race threatened to deadlock the convention and deny the nomination to the front-runner, as they had done so often in the past. Roosevelt had difficulty with his own region of the country because of his opposition to the Tammany machine in New York. Acquiring the required two-thirds vote of delegates for the nomination was difficult for Roosevelt or any other candidate, but FDR eventually won on the fourth ballot when he promised the vice-presidential slot to Garner.

In U.S. political history, Franklin Roosevelt was the first candidate to appear before the convention that nominated him. In an acceptance speech to the conventioneers who had staged wild rallies in his support, Roosevelt made passing reference to the "new deal" that his administration would offer Americans. That phrase, picked up in a newspaper cartoon the next day, came to symbolize the renewal for which Americans yearned as riots and radicalism seemed to threaten the nation's spirit and the legitimacy of its institutions.

Roosevelt conducted an active fall campaign, traveling twenty-three thousand miles in forty-one states to quell suspicions that his physical handicaps would deter him from performing his job. Besides barnstorming the nation, Roosevelt took to the radio airwaves—he was the first sophisticated electronic media candidate—where he conveyed a sense of warmth and confidence. He also showed an intellectual bent and an open mind when he called on academics and professionals—the famed "brain trust"—for their expert advice on the issues.

Franklin D. Roosevelt campaigns by car in West Virginia, October 19, 1932.

Roosevelt won 22.8 million votes (57.4 percent) to Hoover's 15.8 million (39.6 percent). Forty-two of the forty-eight states and 472 of the 531 electoral votes went for Roosevelt. The election was a landslide and a realignment of the major forces in U.S. politics.

The New Deal Coalition

The profound effect of Roosevelt's victory on U.S. politics can hardly be overstated. The New Deal coalition that Roosevelt assembled shaped the political discourse and electoral competition of the United States until the late 1960s. In many respects, that coalition is a central element of politics today.

The new Democratic coalition brought together a disparate group of interests: southerners, African Americans, immigrants, farmers, capital-intensive producers, international businessmen, financiers, urbanites, trade unions, intellectuals, Catholics, and Jews. Rexford Tugwell called it "the most miscellaneous coalition in history."[85] These blocs were not always in perfect harmony—for example, the Democrats juggled the demands of blacks and white southerners with great difficulty—but they were solid building blocks for national political dominance.

The dominance was impressive. Between 1932 and 1964, the Democrats won seven of nine presidential elections. The only successful Republican, Dwight Eisenhower, could just as easily have run as a Democrat. Party leaders in fact asked him to run as a Democrat in 1948 and 1952, and his name was entered in some Democratic primaries in 1952.

The strength of Roosevelt's rule was attributable partly to the president's personality. He could be soothing. When he gave his first "fireside chat" about the banking crisis, the nation responded with cooperation; the raids and violence at banks ended in a matter of weeks. More important than his soothing nature was his ability to experiment and shift gears. Professor James David Barber described Roosevelt's many public postures:

Founder of the New Deal, modern American democracy's closest approximation to a common political philosophy, Roosevelt came on the scene as the least philosophical of men—"a chameleon in plaid," Hoover called him. Firm fighter of yet another Great War, Roosevelt appeared to H. L. Mencken in 1932 as "far too feeble and wishy-washy a fellow to make a really effective fight." Architect of world organization, he introduced himself as totally concerned with America's domestic drama. His name is inseparable from his generation's great social revolution; in 1932, nearly all the heavy thinkers scoffed at him as just another placebo politician—a "pill to cure an earthquake," said Professor [Harold] Laski.[86]

More important than personality was what Roosevelt had to offer the many groups in his coalition. As historian Richard Hofstadter has noted, the New Deal was "a series of improvisations, many adopted very suddenly, many contradictory."[87] The Roosevelt credo was: "Save the people and the nation, and if we have to change our minds twice a day to accomplish that end, we should do it."[88]

Until the vast expenditures of World War II, there was not enough pump-priming to end the Depression, but Roosevelt's initiatives touched almost everyone affected by the slump.[89] For the jobless, there were unemployment insurance and public works programs such as the Works Progress Administration and the Civilian Conservation Corps. For the poor, there were categorical aid programs. For westerners, there were conservation measures. For the banks, there was the famous holiday that stopped runs on holdings, and there were currency and securities reforms. For farmers, there were incentives and price supports and cooperatives. For the aged, there was Social Security. For southeasterners, there was the Tennessee Valley Authority. For southern whites, there was a hands-off policy on race matters. For blacks, there were sympathy and jobs programs. For those living in rural areas, there was electrification. For families, there were home loans. For the weary worker eager for a few rounds at the local tavern, there was the repeal of Prohibition. For laborers, there was acknowledgment of the right to negotiate for their share of the national wealth. For business, there were the Federal Emergency Relief Act and the National Industrial Recovery Act, as well as diplomatic negotiation to reduce trade barriers.

The remarkably divergent interests in the coalition were underscored by the politics of race. Blacks moved en masse to the Democratic Party from their traditional position in the "Party of Lincoln," partly because of Hoover's failure but also because of the inclusive rhetoric of the New Deal. Yet Roosevelt was too concerned about his bloc of southern support to accept even antilynching legislation.

Scholars have argued that the New Deal coalition did not indicate a wholesale shift in existing political loyalties, but rather that new groups such as urbanites and blacks had joined an already stable alliance to tip the competitive balance of U.S. parties. The political discourse in the United States changed not because all or even most groups changed their behavior but because new groups and issues became involved.[90]

The core of Roosevelt's winning coalition was easy to describe: "Southern white Protestants, Catholics, and non-Southern white Protestants of the lowest socioeconomic stratum together accounted for roughly three-fourths of all Americans of voting age in 1940 who thought of themselves as Democrats. By way of contrast, these three groups provided only about 40 percent of the smaller cadre of Republican identifiers."[91] Within the Democratic coalition, there were both new and old elements.

Although the Democratic Party encompassed new constituencies and addressed new issues, it retained many of its traditional supporters. The segregated "Jim Crow" South had consistently been in the Democratic column; in 1896, for example, the South's percentage support for Democrat William Jennings Bryan exceeded that of the rest of the nation by 15.3 points. Even in 1928, when Al Smith's Catholicism reduced support for the Democrats to under 50 percent for the first time, the Deep South supported the Democrats more than the border South did.[92] To the South, the Democrats were reliably the party of white supremacy and agricultural interests, while Republicans favored the industrial interests of the North.

Outside the South, the Democratic Party was the party of immigrants and Catholics. Since Andrew Jackson's day, the overwhelmingly Democratic voting patterns of Catholics had contrasted with the split vote of Protestants in the United States. The Catholic-Protestant divisions represented "not so much religious as more general ethnocultural traditions."[93] The Democratic hold on the Catholic vote was reinforced by the heavy immigration into northern cities in the last half of the nineteenth century. While the anti-Catholic Ku Klux Klan received Democratic backing in the South, it received Republican backing in the North, pushing northern Catholics decisively into the Democratic Party.

A steady base in the Democratic Party consisted of laborers and the poor. From the first party machines in the early nineteenth century to William Jennings Bryan's campaign on behalf of the depressed farm belt in 1896 to Woodrow Wilson's acceptance of labor bargaining in 1914, the Democrats had shown sympathy for the less-privileged classes. Such sympathies often were constricted by prejudice or conservatism, but the Democrats offered more hope of representation than the business-oriented Republicans. Roosevelt solidified the support of the poor and laboring classes.[94] Sundquist has written: "The party system undoubtedly reflected some degree of class before the realignment, but there can be little doubt that it was accentuated by the event. It was in the New Deal era that tight bonds were formed between organized labor and the Democratic Party, that ties equally close if less formal and overt were formed between business and the GOP, and that politics for the first time since 1896 sharply accented class issues."[95] Roosevelt consistently received the support of more than two-thirds of the voters of low socioeconomic status.[96]

New converts to the Democratic Party included blacks and Jews. The inclusion of blacks into the New Deal coalition underscored a "multiplier effect" at work within thriving interest group politics. The Republicans received the black vote in the seventeen elections from Reconstruction to 1932. That year, Roosevelt received 35 percent of the black vote, but his black support was as low as 23 percent in Chicago and 29 percent in Cincinnati.[97] Even though Roosevelt did little to promote black interests in the South, where most blacks lived but could not vote, the black vote for him increased to 70 percent in 1936 and 1940. Migration of blacks to the North and the spillover effects of Roosevelt's many domestic programs brought blacks to the Democratic Party.

Jews, who had voted Republican since their numbers swelled during immigration around the turn of the century, turned to the Democrats as they became the more liberal party. Roosevelt got 85 percent of the Jewish vote in 1936 and 84 percent in 1940. New Deal assistance programs and Roosevelt's efforts to fight Nazism appealed to Jews, but perhaps more important was "the historic pattern of discrimination which forced or disposed Jews to oppose conservative parties."[98] The class division that split other social groups was absent in the Jewish population.

In many ways, the whole of the New Deal was greater than the sum of its parts. Political scientist Samuel Beer has argued that two long-competing visions of U.S. politics—the national idea and the democratic idea—at last came together during Roosevelt's administration. With the New Deal, the Democratic Party was able to combine its traditional concern for local, individualistic interests with a national vision. By bringing "locked-out" groups into the system, the Democrats enhanced both nation building and individual freedoms. The parts, put together, created a stronger whole. Beer quotes the French sociologist Emile Durkheim: "The image of the one who completes us becomes inseparable from ours. . . . It thus becomes an integral and permanent part of our conscience. . . ."[99]

The political genius of "interest-group liberalism"[100] was not just that it offered something to everyone, but that it created a new age of consumerism in which everyone's interest was in economic growth rather than structural change. The general good was defined as growth. The potentially divisive competition over restricted and unequally distributed resources was avoided with a general acceptance of growth as the common goal. When there was growth, everyone could get a little more. That public philosophy became a permanent part of American political discourse.

ROOSEVELT'S FIRST REELECTION: 1936

Roosevelt's coalition and leadership were so strong that he became the only president to win more than two elections. He won four elections and served a little more than twelve years in the White House before dying in office.

Roosevelt's four electoral triumphs caused Republicans to fume about his "imperial" presidency; all they could do in response to FDR was to promote a constitutional amendment to limit presidents to two terms. But more important than this perception was the way Roosevelt shaped the American political agenda. For many people of the time, it was difficult to imagine the United States under any other leader.

It is possible that Roosevelt could have forged an even stronger liberal coalition than he did. But Roosevelt was a pragmatist above all else and alternately angered and wooed such groups as business, labor, farmers, and the military. For example, Roosevelt kept his distance from Upton Sinclair's populist campaign for governor of California in 1934. Because he threatened business interests, Sinclair was the target of a sustained personal attack by business and other conservative forces in the state in what one authority has called the first media campaign in American history. Sinclair's losing effort, the historian Greg Mitchell argued, undermined the power of reformers nationally.[101]

Roosevelt's three successful reelection drives evoked a changing response from Republicans. Roosevelt's first reelection opponent, in 1936, was Gov. Alfred M. Landon of Kansas, who strongly criticized every aspect of the New Deal. After 1936, Republican candidates did not criticize federal intervention in economic and social affairs but rather the speed and the skill of Democratic intervention. In the third election the Republicans argued that Roosevelt was a "warmonger" because he tilted toward Great Britain in World War II. The GOP argued in the third and fourth elections that Roosevelt threatened to become a "dictator" by exceeding the traditional two-term limit.

Landon was the early favorite for the Republican nomination in 1936. Sen. Charles McNary of Oregon, Sen. Arthur Vandenberg of Michigan, and *Chicago Daily News* publisher Frank Knox provided weak opposition. A Republican bolter for Theodore Roosevelt's "Bull Moose" candidacy in 1912, Landon was consistently to the left of the GOP. Historian James MacGregor Burns observed: "Landon had just the qualities of common sense, homely competence, cautious liberalism and rocklike 'soundness' that the Republicans hoped would appeal to a people tiring, it was hoped, of the antics and heroics in the White House."[102]

In 1936 the Republicans could not have stated their opposition to the popular New Deal in any stronger terms. The platform read: "America is in peril. The welfare of American men and women and the future of our youth are at stake. We dedicate ourselves to the preservation of their political liberty, their individual opportunity, and their character as free citizens, which today for the first time are threatened by government itself."[103]

The Republicans called for ending a wide range of government regulations, returning relief to state and local governments, replacing Social Security, balancing the budget, and changing tariff and currency policies. Landon's only innovation was to call for a constitutional amendment allowing the states to regulate the labor of women and children; the Supreme Court had struck down a New York minimum wage law in 1935. After Landon won the nomination on the first ballot, he selected Knox as his running mate.

The only time the two presidential candidates met was at a meeting Roosevelt called with state governors in Des Moines to discuss farm relief and a recent drought. FDR hoped to put Landon on the spot about farm relief. But Landon turned out to be the aggressor, demanding that FDR say what to tell 100,000 starving farmers in Oklahoma. FDR responded that he had some federal agencies working on programs "just as fast as the Lord will let them." When Landon said that such an answer was small consolation, Roosevelt retorted: "What more can you say to the hungry farmer, governor? The machinery will be put in gear just as fast as the Lord will let *you*?"[104]

Landon's campaign possessed a lavish war chest of $9 million, benefited from the defections of Democratic stalwarts such as John Davis and Al Smith (the party's presidential nominees in 1924 and 1928) and well-coordinated campaign work by business lobbies, and engaged in smear campaigns that portrayed Social Security as a simple "pay reduction" measure and Roosevelt as physically and mentally ill. Landon also argued that New Deal spending was just another form of spoils politics, a charge Roosevelt addressed by folding postmasters into the civil service system.

The only important innovation at the Democratic convention was the repeal of the party's requirement that a candidate receive two-thirds of the delegates to win the nomination. After some arm twisting, southern delegates backed the change, but the governor of Texas wondered aloud if the change was designed for a third Roosevelt run in 1940. Roosevelt was renominated without opposition. He asked Garner to run with him a second time.

In response to Landon's GOP nomination and agitation by leaders of the left and right—including Huey Long of Louisiana, Father Charles E. Coughlin of Detroit, Dr. Francis Townsend of California (who espoused a federal pension plan for senior citizens), and the Socialist Norman Thomas of New York—President Roosevelt in his acceptance speech launched a rhetorical war against "economic royalists" who opposed his programs. He dropped the idea of a "unity" campaign in favor of a partisan ideological attack intended to gain a mandate for a variety of stalled programs rather than a personal vote of confidence.[105]

President Franklin D. Roosevelt's Republican opponents during his three successful reelection campaigns were, from left: Gov. Alfred M. Landon of Kansas in 1936; former Democrat and business executive Wendell L. Willkie in 1940; and Gov. Thomas E. Dewey of New York in 1944. Dewey ran again and lost against President Truman in 1948.

At first, Roosevelt had planned a low-key campaign of "conciliation," but when Landon got the GOP nomination he decided to wage the more aggressive campaign. After all, Landon had run an impressive nominating campaign and was thought to appeal to American pinings for governmental stability. In the early stages of the fall campaign, Roosevelt pretended not to be a partisan politician. He crisscrossed the country making "official" inspections of drought states and public works programs and delivering speeches on electrical power, conservation, and social welfare programs, among other topics. Roosevelt assigned Postmaster General James Farley the task of addressing party rifts and Republican charges of spoils.

At the end of September, Roosevelt assumed the role of partisan leader. The president answered Republican charges point by point, then lashed out at the Republicans in biting, sarcastic terms. As the campaign progressed and Roosevelt sensed a strong response from the large crowds to his attacks, the attacks became stronger. At the close of the campaign, he said:

We have not come this far without a struggle and I assure you that we cannot go further without a struggle. For twelve years, our nation was afflicted with a hear-nothing, see-nothing, do-nothing government. The nation looked to the government but the government looked away. Nine mocking years with the golden calf and three long years of the scourge! Nine crazy years at the ticker and three long years at the breadlines! Nine mad years of mirage and three long years of despair! And, my friends, powerful influences strive today to restore that kind of government with its doctrine that that government is best which is most indifferent to mankind. . . . Never before in all of our history have these forces been so united against one candidate as they stand today. They are unanimous in their hate for me—and I welcome their hatred.[106]

Especially to sophisticated campaign technicians of the modern age, a poll that predicted a big Landon victory provides some amusement. The *Literary Digest*, which had predicted past elections with accuracy, conducted a postcard poll of its readers

that pointed toward a Landon landslide. But the heavy middle- and upper-class bias of the magazine's readership meant that the views of the voters on the lower rungs of the economic ladder were left out of the sample. To this day, the poll is cited as the prime example of bad survey group selection.

The failure of the *Literary Digest*'s survey pointed to the most salient aspect of the election results: the heavy class divisions among the voters. Polls showed that class divisions widened starting around the midpoint of Roosevelt's first term. The broad support Roosevelt had enjoyed because of a common economic disaster had hardened along class lines by the time of the 1936 election.

In the 1936 election, Roosevelt won 27.7 million popular votes (60.8 percent) to Landon's 16.7 million (36.5 percent). Roosevelt carried all but two of the forty-eight states, and he took 523 of the 531 electoral votes. In addition, the Senate's Democratic majority increased to 75 of 96 seats, and the House majority increased to 333 of 435 seats. Roosevelt even ran ahead of candidates—such as gubernatorial candidate Herbert Lehman of New York—who had been recruited to boost his vote totals in various states. In fact, the Democratic victory was almost too overwhelming, Roosevelt suggested, because it would encourage Democrats to fight among themselves rather than with Republicans.

ROOSEVELT'S THIRD TERM: 1940

Soon after his 1936 landslide, Roosevelt tempted fate with a proposal that would have increased the size of the Supreme Court from nine to fifteen members in order to "pack" the Court with justices closer to the president's political philosophy. In 1935 and 1936, the high court had struck down important New Deal initiatives such as the Agriculture Adjustment Act, the National Recovery Administration, and the tax on food processing.

Roosevelt shrouded his proposal in statements of concern about the capacities of some of the Court's older justices. In a fireside speech, Roosevelt said the Court's failure to keep pace with the other "horses" in the "three-horse team" of the federal government constituted a "quiet crisis."[107] The elderly chief justice, Charles Evans Hughes, belied that charge with the energy he brought to the tribunal. But Roosevelt refused to compromise on the bill, and it became an executive-legislative dispute. The proposal was widely seen as a brazen power play, and Congress defeated it by the summer of 1937.

Nevertheless, President Roosevelt eventually got the judicial approval he wanted for his initiatives—what wags called "the switch in time that saved nine." The Court appeared to shift its philosophy during the court-packing affair, and, before long, enough justices had retired so that Roosevelt could put his own stamp on the Court.

Other problems awaited Roosevelt in the second term. Splits in the labor movement gave rise to violence during organizing drives, and the president responded haltingly. After his rift with business over the full range of New Deal policies, Roosevelt appeared to be drifting. Conservatives in Congress were more assertive than ever in opposing the "socialist" measures of the Roosevelt years. The only major New Deal legislation in the second term was the Fair Labor Standards Act of 1938, which abolished child labor and set a minimum wage and an official rate of time-and-a-half for overtime.

As Roosevelt looked toward a third term in 1940, the widening war in Europe posed a difficult problem. Nazi Germany had invaded the Rhineland, Poland, France, Norway, Denmark, Holland, Belgium, and Luxembourg and had made alliances with Italy and the Soviet Union. Japan had invaded China. Adolf Hitler launched the Battle of Britain in the summer of 1940; all-night air raids of London came soon afterward.

British prime minister Winston Churchill desperately petitioned President Roosevelt to provide fifty naval destroyers. Britain's need for the destroyers was so great that Roosevelt balked at asking Congress for help. He reasoned that congressional action probably would take three months, and isolationists might even block action, dealing a crippling blow to Britain. After lengthy debate within the administration, Roosevelt agreed to send Churchill the destroyers as part of a "lend-lease" agreement. The United States would receive British bases in the Caribbean as part of the deal.

A favorite parlor game as the 1940 election approached was guessing whom Roosevelt might tap as his successor. Roosevelt publicly maintained that he did not want another term, but he refused to issue a definitive statement begging off the race. Despite the historic precedent against third terms, Roosevelt wanted to remain president. And to avoid the appearance of overzealousness, Roosevelt wanted the Democrats to draft him in 1940.

While the nation waited for Roosevelt to act, Vice President Garner announced his candidacy. Postmaster General Farley and Secretary of State Cordell Hull also wanted to be president, and Roosevelt gave both vague assurances of support. Roosevelt, whose relations with Garner had been soured since the court-packing episode (which Garner opposed), simply watched the vice president struggle to gain a respectable public profile. The Farley and Hull prospects withered without the help of the old master.

From a distance, Roosevelt watched state Democratic delegations declare their support. Polls showed Roosevelt's fortunes rising with the deepening European crisis. Just before the GOP convention, Roosevelt appointed Republicans Henry Stimson and Frank Knox to his cabinet. But Roosevelt did not reveal his plans for 1940, even to his closest aides. The president did not forbid aides such as Harry Hopkins to work on a draft, but he did not get involved because he wanted the Democrats to call on him and not the other way around.

At the Chicago convention, Sen. Alben Barkley told the delegates: "The president has never had, and has not today, any desire or purpose to continue in the office of president.... He wishes in all earnestness and sincerity to make it clear that all the delegates of this convention are free to vote for any candidate."[108] The statement was followed by an hour-long demonstration and Roosevelt's first-ballot nomination.

The convention mood turned sour, however, when Roosevelt announced that he wanted the liberal secretary of agriculture, Henry Wallace, as his running mate. The announcement disgruntled delegates who already had lined up behind other candidates. But Wallace eventually beat Alabama representative William Bankhead, his strongest opponent for the nomination.

The Republicans mounted their strongest challenge to Roosevelt in 1940, largely based on the charge that Roosevelt was moving the United States toward involvement in the world war. Several moves toward military preparedness had failed at the hands of isolationists in Congress. When Roosevelt asked for increases in defense spending after Gen. Francisco Franco's victory in Spain and Hitler's invasion of Austria in 1938, critics asserted that the president was attempting to cover up domestic failures with foreign adventures. Roosevelt pressed on, however, and Congress passed the Selective Service Act and increases in military spending in 1940.

The Republican field in 1940 included several fresh faces: Sen. Robert A. Taft of Ohio, son of the former president; District Attorney Thomas E. Dewey of New York City; and Sen. Charles L. McNary of Oregon and Sen. Arthur H. Vandenberg of Michigan who had been considered long shots for the Republican nomination in 1936. The freshest face of all was Wendell L. Willkie, a utility executive who had never run for political office. A large, affable man, former Democrat Willkie had barnstormed the country for seven years speaking in opposition to the New Deal.[109] Hundreds of "Willkie clubs" sprang up in the summer of 1940, and a number of publications, including Henry Luce's *Time* magazine, chronicled Willkie's career and encouraged the Willkie groundswell. Despite concern about Willkie's lack of political experience, which led to a "stop Willkie" movement, the Indianan won a sixth-ballot nomination by acclamation. Senator McNary, the Republicans' Senate floor leader, reluctantly accepted the vice-presidential nomination.

Traveling thirty thousand miles in thirty-four states, Willkie gave some 540 speeches. By the time his campaign ended, his already husky voice had turned hoarse. The Republicans spent lavishly and organized grassroots clubs for Willkie across the country. Charges against Roosevelt of managerial incompetence, "warmongering," and imperial ambitions punctuated the Willkie effort. A dramatic moment came when labor leader John L. Lewis called on workers to back Willkie.

After a period of strictly "presidential" behavior, Roosevelt took to the campaign trail with partisan vigor. He answered Willkie's warmongering charges with a promise never to involve the United States in "foreign wars" (which left Roosevelt free to respond to a direct attack).

The alienation of some Democratic and independent voters was symbolized by Vice President Garner, who did not even vote. Roosevelt won, but by the slimmest popular vote margin of any race since 1912. He received 27.3 million popular votes (54.7 percent) to Willkie's 22.3 million (44.8 percent). The electoral vote tally was 449–82.

THE WAR AND ITS LEGACY: 1944

Roosevelt's third term and fourth election were dominated by World War II. Japan attacked U.S. bases at Pearl Harbor, Hawaii, on December 7, 1941. The president, speaking before Congress, declared the date of the surprise attack "a day that will live in infamy." Congress shook off its isolationist inclinations and declared war. A few days after Pearl Harbor, Germany and Italy declared war on the United States, confronting the nation with a two-front war.

The war did for the economy what the New Deal, by itself, could not: it brought economic prosperity. The number of unemployed workers fell from eight million to one million between 1940 and 1944. The boom brought seven million more people, half of them women, into the job market. Inflation, worker shortages, and occasional shortages in raw materials posed problems for wartime agencies. The number of U.S. families paying taxes quadrupled, and by 1945 tax revenues were twenty times their 1940 level. Budget deficits reached new heights.[110]

The fighting in Europe and Asia was grim for the first two years of the president's new term. Isolationist sentiment again built up in Congress, with the Midwest proving the region most resistant to Roosevelt's foreign policy. Criticism of how the Roosevelt administration was managing U.S. participation in the wars on both fronts was rampant. The administration won key congressional votes on the war but faced stubborn resistance on domestic measures. In the 1942 midterm elections, the Republicans gained ten seats in the Senate and forty-seven seats in the House—a major repudiation of Roosevelt.

After several setbacks, the Allied forces won impressive victories. Roosevelt and Churchill worked together closely. Allied forces, led by Gen. Dwight Eisenhower, routed the Axis powers in North Africa in 1942. The Soviet Union beat back a Nazi assault on Stalingrad in the winter of 1942–1943. The Allies took over Italy in 1943 and struggled with the Nazis in France in 1944. In September 1944, British and American troops entered Germany. In the Pacific war, American offensives protected Australia in 1942 and secured the Philippines in 1944.

Despite the bitter opposition that prevailed through much of his third term, Roosevelt had no trouble winning a fourth term in 1944. The Allies found greater success on the battlefield and

on the sea, and the nation did not appear willing to risk untested leadership to prosecute the war. The Republicans turned to the governor of New York, Thomas Dewey. Willkie wanted another shot at the White House, and his best-selling book *One World* put him in the public eye, but old-line conservatives blamed him for the 1940 election defeat. Governors John Bricker of Ohio and Harold Stassen of Minnesota and Gen. Douglas MacArthur were the other hopefuls.

Dewey's primary victories over Willkie in the Wisconsin, Nebraska, and Oregon primaries ended Willkie's public career. Dewey was too far in front to stop. At the convention he won a nearly unanimous first-ballot nomination after Bricker and Stassen dropped out. After Gov. Earl Warren of California refused the vice-presidential nomination, Bricker accepted it.

The party platform extolled the virtues of free enterprise but did not criticize the concept of the New Deal and even made bids for the votes of blacks and women. In his acceptance speech Dewey criticized "stubborn men grown old and tired and quarrelsome in office."[111]

The 1944 election marked the early resistance of the South to the modern Democratic Party. Roosevelt was a shoo-in for the nomination, but southerners wanted a replacement for Wallace as vice president, restoration of the two-thirds nominating rule, and a platform declaration of white supremacy. Dissatisfied southerners threatened to bolt the party in November, but when the party adopted only a vague civil rights plank in its platform, southern discontent dissipated. The rest of the platform called for an internationalist thrust in foreign policy and further New Deal-style reforms domestically.

Roosevelt expressed support for Wallace but said he would allow the convention to pick his running mate. Wallace gave a stirring convention speech but disturbed conservatives with his stand against the poll tax and for equal opportunity for all "regardless of race or sex." Sen. Harry S. Truman of Missouri, who had won fame as a critic of defense spending, beat Wallace for the vice-presidential nomination on the second ballot.

The Democratic campaign was dominated by references to the need for wartime unity and reminders of the Republican rule under Hoover. One leaflet bore the words "Lest We Forget" and a photograph of an unemployed man selling apples in front of a "Hoover Club"; an inset photograph showed Dewey conferring with former president Hoover. The Republicans spent nearly as much money in 1944 as they had in the record-setting 1936 election.

Roosevelt won with 25.6 million popular votes (53.4 percent) to Dewey's 22.0 million (45.9 percent). The electoral vote was 432 to 99. But President Roosevelt, who reshaped U.S. politics at all levels, did not have the opportunity to see the end of the war or to participate in the making of the postwar world. On April 12, 1945, less than three months after his fourth inauguration, he collapsed while sitting for a portrait in Warm Springs, Georgia, and died a few hours later.

THE TRUMAN PRESIDENCY: 1948

The shock of President Roosevelt's death was perhaps greatest for the former haberdasher and machine politician who succeeded him. Truman had been a last-minute choice as FDR's running mate the previous year, and he never became a part of Roosevelt's inner circle. Truman did not know about the most important military program of the age—the Manhattan Project, which, in a race with the Nazis, was developing a nuclear bomb in the secrecy of the brand-new town of Oak Ridge, Tennessee.

Truman also faced a problem of stature. Roosevelt had done nothing less than redefine the presidency in his twelve years in office. He not only effected a partisan realignment in U.S. politics, but he changed the very scope of government activity. As would become clear during the Eisenhower presidency, even Republicans had come to accept, grudgingly, the notion that the government ought to play an active role in stimulating the economy and addressing the needs of specific constituency groups.

Another problem facing Truman: many people could not fathom a presidency without Roosevelt. One member of the White House staff said later: "It was all so sudden, I had completely forgotten about Mr. Truman. Stunned, I realized that I simply couldn't comprehend the presidency as something separate from Roosevelt. The presidency, the White House, the war, our lives—they were all Roosevelt."[112] Other aides could not bring themselves to call Truman "Mr. President," as if so doing would dishonor the late president.

Truman's personality could not have presented a greater contrast to that of Roosevelt. Plain-speaking, blunt, middle-class, midwestern, high school educated, wheeling-and-dealing, and surrounded by old pals from the Pendergast machine of Missouri (the Democratic organization that dominated politics in the state), Truman offended people who had been accustomed to the charisma of Roosevelt. Truman's wife, Bess, also paled in comparison to the dynamic, more public Eleanor Roosevelt as first lady. Nevertheless, Truman showed absolute loyalty to the New Deal, but that would never be enough for many old Roosevelt hands and a nation entering a difficult period of postwar readjustment.

By the time the 1948 election neared, Truman was in grave political shape. He brought former president Hoover back from exile for special projects—one of the many ways he rankled the sensibilities of former Roosevelt aides and Mrs. Roosevelt. Truman also professed a desire to "keep my feet on the ground" and avoid the "crackpots and lunatic fringe" that had surrounded FDR.[113] Toward that end he got rid of Commerce Secretary Henry Wallace and others. The independent journalist I. F. Stone wrote of Truman's personnel moves: "The little nameplates outside the little doors . . . began to change. In Justice, Treasury, Commerce and elsewhere, the New Dealers began to be replaced by the kind of men one was accustomed to meeting in county court-houses."[114]

The politics of postwar adjustment was difficult. The Republican 80th Congress, elected in 1946, sought to dismantle many New Deal programs, and it frustrated anti-inflation efforts. Truman, then, had to duel with Congress, vetoing 250 bills (eleven vetoes were overridden). Tentative civil rights initiatives disgruntled the South. Labor unrest was on the rise. Truman's efforts to "contain" Soviet geopolitical ambitions not only created splits among Democrats but also brought attacks from Republi-

can isolationists. And to make matters worse, Truman was said to have performed inadequately at Potsdam, the conference of World War II victors held in the summer of 1945 that established many geographic borders in Europe.

The situation was so bad that Roosevelt's own son promoted General Eisenhower and Supreme Court Justice William O. Douglas for a 1948 run for the Democratic nomination against Truman. Truman, in other words, was doing a good job antagonizing both the left and the right. In August 1948 the Democratic convention appeared to reflect a dangerously polarized nation. The convention began with a feeling of desperation when Eisenhower and Douglas refused to run. Then a "states' rights" plank offered by southern delegates was defeated, and, after strong speeches by Minneapolis mayor Hubert H. Humphrey and others, a strong northern civil rights plank passed. The party's New Deal and northern machine elements decided that southern defection would be less damaging than northern defection.

Defect is just what some southerners did. The "Dixiecrats," under the leadership of South Carolina's governor J. Strom Thurmond, left the convention to conduct their own fall campaign. Thurmond's candidacy ran under the Democratic Party label in four states (Alabama, Louisiana, Mississippi, and South Carolina) and under the States' Rights Democratic Party elsewhere in the South. Meanwhile, the party's left wing, behind Henry Wallace, protested Truman's Marshall Plan (a multimillion-dollar program to rebuild the economies of western Europe), military buildup, and confrontational stance toward the Soviet Union. It, too, ran its own fall campaign under the banner of the Progressive Citizens of America (the Progressive Party).

The seeds of Dixie defection were planted long before the convention. In 1947 the President's Committee on Civil Rights issued a report calling for the protection of the rights of all minorities. It was just the kind of spark southern segregationists needed to begin a dump-Truman drive and to organize their own campaign in 1948. The Southern Governors Conference in March 1948 recommended that southern states send delegates to the Democratic convention and electors to the electoral college who would refuse to back a pro–civil rights candidate.

As political scientist V. O. Key Jr. has shown, the degree of resistance to civil rights in southern states depended on two basic factors: the proportion of blacks in the population and the strength of the two-party system. Key argued that the existence of a large black population led to stronger Democratic measures against black enfranchisement and led whites to support the Democratic Party in greater numbers. "To them [the whites in such districts], a single Negro vote threatened the whole caste system."[115] Alabama, Louisiana, Mississippi, and South Carolina ended up voting for the Thurmond ticket. Other southern states found broader economic and political issues more compelling than race and voted for Truman.[116]

Many of FDR's old political allies eventually got behind the new man, but Truman's election prospects looked bleak. Some support was grudging—Mrs. Roosevelt offered a straightforward endorsement only to rebut newspaper reports that she fa-

In 1948 pollsters and the media fed Republican candidate Thomas E. Dewey's overconfidence in his campaign to unseat President Harry S. Truman. Truman had the last laugh on the press and his opponent.

vored the Republicans. While the Democratic Party was badly fractured, the Republican Party united behind Dewey.

Dewey, who had been the 1944 GOP candidate, survived a large field in 1948 to become the nominee once again. Senator Taft of Ohio was the main threat, but his isolationism and dull public demeanor were liabilities. The most spirited opposition came from Governor Stassen of Minnesota, who appealed to the more liberal and internationalist wing of the party. An anathema to party bosses, Stassen proved his strength in a series of primary victories. Other candidates or potential convention contenders included Generals Eisenhower and MacArthur, Governor Warren, and Senator Vandenberg. Polls showed all of the Republicans but Taft beating Truman.[117]

Dewey gained the preconvention momentum he needed with an impressive primary victory over Stassen in Oregon. He spent three weeks in the state, while Stassen frittered away his time and resources with a hopeless challenge to Taft in the Ohio primary. Dewey was especially tough in a primary debate with Stassen about communism. With these successes, as well as his impressive organizational strength and mastery over convention mechanics, Dewey won the presidential nomination on the third ballot. Warren was selected as the vice-presidential nominee.

Dewey was part of a new breed of Republican leaders—pragmatic and accepting of the New Deal and the international role that the United States would play in the postwar era. He expressed support for the basic tenets of postwar liberalism, including Social Security, civil rights, and the United Nations. In the 1948 campaign, Dewey planned to put himself above the slashing attack style of President Truman. His constant calls for national unity—spoken in a baritone voice and perfect Eng-

lish—expressed broad public acceptance of the vast changes in U.S. politics over the previous twenty years.

From the beginning of the campaign, the media and professional politicians gave Truman little chance of retaining the White House. Early polls showed Dewey with such a strong lead that pollsters simply stopped surveying voters. But the polls failed because of a bias in the way the questions were asked and a presumption that the large undecided vote would cast their ballots in the same way as the rest of the population, when it in fact heavily favored Truman.[118]

Dewey was so certain of victory that he ran as if he were the incumbent. He made a series of bland, almost diplomatic statements rather than energetic campaign speeches. Dewey appeared confident that his advice to one audience—"Vote your own interests"—would attract an amalgam of disaffected groups. Never even mentioning the president's name, Dewey calmly canvassed the country and just smiled when people called him "President Dewey." Dewey was careful to avoid the overaggressive posture that he thought had ruined his 1944 campaign against Roosevelt. He even made some initial cabinet and policy decisions.

Truman's strategy from the beginning was simply to mobilize the New Deal coalition. The biggest danger was apathy, he and campaign aide Clark Clifford reasoned, so the best strategy was to give the voters a reason to go to the polling booths. Because the Democrats were the majority party, they had to concentrate mainly on getting their longtime supporters to the polls.

Truman ran a scrappy and blunt underdog campaign that could have been mistaken for an outsider's effort. Truman was the president, but he ran against the Washington establishment.

Crisscrossing the nation on a whistle-stop train tour, Truman traveled some 31,000 miles and spoke before six million people. He turned his record of vetoes into an asset, claiming that the "do-nothing" Republican Eightieth Congress made him do it. He assailed the conservative Republican record on inflation, housing, labor, farm issues, and foreign affairs. The president drew large crowds—sometimes many times the size of Dewey's crowds—but he was virtually the only political professional who thought he would win.

Truman himself predicted in October that he had 229 solid electoral votes to Dewey's 109 and Thurmond's 9; 189 votes, he said, could go either way. The best anyone would say about the Truman campaign was that its fighting spirit improved the Democrats' chances to win the Senate. Truman answered the Republicans' claims of liberalism and reformism by criticizing the GOP for obstructing his policies. Truman's outsider taunt was constant: "that no-account, do-nothing, Republican 80th Congress!"[119]

Despite the *Chicago Tribune*'s now-famous headline—"Dewey Defeats Truman"—President Truman prevailed. Early returns put Truman in front, but it was expected that the later-reporting western states would give Dewey the win. When California and Ohio went into the Truman column mid-morning on Wednesday, Dewey conceded defeat.

Considering the Democratic defections, Truman's appeal was widespread. He won twenty-eight states with 24.11 million votes (49.51 percent) and might have won more in the South and North with a united party—as it was, Thurmond won 22 percent of the vote in the South. Dewey won 21.97 million votes (45.12 percent), and Thurmond polled 1.17 million votes (2.40 percent). Henry Wallace won some 1.16 million votes (2.38 percent) but no electoral votes. Wallace's candidacy may have cost Truman New York, Michigan, and Maryland. Yet Wallace may have done Truman a favor by freeing him from the taint of being the most liberal candidate in a time when the electorate was weary of liberalism. Particularly because the Republicans did not have a midwesterner on their ticket and talked about cutting back agricultural subsidies, farmers felt safer with Truman. In all, Truman won 303 electoral votes, Dewey 189, and Thurmond 39.

The Democratic defections may have helped Truman by making him the candidate of the center. The Wallace campaign freed the president from suspicions on the right, and the Thurmond defection strengthened Truman's more liberal northern constituency. In addition, the defections may have inspired Democratic voters to turn out in larger numbers than they would have had victory seemed certain.

In the end the election mostly confirmed long-held partisan allegiances. In the words of political scientist Angus Campbell and his colleagues, it was a "maintaining" election: "The electorate responded to current elements in politics very much in terms of its existing partisan loyalties. Apparently very little of the political landscape attracted strong feeling in that year. But what feeling there was seemed to be governed largely by antecedent attachments to one of the two major parties."[120]

"I LIKE IKE": 1952

Truman's political fortunes worsened during his second term to the extent that he decided belatedly against making a bid for the Democratic nomination. In 1952, for the first time in twenty-four years, neither party had an incumbent president as its nominee.

The Democrats suffered from a weariness that is bound to affect any party that has been in power for twenty years. Problems and opponents' frustrated ambitions were piling up, and in Dwight Eisenhower the Republicans were able to recruit a candidate with universal appeal who was coveted by both parties. The national mood in the years before the 1952 election was sour. The nation was tiring of price controls, recurring scandals among members of the White House staff, and the Korean War, which the Truman administration had begun in 1950 but did not appear interested in either winning or pulling out U.S. troops. The Republicans asked for a chance to "clean up the mess" in Washington and punctuated their appeals with the question: "Had enough?"

The Truman administration had met with repeated frustration in dealing with Congress. On civil rights, tariffs, taxes, labor reform, and the sensationalized question of communist sympathizers in the government, Truman had had to cope with a stubborn Democratic Congress, which, in turn, became more stubborn after Republican gains in the 1950 midterm elections. When Truman seized control of the steel mills because he said the steelworkers' strike threatened the nation's security, he was rebuffed by the Supreme Court.[121]

Truman's biggest problems, however, had concerned cronyism and war. Republicans in congressional investigations and on the stump had hammered away at conflict-of-interest scandals in Truman's administration, creating nationwide sentiment to "clean up" Washington with a new administration. Meanwhile, the United States was mired in a stalemate in Korea—a distant war that was being fought inconclusively under the aegis of the United Nations, with uncertain goals (was it to protect South Korea or to defeat North Korea as well?) and uncertain enemies (was the People's Republic of China an opponent as well as North Korea?). Truman evoked ire with his firing of General MacArthur, who wanted to take the war into China, and with the slow movement toward a settlement. Just as the nation had tired of sacrifices in World War I under Woodrow Wilson, it had tired of sacrifices under Truman.

General Eisenhower—who had just left the presidency of Columbia University to take charge of the forces of the North Atlantic Treaty Organization (NATO)—was recruited by Republicans to run when it appeared that other GOP candidates lacked the national appeal to win the White House. Senator Taft was running again, but his isolationism was considered a liability in the postwar age of internationalism. Stassen, MacArthur, and Warren were other likely Republican candidates.

Eisenhower's popular appeal was revealed when he attracted 50.4 percent of the vote in the New Hampshire primary to Taft's 38.7 percent and Stassen's 7.1 percent. Eisenhower performed well in the northeast area primaries, and Taft generally performed well in the Midwest. A write-in campaign for Eisenhower almost upset Stassen in his home state of Minnesota.

When the GOP convention finally met in Chicago, Taft had the lead in convention delegates. In crucial delegate-seating contests, many of them played out on national television, Eisenhower defeated Taft and won the right to seat pro-Eisenhower insurgents from the South. Taft had relied on the old strategy of mobilizing state machines, but such tactics looked unsavory on television. Eisenhower had undisputed popular appeal, and he won on the first ballot after his early lead turned into a stampede.

Eisenhower selected Sen. Richard Nixon of California as his running mate. The thirty-nine-year-old conservative had won national recognition with his activities on the controversial House Committee on Un-American Activities, which investigated the alleged Soviet ties of Alger Hiss, a former State Department official. Hiss served time for a perjury conviction.

The Democrats moved haltingly toward putting together a ticket. Truman did not announce his decision to stay out of the race until April, after two primary losses. Sen. Estes Kefauver of Tennessee, who had gained fame with his televised hearings on organized crime, ran an aggressive primary campaign and entered the convention with the lead in delegates. Other candidates included Gov. Averell Harriman of New York, Vice President Alben Barkley, Sen. Robert Kerr of Oklahoma, and Sen. Richard Russell of Georgia.

The eventual nominee was Gov. Adlai Stevenson of Illinois, grandson of Grover Cleveland's second vice president. Stevenson had had experience in the navy and State departments before running for governor. President Truman had privately recruited Stevenson for the race—at first unsuccessfully. Then Truman and Illinois backers set up a draft movement for Stevenson, which the governor disavowed until the last minute. Kefauver was the early leader in convention balloting, but Stevenson, always close, pulled into the lead on the third ballot.

Stevenson's campaign was an eloquent call to arms for liberals and reformers. Years later Democrats would recall that the campaign had inspired the generation that would take the reins of power under John F. Kennedy in 1960. Democratic politics at all levels in the 1950s and 1960s would revolve around battles between party regulars and reformers.

Stevenson did not have a chance, however, against the popular Eisenhower. Some southern states bolted the Democratic Party, and the Republicans hammered away at the misdeeds of the Democratic administration under Truman. Such issues as the 1949 communist revolution in China ("Who lost China?"), the protracted Korean War, administration corruption, and the alleged communist infiltration of the government captured the nation's attention more than Stevenson's oratory.

More than anything, however, the desire for party change rather than policy change determined the election. The Republican evocation of the theme of "Corruption, Korea, and Communism" did not challenge the policies that the Democrats offered the nation as much as the way they executed those policies. Eisenhower was a proven administrator and was free of the taint of everyday U.S. politics. Stevenson was a reformer him-

self, but his campaign had the conspicuous backing of President Truman. Stevenson's divorce and his public support of Hiss were constant if only vaguely stated issues.

The campaign's biggest controversy developed when newspaper reports alleged that Nixon had used a "secret fund" provided by California millionaires to pay for travel and other expenses. To a Democratic Party weary of charges of impropriety, the revelation offered an opportunity to accuse Nixon of being beholden to special interests. Nixon admitted the existence of the fund but maintained that he used the money solely for travel and that his family did not accept personal gifts.

Nixon originally reacted to the story by asserting that it was a communist smear. When Eisenhower would not publicly back his running mate, speculation developed that Ike would ask Nixon to leave the ticket—and the Republican *New York Herald Tribune* openly called for him to drop out. When Nixon decided to confront his accusers with a television speech, campaign aides told him he would be dropped if the public reaction was not favorable.

Nixon's speech was remarkable. He denied any impropriety and stated that the Stevenson campaign was hypocritical in its criticisms because it had similar funds. More specifically, Nixon denied that he had accepted such gifts as a mink coat for his wife, Pat; he said that his wife wore a "Republican cloth coat." He acknowledged, however, receiving a pet dog named Checkers from a Texas admirer: "And you know, the kids love that dog, and I just want to say this right now, that regardless of what they say about it, we're going to keep it."[122] His folksy message and appeal for telegrams created a wave of sympathy, which Eisenhower rewarded with a pledge of support. The crisis was over.

In a personal victory—surveys showed that the nation still favored the programs of the New Deal but simply wanted to put the cronyism, sacrifices, and Korean War behind it—Eisenhower swept to the White House. Ike won the entire North and West, parts of the South, and some border states—a total of thirty-nine states to Stevenson's nine. His 442 electoral votes and 33.9 million popular votes (55.1 percent) overwhelmed Stevenson's 89 electoral votes and 27.3 million popular votes (44.4 percent). The election of 1956 would bring more of the same.

EISENHOWER'S REELECTION: 1956

Despite his age (sixty-six) and having had a heart attack in 1955, Eisenhower was the strong favorite to be the GOP nominee for another term. Close cooperation with the Democratic congressional leadership and a "hidden-hand" leadership style seemed to comport with the electorate's wishes for normalcy.[123] The White House staff was ably run by the chief of staff, Sherman Adams, and foreign policy was supervised by Secretary of State John Foster Dulles. The genius of Eisenhower's management style was his use of aides as "lightning rods" for unpopular policies.

Even without lightning rods, Eisenhower probably would have fared well. The economy was booming, and Eisenhower had quickly brought the Korean War to a close. His nuclear policy gave the nation a "bigger bang for the buck" in defense spending and kept the troop requirements low. Federal housing and highway programs gave impetus to suburbanization, now considered part of the middle-class American Dream. Issues that would in the future become divisive, such as civil rights, were muffled.

The only unsettled Republican issue was whether Nixon would again be the vice-presidential candidate. Eisenhower offered him a cabinet post, and Stassen mounted a campaign to replace Nixon with Massachusetts governor Christian Herter. After some hesitation, however, Eisenhower stood by his controversial running mate.

In the Democratic camp, Kefauver challenged Stevenson for the right to face Eisenhower in the fall. After impressive primary victories in New Hampshire and Minnesota for Kefauver, the Stevenson campaign fought back with a string of primary wins in states as varied as California, Florida, and Oregon.

Former president Truman endorsed New York governor Harriman—not Stevenson—at the opening of the Democratic convention. A variety of other favorite sons entered the race. But with the help of Eleanor Roosevelt, Stevenson was able to win the nomination for a second time. Stevenson won on the first ballot.

Stevenson left the vice-presidential slot open to the convention delegates. Kefauver, after battling Senators John Kennedy, Albert A. Gore of Tennessee, and Hubert Humphrey and New York mayor Robert Wagner, eventually won. The open contest highlighted the future national political potential of Kennedy, who, according to later accounts, mainly intended not to win the second spot on the ticket but to gain visibility for a 1960 presidential run.

The campaign was bereft of real issues. Eisenhower's campaigning was a tempered appeal to American values and bipartisan consensus. Nixon was left the job of hacking away at the opposition; he called Stevenson "Adlai the Appeaser" and a "Ph.D. graduate of Dean Acheson's cowardly College of Communist Containment."[124] Overall, however, the campaign was an example of what James David Barber has called "the politics of conciliation," with little conflict or desire for change.

Whether or not the electorate was "asleep," as frustrated critics charged, Eisenhower nailed down another strong victory. He won forty-two states, 457 electoral votes, and 35.6 million popular votes (57.4 percent), compared with Stevenson's six states, 73 electoral votes, and 26.0 million popular votes (42.0 percent). In an unprecedented development, however, both houses of Congress went to the opposition.

KENNEDY AND THE POLITICS OF CHANGE: 1960

The periodic national desire for change came at the expense of the Republicans in 1960, when Sen. John F. Kennedy of Massachusetts became the youngest person ever elected president by defeating Vice President Richard Nixon.

The presidential election was foreshadowed by the 1958 midterm election, when the Democrats made impressive gains in Congress. An economic recession and generational politics created the first major shift toward liberalism since the administration of Franklin Roosevelt. The "Class of '58" decisively changed the discourse of U.S. politics. After the election the Democrats held 64 of 98 Senate seats and 283 of 436 House seats, and thirty-five states had Democratic governors. The time appeared ripe for reopening issues that had long been stifled such as civil rights, urban problems, and education.[125]

The 1960 Democratic field was dominated by senators—Kennedy, Lyndon B. Johnson of Texas, Hubert Humphrey of Minnesota, and Stuart Symington of Missouri. Each had important advantages and disadvantages. Kennedy was from a wealthy and politically minded family, but his Catholicism and undistinguished Senate record were liabilities. Johnson was a masterful majority leader, but no southerner had won the White House since James K. Polk in 1844. Humphrey was popular in the Midwest, but he lacked financial backing and was considered too loquacious and liberal. Symington had a strong Senate record and Harry Truman's backing, but he was considered colorless, and Truman's backing carried liabilities.

Former Illinois governor Adlai Stevenson, the party's nominee in 1952 and 1956, stood on the sidelines, hoping that a convention deadlock or draft movement would finally bring him a ticket to the White House. Early speculation was that the convention would be deadlocked and a compromise candidate would have to emerge. It appeared likely that the nomination would go to Symington, Johnson, Humphrey, or to one of the two senior candidates, Stevenson and Kefauver; the other candidates were good bets for the vice-presidential slot.

Kennedy presented the most intriguing candidacy. He was the son of Joseph P. Kennedy, the millionaire who had been Franklin Roosevelt's ambassador to Britain before their bitter break over U.S. involvement in World War II. John Kennedy also was an Ivy League graduate (of Harvard University), a war hero (described in the book *P.T. 109*), and a Pulitzer Prize winner (for *Profiles in Courage*). With an experienced campaign staff, he had won an overwhelming reelection to the Senate in 1958. Moreover, he had been planning a run for the White House for years.

There were Kennedy skeptics, however. No Catholic except Alfred Smith had been a major-party nominee, and Smith's bitter loss and the anti-Catholic sentiments he aroused in 1928 made political professionals wary of naming another Catholic. Some considered Kennedy, at age forty-three, to be too young. Others focused on the influence of Joseph Kennedy, who had bankrolled his son's political career.[126] Truman's comment captured the crux of Kennedy's liabilities: "It's not the Pope I'm afraid of, it's the Pop."[127]

To address the doubts, Kennedy entered political primaries that would enable him to demonstrate vote-getting ability and to confront the religion problem. The two key primaries were Wisconsin and West Virginia. In Wisconsin, Kennedy would answer the charge that he was too conservative. But the Kennedy strategists were divided about whether he should oppose Senator Humphrey of neighboring Minnesota. Wisconsin's growing independence in party politics eventually convinced them, however, that it would present a low risk in return for the possibility of beating Humphrey in his native region. In West Virginia, Kennedy would attempt to blunt the religion issue by attracting the votes of an overwhelmingly Protestant electorate.

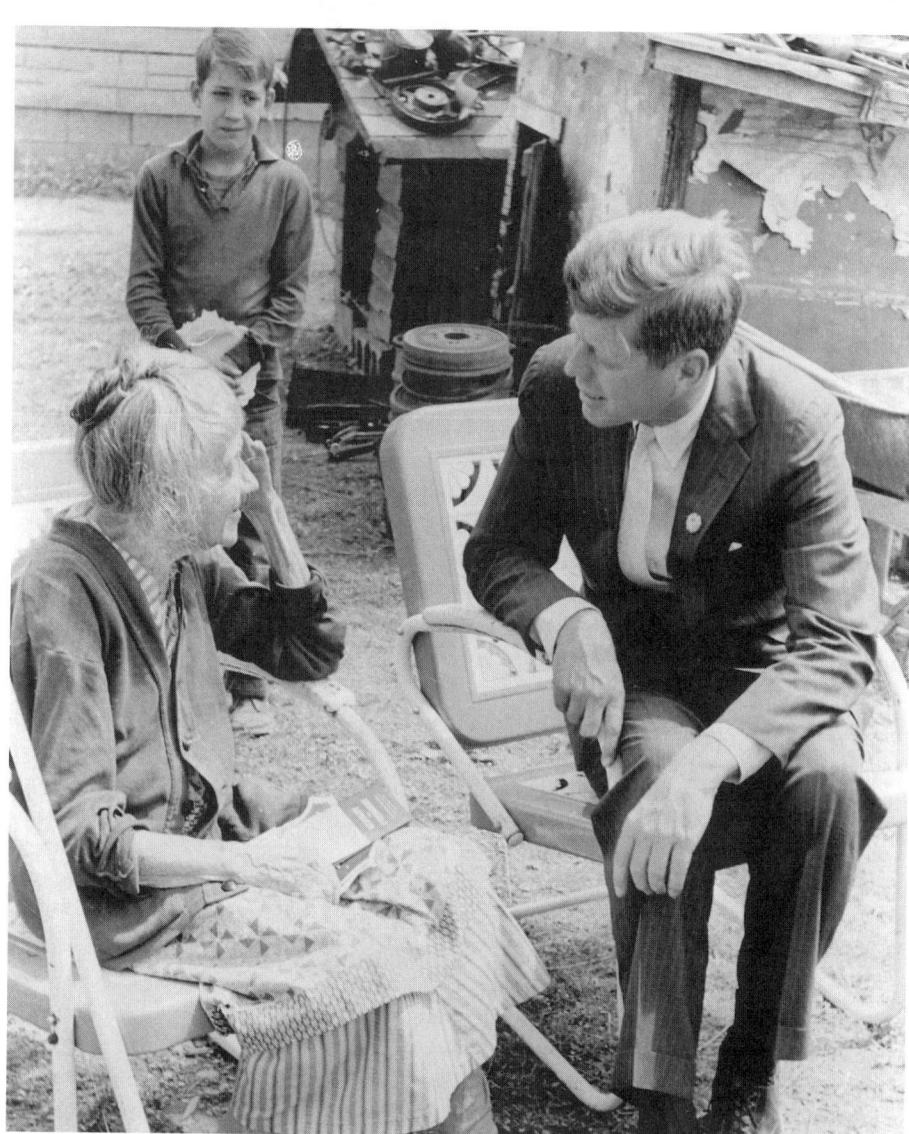

In the 1960 presidential campaign John F. Kennedy worked hard to win the West Virginia primary. His victory in this overwhelmingly Protestant state blunted the issue of his Catholicism and set him on the way to a first-ballot nomination.

In the end, Kennedy defeated Humphrey in Wisconsin. Kennedy's impressive campaign treasury enabled him to staff offices in eight of the ten congressional districts in the state; Humphrey had only two offices. Humphrey maintained that the defeat stemmed from crossover Republican Catholic votes and was therefore illegitimate. (Most of the state's Catholics, who made up 31 percent of the population, belonged to the GOP.) But to Kennedy and many political observers, it was still an important victory.

Humphrey wanted to even the score in West Virginia. If Humphrey had quit the campaign and left Kennedy with no opponents, as many advised him to do, a Kennedy victory would have attracted little attention.[128] But Kennedy was able to use the Appalachian state as a way to deflect the religion issue as well as the "can't win" problem. Kennedy had a thorough organization in West Virginia, and he worked hard. He had commissioned polls in the state as far back as 1958 in anticipation of the presidential race.

Kennedy's handling of the religion question in the primaries was shrewd and would be repeated in the fall campaign. He framed the question as one of tolerance—which put Humphrey

on the defensive because he had never tried to exploit the religion issue. Kennedy had his campaign workers plant questions about how his religious beliefs would affect his loyalty to the nation, to which the candidate replied with a stock answer: "When any man stands on the steps of the Capitol and takes the oath of office as president, he is swearing to uphold the separation of church and state; he puts one hand on the Bible and raises the other hand to God as he takes the oath. And if he breaks the oath, he is not only committing a crime against the Constitution, for which the Congress can impeach him—but he is committing a sin against God."[129]

Kennedy's direct confrontation of the religion issue worked to his benefit. Kennedy had the money to get his message across: his television expenditures alone in the state totaled $34,000, while Humphrey had only $25,000 for the whole primary campaign in West Virginia.[130] Early polls gave Humphrey wide leads, and interviews elicited strong reservations about Kennedy's Catholicism. As the commercials aired and the primary neared, the lead became smaller, and voters privately said they would vote for Kennedy.

JFK, as he asked headline writers to call him instead of the youthful-sounding "Jack," easily won the primary, taking 61 percent of the vote to Humphrey's 39 percent. He was on his way to a first-ballot nomination.

The Kennedy campaign staffers managed the Democratic convention with consummate skill. Had they failed to gain a majority on the first ballot, pressure might have developed for another candidate. But the Kennedy team efficiently lobbied delegations to augment support; the vice-presidential slot was vaguely offered to several politicians. In the end, Lyndon Johnson was the surprise choice for running mate. Even Kennedy supporters had doubts about Johnson, but the selection of the southerner was a classic ticket-balancing move.[131]

Central to Kennedy's winning campaign was his younger brother Robert F. Kennedy. A former counsel to Republican senator Joseph McCarthy, Robert developed into the consummate political operative. He was JFK's confidant, chief strategist, delegate counter, fund-raiser, taskmaster, and persuader. Biographer Arthur M. Schlesinger Jr. wrote that Robert Kennedy's strength "lay in his capacity to address a specific situation, to assemble an able staff, to inspire and flog them into exceptional deeds, and to prevail through sheer force of momentum."[132]

Vice President Richard Nixon was the overwhelming choice for the Republican nomination. Nelson A. Rockefeller, elected governor of New York in 1958, was a liberal alternative, but he announced in 1959 that he would not run. There was a brief surge for Rockefeller when he criticized the party and its "leading candidate," but meetings with Nixon settled the differences. Some conservatives were disgruntled with Nixon, but their efforts for Sen. Barry Goldwater of Arizona would have to wait until 1964.

Nixon selected United Nations Ambassador Henry Cabot Lodge as his running mate, and the party platform and rhetoric stressed the need for experience in a dangerous world. Nixon promised to continue President Dwight Eisenhower's policies. He attempted to portray Kennedy as an inexperienced upstart, even though he was Kennedy's senior by only four years and the two had entered Congress the same year. Nixon led in the polls at the traditional Labor Day start of the fall campaign.

Kennedy's campaign was based on a promise to "get the nation moving again" after eight years of calm Republican rule. Specifically, he assured voters that he would lead the nation out of a recession. The gross national product increased at a rate of only 2.25 percent annually between 1955 and 1959. Economists puzzled over the simultaneously high unemployment and high inflation rates.[133] Kennedy repeatedly called for two related changes in national policy: pump up the economy and increase defense spending dramatically.

The Democrat faced up to the religion issue again with an eloquent speech before the Greater Houston Ministerial Association, and he attracted attention from civil rights leaders when he offered moral and legal support to the Reverend Martin Luther King Jr. after King was arrested for taking part in a sit-in at an Atlanta restaurant. While Kennedy appealed to the party's more liberal and moderate wing, Johnson toured the South to appeal to regional pride and to assuage fears about an activist government.

The high point of the campaign came on September 26, 1960, when the candidates debated on national television before seventy million viewers. Kennedy was well rested and tanned; he had spent the week before the debate with friends and associates. Nixon was tired from two solid weeks of campaigning; he had spent the preparation period by himself. Their appearances alone greatly influenced the outcome of the debates.

Kennedy's main objective had been simply to look relaxed and "up to" the presidency. He had little to lose. Nixon was always confident of his debating skills, and he performed well in the give-and-take of the debate. But the rules of debating—the way "points" are allocated—are not the same for formal debating and televised encounters. Kennedy's managers prepared their candidate better for the staging of the debate. Nixon's five-o'clock shadow reinforced the cartoon image of him as darkly sinister. As a result of all these factors, polls of radio listeners found that Nixon had "won" the debate, but polls of the more numerous television viewers found that Kennedy had "won." Historian Theodore H. White wrote: "It was the picture image that had done it—and in 1960 it was television that had won the nation away from sound to images, and that was that."[134]

While Kennedy called for a more activist and imaginative approach to world problems, Nixon stressed the candidates' similarities so much that their differences paled into insignificance. Kennedy called for a crusade to eliminate want and to confront tyranny. Nixon responded: "I can subscribe completely to the spirit that Sen. Kennedy has expressed tonight."[135] With ideology an unimportant part of the debate, the images of personal character the candidates were able to project gained in importance.

The candidates held three more debates, addressing issues such as Fidel Castro's Cuba, whether the United States should defend the Chinese offshore islands of Quemoy and Matsu in the event of a military strike by China, and relations with Nikita Khrushchev's Soviet Union. None of the debates had the effect of the first, which neutralized Nixon's quasi-incumbency advantage. Nor was Nixon greatly helped by President Eisenhower, who did not campaign for his protégé until late in the campaign.

The election results were so close that Nixon did not concede his defeat until the afternoon of the day after the election. After a vacation in Florida and Nassau, Nixon returned to Washington on November 19 to consider a series of charges that voter fraud had cost him the election. A shift of between eleven thousand and thirteen thousand votes in a total of five or six states could have given Nixon the electoral vote triumph. Nixon said he decided against demanding a recount because it would take "at least a year and a half" and would throw the federal government into turmoil.[136] Other commentators have pointed out that had Nixon, for instance, challenged voting irregularities in Illinois in Democratic precincts in Chicago, irregularities in Republican rural areas of the state could have been challenged by Kennedy.

When the electoral college voted, Kennedy won 303 electoral votes to Nixon's 219. Democratic senator Harry F. Byrd of Virginia attracted 15 electoral votes. Kennedy won twenty-three states to Nixon's twenty-six. (Six Alabama electors and all eight Mississippi electors, elected as "unpledged Democrats," as well as one Republican elector from Oklahoma, cast their votes for Byrd.) The overall popular vote went 34.2 million for Kennedy and 34.1 million for Nixon. The margin was about two-tenths of 1 percent, or 118,574 votes. Moreover, the margins in many states were very close. Kennedy won Illinois by 8,858 votes and Texas by 46,242 votes. Despite statements that the religion question would hurt Kennedy, it probably helped him by mobilizing Catholics on his behalf. Gallup polls showed that 78 percent of Catholics voted for JFK. Although Catholics were a traditional Democratic constituent group—supporting the party by margins of three or four to one—they had shown support for Republicans Eisenhower and Sen. Joseph McCarthy.[137] In addition, Kennedy put together a predictable coalition: he won the support of voters in the Northeast, in most of the South, and in cities, plus blacks and union workers. Upper New England, the Midwest, and the West went primarily to Nixon.

After the election, Kennedy and Goldwater discussed, in an informal way, how they would conduct their campaigns for the presidency in 1964. The two expected to win their parties' nominations easily, and they talked about crisscrossing the nation in head-to-head debates, which would set a new standard for national campaigns.[138]

The Kennedy-Goldwater campaign never came to be, however. On November 22, 1963, while riding in a motorcade in Dallas, Texas, President Kennedy was assassinated by a gunman named Lee Harvey Oswald.[139] Vice President Johnson assumed the presidency.[140]

In his brief administration, Kennedy had compiled a record disappointing even to many of his supporters. The Bay of Pigs fiasco in which a Central Intelligence Agency plan to overthrow the Cuban government failed miserably, the inability to obtain passage of landmark civil rights legislation, budget deficits and a drain of gold supplies from the United States, confrontations with the Soviet Union in Cuba, Hungary, and Berlin, and the nascent U.S. involvement in the Vietnam War created doubts about the young president's control of the government.

Kennedy had, however, made a start on many important issues. Arms control initiatives such as the test ban treaty, economic growth through tax cuts, modernization of the military, the successful management of the Cuban Missile Crisis, civil rights and other domestic initiatives, the Peace Corps and Alliance for Progress, and growing world stature all offered hope for the second term. It would fall to Johnson, the legendary former Senate majority leader, to bring the Kennedy plans to fruition. First acting as the loyal servant of the slain president, then as his own man, Johnson was able to bring to legislative enactment many of the initiatives long-cherished by liberals—most notably the Civil Rights Act of 1964, which was considerably stronger than the Kennedy bill that had stalled in Congress.

"ALL THE WAY WITH LBJ": 1964

From the time of his sad but graceful ascension to the White House, Johnson was never in doubt as the Democrats' 1964 nominee. He was expected to select an eastern or midwestern liberal as his running mate, and he did so when he tapped Senator Humphrey of Minnesota at the convention, which his campaign organization stage-managed down to the last detail. The only dissent from Democratic unity was provided by Gov.

George C. Wallace of Alabama, whose segregationist campaign took advantage of a backlash against the civil rights movement. Wallace entered three primaries against Johnson-allied favorite sons, and he polled 43 percent of the vote in Maryland. Wallace talked about mounting a third-party bid in the fall, but he backed off.

The Republicans were divided into two bitter camps led by Senator Goldwater of Arizona, the eventual nominee, and by Governor Rockefeller of New York. The nomination contest was a struggle for the soul of the party. Other active and inactive candidates included Ambassador to Vietnam Henry Cabot Lodge, former vice president Nixon, and Gov. William Scranton of Pennsylvania. After a New Hampshire primary victory by Lodge, achieved through a well-organized write-in drive while he was still ambassador to Vietnam, Goldwater and Rockefeller scrapped through a series of primaries. The moderate Lodge later helped Scranton in a late effort to recruit uncommitted delegates to stop Goldwater, but by then it was too late. Goldwater lined up strong delegate support to get the nomination before the primary season even began, but he needed to use the primaries to show that he had vote-getting ability. And the state organizations that backed him needed evidence that his conservative message would find popular acceptance.

In the "mixed" nominating system then in place, candidates were able to pick and choose the primaries that best suited their strategies. Front-runners avoided risks, and long shots entered high-visibility and often risky contests as a way to attract the attention of party professionals. As expected, Goldwater won widespread support in the southern state conventions and had strong primary showings in Illinois and Indiana. Rockefeller beat Lodge in Oregon, but the decisive test came when Goldwater narrowly upset Rockefeller in California.

More important than the confusing preconvention contests was the rhetoric. Both the conservative Goldwater and the liberal Rockefeller vowed to save the party from the other's ideology. Goldwater, who rode the bestseller success of his *Conscience of a Conservative* to hero worship among conservatives, made a vigorous case against New Deal politics and for American sway in world politics: "I don't give a tinker's damn what the rest of the world thinks about the United States, as long as we keep strong militarily."[141] Rockefeller implied that Goldwater would risk nuclear war and would recklessly dismantle basic social programs.

The nominating contest was a regional as well as an ideological struggle. The westerner Goldwater—backed by labor-intensive manufacturers, small business and agricultural enterprises, and domestic oil producers—opposed internationalist banking and commercial interests.[142] Goldwater made eastern media the objects of scorn. Rockefeller and his family, of course, represented the apex of the eastern establishment. Because of his strategy, Goldwater isolated his campaign from the manufacturing and financial interests that were at the center of American economic growth for a generation.

Bitter battles over the party platform and unseemly heckling of Rockefeller displayed the party's divisions at the convention. When the conservatives won the nomination and the platform, there was no reconciliation. Goldwater selected Rep. William

Miller of New York, another conservative, as his running mate and vowed to purge the party of liberal and moderate elements.

In a defiant acceptance speech, Goldwater painted a picture of the United States as inept in international affairs and morally corrupt in domestic pursuits, and he vowed an all-out crusade to change the situation: "Tonight there is violence in our streets, corruption in our highest offices, aimlessness among our youth, anxiety among our elderly, and there's a virtual despair among the many who look beyond the material successes toward the inner meaning of their lives. . . . Extremism in defense of liberty is no vice; moderation in pursuit of justice is no virtue."[143]

To a nation experiencing prosperity and unaware of the true proportions of its involvement in Vietnam, the "choice, not an echo" that Goldwater offered was a moral crusade. But the American consensus was built on material, consumer foundations, and an "outsider" appeal would have to wait until the system's foundations became unstable.

The divided GOP made for easy pickings for Johnson. The fall campaign was dominated by Goldwater's gaffes, which started long before the campaign began. He said, for example, that troops committed to the North Atlantic Treaty Organization (NATO) in Europe probably could be cut by at least one-third if NATO "commanders" had the authority to use tactical nuclear weapons in an emergency.[144] Goldwater also proposed a number of changes in the Social Security system, called for selling off the Tennessee Valley Authority, criticized the civil rights movement, and denounced the Supreme Court, the National Labor Relations Board, and the federal bureaucracy. Except for the use of nuclear weapons and changes in Social Security, most of Goldwater's proposals when taken alone were not shocking. But the sum of his proposals—and his sometimes halting explanations—scared many voters.

President Johnson campaigned very actively to win a mandate for an activist new term. He traveled throughout the country making speeches to build a consensus for his domestic programs as well as his reelection. Johnson resisted Goldwater's frequent calls for televised debates. The nation's prosperity was probably enough to keep the president in the White House.[145]

Johnson desperately wanted a personal mandate to pursue a variety of domestic programs that fell under the rubric of the "Great Society"—a term that Johnson used in a 1964 commencement address (borrowed from a book of the same title by British socialist Graham Wallas). The desired landslide—underscored by his campaign slogan, "All the Way with LBJ"—was essential to initiatives in civil rights, health care, community action, education, welfare, housing, and jobs creation. Central to the landslide was not only economic prosperity but also peace in the world's trouble spots. Johnson therefore ran as a "peace" candidate.

But while he was trying to build a coalition that would sustain his domestic initiatives, Johnson faced an increasingly difficult dilemma about the U.S. role in Vietnam. The United States had been involved in opposing Ho Chi Minh's revolution against French colonial rule in the 1940s and 1950s, and under Presidents Eisenhower and Kennedy the United States had made a commitment to the leaders of South Vietnam (created after

In accepting the 1964 Republican nomination, Sen. Barry Goldwater called for a moral crusade, declaring, "Extremism in defense of liberty is no vice; moderation in pursuit of justice is no virtue."

the failure of the 1954 Geneva accord) as a bastion against communist expansion in Asia. But talk of war would likely imperil the domestic initiatives of the Great Society.

So while Johnson was campaigning as the peace candidate in 1964, he also was preparing for a major increase in U.S. involvement in Vietnam. As early as February 1964, the administration began elaborate covert operations in Southeast Asia and prepared a resolution to give the president a "blank check" in Vietnam.[146] By June, the resolution was ready, and the Pentagon had chosen ninety-four bombing targets in North Vietnam and made provisions for bombing support systems on the ground. But on June 15, Johnson decided to delay major offensives until after the election.[147] In August Johnson sent to Congress what would be known as the Tonkin Gulf resolution, which granted the president broad authority to wage war in Vietnam. The resolution passed quickly and nearly unanimously—after all, the president had instructed congressional leaders to get an overwhelming majority so his policy would be bipartisan.

Johnson also seized on Rockefeller's use of the peace issue during the Republican primaries against Goldwater. He alluded to some of Goldwater's scarier statements about war, and he pledged that "we are not about to send American boys nine or ten thousand miles away from home to do what Asian boys ought to be doing for themselves."[148] A week before the election Johnson said: "The only real issue in this campaign, the only one you ought to get concerned about, is who can best keep the peace."[149]

Johnson's popular vote landslide was the largest in U.S. history. He won 61 percent of the popular vote to Goldwater's

38 percent (or 43.1 million to 27.2 million votes). In the electoral college Johnson received 486 votes to Goldwater's 52, and he carried forty-four states—all but Goldwater's home state of Arizona and five deep South states. In addition, the Democratic Party amassed huge majorities in both the Senate (67–33) and the House of Representatives (295–140).

On election day, Johnson created a working group to study "immediately and intensively" the U.S. options in Southeast Asia.[150] The war was increasing far beyond what most supporters of the Tonkin Gulf resolution or "peace" supporters of the president imagined. In 1965 alone the number of U.S. troops in Vietnam increased from 15,000 to nearly 200,000.[151]

The Breakup of Consensus

A long period of uncertainty in American politics began sometime after Johnson's landslide victory over Goldwater in 1964.

By 1968, some thirty thousand Americans had been killed in action in Vietnam, and television was bringing the war into the living rooms of American families. Despite repeated assertions that the United States was defeating the North Vietnamese enemy, U.S. bombing efforts and ground troops did not break the resolve of the communists in the North or their sympathizers who had infiltrated the South. The corrupt South Vietnamese government and army appeared to lack the will to fight the war on their own.

In the United States, the opposition to the war developed as the casualties mounted, and the administration experienced a "credibility gap" because of its statements about the war. Before the United States left Vietnam in 1975, fifty-five thousand Americans had died in combat. Perhaps more important than the number of casualties—about the same as in the Korean War—was the long-term commitment that the United States appeared to have made with little evidence of progress. The "quagmire," as *New York Times* reporter David Halberstam called the war, was perhaps typified by the program of intense U.S. bombing raids that were judged by many experts to be ineffectual against the North's guerrilla warfare strategy.[152]

As opposition to the war grew among an increasingly vocal and well-organized minority, strains developed in Johnson's economic and domestic programs. Starting with the riots in the Watts section of Los Angeles in 1965, urban areas sizzled with resentment of the mainstream liberal establishment. Detroit, Newark, and many major U.S. cities erupted in other riots that burned miles of city streets and caused millions of dollars in damage. The assassination of civil rights leader Martin Luther King Jr. in Memphis in April 1968, led to riots throughout the nation. Even before the riots, however, a conservative reaction against the Great Society had developed.

The activities of the Great Society were many and varied: the Civil Rights Act of 1964, the Voting Rights Act of 1965, Head Start, Model Cities, mass transit legislation, food stamps, Medicaid, the Elementary and Secondary Education Act, college loans, and housing programs that included subsidies for poor, to name just the most prominent programs.

The conservative backlash was apparent before many programs had time to do their work. Efforts such as the Model Cities program and the Community Action Program, which mandated that poverty programs promote "maximum feasible participation" by the poor themselves, often were badly organized. They also created new struggles over jurisdiction in cities that already were notorious for divisive politics. Liberal efforts that predated the Great Society, such as school desegregation, only added to the tensions in cities.

One of the greatest sources of backlash in the late 1960s was an alarming increase in street crime. Even though blacks and the poor were the chief victims of the increase, the issue was most salient for conservative whites. Many tied the breakdown in order to the growth of the welfare state caused by the Great Society. The crime rate seemed to many to be nothing less than ingratitude on the part of the poor. James Sundquist wrote: "While increasing millions were supported by welfare, rising state and local taxes made the citizen more and more aware of who paid the bill. And while he armed himself for protection against thieves or militants, the liberals were trying to pass legislation to take away his guns."[153]

The crime problem was an important element in both national and metropolitan politics. Polls taken in the late 1960s showed that half the women and a fifth of the men in the country were afraid to walk alone in their own neighborhoods at night.[154] In Alabama, Gov. George Wallace was whipping up his supporters in a frenzy of prejudice and resentment. The fear of crime also would be an important element in Richard Nixon's 1968 campaign.

"NIXON NOW": 1968

With the nation divided over the war and domestic policy, the Democrats entered the 1968 campaign in an increasingly perilous state. In December 1967 Sen. Eugene McCarthy of Minnesota challenged President Johnson for the Democratic nomination, a move based almost entirely on McCarthy's antiwar stance. McCarthy did unexpectedly well against Johnson's write-in candidacy in the New Hampshire primary on March 12, 1968, drawing 42.4 percent of the vote to Johnson's 49.5 percent. Anticipating a devastating defeat in the Wisconsin primary on April 2, Johnson dramatically announced his withdrawal from the campaign in a televised address March 31.

After the New Hampshire primary, New York senator Robert F. Kennedy declared his antiwar candidacy, which put in place all the elements for a Democratic fight of historic proportions. Vice President Humphrey took Johnson's place as the administration's candidate.

McCarthy and Kennedy fought each other in the primaries, and Kennedy appeared to have the upper hand when he closed the primary season with a victory in California on June 5. But after making his acceptance speech, he was assassinated, and the party was in greater turmoil than ever.

At the party convention in Chicago, a site Johnson had chosen for what he thought would be his renomination, Humphrey became the Democratic Party's candidate. He had eschewed the primaries; he won the nomination on the strength of endorsements from state party organizations. The vice president took the nomination on the first ballot after Mayor Richard Daley of Chicago committed the Illinois delegation to his effort. Humphrey won with support from the traditional elements of the Democratic coalition—labor, African Americans, urban voters—plus the backers of President Johnson. Humphrey appealed to many of the party's "moderates" on the issue of the Vietnam War.

Preliminary battles over rules and delegate seating, the representativeness of the party, and the Vietnam War caused ugly skirmishes on the convention floor. The party's platform eventually endorsed the administration's war policy, including bombing, but strong opposition to this plank left the Democrats divided.[155]

Outside the convention halls, demonstrations for civil rights and an end to the war met brutal rejection from the police. After three days of sometimes harsh verbal and physical battles with antiwar demonstrators in city parks, the police charged a group of protesters who planned a march on the convention. Theodore H. White described the scene that played on national television:

Like a fist jolting, like a piston exploding from its chamber, comes a hurtling column of police from off Balbo into the intersection, and all things happen too fast: first the charge as the police wedge cleaves through the mob; then screams, whistles, confusion, people running off into Grant Park, across bridges, into hotel lobbies. And as the scene clears, there are little knots in the open clearing—police clubbing youngsters, police dragging youngsters, police rushing them by their elbows, their heels dragging, to patrol wagons, prodding recalcitrants who refuse to enter quietly.[156]

Humphrey and his running mate, Sen. Edmund S. Muskie of Maine, faced an uphill fight.

The Republicans united behind Richard Nixon, the 1960 nominee whose political career had seemed at an end after he lost in the 1962 California gubernatorial election. The GOP did not have to deal with any of the divisiveness of the 1964 Goldwater-Rockefeller battle.

Nixon outspent Humphrey two-to-one. He also followed a carefully devised script that avoided the exhausting schedule of his 1960 campaign and capitalized on the national discontent created by the Vietnam War, urban riots, political assassinations, and general concern about the speed of change wrought by the Great Society. Nixon traveled the high road in his own campaign by calling for the nation to unite and heal its wounds. Promising an "open administration," Nixon's main offer was change. "I must say the man who helped us get into trouble is not the man to get us out."[157] To avoid scrutiny by the national media, Nixon gave few major addresses, preferring instead a series of interviews with local newspapers and broadcasters.

As President Johnson resisted calls for a halt in the bombing of North Vietnam, Nixon said he had a "secret plan" to end the war. He appealed to weary Democrats with his pledge of an activist administration and alternative approaches to dealing with some of the problems the Great Society addressed. Nixon promised to give blacks, in his words, "a piece of the action with a program to encourage entrepreneurial activity in cities." The

Former vice president Richard Nixon tapped into widespread discontent over the Vietnam War and domestic turmoil to win the 1968 presidential election, one of the closest in U.S. history.

"new Nixon" appeared willing to deal with the Soviet Union, which he had scorned earlier in his career. Meanwhile, his vice-presidential nominee, Gov. Spiro T. Agnew of Maryland, offered a slashing critique of the Democrats to middle-class and blue-collar Americans who resented the civil rights laws, government bureaucracy, Vietnam War protesters, and the young protest generation.

Gov. Wallace of Alabama, heading up one of the strongest third party campaigns in U.S. history, ran as an antiestablishment conservative, railing away at desegregation, crime, taxes, opponents of the war in Vietnam, social programs, and "pointy-head" bureaucrats and "intellectual morons." His American Independent Party was the strongest effort since Robert La Follette's Progressive run in 1924. Like the earlier third-party campaigns, the Wallace run caused concern about the soundness of the electoral college system. Because the race was so close, it was conceivable that no candidate would win an electoral college victory. In that event, Wallace could have held the balance of power.[158]

Despite his early disadvantage, Humphrey made steady inroads into Nixon's support by disassociating himself from Johnson's Vietnam policies. When Johnson on November 1 ordered a halt to all bombing of North Vietnam, Humphrey appeared to be free at last from the stigma of the administration. But this change in policy was not enough to win the election for Humphrey.

The 1968 election was one of the closest in U.S. history. Nixon's victory was not confirmed until the day after the election when California, Ohio, and Illinois—each with very close counts—finally went into the Nixon column. Nixon attracted 31.8 million votes (43.4 percent of all votes cast); Humphrey, 31.3 million votes (42.7 percent); and Wallace, 9.9 million votes (13.5 percent). Nixon won thirty-two states and 301 electoral votes, compared with Humphrey's thirteen states and 191 electoral votes. Nixon won six southern states (Wallace won five others), all of the West except Texas, Washington, and Hawaii, and all the midwestern states except Michigan and Minnesota. Humphrey won all of the East except New Hampshire, Vermont, New Jersey, and Delaware, plus West Virginia, Maryland, and the District of Columbia.

One long-lasting effect of 1968 was a transformation of the nominating process. In response to the bitter complaints about their 1968 convention, the Democratic Party adopted rules that would make the primaries the center of the nominating process. The Chicago convention, dominated by party professionals at the expense of many important constituencies—African Americans, women, youth—had nominated a candidate who did not compete in any primaries. The key reform was a limit on the number of delegates that state committees could choose—after 1968, no more than 10 percent of the delegation.

NIXON'S REELECTION: 1972

Sen. George S. McGovern of South Dakota was the miracle candidate of 1972, but his miracle did not last long enough. Edmund Muskie, a veteran of the U.S. Senate and the vice-presidential nominee in 1968, was the early favorite to win the Democratic nomination. But because of party reforms enacted in response to the disastrous 1968 convention, the nominating process was bound to create surprises and confusion.

No fewer than fifteen contenders announced their candidacy, twelve with serious hopes of winning or influencing the final selection. Some twenty-two primaries to choose 60 percent of the party's delegates—a third more than in 1968—were to take place over four months. The marathon would be decided by accidents, media strategy, and a confusing array of voter choices that changed with each new development.

Muskie was badly damaged before the New Hampshire primary when he appeared to cry while lashing back at the *Manchester Union Leader*'s vicious and unrelenting attacks on his campaign and on his outspoken wife, Jane. The *Union Leader* had printed a series of attacks on Jane and then falsely reported that Muskie had laughed at a derogatory joke about French Canadians. Muskie later said of the incident: "It changed people's minds about me, of what kind of a guy I was. They were looking for a strong, steady man, and here I was weak."[159]

Muskie won the first-in-the-nation New Hampshire primary, but his 46.4 percent of the vote was considered a "disappointing" showing. Senator McGovern, the antiwar candidate who won 37.1 percent of the vote, was pronounced the real winner by media and pundits. He had attracted a corps of youthful volunteers and his strong showing—engineered by imaginative young political operatives led by Gary Hart—was a surprise.

After New Hampshire, the Democrats battled through the summer. Wallace parlayed his antibusing rhetoric into an im-

pressive victory in the Florida primary (41.6 percent). Better organized than the others, McGovern won the Wisconsin delegation by winning 29.6 percent of the state vote. McGovern then won an easy Massachusetts victory with 52.7 percent of the vote to Muskie's 21.3 percent. Humphrey edged McGovern in Ohio by 41.2 to 39.6 percent, but McGovern claimed a moral victory.

In the popular primary vote before the late summer California primary, McGovern actually stood in third place behind Wallace and Humphrey. But the delegate allocation rules gave the edge to the candidate who could squeeze out narrow victories in congressional districts, and that was McGovern. McGovern had 560 delegates to Humphrey's 311. Wallace had 324 delegates, but he was paralyzed after being shot in a Maryland shopping center on May 15, 1972, and therefore no longer appeared to have a chance at the nomination.

The big McGovern-Humphrey showdown was California, which offered 271 delegates to the winner. It was a spirited campaign that included a head-to-head debate and strong Humphrey assaults on McGovern's positions on welfare and defense spending. McGovern went on to beat Humphrey by five percentage points in the winner-take-all primary. McGovern also won a majority of the delegates in New Jersey, South Dakota, and New Mexico on the last day of the primary season.[160]

After platform battles over welfare, busing, and the Vietnam War, McGovern won the nomination handily. He then selected Sen. Thomas Eagleton of Missouri as his running mate after several others declined. McGovern did not get to deliver his acceptance speech—perhaps the best speech of his career—until almost three o'clock in the morning, when most television viewers already were in bed.

President Nixon and Vice President Agnew were renominated with barely a peep out of other Republicans. Rep. Paul N. "Pete" McCloskey Jr. of California opposed Nixon in the primaries but won only one delegate (from New Mexico). Rep. John M. Ashbrook of Ohio also ran in the primaries.

McGovern would have been an underdog in the best of circumstances, but his chances were badly damaged by what came to be known as the "Eagleton affair." As the McGovernites celebrated their hard-won nomination, rumors circulated that Eagleton had been hospitalized for exhaustion in the early 1960s. Eagleton finally told McGovern operatives that he had been hospitalized three times for nervous exhaustion and fatigue, and his treatment included electroshock therapy. Despite McGovern's public statement that he was "1,000 percent for Tom Eagleton, and I have no intention of dropping him," Eagleton left the ticket less than two weeks after his nomination.

McGovern eventually replaced Eagleton with his sixth choice, R. Sargent Shriver, former executive of the Peace Corps and Office of Economic Opportunity. But the aura of confusion that surrounded the Eagleton affair and the search for a new vice-presidential candidate hurt the campaign badly. The columnist Tom Braden likened it to a school teacher who could not control the class: "Nice people, too. One looks back with sympathy and a sense of shame. But at the time—was it that they were too nice?—their classes were a shambles. The erasers flew when they turned their backs."[161]

Nixon was in command of the fall campaign. He paraded a litany of accomplishments—the Paris peace talks over the Vietnam War, the diplomatic opening to China, the arms limitation treaty with the Soviet Union, and a number of domestic initiatives. Most of all, he was a strong figure. And if he still aroused suspicion, he was at least a known commodity.

Nixon won all but Massachusetts and the District of Columbia in the fall election. His popular vote margin was 47.2 million to McGovern's 29.2 million; the electoral college cast 520 votes for Nixon and only 17 for McGovern. Nixon's 60.7 percent share of the popular vote stood second only to Johnson's 61.1 percent in 1964.

On the surface, it appeared in 1972 that American politics was entering an age of calm consensus. At the time of the election, the economy was temporarily strong. Moreover, opposition to the Vietnam War had faded as the two sides negotiated in Paris for an end to the war, and the United States had signed an important nuclear arms treaty with the Soviet Union and had made important diplomatic moves with that country and the People's Republic of China. Nixon's landslide victory appeared to be a mandate and a vote of confidence.

But trouble loomed behind the apparent stability and consensus. The war in Vietnam continued, as did the antiwar protests, and generational cleavages remained. The economy experienced the first of many "shocks" in 1973 when the Organization of Petroleum Exporting Countries agreed to ban oil exports to the United States. The economic turmoil that resulted in the United States was topped off with a wage and price freeze. In addition, a warlike atmosphere between the White House and the media (as well as other perceived enemies of the administration who appeared on Nixon's "enemies list") and the mushrooming Watergate scandal combined to create a dark side to U.S. politics in the 1970s.[162]

The Watergate affair was perhaps the greatest political scandal in U.S. history. For the first time, a president was forced to leave office before his term expired. President Nixon resigned on August 9, 1974, when it became apparent that the House of Representatives would impeach him for "high crimes and misdemeanors" and the Senate would convict him. In addition, a number of Nixon aides, including his first attorney general and campaign manager, John Mitchell, would spend time in jail because of the scandal.

At its simplest, the Watergate affair was "a third-rate burglary," followed by a cover-up by President Nixon and his aides. In the summer of 1972, several employees of the Committee to Re-elect the President (dubbed "CREEP") were arrested after they were discovered breaking into and bugging the Democratic National Committee's offices at the posh Watergate complex in Washington. The break-in was not a major issue in the 1972 election, but the next year a Senate committee began an investigation of the entire affair.

During the investigation, a presidential aide revealed that Nixon had secretly taped Oval Office conversations with aides. When the Watergate special prosecutor, Archibald Cox, ordered Nixon to surrender the tapes in October 1973, Nixon ordered Cox fired. But because Nixon's attorney general, Elliot Richard-son, and assistant attorney general, William D. Ruckelshaus, refused to fire Cox, the task was carried out by Solicitor General Robert Bork, igniting a constitutional crisis dubbed the "Saturday night massacre."

Nixon soon handed over the tapes Cox had sought. In the summer of 1974, the Supreme Court ruled that Nixon had to surrender even more tapes, which indicated that he had played an active role in covering up the Watergate scandal. Nixon resigned the presidency when his impeachment and conviction appeared certain. The impeachment articles charged him with obstruction of justice, abuse of presidential powers, and contempt of Congress.

Many students of the Watergate affair maintain that the illegal campaign activities were just part of a tapestry of illegal activities in the Nixon administration—including secretly bombing Cambodia, accepting millions of dollars in illegal campaign contributions, offering government favors in return for contributions, "laundering" money through third parties, wiretapping and burglarizing a wide variety of people thought to be unsupportive of the president, offering executive clemency to convicted campaign workers, engaging in "dirty tricks" to discredit other political figures, compromising criminal investigations by giving information to the people under scrutiny, and using government funds to renovate the president's private residence.[163]

In 1973 Nixon's vice president, Spiro Agnew, resigned after pleading "no contest" to charges of taking bribes while he was governor of Maryland. After Agnew's resignation on October 10, 1973, Nixon named House Minority Leader Gerald Ford, a longtime GOP stalwart, to become vice president under the Twenty-fifth Amendment. Ford, who had never entered a national election, then became president upon Nixon's resignation and quickly attracted the support of the American public with his modest, earnest disposition. He responded to the widespread feeling that Nixon's isolation in the Oval Office had contributed to his downfall by promising to work closely with Congress and to meet with the press regularly.

One month after becoming president, however, Ford ignited a firestorm of criticism with his full pardon of Nixon for all crimes he may have committed while president. Ford testified before Congress that he believed Nixon had suffered enough and that the nation would have been badly torn if a former president were brought to court to face criminal charges. Critics asserted that Ford had made a "deal" in which Nixon resigned the presidency in exchange for the pardon.[164]

Ford selected former New York governor Nelson Rockefeller to be his vice president. Rockefeller received Senate and House confirmation on December 10 and 19, respectively, after long, difficult hearings that centered on his financial dealings.

THE ELECTION OF 1976: JIMMY WHO?

With the benefit of the Watergate scandal and Ford's pardon of Nixon, the Democrats won resounding victories in the 1974 midterm elections. The Democrats' gains of fifty-two House seats and four Senate seats not only created stronger majorities but also reduced the number of members with allegiance to the old system of organizing congressional business.

Virtually unknown to the country at the outset of the campaign, former Georgia governor Jimmy Carter emerged from a field of candidates to win the Democratic nomination and the presidency. His casual and honest approach appealed to many voters.

The moralistic zeal of the "Watergate class" forced major changes on Congress as well as on the presidency and the nation's process of pluralistic political bargaining. The new crop of legislators was so large that it was able to undermine the seniority system that had ordered the way Congress had operated for years. The new system of committee assignments led to a proliferation of subcommittees on which most members had prominent roles. That, in turn, created a fragmented policy-making process—less susceptible to coercion by presidents and party leaders but more susceptible to interest group politics.[165]

The 1976 campaign was the first governed by campaign finance reform legislation enacted in 1971 and 1974. The Federal Election Campaign Act (FECA) of 1971 limited campaign expenditures and required disclosure of campaign receipts and expenditures. The Revenue Act of 1971 created a tax check-off that enabled taxpayers to allocate $1.00 of their taxes for public financing of elections. The FECA amendments of 1974 limited spending and donations for both primary and general election campaigns, established a system of partial public funding of elections, and created the Federal Election Commission to monitor campaign activities.

The Democrats and their eventual nominee, Jimmy Carter, continued to exploit the nation's discontent through the 1976 election. Ronald Reagan, a former movie actor and California governor, added to the Republican Party's vulnerability by waging a stubborn primary campaign against President Ford.

The Democrats appeared headed for a long and bitter nomination struggle for the third time in a row. A few candidates—such as Senators Henry Jackson of Washington and Birch Bayh of Indiana and Governor Wallace of Alabama—had greater stature than others, but their appeal was limited to specific factions of the Democratic coalition. Other candidates included Rep. Morris Udall of Arizona, Sen. Fred Harris of Oklahoma, Sen. Frank Church of Idaho, and Gov. Edmund G. "Jerry" Brown Jr. of California. Church and Brown entered the race late, and Senators Humphrey of Minnesota and Edward M. Kennedy of Massachusetts awaited a draft in the event of a deadlocked convention.

The moderate Carter, whose name recognition in polls stood in single figures when the campaign began, executed a brilliant campaign strategy to win the nomination on the first ballot. Constructing strong organizations for the Iowa caucuses and the New Hampshire primary, Carter won both contests by slim margins. Although liberal candidates Udall and Bayh together polled more votes than Carter, it was Carter who received cover billings on national magazines and live interviews on morning television talk shows.[166] Within a matter of days, Carter went from long shot to front-runner.

Udall performed well in the primaries but never won a single state; he and other liberals were splitting the liberal vote. Udall's chance for a Wisconsin primary win fizzled when Harris refused to back out to create a one-on-one matchup of a liberal with Carter.[167] Carter ran into strong challenges from Church and Brown in later primaries, but he had the delegates and endorsements by the time of the Democratic convention in New York for a first-ballot nomination. The convention itself was a "love fest" with the Democrats united behind Carter and his running mate, Sen. Walter F. Mondale of Minnesota.

The GOP was divided between Ford and Reagan. Ford won the early contests, but Reagan scored big wins in the North Carolina and Texas primaries. Reagan was put on the defensive with his proposals for transferring welfare obligations to the states, but when he focused on foreign policy he had success. For example, he attacked Ford for his policy of détente with the Soviet Union and his negotiation of a treaty that would forfeit U.S. control of the Panama Canal.

In the late summer, with Ford and Reagan locked in a close contest for delegates, Reagan tried to gain the advantage by breaking precedent and naming his vice-presidential candidate before the convention. Reagan's choice—Sen. Richard S. Schweiker of Pennsylvania, a moderate—widened Reagan's ideological appeal but angered many of his conservative supporters. When Reagan tried to force Ford to name a vice-presidential candidate in advance as well, the convention vote on the issue became a crucial test of the candidates' delegate strength. But Ford won that test and the nomination. He selected the acerbic senator Bob Dole of Kansas as his running mate as a consolation prize for disappointed conservatives.

Carter emerged from the Democratic convention with a wide lead over Ford, but the race was too close to call by election day. A number of gaffes—such as Carter's interview with *Playboy* magazine, his ambiguous statements about abortion, and his confused observations on tax reform—hurt the Democratic contender.[168] Ford also gained in the polls when he began to use the patronage powers of the presidency and effectively contrasted his twenty-seven years of Washington experience to Carter's four years as governor of Georgia.

For the first time since 1960, the major candidates took part in televised debates. As the outsider, Carter helped himself by demonstrating a good grasp of national issues and by appealing to Democrats to vote the party line. Ford hurt himself with a claim that Eastern European nations did not consider themselves to be under the control of the Soviet Union.[169] The remark was intended to be testimony to the Europeans' sense of national identity, but it was interpreted as evidence of the president's naiveté.

Carter's main advantage was regional pride. The Democrats had long since lost their hold over the South, but Carter gained widespread support as the first candidate nominated from the region on his own in more than a century. The Democratic Party's many factions—including such big-city mayors as Richard Daley of Chicago and Abraham Beame of New York, civil rights activists, and organized labor—put on a rare display of unity.

Carter defeated Ford by a slim margin, winning 40.8 million votes (50.1 percent) to Ford's 39.1 million (48.0 percent). In the electoral college, 297 votes went to Carter, 240 to Ford. Carter won by pulling together the frazzled New Deal coalition of industrial and urban voters, African Americans, Jews, and southerners. Ford won the West, and Carter won the South, except Virginia. Ford won all the states from the Mississippi River westward except Texas and Hawaii, plus states in his native Midwest like Iowa, Illinois, Michigan, and Indiana. Ford also won Connecticut and the three northernmost New England states—New Hampshire, Vermont, and Maine.

CARTER'S UNCERTAIN LEADERSHIP: 1980

After his election, President Carter's ability to hold the coalition together was limited. The growing influence of the mass media, the fragmenting effects of interest groups, poor relations with Congress, and difficult issues that cut across many different sectors—inflation and unemployment, oil shocks and the more general energy crisis, the Iran hostage crisis, relations with the Soviet Union, and budget austerity moves such as proposed cutbacks in water projects and social welfare—all damaged Carter's governing ability.

As the 1980 election approached, Carter appeared to have lost all but his institutional strength and the reluctance of voters to reject a president for the fourth time in a row. Carter controlled party processes, such as the primary schedule; he had access to key financial support and skilled political operatives; and he shaped much of the political agenda. But Kennedy was hitting him hard from the left, and Reagan and others were hitting him hard from the right. As a result, Carter was unable to forge a lasting consensus on important issues. Kennedy was leading Carter in the polls by a two-to-one margin when he announced

his challenge to the incumbent president in November 1979. But Carter overcame that lead by the start of the nominating season when the seizure of American hostages in Iran rallied the nation around the president and Kennedy made a series of political mistakes. Kennedy was unable to develop campaign themes or answer questions about his personal conduct in the 1969 Chappaquiddick incident in which a woman died after a car he was driving went off a bridge. Other "character" issues, such as Kennedy's alleged "womanizing," and more substantive issues, such as his liberal voting record, also hurt him in a year dominated by conservative themes. Finally, Kennedy's campaign was in financial jeopardy early because of lavish spending on transportation, headquarters, and other expenses.

The campaign of Gov. Jerry Brown of California was unable to find much support for his appeal for recognition of economic and environmental limits. He dropped out of the race in April.

The president was able to manipulate the primary and caucus schedule to bunch together states favorable to him and to match pro-Kennedy states with pro-Carter states. The result was an early, strong Carter lead in delegates. Kennedy came back with some solid primary wins in New York and Pennsylvania, but his campaign by then had been reduced to a vehicle for anti-Carter expressions. Many Kennedy voters hoped for a deadlocked convention at which a third candidate would win the nomination.

Carter won the nomination on the first ballot despite a variety of stop-Carter efforts and Kennedy's attempt to free delegates to vote for any candidate. When Carter won the crucial floor vote on the "open convention" question, Kennedy did not have a chance. The Carter-Mondale ticket entered the fall campaign as a wounded army unable to generate much enthusiasm from the troops.

The Republicans united early behind Reagan. By April 22, 1980, less than two months after the New Hampshire primary, six candidates had dropped out of the race, and George Bush, Reagan's only surviving competitor, was desperately behind in the delegate count. Reagan's campaign experienced an early scare when Bush beat Reagan in the Iowa caucus, but Reagan rebounded, changed campaign managers and tactics, and won a string of primaries and caucuses. By the time of the convention, Reagan was the consensus candidate, and he improved party unity by adding Bush to the fall ticket.

Reagan called on the electorate to replace politics that he said was marked by "pastels," or compromising and uncertain policies, with "bold colors." Reagan's proposed bold strokes included a 30 percent reduction in marginal income tax rates based on a "supply-side" economic theory—which even Bush had said was a dangerous kind of "voodoo economics"—and massive increases in military expenditures. At the same time Reagan criticized Carter's alleged vacillation and his commitment to liberal policies.

President Carter, who was vulnerable as the hostage crisis neared its first anniversary (on November 4, election day) and high inflation and unemployment rates persisted, attempted to portray Reagan as a dangerous, heartless, and inexperienced amateur. Reagan managed to use Carter's attacks to his own advantage by assuming a posture of hurt feelings at the unfair criticism. When in a televised debate Carter attacked Reagan's previous opposition to social welfare programs, Reagan cut him off with a line, "There you go again," that suggested Carter was unfairly and relentlessly distorting Reagan's record.

The greatest controversy of the campaign did not emerge until years later. Books published after the Reagan years charged that the Reagan-Bush campaign negotiated a deal with Iran to delay release of the hostages until after the campaign to embarrass President Carter. Gary Sick, a national security aide for Carter, charged that Reagan campaign officials met with Iranian officials in Europe in the summer of 1980 to arrange weapons sales in exchange for holding the hostages. If true—and many disputed the charges—the deal could have cost Carter the presidency.[170]

Carter strategists also were concerned about the independent candidacy of Rep. John B. Anderson of Illinois, a moderate who dropped out of the Republican race when it became clear that conservatives would dominate that party. After some stronger support in the polls, Anderson stood at about 10 percent for the final two months of the campaign. Carter was concerned that Anderson would take more votes from him than from Reagan, even though analysis of Anderson support suggested otherwise.[171]

Private money almost doubled the amount that Reagan was legally entitled to spend under the federal campaign financing system. Well-organized groups from the "new right," which opposed abortion, gun control, détente, and many social welfare programs, spent lavishly on television commercials and efforts to register like-minded voters. These groups also made a "hit list" of leading liberals in Congress. These candidates were so weakened by the new right's attacks that they put a local and regional drag on an already dragging Democratic ticket.[172]

Polls before election day predicted a close race. Reagan, however, won all but six states and took the White House in an electoral landslide, 489 electoral votes to 49. Reagan won 51 percent of the vote, while Carter managed 41 percent and Anderson 7 percent. Carter ran tight races in ten additional states that could have gone his way with a shift of less than one and a half percentage points. In twenty-one states, Anderson's vote totals made up most or all of the difference between Reagan and Carter. Despite these factors and polls that regularly showed preference for Carter's policy positions, Reagan's victory was impressive. He beat Carter by a better than two-to-one margin in nine states.

Even more surprising than Reagan's electoral landslide was the Republican takeover of the Senate. The new right's targeting of several Senate liberals—such as McGovern, Bayh, Gaylord Nelson of Wisconsin, and John Culver of Iowa—created the biggest Senate turnover since 1958. The Republicans now held the Senate by a 53–46 margin.

President Reagan was able to parlay his claims of an electoral mandate into wide-ranging changes in tax, budget, and military policies. Among other things, he won passage of a three-year, 25 percent cut in tax rates that would reduce federal revenues by $196 billion annually by the time the three-stage program was in place. He also secured omnibus legislation that cut the domestic budget by $140 billion over four years and increased defense spending by $181 billion over the same period. The media hailed

Reagan as the most successful handler of Congress since Lyndon Johnson.

The New Conservative Discourse

Reagan's rise ushered in a new age of conservatism in the American political discourse. The vigorous conservative campaigns for the presidency and Congress were accompanied by a host of new "think tanks" and publications with a restyled set of philosophical and policy pronouncements.

The most celebrated event of the conservative revival was the publication in 1980 of George Gilder's *Wealth and Poverty*, a far-reaching attack on welfare state policies that rested on supply-side economic theory. Gilder argued that free markets and low taxes promoted not only economic efficiency and growth but also other benefits such as family strength and artistic creativity. Gilder's book was a central element of Reagan's campaign for major tax cuts.[173] But the supply-side tracts of Gilder and others were only the most visible signs of the conservative movement. Reagan's criticism of the Supreme Court decisions on abortion and school prayer helped to bring evangelical Christians into the political process. Businesses and conservative philanthropists, meanwhile, sponsored an unprecedented level of public policy research that shaped the debate of elections and government policy.[174]

Reagan's political appeal, according to scholar Garry Wills, turned on his ability to blend contradictory elements of American culture such as capitalism, conservatism, and individualism. While Reagan decried the decline of "traditional American values," for example, he extolled the dynamic economic system that demanded constant change. Wills wrote: "There are so many contradictions in this larger construct that one cannot risk entertaining serious challenge to any of its details. In Reagan, luckily, all these clashes are resolved. He is the ideal past, the successful present, the hopeful future all in one."[175]

Using the "bully pulpit" of the presidency, Reagan was able to overwhelm his opponents with his vision. When Democrats criticized specific Reagan policies, Reagan deflated them with expressions of disdain for "little men with loud voices [that] cry doom."[176] Jeane Kirkpatrick's depiction of Democrats as the "blame America first crowd" neatly expressed the way the Reagan rhetoric foreclosed debate on major policy issues such as the budget and trade deficits, military spending, the U.S. role in the third world, and U.S.-Soviet relations.

By the time the 1984 campaign took place, much of the nation had adopted Reagan's terms of debate. Mondale's strongest performance, in fact, was in the first debate when he congratulated Reagan for restoring national pride and suggested not that Reagan should be ousted but rather that he be given a graceful retirement. Mondale's campaign was basically conservative: he did not propose a single new social program and called the federal budget deficit the nation's top problem.

REAGAN'S 1984 LANDSLIDE

Reagan's popularity dipped to 44 percent in 1983—about the average for modern presidents—but it rebounded when the

Democratic presidential candidate Walter F. Mondale and his running mate, Geraldine Ferraro, the first woman to receive a major party nomination for national office, campaign in the 1984 presidential race.

economy later picked up.[177] As the 1984 election approached, Reagan faced no opposition from Republicans, but a large field of Democrats sought the right to oppose him in the fall.

The Democrats' early front-runner was former vice president Mondale, who had accumulated a wide range of endorsements (AFL-CIO, National Education Association, United Mine Workers, and the National Organization for Women) and an impressive campaign treasury. The more conservative senator John Glenn of Ohio, the first American to orbit the earth, was considered a strong challenger. Other candidates included Senators Gary Hart of Colorado, Alan Cranston of California, and Ernest Hollings of South Carolina, civil rights leader Jesse Jackson, former presidential candidate George McGovern, and former governor Reubin Askew of Florida.

The early results eliminated all but Mondale, Hart, and Jackson just sixteen days after the New Hampshire primary. Hart became the serious challenger to Mondale when he finished second in Iowa and first in New Hampshire, creating an explosion of media coverage. After Mondale recovered, the two fought head-to-head until the convention. Jackson, the second African American to run for the presidency, stayed in the race to promote his liberal party agenda.[178]

After interviewing a wide range of candidates, Mondale selected Rep. Geraldine A. Ferraro of New York as his running mate—the first woman ever to receive a major-party nomination for national office. Representative Ferraro's vice-presidential candidacy probably was a drag on the ticket, not so much because she was a woman but because of the controversy created by her husband's finances and her stand on the abortion question. The controversies hindered the Democratic campaign's effort to articulate its own vision for the nation.[179]

Ferraro appeared knowledgeable and strong in her debate with Vice President Bush, and she often drew large and enthusiastic crowds. But she was stuck in controversy when details of

her husband's questionable real estate, trusteeship, and tax practices became public. Opponents of abortion held prominent and often loud protests at the sites of her speeches, and she got involved in a lengthy public dispute over abortion with Catholic archbishop John O'Connor. Ferraro also did not help the ticket in regions where the Democrats were weak, such as the South and West.

Mondale ran a generally conservative campaign, concentrating on a proposed tax increase to address the unprecedented budget deficit of more than $200 billion and proposing no new social programs. Mondale criticized Reagan's record on the arms race, but he did not outline basic disagreements on other foreign affairs issues. He charged that Reagan, the oldest president in history, was lazy and out of touch. Only late in the campaign, when his speeches became unabashedly liberal and combative, did Mondale create any excitement.

Just once—in the period after the first presidential debate—did Mondale appear to have a chance to defeat President Reagan. Political pundits had marked Mondale as a poor television performer, but the challenger outfoxed Reagan in the debate and afterward appeared to be gaining ground for a few days. Before the debate, Mondale aides had leaked erroneous information that suggested he would make a slashing attack. But Mondale surprised Reagan by adopting a "gold-watch approach" suitable to a family business retiring an old-timer—"sort of embracing a grandfather, and gently pushing him aside."[180] Mondale gave the president credit for helping to restore national patriotism and beginning a national debate on education reform, but he said it was time for new leadership. Reagan appeared confused and, in the rush to demonstrate statistical knowledge of policies, he failed to outline broad themes.

Although the first debate boosted the Mondale campaign's morale, it never brought Mondale within striking range of Reagan—he never came within ten percentage points of Reagan in the polls. Reagan's campaign was a series of rallies with masses of colorful balloons and confident talk about the United States "standing tall" in domestic and world affairs. Reagan was so sure of victory that he made a last-minute trip to Mondale's home state of Minnesota with the hope of completing a fifty-state sweep of the nation.

As it was, Reagan won forty-nine states, with 2-to-1 margins in eight states. Idaho, Nebraska, and Utah each gave Reagan more than 70 percent of the vote. Mondale won only the District of Columbia and his home state of Minnesota, where he beat Reagan by only two-tenths of a percentage point. As for the popular vote, Reagan won 54.5 million votes (58.8 percent) to Mondale's 37.6 million (40.6 percent). In the electoral college, he received 525 votes to Mondale's 13 votes.

Reagan's two landslides and the conservative discourse of his administration led many experts to wonder if they were witnessing a "realignment"—a major shift in political alliances among a variety of social, economic, and ethnic groups.[181] The trend during the 1970s and 1980s appeared to be one of a Democratic hold on congressional and state elections and Republican dominance of presidential elections. Some experts pointed to the electorate's ticket-splitting tendencies as evidence of "dealignment"—a breakdown of the old system without development of an entirely new system.[182]

Perhaps the most noteworthy development of recent years, which fits the dealignment thesis, has been the convergence of the appeal of the two parties. Michael Barone, in *The Almanac of American Politics,* wrote:

Political preferences in the America of the 1940's correlated to a fair degree with income. Republican strength was greater than average in high income states . . . while Roosevelt and Truman carried virtually every state with incomes below the national average. But today there is virtually no correlation between income level and political preference. Utah, with one of the lowest per capita incomes, was one of the nation's most Republican states in 1980. . . . In the Midwest, high income Illinois is more Democratic than low income Indiana.[183]

BUSH'S ASCENDANCY: 1988

The election of 1988 was the first after 1968 in which an incumbent president did not run. With no major figure and no major issues, the campaign was a tumultuous affair. Fourteen candidates struggled to develop an identity with the voters, and the campaign lurched from one symbolic issue to the next, never developing the overarching themes of previous campaigns.

In the absence of any major new issues, and in a time of general peace and prosperity, Republican vice president George Bush won the presidency. Bush defeated Democratic Massachusetts governor Michael S. Dukakis by a margin of 54 percent to 46 percent—48.9 million votes to 41.8 million votes. Bush's electoral vote margin was more impressive, 426–111. A negative campaign and limited voter registration efforts resulted in the lowest voter turnout rate since the 1920 and 1924 race percentages of 49 percent of all eligible voters. Just a little more than 50 percent of all eligible citizens voted for president in 1988.

Bush, benefiting from the Nixon-Reagan presidential coalition, won all the states of the old Confederacy, the entire West except Oregon and Washington, and several northern industrial states. Dukakis originally had hoped to crack the South by selecting a favorite son, Sen. Lloyd M. Bentsen Jr. of Texas, as his running mate, but that tactic failed. Dukakis lost crucial states that he had fought for to the end, such as California, Pennsylvania, Illinois, Ohio, and Missouri. He won New York, Massachusetts, Wisconsin, Minnesota, Oregon, Washington, West Virginia, Iowa, Rhode Island, Hawaii, and the District of Columbia.

President Ronald Reagan's retirement after two full terms created a political void. By most accounts, Reagan was the most popular president since Dwight Eisenhower. His dominance of national politics left little room for other figures to establish presidential stature.

Reagan's fiscal and social policies reduced the possibility for candidates to offer ambitious new programs. The national government's huge budget deficits—which exceeded $200 billion, compared with about $73 billion in the last year of the Carter administration—checked any grandiose new spending plans. The Reagan debt had exceeded the debt of the previous thirty-eight presidents.

President Reagan also had reshaped the dialogue on foreign affairs. He maintained strong opposition to the Soviet Union and other "Marxist" nations with his policies in Nicaragua, Afghanistan, and Angola. He also had projected an image of strength with military action in Libya and Grenada. At the same time, however, he had co-opted his critics by meeting with Soviet leader Mikhail Gorbachev several times and signing a nuclear arms control agreement. Reagan even asserted that the Gorbachev regime was fundamentally different from previous Soviet regimes, which he had called the "evil empire."

The early Republican front-runners were Bush and Sen. Bob Dole of Kansas; former senator Gary Hart of Colorado was considered the early Democratic leader. The campaign got scrambled before it began, however. Hart left the race in 1987 when the Miami *Herald* augmented rumors of Hart's infidelity with a report that he had spent the night with a young model. The newspaper had staked out Hart's Washington townhouse with two reporters, two editors, and a photographer. The investigators sat in a rental car, loitered nearby, and jogged down the street. Hart, considered by many to be the brightest and most issue-oriented candidate, had long faced criticism about his "character."

The Hart story dominated the political news in 1987. Network news programs devoted 132 minutes to Hart, mostly in the first half of the year and, on the GOP side, 32 minutes to the long-shot television evangelist Marion G. "Pat" Robertson. The two front-runners and eventual nominees, Bush and Dukakis, got 28 and 20 minutes, respectively.[184]

Sen. Joseph R. Biden Jr. of Delaware was the next casualty of the media's 1987 concern with character issues.[185] Media reports that he had committed plagiarism on a law school paper and in campaign speeches led to Biden's early exit from the campaign. Biden had been considered a leading candidate because of his experience and strong speaking style.

With Hart and Biden out of the race, the Democrats were in disarray. Dubbed "dwarfs," the remaining candidates—Rev. Jesse Jackson of Illinois, Gov. Dukakis, Rep. Richard A.

After two popular terms as president, Ronald Reagan and wife Nancy pass leadership of the "Reagan Revolution" to newly inaugurated President George Bush and wife Barbara in 1989.

Gephardt of Missouri, Sen. Albert A. Gore Jr. of Tennessee, Sen. Paul M. Simon of Illinois, and former Arizona governor Bruce Babbitt—lacked the combination of extensive government experience and strong national bases many observers thought necessary to win the presidency.

The Republicans had problems of their own. Vice President Bush was the early favorite, and he benefited from his association with President Reagan. But Bush's public fealty to Reagan also created a problem: he was considered a "wimp," unable to stand on his own. Almost every major position Bush had held in his political career was the result of an appointment: ambassador to the United Nations, chair of the Republican National Committee, envoy to China, director of the Central Intelligence Agency, and vice president. Bush had represented Texas for two terms in the House of Representatives and lost two Senate races.

At the outset of the race, Dole was considered a strong contender. As Republican leader in the Senate, he had a high profile in national politics and proven fund-raising abilities. His wife, Elizabeth, was prominent as secretary of transportation. Dole also had a biting wit, which gave spark to his campaigning style but irritated some voters. Other GOP candidates were Rep. Jack Kemp of New York, former secretary of state Alexander M. Haig Jr. of Pennsylvania, former Delaware governor Pierre S. "Pete" du Pont IV, and television evangelist Pat Robertson of Virginia.

The marathon campaign for the nomination began with the Iowa caucuses, a significant event only because of intense media attention. Gephardt barely edged Simon in the Democratic contests, and Dole won the Republican race. The big story was how badly Bush performed: he finished third behind Dole and Robertson.

The Iowa loss caused Bush to emerge from his isolation and confront his rivals for the nomination. (Bush had been the most restrained and cautious candidate as he tried to benefit from the prestige of the White House.) Bush also became more animated

on the campaign trail. As a result of these changes—and a series of television advertisements charging that Dole would raise taxes—Bush beat Dole in the New Hampshire primary. Dole had failed to respond quickly to the Bush offensive, and when he snapped on national television about Bush's "lying about my record," he reinforced his image as a mean-spirited candidate.

Among the Democrats, Governor Dukakis easily won the New Hampshire primary, capitalizing on his regional popularity. Most of the Democratic fire in that race took place between the two runners-up, Gephardt and Simon. Dukakis escaped without any major criticism, and his already strong fund-raising machine went into high gear.

The decisive stage of the GOP campaign was Super Tuesday—March 8—when twenty-two states held presidential primaries or caucuses. Benefiting from a well-organized campaign and his new aggressiveness on the campaign trail, Bush won seventeen of the eighteen GOP contests. Dole staked his campaign on the ensuing Illinois primary, but he lost badly, and Bush was virtually ensured the Republican nomination.

The one issue that threatened Bush throughout 1988 was the Iran-contra scandal. Revelations that the Reagan administration had traded arms to Iran in exchange for the release of hostages held in Lebanon, then used the proceeds illegally to fund the war in Nicaragua, raised questions about Bush's role in the matter. Administration officials admitted lying to Congress, destroying evidence, and operating outside normal government channels; one top official even attempted suicide. The question of Bush's involvement in the affair, however, fizzled after months of inconclusive questioning.

On Super Tuesday, Democratic front-runner Dukakis won Texas and Florida and five northern states, thereby confirming his shaky front-runner status. Civil rights leader Jesse Jackson was the big surprise, however, winning five southern states. Gore won seven states. Even though it was designed to help conservative candidates, Super Tuesday fit Jackson's strengths. Six of the nine states in which Jackson had scored best in 1984 held their contests on Super Tuesday in 1988. Super Tuesday also was supposed to put the South in the national spotlight, but the region received only a few more candidate visits in 1988 (149) than it had in 1976 (145).[186]

The Democratic marathon continued into Illinois, Michigan, and New York. Dukakis took and maintained the lead in delegates with steady wins over Jackson and Gore. Gore finally dropped out after finishing third in a divisive New York primary, and the rest of the campaign was a one-on-one race between Dukakis and Jackson. Only once—after his victory over Dukakis in the Michigan caucuses—did Jackson appear to have a chance to win the Democratic nomination. But in their next encounter, the Wisconsin primary, Dukakis defeated Jackson.

Jackson was a mixed blessing for the party. An energetic campaigner, he attracted support from blacks and from farmers and blue-collar workers who were disgruntled by the uneven rewards of economic growth. But Jackson was considerably to the left of the rest of the party and never had held any government office. Race also was a factor: no political professional believed that a liberal black could be elected president.

Dukakis practically clinched the nomination with his victory over Jackson in the New York primary. The issue of race was at the center of the campaign. New York City mayor Edward I. Koch, a Gore supporter, called Jackson a "radical" and said Jews would be "crazy" to vote for him. Such remarks aggravated tensions between blacks and Jews that had festered since the 1960s. Dukakis avoided the race issue and won the primary.

As the summer conventions approached, Bush and Dukakis each had the full support of his party. The parties' internal divisions were on display as the prospective nominees considered possible vice-presidential candidates. Blacks lobbied for Jackson's selection by Dukakis, while "new right" GOP leaders lobbied against a "moderate" running mate for Bush.

Dukakis selected conservative senator Lloyd Bentsen of Texas as his running mate before the Atlanta Democratic convention. Jackson complained publicly and privately about the decision, but he eventually embraced Bentsen for the sake of party unity. Dukakis hoped Bentsen would be able to help carry Texas: no Democrat had won the presidency without winning Texas since the state became part of the nation in 1845.

The July convention was a success for the Democrats. After a week of Bush-bashing and Democratic conciliation, Dukakis gave an effective acceptance speech peppered with statements in Spanish and Greek. Dukakis left the convention with a double-digit lead over Bush in the polls.

The Republican convention in August did not start out as well. Bush announced his vice-presidential selection, Sen. James Danforth "Dan" Quayle of Indiana, when he arrived in New Orleans. After revelations that Quayle had avoided military service in the Vietnam War by enlisting in the Indiana National Guard, many Republicans criticized Bush's choice. Some even said that Quayle might have to be dropped from the ticket.[187] By the end of the convention, however, the Republicans had weathered the storm. Bush delivered a crisp address, which provided the appealing self-portrait the vice president needed, and moved into the fall campaign for a close battle with Dukakis.

Bush took the offensive immediately after the August GOP convention and hit Dukakis as a "liberal" out of touch with American "values." More specifically, Bush attacked Dukakis for his membership in the American Civil Liberties Union, his veto of a bill requiring Massachusetts teachers to lead children in the Pledge of Allegiance, and a Massachusetts program allowing prisoners time off for weekends. The Bush campaign's "Willie Horton" commercial—which told of a black prisoner raping a woman while out on a weekend release program—was particularly controversial. As Bush pounded away at these symbolic issues (effectively drowning out other major issues such as the national debt, trade deficit, housing, education, U.S.-Soviet relations, the environment, and ethics in government), Dukakis's "negative" ratings with voters soared. Roger Ailes, Bush's media adviser, admitted that the Bush camp knew it would have to define Dukakis. The media themselves had no interest in substance, Ailes pointed out, leaving candidates "three ways to get on the air: pictures, attacks, and mistakes." Thus the Bush campaign spent its time "avoiding mistakes, staying on the attack, and giving them pictures."[188]

Not believing the attacks would affect his standing with undecided voters—and believing they might even hurt Bush—Dukakis did not respond forcefully to the frontal assault until October. By then, however, Bush had effectively defined Dukakis as a newcomer to national politics. Dukakis's counteroffensive in the last two weeks of the campaign came too late.

As Dukakis fell behind Bush, his campaign pinned its hopes on two nationally televised debates. Dukakis performed well in the first debate, but Bush appeared to "win" the second debate. Dukakis failed to gain on Bush.

The only major problem for Bush was Quayle. Most political professionals considered Quayle a "lightweight." The forty-one-year-old Quayle had been a poor student and was a marginal member of Congress.[189] Dukakis said Bush's selection of Quayle amounted to failure in his "first presidential decision." Dukakis compared Quayle to the more experienced Bentsen, who performed much better in a vice-presidential debate. Indeed, in that debate Bentsen gave the campaign perhaps its most memorable moment. Responding to Quayle's assertion that he had as much congressional experience as Jack Kennedy had when he sought the presidency, Bentsen said, "Senator, I served with Jack Kennedy. I knew Jack Kennedy. Jack Kennedy was a friend of mine. Senator, you're no Jack Kennedy."[190]

Public polls revealed that most voters thought that Quayle was a bad choice. The Bush campaign tried to minimize the damage by limiting Quayle's public exposure and carefully scripting his statements. Quayle rarely spoke in major media markets; many of his campaign stops were accessible only by bus. While Bush delivered speeches in several states each day, Quayle often made just one speech before schoolchildren or partisan audiences.

After months of inconsistent and confusing strategy, Dukakis finally developed a strong appeal in the last two weeks of the campaign. He told voters he was on their side and portrayed Bush as a toady to the wealthy. Dukakis said the middle class had been "squeezed" by the policies of the Reagan administration and that the Democrats would provide good jobs, affordable housing and health care, and tough enforcement of environmental protection laws.

But it was not enough. Bush, who had made a fortune in the oil business before entering politics and was the son of a former U.S. senator, persuaded more voters that his experience and values were what they wanted in the very personal choice of a president.

Democrats Regain the White House

In March 1991, in the aftermath of the U.S.-led victory over Iraq in the Persian Gulf War, President George Bush received the highest approval ratings since opinion polling began: around 90 percent of respondents said they approved of his performance as president. But just a year later, Bush was struggling to keep his job—and he failed.

Bill Clinton's victory over Bush in 1992 could have been viewed, on the one hand, as a dramatic shift in American politics. Touting his campaign slogan of "change," the forty-six-year-old Arkansas governor repeatedly blasted the Republican White House for its inattention to domestic problems such as the budget deficit, health care, welfare, civil rights, crime, trade, and economic investment. President Bush, Clinton said, was too obsessed with foreign policy and unconcerned with domestic affairs.

On the other hand, Clinton's election could have been viewed as an aberration. Only the second Democrat elected president since 1968, Clinton got only 43 percent of the vote in a three-candidate race. Voters said they voted against Bush, not for Clinton. The independent candidacy of Texas billionaire H. Ross Perot may have cost Bush the election, as much by tarnishing his reputation as by taking away the votes of the angry middle class. Even people who supported Clinton expressed reservations about his character. Voters reacted warily to reports of Clinton's avoidance of military service in Vietnam, marital infidelity, and conflicts of interest while governor, and to his evasiveness about smoking marijuana as a student. On policy questions, Clinton was well informed, but sometimes he appeared insincere. A label pinned on Clinton in Arkansas—"Slick Willie"—stuck.

THE BUSH STRATEGY

President Bush began the election cycle looking unbeatable. Coasting on the apparent success of his leadership during the Gulf War, Bush appeared to have the strength to lead the United States into what he called the "new world order." In 1989 the countries of the so-called Soviet bloc—East Germany, Poland, Czechoslovakia, Romania, Hungary—had broken from communist rule in a series of nonviolent revolutions. In August 1991 an attempted coup against Mikhail Gorbachev's "perestroika" government in the Soviet Union had failed. Afterward, the Soviet regime—Communist Party and all—had collapsed. The Bush presidency had overseen the most remarkable realignment of world politics since World War II.

Indeed, Bush took credit for presiding over the dramatic changes, but those American "victories" also undermined his position. The Republican Party had dominated recent presidential politics at least partly because of its hawkish policies during the cold war. With the end of the Soviet threat, the GOP no longer had a "gut" issue to use against the Democrats. According to journalist Sidney Blumenthal, "The Cold War's end was not a photo opportunity, a sound bite, a revelation of 'character,' a political consultant's tactic, or even a theme. It was a global sea change as profound as the Cold War's beginning."[191] Bush had a hard time adjusting.

For a while, President Bush looked so strong that many Democrats were reluctant to take him on. The party's leading figures—Gov. Mario Cuomo of New York; Senators Bill Bradley of New Jersey, Al Gore of Tennessee, and Jay Rockefeller of West Virginia; and Rep. Richard Gephardt of Missouri—announced they would not run. Only former senator Paul E. Tsongas of Massachusetts, recently recovered from a bout with cancer, announced his candidacy in spring 1991.

Despite high polling numbers, President Bush might have been doomed from the start. Despite three decades in public life, Bush had never conveyed a coherent identity or campaign theme. His advisers planned to "narrowcast" messages to selected groups until the summer, when Bush would deliver his big "what-I-stand-for" speech. But by that time, Bush's opponent had defined him as weak and unprincipled. His attempt to divert attention to Clinton's foibles only intensified Bush's image as uncertain of his own values and goals.[192]

By the spring of 1992 Bush's base had crumbled. The president had decided to "sit" on his high popularity ratings and win reelection by avoiding mistakes. Bush's chief of staff, John Sununu, summed up the strategy: "There's not another single piece of legislation that needs to be passed in the next two years for this president. In fact, if Congress wants to come together, adjourn, and leave, it's all right with us."[193] The results of this strategy were devastating. In May 1992 a poll found that 76 percent of the public disapproved of the way Bush was handling the economy.[194] His overall approval rating dropped an unprecedented 57 percentage points from the end of the Gulf War to the beginning of the 1992 GOP convention.

A bitter anti-incumbent mood dominated the new campaign year. Nationwide, reformers promoted the idea of term limits for elected officials as a way to sweep out career politicians.[195] Perot, who had parlayed his wealth into a number of headline-grabbing exploits over the years, became a viable independent candidate.[196] His pithy statements about how to "fix" government captured the imagination of the public.

Pennsylvania voters sent a warning shot to the White House when they rejected the 1991 Senate candidacy of Bush's friend and first attorney general, Richard Thornburgh. Democrat Harris Wofford, appointed to the seat that had opened with the death of Sen. John Heinz in April 1991, won on a platform of national health care and a return to domestic priorities—themes that Bill Clinton reprised in 1992. Wofford, a former college president and Kennedy administration official, came from 30 points behind in the polls to win with 55 percent of the vote. It was the highest percentage that any Democrat had received in Pennsylvania senatorial elections. Wofford's campaign was run by a young operative named James Carville.

Bush's major domestic initiative—the budget law passed in October 1990—angered the Republican Party's right wing. Conservatives had long distrusted Bush because of his past moderate positions on taxes, abortion, civil rights, and social programs. The budget act, which increased taxes by $150 billion, broke the pledge of "no new taxes" that Bush had taken in the 1988 presidential campaign.

As the recession and other domestic crises deepened, the president seemed increasingly out of touch. Bush's reported confusion over the use of bar codes at a grocery store symbolized his elite background and isolation. After race riots in Los Angeles drew the nation's attention to the severity of poverty, Bush was photographed teaching baffled-looking urban youths how to use a fishing pole. In a political environment couched in symbolism, these images were ruinous.

Bush had begun his term with less party support than any president in history—the Democrats controlled the Senate by ten seats and the House by eighty-five seats. As a result, Bush's legislative initiatives were routinely labeled "dead on arrival." In 1989, for the first time, the Senate rejected an incoming president's cabinet nominee when it voted down former senator John G. Tower's bid to be secretary of defense. In his dealings with Capitol Hill, Bush had vacillated between confrontation and compromise. In fact, Bush regularly tussled with Congress, vetoing forty-four bills between 1989 and 1992.

THE 1992 PRIMARY SEASON

The Democratic field grew slowly. Besides Clinton and Tsongas, the field included former governor Jerry Brown of California, Senators Thomas Harkin of Iowa and Robert Kerrey of Nebraska, and Gov. L. Douglas Wilder of Virginia. Wilder dropped out, however, before the first contest.

Clinton won the "invisible primaries" before the formal balloting began; he attracted $3.3 million in contributions by the end of 1991. Harkin was second best with a little more than $2 million.[197] The Clinton campaign then organized supporters in most states holding early contests.

By calling himself a "new Democrat," Clinton hoped to separate himself from some of the rejected Democratic candidates of the past: Jimmy Carter, Walter Mondale, and Michael Dukakis. In keeping with this strategy, Clinton promised to move beyond liberal orthodoxy and "reinvent government."[198] His record in Arkansas suggested a willingness to oppose liberal nostrums on issues such as the death penalty, economic growth, and public education.

The centerpiece of Clinton's strategy was to appeal to the "forgotten middle class." Suburbanites, the working class, and southerners and westerners had abandoned the Democratic Party since the late 1960s. Unfortunately for the Democrats, these groups composed a growing part of the electorate. In fact, many pundits argued that these groups gave the Republicans a

"lock" on the presidency.[199] Clinton's goal, then, was to forge a new ideological center and "pick" the lock.

As expected, "favorite-son" Harkin won the Iowa caucuses, winning 76.4 percent of the delegates selected on February 10. Early on, Clinton had led the polling in New Hampshire, but he ran into trouble when the media questioned his character. A woman claimed that she and Clinton had had an affair and that Clinton had helped her to get a state job. Meanwhile, Clinton was reported to have misled an Army Reserves recruiter as part of a scheme to avoid service in Vietnam. And, to make matters worse, at one point Clinton's campaign was almost broke.

But Clinton hit back. Appearing on the television news magazine "60 Minutes" after the January 1992 Super Bowl game, Clinton admitted he had "caused pain" in his marriage but said he and his wife had solved their problems. Hillary Clinton's appearance with her husband seemed to close the matter. Skeptics should vote against Clinton, she said, but they also should drop the character charges.

Tsongas won the New Hampshire primary on February 18 with 33.2 percent of the vote to Clinton's 24.7 percent. Tsongas offered the policy equivalent of castor oil. He said the nation needed to make difficult economic choices such as higher taxes and program cutbacks. He called Clinton, who spoke in favor of a tax cut and the costly Connecticut-built Polaris Navy submarine, a "pander bear."

Clinton, who fell some 20 points in the polls in a month, exuberantly called his second-place finish a victory by noting Tsongas's regional ties and declaring himself the "Comeback Kid." His campaign, however, was out of money and had to be rescued by a $3.5 million line of credit from an Arkansas bank.

Tsongas and Brown won the occasional contest after New Hampshire, but Clinton rolled to the nomination starting with his March 3 victory in the Georgia primary. Kerrey and Harkin dropped out in early March. Clinton's sweep of southern states on "Super Tuesday," March 10, and his decisive wins in Michigan and Illinois on March 17 practically clinched the nomination. But he had a scare when Brown beat him in Connecticut on March 24. He then beat Brown decisively in New York on April 7. Tsongas, by that time an inactive candidate, finished ahead of Brown in New York.

Clinton won thirty-one state primaries with 51.8 percent of the vote; Tsongas, four states with 18.1 percent; and Brown, two states with 20.1 percent.[200] Even as Clinton won state after state and Bush plummeted in the polls, Democratic leaders searched for an alternative; they had grown nervous about Clinton's ability to confront the character issue. In March almost half the Democratic voters in Connecticut's primary said Clinton lacked the "honesty or integrity" to be president.[201] Former governor Brown fed the uncertainty with his relentless attacks on Clinton's ties to special interests. Talk of drafting another candidate continued, but party professionals became resigned to Clinton's nomination.

President Bush faced an unusually pointed challenge from conservative columnist and former White House aide Patrick J. Buchanan, who charged that Bush had betrayed the conservative faith. His main point of attack was the 1990 tax increase. But he also criticized Bush's activism in world affairs, federal support of arts projects that he called "blasphemous," and the nationwide recession.

Buchanan's campaign in New Hampshire, run by his sister, was simple. He wrote his own speeches, showed roughly designed television ads in which people mimicked Bush's "no new taxes" pledge, and mocked Bush's superior campaign organization and resources. According to Buchanan, the "Buchanan brigades" would defeat "King George and his armies." Bush, however, ignored Buchanan's campaign. He sent his wife and other administration representatives to campaign in New Hampshire.

Although in the end Bush won New Hampshire, the media focused on the 37 percent of the vote that the underdog Buchanan received. Buchanan then made a vigorous effort to win some of the southern contests in early March, but he never matched his New Hampshire numbers. Buchanan continued his campaign until June, assured of media attention by virtue of his quixotic quest and uncompromising rhetoric. In the final analysis, however, he did not win any states with his 22 percent of the total primary vote.[202]

Ironically, in taking his hard hits at Bush, Buchanan may have helped to neutralize another protest candidate, former Ku Klux Klan leader David Duke, who had finished second in the Louisiana gubernatorial contest in 1991. Republican leaders were embarrassed by Duke's GOP membership, but he disappeared after a poor showing in New Hampshire.

Perot's on-and-off campaign unsettled Republicans' plans to build on their base in the South and West. Perot's folksy antigovernment rhetoric appealed to voters in the suburbs and high-growth areas of the 1980s—the heart of the GOP base since Richard Nixon's 1968 campaign.

Perot's campaign began where much of the 1992 campaign was waged: on the television talk-show circuit. On the cable TV show "Larry King Live," Perot said in February that he would run for president if volunteers put him on the ballot in all fifty states. He also said he would spend up to $100 million of his own money to fund a "world-class campaign." At one point, Perot appeared to have a chance to win the presidency. Polls in May showed him in second place nationally behind President Bush and winning some southern and western states outright.

As Perot's unofficial campaign progressed, the media raised doubts about his background and grasp of government. For example, Perot had made his fortune by gaining rights to a computer accounting system for government health programs, and it was only his behind-the-scenes lobbying that prompted the Nixon administration to halt a government battle for control of the computer system. On a more personal level, Perot's conspiracy theories about issues such as prisoners of war in Vietnam and political opponents led to speculation about possible paranoia. When asked about the details for his plans to address the budget deficit, improve government efficiency, improve U.S. trade, and address foreign affairs, Perot appeared ill-informed and irritable. Thus by summer more people viewed Perot unfavorably than favorably.

Perot dropped out of the campaign before he had a chance to announce his entry formally. He pointed out that Clinton's se-

Independent H. Ross Perot mounted his 1992 campaign for the presidency by relying on his own money and appearing on the television talk shows, such as here with Larry King.

lection of Sen. Al Gore of Tennessee as his running mate indicated that the Democrats were "getting their act together." He also recognized that his campaign might split the vote badly and send the election into the House of Representatives.

Perot resumed his campaign in the fall, blaming his temporary exit on a Republican "dirty tricks" effort to smear his family. By then the critical reporting had faded. But it was too late for Perot because his erratic behavior had driven away supporters and curious voters alike. Perot also had difficulty finding a credible running mate. His selection of retired admiral James Stockdale became the subject of parody when Stockdale appeared confused and poorly informed during the debate of the vice-presidential candidates.

Even though Perot had no real chance to win, his campaign was significant. He spent $60 million of his own money, mostly to purchase half-hour television advertisements. Some of the ads, dubbed "infomercials," won critical acclaim for their plain talk about the dangers of the federal budget deficit. Perot's bluntness lent credibility to his relentless attacks on Bush.

THE 1992 ELECTION

The communications revolution changed the way the candidates reached voters. For example, candidates appeared in settings once considered undignified for potential presidents. Television talk shows such as "Larry King Live" and "The Arsenio Hall Show," as well as radio programs such as "Imus in the Morning," provided a way for candidates to bypass the establishment media. The blurred lines between news and entertainment were perhaps most evident on cable television in the rock music MTV channel's ongoing coverage of the presidential campaign. New outlets were especially important for candidates facing credibility problems in mainstream media (Clinton) and for the insurgents (Perot and Brown).

Bush's campaign was on the defensive early for using "dirty" campaign tactics. Democrats cited Bush's 1988 "Willie Horton" commercials as evidence of a Republican willingness to appeal to racism and fear. Newspaper citations of the Horton campaign were greater in 1992 than 1988, suggesting that the Democrats eventually got more from the ad's backlash than Republicans got from the original campaign.

Clinton parroted Perot's rhetoric about the evils of special-interest influence in Washington and promised reforms of the campaign finance system. But he also raised money aggressively. The Democrats raised $71 million in 1992, $9 million more than the Republicans.[203] Clinton's selection of moderate senator Gore of Tennessee as a running mate was central to his fall strategy. Gore's service in Vietnam and military expertise countered Clinton's suspect status in foreign policy. Moreover, Gore's Washington experience going back to 1976 helped Clinton to compensate for his own lack of experience. Finally, Gore's reputation as an intellectual—he wrote an acclaimed book about the environment in 1992[204]—contrasted with Vice President Quayle's lightweight reputation.

In his campaign, Clinton benefited from the "year of the woman." Women had supported Democratic candidates in greater numbers than men since the Republican Party dropped its support for the Equal Rights Amendment and abortion rights in 1980. But the Democrats were not able to exploit the "gender gap" until 1992. The galvanizing issue was the allegation that Clarence Thomas, a Bush appointee to the Supreme Court, had sexually harassed a former colleague named Anita Hill. Women were outraged with the Senate Judiciary Committee's handling of the matter, and feminist groups mobilized to increase female representation in politics. The issue put President Bush on the defensive, while Clinton rallied liberals and libertarians alike with his calls for equal opportunity and abortion rights.

The Republican convention in Houston was a turning point in the campaign. Strategists decided to shore up Bush's right-wing support and raise doubts about Clinton's character. The party's platform committee was dominated by the right-wing Christian Coalition. Speeches by Patrick Buchanan, Pat Robertson, and Marilyn Quayle, questioning the Democrats' patriotism and arguing for a rollback of civil liberties, played badly. Bush's lost convention opportunity was apparent in the meager 3 percentage point "bounce" in poll support, compared with Clinton's 17 to 20 percent increase after the Democratic convention.[205]

Clinton ran a sophisticated general election campaign, coordinated from the "war room" in Little Rock by strategists, led by James Carville, who choreographed every aspect of the campaign, from television commercials to talk-show appearances to speechwriting to the bus tours of small towns. The campaign professionals were especially adept at answering charges from the opposition. When Bush attacked, Clintonites issued instant, detailed responses. The quick response prevented Bush's charges from dominating the news cycle.

The Bush-Quayle fall campaign was erratic. Early on, it focused on "family values," critiquing the Democrats as elitists out of touch with ordinary people. Then Bush used the powers of incumbency by announcing billions of dollars in grants to different states. All along, Bush criticized Clinton's character and experience. But the personal attacks often appeared shrill; at one

point, he called Clinton and Gore "bozos" and said "my dog Millie" would be better at foreign policy than they. Bush criticized Clinton's visit to the Soviet Union as a student and suggested that he wanted to import British-style socialism to the United States.

Bush's credibility came under fire in the campaign's final days when a special prosecutor indicted former defense secretary Caspar Weinberger and released a memorandum that indicated Bush had participated in the Iran-contra scandal much more actively than he had acknowledged.

The Clinton-Gore ticket gave the Democrats a solid base in the border states to build on. With Arkansas and Tennessee in the Democratic camp, the Democrats could build outward into the old Confederacy (Georgia, Louisiana, Kentucky), north into the industrial states (Illinois, Michigan, Ohio) and west and north into the farm states (Iowa, Minnesota, Wisconsin). The Democrats had consistently lost those states in presidential elections in the past generation, despite strong support in congressional and statewide races.

The Democrats also built on their core of support in the Northeast (winning all the states from Maine to West Virginia) and capitalized on disgruntlement with Bush in the West (California, Colorado, Hawaii, Montana, Nevada, New Mexico, Oregon, and Washington went for Clinton). That was enough to "pick" the Republican "lock" on the electoral college.

Clinton took only 43 percent of the popular vote but garnered 370 electoral votes. This compared with Bush's 38 percent of the popular vote and 168 electoral votes. Perot's 19 percent share of the vote did not win any states.

The hard anti-incumbent mood of the electorate, stoked by Perot, helped to produce the highest voter turnout rate since 1960. Some 55 percent of eligible voters participated in the election. That participation rate was far below rates of other countries and earlier periods in U.S. history. But it seemed to stem, momentarily, the apathy and resignation of American politics.

SETTING THE STAGE FOR 1996

In 1994 many voters sent a strong message of disapproval with President Clinton's record by electing a Republican Congress. That dramatic event led many political analysts to conclude that Clinton would be a one-term president. But what many had not anticipated was that the new GOP Congress, led prominently by controversial House Speaker Newt Gingrich (Georgia), would incorrectly interpret the 1994 elections results as a mandate for their conservative ideological agenda and then push for substantial—and unpopular—policy reform. This miscalculation provided President Clinton with a new opportunity to redefine himself and to rehabilitate his political future.

While the Republicans strove hard for conservative policy change, Clinton adopted more moderate positions and portrayed himself as a check against the "extremism" of the GOP agenda. That tack proved successful by the end of 1995. With the president and Republican legislators feuding over spending priorities, Congress failed to pass a budget in time to avoid two temporary government shutdowns. As the impasse persisted, the Republican Congress began to appear unreason-

Democratic presidential candidate Bill Clinton talks with young people on a program hosted by the MTV cable channel. The 1992 campaign was revolutionary in the way candidates used nontraditional media to reach voters.

able in the public's eye, and the president benefited from the comparison. This budgetary standoff against Congress was perhaps the single most important event to Clinton's political rehabilitation.

The president entered the 1996 election season with renewed political strength and high approval ratings. In addition to the political miscalculations of the majority in Congress, Clinton benefited from a strengthening economy. A third factor also began to weigh in the president's favor: he lacked an intraparty challenge for renomination, while the GOP nomination contest was an expensive, highly negative, and divisive process.

From the beginning Senate Majority Leader Bob Dole (Kansas) was the clear front-runner for the Republican Party's nomination. He had the broadest party support of any announced candidate, the most prominent endorsements, and the best grassroots campaign organization. Although there never was any serious doubt that he would be the Republican nominee, for several months Dole had to fight off a large group of presidential aspirants including television commentator Pat Buchanan, former Department of Education secretary Lamar Alexander, Texas senator Phil Gramm, Indiana senator Richard Lugar, California representative Robert Dornan, and multimillionaire publisher Malcolm S. "Steve" Forbes Jr.

Of these candidates, initially Gramm appeared to be the most formidable because of his status in the Senate and ability to raise huge sums of money for a campaign. Yet Gramm lacked grassroots support and his campaign faded quickly. Colleague Lugar was highly regarded by party moderates and many opinion leaders, but he ran a bland campaign that dwelt on foreign policy issues that were not driving the Republican electorate. Buchanan had support among many of the dedicated antiabortion conservatives in the party, and he fared surprisingly well in some of the early caucuses and primaries, but most in the GOP considered him too extreme and his campaign too faltered.

The most important opponent to Dole ultimately was the publishing tycoon Forbes, who spent an extraordinary sum of his personal fortune to challenge the front-runner with extensive negative television ads. Although Forbes's campaign failed to dislodge Dole from the front of the pack, it succeeded at raising serious doubts about the senator's ability to beat Clinton. The negative ads also hurt Dole's standing with the wider public and forced him to spend his campaign resources on the nomination battle as Clinton amassed campaign funds for the general election.

Dole's eventual nomination—even after losing the traditionally crucial battleground primary in New Hampshire to Buchanan—did not ensure a united Republican Party to challenge the president. Although Dole had long supported the antiabortion stance of many in his party, social conservatives who made up a crucial bloc of the Republican vote were not convinced of his commitment to their cause. Many considered him too moderate in temperament and too willing to compromise principles. Party moderates worried that Dole would allow the Christian right to force his campaign to adopt positions that would enable the Democrats to once again capitalize on the "extremism" charge.[206]

Even after his nomination was ensured, Dole's campaign failed for weeks to capture the public's attention. In part he appeared too much a part of the GOP agenda in Congress that Democrats had successfully defined as harshly conservative. As senate majority leader Dole had found himself in the difficult position of having to manage his official duties while campaigning for president. This involved promoting the GOP agenda in Congress while at the same time trying to distance himself from its less popular elements. Dole made a bold strategic gamble when he decided to resign from the Senate altogether to campaign full time for the presidency. His emotional departure from the Senate on June 11 temporarily energized his campaign.

At his nominating convention in San Diego, Dole performed a tough balancing act in keeping warring moderates and social conservatives from dividing the party. Dole especially sought to avoid the kind of negative publicity that had surrounded "family values night" at the 1992 GOP convention in Houston.[207] The Republicans struck an awkward compromise: although the party platform was very conservative and kept the antiabortion plank, the convention that the country saw on television was moderate in tone and did not feature prime-time addresses by controversial figures such as Buchanan and television evangelist Pat Robertson.

Dole surprised many with two bold campaign moves. First, he selected as his running mate former New York representative and secretary of Housing and Urban Development Jack Kemp, who earlier had endorsed Forbes. Second, Dole proposed an across-the-board 15 percent income tax cut. This proposal was especially surprising because Dole had cultivated a well-deserved reputation as a "deficit hawk" who opposed supply-side economic theory. Yet to energize his lagging campaign, Dole abandoned his lifelong approach to economic policy. Although Dole succeeded in attracting attention with this move, not all of it was positive as many political analysts focused on the contradictions between his tax cut proposal and earlier statements.

CLINTON'S REELECTION

Although polls throughout 1996 showed Clinton with a commanding lead against Dole, those same polls pointed to voter uneasiness with the president's character. Because of continued negative media coverage resulting from Whitewater-related charges, the badly handled White House firing of its travel office staff, and a sexual harassment lawsuit against Clinton, most of the public believed that their president was an individual of unsatisfactory personal character. Yet the polls also indicated that Americans would reelect a flawed president because of their uneasiness with the Republican nominee, their low opinion of the Republican majority in Congress, and their general satisfaction with the state of the economy.

Throughout the campaign season, Clinton often seemed to be running against the unpopular Gingrich and the Republican Congress more than he was taking on Dole. What made Clinton's campaign so strong, in part, was his governing strategy of what one key aide called "triangulation": that is, separating himself from the unpopular elements of both political parties and establishing a less partisan identity at the center of the political spectrum. To achieve that end, Clinton adopted a number of policy initiatives that were conservative, but also largely popular. He signed a welfare reform bill that liberals in his party detested, pushed for imposition of a V-chip in televisions to allow parents to screen program content for children and for a television program rating system, advocated curfews for teenagers and school uniforms as well as mandatory drug tests for sixteen-year-olds applying for driving licenses, proposed a balanced budget by the year 2002, and extolled his record in reducing the federal budget deficit. Clinton also stayed true to his Democratic roots by opposing congressional efforts to reduce Medicare spending and weaken environmental regulation and

by proposing new government programs to make college education more affordable.

Clinton's strategy was brilliant. He effectively took away from Dole's campaign a number of issues that usually help Republican presidential candidates, such as welfare reform, deficit reduction, and family values. He kept his Democratic base by positioning himself as the only viable check against the "extremism" of the Republican Congress.

From a stylistic standpoint, the Clinton and Dole campaigns could not have been more different. Admirers and critics alike agree that Clinton was an effective campaigner and a strong communicator. By contrast, despite protestations by those who know him to be a warm and humorous person, Dole projected the image of a threatening and humorless politician. Despite a vigorous campaign, Dole never overcame the uneasiness that most voters felt about him personally. In past campaigns he had acquired the negative persona of a political "hatchet man" and that image stuck with him throughout the 1996 race. Indeed, Dole tried so hard to change that image that he spent months refusing to attack Clinton's most serious political weakness: his character. When implored by partisan Republicans to attack the president, Dole would reply that he considered Clinton "my opponent, not my enemy." In his two debates with Clinton, Dole did little to improve his public image, as his presentational style was stiff and somewhat harsh—in large contrast to Clinton who projected a much more assuring image.

In the last weeks of the campaign, when it was clear that Dole had no realistic chance of winning, the Republican candidate made a final gamble: he decided finally to attack the president's character and to make it an overriding theme of the campaign. Dole's attacks on the president made a difference in the campaign polls when the news media began to report on questionable fund-raising practices by the Democratic National Committee (DNC) and meetings between foreign lobbyists and Clinton. Stories of unethical and possibly illegal Democratic campaign contributions dovetailed with the Dole message that Clinton lacked good character—and that such a fault was unsuitable for the person serving as president.

Clinton perhaps further hurt himself when he avoided directly confronting the negative stories about the fund-raising practices of his party. Instead, he protested that candidates had no choice but to raise funds and campaign under a flawed system and that, if reelected, he would propose fundamental campaign finance reform. Although this negative publicity and the Dole charges were not enough to deny Clinton's victory, just days before the election one major poll by the Zogby Group for Reuters News Agency placed Clinton's lead at only 7 percent, significantly below the double-digit margins he had maintained throughout the race.[208]

The Reform Party candidate, billionaire Perot, also benefited somewhat from the negative Clinton press. Although he had never been a serious factor in 1996 as he had been as an independent candidate in 1992—and as a result was excluded from the presidential debates—Perot's support increased by several percentage points in the late polls. But in the end, Perot had little impact on the elections. Because of a perceived strong econo-

President Bill Clinton and Vice President Al Gore accept their renomination at the Democratic National Convention in August 1996. In the general election Clinton became the first Democratic president reelected to a second term since Franklin Roosevelt in 1936.

my and a substantial reduction in the federal debt, the public frustration with the two major parties that had given growth to Perot's candidacy in 1992 simply did not exist in 1996.

As the Dole campaign emphasized the character issue, his senior staff were aware that the *Washington Post* was investigating a story about a past marital indiscretion by their candidate. In a controversial decision, the *Post* decided not to publish the information it had gathered about an extramarital affair Dole had in 1969. The newspaper's decision to not publish even after confirming beyond any doubt all the facts angered Clinton partisans who felt that the *Post* had displayed a double standard. Clinton, of course, had been subjected to unrelenting coverage of allegations of extramarital affairs, and these stories had always played a key role in the president's reputation for poor character. Had the newspaper published the story late in the campaign there is little doubt that it would have had an adverse impact on Dole's late surge in the polls that had largely been driven by the character issue. The *Post*'s editor concluded that the story had no relevance to the issue of Dole's qualification to be president—a decision that most journalists thought should have been left to an informed electorate.[209]

Clinton easily won reelection with 49.2 percent of the popular vote and 379 electoral votes to Dole's 40.7 percent and 159 electoral votes. Reform Party candidate Perot polled 8.4 percent of the vote, less than half of his 1992 total, and received no electoral votes.[210] Clinton's victory made him the first Democrat to win reelection since Franklin Roosevelt won his second term in 1936. He became the first Democrat to be elected to the presidency along with a Republican-controlled Congress. Clinton won every state he had captured in 1992, except for Georgia, Montana, and Colorado. However, he picked up Florida and Arizona—becoming the first Democratic presidential candidate to win Florida since 1976 and first to win Arizona since 1948. The so-called gender gap was key to Clinton's victory: while the male vote was evenly split between the two candidates, Clinton won

the female vote by 16 percent, the largest margin ever. Clinton also beat Dole among every age group and was the clear choice of minorities: he received 80 percent of the black vote and 70 percent of the Hispanic vote.[211]

Yet three facts remained discouraging for Clinton. First, for the second straight election he had failed to win a majority of the popular vote. Second, voter turnout was less than 50 percent, the lowest since 1924. Third, Democrats failed to regain control of the Congress, despite the unpopularity of Gingrich and many of his Republican colleagues. Given this scenario, it was difficult for the president to credibly claim that he had achieved any kind of mandate from the American people.

Exit polling data suggested that the incumbent Clinton indeed benefited from positive public feelings about the economy. In one voter poll conducted by numerous news organizations about 60 percent of the respondents said that the economy was doing well. Those respondents heavily favored Clinton. In 1992 the exit polls found that less than 20 percent said the economy was doing well, a situation that had benefited the challenger Clinton.[212]

Perhaps what was most remarkable about the 1996 national elections was just how little had actually changed, despite the two major parties having spent about $500 million on campaign activities. Political analysts have aptly referred to the 1996 elections as reaffirming the status quo, a dramatic difference from both the 1992 and 1994 elections in which voters expressed frustration with the existing political arrangement and sought substantial changes in their government.

2000 Cliffhanger: GOP Retakes the Presidency

The last presidential election of the twentieth century, the closest in forty years, brought the nation to the brink of a constitutional crisis that was narrowly averted only after an unprecedented thirty-six days of rancorous arguing and litigation over who won, Democrat Al Gore or Republican George W. Bush. The eventual outcome, with Texas governor Bush the official winner, did little to unite the electorate, which had split a hundred million votes almost evenly between the two major party candidates. The lingering bitterness put a damper on the January 20, 2001, inauguration of Bush as the forty-third U.S. president.

Although Gore, the departing vice president, clearly won the national popular vote in the 2000 race by more than a half-million votes, Bush claimed the 25 electoral votes of Florida, where the election had been extremely close. Ultimately the state's Republican administration, headed by Gov. Jeb Bush, certified his brother as the popular vote winner in Florida, raising the GOP candidate's nationwide electoral vote total to 271—one more than he needed to win. Gore unsuccessfully contested the election on grounds that the state had stopped the recounts prematurely, leaving thousands of machine-processed ballots not subjected to the scrutiny of human eyes in a hand recount.

In the end, a sharply divided U.S. Supreme Court halted the Florida count, effectively deciding the election in Bush's favor. It was the first time the Court had taken up a disputed presidential election, let alone the first time it had gone against its traditional states' rights principles to overturn a state judiciary in such a matter. And in a historic election studded with anomalies, "firsts," and ironies, the Court for the first time immediately released audio tapes of its hearings on the suit, *Bush v. Gore.*

The tumult focused new attention on proposals to abolish or reform the electoral college system. It also brought to light the need to modernize the problem-prone voting systems still in use in many states besides Florida. And it exposed serious flaws in the technology that broadcast media rely on to project election results minutes after the polls have closed. Repercussions of the event would be felt for many years to come. *(See box, In Wake of 2000 Election "News Disaster," p. 218.)*

During the weeks of contentious legal maneuvering over the Florida vote, partisan tempers flared throughout the United States. Large groups of demonstrators in Florida and Washington, D.C., shouted at the television cameras and waved signs supporting Bush and his vice-presidential choice, Richard B. Cheney, or Gore and his running mate, Joseph I. Lieberman. In a play on the Gore-Lieberman campaign signs, Bush supporters held up "Sore-Loserman" placards. Gore stalwarts retaliated with "Count the Vote" chants and signs.

In the midst of the uproar, Cheney experienced his fourth (an apparently mild) heart attack. Doctors at George Washington University Hospital in Washington used angioplasty to install a stent, an expandable metal tube, in Cheney's heart to open a blocked artery. Within a few days Cheney was back on the job as head of Bush's transition team.

Bush's victory marked the fourth time in U.S. history that the popular vote loser gained the presidency. The first such election, in 1824, was won by John Quincy Adams, who, like Bush (son of former president George Bush), was the son of a president, John Adams. Although Andrew Jackson won the 1824 popular vote, none of the four candidates received the required electoral vote majority and the House of Representatives decided the election in Adams's favor. All four candidates represented factions of the Democratic-Republican Party. In an 1828 rematch with Adams, Jackson won the presidency and changed his party's name to Democratic.

The second contested presidential election, in 1876, was more analogous to the Bush-Gore dispute in that it too involved charges of irregularities in the election process. New York Democrat Samuel J. Tilden won the national vote against Ohio Republican Rutherford B. Hayes, but controversies over the popular votes in three southern states, including Florida, led to rival sets of electoral vote results being sent to Congress from the three states. Lacking a procedure for resolving the dispute, Congress formed a bipartisan special commission, including Supreme Court justices, that gave the votes to Hayes in return for concessions to the South. Hayes thereby won the presidency by a single electoral vote, a margin only one vote lower than Bush's.

In 1887 Congress enacted the Electoral Vote Count Act, specifying procedures for settling electoral vote disputes. One year later Republican Benjamin Harrison won the 1888 presidential election even though Democrat Grover Cleveland received more popular votes. The 1887 act did not come into play, however, because Harrison decisively won the electoral college vote, 233 to 168. *(See "Last of the Old Order: 1824," p. 232; "The Compromise of 1876," p. 248; "The 1888 Republican Recovery," p. 251; and Chapter 18, The Electoral College.)*

Had the Supreme Court not intervened in 2000, it was conceivable that Florida might have sent competing sets of electors' votes to Congress. Although that did not happen, the rules of the 1887 act thwarted efforts by some House members to challenge Florida's electoral votes. In one of the ironies of the election, it fell to Gore as Senate president to reject his supporters' objections.

It was the first time in U.S. history that the outcome of a presidential election had been contested in the courts. And it was the first time that the U.S. Supreme Court had taken up a lawsuit, brought by Bush, related to a presidential election. The Court traditionally had left such matters to Congress or to the states. *(See Bush v. Gore, p. 1557 in Vol. II.)*

THE PRELIMINARIES

The prolonged dispute over Florida's crucial vote overshadowed all other aspects of the 2000 presidential election, including a rather lackluster primary season dominated throughout by Gore on the Democratic side and Bush on the GOP's. Both locked up their nominations early, despite some strong opposition, primarily from Arizona senator John McCain against Bush and former New Jersey senator Bill Bradley against Gore.

Bush entered the race in early 1999 and quickly established himself as the favorite of the Republican establishment and its campaign donors. Without a sitting Democratic president to compete against, the contest attracted a dozen hopefuls for the GOP nomination. But even before the kickoff Iowa caucuses in January 2000 half of the field dropped out, including former vice president Dan Quayle, former Tennessee governor Lamar Alexander, and Elizabeth Dole, head of the Red Cross and wife of 1996 nominee Bob Dole, who said she was unable to compete with Bush's fund-raising prowess. Conservative commentator Pat Buchanan, a past contender, decided instead to seek the Reform Party nomination.

By early February, Bush and McCain remained the only serious contenders. McCain upset Bush in the New Hampshire and Michigan primaries, but Bush went on to win a cluster of March 7 primaries and enough convention delegates to clinch the nomination. Publisher Malcolm S. "Steve" Forbes Jr., who finished third in New Hampshire, ended his campaign after a less impressive showing in Delaware.

McCain, a former Vietnam prisoner of war and cosponsor with Sen. Russell Feingold of Wisconsin of the bipartisan campaign finance reform legislation, was perceived as a moderate despite his solid conservative voting record in the Senate. This, and his penchant for bluntness, appealed to many non-Republicans, who could vote in the growing number of open or semi-open GOP primaries. In all, McCain defeated Bush in seven of the eighteen primaries he entered. But McCain eventually endorsed Bush and was the only member of Congress accorded a

George W. Bush and Al Gore compete for moderator Jim Lehrer's attention during the final presidential debate held October 17 in St. Louis. Although Gore was given a slight edge in most disinterested postdebate analyses of who won or lost, Bush did better than expected, and, presenting a more likable persona, improved his standing with voters over the course of the three debates.

prime-time speaker's slot at the party's nominating convention in Philadelphia.

For Gore, the nomination challenge from Bradley was short and sweet. Bradley failed to win a single primary and dropped out of the race in early March. In a speech to the Democratic convention at Los Angeles, Bradley expressed his support for Gore.

After the conventions Gore, more so than Bush, faced a vote-siphoning threat from the Green Party candidate, consumer advocate Ralph Nader, who received almost 1 percent of the presidential vote in 1996 and was aiming for 5 percent in 2000—a level that would ensure federal campaign funding for the Greens in the 2004 election. Although Republican swing voters were unlikely to switch to corporation-basher Nader, disaffected liberals who supported Bradley found Nader an attractive alternative.

With polls continuing to show the electorate almost evenly divided, the major party race settled down to basically a personality contest between two Ivy Leaguers—Gore (Harvard) and Bush (Yale). The public perceived Bush as personable but perhaps not so intelligent as Gore, despite Bush's master's degree from Harvard's business school. Although known privately as humorous, Gore was seen publicly as somewhat wooden. In the first of their three debates, Gore came off as smart-alecky against Bush, the self-styled "compassionate conservative." In their subsequent debates, Gore toned down his grimacing and head-shaking at Bush's remarks.

Gore's greatest asset was his experience, sixteen years in Congress and eight years in the vice presidency, against Bush's six years as Texas governor. But being vice president was no guarantee of success. Only four sitting vice presidents, including Bush's father in 1988, had been elected president. And the vice presidency was not a compelling qualification for promotion. As political scientist George O. Jones observed, "Most of them couldn't win the nomination on their own without being the vice president."[213]

Both candidates took a lot of negative press and ribbing from late-night comedians about their speaking habits—Bush for malapropisms and Gore for exaggerations. Bush, for example, in one off-hand statement derided people who regard Social Security as "some kind of federal program," which of course it was. Among Bush's other bloopers, as quoted by *Washington Post* columnist Michael Kelly:

On education: "My education program will resignate among all parents." On foreign policy: "A key to foreign policy is to rely on reliance." On whether Social Security recipients will receive the same benefits under his plan as under the current system: "Maybe, maybe not." On his budget proposal: "It's clearly a budget. It's got a lot of numbers in it."[214]

Gore's most ridiculed statement was about his purported claim of "inventing" the Internet. What he actually said on a CNN program, however, was: "During my service in Congress I took the initiative in creating the Internet"—referring to his sponsorship of legislation that funded the early development of the technology. Despite the alleged "liberal bias" of the news media, a preconvention study by the Pew Research Center and the Project for Excellence in Journalism found that most news coverage portrayed Gore as an exaggerator or as scandal tainted (for his role in the Democrats' 1996 fund-raising practices), while Bush was usually referred to more positively as "a different kind of Republican."[215]

The election had been expected to be close. Bush and Gore ran neck-and-neck in public opinion polls, right up to election day. Conditions were also ripe for a tight race. "Not since 1960 has there been a similar convergence of voting trends," political analyst Rhodes Cook wrote two months before the election. He noted that John F. Kennedy won the 1960 popular vote against Richard Nixon by two-tenths of a percentage point (even closer than Gore's five-tenths of a percentage point), although Kennedy had a comfortable lead in electoral votes. "This time the roles of the two parties are reversed," Cook wrote, "as it is the Republicans who are trying to regain the White House after an eight-year absence. And they begin with a larger cache of electoral votes than the Democrats."[216]

From the outset, the election was Gore's to lose. It is almost axiomatic that the party in power retains the White House in times of peace and prosperity. With President Clinton ineligible to succeed himself, Gore stood to inherit the advantage of running on Clinton's successes, especially an economy that had gone from record federal deficits to record surpluses, which opened the prospect of retiring the $3.7 trillion national debt while safeguarding Social Security, Medicare, and other popular but expensive social programs. Clinton could also claim legislative successes in welfare reform and the North American Free Trade Act as well as foreign policy efforts in Bosnia, Kosovo, Northern Ireland, and the Middle East. On the other hand, Republicans controlled Congress for six of Clinton's eight years in office.

Despite his high job approval ratings, Clinton himself was perhaps Gore's biggest handicap. Bush and other Republican candidates tried to saddle Gore with the sins of the Clinton administration, particularly Clinton's December 1998 impeachment for lying under oath about his affair with Monica Lewinsky

Countdown in Florida

The following is a day-by-day chronology of the events surrounding the disputed presidential election results from Florida in the 2000 race between Republican candidate George W. Bush and Democrat Al Gore.

November 7, 2000. Election in Florida too close to call, with Bush holding narrow lead. TV networks retract premature reports declaring Gore winner of state's twenty-five electoral votes.

November 8–10. Gore calls Bush to concede early November 8, then calls back to withdraw concession. Gore seeks hand recounts in four largely Democratic counties. Bush has unofficial 1,784-vote lead November 9. After all but one of Florida's sixty-seven counties complete machine recount required by state law, Bush lead falls to 327 votes.

November 11–14. Broward, Miami-Dade, Palm Beach, and Volusia Counties undertake manual recounts requested by Gore; federal court on November 13 rejects Bush bid to block hand counts; Volusia finishes recount November 14.

November 13. Florida secretary of state Katherine Harris says she will enforce state law deadline of November 14 for counties to submit returns and will not include manual recounts; election boards in Volusia and Palm Beach Counties ask state court judge to overturn deadline.

November 14–16. Leon County Circuit Judge Terry P. Lewis says Harris must justify her position on deadline; Harris reaffirms decision November 15; Lewis hears new round of arguments November 16.

November 17. Lewis upholds Harris's decision to disregard manual recounts, but Florida supreme court bars certification of state results pending oral arguments on November 20; federal appeals court rejects Bush suit over manual recounts.

November 18. Bush lead grows to 930 votes with absentee ballots; Bush campaign criticizes Democrats for challenging absentee votes from military.

November 21. Florida supreme court rules manual recounts must be included in presidential race if submitted to Harris by 5:00 p.m. Sunday, November 26.

November 22–24. Bush running mate Richard Cheney has heart attack, leaves Washington hospital two days later after surgery to insert stent in artery. Shouting, fist-waving crowd, including Republican congressional aides, tries to enter private room where recounts resume in Miami-Dade. County stops recount, pleading too little time and denying intimidation by the demonstrators. State supreme court on November 23 rejects Gore suit to force Miami-Dade to resume counting. U.S. Supreme Court agrees to hear Bush appeal of Florida supreme court action allowing extended deadline for certifying presidential race.

November 25–26. Manual recounts: Broward finishes November 25; Palm Beach falls just short of completion November

when she was a White House intern. The Republicans' strategy was to run against "Clinton-Gore" rather than against Gore alone—even though Gore's marital fidelity was not at issue.

Conservative congressional Republicans were still angry at Clinton for escaping removal from office through the impeachment process. In November 1998, with impeachment looming, Clinton became the first president since Franklin D. Roosevelt in 1934 to gain House seats at a midterm election. He made a net gain of five seats and got rid of his nemesis, Speaker Newt Gingrich, who resigned from Congress in reaction to the GOP setback. The Speaker-designate, Robert L. Livingston of Louisiana, also resigned after admitting an extra-marital affair. Then, in a political twist of the knife, Clinton handily won acquittal from the Senate in his impeachment trial.

In the 2000 campaign, however, neither the Republicans nor the Democrats openly raised the "character issue." (The *Washington Post* called impeachment "2000's Stealth Issue.").[217] But Gore's need to distance himself from Clinton's indiscretions was implicit in his choice of Lieberman as his running mate. An Orthodox Jew, the first of his faith to run on a major party ticket, Lieberman was known for speaking out on moral issues and family values. Although he voted in the Senate to acquit Clinton, Lieberman had publicly taken the president to task for his dalliance with Lewinsky. On the Republican side, Bush's frequent pledges to "restore the honor and dignity" of the presidency also were a thinly veiled reference to impeachment.

Some Gore supporters felt that he perhaps distanced himself from Clinton too much, thereby sacrificing the opportunity to take his share of the credit for the booming economy and other positive aspects of the Clinton legacy. Clinton himself was said to feel "underused" by the Gore campaign. By the final weeks of the campaign Gore became less reluctant to run on Clinton's record, but it was too late to make much of an impression on undecided voters.

With the cold war over and most people better off than they were eight years earlier, traditionally Democratic pocketbook and social issues dominated the campaign—Social Security, education, health care, abortion rights, and gun control. The huge federal surpluses fueled the money issues, with Bush pushing for tax cuts and heavier outlays for antimissile research and development. Gore pledged a "lockbox" for Social Security and criticized Bush's concept of allowing workers to divert part of their trust fund contributions to private investment accounts.

26. Harris announces November 26 that state elections canvassing board certifies Bush as winner by 537-vote margin; Bush claims victory, says he and Cheney are "honored and humbled" to have won Florida's electoral votes.

November 27–29. Gore formally contests the Florida election on November 27. He sues in Leon County Circuit Court, in Tallahassee, claiming the number of legal votes "improperly rejected" and illegal votes counted in Nassau, Palm Beach, and Miami-Dade Counties is enough to change outcome. Judge N. Sanders Sauls orders ballots brought to Tallahassee for possible counting. More than one million ballots are trucked with police escort to the state capital.

December 1. U.S. Supreme Court hears Bush appeal of deadline extension. Florida justices refuse to order revote requested in Palm Beach County because of controversial "butterfly ballot" used there.

December 2–3. Judge Sauls hears testimony on whether 13,000 ballots from Miami-Dade and Palm Beach Counties should be manually counted. Both sides call witnesses on reliability of punch-card voting systems.

December 4. Sauls rejects Gore's request for manual recount and refuses to decertify Bush as winner. U.S. Supreme Court asks state high court to explain its November 21 action allowing manual recounting and extending deadlines.

December 8–9. Florida justices order hand count of ballots on which machines found no vote for president. U.S. Supreme Court unexpectedly halts the hand counts the next day.

December 10–11. U.S. Supreme Court receives briefs and hears arguments in *Bush v. Gore.*

December 12. U.S. Supreme Court splits 5–4 in ruling for Bush against further hand counts. Florida legislature convenes special session to meet the federal deadline for designating presidential electors. Twenty states miss the deadline by a few days.

December 13. Gore concedes election, congratulates Bush and jokingly adds "and I promised him that this time I wouldn't call him back."

December 18. Presidential electors meet in state capitals to cast votes.

January 6, 2001. Congress meets in joint session to count electoral votes. As Senate president, Vice President Gore presides over his own defeat. Twenty Gore supporters, mostly Congressional Black Caucus members, try to block Florida's votes but Gore rejects each representative's objection because none has also been signed by a senator as the 1887 Electoral Vote Count Act requires. One District of Columbia elector, Barbara Lett-Simmons, withholds her vote from Gore in protest of the District's lack of representation in Congress. Final electoral vote tally is 271 for Bush, 266 for Gore with one abstention.

January 20. Inauguration of Bush as president and Cheney as vice president. Protests, largely nonviolent, mar—but do not disrupt—the inaugural parade.

Bush's conservative stance on gun control brought him $1.7 million in support from the National Rifle Association (more than the NRA's independent expenditures for all candidates in 1996). In all, the Bush campaign raised almost $100 million, mostly from individuals, allowing it to decline federal grants and the spending limits that go with them. The Gore campaign accepted federal funding.

THE LONG ELECTION NIGHT

Problems with the crucial Florida vote erupted almost immediately on election day November 7, 2000. Voters in Palm Beach County reported difficulties with an unusual "butterfly" punch-card ballot. Some Democratic voters there thought that they had inadvertently voted for Reform Party nominee Pat Buchanan instead of for Gore. In some of the other twenty-four counties using outmoded punch-card systems, but with regular ballot forms, voters said they were unable to punch out the hole for the candidate of their choice.

Within hours, as news of the problems spread, people around the world became familiar with the obscure noun *chad*, singular or plural, meaning the tiny piece of paper that is pushed out in a punch-card system. If the chad is only dented (dimpled) or partially dislodged, the voting machine may not register the punch as a vote. Therein lay the basis for much of the contention in the days and weeks that were to follow.

Another serious problem emerged shortly after the polls closed, this one having to do with the system—based on exit polling—devised by the news media to project election winners before the votes are counted. The system is uncannily accurate, but its worst and most embarrassing mistake happened at 7:47 p.m. EST when the broadcast networks, using Voter News Service (VNS) data, projected Gore as the winner in Florida. People were still voting in Florida's western panhandle, in the central time zone, when the election was called for Gore. A short time later, the networks retracted and said Florida was too close to call. (*See box, "Countdown in Florida,"* p. 298.)

In the early hours of November 8 the news reports put Bush ahead. Gore called Bush from Nashville and told him he was prepared to concede. Later, after being advised that there might be a recount in Florida, Gore called again to Bush in Austin. "You mean you're retracting your concession?" a surprised Bush reportedly asked. "You don't have to get snippy about it," Gore is said to have replied.

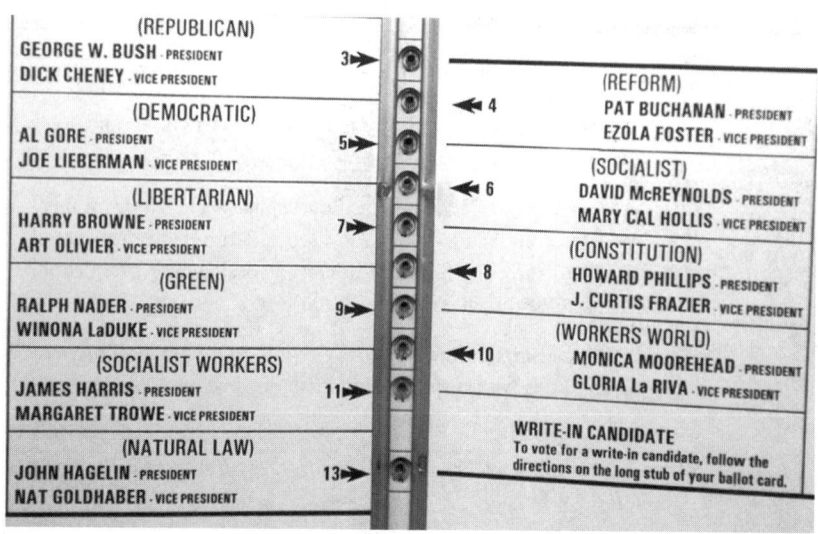

The "butterfly" ballot used in Palm Beach, Florida, confused some voters who, intent on voting for Al Gore, punched out the second hole from the top, recording a vote instead for Reform Party candidate Patrick J. Buchanan (listed on the right side). The confusion probably cost Gore enough votes to swing the state, and thus the electoral college majority to Bush.

Weary television journalists apologized repeatedly for confusing their viewers during the long election night, which finally extended into weeks. "We don't just have egg on our face," said NBC's Tom Brokaw, "we have an omelet." CBS's Dan Rather said, "If you're disgusted with us, frankly I don't blame you."

Besides leading nationwide in the popular vote, Gore outside of Florida led in the electoral college vote, 267 to 246 (after the counting of the absentee vote in Oregon and New Mexico concluded several days later). The entire 2000 presidential election therefore hung on the final results of the popular vote in Florida, which would determine the winner of the state's twenty-five electoral votes.

The close election triggered an automatic machine recount, showing Bush ahead by about 300 votes in Florida. But the Gore camp focused on the thousands of votes that the machines rejected as undervoted, showing no vote for president, or overvoted, showing more than one vote for presidential candidates. Only a manual count of those ballots could discern votes that the machines could not detect, Gore lawyers argued. The Democrats' war cry became, "Every vote counts; count every vote."

In what may have been a tactical mistake, Gore did not request an immediate statewide revote or recount. Instead his lawyers fought to keep hand counts going where Gore was picking up votes, in mostly Democratic counties such as Broward, Miami-Dade, and Volusia, and in Palm Beach County where the butterfly-ballot had recorded an unlikely 3,407 votes for Pat Buchanan, three times more than he received elsewhere in the state. Buchanan himself said it appeared he received votes meant for Gore. Just as fiercely, the Bush forces fought to stop the hand counts. They argued that the votes had been legally counted and recounted, including military and other absentee ballots that favored Bush, and that the canvassers had no uniform standards for gauging the difference between a vote and a nonvote on a punch-card ballot. Allowing more time for recounts, they said, would be changing the rules after the game started.

Both sides assembled high-powered legal teams, each headed by a former secretary of state, James A. Baker III for Bush and Warren N. Christopher for Gore. Both served as above-the-fray

spokespeople while the trench warfare fell chiefly to lawyers Barry Richard for Bush and David Boies for Gore. U.S. Supreme Court arguments for Bush were presented by Ted Olson and for Gore initially by Laurence Tribe of Harvard Law School and later by Boies.

But it was a race against the calendar and Katherine Harris was the timekeeper. Harris, Florida's secretary of state and former cochair of Bush's campaign in the state, announced November 13 that counties had until the following day, the date set in state law, to submit their returns, without any manual recount figures. Lawsuits stayed Harris's hand, however, and the manual counts proceeded by fits and starts until Sunday, November 26, under an extension granted by the seven-member Florida supreme court, made up mostly of Democratic appointees. That evening Harris ceremoniously "certified" Bush as the Florida winner by 537 votes out of six million cast.

The battle was by no means over, however. Gore formally contested the election and Bush meanwhile had protested the deadline extension to the U.S. Supreme Court, which heard the arguments December 1. In Tallahassee, after hearing two days of televised testimony, Leon County Circuit Judge N. Sanders Sauls ruled that Gore failed to prove the need for manual recounts. Gore's witnesses had testified that "chad buildup" and poorly maintained equipment could prevent voters from cleanly punching out a machine-read ballot. Gore received another setback the same day, December 4, when the U.S. Supreme Court returned the deadline-extension case to the Florida high court for clarification.

Gore scored a short-lived victory December 8 when the Florida court by a 4–3 vote ordered a resumption of the hand counts, only to have the U.S. Supreme Court quickly halt them the following day, pending its decision in *Bush v. Gore*. In its 5–4 decision, handed down December 12, the Court majority ruled for Bush that the lack of uniform standards for manual recounts denied "equal protection of the laws" to Florida voters. The Court split along ideological lines in the unsigned decision. In the majority were conservatives William Rehnquist, Antonin Scalia, Clarence Thomas, Anthony Kennedy, and Sandra Day O'Connor. Dissenting were liberals or moderates

Stephen Breyer, Ruth Bader Ginsburg, David Souter, and John Paul Stevens.

The Court action left 42,000 Florida undervotes unexamined, including 35,000 from the punch-card counties, but it effectively resolved the 2000 presidential race and possibly averted a constitutional crisis that might have arisen had the dispute resulted in Florida's sending two sets of electoral votes to Congress. The state legislature had already designated a slate of electors committed to Bush. Faced with a hopeless situation, Gore folded his campaign and conceded December 13.

When the presidential electors met in their states December 18 to cast their ballots, one District of Columbia elector, Barbara Lett-Simmons, withheld her vote from Gore in protest of the District's lack of representation in Congress. This reduced Gore's electoral vote total to 266 against 271 for Bush. Gore received 51.0 million votes (48.4 percent) to 50.5 million (47.9 percent) for Bush. Gore's lead in the popular vote was 539,947. Nader"s 2.8 million votes amounted to 2.7 percent of the total. Buchanan received less than 1 percent with 447,798 votes.

An embarrassing loss to Gore was his home state of Tennessee and its eleven electoral votes. Had he won there he would have had an electoral vote majority and the Florida vote would have been irrelevant. Likewise, had Gore received a fraction of the Nader vote in several close states, including Florida, he would have been over the top in electoral votes. Rhodes Cook, however, pointed out while Nader may have siphoned off Gore voters in Florida and elsewhere, Reform Party candidate Pat Buchanan, whose supporters traditionally lean Republican, may have prevented Bush from winning a few states that went closely for Gore. "[T]here were 30 additional electoral votes that Bush may have won if Buchanan had not been in the race, compared to 29 more electoral votes that may have gone to Gore if Nader had not run. In short, the effect of the two third-party candidates on the electoral vote was essentially a wash."[218]

Nationwide, African Americans voted 9 to 1 for Gore. On January 6, 2001, twenty House members, mostly members of the Congressional Black Caucus, tried to disqualify Florida's electoral votes as Congress met in joint session to count the electoral votes. As Senate president by virtue of his being U.S. vice president, Gore one by one ruled the objections out of order because they had not been signed by a senator as required by law. None of the 100 members of the new Senate, evenly divided between Republicans and Democrats, including presidential spouse Hillary Rodham Clinton of New York, had signed a challenge to the Florida votes. Gore in his concession had asked his supporters to accept the Court verdict and the "finality of the outcome."

AFTERMATH

Protests marred President Bush's inauguration on a cold, rainy Saturday January 20, 2001. Thousands of protesters, under tight security, lined the Pennsylvania Avenue parade route to the White House. They were noisy and visible, but there were relatively few arrests and clashes with the police.

Long and bitter as it was, the thirty-six-day 2000 election "night" was shorter and perhaps less vitriolic than its 1876 counterpart, which extended from November 7 to two days before inauguration, then in March. Because March 4, 1877, fell on a Sunday, President Hayes was sworn in privately at the White House and the public ceremonies took place quietly on Monday.

Similarly, the nation witnessed another peaceful transfer of power with the Bush-Cheney inauguration. As historian David McCullough phrased it, the peacefulness was typical of past inaugurations but perhaps for a different reason. "As close as it was, this election was not about visceral issues like slavery or war—things people are really passionate about," McCullough said. "The nation is closely divided, certainly, but we seem to be divided over which party controls the middle of the political spectrum. I'm not sure it's happened quite like that before."[219]

NOTES

1. A. James Reichley, *The Life of the Parties: A History of American Political Parties* (New York: Free Press, 1992), 17.

2. Richard P. McCormick, *The Presidential Game: The Origins of American Presidential Politics* (New York: Oxford University Press, 1982), chap. 1.

3. Ibid., 33–34.

4. Reichley, *Life of the Parties,* 42.

5. Ibid., 49.

6. Robert J. Dinkin, *Campaigning in America: A History of Election Practices* (New York: Greenwood Press, 1989), 18.

7. Roy F. Nichols, *The Invention of the American Political Parties* (New York: Macmillan, 1967), 192.

8. Bruce L. Felkner, *Political Mischief: Smear, Sabotage, and Reform in U.S. Elections* (New York: Praeger, 1992), 31.

9. Dinkin, *Campaigning in America,* 15, 18.

10. Edward Stanwood, *A History of the Presidency* (Boston: Houghton Mifflin, 1898), 63.

11. John F. Hoadley, *Origins of American Party Politics, 1789–1803* (Lexington: University Press of Kentucky, 1986), 191.

12. T. Harry Williams, *The History of American Wars: From Colonial Times to World War I* (New York: Knopf, 1981), 134.

13. Stanwood, *History of the Presidency,* 110.

14. Matthew A. Crenson, *The Federal Machine* (Baltimore: Johns Hopkins University Press, 1971), 11–30.

15. Jackson biographer Robert V. Remini explains the nickname "Old Hickory." In an arduous five-hundred-mile march, Jackson gave his three horses to wounded soldiers and marched on foot with his troops to give them moral support. The soldiers serving under him agreed that their general was as tough as hickory. "Not much later," Remini writes, "they started calling him 'Hickory' as a sign of their respect and regard; then the affectionate 'Old' was added to give Jackson a nickname . . . that admirably served him thereafter throughout his military and political wars" (Robert V. Remini, *Andrew Jackson* [New York: Harper and Row, 1969], 54).

16. Arthur M. Schlesinger Jr., *The Age of Jackson* (New York: New American Library, 1945), 34.

17. *Guide to Congress,* 2nd ed. (Washington, D.C.: Congressional Quarterly, 1982), 613.

18. Russell L. Hanson, *The Democratic Imagination in America: Conversations with Our Past* (Princeton, N.J.: Princeton University Press, 1985), 125.

19. Eugene H. Roseboom, *A History of Presidential Elections* (New York: Macmillan, 1970), 106.

20. Schlesinger, *Age of Jackson,* 55.

21. Estimates of vote totals vary, especially in the years before standardized methods of balloting. Discrepancies developed because of disputes about stuffing ballot boxes, the eligibility of some voters, absentee ballots, and simple counting and reporting difficulties in the premedia age.

22. Roseboom, *History of Presidential Elections,* 112.

23. Hanson, *Democratic Imagination,* 54–120.

24. Ibid., 140–141.

25. Ibid., 136.

26. See Albert O. Hirschman, *Exit, Voice, and Loyalty* (Cambridge, Mass.: Harvard University Press, 1970).

27. Hanson, *Democratic Imagination*, 138.

28. Richard P. McCormick, "Political Development and the Second Party System," in *The American Party Systems: Stages of Development*, ed. William Nisbet Chambers and Walter Dean Burnham (New York: Oxford University Press, 1967), 102.

29. Paul Taylor, *See How They Run: Electing a President in the Age of Mediaocracy* (New York: Knopf, 1991), 4.

30. James L. Sundquist, *Dynamics of the Party System*, rev. ed. (Washington, D.C.: Brookings, 1983), 51.

31. Roseboom, *Presidential Elections*, 143.

32. Richard Hofstadter, *The American Political Tradition* (New York: Vintage, 1948), 113.

33. Ibid.

34. Hanson, *Democratic Imagination*, 176.

35. Roseboom, *History of Presidential Elections*, 177–181.

36. Paul N. Angle, ed., *The Lincoln Reader* (New York: Pocket Books, 1954), 523.

37. Ibid., 531.

38. Roseboom, *History of Presidential Elections*, 201.

39. Eric Foner, *Reconstruction: America's Unfinished Revolution, 1863–1877* (New York: Harper and Row, 1988).

40. William S. McFeely, *Grant* (New York: Norton, 1981), 283.

41. Ibid., 288–289.

42. Ibid., 381.

43. Bernhard Bailyn et al., *The Great Republic: A History of the American People* (Boston: Little, Brown, 1977), 802.

44. C. Vann Woodward, *Reunion and Reaction* (New York: Doubleday Anchor Books, 1951).

45. Kenneth M. Stampp, *The Era of Reconstruction, 1865–1877* (New York: Vintage, 1965), 210–211.

46. Michael Nelson, "A Short, Ironic History of American National Bureaucracy," *Journal of Politics* 44 (winter 1982): 747–777.

47. Roseboom, *History of Presidential Elections*, 264.

48. Harry Thurston Peck, *Twenty Years of the Republic, 1885–1905* (New York: Dodd, Mead, 1906), 20.

49. Michael E. McGerr, *The Decline of Popular Politics: The American North, 1865–1928* (New York: Oxford University Press), 82–106.

50. Peck, *Twenty Years of the Republic*, 41.

51. Ibid., 78.

52. Ibid., 144.

53. Ibid., 169.

54. Roseboom, *History of Presidential Elections*, 290.

55. Bailyn et al., *Great Republic*, 786.

56. Sundquist, *Dynamics of the Party System*, 107.

57. For a concise account of the machine reform struggle, see Dennis R. Judd, *The Politics of American Cities* (Boston: Little, Brown, 1984), 50–110.

58. See David Montgomery, *The Fall of the House of Labor* (New York: Cambridge University Press, 1987).

59. Sundquist, *Dynamics of the Party System*, 116–118.

60. Ibid., 143, 152.

61. Hofstadter, *American Political Tradition*, 187.

62. Sundquist, *Dynamics of the Party System*, 149–152.

63. Hofstadter, *American Political Tradition*, 192–193.

64. See "William Jennings Bryan, Cross of Gold Speech," in *Great Issues in American History: From Reconstruction to the Present Day, 1864–1969*, ed. Richard Hofstadter (New York: Vintage, 1969), 166–173.

65. Jasper B. Shannon, *Money and Politics* (New York: Random House, 1959), 30–32.

66. Sundquist, *Dynamics of the Party System*, 158.

67. Ibid., 169; for a general discussion of the 1896 election's resulting realignment, see pages 160–169.

68. E. E. Schattschneider, *The Semisovereign People* (Hinsdale, Ill.: Dryden Press, 1975), 76–77.

69. Edmund Morris, *The Rise of Theodore Roosevelt* (New York: Ballantine, 1979), 718.

70. See Gabriel Kolko, *The Triumph of Conservatism* (New York: Free Press, 1963).

71. Sundquist, *Dynamics of the Party System*, 176.

72. See Alpheus I. Mason, *Bureaucracy Convicts Itself* (New York: Viking Press, 1941); and James Penick Jr., *Progressive Politics and Conservation* (Chicago: University of Chicago Press, 1968).

73. August Hecksher, *Woodrow Wilson* (New York: Scribner's, 1991), 231–232.

74. Ibid., 259.

75. J. Leonard Bates, *The United States, 1898–1928* (New York: McGraw-Hill, 1976), 187.

76. Roseboom, *History of Presidential Elections*, 384.

77. John L. Shover, ed., *Politics of the Nineteen Twenties* (Waltham, Mass.: Ginn-Blaisdell, 1970), 148.

78. Ibid., 4.

79. Ibid., 12.

80. Ibid., 10.

81. James David Barber, *The Pulse of Politics: Electing Presidents in the Media Age* (New York: Norton, 1980), 239.

82. William E. Leuchtenberg, *Franklin D. Roosevelt and the New Deal* (New York: Harper and Row, 1963), 13.

83. Frank Friedel, *Franklin D. Roosevelt: The Triumph* (Boston: Little, Brown, 1956), 248–249.

84. Barber, *Pulse of Politics*, 243.

85. Ibid., 244.

86. Ibid., 238.

87. Hofstadter, *American Political Tradition*, 332.

88. Barber, *Pulse of Politics*, 244.

89. See Robert Lekachman, *The Age of Keynes* (New York: Random House, 1966).

90. Schattschneider argues in *The Semisovereign People* that the key element of any conflict is the extent to which the protagonists are able to control how many people get involved. Every "scope of conflict" has a bias. The size of the group involved in the conflict is almost always open to change. Schattschneider writes: "A look at political literature shows that there has indeed been a long-standing struggle between the conflicting tendencies toward the privatization and socialization of conflict" (p. 7). The New Deal was a stage of socialization of conflict.

91. Everett Carll Ladd Jr. and Charles D. Hadley, *Transformations of the American Party System* (New York: Norton, 1978), 86.

92. Ibid., 43.

93. Ibid., 46.

94. Ibid., 64–74, 112; Sundquist, *Dynamics of the Party System*, 214–224.

95. Sundquist, *Dynamics of the Party System*, 217.

96. Ladd and Hadley, *Transformations*, 82.

97. Ibid., 58–59.

98. Ibid., 63.

99. Samuel H. Beer, "Liberalism and the National Interest," *Public Interest*, no. 1 (fall 1966): 81.

100. Theodore J. Lowi, *The End of Liberalism* (New York: Norton, 1969). See also Hanson, *Democratic Imagination*, 257–292.

101. Greg Mitchell, *The Campaign of the Century: Upton Sinclair's Race for Governor of California and the Birth of Modern Media Politics* (New York: Random House, 1992).

102. James MacGregor Burns, *Roosevelt: The Lion and the Fox* (New York: Harcourt Brace and World, 1956), 282–283.

103. Roseboom, *History of Presidential Elections*, 447.

104. Burns, *Roosevelt*, 277–278.

105. Ibid., 269–271.

106. Ibid., 282–283.

107. Ibid., 300.

108. Ibid., 427.

109. Barber, *Pulse of Politics*. This book tells the story behind the Willkie movement and the role played by Henry R. Luce, the founder of Time Inc.

110. See Lekachman, *Age of Keynes,* esp. chaps. 5 and 6.

111. Roseboom, *History of Presidential Elections,* 483.

112. William E. Leuchtenberg, *In the Shadow of F.D.R.: From Harry Truman to Ronald Reagan* (Ithaca, N.Y.: Cornell University Press, 1983), 1–2.

113. Ibid., 15.

114. Ibid., 21.

115. V. O. Key Jr., *Southern Politics in State and Nation* (Knoxville: University of Tennessee Press, 1984), 649.

116. Ibid., 330–344.

117. Barber, *Pulse of Politics,* 50.

118. Nelson W. Polsby and Aaron Wildavsky, *Presidential Elections* (New York: Scribner's, 1984), 205–206.

119. Barber, *Pulse of Politics,* 61.

120. Angus Campbell, Philip E. Convers, Warren E. Miller, and Donald E. Stokes, *The American Voter* (New York: Wiley, 1960), 532.

121. Richard Neustadt, *Presidential Power* (New York: Wiley, 1980), 10, 12–14, 16, 18, 19, 22–25, 43, 67–68, 178.

122. Garry Wills, *Nixon Agonistes* (New York: New American Library, 1969), 91.

123. Fred Greenstein, *The Hidden-Hand Presidency* (New York: Basic Books, 1982).

124. Barber, *Pulse of Politics,* 269.

125. Eric F. Goldman quipped, "The returns, as the gangsters said, made even Alf Landon look good," in *The Crucial Decade* (New York: Vintage, 1960), 326.

126. The elder Kennedy always had planned for his sons to enter national politics. He originally pushed his eldest son, Joseph Jr., but the son died in combat in World War II. John was next; he ran for Congress in 1946. Robert, the third Kennedy son, served as an aide to Sen. Joseph McCarthy before managing John's 1960 presidential campaign and serving as his attorney general. Edward, the youngest, worked on the 1960 campaign and won a Senate seat in 1962.

127. Merle Miller, *Plain Speaking* (New York: Berkeley, 1974), 199.

128. Theodore H. White, *The Making of the President 1960* (New York: Atheneum, 1961), 114–116.

129. Ibid., 128.

130. Ibid., 130.

131. Ibid., 198–204.

132. Arthur M. Schlesinger Jr., *Robert F. Kennedy and His Times* (Boston: Houghton Mifflin, 1978), 193.

133. Henry Fairlie, *The Kennedy Promise* (New York: Dell, 1972), 30–31.

134. White, *Making of the President 1960,* 329.

135. Ibid., 327.

136. Richard M. Nixon, *Six Crises* (Garden City, N.Y.: Doubleday, 1962), 412.

137. White, *Making of the President 1960,* 397–401.

138. Sen. Barry Goldwater, letter to the author, January 25, 1988.

139. The Warren Commission, appointed by Johnson, concluded that Oswald acted alone, but Oswald himself was killed before he had a chance to give full testimony. Many experts dispute the Warren Commission conclusion.

140. The Kennedy assassination fomented passage of the Twenty-fifth Amendment, which provides for a more orderly system of replacement. Previously, when a vice president ascended to the White House after the death or removal of a president, the vice presidency was left vacant. The amendment provides for presidential appointment of a vice president to fill the vacant spot. It also provides for at least temporary replacement of the president in the case of disability. The latter provision developed out of a concern that the country could have become leaderless had Kennedy been physically or mentally impaired but not killed.

141. Barber, *Pulse of Politics,* 167.

142. Thomas Ferguson and Joel Rogers, *Right Turn: The Decline of the Democrats and the Future of American Politics* (New York: Hill and Wang, 1986), 53.

143. Theodore H. White, *The Making of the President 1964* (New York: New American Library, 1965), 261.

144. Ibid., 353.

145. The central importance of economic conditions to electoral politics is widely documented. See, for example, Stanley Kelley Jr., *Interpreting Elections* (Princeton, N.J.: Princeton University Press, 1983); Edward R. Tufte, *Political Control of the Economy* (Princeton, N.J.: Princeton University Press, 1978); and Campbell, et al., *The American Voter.* On the link between economic conditions and the 1964 election, see Kelley, *Interpreting Elections,* 194.

146. Stanley Karnow, *Vietnam: A History* (New York: Viking, 1983), 358.

147. Ibid., 362.

148. Ibid., 395.

149. James David Barber, *The Presidential Character* (Englewood Cliffs, N.J.: Prentice-Hall, 1972), 34.

150. Karnow, *Vietnam,* 403.

151. Ibid., 479.

152. David Halberstam, *The Best and the Brightest* (New York: Random House, 1969).

153. Sundquist, *Dynamics of the Party System,* 384.

154. Ibid., 383.

155. The administration plank supported a bombing halt only when it "would not endanger the lives of our troops in the field," did not call for a reduction in search-and-destroy missions or a withdrawal of troops until the end of the war, and advocated a new government in Saigon only after the war had ended. The minority plank, drafted by McCarthy and McGovern, called for an immediate halt to the bombing, reduction of offensive operations in the South Vietnamese countryside, a negotiated troop withdrawal, and encouragement of the South Vietnamese government to negotiate with communist insurgents. After nearly three hours of debate, the minority plank was defeated, 1,567¾ to 1,041¼.

156. Theodore H. White, *The Making of the President 1968* (New York, Atheneum, 1969), 371.

157. Roseboom, *History of Presidential Elections,* 603.

158. See Russell Baker, *The Next President* (New York: Dell, 1968).

159. David Broder, "The Story That Still Nags at Me," *Washington Monthly,* February 1987, 29–32 .See also Theodore H. White, *Making of the President 1972* (New York: New American Library, 1973), 82.

160. White, *Making of the President 1972,* 129.

161. Ibid., 207.

162. On the politics of the period, see Sundquist, *Dynamics of the Party System,* 393–411; and Theodore H. White, *America in Search of Itself* (New York: Harper and Row, 1981). Good accounts of the Watergate scandal include those by Theodore H. White, *Breach of Faith* (New York: Atheneum, 1975); Jonathan Schell, *The Time of Illusion* (New York: Knopf, 1976); and Lewis Chester et al., *Watergate* (New York: Ballantine, 1973).

163. See Bruce Odes, ed., *From the President: Richard Nixon's Secret Files* (New York: Harper and Row, 1989).

164. Seymour Hersch, "The Pardon," *Atlantic,* August 1983, 55–78.

165. David J. Vogler, *The Politics of Congress* (Boston: Allyn and Bacon, 1977), 15–20, 25–26, 34, 147–155, 243–245.

166. For a good account of Jimmy Carter's 1976 Iowa victory, see Hugh Winebrenner, *The Iowa Precinct Caucuses* (Ames: University of Iowa Press, 1987), 67–93.

167. Jules Witcover, *Marathon* (New York: Viking, 1977), 274–288.

168. Ibid., 545–560.

169. Responding to a question during a debate, Ford said: "There is no Soviet domination of Eastern Europe, and there never will be under a Ford administration. . . . I don't believe . . . that the Yugoslavians consider themselves dominated by the Soviet Union. I don't believe that the Romanians consider themselves dominated by the Soviet Union. I don't believe that the Poles consider themselves dominated by the Soviet Union" (ibid., 597, 598).

170. See Gary Sick, *October Surprise: America's Hostages in Iran and the Election of Ronald Reagan* (New York: Times Books, 1992).

171. Richard Harwood, ed., *The Pursuit of the Presidency 1980* (New York: Berkeley, 1980), 305–307.

172. Thomas Byrne Edsall, *The New Politics of Inequality* (New York: Norton, 1984), 77–78.

173. George Gilder, *Wealth and Poverty* (New York: Basic Books, 1980). Another prominent supply-side tract is that by Jude Wanniski, *The Way the World Works* (New York: Basic Books, 1978). A sympathetic summary of the whole movement can be found in Robert Craig Paul, *The Supply-Side Revolution* (Cambridge, Mass.: Harvard University Press, 1984).

174. Ferguson and Rogers, *Right Turn*, 86–88, n. 245.

175. Garry Wills, *Reagan's America: Innocents at Home* (Garden City, N.Y.: Doubleday, 1987), 387.

176. Ibid., 385.

177. Ferguson and Rogers, *Right Turn*.

178. Rep. Shirley Chisholm of Brooklyn, New York, was the first African American to seek a major-party nomination. Her participation in the 1972 Democratic primaries won 151 delegates.

179. Geraldine Ferraro, with Linda Bird Francke, *Ferraro: My Story* (New York: Bantam, 1985), 164.

180. Paul R. Abramson, John H. Aldrich, and David W. Rohde, *Change and Continuity in the 1984 Elections*, rev. ed. (Washington, D.C.: CQ Press, 1986), 58.

181. V. O. Key Jr., "A Theory of Critical Elections," *Journal of Politics* 17 (February 1955): 3–18.

182. Abramson et al., *Change and Continuity*, 286–287.

183. Michael Barone and Grant Ujifusa, *The Almanac of American Politics: 1984* (Washington, D.C.: National Journal, 1983), xiv. See also Ladd and Hadley, *American Party System*, 237–249.

184. Taylor, *See How They Run*, 76.

185. Also that year, two Supreme Court nominees, Robert H. Bork and Douglas H. Ginsburg, failed to win Senate confirmation. Bork lost because of his views on a wide variety of social issues, but many criticisms focused on his personality. Ginsburg withdrew from consideration after revelations that he had smoked marijuana as a student and law school professor.

186. Barbara Norrander, *Super Tuesday: Regional Politics and Presidential Primaries* (Lexington: University Press of Kentucky, 1992), 101.

187. In the twelve days after Bush picked Quayle, ABC, CBS, and NBC aired ninety-three stories about him—more than Michael Dukakis received during the whole primary season. Two-thirds of the stories were negative. See Taylor, *See How They Run*, 162.

188. Nelson W. Polsby and Aaron Wildavsky, *Presidential Elections: Contemporary Strategies of American Electoral Politics*, 8th ed. (New York: Basic Books, 1991), 248.

189. Quayle did not meet the requirements set for political science majors and failed the first general examination at DePauw University in Indiana. He also failed to gain admission to law school under the usual application procedure. A study of Quayle's congressional career concludes that Quayle had no policy achievements in the House of Representatives but mastered some policy issues in the Senate. See Anthony Lewis, "The Intimidated Press," *New York Times*, January 19, 1989, 27; and Richard F. Fenno Jr., *The Making of a Senator: Dan Quayle* (Washington, D.C.: CQ Press, 1988).

190. *The Presidency A to Z* (Washington, D.C.: Congressional Quarterly, 1992), 29.

191. Sidney Blumenthal, *Pledging Allegiance: The Last Campaign of the Cold War* (New York: HarperCollins, 1990), 317.

192. Michael Duffy and Dan Goodgame, *Marching in Place: The Status Quo Presidency of George Bush* (New York: Simon and Schuster, 1992), 267–268.

193. Quoted in Michael Nelson, "The Presidency: Clinton and the Cycle of Politics and Policy," in *The Elections of 1992*, ed. Michael Nelson (Washington, D.C.: CQ Press, 1993), 144.

194. Paul J. Quirk and Jon K. Dalager, "The Election: A 'New Democrat' and a New Kind of Presidential Campaign," in Nelson, *Elections of 1992*, 61.

195. The unofficial manifesto of this movement is that by George F. Will, *Restoration: Congress, Term Limits, and the Recovery of Deliberative Democracy* (New York: Free Press, 1993).

196. Perot's rescue of his employees from Tehran during the 1979 Iranian revolution, for example, resulted in a best-selling book—Ken Follett's *On Wings of Eagles* (New York: Morrow, 1983)—and a made-for-TV movie. Earlier, he had founded a national organization to support President Nixon's Vietnam policy. Later, his company's merger with General Motors provoked a public dispute that cast him as the problem solver and GM officials as entrenched bureaucrats.

197. Ryan J. Barilleaux and Randall E. Adkins, "The Nominations: Process and Patterns," in Nelson, *Elections of 1992*, 38–39.

198. See David Osborne and Ted Gaebler, *Reinventing Government: How the Entrepreneurial Spirit Is Transforming the Public Sector* (Reading, Mass.: Addison-Wesley, 1992), for a manifesto of Clinton's approach to government reform.

199. For an excellent treatment of the importance of the middle class and suburbanism on modern American politics, see Thomas Byrne Edsall and Mary D. Edsall, *Chain Reaction: The Impact of Race, Rights, and Taxes on American Politics* (New York: Norton, 1991).

200. Barilleaux and Adkins, "The Nominations," 48–49.

201. Duffy and Goodgame, *Marching in Place*.

202. *Congressional Quarterly Weekly Report*, supplements, July 4, 1992, 71, and August 8, 1992, 67.

203. Daniel Hellinger and Dennis R. Judd, *The Democratic Facade* (Belmont, Calif.: Wadsworth, 1994), 180.

204. Al Gore, *Earth in the Balance: Ecology and the Human Spirit* (Boston: Houghton Mifflin, 1992).

205. Ross K. Barker, "Sorting Out and Suiting Up: The Presidential Nominations," in *The Election of 1992*, ed. Gerald M. Pomper (Chatham, N.J.: Chatham House, 1993), 67.

206. See Mark J. Rozell and Clyde Wilcox, "It Isn't the Old Christian Right Anymore," *Los Angeles Times*, April 29, 1996, B5.

207. See Clyde Wilcox and Mark J. Rozell, "Dole's Delicate Balancing Act," *Christian Science Monitor*, June 4, 1996, 20.

208 ."Polls and the Election," *The Public Perspective*, December 1996/January 1997, 58.

209. Howard Kurtz, "A Big Story: But Only Behind the Scenes; Media Fretted Over Reporting Dole Affair," *Washington Post*, November 13, 1996, D1.

210. Green Party candidate Ralph Nader polled 0.7 percent and Libertarian Harry Browne polled 0.5 percent. Rhodes Cook, "Even with Higher Vote, Clinton Remains Minority President," *Congressional Quarterly Weekly Report*, January 18, 1997, 185–188.

211. Howard Fineman, "Clinton's Big Win," *Newsweek*, November 18, 1996, 8–13; Rhodes Cook, "Clinton's Easy Second-Term Win Riddles GOP Electoral Map," *Congressional Quarterly Weekly Report*, November 9, 1996, 3189–3194.

212. See Richard L. Berke, "Clinton Wins Second Term by Solid Margin," *New York Times*, November 6, 1996.

213. See Gregory L. Giroux, "In His Own Right," *Congressional Quarterly Democratic Convention Guide*, August 12, 2000, 9.

214. Michael Kelly, "The Democrats' Delusion," *Washington Post*, November 1, 2000, A33.

215. Jane Hall, "Gore Media Coverage: Playing Hardball," *Columbia Journalism Review*, September/October 2000, 30.

216. Rhodes Cook, "A Reprise of '60?" *The Rhodes Cook Letter*, September 2000, 4.

217. Matthew Vita, "2000's Stealth Issue: Impeachment's Effects Are Playing Out in Races from National to District Level," *Washington Post*, November 1, 2000, A1.

218. Rhodes Cook, "The Nader Factor: Overrated?" *The Rhodes Cook Letter*, January 2001, 7.

219. See Ken Ringle, "For Jan. 20, a Peaceful Precedent," *Washington Post*, January 10, 2001, C9.

CHAPTER 10

Presidential Primaries

THE QUADRENNIAL PROCESS of electing a president has two distinct parts—the nominating process and the general election. Yet while the latter has been generally static in form—a one-day nationwide vote on the first Tuesday after the first Monday in November—the former is constantly evolving.

The changes in the nominating process over the course of the nation's history have been dramatic—from congressional caucuses in the early nineteenth century, through the heyday of the national conventions over the next century and a half, to the present nominating system, where conventions merely ratify the choices made months earlier in the election year by Democratic and Republican primary voters.

Nominations are now decided in the presidential primaries. And they have been since the Democrats' tumultuous convention in Chicago in 1968 encouraged both parties, but the Democrats in particular, to look for ways to open the nominating process to greater grass-roots participation.

The principal way to more voter involvement has been through the proliferation of presidential primaries. While a product of the Progressive Era in the early twentieth century, primaries were few and far between until the late 1960s. But after that, they quickly mushroomed in number—from fifteen in 1968, to thirty-six in 1980, to more than forty in 1996.

As the number of primaries grew, power in the nominating process quickly shifted from party kingmakers at the national conventions to voters in the primary states. Gone were the days when candidates could win their party's nomination without entering the primaries. No nominee of either major party has done so since Democrat Hubert H. Humphrey in 1968. Gone too were the days when candidates could win their party's nomination without first proving broad-based popularity among millions of voters. Since Democrat George McGovern in 1972, every major-party nominee has first been their party's highest vote-getter in the primaries. In the process, the once climactic conventions have become little more than giant pep rallies, ratifying the choices of Democratic and Republican primary voters.

"Front-Loaded" Process

As the number of primaries has grown, nominations have been settled earlier and earlier as more and more states have moved their primaries forward to dates near the beginning of the election year in a bid to heighten their influence (a process that has become known as "front-loading.")

In 1968 only one presidential primary (New Hampshire's) was held before the end of March. In 1980 ten states held pri-

maries so early. By 1988 the number surpassed twenty, and in 2000, more than half the country held primary elections before the end of March.

The result has been an increasingly truncated nominating process that has followed a clear pattern. Early votes in Iowa and New Hampshire have winnowed the field to a handful of candidates. Then, after a short period of unpredictability, one candidate has scored a knockout in the glut of March primaries, with their victory ratified by a string of essentially meaningless primary votes over the spring months.

That is what happened in the campaign for the Republican nomination in 2000. Sen. John McCain of Arizona routed the GOP front-runner, Gov. George W. Bush of Texas, in New Hampshire, and battled him ballot for ballot in the array of Republican primaries scattered across the rest of February. But once the calendar flipped to March, Bush's superior organization and resources kicked in. On March 7 alone, eleven primaries were held from Maine to California. Bush triumphed convincingly in most of them—including the featured events in California, New York, and Ohio—driving McCain from the race and essentially wrapping up the nomination.

The Democratic presidential contest ended at the same time, as Vice President Al Gore defeated former Sen. Bill Bradley of New Jersey in all eleven of the day's Democratic primaries. Roughly five months remained before both parties' national conventions, but the nominations for both parties were settled.

Cut out of any meaningful role in the year's nominating process were Florida, Illinois, New Jersey, North Carolina, Pennsylvania, Wisconsin, and more than a dozen other states, which held their primaries after the competitive stage of the primary season had ended.

The last time that either the Democratic or Republican party had an elongated tug-of-war for its presidential nomination was 1984, when former vice president Walter F. Mondale and Sen. Gary Hart of Colorado battled into the final week of Democratic primaries before Mondale won the final delegates needed to nail down his nomination. Neither party has had a nominating contest that was even vaguely competitive at the time of its national convention since the 1976 Republican race between President Gerald R. Ford and actor and former Gov. Ronald Reagan of California.

REVERSAL OF FORTUNE

When they were regularly winning the White House in the 1970s and 1980s, Republicans showed little interest in tinkering with the nominating process; they were happy to leave that as a concern of the Democrats. But once the GOP began to lose

Types of Primaries and Procedures

In many respects, the presidential nominating process is like a modern-day Alice in Wonderland. Its basic dynamics do not always appear very logical. Primaries and caucuses are strewn across the calendar from January to June, culminating with party conventions in the summer. A nomination is won by a candidate attaining a majority of delegates, an honor that is formally bestowed at the conventions but for years has informally occurred much earlier during the primary season.

Size is less important in determining a state's importance in the nominating process than its tradition and place on the calendar (early is best). Hence, the quadrennial starring role for Iowa and New Hampshire, and the bit parts frequently assigned California and New York.

States have different ground rules in the nominating process. Some have caucuses, many more have primaries. Most primaries allocate a state's delegates, but some are nonbinding "beauty contests," with the delegates elected independently of the preference vote for presidential candidates.

Rules on voter participation vary from state to state. Some states hold "closed" contests, which are open only to a party's registered voters. Some hold "semi-open" events, which allow independent voters to participate along with registered members of the party. About half the states have "open" primaries or caucuses, in which any registered voter can participate. (The bulk of these states do not have party registration to begin with.)

The parties themselves also have different playing fields. Since 1980, Democrats have not allowed any states except Iowa, New Hampshire, and sometimes Maine, to hold a primary or caucus before early March. Republicans have had no such restriction, and in some years a state or two on the GOP side has voted in advance of Iowa and New Hampshire.

Since 1984, Democrats have reserved between 10 and 20 percent of their delegate seats for high-level party and elected officials (such as Democratic governors, members of Congress, and members of the party's national committee). Often called "superdelegates," these automatic delegates do not have to declare a presidential preference. (Republicans did not have "superdelegates" until the 2000 GOP convention approved automatic delegate seats for RNC members in 2004.) Since 1992, Democrats have required states to distribute delegates among their candidates in

proportion to their vote, statewide and in congressional districts, with 15 percent required to win a share.

Republicans, in contrast, allow a variety of delegate allocation methods, including proportional representation, statewide winner-take-all (in which the candidate winning the most votes statewide wins all the delegates), congressional district, and statewide winner-take-all (in which the high vote-getter in a district wins that district's delegates and the high vote-getter statewide wins all the at-large delegates), or some combination of the three.

Still another method is the selection of individual delegates in a "loophole," or direct election, primary. And in Republican caucus states, delegates often run as individuals and frequently are not officially allocated to any candidate.

How delegates are actually elected can vary from state to state. Most primary states hold presidential preference votes, in which voters choose among the candidates who have qualified for the ballot in their states. Although preference votes may be binding or nonbinding, in most states the vote is binding on the delegates, who are elected in the primary itself or chosen outside of it by a caucus process, by a state committee or by the candidates who have qualified to win delegates.

For those primaries in which the preference vote is binding upon delegates, state laws may vary as to the number of ballots through which delegates at the convention must remain committed. Delegates may be bound for as short as one ballot or as long as a candidate remains in the race. National Democratic rules were changed in 1980 to bind delegates for one ballot unless released by the candidate they were elected to support. The rule, though, became a flash point of controversy between the front-runner, President Jimmy Carter, and his major challenger, Sen. Edward M. Kennedy of Massachusetts. The Carter forces prevailed in having the rule sustained at the 1980 convention, but it was subsequently dropped during the quadrennial review of party rules after the election.

Until 1980 the Republicans had a rule requiring delegates bound to a specific candidate by state law in primary states to vote for that candidate at the convention regardless of their personal presidential preferences. That rule was repealed at the party's July 1980 convention.

presidential elections in the 1990s, many Republicans began to decry the "front-loaded" primary calendar that produced nominees within a few weeks of voting.

At their convention in San Diego in 1996, Republicans approved a rules change designed to help spread out the calendar. States were offered bonus delegates the later they held their primary or caucus. It did not get many takers, though, in 2000.

But in the wake of that year's Bush-McCain contest, a party commission headed by former Tennessee senator and national GOP chairman Bill Brock recommended that the presidential primary calendar be dramatically overhauled, so that small

states would vote first in 2004 and large states would vote last.

States were to be grouped into four "pods" of roughly equal number, with each pod voting over the course of a month. The initial calendar called for voting from March to June, but in the course of discussion the calendar was moved up a month to start in February and end in May. Still, the fourth pod was to be comprised of the largest states, holding roughly half the delegates. The idea was to slow the rush to judgment evident in the "front-loaded" primary system by making it mathematically impossible for a candidate to amass a majority of delegates before most, if not all, of the states had voted.

Table 10-1
Votes Cast and Delegates Selected in Presidential Primaries, 1912–2000

	Democratic Party			Republican Party			Total	
Year	Number of primaries	Votes cast	Delegates selected through primaries (%)	Number of primaries	Votes cast	Delegates selected through primaries (%)	Votes cast	Delegates selected through primaries (%)
1912	12	974,775	32.9	13	2,261,240	41.7	3,236,015	37.3
1916	20	1,187,691	53.5	20	1,923,374	58.9	3,111,065	56.2
1920	16	571,671	44.6	20	3,186,248	57.8	3,757,919	51.2
1924	14	763,858	35.5	17	3,525,185	45.3	4,289,043	40.4
1928	16	1,264,220	42.2	15	4,110,288	44.9	5,374,508	43.5
1932	16	2,952,933	40.0	14	2,346,996	37.7	5,299,929	38.8
1936	14	5,181,808	36.5	12	3,319,810	37.5	8,501,618	37.0
1940	13	4,468,631	35.8	13	3,227,875	38.8	7,696,506	37.3
1944	14	1,867,609	36.7	13	2,271,605	38.7	4,139,214	37.7
1948	14	2,151,865	36.3	12	2,653,255	36.0	4,805,120	36.1
1952	16	4,928,006	38.7	13	7,801,413	39.0	12,729,419	38.8
1956	19	5,832,592	42.7	19	5,828,272	44.8	11,660,864	43.7
1960	16	5,687,742	38.3	15	5,537,967	38.6	11,224,631	38.5
1964	16	6,247,435	45.7	16	5,935,339	45.6	12,182,774	45.6
1968	15	7,535,069	40.2	15	4,473,551	38.1	12,008,620	39.1
1972	21	15,993,965	65.3	20	6,188,281	56.8	22,182,246	61.0
1976	27	16,052,652	76.0	26	10,374,125	71.0	26,426,777	73.5
1980	34	18,747,825	71.8	34	12,690,451	76.0	31,438,276	73.7
1984	29	18,009,217	52.4	25	6,575,651	71.0	24,584,868	59.6
1988	36	22,961,936	66.6	36	12,165,115	76.9	35,127,051	70.2
1992	39	20,239,385	66.9	38	12,696,547	83.9	32,935,932	72.7
1996	35	10,996,395	65.3	42	14,233,939	84.6	25,230,334	69.2
2000	40	14,045,745	64.6	43	17,156,117	83.8	31,201,862	70.8

Source: Percentages of delegates selected are from Congressional Quarterly.

The idea, dubbed the "Delaware Plan" because of its state of origin, was controversial, particularly among the larger states, who feared a loss of influence if they were required to vote en masse at the end of the primary season. The "Delaware Plan," though, did win the approval of the rules committee of the Republican National Committee (RNC) in May 2000 and the full RNC itself on the eve of the party's convention that summer.

But the plan was defeated in the convention rules committee July 28, after the Bush campaign shifted from a position of neutrality to opposition. Several reasons were cited for the eleventh hour change of heart, including complaints from the big states over their potential loss of influence, the lack of an agreement with the Democrats over a common course of action, and a loss of control by the states over their primary or caucus dates if the "Delaware Plan" were imposed. But it was also obvious that the Bush campaign wanted an harmonious convention without any contested issues on the floor.

CHANGE CERTAIN IN FUTURE

Even if the "Delaware Plan" had been approved by the Republican convention, it still would have faced an uncertain future. Earlier in 2000, the rules committee of the Democratic Party had expressed support for the status quo and urged Republicans to embrace the Democratic primary calendar, which allowed Iowa and New Hampshire to vote first but prohibited other states from voting before the first Tuesday in March. Meanwhile, the nation's secretaries of state recommended a different solution, a system of regional primaries, whose order would be rotated every four years. Yet with neither of the major parties rallying behind it, the secretaries' plan had little chance of being embraced.

Still, even without the Democrats or Republicans opting for bold changes, the nominating process is by nature evolutionary. Every four years at least a few states move their primary or caucus date, creating a new calendar. And nearly every four years, at least one of the parties makes a change in their rules that proves significant. In 2000 Republicans added four delegates to each state's total in 2004 and created automatic delegate seats for the members of the RNC.

An Evolutionary Process

During the early years of the nation, presidential nominations were decided by party caucuses in Congress (derided by their critics as "King Caucus"). At the dawn of the Jacksonian era in the 1830s, though, the nominating role shifted to national conventions, a broader-based venue where party leaders from around the country held sway.

In the early twentieth century, presidential primaries appeared on the scene, adding a new element of grass-roots democracy and voter input. But for the next half century, the primaries were relatively few in number and played a limited advisory role. Nominations continued to be settled in the party conventions.

After World War II American society became more mobile and media-oriented, and once-powerful party organizations began to lose their clout. An increasing number of presidential as-

Democrat Hubert H. Humphrey in 1968 was the last candidate to win a major party's presidential nomination without entering the primaries.

pirants saw the primaries as a way to generate popular support that might overcome the resistance of party leaders. Both Republican Dwight D. Eisenhower in 1952 and Democrat John F. Kennedy in 1960 scored a string of primary victories that demonstrated their vote-getting appeal and made their nominations possible.

Yet the conventions continued to reign supreme through the 1960s, although 1968 proved to be a watershed year in the evolution of the nominating process. Sens. Eugene McCarthy of Minnesota and Robert F. Kennedy of New York used the handful of Democratic primaries that spring to protest the war in Vietnam, together taking more than two-thirds of the party's primary vote and driving President Lyndon B. Johnson from the race.

History might have been different if Kennedy had not been assassinated after his victory in the California primary that June. But without Kennedy on the scene, the party's embattled leadership was able to maintain a tenuous control of the convention that August in Chicago, nominating Vice President Humphrey, who had not competed in a single primary state.

But Humphrey's nomination came at a price. For the first time in several generations, the legitimacy of the convention itself was thrown into question. And as an outgrowth, a series of Democratic rules review commissions began to overhaul the presidential nominating process to encourage much greater grass-roots participation.

CHANGE COMES QUICKLY

The immediate result was a dramatic increase in presidential primaries that enhanced the chances of long-shot outsiders, such as George McGovern and Jimmy Carter, who captured the Democratic nomination in 1972 and 1976, respectively.

In the 1970s, the primary calendar started slowly, giving little-known candidates the time to raise money and momentum after doing well in the early rounds. Most of the primaries then were held in May and June.

But the layout of the nominating process has been less favorable to dark horses since then. In the 1980s Democrats reinserted party and elected officials into the process, creating a new category of automatic delegate seats for them that have come to be known as "superdelegates." And states began to move forward on the calendar in a bid to increase their influence, heightening the need for candidates to be well organized and well funded at the beginning of the primary season.

Democrats sought to put a brake on the calendar sprawl toward the beginning of the election year by instituting the "window," which prohibited any of the party's primaries or caucuses from being held before early March, with the exception of Iowa, New Hampshire, and for a while, Maine.

With the creation of that early March firewall, many states parked their primary in March—gradually at first, but then in tidal wave proportions in 1988, with the creation of a full-scale primary vote across the South on the second Tuesday in March that came to be known as "Super Tuesday."

The event did not have the effect that its Democratic sponsors had hoped for, in terms of steering the nomination toward a centrist son of the South, such as Sen. Al Gore of Tennessee. In the early 1990s, the early March southern primary lost some of its members.

But the concept of early regional primaries took hold elsewhere. In 1996 all of New England except New Hampshire voted on the first Tuesday in March. Six southern states, led by Texas and Florida, voted on the second Tuesday. Four states in the industrial Midwest—Illinois, Michigan, Ohio, and Wisconsin—voted on the third Tuesday in March. And California anchored a three-state western primary on the fourth Tuesday.

In 2000 the bulk of the New England states continued to vote on the first Tuesday in March, and much of the South on the second Tuesday. But the big story was the dramatic movement toward a broad-based, coast-to-coast vote on the first Tuesday in March. The day's primaries and caucuses involved states with nearly 40 percent of the nation's population, including three of the seven most populous states—California, New York, and Ohio.

Current Arrangement

Even though much of the primary calendar has changed dramatically over the last few decades, the accepted starting points have remained Iowa and New Hampshire (even though other states have occasionally voted before them).

Both states have made their early events into cottage industries, but the candidates and the media have helped make them so. More than ever, Iowa and New Hampshire are about the only places left where candidates have some control over their destinies. They can woo voters one-on-one, whether in bowling alleys, coffee shops, or the frequent gatherings in neighborhood living rooms.

For if there is one thing that has become certain in recent years, once the New Hampshire primary is over and candidates must compete in several states simultaneously, there is a frenetic burst of tarmac-to-tarmac campaigning heavily dependent on media advertising.

With one exception, every presidential nominee since 1976 has won either Iowa or New Hampshire, and finished no lower than third in the other. The exception was Bill Clinton in 1992, who did not seriously contest Iowa in deference to the home-state appeal of Sen. Tom Harkin and finished second in New Hampshire behind former Sen. Paul E. Tsongas of Massachusetts.

Iowa and New Hampshire illustrate the two different types of delegate-selection processes that states have to choose from. Iowa is a caucus; New Hampshire is a primary. Primaries require voters only to cast a ballot, an exercise that usually takes just a few minutes. The deliberative nature of a neighborhood caucus, though, often requires the commitment of an afternoon or evening.

A SMALL SLICE OF THE ELECTORATE

Voter turnout is usually much higher in a primary than a caucus, but even in primaries the turnout is much lower than a general election. In New Hampshire, for instance, where interest in the presidential primary is probably greater than any other state, nearly 400,000 voters turned out in February 2000 for the presidential primary.

The disparity is much greater in many other states. Roughly 35 million votes were cast in all the presidential primaries in 2000. Meanwhile, turnout in the handful of states that held caucuses was no more than several hundred thousand more voters. By comparison, 96 million voters turned out for the 1996 general election.

Rules governing voter participation play a role in the comparatively low turnouts for the nominating process. Every primary is not as open as a general election, where any registered voter can participate. A number of states limit participation to registered Democratic and Republican voters. Some others allow independents to participate, but list them on the voting rolls afterward as members of the party in which they cast their primary ballot.

Still, the vast majority of registered voters across the country can participate in a presidential primary or caucus if they want. The fact that more do not has generated the conventional wisdom that the nominating process is dominated by ideological activists—liberals on the Democratic side, conservatives on the Republican.

That is debatable in the primaries, where the winners in recent years have been from the mainstreams of both parties. An ideological bent is usually more evident in the low-turnout world of the caucuses, where a small cadre of dedicated voters can significantly affect the outcome.

When religious broadcaster Pat Robertson tried for the Republican presidential nomination in 1988, for instance, he won first-round caucus voting in three states and finished second in three others, including Iowa. But Robertson did not come close that year to winning a presidential primary.

CLUES TO THE FALL

It has been a matter of debate within the political community whether the current primary-dominated nominating process is better than the old system, in which party leaders controlled the selection process.

But it is a fact that the increased number of primaries helps provide valuable clues about the vote-getting potential of candidates in the general election. Nominees that have exhibited broad-based appeal among the diverse array of primary voters in the winter and spring have gone on to be quite competitive in the fall, while those nominees who have struggled through the primaries showing limited appeal among one or two of their party's major constituency groups have usually been buried under landslides in November.

A less reliable indicator of what will happen in the fall is the number of votes cast in each party's primaries. In every year from 1956 through 1992, more ballots were cast in Democratic than Republican primaries. In part, it was due to the simple fact that through much of this period, Democrats outnumbered Republicans.

But it also reflected the fact that the Democratic primaries drew more voter interest because they often exhibited more conflict between competing constituencies within the party. That kind of political drama and angst was good for primary turnout, but not for the party's chances in the fall elections, as Republicans won most of the presidential contests in this period.

Legacy of the Progressive Era

Yet, entrenched as they now are in the electoral process, primaries are still relatively recent replacements for the old smoke-filled rooms where party bosses once dictated the choice of presidential nominees.

Presidential primaries originated as an outgrowth of the Progressive movement in the early twentieth century. Progressives, populists, and reformers in general were fighting state and municipal corruption. They objected to the links between political bosses and big business and advocated returning the government to the people.

Part of this "return to the people" was a turn away from what were looked upon as boss-dominated conventions. It was only a matter of time before the primary idea spread from state and local elections to presidential contests. Because there was no provision for a nationwide primary, state primaries were initiated to choose delegates to the national party conventions (delegate-selection primaries) and to register voters' preferences on their parties' eventual presidential nominees (preference primaries).

Florida enacted the first presidential primary law in 1901. The law gave party officials an option of holding a party primary to choose any party candidate for public office, as well as del-

Selection by Caucus Method

In the current primary-dominated era of presidential politics, which began two decades ago, caucuses have survived in the quiet backwater of the nominating process.

The impact of caucuses decreased in the 1970s as the number of primaries grew dramatically. Previously, a candidate sought to run well in primary states mainly to have a bargaining chip with which to deal with powerful leaders in the caucus states. Republicans Barry Goldwater in 1964 and Richard Nixon in 1968 and Democrat Hubert H. Humphrey in 1968 all built up solid majorities among caucus state delegates that carried them to their parties' nominations. Humphrey did not compete in a single primary state in 1968.

After 1968, candidates placed their principal emphasis on primaries. First George McGovern in 1972—and then incumbent Republican President Gerald R. Ford and Democratic challenger Jimmy Carter in 1976—won nomination by securing large majorities of the primary state delegates. Neither McGovern nor Ford won a majority of the caucus state delegates. Carter was able to win a majority only after his opponents' campaigns collapsed.

Complex Method

Compared with a primary, the caucus system is complicated. Instead of focusing on a single primary election ballot, the caucus presents a multitiered system that involves meetings scheduled over several weeks, sometimes even months. There is mass participation at the first level only, with meetings often lasting several hours and attracting only the most enthusiastic and dedicated party members.

The operation of the caucus varies from state to state, and each party has its own set of rules. Most begin with precinct caucuses or some other type of local mass meeting open to all party voters.

Participants, often publicly declaring their votes, elect delegates to the next stage in the process.

In smaller states such as Delaware and Hawaii, delegates are elected directly to a state convention, where the national convention delegates are chosen. In larger states such as Iowa, there is at least one, sometimes two, more steps. Delegates in Iowa are elected at the precinct caucuses to county conventions, which are followed by congressional district conventions and the state convention, the two levels where the national convention delegates are chosen.

Participation, even at the first level of the caucus process, is much lower than in primaries. Caucus participants usually are local party leaders and activists. Many rank-and-file voters find a caucus complex, confusing, or intimidating.

As a result, caucuses are usually considered tailor-made for candidates with a cadre of passionately dedicated supporters. That was evident as long ago as 1972, when a surprisingly strong showing in the Iowa precinct caucuses helped to propel Sen. George McGovern of South Dakota, an ardent foe of the Vietnam War, toward the Democratic nomination.

In a caucus state the focus is on one-on-one campaigning. Time, not money, is usually the most valuable resource. Because organization and personal campaigning are so important, an early start is far more crucial in a caucus state than in a primary. And because only a small segment of the electorate is targeted in most caucus states, candidates usually use media advertising sparingly.

The lone exception is Iowa. As the kick-off point for the quadrennial nominating process, Iowa has recently become a more expensive stop for ambitious presidential candidates, as they must shell out money for everything from straw votes to radio and TV advertising. But the accent in Iowa, as in other caucus states, is

egates to the national conventions. However, there was no provision for placing names of presidential candidates on the ballot—either in the form of a preference vote or with information indicating the preference of the candidates for convention delegates.

Wisconsin's progressive Republican politician, Gov. Robert M. La Follette, gave a major boost to the presidential primary following the 1904 Republican National Convention. It was at that convention that the credentials of La Follette's progressive delegation were rejected and a regular Republican delegation from Wisconsin was seated. Angered by what he considered his unfair treatment, La Follette returned to his home state and began pushing for a presidential primary law. The result was the Wisconsin law of 1905 mandating the direct election of national convention delegates. The law, however, did not include a provision for indicating the delegates' presidential preference.

Pennsylvania followed Wisconsin in 1906 with a statute providing that each candidate for delegate to a national convention

could have printed beside his name on the official primary ballot the name of the presidential candidate he would support at the convention. However, no member of either party exercised this option in the 1908 primary.

La Follette's sponsorship of the delegate-selection primary helped make the concept a part of the progressive political program. The growth of the Progressive movement rapidly resulted in the enactment of presidential primary laws in other states.

The next step in presidential primaries—the preferential vote for president—took place in Oregon. There, in 1910, Sen. Jonathan Bourne, a progressive Republican colleague of La Follette (then a senator), sponsored a referendum to establish a presidential preference primary, with delegates legally bound to support the primary winner. By 1912, with Oregon in the lead, fully a dozen states had enacted presidential primary laws that provided for either direct election of delegates, a preferential vote, or both. The number had expanded to twenty-six states by 1916.

still on grass-roots organization. That was underscored in 1996, when the late-starting campaign of wealthy publisher Steve Forbes spent lavishly on an Iowa media blitz that netted only 10 percent of the Republican caucus vote.

Although the basic steps in the caucus process are the same for both parties, the rules that govern them are vastly different. Democratic rules have been revamped substantially since 1968, establishing national standards for grass-roots participation. Republican rules have remained largely unchanged, with the states given wide latitude in drawing up their delegate-selection plans.

Caucuses

For both the Republican and Democratic parties, the percentage of delegates elected from caucus states was on a sharp decline throughout the 1970s. But the Democrats broke the downward trend and elected more delegates by the caucus process in 1980 than in 1976.

Between 1980 and 1984 six states switched from a primary to a caucus system; none the other way. Since 1984 the trend has turned back toward primaries. In 1996 primaries were held in forty-one states, the District of Columbia, and Puerto Rico. The Democrats elected 65.3 percent of their national convention delegates in primaries, against only 16.8 percent in caucuses. (The remaining 17.9 percent were "superdelegate" party and elected officials.) The Republicans in 1992 chose 84.6 percent of delegates in primaries and the rest by caucus or state committee, with no superdelegates. And the proportions have stayed roughly the same since then.

A strong showing in the caucuses by Walter F. Mondale in 1984 led many Democrats—and not only supporters of his rivals—to conclude that caucuses are inherently unfair. The mainstream Democratic coalition of party activists, labor union members, and teachers dominated the caucuses in Mondale's behalf.

The caucus also came in for criticism in 1988. The Iowa Democratic caucuses were seen as an unrepresentative test dominated by liberal interest groups. And the credibility of the caucuses was shaken by the withdrawal from the race of the two winners—Democrat Richard A. Gephardt and Republican Robert Dole—within a month after the caucuses were held. Furthermore, several other state caucuses featured vicious infighting between supporters of various candidates.

In 1992 the presence of a favorite son, Sen. Tom Harkin, among the leading Democratic candidates for president, further diminished the Iowa caucus' significance as a rival to the New Hampshire primary as an early indicator of the candidate to beat for the nomination. Harkin easily won his state's party caucus, but he soon dropped out after fading in the primaries elsewhere.

Yet in 1996 and again in 2000, Iowa was back enjoying center stage. And in both years, the campaigns of the Republican nominee—Dole and Gov. George W. Bush of Texas, respectively—were successfully launched in Iowa, as was the campaign of Vice President Al Gore in 2000 on the Democratic side.

The major complaint about the caucus process is that it does not involve enough voters, and that the low turnouts are not so representative of voter sentiment as a higher-turnout primary. The combined turnout for both parties for the Iowa caucuses in 2000, for example, was roughly 150,000, less than half the number that turned out for the New Hampshire primary a week later.

Staunch defenders, however, believe a caucus has party-building attributes a primary cannot match. They note that several hours at a caucus can involve voters in a way that quickly casting a primary ballot does not. Following caucus meetings, the state party comes away with lists of thousands of voters who can be tapped to volunteer time or money, or even to run for local office. And, while the multitiered caucus process is often a chore for the state party to organize, a primary is substantially more expensive.

PRIMARIES AND CONVENTIONS

The first major test of the impact of presidential primary laws—in 1912—demonstrated that victories in the primaries did not ensure a candidate's nomination. Former President Theodore Roosevelt, campaigning in twelve Republican primaries, won nine of them, including Ohio, the home state of incumbent Republican president William Howard Taft. Roosevelt lost to Taft by a narrow margin in Massachusetts and to La Follette in North Dakota and Wisconsin.

Despite this impressive string of primary victories, the convention rejected Roosevelt in favor of Taft. Taft supporters dominated the Republican National Committee, which ran the convention, and the convention's credentials committee, which ruled on contested delegates. Moreover, Taft was backed by many state organizations, especially in the South, where most delegates were chosen by caucuses or conventions dominated by party leaders.

On the Democratic side, the convention more closely reflected the primary results. Gov. Woodrow Wilson of New Jersey and Speaker of the House Champ Clark of Missouri were closely matched in total primary votes, with Wilson only 29,632 votes ahead of Clark. Wilson emerged with the nomination after a long convention struggle with Clark.

Likewise, in 1916, Democratic primary results foreshadowed the winner of the nomination, although Wilson, who was then the incumbent, had no major opposition for renomination. But once again, Republican presidential primaries had little impact upon the nominating process at the convention. The eventual nominee, Supreme Court Justice Charles Evans Hughes, had won only two primaries.

In 1920 presidential primaries did not play a major role in determining the winner of either party's nomination. James M. Cox, the eventual Democratic nominee, ran in only one primary, his home state of Ohio. Most of the Democratic primaries featured favorite-son candidates, unpledged delegate slates, or write-in votes. And at the convention Democrats took forty-four ballots to settle on Cox.

Choosing a Running Mate: The Balancing Act

In modern times, with presidential candidates wrapping up their party's nominations early in the primary season, the greatest suspense before a national convention has centered on the selection of a running mate. But this closely watched selection process is a recent development.

During the country's first years, the runner-up for the presidency automatically took the second slot, although that system did not last long. In 1800 Thomas Jefferson and Aaron Burr found themselves in a tie for electoral votes. Neither man's supporters were willing to settle for the lesser office. The deadlock went to the House of Representatives, where Jefferson needed thirty-six ballots to clinch the presidency. It also led to the Twelfth Amendment to the U.S. Constitution, ratified in 1804, providing for separate Electoral College balloting for president and vice president. With the emergence of political parties after 1800, candidates ran as teams. Once party conventions began in 1831, delegates, with the guidance of party bosses, began to do the choosing.

In fact, it was only in 1940 that presidential nominees began regularly hand-picking their running mates. That year, after failing to persuade Secretary of State Cordell Hull to accept the vice presidency, Franklin D. Roosevelt forced Henry A. Wallace on a reluctant Democratic convention by threatening to not run a third time if Wallace was rejected. The only exception to the practice Roosevelt established came in 1956, when Democrat Adlai E. Stevenson left the choice up to the convention.

If the selection of a running mate often seemed like something of an afterthought, it could be because the position itself was not especially coveted. John Adams, the first to hold the job, once complained, "My country has in its wisdom contrived for me the most insignificant office that ever the intention of man contrived or his imagination conceived." More than a century later Thomas R. Marshall, Woodrow Wilson's vice president, expressed a similarly dismal view: "Once there were two brothers. One ran away to sea; the other was elected Vice President. And nothing was ever heard of either of them again."

Writing in *Atlantic* in 1974, historian Arthur Schlesinger Jr. suggested the office be done away with. "It is a doomed office," he commented. "The Vice President has only one serious thing to do: that is, to wait around for the President to die." But there is a reasonable chance that whoever fills the position will get a chance to move up, either by succession or election. As of 2000, fourteen presidents had held the second-ranking post, seven in the twentieth century.

Also, since the 1970s the vice presidency has evolved from the somnolent office it once was; during this period four vice presidents enjoyed responsibility their predecessors did not. Nelson A. Rockefeller, who served under Gerald R. Ford, was given considerable authority in domestic policy coordination. Walter F. Mondale and George Bush helped to set policy for their respective presidents. And Bill Clinton placed Al Gore in charge of a "reinventing government" task force as well as environmental and high-tech initiatives. Many aspiring politicians now see the office as the premier base from which to campaign for the presidency.

Yet whoever is selected is often scrutinized for how well the choice balances (or unbalances) the ticket. One important factor is geography, which Clinton of Arkansas used unconventionally in choosing Sen. Gore of Tennessee to form the first successful all-southern ticket in 164 years. Other traditional factors weighed by nominees are religion and ethnicity. In modern national politics, however, those considerations seemed to be losing their place to race, gender, and age. In 1984, for example, the Democrats chose Rep. Geraldine A. Ferraro of New York to be their vice-presidential candidate, the first woman to receive a major party nomination.

Although no African American has so far been selected by either party, many Democrats thought that Jesse Jackson deserved second place on the ticket in 1988. Jackson had received 29 percent of the primary vote to 43 percent for Michael Dukakis. Instead, the fifty-four-year-old Dukakis chose Sen. Lloyd Bentsen of Texas, then sixty-seven, balancing the Democratic ticket by age as well as geographically and philosophically.

In 1988 George Bush surprised many by selecting Sen. Dan Quayle of Indiana. Quayle was forty-one years old and had a relatively brief career in politics—two terms in the House of Representatives before his election to the Senate in 1980. Because of Quayle's youth and good looks, it was even suggested by some critics that Bush had selected him to appeal to young voters and women. Some disturbing revelations about Quayle's education and National Guard service along with his tendency to misspeak fostered doubts that he was qualified to serve a "heartbeat" away from the presidency. But Bush vigorously defended his choice, and the two won in 1988, before losing their bid for reelection in 1992.

For his running mate, the forty-six-year-old Clinton, in another unbalancing act, selected someone in his own age group (Gore, forty-four) rather than an elder statesman like Bentsen (who served as Clinton's first secretary of the Treasury). But what the Clinton-Gore ticket lacked in the traditional sense, it made up with a balance of the candidate's other attributes. As governor of Arkansas, Clinton lacked foreign policy experience and had a mixed environmental record. Gore had a strong foreign policy and environmental record in Congress.

In 2000 Vice President Gore ran for the White House against Bush's son, Texas governor George W. Bush, who went a different direction from his father in choosing a running mate. The younger Bush chose an experienced Washington hand, Richard B. Cheney, who was a former Wyoming representative and defense secretary in the elder Bush's administration.

As for Gore, he too broke new ground. Rather than pick a southern baby-boomer as Clinton had, he chose Connecticut Senator Joseph I. Lieberman, the fifty-eight-year-old chair of the centrist Democratic Leadership Council and the first member of the Jewish faith to win a place on the national ticket of either major party.

Similarly, the main entrants in the Republican presidential primaries that year failed to capture their party's nomination. Sen. Warren G. Harding of Ohio, the compromise choice, won the primary in his home state but lost badly in Indiana and garnered only a handful of votes elsewhere. The three primary leaders—Sen. Hiram Johnson of California, Gen. Leonard Wood of New Hampshire, and Gov. Frank O. Lowden of Illinois—lost out in the end.

After the first wave of enthusiasm for presidential primaries, interest in them waned. By 1935, eight states had repealed their presidential primary laws. The diminution of reform zeal during the 1920s, the preoccupation of the country with the Great Depression in the 1930s, and war in the 1940s appeared to have been leading factors in this decline. Also, party leaders were not enthusiastic about primaries; the cost of conducting them was relatively high, both for the candidates and the states. Many presidential candidates ignored the primaries, and voter participation often was low.

But after World War II, interest picked up again. Some politicians with presidential ambitions, knowing the party leadership was not enthusiastic about their candidacies, entered the primaries to try to generate a bandwagon effect. In 1948 Harold Stassen, Republican governor of Minnesota from 1939 to 1943, entered presidential primaries in opposition to the Republican organization and made some headway before losing in Oregon to Gov. Thomas E. Dewey of New York. And in 1952, Sen. Estes Kefauver, D-Tenn., riding a wave of public recognition as head of the Senate Organized Crime Investigating Committee, challenged Democratic Party leaders by winning several primaries, including an upset of President Harry S. Truman in New Hampshire. The Eisenhower-Taft struggle for the Republican Party nomination that year also stimulated interest in the primaries.

In 1960 Sen. John F. Kennedy of Massachusetts challenged Sen. Hubert Humphrey of Minnesota in two primaries: Wisconsin, which bordered on Humphrey's home state, and West Virginia, a labor state with few Catholic voters. (Kennedy was Roman Catholic, and some questioned whether voters would elect a Catholic president.) After Kennedy won both primaries, Humphrey withdrew from the race. The efforts of party leaders to draft an alternative to Kennedy came to be viewed as undemocratic by rank-and-file voters. The primary now significantly challenged approval by party leaders as the preferred route to the nomination.

Similarly, Sen. Barry M. Goldwater, R-Ariz., in 1964, former vice president Richard Nixon in 1968, and Sen. George S. McGovern, D-S.D., in 1972, were able to use the primaries to show their vote-getting and organizational abilities on the way to becoming their party's presidential nominees.

THE DEMOCRATS BEGIN TO TINKER

Despite the growing importance of primaries, party leaders until 1968 maintained some control of the nominating process. With only a handful of the fifteen to twenty primaries regularly contested, candidates could count on a short primary season. They began in New Hampshire in March, then tested their appeal during the spring in Wisconsin, Nebraska, Oregon, and

Presidents' Reelection Chances

The record of twentieth-century U.S. presidential elections indicates that a smooth path to renomination is essential for incumbents seeking reelection. Every president who actively sought renomination this century was successful. And those who were virtually unopposed within their own party won another term. But all the presidents who faced significant opposition for renomination ended up losing in the general election.

The following chart shows the presidents who sought reelection to a second term since 1900, whether they had "clear sailing" or "tough sledding" for renomination and their fate in the general election.

A president with an asterisk (*) next to his name was, like Ronald Reagan in 1984, completing his first full four-year term when he sought reelection. A dash (—) indicates there were no presidential preference primaries. The primary vote for President Lyndon B. Johnson in 1964 included the vote cast for favorite sons and uncommitted delegate slates; Johnson was subsequently nominated by acclamation at the Democratic convention. George Bush in 1992 had to fight off a significant challenge by Patrick J. Buchanan in the Republican primaries before he went on to win 95 percent of the convention delegates.

	Primary vote	Convention delegates	General election result
'Clear Sailing'			
William McKinley (1900) *	—	100%	Won
Theodore Roosevelt (1904)	—	100	Won
Woodrow Wilson (1916) *	99%	99	Won
Calvin Coolidge (1924)	68	96	Won
Franklin D. Roosevelt (1936) *	93	100	Won
Franklin D. Roosevelt (1940)	72	86	Won
Franklin D. Roosevelt (1944)	71	92	Won
Harry S. Truman (1948)	64	75	Won
Dwight D. Eisenhower (1956) *	86	100	Won
Lyndon B. Johnson (1964)	88	100	Won
Richard Nixon (1972) *	87	99	Won
Ronald Reagan (1984) *	99	100	Won
Bill Clinton (1996) *	88	100	Won
'Tough Sledding'			
William H. Taft (1912) *	34%	52%	Lost
Herbert Hoover (1932) *	33	98	Lost
Gerald R. Ford (1976)	53	53	Lost
Jimmy Carter (1980) *	51	64	Lost
George Bush (1992) *	72	95	Lost

Incumbent's Percentage of:

California before resuming their courtship of party leaders. In 1968—admittedly an unusual year, with incumbent Democratic president Lyndon B. Johnson suddenly withdrawing from his race for reelection, and the leading Democratic candidate (Sen. Robert F. Kennedy of New York) assassinated a few weeks before the convention—Vice President Humphrey was able to gain the party's nomination without entering a single primary.

But after 1968, the Democrats began tinkering with the nominating rules, in an effort to reduce the alienation of liberals and minorities from the political system and to allow the people to

VPs Who Have Become President

Fourteen men who served as vice president have become president: John Adams, Thomas Jefferson, Martin Van Buren, John Tyler, Millard Fillmore, Andrew Johnson, Chester A. Arthur, Theodore Roosevelt, Calvin Coolidge, Harry S. Truman, Richard M. Nixon, Lyndon B. Johnson, Gerald R. Ford, and George Bush.

Of those, all but Adams, Jefferson, Van Buren, Nixon, and Bush first became president on the death or resignation of their predecessor. Nine vice presidents since 1900 have run unsuccessfully for president:

• Thomas R. Marshall, Democratic vice president under Woodrow Wilson from 1913 to 1921, failed to win the nomination in 1920.

• Charles G. Dawes, Republican vice president under Coolidge from 1925 to 1929, unsuccessfully sought the nomination in 1928 and 1932.

• John Nance Garner, Democratic vice president under Franklin D. Roosevelt from 1933 to 1941, ran unsuccessfully for the nomination in 1940.

• Henry A. Wallace, Democratic vice president under Roosevelt from 1941 to 1945, was Progressive Party nominee in 1948.

• Alben W. Barkley, Democratic vice president under Truman from 1949 to 1953, failed to win the 1952 nomination.

• Nixon, Republican vice president under Dwight D. Eisenhower from 1953 to 1961, was the GOP nominee in 1960. (He won in 1968 and 1972.)

• Hubert H. Humphrey, Democratic vice president under Lyndon Johnson from 1965 to 1969, was the Democratic nominee in 1968.

• Walter F. Mondale, Democratic vice president under Jimmy Carter from 1977 to 1981, was the Democratic nominee in 1984.

• Al Gore, Democratic vice president under Bill Clinton from 1993 to 2001, was the Democratic nominee in 2000.

choose their own leaders. Victors in 1968, and four of the five presidential elections that followed, the Republicans were slow to make any changes in their rules. *(See boxes, Changes in Democrats' Nominating Rules, p. 00; GOP Primary Rules, p. 00.)* This era of grass-roots control produced for the Democrats presidential candidates such as McGovern, a liberal from South Dakota who lost in a landslide to Nixon in 1972, and Jimmy Carter, a former governor of Georgia, who beat incumbent President Gerald R. Ford in 1976 but lost to Ronald Reagan in 1980.

With a then-record high of thirty-seven primaries held in 1980 (including the District of Columbia and Puerto Rico), the opportunity for mass participation in the nominating process was greater than ever before. President Carter and Republican nominee Reagan were the clear winners of the long 1980 primary season. Although Carter received a bare majority of the cumulative Democratic primary vote, he amassed a plurality of more than two and one-half million votes over his major rival,

Sen. Edward M. Kennedy of Massachusetts. With no opposition in the late primary contests, Reagan emerged as a more one-sided choice of GOP primary voters. He finished nearly 4.8 million votes ahead of his closest competitor, George Bush.

Disheartened by Carter's massive defeat in 1980, the Democrats revised their nominating rules for the 1984 election. The party created a new bloc of so-called "superdelegates"—that is, delegate seats were reserved for party leaders who were not formally committed to any presidential candidate. This reform had two main goals. First, Democratic leaders wanted to ensure that the party's elected officials would participate at the convention. Second, they wanted to ensure that these uncommitted party leaders could play a major role in selecting the presidential nominee if no candidate was a clear front-runner.

While the reforms of the 1970s were designed to give more influence to grass-roots activists and less to party regulars, this revision was intended to bring about a deliberative process in which experienced party leaders could help select a consensus Democratic nominee with a strong chance to win the presidency.

The Democrats' new rules had some expected, as well as unexpected, results. For the first time since 1968, the number of primaries declined and the number of caucuses increased. The Democrats held only thirty primaries in 1984 (including the District of Columbia and Puerto Rico). Yet, like McGovern in 1972 and Carter in 1976, Colorado Sen. Gary Hart used the primaries to pull ahead (temporarily) of former vice president Walter F. Mondale, an early front-runner whose strongest ties were to the party leadership and its traditional core elements. In 1984 the presence of superdelegates was important because about four out of five backed Mondale. (But Mondale did wind up with more primary votes than Hart.)

A few critics regarded the seating of superdelegates as undemocratic, and there were calls for reducing their numbers. Yet to those of most influence within the party, the superdelegates had served their purpose. The Democratic National Committee (DNC) set aside additional seats for party leaders, increasing the number of superdelegates from 14 percent of the delegates in 1984 to 18 percent in 1996. All members of the DNC were guaranteed convention seats, as were all Democratic governors and members of Congress.

The Republican Party did not guarantee delegate seats to its leaders until the 2000 convention voted to make members of the RNC automatic "superdelegates" at the party's convention in 2004. Republicans had not acted before that, in part because their rules permit less rigid pledging of delegates, which generally has led to substantial participation by Republican leaders, despite the absence of such guarantees.

Regional Primaries and Super Tuesday

In addition to the Democrats' internal party concerns with the nominating process, other critics often cited the length of the primary season (nearly twice as long as the general election campaign), the expense, the physical strain on the candidates and the variations and complexities of state laws as problems of presidential primaries.

Republican presidential candidates face off in debate before the 1996 primaries. Left to right: Alan Keyes, Morry Taylor, Steve Forbes, Robert Dornan, Bob Dole, Richard Lugar, Lamar Alexander, and Pat Buchanan.

To deal with these problems, several states in 1974 and 1975 discussed the feasibility of creating regional primaries, in which individual states within a geographical region would hold their primaries on the same day. Supporters of the concept believed it would reduce candidate expenses and strain and would permit concentration on regional issues.

The idea achieved some limited success in 1976 when three western states (Idaho, Nevada, and Oregon) and three southern states (Arkansas, Kentucky, and Tennessee)—decided to organize regional primaries in each of their areas. However, the two groups chose May 25 to hold their primaries, thus defeating one of the main purposes of the plan by forcing candidates to shuttle across the country to cover both areas.

Attempts also were made in New England to construct a regional primary. But New Hampshire would not participate because its law required the state to hold its primary at least one week before any other state. Hesitancy by the other New England state legislatures defeated the idea. Only Vermont joined Massachusetts, on March 2, in holding a simultaneous presidential primary, although New Hampshire voted only one week earlier.

In 1980 and 1984, limited regional primaries were held again in several areas of the country. Probably the most noteworthy was the trio of southern states (Alabama, Florida, and Georgia) that voted on the second Tuesday in March—first, in 1980; then again in 1984. It became the basis for "Super Tuesday," which became a full-blown southern-oriented regional primary in 1988.

But the biggest change was that more and more states, hoping to increase their impact on the presidential campaign, decided to hold their primaries early. When South Dakota announced that it would hold its presidential primary in 1988 on Feb. 23, New Hampshire moved its date to Feb. 16.

Sixteen states—a dozen from the South—held primaries on Super Tuesday, March 8, 1988. The long-held goal of many southern political leaders to hold an early regional primary was finally realized. Most of the GOP primaries were winner-take-all, and when Vice President George Bush swept every Republican primary on Super Tuesday, he effectively locked up the GOP nomination. His major opponent, Sen. Robert Dole of Kansas, withdrew by the end of the month. For the Democrats, Massachusetts Gov. Michael S. Dukakis also fared well on Super Tuesday. But the Rev. Jesse Jackson—the first serious black candidate for a major-party presidential nomination—kept the contest going into June.

'MARCH MADNESS'

In 1992 Super Tuesday had become part of a general rush among states to hold their primaries as early as possible. Dubbed "March Madness," the early clustering of primaries—seventeen states held primaries in February or March—was viewed with dismay by some political analysts. They said it could lead to nominees being locked in before most voters knew what was happening, resulting in less informed and deliberative voting in the general election.

As winner in the eight Super Tuesday primaries (six of which were again in the South) on March 10, 1992, President Bush was well on his way to renomination on the GOP side. Although he lost the two New England primaries (Massachusetts and Rhode Island) that day, Bill Clinton by winning all six southern primaries (Florida, Louisiana, Mississippi, Oklahoma, Tennessee, and Texas) established himself as the Democratic front-runner. Most of his competitors had dropped out of the race by the end of the following week. Former Gov. Jerry Brown of California held out until the Democratic convention, but Brown was never able to establish any sort of momentum to overtake Clinton.

In 1996 the process was even more heavily weighted in favor of early primaries, as more than two-thirds of them were held before the end of March. The idea of regional primaries also came the closest to fruition in 1996. "Junior Tuesday Week"

Growth of Presidential Primaries: More and More, Earlier and Earlier

Over the years, there have been more and more states holding primaries earlier and earlier in the presidential election year. The result is that a nominating system that once featured primaries sprinkled across the spring is now front-loaded with the bulk of the primaries held during the winter months of February and March.

Following is a list of primaries held in each month of every nominating season from 1968 through 2000. Primaries included are those in the fifty states and the District of Columbia in which at least one of the parties permitted a direct vote for presidential candidates, or there was an aggregated statewide vote for delegates.

	1968	1972	1976	1980	1984	1988	1992	1996	2000
February	0	0	1	1	1	2	2	5	7
March	1	3	5	9	8	20	15	24	20
April	3	3	2	4	3	3	5	1	2
May	7	11	13	13	11	7	10	8	9
June	4	4	6	9	7	5	7	4	5
Total	15	21	27	36	30	37	39	42	43

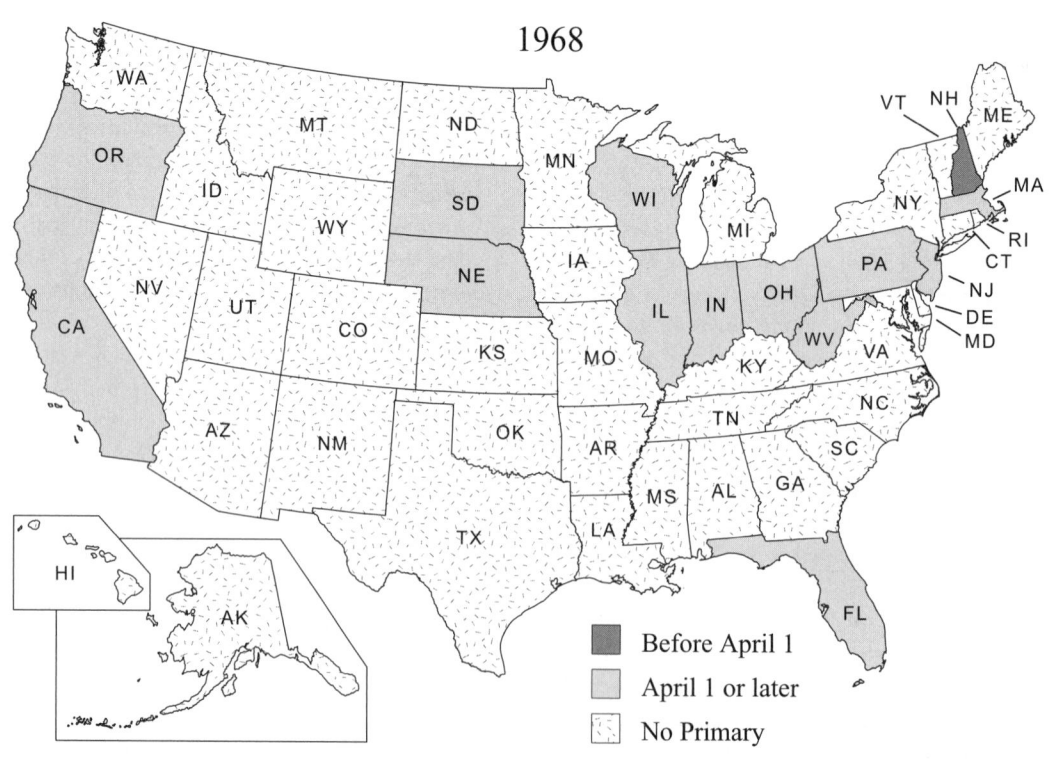

1968

Before April 1

April 1 or later

No Primary

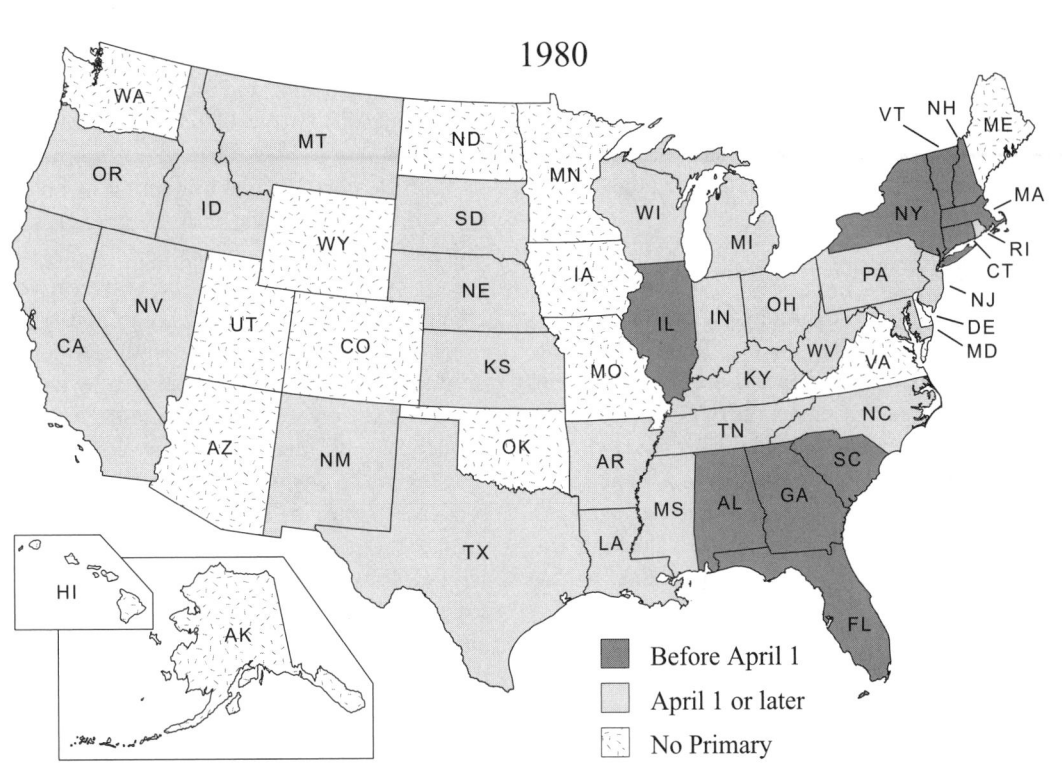

1980

Before April 1
April 1 or later
No Primary

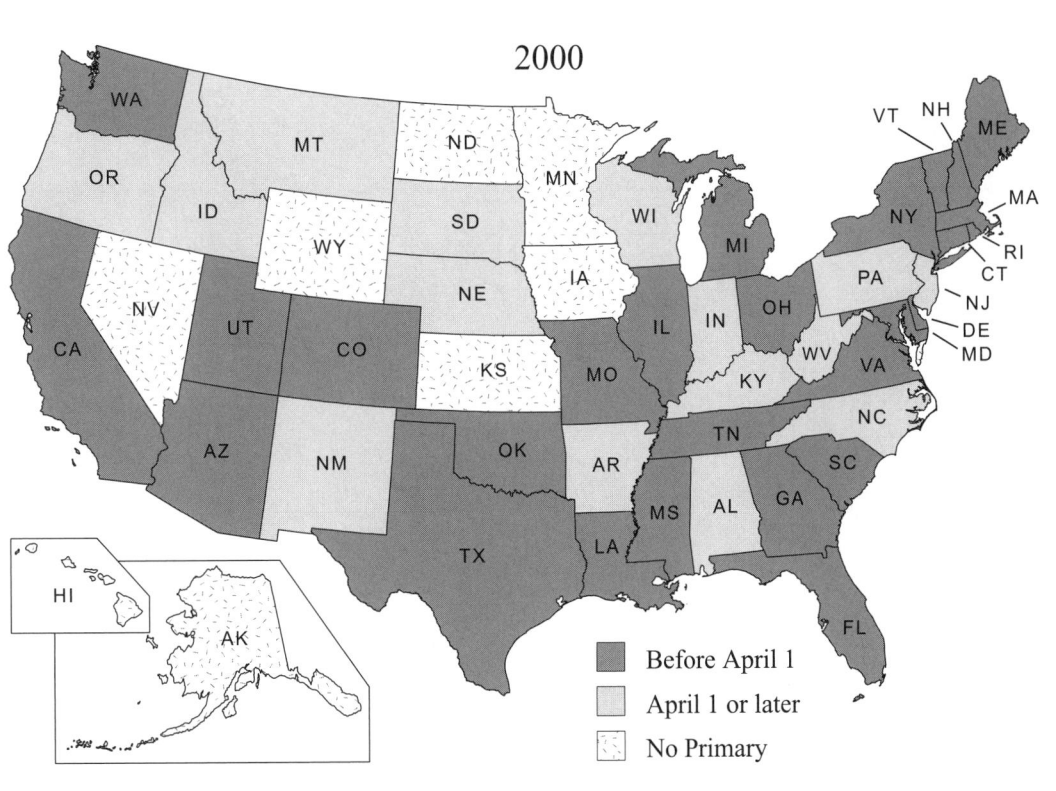

2000

Before April 1
April 1 or later
No Primary

(March 2–7) featured primary voting in ten states (five of which were in New England); Super Tuesday (March 12) had seven primaries (six of which were in the South); and "Big Ten" Tuesday (March 19) had four primaries in important midwestern states. By the time California (which had moved it primary forward in the hope of increasing its sway on the nominating process) had its primary on March 26 (along with two other western states—Nevada and Washington), Dole had all but clinched the Republican nomination.

2000 OUTCOME

In 2000 there were not only a glut of early primaries, but a large concentration on a single day, the first Tuesday in March (March 7). The clustering on this date was not coincidental. It was the earliest date allowed by Democratic rules for states other than Iowa and New Hampshire to hold their primary or caucus. Eleven states scheduled primaries on March 7, 2000, creating a de facto national primary that became variously known as "Titanic Tuesday" or the new "Super Tuesday," although the large southern-oriented vote of the same name remained on the second Tuesday in March.

Political analysts predicted the huge volume of early primaries would result in both parties' nominations being decided by the ides of March. And they were right. George W. Bush and John McCain battled almost evenly through the seven states that held Republican primaries in February—Bush winning four, McCain, three. But once the calendar turned to March, Bush's superior organization and financial resources proved decisive as he dominated the vote March 7 and drove McCain from the race.

With Democratic rules preventing a wholesale movement of states into February, the early Democratic calendar was quite different from the Republican one. The Democratic campaign essentially went "dark" from the early February voting in New Hampshire until the huge array of primaries March 7.

But the result was the same on the Democratic side as it was on the Republican, an early knockout by the front-runner. Vice President Al Gore was closely contested by his major challenger, former Sen. Bill Bradley of New Jersey, in raising funds and drawing media attention during the long stretch before the primaries. But once the balloting began, Bradley proved no match for Gore. The vice president won the late January caucuses in Iowa decisively, the New Hampshire primary narrowly, and swept all the Democratic primaries and caucuses March 7, driving Bradley to the sidelines. Only half the states had voted by then, but the Democratic and Republican races were over.

CHAPTER 11

Presidential Primary Returns, 1912–2000

PRESIDENTIAL PRIMARY RETURNS for all elections from 1912 to 2000 are presented in this chapter (pages 320–410). The main source for the primary returns from 1912 through 1952 is James W. Davis, *Presidential Primaries: Road to the White House* (Westport, Conn.: Greenwood Press, 1980). Congressional Quarterly has supplemented Davis' material with the following sources: Louise Overacker, *The Presidential Primary* (New York: Arno, 1974)—the source used by Davis for the 1912–1924 returns; Walter Kravitz, "Presidential Preference Primaries, 1928–1956," a 1960 Library of Congress study; Paul Davis, Malcolm Moos, and Ralph Goldman, *Presidential Nominating Politics in 1952* (Baltimore: Johns Hopkins Press, 1954); the offices of the secretaries of state; and state handbooks and newspapers. All statistics and footnotes are from Davis, unless otherwise indicated.

The basic source for the primary returns from 1956 to 2000 is the *America Votes* series, compiled biennially by Congressional Quarterly in Washington, D.C. Richard M. Scammon and Alice V. McGillivray of the Elections Research Center, Washington, D.C., created the series first published in 1956. Since 1996 the series has been compiled under the direction of Rhodes Cook. All statistics and footnotes are from Scammon-McGillivray or Cook, unless otherwise indicated.

Figures in the following charts represent one of three types of votes:

• Votes cast directly for a presidential candidate.
• Votes cast for delegates whose candidate preference was indicated on the ballot.
• Votes cast for unpledged delegates. (Included in the "unpledged" category were delegates designated on the ballot as "uninstructed" and "no preference.")

For the delegate-at-large vote in 1912–1924 primaries, Overacker listed the average vote for delegates at large. For the 1928–1952 delegate-at-large vote, Davis listed the highest vote received by any one delegate at large. Congressional Quarterly followed Davis's style for subsequent years.

Percentages in the following tables have been calculated to two decimal points and then rounded; 0.05 percent appears as 0.1 percent. Therefore, columns of percentages do not always total 100 percent. Major presidential candidates, primary winners, favorite sons, members of Congress, and prominent national and state political figures are included in the state-by-state primary results. Minor candidates, including most write-ins, have been grouped in the "Others" category.

The primary tables show only Republican and Democratic contests; other candidates receiving votes in third-party presidential primaries are listed in the footnotes.

1912 Primaries

Republican	Votes	%	Democratic	Votes	%
March 19 North Dakota					
Robert M. La Follette (Wis.)	34,123	57.2	John Burke (N.D.)[1]	9,357	100.0
Theodore Roosevelt (N.Y.)	23,669	39.7			
William H. Taft (Ohio)	1,876	3.1			
March 26 New York[2]					
April 2 Wisconsin					
La Follette	133,354	73.2	Woodrow Wilson (N.J.)	45,945	55.7
Taft	47,514	26.1	Champ Clark (Mo.)	36,464	44.2
Roosevelt	628	0.3	Others	148	0.2
Others	643	0.4			
April 9 Illinois					
Roosevelt	266,917	61.1	Clark	218,483	74.3
Taft	127,481	29.2	Wilson	75,527	25.7
La Follette	42,692	9.8			
April 13 Pennsylvania					
Roosevelt	282,853[3]	59.7	Wilson	98,000[3]	100.0
Taft	191,179[3]	40.3			
April 19 Nebraska					
Roosevelt	45,795	58.7	Clark	21,027	41.0
La Follette	16,785	21.5	Wilson	14,289	27.9
Taft	13,341	17.1	Judson Harmon (Ohio)	12,454	24.3
Others	2,036	2.6	Others	3,499	6.8
April 19 Oregon					
Roosevelt	28,905	40.2	Wilson	9,588	53.0
La Follette	22,491	31.3	Clark	7,857	43.4
Taft	20,517	28.5	Harmon	606	3.3
Others	14	—	Others	49	0.3
April 30 Massachusetts					
Taft	86,722	50.4	Clark	34,575	68.9
Roosevelt	83,099	48.3	Wilson	15,002	29.9
La Follette	2,058	1.2	Others	627	1.2
Others	99	0.1			
May 6 Maryland					
Roosevelt	29,124	52.8	Clark	34,021	54.4
Taft	25,995	47.2	Wilson	21,490	34.3
			Harmon	7,070	11.3
May 14 California					
Roosevelt	138,563	54.6	Clark	43,163	71.5
Taft	69,345	27.3	Wilson	17,214	28.5
La Follette	45,876	18.1			

Republican	**Votes**	**%**		**Democratic**	**Votes**	**%**
May 21 Ohio						
Roosevelt	165,809	55.3	Harmon		96,164	51.7
Taft	118,362	39.5	Wilson		85,084	45.7
La Follette	15,570	5.2	Clark		2,428	1.3
			Others		2,440	1.3
May 28 New Jersey						
Roosevelt	61,297	56.3	Wilson		48,336	98.9
Taft	44,034	40.5	Clark[4]		522	1.1
La Follette	3,464	3.2				
June 4 South Dakota						
Roosevelt	38,106	55.2	Wilson[5]		4,694	35.2
Taft	19,960	28.9	Clark[5]		4,275	32.0
La Follette	10,944	15.9	Clark[5]		2,722	20.4
			Others		1,655	12.4
TOTALS						
Roosevelt	1,164,765	51.5	Wilson		435,169	44.6
Taft	766,326	33.9	Clark		405,537	41.6
La Follette	327,357	14.5	Harmon		116,294	11.9
Others	2,792	0.1	Burke		9,357	1.0
	2,261,240		Others		8,418	0.9
					974,775	

1. Burke was the "favorite son" candidate, according to the North Dakota secretary of state.
2. Primary law optional in 1912. Republicans elected pledged delegates but figures not available.
3. Unofficial figures.
4. Write-in.

5. No presidential preference. Three sets of delegates ran: one labelled "Wilson-Bryan" which came out openly for Wilson; one "Wilson-Clark-Bryan" which became Identified with Clark; one Champ Clark which was accused by the Clark people of being a scheme to split the Clark vote. The "Wilson-Clark-Bryan" list polled 4,275 and the Champ Clark list 2,722. The delegates were given to Wilson by the convention.

1916 Primaries

Republican	Votes	%	Democratic	Votes	%
March 7 Indiana					
Charles W. Fairbanks (Ind.)[1]	176,078	100.0	Woodrow Wilson (N.J.)	160,423	100.0
March 14 Minnesota					
Albert B. Cummins (Iowa)	54,214	76.8	Wilson	45,136	100.0
Others	16,403	23.2			
March 14 New Hampshire					
Unpledged delegates	9,687	100.0	Wilson	5,684	100.0
March 21 North Dakota					
Robert M. La Follette (Wis.)	23,374[2]	70.4	Wilson	12,341	100.0
Others	9,851[2]	29.6			
April 3 Michigan					
Henry Ford (Mich.)	83,057	47.4	Wilson	84,972	100.0
William A. Smith (Mich.)	77,872	44.4			
William O. Simpson (Mich.)	14,365	8.2			
April 4 New York					
Unpledged delegates	147,038	100.0	Wilson	112,538	100.0
April 4 Wisconsin					
La Follette[1]	110,052	98.8	Wilson	109,462	99.8
Others	1,347	1.2	Others	231	0.2
April 11 Illinois					
Lawrence Y. Sherman (Ill.)[1]	155,945	90.2	Wilson	136,839	99.8
Theodore Roosevelt (N.Y.)[3]	15,348	8.9	Others	219	0.2
Others	1,689	1.0			
April 18 Nebraska					
Cummins	29,850	33.7	Wilson	69,506	87.7
Ford	26,884	30.3	Others	9,744	12.3
Charles E. Hughes (N.Y.)[3]	15,837	17.9			
Roosevelt[3]	2,256	2.5			
Others	13,780	15.6			
April 21 Montana					
Cummins	10,415	89.9	Wilson	17,960	100.0
Others	1,173	10.1			
April 25 Iowa					
Cummins	40,257	100.0	Wilson	31,447	100.0
April 25 Massachusetts					
Unpledged delegates at large[4]	60,462	57.3	Wilson	19,580	100.0
Roosevelt[4]	45,117	42.7			
April 25 New Jersey					
Roosevelt[3]	1,076	73.7	Wilson	25,407	100.0
Hughes[3]	383	26.3			

Republican	Votes	%	Democratic	Votes	%

April 25 Ohio

Theodore E. Burton (Ohio)[1]	122,165	86.8	Wilson	82,688	97.2
Roosevelt[3]	1,932	1.4	Others	2,415	2.8
Ford[3]	1,683	1.2			
Hughes[3]	469	0.3			
Others	14,428	10.3			

May 2 California

Unpledged delegates	236,277	100.0	Wilson	75,085	100.0

May 16 Pennsylvania

Martin G. Brumbaugh (Pa.)[1]	233,095	86.3	Wilson	142,202	98.7
Ford[3]	20,265	7.5	Others	1,839	1.3
Roosevelt[3]	12,359	4.6			
Hughes[3]	1,804	0.7			
Others	2,682	1.0			

May 16 Vermont

Hughes[3]	5,480	70.0	Wilson	3,711	99.4
Roosevelt[3]	1,931	24.6	Others	23	0.6
Others	423	5.4			

May 19 Oregon

Hughes	56,764	59.8	Wilson	27,898	100.0
Cummins	27,558	29.0			
Others	10,593	11.2			

May 23 South Dakota

Cummins	29,656	100.0	Wilson	10,341	100.0

June 6 West Virginia

[5]			[5]		

TOTALS

Unpledged delegates	453,464	23.6	Wilson	1,173,220	98.8
Brumbaugh	233,095	12.1	Others	14,471	1.2
Cummins	191,950	10.0		1,187,691	
Fairbanks	176,078	9.2			
Sherman	155,945	8.1			
La Follette	133,426	6.9			
Ford	131,889	6.9			
Burton	122,165	6.4			
Hughes	80,737	4.2			
Roosevelt	80,019	4.2			
Smith	77,872	4.0			
Simpson	14,365	0.7			
Others[5, 6]	72,369	3.8			
	1,923,374				

1. Source for names of "favorite son" candidates: *The New York Times*.

2. Source for vote breakdown: North Dakota secretary of state.

3. Write-in.

4. No presidential preference vote but one set of delegates at large was for Roosevelt and the other set unpledged.

5. Figures not available. Republican winner was Sen. Theodore E. Burton (R Ohio) and Democratic winner was Woodrow Wilson, according to *The New York Times*.

6. In addition to scattered votes, "others" includes Robert G. Ross who received 5,506 votes in the Nebraska primary; Henry D. Estabrook who received 9,851 in the North Dakota primary and 8,132 in the Nebraska primary.

1920 Primaries

Republican	Votes	%	Democratic	Votes	%
March 9 New Hampshire					
Leonard Wood (N.H.)[1]	8,591	53.0	Unpledged delegates[1]	7,103	100.0
Unpledged delegates	5,604	34.6			
Hiram Johnson (Calif.)[1]	2,000	12.3			
March 16 North Dakota					
Johnson	30,573	96.1	William G. McAdoo (N.Y.)[2]	49	12.6
Leonard Wood[2]	987	3.1	Others[2]	340	87.4
Frank O. Lowden (Ill.)[2]	265	0.2			
March 23 South Dakota					
Leonard Wood	31,265	36.5	Others	6,612	100.0
Lowden	26,981	31.5			
Johnson	26,301	30.7			
Others	1,144	1.3			
April 5 Michigan					
Johnson	156,939	38.4	McAdoo	18,665	21.1
Leonard Wood	112,568[3]	27.5	Edward I. Edwards (N.J.)	16,642	18.8
Lowden	62,418	15.3	A. Mitchell Palmer (Pa.)	11,187	12.6
Herbert C. Hoover (Calif.)	52,503	12.8	Others	42,000	47.5
Others	24,729	6.0			
April 6 New York					
Unpledged delegates	199,149	100.0	Unpledged delegates	113,300	100.0
April 6 Wisconsin[4]					
Leonard Wood[2]	4,505	15.0	James M. Cox (Ohio)[2]	76	2.2
Hoover[2]	3,910	13.0	Others	3,391	97.8
Johnson[2]	2,413	8.0			
Lowden[2]	921	3.1			
Others	18,350	60.9			
April 13 Illinois					
Lowden	236,802	51.1	Edwards[2]	6,933	32.3
Leonard Wood	156,719	33.8	McAdoo[2]	3,838	17.9
Johnson	64,201	13.8	Cox[2]	266	1.2
Hoover[2]	3,401	0.7	Others	10,418	48.6
Others	2,674	0.6			
April 20 Nebraska					
Johnson	63,161	46.2	Gilbert M. Hitchcock (Neb.)	37,452	67.3
Leonard Wood	42,385	31.0	Others	18,230	32.7
John J. Pershing (Mo.)	27,669	20.3			
Others	3,432	2.5			
April 23 Montana					
Johnson	21,034	52.4	Others[2]	2,994	100.0
Leonard Wood	6,804	17.0			
Lowden	6,503	16.2			
Hoover	5,076	12.6			
Warren G. Harding (Ohio)	723	1.8			

Republican	Votes	%	Democratic	Votes	%

April 27 Massachusetts

Unpledged delegates	93,356	100.0	Unpledged delegates	21,226	100.0

April 27 New Jersey

Leonard Wood	52,909	50.2	Edwards	4,163	91.4
Johnson	51,685	49.0	McAdoo[2]	180	4.0
Hoover	900	0.9	Others	213	4.7

April 27 Ohio

Harding	123,257	47.6	Cox	85,838	97.8
Leonard Wood	108,565	41.9	McAdoo[2]	292	0.3
Johnson[2]	16,783	6.5	Others	1,647	1.9
Hoover[2]	10,467	4.0			

May 3 Maryland

Leonard Wood	15,900	66.4	[5]		
Johnson	8,059	33.6			

May 4 California

Johnson	369,853	63.9	Unpledged delegates	23,831	100.0
Hoover	209,009	36.1			

May 4 Indiana

Leonard Wood	85,708	37.9	[5]		
Johnson	79,840	35.3			
Lowden	39,627	17.5			
Harding	20,782	9.2			

May 18 Pennsylvania

Edward R. Wood (Pa.)	257,841	92.3	Palmer[6]	80,356	73.7
Johnson[2]	10,869	3.8	McAdoo	26,875	24.6
Leonard Wood[2]	3,878	1.4	Edwards[2]	674	0.6
Hoover[2]	2,825	1.0	Others	1,132	1.0
Others[2]	4,059	1.5			

May 18 Vermont

Leonard Wood	3,451	66.1	McAdoo[2]	137	31.4
Hoover[2]	564	10.8	Edwards[2]	58	13.3
Johnson[2]	402	7.7	Cox[2]	14	3.2
Lowden[2]	29	0.5	Others	227	52.1
Others	777	14.9			

May 21 Oregon

Johnson	46,163	38.4	McAdoo	24,951	98.6
Leonard Wood	43,770	36.5	Others	361	1.4
Lowden	15,581	13.0			
Hoover	14,557	12.1			

May 25 West Virginia

Leonard Wood	27,255	44.6	[5]		
Others	33,849[7]	55.4			

June 5 North Carolina

Johnson	15,375	73.3	[5]		
Leonard Wood	5,603	26.7			

Republican

TOTALS	Votes	%
Johnson	965,651	30.3
Leonard Wood	710,863	22.3
Lowden	389,127	12.2
Hoover	303,212	9.5
Unpledged delegates	298,109	9.4
Edward R. Wood	257,841	8.1
Harding	144,762	4.5
Pershing	27,669	0.9
Others[8]	89,014	2.8
	3,186,248	

Democratic

	Votes	%
Unpledged delegates	165,460	28.9
Palmer	91,543	16.0
Cox	86,194	15.0
McAdoo	74,987	13.1
Hitchcock	37,452	6.6
Edwards	28,470	5.0
Others[9]	87,565	15.3
	571,671	

1. Source: Louise Overacker, *The Presidential Primaries* (1926), p. 238–39. There was no preference vote. In the Republican primary, figures given were for delegates at large favoring Wood and Johnson. In the Democratic primary, although delegates were unpledged, the organization (Robert Charles Murchie) group was understood to be for Hoover. The highest Democratic Hoover delegate received 3,714 votes.

2. Write-in.

3. Source: Overacker, *op. cit.,* p. 238.

4. No names entered for presidential preference in the Republican primary. The real contest lay between two lists of delegates, one headed by Robert M. La Follette and the other by Emanuel L. Philipp.

5. No names entered and no preference vote recorded.

6. Source for name of "favorite son" candidate: the *New York Times.*

7. Most of these votes were received by Sen. Howard Sutherland (R W. Va.). The figure is unofficial.

8. In addition to scattered votes, "others" includes Robert G. Ross who received 1,698 votes in the Nebraska primary.

9. In addition to scattered votes, "others" Includes Robert G. Ross who received 13,179 votes in the Nebraska primary.

1924 Primaries

Republican	Votes	%	Democratic	Votes	%
March 11 New Hampshire					
Calvin Coolidge (Mass.)	17,170	100.0	Unpledged delegates	6,687	100.0
March 18 North Dakota					
Coolidge	52,815	42.1	William G. McAdoo (Calif.)	11,273	100.0
Robert M. La Follette (Wis.)	40,252	32.1			
Hiram Johnson (Calif.)	32,363	25.8			
March 25 South Dakota					
Johnson	40,935	50.7	McAdoo[1]	6,983	77.4
Coolidge	39,791	49.3	Unpledged delegates[1]	2,040	22.6
April 1 Wisconsin[2]					
La Follette[3]	40,738	62.5	McAdoo	54,922	68.2
Coolidge[3]	23,324	35.8	Alfred E. Smith (N.Y.)[3]	5,774	7.2
Johnson[3]	411	0.6	Others	19,827	24.6
Others	688	1.1			
April 7 Michigan					
Coolidge	236,191	67.2	Henry Ford (Mich.)[4]	48,567	53.4
Johnson	103,739	29.5	Woodbridge N. Ferris (Mich.)[4]	42,028	46.2
Others	11,312	3.2	Others	435	0.5
April 8 Illinois					
Coolidge	533,193	58.0	McAdoo	180,544	98.9
Johnson	385,590	42.0	Smith[3]	235	0.1
La Follette[3]	278	—	Others	1,724	0.9
Others	21	—			
April 8 Nebraska					
Coolidge	79,676	63.6	McAdoo[3]	9,342	57.3
Johnson	45,032	35.9	Smith[3]	700	4.3
Others	627	0.5	Others[3]	6,268	38.4
April 22 New Jersey					
Coolidge	111,739	89.1	George S. Silzer (N.J.)[5]	35,601	97.7
Johnson	13,626	10.9	Smith[3]	721	2.0
			McAdoo[3]	69	0.2
			Others	38	0.1
April 22 Pennsylvania					
Coolidge[3]	117,262	87.9	McAdoo[3]	10,376	43.7
Johnson[3]	4,345	3.3	Smith[3]	9,029	38.0
La Follette[3]	1,224	0.9	Others[3]	4,341	18.3
Others	10,523	7.9			
April 29 Massachusetts					
Coolidge	84,840	100.0	Unpledged delegates at large[6]	30,341	100.0
April 29 Ohio					
Coolidge	173,613	86.3	James M. Cox (Ohio)[5]	74,183	71.7
Johnson	27,578	13.7	McAdoo	29,267	28.3

	Republican Votes	%		**Democratic** Votes	%
May 5 Maryland					
Coolidge	19,657	93.7	[7]		
Unpledged delegates	1,326	6.3			
Johnson[3]	3	—			
May 6 California					
Coolidge	310,618	54.3	McAdoo	110,235	85.6
Johnson	261,566	45.7	Unpledged delegates	18,586	14.4
May 6 Indiana					
Coolidge	330,045	84.1	[7]		
Johnson	62,603	15.9			
May 16 Oregon					
Coolidge	99,187	76.8	McAdoo	33,664	100.0
Johnson	30,042	23.2			
May 27 West Virginia					
Coolidge	162,042	100.0	[7]		
May 28 Montana					
Coolidge	19,200	100.0	McAdoo	10,058	100.0
TOTALS					
Coolidge	2,410,363	68.4	McAdoo	456,733	59.8
Johnson	1,007,833	28.6	Cox	74,183	9.7
La Follette	82,492	2.3	Unpledged delegates	57,654	7.5
Unpledged delegates	1,326	—	Ford	48,567	6.4
Others	23,171	0.7	Ferris	42,028	5.5
	3,525,185		Silzer	35,601	4.7
			Smith	16,459	2.2
			Others	32,633	4.3
				763,858	

1. No presidential preference vote, as McAdoo's was the only name entered, but a contest developed between "McAdoo" and "anti-McAdoo" lists of delegates. Figures are average votes cast for these lists.

2. In Wisconsin the real contest in the Republican primary was between two lists of delegates, one led by La Follette and one by Emanuel L. Philipp. In the Democratic primary, the real contest was between two lists of delegates, one favoring Smith and one favoring McAdoo.

3. Write-in.

4. Source for names of "favorite son" candidates: *Michigan Manual*, 1925.

5. Source for names of "favorite son" candidates: *The New York Times*.

6. No presidential preference vote provided for. There were nine candidates for the eight places as delegates at large, one of whom announced his preference for Smith during the campaign and received the second highest number of votes.

7. No names entered and no presidential preference vote taken.

1928 Primaries

Republican	Votes	%	Democratic	Votes	%
March 13 New Hampshire					
Unpledged delegates at large[1]	25,603	100.0	Unpledged delegates at large[1]	9,716	100.0
March 20 North Dakota					
Frank O. Lowden (Ill.)	95,857	100.0	Alfred E. Smith (N.Y.)	10,822	100.0
April 2 Michigan					
Herbert C. Hoover (Calif.)	282,809	97.6	Smith	77,276	98.3
Lowden	5,349	1.8	Thomas Walsh (Mont.)	1,034	1.3
Calvin Coolidge (Mass.)	1,666	0.6	James A. Reed (Mo.)	324	0.4
April 3 Wisconsin					
George W. Norris (Neb.)	162,822	87.1	Reed	61,097	75.0
Hoover	17,659	9.4	Smith	19,781	24.3
Lowden	3,302	1.8	Walsh	541	0.7
Coolidge	680	0.4			
Charles G. Dawes (Ill.)	505	0.3			
Others	1,894	1.0			
April 10 Illinois					
Lowden	1,172,278	99.3	Smith	44,212	91.7
Hoover	4,368	0.4	Reed	3,786	7.9
Coolidge	2,420	0.2	William G. McAdoo (Calif.)	213	0.4
Dawes	756	0.1			
Others	946	0.1			
April 10 Nebraska					
Norris	96,726	91.8	Gilbert M. Hitchcock (Neb.)	51,019	91.5
Hoover	6,815	6.5	Smith	4,755	8.5
Lowden	711	0.7			
Dawes	679	0.7			
Coolidge	452	0.4			
April 24 Ohio					
Hoover	217,430	68.1	Smith	42,365	65.9
Frank B. Willis (Ohio)	84,461	26.5	Atlee Pomerene (Ohio)	13,957	21.7
Dawes	4,311	1.4	Victor Donahey (Ohio)	7,935	12.3
Lowden	3,676	1.2			
Others	9,190	2.9			
April 24 Pennsylvania					
[2]			[2]		
April 28 Massachusetts					
Hoover[3]	100,279	85.2	Smith	38,081	98.1
Coolidge[3]	7,767	6.6	Walsh	254	0.7
Alvan Fuller (Mass.)	1,686	1.4	Others	478	1.2
Lowden[3]	1,040	0.9			
Others	6,950	5.9			
May 1 California					
Hoover	567,219	100.0	Smith	134,471	54.1
			Reed	60,004	24.1
			Walsh	46,770	18.8
			Others	7,263	2.9

Republican	Votes	%	Democratic	Votes	%

May 7 Indiana

| James E. Watson (Ind.) | 228,795 | 53.0 | Evans Woollen (Ind.) | 146,934 | 100.0 |
| Hoover | 203,279 | 47.0 | | | |

May 7 Maryland[4]

| Hoover | 27,128 | 83.3 | [5] | | |
| Unpledged delegates | 5,426 | 16.7 | | | |

May 8 Alabama

| [5] | | | Unpledged delegates at large[6] | 138,957 | 100.0 |

May 15 New Jersey

| Hoover | 382,907 | 100.0 | Smith[3] | 28,506 | 100.0 |

May 18 Oregon

Hoover	101,129	98.7	Smith	17,444	48.5
Lowden	1,322	1.3	Walsh	11,272	31.3
			Reed	6,360	17.7
			Others	881	2.5

May 22 South Dakota

| Unpledged delegates at large[7] | 34,264 | 100.0 | Unpledged delegates at large[7] | 6,221 | 100.0 |

May 29 West Virginia

Guy D. Goff (W.Va.)	128,429	54.0	Smith	81,739	50.0
Hoover	109,303	46.0	Reed	75,796	46.4
			Others	5,789	3.5

June 5 Florida

| [5] | | | Unpledged delegates at large[8] | 108,167 | 100.0 |

TOTALS

Hoover	2,020,325	49.2	Smith	499,452	39.5
Lowden	1,283,535	31.2	Unpledged delegates	263,061	20.8
Norris	259,548	6.3	Reed	207,367	16.4
Watson	228,795	5.6	Woollen	146,934	11.6
Goff	128,429	3.1	Walsh	59,871	4.7
Willis	84,461	2.1	Hitchcock	51,019	4.0
Unpledged delegates	65,293	1.6	Pomerene	13,957	1.1
Coolidge	12,985	0.3	Donahey	7,935	0.6
Dawes	6,251	0.2	McAdoo	213	—
Fuller	1,686	—	Others[10]	14,411	1.1
Others[9]	18,980	0.5			
	4,110,288			1,264,220	

1. Winning Republican delegates were unofficially pledged to Hoover and winning Democratic delegates were unofficially pledged to Smith, according to Walter Kravitz, "Presidential Preferential Primaries: Results 1928–1956" (1960), p. 4.
2. No figures available.
3. Write-in.
4. Source: Kravitz, op. cit., p. 5.
5. No primary.
6. The Montgomery Advertiser of May 3, 1928, described the delegates as independent and anti-Smith.

7. Winning Republican delegates favored Lowden and winning Democratic delegates favored Smith, according to Kravitz, op. cit., p. 5.
8. The Miami Herald of June 6, 1928, described the delegates as unpledged and anti-Smith.
9. In addition to scattered votes, "others" includes Robert G. Ross who received 8,280 votes in the Ohio primary.
10. In addition to scattered votes, "others" includes Poling who received 7,263 votes in the California primary; and Workman who received 881 in the Oregon primary and 5,789 in the West Virginia primary.

1932 Primaries

Republican	Votes	%	Democratic	Votes	%
March 8 New Hampshire					
Unpledged delegates at large[1]	22,903	100.0	Unpledged delegates at large[1]	15,401	100.0
March 15 North Dakota					
Joseph I. France (Md.)	36,000[2]	59.0	Franklin D. Roosevelt (N.Y.)	52,000[2]	61.9
Jacob S. Coxey (Ohio)	25,000[2]	41.0	William H. Murray (Okla.)	32,000[2]	38.1
March 23 Georgia					
[3]			Roosevelt	51,498	90.3
			Others	5,541	9.7
April 5 Wisconsin					
George W. Norris (Neb.)	139,514	95.5	Roosevelt	241,742	98.6
Herbert C. Hoover (Calif.)	6,588	4.5	Alfred E. Smith (N.Y.)[4]	3,502	1.4
April 12 Nebraska					
France	40,481	74.4	Roosevelt	91,393	63.5
Hoover	13,934	25.6	John N. Garner (Texas)	27,359	19.0
			Murray	25,214	17.5
April 13 Illinois					
France	345,498	98.7	James H. Lewis (Ill.)	590,130	99.8
Hoover	4,368	1.2	Roosevelt	1,084	0.2
Charles G. Dawes (Ill.)	129	—	Smith	266	—
			Others[4]	72	—
April 26 Massachusetts					
Unpledged delegates at large[5]	57,534	100.0	Smith[5]	153,465	73.1
			Roosevelt[5]	56,454	26.9
April 26 Pennsylvania					
France	352,092	92.9	Roosevelt	133,002	56.6
Hoover	20,662	5.5	Smith	101,227	43.1
Others	6,126	1.6	Others	563	0.2
May 2 Maryland					
Hoover	27,324	60.0	[6]		
France	17,008	37.3			
Unpledged delegates	1,236	2.7			
May 3 Alabama					
[3]			Unpledged delegates[7]	134,781	100.0
May 3 California					
Hoover	657,420	100.0	Garner	222,385	41.3
			Roosevelt	175,008	32.5
			Smith	141,517	26.3
May 3 South Dakota					
Johnson[8]	64,464	64.7	Roosevelt	35,370	100.0
Others	35,133	35.3			

Republican	Votes	%	**Democratic**	Votes	%
May 10 Ohio					
Coxey	75,844	58.9	Murray	112,512	96.4
France	44,853	34.8	Roosevelt[4]	1,999	1.7
Hoover	8,154	6.3	Smith[4]	951	0.8
			George White (Ohio)	834	0.7
			Newton D. Baker (Ohio)	289	0.2
			Garner[4]	72	—
May 10 West Virginia					
France	88,005	100.0	Roosevelt	219,671	90.3
			Murray	19,826	8.2
			Others	3,727	1.5
May 17 New Jersey					
France	141,330	93.3	Smith	5,234	61.9
Hoover	10,116	6.7	Roosevelt	3,219	38.1
May 20 Oregon					
France	72,681	69.0	Roosevelt	48,554	78.6
Hoover	32,599	31.0	Murray	11,993	19.4
			Others	1,214	2.0
June 7 Florida					
[3]			Roosevelt	203,372	87.7
			Murray	24,847	10.7
			Others	3,645	1.6
TOTALS					
France	1,137,948	48.5	Roosevelt	1,314,366	44.5
Hoover	781,165	33.3	Lewis	590,130	20.0
Norris	139,514	5.9	Smith	406,162	13.8
Coxey	100,844	4.3	Garner	249,816	8.5
Unpledged delegates	81,673	3.5	Murray	226,392	7.7
Johnson	64,464	2.7	Unpledged delegates	150,182	5.1
Dawes	129	—	White	834	—
Others[9]	41,259	1.8	Baker	289	—
	2,346,996		Others[10]	14,762	0.5
				2,952,933	

1. Hoover delegates won the Republican primary and Roosevelt delegates won the Democratic primary, according to Kravitz, *op. cit.*, p. 6.

2. Unofficial figures.

3. No primary.

4. Write-in.

5. Delegate-at-large vote in Republican and Democratic primaries. Hoover delegates won the Republican primary, according to Kravitz, *op. cit.*, p. 6. *The New York Times* of April 28, 1932, also reported that the Republican delegates were pledged to Hoover.

6. No names entered, according to the Maryland Record of Election Returns.

7. These were unpledged delegates who favored Roosevelt, according to Kravitz, *op. cit.*, p. 6.

8. The winning Republican delegation supported Hoover, according to Kravitz, *op. cit.*, p. 7.

9. In addition to scattered votes, "others" includes Bogue who received 35,133 in the South Dakota primary.

10. In addition to scattered votes, "others" includes Leo J. Chassee who received 3,645 in the Florida primary and 3,727 in the West Virginia primary; and Howard who received 5,541 votes in the Georgia primary.

1936 Primaries

Republican	Votes	%	Democratic	Votes	%

March 10 New Hampshire

Republican	Votes	%	Democratic	Votes	%
Unpledged delegates at large[1]	32,992	100.0	Unpledged delegates at large[1]	15,752	100.0

April 7 Wisconsin

Republican	Votes	%	Democratic	Votes	%
William E. Borah (Idaho)	187,334	98.2	Franklin D. Roosevelt (N.Y.)	401,773	100.0
Alfred M. Landon (Kan.)	3,360	1.8	John N. Garner (Texas)	108	—
			Alfred E. Smith (N.Y.)	46	—

April 14 Illinois

Republican	Votes	%	Democratic	Votes	%
Frank Knox (Ill.)	491,575	53.7	Roosevelt	1,416,411	100.0
Borah	419,220	45.8	Others[2]	411	—
Landon	3,775	0.4			
Others[2]	205	—			

April 14 Nebraska

Republican	Votes	%	Democratic	Votes	%
Borah	70,240	74.5	Roosevelt	139,743	100.0
Landon	23,117	24.5			
Others	973	1.0			

April 28 Massachusetts

Republican	Votes	%	Democratic	Votes	%
Landon[2]	76,862	80.6	Roosevelt[2]	51,924	85.9
Herbert C. Hoover (Calif.)[2]	7,276	7.6	Smith[2]	2,928	4.8
Borah[2]	4,259	4.5	Charles E. Coughlin (Mich.)[2]	2,854	4.7
Knox[2]	1,987	2.1	Others[2]	2,774	4.6
Others[2]	5,032	5.3			

April 28 Pennsylvania

Republican	Votes	%	Democratic	Votes	%
Borah	459,982	100.0	Roosevelt	720,309	95.3
			Henry Breckinridge (N.Y.)	35,351	4.7

May 4 Maryland

Republican	Votes	%	Democratic	Votes	%
[3]			Roosevelt	100,269	83.4
			Breckinridge	18,150	15.1
			Unpledged delegates	1,739	1.4

May 5 California

Republican	Votes	%	Democratic	Votes	%
Earl Warren (Calif.)	350,917	57.4	Roosevelt	790,235	82.5
Landon	260,170	42.6	Upton Sinclair (Calif.)	106,068	11.1
			John S. McGroarty (Calif.)	61,391	6.4

May 5 South Dakota

Republican	Votes	%	Democratic	Votes	%
Warren E. Green[4]	44,518	50.1	Roosevelt	48,262	100.0
Borah	44,261	49.9			

May 12 Ohio

Republican	Votes	%	Democratic	Votes	%
Stephen A. Day (Ohio)	155,732	93.4	Roosevelt	514,366	94.0
Landon	11,015	6.6	Breckinridge	32,950	6.0

May 12 West Virginia

Republican	Votes	%	Democratic	Votes	%
Borah	105,855	84.8	Roosevelt	288,799	97.3
Others	18,986	15.2	Others	8,162	2.7

Republican				**Democratic**	
	Votes	%		Votes	%
May 15 Oregon					
Borah	91,949	90.2	Roosevelt	88,305	99.8
Landon	4,467	4.4	Others	208	0.2
Others	5,557	5.4			
May 19 New Jersey					
Landon	347,142	79.2	Breckinridge	49,956	81.1
Borah	91,052	20.8	Roosevelt[2]	11,676	18.9
June 6 Florida					
[3]			Roosevelt	242,906	89.7
			Others	27,982	10.3
TOTALS					
Borah	1,474,152	44.4	Roosevelt	4,814,978	92.9
Landon	729,908	22.0	Breckinridge	136,407	2.6
Knox	493,562	14.9	Sinclair	106,068	2.0
Warren	350,917	10.6	McGroarty	61,391	1.2
Day	155,732	4.7	Unpledged delegates	17,491	0.3
Green	44,518	1.3	Smith	2,974	0.1
Unpledged delegates	32,992	1.0	Coughlin	2,854	0.1
Hoover	7,276	0.2	Garner	108	—
Others[5]	30,753	0.9	Others[6]	39,537	0.8
	3,319,810			5,181,808	

1. Delegates favorable to Knox won the Republican primary and Roosevelt delegates won the Democratic primary, according to Kravitz, *op. cit.,* p. 8.
2. Write-in.
3. No preferential primary held.
4. These delegates were unpledged but favored Landon, according to Kravitz, *op. cit.,* p. 9.

5. In addition to scattered votes, "others" includes Leo J. Chassee who received 18,986 votes in the West Virginia primary.
6. In addition to scattered votes, "others" includes Joseph A. Coutremarsh who received 27,982 votes in the Florida primary and 8,162 votes in the West Virginia primary.

1940 Primaries

Republican	Vote	%	Democratic	Vote	%

March 12 New Hampshire

Unpledged delegates at large	34,616	100.0	Unpledged delegates at large[1]	10,501	100.0

April 2 Wisconsin

Thomas E. Dewey (N.Y.)	70,168	72.6	Franklin D. Roosevelt (N.Y.)	322,991	75.4
Arthur Vandenberg (Mich.)	26,182	27.1	John N. Garner (Texas)	105,662	24.6
Robert A. Taft (Ohio)	341	0.4			

April 9 Illinois

Dewey	977,225	99.9	Roosevelt	1,176,531	86.0
Others[2]	552	0.1	Garner	190,801	14.0
			Others[2]	35	—

April 9 Nebraska

Dewey	102,915	58.9	Roosevelt	111,902	100.0
Vandenberg	71,798	41.1			

April 23 Pennsylvania

Dewey	52,661	66. 7	Roosevelt	724,657	100.0
Franklin D. Roosevelt (N.Y.)	8,294	10.5			
Arthur H. James (Pa.)	8,172	10.3			
Taft	5,213	6.6			
Vandenberg	2,384	3.0			
Herbert C. Hoover (Calif.)	1,082	1.4			
Wendell Willkie (N.Y.)	707	0.9			
Others	463	0.6			

April 30 Massachusetts

Unpledged delegates at large[3]	98,975	100.0	Unpledged delegates at large[3]	76,919	100.0

May 5 South Dakota

Unpledged delegates	52,566	100.0	Unpledged delegates	27,636	100.0

May 6 Maryland

Dewey	54,802	100.0	[4]		

May 7 Alabama

[4]			Unpledged delegates at large[5]	196,508	100.0

May 7 California

Jerrold L. Seawell[6]	538,112	100.0	Roosevelt	723,782	74.0
			Garner	114,594	11.7
			Unpledged delegates[6]	139,055	14.2

May 14 Ohio

Taft	510,025	99.5	Unpledged delegates at large[7]	283,952	100.0
Dewey[2]	2,059	0.4			
John W. Bricker (Ohio)	188	—			
Vandenberg[2]	83	—			
Willkie	53	—			
Others	69	—			

May 14 West Virginia

R. N. Davis (W.Va.)	106,123	100.0	H. C. Allen (W.Va.)	102,729	100.0

Republican	Votes	%	**Democratic**	Votes	%
May 17 Oregon					
Charles L. McNary (Ore.)	133,488	95.9	Roosevelt	109,913	87.2
Dewey	5,190	3.7	Garner	15,584	12.4
Taft	254	0.2	Others	601	0.5
Willkie	237	0.2			
Vandenberg	36	—			
May 21 New Jersey					
Dewey	340,734	93.9	Roosevelt[2]	34,278	100.0
Willkie[2]	20,143	5.6			
Roosevelt[2]	1,202	0.3			
Taft[2]	595	0.2			
Vandenberg[2]	168	—			
TOTALS					
Dewey	1,605,754	49.7	Roosevelt	3,240,054	71.7
Seawell	538,112	16.7	Unpledged delegates	734,571	16.4
Taft	516,428	16.0	Garner	426,641	9.5
Unpledged delegates	186,157	5.8	Allen	102,729	2.3
McNary	133,488	4.1	Others	636	—
Davis	106,123	3.3			
Vandenberg	100,651	3.1		4,468,631	
Willkie	21,140	0.7			
Roosevelt	9,496	0.3			
James	8,172	0.3			
Hoover	1,082	—			
Bricker	188	—			
Others	1,084	—			
	3,227,875				

1. Roosevelt delegates won, according to Kravitz, *op. cit.,* p. 10.

2. Write-in.

3. An unpledged Republican slate defeated a slate of delegates pledged to Dewey, according to Kravitz, *op. cit.,* p. 10. Sixty-nine James A. Farley delegates and three unpledged delegates won in the Democratic primary, according to Kravitz, Ibid. *The New York Times* of May 1, 1940, also reported that most Democratic delegates favored Farley.

4. No primary.

5. Winning delegates were pledged to "favorite son" candidate William B. Bankhead, then Speaker of the U.S. House of Representa-

tives, according to Kravitz, *op. cit.,* p. 10, and the *Montgomery Advertiser* of May 8, 1940.

6. *The Los Angeles Times* of May 8, 1940, reported that the Republican delegation was unpledged. In the Democratic primary, according to Davis, p. 293, unpledged slates were headed by Willis Alien, head of the California "Ham and Eggs" pension ticket which received 90,718 votes; and by Lt. Gov. Ellis E. Patterson, whose slate, backed by Labor's Non-Partisan League, received 48,337 votes.

7. Democratic delegates were pledged to Charles Sawyer (Ohio), according to *Ohio Election Statistics, 1940,* and Kravitz, *op. cit.,* p. 10.

1944 Primaries

Republican	Votes	%	Democratic	Votes	%

March 14 New Hampshire

Unpledged delegates at large[1]	16,723	100.0	Unpledged delegates at large[1]	6,772	100.0

April 5 Wisconsin

Douglas MacArthur (Wis.)	102,421	72.6	Franklin D. Roosevelt (N.Y.)	49,632	94.3
Thomas E. Dewey (N.Y.)	21,036	14.9	Others	3,014	5.7
Harold E. Stassen (Minn.)	7,928	5.6			
Wendell Willkie (N.Y.)	6,439	4.6			
Others	3,307	2.3			

April 11 Illinois

MacArthur	550,354	92.0	Roosevelt	47,561	99.3
Dewey	9,192	1.5	Others	343	0.7
Everett M. Dirksen (Ill.)	581	0.1			
John W. Bricker (Ohio)	148	—			
Stassen	111	—			
Willkie	107	—			
Others	37,575	6.3			

April 11 Nebraska

Stassen	51,800	65.7	Roosevelt	37,405	99.2
Dewey	18,418	23.3	Others	319	0.8
Willkie	8,249	10.5			
Others	432	0.5			

April 25 Massachusetts

Unpledged delegates at large	53,511	100.0	Unpledged delegates at large[1]	57,299	100.0

April 25 Pennsylvania

Dewey[2]	146,706	83.8	Roosevelt	322,469	99.7
MacArthur[2]	9,032	5.2	Others	961	0.3
Franklin D. Roosevelt (N.Y.)	8,815	5.0			
Willkie[2]	3,650	2.1			
Bricker[2]	2,936	1.7			
Edward Martin (Pa.)	2,406	1.4			
Stassen[2]	1,502	0.9			

May 1 Maryland

Unpledged delegates	17,600	78.9	[3]		
Willkie	4,701	21.1			

May 2 Alabama

[3]			Unpledged delegates at large[4]	116,922	100.0

May 2 Florida

[3]			Unpledged delegates at large[5]	118,518	100.0

May 2 South Dakota

Charles A. Christopherson[6]	33,497	60.2	Fred Hildebrandt (S.D.)[6]	7,414	52.4
Others[6]	22,135	39.8	Others[6]	6,727	47.6

May 9 Ohio

Unpledged delegates at large[7]	360,139	100.0	Unpledged delegates at large[7]	164,915	100.0

Republican	Votes	%	**Democratic**	Votes	%
May 9 West Virginia					
Unpledged delegates at large	91,602	100.0	Claude R. Linger (W.Va.)	59,282	100.0
May 16 California					
Earl Warren (Calif.)	594,439	100.0	Roosevelt	770,222	100.0
May 16 New Jersey					
Dewey	17,393	86.2	Roosevelt	16,884	99.6
Roosevelt[2]	1,720	8.5	Thomas E. Dewey (N.Y.)	60	0.4
Willkie	618	3.1			
Bricker	203	1.0			
MacArthur	129	0.6			
Stassen	106	0.5			
May 19 Oregon					
Dewey[2]	50,001	78.2	Roosevelt	79,833	98.7
Stassen[2]	6,061	9.5	Others	1,057	1.3
Willkie[2]	3,333	5.2			
Bricker[2]	3,018	4.7			
MacArthur[2]	191	0.3			
Others	1,340	2.1			
TOTALS					
MacArthur	662,127	29.1	Roosevelt	1,324,006	70.9
Warren	594,439	26.2	Unpledged delegates	464,426	24.9
Unpledged delegates	539,575	23.8	Linger	59,282	3.2
Dewey	262,746	11.6	Hildebrandt	7,414	0.4
Stassen	67,508	3.0	Dewey	60	—
Christopherson	33,497	1.5	Others[9]	12,421	0.7
Willkie	27,097	1.2		1,867,609	
Roosevelt	10,535	0.5			
Bricker	6,305	0.3			
Martin	2,406	0.1			
Dirksen	581	—			
Others[8]	64,789	2.9			
	2,271,605				

1. Nine unpledged and two Dewey delegates won the Republican primary, and Roosevelt delegates won the Democratic primary, according to Kravitz, *op. cit.*, p. 12.

2. Write-in.

3. No primary.

4. The *Montgomery Advertiser* of May 3, 1944, reported that these delegates were pro-Roosevelt but uninstructed.

5. *The New York Times* of May 3,1944, reported that a contest for delegates took place between supporters of Roosevelt and supporters of Sen. Harry F. Byrd (D Va.). A vote breakdown showing Roosevelt and Byrd strength is unavailable.

6. The winning Republican state was pledged to Stassen, the losing Republican state to Dewey and the two Democratic states to Roo-

sevelt, according to the office of the South Dakota secretary of state and Kravitz, *op. cit.*, p. 12.

7. Bricker delegates won the Republican primary and Joseph T. Ferguson delegates won the Democratic primary, according to Kravitz, *op. cit.*, p. 13.

8. In addition to scattered votes, "others" includes Riley A. Bender who received 37,575 votes in the Illinois primary and Joe H. Bottum who received 22,135 in the South Dakota primary.

9. In addition to scattered votes, "others" includes Powell who received 6,727 votes in the South Dakota primary.

1948 Primaries

Republican	Votes	%	Democratic	Votes	%

March 9 New Hampshire

Unpledged delegates at large[1]	28,854	100.0	Unpledged delegates at large[1]	4,409	100.0

April 6 Wisconsin

Harold E. Stassen (Minn.)	64,076	39.4	Harry S Truman (Mo.)	25,415	83.8
Douglas MacArthur (Wis.)	55,302	34.0	Others	4,906	16.2
Thomas E. Dewey (N.Y.)	40,943	25.2			
Others	2,429	1.5			

April 13 Illinois

Riley A. Bender (Ill.)	324,029	96.9	Truman	16,299	81.7
MacArthur	6,672	2.0	Dwight D. Eisenhower (N.Y.)	1,709	8.6
Stassen	1,572	0.5	Scott Lucas (Ill.)	427	2.1
Dewey	953	0.3	Others[2]	1,513	7.6
Robert A. Taft (Ohio)	705	0.2			
Others[2]	475	0.1			

April 13 Nebraska

Stassen	80,979	43.5	Truman	67,672	98.7
Dewey	64,242	34.5	Others	894	1.3
Taft	21,608	11.6			
Arthur Vandenberg (Mich.)	9,590	5.2			
MacArthur	6,893	3.7			
Earl Warren (Calif.)	1,761	0.9			
Joseph W. Martin (Mass.)	910	0.5			
Others	24	—			

April 20 New Jersey[3]

Dewey	3,714	41.4	Truman	1,100	92.5
Stassen	3,123	34.8	Henry A. Wallace (Iowa)	87	7.3
MacArthur	718	8.0	Others	2	0.2
Vandenberg	516	5.8			
Taft	495	5.5			
Dwight D. Eisenhower (N.Y.)	288	3.2			
Joseph W. Martin	64	0.7			
Alfred E. Driscoll (N.J.)	44	0.5			
Warren	14	0.2			

April 27 Massachusetts

Unpledged delegates at large[4]	72,191	100.0	Unpledged delegates at large[4]	51,207	100.0

April 27 Pennsylvania

Stassen[2]	81,242	31.5	Truman	328,891	96.0
Dewey[2]	76,988	29.8	Eisenhower	4,502	1.3
Edward Martin (Pa.)	45,072	17.5	Wallace	4,329	1.3
MacArthur[2]	18,254	7.1	Harold E. Stassen (Minn.)	1,301	0.4
Taft[2]	15,166	5.9	Douglas MacArthur (Wis.)	1,220	0.4
Vandenberg	8,818	3.4	Others	2,409	0.7
Harry S Truman (Mo.)	4,907	1.9			
Eisenhower	4,726	1.8			
Henry A. Wallace (Iowa)	1,452	0.6			
Others	1,537	0.6			

Republican			**Democratic**		
	Votes	%		Votes	%
May 4 Alabama					
[5]			Unpledged delegates at large[6]	161,629	100.0
May 4 Florida					
[5]			Others[7]	92,169	100.0
May 4 Ohio					
Unpledged delegates at large[8]	426,767	100.0	Unpledged delegates at large[8]	271,146	100.0
May 11 West Virginia					
Stassen	110,775	83.2	Unpledged delegates at large	157,102	100.0
Others	22,410	16.8			
May 21 Oregon					
Dewey	117,554	51.8	Truman	112,962	93.8
Stassen	107,946	47.6	Others	7,436	6.2
Others	1,474	0.6			
June 1 California					
Warren	769,520	100.0	Truman	811,920	100.0
June 1 South Dakota					
Hitchcock[9]	45,463	100.0	Truman[9]	11,193	58.3
			Unpledged Delegates[9]	8,016	41.7
TOTALS					
Warren	771,295	29.1	Truman	1,375,452	63.9
Unpledged delegates	527,812	19.9	Unpledged delegates	653,509	30.4
Stassen	449,713	16.9	Eisenhower	6,211	0.3
Bender	324,029	12.2	Wallace	4,416	0.2
Dewey	304,394	11.5	Stassen	1,301	0.1
MacArthur	87,839	3.3	MacArthur	1,220	0.1
Hitchcock	45,463	1.7	Lucas	427	—
Edward Martin	45,072	1.7	Others	109,329	5.1
Taft	37,974	1.4		2,151,865	
Vandenberg	18,924	0.7			
Eisenhower	5,014	0.2			
Truman	4,907	0.2			
Wallace	1,452	0.1			
Joseph W. Martin	974	—			
Driscoll	44	—			
Others[10]	28,349	1.1			
	2,653,255				

1. Six unpledged and two Dewey delegates won in the Republican primary, and Truman delegates won in the Democratic primary, according to Kravitz, *op. cit.*, p. 14.

2. Write-in.

3. Source: Kravitz, *op. cit.*, p. 14.

4. The *Boston Globe* of April 28, 1948, reported that the Republican delegation was "generally unpledged" but was expected to support the "favorite son" candidacy of Sen. Leverett Saltonstall (R Mass.) on the first convention ballot. The Globe reported that Democratic delegates were presumed to favor Truman's nomination.

5. No primary.

6. Unpledged, anti-Truman slate, according to Kravitz, *op. cit.*, p. 15.

7. Unpledged slate, according to Kravitz, *ibid.*

8. Taft won 44 delegates and Stassen nine in the Republican primary, and W.A. Julian won 55 delegates and Bixler one in the Democratic primary, according to Kravitz., *ibid.*

9. Republican delegates were unpledged, according to Kravitz, *op. cit.*, p. 15. In the Democratic primary, according to Davis, p. 297, the slate led by South Dakota Democratic Party Chairman Lynn Fellows endorsed Truman and the slate headed by former Rep. Fred Hildebrandt (D S.D.) ran uninstructed.

10. In addition to scattered votes, "others" includes Byer who received 15,675 votes and Vander Pyl who received 6,735 votes in the West Virginia primary.

1952 Primaries

Republican	Votes	%	Democratic	Votes	%
March 11 New Hampshire					
Dwight D. Eisenhower (N.Y.)	46,661	50.4	Estes Kefauver (Tenn.)	19,800	55.0
Robert A. Taft (Ohio)	35,838	38.7	Harry S Truman (Mo.)	15,927	44.2
Harold E. Stassen (Minn.)	6,574	7.1	Douglas MacArthur (Wis.)	151	0.4
Douglas MacArthur (Wis.)[1]	3,227	3.5	James A. Farley (N.Y.)	77	0.2
Others	230	0.3	Adlai E. Stevenson (Ill.)	40	0.1
March 18 Minnesota					
Stassen	129,706	44.4	Hubert H. Humphrey (Minn.)	102,527	80.0
Eisenhower[1]	108,692	37.2	Kefauver[1]	20,182	15.8
Taft[1]	24,093	8.2	Truman[1]	3,634	2.8
Earl Warren (Calif.)[1]	5,365	1.8	Dwight D. Eisenhower (N.Y.)	1,753	1.4
MacArthur[1]	1,369	0.5			
Estes Kefauver (Tenn.)	386	0.1			
Others	22,712	7.8			
April 1 Nebraska					
Taft[1]	79,357	36.2	Kefauver	64,531	60.3
Eisenhower[1]	66,078	30.1	Robert S. Kerr (Okla.)	42,467	39.7
Stassen	53,238	24.3			
MacArthur[1]	7,478	3.4			
Warren[1]	1,872	0.9			
Others	11,178	5.1			
April 1 Wisconsin					
Taft	315,541	40.6	Kefauver	207,520	85.9
Warren	262,271	33.8	Others	34,005	14.1
Stassen	169,679	21.8			
Others	29,133	3.8			
April 8 Illinois					
Taft	935,867	73.6	Kefauver	526,301	87.7
Stassen	155,041	12.2	Stevenson	54,336	9.1
Eisenhower[1]	147,518	11.6	Truman	9,024	1.5
MacArthur[1]	7,504	0.6	Eisenhower	6,655	1.1
Warren	2,841	0.2	Others[1]	3,798	0.6
Others	23,550	1.9			
April 15 New Jersey					
Eisenhower	390,591	60.7	Kefauver	154,964	100.0
Taft	228,916	35.6			
Stassen	23,559	3.7			
April 22 Pennsylvania					
Eisenhower	863,785	73.6	Kefauver[1]	93,160	53.3
Taft[1]	178,629	15.2	Eisenhower[1]	28,660	16.4
Stassen	120,305	10.3	Truman[1]	26,504	15.2
MacArthur[1]	6,028	0.5	Robert A. Taft (Ohio)	8,311	4.8
Warren	3,158	0.3	Averell Harriman (N.Y.)[1]	3,745	2.1
Harry S Truman (Mo.)	267	—	Stevenson[1]	3,678	2.1
Others	1,121	0.1	Richard B. Russell (Ga.)[1]	1,691	1.0
			Others	9,026	5.2

Republican				Democratic		
	Votes	**%**			**Votes**	**%**
April 29 Massachusetts						
Eisenhower[1]	254,898	69.8	Kefauver		29,287	55.7
Taft[1]	110,188	30.2	Eisenhower		16,007	30.5
			Truman		7,256	13.8
May 5 Maryland[2]						
[3]			Kefauver		137,885	74.8
			Unpledged delegates		46,361	25.2
May 6 Florida						
[3]			Russell		367,980	54.5
			Kefauver		285,358	42.3
			Others		21,296	3.2
May 6 Ohio						
Taft[4]	663,791	78.8	Kefauver[4]		305,992	62.3
Stassen[4]	178,739	21.2	Robert J. Bulkley (Ohio)[4]		184,880	37.7
May 13 West Virginia						
Taft	139,812	78.5	Unpledged delegates at large		191,471	100.0
Stassen	38,251	21.5				
May 16 Oregon						
Eisenhower	172,486	64.6	Kefauver		142,440	72.3
Warren	44,034	16.5	William O. Douglas (Wash.)		29,532	15.0
MacArthur	18,603	7.0	Stevenson		20,353	10.3
Taft[1]	18,009	6.7	Eisenhower[1]		4,690	2.4
Wayne L. Morse (Ore.)	7,105	2.7				
Stassen	6,610	2.5				
Others	350	0.1				
June 3 California						
Warren	1,029,495	66.4	Kefauver		1,155,839	70.4
Thomas H. Werdel (Calif.)	521,110	33.6	Edmund G. Brown (Calif.)		485,578	29.6
June 3 South Dakota						
Taft	64,695	50.3	Kefauver		22,812	66.0
Eisenhower	63,879	49.7	Others[5]		11,741	34.0
June 17 District of Columbia[6]						
[3]			Harriman		14,075	74.9
			Kefauver		3,377	18.0
			Others[1]		1,329	7.1

Republican	Votes	%	Democratic	Votes	%
TOTALS					
Taft	2,794,736	35.8	Kefauver	3,169,448	64.3
Eisenhower	2,114,588	27.1	Brown	485,578	9.9
Warren	1,349,036	17.3	Russell	369,671	7.5
Stassen	881,702	11.3	Unpledged delegates	237,832	4.8
Werdel	521,110	6.7	Bulkley	184,880	3.8
MacArthur	44,209	0.6	Humphrey	102,527	2.1
Morse	7,105	0.1	Stevenson	78,583	1.6
Kefauver	386	—	Truman	62,345	1.3
Truman	267	—	Eisenhower	57,765	1.2
Others[7]	88,274	1.1	Kerr	42,467	0.9
	7,801,413		Douglas	29,532	0.6
			Harriman	17,820	0.4
			Taft	8,311	0.2
			MacArthur	151	—
			Farley	77	—
			Others[8]	81,019	1.6
				4,928,006	

1. Write-in.
2. Source: Kravitz, *op. cit.,* p. 18, and the office of the Maryland secretary of state.
3. No primary.
4. Delegate-at-large vote.
5. These delegates ran on an uninstructed slate, according to Kravitz, *op. cit.,* p. 19.
6. Source: David, Moos, and Goldman, *Nominating Politics in 1952,* Vol. 2, pp. 331–332.

7. In addition to scattered votes, "others" includes Schneider who received 230 votes and received 10,411 in the Nebraska primary; Ritter who received 26,208 and Stearns who received 2,925 in the Wisconsin primary; Slettandahl who received 22,712 in the Minnesota primary and Riley Bender who received 22,321 votes in the Illinois primary.
8. In addition to scattered votes, "others" includes Fox who received 18,322 votes and Charles Broughton who received 15,683 votes in the Wisconsin primary; Compton who received 11,331 and Shaw who received 9,965 in the Florida primary.

1956 Primaries

Republican	Votes	%	Democratic	Votes	%
March 13 New Hampshire					
Dwight D. Eisenhower (Pa.)	56,464	98.9	Estes Kefauver (Tenn.)	21,701	84.6
Others	600	1.1	Others	3,945	15.4
March 20 Minnesota					
Eisenhower	198,111	98.4	Kefauver	245,885	56.8
William F. Knowland (Calif.)	3,209	1.6	Adlai E. Stevenson (Ill.)	186,723	43.2
Others	51	—	Others	48	—
April 3 Wisconsin					
Eisenhower	437,089	95.9	Kefauver	330,665[1]	100.0
Others	18,743	4.1			
April 10 Illinois					
Eisenhower	781,710	94.9	Stevenson	717,742	95.3
Knowland	33,534	4.1	Kefauver[2]	34,092	4.5
Others	8,455	1.0	Others	1,640	0.2
April 17 New Jersey					
Eisenhower	357,066	100.0	Kefauver	117,056	95.7
Others	23	—	Others	5,230	4.3
April 24 Alaska (Territory)					
Eisenhower	8,291	94.4	Stevenson	7,123	61.1
Knowland	488	5.6	Kefauver	4,536	38.9
April 24 Massachusetts					
Eisenhower[2]	51,951	95.1	John W. McCormack (Mass.)[2]	26,128	47.9
Adlai E. Stevenson (Ill.)[2]	604	1.1	Stevenson[2]	19,024	34.9
Christian A. Herter (Mass.)[2]	550	1.0	Kefauver[2]	4,547	8.3
Richard M. Nixon (N.Y.)[2]	316	0.6	Dwight D. Eisenhower (Pa.)[2]	1,850	3.4
John W. McCormack (Mass.)[2]	268	0.5	John F. Kennedy (Mass.)[2]	949	1.7
Knowland[2]	250	0.5	Averell Harriman (N.Y.)[2]	394	0.7
Others[2]	700	1.3	Frank J. Lausche (Ohio)[2]	253	0.5
			Others[2]	1,379	2.5
April 24 Pennsylvania					
Eisenhower	951,932	95.5	Stevenson	642,172	93.6
Knowland	43,508	4.4	Kefauver[2]	36,552	5.3
Others	976	0.1	Others	7,482	1.1
May 1 District of Columbia[3]					
Eisenhower	18,101	100.0	Stevenson	17,306	66.2
			Kefauver	8,837	33.8
May 7 Maryland					
Eisenhower	66,904	95.5	Kefauver	112,768	65.9
Unpledged delegates	3,131	4.5	Unpledged delegates	58,366	34.1
May 8 Indiana					
Eisenhower	351,903	96.4	Kefauver	242,842[1]	100.0
Others	13,320	3.6			
May 8 Ohio					
John W. Bricker (Ohio)	478,453[1]	100.0	Lausche	276,670[1]	100.0

Republican	Votes	%	Democratic	Votes	%

May 8 West Virginia

Unpledged delegates at large	111,883[1]	100.0	Unpledged delegates at large	112,832[1]	100.0

May 15 Nebraska

Eisenhower	102,576	99.8	Kefauver	55,265	94.0
Others	230	0.2	Others	3,556	6.0

May 18 Oregon

Eisenhower	231,418[1]	100.0	Stevenson[2]	98,131	60.2
			Kefauver[2]	62,987	38.6
			Harriman[2]	1,887	1.2

May 29 Florida

Eisenhower	39,690	92.0	Stevenson	230,285	51.5
Knowland	3,457	8.0	Kefauver	216,549	48.5

June 5 California

Eisenhower	1,354,764[1]	100.0	Stevenson	1,139,964	62.6
			Kefauver	680,722	37.4

June 5 Montana

S. C. Arnold[4]	32,732	85.7	Kefauver	77,228[1]	100.0
Others	5,447	14.3			

June 5 South Dakota

Unpledged delegates[5]	59,374[1]	100.0	Kefauver	30,940[1]	100.0

TOTALS

Eisenhower	5,007,970	85.9	Stevenson	3,051,347	52.3
Bricker	478,453	8.2	Kefauver	2,278,636	39.1
Unpledged delegates	174,388	3.0	Lausche	276,923	4.7
Knowland	84,446	1.4	Unpledged delegates	171,198	2.9
S. C. Arnold	32,732	0.6	McCormack	26,128	0.4
Stevenson	604	—	Harriman	2,281	—
Herter	550	—	Eisenhower	1,850	—
Nixon	316	—	Kennedy	949	—
McCormack	268	—	Others	23,280	0.4
Others[6]	48,545	0.8		5,832,592	
	5,828,272				

1. Figures obtained from Scammon's office. In *America Votes*, Scammon did not record vote totals if a candidate was unopposed or if the primary was strictly for delegate selection.
2. Write-in.
3. Source: Davis, *op. cit.*, pp. 300–301.
4. Voters cast their ballots for S. C. Arnold, "stand-in" candidate for Eisenhower.

5. Slate unofficially pledged to Eisenhower but appeared on the ballot as "No preference."
6. In addition to scattered votes, "others" includes Lar Daly who received 8,364 votes in the Illinois primary, 13,320 votes in the Indiana primary and 5,447 votes in the Montana primary; and John Bowman Chapple who received 18,743 votes in the Wisconsin primary.

1960 Primaries

Republican	Votes	%	Democratic	Votes	%

March 8 New Hampshire

Republican	Votes	%	Democratic	Votes	%
Richard M. Nixon (N.Y.)	65,204	89.3	John F. Kennedy (Mass.)	43,372	85.2
Nelson A. Rockefeller (N.Y.)[1]	2,745	3.8	Others	7,527	14.8
John F. Kennedy (Mass.)[1]	2,196	3.0			
Others	2,886	4.0			

April 5 Wisconsin

Nixon	339,383[2]	100.0	Kennedy	476,024	56.5
			Hubert H. Humphrey (Minn.)	366,753	43.5

April 12 Illinois

Nixon	782,849[2]	99.9	Kennedy[1]	34,332	64.6
Others[1]	442[2]	0.1	Adlai E. Stevenson (Ill.)[1]	8,029	15.1
			Stuart Symington (Mo.)[1]	5,744	10.8
			Humphrey[1]	4,283	8.1
			Lyndon B. Johnson (Texas)[1]	442	0.8
			Others[1]	337	0.6

April 19 New Jersey

Unpledged delegates at large	304,766[2]	100.0	Unpledged delegates at large	217,608[2]	100.0

April 26 Massachusetts

Nixon[1]	53,164	86.0	Kennedy[1]	91,607	92.4
Rockefeller[1]	4,068	6.6	Stevenson[1]	4,684	4.7
Kennedy[1]	2,989	4.8	Humphrey[1]	794	0.8
Henry Cabot Lodge (Mass.)[1]	373	0.6	Richard M. Nixon (Calif.)[1]	646	0.7
Adlai E. Stevenson (Ill.)[1]	266	0.4	Symington[1]	443	0.4
Barry Goldwater (Ariz.)[1]	221	0.4	Johnson[1]	268	0.3
Dwight D. Eisenhower (Pa.)[1]	172	0.3	Others[1]	721	0.7
Others[1]	592	1.0			

April 26 Pennsylvania

Nixon	968,538	98.1	Kennedy[1]	183,073	71.3
Rockefeller[1]	12,491	1.3	Stevenson[1]	29,660	11.5
Kennedy[1]	3,886	0.4	Nixon[1]	15,136	5.9
Stevenson[1]	428	—	Humphrey[1]	13,860	5.4
Goldwater[1]	286	—	Symington[1]	6,791	2.6
Others[1]	1,202	0.1	Johnson[1]	2,918	1.1
			Rockefeller[1]	1,078	0.4
			Others[1]	4,297	1.7

May 3 District of Columbia[3]

Unpledged delegates	9,468	100.0	Humphrey	8,239	57.4
			Wayne L. Morse (Ore.)	6,127	42.6

May 3 Indiana

Nixon	408,408	95.4	Kennedy	353,832	81.0
Others	19,677	4.6	Others	82,937	19.0

May 3 Ohio

Nixon	504,072[2]	100.0	Michael V. DiSalle (Ohio)	315,312[2]	100.0

May 10 Nebraska

Nixon	74,356	93.8	Kennedy	80,408	88.7
Rockefeller[1]	2,028	2.6	Symington[1]	4,083	4.5

Republican	Votes	%	Democratic	Votes	%
Goldwater[1]	1,068	1.3	Humphrey[1]	3,202	3.5
Others[1]	1,805	2.3	Stevenson[1]	1,368	1.5
			Johnson[1]	962	1.1
			Others[1]	669	0.7

May 10 West Virginia

	Votes	%		Votes	%
Unpledged delegates at large	123,756[2]	100.0	Kennedy	236,510	60.8
			Humphrey	152,187	39.2

May 17 Maryland

				Votes	%
[4]			Kennedy	201,769	70.3
			Morse	49,420	17.2
			Unpledged delegates	24,350	8.5
			Others	11,417	4.0

May 20 Oregon

	Votes	%		Votes	%
Nixon	211,276	93.1	Kennedy	146,332	51.0
Rockefeller[1]	9,307	4.1	Morse	91,715	31.9
Kennedy[1]	2,864	1.3	Humphrey	16,319	5.7
Goldwater[1]	1,571	0.7	Symington	12,496	4.4
Others[1]	2,015	0.9	Johnson	11,101	3.9
			Stevenson[1]	7,924	2.8
			Others[1]	1,210	0.4

May 24 Florida

	Votes	%		Votes	%
Nixon	51,036[2]	100.0	George A. Smathers (Fla.)	322,235[2]	100.0

June 7 California

	Votes	%		Votes	%
Nixon	1,517,652[2]	100.0	Edmund G. Brown (Calif.)	1,354,031	67.7
			George H. McLain (Calif.)	646,387	32.3

June 7 South Dakota

	Votes	%		Votes	%
Unpledged delegates	48,461[2]	100.0	Humphrey	24,773[2]	100.0

TOTALS

	Votes	%		Votes	%
Nixon	4,975,938	89.9	Kennedy	1,847,259	32.5
Unpledged delegates	486,451	8.8	Brown	1,354,031	23.8
Rockefeller	30,639	0.6	McLain	646,387	11.4
Kennedy	11,935	0.2	Humphrey	590,410	10.4
Goldwater	3,146	0.1	Smathers	322,235	5.7
Stevenson	694	—	DiSalle	315,312	5.5
Lodge	373	—	Unpledged delegates	241,958	4.3
Eisenhower	172	—	Morse	147,262	2.6
Others[5]	28,619	0.5	Stevenson	51,665	0.9
	5,537,967		Symington	29,557	0.5
			Nixon	15,782	0.3
			Johnson	15,691	0.3
			Others[6]	110,192	1.9
				5,687,742	

1. Write-in.
2. Figures obtained from Scammon's office. In *America Votes*, Scammon did not record vote totals if a candidate was unopposed or if the primary was strictly for delegate selection.
3. Source: District of Columbia Board of Elections.
4. No primary.
5. In addition to scattered votes, "others" includes Paul C. Fisher who received 2,388 votes in the New Hampshire primary and Frank R. Beckwith who received 19,677 in the Indiana primary.

6. In addition to scattered votes, "others" includes Lar Daly who received 40,853 votes in the Indiana primary and 7,536 in the Maryland primary; Paul C. Fisher who received 6,853 votes in the New Hampshire primary; John H. Latham who received 42,084 in the Indiana primary and Andrew J. Easter who received 3,881 votes in the Maryland primary.

1964 Primaries

Republican	Votes	%	Democratic	Votes	%
March 10 New Hampshire					
Henry Cabot Lodge (Mass.)[1]	33,007	35.5	Lyndon B. Johnson (Texas)[1]	29,317	95.3
Barry M. Goldwater (Ariz.)	20,692	22.3	Robert F. Kennedy (N.Y.)[1]	487	1.6
Nelson A. Rockefeller (N.Y.)	19,504	21.0	Henry Cabot Lodge (Mass.)[4]	280	0.9
Richard M. Nixon (Calif.)[1]	15,587	16.8	Richard M. Nixon (Calif.)[1]	232	0.8
Margaret Chase Smith (Maine)	2,120	2.3	Barry M. Goldwater (Ariz.)[1]	193	0.6
Harold E. Stassen (Pa.)	1,373	1.5	Nelson A. Rockefeller (N.Y.)[1]	109	0.4
William W. Scranton (Pa.)[1]	105	0.1	Others[1]	159	0.5
Others	465	0.5			
April 7 Wisconsin					
John W. Byrnes (Wis.)	299,612	99.7	John W. Reynolds (Wis.)	522,405	66.2
Unpledged delegates	816	0.3	George C. Wallace (Ala.)	266,136	33.8
April 14 Illinois					
Goldwater	512,840	62.0	Johnson[1]	82,027	91.6
Smith	209,521	25.3	Wallace[1]	3,761	4.2
Henry Cabot Lodge[1]	68,122	8.2	Robert F. Kennedy[1]	2,894	3.2
Nixon[1]	30,313	3.7	Others[1]	841	0.9
George C. Wallace (Ala.)[1]	2,203	0.3			
Rockefeller[1]	2,048	0.2			
Scranton[1]	1,842	0.2			
George W. Romney (Mich.)[1]	465	0.1			
Others[1]	437	0.1			
April 21 New Jersey					
Henry Cabot Lodge[1]	7,896	41.7	Johnson[1]	4,863	82.3
Goldwater[1]	5,309	28.0	Wallace[1]	491	8.3
Nixon[1]	4,179	22.1	Robert F. Kennedy[1]	431	7.3
Scranton[1]	633	3.3	Others[1]	124	2.1
Rockefeller[1]	612	3.2			
Others[1]	304	1.6			
April 28 Massachusetts					
Henry Cabot Lodge[1]	70,809	76.9	Johnson[1]	61,035	73.4
Goldwater[1]	9,338	10.1	Robert F. Kennedy[1]	15,870	19.1
Nixon[1]	5,460	5.9	Lodge[1]	2,269	2.7
Rockefeller[1]	2,454	2.7	Edward M. Kennedy (Mass.)[1]	1,259	1.5
Scranton[1]	1,709	1.9	Wallace[1]	565	0.7
Lyndon B. Johnson (Texas)[1]	600	0.7	Adlai E. Stevenson (Ill.)[1]	452	0.5
Smith[1]	426	0.5	Hubert H. Humphrey (Minn.)[1]	323	0.4
George C. Lodge (Mass.)[1]	365	0.4	Others[1]	1,436	1.7
Romney[1]	262	0.3			
Others[1]	711	0.8			
April 28 Pennsylvania					
Scranton[1]	235,222	51.9	Johnson[1]	209,606	82.8
Henry Cabot Lodge[1]	92,712	20.5	Wallace[1]	12,104	4.8
Nixon[1]	44,396	9.8	Robert F. Kennedy[1]	12,029	4.8
Goldwater[1]	38,669	8.5	William W. Scranton (Pa.)[1]	8,156	3.2
Johnson[1]	22,372	4.9	Lodge[1]	4,895	1.9
Rockefeller[1]	9,123	2.0	Others[1]	6,438	2.5
Wallace[1]	5,105	1.1			
Others[1]	5,269	1.2			

Republican	Votes	%	Democratic	Votes	%

May 2 **Texas**

Republican	Votes	%	Democratic	Votes	%
Goldwater	104,137	74.7	[2]		
Henry Cabot Lodge[1]	12,324	8.8			
Rockefeller	6,207	4.5			
Nixon[1]	5,390	3.9			
Stassen	5,273	3.8			
Smith	4,816	3.5			
Scranton[1]	803	0.6			
Others[1]	373	0.3			

May 5 **District of Columbia**[3]

Republican	Votes	%	Democratic	Votes	%
[3]			Unpledged delegates	41,095	100.0

May 5 **Indiana**

Republican	Votes	%	Democratic	Votes	%
Goldwater	267,935	67.0	Matthew E. Welsh (Ind.)	376,023	64.9
Stassen	107,157	26.8	Wallace	172,646	29.8
Others	24,588	6.2	Others	30,367	5.2

May 5 **Ohio**

Republican	Votes	%	Democratic	Votes	%
James A. Rhodes (Ohio)	615,754[4]	100.0	Albert S. Porter (Ohio)	493,619[4]	100.0

May 12 **Nebraska**

Republican	Votes	%	Democratic	Votes	%
Goldwater	68,050	49.1	Johnson[1]	54,713	89.3
Nixon[1]	43,613	31.5	Robert F. Kennedy[1]	2,099	3.4
Henry Cabot Lodge[1]	22,622	16.3	Wallace[1]	1,067	1.7
Rockefeller[1]	2,333	1.7	Lodge[1]	1,051	1.7
Scranton[1]	578	0.4	Nixon[1]	833	1.4
Johnson[1]	316	0.2	Goldwater[1]	603	1.0
Others[1]	1,010	0.7	Others[1]	904	1.5

May 12 **West Virginia**

Republican	Votes	%	Democratic	Votes	%
Rockefeller	115,680[4]	100.0	Unpledged delegates at large	131,432[4]	100.0

May 15 **Oregon**

Republican	Votes	%	Democratic	Votes	%
Rockefeller	94,190	33.0	Johnson	272,099[4]	99.5
Henry Cabot Lodge	79,169	27.7	Wallace[1]	1,365[4]	0.5
Goldwater	50,105	17.6			
Nixon	48,274	16.9			
Smith	8,087	2.8			
Scranton	4,509	1.6			
Others	1,152	0.4			

May 19 **Maryland**

Republican	Votes	%	Democratic	Votes	%
Unpledged delegates	57,004	58.2	Daniel B. Brewster (Md.)	267,106	53.1
Others	40,994	41.8	Wallace	214,849	42.7
			Unpledged delegates	12,377	2.5
			Others	8,275	1.6

May 26 **Florida**

Republican	Votes	%	Democratic	Votes	%
Unpledged delegates	58,179	57.8	Johnson	393,339[4]	100.0
Goldwater	42,525	42.2			

June 2 **California**

Republican	Votes	%	Democratic	Votes	%
Goldwater	1,120,403	51.6	Unpledged delegates[5]	1,693,813	68.0
Rockefeller	1,052,053	48.4	Unpledged delegates[5]	798,431	32.0

Republican	Votes	%	Democratic	Votes	%
June 2 South Dakota					
Unpledged delegates	57,653	68.0	Unpledged delegates	28,142[4]	100.0
Goldwater	27,076	32.0			
TOTALS					
Goldwater	2,267,079	38.2	Unpledged delegates	2,705,290	43.3
Rockefeller	1,304,204	22.0	Johnson	1,106,999	17.7
Rhodes	615,754	10.4	Wallace	672,984	10.8
Henry Cabot Lodge	386,661	6.5	Reynolds	522,405	8.4
Byrnes	299,612	5.0	Porter	493,619	7.9
Scranton	245,401	4.1	Welsh	376,023	6.0
Smith	224,970	3.8	Brewster	267,106	4.3
Nixon	197,212	3.3	Robert F. Kennedy	33,810	0.5
Unpledged delegates	173,652	2.9	Henry Cabot Lodge	8,495	0.1
Stassen	113,803	1.9	Scranton	8,156	0.1
Johnson	23,288	0.4	Edward M. Kennedy	1,259	—
Wallace	7,308	0.1	Nixon	1,065	—
Romney	727	—	Goldwater	796	—
George C. Lodge	365	—	Stevenson	452	—
Others[6]	75,303	1.3	Humphrey	323	—
	5,935,339		Rockefeller	109	—
			Others[7]	48,544	0.8
				6,247,435	

1. Write-in.

2. No primary authorized.

3. Source: District of Columbia Board of Elections. No figures available for vote for delegates to Republican convention.

4. Figures obtained from Scammon's office. In *America Votes*, Scammon did not record vote totals if a candidate was unopposed or if the primary was strictly for delegate selection.

5. Gov. Edmund G. Brown (D Calif.) headed the winning state of delegates and Mayor Sam Yorty of Los Angeles headed the losing slate.

6. In addition to scattered votes, "others" includes Norman LePage who received 82 votes in the New Hampshire primary; Frank R. Beck-with who received 17,884 votes and Joseph G. Ettl who received 6,704 votes in the Indiana primary; John W. Steffey who received 22,135 votes and Robert E. Ennis who received 18,859 votes in the Maryland primary.

7. In addition to scattered votes, "others" includes Lar Daly who received 15,160 votes, John H. Latham who received 8,067 votes and Fay T. Carpenter Swain who received 7,140 votes in the Indiana primary; and Andrew J. Easter who received 8,275 votes in the Maryland primary.

1968 Primaries*

Republican	Votes	%	Democratic	Votes	%
March 12 New Hampshire					
Richard M. Nixon (N.Y.)	80,666	77.6	Lyndon B. Johnson (Texas)[1]	27,520	49.6
Nelson A. Rockefeller (N.Y.)[1]	11,241	10.8	Eugene J. McCarthy (Minn.)	23,263	41.9
Eugene J. McCarthy (Minn.)[1]	5,511	5.3	Richard M. Nixon (N.Y.)[1]	2,532	4.6
Lyndon B. Johnson (Texas)[1]	1,778	1.7	Others	2,149	3.9
George W. Romney (Mich.)	1,743	1.7			
Harold E. Stassen (Pa.)	429	0.4			
Others	2,570	2.5			
April 2 Wisconsin					
Nixon	390,368	79.7	McCarthy	412,160	56.2
Ronald Reagan (Calif.)	50,727	10.4	Johnson	253,696	34.6
Stassen	28,531	5.8	Robert F. Kennedy (N.Y.)[1]	46,507	6.3
Rockefeller[1]	7,995	1.6	Unpledged delegates	11,861	1.6
Unpledged delegates	6,763	1.4	George C. Wallace (Ala.)[1]	4,031	0.5
Romney[1]	2,087	0.4	Hubert H. Humphrey (Minn.)[1]	3,605	0.5
Others	3,382	0.7	Others	1,142	0.2
April 23 Pennsylvania					
Nixon[1]	171,815	59.7	McCarthy	428,259	71.7
Rockefeller[1]	52,915	18.4	Robert F. Kennedy[1]	65,430	11.0
McCarthy[1]	18,800	6.5	Humphrey[1]	51,998	8.7
George C. Wallace (Ala.)[1]	13,290	4.6	Wallace[1]	24,147	4.0
Robert F. Kennedy (N.Y.)[1]	10,431	3.6	Johnson[1]	21,265	3.6
Reagan[1]	7,934	2.8	Nixon[1]	3,434	0.6
Hubert H. Humphrey (Minn.)[1]	4,651	1.6	Others[1]	2,556	0.4
Johnson[1]	3,027	1.1			
Raymond P. Shafer (Pa.)[1]	1,223	0.4			
Others[1]	3,487	1.2			
April 30 Massachusetts					
Rockefeller[1]	31,964	30.0	McCarthy	122,697	49.3
John A. Volpe (Mass.)	31,465	29.5	Robert F. Kennedy[1]	68,604	27.6
Nixon[1]	27,447	25.8	Humphrey[1]	44,156	17.7
McCarthy[1]	9,758	9.2	Johnson[1]	6,890	2.8
Reagan[1]	1,770	1.7	Nelson A. Rockefeller (N.Y.)[1]	2,275	1.0
Kennedy[1]	1,184	1.1	Wallace[1]	1,688	0.7
Others[1]	2,933	2.8	Others[1]	2,593	1.0
May 7 District of Columbia					
Nixon-Rockefeller[2]	12,102	90.1	Robert F. Kennedy[3]	57,555	62.5
Unpledged delegates[2]	1,328	9.9	Humphrey[3]	32,309	35.1
			Humphrey[3]	2,250	2.4
May 7 Indiana					
Nixon	508,362[4]	100.0	Robert F. Kennedy	328,118	42.3
			Roger D. Branigin (Ind.)	238,700	30.7
			McCarthy	209,695	27.0
May 7 Ohio					
James A. Rhodes (Ohio)	614,492[4]	100.0	Stephen M. Young (Ohio)	549,140[4]	100.0
May 14 Nebraska[5]					
Nixon	140,336	70.0	Robert F. Kennedy	84,102	51.7
Reagan	42,703	21.3	McCarthy	50,655	31.2

Republican	Votes	%	Democratic	Votes	%
Rockefeller[1]	10,225	5.1	Humphrey[1]	12,087	7.4
Stassen	2,638	1.3	Johnson	9,187	5.6
McCarthy[1]	1,544	0.8	Nixon[1]	2,731	1.7
Others	3,030	1.5	Ronald Reagan (Calif.)[1]	1,905	1.2
			Wallace[1]	1,298	0.8
			Others	646	0.4

May 14 West Virginia

	Votes	%		Votes	%
Unpledged delegates at large	81,039[4]	100.0	Unpledged delegates at large	149,282[4]	100.0

May 28 Florida

	Votes	%		Votes	%
Unpledged delegates	51,509[4]	100.0	George A. Smathers (Fla.)	236,242	46.1
			McCarthy	147,216	28.7
			Unpledged delegates	128,899	25.2

May 28 Oregon

	Votes	%		Votes	%
Nixon	203,037	65.0	McCarthy	163,990	44.0
Reagan	63,707	20.4	Robert F. Kennedy	141,631	38.0
Rockefeller[1]	36,305	11.6	Johnson	45,174	12.1
McCarthy[1]	7,387	2.4	Humphrey[1]	12,421	3.3
Kennedy[1]	1,723	0.6	Reagan[1]	3,082	0.8
			Nixon[1]	2,974	0.8
			Rockefeller[1]	2,841	0.8
			Wallace[1]	957	0.3

June 4 California

	Votes	%		Votes	%
Reagan	1,525,091[4]	100.0	Robert F. Kennedy	1,472,166	46.3
			McCarthy	1,329,301	41.8
			Unpledged delegates	380,286	12.0

June 4 New Jersey

	Votes	%		Votes	%
Nixon[1]	71,809	81.1	McCarthy[1]	9,906	36.1
Rockefeller[1]	11,530	13.0	Robert F. Kennedy[1]	8,603	31.3
Reagan[1]	2,737	3.1	Humphrey[1]	5,578	20.3
McCarthy[1]	1,358	1.5	Wallace[1]	1,399	5.1
Others[1]	1,158	1.3	Nixon[1]	1,364	5.0
			Others[1]	596	2.2

June 4 South Dakota

	Votes	%		Votes	%
Nixon	68,113[4]	100.0	Robert F. Kennedy	31,826	49.5
			Johnson	19,316	30.0
			McCarthy	13,145	20.4

June 11 Illinois

	Votes	%		Votes	%
Nixon[1]	17,490	78.1	McCarthy[1]	4,646	38.6
Rockefeller[1]	2,165	9.7	Edward M. Kennedy (Mass.)[1]	4,052	33.7
Reagan[1]	1,601	7.1	Humphrey[1]	2,059	17.1
Others[1]	1,147	5.1	Others[1]	1,281	10.6

	Republican Votes	%		**Democratic** Votes	%
TOTALS					
Reagan	1,696,270	*37.9*	McCarthy	2,914,933	*38.7*
Nixon	1,679,443	*37.5*	Robert F. Kennedy	2,304,542	*30.6*
Rhodes	614,492	*13.7*	Unpledged delegates	670,328	*8.9*
Rockefeller	164,340	*3.7*	Young	549,140	*7.3*
Unpledged delegates	140,639	*3.1*	Johnson	383,048	*5.1*
McCarthy	44,358	*1.0*	Branigin	238,700	*3.2*
Stassen	31,598	*0.7*	Smathers	236,242	*3.1*
Volpe	31,465	*0.7*	Humphrey	166,463	*2.2*
Robert F. Kennedy	13,338	*0.3*	Wallace	33,520	*0.4*
Wallace	13,290	*0.3*	Nixon	13,035	*0.2*
Nixon-Rockefeller[2]	12,102	*0.3*	Rockefeller	5,116	*0.1*
Johnson	4,805	*0.1*	Reagan	4,987	*0.1*
Humphrey	4,651	*0.1*	Edward M. Kennedy	4,052	*0.1*
Romney	3,830	*0.1*	Others[7]	10,963	*0.1*
Shafer	1,223	—			
Others[6]	17,707	*0.4*		7,535,069	
	4,473,551				

* Delegate selection primaries were held in Alabama and New York. In *America Votes,* Scammon did not record vote totals if the primary was strictly for delegate selection and there was no presidential preference voting.

1. Write-in.
2. Prior to the primary, the District Republican organization agreed to divide the nine delegate votes, with six going to Nixon and three going to Rockefeller, according to the *1968 Congressional Quarterly Almanac,* Vol. XXIV. Figures obtained from Scammon's office.
3. Figures obtained from Scammon's office. Two slates favored Humphrey; a member of an "independent" Humphrey slate received 2,250 votes.
4. Figures obtained from Scammon's office. In *America Votes,* Scammon did not record vote totals if a candidate was unopposed or if the primary was strictly for delegate selection.

5. In the American Party presidential primary, Wallace received 493 of the 504 votes cast, or 97.8% of the vote, according to the office of the Nebraska secretary of state.
6. In addition to scattered votes, "others" includes Willis E. Stone who received 527 votes, Herbert F. Hoover who received 247 votes, David Watumull who received 161 votes, William W. Evans who received 151 votes, Elmer W. Coy who received 73 votes and Don Du-Mont who received 39 votes in the New Hampshire primary; and Americus Liberator who received 1,302 votes in the Nebraska primary.
7. In addition to scattered votes, "others" includes John G. Crommelin who received 186 votes, Richard E. Lee who received 170 votes and Jacob J. Gordon who received 77 votes in the New Hampshire primary.

1972 Primaries*

Republican	Votes	%	Democratic	Votes	%
March 7 New Hampshire					
Richard M. Nixon (Calif.)	79,239	67.6	Edmund S. Muskie (Maine)	41,235	46.4
Paul N. McCloskey (Calif.)	23,190	19.8	George S. McGovern (S.D.)	33,007	37.1
John M. Ashbrook (Ohio)	11,362	9.7	Sam Yorty (Calif.)	5,401	6.1
Others	3,417	2.9	Wilbur D. Mills (Ark.)[1]	3,563	4.0
			Vance Hartke (Ind.)	2,417	2.7
			Edward M. Kennedy (Mass.)[1]	954	1.1
			Hubert H. Humphrey (Minn.)[1]	348	0.4
			Henry M. Jackson (Wash.)[1]	197	0.2
			George C. Wallace (Ala.)[1]	175	0.2
			Others	1,557	1.8
March 14 Florida					
Nixon	360,278	87.0	Wallace	526,651	41.6
Ashbrook	36,617	8.8	Humphrey	234,658	18.6
McCloskey	17,312	4.2	Jackson	170,156	13.5
			Muskie	112,523	8.9
			John V. Lindsay (N.Y.)	82,386	6.5
			McGovern	78,232	6.2
			Shirley Chisholm (N.Y.)	43,989	3.5
			Eugene J. McCarthy (Minn.)	5,847	0.5
			Mills	4,539	0.4
			Hartke	3,009	0.2
			Yorty	2,564	0.2
March 21 Illinois					
Nixon[1]	32,550	97.0	Muskie	766,914	62.6
Ashbrook[1]	170	0.5	McCarthy	444,260	36.3
McCloskey[1]	47	0.1	Wallace[1]	7,017	0.6
Others[1]	802	2.4	McGovern[1]	3,687	0.3
			Humphrey[1]	1,476	0.1
			Chisholm[1]	777	0.1
			Jackson[1]	442	—
			Kennedy[1]	242	—
			Lindsay[1]	118	—
			Others	211	—
April 4 Wisconsin					
Nixon	277,601	96.9	McGovern	333,528	29.6
McCloskey	3,651	1.3	Wallace	248,676	22.0
Ashbrook	2,604	0.9	Humphrey	233,748	20.7
None of the names shown	2,315	0.8	Muskie	115,811	10.3
Others	273	0.1	Jackson	88,068	7.8
			Lindsay	75,579	6.7
			McCarthy	15,543	1.4
			Chisholm	9,198	0.8
			None of the names shown	2,450	0.2
			Yorty	2,349	0.2
			Patsy T. Mink (Hawaii)	1,213	0.1
			Mills	913	0.1
			Hartke	766	0.1
			Kennedy[1]	183	—
			Others	559	—
April 25 Massachusetts					
Nixon	99,150	81.2	McGovern	325,673	52.7
McCloskey	16,435	13.5	Muskie	131,709	21.3

Republican	Votes	%	**Democratic**	Votes	%
Ashbrook	4,864	4.0	Humphrey	48,929	7.9
Others	1,690	1.4	Wallace	45,807	7.4
			Chisholm	22,398	3.6
			Mills	19,441	3.1
			McCarthy	8,736	1.4
			Jackson	8,499	1.4
			Kennedy[1]	2,348	0.4
			Lindsay	2,107	0.3
			Hartke	874	0.1
			Yorty	646	0.1
			Others	1,349	0.2

April 25 Pennsylvania

	Votes	%		Votes	%
Nixon[1]	153,886	83.3	Humphrey	481,900	35.1
George C. Wallace (Ala.)[1]	20,472	11.1	Wallace	292,437	21.3
Others[1]	10,443	5.7	McGovern	280,861	20.4
			Muskie	279,983	20.4
			Jackson	38,767	2.8
			Chisholm[1]	306	—
			Others	585	—

May 2 District of Columbia

				Votes	%
[2]			Walter E. Fauntroy (D.C.)	21,217	71.8
			Unpledged delegates	8,343	28.2

May 2 Indiana

	Votes	%		Votes	%
Nixon	417,069	100.0	Humphrey	354,244	47.1
			Wallace	309,495	41.2
			Muskie	87,719	11.7

May 2 Ohio

	Votes	%		Votes	%
Nixon	692,828	100.0	Humphrey	499,680	41.2
			McGovern	480,320	39.6
			Muskie	107,806	8.9
			Jackson	98,498	8.1
			McCarthy	26,026	2.1

May 4 Tennessee

	Votes	%		Votes	%
Nixon	109,696	95.8	Wallace	335,858	68.2
Ashbrook	2,419	2.1	Humphrey	78,350	15.9
McCloskey	2,370	2.1	McGovern	35,551	7.2
Others	4	—	Chisholm	18,809	3.8
			Muskie	9,634	2.0
			Jackson	5,896	1.2
			Mills	2,543	0.5
			McCarthy	2,267	0.5
			Hartke	1,621	0.3
			Lindsay	1,476	0.3
			Yorty	692	0.1
			Others	24	—

May 6 North Carolina

	Votes	%		Votes	%
Nixon	159,167	94.8	Wallace	413,518	50.3
McCloskey	8,732	5.2	Terry Sanford (N.C.)	306,014	37.3
			Chisholm	61,723	7.5
			Muskie	30,739	3.7
			Jackson	9,416	1.1

	Republican			**Democratic**	
	Votes	%		Votes	%

May 9 **Nebraska**

Nixon	179,464	92.4	McGovern	79,309	41.3
McCloskey	9,011	4.6	Humphrey	65,968	34.3
Ashbrook	4,996	2.6	Wallace	23,912	12.4
Others	801	0.4	Muskie	6,886	3.6
			Jackson	5,276	2.7
			Yorty	3,459	1.8
			McCarthy	3,194	1.7
			Chisholm	1,763	0.9
			Lindsay	1,244	0.6
			Mills	377	0.2
			Kennedy[1]	293	0.2
			Hartke	249	0.1
			Others	207	0.1

May 9 **West Virginia**

Unpledged delegates at large	95,813[3]	100.0	Humphrey	246,596	66.9
			Wallace	121,888	33.1

May 16 **Maryland**

Nixon	99,308	86.2	Wallace	219,687	38.7
McCloskey	9,223	8.0	Humphrey	151,981	26.8
Ashbrook	6,718	5.8	McGovern	126,978	22.4
			Jackson	17,728	3.1
			Yorty	13,584	2.4
			Muskie	13,363	2.4
			Chisholm	12,602	2.2
			Mills	4,776	0.8
			McCarthy	4,691	0.8
			Lindsay	2,168	0.4
			Mink	573	0.1

May 16 **Michigan**

Nixon	321,652	95.5	Wallace	809,239	51.0
McCloskey	9,691	2.9	McGovern	425,694	26.8
Unpledged delegates	5,370	1.6	Humphrey	249,798	15.7
Others	30	—	Chisholm	44,090	2.8
			Muskie	38,701	2.4
			Unpledged delegates	10,700	0.7
			Jackson	6,938	0.4
			Hartke	2,862	0.2
			Others	51	—

May 23 **Oregon**

Nixon	231,151	82.0	McGovern	205,328	50.2
McCloskey	29,365	10.4	Wallace	81,868	20.0
Ashbrook	16,696	5.9	Humphrey	51,163	12.5
Others	4,798	1.7	Jackson	22,042	5.4
			Kennedy	12,673	3.1
			Muskie	10,244	2.5
			McCarthy	8,943	2.2
			Mink	6,500	1.6
			Lindsay	5,082	1.2
			Chisholm	2,975	0.7
			Mills	1,208	0.3
			Others	618	0.2

Republican	Votes	%	Democratic	Votes	%

May 23 Rhode Island

Nixon	4,953	88.3	McGovern	15,603	41.2
McCloskey	337	6.0	Muskie	7,838	20.7
Ashbrook	175	3.1	Humphrey	7,701	20.3
Unpledged delegates	146	2.6	Wallace	5,802	15.3
			Unpledged delegates	490	1.3
			McCarthy	245	0.6
			Jackson	138	0.4
			Mills	41	0.1
			Yorty	6	—

June 6 California

Nixon	2,058,825	90.1	McGovern	1,550,652	43.5
Ashbrook	224,922	9.8	Humphrey	1,375,064	38.6
Others	175	—	Wallace[1]	268,551	7.5
			Chisholm	157,435	4.4
			Muskie	72,701	2.0
			Yorty	50,745	1.4
			McCarthy	34,203	1.0
			Jackson	28,901	0.8
			Lindsay	26,246	0.7
			Others	20	—

June 6 New Jersey

| Unpledged delegates at large | 215,719[3] | 100.0 | Chisholm | 51,433 | 66.9 |
| | | | Sanford | 25,401 | 33.1 |

June 6 New Mexico

Nixon	49,067	88.5	McGovern	51,011	33.3
McCloskey	3,367	6.1	Wallace	44,843	29.3
None of the names shown	3,035	5.5	Humphrey	39,768	25.9
			Muskie	6,411	4.2
			Jackson	4,236	2.8
			None of the names shown	3,819	2.5
			Chisholm	3,205	2.1

June 6 South Dakota

| Nixon | 52,820 | 100.0 | McGovern | 28,017 | 100.0 |

TOTALS

Nixon	5,378,704	86.9	Humphrey	4,121,372	25.8
Unpledged delegates	317,048	5.1	McGovern	4,053,451	25.3
Ashbrook	311,543	5.0	Wallace	3,755,424	23.5
McCloskey	132,731	2.1	Muskie	1,840,217	11.5
Wallace	20,472	0.3	McCarthy	553,955	3.5
None of the names shown	5,350	0.1	Jackson	505,198	3.2
Others[4]	22,433	0.4	Chisholm	430,703	2.7
	6,188,281		Sanford	331,415	2.1
			Lindsay	196,406	1.2
			Yorty	79,446	0.5
			Mills	37,401	0.2
			Fauntroy	21,217	0.1
			Unpledged delegates	19,533	0.1
			Kennedy	16,693	0.1
			Hartke	11,798	0.1
			Mink	8,286	0.1
			None of the names shown	6,269	—
			Others[5]	5,181	—
				15,993,965	

* Delegate selection primaries were held in Alabama and New York. In *America Votes*, Scammon did not record vote totals if the primary was strictly for delegate selection and there was no presidential preference voting.

1. Write-in.
2. No Republican primary in 1972.
3. Figures obtained from Scammon's office. In *America Votes*, Scammon did not record vote totals if the primary was strictly for delegate selection.

4. In addition to scattered votes, "others" includes Patrick Paulsen, who received 1,211 votes in the New Hampshire primary.
5. In addition to scattered votes, "others" includes Edward T. Coll, who received 280 votes in the New Hampshire primary and 589 votes in the Massachusetts primary.

1976 Primaries*

Republican	Votes	%	Democratic	Votes	%

February 24 New Hampshire

Republican	Votes	%	Democratic	Votes	%
Gerald R. Ford (Mich.)	55,156	49.4	Jimmy Carter (Ga.)	23,373	28.4
Ronald Reagan (Calif.)	53,569	48.0	Morris K. Udall (Ariz.)	18,710	22.7
Others[1]	2,949	2.6	Birch Bayh (Ind.)	12,510	15.2
			Fred R. Harris (Okla.)	8,863	10.8
			Sargent Shriver (Md.)	6,743	8.2
			Hubert H. Humphrey (Minn.)	4,596	5.6
			Henry M. Jackson (Wash.)	1,857	2.3
			George C. Wallace (Ala.)	1,061	1.3
			Ellen McCormack (N.Y.)	1,007	1.2
			Others	3,661	4.8

March 2 Massachusetts

Republican	Votes	%	Democratic	Votes	%
Ford	115,375	61.2	Jackson	164,393	22.3
Reagan	63,555	33.7	Udall	130,440	17.7
None of the names shown	6,000	3.2	Wallace	123,112	16.7
Others[1]	3,519	1.8	Carter	101,948	13.9
			Harris	55,701	7.6
			Shriver	53,252	7.2
			Bayh	34,963	4.8
			McCormack	25,772	3.5
			Milton J. Shapp (Pa.)	21,693	2.9
			None of the names shown	9,804	1.3
			Humphrey[1]	7,851	1.1
			Edward M. Kennedy (Mass.)[1]	1,623	0.2
			Lloyd Bentsen (Texas)	364	—
			Others	4,905	0.7

March 2 Vermont

Republican	Votes	%	Democratic	Votes	%
Ford	27,014	84.0	Carter	16,335	42.2
Reagan[1]	4,892	15.2	Shriver	10,699	27.6
Others[1]	251	—	Harris	4,893	12.6
			McCormack	3,324	8.6
			Others	3,463	9.0

March 9 Florida

Republican	Votes	%	Democratic	Votes	%
Ford	321,982	52.8	Carter	448,844	34.5
Reagan	287,837	47.2	Wallace	396,820	30.5
			Jackson	310,944	23.9
			None of the names shown	37,626	2.9
			Shapp	32,198	2.5
			Udall	27,235	2.1
			Bayh	8,750	0.7
			McCormack	7,595	0.6
			Shriver	7,084	0.5
			Harris	5,397	0.4
			Robert C. Byrd (W.Va.)	5,042	0.4
			Frank Church (Idaho)	4,906	0.4
			Others	7,889	0.6

March 16 Illinois

Republican	Votes	%	Democratic	Votes	%
Ford	456,750	58.9	Carter	630,915	48.1
Reagan	311,295	40.1	Wallace	361,798	27.6
Lar Daly (Ill.)	7,582	1.0	Shriver	214,024	16.3
Others[1]	266	—	Harris	98,862	7.5
			Others[1]	6,315	0.5

Republican	Votes	%	**Democratic**	Votes	%

March 23 North Carolina

Republican	Votes	%	Democratic	Votes	%
Reagan	101,468	52.4	Carter	324,437	53.6
Ford	88,897	45.9	Wallace	210,166	34.7
None of the names shown	3,362	1.7	Jackson	25,749	4.3
			None of the names shown	22,850	3.8
			Udall	14,032	2.3
			Harris	5,923	1.0
			Bentsen	1,675	0.3

April 6 Wisconsin

Republican	Votes	%	Democratic	Votes	%
Ford	326,869	55.2	Carter	271,220	36.6
Reagan	262,126	44.3	Udall	263,771	35.6
None of the names shown	2,234	0.3	Wallace	92,460	12.5
Others[1]	583	—	Jackson	47,605	6.4
			McCormack	26,982	3.6
			Harris	8,185	1.1
			None of the names shown	7,154	1.0
			Shriver	5,097	0.7
			Bentsen	1,730	0.2
			Bayh	1,255	0.2
			Shapp	596	0.1
			Others[1]	14,473	2.0

April 27 Pennsylvania

Republican	Votes	%	Democratic	Votes	%
Ford	733,472	92.1	Carter	511,905	37.0
Reagan[1]	40,510	5.1	Jackson	340,340	24.6
Others[1]	22,678	2.8	Udall	259,166	18.7
			Wallace	155,902	11.3
			McCormack	38,800	2.8
			Shapp	32,947	2.4
			Bayh	15,320	1.1
			Harris	13,067	0.9
			Humphrey[1]	12,563	0.9
			Others	5,032	0.3

May 4 District of Columbia

[2]

Republican	Votes	%	Democratic	Votes	%
			Carter	10,521	31.6
			Walter E. Fauntroy (unpledged delegates)	10,149	30.5
			Udall	6,999	21.0
			Walter E. Washington (unpledged delegates)	5,161	15.5
			Harris	461	1.4

May 4 Georgia

Republican	Votes	%	Democratic	Votes	%
Reagan	128,671	68.3	Carter	419,272	83.4
Ford	59,801	31.7	Wallace	57,594	11.5
			Udall	9,755	1.9
			Byrd	3,628	0.7
			Jackson	3,358	0.7
			Church	2,477	0.5
			Shriver	1,378	0.3
			Bayh	824	0.2
			Harris	699	0.1
			McCormack	635	0.1
			Bentsen	277	0.1
			Shapp	181	—
			Others	2,393	0.5

Republican	Votes	%	Democratic	Votes	%
May 4 Indiana					
Reagan	323,779	*51.3*	Carter	417,480	*68.0*
Ford	307,513	*48.7*	Wallace	93,121	*15.2*
			Jackson	72,080	*11.7*
			McCormack	31,708	*5.2*
May 11 Nebraska					
Reagan	113,493	*54.5*	Church	67,297	*38.5*
Ford	94,542	*45.4*	Carter	65,833	*37.6*
Others	379	*0.1*	Humphrey	12,685	*7.2*
			Kennedy	7,199	*4.1*
			McCormack	6,033	*3.4*
			Wallace	5,567	*3.2*
			Udall	4,688	*2.7*
			Jackson	2,642	*1.5*
			Harris	811	*0.5*
			Bayh	407	*0.2*
			Shriver	384	*0.2*
			Others[1]	1,467	*0.8*
May 11 West Virginia					
Ford	88,386	*56.8*	Byrd	331,639	*89.0*
Reagan	67,306	*43.2*	Wallace	40,938	*11.0*
May 18 Maryland					
Ford	96,291	*58.0*	Edmund G. Brown Jr. (Calif.)	286,672	*48.4*
Reagan	69,680	*42.0*	Carter	219,404	*37.1*
			Udall	32,790	*5.5*
			Wallace	24,176	*4.1*
			Jackson	13,956	*2.4*
			McCormack	7,907	*1.3*
			Harris	6,841	*1.2*
May 18 Michigan					
Ford	690,180	*64.9*	Carter	307,559	*43.4*
Reagan	364,052	*34.3*	Udall	305,134	*43.1*
Unpledged delegates	8,473	*0.8*	Wallace	49,204	*6.9*
Others[1]	109	—	Unpledged delegates	15,853	*2.2*
			Jackson	10,332	*1.5*
			McCormack	7,623	*1.1*
			Shriver	5,738	*0.8*
			Harris	4,081	*0.6*
			Others[1]	3,142	*0.4*
May 25 Arkansas					
Reagan	20,628	*63.4*	Carter	314,306	*62.6*
Ford	11,430	*35.1*	Wallace	83,005	*16.5*
Unpledged delegates	483	*1.5*	Unpledged delegates	57,152	*11.4*
			Udall	37,783	*7.5*
			Jackson	9,554	*1.9*
May 25 Idaho					
Reagan	66,743	*74.3*	Church	58,570	*78.7*
Ford	22,323	*24.9*	Carter	8,818	*11.9*
Unpledged delegates	727	*0.8*	Humphrey	1,700	*2.3*
			Brown[1]	1,453	*2.0*
			Wallace	1,115	*1.5*

	Republican			**Democratic**		
	Votes	%			Votes	%
			Udall		981	1.3
			Unpledged delegates		964	1.3
			Jackson		485	0.7
			Harris		319	0.4

May 25 **Kentucky**

	Republican Votes	%			Democratic Votes	%
Ford	67,976	50.9	Carter		181,690	59.4
Reagan	62,683	46.9	Wallace		51,540	16.8
Unpledged delegates	1,781	1.3	Udall		33,262	10.9
Others	1,088	0.8	McCormack		17,061	5.6
			Unpledged delegates		11,962	3.9
			Jackson		8,186	2.7
			Others		2,305	0.8

May 25 **Nevada**

	Republican Votes	%			Democratic Votes	%
Reagan	31,637	66.3	Brown		39,671	52.7
Ford	13,747	28.8	Carter		17,567	23.3
None of the names shown	2,365	5.0	Church		6,778	9.0
			None of the names shown		4,603	6.1
			Wallace		2,490	3.3
			Udall		2,237	3.0
			Jackson		1,896	2.5

May 25 **Oregon**

	Republican Votes	%			Democratic Votes	%
Ford	150,181	50.3	Church		145,394	33.6
Reagan	136,691	45.8	Carter		115,310	26.7
Others[1]	11,663	3.9	Brown[1]		106,812	24.7
			Humphrey		22,488	5.2
			Udall		11,747	2.7
			Kennedy		10,983	2.5
			Wallace		5,797	1.3
			Jackson		5,298	1.2
			McCormack		3,753	0.9
			Harris		1,344	0.3
			Bayh		743	0.2
			Others[1]		2,963	0.7

May 25 **Tennessee**

	Republican Votes	%			Democratic Votes	%
Ford	120,685	49.8	Carter		259,243	77.6
Reagan	118,997	49.1	Wallace		36,495	10.9
Unpledged delegates	2,756	1.1	Udall		12,420	3.7
Others[1]	97	—	Church		8,026	2.4
			Unpledged delegates		6,148	1.8
			Jackson		5,672	1.7
			McCormack		1,782	0.5
			Harris		1,628	0.5
			Brown[1]		1,556	0.5
			Shapp		507	0.2
			Humphrey[1]		109	—
			Others[1]		492	0.1

June 1 **Montana**

	Republican Votes	%			Democratic Votes	%
Reagan	56,683	63.1	Church		63,448	59.4
Ford	31,100	34.6	Carter		26,329	24.6
None of the names shown	1,996	2.2	Udall		6,708	6.3
			None of the names shown		3,820	3.6
			Wallace		3,680	3.4
			Jackson		2,856	2.7

Republican				Democratic	
	Votes	**%**		**Votes**	**%**

June 1   Rhode Island

Republican	Votes	%	Democratic	Votes	%
Ford	9,365	65.3	Unpledged delegates	19,035	31.5
Reagan	4,480	31.2	Carter	18,237	30.2
Unpledged delegates	507	3.5	Church	16,423	27.2
			Udall	2,543	4.2
			McCormack	2,468	4.1
			Jackson	756	1.3
			Wallace	507	0.8
			Bayh	247	0.4
			Shapp	132	0.2

June 1   South Dakota

Republican	Votes	%	Democratic	Votes	%
Reagan	43,068	51.2	Carter	24,186	41.2
Ford	36,976	44.0	Udall	19,510	33.3
None of the names shown	4,033	4.8	None of the names shown	7,871	13.4
			McCormack	4,561	7.8
			Wallace	1,412	2.4
			Harris	573	1.0
			Jackson	558	1.0

June 8   California

Republican	Votes	%	Democratic	Votes	%
Reagan	1,604,836	65.5	Brown	2,013,210	59.0
Ford	845,655	34.5	Carter	697,092	20.4
Others[1]	20	—	Church	250,581	7.3
			Udall	171,501	5.0
			Wallace	102,292	3.0
			Unpledged delegates	78,595	2.3
			Jackson	38,634	1.1
			McCormack	29,242	0.9
			Harris	16,920	0.5
			Bayh	11,419	0.3
			Others[1]	215	—

June 8   New Jersey

Republican	Votes	%	Democratic	Votes	%
Ford	242,122	100.00	Carter	210,655	58.4
			Church	49,034	13.6
			Jackson	31,820	8.8
			Wallace	31,183	8.6
			McCormack	21,774	6.0
			Others	16,373	4.5

June 8   Ohio

Republican	Votes	%	Democratic	Votes	%
Ford	516,111	55.2	Carter	593,130	52.3
Reagan	419,646	44.8	Udall	240,342	21.2
			Church	157,884	13.9
			Wallace	63,953	5.6
			Gertrude W. Donahey (unpledged delegates)	43,661	3.9
			Jackson	35,404	3.1

Republican

TOTALS	Votes	%
Ford	5,529,899	53.3
Reagan	4,758,325	45.9
None of the names shown	19,990	0.2
Unpledged delegates	14,727	0.1
Daly	7,582	0.1
Others[1]	43,602	0.4
	10,374,125	

Democratic

	Votes	%
Carter	6,235,609	38.8
Brown	2,449,374	15.3
Wallace	1,995,388	12.4
Udall	1,611,754	10.0
Jackson	1,134,375	7.1
Church	830,818	5.2
Byrd	340,309	2.1
Shriver	304,399	1.9
Unpledged delegates	248,680	1.5
McCormack	238,027	1.5
Harris	234,568	1.5
None of the names shown	93,728	0.6
Shapp	88,254	0.5
Bayh	86,438	0.5
Humphrey	61,992	0.4
Kennedy	19,805	0.1
Bentsen	4,046	—
Others[4]	75,088	0.5
	16,052,652	

* Delegate selection primaries were held in Alabama, New York, and Texas. In *America Votes,* Scammon did not record vote totals if the primary was strictly for delegate selection and there was no presidential preference voting.

1. Write-in.
2. Ford unopposed. No primary held.
3. In addition to scattered write-in votes, "others" include Tommy Klein, who received 1,088 votes in Kentucky.
4. In addition to scattered write-in votes, "others" include Frank Ahern who received 1,487 votes in Georgia; Stanley Arnold, 371 votes in New Hampshire; Arthur O. Blessitt, 828 votes in New Hampshire and 7,889 in Georgia: Frank Bona, 135 votes in New Hampshire and 263 in Georgia; Billy Joe Clegg, 174 votes in New Hampshire; Abram Eisenman, 351 votes in Georgia; John S. Gonas, 2,288 votes in New Jersey; Jesse Gray, 3,574 votes in New Jersey; Robert L. Kelleher, 87 votes in New Hampshire, 1,603 in Massachusetts and 139 in Georgia; Rick Loewenherz, 49 votes in New Hampshire; Frank Lomento, 3,555 votes in New Jersey, Floyd L. Lunger, 3,935 votes in New Jersey; H. R. H. "Fifi" Rockefeller, 2,305 votes in Kentucky; George Roden, 153 votes in Georgia; Ray Rollinson, 3,021 votes in New Jersey; Terry Sanford, 53 votes in New Hampshire and 351 votes in Massachusetts; Bernard B. Schechter, 173 votes in New Hampshire.

1980 Primaries[1]

Republican			Democratic		
	Votes	**%**		**Votes**	**%**
February 17 Puerto Rico[1]			March 16		
George Bush (Texas)[2]	111,940	60.1	Jimmy Carter (Ga.)	449,681	51.7
Howard H. Baker Jr. (Tenn.)[3]	68,934	37.0	Edward M. Kennedy (Mass.)	418,068	48.0
Benjamin Fernandez (Calif.)	2,097	1.1	Edmund G. Brown Jr. (Calif.)[5]	1,660	0.2
John B. Connally (Texas)[4]	1,964	1.1	Others	826	0.1
Harold Stassen (N.Y.)	672	0.4			
Robert Dole (Kan.)	483	0.3			
Others	281	0.1			
February 26 New Hampshire					
Ronald Reagan (Calif.)	72,983	49.6	Carter	52,692	47.1
Bush	33,443	22.7	Kennedy	41,745	37.3
Baker	18,943	12.1	Brown	10,743	9.6
John B. Anderson (Ill.)[6]	14,458	9.8	Lyndon LaRouche (N.Y.)	2,326	2.1
Philip M. Crane (Ill.)	2,618	1.8	Richard Kay (Ohio)	566	0.5
Connally	2,239	1.5	Others[7]	3,858	3.4
Dole	597	—			
Others[7]	1,876	1.3			
March 4 Massachusetts					
Bush	124,365	31.0	Kennedy	590,393	65.1
Anderson	122,987	30.7	Carter	260,401	28.7
Reagan	115,334	28.8	Brown	31,498	3.5
Baker	19,366	4.8	Others[7]	5,368	0.6
Connally	4,714	1.2	No preference	19,663	2.2
Crane	4,669	1.2			
Gerald R. Ford (Mich.)[7]	3,398	0.8			
Dole	577	—			
Fernandez	374	0.1			
Stassen	218	0.1			
Others[7]	2,581	0.6			
No preference	2,243	0.6			
March 4 Vermont					
Reagan	19,720	30.1	Carter	29,015	73.1
Anderson	19,030	29.0	Kennedy	10,135	25.5
Bush	14,226	21.7	Brown[7]	358	0.9
Baker	8,055	12.3	LaRouche[7]	6	—
Ford[7]	2,300	3.5	Others	189	0.5
Crane	1,238	1.9			
Connally	884	1.3			
Stassen	105	0.2			
Others[7]	53	—			
March 8 South Carolina					
Reagan	79,549	54.7			
Connally	43,113	29.6			
Bush	21,569	14.8			
Baker	773	0.5			
Fernandez	171	0.1			
Stassen	150	0.1			
Dole	117	0.1			
Nick Belluso	59	—			
March 11 Alabama					
Reagan	147,352	69.7	Carter	193,734	81.6
Bush	54,730	25.9	Kennedy	31,382	13.2

Republican			**Democratic**		
	Votes	**%**		**Votes**	**%**
Crane	5,099	2.4	Brown	9,529	4.0
Baker	1,963	0.9	William L. Nuckols	609	—
Connally	1,077	0.5	Bob Maddox	540	—
Stassen	544	0.3	Unpledged delegates	1,670	0.7
Dole	447	0.2			
Belluso	141	—			

March 11 **Florida**

Reagan	345,699	56.2	Carter	666,321	60.7
Bush	185,996	30.2	Kennedy	254,727	23.2
Anderson	56,636	9.2	Brown	53,474	4.9
Crane	12,000	2.0	Kay	19,160	1.7
Baker	6,345	1.0	No preference	104,321	9.5
Connally	4,958	0.8			
Stassen	1,377	0.2			
Dole	1,086	0.2			
Fernandez	898	0.1			

March 11 **Georgia**

Reagan	146,500	73.2	Carter	338,772	88.0
Bush	25,293	12.6	Kennedy	32,315	8.4
Anderson	16,853	8.4	Brown	7,255	1.9
Crane	6,308	3.2	Cliff Finch (Miss.)	1,378	0.4
Connally	2,388	1.2	Kay	840	0.2
Baker	1,571	0.8	LaRouche	513	0.1
Fernandez	809	0.4	Unpledged delegates	3,707	1.0
Dole	249	0.1			
Stassen	200	0.1			

March 18 **Illinois**

Reagan	547,355	48.4	Carter	780,787	65.0
Anderson	415,193	36.7	Kennedy	359,875	30.0
Bush	124,057	11.0	Brown	39,168	3.3
Crane	24,865	2.2	LaRouche	19,192	1.6
Baker	7,051	0.6	Anderson[7]	1,643	0.1
Connally	4,548	0.4	Others[7]	402	—
V. A. Kelley	3,757	0.3			
Dole	1,843	0.2			
Ford[7]	1,106	0.1			
Others	306	—			

March 25 **Connecticut**

Bush	70,367	38.6	Kennedy	98,662	46.9
Reagan	61,735	33.9	Carter	87,207	41.5
Anderson	40,354	22.1	LaRouche	5,617	2.7
Baker	2,446	1.3	Brown	5,386	2.6
Crane	1,887	1.0	Unpledged delegates	13,403	6.4
Connally	598	0.3			
Dole	333	0.2			
Fernandez	308	0.2			
Unpledged delegates	4,256	2.3			

March 25 **New York**[1]

			Kennedy	582,757	58.9
			Carter	406,305	41.1

April 1 **Kansas**

Reagan	179,739	63.0	Carter	109,807	56.6
Anderson	51,924	18.2	Kennedy	61,318	31.6

Republican	Votes	%	**Democratic**	Votes	%
Bush	35,838	12.6	Brown	9,434	4.9
Baker	3,603	1.3	Finch	629	0.3
Connally	2,067	0.7	Maddox	632	0.3
Fernandez	1,650	0.6	Frank Ahern	571	0.2
Crane	1,367	0.5	Ray Rollinson	364	—
R.W. Yeager	1,063	0.4	None of the names shown	11,163	5.8
Alvin G. Carris	483	0.2			
Stassen	383	0.1			
William E. Carlson	311	—			
Donald Badgley	244	—			
None of the names shown	6,726	2.4			

April 1 Wisconsin

	Votes	%		Votes	%
Reagan	364,898	40.2	Carter	353,662	56.2
Bush	276,164	30.4	Kennedy	189,520	30.1
Anderson	248,623	27.4	Brown	74,496	11.8
Baker	3,298	0.4	LaRouche	6,896	1.1
Crane	2,951	0.3	Finch	1,842	0.3
Connally	2,312	0.3	Others[7]	509	0.1
Fernandez	1,051	0.1	None of the names shown	2,694	0.4
Stassen	1,010	0.1			
Others[7]	4,951	0.5			
None of the names shown	2,595	0.3			

April 5 Louisiana

	Votes	%		Votes	%
Reagan	31,212	74.9	Carter	199,956	55.7
Bush	7,818	18.8	Kennedy	80,797	22.5
Stassen	126	0.3	Brown	16,774	4.7
Belluso	155	0.3	Finch	11,153	3.1
Fernandez	84	0.2	Kay	3,362	0.9
C. Leon Pickett	67	—	Maddox	2,830	0.8
None of the names shown	2,221	5.3	Don Reaux	2,255	0.6
			Unpledged delegates	41,614	11.6

April 22 Pennsylvania

	Votes	%		Votes	%
Bush	626,759	50.5	Kennedy	736,854	45.7
Reagan	527,916	42.5	Carter	732,332	45.4
Baker	30,846	2.5	Brown	37,669	2.3
Anderson	26,890	2.1	Anderson[7]	9,182	0.6
Connally	10,656	0.9	Bush[7]	2,074	0.1
Stassen	6,767	0.5	Reagan[7]	1,097	0.1
Alvin J. Jacobson	4,357	0.4	Ford[7]	150	—
Fernandez	2,521	0.2	No preference	93,865	5.8
Others	4,699	0.4			

May 3 Texas

	Votes	%		Votes	%
Reagan	268,798	51.0	Carter	770,390	55.9
Bush	249,819	47.4	Kennedy	314,129	22.8
Unpledged delegates	8,152	1.5	Brown	35,585	2.6
			Unpledged delegates	257,250	18.7

May 6 District of Columbia

	Votes	%		Votes	%
Bush	4,973	66.1	Kennedy	39,561	61.7
Anderson	2,025	26.9	Carter	23,697	36.9
Crane	270	3.6	LaRouche	892	1.4
Stassen	201	2.7			
Fernandez	60	0.8			

Republican			**Democratic**		
	Votes	%		Votes	%

May 6 Indiana

Republican	Votes	%	Democratic	Votes	%
Reagan	419,016	73.7	Carter	398,949	67.7
Bush	92,955	16.4	Kennedy	190,492	32.3
Anderson	56,342	9.9			

May 6 North Carolina

Republican	Votes	%	Democratic	Votes	%
Reagan	113,854	67.6	Carter	516,778	70.1
Bush	36,631	21.8	Kennedy	130,684	17.7
Anderson	8,542	5.1	Brown	21,420	2.9
Baker	2,543	1.5	No preference	68,380	9.3
Connally	1,107	0.7			
Dole	629	0.4			
Crane	547	0.3			
No preference	4,538	2.7			

May 6 Tennessee

Republican	Votes	%	Democratic	Votes	%
Reagan	144,625	74.1	Carter	221,658	75.2
Bush	35,274	18.1	Kennedy	53,258	18.1
Anderson	8,722	4.5	Brown	5,612	1.9
Crane	1,574	0.8	Finch	1,663	0.6
Baker[7]	16	—	LaRouche	925	0.3
Ford[7]	14	—	Others[7]	49	—
Connally[7]	1	—	Unpledged delegates	11,515	3.9
Others[7]	8	—			
Unpledged delegates	4,976	2.5			

May 13 Maryland

Republican	Votes	%	Democratic	Votes	%
Reagan	80,557	48.2	Carter	226,528	47.5
Bush	68,389	40.9	Kennedy	181,091	38.0
Anderson	16,244	9.7	Brown	14,313	3.0
Crane	2,113	1.3	Finch	4,891	1.0
			LaRouche	4,388	0.9
			Unpledged delegates	45,879	9.6

May 13 Nebraska

Republican	Votes	%	Democratic	Votes	%
Reagan	155,995	76.0	Carter	72,120	46.9
Bush	31,380	15.3	Kennedy	57,826	37.6
Anderson	11,879	5.8	Brown	5,478	3.6
Dole	1,420	0.7	LaRouche	1,169	0.8
Crane	1,062	0.5	Others[7]	1,247	0.8
Stassen	799	0.4	Unpledged delegates	16,041	10.4
Fernandez	400	0.2			
Others[7]	2,268	1.1			

May 20 Michigan

Republican	Votes	%	Democratic	Votes	%
Bush	341,998	57.5	Brown	23,043	29.4
Reagan	189,184	31.8	LaRouche	8,948	11.4
Anderson	48,947	8.2	Others[7]	10,048	12.8
Fernandez	2,248	0.4	Unpledged delegates	36,385	46.4
Stassen	1,938	0.3			
Others[7]	596	0.1			
Unpledged delegates	10,265	1.7			

May 20 Oregon

Republican	Votes	%	Democratic	Votes	%
Reagan	170,449	54.0	Carter	208,693	56.7
Bush	109,210	34.6	Kennedy	114,651	31.1
Anderson	32,118	10.2	Brown	34,409	9.3
Crane	2,324	0.7	Anderson[7]	5,407	1.5

Republican	Votes	%	Democratic	Votes	%
Others[7]	1,265	0.4	Reagan[7]	2,206	0.6
			Bush[7]	1,838	0.5

May 27 Arkansas[1]

Republican	Votes	%	Democratic	Votes	%
			Carter	269,375	60.1
			Kennedy	78,542	17.5
			Finch	19,469	4.3
			Unpledged delegates	80,904	18.0

May 27 Idaho

Republican	Votes	%	Democratic	Votes	%
Reagan	111,868	82.9	Carter	31,383	62.2
Anderson	13,130	9.7	Kennedy	11,087	22.0
Bush	5,416	4.0	Brown	2,078	4.1
Crane	1,024	0.8	Unpledged delegates	5,934	11.8
Unpledged delegates	3,441	2.6			

May 27 Kentucky

Republican	Votes	%	Democratic	Votes	%
Reagan	78,072	82.4	Carter	160,819	66.9
Bush	6,861	7.2	Kennedy	55,167	23.0
Anderson	4,791	5.1	Kay	2,609	1.1
Stassen	1,223	1.3	Finch	2,517	1.0
Fernandez	764	0.8	Unpledged delegates	19,219	8.0
Unpledged delegates	3,084	3.3			

May 27 Nevada

Republican	Votes	%	Democratic	Votes	%
Reagan	39,352	83.0	Carter	25,159	37.6
Bush	3,078	6.5	Kennedy	19,296	28.8
None of the names shown	4,965	10.5	None of the names shown	22,493	33.6

June 3 California[1]

Republican	Votes	%	Democratic	Votes	%
Reagan	2,057,923	80.3	Kennedy slate	1,507,142	44.8
Anderson	349,315	13.6	Carter slate	1,266,276	37.6
Bush	125,113	4.9	Brown slate	135,962	4.0
Crane	21,465	0.8	LaRouche slate	71,779	2.1
Fernandez	10,242	0.4	Others[7]	51	—
Others[7]	14	—	Unpledged slate	382,759	11.4

June 3 New Mexico

Republican	Votes	%	Democratic	Votes	%
Reagan	37,982	63.8	Kennedy	73,721	46.3
Anderson	7,171	12.0	Carter	66,621	41.8
Bush	5,892	9.9	LaRouche	4,798	3.0
Crane	4,412	7.4	Finch	4,490	2.8
Fernandez	1,795	3.0	Unpledged delegates	9,734	6.1
Stassen	947	1.6			
Unpledged delegates	1,347	2.3			

June 3 New Jersey

Republican	Votes	%	Democratic	Votes	%
Reagan	225,959	81.3	Kennedy	315,109	56.2
Bush	47,447	17.1	Carter	212,387	37.9
Stassen	4,571	1.6	LaRouche	13,913	2.5
			Unpledged delegates	19,499	3.5

June 3 Montana

Republican	Votes	%	Democratic	Votes	%
Reagan	68,744	86.6	Carter	66,922	51.5
Bush	7,665	9.7	Kennedy	47,671	36.7
No preference	3,014	3.8	No preference	15,466	11.9

Republican	Votes	%		**Democratic**	Votes	%

June 3 Ohio[1]

Reagan	692,288	80.8	Carter		605,744	51.1
Bush	164,485	19.2	Kennedy		523,874	44.4
			LaRouche		35,268	3.0
			Kay		21,524	1.8

June 3 Rhode Island

Reagan	3,839	72.0	Kennedy		26,179	68.3
Bush	993	18.6	Carter		9,907	25.8
Stassen	107	2.0	LaRouche		1,160	3.0
Fernandez	48	0.9	Brown		310	0.8
Unpledged delegates	348	6.5	Unpledged delegates		771	2.0

June 3 South Dakota[1]

Reagan slate	72,861	82.2	Kennedy slate		33,418	48.6
Bush	3,691	4.2	Carter slate		31,251	45.4
Stassen	987	1.1	Uncommitted slate		4,094	6.0
No preference	5,366	6.1				

June 3 West Virginia

Reagan	115,407	83.6	Carter		197,687	62.2
Bush	19,509	14.1	Kennedy		120,247	37.8
Stassen	3,100	2.2				

June 3 Mississippi[1]

Reagan slate	23,028	89.4				
Bush slate	2,105	8.2				
Unslated	618	2.4				

TOTALS[8]

Reagan	7,709,793	60.8	Carter		9,593,335	51.2
Bush	2,958,093	23.3	Kennedy		6,963,625	37.1
Anderson	1,572,174	12.4	Brown		573,636	3.1
Baker	112,219	0.9	LaRouche		177,784	1.0
Crane	97,793	0.8	Kay		48,061	0.3
Connally	80,661	0.6	Finch		48,032	0.3
Stassen	24,753	0.2	Maddox		4,002	—
Fernandez	23,423	0.2	Reaux		2,255	—
Dole	7,298	0.1	Nuckols		609	—
Jacobsen	4,357	—	Ahern		571	—
Kelley	3,757	—	Rollinson		364	—
Yeager	1,063	—	Unpledged delegates		950,378	5.1
Carris	483	—	No preference		301,695	1.6
Belluso	355	—	None of the names shown		36,350	0.1
Carlson	311	—	Others		47,128	0.2
Badgley	244	—				
Pickett	67	—			18,747,825	
Unpledged delegates	38,708	0.3				
No preference	15,161	0.1				
None of the names shown	14,286	0.1				
Others	25,452	0.2				
	12,690,451					

1. In 1980, 35 states, the District of Columbia, and Puerto Rico held presidential primaries. California Democrats and South Dakota Republicans and Democrats held state-type preference primaries. In New York, Democrats had a presidential preference, but Republicans held primaries for the selection of delegates only, without indication of presidential preference. In Mississippi, Republicans elected delegates by congressional districts pledged to candidates and the vote indicated is for the highest of each slate's candidates in each congressional district. In Arkansas, the Republicans did not hold a primary although Democrats did. In South Carolina, the Democrats did not hold a primary but Republicans did. The vote in Ohio is for at-large delegates pledged to specific candidates and elected as a group. The Republican and Democratic primaries in Puerto Rico were held on two different dates: February 17 and March 16, respectively.

2. Bush withdrew May 26.

3. Baker withdrew March 5.

4. Connally withdrew March 9.

5. Brown withdrew April 1.

6. Anderson withdrew April 24.

7. Write-in vote.

8. Totals exclude Puerto Rico, where citizens are unable to vote in the general election.

1984 Primaries

Republican	Votes	%	Democratic	Votes	%

February 28 New Hampshire

Republican	Votes	%	Democratic	Votes	%
Ronald Reagan (Calif.)	65,033	86.1	Gary Hart (Colo.)	37,702	37.3
Harold E. Stassen (Pa.)	1,543	2.0	Walter F. Mondale (Minn.)	28,173	27.9
David Kelly (La.)	360	0.5	John Glenn (Ohio)	12,088	12.0
Gary Arnold (Minn.)	252	0.3	Jesse Jackson (Ill.)	5,311	5.3
Benjamin Fernandez (Calif.)	202	0.3	George McGovern (S.D.)	5,217	5.2
Others[1]	8,180	10.8	Ernest F. Hollings (S.C.)	3,583	3.5
			Alan Cranston (Calif.)	2,136	2.1
			Reubin Askew (Fla.)	1,025	1.0
			Stephen A. Koczak (D.C.)	155	0.2
			Gerald Willis (Ala.)	50	—
			Richard B. Kay (Fla.)	27	—
			Others[1]	5,664	5.6

March 6 Vermont[2]

Republican	Votes	%	Democratic	Votes	%
Reagan	33,218	98.7	Hart	51,873	70.0
Others	425	1.3	Mondale	14,834	20.0
			Jackson	5,761	7.8
			Askew	444	0.6
			Others	1,147	1.5

March 13 Alabama

[3]

Republican	Votes	%	Democratic	Votes	%
			Mondale	148,165	34.6
			Glenn	89,286	20.8
			Hart	88,465	20.7
			Jackson	83,787	19.6
			Willis	6,153	1.4
			Hollings	4,759	1.1
			Unpledged delegates	4,464	1.0
			Askew	1,827	0.4
			Cranston	1,377	0.3

March 13 Florida

Republican	Votes	%	Democratic	Votes	%
Reagan	344,150	100.0	Hart	463,799	39.2
			Mondale	394,350	33.4
			Jackson	144,263	12.2
			Glenn	128,209	10.8
			Askew	26,258	2.2
			McGovern	17,614	1.5
			Hollings	3,115	0.3
			Cranston	2,097	0.2
			Kay	1,328	0.1
			Koczak	1,157	0.1

March 13 Georgia

Republican	Votes	%	Democratic	Votes	%
Reagan	50,793	100.0	Mondale	208,588	30.5
			Hart	186,903	27.3
			Jackson	143,730	21.0
			Glenn	122,744	17.9
			McGovern	11,321	1.7
			Hollings	3,800	0.6
			Unpledged delegates	3,068	0.4
			Willis	1,804	0.3
			Askew	1,660	0.2
			Cranston	923	0.1

	Republican			Democratic		
	Votes	%			Votes	%
March 13 Massachusetts						
Reagan	58,996	89.5	Hart		245,943	39.0
No preference	5,005	7.6	Mondale		160,893	25.5
Others	1,936	2.9	McGovern		134,341	21.3
			Glenn		45,456	7.2
			Jackson		31,824	5.0
			No preference		5,080	0.8
			Askew		1,394	0.2
			Hollings		1,203	0.2
			Cranston		853	0.1
			Others		3,975	0.6
March 13 Rhode Island						
Reagan	2,028	90.7	Hart		20,011	45.0
Unpledged delegates	207	9.3	Mondale		15,338	34.5
			Jackson		3,875	8.7
			Glenn		2,249	5.0
			McGovern		2,146	4.8
			Unpledged delegates		439	1.0
			Cranston		273	0.6
			Askew		96	0.2
			Hollings		84	0.2
March 18 Puerto Rico						
3			Mondale		141,698	99.1
			Hart		874	0.6
			Glenn		436	0.3
			Sterling P. Davis (Miss.)		31	—
March 20 Illinois						
Reagan	594,742	99.9	Mondale		670,951	40.4
Others	336	0.1	Hart		584,579	35.2
			Jackson		348,843	21.0
			McGovern		25,336	1.5
			Glenn		19,800	1.2
			Betty Jean Williams (Ill.)		4,797	0.3
			Cranston		2,786	0.2
			Askew		2,182	0.1
			Others		151	—
March 27 Connecticut						
3			Hart		116,286	52.7
			Mondale		64,230	29.1
			Jackson		26,395	12.0
			Askew		6,098	2.8
			McGovern		2,426	1.1
			Hollings		2,283	1.0
			Unpledged delegates		1,973	0.9
			Glenn		955	0.4
			Cranston		196	0.1
April 3 New York						
3			Mondale		621,581	44.8
			Hart		380,564	27.4
			Jackson		355,541	25.6
			Glenn		15,941	1.1
			Cranston		6,815	0.5
			McGovern		4,547	0.3

Republican				Democratic		
	Votes	**%**			**Votes**	**%**
			Askew		2,877	0.2
			Others		84	—

April 3 Wisconsin[4]

"Ronald Reagan Yes"	280,608	95.2	Hart		282,435	44.4
"Ronald Reagan No"	14,047	4.7	Mondale		261,374	41.1
Others[1]	158	0.1	Jackson		62,524	9.8
			McGovern		10,166	1.6
			"None of the names shown"		7,036	1.1
			Glenn		6,398	1.0
			Cranston		2,984	0.5
			Hollings		1,650	0.3
			Askew		683	0.1
			Others		518	0.1

April 10 Pennsylvania

Reagan	616,916	99.3	Mondale		747,267	45.1
Others	4,290	0.7	Hart		551,335	33.3
			Jackson		264,463	16.0
			Cranston		22,829	1.4
			Glenn		22,605	1.4
			Lyndon H. LaRouche Jr. (Va.)		19,180	1.2
			McGovern		13,139	0.8
			Robert K. Griser (Pa.)		6,090	0.4
			Askew		5,071	0.3
			Hollings		2,972	0.2
			Others		1,343	0.1

May 1 District of Columbia

Reagan	5,692	100.0	Jackson		69,106	67.3
			Mondale		26,320	25.6
			Hart		7,305	7.1

May 1 Tennessee

Reagan	75,367	90.9	Mondale		132,201	41.0
Unpledged delegates	7,546	9.1	Hart		93,710	29.1
Others	8	—	Jackson		81,418	25.3
			Unpledged delegates		6,682	2.1
			Glenn		4,198	1.3
			McGovern		3,824	1.2
			Others		30	—

May 5 Louisiana

Reagan	14,964	89.7	Jackson		136,707	42.9
Unpledged delegates	1,723	10.3	Hart		79,593	25.0
			Mondale		71,162	22.3
			Unpledged delegates		19,409	6.1
			LaRouche		4,970	1.6
			McGovern		3,158	1.0
			Griser		1,924	0.6
			Kay		1,344	0.4
			Koczak		543	0.2

May 5 Texas

Reagan	308,713	96.5	[3]			
Unpledged delegates	11,126	3.5				

	Republican				Democratic	
	Votes	**%**			**Votes**	**%**
May 8 Indiana						
Reagan	428,559	100.0		Hart	299,491	41.8
				Mondale	293,413	40.9
				Jackson	98,190	13.7
				Glenn	16,046	2.2
				Bob Brewster (Fla.)	9,815	1.4
May 8 Maryland						
Reagan	73,663	100.0		Mondale	215,222	42.5
				Jackson	129,387	25.5
				Hart	123,365	24.3
				Unpledged delegates	15,807	3.1
				LaRouche	7,836	1.5
				Glenn	6,238	1.2
				McGovern	5,796	1.1
				Cranston	1,768	0.3
				Hollings	1,467	0.3
May 8 North Carolina						
[3]				Mondale	342,324	35.6
				Hart	289,877	30.2
				Jackson	243,945	25.4
				No preference	44,232	4.6
				Glenn	17,659	1.8
				McGovern	10,149	1.1
				Hollings	8,318	0.9
				Askew	3,144	0.3
				Cranston	1,209	0.1
May 8 Ohio						
Reagan	658,169	100.0		Hart	608,528	42.0
				Mondale	583,595	40.3
				Jackson	237,133	16.4
				McGovern	8,991	0.6
				Cranston	4,653	0.3
				LaRouche	4,336	0.3
May 15 Nebraska						
Reagan	145,245	99.9		Hart	86,582	58.2
Others	1,403	1.0		Mondale	39,635	26.6
				Jackson	13,495	9.1
				Unpledged delegates	4,631	3.1
				McGovern	1,561	1.0
				LaRouche	1,227	0.8
				Cranston	538	0.4
				Hollings	450	0.3
				Others	736	0.5
May 15 Oregon						
Reagan	238,594	98.0		Hart	233,638	58.5
Others[1]	4,752	2.0		Mondale	110,374	27.6
				Jackson	37,106	9.3
				Glenn	10,831	2.7
				LaRouche	5,943	1.5
				Others	1,787	0.5

Republican	Votes	%	Democratic	Votes	%

May 15 Idaho

Republican	Votes	%	Democratic	Votes	%
Reagan	97,450	92.2	Hart	31,737	58.0
"None of the names shown"	8,237	7.8	Mondale	16,460	30.1
			Jackson	3,104	5.7
			"None of the names shown"	2,225	4.1
			LaRouche	1,196	2.2

June 5 California

Republican	Votes	%	Democratic	Votes	%
Reagan	1,874,897	100.0	Hart	1,155,499	38.9
Others[1]	78		Mondale	1,049,342	35.3
			Jackson	546,693	18.4
			Glenn	96,770	3.3
			McGovern	69,926	2.4
			LaRouche	52,647	1.8
			Others[1]	26	-

June 5 Montana

Republican	Votes	%	Democratic	Votes	%
Reagan	66,432	92.4	No preference	28,385	83.0
No preference	5,378	7.5	Hart[1]	3,080	9.0
Others	77	0.1	Mondale[1]	2,026	5.9
			Jackson[1]	388	1.1
			Others	335	1.0

June 5 New Jersey

Republican	Votes	%	Democratic	Votes	%
Reagan	240,054	100.0	Mondale	305,516	45.2
			Hart	200,948	29.7
			Jackson	159,788	23.6
			LaRouche	10,309	1.5

June 5 New Mexico

Republican	Votes	%	Democratic	Votes	%
Reagan	40,805	94.9	Hart	87,610	46.7
Unpledged delegates	2,189	5.1	Mondale	67,675	36.1
			Jackson	22,168	11.8
			McGovern	5,143	2.7
			LaRouche	3,330	1.8
			Unpledged delegates	1,477	0.8

June 5 South Dakota

[3]

Republican	Votes	%	Democratic	Votes	%
			Hart	26,641	50.7
			Mondale	20,495	39.0
			Jackson	2,738	5.2
			LaRouche	1,383	2.6
			Unpledged delegates	1,304	2.5

June 5 West Virginia

Republican	Votes	%	Democratic	Votes	%
Reagan	125,790	91.8	Mondale	198,776	53.8
Stassen	11,206	8.2	Hart	137,866	37.3
			Jackson	24,697	6.7
			LaRouche	7,274	2.0
			Alfred Timinski (N.J.)	632	0.2

June 12 North Dakota

Republican	Votes	%	Democratic	Votes	%
Reagan	44,109	100.0	Hart	28,603	85.1
			LaRouche	4,018	12.0
			Mondale[1]	934	2.8

Republican	Votes	%
TOTALS[5]		
Reagan	6,484,987	98.6
"Ronald Reagan No"	14,047	0.2
Stassen	12,749	0.2
Kelly	360	—
Arnold	252	—
Fernandez	202	—
Uncommitted[6]	41,411	0.6
Others	21,643	0.3
	6,575,651	

Democratic	Votes	%
Mondale	6,811,214	37.8
Hart	6,503,968	36.1
Jackson	3,282,431	18.2
Glenn	617,380	3.4
McGovern	334,801	1.9
LaRouche	123,649	0.7
Askew	52,759	0.3
Cranston	51,437	0.3
Hollings	33,684	0.2
Brewster	9,815	0.1
Griser	8,014	—
Willis	8,007	—
Williams	4,797	—
Kay	2,699	—
Koczak	1,855	—
Timinski	632	—
Uncommitted[6]	146,212	0.8
Others	15,796	0.1
	18,009,217	

1. Write-in vote.
2. In Vermont's Liberty Union presidential primary, Dennis L. Serrette received 276 of the 309 votes cast, or 89.3 percent of the vote.
3. No primary.
4. Delegates could vote for or against Reagan within the Republican ticket.

5. Totals exclude Puerto Rico, where citizens are unable to vote in the general election.
6. The Uncommitted category includes votes cast on the following ballot lines: No preference, Unpledged delegates, and "None of the names shown."

1988 Primaries

Republican	Votes	%	Democratic	Votes	%
February 16 New Hampshire					
George Bush (Maine)	59,290	37.6	Michael S. Dukakis (Mass.)	44,112	35.7
Robert Dole (Kan.)	44,797	28.4	Richard A. Gephardt (Mo.)	24,513	19.8
Jack F. Kemp (N.Y.)	20,114	12.8	Paul Simon (Ill.)	21,094	17.1
Pierre S. du Pont IV (Del.)	15,885	10.1	Jesse Jackson (Ill.)	9,615	7.8
Pat Robertson (Va.)	14,775	9.4	Albert Gore Jr. (Tenn.)	8,400	6.8
Alexander M. Haig Jr. (Pa.)	481	0.3	Bruce Babbitt (Ariz.)	5,644	4.6
Harold E. Stassen (Pa.)	130	—	Gary Hart (Colo.)	4,888	4.0
Paul B. Conley (N.Y.)	107	—	William J. du Pont IV (Ill.)	1,349	1.1
Mary Jane Rachner (Minn.)	107	—	David E. Duke (D.C.)	264	0.2
Others[1]	1,958	1.2	Lyndon H. LaRouche Jr. (Va.)	188	0.2
			William A. Marra (N.J.)	142	0.1
			Florenzo DiDonato	84	0.1
			Stephen A. Koczak (D.C.)	47	—
			Norbert G. Dennerll (Ohio)	18	—
			Others[1]	3,154	2.5
February 23 South Dakota					
Dole slate	51,599	55.2	Gephardt	31,184	43.6
Robertson slate	18,310	19.6	Dukakis	22,349	31.2
Bush slate	17,404	18.6	Gore	5,993	8.4
Kemp slate	4,290	4.6	Simon	3,992	5.6
Unpledged delegates slate	1,226	1.3	Hart	3,875	5.4
du Pont slate	576	0.6	Jackson	3,867	5.4
			Babbitt	346	0.5
March 1 Vermont[2]					
Bush	23,565	49.3	Dukakis	28,353	55.8
Dole	18,655	39.0	Jackson	13,044	25.7
Robertson	2,452	5.1	Gephardt	3,910	7.7
Kemp	1,877	3.9	Simon	2,620	5.2
du Pont	808	1.7	Hart	2,055	4.0
Haig	324	0.7	Others[1]	809	1.6
Others[1]	151	0.3			
March 5 South Carolina			[3]		
Bush	94,738	48.5			
Dole	40,265	20.6			
Robertson	37,261	19.1			
Kemp	22,431	11.5			
du Pont	316	0.2			
Haig	177	0.1			
Stassen	104	0.1			
March 8 Alabama					
Bush	137,807	64.5	Jackson	176,764	43.6
Dole	34,733	16.2	Gore	151,739	37.4
Robertson	29,772	13.9	Dukakis	31,306	7.7
Kemp	10,557	4.9	Gephardt	30,214	7.4
du Pont	392	0.2	Hart	7,530	1.9
Haig	300	0.1	Simon	3,063	0.8
			Babbitt	2,410	0.6
			Unpledged delegates	1,771	0.4
			LaRouche	845	0.2

Republican	Votes	%	Democratic	Votes	%

March 8 Arkansas

Republican	Votes	%	Democratic	Votes	%
Bush	32,114	47.0	Gore	185,758	37.3
Dole	17,667	25.9	Dukakis	94,103	18.9
Robertson	12,918	18.9	Jackson	85,003	17.1
Kemp	3,499	5.1	Gephardt	59,711	12.0
Unpledged delegates	1,402	2.1	Unpledged delegates	35,553	7.1
du Pont	359	0.5	Hart	18,630	3.7
Haig	346	0.5	Simon	9,020	1.8
			Duke	4,805	1.0
			Babbitt	2,614	0.5
			LaRouche	2,347	0.5

March 8 Florida

Republican	Votes	%	Democratic	Votes	%
Bush	559,820	62.1	Dukakis	521,041	40.9
Dole	191,197	21.2	Jackson	254,912	20.0
Robertson	95,826	10.6	Gephardt	182,861	14.4
Kemp	41,795	4.6	Gore	161,165	12.7
du Pont	6,726	0.7	Undecided	79,088	6.2
Haig	5,858	0.7	Hart	36,315	2.9
			Simon	27,620	2.2
			Babbitt	10,296	0.8

March 8 Georgia

Republican	Votes	%	Democratic	Votes	%
Bush	215,516	53.8	Jackson	247,831	39.8
Dole	94,749	23.6	Gore	201,490	32.6
Robertson	65,163	16.3	Dukakis	97,179	15.6
Kemp	23,409	5.8	Gephardt	41,489	6.7
du Pont	1,309	0.3	Hart	15,852	2.5
Haig	782	0.2	Simon	8,388	1.3
			Unpledged delegates	7,276	1.2
			Babbitt	3,247	0.5

March 8 Kentucky

Republican	Votes	%	Democratic	Votes	%
Bush	72,020	59.3	Gore	145,988	45.8
Dole	27,868	23.0	Dukakis	59,433	18.6
Robertson	13,526	11.1	Jackson	49,667	15.6
Kemp	4,020	3.3	Gephardt	28,982	9.1
Unpledged delegates	2,245	1.8	Hart	11,798	3.7
Stassen	844	0.7	Unpledged delegates	10,465	3.3
du Pont	457	0.4	Simon	9,393	2.9
Haig	422	0.3	Babbitt	1,290	0.4
			LaRouche	681	0.2
			Richard B. Kay (Fla.)	487	0.2
			Others[1]	537	0.2

March 8 Louisiana

Republican	Votes	%	Democratic	Votes	%
Bush	83,687	57.8	Jackson	221,532	35.5
Robertson	26,295	18.2	Gore	174,974	28.0
Dole	25,626	17.7	Dukakis	95,667	15.3
Kemp	7,722	5.3	Gephardt	66,434	10.6
du Pont	853	0.6	Hart	26,442	4.2
Haig	598	0.4	Duke	23,390	3.7
			Simon	5,155	0.8
			Frank Ahern (La.)	3,701	0.6
			Babbitt	3,076	0.5
			LaRouche	1,681	0.3
			Dennerll	1,575	0.3
			Kay	823	0.1

Republican			**Democratic**		
	Votes	**%**		**Votes**	**%**

March 8 **Maryland**

Republican	Votes	%	Democratic	Votes	%
Bush	107,026	53.3	Dukakis	242,479	45.6
Dole	64,987	32.8	Jackson	152,642	28.7
Robertson	12,860	6.5	Gore	46,063	8.7
Kemp	11,909	5.9	Gephardt	42,059	8.0
du Pont	2,551	1.8	Simon	16,513	3.1
Haig	1,421	0.7	Unpledged delegates	14,948	2.8
			Hart	9,732	1.8
			Babbitt	4,750	0.9
			LaRouche	2,149	0.4

March 8 **Massachusetts**

Republican	Votes	%	Democratic	Votes	%
Bush	141,113	58.6	Dukakis	418,256	58.6
Dole	63,392	26.3	Jackson	133,141	18.7
Kemp	16,791	7.0	Gephardt	72,944	10.2
Robertson	10,891	4.5	Gore	31,631	4.4
du Pont	3,522	1.5	Simon	26,176	3.6
No preference	3,416	1.4	No preference	11,866	1.7
Haig	1,705	0.7	Hart	10,837	1.5
Others[1]	351	0.1	Babbitt	4,222	0.6
			DiDonato	1,971	0.3
			LaRouche	998	0.1
			Others[1]	1,405	0.2

March 8 **Mississippi**

Republican	Votes	%	Democratic	Votes	%
Bush	104,814	66.1	Jackson	160,651	44.7
Dole	26,855	16.9	Gore	120,364	33.5
Robertson	21,378	13.5	Dukakis	29,941	8.3
Kemp	5,479	3.5	Gephardt	19,693	5.5
			Hart	13,934	3.9
			Unpledged delegates	9,384	2.6
			Simon	2,118	0.6
			Babbitt	2,037	0.6
			LaRouche	1,295	0.4

March 8 **Missouri**

Republican	Votes	%	Democratic	Votes	%
Bush	168,812	42.2	Gephardt	305,287	57.8
Dole	164,394	41.1	Jackson	106,386	20.2
Robertson	44,705	11.2	Dukakis	61,303	11.7
Kemp	14,180	3.5	Simon	21,433	4.1
Unpledged delegates	5,563	1.4	Gore	14,549	2.8
du Pont	1,788	0.4	Hart	7,607	1.4
Haig	858	0.2	Unpledged delegates	6,635	1.3
			Duke	1,760	0.3
			Babbitt	1,377	0.3
			LaRouche	664	0.1
			Kay	372	—
			Koczak	241	—
			Dennerll	191	—

March 8 **North Carolina**

Republican	Votes	%	Democratic	Votes	%
Bush	124,260	45.4	Gore	235,669	34.7
Dole	107,032	39.1	Jackson	224,177	33.0
Robertson	26,861	9.8	Dukakis	137,993	20.3
Kemp	11,361	4.1	Gephardt	37,553	5.5
No preference	2,797	1.0	Hart	16,381	2.4
du Pont	944	0.3	No preference	16,337	2.4
Haig	546	0.2	Simon	8,032	1.2
			Babbitt	3,816	0.6

Republican	Votes	%	Democratic	Votes	%

March 8 Oklahoma

Republican	Votes	%	Democratic	Votes	%
Bush	78,224	37.4	Gore	162,584	41.4
Dole	73,016	34.9	Gephardt	82,596	21.0
Robertson	44,067	21.0	Dukakis	66,278	16.9
Kemp	11,439	5.5	Jackson	52,417	13.3
du Pont	938	0.4	Hart	14,336	3.7
Haig	715	0.3	Simon	6,901	1.8
Others[1]	539	0.3	Duke	2,388	0.6
			Babbitt	1,601	0.4
			LaRouche	1,078	0.3
			Koczak	1,068	0.3
			Charles R. Doty (Okla.)	1,005	0.3
			Dennerll	475	0.1

March 8 Rhode Island

Republican	Votes	%	Democratic	Votes	%
Bush	10,401	64.9	Dukakis	34,211	69.7
Dole	3,628	22.6	Jackson	7,445	15.2
Robertson	911	5.7	Gephardt	2,028	4.1
Kemp	792	4.9	Gore	1,939	4.0
Unpledged delegates	174	1.1	Simon	1,395	2.8
du Pont	80	0.5	Unpledged delegates	809	1.7
Haig	49	0.3	Hart	733	1.5
			Babbitt	469	1.0

March 8 Tennessee

Republican	Votes	%	Democratic	Votes	%
Bush	152,515	60.0	Gore	416,861	72.3
Dole	55,027	21.6	Jackson	119,248	20.7
Robertson	32,015	12.6	Dukakis	19,348	3.3
Kemp	10,911	4.3	Gephardt	8,470	1.5
Unpledged delegates	2,340	0.9	Hart	4,706	0.8
Haig	777	0.3	Unpledged delegates	3,032	0.5
du Pont	646	0.3	Simon	2,647	0.5
Others[1]	21	—	Babbitt	1,946	0.3
			Others[1]	56	—

March 8 Texas

Republican	Votes	%	Democratic	Votes	%
Bush	648,178	63.9	Dukakis	579,713	32.8
Robertson	155,449	15.3	Jackson	433,335	24.5
Dole	140,795	13.9	Gore	357,764	20.2
Kemp	50,586	5.0	Gephardt	240,158	13.6
Unpledged delegates	12,563	1.2	Hart	82,199	4.7
du Pont	4,245	0.4	Simon	34,499	1.9
Haig	3,140	0.3	Babbitt	11,618	0.7
			LaRouche	9,013	0.5
			Duke	8,808	0.5
			W. A. Williams	6,238	0.4
			Dennerll	3,700	0.2

March 8 Virginia

Republican	Votes	%	Democratic	Votes	%
Bush	124,738	53.7	Jackson	164,709	45.1
Dole	60,921	26.0	Gore	81,419	22.3
Robertson	32,173	13.7	Dukakis	80,183	22.0
Kemp	10,809	4.6	Gephardt	15,935	4.4
Unpledged delegates	3,675	1.6	Simon	7,045	1.9
du Pont	1,229	0.5	Hart	6,266	1.7
Haig	597	0.3	Unpledged delegates	6,142	1.7
			Babbitt	2,454	0.7
			LaRouche	746	0.2

Republican			**Democratic**		
	Votes	%		Votes	%
March 15 Illinois[4]					
Bush	469,151	54.6	Simon	635,219	42.3
Dole	309,253	36.0	Jackson	484,233	32.3
Robertson	59,087	6.9	Dukakis	245,289	16.3
Kemp	12,687	1.5	Gore	77,265	5.1
du Pont	4,653	0.5	Gephardt	35,108	2.3
Haig	3,806	0.4	Hart	12,769	0.9
			LaRouche	6,094	0.4
			Babbitt	4,953	0.3
March 29 Connecticut					
Bush	73,501	70.6	Dukakis	140,291	58.1
Dole	21,005	20.2	Jackson	68,372	28.3
Kemp	3,281	3.1	Gore	18,501	7.7
Unpledged delegates	3,193	3.1	Hart	5,761	2.4
Robertson	3,191	3.1	Simon	3,140	1.3
			Babbitt	2,370	1.0
			Unpledged delegates	1,951	0.8
			Gephardt	1,009	0.4
April 5 Wisconsin					
Bush	295,295	82.2	Dukakis	483,172	47.6
Dole	28,460	7.9	Jackson	285,995	28.2
Robertson	24,798	6.9	Gore	176,712	17.4
Kemp	4,915	1.4	Simon	48,419	4.8
Uninstructed delegation	2,372	0.7	Gephardt	7,996	0.8
Haig	1,554	0.4	Hart	7,068	0.7
du Pont	1,504	0.4	Uninstructed delegation	2,554	0.3
Others[1]	396	0.1	Babbitt	2,353	0.2
			Others[1]	513	0.1
April 19 New York					
[3]			Dukakis	801,457	50.9
			Jackson	585,076	37.1
			Gore	157,559	10.0
			Simon	17,011	1.1
			Unpledged delegates	10,258	0.7
			Gephardt	2,672	0.2
			LaRouche	1,153	0.1
April 26 Pennsylvania					
Bush	687,323	79.0	Dukakis	1,002,480	66.5
Dole	103,763	11.9	Jackson	411,260	27.3
Robertson	79,463	9.1	Gore	44,542	3.0
			Hart	20,473	1.4
			Simon	9,692	0.6
			Jennifer Alden Wesner (Pa.)	7,546	0.5
			Gephardt	7,254	0.5
			LaRouche	4,443	0.3
May 3 District of Columbia					
Bush	5,890	87.6	Jackson	68,840	80.0
Dole	469	7.0	Dukakis	15,415	17.9
Robertson	268	4.0	Simon	769	0.9
Others[1]	93	1.4	Gore	648	0.8
			Gephardt	300	0.3
			Others[1]	80	0.1

Republican	Votes	%	Democratic	Votes	%
May 3 Indiana					
Bush	351,829	80.4	Dukakis	449,495	69.6
Dole	42,878	9.8	Jackson	145,021	22.5
Robertson	28,712	6.6	Gore	21,865	3.4
Kemp	14,236	3.6	Gephardt	16,777	2.6
			Simon	12,550	1.9
May 3 Ohio					
Bush slate	643,907	81.0	Dukakis slate	869,792	62.9
Dole slate	94,650	11.9	Jackson slate	378,866	27.4
Robertson slate	56,347	7.1	Gore slate	29,931	2.2
			James A. Traficant slate (Ohio)	29,912	2.2
			Hart slate	28,414	2.1
			Douglas Applegate slate (Ohio)	25,068	1.8
			Simon slate	15,524	1.1
			LaRouche slate	6,065	0.4
May 10 Nebraska[5]					
Bush	138,784	68.0	Dukakis	106,334	62.9
Dole	45,572	22.3	Jackson	43,380	25.7
Robertson	10,334	5.1	Gephardt	4,948	2.9
Kemp	8,423	4.1	Unpledged delegates	4,763	2.8
Others[1]	936	0.5	Hart	4,220	2.5
			Gore	2,519	1.5
			Simon	2,104	1.2
			LaRouche	416	0.2
			Others[1]	324	0.2
May 10 West Virginia					
Bush	110,705	77.3	Dukakis	254,289	74.8
Dole	15,600	10.9	Jackson	45,788	13.5
Robertson	10,417	7.3	Gore	11,573	3.4
Kemp	3,820	2.7	Hart	9,284	2.7
Stassen	1,604	1.1	Gephardt	6,130	1.8
Conley	994	0.7	Angus W. McDonald (W.Va.)	3,604	1.1
			Simon	2,280	0.7
			Babbitt	1,978	0.6
			LaRouche	1,482	0.4
			Duke	1,383	0.4
			Dennerll	1,339	0.4
			Traficant	967	0.3
May 17 Oregon					
Bush	199,938	72.8	Dukakis	221,048	56.8
Dole	49,128	17.9	Jackson	148,207	38.1
Robertson	21,212	7.7	Gephardt	6,772	1.7
Others[1]	4,208	1.5	Gore	5,445	1.4
			Simon	4,757	1.2
			LaRouche	1,562	0.4
			Others[1]	1,141	0.3
May 24 Idaho					
Bush	55,464	81.2	Dukakis	37,696	73.4
"None of the names shown"	6,935	10.2	Jackson	8,066	15.7
Robertson	5,876	8.6	"None of the names shown"	2,308	4.5
			Gore	1,891	3.7
			Simon	1,409	2.7

	Republican			**Democratic**	
	Votes	**%**		**Votes**	**%**

June 7 California[6]

Bush	1,856,273	82.9	Dukakis	1,910,808	60.9
Dole	289,220	12.9	Jackson	1,102,093	35.1
Robertson	94,779	4.2	Gore	56,645	1.8
Others[1]	115	—	Simon	43,771	1.4
			LaRouche	25,417	0.8

June 7 Montana

Bush	63,098	73.0	Dukakis	83,684	68.7
Dole	16,762	19.4	Jackson	26,908	22.1
No preference	6,520	7.5	No preference	4,083	3.4
			Gephardt	3,369	2.8
			Gore	2,261	1.9
			Simon	1,566	1.3

June 7 New Jersey

Bush	241,033	100.0	Dukakis	414,829	63.4
			Jackson	213,705	32.7
			Gore	18,062	2.8
			LaRouche	2,621	0.4
			Marra	2,594	0.4
			Duke	2,491	0.4

June 7 New Mexico

Bush	69,359	78.2	Dukakis	114,968	61.0
Dole	9,305	10.5	Jackson	52,988	28.1
Robertson	5,350	6.0	Hart	6,898	3.7
Unpledged delegates	2,569	2.9	Gore	4,747	2.6
Haig	2,161	2.4	Unpledged delegates	3,275	1.7
			Babbitt	2,913	1.5
			Simon	2,821	1.5

June 14 North Dakota

Bush	37,062	94.0	[7]		
Rachner	2,372	6.0			

Republican

TOTALS	Votes	%
Bush	8,254,654	67.9
Dole	2,333,268	19.2
Robertson	1,097,442	9.0
Kemp	331,333	2.7
du Pont	49,781	0.4
Haig	26,617	0.2
Stassen	2,682	—
Rachner	2,479	—
Conley	1,101	—
Uncommitted[8]	57,990	0.5
Others[9]	8,768	0.1
	12,165,115	

Democratic

	Votes	%
Dukakis	9,817,185	42.8
Jackson	6,685,699	29.1
Gore	3,134,516	13.7
Gephardt	1,388,356	6.0
Simon	1,018,136	4.4
Hart	389,003	1.7
Babbitt	77,780	0.3
LaRouche	70,938	0.3
Duke	45,289	0.2
Traficant	30,879	0.1
Applegate	25,068	0.1
Wesner	7,546	—
Dennerll	7,298	—
Williams	6,238	—
Ahern	3,701	—
McDonald	3,604	—
Marra	2,736	—
DiDonato	2,055	—
Kay	1,682	—
Koczak	1,356	—
du Pont	1,349	—
Doty	1,005	—
Uncommitted[8]	232,498	1.0
Others[10]	8,019	—
	22,961,936	

1. Includes write-in votes.

2. In Vermont's Liberty Union presidential primary, Willa Kenoyer received 199 votes (68.9 percent), Herb Lewin received 65 votes (22.5 percent), and there were 25 scattered write-in votes (8.7 percent).

3. No primary.

4. In Illinois's Solidarity presidential primary, Lenora B. Fulani received 170 votes (100 percent).

5. In Nebraska's New Alliance presidential primary, Lenora B. Fulani received 10 votes (100 percent).

6. In California's American Independent presidential primary, James C. Griffin received 9,762 votes (64.4 percent), James Gritz received 5,401 votes (35.6 percent), and there were 3 scattered write-in votes (0.0 percent). In the Peace and Freedom presidential primary, Lenora B. Fulani received 2,117 votes (35.7 percent), Shirley Isaacson received 1,222 votes (20.6 percent), Larry Holmes received 1,042 votes (17.6 percent), Herb Lewin received 778 votes (13.1 percent), Willa Kenoyer received 411 votes (6.9 percent), Al Hamburg received 353 votes (6.0 percent), and there were 6 scattered write-in votes (0.1 percent).

7. No candidates' names appeared on the Democratic ballot. Tallied write-in votes were for Dukakis (2,890) and Jackson (515).

8. The Uncommitted category includes votes cast on the following ballot lines: Unpledged delegates, Undecided, No preference, Uninstructed delegation and "None of the names shown."

9. In addition to scattered write-in votes, "others" include Isabell Masters who received 539 votes in the Oklahoma primary; Robert F. Drucker who received 83 votes in the New Hampshire primary; William Horrigan who received 76 votes in the New Hampshire primary; Michael S. Levinson who received 43 votes in the New Hampshire primary.

10. In addition to scattered write-in votes, "others" include Anthony R. Martin-Trigona who received 598 votes — 537 votes in the Kentucky primary and 61 votes in the New Hampshire primary; Conrad W. Roy who received 122 votes in the New Hampshire primary; Osie Thorpe who received 96 votes — 80 votes in the District of Columbia primary and 16 votes in the New Hampshire primary; William King who received 36 votes in the New Hampshire primary; Edward T. O'Donnell who received 33 votes in the New Hampshire primary; Cyril E. Sagan who received 33 votes in the New Hampshire primary; Frank L. Thomas who received 28 votes in the New Hampshire primary; Claude R. Kirk who received 25 votes in the New Hampshire primary; Irwin Zucker who received 22 votes in the New Hampshire primary; A. A. Van Petten who received 10 votes in the New Hampshire primary; Stanley Lock who received 9 votes in the New Hampshire primary.

1992 Primaries

Republican	Votes	%	Democratic	Votes	%
February 18 New Hampshire[1]					
George Bush (Texas)	92,233	53.0	Paul E. Tsongas (Mass.)	55,638	33.2
Patrick J. Buchanan (Va.)	65,087	37.4	Bill Clinton (Ark.)	41,522	24.7
James P. Lennane (Fla.)	1,684	1.0	Bob Kerrey (Neb.)	18,575	11.1
Pat Paulsen (Calif.)	600	0.3	Torn Harkin (Iowa)	17,057	10.2
Harold E. Stassen (Minn.)	206	0.1	Edmund G. Brown Jr. (Calif.)	13,654	8.1
Jack Fellure (W.Va.)	36	—	Tom Laughlin (Calif.)	3,251	1.9
George Zimmermann (Texas)	31	—	Charles Woods (Nev.)	2,862	1.7
Tennie Rogers (Calif.)	20	—	Lawrence A. Agran (Calif.)	332	0.2
Others[2]	14,268	8.1	Eugene J. McCarthy (Va.)	211	0.1
			Lyndon H. LaRouche Jr. (Va.)	115	0.1
			Stephen Burke (N.Y.)	39	—
			Rufus T. Higginbotham (Texas)	31	—
			Tom Shiekman (Fla.)	23	—
			George W. Benns (N.Y.)	11	—
			Others[2]	14,498	8.7
February 25 South Dakota					
Bush	30,964	69.3	Kerrey	23,892	40.2
Uncommitted	13,707	30.7	Harkin	15,023	25.2
			Clinton	11,375	19.1
			Tsongas	5,729	9.6
			Brown	2,300	3.9
			Agran	606	1.0
			LaRouche	441	0.7
			Others	137	0.2
March 3 Colorado					
Bush	132,100	67.5	Brown	69,073	28.8
Buchanan	58,753	30.0	Clinton	64,470	26.9
Zimmermann	1,592	0.8	Tsongas	61,360	25.6
Paul S. Jensen (Colo.)	1,332	0.7	Kerrey	29,572	12.3
Rogers	535	0.3	Harkin	5,866	2.4
Others	1,378	0.7	Noncommitted	5,356	2.2
			Woods	1,051	0.4
			Agran	672	0.3
			Burke	532	0.2
			McCarthy	488	0.2
			LaRouche	328	0.1
			Tod H. Hawks	165	0.1
			Shiekman	76	—
			Jeffrey Marsh	59	—
			Louis McAlpine	48	—
			Ray Rollinson	46	—
			Others	481	0.2
March 3 Georgia					
Bush	291,905	64.3	Clinton	259,907	57.2
Buchanan	162,085	35.7	Tsongas	109,148	24.0
			Brown	36,808	8.1
			Kerrey	22,033	4.8
			Uncommitted	17,256	3.8
			Harkin	9,479	2.1
March 3 Maryland					
Bush	168,374	70.1	Tsongas	230,490	40.6
Buchanan	71,647	29.9	Clinton	189,905	33.5

Republican	Votes	%	Democratic	Votes	%
			Brown	46,500	8.2
			Uncommitted	36,155	6.4
			Harkin	32,899	5.8
			Kerrey	27,035	4.8
			LaRouche	4,259	0.8

March 7 South Carolina

Republican	Votes	%	Democratic	Votes	%
Bush	99,558	66.9	Clinton	73,221	62.9
Buchanan	38,247	25.7	Tsongas	21,338	18.3
David Duke (La.)	10,553	7.1	Harkin	7,657	6.6
Others	482	0.3	Brown	6,961	6.0
			Uncommitted	3,640	3.1
			Bob Cunningham	1,369	1.2
			Woods	854	0.7
			Kerrey	566	0.5
			Angus W. McDonald	268	0.2
			LaRouche	204	0.2
			Others	336	0.3

March 10 Florida

Republican	Votes	%	Democratic	Votes	%
Bush	608,077	68.1	Clinton	570,566	50.8
Buchanan	285,386	31.9	Tsongas	388,124	34.5
			Brown	139,569	12.4
			Harkin	13,587	1.2
			Kerrey	12,011	1.1

March 10 Louisiana

Republican	Votes	%	Democratic	Votes	%
Bush	83,744	62.0	Clinton	267,002	69.5
Buchanan	36,525	27.0	Tsongas	42,508	11.1
Duke	11,955	8.8	Brown	25,480	6.6
Paulsen	1,186	0.9	McCarthy	15,129	3.9
Rogers	1,111	0.8	Woods	8,989	2.3
Zimmermann	474	0.4	Burke	4,294	1.1
Others	114	0.1	Harkin	4,033	1.0
			Agran	3,511	0.9
			LaRouche	3,082	0.8
			Kerrey	2,984	0.8
			Marsh	2,120	0.6
			Laughlin	1,857	0.5
			Hawks	1,469	0.4
			Rollinson	1,069	0.3
			McAlpine	870	0.2

March 10 Massachusetts[3]

Republican	Votes	%	Democratic	Votes	%
Bush	176,868	65.6	Tsongas	526,297	66.4
Buchanan	74,797	27.7	Brown	115,746	14.6
No preference	10,132	3.8	Clinton	86,817	10.9
Duke	5,557	2.1	Ralph Nader	32,881	4.1
Others[2]	2,347	0.9	No preference	12,198	1.5
			Kerrey	5,409	0.7
			Harkin	3,764	0.5
			McCarthy	3,127	0.4
			Agran	2,224	0.3
			LaRouche	2,167	0.3
			Others[2]	2,255	0.3

March 10 Mississippi

Republican	Votes	%	Democratic	Votes	%
Bush	111,794	72.3	Clinton	139,893	73.1
Buchanan	25,891	16.7	Brown	18,396	9.6

Republican			**Democratic**		
	Votes	**%**		**Votes**	**%**
Duke	16,426	10.6	Tsongas	15,538	8.1
Rogers	189	0.1	Uncommitted	11,796	6.2
Others[2]	408	0.3	Harkin	2,509	1.3
			Kerrey	1,660	0.9
			LaRouche	1,394	0.7
			Others[2]	171	0.1

March 10 Oklahoma

	Votes	**%**		**Votes**	**%**
Bush	151,612	69.6	Clinton	293,266	70.5
Buchanan	57,933	26.6	Brown	69,624	16.7
Duke	5,672	2.6	Woods	16,828	4.0
Isabell Masters (Kan.)	1,830	0.8	Harkin	14,015	3.4
Rogers	674	0.3	Kerrey	13,252	3.2
			LaRouche	6,474	1.6
			McAlpine	2,670	0.6

March 10 Rhode Island

	Votes	**%**		**Votes**	**%**
Bush	9,853	63.0	Tsongas	26,825	52.9
Buchanan	4,967	31.8	Clinton	10,762	21.2
Uncommitted	444	2.8	Brown	9,541	18.8
Duke	326	2.1	Uncommitted	703	1.4
Others[2]	46	0.3	Kerrey	469	0.9
			Woods	408	0.8
			Harkin	319	0.6
			LaRouche	300	0.6
			McCarthy	235	0.5
			Laughlin	94	0.2
			Rollinson	91	0.2
			Agran	79	0.2
			Burke	48	0.1
			Others[2]	835	1.6

March 10 Tennessee

	Votes	**%**		**Votes**	**%**
Bush	178,219	72.5	Clinton	214,485	67.3
Buchanan	54,585	22.2	Tsongas	61,717	19.4
Duke	7,709	3.1	Brown	25,560	8.0
Uncommitted	5,022	2.0	Uncommitted	12,551	3.9
Others[2]	118	—	Harkin	2,099	0.7
			Kerrey	1,638	0.5
			Others[2]	432	0.1

March 10 Texas

	Votes	**%**		**Votes**	**%**
Bush	556,280	69.8	Clinton	972,151	65.6
Buchanan	190,572	23.9	Tsongas	285,191	19.2
Uncommitted	27,936	3.5	Brown	118,923	8.0
Duke	20,255	2.5	Woods	30,092	2.0
Zimmermann	1,349	0.2	Kerrey	20,298	1.4
Rogers	754	0.1	Harkin	19,617	1.3
			LaRouche	12,220	0.8
			Benns	7,876	0.5
			Higginbotham	7,674	0.5
			Hawks	4,924	0.3
			McAlpine	4,009	0.3

March 17 Illinois

	Votes	**%**		**Votes**	**%**
Bush	634,588	76.4	Clinton	776,829	51.6
Buchanan	186,915	22.5	Tsongas	387,891	25.8
Maurice Horton (Ill.)	9,637	1.2	Brown	220,346	14.6

Republican	Votes	%	**Democratic**	Votes	%
			Uncommitted	67,612	4.5
			Harkin	30,710	2.0
			Kerrey	10,916	0.7
			LaRouche	6,599	0.4
			Agran	3,227	0.2

March 17 **Michigan**

Republican	Votes	%	Democratic	Votes	%
Bush	301,948	67.2	Clinton	297,280	50.7
Buchanan	112,122	25.0	Brown	151,400	25.8
Uncommitted	23,809	5.3	Tsongas	97,017	16.6
Duke	10,688	2.4	Uncommitted	27,836	4.8
Others[2]	566	0.1	Harkin	6,265	1.1
			Kerrey	3,219	0.5
			LaRouche	2,049	0.3
			Others[2]	906	0.2

March 24 **Connecticut**

Republican	Votes	%	Democratic	Votes	%
Bush	66,356	66.7	Brown	64,472	37.2
Buchanan	21,815	21.9	Clinton	61,698	35.6
Uncommitted	9,008	9.1	Tsongas	33,811	19.5
Duke	2,294	2.3	Uncommitted	5,430	3.1
			Agran	2,688	1.6
			Harkin	1,919	1.1
			Kerrey	1,169	0.7
			McCarthy	1,036	0.6
			LaRouche	896	0.5

April 7 **Kansas**

Republican	Votes	%	Democratic	Votes	%
Bush	132,131	62.0	Clinton	82,145	51.3
"None of the names shown"	35,450	16.6	Tsongas	24,413	15.2
Buchanan	31,494	14.8	"None of the names shown"	22,159	13.8
Paulsen	5,105	2.4	Brown	20,811	13.0
Duke	3,837	1.8	Kerrey	2,215	1.4
Masters	1,303	0.6	Gary Hauptli	1,303	0.8
Philip Skow	1,105	0.5	Woods	1,119	0.7
Zimmermann	766	0.4	Don Beamgard	1,009	0.6
Fellure	164	0.1	Harkin	940	0.6
Rogers	85	—	Hawks	765	0.5
Others	1,756	0.8	LaRouche	631	0.4
			Ralph Spelbring	537	0.3
			Marsh	160	0.1
			Agran	147	0.1
			McAlpine	131	0.1
			Others	1,766	1.1

April 7 **Minnesota**

Republican	Votes	%	Democratic	Votes	%
Bush	84,841	63.9	Clinton	63,584	31.1
Buchanan	32,094	24.2	Brown	62,474	30.6
Uncommitted	4,098	3.1	Tsongas	43,588	21.3
Stassen	4,074	3.1	Uncommitted	11,366	5.6
Ross Perot (Texas)[4]	3,558	2.7	Ross Perot (Texas)[4]	4,250	2.1
Zimmermann	135	0.1	Harkin	4,077	2.0
Rogers	61	—	McCarthy	3,704	1.8
Others[2]	3,895	2.9	Kerrey	1,191	0.6
			Agran	1,042	0.5
			Woods	990	0.5
			LaRouche	532	0.3
			Burke	348	0.2
			McAlpine	183	0.1

	Republican			**Democratic**	
	Votes	**%**		**Votes**	**%**
			Hawks	111	0.1
			Marsh	106	0.1
			Others[2]	6,624	3.2

April 7 **New York**

[5]

			Clinton	412,349	40.9
			Tsongas	288,330	28.6
			Brown	264,278	26.2
			Harkin	11,535	1.1
			Kerrey	11,147	1.1
			Agran	10,733	1.1
			McCarthy	9,354	0.9

April 7 **Wisconsin**

Bush	364,507	75.6	Clinton	287,356	37.2
Buchanan	78,516	16.3	Brown	266,207	34.5
Duke	12,867	2.7	Tsongas	168,619	21.8
Uninstructed	8,725	1.8	Uninstructed	15,487	2.0
Stassen	3,819	0.8	McCarthy	6,525	0.8
Emmanuel L. Branch	1,013	0.2	Harkin	5,395	0.7
Others[2]	12,801	2.7	Agran	3,193	0.4
			LaRouche	3,120	0.4
			Kerrey	3,044	0.4
			Others[2]	13,650	1.8

April 28 **Pennsylvania**

Bush	774,865	76.8	Clinton	715,031	56.5
Buchanan	233,912	23.2	Brown	325,543	25.7
			Tsongas	161,572	12.8
			LaRouche	21,534	1.7
			Harkin	21,013	1.7
			Kerrey	20,802	1.6

May 5 **District of Columbia**

Bush	4,265	81.5	Clinton	45,716	73.8
Buchanan	970	18.5	Tsongas	6,452	10.4
			Uncommitted	5,292	8.5
			Brown	4,444	7.2

May 5 **Indiana**

Bush	374,666	80.1	Clinton	301,905	63.3
Buchanan	92,949	19.9	Brown	102,379	21.5
			Tsongas	58,215	12.2
			Kerrey	14,350	3.0

May 5 **North Carolina**

Bush	200,387	70.7	Clinton	443,498	64.1
Buchanan	55,420	19.5	No preference	106,697	15.4
No preference	27,764	9.8	Brown	71,984	10.4
			Tsongas	57,589	8.3
			Kerrey	6,216	0.9
			Harkin	5,891	0.9

May 12 **Nebraska**

Bush	156,346	81.4	Clinton	68,562	45.5
Buchanan	25,847	13.5	Brown	31,673	21.0
Duke	2,808	1.5	Uncommitted	24,714	16.4
Zimmermann	1,313	0.7	Tsongas	10,707	7.1

Republican	Votes	%	**Democratic**	Votes	%
Rogers	751	0.4	Harkin	4,239	2.8
Others[2]	5,033	2.6	McCarthy	1,520	1.0
			LaRouche	1,148	0.8
			Woods	485	0.3
			Agran	280	0.2
			Others[2]	7,259	4.8

May 12 West Virginia

Bush	99,994	80.5	Clinton	227,815	74.2
Buchanan	18,067	14.6	Brown	36,505	11.9
Fellure	6,096	4.9	Tsongas	21,271	6.9
			McDonald	9,632	3.1
			Kerrey	3,152	1.0
			LaRouche	3,141	1.0
			Harkin	2,774	0.9
			Woods	1,487	0.5
			Spelbring	1,089	0.4

May 19 Oregon

Bush	203,957	67.1	Clinton	159,802	45.1
Buchanan	57,730	19.0	Brown	110,494	31.2
Duke	6,667	2.2	Tsongas	37,139	10.5
Others[2]	35,805	11.8	McCarthy	6,714	1.9
			LaRouche	3,096	0.9
			Woods	1,895	0.5
			Agran	1,652	0.5
			Others[2]	33,540	9.5

May 19 Washington

Bush	86,839	67.0	Clinton	62,171	42.0
Perot[4]	25,423	19.6	Brown	34,111	23.1
Buchanan	13,273	10.2	Perot[4]	28,311	19.1
Stephen D. Michael	2,619	2.0	Tsongas	18,981	12.8
Duke	1,501	1.2	Harkin	1,858	1.3
			Kerrey	1,489	1.0
			LaRouche	1,060	0.7

May 26 Arkansas

Bush	45,590	87.4	Clinton	342,017	68.0
Buchanan	6,551	12.6	Uncommitted	90,710	18.0
			Brown	55,234	11.0
			LaRouche	14,656	2.9

May 26 Idaho

Bush	73,297	63.5	Clinton	27,004	49.0
"None of the names shown"	27,038	23.4	"None of the names shown"	16,029	29.1
Buchanan	15,167	13.1	Brown	9,212	16.7
			LaRouche	2,011	3.6
			Agran	868	1.6

May 26 Kentucky

Bush	75,371	74.5	Clinton	207,804	56.1
Uncommitted	25,748	25.5	Uncommitted	103,590	28.0
			Brown	30,709	8.3
			Tsongas	18,097	4.9
			Harkin	7,136	1.9
			Kerrey	3,242	0.9

Republican				**Democratic**	
	Votes	%		Votes	%

June 2 **Alabama**

	Votes	%		Votes	%
Bush	122,703	74.3	Clinton	307,621	68.2
Uncommitted	29,830	18.1	Uncommitted	90,863	20.2
Buchanan	12,588	7.6	Brown	30,626	6.8
			Woods	15,247	3.4
			LaRouche	6,542	1.4

June 2 **California**[6]

	Votes	%		Votes	%
Bush	1,587,369	73.6	Clinton	1,359,112	47.5
Buchanan	568,892	26.4	Brown	1,150,460	40.2
Others[2]	203	—	Tsongas	212,522	7.4
			McCarthy	60,635	2.1
			Kerrey	33,935	1.2
			Agran	24,784	0.9
			LaRouche	21,971	0.8
			Others[2]	190	—

June 2 **Montana**

	Votes	%		Votes	%
Bush	65,176	71.6	Clinton	54,989	46.8
No preference	15,098	16.6	No preference	28,164	24.0
Buchanan	10,701	11.8	Brown	21,704	18.5
			Tsongas	12,614	10.7

June 2 **New Jersey**

	Votes	%		Votes	%
Bush	240,535	77.5	Clinton	243,741	62.1
Buchanan	46,432	15.0	Brown	79,877	20.3
Perot[4]	23,303	7.5	Tsongas	45,191	11.5
			Perot[4]	12,478	3.2
			LaRouche	7,799	2.0
			George H. Ballard	2,067	0.5
			Robert F. Hanson	1,473	0.4

June 2 **New Mexico**

	Votes	%		Votes	%
Bush	55,522	63.8	Clinton	95,933	52.9
Uncommitted	23,574	27.1	Uncommitted	35,269	19.4
Buchanan	7,871	9.1	Brown	30,705	16.9
			Tsongas	11,315	6.2
			Harkin	3,233	1.8
			Agran	2,573	1.4
			LaRouche	2,415	1.3

June 2 **Ohio**

	Votes	%		Votes	%
Bush	716,766	83.3	Clinton	638,347	61.2
Buchanan	143,687	16.7	Brown	197,449	18.9
			Tsongas	110,773	10.6
			Louis Stokes (Ohio)	29,983	2.9
			Harkin	25,395	2.4
			Kerrey	22,976	2.2
			LaRouche	17,412	1.7

June 9 **North Dakota**

	Votes	%		Votes	%
Bush	39,863	83.4	Perot[4]	9,516	29.0
Paulsen	4,093	8.6	LaRouche	7,003	21.4
Perot[4]	3,852	8.1	Woods	6,641	20.3
			Shiekman	4,866	14.8
			Clinton[4]	4,760	14.5

Republican

TOTALS	Votes	%
Bush	9,199,463	72.5
Buchanan	2,899,488	22.8
Duke	119,115	0.9
Perot[4]	56,136	0.4
Paulsen	10,984	0.1
Horton	9,637	0.1
Stassen	8,099	0.1
Fellure	6,296	—
Zimmermann	5,660	—
Rogers	4,180	—
Masters	3,133	—
Michael	2,619	—
Lennane	1,684	—
Jensen	1,332	—
Skow	1,105	—
Branch	1,013	—
Uncommitted[7]	287,383	2.3
Others[8]	79,220	0.6
	12,696,547	

Democratic

	Votes	%
Clinton	10,482,411	51.8
Brown	4,071,232	20.1
Tsongas	3,656,010	18.1
Kerry	318,457	1.6
Harkin	280,304	1.4
LaRouche	154,599	0.8
McCarthy	108,678	0.5
Woods	88,948	0.4
Agran	58,611	0.3
Perot[4]	54,755	0.3
Nader	32,881	0.2
Stokes	29,983	0.1
McDonald	9,900	—
McAlpine	7,911	—
Benns	7,887	—
Higginbotham	7,705	—
Hawks	7,434	—
Burke	5,261	—
Laughlin	5,202	—
Shiekman	4,965	—
Marsh	2,445	—
Ballard	2,067	—
Spelbring	1,626	—
Hanson	1,473	—
Cunningham	1,369	—
Hauptli	1,303	—
Rollinson	1,206	—
Beamgard	1,009	—
Uncommitted[7]	750,873	3.7
Others[9]	82,880	0.4
	20,239,385	

1. In New Hampshire's Libertarian presidential primary, Andre V. Marrou received 3,219 votes (95.0 percent) and there were 168 scattered write-in votes (5.0 percent).

2. Includes write-in votes.

3. In Massachusetts' independent presidential primary, Howard Phillips received 352 votes (25.4 percent), "No preference" received 269 votes (19.4 percent), James Gritz received 177 votes (12.8 percent), Robert J. Smith received 54 votes (3.9 percent), Darcy G. Richardson received 36 votes (2.6 percent), Erik Thompson received 35 votes (2.5 percent), Earl F. Dodge received 26 votes (1.9 percent), J. Quinn Brisben received 24 votes (1.7 percent), Michael S. Levinson received 21 votes (1.5 percent), and there were 391 scattered write-in votes (28.2 percent).

4. Write-in votes.

5. No primary.

6. In California's American Independent presidential primary, Howard Phillips received 15,456 votes (99.9 percent) and there were 13 scattered write-in votes. In the Libertarian presidential primary, Andre V. Marrou received 15,002 votes (99.9 percent) and there were 12 scattered write-in votes. In the Peace & Freedom presidential primary, Lenora B. Fulani received 4,586 votes (51.6 percent), Ron Daniels received 2,868 votes (32.2 percent), R. Alison Star-Martinez received 1,434 votes (16.1 percent), and there were 6 scattered write-in votes.

7. The Uncommitted category includes votes cast on the following ballot lines: Uncommitted, Noncommitted, No preference, Uninstructed and "None of the names shown."

8. In addition to scattered write-in votes, "others" include Stephen A. Koczak who received 950 votes—659 votes in the Colorado primary, 262 in the Kansas primary and 29 votes in the New Hampshire pri-

mary; Paul C. Daugherty who received 771 votes — 236 votes in the Kansas primary, 53 votes in the New Hampshire primary and 482 votes in the South Carolina primary; Jack J. H. Beemont who received 735 votes in the Kansas primary; Terrance R. Scott who received 719 votes in the Colorado primary; Billy Joe Clegg who received 518 votes—408 votes in the Mississippi primary and 110 votes in the New Hampshire primary; Charles Doty who received 417 votes in the Kansas primary; Richard P. Bosa who received 349 votes in the New Hampshire primary; Sharon Anderson who received 300 votes in the Minnesota primary; John D. Merwin who received 223 votes in the New Hampshire primary; Beatrice Mooney who received 196 votes in the Minnesota primary; Thomas S. Fabish who received 183 votes— 44 votes in the Kansas primary, 114 votes in the Louisiana primary and 25 votes in the New Hampshire primary; Paul B. Conley who received 115 votes in the New Hampshire primary; Hubert D. Patty who received 93 votes—62 votes in the Kansas primary and 31 votes in the New Hampshire primary; Georgiana Doerschuck who received 57 votes in the New Hampshire primary; Michael Levinson who received 44 votes in the New Hampshire primary; Vincent Latchford who received 32 votes in the New Hampshire primary; F. Dean Johnson who received 24 votes in the New Hampshire primary; Norm Bertasavage who received 23 votes in the New Hampshire primary; Jack Trinsey who received 22 votes in the New Hampshire primary; Conrad A. Ryden who received 20 votes in the New Hampshire primary; Oscar A. Erickson who received 16 votes in the New Hampshire primary; Richard F. Reber who received 14 votes in the New Hampshire primary.

9. In addition to scattered write-in votes, "others" include John A. Barnes who received 892 votes in the Kansas primary; Mary Jane Rachner who received 620 votes in the Minnesota primary; Raymond

Vanskiver who received 510 votes in the Kansas primary; Lenora B. Fulani who received 402 votes in the New Hampshire primary; William D. Pawley who received 364 votes in the Kansas primary; William P. Kreml who received 336 votes in the South Carolina primary; Susan C. Fey who received 308 votes in the Rhode Island primary; Patrick J. Mahoney who received 303 votes in the New Hampshire primary; Jim Hayes who received 279 votes in the Colorado primary; L. Douglas Wilder who received 240 votes—103 votes in the New Hampshire primary and 137 votes in the South Dakota primary; Leonard Talbow who received 202 votes in the Colorado primary; John D. Rigazio who received 186 votes in the New Hampshire primary; Curly Thornton who received 177 votes—125 votes in the New Hampshire primary and 52 votes in the Rhode Island primary; John J. Staradumsky who received 168 votes in the Rhode Island primary; Nathan Averick who received 112 votes—105 votes in the Minnesota primary and 7 votes in the New Hampshire primary; Caroline P. Killeen who received 93 votes in the New Hampshire primary; John P. Cahill who received 83 votes in the New Hampshire primary; Paul Fisher who received 82 votes in the New Hampshire primary; Frank J. Bona who received 65 votes in the New Hampshire primary; Karl J. Hegger who received 61 votes in the New Hampshire primary; William Horrigan who received 53 votes in the New Hampshire primary; Dean A. Curtis who received 43 votes in the New Hampshire primary; Gilbert H. Holmes who received 39 votes in the New Hampshire primary; Ron Kovic who received 36 votes in the New Hampshire primary; Chris Norton who received 31 votes in the New Hampshire primary; Fanny R. Z. Monyek who received 29 votes in the New Hampshire primary; James B. Gay who received 28 votes in the New Hampshire primary; Barry J. Deutsch who received 26 votes in the New Hampshire primary; Cyril E. Sagan who received 26 votes in the New Hampshire primary; Edward T. O'Donnell who received 24 votes in the New Hampshire primary; Stephen H. Schwartz who received 17 votes in the New Hampshire primary.

1996 Primaries

Republican	Votes	%	Democratic	Votes	%
February 20 New Hampshire[1]					
Patrick J. Buchanan (Va.)	56,874	27.2	Bill Clinton (Ark.)	76,797	83.9
Bob Dole (Kan.)	54,738	26.2	Pat Paulsen (Calif.)	1,007	1.1
Lamar Alexander (Tenn.)	47,148	22.6	Lyndon H. LaRouche Jr. (Va.)	433	0.5
Malcolm S. "Steve" Forbes Jr. (N.J.)	25,505	12.2	Heather Anne Harder (Ind.)	369	0.4
Richard G. Lugar (Ind.)	10,838	5.2	Ted L. Gunderson (Nev.)	70	—
Alan Keyes (Md.)	5,572	2.7	Sal Casamassima (Texas)	45	—
Maurice "Morry" Taylor (Ill.)	2,944	1.4	Others[2]	12,841	14.1
Phil Gramm (Texas)	752	0.4			
Robert K. Dornan (Calif.)	529	0.3			
Susan Ducey (Pa.)	151	0.1			
Charles E. Collins (Fla.)	42	—			
Others[2]	3,845	1.8			
February 24 Delaware					
Forbes	10,709	32.7	Clinton	9,694	90.3
Dole	8,909	27.2	LaRouche	1,046	9.7
Buchanan	6,118	18.7			
Alexander	4,375	13.3			
Keyes	1,729	5.3			
Lugar	717	2.2			
Gramm	216	0.7			
February 27 Arizona[3]					
Forbes	115,962	33.4	Clinton	12,303	95.5
Dole	102,980	29.6	No preference	581	4.5
Buchanan	95,742	27.6			
Alexander	24,765	7.1			
Keyes	2,790	0.8			
Lugar	2,064	0.6			
Gramm	857	0.2			
Dornan	735	0.2			
Ducey	539	0.2			
Taylor	148	—			
Others	900	0.3			
February 27 North Dakota[4]					
Dole	26,832	42.1	Roland Riemers (N.D.)	651	41.1
Forbes	12,455	19.5	LaRouche	549	34.7
Buchanan	11,653	18.3	Vernon Clemenson (N.D.)	384	24.2
Gramm	5,997	9.4			
Alexander	4,008	6.3			
Keyes	2,030	3.2			
Lugar	559	0.9			
Taylor	200	0.3			
February 27 South Dakota[5]					
Dole	30,918	44.7	[6]		
Buchanan	19,780	28.6			
Forbes	8,831	12.8			
Alexander	6,037	8.7			
Keyes	2,378	3.4			
Uncommitted	677	1.0			
Gramm	387	0.6			
Taylor	162	0.2			

Republican				Democratic		
	Votes	**%**			**Votes**	**%**

March 2 South Carolina

Dole	124,904	45.1	[6]
Buchanan	80,824	29.2	
Forbes	35,039	12.7	
Alexander	28,647	10.4	
Keyes	5,752	2.1	
Lugar	1,017	0.4	
Gramm	467	0.2	
Taylor	91	—	

March 3 Puerto Rico

Dole	233,742	97.9	[6]
Gramm	1,454	0.6	
Alexander	1,273	0.5	
Forbes	1,078	0.5	
Buchanan	844	0.4	
Keyes	77	—	
Others	280	0.1	

March 5 Colorado

	Votes	%		Votes	%
Dole	108,123	43.6	Clinton	48,454	88.9
Buchanan	53,376	21.5	LaRouche	5,981	11.0
Forbes	51,592	20.8	Gunderson[7]	92	0.2
Alexander	24,184	9.8			
Keyes	9,052	3.7			
Lugar	1,603	0.6			

March 5 Connecticut

Dole	70,998	54.4	[6]
Forbes	26,253	20.1	
Buchanan	19,664	15.1	
Alexander	6,985	5.4	
Keyes	2,209	1.7	
Uncommitted	1,699	1.3	
Lugar	1,495	1.1	
Taylor	430	0.3	
Dornan	401	0.3	
Gramm	284	0.2	

March 5 Georgia

	Votes	%		Votes	%
Dole	226,732	40.6	Clinton	95,103	100.0
Buchanan	162,627	29.1			
Alexander	75,855	13.6			
Forbes	71,276	12.7			
Keyes	17,538	3.1			
Lugar	1,971	0.4			
Gramm	1,095	0.2			
Dornan	1,005	0.2			
Collins	661	0.1			
Taylor	307	0.1			

March 5 Maine

	Votes	%		Votes	%
Dole	31,147	46.3	Clinton	23,879	88.4
Buchanan	16,478	24.5	Uncommitted	2,433	9.0
Forbes	9,991	14.8	LaRouche	715	2.6
Alexander	4,450	6.6			
Lugar	1,934	2.9			
Uncommitted	1,741	2.6			
Keyes	1,229	1.8			

Republican			Democratic		
	Votes	**%**		**Votes**	**%**
Gramm	163	0.2			
Taylor	147	0.2			

March 5 **Maryland**

Republican			Democratic		
Dole	135,522	53.3	Clinton	247,492	84.2
Buchanan	53,585	21.1	Uncommitted	33,417	11.4
Forbes	32,207	12.7	LaRouche	12,290	4.4
Alexander	14,061	5.5			
Keyes	13,718	5.4			
Lugar	2,872	1.1			
Gramm	1,174	0.5			
Dornan	757	0.3			
Taylor	350	0.1			

March 5 **Massachusetts**[8]

Republican			Democratic		
Dole	135,946	47.7	Clinton	135,360	87.1
Buchanan	71,688	25.2	No preference	12,623	8.1
Forbes	39,605	13.9	LaRouche	5,212	3.4
Alexander	21,456	7.5	Others[2]	2,275	1.5
Keyes	5,224	1.8			
Lugar	4,743	1.7			
No preference	3,303	1.2			
Gramm	673	0.2			
Dornan	544	0.2			
Taylor	433	0.2			
Others[2]	1,218	0.4			

March 5 **Rhode Island**

Republican			Democratic		
Dole	9,664	64.4	Clinton	7,825	89.1
Alexander	2,859	19.0	Uncommitted	535	6.1
Uncommitted	1,252	8.3	LaRouche	392	4.5
Lugar	487	3.2	Others[2]	28	0.3
Buchanan[7]	387	2.6			
Taylor	165	1.1			
Forbes[7]	128	0.9			
Keyes[7]	31	0.2			
Dornan[7]	1	—			
Gramm[7]	1	—			
Others[2]	34	0.2			

March 5 **Vermont**[9]

Republican			Democratic		
Dole	23,419	40.3	Clinton	29,763	96.5
Buchanan	9,730	16.7	LaRouche	699	2.3
Forbes	9,066	15.6	Others[2]	376	1.2
Lugar	7,881	13.6			
Alexander	6,145	10.6			
Gramm	291	0.5			
Taylor	257	0.4			
Others[2]	1,324	2.3			

March 7 **New York**[10]

Republican				
Dole	599,748	55.1	[6]	
Forbes	325,211	29.9		
Buchanan	163,365	15.0		

March 12 **Florida**

Republican				
Dole	511,377	56.9	[6]	
Forbes	181,768	20.2		
Buchanan	162,770	18.1		

Republican			**Democratic**		
	Votes	**%**		**Votes**	**%**
Keyes	16,631	1.9			
Alexander	14,142	1.6			
Dornan	4,465	0.5			
Lugar	3,236	0.4			
Gramm	2,994	0.3			
Taylor	1,133	0.1			

March 12 **Louisiana**

Dole	37,170	47.8	Clinton	124,931	80.8
Buchanan	25,757	33.1	LaRouche	18,150	11.7
Forbes	10,265	13.2	Elvena E. Lloyd-Duffie (Ill.)	11,620	7.5
Keyes	2,464	3.2			
Alexander	1,642	2.1			
Taylor	491	0.6			

March 12 **Mississippi**

Dole	91,639	60.3	Clinton	86,716	92.5
Buchanan	39,324	25.9	LaRouche	7,072	7.5
Forbes	12,119	8.0			
Keyes	2,907	1.9			
Alexander	2,781	1.8			
Dornan	2,123	1.4			
Gramm	475	0.3			
Lugar	141	0.1			
Taylor	84	0.1			
Others	332	0.2			

March 12 **Oklahoma**

Dole	156,829	59.3	Clinton	279,454	76.2
Buchanan	56,949	21.5	LaRouche	46,392	12.7
Forbes	37,213	14.1	Lloyd-Duffie	40,758	11.1
Keyes	6,306	2.4			
Alexander	3,436	1.3			
Gramm	1,490	0.6			
Isabell Masters (Kan.)	1,052	0.4			
Lugar	538	0.2			
Collins	451	0.2			
Taylor	278	0.1			

March 12 **Oregon**

Dole	206,938	50.8	Clinton	349,871	94.8
Buchanan	86,987	21.3	Others[2]	19,307	5.2
Forbes	54,121	13.3			
Alexander	28,332	7.0			
Keyes	14,340	3.5			
Lugar	4,971	1.2			
Gramm	2,117	0.5			
Dornan	1,872	0.5			
Taylor	1,344	0.3			
Others[2]	6,492	1.6			

March 12 **Tennessee**

Dole	148,063	51.2	Clinton	122,538	88.9
Buchanan	72,928	25.2	Uncommitted	15,144	11.0
Alexander	32,742	11.3	Others[2]	115	0.1
Forbes	22,171	7.7			
Keyes	7,661	2.6			
Uncommitted	3,078	1.1			
Dornan	898	0.3			

Republican				**Democratic**		
	Votes	**%**			**Votes**	**%**
Gramm	688	0.2				
Lugar	531	0.2				
Taylor	210	0.1				
Others[2]	416	0.1				

March 12 Texas

	Votes	%			Votes	%
Dole	567,164	55.6		Clinton	796,041	86.4
Buchanan	217,974	21.4		Fred Hudson (Texas)	32,232	3.5
Forbes	130,938	12.8		Harder	28,772	3.1
Keyes	41,746	4.1		LaRouche	28,137	3.1
Uncommitted	19,507	1.9		Gunderson	15,550	1.7
Alexander	18,745	1.8		Lloyd-Duffie	10,876	1.2
Gramm	18,629	1.8		Casamassima	9,648	1.0
Lugar	2,266	0.2				
Ducey	1,093	0.1				
Collins	633	0.1				
Taylor	458	—				
Others	650	0.1				

March 19 Illinois[11]

	Votes	%			Votes	%
Dole	532,467	65.1		Clinton	770,001	96.2
Buchanan	186,177	22.7		Lloyd-Duffie	16,045	2.0
Forbes	39,906	4.9		LaRouche	14,624	1.8
Keyes	30,052	3.7		Harder	6	—
Alexander	12,585	1.5				
Lugar	8,286	1.0				
Gramm	6,696	0.8				
Taylor	2,189	0.3				
Others[2]	6	—				

March 19 Michigan

	Votes	%			Votes	%
Dole	265,425	50.6		Uncommitted	123,640	86.6
Buchanan	177,562	33.9		Others[2]	19,110	13.4
Forbes	26,610	5.1				
Uncommitted	23,109	4.4				
Keyes	15,995	3.1				
Alexander	7,631	1.5				
Lugar	2,175	0.4				
Gramm	1,755	0.3				
Dornan	1,723	0.3				
Taylor	1,018	0.2				
Others[2]	1,158	0.2				

March 19 Ohio

	Votes	%			Votes	%
Dole	640,954	66.5		Clinton	713,153	91.8
Buchanan	208,012	21.6		LaRouche	63,377	8.2
Forbes	58,131	6.0				
Keyes	27,197	2.8				
Alexander	19,530	2.0				
Lugar	9,598	1.0				

March 19 Wisconsin

	Votes	%			Votes	%
Dole	301,628	52.3		Clinton	347,629	97.6
Buchanan	194,733	33.8		Uninstructed	7,005	2.0
Forbes	32,205	5.6		Others[2]	1,534	0.4
Keyes	18,028	3.1				
Alexander	11,213	1.9				
Uninstructed	7,504	1.3				
Lugar	3,215	0.6				

Republican			**Democratic**		
	Votes	**%**		**Votes**	**%**
Gramm	2,682	0.5			
Dornan	1,645	0.3			
Taylor	916	0.2			
Others[2]	2,806	0.5			

March 26 California[12]

	Votes	%		Votes	%
Dole	1,619,931	66.1	Clinton	2,342,185	92.8
Buchanan	450,695	18.4	LaRouche	173,953	6.9
Forbes	183,367	7.5	Paulsen[7]	310	—
Keyes	93,577	3.8	Others[2]	6,924	0.3
Alexander	44,130	1.8			
Dornan	23,215	0.9			
Gramm	15,232	0.6			
Lugar	14,801	0.6			
Taylor	5,778	0.2			
Others[2]	1,586	0.1			

March 26 Nevada

	Votes	%			
Dole	72,932	51.9	[6]		
Forbes	27,063	19.2			
Buchanan	21,321	15.2			
"None of these candidates"	12,026	8.6			
Alexander	3,289	2.3			
Keyes	1,999	1.4			
Gramm	745	0.5			
Lugar	464	0.3			
Collins	305	0.2			
Taylor	94	0.1			
Others	399	0.3			

March 26 Washington

	Votes	%		Votes	%
Dole	76,155	63.1	Clinton	97,495	98.5
Buchanan	25,247	20.9	LaRouche	1,451	1.5
Forbes	10,339	8.6			
Keyes	5,610	4.6			
Alexander	1,600	1.3			
Gramm	630	0.5			
Lugar	587	0.5			
Dornan	516	0.4			

April 23 Pennsylvania

	Votes	%		Votes	%
Dole	435,031	63.6	Clinton	666,486	92.0
Buchanan	123,011	18.0	LaRouche	57,583	8.0
Forbes	55,018	8.0			
Keyes	40,025	5.8			
Lugar	31,119	4.5			

May 7 District of Columbia

	Votes	%		Votes	%
Dole	2,256	75.5	Clinton	20,568	98.1
Uncommitted	381	12.8	LaRouche	391	1.9
Buchanan	283	9.4			
Others[2]	67	2.2			

May 7 Indiana

	Votes	%		Votes	%
Dole	365,860	70.8	Clinton	329,536	100.0
Buchanan	100,245	19.4			
Forbes	50,802	9.8			

Republican			**Democratic**		
	Votes	%		Votes	%

May 7 North Carolina

Republican	Votes	%	Democratic	Votes	%
Dole	202,863	71.4	Clinton	461,434	80.6
Buchanan	37,126	13.1	No preference	69,790	12.2
Keyes	11,759	4.1	LaRouche	40,936	7.2
Forbes	11,588	4.1			
No preference	10,918	3.8			
Alexander	7,400	2.6			
Lugar	2,558	0.9			

May 14 Nebraska[13]

Republican	Votes	%	Democratic	Votes	%
Dole	129,131	75.7	Clinton	81,854	86.9
Buchanan	17,741	10.4	LaRouche	10,228	10.9
Forbes	10,612	6.2	Others[2]	2,094	2.2
Keyes	5,132	3.0			
Alexander	4,423	2.6			
Lugar	1,127	0.7			
Dornan	847	0.5			
Taylor	460	0.3			
Others[2]	1,118	0.7			

May 14 West Virginia

Republican	Votes	%	Democratic	Votes	%
Dole	87,534	68.7	Clinton	257,087	86.5
Buchanan	20,928	16.4	LaRouche	40,034	13.5
Forbes	6,222	4.9			
Keyes	4,822	3.8			
Alexander	3,773	3.0			
Gramm	2,391	1.9			
Lugar	1,082	0.8			
Taylor	702	0.6			

May 21 Arkansas

Republican	Votes	%	Democratic	Votes	%
Dole	32,759	76.2	Clinton	239,287	75.8
Buchanan	10,067	23.4	Uncommitted	42,411	13.4
Uncommitted	150	0.3	LaRouche	20,669	6.6
			Lloyd-Duffie	13,136	4.2

May 28 Idaho

Republican	Votes	%	Democratic	Votes	%
Dole	74,011	62.3	Clinton	35,277	87.7
Buchanan	26,461	22.3	"None of the names shown"	4,951	12.3
"None of the names shown"	12,339	10.4			
Keyes	5,904	5.0			

May 28 Kentucky

Republican	Votes	%	Democratic	Votes	%
Dole	76,669	73.8	Clinton	211,667	76.7
Buchanan	8,526	8.2	Uncommitted	44,028	16.0
Uncommitted	4,793	4.6	LaRouche	20,324	7.4
Keyes	3,822	3.7			
Forbes	3,400	3.3			
Alexander	3,272	3.2			
Lugar	2,235	2.2			
Gramm	1,122	1.1			

June 4 Alabama

Republican	Votes	%	Democratic	Votes	%
Dole	160,097	75.5	Clinton	243,588	80.6
Buchanan	33,409	15.8	Uncommitted	45,764	15.2
Uncommitted	11,073	5.2	LaRouche	12,686	4.2
Keyes	7,354	3.5			

Republican	Votes	%	**Democratic**	Votes	%

June 4 Montana

Dole	72,176	61.3	Clinton	82,549	90.0
Buchanan	28,581	24.3	No preference	9,176	10.0
No preference	8,533	7.2			
Forbes	8,456	7.2			

June 4 New Jersey

Dole	180,412	82.5	Clinton	254,004	95.2
Buchanan	23,789	10.9	LaRouche	12,736	4.8
Keyes	14,611	6.7			

June 4 New Mexico[14]

Dole	53,300	75.6	Clinton	109,595	90.3
Buchanan	5,679	8.1	Uncommitted	11,767	9.7
Forbes	3,987	5.7			
Alexander	2,676	3.8			
Keyes	2,265	3.2			
Uncommitted	1,301	1.8			
Dornan	865	1.2			
Taylor	391	0.6			

TOTALS

Dole	8,427,601	59.2	Clinton	9,730,184	88.5
Buchanan	3,021,935	21.2	LaRouche	597,081	5.4
Forbes	1,425,998	10.0	Lloyd-Duffie	92,435	0.8
Alexander	495,590	3.5	Hudson	32,232	0.3
Keyes	449,536	3.2	Harder	29,147	0.3
Lugar	127,111	0.9	Gunderson	15,712	0.1
Gramm	71,457	0.5	Casamassima	9,693	0.1
Dornan	42,141	0.3	Paulsen	1,317	—
Taylor	21,180	0.1	Riemers	651	—
Collins	2,092	—	Clemenson	384	—
Ducey	1,783	—	Uncommitted	423,265	3.8
Masters	1,052	—	Others[17]	64,294	0.6
Uncommitted[15]	123,765	0.9			
Others[16]	22,698	0.2		10,996,395	
	14,233,939				

1. In New Hampshire's Libertarian presidential primary, Harry Browne received 653 votes (40.5 percent), Irwin A. Schiff received 336 votes (20.8 percent) and there were 624 scattered write-in votes (38.6 percent).

2. Includes write-in votes.

3. The Arizona Democratic Party held its primary on March 9, 1996.

4. The North Dakota Democratic primary was nonbinding and did not elect delegates. In North Dakota's Libertarian presidential primary, Harry Browne received 147 votes (100.0 percent). In the Natural Law primary John Hagelin received 119 votes (100.0 percent).

5. In South Dakota's Libertarian presidential primary, Harry Browne received 325 votes (65.4 percent) and Irwin A. Schiff received 172 votes (34.6 percent).

6. No primary

7. Write-in votes.

8. In Massachusetts' Libertarian presidential primary, Harry Browne received 386 votes (44.4 percent), No preference received 237 votes (27.2 percent), Rick Tompkins received 111 votes (12.8 percent), Irwin A. Schiff received 66 votes (7.6 percent) and there were 70 scattered write-in votes (8.0 percent).

9. In Vermont's Liberty Union presidential primary, Mary Cal Hollis received 665 votes (80.1 percent) and there were 165 scattered write-in votes (19.9 percent).

10. Vote was for delegates only; there was no direct vote for candidates.

11. In Illinois' Libertarian presidential primary, Harry Browne received 1,278 votes (74.0 percent) and Irwin A. Schiff received 450 votes (26.0 percent).

12. In California's American Independent presidential primary, Howard Phillips received 19,204 votes (100.0 percent). In the Green presidential primary, Ralph Nader received 22,649 votes (100.0 percent). In the Libertarian presidential primary, Harry Browne received 7,258 votes (50.0 percent), Rick Tompkins received 3,400 votes (23.4 percent), Irwin A. Schiff received 2,215 votes (15.3 percent), Douglass J. Ohmen received 1,517 votes (10.5 percent) and there were 115 write-in votes (0.8 percent). In the Natural Law presidential primary, John Hagelin received 3,779 votes (100.0 percent). In the Peace and Freedom presidential primary, Monica Moorehead received 2,153 votes (33.9 percent), Jan Tucker received 1,512 votes (23.8 percent), Gerald Horne received 1,430 votes (22.5 percent), Mary Cal Hollis received 1,068 votes (16.8 percent), and there were 187 write-in votes (2.9 percent).

13. In Nebraska's Libertarian presidential primary, Harry Browne received 80 votes (89.9 percent) and there were 10 scattered write-in votes (11.1 percent). In the Libertarian Party of Iowa presidential primary, Harry Browne received 49 votes (77.8 percent) and there were 14 scattered write-in votes (22.2 percent).

14. In New Mexico's Green presidential primary, Ralph Nader received 976 votes (65.9 percent), Mary Cal Hollis received 395 votes (26.7 percent) and uncommitted delegates received 110 votes (7.4 percent).

15. The Uncommitted category includes votes cast on the following ballot lines: Uncommitted, No preference, Uninstructed, "None of these candidates" and "None of the names shown."

16. In addition to scattered write-in votes, "others" include Mary "France" Le Tulle who received 940 votes—290 votes in the Nevada primary and 650 votes in the Texas primary; Billy Joe Clegg who received 415 votes—297 votes in the Mississippi primary and 118 votes in the New Hampshire primary; Ann Jennings who received 304 votes in the Arizona primary; Richard P. Bosa who received 216 votes in the New Hampshire primary; Paul Jensen who received 172 votes—99 votes in the Arizona primary and 73 votes in the Puerto Rico primary; Georgiana H. Doerschuck who received 154 votes in the New Hampshire primary; Joann V. Pharr who received 125 votes in the Arizona primary; Hilary Michael Milko who received 109 votes in the Nevada primary; Kenneth Hewitt who received 104 votes in the Arizona primary; Michael Stephen Levinson who received 94 votes—59 votes in the Arizona primary and 35 votes in the New Hampshire primary; Richard D. Skillen who received 80 votes in the New Hampshire primary; Hubert David Patty who received 72 votes—55 votes in the Arizona primary and 17 votes in the New Hampshire primary; Doug Fricke who received 64 votes in the Arizona primary; William James Flanagan who received 48 votes in the New Hampshire primary; Tennie Rogers who received 47 votes—35 votes in the Mississippi primary and 12 in the New Hampshire primary; Charles Holden who received 38 votes in the Arizona primary; Russell J. Fornwalt who received 37 votes in the New Hampshire primary; Clyde Staggs who received 33 votes in the Arizona primary; John B. Hurd who received 26 votes in the New Hampshire primary; Gerald J. McManus who received 20 votes in the New Hampshire primary; C. A. Aldrich who received 19 votes in the Arizona primary.

17. In addition to scattered write-in votes, "others" include Carmen C. Chimento who received 656 votes in the New Hampshire primary; Caroline P. Killeen who received 391 votes in the New Hampshire primary; Bruce C. Daniels who received 312 votes in the New Hampshire primary; James D. Griffin who received 307 votes in the New Hampshire primary; Stephen Michael who received 94 votes in the New Hampshire primary; Willie Felix Carter who received 85 votes in the New Hampshire primary; Robert F. Drucker who received 81 votes in the New Hampshire primary; David Pauling who received 74 votes in the New Hampshire primary; Vincent S. Hamm who received 72 votes in the New Hampshire primary; Ronald W. Spangler who received 72 votes—10 write-in votes in the California primary and 62 votes in the New Hampshire primary; Frank Legas who received 63 votes in the New Hampshire primary; Michael E. Dass who received 57 votes in the New Hampshire primary; Osie Thorpe who received 50 votes in the New Hampshire primary; Ben J. Tomeo who received 47 votes in the New Hampshire primary; John Safran who received 42 votes in the New Hampshire primary.

2000 Primaries

Republican	Votes	%	Democratic	Votes	%
February 1 New Hampshire					
John McCain (Ariz.)	115,606	48.5			
George W. Bush (Texas)	72,330	30.4	Al Gore (Tenn.)	76,897	49.7
Malcom S. "Steve" Forbes Jr. (N.J.)	30,166	12.7	Bill Bradley (N.J.)	70,502	45.6
Alan Keyes (Md.)	15,179	6.4	Charles Buckley (N.H.)	322	0.2
Gary Bauer (Va.)	1,640	0.7	Heather Anne Harder (Ind.)	192	0.1
Orrin G. Hatch (Utah)	163	0.1	Jeffrey B. Peters (N.H.)	156	0.1
Dorian Yeager (N.H.)	98	0.0	John B. Eaton (Mass.)	134	0.1
Anthony R. "Andy" Martin (Fla.)	81	0.0	Lyndon LaRouche (Va.)	124	0.1
Samuel H. Berry Jr. (Ore.)	61	0.0	Jim Taylor (Minn.)	87	0.1
Kenneth A. Capalbo (R.I.)	51	0.0	Mark Greenstein (Calif.)	75	0.0
Timothy L. Mosby (Calif.)	41	0.0	Nathaniel T. Mullins (Mass.)	35	0.0
Mark "Dick" Harnes (N.Y.)	34	0.0	Edward T. O'Donnell Jr. (Del.)	35	0.0
Richard C. Peet (Va.)	23	0.0	Willie F. Carter (Calif.)	30	0.0
Tom Oyler (Kan.)	14	0.0	Randolph "Randy" W. Crow (N.C.)	29	0.0
Others[1]	2,719	1.1	Vincent S. Hamm (Colo.)	22	0.0
			Thomas Koos (Calif.)	19	0.0
			Michael Skok (N.Y.)	18	0.0
			Others[1]	5,962	3.9
February 8 Delaware[2]			**February 5**		
Bush	15,250	50.7	Gore	6,377	57.2
McCain	7,638	25.4	Bradley	4,476	40.2
Forbes	5,883	19.6	LaRouche	288	2.6
Keyes	1,148	3.8			
Bauer	120	0.4			
Hatch	21	0.1			
February 19 (R) South Carolina					
Bush	305,998	53.4			
McCain	239,964	41.9			
Keyes	25,996	4.5			
Bauer	618	0.1			
Forbes	449	0.1			
Hatch	76	0.0			
February 22 Arizona[3]			**March 11**		
McCain	193,708	60.0	Gore	67,582	77.9
Bush	115,115	35.7	Bradley	16,383	18.9
Keyes	11,500	3.6	No preference	1,439	1.7
Forbes	1,211	0.4	Harder	1,358	1.6
Hatch	637	0.2			
John R. McGrath (Ariz.)	239	0.1			
Bauer	177	0.1			
James T. Zanon (Ariz.)	54	0.0			
Chuck See (Ariz.)	28	0.0			
February 22 Michigan					
McCain	650,805	51.0	Uncommitted	31,655	70.6
Bush	549,665	43.1	LaRouche	13,195	29.4
Keyes	59,032	4.6			
Uncommitted	8,714	0.7			
Forbes	4,894	0.4			
Bauer	2,733	0.2			
Hatch	905	0.1			
Joe C. Schriner (Ohio)	22	0.0			

Republican	Votes	%	Democratic	Votes	%
February 29 Virginia					
Bush	350,588	52.8			
McCain	291,488	43.9			
Keyes	20,356	3.1			
Bauer	852	0.1			
Forbes	809	0.1			
February 29 Washington					
Bush	284,053	57.8	Gore	202,456	68.2
McCain	191,101	38.9	Bradley	93,375	31.4
Keyes	11,753	2.4	LaRouche	1,170	0.4
Forbes	1,749	0.4			
Bauer	1,469	0.3			
Hatch	1,023	0.2			
March 7 California					
Bush	1,725,162	60.6	Gore	2,155,321	81.2
McCain	988,706	34.7	Bradley	482,882	18.2
Keyes	112,747	4.0	LaRouche	15,911	0.6
Forbes	8,449	0.3			
Bauer	6,860	0.2			
Hatch	5,997	0.2			
March 7 Connecticut					
McCain	87,176	48.7	Gore	98,312	55.4
Bush	82,881	46.3	Bradley	73,589	41.5
Keyes	5,913	3.3	Uncommitted	5,400	3.0
Forbes	1,242	0.7			
Uncommitted	1,222	0.7			
Bauer	373	0.2			
Hatch	178	0.1			
March 7 Georgia					
Bush	430,480	66.9	Gore	238,396	83.8
McCain	179,046	27.8	Bradley	46,035	16.2
Keyes	29,640	4.6			
Bauer	1,962	0.3			
Forbes	1,647	0.3			
Hatch	413	0.1			
March 7 Maine					
Bush	49,308	51.0	Gore	34,725	54.0
McCain	42,510	44.0	Bradley	26,520	41.3
Keyes	2,989	3.1	LaRouche	208	0.3
Uncommitted	1,038	1.1	Richard J. Epstein (Maine)	192	0.3
Forbes	455	0.5	Uncommitted	2,634	4.1
Bauer	324	0.3			
March 7 Maryland					
Bush	211,439	56.2	Gore	341,630	67.3
McCain	135,981	36.2	Bradley	144,387	28.5
Keyes	25,020	6.7	Uncommitted	16,935	3.3
Forbes	1,678	0.4	LaRouche	4,510	0.9
Bauer	1,328	0.4			
Hatch	588	0.2			

	Republican			**Democratic**	
	Votes	%		Votes	%
March 7 Massachusetts					
McCain	324,708	64.7	Gore	341,586	59.9
Bush	159,534	31.8	Bradley	212,452	37.3
Keyes	12,630	2.5	No preference	11,281	2.0
Bauer	1,744	0.3	LaRouche	2,135	0.4
Forbes	1,407	0.3	Others[1]	2,620	0.5
No preference	1,292	0.3			
Hatch	262	0.1			
Others[1]	374	0.1			
March 7 Missouri					
Bush	275,366	57.9	Gore	171,562	64.6
McCain	167,831	35.3	Bradley	89,092	33.6
Keyes	27,282	5.7	Uncommitted	3,364	1.3
Forbes	2,044	0.4	LaRouche	906	0.3
Uncommitted	1,345	0.3	Pat Price (Mo.)	565	0.2
Bauer	1,038	0.2			
Hatch	363	0.1			
Lawrence L. Hornung (Mo.)	94	0.0			
March 7 New York[4]					
Bush	-	51.0	Gore	639,417	65.6
McCain	-	43.4	Bradley	326,038	33.5
Keyes	-	3.3	LaRouche	9,008	0.9
Forbes	-	2.3			
March 7 Ohio					
Bush	810,369	58.0	Gore	720,311	73.6
McCain	516,790	37.0	Bradley	241,688	24.7
Keyes	55,266	4.0	LaRouche	16,513	1.7
Forbes	8,934	0.6			
Bauer	6,169	0.4			
March 7 Rhode Island					
McCain	21,754	60.2	Gore	26,801	57.2
Bush	13,170	36.5	Bradley	19,000	40.6
Keyes	923	2.6	Uncommitted	844	1.8
Uncommitted	114	0.3	LaRouche	199	0.4
Forbes	89	0.2	Others[1]	235	0.5
Bauer	35	0.1			
Hatch	35	0.1			
Others[1]	23	—			
March 7 Vermont					
McCain	49,045	60.3	Gore	26,774	54.3
Bush	28,741	35.3	Bradley	21,629	43.9
Keyes	2,164	2.7	LaRouche	355	0.7
Forbes	616	0.8	Others[1]	525	1.1
Bauer	293	0.4			
Others[1]	496	0.6			
March 10 Colorado					
Bush	116,897	64.7	Gore	63,384	71.4
McCain	48,996	27.1	Bradley	20,663	23.3
Keyes	11,871	6.6	Uncommitted	3,867	4.3
Forbes	1,197	0.7	LaRouche	821	0.9
Bauer	1,190	0.7			
Hatch	504	0.3			

Republican	Votes	%	Democratic	Votes	%
March 10 Utah					
Bush	57,617	63.3	Gore	12,527	79.9
Keyes	19,367	21.3	Bradley	3,160	20.1
McCain	12,784	14.0			
Forbes	859	0.9			
Bauer	426	0.5			
March 14 Florida					
Bush	516,263	73.8	Gore	451,718	81.8
McCain	139,465	19.9	Bradley	100,277	18.2
Keyes	32,354	4.6			
Forbes	6,553	0.9			
Bauer	3,496	0.5			
Hatch	1,372	0.2			
March 14 Louisiana					
Bush	86,038	83.6	Gore	114,942	73.0
McCain	9,165	8.9	Bradley	31,385	19.9
Keyes	5,900	5.7	LaRouche	6,127	3.9
Forbes	1,041	1.0	Crow	5,097	3.2
Bauer	768	0.7			
March 14 Mississippi					
Bush	101,042	87.9	Gore	79,408	89.6
Keyes	6,478	5.6	Bradley	7,621	8.6
McCain	6,263	5.4	LaRouche	1,573	1.8
Forbes	588	0.5			
Bauer	475	0.4			
Hatch	133	0.1			
March 14 Oklahoma					
Bush	98,781	79.1	Gore	92,654	68.7
McCain	12,973	10.4	Bradley	34,311	25.4
Keyes	11,595	9.3	LaRouche	7,885	5.8
Forbes	1,066	0.9			
Bauer	394	0.3			
March 14 Tennessee					
Bush	193,166	77.0	Gore	198,264	92.1
McCain	36,436	14.5	Bradley	11,323	5.3
Keyes	16,916	6.7	Uncommitted	4,407	2.0
Uncommitted	1,623	0.6	LaRouche	1,031	0.5
Bauer	1,305	0.5	Others[1]	178	0.1
Forbes	1,018	0.4			
Hatch	252	0.1			
Others[1]	75	0.0			
March 14 Texas					
Bush	986,416	87.5	Gore	631,428	80.2
McCain	80,082	7.1	Bradley	128,564	16.3
Keyes	43,518	3.9	LaRouche	26,898	3.4
Uncommitted	9,570	0.8			
Forbes	2,865	0.3			
Bauer	2,189	0.2			
Hatch	1,324	0.1			
Charles Urban (Texas)	793	0.1			

	Republican			**Democratic**		
	Votes	**%**			**Votes**	**%**
March 21 Illinois						
Bush	496,685	67.4	Gore		682,932	84.3
McCain	158,768	21.5	Bradley		115,320	14.2
Keyes	66,066	9.0	LaRouche		11,415	1.4
Forbes	10,334	1.4				
Bauer	5,068	0.7				
April 4 Pennsylvania						
Bush	472,398	73.5	Gore		525,306	74.6
McCain	145,719	22.7	Bradley		146,797	20.8
Forbes	16,162	2.5	LaRouche		32,047	4.6
Bauer	8,806	1.4	Others[1]		3,840	0.5
Keyes	7,100	1.1				
Others[1]	1,624	0.2				
April 4 Wisconsin						
Bush	343,292	69.2	Gore		328,682	88.5
McCain	89,684	18.1	Bradley		32,560	8.8
Keyes	48,919	9.9	Uninstructed delegation		4,105	1.1
Forbes	5,505	1.1	LaRouche		3,743	1.0
Uninstructed delegation	3,452	0.7	Others[1]		2,106	0.6
Bauer	1,813	0.4				
Hatch	1,712	0.3				
Others[1]	1,392	0.3				
May 2 District of Columbia						
Bush	1,771	72.8	Gore		18,621	95.9
McCain	593	24.4	LaRouche		796	4.1
Others[1]	69	2.8				
May 2 Indiana						
Bush	330,095	81.2	Gore		219,604	74.9
McCain	76,569	18.8	Bradley		64,339	21.9
			LaRouche		9,229	3.1
May 2 North Carolina						
Bush	253,485	78.6	Gore		383,696	70.4
McCain	35,018	10.9	Bradley		99,796	18.3
Keyes	25,320	7.9	No preference		49,905	9.2
No preference	5,383	1.7	LaRouche		11,525	2.1
Bauer	3,311	1.0				
May 9 Nebraska						
Bush	145,176	78.2	Gore		73,639	70.0
McCain	28,065	15.1	Bradley		27,884	26.5
Keyes	12,073	6.5	LaRouche		3,191	3.0
Others[1]	444	0.2	Others[1]		557	0.5
May 9 West Virginia						
Bush	87,050	79.6	Gore		182,403	72.0
McCain	14,121	12.9	Bradley		46,710	18.4
Keyes	5,210	4.8	Angus W. McDonald (W.Va.)		19,374	7.6
Forbes	1,733	1.6	LaRouche		4,823	1.9
Bauer	1,290	1.2				

Republican	Votes	%	Democratic	Votes	%
May 16 Oregon					
Bush	292,522	83.6	Gore	300,922	84.9
Keyes	46,764	13.4	LaRouche	38,521	10.9
Others[1]	10,545	3.0	Others[1]	15,151	4.3
May 23 Arkansas					
Bush	35,759	80.2	Gore	193,750	78.5
Keyes	8,814	19.8	LaRouche	53,150	21.5
May 23 Idaho					
Bush	116,385	73.5	Gore	27,025	75.7
Keyes	30,263	19.1	"None of the names shown"	5,722	16.0
"None of the names shown"	11,798	7.4	LaRouche	2,941	8.2
May 23 Kentucky					
Bush	75,783	83.0	Gore	156,966	71.3
McCain	5,780	6.3	Bradley	32,340	14.7
Keyes	4,337	4.7	Uncommitted	26,046	11.8
Bauer	2,408	2.6	LaRouche	4,927	2.2
Uncommitted	1,829	2.0			
Forbes	1,186	1.3			
June 6 Alabama					
Bush	171,077	84.2	Gore	214,541	77.0
Keyes	23,394	11.5	Uncommitted	48,521	17.4
Uncommitted	8,608	4.2	LaRouche	15,465	5.6
June 6 Montana					
Bush	88,194	77.6	Gore	68,420	77.9
Keyes	20,822	18.3	No preference	19,447	22.1
No preference	4,655	4.1			
McCain	2	—			
June 6 New Jersey					
Bush	201,209	83.6	Gore	358,951	94.9
Keyes	39,601	16.4	LaRouche	19,321	5.1
June 6 New Mexico					
Bush	62,161	82.6	Gore	98,715	74.6
McCain	7,619	10.1	Bradley	27,204	20.6
Keyes	4,850	6.4	Uncommitted	3,298	2.5
Uncommitted	600	0.8	LaRouche	3,063	2.3
June 6 South Dakota					
Bush	35,418	78.2			
McCain	6,228	13.8			
Keyes	3,478	7.7			
James Attia (S.D.)	155	0.3			

Republican	Votes	%	**Democratic**	Votes	%
TOTALS					
George W. Bush	10,844,129	63.2	Al Gore	10,626,645	75.7
John McCain	5,118,187	29.8	Bill Bradley	2,798,302	19.9
Alan Keyes	914,548	5.3	Lyndon LaRouche	323,014	2.3
Malcom S. "Steve" Forbes Jr.	121,829	0.7	Angus W. McDonald	19,374	0.1
Gary Bauer	60,674	0.4	Randolph "Randy" W. Crow	5,126	—
Orrin G. Hatch	15,958	0.1	Heather Anne Harder	1,550	—
Uncommitted[5]	61,243	0.4	Uncommitted[5]	238,870	1.7
Others[6]	19,549	0.1	Others[7]	32,864	0.2
	17,156,117			14,045,745	

Notes: The Democratic Party did not hold primaries in South Carolina, South Dakota, and Virginia.

1. Write-in votes.

2. The Delaware Republican Party held its primary on February 8, 2000.

3. The Arizona Democratic Party held its primary on March 11, 2000.

4. Vote percentages were for delegates only; there was no direct vote for candidates.

5. The Uncommitted category includes votes cast on the following ballot lines: Uncommitted, No preference, Uninstructed, "None of these candidates," and "None of the names shown."

6. In addition to scattered write-in votes, "others" include Charles Urban who received 793 votes in the Texas primary; John R. McGrath who received 239 votes in the Arizona primary; James Attia who received 155 votes in the South Dakota primary; Dorian Yeager who received 98 votes in the New Hampshire primary; Lawrence L. Hornung who received 94 votes in the Missouri primary; Anthony R. "Andy" Martin who received 81 votes in the New Hampshire primary; Samuel H. Berry Jr. who received 61 votes in the New Hampshire primary; James T. Zanon who received 54 votes in the Arizona primary; Kenneth A. Capalbo who received 51 votes in the New Hamp-

shire primary; Timothy L. Mosby who received 41 votes in the New Hampshire primary; Mark "Dick" Harnes who received 34 votes in the New Hampshire primary; Chuck See who received 28 votes in the Arizona primary; Richard C. Peet who received 23 votes in the New Hampshire primary; Joe C. Schriner who received 22 votes in the Michigan primary; Tom Oyler who received 14 in the New Hampshire primary.

7. In addition to scattered write-in votes, "others" include Pat Price who received 565 votes in the Missouri primary; Charles Buckley who received 322 votes in the New Hampshire primary; Richard J. Epstein who received 192 votes in the Maine primary; Jeffrey B. Peters who received 156 votes in the New Hampshire primary; John B. Eaton who received 134 votes in the New Hampshire primary; Jim Taylor who received 87 votes in the New Hampshire primary; Mark Greenstein who received 75 votes in the New Hampshire primary; Nathaniel T. Mullins who received 35 votes in the New Hampshire primary; Edward T. O'Donnell Jr. who received 35 votes in the New Hampshire primary; Willie F. Carter who received 30 votes in the New Hampshire primary; Vincent S. Hamm who received 22 votes in the New Hampshire primary; Thomas Koos who received 19 votes in the New Hampshire primary; Michael Skok who received 18 votes in the New Hampshire primary.

CHAPTER 12

Nominating Conventions

Although the presidential nominating convention has been a target of criticism throughout its existence, it has survived to become a traditional fixture of American politics. The convention owes its longevity and general acceptance in large part to the multiplicity of functions that the convention uniquely combines.

The convention is a nominating body that the Democrats, Republicans, and most of the principal third parties have used since the early 1830s to choose their candidates for president and vice president. The convention also produces a platform containing the party's positions on issues of the campaign. Convention delegates form the supreme governing body of the party and as such they make major decisions on party affairs. Between conventions such decisions are made by the national committee with the guidance of the party chair.

The convention provides a forum for compromise among the diverse elements within a party, allowing the discussion and often the satisfactory solution of differing points of view. As the ultimate campaign rally, the convention also gathers together thousands of party leaders and rank-and-file members from across the country in an atmosphere that varies widely, sometimes encouraging sober discussion but often resembling a carnival. But even though the process has drawn heavy criticism, the convention has endured because it successfully performs a variety of actions.

The convention is an outgrowth of the American political experience. Nowhere is it mentioned in the Constitution nor has the authority of the convention ever been a subject of congressional legislation. Rather, the convention has evolved along with the presidential selection process. The convention has been the accepted nominating method of the major political parties since the election of 1832, but internal changes within the convention system have been massive since the early, formative years.

Convention Sites

Before the Civil War, conventions frequently were held in small buildings, even churches, and attracted only several hundred delegates and a minimum of spectators. Transportation and communications were slow, so most conventions were held in the late spring in a city with a central geographical location. Baltimore, Maryland, was the most popular convention city in this initial period, playing host to the first six Democratic conventions (1832 through 1852), two Whig conventions, one National Republican convention, and the 1831 Anti-Masonic gathering—America's first national nominating convention. With

the nation's westward expansion, the heartland city of Chicago, emerged as the most frequent convention center. Since its first one in 1860, Chicago has been the site of twenty-five major party conventions (fourteen Republican, eleven Democratic). The Democrats held their national convention in Chicago as recently as 1996. In 2000 Republicans held their national convention in Philadelphia, which has hosted eight conventions. Democrats chose that year to meet in Los Angeles—the second time that the California city hosted a national party convention.

LOCATING AND FINANCING CONVENTIONS

Since 1976, presidential elections have been publicly funded. Early on, the newly created Federal Election Commission (FEC) ruled that host-city contributions to conventions are allowable, enabling the parties to far exceed the technical limit on convention spending. In 1988, for example, the FEC allotted the two major parties $9.2 million each in public funds for their conventions. The money came from an optional checkoff for publicly financing presidential campaigns on federal income tax forms. (Congress raised the original $1 checkoff to $3 per taxpayer, beginning in 1993.) In 1988 the Republicans, however, spent a total of $18 million on their New Orleans convention, while the Democrats spent $22.5 million in Atlanta. To attract the Democratic convention, Atlanta levied a special tax on hotel guests, which enabled the host committee to offer a package of $5 million in borrowed money. For both conventions, General Motors (with FEC permission) provided fleets of cars at an estimated cost of $350,000.

In 1992 the Democrats spent a record $38.6 million on their New York City meeting, according to political scientist Herbert E. Alexander. For the 1996 conventions, the FEC allotted the two major parties $12.4 million each in public funds, but the total spending for both parties, according to Alexander, was at least twice that amount. In 2000, the federal money given each of the two major parties for their conventions reached $13.5 million. The Reform Party was given $2.5 million.

Major outlays typically go for construction, administration, office space, convention committees, and police and fire protection. Besides adequate hotel and convention hall facilities, safety of the delegates and other attendees is increasingly a major consideration in selection of a national party convention site. The island location of Miami Beach, for example, made it easier to contain protest demonstrators and reportedly was a factor in its selection by the Republicans in 1968 and by both parties in 1972.

For the party that controls the White House, often the overriding factor in site selection is the president's personal prefer-

Sites of Major Party Conventions, 1832–2000

The following chart lists the twenty-one cities selected as the sites of major party conventions and the number of conventions they have hosted from the first national gathering for the Democrats (1832) and the Republicans (1856) through the 2000 conventions. The Democrats have hosted a total of forty-four conventions; the Republicans thirty-seven.

	Total conventions	Democratic conventions		Republican conventions	
		Number	Last hosted	Number	Last hosted
Chicago, Ill.	25	11	1996	14	1960
Baltimore, Md.	10	9	1912	1	1864
Philadelphia, Pa.	8	2	1948	6	2000
St. Louis, Mo.	5	4	1916	1	1896
New York, N.Y.	5	5	1992	0	—
San Francisco, Calif.	4	2	1984	2	1964
Cincinnati, Ohio	3	2	1880	1	1876
Kansas City, Mo.	3	1	1900	2	1976
Miami Beach, Fla.	3	1	1972	2	1972
Cleveland, Ohio	2	0	—	2	1936
Houston, Texas	2	1	1928	1	1992
Los Angeles, Calif.	2	2	2000	0	—
Atlanta, Ga.	1	1	1988	0	—
Atlantic City, N.J.	1	1	1964	0	—
Charleston, S.C.	1	1	1860	0	—
Dallas, Texas	1	0	—	1	1984
Denver, Colo.	1	1	1908	0	—
Detroit, Mich.	1	0	—	1	1980
Minneapolis, Minn.	1	0	—	1	1892
New Orleans, La.	1	0	—	1	1988
San Diego, Calif.	1	0	—	1	1996

ence—as in the GOP's decision to meet in 1992 in President George Bush's adopted home city of Houston, or the Democrats' decision to meet in Atlantic City in 1964, because President Lyndon Johnson wanted a site within helicopter distance of Washington, and convenient to New York City.

The national committees of the two parties select the sites about one year before the conventions are to take place.

CALL OF THE CONVENTION

The second major step in the quadrennial convention process follows several months after the site selection with the announcement of the convention call, the establishment of the three major convention committees—credentials, rules, and platform (resolutions)—the appointment of convention officers, and finally the holding of the convention itself. While these basic steps have undergone little change during the past 170 years, there have been major alterations within the nominating convention system.

The call to the convention sets the date and site of the meeting and is issued early in each election year, if not before. The call to the first Democratic convention, held in 1832, was issued by the New Hampshire Legislature. Early Whig conventions were called by party members in Congress. With the establishment of national committees later in the nineteenth century, the function of issuing the convention call fell to these new party organizations. Each national committee currently has the responsibility for allocating delegates to each state.

Delegate Selection

Both parties have modified the method of allocating delegates to the individual states and territories. From the beginning of the convention system in the nineteenth century, both the Democrats and Republicans distributed votes to the states based on their Electoral College strength.

The first major deviation from this procedure was made by the Republicans after their divisive 1912 convention, in which President William Howard Taft won renomination over former President Theodore Roosevelt. Taft's nomination was due largely to almost solid support from the South—a region vastly overrepresented in relation to its number of Republican voters. Before their 1916 convention the Republicans reduced the allocation of votes to the southern states. At their 1924 convention the Republicans applied the first bonus system, by which states were awarded extra votes for supporting the Republican presidential candidate in the previous election. The concept of bonus votes, applied as a reward to the states for supporting the party ticket, has been used and expanded by both parties since that time.

The Democrats first used a bonus system in 1944, completing a compromise arrangement with southern states for abolishing the party's controversial two-thirds nominating rule. Since then both parties have used various delegate-allocation formulas. At their 1972 convention the Republicans revised the formula and added more than 900 new delegate slots for 1976, increasing the size of the convention by two-thirds. The Ripon Society, an

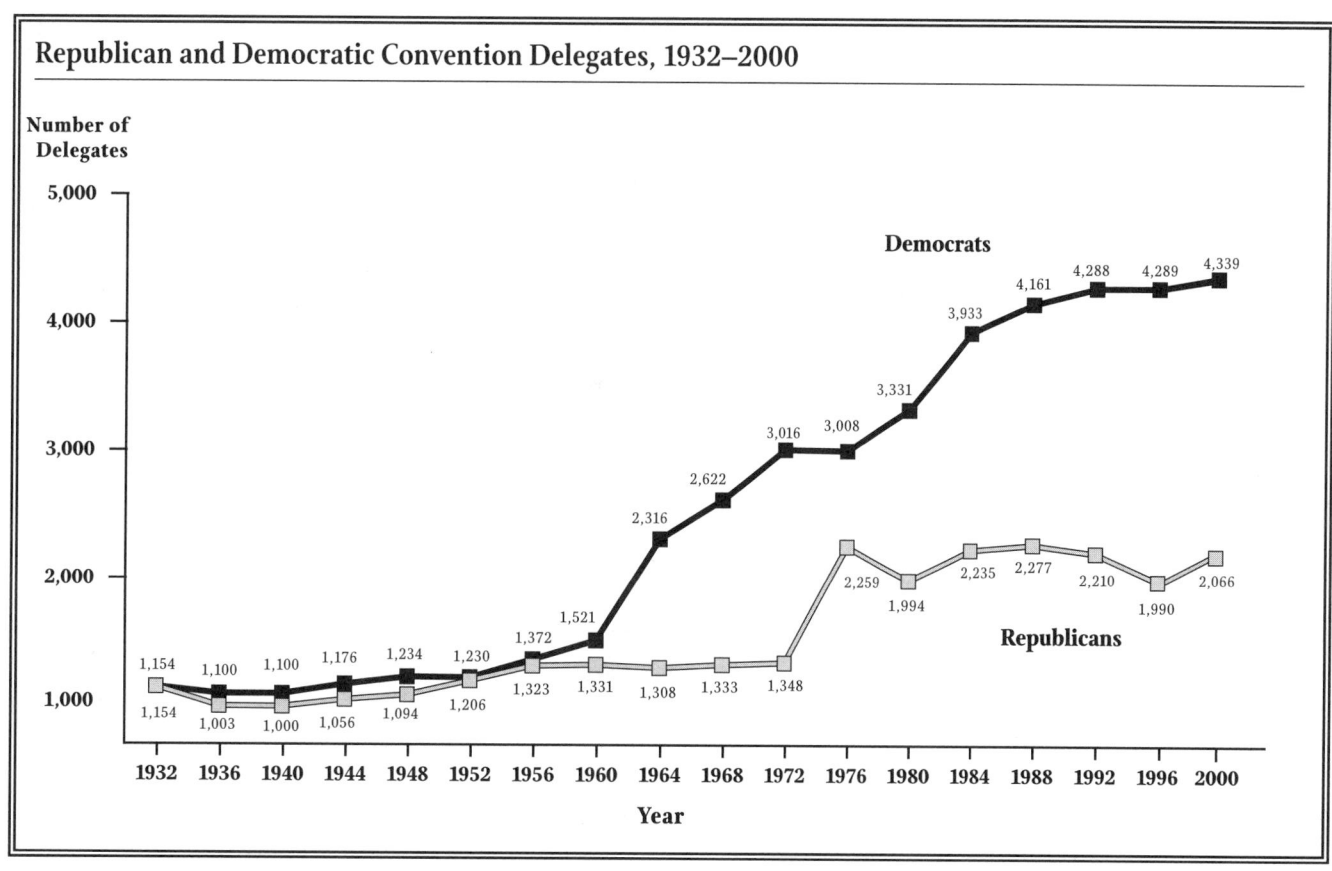

Republican and Democratic Convention Delegates, 1932–2000

Number of Delegates

organization of liberal Republicans, sued to have the new rules overturned. They argued that, because of the extra delegates awarded to states that voted Republican in the previous presidential election, small southern and western states were favored at the expense of the more populous but less Republican eastern states. The challenge failed when the Supreme Court in February 1976 refused to hear the case and thus let stand a U.S. Court of Appeals decision upholding the rules.

Only 116 delegates from thirteen states attended the initial national nominating convention held by the Anti-Masons in 1831, but with the addition of more states and the adoption of increasingly complex voting-allocation formulas by the major parties, the size of conventions spiraled. The 1976 Republican convention had 2,259 delegates, while the Democrats in the same year had 3,075 delegates casting 3,008 votes. (The number of delegate votes was smaller than the number of delegates because Democratic Party rules provide for fractional voting.)

The expanded size of modern conventions in part reflected their democratization, with less command by a few party leaders and dramatic growth among youth, women, and minority delegations. Increased representation for such groups was one of the major reasons given by the Republicans for the huge increase in delegate strength authorized by the 1972 convention (and effective for the 1976 gathering).

The Democrats adopted new rules in June 1978, expanding the number of delegates by 10 percent to provide extra representation for state and local officials. The new Democratic rules also required that women account for at least 50 percent of the delegates beginning with the 1980 convention. That party's national convention continued to grow throughout the next decade—from 3,331 delegate votes in 1980 to 4,339 in 2000. An Associated Press (AP) survey in 2000 found that nearly one-half of the Democratic delegates were women, and fully one-quarter were from minority groups.

In contrast, 2,066 delegates attended the 2000 Republican convention in Philadelphia. Unlike the Democrats, the Republican Party had no rules mandating the makeup of its convention delegates. Barely one-third of the convention delegates were women, according to the AP, and less than 10 percent were from minority groups.

With the increased size of conventions has come a formalization in the method of delegate selection, which at first was often haphazard and informal. At the Democratic convention in 1835, for example, Maryland had 188 delegates to cast the state's ten votes. In contrast, Tennessee's fifteen votes were cast by a traveling businessman who happened to be in the convention city at the time. While the number of delegates and the number of votes allocated tended to be equal or nearly so later in the nineteenth century, a few party bosses frequently exercised domination of national conventions.

Two basic methods of delegate selection were employed in the nineteenth century and continued to be used into the twentieth: the caucus method, by which delegates were chosen by meetings at the local or state level, and the appointment method, by which delegates were appointed by the governor or a powerful state leader.

Democratic Conventions, 1832–2000

Year	City	Dates	Presidential nominee	Vice-presidential nominee	No. of pres. ballots
1832	Baltimore	May 21–23	Andrew Jackson	Martin Van Buren	1
1835	Baltimore	May 20–23	Martin Van Buren	Richard M. Johnson	1
1840	Baltimore	May 5–6	Martin Van Buren	—[1]	1
1844	Baltimore	May 27–29	James K. Polk	George M. Dallas	9
1848	Baltimore	May 22–25	Lewis Cass	William O. Butler	4
1852	Baltimore	June 1–5	Franklin Pierce	William R. King	49
1856	Cincinnati	June 2–6	James Buchanan	John C. Breckinridge	17
1860	Charleston	April 23–May 3	Deadlocked		57
	Baltimore	June 18–23	Stephen A. Douglas	Benjamin Fitzpatrick Herschel V. Johnson[2]	2
1864	Chicago	Aug. 29–31	George B. McClellan	George H. Pendleton	1
1868	New York	July 4–9	Horatio Seymour	Francis P. Blair	22
1872	Baltimore	July 9–10	Horace Greeley	Benjamin G. Brown	1
1876	St. Louis	June 27–29	Samuel J. Tilden	Thomas A. Hendricks	2
1880	Cincinnati	June 22–24	Winfield S. Hancock	William H. English	2
1884	Chicago	July 8–11	Grover Cleveland	Thomas A. Hendricks	2
1888	St. Louis	June 5–7	Grover Cleveland	Allen G. Thurman	1
1892	Chicago	June 21–23	Grover Cleveland	Adlai E. Stevenson	1
1896	Chicago	July 7–11	William J. Bryan	Arthur Sewall	5
1900	Kansas City	July 4–6	William J. Bryan	Adlai E. Stevenson	1
1904	St. Louis	July 6–9	Alton S. Parker	Henry G. Davis	1
1908	Denver	July 7–10	William J. Bryan	John W. Kern	1
1912	Baltimore	June 25–July 2	Woodrow Wilson	Thomas R. Marshall	46
1916	St. Louis	June 14–16	Woodrow Wilson	Thomas R. Marshall	1
1920	San Francisco	June 28–July 6	James M. Cox	Franklin D. Roosevelt	44
1924	New York	June 24–July 9	John W. Davis	Charles W. Bryan	103
1928	Houston	June 26–29	Alfred E. Smith	Joseph T. Robinson	1
1932	Chicago	June 27–July 2	Franklin D. Roosevelt	John N. Garner	4
1936	Philadelphia	June 23–27	Franklin D. Roosevelt	John N. Garner	Acclamation
1940	Chicago	July 15–18	Franklin D. Roosevelt	Henry A. Wallace	1
1944	Chicago	July 19–21	Franklin D. Roosevelt	Harry S. Truman	1
1948	Philadelphia	July 12–14	Harry S. Truman	Alben W. Barkley	1
1952	Chicago	July 21–26	Adlai E. Stevenson	John J. Sparkman	3
1956	Chicago	Aug. 13–17	Adlai E. Stevenson	Estes Kefauver	1
1960	Los Angeles	July 11–15	John F. Kennedy	Lyndon B. Johnson	1
1964	Atlantic City	Aug. 24–27	Lyndon B. Johnson	Hubert H. Humphrey	Acclamation
1968	Chicago	Aug. 26–29	Hubert H. Humphrey	Edmund S. Muskie	1
1972	Miami Beach	July 10–13	George McGovern	Thomas F. Eagleton R. Sargent Shriver[3]	1
1976	New York	July 12–15	Jimmy Carter	Walter F. Mondale	1
1980	New York	Aug. 11–14	Jimmy Carter	Walter F. Mondale	1
1984	San Francisco	July 16–19	Walter F. Mondale	Geraldine A. Ferraro	1
1988	Atlanta	July 18–21	Michael S. Dukakis	Lloyd Bentsen	1
1992	New York	July 13–16	Bill Clinton	Al Gore	1
1996	Chicago	Aug. 26–29	Bill Clinton	Al Gore	1
2000	Los Angeles	Aug. 14–17	Al Gore	Joseph Lieberman	1

1. The 1840 Democratic convention did not nominate a candidate for vice president.

2. The 1860 Democratic convention nominated Benjamin Fitzpatrick, who declined the nomination shortly after the convention adjourned. On June 25 the Democratic National Committee selected Herschel V. Johnson as the party's candidate for vice president.

3. The 1972 Democratic convention nominated Thomas F. Eagleton, who withdrew from the ticket on July 31. On Aug. 8 the Democratic National Committee selected R. Sargent Shriver as the party's candidate for vice president.

PRESIDENTIAL PRIMARIES

A revolutionary new mechanism for delegate selection emerged during the early 1900s: the presidential primary election in which the voters directly elected convention delegates.

Initiated in Florida at the turn of the century, the presidential primary by 1912 was used by thirteen states. In his first annual message to Congress the following year, President Woodrow Wilson advocated the establishment of a national primary to select presidential candidates: "I feel confident that I do not misinterpret the wishes or the expectations of the country when I urge the prompt enactment of legislation which will provide for primary elections throughout the country at which the voters of several parties may choose their nominees for the presidency without the intervention of nominating conventions." Wilson went on to suggest the retention of conventions for the purpose of declaring the results of the primaries and formulating the parties' platforms.

Before any action was taken on Wilson's proposal, the progressive spirit that spurred the growth of presidential primaries died out. Not until the late 1960s and early 1970s, when widespread pressures for change touched both parties but especially

Chief Officers and Keynote Speakers at Democratic National Conventions, 1832–2000

Year	Chair national committee	Temporary chair	Permanent chair	Keynote speaker
1832		Robert Lucas, Ohio	Robert Lucas, Ohio	
1836		Andrew Stevenson, Va.	Andrew Stevenson, Va.	
1840		Isaac Hill, N.H.	William Carroll, Tenn.	
1844		Hendrick B. Wright, Pa.	Hendrick B. Wright, Pa.	
1848	Benjamin Hallet, Mass.	J.S. Bryce, La.	Andrew Stevenson, Va.	
1852	Robert M. McLane, Md.	Gen. Romulus M. Saunders, N.C.	John W. Davis, Ind.	
1856	David A. Smalley, Vt.	Samuel Medary, Ohio	John E. Ward, Ga.	
1860	August Belmont, N.Y.	Francis B. Flournoy, Ark.	Caleb Cushing, Mass.	
1864	August Belmont, N.Y.	William Bigler, Pa.	Horatio Seymour, N.Y.	
1868	August Belmont, N.Y.	Henry L. Palmer, Wis.	Horatio Seymour, N.Y.	
1872	Augustus Schell, N.Y.	Thomas Jefferson Randolph, Va.	James R. Doolittle, Wis.	
1876	Abram Stevens Hewitt, N.Y.	Henry M. Watterson, Ky.	John A. McClernand, Ill.	
1880	William H. Barnum, Conn.	George Hoadly, Ohio	John W. Stevenson, Ky.	
1884	William H. Barnum, Conn.	Richard B. Hubbard, Texas	William F. Vilas, Wis.	
1888	William H. Barnum, Conn.	Stephen M. White, Calif.	Patrick A. Collins, Mass.	
1892	William F. Harrity, Penn.	William C. Owens, Ky.	William L. Wilson, W.Va.	
1896	James K. Jones, Ark.	John W. Daniel, Va.	Stephen M. White, Calif.	
1900	James K. Jones, Ark.	Charles S. Thomas, Colo.	James D. Richardson, Tenn.	
1904	Thomas Taggart, Ind.	John Sharp Williams, Miss.	Champ Clark, Mo.	
1908	Norman E. Mack, N.Y.	Theodore A. Bell, Calif.	Henry D. Clayton, Ala.	
1912	William F. McCombs, N.Y.	Alton B. Parker, N.Y.	Ollie M. James, Ky.	
1916	Vance C. McCormick, Pa.	Martin H. Glynn, N.Y.	Ollie M. James, Ky.	
1920	George H. White, Ohio	Homer S. Cummings, Conn.	Joseph T. Robinson, Ark.	
1924	Clem Shaver, W.Va.	Pat Harrison, Miss.	Thomas J. Walsh, Mont.	
1928	John J. Raskob, Md.	Claude G. Bowers, Ind.	Joseph T. Robinson, Ark.	
1932	James A. Farley, N.Y.	Alben W. Barkley, Ky.	Thomas J. Walsh, Mont.	
1936	James A. Farley, N.Y.	Alben W. Barkley, Ky.	Joseph T. Robinson, Ark.	Alben W. Barkley, Ky.
1940	Edward J. Flynn, N.Y.	William B. Bankhead, Ala.	Alben W. Barkley, Ky.	William B. Bankhead, Ala.
1944	Robert E. Hannegan, Mo.	Robert S. Kerr, Okla.	Samuel D. Jackson, Ind.	Robert S. Kerr, Okla.
1948	J. Howard McGrath, R.I.	Alben W. Barkley, Ky.	Sam Rayburn, Texas	Alben W. Barkley, Ky.
1952	Stephen A. Mitchell, Ill.	Paul A. Dever, Mass.	Sam Rayburn, Texas	Paul A. Dever, Mass.
1956	Paul M. Butler, Ind.	Frank G. Clement, Tenn.	Sam Rayburn, Texas	Frank Clement, Tenn.
1960	Henry Jackson, Wash.	Frank Church, Idaho	LeRoy Collins, Fla.	Frank Church, Idaho
1964	John M. Bailey, Conn.	John O. Pastore, R.I.	John W. McCormack, Mass.	John O. Pastore, R.I.
1968	Lawrence F. O'Brien, Mass.	Daniel K. Inouye, Hawaii	Carl B. Albert, Okla.	Daniel K. Inouye, Hawaii
1972[1]	Lawrence F. O'Brien, Mass.		Lawrence F. O'Brien, Mass.	Reubin Askew, Fla.
1976	Robert S. Strauss, Texas		Lindy Boggs, La.	John Glenn, Ohio
				Barbara C. Jordan, Texas
1980	John C. White, Texas		Thomas P. O'Neill Jr., Mass.	Morris K. Udall, Ariz.
1984	Charles T. Manatt, Calif.		Martha Layne Collins, Ky.	Mario M. Cuomo, N.Y.
1988	Paul G. Kirk Jr., Mass.		Jim Wright, Texas	Ann W. Richards, Texas
1992	Ronald H. Brown, D.C.		Ann W. Richards, Texas	Bill Bradley, N.J.
				Zell Miller, Ga.
				Barbara C. Jordan, Texas
1996	Donald Fowler, S.C.		Thomas A. Daschle, S.D.	Evan Bayh, Ind.
			Richard A. Gephardt, Mo.	
2000	Joe Andrew, Ind.		Barbara Boxer, Calif.	Harold E. Ford Jr., Tenn.
			Dianne Feinstein, Calif.	

1. A rule change eliminated the position of temporary chair.

the Democratic, was there a rapid growth in presidential primaries. In the mid-1980s some states reverted to the caucus method of delegate selection, but their revival soon abated. A record forty-four primaries were held in 2000, including those in the District of Columbia and Puerto Rico.

In many states participation in the presidential primary is restricted to voters belonging to the party holding the primary. In some states, however, participation by voters outside the party is allowed by state-mandated open primaries, usually with the caveat, though, that the party in which they cast a primary ballot is publicly recorded.

DEMOCRATIC RULES IN THE 1980s AND 1990s

In June 1982 the Democratic National Committee (DNC) adopted several changes in the presidential nominating process recommended by the party's Commission on Presidential Nominations, chaired by Gov. James B. Hunt Jr. of North Carolina. The Hunt Commission, as it came to be known, suggested revisions to increase the power of party regulars and give the convention more freedom to act on its own. It was the fourth time in twelve years that the Democrats, struggling to repair their nominating process without repudiating earlier reforms, had

Republican Conventions, 1856–2000

Year	City	Dates	Presidential nominee	Vice-presidential nominee	No. of pres. ballots
1856	Philadelphia	June 17–19	John C. Fremont	William L. Dayton	2
1860	Chicago	May 16–18	Abraham Lincoln	Hannibal Hamlin	3
1864	Baltimore	June 7–8	Abraham Lincoln	Andrew Johnson	1
1868	Chicago	May 20–21	Ulysses S. Grant	Schuyler Colfax	1
1872	Philadelphia	June 5–6	Ulysses S. Grant	Henry Wilson	1
1876	Cincinnati	June 14–16	Rutherford B. Hayes	William A. Wheeler	7
1880	Chicago	June 2–8	James A. Garfield	Chester A. Arthur	36
1884	Chicago	June 3–6	James G. Blaine	John A. Logan	4
1888	Chicago	June 19–25	Benjamin Harrison	Levi P. Morton	8
1892	Minneapolis	June 7–10	Benjamin Harrison	Whitelaw Reid	1
1896	St. Louis	June 16–18	William McKinley	Garret A. Hobart	1
1900	Philadelphia	June 19–21	William McKinley	Theodore Roosevelt	1
1904	Chicago	June 21–23	Theodore Roosevelt	Charles W. Fairbanks	1
1908	Chicago	June 16–19	William H. Taft	James S. Sherman	1
1912	Chicago	June 18–22	William H. Taft	James S. Sherman Nicholas Murray Butler[1]	1
1916	Chicago	June 7–10	Charles E. Hughes	Charles W. Fairbanks	3
1920	Chicago	June 8–12	Warren G. Harding	Calvin Coolidge	10
1924	Cleveland	June 10–12	Calvin Coolidge	Charles G. Dawes	1
1928	Kansas City	June 12–15	Herbert Hoover	Charles Curtis	1
1932	Chicago	June 14–16	Herbert Hoover	Charles Curtis	1
1936	Cleveland	June 9–12	Alfred M. Landon	Frank Knox	1
1940	Philadelphia	June 24–28	Wendell L. Willkie	Charles L. McNary	6
1944	Chicago	June 26–28	Thomas E. Dewey	John W. Bricker	1
1948	Philadelphia	June 21–25	Thomas E. Dewey	Earl Warren	3
1952	Chicago	July 7–11	Dwight D. Eisenhower	Richard M. Nixon	1
1956	San Francisco	Aug. 20–23	Dwight D. Eisenhower	Richard M. Nixon	1
1960	Chicago	July 25–28	Richard M. Nixon	Henry Cabot Lodge	1
1964	San Francisco	July 13–16	Barry Goldwater	William E. Miller	1
1968	Miami Beach	Aug. 5–8	Richard M. Nixon	Spiro T. Agnew	1
1972	Miami Beach	Aug. 21–23	Richard M. Nixon	Spiro T. Agnew	1
1976	Kansas City	Aug. 16–19	Gerald R. Ford	Robert Dole	1
1980	Detroit	July 14–17	Ronald Reagan	George Bush	1
1984	Dallas	Aug. 20–23	Ronald Reagan	George Bush	1
1988	New Orleans	Aug. 15–18	George Bush	Dan Quayle	1
1992	Houston	Aug. 17–20	George Bush	Dan Quayle	1
1996	San Diego	Aug. 12–15	Robert Dole	Jack Kemp	1
2000	Philadelphia	July 31–Aug. 3	George W. Bush	Richard Cheney	1

1. The 1912 Republican convention nominated James S. Sherman, who died on Oct. 30. The Republican National Committee subsequently selected Nicholas Murray Butler to receive the Republican electoral votes for vice president.

rewritten their party rules. (See box, Changes in Democrats' Nominating Rules, p. 419.)

One major change in the Democrats' rules was the creation of a new group of "superdelegates," party and elected officials who would go to the 1984 convention uncommitted and would cast about 14 percent of the ballots. The DNC also adopted a Hunt Commission proposal to weaken the rule binding delegates to vote for their original presidential preference on the first convention ballot. But the new rule also allowed a presidential candidate to replace any disloyal delegate with a more faithful one.

One of the most significant revisions was the Democrats' decision to relax proportional representation at the convention and end the ban on the "loophole" primary-winner-take-all by district. Proportional representation is the distribution of delegates among candidates to reflect their share of the primary or caucus vote, both statewide and in congressional districts. Mandated by party rules in 1980, it was blamed by some Democrats for the protracted primary fight between President Jimmy Carter and Sen. Edward M. Kennedy of Massachusetts. Because candidates needed only about 20 percent of the vote in most places to qualify for a share of the delegates, Kennedy was able to remain in contention. But while the system kept Kennedy going, it did nothing to help his chances of winning the nomination.

Although the Democrats' 1984 rules permitted states to retain proportional representation, they also allowed states to take advantage of two options that could help a front-running candidate build the momentum to wrap up the nomination early in the year.

One was a winner-take-more system. States could elect to keep proportional representation but adopt a winner bonus plan that would award the top vote-getter in each district one extra delegate.

The other option was a return to the loophole primary, which party rules outlawed in 1980 (with exemptions allowing Illinois and West Virginia to retain their loophole voting systems). In the loophole states, voters balloted directly for dele-

Chief Officers and Keynote Speakers at Republican National Conventions, 1856–2000

Year	Chair national committee	Temporary chair	Permanent chair	Keynote speaker
1856	Edwin D. Morgan, N.Y.	Robert Emmet, N.Y.	Henry S. Lane, Ind.	
1860	Edwin D. Morgan, N.Y.	David Wilmot, Pa.	George Ashmun, Mass.	
1864	Edwin D. Morgan, N.Y.	Robert J. Breckinridge, Ky.	William Dennison, Ohio	
1868	Marcus L. Ward, N.J.	Carl Schurz, Mo.	Joseph R. Hawley, Conn.	
1872	William Claflin, Mass.	Morton McMichael, Pa.	Thomas Settle, N.C.	
1876	Edwin D. Morgan, N.Y.	Theodore M. Pomeroy, N.Y.	Edward McPherson, Pa.	
1880	J. Donald Cameron, Pa.	George F. Hoar, Mass.	George F. Hoar, Mass.	
1884	Dwight M. Sabin, Minn.	John R. Lynch, Miss.	John B. Henderson, Mo.	
1888	B.F. Jones, Pa.	John M. Thurston, Neb.	Morris M. Estee, Calif.	
1892	James S. Clarkson, Iowa	J. Sloat Fassett, N.Y.	William McKinley Jr., Ohio	
1896	Thomas H. Carter, Mont.	Charles W. Fairbanks, Ind.	John M. Thurston, Neb.	
1900	Marcus A. Hanna, Ohio	Edward O. Wolcott, Colo.	Henry Cabot Lodge, Mass.	
1904	Henry C. Payne, Wis.	Elihu Root, N.Y.	Joseph G. Cannon, Ill.	
1908	Harry S. New, Ind.	Julius C. Burrows, Mich.	Henry Cabot Lodge, Mass.	
1912	Victor Rosewater, Neb.	Elihu Root, N.Y.	Elihu Root, N.Y.	
1916	Charles D. Hilles, N.Y.	Warren G. Harding, Ohio	Warren G. Harding, Ohio	
1920	Will H. Hays, Ind.	Henry Cabot Lodge, Mass.	Henry Cabot Lodge, Mass.	Henry Cabot Lodge, Mass.
1924	John T. Adams, Iowa	Theodore E. Burton, Ohio	Frank W. Mortdell, Wyo.	
1928	William M. Butler, Mass.	Simeon D. Fess, Ohio	George H. Moses, N.H.	
1932	Simeon D. Fess, Ohio	L. J. Dickinson, Iowa	Bertrand H. Snell, N.Y.	
1936	Henry P. Fletcher, Pa.	Frederick Steiwer, Ore.	Bertrand H. Snell, N.Y.	Frederick Steiwer, Ore.
1940	John Hamilton, Kan.	Harold E. Stassen, Minn.	Joseph W. Martin Jr., Mass.	Harold E. Stassen, Minn.
1944	Harrison E. Spangler, Iowa	Earl Warren, Calif.	Joseph W. Martin Jr., Mass.	Earl Warren, Calif.
1948	Carroll Reece, Tenn.	Dwight H. Green, Ill.	Joseph W. Martin Jr., Mass.	Dwight H. Green, Ill.
1952	Guy George Gabrielson, N.J.	Walter S. Hallanan, W.Va.	Joseph W. Martin Jr., Mass.	Douglas MacArthur
1956	Leonard W. Hall, N.Y.	William F. Knowland, Calif.	Joseph W. Martin Jr., Mass.	Arthur B. Langlie, Wash.
1960	Thruston B. Morton. Ky.	Cecil H. Underwood, W.Va.	Charles A. Halleck, Ind.	Walter H. Judd, Minn.
1964	William E. Miller, N.Y.	Mark O. Hatfield, Ore.	Thruston B. Morton, Ky.	Mark O. Hatfield, Ore.
1968	Ray C. Bliss, Ohio	Edward W. Brooke, Mass.	Gerald R. Ford, Mich.	Daniel J. Evans, Wash.
1972	Robert Dole, Kan.	Ronald Reagan, Calif.	Gerald R. Ford, Mich.	Richard G. Lugar, Ind. Anne L. Armstrong, Texas
1976	Mary Louise Smith, Iowa	Robert Dole, Kan.	John J. Rhodes, Ariz.	Howard H. Baker Jr., Tenn.
1980	Bill Brock, Tenn.	Nancy Landon Kassebaum, Kan.	John J. Rhodes, Ariz.	Guy Vander Jagt, Mich.
1984	Frank J. Fahrenkopf Jr., Nev.	Howard H. Baker Jr., Tenn.	Robert H. Michel, Ill.	Katherine Ortega, N.M.
1988	Lee Atwater, S.C.	Elizabeth Hanford Dole, N.C.	Robert H. Michel, Ill.	Thomas H. Kean, N.J.
1992	Richard N. Bond, N.Y.	Kay Bailey Hutchison, Texas	Robert H. Michel, Ill.	Phil Gramm, Texas
1996	Haley Barbour, Miss.	Christine Todd Whitman, N.J. George W. Bush, Texas	Newt Gingrich, Ga.	Susan Molinari, N.Y.
2000	Jim Nicholson, Colo.	Trent Lott, Miss.	J. Dennis Hastert, Ill.	Colin Powell, D.C.

gates, with each delegate candidate identified by presidential preference. Sometimes several presidential contenders would win at least a fraction of the delegates in a given district, but the most common result is a sweep by the presidential front-runner, even if he has less than an absolute majority. Loophole primaries aid the building of a consensus behind the front-runner, while still giving other candidates a chance to inject themselves back into the race by winning a major loophole state decisively.

The DNC retained the delegate-selection season adopted in 1978, a three-month period stretching from the second Tuesday in March to the second Tuesday in June. But, in an effort to reduce the growing influence of early states in the nominating process, the Democrats required Iowa and New Hampshire to move their highly publicized elections to late winter. Party rules maintained the privileged status of Iowa and New Hampshire before other states but mandated that their initial nominating rounds be held only eight days apart in 1984. Five weeks had intervened between the Iowa caucuses and New Hampshire primary in 1980.

The DNC also retained rules requiring primary states to set candidate filing deadlines thirty to ninety days before the election and limiting participation in the delegate selection process to Democrats only. This last rule eliminated cross-over primaries where voters could participate in the Democratic primary without designating their party affiliation. African Americans and Hispanics won continued endorsement of affirmative action in the new party rules. Women gained renewed support for the equal division rule, which required state delegations at the national convention to be divided equally between men and women.

The Democratic Party's 1988 presidential nominating process remained basically the same as that used in 1984. The rules adopted by the national committee included only minor modifications suggested by the party's rules review panel, the Fairness Commission.

The bloc of uncommitted party and elected officials (superdelegates) was expanded slightly to 16 percent and rearranged to reserve more convention seats for members of Congress,

Political Party Organization and Rules

Political parties in the United States are loosely organized. Anyone of voting age can become a party member simply by signing up. Millions of Americans do just that, while many others shun formal partisan affiliations but think of themselves as Democrats or Republicans nonetheless.

Cowboy humorist Will Rogers used to get laughs by saying, "I am not a member of any organized party. I am a Democrat." But the same line could also be applied to the Republicans, even if they sometimes seemed to be less disorganized than their major rivals.

Both parties have the same fluidity of membership, with the rolls open to independents as well as to supporters of the other party. Formally registering as a Democrat or Republican has the advantage of permitting the member to participate in the party's nominating primaries and caucuses. Most states bar crossover voting in the other party's elections, largely for fear that Democrats would try to nominate the weakest Republican candidates, and vice versa.

There is little evidence, however, that most rank-and-file voters are as concerned about parties as such. In recent elections, roughly three times as many voters have participated in the presidential election as have taken part in the parties' presidential primaries. And in 1995, for the first time ever, a plurality of voters surveyed by the Gallup poll identified themselves as "other" (36 percent) rather than as Republican or Democratic (32 percent each).

Party Structure

Loose though it is, each major party has an organizational structure—a necessity for continuity as an institution, fund raising, and conducting election campaigns. Congress has officially recognized the role of the parties and public funding is provided for their presidential nominating conventions. Some states also provide funding for election campaigns.

Beginning at the precinct or neighborhood level, a series of progressively larger units make up the national organization. Next up the line are city, county, legislative district, congressional district and, just below the national committee, the state organizations.

There is no "chain of command." Each unit is more or less independent. The national chair exerts influence mainly through prestige and force of personality, rather than through any specified powers. The national committee elects the chair, but the president actually designates the chair of the party controlling the White House.

With approximately 450 members, the DNC is more than twice the size of the 165-member Republican National Committee. Roughly 55 members make up the DNC executive committee—a mix of party officers, regional representatives, "at-large" members elected by the DNC, and others representing Democratic affiliates.

Since 1984, the Democrats have occupied their $6.4 million national headquarters at 430 South Capitol Street, S.E., in Washington. Previous locations in New York and Washington (including the Watergate offices burglarized by the Republicans in 1972) were rented.

Besides the chair, eight other DNC officers are specified in the party charter and elected by the national committee: five vice chairs, treasurer, secretary, and national finance chair. Party organizations in the states and territories elect their DNC members for four-year terms, ending with the next convention. They are the state chair and the next highest-ranking member of the opposite sex. Another 200 votes are distributed on a population basis, with each state or territory guaranteed at least two, equally divided among men and women.

Other DNC members are two U.S. senators, two House members, two members of the College Democrats, and three representatives each from among Democratic governors, mayors, state legislators, county officials, municipal officials, Young Democrats, and the National Federation of Democratic Women, as well as two representatives each from among lieutenant governors, secretaries of state and state treasurers, and several dozen at-large members.

The RNC elects at least a dozen officers for two-year terms—the chair, cochair, eight vice chairs, secretary, treasurer, and any other officer deemed necessary. The party owns its national headquarters at 310 First Street, S.E., in Washington. The Republicans maintain a large field staff and generally have more money than the Democrats to dispense to campaigns.

Because of their large sizes, the full national committees seldom meet more than a few times during the four years between the national conventions, which are the parties' supreme governing bodies. In both parties, the day-to-day work of the national organization is done by the chair and the headquarters staff, under direction of the executive committee.

Operating Rules

The most important rules of both major parties deal largely with the selection of delegates to the quadrennial national nominating conventions. While the Democrats in the 1970s and 1980s experimented widely with these rules, mainly to give more representation to women, youth and minorities, Republicans left their rules largely unchanged until the 1990s. (*GOP Primary Rules, box, p. 420.*)

Beginning with reforms proposed by Sen. George S. McGovern of South Dakota, who won the nomination himself in 1972, the Democratic Party attempted to "democratize" the process. A succession of commissions headed by Barbara A. Mikulski of Maryland (1972), Morley Winograd of Michigan (1976), Gov. James B. Hunt Jr. of North Carolina (1980), and Donald L. Fowler of South Carolina (1984), succeeded in gaining equal representation for women, requiring proportional representation of delegates among primary vote-getters and giving convention votes to "superdelegate" party and elected officials.

For the 1992 convention, Democrats for the first time in two decades did not have a special commission intensively examining the nominating process. And since then, the Democratic Party has left its rules largely unchanged. (*Democratic Rules in the 1980s and 1990s, p. 415.*)

Changes in Democrats' Nominating Rules

Between 1972 and 1992 Democrats tinkered with their nominating rules every four years, producing a system that, if not better than before, was always different. Since 1992, however, the party left its rules basically unchanged. The following chart shows the ebb and flow of the Democratic Party's rules changes, with a "✔" indicating the years these major rules were in effect.

	1972	1976	1980	1984	1988	1992	1996	2000
Timing: Restrict delegate-selection events to a three-month period (the "window").			✔	✔	✔	✔	✔	✔
Conditions of Participation: Restrict participation in delegate-selection events to voters who declare themselves Democrats.		✔	✔	✔	✔	✔	✔	✔
Proportional Representation: Ban all types of winner-take-all contests.				✔		✔	✔	✔
Ban all types of winner-reward contests (where winner receives extra delegates).						✔	✔	✔
Delegate Loyalty: Give candidates the right to approve delegates identifying with their candidacy.		✔	✔	✔	✔	✔	✔	✔
Bind delegates to vote for their original presidential preference at convention on first ballot.			✔					
Party and Elected Officials: Expand each delegation to include pledged party and elected officials.			✔	✔	✔	✔	✔	✔
Further expand each delegation to include unpledged party and elected officials ("superdelegates").				✔	✔	✔	✔	✔
Demographic Representation: Encourage participation and representation of minorities and historically underrepresented groups (affirmative action).			✔	✔	✔	✔	✔	✔
Require delegations to be equally divided between men and women.			✔	✔	✔	✔	✔	✔

governors, and the DNC; the rules restricting participation in Democratic primaries and caucuses to Democrats only was relaxed so the open primaries in Wisconsin and Montana could be conducted with the approval of the national party; and the share of the vote a candidate needed to win in a primary or caucus to qualify for delegates was lowered from the 20 percent level used in most places in 1984 to 15 percent.

Only the rule regarding the 15 percent "threshold" spawned much debate during the rules-writing process, and though the discussion of the issue seldom was acrimonious, it did reveal a yawning chasm in the party on what the proper role of the national convention should be.

Most party leaders, including DNC Chairman Paul G. Kirk Jr., wanted a threshold of at least 15 percent because they thought it would help steadily shrink the field of presidential candidates during the primary and caucus season and ensure that the convention would be a "ratifying" body that confirmed the choice of the party's voters.

But civil rights leader and presidential candidate Jesse L. Jackson saw it differently, as did a cadre of liberal activists. They wanted a convention that was more "deliberative," and they complained that getting one was virtually impossible under the system as it existed because it discriminated against long-shot candidates and produced an artificial consensus behind one candidate.

Most Democratic leaders were satisfied with the way the nominating process operated in 1984, and they felt it would be a disaster for the party to go through a free-wheeling, multiballot convention. Not since 1952—at the beginning of the television age—has a national party taken more than one ballot to nominate its presidential candidate.

At the DNC meeting where the new rules were approved, some African-American committee members joined with a few white liberal activists in proposing to eliminate the 15 percent threshold altogether. The proposal was rejected by voice vote. A second proposal to lower the threshold to 10 percent was defeated 92 to 178.

In 1990 the DNC made two basic changes that directly affected the delegate-selection process for the 1992 convention. One change moved forward the officially sanctioned start of the presidential primary season by one week, from the second Tuesday in March to the first. This was an invitation to California to

GOP Primary Rules

The Republican Party, wrote political scientist Nelson W. Polsby, "in many respects remains unreformed." Virtually anything has been permitted in the nominating process so long as it was not baldly discriminatory. And that has been the way GOP leaders have wanted it—at least until the past few years.

While the Democratic Party has a tightly crafted, nationalized set of rules that govern its nominating process, Republicans historically have shunned control by a central authority. The individual GOP state parties have been given wide latitude to determine how their delegates are selected, with guidelines from the national party kept to a minimum.

The result has been a nominating procedure with a simplicity and continuity that the Democrats lack. A more homogeneous party than the Democrats, the Republicans until the late 1990s had not felt the pressure for rules reform that had engulfed the Democrats as long as the GOP was winning presidential elections. No major rules changes were made by the Republicans between 1974 and 1996.

For the year 2000, though, the Republicans instituted bonus delegates for those states that chose their delegates to the national convention after the middle of March. The quickness of the 1996 decision convinced many party leaders that a longer selection process would be more desirable.

At the 2000 GOP convention, the party voted to eliminate the bonus delegates but added automatic "superdelegate" seats for Republican National Committee members at the 2004 convention as well as increasing the base delegate vote total of every state.

Yet even in earlier years when Republicans had a laissez faire approach to their nominating process, they were not able to operate totally in their own world. Campaign finance laws and the rising influence of mass media affected Republicans as well as Democrats. In states where legislatures accommodated the Democrats and created a presidential primary, the Republicans were dragged along.

The Republican Party held twenty primaries in 1972, but during the next twenty-four years the number of primaries has steadily increased. In 2000 the party held a record forty-four primaries, including those in the District of Columbia and Puerto Rico (the Democrats' record was forty primaries in 1992 and 2000). Primaries helped to select roughly 85 percent of delegates to the GOP convention in 2000.

The Democrats required all states in 1992 and thereafter to divide their publicly elected delegates proportionally among candidates who drew at least 15 percent of the primary or caucus vote.

The Democratic Party also continued to steadily increase the number of superdelegates, expanding their number to 802 for the 2000 convention (or 18 percent of the 4,339 delegate votes).

During the 1972–1996 period the Republican Party followed an entirely different approach and made few changes in its nominating rules. While the Democratic rules were revised somewhat for each presidential cycle, the GOP rules remained stable. For the year 2000, however, the Republicans changed their minds on the desirability of deciding the nomination contest by March or April; they provided a bonus for those states that choose their delegates to the 2000 GOP convention after the ides of March.

Before the 2000 convention was even held, though, Republicans were considering even more controversial solutions to spread out the primary calendar, which had become congested with events in February and March. The so-called "Delaware Plan" would have put the smallest states at the beginning of the nominating season in 2004, the largest states at the end. But after winning the approval of the Republican National Committee (RNC) at its preconvention meeting, the proposal was killed by the convention rules committee at the behest of the party standard-bearer, Gov. George W. Bush of Texas, who wanted to remove any semblance of controversy.

Republicans, though, did make several changes in delegate-selection rules for 2004, including elimination of the bonus delegates and creation of automatic "superdelegate" seats for members of the RNC. (See box, GOP Primary Rules, this page.)

CREDENTIALS DISPUTES

Before the opening of a convention the national committee compiles a temporary roll of delegates. The roll is referred to the convention's credentials committee, which holds hearings on the challenges and makes recommendations to the convention, the final arbiter of all disputes.

Some of the most bitter convention battles have concerned the seating of contested delegations. In the twentieth century most of the heated credentials fights have concerned delegations from the South. In the Republican Party the challenges focused on the power of the Republican state organizations to dictate the selection of delegates.

The issue was hottest in 1912 and 1952, when the party throughout most of the South was a skeletal structure whose power was restricted largely to selection of convention delegates. Within the Democratic Party the question of southern credentials emerged after World War II on the volatile issues of civil rights and party loyalty. Important credentials challenges on these issues occurred at the 1948, 1952, 1964, and 1968 Democratic conventions.

There were numerous credentials challenges at the 1972 Democratic convention, but, unlike those at its immediate predecessors, the challenges involved delegations from across the

move its 1992 primary from June to March 3. (California declined in 1992, but in 1996 moved its primary from June to late March. This was part of a desire by both parties in 1992 to speed up the nominating contest and settle it by April or early May, so that united parties could organize their conventions with eyes focused on the November election.) The second change banned winner-reward systems, which gave extra delegates to the winner of a primary or caucus. Fifteen states had used some form of winner-reward system in 1988.

nation and focused on violations of the party's newly adopted guidelines.

After their 1952 credentials battle, the Republicans established a contest committee within the national committee to review credentials challenges before the convention. After their divisive 1968 convention the Democrats also created a formal credentials procedure to review all challenges before the opening of the convention.

Equally important to the settlement of credentials challenges are the rules under which the convention operates. The Republican Party adopts a completely new set of rules at every convention. Although large portions of the existing rules are enacted each time, general revision is always possible.

After its 1968 convention the Democratic Party set out to reform itself and the convention system. The Commission on Rules and the Commission on Party Structure and Delegate Selection, both created by the 1968 convention, proposed many changes that were accepted by the national committee. As a result, a formal set of rules was adopted for the first time at the party's 1972 convention.

Controversial Rules

Although it did not have a formal set of rules before 1972, the Democratic Party had long operated with two controversial rules never used by the Republicans: the unit rule and the two-thirds nominating rule. The unit rule enabled the majority of a delegation, if authorized by its state party, to cast the entire vote of the delegation for one candidate or position. In use since the earliest Democratic conventions, the unit rule was abolished by the 1968 convention.

From their first convention in 1832 until the 1936 convention, the Democrats employed the two-thirds nominating rule, which required any candidate for president or vice president to win not just a simple majority but a two-thirds majority. Viewed as a boon to the South since it allowed that region a virtual veto power over any possible nominee, the rule was abolished with the stipulation that the South would receive an increased vote allocation at later conventions.

In its century of use the two-thirds rule frequently produced protracted, multiballot conventions, often giving the Democrats a degree of turbulence the Republicans, requiring only a simple majority, did not have. Between 1832 and 1932, seven Democratic conventions took more than ten ballots to select a presidential candidate. In contrast, in their entire convention history, the Republicans have had just one convention that required more than ten ballots to select a presidential candidate. *(See box, Democrats' Two-Thirds Rule, this page.)*

One controversy that surfaced during the 1980 Democratic Party convention concerned a rule that bound delegates to vote on the first ballot for the candidates under whose banner they had been elected. Supporters of Sen. Ted Kennedy had devoted their energy to prying the nomination from incumbent President Carter by defeating that rule. But the final tally showed 1,936.42 delegates favoring the binding rule and 1,390.58 opposing it. Passage of the binding rule ensured Carter's renomina-

---

Democrats' Two-Thirds Rule

At their first convention in 1832 the Democrats adopted a rule requiring a two-thirds majority for nomination. Two presidential candidates—Martin Van Buren in 1844 and Champ Clark in 1912—received majorities but failed to attain the two-thirds requirement.

On the first ballot in 1844 Van Buren received 146 of the 266 convention votes, 54.9 percent of the total. His total fell under a simple majority on succeeding roll calls and on the ninth ballot the nomination went to a dark-horse candidate, former governor James K. Polk of Tennessee.

In 1912 from the tenth through the sixteenth ballots Clark recorded a simple majority. He reached his peak on the tenth ballot, receiving 556 of the 1,094 convention votes, 50.8 percent of the total. The nomination, however, ultimately went to New Jersey governor Woodrow Wilson, who was selected on the forty-sixth ballot.

At their 1936 convention the Democrats voted to end the requirement for a two-thirds majority for nomination.

---

tion, and shortly after the vote Kennedy announced that his name would not be placed in nomination.

Convention Officers

Credentials, rules, and platform are three of the major convention committees.

Within the Republican Party, though, the committee on permanent organization ratifies the slate of convention officials. In the Democratic Party, this function is performed by the rules committee.

In both the Democratic and Republican parties, the presiding officer during the bulk of the convention is the permanent chairman. For much of the postwar period, the position has gone to the party's leader in the House of Representatives, particularly at the GOP convention. *(See table, National Party Chairs, 1848–2001, p. 426.)*

However, this loose precedent was broken in the Democratic Party by a rule adopted at the 1972 convention requiring that the presiding officer position alternate every four years between the sexes.

Party Platforms

The adoption of a party platform is one of the principal functions of a convention. The platform committee is charged with the responsibility of writing a party platform to be presented to the convention for its approval.

The main challenge before the platform committee has traditionally been to write a platform all party candidates can use in their campaigns. For this reason, platforms often fit the description given them by Wendell L. Willkie, Republican presidential candidate in 1940: "fusions of ambiguity."

Notable Credentials Fights

1848, Democratic. Two rival New York state factions, known as the Barnburners and the Hunkers, sent separate delegations. By a vote of 126 to 125, the convention decided to seat both delegations and split New York's vote between them. This compromise suited neither faction: the Barnburners bolted the convention; the Hunkers remained but refused to vote.

1860, Democratic. Dissatisfaction with the slavery plank in the party platform spurred a walkout by several dozen southern delegates from the Charleston convention. When the tumultuous convention reconvened in Baltimore six weeks later, a credentials controversy developed on the status of the bolting delegates. The majority report of the credentials committee recommended that the delegates in question, except those from Alabama and Louisiana, be reseated. The minority report recommended that a larger majority of the withdrawing Charleston delegates be allowed to return. The minority report was defeated, 100½ to 150, prompting a walkout by the majority of delegates from nine states.

1880, Republican. Factions for and against the candidacy of former president Ulysses S. Grant clashed on the credentials of the Illinois delegation. By a margin of 387 to 353, the convention rejected a minority report that proposed seating pro-Grant delegates elected at the state convention over other delegates elected at a congressional district caucus. Three other votes were taken on disputed credentials from different Illinois districts, but all were decided in favor of the anti-Grant forces by a similar margin. The votes indicated the weakness of the Grant candidacy. The nomination went to a dark-horse candidate, Rep. James A. Garfield of Ohio, on the thirty-sixth ballot.

1912, Republican. The furious struggle between President William Howard Taft and Theodore Roosevelt for the presidential nomination centered on credentials. The Roosevelt forces brought seventy-two delegate challenges to the floor of the convention, but the test of strength between the two candidates came on a procedural motion. By a vote of 567 to 507, the convention tabled a motion presented by the Roosevelt forces barring any of the delegates under challenge from voting on any of the credentials contests. This procedural vote clearly indicated Taft's control of the convention. All the credentials cases were settled in favor of the Taft delegates, and the presidential nomination ultimately went to the incumbent president.

1932, Democratic. Two delegations favorable to the front-runner for the presidential nomination, Franklin D. Roosevelt, came under challenge. However, in a show of strength, the Roosevelt forces won both contests: seating a Louisiana delegation headed by Sen. Huey P. Long by a vote of 638¾ to 514¼ and a Roosevelt delegation from Minnesota by an even wider margin, 658¼ to 492¾. Roosevelt won the nomination on the fourth ballot.

1952, Democratic. The refusal of three southern states—Louisiana, South Carolina, and Virginia—to agree to a party loyalty pledge brought their credentials into question. The Virginia delegation argued that the problem prompting the loyalty pledge was covered by state law. By a vote of 650½ to 518, the convention approved the seating of the Virginia delegation. After Louisiana and South Carolina took positions similar to that of Virginia, they were seated by a voice vote.

1952, Republican. Sixty-eight delegates from three southern states (Georgia, Louisiana, and Texas) were the focal point of the fight for the presidential nomination between Gen. Dwight D. Eisenhower and Sen. Robert A. Taft of Ohio. The national committee, controlled by forces favorable to Taft, had voted to seat delegations friendly to the Ohio senator from these three states. But by a vote of 607 to 531 the convention seated the Georgia delegation favorable to Eisenhower. It seated the Eisenhower delegates from Louisiana and Texas without roll calls. The general went on to win the presidential nomination on the first ballot.

1968, Democratic. A struggle between the anti–Vietnam War forces, led by Sen. Eugene J. McCarthy of Minnesota, and the party regulars, headed by Vice President Hubert H. Humphrey, dominated the seventeen cases considered by the credentials committee. Three of the cases, involving the Texas, Georgia, and Alabama delegations, required roll calls on the convention floor. All were won by the Humphrey forces. By a vote of 1,368¼ to 956¾, the regular Texas delegation headed by Gov. John B. Connally was seated. A minority report to seat the entire Georgia delegation led by black leader Julian Bond was defeated, 1,043.55 to 1,415.45. And a minority report to seat a McCarthy-backed, largely black delegation from Alabama was also rejected, 880¾ to 1,607. Humphrey, having shown his strength during the credentials contests, went on to win an easy first ballot nomination.

1972, Democratic. The first test of strength at the convention between South Dakota senator George McGovern's delegates and party regulars came over credentials. Key challenges brought to the convention floor concerned the South Carolina, California and Illinois delegations. The South Carolina challenge was brought by the National Women's Political Caucus in response to alleged underrepresentation of women in the delegation. Although the caucus' position was supposedly supported by the McGovern camp, votes were withheld to avoid jeopardizing McGovern's chances of winning the important California contest. The caucus' challenge lost 1,429.05 to 1,555.75. The California challenge was of crucial importance to McGovern, since it involved 151 delegates initially won by the South Dakota senator in the state's winner-take-all primary, but stripped from him by the credentials committee. By a vote of 1,618.28 to 1,238.22, McGovern regained the contested delegates, thereby nailing down his nomination. With victory in hand, the dominant McGovern camp sought a compromise on the Illinois case, which pitted a delegation headed by Chicago's powerful mayor Richard Daley against an insurgent delegation composed of party reformers. Compromise was unattainable and with the bulk of McGovern delegates voting for the reformers, a minority report to seat the Daley delegates was rejected.

Major Platform Fights

1860, Democratic. A minority report on the slavery plank, stating that the decision on allowing slavery in the territories should be left to the Supreme Court, was approved, 165 to 138. The majority report (favored by the South) declared that no government—local, state, or federal—could outlaw slavery in the territories. The acceptance of the minority report precipitated a walkout by several dozen southern delegates and the eventual sectional split in the party.

1896, Democratic. The monetary plank of the platform committee, favoring free and unlimited coinage of silver at a ratio of 16 to 1 with gold, was accepted by the convention, which defeated a proposed gold plank, 626 to 303. During debate William Jennings Bryan made his famous "Cross of Gold" speech supporting the platform committee plank, bringing him to the attention of the convention and resulting in his nomination for president.

1908, Republican. A minority report, proposing a substitute platform, was presented by Sen. Robert M. La Follette of Wisconsin. Minority proposals included increased antitrust activities, enactment of a law requiring publication of campaign expenditures and popular election of senators. All the proposed planks were defeated by wide margins; the closest vote, on direct election of senators, was 114 for, 866 against.

1924, Democratic. A minority plank was presented that condemned the activities of the Ku Klux Klan, then enjoying a resurgence in the South and some states in the Midwest. The plank was defeated $542^7/_{20}$ to $543^3/_{20}$, the closest vote in Democratic convention history.

1932, Republican. A minority plank favoring repeal of the Eighteenth Amendment (Prohibition) in favor of a state-option arrangement was defeated, $460^2/_9$ to $690^{19}/_{36}$.

1948, Democratic. An amendment to the platform, strengthening the civil rights plank by guaranteeing full and equal political participation, equal employment opportunity, personal security, and equal treatment in the military service, was accepted, $651^1/_2$ to $582^1/_2$.

1964, Republican. An amendment offered by Sen. Hugh Scott of Pennsylvania to strengthen the civil rights plank by including voting guarantees in state as well as in federal elections and by eliminating job bias was defeated, 409 to 897.

1968, Democratic. A minority report on Vietnam called for cessation of the bombing of North Vietnam, halting of offensive and search-and-destroy missions by American combat units, a negotiated withdrawal of American troops, and establishment of a coalition government in South Vietnam. It was defeated, $1,041^1/_4$ to $1,567^3/_4$.

1972, Democratic. By a vote of 1,852.86 to 999.34, the convention rejected a minority report proposing a government guaranteed annual income of $6,500 for a family of four. By a vote of 1,101.37 to 1,572.80, a women's rights plank supporting abortion rights was defeated.

1980, Democratic. The platform battle, one of the longest in party history, pitted President Jimmy Carter against his persistent rival, Sen. Edward M. Kennedy of Massachusetts. Stretching over seventeen hours, the debate focused on Kennedy's economics plank, which finally was defeated by a voice vote. Yet Carter was forced to concede on so many specific points, including Kennedy's $12 billion antirecession jobs programs, that the final document bore little resemblance to the draft initially drawn up by Carter's operatives.

1992, Democratic. A tax fairness plank offered by former senator Paul E. Tsongas of Massachusetts was defeated by a vote of 953 to 2,287. The plank called for a delay in any middle-class tax cut and tax credit for families with children until the deficit was under control.

Despite the best efforts of platform-builders to resolve their differences in the comparative privacy of the committee room, they sometimes encounter so controversial a subject that it cannot be compromised. Under these conditions dissident committee members often submit a minority report to the convention floor. Open floor fights are not unusual and, like credentials battles, often reflect the strength of the various candidates.

When the party has an incumbent president, the platform often is drafted in the White House or at least has the approval of the president. Rarely does a party adopt a platform that is critical of an incumbent president of the same party. When Democratic delegates at their 1896 convention, inspired by William Jennings Bryan's "Cross of Gold" speech, repudiated President Grover Cleveland and his support for a gold standard for hard currency, and nominated Bryan for president on a "free silver" platform, they signaled a major sea change in American politics. A similar change took place in 1948, when Democratic delegates led by Mayor Hubert Humphrey of Minneapolis overturned a recommendation by the platform committee and precipitated a walkout of southern delegates by adopting a strong civil rights plank. Although overridden, President Harry S. Truman accepted the Humphrey plank—and won with it.

The first platform was adopted by the Democrats in 1840. It was a short document, fewer than 1,000 words. Since then the platforms with few exceptions have grown longer and longer, covering more issues and appealing to more and more interest groups. One of the exceptions to the growth trend was the 4,500-word Democratic platform of 1988—about one-tenth the length of the 1984 platform. But by 2000 the Democrats' platform had grown again, to more than 24,000 words, compared with about 33,000 words in its Republican counterpart.

The 1996 GOP platform was characterized by hard-line conservative stands on abortion and other social issues. Sen. Robert Dole, the party's nominee, sought to soften its stance and appeal to more middle-road nonparty voters by giving prime time convention speaking slots to more moderate Republicans who pub-

Third Parties Usually Fade Rapidly

Most third-party movements are like shooting stars, shining brightly in one election and then quickly disappearing. In the last century and a half, eleven third parties—plus independents John B. Anderson in 1980 and Ross Perot in 1992—have drawn at least 5 percent of the popular vote in a presidential election.

As of 2000 not one of the third parties was able to maintain its foothold in the electoral process. Four had disappeared by the next election, five others drew a smaller vote total, and two merged with one of the major parties. The Reform Party con-

firmed this pattern in 2000 as its candidate Pat Buchanan received less than 1 percent of the popular vote that year.

Each of these significant third parties, except the Socialists in 1912, made its best showing in its first election. (The Socialists, led by Eugene V. Debs, first ran in 1900, winning just 0.62 percent of the vote.) The following chart lists each party's presidential candidate and the percentage of the vote the party received in its most successful race and in the following election. A dash (–) indicates that the party had disappeared.

Party (candidate)	Year	Percentage of vote	Next election
Anti-Mason (William Wirt)	1832	7.8%	endorsed Whig
Free Soil (Martin Van Buren)	1848	10.1	4.9%
Whig-American (Millard Fillmore)	1856	21.5	–
Southern Democrats (John C. Breckinridge)	1860	18.1	–
Constitutional Union (John Bell)	1860	12.6	–
Populist (James B. Weaver)	1892	8.5	endorsed Democrat
Progressive (Bull Moose) (Theodore Roosevelt)	1912	27.4	0.2
Socialist (Eugene V. Debs)	1912	6.0	3.2
Progressive (Robert M. La Follette)	1924	16.6	–
American Independent (George C. Wallace)	1968	13.5	1.4
John B. Anderson	1980	6.6	endorsed Democrat
Ross Perot	1992	18.9	created Reform Party
Reform Party (Ross Perot)	1996	8.5	0.4

licly expressed disapproval with some of the platform, while affirming their support for a GOP victory in November.

THIRD PARTIES: RADICAL IDEAS

Throughout American history, many daring and controversial political platforms adopted by third parties have been rejected as too radical by the major parties. Yet many of these proposals later have won popular acceptance and have made their way into the major party platforms—and into law. Ideas such as the abolition of slavery, prohibition, the graduated income tax, the popular election of senators, women's suffrage, minimum wages, Social Security, and the eighteen-year-old vote were advocated by Populists, Progressives, and other third parties long before they were finally accepted by the nation as a whole.

The radical third parties and their platforms have been anathema to the established wisdom of the day, denounced as impractical, dangerous, destructive of moral virtues and even traitorous. They have been anti-establishment and more far-

reaching in their proposed solutions to problems than the major parties have dared to be.

MAJOR PARTIES: BROADER APPEAL

In contrast with the third parties, Democrats and Republicans traditionally have been much more cautious against adopting radical platform planks. Trying to appeal to a broad range of voters, the two major parties have tended to compromise differences or to reject controversial platform planks.

The Democratic Party has been more ready than the Republicans to adopt once-radical ideas, but there is usually a considerable time lag between their origin in third parties and their eventual adoption in Democratic platforms. For example, while the Democrats by 1912 had adopted many of the Populist planks of the 1890s, the Bull Moose Progressives of that year already were way ahead of them in proposals for social legislation. Not until 1932 were many of the 1912 Progressive planks adopted by the Democrats.

Chief Officers at Other National Party Conventions, 1831–1892

Year	Party	Temporary chair	Chair
1831	Anti-Masonic		John C. Spencer, N.Y.
1831	National Republican	Abner Lacock, Pa.	James Barbour, Va.
1839	Whig	Isaac Bates, Mass.	James Barbour, Va.
1844	Whig	Andrew F. Hopkins, Ala.	Ambrose Spencer, N.Y.
1848	Whig	John A. Collier, N.Y.	John M. Morehead, N.C.
1852	Whig	George C. Evans, Maine	John G. Chapman, Md.
1843	Liberty		Leicester King
1848	Free Soiler		Charles Francis Adams, Mass.
1852	Free Soiler (Free Democrats)		Henry Wilson, Mass.
1856	American (Know-Nothing)		Ephraim Marsh
1860	Southern Democrat (Breckinridge Factor)		Caleb Cushing, Mass.
1860	Constitutional Union		Washington Hunt, N.Y.
1872	Liberal Republican	Stanley Matthews, Ohio	Carl Schurz, Mo.
1880	Greenback	Gilbert De La Matyr, Ind.	Richard Trevellick, Mich.
1888	Prohibition	H. A. Delano, Conn.	John P. St. John, Kans.
1892	Prohibition	John P. St. John, Kans.	Eli Ritter, Ind.
1892	People's (Populist)	C. H. Ellington, Ga.	H. L. Loricks, S.D.

Similarly, it was not until the 1960s that Democratic platforms incorporated many of the more far-reaching proposals originally put forward by the 1948 Progressive Party in that year.

Filling Vacancies

Starting with the Democratic convention of 1848, and the Republican Party's first national organizing meeting in 1856, both major parties have elected national committees to run the day-to-day business of the parties between conventions.

Since their beginning, one of the most important functions of national committees has been to replace a candidate who dies or resigns after the convention adjourns, or after election day but before the electors cast their votes for president and vice president. This replacement power was assumed informally, but without controversy, at first. It was granted by several national conventions during the Progressive Era (1900–1912), and was made part of both parties' permanent standing rules by the 1920s.

There have been four such vacancies.

In 1860 the Democratic designee for vice president, Sen. Benjamin Fitzpatrick of Alabama, declined the nomination after the ruinously chaotic Baltimore convention of that year finally adjourned. The national committee then nominated former Gov. Herschel V. Johnson of Georgia as Sen. Stephen A. Douglas's running mate.

In 1872 the Democratic nominee for president, Horace Greeley, founder of the *New York Tribune,* died shortly after election day. (Incumbent Republican President Ulysses S. Grant had won the election.) Greeley's dispirited party's national committee declined to select a replacement candidate, and the Democratic electors voted for four different candidates.

In 1912 Vice President James S. Sherman of New York died in office the week before election day. The Republican convention of that year had authorized the national committee to fill vacancies, and the committee quickly replaced Sherman. His name remained on state ballots as President William Howard Taft's running mate, but the eight Republican electors voted, as recommended by the committee, for the replacement candidate, Nicholas Murray Butler of New York, president of Columbia University.

Finally, in 1972, the Democratic nominee for vice president, Sen. Thomas Eagleton of Missouri, resigned his candidacy after the convention adjourned. The nominee for president, Sen. George McGovern, recommended R. Sargent Shriver of Illinois, former head of the Peace Corps, as his replacement running mate, and Shriver was selected by a special meeting of an expanded national committee. *(See box, Political Party Organization and Rules, p. 418.)*

Communications and the Media

Major changes in the national nominating convention have resulted from the massive advances in transportation and communication technologies during the twentieth century.

The revolution in transportation has affected the scheduling of conventions. In the nineteenth century, conventions were

National Party Chairs, 1848–2001

Name	State	Years of service	Name	State	Years of service
Democratic Party			**Republican Party (continued)**		
B. F. Hallett	Massachusetts	1848–1852	Edwin D. Morgan	New York	1872–1876
Robert McLane	Maryland	1852–1856	Zachariah Chandler	Michigan	1876–1879
David A. Smalley	Virginia	1856–1860	J. Donald Cameron	Pennsylvania	1879–1880
August Belmont	New York	1860–1872	Marshall Jewell	Connecticut	1880–1883
Augustus Schell	New York	1872–1876	D. M. Sabin	Minnesota	1883–1884
Abram S. Hewitt	New York	1876–1877	B. F. Jones	Pennsylvania	1884–1888
William H. Barnum	Connecticut	1877–1889	Matthew S. Quay	Pennsylvania	1888–1891
Calvin S. Brice	Ohio	1889–1892	James S. Clarkson	Iowa	1891–1892
William F. Harrity	Pennsylvania	1892–1896	Thomas H. Carter	Montana	1892–1896
James K. Jones	Arkansas	1896–1904	Mark A. Hanna	Ohio	1896–1904
Thomas Taggart	Indiana	1904–1908	Henry C. Payne	Wisconsin	1904
Norman E. Mack	New York	1908–1912	George B. Cortelyou	New York	1904–1907
William F. McCombs	New York	1912–1916	Harry S. New	Indiana	1907–1908
Vance C. McCormick	Pennsylvania	1916–1919	Frank H. Hitchcock	Massachusetts	1908–1909
Homer S. Cummings	Connecticut	1919–1920	John F. Hill	Maine	1909–1912
George White	Ohio	1920–1921	Victor Rosewater	Nebraska	1912
Cordell Hull	Tennessee	1921–1924	Charles D. Hilles	New York	1912–1916
Clem Shaver	West Virginia	1924–1928	William R. Willcox	New York	1916–1918
John J. Raskob	Maryland	1928–1932	Will Hays	Indiana	1918–1921
James A. Farley	New York	1932–1940	John T. Adams	Iowa	1921–1924
Edward J. Flynn	New York	1940–1943	William M. Butler	Massachusetts	1924–1928
Frank C. Walker	Pennsylvania	1943–1944	Hubert Work	Colorado	1928–1929
Robert E. Hannegan	Missouri	1944–1947	Claudius H. Huston	Tennessee	1929–1930
J. Howard McGrath	Rhode Island	1947–1949	Simeon D. Fess	Ohio	1930–1932
William M. Boyle Jr.	Missouri	1949–1951	Everett Sanders	Indiana	1932–1934
Frank E. McKinney	Indiana	1951–1952	Henry P. Fletcher	Pennsylvania	1934–1936
Stephen A. Mitchell	Illinois	1952–1954	John Hamilton	Kansas	1936–1940
Paul M. Butler	Indiana	1955–1960	Joseph W. Martin Jr.	Massachusetts	1940–1942
Henry M. Jackson	Washington	1960–1961	Harrison E. Spangler	Iowa	1942–1944
John M. Bailey	Connecticut	1961–1968	Herbert Brownell Jr.	New York	1944–1946
Lawrence F. O'Brien	Massachusetts	1968–1969	B. Carroll Reece	Tennessee	1946–1948
Fred Harris	Oklahoma	1969–1970	Hugh D. Scott Jr.	Pennsylvania	1948–1949
Lawrence F. O'Brien	Massachusetts	1970–1972	Guy George Gabrielson	New Jersey	1949–1952
Jean Westwood	Utah	1972	Arthur E. Summerfield	Michigan	1952–1953
Robert Straus	Texas	1972–1977	C. Wesley Roberts	Kansas	1953
Kenneth Curtis	Maine	1977–1978	Leonard W. Hall	New York	1953–1957
John White	Texas	1978–1981	H. Meade Alcorn Jr.	Connecticut	1957–1959
Charles Manatt	California	1981–1985	Thruston B. Morton	Kentucky	1959–1961
Paul Kirk	Massachusetts	1985–1989	William E. Miller	New York	1961–1964
Ronald H. Brown	Washington, D.C.	1989–1993	Dean Burch	Arizona	1964–1965
David Wilhelm	Illinois	1993–1994	Ray C. Bliss	Ohio	1965–1969
Christopher Dodd (general chair)	Connecticut	1994–1997	Rogers C. B. Morton	Maryland	1969–1971
			Robert Dole	Kansas	1971–1973
Donald Fowler	South Carolina	1994–1997	George Bush	Texas	1973–1974
Roy Romer (general chair)	Colorado	1997–1999	Mary Louise Smith	Iowa	1974–1977
			William Brock	Tennessee	1977–1981
Steven Grossman	Massachusetts	1997–1999	Richard Richards	Utah	1981–1983
Ed Rendell (general chair)	Pennsylvania	1999–2001	Paul Laxalt (general chair)	Nevada	1983–1986
Joe Andrew	Indiana	1999–2001	Frank Fahrenkopf Jr.	Nevada	1983–1989
Terrence McAuliffe	New York	2001–	Lee Atwater	South Carolina	1989–1991
			Clayton Yeutter	Nebraska	1991–1992
Republican Party			Rich Bond	New York	1992–1993
Edwin D. Morgan	New York	1856–1864	Haley Barbour	Mississippi	1993–1997
Henry J. Raymond	New York	1864–1866	Jim Nicholson	Colorado	1997–2001
Marcus L. Ward	New Jersey	1866–1868	James Gilmore	Virginia	2001–
William Claflin	Massachusetts	1868–1872			

Sources: Hugh A. Bone, *Party Committees and National Politics* (Seattle: University of Washington, 1958), 241–243; Congressional Quarterly, *The President, the Public, and the Parties*, 2nd ed. (Washington, D.C.: Congressional Quarterly, 1997), 21; and various issues of *CQ Weekly Report*.

sometimes held a year or more before the election and at the latest were completed by late spring of the election year. With the ability of people to assemble quickly, conventions in recent years have been held later in the election year, usually in July or Au-

gust. Advances in transportation also have affected site location. Geographic centrality is no longer a primary consideration in the selection of a convention city.

Radio coverage of conventions began in 1924; television cov-

A scene from the 1992 Democratic convention in New York City that nominated Bill Clinton for president.

erage sixteen years later. One of the first changes inspired by the media age was the termination of the custom that a presidential candidate not appear at the convention but accept his nomination in a ceremony several weeks later. Franklin D. Roosevelt was the first major party candidate to break this tradition when in 1932 he delivered his acceptance speech in person before the Democratic convention. Twelve years later, Thomas E. Dewey became the first Republican nominee to give his acceptance speech to the convention. Since then, the final activity of every Democratic and Republican convention has been the delivery of the acceptance speech by the presidential nominee.

Party leaders have also, in recent years, streamlined the schedule, with the assumption that the interest level of most of the viewing public for politics is limited. The result has been shorter speeches and generally fewer roll calls than at those conventions in the pretelevision era. And at both conventions in 2000, the address of the vice-presidential candidate was delivered on the night before that of the presidential nominee.

Party leaders desire to put on a good show for the viewing public with the hope of winning votes for their party in November. The convention is a showcase, designed to present the party as both a model of democracy and an efficient, harmonious body. The schedule of convention activities is drawn up with an eye on the peak evening television viewing hours. There is an attempt to put the party's major selling points—the highly partisan keynote speech, the nominating ballots, and the candidates' acceptance speeches—on in prime time. (The effort to put acceptance speeches on in prime time has been especially strong since 1972, when Democratic nominee George S. McGovern was forced to wait until the wee hours of the morning to make his speech.) Conversely, party leaders try to keep evidence of bitter party factionalism—such as explosive credentials and platform battles—out of the peak viewing period.

Both the Republicans and Democrats went to extraordinary lengths to turn their 2000 conventions into tightly scripted, visually appealing television shows. But it seems that the harder the political parties try to win over American audiences, the less they have to show for their efforts. Many TV viewers voted with their remote controls—tuning out the 2000 conventions. By and large, ratings for the three major networks' broadcasts of the conventions have been on a steady decline for the past two decades.

In the media age the appearance of fairness is important, and in a sense this need to look fair and open has assisted the movement for party reform. Some influential party leaders, skeptical of reform of the convention, have found resistance difficult in the glare of television.

Before the revolution in the means of transportation and communication, conventions met in relative anonymity. Today conventions are held in all the privacy of a fishbowl, with every action and every rumor closely scrutinized. They have become media events and as such are targets for political demonstrations that can be not only an embarrassment to the party but a security problem as well.

In spite of its difficulties, the convention system has survived. As the nation has developed during the past century and a half, the convention has evolved as well, changing its form but retaining its variety of functions. Criticism has been leveled at the convention, but no substitute has yet been offered that would nominate a presidential ticket, adopt a party platform, act as the supreme governing body of the party, and serve as a massive campaign rally and propaganda forum. In addition to these functions, a convention is a place where compromise can take place—compromise often mandatory in a major political party that combines varying viewpoints.

Highlights of National Party Conventions, 1831–2000

1831 First national political convention held in Baltimore by Anti-Masonic Party.

1832 Democratic Party met in Baltimore for its first national convention.

1839 Whig Party held its first national convention.

1840 Democrats set up committee to select vice presidential nominees, subject to approval of convention.

1844 Democrats nominated James K. Polk—first "dark-horse" candidate—after nine ballots. Silas Wright declined the vice-presidential nomination. First time a convention nominee refused nomination.

1848 Democrats established continuing committee, known as "Democratic National Committee."

1852 Democrats and Whigs both adopted platforms before nominating candidates for president, setting precedent followed almost uniformly ever since.

1856 First Republican national convention held in Philadelphia.

1860 Democrats met in Charleston, S.C. After ten days and deadlocked on a presidential nominee, delegates adjourned and reconvened in Baltimore. Benjamin Fitzpatrick, the Democrats' choice for vice president, became the first candidate to withdraw after convention adjournment and be replaced by a selection of the national committee.

First Republican credentials dispute took place over seating delegates from slave states and voting strength of delegates from states where party was comparatively weak.

1864 In attempt to close ranks during Civil War, Republicans used the name "Union Party" at convention.

1868 For the first time, Republicans gave a candidate (Ulysses S. Grant) 100 percent of vote on first ballot.

A letter from Susan B. Anthony was read before Democratic convention urging support of women's suffrage.

1872 Victoria Clafin Woodhull, nominated by the Equal Rights Party, was the first woman presidential candidate. Black leader Frederick Douglass was her running mate.

1880 Republicans nominated James A. Garfield for president on 36th ballot—party's all-time record number of ballots.

1884 Republican Rep. John Roy Lynch of Mississippi became first black elected temporary chairman of national nominating convention.

1888 Frederick Douglass was first black to receive a vote in presidential balloting at a major party political convention (Republican).

1900 Each party had one woman delegate.

1904 Florida Democrats selected delegates in first-ever presidential primary election.

1920 For first time, women attended conventions in significant numbers.

1924 Republicans adopted bonus votes for states that went Republican in previous election. GOP convention was first to be broadcast on radio.

John W. Davis was nominated by Democrats on record 103rd ballot.

1928 Democrats nominated Gov. Alfred E. Smith of New York for president—first time a Roman Catholic placed on national ticket by a major party.

1932 Republicans began tradition of appointing their party leader from House of Representatives as permanent convention chairman.

Democrat Franklin D. Roosevelt became first major party candidate to accept presidential nomination in person.

1936 Democratic Party voted to end requirement of two-thirds delegate majority for nomination.

1940 Republican convention was first to be televised.

1944 Democrats adopted bonus votes for states that went Democratic in previous election.

Thomas E. Dewey became first Republican candidate to accept nomination in person.

1948 Democrats began appointing Speaker of the House as permanent chairman. Republicans renominated Thomas E. Dewey—first time GOP renominated a defeated presidential candidate.

1952 Adlai E. Stevenson was chosen as Democratic nominee in one of few genuine "drafts" in history.

1956 Democrats used party loyalty provision in selecting delegates for first time.

1960 Democrats adopted civil rights plank that was strongest in party history.

Republican nominee Richard Nixon was party's first vice president nominated for president at completion of his term.

1964 Sen. Margaret Chase Smith was nominated for presidency at Republican convention—first time a woman placed in nomination by a major party.

1968 Democratic Party voted to end unit rule. Outside the Chicago convention, antiwar protests erupt in violence.

1980 Democratic delegates were composed of an equal number of men and women.

1984 Democrats nominated Rep. Geraldine A. Ferraro of New York for vice president—the first woman placed on national ticket by a major party.

1996 The Reform Party conducted its first convention in a two-stage process that allowed bailoting by mail, electronic mail, or phone.

2000 Democrats nominated Sen. Joseph Lieberman of Connecticut for vice president—first time a person of Jewish descent placed on national ticket by a major party.

CHAPTER 13

Political Party Nominees, 1831–2000

F ollowing is a comprehensive list of major and minor party nominees for president and vice president from 1831, when the first nominating convention was held by the Anti-Masonic Party, to 1996. In many cases, minor parties made only token efforts at a presidential campaign. Often, third-party candidates declined to run after being nominated by the convention, or their names appeared on the ballots of only a few states. In some cases the names of minor candidates did not appear on any state ballots and they received only a scattering of write-in votes, if any.

The basic source for the 1832 to 1972 elections was Joseph Nathan Kane, *Facts About the Presidents,* 6th ed. (New York: H. W. Wilson Co., 1993). To verify the names appearing in Kane, Congressional Quarterly consulted the following additional sources: Richard M. Scammon, *America at the Polls* (Pittsburgh: University of Pittsburgh Press, 1965); Richard M. Scammon, *America Votes 8* (Washington,

D.C.: Congressional Quarterly, 1969); Richard M. Scammon, *America Votes 10* (Washington, D.C.: Congressional Quarterly, 1973); Richard B. Morris, ed. *Encyclopedia of American History,* (New York: Harper and Row, 1965); *Dictionary of American Biography,* (New York: Scribner's, 1928–1936); *Facts on File* (New York: Facts on File Inc., 1945–1975); Arthur M. Schlesinger, ed., *History of U.S. Political Parties,* Vols. I–IV, (New York: McGraw Hill, 1971); and *Who Was Who in America, 1607–1968,* Vols. I–V (Chicago: Marquis Co., 1943–1968). The source for the 1976 to 1996 elections was Congressional Quarterly's *America Votes* series, Vols. 12 (1977), 14 (1981), 16 (1985), 18 (1989), 20 (1993), 22 (1997), and 24 (2001) published in Washington, D.C.

In cases where these sources contain information in conflict with Kane, the conflicting information is included in a footnote. Where a candidate appears in Kane *but could not be verified in another source,* an asterisk appears beside the candidate's name on the list.

1832 ELECTION

Democratic Party
President: Andrew Jackson, Tennessee
Vice president: Martin Van Buren, New York

National Republican Party
President: Henry Clay, Kentucky
Vice president: John Sergeant, Pennsylvania

Independent Party
President: John Floyd, Virginia
Vice president: Henry Lee, Massachusetts

Anti-Masonic Party
President: William Wirt, Maryland
Vice president: Amos Ellmaker, Pennsylvania

1836 ELECTION

Democratic Party
President: Martin Van Buren, New York
Vice president: Richard Mentor Johnson, Kentucky

Whig Party
President: William Henry Harrison, Hugh Lawson White, Daniel Webster
Vice president: Francis Granger, John Tyler
  The Whigs nominated regional candidates in 1836 hoping that each candidate would carry his region and deny Democrat Van Buren an electoral vote majority. Webster was the Whig candidate in Massachusetts; Harrison in the rest of New England, the Middle Atlantic states, and the West; and White in the South.
  Granger was the running mate of Harrison and Webster. Tyler was White's running mate.

1840 ELECTION

Whig Party
President: William Henry Harrison, Ohio
Vice president: John Tyler, Virginia

Democratic Party
President: Martin Van Buren, New York
  The Democratic convention adopted a resolution that left the choice of vice-presidential candidates to the states. Democratic electors divided their vice-presidential votes among incumbent Richard M. Johnson (forty-eight votes), Littleton W. Tazewell (eleven votes), and James K. Polk (one vote).

Liberty Party
President: James Gillespie Birney, New York
Vice president: Thomas Earle, Pennsylvania

1844 ELECTION

Democratic Party
President: James Knox Polk, Tennessee
Vice president: George Mifflin Dallas, Pennsylvania

Whig Party
President: Henry Clay, Kentucky
Vice president: Theodore Frelinghuysen, New Jersey

Liberty Party
President: James Gillespie Birney, New York
Vice president: Thomas Morris, Ohio

National Democratic Party
President: John Tyler, Virginia
Vice president: None
  Tyler withdrew in favor of the Democrat, Polk.

1848 ELECTION

Whig Party
President: Zachary Taylor, Louisiana
Vice president: Millard Fillmore, New York

Democratic Party
President: Lewis Cass, Michigan
Vice president: William Orlando Butler, Kentucky

Free Soil Party
President: Martin Van Buren, New York
Vice president: Charles Francis Adams, Massachusetts

Free Soil (Barnburners—Liberty Party)
President: John Parker Hale, New Hampshire
Vice president: Leicester King, Ohio
    Later John Parker Hale relinquished the nomination.

National Liberty Party
President: Gerrit Smith, New York
Vice president: Charles C. Foote, Michigan

1852 ELECTION

Democratic Party
President: Franklin Pierce, New Hampshire
Vice president: William Rufus De Vane King, Alabama

Whig Party
President: Winfield Scott, New Jersey
Vice president: William Alexander Graham, North Carolina

Free Soil
President: John Parker Hale, New Hampshire
Vice president: George Washington Julian, Indiana

1856 ELECTION

Democratic Party
President: James Buchanan, Pennsylvania
Vice president: John Cabell Breckinridge, Kentucky

Republican Party
President: John Charles Fremont, California
Vice president: William Lewis Dayton, New Jersey

American (Know-Nothing) Party
President: Millard Fillmore, New York
Vice president: Andrew Jackson Donelson, Tennessee

Whig Party (the "Silver Grays")
President: Millard Fillmore, New York
Vice president: Andrew Jackson Donelson, Tennessee

North American Party
President: Nathaniel Prentice Banks, Massachusetts
Vice president: William Freame Johnson, Pennsylvania
    Banks and Johnson declined the nominations and gave their support to the Republicans.

1860 ELECTION

Republican Party
President: Abraham Lincoln, Illinois
Vice president: Hannibal Hamlin, Maine

Democratic Party
President: Stephen Arnold Douglas, Illinois
Vice president: Herschel Vespasian Johnson, Georgia

Southern Democratic Party
President: John Cabell Breckinridge, Kentucky
Vice president: Joseph Lane, Oregon

Constitutional Union Party
President: John Bell, Tennessee
Vice president: Edward Everett, Massachusetts

1864 ELECTION

Republican Party
President: Abraham Lincoln, Illinois
Vice president: Andrew Johnson, Tennessee

Democratic Party
President: George Brinton McClellan, New York
Vice president: George Hunt Pendleton, Ohio

Independent Republican Party
President: John Charles Fremont, California
Vice president: John Cochrane, New York

Fremont and Cochrane declined the nominations and gave their support to the Republicans.

1868 ELECTION

Republican Party
President: Ulysses Simpson Grant, Illinois
Vice president: Schuyler Colfax, Indiana

Democratic Party
President: Horatio Seymour, New York
Vice president: Francis Preston Blair Jr., Missouri

1872 ELECTION

Republican Party
President: Ulysses Simpson Grant, Illinois
Vice president: Henry Wilson, Massachusetts

Liberal Republican Party
President: Horace Greeley, New York
Vice president: Benjamin Gratz Brown, Missouri

Independent Liberal Republican Party (Opposition Party)
President: William Slocum Groesbeck, Ohio
Vice president: Frederick Law Olmsted, New York

Democratic Party
President: Horace Greeley, New York
Vice president: Benjamin Gratz Brown, Missouri

Straight-Out Democratic Party
President: Charles O'Conor, New York
Vice president: John Quincy Adams, Massachusetts

Prohibition Party
President: James Black, Pennsylvania
Vice president: John Russell, Michigan

People's Party (Equal Rights Party)
President: Victoria Claflin Woodhull, New York
Vice president: Frederick Douglass

Labor Reform Party
President: David Davis, Illinois
Vice president: Joel Parker, New Jersey

Liberal Republican Party of Colored Men
President: Horace Greeley, New York
Vice president: Benjamin Gratz Brown, Missouri

National Working Men's Party
President: Ulysses Simpson Grant, Illinois
Vice president: Henry Wilson, Massachusetts

1876 ELECTION

Republican Party
President: Rutherford Birchard Hayes, Ohio
Vice president: William Almon Wheeler, New York

Democratic Party
President: Samuel Jones Tilden, New York
Vice president: Thomas Andrews Hendricks, Indiana

Greenback Party
President: Peter Cooper, New York
Vice president: Samuel Fenton Cary, Ohio

Prohibition Party
President: Green Clay Smith, Kentucky
Vice president: Gideon Tabor Stewart, Ohio

American National Party
President: James B. Walker, Illinois
Vice president: Donald Kirkpatrick, New York

1880 ELECTION

Republican Party
President: James Abram Garfield, Ohio
Vice president: Chester Alan Arthur, New York

Democratic Party
President: Winfield Scott Hancock, Pennsylvania
Vice president: William Hayden English, Indiana

Greenback Labor Party
President: James Baird Weaver, Iowa
Vice president: Benjamin J. Chambers, Texas

Prohibition Party
President: Neal Dow, Maine
Vice president: Henry Adams Thompson, Ohio

American Party
President: John Wolcott Phelps, Vermont
Vice president: Samuel Clarke Pomeroy, Kansas *

1884 ELECTION

Democratic Party
President: Grover Cleveland, New York
Vice president: Thomas Andrews Hendricks, Indiana

Republican Party
President: James Gillespie Blaine, Maine
Vice president: John Alexander Logan, Illinois

Anti-Monopoly Party
President: Benjamin Franklin Butler, Massachusetts
Vice president: Absolom Madden West, Mississippi

Greenback Party
President: Benjamin Franklin Butler, Massachusetts
Vice president: Absolom Madden West, Mississippi

Prohibition Party
President: John Pierce St. John, Kansas
Vice president: William Daniel, Maryland

American Prohibition Party
President: Samuel Clarke Pomeroy, Kansas
Vice president: John A. Conant, Connecticut

Equal Rights Party
President: Belva Ann Bennett Lockwood, District of Columbia
Vice president: Marietta Lizzie Bell Stow, California

1888 ELECTION

Republican Party
President: Benjamin Harrison, Indiana
Vice president: Levi Parsons Morton, New York

Democratic Party
President: Grover Cleveland, New York
Vice president: Allen Granberry Thurman, Ohio

Prohibition Party
President: Clinton Bowen Fisk, New Jersey
Vice president: John Anderson Brooks, Missouri *

Union Labor Party
President: Alson Jenness Streeter, Illinois
Vice president: Charles E. Cunningham, Arkansas *

United Labor Party
President: Robert Hall Cowdrey, Illinois
Vice president: William H. T. Wakefield, Kansas *

American Party
President: James Langdon Curtis, New York
Vice president: Peter Dinwiddie Wigginton, California *

Equal Rights Party
President: Belva Ann Bennett Lockwood, District of Columbia
Vice president: Alfred Henry Love, Pennsylvania *

Industrial Reform Party
President: Albert E. Redstone, California *
Vice president: John Colvin, Kansas *

1892 ELECTION

Democratic Party
President: Grover Cleveland, New York
Vice president: Adlai Ewing Stevenson, Illinois

Republican Party
President: Benjamin Harrison, Indiana
Vice president: Whitelaw Reid, New York

People's Party of America
President: James Baird Weaver, Iowa
Vice president: James Gaven Field, Virginia

Prohibition Party
President: John Bidwell, California
Vice president: James Britton Cranfill, Texas

Socialist Labor Party
President: Simon Wing, Massachusetts
Vice president: Charles Horatio Matchett, New York *

1896 ELECTION

Republican Party
President: William McKinley, Ohio
Vice president: Garret Augustus Hobart, New Jersey

Democratic Party
President: William Jennings Bryan, Nebraska
Vice president: Arthur Sewall, Maine

People's Party (Populist)
President: William Jennings Bryan, Nebraska
Vice president: Thomas Edward Watson, Georgia

National Democratic Party
President: John McAuley Palmer, Illinois
Vice president: Simon Bolivar Buckner, Kentucky

Prohibition Party
President: Joshua Levering, Maryland
Vice president: Hale Johnson, Illinois *

Socialist Labor Party
President: Charles Horatio Matchett, New York
Vice president: Matthew Maguire, New Jersey

National Party
President: Charles Eugene Bentley, Nebraska
Vice president: James Haywood Southgate, North Carolina *

National Silver Party (Bi-Metallic League)
President: William Jennings Bryan, Nebraska
Vice president: Arthur Sewall, Maine

1900 ELECTION

Republican Party
President: William McKinley, Ohio
Vice president: Theodore Roosevelt, New York

Democratic Party
President: William Jennings Bryan, Nebraska
Vice president: Adlai Ewing Stevenson, Illinois

Prohibition Party
President: John Granville Wooley, Illinois
Vice president: Henry Brewer Metcalf, Rhode Island

Social-Democratic Party
President: Eugene Victor Debs, Indiana
Vice president: Job Harriman, California

People's Party (Populist—Anti-Fusionist faction)
President: Wharton Barker, Pennsylvania
Vice president: Ignatius Donnelly, Minnesota

Socialist Labor Party
President: Joseph Francis Malloney, Massachusetts
Vice president: Valentine Remmel, Pennsylvania
Union Reform Party
President: Seth Hockett Ellis, Ohio
Vice president: Samuel T. Nicholson, Pennsylvania
United Christian Party
President: Jonah Fitz Randolph Leonard, Iowa
Vice president: David H. Martin, Pennsylvania
People's Party (Populist—Fusionist faction)
President: William Jennings Bryan, Nebraska
Vice president: Adlai Ewing Stevenson, Illinois
Silver Republican Party
President: William Jennings Bryan, Nebraska
Vice president: Adlai Ewing Stevenson, Illinois
National Party
President: Donelson Caffery, Louisiana
Vice president: Archibald Murray Howe, Massachusetts *

1904 ELECTION

Republican Party
President: Theodore Roosevelt, New York
Vice president: Charles Warren Fairbanks, Indiana
Democratic Party
President: Alton Brooks Parker, New York
Vice president: Henry Gassaway Davis, West Virginia
Socialist Party
President: Eugene Victor Debs, Indiana
Vice president: Benjamin Hanford, New York
Prohibition Party
President: Silas Comfort Swallow, Pennsylvania
Vice president: George W. Carroll, Texas
People's Party (Populist)
President: Thomas Edward Watson, Georgia
Vice president: Thomas Henry Tibbles, Nebraska
Socialist Labor Party
President: Charles Hunter Corregan, New York
Vice president: William Wesley Cox, Illinois
Continental Party
President: Austin Holcomb
Vice president: A. King, Missouri

1908 ELECTION

Republican Party
President: William Howard Taft, Ohio
Vice president: James Schoolcraft Sherman, New York
Democratic Party
President: William Jennings Bryan, Nebraska
Vice president: John Worth Kern, Indiana
Socialist Party
President: Eugene Victor Debs, Indiana
Vice president: Benjamin Hanford, New York
Prohibition Party
President: Eugene Wilder Chafin, Illinois
Vice president: Aaron Sherman Watkins, Ohio
Independence Party
President: Thomas Louis Hisgen, Massachusetts
Vice president: John Temple Graves, Georgia
People's Party (Populist)
President: Thomas Edward Watson, Georgia
Vice president: Samuel Williams, Indiana

Socialist Labor Party
President: August Gillhaus, New York
Vice president: Donald L. Munro, Virginia
United Christian Party
President: Daniel Braxton Turney, Illinois
Vice president: Lorenzo S. Coffin, Iowa

1912 ELECTION

Democratic Party
President: Woodrow Wilson, New Jersey
Vice president: Thomas Riley Marshall, Indiana
Progressive Party ("Bull Moose" Party)
President: Theodore Roosevelt, New York
Vice president: Hiram Warren Johnson, California
Republican Party
President: William Howard Taft, Ohio
Vice president: James Schoolcraft Sherman, New York
    Sherman died October 30; he was replaced by Nicholas Murray
    Butler, New York.
Socialist Party
President: Eugene Victor Debs, Indiana
Vice president: Emil Seidel, Wisconsin
Prohibition Party
President: Eugene Wilder Chafin, Illinois
Vice president: Aaron Sherman Watkins, Ohio
Socialist Labor Party
President: Arthur Elmer Reimer, Massachusetts
Vice president: August Gillhaus, New York[1]

1916 ELECTION

Democratic Party
President: Woodrow Wilson, New Jersey
Vice president: Thomas Riley Marshall, Indiana
Republican Party
President: Charles Evans Hughes, New York
Vice president: Charles Warren Fairbanks, Indiana
Socialist Party
President: Allan Louis Benson, New York
Vice president: George Ross Kirkpatrick, New Jersey
Prohibition Party
President: James Franklin Hanly, Indiana
Vice president: Ira Landrith, Tennessee
Socialist Labor Party
President: Arthur Elmer Reimer, Massachusetts *
Vice president: Caleb Harrison, Illinois *
Progressive Party
President: Theodore Roosevelt, New York
Vice president: John Milliken Parker, Louisiana

1920 ELECTION

Republican Party
President: Warren Gamaliel Harding, Ohio
Vice president: Calvin Coolidge, Massachusetts
Democratic Party
President: James Middleton Cox, Ohio
Vice president: Franklin Delano Roosevelt, New York
Socialist Party
President: Eugene Victor Debs, Indiana
Vice president: Seymour Stedman, Illinois
Farmer Labor Party
President: Parley Parker Christensen, Utah
Vice president: Maximilian Sebastian Hayes, Ohio

Prohibition Party
President: Aaron Sherman Watkins, Ohio
Vice president: David Leigh Colvin, New York
Socialist Labor Party
President: William Wesley Cox, Missouri
Vice president: August Gillhaus, New York
Single Tax Party
President: Robert Colvin Macauley, Pennsylvania
Vice president: R. G. Barnum, Ohio
American Party
President: James Edward Ferguson, Texas
Vice president: William J. Hough

1924 ELECTION

Republican Party
President: Calvin Coolidge, Massachusetts
Vice president: Charles Gates Dawes, Illinois
Democratic Party
President: John William Davis, West Virginia
Vice president: Charles Wayland Bryan, Nebraska
Progressive Party
President: Robert La Follette, Wisconsin
Vice president: Burton Kendall Wheeler, Montana
Prohibition Party
President: Herman Preston Faris, Missouri
Vice president: Marie Caroline Brehm, California
Socialist Labor Party
President: Frank T. Johns, Oregon
Vice president: Verne L. Reynolds, New York
Socialist Party
President: Robert La Follette, New York
Vice president: Burton Kendall Wheeler, Montana
Workers Party (Communist Party)
President: William Zebulon Foster, Illinois
Vice president: Benjamin Gitlow, New York
American Party
President: Gilbert Owen Nations, District of Columbia
Vice president: Charles Hiram Randall, California[2]
Commonwealth Land Party
President: William J. Wallace, New Jersey
Vice president: John Cromwell Lincoln, Ohio
Farmer Labor Party
President: Duncan McDonald, Illinois *
Vice president: William Bouck, Washington *
Greenback Party
President: John Zahnd, Indiana *
Vice president: Roy M. Harrop, Nebraska *

1928 ELECTION

Republican Party
President: Herbert Clark Hoover, California
Vice president: Charles Curtis, Kansas
Democratic Party
President: Alfred Emanuel Smith, New York
Vice president: Joseph Taylor Robinson, Arkansas
Socialist Party
President: Norman Mattoon Thomas, New York
Vice president: James Hudson Maurer, Pennsylvania
Workers Party (Communist Party)
President: William Zebulon Foster, Illinois
Vice president: Benjamin Gitlow, New York

Socialist Labor Party
President: Verne L. Reynolds, Michigan
Vice president: Jeremiah D. Crowley, New York
Prohibition Party
President: William Frederick Varney, New York
Vice president: James Arthur Edgerton, Virginia
Farmer Labor Party
President: Frank Elbridge Webb, California
Vice president: Will Vereen, Georgia[3]
Greenback Party
President: John Zahnd, Indiana *
Vice president: Wesley Henry Bennington, Ohio *

1932 ELECTION

Democratic Party
President: Franklin Delano Roosevelt, New York
Vice president: John Nance Garner, Texas
Republican Party
President: Herbert Clark Hoover, California
Vice president: Charles Curtis, Kansas
Socialist Party
President: Norman Mattoon Thomas, New York
Vice president: James Hudson Maurer, Pennsylvania
Communist Party
President: William Zebulon Foster, Illinois
Vice president: James William Ford, New York
Prohibition Party
President: William David Upshaw, Georgia
Vice president: Frank Stewart Regan, Illinois
Liberty Party
President: William Hope Harvey, Arkansas
Vice president: Frank B. Hemenway, Washington
Socialist Labor Party
President: Verne L. Reynolds, New York
Vice president: John W. Aiken, Massachusetts
Farmer Labor Party
President: Jacob Sechler Coxey, Ohio
Vice president: Julius J. Reiter, Minnesota
Jobless Party
President: James Renshaw Cox, Pennsylvania
Vice president: V. C. Tisdal, Oklahoma
National Party
President: Seymour E. Allen, Massachusetts

1936 ELECTION

Democratic Party
President: Franklin Delano Roosevelt, New York
Vice president: John Nance Garner, Texas
Republican Party
President: Alfred Mossman Landon, Kansas
Vice president: Frank Knox, Illinois
Union Party
President: William Lemke, North Dakota
Vice president: Thomas Charles O'Brien, Massachusetts
Socialist Party
President: Norman Mattoon Thomas, New York
Vice president: George A. Nelson, Wisconsin
Communist Party
President: Earl Russell Browder, Kansas
Vice president: James William Ford, New York

Prohibition Party
President: David Leigh Colvin, New York
Vice president: Alvin York, Tennessee
Socialist Labor Party
President: John W. Aiken, Massachusetts
Vice president: Emil F. Teichert, New York
National Greenback Party
President: John Zahnd, Indiana *
Vice president: Florence Garvin, Rhode Island *

1940 ELECTION

Democratic Party
President: Franklin Delano Roosevelt, New York
Vice president: Henry Agard Wallace, Iowa
Republican Party
President: Wendell Lewis Willkie, New York
Vice president: Charles Linza McNary, Oregon
Socialist Party
President: Norman Mattoon Thomas, New York
Vice president: Maynard C. Krueger, Illinois
Prohibition Party
President: Roger Ward Babson, Massachusetts
Vice president: Edgar V. Moorman, Illinois
Communist Party (Workers Party)
President: Earl Russell Browder, Kansas
Vice president: James William Ford, New York
Socialist Labor Party
President: John W. Aiken, Massachusetts
Vice president: Aaron M. Orange, New York
Greenback Party
President: John Zahnd, Indiana *
Vice president: James Elmer Yates, Arizona *

1944 ELECTION

Democratic Party
President: Franklin Delano Roosevelt, New York
Vice president: Harry S. Truman, Missouri
Republican Party
President: Thomas Edmund Dewey, New York
Vice president: John William Bricker, Ohio
Socialist Party
President: Norman Mattoon Thomas, New York
Vice president: Darlington Hoopes, Pennsylvania
Prohibition Party
President: Claude A. Watson, California
Vice president: Andrew Johnson, Kentucky
Socialist Labor Party
President: Edward A. Teichert, Pennsylvania
Vice president: Arla A. Albaugh, Ohio
America First Party
President: Gerald Lyman Kenneth Smith, Michigan
Vice president: Henry A. Romer, Ohio

1948 ELECTION

Democratic Party
President: Harry S. Truman, Missouri
Vice president: Alben William Barkley, Kentucky
Republican Party
President: Thomas Edmund Dewey, New York
Vice president: Earl Warren, California

States' Rights Democratic Party
President: James Strom Thurmond, South Carolina
Vice president: Fielding Lewis Wright, Mississippi
Progressive Party
President: Henry Agard Wallace, Iowa
Vice president: Glen Hearst Taylor, Idaho
Socialist Party
President: Norman Mattoon Thomas, New York
Vice president: Tucker Powell Smith, Michigan
Prohibition Party
President: Claude A. Watson, California
Vice president: Dale Learn, Pennsylvania
Socialist Labor Party
President: Edward A. Teichert, Pennsylvania
Vice president: Stephen Emery, New York
Socialist Workers Party
President: Farrell Dobbs, New York
Vice president: Grace Carlson, Minnesota
Christian Nationalist Party
President: Gerald Lyman Kenneth Smith, Missouri
Vice president: Henry A. Romer, Ohio
Greenback Party
President: John G. Scott, New York
Vice president: Granville B. Leeke, Indiana *
Vegetarian Party
President: John Maxwell, Illinois
Vice president: Symon Gould, New York *

1952 ELECTION

Republican Party
President: Dwight David Eisenhower, New York
Vice president: Richard Milhous Nixon, California
Democratic Party
President: Adlai Ewing Stevenson II, Illinois
Vice president: John Jackson Sparkman, Alabama
Progressive Party
President: Vincent William Hallinan, California
Vice president: Charlotta A. Bass, New York
Prohibition Party
President: Stuart Hamblen, California
Vice president: Enoch Arden Holtwick, Illinois
Socialist Labor Party
President: Eric Hass, New York
Vice president: Stephen Emery, New York
Socialist Party
President: Darlington Hoopes, Pennsylvania
Vice president: Samuel Herman Friedman, New York
Socialist Workers Party
President: Farrell Dobbs, New York
Vice president: Myra Tanner Weiss, New York
America First Party
President: Douglas MacArthur, Wisconsin
Vice president: Harry Flood Byrd, Virginia
American Labor Party
President: Vincent William Hallinan, California
Vice president: Charlotta A. Bass, New York
American Vegetarian Party
President: Daniel J. Murphy, California
Vice president: Symon Gould, New York *
Church of God Party
President: Homer Aubrey Tomlinson, New York
Vice president: Willie Isaac Bass, North Carolina *

Constitution Party
President: Douglas MacArthur, Wisconsin
Vice president: Harry Flood Byrd, Virginia
Greenback Party
President: Frederick C. Proehl, Washington
Vice president: Edward J. Bedell, Indiana
Poor Man's Party
President: Henry B. Krajewski, New Jersey
Vice president: Frank Jenkins, New Jersey

1956 ELECTION

Republican Party
President: Dwight David Eisenhower, Pennsylvania
Vice president: Richard Milhous Nixon, California
Democratic Party
President: Adlai Ewing Stevenson II, Illinois
Vice president: Estes Kefauver, Tennessee
States' Rights Party
President: Thomas Coleman Andrews, Virginia
Vice president: Thomas Harold Werdel, California
Ticket also favored by Constitution Party.
Prohibition Party
President: Enoch Arden Holtwick, Illinois
Vice president: Edward M. Cooper, California
Socialist Labor Party
President: Eric Hass, New York
Vice president: Georgia Cozzini, Wisconsin
Texas Constitution Party
President: William Ezra Jenner, Indiana *
Vice president: Joseph Bracken Lee, Utah *
Socialist Workers Party
President: Farrell Dobbs, New York
Vice president: Myra Tanner Weiss, New York
American Third Party
President: Henry Krajewski, New Jersey
Vice president: Ann Marie Yezo, New Jersey
Socialist Party
President: Darlington Hoopes, Pennsylvania
Vice president: Samuel Herman Friedman, New York
Pioneer Party
President: William Langer, North Dakota *
Vice president: Burr McCloskey, Illinois *
American Vegetarian Party
President: Herbert M. Shelton, California *
Vice president: Symon Gould, New York *
Greenback Party
President: Frederick C. Proehl, Washington
Vice president: Edward Kirby Meador, Massachusetts *
States' Rights Party of Kentucky
President: Harry Flood Byrd, Virginia
Vice president: William Ezra Jenner, Indiana
South Carolinians for Independent Electors
President: Harry Flood Byrd, Virginia
Christian National Party
President: Gerald Lyman Kenneth Smith
Vice president: Charles I. Robertson

1960 ELECTION

Democratic Party
President: John Fitzgerald Kennedy, Massachusetts
Vice president: Lyndon Baines Johnson, Texas

Republican Party
President: Richard Milhous Nixon, California
Vice president: Henry Cabot Lodge, Massachusetts
National States' Rights Party
President: Orval Eugene Faubus, Arkansas
Vice president: John Geraerdt Crommelin, Alabama
Socialist Labor Party
President: Eric Hass, New York
Vice president: Georgia Cozzini, Wisconsin
Prohibition Party
President: Rutherford Losey Decker, Missouri
Vice president: Earle Harold Munn, Michigan
Socialist Workers Party
President: Farrell Dobbs, New York
Vice president: Myra Tanner Weiss, New York
Conservative Party of New Jersey
President: Joseph Bracken Lee, Utah
Vice president: Kent H. Courtney, Louisiana
Conservative Party of Virginia
President: C. Benton Coiner, Virginia
Vice president: Edward M. Silverman, Virginia
Constitution Party (Texas)
President: Charles Loten Sullivan, Mississippi
Vice president: Merritt B. Curtis, District of Columbia
Constitution Party (Washington)
President: Merritt B. Curtis, District of Columbia
Vice president: B. N. Miller
Greenback Party
President: Whitney Hart Slocomb, California *
Vice president: Edward Kirby Meador, Massachusetts *
Independent Afro-American Party
President: Clennon King, Georgia
Vice president: Reginald Carter
Tax Cut Party (America First Party; American Party)
President: Lar Daly, Illinois
Vice president: Merritt Barton Curtis, District of Columbia
Theocratic Party
President: Homer Aubrey Tomlinson, New York
Vice president: Raymond L. Teague, Alaska *
Vegetarian Party
President: Symon Gould, New York
Vice president: Christopher Gian-Cursio, Florida

1964 ELECTION

Democratic Party
President: Lyndon Baines Johnson, Texas
Vice president: Hubert Horatio Humphrey, Minnesota
Republican Party
President: Barry Morris Goldwater, Arizona
Vice president: William Edward Miller, New York
Socialist Labor Party
President: Eric Hass, New York
Vice president: Henning A. Blomen, Massachusetts
Prohibition Party
President: Earle Harold Munn, Michigan
Vice president: Mark Shaw, Massachusetts
Socialist Workers Party
President: Clifton DeBerry, New York
Vice president: Edward Shaw, New York
National States' Rights Party
President: John Kasper, Tennessee
Vice president: J. B. Stoner, Georgia

Constitution Party
    President: Joseph B. Lightburn, West Virginia
    Vice president: Theodore C. Billings, Colorado
Independent States' Rights Party
    President: Thomas Coleman Andrews, Virginia
    Vice president: Thomas H. Werdel, California *
Theocratic Party
    President: Homer Aubrey Tomlinson, New York
    Vice president: William R. Rogers, Missouri *
Universal Party
    President: Kirby James Hensley, California
    Vice president: John O. Hopkins, Iowa

1968 ELECTION

Republican Party
    President: Richard Milhous Nixon, New York
    Vice president: Spiro Theodore Agnew, Maryland
Democratic Party
    President: Hubert Horatio Humphrey, Minnesota
    Vice president: Edmund Sixtus Muskie, Maine
American Independent Party
    President: George Corley Wallace, Alabama
    Vice president: Curtis Emerson LeMay, Ohio
        LeMay replaced S. Marvin Griffin, who originally had been
        selected.
Peace and Freedom Party
    President: Eldridge Cleaver
    Vice president: Judith Mage, New York
Socialist Labor Party
    President: Henning A. Blomen, Massachusetts
    Vice president: George Sam Taylor, Pennsylvania
Socialist Workers Party
    President: Fred Halstead, New York
    Vice president: Paul Boutelle, New Jersey
Prohibition Party
    President: Earle Harold Munn Sr., Michigan
    Vice president: Rolland E. Fisher, Kansas
Communist Party
    President: Charlene Mitchell, California
    Vice president: Michael Zagarell, New York
Constitution Party
    President: Richard K. Troxell, Texas
    Vice president: Merle Thayer, Iowa
Freedom and Peace Party
    President: Richard Claxton (Dick) Gregory, Illinois
    Vice president: Mark Lane, New York
Patriotic Party
    President: George Corley Wallace, Alabama
    Vice president: William Penn Patrick, California
Theocratic Party
    President: William R. Rogers, Missouri
Universal Party
    President: Kirby James Hensley, California
    Vice president: Roscoe B. MacKenna

1972 ELECTION

Republican Party
    President: Richard Milhous Nixon, California
    Vice president: Spiro Theodore Agnew, Maryland
Democratic Party
    President: George Stanley McGovern, South Dakota
    Vice president: Thomas Francis Eagleton, Missouri

Eagleton resigned and was replaced on August 8, 1972, by Robert
Sargent Shriver Jr., Maryland, selected by the Democratic National
Committee.

American Independent Party
    President: John George Schmitz, California
    Vice president: Thomas Jefferson Anderson, Tennessee
Socialist Workers Party
    President: Louis Fisher, Illinois
    Vice president: Genevieve Gunderson, Minnesota
Socialist Labor Party
    President: Linda Jenness, Georgia
    Vice president: Andrew Pulley, Illinois
Communist Party
    President: Gus Hall, New York
    Vice president: Jarvis Tyner
Prohibition Party
    President: Earle Harold Munn Sr., Michigan
    Vice president: Marshall Uncapher
Libertarian Party
    President: John Hospers, California
    Vice president: Theodora Nathan, Oregon
People's Party
    President: Benjamin McLane Spock
    Vice president: Julius Hobson, District of Columbia
America First Party
    President: John V. Mahalchik
    Vice president: Irving Homer
Universal Party
    President: Gabriel Green
    Vice president: Daniel Fry

1976 ELECTION

Democratic Party
    President: James Earl (Jimmy) Carter Jr., Georgia
    Vice president: Walter Frederick Mondale, Minnesota
Republican Party
    President: Gerald Rudolph Ford, Michigan
    Vice president: Robert Joseph Dole, Kansas
Independent candidate
    President: Eugene Joseph McCarthy, Minnesota
    Vice president: none[4]
Libertarian Party
    President: Roger MacBride, Virginia
    Vice president: David P. Bergland, California
American Independent Party
    President: Lester Maddox, Georgia
    Vice president: William Dyke, Wisconsin
American Party
    President: Thomas J. Anderson, Tennessee
    Vice president: Rufus Shackleford, Florida
Socialist Workers Party
    President: Peter Camejo, California
    Vice president: Willie Mae Reid, California
Communist Party
    President: Gus Hall, New York
    Vice president: Jarvis Tyner, New York
People's Party
    President: Margaret Wright, California
    Vice president: Benjamin Spock, New York
U.S. Labor Party
    President: Lyndon H. LaRouche Jr., New York
    Vice president: R. W. Evans, Michigan

Prohibition Party
President: Benjamin C. Bubar, Maine
Vice president: Earl F. Dodge, Colorado
Socialist Labor Party
President: Jules Levin, New Jersey
Vice president: Constance Blomen, Massachusetts
Socialist Party
President: Frank P. Zeidler, Wisconsin
Vice president: J. Quinn Brisben, Illinois
Restoration Party
President: Ernest L. Miller
Vice president: Roy N. Eddy
United American Party
President: Frank Taylor
Vice president: Henry Swan

1980 ELECTION[5]

Republican Party
President: Ronald Wilson Reagan, California
Vice president: George Herbert Walker Bush, Texas
Democratic Party
President: James Earl (Jimmy) Carter Jr., Georgia
Vice president: Walter Frederick Mondale, Minnesota
National Unity Campaign
President: John B. Anderson, Illinois
Vice president: Patrick Joseph Lucey, Wisconsin
Libertarian Party
President: Edward E. Clark, California
Vice president: David Koch, New York
Citizens Party
President: Barry Commoner, New York
Vice president: LaDonna Harris, New Mexico
Communist Party
President: Gus Hall, New York
Vice president: Angela Davis, California
American Independent Party
President: John Richard Rarick, Louisiana
Vice president: Eileen M. Shearer, California
Socialist Workers Party
President: Andrew Pulley, Illinois
Vice president: Matilde Zimmermann
President: Clifton DeBerry, California
Vice president: Matilde Zimmermann
President: Richard Congress, Ohio
Vice president: Matilde Zimmermann
Right to Life Party
President: Ellen McCormack, New York
Vice president: Carroll Driscoll, New Jersey
Peace and Freedom Party
President: Maureen Smith, California
Vice president: Elizabeth Barron
Workers World Party
President: Deirdre Griswold, New Jersey
Vice president: Larry Holmes, New York
Statesman Party
President: Benjamin C. Bubar, Maine
Vice president: Earl F. Dodge, Colorado
Socialist Party
President: David McReynolds, New York
Vice president: Diane Drufenbrock, Wisconsin
American Party
President: Percy L. Greaves, New York
Vice president: Frank L. Varnum, California

President: Frank W. Shelton, Utah
Vice president: George E. Jackson
Middle Class Party
President: Kurt Lynen, New Jersey
Vice president: Harry Kieve, New Jersey
Down With Lawyers Party
President: Bill Gahres, New Jersey
Vice president: J. F. Loghlin, New Jersey
Independent Party
President: Martin E. Wendelken
Natural Peoples Party
President: Harley McLain, North Dakota
Vice president: Jewelie Goeller, North Dakota

1984 ELECTION[6]

Republican Party
President: Ronald Wilson Reagan, California
Vice president: George Herbert Walker Bush, Texas
Democratic Party
President: Walter Fritz Mondale, Minnesota
Vice president: Geraldine Anne Ferraro, New York
Libertarian Party
President: David P. Bergland, California
Vice president: Jim Lewis, Connecticut
Independent Party
President: Lyndon H. LaRouche Jr., Virginia
Vice president: Billy Davis, Mississippi
Citizens Party
President: Sonia Johnson, Virginia
Vice president: Richard Walton, Rhode Island
Populist Party
President: Bob Richards, Texas
Vice president: Maureen Kennedy Salaman, California
Independent Alliance Party
President: Dennis L. Serrette, New Jersey
Vice president: Nancy Ross, New York
Communist Party
President: Gus Hall, New York
Vice president: Angela Davis, California
Socialist Workers Party
President: Mel Mason, California
Vice president: Andrea Gonzalez, New York
Workers World Party
President: Larry Holmes, New York
Vice president: Gloria La Riva, California
President: Gavrielle Holmes, New York
Vice president: Milton Vera
American Party
President: Delmar Dennis, Tennessee
Vice president: Traves Brownlee, Delaware
Workers League Party
President: Ed Winn, New York
Vice presidents: Jean T. Brust, Helen Halyard, Edward Bergonzi
Prohibition Party
President: Earl F. Dodge, Colorado
Vice president: Warren C. Martin, Kansas

1988 ELECTION[7]

Republican Party
President: George Herbert Walker Bush, Texas
Vice president: James "Dan" Quayle, Indiana

Democratic Party
President: Michael Stanley Dukakis, Massachusetts
Vice president: Lloyd Millard Bentsen Jr., Texas

Libertarian Party
President: Ronald E. Paul, Texas
Vice president: Andre V. Marrou, Nevada

New Alliance Party
President: Lenora B. Fulani, New York
Vice president: Joyce Dattner

Populist Party
President: David E. Duke, Louisiana
Vice president: Floyd C. Parker

Consumer Party
President: Eugene Joseph McCarthy, Minnesota
Vice president: Florence Rice

American Independent Party
President: James C. Griffin, California
Vice president: Charles J. Morsa

National Economic Recovery Party
President: Lyndon H. LaRouche Jr., Virginia
Vice president: Debra H. Freeman

Right to Life Party
President: William A. Marra, New Jersey
Vice president: Joan Andrews

Workers League Party
President: Edward Winn, New York
Vice president: Barry Porster

Socialist Workers Party
President: James Warren, New Jersey
Vice president: Kathleen Mickells

Peace and Freedom Party
President: Herbert Lewin
Vice president: Vikki Murdock

Prohibition Party
President: Earl F. Dodge, Colorado
Vice president: George D. Ormsby

Workers World Party
President: Larry Holmes, New York
Vice president: Gloria La Riva, California

Socialist Party
President: Willa Kenoyer, Minnesota
Vice president: Ron Ehrenreich

American Party
President: Delmar Dennis, Tennessee
Vice president: Earl Jepson

Grassroots Party
President: Jack E. Herer, California
Vice president: Dana Beal

Independent Party
President: Louie Youngkeit, Utah

Third World Assembly
President: John G. Martin, District of Columbia
Vice president: Cleveland Sparrow

1992 ELECTION[8]

Democratic Party
President: Bill Clinton, Arkansas
Vice president: Albert Gore Jr., Tennessee

Republican Party
President: George Herbert Walker Bush, Texas
Vice president: James "Dan" Quayle, Indiana

Independent
President: H. Ross Perot, Texas
Vice president: James Stockdale, California

Libertarian Party
President: Andre V. Marrou, Nevada
Vice president: Nancy Lord, Georgia

America First Party (Populist)
President: James "Bo" Gritz, Nevada
Vice president: Cyril Minett

New Alliance Party
President: Lenora B. Fulani, New York
Vice president: Maria E. Munoz, California

U.S. Taxpayers Party
President: Howard Phillips, Virginia
Vice president: Albion W. Knight, Maryland

Natural Law Party
President: John Hagelin, Iowa
Vice president: Mike Tompkins, Iowa

Peace and Freedom Party
President: Ron Daniels, California
Vice president: Asiba Tupahache

Independent
President: Lyndon H. LaRouche Jr., Virginia
Vice president: James L. Bevel

Socialist Workers Party
President: James Warren, New Jersey
Vice president: Willie Mae Reid

Independent
President: Drew Bradford

Grassroots Party
President: Jack E. Herer, California
Vice president: Derrick P. Grimmer

Socialist Party
President: J. Quinn Brisben, Illinois
Vice president: Barbara Garson

Workers League Party
President: Helen Halyard, Michigan
Vice president: Fred Mazelis, Michigan

Take Back America Party
President: John Yiamouyiannas
Vice president: Allen C. McCone

Independent
President: Delbert L. Ehlers
Vice president: Rick Wendt

Prohibition Party
President: Earl F. Dodge, Colorado
Vice president: George D. Ormsby

Apathy Party
President: Jim Boren
Vice president: Will Weidman

Third Party
President: Eugene A. Hem
Vice president: Joanne Roland

Looking Back Party
President: Isabell Masters, Oklahoma
Vice president: Walter Masters, Florida

American Party
President: Robert J. Smith
Vice president: Doris Feimer

Workers World Party
President: Gloria La Riva, California
Vice president: Larry Holmes, New York

1996 ELECTION[9]

Democratic Party
    President: Bill Clinton, Arkansas
    Vice president: Albert Gore Jr., Tennessee

Republican Party
    President: Robert Dole, Kansas
    Vice president: Jack Kemp, New York

Reform Party
    President: H. Ross Perot, Texas
    Vice president: Pat Choate, District of Columbia

Green Party
    President: Ralph Nader, District of Columbia
    Vice president: Winona LaDuke, Minnesota

Libertarian Party
    President: Harry Browne, Tennessee
    Vice president: Jo Anne Jorgensen, South
        Carolina

U.S. Taxpayers Party
    President: Howard Phillips, Virginia
    Vice president: Herbert W. Titus, Virginia

Natural Law Party
    President: John Hagelin, Iowa
    Vice president: Mike Tompkins, North Carolina

Workers World Party
    President: Monica Moorehead, New York
    Vice president: Gloria La Riva, California

Peace and Freedom Party
    President: Marsha Feinland, California
    Vice president: Kate McClatchy, Massachusetts

Independent
    President: Charles E. Collins, Florida
    Vice president: Rosemary Giumarra

Socialist Workers Party
    President: James E. Harris Jr., Georgia
    Vice president: Laura Garza, New York

Grassroots Party
    President: Dennis Peron, Minnesota
    Vice president: Arlin Troutt, Arizona

Socialist Party
    President: Mary Cal Hollis, Colorado
    Vice president: Eric Chester, Massachusetts

Socialist Equality Party
    President: Jerome White, Michigan
    Vice president: Fred Mazelis, Michigan

American Party
    President: Diane Beall Templin, California
    Vice president: Gary Van Horn, Utah

Prohibition Party
    President: Earl F. Dodge, Colorado
    Vice president: Rachel Bubar Kelly, Maine

Independent Party of Utah
    President: A. Peter Crane, Utah
    Vice president: Connie Chandler, Utah

America First Party
    President: Ralph Forbes, Arkansas

Independent Grassroots Party
    President: John Birrenbach, Minnesota
    Vice president: George McMahon, Iowa

Looking Back Party
    President: Isabell Masters, Oklahoma
    Vice president: Shirley Jean Masters, California

Independent
    President: Steve Michael, District of Columbia

2000 ELECTION

Republican Party
    President: George W. Bush, Texas
    Vice president: Richard Cheney, Wyoming

Democratic Party
    President: Albert Gore Jr., Tennessee
    Vice president: Joseph Lieberman, Connecticut

Green Party
    President: Ralph Nader, District of Columbia
    Vice president: Winona LaDuke, Minnesota

Reform Party
    President: Patrick J. Buchanan, Virginia
    Vice president: Ezola Foster, California

Libertarian Party[10]
    President: Harry Browne, Tennessee
    Vice president: Art Olivier, California
    President: L. Neil Smith, Arizona

Constitution Party
    President: Howard Phillips, Virginia
    Vice president: J. Curtis Frazier II, Missouri

Natural Law Party
    President: John Hagelin, Iowa
    Vice president: Nat Goldhaber, California

Socialist Workers Party
    President: James E. Harris Jr., Georgia
    Vice president: Margaret Trowe, Minnesota

Socialist Party
    President: David McReynolds, New York
    Vice president: Mary Cal Hollis, Colorado

Workers World Party
    President: Monica Moorehead, New Jersey
    Vice president: Gloria La Riva, California

Independent
    President: Cathy Gordon Brown, Tennessee
    Vice president: Sabrina R. Allen, Tennessee

Vermont Grassroots Party
    President: Dennis I. Lane, Vermont
    Vice president: Dale Wilkinson, Minnesota

Independent
    President: Randall A. Venson, Tennessee
    Vice president: Gene Kelley, Tennessee

Prohibition Party
    President: Earl F. Dodge, Colorado
    Vice president: W. Dean Watkins, Arizona

Independent
    President: Louie Youngkeit, Utah
    Vice president: Robert Leo Beck, Utah

NOTES

* Candidates appeared in Joseph Nathan Kane, *Facts About the Presidents,* 4th ed. (New York: H. W. Wilson, 1981), but could not be verified in another source.

1. 1912: Arthur M. Schlesinger's History of American Presidential Elections (New York: McGraw-Hill, 1971) lists the Socialist Labor Party vice-presidential candidate as Francis. No first name is given.

2. 1924: Richard M. Scammon's *America at the Polls* (Pittsburgh: University of Pittsburgh Press, 1965) lists the American Party vice-presidential candidate as Leander L. Pickett.

3. 1928: *America at the Polls* lists the Farmer Labor Party vice-presidential candidate as L. R. Tillman.

4. 1976: McCarthy, who ran as an independent with no party designation, had no national running mate, favoring the elimination of the office. But as various state laws required a running mate, he had different ones in different states, amounting to nearly two dozen, all political unknowns.

5. 1980: In several cases vice-presidential nominees were different from those listed for most states, and the Socialist Workers and American Party nominees for president varied from state to state. For example, because Pulley, the major standard-bearer for the Socialist Workers Party was only twenty-nine years old, his name was not allowed on the ballot in some states (the Constitution requires presidential candidates to be at least thirty-five years old). Hence, the party ran other candidates in those states. In a number of states, candidates appeared on the ballot with variants of the party designations listed, without any party designation, or with entirely different party names.

6. 1984: Both Larry Holmes and Gavrielle Holmes were standard-bearers of the Workers World Party. Of the two, Larry Holmes was listed on more state ballots. Milton Vera was Gavrielle Holmes's vice-presidential running mate in Ohio and Rhode Island. The Workers League Party had three vice-presidential candidates: Jean T. Brust in Illinois; Helen Halyard in Michigan, New Jersey, and Pennsylvania; and Edward Bergonzi in Minnesota and Ohio.

7. 1988: The candidates listed include all those who appeared on the ballot in at least one state. In some cases, a party's vice-presidential candidate varied from state to state. Candidates' full names and states were not available from some parties.

8. 1992: The candidates listed include all those who appeared on the ballot in at least one state. In some cases a party's vice-presidential candidate varied from state to state. Candidates' states were not available from some parties.

9. 1996: The candidates listed include all those who appeared on the ballot in at least one state. In some cases a party's vice-presidential candidate varied from state to state. Candidates' states were not available from some parties.

10. 2000: L. Neil Smith ran as the Libertarian Party's presidential candidate in Arizona only. Harry Browne ran as the party's candidate in the other forty-nine states.

CHAPTER 14

Convention Chronology, 1831–2000

THIS CHAPTER contains brief descriptions of all presidential nominating conventions of major American political parties and excerpts from party platforms. The chronology begins in 1831, when the Anti-Masonic Party held the first nominating convention in American history, and concludes with the national conventions of the Republican and Democratic parties in 2000.

The narrative includes conventions for all parties receiving at least 2 percent of the popular vote in the presidential election. Thus, conventions for the Socialist Party, which received at least 2 percent of the presidential popular vote in 1904, 1908, 1912, 1920, and 1932, are included. Socialist Party conventions for other presidential election years when the party received less than 2 percent of the popular vote do not appear. In 2000 the Green Party received 2.7 percent of the popular vote so its convention is included here.

The source most frequently consulted in preparing the narrative was Richard C. Bain and Judith H. Parris, *Convention Decisions and Voting Records,* (Washington, D.C.: Brookings Institution, 1973).

BALLOT VOTE TOTALS

Throughout the narrative, vote totals appear for significant ballots on platform disputes and procedural issues and for presidential and vice-presidential balloting.

The source used for 1835–1972 vote totals was *Convention Decisions and Voting Records.* The sources for the 1976 through 2000 vote totals were *The Official Proceedings of the Democratic National Convention* and the Republican National Committee. Charts showing state-by-state voting on selected ballots appear in Chapter 15, Key Convention Ballots, pages 574–641. *(For details on these charts, see p. 573.)*

PLATFORM EXCERPTS

The source for the party platform excerpts that appear in the convention chronology was Kirk H. Porter and Donald Bruce Johnson, *National Party Platforms, 1840–1972* (Urbana: University of Illinois Press, 1973). For the Democratic and Republican platform excerpts for 1976 to 2000, the official texts of the platforms adopted by the two parties were used.

In adopting the material from *National Party Platforms, 1840–1968,* Congressional Quarterly has added boldface subheadings to highlight the organization of the texts. For example, excerpts from the 1844 Democratic Party platform appear on page 447. The boldface headings—Appeal to the Masses, Internal Improvements, Government Spending, etc.—do not appear in the text of the party platform as it was published in *National Party Platforms, 1840–1972.* In all other respects, Congressional Quarterly has followed the style and typography of the platform texts appearing in *National Party Platforms, 1840–1968.* In excerpting the material from the Democratic and Republican platforms from 1976 to 2000, Congressional Quarterly has also edited the boldface subheadings from the original platform documents.

1831–1832 Conventions

PRESIDENTIAL CANDIDATES

William Wirt
Anti-Mason

Henry Clay
National Republican

Andrew Jackson
Democrat

ANTI-MASONS

In September 1831 the Anti-Masonic Party held the first national nominating convention in American history. Thirteen states, none south of Maryland, sent 116 delegates to the gathering in Baltimore. They selected the party's presidential and vice-presidential candidates, adopted an address to the people (a precursor of the party platform), and established a national corresponding committee that created the framework for a national campaign organization.

Ironically, the Anti-Masons, whose keystone was opposition to Masonry, nominated a former Mason, William Wirt of Maryland, as their presidential standard-bearer. In spite of a rule requiring a three-fourths nominating majority, Wirt was an easy first-ballot winner and the nearly unanimous nominee of the convention.

He was not, however, the first choice of party leaders, who had been rebuffed in their earlier efforts to persuade Henry Clay and later Supreme Court Justice John McLean to take the presidential nomination. Wirt himself was not an enthusiastic candidate, stating that he saw nothing repugnant about Masonry and that if his views did not suit the convention, he would willingly withdraw from the ticket. The delegates supported Wirt and chose Amos Ellmaker of Pennsylvania as his vice-presidential running mate.

NATIONAL REPUBLICANS

In December 1831 the National Republicans held a national convention in Baltimore. The National Republicans were united primarily in their opposition to incumbent President Andrew Jackson. The idea of a convention had been proposed by an anti-Jackson committee in New York City and approved by the leading National Republican newspaper, the *National Intelligencer*. There was no uniform method of delegate selection, with state conventions, legislative caucuses, and local meetings all being used.

Eighteen states sent 168 delegates to the National Republican convention, although nearly one-quarter were late in arriving due to inclement winter weather. Without any preestablished rules, it was agreed that the roll calls would be taken by announcing each delegate's name. Henry Clay of Kentucky was the convention's unanimous choice for president, and former representative John Sergeant of Pennsylvania was selected without opposition for vice president. Letters accepting their nominations were received from both candidates.

There was no formal platform, although the convention adopted an address to the people that criticized Jackson for dividing a previously harmonious country.

In May 1832 a convention of young National Republicans met in Washington, D.C., and passed a series of resolutions calling for a protective tariff, federal support of internal improvements, and recognition of the Supreme Court as the ultimate authority on constitutional questions. The last was a rebuke of Jackson for disregarding Supreme Court decisions concerning the Cherokee American Indians. Other resolutions criticized Jackson's use of the spoils system in distributing patronage and his handling of foreign policy with Great Britain. Although not a formal platform, the resolutions adopted by the convention of young National Republicans were the most definitive discussion of issues during the 1832 campaign.

DEMOCRATS

The Democrats held their first national convention in Baltimore in late May 1832. Representatives from twenty-three states attended. The call for a Democratic national convention had been made by Jacksonian members of the New Hampshire legislature, and their proposal was approved by prominent members of President Andrew Jackson's administration. The convention was called to order by a member of the New Hampshire legislature, who explained the intent of the gathering in these words:

... [The] object of the people of New Hampshire who called this convention was, not to impose on the people, as candidates for either of the two first offices of the government, any local favorite; but to concentrate the opinions of all the states. . . . They believed that the example of this convention would operate favorably in future elections; that the people would be disposed, after seeing the good effects of this convention in conciliating the different and distant sections of the country, to continue this mode of nomination." *(Reprinted from* Convention Decisions and Voting Records, *by Richard C. Bain, p. 17.)*

The convention adopted two rules that Democratic conventions retained well into the twentieth century. One based each state's convention vote on its electoral vote, an apportionment method unchanged until 1940.

A second rule established a two-thirds nominating majority, a controversial measure that remained a feature of Democratic conventions until 1936. The 1832 convention also adopted the procedure of having one person from each delegation announce the vote of his state.

The delegates did not formally nominate Jackson for the presidency. Instead they concurred in the various nominations he had received earlier from state legislatures. Jackson's choice for vice president, Martin Van Buren of New York, was easily nominated on the first ballot, receiving 208 of the 283 votes cast.

Instead of adopting a platform or address to the people, the convention decided that each state delegation should write its own report to its constituents. The convention also determined to establish in each state general corresponding committees that together would provide a nationwide organization for the campaign.

1835–1836 Conventions

PRESIDENTIAL CANDIDATES

Martin Van Buren
Democrat

Daniel Webster
Whig

Hugh L. White
Whig

William Henry Harrison
Whig

DEMOCRATS

The Democrats held their second national convention in Baltimore in May 1835. The early date had been set by President Andrew Jackson to prevent the emergence of opposition to his hand picked successor, Vice President Martin Van Buren. Delegates from twenty-two states and two territories attended, and the size of the delegations was generally related to their distance from Baltimore. One hundred eighty-eight individuals were on hand from Maryland to cast the state's ten votes, but only one person attended from Tennessee—a visiting businessman who cast fifteen votes. Alabama, Illinois, and South Carolina were unrepresented.

Two rival Pennsylvania delegations arrived, precipitating the first credentials dispute in convention history. It was decided to seat both delegations and let them share the Pennsylvania vote.

An effort to eliminate the rule requiring a two-thirds nominating majority initially passed by a margin of 231 to 210 (apparently counting individual delegates instead of state convention votes), but the two-thirds rule was reimposed by a voice vote. A question developed whether the nominating majority should be based on only the states represented or on all the states in the union. It was decided to base the majority on only those present.

Vice President Van Buren won the presidential nomination, winning all 265 votes. Richard M. Johnson of Kentucky barely reached the necessary two-thirds majority on the first vice-presidential ballot, receiving 178 votes, just one vote more than the required minimum. *(Table, p. 574.)*

Johnson, famous as the alleged slayer of the American Indian chief Tecumseh, had aroused some disapproval because of his personal life. Johnson had lived with a mulatto mistress by whom he had two daughters.

Once again the Democrats did not write a formal platform, although an address to the people was published in the party newspaper, the *Washington Globe.* Van Buren wrote a letter of acceptance in which he promised to "tread generally in the footsteps of President Jackson."

WHIGS

During Jackson's second term, a new party, the Whigs, emerged as the Democrats' primary opposition. It contained remnants of the short-lived National Republican Party, as well as anti-Jackson elements in the Democratic and Anti-Masonic parties. Although the Whigs were a rising political force, the party lacked national cohesion in 1836. Instead of holding a convention and nominating national candidates, the Whigs ran regional candidates nominated by state legislatures. It was the hope of Whig strategists that the regional candidates would re-

ceive enough electoral votes to throw the election into the House of Representatives, where the party could unite behind the leading prospect.

Sen. Daniel Webster of New Hampshire ran as the Whig candidate in Massachusetts; Sen. Hugh L. White of Tennessee was the party standard-bearer in the South; Gen. William Henry Harrison of Ohio was the Whig candidate in the rest of the country. The Whigs chose Francis Granger of New York as Harrison and Webster's running mate and John Tyler of Virginia to run with White.

1839–1840 Conventions

PRESIDENTIAL CANDIDATES

William Henry Harrison
Whig

Martin Van Buren
Democrat

WHIGS

By 1839 the Whigs had established themselves as a powerful opposition party, unified enough to run a national candidate against the Democratic president, Martin Van Buren. The call for the Whigs' first national convention was issued by a group of party members in Congress. Nearly 250 delegates responded, gathering in Harrisburg, Pa., in December 1839.

Three candidates were in contention for the presidential nomination: Generals William Henry Harrison of Ohio and Winfield Scott of Virginia and Sen. Henry Clay of Kentucky. After long debate, it was decided that each state would ballot separately, then select representatives who would meet and discuss the views and results of their delegation meetings with representatives of the other states. The unit rule would be in effect, binding the entire vote of each state to the candidate who received a majority of the state's delegates.

The nominating rules agreed to by the convention strongly favored the forces opposed to Clay. First, they negated substantial Clay strength in state delegations in which he did not hold a majority of the vote. Second, they permitted balloting in relative anonymity, so that delegates would be more likely to defect from the popular Kentuckian than they would if the balloting were public.

Clay led on the first ballot, but switches by Scott delegates on subsequent roll calls gave the nomination to Harrison. On the final ballot, Harrison received 148 votes to ninety for Clay and sixteen for Scott. Harrison's vote was short of a two-thirds majority, but under Whig rules only a simple majority was needed to nominate.

To give the ticket factional and geographic balance, a friend of Clay, former Democrat John Tyler of Virginia, was the unanimous selection for vice president. The convention did not risk destruction of the tenuous unity of its anti-Democratic coalition by adopting a party platform or statement of principles.

DEMOCRATS

In May 1840 the Democrats held their national convention in Baltimore. The call once again was initiated by members of the New Hampshire legislature. Delegates from twenty-one states attended, while five states were unrepresented. Again, the size of the state delegations was largely determined by their distance from Baltimore. New Jersey sent fifty-nine people to cast the state's eight votes, while only one delegate came from Massachusetts to decide that state's fourteen votes.

To avoid a bitter dispute over the vice-presidential nomination, the convention appointed a committee to recommend nominees for both spots on the ticket. The committee's recommendation that Van Buren be renominated for president was passed by acclamation. On the touchier problem of the vice presidency, the committee recommended that no nomination be made, a suggestion that was also agreed to by the convention. Dissatisfaction with the personal life of Vice President Johnson had increased, leading to the decision that state Democratic leaders determine who would run as the vice-presidential candidate in their own states.

Before the nominating process had begun, the convention had approved the first party platform in American history. A platform committee was appointed "to prepare resolutions declaratory of the principles of the . . . party." The committee report was approved without discussion.

The first Democratic platform was a short document, fewer than 1,000 words long. Although brief by modern standards, the platform clearly emphasized the party's belief in a strict reading of the Constitution. It began by stating "that the federal government is one of limited powers" and spelled out in detail what the federal government could not do. The platform stated that the federal government did not have the power to finance internal improvements, assume state debts, charter a national bank or interfere with the rights of the states, especially relating to slavery. The platform criticized the abolitionists for stirring up the explosive slavery question. The Democrats urged the government to practice economy, supported President Van Buren's independent treasury plan, and affirmed their belief in the principles expressed in the Declaration of Independence.

In addition to the platform, the convention adopted an address to the people, which was written by a separate committee. Much longer than the platform, the address discussed party principles, lauded Van Buren and Jackson for following these principles and warned of dire consequences if the opposition should be elected.

Following are excerpts from the Democratic platform of 1840:

Strict Construction. That the federal government is one of limited powers, derived solely from the constitution, and the grants of power shown therein, ought to be strictly construed by all the departments and agents of the government, and that it is inexpedient and dangerous to exercise doubtful constitutional powers.

Internal Improvements. That the constitution does not confer upon the general government the power to commence and carry on, a general system of internal improvements.

State Debts. That the constitution does not confer authority upon the federal government, directly or indirectly, to assume the debts of the several states, contracted for local internal improvements, or other state purposes; nor would such assumption be just or expedient.

Equality of Rights. That justice and sound policy forbid the federal government to foster one branch of industry to the detriment of another, or to cherish the interests of one portion to the injury of another portion of our common country—that every citizen and every section of the country, has a right to demand and insist upon an equality of rights and privileges, and to complete and ample protection of person and property from domestic violence, or foreign aggression.

Government Spending. That it is the duty of every branch of the government, to enforce and practice the most rigid economy, in conducting our public affairs, and that no more revenue ought to be raised, than is required to defray the necessary expenses of the government.

National Bank. That congress has no power to charter a national bank; that we believe such an institution one of deadly hostility to the best interests of the country, dangerous to our republican institutions and the liberties of the people, and calculated to place the business of the country within the control of a concentrated money power, and above the laws and the will of the people.

States' Rights, Slavery. That congress has no power, under the constitution, to interfere with or control the domestic institutions of the several states, and that such states are the sole and proper judges of everything appertaining to their own affairs, not prohibited by the constitution; that all efforts by abolitionists or others, made to induce congress to interfere with questions of slavery, or to take incipient steps in relation thereto, are calculated to lead to the most alarming and dangerous consequences, and that all such efforts have an inevitable tendency to diminish the happiness of the people, and endanger the stability and permanency of the union, and ought not to be countenanced by any friend to our political institutions.

Independent Treasury. That the separation of the moneys of the government from banking institutions, is indispensable for the safety of the funds of the government, and the rights of the people.

Democratic Principles. That the liberal principles embodied by Jefferson in the Declaration of Independence, and sanctioned in the constitution, which makes ours the land of liberty, and the asylum of the oppressed of every nation, have ever been cardinal principles in the democratic faith; and every attempt to abridge the present privilege of becoming citizens, and the owners of soil among us, ought to be resisted with the same spirit which swept the alien and sedition laws from our statute-book.

1843–1844 Conventions

PRESIDENTIAL CANDIDATES

James G. Birney
Liberty

Henry Clay
Whig

James K. Polk
Democrat

LIBERTY PARTY

The Liberty Party held its second national convention in Buffalo, N.Y., in August 1843. The party, born of the failure of the Whigs and the Democrats to make a strong appeal to abolitionist voters, had held its first national convention in April 1840 in Albany, New York. James G. Birney of Michigan, a former slave owner, was nominated for president and Thomas Earle of Ohio was chosen as his running mate. In the 1840 election the party polled 0.29 percent of the national popular vote.

At the 1843 convention, 148 delegates from twelve states assembled in Buffalo and renominated Birney for the presidency and chose Thomas Morris of Ohio as his running mate. The party platform was more than 3,000 words long, the lengthiest platform written by any party in the nineteenth century. In spite of its length, the platform discussed only one issue, slavery. In the 1844 election, the party received 2.3 percent of the national popular vote, its highest total in any presidential election. By 1848, most members of the party joined the newly formed Free Soil Party.

Following are excerpts from the Liberty Party platform of 1844:

Resolved, That the Liberty party . . . will demand the absolute and unqualified divorce of the General Government from Slavery, and also the restoration of equality of rights, among men, in every State where the party exists, or may exist.

Therefore, Resolved, That we hereby give it to be distinctly understood, by this nation and the world, that, as abolitionists, considering that the strength of our cause lies in its righteousness—and our hope for it in our conformity to the LAWS of GOD, and our respect for the RIGHTS OF MAN, we owe it to the Sovereign Ruler of the Universe, as a proof of our allegiance to Him, in all our civil relations and offices, whether as private citizens, or as public functionaries sworn to support the Constitution of the United States, to regard and to treat the third clause of the second section of the fourth article of that instrument, whenever applied to the case of a fugitive slave, as utterly null and void, and consequently as forming no part of the Constitution of the United States, whenever we are called upon, or sworn, to support it.

WHIGS

In a harmonious one-day session, the Whigs' national convention nominated for the presidency the party's former leader in Congress, Henry Clay. It was a final rebuff for President John Tyler from the party that had nominated him for the second spot on its ticket in 1840. Three years of bickering between the White House and Whig leaders in Congress had made Tyler, former Democrat, persona non grata in the Whig Party.

Delegates from every state were represented at the Whig convention, held in Baltimore on May 1, 1844. Clay was the unanimous nominee, and it was proposed that he be invited to address the convention the next day. However, the Kentuckian declined this opportunity to make the first acceptance speech in American political history, stating in a letter that he was unable to reconcile an appearance with his "sense of delicacy and propriety." *(Table, p. 515.)*

Three potential candidates for the vice presidency sent letters of withdrawal before balloting for second place on the ticket began. Unlike the convention four years earlier, the Whigs abandoned their relatively secret state caucus method of voting and adopted a public roll call, with the chair calling the name of each delegate. Theodore Frelinghuysen of New Jersey won a plurality of the convention vote for vice president on the first ballot and went on to gain, on the third ballot, the required majority.

After the nominations, several resolutions were adopted, including one that defined Whig principles and served as the party's first platform. It was a brief document, fewer than 100 words long, and the only clear difference between it and the platform adopted later by the Democratic convention was on the issue of distributing proceeds from the sale of public land. The Whigs favored distribution of these revenues to the states; the Democrats opposed it believing the proceeds should be retained by the federal government. In a continued reaction to the Jackson administration, the Whigs criticized "executive usurpations" and proposed a single-term presidency. The rest of the Whig platform called for government efficiency, "a well-regulated currency" and a tariff for revenue and the protection of American labor.

Westward territorial expansion, particularly the annexation of Texas, was not mentioned in the Whig platform, but it was an explosive issue by 1844 that made a significant impact on the Democratic convention.

Following is an excerpt from the Whig platform of 1844:

Resolved, That these principles may be summed as comprising, a well-regulated currency; a tariff for revenue to defray the necessary expenses of the government, and discriminating with special reference to protection of the domestic labor of the country; the distribution of the proceeds of the sales of the public lands; a single term for the presidency; a reform of executive usurpations;—and, generally—such an administration of the affairs of the country as shall impart to every branch of the public service the greatest practicable efficiency, controlled by a well regulated and wise economy.

DEMOCRATS

Delegates from every state except South Carolina assembled in Baltimore in late May 1844 for the Democratic convention. The front-runner for the presidential nomination was former president Martin Van Buren, whose status was threatened on the eve of the convention by his statement against the annexation of Texas. Van Buren's position jeopardized his support in the South, and with a two-thirds majority apparently necessary, dimmed his chances of obtaining the presidential nomination. The question of requiring a two-thirds nominating majority was debated in the early sessions of the convention, and by a vote of 148 to 118 the two-thirds majority rule, initially adopted by the party in 1832, was ratified. (*Table, p. 574.*)

Van Buren led the early presidential balloting, actually receiving a simple majority of the vote on the first ballot. On succeeding roll calls, however, his principal opponent, Lewis Cass of Michigan, gained strength and took the lead. But neither candidate approached the 178 votes needed for nomination.

With a deadlock developing, sentiment for a compromise candidate appeared. James K. Polk, former speaker of the Tennessee House and former governor of Tennessee, emerged as an acceptable choice and won the nomination on the ninth ballot. It marked the first time in American history that a dark-horse candidate won a presidential nomination. (*Table, p. 574.*)

A friend of Van Buren, Sen. Silas Wright of New York, was the nearly unanimous nominee of the convention for vice president. But Wright refused the nomination, quickly notifying the delegates by way of Samuel Morse's new invention, the telegraph. After two more ballots, George M. Dallas of Pennsylvania was chosen as Polk's running mate.

Among its final actions, the convention appointed a central committee and recommended that a nationwide party organization be established—a forerunner of the national committee. The delegates did not adopt a platform but appointed a committee to draft resolutions.

The resulting document contained the same resolutions included in the party's 1840 platform, plus several new planks. The Democrats opposed the distribution of the proceeds from the sale of public lands; were against placing any restrictions on the executive veto power; and, to alleviate the sectional bitterness aroused by the prospect of Western expansion, recommended the annexation of both Texas and Oregon.

President Tyler, although abandoned by the major parties, wanted to remain in office. Friends and federal officeholders gathered in Baltimore at the same time as the Democrats and nominated Tyler. However, it became apparent that the president's national vote-getting appeal was limited, and he withdrew from the race in favor of the Democrat, Polk.

Following are excerpts from the Democratic resolutions of 1844:

Appeal to the Masses. That the American Democracy place their trust, not in factitious symbols, not in displays and appeals insulting to the judgment and subversive of the intellect of the people, but in a clear reliance upon the intelligence, patriotism, and the discriminating justice of the American masses.

That we regard this as a distinctive feature of our political creed, which we are proud to maintain before the world, as the great moral element in a form of government springing from and upheld by the popular will; and we contrast it with the creed and practice of Federalism, under whatever name or form, which seeks to palsy the will of the constituent, and which conceives no imposture too monstrous for the popular credulity.

Internal Improvements. That the Constitution does not confer upon the General Government the power to commence or carry on a general system of internal improvements.

State Debts. That the Constitution does not confer authority upon the Federal Government, directly or indirectly, to assume the debts of the several states.

Government Spending. That it is the duty of every branch of the government to enforce and practice the most rigid economy in conducting our public affairs, and that no more revenue ought to be raised than is required to defray the necessary expenses of the government.

National Bank. That Congress has no power to charter a United States Bank, that we believe such an institution one of deadly hostility to the best interests of the country, dangerous to our republican institutions and the liberties of the people.

States' Rights. That Congress has no power, under the Constitution, to interfere with or control the domestic institutions of the several States; and that such States are the sole and proper judges of everything pertaining to their own affairs, not prohibited by the Constitution; that all efforts, by abolitionists or others, made to induce Congress to interfere with questions of slavery, or to take incipient steps in relation thereto, are calculated to lead to the most alarming and dangerous consequences.

Public Lands. That the proceeds of the Public Lands ought to be sacredly applied to the national objects specified in the Constitution, and that we are opposed to the laws lately adopted, and to any law for the distribution of such proceeds among the States, as alike inexpedient in policy and repugnant to the Constitution.

Executive Veto Power. That we are decidedly opposed to taking from the President the qualified veto power by which he is enabled, under restrictions and responsibilities amply sufficient to guard the public interest.

Western Expansion. That our title to the whole of the Territory of Oregon is clear and unquestionable; that no portion of the same ought to be ceded to England or any other power, and that the reoccupation of Oregon and the reannexation of Texas at the earliest practicable period are great American measures, which this Convention recommends to the cordial support of the Democracy of the Union.

1848 Conventions

PRESIDENTIAL CANDIDATES

Lewis Cass
Democrat

Zachary Taylor
Whig

Martin Van Buren
Free Soil

DEMOCRATS

Delegates from every state gathered in Baltimore in May 1848 for the Democratic Party's fifth national convention. A seating dispute between two rival New York delegations enlivened the early convention sessions. The conflict reflected a factional fight in the state Democratic Party between a more liberal antislavery faction, known as the Barnburners, and a more conservative faction, known as the Hunkers. By a vote of 126 to 125, the convention adopted a compromise by which both delegations were seated and shared New York's vote. However, this compromise satisfied neither of the contesting delegations. The Barnburners bolted the convention. The Hunkers remained but refused to vote. *(Table, p. 575.)*

Before the presidential balloting could begin, the convention had to decide whether to use the controversial two-thirds rule. Consideration of the rule preceded the credentials controversy, which brought an objection from New York delegates who wanted their seating dispute settled first. But, by a vote of 133 to 121, the convention refused to table the issue. A second vote on adoption of the two-thirds rule was approved, 176 to 78. *(Table, p. 575.)*

The front-runner for the presidential nomination was Sen. Lewis Cass of Michigan. Although Cass was from the North, his view that the existence of slavery in the territories should be determined by their inhabitants (a forerunner of Stephen Douglas' "popular sovereignty") was a position acceptable to the South.

Cass received 125 votes on the first ballot, more than double the total of his two principal rivals, James Buchanan of Pennsylvania and Levi Woodbury of New Hampshire. Cass's vote total steadily increased during the next three roll calls, and on the fourth ballot he received 179 votes and was nominated. His vote was actually short of a two-thirds majority of the allotted convention votes, but the chair ruled that, with New York not voting, the required majority was reduced. *(Table, p. 575.)*

The vice-presidential nomination went on the second ballot to Gen. William O. Butler of Kentucky, who had 169 of the 253

votes cast. As in the earlier presidential balloting, Butler's two-thirds majority was based on votes cast rather than votes allotted. Butler's primary rival for the nomination was a military colleague, Gen. John A. Quitman of Mississippi.

One of the most significant acts of the convention was the formation of a national committee, with one member from each state, that would handle party affairs until the next convention four years later.

As in 1840 and 1844, the heart of the Democratic platform was a series of resolutions describing the party's concept of a federal government with limited powers. New resolutions emphasized Democratic opposition to a national bank and the distribution of land sales to the states, while applauding the independent treasury plan, the lower tariff bill passed in 1846, and the successful war against Mexico. An effort by William L. Yancey of Alabama to insert in the platform a plank on slavery that would prevent interference with the rights of slaveholders in states or territories was defeated, 216 to 36. The slavery plank written in the platform had the same wording as earlier versions in the 1840 and 1844 Democratic platforms. The plank was milder than Yancey's proposal, stating simply that Congress did not have the power to interfere with slavery in the states. The convention adopted the complete platform by a vote of 247 to 0.

Following are excerpts from the 1848 Democratic platform:

Mexican War. That the war with Mexico, provoked on her part by years of insult and injury, was commenced by her army crossing the Rio Grande, attacking the American troops, and invading our sister State of Texas; and that, upon all the principles of patriotism and laws of nations, it is a just and necessary war on our part, in which every American citizen should have shown himself on the side of his country, and neither morally nor physically, by word or by deed, have given "aid and comfort to the enemy."

Democratic Accomplishments. That the fruits of the great political triumph of 1844, which elected James K. Polk and George M. Dallas President and Vice President of the United States, have fulfilled the hopes of the Democracy of the Union—in defeating the declared purposes of their opponents to create a national bank; in preventing the corrupt and unconstitutional distribution of the land proceeds, from the common treasury of the Union, for local purposes; in protecting the currency and the labor of the country from ruinous fluctuations, and guarding the money of the people for the use of the people, by the establishment of the constitutional treasury; in the noble impulse given to the cause of free trade, by the repeal of the tariff in 1842 and the creation of the more equal, honest, and productive tariff of 1846.

WHIGS

Whig delegates from every state except Texas gathered in Philadelphia in June 1848. Although the Lone Star state was unrepresented, a Texas Whig state convention had earlier given a proxy for its votes to the Louisiana delegates. There was debate in the convention about the legality of the proxy, but it was ultimately accepted by the delegates.

The battle for the Whig's presidential nomination involved three major contenders, the party's respected aging statesman, Henry Clay of Kentucky; and two generals—Zachary Taylor and Winfield Scott, both of Virginia—whose political appeal was significantly increased by their military exploits in the recently completed Mexican War. Taylor led throughout the balloting, taking the lead on the first ballot with 111 votes, compared with 97 for Clay and 43 for Scott. Taylor increased his lead on subsequent roll calls, winning the nomination on the fourth ballot with 171 of the 280 votes cast. (Table, p. 576.)

Millard Fillmore of New York and Abbott Lawrence of Massachusetts were the prime contenders for the vice-presidential nomination. Fillmore led Lawrence, 115 to 109, on the first ballot and pulled away to win on the second ballot with 173 of the 266 votes cast.

A motion to make the presidential and vice-presidential nominations unanimous failed when several delegates objected, doubting Taylor's support of Whig principles.

The Whig convention did not formally adopt a party platform, although a ratification meeting held in Philadelphia after the convention adopted a series of resolutions. The resolutions avoided a discussion of issues, instead lauding the party's presidential nominee, Zachary Taylor, and affirming his faithfulness to the tenets of the party.

FREE SOILERS

Antislavery Whigs, New York Barnburners, and members of the Liberty Party gathered in Buffalo, New York, in August 1848 to form a new third party, the Free Soilers. While opposition to slavery was a common denominator of the various elements in the new party, the dissident Democrats and Whigs also were attracted to the Free Soil Party by the lack of influence they exerted in their former parties. The call for a Free Soil convention was made by the New York Barnburners at their state conclave in June 1848 and by a nonpartisan gathering in Columbus, Ohio, the same month. The latter assembly, organized by Salmon P. Chase, was entitled a People's Convention of Friends of Free Territory and was designed to set the stage for a national Free Soil convention.

Eighteen states (including the slave states of Delaware, Maryland, and Virginia) sent 465 delegates to Buffalo for the birth of the Free Soil Party. Because of the large number of delegates,

convention leaders determined that delegates from each state would select several members to form a Committee on Conference, which would conduct convention business. The rest of the delegates would sit in a large tent and listen to campaign oratory.

Martin Van Buren, the former Democratic president and a favorite of the Barnburners, was chosen as the new party's standard-bearer on the first ballot. Van Buren received 244 votes to defeat John P. Hale of New Hampshire, who had 181 votes. Hale had been nominated by the Liberty Party in October 1847, but with Van Buren's nomination he withdrew from the race. The vice-presidential nomination went to a former Whig, Charles Francis Adams of Massachusetts.

The platform adopted by the Free Soil Party focused on the slavery issue, but its opposition to slavery was milder than earlier Liberty Party platforms. The Free Soilers also declared themselves on other issues besides slavery, further distinguishing themselves from the single-minded Liberty Party.

While the Free Soilers opposed the extension of slavery into the territories, they did not feel the federal government had the power to interfere with slavery in the states. Although this position was significantly stronger than the position adopted by the Democrats, it was milder than the all-out opposition to slavery expressed by the Liberty Party four years earlier.

The Free Soilers also adopted positions on a variety of other issues, supporting free land for settlers, a tariff for revenue purposes, cheap postage, and federal spending for river and harbor improvements. Basically, the Free Soil platform expressed belief in a federal government with broader powers than that conceived by the Democrats.

Following are excerpts from the 1848 Free Soil Party platform:

Slavery. That Slavery in the several States of this Union which recognize its existence, depends upon the State laws alone, which cannot be repealed or modified by the Federal Government, and for which laws that Government is not responsible. We therefore propose no interference by Congress with Slavery within the limits of any State.

Resolved, THAT IT IS THE DUTY OF THE FEDERAL GOVERNMENT TO RELIEVE ITSELF FROM ALL RESPONSIBILITY FOR THE EXISTENCE OR CONTINUANCE OF SLAVERY WHEREVER THAT GOVERNMENT POSSESS CONSTITUTIONAL POWER TO LEGISLATE ON THAT SUBJECT, AND IS THUS RESPONSIBLE FOR ITS EXISTENCE.

Resolved, That the true, and, in the judgment of this Convention, the *only* safe means of preventing the extension of Slavery into territory now free, is to prohibit its existence in all such territory by *an act of Congress.*

Government Administration. That we demand CHEAP POSTAGE for the people; a retrenchment of the expenses and patronage of the Federal Government; the *abolition* of all *unnecessary* offices and salaries; and the election by the People of all civil officers in the service of the Government, so far as the same may be practicable.

Internal Improvements. That *river* and *harbor improvements,* when demanded by the safety and convenience of commerce with foreign nations, or among the several States, are objects of *national concern;* and that it is the duty of Congress, in the exercise of its constitutional powers, to provide therefor.

Homesteading. That the FREE GRANT TO ACTUAL SETTLERS, in consideration of the expenses they incur in making settlements in the wilderness, which are usually fully equal to their actual cost, and of the public benefits resulting therefrom, of reasonable portions of the public lands, under suitable limitations, is a wise and just measure of public policy, which will promote, in various ways, the interest of all the States of this Union; and we therefore recommend it to the favorable consideration of the American People.

Tariff. That the obligations of honor and patriotism require the

earliest practical payment of the national debt, and we are therefore in favor of such a tariff of duties as will raise revenue adequate to defray the necessary expenses of the Federal Government, and to pay annual installments of our debt and the interest thereon.

Party Motto. *Resolved,* That we inscribe on our banner, "FREE SOIL, FREE SPEECH, FREE LABOR, AND FREE MEN."

1852 Conventions

PRESIDENTIAL CANDIDATES

Franklin Pierce
Democrat

Winfield Scott
Whig

John P. Hale
Free Soil

DEMOCRATS

In spite of the efforts of the major politicians of both parties, the explosive slavery question was fast becoming the dominant issue in American politics and was threatening the tenuous intersectional alliances that held together both the Democratic and Whig parties. Under the cloud of this volatile issue, the Democratic convention convened in Baltimore in June 1852.

The delegates were called to order by the party's first national chairman, Benjamin F. Hallett of Massachusetts. Hallett's first action was to limit the size of each state delegation to its electoral vote, dispatching members of oversized delegations to the rear of the hall. Retention of the two-thirds rule provoked little opposition, unlike the disputes at the 1844 and 1848 conventions, and an effort to table the rule was soundly beaten, 269 to 13.

With a degree of orderliness, the convention disposed of procedural matters, clearing the way for the presidential balloting. There were four major contenders for the nomination: Sen. Lewis Cass of Michigan, James Buchanan of Pennsylvania, and William L. Marcy of New York—all three more than sixty years old—and the rising young senator from Illinois, Stephen A. Douglas, thirty-nine. Each of the four challengers led at one point during the numerous ballots that followed.

Cass jumped in front initially, receiving 116 votes on the first ballot. Buchanan trailed with 93, while Marcy and Douglas were far back with 27 and 20 votes, respectively. Cass's vote dropped after the first few roll calls, but he was able to hold the lead until the twentieth ballot, when Buchanan moved in front. Buchanan led for several roll calls, followed by Douglas, who edged into

the lead on the thirtieth ballot, only to be quickly displaced by Cass on the thirty-second ballot. Marcy made his spurt between the thirty-sixth and forty-eighth ballots, and took the lead on the forty-fifth and forty-sixth ballots. But in spite of the quick changes in fortune, none of the four contenders could win a simple majority of the votes, let alone the two-thirds required. *(Table, p. 577.)*

With a deadlock developing, on the thirty-fifth ballot the Virginia delegation introduced a new name, Franklin Pierce of New Hampshire. Although formerly a member of both houses of Congress, Pierce was little known nationally and not identified with any party faction. Pierce's relative anonymity made him an acceptable alternative in the volatile convention. Pierce received fifteen votes on the thirty-fifth ballot and gradually gained strength on subsequent ballots, with the big break coming on the forty-ninth roll call. Nearly unanimous votes for Pierce in the New England states created a bandwagon effect that resulted in his nomination on this ballot with 279 of the 288 votes cast. The forty-nine ballots took two days.

Beginning the vice-presidential roll call, a spokesman for the Maine delegation suggested that second place on the ticket go to a representative of the South, specifically mentioning Sen. William R. King of Alabama. King moved into a strong lead on the first ballot with 125 votes and easily won nomination on the second roll call with 277 of the 288 votes cast.

The platform adopted by the Democratic convention contained the same nine resolutions that had been in all party platforms since 1840, detailing the Democratic concept of a limited federal government. The platform included a plank supporting the Compromise of 1850, the congressional solution to the slavery question. Actually, both the Whigs and Democrats endorsed the compromise of 1850. The major point of dispute between the two parties was over the issue of internal improvements, with the Whigs taking a broader view of federal power in this sphere.

Following are excerpts from the Democratic platform of 1852:

Compromise of 1850. *Resolved,* . . . the democratic party of the Union, standing on this national platform, will abide by and adhere to a faithful execution of the acts known as the compromise measures settled by the last Congress—"the act for reclaiming fugitives from service or labor" included; which act, being designed to carry out an express provision of the constitution, cannot, with fidelity thereto be repealed nor so changed as to destroy or impair its efficiency.

Resolved, That the democratic party will resist all attempts at renewing, in congress or out of it, the agitation of the slavery question, under whatever shape or color the attempt may be made.

Democratic Principles. That, in view of the condition of popular institutions in the Old World, a high and sacred duty is devolved, with increased responsibility upon the democratic party of this country, as the party of the people, to uphold and maintain the rights of every State, and thereby the Union of the States, and to sustain and advance among us constitutional liberty, by continuing to resist all monopolies and exclusive legislation for the benefit of the few at the expense of the many, and by a vigilant and constant adherence to those principles and compromises of the constitution, which are broad enough and strong enough to embrace and uphold the Union as it was, the Union as it is, and the Union as it shall be, in the full expansion of the energies and capacity of this great and progressive people.

WHIGS

Although in control of the White House, the Whigs were more sharply divided by the Compromise of 1850 than were the Democrats. The majority of northern Whigs in Congress opposed the Compromise, while most southern members of the party favored it. Faced with widening division in their ranks, Whig delegates convened in Baltimore in June 1852. The call for this national convention had been issued by Whig members of Congress, and delegates from all thirty-one states attended.

The convention sessions were often lively and sometimes raucous. When asked to present its report the first day, the credentials committee responded that it was not ready to report and "didn't know when—maybe for days." A minister, invited to the hall to deliver a prayer to the convention, never had his chance. The delegates debated when the prayer should be delivered and finally decided to omit it.

A heated debate occurred on how many votes each state would be apportioned on the platform committee. By a vote of 149 to 144, the delegates adopted a plan whereby each state's vote on the committee would reflect its strength in the electoral college. Strong protests from southern and small northern states, however, brought a reversal of this decision, and although no formal vote was recorded, representation on the platform committee was changed so that each state received one vote.

The northern and southern wings of the Whig Party were nearly equally represented at the Baltimore convention, and the close split produced a prolonged battle for the party's presidential nomination. The two major rivals for the nomination, President Millard Fillmore and Winfield Scott, had nearly equal strength. Ironically, the basic appeal of Fillmore of New York was among southern delegates, who appreciated his support of the Compromise of 1850.

Although a native of Virginia, Scott was not popular in the South because of his ambivalence on the Compromise and the active support given him by a leading antislavery northerner, Sen. William H. Seward of New York. Scott's strength was in the northern and western states. A third candidate in the field was Daniel Webster, the party's elder statesman, whose appeal was centered in his native New England.

On the first ballot, Fillmore received 133 votes, Scott had 132, and Webster collected 29. This nearly equal distribution of the vote between Fillmore and Scott continued with little fluctuation through the first two days of balloting. Midway through the second day, after the thirty-fourth ballot, a motion was made to adjourn. Although it was defeated by a vote of 126 to 76, other motions were made to adjourn throughout the rest of the session. Finally, amid increasing confusion, after the forty-sixth ballot, delegates voted by a margin of 176 to 116 to adjourn. *(Table, p. 578.)*

Commotion continued the next day, with southern delegates trying unsuccessfully to expel Henry J. Raymond, the editor of the *New York Times,* who was also a delegate by proxy. In an article, Raymond had charged collusion between party managers and southern delegates, with the South getting its way on the platform while Scott received the presidential nomination.

Amid this uproar, the leaders of the Fillmore and Webster forces were negotiating. Fillmore was willing to release his delegates to Webster, if Webster could muster 41 votes on his own. As the balloting continued, it was apparent that Webster could not; and enough delegates defected to Scott to give the Mexican War hero a simple majority and the nomination on the fifty-third ballot. On the final roll call, Scott received 159 votes, compared with 112 for Fillmore, and 21 for Webster.

Several individuals placed in nomination for the vice presidency refused it immediately. The chairman of the convention finally declared Secretary of the Navy William A. Graham of North Carolina to be the unanimous selection. No formal roll-call vote was recorded.

For only the second time in their history, the Whigs adopted a party platform. Like their Democratic adversaries, the Whigs supported the Compromise of 1850 and perceived the federal government as having limited powers. Additional planks called for a tariff on imports to raise revenue and for an isolationist foreign policy that avoided "entangling alliances." The platform was adopted by a vote of 227 to 66, with all the dissenting votes cast by delegates from the North and West.

Following are excerpts from the Whig platform of 1852:

Strict Construction. The Government of the United States is of a limited character, and it is confined to the exercise of powers expressly granted by the Constitution, and such as may be necessary and proper for carrying the granted powers into full execution, and that all powers not granted or necessarily implied are expressly reserved to the States respectively and to the people.

Foreign Policy. That while struggling freedom everywhere enlists the warmest sympathy of the Whig party, we still adhere to the doctrines of the Father of his Country, as announced in his Farewell Address, of keeping ourselves free from all entangling alliances with foreign countries, and of never quitting our own to stand upon foreign ground, that our mission as a republic is not to propagate our opinions, or impose on other countries our form of government by artifice or force; but to teach, by example, and show by our success, moderation and justice, the blessings of self-government, and the advantages of free institutions.

Tariff. Revenue sufficient for the expenses of an economical administration of the Government in time of peace ought to be derived from a duty on imports, and not from direct taxation.

Internal Improvements. The Constitution vests in Congress the power to open and repair harbors, and remove obstructions from navigable rivers, whenever such improvements are necessary for the common defense, and for the protection and facility of commerce with foreign nations, or among the States, said improvements being, in every instance, national and general in their character.

Compromise of 1850. That the series of acts of the Thirty-first Congress—the act known as the Fugitive Slave Law, included—are received and acquiesced in by the Whig Party of the United States as a settlement in principle and substance, of the dangerous and exciting question which they embrace; and, so far as they are concerned, we will maintain them, and insist upon their strict enforcement, until time and experience shall demonstrate the necessity of further legislation.

FREE DEMOCRATS (FREE SOILERS)

After the 1848 election, the New York Barnburners returned to the Democratic Party, and the rest of the Free Soilers were ready to coalesce with either the Democrats or the Whigs. But the process of absorption was delayed by the Compromise of 1850. It was viewed as a solution to the slavery question by the two major parties but was regarded as a sellout by most antislavery groups.

Responding to a call for a national convention issued by a Cleveland, Ohio, antislavery meeting, delegates gathered in Pittsburgh in August 1852. Antislavery Whigs and remnants of the Liberty Party were in attendance at what was termed the Free Soil Democratic Convention.

John P. Hale of New Hampshire unanimously won the presi-

dential nomination, and George W. Julian of Indiana was selected as his running mate.

Although the platform covered a number of issues, the document focused on the slavery question. The Free Soil Democrats opposed the Compromise of 1850 and called for the abolition of slavery. Like both major parties, the Free Democrats expressed the concept of a limited federal government, but they agreed with the Whigs that the government should undertake certain river and harbor improvements. The Free Democrats went beyond the other parties in advocating a homestead policy, extending a welcome to immigrants and voicing support for new republican governments in Europe and the Caribbean.

Following are excerpts from the Free Democratic platform of 1852:

Strict Construction. That the Federal Government is one of limited powers, derived solely from the Constitution, and the grants of power therein ought to be strictly construed by all the departments and agents of the Government, and it is inexpedient and dangerous to exercise doubtful constitutional powers.

Compromise of 1850. That, to the persevering and importunate demands of the slave power for more slave States, new slave Territories, and the nationalization of slavery, our distinct and final answer is—no more slave States, no slave Territory, no nationalized slavery, and no national legislation for the extradition of slaves.

That slavery is a sin against God and a crime against man, which no human enactment nor usage can make right; and that Christianity, humanity, and patriotism, alike demand its abolition.

That the Fugitive Slave Act of 1850 is repugnant to the Constitution, to the principles of the common law, to the spirit of Christianity, and to the sentiments of the civilized world. We therefore deny its binding force upon the American People, and demand its immediate and total repeal.

Homesteading. That the public lands of the United States belong to the people, and should not be sold to individuals nor granted to corporations, but should be held as a sacred trust for the benefit of the people, and should be granted in limited quantities, free of cost, to landless settlers.

Internal Improvements. That river and harbor improvements, when necessary to the safety and convenience of commerce with foreign nations or among the several States, are objects of national concern, and it is the duty of Congress in the exercise of its constitutional powers to provide for the same.

1856 Conventions

PRESIDENTIAL CANDIDATES

John C. Fremont
Republican

Millard Fillmore
Know-Nothing

James Buchanan
Democrat

REPUBLICANS

With the decline of the Whigs and the increasing importance of the slavery issue, there was room for a new political party. Officially born in 1854, the new Republican Party moved to fill the vacuum.

The party's first meeting was held in Pittsburgh in February 1856, with delegates from twenty-four states attending. United in their opposition to the extension of slavery and the policies of the Pierce administration, the gathering selected a national committee (with one representative from each state), which was empowered to call the party's first national convention.

The subsequent call was addressed not to Republicans but "to the people of the United States" who were opposed to the Pierce administration and the congressional compromises on slavery. Each state was allocated six delegates at the forthcoming convention, with three additional delegates for each congressional district.

When the first Republican National Convention assembled in Philadelphia in June 1856, the gathering was clearly sectional. There were nearly 600 delegates present, representing all the northern states, the border slave states of Delaware, Maryland, Virginia, and Kentucky, and the District of Columbia. The territory of Kansas, symbolically important in the slavery struggle, was treated as a state and given full representation. There were no delegations from the remaining southern slave states.

Under convention rules, the roll call was to proceed in alphabetical order, with each state allocated three times its electoral vote. In response to a question, the chair decided that a simple majority would be required and not the two-thirds majority mandated by the Democratic convention. This was an important rule that distinguished the conventions of the two major parties well into the twentieth century.

Two major contenders for the Republican presidential nomination, Salmon P. Chase of Ohio and William H. Seward of New York, both withdrew before the balloting began. Another contender, Supreme Court Justice John McLean of Ohio, withdrew briefly, but then reentered the race. However, McLean could not catch the front-runner, John C. Fremont of California. Although briefly a U.S. senator, Fremont was most famous as an explorer, and he benefited from being free of any ideological identification.

The other contenders were all identified with one of the factions that had come to make up the new party. Fremont won a preliminary, informal ballot, receiving 359 votes to 190 for McLean. On the formal roll call, Fremont won easily, winning 520 of the 567 votes. *(Table, p. 579.)*

A preliminary, informal ballot was taken for the vice presidency as well. William L. Dayton, a former senator from New Jersey, led with 253 votes, more than twice the total received by an Illinois lawyer, Abraham Lincoln, who had served in the House of Representatives 1847–1849. On the formal ballot, Dayton swept to victory with 523 votes. His nomination was quickly made unanimous.

The Republican platform was approved by a voice vote. It was a document with sectional appeal, written by northern delegates for the North. Unlike the Democrats, the Republicans opposed the concept of popular sovereignty and believed that slavery should be prohibited in the territories. Specifically, the platform called for the admission of Kansas as a free state.

The Republicans also differed with the Democrats on the question of internal improvements, supporting the view that Congress should undertake river and harbor improvements. The Republican platform denounced the Ostend Manifesto, a document secretly drawn up by three of Pierce's ambassadors in Europe, that suggested the United States either buy or take Cuba from Spain. The Republicans termed the manifesto a "highwayman's plea, that 'might makes right.'"

Both parties advocated the building of a transcontinental transportation system, with the Republicans supporting the construction of a railroad.

Following are excerpts from the Republican platform of 1856:

Slavery. This Convention of Delegates, assembled in pursuance of a call addressed to the people of the United States, without regard to past political differences or divisions, who are opposed to the repeal of the Missouri Compromise; to the policy of the present Administration; to the extension of Slavery into Free Territory; in favor of the admission of Kansas as a Free State; of restoring the action of the Federal Government to the principles of Washington and Jefferson. . . .

That the Constitution confers upon Congress sovereign powers over the Territories of the United States for their government; and that in the exercise of this power, it is both the right and the imperative duty of Congress to prohibit in the Territories those twin relics of barbarism—Polygamy, and Slavery.

Cuba. That the highwayman's plea, that "might makes right," embodied in the Ostend Circular, was in every respect unworthy of American diplomacy, and would bring shame and dishonor upon any Government or people that gave it their sanction.

Transcontinental Railroad. That a railroad to the Pacific Ocean by the most central and practicable route is imperatively demanded by the interests of the whole country.

Internal Improvements. That appropriations by Congress for the improvement of rivers and harbors, of a national character, required for the accommodation and security of our existing commerce, are authorized by the Constitution, and justified by the obligation of the Government to protect the lives and property of its citizens.

AMERICAN (KNOW-NOTHINGS)

In addition to the Republicans, the American Party or Know-Nothings aspired to replace the Whigs as the nation's second major party. However, unlike the Republicans, the Know-Nothings were a national political organization, and the slavery issue that helped unite the Republicans divided the Know-Nothings. The main Know-Nothing concern was to place restrictions on the large number of European immigrants who arrived in the 1840s and 1850s.

The party held its first and only national convention in Philadelphia in February 1856. Several days before the convention began, the American Party's national council met and drew up the party platform. When the convention assembled, antislavery delegates objected to the platform, with its espousal of popular sovereignty, and called for the nomination of candidates who would outlaw slavery in the new territories. When their resolution was defeated, 141 to 59, these antislavery delegates—mainly from New England and Ohio—bolted the convention.

The remaining delegates nominated former president Millard Fillmore (1850–1853) of New York for president. Fillmore was popular in the South for his support of compromise slavery measures during his administration and was nominated on the second ballot. Andrew Jackson Donelson of Tennessee was chosen as the vice-presidential candidate.

In June 1856 several days before the Republican convention was scheduled to begin, the antislavery Know-Nothings assembled in New York and nominated Speaker of the House Nathaniel P. Banks of Massachusetts for the presidency and former governor William F. Johnston of Pennsylvania as his running mate. Banks, who actually favored Fremont's nomination, withdrew from the race when Fremont was chosen as the Republican candidate. Johnston bowed out in favor of Fremont's running mate, William L. Dayton, later in the campaign.

The Know-Nothing convention that had met earlier in Philadelphia adopted a platform similar to that of the Democrats on the slavery question. The document advocated noninterference in the affairs of the states and the concept of popular sovereignty for deciding slavery in the territories. Although also calling for economy in government spending, the bulk of the Know-Nothing platform dealt with restricting immigrants. Among the nativistic planks were proposals that native-born citizens be given the first chance for all government offices, that the naturalization period for immigrants be extended to twenty-one years and that paupers and convicted criminals be kept from entering the United States.

Following are excerpts from the Know-Nothing platform of 1856:

Slavery, States' Rights. The unequalled recognition and maintenance of the reserved rights of the several states, and the cultivation of harmony and fraternal good-will between the citizens of the several states, and to this end, non-interference by Congress with questions appertaining solely to the individual states, and non-intervention by each state with the affairs of any other state.

The recognition of the right of the native-born and naturalized citizens of the United States, permanently residing in any territory thereof, to frame their constitutions and laws, and to regulate their domestic and social affairs in their own mode, subject only to the provisions of the federal Constitution, with the right of admission into the Union whenever they have the requisite population for one representative in Congress.

Nativism. *Americans must rule America;* and to this end, *native*-born citizens should be selected for all state, federal, or municipal offices of government employment, in preference to naturalized citizens. . . .

No person should be selected for political station (whether of native or foreign birth), who recognizes any alliance or obligation of any description to any foreign prince, potentate or power, who refuses to recognize the federal and state constitutions (each within its own sphere), as paramount to all other laws, as rules of particular [political] action.

A change in the laws of naturalization, making a continued residence of twenty-one years, of all not heretofore provided for, an indispensable requisite for citizenship hereafter, and excluding all paupers or persons convicted of crime from landing upon our shores.

DEMOCRATS

In June 1856 delegates from all thirty-one states gathered in Cincinnati, Ohio, for the party's seventh quadrennial convention. It was the first Democratic convention to be held outside Baltimore.

Roll-call votes were taken during the first two days on the establishment of a platform committee and on the method of ticket allocation for the galleries. The first close vote came on the credentials committee report concerning the seating of two contesting New York delegations. By a vote of 136 to 123, the convention agreed to a minority report seating both contending factions and splitting the state's vote between them.

Three men were in contention for the party's presidential nomination: President Franklin Pierce of New Hampshire, James Buchanan of Pennsylvania, and Sen. Stephen A. Douglas of Illinois. All three had actively sought the nomination before.

Ironically, Buchanan, who had spent the previous three years as ambassador to Great Britain, was in the most enviable position. Having been abroad, Buchanan had largely avoided the increasing slavery controversy that bedeviled his major rivals.

Buchanan led on the first ballot with 135½ votes with Pierce receiving 122½, and Douglas 33. As the balloting continued, Pierce lost strength, while both Buchanan and Douglas gained. After the fifteenth roll call, the vote stood: Buchanan, 168½, Douglas, 118½, Pierce 3½. (*Table, p. 579.*)

While the two front-runners had substantial strength, neither of them was a sectional candidate. Both received votes from northern and southern delegations. With the possibility of a stalemate looming, Douglas withdrew after the sixteenth ballot. On the seventeenth roll call, Buchanan received all 296 votes, and the nomination.

On the first ballot for the vice presidency, eleven different individuals received votes. Rep. John A. Quitman of Mississippi led with 59 votes, followed by Rep. John C. Breckinridge of Kentucky, with 50. At the beginning of the second ballot, the New England delegations cast a nearly unanimous vote for Breckinridge, creating a bandwagon effect that resulted in the nomination of the Kentuckian. Ironically, before the vice-presidential balloting began, Breckinridge had asked that his name be withdrawn from consideration. Believing himself too young (he was thirty-five), Breckinridge stated that "promotion should follow seniority."

In spite of his earlier demurrer, Breckinridge was in the convention hall and announced his acceptance of the nomination. It marked one of the few times in American political history that a candidate was present for his own nomination.

The party platform was considered in two segments, with the domestic and foreign policy sections debated separately. The theme of the domestic section, as in past platforms, was the Democrats' concept of a limited federal government. The unconstitutionality of a national bank, federal support for internal improvements, and distribution of proceeds from the sale of public land were again mentioned.

Nearly one-third of the entire platform was devoted to the slavery question, with support for the various congressional compromise measures stressed. The Democratic position was underscored in a passage that was capitalized in the convention *Proceedings:* "non-interference by Congress with slavery in state and territory, or in the District of Columbia."

In another domestic area, the Democrats denounced the Know-Nothings for being un-American. The convention approved the domestic policy section of the platform by a vote of 261 to 35, with only the New York delegation voting in opposition.

The foreign policy section expressed a nationalistic and expansionist spirit that was absent from previous Democratic platforms.

There were six different foreign policy planks, each voted on separately. The first plank, calling for free trade, passed 210 to 29. The second, favoring implementation of the Monroe Doctrine, passed 240 to 21. The third plank, backing westward continental expansion, was approved 203 to 56. The fourth plank, which expressed sympathy with the people of Central America, grew out of the United States' dispute with Great Britain over

control of that area. The plank was approved, 221 to 38. The fifth plank, calling for United States "ascendency in the Gulf of Mexico," passed 229 to 33. A final resolution, presented separately, called for the construction of roads to the Pacific Ocean. The resolution was at first tabled, 154 to 120, and a second vote to reconsider failed, 175 to 121. But when the resolution was raised a third time after the presidential nomination, it passed, 205 to 87.

Following are excerpts from the Democratic platform of 1856:

Slavery. That claiming fellowship with, and desiring the co-operation of all who regard the preservation of the Union under the Constitution as the paramount issue—and repudiating all sectional parties and platforms concerning domestic slavery, which seek to embroil the States and incite to treason and armed resistance to law in the Territories; and whose avowed purposes, if consummated, must end in civil war and disunion, the American Democracy recognize and adopt the principles contained in the organic laws establishing the Territories of Kansas and Nebraska as embodying the only sound and safe solution of the "slavery question" upon which the great national idea of the people of this whole country can repose in its determined conservatism of the Union—NON-INTERFERENCE BY CONGRESS WITH SLAVERY IN STATE AND TERRITORY, OR IN THE DISTRICT OF COLUMBIA.

Know-Nothings. [T]he liberal principles embodied in the Declaration of Independence . . . makes ours the land of liberty and the asylum of the oppressed . . . every attempt to abridge the privilege of becoming citizens . . . ought to be resisted.

Since the foregoing declaration was uniformly adopted by our predecessors in National Conventions, an adverse political and religious test has been secretly organized by a party claiming to be exclusively American, it is proper that the American Democracy should clearly define its relation thereto, and declare its determined opposition to all secret political societies, by whatever name they may be called.

Free Trade. That there are questions connected with the foreign policy of this country, which are inferior to no domestic question whatever. The time has come for the people of the United States to declare themselves in favor of free seas and progressive free trade.

Latin America. [W]e should hold as sacred the principles involved in the Monroe Doctrine: their bearing and import admit of no misconstruction; they should be applied with unbending rigidity.

Gulf of Mexico. That the Democratic party will expect of the next Administration that every proper effort be made to insure our ascendency in the Gulf of Mexico.

Transcontinental Roads. That the Democratic party recognizes the great importance, in a political and commercial point of view, of a safe and speedy communication, by military and postal roads, through our own territory, between the Atlantic and Pacific coasts.

WHIGS

On the verge of extinction, the Whig Party held its last national convention in September 1856. Delegates assembled in Baltimore from twenty-one states and endorsed the Know-Nothing ticket of Fillmore and Donelson.

However, the Whigs adopted their own platform. It avoided specific issues, instead calling for preservation of the Union. The platform criticized both the Democrats and Republicans for appealing to sectional passions and argued for the presidential candidacy of the former Whig, Millard Fillmore.

Following is an excerpt from the Whig platform of 1856:

Preserving the Union. That the Whigs of the United States are assembled here by reverence for the Constitution, and unalterable attachment to the National Union, and a fixed determination to do all in

their power to preserve it for themselves and posterity. They have no new principles to announce—no new platform to establish, but are content broadly to rest where their fathers have rested upon the Constitution of the United States, wishing no safer guide, no higher law.

1860 Conventions

PRESIDENTIAL CANDIDATES

Stephen A. Douglas
Democrat

John C. Breckinridge
Southern Democrat

Abraham Lincoln
Republican

John Bell
Constitutional Union

DEMOCRATS

Rarely in American history has there been a convention as tumultuous as the one that assembled in Charleston, South Carolina, in April 1860. The Democrats met at a time when their party was threatened by sectional division, caused by the explosive slavery question. The issue had grown increasingly inflammatory during the 1850s, and, because of rising emotions, the chances of a successful compromise solution decreased.

From the outset of the convention, there was little visible effort to obtain party unity. Parliamentary squabbling with frequent appeals to the chair marked the early sessions. Before the presidential balloting even began, twenty-seven separate roll calls on procedural and platform matters were taken.

A bitter dispute between northern and southern delegates over the wording of the platform's slavery plank precipitated a walkout by several dozen southern delegates. Both the majority and minority reports submitted to the convention called for a reaffirmation of the Democratic platform of 1856. In addition, however, the majority report (favored by the South) declared that no government—local, state, or federal—could outlaw slavery in the territories. The minority report took a more moderate position, stating that the decision on allowing slavery in the territories should be left to the Supreme Court.

After a day of debate, the convention agreed, by a vote of 152 to 151, to recommit both reports to the platform committee. Basically, the vote followed sectional lines, with southern delegates approving recommittal. However, the revised majority and minority reports subsequently presented to the convention were similar to the originals.

An amendment by Benjamin F. Butler of Massachusetts, to endorse the 1856 platform without any mention of slavery, was defeated, 198 to 105. After two procedural roll calls, the delegates voted, 165 to 138, to accept the minority report. The vote followed sectional lines, with the northern delegates victorious. (*Table, p. 580.*)

Unhappy with the platform and unwilling to accept it, forty-five delegates from nine states bolted the convention. The majority of six southern delegations withdrew (Alabama, Mississippi, Florida, Texas, South Carolina, and Louisiana), along with scattered delegates from three other states (Arkansas, Delaware, and North Carolina).

With the size of the convention reduced, chairman Caleb Cushing of Massachusetts made an important decision. He ruled that the two-thirds nominating majority would be based on the total votes allocated (303) rather than the number of delegates present and voting. Although Cushing's ruling was approved by a vote of 141 to 112, it countered precedents established at the 1840 and 1848 Democratic conventions, when the nominating majority was based on those present and voting.

Cushing's ruling made it nearly impossible for any candidate to amass the necessary two-thirds majority. Particularly affected was the front-runner, Sen. Stephen A. Douglas of Illinois, whose standing in the South had diminished with his continued support of popular sovereignty. Douglas moved into a big lead on the first ballot, receiving 145½ votes to 42 for Sen. Robert M. T. Hunter of Virginia and 35½ for James Guthrie of Kentucky. Despite his large lead over the rest of the field, Douglas was well short of the 202 votes needed for nomination and, with his limited sectional appeal, had little chance of gaining the needed delegates.

After three days of balloting and fifty-seven presidential roll calls, the standing of the three candidates had undergone little change. Douglas led with 151½ votes, followed by Guthrie with 65½, and Hunter with 16. The delegates, in session for ten days and wearied by the presidential deadlock, voted 194½ to 55½ to recess for six weeks and reconvene in Baltimore. This marked the first and only time that a major party adjourned its convention and moved it from one city to another.

Reconvening in Baltimore in June, the delegates were faced with another sticky question: whether or not to seat the delegates who had bolted the Charleston convention. The majority report presented by the credentials committee reviewed each case individually and recommended that the bolting southern delegates, except those from Alabama and Louisiana, be reseated. The minority report recommended that a larger majority of the withdrawing Charleston delegates be reseated. The minority report was defeated, 150 to 100½. Ten more roll calls followed on various aspects of the credentials dispute, but they did not change the result of the first vote. *(Table, p. 580.)*

The convention vote on credentials produced a new walkout, involving the majority of delegates from Virginia, North Carolina, Tennessee, Maryland, Kentucky, Missouri, Arkansas, California, and Oregon, and anti-Douglas delegates from Massachusetts. With the presidential balloting ready to resume, less than two-thirds of the original convention was present.

On the first ballot, Douglas received 173½ of the 190½ votes cast. On the second ballot, his total increased to 190½, but it was obviously impossible for him to gain two-thirds (202) of the votes allocated (303). After the second roll call, a delegate moved that Douglas, having obtained a two-thirds majority of the votes cast, be declared the Democratic presidential nominee. The motion passed unanimously on a voice vote. *(Table, p. 580.)*

The convention left the selection of the vice-presidential candidate to a caucus of the remaining southern delegates. They chose Sen. Benjamin Fitzpatrick of Alabama, who received all 198½ votes cast on the vice-presidential roll call.

Shortly after the convention adjourned, Fitzpatrick declined the nomination. For the first time in American history, a national committee was called upon to fill a vacancy on the ticket. By a unanimous vote of committee members, the former governor of Georgia, Herschel V. Johnson, was chosen to be Douglas's running mate.

The Democratic platform, in addition to the controversial slavery plank, provided a reaffirmation of the 1856 platform, with its proposals for a limited federal government but an expansionist foreign policy. The 1860 platform added planks that continued the expansionist spirit, calling for the construction of a transcontinental railroad and acquisition of the island of Cuba.

Following are excerpts from the 1860 Democratic platform:

Slavery. Inasmuch as difference of opinion exists in the Democratic party as to the nature and extent of the powers of a territorial legislature, and as to the powers and duties of Congress, under the Constitution of the United States, over the institution of slavery within the Territories,

Resolved, That the Democratic party will abide by the decision of the Supreme Court of the United States upon these questions of Constitutional law.

Transcontinental Railroad. That one of the necessities of the age, in a military, commercial, and postal point of view, is speedy communication between the Atlantic and Pacific States; and the Democratic party pledge such Constitutional Government aid as will insure the construction of a Railroad to the Pacific coast, at the earliest practicable period.

Cuba. That the Democratic party are in favor of the acquisition of the Island of Cuba on such terms as shall be honorable to ourselves and just to Spain.

SOUTHERN DEMOCRATS (BRECKINRIDGE FACTION)

A small group of Southern delegates that bolted the Charleston convention met in Richmond, Virginia, in early June. They decided to delay action until after the resumed Democratic convention had concluded. In late June they met in Baltimore with bolters from the regular Democratic convention. There were representatives from nineteen states among the more than 200 delegates attending, but most of the fifty-eight northern delegates were officeholders in the Buchanan administration. Vice President John C. Breckinridge of Kentucky won the presidential nomination, and Sen. Joseph Lane of Oregon was chosen as his running mate.

The platform adopted by the southern Democrats was similar to the one approved by the Democratic convention at Charleston. The bolters reaffirmed the Democrats' 1856 platform, which called for the construction of a transcontinental railroad and acquisition of Cuba. But on the controversial slavery issue, the rump assemblage adopted the southerners' plank defeated at the Charleston convention. The failure to reach agreement on this one issue, the most disruptive sectional split in the history of American political parties, presaged the Civil War.

Following are excerpts from the platform adopted by the Southern (or Breckinridge faction) Democrats in 1860:

Resolved, that the platform adopted by the Democratic party at Cincinnati be affirmed, with the following explanatory resolutions:

1. That the Government of a Territory organized by an act of Congress is provisional and temporary, and during its existence all citizens of the United States have an equal right to settle with their property in the Territory, without their rights, either of person or property, being destroyed or impaired by Congressional or Territorial legislation.

2. That it is the duty of the Federal Government, in all its departments, to protect, when necessary, the rights of persons and property in the Territories, and wherever else its constitutional authority extends.

REPUBLICANS

With their major opposition split along sectional lines, the Republicans gathered for their convention in Chicago in a mood of optimism. The Democrats had already broken up at Charleston before the Republican delegates convened in May 1860.

The call for the convention was addressed not only to faithful party members but to other groups that shared the Republicans' dissatisfaction with the policies of the Buchanan administration. The call to the convention particularly emphasized the party's opposition to any extension of slavery into the territories.

Delegates from all the northern states and the territories of Kansas and Nebraska, the District of Columbia, and the slave states of Maryland, Delaware, Virginia, Kentucky, Missouri, and Texas assembled at Chicago's new 10,000-seat convention hall, known as the Wigwam. A carnival-like atmosphere enveloped Chicago, with bands marching through the streets and thousands of enthusiastic Republicans ringing the overcrowded convention hall.

Inside, the delegates' first debate concerned the credentials report. The question was raised whether the represented southern states should be allocated votes reflecting their electoral college strength, when there were very few Republicans in these states. By a vote of 275½ to 171½, the convention recommitted the credentials report for the purpose of scaling down the vote allocation of the southern states.

A second debate arose over what constituted a nominating majority. The rules committee recommended that the nominating majority reflect the total electoral vote of all the states in the Union. The minority report argued that, since all the states were not represented, the nominating majority suggested by the rules committee would in fact require nearly a two-thirds majority. The minority report recommended instead that nominations be based on a simple majority of votes allocated for the states represented. The minority report passed, 349½ to 88½.

Sen. William H. Seward of New York was the front-runner for the presidential nomination and led on the first ballot. Seward received 173½ votes to lead runner-up Abraham Lincoln of Illinois, who had 102. Sen. Simon Cameron of Pennsylvania followed with 50½ votes, Salmon P. Chase of Ohio with 49, and Edward Bates of Missouri with 48. *(Table, p. 581.)*

With the packed galleries cheering their native son, Lincoln closed the gap on the second roll call. After two ballots, the voting stood: Seward, 184½; Lincoln, 181; Chase, 42½; Bates, 35. Lincoln, who had gained national prominence two years earlier as a result of his debates on slavery with Democrat Stephen A. Douglas in the 1858 campaign for the U.S. Senate, emerged as the candidate of the anti-Seward forces. On the third ballot, he won the nomination. When the third roll call was completed, Lincoln's vote total stood at 231½, 1½ votes short of a majority. But Ohio quickly shifted four votes to Lincoln, giving him the nomination. After changes by other states, the final vote was Lincoln, 340; Seward, 121½.

The primary contenders for the vice-presidential nomination were Sen. Hannibal Hamlin of Maine and Cassius M. Clay of Kentucky. Hamlin assumed a strong lead on the first ballot, receiving 194 votes to 100½ for Clay. On the second roll call, an increased vote for Hamlin from states in his native New England created a bandwagon for the Maine senator. Hamlin won the nomination on the second ballot with 367 votes, far outdistancing Clay, who received 86. After the roll call was completed, Hamlin's nomination was declared unanimous.

About half of the platform adopted by the Republican convention dealt with the slavery question. Unlike the Democrats, the Republicans clearly opposed the extension of slavery into the territories. However, the Republican platform also expressed support for states' rights, which served as a rebuke to radical abolitionism.

The Republican and Democratic platforms again were opposed on the question of internal improvements. The Republicans supported river and harbor improvements, while the Democrats, by reaffirming their 1856 platform, opposed any federal support for internal improvements. Both parties favored construction of a transcontinental railroad and opposed restrictions on immigration.

However, on two major issues, the Republicans went beyond the Democrats, advocating a protective tariff and homestead legislation.

Following are excerpts from the 1860 Republican platform:

Slavery. That the new dogma that the Constitution, of its own force, carries slavery into any or all of the territories of the United States, is a dangerous political heresy, at variance with the explicit provisions of that instrument itself, with contemporaneous exposition, and with legislative and judicial precedent; is revolutionary in its tendency, and subversive of the peace and harmony of the country.

That the normal condition of all the territory of the United States is that of freedom. . . . we deny the authority of Congress, of a territorial legislature, or of any individuals, to give legal existence to slavery in any territory of the United States.

States' Rights. That the maintenance inviolate of the rights of the states, and especially the right of each state to order and control its own domestic institutions according to its own judgment exclusively, is essential to that balance of powers on which the perfection and endurance of our political fabric depends; and we denounce the lawless invasion by armed force of the soil of any state or territory, no matter under what pretext, as among the gravest of crimes.

Tariff. That, while providing revenue for the support of the general government by duties upon imports, sound policy requires such an adjustment of these imports as to encourage the development of the industrial interests of the whole country.

Transcontinental Railroad. That a railroad to the Pacific Ocean is imperatively demanded by the interests of the whole country; that the federal government ought to render immediate and efficient aid in its construction; and that, as preliminary thereto, a daily overland mail should be promptly established.

CONSTITUTIONAL UNION

At the invitation of a group of southern Know-Nothing congressmen, the remnants of the 1856 Fillmore campaign, conservative Whigs and Know-Nothings, met in Baltimore in May 1860 to form the Constitutional Union Party.

The chief rivals for the presidential nomination were former Sen. John Bell of Tennessee and Gov. Sam Houston of Texas. Bell won on the second ballot, and Edward Everett of Massachusetts was selected as his running mate.

The Constitutional Union Party saw itself as a national unifying force in a time of crisis. The brief platform did not discuss issues, instead denouncing the sectionalism of the existing parties and calling for national unity.

Following are excerpts from the 1860 Constitutional Union platform:

Whereas, Experience has demonstrated that Platforms adopted by the partisan Conventions of the country have had the effect to mislead and deceive the people, and at the same time to widen the political divisions of the country, by the creation and encouragement of geographical and sectional parties; therefore

Resolved, that it is both the part of patriotism and of duty to *recognize* no political principle other than THE CONSTITUTION OF THE COUNTRY, THE UNION OF THE STATES, AND THE ENFORCEMENT OF THE LAWS.

1864 Conventions

PRESIDENTIAL CANDIDATES

Abraham Lincoln
Republican

George McClellan
Democrat

REPUBLICANS (UNION PARTY)

Although elements in the Republican Party were dissatisfied with the conduct of the Civil War, President Abraham Lincoln was in firm control of his party's convention, which met in Baltimore in June 1864. As with previous Republican conventions, the call was not limited to the party faithful. Democrats in support of the Lincoln war policy were encouraged to attend, and the name "Union Party" was used to describe the wartime coalition.

Delegates were present from all the Northern states, the territories, the District of Columbia, and the slave states of Arkansas, Florida, Louisiana, Tennessee, South Carolina, and Virginia. Credentials disputes occupied the early sessions. The credentials committee recommended that all the Southern states except South Carolina be admitted, but denied the right to vote. A minority report, advocating voting privileges for the Tennessee delegation, was passed, 310 to 151. A second minority report favoring voting privileges for Arkansas and Louisiana was approved, 307 to 167. However, the credentials committee recommendation that Florida and Virginia be denied voting rights, and South Carolina be excluded entirely, were accepted without a roll call.

Although dissatisfaction with the administration's war policy had spawned opposition to Lincoln, the boomlets for such presidential hopefuls as Treasury Secretary Salmon P. Chase petered out. The Lincoln forces controlled the convention, and the president was easily renominated on the first ballot. Lincoln received 494 of the 516 votes cast, losing only Missouri's 22 votes, which were committed to Gen. Ulysses S. Grant. After the roll call, Missouri moved that the vote be made unanimous. *(Table, p. 582.)*

Lincoln did not publicly declare his preference for a vice-presidential running mate, leaving the selection to the convention. The main contenders included incumbent vice president, Hannibal Hamlin of Maine; former senator and military governor of Tennessee, Democrat Andrew Johnson; and former senator Daniel S. Dickinson of New York. Johnson led on the first ballot with 200 votes, followed by Hamlin with 150 and Dickinson with 108. After completion of the roll call, a switch to Johnson by the Kentucky delegation ignited a surge to the Tennessean that delivered him 492 votes and the nomination.

The Republican (Union) platform was approved without debate. Unlike the Democrats, who criticized the war effort and called for a quick, negotiated peace, the Republicans favored a vigorous prosecution of the war until the South surrendered unconditionally. The Republicans called for the eradication of slavery, with its elimination embodied in a constitutional amendment.

Although the Republican document focused on the Civil War, it also included planks encouraging immigration, urging the speedy construction of a transcontinental railroad and reaffirming the Monroe Doctrine.

Following are excerpts from the Republican (Union) platform of 1864:

Resolved, . . . we pledge ourselves, as Union men, animated by a common sentiment and aiming at a common object, to do everything in our power to aid the Government in quelling by force of arms the Rebellion now raging against its authority, and in bringing to the punishment due to their crimes the Rebels and traitors arrayed against it.

Resolved, That we approve the determination of the Government of the United States not to compromise with Rebels, or to offer them any terms of peace, except such as may be based upon an unconditional surrender of their hostility and a return to their just allegiance to the Constitution and laws of the United States, and that we call upon the Government to maintain this position and to prosecute the war with the utmost possible vigor to the complete suppression of the Rebellion, in full reliance upon the self-sacrificing patriotism, the heroic valor and the undying devotion of the American people to the country and its free institutions.

Resolved, That as slavery was the cause, and now constitutes the strength of this Rebellion, and as it must be, always and everywhere, hostile to the principles of Republican Government, justice and the National safety demand its utter and complete extirpation from the soil of the Republic . . . we are in favor, furthermore, of such an amendment to the Constitution, to be made by the people in conformity with its provisions, as shall terminate and forever prohibit the existence of Slavery within the limits of the jurisdiction of the United States.

Resolved, That the thanks of the American people are due to the soldiers and sailors of the Army and Navy, who have periled their lives in defense of the country and in vindication of the honor of its flag.

DEMOCRATS

The Democrats originally scheduled their convention for early summer but postponed it until late August to gauge the significance of military developments.

The party, badly split during the 1860 campaign, no longer had the Southern faction with which to contend. But while there was no longer a regional split, new divisions arose over the continuing war. There was a large peace faction, known as the Copperheads, that favored a quick, negotiated peace with the South. Another faction supported the war but criticized its handling by the Lincoln administration. A third faction supported Lincoln's conduct of the war and defected to support the Republican president.

Although factionalized, the Democratic delegates who assembled in Chicago were optimistic about their party's chances. The war-weary nation, they thought, was ready to vote out the Lincoln administration if there was not a quick change in Northern military fortunes.

Although the border states were represented at the Democratic convention, the territories and seceded Southern states were not. In spite of the party's internal divisions, there was little opposition to the presidential candidacy of Gen. George B. McClellan of New Jersey. The former commander of the Union Army won on the first ballot, receiving 174 of the 226

votes cast. Former governor Thomas H. Seymour of Connecticut trailed with 38 votes. A switch to McClellan by several Ohio delegates prompted shifts by other delegations and brought his total to 202½. Clement Vallandigham, a leader of the Copperhead faction, moved that McClellan's nomination be made unanimous.

Eight candidates were placed in nomination for the vice presidency. James Guthrie of Kentucky led Rep. George H. Pendleton of Ohio, the favorite of the Copperheads, on the first ballot, 65½ to 55. However, shifts to Pendleton by Illinois, Kentucky, and New York after completion of the roll call created a bandwagon that led quickly to his unanimous nomination. In the convention hall at the time of his selection, Pendleton made a short speech of acceptance. (*Table, p. 582.*)

The platform adopted by the Democrats reflected the views of the Copperhead faction. The Lincoln administration's conduct of the Civil War was denounced, with particular criticism of the use of martial law and the abridgement of state and civil rights. The platform called for an immediate end to hostilities and a negotiated peace. The "sympathy" of the party was extended to soldiers and sailors involved in the war. Besides a criticism of the war and its conduct by the Lincoln administration, there were no other issues discussed in the platform.

Following are excerpts from the Democratic platform of 1864:

Resolved, That this convention does explicitly declare, as the sense of the American people, that after four years of failure to restore the Union by the experiment of war, during which, under the pretense of a military necessity of war-power higher than the Constitution, the Constitution itself has been disregarded in every part, and public liberty and private right alike trodden down, and the material prosperity of the country essentially impaired, justice, humanity, liberty, and the public welfare demand that immediate efforts be made for a cessation of hostilities, with a view of an ultimate convention of the States, or other peaceable means, to the end that, at the earliest practicable moment, peace may be restored on the basis of the Federal Union of the States.

Resolved, That the sympathy of the Democratic party is heartily and earnestly extended to the soldiery of our army and sailors of our navy, who are and have been in the field and on the sea under the flag of our country, and, in the events of its attaining power, they will receive all the care, protection, and regard that the brave soldiers and sailors of the republic have so nobly earned.

1868 Conventions

PRESIDENTIAL CANDIDATES

Ulysses S. Grant
Republican

Horatio Seymour
Democrat

REPUBLICANS

The "National Union Republican Party," as the political organization was termed in its platform, held its first postwar convention in Chicago in May 1868. Delegations from the states of the old Confederacy were accepted; several included blacks.

The turbulent nature of postwar politics was evident in the fact that Gen. Ulysses S. Grant, the clear front-runner for the Republican nomination, had been considered a possible contender for the Democratic nomination barely a year earlier. Less than six months before the convention, the basically apolitical Grant had broken with Andrew Johnson, who had become president following the assassination of Abraham Lincoln in 1865.

Grant's was the only name placed in nomination, and on the ensuing roll call he received all 650 votes. *(Table, p. 583.)*

While the presidential race was cut and dried, the balloting for vice president was wide open, with eleven candidates receiving votes on the initial roll call. Sen. Benjamin F. Wade of Ohio led on the first ballot with 147 votes, followed by Gov. Reuben E. Fenton of New York with 126, Sen. Henry Wilson of Massachusetts with 119, and Speaker of the House Schuyler Colfax of Indiana with 115.

Over the next four ballots, Wade and Colfax were the front-runners, with Colfax finally moving ahead on the fifth ballot. His lead over Wade at this point was only 226 to 207, but numerous vote shifts after the roll call quickly pushed the Indiana representative over the top and gave him the nomination. After all the vote changes, Colfax's total stood at 541, followed by Fenton with 69 and Wade with 38.

Not surprisingly, the platform adopted by the Republicans differed sharply with the Democrats over reconstruction and Johnson's presidency. The Republican platform applauded the radical reconstruction program passed by Congress and denounced Johnson as "treacherous" and deserving of impeachment. The Republican platform approved of voting rights for black men in the South but determined that this was a subject for each state to decide in the rest of the nation.

The two parties also differed on their response to the currency question. While the Democrats favored a "soft-money" policy, the Republicans supported a continued "hard-money" approach, rejecting the Democratic proposal that the economic crisis could be eased by an increased supply of greenbacks.

Following are excerpts from the Republican platform of 1868:

Reconstruction. We congratulate the country on the assured success of the reconstruction policy of Congress, as evinced by the adoption, in the majority of the States lately in rebellion, of constitutions securing equal civil and political rights to all, and regard it as the duty of the Government to sustain those constitutions, and to prevent the people of such States from being remitted to a state of anarchy or military rule.

The guaranty by Congress of equal suffrage to all loyal men at the South was demanded by every consideration of public safety, of gratitude, and of justice, and must be maintained; while the question of suffrage in all the loyal States properly belongs to the people of those States.

President Andrew Johnson. We profoundly deplore the untimely and tragic death of Abraham Lincoln, and regret the accession of Andrew Johnson to the Presidency, who has acted treacherously to the people who elected him and the cause he was pledged to support; has usurped high legislative and judicial functions; has refused to execute the laws; has used his high office to induce other officers to ignore and violate the laws; has employed his executive powers to render insecure the property, the peace, the liberty, and life of the citizen; has abused the pardoning power; has denounced the National Legislature as unconstitutional; has persistently and corruptly resisted, by every means in his power, every proper attempt at the reconstruction of the States lately in rebellion; has perverted the public patronage into an engine of wholesale corruption; and has been justly impeached for high crimes and misdemeanors, and properly pronounced guilty thereof by the vote of thirty-five senators.

Currency. We denounce all forms of repudiation as a national crime; and national honor requires the payment of the public indebtedness in the utmost good faith to all creditors at home and abroad, not only according to the letter, but the spirit of the laws under which it was contracted.

DEMOCRATS

Reunited after the Civil War, the Democratic Party held its first postwar convention in New York's newly constructed Tammany Hall. It was no accident that convention proceedings began on July 4, 1868. The Democratic National Committee had set the date, and its chairman, August Belmont of New York, opened the first session with a harsh criticism of Republican reconstruction policy and the abridgement of civil rights.

Delegates from Southern states were voting members of the convention, but an effort to extend representation to the territories was defeated, 184 to 106.

Before the presidential balloting began, the convention chairman ruled that, as at the 1860 Charleston assembly, a nominating majority would be based on two-thirds of the total votes allocated (317) and not votes cast. On the opening ballot, the party's vice-presidential candidate four years earlier, George H. Pendleton of Ohio, took the lead. Pendleton, although popular in the economically depressed Midwest because of his plan to inflate the currency by printing more greenbacks, had little appeal in the eastern states. Nonetheless, he led on the first ballot with 105 votes. President Andrew Johnson was next, with 65 votes. Johnson's vote was largely complimentary and declined after the first roll call. Pendleton, however, showed increased strength, rising to a peak of 156½ votes on the eighth ballot. But Pendleton's total was well short of the 212 votes required to nominate, and his total steadily decreased after the eighth roll call. (*Table, p. 584.*)

The collapse of the Pendleton and Johnson candidacies produced a boom for Gen. Winfield Scott Hancock of Pennsylvania. Opponents of Hancock attempted to break his surge by calling for adjournment after the sixteenth ballot. Although the move for adjournment was defeated, 174½ to 14½, the Hancock boom began to lose momentum. The Civil War general peaked at 144½ votes on the eighteenth ballot, well short of a two-thirds majority.

With Hancock stymied, a new contender, Sen. Thomas A. Hendricks of Indiana, gained strength. Hendricks' vote rose to 132 on the twenty-first ballot, and the trend to the Indiana senator continued on the twenty-second ballot until the roll call reached Ohio. However, Ohio shifted its entire vote to Horatio Seymour, the permanent chairman of the convention and a former governor of New York. Seymour declined to be a candidate, and so announced to the convention, but Ohio did not change its vote, and friends of Seymour hustled the reluctant candidate from the hall. The bandwagon had begun, and when the vote switches were completed, Seymour had received all 317 votes.

The vice-presidential nomination went to Gen. Francis P. Blair Jr. of Missouri, a former Republican, who was unanimously selected on the first ballot. The names of several other candidates were placed in nomination, but the announcement of Blair's candidacy created a bandwagon that led to the withdrawal of the others.

The Democratic platform was accepted by a voice vote without debate. The platform began by declaring the questions of slavery and secession to be permanently settled by the Civil War. Several planks criticized the Republican reconstruction program, passed by the party's Radical wing in Congress. The Radicals themselves were scathingly denounced for their "unparalleled oppression and tyranny." The Democratic platform expressed its support for Andrew Johnson's conduct as president and decried the attempts to impeach him.

For the first time, the question of the coinage and printing of money was discussed in the party platform. Two planks were included that could be generally interpreted as supporting Pendleton's inflationary greenback plan.

On the tariff issue, the Democrats called for a tariff that would primarily raise revenue but also protect American industry.

Following are excerpts from the Democratic platform of 1868:

Reconstruction. . . . [W]e arraign the Radical party for its disregard of right, and the unparalleled oppression and tyranny which have marked its career.

Instead of restoring the Union, it has, so far as in its power, dissolved it, and subjected ten States, in time of profound peace, to military despotism and negro supremacy.

President Andrew Johnson. That the President of the United States, Andrew Johnson, in exercising the power of his high office in resisting the aggressions of Congress upon the Constitutional rights of the States and the people, is entitled to the gratitude of the whole American people; and in behalf of the Democratic party, we tender him our thanks for his patriotic efforts in that regard.

Currency. . . . where the obligations of the government do not expressly state upon their face, or the law under which they were issued does not provide, that they shall be paid in coin, they ought, in right and in justice, to be paid in the lawful money of the United States. . . . One currency for the government and the people, the laborer and the officeholder, the pensioner and the soldier, the producer and the bondholder.

1872 Conventions

PRESIDENTIAL CANDIDATES

Horace Greeley
Liberal Republican, Democrat

Ulysses S. Grant
Republican

LIBERAL REPUBLICANS

The short-lived Liberal Republican Party grew out of grievances that elements in the Republican Party had with the policies of the Grant administration. There was particular dissatisfaction with the "carpetbag" governments in the South, support for extensive civil service reform and a general distaste for the corrupt administration of President Ulysses S. Grant.

The idea for the Liberal Republican movement originated in Missouri, where, in the 1870 state elections, a coalition of reform Republicans and Democrats swept to victory. In January 1872 a state convention of this new coalition issued the call for a national convention to be held that May in Cincinnati, Ohio.

Without a formal, nationwide organization, the delegate selection process was haphazard. Some of the delegates were self-appointed, but generally the size of each delegation reflected twice a state's electoral vote.

Three separate groups—reformers, anti-Grant politicians, and a coalition of four influential newspaper editors known as "the Quadrilateral"—vied for control of the convention. For the presidential nomination, the reformers favored either Charles Francis Adams of Massachusetts or Sen. Lyman Trumbull of Illinois. The professional politicians were inclined to Supreme Court Justice David Davis of Illinois or Horace Greeley of New York. The newspaper editors opposed Davis.

On the first ballot, Adams led with 203 votes, followed by Greeley with 147, Trumbull with 110, Gov. B. Gratz Brown of Missouri with 95, and Davis with 92½. After the roll call, Brown announced his withdrawal from the race and his support for Greeley. For the next five ballots, Greeley and Adams battled for the lead. But on the sixth ballot, the professional politicians were able to ignite a stampede for Greeley that resulted in his nomination.

Many of the reform-minded delegates, disgusted with the selection of the New York editor, left the convention. The vice-presidential nomination went on the second ballot to a Greeley supporter, Gov. Brown of Missouri.

The platform adopted by the Liberal Republicans differed with the one later accepted by the Republicans on three main points: reconstruction, civil service reform, and the tariff.

The Liberal Republicans called for an end to reconstruction with its "carpetbag" governments, a grant of universal amnesty to southern citizens, and a return to home rule in the South. The Liberal Republicans sharply criticized the corruption of civil service under the Grant administration and labeled its reform one of the leading issues of the day. The civil service plank advocated a one-term limit on the presidency.

The presence of delegates supporting both protection and free trade led to a tariff plank that frankly stated the party's position on the issue should be left to local determination.

Following are excerpts from the Liberal Republican platform of 1872:

Reconstruction. We demand the immediate and absolute removal of all disabilities imposed on account of the Rebellion, which was finally subdued seven years ago, believing that universal amnesty will result in complete pacification in all sections of the country.

Local self-government, with impartial suffrage, will guard the rights of all citizens more securely than any centralized power. The public welfare requires the supremacy of the civil over the military authority, and freedom of person under the protection of the *habeas corpus*.

Civil Rights. We recognize the equality of all men before the law, and hold that it is the duty of Government in its dealings with the people to mete out equal and exact justice to all of whatever nativity, race, color, or persuasion, religious or political.

Civil Service Reform. The Civil Service of the Government has become a mere instrument of partisan tyranny and personal ambition and an object of selfish greed. It is a scandal and reproach upon free institutions and breeds a demoralization dangerous to the perpetuity of republican government. We therefore regard such thorough reforms of the Civil Service as one of the most pressing necessities of the hour; that honesty, capacity, and fidelity constitute the only valid claim to public employment; that the offices of the Government cease to be a matter of arbitrary favoritism and patronage, and that public station become again a pest of honor. To this end it is imperatively required that no President shall be a candidate for reelection.

Tariff. . . . recognizing that there are in our midst honest but irreconcilable differences of opinion with regard to the respective systems of Protection and Free Trade, we remit the discussion of the subject to the people in their Congress Districts, and to the decision of Congress thereon, wholly free of Executive interference or dictation.

Homesteading. We are opposed to all further grants of lands to railroads or other corporations. The public domain should be held sacred to actual settlers.

DEMOCRATS

The Democratic convention that met in Baltimore in July 1872 was one of the most bizarre in American political history. In sessions totaling only six hours, the delegates endorsed the decisions on candidates and platform made at a convention one month earlier by the Liberal Republicans. The Democratic convention merely rubber-stamped the creation of a coalition of Liberal Republicans and the core of the Democratic Party. (*Table, p. 585.*)

This new coalition was established with little dissent. When it came time for the presidential balloting, nominating speeches were not allowed. On the subsequent roll call, Greeley, the nominee of the Liberal Republicans, received 686 of the allotted 732 votes. It was an ironic choice, because in earlier decades Greeley, as editor of the *New York Tribune,* had been a frequent critic of the Democratic Party. More than anything else, however, Greeley's selection underscored the lack of strong leadership in the post–Civil War Democratic Party.

In similar fashion, the convention endorsed the nomination of B. Gratz Brown for vice president. Brown, the governor of Missouri and the choice of the Liberal Republicans, was the early unanimous nominee of the Democrats, with 713 votes.

By a vote of 574 to 158, the delegates agreed to limit debate on the platform to one hour. Except for a brief introduction, the Democrats approved the same platform that had been adopted by the Liberal Republicans a month earlier. Key planks called for an end to reconstruction and complete amnesty for Southern citizens, a return to a federal government with limited powers, civil service reform, and the halt of grants of public land to railroads and other corporations. Ironically, the platform also favored a hard-money policy, a reversal of the Democrats' soft-money stand in 1868. Although there was some objection to the point-by-point acceptance of the Liberal Republican platform, it was adopted by a vote of 671 to 62. (*For platform excerpts, see the Liberal Republicans section, p. 463.*)

REPUBLICANS

With the reform wing of the Republican Party already having bolted, the remaining elements of the party gathered in relative harmony in Philadelphia in June 1872. President Ulysses S. Grant was renominated without opposition, receiving all 752 votes cast. (*Table, p. 585.*)

The only contest at the convention centered around the vice-presidential nomination, with the incumbent, Schuyler Colfax of Indiana, and Sen. Henry Wilson of Massachusetts the two major rivals. Wilson took a slim plurality over Colfax on the first roll call, 364½ to 321½, but a vote shift by Virginia after completion of the roll gave Wilson the necessary majority with 399½ votes.

Without debate or opposition, the platform was adopted. It lauded the eleven years of Republican rule, noting the success of Reconstruction, the hard-money policy, and the homestead program. A tariff plank called for a duty on imports to raise revenue as well as to protect American business.

The platform also included several progressive planks, including a recommendation that the franking privilege be abolished, an extension of rights to women, and a call for federal and state legislation that would ensure equal rights for all races throughout the nation. The last plank was a significant change from the 1868 platform, which called for black suffrage in the South but left the decision on black voting rights to the individual states elsewhere.

Following are excerpts from the Republican platform of 1872:

Reconstruction. We hold that Congress and the President have only fulfilled an imperative duty in their measures for the suppression of violent and treasonable organizations in certain lately rebellious regions, and for the protection of the ballot-box, and therefore they are entitled to the thanks of the nation.

Civil Rights. Complete liberty and exact equality in the enjoyment of all civil, political, and public rights should be established and effectually maintained throughout the Union, by efficient and appropriate State and Federal legislation. Neither the law nor its administration should admit any discrimination in respect of citizens by reason of race, creed, color, or previous condition of servitude.

Civil Service Reform. Any system of the civil service under which the subordinate positions of the government are considered rewards for mere party zeal is fatally demoralizing, and we therefore favor a reform of the system by laws which shall abolish the evils of patronage, and make honesty, efficiency, and fidelity the essential qualifications for public positions, without practically creating a life-tenure of office.

Tariff. . . . [R]evenue . . . should be raised by duties upon importations, the details of which should be so adjusted as to aid in securing remunerative wages to labor, and to promote the industries, prosperity, and growth of the whole country.

Homesteading. We are opposed to further grants of the public lands to corporations and monopolies, and demand that the national domain be set apart for free homes for the people.

Women's Rights. The Republican party is mindful of its obligations to the loyal women of America for their noble devotion to the cause of freedom. Their admission to wider fields of usefulness is viewed with satisfaction, and the honest demand of any class of citizens for additional rights should be treated with respectful consideration.

1876 Conventions

PRESIDENTIAL CANDIDATES

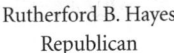

Rutherford B. Hayes
Republican

Samuel J. Tilden
Democrat

REPUBLICANS

The Republican convention assembled in Cincinnati, Ohio, in mid-June 1876. The call to the convention extended the olive branch to the dissident Liberal Republicans, who in large measure had rejoined their original party.

One of the highlights of the early sessions was a speech by the prominent black leader Frederick Douglass, who lambasted the Republicans for freeing the slaves without providing means for their economic or physical security.

A dispute developed over the seating of two contesting Alabama delegations. It was a candidate-oriented dispute, with the majority report favoring a delegation strongly for House Speaker James G. Blaine of Maine. The minority report supported a delegation pledged to Sen. Oliver P. Morton of Indiana. In the subsequent roll call, the convention decided in favor of the Blaine delegation by a vote of 369 to 360.

The presidential race was contested by the champions of the three nearly equal wings of the party. The Radicals were led by senators Roscoe Conkling of New York and Morton; the Half-Breeds, by Blaine; and the reformers, by former Treasury secretary Benjamin H. Bristow of Kentucky.

A fiery nominating speech for Blaine, delivered by Col. Robert G. Ingersoll, referred to the House Speaker as the "plumed knight," an appellation that stuck with Blaine the rest of his political career. Although it was a compelling speech, its effect was reduced by a failure in the hall's lighting system, which forced an early adjournment.

Nonetheless, when balloting commenced the next morning, Blaine had a wide lead, receiving 285 votes on the first ballot, compared with 124 for Morton, 113 for Bristow, and 99 for Conkling. (*Table, p. 586.*)

In the middle of the second ballot, a procedural dispute arose over the legality of the unit rule. Three delegates in the Pennsylvania delegation wished to vote for another candidate and appealed to the chair. The chair ruled that their votes should be counted, even though Pennsylvania was bound by the state con-

vention to vote as a unit. The ruling of the chair was upheld on a voice vote, but subsequent debate brought a roll call on reconsidering the decision. The motion to reconsider passed, 381 to 359. However, by a margin of 395 to 353, another roll call upheld the power of the convention chairman to abolish the unit rule.

Although the vote had long-range significance for future Republican conventions, in the short run it provided a slight boost for Blaine, who gained several delegates in Pennsylvania. On the next four ballots, Blaine retained his large lead but could not come close to the necessary 379 votes needed for nomination. The only candidate to show increased strength was Gov. Rutherford B. Hayes of Ohio, who jumped from 68 votes on the fourth roll call to 104 on the fifth.

On the sixth ballot, however, Blaine showed renewed strength, rising to 308 votes, while Hayes assumed second place with 113. The House Speaker continued to gain on the seventh ballot, but the anti-Blaine forces quickly and successfully united behind Hayes. The Ohio governor, a viable compromise choice who had not alienated any of the party factions, won the nomination with 384 votes to 351 for Blaine.

Five candidates were placed in nomination for the vice presidency. However, Rep. William A. Wheeler of New York was so far in the lead that the roll call was suspended after South Carolina voted, and Wheeler was declared the nominee by acclamation.

Platform debate centered on the party's immigration plank. A Massachusetts delegate proposed deletion of the plank, which called for a congressional investigation of oriental immigration. The delegate argued that the plank was inconsistent with the Republican principle that favored the equality of all races. However, by a vote of 518 to 229, the plank was retained as written.

The Republican platform included a scathing denunciation of the Democratic Party, but only on the issues of currency and tariff was it markedly different from the opposition. The Republicans, unlike the Democrats, favored complete payment of Civil War bonds in hard money as quickly as possible. While the

Democrats supported a tariff for revenue purposes only, the Republicans implied that the tariff should protect American industry as well as raise revenue.

As in past platforms, the Republicans called for the extension of civil rights, civil service reform, increased rights for women, the abolition of polygamy, and the distribution of public land to homesteaders. A new plank proposed that a constitutional amendment be passed forbidding the use of federal funds for non-public schools.

Following are excerpts from the Republican platform of 1876:

Currency. In the first act of congress, signed by President Grant, the national government . . . solemnly pledged its faith "to make provisions at the earliest practicable period, for the redemption of the United States notes in coin." Commercial prosperity, public morals, and the national credit demand that this promise be fulfilled by a continuous and steady progress to specie payment.

Tariff. The revenue necessary for current expenditures and the obligations of the public debt must be largely derived from duties upon importations, which, so far as possible, should be so adjusted as to promote the interests of American labor and advance the prosperity of the whole country.

Immigration. It is the immediate duty of congress fully to investigate the effects of the immigration and importation of Mongolians on the moral and material interests of the country.

Education. The public school system of the several states is the bulwark of the American republic; and, with a view to its security and permanence, we recommend an amendment to the constitution of the United States, forbidding the application of any public funds or property for the benefit of any school or institution under sectarian control.

Democratic Party. We therefore note with deep solicitude that the Democratic party counts, as its chief hope of success, upon the electoral vote of a united South, secured through the efforts of those who were recently arrayed against the nation; and we invoke the earnest attention of the country to the grave truth, that a success thus achieved would reopen sectional strife and imperil national honor and human rights.

We charge the Democratic party with being the same in character and spirit as when it sympathized with treason; with making its control of the house of representatives the triumph and opportunity of the nation's recent foes; with reasserting and applauding in the national capitol the sentiments of unrepentant rebellion; with sending Union soldiers to the rear, and promoting Confederate soldiers to the front; with deliberately proposing to repudiate the plighted faith of the government; with being equally false and imbecile upon the over-shadowing financial question; with thwarting the ends of justice, by its partisan mismanagements and obstruction of investigation; with proving itself, through the period of its ascendancy in the lower house of Congress, utterly incompetent to administer the government;—and we warn the country against trusting a party thus alike unworthy, recreant, and incapable.

DEMOCRATS

America's rapid westward expansion was typified by the site of the Democratic Party's 1876 convention—St. Louis, Missouri. It marked the first time that a national convention was held west of the Mississippi River.

The Democratic delegates assembled in late June. The one procedural matter debated was a proposal that the two-thirds rule be abolished at the 1880 convention and that the Democratic National Committee include such a recommendation in its next convention call. A move to table the proposal was defeated, 379 to 359. However, the national committee took no action on the proposal.

Two governors, Samuel J. Tilden of New York and Thomas A. Hendricks of Indiana, were the principal contenders for the presidential nomination, with Tilden having a substantial lead in delegates as the convention opened. Ironically, Tilden's most vocal opposition came from his New York delegation, where John Kelly of Tammany Hall spearheaded an effort to undermine Tilden's candidacy. Tilden's reform moves as governor had alienated Tammany Hall, and several times during the convention, Kelly took the floor to denounce Tilden.

Nonetheless, Tilden had a substantial lead on the first ballot, receiving 401½ votes to 140½ for Hendricks. Although short of the 492 votes needed to nominate, Tilden moved closer when Missouri switched its votes to him after the first roll call. The movement to Tilden continued on the second ballot, and he finished the roll call with 535 votes, more than enough to ensure his nomination. *(Table, p. 587.)*

Hendricks, the runner-up for the presidential nomination, was the nearly unanimous choice of the delegates for the vice presidency. Hendricks received 730 votes, with the other eight votes not being cast.

The Democratic platform was an unusual one. Rather than being arranged in usual fashion with a series of numbered planks, it was written in paragraph form in language unusually powerful for a party platform. The theme of the document was the need for reform, and nearly half the paragraphs began with the phrase, "Reform is necessary. . . ."

Debate focused on the party's stand on the currency issue. The majority report proposed repeal of the Resumption Act of 1875, a hard-money measure that called for the payment of Civil War bonds in coin. A minority report sponsored by delegates from five eastern states proposing deletion of this position was defeated, 550 to 219. A second minority report, introduced by Midwestern delegates, favored a more strongly worded opposition to the Resumption Act. It too was defeated, 505 to 229, with Midwestern delegations providing the bulk of the minority vote. The platform as a whole was approved, 651 to 83, again with most of the dissenting votes coming from the Midwest.

Besides the currency proposal, the platform called for extensive civil service reform, a tariff for revenue purposes only, restrictions on Chinese immigration, and a new policy on the distribution of public land that would benefit the homesteaders and not the railroads. In addition to its reform theme, the platform was filled with sharp criticisms of Republican rule.

Following are excerpts from the Democratic platform of 1876:

Civil Service Reform. Reform is necessary in the civil service. Experience proves that efficient economical conduct of the government is not possible if its civil service be subject to change at every election, be a prize fought for at the ballot-box, be an approved reward of party zeal instead of posts of honor assigned for proved competency and held for fidelity in the public employ; that the dispensing of patronage should neither be a tax upon the time of our public men nor an instrument of their ambition. Here again, profession falsified in the performance attest that the party in power can work out no practical or salutary reform. Reform is necessary even more in the higher grades of the public service. President, Vice-President, judges, senators, representatives, cabinet officers—these and all others in authority are the people's servants. Their offices are not a private perquisite; they are a public trust. When the annals of this Republic show disgrace and censure of a Vice-President; a late Speaker of the House of Representatives marketing his rulings as a presiding officer; three Senators profiting secretly by their votes as law-makers; five chairmen of the leading committees of the late House of Representatives exposed in jobbery; a late Secretary of the Treasury forcing balances in the public accounts; a late Attorney-General misappropriating public funds; a Secretary of the Navy enriched and enriching friends by a percentage levied off the profits of contractors with his department; an Ambassador to England censured in a dishonorable speculation; the President's Private Secretary barely escaping conviction upon trial for guilty complicity in frauds upon the revenue; a Secretary of War impeached for high crimes and misdemeanors—the demonstration is complete, that the first step in reform must be the people's choice of honest men from another party, lest the disease of one political organization infect the body politic, and lest by making no change of men or parties, we get no change of measures and no real reform.

Currency. We denounce the improvidence which, in eleven years of peace, has taken from the people in Federal taxes thirteen times the whole amount of the legal-tender notes and squandered four times their sum in useless expense, without accumulating any reserve for their redemption. We denounce the financial imbecility and immorality of that party, which, during eleven years of peace, has made no advance toward resumption, no preparation for resumption, but instead has obstructed resumption by wasting our resources and exhausting all our surplus income, and while annually professing to intend a speedy return to specie payments, has annually enacted fresh hindrances thereto. As such hindrance we denounce the resumption clause of the act of 1875 and we here demand its repeal.

Tariff. We denounce the present tariff levied upon nearly four thousand articles as a masterpiece of injustice, inequality and false pretense, which yields a dwindling and not a yearly rising revenue, has impoverished many industries to subsidize a few. . . . We demand that all customhouse taxation shall be only for revenue.

Homesteading. Reform is necessary to put a stop to the profligate waste of public lands and their diversion from actual settlers by the party in power, which has squandered two hundred millions of acres upon railroads alone, and out of more than thrice that aggregate has disposed of less than a sixth directly to the tillers of the soil.

Immigration. . . . [W]e denounce the policy which thus discards the liberty-loving German and tolerates the revival of the coolie-trade in Mongolian women for immoral purposes, and Mongolian men held to perform servile labor contracts, and demand such modification of the treaty with the Chinese Empire, or such legislation within constitutional limitations, as shall prevent further importation or immigration of the Mongolian race.

1880 Conventions

PRESIDENTIAL CANDIDATES

James A. Garfield
Republican

James B. Weaver
Greenback

Winfield Hancock
Democrat

REPUBLICANS

The Republicans gathered in Chicago beginning June 2, 1880, for their seventh quadrennial nominating convention. For the first time, the convention call was addressed only to Republicans and not more broadly to others who sympathized with party principles.

The convention was divided into two factions. One, headed by Sen. Roscoe Conkling of New York, favored the nomination of former president Ulysses S. Grant for a third term. The anti-Grant faction, although not united around one candidate, included the eventual nominee, Rep. James A. Garfield of Ohio, among its leaders.

Preconvention skirmishing focused on the selection of a temporary chairman. The Grant forces desired one from their own ranks who would uphold the unit rule—a rule important to Grant, because he had the support of a majority of delegates in several large states. However, the Grant strategy was blocked, and a temporary chairman neutral to both sides was chosen by the Republican National Committee, leaving the ultimate decision on the unit rule to the convention.

A test of strength between the two factions came early in the convention on an amended motion by Conkling directing the credentials committee to report to the convention prior to the rules committee. Conkling's amended motion was defeated, 406 to 318.

In spite of the defeat of the amended motion, much time was spent debating delegate credentials. More than fifty cases were presented in committee, and seven of them came to the floor for a vote. Five of the cases featured seating disputes among delegates selected in district caucuses and those chosen for the same seats in state conventions. In each case—involving delegates from the states of Illinois, Kansas, and West Virginia—the convention supported the claim of the delegates elected at the district level.

The Illinois credentials fight produced the only candidate-oriented division, with the Grant forces favoring the seating of the delegates selected at the state convention. But by a margin of 387 to 353, the convention voted to seat the delegates selected in the district caucuses. Three other votes were taken on disputed credentials from different Illinois districts, but all were decided in favor of the anti-Grant forces by a similar margin. *(Table, p. 588.)*

The majority report of the rules committee advocated that the controversial unit rule not be used. A motion by the Grant forces that the presidential nominations begin without passage of the rules committee report was defeated, 479 to 276. The vote was a key setback for the supporters of the former president, as the majority report was subsequently adopted by acclamation.

While the Grant forces suffered defeat on adoption of the unit rule, their candidate assumed the lead on the first ballot for president, with 304 votes. Sen. James G. Blaine of Maine followed closely with 284, and Treasury Secretary John Sherman of Ohio, the candidate nominated by Rep. Garfield, trailed with 93 votes.

Ballot after ballot was taken throughout the day, but after the twenty-eighth roll call, the last of the night, there was little change in the vote totals of the leading candidates. Grant led with 307 votes; Blaine had 279, and Sherman, 91.

When balloting resumed the next morning, Sherman's vote total jumped to 116, the biggest gain among the contenders, but still well behind Grant and Blaine. Grant gained votes on the thirty-fourth ballot, rising to a new high of 312, but on the same roll call a boom for Garfield began, with the Ohio representative collecting 16 votes from Wisconsin. Garfield protested that he was not a candidate but was ruled out of order by the chairman.

The Ohio representative continued to gain on the thirty-fifth ballot, his vote total rising to 50. On the next ballot, Garfield won the nomination, receiving the votes of nearly all the anti-Grant delegates. At the end of the roll call, Garfield had 399 votes; Grant, 306, and Blaine, 42, with nine votes distributed among other candidates.

Four men were placed in nomination for the vice presidency, but Chester A. Arthur of New York was the easy winner on the first ballot. Arthur, the former collector of the port of New York, received 468 votes to 193 for former representative Elihu B. Washburne of Illinois. Most of Arthur's support came from delegates who had backed Grant.

The Republican platform was passed by a voice vote without debate. For the first time, the platform included planks that clearly called for the exercise of federal power, emphasizing that the Constitution was "a supreme law, and not a mere contract." This philosophy contrasted with the Democratic platform, which favored home rule and government decentralization.

The two parties also differed on the tariff issue. The Republicans favored a revenue tariff that would also protect American industry, while the Democrats explicitly called for a revenue tariff only.

In its original form, the Republican platform did not include a civil service plank. An amendment from the floor, however, calling for a "thorough, radical and complete" reform of the civil service, was passed by a voice vote.

Following are excerpts from the Republican platform of 1880:

Federal Power. The Constitution of the United States is a supreme law, and not a mere contract. Out of confederated States it made a sovereign nation. Some powers are denied to the Nation, while others are denied to the States; but the boundary between the powers delegated and those reserved is to be determined by the National and not by the State tribunal.

The work of popular education is one left to the care of the several States, but it is the duty of the National Government to aid that work to the extent of its constitutional power. The intelligence of the Nation is but the aggregate of the intelligence in the several States, and the destiny of the Nation must be guided, not by the genius of any one State, but by the aggregate genius of all.

Tariff. We affirm the belief, avowed in 1876, that the duties levied for the purpose of revenue should so discriminate as to favor American labor. . . .

Civil Service Reform. The Republican party, . . . adopts the declaration of President Hayes that the reform of the civil service should be thorough, radical and complete.

Chinese Immigration. . . . [T]he Republican party, regarding the unrestricted immigration of the Chinese as a matter of grave concernment . . . would limit and restrict that immigration by the enactment of such just, humane and reasonable laws and treaties as will produce that result.

GREENBACK PARTY

A coalition of farmer and labor groups met in Chicago beginning June 9, 1880, to hold the second national Greenback Party convention. The party's first convention was held four years earlier, but it was not until 1880 that the Greenback Party received more than 2 percent of the popular vote. The party held its third and final convention four years later, but was unable in 1884 to attain 2 percent of the popular vote.

The 1880 convention attracted representatives of the various Greenback Party factions, as well as forty-four delegates from the Socialist Labor Party. Rep. James B. Weaver of Iowa was nominated for the presidency, and B. J. Chambers of Texas was chosen as his running mate.

The platform adopted was far broader than the one conceived by the Greenbacks at their first convention in 1876. That year they focused solely on the currency issue. For the agrarian interests, currency planks remained that called for the unlimited coinage of silver and gold and the issuance of currency by the federal government and not private banks. Also adopted for the farm elements were planks advocating increased public land for settlers, denouncing large monopolies and proposing that Congress control passenger and freight rates.

Included for the labor groups were proposals for an eight-hour day, the abolition of child labor, the improvement of working conditions and the curtailment of Chinese immigration.

The Greenback platform also included planks that favored a graduated income tax and women's suffrage.

Following are excerpts from the Greenback platform of 1880:

Currency. . . . All money, whether metallic or paper, should be issued and its volume controlled by the Government, and not by or through banking corporations, and when so issued should be a full legal-tender for all debts, public and private.

That the bonds of the United States should not be refunded, but paid as rapidly as practicable, according to contract. To enable the Government to meet these obligations, legal-tender currency should be substituted for the notes of the National banks, the National banking system abolished, and the unlimited coinage of silver, as well as gold, established by law.

Labor. That labor should be so protected by National and State authority as to equalize the burdens and insure a just distribution of its results; the eight-hour law of Congress should be enforced, the sanitary condition of industrial establishments placed under rigid control; the competition of contract labor abolished, a bureau of labor statistics established, factories, mines, and workshops inspected, the employment of children under fourteen years of age forbidden, and wages paid in cash.

Chinese Immigration. Slavery being simply cheap labor, and cheap labor being simple slavery, the importation and presence of Chinese serfs necessarily tends to brutalize and degrade American labor.

Homesteading. Railroad and land grants forfeited by reason of non-fulfillment of contract should be immediately reclaimed by the Government, and henceforth the public domain reserved exclusively as homes for actual settlers.

Regulation of Monopolies. It is the duty of Congress to regulate inter-state commerce. All lines of communication and transportation should be brought under such legislative control as shall secure moderate, fair and uniform rates for passenger and freight traffic.

We denounce as destructive to prosperity and dangerous to liberty, the action of the old parties in fostering and sustaining gigantic land, railroad, and money corporations and monopolies, invested with, and exercising powers belonging to the Government, and yet not responsible to it for the manner of their exercise.

Income Tax. All property should bear its just proportion of taxation, and we demand a graduated income tax.

Women's Suffrage. That every citizen of due age, sound mind, and not a felon, be fully enfranchised, and that this resolution be referred to the States, with recommendation for their favorable consideration.

DEMOCRATS

The Democrats held their thirteenth quadrennial nominating convention in Cincinnati, Ohio, in late June 1880. Credentials disputes enlivened the early sessions, with two competing New York delegations the focus of attention. The challenging group, controlled by Tammany Hall, requested 20 of New York's 70 votes. But by a margin of 457 to 205½, the convention refused the request.

Samuel J. Tilden, the Democratic standard-bearer in 1876 and the narrow loser in that controversial election, was not a candidate in 1880, although he did not officially notify his supporters of this fact until the presidential balloting had begun. Tilden's indecision, however, had long before opened the door for other prospective candidates.

On the first ballot, Gen. Winfield Scott Hancock of Pennsylvania, a candidate for the nomination in both 1868 and 1876, led with 171 votes, followed by Sen. Thomas F. Bayard of Delaware with 153½ and former representative Henry G. Payne of Ohio (who served as a stalking horse for the Tilden forces), with 81. (*Table, p. 589.*)

Tilden's declaration of noncandidacy was announced before the second ballot, and the Tilden forces shifted their strength to House Speaker Samuel J. Randall of Pennsylvania. Nonetheless, Hancock was the big gainer on the second ballot, his vote total jumping to 320. Randall followed with 128½, and Bayard slipped to third place with 112. Although Hancock was well short of the 492 votes needed for nomination, Wisconsin began a string of vote switches to Hancock that resulted in the military leader's selection. After all the changes, Hancock received 705 of the 738 votes cast.

The vice-presidential nomination went by acclamation to former representative William H. English of Indiana, the only candidate.

The platform was accepted without debate or opposition. Its style of short, sharp phrases contrasted with the 1876 platform, which was written in flowing sentences built around the theme of the necessity of reform.

The 1880 platform called for decentralization of the federal government with increased local government, currency based on hard money, a tariff for revenue only, civil service reform, and an end to Chinese immigration. The platform saved its harshest language to describe the party's reaction to the controversial election of 1876, which it labeled "the great fraud."

Following are excerpts from the Democratic platform of 1880:

Government Centralization. Opposition to centralization and to that dangerous spirit of encroachment which tends to consolidate the powers of all departments in one, and thus to create whatever be the form of government, a real despotism. No sumptuary laws; separation of Church and State, for the good of each; common schools fostered and protected.

Currency. Home rule; honest money, consisting of gold and silver, and paper convertible into coin on demand.

Tariff. [A] tariff for revenue only.

Civil Service Reform. We execrate the course of this administration in making places in the civil service a reward for political crime, and demand a reform by statute which shall make it forever impossible for a defeated candidate to bribe his way to the seat of the usurper by billeting villains upon the people.

Chinese Immigration. No more Chinese immigration, except for travel, education, and foreign commerce, and that even carefully guarded.

Election of 1876. The great fraud of 1876–1877, by which, upon a false count of the electoral voters of two States, the candidate defeated at the polls was declared to be President, and for the first time in American history, the will of the people was set aside under a threat of military violence, struck a deadly blow at our system of representative government. The Democratic party, to preserve the country from the horrors of a civil war, submitted for the time in firm and patriotic faith that the people would punish this crime in 1880. This issue precedes and dwarfs every other. It imposes a more sacred duty upon the people of the Union than ever addressed the conscience of a nation of free men.

1884 Conventions

PRESIDENTIAL CANDIDATES

James G. Blaine
Republican

Grover Cleveland
Democrat

REPUBLICANS

The Republicans gathered in Chicago in June 1884 for their convention. For the first time, the call to the convention prescribed how and when delegates should be selected, an effort to avoid the credentials disputes that had besieged the convention four years earlier.

The assassination of President James A. Garfield three years earlier had opened up the Republican presidential race, and the party war horse, James G. Blaine of Maine, emerged as the front-runner for the nomination. However, there was strong opposition to Blaine from several candidates, including the incumbent president, Chester A. Arthur of New York.

The first test between the two sides was over the choice of a temporary chairman. The Blaine forces supported former senator Powell Clayton of Arkansas, while the anti-Blaine coalition favored a black delegate from Mississippi, John R. Lynch. Lynch won by a vote of 424 to 384. *(Table, p. 590.)*

A motion by the Blaine forces to adjourn after the presidential nominating speeches was also beaten, 412 to 391. But on the first ballot Blaine assumed the lead with 334½ votes, followed by President Arthur with 278 and Sen. George F. Edmunds of Vermont with 93. Most of Arthur's strength was in the South, where the administration's patronage power had great effect.

Blaine gained votes on the next two ballots, his total rising to 375 on the third ballot, while Arthur dropped slightly to 274. After this roll call, the anti-Blaine forces tried to force adjournment but were defeated, 458 to 356. On the fourth ballot, Blaine received the nomination, winning 541 votes to 207 for Arthur and 41 for Edmunds.

Sen. John A. Logan of Illinois was the only person placed in nomination for vice president. Logan, who earlier had been in contention for the presidential nomination, received 779 of the 820 votes in the convention for second place on the ticket.

The party platform was adopted without dissent, and on major issues was little different from the planks presented by the Democrats. The Republicans proposed a tariff that would both protect American industry and raise revenue, called for civil service reform, advocated restrictions on Chinese immigration, and favored increased availability of public lands for settlers. In addition, the Republicans adopted features of the Greenback Party platform, calling for government regulation of railroads and an eight-hour workday.

Following are excerpts from the Republican platform of 1884:

Tariff. We . . . demand that the imposition of duties on foreign imports shall be made, not "for revenue only," but that in raising the requisite revenues for the government, such duties shall be so levied as to afford security to our diversified industries and protection to the rights and wages of the laborer; to the end that active and intelligent labor, as well as capital, may have its just reward, and the laboring man his full share in the national prosperity.

Chinese Immigration. [W]e denounce the importation of contract labor, whether from Europe or Asia, as an offense against the spirit of American institutions; and we pledge ourselves to sustain the present law restricting Chinese immigration, and to provide such further legislation as is necessary to carry out its purposes.

Labor. We favor the establishment of a national bureau of labor; the enforcement of the eight hour law.

Regulation of Railroads. The principle of public regulation of railway corporations is a wise and salutary one for the protection of all classes of the people; and we favor legislation that shall prevent unjust discrimination and excessive charges for transportation, and that shall secure to the people, and the railways alike, the fair and equal protection of the laws.

DEMOCRATS

The 1884 Democratic convention was held in Chicago in July. For the first time, the party extended delegate voting rights to the territories and the District of Columbia.

A debate over the unit rule highlighted the first day of the convention. Delegates from Tammany Hall, a minority of the New York delegation, presented an amendment to the temporary rules designed to abolish the unit rule. All the New York delegates were bound by their state convention to vote as a unit. However, the national convention defeated the amendment by a vote of 463 to 332, thus limiting the power of the Tammany delegates.

A resolution was passed opening the position of party chairman to individuals who were not members of the Democratic National Committee. Another resolution, to eliminate the two-thirds rule at future conventions, was put to a vote, but the roll call was suspended when it became apparent the resolution would not pass.

Several peculiarities were evident during the presidential nominating speeches. Sen. Thomas A. Hendricks of Indiana, the favorite of the Hoosier delegation, nominated former senator Joseph E. McDonald as the state's favorite son in a speech listing attributes that easily could have described Hendricks. Two seconding speeches for Gov. Grover Cleveland of New York were delivered by Tammany delegates who actually used the time to denounce Cleveland.

In spite of the opposition within his own delegation, Cleveland was the front-runner for the nomination and had a big lead on the first ballot. Cleveland received 392 votes, easily outdistancing Sen. Thomas F. Bayard of Delaware, who had 170. Former senator Allen G. Thurman of Ohio was next, with 88. Hendricks received one vote but protested to the convention that he was not a candidate.

A boom for Hendricks was undertaken on the second ballot, with the Indiana delegation shifting its support from McDonald to Hendricks. However, Cleveland also gained and continued to hold a large lead over the rest of the field. After two roll calls, these vote totals stood: Cleveland, 475; Bayard, 151½; Hendricks, 123½; Thurman, 60. With the New York governor holding a majority of the vote, North Carolina switched to Cleveland, and this started a bandwagon that gave him the required two-thirds majority. After the shifts, Cleveland received 683 of the 820 votes in the convention. *(Table, p. 591.)*

Over the objections of the Indiana delegation, Hendricks was nominated for the vice presidency. The Indiana leaders were a bit upset that Hendricks did not receive the presidential nomination but did contribute to his nearly unanimous total for second place on the ticket. When the roll call was completed, Hendricks had received all but four votes.

The Democratic platform of 1884 was one of the longest documents adopted by the party in the nineteenth century. The platform was about 3,000 words long, with the first third devoted to a description of alleged Republican failures.

The platform straddled the increasingly important tariff issue. In 1880 the Democrats clearly favored a revenue tariff only, but the 1884 document called for both revenue and protection of American industry.

A minority report introduced by Benjamin F. Butler, former governor of Massachusetts, focused on the tariff issue. Butler advocated a duty on imports that would hit harder at luxury items and less on necessities than the tariff favored by the majority report and would ensure more protection for American labor. The minority report was defeated, 721½ to 96½.

Butler, a former Republican and, earlier in 1884, nominated for president by the Greenback and Anti-Monopoly parties, also introduced substitute planks on labor, monopoly, public corporations, currency, and civil service reform. These other planks were defeated by a voice vote, and the platform as written was adopted by acclamation.

Following are excerpts from the Democratic platform of 1884:

Tariff. Knowing full well, . . . that legislation affecting the operations of the people should be cautious and conservative in method, not in advance of public opinion, but responsive to its demands, the Democratic party is pledged to revise the tariff in a spirit of fairness to all interests.

But in making reduction in taxes, it is not proposed to injure any domestic industries, but rather to promote their healthy growth. From the foundation of this Government, taxes collected at the Custom House have been the chief source of Federal Revenue. Such they must continue to be. Moreover, many industries have come to rely upon legislation for successful continuance, so that any change of law must be at every step regardful of the labor and capital thus involved. The process of reform must be subject in the execution to this plain dictate of justice. . . .

Sufficient revenue to pay all the expenses of the Federal Government . . . can be got, under our present system of taxation, from the custom house taxes on fewer imported articles, bearing heaviest on articles of luxury, and bearing lightest on articles of necessity.

Civil Liberties—Civil Service Reform. We oppose sumptuary laws which vex the citizen and interfere with individual liberty; we favor honest Civil Service Reform, and the compensation of all United States officers by fixed salaries; the separation of Church and State; and the diffusion of free education by common schools, so that every child in the land may be taught the rights and duties of citizenship.

Chinese Immigration. [W]e . . . do not sanction the importation of foreign labor, or the admission of servile races, unfitted by habits, training, religion, or kindred, for absorption into the great body of our people, or for the citizenship which our laws confer. American civilization demands that against the immigration or importation of Mongolians to these shores our gates be closed.

1888 Conventions

PRESIDENTIAL CANDIDATES

Clinton B. Fisk
Prohibitionist

Grover Cleveland
Democrat

Benjamin Harrison
Republican

PROHIBITION

The Prohibition Party held its fifth national convention in Indianapolis in late May 1888. The party had held conventions since the 1872 campaign, but not until 1888 did the Prohibitionists receive at least 2 percent of the popular vote.

The 1888 convention selected Clinton B. Fisk of New Jersey for president and John A. Brooks of Missouri as his running mate. While the platform focused on the need for prohibition, planks were included that covered other issues. The Prohibition Party favored a tariff that would both protect American industry and raise revenue, supported the extension of voting rights, favored immigration restrictions, and proposed the abolition of polygamy.

Following are excerpts from the Prohibition Party platform of 1888:

Prohibition. That the manufacture, importation, exportation, transportation and sale of alcoholic beverages should be made public crimes, and prohibited as such.

Tariff. That an adequate public revenue being necessary, it may properly be raised by import duties; but import duties should be so reduced that no surplus shall be accumulated in the Treasury, and that the burdens of taxation shall be removed from foods, clothing and other comforts and necessaries of life, and imposed on such articles of import as will give protection both to the manufacturing employer and producing laborer against the competition of the world.

DEMOCRATS

When the Democratic convention assembled in St. Louis in early June 1888, the party, for the first time since the outset of the Civil War, was in control of the White House. There was no contest for the presidential nomination, with the incumbent, Grover Cleveland, renominated by acclamation. However, the death of Vice President Thomas A. Hendricks in 1885 left open the second place on the ticket.

Former senator Allen G. Thurman of Ohio was the favorite for the vice-presidential nomination and won easily on the first

ballot with 684 votes. Gov. Isaac P. Gray of Indiana had 101 votes, and Gen. John C. Black of Illinois trailed with 36. After the nomination of the seventy-five-year-old Thurman, red bandannas were strung up around the hall. The bandanna was Thurman's political symbol, used extensively in his public habit of pinching snuff.

The platform was adopted by acclamation. It reaffirmed the Democratic platform written four years earlier, but in addition lauded the policies of President Cleveland and the achievements of Democratic rule, opposed the existing protective tariff and supported legislation to modify it and proposed a reformation of tax laws. A plank introduced from the floor favoring Irish home rule was included in the platform.

Following are excerpts from the Democratic platform of 1888:

Tariff. The Democratic party of the United States, in National Convention assembled, renews the pledge of its fidelity to Democratic faith and reaffirms the platform adopted by its representatives in the Convention of 1884, and indorses the views expressed by President Cleveland in his last annual message to Congress as the correct interpretation of that platform upon the question of Tariff reduction; and also indorses the efforts of our Democratic Representatives in Congress to secure a reduction of excessive taxation. . . .

Resolved, That this convention hereby indorses and recommends the early passage of the bill for the reduction of the revenue now pending in the House of Representatives.

Tax Reform. All unnecessary taxation is unjust taxation. . . . Every Democratic rule of governmental action is violated when through unnecessary taxation a vast sum of money, far beyond the needs of an economical administration, is drawn from the people and the channels of trade, and accumulated as a demoralizing surplus in the National Treasury. . . . The Democratic remedy is to enforce frugality in public expense and abolish needless taxation.

Federal Power. Chief among its principles of party faith are the maintenance of an indissoluble Union of free and indestructible States, now about to enter upon its second century of unexampled progress and renown; devotion to a plan of government regulated by a written Constitution, strictly specifying every granted power and expressly reserving to the States or people the entire ungranted residue of power.

REPUBLICANS

The Republicans assembled for their convention in Chicago in late June 1888. Not only was the party out of the White House for the first time since the Civil War, but a perennial contender for the presidential nomination, James G. Blaine, had taken himself out of the running. Although this encouraged a number of candidates to seek the nomination, none came near to mustering the needed majority as the balloting for president began.

The 832 convention votes were distributed among fourteen candidates, with Sen. John Sherman of Ohio leading the field with 229 votes. Circuit Judge Walter Q. Gresham of Indiana followed with 107 votes, while four other candidates received more than 70 votes. During the rest of the day, two more ballots were taken, with little appreciable change in the strength of the candidates. After the third roll call, Sherman led with 244 votes, followed by Gresham with 123 and former governor Russell A. Alger of Michigan with 122.

The unexpected withdrawal from the race of Chauncey Depew of New York, the favorite of that state's delegation, prompted a call for adjournment after the third ballot. The motion passed, 531 to 287.

When balloting resumed the next morning, the biggest gainer was former Sen. Benjamin Harrison of Indiana. Although Sherman still held the lead with 235 votes on the fourth ballot, Harrison's vote total had leaped from 94 votes on the third to 216 on the fourth. There was little change on the fifth ballot, taken on a Saturday, and after the roll call the delegates approved, 492 to 320, a motion to adjourn until Monday. The motion was generally supported by delegates opposed to Harrison.

When the convention reconvened, both Sherman and Harrison showed small gains—Sherman rising to 244 votes and Harrison to 231. On the next roll call, the seventh, Harrison took the lead for the first time, thanks largely to a shift of votes from delegates previously holding out for Blaine. Harrison led, 279 to 230, and the trend to the Indianan accelerated to a bandwagon the next ballot. Harrison easily achieved a majority on the eighth roll call, winning 544 votes to 118 for Sherman. *(Table, p. 592.)*

Three individuals were placed in nomination for vice president, but former representative Levi P. Morton of New York was the runaway winner on the first ballot. Morton received 592 votes to easily outdistance Rep. William Walter Phelps of New Jersey, 119 votes, and William O. Bradley of Kentucky, 103.

The platform sharply differed from that of the Democrats on the important tariff issue, strongly supporting the protective tariff and opposing the legislation favored by the Democrats. Like the Democrats, the Republicans called for a reduction in taxes, specifically recommending repeal of taxes on tobacco and on alcohol used in the arts and for mechanical purposes. In other areas, the Republicans favored the use of both gold and silver as currency, strongly opposed the Mormon practice of polygamy, and called for veterans' pensions.

Following are excerpts from the Republican platform of 1888:

Tariff. We are uncompromisingly in favor of the American system of protection; we protest against its destruction as proposed by the President and his party. They serve the interests of Europe; we will support the interests of America. . . . The protective system must be maintained. Its abandonment has always been followed by general disaster to all interests, except those of the usurer and the sheriff. We denounce the Mills bill as destructive to the general business, the labor and the farming interests of the country, and we heartily indorse the consistent and patriotic action of the Republican Representatives in Congress in opposing its passage.

Tax Reform. The Republican party would effect all needed reduction of the National revenue by repealing the taxes upon tobacco, which are an annoyance and burden to agriculture, and the tax upon spirits used in the arts, and for mechanical purposes, and by such revision of the tariff laws as will tend to check imports of such articles as are produced by our people, the production of which gives employment to our labor, and releases from import duties those articles of foreign production (except luxuries), the like of which cannot be produced at home. If there shall remain a larger revenue than is requisite for the wants of the government we favor the entire repeal of internal taxes rather than the surrender of any part of our protective system at the joint behests of the whiskey trusts and the agents of foreign manufacturers.

Currency. The Republican party is in favor of the use of both gold and silver as money, and condemns the policy of the Democratic Administration in its efforts to demonetize silver.

Veterans' Benefits. The gratitude of the Nation to the defenders of the Union cannot be measured by laws. . . . We denounce the hostile spirit shown by President Cleveland in his numerous vetoes of measures for pension relief, and the action of the Democratic House of Representatives in refusing even a consideration of general pension legislation.

Polygamy. The political power of the Mormon Church in the Territories as exercised in the past is a menace to free institutions too dangerous to be longer suffered. Therefore we pledge the Republican party to appropriate legislation asserting the sovereignty of the Nation in all Territories where the same is questioned, and in furtherance of that end to place upon the statute books legislation stringent enough to divorce the political from the ecclesiastical power, and thus stamp out the attendant wickedness of polygamy.

1892 Conventions

PRESIDENTIAL CANDIDATES

Benjamin Harrison
Republican

Grover Cleveland
Democrat

James B. Weaver
Populist

REPUBLICANS

Although President Benjamin Harrison was unpopular with various elements in the Republican Party, administration forces were in control of the convention that assembled in early June 1892 in Minneapolis, Minnesota. A Harrison supporter, former representative William McKinley of Ohio, was elected without opposition as the convention's permanent chairman.

A question concerning the credentials of six Alabama delegates resulted in a protracted debate on whether the six delegates in question could vote on their own case. The situation was resolved when the Alabama delegates voluntarily abstained from voting. The minority report, which proposed seating the six Alabama delegates on the original roll, was defeated, 463 to 423½, and the majority report was subsequently adopted, 476 to 365½. The two votes were candidate-oriented, with the winning side in each case composed largely of Harrison voters.

Harrison's chances of renomination were so strong that two other possibilities, James G. Blaine and William McKinley, never publicly announced as candidates for the presidency. Harrison won easily on the first ballot, receiving 535⅙ votes to 182⅙ for Blaine and 182 for McKinley. McKinley was in the ironic position of presiding over the convention at the same time he was receiving votes on the presidential ballot. The Ohioan withdrew briefly as permanent chairman and moved that Harrison's nomination be made unanimous. The motion was withdrawn after objections but placed McKinley publicly on the Harrison bandwagon. (*Table, p. 593.*)

While the Republican Party had an incumbent vice president in Levi P. Morton, the New York delegation supported Whitelaw Reid, the former editor of the *New York Tribune* and ambassador to France. With Morton making little effort to retain his position, Reid was nominated by acclamation, the first time a Republican convention had dispensed with a roll call in choosing a member of its national ticket.

The platform was adopted by a voice vote, and on only two major issues did it differ from that of the Democrats. The Republicans supported a protective tariff, clearly diverging from the Democrats, who supported import duties for revenue only. The Republicans also included a plank that sympathized with the prohibition effort, while the Democrats announced their opposition "to all sumptuary laws."

Both parties favored a bimetallic currency, with gold and silver of equal value, and supported the construction of a canal across Nicaragua. In addition, the Republicans advocated an expansionist foreign policy.

Following are excerpts from the Republican platform of 1892:

Tariff. We reaffirm the American doctrine of protection. We call attention to its growth abroad. We maintain that the prosperous condition of our country is largely due to the wise revenue legislation of the Republican congress.

We believe that all articles which cannot be produced in the United States, except luxuries, should be admitted free of duty, and that on all imports coming into competition with the products of American labor, there should be levied duties equal to the difference between wages abroad and at home.

Currency. The American people, from tradition and interest, favor bi-metallism, and the Republican party demands the use of both gold and silver as standard money, with such restrictions and under such provisions, to be determined by legislation, as will secure the maintenance of the parity of values of the two metals so that the purchasing and debt-paying power of the dollar, whether of silver, gold, or paper, shall be at all times equal. The interests of the producers of the country, its farmers and its workingmen, demand that every dollar, paper or coin, issued by the government, shall be as good as any other.

Foreign Policy. We reaffirm our approval of the Monroe doctrine and believe in the achievement of the manifest destiny of the Republic in its broadest sense.

Central American Canal. The construction of the Nicaragua Canal is of the highest importance to the American people, both as a measure of National defense and to build up and maintain American commerce, and it should be controlled by the United States Government.

Prohibition. We sympathize with all wise and legitimate efforts to lessen and prevent the evils of intemperance and promote morality.

DEMOCRATS

One of the strangest conventions in party annals was held by the Democrats in Chicago in late June 1892. Much of the disturbance was due to stormy weather, with the accompanying noise and leaks in the roof frequently interrupting the proceedings. Inside the hall, the discomfort of the delegates was increased by the vocal opposition of 600 Tammany Hall workers to the renomination of former president Grover Cleveland of New York.

Although Cleveland was a solid favorite for renomination, he was opposed by his home state delegation. The Tammany forces engineered an early state convention that chose a delegation committed to Gov. David B. Hill. But in spite of the hostility of the New York delegation, Cleveland was able to win renomination on the first ballot, receiving 617⅓ votes to 114 for Hill and 103 for Gov. Horace Boles of Iowa. (*Table, p. 593.*)

Four individuals were placed in nomination for the vice presidency, with Adlai E. Stevenson of Illinois assuming the lead on the first ballot. Stevenson, a former representative and later assistant postmaster general during Cleveland's first administration, led former governor Isaac P. Gray of Indiana, 402 to 343. After the first roll call was completed, Iowa switched to Stevenson, starting a bandwagon that led quickly to his nomination. After all the switches had been tallied, Stevenson was the winner with 652 votes, followed by Gray with 185.

The platform debate centered around the tariff plank. The plank, as originally written, straddled the issue. But a sharply worded substitute proposed from the floor, calling for a tariff for revenue only, passed easily, 564 to 342. The currency section called for stable money, with the coinage of both gold and silver in equal amounts. The platform also included a plank that called for the construction of a canal through Nicaragua.

Following are excerpts from the Democratic platform of 1892:

Tariff. We denounce Republican protection as a fraud, a robbery of the great majority of the American people for the benefit of the few. We declare it to be a fundamental principle of the Democratic party that the Federal Government has no constitutional power to impose and collect tariff duties, except for the purpose of revenue only, and we demand that the collection of such taxes shall be limited to the necessities of the Government when honestly and economically administered.

Currency. We hold to the use of both gold and silver as the standard money of the country, and to the coinage of both gold and silver without discriminating against either metal or charge for mintage, but the dollar unit of coinage of both metals must be of equal intrinsic and exchangeable value, or be adjusted through international agreement or by such safeguards of legislation as shall insure the maintenance of the parity of the two metals and the equal power of every dollar at all times in the markets and in the payment of debts; and we demand that all paper currency shall be kept at par with and redeemable in such coin.

Central American Canal. For purposes of national defense and the promotion of commerce between the States, we recognize the early construction of the Nicaragua Canal and its protection against foreign control as of great importance to the United States.

Prohibition. We are opposed to all sumptuary laws, as an interference with the individual rights of the citizen.

Federal Power. [W]e solemnly declare that the need of a return to these fundamental principles of free popular government, based on home rule and individual liberty, was never more urgent than now, when the tendency to centralize all power at the Federal capital has become a menace to the reserved rights of the States that strikes at the very roots of our Government under the Constitution as framed by the fathers of the Republic.

PROHIBITION

The Prohibition Party's sixth convention was held in Cincinnati in late June 1892 and nominated John Bidwell of California for president and James B. Cranfill of Texas as his running mate. While the Prohibition Party continued to run a national ticket through the 1972 election, 1892 marked the last year that the party received more than 2 percent of the popular vote.

Although beginning and ending with calls for prohibition, the 1892 platform as a whole was a reform-minded document, favoring women's suffrage and equal wages for women, an inflated currency and the nationalization of railroad, telegraph, and other public corporations.

Following are excerpts from the Prohibition platform of 1892:

Prohibition. . . . We declare anew for the entire suppression of the manufacture, sale, importation, exportation and transportation of alcoholic liquors as a beverage by Federal and State legislation, and the full powers of Government should be exerted to secure this result. Any party that fails to recognize the dominant nature of this issue in American politics is undeserving of the support of the people.

Women's Rights. No citizen should be denied the right to vote on account of sex, and equal labor should receive equal wages, without regard to sex.

Currency. The money of the country should consist of gold, silver, and paper, and be issued by the General Government only, and in sufficient quantity to meet the demands of business and give full opportunity for the employment of labor. To this end an increase in the volume of money is demanded, and no individual or corporation should be allowed to make any profit through its issue. It should be made a legal tender for the payment of all debts, public and private. Its volume should be fixed at a definite sum per capita and made to increase with our increase in population.

Tariff. Tariff should be levied only as a defense against foreign governments which levy tariff upon or bar out our products from their markets, revenue being incidental.

Government Nationalization. Railroad, telegraph, and other public corporations should be controlled by the Government in the interest of the people.

PEOPLE'S PARTY (POPULISTS)

The most successful of the nineteenth century farmer-labor coalitions was the People's Party, commonly known as the Populists, which formally organized as a political party at a convention in Cincinnati in May 1891. Further organization was accomplished at a convention in St. Louis the next February, from which emanated the call to the party's first national nominating convention, to be held that summer in Omaha, Nebraska. The election of 1892 was the only one in which the Populists received more than 2 percent of the national vote. Four years later the party endorsed the Democratic ticket, and from 1900 through 1908 the Populists ran separate tickets, but failed to receive 2 percent of the popular vote.

The call to the 1892 convention specified procedures for the selection of delegates and set the size of the convention at 1,776 delegates. Thirteen hundred to fourteen hundred delegates actually assembled in Omaha for the Populist convention, which opened July 2. The field for the presidential nomination was reduced by the death early in 1892 of southern agrarian leader Leonidas L. Polk of North Carolina and the refusal of Judge Walter Q. Gresham of Indiana to seek the nomination. First place on the ticket went to former representative James B. Weaver of Iowa, who defeated Sen. James H. Kyle of South Dakota, 995 to 275.

James G. Field of Virginia won the vice-presidential nomination over Ben Terrell of Texas by a vote of 733 to 554. The ticket bridged any sectional division, pairing a former Union general (Weaver) with a former Confederate major (Field).

On July 4 the delegates enthusiastically adopted the platform. It contained few ideas that were not contained in the earlier platforms of other farmer-labor parties. But the document adopted by the Populists brought these proposals together into one forcefully written platform. More than half the platform was devoted to the preamble, which demanded widespread reform and sharply criticized the two major parties. It attacked the Democrats and Republicans for waging "a sham battle over the tariff," while ignoring more important issues.

The remainder of the platform was divided into three major parts that discussed finance, transportation, and land policy. The Populists proposed that the currency be inflated, with the unlimited coinage of silver and a substantial increase in the circulating medium to at least $50 per capita. The Populists' currency plank was sharply different from those of the two major parties, which favored a stable, bimetallic currency.

The Populists also went well beyond the two major parties in advocating the nationalization of the railroads and telegraph and telephone companies. Both the Populists and Democrats advocated land reform, although the proposals received greater emphasis in the Populist platform.

The Populists included a call for a graduated income tax and expanded government power.

Although not considered part of the platform, supplementary resolutions were passed that favored the initiative and referendum, a limit of one term for the president, the direct election of senators, the secret ballot and additional labor-oriented proposals that called for improvement in working conditions.

Following are excerpts from the Populist platform of 1892:

Preamble. The conditions which surround us best justify our cooperation; we meet in the midst of a nation brought to the verge of moral, political, and material ruin. Corruption dominates the ballot-box, the Legislatures, the Congress, and touches even the ermine of the bench. The people are demoralized; most of the states have been compelled to isolate the voters at the polling places to prevent universal intimidation and bribery. The newspapers are largely subsidized or muzzled, public opinion silenced, business prostrated, homes covered with mortgages, labor impoverished, and the land concentrating in the hands of capitalists. The urban workmen are denied the right to organize for self-protection; imported pauperized labor beats down their wages, a hireling standing army, unrecognized by our laws, is established to shoot them down, and they are rapidly degenerating into European conditions. The fruits of the toil of millions are boldly stolen to build up colossal fortunes for a few, unprecedented in the history of mankind; and the possessors of these, in turn despise the Republic and endanger liberty. From the same prolific womb of governmental injustice we breed the two great classes—tramps and millionaires. . . .

We have witnessed for more than a quarter of a century the struggles of the two great political parties for power and plunder, while grievous wrongs have been inflicted upon the suffering people. We charge that the controlling influence dominating both these parties have permitted the existing dreadful conditions to develop without serious effort to prevent or restrain them. Neither do they now promise us any substantial reform. They have agreed together to ignore, in the coming campaign, every issue but one. They propose to drown the outcries of a plundered people with the uproar of a sham battle over the tariff, so that capitalists, corporations, national banks, rings, trusts, watered stock, the demonetization of silver and the oppressions of the usurers may all be lost sight of. They propose to sacrifice our homes, lives, and children on the altar of mammon; to destroy the multitude in order to secure corruption funds from the millionaires. . . .

We believe that the power of government—in other words, of the people—should be expanded (as in the case of the postal service) as rapidly and as far as the good sense of an intelligent people and the teachings of experience shall justify, to the end that oppression, injustice and poverty, shall eventually cease in the land.

While our sympathies as a party of reform are naturally upon the side of every proposition which will tend to make men intelligent, virtuous and temperate, we nevertheless regard these questions, important as they are, as secondary to the great issues now pressing for solution, and upon which not only our individual prosperity, but the very existence of free institutions depend; and we ask all men to first help us to determine whether we are to have a republic to administer, before we differ as to the conditions upon which it is to be administered, believing that the forces of reform this day organized will never cease to move forward, until every wrong is remedied, and equal rights and equal privileges securely established for all the men and women of this country.

Currency. We demand free and unlimited coinage of silver and gold at the present legal ratio of 16 to 1.

We demand that the amount of circulating medium be speedily increased to not less than $50 per capita.

We demand that postal savings banks be established by the government for the safe deposit of the earnings of the people and to facilitate exchange.

Transportation. Transportation being a means of exchange and a public necessity, the government should own and operate the railroads in the interest of the people. The telegraph and telephone, like the post office system, being a necessity for the transmission of news, should be owned and operated by the government in the interest of the people.

Land. The land, including all the natural sources of wealth, is the heritage of the people, and should not be monopolized for speculative purposes, and alien ownership of land should be prohibited. All land now held by railroad and other corporations in excess of their actual needs, and all lands now owned by aliens, should be reclaimed by the government and held for actual settlers only.

1896 Conventions

PRESIDENTIAL CANDIDATES

William McKinley
Republican

William J. Bryan
Democrat

REPUBLICANS

The currency issue, which spawned several third-party efforts in the late nineteenth century, emerged as the dominant issue of contention between the Republican and Democratic parties in the campaign of 1896. The forces in favor of the gold standard were firmly in control of the Republican convention that was held in St. Louis in early June 1896.

Actually, the convention was less a forum for the discussion of issues than a showcase for the political acumen of Mark Hanna of Ohio. Hanna, William McKinley's campaign manager, had been intensely courting delegates across the country, especially in the South, for more than a year before the convention. Before the rap of the opening gavel, Hanna had amassed a majority of the delegates for the popular Ohio governor.

The first evidence of McKinley strength came on a credentials question. A minority report was introduced claiming the credentials committee had held hearings on only two of 160 cases and proposing that the committee resume hearings. A maneuver to squelch the minority report was made when a delegate moved to cut off debate. With the McKinley forces providing most of the majority, the motion passed, 551½ to 359½.

Four other candidates in addition to McKinley were in contention for the presidential nomination, but McKinley was the runaway winner on the first ballot. He received 661½ votes to 84½ for the runner-up, House Speaker Thomas B. Reed of Maine. (*Table, p. 594.*)

There were two serious contenders for the vice-presidential nomination: Garret A. Hobart, a McKinley supporter and former state legislator from New Jersey, and Henry Clay Evans, a former candidate for governor of Tennessee. Hobart won, winning 523½ votes on the first ballot to 287½ for Evans.

As at the Democratic convention, the platform debate centered around the currency issue. The gold forces, firmly in control of the Republican convention, produced a majority report that called for maintenance of the gold standard until the time when bimetallism could be effected by an international agree-

ment. This plank did not satisfy the silver minority. Led by Sen. Henry M. Teller of Colorado, a minority plank was introduced favoring the unlimited coinage of silver and gold at the ratio of 16 to 1. Teller's plank, similar to the currency plank adopted later by the Democrats, was defeated, 818½ to 105½. A second roll call on adoption of the majority plank resulted in another decisive defeat for the silver forces. The majority plank carried, 812½ to 110½.

With the decisive defeat of the minority plank, Teller led a walkout by twenty-four silver delegates, including the entire Colorado and Idaho delegations and members of the Montana, South Dakota, and Utah delegations. The rest of the platform was adopted by a voice vote.

The currency plank that caused the commotion was buried deep in the middle of the Republican platform. The document began with a denunciation of Democratic rule and proceeded into a discussion of the merits of a protective tariff. A tariff for revenue purposes only was advocated in the Democratic platform, but the issue in the Republican document was clearly considered to be of secondary importance.

The Republican platform was also distinguishable from that of the Democrats in recommending a more expansionistic foreign policy, proposing stricter immigration restrictions and, for the first time, specifically denouncing the practice of lynching.

Following are excerpts from the Republican platform of 1896:

Currency. The Republican party is unreservedly for sound money. . . . We are unalterably opposed to every measure calculated to debase our currency or impair the credit of our country. We are therefore opposed to the free coinage of silver, except by international agreement with the leading commercial nations of the earth, which agreement we pledge ourselves to promote, and until such agreement can be obtained the existing gold standard must be maintained.

Tariff. We renew and emphasize our allegiance to the policy of protection, as the bulwark of American industrial independence, and the foundation of American development and prosperity. . . . Protection and Reciprocity are twin measures of American policy and go hand in hand. Democratic rule has recklessly struck down both, and both must be re-established. Protection for what we produce; free admission for the necessaries of life which we do not produce; reciprocal agreement of mutual interests, which gain open markets for us in return for our open markets for others. Protection builds up domestic industry and trade and secures our own market for ourselves; reciprocity builds up foreign trade and finds an outlet for our surplus.

Foreign Policy. Our foreign policy should be at all times firm, vigorous and dignified, and all our interests in the western hemisphere should be carefully watched and guarded.

The Hawaiian Islands should be controlled by the United States, and no foreign power should be permitted to interfere with them. The Nicaragua Canal should be built, owned and operated by the United States. And, by the purchase of the Danish Islands we should secure a much needed Naval station in the West Indies. . . . We therefore, favor the continued enlargement of the navy, and a complete system of harbor and sea-coast defenses.

Immigration. For the protection of the equality of our American citizenship and of the wages of our workingmen, against the fatal competition of low priced labor, we demand that the immigration laws be thoroughly enforced, and so extended as to exclude from entrance to the United States those who can neither read nor write.

Lynching. We proclaim our unqualified condemnation of the uncivilized and preposterous [barbarous] practice well known as lynching, and the killing of human beings suspected or charged with crime without process of law.

DEMOCRATS

The Democratic convention that assembled in Chicago in July 1896 was dominated by one issue—currency. A delegate's viewpoint on this single issue influenced his position on every vote taken. Generally, the party was split along regional lines, with eastern delegations favoring a hard-money policy with maintenance of the gold standard, and most southern and western delegations supporting a soft-money policy with the unlimited coinage of silver.

Division in the convention was apparent on the first day, when the silver forces challenged the national committee's selection of Gov. David B. Hill of New York as temporary chairman. The pro-silver delegates put up Sen. John W. Daniel of Virginia for the post, and Daniel won easily, 556 to 349. His victory indicated the dominance of the silver forces and presaged their ability to control the convention.

Two sets of credentials challenges were next on the agenda. By a voice vote, the convention agreed to seat a Nebraska delegation headed by a young silver supporter, William Jennings Bryan. And, by a vote of 558 to 368, the convention defeated a recommendation to seat Michigan delegates supported by the hard-money-dominated national committee.

With their lack of strength apparent, the gold forces declined to run a candidate for president. However, the silver delegates could not initially coalesce behind one candidate, and fourteen individuals received votes on the first ballot. Rep. Richard P. "Silver Dick" Bland of Missouri was the pacesetter, with 235 votes, followed by Bryan, a former House member, with 137 and Robert E. Pattison, former Pennsylvania governor, with 97. Bryan, thirty-six years old, earlier had electrified the convention during the platform debate on currency, with his memorable

"Cross of Gold" speech, which had elevated him to the position of a major contender. *(Table, p. 595.)*

On the next two roll calls, both candidates showed gains. Bland's total climbed to 291 on the third ballot and Bryan's rose to 219. Bryan continued to gain on the next ballot and assumed the lead over Bland, 280 to 241. The movement to Bryan accelerated on the fifth ballot, and he won the nomination easily, receiving 652 of the 930 convention votes. Although Bryan was the nearly unanimous choice of the silver forces, 162 gold delegates indicated their dissatisfaction with the proceedings by refusing to vote.

With Bryan declining to indicate a preference for vice president, sixteen candidates received votes for the office on the first ballot. The Nebraska delegation, following Bryan's example, declined to participate in the vice-presidential balloting.

Former representative John C. Sibley of Pennsylvania took the lead on the first ballot with 163 votes, followed by Ohio editor and publisher John R. McLean with 111, and Maine shipbuilder Arthur Sewall with 100.

Bland spurted into the lead on the second ballot with 294 votes, followed by McLean and Sibley. After the roll call, Sibley withdrew, and on the third ballot the race between Bland and McLean tightened. The Missourian led, 255 to 210, but he too withdrew after the roll call. Sewall emerged as McLean's major competitor on the fourth ballot, and with the withdrawal of the Ohio journalist from the race, the nomination was Sewall's on the fifth ballot. Actually, Sewall's vote total of 602 on the final roll call was less than two-thirds of the convention vote, but with 251 disgruntled gold delegates refusing to vote, the required majority was reduced to only those voting.

Not surprisingly, the platform debate centered around the currency plank. The Eastern delegations proposed that, until silver coinage could be arranged by international agreement, the gold standard should be maintained. The southern and western delegations countered by demanding that the unlimited coinage of silver should begin without requiring a delay to reach an international agreement. Bryan managed the platform debate for the silver forces and scheduled himself as the final speaker, an enviable position from which to make a deep impression on the emotion-packed convention.

Bryan made the most of his opportunity, ending his dramatic speech with the famous peroration: "You shall not press down upon the brow of labor this crown of thorns, you shall not crucify mankind upon a cross of gold." The gold plank was defeated, 626 to 303. Although the speech was a key factor in Bryan's nomination, it was not influential in defeating the gold plank, which was already doomed to defeat. *(Table, p. 595.)*

A resolution commending the Cleveland administration was also defeated, 564 to 357, and after several attempts to modify the currency plank were rejected by voice votes, the platform as a whole was adopted, 622 to 307.

Following are excerpts from the Democratic platform of 1896:

Currency. We demand the free and unlimited coinage of both silver and gold at the present legal ratio of 16 to 1 without waiting for the aid or consent of any other nation.

Railroads. The absorption of wealth by the few, the consolidation of our leading railroad systems, and the formation of trusts and pools require a stricter control by the Federal Government of those arteries of commerce. We demand the enlargement of the powers of the Interstate Commerce Commission and such restriction and guarantees in the control of railroads as will protect the people from robbery and oppression.

No Third Term. We declare it to be the unwritten law of this Republic, established by custom and usage of 100 years, and sanctioned by the examples of the greatest and wisest of those who founded and have maintained our Government that no man should be eligible for a third term of the Presidential office.

Federal Power. During all these years the Democratic Party has resisted the tendency of selfish interests to the centralization of governmental power, and steadfastly maintained the integrity of the dual scheme of government established by the founders of this Republic of republics.

Under its guidance and teachings the great principle of local self-government has found its best expression in the maintenance of the rights of the States and in its assertion of the necessity of confining the general government to the exercise of the powers granted by the Constitution of the United States.

1900 Conventions

PRESIDENTIAL CANDIDATES

William McKinley
Republican

William J. Bryan
Democrat

REPUBLICANS

Surface harmony was the hallmark of the Republican conclave held in Philadelphia in June 1900. The Colorado delegation, which had walked out of the 1896 convention, was honored by having one of its members, Sen. Edward O. Wolcott, chosen as temporary chairman.

There was no opposition to President William McKinley, and he won all 926 votes on the first roll call. However, the death of Vice President Garret A. Hobart in 1899 had left the second spot on the ticket open. McKinley did not have a preference and asked his campaign manager, Mark Hanna, not to influence the convention. McKinley's hands-off policy worked to the advantage of the popular governor of New York and hero of the Spanish-American War, Theodore Roosevelt, whom Hanna disliked. *(Table, p. 596.)*

Roosevelt's popularity, coupled with the desire of New York boss Thomas C. Platt to eliminate a powerful state rival, enabled the forty-one-year-old governor to clinch the nomination before balloting began. On the vice-presidential roll call, Roosevelt received all but one vote. The single uncast vote came from Roosevelt's New York delegation, which cast 71 of its 72 votes for Roosevelt.

The Republicans adopted a platform that applauded the four years of Republican rule and credited McKinley's policies

with improving business conditions and winning the Spanish-American War. The platform defended postwar expansionism and called for increased foreign trade and the creation of a Department of Commerce.

As in 1896, the Republican platform opposed the unlimited coinage of silver and supported maintenance of the gold standard. On the tariff issue, the Republicans continued to laud the protective duty on imports.

Following are excerpts from the Republican platform of 1900:

Foreign Trade, Panama Canal. We favor the construction, ownership, control and protection of an Isthmian Canal by the Government of the United States. New markets are necessary for the increasing surplus of our farm products. Every effort should be made to open and obtain new markets, especially in the Orient, and the Administration is warmly to be commended for its successful efforts to commit all trading and colonizing nations to the policy of the open door in China.

International Expansion. In accepting by the Treaty of Paris the just responsibility of our victories in the Spanish war, the President and the Senate won the undoubted approval of the American people. No other course was possible than to destroy Spain's sovereignty throughout the West Indies and in the Philippine Islands. That course created our responsibility before the world, and with the unorganized population whom our intervention had freed from Spain, to provide for the maintenance of law and order, and for the establishment of good government and for the performance of international obligations. Our authority could not be less than our responsibility; and whenever sovereign rights were extended it became the high duty of the Government to maintain its authority, to put down armed insurrection and to confer the blessings of liberty and civilization upon all the rescued peoples.

Antitrust. We recognize the necessity and propriety of the honest co-operation of capital to meet new business conditions and especially to extend our rapidly increasing foreign trade, but we condemn all conspiracies and combinations intended to restrict business, to create monopolies, to limit production, or to control prices; and favor such legislation as will effectively restrain and prevent all such abuses, protect and promote competition and secure the rights of producers, laborers, and all who are engaged in industry and commerce.

Currency. We renew our allegiance to the principle of the gold standard and declare our confidence in the wisdom of the legislation of the Fifty-sixth Congress, by which the parity of all our money and the stability of our currency upon a gold basis has been secured. . . .

We declare our steadfast opposition to the free and unlimited coinage of silver.

Tariff. We renew our faith in the policy of Protection to American labor. In that policy our industries have been established, diversified and maintained. By protecting the home market competition has been stimulated and production cheapened.

DEMOCRATS

The Democrats opened their 1900 convention in Kansas City, Missouri, on July 4, and showed a degree of party harmony not evident at their convention four years earlier. After the party factionalism of 1896, the delegates made a conscious effort to display a unified front—an effort aided by the decline of the controversial silver issue. The discovery of new gold deposits in North America and the subsequent increase in currency had lessened the divisive impact of the silver issue.

William Jennings Bryan, the Democratic standard-bearer in 1896, was renominated without opposition, receiving all 936 votes. The harmony in the convention was evident when former New York senator David B. Hill, a leader of the gold forces four years earlier, gave a seconding speech for Bryan. *(Table, p. 596.)*

Seven names were placed in nomination for the vice presidency. However, two withdrew before the balloting began. Adlai E. Stevenson of Illinois, vice president under Grover Cleveland, led on the first roll call with 559½ votes, followed by Hill, who received 200 votes in spite of withdrawing from the race before the voting started. After completion of the ballot, a series of vote switches resulted in Stevenson's unanimous nomination.

The platform was adopted without floor debate. The major theme of the document was anti-imperialism, although an attack on trusts and a discussion of the currency question also were emphasized.

The anti-imperialism section was placed at the beginning of the platform and was labeled the most important issue of the campaign. The delegates enthusiastically accepted the plank, which forcefully criticized American international expansion after the Spanish-American War. The platform asserted "that no nation can long endure half republic and half empire" and denounced increasing U.S. militarism. The Democratic position

sharply differed from the one advocated by the Republicans, whose platform defended postwar expansionism.

After the anti-imperialism section was a sharp attack on monopolies, the most detailed antitrust section that had yet appeared in a Democratic platform. The plank called for more comprehensive antitrust legislation and more rigid enforcement of the laws already enacted. Although the Republicans also condemned monopolies, the issue received a mere one-sentence mention in their platform.

With the decline of the silver issue, the necessity of a pro-silver plank was a matter of debate in the resolutions committee. However, Bryan threatened to withdraw his candidacy if a plank calling for the unlimited coinage of silver was not included in the platform. By a majority of one vote, the resolutions committee included the silver plank, and it was accepted without dissent by the convention. The Democratic position set up another distinction with the Republicans, who, as four years earlier, favored maintenance of the gold standard.

In addition to the anti-imperialism, antitrust, and currency sections of the platform, the Democrats proposed the creation of a Department of Labor, favored the direct election of senators and, unlike the Republicans, supported the construction and ownership of a Nicaraguan canal. The Republican platform advocated construction and ownership of a canal across the Isthmus of Panama.

Following are excerpts from the Democratic platform of 1900:

Anti-imperialism. We hold that the Constitution follows the flag, and denounce the doctrine that an Executive or Congress deriving their existence and their powers from the Constitution can exercise lawful authority beyond it or in violation of it. We assert that no nation can long endure half republic and half empire, and we warn the American people that imperialism abroad will lead quickly and inevitably to despotism at home. . . .

We are not opposed to territorial expansion when it takes in desirable territory which can be erected into States in the Union, and whose people are willing and fit to become American citizens. We favor trade expansion by every peaceful and legitimate means. But we are unalterably opposed to seizing or purchasing distant islands to be governed outside the Constitution, and whose people can never become citizens. . . .

The importance of other questions, now pending before the American people is no wise diminished and the Democratic party takes no backward step from its position on them, but the burning issue of imperialism growing out of the Spanish war involves the very existence of the Republic and the destruction of our free institutions. We regard it as the paramount issue of the campaign. . . .

We oppose militarism. It means conquest abroad and intimidation and oppression at home. It means the strong arm which has ever been fatal to free institutions. . . . This republic has no place for a vast military establishment, a sure forerunner of compulsory military service and conscription. When the nation is in danger the volunteer soldier is his country's best defender.

Antitrust. We pledge the Democratic party to an unceasing warfare in nation, State and city against private monopoly in every form. Existing laws against trusts must be enforced and more stringent ones must be enacted. . . . Tariff laws should be amended by putting the products of trusts upon the free list, to prevent monopoly under the plea of protection.

Currency. We reaffirm and indorse the principles of the National Democratic Platform adopted at Chicago in 1896, and we reiterate the demand of that platform for an American financial system made by the American people for themselves, and which shall restore and maintain a bimetallic price-level, and as part of such system the immediate restoration of the free and unlimited coinage of silver and gold at the present legal ratio of 16 to 1, without waiting for the aid or consent of any other nation.

1904 Conventions

PRESIDENTIAL CANDIDATES

Eugene V. Debs
Socialist

Theodore Roosevelt
Republican

Alton B. Parker
Democrat

SOCIALISTS

The Socialist Party held its first national nominating convention in Chicago in early May 1904 and nominated Eugene V. Debs of Indiana for president and Benjamin Hanford of New York as his running mate. Debs ran in 1900 as the presidential candidate of two socialist groups, the Social Democratic Party and a moderate faction of the Socialist Labor Party.

The bulk of the platform was devoted to the philosophy of the international Socialist movement, with its belief in the eventual demise of capitalism and the ultimate achievement of a classless, worker-oriented society. To hasten the creation of a Socialist society, the platform favored many reforms advocated by the Populists and earlier agrarian-labor movements: the initiative, referendum, and recall; women's suffrage; tax reform, including the graduated income tax; the public ownership of transportation, communication and exchange; and various labor benefits, including higher wages and shorter hours.

Following are excerpts from the Socialist platform of 1904:

To the end that the workers may seize every possible advantage that may strengthen them to gain complete control of the powers of government, and thereby the sooner establish the cooperative commonwealth, the Socialist Party pledges itself to watch and work, in both the economic and the political struggle, for each successive immediate interest of the working class; for shortened days of labor and increases of wages; for the insurance of the workers against accident, sickness and lack of employment; for pensions for aged and exhausted workers; for the public ownership of the means of transportation, communication and exchange; for the graduated taxation of incomes, inheritances, franchises and land values, the proceeds to be applied to the public employment and improvement of the conditions of the workers; for the complete education of children, and their freedom from the workshop; for the prevention of the use of the military against labor in the settlement of strikes; for the free administration of justice; for popular government, including initiative, referendum, proportional representation, equal suffrage of men and women, municipal home rule, and the recall of officers by their constituents; and for every gain or advantage for the workers that may be wrested from the capitalist system, and that may relieve the suffering and strengthen the hands of labor. We lay upon every man elected to any executive or legislative office the first duty of striving to procure whatever is for the workers' most immediate interest, and for whatever will lessen the economic and political powers of the capitalist, and increase the like powers of the worker.

REPUBLICANS

President Theodore Roosevelt was totally in command of the Republican convention held in Chicago in June 1904. His most dangerous potential rival for the nomination, Sen. Mark Hanna of Ohio, had died in February, leaving the field clear for Roosevelt.

The rather trivial matter of most interest before the presidential balloting began was Hawaii's vote allocation. The rules committee recommended that the votes of the territory be reduced from six to two. A substitute amendment proposed that Hawaii retain its six votes for the 1904 convention but that its vote allocation be reviewed by the national committee for future conventions. The substitute was accepted by the narrow margin of 495 to 490.

Roosevelt's nomination caused less commotion. On the first ballot, he received all 994 votes. The party leadership favored Sen. Charles W. Fairbanks of Indiana for the vice presidency. Although the Georgia, Illinois, Missouri, and Nebraska delegations noted that they preferred other candidates, Fairbanks was nominated by acclamation. *(Table, p. 598.)*

The party platform was adopted without dissent. In the document the Republicans charted little new ground, instead detailing the benefits of Republican rule and restating old positions. America's expansionistic foreign policy was praised, as was the protective tariff and the gold standard.

A display of Roosevelt theatrics followed the adoption of the platform. The convention chairman was instructed to read a message from the secretary of state to the American consul in Morocco: "We want either Perdicaris alive or Raisuli dead." The message referred to an alleged American citizen, Ion Perdicaris, who had been captured by the Moroccan chieftain, Raisuli. The American ultimatum read to the convention followed the dispatch of several ships to Morocco. The reading of the message roused the delegates, as it was no doubt intended to do.

Following are excerpts from the Republican platform in 1904:

Shipbuilding. We . . . favor legislation which will encourage and build up the American merchant marine, and we cordially approve the legislation of the last Congress which created the Merchant Marine Commission to investigate and report upon this subject.

Monopoly. Combinations of capital and of labor are the results of the economic movement of the age, but neither must be permitted to infringe upon the rights and interests of the people. Such combinations, when lawfully formed for lawful purposes, are alike entitled to the protection of the laws, but both are subject to the laws and neither can be permitted to break them.

DEMOCRATS

William Jennings Bryan, after two unsuccessful campaigns for the presidency, was not a candidate for the Democratic nomination in 1904. However, he was present at the party's convention in St. Louis that July and was a prominent factor in the proceedings.

Bryan's first appearance before the convention came during a credentials dispute, featuring a challenge by Bryan supporters in Illinois to the state delegation approved by the credentials committee. Bryan spoke in behalf of his supporters, but their minority report was beaten, 647 to 299.

Bryan appeared again to second the presidential nomination of Sen. Francis M. Cockrell of Missouri, one of eight candidates nominated. Much of his speech, however, was devoted to criticizing the conservative front-runner, Alton B. Parker, chief justice of the New York Court of Appeals, while boosting more progressive candidates. In spite of Bryan's opposition, Parker came within nine votes of receiving the necessary two-thirds majority on the first ballot. Parker had 658 votes, followed by Rep. William Randolph Hearst of New York, with 200, and Cockrell, who trailed with 42. Although Hearst had progressive credentials, Bryan hesitated to support him and jeopardize his own leadership of the progressive wing of the party.

With Parker so close to victory, Idaho shifted its votes to the New York judge, prompting enough switches by other states to give Parker 679 votes and the nomination. Hearst, with his strength in the Middle West and West, finished with 181 votes. *(Table, p. 597.)*

With the nomination in hand, Parker stunned the convention by sending a telegram to the New York delegation, announcing his support of the gold standard and advising the convention to select a new candidate if they found his position unacceptable. Parker supporters drafted a response stating that there was nothing to preclude his nomination, because the platform was silent on the currency issue.

Bryan, ill with a fever in his hotel but still a supporter of the silver cause, rose from his sickbed to join several southern leaders on the floor of the convention in denouncing Parker's telegram and the drafted response. Nonetheless, the response recommended by the Parker forces was approved, 794 to 191, with opposition principally from the Middle West and West.

For vice president, the convention chose former West Virginia senator Henry G. Davis. He nearly achieved a two-thirds majority on the first ballot, receiving 654 votes. With Davis's nomination so near, a motion to declare him the vice-presidential candidate was approved. Davis, at age eighty, was the oldest candidate ever put on a national ticket by a major party. He was a man of great wealth, and the Democrats hoped that he would give freely to their campaign.

Although the platform was accepted without debate by a voice vote, there was maneuvering behind the scenes to meet the objections of Bryan. The initial platform draft before the resolutions committee included a plank that declared that recent gold discoveries had removed the currency question as a political issue. Bryan found this plank objectionable and successfully fought in the resolutions committee for its deletion. Bryan was less successful in having an income tax plank included but was able to get a more strongly worded antitrust resolution.

Unlike the Democratic platform of 1900, which focused on anti-imperialism, antimonopoly, and currency, the 1904 platform covered about two dozen topics with nearly equal emphasis.

The Democrats and Republicans disagreed on one new issue: federal support for private shipping firms. The Democrats opposed government assistance; the Republicans favored it. But on other issues the platform of the Democrats, like that of the Republicans, broke little new ground, instead restating positions that had been included in earlier Democratic platforms. There was a continued attack on American imperialism and a call for a smaller army. There were planks that urged less international involvement and more emphasis on domestic improvements.

Following are excerpts from the Democratic platform of 1904:

Roosevelt Administration. The existing Republican administration has been spasmodic, erratic, sensational, spectacular and arbitrary. It has made itself a satire upon the Congress, courts, and upon the settled practices and usages of national and international law . . . the necessity of reform and the rescue of the administration of Government from the headstrong, arbitrary and spasmodic methods which distract business by uncertainty, and pervade the public mind with dread, distrust and perturbation.

Shipbuilding. We denounce the ship subsidy bill recently passed by the United States Senate as an iniquitous appropriation of public funds for private purposes and a wasteful, illogical and useless attempt to overcome by subsidy the obstructions raised by Republican legislation to the growth and development of American commerce on the sea.

We favor the upbuilding of a merchant marine without new or additional burdens upon the people and without bounties from the public treasury.

1908 Conventions

PRESIDENTIAL CANDIDATES

Eugene V. Debs
Socialist

William H. Taft
Republican

William J. Bryan
Democrat

SOCIALISTS

The Socialists met in Chicago in May 1908 and renominated the ticket that had represented the party four years earlier: Eugene V. Debs of Indiana for president and Benjamin Hanford of New York as his running mate.

The platform was divided into several major sections, including a discussion of principles, and topics entitled general demands, industrial demands, and political demands. The Socialists' goal was the creation of a classless society, and in pursuance of this goal the movement was identified as a party of the working class.

Among the general demands were proposals for public works programs to aid the unemployed and public ownership of land, means of transportation and communication, and monopolies.

Industrial demands included calls for reduced working hours, the abolition of child labor, and more effective inspections of working areas.

The section on political demands began with a restatement of earlier positions, with a call for tax reform; women's suffrage; and the initiative, referendum, and recall. However, the section also included more radical demands, such as the abolition of the Senate, the amendment of the Constitution by popular vote, the direct election of all judges and the removal of power from the Supreme Court to declare legislation passed by Congress unconstitutional.

Following are excerpts from the Socialist platform of 1908:

Public Works Projects. The immediate government relief for the unemployed workers by building schools, by reforesting of cutover and waste lands, by reclamation of arid tracts, and the building of canals, and by extending all other useful public works. All persons employed on such works shall be employed directly by the government under an eight hour work day and at the prevailing union wages. The government shall also loan money to states and municipalities without interest for the purpose of carrying on public works. It shall contribute to the funds of labor organizations for the purpose of assisting their un-

employed members, and shall take such other measures within its power as will lessen the widespread misery of the workers caused by the misrule of the capitalist class.

Public Ownership. The collective ownership of railroads, telegraphs, telephones, steamship lines and all other means of social transportation and communication, and all land.

The collective ownership of all industries which are organized on a national scale and in which competition has virtually ceased to exist.

Labor. The improvement of the industrial condition of the workers.

(a) By shortening the workday in keeping with the increased productiveness of machinery.

(b) By securing to every worker a rest period of not less than a day and a half in each week.

(c) By securing a more effective inspection of workshops and factories.

(d) By forbidding the employment of children under sixteen years of age.

(e) By forbidding the interstate transportation of the products of child labor, of convict labor and of all uninspected factories.

(f) By abolishing official charity and substituting in its place compulsory insurance against unemployment, illness, accident, invalidism, old age and death.

Tax Reform. The extension of inheritance taxes, graduated in proportion to the amount of the bequests and the nearness of kin.

A graduated income tax.

Women's Suffrage. Unrestricted and equal suffrage for men and women. . . .

Senate. The abolition of the senate.

Constitutional and Judicial Reforms. The abolition of the power usurped by the supreme court of the United States to pass upon the constitutionality of legislation enacted by Congress. National laws to be repealed or abrogated only by act of Congress or by a referendum of the whole people.

That the constitution be made amendable by majority vote.

That all judges be elected by the people for short terms, and that the power to issue injunctions shall be curbed by immediate legislation.

REPUBLICANS

The Republicans held their convention in Chicago in June 1908. Although President Roosevelt declined to be a candidate for reelection, his choice for the presidency, Secretary of War William Howard Taft, was assured of nomination before the convention began.

Of the 980 seats at the convention, 223 were contested, but all the challenges were settled before the convention assembled. However, a dispute arose over the vote-allocation formula for the next convention. An amendment to the rules committee report proposed that the vote allocation be based on population rather than the electoral vote, as was currently in effect. Essentially, the amendment would have reduced the power of the southern delegations. But a combination of southern delegates and Taft supporters from other states defeated the amendment, 506 to 471. *(Table, p. 599.)*

Seven names were placed in nomination for the presidency, but Taft was a landslide winner on the first ballot, receiving 702 votes. Sen. Philander C. Knox of Pennsylvania was a distant runner-up with 68 votes.

For vice president, the convention selected Rep. James S. Sherman, a conservative New Yorker. Sherman won 816 votes on the first ballot, easily outdistancing former New Jersey governor Franklin Murphy, who had 77 votes.

The Wisconsin delegation, led by Sen. Robert M. La Follette, introduced a detailed minority report to the party platform. The Wisconsin proposals were considered in several separate sections. The first section included proposals for the establishment of a permanent tariff commission, the creation of a Department of Labor and the limitation of an eight-hour day for government workers. It was defeated, 952 to 28.

The second section recommended legislation to require the publication of campaign contributions. It was defeated, 880 to 94. Further sections of the minority report proposed the physical valuation of railroad property to help determine reasonable rates, and the direct election of senators. The railroad reform plank was beaten, 917 to 63, while the senatorial election plank was rejected, 866 to 114. After these votes, the majority report on the platform was adopted by a voice vote.

The platform approved by the delegates applauded the benefits of Republican rule, noting that under the party's guidance the United States had become the wealthiest nation on Earth. The principle of a protective tariff was applauded, as was the gold standard, an expansionist foreign policy and support for America's merchant marine.

Following are excerpts from the Republican platform of 1908:

Party Differences. In history, the difference between Democracy and Republicanism is that the one stood for debased currency, the other for honest currency; the one for free silver, the other for sound money; the one for free trade, the other for protection; the one for the contraction of American influence, the other for its expansion; the one has been forced to abandon every position taken on the great issues before the people, the other has held and vindicated all.

The present tendencies of the two parties are even more marked by inherent differences. The trend of Democracy is toward socialism, while the Republican party stands for a wise and regulated individualism. . . . Ultimately Democracy would have the nation own the people, while Republicanism would have the people own the nation.

DEMOCRATS

The Democratic convention of 1908 was held in July in Denver, Colorado—the first convention held by a major party in a western state. The convention was dominated by the Bryan forces, who regained control of the party after the conservative Alton B. Parker's landslide defeat in 1904.

Bryan's strength was evident on the first roll-call vote, concerning a Pennsylvania credentials dispute. The majority report claimed there were voting irregularities in five Philadelphia districts and urged the seating of Bryan delegates in place of those elected. By a vote of 604½ to 386½, the convention defeated the minority report, which argued for the delegates initially elected in the primary. The majority report then passed by a voice vote.

Bryan's presidential nomination was never in doubt. He was an easy winner on the first ballot, receiving 888½ votes to 59½ for Judge George Gray of Delaware and 46 for Gov. John A. Johnson of Minnesota. *(Table, p. 598.)*

Bryan left the choice of his running mate to the delegates. Although four names were placed in nomination, former Indiana gubernatorial candidate John W. Kern was chosen by acclamation. The *New York Times* sarcastically described the consistency of the Bryan-Kern ticket: "For a man twice defeated for the Presidency was at the head of it, and a man twice defeated for governor of his state was at the tail of it."

The platform adopted by the convention was tailored to Bryan's liking and had as its theme, "Shall the people rule?" The first portion of the document criticized Republican rule, specifically denouncing government overspending, a growing Republican-oriented bureaucracy, and an unethical link between big business and the Republican Party characterized by large, unreported campaign contributions.

Meeting three weeks after the Republicans, the Democrats adopted most of the minority planks rejected earlier by the Republicans. Included in the Democratic platform were calls for the physical valuation of railroads, the creation of a Department of Labor, eight-hour work days for government employees, the direct election of senators, and a prohibition against corporate campaign contributions and individual contributions over "a reasonable amount." The two parties continued to disagree on support of the American merchant marine, the nature of tariff revision, and the direction of foreign policy, particularly regarding the lands acquired after the Spanish-American War.

The Democratic platform restated the party's support of a lower tariff, more extensive antitrust legislation with more rigid enforcement, a graduated income tax, increased power for the Interstate Commerce Commission to regulate railroads, telephone and telegraph companies, and a recommendation of prompt independence for the Philippines.

The Democrats included a plank abhorring Roosevelt's attempt to create a "dynasty," a direct reference to the outgoing president's hand-picking his war secretary, William Howard Taft, as the next Republican presidential candidate.

Following are excerpts from the Democratic platform of 1908:

Appeal to the Masses. The conscience of the nation is now aroused to free the Government from the grip of those who have made it a business asset of the favor-seeking corporations. It must become again a people's government, and be administered in all its departments according to the Jeffersonian maxim, "equal rights to all; special privileges to none."

"Shall the people rule?" is the overshadowing issue which manifests itself in all the questions now under discussion.

Campaign Contributions. We demand Federal legislation forever terminating the partnership which has existed between corporations of the country and the Republican party under the expressed or implied agreement that in return for the contribution of great sums of money wherewith to purchase elections, they should be allowed to continue substantially unmolested in their efforts to encroach upon the rights of the people. . . .

We pledge the Democratic party to the enactment of a law prohibiting any corporation from contributing to a campaign fund and any individual from contributing an amount above a reasonable maximum, and providing for the publication before election of all such contributions.

Labor. Questions of judicial practice have arisen especially in connection with industrial disputes. We deem that the parties to all judicial proceedings should be treated with rigid impartiality, and that injunctions should not be issued in any cases in which injunctions would not issue if no industrial dispute were involved. . . .

We favor the eight hour day on all Government work.

We pledge the Democratic party to the enactment of a law by Congress, as far as the Federal jurisdiction extends, for a general employer's liability act covering injury to body or loss of life of employees.

We pledge the Democratic party to the enactment of a law creating a Department of Labor, represented separately in the President's Cabinet, in which Department shall be included the subject of mines and mining.

1912 Conventions

PRESIDENTIAL CANDIDATES

Eugene V. Debs
Socialist

William H. Taft
Republican

Woodrow Wilson
Democrat

Theodore Roosevelt
Progressive

SOCIALISTS

Eugene V. Debs of Indiana was nominated by the Socialists in 1912 to make his fourth run for the presidency. The convention, which met in Indianapolis in May, chose Emil Seidel of Wisconsin as his running mate.

The platform adopted by the Socialists was similar to the one written four years earlier, with calls for increased worker benefits, public works jobs for the unemployed, public ownership of land and the means of transportation and communication, tax reform, widespread political reform, and a social insurance program.

The Socialists also added new proposals, advocating public ownership of the banking and currency system, the introduction of minimum wage scales, the elimination of the profit system in government contracts, an increase in corporation taxes, and the direct election of the president and vice president.

Following are excerpts from the Socialist platform of 1912:

Social Insurance. By abolishing official charity and substituting a non-contributory system of old age pensions, a general system of insurance by the State of all its members against unemployment and invalidism and a system of compulsory insurance by employers of their workers, without cost to the latter, against industrial diseases, accidents and death.

Government Contracts. By abolishing the profit system in government work and substituting either the direct hire of labor or the awarding of contracts to cooperative groups of workers.

Minimum Wage. By establishing minimum wage scales.

Tax Reform. The adoption of a graduated income tax, the increase of the rates of the present corporation tax and the extension of inheritance taxes, graduated in proportion to the value of the estate and to nearness of kin—the proceeds of these taxes to be employed in the socialization of industry.

Banking and Currency. The collective ownership and democratic management of the banking and currency system.

Direct Election of President. The election of the President and Vice-President by direct vote of the people.

REPUBLICANS

The 1912 Republican convention was one of the most tumultuous ever. It was held in Chicago in June and served as a fiery culmination to the bitter contest between President William Howard Taft and former president Theodore Roosevelt for the party's presidential nomination.

Roosevelt had overwhelmed Taft in the presidential primaries, but Roosevelt's popular strength was more than offset by Taft's control of the national committee and southern delegations. Taft supporters held thirty-seven of fifty-three seats on the national committee, an edge that the incumbent president's managers used to advantage in settling seating disputes. Of the 1,078 convention seats, 254 were contested before the national committee, and 235 were settled in favor of Taft delegates. Although a number of Roosevelt challenges were made with little justification, the dispensation of the challenges showed Taft's control of the convention organization.

With the conservative Republicans united behind Taft, Roosevelt faced the additional problem of sharing support from the progressive wing of the party with another candidate, Sen. Robert M. La Follette of Wisconsin. La Follette had only forty-one delegates; but, angered by Roosevelt's bid to control the progressive forces, refused to withdraw as a candidate.

The first skirmish at the convention was over the choice of a temporary chairman. The Taft forces favored Sen. Elihu Root of New York, while the Roosevelt delegates supported Gov. Francis E. McGovern of Wisconsin.

On a prolonged roll call, during which the vote of each delegate was taken individually, Root defeated McGovern, 558 to 501. (*Table, p. 600.*)

With the contest for the temporary chairmanship settled, the battle shifted to credentials. Virtually shut out in the settlement of credentials cases by the national committee, the Roosevelt forces brought seventy-two delegate challenges to the floor of the convention. Before consideration of the cases, the Roosevelt leaders moved that none of the challenged delegates (favorable to Taft) be allowed to vote on any of the credentials contests. However, a motion to table this proposal carried, 567 to 507, and the challenged delegates were allowed to vote on all cases except their own. Although the Taft forces were clearly in control of the convention, four credentials cases were presented for a vote, and all were decided in favor of the Taft delegates. The rest of the contests were settled by voice votes.

At this point, Roosevelt, who had dramatically come to Chicago to direct his forces, advised his delegates to abstain from voting but to remain in the convention as a silent protest to what he regarded as steamroller tactics. In the convention hall itself, the pro-Roosevelt galleries emphasized the feelings of their leader by rubbing sandpaper and blowing horns to imitate the sounds of a steamroller.

Only two names were placed in nomination for the presidency—Taft's and La Follette's. Taft was nominated by Warren G. Harding of Ohio, who himself would be president less than a

decade later but at the time was merely a former lieutenant governor. With most of the Roosevelt delegates abstaining, Taft won easily on the first ballot with 556 votes. Roosevelt received 107 votes and La Follette 41, while 348 delegates were present and did not vote.

Vice President James S. Sherman was easily renominated, collecting 596 votes to 21 for the runner-up, Sen. William E. Borah of Idaho. However, 352 delegates were present but refused to vote, and 72 others were absent. In recognition of Sherman's failing health, the convention passed a resolution empowering the national committee to fill any vacancy on the ticket that might occur.

As in 1908, a progressive minority report to the platform was submitted. However, instead of taking individual votes on the various planks, the convention tabled the whole report by a voice vote. Subsequently, the majority report was accepted by a vote of 666 to 53, with 343 delegates present but not voting.

The platform lauded the accomplishments of the McKinley, Roosevelt, and Taft administrations but contained few major positions different from the Democrats' platform. The Republican platform included, however, new planks favoring judicial reform and legislation publicizing campaign contributions and outlawing corporate campaign donations.

Although the Roosevelt delegates had remained in the convention hall as a silent protest to the renomination of Taft and Sherman, the groundwork for the creation of a Roosevelt-led third party had begun as soon as the credentials contests were settled in favor of Taft. Before the Republican convention even began its presidential balloting, Roosevelt announced that he would accept the nomination of the "honestly elected majority" of the Republican convention or a new progressive party. The next day, June 22, after final adjournment of the Republican convention, many of the Roosevelt delegates assembled in a Chicago auditorium to hear their leader announce his availability as a candidate of an honestly elected progressive convention. Gov. Hiram Johnson of California was named temporary chairman of the new party, and planning was begun to hold a national convention later in the summer.

Following are excerpts from the Republican platform of 1912:

Tariff. The protective tariff is so woven into the fabric of our industrial and agricultural life that to substitute for it a tariff for revenue only would destroy many industries and throw millions of our people out of employment. The products of the farm and of the mine should receive the same measure of protection as other products of American labor.

Campaign Contributions. We favor such additional legislation as may be necessary more effectually to prohibit corporations from contributing funds, directly or indirectly, to campaigns for the nomination or election of the President, the Vice-President, Senators, and Representatives in Congress.

We heartily approve the recent Act of Congress requiring the fullest publicity in regard to all campaign contributions, whether made in connection with primaries, conventions, or elections.

Judicial Reform. That the Courts, both Federal and State, may bear the heavy burden laid upon them to the complete satisfaction of public opinion, we favor legislation to prevent long delays and the tedious and costly appeals which have so often amounted to a denial of justice in civil cases and to a failure to protect the public at large in criminal cases.

DEMOCRATS

For the first time since 1872, the Democratic convention was held in Baltimore. The delegates, who assembled in the Maryland city in June, one week after the Republicans began their convention in Chicago, had a number of presidential candidates to choose from, although House Speaker Champ Clark of Missouri and Gov. Woodrow Wilson of New Jersey were the major contenders.

Once again, William Jennings Bryan had a major impact on the proceedings of a Democratic convention. His first appearance came in opposition to the national committee's selection of Judge Alton B. Parker of New York, the party's standard-bearer in 1904, as temporary chairman. Bryan nominated Sen. John W. Kern of Indiana for the post. In declining to be a candidate for temporary chairman, Kern recommended that Parker also withdraw as a candidate. But when Parker refused, Kern nominated Bryan for the post. Parker won on the roll call that followed, 579 to 508, with most of the Wilson delegates voting for Bryan, the Clark delegates splitting their support and delegates for other candidates favoring Parker. (Table, p. 601.)

The defeat of Bryan produced an avalanche of telegrams from across the country, with a contemporary estimate of more than 100,000 flooding the delegates in Baltimore. Most of the telegrams were written by progressives and served to weaken the candidacy of the more conservative Clark.

In an attempt to appease Bryan, Parker urged members of the platform committee to select the Nebraskan as their chairman. Bryan, however, refused this overture. Subsequently, the platform committee announced that, by a margin of 41 to 11, the committee had voted to delay presentation of the platform until after selection of the candidates.

The Wilson forces won their first key vote on a question involving the unit rule. The vote specifically concerned the Ohio delegation, where district delegates, elected for Wilson, were bound by the state convention to vote for Gov. Judson Harmon of Ohio. By a vote of 565½ to 491⅓, the convention approved the right of the district delegates to vote for Wilson.

The Wilson forces won another test on a credentials dispute concerning the South Dakota delegation. The credentials committee recommended seating a delegation pledged to Clark; but the convention, by a vote of 639½ to 437, supported the minority report, which called for seating delegates pledged to Wilson.

Bryan reappeared before the presidential balloting and introduced a resolution opposing the nomination of any candidate "who is the representative of or under obligation to J. Pierpont Morgan, Thomas F. Ryan, August Belmont, or any other member of the privilege-hunting and favor-seeking class." Bryan's resolution passed easily, 883 to 202½.

Six names were placed in nomination for the presidency. Clark led on the first ballot with 440½ votes, followed by Wilson with 324, Harmon with 148, and Rep. Oscar W. Underwood of Alabama with 117½. Under the two-thirds rule, 730 votes were needed to nominate. (Table, p. 601.)

For nine ballots, there was little change in the vote totals, but on the tenth roll call New York shifted its 90 votes from Harmon to Clark. Expecting a quick triumph, the Clark forces unleashed an hour-long demonstration. However, their celebration was premature. While Clark had 556 votes, a majority, his total was well short of the two-thirds majority required by the rules.

The tenth ballot proved to be the high-water mark for Clark. On succeeding roll calls, he slowly began to lose strength. During the fourteenth ballot, Bryan received permission to address the convention again, this time to explain his vote. "The Great Commoner" announced that he could not support a candidate endorsed by the Tammany-controlled New York delegation and, although bound earlier by state primary results to support Clark, was now switching his vote to Wilson. Most of the Nebraska delegation followed Bryan in voting for Wilson. After the fourteenth ballot, the vote totals stood: Clark, 553; Wilson, 361; Underwood, 111.

There were long intervals between other major vote switches. On the twentieth ballot, Kansas shifted 20 of its votes from Clark to Wilson. On the twenty-eighth ballot, after a weekend recess, Indiana's favorite son, Gov. Thomas R. Marshall, withdrew in favor of Wilson. The slow trend in favor of the New Jersey governor finally enabled Wilson to pass Clark on the thirtieth roll call, 450 to 455; Underwood remained a distant third with 121½ votes. (Table, p. 601.)

The convention adjourned for the evening after the forty-second ballot, but the Wilson momentum continued the next day. Illinois switched its 58 votes to Wilson on the forty-third ballot, giving him a simple majority with 602 votes. Clark continued to decline, slipping to 329 votes.

Wilson showed slight gains on the next two ballots, but the big break came on the forty-sixth roll call, when Underwood withdrew. This was followed by the withdrawal of Clark and the other remaining candidates. Wilson received 990 votes on the forty-sixth ballot, followed by Clark with 84.

Clark's failure to win the nomination marked the first occasion since 1844 that a candidate achieved a simple majority of the votes, without subsequently winning the necessary two-thirds majority. The forty-six roll calls also represented the highest number of presidential ballots taken at any convention, Republican or Democratic, since 1860.

Wilson preferred Underwood as his running mate, but the Alabama representative was not interested in second place on the ticket. On the vice-presidential roll call that followed, nine candidates received votes, led by Marshall with 389 votes and Gov. John Burke of North Dakota with 304⅔. Marshall lengthened his lead over Burke on the second ballot, 644½ to 386⅓. After the roll call was completed, a New Jersey delegate moved that Marshall's nomination be made unanimous, and the motion passed.

The Democratic platform was approved without debate before selection of the vice-presidential candidate. The platform restated a number of positions included in earlier party documents. It blamed the high cost of living on the protective tariff and the existence of trusts, and it called for a lower, revenue-only tariff and the passage of stronger antitrust legislation. The tariff issue was one of the major areas on which there was a marked difference between the parties, as the Republicans continued to support a protective tariff.

As in 1908, planks were included favoring the publicizing of campaign contributions and calling for the prohibition of corporate contributions and a limit on individual contributions.

The Democrats' labor plank was also virtually a restatement of the party's position four years earlier, supporting creation of a Department of Labor, a more limited use of injunctions, the guaranteed right of workers to organize and passage of an employees' compensation law. In contrast to the Democrats' support of employers' liability, the Republicans advocated workmen's compensation legislation.

Unlike the Republicans, the Democrats called for federal legislation to regulate the rates of railroad, telegraph, telephone, and express companies based on valuation by the Interstate Commerce Commission. A plank was also included in the Democratic platform calling for the ratification of constitutional amendments establishing a graduated income tax and the direct election of senators—issues on which the Republican platform was silent. Imperialism was again denounced, as it had been in every Democratic platform since 1900.

New planks advocated a single-term presidency, the extension of presidential primaries to all states, reform of the judicial system to eliminate delays and cut expenses in court proceedings, and the strengthening of the government's pure food and public health agencies.

Following are excerpts from the Democratic platform of 1912:

Single-term Presidency. We favor a single Presidential term, and to that end urge the adoption of an amendment to the Constitution making the President of the United States ineligible to reelection, and we pledge the candidates of this Convention to this principle.

Presidential Primaries. The movement toward more popular government should be promoted through legislation in each State which will permit the expression of the preference of the electors for national candidates at presidential primaries.

Judicial Reform. We recognize the urgent need of reform in the administration of civil and criminal law in the United States, and we recommend the enactment of such legislation and the promotion of such measures as will rid the present legal system of the delays, expense, and uncertainties incident to the system as now administered.

States' Rights. Believing that the most efficient results under our system of government are to be attained by the full exercise by the States of their reserved sovereign powers, we denounce as usurpation the efforts of our opponents to deprive the States of any of the rights reserved to them, and to enlarge and magnify by indirection the powers of the Federal government.

PROGRESSIVES

Early in August 1912 the bolting Roosevelt forces assembled in Chicago and nominated their leader to guide a new party, the Progressives. More than 2,000 delegates, representing every state except South Carolina, gathered for the three-day convention. It was a diverse assembly that matched the Populists in crusading idealism and included, for the first time, women as well as men politicians and social workers as well as businessmen.

While the delegates enthusiastically sang "Onward, Christian Soldiers" and "The Battle Hymn of the Republic" and cheered the appearance of Roosevelt before the convention, there was some dissension caused by the party's racial policy.

During the campaign for the Republican presidential nomination, Taft had the support of party organizations in the South, which included blacks. As a result, Roosevelt directed his appeal strictly to white leaders in the region. Describing southern black delegates as uneducated and purchasable, Roosevelt insisted that only "lily white" delegations from the South be seated at the Progressive convention, but he allowed blacks to be included in delegations from other states. Although there was no floor debate on this policy, a number of liberal delegates were dissatisfied with Roosevelt's decision.

Both Roosevelt and his handpicked choice for vice president, Gov. Hiram W. Johnson of California, were nominated by acclamation. Jane Addams, a Chicago social worker and leader in the women's rights movement, gave evidence of the role of women in the Progressive Party by delivering a seconding speech for Roosevelt.

Like the nominations of the Progressive standard-bearers, the party platform was adopted by acclamation. But the voice vote hid the dissatisfaction felt by midwestern and western Progressives over the antitrust plank. Most of the Progressives from these regions favored the busting of trusts through enforcement of the Sherman Antitrust Act. Roosevelt, however, favored government regulation rather than trust-busting.

The platform approved by the convention included the trust-busting position. However, Roosevelt and his close advisers deleted the section in the official report. While there was obvious disagreement in the party on this issue, there was no floor debate or roll-call vote on the subject.

With the theme "A Covenant with the People," the platform argued for increased democratization coupled with more people-oriented federal programs. The party favored nationwide presidential primaries; the direct election of senators; the initiative, referendum, and recall; and women's suffrage. Additionally, the Progressives proposed that state laws ruled unconstitutional be submitted to a vote of the state electorate.

The platform also advocated congressional reforms: the registration of lobbyists, the publicizing of committee hearings except in foreign affairs, and the recording of committee votes.

Like the Democrats, the Progressives favored creation of a Department of Labor and a more limited use of labor injunctions, but additionally the new party called for a prohibition of child labor and convict contract labor.

The Progressives went beyond both major parties in proposing the union of government health agencies into a single national health service and the creation of a social insurance system that would assist both the elderly and workers who were ill or unemployed. To help support their proposed federal programs, the Progressives recommended passage of the income tax amendment and establishment of a graduated inheritance tax.

Having adopted their platform and selected their candidates, the delegates to the Progressive convention adjourned by singing the "Doxology."

Following are excerpts from the Progressive platform of 1912:

Electoral Reform. In particular, the party declares for direct primaries of the nomination of State and National officers, for nationwide preferential primaries for candidates for the presidency; for the direct election of United States Senators by the people; and we urge on the States the policy of the short ballot, with responsibility to the people secured by the initiative, referendum and recall.

Women's Suffrage. The Progressive party, believing that no people can justly claim to be a true democracy which denies political rights on account of sex, pledges itself to the task of securing equal suffrage to men and women alike.

Judicial Reform. That when an Act, passed under the police power of the State, is held unconstitutional under the State Constitution, by the courts, the people, after an ample interval for deliberation, shall have an opportunity to vote on the question whether they desire the Act to become law, notwithstanding such decision.

Campaign Contributions. We pledge our party to legislation that will compel strict limitation of all campaign contributions and expenditures, and detailed publicity of both before as well as after primaries and elections.

Congressional Reform. We pledge our party to legislation compelling the registration of lobbyists; publicity of committee hearings except on foreign affairs, and recording of all votes in committee. . . .

National Health Service. We favor the union of all the existing agencies of the Federal Government dealing with the public health into a single national health service without discrimination against or for any one set of therapeutic methods, school of medicine, or school of healing with such additional powers as may be necessary to enable it to perform efficiently such duties in the protection of the public from preventable diseases as may be properly undertaken by the Federal authorities, including the executing of existing laws regarding pure food, quarantine and cognate subjects, the promotion of vital statistics and the extension of the registration area of such statistics, and cooperation with the health activities of the various States and cities of the Nation.

Social Insurance. The protection of home life against the hazards of sickness, irregular employment and old age through the adoption of a system of social insurance adapted to American use. . . .

Antitrust Action. We therefore demand a strong National regulation of inter-State corporations . . . we urge the establishment of a strong Federal administrative commission of high standing, which shall maintain permanent active supervision over industrial corporations engaged in inter-State commerce, or such of them as are of public importance, doing for them what the Government now does for the National banks, and what is now done for the railroads by the Inter-State Commerce Commission.

Income and Inheritance Taxes. We believe in a graduated inheritance tax as a National means of equalizing the obligations of holders of property to Government, and we hereby pledge our party to enact such a Federal law as will tax large inheritances, returning to the States an equitable percentage of all amounts collected.

We favor the ratification of the pending amendment to the Constitution giving the Government power to levy an income tax.

Tariff. We demand tariff revision because the present tariff is unjust to the people of the United States. Fair dealing toward the people requires an immediate downward revision of those schedules wherein duties are shown to be unjust or excessive. . . .

The Democratic party is committed to the destruction of the protective system through a tariff for revenue only—a policy which would inevitably produce widespread industrial and commercial disaster.

Republicans and Democrats. Political parties exist to secure responsible government and to execute the will of the people.

From these great tasks both of the old parties have turned aside. Instead of instruments to promote the general welfare, they have become the tools of corrupt interests which use them impartially to serve their selfish purposes. Behind the ostensible government sits enthroned an invisible government owing no allegiance and acknowledging no responsibility to the people.

To destroy this invisible government, to dissolve the unholy alliance between corrupt business and corrupt politics is the first task of the statesmanship of the day.

States' Rights. The extreme insistence on States' rights by the Democratic party in the Baltimore platform demonstrates anew its ability to understand the world into which it has survived or to administer the affairs of a union of States which have in all essential respects become one people.

1916 Conventions

PRESIDENTIAL CANDIDATES

Charles E. Hughes
Republican

Woodrow Wilson
Democrat

REPUBLICANS

The Republicans and Progressives both held their conventions in Chicago in early June 1916. Leaders of both parties were ready to negotiate to heal the split that had divided the Republican Party in 1912.

Before the convention began, the Republican National Committee already had effected reform in the vote-allocation formula. To meet the objection raised in 1912 that the South was overrepresented, the national committee adopted a new method of vote allocation that considered a state's Republican voting strength as well as its electoral vote. Under the new formula, the southern states lost seventy-eight delegate seats, or more than a third of their 1912 total.

But while the Republicans were willing to make some internal reforms, most party leaders were adamantly opposed to nominating the hero of the Progressives, Theodore Roosevelt. Before the presidential balloting began, the Republican convention approved by voice vote the selection of a five-man committee to meet jointly with representatives of the Progressive convention, with the hope of finding a course of action that would unify the two parties.

However, the Republican representatives reported back that the Progressives, while desiring unity with the Republicans, firmly favored the nomination of Roosevelt. The Republican convention chairman, Sen. Warren G. Harding of Ohio, instructed the conferees to continue negotiations but allowed the presidential balloting to begin.

Charles Evans Hughes, a Supreme Court justice and former governor of New York, was the front-runner for the Republican nomination. Hughes did not actively seek the nomination and remained on the Supreme Court during the preconvention period. But he was viewed by many party leaders as an ideal compromise candidate, because of his progressive credentials and lack of involvement in the divisive 1912 campaign.

However, some conservative party leaders felt Hughes was too progressive and sought other candidates. Seventeen men received

votes on the first ballot, led by Hughes with 253½. Next were Sen. John W. Weeks of Massachusetts with 105 votes and former senator Elihu Root of New York with 103. Five of the other vote recipients had at least 65 votes each. The justice widened his lead on the second ballot, receiving 328½ votes to 98½ for Root. After the second roll call the convention voted 694½ to 286½ to recess for the evening. Most of the votes for adjournment came from delegates outside the Hughes column. (*Table, p. 602.*)

While the Republican convention was in recess, the joint committee of Republicans and Progressives continued to negotiate. The Republican members proposed Hughes as a compromise candidate, but in a message from his home in Oyster Bay, New York, Roosevelt stunned both parties by suggesting the name of Henry Cabot Lodge, a conservative senator from Massachusetts.

The Progressive delegates reacted defiantly to this recommendation by nominating Roosevelt by acclamation and selecting John M. Parker of Louisiana as his running mate. Roosevelt, however, immediately scotched the enthusiasm of the Progressive delegates by conditionally declining the nomination. Roosevelt informed the convention that he would support Hughes if the latter's positions on major issues were acceptable.

When the Republican convention reconvened the next day, the opposition to Hughes had evaporated. The New Yorker received 949½ of the 987 convention votes on the third ballot, and his nomination was subsequently declared unanimous.

Charles W. Fairbanks of Indiana, vice president under Roosevelt, was the convention's choice to fill out the Republican ticket. Fairbanks won on the first ballot by 863 votes to 108 for former Nebraska senator Elmer J. Burkett.

The Wisconsin delegation again presented its own minority platform report, which included planks that denounced "dollar diplomacy" and called for women's suffrage, a referendum before any declaration of war, and constitutional amendments to establish the initiative, referendum, and recall. The minority report was defeated and the majority report was approved by voice votes.

The adopted platform harshly criticized the policies of the Wilson administration. In foreign policy, the Republicans denounced the Wilson government for "shifty expedients" and "phrase making" and promised "strict and honest neutrality." The platform condemned the administration for its intervention in Mexico and noninvolvement in the Philippines. The Republicans also called for a stronger national defense.

The two parties continued to disagree on the tariff issue, with the Republicans criticizing the lower (Democratic-passed) Underwood tariff and arguing for a higher, protective tariff. The Republican platform lauded the party's efforts in passing antitrust and transportation rate regulation, but it criticized the Democrats for harassing business.

Following are excerpts from the Republican platform of 1916:

Foreign Policy. We desire peace, the peace of justice and right, and believe in maintaining a strict and honest neutrality between the belligerents in the great war in Europe. We must perform all our duties and insist upon all our rights as neutrals without fear and without favor. We believe that peace and neutrality, as well as the dignity and influence of the United States, cannot be preserved by shifty expedients, by phrase making, by performances in language, or by attitudes ever changing in an effort to secure votes or voters.

National Defense. We must have a Navy so strong and so well proportioned and equipped, so thoroughly ready and prepared, that no enemy can gain command of the sea and effect a landing in force on either our Western or our Eastern coast. To secure these results we must have a coherent continuous policy of national defense, which even in these perilous days the Democratic party has utterly failed to develop, but which we promise to give to the country.

Merchant Marine. We are utterly opposed to the Government ownership of vessels as proposed by the Democratic party, because Government-owned ships, while effectively preventing the development of the American Merchant Marine by private capital, will be entirely unable to provide for the vast volume of American freights and will leave us more helpless than ever in the hard grip of foreign syndicates.

Tariff. The Republican party stands now, as always, in the fullest sense for the policy of tariff protection to American industries and American labor.

Business. The Republican party firmly believes that all who violate the laws in regulation of business, should be individually punished. But prosecution is very different from persecution, and business success, no matter how honestly attained, is apparently regarded by the Democratic party as in itself a crime. Such doctrines and beliefs choke enterprise and stifle prosperity. The Republican party believes in encouraging American business as it believes in and will seek to advance all American interests.

Women's Suffrage. The Republican party, reaffirming its faith in government of the people, by the people, for the people, as a measure of justice to one-half the adult people of this country, favors the extension of the suffrage to women, but recognizes the right of each state to settle this question for itself.

DEMOCRATS

The Democratic convention of 1916 was held in St. Louis in mid-June. The delegates were nearly unanimous in their support for President Woodrow Wilson, who was renominated by the vote of 1,092 to 1—the lone dissenting vote coming from an Illinois delegate who disapproved of a motion to nominate Wilson by acclamation. With Wilson's approval, Vice President Thomas R. Marshall was renominated by acclamation.

For the first time in more than two decades, William Jennings Bryan was not a major convention force. Bryan was defeated in his bid to be a delegate-at-large from Nebraska and attended the convention as a reporter. He was invited to address the delegates and echoed the theme stressed by other speakers, that Wilson would keep the nation out of war.

Wilson was the recognized leader of the Democratic Party, but the pacifistic theme, emphasized by Bryan and other convention orators, struck a responsive chord among the delegates that was mildly alarming to Wilson and his managers. They initially had planned to accent the theme of Americanism and national unity.

The wording of the national unity plank was a matter of debate within the platform committee. The Democratic senators from Missouri warned that Wilson's strongly worded plank might offend German-American citizens. Nonetheless, the Wilson plank was retained and placed prominently near the beginning of the platform.

The only section of the platform brought to a floor vote was the plank on women's suffrage. The majority plank favored extending the vote to women, while a minority plank advocated leaving the matter to the individual states. The minority plank was defeated, 888½ to 181½. The rest of the platform was then adopted by a voice vote. The Democratic position on women's suffrage contrasted with that of the Republicans, who proposed leaving the matter up to the individual states. *(Table, p. 603.)*

The platform's inclusion of national unity and military preparedness planks was a contrast with earlier Democratic platforms around the turn of the century, which had consistently denounced imperialism and denied the need for a stronger military. Even though spurred by the war in Europe, the new planks were a notable change.

The rest of the platform focused on the progressive reforms of the Wilson administration, particularly in tariff, banking, labor, and agriculture. Wilson himself was lauded as "the greatest American of his generation."

Noticeably absent from the platform were two planks in the party's document four years earlier: a call for a single-term presidency and a defense of states' rights.

Following are excerpts from the Democratic platform of 1916:

National Unity. In this day of test, America must show itself not a nation of partisans but a nation of patriots. There is gathered here in America the best of the blood, the industry and the genius of the whole world, the elements of a great race and a magnificent society to be welded into a mighty and splendid Nation. Whoever, actuated by the purpose to promote the industry of a foreign power, in disregard of our own country's welfare or to injure this government in its foreign relations or cripple or destroy its industries at home, and whoever by arousing prejudices of a racial, religious or other nature creates discord and strife among our people so as to obstruct the wholesome process of unification, is faithless to the trust which the privileges of citizenship repose in him and is disloyal to his country.

Military Preparedness. We therefore favor the maintenance of an army fully adequate to the requirements of order, of safety, and of the protection of the nation's rights, the fullest development of modern methods of seacoast defence and the maintenance of an adequate reserve of citizens trained to arms and prepared to safeguard the people and territory of the United States against any danger of hostile action which may unexpectedly arise; and a fixed policy for the continuous development of a navy, worthy to support the great naval traditions of the United States and fully equal to the international tasks which this Nation hopes and expects to take a part in performing.

Tariff. We reaffirm our belief in the doctrine of a tariff for the purpose of providing sufficient revenue for the operation of the government economically administered, and unreservedly endorse the Underwood tariff law as truly exemplifying that doctrine.

Women's Suffrage. We recommend the extension of the franchise to the women of the country by the States upon the same terms as to men.

SOCIALISTS

The Socialists did not hold a convention in 1916 but did nominate candidates and adopt a platform. The candidates were chosen in a unique mail referendum. With Eugene V. Debs's refusal to run, the presidential nomination went to Allan L. Benson of New York. George R. Kirkpatrick of New Jersey was selected as his running mate.

More than half of the Socialist platform was devoted to criticizing the U.S. preparations for war. The Socialists opposed the war in Europe and viewed the American drive for preparedness as an effort by ruling capitalists to protect the system and their profits.

The Socialist platform specifically advocated no increase in military appropriations, a national referendum on any declaration of war, the shifting of the power to make foreign policy from the president to Congress, the abandonment of the Monroe Doctrine and immediate independence for the Philippines.

The rest of the platform was divided into sections entitled political demands, industrial demands, and collective ownership. The proposals in these sections paralleled earlier Socialist platforms, although there was a new plank, advocating lending by the federal government to local governments, which was an early expression of the concept of revenue-sharing.

Following are excerpts from the Socialist platform of 1916:

Militarism and Preparedness. The working class must recognize militarism as the greatest menace to all efforts toward industrial freedom, and regardless of political or industrial affiliations must present a united front in the fight against preparedness and militarism. . . . The war in Europe, which diminished and is still diminishing the remote possibility of European attack upon the United States, was nevertheless seized upon by capitalists and by unscrupulous politicians as a means of spreading fear throughout the country, to the end that, by false pretenses, great military establishments might be obtained. We denounce such "preparedness" as both false in principle, unnecessary in character and dangerous in its plain tendencies toward militarism.

Foreign Policy. We, therefore, demand that the power to fix foreign policies and conduct diplomatic negotiations shall be lodged in congress and shall be exercised publicly, the people reserving the right to order congress, at any time, to change its foreign policy.

Referendum on War. That no war shall be declared or waged by the United States without a referendum vote of the entire people, except for the purpose of repelling invasion.

Federal Loans to Local Governments. The government shall lend money on bonds to counties and municipalities at a nominal rate of interest for the purpose of taking over or establishing public utilities and for building or maintaining public roads or highways and public schools.

1920 Conventions

PRESIDENTIAL CANDIDATES

Eugene V. Debs
Socialist

Warren G. Harding
Republican

James M. Cox
Democrat

SOCIALISTS

The Socialists held their convention in New York in May and for the fifth time nominated Eugene V. Debs of Indiana for president. It was one of the strangest candidacies in American polit-

ical history, because at the time Debs was serving a ten-year prison term in the Atlanta federal penitentiary for his outspoken opposition to the American war effort. Seymour Stedman of Ohio was chosen as his running mate.

The Socialist platform was again a distinctive document, going far beyond the platforms of the two major parties in the radical nature of the reforms proposed. The platform characterized the war policies and peace proposals of the Wilson administration as "despotism, reaction and oppression unsurpassed in the annals of the republic." It called for the replacement of the "mischievous" League of Nations with an international parliament. It favored recognition of both the newly established Irish Republic and the Soviet Union.

The Socialists continued to advocate extensive tax reform and included new calls for a tax on unused land and a progressive property tax on wartime profits that would help pay off government debts. The platform warned that the continuing militaristic mood of both major parties could lead to another war.

The Socialists continued to recommend extensive labor benefits, but for the first time they specifically mentioned migratory workers as needing government assistance.

Following are excerpts from the Socialist platform of 1920:

League of Nations. The Government of the United States should initiate a movement to dissolve the mischievous organization called the "League of Nations" and to create an international parliament, composed of democratically elected representatives of all nations of the world based upon the recognition of their equal rights, the principles of self determination, the right to national existence of colonies and other dependencies, freedom of international trade and trade routes by land and sea, and universal disarmament, and be charged with revising the Treaty of Peace on the principles of justice and conciliation.

Labor. Congress should enact effective laws to abolish child labor, to fix minimum wages, based on an ascertained cost of a decent standard of life, to protect migratory and unemployed workers from oppression, to abolish detective and strike-breaking agencies and to establish a shorter work-day in keeping with increased industrial productivity.

Blacks. Congress should enforce the provisions of the Thirteenth, Fourteenth and Fifteenth Amendments with reference to the Negroes, and effective federal legislation should be enacted to secure the Negroes full civil, political, industrial and educational rights.

REPUBLICANS

In mid-June, Republicans met for the fifth straight time in Chicago for their quadrennial convention. For the first time, women were on the floor in large numbers as delegates. With the constitutional amendment granting women the vote on the verge of passage, Republicans, especially in the Midwest and West, were quick to include women in their delegations.

The Republicans, like the Democrats two weeks later, entered their convention with no clear front-runner for the presidential nomination. Three candidates were at the top of the list, but two of them, Maj. Gen. Leonard Wood of New Hampshire and Sen. Hiram Johnson of California, split the party's progressive wing, while the third entry, Gov. Frank Lowden of Illinois, ran poorly in the presidential primaries and was accused of campaign spending irregularities.

The names of eleven men were placed in nomination for the presidency, but none came close during the first day of balloting to the 493 votes needed to nominate. Wood led on the initial roll call with 287½ votes, trailed by Lowden with 211½ and Johnson

with 133½. Sen. Warren G. Harding of Ohio, who had not campaigned for the nomination as extensively as the three pacesetters, placed sixth with 65½ votes. Wood, Lowden, and Johnson all gained strength during the first three ballots. *(Table, p. 604.)*

After the third roll call, the Johnson delegates moved for adjournment but were defeated, 701½ to 275½. On the fourth ballot, Wood's vote total rose to 314½, well short of a majority but the highest mark attained yet by any candidate. At this point, Harding stood in fifth place with 61½ votes. Although a motion to adjourn had been soundly defeated after the previous roll call, the permanent chairman, Sen. Henry Cabot Lodge of Massachusetts, entertained a new motion to adjourn and declared it passed on a closely divided voice vote.

The adjournment gave Republican leaders a chance to confer and discuss the various presidential possibilities. Much is made in history books about Harding's selection that night in the legendary "smoke-filled room," when Harding was allegedly interviewed at 2 o'clock by Republican leaders and, answering their questions satisfactorily, was chosen as the nominee. The authenticity of the meeting has been questioned, as has the power of the politicians who made the designation. But, nonetheless, it was clear that Harding was a viable compromise choice who was both acceptable to the conservative party leadership and could be nominated by the delegates.

Harding's vote total rose slowly in the next day's balloting until the ninth ballot, when a large shift, primarily of Lowden delegates, boosted the Ohio senator's vote from 133 to 374½. This was the highest total for any candidate to this point and started a bandwagon that produced Harding's nomination on the tenth ballot. After the various switches, the final vote stood: Harding, 692⅕; Wood, 156, and Johnson, 80⅘, with the rest of the vote scattered.

Immediately after Harding's nomination, the vice-presidential balloting began. After the nomination of Sen. Irvine L. Lenroot of Wisconsin, a delegate from Oregon rose and, standing on his chair, nominated Gov. Calvin Coolidge of Massachusetts. An enthusiastic demonstration followed, showing the wide delegate support for Coolidge. The governor, who had risen to national prominence less than a year earlier with his handling of a Boston police strike, was a runaway winner on the one vice-presidential ballot. Coolidge received 674½ votes to Lenroot's 146½.

The Wisconsin delegation again presented a detailed minority report to the platform. It included planks that opposed entry into the League of Nations under the terms of the proposed treaty, objected to compulsory military service, called for the quick conclusion of peace negotiations and normalization of foreign relations and recommended a bonus for servicemen to match the wages of wartime civilian workers.

In domestic reforms, the Wisconsin report advocated the election of federal judges and the passage of a constitutional amendment that would establish the initiative, referendum, and recall. The entire minority report was rejected by a voice vote, and the platform as written was adopted in a similar manner.

The platform began by denouncing the Wilson administration for being completely unprepared for both war and peace. It went on to criticize Wilson for establishing an "executive autocracy" by arrogating to himself power that belonged to other branches of government.

The platform included a League of Nations plank that intentionally straddled the controversial issue, applauding the Republican-controlled Senate for defeating Wilson's League but pledging the party "to such agreements with the other nations of the world as shall meet the full duty of America to civilization and humanity."

To help cut federal spending, the Republicans favored consolidating some departments and bureaus and establishing an executive budget.

Both parties continued to differ on the tariff, with the Democrats reiterating their belief in a revenue tariff and the Republicans restating their support of a protective tariff.

Following are excerpts from the Republican platform of 1920:

League of Nations. The Republican party stands for agreement among the nations to preserve the peace of the world. . . .

The covenant signed by the President at Paris failed signally . . . and contains stipulations, not only intolerable for an independent people, but certain to produce the injustice, hostility and controversy among nations which it proposed to prevent.

[W]e pledge the coming Republican administration to such agreements with the other nations of the world as shall meet the full duty of America to civilization and humanity, in accordance with American ideals, and without surrendering the right of the American people to exercise its judgment and its power in favor of justice and peace.

DEMOCRATS

San Francisco was the host city for the 1920 Democratic convention, marking the first time a convention of one of the major parties was held west of the Rockies. Not only was the site a new one, but when the convention opened in late June, for the first time in a generation the Democratic Party had no recognized leader such as Cleveland, Bryan, or Wilson.

President Woodrow Wilson had some hope of a third nomination, but his failing health and skidding popularity made this an unrealistic prospect. But Wilson's refusal to endorse another candidate prevented the emergence of any presidential hopeful as a front-runner for the nomination. In all, twenty-four candidates received votes on the first presidential roll call, but none approached the 729 votes needed for nomination. William Gibbs McAdoo, Wilson's son-in-law and former treasury secretary, led with 266 votes, in spite of having withdrawn from the race several days before the convention began. Attorney General A. Mitchell Palmer, famed for his efforts during the "Red Scare," followed closely with 254 votes. Two governors, Ohio's James M. Cox and New York's Alfred E. Smith, trailed with 134 and 109 votes respectively. *(Table, p. 605.)*

Another ballot was taken before evening adjournment, with the top four candidates retaining the same order and nearly the same vote.

During the next day's balloting, Cox gained steadily and passed both McAdoo and Palmer. When the majority of McAdoo and Palmer delegates successfully carried a motion to recess after the sixteenth ballot, Cox held the lead with 454½ votes. McAdoo was next with 337 votes and Palmer trailed with 164½.

Six more ballots were taken during the evening session, and although Cox's lead narrowed, he still led McAdoo after the 22nd ballot, 430 to 372½. In the next day's balloting, McAdoo gradually gained ground until he finally passed Cox on the 30th ballot, 403½ to 400½. After completion of the roll call, the motion was made to eliminate the lowest candidate on each succeeding ballot until a nominee had been selected. This drastic proposal to shorten the convention was defeated, 812½ to 264.

Balloting continued without interruption through the 36th roll call. McAdoo still led with 399 votes, but his margin over Cox was reduced to 22 votes, and Palmer with 241 votes achieved his highest total since the 11th ballot.

A candidate was finally nominated during the evening session of the convention's third day of presidential balloting. The Palmer revival fizzled quickly, with most of his delegates going to either McAdoo or Cox. The Ohio governor regained the lead on the thirty-ninth ballot, when the majority of the Indiana delegation shifted from McAdoo to Cox. After this roll call, Cox led McAdoo, 468½ to 440, Palmer having slipped to 74. Cox continued to gain, and a last-ditch effort by McAdoo delegates to force an adjournment failed, 637 to 406. Cox's vote total reached 699½ votes on the forty-fourth ballot, and, with victory imminent, a motion was adopted to declare the Ohio governor the unanimous nominee of the convention. *(Table, p. 605.)*

Cox's choice for the vice-presidential nomination was Franklin D. Roosevelt of New York, the thirty-eight-year-old assistant secretary of the Navy. Roosevelt was nominated by acclamation.

William Jennings Bryan attended the convention and proposed five planks as amendments to the platform. Only his plank endorsing prohibition, however, was submitted for a roll-call vote, and it was soundly beaten, 929½ to 155½. A counterproposal by a New York delegate, recognizing the legality of the prohibition amendment to the Constitution but favoring the manufacture of beer and light wines for home use, was also defeated, 724½ to 356. The platform finally adopted did not discuss the prohibition question.

Bryan's four other planks covered a wide range of issues. He favored establishing a national newspaper, reducing from two-thirds to a simple majority the vote needed to approve treaties in the Senate, expressed opposition to peacetime universal compulsory military training and recommended that interstate companies reveal the difference between the cost and selling price of their products. All four planks were defeated by voice votes.

One other amendment, calling for the recognition of Irish independence, came to the floor for a roll-call vote. It was beaten, 674 to 402½. Included instead was a milder plank sympathizing with the Irish struggle for independence. Subsequently, the delegates approved by voice vote the entire platform as it was first written.

Although the delegates were unwilling to renominate Wilson, the platform was largely devoted to praise of his leadership and legislation passed during his presidency. The platform reflected Wilson's thinking by placing the League of Nations plank prominently at the beginning and supporting the president's call for American membership. The plank did allow for reservations to the treaty, but none that would prevent American participation in the League.

Following are excerpts from the Democratic platform of 1920:

League of Nations. The Democratic Party favors the League of Nations as the surest, if not the only, practicable means of maintaining the permanent peace of the world and terminating the insufferable burden of great military and naval establishments. . . .

We commend the President for his courage and his high conception of good faith in steadfastly standing for the covenant agreed to by all the associated and allied nations at war with Germany, and we condemn the Republican Senate for its refusal to ratify the treaty merely because it was the product of Democratic statesmanship, thus inter-posing partisan envy and personal hatred in the way of the peace and renewed prosperity of the world. . . .

We advocate the immediate ratification of the treaty without reservations which would impair its essential integrity, but do not oppose the acceptance of any reservations making clearer or more specific the obligations of the United States to the league associates.

Irish Independence. The great principle of national self-determination has received constant reiteration as one of the chief objectives for which this country entered the war and victory established this principle.

Within the limitations of international comity and usage, this Convention repeats the several previous expressions of the sympathy of the Democratic Party of the United States for the aspirations of Ireland for self-government.

1924 Conventions

PRESIDENTIAL CANDIDATES

Calvin Coolidge
Republican

John W. Davis
Democrat

Robert M. La Follette
Progressive

REPUBLICANS

The Republicans gathered for their convention in Cleveland, Ohio, in June. For the first time, a convention was broadcast by radio. Also for the first time, Republican Party rules were changed to elect women to the national committee, with one man and one woman to be chosen from each state and territory.

Unlike the Democratic marathon that began two weeks later in New York, there was surface harmony at the Republican convention. President Calvin Coolidge's success in the spring primaries, and his ability to defuse the corruption issue, eliminated any major opposition. Coolidge was easily nominated on the first ballot, receiving 1,065 votes. Sen. Robert M. La Follette of Wisconsin was a distant second with 34 votes, while Sen. Hiram W. Johnson of California collected the remaining 10. *(Table, p. 608.)*

The vice-presidential nomination was a confused matter. Eight candidates were nominated, and on the first ballot former Illinois governor Frank O. Lowden led with 222 votes. Although Lowden publicly stated that he would not accept the nomination, he received a majority of the vote on the second roll call. A recess was taken to see if Lowden had changed his mind, but when it was certain that he had not the delegates resumed balloting.

On the third roll call, former budget bureau director Charles G. Dawes received 682½ votes to win nomination. Secretary of Commerce Herbert Hoover was second with 234½ votes.

As was its custom throughout the early twentieth century, the Wisconsin delegation proposed a detailed minority report to the platform. Proposals included government ownership of railroads and water power, an increased excess profits tax and reduced taxes on individuals with low incomes. The Wisconsin platform was rejected without a roll-call vote.

The platform that was adopted lauded the economy in government shown by the Republican administration and promised a reduction in taxes.

The Democrats and Republicans continued to differ on the tariff issue, with the Republicans again defending the protective tariff. The Ku Klux Klan was not mentioned in the Republican platform, nor was it discussed on the floor. The controversial organization was the subject of a divisive floor fight at the Democratic convention.

The Republican platform criticized the corruption found to exist in the Harding administration, but it also denounced efforts "to besmirch the names of the innocent and undermine the confidence of the people in the government under which they live."

In the area of foreign policy, the Republicans opposed membership in the League of Nations, although favoring participation in the World Court. While applauding the return of peace and reflecting the nation's increasing mood of isolationism, the Republicans opposed cutbacks in the Army and Navy.

Following are excerpts from the Republican platform of 1924:

Corruption. We demand the speedy, fearless and impartial prosecution of all wrong doers, without regard for political affiliations; but we declare no greater wrong can be committed against the people than the attempt to destroy their trust in the great body of their public servants. Admitting the deep humiliation which all good citizens share that our public life should have harbored some dishonest men, we assert that these undesirables do not represent the standard of our national integrity.

Taxes. We pledge ourselves to the progressive reduction of taxes of all the people as rapidly as may be done with due regard for the essential expenditures for the government administered with rigid economy and to place our tax system on a sound peace time basis.

League of Nations. This government has definitely refused membership in the league of nations or to assume any obligations under the covenant of the league. On this we stand.

Military. There must be no further weakening of our regular army and we advocate appropriations sufficient to provide for the training of all members of the national guard, the citizens' military training camps, the reserve officers' training camps and the reserves who may offer themselves for service. We pledge ourselves for service. We pledge ourselves to round out and maintain the navy to the full strength provided the United States by the letter and spirit of the limitation of armament conference.

War Profiteering. [S]hould the United States ever again be called upon to defend itself by arms the president be empowered to draft such material resources and such services as may be required, and to stabilize the prices of services and essential commodities, whether used in actual warfare or private activities.

Republican Philosophy. The prosperity of the American nation rests on the vigor of private initiative which has bred a spirit of independence and self-reliance. The republican party stands now, as always, against all attempts to put the government into business.

American industry should not be compelled to struggle against government competition. The right of the government to regulate, supervise and control public utilities and public interests, we believe, should be strengthened, but we are firmly opposed to the nationalization or government ownership of public utilities.

DEMOCRATS

The 1924 Democratic convention in New York's old Madison Square Garden was the longest in American history. From the opening gavel on June 24 through final adjournment on July 10, the convention spanned seventeen days. The reason for the convention's unprecedented length was an almost unbreakable deadlock between the party's rural and urban factions that ex-

tended the presidential balloting for a record 103 roll calls. (*Table, pp. 606–607.*)

Gov. Alfred E. Smith of New York was the candidate of the urban delegates, while William Gibbs McAdoo of California led the rural forces. But beyond any ideological differences between the two candidates was a bitter struggle between the urban and rural wings for control of the party. Smith, a Roman Catholic of Irish ancestry and an opponent of Prohibition and the Ku Klux Klan, embodied characteristics loathed by the rural leaders. McAdoo, a Protestant, a supporter of Prohibition and tolerant of the Ku Klux Klan, was equally unacceptable to the urban forces. Without a strong leader to unite the two factions, and with the two-thirds rule in effect, a long deadlock was inevitable.

Besides Smith and McAdoo, fourteen other candidates were nominated. The most memorable speech was delivered by Franklin D. Roosevelt, who, in nominating Smith, referred to him as "the happy warrior," a description that remained with Smith the rest of his career.

Presidential balloting commenced on Monday, June 30. McAdoo led on the first roll call with 431½ votes, followed by Smith with 241, with 733 votes needed for nomination. Through the week, 77 ballots were taken, but none of the candidates approached the required two-thirds majority. At the end of the week, after the seventy-seventh ballot, McAdoo led with 513 votes; Smith had 367; John W. Davis of New York, the eventual nominee, was a distant third with 76½, an improvement of 45½ votes over his first-ballot total. McAdoo had reached the highest total for any candidate, 530 votes, on the sixty-ninth ballot.

William Jennings Bryan, making his last appearance at a Democratic convention, as a delegate from Florida, was given permission to explain his opposition to Smith during the thirty-eighth ballot. But Bryan's final convention oration was lost in a chorus of boos from the urban forces who found his rural philosophy increasingly objectionable.

After the sixty-sixth ballot, the first of a series of proposals was introduced to break the deadlock. It was recommended that the convention meet in executive session and listen to each of the candidates. This received majority approval, 551 to 538, but a two-thirds majority was needed to change the rules. A second proposal, to invite Smith alone to address the convention, also fell short of the necessary two-thirds, although achieving a majority, 604½ to 473.

After the seventy-third ballot, it was recommended that the lowest vote-getter be dropped after each roll call until only five candidates remained, a proposal to be in effect for one day only. This recommendation was defeated, 589½ to 496. A more drastic motion, to adjourn after the seventy-fifth ballot and reconvene two weeks later in Kansas City, was decisively beaten, 1,007.3 to 82.7. The delegates did agree, however, to have representatives of each candidate hold a conference over the weekend.

Balloting resumed on Monday, July 7, with the seventy-eighth roll call. After the eighty-second ballot, a resolution was passed, 985 to 105, releasing all delegates from their commitments.

McAdoo's vote dropped sharply as the balloting progressed, and for the first time, on the eighty-sixth roll call, Smith passed him, 360 to 353½. A boom for Sen. Samuel M. Ralston of Indiana, which had begun on the eighty-fourth ballot, petered out on the ninety-third roll call when Ralston quit the race. At the time of his withdrawal, Ralston was in third place with 196¼ votes.

After the ballot, Roosevelt announced that Smith was willing to withdraw from the race if McAdoo would also. McAdoo rejected this suggestion. McAdoo did regain the lead from Smith on the ninety-fourth ballot, 395 to 364½, but with victory beyond reach, released his delegates after the ninety-ninth ballot.

Davis was the principal beneficiary of the McAdoo withdrawal, moving into second place on the one-hundredth ballot and gaining the lead on the next roll call with 316 votes. Most of Smith's strength moved to Alabama's anti-Klan, anti-Prohibition senator, Oscar W. Underwood, who took second place on the one hundred and first ballot with 229½ votes. Underwood, however, could not keep pace with Davis, who stretched his lead on the next two ballots. After the one hundred and third ballot, Davis's total stood at 575½ votes to 250½ for the Alabama senator.

Before the next ballot could begin, Iowa switched its vote to Davis, causing other shifts that brought Davis the nomination. After the changes had been recorded, Davis had 844 votes to 102½ for Underwood. The West Virginian's nomination was then declared unanimous.

The core of Davis's vote had come from the rural delegates; urban delegates gave him the necessary votes to win the nomination. After nine days of balloting, the Democrats had a presidential candidate.

The party leadership preferred Gov. Charles W. Bryan of Nebraska, William Jennings Bryan's younger brother, as Davis's running mate. Bryan trailed Tennessee labor leader George L. Berry on the first ballot, 263½ to 238, but vote switches begun by Illinois after the roll call brought Bryan the nomination. After the changes Bryan had 740 votes, barely beyond the two-thirds majority necessary.

The discord evident in the presidential and vice-presidential balloting had its roots in the spirited platform battle that preceded the nominations. The first subject of debate was the League of Nations, with the majority report recommending that American entry be determined by a national referendum. The minority plank argued that this was an unwieldy solution that would put the issue aside. Instead, the minority report favored entry into the League of Nations and World Court without reservation. The minority position was rejected, 742½ to 353½. Nonetheless, the Democrats differed markedly in their position from the Republicans, who flatly opposed membership in the League, although favoring participation in the World Court.

The League of Nations debate proved to be merely a warm-up for the controversial religious liberties plank. The focus of debate was the Ku Klux Klan, which was opposed by name in the minority report but was not mentioned in the majority report. In one of the closest votes in convention history, the minority plank was defeated, 543³⁄₂₀ to 542⁷⁄₂₀. The vote closely followed factional lines, with most rural delegates opposing condemnation of the Klan and urban delegates supporting the minority plank.

The rest of the platform stressed Democratic accomplishments during the Wilson presidency, in contrast to Republican corruption. Democratic links with the common man were emphasized, while the Republicans were denounced as the party of the rich. The Democratic platform advocated increased taxes on the wealthy in contrast to the Republicans, who promised a reduction in taxes.

The Democrats continued to advocate a low tariff that would encourage competition. A plank demanding states' rights appeared in the platform, but there were also calls for government regulation of the anthracite coal industry, federal support of the American merchant marine and legislation that would restrict and publicize individual campaign contributions.

There were planks favoring a cutback in the American military, a national referendum before any declaration of war (except outright aggression against the United States) and the drafting of resources as well as men during wartime. The anti-militaristic planks were a return to the position the party had held earlier in the twentieth century.

Following are excerpts from the Democratic platform of 1924:

Republican Corruption. Such are the exigencies of partisan politics that republican leaders are teaching the strange doctrine that public censure should be directed against those who expose crime rather than against criminals who have committed the offenses. If only three cabinet officers out of ten are disgraced, the country is asked to marvel at how many are free from taint. Long boastful that it was the only party "fit to govern," the republican party has proven its inability to govern even itself. It is at war with itself. As an agency of government it has ceased to function.

Income Tax. The income tax was intended as a tax upon wealth. It was not intended to take from the poor any part of the necessities of life. We hold that the fairest tax with which to raise revenue for the federal government is the income tax. We favor a graduated tax upon incomes, so adjusted as to lay the burdens of government upon the taxpayers in proportion to the benefits they enjoy and their ability to pay.

Campaign Contributions. We favor the prohibition of individual contributions, direct and indirect, to the campaign funds of congressmen, senators or presidential candidates, beyond a reasonable sum to be fixed in the law, for both individual contributions and total expenditures, with requirements for full publicity.

States' Rights. We demand that the states of the union shall be preserved in all their vigor and power. They constitute a bulwark against the centralizing and destructive tendencies of the republican party.

Anti-militarism. We demand a strict and sweeping reduction of armaments by land and sea, so that there shall be no competitive military program or naval building. Until international agreements to this end have been made we advocate an army and navy adequate for our national safety. . . .

War is a relic of barbarism and it is justifiable only as a measure of defense.

War Profiteering. In the event of war in which the manpower of the nation is drafted, all other resources should likewise be drafted. This will tend to discourage war by depriving it of its profits.

PROGRESSIVES

Under the sponsorship of the Conference of Progressive Political Action, representatives of various liberal, labor and agrarian groups met in Cleveland on July 4 to launch the Progressive Party and ratify the ticket of Wisconsin senator Robert M. La Follette for president and Montana senator Burton K. Wheeler for vice president. The conference earlier had designated La Follette as its presidential nominee and had given him the power to choose his running mate. The national ticket of the Progressives crossed party lines, joining a Republican, La Follette, with a Democrat, Wheeler. The ticket was endorsed by the Socialists, who supported the Progressive candidates rather than run a separate national ticket.

In large part the Progressive platform advocated measures that had been proposed earlier by the Populists, Socialists, and Progressives before World War I. The key issue, as viewed by the La Follette Progressives, was "the control of government and industry by private monopoly." The platform favored the government ownership of railroads and water power, rigid federal control over natural resources, the outlawing of injunctions in labor disputes, a cutback in military spending, tax reform and political reform—including the direct election of the president, a national referendum before a declaration of war (except in cases of invasion), election of federal judges and congressional power to override the Supreme Court.

Following are excerpts from the Progressive platform of 1924:

Anti-monopoly. The great issue before the American people today is the control of government and industry by private monopoly.

For a generation the people have struggled patiently, in the face of repeated betrayals by successive administrations, to free themselves from this intolerable power which has been undermining representative government.

Through control of government, monopoly has steadily extended its absolute dominion to every basic industry.

In violation of law, monopoly has crushed competition, stifled private initiative and independent enterprise. . . .

The equality of opportunity proclaimed by the Declaration of Independence and asserted and defended by Jefferson and Lincoln as the heritage of every American citizen has been displaced by special privilege for the few, wrested from the government of the many.

Tax Reform. We . . . favor a taxation policy providing for immediate reductions upon moderate incomes, large increases in the inheritance tax rates upon large estates to prevent the indefinite accumulation by inheritance of great fortunes in a few hands, taxes upon excess profits to penalize profiteering, and complete publicity, under proper safeguards, of all Federal tax returns.

Court Reform. We favor submitting to the people, for their considerate judgment, a constitutional amendment providing that Congress may by enacting a statute make it effective over a judicial vote.

We favor such amendment to the constitution as may be necessary to provide for the election of all Federal Judges, without party designation, for fixed terms not exceeding ten years, by direct vote of the people.

National Referendums. Over and above constitutions and statutes and greater than all is the supreme sovereignty of the people, and with them should rest the final decision of all great questions of national policy. We favor such amendments to the Federal Constitution as may be necessary to provide for the direct nomination and election of the President, to extend the initiative and referendum to the federal government, and to insure a popular referendum for or against war except in cases of actual invasion.

1928 Conventions

PRESIDENTIAL CANDIDATES

Herbert Hoover
Republican

Alfred E. Smith
Democrat

REPUBLICANS

The Republicans held their convention in Kansas City, Missouri, in mid-June 1928. Nearly a year earlier, President Calvin Coolidge had declared his intention not to seek reelection with a typically brief statement: "I do not choose to run for President in 1928." While some business leaders hoped that Coolidge

would be open to a draft, the taciturn incumbent made no effort to encourage them. The vacuum caused by Coolidge's absence was quickly filled by Commerce Secretary Herbert Hoover of California, whose success in the spring primaries solidified his position as the front-runner.

Hoover's strength was evident on the first roll call of the convention, a credentials challenge to eighteen Hoover delegates from Texas. In a vote that revealed candidate strength, the move to unseat the Hoover delegates was defeated, 659½ to 399½. In the presidential balloting that followed, he gained more votes to win the nomination easily on the first ballot. Hoover's vote total was swelled before the balloting began by the withdrawal of his principal opponent, former Illinois governor Frank O. Lowden, who declared in a letter that he could not accept the party platform's stand on agriculture. Six names were placed in nomination, but Hoover was a landslide winner, receiving 837 of the 1,089 convention votes. Lowden finished second with 74 votes. *(Table, p. 609.)*

Sen. Charles Curtis of Kansas was virtually unopposed for the vice-presidential nomination, receiving 1,052 votes.

Although Wisconsin's prominent progressive leader, Robert M. La Follette, had died in 1925, his state's delegation again presented a minority platform. The report was presented by Sen. Robert M. La Follette Jr., who had taken over his father's Senate seat. Among the planks of the Wisconsin report were proposals favoring enactment of the McNary-Haugen farm bill, government operation of major water power projects, increased income taxes on the rich and liberalization of Prohibition. No vote was taken on the Wisconsin proposals.

A resolution favoring repeal of Prohibition was tabled by a voice vote.

A separate agricultural resolution was proposed that advocated the basic provisions of the McNary-Haugen bill (twice vetoed by Coolidge), without mentioning the controversial bill by name. On a roll-call vote, the resolution was defeated, 807 to 277, with support centered in the farm states but with most Hoover delegates voting against it.

The platform as originally written was adopted by a voice vote. The platform promised continued prosperity and government economy. The belief in a protective tariff was reiterated. The document concluded with a plank entitled "home rule," which expressed the party's belief in self-reliance and strong local government.

Following are excerpts from the Republican platform of 1928:

Tariff. We reaffirm our belief in the protective tariff as a fundamental and essential principle of the economic life of this nation. . . . However, we realize that there are certain industries which cannot now successfully compete with foreign producers because of lower foreign wages and a lower cost of living abroad, and we pledge the next Republican Congress to an examination and where necessary a revision of these schedules to the end that American labor in these industries may again command the home market, may maintain its standard of living, and may count upon steady employment in its accustomed field.

Outlaw War. We endorse the proposal of the Secretary of State for a multilateral treaty proposed to the principal powers of the world and open to the signatures of all nations, to renounce war as an instrument of national policy and declaring in favor of pacific settlement of international disputes, the first step in outlawing war.

Agriculture. We promise every assistance in the reorganization of the market system on sounder and more economical lines and, where diversification is needed, Government financial assistance during the period of transition.

The Republican Party pledges itself to the enactment of legislation creating a Federal Farm Board clothed with the necessary powers to promote the establishment of a farm marketing system of farmer-owned and controlled stabilization corporations or associations to prevent and control surpluses through orderly distribution. . . .

We favor, without putting the Government into business, the establishment of a Federal system of organization for co-operative and orderly marketing of farm products.

Prohibition. The people through the method provided by the Constitution have written the Eighteenth Amendment into the Constitution. The Republican Party pledges itself and its nominees to the observance and vigorous enforcement of this provision of the Constitution.

Republican Philosophy. There is a real need of restoring the individual and local sense of responsibility and self-reliance; there is a real need for the people once more to grasp the fundamental fact that under our system of government they are expected to solve many problems themselves through their municipal and State governments, and to combat the tendency that is all too common to turn to the Federal Government as the easiest and least burdensome method of lightening their own responsibilities.

DEMOCRATS

The Democratic convention was held in late June in Houston, Texas, the first time since 1860 that the party's nominating convention had been conducted in a southern city. The rural and urban wings of the party, which had produced the fiasco in Madison Square Garden four years earlier, wanted no more bloodletting. This explained the acceptance of Houston as the convention site by the urban forces, whose presidential candidate, Gov. Alfred E. Smith of New York, was the front-runner for the nomination. Smith's path to the nomination was largely unobstructed, thanks to the decision of William Gibbs McAdoo not to run. McAdoo, the rural favorite in 1924, feared the possibility of another bitter deadlock that would destroy party unity.

The convention broke with tradition by bypassing politicians and selecting Claude G. Bowers of Indiana, a historian and an editorial writer for the *New York World*, as temporary chairman.

When it came time for the selection of a presidential candidate, Franklin D. Roosevelt once again placed Smith's name in nomination. On the roll call that followed, the New York governor came within 10 votes of the required two-thirds. Ohio quickly switched 44 of its votes to Smith, and the switch pushed "the happy warrior" over the top. When the vote switches were completed, Smith had received 849⅙ of the 1,100 convention votes. No other candidate's vote had totaled more than 100. *(Table, p. 609.)*

Senate Minority Leader Joseph T. Robinson of Arkansas had little opposition for the vice presidency and was nominated on the first ballot with 914⅙ votes. Sen. Alben W. Barkley of Kentucky finished a distant second with 77 votes. After a vote switch, Robinson had 1,035⅙ votes. As a "dry" Protestant from the South, Robinson balanced the ticket. He was the first southerner to be nominated for national office by either major party since the Civil War.

For the first time since 1912, there were no roll-call votes on amendments to the Democratic platform. A minority plank was introduced calling for the party's complete support of Prohibition, but there was no effort to force a roll-call vote. The platform included a milder Prohibition plank that promised "an honest effort to enforce the eighteenth Amendment (Prohibition)." On the surface there was little difference from the Republican plank, which pledged "vigorous enforcement" of Prohibition. But in a telegram read to the convention shortly before its final adjournment, Smith negated the effect of the milder plank by declaring there should be "fundamental changes in the present provisions for national Prohibition." Smith's statement was disappointing to many "dry" delegates and lessened whatever enthusiasm they felt for the New York governor. No other issues were discussed, and the platform as written was approved by a voice vote.

Agriculture, the most depressed part of the economy in the 1920s, received more space in the platform than any other issue. The Democrats opposed federal subsidies to farmers, but they advocated government loans to cooperatives and the creation of a federal farm board that would operate similarly to the Federal Reserve Board. While the Republican platform also favored creation of a farm board, as a whole it called for more initiative by the farmers themselves and less direct government help than did the Democratic platform.

Since the late nineteenth century, Democratic platforms had favored a low tariff. The 1928 tariff plank represented a change, expressing as much interest in ensuring competition and protecting the American wage-earner as in raising revenue. Instead of being consistently low, tariff rates were to be based on the difference between the cost of production in the United States and abroad. As a result of the Democrats' altered stand on the tariff, the positions of the two parties on this issue were the closest they had been in a generation.

The Democrats' 1928 platform did not mention the League of Nations, in contrast to the Republicans, who restated their opposition to the League. Both parties called for maintenance of American military strength until international disarmament agreements could be reached. A section of the Democratic foreign policy plank questioned the extent of presidential power in the area of international affairs. President Coolidge was specifically criticized for authorizing American military intervention in Nicaragua without congressional approval.

An unemployment plank was included in the Democratic platform that proposed the creation of public works jobs in times of economic hardship.

As was the case with most Democratic platforms since the early nineteenth century, there was a defense of states' rights and a plank that recognized education as an area of state responsibility. The Democrats made no mention of civil rights in contrast to the Republicans, who, as in 1920, proposed federal anti-lynching legislation.

Following are excerpts from the Democratic platform of 1928:

Prohibition. Speaking for the national Democracy, this convention pledges the party and its nominees to an honest effort to enforce the eighteenth amendment.

Agriculture. Farm relief must rest on the basis of an economic equality of agriculture with other industries. To give this equality a remedy must be found which will include among other things:

(a) Credit aid by loans to co-operatives on at least as favorable a basis as the government aid to the merchant marine.

(b) Creation of a federal farm board to assist the farmer and stock raiser in the marketing of their products, as the Federal Reserve Board has done for the banker and business man.

Presidential War Power. Abolition of the practice of the president of entering into and carrying out agreements with a foreign government, either de facto or de jure, for the protection of such government against revolution or foreign attack, or for the supervision of its internal affairs, when such agreements have not been advised and consented to by the Senate, as provided in the Constitution of the United States, and we condemn the administration for carrying out such an unratified agreement that requires us to use our armed forces in Nicaragua.

Tariff. Duties that will permit effective competition, insure against monopoly and at the same time produce a fair revenue for the support of government. Actual difference between the cost of production at home and abroad, with adequate safeguard for the wage of the American laborer must be the extreme measure of every tariff rate.

Unemployment and Public Works. We favor the adoption by the government, after a study of this subject, of a scientific plan whereby during periods of unemployment appropriations shall be made available for the construction of necessary public works and the lessening, as far as consistent with public interests, of government construction work when labor is generally and satisfactorily employed in private enterprise.

Education. We believe with Jefferson and other founders of the Republic that ignorance is the enemy of freedom and that each state, being responsible for the intellectual and moral qualifications of its citizens and for the expenditure of the moneys collected by taxation for the support of its schools, shall use its sovereign right in all matters pertaining to education.

1932 Conventions

PRESIDENTIAL CANDIDATES

Norman Thomas
Socialist

Herbert Hoover
Republican

Franklin D. Roosevelt
Democrat

SOCIALISTS

The Socialist Party held its convention in Milwaukee, Wisconsin, in May and renominated the same ticket that had represented the party in 1928: Norman Thomas of New York for president and James H. Maurer of Pennsylvania for vice president. Aided by the deepening economic depression, the Socialists received more than 2 percent of the popular vote for the first time since 1920. The party continued to run a national ticket until 1956, but 1932 was the last election in which the Socialists received at least 2 percent of the vote.

By a vote of 117 to 64, the convention adopted a resolution supporting the efforts of the Soviet Union to create a Socialist society. An attempt to oust Morris Hillquit as national chairman of the party was beaten, 108 to 81.

The Socialist platform of 1932 contained a number of proposals that had been set forth in earlier party platforms, such as public ownership of natural resources and the means of transportation and communication, increased taxes on the wealthy, an end to the Supreme Court's power to rule congressional legislation unconstitutional, and a reduction in the size and expenditures of the military.

The platform also advocated United States recognition of the Soviet Union and American entry into the League of Nations. Repeal of Prohibition was recommended, as was the creation of a federal marketing system that would buy and market farm commodities.

To meet the hardship of the Depression, the Socialists listed a series of proposals, which included the expenditure of $10 billion for unemployment relief and public works projects.

Following are excerpts from the Socialist platform of 1932:

Unemployment Relief. 1. A Federal appropriation of $5,000,000,000 for immediate relief for those in need to supplement State and local appropriations.

2. A Federal appropriation of $5,000,000,000 for public works and roads, reforestation, slum clearance, and decent homes for the workers, by Federal Government, States and cities.

3. Legislation providing for the acquisition of land, buildings, and equipment necessary to put the unemployed to work producing food, fuel, and clothing and for the erection of houses for their own use.

4. The 6-hour day and the 5-day week without reduction of wages.

5. A comprehensive and efficient system of free public employment agencies.

6. A compulsory system of unemployment compensation with adequate benefits, based on contributions by the Government and by employers.

7. Old-age pensions for men and women 60 years of age and over.

8. Health and maternity insurance.

REPUBLICANS

As the incumbent party during the outset of the Depression, the Republicans bore the major political blame for the worsening economy. In a subdued mood, the party gathered in Chicago in June 1932 for its national convention.

Republican leaders did not view their electoral prospects optimistically for the fall election, but saw no realistic alternative to President Herbert Hoover.

Hoover was easily if unenthusiastically renominated, receiving 1,126½ of the 1,154 convention votes. The highlight of the presidential balloting was the attempt by former Maryland senator Joseph I. France, who ran in several spring primaries, to gain the rostrum and nominate former president Coolidge. France's dramatic plan, however, was foiled by convention managers, who refused him permission to speak and had him escorted from the hall. *(Table, p. 610.)*

Vice President Charles Curtis had stiff opposition in his bid for renomination. The incumbent was seriously challenged by Maj. Gen. James G. Harbord of New York and the national commander of the American Legion, Hanford MacNider of Iowa. Curtis was short of a majority after the first ballot, but Pennsylvania quickly shifted its 75 votes to the vice president and this pushed him over the top. With the vote standing at Curtis, 634¼; MacNider, 182¾, and Harbord, 161¾, Curtis' renomination was made unanimous.

The major platform controversy surrounded the Prohibition plank. The majority plank, supported by Hoover, was ambiguous. It called for the enforcement of Prohibition but advocated a national referendum that would permit each state to determine whether or not it wanted Prohibition. A more clear-cut minority plank favored repeal of Prohibition. The minority proposal was defeated, however, $690\frac{19}{36}$ to $460\frac{2}{9}$. Following this roll call, the rest of the platform was approved by a voice vote.

The document approved by the Republicans was the longest in the party's history—nearly 9,000 words. It blamed the nation's continued economic problems on a worldwide depression, but lauded Hoover's leadership in meeting the crisis. The Republicans saw reduced government spending and a balanced budget as keys to ending the Depression. The party platform viewed unemployment relief as a matter for private agencies and local governments to handle.

The Republicans continued their support of a protective tariff. On the agricultural issue, the party proposed acreage controls to help balance supply and demand.

The final plank of the Republican platform urged party members in Congress to demonstrate party loyalty by supporting the Republican program. The plank warned that the party's strength was jeopardized by internal dissent.

Following are excerpts from the Republican platform of 1932:

Unemployment Relief. The people themselves, by their own courage, their own patient and resolute effort in the readjustments of their own affairs, can and will work out the cure. It is our task as a party, by leadership and a wise determination of policy, to assist that recovery. . . .

True to American traditions and principles of government, the administration has regarded the relief problem as one of State and local responsibility. The work of local agencies, public and private has been coordinated and enlarged on a nation-wide scale under the leadership of the President.

Government Spending. We urge prompt and drastic reduction of public expenditure and resistance to every appropriation not demonstrably necessary to the performance of government, national or local.

Agriculture. The fundamental problem of American agriculture is the control of production to such volume as will balance supply with demand. In the solution of this problem the cooperative organization of farmers to plan production, and the tariff, to hold the home market for American farmers, are vital elements. A third element equally as vital is the control of the acreage of land under cultivation, as an aid to the efforts of the farmer to balance production.

Prohibition. We . . . believe that the people should have an opportunity to pass upon a proposed amendment the provision of which, while retaining in the Federal Government power to preserve the gains already made in dealing with the evils inherent in the liquor traffic, shall allow the States to deal with the problem as their citizens may determine, but subject always to the power of the Federal Government to protect those States where prohibition may exist and safeguard our citizens everywhere from the return of the saloon and attendant abuses.

DEMOCRATS

With the nation in the midst of the Great Depression, the Democratic Party had its best chance for victory since 1912. The delegates assembled in Chicago in late June 1932, confident that the convention's nominee would defeat President Hoover.

Gov. Franklin D. Roosevelt of New York entered the convention with a majority of the votes, but was well short of the two-thirds majority needed for nomination. Ironically, his principal opponent was the man he had nominated for the presidency three times, former New York governor Alfred E. Smith.

Roosevelt's strength was tested on several key roll calls before the presidential balloting began. Two of the votes involved credentials challenges to Roosevelt delegations from Louisiana and Minnesota. By a vote of $638\frac{3}{4}$ to $514\frac{1}{4}$, the delegates seated the Roosevelt forces from Louisiana, headed by Sen. Huey P. Long. And by a wider margin of $658\frac{1}{4}$ to $492\frac{3}{4}$ the convention seated the Roosevelt delegates from Minnesota. *(Table, p. 611.)*

After settlement of the credentials cases, the battleground shifted to the selection of the permanent convention chairman. The Roosevelt forces backed Sen. Thomas J. Walsh of Montana, who was recommended by the committee on permanent organization. The Smith and other anti-Roosevelt factions coalesced behind Jouett Shouse of Kansas, chairman of the executive committee of the Democratic National Committee, who was recommended for permanent chairman by the national committee. But by a vote of 626 to 528, the Roosevelt forces won again, and Walsh assumed the gavel as permanent chairman.

The Roosevelt managers considered challenging the two-thirds rule; but, realizing that a bruising fight could alienate some of their own delegates, particularly in the South, they dropped the idea. Instead, the report of the rules committee recommended that a change in the two-thirds rule be delayed until the 1936 convention.

The presidential balloting began in the middle of an all-night session. After a motion to adjourn was defeated, $863\frac{1}{2}$ to $281\frac{1}{2}$, the first roll call began at 4:30 a.m. Roosevelt received a clear majority of $666\frac{1}{4}$ votes on the first ballot, compared with $201\frac{3}{4}$ for Smith and $90\frac{1}{4}$ for House Speaker John Nance Garner of Texas. Seven hundred and seventy votes were necessary for nomination. *(Table, p. 611.)*

Roosevelt gained slightly on the second ballot, advancing to $677\frac{3}{4}$ votes, while Smith dropped to $194\frac{1}{4}$ and Garner remained constant. Of side interest was the shift of Oklahoma's votes from its governor to Will Rogers, the state's famous humorist.

There were few changes on the next roll call, and at 9:15 a.m. the delegates agreed to adjourn. The vote totals after three ballots: Roosevelt, 682.79; Smith, $190\frac{1}{4}$; Garner, $101\frac{1}{4}$.

When balloting resumed the next evening, William Gibbs McAdoo of California quickly launched the bandwagon for Roosevelt by announcing that his state's 44 votes were switching from Garner to the New York governor. Other states followed California's lead, and when the fourth ballot was completed Roosevelt had 945 votes and the nomination. With the Smith vote holding at $190\frac{1}{2}$, no effort was made to make the nomination unanimous.

Although it is not clear whether there was a formal deal struck before the fourth ballot between the Garner and Roosevelt forces, the Texas representative was the unanimous choice of the convention for vice president. Forty states seconded his nomination, and no roll call was taken.

In an effort to break what he described as "absurd traditions," Roosevelt flew from Albany to Chicago to accept the presidential nomination personally. (Previously, a major party candidate would be formally notified of his nomination in a ceremony several weeks after the convention.) In his speech of acceptance, Roosevelt struck a liberal tone and issued his memorable pledge of "a new deal for the American people."

The platform adopted by the convention was not a blueprint for the New Deal to follow. It was fewer than 2,000 words long, the party's shortest platform since 1888, and less than one-fourth as long as the document adopted by the Republicans. It blamed the Depression on the "disastrous policies" practiced by the Republicans but made few new proposals, instead forcefully restating positions that had appeared in earlier party platforms.

The Democrats advocated a balanced budget with a cut of at least 25 percent in federal spending and called for removal of the federal government from competition with private enterprise in all areas except public works and natural resources.

The Democratic platform, unlike its Republican counterpart, advocated extensive unemployment relief and public works projects, regulation of holding companies and securities exchanges, "a competitive tariff for revenue," and the extension of farm cooperatives.

The plank that sparked the most enthusiasm among the delegates was the call for the repeal of Prohibition. A milder plank favored by "dry" delegates was resoundingly defeated, 934¾ to 213¾.

The only measure added from the floor of the convention favored "continuous responsibility of government for human welfare, especially for the protection of children." It was approved by a standing vote.

Following are excerpts from the Democratic platform of 1932:

Government Spending. We advocate an immediate and drastic reduction of governmental expenditures by abolishing useless commissions and offices, consolidating departments and bureaus, and eliminating extravagance to accomplish a saving of not less than twenty-five percent in the cost of the Federal Government. And we call upon the Democratic Party in the states to make a zealous effort to achieve a proportionate result.

We favor maintenance of the national credit by a federal budget annually balanced on the basis of accurate executive estimates within revenues, raised by a system of taxation levied on the principle of ability to pay.

Unemployment Relief, Public Works Projects. We advocate the extension of federal credit to the states to provide unemployment relief wherever the diminishing resources of the states makes it impossible for them to provide for the needy; expansion of the federal program of necessary and useful construction effected with a public interest, such as adequate flood control and waterways.

We advocate the spread of employment by a substantial reduction in the hours of labor, the encouragement of the shorter week by applying that principle in government service; we advocate advance planning of public works.

We advocate unemployment and old-age insurance under state laws.

Prohibition. We advocate the repeal of the Eighteenth Amendment. To effect such repeal we demand that the Congress immediately propose a Constitutional Amendment to truly represent [sic] the conventions in the states called to act solely on that proposal; we urge the enactment of such measures by the several states as will actually promote temperance, effectively prevent the return of the saloon, and bring the liquor traffic into the open under complete supervision and control by the states.

Agriculture. Extension and development of the Farm Cooperative movement and effective control of crop surpluses so that our farmers may have the full benefit of the domestic market.

The enactment of every constitutional measure that will aid the farmers to receive for their basic farm commodities prices in excess of cost.

1936 Conventions

PRESIDENTIAL CANDIDATES

Alfred M. Landon
Republican

Franklin D. Roosevelt
Democrat

William Lemke
Union

REPUBLICANS

The Republican convention, held in Cleveland in early June, was an unusually harmonious gathering for a party out of power. There were only two roll-call votes on the convention floor, for president and vice president, and both were one-sided.

The only matter of debate was the vote allocation for Alaska, Hawaii, and the District of Columbia. By a voice vote, the convention approved the minority report of the rules committee, which sliced the vote for these three from six to three votes apiece.

Former president Herbert Hoover received an enthusiastic reception when he spoke, but by that time Kansas governor Alfred M. Landon had the presidential nomination sewed up. Landon, one of the few Republican governors to be reelected during the Depression, received 984 votes on the first ballot, compared with 19 for Sen. William E. Borah of Idaho. *(Table, p. 612.)*

Before the balloting began, Landon had sent a telegram to the convention that expressed his agreement with the "word and spirit" of the party platform but elaborated his position on several points. The Kansan advocated the passage of a constitutional amendment to ensure women and children safe working conditions and to establish guidelines for wages and hours in the event that legislation passed by Congress was ruled unconstitutional. Landon's message also proposed extending the civil service to include all workers in federal departments and agencies below the rank of assistant secretary, and it defined "sound currency" as currency that could be exchanged for gold. Landon's pronouncements were met with thirty minutes of cheering.

For vice president, the convention selected Col. Frank Knox of Illinois, publisher of the *Chicago Daily News*. Knox, who earlier had campaigned energetically, if not successfully, for the presidential nomination, received all 1,003 votes on the first ballot.

The Republican platform, which began with the sentence, "America is in peril," focused on the alleged threat of New Deal policies to American constitutional government. The platform assailed the Roosevelt administration for "dishonoring Ameri-

can traditions" and promised to protect local self-government and the power of the Supreme Court.

The Republicans promised a balanced budget, reduced federal expenditures, a "sound currency," a more discriminating public works program, and the administration of unemployment relief by "non-political local agencies" that would be financed jointly by the various states and the federal government.

The Republicans shared with the Democrats the belief in an isolationist foreign policy and the concepts of social security, unemployment insurance and crop control.

Following are excerpts from the Republican platform of 1936:

Roosevelt's "New Deal." America is in peril. The welfare of American men and women and the future of our youth are at stake. We dedicate ourselves to the preservation of their political liberty, their individual opportunity and their character as free citizens, which today for the first time are threatened by Government itself. . . .

The powers of Congress have been usurped by the President.

The integrity and authority of the Supreme Court have been flouted.

The rights and liberties of American citizens have been violated.

Regulated monopoly has displaced free enterprise.

The New Deal Administration constantly seeks to usurp the rights reserved to the States and to the people.

Unemployment Relief. The return of responsibility for relief administration to nonpolitical local agencies familiar with community problems. . . .

Undertaking of Federal public works only on their merits and separate from the administration of relief.

Government Spending, Currency. Balance the budget—not by increasing taxes but by cutting expenditures, drastically and immediately. . . .

We advocate a sound currency to be preserved at all hazards.

The first requisite to a sound and stable currency is a balanced budget.

Foreign Policy. We pledge ourselves to promote and maintain peace by all honorable means not leading to foreign alliances or political commitments.

Obedient to the traditional foreign policy of America and to the repeatedly expressed will of the American people, we pledge that America shall not become a member of the League of Nations nor of the World Court nor shall America take on any entangling alliances in foreign affairs.

DEMOCRATS

The 1936 Democratic convention, held in Philadelphia in late June, was one of the most harmonious in party history. There were no floor debates, and, for the first time since 1840, there were no roll-call votes.

The only matter that required discussion—elimination of the century-old two-thirds rule—was settled in the rules committee. There, by a vote of 36 to 13, the committee agreed to abrogate the rule, which had been a controversial part of Democratic conventions since 1832. To mollify the South, which was particularly threatened by elimination of the two-thirds rule, the rules committee added a provision that would include consideration of a state's Democratic voting strength in determining its future convention vote allocation. The rules committee report was approved by a voice vote.

Both President Franklin D. Roosevelt and Vice President John Nance Garner were renominated by acclamation, but more than a full day of oratory was expended in eulogizing the Democratic standard-bearers. Roosevelt was seconded by delegates from each of the states and territories—more than fifty separate speakers. Seventeen delegates spoke on behalf of Garner.

Both Roosevelt and Garner personally accepted their nominations in ceremonies at the University of Pennsylvania's Franklin Field. Before a crowd estimated as large as 100,000, Roosevelt electrified his listeners with a speech that blasted his adversaries among the rich as "economic royalists" and included the sentence: "This generation of Americans has a rendezvous with destiny."

As in 1932 the platform adopted by the Democrats was a short one, about 3,000 words. The document paid lip service to the concept of a balanced budget and reduced government spending, but it supported continuation of the extensive federal programs undertaken by the Roosevelt administration.

The platform did not, as many in past years had, mention states' rights; this reflected the party's changing view toward federal power. To counter what was viewed as obstructionism by the Supreme Court, the Democrats suggested the possibility of passing a "clarifying amendment" to the Constitution that would enable Congress and state legislatures to enact bills without the fear of an unfavorable decision from the Supreme Court.

The foreign policy plank recognized the isolationist mood of the period, calling for neutrality in foreign disputes and the avoidance of international commitments that would draw the United States into war.

Following are excerpts from the Democratic platform of 1936:

Federal Power. The Republican platform proposes to meet many pressing national problems solely by action of the separate States. We know that drought, dust storms, floods, minimum wages, maximum hours, child labor, and working conditions in industry, monopolistic and unfair business practices cannot be adequately handled exclusively by 48 separate State legislatures, 48 separate State administrations, and 48 separate State courts. Transactions and activities which inevitably overflow State boundaries call for both State and Federal treatment.

We have sought and will continue to seek to meet these problems through legislation within the Constitution.

If these problems cannot be effectively solved by legislation within the Constitution, we shall seek such clarifying amendment as will assure to the legislatures of the several States and to the Congress of the United States, each within its proper jurisdiction, the power to enact those laws which the State and Federal legislatures, within their respective spheres, shall find necessary, in order adequately to regulate commerce, protect public health and safety and safeguard economic security. Thus we propose to maintain the letter and spirit of the Constitution.

Government Spending. We are determined to reduce the expenses of government. We are being aided therein by the recession in unemployment. As the requirements of relief decline and national income advances, an increasing percentage of Federal expenditures can and will be met from current revenues, secured from taxes levied in accordance with ability to pay. Our retrenchment, tax and recovery programs thus reflect our firm determination to achieve a balanced budget and the reduction of the national debt at the earliest possible moment.

Foreign Policy. We reaffirm our opposition to war as an instrument of national policy, and declare that disputes between nations should be settled by peaceful means. We shall continue to observe a true neutrality in the disputes of others; to be prepared resolutely to resist aggression against ourselves; to work for peace and to take the profits out of war; to guard against being drawn, by political commitments, international banking or private trading, into any war which may develop anywhere.

UNION PARTY

With the support of Father Charles E. Coughlin and his National Union for Social Justice, on June 19, 1936, Rep. William Lemke of North Dakota, a Republican, declared his presidential candidacy on the newly formed Union Party ticket. Thomas O'Brien, a Boston railroad union lawyer, was announced as Lemke's running mate. The fledgling political organization had a brief existence, running a national ticket only in the 1936 election.

The Union Party was basically an extension of Coughlin's organization, and the Lemke-O'Brien ticket was endorsed at the National Union for Social Justice convention in August by a vote of 8,152 to 1.

The Union Party platform reportedly was written by Coughlin, Lemke, and O'Brien at the Roman Catholic priest's church in Royal Oak, Michigan. It was a brief document, fewer than 1,000 words, that contained fifteen points similar to the sixteen-point program favored by Coughlin's National Union. The primary distinctions between the Union Party and the two major parties were in currency expansion, civil service reform, and restrictions on wealth. The Union Party called for the creation of a central bank, regulated by Congress, that would issue currency to help pay off the federal debt and refinance agricultural and home mortgage indebtedness. The Union Party platform also proposed extending the civil service to all levels of the federal government and advocated placing restrictions on annual individual income coupled with a ceiling on gifts and inheritances. The new party differed from the Socialists by emphasizing that private property should not be confiscated.

Following are excerpts from the Union Party platform of 1936:

Currency Expansion. Congress and Congress alone shall coin and issue the currency and regulate the value of all money and credit in the United States through a central bank of issue.

Immediately following the establishment of the central bank of issue Congress shall provide for the retirement of all tax-exempt, interest-bearing bonds and certificates of indebtedness of the Federal Government and shall refinance all the present agricultural mortgage indebtedness for the farmer and all the home mortgage indebtedness for the farmer and all the home mortgage indebtedness for the city owner by the use of its money and credit which it now gives to the private bankers.

Civil Service Reform. Congress shall so legislate that all Federal offices and positions of every nature shall be distributed through civil-service qualifications and not through a system of party spoils and corrupt patronage.

Restrictions on Wealth. Congress shall set a limitation upon the net income of any individual in any one year and a limitation of the amount that such an individual may receive as a gift or as an inheritance, which limitation shall be executed through taxation.

Foreign Policy. Congress shall establish an adequate and perfect defense for our country from foreign aggression either by air, by land, or by sea, but with the understanding that our naval, air, and military forces must not be used under any consideration in foreign fields or in foreign waters either alone or in conjunction with any foreign power. If there must be conscription, there shall be a conscription of wealth as well as a conscription of men.

1940 Conventions

PRESIDENTIAL CANDIDATES

Wendell L. Willkie
Republican

Franklin D. Roosevelt
Democrat

REPUBLICANS

The Republican convention was held in Philadelphia in late June, and it culminated one of the most successful of all campaign blitzes. Wendell L. Willkie, an Indiana native who had never before run for public office, was nominated by the Republicans to run for president. A Democrat until 1938, Willkie had gained fame as a defender of private enterprise in opposition to Roosevelt's public power projects. Although Willkie had broad personal appeal, he and his well-financed group of political "amateurs" did not launch their presidential bid until late spring and missed the presidential primaries. Willkie's momentum came from his rapid rise in the Republican preference polls, as he soared from only 3 percent in early May to 29 percent six weeks later.

At the Republican convention, ten names were placed in nomination for the presidency. Willkie's principal rivals were Manhattan District Attorney Thomas E. Dewey, making his first presidential bid at age thirty-eight, and Sen. Robert A. Taft of Ohio. On the first ballot, Dewey led with 360 votes, followed by Taft with 189, and Willkie with 105. For nomination 501 votes were needed. *(Table, p. 613.)*

After the first roll call, Dewey steadily lost strength, while Willkie and Taft gained. Willkie assumed the lead on the fourth ballot, passing both Dewey and Taft. Willkie's vote was 306, while Taft moved into second place with 254. Dewey dropped to third with 250.

On the fifth ballot, the contest narrowed to just Willkie and Taft, as both candidates continued to gain—Willkie jumping to 429 votes and Taft to 377. The shift of Michigan's votes to Willkie on the sixth ballot started a bandwagon for the Indianan that pushed him over the top. When the roll call was completed, Willkie was nominated with 655 votes, and a motion to make his nomination unanimous was adopted.

As his running mate, Willkie favored Senate Minority Leader Charles L. McNary of Oregon. McNary, a supporter of some New Deal measures, was opposed by Rep. Dewey Short of Missouri, a vocal anti–New Dealer. McNary, however, was able to win easily on a single ballot, receiving 890 votes to 108 for Short.

The Republican platform was adopted without debate, although an Illinois member of the platform committee commented that his state would have preferred a stronger antiwar plank. As it was, the Republican foreign policy plank sharply criticized the Roosevelt administration for not adequately preparing the nation's defense. However, the rest of the plank was similar to the one adopted three weeks later by the Democrats at the convention: opposing involvement in war but stressing national defense, and advocating aid to the Allies that would not be "inconsistent with the requirements of our own national defense."

In domestic affairs, the Republicans lambasted the extension of federal power under the New Deal and promised cuts in government spending and the reduction of federal competition with private enterprise. The Republican platform agreed with the concept of unemployment relief and Social Security initiated by the Roosevelt administration, but it proposed the administration of these programs by the states and not the federal government.

The Republicans attacked Roosevelt's monetary measures and advocated currency reforms that included congressional control.

The platform also proposed new amendments to the Constitution that would provide equal rights for men and women and would limit a president to two terms in office.

Following are excerpts from the Republican platform of 1940:

Foreign Policy. The Republican Party is firmly opposed to involving this Nation in foreign war. . . .

The Republican Party stands for Americanism, preparedness and peace. We accordingly fasten upon the New Deal full responsibility for our unpreparedness and for the consequent danger of involvement in war. . . .

Our sympathies have been profoundly stirred by invasion of unoffending countries and by disaster to nations whole [whose] ideals most closely resemble our own. We favor the extension to all peoples fighting for liberty, or whose liberty is threatened, of such aid as shall not be in violation of international law or inconsistent with the requirements of our own national defense.

Unemployment Relief. We shall remove waste, discrimination, and politics from relief-through administration by the States with federal grants-in-aid on a fair and nonpolitical basis, thus giving the man and woman on relief a larger share of the funds appropriated.

Currency. The Congress should reclaim its constitutional powers over money, and withdraw the President's arbitrary authority to manipulate the currency, establish bimetallism, issue irredeemable paper money, and debase the gold and silver coinage. We shall repeal the Thomas Inflation Amendment of 1933 and the (foreign) Silver Purchase Act of 1934, and take all possible steps to preserve the value of the Government's huge holdings of gold and reintroduce gold into circulation.

Women's Rights. We favor submission by Congress to the States of an amendment to the Constitution providing for equal rights for men and women.

No Third Term. To insure against the overthrow of our American system of government we favor an amendment to the Constitution providing that no person shall be President of the United States for more than two terms.

DEMOCRATS

At the time of both major party conventions in the summer of 1940, Hitler's forces were moving quickly and relentlessly across western Europe. International events assumed a major importance in political decisions. President Franklin D. Roosevelt, who gave evidence before 1940 that he would not seek a third term, became increasingly receptive to the idea of a draft as the Democratic convention drew nearer. The threat to American security caused by the awesomely successful Nazi military machine, coupled with Roosevelt's inability to find an adequate New Deal–style successor, seemed to spur the president's decision to accept renomination.

The Democratic convention was held in Chicago in mid-July. On the second night of the convention, a message from Roosevelt was read stating that he did not desire to run for reelection and urging the delegates to vote for any candidate they wished. Although worded in a negative way, the message did not shut the door on a draft. The delegates reacted, however, by sitting in stunned silence until a Chicago city official began shouting over the public address system, "We want Roosevelt." The cheerleading galvanized the delegates into an hour-long demonstration.

Presidential balloting was held the next day. Roosevelt won easily on the first roll call, although two members of his administration, Vice President John Nance Garner and Postmaster General James A. Farley of New York, ran against him. Roosevelt received $945^{13}/_{30}$ of the 1,100 votes. Farley had $72^{9}/_{10}$ and Garner had 61. *(Table, p. 612.)*

While the delegates were satisfied to have Roosevelt at the top of the ticket again, many balked at his choice for vice president, Agriculture Secretary Henry A. Wallace of Iowa. Wallace, a leading liberal in the administration and a former Republican, was particularly distasteful to conservative Democrats. Many delegates were expecting Roosevelt to leave the vice-presidential choice to the convention and were unhappy to have the candidate dictated to them.

It took a personal appearance at the convention by the president's wife, Eleanor Roosevelt, and a threat by the president that he would not accept the presidential nomination without his handpicked running mate, to steer the delegates toward Wallace. In spite of the pressure by the Roosevelt forces, the vote was scattered among 13 candidates on the vice-presidential ballot. Wallace, though, was able to obtain a slim majority, $626^{11}/_{30}$ votes to $329^{3}/_{5}$ for the runner-up, House Speaker William B. Bankhead of Alabama. Because of the displeasure of many of the delegates, Wallace was asked not to address the convention.

The convention closed by hearing a radio address by Roosevelt, who stated that he had not wanted the nomination but accepted it because the existing world crisis called for personal sacrifice.

The party platform was adopted without a roll call, although there was an amendment presented by a Minnesota representative that opposed any violation of the two-term tradition. It was rejected by a voice vote. The platform as adopted was divided into three sections. The first discussed American military preparedness and foreign policy; the second detailed the New Deal's benefits for various segments of the economy (agriculture, labor, business); the third listed New Deal welfare measures, ranging from unemployment relief to low-cost housing.

As a concession to the party's isolationist wing, the first section contained the administration's promise not to participate in foreign wars or fight in foreign lands, except in case of an attack on the United States. The plank stressed the need of a strong national defense to discourage aggression, but also pledged to provide to free nations (such as Great Britain) material aid "not inconsistent with the interests of our own national self-defense."

An electric power plank was included in the second section of the platform as a direct result of the Republicans' selection of Wendell L. Willkie, a former utilities executive, as their presidential candidate. The Democrats argued in favor of the massive public power projects constructed during the New Deal and criticized private utilities such as the one formerly headed by Willkie.

The third section of the platform drew a sharp distinction from the Republicans on the issue of unemployment relief, opposing any efforts to turn the administration of relief over to the states or local governments.

Following are excerpts from the Democratic platform of 1940:

Democratic Achievements. Toward the modern fulfillment of the American ideal, the Democratic Party, during the last seven years, has labored successfully:

1. To strengthen democracy by defensive preparedness against aggression, whether by open attack or secret infiltration;

2. To strengthen democracy by increasing our economic efficiency; and

3. To strengthen democracy by improving the welfare of the people.

Foreign Policy. We will not participate in foreign wars, and we will not send our army, naval or air forces to fight in foreign lands outside of the Americas, except in case of attack. . . .

Weakness and unpreparedness invite aggression. We must be so strong that no possible combination of powers would dare to attack us. We propose to provide America with an invincible air force, a navy strong enough to protect all our seacoasts and our national interests, and a fully-equipped and mechanized army.

Unemployment Relief. We shall continue to recognize the obligation of Government to provide work for deserving workers who cannot be absorbed by private industry.

We are opposed to vesting in the states and local authorities the control of Federally-financed work relief. We believe that this Republican proposal is a thinly disguised plan to put the unemployed back on the dole.

Electric Power. The nomination of a utility executive by the Republican Party as its presidential candidate raises squarely the issue, whether the nation's water power shall be used for all the people or for the selfish interests of a few. We accept that issue.

1944 Conventions

PRESIDENTIAL CANDIDATES

Thomas E. Dewey
Republican

Franklin D. Roosevelt
Democrat

REPUBLICANS

For the first time since 1864, the nation was at war during a presidential election year. The Republicans held their convention first, meeting in Chicago in late June 1944. With a minimum of discord, the delegates selected a national ticket and adopted a platform. Gov. Thomas E. Dewey of New York, the front-runner for the presidential nomination, was the nearly unanimous selection when his last two rivals, Gov. John W.

Bricker of Ohio and former Minnesota governor Harold E. Stassen, both withdrew from the race before the roll call. On the single ballot, Dewey received 1,056 of the 1,057 votes cast. The one dissenting vote was cast by a Wisconsin delegate for Gen. Douglas MacArthur. *(Table, p. 614.)*

As Dewey's running mate, the delegates unanimously selected Gov. Bricker, an isolationist and party regular, who received all 1,057 votes cast. During the nominating speeches, Rep. Charles A. Halleck of Indiana made the unusual move of recommending his state's first choice for vice president, William L. Hutcheson, for secretary of labor.

Dewey came to Chicago personally to accept the nomination, becoming the first Republican presidential candidate to break the tradition of waiting to accept the nomination in a formal notification ceremony. The thrust of Dewey's speech was an attack on the Roosevelt administration, which he referred to as "stubborn men grown old and tired and quarrelsome in office."

The platform was approved without dissent. The international section was written in a guarded tone. It favored "responsible participation by the United States in postwar cooperative organization" but declared that any agreement must be approved by a two-thirds vote of the Senate. The Republicans favored the establishment of a postwar Jewish state in Palestine.

The domestic section of the platform denounced the New Deal's centralization of power in the federal government, with its increased government spending and deficits. The Republicans proposed to stabilize the economy through the encouragement of private enterprise.

The platform restated several of the planks included four years earlier, among which were the call for an equal rights amendment, a two-term limitation on the president and the return of control over currency matters from the president to Congress.

The Republicans adopted a civil rights plank that called for a congressional investigation of the treatment of blacks in the military, passage of a constitutional amendment to eliminate the poll tax, and legislation that would outlaw lynching and permanently establish a Fair Employment Practice Commission.

Following are excerpts from the Republican platform of 1944:

Postwar International Organization. We favor responsible participation by the United States in post-war cooperative organization among sovereign nations to prevent military aggression and to attain permanent peace with organized justice in a free world.

Such organization should develop effective cooperative means to direct peace forces to prevent or repel military aggression. Pending this, we pledge continuing collaboration with the United Nations to assure these ultimate objectives....

We shall sustain the Constitution of the United States in the attainment of our international aims; and pursuant to the Constitution of the United States any treaty or agreement to attain such aims made on behalf of the United States with any other nation or any association of nations, shall be made only by and with the advice and consent of the Senate of the United States provided two-thirds of the Senators present concur.

Israel. In order to give refuge to millions of distressed Jewish men, women and children driven from their homes by tyranny, we call for the opening of Palestine to their unrestricted immigration and land ownership, so that in accordance with the full intent and purpose of the Balfour Declaration of 1917 and the Resolution of a Republican Congress in 1922, Palestine may be constituted as a free and democratic Commonwealth. We condemn the failure of the President to insist that the mandatory of Palestine carry out the provision of the Balfour Declaration and of the mandate while he pretends to support them.

New Deal. Four more years of New Deal policy would centralize all power in the President, and would daily subject every act of every citizen to regulation by his henchmen; and this country could remain a Republic only in name. No problem exists which cannot be solved by

American methods. We have no need of either the communistic or the fascist technique.

... The National Administration has become a sprawling, overlapping bureaucracy. It is undermined by executive abuse of power, confused lines of authority, duplication of effort, inadequate fiscal controls, loose personnel practices and an attitude of arrogance previously unknown in our history.

Economy. We reject the theory of restoring prosperity through government spending and deficit financing.

We shall promote the fullest stable employment through private enterprise.

Civil Rights. We pledge an immediate Congressional inquiry to ascertain the extent to which mistreatment, segregation and discrimination against Negroes who are in our armed forces are impairing morale and efficiency, and the adoption of corrective legislation.

We pledge the establishment by Federal legislation of a permanent Fair Employment Practice Commission.

The payment of any poll tax should not be a condition of voting in Federal elections and we favor immediate submission of a Constitutional amendment for its abolition.

We favor legislation against lynching and pledge our sincere efforts in behalf of its early enactment.

Agriculture. An American market price to the American farmer and the protection of such price by means of support prices, commodity loans, or a combination thereof, together with such other economic means as will assure an income to agriculture that is fair and equitable in comparison with labor, business and industry. We oppose subsidies as a substitute for fair markets.

Serious study of and search for a sound program of crop insurance with emphasis upon establishing a serf-supporting program.

DEMOCRATS

President Franklin D. Roosevelt, who four years earlier did not make a final decision about accepting a third nomination until the last moment, clearly stated his intention to run for a fourth term a week before the 1944 convention was to open in Chicago. In a message to Democratic National Chairman Robert E. Hannegan of Missouri released July 11, Roosevelt declared that while he did not desire to run, he would accept renomination reluctantly as a "good soldier."

The early sessions of the convention were highlighted by approval of the rules committee report and settlement of a credentials challenge. The rules committee mandated the national committee to revamp the convention's vote-allocation formula in a way that would take into account Democratic voting strength. This measure was adopted to appease southern delegates, who in 1936 were promised an increased proportion of the convention vote in return for elimination of the two-thirds rule. No action had been taken to implement the pledge in the intervening eight years.

The credentials dispute involved the Texas delegation, which was represented by two competing groups. By a voice vote, the convention agreed to seat both groups.

Vice President Henry A. Wallace enlivened the presidential nominations by appearing before the convention to urge Roosevelt's renomination. Wallace termed the president the "greatest liberal in the history of the U.S." In the balloting that followed, Roosevelt easily defeated Sen. Harry F. Byrd of Virginia, who was supported by some conservative southern delegates unhappy with the domestic legislation favored by the New Deal. The final tally: Roosevelt, 1,086; Byrd, 89; former postmaster general James A. Farley, 1. *(Table, p. 614.)*

Roosevelt accepted the nomination in a radio address delivered from the San Diego Naval Base, where he had stopped off en route to a wartime conference.

The real drama of the convention, the selection of the vice-presidential nominee, came next. Roosevelt had been ambivalent about the choice of his running mate, encouraging several people to run but not publicly endorsing any of them. The president wrote an ambiguous letter to the convention chairman, which was read to the delegates. Roosevelt stated that if he were a delegate himself he would vote for Wallace's renomination, but that the ultimate choice was the convention's and it must consider the pros and cons of its selection.

In another message, written privately for National Chairman Hannegan, Roosevelt declared that he would be happy to run with either Missouri senator Harry S. Truman or Supreme Court Justice William O. Douglas. Most of the party bosses preferred Truman to the more liberal alternatives, Wallace and Douglas. Truman originally was slated to nominate former South Carolina senator and Supreme Court Justice James F. Byrnes for vice president. But, spurred by his political advisers, Roosevelt telephoned Truman in Chicago and urged him to accept the nomination. Truman reluctantly agreed.

Roosevelt's final preference for Truman was not publicly announced, and twelve names were placed before the convention. Wallace led on the first roll call with 429½ votes, followed by Truman with 319½. Favorite sons and other hopefuls shared the remaining votes cast.

Truman passed Wallace on the second ballot, 477½ to 473, and, immediately after completion of the roll call, Alabama began the bandwagon for the Missouri senator by switching its votes to him. When all the shifts had been made, Truman was an easy winner with 1,031 votes, while Wallace finished with 105.

The platform adopted by the convention was a short one, only 1,360 words. The first third of the platform lauded the accomplishments of Roosevelt's first three terms. The rest of the document outlined the party's proposals for the future. In foreign affairs, the Democrats advocated the creation of a postwar international organization that would have adequate forces available to prevent future wars. The party also called for American membership in an international court of justice. The Democrats joined their Republican opponents in favoring the establishment of an independent Jewish state in Palestine.

The domestic section of the platform proposed a continuation of New Deal liberalism, with passage of an equal rights amendment for women, price guarantees and crop insurance for farmers, and the establishment of federal aid to education that would be administered by the states.

A minority report concerning foreign policy called for the establishment of an international air force to help keep peace. The proposal was rejected, however, when the platform committee chairman indicated that the existence of an air force was included in the majority report's call for "adequate forces" to be at the disposal of the proposed international organization.

Following are excerpts from the Democratic platform of 1944:

Postwar International Organizations. That the world may not again be drenched in blood by international outlaws and criminals, we pledge:

To join with the other United Nations in the establishment of an international organization based on the principle of the sovereign equality of all peace-loving states, open to membership by all such states, large and small, for the prevention of aggression and the maintenance of international peace and security.

To make all necessary and effective agreements and arrangements through which the nations would maintain adequate forces to meet the needs of preventing war and of making impossible the preparation for war and which would have such forces available for joint action when necessary.

Such organization must be endowed with power to employ armed forces when necessary to prevent aggression and preserve peace.

Israel. We favor the opening of Palestine to unrestricted Jewish immigration and colonization, and such a policy as to result in the establishment there of a free and democratic Jewish commonwealth.

Women's Rights. We favor legislation assuring equal pay for equal work, regardless of sex.

We recommend to Congress the submission of a Constitutional amendment on equal rights for women.

Education. We favor Federal aid to education administered by the states without interference by the Federal Government.

Agriculture. Price guarantees and crop insurance to farmers with all practical steps:

To keep agriculture on a parity with industry and labor.

To foster the success of the small independent farmer.

To aid the home ownership of family-sized farms.

To extend rural electrification and develop broader domestic and foreign markets for agricultural products.

Civil Rights. We believe that racial and religious minorities have the right to live, develop and vote equally with all citizens and share the rights that are guaranteed by our Constitution. Congress should exert its full constitutional powers to protect those rights.

1948 Conventions

PRESIDENTIAL CANDIDATES

Thomas E. Dewey
Republican

Harry S. Truman
Democrat

J. Strom Thurmond
States' Rights

Henry A. Wallace
Progressive

REPUBLICANS

The Republican convention was held in Philadelphia in late June. As in 1944, New York governor Thomas E. Dewey entered the convention as the front-runner for the nomination. But unlike four years earlier, when he was virtually handed the nomination, Dewey was contested by several candidates, including Ohio senator Robert A. Taft and former Minnesota governor Harold E. Stassen.

In all, seven names were placed in nomination, with 548 votes needed to determine a winner. Dewey led on the first roll call with 434 votes, followed by Taft with 224 and Stassen with 157. Each of the other candidates received fewer than 100 votes. (*Table, p. 615.*)

On the second roll call, Dewey moved closer to the nomination, receiving 515 votes. Taft and Stassen continued to trail, with 274 and 149 votes respectively. At this point, the anti-Dewey forces requested a recess, which was agreed to by the confident Dewey organization.

Unable to form a coalition that could stop Dewey, all his opponents withdrew before the third ballot. On the subsequent roll call, the New York governor was the unanimous choice of the convention, receiving all 1,094 votes.

Dewey's choice for vice president was California governor Earl Warren, who was nominated by acclamation. Warren had been a favorite-son candidate for the presidency and agreed to take second place on the ticket only after receiving assurances that the responsibilities of the vice presidency would be increased if Dewey were elected.

The Republican platform was adopted without dissent. The wording of the platform was unusually positive for a party out of the White House. The failures of the Truman administration were dismissed in a short paragraph, with the rest of the document praising the accomplishments of the Republican 80th Congress and detailing the party's proposals for the future.

One of the major issues of the 1948 campaign was the controversial Taft-Hartley labor law, a measure supported by the Republicans, but which most Democratic leaders felt should be repealed. The Republicans were silent on national health insurance, and the party's housing position stressed private initiative rather than federal legislation. As in 1944 the Republicans opposed the poll tax and segregation in the military and favored legislation to outlaw lynching.

The Republican platform accepted the concept of a bipartisan foreign policy. Paragraphs were inserted that supported the Marshall Plan for European recovery, the United Nations and recognition of Israel.

Following are excerpts from the Republican platform of 1948:

Civil Rights. This right of equal opportunity to work and to advance in life should never be limited in any individual because of race, religion, color, or country of origin. We favor the enactment and just enforcement of such Federal legislation as may be necessary to maintain this right at all times in every part of this Republic. . . .

Lynching or any other form of mob violence anywhere is a disgrace to any civilized state, and we favor the prompt enactment of legislation to end this infamy. . . .

We favor the abolition of the poll tax as a requisite to voting.

We are opposed to the idea of racial segregation in the armed services of the United States.

Housing. Housing can best be supplied and financed by private enterprise; but government can and should encourage the building of better homes at less cost. We recommend Federal aid to the States for local slum clearance and low-rental housing programs only where there is a need that cannot be met either by private enterprise or by the States and localities.

Labor. Here are some of the accomplishments of this Republican Congress: a sensible reform of the labor law, protecting all rights of Labor while safeguarding the entire community, against those breakdowns in essential industries which endanger the health and livelihood of all. . . .

We pledge continuing study to improve labor-management legislation in the light of experience and changing conditions. . . .

We favor equal pay for equal work regardless of sex.

Internal Security. We pledge a vigorous enforcement of existing laws against Communists and enactment of such new legislation as may be necessary to expose the treasonable activities of Communists and defeat their objective of establishing here a godless dictatorship controlled from abroad.

Foreign Policy. We are proud of the part that Republicans have taken in those limited areas of foreign policy in which they have been permitted to participate. We shall invite the Minority Party to join us under the next Republican Administration in stopping partisan politics at the water's edge.

United Nations. We believe in collective security against aggression and in behalf of justice and freedom. We shall support the United Nations as the world's best hope in this direction, striving to strengthen it and promote its effective evolution and use. The United Nations should progressively establish international law, be freed of any veto in the peaceful settlement of international disputes, and be provided with the armed forces contemplated by the Charter.

Israel. We welcome Israel into the family of nations and take pride in the fact that the Republican Party was the first to call for the establishment of a free and independent Jewish Commonwealth.

DEMOCRATS

The Democratic delegates were in a melancholy mood when they gathered in Philadelphia in mid-July 1948. Franklin D. Roosevelt was dead; the Republicans had regained control of Congress in 1947; Roosevelt's successor, Harry S. Truman, appeared unable to stem massive defections of liberals and southern conservatives from the New Deal coalition.

The dissatisfaction of southern delegates with policies of the national party was a prominent feature of the 1948 convention. Although the national committee had been mandated by the 1944 convention to devise a new vote-allocation procedure that would appease the South, the redistribution of votes for the 1948 convention merely added two votes to each of the thirty-six states that backed Roosevelt in the 1944 election. This did not appreciably bolster southern strength.

As the convention progressed, southern displeasure focused on the civil rights issue. The Mississippi delegation included in its credentials resolutions against civil rights that bound the delegation to bolt the convention if a states' rights plank was not included in the platform. The Mississippi resolutions also denied the power of the national convention to require the Democratic Party of Mississippi to support any candidate who favored President Truman's civil rights program or any candidate who failed to denounce that program.

A minority report was introduced that recommended the Mississippi delegation not be seated. This proposal was defeated by a voice vote, and, in the interest of party harmony, no roll-call vote was taken. However, in an unusual move, several delegations, including those of California and New York, asked that they be recorded in favor of the minority report.

Joined by several other southern states, Texas presented a minority proposal to the rules committee report, which favored reestablishment of the two-thirds rule. The minority proposal, however, was beaten by a voice vote.

When the presidential balloting began, the entire Mississippi delegation and thirteen members of the Alabama delegation withdrew in opposition to the convention's stand on civil rights. However, their withdrawal in no way jeopardized the nomination of Truman. Some party leaders had earlier flirted with the possibility of drafting Gen. Dwight D. Eisenhower or even Supreme Court Justice William O. Douglas. But the lack of interest of these two men in the Democratic nomination left the field clear for Truman.

The incumbent won a clear majority on the first ballot, receiving 926 votes to 266 for Georgia senator Richard B. Russell, who received the votes of more than 90 percent of the remaining southern delegates. Among the states of the Old Confederacy, Truman received only 13 votes, all from North Carolina. After several small vote switches, the final tally stood: Truman, 947½; Russell, 263. *(Table, p. 616.)*

Veteran Kentucky senator Alben W. Barley, the convention's keynoter, was nominated by acclamation for vice president.

Truman appeared before the convention to accept the nomination and aroused the dispirited delegates with a lively speech attacking the Republican Congress. Referring to it as the "worst 80th Congress," Truman announced that he would call a special session so that the Republicans could pass the legislation they said they favored in their platform.

The Democratic platform was adopted by a voice vote, after a heated discussion of the civil rights section. As presented to the convention by the platform committee, the plank favored equal rights for all citizens but was couched in generalities such as those in the 1944 plank. Southern delegates wanted a weaker commitment to civil rights, and various southern delegations offered three different amendments.

One, presented by former governor Dan Moody of Texas and signed by fifteen members of the platform committee, was a broadly worded statement that emphasized the power of the states. A second amendment, sponsored by two Tennessee members of the platform committee, was a brief, emphatic statement declaring the rights of the states. The third amendment, introduced by the Mississippi delegation as a substitute for the Moody amendment, specifically listed the powers of the states to maintain segregation. The Moody amendment was beaten, 924 to 310, with nearly all the support limited to the South. The other two amendments were rejected by voice vote. *(Table, p. 616.)*

Northern liberals countered by proposing to strengthen the civil rights plank. Introduced by former representative Andrew J. Biemiller of Wisconsin and championed by Mayor Hubert H. Humphrey of Minneapolis, the amendment commended Truman's civil rights program and called for congressional action to guarantee equal rights in voting participation, employment opportunity, personal security and military service. The Biemiller amendment was passed, 651½ to 582½, with delegations from the larger northern states supporting it. Delegations from the South were in solid opposition and were joined by delegates from border and small northern states. *(Table, p. 616.)*

The rest of the platform lauded Truman's legislative program and blamed the Republican Congress for obstructing beneficial legislation. In the New Deal tradition, the platform advocated the extension of Social Security, raising of the minimum wage, establishment of national health insurance, and the creation of a permanent flexible price support system for farmers. Congress was blamed for obstructing passage of federal aid to education, comprehensive housing legislation and funding for the Marshall Plan to help rebuild Europe. The Republicans were also criticized for crippling reciprocal trade agreements, passage of the Taft-Hartley Act, and even the rising rate of inflation.

The development of the cold war with the communist world produced a new issue, internal security, on which the two major parties differed sharply. While the Republican position stressed the pursuit of subversives, the Democrats placed more emphasis on the protection of individual rights.

In foreign affairs, the Democratic platform called for the establishment of a United Nations military force, international control of the atomic bomb, and recognition of the state of Israel.

Following are excerpts from the Democratic platform of 1948:

Civil Rights. We highly commend President Harry S Truman for his courageous stand on the issue of civil rights.

We call upon the Congress to support our President in guaranteeing these basic and fundamental American Principles: (1) the right of full and equal political participation; (2) the right to equal opportunity of employment; (3) the right of security of person; (4) and the right of equal treatment in the service and defense of our nation.

Housing. We shall enact comprehensive housing legislation, including provisions for slum clearance and low-rent housing projects initiated by local agencies. This nation is shamed by the failure of the Republican 80th Congress to pass the vitally needed general housing legislation as recommended by the President. Adequate housing will end the need for rent control. Until then, it must be continued.

Social Security, Health Insurance. We favor the extension of the Social Security program established under Democratic leadership, to provide additional protection against the hazards of old age, disability, disease or death. We believe that this program should include:

Increases in old-age and survivors' insurance benefits by at least 50 percent, and reduction of the eligibility age for women from 65 to 60 years; extension of old-age and survivors' and unemployment insurance to all workers not now covered; insurance against loss of earnings on account of illness or disability; improved public assistance for the needy.

Labor. We advocate the repeal of the Taft-Hartley Act. It was enacted by the Republican 80th Congress over the President's veto. . . .

We favor the extension of the coverage of the Fair Labor Standards Act as recommended by President Truman, and the adoption of a minimum wage of at least 75 cents an hour in place of the present obsolete and inadequate minimum of 40 cents an hour.

We favor legislation assuring that the workers of our nation receive equal pay for equal work, regardless of sex.

United Nations. We will continue to lead the way toward curtailment of the use of the veto. We shall favor such amendments and modifications of the charter as experience may justify. We will continue our efforts toward the establishment of an international armed force to aid its authority. We advocate the grant of a loan to the United Nations recommended by the President, but denied by the Republican Congress, for the construction of the United Nations headquarters in this country.

Disarmament. We advocate the effective international control of weapons of mass destruction, including the atomic bomb, and we approve continued and vigorous efforts within the United Nations to bring about the successful consummation of the proposals which our Government has advanced.

Israel. We pledge full recognition to the State of Israel. We affirm our pride that the United States under the leadership of President Truman played a leading role in the adoption of the resolution of November 29, 1947, by the United Nations General Assembly for the creation of a Jewish State.

Internal Security. We shall continue vigorously to enforce the laws against subversive activities, observing at all times the constitutional guarantees which protect free speech, the free press and honest political activity. We shall strengthen our laws against subversion to the full extent necessary, protecting at all times our traditional individual freedoms.

STATES' RIGHTS (DIXIECRATS)

Provoked by the Democratic convention's adoption of a strong civil rights plank, Gov. Fielding L. Wright of Mississippi invited other southern Democrats to meet in Birmingham, Alabama, on July 17 to select a regional ticket that would reflect southern views.

It was a disgruntled group that gathered in Birmingham, just three days after the close of the Democratic convention. Placards on the floor of the convention hall identified thirteen states, yet there were no delegates from Georgia, Kentucky, or North Carolina, and Virginia was represented by four University of Virginia students and an Alexandria woman who was returning home from a trip south. Most major southern politicians shied away from the bolters, fearing that involvement would jeopardize their standing with the national party and their seniority in Congress.

Former Alabama governor Frank M. Dixon with a keynote address vocalized the mood of the convention by charging that Truman's civil rights program would "reduce us to the status of a mongrel, inferior race, mixed in blood, our Anglo-Saxon heritage a mockery."

As its standard-bearers, the convention chose Gov. J. Strom Thurmond of South Carolina for president and Gov. Wright for vice president. Thurmond's acceptance speech touched on another grievance of bolting southern Democrats: their decreasing power within the Democratic Party. Thurmond warned: "If the South should vote for Truman this year, we might just as well petition the Government to give us a colonial status."

The platform adopted by the Dixiecrats was barely 1,000 words long, but it forcefully presented the case for states' rights. The platform warned that the tendency toward greater federal power ultimately would establish a totalitarian police state.

The Dixiecrats saved their most vitriolic passages to describe the civil rights plank adopted by the Democratic convention. They declared their support for segregation and charged that the plank adopted by the Democrats was meant "to embarrass and humiliate the South."

The platform also charged the national Democratic Party with ingratitude, claiming that the South had supported the Democratic ticket with "clock-like regularity" for nearly 100 years, but that now the national party was being dominated by states controlled by the Republicans.

Following are excerpts from the States' Rights platform of 1948:

States' Rights. We believe that the protection of the American people against the onward march of totalitarian government requires a faithful observance of Article X of the American Bill of Rights which provides that: "The powers not delegated to the United States by the Constitution, nor prohibited by it to the states, are reserved to the states respectively, or to the people."

Civil Rights. We stand for the segregation of the races and the racial integrity of each race; the constitutional right to choose one's associates; to accept private employment without governmental interference, and to earn one's living in any lawful way. We oppose the elimination of segregation employment by Federal bureaucrats called for by the misnamed civil rights program. We favor home rule, local self-government, and a minimum interference with individual rights.

We oppose and condemn the action of the Democratic convention in sponsoring a civil rights program calling for the elimination of segregation, social equality by Federal fiat, regulation of private employment practices, voting and local law enforcement.

We affirm that the effective enforcement of such a program would be utterly destructive of the social, economic and political life of the Southern people, and of other localities in which there may be differences in race, creed or national origin in appreciable numbers.

PROGRESSIVES

On December 29, 1947, former vice president Henry A. Wallace announced his presidential candidacy at the head of a new liberal party. Officially named the Progressive Party at its convention in Philadelphia in late July 1948, the new party was composed of some liberal Democrats as well as more radical groups and individuals that included some communists.

Nearly 3,200 delegates nominated Wallace for the presidency and Democratic senator Glen H. Taylor of Idaho as his running mate. The colorful Taylor and his family regaled the delegates with their rendition of "When You Were Sweet Sixteen."

On the final night of the convention, 32,000 spectators assembled to hear Wallace deliver his acceptance speech at Shibe Park. The Progressive standard-bearer expressed his belief in "progressive capitalism," which would place "human rights above property rights," and envisioned "a new frontier. . . . across the wilderness of poverty and sickness."

Former Roosevelt associate Rexford G. Tugwell chaired the seventy-four-member platform committee that drafted a detailed platform, about 9,000 words in length, that was adopted by the convention. The platform denounced the two major parties as champions of big business and claimed the new party to be the true "political heirs of Jefferson, Jackson and Lincoln." However, many political observers and opponents of the Progressives dismissed the new party as a Communist-front organization.

Although numerous positions taken by the Progressives in 1948 were considered radical, many were later adopted or seriously considered by the major parties.

The foreign policy plank advocated negotiations between the United States and the Soviet Union ultimately leading to a peace agreement, and it sharply criticized the "anti-Soviet hysteria" of the period. The platform called for repeal of the draft, repudiation of the Marshall Plan, worldwide disarmament featuring

abolition of the atomic bomb, amnesty for conscientious objectors imprisoned in World War II, recognition and aid to Israel, extension of United Nations humanitarian programs, and the establishment of a world legislature.

In the domestic area, the Progressives opposed internal security legislation, advocated the eighteen-year-old vote, favored the creation of a Department of Culture, called for food stamp and school hot lunch programs, and proposed a federal housing plan that would build 25 million homes in ten years and subsidize low-income housing.

The Progressives also reiterated the proposals of earlier third parties by favoring the direct election of the president and vice president, extensive tax reform, stricter control of monopolies, and the nationalization of the principal means of communication, transportation, and finance.

The Progressives joined the Democrats and Republicans in proposing strong civil rights legislation and an equal rights amendment for women.

Following are excerpts from the Progressive platform of 1948:

Soviet Union. The Progressive Party . . . demands negotiation and discussion with the Soviet Union to find areas of agreement to win the peace.

Disarmament. The Progressive Party will work through the United Nations for a world disarmament agreement to outlaw the atomic bomb, bacteriological warfare, and all other instruments of mass destruction; to destroy existing stockpiles of atomic bombs and to establish United Nations controls, including inspection, over the production of atomic energy; and to reduce conventional armaments drastically in accordance with resolutions already passed by the United Nations General Assembly.

World Legislation. The only ultimate alternative to war is the abandonment of the principle of the coercion of sovereignties by sovereignties and the adoption of the principle of the just enforcement upon individuals of world federal law, enacted by a world federal legislature with limited but adequate powers to safeguard the common defense and the general welfare of all mankind.

Draft. The Progressive Party calls for the repeal of the peacetime draft and the rejection of Universal Military Training.

Amnesty. We demand amnesty for conscientious objectors imprisoned in World War II.

Internal Security. We denounce anti-Soviet hysteria as a mask for monopoly, militarism, and reaction. . . .

The Progressive Party will fight for the constitutional rights of Communists and all other political groups to express their views as the first line in the defense of the liberties of a democratic people.

Civil Rights. The Progressive Party condemns segregation and discrimination in all its forms and in all places. . . .

We call for a Presidential proclamation ending segregation and all forms of discrimination in the armed services and Federal employment.

We demand Federal anti-lynch, anti-discrimination, and fair-employment-practices legislation, and legislation abolishing segregation in interstate travel.

We call for immediate passage of anti–poll tax legislation, enactment of a universal suffrage law to permit all citizens to vote in Federal elections, and the full use of Federal enforcement powers to assure free exercise of the right to franchise.

Food Stamps, School Lunches. We also call for assistance to low-income consumers through such programs as the food stamp plan and the school hot-lunch program.

Housing. We pledge an attack on the chronic housing shortage and the slums through a long-range program to build 25 million new homes during the next ten years. This program will include public subsidized housing for low-income families.

Nationalization. As a first step, the largest banks, the railroads, the merchant marine, the electric power and gas industry, and industries primarily dependent on government funds or government purchases such as the aircraft, the synthetic rubber and synthetic oil industries must be placed under public ownership.

Youth Vote. We call for the right to vote at eighteen.

1952 Conventions

PRESIDENTIAL CANDIDATES

Dwight D. Eisenhower
Republican

Adlai E. Stevenson
Democrat

REPUBLICANS

For the third straight time, both major parties held their conventions in the same city. In 1952 the site was Chicago; the Republicans met there in early July two weeks before the Democrats. The battle for the presidential nomination pitted the hero of the party's conservative wing, Sen. Robert A. Taft of Ohio, against the favorite of most moderate and liberal Republicans, Gen. Dwight D. Eisenhower. The general, a Texas native, had resigned as supreme commander of the North Atlantic Treaty Organization (NATO) less than six weeks before the convention to pursue the nomination actively.

As in 1912, when Taft's father had engaged in a bitter struggle with Theodore Roosevelt for the nomination, the outcome of the presidential race was determined in preliminary battles over convention rules and credentials.

The first confrontation came on the issue of the voting rights of challenged delegates. The Taft forces proposed adoption of the 1948 rules, which would have allowed contested delegates to vote on all credentials challenges except their own. The Eisenhower forces countered by proposing what they called a "fair play amendment," which would seat only those contested delegates who were approved by at least a two-thirds vote of the national committee. At stake were a total of sixty-eight delegates from Georgia, Louisiana, and Texas, with the large majority of the challenged delegates in favor of Taft. The Taft forces introduced a substitute to the "fair play amendment," designed to exempt seven delegates from Louisiana. On the first test of

strength between the two candidates, the Eisenhower forces were victorious, as the substitute amendment was defeated, 658 to 548. The "fair play amendment" was subsequently approved by a voice vote. *(Table, p. 617.)*

The second confrontation developed with the report of the credentials committee. The Eisenhower forces presented a minority report concerning the contested Georgia, Louisiana, and Texas seats. After a bitter debate, a roll-call vote was taken on the Georgia challenge, with the Eisenhower forces winning again, 607 to 531.

The Louisiana and Texas challenges were settled in favor of the Eisenhower forces without a roll-call vote. The favorable settlement of the credentials challenges increased the momentum behind the Eisenhower candidacy.

Before the presidential balloting began, a nonpartisan debate was held on a proposal to add state chairmen to the national committee from states recording Republican electoral majorities and to remove the requirement that women hold one of each state's seats on the national committee. The proposal was primarily intended to decrease southern influence on the national committee. But the major opposition was raised by a number of women delegates who objected to the rule change; however, their effort to defeat it was rejected by voice vote.

Five men were nominated for the presidency, but on completion of the first roll call Eisenhower had 595 votes and was within nine votes of victory. Taft was a strong second with 500 votes. However, before a second ballot could begin, Minnesota switched

19 votes from favorite son Harold E. Stassen to Eisenhower, giving the latter the nomination. After a series of vote changes, the final tally stood: Eisenhower, 845; Taft, 280; other candidates, 81. The general's nomination was subsequently made unanimous.

Eisenhower's choice as a running mate, thirty-nine-year-old senator Richard Nixon of California, was nominated by acclamation. Eisenhower promised in his acceptance speech to lead a "crusade" against "a party too long in power."

The 6,000-word platform was adopted by a voice vote. The document included a sharp attack on the Democrats, charging the Roosevelt and Truman administrations with "violating our liberties . . . by seizing powers never granted," "shielding traitors" and attempting to establish "national socialism." The foreign policy section, written by John Foster Dulles, supported the concept of collective security but denounced the Truman policy of containment and blamed the administration for the communist takeover of China. The Republican platform advocated increased national preparedness.

As well as castigating the Democrats for an incompetent foreign policy, the Republicans denounced their opposition for laxness in maintaining internal security. A plank asserted: "There are no Communists in the Republican Party."

On most domestic issues the platform advocated a reduction in federal power. The civil rights plank proposed federal action to outlaw lynching, poll taxes, and discriminatory employment practices. However, unlike the plank four years earlier, the Republican position included a paragraph that declared the individual states had primary responsibility for their own domestic institutions. On a related issue of states' rights, the Republicans, as in 1948, favored state control of tideland resources.

Following are excerpts from the Republican platform of 1952:

Democratic Failures. We charge that they have arrogantly deprived our citizens of precious liberties by seizing powers never granted.

We charge that they work unceasingly to achieve their goal of national socialism. . . .

We charge that they have shielded traitors to the Nation in high places, and that they have created enemies abroad where we should have friends.

We charge that they have violated our liberties by turning loose upon the country a swarm of arrogant bureaucrats and their agents who meddle intolerably in the lives and occupations of our citizens.

We charge that there has been corruption in high places, and that examples of dishonesty and dishonor have shamed the moral standards of the American people.

We charge that they have plunged us into war in Korea without the consent of our citizens through their authorized representatives in the Congress, and have carried on the war without will to victory. . . .

Tehran, Yalta and Potsdam were the scenes of those tragic blunders with others to follow. The leaders of the Administration in power acted without the knowledge or consent of Congress or of the American people. They traded our overwhelming victory for a new enemy and for new oppressions and new wars which were quick to come.

. . . And finally they denied the military aid that had been authorized by Congress and which was crucially needed if China were to be saved. Thus they substituted on our Pacific flank a murderous enemy for an ally and friend.

Internal Security. By the Administration's appeasement of Communism at home and abroad it has permitted Communists and their fellow travelers to serve in many key agencies and to infiltrate our American life. . . .

There are no Communists in the Republican Party. We have always recognized Communism to be a world conspiracy against freedom and religion. We never compromised with Communism and we have fought to expose it and to eliminate it in government and American life.

Civil Rights. We believe that it is the primary responsibility of each State to order and control its own domestic institutions, and this power, reserved to the states, is essential to the maintenance of our Federal Republic. However, we believe that the Federal Government should take supplemental action within its constitutional jurisdiction to oppose discrimination against race, religion or national origin.

We will prove our good faith by:

Appointing qualified persons, without distinction of race, religion or national origin, to responsible positions in the Government.

Federal action toward the elimination of lynching.

Federal action toward the elimination of poll taxes as a prerequisite to voting.

Appropriate action to end segregation in the District of Columbia.

Enacting Federal legislation to further just and equitable treatment in the area of discriminatory employment practices. Federal action should not duplicate state efforts to end such practices; should not set up another huge bureaucracy.

Labor. We favor the retention of the Taft-Hartley Act.

. . . We urge the adoption of such amendments to the Taft-Hartley Act as time and experience show to be desirable, and which further protect the rights of labor, management and the public.

DEMOCRATS

The Democrats held their 1952 convention in Chicago in late July. The convention lasted six days, the longest by either party in the post–World War II years. The proceedings were enlivened by disputes over credentials and a party loyalty pledge and a wide-open race for the presidential nomination.

The legitimately selected Texas delegation, dominated by the Dixiecrat wing of the state party, was challenged by a delegation loyal to the national party, but chosen in a rump assembly. Without a roll-call vote, the convention approved the credentials of the Dixiecrat-oriented delegates, although their seating was protested by Northern liberals.

The Dixiecrat bolt of 1948 resulted in the introduction of a party loyalty pledge at the 1952 convention. The resolution, introduced by Sen. Blair Moody of Michigan, proposed that no delegate be seated who would not assure the credentials committee that he would work to have the Democratic national ticket placed on the ballot in his state under the party's name. This resolution was aimed at several southern states that had listed the Thurmond-Wright ticket under the Democratic Party label on their state ballots in 1948.

Sen. Spessard L. Holland of Florida introduced a substitute resolution that simply declared it would be "honorable" for each delegate to adhere to the decisions reached in the convention. Holland's resolution, however, was defeated and Moody's was approved, both by voice votes.

The report of the credentials committee listed three southern states—Louisiana, South Carolina, and Virginia—that declined to abide by the Moody resolution. The question of their seating rights came to a head during the roll call for presidential nominations, when Virginia questioned its own status in the convention. A motion to seat the Virginia delegation in spite of its nonobservance of the resolution was presented for a vote. Although not agreeing to the pledge, the chairman of the Virginia delegation indicated that the problem prompting the Moody resolution was covered by state law. After a long, confusing roll call, interrupted frequently by demands to poll individual delegates, the motion to seat the Virginia delegation passed, 650½ to 518. *(Table, p. 618.)*

After efforts to adjourn were defeated, the Louisiana and South Carolina delegations offered assurances similar to those presented by Virginia and were seated by a voice vote.

Eleven names were placed in nomination for the presidency, although the favorite of most party leaders, Illinois governor Adlai E. Stevenson, was a reluctant candidate. Stevenson expressed interest only in running for reelection as governor, but a draft-Stevenson movement developed and gained strength quickly as the convention proceeded.

Sen. Estes Kefauver of Tennessee, a powerful vote-getter in the primaries, was the leader on the first ballot, with 340 votes. He was followed by Stevenson with 273; Sen. Richard B. Russell of Georgia, the southern favorite, with 268; and W. Averell Harriman of New York with 123½.

The second ballot saw gains by the three front-runners, with Kefauver's vote rising to 362½, Stevenson's to 324½ and Russell's to 294. A recess was taken during which Harriman and Massachusetts' favorite son, Gov. Paul A. Dever, both withdrew in favor of Stevenson.

The Illinois governor won a narrow majority on the third ballot, receiving 617½ of the 1,230 convention votes. Kefauver finished with 275½ and Russell with 261. The selection of Stevenson represented the first success for a presidential draft movement of a reluctant candidate since the nomination of James A. Garfield by the Republicans in 1880. *(Table, p. 618.)*

For vice president, Stevenson chose Sen. John J. Sparkman of Alabama, who was nominated by acclamation.

Although a reluctant candidate, Stevenson promised the delegates a fighting campaign but warned: "Better we lose the election than mislead the people; and better we lose than misgovern the people."

The Democratic platform was adopted without the rancor that had accompanied consideration of the party platform four years earlier. The document was approved by a voice vote, although both the Georgia and Mississippi delegations asked that they be recorded in opposition.

The platform promised extension and improvement of New Deal and Fair Deal policies that had been proposed and enacted over the previous 20 years. The party's foremost goal was stated to be "peace with honor," which could be achieved by support for a strengthened United Nations, coupled with the policy of collective security in the form of American assistance for allies around the world. The peaceful use of atomic energy was pledged, as were efforts to establish an international control system. However, the platform also promised the use of atomic weapons, if needed, for national defense.

The civil rights plank was nearly identical to the one that appeared in the 1948 platform. Federal legislation was called for to guarantee equal rights in voting participation, employment opportunity, and personal security.

The platform called for extending and changing the Social Security system. A plank favored elimination of the work clause so that the elderly could collect benefits and still work.

Political reform was recommended that would require the disclosure of campaign expenses in federal elections.

The Democrats and Republicans took different stands on several major domestic issues. The Democrats favored repeal of the Taft-Hartley Act; the Republicans proposed to retain the act but make modifications where necessary. The Democrats advocated closing tax loopholes and, after defense needs were met, reducing taxes. The Republicans called for tax reduction based on a cut in government spending. In education, the Democrats favored federal assistance to state and local units; the Republicans viewed education solely as the responsibility of local and state governments.

The Democrats favored continuation of federal power projects, while the Republicans opposed "all-powerful federal socialistic valley authorities."

Both parties favored a parity price program for farmers. The Democrats advocated a mandatory price support program for basic agricultural products at not less than 90 percent of parity, and the Republicans proposing a program that would establish "full parity prices for all farm products."

Following are excerpts from the Democratic platform of 1952:

Atomic Energy. In the field of atomic energy, we pledge ourselves:
(1) to maintain vigorous and non-partisan civilian administrations, with adequate security safeguards;
(2) to promote the development of nuclear energy for peaceful purposes in the interests of America and mankind;
(3) to build all the atomic and hydrogen firepower needed to defend our country, deter aggression, and promote world peace;
(4) to exert every effort to bring about bona fide international control and inspection of all atomic weapons.

Civil Rights. We will continue our efforts to eradicate discrimination based on race, religion or national origin. . . .
We are proud of the progress that has been made in securing equality of treatment and opportunity in the Nation's armed forces and the civil service and all areas under Federal jurisdiction. . . .
At the same time, we favor Federal legislation effectively to secure these rights to everyone:
(1) the right to equal opportunity for employment;
(2) the right to security of persons;
(3) the right to full and equal participation in the Nation's political life, free from arbitrary restraints.

Agriculture. We will continue to protect the producers of basic agricultural commodities under the terms of a mandatory price support program at not less than ninety percent of parity. We continue to advocate practical methods for extending price supports to other storables and to the producers of perishable commodities, which account for three-fourths of all farm income.

Campaign Finance. We advocate new legislation to provide effective regulation and full disclosure of campaign expenditures in elections to Federal office, including political advertising from any source.

Labor. We strongly advocate the repeal of the Taft-Hartley Act.

Tax Reform. We believe in fair and equitable taxation. We oppose a Federal general sales tax. We adhere to the principle of ability to pay. We have enacted an emergency excess profits tax to prevent profiteering from the defense program and have vigorously attacked special tax privileges. . . . As rapidly as defense requirements permit, we favor reducing taxes, especially for people with lower incomes. . . .

Justice requires the elimination of tax loopholes which favor special groups. We pledge continued efforts to the elimination of remaining loopholes.

Social Security. We favor the complete elimination of the work clause for the reason that those contributing to the Social Security program should be permitted to draw benefits, upon reaching the age of eligibility, and still continue to work.

Education. Local, State and Federal governments have shared responsibility to contribute appropriately to the pressing needs of our educational system. We urge that Federal contributions be made available to State and local units which adhere to basic minimum standards.

The Federal Government should not dictate nor control educational policy.

1956 Conventions

PRESIDENTIAL CANDIDATES

Adlai E. Stevenson
Democrat

Dwight D. Eisenhower
Republican

DEMOCRATS

Both parties held their conventions in August, the latest date ever for the Republicans and the latest for the Democrats since the wartime convention of 1864. For the first time since 1888 the date of the Democratic convention preceded that of the Republicans. The Democrats met in mid-August in Chicago with an allotment of 1,372 votes, the largest in party history. The increased allotment was the result of a new distribution formula, which for the first time rewarded states for electing Democratic governors and senators in addition to supporting the party's presidential candidate.

A provision of the convention call handled the party loyalty question, a thorny issue at the 1952 convention, by assuming that, in the absence of a challenge, any delegate would be understood to have the best interests of the party at heart. Another provision of the call threatened any national committeeman who did not support the party's national ticket with removal from the Democratic National Committee.

In an unusual occurrence, nominating speeches were delivered by a past and a future president for men who would not attain the office themselves. Sen. John F. Kennedy of Massachu-

setts placed Adlai E. Stevenson's name in nomination, while former president Harry S. Truman seconded the nomination of New York governor W. Averell Harriman. Truman criticized Stevenson as a "defeatist," but was countered by Eleanor Roosevelt, who appeared before the convention in support of the former Illinois governor.

In spite of the oratorical byplay, Stevenson was in good position to win the nomination before the convention even began, having eliminated his principal rival, Sen. Estes Kefauver of Tennessee, in the primaries. Stevenson won a majority on the first ballot, receiving 905½ votes to easily defeat Harriman, who had 210. Sen. Lyndon B. Johnson of Texas finished third, with 80 votes. Upon completion of the roll call, a motion was approved to make Stevenson's nomination unanimous. *(Table, p. 619.)*

In an unusual move, Stevenson announced that he would not personally select his running mate but would leave the choice to the convention. Stevenson's desire for an open selection was designed to contrast with the expected cut-and-dried nature of the upcoming Republican convention. But the unusual move caught both delegates and prospective candidates off guard.

Numerous delegations passed on the first ballot, and upon completion of the roll call votes were scattered among thirteen different candidates. When the vote totals were announced at the end of the roll call, Kefauver led with 483½ votes, followed by Kennedy with 304, Sen. Albert A. Gore of Tennessee with 178, Mayor Robert F. Wagner of New York City with 162½, and Sen. Hubert H. Humphrey of Minnesota with 134½. A total of 687 votes were needed to nominate.

With a coalition that included most of the southern and eastern delegates, Kennedy drew into the lead on the second ballot. After the roll call but before the chair recognized vote changes, the totals stood: Kennedy, 618; Kefauver, 551½; Gore, 110½. Kentucky, the first state to be recognized, shifted its 30 votes to Kennedy, leaving the thirty-nine-year-old senator fewer than 40 votes short of the nomination.

But Gore was recognized next and began a bandwagon for Kefauver by withdrawing in favor of his Tennessee colleague. Other states followed Gore's lead, and at the conclusion of the vote shifts Kefauver had a clear majority. The final tally was Kefauver, 755½ and Kennedy, 589. Kennedy moved that his opponent's nomination be made unanimous.

Ironically, Kefauver won a majority of the votes in only two states in his home region, Tennessee and Florida. His strength lay in midwestern and western delegations.

As in 1948 platform debate focused on the civil rights issue. A Minnesota member of the platform committee introduced a minority report that advocated a civil rights plank stronger than that in the majority report. The plank presented by the platform committee pledged to carry out Supreme Court decisions on desegregation, but not through the use of force. The party promised to continue to work for equal rights in voting, employment, personal security, and education. The Minnesota substitute was more specific, as it favored federal legislation to achieve equal voting rights and employment opportunities and to guarantee personal safety. The minority plank also favored more rigid enforcement of civil rights legislation. Although several states clamored for a roll-call vote, the chair took a voice vote, which went against the Minnesota substitute.

The entire platform was the longest yet approved by a Democratic convention, about 12,000 words. The document was divided into eleven sections, the first dealing with defense and foreign policy and the remainder with domestic issues.

The platform described President Eisenhower as a "political amateur . . . dominated . . . by special privilege." It applauded the legislative accomplishments of the Democratic Congress elected in 1954 and proposed a continuation of the social and economic legislation begun during the New Deal.

The foreign policy of the Eisenhower administration was criticized in a plank that accused the Republicans of cutting funds for the military in an attempt to balance the budget. The Democrats declared that the United States must have the strongest military in the world to discourage aggression by America's enemies. The foreign policy plank also pledged to strengthen the United Nations as a peacekeeping organization and promised to work diligently for worldwide disarmament.

The platform blamed the Republicans for allowing big business to dominate the economy and promised tax relief and other government assistance to help small business. The Democrats advocated repeal of the Taft-Hartley Act, as the party had done in every platform since 1948, and favored an increase in the minimum wage. Tax reductions were proposed for lower-income taxpayers, and an increase of at least $200 in the personal tax exemption was recommended.

For farmers, the Democrats proposed price supports at 90 percent of parity on basic crops, as opposed to the Republican program of flexible price supports.

For the first time since the beginning of the New Deal, the Democratic platform mentioned the importance of states' rights. The party also reiterated its position on education, which advocated federal assistance, but stated that ultimate control of the schools lay in the hands of state and local governments.

In political reform the platform proposed restrictions on government secrecy and repeated the party's call for the passage of an equal rights amendment.

Following are excerpts from the Democratic platform of 1956:

Foreign Policy. *The Failure at Home.* Political considerations of budget balancing and tax reduction now come before the wants of our national security and the needs of our Allies. The Republicans have slashed our own armed strength, weakened our capacity to deal with military threats, stifled our air force, starved our army and weakened our capacity to deal with aggression of any sort save by retreat or by the alternatives, "massive retaliation" and global atomic war. Yet, while our troubles mount, they tell us our prestige was never higher, they tell us we were never more secure.

Disarmament. To eliminate the danger of atomic war, a universal, effective and enforced disarmament system must be the goal of responsible men and women everywhere. So long as we lack enforceable international control of weapons, we must maintain armed strength to avoid war. But technological advances in the field of nuclear weapons make disarmament an ever more urgent problem. Time and distance can never again protect any nation of the world.

Labor. We unequivocally advocate repeal of the Taft-Hartley Act. The Act must be repealed because State "right-to-work" laws have their genesis in its discriminatory anti-labor provisions. . . .

The Taft-Hartley Act has been proven to be inadequate, unworkable and unfair. It interferes in an arbitrary manner with collective bargaining, causing imbalance in the relationship between management and labor.

Agriculture. Undertake immediately by appropriate action to endeavor to regain the full 100 percent of parity the farmers received under the Democratic Administrations. We will achieve this by means of supports on basic commodities at 90 percent of parity and by means of commodity loans, direct purchases, direct payments to producers, marketing agreements and orders, production adjustments, or a combination of these, including legislation, to bring order and stability into the relationship between the producer, the processor and the consumer.

Education. We are now faced with shortages of educational facilities that threaten national security, economic prosperity and human well-being. The resources of our States and localities are already strained to the limit. Federal aid and action should be provided, within the traditional framework of State and local control.

Tax Reform. We favor realistic tax adjustments, giving first consideration to small independent business and the small individual taxpayer.

Lower-income families need tax relief; only a Democratic victory will assure this. We favor an increase in the present personal tax exemption of $600 to a minimum of at least $800.

Government Secrecy. *Freedom of Information.* During recent years there has developed a practice on the part of Federal agencies to delay and withhold information which is needed by Congress and the general public to make important decisions affecting their lives and destinies. We believe that this trend toward secrecy in Government should be reversed and that the Federal Government should return to its basic tradition of exchanging and promoting the freest flow of information possible in those unclassified areas where secrets involving weapons development and bona fide national security are not involved.

States' Rights. While we recognize the existence of honest differences of opinion as to the true location of a Constitutional line of demarcation between the Federal Government and the States, the Democratic Party expressly recognizes the vital importance of the respective States in our Federal Union. The Party of Jefferson and Jackson pledges itself to continued support of those sound principles of local government which will best serve the welfare of our people and the safety of our democratic rights.

Civil Rights. We are proud of the record of the Democratic Party in securing equality of treatment and opportunity in the nation's armed forces, the Civil Service, and in all areas under Federal jurisdiction. The Democratic Party pledges itself to continue its efforts to eliminate illegal discriminations of all kinds, in relation to (1) full rights to vote, (2) full rights to engage in gainful occupations, (3) full rights to enjoy security of the person, and (4) full rights to education in all publicly supported institutions.

Recent decisions of the Supreme Court of the United States relating to segregation in publicly supported schools and elsewhere have brought consequences of vast importance to our Nation as a whole and especially to communities directly affected. We reject all proposals for the use of force to interfere with the orderly determination of these matters by the courts.

REPUBLICANS

The Republicans opened their convention in San Francisco three days after the close of the Democratic convention in Chicago. In contrast to the turbulent convention of their adversaries, the Republicans' renomination of Dwight D. Eisenhower and Richard Nixon was a formality. The only possible obstacle to Eisenhower's candidacy was his health, but by August 1956 his recovery from a heart attack and an ileitis operation was complete enough to allow him to seek a second term. On the convention's single roll call for president, Eisenhower received all 1,323 votes. *(Table, p. 619.)*

What drama occurred at the Republican convention surrounded the vice-presidential nomination. Several weeks before the opening of the convention, former Minnesota governor Harold Stassen, the disarmament adviser to Eisenhower, had begun a movement to replace Vice President Nixon with Massachusetts governor Christian A. Herter. However, with lack of interest from party leaders, this movement petered out. At the convention both Herter and Stassen gave nominating speeches for Nixon. During the roll call, a commotion was caused by a Nebraska delegate, who attempted to nominate "Joe Smith." After some discussion, it was determined that "Joe Smith" was a fictitious individual, and the offending delegate was escorted from the hall. On the one ballot for vice president, a unanimous vote was recorded for Nixon.

While no opposition to the platform was expressed on the floor of the convention, several southern delegates were unhappy with the civil rights plank and withdrew from the convention. The plank in question listed advances in desegregation under the Republican administration, voiced acceptance of the Supreme Court ruling on school desegregation, and pledged to enforce existing civil rights statutes.

The platform as a whole was slightly longer than the Democratic document and was dedicated to Eisenhower and "the youth of America." Unlike the Democratic platform, which began with a discussion of foreign policy and national defense, the first issue pursued by the Republicans was the economy.

The Eisenhower administration was praised for balancing the budget, reducing taxes, and halting inflation. The platform promised continued balanced budgets, gradual reduction of the national debt, and cuts in government spending consistent with the maintenance of a strong military. Two measures favored by the Democrats, tax relief for small businesses and tax reductions for low-income and middle-income families, were both mentioned as secondary economic goals in the Republican platform.

The labor plank advocated revision but not repeal of the Taft-Hartley Act. The agricultural section favored elimination of price-depressing surpluses and continuation of the flexible price-support program. As they had for the past quarter century, the Republicans joined the Democrats in recommending passage of an equal rights amendment.

The foreign policy section of the Republican platform praised the Eisenhower administration for ending the Korean War, stemming the worldwide advance of communism and entering new collective security agreements. The plank also emphasized the necessity of a bipartisan foreign policy. The "preservation" of Israel was viewed as an "important tenet of American foreign policy," a notable difference from the Democratic platform, which took a more even-handed approach toward both Israel and the Arab states.

The national defense section emphasized the nation's possession of "the strongest striking force in the world," a rebuttal to Democratic charges that the Republicans had jeopardized the efficiency of the armed forces in an effort to balance the budget.

Following are excerpts from the Republican platform of 1956:

Economy. We pledge to pursue the following objectives:
Further reductions in Government spending as recommended in the Hoover Commission Report, without weakening the support of a superior defense program or depreciating the quality of essential services of government to our people.

Continued balancing of the budget, to assure the financial strength of the country which is so vital to the struggle of the free world in its battle against Communism; and to maintain the purchasing power of a sound dollar, and the value of savings, pensions and insurance.

Gradual reduction of the national debt.

Then, insofar as consistent with a balanced budget, we pledge to work toward these additional objectives:

Further reductions in taxes with particular consideration for low and middle income families.

Initiation of a sound policy of tax reductions which will encourage small independent businesses to modernize and progress.

Labor. Revise and improve the Taft-Hartley Act so as to protect more effectively the rights of labor unions, management, the individual worker, and the public. The protection of the right of workers to organize into unions and to bargain collectively is the firm and permanent policy of the Eisenhower Administration.

Agriculture. This program must be versatile and flexible to meet effectively the impact of rapidly changing conditions. It does not envision making farmers dependent upon direct governmental payments for their incomes. Our objective is markets which return full parity to our farm and ranch people when they sell their products.

Civil Rights. The Republican Party accepts the decision of the U.S. Supreme Court that racial discrimination in publicly supported schools must be progressively eliminated. We concur in the conclusion of the Supreme Court that its decision directing school desegregation should be accomplished with "all deliberate speed" locally through Federal District Courts. The implementation order of the Supreme Court recognizes the complex and acutely emotional problems created by its decision in certain sections of our country where racial patterns have been developed in accordance with prior and long-standing decisions of the same tribunal.

We believe that true progress can be attained through intelligent study, understanding, education and good will. Use of force or violence by any group or agency will tend only to worsen the many problems inherent in the situation. This progress must be encouraged and the work of the courts supported in every legal manner by all branches of the Federal Government to the end that the constitutional ideal of equality before the law, regardless of race, creed or color, will be steadily achieved.

Foreign Policy. The advance of Communism has been checked, and, at key points, thrown back. The once-monolithic structure of International Communism, denied the stimulant of successive conquests, has shown hesitancy both internally and abroad.

National Defense. We *have* the strongest striking force in the world—in the air—on the sea—and a magnificent supporting land force in our Army and Marine Corps.

Israel. We regard the preservation of Israel as an important tenet of American foreign policy. We are determined that the integrity of an independent Jewish State shall be maintained. We shall support the independence of Israel against armed aggression. The best hope for peace in the Middle East lies in the United Nations. We pledge our continued efforts to eliminate the obstacles to a lasting peace in this area.

1960 Conventions

PRESIDENTIAL CANDIDATES

John F. Kennedy
Democrat

Richard M. Nixon
Republican

DEMOCRATS

For the first time, a national political convention was held in Los Angeles. More than 4,000 delegates and alternates converged on the California metropolis in July to select the Democratic standard-bearers for 1960. The delegate-allocation method had been changed since 1956 by the Democratic National Committee, from a formula that included Democratic voting strength to a system that emphasized population only. No states lost seats, but the new formula tended to strengthen populous northern states.

The early sessions of the convention dealt with rules and credentials. The convention rules, approved without debate, included the compromise loyalty pledge adopted by the 1956 con-

vention. The only credentials dispute involved two contesting delegations from the Commonwealth of Puerto Rico. By a voice vote, the convention agreed to seat both delegations while splitting the vote of the Commonwealth.

The front-runner for the presidential nomination was Massachusetts senator John F. Kennedy, whose success in the primaries and support from many of the party's urban leaders put him on the verge of a nominating majority. His principal rival was Senate Majority Leader Lyndon B. Johnson of Texas, although the favorite of the convention galleries was Adlai E. Stevenson, the party's unsuccessful standard-bearer in 1952 and 1956. Johnson challenged Kennedy to a debate, which was held before a joint gathering of the Massachusetts and Texas delegations. Coming the day before the balloting, the debate had little effect on the ultimate outcome.

Nine men were nominated, but Kennedy received a clear majority on the first ballot. At the end of the roll call, the Massachusetts senator had 806 votes, to easily outdistance Johnson, who received 409. Sen. Stuart Symington of Missouri was a distant third with 86 votes, and Stevenson followed with 79½. A motion to make Kennedy's nomination unanimous was approved by a voice vote. Kennedy's selection marked the first time since 1920 that a senator had been nominated for the presidency by Democrats or Republicans and the first time since 1928 that a Roman Catholic had been represented on a national ticket of one of the two major parties. (*Table, p. 620.*)

Kennedy surprised some supporters and political observers by choosing his erstwhile adversary, Lyndon Johnson, as his running mate. A motion to nominate Johnson by acclamation was approved by a voice vote.

Kennedy delivered his acceptance speech to 80,000 spectators at the Los Angeles Coliseum. He envisioned the United States as "on the edge of a new frontier—the frontier of the 1960s—a frontier of unknown opportunities and perils—a frontier of unfulfilled hopes and threats," adding that this "new frontier . . . is not a set of promises—it is a set of challenges."

The Democratic platform was easily the longest yet written by the party, about 20,000 words. The platform itself was approved by a voice vote, although the civil rights and fiscal responsibility planks were debated on the convention floor, and roll-call votes had been taken in committee.

Regional hearings had been held by subcommittees of the 108-member platform committee in the spring, but votes on controversial issues were not taken by the full committee until the convention. A plank that urged elimination of the immigration quota system was approved, 66 to 28, with opposition led by Sen. James O. Eastland of Mississippi. An agricultural plank recommending price supports at 90 percent of parity was passed, 66 to 22, with opponents claiming that it was a restatement of the liberal program proposed by the National Farmers Union. A motion to reconsider the plank was defeated, 38 to 32. An Eastland motion to delete condemnation of "right-to-work" laws was defeated without a recorded vote.

The civil rights plank caused the greatest controversy. Sen. Sam J. Ervin Jr. of North Carolina introduced motions to delete portions that proposed establishing a Fair Employment Practices Commission, continuing the Civil Rights Commission as a permanent agency, granting the attorney general the power to file civil injunction suits to prevent discrimination, and setting 1963 as the deadline for the initiation of school desegregation plans. Ervin's motions were defeated by a voice vote, and the entire plank was approved, 66 to 24.

Delegates from nine southern states signed a statement that repudiated the civil rights plank. Led by Georgia Democratic Chairman James H. Gray and Ervin, these nine states introduced a minority report on the convention floor calling for elimination of the platform's civil rights plank. After an hour's debate, the minority report was rejected by a voice vote.

As approved by the convention, the platform began with a discussion of foreign policy. The Democrats blamed the Republican administration for allowing the United States military strength to deteriorate. The national defense plank declared there was a "missile gap, space gap, and limited-war gap," and promised to improve America's military position so that it would be second to none. The Democrats recommended creation of "a national peace agency for disarmament planning and research." The money saved by international disarmament, the plank stated, could be used to attack world poverty.

Foreign military aid was viewed as a short-range necessity that should be replaced by economic aid "as rapidly as security considerations permit." At the same time, the platform proposed that development programs be placed on a "long-term basis to permit more effective planning."

The Democrats' economic plank called for an average national growth rate of 5 percent annually. Economic growth at this rate would create needed tax revenue, the Democrats believed, which—coupled with cuts in government waste, closing of tax loopholes and more extensive efforts to catch tax evaders—would help balance the budget. The Democrats promised to use measures such as public works projects and temporary tax cuts to combat recessions or depressions.

The platform promised an increase in the minimum wage to $1.25 an hour and pledged to extend coverage to include more workers. There was a pledge to amend the Social Security program so the elderly could continue working without sacrificing basic benefits.

Equal rights legislation was favored, although the platform did not call for passage of a constitutional amendment of 1960.

Following are excerpts from the Democratic platform of 1960:

National Defense. Our military position today is measured in terms of gaps—missile gap, space gap, limited-war gap. . . .

This is the strength that must be erected:

1. Deterrent military power such that the Soviet and Chinese leaders will have no doubt that an attack on the United States would surely be followed by their own destruction.

2. Balanced conventional military forces which will permit a response graded to the intensity of any threats of aggressive force.

3. Continuous modernization of these forces through intensified research and development, including essential programs now slowed down, terminated, suspended or neglected for lack of budgetary support.

Disarmament. This requires a national peace agency for disarmament planning and research to muster the scientific ingenuity, coordination, continuity, and seriousness of purpose which are now lacking in our arms control efforts. . . .

As world-wide disarmament proceeds, it will free vast resources for a new international attack on the problem of world poverty.

Immigration. The national-origins quota system of limiting immigration contradicts the founding principles of this nation. It is inconsistent with our belief in the rights of man. This system was instituted after World War I as a policy of deliberate discrimination by a Republican Administration and Congress.

Foreign Aid. Where military assistance remains essential for the common defense, we shall see that the requirements are fully met. But as rapidly as security considerations permit, we will replace tanks with tractors, bombers with bulldozers, and tacticians with technicians.

Civil Rights. We believe that every school district affected by the Supreme Court's school desegregation decision should submit a plan providing for at least first-step compliance by 1963, the 100th anniversary of the Emancipation Proclamation.

For this and for the protection of all other Constitutional rights of Americans, the Attorney General should be empowered and directed to file civil injunction suits in Federal courts to prevent the denial of any civil right on grounds of race, creed or color.

Economy. We Democrats believe that our economy can and must grow at an average rate of 5 percent annually, almost twice as fast as our average annual rate since 1953. We pledge ourselves to policies that will achieve this goal without inflation. . . .

The policies of a Democratic Administration to restore economic growth will reduce current unemployment to a minimum.

Tax Reform. We shall close the loopholes in the tax laws by which certain privileged groups legally escape their fair share of taxation.

Labor. We pledge to raise the minimum wage to $1.25 an hour and to extend coverage to several million workers not now protected.

Agriculture. The Democratic Administration will work to bring about full parity income for farmers in all segments of agriculture by helping them to balance farm production with the expanding needs of the nation and the world.

Measures to this end include production and marketing quotas measured in terms of barrels, bushels and bales, loans on basic commodities at not less than 90 percent of parity, production payments, commodity purchases, and marketing orders and agreements.

Government Spending. The Democratic Party believes that state and local governments are strengthened—not weakened—by financial assistance from the Federal Government. We will extend such aid without impairing local administration through unnecessary Federal interference or red tape.

REPUBLICANS

On July 25, ten days after the close of the Democratic convention, the Republican convention opened in Chicago. Although Vice President Richard M. Nixon had a lock on the presidential nomination, the party's two major figures four years later, Arizona senator Barry Goldwater and New York governor Nelson A. Rockefeller, both had major roles in convention activities.

Both Goldwater and Rockefeller announced that they did not want their names placed in nomination, but the Arizona delegation disregarded Goldwater's request and nominated him anyway. In a convention speech, the Arizona senator withdrew his name and went on to advise conservative Republicans to work within the party: "Let's grow up conservatives. . . . If we want to take this party back—and I think we can someday—let's get to work."

On the roll call that followed, Nixon was a nearly unanimous choice, receiving 1,321 votes to 10 for Goldwater (all from Louisiana). On a voice vote, Nixon's nomination was made unanimous. *(Table, p. 620.)*

Nixon reportedly wanted Rockefeller as his running mate, but was unable to persuade the New Yorker to join the ticket. The Republican standard-bearer subsequently turned to United Nations Ambassador Henry Cabot Lodge Jr., a former senator from Massachusetts who had been beaten for reelection by John Kennedy in 1952. On the vice-presidential ballot, Lodge received all but one vote. The lone dissenter, a Texas delegate, initially abstained but switched his vote to Lodge at the end of the roll call.

In his acceptance speech, Nixon promised to campaign in all fifty states and rebutted a theme in Kennedy's acceptance speech. "Our primary aim must be not to help government, but to help people—to help people attain the life they deserve," said Nixon.

Much of the drama of the 1960 Republican convention surrounded the party platform. And the highlight of the platform maneuvering was a late-night meeting involving Nixon and Rockefeller, held at Rockefeller's New York City apartment two days before the opening of the convention. The meeting, a secret to most of Nixon's closest aides, resulted in a fourteen-point agreement between the two Republican leaders on major issues contained in the platform. The agreement, informally dubbed the "compact of Fifth Avenue," was issued by Rockefeller, who declared that the meeting was held at Nixon's insistence.

Half of the fourteen points dealt with national security and foreign policy. The other half discussed domestic issues, including government reorganization, civil rights, agriculture, economic growth, and medical care for the elderly. Although not markedly different in wording from the draft of the platform committee, the "compact" expressed a tone of urgency that was not evident in the draft.

The Nixon-Rockefeller agreement was made with the knowledge of the platform committee chairman, Charles H. Percy of Illinois, but was greeted with hostility by many members of the committee and by party conservatives. Goldwater termed the "compact" a "surrender" and the "Munich of the Republican Party" that would ensure the party's defeat that fall.

The two issues of greatest controversy were civil rights and national defense. The original civil rights plank, drafted by the platform committee, did not express support for civil rights demonstrations or promise federal efforts to gain job equality for blacks. The Nixon-Rockefeller agreement did both. Nixon threatened to wage a floor fight if the stronger civil rights plank was not inserted in the platform. By a vote of 50 to 35, the platform committee agreed to reconsider the original civil rights plank; by a margin of 56 to 28, the stronger plank was approved.

With the approval of both Rockefeller and President Dwight D. Eisenhower, several changes were made in the national security plank that emphasized the necessity of quickly upgrading America's armed forces. The platform committee approved reconsideration of the original defense plank by a voice vote, and the whole platform was adopted unanimously.

With disagreements resolved in the committee, there were neither minority reports nor floor fights. The convention approved the platform by a voice vote.

In its final form, the Republican platform was shorter than its Democratic counterpart, although still nearly 15,000 words in length. The foreign policy section asserted that the nation's greatest task was "to nullify the Soviet conspiracy." The platform claimed that America's military strength was second to none but, in line with the Nixon-Rockefeller "compact," indicated that improvements were needed in some parts of the armed forces.

The Republicans joined their Democratic opposition in favoring a workable disarmament program but did not advocate a phaseout of foreign military aid, as did the Democrats. However, the Republicans proposed a change in the funding of foreign aid that emphasized "the increasing use of private capital and government loans, rather than outright grants."

The Republicans agreed with the Democrats that the nation should experience more rapid economic growth but did not adopt the 5 percent annual growth rate favored by the Democrats. The Republicans stressed the virtues of a balanced budget and regarded free enterprise, rather than massive government programs, as the key to economic growth.

As in 1956, the two parties differed on farm price supports. The Republicans supported a program of flexible support payments, while the Democrats recommended setting price supports at 90 percent of parity.

Both parties proposed allowing individuals to work beyond their mandatory retirement age, although the Democrats tied their proposal to amendment of the Social Security program.

The Republicans did not urge elimination of the immigration quota system, as did their opponents, but they favored overhaul of the system to allow an increase in immigration.

On the issue of equal rights, the Republicans continued to favor passage of a constitutional amendment. The Democrats had backed away from this position, which they had held in earlier platforms, instead proposing the passage of equal rights legislation in Congress.

As they had since the beginning of the New Deal, the Republican and Democratic platforms differed noticeably as to the extent and desirability of federal spending. The Democrats viewed federal assistance to state and local governments as beneficial. The Republicans believed the federal government could help meet the problems of urban growth, but that state and local governments should administer all the programs they could best handle.

Following are excerpts from the Republican platform of 1960:

National Defense. The future of freedom depends heavily upon America's military might and that of her allies. Under the Eisenhower-Nixon Administration, our military might has been forged into a power second to none. . . .

The strategic imperatives of our national defense policy are these:

A second-strike capability, that is, a nuclear retaliatory power that can survive surprise attack, strike back, and destroy any possible enemy.

Highly mobile and versatile forces, including forces deployed, to deter or check local aggressions and "brush fire wars" which might bring on all-out nuclear war.

Disarmament. We are similarly ready to negotiate and to institute realistic methods and safeguards for disarmament, and for the suspension of nuclear tests. We advocate an early agreement by all nations to forego nuclear tests in the atmosphere, and the suspension of other tests as verification techniques permit.

Immigration. The annual number of immigrants we accept be at least doubled.

Obsolete immigration laws be amended by abandoning the outdated 1920 census data as a base and substituting the 1960 census.

The guidelines of our immigration policy be based upon judgment of the individual merit of each applicant for admission and citizenship.

Foreign Aid. Agreeable to the developing nations, we would join with them in inviting countries with advanced economies to share with us a proportionate part of the capital and technical aid required. We would emphasize the increasing use of private capital and government loans, rather than outright grants, as a means of fostering independence and mutual respect.

Civil Rights. *Voting.* We pledge:
Continued vigorous enforcement of the civil rights laws to guarantee the right to vote to all citizens in all areas of the country. . . .
Public Schools. We pledge:
The Department of Justice will continue its vigorous support of court orders for school desegregation . . .

We oppose the pretense of fixing a target date 3 years from now for the mere submission of plans for school desegregation. Slow-moving school districts would construe it as a three-year moratorium during which progress would cease, postponing until 1963 the legal process to enforce compliance. We believe that each of the pending court actions should proceed as the Supreme Court has directed and that in no district should there be any such delay.
Employment. We pledge:
Continued support for legislation to establish a Commission on Equal Job Opportunity to make permanent and to expand with legislative backing the excellent work being performed by the President's Committee on Government Contracts. . . .
Housing. We pledge:
Action to prohibit discrimination in housing constructed with the aid of federal subsidies.

Economy. We reject the concept of artificial growth forced by massive new federal spending and loose money policies. The only effective way to accelerate economic growth is to increase the traditional strengths of our free economy—initiative and investment, productivity and efficiency.

Agriculture. Use of price supports at levels best fitted to specific commodities, in order to widen markets, ease production controls, and help achieve increased farm family income.

Government Reorganization. The President must continue to be able to reorganize and streamline executive operations to keep the executive branch capable of responding effectively to rapidly changing conditions in both foreign and domestic fields. . . .

Government Spending. Vigorous state and local governments are a vital part of our federal union. The federal government should leave to state and local governments those programs and problems which they can best handle and tax sources adequate to finance them. We must continue to improve liaison between federal, state and local governments. We believe that the federal government, when appropriate, should render significant assistance in dealing with our urgent problems of urban growth and change. No vast new bureaucracy is needed to achieve this objective.

1964 Conventions

PRESIDENTIAL CANDIDATES

Barry Goldwater
Republican

Lyndon B. Johnson
Democrat

REPUBLICANS

Division between the party's conservative and moderate wings, muted during the Eisenhower administration, exploded at the Republicans' July 13–16 convention in San Francisco.

Although Sen. Barry Goldwater of Arizona, the hero of Republican conservatives, had a commanding lead as the convention opened, he was vigorously challenged by Pennsylvania governor William W. Scranton, the belated leader of the moderate forces. Two days before the presidential balloting, a letter in Scranton's name was sent to Goldwater. It charged the Goldwater organization with regarding the delegates as "little more than a flock of chickens whose necks will be wrung at will." The message continued, describing Goldwater's political philosophy as a "crazy-quilt collection of absurd and dangerous positions." The letter concluded by challenging the Arizona senator to a debate before the convention. Although the message was written by Scranton's staff without his knowledge, the Pennsylvania governor supported the substance of the letter. Goldwater declined the invitation to debate.

Although seven names were placed in nomination for the presidency, the outcome was a foregone conclusion. Goldwater was an easy winner on the first ballot, receiving 883 of the 1,308 votes. Scranton was a distant second with 214 votes; New York governor Nelson A. Rockefeller followed with 114. Scranton moved that Goldwater's nomination be made unanimous, and his motion was approved by a voice vote. Support for the major moderate candidates, Scranton and Rockefeller, was centered in the Northeast. Goldwater had an overwhelming majority of the delegates from other regions. *(Table, p. 621.)*

As his running mate, Goldwater selected the Republican national chairman, Rep. William E. Miller of New York. On disclosing his choice of Miller, Goldwater stated that "one of the reasons I chose Miller is that he drives Johnson nuts." On the vice-presidential roll call, the conservative New York representative received 1,305 votes, with three delegates from Tennessee abstaining. A Roman Catholic, Miller became the first member of that faith ever to run on a Republican Party national ticket.

Goldwater's acceptance speech was uncompromising and did not attempt to dilute his conservatism in an effort to gain votes: "Anyone who joins us in all sincerity we welcome. Those who do not care for our cause, we don't expect to enter our ranks in any case. And let our Republicanism so focused and so dedicated not be made fuzzy and futile by unthinking and stupid labels. I would remind you that extremism in the defense of liberty is no vice. And let me remind you also that moderation in the pursuit of justice is no virtue."

By a voice vote, the convention adopted the party platform, but not before the moderate forces waged floor fights on three issues—extremism, civil rights, and control of nuclear weapons. Within the platform committee, 70 to 80 different amendments were presented, but when the platform reached the floor the moderates concentrated on these three specific issues.

Extremism was the first issue considered, with Sen. Hugh Scott of Pennsylvania introducing an amendment that specifically denounced efforts of the John Birch Society, the Ku Klux Klan, and the Communist Party to infiltrate the Republican Party. Rockefeller spoke on behalf of the amendment but was booed throughout his speech. Rockefeller argued that a "radical, high-financed, disciplined minority" was trying to take over the Republican Party, a minority "wholly alien to the middle course . . . the mainstream." The amendment was rejected on a standing vote, by a margin estimated at two to one.

A second amendment on extremism, proposed by Michigan governor George W. Romney, condemned extremist groups but not by name. The Romney amendment was similarly rejected on a standing vote by about the same margin. Scott introduced a civil rights amendment adding additional pledges to the existing plank, including more manpower for the Justice Department's Civil Rights Division; a statement of pride in Republican support of the 1964 Civil Rights Act; requirements for first-step compliance with school desegregation by all school districts in one year; voting guarantees to state as well as federal elections, and promises to eliminate job bias. The platform's brief plank on civil rights called for "full implementation and faithful execution" of the 1964 act, but it also stated that "the elimination of any such discrimination is a matter of heart, conscience and education as well as of equal rights under law." On a roll-call vote, the Scott amendment was defeated, 897 to 409. The pattern of the vote closely followed the presidential ballot, with support for the amendment centered in the Northeast. (*Table, p. 621.*)

Romney offered a brief, alternative civil rights plank that pledged action at the state, local, and private levels to eliminate discrimination in all fields. It was defeated by a voice vote.

Scott proposed another amendment, declaring the president to have sole authority to control the use of nuclear weapons. This contrasted with Goldwater's position advocating that North Atlantic Treaty Organization (NATO) commanders be given greater authority in the use of tactical nuclear weapons. The Scott amendment was rejected on a standing vote.

In its final form, the Republican platform was barely half as long as its Democratic counterpart. The Republican platform was divided into four sections, the first two enumerating Democratic failures in foreign policy and domestic affairs. The last two sections detailed Republican proposals.

The Republicans were suspicious of any détente with the communist world, instead calling for "a dynamic strategy of victory . . . for freedom." The platform contended that American military strength was deteriorating and promised the establishment of a military force superior to that of the nation's enemies. The Republicans expressed distrust of the 1963 nuclear test ban treaty and vowed to "never unilaterally disarm America." The platform promised to revitalize NATO, which was viewed as a keystone of Republican foreign policy.

Coupled with the anticommunism of the foreign policy sections was the central theme of the domestic sections—the need to trim the power of the federal government and to relocate it in state and local governments. This conservative philosophy was evident in various domestic planks. The Republicans promised a reduction of at least $5 billion in federal spending and pledged to end budget deficits.

The "one person, one vote" ruling of the Supreme Court brought the recommendation by the Republicans that a constitutional amendment be passed to allow states with bicameral legislatures to use a measurement other than population.

Following are excerpts from the Republican platform of 1964:

Peace. This Administration has sought accommodations with Communism without adequate safeguards and compensating gains for freedom. It has alienated proven allies by opening a "hot line" first with a sworn enemy rather than with a proven friend, and in general pursued a risky path such as began at Munich a quarter century ago. . . .

The supreme challenge to this policy is an atheistic imperialism—Communism. . . .

National Defense. This Administration has adopted policies which will lead to a potentially fatal parity of power with Communism instead of continued military superiority for the United States.

It has permitted disarmament negotiations to proceed without adequate consideration of military judgment. . . . It has failed to take minimum safeguards against possible consequences of the limited nuclear

test ban treaty, including advanced underground tests where permissible and full readiness to test elsewhere should the need arise. . . .

We will maintain a superior, not merely equal, military capability as long as the Communist drive for world domination continues. It will be a capability of balanced force, superior in all its arms, maintaining flexibility for effective performance in the rapidly changing science of war.

Republicans will never unilaterally disarm America.

Berlin. We will demand that the Berlin Wall be taken down prior to the resumption of any negotiations with the Soviet Union on the status of forces in, or treaties affecting, Germany.

Cuba. We Republicans will recognize a Cuban government in exile; we will support its efforts to regain the independence of its homeland; we will assist Cuban freedom fighters in carrying on guerrilla warfare against the Communist regime; we will work for an economic boycott by all nations of the free world in trade with Cuba. . . .

Vietnam. We will move decisively to assure victory in South Vietnam. While confining the conflict as closely as possible, America must move to end the fighting in a reasonable time and provide guarantees against further aggression. We must make it clear to the Communist world that, when conflict is forced with America, it will end only in victory for freedom.

Federal Power. Humanity is tormented once again by an age-old issue—is man to live in dignity and freedom under God or to be enslaved—are men in government to serve, or are they to master, their fellow men? . . .

1. Every person has the right to govern himself, to fix his own goals, and to make his own way with a minimum of governmental interference.

2. It is for government to foster and maintain an environment of freedom encouraging every individual to develop to the fullest his God-given powers of mind, heart and body; and, beyond this, government should undertake only needful things, rightly of public concern, which the citizen cannot himself accomplish.

We Republicans hold that these two principles must regain their primacy in our government's relations, not only with the American people, but also with nations and peoples everywhere in the world.

Economy. In furtherance of our faith in the individual, we also pledge prudent, responsible management of the government's fiscal affairs to protect the individual against the evils of spendthrift government—protecting most of all the needy and fixed-income families against the cruelest tax, inflation—and protecting every citizen against the high taxes forced by excessive spending, in order that each individual may keep more of his earning for his own and his family's use.

Tax Reform. In furtherance of our faith in limited, frugal and efficient government we also pledge: credit against Federal taxes for specified State and local taxes paid, and a transfer to the States of excise and other Federal tax sources. . . .

Civil Rights. Full implementation and faithful execution of the Civil Rights Act of 1964, and all other civil rights statutes, to assure equal rights and opportunities guaranteed by the Constitution to every citizen; . . . continued opposition to discrimination based on race, creed, national origin or sex. We recognize that the elimination of any such discrimination is a matter of heart, conscience, and education, as well as of equal rights under law.

Education. To continue the advancement of education on all levels, through such programs as selective aid to higher education, strengthened State and local tax resources, including tax credits for college education, while resisting the Democratic efforts which endanger local control of schools. . . .

School Prayer. Support of a Constitutional amendment permitting those individuals and groups who choose to do so to exercise their religion freely in public places, provided religious exercises are not prepared or prescribed by the state or political subdivision thereof and no person's participation therein is coerced, thus preserving the traditional separation of church and state. . . .

Obscenity. Enactment of legislation, despite Democratic opposition, to curb the flow through the mails of obscene materials which has flourished into a multimillion dollar obscenity racket. . . .

Medical Care for Elderly. Full coverage of all medical and hospital costs for the needy elderly people, financed by general revenues through broader implementation of Federal-State plans. . . .

Reapportionment. Support of a Constitutional amendment, as well as legislation, enabling States having bicameral legislatures to apportion one House on bases of their choosing, including factors other than population. . . .

DEMOCRATS

In late August in Atlantic City, New Jersey, the Democratic convention nominated President Lyndon B. Johnson for a full term in the White House. The proceedings were stage-managed by the president and were met with little visible dissent on the convention floor. The four-day event August 24–27 was a political triumph for the veteran politician from Texas, who less than a year earlier had been the assassinated John F. Kennedy's vice president.

The Democratic convention was larger than any previous convention of an American political party, with 5,260 delegates and alternates. A new vote-allocation formula was in effect that combined consideration of a state's electoral vote with its support for the Kennedy-Johnson ticket in 1960. While no states lost votes from four years earlier, many of the larger states gained significantly. As a result, there were 2,316 votes at the 1964 convention, compared with 1,521 in 1960.

With no controversy surrounding either the party nominee or platform, attention focused on the credentials challenge brought by the integrated Mississippi Freedom Democratic Party against the all-white delegation sent by the regular state party. By a voice vote, the convention approved a compromise negotiated by Minnesota senator Hubert H. Humphrey. The settlement called for seating of the Mississippi regulars, provided they signed a written pledge to back the national ticket and urged the state's presidential electors to do likewise. It also proposed the seating of Democrats as delegates at large, and the remainder of the delegation as honored guests; and it stipulated that at future conventions delegations would be barred from states that allowed racial discrimination in voting. Although the convention approved this solution, the Freedom Democrats rejected the compromise, and all but four members of the regular Mississippi delegation refused to sign the pledge and left the convention.

The convention also approved a recommendation requiring the Alabama delegation to sign a personal loyalty oath, the result of the state party's placing "unpledged" (anti-Johnson) electors on the Alabama ballot. Eleven Alabama members signed the loyalty oath; the remaining forty-two delegates and alternates withdrew from the convention.

The roll-call vote for president was dispensed with, and Johnson was nominated by acclamation. Immediately after his selection, Johnson made the unprecedented move of appearing before the delegates to announce his choice for vice president, Humphrey. Johnson had tried to make his selection as suspenseful and dramatic as possible. Although most observers felt Humphrey would be the choice, earlier that day Johnson had called both the Minnesota senator and Connecticut senator Thomas J. Dodd to the White House. However, at this meeting Johnson invited Humphrey to be on the ticket, and later that night the delegates nominated Humphrey by acclamation. (The 1964 Democratic convention was only the second in party history in which there were no roll-call votes—the other time was 1936.)

On the final day of the convention, the two nominees delivered their acceptance speeches. Humphrey frequently referred to the Republican candidate, Sen. Goldwater, as "the temporary Republican spokesman," and listed major legislation supported by a majority of both parties in the Senate, "but not Sen. Goldwater."

The emotional highlight of the convention was the appearance of Attorney General Robert F. Kennedy, who introduced a film about the presidency of his late brother.

By a voice vote, the convention approved the party platform. Following the trend toward longer and longer documents, the platform was 22,000 words in length. Although the document was adopted without debate on the convention floor, several roll-call votes were taken in the platform committee. By a vote of 53 to 16, the committee rejected a proposal by Sen. Joseph S. Clark of Pennsylvania to strengthen the disarmament plank. Clark's proposal called for further disarmament "under world law," wording that the committee majority did not want to include.

By a margin of 39 to 38, the platform committee pledged to support a constitutional amendment giving the District of Columbia representation in Congress. On another roll-call vote (52 to 19), the committee promised to repeal the Taft-Hartley Act provision permitting state right-to-work laws.

Without a recorded vote, the committee adopted another provision by Sen. Clark proposing revision of congressional rules and procedures to "assure majority rule after reasonable debate and to guarantee that major legislative proposals of the President can be brought to a vote after reasonable consideration in committee." The proposal was a reference to the Senate cloture rule, requiring a two-thirds vote to cut off debate, and to the power of the House Rules Committee to keep legislation from the floor.

The entire platform was a wide-ranging document designed to appeal to as many segments of the electorate as possible. Self-described as a "covenant of unity," the platform was written in a moderate tone to contrast with the unqualified conservatism expressed in the Republican platform.

The latter three-quarters of the Democratic platform was a section entitled "An Accounting of Stewardship, 1961–1964," which described the accomplishments of the Kennedy-Johnson administration in thirty-eight areas of public policy. The first quarter of the platform discussed the party's position on major issues of the day, from peace and national defense to civil rights, the economy, agriculture, natural resources, urban affairs, federal power and government reform, and extremism.

In view of the militant anticommunism of Sen. Goldwater and the Republican platform, the Democrats viewed peace and national defense as winning issues with a majority of the electorate. The Democrats claimed that the world was closer to peace than in 1960, due in part to the United States' overwhelming nuclear superiority and internal splits in the communist world, as well as the success of international negotiations such as those resulting in the nuclear test ban treaty. But, in an allusion to Goldwater's stance, the platform warned that recklessness by a president in foreign policy could result in nuclear disaster. The Democratic platform included a provision rejected by the Republicans, insisting that control of nuclear weapons must be kept in the hands of the president.

While peace and national defense were stressed by the Democrats, the Republican platform concentrated on the need to limit the power of the federal government. On this issue, the Democratic platform contained a recommendation to help state and local governments develop new revenue sources. But the Democratic plank also included an assertion that contradicted the Republicans' criticism of expanding federal power: "No government at any level can properly complain of violation of its power, if it fails to meet its responsibilities."

Neither party had a civil rights plank containing specifics. The difference was wording, with the Democrats promising "fair, effective enforcement" of the 1964 Civil Rights Act, but precluding the use of quotas in combating racial discrimination. The Republicans pledged "full implementation and faithful execution" of civil rights laws.

Without dissent, the Democratic platform included a provision that condemned extremism of the right and left, especially the Communist Party, the Ku Klux Klan and the John Birch Society.

The two parties differed in their opinion of the health of the economy. The Republicans blamed their opposition for inflation and continuing unemployment and promised a reduction of at least $5 billion in federal spending. The Democrats countered by claiming the Kennedy-Johnson administration had engineered "the longest and strongest peacetime prosperity in modern history."

Following are excerpts from the Democratic platform of 1964:

Peace. At the start of the third decade of the nuclear age, the preservation of peace requires the strength to wage war and the wisdom to avoid it. The search for peace requires the utmost intelligence, the clearest vision, and a strong sense of reality. . . . Battered by economic failures, challenged by recent American achievements in space, torn by the Chinese-Russian rift, and faced with American strength and courage—international Communism has lost its unity and momentum.

National Defense. Specifically, we must and we will:
—Continue the overwhelming supremacy of our Strategic Nuclear Forces.
—Strengthen further our forces for discouraging limited wars and fighting subversion.
—Maintain the world's largest research and development effort, which has initiated more than 200 new programs since 1961, to ensure continued American leadership in weapons systems and equipment. . . .

Control of the use of nuclear weapons must remain solely with the highest elected official in the country—the President of the United States. . . .

The complications and dangers in our restless, constantly changing world require of us consummate understanding and experience. One rash act, one thoughtless decision, one unchecked reaction—and cities could become smouldering ruins and farms parched wasteland.

Civil Rights. The Civil Rights Act of 1964 deserves and requires full observance by every American and fair, effective enforcement if there is any default. . . .

Extremism. We condemn extremism, whether from the Right or Left, including the extreme tactics of such organizations as the Communist Party, the Ku Klux Klan and the John Birch Society.

Federal Power. The Democratic Party holds to the belief that government in the United States—local, state and federal—was created in order to serve the people. Each level of government has appropriate powers and each has specific responsibilities. The first responsibility of government at every level is to protect the basic freedoms of the people. No government at any level can properly complain of violation of its power, if it fails to meet its responsibilities.

The federal government exists not to grow larger, but to enlarge the individual potential and achievement of the people.

The federal government exists not to subordinate the states, but to support them.

Economy. In 42 months of uninterrupted expansion under Presidents Kennedy and Johnson, we have achieved the longest and strongest peacetime prosperity in modern history. . . .

It is the national purpose, and our commitment, that every man or woman who is willing and able to work is entitled to a job and to a fair wage for doing it.

1968 Conventions

PRESIDENTIAL CANDIDATES

Richard M. Nixon
Republican

Hubert H. Humphrey
Democrat

George C. Wallace
American Independent

REPUBLICANS

The Republican convention, held August 5–8 in Miami Beach, Florida, had a surface tranquility that the later Democratic convention lacked. Only two roll-call votes were taken to nominate presidential and vice-presidential candidates.

The credentials committee considered only one serious challenge, and that involved a single delegate. By a 32–32 vote, the committee defeated an unexpectedly strong attempt to overturn the preconvention decision to seat Rep. H. R. Gross of Iowa rather than a Des Moines housewife. The full convention approved the credentials committee report without a roll-call vote.

Delegates approved the rules committee report without comment. It contained recommendations to prohibit discrimination in the selection of future convention delegates and to add the Republican state chairmen as members of the Republican National Committee.

Twelve names were placed in nomination for the presidency, although the contest was clearly among three candidates: the front-runner, former vice president Richard Nixon, and two governors, Nelson A. Rockefeller of New York and Ronald Reagan of California. The ideological gulf between the more liberal Rockefeller and the more conservative Reagan made it difficult for them to agree on a common strategy to stop Nixon, even when Reagan abandoned his favorite-son status for active candidacy two days before the balloting.

To head off the defection to Reagan of his more conservative supporters, Nixon seemed to take a sharp tack to the right the day before the balloting. He told southern delegations he would not run an administration that would "ram anything down your throats," that he opposed school busing, that he would appoint "strict constitutionalists" to the Supreme Court, and that he was critical of federal intervention in local school board affairs.

Nixon won the nomination on the first ballot, receiving 692 votes (25 more than necessary) to easily outdistance Rockefeller, who had 277, and Reagan, who had 182. After vote switches, the final totals were Nixon, 1,238, Rockefeller, 93, and Reagan, 2. In a

brief speech, Reagan moved that Nixon's nomination be made unanimous, but his motion was never put to a vote. (*Table, p. 622.*)

In his selection of a running mate, Nixon surprised many observers by tapping Gov. Spiro T. Agnew of Maryland. Agnew, who had delivered the major nominating speech for Nixon, had, ironically, been one of Rockefeller's earliest and strongest supporters. But Agnew ceased his active support of Rockefeller in March, irked by the New York governor's indecision about entering the race, and, at the beginning of convention week, announced his support for Nixon.

The name of Michigan governor George Romney also was placed in nomination for vice president. Agnew was an easy winner, receiving 1,119 votes to 186 for Romney, who made no effort to withdraw his name. After completion of the roll call, a Romney motion to make Agnew's nomination unanimous was approved.

The delegates approved without debate the 1968 Republican platform, which steered a careful middle course between conservatives and liberals on domestic policy and between "doves" and "hawks" on the touchy Vietnam issue. The 11,500-word document was somewhat more liberal in tone than that of 1960 and was far removed from the militantly conservative tone of the 1964 document.

A major floor fight on the platform was averted when platform committee members, led by Senate Minority Leader Everett McKinley Dirksen of Illinois, substituted for the original hard-line war plank new language stressing the need for de-Americanization of both the military and civilian efforts in Vietnam. "Doves" and "hawks" alike went along with the revised version.

As originally written, the plank criticized the Johnson administration for not leaving key Vietnam decisions to the military and for the administration's policy of military gradualism. Both Nixon and Rockefeller backers opposed the strong language, and a compromise Vietnam plank was accepted. As well as advocating the de-Americanization of the war, it proposed concentrating on protection of the South Vietnamese population rather than on capturing territory, and on efforts to strengthen local forces and responsibility. Although the adopted platform endorsed continued negotiations with Hanoi, it remained silent on the important issues of a bombing pause and of a possible Saigon coalition that would include the communists.

In its discussion of national defense, the platform criticized the administration for failure to develop superior new weaponry. The document indicated that, when the Vietnam War was over, a reduced defense budget might make possible increased federal spending on social welfare programs. But it neither suggested how much more spending nor recommended any substantial increases in the near future.

The platform treated rioting and crime in militant fashion: "We will not tolerate violence!" The crime plank criticized the Johnson administration for not taking effective action against crime and pledged "an all-out federal-state-local crusade."

In its youth plank, the Republicans urged the states to lower the voting age to eighteen but did not endorse proposals for a constitutional amendment to lower the federal voting age. The plank also advocated action to shorten the period in which young men were eligible for the draft and proposed to develop eventually a voluntary force.

Following are excerpts from the Republican platform of 1968:

Vietnam. The Administration's Vietnam policy has failed—militarily, politically, diplomatically, and with relation to our own people.

We condemn the Administration's breach of faith with the American people respecting our heavy involvement in Vietnam. Every citizen bitterly recalls the Democrat campaign oratory of 1964: "We are not about to send American boys 9–10,000 miles away from home to do what Asian boys ought to be doing for themselves."

The entire nation has been profoundly concerned by hastily-extemporized, undeclared land wars which embroil massive U.S. Army forces thousands of miles from our shores. It is time to realize that not every international conflict is susceptible of solution by American ground forces. . . .

We pledge to adopt a strategy relevant to the real problems of the war, concentrating on the security of the population, on developing a greater sense of nationhood, and on strengthening the local forces. It will be a strategy permitting a progressive de-Americanization of the war, both military and civilian. . . .

National Defense. Grave errors, many now irretrievable, have characterized the direction of our nation's defense.

A singular notion—that salvation for America lies in standing still—has pervaded the entire effort. Not retention of American superiority but parity with the Soviet Union has been made the controlling doctrine in many critical areas. We have frittered away superior military capabilities, enabling the Soviets to narrow their defense gap, in some areas to outstrip us, and to move to cancel our lead entirely by the early Seventies.

China. Improved relations with Communist nations can come only when they cease to endanger other states by force or threat. Under existing conditions, we cannot favor recognition of Communist China or its admission to the United Nations.

Crime. Fire and looting, causing millions of dollars of property damage, have brought great suffering to home owners and small businessmen, particularly in black communities least able to absorb catastrophic losses. The Republican Party strongly advocates measures to alleviate and remove the frustrations that contribute to riots. We simultaneously support decisive action to quell civil disorder, relying primarily on state and local governments to deal with these conditions.

America has adequate peaceful and lawful means for achieving even fundamental social change if the people wish it. *We will not tolerate violence!*

For the future, we pledge an all-out, federal-state-local crusade against crime, including:

—Leadership by an Attorney General who will restore stature and respect to that office. . . .

—Enactment of legislation to control indiscriminate availability of firearms, safeguarding the right of responsible citizens to collect, own and use firearms for legitimate purposes, retaining primary responsibility at the state level, with such federal laws as necessary to better enable the states to meet their responsibilities.

DEMOCRATS

While violence flared in the streets and thousands of police and guards imposed security precautions unprecedented at presidential nominating conventions, the 1968 Democratic convention met August 26–29 in Chicago to nominate Hubert H. Humphrey of Minnesota for the presidency and to endorse the controversial Vietnam policies of the Johnson-Humphrey administration.

Twin themes—physical force to keep order and political force to overrule minority sentiment in the Democratic Party—were apparent throughout the convention.

The physical force, supplied by 11,900 Chicago police, 7,500 army regulars, 7,500 Illinois National Guardsmen, and 1,000 FBI and Secret Service agents, was exerted to keep vociferous Vietnam War critics away from the convention headquarters hotels and the International Amphitheatre where official sessions were held. A security ring several blocks wide guarded the Amphitheatre, itself surrounded by a barbed wire fence and multiple security checkpoints for entering delegates, reporters, and guests. No violence erupted in the Amphitheatre area, but near the downtown hotels there were days of bitter demonstrations that ended with repeated police use of tear gas. At the end of convention week, the Chicago police announced that 589 persons had been arrested, with more than 119 police and 100 demonstrators injured.

The political force was exerted by the Johnson administration organization backing Vice President Humphrey, whose supporters enjoyed clear control of convention proceedings from start to end. In a distinct minority were the antiwar factions that rallied around the candidacies of Senators Eugene J. McCarthy of Minnesota and George McGovern of South Dakota. The McCarthy forces mounted a series of challenges to the Humphrey faction—on credentials, rules, the platform, and finally the nomination itself.

In the first business of the convention, the Humphrey and McCarthy forces joined to ban the 136-year-old unit rule, which enabled the majority of a split delegation to cast the delegation's entire vote for the candidate favored by the majority. Delegates rejected by voice vote a motion by the Texas delegation to retain the rule through the 1968 convention. However, as expected, the brief moments of unity ended when the convention moved on to consider credentials challenges.

The credentials committee had considered an unprecedented number of challenges, involving delegates from fifteen states. Although McCarthy supported almost all the challenges, his candidacy was not always the paramount issue. In the case of the disputed southern delegations, racial imbalance, the party loyalty issue, or a combination of both, were more important. Of the seventeen different challenges, McCarthy supported all but one (in Wisconsin); McGovern backed all the southern challenges; Humphrey supported only the Mississippi challenge publicly.

In a historic move, the convention by a voice vote seated a new loyalist Democratic faction from Mississippi and unseated the delegation of the traditionally segregationist, conservative regular party. The credentials committee decided all other challenges in favor of the regular delegations, but minority reports were filed for the Alabama, Georgia, North Carolina, and Texas challengers. The North Carolina case was decided by a voice vote supporting the regular delegation, but the other three cases were settled by roll-call votes.

The first state to be considered was Texas, and, by a vote of 1,368¼ to 956¾, the convention approved the seating of the regular delegation led by Gov. John B. Connally. The rival McCarthy-supported Texas faction was led by Sen. Ralph Yarborough. (Table, p. 623.)

The Georgia case was considered next, with the credentials committee recommending that both rival delegations be seated and the Georgia vote split evenly between them. However, both delegations found this to be an unsatisfactory solution and presented reports to have their entire delegation seated alone. A minority report to seat the challenging Loyal National Democrats, led by black state representative Julian Bond, was defeated 1,415.45 to 1,043.55. A minority report to seat the regular delegation, hand picked by Gov. Lester G. Maddox and Democratic state chairman James H. Gray, was rejected by a voice vote. The solution recommended by the credentials committee was subsequently approved by a voice vote.

The Alabama case involved three competing factions: the regulars, the largely black National Democratic Party of Alabama (NDPA), and the integrated Alabama Independent Democratic Party (AIDP), created solely to run a slate of presidential electors loyal to the national party against the third-party candidacy of Alabama governor George C. Wallace. The credentials committee proposed seating all members of the regular delegation who would sign a loyalty pledge and replacing those who would not sign with loyal members of the AIDP delegation. However, the McCarthy-backed NDPA introduced a minority report to seat its entire delegation. By a vote of 1,607 to 880¾, the convention rejected this minority report and by a voice vote approved the recommendation of the credentials committee.

The remainder of the credentials committee report was approved, including a resolution instructing the Democratic National Committee to include, in the call for the 1972 convention, encouragement to state parties to ensure that all Democrats in each state have a "meaningful and timely" opportunity to participate in delegate selection.

McCarthy, McGovern, and other liberal factions won their greatest breakthrough on convention rules, obtaining by a vote of 1,351¼ to 1,209 elimination of the unit rule at every level of party activity leading up to and including the 1972 convention. Many Humphrey-pledged delegates also backed the unit rule change. Also a part of this successful minority report was the requirement that the delegate-selection process in 1972 be public and held within the calendar year of the convention.

On Wednesday night, on the third day of the convention, while nominations and balloting for president took place at the Amphitheatre, the worst violence of the convention broke out downtown, and television screens carried pictures of phalanxes of Chicago police advancing on demonstrators. At the same time, hundreds of Chicago mayor Richard J. Daley's workers were brought into the galleries with apparent improper credentials. Some delegates, apparently refusing to show their credentials to the omnipresent security guards, were physically ejected from the convention floor. The McCarthy and McGovern forces charged "atrocities" and tried to adjourn the convention for two weeks. House Majority Leader Carl Albert of Oklahoma, the convention chairman, refused to accept their motions.

In addition to Humphrey, McCarthy, and McGovern, only two other candidates were placed in nomination—the Rev. Channing E. Phillips of the District of Columbia, who became the first black ever nominated for the presidency at a national convention, and North Carolina governor Dan K. Moore.

The emotional highlight of the session was provided by McGovern's nominator, Connecticut senator Abraham A. Ribicoff, who charged that "with George McGovern as president of the United States we wouldn't have to have Gestapo tactics in the streets of Chicago."

Humphrey was an easy winner on the first ballot, receiving 1,759¼ votes to 601 for McCarthy, 146½ for McGovern, and 67½ for Phillips. Humphrey's winning majority included the bulk of party moderates, big-city organizations of the North (including Daley's), and southern conservatives. In a tumultuous ending to one of the wildest nights in American politics, Chairman Albert gaveled through a motion to make the nomination unanimous (despite major opposition on the floor) and adjourned the session. (Table, p. 623.)

As his running mate, Humphrey chose Maine senator Edmund S. Muskie. Julian Bond's name also was placed in nomination, but Bond, then twenty-eight, withdrew, explaining that he was under the "legal age" to be president (the constitutional minimum is thirty-five). Before the end of the first ballot, Albert recognized Mayor Daley, who moved that Muskie be declared the vice-presidential nominee by acclamation. With the convention in a particularly unruly state, the Daley motion was quickly adopted. At the time the roll call was suspended, Muskie already had received 1,942½ votes, a majority. Bond was a distant second with 48½.

The 18,000-word platform, adopted by a voice vote, was a document that met the demands of the Democratic Party's liberals word for word in almost every section except that which dealt with U.S. policy in Vietnam. At one point during the platform-writing sessions, it appeared that Humphrey might assent to a plank calling for a halt in U.S. bombing of North Vietnam. But President Johnson reportedly sent personal instructions that the plank should support administration policy.

The administration plank, approved 62–35 in the platform committee, supported a bombing halt only when it "would not endanger the lives of our troops in the field," did not call for a reduction in search-and-destroy missions or a withdrawal of troops until the end of the war, and advocated a new government in Saigon only after the war had ended. The minority plank, drafted by McCarthy and McGovern, called for an immediate halt to the bombing, reduction of offensive operations in the South Vietnamese countryside, a negotiated troop withdrawal, and encouragement of the South Vietnamese government to negotiate with communist insurgents.

Following nearly three hours of debate the minority plank was defeated, 1,567¾ to 1,041¼. After the result was announced, members of the New York delegation and others slipped on black armbands and sang "We Shall Overcome." (*Table, p. 623.*)

Unlike the Republican platform, which called for decreased United States involvement in Vietnam, Democrats adopted a plan that called for a continued strong American war effort. Although the Democrats agreed with Republicans that the South Vietnamese eventually should take over their nation's defense, they gave no indication that an expanded Vietnamese role could lead to U.S. troop reductions in the near future.

Following are excerpts from the Democratic platform of 1968:

Vietnam. Recognizing that events in Vietnam and the negotiations in Paris may affect the timing and the actions we recommend we would support our Government in the following steps:

Bombing—Stop all bombing of North Vietnam when this action would not endanger the lives of our troops in the field; this action should take into account the response from Hanoi.

Troop Withdrawal—Negotiate with Hanoi an immediate end or limitation of hostilities and the withdrawal from South Vietnam of all foreign forces—both United States and allied forces, and forces infiltrated from North Vietnam. . . .

National Defense. We must and will maintain a strong and balanced defense establishment adequate to the task of security and peace. There must be no doubt about our strategic nuclear capacity, our capacity to meet limited challenges, and our willingness to act when our vital interests are threatened. . . .

We face difficult and trying times in Asia and in Europe. We have responsibilities and commitments we cannot escape with honor.

China. The immediate prospects that China will emerge from its self-imposed isolation are dim. But both Asians and Americans will have to coexist with the 750 million Chinese on the mainland. We shall continue to make it clear that we are prepared to cooperate with China whenever it is ready to become a responsible member of the international community. We would actively encourage economic, social and cultural exchange with mainland China as a means of freeing that nation and her people from their narrow isolation.

Crime. In fighting crime we must not foster injustice. Lawlessness cannot be ended by curtailing the hard-won liberties of all Americans. The right of privacy must be safeguarded. Court procedures must be expedited. Justice delayed is justice denied.

A respect for civil peace requires also a proper respect for the legitimate means of expressing dissent. A democratic society welcomes criticism within the limits of the law. Freedom of speech, press, assembly

and association, together with free exercise of the franchise, are among the legitimate means to achieve change in a democratic society. But when the dissenter resorts to violence, he erodes the institutions and values which are the underpinnings of our democratic society. We must not and will not tolerate violence.

Electoral Reform. We fully recognize the principle of one man, one vote in all elections. We urge that due consideration be given to the question of Presidential primaries throughout the nation. We urge reform of the electoral college and election procedures to assure that the votes of the people are fully reflected.

AMERICAN INDEPENDENT PARTY

Former Alabama governor George C. Wallace declared his third-party presidential candidacy on February 8, 1968. The vehicle for his candidacy was his personally created American Independent Party. No convention was held by the party to ratify his selection. (A descendant of the 1968 Wallace campaign, the American Party ran a national ticket in 1972 but received less than 2 percent of the vote.)

On February 14 Wallace announced the choice of former Georgia governor Marvin Griffin as his "interim" vice-presidential running mate, but he made clear that an official candidate would be chosen later in the campaign. Griffin's tentative candidacy was necessary to allow the American Independent Party to get on the ballot in several states. On October 3 Wallace announced his choice of retired air force general Curtis E. LeMay, an Ohio native, as his official running mate.

Ten days later, Wallace released the text of his party's platform. The document generally took a harder line toward domestic and international problems than did the Democratic and Republican platforms. Wallace favored termination of the Vietnam War through negotiations but added that, if negotiations failed, the United States should seek a military solution.

As expected, the emphasis of the platform on domestic issues centered on returning control of local affairs to the states and communities, with the federal government serving in an assisting role rather than an authoritarian manner.

Following are excerpts from the American Independent Party platform of 1968:

Vietnam. We earnestly desire that the conflict be terminated through peaceful negotiations and we will lend all aid, support, effort, sincerity and prayer to the efforts of our negotiators. Negotiation will be given every reasonable and logical chance for success and we will be patient to an extreme in seeking an end to the war through this means. If it becomes evident that the enemy does not desire to negotiate in good faith, that our hopes of termination of hostilities are not being realized and that the lives and safety of our committed troops are being further endangered, we must seek a military conclusion.

Crime. Lawlessness has become commonplace in our present society. The permissive attitude of the executive and judiciary at the national level sets the tone for this moral decay. The criminal and anarchist who preys on the decent law abiding citizen is rewarded for his misconduct through never ending justification and platitudes from those in high places who seem to have lost their concern for that vast segment of America that so strongly believes in law and order. . . .

We will appoint as Attorney General a person interested in the enforcement rather than the disruption of legal processes and restore that office to the dignity and stature it deserves and requires.

Federal Power. The Federal Government, in derogation and flagrant violation of this Article [X] of the Bill of Rights, has in the past three decades seized and usurped many powers not delegated to it, such as, among others: the operation and control of the public school system of the several states; the power to prescribe the eligibility and qualifications of those who would vote in our state and local elections; the power to intrude upon and control the farmer in the operation of his farm; the power to tell the property owner to whom he can and cannot sell or rent his property; and, many other rights and privileges of the individual citizen, which are properly subject to state or local control, as distinguished from federal control. The Federal Government has forced the states to reapportion their legislatures, a prerogative of the states alone. The Federal Government has attempted to take over and control the seniority and apprenticeship lists of the labor unions; the Federal Government has adopted so-called "Civil Rights Acts," particularly the one adopted in 1964, which have set race against race and class against class, all of which we condemn.

The Judiciary. In the period of the past three decades, we have seen the Federal judiciary, primarily the Supreme Court, transgress repeatedly upon the prerogatives of the Congress and exceed its authority by enacting judicial legislation, in the form of decisions based upon political and sociological considerations, which would never have been enacted by the Congress. We have seen them, in their solicitude for the criminal and lawless element of our society, shackle the police and other law enforcement agencies; and, as a result, they have made it increasingly difficult to protect the law-abiding citizen from crime and criminals. This is one of the principal reasons for the turmoil and the near revolutionary conditions which prevail in our country today, and particularly in our national capital. The Federal judiciary, feeling secure in their knowledge that their appointment is for life, have far exceeded their constitutional authority, which is limited to interpreting or construing the law.

It shall be our policy and our purpose, at the earliest possible time, to propose and advocate and urge the adoption of an amendment to the United States Constitution whereby members of the Federal judiciary at District level be required to face the electorate on his record at periodical intervals; and, in the event he receives a negative vote upon such election, his office shall thereupon become vacant, and a successor shall be appointed to succeed him.

With respect to the Supreme Court and the Courts of Appeals I [George Wallace] would propose that this amendment require reconfirmation of the office holder by the United States Senate at reasonable intervals.

1972 Conventions

PRESIDENTIAL CANDIDATES

George McGovern
Democrat

Richard M. Nixon
Republican

DEMOCRATS

Massive reforms in convention rules and delegate-selection procedures made the 1972 Democratic convention, held in Miami Beach, Florida, July 10–13, significantly different from the violence-plagued assembly in Chicago four years earlier.

Two special commissions created by the 1968 convention drafted the reforms. The Commission on Rules, chaired by Rep. James G. O'Hara of Michigan, composed the first set of rules ever written on Democratic convention procedure. Among the reforms that the Democratic National Committee adopted were:

• A new vote-allocation formula based nearly equally on electoral college strength and the Democratic vote in recent presidential elections.

• An expansion of the convention rules, platform, and credentials committees so that their make-up would reflect state population differences rather than the previous method of allocating two seats to each state.

• The assurance that women and men be equally represented on committees and among convention officers.

• The requirement that the meetings and votes of all convention committees be open to the public.

• The requirement that the reports and minority views of all the committees be released at specified dates before the opening of the convention.

• The banning of floor demonstrations for candidates.

• The arrangement of the states and territories for roll calls in random sequence determined by lot rather than in the traditional alphabetical order.

The Commission on Party Structure and Delegate Selection, first chaired by Sen. George McGovern of South Dakota and later by Rep. Donald M. Fraser of Minnesota, formulated eighteen guidelines to be met by the states in the delegate-selection process. With the approval of these guidelines by the Democratic National Committee, they became part of the 1972 convention call, thus requiring the states to be in full compliance with the guidelines before they would be seated.

Among the important features of the eighteen guidelines were the elimination of the unit rule; the restriction that no more than 10 percent of a state's delegation be named by its state committee; the requirement that all steps in the delegate-selection process be publicly advertised and held in easily accessible public places within the calendar year of the convention; the requirement that women, youth, and minority groups be included in delegations "in reasonable relationship" to their presence in the state's population; and the establishment of a detailed, public method of hearing delegate challenges.

The reforms encouraged an unprecedented number of challenges. The credentials committee opened hearings in Washington, D.C., two weeks before the start of the convention, faced with eighty-two challenges from thirty states and one territory. A total of 1,289 delegates were challenged, representing more than 40 percent of the convention delegates. More than four-fifths of the challenges were filed on grounds of noncompliance with reform commission guidelines regarding adequate representation of women, youth, and minorities.

The most controversial challenges involved the California delegation and the part of the Illinois delegation controlled by Mayor Richard J. Daley of Chicago. The credentials committee, in a move that surprised supporters of McGovern, a candidate for the presidential nomination, upheld a challenge of California's winner-take-all primary law, stripping McGovern of 151 of the 271 delegate votes he had won in the primary.

The committee voted 72 to 66 to award the 151 convention seats to Sen. Hubert H. Humphrey of Minnesota and seven other candidates in proportion to their share of the popular ballots cast in the state's June primary. Although McGovern was clearly the front-runner for the nomination, the decision, if not overturned by the full convention, threatened his chances of being selected.

In a tense and dramatic balloting session the next day, the committee voted 71 to 61 to unseat fifty-nine Chicago delegates, including Daley, on grounds that the procedures under which they had been selected violated five of the party's reform guidelines. Most of the Illinois delegates challenging Daley supported McGovern.

The emotional credentials challenges were considered on the first night of the convention. Twenty-three challenges from fifteen states were brought to the convention floor, but the spotlight was on the California and Illinois cases. A key preliminary vote took place on a challenge to the South Carolina delegation brought by the National Women's Political Caucus. The challenge, seeking to increase the number of women in the state delegation, was rejected by a vote of 1,555.75 to 1,429.05. *(Table p. 624.)*

The outcome of the vote could have set an important precedent on what constituted a majority on subsequent challenges. Anti-McGovern forces had hoped to get a ruling from the chair allowing an absolute majority of 1,509 delegates to prevail rather than a simple majority of delegates actually voting.

Convention Chairman Lawrence F. O'Brien (also chairman of the Democratic National Committee) had announced earlier that a majority would consist of one-half plus one of the number of eligible voters. The rules provided that no delegates could vote on their own credentials challenges.

Because the winning total on the South Carolina vote exceeded by a wide margin both the eligible majority and the absolute majority of the convention's 3,016 votes, the anti-McGovern coalition was unable to force a test of what constituted a majority. Thus the vote, although it rejected the position of South Carolina challengers favorable to McGovern, set the stage for returning the 151 California delegates to McGovern. The McGovern forces subsequently won the crucial California challenge, 1,618.28 to 1,238.22. *(Table p. 624.)*

Following the defeat of a compromise in the Chicago case, a minority report asking for seating of the Daley delegates alone, was defeated 1,486.04 to 1,371.56. The vote seated a group, a majority of which supported McGovern, headed by Chicago alderman William Singer and black activist Jesse Jackson. *(Table p. 624.)*

No other roll-call votes were needed to resolve the remaining credentials challenges. After the settlement of all the delegate contests, the convention had a composition unlike that of any previous major party convention. The 1972 Democratic assembly was the largest in major party history, with 3,203 delegates casting 3,016 votes. Unlike the situation in 1968, most delegates were chosen in state primary elections rather than in state conventions or caucuses. Nearly two-thirds of the delegates to the 1972 convention were selected in primaries, while only 41 percent had been elected by the primary system four years earlier, when Humphrey won the Democratic nomination without entering any primaries.

There were also large increases in the number of women, youth, and racial minorities at the 1972 convention. The proportion of women delegates rose from 13 percent in 1968 to 40 percent in 1972; the number of youth delegates (age thirty and under) dramatically jumped from 2.6 percent in 1968 to 21 percent four years later; and black delegates made up 15 percent of the 1972 convention, compared with 5.5 percent in 1968. But while women, youth, and blacks were better represented than at earlier conventions, there was a lower level of participation by elected party officials. Only thirty of the 255 Democratic U.S. House members were present in Miami Beach.

The report of the rules committee was approved on the second day of the convention by a voice vote. The report proposed the abolition of winner-take-all primaries in 1976; the abolition of cross-over voting by Republicans in future Democratic presidential primaries; the selection of a woman as chairman of the 1976 convention, with the job rotating between the sexes thereafter; the creation of a special fund in the Democratic National Committee to subsidize the expenses of poor delegates at future national conventions and other party councils, and the appointment of a commission to make "appropriate revisions" in the reform guidelines.

Although the delegates overwhelmingly accepted these reforms, they balked at approving the party charter drafted by the rules committee. The new charter, the first ever written for a major party, was intended to free the national party of four-year presidential election cycles and to broaden public involvement in major national policy questions. But the charter was opposed by some party leaders, particularly members of Congress, who viewed the document as shifting power from elected politicians to the grass-roots level. By a vote of 2,408.45 to 195.10, the convention approved a compromise resolution to delay consideration of the charter until a proposed midterm policy conference in 1974. The compromise also enlarged the Democratic National Committee and revised its membership to reflect Democratic strength in the various states.

The settlement of the California challenge on the opening night of the convention in favor of the McGovern forces effectively locked up the presidential nomination for the South Dakota senator. The next day, two of his major rivals in the primaries, Senators Humphrey and Muskie, withdrew from the race. In the balloting on the third day of the convention, McGovern was an easy winner on the first roll call. Before switches, McGovern had received 1,728.35 votes to 525 for Sen. Henry M. Jackson of Washington, 381.7 for Gov. George C. Wallace of Alabama, and 151.95 for Rep. Shirley Chisholm of New York. After vote changes, McGovern's vote total rose to 1,864.95, but no attempt was made to make his nomination unanimous. *(Table p. 219.)*

With McGovern's first choice for vice president, Sen. Edward M. Kennedy of Massachusetts, rebuffing all overtures, McGovern selected Sen. Thomas F. Eagleton of Missouri. The vice-presidential balloting was prolonged by the nomination of six other candidates, and, by the time the roll call was suspended, votes were distributed among more than seventy different "candidates." Eagleton received 1,741.81 votes, a majority. On the motion of Frances T. "Sissy" Farenthold, the runner-up, the roll call was suspended and Eagleton was nominated by acclamation.

Because of the long vice-presidential roll call, it was nearly 3 A.M. before McGovern was able to deliver his acceptance speech, costing him the prime-time television audience. In the speech, he stressed the antiwar theme that was a basic part of his campaign and implored the nation to "come home" to its founding ideals.

Barely ten days after selection of the Democratic ticket, on July 25, Eagleton disclosed that he voluntarily had hospitalized himself three times between 1960 and 1966 for "nervous exhaustion and fatigue." McGovern strongly supported his running mate at the time, but in the following days, his support for the Missouri senator began to wane. After meeting with McGovern on July 31, Eagleton withdrew from the ticket. It marked the first time since 1860 that a major party candidate had withdrawn from a national ticket after the convention had adjourned.

On August 5 McGovern announced that his choice to replace Eagleton was R. Sargent Shriver of Maryland, U.S. ambassador to France and the former director of the Peace Corps and the Office of Economic Opportunity. The newly enlarged Democratic National Committee formally nominated Shriver in an August 8 meeting in Washington.

The 1972 Democratic platform was probably the most liberal and the longest (about twenty-five thousand words) ever offered by a major political party. The platform was more a collection of independent reform proposals than a unified plan of action. Its recommendations, largely written by separate subject-area task forces, did not translate into a compact program for Congress to consider or for a president to propose. But the platform's common themes reflected the changes in the party since 1968 and set it off from all other Democratic platforms of the previous generation.

The National Welfare Rights Organization sponsored a measure requiring the federal government to guarantee every family of four an annual income of $6,500. It lost, 1,852.86 to 999.34. *(Table p. 625.)*

The platform's position on the Vietnam War was blunt and unequivocal. As "the first order of business" of a Democratic administration, the platform pledged "immediate and complete withdrawal of all U.S. forces in Indochina." The plank also promised an end to military aid to the Saigon regime but pledged economic assistance to Vietnam to help the nation emerge from the war. Amnesty for war resisters was recommended after the return of American prisoners of war.

Following are excerpts from the Democratic platform of 1972:

Vietnam. We believe that war is a waste of human life. We are determined to end forthwith a war which has cost 50,000 American lives, $150 billion of our resources, that has divided us from each other, drained our national will and inflicted incalculable damage to countless people. We will end that war by a simple plan that need not be kept secret: The immediate total withdrawal of all Americans from Southeast Asia.

Vietnam Amnesty. To those who for reasons of conscience refused to serve in this war and were prosecuted or sought refuge abroad, we state our firm intention to declare an amnesty, on an appropriate basis, when the fighting has ceased and our troops and prisoners of war have returned.

Poverty. The next Democratic Administration must end the present welfare system and replace it with an income security program which places cash assistance in an appropriate context with all of the measures outlined above, adding up to an earned income approach to ensure each family an income substantially more than the poverty level defined in the area. Federal income assistance will supplement the income of working poor people and assure an adequate income for those unable to work.

Crime. There must be laws to control the improper use of hand guns. Four years ago a candidate for the presidency was slain by a hand gun. Two months ago, another candidate for that office was gravely wounded. Three out of four police officers killed in the line of duty are slain with hand guns. Effective legislation must include a ban on sale of hand guns known as Saturday night specials which are unsuitable for sporting purposes.

Free Expression and Privacy. The new Democratic Administration should bring an end to the pattern of political persecution and investigation, the use of high office as a pulpit for unfair attack and intimidation and the blatant efforts to control the poor and to keep them from acquiring additional economic security or political power.

The epidemic of wiretapping and electronic surveillance engaged in by the Nixon Administration and the use of grand juries for purposes of political intimidation must be ended. The rule of law and the supremacy of the Constitution, as these concepts have traditionally been understood, must be restored.

Rights of Women. Women historically have been denied a full voice in the evolution of the political and social institutions of this country and are therefore allied with all underrepresented groups in a common desire to form a more humane and compassionate society. The Democratic Party pledges the following:

· A priority effort to ratify the Equal Rights Amendment. . . .
· Appointment of women to positions of top responsibilities in all branches of the federal government, to achieve an equitable ratio of women and men.

Presidential Elections. We favor a Constitutional change to abolish the Electoral College and to give every voter a direct and equal voice in Presidential elections. The amendment should provide for a runoff election, if no candidate received more than 40 percent of the popular vote.

REPUBLICANS

Six weeks after the Democratic convention, the Republicans gathered in the same Miami Beach convention hall. The August 21–23 convention, precisely programmed to make the most of free prime time, was a gigantic television spectacular from start to finish. The main business of the convention, the nomination of President Richard Nixon and Vice President Spiro T. Agnew to a second term, was a carefully planned ritual.

The selection of Miami Beach as the convention city provided as much drama as the convention itself. Initially the Republicans had chosen San Diego, California, as the host city, but the reluctance of that city to provide necessary facilities on schedule, coupled with the revelation that the International Telephone and Telegraph Corp. had pledged as much as $400,000 in local contributions, led the Republican National Committee to move the convention to Miami Beach.

Despite the preliminary organizational problems, the atmosphere of the convention itself was almost euphoric, and the sessions proceeded with dispatch. The five sessions lasted only sixteen hours and fifty-nine minutes, compared with the thirty hours and eighteen minutes of the Democratic convention.

The one debate, which lasted only an hour, occurred over the adoption of new procedures for selecting national convention delegates. The Republican National Committee's preconvention rules committee approved a 1976 delegate-allocation plan initiated by Sen. John G. Tower of Texas and Rep. Jack F. Kemp of New York. The plan emphasized a state's Republican presidential vote in awarding bonus delegates. It was viewed as especially beneficial to small southern and western states. The convention rules committee amended the Tower-Kemp plan to make it more palatable to larger states by adding some bonus delegates for states electing Republican governors and members of Congress.

However, Rep. William A. Steiger of Wisconsin introduced a different plan, weighted more toward states electing Republican governors and members of Congress—a plan that would work to the advantage of the larger states. The debate on the contrasting plans focused on the question of whether states should be rewarded chiefly for delivering their electoral votes to a Republican presidential candidate or whether the bonus should be based to some extent on gubernatorial and congressional contests.

The dispute was in part a battle between liberals and conservatives. Final victory for the conservatives was achieved on a 910 to 434 roll-call vote that defeated the Steiger amendment. The reallocation formula adopted by the delegates would expand the 1976 convention to more than 2,000 delegates, compared with the 1,348 who went to Miami Beach in 1972.

The struggle over the delegate-allocation formula was the only sign of party division at the convention. Nixon was renominated on the third night, receiving 1,347 of the 1,348 votes. The only opposing vote was cast reluctantly by a delegate from New Mexico for Rep. Paul N. McCloskey Jr. of California, whose antiwar challenge of the president had fizzled after the year's first primary in New Hampshire. *(Table p. 626.)*

One measure of the unity that surrounded the festive proceedings was the appearance of Gov. Nelson A. Rockefeller of New York to deliver Nixon's nominating speech. Rockefeller had become a loyal supporter of the president after having been his chief rival for the Republican nomination in 1960 and 1968.

Agnew was nominated the next night with 1,345 votes. There were two abstentions and one waggish vote for newscaster David Brinkley.

In his acceptance speech, Nixon combined a review of his first four years with promises for the next four and indirect but highly partisan attacks on his Democratic opponent, George McGovern. Nixon stressed that the choice in the upcoming election was "not between radical change and no change, the choice . . . is between change that works and change that won't work."

The Republican platform provoked little discussion and was approved by a voice vote. Two amendments were offered. The first, which would have pledged a prohibition on deficit federal spending, was defeated by voice vote. The second, advocating self-determination for American Indians, was approved by voice vote with the consent of the platform committee chairman, Rep. John J. Rhodes of Arizona.

The document, approximately twenty-thousand words long, was generally moderate in its proposals and conservative in language, in contrast to the Democrats' liberal platform.

The actual drafting of the Republican platform was heavily influenced by the White House, and platform committee sessions were held behind closed doors. In contrast, the Democrats held ten regional hearings around the country, drafted their platform in public, and were required by party rules to produce a final version at least ten days before the convention opened.

Following are excerpts from the Republican platform of 1972:

Vietnam. We will continue to seek a settlement of the Vietnam War which will permit the people of Southeast Asia to live in peace under political arrangements of their own choosing. We take specific note of the remaining major obstacle to settlement—Hanoi's demand that the United States overthrow the Saigon government and impose a Communist-dominated government on the South Vietnamese. We stand unequivocally at the side of the President in his effort to negotiate honorable terms, and in his refusal to accept terms which would dishonor this country.

Vietnam Amnesty. We are proud of the men and women who wear our country's uniform, especially of those who have borne the burden of fighting a difficult and unpopular war. Here and now we reject all proposals to grant amnesty to those who have broken the law by evading military service. We reject the claim that those who fled are more deserving, or obeyed a higher morality, than those next in line who served in their places.

Tax Reform. We reject the deceitful tax "reform" cynically represented as one that would soak the rich, but in fact one that would sharply raise the taxes of millions of families in middle-income brackets as well. We reject as well the lavish spending promised by the opposition Party which would more than double the present budget of the United States Government. This, too, would cause runaway inflation or force heavy increases in personal taxes.

Gun Control. [We pledge to] safeguard the right of responsible citizens to collect, own and use firearms for legitimate purposes, including hunting, target shooting and self-defense. We will strongly support efforts of all law enforcement agencies to apprehend and prosecute to the limit of the law all those who use firearms in the commission of crimes.

Women's Rights. Continued . . . support of the Equal Rights Amendment to the Constitution, our Party being the first national party to back this Amendment.

School Prayer. We reaffirm our view that voluntary prayer should be freely permitted in public places—particularly, by school children while attending public schools—provided that such prayers are not prepared or prescribed by the state or any of its political subdivisions and that no person's participation is coerced, thus preserving the traditional separation of church and state.

Health. To assure access to basic medical care for all our people, we support a program financed by employers, employees and the Federal Government to provide comprehensive health insurance coverage, including insurance against the cost of long-term and catastrophic illnesses and accidents and renal failure which necessitates dialysis, at a cost which all Americans can afford. . . .

We oppose nationalized compulsory health insurance. This approach would at least triple in taxes the amount the average citizen now pays for health and would deny families the right to choose the kind of care they prefer. Ultimately it would lower the overall quality of health care for all Americans.

1976 Conventions

PRESIDENTIAL CANDIDATES

Jimmy Carter
Democrat

Gerald R. Ford
Republican

DEMOCRATS

Jimmy Carter, whose presidential primary campaign flouted Democratic Party regulars, brought the party's diverse elements together July 12–15 in a show of unaccustomed unity. The four-day 1976 convention in New York City was the party's most harmonious in twelve years and a stark contrast to the bitter and divisive conventions of 1968 and 1972.

The spirit of harmony was evident in the committee reports. No credentials challenges were carried to the convention floor and just one minority plank to the platform was offered. Only the rules committee report sparked much debate, and it was muted compared with the emotional struggles in the previous two conventions.

The lack of a spirited competition for the presidential nomination was an important factor in the absence of credentials challenges. However, the groundwork for the harmonious atmosphere had been established months earlier, when the Democratic National Committee adopted new delegate-selection and convention rules.

The delegate-selection rules abolished the implicit quota system that had been the basis of most challenges in 1972. The only basis for a challenge in 1976 was the violation of a state's delegate-selection or affirmative action plan to ensure the fair representation of minorities. Because all states had their plans approved by the national committee's Compliance Review Commission, the credentials committee was not weighing the fairness of the plan but merely whether the state party had implemented it. In reverse of the 1972 system, the burden of proof was on the challenging individual or group, not on the state parties.

The task of challengers was further impeded by the action of the national committee in October 1975, raising the petition requirement for convention minority reports from 10 percent to 25 percent of credentials committee members.

The stringent new rules had an effect on the demographic composition of the convention. A postconvention survey by the national committee indicated that 36 percent of the delegates in 1976 were women, compared with 38 percent in 1972; 7 percent were black compared with 15 percent four years earlier, and 14 percent were youths, compared with 21 percent in 1972.

The first roll call of the convention came on a rules committee minority report that would have permitted extended debate on the platform. The measure was promoted by party liberals, who complained that the restrictive convention rules cut off their chance for full debate. They urged platform debate on a maximum of three issues for a total of one hour, if at least three hundred delegates from ten states signed a petition for such issues. The proposal called for debate only; no votes would have been taken.

Carter delegates, though, were nearly unanimous in their opposition, fearing that adoption of the minority report would unduly lengthen the proceedings. The convention rejected the minority report by a vote of 735 to 1,957½.

Liberals had better luck when the rules relating to future conventions were considered. By voice votes, they won approval of majority reports to establish the party's new Judicial Council as an arbiter of party rules and to eliminate the controversial loophole primary.

A loophole primary permitted election of delegates on a winner-take-all basis at the congressional district level. Carter and Democratic National Chairman Robert S. Strauss both favored the minority report, which called simply for review of the loophole primary by the newly established Commission on the Role and Future of Presidential Primaries, headed by Michigan state chairman Morley Winograd.

Liberals argued that this was not enough. They claimed that the loophole primary violated the party charter, which required proportional representation. Their position prevailed in the rules committee by a razor-thin margin of 58½ to 58¼. Although Carter managers were unhappy with the majority report, they did not press for a roll call and the convention approved it by voice vote.

But the convention rejected on roll-call votes liberal amendments to mandate the size and agenda of the party's 1978 midterm conference and to lower the minority report requirement at future conventions. The minority report on the 1978 conference would have required a prescribed agenda that included the discussion of policy matters. It also would have mandated a conference of at least two thousand delegates, two-thirds of them elected at the congressional district level. On the roll call the proposal ran ahead 1,240 to 1,128, but it failed because of convention rules requiring a constitutional majority of 1,505 votes.

Another roll call came on the unsuccessful attempt by liberal delegates to have the minority report requirement at future conventions lowered from 25 percent to 15 percent of convention committee members. It was rejected, 1,249 to 1,354½.

Potentially the most explosive of the rules issues, regarding a "female quota" at future conventions, was settled in behind-the-scenes meetings between Carter and representatives of the women's caucus. At a rules committee meeting in Washington, D.C., in late June, the women's caucus had demanded equal representation with men in state delegations at future conventions. The Carter forces balked at this. Carter's views prevailed in the rules committee, which urged each state to promote equal division between the sexes but left the implementation of the rule to each state party. The women's caucus filed a minority report.

Both sides expressed a willingness to compromise, and in New York City July 11 and 12 Carter met with representatives of the women's caucus. They reached a compromise that encouraged—but did not require—equal representation for women at the party's midterm conference and at future conventions. Language was inserted calling for the national committee to "encourage and assist" state parties in achieving equal division.

The compromise also included agreements between Carter and the women on other questions. Carter promised to establish an independent women's division in the party outside the realm of the chairman and pledged full party representation for women. The candidate promised to work for the ratification of the Equal Rights Amendment and pledged high government positions for women. With acceptance of this compromise by the women's caucus, the minority report was withdrawn and the compromise language on equal division was worked into the majority report.

Balloting for president came on July 14, the third day of the convention, but it was merely a formality. Carter had locked up the nomination more than a month earlier when he won the June 8 Ohio primary, a victory that prompted a cascade of endorsements and stymied his remaining opposition. Besides Carter, three other names were placed in nomination: Rep. Morris K. Udall of Arizona, Carter's most persistent primary challenger; Gov. Edmund G. Brown Jr. of California; and antiabortion crusader Ellen McCormack. The proceedings, though, turned into a love-feast as Udall before the balloting and Brown afterwards appeared at the convention to declare their support for Carter.

On the presidential roll call, Carter received 2,238½ of the convention's 3,008 votes, topping the needed majority little more than halfway through the balloting with the vote from Ohio. Udall finished second with 329½ votes, followed by Brown with 300½, Gov. George C. Wallace of Alabama with 57, and McCormack with 22. The rest of the vote was scattered. After completion of the roll call—and vote switches in California, Rhode Island, and Louisiana—a motion to make the nomination unanimous was approved by voice vote. *(Table, p. 627.)*

The following morning Carter announced that his choice for vice president was Sen. Walter F. Mondale of Minnesota. Carter noted that it was a difficult decision, admitting that he had changed his mind three times in the previous thirty days.

In explaining his choice, Carter cited Mondale's experience and political philosophy, his concept of the presidency, and the preparation Mondale had made for his interview with Carter. Most of all, Carter emphasized compatibility, saying, "It's a very sure feeling that I have."

Mondale was one of seven prospective running mates Carter had personally interviewed. At his home in Plains, Georgia, Carter had interviewed, besides Mondale, Sens. Edmund S. Muskie (Maine) and John Glenn (Ohio). At the New York convention he interviewed Sens. Henry M. Jackson (Washington), Frank Church (Idaho), and Adlai E. Stevenson III (Illinois), and Rep. Peter W. Rodino Jr. (New Jersey). Rodino withdrew his name from consideration shortly after his interview.

Like the presidential roll call the previous night, the balloting for vice president on July 15 was a formality. Mondale had only one declared opponent, Gary Benoit, a Massachusetts college student and a Wallace delegate. Two others were nominated but withdrew—Rep. Ronald V. Dellums of California and Vietnam War resister Fritz Efaw of Oklahoma. Dellums, an African American from Oakland, appeared personally to withdraw his name and used the opportunity to plead with Carter to pay attention to the needs of minorities at home and to Third World aspirations abroad.

On the roll call, Mondale swamped his rivals, receiving 2,817 votes, more than 90 percent of the convention total. Retiring House Speaker Carl Albert (Oklahoma) finished a distant second with 36 votes, all cast as a complimentary gesture by his home state delegation. Rep. Barbara C. Jordan (Texas), an African American from Houston, followed with 28 votes, an apparent tribute to her dramatic keynote address.

Following the balloting, Mondale delivered his acceptance speech and succeeded in arousing the delegates with a partisan oratorical style reminiscent of his Minnesota mentor, Sen. Hubert H. Humphrey.

"We have just lived through the worst scandal in American history," Mondale declared, "and are now led by a president who pardoned the person who did it." His reference to the Watergate affair and to the Nixon pardon brought the delegates to their feet.

Carter's acceptance speech, unlike Mondale's, was not a rousing one in the traditional sense. But Carter was able to begin his address before 11 P.M., in the prime television slot that Strauss had promised as a contrast to George McGovern's nearly unheard 3 A.M. acceptance speech in 1972.

The 1976 platform had been carefully constructed by the Carter forces at platform committee meetings in Washington, D.C., in June. The ninety-page document was something of a throwback to earlier years—a broad statement of party goals rather than a list of legislative programs and controversial stands on issues. The platform and the care with which it was written reflected the Democrats' determination to avoid the platform fights and issues that proved costly to the party in the previous two elections.

Unlike 1972, when there was sharp, divisive debate on twenty minority planks, only one minority plank—on revising the 1939 Hatch Act to allow federal employees to run for political office and participate in partisan campaigns—was presented to the delegates in Madison Square Garden. It was approved by the Carter forces and was adopted by a voice vote after minimal debate.

Following are excerpts from the Democratic platform of 1976:

Economy. To meet our goals we must set annual targets for employment, production and price stability; the Federal Reserve must be made a full partner in national economic decisions and become responsive to the economic goals of Congress and the President. . . .

Full Employment. We have met the goals of full employment with stable prices in the past and can do it again. The Democratic Party is committed to the right of all adult Americans willing, able and seeking work to have opportunities for useful jobs at living wages. To make that commitment meaningful, we pledge ourselves to the support of legislation that will make every responsible effort to reduce adult unemployment to 3 percent within 4 years. . . .

Government Reform. The Democratic Party is committed to the adoption of reforms such as zero-based budgeting, mandatory reorganization timetables, and sunset laws which do not jeopardize the implementation of basic human and political rights.

An Office of Citizen Advocacy should be established as part of the executive branch, independent of any agency, with full access to agency records and with both the power and the responsibility to investigate complaints.

We support the revision of the Hatch Act so as to extend to federal workers the same political rights enjoyed by other Americans as a birthright, while still protecting the Civil Service from political abuse.

We call for legislative action to provide for partial public financing on a matching basis of the congressional elections, and the exploration of further reforms to insure the integrity of the electoral process.

Health. We need a comprehensive national health insurance system with universal and mandatory coverage. Such a national health insurance system should be financed by a combination of employer-employee shared payroll taxes and general tax revenues. Consideration should be given to developing a means of support for national health insurance that taxes all forms of economic income.

Welfare Reform. We should move toward replacement of our existing inadequate and wasteful system with a simplified system of income maintenance, substantially financed by the federal government, which includes a requirement that those able to work be provided with appropriate available jobs or job training opportunities. Those persons who are physically able to work (other than mothers with dependent children) should be required to accept appropriate available jobs or job training.

As an interim step, and as a means of providing immediate federal fiscal relief to state and local governments, local governments should no longer be required to bear the burden of welfare costs. Further, there should be a phased reduction in the states' share of welfare costs.

Civil Rights and Liberties. We pledge effective and vigorous action to protect citizens' privacy from bureaucratic and technological intrusions, such as wiretapping and bugging without judicial scrutiny and supervision; and a full and complete pardon for those who are in legal or financial jeopardy because of their peaceful opposition to the Vietnam War, with deserters to be considered on a case-by-case basis.

We fully recognize the religious and ethical nature of the concerns which many Americans have on the subject of abortion. We feel, however, that it is undesirable to attempt to amend the U.S. Constitution to overturn the Supreme Court decision in this area.

Gun Control. Handguns simplify and intensify violent crime. Ways must be found to curtail the availability of these weapons. The Democratic Party must provide the leadership for a coordinated federal and state effort to strengthen the presently inadequate controls over the manufacture, assembly, distribution and possession of handguns and to ban Saturday night specials.

Furthermore, since people and not guns commit crimes, we support mandatory sentencing for individuals convicted of committing a felony with a gun.

The Democratic Party, however, affirms the right of sportsmen to possess guns for purely hunting and target-shooting purposes.

Energy. The Democratic energy platform begins with a recognition that the federal government has an important role to play in insuring the nation's energy future, and that it must be given the tools it needs to protect the economy and the nation's consumers from arbitrary and excessive energy price increases and help the nation embark on a massive domestic energy program focusing on conservation, coal conversion, exploration and development of new technologies to insure an adequate short-term and long-term supply of energy for the nation's needs. . . .

The huge reserves of oil, gas and coal on federal territory, including the outer continental shelf, belong to all the people. The Republicans have pursued leasing policies which give the public treasury the least benefit and the energy industry the most benefit from these public resources. Consistent with environmentally sound practices, new leasing procedures must be adopted to correct these policies, as well as insure the timely development of existing leases. . . .

We also support the legal prohibition against corporate ownership of competing types of energy, such as oil and coal. We believe such "horizontal" concentration of economic power to be dangerous both to the national interest and to the functioning of the competitive system.

Environment. The Democratic Party's strong commitment to environmental quality is based on its conviction that environmental protection is not simply an aesthetic goal, but is necessary to achieve a more just society. Cleaning up air and water supplies and controlling the proliferation of dangerous chemicals is a necessary part of a successful national health program. Protecting the worker from workplace hazards is a key element of our full employment program. . . .

Latin America. We must make clear our revulsion at the systematic violations of basic human rights that have occurred under some Latin American military regimes.

We pledge support for a new Panama Canal treaty, which insures the interests of the United States in that waterway, recognizes the principles already agreed upon, takes into account the interests of the Canal work force, and which will have wide hemispheric support.

REPUBLICANS

After four boisterous, raucous, and sometimes tearful days, Republicans ended their 1976 national convention on a positive note absent during most of a gathering characterized by strident attacks on the Democrats and the Congress they controlled. Delegates arrived in Kansas City, Missouri, for the August 16–19 convention more evenly split than they had been since 1952, when Dwight D. Eisenhower edged Sen. Robert A. Taft of Ohio (1939–1953) for the GOP nomination. Both major rivals for the nomination, President Gerald R. Ford (breaking with tradition) and former California governor Ronald Reagan, arrived in town three days before the balloting to continue their pursuit of delegates.

Ford, relying heavily on the prestige of the presidency that sometimes had failed to produce results during the seven-month campaign, invited a number of wavering delegates to his hotel suite in the new Crown Center Hotel while Reagan also courted delegates personally.

By a margin of 111 votes on August 17, the Reagan forces lost the first and probably the most important roll call of the convention. The vote came on a Reagan-sponsored amendment to the rules committee report that would have required all presidential candidates to name their running mates before the presidential balloting the next night.

The idea of a test vote on the vice-presidential question was sprung by Reagan's campaign manager, John Sears, barely a week before the convention, when on August 9 he appeared before the rules committee and urged that the proposal be included as Section C of Rule 16. The amendment was clearly aimed at throwing Ford on the defensive, because Reagan had designated Sen. Richard S. Schweiker of Pennsylvania as his running mate on July 26. Under the proposal, failure of a candidate to comply would have freed all delegates from any commitments to vote for him.

The convention debate and vote on Rule 16C was the focal point of the August 17 session. Supporters characterized the proposal as a "right-to-know" amendment. "A presidential candidate must tell us who's on his team before we are expected to join him," argued former Missouri representative Thomas B. Curtis, the sponsor of the amendment. "The delegates have the right to be consulted for a day of decision that will have an impact for years to come."

Speakers against the amendment countered that it was solely a maneuver of the Reagan forces and that any vice-presidential selection reform should be deliberately considered on its merits.

The final court stood at 1,069 in favor of the amendment and 1,180 against, with ten abstentions. The vote was the first tangible evidence of Ford strength at the convention and paved the way for his nomination. (*Table, p. 628.*)

On the presidential roll call August 18, the final vote was 1,187 for Ford, 1,070 for Reagan, one vote from the New York delegation for Commerce Secretary Elliot L. Richardson, and one abstention. (*Table, p. 628.*) On a voice vote the convention made the nomination unanimous.

Ford added to the partisan style of the Republican ticket the next day by selecting Sen. Robert Dole of Kansas as his running mate after Reagan ruled out his acceptance of the second spot. While little mentioned during speculation about Ford's vice presidential choice, Dole, a former chairman of the Republican National Committee, was seen as an effective gut fighter who would allow Ford to keep his campaign style presidential in the battle against Carter.

Vice President Nelson A. Rockefeller nominated his own potential successor, telling the crowd that the Kansas senator not only could stand the heat of political battle, but also could "really dole it out." Rockefeller, unpopular with conservatives, had not sought to continue in the job he had gained through appointment in 1974.

On the vice-presidential roll call, Dole received 1,921 of the convention's 2,259 votes. Sen. Jesse A. Helms of North Carolina, a hero of the conservatives, finished a distant second with 103 votes. The remaining votes were scattered among twenty-nine other "candidates."

Ford's acceptance speech concentrated on his record since taking office in mid-1974. The president took credit for cutting inflation in half, increasing employment to a record level, and bringing the country to peace.

Ford diverged from his prepared text to issue a direct challenge to Carter. "I'm ready, eager to go before the American people and debate the real issues face to face with Jimmy Carter," the president said. "The American people have the right to know first-hand exactly where both of us stand." No major party presidential nominees had debated since the Kennedy-Nixon debates in 1960.

By the time the convention got around to debating the platform the night of August 17, an expected bitter struggle between Ford and Reagan forces had been deflated by the earlier vote on rules. The arena, which had been packed two hours earlier, held a somewhat smaller crowd after midnight. Many Ford delegates in particular, confident that they had won the main event, left while members of the platform committee presented the sixty-five-page document.

Two minority planks were offered, in accordance with platform committee rules that required petitions signed by 25 percent of the members. The first, sponsored by Ann F. Peckham of Wisconsin, called for deleting all platform references to abortion. The committee-approved section supported a constitutional amendment "to restore protection of the right to life of unborn children." After a twelve-minute debate, the minority plank was defeated by voice vote and the abortion language stayed in.

The second minority report, a six-paragraph addition to the foreign policy section, was sponsored by thirty-four Reagan supporters on the platform committee. Without mentioning names, it criticized President Ford and Secretary of State Henry A. Kissinger for losing public confidence, making secret international agreements, and discouraging the hope of freedom for those who did not have it—presumably captive nations.

Many of Ford's supporters, including Rep. John B. Anderson of Illinois and Senate Minority Leader Hugh Scott of Pennsylvania, earlier had expressed strong opposition to the "morality in foreign policy" plank, as it came to be called. Ford's floor leader, Sen. Robert P. Griffin of Michigan, and Rep. David C. Treen of Louisiana sought compromise language in informal negotiations on the floor. But the Reagan forces, led by Senator Helms, were adamant.

Not wishing to offend the Reagan contingent further, Ford's supporters decided not to fight. Sen. Roman L. Hruska of Nebraska, chairman of the foreign policy subcommittee, announced from the podium that there would be no organized opposition to the plank. It was passed by voice vote. The convention then approved the platform.

The document reflected the nearly equal influence of President Ford and Ronald Reagan at the convention. It was a traditional Republican blueprint for limited government—a clear contrast with the Democratic platform.

Ordinarily, the platform of the party holding the White House heaps praise on the incumbent president and boasts of the way he has led the nation. This Republican platform did not. With Ford embroiled in a contest for the nomination, the platform writers chose to mention him by name only a few times. Richard Nixon was never mentioned. There were only vague references to Watergate.

Following are excerpts from the Republican Party platform of 1976:

Economy. We believe it is of paramount importance that the American people understand that the number one destroyer of jobs is inflation.

Republicans hope every American realizes that if we are to permanently eliminate high unemployment, it is essential to protect the integrity of our money. That means putting an end to deficit spending.

Wage and price controls are not the solution to inflation. They attempt to treat only the symptom—rising prices—not the cause. Historically, controls have always been a dismal failure, and in the end they create only shortages, black markets and higher prices. For these reasons the Republican Party strongly opposes any reimposition of such controls, on a standby basis or otherwise. . . .

Government Reform. There must be functional realignment of government, instead of the current arrangement by subject areas or constituencies.

Revenue Sharing is an effort to reverse the trend toward centralization. Revenue Sharing must continue without unwarranted federal strictures and regulations.

Block grant programs should be extended to replace many existing categorical health, education, child nutrition and social programs.

While we oppose a uniform national primary, we encourage the concept of regional presidential primaries, which would group those states which voluntarily agree to have presidential primaries in a geographical area on a common date.

Criminal Justice. Each state should have the power to decide whether it wishes to impose the death penalty for certain crimes. All localities are urged to tighten their bail practices and to review their sentencing and parole procedures.

Gun Control. We support the right of citizens to keep and bear arms. We oppose federal registration of firearms. Mandatory sentences for crimes committed with a lethal weapon are the only effective solution to this problem.

Civil Rights and Liberties. The Republican Party reaffirms its support for ratification of the Equal Rights Amendment. Our Party was the first national party to endorse the E.R.A. in 1940. We continue to believe its ratification is essential to insure equal rights for all Americans.

The Republican Party favors a continuance of the public dialogue on abortion and supports the efforts of those who seek enactment of a constitutional amendment to restore protection of the right to life for unborn children.

Welfare Reform. We oppose federalizing the welfare system; local levels of government are most aware of the needs of their communities.

We also oppose the guaranteed annual income concept or any programs that reduce the incentive to work.

Those features of the present law, particularly the food stamp program, that draw into assistance programs people who are capable of paying for their own needs should be corrected. The humanitarian purpose of such programs must not be corrupted by eligibility loopholes.

Health. We support extension of catastrophic illness protection to all who cannot obtain it. We should utilize our private health insurance system to assure adequate protection for those who do not have it. Such an approach will eliminate the red tape and high bureaucratic costs inevitable in a comprehensive national program.

The Republican Party opposes compulsory national health insurance.

Energy. One fact should now be clear: We must reduce sharply our dependence on other nations for energy and strive to achieve energy independence at the earliest possible date. We cannot allow the economic destiny and international policy of the United States to be dictated by the sovereign powers that control major portions of the world's petroleum supplies. . . .

Foreign Policy. We recognize and commend that great beacon of human courage and morality, Alexander Solzhenitsyn, for his compelling message that we must face the world with no illusions about the nature of tyranny. Ours will be a foreign policy that keeps this ever in mind.

Ours will be a foreign policy which recognizes that in international negotiations we must make no undue concessions; that in pursuing

détente we must not grant unilateral favors with only the hope of getting future favors in return.

Agreements that are negotiated, such as the one signed in Helsinki, must not take from those who do not have freedom the hope of one day gaining it.

Finally, we are firmly committed to a foreign policy in which secret agreements, hidden from our people, will have no part.

Latin America. By continuing its policies of exporting subversion and violence, Cuba remains outside the Inter-American family of nations. We condemn attempts by the Cuban dictatorship to intervene in the affairs of other nations; and, as long as such conduct continues, it shall remain ineligible for admission to the Organization of American States.

The United States intends that the Panama Canal be preserved as an international waterway for the ships of all nations. . . . In any talks with Panama, however, the United States negotiators should in no way cede, dilute, forfeit, negotiate or transfer any rights, power, authority, jurisdiction, territory or property that are necessary for the protection and security of the United States and the entire Western Hemisphere.

1980 Conventions

PRESIDENTIAL CANDIDATES

Jimmy Carter
Democrat

Ronald Reagan
Republican

John B. Anderson
Independent

REPUBLICANS

Ronald Reagan, the sixty-nine-year-old former California governor, was installed as the Republican presidential nominee at the party's national convention, but his moment of glory nearly was overshadowed by an unusual flap over the number-two spot. The choosing of Reagan's running mate provided the only suspense at the GOP convention, held July 14–17 in Detroit's Joe Louis Arena.

Who would fill the number-one spot had been determined long before when Reagan won twenty-eight of the thirty-four Republican presidential primaries and eliminated all of his major rivals. The last to withdraw—George Bush—was tapped by Reagan July 16 as his ticket mate in a dramatic postmidnight appearance before the delegates.

For most of the evening of July 16, it looked as though Gerald R. Ford would occupy the second spot on the ticket, which would have made him the first former president to run for vice president. A number of Republicans had described the combination as a "dream ticket." Groups of Reagan and Ford supporters had met four times to "discuss" the possibility of forging a Reagan-Ford ticket.

The discussions reportedly centered around providing a role for Ford somewhat akin to the White House chief of staff's. Ford further fed the speculation, offering a simple solution to the temporary problem that would have been posed by the Twelfth Amendment to the Constitution. The amendment would have had the effect of prohibiting the members of the electoral college from California from voting for both Reagan and Ford because both were California residents. The amendment says that the electors from any state must vote for at least one person who is not from that state. Ford said Reagan's lawyers had researched the residency question and determined that legally there would be no problem if the former president changed his residence to Michigan, which he represented in the House for twenty-five years, or to Colorado, where he owned a home.

As the evening of July 16 wore on, the speculation heightened. About 9:15 P.M. Reagan telephoned Ford to ask him to make up his mind whether he wanted the vice president's job. Meanwhile, convention officials proceeded to call the roll of the states, and Reagan received enough votes to become the official nominee.

But at about 11:15 P.M. the Reagan-Ford arrangement fell apart. Ford went to Reagan's suite in the Detroit Plaza Hotel and the two men agreed that it would be better for Ford to campaign for the GOP ticket rather than be a member of it. "His [Ford's] instinct told him it was not the thing to do," Reagan said later.

When it became apparent that efforts to persuade Ford to join the ticket had failed, Reagan turned to Bush, a moderate with proven vote-getting ability. The Reagan camp refused to acknowledge that Bush had been the second choice, even though it was widely perceived that way. "There was everybody else and then the Ford option," Edwin Meese, Reagan's chief of staff, said later.

Bush had been Reagan's most persistent competitor through the long primary season, but he won only six primaries—Michigan, Massachusetts, Connecticut, Pennsylvania, the District of Columbia, and Puerto Rico. Bush was one of the vice-presidential possibilities favored by those in the party who believed that Reagan had to reach outside the GOP's conservative wing if he were to have broad appeal in November.

Bush supporters said that his Texas residency would balance the ticket geographically and that his extensive government service would overcome criticism that Reagan did not have any Washington experience. Bush served from 1967 to 1971 in the U.S. House and had been ambassador to the United Nations, head of the U.S. liaison office in Peking, and director of the Central Intelligence Agency.

The Republican Party's 1980 platform was more a blueprint for victory in November than a definitive statement of party views. Rather than slug it out over specifics, the party's moderate and conservative wings agreed to blur their differences to appear united, to broaden the party's appeal and to smooth Reagan's way to the White House.

Overwhelmingly, platform committee members agreed the document should be consistent with Reagan's positions. Thus, though one media poll found delegates overwhelmingly in favor of resuming a peacetime draft, the platform bowed to the view of its nominee and stated its opposition to a renewal of the draft "at this time." In the same manner, the party's platform took no position on ratification of the Equal Rights Amendment (ERA) to the Constitution. Since 1940 Republican platforms had supported an ERA amendment. Reagan, however, opposed ratification, and ERA opponents far outnumbered the amendment's supporters on the platform committee. Yet Reagan, in a gesture

to moderates, suggested that the platform not take a position on the issue, and the committee agreed.

Most of the platform document consisted of policy statements on which most Republicans agreed. There were calls for tax cuts, pleas for less government regulation, and harsh criticisms of the Carter administration. In two areas, however, the platform took a particularly hard-line position. The platform supported a constitutional amendment that would outlaw abortion and called on a Reagan administration to appoint federal judges who opposed abortion. On defense, platform writers took an already hard-line plank that had been drafted by party staff and moved it sharply to the right. The platform called for massive increases in defense spending and scoffed at the Carter administration's proposed Strategic Arms Limitation Treaty (SALT II).

On the other hand, to pick up votes from organized labor, blacks, and the poor, the platform made some new overtures to those traditionally non-Republican groups. It pledged to strengthen enforcement of the civil rights laws, made overtures to U.S. workers put out of their jobs by competition from foreign imports, and promised to save America's inner cities.

The platform was adopted by the convention July 15 without change, but not before an unsuccessful attempt was made to reopen on the floor one of its more controversial sections: the section suggesting that Reagan appoint federal judges who oppose abortion. Sen. Charles H. Percy of Illinois called it "the worst plank I have ever seen in any platform by the Republican Party." The moderates sought to round up support for reopening the platform on the floor, but their efforts failed.

Ronald Reagan received the Republican nomination on the first ballot. (Table, p. 629.)

In his acceptance speech, Reagan combined sharp jabs at the alleged shortcomings of the Carter administration with a reaffirmation of his own conservative credo. Reagan cited three grave threats to the nation's existence—"a disintegrating economy, a weakened defense, and an energy policy based on the sharing of scarcity." The culprits, Reagan contended, were President Carter and the Democratic Congress. He said they had preached that the American people needed to tighten their belts. "I utterly reject that view," he declared.

Following are excerpts from the Republican Party platform of 1980:

Taxes. . . . [W]e believe it is essential to cut personal tax rates out of fairness to the individual. . . .

Therefore, the Republican Party supports across-the-board reductions in personal income tax rates, phased in over three years, which will reduce tax rates from the range of 14 to 70 percent to a range of from 10 to 50 percent.

. . . Republicans will move to end tax bracket creep caused by inflation. We support tax indexing to protect taxpayers from the automatic tax increases caused when cost-of-living wage increases move them into higher tax brackets.

Black Americans. During the next four years we are committed to policies that will:

• encourage local governments to designate specific enterprise zones within depressed areas that will promote new jobs, new and expanded businesses and new economic vitality;

• open new opportunities for black men and women to begin small businesses of their own by, among other steps, removing excessive regulations, disincentives for venture capital and other barriers erected by the government;

• bring strong, effective enforcement of federal civil rights statutes, especially those dealing with threats to physical safety and security which have recently been increasing; and

• ensure that the federal government follows a nondiscriminatory system of appointments . . . with a careful eye for qualified minority aspirants.

Women's Rights. We acknowledge the legitimate efforts of those who support or oppose ratification of the Equal Rights Amendment.

We reaffirm our Party's historic commitment to equal rights and equality for women.

We support equal rights and equal opportunities for women, without taking away traditional rights of women such as exemption from the military draft. We support the enforcement of all equal opportunity laws and urge the elimination of discrimination against women.

We reaffirm our belief in the traditional role and values of the family in our society. . . . The importance of support for the mother and homemaker in maintaining the values of this country cannot be over-emphasized.

Abortion. While we recognize differing views on this question among Americans in general—and in our own Party—we affirm our support of a constitutional amendment to restore protection of the right to life for unborn children. We also support the Congressional efforts to restrict the use of taxpayers' dollars for abortion.

Education. . . . [T]he Republican Party supports deregulation by the federal government of public education, and encourages the elimination of the federal Department of Education.

We support Republican initiatives in the Congress to restore the right of individuals to participate in voluntary, non-denominational prayer in schools and other public facilities. . . .

Crime. We believe that the death penalty serves as an effective deterrent to capital crime and should be applied by the federal government and by states which approve it as an appropriate penalty for certain major crimes.

We believe the right of citizens to keep and bear arms must be preserved. Accordingly, we oppose federal registration of firearms. Mandatory sentences for commission of armed felonies are the most effective means to deter abuse of this right.

Foreign Competition. The Republican Party recognizes the need to provide workers who have lost their jobs because of technological obsolescence or imports the opportunity to adjust to changing economic conditions. In particular, we will seek ways to assist workers threatened by foreign competition.

The Republican Party believes that protectionist tariffs and quotas are detrimental to our economic well-being. Nevertheless, we insist that our trading partners offer our nation the same level of equity, access, and fairness that we have shown them.

Big Government. The Republican Party reaffirms its belief in the decentralization of the federal government and in the traditional American principle that the best government is the one closest to the people. There, it is less costly, more accountable, and more responsive to people's needs. . . .

Energy. We are committed to . . . a strategy of aggressively boosting the nation's energy supplies; stimulating new energy technology and more efficient energy use; restoring maximum feasible choice and freedom in the marketplace for energy consumers and producers alike; and eliminating energy shortages and disruptions. . . .

Balanced Budget. If federal spending is reduced as tax cuts are phased in, there will be sufficient budget surpluses to fund the tax cuts, and allow for reasonable growth in necessary program spending.

. . . We believe a Republican President and a Republican Congress can balance the budget and reduce spending through legislative actions, eliminating the necessity for a Constitutional amendment to compel it. However, if necessary, the Republican Party will seek to adopt a Constitutional amendment to limit federal spending and balance the budget, except in time of national emergency as determined by a two-thirds vote of Congress.

National Security. Republicans commit themselves to an immediate increase in defense spending to be applied judiciously to critically needed programs. We will build toward a sustained defense expenditure sufficient to close the gap with the Soviets. Republicans approve and endorse a national strategy of peace through strength. . . .

Nuclear Forces. . . . We reject the mutual-assured-destruction (MAD) strategy of the Carter Administration. . . . We propose, instead, a credible strategy which will deter a Soviet attack by the clear capability of our forces to survive and ultimately to destroy Soviet military targets.

A Republican Administration will strive for early modernization of our theater nuclear forces so that a seamless web of deterrence can be maintained against all levels of attack, and our credibility with our European allies is restored.

Defense Manpower and the Draft. The Republican Party is not prepared to accept a peacetime draft at this time. . . . We will not consider a peacetime draft unless a well-managed, Congressionally-funded, full-scale effort to improve the all-volunteer force does not meet expectations.

The Americas. We deplore the Marxist Sandinista takeover of Nicaragua and the Marxist attempts to destabilize El Salvador, Guatemala, and Honduras. We do not support United States assistance to any Marxist government in this hemisphere and we oppose the Carter Administration aid program for the government of Nicaragua. However, we will support the efforts of the Nicaraguan people to establish a free and independent government.

DEMOCRATS

President Jimmy Carter emerged victorious from a deeply divided Democratic National Convention unsure whether his plea for unity to supporters of rival Sen. Edward M. Kennedy of Massachusetts had succeeded. Kennedy had been Carter's main opponent in his quest for renomination throughout the spring primary season. When it became apparent that Kennedy had not won in the primaries and caucuses the delegate support he needed, he turned his efforts to prying the nomination away from the president at the convention.

Kennedy's presence was strong throughout the convention week and expressions of support for the senator sometimes upstaged those for the incumbent president. Chants of "We want Ted" rocked off the walls of New York's Madison Square Garden during the convention's four days, August 11–14. And their echo faintly followed the president as he left the podium following his acceptance speech.

Kennedy's efforts to wrest the nomination from Carter centered around a proposed new convention rule that bound delegates to vote on the first ballot for the candidates under whose banner they were elected. When the convention opened, Carter could count 315 more votes than he needed for the nomination—votes that he had won in nominating caucuses and presidential primaries. As a result, Kennedy's only chance to gain the nomination was to defeat the binding rule.

Opponents of the binding rule argued that political conditions had changed since the delegates were elected months earlier and that to bind them would break with a century and a half of Democratic tradition.

But most Carter supporters scoffed at that contention, stressing that delegates were free to vote their conscience on all roll calls but the first one for president. Passage of the rule was simply fair play, they added. It had been adopted in 1978 without opposition by the party's most recent rules-review commission and the Democratic National Committee. Only when it was apparent that Carter was winning, claimed Atlanta mayor Maynard Jackson, did the Kennedy camp want to change the rules to allow a "fifth ball, a fourth out, or a tenth inning."

When the measure finally came to a vote, Carter forces turned back the attempt to overturn the proposed rule. The vote was 1,936.418 to 1,390.580 against Kennedy's position. *(Table, p. 630.)*

Shortly after the vote, Kennedy ended his nine-month challenge to the president by announcing that his name would not be placed in nomination August 13. Passage of the binding rule ensured Carter's renomination.

Despite the loss on the binding rule, the Kennedy camp succeeded in molding the party platform more to their liking. The final document was filled with so many concessions to the Kennedy forces that it won only a half-hearted endorsement from the president. The platform battle, one of the longest in party history, filled seventeen hours of debate and roll calls that stretched over two days, August 12 and 13.

Most of Carter's concessions and outright defeats came on the economic and human needs sections of the forty-thousand-word document. It was these revisions that Carter rejected—as diplomatically as possible—in a statement issued several hours after the debate wound to a close.

The marathon platform debate reached its high point on Tuesday evening, August 12, when Kennedy addressed the delegates in behalf of his minority report on the economic chapter. Kennedy's speech provided the Democratic convention with its most exciting moments. The address, which sparked a forty-minute emotional demonstration when it was over, called for Democratic unity and laced into the Republican nominee, Ronald Reagan.

Kennedy defended his liberal ideology, supporting national health insurance and federal spending to restore deteriorated urban areas. He lashed out at Reagan's proposal for a massive tax cut, labeling it as beneficial only to the wealthy. Buoyed by the Kennedy oratory, the convention went on to pass by voice vote three liberal Kennedy platform planks on the economy, thereby rejecting the more moderate versions favored by Carter.

The first of the Kennedy-sponsored planks was a statement pledging that fairness would be the overriding principle of the Democrats' economic policy and that no actions would be taken that would "significantly increase" unemployment. The convention next approved a Kennedy plank seeking a $12 billion antirecession jobs program, a $1 billion rail renewal plan, and an expanded housing program for low- and moderate-income families. The final Kennedy economic plank was a statement of opposition to fighting inflation through a policy of high interest rates and unemployment. Carter had agreed to this plank the day before the convention opened.

Carter floor managers realized that it would be difficult to block passage of the Kennedy economic proposals. After the senator's emotion-filled speech, Carter advisers—realizing their position could not prevail—quickly sought to change from a roll call to a voice vote on the economic planks.

During the floor demonstration that followed Kennedy's speech, a series of telephone calls ricocheted between the podium and the senator's campaign trailer located off the convention floor. The negotiations involved how many elements of the Kennedy program would be accepted by voice vote. In the end, Carter prevailed on only one of Kennedy's economic minority reports, the call for an immediate wage and price freeze followed by controls.

Shortly after Carter's renomination August 13, Kennedy issued a statement endorsing the platform and pledging his support for Carter. In the final moments before adjournment, Kennedy made a stiff and brief appearance on the platform with Carter, Vice President Walter F. Mondale, and a host of Democratic office-holders. But the coolness of his appearance—accompanied by the warmest reception of the night—left questionable the commitment of the senator and his supporters to work strenuously for Carter's reelection.

Carter won the Democratic nomination with 2,123 votes compared with Kennedy's 1,150.5. Other candidates split 54.5 votes. *(Table, p. 630.)*

In his acceptance speech, Carter alluded to the convention's divisions. He led off with praise for Kennedy's tough campaign, thanks for his concessions during the convention, and an appeal for future help. "Ted, your party needs—and I need—you, and your idealism and dedication working for us." Carter spent much of the speech characterizing Reagan's programs as a disastrous "fantasy world" of easy answers. He avoided detailed comments on the economic issues over which he and Kennedy had split, confining himself to statements that he wanted jobs for all who needed them.

As expected, Mondale was renominated for vice president. The vice president's acceptance speech set delegates chanting "Not Ronald Reagan" as Mondale reeled off a list of liberal values and programs that, he said, most Americans agreed with. Mondale was one of the few speakers to unequivocally praise Carter's record, which he did at some length. The speech ended with a warning not to "let anyone make us less than what we can be."

Following are excerpts from the Democratic Party platform of 1980:

Employment. We specifically reaffirm our commitment to achieve all the goals of the Humphrey-Hawkins Full Employment Act within the currently prescribed dates in the Act, especially those relating to a joint reduction in unemployment and inflation. Full employment is important to the achievement of a rising standard of living, to the pursuit of sound justice, and to the strength and vitality of America.

Antirecession Assistance. A Democratic antirecession program must recognize that Blacks, Hispanics, other minorities, women, and older workers bear the brunt of recession. We pledge a $12 billion antirecession jobs program, providing at least 800,000 additional jobs, including full funding of the counter-cyclical assistance program for the cities, a major expansion of the youth employment and training program to give young people in our inner cities new hope, expanded training programs for women and displaced homemakers to give these workers a fair chance in the workplace, and new opportunities for the elderly to contribute their talents and skills.

Tax Reductions. We commit ourselves to targeted tax reductions designed to stimulate production and combat recession as soon as it appears so that tax reductions will not have a disproportionately inflationary effect. We must avoid untargeted tax cuts which would increase inflation.

Federal Spending. Spending restraint must be sensitive to those who look to the federal government for aid and assistance, especially to our nation's workers in times of high unemployment. At the same time, as long as inflationary pressures remain strong, fiscal prudence is essential to avoid destroying the progress made to date in reducing the inflation rate.

Fiscal policy must remain a flexible economic tool. We oppose a Constitutional amendment requiring a balanced budget.

Interest Rates. . . . [W]e must continue to pursue a tough antiinflationary policy which will lead to an across-the-board reduction in interest rates on loans.

In using monetary policy to fight inflation, the government should be sensitive to the special needs of areas of our economy most affected by high interest rates.

Worker Protection. The Democratic Party will not pursue a policy of high interest rates and unemployment as the means to fight inflation. We will take no action whose effect will be a significant increase in unemployment, no fiscal action, no monetary action, no budgetary action. The Democratic Party remains committed to policies that will not produce high interest rates or high unemployment.

OSHA protections should be properly administered, with the concern of the worker being the highest priority; legislative or administrative efforts to weaken OSHA's basic worker protection responsibilities are unacceptable.

We will continue to oppose a sub-minimum wage for youth and other workers and to support increases in the minimum wage so as to ensure an adequate income for all workers.

Human Needs. While we recognize the need for fiscal restraint . . . we pledge as Democrats that for the sole and primary purpose of fiscal restraint alone, we will *not* support reductions in the funding of any program whose purpose is to serve the basic human needs of the most needy in our society—programs such as unemployment, income maintenance, food stamps, and efforts to enhance the educational, nutritional or health needs of children.

Education. . . . [W]e will continue to support the Department of Education and assist in its all-important educational enterprise. . . .

. . . The federal government and the states should be encouraged to equalize or take over educational expenses, relieving the overburdened . . . taxpayer. . . . The Democratic Party continues to support programs aimed at achieving communities integrated both in terms of race and economic class. . . .

Equal Rights Amendment. . . . [T]he Democratic Party must ensure that ERA at last becomes the 27 Amendment to the Constitution. We oppose efforts to rescind ERA in states which have already ratified the amendment, and we shall insist that past rescissions are invalid.

Abortion. The Democratic Party recognizes reproductive freedom as a fundamental human right. We therefore oppose government interference in the reproductive decisions of Americans, especially those government programs or legislative restrictions that deny poor Americans their right to privacy by funding or advocating one or a limited number of reproductive choices only. Specifically, the Democratic Party opposes . . . restrictions on funding for health services for the poor that deny poor women especially the right to exercise a constitutionally-guaranteed right to privacy.

Gun Control. The Democratic Party affirms the right of sportsmen to possess guns for purely hunting and target-shooting purposes. However, handguns simplify and intensify violent crime. . . . The Democratic Party supports enactment of federal legislation to strengthen the presently inadequate regulations over the manufacture, assembly, distribution, and possession of handguns and to ban "Saturday night specials."

Energy. We must make energy conservation our highest priority, not only to reduce our dependence on foreign oil, but also to guarantee that our children and grandchildren have an adequate supply of energy. . . .

National Security. Our fourth major objective is to strengthen the military security of the United States and our Allies at a time when trends in the military balance have become increasingly adverse. America is now, and will continue to be, the strongest power on earth. It was the Democratic Party's greatest hope that we could, in fact, reduce our military effort. But realities of the world situation, including the unremitting buildup of Soviet military forces, required that we begin early to reverse the decade-long decline in American defense efforts.

NATIONAL UNITY CAMPAIGN

Rep. John B. Anderson of Illinois, a Republican, declared himself an independent candidate for the presidency April 24, 1980, after it became clear that he could not obtain his party's presidential nomination. Anderson created the National Unity Campaign as the vehicle for his third-party candidacy. No party convention was held to select Anderson or to ratify the selection.

On August 25 Anderson announced he had tapped former Wisconsin governor Patrick J. Lucey, a Democrat, to be his running mate. The selection of Lucey was seen as a move by Anderson to attract liberal Democrats disgruntled by President Jimmy Carter's renomination. Anderson's choice of a running mate and the August 30 release of a National Unity Campaign platform helped establish him as a genuine contender in the presidential race.

The 317-page platform put forth specific proposals on a variety of national issues, emphasizing domestic questions. The positions taken generally were fiscally conservative and socially liberal, remaining true to Anderson's "wallet on the right, heart on the left" philosophy.

The platform made clear that Anderson's primary goal was to restore the nation's economic health by adopting fiscal and tax policies that would "generate a substantial pool of investment capital," which then would be used to increase productivity and create jobs. Anderson proposed countercyclical revenue sharing to direct federal funds to areas hardest hit by the election year recession. He rejected mandatory wage and price controls as a cure for inflation, proposing instead a program under which the government would encourage labor and management to work toward agreement on proper levels for wages and prices and use tax incentives to encourage compliance with the standards set. In contrast to both Carter and Reagan, Anderson opposed tax cuts for individuals. He also criticized constitutional amendments to balance the federal budget, saying that while the budget should be balanced "in ordinary times," it could be expected to run a deficit in times of "economic difficulty."

Anderson's energy policy made reducing oil imports the top priority. His platform proposed a 50-cent-a-gallon excise tax on gasoline to discourage consumption, with the revenue to be used to cut Social Security taxes. Anderson favored the decontrol of oil prices begun under Carter and proposed a 40-mile-per-gallon fuel economy standard for new autos.

For American cities, Anderson proposed using about 90 percent of alcohol and tobacco taxes to help build mass transit systems and fight deterioration of public facilities. He also favored offering tax incentives to encourage businesses to locate in blighted urban areas.

Following are excerpts from the National Unity Campaign platform of 1980:

Economy. We will construct a Wage-Price Incentives Program. Our administration will invite labor and management leaders to agree upon fair and realistic guidelines and to determine appropriate tax-based incentives to encourage compliance. . . .

In the absence of sharp and prolonged increases in the rate of inflation, we will oppose mandatory wage and price standards.

Gasoline Tax. We would couple decontrol of oil and gas prices with an excise tax of 50 cents per gallon on gasoline, the full revenues of that tax being returned to individuals through reductions in payroll taxes and increased Social Security benefits. . . . We will employ tax credits and other incentives to promote substitution of nonpetroleum energy for oil, adoption of energy-efficient systems in industry and elsewhere,

improvements in transportation and energy production technologies, and development of less wasteful structures for home and commerce.

Cities. . . . [A]n Anderson-Lucey Administration will propose an Urban Reinvestment Trust Fund. Funded through. . . revenues from the Federal alcohol and tobacco excise taxes and phased in over three years, it will disburse approximately $3.9 billion annually. It will be used for upgrading, repair and replacement of [urban] capital plant and equipment.

Within our distressed older cities, there are zones of devastation, blighted by crime, arson and population flight. . . . We favor legislation that would create "enterprise zones" in these areas, by lowering corporate, capital gains, payroll and property taxes and by furnishing new tax incentives. . . .

Social Issues. We are committed to ratification of the Equal Rights Amendment. We oppose government intrusion in the most intimate of family decisions-the right to bear or not to bear children-and will fight against any constitutional amendment prohibiting abortion. We support public funding of family planning services and other efforts to enable women to find. . . alternatives to abortion.

National Defense and Arms Control. In strategic forces, we will maintain a stable balance by preserving essential equivalence with the Soviet Union. To meet an evolving threat to our deterrent, we will modernize and diversify our strategic arsenal.

The growing concern over the threat to fixed, land-based missiles poses an urgent problem to both the United States and the Soviet Union. Economically, environmentally and strategically, the . . . cure proposed by the Carter Administration-the MX system-is unsound. . . .

We favor. . . a short-term. . . nuclear test ban treaty between the United States, the Soviet Union and the United Kingdom. . . .

For a more effective defense, we will rely heavily on collective security arrangements with our principal allies in NATO and Japan. We will work to reinforce and enhance our historic partnership with our Western European allies.

We will propose to Moscow supplementary measures that could make possible the ratification of the SALT II Treaty and the start of SALT III negotiations. These proposals will respond to concerns expressed in the U.S. Senate regarding such issues as verification and future force reductions.

1984 Conventions

PRESIDENTIAL CANDIDATES

Walter F. Mondale
Democrat

Ronald Reagan
Republican

DEMOCRATS

Ending a long and difficult nomination campaign with a display of party unity and a historic vice-presidential choice, Walter F. Mondale used the 1984 Democratic convention to sound the opening themes of his challenge to President Ronald Reagan: family, fairness, the flag, and the future.

Accepting their nominations July 19 before cheering, flag-waving delegates at the San Francisco convention, the presidential candidate and his running mate, Rep. Geraldine A. Ferraro of New York, served notice that they would hold Reagan to account for his policies in their uphill battle to capture the White House. "Here is the truth about the [nation's] future," Mondale told the Democrats as they wrapped up their four-day convention. "We are living on borrowed money and borrowed time."

The spectacle of Mondale and Ferraro, with their families, celebrating with delegates in the jammed Moscone Center capped a week in which the Democrats came together to choose their ticket and shore up party unity. Toward that end, the convention succeeded to a greater degree than had seemed possible when the former vice president was battling Sen. Gary Hart of Colorado and Jesse Jackson in the primaries and caucuses. There was little acrimony over consideration of the party platform. And, once Mondale was nominated, the three rivals seemed to put aside their most visible differences.

The fifty-six-year-old Minnesotan had been the apparent winner since the final round of primaries on June 5, when he took New Jersey, which gave him the 1,967 pledged delegates needed to take the nomination. Mondale finished the convention balloting with nearly a thousand votes more than Hart, his closest competitor, yet he was by no means an overwhelming choice. He polled 2,191 votes—about 56 percent of a possible 3,933. Jackson received 465.5 votes. (*Table, p. 633.*)

The Democratic unity displayed in San Francisco—so different from the 1980 convention, when the struggle between President Jimmy Carter and Sen. Edward M. Kennedy of Massachusetts left the party torn and battered—was due largely to delegates' deeply felt antipathy to the policies of the Reagan administration. The unusual harmony was also due, at least in part, to Gov. Mario M. Cuomo of New York, who electrified delegates with his keynote address on the opening night, July 16. In an eloquent appeal for family values and compassion for the poor, he set the tone for the rest of the convention. His speech was rivaled in intensity only by Ferraro's nomination by acclamation July 19 and an impassioned speech given by Jackson on July 17.

Speaking forcefully but without dramatic oratorical flourishes, and repeatedly interrupted by emotional applause, Cuomo combined an appeal to Democratic traditions with specific attacks on the domestic and foreign policies of the Reagan administration. Noting Reagan's reference to America as "a shining city on a hill," Cuomo said that "the hard truth is that not everyone is sharing in this city's splendor and glory. There is despair, Mr. President, in the faces that you don't see, in the places that you don't visit in your shining city."

Pledging a government of "new realism" that would combine strong but conciliatory foreign policies with tough economic initiatives, Mondale vowed in his acceptance speech to squeeze the budget and raise taxes to reduce soaring deficits, then approaching $200 billion a year. "Let's tell the truth. . . . Mr. Reagan will raise taxes, and so will I," Mondale said. "He won't tell you. I just did."

To Ferraro, the first woman put on the national ticket by a major party, her nomination by acclamation was a special honor. Quoting the late Rev. Martin Luther King Jr., she said that " 'Occasionally in life there are moments which cannot be completely explained in words. Their meaning can only be articulated by the inaudible language of the heart.' Tonight is such a moment for me. My heart is filled with pride."

The forty-five thousand-word platform adopted at the convention created few divisions in the party, but few candidates were enthusiastic about using it in their fall campaigns. Adopted in an emphatic but seldom angry four-hour debate July 17, the platform drew heavily from Mondale's campaign themes. It also contained significant contributions from Hart and Jackson.

The debate on five minority planks offered by Hart and Jackson was lackluster compared with the heated platform struggles between Carter and Kennedy at the 1980 convention. The first sign that Mondale would surmount the Jackson challenges came on the plank pledging "no first use" of nuclear weapons. After a brief debate, it was defeated, with 1,405.7 delegates voting for it and 2,216.3 against. *(Table, p. 632.)*

Jackson supporters said it was "morally and militarily insane" even to consider using nuclear weapons, but Mondale's backers said the platform's arms control language was strong enough in promising movement toward a "no-first-use" stance.

In contrast to the opposition to Jackson's national security planks, Hart's "peace plank" was readily accepted by Mondale. Delegates adopted it, 3,271.8 to 351.2. The plank said a Democratic president would not "hazard American lives or engage in unilateral military involvement" in areas such as the Persian Gulf or Central America unless American objectives were clear and diplomatic efforts had been exhausted. *(Table, p. 632.)*

Jackson's two other minority reports dealt with issues of special interest to his black constituency: runoff primaries in the South and affirmative action. His call to abolish runoff primaries was defeated, but a compromise version of the affirmative action plank was accepted.

Ten southern states used runoff primaries when no candidate received a majority in the fast primary. Jackson claimed these second elections diluted minority voting strength because white voters often reverted to racial loyalty when a runoff choice was between a white and a black candidate. Supporters of second primaries argued that they prevented the nomination of fringe candidates who could receive a plurality in first-round primaries when more credible candidates split the vote. The dual primaries plank was defeated 2,500.8 to 1,253.2. *(Table, p. 632.)*

The other dispute was whether the platform should reject the use of quotas to overturn discrimination in employment and education. As adopted in June, the platform specifically rejected quotas but called for affirmative action goals and timetables to end discrimination in hiring, promotions, and education.

Following are excerpts from the Democratic platform of 1984:

Budget Deficits. . . . The Democratic Party is pledged to reducing these intolerable deficits. We will reassess defense expenditures; create a tax system that is both adequate and fair; control skyrocketing health costs without sacrificing quality of care; and eliminate other unnecessary expenditures.

We oppose the artificial and rigid Constitutional restraint of a balanced budget amendment. Further we oppose efforts to call a federal constitutional convention for this purpose.

Tax Reform. We will cap the effect of the Reagan tax cuts for wealthy Americans and enhance the progressivity of our personal income tax code, limiting the benefits of the third year of the Reagan tax cuts to the level of those with incomes of less than $60,000. We will partially defer indexation while protecting average Americans. We will close loopholes, eliminate the preferences and write-offs, exemptions,

and deductions which skew the code toward the rich and toward unproductive tax shelters. Given the fact that there has been a veritable hemorrhage of capital out of the federal budget, reflected in part by the huge budget deficit, there must be a return to a fair tax on corporate income. . . .

Controlling Domestic Spending. Social Security is one of the most important and successful initiatives in the history of our country, and it is an essential element of the social compact that binds us together as a community. There is no excuse—as the Reagan Administration has repeatedly suggested—for slashing Social Security to pay for excesses in other areas of the budget. We will steadfastly oppose such efforts, now and in the future.

It is rather in the area of health care costs that reform is urgently needed. By 1988, Medicare costs will rise to $106 billion; by the turn of the century, the debt of the trust fund may be as great as $1 trillion. In the Republican view, the problem is the level of benefits which senior citizens and the needy receive. As Democrats, we will protect the interests of health care beneficiaries. The real problem is the growing cost of health care services. . . .

Affirmative Action. The Democratic Party firmly commits itself to protect the civil rights of every citizen and to pursue justice and equal treatment under the law for all citizens. The Party reaffirms its longstanding commitment to the eradication of discrimination in all aspects of American life through the use of affirmative action goals, timetables, and other verifiable measurements to overturn historic patterns and historic burdens of discrimination in hiring, training, promotions, contract procurement, education, and the administration of all Federal programs. . . .

Equal Rights for Women. A top priority of a Democratic Administration will be ratification of the unamended Equal Rights Amendment. . . . The Democratic Party defines nondiscrimination to encompass both equal pay for equal work and equal pay for work of comparable worth, and we pledge to take every step, including enforcement of current law and amending the Constitution to include the unamended ERA, to close the wage gap.

Abortion. . . . The Democratic Party recognizes reproductive freedom as a fundamental human right. We therefore oppose government interference in the reproductive decisions of Americans, especially government interference which denies poor Americans their right to privacy by funding or advocating one or a limited number of reproductive choices only. . . .

Voting Rights Act. A Democratic President and Administration pledge to eliminate any and all discriminatory barriers to full voting rights, whether they be at-large requirements, second-primaries, gerrymandering, annexation, dual registration, dual voting or other practices. Whatever law, practice, or regulation discriminates against the voting rights of minority citizens, a Democratic President and Administration will move to strike it down. . . .

Homosexual Rights. . . . All groups must be protected from discrimination based on race, color, sex, religion, national origin, language, age, or sexual orientation. We will support legislation to prohibit discrimination in the workplace based on sexual orientation. We will assure that sexual orientation per se does not serve as a bar to participation in the military. . . .

Gun Control. We support tough restraints on the manufacture, transportation, and sale of snubnosed handguns, which have no legitimate sporting use and are used in a high proportion of violent crimes.

Arms Control. . . . A Democratic President will propose an early summit with regular, annual summits to follow, with the Soviet leaders, and meetings between senior civilian and military officials, in order to reduce tensions and explore possible formal agreements.... A new Democratic Administration will implement a strategy for peace which makes arms control an integral part of our national security policy. We must move the world back from the brink of nuclear holocaust and set a new direction toward an enduring peace, in which lower levels of military spending will be possible. Our ultimate aim must be to abolish all nuclear weapons in a world safe for peace and freedom....

These steps should lead promptly to the negotiation of a comprehensive, mutual and verifiable freeze on the testing, production, and deployment of all nuclear weapons. Building on this initiative, the Democratic President will update and resubmit the SALT II Treaty to the Senate for its advice and consent....

Defense Policy. The Reagan Administration measures military might by dollars spent. The Democratic Party seeks prudent defense based on sound planning and a realistic assessment of threats....

A Democratic President will be prepared to apply military force when vital American interests are threatened, particularly in the event of an attack upon the United States or its immediate allies. But he or she will not hazard American lives or engage in unilateral military involvement:

• Where our objectives are not clear;

• Until all instruments of diplomacy and non-military leverage, as appropriate, have been exhausted;

• Where our objectives threaten unacceptable costs or unreasonable levels of military force;

• Where the local forces supported are not working to resolve the causes of conflict;

• Where multilateral or allied options for the resolution of conflict are available....

The Middle East. ... The Democratic Party opposes any consideration of negotiations with the PLO, unless the PLO abandons terrorism, recognizes the state of Israel, and adheres to U.N. Resolutions 242 and 338.

Jerusalem should remain forever undivided with free access to the holy places for people of all faiths. As stated in the 1976 and 1980 platforms, the Democratic Party recognizes and supports the established status of Jerusalem as the capital of Israel. As a symbol of this stand, the U.S. Embassy should be moved from Tel Aviv to Jerusalem.

Central America. ... We must terminate our support for the contras and other paramilitary groups fighting in Nicaragua. We must halt those U.S. military exercises in the region which are being conducted for no other real purpose than to intimidate or provoke the Nicaraguan government or which may be used as a pretext for deeper U.S. military involvement in the area.

REPUBLICANS

A jubilant Republican Party wound up its August 20–23 convention in Dallas, Texas, confident that President Ronald Reagan and Vice President George Bush would be the winning team in November. With the ticket's renomination certain beforehand, the convention was more a celebration than a business meeting of GOP activists. Behind the cheering and display of party unity, however, ran a current of dissent: moderates, who were greatly outnumbered, voiced unhappiness with the party's direction and its platform.

During convention week, speaker after speaker criticized the Democrats, saying they represented a legacy of "malaise" from Jimmy Carter's administration and promised only a future of fear. Reagan, too, emphasized that theme in his fifty-five-minute

acceptance speech. To repeated interruptions of applause and cheers, he drew sharp differences between Republicans and Democrats and between himself and the Democratic presidential nominee, Walter F. Mondale. "The choices this year are not just between two different personalities or between two political parties," Reagan said. "They are between two different visions of the future, two fundamentally different ways of governing—their government of pessimism, fear and limits ... or ours of hope, confidence and growth."

In his acceptance speech, Bush vigorously touted the Reagan administration's record. "Under this president, more lands have been acquired for parks, more for wilderness," he said. "The quality of life is better—and that's a fact." In foreign affairs, Bush said, "... there is new confidence in the U.S. leadership around the world. ... Because our president stood firm in defense of freedom, America has regained respect throughout the world. ..."

Speakers in previous sessions had sought to make the same points. They tried to link former vice president Mondale to the policies and problems of the administration in which he had served. "Carter-Mondale" became their shorthand for a list of evils: inflation, high interest rates, foreign policy failures, and sagging national spirit.

GOP leaders also were eager to portray the Democratic ticket and the party's leadership as out of step with most Democrats. They gave the spotlight to Democrats-turned-Republicans and issued one of their warmest welcomes to Jeane J. Kirkpatrick, the U.S. representative to the United Nations, whom one party leader referred to as an "enlightened Democrat." Kirkpatrick delivered a foreign policy speech during the opening session.

Yet the convention was clearly a Republican event, with the administration firmly in control and many of its members on hand. The party's leaders also made clear they were making a pitch for women voters, in response to the candidacy of Rep. Geraldine A. Ferraro, D-N.Y., Mondale's running mate.

The delegates moved to renominate Reagan and Bush. Although the outcome came as no surprise, there was an unusual joint roll call on the nominations, with Reagan receiving 2,233 votes and Bush, 2,235. *(Table, p. 631.)*

Earlier, after spirited debate, the 106-member platform committee adopted a 1984 campaign document that conformed in virtually all respects to the themes Reagan had sounded during his first term in office. The convention itself ratified the thirty-thousand-word platform with no debate August 21. On almost every aspect of public policy, the document stood in stark contrast to the platform the Democrats had adopted in San Francisco.

However, in its strong stand against tax increases and its criticism of the independent Federal Reserve Board, the Republican platform went further than the White House wanted. Administration representatives led by former transportation secretary Drew Lewis sought to soften the tax plank, but, while they succeeded in modifying some of the language, they were unable to alter it substantially. The tax section of the Republican platform pledged that the party would continue efforts to lower tax rates and would support tax reform that "will lead to a fair and simple tax system." The platform said the party believed that a "modified flat tax—with specific exemptions for such items as mortgage interest—is a most promising approach."

Taxes had mushroomed as an election issue when Mondale said in his acceptance speech at the Democratic National Convention that, regardless of who won in November, tax increases would be necessary in 1985 to combat record federal budget deficits. Mondale also accused Reagan of having a secret plan to raise taxes.

Despite an hour-long debate, the GOP platform committee had refused to endorse the proposed Equal Rights Amendment (ERA)—which Reagan opposed—or compromise language stating that the Republicans respected those who supported the amendment. The committee also turned aside challenges by party moderates to language endorsing voluntary prayer in public schools and opposing federal financing for abortions under any circumstances.

Following are excerpts from the Republican platform of 1984:

Economic Policy. Our most important economic goal is to expand and continue the economic recovery and move the nation to full employment without inflation. We therefore oppose any attempts to increase taxes, which would harm the recovery and reverse the trend to restoring control of the economy to individual Americans. We favor reducing deficits by continuing and expanding the strong economic recovery brought about by the policies of this Administration and by eliminating wasteful and unnecessary government spending. . . .

Tax Policy. The Republican Party pledges to continue our efforts to lower tax rates, change and modernize the tax system, and eliminate the incentive-destroying effects of graduated tax rates. We therefore support tax reform that will lead to a fair and simple tax system and believe a modified flat tax—with specific exemptions for such items as mortgage interest—is a most promising approach.

Balancing the Budget. The congressional budget process is bankrupt. Its implementation has not brought spending under control, and it must be thoroughly reformed. We will work for the constitutional amendment requiring a balanced federal budget passed by the Republican Senate but blocked by the Democrat-controlled House and denounced by the Democrat Platform. If Congress fails to act on this issue, a constitutional convention should be convened to address only this issue in order to bring deficit spending under control.

The President is denied proper control over the federal budget. To remedy this, we support enhanced authority to prevent wasteful spending, including a line-item veto. . . .

Monetary Policy. Just as our tax policy has only laid the groundwork for a new era of prosperity, reducing inflation is only the first step in restoring a stable currency. A dollar now should be worth a dollar in the future. This allows real economic growth without inflation and is the primary goal of our monetary policy.

The Federal Reserve Board's destabilizing actions must therefore stop. We need coordination between fiscal and monetary policy, timely information about Fed decisions, and an end to the uncertainties people face in obtaining money and credit. The Gold Standard may be a useful mechanism for realizing the Federal Reserve's determination to adopt monetary policies needed to sustain price stability.

Energy. We will complete America's energy agenda. Natural gas should be responsibly decontrolled as rapidly as possible so that families and businesses can enjoy the full benefits of lower prices and greater production, as with decontrolled oil. We are committed to the repeal of the confiscatory windfall profits tax, which has forced the American consumer to pay more for less and left us vulnerable to the energy and economic stranglehold of foreign producers. . . .

We are committed to the termination of the Department of Energy. President Reagan has succeeded in abolishing that part which was telling Americans what to buy, where to buy it, and at what price—the regulatory part of DOE. Then he reduced the number of bureaucrats by 25 percent. Now is the time to complete the job.

Education. We believe that education is a local function, a State responsibility, and a federal concern. The federal role in education should be limited. It includes helping parents and local authorities ensure high standards, protecting civil rights, and ensuring family rights. . . .

We have enacted legislation to guarantee equal access to school facilities by student religious groups. Mindful of our religious diversity, we reaffirm our commitment to the freedoms of religion and speech guaranteed by the Constitution of the United States and firmly support the rights of students to openly practice the same, including the right to engage in voluntary prayer in schools. . . .

Crime and Gun Control. . . . Republicans will continue to defend the constitutional right to keep and bear arms. When this right is abused and armed felonies are committed, we believe in stiff, mandatory sentencing. . . .

Abortion. The unborn child has a fundamental individual right to life which cannot be infringed. We therefore reaffirm our support for a human life amendment to the Constitution, and we endorse legislation to make clear that the Fourteenth Amendment's protections apply to unborn children. We oppose the use of public revenues for abortion and will eliminate funding for organizations which advocate or support abortions. . . .

We applaud President Reagan's fine record of judicial appointments, and we reaffirm our support for the appointment of judges at all levels of the judiciary who respect traditional family values and the sanctity of innocent human life. . . .

Central America. Today, democracy is under assault throughout [Central America]. Marxist Nicaragua threatens not only Costa Rica and Honduras, but also El Salvador and Guatemala. The Sandinista regime is building the largest military force in Central America, importing Soviet equipment, Eastern bloc and PLO advisers, and thousands of Cuban mercenaries. The Sandinista government has been increasingly brazen in its embrace of Marxism-Leninism. The Sandinistas have systematically persecuted free institutions, including synagogue and church, schools, the private sector, the free press, minorities, and families and tribes throughout Nicaragua. We support continued assistance to the democratic freedom fighters in Nicaragua. Nicaragua cannot be allowed to remain a Communist sanctuary, exporting terror and arms throughout the region. . . .

The Soviet Union. Stable and peaceful relations with the Soviet Union are possible and desirable, but they depend upon the credibility of American strength and determination. . . . Our policy of peace through strength encourages freedom-loving people everywhere and provides hope for those who look forward one day to enjoying the fruits of self-government. . . .

1988 Conventions

PRESIDENTIAL CANDIDATES

Michael S. Dukakis
Democrat

George Bush
Republican

DEMOCRATS

After years of internal warfare, the Democrats staged a remarkable show of unity at their 1988 national convention, held July 18–21 in Atlanta, Georgia. For once, the issue-oriented activists who dominated the Democratic nominating process for nearly two decades subordinated their agendas to the goal of party victory, avoiding the self-inflicted wounds that had marred so many conventions since the 1968 Chicago debacle.

Massachusetts governor Michael S. Dukakis arrived at the convention with enough delegate support to ensure his nomination as the Democratic presidential candidate. Earlier, on July 12, he had announced his choice of running mate, Sen. Lloyd Bentsen of Texas.

The only risk of serious political conflict at the convention came from Jesse Jackson, who finished second in the delegate race. The convention approached with some of Jackson's hardcore supporters threatening boycotts, protest marches, and walkouts. Some saw Dukakis's selection of Bentsen as a snub to Jackson. A breakthrough, however, came at a three-hour morning meeting July 18 of Dukakis, Jackson, and Bentsen. Afterward, Jackson said he was committed to helping elect the ticket, although he would still allow his name to be placed in nomination. In answer to a reporter's question, he said he no longer sought the vice presidency.

With the Dukakis-Jackson agreement reached, the atmosphere inside Atlanta's Omni Coliseum on opening night was remarkably fraternal. Democratic National Committee Chairman Paul G. Kirk Jr. persistently underlined the theme of unity, pointing to the fact that the credentials and rules reports—sources of numerous battles and test votes at past conventions—had been previously ratified by the Dukakis and Jackson campaigns. Both were adopted without discussion. Texas state treasurer Ann Richards delivered a folksy keynote address that included one of the more memorable quips in convention oratory. "Poor George," she said. "He can't help it. He was born with a silver foot in his mouth."

In the afternoon of the second day of the convention, the candidates' campaigns eliminated their last major grounds for argument—the minority planks of the Democratic platform—with a minimum of rancor.

In the debate on what the Jackson campaign called the "fair tax" plank, Manhattan Borough president David Dinkins said that "the rich and the corporations" received the bulk of the Reagan administration tax cuts, which he blamed for the large federal deficits. But Denver mayor Federico Pena warned that passage of the plank would be campaign fodder for Republicans, who persistently portrayed the Democrats as the "tax-and-spend" party. Delegates defeated it 1,091.5 to 2,499. (Table, p. 634.)

More emotion was expressed over the nuclear-strategy plank, with Jackson supporters waving placards and changing, "No first use!" Supporters said the plank would show Democratic commitment to world peace. But Dukakis supporters, while expressing solidarity with the cause of nuclear disarmament, said the defense strategy that called for use of nuclear weapons in the event of an invasion of western Europe was a bedrock of the NATO alliance. They also said that, should Dukakis be elected president, the plank could deprive him of an effective tool to force the Soviets to the bargaining table. The minority plank was defeated, 1,220.59 to 2,474.13. (Table, p. 228.)

Without debate the delegates adopted a compromise package of nine other amendments pressed by the Jackson camp and accepted by Dukakis. These embodied much of the spirit and some of the specifics that Jackson had tried to insert into the platform all along—a denunciation of aid to "irregular" forces in Central America, a national health program, sharply higher spending for education, and a moratorium on missile flight testing.

Notwithstanding the concessions to Jackson, the platform drafted by the Dukakis forces remained a general statement of party themes, rather than a series of promises to constituency groups. At forty-five hundred words, the platform was one-tenth the length of its 1984 counterpart.

Rousing speeches by Sen. Edward M. Kennedy and Jackson topped the evening schedule. Kennedy, introduced by his nephew John F. Kennedy Jr., accused Bush of "burying his head in his hands and hiding from the record of Reagan-Bush mistakes." Kennedy then listed a series of issues—Iran-contra, the Noriega drug connection, domestic budget cuts, civil rights—on which he said the Reagan administration had made wrong choices, following each example with the refrain, "Where was George?" The delegates spontaneously picked up the slogan as a chant.

In his fifty-five-minute speech, Jackson invoked the heroes of the civil rights movement, including Martin Luther King Jr., and briefly shared the stage with Rosa Parks, heroine of the 1955 Montgomery, Alabama, bus boycott. He said that his campaign was a historic culmination of earlier black struggles. The speech was climaxed by Jackson's call for Americans to "never surrender" to poverty, drugs, malnutrition, inequality, disease, or physical handicaps. "Keep hope alive," he concluded. "Keep hope alive."

Arkansas governor Bill Clinton nominated Dukakis the evening of July 20 with a thirty-five-minute speech that will be remembered more for its duration than its content. Clinton praised Dukakis as "a man with vision, a shining vision for this country."

The roll call, marked by the usual "Great State of . . ." boosterism, went as predetermined by the primary-and-caucus process. The one surprise came from Minnesota, where three antiabortion delegates registered support for Rep. Richard H. Stallings, Idaho, who shared their opposition to abortion. Four other candidates received one or two votes each.

The only apparent suspense was which state would put Dukakis over the 2,082-vote total he needed to clinch the nomination. But the Dukakis campaign—cognizant of California's importance in November—had even taken care of that detail. They arranged for several delegations to pass on the first call to ensure that California would have the honor. The final tally was Dukakis 2,876.25 delegate votes; Jackson, 1,218.5. *(Table, p. 228.)*

For his acceptance speech on the final night of the convention, Dukakis was introduced by his cousin, Olympia Dukakis, an Oscar-winning actress and New Jersey delegate. Dukakis described himself as a product of the American dream. He paid tribute to his immigrant parents, and tears welled in his eyes when he talked about how proud his father would have been of his son, and of his adopted country. He cited individuals who represented America's cultural diversity, including Jackson.

Following are excerpts from the Democratic platform of 1988:

Economy. . . . We believe that all Americans have a fundamental right to economic justice in a stronger, surer national economy, an economy that must grow steadily without inflation, that can generate a rising standard of living for all and fulfill the desire of all to work in dignity up to their full potential in good health with good jobs at good wages, an economy that is prosperous in every region, from coast to coast, including our rural towns and our older industrial communities, our mining towns, our energy producing areas and the urban areas that have been neglected for the past seven years.

Education. . . . [T]he education of our citizens, from Head Start to institutions of higher learning, deserves our highest priority. . . . We pledge to better balance our national priorities by significantly increasing federal funding for education. . . .

Drugs. . . . [I]llegal drugs pose a direct threat to the security of our nation from coast to coast. . . . [E]very arm and agency of government at every federal, state and local level—including every useful diplomatic, military, educational, medical and law enforcement effort necessary—should at long last be mobilized and coordinated with private efforts under the direction of a National Drug "Czar" to halt both the international supply and the domestic demand for illegal drugs now ravaging our country; and that the legalization of illicit drugs would represent a tragic surrender in a war we intend to win. . . .

Criminal Justice. . . . [T]he federal government should provide increased assistance to local criminal justice agencies, enforce a ban on "cop killer" bullets that have no purpose other than the killing and maiming of law enforcement officers, reinforce our commitment to help crime victims, and assume a leadership role in securing the safety of our neighborhoods and homes.

Individual Rights. . . . [W]e must work for the adoption of the Equal Rights Amendment to the Constitution; that the fundamental right of reproductive choice should be guaranteed regardless of ability to pay; that our machinery for civil rights enforcement and legal services to the poor should be rebuilt and vigorously utilized; and that our immigration policy should be reformed to promote fairness, non-discrimination and family reunification and to reflect our constitutional freedoms of speech, association and travel. We further believe that the voting rights of all minorities should be protected, the recent surge in hate violence and negative stereotyping combatted, the discriminatory English-only pressure groups resisted, our treaty commitments with Native Americans enforced by culturally sensitive officials, and the lingering effects of past discrimination eliminated by affirmative action, including goals, timetables, and procurement set-asides.

Health Care. . . . We believe that all Americans should enjoy access to affordable, comprehensive health services for both the physically and mentally ill, from prenatal care for pregnant women at risk to more adequate care for our Vietnam and other veterans, from well-baby care to childhood immunization to Medicare; that a national health program providing federal coordination and leadership is necessary to restrain health care costs while assuring quality care and advanced medical research; that quality, affordable, long-term home and health care should be available to all senior and disabled citizens, allowing them to live with dignity in the most appropriate setting; that an important first step toward comprehensive health services is to ensure that every family should have the security of basic health insurance; and that the HIV/AIDS epidemic is an unprecedented public health emergency requiring increased support for accelerated research on, and expedited FDA approval of, treatments and vaccines. . . .

Voting Rights. . . . [T]his country's democratic processes must be revitalized: by securing universal, same day and mail-in voter registration as well as registration on the premises of appropriate government agencies; by preventing the misuse of at-large elections, the abuse of election day challenges and registration roll purges, any undercounting in the national census, and any dilution of the one-person, one-vote principle; by ending discrimination against public employees who are denied the right to full political participation; by supporting statehood for the District of Columbia; by treating the offshore territories under our flag equitably and sensitively under federal policies, assisting their economic and social development and respecting their right to decide their future in their relationship with the United States; by empowering the commonwealth of Puerto Rico with greater autonomy within its relationship with the United States to achieve the economic, social and political goals of its people, and by giving it just and fair participation in federal programs; by assuring and pledging the full and equal access of women and minorities to elective office and party endorsement; and by minimizing the domination and distortion of our elections by moneyed interests. . . .

Defense. We believe that our national strength has been sapped by a defense establishment wasting money on duplicative and dubious new weapons instead of investing more in readiness and mobility; that our national strength will be enhanced by more stable defense budgets and by a commitment from our allies to assume a greater share of the costs and responsibilities required to maintain peace and liberty. . . .

Arms Control. We believe in following up the INF [intermediate-range nuclear force] Treaty, a commendable first step, with mutual, verifiable and enforceable agreements that will make significant reductions in strategic weapons in a way that diminishes the risk of nuclear attack by either superpower; reduce conventional forces to lower and equivalent levels in Europe, requiring deeper cuts on the Warsaw Pact side; ban chemical and space weapons in their entirety; promptly initiate a mutual moratorium on missile flight testing and halt all nuclear weapons testing while strengthening our efforts to prevent the spread of these weapons to other nations before the nightmare of nuclear terrorism engulfs us all.

International Relations. . . . [W]e believe that this country, maintaining the special relationship with Israel founded upon mutually shared values and strategic interests, should provide new leadership to deliver the promise of peace and security through negotiations that has been held out to Israel and its neighbors by the Camp David Accords. . . . We further believe that the United States must fully support the Arias Peace Plan, which calls for an end to the fighting, national reconciliation, guarantees of justice, freedom, human rights and democracy, an end to support for irregular forces, and a commitment by the Central American governments to prevent the use of their territory to destabilize others in the region. . . .

REPUBLICANS

On the opening day of the Republican national convention, held August 15–18 in New Orleans's Louisiana Superdome, the delegates hailed Ronald Reagan's valedictory, a swan song from a politician who had carried GOP conservatives to unprecedented levels of power. The delegates greeted Reagan as a conquering hero, and they cheered enthusiastically at many of his applause lines. But the mood was tempered by the poignancy of the moment—a realization that Reagan was making his last convention speech as leader of his party and his country, and that the future for Republicans was uncertain.

For his part, Reagan was firm if slightly subdued in his farewell speech. He offered again his optimistic vision of America and took some predictable jabs at his Democratic critics. But the most pertinent symbol of Reagan's role in the 1988 campaign was his strong praise of Vice President George Bush, saying "George played a major role in everything that we have accomplished in these eight years." Reagan responded to the Democrats' "Where was George?" chant by intoning, "George was there." Reagan's promise of campaign assistance and his call for Bush to "win one for the Gipper" was a lift for Bush supporters, who had been disturbed by Reagan's previously pallid endorsement of their candidate.

The Republicans had plenty of theater scheduled for August 16, with an agenda that included New Jersey governor Thomas H. Kean's keynote address and speeches by evangelist and former GOP presidential candidate Pat Robertson, former United Nations representative Jeane J. Kirkpatrick, and former president Gerald R. Ford. But Bush himself stole the show with his midafternoon announcement that he had selected dark-horse prospect Sen. Dan Quayle of Indiana as his running mate.

Bush made the choice public at a welcoming ceremony on the New Orleans riverfront. He praised Quayle, who was a generation younger than Bush, as "a man of the future." News reporters, meanwhile, had little to distract them from their rounds on the vice-presidential rumor circuit as the reports of the credentials, rules, and platform committees were approved without debate in the morning session.

But there was no press "honeymoon" for the prospective vice-presidential nominee. A series of tough questions asked at an August 17 news conference with Bush made the afternoon difficult for Quayle—and, by extension, for Bush. Quayle's first problem was with a question about a 1980 Florida incident in which Quayle, then a House member, and two colleagues were seen in the company of lobbyist Paula Parkinson, who later posed nude in *Playboy* magazine and said she had had sexual relationships with members of Congress. Quayle's defense at the time, that he had no involvement with Parkinson, never was refuted.

The most potentially explosive issue raised at the news conference was whether Quayle, a member of Indiana's Pulliam publishing family, had used family influence to gain enlistment in the Indiana National Guard in 1969 to avoid service in the Vietnam War. Quayle first referred to the question as "a cheap shot." Then he dismissed it, saying his thoughts at the time centered on plans for law school, marriage, and family. The controversy, however, did not subdue the enthusiasm of convention delegates—for their soon-to-be presidential nominee George Bush or his choice of vice president. In the evening session, after a lengthy roll call, George W. Bush announced the Texas delegation votes that put his father over the top unopposed. (*Table, p. 635.*)

The Indiana senator was nominated by acclamation. A new party rule had eliminated the necessity of a roll call and made it difficult for dissident delegates to call for one had there been opposition to Bush's choice.

Early on in his acceptance speech Quayle confronted the National Guard issue briefly and with a somewhat defiant tone. After expressing pride in his congressional service, he said, "As a young man, I served six years in the National Guard, and like the millions of Americans who have served in the Guard . . . I am proud of it."

With Bush trailing his Democratic opponent, Michael S. Dukakis, in public opinion polls, media commentators and Bush supporters alike said he had to make the "speech of his life" in accepting the presidential nomination on the night of August 18. Bush did not waste the opportunity.

He hit on the conservative hot-button issues—the Pledge of Allegiance (Dukakis had vetoed, on constitutional grounds, a bill requiring Massachusetts public school students to recite the pledge), the death penalty, voluntary school prayer, gun owner-ship, opposition to abortion, prison furloughs—that had been raised by speaker after speaker during the convention.

Restating his promise not to raise taxes, which he said Dukakis would not rule out, Bush said he would tell persistent tax proponents to "Read my lips. 'No new taxes.' " Bush finished his speech by leading the convention in the Pledge of Allegiance, ending a week in which a record may have been set for mentions of the pledge.

Following are excerpts from the Republican platform of 1988:

Jobs. . . . The Republican Party puts the creation of jobs and opportunity first. . . . We will use new technologies, such as computer data bases and telecommunications, to strengthen and streamline job banks matching people who want work with available jobs.

We advocate incentives for educating, training, and retraining workers for new and better jobs—through programs like the Job Training Partnership Act, which provides for a public/private partnership. . . .

With its message of economic growth and opportunity, the GOP is the natural champion of blacks, minorities, women and ethnic Americans. . . . We are the party of real social progress. Republicans welcome the millions of forward-looking Americans who want an "opportunity society," not a welfare state. . . .

Taxes. *We oppose any attempts to increase taxes.* Tax increases harm the economic expansion and reverse the trend to restoring control of the economy to individual Americans.

We reject calls for higher taxes from all quarters—including "bipartisan commissions." The decisions of our government should not be left to a body of unelected officials. . . .

Health. Republicans believe in reduced government control of health care while maintaining an unequivocal commitment to quality health care. . . .

AIDS. We will vigorously fight against AIDS. . . . Continued research on the virus is vital. We will continue as well to provide experimental drugs that may prolong life. We will establish within the Food and Drug Administration a process for expedited review of drugs which may benefit AIDS patients. We will allow supervised usage of experimental treatments.

We must not only marshal our scientific resources against AIDS, but must also protect those who do not have the disease. In this regard, education plays a critical role. AIDS education should emphasize that abstinence from drug abuse and sexual activity outside of marriage is the safest way to avoid infection with the AIDS virus. . . .

Social Security. We pledge to preserve the integrity of the Social Security trust funds. We encourage public officials at all levels to safeguard the integrity of public and private pension funds against raiding. . . .

Equal Rights, Religious Rights, Abortion. "Deep in our hearts, we do believe":

• That bigotry has no place in American life. We denounce those persons, organizations, publications and movements which practice or promote racism, anti-Semitism or religious intolerance.

• That the Pledge of Allegiance should be recited daily in schools in all States. . . .

• In defending religious freedom. Mindful of our religious diversity, we firmly support the right of students to engage in voluntary prayer in schools. We call for full enforcement of the Republican legislation that now guarantees equal access to school facilities by student religious groups.

• That the unborn child has a fundamental right to life which can-

not be infringed. We therefore reaffirm our support for a human life amendment to the Constitution, and we endorse legislation to make clear that the Fourteenth Amendment's protections apply to unborn children. We oppose the use of public revenues for abortion and will eliminate funding for organizations which advocate or support abortion. . . .

Disabled. We support efforts to provide disabled voters full access to the polls and opportunity to participate in all aspects of the political process. . . .

Gun Ownership. Republicans defend the constitutional right to keep and bear arms. . . .

Workers' Rights. We affirm the right of all freely to form, join or assist labor organizations to bargain collectively, consistent with state laws. . . . We renew our longstanding support for the right of states to enact "Right-to-Work" laws. To protect the political rights of every worker, we oppose the use of compulsory dues or fees for partisan purposes. . . .

Crime. We will forge ahead with the Republican anti-crime agenda:

• Republicans oppose furloughs for those criminals convicted of first degree murder and others who are serving a life sentence without possibility of parole. We believe that victims' rights should not be accorded less importance than those of convicted felons.

• We will re-establish the federal death penalty. . . .

Drugs. The Republican Party is committed to a drug-free America. Our policy is strict accountability, for users of illegal drugs as well as for those who profit by that usage. . . .

• The Republican Party unequivocally opposes legalizing or decriminalizing any illicit drug.

• We support strong penalties, including the death penalty for major drug traffickers. . . .

Oil. We will set an energy policy for the United States to maintain a viable core industry and to ensure greater energy self sufficiency through private initiatives. We will adopt forceful initiatives to reverse the decline of our domestic oil production. Republicans support:

• Repeal of the counterproductive Windfall Profits Tax.

• Maintenance of our schedule for filling the Strategic Petroleum Reserve to reach 750 million barrels by 1993 and encouragement of our allies to maintain similar reserves. . . .

Environment. Republicans propose the following program for the environment in the 1990s:

• We will work for further reductions in air and water pollution and effective actions against the threats posed by acid rain. . . .

• A top priority of our country must be the continued improvement of our National Parks and wildlife areas. . . .

The Americas. The Republican party reaffirms its strong support of the Monroe Doctrine as the foundation for our policy throughout the Hemisphere, and pledges to conduct foreign policy in accord with its principles. . . .

Republicans will continue to oppose any normalization of relations with the government of Cuba as long as Fidel Castro continues to oppress the Cuban people at home and to support international terrorism and drug trafficking abroad. We will vigorously continue our support for establishment of a genuinely representative government directly elected by the Cuban people. We reiterate our support of Radio Marti and urge the creation of TV Marti to better reach the oppressed people of Cuba. . . .

Soviet Union. Steady American leadership is needed now more than ever to deal with the challenges posed by a rapidly changing Soviet Union. Americans cannot afford a future administration which eagerly attempts to embrace perceived, but as yet unproven, changes in Soviet policy. Nor can we indulge naive inexperience or an overly enthusiastic endorsement of current Soviet rhetoric. . . .

Republicans proudly reaffirm the Reagan Doctrine: America's commitment to aid freedom-fighters against the communist oppression which destroys freedom and the human spirit. . . .

The Middle East. The foundation of our policy in the Middle East has been and must remain the promotion of a stable and lasting peace, recognizing our moral and strategic relationship with Israel. . . .

We will continue to maintain Israel's qualitative advantage over any adversary or coalition of adversaries.

We will continue to solidify our strategic relationship with Israel. . . .

We oppose the creation of an independent Palestinian state; its establishment is inimical to the security interests of Israel, Jordan and the U.S. . . .

Strategic Defense Initiative (SDI). We are committed to rapid and certain deployment of SDI as technologies permit, and we will determine the exact architecture of the system as technologies are tested and proven. . . .

Arms Control. Arms reduction can be an important aspect of our national policy only when agreements enhance the security of the United States and its allies. [T]rue arms reductions as a means to improve U.S. security, not just the perception of East-West détente. . . .

• We will consistently undertake necessary improvements in our forces to maintain the effectiveness of our deterrent.

• We will not negotiate in areas which jeopardize our security. In particular, we will not compromise plans for the research, testing, or the rapid and certain deployment of SDI. . . .

1992 Conventions

PRESIDENTIAL CANDIDATES

Bill Clinton
Democrat

George Bush
Republican

Ross Perot
Independent

DEMOCRATS

The Democrats, meeting at Madison Square Garden in New York July 13–16, nominated a national ticket of party moderates and adopted a 1992 platform heavily influenced by the centrist ideas of the Democratic Leadership Council (DLC) and its think tank, the Progressive Policy Institute.

The convention stressed the themes Democrats planned to push in the fall campaign: redefining the party in the centrist vein, emphasizing youth, traditional family values, and mainstream policy views—as desired by its nominee, Arkansas governor and DLC leader, Bill Clinton. Every bit as unsubtle were the efforts to redefine the nominee's personal image. In appealing to youth, as in much else, Clinton, forty-five, was assisted by his running mate, Sen. Albert Gore, forty-four, of Tennessee, making their ticket the youngest in the twentieth century.

Despite the refusal of former California governor Edmund G. "Jerry" Brown Jr. to hop on the bandwagon or the stunning July 16 announcement from independent presidential candidate Ross Perot that he was bowing out (a decision he later reversed),

Clinton controlled the focus and direction of the convention. He declined to yield to the tough tactics of black activist and former presidential candidate Jesse L. Jackson, demonstrating a tough-mindedness of his own.

The convention was marked by relatively few fractional disputes. Controversy involved primarily the question of whether Brown would be allowed to address the convention from the podium. Brown arrived with more than six hundred delegates, enough to cause some disturbance. For most of the first session, they milled in the well beneath the main stage, heckling speakers and waving signs. Some covered their mouths with labels or duct tape.

In the end, Brown was allowed to give his own seconding speech on July 15. But that meant he spoke at shortly after 8 P.M. (5 P.M. in California), well before the commercial broadcast networks had switched from their regular programming to convention coverage. Gradually, the Brown delegates softened their protest and ended any serious attempt to disrupt the convention.

A large section of the opening program was designed to give exposure to six of the Democrats' leading female Senate candidates, all of whom spoke briefly from the convention floor. Dianne Feinstein of California, the last to speak, dismissed Republicans who referred to the wave of female candidates as "just gender politics." "It's not just about gender. It's about an agenda, an agenda of change," Feinstein said.

Heralding the "Year of the Woman," Democratic women played a major role at the convention, and issues women had highlighted—abortion rights, women's health care, and the Clarence Thomas-Anita F. Hill hearings—were discussed from the podium, always to loud cheers from the floor.

Instead of the usual keynote speaker, the Democrats opted for three: Sen. Bill Bradley of New Jersey, Gov. Zell Miller of Georgia, and former Texas representative Barbara Jordan. They stressed that the party had changed, blasted the Bush administration for economic policies that favored the rich, and portrayed Clinton as a candidate from modest roots who was in touch with the people.

The Democrats later solidified their move to the center by adopting a platform devoid of many of the liberal planks and slogans that characterized previous documents. The debate over the party's manifesto was brief and uninspired. Clinton's overwhelming delegate strength and Democrats' frustration with three straight presidential losses helped mute any complaints over the centrist platform that clearly reflected the Clinton view of how the Democratic Party should present itself to voters.

The platform emphasized the need for economic growth and pledged efforts to uphold law and order, use of military force overseas where necessary, a cutoff in welfare benefits after two years, and support for the right of states to enact death penalty statutes. The platform did include more traditional Democratic viewpoints, such as protecting abortion rights, providing civil rights for homosexuals, and taxing wealthy people at higher rates.

By prior agreement, delegates pledged to former senator Paul E. Tsongas of Massachusetts were allowed to offer and debate four minority planks. Three of the planks ultimately were rejected by voice vote. One called for investment-related tax breaks. Another, on the deficit, called for limits on government spending, including Medicare and other politically sensitive entitlements. And a third proposed increasing the gasoline tax by five cents per gallon to benefit new spending on roads and bridges. A roll-call vote was held on the fourth plank, which said that a middle-class tax cut and a tax credit for families with children ought to be delayed until the deficit was under control. This had a been a key difference between Tsongas and Clinton during the campaign. Delegates defeated the plank, 953 to 2,287. (*Table, p. 636.*)

New York governor Mario M. Cuomo formally nominated Clinton, saluting him as the "comeback kid." The final roll-call tally was Clinton, 3,372; Brown, 596; and Tsongas, 209, and subsequently the nomination was approved by acclamation.

After the vote, Clinton paid a surprise "thank you" visit to the convention, as John F. Kennedy had done in 1960.

The next day, in his fifty-four-minute acceptance speech, some twenty minutes longer than the seemingly interminable nominating speech he gave in 1988, Clinton described himself as "a product of the American middle class" who would accept the nomination "in the name of all the people who do the work, pay the taxes, raise the kids, and play by the rules. . . ." Pledging a "government that is leaner, not meaner," he called for "a New Covenant, based not simply on what each of us can take, but on what all of us must give to our nation." Clinton and Gore paid respect to the intensity of women's political feeling. They endorsed abortion rights and equal rights in the workplace. Both lavished praise on their wives, receiving roars of approval from the audience. And when Clinton talked of a notional child "somewhere at this very moment . . . born in America," he deliberately used female pronouns to refer to her.

Clinton often referred to himself as "the comeback kid." He claimed the title after rebounding from loss of the New Hampshire primary (to Tsongas) and damaging stories about his alleged relationship with a singer and about the means by which he avoided the Vietnam War draft.

Following are excerpts from the Democratic platform of 1992:

Economic Opportunity. Our party's first priority is opportunity-broad-based, non-inflationary economic growth and the opportunity that flows from it. Democrats in 1992 hold nothing more important for America than an economy that offers growth and jobs for all. . . . We reject both the do-nothing government of the last 12 years and the big government theory that says we can hamstring business and tax and spend our way to prosperity. . . .

The Deficit. Addressing the deficit requires fair and shared sacrifice of all Americans for the common good. . . . In place of the Republican supply side disaster, the Democratic investment, economic conversion and growth strategy will generate more revenues from a growing economy. We must also tackle spending by putting everything on the table. . . .

Education. A competitive American economy requires the global market's best-educated, best-trained, most flexible work force. It's not enough to spend more on our schools; we must insist on results. We oppose the Bush administration's efforts to bankrupt the public school system-the bedrock of democracy-through private school vouchers. . . .

Health Care. All Americans should have universal access to quality, affordable health care-not as a privilege but as a right. That requires tough controls on health costs, which are rising at two to three times the rate of inflation, terrorizing American families and businesses and depriving millions of the care they need. We will enact a uniquely American reform of the health-care system. . . . We must be united in declaring war on AIDS and HIV disease, implement the recommendations of the National Commission on AIDS and fully fund the Ryan White Care Act; provide targeted and honest prevention campaigns; combat HIV-related discrimination; make drug treatment available for all addicts who seek it; guarantee access to quality care; expand clinical trials for treatments and vaccines; and speed up the FDA [Food and Drug Administration] drug approval process.

Energy. We reject the Republican myth that energy efficiency and environmental protection are enemies of economic growth. We will make our economy more efficient, using less energy, reducing our dependence on foreign oil, and producing less solid and toxic waste. . . .

Civil and Equal Rights. We don't have an American to waste. Democrats will continue to lead the fight to ensure that no Americans suffer discrimination or deprivation of rights on the basis of race, gender, language, national origin, religion, age, disability, sexual orientation or other characteristics irrelevant to ability. We support ratification of the

Equal Rights Amendment, affirmative action, stronger protection of voting rights for racial and ethnic minorities, including language access to voting, and continued resistance to discriminatory English-only pressure groups.... . provide civil rights protection for gay men and lesbians and an end to Defense Department discrimination; respect Native American culture and our treaty commitments; require the United States government to recognize its trustee obligations to the inhabitants of Hawaii generally and to Native Hawaiians in particular; and fully enforce the Americans with Disability Act to enable people with disabilities to achieve independence and function at their highest possible level.

Welfare Reform. Welfare should be a second chance, not a way of life. We want to break the cycle of welfare by adhering to two simple principles: No one who is able to work can stay on welfare forever, and no one who works should live in poverty.... . We will give them the help they need to make the transition from welfare to work, and require people who can work to go to work within two years in available jobs either in the private sector or in community service to meet unmet needs. That will restore the covenant that welfare was meant to be: A promise of temporary help for people who have fallen on hard times.

Abortion. Democrats stand behind the right of every woman to choose, consistent with *Roe v. Wade,* regardless of ability to pay, and support a national law to protect that right....

Environment ... We will oppose Republican efforts to gut the Clean Air Act in the guise of competitiveness. We will reduce the volume of solid waste and encourage the use of recycled materials while discouraging excess packaging. To avoid the mistakes of the past, we will actively support energy efficiency, recycling and pollution-prevention strategies.

Government Reform. Democrats in 1992 intend to lead a revolution in government, challenging it to act responsibly and be accountable, starting with the hardest and most urgent problems of the deficit and economic growth....

Crime and Drugs. To empower America's communities, Democrats pledge to restore government as upholder of basic law and order for crime-ravaged communities. The simplest and most direct way to restore order in our cities is to put more police on the streets.... We support a reasonable waiting period to permit background checks for purchases of handguns, as well as assault weapons controls to ban the possession, sale, importation and manufacture of the most deadly assault weapons....

Defense.... The United States must be prepared to use military force decisively when necessary to defend our vital interests. The burdens of collective security in a new era must be shared fairly, and we should encourage multilateral peacekeeping through the United Nations and other international efforts....

Middle East Peace. Support for the peace process now under way in the Middle East, rooted in the tradition of the Camp David accords. Direct negotiations between Israel, her Arab neighbors and Palestinians, with no imposed solutions, are the only way to achieve enduring security for Israel and full peace for all parties in the region....

Human Rights. Standing everywhere for the rights of individuals and respect for ethnic minorities against the repressive acts of governments-against torture, political imprisonment and all attacks on civilized standards of human freedom. This is a proud tradition of the Democratic Party, which has stood for freedom in South Africa and continues to resist oppression in Cuba. Our nation should once again promote the principle of sanctuary for politically oppressed people

everywhere, be they Haitian refugees, Soviet Jews seeking U.S. help in their successful absorption into Israeli society or Vietnamese fleeing communism. Forcible return of anyone fleeing political repression is a betrayal of American values.

REPUBLICANS

Five weeks after the Democratic convention, the Republicans convened in Houston August 17–20 and did their best to persuade voters to remember the past and trust in experience. From the rousing opening night performance of former president Ronald Reagan to the repeated calls to honor traditional family values, the Republican National Convention looked backward as much as it looked ahead.

There were frequent references to having defeated communism and having won the Persian Gulf War. Voters were asked to ignore the Democrats' attempt to remake themselves in a more moderate image and to remember instead what life was like under Jimmy Carter, the most recent Democratic president.

There was little moderation evident in the party platform adopted for George Bush's second term. The GOP approved a hard-line approach opposing abortion rights and any attempt to increase taxes. On the social issues front, there were planks favoring school choice, school prayer, and family unity.

Finally, the delegates needed little prompting to vent their frustrations at the "liberal media" for praising Democratic nominee Bill Clinton, dwelling on dissension over the GOP's antiabortion stance, and overemphasizing the weak economy. Bush sought to link Clinton to the Democratic Congress, which he blamed for the nation's problems—a refrain that would be played over and over throughout the week.

This was a homecoming of sorts for Bush. A New Englander by birth who went to Texas to work in the oil business, he retained his residency at a Houston hotel.

Party activists also sought a fresh start for Dan Quayle, widely perceived as being bumbling, gaffe-prone, and ineffective. But many conservatives still viewed the vice president as a hero, and because Quayle survived attempts to dump him from the ticket during the weeks leading up to the convention, GOP strategists looked forward to remaking his image as a thoughtful, middle-class American fighting for family values.

When the convention opened it already had become clear that efforts to force a debate on abortion had fallen short. A majority in six delegations was required to challenge the platform's call for a constitutional ban on all abortions, but abortion rights supporters said they could muster majorities in only four delegations—Maine, Massachusetts, New Mexico, and the Virgin Islands. The reason, they said, was that delegates felt it was more important to avoid embarrassing Bush than to force an open debate. In the end the platform was approved by voice vote. There were cries of "no!" when the document was put to delegates, but no public challenge.

In his speech conservative columnist Patrick J. Buchanan, who had unsuccessfully challenged Bush in the primaries, appealed to his supporters to throw their support to the president. He acknowledged the disagreements that led him to challenge Bush but said the convention marked the time to unite.

Buchanan's remarks were enthusiastically received in the hall, but the biggest response came for President Reagan, who described his speech as the "last chapter" in his political career. At eighty-one, the grand patriarch of the Republican Party showed all the oratorical skills and political spirit that had made him the hero of GOP conservatives.

"We stood tall and proclaimed that communism was destined for the ash heap of history," he said. "We never heard so much ridicule from our liberal friends. But we knew then what the liberal Democrat leaders just couldn't figure out: The sky would not fall if America restored her strength and resolve. The sky would not fall if an American president spoke the truth. The only thing that would fall was the Berlin Wall."

The nomination roll call was arranged so that Texas, the convention's host state and technically Bush's home, put him over the top. The final tally was 2,166 votes for Bush, 18 for Buchanan, and three for others, before the nomination was approved by acclamation. New Hampshire never cast its 23 votes. (Table, p. 637.)

In their acceptance speeches, Bush and Quayle sought to offset negative publicity against them while hurling their own negativity at the Democrats. Speaking first, Quayle defiantly answered his legion of detractors. "I know my critics wish I were not standing here tonight," he said. "They don't like our values. They look down on our beliefs. They're afraid of our ideas. And they know the American people stand on our side."

Bush came out fighting against the Democratic-controlled Congress and Clinton. Responding to the concerns of delegates still angry over his broken "no-new-taxes" pledge, Bush admitted that it had been a mistake but posed a question to the electorate. "Who do you trust in this election—the candidate who has raised taxes one time and regrets it, or the other candidate who raised taxes and fees 128 times and enjoyed it every time?"

Trust was again the issue as Bush highlighted his role as commander in chief in winning the Persian Gulf War against Iraq. His success and the remaining threats to peace allowed Bush to raise questions about what his opponent would have done.

Following are excerpts from the Republican platform of 1992:

Family Values. Our greatness starts at home—literally. So Republicans believe government should strengthen families, not replace them. Today, more than ever, the traditional family is under assault. We believe our laws should reflect what makes our nation prosperous and wholesome: faith in God, hard work, service to others and limited government. . . . [W]e want to expand the Young Child Tax Credit to $500 per child and make it available to all families with children under the age of 10. . . .

Education. The Republican strategy is based on sound principle. Parents have the right to choose the best school for their children. Schools should teach right from wrong. Schools should reinforce parental authority, not replace it. . . .

[W]e support the right of students to engage in voluntary prayer in schools and the right of the community to do so at commencements or other occasions. We will strongly enforce the law guaranteeing equal access to school facilities. We also advocate recitation of the Pledge of Allegiance in schools as a reminder of the principles that sustain us as one nation under God. . . .

AIDS. We are committed to ensure that our nation's response to AIDS is shaped by compassion, not fear or ignorance and will oppose,

as a matter of decency and honor, any discrimination against Americans who are its victims. . . . Above all, a cure must be found. We have committed enormous resources—$4.2 billion over the past four years for research alone, more than for any disease except cancer. . . .

Social Security. We reaffirm our commitment to a strong Social Security system. To stop penalizing grandparents and other seniors who care for children, we pledge to continue the Republican crusade to end the earnings limitation for Social Security recipients...

Cultural Values. We oppose any legislation or law that legally recognizes same-sex marriages and allows such couples to adopt children or provide foster care. . . .

Welfare Reform. Today's welfare system is anti-work and anti-marriage. It taxes families to subsidize illegitimacy. It rewards unethical behavior and penalizes initiative. It cannot be merely tinkered with by Congress; it must be re-created by states and localities. Republican governors and legislators in several states have already launched dramatic reforms, especially with workfare and learnfare. Welfare can no longer be a check in the mail with no responsibility. . . .

Individual Rights. The protection of individual rights is the foundation for opportunity and security. . . .

We believe the unborn child has a fundamental individual right to life that cannot be infringed. We therefore reaffirm our support for a human life amendment to the Constitution, and we endorse legislation to make clear that the 14th Amendment's protections apply to unborn children. We oppose using public revenues for abortion and will not fund organizations that advocate it. . . .

Republicans defend the constitutional right to keep and bear arms. We call for stiff mandatory sentences for those who use firearms in a crime. . . .

Taxes. We will oppose any effort to increase taxes. . . . We believe the tax increases of 1990 should ultimately be repealed. . . . As the deficit comes under control, we aspire to further tax rate cuts, strengthening incentives to work, save, invest and innovate. We also support President Bush's efforts to reduce federal spending and to cap the growth of non-Social Security entitlements. . . . We support further tax simplification. . . .

Government Reform. We reaffirm our support for a constitutional amendment to limit the number of terms House members and senators may serve. . . .

Congress must stop exempting itself from laws such as the minimum wage and the civil rights statutes, as well as laws that apply to the executive branch. The Independent Counsel Act is a case in point. . . . If that act is reauthorized, it must be extended to Congress as well. Safety and health regulations, civil rights and minimum wage laws are further examples of areas where Congress has set itself apart from the people. This practice must end. . . .

Budget Reform. Republicans vigorously support a balanced budget, a balanced-budget constitutional amendment and a line-item veto for the president.

Republicans believe this balancing of the budget should be achieved, not by increasing taxes to match spending, but by cutting spending to current levels of revenue. We prefer a balanced-budget amendment that contains a supermajority requirement to raise taxes. . . .

Campaign Reform. We will require congressional candidates to raise most of their funds from individuals within their home constituencies. This will limit outside special-interest money and result in less expensive campaigns, with less padding for incumbents. To the same end, we will strengthen the role of political parties to remove pressure on candidates to spend so much time soliciting funds. We will eliminate political action committees supported by corporations, unions or trade associations, and restrict the practice of bundling.

Energy. We will. . . . [allow] access, under environmental safeguards, to the coastal plain of the Arctic National Wildlife Refuge, possibly one of the largest petroleum reserves in our country, and to selected areas of the outer continental shelf (OCS). . . .

Public Lands. The millions of acres that constitute this nation's public lands must continue to provide for a number of uses. We are committed to the multiple use of our public lands. We believe that recreation, forestry, ranching, mining, oil and gas exploration, and production on our public lands can be conducted in a way compatible with their conservation. . . .

Transportation. To keep America on the move, we assert the same principle that guides us in all other sectors of the economy: consumers benefit through competition within the private sector. That is why we will complete the job of trucking deregulation. We will also abolish the Interstate Commerce Commission, finally freeing shippers and consumers from horse-and-buggy regulation. . . .

Middle East Peace. The basis for negotiations must be U.N. Security Council Resolutions 242 and 338. Peace must come from direct negotiations.

A meaningful peace must assure Israel's security while recognizing the legitimate rights of the Palestinian people. We oppose the creation of an independent Palestinian state. Nor will we support the creation of any political entity that would jeopardize Israel's security. . . .

Disarmament. We will banish the threat of nuclear annihilation from the face of the earth-not by savaging our military, as some Democrats might insist but by building on the historic diplomatic achievements of Presidents Bush and Reagan.

This means ensuring stable command and control of the former Soviet arsenal, complete acceptance and verified implementation of all treaty obligations by the successor states to the Soviet Union, and achieving the additional 50 percent reduction in strategic forces now agreed upon. . . .

Defense. Republicans call for a controlled defense drawdown, not a free fall. That is why President Bush proposes to carefully reduce defense spending over the next four years by an additional $34 billion, including $18 billion in outlays, with a 25 percent reduction in personnel. He has already eliminated over 100 weapon systems. Around the world, American forces are coming home from the frontiers of the Cold War. More than 550 overseas bases are being closed or realigned. Yet U.S. forces retain the ability to meet the challenge of another Desert Storm with equal success. . . .

We applaud the president's efforts to assist all individuals and communities adversely affected by the ongoing defense build-down, with more than 30 defense adjustment programs already in place and more than $7 billion committed to the effort in just the next two years. . . .

ROSS PEROT, INDEPENDENT

The 1992 independent candidacy of Texas billionaire Ross Perot began with a call-in television show rather than with a nominating convention. Undeclared at first, the Perot candidacy began February 20 with his appearance on CNN's *Larry King Live* when Perot expressed a willingness to run for president. Under King's prodding, Perot said that if the people "register me in fifty states" he would use his own money for a "world-class campaign."

Perot, a Naval Academy graduate who founded his computer company after leaving IBM, had been in the public eye for years, financing expeditions to help find American prisoners in Vietnam and rescue his employees in Iran, reforming the Texas school system, trying to shake up General Motors' management, and appearing on radio and TV talk shows to warn about the mounting federal deficit.

Tens of thousands of volunteers responded to Perot's challenge and began circulating petitions to place his name on the ballot in states from coast to coast. Meanwhile, Perot began forming a campaign organization. Polls in early spring showed him leading both President George Bush and challenger Bill Clinton. In June he hired as strategists Hamilton Jordan, manager of Jimmy Carter's 1976 and 1980 campaigns, and Edward J. Rollins, manager of Ronald Reagan's 1984 reelection campaign.

But Perot's standing in the polls began to fall as the media spotlight produced a spate of negative publicity about his quirky personality and fitness to operate within the political system he pledged to reform. On July 16 Perot abruptly announced he was dropping out of the race and closing down his operation.

Perot gave several reasons for his decision. He said he "didn't have any drive to be president" and that he was concerned the election would be thrown to the House of Representatives if he took enough votes from Bush and Clinton to deny both the required electoral vote majority. Earlier he had complained that Republican dirty tricks were undermining his campaign.

By this time Perot had qualified for the ballot in twenty-four states and was well on his way to the goal of qualifying in all fifty states. His disappointed followers felt betrayed by the sudden withdrawal.

But just as suddenly, Perot was back in the race. On October 16 he said he was returning because the major parties had failed to address the problems he had been highlighting in his speeches, both as a private citizen and a political candidate. "We gave them a chance," he said, "They didn't do it."

With the campaign revived, volunteers succeeded in getting Perot on the ballot in every state. Because some states required that he have a running mate, Perot chose retired admiral and former Vietnam War prisoner James B. Stockdale of California. The campaign, which Perot called United We Stand America, later became the Reform Party, which nominated Perot for president in 1996. The organization had no formal platform in 1992 or 1996.

1996 Conventions

PRESIDENTIAL CANDIDATES

Bill Clinton
Democrat

Bob Dole
Republican

Ross Perot
Reform

REPUBLICANS

The Republican Party on August 12–15 showcased GOP presidential nominee Bob Dole, the former Senate majority leader from Kansas, and his vice-presidential selection, former New York representative Jack F. Kemp, at the party's nominating convention in San Diego, California. Seeking to energize loyalists while also expanding its base, the convention's carefully orchestrated moments melded the twin themes of compassion and conservatism.

Organizers succeeded in tightly scripting the convention, banishing any hint of controversy and leaving the delegates with little to do but wave their colorful Dole-Kemp placards and present a picture of enthusiastic party unity for the network television cameras. The paucity of controversy cheered Republicans, who still remembered the 1992 convention in Houston that was marked by strident speeches on abortion and other hot-button social issues. In contrast, San Diego conventioneers were treated to speech after speech that stressed inclusion and moderation.

The Republican platform—as rigidly conservative as any in recent memory—was the designated forum for the party's sharper ideological right wing. Party moderates were kept happy during convention week with prime-time speaking slots. The social conservatives—who were at least a plurality in the ranks of the delegates—were rarely on stage during prime time.

On Monday, August 17, the delegates formally adopted the 1996 party platform by voice vote at the convention's sparsely attended opening morning session. The smooth and swift approval belied the fierce, prolonged struggle over the plank calling for a constitutional amendment to ban abortion. During platform deliberations the week before the convention, social conservatives who dominated the platform-writing process soundly defeated multiple amendments to soften the abortion plank or acknowledge differing views of the issue within the party. At the urging of the Dole campaign, however, the platform committee agreed to add the texts of defeated amendments as an appendix headed "Minority Views." Thereafter, also

at the urging of the Dole camp, abortion rights advocates dropped their planned protest on the convention floor.

Even most of the delegates pledged to conservative commentator Patrick J. Buchanan seemed to approve of the deal. Although Buchanan was denied a podium speech and his delegates were not allowed to place his name in nomination, his supporters said they appreciated the tone of unity and found plenty of reasons to rally around the Dole-Kemp ticket.

A highlight of the first evening came when Nancy Reagan delivered a tribute to her husband, former president Ronald Reagan, who, suffering from Alzheimer's disease, did not attend the GOP convention for the first time in more than three decades. The audience barely had a chance to collect its emotions before retired Army general Colin L. Powell marched to the podium and confirmed his status as a rising GOP star. Sounding the theme of the evening—and indeed the convention itself—Powell said the GOP "must always be the party of inclusion." In a rare acknowledgment of the party's tensions over social issues that lurked out of sight of the cameras, Powell declared his support for abortion rights and affirmative action.

Reflecting the party's new emphasis on diversity, female and minority speakers dominated the podium, even though their numbers were disproportionately low among the 1,990 delegates. The selection of New York representative Susan Molinari, an abortion rights supporter, as keynote speaker was another signal to moderates that they were welcome in the party. However, Molinari avoided mentioning abortion in her speech.

In the convention's most intriguing role reversal, House Speaker and convention chair Newt Gingrich, who rose to power and to controversy as a partisan firebrand, used his one short speaking slot Tuesday to praise volunteer efforts—presenting a softer, warmer side of the Republican Party. Wednesday, August 14, was highlighted by an unconventional appearance by Elizabeth Hanford Dole, the nominee's wife, who took a hand-held microphone to the convention floor to praise her husband's personal and political qualities.

The delegates formally made Bob Dole their presidential candidate following a nominating speech by Sen. John McCain of Arizona. The roll call of the states proved anticlimactic. It lasted about an hour and a half, yet the balloting was not unanimous. Dole ended up with 1,928 of the 1,990 delegate votes; Buchanan received 43 votes. (Table, p. 638.)

On the final evening, Dole and Kemp delivered acceptance speeches that laid the basis for their campaign against President Bill Clinton. Kemp, a fervent and enthusiastic promoter of the GOP as the party of opportunity, promised that Republican policies—including tax cuts and reduced regulation—would unleash a burst of economic activity benefiting all Americans.

In his speech, Dole prominently mentioned his proposed across-the-board, 15 percent income tax cut that had become the centerpiece of his campaign. But he also prescribed racial and ethnic tolerance as a dictum for the party. "If there is anyone who has mistakenly attached himself to our party in the belief that we are not open to citizens of every race and religion, then let me remind you," Dole said sternly, "tonight this hall belongs to the party of Lincoln, and the exits, which are clearly marked, are for you to walk out of as I stand this ground without compromise."

Yet, no matter how well Dole and the Republicans papered over differences at the convention, the party remained split between its traditional base of fiscal conservatives and its new base of social-issue activists who wanted to see their positions turned into policy.

Following are excerpts from the Republican platform of 1996:

Tax Relief. American families are suffering from the twin burdens of stagnant incomes and near-record taxes. . . . American families deserve better. They should be allowed to keep more of their hard-earned money so they can spend on their priorities. . . .

In response to this unprecedented burden confronting America, we support an across-the-board, 15-percent tax cut to marginal tax rates. . . . To remove impediments to job creation and economic growth, we support reducing the top tax rate on capital gains by 50 percent. . . . The income tax on Social Security benefits. . . must be repealed. . . .

To protect the American people from those who would undo their forthcoming victory over big government, we support legislation requiring a super-majority vote in both houses of Congress to raise taxes. . . .

Balancing the Budget. . . . Republicans support a Balanced Budget Amendment to the Constitution, phased in over a short period and with appropriate safeguards for national emergencies. . . .

Homeownership. . . . We support transforming public housing into private housing, converting low-income families into proud homeowners. Resident management of public housing is a first step toward that goal, which includes eliminating the Department of Housing and Urban Development (HUD). HUD's core functions will be turned over to the states. . . .

Changing Washington from the Ground Up. . . . We support elimination of the Departments of Commerce, Housing and Urban Development, Education, and Energy, and the elimination, defunding or privatization of agencies which are obsolete, redundant, of limited value, or too regional in focus. Examples of agencies. . . . are the National Endowment for the Arts, the National Endowment for the Humanities, the Corporation for Public Broadcasting and the Legal Services Corporation. . . .

Government Reform. . . . True reform is indeed needed: ending taxpayer subsidies for campaigns, strengthening party structures to guard against rogue operations, requiring full and immediate disclosure of all contributions, and cracking down on the indirect support, or "soft money," by which special interest groups underwrite their favored candidates. . . .

Regulatory Reform. . . . A Republican administration will require periodic review of existing regulations to ensure they are effective and do away with obsolete and conflicting rules. We will encourage civil servants to find ways to reduce regulatory burdens on the public and will require federal agencies to disclose the costs of new regulations on individuals and small businesses. . . . We will require agencies to conduct cost-benefit analyses of their regulations. . . .

Restoring Justice to the Courts. . . . The federal judiciary, including the U.S. Supreme Court, has overstepped its authority under the Constitution. It has usurped the right of citizen legislators and popularly elected executives to make law by declaring duly enacted laws to be "unconstitutional" through the misapplication of the principle of judicial review. . . . A Republican president will ensure that a process is established to select for the federal judiciary nominees who understand that their task is first and foremost to be faithful to the Constitution and to the intent of those who framed it. . . .

The Nation's Capital. . . . We reaffirm the constitutional status of the District of Columbia as the seat of government of the United States and reject calls for statehood for the District. . . . We call for structural reform of the city's government and its education system. . . .

Upholding the Rights of All. . . . We oppose discrimination based on sex, race, age, creed, or national origin and will vigorously enforce anti-discrimination statutes. We reject the distortion of those laws to cover sexual preference, and we endorse the Defense of Marriage Act to prevent states from being forced to recognize same-sex unions. Because we believe rights inhere in individuals, not in groups, we will attain our nation's goal of equal rights without quotas or other forms of preferential treatment. . . .

The unborn child has a fundamental individual right to life which cannot be infringed. We support a human life amendment to the Constitution and we endorse legislation to make clear that the Fourteenth Amendment's protections apply to unborn children. Our purpose is to have legislative and judicial protection of that right against those who perform abortions. . . .

We applaud Bob Dole's commitment to revoke the Clinton executive orders concerning abortion and to sign into law an end to partial-birth abortions. . . .

We defend the constitutional right to keep and bear arms. . . .

A Sensible Immigration Policy. . . . Illegal aliens should not receive public benefits other than emergency aid, and those who become parents while illegally in the United States should not be qualified to claim benefits for their offspring. Legal immigrants should depend for assistance on their sponsors, who are legally responsible for their financial well-being, not the American taxpayers. . . .

From Many, One. . . . While we benefit from our differences, we must also strengthen the ties that bind us to one another. Foremost among those is the flag. Its deliberate desecration is not "free speech," but an assault against our history and our hopes. We support a constitutional amendment that will restore to the people, through their elected representatives, their right to safeguard Old Glory. . . .

We support the official recognition of English as the nation's common language. . . .

Improving Education. . . . The federal government has no constitutional authority to be involved in school curricula or to control jobs in the workplace. That is why we will abolish the Department of Education, end federal meddling in our schools and promote family choice at all levels of learning. . . .

We will continue to work for the return of voluntary prayer to our schools. . . .

Health Care. Our goal is to maintain the quality of America's health care—the best in the world, bar none—while making health care and health insurance more accessible and more affordable. . . .

We reaffirm our determination to protect Medicare. We will ensure a significant annual expansion in Medicare. That isn't "cutting Medicare." It's a projected average annual rate of growth of 7.1 percent a year—more than twice the rate of inflation—to ensure coverage for those who need it now and those who will need it in the future. . .

The Middle East. . . . We applaud the Republican Congress for enacting legislation to recognize Jerusalem as the undivided capital of Israel. A Republican administration will ensure that the U.S. Embassy is moved to Jerusalem by May 1999. . . .

The Men and Women of Defense. . . . We affirm that homosexuality is incompatible with military service. . . . We reaffirm our support for the exemption of women from ground combat units and are concerned about the current policy of involuntarily assigning women to combat or near-combat units. . . .

REFORM PARTY

Founded in the fall of 1995 by Texas billionaire and presidential aspirant Ross Perot, the Reform Party conducted its first presidential nominating convention in an unusual two-stage process. The first session convened in Long Beach, California, on August 11, 1996, and the second session met one week later across the country at Valley Forge, Pennsylvania, on August 18. During the intervening week, ballots were sent to 1.3 million Reform Party members who voted in a "national primary" for the candidate of their choice by mail, electronic mail, or phone—an array of methods that party officials clearly saw as the election system of the future.

Perot had spent an estimated $6 million of his own money in bankrolling the party. After winning 19 percent of the popular vote in his unsuccessful independent bid against Democrat Bill Clinton and Republican President George Bush in the 1992 presidential election, Perot had formed the nonpartisan education organization, United We Stand America (UWSA), to promote his ideas on the national agenda. In 1995 Perot and UWSA supporters spun off the Reform Party as a full-fledged political party.

The California session drew roughly two thousand members—a fairly homogeneous group demographically, overwhelmingly white, and predominantly middle-aged or older. In the main, they tended to be politically disenchanted, strong proponents of the military, and strong supporters of reform in the mechanics of government and electoral politics.

Speeches by the party's two presidential candidates—Perot and former Democratic governor Richard D. Lamm of Colorado—highlighted the first session, which was televised nationally on C-SPAN and CNN. Lamm took a number of swipes at the Democrats and Republicans, saying "They do not enjoy a right of perpetual existence." But he also made it clear he was an alternative to Perot. "The torch must pass," said Lamm. "The Reform Party is larger than any one individual."

Lamm echoed Perot in urging the party to build on the need for campaign reform, fiscal responsibility, and increased immigration controls. The latter issue, in particular, struck a chord with the Long Beach audience, which responded with cheers when Lamm declared that "the Statue of Liberty stands for liberty, not unlimited immigration."

But if Lamm spoke politely, like an invited guest, Perot played the garrulous host. Perot had every reason to be optimistic. He led Lamm by a ratio of more than 2-to-1 in the first round of nomination balloting that determined the party's primary finalists. "I want to be your president," Perot declared, trying to dispel memories of 1992, when he abruptly quit the presidential race in July, only to reenter in October.

During the following week, Lamm criticized the ground rules of the party's nominating process, which were devised by Perot operatives. "I don't think it has been a fair playing field or party-building endeavor as I was promised," he said.

The modern balloting system had its snags, too. Some participants complained that they did not receive ballots in time to vote. Even Lamm had trouble obtaining a ballot for himself. In the final tally, only 5 percent of the party's declared membership voted. On August 17, national coordinator Russell Verney announced that Perot had won the nomination by taking 65 percent of the primary vote to Lamm's 35 percent.

In his acceptance speech the following day at the Valley Forge convention center, Perot stressed the issues he was known for—reduced federal debt, lobbying reform, and higher ethical standards for elected officials. Perot especially ripped both parties for not following through on promising to form a task force to reform campaign finance. Despite his earlier criticism of public financing—Perot had spent more than $60 million of his own money to self-finance his 1992 campaign—he announced that he would accept federal matching funds in 1996. But in accepting the nearly $30 million in public matching funds for which he qualified, Perot had to limit his personal funding to $50,000. At the end of his speech, Perot urged supporters to contribute to his campaign, as a telephone number flashed on screens behind him. Perot then hastened from the stage for an appearance on CNN's *Larry King Live*, the program on which he made many of his campaign announcements in 1992 and 1996.

The Reform Party did not have a formal 1996 platform.

DEMOCRATS

Meeting in Chicago for the eleventh time in the party's history, the Democratic Party on August 26–29 jubilantly renominated President Bill Clinton and Vice President Al Gore. Democratic officials produced a convention designed to stir the viewing public's emotions. Speakers and videos highlighted the party's racial and ethnic diversity while drawing attention to Clinton's efforts to ease the burdens on middle-class families. Taking advantage of meeting two weeks after the Republicans nominated Bob Dole, Democrats repeatedly hammered away at Dole's offer to be "a bridge to the past" as proof that the GOP wanted to turn back the clock on economic, social, and cultural change.

Despite the apparent unity, the convention exposed the unresolved philosophical divisions between the party's liberal and centrist wings. Members of centrist Democratic Party groups such as the Blue Dogs, a group of House deficit hawks, and the Democratic Leadership Council insisted that their blueprint for smaller government was gradually becoming the party's dominant position. They pointed to the 1996 platform, adopted without dissent August 27, which was generally more conservative than past documents. "Our platform calls for a balanced budget," said Rep. Charles W. Stenholm of Texas. "That's a first."

Some veteran liberals, such as Rep. Charles B. Rangel of New York, acknowledged the party's move to the center. "America has shifted on us," Rangel said. "Americans should be prepared to raise the taxes, invest in productivity, and create the jobs. But they can't support that. They'd rather cut taxes, invest in defense, and build jails."

The high point of the first evening was the appearance of a pair of lifelong Republicans: former Ronald Reagan press secretary James S. Brady, and his wife, Sarah. In a reference to the Republican convention, Sarah Brady said, "Jim, we must have made a wrong turn. This isn't San Diego." The Bradys, who had become gun control proponents after James Brady was partially paralyzed from being shot during the 1981 attempt to assassinate President Reagan, called for increased efforts to reduce gun violence. They praised Clinton for enacting the Brady bill, which imposed a seven-day waiting period for handgun purchases.

Actor Christopher Reeve, paralyzed from a horse-riding accident in 1995, capped the evening's speeches with a plea for compassion and assistance to Americans with disabilities. Reeve, speaking from a wheelchair, held the hushed audience's attention as he called for increased research funding for multiple sclerosis, Parkinson's disease, spinal cord injuries, and AIDS.

On Tuesday former New York governor Mario M. Cuomo and civil rights leader Jesse Jackson from the liberal wing of the party spoke to the convention—although before the late-night portion of the broadcast by the three major television networks. While the two men agreed to disagree with the president over welfare reform, they launched some of the harshest partisan attacks of the convention. Cuomo proclaimed a need to elect a Democratic majority to Congress to fend off the Republicans' conservative agenda. "They are the real threat," he said. Jackson focused on the need to improve conditions in economically deprived sections of the United States. His repeated plea to "keep that faith" with poor and struggling Americans became a chant echoed by the rapt audience.

Following the keynote speech by Gov. Evan Bayh of Indiana, the evening's theme was "Families First." Speakers included an opponent of abortion, Rep. Tony P. Hall of Ohio. "Many of us have felt left out [in the past]," Hall said. "This year it's different." In 1992 Pennsylvania's antiabortion governor, Robert P. Casey, had not been permitted to speak at the Democratic convention. The final speaker, first lady Hillary Rodham Clinton, closed out the evening with a passionate explanation of her view of family values.

On Wednesday, Gore's speech broke tradition by being scheduled the day before the president's acceptance speech. Gore rallied the convention with sharp jabs at the Republican nominee. "In his speech from San Diego, Senator Dole offered himself as a bridge to the past," said Gore. "Tonight, Bill Clinton and I offer ourselves as a bridge to the future."

But the most memorable part of his speech was a deeply personal glimpse at a family tragedy. Seeking to underscore the dangers of underage smoking, Gore recounted the final, painful days and hours of his sister who began smoking at age thirteen and ultimately died of lung cancer.

The nomination of Clinton followed, with Sen. Christopher J. Dodd of Connecticut, the DNC general chairman, hailing the president for leading the nation into an era of prosperity, while courageously taking on powerful special interests such as the gun lobby and the tobacco industry. The formality of the presidential roll call culminated the evening. The final tally was announced as a unanimous 4,289 votes for Clinton, although there appeared to be roughly a dozen votes that were not cast during the roll call. (Table, p. 639.)

President Clinton capped the Democratic convention with a sixty-six-minute policy address that chronicled his administration's accomplishments. The president's speech was designed to burnish his centrist image and lay the foundation for a second term. In his address, the president resolved to "build a bridge to the twenty-first century, to meet our values and protect our values."

Clinton promised to balance the budget without threatening Medicare and Medicaid, education programs, or environmental protection. He also proposed a series of modest initiatives including deploying of thirty thousand reading specialists to help enlist one million volunteer reading tutors, expanding controls on handgun sales, providing targeted tax cuts such as tax credits and deductions for college tuition and tax breaks for first-time home buyers, and increasing funding for cleaning up superfund toxic waste sites.

Following are excerpts from the Democratic platform of 1996:

Balancing the Budget. . . . In 1992, we promised to cut the deficit in half over four years. We did. Our 1993 economic plan cut spending by over a quarter trillion dollars in five years. . . . Now the Democratic Party is determined to finish the job and balance the budget. President Clinton has put forward a plan to balance the budget by 2002 while living up to our commitments to our elderly and our children and maintaining strong economic growth. . . . Today's Democratic Party believes we have a duty to care for our parents, so they can live their lives in dignity. That duty includes securing Medicare and Medicaid, finding savings without reducing quality or benefits, and protecting Social Security for future generations. . . .

Tax Relief. . . . Today's Democratic Party is committed to targeted tax cuts that help working Americans invest in their future, and we insist that any tax cuts are completely paid for, because we are determined to balance the budget. . . .

Foreign Trade. We believe that if we want the American economy to continue strong growth, we must continue to expand trade, and not retreat from the world. . . . We must continue to work to lower foreign trade barriers. . . .

Education. . . . In the next four years, we must do even more to make sure America has the best public schools on earth. . . . We must hold students, teachers, and schools to the highest standards. Every child should be able to read by the end of the third grade. Students should be required to demonstrate competency and achievement for promotion or graduation. Teachers should be required to meet high standards for professional performance and be rewarded for the good jobs they do—and there should be a fair, timely, cost-effective process to remove those who do not measure up. . . . We should expand public school choice, but we should not take American tax dollars from public schools and give them to private schools. We should promote public charter schools that are held to the highest standards of accountability and access. . . .

Health Care. The Democratic Party is committed to ensuring that Americans have access to affordable, high-quality health care. . . . In the next four years, we must take further steps to ensure that Americans have access to quality, affordable health care. We should start by making sure that people get help paying premiums so they do not lose health care while they're looking for a new job. We support expanded coverage of home care, hospice, and community-based services, so the elderly and people with disabilities of all ages can live in their own communities and as independently as possible. We . . . believe health insurance coverage for mental health care is vitally important and we support parity for mental health care.

Retirement. . . . We want . . . to make sure people can carry their pensions with them when they change jobs, protect pensions even further, and expand the number of workers with pension coverage. Democrats created Social Security, we oppose efforts to dismantle it, and we will fight to save it. We must ensure that it is on firm financial footing well into the next century. . . .

Fighting Crime. . . . President Clinton beat back fierce Republican opposition. . . . to answer the call of America's police officers and pass the toughest Crime Bill in history. . . . And it is making a difference. In city after city and town after town, crime rates are finally coming down. . . . Any attempt to repeal the Brady Bill or assault weapons ban will be met with a veto. We must do everything we can to stand behind our police officers, and the first thing we should do is pass a ban on cop-killer bullets. . . .

Immigration. . . . We support a legal immigration policy that is pro-family, pro-work, pro-responsibility, and pro-citizenship, and we deplore those who blame immigrants for economic and social problems. . . .We cannot tolerate illegal immigration and we must stop it. . . .

We deplore those who use the need to stop illegal immigration as a pretext for discrimination. And we applaud the wisdom of Republicans . . . who oppose the mean-spirited and shortsighted effort of Republicans in Congress to bar the children of illegal immigrants from schools. . . .

Welfare Reform. . . . Over the past four years, President Clinton has dramatically transformed the welfare system. . . . Welfare rolls are finally coming down—there are 1.3 million fewer people on welfare today than there were when President Clinton took office in January 1993.

. . . . Thanks to President Clinton and the Democrats, the new welfare bill includes the health care and child care people need so they can go to work confident their children will be cared for. Thanks to President Clinton and the Democrats, the new welfare bill imposes time limits and real work requirements. . . . Thanks to President Clinton and the Democrats, the new welfare bill cracks down on deadbeat parents and requires minor mothers to live at home with their parents or with another responsible adult. . . .

We know the new bill passed by Congress is far from perfect—parts of it should be fixed because they go too far and have nothing to do with welfare reform. . . .

Abortion. The Democratic Party stands behind the right of every woman to choose, consistent with *Roe v. Wade*, and regardless of ability to pay. President Clinton took executive action to make sure that the right to make such decisions is protected for all Americans. Over the last four years, we have taken action to end the gag rule and ensure safety at family planning and women's health clinics. We believe it is a fundamental constitutional liberty that individual Americans—not government—can best take responsibility for making the most difficult and intensely personal decisions regarding reproduction. . . .

Political Reform. . . . The President and the Democratic Party support the bipartisan McCain-Feingold campaign finance reform bill. It will limit campaign spending, curb the influence of PACs and lobbyists, and end the soft money system. Perhaps most important of all, this bill provides free TV time for candidates, so they can talk directly to citizens about real issues and real ideas. . . . It is time to take the reins of democracy away from big money and put them back in the hands of the American people, where they belong. We applaud efforts by broadcasters and private citizens alike, to increase candidates' direct access to voters through free TV. . . .

The Middle East. . . . Jerusalem is the capital of Israel and should remain an undivided city accessible to people of all faiths. We are also committed to working with our Arab partners for peace to build a brighter, more secure and prosperous future for all the people of the Middle East. . . .

Protecting Our Environment. . . . We are committed to protecting the majestic legacy of our National Parks. . . . We will be good stewards of our old-growth forests, oppose new offshore oil drilling and mineral exploration and production in our nation's many environmentally critical areas, and protect our oceans from oil spills and the dumping of toxic and radioactive waste. . . .

Fighting Discrimination. Today's Democratic Party knows we must renew our efforts to stamp out discrimination and hatred of every kind, wherever and whenever we see it. . . . We believe everyone in America should learn English so they can fully share in our daily life, but we strongly oppose divisive efforts like English-only legislation. . . .

Religious Freedom. Today's Democratic Party understands that all Americans have a right to express their faith. . . . Americans have a right to express their love of God in public, and we applaud the President's work to ensure that children are not denied private religious expression in school. . . .

2000 Conventions

PRESIDENTIAL CANDIDATES

George W. Bush
Republican

Al Gore
Democrat

Ralph Nader
Green

REPUBLICANS

Meeting July 31–August 3 in Philadelphia, birthplace of the U.S. Constitution, the Republican Party made history of its own by naming George W. Bush, the son of a president, as the GOP standard-bearer for 2000. The proud father, former president George Bush, was among the many family members applauding the party's choice.

Delegates hoped a victory by Texas governor Bush would give the nation its second father-son presidential pair. The first was Federalist John Adams (1797–1801) and Democrat John Quincy Adams (1825–1829). Both were one-term presidents, as was the senior Bush, who lost to Democrat Bill Clinton in 1992.

In another historical irony, the nomination pitted Bush against Vice President Al Gore, who with Clinton halted twelve years of Republican control of the White House and who hoped to extend the Democrats' eight-year administration, just as George Bush had done for the GOP on Ronald Reagan's retirement in 1988.

The overriding difference between the two situations, as the Clinton-Gore strategists put it back then, was "the economy, stupid." Where Bush was washed out of office in a sea of red ink, Gore was riding a crest of unprecedented prosperity and federal budget surpluses. The year 2000 was a time of plenty that both parties sought to exploit.

In their acceptance speeches Bush and his running mate, former defense secretary Richard B. Cheney, assailed the Democrats for overlooking the opportunities of an overflowing treasury. "For eight years the Clinton-Gore administration has coasted through prosperity," Bush said. "So much promise to no great purpose. Instead of seizing this moment, the . . . administration has squandered it."

Similarly the party's 32,000-word platform was replete with references to prosperity and ways to use it, chiefly through tax cuts, which Bush said would benefit all taxpayers and not just the rich.

Bush's nomination at Philadelphia's First Union Center was strictly a formality. He, like Gore, had secured the nomination months earlier through primary victories that won him enough delegates to eliminate the competition. The next strongest primary candidate, Sen. John McCain of Arizona, endorsed Bush and released his delegates to him. For the vote, the convention planners used a novel "rolling roll call" that took several days. Bush and Cheney won the votes of all 2,066 delegates. (Table, p. 640.)

In keeping with the convention's themes of unity and inclusion, there were no floor fights on rules or on platform planks. Averting one such fight, the rules committee rejected, 66–33, the so-called Delaware plan to limit the GOP presidential primary schedule to four months, with smaller states voting first. The Republican National Committee approved the plan, but big states objected that it would weaken their strength in the delegate-selection process.

A floor fight was also avoided over the issue of abortion. Moderates tried unsuccessfully to remove platform language supporting a constitutional ban on abortion, fearing that it would hurt GOP candidates, especially among women voters. Bush told the delegates that as president he would sign a ban on partial-birth abortions if Congress sent him one.

Although only 4 percent of the delegates were black, the convention gave prominent roles to minorities. African American retired general Colin L. Powell gave the keynote address. Among other speakers were the nominee's wife, Laura, as well as Hispanics and a gay House member, Jim Kolbe of Arizona. As Kolbe spoke several Texas delegates removed their cowboy hats and bowed heads to show, as one put it, that they were not "condoning perversion."

The platform reaffirmed the party's opposition to homosexuality in the military, but in other ways it reflected Bush's self-described "compassionate conservatism." Missing were past GOP calls for eliminating the Education and Energy departments and federal agencies supporting the arts and humanities.

Added was a new women's health section supporting more research on diseases that disproportionately affect women. The document also welcomed "New Americans" in a softened stance on immigration.

Following are excerpts from the Republican platform of 2000:

Taxes and Budget. . . . When the average American family has to work more than four months out of every year to fund all levels of government, it's time to change the tax system, to make it simpler, flatter, and fairer for everyone. It's time for an economics of inclusion that will let people keep more of what they earn and accelerate movement up the opportunity ladder.

We therefore enthusiastically endorse the principles of Governor Bush's Tax Cut with a Purpose:

• Replace the five current tax brackets with four lower ones, ensuring all taxpayers significant tax relief while targeting it especially toward low-income workers.

• Help families by doubling the child tax credit to $1,000, making it available to more families, and eliminating the marriage penalty.

• Encourage entrepreneurship and growth by capping the top marginal rate, ending the death tax, and making permanent the Research and Development credit.

• Promote charitable giving and education. Foster capital investment and savings to boost today's dangerously low personal savings rate. . . .

Family Matters. We support the traditional definition of "marriage" as the legal union of one man and one woman, and we believe that federal judges and bureaucrats should not force states to recognize other living arrangements as marriages. . . . We do not believe sexual preference should be given special legal protection or standing in law.

Education. . . . Raise academic standards through increased local control and accountability to parents, shrinking a multitude of federal programs into five flexible grants in exchange for real, measured progress in student achievement.

Assist states in closing the achievement gap and empower needy families to escape persistently failing schools by allowing federal dollars to follow their children to the school of their choice.

. . . . We recognize that. . . . the role of the federal government must be progressively limited as we return control to parents, teachers, and local school boards. . . . The Republican Congress rightly opposed attempts by the Department of Education to establish federal testing that would set the stage for a national curriculum. We believe it's time to test the Department, and each of its programs, instead. . . .

Abortion. . . . The Supreme Court's recent decision, prohibiting states from banning partial-birth abortions—a procedure denounced by a committee of the American Medical Association and rightly branded as four-fifths infanticide—shocks the conscience of the nation. As a country, we must keep our pledge to the first guarantee of the Declaration of Independence. That is why we say the unborn child has a fundamental individual right to life which cannot be infringed. We support a human life amendment to the Constitution and we endorse legislation to make clear that the Fourteenth Amendment's protections apply to unborn children. . . .

Gun Laws. . . . We defend the constitutional right to keep and bear arms, and we affirm the individual responsibility to safely use and store firearms.

Because self-defense is a basic human right, we will promote training in their safe usage, especially in federal programs for women and the elderly. A Republican administration will vigorously enforce current gun laws, neglected by the Democrats, especially by prosecuting

dangerous offenders identified as felons in instant background checks. Although we support background checks to ensure that guns do not fall into the hands of criminals, we oppose federal licensing of law-abiding gun owners and national gun registration as a violation of the Second Amendment and an invasion of privacy of honest citizens. . . .

New Americans. . . . Our country's ethnic diversity within a shared national culture is unique in all the world. We benefit from our differences, but we must also strengthen the ties that bind us to one another. Foremost among those is the flag. Its deliberate desecration is not "free speech" but an assault against both our proud history and our greatest hopes. We therefore support a constitutional amendment that will restore to the people, through their elected representatives, their right to safeguard Old Glory.

Another sign of our unity is the role of English as our common language. . . . For newcomers, it has always been the fastest route to the mainstream of American life. English empowers. That is why fluency in English must be the goal of bilingual education programs. We support the recognition of English as the nation's common language. At the same time, mastery of other languages is important for America's competitiveness in the world market. . . .

As a nation of immigrants, we welcome all new Americans who have entered lawfully and are prepared to follow our laws and provide for themselves and their families. In their search for a better life, they strengthen our economy, enrich our culture, and defend the nation in war and in peace. To ensure fairness for those wishing to reside in this country, and to meet the manpower needs of our expanding economy, a total overhaul of the immigration system is sorely needed. . . .

Saving Social Security. . . . Anyone currently receiving Social Security, or close to being eligible for it, will not be impacted by any changes. Key changes should merit bipartisan agreement so any reforms will be a win for the American people rather than a political victory for any one party.

Real reform does not require, and will not include, tax increases.

Personal savings accounts must be the cornerstone of restructuring. Each of today's workers should be free to direct a portion of their payroll taxes to personal investments for their retirement future. . . . Today's financial markets offer a variety of investment options, including some that guarantee a rate of return higher than the current Social Security system with no risk to the investor. Choice is the key. Any new options for retirement security should be voluntary, so workers can choose to remain in the current system or opt for something different. . . .

Health Care. . . . Medicare, at age 35, needs a new lease on life. It's time to bring this program, so critical for 39 million seniors and individuals with disabilities, into the Twenty-first Century. It's time to modernize the benefit package to match current medical science, improve the program's financial stability, and cut back the bureaucratic jungle that is smothering it. It's time to give older Americans access to the same health insurance plan the Congress has created for itself, so that seniors will have the same choices and security as Members of Congress, including elimination of all current limitations and restrictions that prevent the establishment of medical savings accounts. . . .

Medicare, the bedrock of care for our elderly, is suffocating under more than 130,000 pages of federal rules, three times the size of the entire IRS code. It pays for only 53 percent of seniors' care, provides no outpatient prescription drugs, and does not cover real long-term care, and it is still headed for bankruptcy in the near future. The doctor-patient relationship has been eroded, and in some instances replaced, by external decision-making and managed care bureaucracy.

We intend to save this beleaguered system with a vision of health care adapted to the changing demands of a new century. It is as simple, and yet as profound, as this: All Americans should have access to high-quality and affordable health care. . . . In achieving that goal, we will promote a health care system that supports, not supplants, the private sector; that promotes personal responsibility in health care decision-making; and that ensures the least intrusive role for the federal government. . . .

Women's Health. . . . Across this country, and at all levels of government, Republicans are at the forefront in aggressively developing health care initiatives targeted specifically at the needs of women. The enormous increases in the NIH [National Institutes of Health] budget brought about by the Republican Congress will make possible aggressive new research and clinical trials into diseases and health issues that disproportionately affect women as well as into conditions that affect the elderly, the majority of whom are women. And we are leading efforts to reach out to underserved and minority female populations, where disparities persist in life expectancy, infant mortality and death rates from cancer, heart disease, and diabetes. . . .

Energy. . . . By any reasonable standard, the Department of Energy has utterly failed in its mission to safeguard America's energy security. The Federal Energy Regulatory Commission has been no better, and the Environmental Protection Agency (EPA) has been shutting off America's energy pipeline with a regulatory blitz that has only just begun. In fact, 36 oil refineries have closed in just the last eight years, while not a single new refinery has been built in this country in the last quarter-century. EPA's patchwork of regulations has driven fuel prices higher in some areas than in others. . . .

A Military for the Twenty-first Century. . . . Over the past seven years, a shrunken American military has been run ragged by a deployment tempo that has eroded its military readiness. Many units have seen their operational requirements increased four-fold, wearing out both people and equipment. Only last fall the Army certified two of its premier combat divisions as unready for war because of underfunding, mismanagement, and over commitment to peacekeeping missions around the globe. More Army units and the other armed services report similar problems. It is a national scandal that almost one quarter of our Army's active combat strength is unfit for wartime duty. . . .

The new Republican government will renew the bond of trust between the Commander-in-Chief, the American military, and the American people. The military is not a civilian police force or a political referee. We believe the military must no longer be the object of social experiments. We affirm traditional military culture. We affirm that homosexuality is incompatible with military service. . . .

The Middle East and Persian Gulf. . . . It is important for the United States to support and honor Israel, the only true democracy in the Middle East. We will ensure that Israel maintains a qualitative edge in defensive technology over any potential adversaries. We will not pick sides in Israeli elections. The United States has a moral and legal obligation to maintain its Embassy and Ambassador in Jerusalem. Immediately upon taking office, the next Republican president will begin the process of moving the U. S. Embassy from Tel Aviv to Israel's capital, Jerusalem. . . .

DEMOCRATS

Declaring himself "my own man," Vice President Al Gore stepped from the shadow of President Bill Clinton and accepted the Democratic Party's nomination for president on the final night of the party's August 14–17 convention at Los Angeles's Staples Center.

Reinforcing the independence he sought to portray, Gore earlier had taken a gamble unprecedented in American politics. He chose as his running mate Sen. Joseph Lieberman of Con-

necticut, making him the first Jew to run on a major party's national ticket. Besides being of a religious minority, Lieberman had at times broken with his party on economic issues and had sternly deplored Clinton's sexual affair with Monica Lewinsky.

But the convention delegates enthusiastically accepted Gore's choice of Lieberman as his partner against George W. Bush and Richard B. Cheney, the Republican ticket named two weeks earlier in Philadelphia. Like Bush and Cheney, Gore and Lieberman won the unanimous approval of their respective delegates. Gore had locked up the presidential nomination by defeating former senator Bill Bradley in the Democratic primaries. In a convention speech, Bradley urged Gore's election.

Most public opinion polls showed Gore trailing Bush before the conventions. Afterward both nominees received a "bounce" from their convention performances, but Gore's choice of running mate and his "my own man" ploy appeared to have been somewhat more popular than Bush's effort. Polls after the Democratic convention showed Gore leading Bush slightly.

Although Gore had been in the public eye for much of his life—as a House member, senator, and eight years as vice president—he devoted much of his acceptance speech to telling the delegates and television audience "who I truly am." He told of growing up in Carthage, Tennessee, and paid tribute to his recently deceased father, former senator Albert A. Gore, and his mother, one of the first woman graduates of Vanderbilt University Law School.

He praised Clinton as "a leader who moved us out of the valley of recession and into the longest period of prosperity in American history." But he also distanced himself from the moral behavior in office that led to Clinton's impeachment and Senate trial. "If you entrust me with the presidency, I know I won't always be the most exciting politician," Gore said, adding, "I will never let you down."

Even Clinton seemed to recognize Gore's need to shake loose the moral baggage of the president he had served for eight years. In his farewell speech to the convention, Clinton praised Gore's character as an adviser, leader, and champion of ordinary Americans. Choosing Gore as his partner, Clinton said, was "one of the very best decisions of my life."

Gore's speech and the party platform stressed the prosperity and budget surpluses achieved during Clinton's two terms. Gore pledged to continue balancing the budget while delivering "the right kind of tax cuts." The Bush kind, he said, would benefit the wealthy and leave little to pay down the national debt or meet the needs of poor and working families. "They're for the powerful," Gore said. "We're for the people."

Although Lieberman voted against conviction of Clinton after earlier criticizing him from the Senate floor, he had been an advocate of moral decency long before the Lewinsky affair came to light. Gore's wife, Tipper, had a similar background as a critic of explicit rock music in the 1980s. And, despite Hollywood's importance as a revenue source for the Democrats, the party platform contained a plank calling on the entertainment industry to assume more responsibility in protecting children from violence and cruelty.

Gore's movie actor friend and Harvard roommate Tommy

Lee Jones nominated Gore. Tipper Gore introduced her husband to the 4,339 delegates. One of Gore's daughters, Karenna Gore Schiff, also spoke to the convention. No other names were placed in nomination, and there were no floor fights over the party rules or platform. (*Table, p. 641.*)

Following are excerpts from the Democratic platform of 2000:

Fiscal Discipline. . . . Today, for most families, the federal tax burden is the lowest it has been in twenty years. The Bush tax slash takes a different course. It is bigger than any cut Newt Gingrich ever dreamed of. It would let the richest one percent of Americans afford a new sports car and middle class Americans afford a warm soda. It is so out-of-step with reality that the Republican Congress refused to enact it. It would undermine the American economy and undercut our prosperity. . . . Democrats seek the right kind of tax relief—tax cuts that are specifically targeted to help those who need them the most.

These tax cuts would let families live their values by helping them save for college, invest in their job skills and lifelong learning, pay for health insurance, afford child care, eliminate the marriage penalty for working families, care for elderly or disabled loved ones, invest in clean cars and clean homes, and build additional security for their retirement.

Retirement Security. . . . The choice for Americans on this vital part of our national heritage has never been more clear: Democrats believe in using our prosperity to save Social Security; the Republicans' tax cut would prevent America from ensuring our senior citizens have a secure retirement. We owe it to America's children and their children to make the strength and solvency of Social Security a major national priority.

That's why Al Gore is committed to making Social Security safe and secure for more than half a century by using the savings from our current unprecedented prosperity to strengthen the Social Security Trust Fund in preparation for the retirement of the Baby Boom generation. . . .

To build on the success of Social Security, Al Gore has proposed the creation of Retirement Savings Plus—voluntary, tax-free, personally-controlled, privately-managed savings accounts with a government match that would help couples build a nest egg of up to $400,000. . . .

Education. . . . George W. Bush and the Republican Party offer neither real accountability nor reasonable investment [in education]. . . . Their version of accountability relies on private school vouchers that would offer too few dollars to too few children to escape their failing schools. These vouchers would pass the buck on accountability while pulling bucks out of the schools that need them most. . . .

By the end of the next presidential term, we should have a fully qualified, well trained teacher in every classroom in every school in every part of this country and every teacher should pass a rigorous test to get there.

By the end of the next presidential term, every failing school in America should be turned around—or shut down and reopened under new public leadership.

By the end of the next presidential term, we should ensure that no high school student graduates unless they have mastered the basics of reading and math—so that the diploma they receive really means something.

By the end of the next presidential term, parents across the nation ought to be able to choose the best public school for their children. . . .

We should make a college education as universal as high school is today. Al Gore has proposed a new National Tuition Savings program to tie together state tuition savings programs in more than 30 states so that parents can save for college tax-free and inflation-free. We propose a tax cut for tuition and fees for post-high school education and training that allows families to choose either a $10,000 a year tax deduction or a $2,800 tax credit. . . .

Fighting Crime. . . . Strong and Sensible Gun Laws. . . . Democrats believe that we should fight gun crime on all fronts—with stronger laws and stronger enforcement. That's why Democrats fought and passed the Brady Law and the Assault Weapons Ban. We increased federal, state, and local gun crime prosecution by 22 percent since 1992. Now gun crime is down by 35 percent.

Now we must do even more. We need mandatory child safety locks, to protect our children. We should require a photo license I.D., a full background check, and a gun safety test to buy a new handgun in America. We support more federal gun prosecutors, ATF agents and inspectors, and giving states and communities another 10,000 prosecutors to fight gun crime.

Hate Crimes. . . . Hate crimes are more than assaults on people, they are assaults on the very idea of America. They should be punished with extra force. Protections should include hate violence based on gender, disability or sexual orientation. And the Republican Congress should stop standing in the way of this pro-civil rights, anti-crime legislation. . . .

Valuing Families. . . . Responsible Entertainment. . . . Parents and the entertainment industry must accept more responsibility. Many parents are not aware of the resources available to them, such as the V-chip technology in television sets and Internet filtering devices, that can help them shield children from violent entertainment. The entertainment industry must accept more responsibility and exercise more self-restraint, by strictly enforcing movie ratings, by taking a close look at violence in its own advertising, and by determining whether the ratings systems are allowing too many children to be exposed to too much violence and cruelty.

Health Care. Universal Health Coverage. There is much more left to do. We must redouble our efforts to bring the uninsured into coverage step-by-step and as soon as possible. We should guarantee access to affordable health care for every child in America. We should expand coverage to working families, including more Medicaid assistance to help with the transition from welfare to work. . . . In addition, Americans aged 55 to 65—the fastest growing group of uninsured—should be allowed to buy into the Medicare program to get the coverage they need. By taking these steps, we can move our nation closer to the goal of providing universal health coverage for all Americans.

. . . . A Real Patients' Bill of Rights. Medical decisions should be made by patients and their doctors and nurses, not accountants and bureaucrats at the end of a phone line a thousand miles away. . . . Americans need a real, enforceable Patients' Bill of Rights with the right to see a specialist, the right to appeal decisions to an outside board, guaranteed coverage of emergency room care, and the right to sue when they are unfairly denied coverage. . . .

Protecting and Strengthening Medicare. It is time we ended the tragedy of elderly Americans being forced to choose between meals and medication. It is time we modernized Medicare with a new prescription drug benefit. This is an essential step in making sure that the best new cures and therapies are available to our seniors and disabled Americans. We cannot afford to permit our seniors to receive only part of the medical care they need. . . .

Abortion. Choice. The Democratic Party stands behind the right of every woman to choose, consistent with *Roe v. Wade*, and regardless of ability to pay. We believe it is a fundamental constitutional liberty that individual Americans—not government—can best take responsibility for making the most difficult and intensely personal decisions regarding reproduction. This year's Supreme Court rulings show to us all that eliminating a woman's right to choose is only one justice away. That's why the stakes in this election are as high as ever. . . .

Campaign Finance Reform. . . . The big-time lobbyists and special interest were so eager [in 2000] to invest in George W. Bush and deliver campaign cash to him hand-over-fist that he became the first major party nominee to pull out of the primary election financing structure and refuse to abide by campaign spending limits.

In this year's presidential primaries it became clear that the Republican establishment is violently opposed to John McCain's call for reforming our democracy. Al Gore supports John McCain's campaign for political reform. In fact, the McCain-Feingold bill is the very first piece of legislation that a President Al Gore will submit to Congress—and he will fight for it until it becomes the law of the land.

Then he will go even further—much further. He will insist on tough new lobbying reform, publicly-guaranteed TV time for debates and advocacy by candidates, and a crackdown on special interest issue ads. . . .

Transforming the Military. . . . The Democratic Party understands that, good as they are, the armed forces must continue to evolve. They must not only remain prepared for conventional military action, but must sharpen their ability to deal with new missions and new kinds of threats. They must become more agile, more versatile, and must more completely incorporate the revolutionary implications and advantages of American supremacy in information technology.

. . . . A high-tech fighting force must recruit, train, and retain a professional all-volunteer force of the highest caliber. . . . While the number of soldiers and families on food stamps is down by two-thirds over the past decade, it is unacceptable that any member of our armed forces should have to rely on food stamps. Al Gore is committed to equal treatment of all service members and believes all patriotic Americans be allowed to serve their country without discrimination, persecution, and violence. . . .

Middle East. . . . Jerusalem is the capital of Israel and should remain an undivided city accessible to people of all faiths. In view of the government of Israel's courageous decision to withdraw from Lebanon, we believe special responsibility now resides with Syria to make a contribution toward peace. The recently-held Camp David summit, while failing to bridge all the gaps between Israel and the Palestinians, demonstrated President Clinton's resolve to do all the United States could do to bring an end to that long conflict. Al Gore, as president, will demonstrate the same resolve. . . .

GREEN PARTY

Building on the modest success of his token candidacy four years earlier, consumer advocate Ralph Nader emerged in 2000 as a full-fledged presidential candidate. He accepted the Green Party nomination at its June 25 convention in Denver, Colorado, with a broad-brush attack on the institutions of power in the United States.

Pledging "government of, by, and for the people—not monied interests," Nader called for a collective understanding of the "inequalities afflicting so many of our citizens. . . . What is so normalized now must be defined as intolerable and unworthy of this great country of ours."

Delegates from thirty-nine state Green parties nominated Nader by a 295–21 vote. They also renominated Native American Winona LaDuke, Nader's 1996 running mate, and ratified a lengthy platform setting forth the party's "key values."

In contrast to 1996, when he won 0.7 percent of the presidential vote as the Greens' nominal candidate in fewer than half the states, with no serious campaigning and only a $5,000 budget, Nader was already an active candidate before the Denver convention. He had barnstormed in all fifty states and had raised $1 million of a projected $5 million war chest. His goal was to win at least 5 percent of the vote, which would entitle the Greens to federal matching campaign funds in 2004.

At age sixty-six, Nader had received widespread respect for his forty-two years of public service in behalf of consumers, the environment, and economic justice. But his candidacy against Republican George W. Bush and Democrat Al Gore soured many in his normal constituency, particularly liberals who feared it would hurt Gore. The *New York Times,* in a June 30 editorial entitled "Mr. Nader's Misguided Crusade," said Nader was engaging in a "self-indulgent exercise" that would distract voters from the clear-cut choices offered by Bush and Gore.

Nader, however, denied being a "spoiler" of Gore's chances. He told reporters, "I'm worried about Gore taking votes away from me."

The candidate devoted much of his nearly two-hour acceptance speech to attacks on "corporate welfare," the "Bush and Gore duopoly," the International Monetary Fund and the World Trade Organization, and "corporatization" that he said is "fast going global" and undermining "our legitimate local state and national sovereignties." He called for universal health insurance, a higher minimum wage, and banning or sharply limiting PACs (political action committees) and "soft money" given to parties.

Nader assailed the Commission on Presidential Debates for excluding third-party candidates from the planned debates between the major party nominees. The shutout, he said, limits "the competitive democratic process on which the American electoral system is supposed to be built."

Following are excerpts from the Green Party platform of 2000:

Democracy. A growing and grave imbalance between the often-converging power of Big Business, Big Government and the citizens of this country has seriously damaged our democracy. . . . It's time to end "corporate welfare" as we know it. . . .

Political Reform. We propose comprehensive campaign finance reform, including caps on spending and contributions, at the national and state level, and/or full public financing of elections to remove undue influence in political campaigns. We will work to ban or greatly limit political action committees and restrict soft money contributions. . . .

We believe in majority rule. Accordingly, we call for the use of instant runoff voting in chief executive races (mayor, governor, president, etc.) where voters can rank their favorite candidates (1,2,3, etc.) to guarantee that the winner has majority support and that voters aren't relegated to choosing between the "lesser of two evils."

The Electoral College is an eighteenth century anachronism. We call for a constitutional amendment abolishing the Electoral College and providing for the direct election of the president by Instant Runoff Voting. Until that time, we call for a proportional allocation of delegates in state primaries.

Foreign Policy. . . . . Greens believe the more than $300 billion defense budget must be cut. The Green Party calls for military spending to be cut by 50 percent over the next 10 years, with increases in spending for social programs. . . .

It is our belief that the massive debt owed by the Third World is causing immense misery and environmental destruction. foreign aid must be addressed in the context of retiring this debt and not forcing "structural adjustments" via the International Monetary Fund (IMF) and World Bank on the economies of the underdeveloped world. . . .

Health Care. . . . . Alongside the many Americans calling for action that makes health care a right, not a privilege, the Green Party states with a clear voice its strong support for universal health care. . . . We call for passage of legislation at the national and state level that guarantees comprehensive benefits for all Americans. A single-insurer system funded by the federal government and administered at the state and local levels remains viable and is an essential barometer of our national health and well-being. . . .

We believe the right of a woman to control her own body is inalienable. It is essential that the option of a safe, legal abortion remains available. . . .

Social Security. . . . . The Green Party opposes the "privatization" of Social Security. The Social Security trust fund, contrary to claims being made by Republican and Democrat candidates, is not about to "go broke" and does not need to be "fixed" by Wall Street. . . . Considering that the bottom 20 percent of American senior citizens get roughly 80 percent of their income from Social Security, and that without Social Security nearly 70 percent of black elderly and 60 percent of Latino elderly households would be in poverty, it is critical that the public protections of Social Security are not privatized and subjected to increased risk based on misleading projections of shortfalls.

Criminal Justice. . . . . We support the 'Brady Bill' and thoughtful, carefully considered gun control.

. . . . We do not support, as a matter of conscience, the death penalty.

Civil and Equal Rights. . . . . We call for an end to official support for any remaining badges and indicia of slavery and specifically call for the immediate removal of the Confederate battle flag from any and all government buildings because we recognize that, to many, this remains a painful reminder of second-class status on the basis of race. . . .

We affirm the right to openly embrace sexual orientation in the intimate choice of who we love. . . . We support the rights of gay, lesbian, bisexual and transgendered people in housing, jobs, civil marriage and benefits, child custody—and in all areas of life, the right to be treated equally with all other people. . . .

We will resist discriminatory English-only pressure groups. We call for a national language policy that would encourage all citizens to be fluent in at least two languages.

Native Americans. . . . . As Greens we feel a special affinity to the respect for community and the Earth that many Native peoples have at their roots. . . . We recognize that Native American land and treaty rights often stand at the front-line against government and multinational corporate attempts to plunder energy, mineral, timber, fish, and game resources, polluting water, air, and land in the service of the military, economic expansion, and the consumption of natural resources. Therefore, we support legal, political, and grassroots efforts by and on behalf of Native Americans to protect their traditions, rights, livelihoods, and their sacred spaces.

Energy Policy. . . . . If we do not alter our energy use soon—and drastically—the ecological crisis may be exacerbated past a point where it can be resolved. A comprehensive energy policy must be a critical element of our environmental thinking. Investing in energy efficiency and renewable energy is key to sustainability. . . . Extensive conservation measures will bring huge resource savings for both the economy and the environment. Conservation, along with energy efficiency and renewables, is an essential part of an effective energy policy. The Greens call for pervasive efforts on the energy conservation front. . .

Nuclear Issues. . . . . The Green Party recognizes that there is no such thing as nuclear waste "disposal." All six of the "low-level" nuclear waste dumps in the United States have leaked. There are no technological quick fixes which can effectively isolate nuclear waste from the biosphere for the duration of its hazardous life. Therefore, it is essential that generation of additional nuclear wastes be stopped. . . .

The Green Party calls for the early retirement of nuclear power reactors as soon as possible (in no more than five years) and for a phaseout of other technologies that use or produce nuclear waste. . . .

Fossil Fuels. . . . . We call for transition energy strategies, including the use of relatively clean-burning natural gas, as a way to reorder our energy priorities and over-reliance on traditional fuels. . . . We call for a gradual phase-out of gasoline and other fossil fuels.

Emissions Reduction. . . . . With only 4 percent of the earth's people, the United States produces more than 20 percent of emissions. From 1990 to 1996, total U.S. emissions grew by an amount equal to what Brazil and Indonesia produce every year. Per capita, the United States emits 85 percent more than Germany, twice as much as England and Japan, and currently nearly ten times as much as China. The Green Party urges the U.S. Congress to act immediately to address the critical global warming and climate change issues. . . .

Trade. . . . . We reject trade agreements negotiated in secret and unduly influenced by corporate attorneys and representatives. In particular, we oppose the North American Free Trade Agreement (NAFTA), the General Agreement On Tariffs And Trade (GATT), and its progeny, the World Trade Organization (WTO) . . . . We demand that these agreements be updated to include more specific environmental, worker, health and safety standards in the text itself, not as "side agreements."

National Debt. . . . . During the 1980s, our national debt grew from approximately $1 trillion to over $5 trillion. During that time, we refused to fund Social Security, food stamps, public housing, higher education, public transportation, etc., etc. In effect when you neglect the economic well-being of the society and refuse to protect the environment, the result can hardly be described as a surplus. . . . To help make up for our nation's neglect, we support tax increases on mega-corporate and wealthy interests; defense budget reductions. . . . and entitlement reductions to those who can afford reductions most. Entitlement spending is over one-half of the federal budget. One way to reduce entitlement costs substantially would be by "means testing," i.e. by scaling back payments to the six million citizens in families with incomes over $50,000 annually.

CHAPTER 15

Key Convention Ballots

THIS SECTION PRESENTS the results of important balloting from the presidential nominating conventions of three major American political parties (Whigs, Democrats, and Republicans) from 1835 to 2000. The balloting results are arranged in chronological order by convention year. Major contenders for the respective party nominations appear in the tables by last name only. Full names and other detailed descriptions of each convention can be found in Chapter 14, Convention Chronology. Each table contains a reference indicating the page where this information appears.

The source for the balloting results for the 1835–1972 conventions is Richard C. Bain and Judith H. Parris, *Convention Decisions and Voting Records* (Washington, D.C.: Brookings Institution, 1973). Permission to use this material was granted by the Brookings Institution, which holds the copyright. The sources for the 1976 to 2000 vote totals are *The Official Proceedings of the Democratic National Convention* and the Republican National Committee. *Convention Decisions and Voting Records* contains ballots for three major parties in American history—the Democrats, the Whigs, and modern Republicans. This section includes ballots from conventions of these three parties alone.

In selecting ballots to include here, Congressional Quarterly followed several criteria:

• To include nominating ballots and selected other critical presidential ballots. The Democratic Party conventions of 1832, 1840, 1888, 1916, 1936, and 1964 nominated presidential candidates by acclamation without balloting.

• To include key ballots on important procedural issues, credentials contests, and platform disputes.

• To exclude all ballots for vice-presidential candidates.

VOTE TOTAL DISCREPANCIES

Bain and Parris note frequent discrepancies between totals given in the published proceedings of the party conventions and the totals reached by adding up the state-by-state delegation votes. They state: "Wherever the discrepancy was obvious and the correct figure could be clearly derived, the record has been printed in corrected form. When the added totals of detailed figures listed differ from the sums printed in the proceedings, both totals are given."

Congressional Quarterly has followed this same procedure. For example, on page 577, the forty-ninth presidential ballot of the 1852 Democratic Party convention appears. Franklin Pierce is listed as receiving 279 votes, the sum of the column. A footnote, however, indicates that the convention proceedings recorded Pierce as receiving 283 votes. Similar examples appear on pages 580, 581, and 582.

1835 Democratic

(Narrative, p. 443)

Delegation	Total Votes	First Pres. Ballot Van Buren
Connecticut	8	8
Delaware	3	3
Georgia	11	11
Indiana	9	9
Kentucky	15	15
Louisiana	5	5
Maine	10	10
Maryland	10	10
Massachusetts	14	14
Mississippi	4	4
Missouri	4	4
New Hampshire	7	7
New Jersey	8	8
New York	42	42
North Carolina	15	15
Ohio	21	21
Pennsylvania	30	30
Rhode Island	4	4
Tennessee	15	15
Vermont	7	7
Virginia	23	23
Total	265	265

1844 Democratic

(Narrative, p. 447)

Delegation	Total Votes	Amendment Ratifying Two-Thirds Rule Yea	Nay	First Pres. Ballot[1] Van Buren	Cass	Fifth Pres. Ballot[2] Van Buren	Cass	Ninth Pres. Ballot (Before shift)[3] Polk	Cass	Ninth Pres. Ballot (After shift) Polk
Alabama	9	9	—	1	8	1	8	9	—	9
Arkansas	3	3	—	—	—	—	—	3	—	3
Connecticut	6	3	3	6	—	—	—	6	—	6
Delaware	3	3	—	—	3	—	3	3	—	3
Georgia	10	10	—	—	9	—	9	9	—	10
Illinois	9	9	—	5	2	2	4	9	—	9
Indiana	12	12	—	3	9	1	11	12	—	12
Kentucky	12	12	—	—	—	—	—	12	—	12
Louisiana	6	6	—	—	—	—	—	6	—	6
Maine	9	—	9	8	—	8	1	7	1	9
Maryland	8	6	2	2	4	2	6	7	1	8
Massachusetts	12	5	7	8	1	7	3	10	2	12
Michigan	5	5	—	1	4	—	5	—	5	5
Mississippi	6	6	—	—	6	—	6	6	—	6
Missouri	7	—	7	7	—	7	—	7	—	7
New Hampshire	6	—	6	6	—	2	—	6	—	6
New Jersey	7	7	—	3	2	—	4	2	5	7
New York	36	—	36	36	—	36	—	35	—	36
North Carolina	11	5	5	2	4	—	7	11	—	11
Ohio	23	—	23	23	—	20	3	18	2	23
Pennsylvania	26	12	13	26	—	16	—	19	7	26
Rhode Island	4	2	2	4	—	1	1	4	—	4
Tennessee	13	13	—	—	13	—	13	13	—	13
Vermont	6	3	3	5	1	—	6	—	6	6
Virginia	17	17	—	—	17	—	17	17	—	17
Total	266	148	118	146	83	103	107	231	29	266

1. Other candidates: Richard M. Johnson, 24; John C. Calhoun, 6; James Buchanan, 4; Levi Woodbury, 2; Commodore Stewart, 1.
2. Other candidates: Johnson, 29; Buchanan, 26; not voting, 1.
3. Not voting, 6.

1844 Whig

(Narrative, p. 446)

Delegation	Total Votes	First Pres. Ballot Clay	Delegation	Total Votes	First Pres. Ballot Clay
Alabama	9	9	Missouri	7	7
Arkansas	3	3	New Hampshire	6	6
Connecticut	6	6	New Jersey	7	7
Delaware	3	3	New York	36	36
Georgia	10	10	North Carolina	11	11
Illinois	9	9	Ohio	23	23
Indiana	12	12	Pennsylvania	26	26
Kentucky	12	12	Rhode Island	4	4
Louisiana	6	6	South Carolina	9	9
Maine	9	9	Tennessee	13	13
Maryland	8	8	Vermont	6	6
Massachusetts	12	12	Virginia	17	17
Michigan	5	5			
Mississippi	6	6	Total	275	275

1848 Democratic

(Narrative, p. 448)

Delegation	Total Votes	Adoption of Two-Thirds Rule Yea	Nay	Not Voting	Amendment on N.Y. Credentials Yea	Nay	Not Voting	First Pres. Ballot[1] Cass	Buchanan	Woodbury	Fourth Pres. Ballot[2] Cass	Buchanan	Woodbury
Alabama	9	9	—	—	—	9	—	—	4	5	—	4	5
Arkansas	3	3	—	—	—	3	—	3	—	—	3	—	—
Connecticut	6	6	—	—	6	—	—	—	—	6	—	—	6
Delaware	3	2	1	—	1	2	—	3	—	—	3	—	—
Florida	3	3	—	—	—	3	—	—	—	—	—	—	3
Georgia	10	10	—	—	—	10	—	—	2	5	10	—	—
Illinois	9	9	—	—	9	—	—	9	—	—	9	—	—
Indiana	12	3	9	—	7	5	—	12	—	—	12	—	—
Iowa	4	4	—	—	4	—	—	1	3	—	4	—	—
Kentucky	12	12	—	—	10	2	—	7	1	1	8	1	1
Louisiana	6	6	—	—	—	6	—	6	—	—	6	—	—
Maine	9	9	—	—	9	—	—	—	—	9	—	—	9
Maryland	8	7	1	—	2	5	1	6	—	2	6	—	2
Massachusetts	12	10	2	—	11	1	—	—	—	12	8	—	4
Michigan	5	5	—	—	—	5	—	5	—	—	5	—	—
Mississippi	6	6	—	—	—	6	—	6	—	—	6	—	—
Missouri	7	1	6	—	1	4	2	7	—	—	7	—	—
New Hampshire	6	6	—	—	6	—	—	—	—	6	—	—	6
New Jersey	7	7	—	—	7	—	—	—	7	—	7	—	—
New York	36	—	—	36	—	—	36	—	—	—	—	—	—
North Carolina	11	11	—	—	—	11	—	—	10	1	11	—	—
Ohio	23	—	23	—	14	9	—	23	—	—	23	—	—
Pennsylvania	26	—	26	—	19	7	—	—	26	—	—	26	—
Rhode Island	4	3	1	—	2	2	—	1	—	3	4	—	—
South Carolina	9	9	—	—	—	9	—	—	—	—	9	—	—
Tennessee	13	13	—	—	9	4	—	7	2	1	7	2	2
Texas	4	4	—	—	4	—	—	4	—	—	4	—	—
Vermont	6	1	5	—	5	1	—	4	—	2	6	—	—
Virginia	17	17	—	—	—	17	—	17	—	—	17	—	—
Wisconsin	4	—	4	—	—	4	—	4	—	—	4	—	—
Total	290	176	78	36	126	125	39	125	55	53	179	33	38

1. Other candidates: John C. Calhoun, 9; W. J. Worth, 6; George M. Dallas, 3; not voting, 39.
2. Other candidates: William O. Butler, 4; Worth, 1; not voting, 35.

1848 Whig

(Narrative, p. 449)

Delegation	Total Votes	First Pres. Ballot[1]			Fourth Pres. Ballot[2]		
		Taylor	Clay	Scott	Taylor	Clay	Scott
Alabama	7	6	1	—	6	1	—
Arkansas	3	3	—	—	3	—	—
Connecticut	6	—	6	—	3	3	—
Delaware	3	—	—	—	2	—	1
Florida	3	3	—	—	3	—	—
Georgia	10	10	—	—	10	—	—
Illinois	8	4	3	1	8	—	—
Indiana	12	1	2	9	7	1	4
Iowa	4	2	1	—	4	—	—
Kentucky	12	7	5	—	11	1	—
Louisiana	6	5	1	—	6	—	—
Maine	9	5	1	—	5	—	3
Maryland	8	—	8	—	8	—	—
Massachusetts	12	—	—	—	1	—	2
Michigan	5	—	3	2	2	—	3
Mississippi	6	6	—	—	6	—	—
Missouri	7	6	—	—	7	—	—
New Hampshire	6	—	—	—	2	—	—
New Jersey	7	3	4	—	4	3	—
New York	36	—	29	5	6	13	17
North Carolina	11	6	5	—	10	1	17
Ohio	23	1	1	20	1	1	21
Pennsylvania	26	8	12	6	12	4	10
Rhode Island	4	—	4	—	4	—	—
South Carolina	2	1	1	—	1	1	—
Tennessee	13	13	—	—	13	—	—
Texas	4	4	—	—	4	—	—
Vermont	6	1	5	—	2	2	2
Virginia	17	15	2	—	16	1	—
Wisconsin	4	1	3	—	4	—	—
Total	280	111	97	43	171	32	63

1. Other candidates: Daniel Webster, 22; John McLean, 2; John M. Clayton, 4.
2. Other candidate: Webster, 14.

1852 Democratic

(Narrative, p. 450)

Delegation	Total Votes	First Pres. Ballot[1]		Twentieth Pres. Ballot[2]			Thirtieth Pres. Ballot[3]			Thirty-Fifth Pres. Ballot[4]				Forty-Eighth Pres. Ballot[5]				Forty-ninth Pres. Ballot[6]
		Cass	Buchanan	Buchanan	Cass	Douglas	Douglas	Buchanan	Cass	Cass	Douglas	Marcy	Buchanan	Marcy	Cass	Pierce	Douglas	Pierce
Alabama	9	—	9	9	—	—	—	9	—	—	—	—	9	9	—	—	—	9
Arkansas	4	—	4	—	—	4	4	—	—	—	4	—	—	—	—	—	4	4
California	4	—	—	1	—	3	3	1	—	2	1	—	1	—	4	—	—	4
Connecticut	6	2	2	2	2	1	6	—	—	3	3	—	—	6	—	—	—	6
Delaware	3	3	—	—	3	—	—	—	—	3	—	—	—	—	3	—	—	3
Florida	3	—	—	—	—	2	2	—	—	—	2	—	—	—	—	—	2	3
Georgia	10	—	10	10	—	—	—	10	—	—	10	—	—	10	—	—	—	10
Illinois	11	—	—	—	—	11	11	—	—	—	11	—	—	—	—	—	11	11
Indiana	13	—	—	—	—	—	—	—	—	13	—	—	—	—	13	—	—	13
Iowa	4	2	—	—	1	3	4	—	—	2	2	—	—	—	2	—	2	4
Kentucky	12	12	—	—	12	—	—	—	—	12	—	—	—	—	—	12	—	12
Louisiana	6	6	—	—	6	—	6	—	—	6	—	—	—	—	6	—	—	6
Maine	8	5	3	1	4	3	5	2	—	2	5	—	1	—	—	8	—	8
Maryland	8	8	—	—	8	—	—	—	8	8	—	—	—	1	1	5	—	5
Massachusetts	13	9	—	—	1	7	7	—	1	7	1	5	—	6	—	6	1	13
Michigan	6	6	—	—	6	—	—	—	6	6	—	—	—	—	6	—	—	6
Mississippi	7	—	7	7	—	—	—	7	—	—	—	7	—	7	—	—	—	7
Missouri	9	9	—	—	—	9	9	—	—	9	—	—	—	—	9	—	—	9
New Hampshire	5	4	—	—	5	—	—	2	—	5	—	—	—	—	—	5	—	5
New Jersey	7	7	—	7	—	—	—	7	—	7	—	—	—	7	—	—	—	7
New York	35	11	—	—	12	—	1	—	11	12	1	22	—	24	10	—	1	35
North Carolina	10	—	10	9	—	1	4	6	—	—	—	10	—	10	—	—	—	10
Ohio	23	16	—	—	13	6	9	—	7	18	3	—	—	—	15	—	4	17
Pennsylvania	27	—	27	27	—	—	—	27	—	—	—	—	27	—	—	—	—	27
Rhode Island	4	3	—	—	—	4	4	—	—	4	—	—	—	—	—	4	—	4
Tennessee	12	6	6	4	5	3	7	5	—	9	2	—	1	9	—	—	1	12
Texas	4	—	—	—	—	—	—	—	—	—	—	—	—	—	—	—	—	4
Vermont	5	5	—	—	—	5	5	—	—	—	5	—	—	—	—	—	5	5
Virginia	15	—	15	15	—	—	—	15	—	—	—	—	—	—	—	15	—	15
Wisconsin	5	2	—	—	3	2	5	—	—	3	2	—	—	—	3	—	2	5
Total	288	116	93	92	81	64	92	91	33	131	52	44	39	89	72	55	33	279[a]

1. Other candidates: William L. Marcy, 27; Stephen A. Douglas, 20; Joseph Lane, 13; Samuel Houston, 8; J. B. Weller, 4; Henry Dodge, 3; William O. Butler, 2; Daniel S. Dickinson, 1; not voting, 1.

2. Other candidates: Marcy, 26; Lane, 13; Houston, 10; Butler, 1; Dickinson, 1.

3. Other candidates: Marcy, 26; Butler, 20; Lane, 13; Houston, 12; Dickinson, 1.

4. Other candidates: Franklin Pierce, 15; Houston, 5; Butler, 1; Dickinson, 1.

5. Other candidates: Buchanan, 28; Houston, 6; Linn Boyd, 2; Butler, 1; R. J. Ingersoll, 1; Dickinson, 1.

6. Other candidates: Cass, 2; Douglas, 2; Butler, 1; Houston, 1; not voting, 3.

a. Sum of column; proceedings record 283.

1852 Whig

(Narrative, p. 451)

Delegation	Total Votes	First Pres. Ballot			50th Pres. Ballot			52nd Pres. Ballot			53rd Pres. Ballot		
		Scott	Fillmore	Webster	Scott	Fillmore	Webster	Scott	Fillmore	Webster	Scott	Fillmore	Webster
Alabama	9	—	9	—	—	9	—	—	9	—	—	9	—
Arkansas	4	—	4	—	—	4	—	—	4	—	—	4	—
California	4	2	1	1	3	1	—	3	—	1	3	—	1
Connecticut	6	2	1	3	2	1	3	2	1	3	2	1	3
Delaware	3	3	—	—	3	—	—	3	—	—	3	—	—
Florida	3	—	3	—	—	3	—	—	3	—	—	3	—
Georgia	10	—	10	—	—	10	—	—	10	—	—	10	—
Illinois	11	11	—	—	11	—	—	11	—	—	11	—	—
Indiana	13	13	—	—	13	—	—	13	—	—	13	—	—
Iowa	4	—	4	—	1	3	—	1	3	—	1	3	—
Kentucky	12	—	12	—	—	12	—	—	12	—	—	11	—
Louisiana	6	—	6	—	—	6	—	—	6	—	—	6	—
Maine	8	8	—	—	8	—	—	8	—	—	8	—	—
Maryland	8	—	8	—	—	8	—	—	8	—	—	8	—
Massachusetts	13	2	—	11	2	—	11	2	—	11	2	—	11
Michigan	6	6	—	—	6	—	—	6	—	—	6	—	—
Mississippi	7	—	7	—	—	7	—	—	7	—	—	7	—
Missouri	9	—	9	—	3	6	—	1	6	—	3	6	—
New Hampshire	5	1	—	4	1	—	4	1	—	4	5	—	—
New Jersey	7	7	—	—	7	—	—	7	—	—	7	—	—
New York	35	24	7	2	25	7	1	25	7	1	25	7	1
North Carolina	10	—	10	—	—	10	—	—	10	—	—	10	—
Ohio	23	22	1	—	23	—	—	23	—	—	23	—	—
Pennsylvania	27	26	1	—	26	1	—	27	—	—	27	—	—
Rhode Island	4	1	1	2	2	—	2	2	—	2	3	—	1
South Carolina	8	—	8	—	—	8	—	—	8	—	—	8	—
Tennessee	12	—	12	—	—	12	—	4	8	—	3	9	—
Texas	4	—	4	—	—	4	—	—	4	—	—	4	—
Vermont	5	1	1	3	2	—	3	2	2	1	5	—	—
Virginia	15	1	13	—	3	10	—	3	10	—	8	6	—
Wisconsin	5	1	1	3	1	1	3	2	—	2	1	—	4
Total	296	132[a]	133	29	142	122[a]	27	148[a]	118	25	159	112	21

a. The sum of the column for Scott on the first ballot is 131 votes, for Fillmore on the 50th ballot 123 votes and for Scott on the 52nd ballot is 146 votes. The source for these discrepancies is the *Baltimore Sun* for June 19, 1852, and June 22, 1852. The *Sun* reported June 19, 1852, total votes for Scott on the first ballot as 132 votes; however, the column of figures for the state-by-state ballots reported in the *Sun* add up to 131 votes. Similarly, on June 22, 1852, the *Sun* reported 122 votes for Fillmore on the 50th ballot and 148 for Scott on the 52nd ballot, but the state-by-state ballots reported in the *Sun* add up to 123 votes and 146 votes, respectively. Bain's *Convention Decisions and Voting Records* used the *Baltimore Sun* as its source for the 1852 Whig convention ballots.

1856 Republican

(Narrative, p. 453)

Delegation	Total Votes	Informal Pres. Ballot[1]		Formal Pres. Ballot[2]
		Fremont	McLean	Fremont
California	12	12	—	12
Connecticut	18	18	—	18
Delaware	9	—	9	9
Illinois	34	14	19	33
Indiana	39	18	21	39
Iowa	12	12	—	12
Kansas	10	9	—	9
Kentucky	5	5	—	5
Maine	24	13	11	24
Maryland	9	4	3	7
Massachusetts	39	39	—	39
Michigan	18	18	—	18
Minnesota	2	—	—	—
New Hampshire	15	15	—	15
New Jersey	21	7	14	21
New York	105	93	3	105
Ohio	69	30	39	55
Pennsylvania	81	10	71	57
Rhode Island	12	12	—	12
Vermont	15	15	—	15
Wisconsin	15	15	—	15
District of Columbia	3	—	—	—
Total	567	359	190	520

1. Other candidates: Nathaniel Banks, 1; Charles Sumner, 2; William Seward, 1; absent or not voting, 14.
2. Other candidates: John McLean, 37; Seward, 1; absent or not voting, 9.

1856 Democratic

(Narrative, p. 454)

Delegation	Total Votes	First Pres. Ballot				Tenth Pres. Ballot				Fifteenth Pres. Ballot			17th Pres. Ballot
		Buchanan	Pierce	Douglas	Other	Buchanan	Pierce	Douglas	Other	Buchanan	Douglas	Other	Buchanan
Alabama	9	—	9	—	—	—	9	—	—	—	9	—	9
Arkansas	4	—	4	—	—	—	—	4	—	—	4	—	4
California	4	—	—	—	4	—	—	—	4	—	—	4	4
Connecticut	6	6	—	—	—	6	—	—	—	6	—	—	6
Delaware	3	3	—	—	—	3	—	—	—	3	—	—	3
Florida	3	—	3	—	—	—	3	—	—	—	3	—	3
Georgia	10	—	10	—	—	3	—	7	—	3	7	—	10
Illinois	11	—	—	11	—	—	—	11	—	—	11	—	11
Indiana	13	13	—	—	—	13	—	—	—	13	—	—	13
Iowa	4	—	—	4	—	2	—	2	—	2	2	—	4
Kentucky	12	4	5	3	—	4½	—	7½	—	4	7	1	12
Louisiana	6	6	—	—	—	6	—	—	—	6	—	—	6
Maine	8	5	3	—	—	6	2	—	—	7	—	1	8
Maryland	8	6	2	—	—	7	1	—	—	8	—	—	8
Massachusetts	13	4	9	—	—	6	7	—	—	10	3	—	13
Michigan	6	6	—	—	—	6	—	—	—	6	—	—	6
Mississippi	7	—	7	—	—	—	7	—	—	—	7	—	7
Missouri	9	—	—	9	—	—	—	9	—	—	9	—	9
New Hampshire	5	—	5	—	—	—	5	—	—	—	5	—	5
New Jersey	7	7	—	—	—	7	—	—	—	7	—	—	7
New York	35	17	18	—	—	18	17	—	—	17	18	—	35
North Carolina	10	—	10	—	—	—	10	—	—	—	10	—	10
Ohio	23	13½	4½	4	1	13	3½	5	1½	13½	6½	3	23
Pennsylvania	27	27	—	—	—	27	—	—	—	27	—	—	27
Rhode Island	4	—	4	—	—	—	4	—	—	4	—	—	4
South Carolina	8	—	8	—	—	—	8	—	—	—	8	—	8
Tennessee	12	—	12	—	—	—	—	12	—	12	—	—	12
Texas	4	—	4	—	—	—	4	—	—	—	4	—	4
Vermont	5	—	5	—	—	—	—	5	—	—	5	—	5
Virginia	15	15	—	—	—	15	—	—	—	15	—	—	15
Wisconsin	5	3	—	2	—	5	—	—	—	5	—	—	5
Total	296	135½	122½	33	5[1]	147½	80½	62½	5½[2]	168½	118½	9[3]	296

1. Other candidate: Lewis Cass, 5.
2. Other candidate: Cass, 5½.
3. Other candidates: Cass, 4½; Franklin Pierce, 3½; not voting, 1.

1860 Democratic

(Narrative, p. 456)

| | | Charleston Convention | | | | | | | | | Baltimore Convention | | | | | | | |
| | | Butler Amend. on 1856 platform | | Minority Report on platform | | First Pres. Ballot[1] | | | 57th Pres. Ballot[2] | | Minority Report on Credentials | | | Reconsider Louisiana Credentials | | | First Pres. Ballot[3] | Second Pres. Ballot[4] |
Delegation	Total Votes	Yea	Nay	Yea	Nay	Douglas	Hunter	Guthrie	Douglas	Guthrie	Yea	Nay	Not Voting	Yea	Nay	Not Voting	Douglas	Douglas
Alabama	9	—	9	—	9	—	—	—	—	—	—	—	9	—	—	9	9	9
Arkansas	4	—	4	—	4	—	1	—	—	—	½	½	3	½	½	3	1	1½
California	4	—	4	—	4	—	—	—	—	—	4	—	—	—	4	—	—	—
Connecticut	6	2½	3½	6	—	3½	—	—	3½	2½	2½	3½	—	3½	2½	—	3½	3½
Delaware	3	3	—	—	3	—	2	—	—	—	2	—	1	—	2	1	—	—
Florida	3	—	3	—	3	—	—	—	—	—	—	—	3	—	—	3	—	—
Georgia	10	10	—	—	10	—	—	—	—	—	—	—	10	—	—	10	—	—
Illinois	11	—	11	11	—	11	—	—	11	—	—	11	—	11	—	—	11	11
Indiana	13	—	13	13	—	13	—	—	13	—	—	13	—	13	—	—	13	13
Iowa	4	—	4	4	—	4	—	—	4	—	—	4	—	4	—	—	4	4
Kentucky	12	9	3	2½	9½	—	—	12	—	12	10	2	—	2	10	—	—	3
Louisiana	6	—	6	—	6	—	—	—	—	—	—	—	6	—	—	6	6	6
Maine	8	3	5	8	—	5	—	3	5	3	2½	5½	—	5½	2½	—	5½	7
Maryland	8	5½	2½	3½	4½	2	5	—	4	4	5½	2	½	2	6	—	2½	2½
Massachusetts	13	8	5	7	6	5½	6	—	6	6	8	5	—	5	8	—	10	10
Michigan	6	—	6	6	—	6	—	—	6	—	—	6	—	6	—	—	6	6
Minnesota	4	1½	2½	4	—	4	—	—	3	—	1½	2½	—	2½	1½	—	2½	4
Mississippi	7	—	7	—	7	—	—	—	—	—	—	—	7	—	—	7	—	—
Missouri	9	4½	4½	4	5	4½	—	4½	4½	4½	5	4	—	4½	4½	—	4½	4½
New Hampshire	5	—	5	5	—	5	—	—	5	—	½	4½	—	4½	½	—	5	5
New Jersey	7	5	2	5	2	—	—	7	2	5	4	3	—	2½	4½	—	2½	2½
New York	35	—	35	35	—	35	—	—	35	—	—	35	—	35	—	—	35	35
North Carolina	10	10	—	—	10	1	9	—	1	—	9	1	—	1	8½	½	1	1
Ohio	23	—	23	23	—	23	—	—	23	—	—	23	—	23	—	—	23	23
Oregon	3	3	—	—	3	—	—	—	—	—	3	—	—	—	3	—	—	—
Pennsylvania	27	16½	10½	12	15	9	3	9	9½	17½	17	10	—	10	17	—	10	19
Rhode Island	4	—	4	4	—	4	—	—	4	—	—	4	—	4	—	—	4	4
South Carolina	8	—	8	—	8	—	—	1	—	—	—	—	8	—	—	8	—	—
Tennessee	12	11	1	1	11	—	—	—	1	11	10	1	1	2	10	—	3	3
Texas	4	—	4	—	4	—	—	—	—	—	—	—	4	—	—	4	—	—
Vermont	5	—	5	5	—	5	—	—	5	—	1½	3½	—	4½	½	—	5	5
Virginia	15	12½	12½	1	14	—	15	—	1	—	14	1	—	—	15	—	1½	3
Wisconsin	5	—	5	5	—	5	—	—	5	—	—	5	—	5	—	—	5	5
Total	303	105	198	165	138	145½	42	35½a	151½	65½	100½	150	52½	151b	100½c	51½	173½	190½d

1. Other candidates: Andrew Johnson, 12; Daniel S. Dickinson, 7; Joseph Lane, 6; Isaac Toucey, 2½; Jefferson Davis, 1½; James A. Pearce, 1; not voting, 50.

2. Other candidates: Robert M. T. Hunter, 16; Lane, 14; Dickinson, 4; Davis, 1; not voting 51.

3. Other candidates: James Guthrie, 9; John C. Breckinridge, 5; Thomas S. Bocock, 1; Horatio Seymour, 1; Henry A. Wise, ½; Dickinson, ½; not voting, 112½.

4. Other candidates: Breckinridge, 7½; Guthrie, 5½; not voting, 99½.

a. Sum of column; proceedings record 35.

b. Sum of column; proceedings record 150½.

c. Sum of column; proceedings record 99.

d. Sum of column; proceedings record 181½.

1860 Republican

(Narrative, p. 457)

Delegation	Total Votes	First Pres. Ballot[1]					Second Pres. Ballot[2]		Third Pres. Ballot[3] (Before shift)		Third Pres. Ballot[4] (After shift)	
		Seward	Lincoln	Cameron	Bates	Chase	Seward	Lincoln	Seward	Lincoln	Seward	Lincoln
California	8	8	½	—	—	—	8	—	8	—	3	5
Connecticut	12	—	2	—	7	2	—	4	1	4	1	8
Delaware	6	—	—	—	6	—	—	6	—	6	—	6
Illinois	22	—	22	—	—	—	—	22	—	22	—	22
Indiana	26	—	26	—	—	—	—	26	—	26	—	26
Iowa	8	2	2	1	1	1	2	5	2	5½	—	8
Kansas	6	6	—	—	—	—	6	—	6	—	—	6
Kentucky	23	5	6	—	—	8	7	9	6	13	—	23
Maine	16	10	6	—	—	—	10	6	10	6	—	16
Maryland	11	13	—	—	8	—	3	—	2	9	2	9
Massachusetts	26	21	4	—	—	—	22	4	18	8	18	8
Michigan	12	12	—	—	—	—	12	—	12	—	12	—
Minnesota	8	8	—	—	—	—	8	—	8	—	—	8
Missouri	18	—	—	—	18	—	—	—	—	—	—	18
Nebraska	6	2	1	1	—	2	3	1	3	1	—	6
New Hampshire	10	—	—	—	—	1	1	9	1	9	—	10
New Jersey	14	1	7	—	—	—	4	—	5	8	5	8
New York	70	70	—	—	—	—	70	—	70	—	70	—
Ohio	46	—	8	—	—	34	—	14	—	29	—	46
Oregon	5	—	—	—	5	—	—	—	1	4	—	5
Pennsylvania	54	1½	4	47½	—	—	2½	48	—	52	½	53
Rhode Island	8	—	—	—	1	1	—	3	1	5	—	8
Texas	6	4	—	—	2	—	6	—	6	—	—	6
Vermont	10	—	—	—	—	—	—	10	—	10	—	10
Virginia	23	8	14	1	—	—	8	14	8	14	—	23
Wisconsin	10	10	—	—	—	—	10	—	10	—	10	—
District of Columbia	2	2	—	—	—	—	2	—	2	—	—	2
Total	466	173½	102	50½	48	49	184½	181	180	231½	121½	340[a]

1. Other candidates: Benjamin F. Wade, 3; John McLean, 12; John M. Reed, 1; William L. Dayton, 14; Charles Sumner, 1; John C. Fremont, 1; Jacob Collamer, 10; absent and not voting, 1.

2. Other candidates: Edward Bates, 35; Simon Cameron, 2; McLean, 8; Salmon P. Chase, 42½; Dayton, 10; Cassius M. Clay, 2; absent and not voting 1.

3. Other candidates: Edward Bates, 22; Chase, 24½; McLean, 5; Dayton, 1; Clay, 1; absent and not voting, 1.

4. Other candidates: Chase, 2; Dayton, 1; Clay, 1; McLean, ½.

a. Sum of column; proceedings record 364.

1864 Republican

(Narrative, p. 459)

Delegation	Total Votes	First Pres. Ballot[1]	
		Lincoln	Grant
Arkansas	10	10	—
California	10	7	—
Colorado	6	6	—
Connecticut	12	12	—
Delaware	6	6	—
Illinois	32	32	—
Indiana	26	26	—
Iowa	16	16	—
Kansas	6	6	—
Kentucky	22	22	—
Louisiana	14	14	—
Maine	14	14	—
Maryland	14	14	—
Massachusetts	24	24	—
Michigan	16	16	—
Minnesota	8	8	—
Missouri	22	—	22
Nebraska	6	6	—
Nevada	6	6	—
New Hampshire	10	10	—
New Jersey	14	14	—
New York	66	66	—
Ohio	42	42	—
Oregon	6	6	—
Pennsylvania	52	52	—
Rhode Island	8	8	—
Tennessee	15	15	—
Vermont	10	10	—
West Virginia	10	10	—
Wisconsin	16	16	—
Total	519	494[a]	22

1. Not voting, 3.
a. Sum of column; proceedings record 484.

1864 Democratic

(Narrative, p. 460)

Delegation	Total Votes	First Pres. Ballot[1]		First Pres. Ballot	
		McClellan	Seymour	McClellan	Seymour
		(Before shift)		(After shift)	
California	5	2½	2½	5	—
Connecticut	6	5½	—	6	—
Delaware	3	—	3	—	3
Illinois	16	16	—	16	—
Indiana	13	9½	3½	9½	3½
Iowa	8	3	—	8	—
Kansas	3	3	—	3	—
Kentucky	11	5½	5½	11	—
Maine	7	4	3	7	—
Maryland	7	—	7	—	7
Massachusetts	12	11½	—	12	—
Michigan	8	6½	—	8	—
Minnesota	4	4	—	4	—
Missouri	11	6½	—	7	4
New Hampshire	5	5	—	5	—
New Jersey	7	7	—	7	—
New York	33	33	—	33	—
Ohio	21	8½	10½	15	6
Oregon	3	2	1	3	—
Pennsylvania	26	26	—	26	—
Rhode Island	4	4	—	4	—
Vermont	5	4	1	5	—
Wisconsin	8	7	1	8	—
Total	226	174	38	202½	23½[a]

1. Other candidates: Horatio Seymour, 12 (votes on table are for Thomas H. Seymour); Charles O'Connor, ½; blank, 1½.
a. Sum of column; proceedings record 28½.

1868 Republican

(Narrative, p. 461)

Delegation	Total Votes	First Pres. Ballot Grant
Alabama	18	18
Arkansas	10	10
California	10	10
Colorado	6	6
Connecticut	12	12
Delaware	6	6
Florida	6	6
Georgia	18	18
Idaho	2	2
Illinois	32	32
Indiana	26	26
Iowa	16	16
Kansas	6	6
Kentucky	22	22
Louisiana	14	14
Maine	14	14
Maryland	14	14
Massachusetts	24	24
Michigan	16	16
Minnesota	8	8
Mississippi	14	14
Missouri	22	22
Montana	2	2
Nebraska	6	6
Nevada	6	6
New Hampshire	10	10
New Jersey	14	14
New York	66	66
North Carolina	18	18
Dakota[a]	2	2
Ohio	42	42
Oregon	6	6
Pennsylvania	52	52
Rhode Island	8	8
South Carolina	12	12
Tennessee	20	20
Texas	12	12
Vermont	10	10
Virginia	20	20
West Virginia	10	10
Wisconsin	16	16
District of Columbia	2	2
Total	650	650

a. Dakota Territory, includes North and South Dakota.

1868 Democratic

(Narrative, p. 462)

| Delegation | Total Votes | First Pres. Ballot[1] | | | | 22nd Pres. Ballot[2] (Before shift) | | 22nd Pres. Ballot (After shift) |
		Pendleton	Hancock	Church	Johnson	Hancock	Hendricks	Seymour
Alabama	8	—	—	—	8	8	—	8
Arkansas	5	—	—	—	—	—	5	5
California	5	2	—	—	—	—	5	5
Connecticut	6	—	—	—	—	—	—	6
Delaware	3	3	—	—	—	3	—	3
Florida	3	—	—	—	3	—	3	3
Georgia	9	—	—	—	9	9	—	9
Illinois	16	16	—	—	—	—	16	16
Indiana	13	13	—	—	—	—	13	13
Iowa	8	8	—	—	—	—	8	8
Kansas	3	2	—	—	—	1	2	3
Kentucky	11	11	—	—	—	—	—	11
Louisiana	7	—	7	—	—	7	—	7
Maine	7	1½	4½	—	1	4½	2½	7
Maryland	7	4½	—	—	2½	6	1	7
Massachusetts	12	1	11	—	—	—	—	12
Michigan	8	—	—	—	—	—	8	8
Minnesota	4	4	—	—	—	—	4	4
Mississippi	7	—	7	—	—	7	—	7
Missouri	11	5	2	1	½	2	8	11
Nebraska	3	3	—	—	—	—	3	3
Nevada	3	—	—	—	—	—	3	3
New Hampshire	5	2	2	—	—	4½	½	5
New Jersey	7	—	—	—	—	—	7	7
New York	33	—	—	33	—	—	33	33
North Carolina	9	—	—	—	9	—	9	9
Ohio	21	21	—	—	—	—	—	21
Oregon	3	3	—	—	—	—	3	3
Pennsylvania	26	—	—	—	—	26	—	26
Rhode Island	4	—	—	—	—	—	—	4
South Carolina	6	—	—	—	6	6	—	6
Tennessee	10	—	—	—	10	3½	1½	10
Texas	6	—	—	—	6	6	—	6
Vermont	5	—	—	—	—	—	5	5
Virginia	10	—	—	—	10	10	—	10
West Virginia	5	5	—	—	—	—	5	5
Wisconsin	8	—	—	—	—	—	—	—
Total	317	105	33½	34	65	103½	145½	317

1. Other candidates: James E. English, 16; Joel Parker, 13; Asa Packer, 26; James R. Doolittle, 13; Thomas A. Hendricks, 2½; Frank P. Blair, ½; Reverdy Johnson, 8½.

2. Other candidates: Horatio Seymour, 22; English, 7; Doolittle, 4; Johnson, 4; not voting, 31.

1872 Democratic

(Narrative, p. 464)

Delegation	Total Votes	First Pres. Ballot[1] Greeley
Alabama	20	20
Arkansas	12	12
California	12	12
Connecticut	12	12
Delaware	6	—
Florida	8	6
Georgia	22	18
Illinois	42	42
Indiana	30	30
Iowa	22	22
Kansas	10	10
Kentucky	24	24
Louisiana	16	16
Maine	14	14
Maryland	16	16
Massachusetts	26	26
Michigan	22	22
Minnesota	10	10
Mississippi	16	16
Missouri	30	30
Nebraska	6	6
Nevada	6	6
New Hampshire	10	10
New Jersey	18	9
New York	70	70
North Carolina	20	20
Ohio	44	44
Oregon	6	6
Pennsylvania	58	58
Rhode Island	8	8
South Carolina	14	14
Tennessee	24	24
Texas	16	16
Vermont	10	10
Virginia	22	22
West Virginia	10	8
Wisconsin	20	20
Total	**732**	**686**

1. Other candidates: Thomas F. Bayard, 15; Jeremiah S. Black, 21; William S. Groesbeck, 2; blank, 8.

1872 Republican

(Narrative, p. 464)

Delegation	Total Votes	First Pres. Ballot[1] Grant
Alabama	20	20
Arizona	2	2
Arkansas	12	12
California	12	12
Colorado	2	2
Connecticut	12	12
Delaware	6	6
Florida	8	8
Georgia	22	22
Idaho	2	2
Illinois	42	42
Indiana	30	30
Iowa	22	22
Kansas	10	10
Kentucky	24	24
Louisiana	16	16
Maine	14	14
Maryland	16	16
Massachusetts	26	26
Michigan	22	22
Minnesota	10	10
Mississippi	16	16
Missouri	30	30
Montana	2	2
Nebraska	6	6
Nevada	6	6
New Hampshire	10	10
New Jersey	18	18
New Mexico	2	2
New York	70	70
North Carolina	20	20
Dakota[a]	2	2
Ohio	44	44
Oregon	6	6
Pennsylvania	58	58
Rhode Island	8	8
South Carolina	14	14
Tennessee	24	24
Texas	16	16
Utah	2	2
Vermont	10	10
Virginia	22	22
Washington	2	2
West Virginia	10	10
Wisconsin	20	20
Wyoming	2	2
District of Columbia	2	2
Total	**752**	**752**

a. Dakota Territory, includes North and South Dakota.

1876 Republican

(Narrative, p. 465)

Delegation	Total Votes	First Pres. Ballot[1]				Abolish Unit Rule			Fifth Pres. Ballot[2]					Sixth Pres. Ballot[3]					Seventh Pres. Ballot[4]	
		Blaine	Morton	Conkling	Bristow	Yea	Nay	Not Voting	Blaine	Bristow	Conkling	Hayes	Morton	Blaine	Morton	Conkling	Bristow	Hayes	Blaine	Hayes
Ala.	20	10	—	—	7	20	—	—	16	4	—	—	—	15	—	—	4	1	17	—
Ariz.	2	2	—	—	—	2	—	—	2	—	—	—	—	2	—	—	—	—	2	—
Ark.	12	—	12	—	—	4	8	—	1	—	—	—	11	1	11	—	—	—	11	—
Calif.	12	9	—	1	2	11	1	—	6	—	3	3	—	6	—	2	—	4	6	6
Colo.	6	6	—	—	—	6	—	—	6	—	—	—	—	6	—	—	—	—	6	1
Conn.	12	—	—	—	2	3	9	—	2	8	—	2	—	2	—	—	7	3	2	3
Del.	6	6	—	—	—	5	1	—	6	—	—	—	—	6	—	—	—	—	6	—
Fla.	8	1	4	3	—	4	4	—	2	—	—	—	3	4	4	—	—	—	8	—
Ga.	22	5	6	8	3	9	13	—	8	2	6	—	5	9	4	6	2	—	14	7
Idaho	2	2	—	—	—	2	—	—	2	—	—	—	—	2	—	—	—	—	2	—
Ill.	42	38	—	—	3	38	4	—	33	5	—	3	—	32	—	—	5	3	35	2
Ind.	30	—	30	—	—	1	29	—	—	—	—	—	30	—	30	—	—	—	—	25
Iowa	22	22	—	—	—	22	—	—	21	—	1	—	—	21	—	—	—	1	22	—
Kan.	10	10	—	—	—	10	—	—	10	—	—	—	—	10	—	—	—	—	10	—
Ky.	24	—	—	—	24	1	23	—	—	24	—	—	—	—	—	—	24	—	—	24
La.	16	2	14	—	—	6	10	—	5	—	—	—	11	6	10	—	—	—	14	2
Maine	14	14	—	—	—	14	—	—	14	—	—	—	—	14	—	—	—	—	14	—
Md.	16	16	—	—	—	16	—	—	16	—	—	—	—	16	—	—	—	—	16	—
Mass.	26	6	—	—	17	15	7	4	5	19	—	—	—	5	—	—	19	—	5	21
Mich.	22	8	—	1	9	3	19	—	—	—	22	—	—	—	—	—	22	—	—	22
Minn.	10	10	—	—	—	7	3	—	9	—	—	—	—	9	—	—	—	—	9	1
Miss.	16	—	11	1	3	9	6	1	—	8	2	2	4	1	5	2	4	4	—	16
Mo.	30	14	12	1	2	25	5	—	20	3	—	2	5	18	7	—	3	2	20	10
Mont.	2	2	—	—	—	2	—	—	1	—	—	1	—	1	—	—	—	1	—	2
Neb.	6	6	—	—	—	6	—	—	6	—	—	—	—	6	—	—	—	—	6	—
Nev.	6	—	—	2	3	—	6	—	—	1	2	1	—	—	—	2	2	1	—	6
N.H.	10	7	—	—	3	10	—	—	7	3	—	—	—	7	—	—	3	—	7	3
N.J.	18	13	—	—	—	15	3	—	12	—	—	6	—	12	—	—	—	6	12	6
N.M.	2	2	—	—	—	2	—	—	2	—	—	—	—	2	—	—	—	—	2	—
N.Y.	70	—	—	69	1	15	54	1	—	2	68	—	—	—	—	68	2	—	9	61
N.C.	20	9	2	7	1	6	13	1	—	—	12	—	1	12	1	—	—	1	—	20
Dak.ª	2	2	—	—	—	2	—	—	2	—	—	—	—	2	—	—	—	—	2	—
Ohio	44	—	—	—	—	14	30	—	—	—	—	44	—	—	—	—	—	44	—	44
Ore.	6	6	—	—	—	6	—	—	6	—	—	—	—	6	—	—	—	—	6	—
Pa.	58	—	—	—	—	1	57	—	5	—	—	—	—	14	—	—	—	—	30	28
R.I.	8	2	—	—	6	1	7	—	2	6	—	—	—	2	—	—	6	—	2	6
S.C.	14	—	13	—	1	2	12	—	5	3	—	1	5	10	2	—	1	1	7	7
Tenn.	24	4	10	—	10	19	5	—	7	10	—	—	7	7	1	—	12	4	6	18
Texas	16	2	5	3	6	4	12	—	3	3	—	1	8	2	4	1	1	7	1	15
Utah	2	2	—	—	—	2	—	—	2	—	—	—	—	2	—	—	—	—	2	—
Vt.	10	1	—	—	8	5	5	—	—	8	—	2	—	—	—	—	8	2	—	10
Va.	22	16	3	3	—	19	2	1	16	—	—	—	3	13	4	—	3	2	14	8
Wash.	2	2	—	—	—	2	—	—	2	—	—	—	—	2	—	—	—	—	2	—
W.Va.	10	8	—	—	—	10	—	—	7	—	—	2	—	6	—	—	—	4	6	4
Wis.	20	20	—	—	—	17	3	—	16	3	—	—	1	16	1	—	3	—	16	4
Wyo.	2	—	—	—	2	—	2	—	—	2	—	—	—	—	—	—	2	—	—	2
D.C.	2	—	2	—	—	2	—	—	1	—	—	—	1	1	1	—	—	—	2	—
Total	756	285	124	99	113	395	353	8	286	114	82	104	95	308	85	81	111	113	351	384

1. Other candidates: Rutherford B. Hayes, 61; John F. Hartranft, 58; Marshall Jewell, 11; William A. Wheeler, 3; not voting, 2.
2. Other candidates: Hartranft, 69; Elihu B. Washburne, 3; Wheeler, 2; not voting, 2.
3. Other candidates: Hartranft, 50; Washburne, 4; Wheeler, 2; not voting, 2.
4. Other candidates: Benjamin H. Bristow, 21.
a. Dakota Territory, includes North and South Dakota.

1876 Democratic

(Narrative, p. 466)

Delegation	Total Votes	First Pres. Ballot[1]			Second Pres. Ballot[2]	
		Tilden	Hendricks	Hancock	Tilden	
Alabama	20	13	5	2	20	—
Arkansas	12	12	—	—	12	—
California	12	12	—	—	12	—
Colorado	6	—	6	—	6	—
Connecticut	12	12	—	—	12	—
Delaware	6	—	—	—	6	—
Florida	8	8	—	—	8	—
Georgia	22	5	—	1	22	—
Illinois	42	19	23	—	26	16
Indiana	30	—	30	—	—	30
Iowa	22	14	6	2	22	—
Kansas	10	—	10	—	2	8
Kentucky	24	24	—	—	24	—
Louisiana	16	9	—	5	16	—
Maine	14	14	—	—	14	—
Maryland	16	11	3	—	14	2
Massachusetts	26	26	—	—	26	—
Michigan	22	14	8	—	19	3
Minnesota	10	10	—	—	10	—
Mississippi	16	16	—	—	16	—
Missouri	30	—	14	—	30	—
Nebraska	6	6	—	—	6	—
Nevada	6	3	3	—	4	—
New Hampshire	10	10	—	—	10	—
New Jersey	18	—	—	—	18	—
New York	70	70	—	—	70	—
North Carolina	20	9	4	5	20	—
Ohio	44	—	—	—	—	—
Oregon	6	6	—	—	6	—
Pennsylvania	58	—	—	58	—	—
Rhode Island	8	8	—	—	8	—
South Carolina	14	14	—	—	14	—
Tennessee	24	—	24	—	—	24
Texas	16	10½	2½	2	16	—
Vermont	10	10	—	—	10	—
Virginia	22	17	1	—	17	1
West Virginia	10	—	—	—	—	—
Wisconsin	20	19	1	—	19	1
Total	738	401½[a]	140½	75	535	85

1. Other candidates: William Allen, 54; Allen G. Thurman, 3; Thomas F. Bayard, 33; Joel Parker, 18; James O. Broadhead, 16.
2. Other candidates: Allen, 54; Bayard, 4; Winfield Scott Hancock, 58; Thurman, 2.
a. Sum of column; proceedings record 404½.

1880 Republican

(Narrative, p. 467)

Column groups: **Minority Report Illinois 1st Dist.** (Yea, Nay, Not Voting) · **First Pres. Ballot[1]** (Grant, Blaine, Sherman, Other) · **34th Pres. Ballot[2]** (Grant, Blaine, Sherman, Other) · **35th Pres. Ballot[3]** (Grant, Blaine, Sherman, Garfield, Other) · **36th Pres. Ballot[4]** (Grant, Blaine, Garfield, Other)

Delegation	Total Votes	Yea	Nay	Not Voting	Grant (1st)	Blaine (1st)	Sherman (1st)	Other (1st)	Grant (34)	Blaine (34)	Sherman (34)	Other (34)	Grant (35)	Blaine (35)	Sherman (35)	Garfield (35)	Other (35)	Grant (36)	Blaine (36)	Garfield (36)	Other (36)
Ala.	20	16	4	—	16	1	3	—	16	4	—	—	16	4	—	—	—	16	4	—	—
Ariz.	2	—	2	—	—	2	—	—	—	2	—	—	—	2	—	—	—	—	—	2	—
Ark.	12	12	—	—	12	—	—	—	12	—	—	—	12	—	—	—	—	12	—	—	—
Calif.	12	—	12	—	—	12	—	—	—	12	—	—	—	12	—	—	—	—	12	—	—
Colo.	6	6	—	—	6	—	—	—	6	—	—	—	6	—	—	—	—	6	—	—	—
Conn.	12	—	10	2	—	3	—	9	—	3	—	9	—	3	—	—	9	—	1	11	—
Del.	6	—	6	—	—	6	—	—	—	6	—	—	—	6	—	—	—	—	6	—	—
Fla.	8	8	—	—	8	—	—	—	8	—	—	—	8	—	—	—	—	8	—	—	—
Ga.	22	6	16	—	6	8	8	—	8	9	5	—	8	9	5	—	—	8	10	1	3
Idaho	2	—	2	—	—	2	—	—	—	2	—	—	—	2	—	—	—	—	2	—	—
Ill.	42	40	—	2	24	10	—	8	24	10	—	8	24	10	—	—	8	24	6	7	5
Ind.	30	5	25	—	1	26	2	1	2	20	2	6	1	2	—	27	—	1	—	29	—
Iowa	22	—	22	—	—	22	—	—	—	22	—	—	—	22	—	—	—	—	—	22	—
Kan.	10	—	—	10	4	6	—	—	4	6	—	—	4	6	—	—	—	4	6	—	—
Ky.	24	21	3	—	20	1	3	—	20	1	3	—	20	1	3	—	—	20	1	3	—
La.	16	8	8	—	8	2	6	—	8	4	4	—	8	4	4	—	—	8	—	8	—
Maine	14	—	14	—	—	14	—	—	—	14	—	—	—	14	—	—	—	—	—	14	—
Md.	16	8	8	—	7	7	2	—	7	2	7	—	7	3	2	4	—	6	—	10	—
Mass.	26	4	22	—	3	—	2	21	4	—	21	1	4	—	21	—	1	4	—	22	—
Mich.	22	1	21	—	1	21	—	—	1	21	—	—	1	21	—	—	—	1	—	21	—
Minn.	10	4	6	—	—	—	—	10	—	6	—	4	1	6	—	—	3	2	—	8	—
Miss.	16	11	5	—	6	4	6	—	8	4	3	1	8	4	3	1	—	7	—	9	—
Mo.	30	29	1	—	29	—	—	1	29	—	—	1	29	—	—	—	1	29	—	1	—
Mont.	2	—	2	—	—	2	—	—	—	2	—	—	—	2	—	—	—	—	2	—	—
Neb.	6	—	6	—	—	6	—	—	—	6	—	—	—	6	—	—	—	—	6	—	—
Nev.	6	—	6	—	—	6	—	—	—	6	—	—	—	6	—	—	—	2	1	3	—
N.H.	10	—	10	—	—	10	—	—	—	10	—	—	—	10	—	—	—	—	—	10	—
N.J.	18	—	18	—	—	16	—	2	—	14	2	2	—	14	2	—	2	—	—	18	—
N.M.	2	—	2	—	—	2	—	—	—	2	—	—	—	2	—	—	—	—	2	—	—
N.Y.	70	47	22	1	51	17	2	—	50	18	2	—	50	18	2	—	—	50	—	20	—
N.C.	20	19	1	—	6	—	14	—	6	—	14	—	6	—	13	1	—	5	—	15	—
Dak.[a]	2	1	1	—	1	1	—	—	1	1	—	—	1	1	—	—	—	—	—	2	—
Ohio	44	16	28	—	—	9	34	1	—	9	34	1	—	9	34	—	1	—	—	43	1
Ore.	6	—	6	—	—	6	—	—	—	6	—	—	—	6	—	—	—	—	—	6	—
Pa.	58	34	24	—	32	23	3	—	35	22	—	1	36	20	—	1	1	37	—	21	—
R.I.	8	—	8	—	—	8	—	—	—	8	—	—	—	8	—	—	—	—	—	8	—
S.C.	14	10	4	—	13	—	1	—	11	1	2	—	11	1	2	—	—	8	—	6	—
Tenn.	24	16	8	—	16	6	1	1	17	4	3	—	17	4	3	—	—	15	1	8	—
Texas	16	11	4	1	11	2	2	1	13	1	1	1	13	1	1	—	1	13	—	3	—
Utah	2	—	2	—	1	1	—	—	1	1	—	—	1	1	—	—	—	—	—	2	—
Vt.	10	4	6	—	—	—	—	10	—	—	—	10	—	—	—	—	10	—	—	10	—
Va.	22	13	9	—	18	3	1	—	16	3	3	—	16	3	3	—	—	19	—	3	—
Wash.	2	—	2	—	—	2	—	—	—	2	—	—	—	2	—	—	—	—	—	2	—
W.Va.	10	—	10	—	1	8	—	1	1	8	1	—	1	8	1	—	—	1	—	9	—
Wis.	20	1	19	—	1	7	3	9	2	1	—	17	2	2	—	16	—	—	—	20	—
Wyo.	2	1	1	—	1	1	—	—	1	1	—	—	1	1	—	—	—	—	—	2	—
D.C.	2	1	1	—	1	1	—	—	1	1	—	—	1	1	—	—	—	—	—	2	—
Total	**756**	353	387	16	304	284	93	75	312	275	107	62	313	257	99	50	37	306	42	399	9

1. Other candidates: George F. Edmunds, 34; Elihu B. Washburne, 30; William Windom, 10; not voting 1.
2. Other candidates: Washburne, 30; James A. Garfield, 17; Edmunds, 11; Windom, 4.
3. Other candidates: Washburne, 23; Edmunds, 11; Windom, 3.
4. Other candidates: Washburne, 5; John Sherman, 3; not voting, 1.
a. Dakota Territory, includes North and South Dakota.

1880 Democratic

(Narrative, p. 469)

Delegation	Total Votes	First Pres. Ballot[1]			Second Pres. Ballot[2] (Before shift)			Second Pres. Ballot[3] (After shift)
		Bayard	Hancock	Payne	Hancock	Bayard	Randall	Hancock
Alabama	20	7	7	—	11	5	—	20
Arkansas	12	—	—	—	—	—	—	12
California	12	—	—	—	5	—	—	12
Colorado	6	—	—	—	—	—	—	6
Connecticut	12	4	—	2	—	1	—	12
Delaware	6	6	—	—	—	6	—	6
Florida	8	8	—	—	—	8	—	8
Georgia	22	5	8	—	7	5	—	22
Illinois	42	—	—	—	—	42	—	42
Indiana	30	—	—	—	—	—	—	—
Iowa	22	3	7	2	9	1	12	21
Kansas	10	—	—	—	10	—	—	10
Kentucky	24	6	1	—	8	7	—	24
Louisiana	16	—	16	—	16	—	—	16
Maine	14	—	14	—	14	—	—	14
Maryland	16	16	—	—	—	16	—	14
Massachusetts	26	11½	6	—	11	7	3½	26
Michigan	22	2	5	1	14	4	1	22
Minnesota	10	—	10	—	10	—	—	10
Mississippi	16	8	5	—	6	8	—	16
Missouri	30	4	12	—	28	2	—	30
Nebraska	6	—	—	6	—	—	6	6
Nevada	6	—	—	—	—	—	1	6
New Hampshire	10	3	4	—	5	—	5	10
New Jersey	18	10	—	—	7	4	4	18
New York	70	—	—	70	—	—	70	70
North Carolina	20	7	9	—	20	—	—	20
Ohio	44	—	—	—	—	—	—	44
Oregon	6	—	—	—	—	—	—	6
Pennsylvania	58	7	28	—	32	—	25	58
Rhode Island	8	2	2	—	6	—	1	8
South Carolina	14	14	—	—	—	14	—	14
Tennessee	24	9	11	—	14	8	—	24
Texas	16	5	9	—	11	5	—	16
Vermont	10	—	10	—	10	—	—	10
Virginia	22	10	3	—	7	8	—	22
West Virginia	10	—	3	—	7	1	—	10
Wisconsin	20	6	1	—	10	2	—	20
Total	738	153½	171	81	320	112	128½	705

1. Other candidates: Allen G. Thurman, 68½; Stephen J. Field, 65; William R. Morrison, 62; Thomas A. Hendricks, 49½; Samuel J. Tilden, 38; Horatio Seymour, 8; W. A. H. Loveland, 5; Samuel J. Randall, 6; Thomas Ewing, 10; Joseph E. McDonald, 3; George B. McClellan, 2; Joel Parker, 1; Jeremiah Black, 1; Hugh J. Jewett, 1; James E. English, 1; Lothrop, 1; not voting, 10½.

2. Other candidates: Hendricks, 31; English, 19; Tilden, 6; Thurman, 50; Parker, 2; Field, 65½; Jewett, 1; not voting, 3.

3. Other candidates: Hendricks, 30; Bayard, 2; Tilden, 1.

1884 Republican
(Narrative, p. 470)

Delegation	Total Votes	Temporary Chairman[1] Lynch	Clayton	First Pres. Ballot[2] Arthur	Blaine	Edmunds	Third Pres. Ballot[3] Arthur	Blaine	Fourth Pres. Ballot[4] Arthur	Blaine
Alabama	20	19	1	17	1	—	17	2	12	8
Arizona	2	—	2	—	2	—	—	2	—	2
Arkansas	14	1	13	4	8	2	3	11	3	11
California	16	—	16	—	16	—	—	16	—	16
Colorado	6	—	6	—	6	—	—	6	—	6
Connecticut	12	6	6	—	—	—	—	—	—	—
Delaware	6	1	5	1	5	—	1	5	1	5
Florida	8	7	1	7	1	—	7	1	5	3
Georgia	24	24	—	24	—	—	24	—	24	—
Idaho	2	2	—	2	—	—	1	1	—	2
Illinois	44	16	28	1	3	—	1	3	3	34
Indiana	30	10	20	9	18	1	10	18	—	30
Iowa	26	3	23	—	26	—	—	26	2	24
Kansas	18	4	14	4	12	—	—	15	—	18
Kentucky	26	20	6	16	5½	—	16	6	15	9
Louisiana	16	11	4	10	2	—	9	4	7	9
Maine	12	—	12	—	12	—	—	12	—	12
Maryland	16	6	10	6	10	—	4	12	1	15
Massachusetts	28	24	4	2	1	25	3	1	7	3
Michigan	26	12	14	2	15	7	4	18	—	26
Minnesota	14	6	8	1	7	6	2	7	—	14
Mississippi	18	16	2	17	1	—	16	1	16	2
Missouri	32	14	16	10	5	6	11	12	—	32
Montana	2	1	1	—	1	1	—	1	—	2
Nebraska	10	2	8	2	8	—	—	10	—	10
Nevada	6	—	6	—	6	—	—	6	—	6
New Hampshire	8	8	—	4	—	4	5	—	2	3
New Jersey	18	9	9	—	9	6	1	11	—	17
New Mexico	2	2	—	2	—	—	2	—	2	—
New York	72	46	26	31	28	12	32	28	30	29
North Carolina	22	17	3	19	2	—	18	4	12	8
Dakota[a]	2	—	2	—	2	—	—	2	—	2
Ohio	46	22	23	—	21	—	—	25	—	46
Oregon	6	—	6	—	6	—	—	6	—	6
Pennsylvania	60	13	45	11	47	1	8	50	8	51
Rhode Island	8	8	—	—	—	8	—	—	1	7
South Carolina	18	18	—	17	1	—	16	2	15	2
Tennessee	24	21	2	16	7	—	17	7	12	11
Texas	26	12	12	11	13	—	11	14	8	15
Utah	2	—	2	2	—	—	2	—	—	2
Vermont	8	8	—	—	—	8	—	—	—	—
Virginia	24	20	4	21	2	—	20	4	20	4
Washington	2	1	1	—	2	—	—	2	—	2
West Virginia	12	—	12	—	12	—	—	12	—	12
Wisconsin	22	11	10	6	10	6	10	11	—	22
Wyoming	2	2	—	2	—	—	2	—	—	2
District of Columbia	2	1	1	1	1	—	1	1	1	1
Total	820	424	384	278	334½	93	274	375	207	541

1. Not voting, 12.
2. Other candidates: John A. Logan, 63½; John Sherman, 30; Joseph R. Hawley, 13; Robert T. Lincoln, 4; William T. Sherman, 2; not voting, 2.
3. Other candidates: George F. Edmunds, 69; Logan, 53; John Sherman, 25; Hawley 13; Lincoln, 8; William T. Sherman, 3; not voting 9, 1.
4. Other candidates: Edmunds, 41; Hawley, 15; Logan, 7; Lincoln, 2; not voting, 7.
a. Dakota Territory, includes North and South Dakota.

1884 Democratic

(Narrative, p. 471)

Delegation	Total Votes	Unit Rule: Amendment to Permit Polling of Delegates			First Pres. Ballot[1]			Second Pres. Ballot[2] (Before shift)			Second Pres. Ballot[3] (After shift)	
		Yea	Nay	Not Voting	Cleveland	Bayard	Thurman	Cleveland	Bayard	Hendricks	Cleveland	Bayard
Alabama	20	15	5	—	4	14	1	5	14	—	5	14
Arizona	2	—	—	2	2	—	—	2	—	—	2	—
Arkansas	14	—	14	—	14	—	—	14	—	—	14	—
California	16	16	—	—	—	—	16	6	—	—	16	—
Colorado	6	4	2	—	—	—	1	6	—	—	6	—
Connecticut	12	2	10	—	12	—	—	12	—	—	12	—
Delaware	6	6	—	—	—	6	—	—	6	—	—	6
Florida	8	2	6	—	8	—	—	6	2	—	8	—
Georgia	24	12	12	—	10	12	—	14	10	—	22	2
Idaho	2	—	—	2	2	—	—	2	—	—	2	—
Illinois	44	22	22	—	28	2	1	38	3	1	43	—
Indiana	30	30	—	—	—	—	—	—	—	30	30	—
Iowa	26	6	20	—	23	1	1	22	—	4	26	—
Kansas	18	3	15	—	11	5	2	12	4	—	17	1
Kentucky	26	20	6	—	—	—	—	3	7	15	4	21
Louisiana	16	—	16	—	13	1	1	15	—	—	15	—
Maine	12	2	10	—	12	—	—	12	—	—	12	—
Maryland	16	—	16	—	6	10	—	10	6	—	16	—
Massachusetts	28	21	7	—	5	21	2	8	7½	12½	8	7½
Michigan	26	12	12	2	14	1	11	13	—	13	23	—
Minnesota	14	—	14	—	14	—	—	14	—	—	14	—
Mississippi	18	18	—	—	1	15	1	2	14	2	2	14
Missouri	32	8	24	—	15	10	3	21	5	6	32	—
Montana	2	—	—	2	2	—	—	2	—	—	2	—
Nebraska	10	5	5	—	8	1	1	9	1	—	9	1
Nevada	6	6	—	—	—	—	6	—	—	5	—	—
New Hampshire	8	—	8	—	8	—	—	8	—	—	8	—
New Jersey	18	14	4	—	4	3	—	5	2	11	5	2
New Mexico	2	—	—	2	2	—	—	1	—	—	2	—
New York	72	—	72	—	72	—	—	72	—	—	72	—
North Carolina	22	10	12	—	—	22	—	—	22	—	22	—
Dakota[a]	2	—	—	2	2	—	—	2	—	—	2	—
Ohio	46	25	21	—	21	—	23	21	—	1	46	—
Oregon	6	—	6	—	2	4	—	2	2	2	6	—
Pennsylvania	60	21	39	—	5	—	—	42	2	11	42	2
Rhode Island	8	—	8	—	6	2	—	6	2	—	7	1
South Carolina	18	3	14	1	8	10	—	8	9	1	10	8
Tennessee	24	17	7	—	2	8	9	2	10	1	24	—
Texas	26	12	10	4	11	10	4	12	12	1	26	—
Utah	2	—	—	2	—	—	—	1	—	1	2	—
Vermont	8	—	8	—	8	—	—	8	—	—	8	—
Virginia	24	6	18	—	13	9	1	13	8	2	23	—
Washington	2	—	—	2	1	—	—	2	—	—	2	—
West Virginia	12	9	3	—	7	2	2	6	3	—	10	2
Wisconsin	22	5	17	—	12	1	2	20	—	2	22	—
Wyoming	2	—	—	2	2	—	—	2	—	—	2	—
District of Columbia	2	—	—	2	2	—	—	—	—	2	2	—
Total	820	332	463	25	392	170	88	475	151½	123½	683	81½

1. Other candidates: Joseph E. McDonald, 56; Samuel J. Randall, 78; John G. Carlisle, 27; George Hoadly, 3; Thomas A. Hendricks, 1; Samuel J. Tilden, 1; Roswell P. Flower, 4.

2. Other candidates: Allen G. Thurman, 60; Randall, 5; McDonald, 2; Tilden, 2; not voting, 1.

3. Other candidates: Hendricks, 45½; Thurman, 4; Randall, 4; McDonald, 2.

a. Dakota Territory, includes North and South Dakota.

1888 Republican

(Narrative, p. 473)

Delegation	Total Votes	First Pres. Ballot[1]						Sixth Pres. Ballot[2]					Seventh Pres. Ballot[3]					Eighth Pres. Ballot[4]			
		Alger	Allison	Depew	Gresham	Harrison	Sherman	Alger	Allison	Gresham	Harrison	Sherman	Alger	Allison	Gresham	Harrison	Sherman	Alger	Gresham	Harrison	Sherman
Ala.	20	6	—	1	—	1	12	6	—	—	1	12	6	—	—	12	—	10	—	3	5
Ariz.	2	2	—	—	—	—	—	2	—	—	—	—	2	—	—	—	—	—	—	2	—
Ark.	14	—	—	—	1	1	2	14	—	—	—	—	14	—	—	—	—	14	—	—	—
Calif.	16	—	—	—	—	—	—	—	—	—	—	—	1	—	—	15	—	—	—	15	—
Colo.	6	—	1	—	3	2	—	—	—	—	—	5	—	6	—	—	—	—	—	6	—
Conn.	12	—	—	—	—	—	—	2	4	—	—	6	2	—	—	4	5	—	—	12	—
Del.	6	—	—	—	6	—	—	—	—	1	5	—	—	—	1	5	—	—	—	6	—
Fla.	8	—	—	—	—	1	4	5	—	—	1	1	3	—	—	4	1	4	—	2	2
Ga.	24	—	—	—	1	2	19	—	—	1	2	19	1	—	1	3	17	3	1	10	9
Idaho	2	—	1	—	1	—	—	—	—	2	—	—	—	—	2	—	—	—	—	2	—
Ill.	44	—	—	44	—	—	—	—	—	41	3	—	1	—	40	3	—	—	40	4	—
Ind.	30	—	—	—	1	29	—	—	—	1	29	—	—	—	1	29	—	—	1	29	—
Iowa	26	—	26	—	—	—	—	—	26	—	—	—	—	26	—	—	—	1	3	22	—
Kan.	18	—	—	—	—	—	—	2	3	3	6	1	1	3	—	12	1	1	—	16	—
Ky.	26	4	—	1	5	4	12	6	—	2	7	9	3	—	2	10	9	1	2	15	7
La.	16	2	3	1	1	—	9	3	2	2	—	9	3	2	2	—	9	4	—	9	3
Maine	12	3	2	3	1	2	1	2	1	2	1	3	1	2	2	2	1	—	1	5	3
Md.	16	—	2	1	1	5	5	—	—	1	6	6	—	—	—	9	6	—	—	11	4
Mass.	28	6	2	1	2	4	9	8	2	1	5	11	2	3	1	9	11	1	—	25	2
Mich.	26	26	—	—	—	—	—	26	—	—	—	—	26	—	—	—	—	26	—	—	—
Minn.	14	1	—	2	11	—	—	3	—	5	6	—	2	—	4	8	—	1	—	13	—
Miss.	18	—	—	1	3	—	14	—	—	3	—	14	—	—	3	—	14	1	3	4	11
Mo.	32	6	3	2	11	3	6	15	1	11	2	2	14	—	12	3	2	15	8	7	2
Mont.	2	—	1	—	1	—	—	—	—	1	1	—	—	1	1	—	—	—	—	2	—
Neb.	10	2	3	—	1	—	3	2	5	—	—	3	2	5	—	2	1	1	—	9	—
Nev.	6	3	3	—	—	—	—	5	—	—	—	—	—	6	—	—	—	2	—	4	—
N.H.	8	—	—	4	—	4	—	—	—	1	6	1	—	—	—	8	—	—	—	8	—
N.J.	18	—	—	—	—	—	—	—	—	1	14	—	1	—	1	10	1	—	—	18	—
N.M.	2	1	—	—	—	—	—	1	—	—	—	—	1	—	—	—	—	—	—	2	—
N.Y.	72	—	—	71	—	—	1	—	—	—	72	—	—	—	—	72	—	—	—	72	—
N.C.	22	2	—	1	2	1	15	9	—	—	2	11	7	—	—	3	12	3	—	8	11
Dak.[a]	10	1	1	2	1	1	1	—	—	—	10	—	—	—	—	10	—	—	—	10	—
Ohio	46	—	—	—	—	—	46	—	—	—	1	45	—	—	—	1	45	—	—	1	45
Ore.	6	—	—	—	4	1	—	—	—	5	—	—	—	6	—	—	—	—	—	6	—
Pa.	60	1	—	5	—	—	29	—	—	—	6	54	—	—	—	9	51	—	—	59	1
R.I.	8	—	8	—	—	—	—	—	8	—	—	—	—	6	—	2	—	—	—	8	—
S.C.	18	3	—	1	—	—	11	11	—	—	1	6	11	—	—	1	6	10	—	4	4
Tenn.	24	9	1	2	1	1	7	6	1	—	1	8	9	1	—	3	5	3	—	20	—
Texas	26	2	7	—	5	1	7	3	8	3	1	7	2	8	1	3	7	—	—	26	—
Utah	2	—	2	—	—	—	—	—	—	2	—	—	—	2	—	—	—	—	—	2	—
Vt.	8	—	—	—	8	—	—	—	—	8	—	—	—	—	8	—	—	—	8	—	—
Va.	24	3	3	—	1	5	11	3	5	—	6	10	3	5	—	6	10	—	—	15	9
Wash.	6	—	1	—	3	1	—	1	—	4	1	—	1	—	4	1	—	—	—	6	—
W.Va.	12	1	—	—	2	2	5	1	—	1	2	5	—	—	5	3	1	—	—	12	—
Wis.	22	—	—	—	—	—	—	—	—	1	21	—	—	—	2	20	—	—	—	22	—
Wyo.	2	—	2	—	—	—	—	—	2	—	—	—	—	2	—	—	—	—	—	2	—
D.C.	2	—	—	—	—	—	—	1	—	—	—	—	1	—	—	—	—	—	—	2	—
Totals	832	84	72	99	107	85	229	137	73	91	231	244	120	76	91	279	230	100	59	544	118

1. Other candidates: James G. Blaine, 35; John J. Ingalls, 28; William W. Phelps, 25; Jeremiah M. Rusk, 25; Edwin H. Fitler, 24; Joseph R. Hawley, 13; Robert T. Lincoln, 3; William McKinley, 2; no voting, 1.

2. Other candidates: Blaine, 40; McKinley, 12; Joseph B. Foraker, 1; Frederick D. Grant, 1; not voting, 2.

3. Other candidates: McKinley, 16; Blaine, 15; Lincoln, 2; Foraker, 1; Creed Haymond, 1; not voting, 1.

4. Other candidates: Blaine, 5; McKinley, 4; not voting, 2.

a. Dakota Territory, includes North and South Dakota.

1892 Republican

(Narrative, p. 474)

First Pres. Ballot[1]

Delegation	Total Votes	Harrison	Blaine	McKinley
Alabama	22	15	—	7
Arizona	2	1	1	—
Arkansas	16	15	—	1
California	18	8	9	1
Colorado	8	—	8	—
Connecticut	12	4	—	8
Delaware	6	4	1	1
Florida	8	8	—	—
Georgia	26	26	—	—
Idaho	6	—	6	—
Illinois	48	34	14	—
Indiana	30	30	—	—
Iowa	26	20	5	1
Kansas	20	11	—	9
Kentucky	26	22	2	1
Louisiana	16	8	8	—
Maine	12	—	12	—
Maryland	16	14	—	2
Massachusetts	30	18	1	11
Michigan	28	7	2	19
Minnesota	18	8	9	1
Mississippi	18	13½	4½	—
Missouri	34	28	4	2
Montana	6	5	1	—
Nebraska	16	15	—	1
Nevada	6	—	6	—
New Hampshire	8	4	2	—
New Jersey	20	18	2	—
New Mexico	6	6	—	—
New York	72	27	35	10
North Carolina	22	17⅔	2⅔	1
North Dakota	6	2	4	—
Ohio	46	1	—	45
Oklahoma	2	2	—	—
Oregon	8	1	—	7
Pennsylvania	64	19	3	42
Rhode Island	8	5	1	1
South Carolina	18	13	3	2
South Dakota	8	8	—	—
Tennessee	24	17	4	3
Texas	30	22	6	—
Utah	2	2	—	—
Vermont	8	8	—	—
Virginia	24	9	13	2
Washington	8	1	6	1
West Virginia	12	12	—	—
Wisconsin	24	19	2	3
Wyoming	6	4	2	—
Alaska	2	2	—	—
District of Columbia	2	—	2	—
Indian Territory	2	1	1	—
Total	906	535⅙	182⅙	182

1. Other candidates: Thomas B. Reed, 4; Robert T. Lincoln, 1; not voting, 1⅔.

* Source: Official Proceeding, 10th Republican Convention.

1892 Democratic

(Narrative, p. 475)

First Pres. Ballot[1]

Delegation	Total Votes	Cleveland	Boies	Hill
Alabama	22	14	1	2
Arizona	6	5	—	—
Arkansas	16	16	—	—
California	18	18	—	—
Colorado	8	—	5	3
Connecticut	12	12	—	—
Delaware	6	6	—	—
Florida	8	5	—	—
Georgia	26	17	—	5
Idaho	6	—	6	—
Illinois	48	48	—	—
Indiana	30	30	—	—
Iowa	26	—	26	—
Kansas	20	20	—	—
Kentucky	26	18	2	—
Louisiana	16	3	11	1
Maine	12	9	—	1
Maryland	16	6	—	—
Massachusetts	30	24	1	4
Michigan	28	28	—	—
Minnesota	18	18	—	—
Mississippi	18	8	3	3
Missouri	34	34	—	—
Montana	6	—	6	—
Nebraska	16	15	—	—
Nevada	6	—	4	—
New Hampshire	8	8	—	—
New Jersey	20	20	—	—
New Mexico	6	4	1	1
New York	72	—	—	72
North Carolina	22	3⅓	1	—
North Dakota	6	6	—	—
Ohio	46	14	16	6
Oklahoma[a]	4	4	—	—
Oregon	8	8	—	—
Pennsylvania	64	64	—	—
Rhode Island	8	8	—	—
South Carolina	18	2	13	3
South Dakota	8	7	1	—
Tennessee	24	24	—	—
Texas	30	23	6	1
Utah	2	2	—	—
Vermont	8	8	—	—
Virginia	24	12	—	11
Washington	8	8	—	—
West Virginia	12	7	—	1
Wisconsin	24	24	—	—
Wyoming	6	3	—	—
Alaska	2	2	—	—
District of Columbia	2	2	—	—
Total	910	617⅓	103	114

1. Other candidates: Arthur P. Gorman, 36½; John G. Carlisle, 14; Adlai E. Stevenson, 16⅔; James E. Campbell, 2; William R. Morrison, 3; William E. Russell, 1; William C. Whitney, 1; Robert E. Pattison, 1; not voting, ½.

a. Including Indian Territory, 2 votes.

1896 Republican

(Narrative, p. 477)

First Pres. Ballot[1]

Delegation	Total Votes	McKinley	Reed	Morton	Allison	Quay
Alabama	22	19	2	1	—	—
Arizona	6	6	—	—	—	—
Arkansas	16	16	—	—	—	—
California	18	18	—	—	—	—
Colorado	8	—	—	—	—	—
Connecticut	12	7	5	—	—	—
Delaware	6	6	—	—	—	—
Florida	8	6	—	2	—	—
Georgia	26	22	2	—	—	2
Idaho	6	—	—	—	—	—
Illinois	48	46	2	—	—	—
Indiana	30	30	—	—	—	—
Iowa	26	—	—	—	26	—
Kansas	20	20	—	—	—	—
Kentucky	26	26	—	—	—	—
Louisiana	16	11	4	—	½	½
Maine	12	—	12	—	—	—
Maryland	16	15	1	—	—	—
Massachusetts	30	1	29	—	—	—
Michigan	28	28	—	—	—	—
Minnesota	18	18	—	—	—	—
Mississippi	18	17	—	—	—	1
Missouri	34	34	—	—	—	—
Montana	6	1	—	—	—	—
Nebraska	16	16	—	—	—	—
Nevada	6	3	—	—	—	—
New Hampshire	8	—	8	—	—	—
New Jersey	20	19	1	—	—	—
New Mexico	6	5	—	—	1	—
New York	72	17	—	55	—	—
North Carolina	22	19½	2½	—	—	—
North Dakota	6	6	—	—	—	—
Ohio	46	46	—	—	—	—
Oklahoma[a]	12	10	1	—	1	—
Oregon	8	8	—	—	—	—
Pennsylvania	64	6	—	—	—	58
Rhode Island	8	—	8	—	—	—
South Carolina	18	18	—	—	—	—
South Dakota	8	8	—	—	—	—
Tennessee	24	24	—	—	—	—
Texas	30	21	5	—	3	—
Utah	6	3	—	—	3	—
Vermont	8	8	—	—	—	—
Virginia	24	23	1	—	—	—
Washington	8	8	—	—	—	—
West Virginia	12	12	—	—	—	—
Wisconsin	24	24	—	—	—	—
Wyoming	6	6	—	—	—	—
Alaska	4	4	—	—	—	—
District of Columbia	2	—	1	—	1	—
Total	924	661½	84½	58	35½	61½

1. Other candidates: J. Donald Cameron, 1; not voting, 22.
a. Including Indian Territory, 6 votes.

1896 Democratic

(Narrative, p. 478)

Delegation	Total Votes	Minority Gold Standard Plank			First Pres. Ballot[1]			Fourth Pres. Ballot[2]			Fifth Pres. Ballot[3]	
		Yea	Nay	Not Voting	Bryan	Bland	Pattison	Bryan	Bland	Pattison	Bryan	Pattison
Alabama	22	—	22	—	—	—	—	22	—	—	22	—
Arizona	6	—	6	—	—	6	—	—	6	—	6	—
Arkansas	16	—	16	—	—	16	—	—	16	—	16	—
California	18	—	18	—	4	—	—	12	2	—	18	—
Colorado	8	—	8	—	—	—	—	8	—	—	8	—
Connecticut	12	12	—	—	—	—	—	—	—	2	—	2
Delaware	6	5	1	—	1	—	3	1	—	3	1	3
Florida	8	3	5	—	1	2	1	5	—	—	8	—
Georgia	26	—	26	—	26	—	—	26	—	—	26	—
Idaho	6	—	6	—	—	6	—	6	—	—	6	—
Illinois	48	—	48	—	—	48	—	—	48	—	48	—
Indiana	30	—	30	—	—	—	—	—	—	—	30	—
Iowa	26	—	26	—	—	—	—	—	—	—	26	—
Kansas	20	—	20	—	—	20	—	20	—	—	20	—
Kentucky	26	—	26	—	—	—	—	—	—	—	26	—
Louisiana	16	—	16	—	16	—	—	16	—	—	16	—
Maine	12	10	2	—	2	2	5	2	2	5	4	4
Maryland	16	12	4	—	4	—	11	5	—	10	5	10
Massachusetts	30	27	3	—	1	2	3	1	2	3	6	3
Michigan	28	—	28	—	9	4	—	28	—	—	28	—
Minnesota	18	11	6	1	2	—	2	10	1	—	11	—
Mississippi	18	—	18	—	18	—	—	18	—	—	18	—
Missouri	34	—	34	—	—	34	—	—	34	—	34	—
Montana	6	—	6	—	—	4	—	—	6	—	6	—
Nebraska	16	—	16	—	16	—	—	16	—	—	16	—
Nevada	6	—	6	—	—	—	—	6	—	—	6	—
New Hampshire	8	8	—	—	—	—	1	—	—	1	—	1
New Jersey	20	20	—	—	—	—	—	—	—	2	—	2
New Mexico	6	—	6	—	—	6	—	—	6	—	6	—
New York	72	72	—	—	—	—	—	—	—	—	—	—
North Carolina	22	—	22	—	22	—	—	22	—	—	22	—
North Dakota	6	—	6	—	—	—	—	—	—	—	4	—
Ohio	46	—	46	—	—	—	—	—	—	—	46	—
Oklahoma[a]	12	—	12	—	—	12	—	—	12	—	12	—
Oregon	8	—	8	—	—	—	—	8	—	—	8	—
Pennsylvania	64	64	—	—	—	—	64	—	—	64	—	64
Rhode Island	8	8	—	—	—	—	6	—	—	6	—	6
South Carolina	18	—	18	—	—	—	—	18	—	—	18	—
South Dakota	8	8	—	—	6	—	1	7	—	1	8	—
Tennessee	24	—	24	—	—	24	—	—	24	—	24	—
Texas	30	—	30	—	—	30	—	—	30	—	30	—
Utah	6	—	6	—	—	6	—	—	6	—	6	—
Vermont	8	8	—	—	4	—	—	4	—	—	4	—
Virginia	24	—	24	—	—	—	—	—	24	—	24	—
Washington	8	3	5	—	1	7	—	2	6	—	4	—
West Virginia	12	—	12	—	—	—	—	1	10	—	2	—
Wisconsin	24	24	—	—	4	—	—	5	—	—	5	—
Wyoming	6	—	6	—	—	—	—	6	—	—	6	—
Alaska	6	6	—	—	—	6	—	—	6	—	6	—
District of Columbia	6	2	4	—	—	—	—	5	—	—	6	—
Total	930	303	626	1	137	235	97	280	241	97	652	95

1. Other candidates: Horace Boies, 67; Claude Matthews, 37; John R. McLean, 54; Joseph C. S. Blackburn, 82; Adlai E. Stevenson, 6; Henry M. Teller, 8; William E. Russell, 2; Benjamin R. Tillman, 17; James E. Campbell, 1; Sylvester Pennoyer, 8; David B. Hill, 1; not voting, 178.

2. Other candidates: Boies, 33; Mathews, 36; Blackburn, 27; McLean, 46; Stevenson, 8; Hill, 1; not voting, 161.

3. Other candidates: Richard P. Bland, 11; Stevenson, 8; Hill, 1; David Turpie, 1; not voting, 162.

a. Including Indian Territory, 6 votes.

1900 Republican

(Narrative, p. 479)

Delegation	Total Votes	First Pres. Ballot McKinley
Alabama	22	22
Arizona	6	6
Arkansas	16	16
California	18	18
Colorado	8	8
Connecticut	12	12
Delaware	6	6
Florida	8	8
Georgia	26	26
Idaho	6	6
Illinois	48	48
Indiana	30	30
Iowa	26	26
Kansas	20	20
Kentucky	26	26
Louisiana	16	16
Maine	12	12
Maryland	16	16
Massachusetts	30	30
Michigan	28	28
Minnesota	18	18
Mississippi	18	18
Missouri	34	34
Montana	6	6
Nebraska	16	16
Nevada	6	6
New Hampshire	8	8
New Jersey	20	20
New Mexico	6	6
New York	72	72
North Carolina	22	22
North Dakota	6	6
Ohio	46	46
Oklahoma[a]	12	12
Oregon	8	8
Pennsylvania	64	64
Rhode Island	8	8
South Carolina	18	18
South Dakota	8	8
Tennessee	24	24
Texas	30	30
Utah	6	6
Vermont	8	8
Virginia	24	24
Washington	8	8
West Virginia	12	12
Wisconsin	24	24
Wyoming	6	6
Alaska	4	4
District of Columbia	2	2
Hawaii	2	2
Total	926	926

a. Including Indian Territory, 6 votes.

1900 Democratic

(Narrative, p. 480)

Delegation	Total Votes	First Pres. Ballot Bryan
Alabama	22	22
Arizona	6	6
Arkansas	16	16
California	18	18
Colorado	8	8
Connecticut	12	12
Delaware	6	6
Florida	8	8
Georgia	26	26
Idaho	6	6
Illinois	48	48
Indiana	30	30
Iowa	26	26
Kansas	20	20
Kentucky	26	26
Louisiana	16	16
Maine	12	12
Maryland	16	16
Massachusetts	30	30
Michigan	28	28
Minnesota	18	18
Mississippi	18	18
Missouri	34	34
Montana	6	6
Nebraska	16	16
Nevada	6	6
New Hampshire	8	8
New Jersey	20	20
New Mexico	6	6
New York	72	72
North Carolina	22	22
North Dakota	6	6
Ohio	46	46
Oklahoma[a]	12	12
Oregon	8	8
Pennsylvania	64	64
Rhode Island	8	8
South Carolina	18	18
South Dakota	8	8
Tennessee	24	24
Texas	30	30
Utah	6	6
Vermont	8	8
Virginia	24	24
Washington	8	8
West Virginia	12	12
Wisconsin	24	24
Wyoming	6	6
Alaska	6	6
District of Columbia	6	6
Hawaii	6	6
Total	936	936

a. Including Indian Territory, 6 votes.

1904 Democratic

(Narrative, p. 482)

Delegation	Total Votes	First Pres. Ballot[1] (Before shift)		First Pres. Ballot[2] (After shift)		Sending Telegram to Parker		
		Parker	Hearst	Parker	Hearst	Yea	Nay	Not Voting
Alabama	22	22	—	22	—	22	—	—
Arizona	6	—	6	—	6	—	6	—
Arkansas	18	18	—	18	—	16	4	—
California	20	—	20	—	20	16	4	—
Colorado	10	4	5	4	5	4	6	—
Connecticut	14	14	—	14	—	14	—	—
Delaware	6	—	—	—	—	6	—	—
Florida	10	6	4	6	4	6	4	—
Georgia	26	26	—	26	—	26	—	—
Idaho	6	—	6	6	—	—	6	—
Illinois	54	—	54	—	54	54	—	—
Indiana	30	30	—	30	—	30	—	—
Iowa	26	—	26	—	26	—	26	—
Kansas	20	7	10	7	10	—	20	—
Kentucky	26	26	—	26	—	26	—	—
Louisiana	18	18	—	18	—	18	—	—
Maine	12	7	1	7	1	7	2	3
Maryland	16	16	—	16	—	16	—	—
Massachusetts	32	—	—	—	—	32	—	—
Michigan	28	28	—	28	—	28	—	—
Minnesota	22	9	9	9	9	9	13	—
Mississippi	20	20	—	20	—	20	—	—
Missouri	36	—	—	—	—	—	36	—
Montana	6	6	—	6	—	—	6	—
Nebraska	16	—	4	—	4	—	16	—
Nevada	6	—	6	2	4	2	4	—
New Hampshire	8	8	—	8	—	8	—	—
New Jersey	24	24	—	24	—	24	—	—
New Mexico	6	—	6	—	6	6	—	—
New York	78	78	—	78	—	78	—	—
North Carolina	24	24	—	24	—	24	—	—
North Dakota	8	—	—	—	—	—	8	—
Ohio	46	46	—	46	—	31	6	9
Oklahoma[a]	12	7	3	7	3	7	5	—
Oregon	8	4	2	4	2	4	4	—
Pennsylvania	68	68	—	68	—	68	—	—
Rhode Island	8	2	6	2	6	2	5	1
South Carolina	18	18	—	18	—	18	—	—
South Dakota	8	—	8	—	8	—	8	—
Tennessee	24	24	—	24	—	24	—	—
Texas	36	36	—	36	—	36	—	—
Utah	6	6	—	6	—	6	—	—
Vermont	8	8	—	8	—	8	—	—
Virginia	24	24	—	24	—	24	—	—
Washington	10	—	10	10	—	10	—	—
West Virginia	14	10	2	13	1	14	—	—
Wisconsin	26	—	—	—	—	26	—	—
Wyoming	6	—	6	—	6	2	2	2
Alaska	6	6	—	6	—	6	—	—
District of Columbia	6	6	—	6	—	6	—	—
Hawaii	6	—	6	—	6	2	4	—
Puerto Rico	6	2	—	2	—	6	—	—
Total	1000	658	200	679	181	794	191	15

1. Other candidates: George Gray, 12; Nelson A. Miles, 3; Francis M. Cockrell, 42; Richard Olney, 38; Edward C. Wall, 27; George B. McClellan, 3; Charles A. Towne, 2; Robert E. Pattison, 4; John S. Williams, 8; Bird S. Coler, 1; Arthur P. Gorman, 2.

2. Other candidates: Gray, 12; Miles, 3; Cockrell, 42; Olney, 38; Wall, 27; McClellan, 3; Towne, 2; Pattison, 4; Williams, 8; Coler, 1.

a. Including Indian Territory, 6 votes.

1904 Republican

(Narrative, p. 481)

Delegation	Total Votes	First Pres. Ballot Roosevelt
Alabama	22	22
Arizona	6	6
Arkansas	18	18
California	20	20
Colorado	10	10
Connecticut	14	14
Delaware	6	6
Florida	10	10
Georgia	26	26
Idaho	6	6
Illinois	54	54
Indiana	30	30
Iowa	26	26
Kansas	20	20
Kentucky	26	26
Louisiana	18	18
Maine	12	12
Maryland	16	16
Massachusetts	32	32
Michigan	28	28
Minnesota	22	22
Mississippi	20	20
Missouri	36	36
Montana	6	6
Nebraska	16	16
Nevada	6	6
New Hampshire	8	8
New Jersey	24	24
New Mexico	6	6
New York	78	78
North Carolina	24	24
North Dakota	8	8
Ohio	46	46
Oklahoma[a]	12	12
Oregon	8	8
Pennsylvania	68	68
Rhode Island	8	8
South Carolina	18	18
South Dakota	8	8
Tennessee	24	24
Texas	36	36
Utah	6	6
Vermont	8	8
Virginia	24	24
Washington	10	10
West Virginia	14	14
Wisconsin	26	26
Wyoming	6	6
Alaska	6	6
District of Columbia	2	2
Hawaii	6	6
Philippine Islands	2	2
Puerto Rico	2	2
Total	994	994

a. Including Indian Territory, 6 votes.

1908 Democratic

(Narrative, p. 484)

Delegation	Total Votes	First Pres. Ballot[1] Bryan
Alabama	22	22
Arizona	6	6
Arkansas	18	18
California	20	20
Colorado	10	10
Connecticut	14	9
Delaware	6	—
Florida	10	10
Georgia	26	4
Idaho	6	6
Illinois	54	54
Indiana	30	30
Iowa	26	26
Kansas	20	20
Kentucky	26	26
Louisiana	18	18
Maine	12	10
Maryland	16	7
Massachusetts	32	32
Michigan	28	28
Minnesota	22	—
Mississippi	20	20
Missouri	36	36
Montana	6	6
Nebraska	16	16
Nevada	6	6
New Hampshire	8	7
New Jersey	24	—
New Mexico	6	6
New York	78	78
North Carolina	24	24
North Dakota	8	8
Ohio	46	46
Oklahoma	14	14
Oregon	8	8
Pennsylvania	68	49½
Rhode Island	8	5
South Carolina	18	18
South Dakota	8	8
Tennessee	24	24
Texas	36	36
Utah	6	6
Vermont	8	7
Virginia	24	24
Washington	10	10
West Virginia	14	14
Wisconsin	26	26
Wyoming	6	6
Alaska	6	6
District of Columbia	6	6
Hawaii	6	6
Puerto Rico	6	6
Total	1002	888½

1. Other candidates: John A. Johnson, 46; George Gray, 59½; not voting, 8.

1908 Republican

(Narrative, p. 484)

Delegation	Total Votes	Minority Report on Changing Delegate Apportionment Formula			Minority Plank for Direct Election of Senators		First Pres. Ballot[1]
		Yea	Nay	Not Voting	Yea	Nay	Taft
Alabama	22	—	22	—	—	22	22
Arizona	2	—	2	—	—	2	2
Arkansas	18	—	18	—	—	18	18
California	20	—	20	—	—	20	20
Colorado	10	10	—	—	—	10	10
Connecticut	14	14	—	—	—	14	14
Delaware	6	—	6	—	—	6	6
Florida	10	—	10	—	—	10	10
Georgia	26	—	26	—	—	26	17
Idaho	6	—	6	—	3	3	6
Illinois	54	54	—	—	1	53	3
Indiana	30	30	—	—	11	19	—
Iowa	26	6	20	—	1	25	26
Kansas	20	—	20	—	—	20	20
Kentucky	26	1	25	—	2	24	24
Louisiana	18	—	18	—	—	18	18
Maine	12	12	—	—	—	12	12
Maryland	16	—	16	—	1	15	16
Massachusetts	32	32	—	—	—	32	32
Michigan	28	18	10	—	5	23	27
Minnesota	22	10	11	1	—	22	22
Mississippi	20	—	20	—	—	20	20
Missouri	36	12	24	—	4	32	36
Montana	6	—	6	—	—	6	6
Nebraska	16	7	9	—	16	—	16
Nevada	6	—	6	—	—	6	6
New Hampshire	8	8	—	—	—	8	5
New Jersey	24	23	1	—	—	24	15
New Mexico	2	—	—	2	—	2	2
New York	78	78	—	—	—	78	10
North Carolina	24	—	24	—	—	24	24
North Dakota	8	—	8	—	—	8	8
Ohio	46	8	38	—	2	44	42
Oklahoma	14	—	14	—	14	—	14
Oregon	8	3	5	—	—	8	8
Pennsylvania	68	68	—	—	13	55	1
Rhode Island	8	8	—	—	—	8	8
South Carolina	18	—	18	—	—	18	13
South Dakota	8	8	—	—	8	—	8
Tennessee	24	—	24	—	—	24	24
Texas	36	—	36	—	—	36	36
Utah	6	6	—	—	2	4	6
Vermont	8	8	—	—	—	8	8
Virginia	24	—	24	—	—	24	21
Washington	10	4	6	—	—	10	10
West Virginia	14	14	—	—	5	9	14
Wisconsin	26	26	—	—	25	1	1
Wyoming	6	—	6	—	—	6	6
Alaska	2	2	—	—	—	2	2
District of Columbia	2	1	1	—	—	2	1
Hawaii	2	—	2	—	1	1	2
Philippine Islands	2	—	2	—	—	2	2
Puerto Rico	2	—	2	—	—	2	2
Total	980	471	506	3	114	866	702

1. Other candidates: Philander C. Knox, 68; Charles E. Hughes, 67; Joseph G. Cannon, 58; Charles W. Fairbanks, 40; Robert M. La Follette, 25; Joseph B. Foraker, 16; Theodore Roosevelt, 3; not voting, 1.

1912 Republican

(Narrative, p. 486)

Delegation	Total Votes	Temporary Chairman[1] Root	McGovern	Table Motion Prohibiting Challenged Taft Delegates from Voting — Yea	Nay	Not Voting	First Pres. Ballot[2] Taft	Roosevelt	Present, Not Voting
Alabama	24	22	2	22	2	—	22	—	2
Arizona	6	6	—	6	—	—	6	—	—
Arkansas	18	17	1	17	1	—	17	—	1
California	26	2	24	2	24	—	2	—	24
Colorado	12	12	—	12	—	—	12	—	—
Connecticut	14	14	—	14	—	—	14	—	—
Delaware	6	6	—	6	—	—	6	—	—
Florida	12	12	—	12	—	—	12	—	—
Georgia	28	22	6	24	4	—	28	—	—
Idaho	8	—	8	—	8	—	1	—	—
Illinois	58	9	49	7	51	—	2	53	1
Indiana	30	20	10	20	9	1	20	3	7
Iowa	26	16	10	16	10	—	16	—	—
Kansas	20	2	18	2	18	—	2	—	18
Kentucky	26	23	3	24	2	—	24	2	—
Louisiana	20	20	—	20	—	—	20	—	—
Maine	12	—	12	—	12	—	—	—	12
Maryland	16	8	8	9	7	—	1	9	5
Massachusetts	36	18	18	18	18	—	15	—	21
Michigan	30	19	10	20	10	—	20	9	1
Minnesota	24	—	24	—	24	—	—	—	24
Mississippi	20	16	4	16	4	—	17	—	3
Missouri	36	16	20	16	20	—	16	—	20
Montana	8	8	—	8	—	—	8	—	—
Nebraska	16	—	16	—	16	—	—	2	14
Nevada	6	6	—	6	—	—	6	—	—
New Hampshire	8	8	—	8	—	—	8	—	—
New Jersey	28	—	28	—	28	—	—	2	26
New Mexico	8	6	2	7	1	—	7	1	—
New York	90	76	13	75	15	—	76	8	6
North Carolina	24	3	21	2	22	—	1	1	22
North Dakota	10	—	9	2	8	—	—	—	—
Ohio	48	14	34	14	34	—	14	—	34
Oklahoma	20	4	16	4	16	—	4	1	15
Oregon	10	3	6	5	5	—	—	8	2
Pennsylvania	76	12	64	12	64	—	9	2	62
Rhode Island	10	10	—	10	—	—	10	—	—
South Carolina	18	11	7	11	6	1	16	—	1
South Dakota	10	—	10	—	10	—	—	5	—
Tennessee	24	23	1	23	1	—	23	1	—
Texas	40	31	8	29	9	2	31	—	8
Utah	8	7	1	7	1	—	8	—	—
Vermont	8	6	2	6	2	—	6	—	2
Virginia	24	22	2	21	3	—	22	—	1
Washington	14	14	—	14	—	—	14	—	—
West Virginia	16	—	16	—	16	—	—	—	16
Wisconsin	26	—	12	—	26	—	—	—	—
Wyoming	6	6	—	6	—	—	6	—	—
Alaska	2	2	—	2	—	—	2	—	—
District of Columbia	2	2	—	2	—	—	2	—	—
Hawaii	6	—	6	6	—	—	6	—	—
Philippine Islands	2	2	—	2	—	—	2	—	—
Puerto Rico	2	2	—	2	—	—	2	—	—
Total	1078	558	501	567	507	4	556[a]	107	348[b]

1. Other candidates: W.S. Lauder, 12; Asle J. Gronna, 1; not voting, 6.
2. Other candidates: Robert M. La Follette, 41; Albert B. Cummins, 17; Charles E. Hughes, 2; absent and not voting, 7.
a. Sum of column; proceedings record 561.
b. Sum of column; proceedings record 349.

1912 Democratic

(Narrative, p. 487)

Delegation	Total Votes	Temporary Chairman[1]		First Pres. Ballot[2]				Tenth Pres. Ballot[3]			Thirtieth Pres. Ballot[4]			43rd Pres. Ballot[5]		45th Pres. Ballot[6]		46th Pres. Ballot[7]
		Bryan	Parker	Clark	Wilson	Harmon	Underwood	Clark	Wilson	Underwood	Clark	Wilson	Underwood	Clark	Wilson	Clark	Wilson	Wilson
Ala.	24	1½	22½	—	—	—	24	—	—	24	—	—	24	—	—	—	—	24
Ariz.	6	4	2	6	—	—	—	6	—	—	4	2	—	3	2	3	3	6
Ark.	18	—	18	18	—	—	—	18	—	—	18	—	—	18	—	18	—	18
Calif.	26	7	18	26	—	—	—	26	—	—	26	—	—	26	—	26	—	2
Colo.	12	6	6	12	—	—	—	12	—	—	12	—	—	11	1	2	10	12
Conn.	14	2	12	—	—	—	—	7	—	7	7	3	4	1	5	2	5	14
Del.	6	6	—	—	6	—	—	—	6	—	—	6	—	—	6	—	6	6
Fla.	12	1	11	—	—	—	12	—	—	12	—	—	12	—	2	—	3	7
Ga.	28	—	28	—	—	—	28	—	—	28	—	—	28	—	—	—	—	28
Idaho	8	8	—	8	—	—	—	8	—	—	2½	5½	—	1	7	1½	6½	8
Ill.	58	—	58	58	—	—	—	58	—	—	58	—	—	—	58	—	58	58
Ind.	30	8	21	—	—	—	—	—	—	—	1	28	—	1	28	—	30	30
Iowa	26	13	13	26	—	—	—	26	—	—	12	14	—	11½	14½	9	17	26
Kan.	20	20	—	20	—	—	—	20	—	—	—	20	—	—	20	—	20	20
Ky.	26	7½	17½	26	—	—	—	26	—	—	26	—	—	26	—	26	—	26
La.	20	10	10	11	9	—	—	10	10	—	7	12	—	6	14	5	15	18
Maine	12	1	11	1	9	—	2	1	11	—	1	9	2	1	11	1	11	12
Md.	16	1½	14½	16	—	—	—	16	—	—	11	4½	—	9	5½	8½	7	16
Mass.	36	18	15	36	—	—	—	33	1	2	—	7	—	—	9	—	9	36
Mich.	30	9	21	12	10	7	—	18	9	—	18	12	—	2	28	2	28	30
Minn.	24	24	—	—	24	—	—	—	24	—	—	24	—	—	24	—	24	24
Miss.	20	—	20	—	—	—	20	—	—	20	—	—	20	—	—	—	—	20
Mo.	36	14	22	36	—	—	—	36	—	—	36	—	—	36	—	36	—	—
Mont.	8	7	1	8	—	—	—	8	—	—	2	6	—	1	7	1	7	8
Neb.	16	13	3	12	—	4	—	13	3	—	3	13	—	3	13	3	13	16
Nev.	6	6	—	6	—	—	—	6	—	—	6	—	—	6	—	6	—	—
N.H.	8	5	3	8	—	—	—	5	3	—	3	5	—	3	5	3	5	8
N.J.	28	24	4	2	24	—	2	4	24	—	4	24	—	4	24	4	24	24
N.M.	8	8	—	8	—	—	—	8	—	—	8	—	—	8	—	8	—	8
N.Y.	90	—	90	—	—	90	—	90	—	—	90	—	—	90	—	90	—	90
N.C.	24	9	15	—	16½	½	7	—	18	6	—	17½	6½	—	22	—	22	24
N.D.	10	10	—	—	10	—	—	—	10	—	—	10	—	—	10	—	10	10
Ohio	48	19	29	1	10	35	—	6	11	—	—	19	10	—	20	—	23	23
Okla.	20	20	—	10	10	—	—	10	10	—	10	10	—	10	10	10	10	20
Ore.	10	9	1	—	10	—	—	—	10	—	—	10	—	—	10	—	10	10
Pa.	76	67	9	—	71	5	—	5	71	—	4	72	—	2	74	—	76	76
R.I.	10	—	10	10	—	—	—	10	—	—	10	—	—	10	—	10	—	10
S.C.	18	18	—	—	18	—	—	—	18	—	—	18	—	—	18	—	18	18
S.D.	10	10	—	—	10	—	—	—	10	—	—	10	—	—	10	—	10	10
Tenn.	24	7	17	6	6	6	6	13	7½	3½	13½	8	2½	10	8	8	10	24
Texas	40	40	—	—	40	—	—	—	40	—	—	40	—	—	40	—	40	40
Utah	8	4	4	1½	6	½	—	1½	6½	—	1½	6½	—	1½	6½	—	8	8
Vt.	8	—	8	—	—	—	—	—	8	—	—	8	—	—	8	—	8	8
Va.	24	10	14	—	9½	—	14½	—	9½	14	3	9½	11½	—	24	—	24	24
Wash.	14	14	—	14	—	—	—	14	—	—	14	—	—	14	—	14	—	14
W.Va.	16	4½	10½	16	—	—	—	16	—	—	16	—	—	—	16	—	16	16
Wis.	26	26	—	6	19	—	—	6	20	—	6	19	—	4	22	—	26	26
Wyo.	6	6	—	6	—	—	—	6	—	—	6	—	—	—	6	—	6	6
Alaska	6	2	4	4	—	—	—	3	3	—	6	—	—	1	5	—	6	6
D.C.	6	—	6	6	—	—	—	6	—	—	6	—	—	6	—	6	—	—
Hawaii	6	2	4	2	3	—	1	2	3	1	2	3	1	2	4	2	4	6
Phil. Is.	6	2	4	—	—	—	—	—	—	—	—	—	—	—	—	—	—	—
P.R.	6	4	2	2	3	—	1	2	4	—	1½	4½	—	1	4½	1	4½	6
Total	1094	508	579	440½	324	148	117½	556	350½	117½	455	460	121½	329	602	306	633	990

1. Other candidates: James A. O'Gorman, 4; John W. Kern, 1; not voting, 2.
2. Other candidates: Simeon E. Baldwin, 22; Thomas R. Marshall, 31; William J. Bryan, 1; William Sulzer, 2; not voting, 8.
3. Other candidates: Judson Harmon, 31; Marshall, 31; Kern, 1; Bryan, 1; not voting, 6.
4. Other candidates: Eugene N. Foss, 30; Harmon, 19; Kern, 2; not voting, ½.
5. Other candidates: Oscar W. Underwood, 98½; Harmon, 28; Foss, 27; Bryan, 1; Kern, 1; not voting, 7½.
6. Other candidates: Underwood, 97; Foss, 27; Harmon, 25; not voting, 6.
7. Other candidates: Champ Clark, 84; Harmon, 12; not voting, 8.

1916 Republican

(Narrative, p. 490)

Delegation	Total Votes	First Pres. Ballot[1]			Second Pres. Ballot[2]		Third Pres. Ballot[3]
		Hughes	Root	Weeks	Hughes	Root	Hughes
Alabama	16	8	—	3	9	—	16
Arizona	6	4	—	—	4	—	6
Arkansas	15	1	3	3	—	2	15
California	26	9	8	3	11	12	26
Colorado	12	—	5	—	—	5	12
Connecticut	14	5	5	1	5	7	14
Delaware	6	—	—	—	—	—	6
Florida	8	8	—	—	8	—	8
Georgia	17	5	—	6	6	—	17
Idaho	8	4	—	—	4	1	8
Illinois	58	—	—	—	—	—	58
Indiana	30	—	—	—	—	—	30
Iowa	26	—	—	—	—	—	26
Kansas	20	10	2	3	10	2	20
Kentucky	26	10	—	—	11	—	26
Louisiana	12	4	1	3	6	1	12
Maine	12	6	1	3	8	1	12
Maryland	16	7	1	5	7	1	15
Massachusetts	36	4	—	28	12	—	32
Michigan	30	—	—	—	28	—	30
Minnesota	24	—	—	—	—	—	24
Mississippi	12	4	—	1½	4	—	8½
Missouri	36	18	—	8	22	—	34
Montana	8	—	—	—	—	—	7
Nebraska	16	—	—	—	2	—	16
Nevada	6	4	2	—	4	2	6
New Hampshire	8	—	—	8	3	3	8
New Jersey	28	12	12	1	16	3	27
New Mexico	6	2	—	2	2	—	5
New York	87	42	43	—	43	42	87
North Carolina	21	6	2	3	6	2	14
North Dakota	10	—	—	—	—	—	10
Ohio	48	—	—	—	—	—	48
Oklahoma	20	5	1	6	5	1	19
Oregon	10	10	—	—	10	—	10
Pennsylvania	76	2	—	—	8	1	72
Rhode Island	10	10	—	—	10	—	10
South Carolina	11	2	1	3	4	—	6
South Dakota	10	—	—	—	—	—	10
Tennessee	21	9	—	3½	8	½	18
Texas	26	1	1	1	3	3	26
Utah	8	4	3	—	5	2	7
Vermont	8	8	—	—	8	—	8
Virginia	15	5½	3	3	8½	5	15
Washington	14	5	8	—	5	—	14
West Virginia	16	1	—	5	4	1	16
Wisconsin	26	11	—	—	11	—	23
Wyoming	6	6	—	—	6	—	6
Alaska	2	1	—	1	1	—	2
Hawaii	2	—	—	1	1	—	2
Philippine Islands	2	—	1	—	—	1	2
Total	987	253½	103	105	328½	98½	949½

1. Other candidates: Albert B. Cummins, 85; Theodore E. Burton, 77½; Charles W. Fairbanks, 74½; Lawrence Y. Sherman, 66; Theodore Roosevelt, 65; Philander C. Knox, 36; Henry Ford, 32; Martin G. Brumbaugh, 29; Robert M. La Follette, 25; William H. Taft, 14; Coleman du Pont, 12; Frank B. Willis, 4; William E. Borah, 2; Samuel W. McCall, 1; not voting, 2½.

2. Other candidates: Fairbanks, 88½; Cummins, 85; Roosevelt, 81; John W. Weeks, 79; Burton, 76½; Sherman, 65; Knox, 36; La Follette, 25; du Pont, 13; John Wanamaker, 5; Willis, 1; Leonard Wood, 1; Warren G. Harding, 1; McCall, 1; not voting, 2.

3. Other candidates: Roosevelt, 18½; La Follette, 3; du Pont, 5; Henry Cabot Lodge, 7; Weeks, 3; not voting, 1.

1916 Democratic

(Narrative, p. 491)

Delegation	Total Votes	Minority Plank on Women's Suffrage		
		Yea	Nay	Not Voting
Alabama	24	1	23	—
Arizona	6	—	6	—
Arkansas	18	—	18	—
California	26	—	26	—
Colorado	12	—	12	—
Connecticut	14	1	13	—
Delaware	6	—	6	—
Florida	12	4	8	—
Georgia	28	23½	4½	—
Idaho	8	—	8	—
Illinois	58	1	57	—
Indiana	30	24	6	—
Iowa	26	—	26	—
Kansas	20	—	20	—
Kentucky	26	—	26	—
Louisiana	20	8	12	—
Maine	12	—	6	6
Maryland	16	16	—	—
Massachusetts	36	6	30	—
Michigan	30	—	30	—
Minnesota	24	9	15	—
Mississippi	20	—	20	—
Missouri	36	4	24	8
Montana	8	—	8	—
Nebraska	16	—	16	—
Nevada	6	—	6	—
New Hampshire	8	1	7	—
New Jersey	28	10	11	7
New Mexico	6	—	6	—
New York	90	—	90	—
North Carolina	24	11	13	—
North Dakota	10	—	10	—
Ohio	48	20	28	—
Oklahoma	20	—	20	—
Oregon	10	—	10	—
Pennsylvania	76	—	76	—
Rhode Island	10	1	9	—
South Carolina	18	—	18	—
South Dakota	10	—	10	—
Tennessee	24	—	24	—
Texas	40	32	8	—
Utah	8	—	8	—
Vermont	8	—	8	—
Virginia	24	—	24	—
Washington	14	—	14	—
West Virginia	16	8	8	—
Wisconsin	26	—	26	—
Wyoming	6	—	6	—
Alaska	6	—	6	—
District of Columbia	6	—	6	—
Hawaii	6	—	6	—
Philippine Islands	6	1	4	1
Puerto Rico	6	—	6	—
Total	1092	181½	888½	22

1920 Republican

(Narrative, p. 493)

Delegation	Total Votes	First Pres. Ballot[1] Wood	Lowden	Johnson	Fourth Pres. Ballot[2] Wood	Lowden	Johnson	Eighth Pres. Ballot[3] Wood	Lowden	Harding	Ninth Pres. Ballot[4] Wood	Lowden	Harding	Tenth Pres. Ballot[5] (Before shift) Wood	Harding	Tenth Pres. Ballot[6] (After shift) Wood	Harding
Alabama	14	4	6	3	4	6	4	4	6	4	4	6	4	3	8	3	8
Arizona	6	6	—	—	6	—	—	6	—	—	6	—	—	6	—	—	6
Arkansas	13	6	6	—	2½	10½	—	1½	11½	—	1½	10½	1	—	13	—	13
California	26	—	—	26	—	—	26	—	—	—	—	—	—	—	—	—	—
Colorado	12	9	2	—	9	2	—	6	3	3	6	1	5	6	5	—	12
Connecticut	14	—	14	—	—	13	1	1	11	—	—	—	13	—	13	—	13
Delaware	6	—	—	—	—	2	—	—	—	3	—	—	3	—	6	—	6
Florida	8	4½	2½	—	6½	1½	—	7	1	—	1	—	7	½	7½	½	7½
Georgia	17	8	9	—	8	9	—	8	9	—	8	8	1	7	10	7	10
Idaho	8	5	—	1	5	1	1	4	2	1	5	1	1	3	2	3	2
Illinois	58	14	41	3	—	41	17	—	41	—	—	41	—	—	22.2	—	38.2
Indiana	30	22	—	8	18	3	6	15	4	11	15	4	11	8	20	9	21
Iowa	26	—	26	—	—	26	—	—	26	—	—	26	—	—	26	—	26
Kansas	20	14	6	—	14	6	—	10	6	4	—	—	20	1	18	1	18
Kentucky	26	—	20	1	—	26	—	—	26	—	—	—	26	—	26	—	26
Louisiana	12	3	3	1	3	6	—	3	7	2	—	—	12	—	12	—	12
Maine	12	11	—	—	11	—	—	12	—	—	12	—	—	12	—	12	—
Maryland	16	16	—	—	16	—	—	16	—	—	16	—	—	10	5	10	5
Massachusetts	35	7	—	—	16	—	—	11	—	—	11	1	1	17	17	17	17
Michigan	30	—	—	30	—	—	30	13	7	—	15	6	1	1	25	1	25
Minnesota	24	19	3	2	17	5	2	16	5	—	17	5	—	21	2	21	2
Mississippi	12	4½	2	—	7½	2½	—	8½	1½	2	7½	—	4½	2½	9½	—	12
Missouri	36	4½	18	3	8½	19	1	2½	15½	17	—	—	36	—	36	—	36
Montana	8	—	—	8	—	—	8	—	—	8	—	—	—	—	—	—	—
Nebraska	16	3	—	13	6	—	10	14	—	—	16	—	—	5	4	5	4
Nevada	6	2	1½	2	2½	2	1½	1½	—	3½	1½	—	3½	—	3½	—	3½
New Hampshire	8	8	—	—	8	—	—	8	—	—	8	—	—	8	—	8	—
New Jersey	28	17	—	11	17	—	11	16	—	2	15	—	4	15	5	15	5
New Mexico	6	6	—	—	6	—	—	6	—	—	6	—	—	6	—	—	6
New York	88	10	2	—	20	32	5	23	45	8	5	4	66	6	68	6	68
North Carolina	22	—	—	1	3	15	2	2	16	4	3	—	18	2	20	2	20
North Dakota	10	2	—	8	3	1	6	3	4	—	3	4	—	1	9	—	10
Ohio	48	9	—	—	9	—	—	9	—	39	9	—	39	—	48	—	48
Oklahoma	20	1½	18½	—	2	18	—	2	18	—	½	—	18	½	18	½	18
Oregon	10	1	—	9	5	—	5	4	—	1	4	—	1	3	2	3	2
Pennsylvania	76	—	—	—	—	—	—	—	—	—	—	—	—	14	60	14	60
Rhode Island	10	10	—	—	10	—	—	10	—	—	10	—	—	—	10	—	10
South Carolina	11	—	8	—	—	11	—	—	11	—	—	—	11	—	11	—	11
South Dakota	10	10	—	—	10	—	—	10	—	—	10	—	—	6	4	6	4
Tennessee	20	20	—	—	19	1	—	10	7	3	6	1	13	—	20	—	20
Texas	23	8½	5	1½	8	9½	1	5	8½	8½	1	1	19½	—	23	—	23
Utah	8	5	2	—	5	2	—	4	2	2	2	2	4	1	5	1	5
Vermont	8	8	—	—	8	—	—	8	—	—	8	—	—	8	—	8	—
Virginia	15	3	12	—	3	12	—	3	10	2	4	—	11	1	14	1	14
Washington	14	—	—	—	—	—	—	—	—	—	—	—	—	5	6	—	14
West Virginia	16	—	—	—	8	—	1	9	—	7	8	—	7	—	16	—	16
Wisconsin	26	1	—	—	1	—	2	1	—	—	1	—	—	—	1	—	1
Wyoming	6	—	3	—	3	3	—	—	—	6	—	—	6	6	—	6	—
Alaska	2	—	—	—	1	—	—	1	—	—	1	—	—	—	2	—	2
District of Columbia	2	2	—	—	2	—	—	2	—	—	—	—	2	2	—	2	—
Hawaii	2	—	—	—	—	2	—	—	2	—	—	—	—	—	2	—	2
Philippine Islands	2	2	—	—	2	—	—	2	—	—	2	—	—	2	—	2	—
Puerto Rico	2	1	1	—	1	1	—	1	1	—	—	—	2	—	2	—	2
Total	984	287½	211½	133½	314½	289	140½	299	307	133[a]	249	121½	374½	181½	644.7	156	692.2

1. Other candidates: Warren G. Harding, 65½; William C. Sproul, 84; Calvin Coolidge, 34; Herbert Hoover, 5½; Coleman du Pont, 7; Jeter C. Pritchard, 21; Robert M. La Follette, 24; Howard Sutherland, 17; William E. Borah, 2; Charles B. Warren, 1; Miles Poindexter, 20; Nicholas M. Butler, 69½; not voting, 1.

2. Other candidates: Harding, 61½; Sproul, 79½; Coolidge, 25; Hoover, 5; du Pont, 2; La Follette, 22; Sutherland, 3; Borah, 1; Poindexter, 15; Butler, 20; James E. Watson, 4; Knox, 2.

3. Other candidates: Hiram W. Johnson, 87; Coolidge, 30; du Pont, 3; Frank B. Kellogg, 1; La Follette, 24; Poindexter, 15; Irvine L. Lenroot, 1; Hoover, 5; Butler, 2; Knox, 1; Sproul, 76.

4. Other candidates: Johnson, 82; Sproul, 78; Coolidge, 28; Hoover, 6; Lenroot, 1; Butler, 2; Knox, 1; La Follette, 24; Poindexter, 14; Will H. Hays, 1; H. F. MacGregor, 1; not voting, 1.

5. Other candidates: Frank Lowden, 28; Johnson, 80⅘; Hoover, 10½; Coolidge, 5; Butler, 2; Lenroot, 1; Hays, 1; Knox, 1; La Follette, 24; Poindexter, 2; not voting, 2½.

6. Other candidates: Lowden, 11; Johnson, 80⅘; Hoover, 9½; Coolidge, 5; Butler, 2; Lenroot, 1; Hays, 1; Knox, 1; La Follette, 24; not voting, ½.

a. Sum of column; proceedings record 133½.

1920 Democratic

(Narrative, p. 494)

Delegation	Total Votes	First Pres. Ballot[1] McAdoo	Cox	Palmer	Smith	Thirtieth Pres. Ballot[2] McAdoo	Cox	Palmer	39th Pres. Ballot[3] McAdoo	Cox	44th Pres. Ballot[4] McAdoo	Cox
Alabama	24	9	3	6	2	12	7	—	8	—	8	13
Arizona	6	4	1	—	—	3	2	—	4	2	2½	3½
Arkansas	18	3	7	2	—	3	14	1	4	14	—	18
California	26	10	4	3	1	10	13	1	14	12	13	13
Colorado	12	3	—	8	—	5	6	—	4	7	3	9
Connecticut	14	—	—	—	—	1	6	4	3	10	2	12
Delaware	6	4	—	—	—	4	2	—	4	2	3	3
Florida	12	1	—	8	—	3	9	—	3	9	—	12
Georgia	28	—	—	28	—	—	—	28	28	—	—	28
Idaho	8	8	—	—	—	8	—	—	8	—	8	—
Illinois	58	9	9	35	5	21	36	1	18	38	13	44
Indiana	30	—	—	—	—	29	—	—	11	19	—	30
Iowa	26	—	—	—	—	—	26	—	—	26	—	26
Kansas	20	20	—	—	—	20	—	—	20	—	20	—
Kentucky	26	3	23	—	—	5	20	—	5	20	—	26
Louisiana	20	5	2	2	—	4	14	—	7	12	—	20
Maine	12	5	—	5	—	7	—	5	12	—	5	5
Maryland	16	5½	5½	—	—	5½	8½	—	5½	8½	—	13½
Massachusetts	36	4	4	17	7	2	15	16	1	33	—	35
Michigan	30	15	—	12	—	15	6	9	14	12	—	—
Minnesota	24	10	2	7	—	14	4	4	16	7	15	8
Mississippi	20	—	—	—	—	—	20	—	—	20	—	20
Missouri	36	15½	2½	10	—	18	6	5	20½	11½	17	18
Montana	8	1	—	—	—	8	—	—	8	—	2	6
Nebraska	16	—	—	—	—	7	—	—	7	—	2	5
Nevada	6	—	6	—	—	—	6	—	—	6	—	6
New Hampshire	8	4	—	1	—	5	2	1	5	2	6	2
New Jersey	28	—	—	—	—	—	28	—	—	28	—	28
New Mexico	6	2	—	1	—	6	—	—	6	—	6	—
New York	90	—	—	—	90	20	70	—	20	70	20	70
North Carolina	24	—	—	—	—	24	—	—	24	—	24	—
North Dakota	10	6	1	2	—	8	2	—	9	1	4	2
Ohio	48	—	48	—	—	—	48	—	—	48	—	48
Oklahoma	20	—	—	—	—	—	—	—	—	—	—	—
Oregon	10	10	—	—	—	10	—	—	10	—	10	—
Pennsylvania	76	2	—	73	—	2	1	73	2	1	4	68
Rhode Island	10	2	—	5	2	3	4	3	1	7	1	9
South Carolina	18	18	—	—	—	18	—	—	18	—	18	—
South Dakota	10	—	—	—	—	6	4	—	6	3	3	5
Tennessee	24	2	8	9	—	40	—	—	40	—	40	—
Texas	40	40	—	—	—	40	—	—	40	—	7	1
Utah	8	8	—	—	—	8	—	—	8	—	—	8
Vermont	8	4	2	1	1	1	6	1	4	4	2½	18½
Virginia	24	—	—	—	—	—	—	—	10	11	—	13
Washington	14	10	—	—	—	14	—	—	11	2½	3	23
West Virginia	16	—	—	—	—	—	—	—	—	—	3	3
Wisconsin	26	11	5	3	1	19	7	—	19	7	—	6
Wyoming	6	6	—	—	—	6	—	—	6	—	2	—
Alaska	6	2	1	3	—	2	1	3	4	2	—	6
Canal Zone	2	1	—	1	—	1	—	1	2	—	2	—
District of Columbia	6	—	—	6	—	—	—	6	—	6	—	6
Hawaii	6	2	—	4	—	1	5	—	1	5	2	4
Philippine Islands	6	—	—	—	—	3	2	1	3	2	1	5
Puerto Rico	6	1	—	2	—	2	—	2	6	—	1	—
Total	1094	266	134	254[a]	109	403½	400½	165	440	468½	270	699½

1. Other candidates: Homer S. Cummings, 25; James W. Gerard, 21; Robert L. Owen, 33; Gilbert M. Hitchcock, 18; Edwin T. Meredith, 27; Edward I. Edwards, 42; John W. Davis, 32; Carter Glass, 26½; Furnifold M. Simmons, 24; Francis B. Harrison, 6; John S. Williams, 20; Thomas R. Marshall, 37; Champ Clark, 9; Oscar W. Underwood, ½; William R. Hearst, 1; William J. Bryan, 1; Bainbridge Colby, 1; Josephus Daniels, 1; Wood, 4.

2. Other candidates: Cummings, 4; Owen, 33; Davis, 58; Glass, 24; Clark, 2; Underwood, 2; not voting, 2.

3. Other candidates: A. Mitchell Palmer, 74; Davis, 71½; Owen, 32; Cummings, 2; Clark, 2; Colby, 1; not voting, 3.

4. Other candidates: Palmer, 1; Davis, 52; Owen, 34; Glass, 1½; Colby, 1; not voting, 36.

a. Sum of column; proceedings record 256.

1924 Democratic

(Narrative, p. 496)

Delegation	Total Votes	Minority Report on League of Nations			Minority Report on Ku Klux Klan			First Pres. Ballot[1]		Fiftieth Pres. Ballot[2]		Ninetieth Pres. Ballot[3]		
		Yea	Nay	Not Voting	Yea	Nay	Not Voting	McAdoo	Smith	McAdoo	Smith	McAdoo	Smith	Ralston
Alabama	24	12½	11½	—	24	—	—	—	—	—	—	—	—	—
Arizona	6	1½	4½	—	1	5	—	4½	—	3½	—	3½	—	—
Arkansas	18	3	15	—	—	18	—	—	—	—	—	—	—	—
California	26	4	22	—	7	19	—	26	—	26	—	26	—	—
Colorado	12	9½	2½	—	6	6	—	—	—	4	3	1	3	½
Connecticut	14	5	9	—	13	1	—	—	6	4	10	2	12	—
Delaware	6	6	—	—	6	—	—	—	—	—	—	—	—	—
Florida	12	5	7	—	1	11	—	12	—	10	1	9	—	3
Georgia	28	—	28	—	1	19½	7½	28	—	28	—	28	—	—
Idaho	8	8	—	—	—	8	—	8	—	8	—	8	—	—
Illinois	58	10	48	—	45	13	—	12	15	13	20	12	36	6
Indiana	30	—	30	—	5	25	—	—	—	—	—	—	—	30
Iowa	26	—	26	—	13½	12½	—	26	—	26	—	—	—	—
Kansas	20	—	20	—	—	20	—	—	—	20	—	—	—	—
Kentucky	26	9½	16½	—	9½	16½	—	26	—	26	—	26	—	—
Louisiana	20	—	20	—	—	20	—	—	—	—	—	—	—	—
Maine	12	11	1	—	8	4	—	2	3½	2½	4½	1½	4½	—
Maryland	16	—	16	—	16	—	—	—	—	—	—	—	—	—
Massachusetts	36	8	28	—	35½	½	—	1½	33	2½	33½	2½	33½	—
Michigan	30	6	24	—	12½	16½	1	—	—	15	15	—	10	20
Minnesota	24	10	14	—	17	7	—	5	10	6	15	6	15	—
Mississippi	20	—	20	—	—	20	—	—	—	—	—	—	—	20
Missouri	36	2	34	—	10½	25½	—	36	—	36	—	—	—	36
Montana	8	—	8	—	1	7	—	7	1	7	—	7	1	—
Nebraska	16	—	16	—	3	13	—	1	—	13	3	1	—	—
Nevada	6	—	6	—	—	6	—	6	—	6	—	—	—	6
New Hampshire	8	8	—	—	2½	5½	—	—	—	4½	3½	3	3½	—
New Jersey	28	—	28	—	28	—	—	—	—	—	28	—	28	—
New Mexico	6	—	6	—	1	5	—	6	—	6	—	6	—	—
New York	90	35	55	—	90	—	—	—	90	2	88	2	88	—
North Carolina	24	6	18	—	3 17/20	20 3/20	—	24	—	17	—	3	—	—
North Dakota	10	1	9	—	10	—	—	10	—	5	5	5	5	—
Ohio	48	48	—	—	32½	15½	—	—	—	—	—	—	20½	17
Oklahoma	20	—	20	—	—	20	—	20	—	—	—	—	—	20
Oregon	10	1	9	—	—	10	—	10	—	10	—	10	—	—
Pennsylvania	76	52	22	2	49½	24½	2	25½	35½	25½	38½	25½	39½	—
Rhode Island	10	—	10	—	10	—	—	—	10	—	10	—	10	—
South Carolina	18	18	—	—	—	18	—	18	—	18	—	18	—	—
South Dakota	10	—	10	—	6	4	—	10	—	9	—	9	—	—
Tennessee	24	15	9	—	3	21	—	24	—	24	—	24	—	—
Texas	40	—	40	—	—	40	—	40	—	40	—	40	—	—
Utah	8	5½	2½	—	4	4	—	8	—	8	—	8	—	—
Vermont	8	2	6	—	8	—	—	1	7	1	7	—	8	—
Virginia	24	24	—	—	2½	21½	—	—	—	—	—	—	—	—
Washington	14	—	14	—	—	14	—	14	—	14	—	14	—	—
West Virginia	16	16	—	—	7	9	—	—	—	—	—	—	—	1
Wisconsin	26	4	22	—	25	1	—	3	23	3	23	1	23	—
Wyoming	6	3	3	—	2	4	—	—	—	1	4½	—	3	—
Alaska	6	—	5	—	6	—	—	1	3	1	3	—	5	—
Canal Zone	6	—	6	—	2	4	—	6	—	6	—	3	3	—
District of Columbia	6	—	6	—	6	—	—	6	—	6	—	6	—	—
Hawaii	6	—	6	—	4	2	—	1	1	1	1	1	—	—
Philippine Islands	6	2	4	—	2	2	2	3	3	3	3	2	2	—
Puerto Rico	6	1	5	—	2	4	—	—	—	—	—	—	1	—
Virgin Islands	—	—	—	—	—	—	—	—	—	—	—	—	—	—
Total	1098	353½	742½	2	542 7/20	543 3/20	12½	431½	241	461½	320½	314	354½	159½

1. Other candidates: Oscar W. Underwood, 42½; Joseph T. Robinson, 21; Willard Saulsbury, 7; Samuel M. Ralston, 30; Jonathan M. Davis, 20; Albert C. Ritchie, 22½; Woodbridge N. Ferris, 30; James M. Cox, 59; Charles W. Bryan, 18; Fred H. Brown, 17; George S. Silzer, 38; Carter Glass, 25; John W. Davis, 31; William E. Sweet, 12; Patrick Harrison, 43½; Houston Thompson, 1; John B. Kendrick, 6.

2. Other candidates: John W. Davis, 64; Ralston, 58; Underwood, 42½; Robinson, 44; Glass, 24; Cox, 54; Ritchie, 16½; Saulsbury, 6; Thomas J. Walsh, 1; Jonathan M. Davis, 2; Owen, 4.

3. Other candidates: Underwood, 42½; Robinson, 20; John W. Davis, 65½; Glass, 30½; Ritchie, 16½; Saulsbury, 6; Walsh, 5; Bryan, 15; Jonathan M. Davis, 22; Josephus Daniels, 19; Edwin T. Meredith, 26; not voting, 2.

1924 Democratic

(Narrative, p. 496)

Delegation	100th Pres. Ballot[4]			101st Pres. Ballot[5]				102nd Pres. Ballot[6]			103rd Pres. Ballot[7] (Before shift)		103rd Pres. Ballot[8] (After shift)	
	McAdoo	Smith	Davis	Underwood	Smith	Davis	Meredith	Underwood	Davis	Walsh	Underwood	Davis	Underwood	Davis
Alabama	—	—	—	24	—	—	—	24	—	—	24	—	—	24
Arizona	3	—	—	3	—	—	—	3	—	—	3	—	3	—
Arkansas	—	—	—	—	—	—	—	—	—	—	—	—	—	—
California	16½	—	—	—	1	—	3	—	—	26	2	2	—	26
Colorado	½	3½	1½	1	3	2½	1	6½	1½	—	5	3	5	3
Connecticut	2	12	—	11	—	1	—	11	—	3	11	—	—	14
Delaware	—	—	—	—	—	6	—	—	—	—	6	—	6	—
Florida	9	—	3	—	—	3	—	—	5	4	—	6	—	6
Georgia	28	—	—	—	—	5	12	1	13	—	—	27	—	27
Idaho	—	—	—	—	—	—	—	—	—	8	—	8	—	8
Illinois	—	35	6	20	—	4	13	20	3	13	19	19	—	58
Indiana	—	—	14	3	—	10	6	10	10	—	5	25	5	25
Iowa	—	—	—	—	—	—	26	—	—	—	—	—	—	26
Kansas	—	—	20	—	—	20	—	—	20	—	—	20	—	20
Kentucky	12	—	8½	1	1	9	½	1	9	6½	1	22½	—	26
Louisiana	—	—	20	—	—	20	—	—	20	—	—	20	—	20
Maine	1	2	8	5	—	6	—	8	4	—	10	2	10	2
Maryland	—	—	—	—	—	16	—	—	16	—	—	16	—	16
Massachusetts	2½	33½	—	—	33	—	—	8	½	2	23½	2	23½	2
Michigan	—	10	15	10	—	12	1	14	16	—	—	29½	—	29½
Minnesota	6	15	1	—	15	1	—	14	2	1	16	3	16	3
Mississippi	—	—	—	—	—	20	—	—	20	—	—	20	—	20
Missouri	—	—	36	—	—	36	—	—	36	—	—	36	—	36
Montana	1	—	—	—	—	—	—	—	—	8	—	—	—	—
Nebraska	—	2	—	—	1	—	11	2	—	4	2	1	2	1
Nevada	—	6	—	—	—	—	—	—	—	6	—	6	—	6
New Hampshire	—	1	2	—	1	1	1½	—	3½	4½	—	3½	—	3½
New Jersey	—	28	—	16	—	—	—	16	2	—	16	1	16	1
New Mexico	6	—	—	—	1½	1	1	—	2½	—	—	2	—	2
New York	2	88	—	86½	—	—	—	84	1	1	44	4	—	60
North Carolina	—	—	—	1	—	20	1	1	23	—	5½	18½	—	24
North Dakota	3	5	—	—	5	—	1	5	—	5	—	—	—	—
Ohio	—	15	23	5	10	23	5	7	25	—	4	41	1	46
Oklahoma	—	—	—	—	—	—	—	—	20	—	—	20	—	20
Oregon	10	—	—	—	1	2	1	1	2	—	1	5	1	5
Pennsylvania	17½	39½	9	6	36½	19½	1	32½	29½	4	31½	37½	—	76
Rhode Island	—	10	—	10	—	—	—	10	—	—	—	10	—	10
South Carolina	18	—	—	—	—	18	—	—	18	—	—	18	—	18
South Dakota	—	—	—	—	—	—	—	2	—	—	2	—	2	—
Tennessee	6	—	8	1	—	15	—	—	19	—	—	19	—	19
Texas	40	—	—	—	—	—	40	—	40	—	—	40	—	40
Utah	—	—	4	—	—	4	—	—	4	4	—	8	—	8
Vermont	—	8	—	4	—	4	—	4	4	—	—	8	—	8
Virginia	—	—	—	—	—	12	—	—	12	—	—	12	—	24
Washington	—	—	—	—	—	—	—	—	—	14	—	14	—	14
West Virginia	—	—	16	—	—	16	—	—	16	—	—	16	—	16
Wisconsin	—	22	—	8	9	—	1	11	—	9	8	1	1	22
Wyoming	—	3	½	—	3	3	—	—	6	—	—	6	—	6
Alaska	—	6	—	6	—	—	—	6	—	—	2	4	2	4
Canal Zone	3	3	—	—	—	—	3	3	3	—	—	6	—	6
District of Columbia	—	—	—	—	—	—	—	—	6	—	6	—	6	—
Hawaii	1	1	3	1	1	4	—	1	4	—	1	4	1	4
Philippine Islands	2	2	—	5	—	—	1	5	—	—	1	4	1	4
Puerto Rico	—	1	5	1	—	5	—	1	5	—	1	5	1	5
Virgin Islands	—	—	—	—	—	—	—	—	—	—	—	—	—	—
Total	190	351½	203½	229½	121	316	130	317	415½	123	250½	575½	102½	844

4. Other candidates: Underwood, 41½; Robinson, 46; Bryan, 2; Saulsbury, 6; Walsh, 52½; Owen, 20; Ritchie, 17½; Meredith 75½; David F. Houston, 9; Glass, 35; Daniels, 24; Newton D. Baker, 4; George L. Berry, 1; James W. Gerard, 19; not voting, 9.

5. Other candidates: Robinson, 22½; William G. McAdoo, 52; Walsh, 98; Ritchie, ½; Berry, 1; A. A. Murphree, 4; Houston, 9; Owen, 23; Cummings, 9; Glass, 59; Gerard, 16; Baker, 1; Daniels, 24; Cordell Hull, 2; not voting, 3½.

6. Other candidates: Robinson, 21; McAdoo, 21; Alfred E. Smith, 44; Thompson, 1; Ritchie, ½; Bryan, 1; Gerard, 7; Glass, 67; Cordell Daniels, 2; Berry, 1½; Meredith, 66½; Henry T. Allen, 1; Hull, 1; not voting, 8.

7. Other candidates: McAdoo, 14½; Robinson, 21; Meredith, 42½; Glass, 79; Hull, 1; Smith, 10½; Daniels, 1; Gerard, 8; Thompson, 1; Walsh, 84½, not voting, 9.

8. Other candidates: Robinson, 20; McAdoo, 11½; Smith, 7½; Walsh, 58; Meredith, 15½; Glass, 23; Gerard, 7; Hull, 1; not voting, 8.

1924 Republican

(Narrative, p. 495)

Delegation	Total Votes	First Pres. Ballot[1] Coolidge
Alabama	16	16
Arizona	9	9
Arkansas	14	14
California	29	29
Colorado	15	15
Connecticut	17	17
Delaware	9	9
Florida	10	10
Georgia	18	18
Idaho	11	11
Illinois	61	61
Indiana	33	33
Iowa	29	29
Kansas	23	23
Kentucky	26	26
Louisiana	13	13
Maine	15	15
Maryland	19	19
Massachusetts	39	39
Michigan	33	33
Minnesota	27	27
Mississippi	12	12
Missouri	39	39
Montana	11	11
Nebraska	19	19
Nevada	9	9
New Hampshire	11	11
New Jersey	31	31
New Mexico	9	9
New York	91	91
North Carolina	22	22
North Dakota	13	7
Ohio	51	51
Oklahoma	23	23
Oregon	13	13
Pennsylvania	79	79
Rhode Island	13	13
South Carolina	11	11
South Dakota	13	3
Tennessee	27	27
Texas	23	23
Utah	11	11
Vermont	11	11
Virginia	17	17
Washington	17	17
West Virginia	19	19
Wisconsin	29	1
Wyoming	9	9
Alaska	2	2
District of Columbia	2	2
Hawaii	2	2
Philippine Islands	2	2
Puerto Rico	2	2
Total	1109	1065

1. Other candidates: Robert M. La Follette, 34; Hiram W. Johnson, 10.

1928 Republican

(Narrative, p. 498)

Delegation	Total Votes	First Pres. Ballot[1] Hoover
Alabama	15	15
Arizona	9	9
Arkansas	11	11
California	29	29
Colorado	15	15
Connecticut	17	17
Delaware	9	9
Florida	10	9
Georgia	16	15
Idaho	11	11
Illinois	61	24
Indiana	33	—
Iowa	29	7
Kansas	23	—
Kentucky	29	29
Louisiana	12	11
Maine	15	15
Maryland	19	19
Massachusetts	39	39
Michigan	33	33
Minnesota	27	11
Mississippi	12	12
Missouri	39	28
Montana	11	10
Nebraska	19	11
Nevada	9	9
New Hampshire	11	11
New Jersey	31	31
New Mexico	9	7
New York	90	90
North Carolina	20	17
North Dakota	13	4
Ohio	51	36
Oklahoma	20	—
Oregon	13	13
Pennsylvania	79	79
Rhode Island	13	12
South Carolina	11	11
South Dakota	13	2
Tennessee	19	19
Texas	26	26
Utah	11	9
Vermont	11	11
Virginia	15	15
Washington	17	17
West Virginia	19	1
Wisconsin	26	9
Wyoming	9	9
Alaska	2	2
District of Columbia	2	2
Hawaii	2	2
Philippine Islands	2	2
Puerto Rico	2	2
Total	1089	837

1. Other candidates: Frank O. Lowden, 74; Charles Curtis, 64; James E. Watson, 45; George W. Norris, 24; Guy D. Goff, 18; Calvin Coolidge, 17; Charles G. Dawes, 4; Charles E. Hughes, 1; not voting, 5.

1928 Democratic

(Narrative, p. 499)

Delegation	Total Votes	First Pres. Ballot[1] (Before shift) Smith	First Pres. Ballot[2] (After shift) Smith
Alabama	24	1	1
Arizona	6	6	6
Arkansas	17	17	17
California	26	26	26
Colorado	12	12	12
Connecticut	14	14	14
Delaware	6	6	6
Florida	12	—	—
Georgia	28	—	—
Idaho	8	8	8
Illinois	58	56	56
Indiana	30	—	25
Iowa	26	26	26
Kansas	20	—	11½
Kentucky	26	26	26
Louisiana	20	20	20
Maine	12	12	12
Maryland	16	16	16
Massachusetts	36	36	36
Michigan	30	30	30
Minnesota	24	24	24
Mississippi	20	—	9½
Missouri	36	—	—
Montana	8	8	8
Nebraska	16	—	12
Nevada	6	6	6
New Hampshire	8	8	8
New Jersey	28	28	28
New Mexico	6	6	6
New York	90	90	90
North Carolina	24	4⅔	4⅔
North Dakota	10	10	10
Ohio	48	1	45
Oklahoma	20	10	10
Oregon	10	10	10
Pennsylvania	76	70½	70½
Rhode Island	10	10	10
South Carolina	18	—	—
South Dakota	10	10	10
Tennessee	24	—	23
Texas	40	—	—
Utah	8	8	8
Vermont	8	8	8
Virginia	24	6	6
Washington	14	14	14
West Virginia	16	10½	10½
Wisconsin	26	26	26
Wyoming	6	6	6
Alaska	6	6	6
Canal Zone	6	6	6
District of Columbia	6	6	6
Hawaii	6	6	6
Philippine Islands	6	6	6
Puerto Rico	6	6	6
Virgin Islands	2	2	2
Total	1100	724⅔	849⅙

1. Other candidates: Cordell Hull, 71⅚; Walter F. George, 52½; James A. Reed, 48; Atlee Pomerene, 47; Jesse H. Jones, 43; Evans Woollen, 32; Patrick Harrison, 20; William A. Ayres, 20; Richard C. Watts, 18; Gilbert M. Hitchcock, 16; Vic Donahey, 5; Houston Thompson, 2.

2. Other candidates: George, 52½; Reed, 52; Hull, 50⅚; Jones, 43; Watts, 18; Harrison, 8½; Woollen, 7; Donahey, 5; Ayres, 3; Pomerene, 3; Hitchcock, 2; Thompson, 2; Theodore G. Bilbo, 1; not voting, 2½.

1932 Republican

(Narrative, p. 501)

Delegation	Total Votes	Repeal of Prohibition Plank		First Pres. Ballot[1]
		Yea	Nay	Hoover
Alabama	19	—	19	19
Arizona	9	9	—	9
Arkansas	15	—	15	15
California	47	6	41	47
Colorado	15	1	14	15
Connecticut	19	19	—	19
Delaware	9	—	9	9
Florida	16	—	16	16
Georgia	16	2	14	16
Idaho	11	—	11	11
Illinois	61	45	15½	54½
Indiana	31	28	3	31
Iowa	25	3	22	25
Kansas	21	4	17	21
Kentucky	25	15	10	25
Louisiana	12	—	12	12
Maine	13	5	8	13
Maryland	19	—	19	19
Massachusetts	34	16	17	34
Michigan	41	25½	15½	41
Minnesota	25	—	25	25
Mississippi	11	11	—	11
Missouri	33	8½	23¾	33
Montana	11	—	11	11
Nebraska	17	1	16	17
Nevada	9	8	1	9
New Hampshire	11	—	11	11
New Jersey	35	35	—	35
New Mexico	9	2	7	8
New York	97	76	21	97
North Carolina	28	3	25	28
North Dakota	11	—	11	9
Ohio	55	12⅔	42⅔	55
Oklahoma	25	—	25	25
Oregon	13	3	10	9
Pennsylvania	75	51	23	73
Rhode Island	8	8	—	8
South Carolina	10	—	10	10
South Dakota	11	3	8	11
Tennessee	24	1	23	24
Texas	49	—	49	49
Utah	11	1	10	11
Vermont	9	9	—	9
Virginia	25	—	25	25
Washington	19	11	8	19
West Virginia	19	4	15	19
Wisconsin	27	22	5	15
Wyoming	9	9	—	9
Alaska	2	—	2	2
District of Columbia	2	—	2	2
Hawaii	2	2	—	2
Philippine Islands	2	1	1	2
Puerto Rico	2	—	2	2
Total	1154	460⅔	690¹⁹⁄₃₆	1126½

1. Other candidates: John J. Blaine, 13; Calvin Coolidge, 4½; Joseph I. France, 4; Charles G. Dawes, 1; James W. Wadsworth, 1; not voting, 4.

1932 Democratic

(Narrative, p. 502)

Delegation	Total Votes	Louisiana Credentials			Minnesota Credentials			Permanent Organization		First Pres. Ballot[1]		Second Pres. Ballot[2]		Third Pres. Ballot[3]		Fourth Pres. Ballot[4]	
		Yea	Nay	Not Voting	Yea	Nay	Not Voting	Yea	Nay	Roosevelt	Smith	Roosevelt	Smith	Roosevelt	Smith	Roosevelt	Smith
Ala.	24	—	24	—	—	24	—	4½	19½	24	—	24	—	24	—	24	—
Ariz.	6	—	6	—	—	6	—	—	6	6	—	6	—	6	—	6	—
Ark.	18	—	18	—	—	18	—	—	18	18	—	18	—	18	—	18	—
Calif.	44	44	—	—	44	—	—	44	—	—	—	—	—	—	—	44	—
Colo.	12	—	12	—	—	12	—	—	12	12	—	12	—	12	—	12	—
Conn.	16	9½	6½	—	9¼	6¾	—	9½	6½	—	16	—	16	—	16	—	16
Del.	6	1	5	—	—	6	—	1	5	6	—	6	—	6	—	6	—
Fla.	14	3	11	—	—	14	—	—	14	14	—	14	—	14	—	14	—
Ga.	28	—	28	—	—	28	—	—	28	28	—	28	—	28	—	28	—
Idaho	8	—	8	—	—	8	—	—	8	8	—	8	—	8	—	8	—
Ill.	58	50¼	7¾	—	48	10	—	42	16	15¼	2¼	15¼	2¼	15¼	2¼	58	—
Ind.	30	30	—	—	30	—	—	30	—	14	2	16	2	16	2	30	—
Iowa	26	13	13	—	—	26	—	10	16	26	—	26	—	26	—	26	—
Kan.	20	—	20	—	—	20	—	6½	13½	20	—	20	—	20	—	20	—
Ky.	26	—	26	—	—	26	—	—	26	26	—	26	—	26	—	26	—
La.	20	—	20	—	—	20	—	—	20	20	—	20	—	20	—	20	—
Maine	12	6	6	—	6	6	—	7	5	12	—	12	—	12	—	12	—
Md.	16	16	—	—	16	—	—	16	—	—	—	—	—	—	—	—	16
Mass.	36	36	—	—	36	—	—	36	—	—	36	—	36	—	36	—	36
Mich.	38	—	38	—	—	38	—	—	38	38	—	38	—	38	—	38	—
Minn.	24	1	23	—	1	23	—	3	21	24	—	24	—	24	—	24	—
Miss.	20	—	20	—	—	20	—	—	20	20	—	20	—	20	—	20	—
Mo.	36	19½	19½	—	16½	19½	—	16½	10½	12	—	18	—	20½	—	36	—
Mont.	8	—	8	—	—	8	—	—	8	8	—	8	—	8	—	8	—
Neb.	16	—	16	—	—	16	—	1	15	16	—	16	—	16	—	16	—
Nev.	6	—	6	—	—	6	—	—	6	6	—	6	—	6	—	6	—
N.H.	8	—	8	—	—	8	—	—	8	8	—	8	—	8	—	8	—
N.J.	32	32	—	—	32	—	—	32	—	—	32	—	32	—	32	—	32
N.M.	6	—	6	—	—	6	—	3	3	6	—	6	—	6	—	6	—
N.Y.	94	65	29	—	65	29	—	67	27	28½	65½	29½	64½	31	63	31	63
N.C.	26	20½	5½	—	—	26	—	4	22	26	—	26	—	25 4/100	—	26	—
N.D.	10	—	10	—	2½	7½	—	1	9	9	—	10	—	9	—	10	—
Ohio	52	40	11	1	48½	2½	1	49½	2½	—	—	½	—	2½	—	29	17
Okla.	22	22	—	—	22	—	—	22	—	—	—	—	—	—	—	22	—
Ore.	10	—	10	—	—	10	—	1	9	10	—	10	—	10	—	10	—
Pa.	76	20½	55½	—	25	49	2	27½	48½	44½	30	44½	23½	45½	21	49	14½
R.I.	10	10	—	—	10	—	—	10	—	—	10	—	10	—	10	—	10
S.C.	18	—	18	—	—	18	—	—	18	18	—	18	—	18	—	18	—
S.D.	10	—	10	—	—	10	—	—	10	10	—	10	—	10	—	10	—
Tenn.	24	—	24	—	—	24	—	—	24	24	—	24	—	24	—	24	—
Texas	46	46	—	—	46	—	—	46	—	—	—	—	—	—	—	46	—
Utah	8	—	8	—	—	8	—	—	8	8	—	8	—	8	—	8	—
Vt.	8	—	8	—	—	8	—	—	8	8	—	8	—	8	—	8	—
Va.	24	24	—	—	24	—	—	24	—	—	—	—	—	—	—	24	—
Wash.	16	—	16	—	—	16	—	—	16	16	—	16	—	16	—	16	—
W.Va.	16	—	16	—	3	13	—	—	16	16	—	16	—	16	—	16	—
Wis.	26	2	24	—	2	24	—	2	24	24	2	24	2	24	2	24	2
Wyo.	6	—	6	—	—	6	—	—	6	6	—	6	—	6	—	6	—
Alaska	6	—	6	—	—	6	—	6	—	5	—	6	—	6	—	6	—
Canal Z.	6	—	6	—	—	6	—	—	6	6	—	6	—	6	—	6	—
D.C.	6	—	6	—	—	6	—	—	6	6	—	6	—	6	—	6	—
Hawaii	6	—	6	—	—	6	—	—	6	6	—	6	—	6	—	6	—
Phil. Is.	6	6	—	—	6	—	—	6	—	—	6	—	6	—	6	—	6
P.R.	6	—	6	—	—	6	—	—	6	6	—	6	—	6	—	6	—
Vir. Is.	2	—	2	—	—	2	—	—	2	—	—	—	—	—	—	—	—
Total	1154	514¼	638¾	1	492¾	658¼	3	528	626	666¼	201¾	677¾	194¼	682 79/100	190¼	945	190½

1. Other candidates: John N. Garner, 90¼; Harry F. Byrd, 25; Melvin A. Traylor, 42¼; Albert C. Ritchie, 21; James A. Reed, 24; George White, 52; William H. Murray, 23; Newton D. Baker, 8½.

2. Other candidates: Garner, 90¼; Byrd, 24; Traylor, 40¼; Ritchie, 23½; Reed, 18; White, 50½; Baker, 8; Will Rogers, 22; not voting, 5½.

3. Other candidates: Garner, 101¼; Byrd, 24 96/100; Traylor, 40¼; Richie, 23½; Reed, 27½; White, 52½; Baker, 8½; not voting, 2½.

4. Other candidates: Ritchie, 3½; White, 3; Baker, 5½; James M. Cox, 1; not voting, 5½.

1936 Republican

(Narrative, p. 504)

Delegation	Total Votes	First Pres. Ballot[1] Landon
Alabama	13	13
Arizona	6	6
Arkansas	11	11
California	44	44
Colorado	12	12
Connecticut	19	19
Delaware	9	9
Florida	12	12
Georgia	14	14
Idaho	8	8
Illinois	57	57
Indiana	28	28
Iowa	22	22
Kansas	18	18
Kentucky	22	22
Louisiana	12	12
Maine	13	13
Maryland	16	16
Massachusetts	33	33
Michigan	38	38
Minnesota	22	22
Mississippi	11	11
Missouri	30	30
Montana	8	8
Nebraska	14	14
Nevada	6	6
New Hampshire	11	11
New Jersey	32	32
New Mexico	6	6
New York	90	90
North Carolina	23	23
North Dakota	8	8
Ohio	52	52
Oklahoma	21	21
Oregon	10	10
Pennsylvania	75	75
Rhode Island	8	8
South Carolina	10	10
South Dakota	8	8
Tennessee	17	17
Texas	25	25
Utah	8	8
Vermont	9	9
Virginia	17	17
Washington	16	16
West Virginia	16	15
Wisconsin	24	6
Wyoming	6	6
Alaska	3	3
District of Columbia	3	3
Hawaii	3	3
Philippine Islands	2	2
Puerto Rico	2	2
Total	1003	984

1. Other candidates: William E. Borah, 19.

1940 Democratic

(Narrative, p. 507)

Delegation	Total Votes	First Pres. Ballot[1] Roosevelt
Alabama	22	20
Arizona	6	6
Arkansas	18	18
California	44	43
Colorado	12	12
Connecticut	16	16
Delaware	6	6
Florida	14	12½
Georgia	24	24
Idaho	8	8
Illinois	58	58
Indiana	28	28
Iowa	22	22
Kansas	18	18
Kentucky	22	22
Louisiana	20	20
Maine	10	10
Maryland	16	7½
Massachusetts	34	21½
Michigan	38	38
Minnesota	22	22
Mississippi	18	18
Missouri	30	26½
Montana	8	8
Nebraska	14	13
Nevada	6	2
New Hampshire	8	8
New Jersey	32	32
New Mexico	6	6
New York	94	64½
North Carolina	26	26
North Dakota	8	8
Ohio	52	52
Oklahoma	22	22
Oregon	10	10
Pennsylvania	72	72
Rhode Island	8	8
South Carolina	16	16
South Dakota	8	3
Tennessee	22	22
Texas	46	—
Utah	8	8
Vermont	6	6
Virginia	22	5¹⁴⁄₁₅
Washington	16	15
West Virginia	16	12
Wisconsin	24	21
Wyoming	6	6
Alaska	6	—
Canal Zone	6	—
District of Columbia	6	6
Hawaii	6	6
Philippine Islands	6	6
Puerto Rico	6	3
Virgin Islands	2	2
Total	1100	946¹³⁄₃₀

1. Other candidates: James A. Farley, 72⁹⁄₁₀; John N. Garner; 61; Millard E. Tydings, 9½; Cordell Hull, 5⅔; not voting, 4½.

1940 Republican

(Narrative, p. 506)

Delegation	Total Votes	First Pres. Ballot[1] Dewey	Taft	Willkie	Fourth Pres. Ballot[2] Dewey	Taft	Willkie	Fifth Pres. Ballot[3] Taft	Willkie	Sixth (before shift)[4] Taft	Willkie	Sixth (after shift)[5] Willkie
Alabama	13	7	6	—	7	5	1	7	5	7	6	13
Arizona	6	—	—	—	—	—	6	—	6	—	6	6
Arkansas	12	2	7	2	3	7	2	10	2	10	2	12
California	44	7	7	7	9	11	10	12	9	22	17	44
Colorado	12	1	4	3	1	4	3	4	4	6	5	12
Connecticut	16	—	—	16	—	—	16	—	16	—	16	16
Delaware	6	—	1	3	—	—	6	—	6	—	6	6
Florida	12	6	1	—	9	2	—	3	7	2	10	12
Georgia	14	7	3	—	6	3	2	7	6	7	6	14
Idaho	8	8	—	—	8	—	—	7	—	6	2	8
Illinois	58	52	2	4	17	27	10	30	17	33	24	58
Indiana	28	7	7	9	5	6	15	7	20	5	23	28
Iowa	22	—	—	—	2	—	—	13	7	15	7	22
Kansas	18	—	—	—	11	2	5	—	18	—	18	18
Kentucky	22	12	8	—	9	13	—	22	—	22	—	22
Louisiana	12	5	5	—	6	6	—	12	—	12	—	12
Maine	13	—	—	—	2	2	9	—	13	—	13	13
Maryland	16	16	—	—	—	—	14	1	14	1	15	16
Massachusetts	34	—	—	1	—	2	28	2	28	2	30	34
Michigan	38	—	—	—	2	—	—	—	—	2	35	38
Minnesota	22	3	4	6	2	9	9	12	9	11	10	22
Mississippi	11	3	8	—	2	9	—	11	—	9	2	11
Missouri	30	10	3	6	4	3	18	7	21	4	26	30
Montana	8	8	—	—	3	3	2	4	4	4	4	8
Nebraska	14	14	—	—	2	5	5	9	5	6	8	14
Nevada	6	—	2	2	—	1	4	2	4	2	4	6
New Hampshire	8	—	—	—	—	—	4	2	6	2	6	8
New Jersey	32	20	—	12	6	1	23	1	26	—	32	32
New Mexico	6	3	1	2	1	1	4	2	4	1	5	6
New York	92	61	—	8	48	5	35	10	75	7	78	92
North Carolina	23	9	7	2	6	6	9	11	12	8	15	23
North Dakota	8	2	1	1	2	1	3	4	4	4	4	8
Ohio	52	—	52	—	—	52	—	52	—	52	—	52
Oklahoma	22	22	—	—	10	6	3	18	4	5	17	22
Oregon	10	—	—	—	1	—	1	—	1	3	7	10
Pennsylvania	72	1	—	1	—	—	19	—	21	—	72	72
Rhode Island	8	1	3	3	—	4	4	4	4	3	5	8
South Carolina	10	10	—	—	8	—	2	—	9	—	10	10
South Dakota	8	—	—	—	4	1	—	7	1	2	6	8
Tennessee	18	8	3	2	5	6	5	9	6	5	10	17
Texas	26	—	26	—	—	26	—	26	—	26	—	26
Utah	8	2	2	1	2	2	1	3	5	1	7	8
Vermont	9	1	3	3	1	3	5	3	6	2	7	9
Virginia	18	2	9	5	—	7	11	7	11	2	16	18
Washington	16	13	3	—	12	3	—	16	—	4	10	16
West Virginia	16	8	5	3	6	3	7	9	6	—	15	15
Wisconsin	24	24	—	—	24	—	—	—	—	2	20	24
Wyoming	6	1	1	2	3	2	1	3	3	—	6	6
Alaska	3	1	2	—	—	2	1	3	—	1	2	3
District of Columbia	3	2	1	—	—	1	2	1	2	—	3	3
Hawaii	3	—	—	—	—	—	—	1	1	—	3	3
Philippine Islands	2	—	1	1	—	1	1	1	1	—	2	2
Puerto Rico	2	1	1	—	1	1	—	2	—	—	2	2
Total	1000	360	189	105	250	254	306	377	429	318	655	998

1. Other candidate: Arthur H. Vandenberg, 76; Arthur H. James, 74; Joseph W. Martin, 44; Hanford MacNider, 34; Frank E. Gannett, 33; H. Styles Bridges, 28; Arthur Capper, 18; Herbert Hoover, 17; Charles L. McNary, 13; Harlan J. Bushfield, 9.

2. Other candidates: Vandenberg, 61; James, 56; Hoover, 31; MacNider, 26; McNary, 8; Gannett, 4; Bridges, 1; not voting, 3.

3. Other candidates: James, 59; Thomas E. Dewey, 57; Vandenberg, 42; Hoover, 20; McNary, 9; MacNider, 4; Gannett, 1; not voting, 2.

4. Other candidates: Dewey, 11; Hoover, 10; Gannett, 1; McNary, 1; not voting, 4.

5. Not voting, 2.

1944 Republican

(Narrative, p. 508)

Delegation	Total Votes	First Pres. Ballot[1] Dewey
Alabama	14	14
Arizona	8	8
Arkansas	12	12
California	50	50
Colorado	15	15
Connecticut	16	16
Delaware	9	9
Florida	15	15
Georgia	14	14
Idaho	11	11
Illinois	59	59
Indiana	29	29
Iowa	23	23
Kansas	19	19
Kentucky	22	22
Louisiana	13	13
Maine	13	13
Maryland	16	16
Massachusetts	35	35
Michigan	41	41
Minnesota	25	25
Mississippi	6	6
Missouri	30	30
Montana	8	8
Nebraska	15	15
Nevada	6	6
New Hampshire	11	11
New Jersey	35	35
New Mexico	8	8
New York	93	93
North Carolina	25	25
North Dakota	11	11
Ohio	50	50
Oklahoma	23	23
Oregon	15	15
Pennsylvania	70	70
Rhode Island	8	8
South Carolina	4	4
South Dakota	11	11
Tennessee	19	19
Texas	33	33
Utah	8	8
Vermont	9	9
Virginia	19	19
Washington	16	16
West Virginia	19	19
Wisconsin	24	23
Wyoming	9	9
Alaska	3	3
District of Columbia	3	3
Hawaii	5	5
Philippine Islands	2	—
Puerto Rico	2	2
Total	1059	1056

1. Other candidates: Douglas MacArthur, 1; absent, 2.

1944 Democratic

(Narrative, p. 509)

Delegation	Total Votes	First Pres. Ballot[1] Roosevelt
Alabama	24	22
Arizona	10	10
Arkansas	20	20
California	52	52
Colorado	12	12
Connecticut	18	18
Delaware	8	8
Florida	18	14
Georgia	26	26
Idaho	10	10
Illinois	58	58
Indiana	26	26
Iowa	20	20
Kansas	16	16
Kentucky	24	24
Louisiana	22	—
Maine	10	10
Maryland	18	18
Massachusetts	34	34
Michigan	38	38
Minnesota	24	24
Mississippi	20	—
Missouri	32	32
Montana	10	10
Nebraska	12	12
Nevada	8	8
New Hampshire	10	10
New Jersey	34	34
New Mexico	10	10
New York	96	94½
North Carolina	30	30
North Dakota	8	8
Ohio	52	52
Oklahoma	22	22
Oregon	14	14
Pennsylvania	72	72
Rhode Island	10	10
South Carolina	18	14½
South Dakota	8	8
Tennessee	26	26
Texas	48	36
Utah	10	10
Vermont	6	6
Virginia	24	—
Washington	18	18
West Virginia	18	17
Wisconsin	26	26
Wyoming	8	8
Alaska	6	6
Canal Zone	6	6
District of Columbia	6	6
Hawaii	6	6
Philippine Islands	6	6
Puerto Rico	6	6
Virgin Islands	2	2
Total	1176	1086

1. Other candidates: Harry F. Byrd, 89; James A. Farley, 1.

1948 Republican

(Narrative, p. 511)

Delegation	Total Votes	First Pres. Ballot[1]			Second Pres. Ballot[2]			Third Pres. Ballot
		Dewey	Stassen	Taft	Dewey	Stassen	Taft	Dewey
Alabama	14	9	—	5	9	—	5	14
Arizona	8	3	2	3	4	2	2	8
Arkansas	14	3	4	7	3	4	7	14
California	53	—	—	—	—	—	—	53
Colorado	15	3	5	7	3	8	4	15
Connecticut	19	—	—	—	—	—	—	19
Delaware	9	5	1	2	6	1	2	9
Florida	16	6	4	6	6	4	6	16
Georgia	16	12	1	—	13	1	—	16
Idaho	11	11	—	—	11	—	—	11
Illinois	56	—	—	—	5	—	50	56
Indiana	29	29	—	—	29	—	—	29
Iowa	23	3	13	5	13	7	2	23
Kansas	19	12	1	2	14	1	2	19
Kentucky	25	10	1	11	11	1	11	25
Louisiana	13	6	—	7	6	—	7	13
Maine	13	5	4	1	5	7	—	13
Maryland	16	8	3	5	13	—	3	16
Massachusetts	35	17	1	2	18	1	3	35
Michigan	41	—	—	—	—	—	—	41
Minnesota	25	—	25	—	—	25	—	25
Mississippi	8	—	—	8	—	—	8	8
Missouri	33	17	6	8	18	6	7	33
Montana	11	5	3	3	6	2	3	11
Nebraska	15	2	13	—	6	9	—	15
Nevada	9	6	1	2	6	1	2	9
New Hampshire	8	6	2	—	6	2	—	8
New Jersey	35	—	—	—	24	6	2	35
New Mexico	8	3	2	3	3	2	3	8
New York	97	96	—	1	96	—	1	97
North Carolina	26	16	2	5	17	2	4	26
North Dakota	11	—	11	—	—	11	—	11
Ohio	53	—	9	44	1	8	44	53
Oklahoma	20	18	—	1	19	—	1	20
Oregon	12	12	—	—	12	—	—	12
Pennsylvania	73	41	1	28	40	1	29	73
Rhode Island	8	1	—	1	4	—	2	8
South Carolina	6	—	—	6	—	—	6	6
South Dakota	11	3	8	—	7	4	—	11
Tennessee	22	6	—	—	8	—	13	22
Texas	33	2	1	30	2	2	29	33
Utah	11	5	2	4	6	2	3	11
Vermont	9	7	2	—	7	2	—	9
Virginia	21	10	—	10	13	—	7	21
Washington	19	14	2	1	14	2	3	19
West Virginia	16	11	5	—	13	3	—	16
Wisconsin	27	—	19	—	2	19	—	27
Wyoming	9	4	3	2	6	3	—	9
Alaska	3	2	—	1	3	—	—	3
District of Columbia	3	2	—	—	3	—	—	3
Hawaii	5	3	—	1	3	—	2	5
Puerto Rico	2	—	—	2	1	—	1	2
Total	1094	434	157	224	515	149	274	1094

1. Other candidates: Arthur H. Vandenberg, 62; Earl Warren, 59; Dwight H. Green, 56; Alfred E. Driscoll, 35; Raymond E. Baldwin, 19; Joseph W. Martin, 18; B. Carroll Reece, 15; Douglas MacArthur, 11; Everett M. Dirksen, 1; not voting, 3.
2. Other candidates: Vandenberg, 62; Warren, 57; Baldwin, 19; Martin, 10; MacArthur, 7; Reece, 1.

1948 Democratic

(Narrative, p. 512)

Delegation	Total Votes	Pro-Southern Amendment to Civil Rights Plank		Plank Endorsing Truman's Civil Rights Policy		First Pres. Ballot[1] (Before shift)		First Pres. Ballot[2] (After shift)	
		Yea	Nay	Yea	Nay	Truman	Russell	Truman	Russell
Alabama	26	26	—	—	26	—	26	—	26
Arizona	12	—	12	—	12	12	—	12	—
Arkansas	22	22	—	—	22	—	22	—	22
California	54	1½	52½	53	1	53½	—	54	—
Colorado	12	3	9	10	2	12	—	12	—
Connecticut	20	—	20	20	—	20	—	20	—
Delaware	10	—	10	—	10	10	—	10	—
Florida	20	20	—	—	20	—	19	—	20
Georgia	28	28	—	—	28	—	28	—	28
Idaho	12	—	12	—	12	12	—	12	—
Illinois	60	—	60	60	—	60	—	60	—
Indiana	26	—	26	17	9	25	—	26	—
Iowa	20	—	20	18	2	20	—	20	—
Kansas	16	—	16	16	—	16	—	16	—
Kentucky	26	—	26	—	26	26	—	26	—
Louisiana	24	24	—	—	24	—	24	—	24
Maine	10	—	10	3	7	10	—	10	—
Maryland	20	—	20	—	20	20	—	20	—
Massachusetts	36	—	36	36	—	36	—	36	—
Michigan	42	—	42	42	—	42	—	42	—
Minnesota	26	—	26	26	—	26	—	26	—
Mississippi	22	22	—	—	22	—	—	—	—
Missouri	34	—	34	—	34	34	—	34	—
Montana	12	—	12	1½	10½	12	—	12	—
Nebraska	12	—	12	3	9	12	—	12	—
Nevada	10	—	10	—	10	10	—	10	—
New Hampshire	12	—	12	1	11	11	—	11	—
New Jersey	36	—	36	36	—	36	—	36	—
New Mexico	12	—	12	—	12	12	—	12	—
New York	98	—	98	98	—	83	—	98	—
North Carolina	32	32	—	—	32	13	19	13	19
North Dakota	8	—	8	—	8	8	—	8	—
Ohio	50	—	50	39	11	50	—	50	—
Oklahoma	24	—	24	—	24	24	—	24	—
Oregon	16	3	13	7	9	16	—	16	—
Pennsylvania	74	—	74	74	—	74	—	74	—
Rhode Island	12	—	12	—	12	12	—	12	—
South Carolina	20	20	—	—	20	—	20	—	20
South Dakota	8	—	8	8	—	8	—	8	—
Tennessee	28	28	—	—	28	—	28	—	28
Texas	50	50	—	—	50	—	50	—	50
Utah	12	—	12	—	12	12	—	12	—
Vermont	6	—	6	6	—	5½	—	5½	—
Virginia	26	26	—	—	26	—	26	—	26
Washington	20	—	20	20	—	20	—	20	—
West Virginia	20	—	20	7	13	15	4	20	—
Wisconsin	24	—	24	24	—	24	—	24	—
Wyoming	6	1½	4½	4	2	6	—	6	—
Alaska	6	3	3	2	4	6	—	6	—
Canal Zone	2	—	2	—	2	2	—	2	—
District of Columbia	6	—	6	6	—	6	—	6	—
Hawaii	6	—	6	6	—	6	—	6	—
Puerto Rico	6	—	6	6	—	6	—	6	—
Virgin Islands	2	—	2	2	—	2	—	2	—
Total	1234	310[a]	924[b]	651½	582½	926	266	947½	263

1. Other candidates: Paul V. McNutt, 2½; James A. Roe, 15; Alben W. Barkley, 1; not voting, 23½.
2. Other candidates: McNutt, ½; not voting, 23.
a. Sum of column; proceedings record 309.
b. Sum of column; proceedings record 925.

1952 Republican

(Narrative, p. 515)

Delegation	Total Votes	Pro-Taft Amendment on Louisiana Delegates		Pro-Eisenhower Report on Georgia Delegates		First Pres. Ballot[1] (Before shift)		First Pres. Ballot[2] (After shift)	
		Yea	Nay	Yea	Nay	Eisenhower	Taft	Eisenhower	Taft
Alabama	14	9	5	5	9	5	9	14	—
Arizona	14	12	2	3	11	4	10	4	10
Arkansas	11	11	—	3	8	4	6	11	—
California	70	—	70	62	8	—	—	—	—
Colorado	18	1	17	17	1	15	2	17	1
Connecticut	22	2	20	21	1	21	1	22	—
Delaware	12	5	7	8	4	7	5	12	—
Florida	18	15	3	5	13	6	12	18	—
Georgia	17	17	—	—	—	14	2	16	1
Idaho	14	14	—	—	14	—	14	14	—
Illinois	60	58	2	1	59	1	59	1	59
Indiana	32	31	1	3	29	2	30	2	30
Iowa	26	11	15	16	10	16	10	20	6
Kansas	22	2	20	20	2	20	2	22	—
Kentucky	20	18	2	2	18	1	19	13	7
Louisiana	15	13	2	—	2	13	2	15	—
Maine	16	5	11	11	5	11	5	15	1
Maryland	24	5	19	15	9	16	8	24	—
Massachusetts	38	5	33	33	5	34	4	38	—
Michigan	46	1	45	32	14	35	11	35	11
Minnesota	28	—	28	28	—	9	—	28	—
Mississippi	5	5	—	—	5	—	5	5	—
Missouri	26	4	22	21	5	21	5	26	—
Montana	8	7	1	1	7	1	7	1	7
Nebraska	18	13	5	7	11	4	13	7	11
Nevada	12	7	5	2	10	5	7	10	2
New Hampshire	14	—	14	14	—	14	—	14	—
New Jersey	38	5	33	32	6	33	5	38	—
New Mexico	14	8	6	5	9	6	8	6	8
New York	96	1	95	92	4	92	4	95	1
North Carolina	26	14	12	10	16	12	14	26	—
North Dakota	14	11	3	3	11	4	8	5	8
Ohio	56	56	—	—	56	—	56	—	56
Oklahoma	16	10	6	4	12	4	7	8	4
Oregon	18	—	18	18	—	18	—	18	—
Pennsylvania	70	13	57	52	18	53	15	70	—
Rhode Island	8	2	6	6	2	6	1	8	—
South Carolina	6	5	1	1	5	2	4	6	—
South Dakota	14	14	—	—	14	—	14	7	7
Tennessee	20	20	—	—	20	—	20	20	—
Texas	38	22	16	—	—	33	5	38	—
Utah	14	14	—	—	14	—	14	14	—
Vermont	12	—	12	12	—	12	—	12	—
Virginia	23	13	10	7	16	9	14	19	4
Washington	24	4	20	19	5	20	4	21	3
West Virginia	16	15	1	1	15	1	14	3	13
Wisconsin	30	24	6	6	24	—	24	—	24
Wyoming	12	8	4	4	8	6	6	12	—
Alaska	3	3	—	—	3	1	2	3	—
Canal Zone	—	—	—	—	—	—	—	—	—
District of Columbia	6	6	—	—	6	—	6	6	—
Hawaii	8	7	1	3	5	3	4	4	4
Puerto Rico	3	2	1	1	2	—	3	1	2
Virgin Islands	1	—	1	1	—	1	—	1	—
Total	1206	548	658	607	531	595	500	845	280

1. Other candidates: Earl Warren, 81; Harold E. Stassen, 20; Douglas MacArthur, 10.
2. Other candidates: Warren, 77; MacArthur, 4.

1952 Democratic

(Narrative, p. 516)

Delegation	Total Votes	Seating Virginia Delegation			Table Motion to Adjourn			First Pres. Ballot[1]				Second Pres. Ballot[2]				Third Pres. Ballot[3]		
		Yea	Nay	Not Voting	Yea	Nay	Not Voting	Harriman	Kefauver	Russell	Stevenson	Harriman	Kefauver	Russell	Stevenson	Kefauver	Russell	Stevenson
Alabama	22	22	—	—	13½	8½	—	—	8	13	—	—	7½	14	½	7½	14	½
Arizona	12	12	—	—	12	—	—	—	—	12	—	—	—	12	—	—	12	—
Arkansas	22	22	—	—	19	3	—	—	—	—	—	1	1½	18	1½	1½	—	20½
California	68	4	61	3	—	68	—	—	68	—	—	—	68	—	—	68	—	—
Colorado	16	4½	11½	—	4	12	—	5	2	8½	½	5	5	2½	3½	4	3½	8½
Connecticut	16	—	16	—	16	—	—	—	—	—	16	—	—	—	16	—	—	16
Delaware	6	6	—	—	6	—	—	—	—	—	6	—	—	—	6	—	—	6
Florida	24	24	—	—	19	5	—	—	5	19	—	—	5	19	—	5	19	—
Georgia	28	28	—	—	28	—	—	—	—	28	—	—	—	28	—	—	28	—
Idaho	12	12	—	—	—	12	—	3½	3	1	1½	—	—	—	12	—	—	12
Illinois	60	52	8	—	53	7	—	1	3	—	53	—	3	—	54	3	—	54
Indiana	25	14½	6½	5	25	1	—	—	1	—	25	—	1	—	25	1	—	25
Iowa	24	17	7	—	8	15	1	½	8	2	8	½	8½	3	9½	8	3	10
Kansas	16	—	16	—	16	—	—	—	—	—	16	—	—	—	16	—	—	16
Kentucky	26	26	—	—	26	—	—	—	—	—	—	—	—	—	—	—	—	—
Louisiana	20	20	—	—	20	—	—	—	—	20	—	—	—	20	—	—	20	—
Maine	10	2½	7½	—	4½	5½	—	1½	1½	2½	3½	1	1	2½	4½	½	2½	7
Maryland	18	18	—	—	18	—	—	—	—	18	—	—	15½	2	—	8½	2½	6
Massachusetts	36	16	19	1	30	4½	1½	—	—	—	—	—	2½	—	—	5	1	25
Michigan	40	—	40	—	—	40	—	—	40	—	—	—	40	—	—	—	—	40
Minnesota	26	—	26	—	—	26	—	—	—	—	—	1½	17	—	7½	13	—	13
Mississippi	18	18	—	—	18	—	—	—	—	18	—	—	—	18	—	—	18	—
Missouri	34	34	—	—	29	5	—	1½	2	—	18	1½	2	—	19½	2	—	22
Montana	12	—	12	—	12	—	—	—	—	—	—	3	3	3	—	—	—	12
Nebraska	12	8	3	1	—	12	—	—	5	1	2	—	5	1	2	3	1	8
Nevada	10	10	—	—	9½	½	—	—	½	8	1	—	½	7½	2	½	7½	2
New Hampshire	8	1	7	—	—	8	—	—	8	—	—	—	8	—	—	8	—	—
New Jersey	32	—	32	—	24	8	—	1	3	—	28	—	4	—	28	4	—	28
New Mexico	12	12	—	—	12	—	—	1	1½	4	1	—	1½	6	4½	1½	3½	7
New York	94	7	87	—	5	89	—	83½	1	—	6½	84½	—	1	6½	4	—	86½
North Carolina	32	32	—	—	32	—	—	—	—	26	5½	—	—	24	7	—	24	7½
North Dakota	8	8	—	—	8	—	—	—	2	2	2	—	—	—	—	—	—	8
Ohio	54	33½	14½	6	26	28	—	1	29½	7	13	1	27½	8	17½	27	1	26
Oklahoma	24	24	—	—	24	—	—	—	—	—	—	—	—	—	—	—	—	—
Oregon	12	4	8	—	—	12	—	—	12	—	—	—	12	—	—	11	—	1
Pennsylvania	70	57	13	—	35	35	—	4½	22½	—	36	2½	21½	—	40	—	—	70
Rhode Island	12	10	2	—	10	2	—	1½	3½	—	5½	—	4	—	8	—	—	12
South Carolina	16	—	—	16	—	—	16	—	—	16	—	—	—	16	—	—	16	—
South Dakota	8	—	8	—	—	8	—	—	8	—	—	—	8	—	—	8	—	—
Tennessee	28	—	28	—	—	28	—	—	28	—	—	—	28	—	—	28	—	—
Texas	52	52	—	—	52	—	—	—	—	52	—	—	—	52	—	—	52	—
Utah	12	3	9	—	—	12	—	6½	½	2	½	9	1½	—	½	—	—	12
Vermont	6	—	6	—	6	—	—	—	—	½	5	—	½	½	5	—	½	5½
Virginia	28	—	—	28	28	—	—	—	—	28	—	—	—	28	—	—	28	—
Washington	22	12½	9½	—	3	10	—	—	12	½	6	2	12½	½	6	11	½	10½
West Virginia	20	13½	5	1½	10	9	1	—	5½	7	1	—	7½	6½	5½	7½	3½	9
Wisconsin	28	1	27	—	—	28	—	—	28	—	—	—	28	—	—	28	—	—
Wyoming	10	5½	4½	—	2½	7½	—	3½	1½	½	3	2½	3	—	4½	—	—	10
Alaska	6	—	6	—	—	6	—	—	6	—	—	—	6	—	—	6	—	—
Canal Zone	2	2	—	—	2	—	—	—	—	2	—	—	—	2	—	—	—	2
D.C.	6	—	6	—	—	6	—	6	—	—	—	6	—	—	—	—	—	6
Hawaii	6	—	6	—	4	2	—	1	1	—	—	—	1	—	5	1	—	5
Puerto Rico	6	2	4	—	1	5	—	—	—	—	6	—	—	—	6	—	—	6
Virgin Islands	2	—	2	—	—	2	—	—	1	—	1	—	1	—	1	—	—	2
Total	1230	650½	518	61½	671	539½a	19½	123½	340	268	273	121	362½	294	324½	275½	261	617½

1. Other candidates: Alben W. Barkley, 48½; Robert S. Kerr, 65; J. William Fulbright, 22; Paul H. Douglas, 3; Oscar R. Ewing, 4; Paul A. Dever, 37½; Hubert H. Humphrey, 26; James E. Murray, 12; Harry S. Truman, 6; William O. Douglas, ½; not voting, 1.

2. Other candidates: Barkley, 78½; Paul H. Douglas, 3; Kerr, 5½; Ewing, 3; Dever, 30½; Truman, 6; not voting, 1½.

3. Other candidates: Barkley, 67½; Paul H. Douglas, 3; Dever, ½; Ewing, 3; not voting, 2.

a. Sum of column; proceedings record 534.

1956 Democratic

(Narrative, p. 518)

Delegation	Total Votes	First Pres. Ballot[1]		
		Stevenson	Harriman	Other
Alabama	26	15½	—	10½
Arizona	16	16	—	—
Arkansas	26	26	—	—
California	68	68	—	—
Colorado	20	13½	6	½
Connecticut	20	20	—	—
Delaware	10	10	—	—
Florida	28	25	—	3
Georgia	32	—	—	32
Idaho	12	12	—	—
Illinois	64	53½	8½	2
Indiana	26	21½	3	1½
Iowa	24	16½	7	½
Kansas	16	16	—	—
Kentucky	30	—	—	30
Louisiana	24	24	—	—
Maine	14	10½	3½	—
Maryland	18	18	—	—
Massachusetts	40	32	7½	½
Michigan	44	39	5	—
Minnesota	30	19	11	—
Mississippi	22	—	—	22
Missouri	38	—	—	38
Montana	16	10	6	—
Nebraska	12	12	—	—
Nevada	14	5½	7	1½
New Hampshire	8	5½	1½	1
New Jersey	36	36	—	—
New Mexico	16	12	3½	½
New York	98	5½	92½	—
North Carolina	36	34½	1	½
North Dakota	8	8	—	—
Ohio	58	52	½	5½
Oklahoma	28	—	28	—
Oregon	16	16	—	—
Pennsylvania	74	67	7	—
Rhode Island	16	16	—	—
South Carolina	20	2	—	18
South Dakota	8	8	—	—
Tennessee	32	32	—	—
Texas	56	—	—	56
Utah	12	12	—	—
Vermont	6	5½	½	—
Virginia	32	—	—	32
Washington	26	19½	6	½
West Virginia	24	24	—	—
Wisconsin	28	22½	5	½
Wyoming	14	14	—	—
Alaska	6	6	—	—
Canal Zone	3	3	—	—
District of Columbia	6	6	—	—
Hawaii	6	6	—	—
Puerto Rico	6	6	—	—
Virgin Islands	3	3	—	—
Total	1372	905½	210	256½

1. Other candidates: Lyndon B. Johnson, 80; James C. Davis, 33; Albert B. Chandler, 36½; John S. Battle, 32½; George B. Timmerman, 23½; W. Stuart Symington, 45½; Frank Lausche, 5½.

1956 Republican

(Narrative, p. 520)

Delegation	Total Votes	First Pres. Ballot Eisenhower
Alabama	21	21
Arizona	14	14
Arkansas	16	16
California	70	70
Colorado	18	18
Connecticut	22	22
Delaware	12	12
Florida	26	26
Georgia	23	23
Idaho	14	14
Illinois	60	60
Indiana	32	32
Iowa	26	26
Kansas	22	22
Kentucky	26	26
Louisiana	20	20
Maine	16	16
Maryland	24	24
Massachusetts	38	38
Michigan	46	46
Minnesota	28	28
Mississippi	15	15
Missouri	32	32
Montana	14	14
Nebraska	18	18
Nevada	12	12
New Hampshire	14	14
New Jersey	38	38
New Mexico	14	14
New York	96	96
North Carolina	28	28
North Dakota	14	14
Ohio	56	56
Oklahoma	22	22
Oregon	18	18
Pennsylvania	70	70
Rhode Island	14	14
South Carolina	16	16
South Dakota	14	14
Tennessee	28	28
Texas	54	54
Utah	14	14
Vermont	12	12
Virginia	30	30
Washington	24	24
West Virginia	16	16
Wisconsin	30	30
Wyoming	12	12
Alaska	4	4
District of Columbia	6	6
Hawaii	10	10
Puerto Rico	3	3
Virgin Islands	1	1
Total	1323	1323

1960 Democratic

(Narrative, p. 521)

First Pres. Ballot[1]

Delegation	Total Votes	Kennedy	Johnson	Stevenson	Symington
Alabama	29	3	20	½	3½
Alaska	9	9	—	—	—
Arizona	17	17	—	—	—
Arkansas	27	—	27	—	—
California	81	33½	7½	31½	8
Colorado	21	13½	—	5½	2
Connecticut	21	21	—	—	—
Delaware	11	—	11	—	—
Florida	29	—	—	—	—
Georgia	33	—	33	—	—
Hawaii	9	1½	3	3½	1
Idaho	13	6	4½	½	2
Illinois	69	61½	—	2	5½
Indiana	34	34	—	—	—
Iowa	26	21½	½	2	½
Kansas	21	21	—	—	—
Kentucky	31	3½	25½	1½	½
Louisiana	26	—	26	—	—
Maine	15	15	—	—	—
Maryland	24	24	—	—	—
Massachusetts	41	41	—	—	—
Michigan	51	42½	—	2½	6
Minnesota	31	—	—	—	—
Mississippi	23	—	—	—	—
Missouri	39	—	—	—	39
Montana	17	10	2	2½	2½
Nebraska	16	11	½	—	4
Nevada	15	5½	6½	2½	½
New Hampshire	11	11	—	—	—
New Jersey	41	—	—	—	—
New Mexico	17	4	13	—	—
New York	114	104½	3½	3½	2½
North Carolina	37	6	27½	3	—
North Dakota	11	11	—	—	—
Ohio	64	64	—	—	—
Oklahoma	29	—	29	—	—
Oregon	17	16½	—	½	—
Pennsylvania	81	68	4	7½	—
Rhode Island	17	17	—	—	—
South Carolina	21	—	21	—	—
South Dakota	11	4	2	1	2½
Tennessee	33	—	33	—	—
Texas	61	—	61	—	—
Utah	13	8	3	—	1½
Vermont	9	9	—	—	—
Virginia	33	—	33	—	—
Washington	27	14½	2½	6½	3
West Virginia	25	15	5½	3	1½
Wisconsin	31	23	—	—	—
Wyoming	15	15	—	—	—
Canal Zone	4	—	4	—	—
District of Columbia	9	9	—	—	—
Puerto Rico	7	7	—	—	—
Virgin Islands	4	4	—	—	—
Total	1521	806	409	79½	86

1960 Republican

(Narrative, p. 523)

First Pres. Ballot

Delegation	Total Votes	Nixon	Goldwater
Alabama	22	22	—
Alaska	6	6	—
Arizona	14	14	—
Arkansas	16	16	—
California	70	70	—
Colorado	18	18	—
Connecticut	22	22	—
Delaware	12	12	—
Florida	26	26	—
Georgia	24	24	—
Hawaii	12	12	—
Idaho	14	14	—
Illinois	60	60	—
Indiana	32	32	—
Iowa	26	26	—
Kansas	22	22	—
Kentucky	26	26	—
Louisiana	26	16	10
Maine	16	16	—
Maryland	24	24	—
Massachusetts	38	38	—
Michigan	46	46	—
Minnesota	28	28	—
Mississippi	12	12	—
Missouri	26	26	—
Montana	14	14	—
Nebraska	18	18	—
Nevada	12	12	—
New Hampshire	14	14	—
New Jersey	38	38	—
New Mexico	14	14	—
New York	96	96	—
North Carolina	28	28	—
North Dakota	14	14	—
Ohio	56	56	—
Oklahoma	22	22	—
Oregon	18	18	—
Pennsylvania	70	70	—
Rhode Island	14	14	—
South Carolina	13	13	—
South Dakota	14	14	—
Tennessee	28	28	—
Texas	54	54	—
Utah	14	14	—
Vermont	12	12	—
Virginia	30	30	—
Washington	24	24	—
West Virginia	22	22	—
Wisconsin	30	30	—
Wyoming	12	12	—
District of Columbia	8	8	—
Puerto Rico	3	3	—
Virgin Islands	1	1	—
Total	1331	1321	10

1. Other candidates: Ross R. Barnett, 23 (Mississippi); George A. Smathers, 30 (29 in Florida, ½ in Alabama, ½ in North Carolina); Hubert H. Humphrey, 42½ (31 in Minnesota, 8 in Wisconsin, 1½ in South Dakota, ½ in Nebraska, ½ in Utah); Robert B. Meyner, 43 (41 in New Jersey, 1½ in Pennsylvania, ½ in Alabama); Herschel C. Loveless, 1½ (Iowa); Orval E. Faubus, ½ (Alabama); Edmund G. Brown, ½ (California); Albert D. Rosellini, ½ (Washington).

1964 Republican

(Narrative, p. 525)

Delegation	Total Votes	Minority Amendment on Civil Rights[1]		First Pres. Ballot[2] (Before shift)			First Pres. Ballot[3] (After shift)		
		Yea	Nay	Goldwater	Rockefeller	Scranton	Goldwater	Rockefeller	Scranton
Alabama	20	—	20	20	—	—	20	—	—
Alaska	12	12	—	—	—	8	—	—	8
Arizona	16	—	16	16	—	—	16	—	—
Arkansas	12	—	12	9	1	2	12	—	—
California	86	—	86	86	—	—	86	—	—
Colorado	18	—	18	15	—	3	18	—	—
Connecticut	16	11	5	4	—	12	16	—	—
Delaware	12	11	1	7	—	5	10	—	2
Florida	34	—	34	34	—	2	34	—	—
Georgia	24	—	24	22	—	2	24	—	—
Hawaii	8	4	4	4	—	—	8	—	—
Idaho	14	—	14	14	—	—	14	—	—
Illinois	58	4	54	56	2	—	56	2	—
Indiana	32	—	32	32	—	—	32	—	—
Iowa	24	2	22	14	—	10	24	—	—
Kansas	20	2	18	18	—	1	18	—	1
Kentucky	24	1	23	21	—	3	22	—	2
Louisiana	20	—	20	20	—	—	20	—	—
Maine	14	11	3	—	—	—	—	—	—
Maryland	20	17	3	6	1	13	7	1	12
Massachusetts	34	27	7	5	—	26	34	—	—
Michigan	48	37	9	8	—	—	48	—	—
Minnesota	26	17	9	8	—	—	26	—	—
Mississippi	13	—	13	13	—	—	13	—	—
Missouri	24	1	23	23	—	1	24	—	—
Montana	14	—	14	14	—	—	14	—	—
Nebraska	16	—	16	16	—	—	16	—	—
Nevada	6	—	6	6	—	—	6	—	—
New Hampshire	14	14	—	—	—	14	—	—	14
New Jersey	40	40	—	20	—	20	38	—	2
New Mexico	14	—	14	14	—	—	14	—	—
New York	92	86	6	5	87	—	87	—	—
North Carolina	26	—	26	26	—	—	26	—	—
North Dakota	14	1	13	7	1	—	14	—	—
Ohio	58	—	58	57	—	—	58	—	—
Oklahoma	22	—	22	22	—	—	22	—	—
Oregon	18	10	8	—	18	—	16	—	—
Pennsylvania	64	62	2	4	—	60	64	—	—
Rhode Island	14	11	3	3	—	11	14	—	—
South Carolina	16	—	16	16	—	—	16	—	—
South Dakota	14	—	14	12	—	2	14	—	—
Tennessee	28	—	28	28	—	—	28	—	—
Texas	56	—	56	56	—	—	56	—	—
Utah	14	—	14	14	—	—	14	—	—
Vermont	12	8	4	3	2	2	3	2	2
Virginia	30	—	30	29	—	1	30	—	—
Washington	24	1	23	22	—	1	22	—	1
West Virginia	14	4	10	10	2	2	12	1	1
Wisconsin	30	—	30	30	—	—	30	—	—
Wyoming	12	—	12	12	—	—	12	—	—
District of Columbia	9	7	2	4	—	5	4	—	5
Puerto Rico	5	5	—	—	—	5	5	—	—
Virgin Islands	3	3	—	—	—	3	3	—	—
Total	1308	409	897	883	114	214	1220	6	50

1. Not voting, 2.

2. Other candidates: George Romney, 41 (40 in Michigan, 1 in Kansas); Margaret C. Smith, 27 (14 in Maine, 5 in Vermont, 3 in North Dakota, 2 in Alaska, 1 in Massachusetts, 1 in Ohio, 1 in Washington); Walter H. Judd, 22 (18 in Minnesota, 3 in North Dakota, 1 in Alaska); Hiram L. Fong, 5 (4 in Hawaii, 1 in Alaska); Henry C. Lodge, 2 (Massachusetts).

3. Other candidates: Smith, 22 (14 in Maine, 5 in Vermont, 2 in Alaska, 1 in Washington); Fong, 1 (Alaska); Judd, 1 (Alaska); Romney, 1 (Kansas); not voting, 7 (5 in New York, 2 in Oregon).

1968 Republican

(Narrative, p. 529)

Delegation	Total Votes	First Pres. Ballot[1] (Before shift)			First Pres. Ballot (After shift)		
		Nixon	Rockefeller	Reagan	Nixon	Rockefeller	Reagan
Alabama	26	14	—	12	26	—	—
Alaska	12	11	1	—	12	—	—
Arizona	16	16	—	—	16	—	—
Arkansas	18	—	—	—	18	—	—
California	86	—	—	86	86	—	—
Colorado	18	14	3	1	18	—	—
Connecticut	16	4	12	—	16	—	—
Delaware	12	9	3	—	12	—	—
Florida	34	32	1	1	34	—	—
Georgia	30	21	2	7	30	—	—
Hawaii	14	—	—	—	14	—	—
Idaho	14	9	—	5	14	—	—
Illinois	58	50	5	3	58	—	—
Indiana	26	26	—	—	26	—	—
Iowa	24	13	8	3	24	—	—
Kansas	20	—	—	—	19	1	—
Kentucky	24	22	2	—	24	—	—
Louisiana	26	19	—	7	26	—	—
Maine	14	7	7	—	14	—	—
Maryland	26	18	8	—	26	—	—
Massachusetts	34	—	34	—	34	—	—
Michigan	48	4	—	—	48	—	—
Minnesota	26	9	15	—	26	—	—
Mississippi	20	20	—	—	20	—	—
Missouri	24	16	5	3	24	—	—
Montana	14	11	—	3	14	—	—
Nebraska	16	16	—	—	16	—	—
Nevada	12	9	3	—	12	—	—
New Hampshire	8	8	—	—	8	—	—
New Jersey	40	18	—	—	40	—	—
New Mexico	14	8	1	5	14	—	—
New York	92	4	88	—	4	88	—
North Carolina	26	9	1	16	26	—	—
North Dakota	8	5	2	1	8	—	—
Ohio	58	2	—	—	58	—	—
Oklahoma	22	14	1	7	22	—	—
Oregon	18	18	—	—	18	—	—
Pennsylvania	64	22	41	1	64	—	—
Rhode Island	14	—	14	—	14	—	—
South Carolina	22	22	—	—	22	—	—
South Dakota	14	14	—	—	14	—	—
Tennessee	28	28	—	—	28	—	—
Texas	56	41	—	15	54	—	2
Utah	8	2	—	—	8	—	—
Vermont	12	9	3	—	12	—	—
Virginia	24	22	2	—	24	—	—
Washington	24	15	3	6	24	—	—
West Virginia	14	11	3	—	13	1	—
Wisconsin	30	30	—	—	30	—	—
Wyoming	12	12	—	—	12	—	—
District of Columbia	9	6	3	—	6	3	—
Puerto Rico	5	—	5	—	5	—	—
Virgin Islands	3	2	1	—	3	—	—
Total	1333	692	277	182	1238	93	2

1. Other candidates: James A. Rhodes, 55 (Ohio); George Romney, 50 (44 in Michigan, 6 in Utah); Clifford P. Case, 22 (New Jersey); Frank Carlson, 20 (Kansas); Winthrop Rockefeller, 18 (Arkansas); Hiram L. Fong, 14 (Hawaii); Harold Stassen, 2 (1 in Minnesota, 1 in Ohio); John V. Lindsay, 1 (Minnesota).

1968 Democratic

(Narrative, p. 530)

Delegation	Total Votes	Texas Credentials[1]		Georgia Credentials[2]		Alabama Credentials[3]		End Unit Rule[4]		Report on Vietnam[5]		First Pres. Ballot[6]			
		Yea	Nay	Yea	Nay	Yea	Nay	Yea	Nay	Yea	Nay	Humphrey	McCarthy	McGovern	Phillips
Ala.	32	32	—	10	22	—	—	5½	24½	1½	30½	23	—	—	—
Alaska	22	17	5	5	17	14	8	22	—	10	12	17	2	3	—
Ariz.	19	1¼	17	17	2	7½	11½	—	19	6½	12½	14½	2½	2	—
Ark.	33	33	—	3	29	8	23	—	32	7	25	30	2	—	—
Calif.	174	1	173	173	1	173	1	173	1	166	6	14	91	51	17
Colo.	35	—	35	30	5	34	1	35	—	21	14	16½	10	5½	3
Conn.	44	30	12	13	27	21	21	9	30	13	30	35	8	—	1
Del.	22	21	—	3	18	2	19	—	21	—	21	21	—	—	—
Fla.	63	58	4	9	54	6	57	11	52	7	56	58	5	—	—
Ga.	43	—	—	—	—	25	17½	39	4	19½	23½	19½	13½	1	3
Hawaii	26	26	—	4	22	—	26	3	23	—	26	26	—	—	—
Idaho	25	22½	2½	4½	20½	2	23	1	24	10	15	21	3½	½	—
Ill.	118	114	4	12	83	18	100	3	115	13	105	112	3	3	—
Ind.	63	34	10	25	38	13	41½	63	—	15	47½	49	11	2	1
Iowa	46	37½	8½	32	12	24½	21½	46	—	36	10	18½	19½	5	—
Kan.	38	38	—	3½	34½	5½	31½	6	20	4½	33½	34	1	3	—
Ky.	46	40½	5½	6	40	6½	39½	6½	39½	7	39	41	5	—	—
La.	36	32	4	7	29	—	36	—	36	2½	33½	35	—	—	—
Maine	27	25	1	5	22	—	26	27	—	4½	22½	23	4	—	—
Md.	49	46	3	3	46	2	47	49	—	12	37	45	2	2	—
Mass.	72	16	47	39	24	29	29	37	31	56	16	2	70	—	—
Mich.	96	70	23	35	58	26	67	43½	44½	52	44	72½	9½	7½	6½
Minn.	52	34½	14½	16	33	23½	28½	16	33½	16½	34½	38	11½	—	2½
Miss.	24	2	18½	18	2	12½	8½	21½	½	19½	2½	9½	6½	4	2
Mo.	60	48	12	12	48	8	52	60	—	10	50	56	3½	—	½
Mont.	26	20	4	2½	21½	3½	22½	12½	12	6	20	23½	2½	—	—
Neb.	30	12	16	11	18	13	15	26	2	19	11	15	6	9	—
Nev.	22	13	7	14	8	12½	9½	22	—	3½	18½	18½	2½	1	—
N.H.	26	6	20	23	2	25	—	23	3	23	3	6	20	—	—
N.J.	82	43	25	22	51	21	61	21	61	24	57	62	19	—	1
N.M.	26	13	13	11	15	11	15	11	15	11½	14½	15	11	—	—
N.Y.	190	—	190	190	—	80[e]	82[e]	190	—	148	42	96½	87	1½	2
N.C.	59	54½	4½	3½	55½	1	58	2	57	7	51	44½	2	½	—
N.D.	25	17	5	5	17	7	18	17	5	6	19	18	7	—	—
Ohio	115	37½	27	21	80	30½	65	23	92	48	67	94	18	2	—
Okla.	41	40	1	1	40	6½	34	6	35	4	37	37½	2½	½	½
Ore.	35	10	23	32	—	31	3	31	—	29	6	—	35	—	—
Pa.	130	80½	42½	31½	90½	22¼	100½	39¾	79½	35¼	92¼	103¾	21½	2½	1½
R.I.	27	24½	2½	12	11	2½	24½	3½	23½	5	22	23½	2½	—	—
S.C.	28	28	—	4	22	—	28	4½	23½	1	27	28	—	—	—
S.D.	26	1	25	26	—	24	2	26	—	26	—	2	—	24	—
Tenn.	51	48½	1	—	51	½	49½	2½	46½	2	49	49½	½	1	—
Texas	104	—	—	2.55	101.45	—	104	5	99	—	104	100½	2½	—	1
Utah	26	18	8	7	19	5	21	26	—	6	20	23	2	—	1
Vt.	22	5	13	17	4	14	7	22	—	17	5	8	6	7	—
Va.	54	21½	22½	8½	35½	1	53	9½	43½		46	42½	5½	—	2
Wash.	47	31½	15½	18	29	16	28	21½	25½	15½	31½	32½	8½	6	—
W.Va.	38	19	12	8	22	9	29	38	—	8	30	34	3	—	—
Wis.	59	5	54	52	7	54	4	58	1	52	7	8	49	1	1
Wyo.	22	18½	3½	2	20	6½	15½	3	19	3½	18½	18½	3½	—	—
Canal Z.	5	4	—	2	3	—	4	1	4	1½	3½	4	—	1	—
D. C.	23	—	22	22	—	23	—	23	—	21	2	2	—	—	21
Guam	5	4½	½	—	5	—	5	½	4½	½	4½	5	—	—	—
P.R.	8	8	—	7½	—	—	8	1	7	—	8	8	—	—	—
Vir. Is.	5	5	—	2½	—	—	5	5	—	—	5	—	—	—	—
Total	2622	1368¼[a]	956¾[b]	1043.55[c]	1415.45[d]	880¾[f]	1607[g]	1351¼[h]	1209[i]	1041¼	1567¾	1759¼[j]	601	146½	67½

1. Not voting, 297.
2. Not voting, 163.
3. Not voting, 134½.
4. Not voting, 61¾.
5. Not voting, 13.
6. Other candidates: Dan K. Moore. 17½ (12 in North Carolina, 3 in Virginia, 2 in Georgia, ½ in Alabama); Edward M. Kennedy, 12¾ (proceedings record, 12½) (3½ in Alabama, 3 in Iowa, 3 in New York, 1 in Ohio, 1 in West Virginia, ¾ in Pennsylvania; ½ in Georgia); Bryant, 1½ (Alabama); George C. Wallace, ½ (Alabama); James H. Gray, ½ (Georgia); not voting, 15 (3 in Alabama, 3 in Georgia, 2 in Mississippi, 1 in Arkansas, 1 in California, 1 in Delaware, 1 in Louisiana, 1 in Rhode Island, 1 in Vermont, 1 in Virginia).

a. Sum of column; proceedings record, 1368.
b. Sum of column; proceedings record, 955.
c. Sum of column; proceedings record, 1041½.
d. Sum of column; proceedings record, 1413.
e. New York vote announced after outcome of roll call.
f. Sum of column; proceedings record (without New York vote), 801½.
g. Sum of column; proceedings record (without New York), 1525.
h. Sum of column; proceedings record,1350.
i. Sum of column; proceedings record, 1206.
j. Sum of column; proceedings record, 1761¾ .

1972 Democratic

(Narrative, p. 533)

Delegation[1]	Total Votes	Minority Report South Carolina Credentials			Minority Report California Credentials			Minority Report Illinois Credentials		
		Yea	Nay	Not Voting	Yea	Nay	Not Voting	Yea	Nay	Not Voting
California	271	120	151	—	120	—	151	84	136	51
South Carolina	32	—	9	23	3	29	—	31	1	—
Ohio	153	63	87	3	75	78	—	69	70	14
Canal Zone	3	1.50	1.50	—	3	—	—	1	2	—
Utah	19	10	8	1	13	6	—	5	14	—
Delaware	13	5.85	7.15	—	6.50	6.50	—	6.50	6.50	—
Rhode Island	22	20	2	—	22	—	—	7.09	14.91	—
Texas	130	34	96	—	34	96	—	96	34	—
West Virginia	35	13	22	—	15	20	—	24	11	—
South Dakota	17	17	—	—	17	—	—	—	17	—
Kansas	35	17	18	—	18	17	—	18	17	—
New York	278	269	9	—	267	11	—	20	256	2
Virginia	53	34.50	18.50	—	38.50	14.50	—	16.50	35.50	1
Wyoming	11	2.20	8.80	—	4.40	6.60	—	7.70	3.30	—
Arkansas	27	13	14	—	8	19	—	13	14	—
Indiana	76	18	58	—	33	43	—	53	23	—
Puerto Rico	7	6.50	0.50	—	6.50	0.50	—	0.50	6.50	—
Tennessee	49	22	27	—	23	26	—	20	29	—
Pennsylvania	182	55.50	126	0.50	72	105	5	106.50	62	13.50
Mississippi	25	20	5	—	19	6	—	—	25	—
Wisconsin	67	39	28	—	55	12	—	12	55	—
Illinois	170	79	90	1	114.50	55.50	—	76	30	64
Maine	20	1	19	—	—	20	—	13	7	—
Florida	81	1	80	—	3	78	—	80	1	—
New Hampshire	18	13.50	4.50	—	9.90	8.10	—	9	8.10	0.90
Arizona	25	15	10	—	12	13	—	4	21	—
North Carolina	64	6	58	—	21	43	—	39	23	2
Massachusetts	102	97	5	—	97	5	—	11	91	—
Nebraska	24	14	9	1	20	4	—	13	11	—
Georgia	53	5.50	47.50	—	21.75	31.25	—	24	27.50	1.50
North Dakota	14	7	6.30	0.70	8.40	5.60	—	2.10	11.90	—
Maryland	53	24	29	—	27.83	25.17	—	28.67	24.33	—
New Jersey	109	79	29	1	85.50	22.50	1	30	75.50	3.50
Vermont	12	7	5	—	11	1	—	2	10	—
Nevada	11	5.75	5.25	—	5.75	5.25	—	6.75	4.25	—
Michigan	132	51	81	—	55	76	1	85	47	—
Iowa	46	23	23	—	27	19	—	20	26	—
Colorado	36	23	13	—	27	9	—	5	31	—
Alabama	37	1	36	—	1	36	—	32	5	—
Alaska	10	6.75	3.25	—	7.25	2.75	—	4.75	5.25	—
Hawaii	17	2	15	—	7	10	—	17	—	—
Washington	52	—	52	—	—	52	—	52	—	—
Minnesota	64	56	8	—	29	35	—	32	32	—
Louisiana	44	25	19	—	22.50	21.50	—	9.50	32.50	2
Idaho	17	12.50	4.50	—	11.50	5.50	—	4	13	—
Montana	17	10	7	—	14.50	1	1.50	2.50	14.50	—
Connecticut	51	8	43	—	21	30	—	40	11	—
District of Columbia	15	12	3	—	13.50	1.50	—	1.50	13.50	—
Virgin Islands	3	1	2	—	2.50	0.50	—	3	—	—
Kentucky	47	10	37	—	11	36	—	36	10	1
Missouri	73	13.50	59.50	—	22.50	50.50	—	59	13	1
New Mexico	18	10	8	—	10	8	—	8	10	—
Guam	3	1.50	1.50	—	1.50	1.50	—	—	3	—
Oregon	34	16	18	—	33	1	—	2	32	—
Oklahoma	39	11	28	—	11	28	—	29	9	1
Total	3016	1429.05	1555.75	31.20	1618.28	1238.22	159.50	1371.56[a]	1486.04[b]	158.40

1. Delegations at this convention are listed in the order in which they voted. All fractional votes are expressed in decimals for consistency.
a. Sum of column; proceedings record, 1371.55.
b. Sum of column; proceedings record, 1486.05.

1972 Democratic

(Narrative, p. 533)

Minority Report Guaranteed Income			First Pres. Ballot[2] (Before shift)					First Pres. Ballot[3] (After shift)				
Yea	Nay	Not Voting	McGovern	Jackson	Wallace	Chisholm	Sanford	McGovern	Jackson	Wallace	Chisholm	Sanford
131	114	26	271	—	—	—	—	271	—	—	—	—
4	21	7	6	10	6	4	6	10	9	6	—	6
39	86	28	77	39	—	23	3	77	39	—	23	3
2.50	0.50	—	3	—	—	—	—	3	—	—	—	—
8	11	—	14	1	—	—	3	14	1	—	—	3
4.55	8.45	—	5.85	6.50	—	0.65	—	5.85	5.85	—	0.65	—
10.86	11.14	—	22	—	—	—	—	22	—	—	—	—
15	115	—	54	23	48	4	—	54	23	48	4	—
3	32	—	16	14	1	—	4	16	14	1	—	4
1	16	—	17	—	—	—	—	17	—	—	—	—
5	30	—	20	10	—	2	1	20	10	—	2	1
152	118	8	263	9	—	6	—	278	—	—	—	—
30	21	2	33.50	4	1	5.50	9	37	5	—	2.50	8.50
0.55	10.45	—	3.30	6.05	—	1.10	—	3.30	6.05	—	1.10	—
10	16	1	1	1	—	—	—	1	1	—	—	—
17	56	3	26	20	26	1	—	28	19	25	—	—
4	3	—	7	—	—	—	—	7	—	—	—	—
21	27	1	—	—	33	10	—	5	—	32	7	—
49.50	117.50	15	81	86.50	2	9.50	1	81	86.50	2	9.50	1
22	—	3	10	—	—	12	3	23	—	—	2	5
29	38	—	55	3	—	5	—	55	3	—	5	—
59	95	16	119	30.50	0.50	4.50	2	155	6	—	1	—
1	19	—	5	—	—	—	—	5	—	—	—	—
4	77	—	2	—	75	2	—	4	—	75	1	—
0.90	14.40	2.70	10.80	5.40	—	—	—	10.80	5.40	—	—	—
6	19	—	21	3	—	—	1	22	3	—	—	—
17	47	—	—	—	37	—	27	—	—	37	—	27
60	40	2	102	—	—	—	—	102	—	—	—	—
2	22	—	21	3	—	—	—	21	3	—	—	—
10.50	34	8.50	14.50	14.50	11	12	1	14.50	14.50	11	12	1
1.40	10.50	2.10	8.40	2.80	0.70	0.70	—	10.50	2.10	—	0.70	—
14.33	38.67	—	13	—	38	2	—	13	—	38	2	—
61.50	35.50	12	89	11.50	—	4	1.50	92.50	11	—	3.50	—
4	8	—	12	—	—	—	—	12	—	—	—	—
2.75	8.25	—	5.75	5.25	—	—	—	5.75	5.25	—	—	—
30.50	96.50	5	50.50	7	67.50	3	1	51.50	7	67.50	2	1
6	39	1	35	—	—	3	4	35	—	—	3	4
15	21	—	27	—	—	7	—	29	2	—	5	—
10	27	—	9	1	24	—	1	9	1	24	—	1
3	5.50	1.50	6.50	3.25	—	—	—	6.50	3.25	—	—	—
1.50	15.50	—	6.50	8.50	—	1	—	6.50	8.50	—	1	—
1	51	—	—	52	—	—	—	—	52	—	—	—
28	33	3	11	—	—	6	—	43	—	—	4	1
22	20	2	10.25	10.25	3	18.50	2	25.75	5.25	3	4	1
5	12	—	12.50	2.50	—	2	—	12.50	2.50	—	2	—
2	14	1	16	—	—	1	—	16	—	—	1	—
22	29	—	30	20	—	—	1	30	20	—	—	1
15	—	—	13.50	1.50	—	—	—	13.50	1.50	—	—	—
2.50	0.50	—	1	1.50	—	0.50	—	1	1.50	—	0.50	—
1	41	5	10	35	—	—	2	10	35	—	—	2
12	55	6	24.50	48.50	—	—	—	24.50	48.50	—	—	—
3	15	—	10	—	8	—	—	10	—	8	—	—
—	3	—	1.50	1.50	—	—	—	1.50	1.50	—	—	—
11	23	—	34	—	—	—	—	34	—	—	—	—
5.50	31.50	2	1.50	23.50	—	1	4	9.50	23.50	—	2	4
999.34	1852.86	163.80	1728.35	525.00	381.70	151.95	77.50	1864.95	485.65	377.50	101.45	69.50

2. Other candidates: Hubert H. Humphrey, 66.70 (46 in Minnesota, 4 in Ohio, 4 in Wisconsin, 3 in Michigan, 2 in Indiana, 2 in Pennsylvania, 2 in Florida, 1 in Utah, 1 in Chicago, 1 in Hawaii, 0.70 in North Dakota); Wilbur D. Mills, 33.80 (25 in Arkansas, 3 in Illinois, 3 in New Jersey, 2 in Alabama, 0.55 in Wyoming, 0.25 in Alaska); Edmund S. Muskie, 24.30 (15 in Maine, 5.50 in Illinois, 1.80 in New Hampshire, 1 in Texas, 1 in Colorado); Edward M. Kennedy, 12.70 (4 in Iowa, 3 in Illinois, 2 in Ohio, 1 in Kansas, 1 in Indiana, 1 in Tennessee, 0.70 in North Dakota); Wayne L. Hays, 5 (Ohio); Eugene J. McCarthy, 2 (Illinois); Mondale, 1 (Kansas); Clark, 1 (Minnesota); not voting, 5 (Tennessee).

3. Humphrey, 35 (16 in Minnesota, 4 in Ohio, 4 in Wisconsin, 3 in Indiana, 3 in Michigan, 2 in Pennsylvania, 1 in Utah, 1 in Florida, 1 in Hawaii); Mills, 32.80 (25 in Arkansas, 2 in Illinois, 2 in New Jersey, 2 in Alabama, 1 in South Carolina, 0.55 in Wyoming, 0.25 in Alaska); Muskie, 20.80 (15 in Maine, 3 in Illinois, 1.80 in New Hampshire, 1 in Texas); Kennedy, 10.65 (4 in Iowa, 2 in Ohio, 1 in Kansas, 1 in Indiana, 1 in Tennessee, 1 in Illinois, 0.65 in Delaware); Hays, 5 (Ohio); McCarthy, 2 (Illinois); Mondale, 1 (Kansas).

1972 Republican

(Narrative, p. 536)

Delegation	Total Votes	First Pres. Ballot	
		Nixon	McCloskey
Alabama	18	18	—
Alaska	12	12	—
Arizona	18	18	—
Arkansas	18	18	—
California	96	96	—
Colorado	20	20	—
Connecticut	22	22	—
Delaware	12	12	—
Florida	40	40	—
Georgia	24	24	—
Hawaii	14	14	—
Idaho	14	14	—
Illinois	58	58	—
Indiana	32	32	—
Iowa	22	22	—
Kansas	20	20	—
Kentucky	24	24	—
Louisiana	20	20	—
Maine	8	8	—
Maryland	26	26	—
Massachusetts	34	34	—
Michigan	48	48	—
Minnesota	26	26	—
Mississippi	14	14	—
Missouri	30	30	—
Montana	14	14	—
Nebraska	16	16	—
Nevada	12	12	—
New Hampshire	14	14	—
New Jersey	40	40	—
New Mexico	14	13	1
New York	88	88	—
North Carolina	32	32	—
North Dakota	12	12	—
Ohio	56	56	—
Oklahoma	22	22	—
Oregon	18	18	—
Pennsylvania	60	60	—
Rhode Island	8	8	—
South Carolina	22	22	—
South Dakota	14	14	—
Tennessee	26	26	—
Texas	52	52	—
Utah	14	14	—
Vermont	12	12	—
Virginia	30	30	—
Washington	24	24	—
West Virginia	18	18	—
Wisconsin	28	28	—
Wyoming	12	12	—
District of Columbia	9	9	—
Guam	3	3	—
Puerto Rico	5	5	—
Virgin Islands	3	3	—
Total	1348	1347	1

1976 Democratic

(Narrative, p. 537)

Delegation	Total Votes	First Pres. Ballot[1] (Before shift)				First Pres. Ballot[2] (After shift)			
		Carter	Udall	Brown	Wallace	Carter	Udall	Brown	Wallace
Alabama	35	30	—	—	5	30	—	—	5
Alaska	10	10	—	—	—	10	—	—	—
Arizona	25	6	19	—	—	6	19	—	—
Arkansas	26	25	1	—	—	25	1	—	—
California	280	73	2	205	—	278	2	—	—
Colorado	35	15	6	11	—	15	6	11	—
Connecticut	51	35	16	—	—	35	16	—	—
Delaware	12	10.50	—	1.50	—	10.50	—	1.50	—
Florida	81	70	—	1	10	70	—	1	10
Georgia	50	50	—	—	—	50	—	—	—
Hawaii	17	17	—	—	—	17	—	—	—
Idaho	16	16	—	—	—	16	—	—	—
Illinois	169	164	1	2	1	164	1	2	1
Indiana	75	72	—	—	3	72	—	—	—
Iowa	47	25	20	1	—	25	20	1	—
Kansas	34	32	2	—	—	32	2	—	—
Kentucky	46	39	2	—	5	29	2	—	5
Louisiana	41	18	—	18	5	35	—	1	5
Maine	20	15	5	—	—	15	5	—	—
Maryland	53	44	6	3	—	44	6	3	—
Massachusetts[3]	104	65	21	—	11	65	21	—	11
Michigan	133	75	58	—	—	75	58	—	—
Minnesota	65	37	2	1	—	37	2	1	—
Mississippi	24	23	—	—	—	23	—	—	—
Missouri	71	58	4	2	—	58	4	2	—
Montana	17	11	2	—	—	11	2	—	—
Nebraska	23	20	—	3	—	20	—	3	—
Nevada	11	3	—	6.50	—	3	—	6.50	—
New Hampshire	17	15	2	—	—	15	2	—	—
New jersey	108	108	—	—	—	108	—	—	—
New Mexico	18	14	4	—	—	14	4	—	—
New York	274	209.50	56.50	4	—	209.50	56.50	4	—
North Carolina	61	56	—	—	3	56	—	—	3
North Dakota	13	13	—	—	—	13	—	—	—
Ohio	152	132	20	—	—	132	20	—	—
Oklahoma	37	32	1	—	—	32	1	—	—
Oregon	34	16	—	10	—	16	—	10	—
Pennsylvania	178	151	21	6	—	151	21	6	—
Rhode Island	22	14	—	8	—	22	—	—	—
South Carolina	31	28	—	1	2	28	—	1	2
South Dakota	17	11	5	—	—	11	5	—	—
Tennessee	46	45	—	—	1	45	—	—	1
Texas	130	124	—	4	1	124	—	4	1
Utah	18	10	—	5	—	10	—	5	—
Vermont	12	5	4	3	—	5	4	3	1
Virginia	54	48	6	—	—	48	6	—	—
Washington	53	36	11	3	—	36	11	3	—
West Virginia	33	30	1	—	—	30	1	—	—
Wisconsin	68	29	25	—	10	29	25	—	10
Wyoming	10	8	1	1	—	8	1	1	—
District of Columbia	17	12	5	—	—	12	5	—	—
Puerto Rico	22	22	—	—	—	22	—	—	—
Canal Zone	3	3	—	—	—	3	—	—	—
Guam	3	3	—	—	—	3	—	—	—
Virgin Island	3	3	—	—	—	3	—	—	—
Democrats Abroad	3	2.50	—	0.50	—	2.50	—	0.50	—
Total	3008	2238.50	329.50	300.50	57.00	2468.50	329.50	70.50	57.00

1. Other candidates: Ellen McCormack, 22 (1 in Illinois, 2 in Massachusetts, 11 in Minnesota, 7 in Missouri, 1 in Wisconsin); Frank Church, 19 (3 in Colorado, 4 in Montana, 1 in Nevada, 8 in Oregon, 1 in Utah, 2 in Washington); Hubert H. Humphrey, 10 (9 in Minnesota, 1 in South Dakota); Henry M. Jackson, 10 (2 in Massachusetts, 4 in New York, 1 in Washington, 3 in Wisconsin); Fred Harris, 9 (2 in Massachusetts, 4 in Minnesota, 3 in Oklahoma); Milton J. Shapp, 2 (1 in Massachusetts, 1 in Utah); receiving one vote each: Robert C. Byrd (West Virginia); Cesar Chavez (Utah); Leon Jaworski (Texas); Barbara C. Jordan (Oklahoma); Edward M. Kennedy (Iowa); Jennings Randolph (West Virginia); Fred Stover (Minnesota); "nobody" (0.5 in Nevada); not voting, 3 (1 in Mississippi, 2 in North Carolina).

2. The rules were suspended after the switches and Carter was nominated by acclamation.

3. Massachusetts passed when originally called on and cast its votes at the end of the roll call, after vote switches.

1976 Republican

(Narrative, p. 540)

Delegation	Total Votes	Rule 16C[1]		First Pres. Ballot[2]	
		Yea	Nay	Ford	Reagan
Alabama	37	37	—	—	37
Alaska	19	2	17	17	2
Arizona	29	25	4	2	27
Arkansas	27	17	10	10	17
California	167	166	1	—	167
Colorado	31	26	5	5	26
Connecticut	35	—	35	35	—
Delaware	17	1	16	15	2
Florida	66	28	38	43	23
Georgia	48	39	7	—	48
Hawaii	19	1	18	18	1
Idaho	21	17	4	4	17
Illinois	101	20	79	86	14
Indiana	54	27	27	9	45
Iowa	36	18	18	19	17
Kansas	34	4	30	30	4
Kentucky	37	26	10	19	18
Louisiana	41	34	6	5	36
Maine	20	5	15	15	5
Maryland	43	8	35	43	—
Massachusetts	43	15	28	28	15
Michigan	84	29	55	55	29
Minnesota	42	5	35	32	10
Mississippi	30	—	30	16	14
Missouri	49	30	18	18	31
Montana	20	20	—	—	20
Nebraska	25	18	7	7	18
Nevada	18	15	3	5	13
New Hampshire	21	3	18	18	3
New Jersey	67	4	62	63	4
New Mexico	21	20	1	—	21
New York	154	20	134	133	20
North Carolina	54	51	3	25	29
North Dakota	18	6	12	11	7
Ohio	97	7	90	91	6
Oklahoma	36	36	—	—	36
Oregon	30	14	16	16	14
Pennsylvania	103	14	89	93	10
Rhode Island	19	—	19	19	—
South Carolina	36	25	11	9	27
South Dakota	20	11	9	9	11
Tennessee	43	17	26	21	22
Texas	100	100	—	—	100
Utah	20	20	—	—	20
Vermont	18	—	18	18	—
Virginia	51	36	15	16	35
Washington	38	31	7	7	31
West Virginia	28	12	16	20	8
Wisconsin	45	—	45	45	—
Wyoming	17	9	8	7	10
District of Columbia	14	—	14	14	—
Puerto Rico	8	—	8	8	—
Guam	4	—	4	4	—
Virgin Islands	4	—	4	4	—
Total	2259	1069	1180	1187	1070

1. Not voting, 10.
2. Other candidate: Elliot L. Richardson, 1 (New York); not voting, 1 (Illinois). The nomination was made unanimous at the end of the balloting.

1980 Republican

(Narrative, p. 542)

Delegation	Total Votes	First Pres. Ballot[1]		
		Reagan	Anderson	Bush
Alabama	27	27	—	—
Alaska	19	19	—	—
Arizona	28	28	—	—
Arkansas	19	19	—	—
California	168	168	—	—
Colorado	31	31	—	—
Connecticut	35	35	—	—
Delaware	12	12	—	—
District of Columbia	14	14	—	—
Florida	51	51	—	—
Georgia	36	36	—	—
Guam	4	4	—	—
Hawaii	14	14	—	—
Idaho	21	21	—	—
Illinois	102	81	21	—
Indiana	54	54	—	—
Iowa	37	37	—	—
Kansas	32	32	—	—
Kentucky	27	27	—	—
Louisiana	31	31	—	—
Maine	21	21	—	—
Maryland	30	30	—	—
Massachusetts	42	33	9	—
Michigan	82	67	—	13
Minnesota	34	33	—	—
Mississippi	22	22	—	—
Missouri	37	37	—	—
Montana	20	20	—	—
Nebraska	25	25	—	—
Nevada	17	17	—	—
New Hampshire	22	22	—	—
New Jersey	66	66	—	—
New Mexico	22	22	—	—
New York	123	121	—	—
North Carolina	40	40	—	—
North Dakota	17	17	—	—
Ohio	77	77	—	—
Oklahoma	34	34	—	—
Oregon	29	29	—	—
Pennsylvania	83	83	—	—
Puerto Rico	14	14	—	—
Rhode Island	13	13	—	—
South Carolina	25	25	—	—
South Dakota	22	22	—	—
Tennessee	32	32	—	—
Texas	80	80	—	—
Utah	21	21	—	—
Vermont	19	19	—	—
Virginia	51	51	—	—
Virgin Islands	4	4	—	—
Washington	37	36	1	—
West Virginia	18	18	—	—
Wisconsin	34	28	6	—
Wyoming	19	19	—	—
Total	1994	1939	37	13

1. Other candidates: Anne Armstrong, 1 (Michigan); not voting, 4.

1980 Democratic

(Narrative, p. 544)

Delegation	Total Votes	Minority Rule #5[1]		First Pres. Ballot[3] (Before shift)		First Pres. Ballot[4] (After shift)	
		Yea	Nay	Carter	Kennedy	Carter	Kennedy
Alabama	45	3	42	43	2	43	2
Alaska	11	6.11	4.89	8.40	2.60	8.40	2.60
Arizona	29	16	13	13	16	13	16
Arkansas	33	9	24	25	6	25	6
California	306	171	132[2]	140	166	140	166
Colorado	40	24	16	27	10	27	10
Connecticut	54	28	26	26	28	26	28
Delaware	14	6.50	7.50	10	4	14	—
District of Columbia	19	12	7	12	5	12	5
Florida	100	25	75	75	25	75	25
Georgia	63	1	62	62	—	62	—
Hawaii	19	4	15	16	2	16	2
Idaho	17	9	8	9	7	9	7
Illinois	179	26	153	163	16	163	16
Indiana	80	27	53	53	27	53	27
Iowa	50	21	29	31	17	33	17
Kansas	37	17	20	23	14	23	14
Kentucky	50	12	38	45	5	45	5
Louisiana	51	15	36	50	1	50	1
Maine	22	12	10	11	11	11	11
Maryland	59	27	32	34	24	34	24
Massachusetts	111	81	30	34	77	34	77
Michigan	141	71	70	102	38	102	38
Minnesota	75	30	45	41	14	41	14
Mississippi	32	—	32	32	—	32	—
Missouri	77	20	57	58	19	58	19
Montana	19	9	10	13	6	13	6
Nebraska	24	11	13	14	10	14	10
Nevada	12	6.47	5.53	8.12	3.88	8.12	3.88
New Hampshire	19	9	10	10	9	10	9
New Jersey	113	68	45	45	68	45	68
New Mexico	20	11	9	10	10	10	10
New York	282	163	118	129	151	129	151
North Carolina	69	13	56	66	3	66	3
North Dakota	14	10	4	5	7	5	7
Ohio	161	81	80	89	72	89	72
Oklahoma	42	9	33	36	3	36	3
Oregon	39	14	25	26	13	26	13
Pennsylvania	185	102	83	95	90	95	90
Puerto Rico	41	20	21	21	20	21	20
Rhode Island	23	17	6	6	17	6	17
South Carolina	37	6	31	37	—	37	—
South Dakota	19	10	9	9	10	9	10
Tennessee	55	8	47	51	4	51	4
Texas	152	47	105	108	38	108	38
Utah	20	12	8	11	4	11	4
Vermont	12	7.50	4.50	5	7	5	7
Virginia	64	7	57	59	5	59	5
Washington	58	24	34	36	22	36	22
West Virginia	35	16	19	21	10	21	10
Wisconsin	75	26	49	48	26	48	26
Wyoming	11	3.50	7.50	8	3	8	3
Virgin Islands	4	—	4	4	—	4	—
Guam	4	—	4	4	—	4	—
Latin America	4	4	—	4	—	4	—
Democrats Abroad	4	2.50	1.50	1.50	2	1.50	2
Total	3331	1390.58	1936.42	2123.02	1150.48	2129.02	1150.48

1. The vote was on a minority report by supporters of Sen. Edward M. Kennedy to overturn a proposed rule that would bind all delegates to vote on the first ballot for the presidential candidate under whose banner they were elected. a "yes" vote supported the Kennedy position while a "no" supported the Carter view that delegates should be bound.

2. Not voting, 1.

3. Other candidates: William Proxmire, 10 (Minnesota); Scott M. Matheson, 5 (Utah); Koryne Horbal, 5 (Minnesota); Ronald V. Dellums, 2.5 (2 in New York, 0.5 from Democrats Abroad); receiving 2 votes each: John C. Culver (Iowa); Warren Spannous (Minnesota); Alice Tripp (Minnesota); Kent Hance (Texas); Robert C. Byrd (West Virginia); receiving 1 vote each: Dale Bumpers (Arkansas); Edmund S. Muskie (Colorado); Walter F. Mondale (Minnesota); Hugh L. Carey (Oklahoma); Tom Steed (Oklahoma); Edmund G. Brown (Wisconsin); uncommitted, 10; not voting, 5: absent, 2.

4. Votes for other candidates remained the same except that Iowa switched its 2 votes for Culver to Carter. After the switches Carter was nominated by acclamation.

1984 Republican

(Narrative, p. 550)

Delegation	Total Votes	First Pres. Ballot[1] Reagan
Alabama	38	38
Alaska	18	18
Arizona	32	32
Arkansas	29	29
California	176	176
Colorado	35	35
Connecticut	35	35
Delaware	19	19
District of Columbia	14	14
Florida	82	82
Georgia	37	37
Guam	4	4
Hawaii	14	14
Idaho	21	21
Illinois	93	92
Indiana	52	52
Iowa	37	37
Kansas	32	32
Kentucky	37	37
Louisiana	41	41
Maine	20	20
Maryland	31	31
Massachusetts	52	52
Michigan	77	77
Minnesota	32	32
Mississippi	30	30
Missouri	47	47
Montana	20	20
Nebraska	24	24
Nevada	22	22
New Hampshire	22	22
New Jersey	64	64
New Mexico	24	24
New York	136	136
North Carolina	53	53
North Dakota	18	18
Ohio	89	89
Oklahoma	35	35
Oregon	32	32
Pennsylvania	98	97
Puerto Rico	14	14
Rhode Island	14	14
South Carolina	35	35
South Dakota	19	19
Tennessee	46	46
Texas	109	109
Utah	26	26
Vermont	19	19
Virginia	50	50
Virgin Islands	4	4
Washington	44	44
West Virginia	19	19
Wisconsin	46	46
Wyoming	18	18
Total	2235	2233

1. Not voting, 2.

1984 Democratic

(Narrative, p. 548)

Delegation	Total Votes	No First Use of Nuclear Weapons			Defense Spending			Dual Primaries			Military Force Restrictions		
		Yea	Nay	Not Voting	Yea	Nay	Not Voting	Yea	Nay	Not Voting	Yea	Nay	Not Voting
Alabama	62	15	46	1	11	49	2	13	49	—	61	1	—
Alaska	14	7	7	—	1	13	—	2	12	—	13	1	—
Arizona	40	20	19	—	18	21	—	20	19	—	39	—	—
Arkansas	42	13	29	—	12	30	—	7	33	2	39	2	1
California	345	149	84	—	99	170	—	129	128	—	285	31	—
Colorado	51	31	16	4	5	45	1	26	24	1	51	—	—
Connecticut	60	28	24	8	32	27	1	27	33	—	60	—	—
Delaware	18	1	17	—	1	17	—	1	17	—	18	—	—
D.C.	19	15	4	—	17	2	—	14	5	—	6	12	—
Florida	143	47	76	20	42	81	20	27	110	6	95	25	23
Georgia	84	40	33	—	38	45	—	39	42	—	67	1	2
Hawaii	27	1	26	—	—	27	—	—	27	—	—	—	—
Idaho	22	9	—	—	10	11	—	9	13	—	22	—	—
Illinois	194	42	145	—	40	147	—	48	143	—	191	—	3
Indiana	88	31	46	—	18	64	—	23	64	—	88	—	—
Iowa	58	22	36	—	7	51	—	5	53	—	58	—	—
Kansas	44	14	29	1	6	38	—	10	34	—	44	—	—
Kentucky	63	14	48	—	10	52	—	15	47	—	55	8	—
Louisiana	69	24	32	—	30	39	—	44	22	—	44	22	—
Maine	27	7	16	—	3	22	—	10	16	—	23	1	—
Maryland	74	20	51	3	20	54	—	18	56	—	51	19	4
Massachusetts	116	89	24	—	69	43	1	82	31	1	112	—	—
Michigan	155	43	105	7	32	118	5	37	111	7	137	—	18
Minnesota	86	37	41	8	30	48	8	25	57	4	73	2	11
Mississippi	43	15	26	2	16	26	1	13	29	1	33	8	2
Missouri	86	20	62	4	22	62	2	24	61	1	70	—	16
Montana	25	8	15	2	4	21	—	5	20	—	25	—	—
Nebraska	30	2	25	3	2	25	3	10	17	3	24	—	6
Nevada	20	6	14	—	3	17	—	5	15	—	19	—	—
New Hampshire	22	10	12	—	5	17	—	1	21	—	22	—	—
New Jersey	122	9	113	—	9	113	—	7	115	—	116	6	—
New Mexico	28	7	19	2	2	26	—	3	25	—	27	1	—
New York	285	134	140	—	131	139	7	125	146	3	196	57	—
North Carolina	88	28	56	—	19	66	—	32	55	—	73	3	—
North Dakota	18	13	5	—	8	10	—	8	10	—	18	—	—
Ohio	175	71	103	—	47	122	6	40	133	2	173	—	2
Oklahoma	53	16	35	2	3	47	3	3	49	1	49	3	1
Oregon	50	32	13	5	26	21	3	24	24	2	49	—	1
Pennsylvania	195	42	153	—	39	156	—	53	142	—	195	—	—
Puerto Rico	53	—	53	—	—	53	—	—	53	—	10	43	—
Rhode Island	27	11	15	1	11	15	1	8	18	1	24	—	2
South Carolina	48	21	23	4	23	19	6	21	25	2	21	19	8
South Dakota	19	7	12	—	7	12	—	7	12	—	—	6	—
Tennessee	76	31	41	4	29	41	6	34	39	3	72	1	3
Texas	200	53	137	10	47	141	12	39	150	11	152	38	10
Utah	27	17	10	—	11	15	1	13	14	—	19	7	1
Vermont	17	11	4	—	10	4	—	10	4	—	12	3	—
Virginia	78	29	48	—	29	48	—	33	43	—	50	23	4
Washington	70	49	18	—	29	39	1	35	35	—	67	—	—
West Virginia	44	12	27	5	12	29	3	17	24	3	—	—	—
Wisconsin	89	28	45	16	26	57	6	31	54	4	83	6	—
Wyoming	15	2	12	—	2	12	—	13	1	—	13	1	—
Latin America	5	—	5	—	.5	4.5	—	—	5	—	5	—	—
Democrats Abroad	5	1.5	3.5	—	1.5	3.5	—	—	5	—	5	—	—
Virgin Islands	6	1.2	4.8	—	2.6	2.6	.6	1.2	4.8	—	4.8	1.2	—
American Samoa	6	—	6	—	—	6	—	—	6	—	6	—	—
Guam	7	—	7	—	—	7	—	7	—	—	7	—	—
Total	3933	1405.7	2216.3	112	1127.6	2591.6	99.6	1253.2	2500.8	58	3271.8	351.2	118

1984 Democratic

(Narrative, p. 548)

Delegation	Total Votes	First Pres. Ballot[1]		
		Mondale	Hart	Jackson
Alabama	62	39	13	9
Alaska	14	9	4	1
Arizona	40	20	16	2
Arkansas	42	26	9	7
California	345	95	190	33
Colorado	51	1	42	1
Connecticut	60	23	36	1
Delaware	18	13	5	0
D.C.	19	5	—	14
Florida	143	82	55	3
Georgia	84	40	24	20
Hawaii	27	27	—	0
Idaho	22	10	12	0
Illinois	194	114	41	39
Indiana	88	42	38	8
Iowa	58	37	18	2
Kansas	44	25	16	3
Kentucky	63	51	5	7
Louisiana	69	26	19	24
Maine	27	13	13	0
Maryland	74	54	3	17
Massachusetts	116	59	49	5
Michigan	155	96	49	10
Minnesota	86	63	3	4
Mississippi	43	26	4	13
Missouri	86	55	14	16
Montana	25	11	13	1
Nebraska	30	12	17	1
Nevada	20	9	10	1
New Hampshire	22	12	10	0
New Jersey	122	115	—	7
New Mexico	28	13	13	2
New York	285	156	75	52
North Carolina	88	53	19	16
North Dakota	18	10	5	1
Ohio	175	84	80	11
Oklahoma	53	24	26	3
Oregon	50	16	31	2
Pennsylvania	195	177	—	18
Puerto Rico	53	53	—	0
Rhode Island	27	14	12	0
South Carolina	48	16	13	19
South Dakota	19	9	10	0
Tennessee	76	39	20	17
Texas	200	119	40	36
Utah	27	8	19	0
Vermont	17	5	8	3
Virginia	78	34	18	25
Washington	70	31	36	3
West Virginia	44	30	14	0
Wisconsin	89	58	25	6
Wyoming	15	7	7	0
Latin American	5	5	—	0
Democrats Abroad	5	3	1.5	0.5
Virgin Islands	6	4	—	2
American Samoa	6	6	—	0
Guam	7	7	—	0
Total	3933	2191	1200.5	465.5

1. Other candidates: Thomas F. Eagleton, 18 (16 in Minnesota, 2 in North Dakota); George McGovern, 4 (3 in Massachusetts, 1 in Iowa); John Glenn, 2 (Texas); Joseph R. Biden Jr., 1 (Maine); Martha Kirkland, 1 (Alabama); not voting, 40 (27 in California, 7 Connecticut, 2 in Arizona, 2 in Florida, 1 in Vermont, 1 in Wyoming); absent, 10.

1988 Democratic

(Narrative, p. 552)

Delegation	Total Votes	Fair Tax[1]		No First Use of Nuclear Weapons[2]		First Pres. Ballot[3]	
		Yea	Nay	Yea	Nay	Dukakis	Jackson
Alabama	65	14	35	19	38	37	28
Alaska	17	5	7	8	8	9	7
Arizona	43	15	21	15	25	28	14
Arkansas	48	11	27	9	25	31	11
California	363	104	240	119.09	192.63	235	122
Colorado	55	20	31	20	32	37	18
Connecticut	63	16	42	21	39	47	16
Delaware	19	8	11	8	11	9	7
Florida	154	33	89	33	100	116	35
Georgia	94	30	43	36	43	50	42
Hawaii	28	8	19	8	19	19	8
Idaho	24	3	18	3	18	20	3
Illinois	200	28	75	40	62	138	57
Indiana	89	18	68	19	66	69.50	18
Iowa	61	11	48	21	38	49	12
Kansas	45	12	29.50	14.50	28.50	30	15
Kentucky	65	6	43	6	46	59	6
Louisiana	76	23	11	26	13	41	33
Maine	29	11	15	11	14	17	12
Maryland	84	21	58	21	58	59	25
Massachusetts	119	20	79	23	86	99	19
Michigan	162	78	77	78	77	80	80
Minnesota	91	36	45	42	46	57	29
Mississippi	47	24	15	27	16	19	26
Missouri	88	31	49	33	50	50	37
Montana	28	5	21	7	19	22	5
Nebraska	30	7	23	7	23	22	8
Nevada	23	5	15	6	15	16	5
New Hampshire	22	0	22	1	21	22	0
New Jersey	126	19	39	19	64	107	19
New Mexico	30	7	19	7	20	22	8
New York	292	90	181	108	173	194	97
North Carolina	95	36	51	37	51	58	35
North Dakota	22	46	131	5	11	17	3
Ohio	183	46	131	48	132	136	46
Oklahoma	56	4	44	4	46	52	4
Oregon	54	18	31	18	34	35	18
Pennsylvania	202	22	177	22	179	179	23
Rhode Island	28	3	15	4	16	24	3
South Carolina	53	29	19	30	23	22	31
South Dakota	20	2	16	2	17	19	1
Tennessee	84	12	54	15	57	63	20
Texas	211	72	123	72	121	135	71
Utah	28	3	18	5	20	25	3
Vermont	20	10	9	11	9	9	9
Virginia	86	37	46	41	44	42	42
Washington	77	27	46	29	42	50	27
West Virginia	47	0	44	1	43	47	0
Wisconsin	91	24	59	25	59	65	25
Wyoming	18	4	12	6	10	14	4
District of Columbia	25	13	6	16	8	7	18
Puerto Rico	57	3	53	8	48	48.50	8
Virgin Islands	5	5	0	5	0	0	5
American Samoa	6	0	6	0	6	6	0
Guam	4	0	4	0	4	4	0
Democrats Abroad	9	0.50	8.50	1	8	8.25	0.50
Total	4,162	1,091.50	2,499.00	1,220.59	2,474.13	2,876.25	1,218.50

1. Not voting, 90.
2. Not voting, 67.
3. Other candidates: Lloyd Bentsen, 1 (Alaska); Joseph R. Biden Jr., 2 (Delaware); Richard A. Gephardt, 2 (1 in Louisiana, 1 in Texas); Richard H. Stallings, 3 (Minnesota); Gary Hart, 1 (Vermont), absent, 44.25.

1988 Republican

(Narrative, p. 554)

Delegation	Total Votes	First Pres. Ballot Bush
Alabama	38	38
Alaska	19	19
Arizona	33	33
Arkansas	27	27
California	175	175
Colorado	36	36
Connecticut	35	35
Delaware	17	17
Florida	82	82
Georgia	48	48
Hawaii	20	20
Idaho	22	22
Illinois	92	92
Indiana	51	51
Iowa	37	37
Kansas	34	34
Kentucky	38	38
Louisiana	41	41
Maine	22	22
Maryland	41	41
Massachusetts	52	52
Michigan	77	77
Minnesota	31	31
Mississippi	31	31
Missouri	47	47
Montana	20	20
Nebraska	25	25
Nevada	20	20
New Hampshire	23	23
New Jersey	64	64
New Mexico	26	26
New York	136	136
North Carolina	54	54
North Dakota	16	16
Ohio	88	88
Oklahoma	36	36
Oregon	32	32
Pennsylvania	96	96
Rhode Island	21	21
South Carolina	37	37
South Dakota	18	18
Tennessee	45	45
Texas	111	111
Utah	26	26
Vermont	17	17
Virginia	50	50
Washington	41	41
West Virginia	28	28
Wisconsin	47	47
Wyoming	18	18
District of Columbia	14	14
Puerto Rico	14	14
Virgin Islands	4	4
Guam	4	4
Total	2,277	2,277

1992 Democratic
(Narrative, p. 556)

Delegation	Total Votes	Tax Fairness[1]		First Pres. Ballot[2]		
		Yes	Nay	Clinton	Brown	Tsongas
Alabama	67	0	67	67	0	0
Alaska	18	0	16	18	0	0
Arizona	49	29	15	23	12	14
Arkansas	48	0	48	48	0	0
California	406	96	176	211	160	0
Colorado	58	31	23	26	19	13
Connecticut	66	23	30	45	21	0
Delaware	21	8	8	17	3	1
Florida	167	50	71	141	3	15
Georgia	96	14	50	96	0	0
Hawaii	28	5	17	24	2	0
Idaho	26	5	17	22	0	1
Illinois	195	51	76	155	9	29
Indiana	93	21	68	73	20	0
Iowa	59	7	43	55	2	0
Kansas	44	5	38	43	0	0
Kentucky	64	3	53	63	0	0
Louisiana	75	0	75	75	0	0
Maine	31	18	2	14	13	4
Maryland	85	27	23	83	0	2
Massachusetts	119	97	0	109	6	1
Michigan	159	43	82	120	35	0
Minnesota	92	23	43	61	8	2
Mississippi	46	0	46	46	0	0
Missouri	92	6	46	91	1	0
Montana	24	0	19	21	2	0
Nebraska	33	10	14	24	9	0
Nevada	27	0	25	23	4	0
New Hampshire	24	10	10	17	0	7
New Jersey	126	12	76	102	24	0
New Mexico	34	3	27	30	3	0
New York	290	116	109	155	67	64
North Carolina	99	0	64	95	1	0
North Dakota	22	3	14	18	0	0
Ohio	178	37	141	144	34	0
Oklahoma	58	0	53	56	2	0
Oregon	57	14	38	38	19	0
Pennsylvania	194	21	78	139	43	4
Rhode Island	29	7	9	27	2	0
South Carolina	54	7	40	54	0	0
South Dakota	21	1	16	21	0	0
Tennessee	85	6	38	85	0	0
Texas	232	33	112	204	4	20
Utah	29	25	0	20	9	0
Vermont	21	11	6	14	7	0
Virginia	97	11	43	94	3	0
Washington	84	30	29	49	18	14
West Virginia	41	0	13	41	0	0
Wisconsin	94	29	61	46	30	18
Wyoming	19	5	8	18	1	0
District of Columbia	31	0	30	31	0	0
Puerto Rico	58	0	58	57	0	0
Virgin Islands	5	0	5	5	0	0
American Samoa	5	0	5	5	0	0
Guam	4	0	4	4	0	0
Democrats Abroad	9	0	8.75	9	0	0
Total	4,288	953.00	2,286.75	3,372	596	209

1. Not voting, 177.
2. Other candidates: Larry Agran, 3 (1 in Idaho, 2 in Minnesota); Robert P. Casey, 10 (Minnesota); Patricia Schroeder, 8 (Colorado); Albert Gore Jr., 1 (Pennsylvania); Joseph Simonetti, 1 (Pennsylvania); Others, 2 (1 in New Mexico, 1 in North Dakota). Not voting, 86.

1992 Republican

(Narrative, p. 558)

Delegation	Total Votes	First Pres. Ballot[1]	
		Bush	Buchanan
Alabama	38	38	0
Alaska	19	19	0
Arizona	37	37	0
Arkansas	27	27	0
California	201	201	0
Colorado	37	31	5
Connecticut	35	35	0
Delaware	19	19	0
Florida	97	97	0
Georgia	52	52	0
Hawaii	14	14	0
Idaho	22	22	0
Illinois	85	85	0
Indiana	51	51	0
Iowa	23	23	0
Kansas	30	30	0
Kentucky	35	35	0
Louisiana	38	38	0
Maine	22	22	0
Maryland	42	42	0
Massachusetts	38	35	1
Michigan	72	72	0
Minnesota	32	32	0
Mississippi	34	34	0
Missouri	47	47	0
Montana	20	20	0
Nebraska	24	24	0
Nevada	21	21	0
New Hampshire[2]	23	—	0
New Jersey	60	60	0
New Mexico	25	25	0
New York	100	100	0
North Carolina	57	57	0
North Dakota	17	17	0
Ohio	83	83	0
Oklahoma	34	34	0
Oregon	23	23	0
Pennsylvania	91	90	1
Rhode Island	15	15	0
South Carolina	36	36	0
South Dakota	19	19	0
Tennessee	45	34	11
Texas	121	121	0
Utah	27	27	0
Vermont	19	19	0
Virginia	55	55	0
Washington	35	35	0
West Virginia	18	18	0
Wisconsin	35	35	0
Wyoming	20	20	0
District of Columbia	14	14	0
Puerto Rico	14	14	0
Virgin Islands	4	4	0
American Samoa	4	4	0
Guam	4	4	0
Total	2,210	2,166	18

1. Other candidates: Howard Phillips, 2 (1 in Colorado; 1 in Massachusetts), Alan Keyes, 1 (Massachusetts).
2. Never voted.

1996 Republican

(Narrative, p. 561)

Delegation	Total Votes	First Pres. Ballot[1]	
		Dole	Buchanan
Alabama	40	40	0
Alaska	19	16	0
Arizona	39	37	0
Arkansas	20	16	0
California	165	165	0
Colorado	27	27	0
Connecticut	27	27	0
Delaware	12	12	0
Florida	98	98	0
Georgia	42	42	0
Hawaii	14	14	0
Idaho	23	19	0
Illinois	69	69	0
Indiana	52	52	0
Iowa	25	25	0
Kansas	31	31	0
Kentucky	26	26	0
Louisiana	30	17	10
Maine	15	15	0
Maryland	32	32	0
Massachusetts	37	37	0
Michigan	57	52	5
Minnesota	33	33	0
Mississippi	33	33	0
Missouri	36	24	11
Montana	14	14	0
Nebraska	24	24	0
Nevada	14	14	0
New Hampshire	16	16	0
New Jersey	48	48	0
New Mexico	18	18	0
New York	102	102	0
North Carolina	58	58	0
North Dakota	18	17	0
Ohio	67	67	0
Oklahoma	38	38	0
Oregon	23	18	5
Pennsylvania	73	73	0
Rhode Island	16	16	0
South Carolina	37	37	0
South Dakota	18	18	0
Tennessee	38	37	0
Texas	123	121	2
Utah	28	27	1
Vermont	12	12	0
Virginia	53	53	0
Washington	36	27	9
West Virginia	18	18	0
Wisconsin	36	36	0
Wyoming	20	20	0
District of Columbia	14	14	0
Puerto Rico	14	14	0
Virgin Islands	4	4	0
American Samoa	4	4	0
Guam	4	4	0
Total	1,990	1,928	43

1. Other candidates: Phil Gramm, 2 (Louisiana); Alan Keyes, 1(Missouri); Robert Bork, 1 (Louisiana); not voting, 15.

1996 Democratic

(Narrative, p. 563)

Delegation	Total Votes	First Pres. Ballot[1] Clinton
Alabama	66	66
Alaska	19	19
Arizona	59	59
Arkansas	47	47
California	422	416
Colorado	56	56
Connecticut	67	67
Delaware	21	21
Florida	178	178
Georgia	91	91
Hawaii	30	29
Idaho	23	23
Illinois	193	193
Indiana	88	88
Iowa	56	56
Kansas	42	42
Kentucky	61	61
Louisiana	71	71
Maine	32	32
Maryland	88	88
Massachusetts	114	114
Michigan	156	156
Minnesota	92	92
Mississippi	47	47
Missouri	93	93
Montana	24	24
Nebraska	34	34
Nevada	26	26
New Hampshire	26	26
New Jersey	122	122
New Mexico	34	34
New York	289	289
North Carolina	99	99
North Dakota	22	21
Ohio	172	172
Oklahoma	52	52
Oregon	57	54
Pennsylvania	195	195
Rhode Island	32	31
South Carolina	51	51
South Dakota	22	22
Tennessee	80	80
Texas	229	229
Utah	31	31
Vermont	22	22
Virginia	97	97
Washington	90	90
West Virginia	43	43
Wisconsin	93	93
Wyoming	19	19
District of Columbia	33	33
Puerto Rico	58	58
Virgin Islands	4	4
American Samoa	6	6
Guam	6	6
Democrats Abroad	9	9
Total	4,289	4,277

1. Not voting, 12.

2000 Republican

(Narrative, p. 566)

Delegation	Total Votes	First Pres. Ballot Bush
Alabama	44	44
Alaska	23	23
Arizona	30	30
Arkansas	24	24
California	162	162
Colorado	40	40
Connecticut	25	25
Delaware	12	12
Florida	80	80
Georgia	54	54
Hawaii	14	14
Idaho	28	28
Illinois	74	74
Indiana	55	55
Iowa	25	25
Kansas	35	35
Kentucky	31	31
Louisiana	29	29
Maine	14	14
Maryland	31	31
Massachusetts	37	37
Michigan	58	58
Minnesota	34	34
Mississippi	33	33
Missouri	35	35
Montana	23	23
Nebraska	30	30
Nevada	17	17
New Hampshire	17	17
New Jersey	54	54
New Mexico	21	21
New York	101	101
North Carolina	62	62
North Dakota	19	19
Ohio	69	69
Oklahoma	38	38
Oregon	24	24
Pennsylvania	78	78
Rhode Island	14	14
South Carolina	37	37
South Dakota	22	22
Tennessee	37	37
Texas	124	124
Utah	29	29
Vermont	12	12
Virginia	56	56
Washington	37	37
West Virginia	18	18
Wisconsin	37	37
Wyoming	22	22
District of Columbia	15	15
Puerto Rico	14	14
Virgin Islands	4	4
American Samoa	4	4
Guam	4	4
Total	2,066	2,066

2000 Democratic

(Narrative, p. 568)

Delegation	Total Votes	First Pres. Ballot[1] Gore
Alabama	64	64
Alaska	19	19
Arizona	55	55
Arkansas	47	47
California	435	435
Colorado	61	61
Connecticut	67	67
Delaware	22	22
Florida	186	186
Georgia	92	92
Hawaii	33	33
Idaho	23	23
Illinois	190	190
Indiana	88	88
Iowa	57	57
Kansas	42	42
Kentucky	58	58
Louisiana	73	73
Maine	33	33
Maryland	95	95
Massachusetts	118	118
Michigan	157	157
Minnesota	91	91
Mississippi	48	48
Missouri	92	92
Montana	24	24
Nebraska	32	32
Nevada	29	29
New Hampshire	29	29
New Jersey	124	124
New Mexico	35	35
New York	294	294
North Carolina	103	103
North Dakota	22	22
Ohio	170	170
Oklahoma	52	52
Oregon	58	58
Pennsylvania	191	191
Rhode Island	33	33
South Carolina	52	52
South Dakota	22	22
Tennessee	81	81
Texas	231	231
Utah	29	29
Vermont	22	22
Virginia	95	95
Washington	94	94
West Virginia	42	42
Wisconsin	93	93
Wyoming	18	18
District of Columbia	33	33
Puerto Rico	58	58
Virgin Islands	6	6
American Samoa	6	6
Guam	6	6
Democrats Abroad	9	9
Total	4,339	4,339

1. Unofficial total. There may have been several delegates not voting.

CHAPTER 16

Popular Vote Returns for President

P OPULAR VOTE RETURNS for all presidential elections from 1824 to 2000 are presented in this section (pages 644–700). The presidential returns, except where indicated by a footnote, were obtained from three sources. The returns for 1824 to 1916 are from Inter-University Consortium for Political and Social Research (ICPSR) at the University of Michigan. The returns from 1920 to 1992 are from Richard M. Scammon and Alice V. McGillivray, *America at the Polls* (Washington, D.C.: Congressional Quarterly, 1994). The returns for 1996 and 2000 are from the *America Votes* series, compiled biennially by Rhodes Cook for Congressional Quarterly in Washington, D.C. For this edition, elections historian Michael J. Dubin supplemented this source material with new elections data research. CQ editors felt the new data was of scholarly merit and worthy of inclusion—much of it filling the gaps or correcting errors in previous editions of *Guide to U.S. Elections*. Dubin's original sources are also listed in the footnotes.

The 1824 starting date for the ICPSR collection was based on factors such as the pronounced trend by 1824 for the election of presidential electors by popular vote, as well as the availability, accessibility, and quality of the returns. The bulk of the ICPSR election data collection consists of returns at the county level in computer-readable form.

TABLE ORGANIZATION

For each presidential election from 1824 to 2000, the following information is provided in the tables for the popular returns:

- Names and party affiliations of major candidates.
- Total state-by-state popular vote for president.
- State-by-state breakdown of the popular vote and the percentage of the vote received by each candidate.
- The aggregate vote and percentage of the total vote received in each state by minor party candidates, minor parties running unpledged electors, or unidentified votes. These figures appear in the column designated "Other"; a complete breakdown of these votes appears on pages 689–700.
- The plurality received by the candidate who carried each state, along with the candidate's party designation.
- The total national popular vote for president, the total national popular vote and percentage of the vote received by each candidate, and the nationwide plurality of the candidate who received the greatest number of votes.

The omission of popular vote returns for a state *after 1824* indicates an absence of popular voting for that election. The South Carolina legislature, for example, chose the state's presidential electors until 1860, and the state did not participate in the 1864 presidential election because of the Civil War. Thus, the first popular vote returns shown for South Carolina are for the 1868 election.

PARTY DESIGNATION

In many cases presidential candidates appeared on state ballots under different, even *multiple* party designations. Thus, in the returns for 1968, George C. Wallace ran for president under a variety of party designations in different states: Democratic, American, American Independent, Independent, George Wallace Party, Conservative, American Party of Missouri, Independent American, Courage, and George Wallace and Independent.

To provide one party designation for presidential candidates for the elections 1824 through 1916, Congressional Quarterly has aggregated under a single party designation the votes of candidates who are listed in the ICPSR data as receiving votes under more than one party designation. The source used for assigning party designation for these years is Svend Petersen, *A Statistical History of the American Presidential Elections* (Westport, Conn.: Greenwood Press, 1981). For the 1920 to 1992 elections, the source for party designation is Scammon and McGillivray, *America at the Polls*. For 1968 Scammon lists Wallace as an American Independent, and Congressional Quarterly follows this usage. For the 1996 and 2000 elections, the source for party designation is Cook, the *America Votes* series.

VOTE TOTALS AND PERCENTAGES

The total popular vote for each candidate in a given election was determined by adding the votes received by that candidate in each state (including write-in votes where available), even though the vote totals for some states may have come from sources other than ICPSR, Scammon, or Cook.

The percentages of the vote received in each state and nationally by any candidate or party has been calculated to two decimal places and rounded to one place; thus, 0.05 percent is listed as 0.1 percent. Due to rounding, state and national percentages do not always equal 100 percent.

PLURALITIES

The plurality column represents the differences between the vote received by the first- and second-place finishers in each state and in the nation. In most cases, most notably in 1912 and 1924, a losing major party candidate finished in third place in a state. In those few cases where votes from the "Other" column were needed to calculate the plurality, a footnote provides an explanation. For a breakdown of "Other" votes, see Popular Returns: Minor Candidates and Parties, pp. 689–700.

1824 Presidential Election

STATE	TOTAL VOTE	JOHN Q. ADAMS (Democratic-Republican)		ANDREW JACKSON (Democratic-Republican)		HENRY CLAY (Democratic-Republican)		WILLIAM H. CRAWFORD (Democratic-Republican)		OTHER[1]		PLURALITY[2]	
		Votes	%	Votes	%	Votes	%	Votes	%	Votes	%		
Alabama	13,603	2,422	17.8	9,429	69.3	96	0.7	1,656	12.2	—	0.0	7,007	AJ
Connecticut	10,647	7,494	70.4	—	0.0	—	0.0	1,965	18.5	1,188	11.2	5,529	JQA
Illinois	4,671	1,516	32.5	1,272	27.2	1,036	22.2	847	18.1	—	0.0	244	JQA
Indiana	15,838	3,071	19.4	7,444	47.0	5,316	33.6	—	0.0	7	0.0	2,128	AJ
Kentucky	23,338	—	0.0	6,356	27.2	16,982	72.8	—	0.0	—	0.0	10,626	HC
Maine[3]	12,625	10,289	81.5	—	0.0	—	0.0	2,336	18.5	—	0.0	7,953	JQA
Maryland[3]	33,214	14,632	44.1	14,523	43.7	695	2.1	3,364	10.1	—	0.0	109	JQA
Massachusetts	42,056	30,687	73.0	—	0.0	—	0.0	—	0.0	11,369	27.0	24,071	JQA[4]
Mississippi	4,894	1,654	33.8	3,121	63.8	—	0.0	119	2.4	—	0.0	1,467	AJ
Missouri	3,432	159	4.6	1,166	34.0	2,042	59.5	32	0.9	33	1.0	876	HC
New Hampshire[3]	10,032	9,389	93.6	—	0.0	—	0.0	643	6.4	—	0.0	8,746	JQA
New Jersey	19,837	8,309	41.9	10,332	52.1	—	0.0	1,196	6.0	—	0.0	2,023	AJ
North Carolina	36,109	—	0.0	20,231	56.0	—	0.0	15,622	43.3	256	0.7	4,609	AJ
Ohio[3]	50,024	12,280	24.5	18,489	37.0	19,255	38.5	—	0.0	—	0.0	766	HC
Pennsylvania	47,073	5,441	11.6	35,736	75.9	1,690	3.6	4,206	8.9	—	0.0	30,295	AJ
Rhode Island	2,344	2,144	91.5	—	0.0	—	0.0	—	0.0	200	8.5	1,944	JQA
Tennessee[3]	20,725	216	1.0	20,197	97.5	—	0.0	312	1.5	—	0.0	19,885	AJ
Virginia	15,371	3,419	22.2	2,975	19.4	419	2.7	8,558	55.7	—	0.0	5,139	WHC
Totals	**365,833**	**113,122**	**30.9**	**151,271**	**41.3**	**47,531**	**13.0**	**40,856**	**11.2**	**13,053**	**3.6**	**38,149**	**AJ**

1. For breakdown of "Other" votes, see minor candidate vote totals, p. 689.
2. For the 1824 plurality winner the designations are JQA (John Quincy Adams), AJ (Andrew Jackson), WHC (William H. Crawford), and HC (Henry Clay). Adams was elected president by the House of Representatives.
3. Figures from Svend Petersen, *A Statistical History of the American Presidential Elections* (Westport, Conn.: Greenwood Press, 1981), 18.
4. Plurality of 24,071 votes is calculated on the basis of 6,616 for unpledged electors.

1828 Presidential Election

STATE	TOTAL VOTE	ANDREW JACKSON (Democratic-Republican)		JOHN Q. ADAMS (National Republican)		OTHER[1]		PLURALITY	
		Votes	%	Votes	%	Votes	%		
Alabama	18,618	16,736	89.9	1,878	10.1	4	0.0	14,858	DR
Connecticut	19,378	4,448	23.0	13,829	71.4	1,101	5.7	9,381	NR
Georgia[2]	20,004	19,362	96.8	642	3.2	—	0.0	18,720	DR
Illinois	14,222	9,560	67.2	4,662	32.8	—	0.0	4,898	DR
Indiana	39,210	22,201	56.6	17,009	43.4	—	0.0	5,192	DR
Kentucky	70,776	39,308	55.5	31,468	44.5	—	0.0	7,840	DR
Louisiana	8,687	4,605	53.0	4,082	47.0	—	0.0	523	DR
Maine	34,789	13,927	40.0	20,773	59.7	89	0.3	6,846	NR
Maryland	45,796	22,782	49.7	23,014	50.3	—	0.0	232	NR
Massachusetts	39,074	6,012	15.4	29,836	76.4	3,226	8.3	23,824	NR
Mississippi	8,344	6,763	81.1	1,581	18.9	—	0.0	5,182	DR
Missouri	11,654	8,232	70.6	3,422	29.4	—	0.0	4,810	DR
New Hampshire	44,035	20,212	45.9	23,823	54.1	—	0.0	3,611	NR
New Jersey	45,570	21,809	47.9	23,753	52.1	8	0.0	1,944	NR
New York	270,975	139,412	51.4	131,563	48.6	—	0.0	7,849	DR
North Carolina	51,747	37,814	73.1	13,918	26.9	15	0.0	23,896	DR
Ohio	131,049	67,596	51.6	63,453	48.4	—	0.0	4,143	DR
Pennsylvania	152,220	101,457	66.7	50,763	33.3	—	0.0	50,694	DR
Rhode Island	3,580	820	22.9	2,755	77.0	5	0.1	1,935	NR
Tennessee[2]	46,533	44,293	95.2	2,240	4.8	—	0.0	42,053	DR
Vermont	32,833	8,350	25.4	24,363	74.2	120	0.4	16,013	NR
Virginia	38,924	26,854	69.0	12,070	31.0	—	0.0	14,784	DR
Totals	1,148,018	642,553	56.0	500,897	43.6	4,568	0.4	141,656	DR

1. For breakdown of "Other" votes, see minor candidate vote totals, p. 689.
2. Figures from Svend Petersen, *A Statistical History of the American Presidential Elections* (Westport, Conn.: Greenwood Press, 1981), 20.

1832 Presidential Election

STATE	TOTAL VOTE	ANDREW JACKSON (Democrat) Votes	%	HENRY CLAY (National Republican) Votes	%	WILLIAM WIRT (Anti-Mason) Votes	%	OTHER[1] Votes	%	PLURALITY	
Alabama	14,291	14,286	100.0	5	0.0	—	0.0	—	0.0	14,281	D
Connecticut	32,833	11,269	34.3	18,155	55.3	3,409	10.4	—	0.0	6,886	NR
Delaware	8,386	4,110	49.0	4,276	51.0	—	0.0	—	0.0	166	NR
Georgia[2]	20,750	20,750	100.0	—	0.0	—	0.0	—	0.0	20,750	D
Illinois	21,481	14,609	68.0	6,745	31.4	97	0.5	30	0.1	7,864	D
Indiana	57,152	31,652	55.4	25,473	44.6	27	0.0	—	0.0	6,179	D
Kentucky	79,741	36,292	45.5	43,449	54.5	—	0.0	—	0.0	7,157	NR
Louisiana	6,337	3,908	61.7	2,429	38.3	—	0.0	—	0.0	1,479	D
Maine	62,153	33,978	54.7	27,331	44.0	844	1.4	—	0.0	6,647	D
Maryland	38,316	19,156	50.0	19,160	50.0	—	0.0	—	0.0	4	NR
Massachusetts	67,619	13,933	20.6	31,963	47.3	14,692	21.7	7,031	10.4	17,271	NR
Mississippi	5,750	5,750	100.0	—	0.0	—	0.0	—	0.0	5,750	D
Missouri[2]	5,192	5,192	100.0	—	0.0	—	0.0	—	0.0	5,192	D
New Hampshire	43,793	24,855	56.8	18,938	43.2	—	0.0	—	0.0	5,917	D
New Jersey	47,760	23,826	49.9	23,466	49.1	468	1.0	—	0.0	360	D
New York	323,393	168,497	52.1	154,896	47.9	—	0.0	—	0.0	13,601	D
North Carolina	29,799	25,261	84.8	4,538	15.2	—	0.0	—	0.0	20,723	D
Ohio	158,350	81,246	51.3	76,566	48.4	538	0.3	—	0.0	4,680	D
Pennsylvania	157,679	90,973	57.7	—	0.0	66,706	42.3	—	0.0	24,267	D
Rhode Island	5,747	2,051	35.7	2,871	50.0	819	14.3	6	0.1	820	NR
Tennessee	29,425	28,078	95.4	1,347	4.6	—	0.0	—	0.0	26,731	D
Vermont	32,344	7,865	24.3	11,161	34.5	13,112	40.5	206	0.6	1,951	AM
Virginia	45,682	34,243	75.0	11,436	25.0	3	0.0	—	0.0	22,807	D
Totals	1,293,973	701,780	54.2	484,205	37.4	100,715	7.8	7,273	0.6	217,575	D

1. For breakdown of "Other" vote, see minor candidate vote totals, p. 689.
2. Figures from Svend Petersen, *A Statistical History of the American Presidential Elections* (Westport, Conn.: Greenwood Press, 1981), 21.

1836 Presidential Election

STATE	TOTAL VOTE	MARTIN VAN BUREN (Democrat)		WILLIAM H. HARRISON (Whig)		HUGH L. WHITE (Whig)		DANIEL WEBSTER (Whig)		OTHER[1]		PLURALITY[2]	
		Votes	%	Votes	%	Votes	%	Votes	%	Votes	%		
Alabama	37,296	20,638	55.3	—	0.0	16,658	44.7	—	0.0	—	0.0	3,980	MBV
Arkansas	3,714	2,380	64.1	—	0.0	1,334	35.9	—	0.0	—	0.0	1,046	MBV
Connecticut	38,093	19,294	50.6	18,799	49.4	—	0.0	—	0.0	—	0.0	495	MBV
Delaware	8,895	4,154	46.7	4,736	53.2	—	0.0	—	0.0	5	0.1	582	WHH
Georgia	47,259	22,778	48.2	—	0.0	24,481	51.8	—	0.0	—	0.0	1,703	HLW
Illinois	33,589	18,369	54.7	15,220	45.3	—	0.0	—	0.0	—	0.0	3,149	MBV
Indiana	74,423	33,084	44.5	41,339	55.5	—	0.0	—	0.0	—	0.0	8,255	WHH
Kentucky	70,090	33,229	47.4	36,861	52.6	—	0.0	—	0.0	—	0.0	3,632	WHH
Louisiana	7,425	3,842	51.7	—	0.0	3,583	48.3	—	0.0	—	0.0	259	MBV
Maine	38,740	22,825	58.9	14,803	38.2	—	0.0	—	0.0	1,112	2.9	8,022	MBV
Maryland	48,119	22,267	46.3	25,852	53.7	—	0.0	—	0.0	—	0.0	3,585	WHH
Massachusetts	74,732	33,486	44.8	—	0.0	—	0.0	41,201	55.1	45	0.1	33,486	DW
Michigan	12,052	6,507	54.0	5,545	46.0	—	0.0	—	0.0	—	0.0	962	MBV
Mississippi	20,079	10,297	51.3	—	0.0	9,782	48.7	—	0.0	—	0.0	515	MBV
Missouri[3]	18,332	10,995	60.0	—	0.0	7,337	40.0	—	0.0	—	0.0	3,658	MBV
New Hampshire	24,925	18,697	75.0	6,228	25.0	—	0.0	—	0.0	—	0.0	12,469	MBV
New Jersey	51,729	25,592	49.5	26,137	50.5	—	0.0	—	0.0	—	0.0	545	WHH
New York	305,343	166,795	54.6	138,548	45.4	—	0.0	—	0.0	—	0.0	28,247	MBV
North Carolina	50,153	26,631	53.1	—	0.0	23,521	46.9	—	0.0	1	0.0	3,110	MBV
Ohio	202,931	97,122	47.9	105,809	52.1	—	0.0	—	0.0	—	0.0	8,687	WHH
Pennsylvania	178,701	91,466	51.2	87,235	48.8	—	0.0	—	0.0	—	0.0	4,231	MBV
Rhode Island	5,673	2,962	52.2	2,710	47.8	—	0.0	—	0.0	1	0.0	252	MBV
Tennessee	62,197	26,170	42.1	—	0.0	36,027	57.9	—	0.0	—	0.0	9,857	HLW
Vermont	35,099	14,040	40.0	20,994	59.8	—	0.0	—	0.0	65	0.2	6,954	WHH
Virginia	53,945	30,556	56.6	—	0.0	23,384	43.3	—	0.0	5	0.0	7,172	MBV
Totals	1,503,534	764,176	50.8	550,816	36.6	146,107	9.7	41,201	2.7	1,234	0.1	213,360	MBV

1. For breakdown of "Other" vote, see minor candidate vote totals, p. 689.
2. For the 1836 plurality winner, the designations are MVB (Martin Van Buren), WHH (William Henry Harrison), HLW (Hugh L. White), and DW (Daniel Webster).
3. Figures from Svend Petersen, *A Statistical History of the American Presidential Elections* (Westport, Conn.: Greenwood Press, 1981), 22.

1840 Presidential Election

STATE	TOTAL VOTE	WILLIAM H. HARRISON (Whig)		MARTIN VAN BUREN (Democrat)		JAMES G. BIRNEY (Liberty)		OTHER[1]		PLURALITY	
		Votes	%	Votes	%	Votes	%	Votes	%		
Alabama	62,511	28,515	45.6	33,996	54.4	—	0.0	—	0.0	5,481	D
Arkansas	11,839	5,160	43.6	6,679	56.4	—	0.0	—	0.0	1,519	D
Connecticut	56,879	31,598	55.6	25,281	44.4	—	0.0	—	0.0	6,317	W
Delaware	10,852	5,967	55.0	4,872	44.9	—	0.0	13	0.1	1,095	W
Georgia	72,322	40,339	55.8	31,983	44.2	—	0.0	—	0.0	8,356	W
Illinois	93,175	45,574	48.9	47,441	50.9	160	0.2	—	0.0	1,867	D
Indiana	117,605	65,280	55.5	51,696	44.0	30	0.0	599	0.5	13,584	W
Kentucky	91,104	58,488	64.2	32,616	35.8	—	0.0	—	0.0	25,872	W
Louisiana	18,912	11,296	59.7	7,616	40.3	—	0.0	—	0.0	3,680	W
Maine	92,802	46,612	50.2	46,190	49.8	—	0.0	—	0.0	422	W
Maryland	62,280	33,528	53.8	28,752	46.2	—	0.0	—	0.0	4,776	W
Massachusetts	126,825	72,852	57.4	52,355	41.3	1,618	1.3	—	0.0	20,497	W
Michigan	44,029	22,933	52.1	21,096	47.9	—	0.0	—	0.0	1,837	W
Mississippi	36,525	19,515	53.4	17,010	46.6	—	0.0	—	0.0	2,505	W
Missouri	52,923	22,954	43.4	29,969	56.6	—	0.0	—	0.0	7,015	D
New Hampshire	59,956	26,310	43.9	32,774	54.7	872	1.5	—	0.0	6,464	D
New Jersey	64,454	33,351	51.7	31,034	48.1	69	0.1	—	0.0	2,317	W
New York	441,543	226,001	51.2	212,733	48.2	2,809	0.6	—	0.0	13,268	W
North Carolina	80,735	46,567	57.7	34,168	42.3	—	0.0	—	0.0	12,399	W
Ohio	272,890	148,043	54.3	123,944	45.4	903	0.3	—	0.0	24,099	W
Pennsylvania	287,695	144,023	50.1	143,672	49.9	—	0.0	—	0.0	351	W
Rhode Island	8,631	5,213	60.4	3,263	37.8	19	0.2	136	1.6	1,950	W
Tennessee	108,145	60,194	55.7	47,951	44.3	—	0.0	—	0.0	12,243	W
Vermont	50,782	32,440	63.9	18,006	35.5	317	0.6	19	0.0	14,434	W
Virginia	86,394	42,637	49.4	43,757	50.6	—	0.0	—	0.0	1,120	D
Totals	2,411,808	1,275,390	52.9	1,128,854	46.8	6,797	0.3	767	0.0	146,536	W

1. For breakdown of "Other" vote, see minor candidate vote totals, p. 689.

1844 Presidential Election

STATE	TOTAL VOTE	JAMES K. POLK (Democrat) Votes	%	HENRY CLAY (Whig) Votes	%	JAMES G. BIRNEY (Liberty) Votes	%	OTHER [1] Votes	%	PLURALITY	
Alabama	63,403	37,401	59.0	26,002	41.0	—	0.0	—	0.0	11,399	D
Arkansas	15,150	9,546	63.0	5,604	37.0	—	0.0	—	0.0	3,942	D
Connecticut	64,616	29,841	46.2	32,832	50.8	1,943	3.0	—	0.0	2,991	W
Delaware	12,247	5,970	48.7	6,271	51.2	—	0.0	6	0.0	301	W
Georgia	86,247	44,147	51.2	42,100	48.8	—	0.0	—	0.0	2,047	D
Illinois	109,057	58,795	53.9	45,854	42.0	3,469	3.2	939	0.9	12,941	D
Indiana	140,157	70,183	50.1	67,866	48.4	2,108	1.5	—	0.0	2,317	D
Kentucky	113,237	51,988	45.9	61,249	54.1	—	0.0	—	0.0	9,261	W
Louisiana	26,865	13,782	51.3	13,083	48.7	—	0.0	—	0.0	699	D
Maine	84,933	45,719	53.8	34,378	40.5	4,836	5.7	—	0.0	11,341	D
Maryland	68,690	32,706	47.6	35,984	52.4	—	0.0	—	0.0	3,278	W
Massachusetts	132,037	53,039	40.2	67,062	50.8	10,830	8.2	1,106	0.8	14,023	W
Michigan	55,560	27,737	49.9	24,185	43.5	3,638	6.5	—	0.0	3,552	D
Mississippi	45,004	25,846	57.4	19,158	42.6	—	0.0	—	0.0	6,688	D
Missouri	72,522	41,322	57.0	31,200	43.0	—	0.0	—	0.0	10,122	D
New Hampshire	49,187	27,160	55.2	17,866	36.3	4,161	8.5	—	0.0	9,294	D
New Jersey	75,944	37,495	49.4	38,318	50.5	131	0.2	—	0.0	823	W
New York	485,882	237,588	48.9	232,482	47.8	15,812	3.3	—	0.0	5,106	D
North Carolina	82,521	39,287	47.6	43,232	52.4	—	0.0	2	0.0	3,945	W
Ohio	312,300	149,127	47.8	155,091	49.7	8,082	2.6	—	0.0	5,964	W
Pennsylvania	331,645	167,311	50.4	161,195	48.6	3,139	0.9	—	0.0	6,116	D
Rhode Island	12,194	4,867	39.9	7,322	60.0	—	0.0	5	0.0	2,455	W
Tennessee	119,957	59,917	49.9	60,040	50.1	—	0.0	—	0.0	123	W
Vermont	48,765	18,041	37.0	26,770	54.9	3,954	8.1	—	0.0	8,729	W
Virginia	95,539	50,679	53.0	44,860	47.0	—	0.0	—	0.0	5,819	D
Totals	2,703,659	1,339,494	49.5	1,300,004	48.1	62,103	2.3	2,058	0.1	39,490	D

1. For breakdown of "Other" vote, see minor candidate vote totals, p. 689.

1848 Presidential Election

STATE	TOTAL VOTE	ZACHARY TAYLOR (Whig)		LEWIS CASS (Democrat)		MARTIN VAN BUREN (Free Soil)		OTHER[1]		PLURALITY	
		Votes	%	Votes	%	Votes	%	Votes	%		
Alabama	61,659	30,482	49.4	31,173	50.6	—	0.0	4	0.0	691	D
Arkansas	16,888	7,587	44.9	9,301	55.1	—	0.0	—	0.0	1,714	D
Connecticut	62,398	30,318	48.6	27,051	43.4	5,005	8.0	24	0.0	3,267	W
Delaware	12,432	6,440	51.8	5,910	47.5	82	0.7	—	0.0	530	W
Florida	7,203	4,120	57.2	3,083	42.8	—	0.0	—	0.0	1,037	W
Georgia	92,317	47,532	51.5	44,785	48.5	—	0.0	—	0.0	2,747	W
Illinois	124,596	52,853	42.4	55,952	44.9	15,702	12.6	89	0.1	3,099	D
Indiana	152,394	69,668	45.7	74,695	49.0	8,031	5.3	—	0.0	5,027	D
Iowa	22,271	9,930	44.6	11,238	50.5	1,103	5.0	—	0.0	1,308	D
Kentucky	116,865	67,145	57.5	49,720	42.5	—	0.0	—	0.0	17,425	W
Louisiana	33,866	18,487	54.6	15,379	45.4	—	0.0	—	0.0	3,108	W
Maine	87,625	35,273	40.3	40,195	45.9	12,157	13.9	—	0.0	4,922	D
Maryland	72,359	37,702	52.1	34,528	47.7	129	0.2	—	0.0	3,174	W
Massachusetts	134,748	61,072	45.3	35,281	26.2	38,333	28.4	62	0.0	22,739	W
Michigan	65,082	23,947	36.8	30,742	47.2	10,393	16.0	—	0.0	6,795	D
Mississippi	52,456	25,911	49.4	26,545	50.6	—	0.0	—	0.0	634	D
Missouri	72,748	32,671	44.9	40,077	55.1	—	0.0	—	0.0	7,406	D
New Hampshire	50,104	14,781	29.5	27,763	55.4	7,560	15.1	—	0.0	12,982	D
New Jersey	77,745	40,015	51.5	36,901	47.5	829	1.1	—	0.0	3,114	W
New York	455,944	218,583	47.9	114,319	25.1	120,497	26.4	2,545	0.6	98,086	W
North Carolina	79,826	44,054	55.2	35,772	44.8	—	0.0	—	0.0	8,282	W
Ohio	328,987	138,656	42.1	154,782	47.0	35,523	10.8	26	0.0	16,126	D
Pennsylvania	369,092	185,730	50.3	172,186	46.7	11,176	3.0	—	0.0	13,544	W
Rhode Island	11,049	6,705	60.7	3,613	32.7	726	6.6	5	0.0	3,092	W
Tennessee	122,463	64,321	52.5	58,142	47.5	—	0.0	—	0.0	6,179	W
Texas	17,000	5,281	31.1	11,644	68.5	—	0.0	75	0.4	6,363	D
Vermont	47,897	23,117	48.3	10,943	22.8	13,837	28.9	—	0.0	9,280	W
Virginia	92,004	45,265	49.2	46,739	50.8	—	0.0	—	0.0	1,474	D
Wisconsin	39,166	13,747	35.1	15,001	38.3	10,418	26.6	—	0.0	1,254	D
Totals	2,879,184	1,361,393	47.3	1,223,460	42.5	291,501	10.1	2,830	0.1	137,933	W

1. For breakdown of "Other" vote, see minor candidate vote totals, p. 690.

1852 Presidential Election

STATE	TOTAL VOTE	FRANKLIN PIERCE (Democrat) Votes	%	WINFIELD SCOTT (Whig) Votes	%	JOHN P. HALE (Free Soil) Votes	%	OTHER[1] Votes	%	PLURALITY	
Alabama	44,147	26,881	60.9	15,061	34.1	—	0.0	2,205	5.0	11,820	D
Arkansas	19,577	12,173	62.2	7,404	37.8	—	0.0	—	0.0	4,769	D
California	76,810	40,721	53.0	35,972	46.8	61	0.1	56	0.1	4,749	D
Connecticut	66,781	33,249	49.8	30,359	45.5	3,161	4.7	12	0.0	2,890	D
Delaware	12,673	6,318	49.9	6,293	49.7	62	0.5	—	0.0	25	D
Florida	7,193	4,318	60.0	2,875	40.0	—	0.0	—	0.0	1,443	D
Georgia[2]	62,626	40,516	64.7	16,660	26.6	—	0.0	5,450	8.7	23,856	D
Illinois	154,974	80,378	51.9	64,733	41.8	9,863	6.4	—	0.0	15,645	D
Indiana	183,176	95,340	52.0	80,907	44.2	6,929	3.8	—	0.0	14,433	D
Iowa	35,364	17,763	50.2	15,856	44.8	1,606	4.5	139	0.4	1,907	D
Kentucky	111,643	53,949	48.3	57,428	51.4	266	0.2	—	0.0	3,479	W
Louisiana	35,902	18,647	51.9	17,255	48.1	—	0.0	—	0.0	1,392	D
Maine	82,182	41,609	50.6	32,543	39.6	8,030	9.8	—	0.0	9,066	D
Maryland	75,120	40,022	53.3	35,077	46.7	21	0.0	—	0.0	4,945	D
Massachusetts	127,103	44,569	35.1	52,683	41.4	28,023	22.0	1,828	1.4	8,114	W
Michigan	82,939	41,842	50.4	33,860	40.8	7,237	8.7	—	0.0	7,982	D
Mississippi	44,454	26,896	60.5	17,558	39.5	—	0.0	—	0.0	9,338	D
Missouri	68,801	38,817	56.4	29,984	43.6	—	0.0	—	0.0	8,833	D
New Hampshire	50,535	28,503	56.4	15,486	30.6	6,546	13.0	—	0.0	13,017	D
New Jersey	83,926	44,301	52.8	38,551	45.9	336	0.4	738	0.9	5,750	D
New York	522,294	262,083	50.2	234,882	45.0	25,329	4.8	—	0.0	27,201	D
North Carolina	78,891	39,788	50.4	39,043	49.5	—	0.0	60	0.1	745	D
Ohio	352,903	169,193	47.9	152,577	43.2	31,133	8.8	—	0.0	16,616	D
Pennsylvania	387,920	198,568	51.2	179,182	46.2	8,500	2.2	1,670	0.4	19,386	D
Rhode Island	17,005	8,735	51.4	7,626	44.8	644	3.8	—	0.0	1,109	D
Tennessee	115,486	56,900	49.3	58,586	50.7	—	0.0	—	0.0	1,686	W
Texas	20,223	14,857	73.5	5,356	26.5	—	0.0	10	0.0	9,501	D
Vermont	43,838	13,044	29.8	22,173	50.6	8,621	19.7	—	0.0	9,129	W
Virginia	132,604	73,872	55.7	58,732	44.3	—	0.0	—	0.0	15,140	D
Wisconsin	64,740	33,658	52.0	22,240	34.4	8,842	13.7	—	0.0	11,418	D
Totals	3,161,830	1,607,510	50.8	1,386,942	43.9	155,210	4.9	12,168	0.4	220,568	D

1. For breakdown of "Other" vote, see minor candidate vote totals, p. 690.
2. Figures from Svend Petersen, *A Statistical History of the American Presidential Elections* (Westport, Conn.: Greenwood Press, 1981), 31.

1856 Presidential Election

STATE	TOTAL VOTE	JAMES BUCHANAN (Democrat) Votes	%	JOHN C. FREMONT (Republican) Votes	%	MILLARD FILLMORE (Whig-American) Votes	%	OTHER [1] Votes	%	PLURALITY	
Alabama	75,291	46,739	62.1	—	0.0	28,552	37.9	—	0.0	18,187	D
Arkansas	32,642	21,910	67.1	—	0.0	10,732	32.9	—	0.0	11,178	D
California	110,255	53,342	48.4	20,704	18.8	36,195	32.8	14	0.0	17,147	D
Connecticut	80,360	35,028	43.6	42,717	53.2	2,615	3.3	—	0.0	7,689	R
Delaware	14,598	8,004	54.8	310	2.1	6,275	43.0	9	0.1	1,729	D
Florida	11,191	6,358	56.8	—	0.0	4,833	43.2	—	0.0	1,525	D
Georgia	99,020	56,581	57.1	—	0.0	42,439	42.9	—	0.0	14,142	D
Illinois	239,334	105,528	44.1	96,275	40.2	37,531	15.7	—	0.0	9,253	D
Indiana	235,401	118,670	50.4	94,375	40.1	22,356	9.5	—	0.0	24,295	D
Iowa	92,310	37,568	40.7	45,073	48.8	9,669	10.5	—	0.0	7,505	R
Kentucky	142,058	74,642	52.5	—	0.0	67,416	47.5	—	0.0	7,226	D
Louisiana	42,873	22,164	51.7	—	0.0	20,709	48.3	—	0.0	1,455	D
Maine	109,689	39,140	35.7	67,279	61.3	3,270	3.0	—	0.0	28,139	R
Maryland	86,860	39,123	45.0	285	0.3	47,452	54.6	—	0.0	8,329	WA
Massachusetts	170,048	39,244	23.1	108,172	63.6	19,626	11.5	3,006	1.8	68,928	R
Michigan	125,558	52,136	41.5	71,762	57.2	1,660	1.3	—	0.0	19,626	R
Mississippi	59,647	35,456	59.4	—	0.0	24,191	40.6	—	0.0	11,265	D
Missouri	106,486	57,964	54.4	—	0.0	48,522	45.6	—	0.0	9,442	D
New Hampshire	69,774	31,891	45.7	37,473	53.7	410	0.6	—	0.0	5,582	R
New Jersey	99,396	46,943	47.2	28,338	28.5	24,115	24.3	—	0.0	18,605	D
New York	596,486	195,878	32.8	276,004	46.3	124,604	20.9	—	0.0	80,126	R
North Carolina	84,963	48,243	56.8	—	0.0	36,720	43.2	—	0.0	11,523	D
Ohio	386,640	170,874	44.2	187,497	48.5	28,121	7.3	148	0.0	16,623	R
Pennsylvania	460,937	230,772	50.1	147,963	32.1	82,202	17.8	—	0.0	82,809	D
Rhode Island	19,822	6,680	33.7	11,467	57.8	1,675	8.5	—	0.0	4,787	R
Tennessee	133,582	69,704	52.2	—	0.0	63,878	47.8	—	0.0	5,826	D
Texas	48,005	31,995	66.6	—	0.0	16,010	33.4	—	0.0	15,985	D
Vermont	50,675	10,569	20.9	39,561	78.1	545	1.1	—	0.0	28,992	R
Virginia	150,233	90,083	60.0	—	0.0	60,150	40.0	—	0.0	29,933	D
Wisconsin	120,513	52,843	43.8	67,090	55.7	580	0.5	—	0.0	14,247	R
Totals	4,054,647	1,836,072	45.3	1,342,345	33.1	873,053	21.5	3,177	0.1	493,727	D

1. For breakdown of "Other" vote, see minor candidate vote totals, p. 690.

1860 Presidential Election

STATE	TOTAL VOTE	ABRAHAM LINCOLN (Republican) Votes	%	STEPHEN A. DOUGLAS (Democrat) Votes	%	JOHN C. BRECKINRIDGE (Southern Democrat) Votes	%	JOHN BELL (Constitutional Union) Votes	%	OTHER[1] Votes	%	PLURALITY	
Alabama	90,122	—	0.0	13,618	15.1	48,669	54.0	27,835	30.9	—	0.0	20,834	SD
Arkansas	54,152	—	0.0	5,357	9.9	28,732	53.1	20,063	37.0	—	0.0	8,669	SD
California	119,827	38,733	32.3	37,999	31.7	33,969	28.3	9,111	7.6	15	0.0	734	R
Connecticut	74,819	43,488	58.1	15,431	20.6	14,372	19.2	1,528	2.0	—	0.0	28,057	R
Delaware	16,115	3,822	23.7	1,066	6.6	7,339	45.5	3,888	24.1	—	0.0	3,451	SD
Florida	13,301	—	0.0	223	1.7	8,277	62.2	4,801	36.1	—	0.0	3,476	SD
Georgia	106,717	—	0.0	11,581	10.9	52,176	48.9	42,960	40.3	—	0.0	9,216	SD
Illinois	339,666	172,171	50.7	160,215	47.2	2,331	0.7	4,914	1.4	35	0.0	11,956	R
Indiana	272,143	139,033	51.1	115,509	42.4	12,295	4.5	5,306	1.9	—	0.0	23,524	R
Iowa	128,739	70,302	54.6	55,639	43.2	1,035	0.8	1,763	1.4	—	0.0	14,663	R
Kentucky[2]	146,216	1,364	0.9	25,651	17.5	53,143	36.3	66,058	45.2	—	0.0	12,915	CU
Louisiana	50,510	—	0.0	7,625	15.1	22,681	44.9	20,204	40.0	—	0.0	2,477	SD
Maine	100,918	62,811	62.2	29,693	29.4	6,368	6.3	2,046	2.0	—	0.0	33,118	R
Maryland	92,502	2,294	2.5	5,966	6.4	42,482	45.9	41,760	45.1	—	0.0	722	SD
Massachusetts	169,876	106,684	62.8	34,370	20.2	6,163	3.6	22,331	13.1	328	0.2	72,314	R
Michigan	154,758	88,481	57.2	65,057	42.0	805	0.5	415	0.3	—	0.0	23,424	R
Minnesota	34,804	22,069	63.4	11,920	34.2	748	2.1	50	0.1	17	0.0	10,149	R
Mississippi	69,095	—	0.0	3,282	4.7	40,768	59.0	25,045	36.2	—	0.0	15,723	SD
Missouri	165,563	17,028	10.3	58,801	35.5	31,362	18.9	58,372	35.3	—	0.0	429	D
New Hampshire	65,943	37,519	56.9	25,887	39.3	2,125	3.2	412	0.6	—	0.0	11,632	R
New Jersey[2]	121,215	58,346	48.1	62,869	51.9	—	0.0	—	0.0	—	0.0	4,523	D
New York	675,156	362,646	53.7	312,510	46.3	—	0.0	—	0.0	—	0.0	50,136	R
North Carolina	96,712	—	0.0	2,737	2.8	48,846	50.5	45,129	46.7	—	0.0	3,717	SD
Ohio	442,866	231,709	52.3	187,421	42.3	11,406	2.6	12,194	2.8	136	0.0	44,288	R
Oregon	14,758	5,329	36.1	4,136	28.0	5,075	34.4	218	1.5	—	0.0	254	R
Pennsylvania	476,442	268,030	56.3	16,765	3.5	178,871	37.5	12,776	2.7	—	0.0	89,159	R
Rhode Island	19,951	12,244	61.4	7,707	38.6	—	0.0	—	0.0	—	0.0	4,537	R
Tennessee	146,106	—	0.0	11,281	7.7	65,097	44.6	69,728	47.7	—	0.0	4,631	CU
Texas	62,855	—	0.0	18	0.0	47,454	75.5	15,383	24.5	—	0.0	32,071	SD
Vermont	44,644	33,808	75.7	8,649	19.4	218	0.5	1,969	4.4	—	0.0	25,159	R
Virginia	166,891	1,887	1.1	16,198	9.7	74,325	44.5	74,481	44.6	—	0.0	156	CU
Wisconsin	152,179	86,110	56.6	65,021	42.7	887	0.6	161	0.1	—	0.0	21,089	R
Totals	**4,685,561**	**1,865,908**	**39.9**	**1,380,202**	**29.5**	**848,019**	**18.1**	**590,901**	**12.6**	**531**	**0.0**	**485,706**	**R**

1. For breakdown of "Other" vote, see minor candidate vote totals, p. 690.
2. Figures from Svend Petersen, *A Statistical History of the American Presidential Elections* (Westport, Conn.: Greenwood Press, 1981), 37.

1864 Presidential Election

STATE[1]	TOTAL VOTE	ABRAHAM LINCOLN (Republican)		GEORGE B. McCLELLAN (Democrat)		OTHER[2]		PLURALITY	
		Votes	%	Votes	%	Votes	%		
California	105,890	62,053	58.6	43,837	41.4	—	0.0	18,216	R
Connecticut	86,958	44,673	51.4	42,285	48.6	—	0.0	2,388	R
Delaware	16,922	8,155	48.2	8,767	51.8	—	0.0	612	D
Illinois	348,236	189,512	54.4	158,724	45.6	—	0.0	30,788	R
Indiana	280,117	149,887	53.5	130,230	46.5	—	0.0	19,657	R
Iowa[3]	138,025	88,500	64.1	49,525	35.9	—	0.0	38,975	R
Kansas	21,580	17,089	79.2	3,836	17.8	655	3.0	13,253	R
Kentucky	92,088	27,787	30.2	64,301	69.8	—	0.0	36,514	D
Maine[4]	115,099	68,104	59.2	46,995	40.8	—	0.0	21,109	R
Maryland	72,892	40,153	55.1	32,739	44.9	—	0.0	7,414	R
Massachusetts	175,493	126,742	72.2	48,745	27.8	6	0.0	77,997	R
Michigan[5]	160,023	88,551	55.3	71,472	44.7	—	0.0	17,079	R
Minnesota	42,433	25,031	59.0	17,376	40.9	26	0.1	7,655	R
Missouri	104,346	72,750	69.7	31,596	30.3	—	0.0	41,154	R
Nevada	16,420	9,826	59.8	6,594	40.2	—	0.0	3,232	R
New Hampshire	69,630	36,596	52.6	33,034	47.4	—	0.0	3,562	R
New Jersey	128,744	60,724	47.2	68,020	52.8	—	0.0	7,296	D
New York	730,721	368,735	50.5	361,986	49.5	—	0.0	6,749	R
Ohio	471,283	265,674	56.4	205,609	43.6	—	0.0	60,065	R
Oregon	18,350	9,888	53.9	8,457	46.1	5	0.0	1,431	R
Pennsylvania[6]	572,707	296,391	51.7	276,316	48.3	—	0.0	20,075	R
Rhode Island	23,067	14,349	62.2	8,718	37.8	—	0.0	5,631	R
Vermont	55,740	42,419	76.1	13,321	23.9	—	0.0	29,098	R
West Virginia	34,877	23,799	68.2	11,078	31.8	—	0.0	12,721	R
Wisconsin	149,342	83,458	55.9	65,884	44.1	—	0.0	17,574	R
Totals	**4,030,291**	**2,220,846**	**55.1**	**1,809,445**	**44.9**	**692**	**0.0**	**411,401**	**R**

1. Eleven Confederate states did not participate in the election because of the Civil War.
2. For breakdown of "Other" vote, see minor candidate vote totals, p. 690.
3. Figures from *Iowa Official Register, 1913–1914*.
4. Figures from Maine's Executive Council minutes.
5. Figures from *Michigan Manual 1913*, p. 689.
6. Figures from Pennsylvania's *Manual*, 1865.

1868 Presidential Election

STATE[1]	TOTAL VOTE	ULYSSES S. GRANT (Republican)		HORATIO SEYMOUR (Democrat)		OTHER[2]		PLURALITY	
		Votes	%	Votes	%	Votes	%		
Alabama	149,594	76,667	51.3	72,921	48.7	6	0.0	3,746	R
Arkansas	41,190	22,112	53.7	19,078	46.3	—	0.0	3,034	R
California	108,656	54,588	50.2	54,068	49.8	—	0.0	520	R
Connecticut	98,570	50,789	51.5	47,781	48.5	—	0.0	3,008	R
Delaware	18,571	7,614	41.0	10,957	59.0	—	0.0	3,343	D
Georgia	159,816	57,109	35.7	102,707	64.3	—	0.0	45,598	D
Illinois	449,420	250,304	55.7	199,116	44.3	—	0.0	51,188	R
Indiana	343,528	176,548	51.4	166,980	48.6	—	0.0	9,568	R
Iowa	194,439	120,399	61.9	74,040	38.1	—	0.0	46,359	R
Kansas	43,630	30,027	68.8	13,600	31.2	3	0.0	16,427	R
Kentucky	155,455	39,566	25.5	115,889	74.5	—	0.0	76,323	D
Louisiana	113,488	33,263	29.3	80,225	70.7	—	0.0	46,962	D
Maine	112,962	70,502	62.4	42,460	37.6	—	0.0	28,042	R
Maryland	92,795	30,438	32.8	62,357	67.2	—	0.0	31,919	D
Massachusetts	195,508	136,379	69.8	59,103	30.2	26	0.0	77,276	R
Michigan	225,632	128,563	57.0	97,069	43.0	—	0.0	31,494	R
Minnesota	71,620	43,545	60.8	28,075	39.2	—	0.0	15,470	R
Missouri	152,488	86,860	57.0	65,628	43.0	—	0.0	21,232	R
Nebraska	15,291	9,772	63.9	5,519	36.1	—	0.0	4,253	R
Nevada	11,689	6,474	55.4	5,215	44.6	—	0.0	1,259	R
New Hampshire	68,304	37,718	55.2	30,575	44.8	11	0.0	7,143	R
New Jersey	163,133	80,132	49.1	83,001	50.9	—	0.0	2,869	D
New York	849,771	419,888	49.4	429,883	50.6	—	0.0	9,995	D
North Carolina	181,498	96,939	53.4	84,559	46.6	—	0.0	12,380	R
Ohio	518,665	280,159	54.0	238,506	46.0	—	0.0	41,653	R
Oregon	22,086	10,961	49.6	11,125	50.4	—	0.0	164	D
Pennsylvania	655,662	342,280	52.2	313,382	47.8	—	0.0	28,898	R
Rhode Island	19,511	13,017	66.7	6,494	33.3	—	0.0	6,523	R
South Carolina	107,538	62,301	57.9	45,237	42.1	—	0.0	17,064	R
Tennessee	82,757	56,628	68.4	26,129	31.6	—	0.0	30,499	R
Vermont	56,224	44,173	78.6	12,051	21.4	—	0.0	32,122	R
West Virginia	49,321	29,015	58.8	20,306	41.2	—	0.0	8,709	R
Wisconsin	193,628	108,920	56.3	84,708	43.7	—	0.0	24,212	R
Totals	5,722,440	3,013,650	52.7	2,708,744	47.3	46		304,906	R

1. Mississippi, Texas, and Virginia did not participate in the election due to Reconstruction. In Florida the state legislature cast the electoral vote.
2. For breakdown of "Other" vote, see minor candidate vote totals, p. 690.

1872 Presidential Election

STATE	TOTAL VOTE	ULYSSES S. GRANT (Republican)		HORACE GREELEY (Democrat, Liberal Republican)		CHARLES O'CONOR (Straight Out Democrat)		OTHER [1]		PLURALITY	
		Votes	%	Votes	%	Votes	%	Votes	%		
Alabama	169,716	90,272	53.2	79,444	46.8	—	0.0	—	0.0	10,828	R
Arkansas	79,300	41,373	52.2	37,927	47.8	—	0.0	—	0.0	3,446	R
California	95,785	54,007	56.4	40,717	42.5	1,061	1.1	—	0.0	13,290	R
Connecticut	95,992	50,307	52.4	45,685	47.6	—	0.0	—	0.0	4,622	R
Delaware	21,822	11,129	51.0	10,205	46.8	488	2.2	—	0.0	924	R
Florida	33,190	17,763	53.5	15,427	46.5	—	0.0	—	0.0	2,336	R
Georgia	138,906	62,550	45.0	76,356	55.0	—	0.0	—	0.0	13,806	D
Illinois	429,971	241,936	56.3	184,884	43.0	3,151	0.7	—	0.0	57,052	R
Indiana	349,779	186,147	53.2	163,632	46.8	—	0.0	—	0.0	22,515	R
Iowa	216,365	131,566	60.8	71,189	32.9	2,221	1.0	11,389	5.3	60,377	R
Kansas	100,512	66,805	66.5	32,970	32.8	156	0.2	581	0.6	33,835	R
Kentucky	191,552	88,970	45.5	100,208	54.5	2,374	1.2	—	0.0	11,238	D
Louisiana	128,692	71,663	55.7	57,029	44.3	—	0.0	—	0.0	14,634	R
Maine	90,523	61,426	67.9	29,097	32.1	—	0.0	—	0.0	32,329	R
Maryland	134,447	66,760	49.7	67,687	50.3	—	0.0	—	0.0	927	D
Massachusetts	192,650	133,455	69.3	59,195	30.7	—	0.0	—	0.0	74,260	R
Michigan	221,569	138,768	62.6	78,651	35.5	2,879	1.3	1,271	0.6	60,117	R
Minnesota	91,339	56,040	61.4	35,131	38.5	—	0.0	168	0.2	20,909	R
Mississippi	129,457	82,175	63.5	47,282	36.5	—	0.0	—	0.0	34,893	R
Missouri	273,059	119,196	43.7	151,434	55.5	2,429	0.9	—	0.0	32,238	D
Nebraska	25,932	18,329	70.7	7,603	29.3	—	0.0	—	0.0	10,726	R
Nevada	14,649	8,413	57.4	6,236	42.6	—	0.0	—	0.0	2,177	R
New Hampshire	68,906	37,168	53.9	31,425	45.6	—	0.0	313	0.5	5,743	R
New Jersey[2]	168,467	91,666	54.5	76,801	45.5	—	0.0	—	0.0	14,865	R
New York	829,692	440,758	53.1	387,279	46.7	1,454	0.2	201	0.0	53,479	R
North Carolina	165,163	94,772	57.4	70,130	42.5	261	0.2	—	0.0	24,642	R
Ohio	529,435	281,852	53.2	244,320	46.1	1,163	0.2	2,100	0.4	37,532	R
Oregon	20,107	11,818	58.8	7,742	38.5	547	2.7	—	0.0	4,076	R
Pennsylvania	561,629	349,589	62.2	212,040	37.8	—	0.0	—	0.0	137,549	R
Rhode Island	18,994	13,665	71.9	5,329	28.1	—	0.0	—	0.0	8,336	R
South Carolina	95,452	72,290	75.7	22,699	23.8	204	0.2	259	0.3	49,591	R
Tennessee	179,046	85,655	47.8	93,391	52.2	—	0.0	—	0.0	7,736	D
Texas	115,700	47,910	41.4	67,675	58.5	115	0.1	—	0.0	19,765	D
Vermont	52,961	41,480	78.3	10,926	20.6	553	1.0	—	0.0	30,554	R
Virginia	185,195	93,463	50.5	91,647	49.5	85	0.0	—	0.0	1,816	R
West Virginia	62,467	32,320	51.7	29,532	47.3	615	1.0	—	0.0	2,788	R
Wisconsin	192,255	105,012	54.6	86,390	44.9	853	0.4	—	0.0	18,622	R
Totals	6,470,674	3,598,468	55.6	2,835,315	43.8	20,609	0.3	16,282	0.3	763,153	R

1. For breakdown of "Other" vote, see minor candidate vote totals, p. 690.
2. Figures from New Jersey's *Manual, 1873*.

1876 Presidential Election

STATE	TOTAL VOTE	RUTHERFORD B. HAYES [1] (Republican)		SAMUEL J. TILDEN [1] (Democrat)		PETER COOPER (Greenback)		OTHER [2]		PLURALITY	
		Votes	%	Votes	%	Votes	%	Votes	%		
Alabama	171,699	68,708	40.0	102,989	60.0	—	0.0	2	0.0	34,281	D
Arkansas	96,946	38,649	39.9	58,086	59.9	211	0.2	—	0.0	19,437	D
California	155,784	79,258	50.9	76,460	49.1	47	0.0	19	0.0	2,798	R
Connecticut	122,134	59,033	48.3	61,927	50.7	774	0.6	400	0.3	2,894	D
Delaware	24,133	10,752	44.6	13,381	55.4	—	0.0	—	0.0	2,629	D
Florida	46,776	23,849	51.0	22,927	49.0	—	0.0	—	0.0	922	R
Georgia	180,690	50,533	28.0	130,157	72.0	—	0.0	—	0.0	79,624	D
Illinois	554,368	278,232	50.2	258,611	46.6	17,207	3.1	318	0.1	19,621	R
Indiana	430,020	206,971	48.1	213,516	49.7	9,533	2.2	—	0.0	6,545	D
Iowa	293,398	171,326	58.4	112,121	38.2	9,431	3.2	520	0.2	59,205	R
Kansas	124,134	78,324	63.1	37,902	30.5	7,770	6.3	138	0.1	40,422	R
Kentucky	259,614	97,156	37.4	159,696	61.5	1,944	0.7	818	0.3	62,540	D
Louisiana	145,823	75,315	51.6	70,508	48.4	—	0.0	—	0.0	4,807	R
Maine[3]	117,045	66,300	56.6	49,917	42.6	662	0.6	166	0.1	16,383	R
Maryland	163,759	71,980	44.0	91,779	56.0	—	0.0	—	0.0	19,799	D
Massachusetts	259,619	150,063	57.8	108,777	41.9	—	0.0	779	0.3	41,286	R
Michigan	318,426	166,901	52.4	141,665	44.5	9,023	2.8	837	0.3	25,236	R
Minnesota[4]	124,119	72,982	58.8	48,816	39.3	2,321	1.9	—	0.0	24,166	R
Mississippi	164,776	52,603	31.9	112,173	68.1	—	0.0	—	0.0	59,570	D
Missouri	350,610	145,027	41.4	202,086	57.6	3,497	1.0	—	0.0	57,059	D
Nebraska	49,258	31,915	64.8	17,343	35.2	—	0.0	—	0.0	14,572	R
Nevada	19,691	10,383	52.7	9,308	47.3	—	0.0	—	0.0	1,075	R
New Hampshire	80,143	41,540	51.8	38,510	48.1	—	0.0	93	0.1	3,030	R
New Jersey	220,193	103,517	47.0	115,962	52.7	714	0.3	—	0.0	12,445	D
New York	1,015,503	489,207	48.2	521,949	51.4	1,978	0.2	2,369	0.2	32,742	D
North Carolina	233,911	108,484	46.4	125,427	53.6	—	0.0	—	0.0	16,943	D
Ohio	658,650	330,698	50.2	323,182	49.1	3,058	0.5	1,712	0.3	7,516	R
Oregon	29,873	15,207	50.9	14,157	47.4	509	1.7	—	0.0	1,050	R
Pennsylvania	758,973	384,157	50.6	366,204	48.2	7,209	0.9	1,403	0.2	17,953	R
Rhode Island	26,499	15,787	59.6	10,712	40.4	—	0.0	—	0.0	5,075	R
South Carolina	182,683	91,786	50.2	90,897	49.8	—	0.0	—	0.0	889	R
Tennessee	222,743	89,566	40.2	133,177	59.8	—	0.0	—	0.0	43,611	D
Texas	151,431	45,013	29.7	106,372	70.2	—	0.0	46	0.0	61,359	D
Vermont	64,460	44,092	68.4	20,254	31.4	—	0.0	114	0.2	23,838	R
Virginia	236,288	95,518	40.4	140,770	59.6	—	0.0	—	0.0	45,252	D
West Virginia	99,647	41,997	42.1	56,546	56.7	1,104	1.1	—	0.0	14,549	D
Wisconsin[5]	257,799	130,668	50.7	123,927	48.1	1,509	0.6	1,695	0.7	6,741	R
Totals	8,411,618	4,033,497	48.0	4,288,191	51.0	78,501	0.9	11,429	0.1	254,694	D

1. Hayes won the election. For resolution of disputed 1876 election, see p. 710.
2. For breakdown of "Other" vote, see minor candidate vote totals, p. 690.
3. Figures from *Maine Register, 1945*.
4. Figures from *Minnesota Votes*.
5. Figures from *Wisconsin Blue Book 1997*, p. 677.

1880 Presidential Election

STATE	TOTAL VOTE	JAMES A. GARFIELD (Republican)		WINFIELD S. HANCOCK (Democrat)		JAMES B. WEAVER (Greenback)		OTHER[1]		PLURALITY	
		Votes	%	Votes	%	Votes	%	Votes	%		
Alabama	151,902	56,350	37.1	91,130	60.0	4,422	2.9	—	0.0	34,780	D
Arkansas[2]	108,870	42,436	39.0	60,775	55.9	4,116	3.8	1,543	1.4	18,339	D
California	164,218	80,282	48.9	80,426	49.0	3,381	2.1	129	0.1	144	D
Colorado	53,546	27,450	51.3	24,647	46.0	1,435	2.7	14	0.0	2,803	R
Connecticut	132,798	67,071	50.5	64,411	48.5	868	0.7	448	0.3	2,660	R
Delaware	29,458	14,148	48.0	15,181	51.5	129	0.4	—	0.0	1,033	D
Florida	51,618	23,654	45.8	27,964	54.2	—	0.0	—	0.0	4,310	D
Georgia	157,451	54,470	34.6	102,981	65.4	—	0.0	—	0.0	48,511	D
Illinois	622,305	318,036	51.1	277,321	44.6	26,358	4.2	590	0.1	40,715	R
Indiana	470,758	232,169	49.3	225,523	47.9	13,066	2.8	—	0.0	6,646	R
Iowa	323,140	183,904	56.9	105,845	32.8	32,327	10.0	1,064	0.3	78,059	R
Kansas	201,054	121,520	60.4	59,789	29.7	19,710	9.8	35	0.0	61,731	R
Kentucky	266,884	106,059	39.7	149,068	55.9	11,499	4.3	258	0.1	43,009	D
Louisiana	104,462	38,978	37.3	65,047	62.3	437	0.4	—	0.0	26,069	D
Maine	143,903	74,052	51.5	65,211	45.3	4,409	3.1	231	0.2	8,841	R
Maryland	173,049	78,515	45.4	93,706	54.1	828	0.5	—	0.0	15,191	D
Massachusetts	282,505	165,198	58.5	111,960	39.6	4,548	1.6	799	0.3	53,238	R
Michigan	353,076	185,335	52.5	131,596	37.3	34,895	9.9	1,250	0.4	53,739	R
Minnesota	150,806	93,939	62.3	53,314	35.4	3,267	2.2	286	0.2	40,625	R
Mississippi	117,068	34,844	29.8	75,750	64.7	5,797	5.0	677	0.6	40,906	D
Missouri	397,289	153,647	38.7	208,600	52.5	35,042	8.8	—	0.0	54,953	D
Nebraska	87,355	54,979	62.9	28,523	32.7	3,853	4.4	—	0.0	26,456	R
Nevada	18,343	8,732	47.6	9,611	52.4	—	0.0	—	0.0	879	D
New Hampshire	86,361	44,856	51.9	40,797	47.2	528	0.6	180	0.2	4,059	R
New Jersey	245,928	120,555	49.0	122,565	49.8	2,617	1.1	191	0.1	2,010	D
New York	1,103,945	555,544	50.3	534,511	48.4	12,373	1.1	1,517	0.1	21,033	R
North Carolina	240,946	115,616	48.0	124,204	51.5	1,126	0.5	—	0.0	8,588	D
Ohio	724,984	375,048	51.7	340,867	47.0	6,456	0.9	2,613	0.4	34,181	R
Oregon	40,841	20,619	50.5	19,955	48.9	267	0.7	—	0.0	664	R
Pennsylvania	874,783	444,704	50.8	407,428	46.6	20,667	2.4	1,984	0.2	37,276	R
Rhode Island	29,235	18,195	62.2	10,779	36.9	236	0.8	25	0.1	7,416	R
South Carolina	169,793	57,954	34.1	111,236	65.5	567	0.3	36	0.0	53,282	D
Tennessee	243,263	107,677	44.3	129,569	53.3	6,017	2.5	—	0.0	21,892	D
Texas[2]	240,659	57,225	23.8	155,963	64.8	27,471	11.4	—	0.0	98,738	D
Vermont	65,098	45,567	70.0	18,316	28.1	1,215	1.9	—	0.0	27,251	R
Virginia[2]	212,660	83,634	39.3	128,647[3]	60.5	—	0.0	379	0.2	45,013	D
West Virginia	112,641	46,243	41.1	57,390	50.9	9,008	8.0	—	0.0	11,147	D
Wisconsin	267,202	144,406	54.0	114,650	42.9	7,986	3.0	160	0.1	29,756	R
Totals	**9,220,197**	**4,453,611**	**48.3**	**4,445,256**	**48.2**	**306,921**	**3.3**	**14,409**	**0.2**	**8,355**	**R**

1. For breakdown of "Other" vote, see minor candidate vote totals, p. 690.
2. Figures from W. Dean Burnham, *Presidential Ballots 1836–1892* (New York: Arno Press, 1976).
3. According to Burnham there were two Democratic slates—regular with 96,594 votes and Readjuster Democrats with 32,053 votes—and he does not combine the two. They are combined here. It is not entirely clear if they ran the same set of electors.

1884 Presidential Election

STATE	TOTAL VOTE	GROVER CLEVELAND (Democrat)		JAMES G. BLAINE (Republican)		BENJAMIN F. BUTLER (Greenback)		JOHN P. ST. JOHN (Prohibition)		OTHER[1]		PLURALITY	
		Votes	%	Votes	%	Votes	%	Votes	%	Votes	%		
Alabama	153,624	92,736	60.4	59,444	38.7	762	0.5	610	0.4	72	0.0	33,292	D
Arkansas	125,779	72,734	57.8	51,198	40.7	1,847	1.5	—	0.0	—	0.0	21,536	D
California	196,988	89,288	45.3	102,369	52.0	2,037	1.0	2,965	1.5	329	0.2	13,081	R
Colorado	66,519	27,723	41.7	36,084	54.2	1,956	2.9	756	1.1	—	0.0	8,361	R
Connecticut	137,221	67,167	48.9	65,879	48.0	1,682	1.2	2,493	1.8	—	0.0	1,288	D
Delaware	29,984	16,957	56.6	12,953	43.2	10	0.0	64	0.2	—	0.0	4,004	D
Florida	59,990	31,769	53.0	28,031	46.7	—	0.0	72	0.1	118	0.2	3,738	D
Georgia	143,610	94,667	65.9	48,603	33.8	145	0.1	195	0.1	—	0.0	46,064	D
Illinois	672,670	312,351	46.4	337,469	50.2	10,776	1.6	12,074	1.8	—	0.0	25,118	R
Indiana[2]	495,423	245,041	49.5	238,511	48.1	8,820	1.8	3,051	0.6	—	0.0	6,530	D
Iowa	393,542	177,316	45.1	197,089	50.1	16,341	4.2	1,499	0.4	1,297	0.3	19,773	R
Kansas	250,991	90,111	35.9	154,410	61.5	1,691	0.7	4,311	1.7	468	0.2	64,299	R
Kentucky	276,503	152,894	55.3	118,822	43.0	1,690	0.6	3,097	1.1	—	0.0	34,072	D
Louisiana	109,399	62,594	57.2	46,347	42.4	120	0.1	338	0.3	—	0.0	16,247	D
Maine[3]	130,489	52,153	40.0	72,217	55.3	3,953	3.0	2,160	1.7	6	0.0	20,064	R
Maryland	185,838	96,941	52.2	85,748	46.1	347	0.2	2,802	1.5	—	0.0	11,193	D
Massachusetts[4]	303,383	122,352	40.3	146,724	48.4	24,382	8.0	9,923	3.3	2	0.0	24,372	R
Michigan[5]	401,186	189,361	47.2	192,669	48.0	753	0.2	18,403	4.6	—	0.0	3,308	R
Minnesota[6]	190,236	70,135	36.7	111,819	58.8	3,583	1.9	4,696	2.5	—	0.0	41,684	R
Mississippi	120,688	77,653	64.3	43,035	35.7	—	0.0	—	0.0	—	0.0	34,618	D
Missouri	441,268	236,023	53.5	203,081	46.0	—	0.0	2,164	0.5	—	0.0	32,942	D
Nebraska	134,202	54,391	40.5	76,912	57.3	—	0.0	2,899	2.2	—	0.0	22,521	R
Nevada	12,779	5,577	43.6	7,176	56.2	26	0.2	—	0.0	—	0.0	1,599	R
New Hampshire	84,586	39,198	46.3	43,254	51.1	554	0.7	1,580	1.9	—	0.0	4,056	R
New Jersey	260,853	127,747	49.0	123,436	47.3	3,486	1.3	6,156	2.4	28	0.0	4,311	D
New York	1,167,003	563,048	48.2	562,001	48.2	16,955	1.5	24,999	2.1	—	0.0	1,047	D
North Carolina	268,356	142,905	53.3	125,021	46.6	—	0.0	430	0.2	—	0.0	17,884	D
Ohio	784,620	368,280	46.9	400,092	51.0	5,179	0.7	11,069	1.4	—	0.0	31,812	R
Oregon	52,683	24,598	46.7	26,845	51.0	726	1.4	479	0.9	35	0.1	2,247	R
Pennsylvania[7]	899,563	392,915	43.7	474,350	52.7	16,992	1.9	15,306	1.7	—	0.0	81,435	R
Rhode Island	32,771	12,391	37.8	19,030	58.1	422	1.3	928	2.8	—	0.0	6,639	R
South Carolina	92,812	69,845	75.3	21,730	23.4	—	0.0	—	0.0	1,237	1.3	48,115	D
Tennessee	259,978	133,770	51.5	124,101	47.7	957	0.4	1,150	0.4	—	0.0	9,669	D
Texas[2]	326,458	226,375	69.3	93,345	28.6	3,221	1.0	3,517	1.1	—	0.0	133,030	D
Vermont	59,409	17,331	29.2	39,514	66.5	785	1.3	1,752	2.9	27	0.0	22,183	R
Virginia	284,977	145,491	51.1	139,356	48.9	—	0.0	130	0.0	—	0.0	6,135	D
West Virginia	132,145	67,311	50.9	63,096	47.7	799	0.6	939	0.7	—	0.0	4,215	D
Wisconsin	319,847	146,447	45.8	161,155	50.4	4,594	1.4	7,651	2.4	—	0.0	14,708	R
Totals	10,058,373	4,915,586	48.9	4,852,916	48.2	135,594	1.3	150,658	1.5	3,619	0.0	62,670	D

1. For breakdown of "Other" vote, see minor candidate vote totals, p. 690.
2. Figures from W. Dean Burnham, *Presidential Ballots 1836–1892* (New York: Arno Press, 1976).
3. Figures from Svend Petersen, *A Statistical History of the American Presidential Elections* (Westport, Conn.: Greenwood Press, 1981); *Maine Register, 1945.*
4. Figures from *Manual, 1885.*
5. Figures from *Michigan Manual, 1913,* p. 689. For Michigan's Democratic total, twelve out of thirteen electors ran on both the Democratic and Greenback ticket (a Fusion slate); the Fusion electors vote is used here. The vote listed under Greenback was solely for the "straight" Greenback slate.
6. Figures from *Minnesota Votes.*
7. Figures from Pennsylvania's *Manual, 1885.*

1888 Presidential Election

STATE	TOTAL VOTE	BENJAMIN HARRISON[1] (Republican)		GROVER CLEVELAND[1] (Democrat)		CLINTON B. FISK (Prohibition)		ALSON J. STREETER (Union Labor)		OTHER[2]		PLURALITY	
		Votes	%	Votes	%	Votes	%	Votes	%	Votes	%		
Alabama	175,085	57,177	32.7	117,314	67.0	594	0.3	—	0.0	—	0.0	60,137	D
Arkansas	157,058	59,752	38.0	86,062	54.8	614	0.4	10,630	6.8	—	0.0	26,310	D
California	251,339	124,816	49.7	117,729	46.8	5,761	2.3	—	0.0	3,033	1.2	7,087	R
Colorado	91,946	50,772	55.2	37,549	40.8	2,182	2.4	1,266	1.4	177	0.2	13,223	R
Connecticut	153,978	74,584	48.4	74,920	48.7	4,234	2.7	240	0.2	—	0.0	336	D
Delaware	29,764	12,950	43.5	16,414	55.1	399	1.3	—	0.0	1	0.0	3,464	D
Florida	66,500	26,529	39.9	39,557	59.5	414	0.6	—	0.0	—	0.0	13,028	D
Georgia	142,936	40,499	28.3	100,493	70.3	1,808	1.3	136	0.1	—	0.0	59,994	D
Illinois	747,813	370,475	49.5	348,351	46.6	21,703	2.9	7,134	1.0	150	0.0	22,124	R
Indiana	536,988	263,366	49.0	260,990	48.6	9,939	1.9	2,693	0.5	—	0.0	2,376	R
Iowa	404,694	211,607	52.3	179,876	44.4	3,550	0.9	9,105	2.2	556	0.1	31,731	R
Kansas	331,133	182,845	55.2	102,739	31.0	6,774	2.0	37,838	11.4	937	0.3	80,106	R
Kentucky	344,868	155,138	45.0	183,830	53.3	5,223	1.5	677	0.2	—	0.0	28,692	D
Louisiana	115,891	30,660	26.5	85,032	73.4	160	0.1	39	0.0	—	0.0	54,372	D
Maine	128,253	73,730	57.5	50,472	39.4	2,691	2.1	1,344	1.0	16	0.0	23,258	R
Maryland	210,941	99,986	47.4	106,188	50.3	4,767	2.3	—	0.0	—	0.0	6,202	D
Massachusetts	344,243	183,892	53.4	151,590	44.0	8,701	2.5	—	0.0	60	0.0	32,302	R
Michigan	475,356	236,387	49.7	213,469	44.9	20,945	4.4	4,555	1.0	—	0.0	22,918	R
Minnesota	263,162	142,492	54.1	104,372	39.7	15,201	5.8	1,097	0.4	—	0.0	38,120	R
Mississippi	115,786	30,095	26.0	85,451	73.8	240	0.2	—	0.0	—	0.0	55,356	D
Missouri	521,359	236,252	45.3	261,943	50.2	4,539	0.9	18,625	3.6	—	0.0	25,691	D
Nebraska	202,630	108,417	53.5	80,552	39.8	9,435	4.7	4,226	2.1	—	0.0	27,865	R
Nevada	12,573	7,229	57.5	5,303	42.2	41	0.3	—	0.0	—	0.0	1,926	R
New Hampshire	90,770	45,734	50.4	43,382	47.8	1,596	1.8	—	0.0	58	0.1	2,352	R
New Jersey[3]	303,801	144,360	47.5	151,508	49.9	7,933	2.6	—	0.0	—	0.0	7,148	D
New York[4]	1,321,270	650,338	49.2	635,965	48.1	30,231	2.3	627	0.0	4,736	0.4	14,373	R
North Carolina[5]	285,946	134,784	47.1	148,336	51.9	2,789	1.0	—	0.0	37	0.0	13,552	D
Ohio	839,357	416,054	49.6	395,456	47.1	24,356	2.9	3,491	0.4	—	0.0	20,598	R
Oregon	61,889	33,291	53.8	26,518	42.8	1,676	2.7	—	0.0	404	0.7	6,773	R
Pennsylvania	997,568	526,091	52.7	446,633	44.8	20,947	2.1	3,873	0.4	24	0.0	79,458	R
Rhode Island	40,775	21,969	53.9	17,530	43.0	1,251	3.1	18	0.0	7	0.0	4,439	R
South Carolina	79,997	13,736	17.2	65,824	82.3	—	0.0	—	0.0	437	0.5	52,088	D
Tennessee[5]	304,313	139,511	45.8	158,779	52.2	5,975	2.0	48	0.0	—	0.0	19,268	D
Texas[6]	363,484	93,991	25.9	236,290	65.0	4,739	1.3	28,459	7.8	—	0.0	142,299	D
Vermont	63,476	45,193	71.2	16,788	26.4	1,460	2.3	—	0.0	35	0.1	28,405	R
Virginia	304,087	150,399	49.5	152,004	50.0	1,684	0.6	—	0.0	—	0.0	1,605	D
West Virginia	159,440	78,171	49.0	78,677	49.3	1,084	0.7	1,508	0.9	—	0.0	506	D
Wisconsin	354,614	176,553	49.8	155,232	43.8	14,277	4.0	8,552	2.4	—	0.0	21,321	R
Totals	11,395,705	5,449,825	47.8	5,539,118	48.6	249,492	2.2	146,602	1.3	10,668	0.1	89,293	D

1. Harrison won the election. See p. 743.
2. For breakdown of "Other" vote, see minor candidate vote totals, p. 690.
3. Figures from *Manual, 1889*.
4. Figures from *New York Legislative Manual, 1889*.
5. Figures from Svend Petersen, *A Statistical History of the American Presidential Elections* (Westport, Conn.: Greenwood Press, 1981).
6. Figures from W. Dean Burnham, *Presidential Ballots 1836–1892* (New York: Arno Press, 1976).

1892 Presidential Election

STATE	TOTAL VOTE	GROVER CLEVELAND (Democrat)		BENJAMIN HARRISON (Republican)		JAMES B. WEAVER (Populist)		JOHN BIDWELL (Prohibition)		OTHER[1]		PLURALITY	
		Votes	%	Votes	%	Votes	%	Votes	%	Votes	%		
Alabama	232,543	138,135	59.4	9,184	3.9	84,984	36.5	240	0.1	—	0.0	53,151	D
Arkansas	148,117	87,834	59.3	47,072	31.8	11,831	8.0	113	0.1	1,267	0.9	40,762	D
California	269,585	118,151	43.8	118,027	43.8	25,311	9.4	8,096	3.0	—	0.0	124	D
Colorado	93,881	—	0.0	38,620	41.1	53,584	57.1	1,677	1.8	—	0.0	14,964	POP
Connecticut	164,593	82,395	50.1	77,030	46.8	809	0.5	4,026	2.4	333	0.2	5,365	D
Delaware	37,235	18,581	49.9	18,077	48.5	—	0.0	564	1.5	13	0.0	504	D
Florida[2]	35,567	30,154	84.8	—	0.0	4,843	13.6	570	1.6	—	0.0	25,311	D
Georgia[2]	223,961	129,386	57.8	48,305	21.6	42,937	19.2	988	0.4	2,345	1.0	81,081	D
Idaho	19,407	—	0.0	8,599	44.3	10,520	54.2	288	1.5	—	0.0	1,921	POP
Illinois	873,667	426,281	48.8	399,308	45.7	22,207	2.5	25,871	3.0	—	0.0	26,973	D
Indiana	553,613	262,740	47.5	255,615	46.2	22,208	4.0	13,050	2.4	—	0.0	7,125	D
Iowa	443,159	196,367	44.3	219,795	49.6	20,595	4.6	6,402	1.4	—	0.0	23,428	R
Kansas	323,591	—	0.0	156,134	48.3	162,888	50.3	4,569	1.4	—	0.0	6,754	POP
Kentucky	340,864	175,461	51.5	135,462	39.7	23,500	6.9	6,441	1.9	—	0.0	39,999	D
Louisiana[2]	118,287	87,922	74.3	27,903	23.6	2,462	2.1	—	0.0	—	0.0	60,023	D
Maine[3]	116,013	48,024	41.4	62,878	54.2	2,045	1.8	3,062	2.6	4	0.0	14,854	R
Maryland	213,275	113,866	53.4	92,736	43.5	796	0.4	5,877	2.8	—	0.0	21,130	D
Massachusetts	391,028	176,813	45.2	202,814	51.9	3,210	0.8	7,539	1.9	652	0.2	26,001	R
Michigan	466,917	202,396	43.3	222,708	47.7	20,031	4.3	20,857	4.5	925	0.2	20,312	R
Minnesota[4]	267,461	101,055	37.8	122,836	45.9	29,336	11.0	14,234	5.3	—	0.0	21,781	R
Mississippi	52,519	40,030	76.2	1,398	2.7	10,118	19.3	973	1.9	—	0.0	29,912	D
Missouri	541,583	268,400	49.6	227,646	42.0	41,204	7.6	4,333	0.8	—	0.0	40,754	D
Montana	44,461	17,690	39.8	18,871	42.4	7,338	16.5	562	1.3	—	0.0	1,181	R
Nebraska	200,205	24,956	12.5	87,213	43.6	83,134	41.5	4,902	2.4	—	0.0	4,079	R
Nevada	10,826	703	6.5	2,811	26.0	7,226	66.7	86	0.8	—	0.0	4,415	POP
New Hampshire	89,328	42,081	47.1	45,658	51.1	292	0.3	1,297	1.5	—	0.0	3,577	R
New Jersey	337,485	170,987	50.7	156,059	46.2	969	0.3	8,133	2.4	1,337	0.4	14,928	D
New York	1,336,793	654,868	49.0	609,350	45.6	16,429	1.2	38,190	2.9	17,956	1.3	45,518	D
North Carolina	280,270	132,951	47.4	100,346	35.8	44,336	15.8	2,637	0.9	—	0.0	32,605	D
North Dakota[2]	36,118	—	0.0	17,519	48.5	17,700	49.0	899	2.5	—	0.0	181	POP
Ohio	850,164	404,115	47.5	405,187	47.7	14,850	1.7	26,012	3.1	—	0.0	1,072	R
Oregon	78,378	14,243	18.2	35,002	44.7	26,875	34.3	2,258	2.9	—	0.0	8,127	R
Pennsylvania	1,003,000	452,264	45.1	516,011	51.4	8,714	0.9	25,123	2.5	888	0.1	63,747	R
Rhode Island	53,196	24,336	45.7	26,975	50.7	228	0.4	1,654	3.1	3	0.0	2,639	R
South Carolina	70,504	54,680	77.6	13,345	18.9	2,407	3.4	—	0.0	72	0.1	41,335	D
South Dakota	70,513	9,081	12.9	34,888	49.5	26,544	37.6	—	0.0	—	0.0	8,344	R
Tennessee	265,732	136,468	51.4	100,537	37.8	23,918	9.0	4,809	1.8	—	0.0	35,931	D
Texas[5]	422,447	239,148	56.6	77,478	18.3	99,688	23.6	2,165	0.5	3,968	1.0	161,670	D
Vermont	55,793	16,325	29.3	37,992	68.1	42	0.1	1,424	2.6	10	0.0	21,667	R
Virginia	292,238	164,136	56.2	113,098	38.7	12,275	4.2	2,729	0.9	—	0.0	51,038	D
Washington	87,968	29,802	33.9	36,459	41.4	19,165	21.8	2,542	2.9	—	0.0	6,657	R
West Virginia	171,079	84,467	49.4	80,292	46.9	4,167	2.4	2,153	1.3	—	0.0	4,175	D
Wisconsin	371,481	177,325	47.7	171,101	46.1	9,919	2.7	13,136	3.5	—	0.0	6,224	D
Wyoming	16,703	—	0.0	8,454	50.6	7,722	46.2	498	3.0	29	0.2	732	R
Totals	12,071,548	5,554,617	46.0	5,186,793	43.0	1,024,280	8.5	270,979	2.2	29,802	0.2	367,824	D

1. For breakdown of "Other" vote, see minor candidate vote totals, p. 690.
2. Figures from Svend Petersen, *A Statistical History of the American Presidential Elections* (Westport, Conn.: Greenwood Press, 1981), p. 60.
3. Figures from *Maine Register, 1945*.
4. Figures from *Minnesota Votes*.
5. Figures from *The Texas Almanac's Political History of Texas*.

1896 Presidential Election

STATE	TOTAL VOTE	WILLIAM McKINLEY (Republican)		WILLIAM J. BRYAN (Democrat, Populist)[1]		JOHN M. PALMER (National Democrat)		JOSHUA LEVERING (Prohibition)		OTHER[2]		PLURALITY	
		Votes	%	Votes	%	Votes	%	Votes	%	Votes	%		
Alabama	194,580	55,673	28.6	130,298	67.0	6,375	3.3	2,234	1.1	—	0.0	74,625	D
Arkansas	149,396	37,512	25.1	110,103	73.7	—	0.0	889	0.6	892	0.6	72,591	D
California[3]	299,374	146,688	49.1	123,143	41.2	2,006	0.7	2,573	0.9	24,285	8.2	23,545	R
Colorado	189,539	26,271	13.9	161,005	84.9	1	0.0	1,717	0.9	545	0.3	134,734	D
Connecticut	174,394	110,285	63.2	56,740	32.5	4,336	2.5	1,806	1.0	1,227	0.7	53,545	R
Delaware[4]	31,538	16,883	53.5	13,425	42.6	877	2.8	355	1.1	—	0.0	3,458	R
Florida[3]	46,468	11,298	24.3	30,683	66.0	1,778	3.8	656	1.4	2,053	4.4	19,385	D
Georgia[5]	163,309	60,107	36.8	94,733	58.0	2,809	1.7	5,613	3.4	47	0.0	34,626	D
Idaho	29,631	6,324	21.3	23,135	78.1	—	0.0	172	0.6	—	0.0	16,811	D
Illinois	1,090,766	607,130	55.7	465,593	42.7	6,307	0.6	9,796	0.9	1,940	0.2	141,537	R
Indiana	637,089	323,754	50.8	305,538	48.0	2,145	0.3	3,061	0.5	2,591	0.4	18,216	R
Iowa	521,550	289,293	55.5	223,744	42.9	4,516	0.9	3,192	0.6	805	0.2	65,549	R
Kansas	336,085	159,484	47.5	173,049	51.5	1,209	0.4	1,723	0.5	620	0.2	13,565	D
Kentucky	445,928	218,171	48.9	217,894	48.9	5,084	1.1	4,779	1.1	—	0.0	277	R
Louisiana	101,046	22,037	21.8	77,175	76.4	1,834	1.8	—	0.0	—	0.0	55,138	D
Maine	118,419	80,403	67.9	34,587	29.2	1,867	1.6	1,562	1.3	—	0.0	45,816	R
Maryland	250,249	136,959	54.7	104,150	41.6	2,499	1.0	5,918	2.4	723	0.3	32,809	R
Massachusetts	401,269	278,976	69.5	105,414	26.3	11,749	2.9	2,998	0.7	2,132	0.5	173,562	R
Michigan	545,583	293,336	53.8	237,164	43.5	6,923	1.3	4,978	0.9	3,182	0.6	56,172	R
Minnesota	341,762	193,503	56.6	139,735	40.9	3,222	0.9	4,348	1.3	954	0.3	53,768	R
Mississippi	69,591	4,819	6.9	63,355	91.0	1,021	1.5	396	0.6	—	0.0	58,536	D
Missouri	674,032	304,940	45.2	363,667	54.0	2,365	0.4	2,169	0.3	891	0.1	58,727	D
Montana	53,330	10,509	19.7	42,628	79.9	—	0.0	193	0.4	—	0.0	32,119	D
Nebraska	223,181	103,064	46.2	115,007	51.5	2,885	1.3	1,242	0.6	983	0.4	11,943	D
Nevada[6]	10,314	1,938	18.8	7,802	75.6	—	0.0	—	0.0	574	5.6	5,864	D
New Hampshire[3]	83,670	57,444	68.7	21,271	25.4	3,520	4.2	779	0.9	656	0.8	36,173	R
New Jersey	371,014	221,367	59.7	133,675	36.0	6,373	1.7	—	0.0	9,599	2.6	87,692	R
New York	1,423,876	819,838	57.6	551,369	38.7	18,950	1.3	16,052	1.1	17,667	1.2	268,469	R
North Carolina	331,337	155,122	46.8	174,408	52.6	578	0.2	635	0.2	594	0.2	19,286	D
North Dakota	47,391	26,335	55.6	20,686	43.6	—	0.0	358	0.8	12	0.0	5,649	R
Ohio[3]	1,014,295	525,991	51.9	474,882	46.8	1,858	0.2	5,068	0.5	6,496	0.6	51,109	R
Oregon	97,335	48,700	50.0	46,739	48.0	977	1.0	919	0.9	—	0.0	1,961	R
Pennsylvania[7]	1,194,355	728,300	61.0	427,125	35.8	11,000	0.9	19,274	1.6	8,656	0.7	301,175	R
Rhode Island	54,785	37,437	68.3	14,459	26.4	1,166	2.1	1,160	2.1	563	1.0	22,978	R
South Carolina	68,938	9,313	13.5	58,801	85.3	824	1.2	—	0.0	—	0.0	49,488	D
South Dakota	82,937	41,040	49.5	41,225	49.7	—	0.0	672	0.8	—	0.0	185	D
Tennessee	320,903	148,683	46.3	167,168	52.1	1,953	0.6	3,099	1.0	—	0.0	18,485	D
Texas[8]	515,987	163,413	31.7	267,803	51.9	4,989	1.0	1,797	0.3	77,985	15.1	104,390	D
Utah	78,098	13,491	17.3	64,607	82.7	—	0.0	—	0.0	—	0.0	51,116	D
Vermont[9]	63831	51,127	80.1	10,179	15.9	1,331	2.1	733	1.1	461	0.7	40,948	R
Virginia	294,674	135,379	45.9	154,708	52.5	2,129	0.7	2,350	0.8	108	0.0	19,329	D
Washington[3]	93,583	39,153	41.8	51,646	55.2	—	0.0	968	1.0	1,668	1.8	12,493	D
West Virginia	201,757	105,379	52.2	94,480	46.8	678	0.3	1,220	0.6	—	0.0	10,899	R
Wisconsin	447,409	268,135	59.9	165,523	37.0	4,584	1.0	7,507	1.7	1,660	0.4	102,612	R
Wyoming[3]	21,093	10,072	47.8	10,376	49.3	—	0.0	159	0.8	486	2.3	304	D
Totals	**13,905,691**	**7,105,144**	**51.1**	**6,370,897**	**45.8**	**132,718**	**1.0**	**125,118**	**0.9**	**171,814**	**1.2**	**734,247**	**R**

1. Bryan was nominated by both the Democrats and the Populists but with different running mates. In several states different slates of electors were entered by each party. It is legally incorrect to combine the vote. The separate vote for Bryan usually under the Populist ticket is listed under "Other." In other states it appears that the two slates of electors were the same and it is correct to combine the vote.
2. For breakdown of "Other" vote, see minor candidate vote totals, p. 691.
3. Figures from Edgar E. Robinson, *The Presidential Vote 1896–1932* (Stanford, Calif.: Stanford University Press, 1934).
4. The vote of Kent County was excluded from the official tally because two sets of returns were sent to the state. The vote of the county as reported would have made the vote: McKinley, 20,685; Bryan, 16,708; Palmer, 968; and Levering, 469.
5. Figures from Svend Petersen, *A Statistical History of the American Presidential Elections* (Westport, Conn.: Greenwood Press, 1981).
6. Figures from *Political History of Nevada* (Secretary of State).
7. Figures from *Manual, 1897*.
8. There were two separate Bryan slates in Texas with various sources offering widely different totals. Figures here are from Robinson, *The Presidential Vote*, supplemented with manuscript returns supplied by the Texas secretary of state.
9. Figures from *Vermont Legislative Directory*.

1900 Presidential Election

STATE	TOTAL VOTE	WILLIAM McKINLEY (Republican)		WILLIAM J. BRYAN (Democrat)		JOHN G. WOOLEY (Prohibition)		EUGENE V. DEBS (Socialist)		OTHER[1]		PLURALITY	
		Votes	%	Votes	%	Votes	%	Votes	%	Votes	%		
Alabama[2]	160,477	55,634	34.7	96,368	60.1	3,796	2.4	928	0.6	3,751	2.3	40,734	D
Arkansas	127,966	44,800	35.0	81,242	63.5	584	0.5	—	0.0	1,340	1.0	36,442	D
California[3]	302,399	164,755	54.5	124,985	41.3	5,087	1.7	7,572	2.50	—	0.0	39,770	R
Colorado	220,895	92,701	42.0	122,705	55.5	3,790	1.7	686	0.3	1,013	0.5	30,004	D
Connecticut	180,195	102,572	56.9	74,014	41.1	1,617	0.9	1,029	0.6	963	0.5	28,558	R
Delaware	41,989	22,535	53.7	18,852	44.9	546	1.3	56	0.1	—	0.0	3,683	R
Florida[2]	39,777	7,463	18.8	28,273	71.1	2,244	5.7	654	1.6	1,143	2.9	20,810	D
Georgia	121,410	34,260	28.2	81,180	66.9	1,402	1.2	—	0.0	4,568	3.8	46,920	D
Idaho[2]	56,760	27,198	47.9	28,260	49.8	857	1.5	—	0.0	445	0.8	1,062	D
Illinois	1,131,898	597,985	52.8	503,061	44.4	17,626	1.6	9,687	0.9	3,539	0.3	94,924	R
Indiana	664,094	336,063	50.6	309,584	46.6	13,718	2.1	2,374	0.4	2,355	0.4	26,479	R
Iowa	530,345	307,799	58.0	209,261	39.5	9,502	1.8	2,743	0.5	1,040	0.2	98,538	R
Kansas[4]	353,766	185,955	52.6	162,601	46.0	3,605	1.0	1,605	0.5	—	0.0	23,354	R
Kentucky[5]	467,580	226,801	48.5	234,889	50.2	2,814	0.6	—	0.0	3,076	0.7	8,008	D
Louisiana	67,906	14,234	21.0	53,668	79.0	—	0.0	—	0.0	4	0.0	39,434	D
Maine[6]	107,698	66,413	61.7	37,822	35.1	2,585	2.4	878	0.8	—	0.0	28,591	R
Maryland	264,386	136,151	51.5	122,237	46.2	4,574	1.7	900	0.3	524	0.2	13,914	R
Massachusetts	414,804	238,866	57.6	156,997	37.8	6,202	1.5	9,607	2.3	3,132	0.8	81,869	R
Michigan	543,789	316,014	58.1	211,432	38.9	11,804	2.2	2,820	0.5	1,719	0.3	104,582	R
Minnesota	316,311	190,461	60.2	112,901	35.7	8,555	2.7	3,065	1.0	1,329	0.4	77,560	R
Mississippi	59,055	5,707	9.7	51,706	87.6	—	0.0	—	0.0	1,642	2.8	45,999	D
Missouri	683,658	314,092	45.9	351,922	51.5	5,965	0.9	6,139	0.9	5,540	0.8	37,830	D
Montana	63,856	25,409	39.8	37,311	58.4	306	0.5	711	1.1	119	0.2	11,902	D
Nebraska	241,430	121,835	50.5	114,013	47.2	3,655	1.5	823	0.3	1,104	0.5	7,822	R
Nevada	10,196	3,849	37.8	6,347	62.2	—	0.0	—	0.0	—	0.0	2,498	D
New Hampshire	92,364	54,799	59.3	35,489	38.4	1,270	1.4	790	0.9	16	0.0	19,310	R
New Jersey	401,050	221,707	55.3	164,808	41.1	7,183	1.8	4,609	1.1	2,743	0.7	56,899	R
New York	1,548,043	822,013	53.1	678,462	43.8	22,077	1.4	12,869	0.8	12,622	0.8	143,551	R
North Carolina	292,518	132,997	45.5	157,733	53.9	990	0.3	—	0.0	798	0.3	24,736	D
North Dakota	57,783	35,898	62.1	20,524	35.5	735	1.3	517	0.9	109	0.2	15,374	R
Ohio	1,040,073	543,918	52.3	474,882	45.7	10,203	1.0	4,847	0.5	6,223	0.6	69,036	R
Oregon[7]	84,216	46,526	55.2	33,385	39.6	2,536	3.1	1,494	1.8	275	0.3	13,141	R
Pennsylvania	1,173,210	712,665	60.7	424,232	36.2	27,908	2.4	4,831	0.4	3,574	0.3	288,433	R
Rhode Island	56,548	33,784	59.7	19,812	35.0	1,529	2.7	—	0.0	1,423	2.5	13,972	R
South Carolina	50,698	3,525	7.0	47,173	93.0	—	0.0	—	0.0	—	0.0	43,648	D
South Dakota	96,169	54,574	56.7	39,538	41.1	1,541	1.6	176	0.2	340	0.4	15,036	R
Tennessee	273,860	123,108	45.0	145,240	53.0	3,844	1.4	346	0.1	1,322	0.5	22,132	D
Texas	424,334	131,174	30.9	267,945	63.1	2,642	0.6	1,846	0.4	20,727	4.9	136,771	D
Utah	93,071	47,089	50.6	44,949	48.3	205	0.2	717	0.8	111	0.1	2,140	R
Vermont	56,212	42,569	75.7	12,849	22.9	383	0.7	39	0.1	372	0.7	29,720	R
Virginia	264,208	115,769	43.8	146,079	55.3	2,130	0.8	—	0.0	230	0.1	30,310	D
Washington	107,523	57,455	53.4	44,833	41.7	2,363	2.2	2,006	1.9	866	0.8	12,622	R
West Virginia	220,796	119,829	54.3	98,807	44.8	1,628	0.7	286	0.1	246	0.1	21,022	R
Wisconsin	442,501	265,760	60.1	159,163	36.0	10,027	2.3	7,048	1.6	503	0.1	106,597	R
Wyoming	24,708	14,482	58.6	10,164	41.1	—	0.0	21	0.1	41	0.2	4,318	R
Totals	13,972,525	7,219,193	51.7	6,357,698	45.5	210,028	1.5	94,719	0.7	90,887	0.7	861,495	R

1. For breakdown of "Other" vote, see minor candidate vote totals, p. 691.
2. Figures from Edgar E. Robinson, *The Presidential Vote 1896–1932* (Stanford, Calif.: Stanford University Press, 1934).
3. Figures from Svend Petersen, *A Statistical History of the American Presidential Elections* (Westport, Conn.: Greenwood Press, 1981); *Blue Book, 1908*, p. 700.
4. Figures from Petersen, *A Statistical History*, p. 67.
5. Figures from *Official Manual, 1904*, pp. 118–121.
6. Figures from *Maine Register*, 1945.
7. Figures from Petersen, *A Statistical History*; Robinson, *The Presidential Vote*.

1904 Presidential Election

STATE	TOTAL VOTE	THEODORE ROOSEVELT (Republican)		ALTON B. PARKER (Democrat)		EUGENE V. DEBS (Socialist)		SILAS C. SWALLOW (Prohibition)		OTHER[1]		PLURALITY	
		Votes	%	Votes	%	Votes	%	Votes	%	Votes	%		
Alabama	108,785	22,472	20.7	79,797	73.4	853	0.8	612	0.6	5,051	4.6	57,325	D
Arkansas	116,328	46,760	40.2	64,434	55.4	1,816	1.6	992	0.9	2,326	2.0	17,674	D
California	331,768	205,226	61.9	89,294	26.9	29,535	8.9	7,380	2.2	333	0.1	115,932	R
Colorado	243,667	134,661	55.3	100,105	41.1	4,304	1.8	3,438	1.4	1,159	0.5	34,556	R
Connecticut	191,136	111,089	58.1	72,909	38.1	Z8	2.4	1,506	0.8	1,089	0.6	38,180	R
Delaware	43,856	23,705	54.1	19,347	44.1	146	0.3	607	1.4	51	0.1	4,358	R
Florida[2]	39,302	8,314	21.2	27,046	68.8	2,337	6.0	—	0.0	1,605	4.1	18,732	D
Georgia	130,986	24,004	18.3	83,466	63.7	196	0.1	685	0.5	22,635	17.3	59,462	D
Idaho	72,577	47,783	65.8	18,480	25.5	4,949	6.8	1,013	1.4	352	0.5	29,303	R
Illinois	1,076,495	632,645	58.8	327,606	30.4	69,225	6.4	34,770	3.2	12,249	1.1	305,039	R
Indiana	682,206	368,289	54.0	274,356	40.2	12,023	1.8	23,496	3.4	4,042	0.6	93,933	R
Iowa	485,703	307,907	63.4	149,141	30.7	14,847	3.1	11,601	2.4	2,207	0.5	158,766	R
Kansas	329,047	213,455	64.9	86,164	26.2	15,869	4.8	7,306	2.2	6,253	1.9	127,291	R
Kentucky	435,946	205,457	47.1	217,170	49.8	3,599	0.8	6,603	1.5	3,117	0.7	11,713	D
Louisiana	53,908	5,205	9.7	47,708	88.5	995	1.8	—	0.0	—	0.0	42,503	D
Maine[3]	96,036	64,438	67.1	27,648	28.8	2,103	2.2	1,510	1.6	337	0.3	36,790	R
Maryland	224,229	109,497	48.8	109,446	48.8	2,247	1.0	3,034	1.4	5	0.0	51	R
Massachusetts	445,100	257,813	57.9	165,746	37.2	13,604	3.1	4,279	1.0	3,658	0.8	92,067	R
Michigan	520,443	361,863	69.5	134,163	25.8	8,942	1.7	13,312	2.6	2,163	0.4	227,700	R
Minnesota	292,860	216,651	74.0	55,187	18.8	11,692	4.0	6,253	2.1	3,077	1.1	161,464	R
Mississippi	58,721	3,280	5.6	53,480	91.1	462	0.8	—	0.0	1,499	2.6	50,200	D
Missouri	643,861	321,449	49.9	296,312	46.0	13,009	2.0	7,191	1.1	5,900	0.9	25,137	R
Montana	63,568	33,994	53.5	21,816	34.3	5,675	8.9	339	0.5	1,744	2.7	12,178	R
Nebraska	225,732	138,558	61.4	52,921	23.4	7,412	3.3	6,323	2.8	20,518	9.1	85,637	R
Nevada	12,115	6,864	56.7	3,982	32.9	925	7.6	—	0.0	344	2.8	2,882	R
New Hampshire	90,151	54,157	60.1	34,071	37.8	1,090	1.2	750	0.8	83	0.1	20,086	R
New Jersey[4]	432,547	245,164	56.7	164,566	38.0	9,587	2.2	6,845	1.6	6,385	1.5	80,598	R
New York	1,617,765	859,533	53.1	683,981	42.3	36,883	2.3	20,787	1.3	16,581	1.0	175,552	R
North Carolina	207,818	82,442	39.7	124,091	59.7	124	0.1	342	0.2	819	0.4	41,649	D
North Dakota[2]	70,279	52,595	74.8	14,273	20.3	2,009	2.9	1,137	1.6	165	0.2	38,322	R
Ohio	1,004,395	600,095	59.7	344,674	34.3	36,260	3.6	19,339	1.9	4,027	0.4	255,421	R
Oregon	89,656	60,309	67.3	17,327	19.3	7,479	8.3	3,795	4.2	746	0.8	42,982	R
Pennsylvania	1,236,738	840,949	68.0	337,998	27.3	21,863	1.8	33,717	2.7	2,211	0.2	502,951	R
Rhode Island	68,656	41,605	60.6	24,839	36.2	956	1.4	768	1.1	488	0.7	16,766	R
South Carolina	55,890	2,570	4.6	53,320	95.4	—	0.0	—	0.0	—	0.0	50,750	D
South Dakota	101,395	72,083	71.1	21,969	21.7	3,138	3.1	2,965	2.9	1,240	1.2	50,114	R
Tennessee	242,750	105,363	43.4	131,653	54.2	1,354	0.6	1,889	0.8	2,491	1.0	26,290	D
Texas	233,609	51,307	22.0	167,088	71.5	2,788	1.2	3,933	1.7	8,493	3.6	115,781	D
Utah	101,626	62,446	61.4	33,413	32.9	5,767	5.7	—	0.0	—	0.0	29,033	R
Vermont	51,888	40,459	78.0	9,777	18.8	859	1.7	792	1.5	1	0.0	30,682	R
Virginia	130,410	48,180	36.9	80,649	61.8	202	0.2	1,379	1.1	—	0.0	32,469	D
Washington	145,151	101,540	70.0	28,098	19.4	10,023	6.9	3,229	2.2	2,261	1.6	73,442	R
West Virginia	239,986	132,620	55.3	100,855	42.0	1,573	0.7	4,599	1.9	339	0.1	31,765	R
Wisconsin	443,440	280,314	63.2	124,205	28.0	28,240	6.4	9,872	2.2	809	0.2	156,109	R
Wyoming	30,614	20,489	66.9	8,930	29.2	987	3.2	208	0.7	—	0.0	11,559	R
Totals	13,519,039	7,625,599	56.4	5,083,501	37.6	402,490	3.0	258,596	1.9	148,853	1.1	2,542,098	R

1. For breakdown of "Other" vote, see minor candidate vote totals, p. 691.
2. Figures from Svend Petersen, *A Statistical History of the American Presidential Elections* (Westport, Conn.: Greenwood Press, 1981).
3. Figures from *Maine Register, 1945*.
4. Figures from *Manual, 1905*.

1908 Presidential Election

STATE	TOTAL VOTE	WILLIAM H. TAFT (Republican) Votes	%	WILLIAM J. BRYAN (Democrat) Votes	%	EUGENE V. DEBS (Socialist) Votes	%	EUGENE W. CHAFIN (Prohibition) Votes	%	OTHER[1] Votes	%	PLURALITY	
Alabama	105,152	25,561	24.3	74,391	70.7	1,450	1.4	690	0.7	3,060	2.9	48,830	D
Arkansas	151,845	56,684	37.3	87,020	57.3	5,842	3.8	1,026	0.7	1,273	0.8	30,336	D
California	386,625	214,398	55.5	127,492	33.0	28,659	7.4	11,770	3.0	4,306	1.1	86,906	R
Colorado	263,858	123,693	46.9	126,644	48.0	7,960	3.0	5,559	2.1	2	0.0	2,951	D
Connecticut	189,903	112,815	59.4	68,255	35.9	5,113	2.7	2,380	1.3	1,340	0.7	44,560	R
Delaware	48,007	25,014	52.1	22,055	45.9	239	0.5	670	1.4	29	0.1	2,959	R
Florida	49,360	10,654	21.6	31,104	63.0	3,747	7.6	1,356	2.7	2,499	5.1	20,450	D
Georgia[2]	132,794	41,692	31.4	72,413	54.5	584	0.4	1,059	0.8	17,046	12.8	30,721	D
Idaho	97,293	52,621	54.1	36,162	37.2	6,400	6.6	1,986	2.0	124	0.1	16,459	R
Illinois	1,155,254	629,932	54.5	450,810	39.0	34,711	3.0	29,364	2.5	10,437	0.9	179,122	R
Indiana	721,117	348,993	48.4	338,262	46.9	13,476	1.9	18,036	2.5	2,350	0.3	10,731	R
Iowa	494,770	275,210	55.6	200,771	40.6	8,287	1.7	9,837	2.0	665	0.1	74,439	R
Kansas	376,043	197,316	52.5	161,209	42.9	12,420	3.3	5,030	1.3	68	0.0	36,107	R
Kentucky	490,719	235,711	48.0	244,092	49.7	4,093	0.8	5,885	1.2	938	0.2	8,381	D
Louisiana	75,117	8,958	11.9	63,568	84.6	2,514	3.3	—	0.0	77	0.1	54,610	D
Maine	106,335	66,987	63.0	35,403	33.3	1,758	1.7	1,487	1.4	700	0.7	31,584	R
Maryland	238,531	116,513	48.8	115,908	48.6	2,323	1.0	3,302	1.4	485	0.2	605	R
Massachusetts	456,905	265,966	58.2	155,533	34.0	10,778	2.4	4,373	1.0	20,255	4.4	110,433	R
Michigan	538,124	333,313	61.9	174,619	32.4	11,527	2.1	16,785	3.1	1,880	0.3	158,694	R
Minnesota[3]	331,328	195,846	59.1	109,411	33.0	14,528	4.4	11,114	3.4	429	0.1	86,435	R
Mississippi	66,904	4,363	6.5	60,287	90.1	978	1.5	—	0.0	1,276	1.9	55,924	D
Missouri	715,841	347,203	48.5	346,574	48.4	15,431	2.2	4,209	0.6	2,424	0.3	629	R
Montana	69,233	32,471	46.9	29,511	42.6	5,920	8.6	838	1.2	493	0.7	2,960	R
Nebraska	266,799	126,997	47.6	131,099	49.1	3,524	1.3	5,179	1.9	—	0.0	4,102	D
Nevada	24,526	10,775	43.9	11,212	45.7	2,103	8.6	—	0.0	436	1.8	437	D
New Hampshire	89,595	53,144	59.3	33,655	37.6	1,299	1.4	905	1.0	592	0.7	19,489	R
New Jersey	467,111	265,298	56.8	182,522	39.1	10,249	2.2	4,930	1.1	4,112	0.9	82,776	R
New York	1,638,350	870,070	53.1	667,468	40.7	38,451	2.3	22,667	1.4	39,694	2.4	202,602	R
North Carolina	252,554	114,887	45.5	136,928	54.2	372	0.1	354	0.1	13	0.0	22,041	D
North Dakota	94,524	57,680	61.0	32,884	34.8	2,421	2.6	1,496	1.6	43	0.0	24,796	R
Ohio	1,121,552	572,312	51.0	502,721	44.8	33,795	3.0	11,402	1.0	1,322	0.1	69,591	R
Oklahoma	254,260	110,473	43.4	122,362	48.1	21,425	8.4	—	0.0	—	0.0	11,889	D
Oregon	110,539	62,454	56.5	37,792	34.2	7,322	6.6	2,682	2.4	289	0.3	24,662	R
Pennsylvania	1,267,450	745,779	58.8	448,782	35.4	33,914	2.7	36,694	2.9	2,281	0.2	296,997	R
Rhode Island	72,317	43,942	60.8	24,706	34.2	1,365	1.9	1,016	1.4	1,288	1.8	19,236	R
South Carolina	66,379	3,945	5.9	62,288	93.8	100	0.2	—	0.0	46	0.1	58,343	D
South Dakota	114,775	67,536	58.8	40,266	35.1	2,846	2.5	4,039	3.5	88	0.1	27,270	R
Tennessee	257,180	117,977	45.9	135,608	52.7	1,870	0.7	301	0.1	1,424	0.6	17,631	D
Texas	292,913	65,605	22.4	216,662	74.0	7,779	2.7	1,626	0.6	1,241	0.4	151,057	D
Utah	108,757	61,165	56.2	42,610	39.2	4,890	4.5	—	0.0	92	0.1	18,555	R
Vermont	52,680	39,552	75.1	11,496	21.8	—	0.0	799	1.5	833	1.6	28,056	R
Virginia	137,065	52,572	38.4	82,946	60.5	255	0.2	1,111	0.8	181	0.1	30,374	D
Washington	183,570	106,062	57.8	58,383	31.8	14,177	7.7	4,700	2.6	248	0.1	47,679	R
West Virginia	258,098	137,869	53.4	111,410	43.2	3,679	1.4	5,140	2.0	—	0.0	26,459	R
Wisconsin	454,438	247,744	54.5	166,662	36.7	28,147	6.2	11,565	2.5	320	0.1	81,082	R
Wyoming	37,608	20,846	55.4	14,918	39.7	1,715	4.6	66	0.2	63	0.2	5,928	R
Totals	14,884,098	7,676,598	51.6	6,406,874	43.0	420,436	2.8	253,428	1.7	126,762	0.9	1,269,724	R

1. For breakdown of "Other" vote, see minor candidate vote totals, p. 691.
2. Figures from Svend Petersen, *A Statistical History of the American Presidential Elections* (Westport, Conn.: Greenwood Press, 1981).
3. Figures from *Minnesota Votes*.

1912 Presidential Election

STATE	TOTAL VOTE	WOODROW WILSON (Democrat)		THEODORE ROOSEVELT (Progressive)		WILLIAM H. TAFT (Republican)		EUGENE V. DEBS (Socialist)		OTHER[1]		PLURALITY	
		Votes	%	Votes	%	Votes	%	Votes	%	Votes	%		
Alabama	117,959	82,438	69.9	22,680	19.2	9,807	8.3	3,029	2.6	5	0.0	59,758	D
Arizona	23,687	10,324	43.6	6,949	29.3	2,986	12.6	3,163	13.4	265	1.1	3,375	D
Arkansas	125,104	68,814	55.0	21,644	17.3	25,585	20.5	8,153	6.5	908	0.7	43,229	D
California	677,877	283,436	41.8	283,610	41.8	3,847	0.6	79,201	11.7	27,783	4.1	174	PR
Colorado	265,954	113,912	42.8	71,752	27.0	58,386	22.0	16,366	6.2	5,538	2.1	42,160	D
Connecticut	190,404	74,561	39.2	34,129	17.9	68,324	35.9	10,056	5.3	3,334	1.8	6,237	D
Delaware	48,690	22,631	46.5	8,886	18.3	15,997	32.9	556	1.1	620	1.3	6,634	D
Florida[2]	51,911	36,417	70.2	4,555	8.8	4,279	8.2	4,806	9.3	1,854	3.6	31,862	D
Georgia	121,470	93,087	76.6	21,985	18.1	5,191	4.3	1,058	0.9	149	0.1	71,102	D
Idaho	105,754	33,921	32.1	25,527	24.1	32,810	31.0	11,960	11.3	1,536	1.5	1,111	D
Illinois	1,146,173	405,048	35.3	386,478	33.7	253,593	22.1	81,278	7.1	19,776	1.7	18,570	D
Indiana	654,474	281,890	43.1	162,007	24.8	151,267	23.1	36,931	5.6	22,379	3.4	119,883	D
Iowa	492,353	185,322	37.6	161,819	32.9	119,805	24.3	16,967	3.4	8,440	1.7	23,503	D
Kansas	365,560	143,663	39.3	120,210	32.9	74,845	20.5	26,779	7.3	63	0.0	23,453	D
Kentucky[3]	453,707	219,585	48.4	102,766	22.7	115,520	25.5	11,647	2.6	4,189	0.9	104,065	D
Louisiana	79,248	60,871	76.8	9,283	11.7	3,833	4.8	5,261	6.6	—	0.0	51,588	D
Maine	129,641	51,113	39.4	48,495	37.4	26,545	20.5	2,541	2.0	947	0.7	2,618	D
Maryland	231,981	112,674	48.6	57,789	24.9	54,956	23.7	3,996	1.7	2,566	1.1	54,885	D
Massachusetts	488,056	173,408	35.5	142,228	29.1	155,948	32.0	12,616	2.6	3,856	0.8	17,460	D
Michigan	547,971	150,201	27.4	213,243	38.9	151,434	27.6	23,060	4.2	10,033	1.8	61,809	PR
Minnesota	334,219	106,426	31.8	125,856	37.7	64,334	19.2	27,505	8.2	10,098	3.0	19,430	PR
Mississippi	64,483	57,324	88.9	3,549	5.5	1,560	2.4	2,050	3.2	—	0.0	53,775	D
Missouri	698,566	330,746	47.3	124,375	17.8	207,821	29.7	28,466	4.1	7,158	1.0	122,925	D
Montana	80,256	28,129	35.0	22,709	28.3	18,575	23.1	10,811	13.5	32	0.0	5,420	D
Nebraska	249,483	109,008	43.7	72,681	29.1	54,226	21.7	10,185	4.1	3,383	1.4	36,327	D
Nevada	20,115	7,986	39.7	5,620	27.9	3,196	15.9	3,313	16.5	—	0.0	2,366	D
New Hampshire	87,961	34,724	39.5	17,794	20.2	32,927	37.4	1,981	2.3	535	0.6	1,797	D
New Jersey	433,663	178,638	41.2	145,679	33.6	89,066	20.5	15,948	3.7	4,332	1.0	32,959	D
New Mexico	48,807	20,437	41.9	8,347	17.1	17,164	35.2	2,859	5.9	—	0.0	3,273	D
New York	1,588,315	655,573	41.3	390,093	24.6	455,487	28.7	63,434	4.0	23,728	1.5	200,086	D
North Carolina	243,776	144,407	59.2	69,135	28.4	29,129	11.9	987	0.4	118	0.0	75,272	D
North Dakota	86,474	29,549	34.2	25,726	29.7	22,990	26.6	6,966	8.1	1,243	1.4	3,823	D
Ohio	1,037,114	424,834	41.0	229,807	22.2	278,168	26.8	90,164	8.7	14,141	1.4	146,666	D
Oklahoma	253,694	119,143	47.0	—	0.0	90,726	35.8	41,630	16.4	2,195	0.9	28,417	D
Oregon	137,040	47,064	34.3	37,600	27.4	34,673	25.3	13,343	9.7	4,360	3.2	9,464	D
Pennsylvania	1,217,736	395,637	32.5	444,894	36.5	273,360	22.4	83,614	6.9	20,231	1.7	49,257	PR
Rhode Island	77,894	30,412	39.0	16,878	21.7	27,703	35.6	2,049	2.6	852	1.1	2,709	D
South Carolina	50,403	48,355	95.9	1,293	2.6	536	1.1	164	0.3	55	0.1	47,062	D
South Dakota	116,327	48,942	42.1	58,811	50.6	—	0.0	4,664	4.0	3,910	3.4	9,869	PR
Tennessee	251,933	133,021	52.8	54,041	21.5	60,475	24.0	3,564	1.4	832	0.3	72,546	D
Texas	300,961	218,921	72.7	26,715	8.9	28,310	9.4	24,884	8.3	2,131	0.7	190,611	D
Utah	112,272	36,576	32.6	24,174	21.5	42,013	37.4	8,999	8.0	510	0.5	5,437	R
Vermont	62,804	15,350	24.4	22,129	35.2	23,303	37.1	928	1.5	1,094	1.7	1,174	R
Virginia	136,975	90,332	65.9	21,776	15.9	23,288	17.0	820	0.6	759	0.6	67,044	D
Washington	322,799	86,840	26.9	113,698	35.2	70,445	21.8	40,134	12.4	11,682	3.6	26,858	PR
West Virginia	268,728	113,097	42.1	79,112	29.4	56,754	21.1	15,248	5.7	4,517	1.7	33,985	D
Wisconsin	399,975	164,230	41.1	62,448	15.6	130,596	32.7	33,476	8.4	9,225	2.3	33,634	D
Wyoming	42,283	15,310	36.2	9,232	21.8	14,560	34.4	2,760	6.5	421	1.0	750	D
Totals	15,043,029	6,294,326	41.8	4,120,207	27.4	3,486,343	23.2	900,370	6.0	241,783	1.6	2,174,119	D

1. For breakdown of "Other" vote, see minor candidate vote totals, p. 691.
2. Figures from Svend Petersen, *A Statistical History of the American Presidential Elections* (Westport, Conn.: Greenwood Press, 1981); Edgar E. Robinson, *The Presidential Vote 1896–1932* (Stanford, Calif.: Stanford University Press, 1934).
3. Figures from *Kentucky Directory 1916,* pp. 145–149.

1916 Presidential Election

STATE	TOTAL VOTE	WOODROW WILSON (Democrat) Votes	%	CHARLES E. HUGHES (Republican) Votes	%	ALLAN L. BENSON (Socialist) Votes	%	J. FRANK HANLY (Prohibition) Votes	%	OTHER[1] Votes	%	PLURALITY	
Alabama[2]	131,142	99,409	75.6	28,809	21.9	1,925	1.5	999	0.8	—	0.0	70,600	D
Arizona	58,019	33,170	57.2	20,522	35.4	3,174	5.5	1,153	2.0	—	0.0	12,648	D
Arkansas[3]	168,348	112,186	66.6	47,148	28.0	6,999	4.2	2,015	1.2	—	0.0	65,038	D
California	999,250	465,936	46.6	462,516	46.3	42,898	4.3	27,713	2.8	187	0.0	3,420	D
Colorado[3]	294,375	178,816	60.5	102,308	34.8	10,049	3.4	2,793	0.9	409	0.1	76,508	D
Connecticut	213,874	99,786	46.7	106,514	49.8	5,179	2.4	1,789	0.8	606	0.3	6,728	R
Delaware	51,810	24,753	47.8	26,011	50.2	480	0.9	566	1.1	—	0.0	1,258	R
Florida	80,734	55,984	69.3	14,611	18.1	5,353	6.6	4,786	5.9	—	0.0	41,373	D
Georgia[4]	158,690	125,845	79.3	11,225	7.1	967	0.6	—	0.0	20,653	12.9	105,192	D
Idaho	134,615	70,054	52.0	55,368	41.1	8,066	6.0	1,127	0.8	—	0.0	14,686	D
Illinois	2,192,707	950,229	43.3	1,152,549	52.6	61,394	2.8	26,047	1.2	2,488	0.1	202,320	R
Indiana	718,853	334,063	46.5	341,005	47.4	21,860	3.0	16,368	2.3	5,557	0.8	6,942	R
Iowa	518,738	221,699	42.7	280,439	54.1	10,976	2.1	3,371	0.6	2,253	0.4	58,740	R
Kansas	629,813	314,588	49.9	277,658	44.1	24,685	3.9	12,882	2.0	—	0.0	36,930	D
Kentucky	520,078	269,990	51.9	241,854	46.5	4,734	0.9	3,039	0.6	461	0.1	28,136	D
Louisiana	92,974	79,875	85.9	6,466	7.0	284	0.3	—	0.0	6,349	6.8	73,409	D
Maine	136,314	64,033	47.0	69,508	51.0	2,177	1.6	596	0.4	—	0.0	5,475	R
Maryland	262,039	138,359	52.8	117,347	44.8	2,674	1.0	2,903	1.1	756	0.3	21,012	D
Massachusetts	531,822	247,885	46.6	268,784	50.5	11,058	2.1	2,993	0.6	1,102	0.2	20,899	R
Michigan	646,873	283,993	43.9	337,952	52.2	16,012	2.5	8,085	1.2	831	0.1	53,959	R
Minnesota	387,367	179,155	46.2	179,544	46.3	20,117	5.2	7,793	2.0	758	0.2	389	R
Mississippi	86,679	80,422	92.8	4,253	4.9	1,484	1.7	—	0.0	520	0.6	76,169	D
Missouri	786,773	398,032	50.6	369,339	46.9	14,612	1.9	3,887	0.5	903	0.1	28,693	D
Montana	178,009	101,104	56.8	66,933	37.6	9,634	5.4	—	0.0	338	0.2	34,171	D
Nebraska	287,315	158,827	55.3	117,771	41.0	7,141	2.5	2,952	1.0	624	0.2	41,056	D
Nevada	33,314	17,776	53.4	12,127	36.4	3,065	9.2	346	1.0	—	0.0	5,649	D
New Hampshire	89,127	43,781	49.1	43,725	49.1	1,318	1.5	303	0.3	—	0.0	56	D
New Jersey	494,442	211,018	42.7	268,982	54.4	10,405	2.1	3,182	0.6	855	0.2	57,964	R
New Mexico	66,879	33,693	50.4	31,097	46.5	1,977	3.0	112	0.2	—	0.0	2,596	D
New York	1,706,305	759,426	44.5	879,238	51.5	45,944	2.7	19,031	1.1	2,666	0.2	119,812	R
North Carolina	289,837	168,383	58.1	120,890	41.7	509	0.2	55	0.0	—	0.0	47,493	D
North Dakota	115,390	55,206	47.8	53,471	46.3	5,716	5.0	997	0.9	—	0.0	1,735	D
Ohio	1,165,091	604,161	51.9	514,753	44.2	38,092	3.3	8,085	0.7	—	0.0	89,408	D
Oklahoma	292,327	148,123	50.7	97,233	33.3	45,091	15.4	1,646	0.6	234	0.1	50,890	D
Oregon	261,650	120,087	45.9	126,813	48.5	9,711	3.7	4,729	1.8	310	0.1	6,726	R
Pennsylvania	1,297,189	521,784	40.2	703,823	54.3	42,638	3.3	28,525	2.2	419	0.0	182,039	R
Rhode Island	87,816	40,394	46.0	44,858	51.1	1,914	2.2	470	0.5	180	0.2	4,464	R
South Carolina	63,950	61,845	96.7	1,550	2.4	135	0.2	—	0.0	420	0.7	60,295	D
South Dakota	128,942	59,191	45.9	64,217	49.8	3,760	2.9	1,774	1.4	—	0.0	5,026	R
Tennessee	272,190	153,280	56.3	116,223	42.7	2,542	0.9	145	0.1	—	0.0	37,057	D
Texas[5]	372,467	286,514	76.9	64,999	17.5	18,969	5.1	1,985	0.5	—	0.0	221,515	D
Utah	143,145	84,145	58.8	54,137	37.8	4,460	3.1	149	0.1	254	0.2	30,008	D
Vermont	64,475	22,708	35.2	40,250	62.4	798	1.2	709	1.1	10	0.0	17,542	R
Virginia[2]	153,993	102,825	66.8	49,358	32.1	1,060	0.7	683	0.4	67	0.0	53,467	D
Washington	380,994	183,388	48.1	167,208	43.9	22,800	6.0	6,868	1.8	730	0.2	16,180	D
West Virginia	289,671	140,403	48.5	143,124	49.4	6,144	2.1	—	0.0	—	0.0	2,721	R
Wisconsin	447,134	191,363	42.8	220,822	49.4	27,631	6.2	7,318	1.6	—	0.0	29,459	R
Wyoming	51,906	28,376	54.7	21,698	41.8	1,459	2.8	373	0.7	—	0.0	6,678	D
Totals	**18,535,445**	**9,126,063**	**49.2**	**8,547,039**	**46.1**	**590,110**	**3.2**	**221,293**	**1.2**	**50,940**	**0.3**	**579,024**	**D**

1. For breakdown of "Other" vote, see minor candidate vote totals, p. 692.
2. Figures from Svend Petersen, *A Statistical History of the American Presidential Elections* (Westport, Conn.: Greenwood Press, 1981); Edgar E. Robinson, *The Presidential Vote 1896–1932* (Stanford, Calif.: Stanford University Press, 1934).
3. Figures from Petersen, *A Statistical History.*
4. Figures from Petersen, *A Statistical History.* Plurality of 105,192 votes is calculated on the basis of 20,653 votes cast for the Progressive Party.
5. Figures from Petersen, *A Statistical History*; *Texas Almanac.*

1920 Presidential Election

STATE	TOTAL VOTE	WARREN G. HARDING (Republican)		JAMES M. COX (Democrat)		EUGENE V. DEBS (Socialist)		PARLEY P. CHRISTENSEN (Farmer-Labor)		OTHER[1]		PLURALITY	
		Votes	%	Votes	%	Votes	%	Votes	%	Votes	%		
Alabama	233,951	74,719	31.9	156,064	66.7	2,402	1.0	—	0.0	766	0.3	81,345	D
Arizona	66,803	37,016	55.4	29,546	44.2	222	0.3	15	0.0	4	0.0	7,470	R
Arkansas[2]	183,637	71,117	38.7	107,409	58.5	5,111	2.8	—	0.0	—	0.0	36,292	D
California	943,463	624,992	66.2	229,191	24.3	64,076	6.8	—	0.0	25,204	2.7	395,801	R
Colorado	292,053	173,248	59.3	104,936	35.9	8,046	2.8	3,016	1.0	2,807	1.0	68,312	R
Connecticut	365,518	229,238	62.7	120,721	33.0	10,350	2.8	1,947	0.5	3,262	0.9	108,517	R
Delaware	94,875	52,858	55.7	39,911	42.1	988	1.0	93	0.1	1,025	1.1	12,947	R
Florida	145,684	44,853	30.8	90,515	62.1	5,189	3.6	—	0.0	5,127	3.5	45,662	D
Georgia	149,558	42,981	28.7	106,112	71.0	465	0.3	—	0.0	—	0.0	63,131	D
Idaho[2]	138,359	91,351	66.0	46,930	33.9	38	0.3	6	0.0	34	0.2	44,421	R
Illinois	2,094,714	1,420,480	67.8	534,395	25.5	74,747	3.6	49,630	2.4	15,462	0.7	886,085	R
Indiana	1,262,974	696,370	55.1	511,364	40.5	24,713	2.0	16,499	1.3	14,028	1.1	185,006	R
Iowa	894,959	634,674	70.9	227,804	25.5	16,981	1.9	10,321	1.2	5,179	0.6	406,870	R
Kansas	570,243	369,268	64.8	185,464	32.5	15,511	2.7	—	0.0	—	0.0	183,804	R
Kentucky	918,636	452,480	49.3	456,497	49.7	6,409	0.7	—	0.0	3,250	0.4	4,017	D
Louisiana	126,397	38,539	30.5	87,519	69.2	—	0.0	—	0.0	339	0.3	48,980	D
Maine	197,840	136,355	68.9	58,961	29.8	2,214	1.1	—	0.0	310	0.2	77,394	R
Maryland	428,443	236,117	55.1	180,626	42.2	8,876	2.1	1,645	0.4	1,179	0.3	55,491	R
Massachusetts	993,718	681,153	68.5	276,691	27.8	32,267	3.2	—	0.0	3,607	0.4	404,462	R
Michigan	1,048,411	762,865	72.8	233,450	22.3	28,947	2.8	10,480	1.0	12,669	1.2	529,415	R
Minnesota	735,838	519,421	70.6	142,994	19.4	56,106	7.6	—	0.0	17,317	2.4	376,427	R
Mississippi	82,351	11,576	14.1	69,136	84.0	1,639	2.0	—	0.0	—	0.0	57,560	D
Missouri	1,332,140	727,252	54.6	574,699	43.1	20,342	1.5	3,108	0.2	6,739	0.5	152,553	R
Montana	179,006	109,430	61.1	57,372	32.1	—	0.0	12,204	6.8	—	0.0	52,058	R
Nebraska	382,743	247,498	64.7	119,608	31.3	9,600	2.5	—	0.0	6,037	1.6	127,890	R
Nevada	27,194	15,479	56.9	9,851	36.2	1,864	6.9	—	0.0	—	0.0	5,628	R
New Hampshire	159,092	95,196	59.8	62,662	39.4	1,234	0.8	—	0.0	—	0.0	32,534	R
New Jersey	910,251	615,333	67.6	258,761	28.4	27,385	3.0	2,264	0.2	6,508	0.7	356,572	R
New Mexico	105,412	57,634	54.7	46,668	44.3	2	0.0	1,104	1.0	4	0.0	10,966	R
New York	2,898,513	1,871,167	64.6	781,238	27.0	203,201	7.0	18,413	0.6	24,494	0.8	1,089,929	R
North Carolina	538,649	232,819	43.2	305,367	56.7	446	0.1	—	0.0	17	0.0	72,548	D
North Dakota	205,786	160,082	77.8	37,422	18.2	8,282	4.0	—	0.0	—	0.0	122,660	R
Ohio	2,021,653	1,182,022	58.5	780,037	38.6	57,147	2.8	—	0.0	2,447	0.1	401,985	R
Oklahoma	485,678	243,840	50.2	216,122	44.5	25,716	5.3	—	0.0	—	0.0	27,718	R
Oregon	238,522	143,592	60.2	80,019	33.5	9,801	4.1	—	0.0	5,110	2.1	63,573	R
Pennsylvania	1,851,248	1,218,215	65.8	503,202	27.2	70,021	3.8	15,642	0.8	44,168	2.4	715,013	R
Rhode Island	167,981	107,463	64.0	55,062	32.8	4,351	2.6	—	0.0	1,105	0.7	52,401	R
South Carolina[3]	66,808	2,610	3.9	64,170	96.1	28	0.0	—	0.0	—	0.0	61,560	D
South Dakota	182,237	110,692	60.7	35,938	19.7	—	0.0	34,707	19.0	900	0.5	74,754	R
Tennessee	428,036	219,229	51.2	206,558	48.3	2,249	0.5	—	0.0	—	0.0	12,671	R
Texas	486,109	114,658	23.6	287,920	59.2	8,124	1.7	—	0.0	75,407	15.5	173,262	D
Utah	145,828	81,555	55.9	56,639	38.8	3,159	2.2	4,475	3.1	—	0.0	24,916	R
Vermont	89,961	68,212	75.8	20,919	23.3	—	0.0	—	0.0	830	0.9	47,293	R
Virginia	231,000	87,456	37.9	141,670	61.3	808	0.3	240	0.1	826	0.4	54,214	D
Washington	398,715	223,137	56.0	84,298	21.1	8,913	2.2	77,246	19.4	5,121	1.3	138,839	R
West Virginia	509,936	282,007	55.3	220,785	43.3	5,618	1.1	—	0.0	1,526	0.3	61,222	R
Wisconsin	701,281	498,576	71.1	113,422	16.2	80,635	11.5	—	0.0	8,648	1.2	385,154	R
Wyoming	56,253	35,091	62.4	17,429	31.0	1,288	2.3	2,180	3.9	265	0.5	17,662	R
Totals	26,768,457	16,151,916	60.3	9,134,074	34.1	915,511	3.4	265,235	1.0	301,721	1.1	7,017,842	R

1. For breakdown of "Other" vote, see minor candidate vote totals, p. 692.
2. Figures from Svend Petersen, *A Statistical History of the American Presidential Elections* (Westport, Conn.: Greenwood Press, 1981); *America at the Polls 1920-1956* (Washington, D.C.: Congressional Quarterly, 1994).
3. Two sets of Harding electors are combined here: Republican, 2,244; Insurgent Referendum, 366.

1924 Presidential Election

STATE	TOTAL VOTE	CALVIN COOLIDGE (Republican)		JOHN W. DAVIS (Democrat)		ROBERT M. LA FOLLETTE (Progressive)		HERMAN P. FARIS (Prohibition)		OTHER[1]		PLURALITY	
		Votes	%	Votes	%	Votes	%	Votes	%	Votes	%		
Alabama[2]	166,593	45,005	27.0	112,966	67.8	8,084	4.9	538	0.3	—	0.0	67,961	D
Arizona	73,961	30,516	41.3	26,235	35.5	17,210	23.3	—	0.0	—	0.0	4,281	R
Arkansas	138,540	40,583	29.3	84,790	61.2	13,167	9.5	—	0.0	—	0.0	44,207	D
California	1,281,778	733,250	57.2	105,514	8.2	424,649	33.1	18,365	1.4	—	0.0	308,601	R
Colorado[3]	342,261	195,171	57.0	75,238	22.0	69,945	20.4	966	0.3	940	0.3	119,933	R
Connecticut	400,396	246,322	61.5	110,184	27.5	42,416	10.6	—	0.0	1,474	0.4	136,138	R
Delaware	90,885	52,441	57.7	33,445	36.8	4,979	5.5	—	0.0	20	0.0	18,996	R
Florida	109,158	30,633	28.1	62,083	56.9	8,625	7.9	5,498	5.0	2,319	2.1	31,450	D
Georgia	166,635	30,300	18.2	123,262	74.0	12,687	7.6	231	0.1	155	0.1	92,962	D
Idaho	147,690	69,791	47.3	23,951	16.2	53,948	36.5	—	0.0	—	0.0	15,843	R
Illinois	2,470,067	1,453,321	58.8	576,975	23.4	432,027	17.5	2,367	0.1	5,377	0.2	876,346	R
Indiana	1,272,390	703,042	55.3	492,245	38.7	71,700	5.6	4,416	0.3	987	0.1	210,797	R
Iowa	976,770	537,458	55.0	160,382	16.4	274,448	28.1	—	0.0	4,482	0.5	263,010	R
Kansas	662,456	407,671	61.5	156,320	23.6	98,461	14.9	—	0.0	4	0.0	251,351	R
Kentucky[4]	816,070	398,966	48.9	375,593	46.0	38,465	4.7	—	0.0	3,046	0.4	23,373	R
Louisiana	121,951	24,670	20.2	93,218	76.4	—	0.0	—	0.0	4,063	3.3	68,548	D
Maine	192,192	138,440	72.0	41,964	21.8	11,382	5.9	—	0.0	406	0.2	96,476	R
Maryland	358,630	162,414	45.3	148,072	41.3	47,157	13.1	—	0.0	987	0.3	14,342	R
Massachusetts	1,129,837	703,476	62.3	280,831	24.9	141,225	12.5	—	0.0	4,305	0.4	422,645	R
Michigan	1,160,419	874,631	75.4	152,359	13.1	122,014	10.5	6,085	0.5	5,330	0.5	722,272	R
Minnesota	822,146	420,759	51.2	55,913	6.8	339,192	41.3	—	0.0	6,282	0.8	81,567	R
Mississippi	112,442	8,494	7.6	100,474	89.4	3,474	3.1	—	0.0	—	0.0	91,980	D
Missouri[5]	1,310,095	648,488	49.5	574,962	43.9	83,986	6.4	1,418	0.1	1,231	0.1	73,526	R
Montana[6]	174,425	74,138	42.5	33,805	19.4	65,876	37.9	—	0.0	358	0.2	8,014	R
Nebraska	463,559	218,985	47.2	137,299	29.6	105,681	22.8	1,594	0.3	—	0.0	81,686	R
Nevada	26,921	11,243	41.8	5,909	21.9	9,769	36.3	—	0.0	—	0.0	1,474	R
New Hampshire	164,769	98,575	59.8	57,201	34.7	8,993	5.5	—	0.0	—	0.0	41,374	R
New Jersey	1,088,054	676,277	62.2	298,043	27.4	109,028	10.0	1,660	0.2	3,046	0.3	378,234	R
New Mexico	112,830	54,745	48.5	48,542	43.0	9,543	8.5	—	0.0	—	0.0	6,203	R
New York[7]	3,263,939	1,820,058	55.8	950,796	29.1	474,913	14.6	—	0.0	18,172	0.6	869,262	R
North Carolina	481,608	190,754	39.6	284,190	59.0	6,651	1.4	13	0.0	—	0.0	93,436	D
North Dakota	199,081	94,931	47.7	13,858	7.0	89,922	45.2	—	0.0	370	0.2	5,009	R
Ohio	2,016,296	1,176,130	58.3	477,887	23.7	358,008	17.8	—	0.0	4,271	0.2	698,243	R
Oklahoma[8]	527,928	225,755	42.8	255,798	48.4	41,141	7.8	—	0.0	5,234	1.0	30,043	D
Oregon	279,488	142,579	51.0	67,589	24.2	68,403	24.5	—	0.0	917	0.3	74,176	R
Pennsylvania[9]	2,144,850	1,401,481	65.3	409,192	19.1	307,567	14.3	9,779	0.5	16,831	0.8	992,289	R
Rhode Island	210,115	125,286	59.6	76,606	36.5	7,628	3.6	—	0.0	595	0.3	48,680	R
South Carolina	50,755	1,123	2.2	49,008	96.6	623	1.2	—	0.0	1	0.0	47,885	D
South Dakota	203,868	101,299	49.7	27,214	13.3	75,355	37.0	—	0.0	—	0.0	25,944	R
Tennessee	301,030	130,831	43.5	159,339	52.9	10,666	3.5	94	0.0	100	0.0	28,508	D
Texas	657,054	130,794	19.9	483,381	73.6	42,879	6.5	—	0.0	—	0.0	352,587	D
Utah	156,990	77,327	49.3	47,001	29.9	32,662	20.8	—	0.0	—	0.0	30,326	R
Vermont	102,917	80,498	78.2	16,124	15.7	5,964	5.8	326	0.3	5	0.0	64,374	R
Virginia	223,603	73,328	32.8	139,717	62.5	10,369	4.6	—	0.0	189	0.1	66,389	D
Washington	421,549	220,224	52.2	42,842	10.2	150,727	35.8	—	0.0	7,756	1.8	69,497	R
West Virginia[10]	583,662	288,635	49.5	257,232	44.1	36,723	6.3	—	0.0	1,072	0.2	31,403	R
Wisconsin	840,827	311,614	37.1	68,115	8.1	453,678	54.0	2,918	0.3	4,502	0.5	142,064	P
Wyoming	79,900	41,858	52.4	12,868	16.1	25,174	31.5	—	0.0	—	0.0	16,684	R
Totals	29,099,380	15,724,310	54.0	8,386,532	28.8	4,827,184	16.6	56,268	0.2	104,827	0.4	7,337,778	R

1. For breakdown of "Other" vote, see minor candidate vote totals, p. 692.
2. Figures from Svend Petersen, *A Statistical History of the American Presidential Elections* (Westport, Conn.: Greenwood Press, 1981); Clerk of the House of Representatives, *Statistics of the Congressional and Presidential Election* (Washington, D.C.: U.S. Government Printing Office, 1924).
3. Two sets of La Follette electors are combined here: Colorado Independent Progressive, 57,368; Farmer-Labor, 12,577.
4. Figures from Petersen, *A Statistical History*; Clerk of the House, *Congressional and Presidential Election*; *Kentucky Directory 1925*, p. 142.
5. Two sets of La Follette electors are combined here: Missouri Socialist, 56,723; Liberal, 27,263.
6. Two sets of La Follette electors are combined here: Montana Independent Progressive, 61,105; Farmer-Labor, 4,771.
7. Two sets of La Follette electors are combined here: New York Socialist, 268,518; Progressive, 206,395.
8. There were two separate slates of electors pledged to La Follette in Oklahoma that could not legally be combined. State Election Board *Directory of Oklahoma 1973*, p. 343.
9. Two sets of La Follette electors are combined here: Pennsylvania Socialist, 93,441; Labor, 214,126.
10. Two sets of La Follette electors are combined here: West Virginia Socialist, 14,903; Farmer-Labor, 21,820.

1928 Presidential Election

STATE	TOTAL VOTE	HERBERT C. HOOVER (Republican)		ALFRED E. SMITH (Democrat)		NORMAN M. THOMAS (Socialist)		WILLIAM Z. FOSTER (Communist)		OTHER[1]		PLURALITY	
		Votes	%	Votes	%	Votes	%	Votes	%	Votes	%		
Alabama	248,981	120,725	48.5	127,796	51.3	460	0.2	—	0.0	—	0.0	7,071	D
Arizona	91,254	52,533	57.6	38,537	42.2	—	0.0	184	0.2	—	0.0	13,996	R
Arkansas	197,726	77,784	39.3	119,196	60.3	429	0.2	317	0.2	—	0.0	41,412	D
California	1,796,656	1,162,323	64.7	614,365	34.2	19,595	1.1	—	0.0	373	0.0	547,958	R
Colorado	392,242	253,872	64.7	133,131	33.9	3,472	0.9	675	0.2	1,092	0.3	120,741	R
Connecticut	553,118	296,641	53.6	252,085	45.6	3,029	0.5	738	0.1	625	0.1	44,556	R
Delaware	104,602	68,860	65.8	35,354	33.8	329	0.3	59	0.1	—	0.0	33,506	R
Florida[2]	253,672	144,168	56.8	101,764	40.1	4,036	1.6	3,704	1.5	—	0.0	42,404	R
Georgia[3]	231,592	101,800	44.0	129,604	56.0	124	0.1	64	0.0	—	0.0	27,804	D
Idaho[4]	154,230	99,848	64.7	53,074	34.4	1,308	0.8	—	0.0	—	0.0	46,774	R
Illinois	3,107,489	1,769,141	56.9	1,313,817	42.3	19,138	0.6	3,581	0.1	1,812	0.1	455,324	R
Indiana	1,421,314	848,290	59.7	562,691	39.6	3,871	0.3	321	0.0	6,141	0.4	285,599	R
Iowa	1,009,189	623,570	61.8	379,011	37.6	2,960	0.3	328	0.0	3,320	0.3	244,559	R
Kansas	713,200	513,672	72.0	193,003	27.1	6,205	0.9	320	0.0	—	0.0	320,669	R
Kentucky	940,521	558,064	59.3	381,070	40.5	783	0.1	288	0.0	316	0.0	176,994	R
Louisiana	215,833	51,160	23.7	164,655	76.3	—	0.0	—	0.0	18	0.0	113,495	D
Maine	262,170	179,923	68.6	81,179	31.0	1,068	0.4	—	0.0	—	0.0	98,744	R
Maryland	528,348	301,479	57.1	223,626	42.3	1,701	0.3	636	0.1	906	0.2	77,853	R
Massachusetts	1,577,823	775,566	49.2	792,758	50.2	6,262	0.4	2,461	0.2	776	0.0	17,192	D
Michigan	1,372,082	965,396	70.4	396,762	28.9	3,516	0.3	2,881	0.2	3,527	0.3	568,634	R
Minnesota	970,976	560,977	57.8	396,451	40.8	6,774	0.7	4,853	0.5	1,921	0.2	164,526	R
Mississippi[5]	151,568	27,030	17.8	124,538	82.2	—	0.0	—	0.0	—	0.0	97,508	D
Missouri	1,500,845	834,080	55.6	662,684	44.2	3,739	0.2	—	0.0	342	0.0	171,396	R
Montana	194,108	113,300	58.4	78,578	40.5	1,667	0.9	563	0.3	—	0.0	34,722	R
Nebraska	547,128	345,745	63.2	197,950	36.2	3,433	0.6	—	0.0	—	0.0	147,795	R
Nevada	32,417	18,327	56.5	14,090	43.5	—	0.0	—	0.0	—	0.0	4,237	R
New Hampshire	196,757	115,404	58.7	80,715	41.0	465	0.2	173	0.1	—	0.0	34,689	R
New Jersey	1,549,381	926,050	59.8	616,517	39.8	4,897	0.3	1,257	0.1	660	0.0	309,533	R
New Mexico	118,077	69,708	59.0	48,211	40.8	—	0.0	158	0.1	—	0.0	21,497	R
New York	4,405,626	2,193,344	49.8	2,089,863	47.4	107,332	2.4	10,876	0.2	4,211	0.1	103,481	R
North Carolina	635,150	348,923	54.9	286,227	45.1	—	0.0	—	0.0	—	0.0	62,696	R
North Dakota	239,845	131,419	54.8	106,648	44.5	936	0.4	842	0.4	—	0.0	24,771	R
Ohio	2,508,346	1,627,546	64.9	864,210	34.5	8,683	0.3	2,836	0.1	5,071	0.2	763,336	R
Oklahoma	618,427	394,046	63.7	219,174	35.4	3,924	0.6	—	0.0	1,283	0.2	174,872	R
Oregon	319,942	205,341	64.2	109,223	34.1	2,720	0.9	1,094	0.3	1,564	0.5	96,118	R
Pennsylvania	3,150,612	2,055,382	65.2	1,067,586	33.9	18,647	0.6	4,726	0.2	4,271	0.1	987,796	R
Rhode Island	237,194	117,522	49.5	118,973	50.2	—	0.0	283	0.1	416	0.2	1,451	D
South Carolina[6]	68,605	5,858	8.5	62,700	91.4	47	0.1	—	0.0	—	0.0	56,842	D
South Dakota	261,857	157,603	60.2	102,660	39.2	443	0.2	224	0.1	927	0.4	54,943	R
Tennessee	353,192	195,388	55.3	157,143	44.5	567	0.2	94	0.0	—	0.0	38,245	R
Texas[7]	708,999	367,036	51.8	341,032	48.1	722	0.1	209	0.0	—	0.0	26,004	R
Utah	176,603	94,618	53.6	80,985	45.9	954	0.5	46	0.0	—	0.0	13,633	R
Vermont	135,191	90,404	66.9	44,440	32.9	—	0.0	—	0.0	347	0.3	45,964	R
Virginia	305,364	164,609	53.9	140,146	45.9	249	0.1	179	0.1	181	0.1	24,463	R
Washington	500,840	335,844	67.1	156,772	31.3	2,615	0.5	1,541	0.3	4,068	0.8	179,072	R
West Virginia	642,752	375,551	58.4	263,784	41.0	1,313	0.2	401	0.1	1,703	0.3	111,767	R
Wisconsin	1,016,831	544,205	53.5	450,259	44.3	18,213	1.8	1,528	0.2	2,626	0.3	93,946	R
Wyoming	82,835	52,748	63.7	29,299	35.4	788	1.0	—	0.0	—	0.0	23,449	R
Totals	36,801,510	21,432,823	58.2	15,004,336	40.8	267,414	0.7	48,440	0.1	48,497	0.1	6,428,487	R

1. For breakdown of "Other" vote, see minor candidate vote totals, p. 692.
2. Figures from Clerk of the House of Representatives, *Statistics of the Congressional and Presidential Election* (Washington, D.C.: U.S. Government Printing Office, 1928).
3. Two sets of Hoover electors are combined here: Republican, 65,423; Anti-Smith, 36,377.
4. Figures from Clerk of the House, *Congressional and Presidential Election.*
5. Three sets of Hoover electors are combined here: Republican, 26,222; Ligon electors, 544; Rogers electors, 264.
6. Two sets of Hoover electors are combined here: Republican, 3,188; Anti-Smith, 2,670.
7. Figures from Svend Petersen, *A Statistical History of the American Presidential Elections* (Westport, Conn.: Greenwood Press, 1981); Clerk of the House, *Congressional and Presidential Election; Texas Almanac.*

1932 Presidential Election

STATE	TOTAL VOTE	FRANKLIN D. ROOSEVELT (Democrat)		HERBERT C. HOOVER (Republican)		NORMAN M. THOMAS (Socialist)		WILLIAM Z. FOSTER (Communist)		OTHER[1]		PLURALITY	
		Votes	%	Votes	%	Votes	%	Votes	%	Votes	%		
Alabama	245,303	207,910	84.8	34,675	14.1	2,030	0.8	675	0.3	13	0.0	173,235	D
Arizona	118,251	79,264	67.0	36,104	30.5	2,618	2.2	256	0.2	9	0.0	43,160	D
Arkansas	216,569	186,829	86.3	27,465	12.7	1,166	0.5	157	0.1	952	0.4	159,364	D
California	2,266,972	1,324,157	58.4	847,902	37.4	63,299	2.8	1,023	0.0	30,591	1.3	476,255	D
Colorado	457,696	250,877	54.8	189,617	41.4	13,591	3.0	787	0.2	2,824	0.6	61,260	D
Connecticut	594,183	281,632	47.4	288,420	48.5	20,480	3.4	1,364	0.2	2,287	0.4	6,788	R
Delaware	112,901	54,319	48.1	57,073	50.6	1,376	1.2	133	0.1	—	0.0	2,754	R
Florida	276,943	206,307	74.5	69,170	25.0	775	0.3	—	0.0	691	0.2	137,137	D
Georgia	255,590	234,118	91.6	19,863	7.8	461	0.2	23	0.0	1,125	0.4	214,255	D
Idaho	186,520	109,479	58.7	71,312	38.2	526	0.3	491	0.3	4,712	2.5	38,167	D
Illinois	3,407,926	1,882,304	55.2	1,432,756	42.0	67,258	2.0	15,582	0.5	10,026	0.3	449,548	D
Indiana	1,576,927	862,054	54.7	677,184	42.9	21,388	1.4	2,187	0.1	14,114	0.9	184,870	D
Iowa	1,036,687	598,019	57.7	414,433	40.0	20,467	2.0	559	0.1	3,209	0.3	183,586	D
Kansas	791,978	424,204	53.6	349,498	44.1	18,276	2.3	—	0.0	—	0.0	74,706	D
Kentucky	983,059	580,574	59.1	394,716	40.2	3,853	0.4	271	0.0	3,645	0.4	185,858	D
Louisiana	268,804	249,418	92.8	18,853	7.0	—	0.0	—	0.0	533	0.2	230,565	D
Maine	298,444	128,907	43.2	166,631	55.8	2,489	0.8	162	0.1	255	0.1	37,724	R
Maryland	511,054	314,314	61.5	184,184	36.0	10,489	2.1	1,031	0.2	1,036	0.2	130,130	D
Massachusetts	1,580,114	800,148	50.6	736,959	46.6	34,305	2.2	4,821	0.3	3,881	0.2	63,189	D
Michigan	1,664,765	871,700	52.4	739,894	44.4	39,205	2.4	9,318	0.6	4,648	0.3	131,806	D
Minnesota	1,002,843	600,806	59.9	363,959	36.3	25,476	2.5	6,101	0.6	6,501	0.6	236,847	D
Mississippi[2]	146,034	140,168	96.0	5,180	3.5	686	0.5	—	0.0	—	0.0	134,988	D
Missouri	1,609,894	1,025,406	63.7	564,713	35.1	16,374	1.0	568	0.0	2,833	0.2	460,693	D
Montana	216,479	127,286	58.8	78,078	36.1	7,891	3.6	1,775	0.8	1,449	0.7	49,208	D
Nebraska	570,135	359,082	63.0	201,177	35.3	9,876	1.7	—	0.0	—	0.0	157,905	D
Nevada	41,430	28,756	69.4	12,674	30.6	—	0.0	—	0.0	—	0.0	16,082	D
New Hampshire	205,520	100,680	49.0	103,629	50.4	947	0.5	264	0.1	—	0.0	2,949	R
New Jersey	1,630,063	806,630	49.5	775,684	47.6	42,998	2.6	2,915	0.2	1,836	0.1	30,946	D
New Mexico	151,606	95,089	62.7	54,217	35.8	1,776	1.2	135	0.1	389	0.3	40,872	D
New York	4,688,614	2,534,959	54.1	1,937,963	41.3	177,397	3.8	27,956	0.6	10,339	0.2	596,996	D
North Carolina	711,498	497,566	69.9	208,344	29.3	5,588	0.8	—	0.0	—	0.0	289,222	D
North Dakota	256,290	178,350	69.6	71,772	28.0	3,521	1.4	830	0.3	1,817	0.7	106,578	D
Ohio	2,609,728	1,301,695	49.9	1,227,319	47.0	64,094	2.5	7,231	0.3	9,389	0.4	74,376	D
Oklahoma	704,633	516,468	73.3	188,165	26.7	—	0.0	—	0.0	—	0.0	328,303	D
Oregon	368,751	213,871	58.0	136,019	36.9	15,450	4.2	1,681	0.5	1,730	0.5	77,852	D
Pennsylvania	2,859,021	1,295,948	45.3	1,453,540	50.8	91,119	3.2	5,658	0.2	12,756	0.4	157,592	R
Rhode Island	266,170	146,604	55.1	115,266	43.3	3,138	1.2	546	0.2	616	0.2	31,338	D
South Carolina	104,407	102,347	98.0	1,978	1.9	82	0.1	—	0.0	—	0.0	100,369	D
South Dakota	288,438	183,515	63.6	99,212	34.4	1,551	0.5	364	0.1	3,796	1.3	84,303	D
Tennessee	390,273	259,473	66.5	126,752	32.5	1,796	0.5	254	0.1	1,998	0.5	132,721	D
Texas[3]	863,406	760,348	88.1	97,959	11.3	4,450	0.5	207	0.0	442	0.0	662,389	D
Utah	206,578	116,750	56.5	84,795	41.0	4,087	2.0	946	0.5	—	0.0	31,955	D
Vermont	136,980	56,266	41.1	78,984	57.7	1,533	1.1	195	0.1	2	0.0	22,718	R
Virginia	297,942	203,979	68.5	89,637	30.1	2,382	0.8	86	0.0	1,858	0.6	114,342	D
Washington	614,814	353,260	57.5	208,645	33.9	17,080	2.8	2,972	0.5	32,857	5.3	144,615	D
West Virginia	743,774	405,124	54.5	330,731	44.5	5,133	0.7	444	0.1	2,342	0.3	74,393	D
Wisconsin	1,114,814	707,410	63.5	347,741	31.2	53,379	4.8	3,105	0.3	3,179	0.3	359,669	D
Wyoming	96,962	54,370	56.1	39,583	40.8	2,829	2.9	180	0.2	—	0.0	14,787	D
Totals	39,747,783	22,818,740	57.4	15,760,425	39.6	884,685	2.2	103,253	0.3	180,680	0.5	7,058,315	D

1. For breakdown of "Other" vote, see minor candidate vote totals, p. 692
2. Two sets of Hoover electors are combined here: Lily White, 3,210; Black and Tan, 1,970.
3. Figures from Svend Petersen, *A Statistical History of the American Presidential Elections* (Westport, Conn.: Greenwood Press, 1981); Clerk of the House of Representatives, *Statistics of the Congressional and Presidential Election* (Washington, D.C.: U.S. Government Printing Office, 1932); *Texas Almanac.*

1936 Presidential Election

STATE	TOTAL VOTE	FRANKLIN D. ROOSEVELT (Democrat)		ALFRED M. LANDON (Republican)		WILLIAM LEMKE (Union)		NORMAN M. THOMAS (Socialist)		OTHER[1]		PLURALITY	
		Votes	%	Votes	%	Votes	%	Votes	%	Votes	%		
Alabama	275,744	238,196	86.4	35,358	12.8	551	0.2	242	0.1	1,397	0.5	202,838	D
Arizona	124,163	86,722	69.8	33,433	26.9	3,307	2.7	317	0.3	384	0.3	53,289	D
Arkansas	179,431	146,765	81.8	32,049	17.9	4	0.0	446	0.2	167	0.1	114,716	D
California	2,638,882	1,766,836	67.0	836,431	31.7	—	0.0	11,331	0.4	24,284	0.9	930,405	D
Colorado	488,685	295,021	60.4	181,267	37.1	9,962	2.0	1,594	0.3	841	0.2	113,754	D
Connecticut	690,723	382,129	55.3	278,685	40.3	21,805	3.2	5,683	0.8	2,421	0.4	103,444	D
Delaware[2]	127,603	69,702	54.6	54,014	42.3	442	0.3	172	0.1	3,273	2.6	15,688	D
Florida	327,436	249,117	76.1	78,248	23.9	—	0.0	—	0.0	71	0.0	170,869	D
Georgia	293,170	255,363	87.1	36,943	12.6	136	0.0	68	0.0	660	0.2	218,420	D
Idaho	199,617	125,683	63.0	66,256	33.2	7,678	3.8	—	0.0	—	0.0	59,427	D
Illinois	3,956,522	2,282,999	57.7	1,570,393	39.7	89,439	2.3	7,530	0.2	6,161	0.2	712,606	D
Indiana	1,650,897	934,974	56.6	691,570	41.9	19,407	1.2	3,856	0.2	1,090	0.1	243,404	D
Iowa	1,142,737	621,756	54.4	487,977	42.7	29,687	2.6	1,373	0.1	1,944	0.2	133,779	D
Kansas	865,507	464,520	53.7	397,727	46.0	494	0.1	2,766	0.3	—	0.0	66,793	D
Kentucky	926,214	541,944	58.5	369,702	39.9	12,501	1.3	627	0.1	1,440	0.2	172,242	D
Louisiana	329,778	292,894	88.8	36,791	11.2	—	0.0	—	0.0	93	0.0	256,103	D
Maine	304,240	126,333	41.5	168,823	55.5	7,581	2.5	783	0.3	720	0.2	42,490	R
Maryland	624,896	389,612	62.3	231,435	37.0	—	0.0	1,629	0.3	2,220	0.4	158,177	D
Massachusetts	1,840,357	942,716	51.2	768,613	41.8	118,639	6.4	5,111	0.3	5,278	0.3	174,103	D
Michigan	1,805,098	1,016,794	56.3	699,733	38.8	75,795	4.2	8,208	0.5	4,568	0.3	317,061	D
Minnesota	1,129,975	698,811	61.8	350,461	31.0	74,296	6.6	2,872	0.3	3,535	0.3	348,350	D
Mississippi	162,142	157,333	97.0	4,467	2.8	—	0.0	342	0.2	—	0.0	152,866	D
Missouri	1,828,635	1,111,043	60.8	697,891	38.2	14,630	0.8	3,454	0.2	1,617	0.1	413,152	D
Montana	230,502	159,690	69.3	63,598	27.6	5,539	2.4	1,066	0.5	609	0.3	96,092	D
Nebraska	608,023	347,445	57.1	247,731	40.7	12,847	2.1	—	0.0	—	0.0	99,714	D
Nevada	43,848	31,925	72.8	11,923	27.2	—	0.0	—	0.0	—	0.0	20,002	D
New Hampshire	218,114	108,460	49.7	104,642	48.0	4,819	2.2	—	0.0	193	0.1	3,818	D
New Jersey	1,820,437	1,083,850	59.5	720,322	39.6	9,407	0.5	3,931	0.2	2,927	0.2	363,528	D
New Mexico	169,135	106,037	62.7	61,727	36.5	924	0.5	343	0.2	104	0.1	44,310	D
New York	5,596,398	3,293,222	58.8	2,180,670	39.0	—	0.0	86,897	1.6	35,609	0.6	1,112,552	D
North Carolina	839,475	616,141	73.4	223,294	26.6	2	0.0	21	0.0	17	0.0	392,847	D
North Dakota	273,716	163,148	59.6	72,751	26.6	36,708	13.4	552	0.2	557	0.2	90,397	D
Ohio	3,012,660	1,747,140	58.0	1,127,855	37.4	132,212	4.4	167	0.0	5,286	0.2	619,285	D
Oklahoma	749,740	501,069	66.8	245,122	32.7	—	0.0	2,221	0.3	1,328	0.2	255,947	D
Oregon	414,021	266,733	64.4	122,706	29.6	21,831	5.3	2,143	0.5	608	0.1	144,027	D
Pennsylvania	4,138,105	2,353,788	56.9	1,690,300	40.8	67,467	1.6	14,375	0.3	12,175	0.3	663,488	D
Rhode Island	310,278	164,338	53.0	125,031	40.3	19,569	6.3	—	0.0	1,340	0.4	39,307	D
South Carolina	115,437	113,791	98.6	1,646	1.4	—	0.0	—	0.0	—	0.0	112,145	D
South Dakota	296,452	160,137	54.0	125,977	42.5	10,338	3.5	—	0.0	—	0.0	34,160	D
Tennessee[3]	475,533	327,083	68.8	146,516	30.8	296	0.1	687	0.1	951	0.2	180,567	D
Texas[4]	843,482	734,485	87.1	103,874	12.3	3,281	0.4	1,075	0.1	767	0.1	630,611	D
Utah	216,679	150,248	69.3	64,555	29.8	1,121	0.5	432	0.2	323	0.1	85,693	D
Vermont	143,689	62,124	43.2	81,023	56.4	—	0.0	—	0.0	542	0.4	18,899	R
Virginia	334,590	234,980	70.2	98,336	29.4	233	0.1	313	0.1	728	0.2	136,644	D
Washington	692,338	459,579	66.4	206,892	29.9	17,463	2.5	3,496	0.5	4,908	0.7	252,687	D
West Virginia	829,945	502,582	60.6	325,358	39.2	—	0.0	832	0.1	1,173	0.1	177,224	D
Wisconsin	1,258,560	802,984	63.8	380,828	30.3	60,297	4.8	10,626	0.8	3,825	0.3	422,156	D
Wyoming	103,382	62,624	60.6	38,739	37.5	1,653	1.6	200	0.2	166	0.2	23,885	D
Totals	45,656,991	27,750,866	60.8	16,679,683	36.5	892,361	2.0	187,781	0.4	136,300	0.3	11,071,183	D

1. For breakdown of "Other" vote, see minor candidate vote totals, p. 693.
2. Figures from Clerk of the House of Representatives, *Statistics of the Congressional and Presidential Election* (Washington, D.C.: U.S. Government Printing Office, 1936). Two sets of Landon electors—Republican and Independent Republican—are combined here.
3. Figures from Svend Petersen, *A Statistical History of the American Presidential Elections* (Westport, Conn.: Greenwood Press, 1981); Clerk of the House, *Congressional and Presidential Election.*
4. Figures from Petersen, *A Statistical History*; Clerk of the House, *Congressional and Presidential Election*; *Texas Almanac.*

1940 Presidential Election

STATES	TOTAL VOTE	FRANKLIN D. ROOSEVELT (Democrat) Votes	%	WENDELL WILLKIE (Republican) Votes	%	NORMAN M. THOMAS (Socialist) Votes	%	ROGER W. BABSON (Prohibition) Votes	%	OTHER [1] Votes	%	PLURALITY	
Alabama	294,219	250,726	85.2	42,184	14.3	100	0.0	700	0.2	509	0.2	208,542	D
Arizona	150,039	95,267	63.5	54,030	36.0	—	0.0	742	0.5	—	0.0	41,237	D
Arkansas	200,429	157,213	78.4	42,122	21.0	301	0.2	793	0.4	—	0.0	115,091	D
California	3,268,791	1,877,618	57.4	1,351,419	41.3	16,506	0.5	9,400	0.3	13,848	0.4	526,199	D
Colorado	549,004	265,554	48.4	279,576	50.9	1,899	0.3	1,597	0.3	378	0.1	14,022	R
Connecticut	781,502	417,621	53.4	361,819	46.3	—	0.0	—	0.0	2,062	0.3	55,802	D
Delaware	136,374	74,599	54.7	61,440	45.1	115	0.1	220	0.2	—	0.0	13,159	D
Florida	485,640	359,334	74.0	126,158	26.0	—	0.0	—	0.0	148	0.0	233,176	D
Georgia[2]	312,686	265,194	84.8	46,495	14.9	—	0.0	983	0.3	14	0.0	218,699	D
Idaho	235,168	127,842	54.4	106,553	45.3	497	0.2	—	0.0	276	0.1	21,289	D
Illinois	4,217,935	2,149,934	51.0	2,047,240	48.5	10,914	0.3	9,190	0.2	657	0.0	102,694	D
Indiana	1,782,747	874,063	49.0	899,466	50.5	2,075	0.1	6,437	0.4	706	0.0	25,403	R
Iowa	1,215,432	578,802	47.6	632,370	52.0	—	0.0	2,284	0.2	1,976	0.2	53,568	R
Kansas	860,297	364,725	42.4	489,169	56.9	2,347	0.3	4,056	0.5	—	0.0	124,444	R
Kentucky	970,163	557,322	57.4	410,384	42.3	1,014	0.1	1,443	0.1	—	0.0	146,938	D
Louisiana	372,305	319,751	85.9	52,446	14.1	—	0.0	—	0.0	108	0.0	267,305	D
Maine	320,840	156,478	48.8	163,951	51.1	—	0.0	—	0.0	411	0.1	7,473	R
Maryland	660,104	384,546	58.3	269,534	40.8	4,093	0.6	—	0.0	1,931	0.3	115,012	D
Massachusetts	2,026,993	1,076,522	53.1	939,700	46.4	4,091	0.2	1,370	0.1	5,310	0.3	136,822	D
Michigan	2,085,929	1,032,991	49.5	1,039,917	49.9	7,593	0.4	1,795	0.1	3,633	0.2	6,926	R
Minnesota	1,251,188	644,196	51.5	596,274	47.7	5,454	0.4	—	0.0	5,264	0.4	47,922	D
Mississippi	175,824	168,267	95.7	7,364	4.2	193	0.1	—	0.0	—	0.0	160,903	D
Missouri	1,833,729	958,476	52.3	871,009	47.5	2,226	0.1	1,809	0.1	209	0.0	87,467	D
Montana	247,873	145,698	58.8	99,579	40.2	1,443	0.6	664	0.3	489	0.2	46,119	D
Nebraska	615,878	263,677	42.8	352,201	57.2	—	0.0	—	0.0	—	0.0	88,524	R
Nevada	53,174	31,945	60.1	21,229	39.9	—	0.0	—	0.0	—	0.0	10,716	D
New Hampshire	235,419	125,292	53.2	110,127	46.8	—	0.0	—	0.0	—	0.0	15,165	D
New Jersey	1,972,552	1,016,808	51.5	945,475	47.9	2,433	0.1	873	0.0	6,963	0.4	71,333	D
New Mexico	183,258	103,699	56.6	79,315	43.3	144	0.1	100	0.1	—	0.0	24,384	D
New York	6,301,596	3,251,918	51.6	3,027,478	48.0	18,950	0.3	3,250	0.1	—	0.0	224,440	D
North Carolina	822,648	609,015	74.0	213,633	26.0	—	0.0	—	0.0	—	0.0	395,382	D
North Dakota	280,775	124,036	44.2	154,590	55.1	1,279	0.5	325	0.1	545	0.2	30,554	R
Ohio	3,319,912	1,733,139	52.2	1,586,773	47.8	—	0.0	—	0.0	—	0.0	146,366	D
Oklahoma	826,212	474,313	57.4	348,872	42.2	—	0.0	3,027	0.4	—	0.0	125,441	D
Oregon	481,240	258,415	53.7	219,555	45.6	398	0.1	154	0.0	2,718	0.6	38,860	D
Pennsylvania	4,078,714	2,171,035	53.2	1,889,848	46.3	10,967	0.3	—	0.0	6,864	0.2	281,187	D
Rhode Island	321,152	182,181	56.7	138,654	43.2	—	0.0	74	0.0	243	0.1	43,527	D
South Carolina	99,830	95,470	95.6	4,360	4.4	—	0.0	—	0.0	—	0.0	91,110	D
South Dakota	308,427	131,362	42.6	177,065	57.4	—	0.0	—	0.0	—	0.0	45,703	R
Tennessee	522,823	351,601	67.3	169,153	32.4	463	0.1	1,606	0.3	—	0.0	182,448	D
Texas[3]	1,041,168	840,151	80.7	199,152	19.1	728	0.1	925	0.1	212	0.0	640,999	D
Utah	247,819	154,277	62.3	93,151	37.6	200	0.1	—	0.0	191	0.1	61,126	D
Vermont	143,062	64,269	44.9	78,371	54.8	—	0.0	—	0.0	422	0.3	14,102	R
Virginia	346,608	235,961	68.1	109,363	31.6	282	0.1	882	0.3	120	0.0	126,598	D
Washington	793,833	462,145	58.2	322,123	40.6	4,586	0.6	1,686	0.2	3,293	0.4	140,022	D
West Virginia	868,076	495,662	57.1	372,414	42.9	—	0.0	—	0.0	—	0.0	123,248	D
Wisconsin	1,405,522	704,821	50.1	679,206	48.3	15,071	1.1	2,148	0.2	4,276	0.3	25,615	D
Wyoming	112,240	59,287	52.8	52,633	46.9	148	0.1	172	0.2	—	0.0	6,654	D
Totals	49,817,149	27,343,218	54.7	22,334,940	44.8	116,510	0.2	58,705	0.1	63,776	0.1	5,008,278	D

1. For breakdown of "Other" vote, see minor candidate vote totals, p. 693.
2. Two sets of Willkie electors are combined here: Republican, 23,934; Independent Democrat, 22,561.
3. Figures from Svend Petersen, *A Statistical History of the American Presidential Elections* (Westport, Conn.: Greenwood Press, 1981); Clerk of the House of Representatives, *Statistical of the Congressional and Presidential Election* (Washington, D.C.: U.S. Government Printing Office, 1940); *Texas Almanac.*

1944 Presidential Election

STATE	TOTAL VOTE	FRANKLIN D. ROOSEVELT (Democrat) Votes	%	THOMAS E. DEWEY (Republican) Votes	%	NORMAN THOMAS (Socialist) Votes	%	CLAUDE A. WATSON (Prohibition) Votes	%	OTHER [1] Votes	%	PLURALITY	
Alabama	244,743	198,918	81.3	44,540	18.2	190	0.1	1,095	0.4	—	0.0	154,378	D
Arizona	137,634	80,926	58.8	56,287	40.9	—	0.0	421	0.3	—	0.0	24,639	D
Arkansas	212,954	148,965	70.0	63,551	29.8	438	0.2	—	0.0	—	0.0	85,414	D
California	3,520,875	1,988,564	56.5	1,512,965	43.0	2,515	0.1	14,770	0.4	2,061	0.1	475,599	D
Colorado	505,039	234,331	46.4	268,731	53.2	1,977	0.4	—	0.0	—	0.0	34,400	R
Connecticut	831,990	435,146	52.3	390,527	46.9	5,097	0.6	—	0.0	1,220	0.1	44,619	D
Delaware	125,361	68,166	54.4	56,747	45.3	154	0.1	294	0.2	—	0.0	11,419	D
Florida	482,803	339,377	70.3	143,215	29.7	—	0.0	—	0.0	211	0.0	196,162	D
Georgia[2]	328,129	268,187	81.7	56,506	17.2	6	0.0	36	0.0	3,373	1.0	211,681	D
Idaho	208,321	107,399	51.6	100,137	48.1	282	0.1	503	0.2	—	0.0	7,262	D
Illinois	4,036,061	2,079,479	51.5	1,939,314	48.0	180	0.0	7,411	0.2	9,677	0.2	140,165	D
Indiana	1,672,091	781,403	46.7	875,891	52.4	2,223	0.1	12,574	0.8	—	0.0	94,488	R
Iowa	1,052,599	499,876	47.5	547,267	52.0	1,511	0.1	3,752	0.4	193	0.0	47,391	R
Kansas	733,776	287,458	39.2	442,096	60.2	1,613	0.2	2,609	0.4	—	0.0	154,638	R
Kentucky	867,924	472,589	54.5	392,448	45.2	535	0.1	2,023	0.2	329	0.0	80,141	D
Louisiana	349,383	281,564	80.6	67,750	19.4	—	0.0	—	0.0	69	0.0	213,814	D
Maine	296,400	140,631	47.4	155,434	52.4	—	0.0	—	0.0	335	0.1	14,803	R
Maryland	608,439	315,490	51.9	292,949	48.1	—	0.0	—	0.0	—	0.0	22,541	D
Massachusetts	1,960,665	1,035,296	52.8	921,350	47.0	—	0.0	973	0.0	3,046	0.2	113,946	D
Michigan	2,205,223	1,106,899	50.2	1,084,423	49.2	4,598	0.2	6,503	0.3	2,800	0.1	22,476	D
Minnesota	1,125,504	589,864	52.4	527,416	46.9	5,048	0.4	—	0.0	3,176	0.3	62,448	D
Mississippi	180,234	168,621	93.6	11,613	6.4	—	0.0	—	0.0	—	0.0	157,008	D
Missouri	1,571,697	807,356	51.4	761,175	48.4	1,751	0.1	1,195	0.1	220	0.0	46,181	D
Montana	207,355	112,556	54.3	93,163	44.9	1,296	0.6	340	0.2	—	0.0	19,393	D
Nebraska	563,126	233,246	41.4	329,880	58.6	—	0.0	—	0.0	—	0.0	96,634	R
Nevada	54,234	29,623	54.6	24,611	45.4	—	0.0	—	0.0	—	0.0	5,012	D
New Hampshire	229,625	119,663	52.1	109,916	47.9	46	0.0	—	0.0	—	0.0	9,747	D
New Jersey	1,963,761	987,874	50.3	961,335	49.0	3,358	0.2	4,255	0.2	6,939	0.4	26,539	D
New Mexico	152,225	81,389	53.5	70,688	46.4	—	0.0	148	0.1	—	0.0	10,701	D
New York	6,316,790	3,304,238	52.3	2,987,647	47.3	10,553	0.2	—	0.0	14,352	0.2	316,591	D
North Carolina	790,554	527,399	66.7	263,155	33.3	—	0.0	—	0.0	—	0.0	264,244	D
North Dakota	220,182	100,144	45.5	118,535	53.8	954	0.4	549	0.2	—	0.0	18,391	R
Ohio	3,153,056	1,570,763	49.8	1,582,293	50.2	—	0.0	—	0.0	—	0.0	11,530	R
Oklahoma	722,636	401,549	55.6	319,424	44.2	—	0.0	1,663	0.2	—	0.0	82,125	D
Oregon	480,147	248,635	51.8	225,365	46.9	3,785	0.8	2,362	0.5	—	0.0	23,270	D
Pennsylvania	3,794,793	1,940,479	51.1	1,835,054	48.4	11,721	0.3	5,750	0.2	1,789	0.0	105,425	D
Rhode Island	299,276	175,356	58.6	123,487	41.3	—	0.0	433	0.1	—	0.0	51,869	D
South Carolina[3]	103,382	90,601	87.6	4,554	4.4	—	0.0	365	0.4	7,862	7.6	82,802	D
South Dakota	232,076	96,711	41.7	135,365	58.3	—	0.0	—	0.0	—	0.0	38,654	R
Tennessee	510,692	308,707	60.4	200,311	39.2	792	0.2	882	0.2	—	0.0	108,396	D
Texas	1,150,334	821,605	71.4	191,423	16.6	594	0.1	1,018	0.1	135,694	11.8	630,182	D
Utah	248,319	150,088	60.4	97,891	39.4	340	0.1	—	0.0	—	0.0	52,197	D
Vermont	125,361	53,820	42.9	71,527	57.1	—	0.0	—	0.0	14	0.0	17,707	R
Virginia	388,485	242,276	62.4	145,243	37.4	417	0.1	459	0.1	90	0.0	97,033	D
Washington	856,328	486,774	56.8	361,689	42.2	3,824	0.4	2,396	0.3	1,645	0.2	125,085	D
West Virginia	715,596	392,777	54.9	322,819	45.1	—	0.0	—	0.0	—	0.0	69,958	D
Wisconsin	1,339,152	650,413	48.6	674,532	50.4	13,205	1.0	—	0.0	1,002	0.1	24,119	R
Wyoming	101,340	49,419	48.8	51,921	51.2	—	0.0	—	0.0	—	0.0	2,502	R
Totals	**47,976,670**	**25,612,610**	**53.4**	**22,021,053**	**45.9**	**79,003**	**0.2**	**74,779**	**0.2**	**196,097**	**0.4**	**3,591,557**	**D**

1. For breakdown of "Other" vote, see minor candidate vote totals, p. 693.
2. Clerk of the House of Representatives, *Statistics of the Congressional and Presidential Election* (Washington, D.C.: U.S. Government Printing Office, 1944). There were two separate slates of electors pledged to Dewey in Georgia that could not legally be combined: Republican, 56,606; Independent Democrat, 3,373.
3. Clerk of the House, *Congressional and Presidential Election*. There were two separate slates of electors pledged to Dewey in South Carolina that could not legally be combined: Republican, 4,554; Tobert Faction, 63. Plurality of 82,802 votes is calculated on the basis of 7,799 votes cast for the Southern Democrats Party.

1948 Presidential Election

STATE	TOTAL VOTE	HARRY S. TRUMAN (Democrat)		THOMAS E. DEWEY (Republican)		J. STROM THURMOND (States' Rights Democrat)		HENRY A. WALLACE (Progressive)		OTHER[1]		PLURALITY
		Votes	%	Votes	%	Votes	%	Votes	%	Votes	%	
Alabama	214,980	—	0.0	40,930	19.0	171,443	79.7	1,522	0.7	1,085	0.5	130,513 SR
Arizona	177,065	95,251	53.8	77,597	43.8	—	0.0	3,310	1.9	907	0.5	17,654 D
Arkansas	242,475	149,659	61.7	50,959	21.0	40,068	16.5	751	0.3	1,038	0.4	98,700 D
California	4,021,538	1,913,134	47.6	1,895,269	47.1	1,228	0.0	190,381	4.7	21,526	0.5	17,865 D
Colorado	515,237	267,288	51.9	239,714	46.5	—	0.0	6,115	1.2	2,120	0.4	27,574 D
Connecticut	883,518	423,297	47.9	437,754	49.5	—	0.0	13,713	1.6	8,754	1.0	14,457 R
Delaware	139,073	67,813	48.8	69,588	50.0	—	0.0	1,050	0.8	622	0.4	1,775 R
Florida	577,643	281,988	48.8	194,280	33.6	89,755	15.5	11,620	2.0	—	0.0	87,708 D
Georgia	418,844	254,646	60.8	76,691	18.3	85,135	20.3	1,636	0.4	736	0.2	169,511 D
Idaho	214,816	107,370	50.0	101,514	47.3	—	0.0	4,972	2.3	960	0.4	5,856 D
Illinois	3,984,046	1,994,715	50.1	1,961,103	49.2	—	0.0	—	0.0	28,228	0.7	33,612 D
Indiana	1,656,212	807,831	48.8	821,079	49.6	—	0.0	9,649	0.6	17,653	1.1	13,248 R
Iowa	1,038,264	522,380	50.3	494,018	47.6	—	0.0	12,125	1.2	9,741	0.9	28,362 D
Kansas	788,819	351,902	44.6	423,039	53.6	—	0.0	4,603	0.6	9,275	1.2	71,137 R
Kentucky	822,658	466,756	56.7	341,210	41.5	10,411	1.3	1,567	0.2	2,714	0.3	125,546 D
Louisiana	416,336	136,344	32.7	72,657	17.5	204,290	49.1	3,035	0.7	10	0.0	67,946 SR
Maine	264,787	111,916	42.3	150,234	56.7	—	0.0	1,884	0.7	753	0.3	38,318 R
Maryland	596,748	286,521	48.0	294,814	49.4	2,489	0.4	9,983	1.7	2,941	0.5	8,293 R
Massachusetts	2,107,146	1,151,788	54.7	909,370	43.2	—	0.0	38,157	1.8	7,831	0.4	242,418 D
Michigan	2,109,609	1,003,448	47.6	1,038,595	49.2	—	0.0	46,515	2.2	21,051	1.0	35,147 R
Minnesota	1,212,226	692,966	57.2	483,617	39.9	—	0.0	27,866	2.3	7,777	0.6	209,349 D
Mississippi	192,190	19,384	10.1	5,043	2.6	167,538	87.2	225	0.1	—	0.0	148,154 SR
Missouri	1,578,628	917,315	58.1	655,039	41.5	—	0.0	3,998	0.3	2,276	0.1	262,276 D
Montana	224,278	119,071	53.1	96,770	43.1	—	0.0	7,313	3.3	1,124	0.5	22,301 D
Nebraska	488,940	224,165	45.8	264,774	54.2	—	0.0	—	0.0	1	0.0	40,609 R
Nevada	62,117	31,291	50.4	29,357	47.3	—	0.0	1,469	2.4	—	0.0	1,934 D
New Hampshire	231,440	107,995	46.7	121,299	52.4	7	0.0	1,970	0.9	169	0.1	13,304 R
New Jersey	1,949,555	895,455	45.9	981,124	50.3	—	0.0	42,683	2.2	30,293	1.6	85,669 R
New Mexico	187,063	105,464	56.4	80,303	42.9	—	0.0	1,037	0.6	259	0.1	25,161 D
New York	6,177,337	2,780,204	45.0	2,841,163	46.0	—	0.0	509,559	8.2	46,411	0.8	60,959 R
North Carolina	791,209	459,070	58.0	258,572	32.7	69,652	8.8	3,915	0.5	—	0.0	200,498 D
North Dakota	220,716	95,812	43.4	115,139	52.2	374	0.2	8,391	3.8	1,000	0.5	19,327 R
Ohio	2,936,071	1,452,791	49.5	1,445,684	49.2	—	0.0	37,596	1.3	—	0.0	7,107 D
Oklahoma	721,599	452,782	62.7	268,817	37.3	—	0.0	—	0.0	—	0.0	183,965 D
Oregon	524,080	243,147	46.4	260,904	49.8	—	0.0	14,978	2.9	5,051	1.0	17,757 R
Pennsylvania	3,735,348	1,752,426	46.9	1,902,197	50.9	—	0.0	55,161	1.5	25,564	0.7	149,771 R
Rhode Island	327,702	188,736	57.6	135,787	41.4	—	0.0	2,619	0.8	560	0.2	52,949 D
South Carolina	142,571	34,423	24.1	5,386	3.8	102,607	72.0	154	0.1	1	0.0	68,184 SR
South Dakota	250,105	117,653	47.0	129,651	51.8	—	0.0	2,801	1.1	—	0.0	11,998 R
Tennessee	550,283	270,402	49.1	202,914	36.9	73,815	13.4	1,864	0.3	1,288	0.2	67,488 D
Texas[2]	1,147,245	750,700	65.4	282,240	24.6	106,909	9.3	3,764	0.3	3,632	0.3	468,460 D
Utah	276,306	149,151	54.0	124,402	45.0	—	0.0	2,679	1.0	74	0.0	24,749 D
Vermont	123,382	45,557	36.9	75,926	61.5	—	0.0	1,279	1.0	620	0.5	30,369 R
Virginia	419,256	200,786	47.9	172,070	41.0	43,393	10.4	2,047	0.5	960	0.2	28,716 D
Washington	905,058	476,165	52.6	386,314	42.7	—	0.0	31,692	3.5	10,887	1.2	89,851 D
West Virginia	748,750	429,188	57.3	316,251	42.2	—	0.0	3,311	0.4	—	0.0	112,937 D
Wisconsin	1,276,800	647,310	50.7	590,959	46.3	—	0.0	25,282	2.0	13,249	1.0	56,351 D
Wyoming	101,425	52,354	51.6	47,947	47.3	—	0.0	931	0.9	193	0.2	4,407 D
Totals	48,691,494	24,105,810	49.5	21,970,064	45.1	1,169,114	2.4	1,157,172	2.4	289,334	0.6	2,135,746 D

1. For breakdown of "Other" vote, see minor candidate vote totals, p. 693.
2. Figures from Svend Petersen, *A Statistical History of the American Presidential Elections* (Westport, Conn.: Greenwood Press, 1981); Clerk of the House of Representatives, *Statistics of the Congressional and Presidential Election* (Washington, D.C.: U.S. Government Printing Office, 1948); *Texas Almanac.* Totals do not include the vote in thirty-five counties that were excluded from the official returns. Had these counties been counted, the vote in Texas would have been as follows: Total, 1,249,577; Truman, 824,235; Dewey, 303,467; Thurmond, 113,920; Wallace, 3,918; Other, 4,037; Plurality, 520,768 D. The totals for the nation would have been as follows: Total, 48,793,826; Truman, 24,179,345; Dewey, 21,991,291; Thurmond, 1,176,125; Wallace, 1,157,326; Other, 289,739; Plurality, 2,188,054 D.

1952 Presidential Election

STATE	TOTAL VOTE	DWIGHT D. EISENHOWER (Republican)		ADLAI E. STEVENSON (Democrat)		VINCENT HALLINAN (Progressive)		STUART HAMBLEN (Prohibition)		OTHER[1]		PLURALITY	
		Votes	%	Votes	%	Votes	%	Votes	%	Votes	%		
Alabama	426,120	149,231	35.0	275,075	64.6	—	0.0	1,814	0.4	—	0.0	125,844	D
Arizona	260,570	152,042	58.3	108,528	41.7	—	0.0	—	0.0	—	0.0	43,514	R
Arkansas	404,800	177,155	43.8	226,300	55.9	—	0.0	886	0.2	459	0.1	49,145	D
California	5,141,849	2,897,310	56.3	2,197,548	42.7	24,106	0.5	15,653	0.3	7,232	0.1	699,762	R
Colorado	630,103	379,782	60.3	245,504	39.0	1,919	0.3	—	0.0	2,898	0.5	134,278	R
Connecticut	1,096,911	611,012	55.7	481,649	43.9	1,466	0.1	—	0.0	2,784	0.3	129,363	R
Delaware	174,025	90,059	51.8	83,315	47.9	155	0.1	234	0.1	262	0.2	6,744	R
Florida	989,337	544,036	55.0	444,950	45.0	—	0.0	—	0.0	351	0.0	99,086	R
Georgia	655,785	198,961	30.3	456,823	69.7	—	0.0	—	0.0	1	0.0	257,862	D
Idaho	276,254	180,707	65.4	95,081	34.4	443	0.2	—	0.0	23	0.0	85,626	R
Illinois	4,481,058	2,457,327	54.8	2,013,920	44.9	—	0.0	—	0.0	9,811	0.2	443,407	R
Indiana	1,955,049	1,136,259	58.1	801,530	41.0	1,085	0.1	15,335	0.8	840	0.0	334,729	R
Iowa	1,268,773	808,906	63.8	451,513	35.6	5,085	0.4	2,882	0.2	387	0.0	357,393	R
Kansas	896,166	616,302	68.8	273,296	30.5	—	0.0	6,038	0.7	530	0.1	343,006	R
Kentucky	993,148	495,029	49.8	495,729	49.9	336	0.0	1,161	0.1	893	0.1	700	D
Louisiana	651,952	306,925	47.1	345,027	52.9	—	0.0	—	0.0	—	0.0	38,102	D
Maine	351,786	232,353	66.0	118,806	33.8	332	0.1	—	0.0	295	0.1	113,547	R
Maryland	902,074	499,424	55.4	395,337	43.8	7,313	0.8	—	0.0	—	0.0	104,087	R
Massachusetts	2,383,398	1,292,325	54.2	1,083,525	45.5	4,636	0.2	886	0.0	2,026	0.1	208,800	R
Michigan	2,798,592	1,551,529	55.4	1,230,657	44.0	3,922	0.1	10,331	0.4	2,153	0.1	320,872	R
Minnesota	1,379,483	763,211	55.3	608,458	44.1	2,666	0.2	2,147	0.2	3,001	0.2	154,753	R
Mississippi	285,532	112,966	39.6	172,566	60.4	—	0.0	—	0.0	—	0.0	59,600	D
Missouri	1,892,062	959,429	50.7	929,830	49.1	987	0.1	885	0.0	931	0.0	29,599	R
Montana	265,037	157,394	59.4	106,213	40.1	723	0.3	548	0.2	159	0.1	51,181	R
Nebraska	609,660	421,603	69.2	188,057	30.8	—	0.0	—	0.0	—	0.0	233,546	R
Nevada	82,190	50,502	61.4	31,688	38.6	—	0.0	—	0.0	—	0.0	18,814	R
New Hampshire	272,950	166,287	60.9	106,663	39.1	—	0.0	—	0.0	—	0.0	59,624	R
New Jersey	2,418,554	1,373,613	56.8	1,015,902	42.0	5,589	0.2	989	0.0	22,461	0.9	357,711	R
New Mexico	238,608	132,170	55.4	105,661	44.3	225	0.1	297	0.1	255	0.1	26,509	R
New York	7,128,239	3,952,813	55.5	3,104,601	43.6	64,211	0.9	—	0.0	6,614	0.1	848,212	R
North Carolina	1,210,910	558,107	46.1	652,803	53.9	—	0.0	—	0.0	—	0.0	94,696	D
North Dakota	270,127	191,712	71.0	76,694	28.4	344	0.1	302	0.1	1,075	0.4	115,018	R
Ohio	3,700,758	2,100,391	56.8	1,600,367	43.2	—	0.0	—	0.0	—	0.0	500,024	R
Oklahoma	948,984	518,045	54.6	430,939	45.4	—	0.0	—	0.0	—	0.0	87,106	R
Oregon	695,059	420,815	60.5	270,579	38.9	3,665	0.5	—	0.0	—	0.0	150,236	R
Pennsylvania	4,580,969	2,415,789	52.7	2,146,269	46.9	4,222	0.1	8,951	0.2	5,738	0.1	269,520	R
Rhode Island	414,498	210,935	50.9	203,293	49.0	187	0.0	—	0.0	83	0.0	7,642	R
South Carolina[2]	341,087	9,793	2.9	173,004	50.7	—	0.0	1	0.0	158,289	46.4	4,922	D
South Dakota	294,283	203,857	69.3	90,426	30.7	—	0.0	—	0.0	—	0.0	113,431	R
Tennessee	892,553	446,147	50.0	443,710	49.7	885	0.1	1,432	0.2	379	0.0	2,437	R
Texas	2,075,946	1,102,878	53.1	969,228	46.7	294	0.0	1,983	0.1	1,563	0.1	133,650	R
Utah	329,554	194,190	58.9	135,364	41.1	—	0.0	—	0.0	—	0.0	58,826	R
Vermont	153,557	109,717	71.5	43,355	28.2	282	0.2	—	0.0	203	0.1	66,362	R
Virginia	619,689	349,037	56.3	268,677	43.4	311	0.1	—	0.0	1,664	0.3	80,360	R
Washington	1,102,708	599,107	54.3	492,845	44.7	2,460	0.2	—	0.0	8,296	0.8	106,262	R
West Virginia	873,548	419,970	48.1	453,578	51.9	—	0.0	—	0.0	—	0.0	33,608	D
Wisconsin	1,607,370	979,744	61.0	622,175	38.7	2,174	0.1	—	0.0	3,277	0.2	357,569	R
Wyoming	129,253	81,049	62.7	47,934	37.1	—	0.0	194	0.2	76	0.1	33,115	R
Totals	61,550,918	33,777,945	54.9	27,314,992	44.4	140,023	0.2	72,949	0.1	245,009	0.4	6,462,953	R

1. For breakdown of "Other" vote, see minor candidate vote totals, p. 694.
2. There were two separate slates of electors pledged to Eisenhower in South Carolina that could not legally be combined: Republican, 9,793; Independent slate, 158,289. Had these two been combined Eisenhower would have totaled 168,082 in the state and 33,936,234 nationally.

1956 Presidential Election

STATE	TOTAL VOTE	DWIGHT D. EISENHOWER (Republican)		ADLAI E. STEVENSON (Democrat)		T. COLEMAN ANDREWS (Constitution)		ERIC HASS (Socialist Labor)		OTHER[1]		PLURALITY	
		Votes	%	Votes	%	Votes	%	Votes	%	Votes	%		
Alabama	496,861	195,694	39.4	280,844	56.5	—	0.0	—	0.0	20,323	4.1	885,150	D
Arizona	290,173	176,990	61.0	112,880	38.9	303	0.1	—	0.0	—	0.0	64,110	R
Arkansas	406,572	186,287	45.8	213,277	52.5	7,008	1.7	—	0.0	—	0.0	26,990	D
California	5,466,355	3,027,668	55.4	2,420,135	44.3	6,087	0.1	300	0.0	12,165	0.2	607,533	R
Colorado	657,074	394,479	60.0	257,997	39.3	759	0.1	3,308	0.5	531	0.1	136,482	R
Connecticut	1,117,121	711,837	63.7	405,079	36.3	—	0.0	—	0.0	205	0.0	306,758	R
Delaware	177,988	98,057	55.1	79,421	44.6	—	0.0	110	0.1	400	0.2	18,636	R
Florida	1,125,762	643,849	57.2	480,371	42.7	—	0.0	—	0.0	1,542	0.1	163,478	R
Georgia	669,655	222,778	33.3	444,688	66.4	2,096	0.3	—	0.0	93	0.0	221,910	D
Idaho	272,989	166,979	61.2	105,868	38.8	126	0.0	—	0.0	16	0.0	61,111	R
Illinois	4,407,407	2,623,327	59.5	1,775,682	40.3	—	0.0	8,342	0.2	56	0.0	847,645	R
Indiana	1,974,607	1,182,811	59.9	783,908	39.7	—	0.0	1,334	0.1	6,554	0.3	398,903	R
Iowa	1,234,564	729,187	59.1	501,858	40.7	3,202	0.3	125	0.0	192	0.0	227,329	R
Kansas	866,243	566,878	65.4	296,317	34.2	—	0.0	—	0.0	3,048	0.4	270,561	R
Kentucky	1,053,805	572,192	54.3	476,453	45.2	—	0.0	358	0.0	4,802	0.5	95,739	R
Louisiana	617,544	329,047	53.3	243,977	39.5	—	0.0	—	0.0	44,520	7.2	85,070	R
Maine	351,706	249,238	70.9	102,468	29.1	—	0.0	—	0.0	—	0.0	146,770	R
Maryland	932,827	559,738	60.0	372,613	39.9	—	0.0	—	0.0	476	0.1	187,125	R
Massachusetts	2,348,506	1,393,197	59.3	948,190	40.4	—	0.0	5,573	0.2	1,546	0.1	445,007	R
Michigan	3,080,468	1,713,647	55.6	1,359,898	44.1	—	0.0	—	0.0	6,923	0.2	353,749	R
Minnesota	1,340,005	719,302	53.7	617,525	46.1	—	0.0	2,080	0.2	1,098	0.1	101,777	R
Mississippi	248,104	60,685	24.5	144,453	58.2	—	0.0	—	0.0	42,966	17.3	83,768	D
Missouri	1,832,562	914,289	49.9	918,273	50.1	—	0.0	—	0.0	—	0.0	3,984	D
Montana	271,171	154,933	57.1	116,238	42.9	—	0.0	—	0.0	—	0.0	38,695	R
Nebraska	577,137	378,108	65.5	199,029	34.5	—	0.0	—	0.0	—	0.0	179,079	R
Nevada	96,689	56,049	58.0	40,640	42.0	—	0.0	—	0.0	—	0.0	15,409	R
New Hampshire	266,994	176,519	66.1	90,364	33.8	111	0.0	—	0.0	—	0.0	86,155	R
New Jersey	2,484,312	1,606,942	64.7	850,337	34.2	5,317	0.2	6,736	0.3	14,980	0.6	756,605	R
New Mexico	253,926	146,788	57.8	106,098	41.8	364	0.1	69	0.0	607	0.2	40,690	R
New York	7,095,971	4,345,506	61.2	2,747,944	38.7	1,027	0.0	150	0.0	1,344	0.0	1,597,562	R
North Carolina	1,165,592	575,062	49.3	590,530	50.7	—	0.0	—	0.0	—	0.0	15,468	D
North Dakota	253,991	156,766	61.7	96,742	38.1	483	0.2	—	0.0	—	0.0	60,024	R
Ohio	3,702,265	2,262,610	61.1	1,439,655	38.9	—	0.0	—	0.0	—	0.0	822,955	R
Oklahoma	859,350	473,769	55.1	385,581	44.9	—	0.0	—	0.0	—	0.0	88,188	R
Oregon	736,132	406,393	55.2	329,204	44.7	—	0.0	—	0.0	535	0.1	77,189	R
Pennsylvania	4,576,503	2,585,252	56.5	1,981,769	43.3	—	0.0	7,447	0.2	2,035	0.0	603,483	R
Rhode Island	387,609	225,819	58.3	161,790	41.7	—	0.0	—	0.0	—	0.0	64,029	R
South Carolina[2]	300,583	75,700	25.2	136,372	45.4	2	0.0	—	0.0	88,509	29.4	47,863	D
South Dakota	293,857	171,569	58.4	122,288	41.6	—	0.0	—	0.0	—	0.0	49,281	R
Tennessee	939,404	462,288	49.2	456,507	48.6	19,820	2.1	—	0.0	789	0.1	5,781	R
Texas	1,955,168	1,080,619	55.3	859,958	44.0	14,591	0.7	—	0.0	—	0.0	220,661	R
Utah	333,995	215,631	64.6	118,364	35.4	—	0.0	—	0.0	—	0.0	97,267	R
Vermont	152,978	110,390	72.2	42,549	27.8	—	0.0	—	0.0	39	0.0	67,841	R
Virginia	697,978	386,459	55.4	267,760	38.4	42,964	6.2	351	0.1	444	0.1	118,699	R
Washington	1,150,889	620,430	53.9	523,002	45.4	—	0.0	7,457	0.6	—	0.0	97,428	R
West Virginia	830,831	449,297	54.1	381,534	45.9	—	0.0	—	0.0	—	0.0	67,763	R
Wisconsin	1,550,558	954,844	61.6	586,768	37.8	6,918	0.4	710	0.0	1,318	0.1	368,076	R
Wyoming	124,127	74,573	60.1	49,554	39.9	—	0.0	—	0.0	—	0.0	25,019	R
Totals	62,026,908	35,590,472	57.4	26,022,752	42.0	111,178	0.2	44,450	0.1	258,056	0.4	9,567,720	R

1. For breakdown of "Other" vote, see minor candidate vote totals, p. 694.
2. Plurality of 47,863 votes is calculated on the basis of Stevenson's vote and the 88,509 votes cast for unpledged electors.

1960 Presidential Election

STATE	TOTAL VOTE	JOHN F. KENNEDY (Democrat)		RICHARD M. NIXON (Republican)		ERIC HASS (Socialist Labor)		(UNPLEDGED)		OTHER[1]		PLURALITY	
		Votes	%	Votes	%	Votes	%	Votes	%	Votes	%		
Alabama D	570,225	324,050	56.8	237,981	41.7	—	0.0	—	0.0	8,194	1.4	86,069	
Alaska	60,762	29,809	49.1	30,953	50.9	—	0.0	—	0.0	—	0.0	1,144	R
Arizona	398,491	176,781	44.4	221,241	55.5	469	0.1	—	0.0	—	0.0	44,460	R
Arkansas	428,509	215,049	50.2	184,508	43.1	—	0.0	—	0.0	28,952	6.8	30,541	D
California	6,506,578	3,224,099	49.6	3,259,722	50.1	1,051	0.0	—	0.0	21,706	0.3	35,623	R
Colorado	736,236	330,629	44.9	402,242	54.6	2,803	0.4	—	0.0	562	0.1	71,613	R
Connecticut	1,222,883	657,055	53.7	565,813	46.3	—	0.0	—	0.0	15	0.0	91,242	D
Delaware	196,683	99,590	50.6	96,373	49.0	82	0.0	—	0.0	638	0.3	3,217	D
Florida	1,544,176	748,700	48.5	795,476	51.5	—	0.0	—	0.0	—	0.0	46,776	R
Georgia	733,349	458,638	62.5	274,472	37.4	—	0.0	—	0.0	239	0.0	184,166	D
Hawaii	184,705	92,410	50.0	92,295	50.0	—	0.0	—	0.0	—	0.0	115	D
Idaho	300,450	138,853	46.2	161,597	53.8	—	0.0	—	0.0	—	0.0	22,744	R
Illinois	4,757,409	2,377,846	50.0	2,368,988	49.8	10,560	0.2	—	0.0	15	0.0	8,858	D
Indiana	2,135,360	952,358	44.6	1,175,120	55.0	1,136	0.1	—	0.0	6,746	0.3	222,762	R
Iowa	1,273,810	550,565	43.2	722,381	56.7	230	0.0	—	0.0	634	0.0	171,816	R
Kansas	928,825	363,213	39.1	561,474	60.4	—	0.0	—	0.0	4,138	0.4	198,261	R
Kentucky	1,124,462	521,855	46.4	602,607	53.6	—	0.0	—	0.0	—	0.0	80,752	R
Louisiana	807,891	407,339	50.4	230,980	28.6	—	0.0	—	0.0	169,572	21.0	176,359	D
Maine	421,767	181,159	43.0	240,608	57.0	—	0.0	—	0.0	—	0.0	59,449	R
Maryland	1,055,349	565,808	53.6	489,538	46.4	—	0.0	—	0.0	3	0.0	76,270	D
Massachusetts	2,469,480	1,487,174	60.2	976,750	39.6	3,892	0.2	—	0.0	1,664	0.1	510,424	D
Michigan	3,318,097	1,687,269	50.9	1,620,428	48.8	1,718	0.1	—	0.0	8,682	0.3	66,841	D
Minnesota	1,541,887	779,933	50.6	757,915	49.2	962	0.1	—	0.0	3,077	0.2	22,018	D
Mississippi[2]	298,171	108,362	36.3	73,561	24.7	—	0.0	116,248	39.0	—	0.0	7,886	U
Missouri	1,934,422	972,201	50.3	962,221	49.7	—	0.0	—	0.0	—	0.0	9,980	D
Montana	277,579	134,891	48.6	141,841	51.1	—	0.0	—	0.0	847	0.3	6,950	R
Nebraska	613,095	232,542	37.9	380,553	62.1	—	0.0	—	0.0	—	0.0	148,011	R
Nevada	107,267	54,880	51.2	52,387	48.8	—	0.0	—	0.0	—	0.0	2,493	D
New Hampshire	295,761	137,772	46.6	157,989	53.4	—	0.0	—	0.0	—	0.0	20,217	R
New Jersey	2,773,111	1,385,415	50.0	1,363,324	49.2	4,262	0.2	—	0.0	20,110	0.7	22,091	D
New Mexico	311,107	156,027	50.2	153,733	49.4	570	0.2	—	0.0	777	0.2	2,294	D
New York	7,291,079	3,830,085	52.5	3,446,419	47.3	—	0.0	—	0.0	14,575	0.2	383,666	D
North Carolina	1,368,556	713,136	52.1	655,420	47.9	—	0.0	—	0.0	—	0.0	57,716	D
North Dakota	278,431	123,963	44.5	154,310	55.4	—	0.0	—	0.0	158	0.1	30,347	R
Ohio	4,161,859	1,944,248	46.7	2,217,611	53.3	—	0.0	—	0.0	—	0.0	273,363	R
Oklahoma	903,150	370,111	41.0	533,039	59.0	—	0.0	—	0.0	—	0.0	162,928	R
Oregon	776,421	367,402	47.3	408,060	52.6	—	0.0	—	0.0	959	0.1	40,658	R
Pennsylvania	5,006,541	2,556,282	51.1	2,439,956	48.7	7,185	0.1	—	0.0	3,118	0.1	116,326	D
Rhode Island	405,535	258,032	63.6	147,502	36.4	—	0.0	—	0.0	1	0.0	110,530	D
South Carolina	386,688	198,129	51.2	188,558	48.8	—	0.0	—	0.0	1	0.0	9,571	D
South Dakota	306,487	128,070	41.8	178,417	58.2	—	0.0	—	0.0	—	0.0	50,347	R
Tennessee	1,051,792	481,453	45.8	556,577	52.9	—	0.0	—	0.0	13,762	1.3	75,124	R
Texas	2,311,084	1,167,567	50.5	1,121,310	48.5	—	0.0	—	0.0	22,207	1.0	46,257	D
Utah	374,709	169,248	45.2	205,361	54.8	—	0.0	—	0.0	100	0.0	36,113	R
Vermont	167,324	69,186	41.3	98,131	58.6	—	0.0	—	0.0	7	0.0	28,945	R
Virginia	771,449	362,327	47.0	404,521	52.4	397	0.1	—	0.0	4,204	0.5	42,194	R
Washington	1,241,572	599,298	48.3	629,273	50.7	10,895	0.9	—	0.0	2,106	0.2	29,975	R
West Virginia	837,781	441,786	52.7	395,995	47.3	—	0.0	—	0.0	—	0.0	45,791	D
Wisconsin	1,729,082	830,805	48.0	895,175	51.8	1,310	0.1	—	0.0	1,792	0.1	64,370	R
Wyoming	140,782	63,331	45.0	77,451	55.0	—	0.0	—	0.0	—	0.0	14,120	R
Totals	68,838,219	34,226,731	49.7	34,108,157	49.5	47,522	0.1	116,248	0.2	339,561	0.5	118,574	D

1. For breakdown of "Other" vote, see minor candidate vote totals, p. 694.
2. Votes for unpledged electors who carried the state and cast electoral votes for Harry F. Byrd (D Va.).

1964 Presidential Election

STATE	TOTAL VOTE	LYNDON B. JOHNSON (Democrat)		BARRY M. GOLDWATER (Republican)		ERIC HASS (Socialist Labor)		CLIFTON DeBERRY (Socialist Workers)		OTHER[1]		PLURALITY	
		Votes	%	Votes	%	Votes	%	Votes	%	Votes	%		
Alabama[2]	689,818	—	0.0	479,085	69.5	—	0.0	—	0.0	210,732	30.5	268,353	R
Alaska	67,259	44,329	65.9	22,930	34.1	—	0.0	—	0.0	—	0.0	21,399	D
Arizona	480,770	237,753	49.5	242,535	50.4	482	0.1	—	0.0	—	0.0	4,782	R
Arkansas	560,426	314,197	56.1	243,264	43.4	—	0.0	—	0.0	2,965	0.5	70,933	D
California	7,057,586	4,171,877	59.1	2,879,108	40.8	489	0.0	378	0.0	5,734	0.1	1,292,769	D
Colorado	776,986	476,024	61.3	296,767	38.2	302	0.0	2,537	0.3	1,356	0.2	179,257	D
Connecticut	1,218,578	826,269	67.8	390,996	32.1	—	0.0	—	0.0	1,313	0.1	435,273	D
Delaware	201,320	122,704	60.9	78,078	38.8	113	0.1	—	0.0	425	0.2	44,626	D
Florida	1,854,481	948,540	51.1	905,941	48.9	—	0.0	—	0.0	—	0.0	42,599	D
Georgia	1,139,335	522,556	45.9	616,584	54.1	—	0.0	—	0.0	195	0.0	94,028	R
Hawaii	207,271	163,249	78.8	44,022	21.2	—	0.0	—	0.0	—	0.0	119,227	D
Idaho	292,477	148,920	50.9	143,557	49.1	—	0.0	—	0.0	—	0.0	5,363	D
Illinois	4,702,841	2,796,833	59.5	1,905,946	40.5	—	0.0	—	0.0	62	0.0	890,887	D
Indiana	2,091,606	1,170,848	56.0	911,118	43.6	1,374	0.1	—	0.0	8,266	0.4	259,730	D
Iowa	1,184,539	733,030	61.9	449,148	37.9	182	0.0	159	0.0	2,020	0.2	283,882	D
Kansas	857,901	464,028	54.1	386,579	45.1	1,901	0.2	—	0.0	5,393	0.6	77,449	D
Kentucky	1,046,105	669,659	64.0	372,977	35.7	—	0.0	—	0.0	3,469	0.3	296,682	D
Louisiana	896,293	387,068	43.2	509,225	56.8	—	0.0	—	0.0	—	0.0	122,157	R
Maine	380,965	262,264	68.8	118,701	31.2	—	0.0	—	0.0	—	0.0	143,563	D
Maryland	1,116,457	730,912	65.5	385,495	34.5	—	0.0	—	0.0	50	0.0	345,417	D
Massachusetts	2,344,798	1,786,422	76.2	549,727	23.4	4,755	0.2	—	0.0	3,894	0.2	1,236,695	D
Michigan	3,203,102	2,136,615	66.7	1,060,152	33.1	1,704	0.1	3,817	0.1	814	0.0	1,076,463	D
Minnesota	1,554,462	991,117	63.8	559,624	36.0	2,544	0.2	1,177	0.1	—	0.0	431,493	D
Mississippi	409,146	52,618	12.9	356,528	87.1	—	0.0	—	0.0	—	0.0	303,910	R
Missouri	1,817,879	1,164,344	64.0	653,535	36.0	—	0.0	—	0.0	—	0.0	510,809	D
Montana	278,628	164,246	58.9	113,032	40.6	—	0.0	332	0.1	1,018	0.4	51,214	D
Nebraska	584,154	307,307	52.6	276,847	47.4	—	0.0	—	0.0	—	0.0	30,460	D
Nevada	135,433	79,339	58.6	56,094	41.4	—	0.0	—	0.0	—	0.0	23,245	D
New Hampshire	288,093	184,064	63.9	104,029	36.1	—	0.0	—	0.0	—	0.0	80,035	D
New Jersey	2,847,663	1,868,231	65.6	964,174	33.9	7,075	0.2	8,183	0.3	—	0.0	904,057	D
New Mexico	328,645	194,015	59.0	132,838	40.4	1,217	0.4	—	0.0	575	0.2	61,177	D
New York	7,166,275	4,913,102	68.6	2,243,559	31.3	6,118	0.1	3,228	0.0	268	0.0	2,669,543	D
North Carolina	1,424,983	800,139	56.2	624,844	43.8	—	0.0	—	0.0	—	0.0	175,295	D
North Dakota	258,389	149,784	58.0	108,207	41.9	—	0.0	224	0.1	174	0.1	41,577	D
Ohio	3,969,196	2,498,331	62.9	1,470,865	37.1	—	0.0	—	0.0	—	0.0	1,027,466	D
Oklahoma	932,499	519,834	55.7	412,665	44.3	—	0.0	—	0.0	—	0.0	107,169	D
Oregon	786,305	501,017	63.7	282,779	36.0	—	0.0	—	0.0	2,509	0.3	218,238	D
Pennsylvania	4,822,690	3,130,954	64.9	1,673,657	34.7	5,092	0.1	10,456	0.2	2,531	0.1	1,457,297	D
Rhode Island	390,091	315,463	80.9	74,615	19.1	—	0.0	—	0.0	13	0.0	240,848	D
South Carolina	524,779	215,723	41.1	309,048	58.9	—	0.0	—	0.0	8	0.0	93,325	R
South Dakota	293,118	163,010	55.6	130,108	44.4	—	0.0	—	0.0	—	0.0	32,902	D
Tennessee	1,143,946	634,947	55.5	508,965	44.5	—	0.0	—	0.0	34	0.0	125,982	D
Texas	2,626,811	1,663,185	63.3	958,566	36.5	—	0.0	—	0.0	5,060	0.2	704,619	D
Utah	401,413	219,628	54.7	181,785	45.3	—	0.0	—	0.0	—	0.0	37,843	D
Vermont	163,089	108,127	66.3	54,942	33.7	—	0.0	—	0.0	20	0.0	53,185	D
Virginia	1,042,267	558,038	53.5	481,334	46.2	2,895	0.3	—	0.0	—	0.0	76,704	D
Washington	1,258,556	779,881	62.0	470,366	37.4	7,772	0.6	537	0.0	—	0.0	309,515	D
West Virginia	792,040	538,087	67.9	253,953	32.1	—	0.0	—	0.0	—	0.0	284,134	D
Wisconsin	1,691,815	1,050,424	62.1	638,495	37.7	1,204	0.1	1,692	0.1	—	0.0	411,929	D
Wyoming	142,716	80,718	56.6	61,998	43.4	—	0.0	—	0.0	—	0.0	18,720	D
Dist. of Col.	198,597	169,796	85.5	28,801	14.5	—	0.0	—	0.0	—	0.0	140,995	D
Totals	70,644,592	43,129,566	61.1	27,178,188	38.5	45,219	0.1	32,720	0.0	258,899	0.4	15,951,378	D

1. For breakdown of "Other" vote, see minor candidate vote totals, p. 694.
2. Plurality of 268,353 votes is calculated on the basis of Goldwater's vote and the 210,732 votes cast for the unpledged Democratic elector ticket.

1968 Presidential Election

STATE	TOTAL VOTE	RICHARD M. NIXON (Republican)		HUBERT H. HUMPHREY (Democrat)		GEORGE C. WALLACE (American Independent)		HENNING A. BLOMEN (Socialist Labor)		OTHER[1]		PLURALITY	
		Votes	%	Votes	%	Votes	%	Votes	%	Votes	%		
Alabama	1,049,922	146,923	14.0	196,579	18.7	691,425	65.9	—	0.0	14,995	1.4	494,846	A
Alaska	83,035	37,600	45.3	35,411	42.6	10,024	12.1	—	0.0	—	0.0	2,189	R
Arizona	486,936	266,721	54.8	170,514	35.0	46,573	9.6	75	0.0	3,053	0.6	96,207	R
Arkansas	619,969	190,759	30.8	188,228	30.4	240,982	38.9	—	0.0	—	0.0	50,223	A
California	7,251,587	3,467,664	47.8	3,244,318	44.7	487,270	6.7	341	0.0	51,994	0.7	223,346	R
Colorado	811,199	409,345	50.5	335,174	41.3	60,813	7.5	3,016	0.4	2,851	0.4	74,171	R
Connecticut	1,256,232	556,721	44.3	621,561	49.5	76,650	6.1	—	0.0	1,300	0.1	64,840	D
Delaware	214,367	96,714	45.1	89,194	41.6	28,459	13.3	—	0.0	—	0.0	7,520	R
Florida	2,187,805	886,804	40.5	676,794	30.9	624,207	28.5	—	0.0	—	0.0	210,010	R
Georgia	1,250,266	380,111	30.4	334,440	26.7	535,550	42.8	—	0.0	165	0.0	155,439	A
Hawaii	236,218	91,425	38.7	141,324	59.8	3,469	1.5	—	0.0	—	0.0	49,899	D
Idaho	291,183	165,369	56.8	89,273	30.7	36,541	12.5	—	0.0	—	0.0	76,096	R
Illinois	4,619,749	2,174,774	47.1	2,039,814	44.2	390,958	8.5	13,878	0.3	325	0.0	134,960	R
Indiana	2,123,597	1,067,885	50.3	806,659	38.0	243,108	11.4	—	0.0	5,945	0.3	261,226	R
Iowa	1,167,931	619,106	53.0	476,699	40.8	66,422	5.7	241	0.0	5,463	0.5	142,407	R
Kansas	872,783	478,674	54.8	302,996	34.7	88,921	10.2	—	0.0	2,192	0.3	175,678	R
Kentucky	1,055,893	462,411	43.8	397,541	37.6	193,098	18.3	—	0.0	2,843	0.3	64,870	R
Louisiana	1,097,450	257,535	23.5	309,615	28.2	530,300	48.3	—	0.0	—	0.0	220,685	A
Maine	392,936	169,254	43.1	217,312	55.3	6,370	1.6	—	0.0	—	0.0	48,058	D
Maryland	1,235,039	517,995	41.9	538,310	43.6	178,734	14.5	—	0.0	—	0.0	20,315	D
Massachusetts	2,331,752	766,844	32.9	1,469,218	63.0	87,088	3.7	6,180	0.3	2,422	0.1	702,374	D
Michigan	3,306,250	1,370,665	41.5	1,593,082	48.2	331,968	10.0	1,762	0.1	8,773	0.3	222,417	D
Minnesota	1,588,506	658,643	41.5	857,738	54.0	68,931	4.3	285	0.0	2,909	0.2	199,095	D
Mississippi	654,509	88,516	13.5	150,644	23.0	415,349	63.5	—	0.0	—	0.0	264,705	A
Missouri	1,809,502	811,932	44.9	791,444	43.7	206,126	11.4	—	0.0	—	0.0	20,488	R
Montana	274,404	138,835	50.6	114,117	41.6	20,015	7.3	—	0.0	1,437	0.5	24,718	R
Nebraska	536,851	321,163	59.8	170,784	31.8	44,904	8.4	—	0.0	—	0.0	150,379	R
Nevada	154,218	73,188	47.5	60,598	39.3	20,432	13.2	—	0.0	—	0.0	12,590	R
New Hampshire	297,298	154,903	52.1	130,589	43.9	11,173	3.8	—	0.0	633	0.2	24,314	R
New Jersey	2,875,395	1,325,467	46.1	1,264,206	44.0	262,187	9.1	6,784	0.2	16,751	0.6	61,261	R
New Mexico	327,350	169,692	51.8	130,081	39.7	25,737	7.9	—	0.0	1,840	0.6	39,611	R
New York	6,791,688	3,007,932	44.3	3,378,470	49.7	358,864	5.3	8,432	0.1	37,990	0.6	370,538	D
North Carolina	1,587,493	627,192	39.5	464,113	29.2	496,188	31.3	—	0.0	—	0.0	131,004	R
North Dakota	247,882	138,669	55.9	94,769	38.2	14,244	5.7	—	0.0	200	0.1	43,900	R
Ohio	3,959,698	1,791,014	45.2	1,700,586	42.9	467,495	11.8	120	0.0	483	0.0	90,428	R
Oklahoma	943,086	449,697	47.7	301,658	32.0	191,731	20.3	—	0.0	—	0.0	148,039	R
Oregon	819,622	408,433	49.8	358,866	43.8	49,683	6.1	—	0.0	2,640	0.3	49,567	R
Pennsylvania	4,747,928	2,090,017	44.0	2,259,405	47.6	378,582	8.0	4,977	0.1	14,947	0.3	169,388	D
Rhode Island	385,000	122,359	31.8	246,518	64.0	15,678	4.1	—	0.0	445	0.1	124,159	D
South Carolina	666,978	254,062	38.1	197,486	29.6	215,430	32.3	—	0.0	—	0.0	38,632	R
South Dakota	281,264	149,841	53.3	118,023	42.0	13,400	4.8	—	0.0	—	0.0	31,818	R
Tennessee	1,248,617	472,592	37.8	351,233	28.1	424,792	34.0	—	0.0	—	0.0	47,800	R
Texas	3,079,216	1,227,844	39.9	1,266,804	41.1	584,269	19.0	—	0.0	299	0.0	38,960	D
Utah	422,568	238,728	56.5	156,665	37.1	26,906	6.4	—	0.0	269	0.1	82,063	R
Vermont	161,404	85,142	52.8	70,255	43.5	5,104	3.2	—	0.0	903	0.6	14,887	R
Virginia	1,361,491	590,319	43.4	442,387	32.5	321,833	23.6	4,671	0.3	2,281	0.2	147,932	R
Washington	1,304,281	588,510	45.1	616,037	47.2	96,990	7.4	488	0.0	2,256	0.2	27,527	D
West Virginia	754,206	307,555	40.8	374,091	49.6	72,560	9.6	—	0.0	—	0.0	66,536	D
Wisconsin	1,691,538	809,997	47.9	748,804	44.3	127,835	7.6	1,338	0.1	3,564	0.2	61,193	R
Wyoming	127,205	70,927	55.8	45,173	35.5	11,105	8.7	—	0.0	—	0.0	25,754	R
Dist. of Col.	170,578	31,012	18.2	139,566	81.8	—	0.0	—	0.0	—	0.0	108,554	D
Totals	73,211,875	31,785,480	43.4	31,275,166	42.7	9,906,473	13.5	52,588	0.1	192,168	0.3	510,314	R

1. For breakdown of "Other" vote, see minor candidate vote totals, p. 694.

1972 Presidential Election

STATE	TOTAL VOTE	RICHARD M. NIXON (Republican)		GEORGE S. McGOVERN (Democrat)		JOHN G. SCHMITZ (American)		BENJAMIN SPOCK (People's)		OTHER [1]		PLURALITY	
		Votes	%	Votes	%	Votes	%	Votes	%	Votes	%		
Alabama	1,006,111	728,701	72.4	256,923	25.5	11,928	1.2	—	0.0	8,559	0.9	471,778	R
Alaska	95,219	55,349	58.1	32,967	34.6	6,903	7.2	—	0.0	—	0.0	22,382	R
Arizona	622,926	402,812	64.7	198,540	31.9	21,208	3.4	—	0.0	366	0.1	204,272	R
Arkansas	651,320	448,541	68.9	199,892	30.7	2,887	0.4	—	0.0	—	0.0	248,649	R
California	8,367,862	4,602,096	55.0	3,475,847	41.5	232,554	2.8	55,167	0.7	2,198	0.0	1,126,249	R
Colorado	953,884	597,189	62.6	329,980	34.6	17,269	1.8	2,403	0.3	7,043	0.7	267,209	R
Connecticut	1,384,277	810,763	58.6	555,498	40.1	17,239	1.2	—	0.0	777	0.1	255,265	R
Delaware	235,516	140,357	59.6	92,283	39.2	2,638	1.1	—	0.0	238	0.1	48,074	R
Florida	2,583,283	1,857,759	71.9	718,117	27.8	—	0.0	—	0.0	7,407	0.3	1,139,642	R
Georgia	1,174,772	881,496	75.0	289,529	24.6	812	0.1	—	0.0	2,935	0.2	591,967	R
Hawaii	270,274	168,865	62.5	101,409	37.5	—	0.0	—	0.0	—	0.0	67,456	R
Idaho	310,379	199,384	64.2	80,826	26.0	28,869	9.3	903	0.3	397	0.1	118,558	R
Illinois	4,723,236	2,788,179	59.0	1,913,472	40.5	2,471	0.1	—	0.0	19,114	0.4	874,707	R
Indiana	2,125,529	1,405,154	66.1	708,568	33.3	—	0.0	4,544	0.2	7,263	0.3	696,586	R
Iowa	1,225,944	706,207	57.6	496,206	40.5	22,056	1.8	—	0.0	1,475	0.1	210,001	R
Kansas	916,095	619,812	67.7	270,287	29.5	21,808	2.4	—	0.0	4,188	0.5	349,525	R
Kentucky	1,067,499	676,446	63.4	371,159	34.8	17,627	1.7	1,118	0.1	1,149	0.1	305,287	R
Louisiana	1,051,491	686,852	65.3	298,142	28.4	52,099	5.0	—	0.0	14,398	1.4	388,710	R
Maine	417,042	256,458	61.5	160,584	38.5	—	0.0	—	0.0	—	0.0	95,874	R
Maryland	1,353,812	829,305	61.3	505,781	37.4	18,726	1.4	—	0.0	—	0.0	323,524	R
Massachusetts	2,458,756	1,112,078	45.2	1,332,540	54.2	2,877	0.1	101	0.0	11,160	0.5	220,462	D
Michigan	3,489,727	1,961,721	56.2	1,459,435	41.8	63,321	1.8	—	0.0	5,250	0.2	502,286	R
Minnesota	1,741,652	898,269	51.6	802,346	46.1	31,407	1.8	2,805	0.2	6,825	0.4	95,923	R
Mississippi	645,963	505,125	78.2	126,782	19.6	11,598	1.8	—	0.0	2,458	0.4	378,343	R
Missouri	1,855,803	1,153,852	62.2	697,147	37.6	—	0.0	—	0.0	4,804	0.3	456,705	R
Montana	317,603	183,976	57.9	120,197	37.8	13,430	4.2	—	0.0	—	0.0	63,779	R
Nebraska	576,289	406,298	70.5	169,991	29.5	—	0.0	—	0.0	—	0.0	236,307	R
Nevada	181,766	115,750	63.7	66,016	36.3	—	0.0	—	0.0	—	0.0	49,734	R
New Hampshire	334,055	213,724	64.0	116,435	34.9	3,386	1.0	—	0.0	510	0.2	97,289	R
New Jersey	2,997,229	1,845,502	61.6	1,102,211	36.8	34,378	1.1	5,355	0.2	9,783	0.3	743,291	R
New Mexico	386,241	235,606	61.0	141,084	36.5	8,767	2.3	—	0.0	784	0.2	94,522	R
New York	7,165,919	4,192,778	58.5	2,951,084	41.2	—	0.0	—	0.0	22,057	0.3	1,241,694	R
North Carolina	1,518,612	1,054,889	69.5	438,705	28.9	25,018	1.6	—	0.0	—	0.0	616,184	R
North Dakota	280,514	174,109	62.1	100,384	35.8	5,646	2.0	—	0.0	375	0.1	73,725	R
Ohio	4,094,787	2,441,827	59.6	1,558,889	38.1	80,067	2.0	—	0.0	14,004	0.3	882,938	R
Oklahoma	1,029,900	759,025	73.7	247,147	24.0	23,728	2.3	—	0.0	—	0.0	511,878	R
Oregon	927,946	486,686	52.4	392,760	42.3	46,211	5.0	—	0.0	2,289	0.2	93,926	R
Pennsylvania	4,592,106	2,714,521	59.1	1,796,951	39.1	70,593	1.5	—	0.0	10,041	0.2	917,570	R
Rhode Island	415,808	220,383	53.0	194,645	46.8	25	0.0	5	0.0	750	0.2	25,738	R
South Carolina	673,960	477,044	70.8	186,824	27.7	10,075	1.5	—	0.0	17	0.0	290,220	R
South Dakota	307,415	166,476	54.2	139,945	45.5	—	0.0	—	0.0	994	0.3	26,531	R
Tennessee	1,201,182	813,147	67.7	357,293	29.7	30,373	2.5	—	0.0	369	0.0	455,854	R
Texas	3,471,281	2,298,896	66.2	1,154,289	33.3	6,039	0.2	—	0.0	12,057	0.3	1,144,607	R
Utah	478,476	323,643	67.6	126,284	26.4	28,549	6.0	—	0.0	—	0.0	197,359	R
Vermont	186,947	117,149	62.7	68,174	36.5	—	0.0	1,010	0.5	614	0.3	48,975	R
Virginia	1,457,019	988,493	67.8	438,887	30.1	19,721	1.4	—	0.0	9,918	0.7	549,606	R
Washington	1,470,847	837,135	56.9	568,334	38.6	58,906	4.0	2,644	0.2	3,828	0.3	268,801	R
West Virginia	762,399	484,964	63.6	277,435	36.4	—	0.0	—	0.0	—	0.0	207,529	R
Wisconsin	1,852,890	989,430	53.4	810,174	43.7	47,525	2.6	2,701	0.1	3,060	0.2	179,256	R
Wyoming	145,570	100,464	69.0	44,358	30.5	748	0.5	—	0.0	—	0.0	56,106	R
Dist. of Col.	163,421	35,226	21.6	127,627	78.1	—	0.0	—	0.0	568	0.3	92,401	D
Totals	77,718,554	47,169,911	60.7	29,170,383	37.5	1,099,482	1.4	78,756	0.1	200,022	0.3	17,999,528	R

1. For breakdown of "Other" vote, see minor candidate vote totals, p. 695.

1976 Presidential Election

STATE	TOTAL VOTE	JIMMY CARTER (Democrat)		GERALD R. FORD (Republican)		EUGENE J. McCARTHY (Independent)		ROGER MacBRIDE (Libertarian)		OTHER[1]		PLURALITY	
		Votes	%	Votes	%	Votes	%	Votes	%	Votes	%		
Alabama	1,182,850	659,170	55.7	504,070	42.6	99	0.0	1,481	0.1	18,030	1.5	155,100	D
Alaska	123,574	44,058	35.7	71,555	57.9	—	0.0	6,785	5.5	1,176	1.0	27,497	R
Arizona	742,719	295,602	39.8	418,642	56.4	19,229	2.6	7,647	1.0	1,599	0.2	123,040	R
Arkansas	767,535	498,604	65.0	267,903	34.9	639	0.1	—	0.0	389	0.1	230,701	D
California	7,867,117	3,742,284	47.6	3,882,244	49.3	58,412	0.7	56,388	0.7	127,789	1.6	139,960	R
Colorado	1,081,554	460,353	42.6	584,367	54.0	26,107	2.4	5,330	0.5	5,397	0.5	124,014	R
Connecticut	1,381,526	647,895	46.9	719,261	52.1	3,759	0.3	209	0.0	10,402	0.8	71,366	R
Delaware	235,834	122,596	52.0	109,831	46.6	2,437	1.0	—	0.0	970	0.4	12,765	D
Florida	3,150,631	1,636,000	51.9	1,469,531	46.6	23,643	0.8	103	0.0	21,354	0.7	166,469	D
Georgia	1,467,458	979,409	66.7	483,743	33.0	991	0.1	175	0.0	3,140	0.2	495,666	D
Hawaii	291,301	147,375	50.6	140,003	48.1	—	0.0	3,923	1.3	—	0.0	7,372	D
Idaho	344,071	126,549	36.8	204,151	59.3	1,194	0.3	3,558	1.0	8,619	2.5	77,602	R
Illinois	4,718,914	2,271,295	48.1	2,364,269	50.1	55,939	1.2	8,057	0.2	19,354	0.4	92,974	R
Indiana	2,220,362	1,014,714	45.7	1,183,958	53.3	—	0.0	—	0.0	21,690	1.0	169,244	R
Iowa	1,279,306	619,931	48.5	632,863	49.5	20,051	1.6	1,452	0.1	5,009	0.4	12,932	R
Kansas	957,845	430,421	44.9	502,752	52.5	13,185	1.4	3,242	0.3	8,245	0.9	72,331	R
Kentucky	1,167,142	615,717	52.8	531,852	45.6	6,837	0.6	814	0.1	11,922	1.0	83,865	D
Louisiana	1,278,439	661,365	51.7	587,446	46.0	6,588	0.5	3,325	0.3	19,715	1.5	73,919	D
Maine	483,216	232,279	48.1	236,320	48.9	10,874	2.3	11	0.0	3,732	0.8	4,041	R
Maryland	1,439,897	759,612	52.8	672,661	46.7	4,541	0.3	255	0.0	2,828	0.2	86,951	D
Massachusetts	2,547,558	1,429,475	56.1	1,030,276	40.4	65,637	2.6	135	0.0	22,035	0.9	399,199	D
Michigan	3,653,749	1,696,714	46.4	1,893,742	51.8	47,905	1.3	5,406	0.1	9,982	0.3	197,028	R
Minnesota	1,949,931	1,070,440	54.9	819,395	42.0	35,490	1.8	3,529	0.2	21,077	1.1	251,045	D
Mississippi	769,361	381,309	49.6	366,846	47.7	4,074	0.5	2,788	0.4	14,344	1.9	14,463	D
Missouri	1,953,600	998,387	51.1	927,443	47.5	24,029	1.2	—	0.0	3,741	0.2	70,944	D
Montana	328,734	149,259	45.4	173,703	52.8	—	0.0	—	0.0	5,772	1.8	24,444	R
Nebraska	607,668	233,692	38.5	359,705	59.2	9,409	1.5	1,482	0.2	3,380	0.6	126,013	R
Nevada	201,876	92,479	45.8	101,273	50.2	—	0.0	1,519	0.8	6,605	3.3	8,794	R
New Hampshire	339,618	147,635	43.5	185,935	54.7	4,095	1.2	936	0.3	1,017	0.3	38,300	R
New Jersey	3,014,472	1,444,653	47.9	1,509,688	50.1	32,717	1.1	9,449	0.3	17,965	0.6	65,035	R
New Mexico	418,409	201,148	48.1	211,419	50.5	1,161	0.3	1,110	0.3	3,571	0.9	10,271	R
New York	6,534,170	3,389,558	51.9	3,100,791	47.5	4,303	0.1	12,197	0.2	27,321	0.4	288,767	D
North Carolina	1,678,914	927,365	55.2	741,960	44.2	780	0.0	2,219	0.1	6,590	0.4	185,405	D
North Dakota	297,188	136,078	45.8	153,470	51.6	2,952	1.0	253	0.1	4,435	1.5	17,392	R
Ohio	4,111,873	2,011,621	48.9	2,000,505	48.7	58,258	1.4	8,961	0.2	32,528	0.8	11,116	D
Oklahoma	1,092,251	532,442	48.7	545,708	50.0	14,101	1.3	—	0.0	—	0.0	13,266	R
Oregon	1,029,876	490,407	47.6	492,120	47.8	40,207	3.9	—	0.0	7,142	0.7	1,713	R
Pennsylvania	4,620,787	2,328,677	50.4	2,205,604	47.7	50,584	1.1	—	0.0	35,922	0.8	123,073	D
Rhode Island	411,170	227,636	55.4	181,249	44.1	479	0.1	715	0.2	1,091	0.3	46,387	D
South Carolina	802,583	450,807	56.2	346,149	43.1	289	0.0	53	0.0	5,285	0.7	104,658	D
South Dakota	300,678	147,068	48.9	151,505	50.4	—	0.0	1,619	0.5	486	0.2	4,437	R
Tennessee	1,476,345	825,879	55.9	633,969	42.9	5,004	0.3	1,375	0.1	10,118	0.7	191,910	D
Texas	4,071,884	2,082,319	51.1	1,953,300	48.0	20,118	0.5	189	0.0	15,958	0.4	129,019	D
Utah	541,198	182,110	33.6	337,908	62.4	3,907	0.7	2,438	0.5	14,835	2.7	155,798	R
Vermont	187,765	80,954	43.1	102,085	54.4	4,001	2.1	—	0.0	725	0.4	21,131	R
Virginia	1,697,094	813,896	48.0	836,554	49.3	—	0.0	4,648	0.3	41,996	2.5	22,658	R
Washington	1,555,534	717,323	46.1	777,732	50.0	36,986	2.4	5,042	0.3	18,451	1.2	60,409	R
West Virginia	750,964	435,914	58.0	314,760	41.9	113	0.0	16	0.0	161	0.0	121,154	D
Wisconsin	2,104,175	1,040,232	49.4	1,004,987	47.8	34,943	1.7	3,814	0.2	20,199	1.0	35,245	D
Wyoming	156,343	62,239	39.8	92,717	59.3	624	0.4	89	0.1	674	0.4	30,478	R
Dist. of Col.	168,830	137,818	81.6	27,873	16.5	—	0.0	274	0.2	2,865	1.7	109,945	D
Totals	81,555,889	40,830,763	50.1	39,147,793	48.0	756,691	0.9	173,011	0.2	647,631	0.8	1,682,970	D

1. For breakdown of "Other" vote, see minor candidate vote totals, p. 695.

1980 Presidential Election

STATE	TOTAL VOTE	RONALD REAGAN (Republican)		JIMMY CARTER (Democrat)		JOHN B. ANDERSON (Independent)		ED CLARK (Libertarian)		OTHER[1]		PLURALITY	
		Votes	%	Votes	%	Votes	%	Votes	%	Votes	%		
Alabama	1,341,929	654,192	48.8	636,730	47.4	16,481	1.2	13,318	1.0	21,208	1.6	17,462	R
Alaska	158,445	86,112	54.3	41,842	26.4	11,155	7.0	18,479	11.7	857	0.5	44,270	R
Arizona	873,945	529,688	60.6	246,843	28.2	76,952	8.8	18,784	2.1	1,678	0.2	282,845	R
Arkansas	837,582	403,164	48.1	398,041	47.5	22,468	2.7	8,970	1.1	4,939	0.6	5,123	R
California	8,587,063	4,524,858	52.7	3,083,661	35.9	739,833	8.6	148,434	1.7	90,277	1.1	1,441,197	R
Colorado	1,184,415	652,264	55.1	367,973	31.1	130,633	11.0	25,744	2.2	7,801	0.7	284,291	R
Connecticut	1,406,285	677,210	48.2	541,732	38.5	171,807	12.2	8,570	0.6	6,966	0.5	135,478	R
Delaware	235,900	111,252	47.2	105,754	44.8	16,288	6.9	1,974	0.8	632	0.3	5,498	R
Florida	3,686,930	2,046,951	55.5	1,419,475	38.5	189,692	5.1	30,524	0.8	288	0.0	627,476	R
Georgia	1,596,695	654,168	41.0	890,733	55.8	36,055	2.3	15,627	1.0	112	0.0	236,565	D
Hawaii	303,287	130,112	42.9	135,879	44.8	32,021	10.6	3,269	1.1	2,006	0.7	5,767	D
Idaho	437,431	290,699	66.5	110,192	25.2	27,058	6.2	8,425	1.9	1,057	0.2	180,507	R
Illinois	4,749,721	2,358,049	49.6	1,981,413	41.7	346,754	7.3	38,939	0.8	24,566	0.5	376,636	R
Indiana	2,242,033	1,255,656	56.0	844,197	37.7	111,639	5.0	19,627	0.9	10,914	0.5	411,459	R
Iowa	1,317,661	676,026	51.3	508,672	38.6	115,633	8.8	13,123	1.0	4,207	0.3	167,354	R
Kansas	979,795	566,812	57.9	326,150	33.3	68,231	7.0	14,470	1.5	4,132	0.4	240,662	R
Kentucky	1,294,627	635,274	49.1	616,417	47.6	31,127	2.4	5,531	0.4	6,278	0.5	18,857	R
Louisiana	1,548,591	792,853	51.2	708,453	45.7	26,345	1.7	8,240	0.5	12,700	0.8	84,400	R
Maine	523,011	238,522	45.6	220,974	42.3	53,327	10.2	5,119	1.0	5,069	1.0	17,548	R
Maryland	1,540,496	680,606	44.2	726,161	47.1	119,537	7.8	14,192	0.9	—	0.0	45,555	D
Massachusetts[2]	2,522,890	1,057,631	41.9	1,053,802	41.7	382,539	15.2	22,038	0.9	6,880	0.3	3,829	R
Michigan	3,909,725	1,915,225	49.0	1,661,532	42.5	275,223	7.0	41,597	1.1	16,148	0.4	253,693	R
Minnesota	2,051,980	873,268	42.6	954,174	46.5	174,990	8.5	31,592	1.5	17,956	0.9	80,906	D
Mississippi	892,620	441,089	49.4	429,281	48.1	12,036	1.3	5,465	0.6	4,749	0.5	11,808	R
Missouri	2,099,824	1,074,181	51.2	931,182	44.3	77,920	3.7	14,422	0.7	2,119	0.1	142,999	R
Montana	363,952	206,814	56.8	118,032	32.4	29,281	8.0	9,825	2.7	—	0.0	88,782	R
Nebraska	640,854	419,937	65.5	166,851	26.0	44,993	7.0	9,073	1.4	—	0.0	253,086	R
Nevada	247,885	155,017	62.5	66,666	26.9	17,651	7.1	4,358	1.8	4,193	1.7	88,351	R
New Hampshire	383,990	221,705	57.7	108,864	28.4	49,693	12.9	2,064	0.5	1,664	0.4	112,841	R
New Jersey	2,975,684	1,546,557	52.0	1,147,364	38.6	234,632	7.9	20,652	0.7	26,479	0.9	399,193	R
New Mexico	456,971	250,779	54.9	167,826	36.7	29,459	6.4	4,365	1.0	4,542	1.0	82,953	R
New York	6,201,959	2,893,831	46.7	2,728,372	44.0	467,801	7.5	52,648	0.8	59,307	1.0	165,459	R
North Carolina	1,855,833	915,018	49.3	875,635	47.2	52,800	2.8	9,677	0.5	2,703	0.1	39,383	R
North Dakota	301,545	193,695	64.2	79,189	26.3	23,640	7.8	3,743	1.2	1,278	0.4	114,506	R
Ohio	4,283,603	2,206,545	51.5	1,752,414	40.9	254,472	5.9	49,033	1.1	21,139	0.5	454,131	R
Oklahoma	1,149,708	695,570	60.5	402,026	35.0	38,284	3.3	13,828	1.2	—	0.0	293,544	R
Oregon	1,181,516	571,044	48.3	456,890	38.7	112,389	9.5	25,838	2.2	15,355	1.3	114,154	R
Pennsylvania	4,561,501	2,261,872	49.6	1,937,540	42.5	292,921	6.4	33,263	0.7	35,905	0.8	324,332	R
Rhode Island	416,072	154,793	37.2	198,342	47.7	59,819	14.4	2,458	0.6	660	0.2	43,549	D
South Carolina	894,071	441,841	49.4	430,385	48.1	14,153	1.6	5,139	0.6	2,553	0.3	11,456	R
South Dakota	327,703	198,343	60.5	103,855	31.7	21,431	6.5	3,824	1.2	250	0.1	94,488	R
Tennessee	1,617,616	787,761	48.7	783,051	48.4	35,991	2.2	7,116	0.4	3,697	0.2	4,710	R
Texas	4,541,636	2,510,705	55.3	1,881,147	41.4	111,613	2.5	37,643	0.8	528	0.0	629,558	R
Utah	604,222	439,687	72.8	124,266	20.6	30,284	5.0	7,226	1.2	2,759	0.5	315,421	R
Vermont	213,299	94,628	44.4	81,952	38.4	31,761	14.9	1,900	0.9	3,058	1.4	12,676	R
Virginia	1,866,032	989,609	53.0	752,174	40.3	95,418	5.1	12,821	0.7	16,010	0.9	237,435	R
Washington	1,742,394	865,244	49.7	650,193	37.3	185,073	10.6	29,213	1.7	12,671	0.7	215,051	R
West Virginia	737,715	334,206	45.3	367,462	49.8	31,691	4.3	4,356	0.6	—	0.0	33,256	D
Wisconsin	2,273,221	1,088,845	47.9	981,584	43.2	160,657	7.1	29,135	1.3	13,000	0.6	107,261	R
Wyoming	176,713	110,700	62.6	49,427	28.0	12,072	6.8	4,514	2.6	—	0.0	61,273	R
Dist. of Col.	175,237	23,545	13.4	131,113	74.8	16,337	9.3	1,114	0.6	3,128	1.8	107,568	D
Totals	86,513,813	43,904,153	50.7	35,483,883	41.0	5,720,060	6.6	921,299	1.1	484,418	0.6	8,420,270	R

1. For breakdown of "Other" vote, see minor candidate vote totals, p. 696.
2. Figures from Clerk of the House of Representatives, *Statistics of the Congressional and Presidential Election* (Washington, D.C.: U.S. Government Printing Office, 1980); *Massachusetts Election Statistics, 1980*.

1984 Presidential Election

STATE	TOTAL VOTE	RONALD REAGAN (Republican)		WALTER F. MONDALE (Democrat)		DAVID BERGLAND (Libertarian)		LYNDON H. LaROUCHE JR. (Independent)		OTHER[1]		PLURALITY	
		Votes	%	Votes	%	Votes	%	Votes	%	Votes	%		
Alabama	1,441,713	872,849	60.5	551,899	38.3	9,504	0.7	—	0.0	7,461	0.5	320,950	R
Alaska	207,605	138,377	66.7	62,007	29.9	6,378	3.1	—	0.0	843	0.4	76,370	R
Arizona	1,025,897	681,416	66.4	333,854	32.5	10,585	1.0	—	0.0	42	0.0	347,562	R
Arkansas	884,406	534,774	60.5	338,646	38.3	2,221	0.3	1,890	0.2	6,875	0.8	196,128	R
California	9,505,423	5,467,009	57.5	3,922,519	41.3	49,951	0.5	—	0.0	65,944	0.7	1,544,490	R
Colorado	1,295,380	821,817	63.4	454,975	35.1	11,257	0.9	4,662	0.4	2,669	0.2	366,842	R
Connecticut	1,466,900	890,877	60.7	569,597	38.8	204	0.0	—	0.0	6,222	0.4	321,280	R
Delaware	254,572	152,190	59.8	101,656	39.9	268	0.1	—	0.0	458	0.2	50,534	R
Florida	4,180,051	2,730,350	65.3	1,448,816	34.7	754	0.0	—	0.0	131	0.0	1,281,534	R
Georgia	1,776,120	1,068,722	60.2	706,628	39.8	152	0.0	34	0.0	584	0.0	362,094	R
Hawaii	335,846	185,050	55.1	147,154	43.8	2,167	0.6	654	0.2	821	0.2	37,896	R
Idaho	411,144	297,523	72.4	108,510	26.4	2,823	0.7	—	0.0	2,288	0.6	189,013	R
Illinois	4,819,088	2,707,103	56.2	2,086,499	43.3	10,086	0.2	—	0.0	15,400	0.3	620,604	R
Indiana	2,233,069	1,377,230	61.7	841,481	37.7	6,741	0.3	—	0.0	7,617	0.3	535,749	R
Iowa	1,319,805	703,088	53.3	605,620	45.9	1,844	0.1	6,248	0.5	3,005	0.2	97,468	R
Kansas	1,021,991	677,296	66.3	333,149	32.6	3,329	0.3	—	0.0	8,217	0.8	344,147	R
Kentucky	1,369,345	821,702	60.0	539,539	39.4	—	0.0	1,776	0.1	6,328	0.5	282,163	R
Louisiana	1,706,822	1,037,299	60.8	651,586	38.2	1,876	0.1	3,552	0.2	12,509	0.7	385,713	R
Maine	553,144	336,500	60.8	214,515	38.8	—	0.0	—	0.0	2,129	0.4	121,985	R
Maryland	1,675,873	879,918	52.5	787,935	47.0	5,721	0.3	—	0.0	2,299	0.1	91,983	R
Massachusetts	2,559,453	1,310,936	51.2	1,239,606	48.4	—	0.0	—	0.0	8,911	0.3	71,330	R
Michigan	3,801,658	2,251,571	59.2	1,529,638	40.2	10,055	0.3	3,862	0.1	6,532	0.2	721,933	R
Minnesota	2,084,449	1,032,603	49.5	1,036,364	49.7	2,996	0.1	3,865	0.2	8,621	0.4	3,761	D
Mississippi	941,104	582,377	61.9	352,192	37.4	2,336	0.2	1,001	0.1	3,198	0.3	230,185	R
Missouri	2,122,783	1,274,188	60.0	848,583	40.0	—	0.0	—	0.0	12	0.0	425,605	R
Montana	384,377	232,450	60.5	146,742	38.2	5,185	1.3	—	0.0	—	0.0	85,708	R
Nebraska	652,090	460,054	70.6	187,866	28.8	2,079	0.3	—	0.0	2,091	0.3	272,188	R
Nevada	286,667	188,770	65.8	91,655	32.0	2,292	0.8	—	0.0	3,950	1.4	97,115	R
New Hampshire	389,066	267,051	68.6	120,395	30.9	735	0.2	467	0.1	418	0.1	146,656	R
New Jersey	3,217,862	1,933,630	60.1	1,261,323	39.2	6,416	0.2	—	0.0	16,493	0.5	672,307	R
New Mexico	514,370	307,101	59.7	201,769	39.2	4,459	0.9	—	0.0	1,041	0.2	105,332	R
New York	6,806,810	3,664,763	53.8	3,119,609	45.8	11,949	0.2	—	0.0	10,489	0.2	545,154	R
North Carolina	2,175,361	1,346,481	61.9	824,287	37.9	3,794	0.2	—	0.0	799	0.0	522,194	R
North Dakota	308,971	200,336	64.8	104,429	33.8	703	0.2	1,278	0.4	2,225	0.7	95,907	R
Ohio	4,547,619	2,678,560	58.9	1,825,440	40.1	5,886	0.1	10,693	0.2	27,040	0.6	853,120	R
Oklahoma	1,255,676	861,530	68.6	385,080	30.7	9,066	0.7	—	0.0	—	0.0	476,450	R
Oregon	1,226,527	685,700	55.9	536,479	43.7	—	0.0	—	0.0	4,348	0.4	149,221	R
Pennsylvania	4,844,903	2,584,323	53.3	2,228,131	46.0	6,982	0.1	—	0.0	25,467	0.5	356,192	R
Rhode Island	410,492	212,080	51.7	197,106	48.0	277	0.1	—	0.0	1,029	0.3	14,974	R
South Carolina	968,529	615,539	63.6	344,459	35.6	4,359	0.5	—	0.0	4,172	0.4	271,080	R
South Dakota	317,867	200,267	63.0	116,113	36.5	—	0.0	—	0.0	1,487	0.5	84,154	R
Tennessee	1,711,994	990,212	57.8	711,714	41.6	3,072	0.2	1,852	0.1	5,144	0.3	278,498	R
Texas	5,397,571	3,433,428	63.6	1,949,276	36.1	—	0.0	14,613	0.3	254	0.0	1,484,152	R
Utah	629,656	469,105	74.5	155,369	24.7	2,447	0.4	—	0.0	2,735	0.4	313,736	R
Vermont	234,561	135,865	57.9	95,730	40.8	1,002	0.4	423	0.2	1,541	0.7	40,135	R
Virginia	2,146,635	1,337,078	62.3	796,250	37.1	—	0.0	13,307	0.6	—	0.0	540,828	R
Washington	1,883,910	1,051,670	55.8	807,352	42.9	8,844	0.5	4,712	0.3	11,332	0.6	244,318	R
West Virginia	735,742	405,483	55.1	328,125	44.6	—	0.0	—	0.0	2,134	0.3	77,358	R
Wisconsin	2,211,689	1,198,584	54.2	995,740	45.0	4,883	0.2	3,791	0.2	8,691	0.4	202,844	R
Wyoming	188,968	133,241	70.5	53,370	28.2	2,357	1.2	—	0.0	—	0.0	79,871	R
Dist. of Col.	211,288	29,009	13.7	180,408	85.4	279	0.1	127	0.1	1,465	0.7	151,399	D
Totals	92,652,842	54,455,075	58.8	37,577,185	40.6	228,314	0.2	78,807	0.1	313,461	0.3	16,877,890	R

1. For breakdown of "Other" vote, see minor candidate vote totals, p. 696.

1988 Presidential Election

STATE	TOTAL VOTE	GEORGE BUSH (Republican)		MICHAEL S. DUKAKIS (Democrat)		RON PAUL (Libertarian)		LENORA B. FULANI (New Alliance)		OTHER[1]		PLURALITY	
		Votes	%	Votes	%	Votes	%	Votes	%	Votes	%		
Alabama	1,378,476	815,576	59.2	549,506	39.9	8,460	0.6	3,311	0.2	1,623	0.1	266,070	R
Alaska	200,116	119,251	59.6	72,584	36.3	5,484	2.7	1,024	0.5	1,773	0.9	46,667	R
Arizona	1,171,873	702,541	60.0	454,029	38.7	13,351	1.1	1,662	0.1	290	0.0	248,512	R
Arkansas	827,738	466,578	56.4	349,237	42.2	3,297	0.4	2,161	0.3	6,465	0.8	117,341	R
California	9,887,065	5,054,917	51.1	4,702,233	47.6	70,105	0.7	31,181	0.3	28,629	0.3	352,684	R
Colorado	1,372,394	728,177	53.1	621,453	45.3	15,482	1.1	2,539	0.2	4,743	0.3	106,724	R
Connecticut	1,443,394	750,241	52.0	676,584	46.9	14,071	1.0	2,491	0.2	7	0.0	73,657	R
Delaware	249,891	139,639	55.9	108,647	43.5	1,162	0.5	443	0.2	—	0.0	30,992	R
Florida	4,302,313	2,618,885	60.9	1,656,701	38.5	19,796	0.5	6,655	0.2	276	0.0	962,184	R
Georgia	1,809,672	1,081,331	59.8	714,792	39.5	8,435	0.5	5,099	0.3	15	0.0	366,539	R
Hawaii	354,461	158,625	44.8	192,364	54.3	1,999	0.6	1,003	0.3	470	0.1	33,739	D
Idaho	408,968	253,881	62.1	147,272	36.0	5,313	1.3	2,502	0.6	—	0.0	106,609	R
Illinois	4,559,120	2,310,939	50.7	2,215,940	48.6	14,944	0.3	10,276	0.2	7,021	0.2	94,999	R
Indiana	2,168,621	1,297,763	59.8	860,643	39.7	—	0.0	10,215	0.5	—	0.0	437,120	R
Iowa	1,225,614	545,355	44.5	670,557	54.7	2,494	0.2	540	0.0	6,668	0.5	125,202	D
Kansas	993,044	554,049	55.8	422,636	42.6	12,553	1.3	3,806	0.4	—	0.0	131,413	R
Kentucky	1,322,517	734,281	55.5	580,368	43.9	2,118	0.2	1,256	0.1	4,494	0.3	153,913	R
Louisiana	1,628,202	883,702	54.3	717,460	44.1	4,115	0.3	2,355	0.1	20,570	1.3	166,242	R
Maine	555,035	307,131	55.3	243,569	43.9	2,700	0.5	1,405	0.3	230	0.0	63,562	R
Maryland	1,714,358	876,167	51.1	826,304	48.2	6,748	0.4	5,115	0.3	24	0.0	49,863	R
Massachusetts	2,632,805	1,194,635	45.4	1,401,415	53.2	24,251	0.9	9,561	0.4	2,943	0.1	206,780	D
Michigan	3,669,163	1,965,486	53.6	1,675,783	45.7	18,336	0.5	2,513	0.1	7,045	0.2	289,703	R
Minnesota	2,096,790	962,337	45.9	1,109,471	52.9	5,109	0.2	1,734	0.1	18,139	0.9	147,134	D
Mississippi	931,527	557,890	59.9	363,921	39.1	3,329	0.4	2,155	0.2	4,232	0.5	193,969	R
Missouri	2,093,713	1,084,953	51.8	1,001,619	47.8	434	0.0	6,656	0.3	51	0.0	83,334	R
Montana	365,674	190,412	52.1	168,936	46.2	5,047	1.4	1,279	0.3	—	0.0	21,476	R
Nebraska	661,465	397,956	60.2	259,235	39.2	2,534	0.4	1,740	0.3	—	0.0	138,721	R
Nevada	350,067	206,040	58.9	132,738	37.9	3,520	1.0	835	0.2	6,934	2.0	73,302	R
New Hampshire	451,074	281,537	62.4	163,696	36.3	4,502	1.0	790	0.2	549	0.1	117,841	R
New Jersey	3,099,553	1,743,192	56.2	1,320,352	42.6	8,421	0.3	5,139	0.2	22,449	0.7	422,840	R
New Mexico	521,287	270,341	51.9	244,497	46.9	3,268	0.6	2,237	0.4	944	0.2	25,844	R
New York	6,485,683	3,081,871	47.5	3,347,882	51.6	12,109	0.2	15,845	0.2	27,976	0.4	266,011	D
North Carolina	2,134,370	1,237,258	58.0	890,167	41.7	1,263	0.1	5,682	0.3	—	0.0	347,091	R
North Dakota	297,261	166,559	56.0	127,739	43.0	1,315	0.4	396	0.1	1,252	0.4	38,820	R
Ohio	4,393,699	2,416,549	55.0	1,939,629	44.1	11,989	0.3	12,017	0.3	13,515	0.3	476,920	R
Oklahoma	1,171,036	678,367	57.9	483,423	41.3	6,261	0.5	2,985	0.3	—	0.0	194,944	R
Oregon	1,201,694	560,126	46.6	616,206	51.3	14,811	1.2	6,487	0.5	4,064	0.3	56,080	D
Pennsylvania	4,536,251	2,300,087	50.7	2,194,944	48.4	12,051	0.3	4,379	0.1	24,790	0.5	105,143	R
Rhode Island	404,620	177,761	43.9	225,123	55.6	825	0.2	280	0.1	631	0.2	47,362	D
South Carolina	986,009	606,443	61.5	370,554	37.6	4,935	0.5	4,077	0.4	—	0.0	235,889	R
South Dakota	312,991	165,415	52.8	145,560	46.5	1,060	0.3	730	0.2	226	0.1	19,855	R
Tennessee	1,636,250	947,233	57.9	679,794	41.5	2,041	0.1	1,334	0.1	5,848	0.4	267,439	R
Texas	5,427,410	3,036,829	56.0	2,352,748	43.3	30,355	0.6	7,208	0.1	270	0.0	684,081	R
Utah	647,008	428,442	66.2	207,343	32.0	7,473	1.2	455	0.1	3,295	0.5	221,099	R
Vermont	243,328	124,331	51.1	115,775	47.6	1,000	0.4	205	0.1	2,017	0.8	8,556	R
Virginia	2,191,609	1,309,162	59.7	859,799	39.2	8,336	0.4	14,312	0.7	—	0.0	449,363	R
Washington	1,865,253	903,835	48.5	933,516	50.0	17,240	0.9	3,520	0.2	7,142	0.4	29,681	D
West Virginia	653,311	310,065	47.5	341,016	52.2	—	0.0	2,230	0.3	—	0.0	30,951	D
Wisconsin	2,191,608	1,047,499	47.8	1,126,794	51.4	5,157	0.2	1,953	0.1	10,205	0.5	79,295	D
Wyoming	176,551	106,867	60.5	67,113	38.0	2,026	1.1	545	0.3	—	0.0	39,754	R
Dist. of Col.	192,877	27,590	14.3	159,407	82.6	554	0.3	2,901	1.5	2,425	1.3	131,817	D
Totals	91,594,809	48,886,097	53.4	41,809,074	45.6	432,179	0.5	217,219	0.2	250,240	0.3	7,077,023	R

1. For breakdown of "Other" vote, see minor candidate vote totals, p. 697.

1992 Presidential Election

STATE	TOTAL VOTE	BILL CLINTON (Democrat) Votes	%	GEORGE BUSH (Republican) Votes	%	ROSS PEROT (Independent) Votes	%	ANDRE V. MARROU (Libertarian) Votes	%	OTHER[1] Votes	%	PLURALITY	
Alabama	1,688,060	690,080	40.9	804,283	47.6	183,109	10.8	5,737	0.3	4,851	0.3	114,203	R
Alaska	258,506	78,294	30.3	102,000	39.5	73,481	28.4	1,378	0.5	3,353	1.3	23,706	R
Arizona	1,486,975	543,050	36.5	572,086	38.5	353,741	23.8	6,759	0.5	11,339	0.8	29,036	R
Arkansas	950,653	505,823	53.2	337,324	35.5	99,132	10.4	1,261	0.1	7,113	0.7	168,499	D
California	11,131,721	5,121,325	46.0	3,630,574	32.6	2,296,006	20.6	48,139	0.4	35,677	0.3	1,490,751	D
Colorado	1,569,180	629,681	40.1	562,850	35.9	366,010	23.3	8,669	0.6	1,970	0.1	66,831	D
Connecticut	1,616,332	682,318	42.2	578,313	35.8	348,771	21.6	5,391	0.3	1,539	0.1	104,005	D
Delaware	289,735	126,054	43.5	102,313	35.3	59,213	20.4	935	0.3	1,220	0.4	23,741	D
Florida	5,314,392	2,072,698	39.0	2,173,310	40.9	1,053,067	19.8	15,079	0.3	238		100,612	R
Georgia	2,321,125	1,008,966	43.5	995,252	42.9	309,657	13.3	7,110	0.3	140		13,714	D
Hawaii	372,842	179,310	48.1	136,822	36.7	53,003	14.2	1,119	0.3	2,588	0.7	42,488	D
Idaho	482,142	137,013	28.4	202,645	42.0	130,395	27.0	1,167	0.2	10,922	2.3	65,632	R
Illinois	5,050,157	2,453,350	48.6	1,734,096	34.3	840,515	16.6	9,218	0.2	12,978	0.3	719,254	D
Indiana	2,305,871	848,420	36.8	989,375	42.9	455,934	19.8	7,936	0.3	4,206	0.2	140,955	R
Iowa	1,354,607	586,353	43.3	504,891	37.3	253,468	18.7	1,076	0.1	8,819	0.7	81,462	D
Kansas	1,157,335	390,434	33.7	449,951	38.9	312,358	27.0	4,314	0.4	278		59,517	R
Kentucky	1,492,900	665,104	44.6	617,178	41.3	203,944	13.7	4,513	0.3	2,161	0.1	47,926	D
Louisiana	1,790,017	815,971	45.6	733,386	41.0	211,478	11.8	3,155	0.2	26,027	1.5	82,585	D
Maine	679,499	263,420	38.8	206,504	30.4	206,820	30.4	1,681	0.2	1,074	0.2	56,600	D
Maryland	1,985,046	988,571	49.8	707,094	35.6	281,414	14.2	4,715	0.2	3,252	0.2	281,477	D
Massachusetts	2,773,700	1,318,662	47.5	805,049	29.0	630,731	22.7	9,024	0.3	10,234	0.4	513,613	D
Michigan	4,274,673	1,871,182	43.8	1,554,940	36.4	824,813	19.3	10,175	0.2	13,563	0.3	316,242	D
Minnesota	2,347,948	1,020,997	43.5	747,841	31.9	562,506	24.0	3,374	0.1	13,230	0.6	273,156	D
Mississippi	981,793	400,258	40.8	487,793	49.7	85,626	8.7	2,154	0.2	5,962	0.6	87,535	R
Missouri	2,391,565	1,053,873	44.1	811,159	33.9	518,741	21.7	7,497	0.3	295		242,714	D
Montana	410,611	154,507	37.6	144,207	35.1	107,225	26.1	986	0.2	3,686	0.9	10,300	D
Nebraska	737,546	216,864	29.4	343,678	46.6	174,104	23.6	1,340	0.2	1,560	0.2	126,814	R
Nevada	506,318	189,148	37.4	175,828	34.7	132,580	26.2	1,835	0.4	6,927	1.4	13,320	D
New Hampshire	537,943	209,040	38.9	202,484	37.6	121,337	22.6	3,548	0.7	1,534	0.3	6,556	D
New Jersey	3,343,594	1,436,206	43.0	1,356,865	40.6	521,829	15.6	6,822	0.2	21,872	0.7	79,341	D
New Mexico	569,986	261,617	45.9	212,824	37.3	91,895	16.1	1,615	0.3	2,035	0.4	48,793	D
New York	6,926,925	3,444,450	49.7	2,346,649	33.9	1,090,721	15.7	13,451	0.2	31,654	0.5	1,097,801	D
North Carolina	2,611,850	1,114,042	42.7	1,134,661	43.4	357,864	13.7	5,171	0.2	112		20,619	R
North Dakota	308,133	99,168	32.2	136,244	44.2	71,084	23.1	416	0.1	1,221	0.4	37,076	R
Ohio	4,939,967	1,984,942	40.2	1,894,310	38.3	1,036,426	21.0	7,252	0.1	17,037	0.3	90,632	D
Oklahoma	1,390,359	473,066	34.0	592,929	42.6	319,878	23.0	4,486	0.3	—		119,863	R
Oregon	1,462,643	621,314	42.5	475,757	32.5	354,091	24.2	4,277	0.3	7,204	0.5	145,557	D
Pennsylvania	4,959,810	2,239,164	45.1	1,791,841	36.1	902,667	18.2	21,477	0.4	4,661	0.1	447,323	D
Rhode Island	453,477	213,299	47.0	131,601	29.0	105,045	23.2	571	0.1	2,961	0.7	81,698	D
South Carolina	1,202,527	479,514	39.9	577,507	48.0	138,872	11.5	2,719	0.2	3,915	0.3	97,993	R
South Dakota	336,254	124,888	37.1	136,718	40.7	73,295	21.8	814	0.2	539	0.2	11,830	R
Tennessee	1,982,638	933,521	47.1	841,300	42.4	199,968	10.1	1,847	0.1	6,002	0.3	92,221	D
Texas	6,154,018	2,281,815	37.1	2,496,071	40.6	1,354,781	22.0	19,699	0.3	1,652		214,256	R
Utah	743,999	183,429	24.7	322,632	43.4	203,400	27.3	1,900	0.3	32,638	4.4	119,232	R
Vermont	289,701	133,592	46.1	88,122	30.4	65,991	22.8	501	0.2	1,495	0.5	45,470	D
Virginia	2,558,665	1,038,650	40.6	1,150,517	45.0	348,639	13.6	5,730	0.2	15,129	0.6	111,867	R
Washington	2,288,230	993,037	43.4	731,234	32.0	541,780	23.7	7,533	0.3	14,646	0.6	261,803	D
West Virginia	683,762	331,001	48.4	241,974	35.4	108,829	15.9	1,873	0.3	85		89,027	D
Wisconsin	2,531,114	1,041,066	41.1	930,855	36.8	544,479	21.5	2,877	0.1	11,837	0.5	110,211	D
Wyoming	200,598	68,160	34.0	79,347	39.6	51,263	25.6	844	0.4	984	0.5	11,187	R
Dist. of Col.	227,572	192,619	84.6	20,698	9.1	9,681	4.3	467	0.2	4,107	1.8	171,921	D
Totals	104,425,014	44,909,326	43.0	39,103,882	37.4	19,741,657	18.9	291,627	0.3	378,522	0.4	5,805,444	D

1. For breakdown of "Other" votes, see minor candidate vote totals, p. 697.

1996 Presidential Election

STATE	TOTAL VOTE	BILL CLINTON (Democrat)		BOB DOLE (Republican)		ROSS PEROT (Reform)		RALPH NADER (Green)		OTHER[1]		PLURALITY	
		Votes	%	Votes	%	Votes	%	Votes	%	Votes	%		
Alabama	1,534,349	662,165	43.2	769,044	50.1	92,149	6.0	—		10,991	0.7	106,879	R
Alaska	241,620	80,380	33.3	122,746	50.8	26,333	10.9	7,597	3.1	4,564	1.9	42,366	R
Arizona	1,404,405	653,288	46.5	622,073	44.3	112,072	8.0	2,062	0.1	14,910	1.1	31,215	D
Arkansas	884,262	475,171	53.7	325,416	36.8	69,884	7.9	3,649	0.4	10,142	1.1	149,755	D
California	10,019,484	5,119,835	51.1	3,828,380	38.2	697,847	7.0	237,016	2.4	136,406	1.4	1,291,455	D
Colorado	1,510,704	671,152	44.4	691,848	45.8	99,629	6.6	25,070	1.7	23,005	1.5	20,696	R
Connecticut	1,392,614	735,740	52.8	483,109	34.7	139,523	10.0	24,321	1.7	9,921	0.7	252,631	D
Delaware	270,845	140,355	51.8	99,062	36.6	28,719	10.6	18		2,691	1.0	41,293	D
Florida	5,303,794	2,546,870	48.0	2,244,536	42.3	483,870	9.1	4,101	0.1	24,417	0.5	302,334	D
Georgia	2,299,071	1,053,849	45.8	1,080,843	47.0	146,337	6.4	—		18,042	0.8	26,994	R
Hawaii	360,120	205,012	56.9	113,943	31.6	27,358	7.6	10,386	2.9	3,421	0.9	91,069	D
Idaho	491,719	165,443	33.6	256,595	52.2	62,518	12.7	—		7,163	1.5	91,152	R
Illinois	4,311,391	2,341,744	54.3	1,587,021	36.8	346,408	8.0	1,447		34,771	0.8	754,723	D
Indiana	2,135,431	887,424	41.6	1,006,693	47.1	224,299	10.5	895		16,120	0.8	119,269	R
Iowa	1,234,075	620,258	50.3	492,644	39.9	105,159	8.5	6,550	0.5	9,464	0.8	127,614	D
Kansas	1,074,300	387,659	36.1	583,245	54.3	92,639	8.6	914	0.1	9,843	0.9	195,586	R
Kentucky	1,388,708	636,614	45.8	623,283	44.9	120,396	8.7	701	0.1	7,714	0.6	13,331	D
Louisiana	1,783,959	927,837	52.0	712,586	39.9	123,293	6.9	4,719	0.3	15,524	0.9	215,251	D
Maine	605,897	312,788	51.6	186,378	30.8	85,970	14.2	15,279	2.5	5,482	0.9	126,410	D
Maryland	1,780,870	966,207	54.3	681,530	38.3	115,812	6.5	2,606	0.1	14,715	0.8	284,677	D
Massachusetts	2,556,786	1,571,763	61.5	718,107	28.1	227,217	8.9	4,565	0.2	35,134	1.4	853,656	D
Michigan	3,848,844	1,989,653	51.7	1,481,212	38.5	336,670	8.7	2,322	0.1	38,987	1.0	508,441	D
Minnesota	2,192,640	1,120,438	51.1	766,476	35.0	257,704	11.8	24,908	1.1	23,114	1.1	353,962	D
Mississippi	893,857	394,022	44.1	439,838	49.2	52,222	5.8	—		7,775	0.9	45,816	R
Missouri	2,158,065	1,025,935	47.5	890,016	41.2	217,188	10.1	534		24,392	1.1	135,919	D
Montana	407,261	167,922	41.3	179,652	44.1	55,229	13.6	—		4,458	1.1	11,730	R
Nebraska	677,415	236,761	35.0	363,467	53.7	71,278	10.5	—		5,909	0.9	126,706	R
Nevada	464,279	203,974	43.9	199,244	42.9	43,986	9.5	4,730	1.0	12,345	2.7	4,730	D
New Hampshire	499,175	246,214	49.3	196,532	39.4	48,390	9.7	—		8,039	1.6	49,682	D
New Jersey	3,075,807	1,652,329	53.7	1,103,078	35.9	262,134	8.5	32,465	1.1	25,801	0.8	549,251	D
New Mexico	556,074	273,495	49.2	232,751	41.9	32,257	5.8	13,218	2.4	4,353	0.8	40,744	D
New York	6,316,129	3,756,177	59.5	1,933,492	30.6	503,458	8.0	75,956	1.2	47,046	0.7	1,822,685	D
North Carolina	2,515,807	1,107,849	44.0	1,225,938	48.7	168,059	6.7	2,108	0.1	11,853	0.4	118,089	R
North Dakota	266,411	106,905	40.1	125,050	46.9	32,515	12.2	—		1,941	0.7	18,145	R
Ohio	4,534,434	2,148,222	47.4	1,859,883	41.0	483,207	10.7	2,962	0.1	40,160	0.9	288,339	D
Oklahoma	1,206,713	488,105	40.4	582,315	48.3	130,788	10.8	—		5,505	0.5	94,210	R
Oregon	1,377,760	649,641	47.2	538,152	39.1	121,221	8.8	49,415	3.6	19,331	1.4	111,489	D
Pennsylvania	4,506,118	2,215,819	49.2	1,801,169	40.0	430,984	9.6	3,086	0.1	55,060	1.2	414,650	D
Rhode Island	390,284	233,050	59.7	104,683	26.8	43,723	11.2	6,040	1.5	2,788	0.7	128,367	D
South Carolina	1,151,689	506,283	44.0	573,458	49.8	64,386	5.6	—		7,562	0.7	67,175	R
South Dakota	323,826	139,333	43.0	150,543	46.5	31,250	9.7	—		2,700	0.8	11,210	R
Tennessee	1,894,105	909,146	48.0	863,530	45.6	105,918	5.6	6,427	0.3	9,084	0.4	45,616	D
Texas	5,611,644	2,459,683	43.8	2,736,167	48.8	378,537	6.7	4,810	0.1	32,447	0.6	276,484	R
Utah	665,629	221,633	33.3	361,911	54.4	66,461	10.0	4,615	0.7	11,009	1.7	140,278	R
Vermont	258,449	137,894	53.4	80,352	31.1	31,024	12.0	5,585	2.2	3,594	1.4	57,542	D
Virginia	2,416,642	1,091,060	45.1	1,138,350	47.1	159,861	6.6	—		27,371	1.1	47,290	R
Washington	2,253,837	1,123,323	49.8	840,712	37.3	201,003	8.9	60,322	2.7	28,477	1.3	282,611	D
West Virginia	636,459	327,812	51.5	233,946	36.8	71,639	11.3	—		3,062	0.5	93,866	D
Wisconsin	2,196,169	1,071,971	48.8	845,029	38.5	227,339	10.4	28,723	1.3	23,107	1.1	226,942	D
Wyoming	211,571	77,934	36.8	105,388	49.8	25,928	12.3	—		2,321	1.1	27,454	R
Dist. of Col.	185,726	158,220	85.2	17,339	9.3	3,611	1.9	4,780	2.6	1,776	1.0	140,881	D
Totals	96,277,223	47,402,357	49.2	39,198,755	40.7	8,085,402	8.4	684,902	0.7	905,807	0.9	8,203,602	D

1. For breakdown of "Other" votes, see minor candidate vote totals, p. 698.

2000 Presidential Election

STATE	TOTAL VOTE	GEORGE W. BUSH (Republican)		AL GORE (Democrat)		RALPH NADER (Green)		PATRICK J. BUCHANAN (Reform)		OTHER[1]		PLURALITY	
		Votes	%	Votes	%	Votes	%	Votes	%	Votes	%		
Alabama	1,666,272	941,173	56.5	692,611	41.6	18,323	1.1	6,351	0.4	7,814	0.5	248,562	R
Alaska	285,560	167,398	58.6	79,004	27.7	28,747	10.1	5,192	1.8	5,219	1.8	88,394	R
Arizona	1,532,016	781,652	51.0	685,341	44.7	45,645	3.0	12,373	0.8	7,005	0.5	96,311	R
Arkansas	921,781	472,940	51.3	422,768	45.9	13,421	1.5	7,358	0.8	5,294	0.6	50,172	R
California	10,965,856	4,567,429	41.7	5,861,203	53.4	418,707	3.8	44,987	0.4	75,530	0.7	1,293,774	D
Colorado	1,741,368	883,748	50.8	738,227	42.4	91,434	5.3	10,465	0.6	17,494	1.0	145,521	R
Connecticut	1,459,525	561,094	38.4	816,015	55.9	64,452	4.4	4,731	0.3	13,233	0.9	254,921	D
Delaware	327,622	137,288	41.9	180,068	55.0	8,307	2.5	777	0.2	1,182	0.4	42,780	D
Florida	5,963,110	2,912,790	48.8	2,912,253	48.8	97,488	1.6	17,484	0.3	23,095	0.4	537	R
Georgia	2,596,645	1,419,720	54.7	1,116,230	43.0	13,273	0.5	10,926	0.4	36,496	1.4	303,490	R
Hawaii	367,951	137,845	37.5	205,286	55.8	21,623	5.9	1,071	0.3	2,126	0.6	67,441	D
Idaho	501,621	336,937	67.2	138,637	27.6	12,292	2.5	7,615	1.5	6,140	1.2	198,300	R
Illinois	4,742,123	2,019,421	42.6	2,589,026	54.6	103,759	2.2	16,106	0.3	13,811	0.3	569,605	D
Indiana	2,199,302	1,245,836	56.6	901,980	41.0	18,531	0.8	16,959	0.8	15,996	0.7	343,856	R
Iowa	1,315,563	634,373	48.2	638,517	48.5	29,374	2.2	5,731	0.4	7,568	0.6	4,144	D
Kansas	1,072,218	622,332	58.0	399,276	37.2	36,086	3.4	7,370	0.7	7,154	0.7	223,056	R
Kentucky	1,544,187	872,492	56.5	638,898	41.4	23,192	1.5	4,173	0.3	5,432	0.4	233,594	R
Louisiana	1,765,656	927,871	52.6	792,344	44.9	20,473	1.2	14,356	0.8	10,612	0.6	135,527	R
Maine	651,817	286,616	44.0	319,951	49.1	37,127	5.7	4,443	0.7	3,680	0.6	33,335	D
Maryland	2,020,480	813,797	40.3	1,140,782	56.5	53,768	2.7	4,248	0.2	7,885	0.4	326,985	D
Massachusetts	2,702,984	878,502	32.5	1,616,487	59.8	173,564	6.4	11,149	0.4	23,282	0.9	737,985	D
Michigan	4,232,711	1,953,139	46.1	2,170,418	51.3	84,165	2.0	2,061	0.0	22,928	0.5	217,279	D
Minnesota	2,438,685	1,109,659	45.5	1,168,266	47.9	126,696	5.2	22,166	0.9	11,898	0.5	58,607	D
Mississippi	994,184	572,844	57.6	404,614	40.7	8,122	0.8	2,265	0.2	6,339	0.6	168,230	R
Missouri	2,359,892	1,189,924	50.4	1,111,138	47.1	38,515	1.6	9,818	0.4	10,497	0.4	78,786	R
Montana	410,997	240,178	58.4	137,126	33.4	24,437	5.9	5,697	1.4	3,559	0.9	103,052	R
Nebraska	697,019	433,862	62.2	231,780	33.3	24,540	3.5	3,646	0.5	3,191	0.5	202,082	R
Nevada	608,970	301,575	49.5	279,978	46.0	15,008	2.5	4,747	0.8	7,662	1.3	21,597	R
New Hampshire	569,081	273,559	48.1	266,348	46.8	22,198	3.9	2,615	0.5	4,361	0.8	7,211	R
New Jersey	3,187,226	1,284,173	40.3	1,788,850	56.1	94,554	3.0	6,989	0.2	12,660	0.4	504,677	D
New Mexico	598,605	286,417	47.8	286,783	47.9	21,251	3.6	1,392	0.2	2,762	0.5	366	D
New York	6,821,999	2,403,374	35.2	4,107,697	60.2	244,030	3.6	31,599	0.5	35,299	0.5	1,704,323	D
North Carolina	2,911,262	1,631,163	56.0	1,257,692	43.2	—	0.0	8,874	0.3	13,533	0.5	373,471	R
North Dakota	288,256	174,852	60.7	95,284	33.1	9,486	3.3	7,288	2.5	1,346	0.5	79,568	R
Ohio	4,701,998	2,350,363	50.0	2,183,628	46.4	117,799	2.5	26,721	0.6	23,484	0.5	166,735	R
Oklahoma	1,234,229	744,337	60.3	474,276	38.4	—	0.0	9,014	0.7	6,602	0.5	270,061	R
Oregon	1,533,968	713,577	46.5	720,342	47.0	77,357	5.0	7,063	0.5	15,629	1.0	6,765	D
Pennsylvania	4,913,119	2,281,127	46.4	2,485,967	50.6	103,392	2.1	16,023	0.3	26,610	0.5	204,840	D
Rhode Island	409,047	130,555	31.9	249,508	61.0	25,052	6.1	2,273	0.6	1,659	0.4	118,953	D
South Carolina	1,382,717	785,937	56.8	565,561	40.9	20,200	1.5	3,519	0.3	7,500	0.5	220,376	R
South Dakota	316,269	190,700	60.3	118,804	37.6	—	0.0	3,322	1.1	3,443	1.1	71,896	R
Tennessee	2,076,181	1,061,949	51.1	981,720	47.3	19,781	1.0	4,250	0.2	8,481	0.4	80,229	R
Texas	6,407,637	3,799,639	59.3	2,433,746	38.0	137,994	2.2	12,394	0.2	23,864	0.4	1,365,893	R
Utah	770,754	515,096	66.8	203,053	26.3	35,850	4.7	9,319	1.2	7,436	1.0	312,043	R
Vermont	294,308	119,775	40.7	149,022	50.6	20,374	6.9	2,192	0.7	2,945	1.0	29,247	D
Virginia	2,739,447	1,437,490	52.5	1,217,290	44.4	59,398	2.2	5,455	0.2	19,814	0.7	220,200	R
Washington	2,487,433	1,108,864	44.6	1,247,652	50.2	103,002	4.1	7,171	0.3	20,744	0.8	138,788	D
West Virginia	648,124	336,475	51.9	295,497	45.6	10,680	1.6	3,169	0.5	2,303	0.4	40,978	R
Wisconsin	2,598,607	1,237,279	47.6	1,242,987	47.8	94,070	3.6	11,446	0.4	12,825	0.5	5,708	D
Wyoming	218,351	147,947	67.8	60,481	27.7	4,625	2.1	2,724	1.2	2,574	1.2	87,466	R
Dist. of Col.	201,894	18,073	9.0	171,923	85.2	10,576	5.2	—	0.0	1,322	0.7	153,850	D
Totals	105,396,627	50,455,156	47.9	50,992,335	48.4	2,882,738	2.7	449,077	0.4	617,321	0.6	537,179	D

1. For breakdown of "Other" votes, see minor candidate vote totals, p. 699.

Presidential Popular Vote Returns: Minor Candidates and Parties, 1824–2000

This section contains popular vote returns for all minor candidates and parties that were aggregated in the columns labeled "Other" in the presidential election returns found on pages 644–688. The source for these data for 1824–1916, except where indicated by a footnote, is the Inter-University Consortium for Political and Social Research (ICPSR). *(See box, ICP-SR Historical Election Returns File, p. 000.)* For the 1920 to 1992 elections, the source is Richard M. Scammon and Alice V. McGillivray, *America at the Polls* (Washington, D.C.: Congressional Quarterly, 1994). For the 1996 and 2000 elections, the source is the *America Votes* series, compiled biennially by Rhodes Cook for CQ Press in Washington, D.C.

For this edition, Congressional Quarterly has supplemented the base source material with new research provided by elections historian Michael J. Dubin. For the state returns marked with an asterisk (*), the sources for the revised data are found in the footnotes to the same states in the corresponding presidential election table found on pages 644–688.

The material in this section is presented in the following order:

• Year of presidential election.
• Name of candidate and party, if available from the ICPSR, Scammon, and Cook data. "Scattered write-ins" is used where votes were recorded but neither the candidate nor a party was known. In nearly all cases, these figures were the total write-in vote.
• State name and number of votes. Percentages may be calculated by using the state vote totals from the presidential election tables found on pages 644–688.

• Nationwide vote totals. Percentages may be calculated by using the national vote total from the presidential election tables.

In the ICPSR data, the distinct party designations appearing in the original sources are preserved. Thus, in the ICPSR returns for 1880, John W. Phelps received votes under the following four party designations: "Anti-Masonic"—California, 5 votes, Illinois, 150 votes, and Pennsylvania, 44 votes; "Anti-Secret"—Kansas, 25 votes; "National American"—Michigan, 312 votes; and "American"—Rhode Island, 4 votes, and Wisconsin, 91 votes.

To provide one party designation for each minor candidate for the elections 1824 to 1916, Congressional Quarterly has aggregated under a single party designation the votes of minor candidates who are listed in the ICPSR data as receiving votes under more than one party designation. The source used for assigning party designations for these years is Svend Petersen, *A Statistical History of the American Presidential Elections* (Westport, Conn.: Greenwood Press, 1981) where Petersen gives a party designation. In the 1880 election cited above, Peterson lists John W. Phelps as an American Party candidate. Where Petersen lists no party designation, Congressional Quarterly selected the party designation for a candidate that appeared most frequently in the ICPSR returns. For the 1920 to 1992 elections, the source for party designations is Scammon and McGillivray, *America at the Polls*. For the 1996 and 2000 elections, the source is Cook, *America Votes*.

1824 Election

Unpledged Republican
Massachusetts, 6,616 votes.
Scattered write-ins
Connecticut, 1,188 votes; Indiana, 7; Massachusetts, 4,753; Missouri, 33; North Carolina, 256; Rhode Island, 200.
Total: 6,437

1828 Election

Scattered write-ins
Alabama, 4 votes; Connecticut, 1,101; Maine, 89; Massachusetts, 3,226; New Jersey, 8; North Carolina, 15; Rhode Island, 5; Vermont, 120.
Total: 4,568

1832 Election

Scattered write-ins
Illinois, 30 votes; Massachusetts, 7,031; Rhode Island, 6; Vermont, 206.
Total: 7,273

1836 Election

Scattered write-ins
Delaware, 5 votes; Maine, 1,112; Massachusetts, 45; North Carolina, 1; Rhode Island, 1; Vermont, 65; Virginia, 5.
Total: 1,234

1840 Election

Scattered write-ins
Delaware, 13 votes; Indiana, 599; Rhode Island, 136; Vermont, 19.
Total: 767

1844 Election

Scattered write-ins
Delaware, 6 votes; Illinois, 939; Massachusetts, 1,106; North Carolina, 2; Rhode Island, 5.
Total: 2,058

1848 Election

Gerrit Smith (Liberty)
New York, 2,545 votes.
Henry Clay (Clay Whig)
Illinois, 89 votes.
Scattered write-ins
Alabama, 4 votes; Connecticut, 24; Massachusetts, 62; North Carolina, 26; Rhode Island, 5; Texas, 75.
Total: 196

1852 Election

Daniel Webster (Whig)[1]
Georgia, 5,324 votes; Massachusetts, 1,670.
Total: 6,994
—Broome (Native American)
Massachusetts, 158 votes; New Jersey, 738; Pennsylvania, 1,670.
Total: 2,566
George Michael Troup (Southern Rights)[2]
Alabama, 2,205 votes; Georgia, 126.
Total: 2,331
Scattered write-ins
California, 56 votes; Connecticut, 12; Iowa, 139; North Carolina, 60; Texas, 10.
Total: 272

1856 Election

Scattered write-ins
California, 14 votes; Delaware, 9; Massachusetts, 3,006; Ohio, 148.
Total: 3,177

1860 Election

Gerrit Smith (Union)
Illinois, 35 votes; Ohio, 136.
Scattered write-ins
California, 15 votes; Massachusetts, 328; Minnesota, 17.
Total: 360

1864 Election

E. Cheeseborough
Kansas, 543 votes.
Kansas, 112 votes; Massachusetts, 6; Minnesota, 26; Oregon, 5.
Total: 149

1868 Election

Scattered write-ins
Alabama, 6 votes; Kansas, 3; Massachusetts, 26; New Hampshire, 11.
Total: 46

1872 Election

James Black (Prohibition)
Michigan, 1,271 votes; New York, 201*; Ohio, 2,100.
Total: 3,572
Liberal Republican Elector
Iowa, 10,447 votes.
Scattered write-ins
Iowa, 942 votes; Kansas, 581; Minnesota, 168; New Hampshire, 313; South Carolina, 259.
Total: 2,263

1876 Election

Green Clay Smith (Prohibition)
Connecticut, 374 votes; Illinois, 141; Kansas, 110; Kentucky, 818*; Michigan, 766; New York, 2,369; Ohio, 1,636; Pennsylvania, 1,320; Wisconsin, 27.
Total: 7,561
James B. Walker (American)
Illinois, 177 votes; Kansas, 23; Michigan, 71; Ohio, 76; Pennsylvania, 83; Wisconsin, 29.
Total: 459
Communist
Wisconsin, 32 votes.
Scattered write-ins
Alabama, 2 votes; California, 19; Connecticut, 26; Iowa, 520; Kansas, 5; Maine, 166*; Massachusetts, 779; New Hampshire, 93; Texas, 46; Vermont, 114; Wisconsin, 1,607.
Total: 3,377

1880 Election

Neal Dow (Prohibition)
California, 54 votes; Connecticut, 409; Illinois, 440; Kansas, 10; Kentucky, 258*; Maine, 92; Massachusetts, 682; Michigan, 938; Minnesota, 286; New Hampshire, 180; New Jersey, 191; New York, 1,517; Ohio, 2,613; Pennsylvania, 1,940; Rhode Island, 20; Wisconsin, 69.
Total: 9,699
John W. Phelps (American)
California, 5 votes; Illinois, 150; Kansas, 25; Michigan, 312; Pennsylvania, 44; Rhode Island, 4; Wisconsin, 91.
Total: 631
A. C. Brewer (Independent Democrat)
Arkansas, 322 votes.
Scattered write-ins
Arkansas, 1,221 votes; California, 70; Colorado, 14; Connecticut, 39; Iowa, 1,064; Maine, 139; Massachusetts, 117; Mississippi, 677; Rhode Island, 1; South Carolina, 36; Virginia, 379*.
Total: 3,757

1884 Election

Scattered write-ins
Alabama, 72 votes; California, 329; Florida, 118; Iowa, 1,297; Kansas, 468; Maine, 6; Massachusetts, 2; New Jersey, 28; Oregon, 35; South Carolina, 1,237; Vermont, 27.
Total: 3,619

1888 Election

Robert H. Cowdrey (United Labor)
Illinois, 150 votes; New York, 2,668*; Oregon, 351.
Total: 3,169
Socialist Labor
New York, 2,068 votes.
James Langdon Curtis (American)
California, 1,591 votes; Pennsylvania, 24.
Total: 1,615
Scattered write-ins
California, 1,442 votes; Colorado, 177; Delaware, 1; Iowa, 556; Kansas, 937; Maine, 16; Massachusetts, 60; New Hampshire, 58; North Carolina, 37; Oregon, 53; Rhode Island, 7; South Carolina, 437; Vermont, 35.
Total: 3,816

1892 Election

Simon Wing (Socialist Labor)
Connecticut, 333 votes; Massachusetts, 649; New Jersey, 1,337; New York, 17,956; Pennsylvania, 888.
Total: 21,163

Scattered write-ins

Arkansas, 1,267 votes; Delaware, 13; Georgia, 2,345; Maine, 4; Massachusetts, 3; Michigan, 925; Rhode Island, 3; South Carolina, 72; Texas, 3,968*; Vermont, 10; Wyoming, 29.

Total: 8,639

1896 Election

William Jennings Bryan (Populist)

California, 21,734* votes; Florida, 2,053*; Nevada, 574*; New Hampshire, 379*; Ohio, 2,615*; Pennsylvania, 6,103*; Texas, 77,985*; Vermont, 461*; Washington, 1,668*, Wyoming, 486*.

Total: 114,558

Charles Horatio Matchett (Socialist Labor)

California, 1,611 votes; Colorado, 159; Connecticut, 1,223; Illinois, 1,147; Indiana, 324; Iowa, 453; Maryland, 587; Massachusetts, 2,112; Michigan, 293; Minnesota, 954; Missouri, 599; Nebraska, 186; New Hampshire, 228; New Jersey, 3,985; New York, 17,667; Ohio, 1,165; Pennsylvania, 1,683; Rhode Island, 558; Virginia, 108; Wisconsin, 1,314.

Total: 36,356

Charles Eugene Bentley (National Prohibition)

Arkansas, 892 votes; California, 1,047; Colorado, 386; Illinois, 793; Indiana, 2,267; Iowa, 352; Kansas, 620; Maryland, 136; Michigan, 1,816; Missouri, 292; Nebraska, 797; New Hampshire, 49; New Jersey, 5,614; North Carolina, 222; Ohio, 2,716; Pennsylvania, 870; Washington, 148; Wisconsin, 346.

Total: 19,363

Scattered write-ins

California, 4 votes; Connecticut, 4; Georgia, 47; Massachusetts, 20; Michigan, 1,073; North Carolina, 372; North Dakota, 12; Rhode Island, 5.

Total: 1,537

1900 Election

Wharton Barker (Populist)

Alabama, 3,751* votes; Arkansas, 972; Colorado, 333; Florida, 1,143; Georgia, 4,568; Idaho, 445; Illinois, 1,141; Indiana, 1,438; Iowa, 615; Kentucky, 1,961; Michigan, 889; Mississippi, 1,642; Missouri, 4,244; Nebraska, 1,104; New Jersey, 669; North Carolina, 798; North Dakota, 109; Ohio, 251; Oregon, 275*; Pennsylvania, 638; South Dakota, 340; Tennessee, 1,322; Texas, 20,981*; Vermont, 367; Virginia, 63; West Virginia, 246; Wyoming, 20.

Total: 50,329

Joseph P. Malloney (Socialist Labor)

Colorado, 654 votes; Connecticut, 908; Illinois, 1,374; Indiana, 663; Iowa, 259; Kentucky, 390; Maryland, 382; Massachusetts, 2,599; Michigan, 830; Minnesota, 1,329; Missouri, 1,296; Montana, 119; New Jersey, 2,074; New York, 12,622; Ohio, 1,688; Pennsylvania, 2,936; Rhode Island, 1,423; Texas, 162; Utah, 102; Virginia, 167; Washington, 866; Wisconsin, 503.

Total: 33,346

Seth Hockett Ellis (Union Reform)

Arkansas, 341 votes; Illinois, 672; Indiana, 254; Maryland, 142; Ohio, 4,284.

Total: 5,693

Alexander Hirschberg (Social Democrat)

Kentucky, 770* votes.

Jonah Fitz Randolph Leonard (United Christian)

Illinois, 352 votes; Iowa, 166.

Total: 518

Anti-Imperialist

Connecticut, 45 votes.

Scattered write-ins

Arkansas, 27 votes; Colorado, 26; Connecticut, 10; Louisiana, 4; Massachusetts, 533, New Hampshire, 16; Utah, 9; Vermont, 5; Wyoming, 21.

Total: 651

1904 Election

Thomas E. Watson (Populist)

Alabama, 5,051 votes; Arkansas, 2,326; Colorado, 824; Connecticut, 495; Delaware, 51; Florida, 1,605; Georgia, 22,635; Idaho, 352; Illinois, 6,725; Indiana, 2,444; Iowa, 2,207; Kansas, 6,253; Kentucky, 2,521; Maine, 337; Maryland, 1; Massachusetts, 1,294; Michigan, 1,145; Minnesota, 2,103; Mississippi, 1,499; Missouri, 4,226; Montana, 1,531; Nebraska, 20,518; Nevada, 344; New Hampshire, 82; New Jersey, 3,705; New York, 7,459; North Carolina, 819; North Dakota, 165*; Ohio, 1,392; Oregon, 746; South Dakota, 1,240; Tennessee, 2,491; Texas, 8,062; Washington, 669; West Virginia, 339; Wisconsin, 560.

Total: 114,216

Charles Hunter Corregan (Socialist Labor)

Colorado, 335 votes; Connecticut, 583; Illinois, 4,698; Indiana, 1,598; Kentucky, 596; Massachusetts, 2,359; Michigan, 1,018; Minnesota, 974; Missouri, 1,674; Montana, 213; New Jersey, 2,680*; New York, 9,122; Ohio, 2,635; Pennsylvania, 2,211; Rhode Island, 488; Texas, 431; Washington, 1,592; Wisconsin, 249.

Total: 33,456

Austin Holcomb (Continental)

Illinois, 826 votes.

Scattered write-ins

California, 333 votes; Connecticut, 11; Maryland, 4; Massachusetts, 5; New Hampshire, 1; Vermont, 1.

Total: 355

1908 Election

Thomas L. Hisgen (Independence)

Alabama, 497 votes; Arkansas, 286; California, 4,278; Connecticut, 728; Delaware, 29; Florida, 553; Georgia, 77*; Idaho, 124; Illinois, 7,724; Indiana, 514; Iowa, 404; Kansas, 68; Kentucky, 200; Louisiana, 77; Maine, 700; Maryland, 485; Massachusetts, 19,235; Michigan, 734; Minnesota, 429*; Missouri, 392; Montana, 493; Nevada, 436; New Hampshire, 584; New Jersey, 2,916; New York, 35,817; North Dakota, 43; Ohio, 439; Oregon, 289; Pennsylvania, 1,057; Rhode Island, 1,105; South Carolina, 46; South Dakota, 88; Tennessee, 332; Texas, 106; Utah, 92; Vermont, 804; Virginia, 51; Washington, 248; Wyoming, 63.

Total: 82,543

Thomas E. Watson (Populist)

Alabama, 1,576 votes; Arkansas, 987; Florida, 1,946; Georgia, 16,969*; Illinois, 633; Indiana, 1,193; Iowa, 261; Kentucky, 333; Mississippi, 1,276; Missouri, 1,165; Ohio, 162; Tennessee, 1,092; Texas, 960; Virginia, 105.

Total: 28,658

August Gillhaus (Socialist Labor)

Connecticut, 608 votes; Illinois, 1,680; Indiana, 643; Kentucky, 405; Massachusetts, 1,011; Michigan, 1,085; Missouri, 867; New Jersey, 1,196; New York, 3,877; Ohio, 721; Pennsylvania, 1,224; Rhode Island, 183; Texas, 175; Virginia, 25; Wisconsin, 318.

Total: 14,018

Daniel Braxton Turney (United Christian)

Illinois, 400 votes; Michigan, 61.

Republican (Davidson Faction)

Alabama, 987 votes.

Scattered write-ins

California, 28 votes; Colorado, 2; Connecticut, 4; Massachusetts, 9; New Hampshire, 8; North Carolina, 13; Vermont, 29; Wisconsin, 2.

Total: 95

1912 Election

Eugene W. Chafin (Prohibition)

Arizona, 265 votes; Arkansas, 908; California, 23,366; Colorado, 5,063; Connecticut, 2,068; Delaware, 620; Florida, 1,854; Georgia, 149; Idaho, 1,536; Illinois, 15,710; Indiana, 19,249; Iowa, 8,440; Kentucky, 3,233*; Maine, 947; Maryland, 2,244; Massachusetts, 2,753; Michigan, 8,794; Minnesota, 7,886; Missouri, 5,380; Montana, 32; Nebraska, 3,383; New Hampshire, 535; New Jersey, 2,936; New York, 19,455; North Carolina, 118; North Dakota, 1,243; Ohio, 11,511; Oklahoma, 2,195; Oregon, 4,360; Pennsylvania, 19,525; Rhode Island,

616; South Dakota, 3,910; Tennessee, 832; Texas, 1,701; Vermont, 1,094; Virginia, 709; Washington, 9,810; West Virginia, 4,517; Wisconsin, 8,584; Wyoming, 421.
Total: 207,952

Arthur E. Reimer (Socialist Labor)
Colorado, 475 votes; Connecticut, 1,260; Illinois, 4,066; Indiana, 3,130; Kentucky, 956*; Maryland, 322; Massachusetts, 1,102; Michigan, 1,239; Minnesota, 2,212; Missouri, 1,778; New Jersey, 1,396; New York, 4,273; Ohio, 2,630; Pennsylvania, 706; Rhode Island, 236; Texas, 430; Utah, 510; Virginia, 50; Washington, 1,872; Wisconsin, 632.
Total: 29,275

Scattered write-ins
Alabama, 5 votes; California, 4,417; Connecticut, 6; Kansas, 63; Massachusetts, 1; South Carolina, 55; Wisconsin, 9.
Total: 4,556

1916 Election

Arthur E. Reimer (Socialist Labor)
Connecticut, 606 votes; Illinois, 2,488; Indiana, 1,659; Iowa, 460; Kentucky, 332; Maryland, 756; Massachusetts, 1,096; Michigan, 831; Minnesota, 468; Missouri, 903; Nebraska, 624; New Jersey, 855; New York; 2,666; Pennsylvania, 419; Rhode Island, 180; Utah, 144; Virginia, 67; Washington, 730.
Total: 15,284

Progressive[3]
Colorado, 409 votes; Georgia, 20,653*; Indiana, 3,898; Iowa, 1,793; Kentucky, 129; Louisiana, 6,349; Minnesota, 290; Mississippi, 520; Montana, 338; Oklahoma, 234; Oregon, 310; South Carolina, 162; Utah, 110.
Total: 35,195

Scattered write-ins
California, 187 votes; Massachusetts, 6; South Carolina, 258; Vermont, 10.
Total: 461

1920 Election

Aaron Sherman Watkins (Prohibition)
Alabama, 766 votes; Arizona, 4; California, 25,204; Colorado, 2,807; Connecticut, 1,771; Delaware, 986; Florida, 5,127; Idaho, 34*; Illinois, 11,216; Indiana, 13,462; Iowa, 4,197; Kentucky, 3,250; Michigan, 9,646; Minnesota, 11,489; Missouri, 5,152; Nebraska, 5,947; New Jersey, 4,895; New York, 19,653; North Carolina, 17; Ohio, 294; Oregon, 3,595; Pennsylvania, 42,612; Rhode Island, 510; South Dakota, 900; Vermont, 774; Virginia, 826; Washington, 3,800; West Virginia, 1,526; Wisconsin, 8,648; Wyoming, 265.
Total: 189,373

James Edward Ferguson (American)
Texas, 48,098 votes.

William W. Cox (Socialist Labor)
Connecticut, 1,491 votes; Illinois, 3,471; Iowa, 982; Maryland, 1,178; Massachusetts, 3,583; Michigan, 2,539; Minnesota, 5,828; Missouri, 1,587; New Jersey, 1,010; New York, 4,841; Oregon, 1,515; Pennsylvania, 753; Rhode Island, 495; Washington, 1,321.
Total: 30,594

Robert Colvin Macauley (Single Tax)
Delaware, 39 votes; Illinois, 775; Indiana, 566; Maine, 310; Michigan, 484; New Jersey, 603; Ohio, 2,153; Pennsylvania, 803; Rhode Island, 100.
Total: 5,833

Black and Tan Republican
Texas, 27,309 votes.

Scattered write-ins
Louisiana, 339 votes; Maryland, 1; Massachusetts, 24; Nebraska, 90; New Mexico, 4; Vermont, 56.
Total: 514

1924 Election

Frank T. Johns (Socialist Labor)
Colorado, 378 votes; Connecticut, 1,373; Illinois, 2,334; Kentucky, 1,499*; Maine, 406; Maryland, 987; Massachusetts, 1,668; Michigan, 5,330; Minnesota, 1,855; Missouri, 1,066; New Jersey, 853;

New York, 9,928; Ohio, 3,025; Oregon, 917; Pennsylvania, 634; Rhode Island, 268; Virginia, 189; Washington, 1,004; Wisconsin, 458.
Total: 34,172

William Z. Foster (Communist)
Colorado, 562 votes; Illinois, 2,622; Indiana, 987; Iowa, 4,037; Massachusetts, 2,635; Minnesota, 4,427; Montana, 358; New Jersey, 1,560; New York, 8,244; North Dakota, 370; Pennsylvania, 2,735; Rhode Island, 289; Washington, 761; Wisconsin, 3,773.
Total: 33,360

Gilbert Owen Nations (American)
Florida, 2,319 votes; Georgia, 155; Kentucky, 1,299*; New Jersey, 368; Pennsylvania, 13,035; Tennessee, 100; Washington, 5,991; West Virginia, 1,072.
Total: 24,339

Robert M. La Follette (Socialist)
Oklahoma, 5,234* votes.

William J. Wallace (Commonwealth Land)
Delaware, 20 votes; Illinois, 421; Kentucky, 248*; Missouri, 165; New Jersey, 265; Ohio, 1,246, Pennsylvania, 296; Rhode Island, 38; Wisconsin, 271.
Total: 2,970

Scattered write-ins
Connecticut, 101 votes; Iowa, 445; Kansas, 4; Louisiana, 4,063; Pennsylvania, 131; South Carolina, 1; Vermont, 5.
Total: 4,752

1928 Election

Verne L. Reynolds (Socialist Labor)
Connecticut, 625 votes; Illinois, 1,812; Indiana, 645; Iowa, 230; Kentucky, 316; Maryland, 906; Massachusetts, 772; Michigan, 799; Minnesota, 1,921; Missouri, 342; New Jersey, 500; New York, 4,211; Ohio, 1,515; Oregon, 1,564; Pennsylvania, 382; Rhode Island, 416; Virginia, 181; Washington, 4,068; Wisconsin, 381.
Total: 21,586

William Frederick Varney (Prohibition)
Indiana, 5,496 votes; Michigan, 2,728; New Jersey, 160; Ohio, 3,556; Pennsylvania, 3,875; Vermont, 338; West Virginia, 1,703; Wisconsin, 2,245.
Total: 20,101

Frank Elbridge Webb (Farmer Labor)
Colorado, 1,092 votes; Iowa, 3,088; Oklahoma, 1,283; South Dakota, 927.
Total: 6,390

Scattered write-ins
California, 373 votes; Iowa, 2; Massachusetts, 4; Pennsylvania, 14; Vermont, 9.
Total: 420

1932 Election

William David Upshaw (Prohibition)
Alabama, 13 votes; California, 20,637; Colorado, 1,928; Georgia, 1,125; Illinois, 6,388; Indiana, 10,399; Iowa, 2,111; Kentucky, 2,252; Massachusetts, 1,142; Michigan, 2,893; Missouri, 2,429; New Jersey, 774; Ohio, 7,421; Pennsylvania, 11,319; Rhode Island, 183; South Dakota, 463; Tennessee, 1,998; Virginia, 1,843; Washington, 1,540; West Virginia, 2,342; Wisconsin, 2,672.
Total: 81,872

William Hope Harvey (Liberty)
Arkansas, 952 votes; California, 9,827; Idaho, 4,712; Michigan, 217; Montana, 1,449; New Mexico, 389; North Dakota, 1,817; South Dakota, 3,333; Texas, 324*; Washington, 30,308.
Total: 53,328

Verne L. Reynolds (Socialist Labor)
Colorado, 427 votes; Connecticut, 2,287; Illinois, 3,638; Indiana, 2,070; Kentucky, 1,393; Maine, 255; Maryland, 1,036; Massachusetts, 2,668; Michigan, 1,401; Minnesota, 770; Missouri, 404; New Jersey, 1,062; New York, 10,339; Ohio, 1,968; Oregon, 1,730; Pennsylvania, 659; Rhode Island, 433; Washington, 1,009; Wisconsin, 494.
Total: 34,043

Jacob S. Coxey (Farmer Labor)
Colorado, 469 votes; Iowa, 1,094; Michigan, 137; Minnesota, 5,731.
Total: 7,431

John Zahnd (National)
Indiana, 1,645 votes.
James R. Cox (Jobless)
Pennsylvania, 725 votes; Virginia, 15.
Total: 740.
Jacksonian
Texas, 104* votes.
Arizona Progressive Democrat
Arizona, 9 votes.
Scattered write-ins
California, 127 votes; Florida, 691; Iowa, 4; Louisiana, 533; Massachusetts, 71; Pennsylvania, 53; Texas, 34; Vermont, 2; Wisconsin, 13.
Total: 1,528

1936 Election

Earl Browder (Communist)
Alabama, 678 votes; Arkansas, 167; California, 10,877; Colorado, 497; Connecticut, 1,193; Delaware, 51; Illinois, 801; Indiana, 1,090; Iowa, 506; Kentucky, 207; Maine, 257; Maryland, 915; Massachusetts, 2,930; Michigan, 3,384; Minnesota, 2,574; Missouri, 417; Montana, 385; New Hampshire, 193; New Jersey, 1,639; New Mexico, 43; New York, 35,609; North Carolina, 11; North Dakota, 360; Ohio, 5,251; Oregon, 104; Pennsylvania, 4,060; Rhode Island, 411; Tennessee, 319*; Texas, 253*; Utah, 280; Vermont, 405; Virginia, 98; Washington, 1,907; Wisconsin, 2,197; Wyoming, 91.
Total: 80,160
D. Leigh Colvin (Prohibition)
Alabama, 719 votes; Arizona, 384; California, 12,917; Georgia, 660; Illinois, 3,439; Iowa, 1,182; Kentucky, 939; Maine, 334; Massachusetts, 1,032; Michigan, 579; Missouri, 908; Montana, 224; New Jersey, 926; New Mexico, 61; North Dakota, 197; Oklahoma, 1,328; Oregon, 4; Pennsylvania, 6,691; Tennessee, 632*; Texas, 514*; Utah, 43; Virginia, 594; Washington, 1,041; West Virginia, 1,173; Wisconsin, 1,071; Wyoming, 75.
Total: 37,667
John W. Aiken (Socialist Labor)
Colorado, 344 votes; Connecticut, 1,228; Illinois, 1,921; Iowa, 252, Kentucky, 294; Maine, 129; Maryland, 1,305; Massachusetts, 1,305; Michigan, 600; Minnesota, 961; Missouri, 292; New Jersey, 362; Ohio, 28; Oregon, 500; Pennsylvania, 1,424; Rhode Island, 929; Virginia, 36; Washington, 362; Wisconsin, 557.
Total: 12,829
Independent Republicans
Delaware, 3,222* votes.
William Dudley Pelley (Christian)
Washington, 1,598 votes.
Scattered write-ins
California, 490 votes; Florida, 71; Iowa, 4; Louisiana, 93; Massachusetts, 11; Michigan, 5; North Carolina, 6; Ohio, 7; Oregon, 108; Vermont, 137.
Total: 824

1940 Election

Earl Browder (Communist)
Alabama, 509 votes; California, 13,586; Colorado, 378; Connecticut, 1,091; Idaho, 276; Iowa, 1,524; Maine, 411; Maryland, 1,274; Massachusetts, 3,806; Michigan, 2,834; Minnesota, 2,711; Montana, 489; New Jersey, 6,508; Oregon, 191; Pennsylvania, 4,519; Rhode Island, 243; Texas, 212*; Utah, 191; Vermont, 411; Virginia, 72; Washington, 2,626; Wisconsin, 2,394.
Total: 46,256
John W. Aiken (Socialist Labor)
Connecticut, 971 votes; Indiana, 706; Iowa, 452; Maryland, 657; Massachusetts, 1,492; Michigan, 795; Minnesota, 2,553; Missouri, 209; New Jersey, 455; Oregon, 2,487; Pennsylvania, 1,518; Virginia, 48; Washington, 667; Wisconsin, 1,882.
Total: 14,892
Alfred Knutson (Independent)
North Dakota, 545 votes.

Scattered write-ins
California, 262 votes; Florida, 148; Georgia, 14; Illinois, 657; Louisiana, 108; Massachusetts, 12; Michigan, 4; Oregon, 40: Pennsylvania, 827; Vermont, 11.
Total: 2,083

1944 Election

Edward A. Teichert (Socialist Labor)
California, 180 votes; Connecticut, 1,220; Illinois, 9,677; Iowa, 193; Kentucky, 329; Maine, 335; Massachusetts, 2,780; Michigan, 1,264; Minnesota, 3,176; Missouri, 220; New Jersey, 6,939; New York, 14,352; Pennsylvania, 1,789; Virginia, 90; Washington, 1,645; Wisconsin, 1,002.
Total: 45,191
Gerald L. K. Smith (America First)
Michigan, 1,530 votes; Texas, 250.
Total: 1,780
Texas Regulars
Texas, 135,444 votes.
Southern Democrat
South Carolina, 7,799 votes.
Independent Democrat
Georgia, 3,373* votes.
Republican (Tobert faction)
South Carolina, 63* votes.
Scattered write-ins
California, 1,881 votes; Florida, 211; Louisiana, 69; Massachusetts, 266; Michigan, 6; Vermont, 14.
Total: 2,447

1948 Election

Norman M. Thomas (Socialist)
Arkansas, 1,037 votes; California, 3,459; Colorado, 1,678; Connecticut, 6,964; Delaware, 250; Georgia, 3; Idaho, 332; Illinois, 11,522; Indiana, 2,179; Iowa, 1,829; Kansas, 2,807; Kentucky, 1,284; Maine, 547; Maryland, 2,941; Michigan, 6,063; Minnesota, 4,646; Missouri, 2,222; Montana, 695; New Hampshire, 86; New Jersey, 10,521; New Mexico, 83; New York, 40,879; North Dakota, 1,000; Oregon, 5,051; Pennsylvania, 11,325; Rhode Island, 429; South Carolina, 1; Tennessee, 1,288; Texas, 874*; Vermont, 585; Virginia, 726; Washington, 3,534; Wisconsin, 12,547; Wyoming, 137.
Total: 139,524
Claude A. Watson (Prohibition)
Alabama, 1,085 votes; Arizona, 786; Arkansas, 1; California, 16,926; Delaware, 343; Georgia, 732; Idaho, 628; Illinois, 11,959; Indiana, 14,711; Iowa, 3,382; Kansas, 6,468; Kentucky, 1,245; Massachusetts, 1,663; Michigan, 13,052; Montana, 429; New Jersey, 10,593; New Mexico, 127; Pennsylvania, 10,538; Texas, 2,758*; Washington, 6,117.
Total: 103,543
Edward A. Teichert (Socialist Labor)
Arizona, 121 votes; California, 195; Colorado, 214; Connecticut, 1,184; Delaware, 29; Illinois, 3,118; Indiana, 763; Iowa, 4,274; Kentucky, 185; Maine, 206; Massachusetts, 5,535; Michigan, 1,263; Minnesota, 2,525; New Hampshire, 83; New Jersey, 3,354; New Mexico, 49; New York, 2,729; Pennsylvania, 1,461; Rhode Island, 131; Virginia, 234; Washington, 1,133; Wisconsin, 399; Wyoming, 56.
Total: 29,241
Farrell Dobbs (Socialist Workers)
California, 133 votes; Colorado, 228; Connecticut, 606; Iowa, 256; Michigan, 672; Minnesota, 606; New Jersey, 5,825; New York, 2,675; Pennsylvania, 2,133; Utah, 74; Washington, 103; Wisconsin, 303.
Total: 13,614
Scattered write-ins
California, 813 votes; Georgia, 1; Illinois, 1,629; Louisiana, 10; Massachusetts, 633; Michigan, 1; Missouri, 54; Nebraska, 1; New York, 128; Pennsylvania, 107; Vermont, 35.
Total: 3,412

1952 Election

Eric Hass (Socialist Labor)
Arkansas, 1 vote; California, 273; Colorado, 352; Connecticut, 535; Delaware, 242; Illinois, 9,363; Indiana, 840; Iowa, 139; Kentucky, 893; Maine, 156; Massachusetts, 1,957; Michigan, 1,495; Minnesota, 2,383; Missouri, 169; New Jersey, 5,815; New Mexico, 35; New York, 1,560; Pennsylvania, 1,377; Rhode Island, 83; Virginia, 1,160; Washington, 633; Wisconsin, 770; Wyoming, 36.
Total: 30,267

Darlington Hoopes (Socialist)
California, 206 votes; Colorado, 365; Connecticut, 2,244; Delaware, 20; Iowa, 219; Kansas, 530; Maine, 138; Missouri, 227; Montana, 159; New Jersey, 8,593; New York, 2,664; Pennsylvania, 2,698; Vermont, 185; Virginia, 504; Washington, 254; Wisconsin, 1,157; Wyoming, 40.
Total: 20,203

Douglas MacArthur (Constitution)[4]
Arkansas, 458 votes; California, 3,504; Colorado, 2,181; Missouri, 535; New Mexico; 220; North Dakota, 1,075; Tennessee, 379; Texas, 1,563; Washington, 7,290.
Total: 17,205

Farrell Dobbs (Socialist Workers)
Michigan, 655 votes; Minnesota, 618; New Jersey, 3,850; New York, 2,212; Pennsylvania, 1,508; Washington, 119; Wisconsin, 1,350.
Total: 10,312

Henry Krajewski (Poor Man's)
New Jersey, 4,203 votes.

Independent Republican
South Carolina, 158,289* votes.

Scattered write-ins
California, 3,249 votes; Connecticut, 5; Florida, 351; Georgia, 1; Idaho, 23; Illinois, 448; Iowa, 29; Maine, 1; Massachusetts, 69; Michigan, 3; New York, 178; Pennsylvania, 155; Vermont, 18.
Total: 4,530

1956 Election

Enoch A. Holtwick (Prohibition)
California, 11,119 votes; Delaware, 400; Indiana, 6,554; Kansas, 3,048; Kentucky, 2,145; Massachusetts, 1,205; Michigan, 6,923; New Jersey, 9,147; New Mexico, 607; Tennessee, 789.
Total: 41,937

Farrell Dobbs (Socialist Workers)
California, 96 votes; Minnesota, 1,098; New Jersey, 4,004; Pennsylvania, 2,035; Wisconsin, 564.
Total: 7,797

Harry F. Byrd (States' Rights)
Kentucky, 2,657 votes.

Darlington Hoopes (Socialist)
California, 123 votes; Colorado, 531; Iowa, 192; New York, 82; Virginia, 444; Wisconsin, 754.
Total: 2,126

Henry Krajewski (American Third Party)
New Jersey, 1,829 votes.

Gerald L. K. Smith (Christian Nationalist)
California, 8 votes.

Independent Electors
Alabama, 20,323 votes; Louisiana, 44,520; Mississippi, 42,966; South Carolina, 88,509.
Total: 196,318

Scattered write-ins
California, 819 votes; Connecticut, 205; Florida, 1,542; Georgia, 93; Idaho, 16; Illinois, 56; Maryland, 476; Massachusetts, 341; New York, 1,262; Oregon, 535; Vermont, 39.
Total: 5,384

1960 Election

Rutherford L. Decker (Prohibition)
Alabama, 2,106 votes; California, 21,706; Delaware, 284; Indiana, 6,746; Kansas, 4,138; Massachusetts, 1,633; Michigan, 2,029; Montana, 456; New Mexico, 777; Tennessee, 2,458; Texas, 3,870.
Total: 46,203

Orval E. Faubus (National States' Rights)
Alabama, 4,367 votes; Arkansas, 28,952; Delaware, 354; Tennessee, 11,296.
Total: 44,977

Farrell Dobbs (Socialist Workers)
Colorado, 562 votes; Iowa, 634; Michigan, 4,347; Minnesota, 3,077; Montana, 391; New Jersey, 11,402; New York, 14,319; North Dakota, 158; Pennsylvania, 2,678; Utah, 100; Washington, 705; Wisconsin, 1,792.
Total: 40,165

Charles L. Sullivan (Constitutional)
Texas, 18,162 votes.

J. Bracken Lee (Conservative)
New Jersey, 8,708 votes.

C. Benton Coiner (Virginia Conservative)
Virginia, 4,204 votes.

Lar Daly (Tax Cut)
Michigan, 1,767 votes.

Clennon King (Independent Afro-American Unity)
Alabama, 1,485 votes.

Merritt B. Curtis (Constitution)
Washington, 1,401 votes.

Independent Electors
Louisiana, 169,572 votes; Michigan, 539.
Total: 170,111

Scattered write-ins
Alabama, 236 votes; Connecticut, 15; Georgia, 239; Illinois, 15; Maryland, 3; Massachusetts, 31; Oregon, 959; Pennsylvania, 440; South Carolina, 1; Texas, 175; Vermont, 7.
Total: 2,378

1964 Election

E. Harold Munn (Prohibition)
California, 305 votes; Colorado, 1,356; Delaware, 425; Indiana, 8,266; Iowa, 1,902; Kansas, 5,393; Massachusetts, 3,735; Michigan, 669; Montana, 499; New Mexico, 543; North Dakota, 174.
Total: 23,267

John Kasper (National States' Rights)
Arkansas, 2,965 votes; Kentucky, 3,469; Montana, 519.
Total: 6,953

Joseph B. Lightburn (Constitution)
Texas, 5,060 votes.

James Hensley (Universal Party)
California, 19 votes.

Unpledged Democrat
Alabama, 210,732 votes.

Scattered write-ins
Alabama, 1 vote; California, 5,410; Connecticut, 1,313; Georgia, 195; Illinois, 62; Iowa, 118; Maryland, 50; Massachusetts, 159; Michigan, 145; New York, 268; Oregon, 2,509; Pennsylvania, 2,531; Rhode Island, 13; South Carolina, 8; Tennessee, 34; Vermont, 20.
Total: 12,868

1968 Election

Dick Gregory (Freedom and Peace)
California, 3,230 votes; Colorado, 1,393; Indiana, 36; New Jersey, 8,084; New York, 24,517; Ohio, 372; Pennsylvania, 7,821; Virginia, 1,680.
Total: 47,133

Fred Halstead (Socialist Workers)
Arizona, 85 votes; Colorado, 235; Indiana, 1,293; Iowa, 3,377; Kentucky, 2,843; Michigan, 4,099; Minnesota, 807; Montana, 457; New Hampshire, 104; New Jersey, 8,667; New Mexico, 252; New York, 11,851; North Dakota, 128; Ohio, 69; Pennsylvania, 4,862; Rhode Island, 383; Utah, 89; Vermont, 295; Washington, 270; Wisconsin, 1,222.
Total: 41,388

Eldridge Cleaver (Peace and Freedom)
Arizona, 217 votes; California, 27,707; Iowa, 1,332; Michigan, 4,585; Minnesota, 933; Utah, 180; Washington, 1,609.
Total: 36,563

Eugene J. McCarthy

Arizona, 2,751 votes; California, 20,721; Minnesota, 584; Oregon, 1,496.

Total: 25,552

E. Harold Munn (Prohibition)

Alabama, 4,022 votes; California, 59; Colorado, 275; Indiana, 4,616; Iowa, 362; Kansas, 2,192; Massachusetts, 2,369; Michigan, 60; Montana, 510; North Dakota, 38; Ohio, 19; Virginia, 601.

Total: 15,123

Ventura Chavez (People's Constitution)

New Mexico, 1,519 votes.

Charlene Mitchell (Communist)

California, 260 votes; Minnesota, 415; Ohio, 23; Washington, 377.

Total: 1,075

James Hensley (Universal)

Iowa, 142 votes.

Richard K. Troxell (Constitution)

North Dakota, 34 votes.

Kent M. Soeters (Berkeley Defense Group)

California, 17 votes.

American Independent Democrat

Alabama, 10,960 votes.

New Party

New Hampshire, 421 votes; Vermont, 579.

Total: 1,000

New Reform

Montana, 470 votes.

Scattered write-ins

Alabama, 13 votes; Colorado, 948; Connecticut, 1,300; Georgia, 165; Illinois, 325; Iowa, 250; Massachusetts, 53; Michigan, 29; Minnesota, 170; New Hampshire, 108; New Mexico, 69; New York, 1,622; Oregon, 1,144; Pennsylvania, 2,264; Rhode Island, 62; Texas, 299; Vermont, 29; Wisconsin, 2,342.

Total: 11,192

1972 Election

Louis Fisher (Socialist Labor)

California, 197 votes; Colorado, 4,361; Georgia, 3; Illinois, 12,344; Indiana, 1,688; Iowa, 195; Massachusetts, 129; Michigan, 2,437; Minnesota, 4,261; New Jersey, 4,544; New York, 4,530; Ohio, 7,107; Virginia, 9,918; Washington, 1,102; Wisconsin, 998.

Total: 53,814

Linda Jenness (Socialist Workers)

Arizona, 366 votes; California, 574; Colorado, 666; District of Columbia, 316; Idaho, 397; Iowa, 488; Kentucky, 685; Louisiana, 14,398; Massachusetts, 10,600; Michigan, 1,603; Minnesota, 940; Mississippi, 2,458; New Hampshire, 368; New Jersey, 2,233; New Mexico, 474; North Dakota, 288; Pennsylvania, 4,639; Rhode Island, 729; South Dakota, 994; Texas, 8,664; Vermont, 296; Washington, 623.

Total: 52,799

Gus Hall (Communist)

California, 373 votes; Colorado, 432; District of Columbia, 252; Illinois, 4,541; Iowa, 272; Kentucky, 464; Massachusetts, 46; Michigan, 1,210; Minnesota, 662; New Jersey, 1,263; New York, 5,641; North Dakota, 87; Ohio, 6,437; Pennsylvania, 2,686; Washington, 566; Wisconsin, 663.

Total: 25,595

Evelyn Reed (Socialist Workers)

Indiana, 5,575 votes; New York, 7,797; Wisconsin, 506.

Total: 13,878

E. Harold Munn (Prohibition)

Alabama, 8,559 votes; California, 53; Colorado, 467; Delaware, 238; Kansas, 4,188.

Total: 13,505

John Hospers (Libertarian)

California, 980 votes; Colorado, 1,111; Massachusetts, 43; Rhode Island, 2; Washington, 1,537.

Total: 3,673

John V. Mahalchik (America First)

New Jersey, 1,743 votes.

Gabriel Green (Universal)

California, 21 votes; Iowa, 199.

Total: 220

Scattered write-ins

Colorado, 6 votes; Connecticut, 777; Florida, 7,407; Georgia, 2,932; Illinois, 2,229; Iowa, 321; Massachusetts, 342; Minnesota, 962; Missouri, 4,804; New Hampshire, 142; New Mexico, 310; New York, 4,089; Ohio, 460; Oregon, 2,289; Pennsylvania, 2,716; Rhode Island, 19; South Carolina, 17; Tennessee, 369; Texas, 3,393; Vermont, 318; Wisconsin, 893.

Total: 34,795

1976 Election

Lester Maddox (American Independent)

Alabama, 9,198 votes; Arizona, 85; California, 51,098; Connecticut, 7,101; Georgia, 1,071; Idaho, 5,935; Kansas, 2,118; Kentucky, 2,328; Louisiana, 10,058; Maine, 8; Maryland, 171; Mississippi, 4,861; Nebraska, 3,380; Nevada, 1,497; New Jersey, 7,716; New Mexico, 31; New York, 97; North Dakota, 269; Ohio, 15,529; Pennsylvania, 25,344; Rhode Island, 1; South Carolina, 1,950; Tennessee, 2,303; Texas, 41; Utah, 1,162; Washington, 8,585; West Virginia, 12; Wisconsin, 8,552; Wyoming; 30.

Total: 170,531

Thomas J. Anderson (American)

Alabama, 70 votes; Arizona, 564; Arkansas, 389; California, 4,565; Colorado, 397; Connecticut, 155; Delaware, 645; Florida, 21,325; Georgia, 1,168; Idaho, 493; Illinois, 387; Indiana, 14,048; Iowa, 3,040; Kansas, 4,724; Kentucky, 8,308; Maine, 28; Maryland, 321; Massachusetts, 7,555; Minnesota, 13,592; Mississippi, 6,678; Montana, 5,772; New Mexico, 106; New York, 451; North Carolina, 5,607; North Dakota, 3,796; Oregon, 1,035; Rhode Island, 24; South Carolina, 2,996; Tennessee, 5,769; Texas, 11,442; Utah, 13,284; Virginia, 16,686; Washington, 5,046; West Virginia, 17; Wyoming, 290.

Total: 160,773

Peter Camejo (Socialist Workers)

Alabama, 1 vote; Arizona, 928; California, 17,259; Colorado, 1,126; Connecticut, 42; District of Columbia, 545; Georgia, 43; Idaho, 14; Illinois, 3,615; Indiana, 5,695; Iowa, 267; Kentucky, 350; Louisiana, 2,240; Maine, 1; Maryland, 261; Massachusetts, 8,138; Michigan, 1,804; Minnesota, 4,149; Mississippi, 2,805; New Hampshire, 161; New Jersey, 1,184; New Mexico, 2,462; New York, 6,996; North Dakota, 43; Ohio, 4,717; Pennsylvania, 3,009; Rhode Island, 462; South Carolina, 8; South Dakota, 168; Texas, 1,723; Utah, 268; Vermont, 430; Virginia, 17,802; Washington, 905; West Virginia, 2; Wisconsin, 1,691.

Total: 91,314

Gus Hall (Communist)

Alabama, 1,954 votes; California, 12,766; Colorado, 403; Connecticut, 186; District of Columbia, 219; Georgia, 3; Idaho, 5; Illinois, 9,250; Iowa, 554; Kentucky, 426; Louisiana, 7,417; Maine, 14; Maryland, 68; Minnesota, 1,092; New Jersey, 1,662; New Mexico, 19; New York, 10,270; North Dakota, 84; Ohio, 7,817; Pennsylvania, 1,891; Rhode Island, 334; South Carolina, 1; South Dakota, 318; Tennessee, 547; Utah, 121; Washington, 817; West Virginia, 5; Wisconsin, 749.

Total: 58,992

Margaret Wright (People's Party)

California, 41,731 votes; Connecticut, 1; Idaho, 1; Maryland, 8; Massachusetts, 33; Michigan, 3,504; Minnesota, 635; New Jersey, 1,044; Washington, 1,124; Wisconsin, 943.

Total: 49,024

Lyndon H. LaRouche Jr. (U.S. Labor)

Alabama, 1 vote; Colorado, 567; Connecticut, 1,789; Delaware, 136; District of Columbia, 157; Georgia, 1; Idaho, 739; Illinois, 2,018; Indiana, 1,947; Iowa, 241; Kentucky, 510; Maryland, 21; Massachusetts, 4,922; Michigan, 1,366; Minnesota, 543; New Hampshire, 186; New Jersey, 1,650; New Mexico, 1; New York, 5,413; North Carolina, 755; North Dakota, 142; Ohio, 4,335; Pennsylvania, 2,744; South Carolina, 2; Tennessee, 512; Vermont, 196; Virginia, 7,508; Washington, 903; Wisconsin, 738.

Total: 40,043

Benjamin C. Bubar (Prohibition)

Alabama, 6,669 votes; California, 34; Colorado, 2,882; Delaware, 103; Kansas, 1,403; Maine, 3,495; Maryland, 2; Massachusetts, 14; New Jersey, 554; New Mexico, 211; North Dakota, 63; Ohio, 62; Tennessee, 442.

Total: 15,934

Jules Levin (Socialist Labor)

California, 222 votes; Colorado, 14; Connecticut, 1; Delaware, 86; Florida, 19; Georgia, 2; Illinois, 2,422; Iowa, 167; Maine, 1; Maryland, 7; Massachusetts, 19; Michigan, 1,148; Minnesota, 370; New Hampshire, 66; New Jersey, 3,686; New York, 28; Ohio, 68; Rhode Island, 188; Washington, 713; Wisconsin, 389.

Total: 9,616

Frank P. Zeidler (Socialist)

Connecticut, 5 votes; Florida, 8; Georgia, 2; Idaho, 2; Iowa, 234; Maryland, 16; Minnesota, 354; New Jersey, 469; New Mexico, 240; New York, 14; North Dakota, 38; Washington, 358; Wisconsin, 4,298.

Total: 6,038

Ernest L. Miller (Restoration)

California, 26 votes; Colorado, 6; Florida, 2; Georgia, 3; Maryland, 8; Tennessee, 316.

Total: 361

Frank Taylor (United American)

Arizona, 22 votes; California, 14.

Total: 36

Scattered write-ins

Alabama, 137 votes; Alaska, 1,176; California, 74; Colorado, 2; Connecticut, 1,122; District of Columbia, 1,944, 1.2; Georgia, 847; Idaho, 1,430; Illinois, 1,662; Iowa, 506; Maine, 185; Maryland, 1,945; Massachusetts, 1,354; Michigan, 2,160; Minnesota, 342; Missouri, 3,741; Nevada, 5,108 (none of the above), 2.5; New Hampshire, 604; New Mexico, 501; New York, 4,052; North Carolina, 228; Oregon, 6,107; Pennsylvania, 2,934; Rhode Island, 82; South Carolina, 328; Tennessee, 229; Texas, 2,752; Vermont, 99; West Virginia, 125; Wisconsin, 2,839; Wyoming, 354.

Total: 44,969

1980 Election

Barry Commoner (Citizens)

Alabama, 517 votes; Arizona, 551; Arkansas, 2,345; California, 61,063; Colorado, 5,614; Connecticut, 6,130; Delaware, 103; District of Columbia, 1,840; Georgia, 104; Hawaii, 1,548; Illinois, 10,692; Indiana, 4,852; Iowa, 2,273; Kentucky, 1,304; Louisiana, 1,584; Maine, 4,394; Massachusetts, 2,056; Michigan, 11,930; Minnesota, 8,407; Missouri, 573; New Hampshire, 1,320; New Jersey, 8,203; New Mexico, 2,202; New York, 23,186; North Carolina, 2,287; North Dakota, 429; Ohio, 8,564; Oregon, 13,642; Pennsylvania, 10,430; Rhode Island, 67; Tennessee, 1,112; Texas, 453; Utah, 1,009; Vermont, 2,316; Virginia, 14,024; Washington, 9,403; Wisconsin, 7,767.

Total: 234,294

Gus Hall (Communist)

Alabama, 1,629 votes; Arizona, 25; Arkansas, 1,244; California, 847; Colorado, 487; Delaware, 13; District of Columbia, 371; Florida, 123; Hawaii, 458; Illinois, 9,711; Indiana, 702; Iowa, 298; Kansas, 967; Kentucky, 348; Maine, 591; Michigan, 3,262; Minnesota, 1,184; Missouri, 26; New Hampshire, 129; New Jersey, 2,555; New York, 7,414; North Dakota, 93; Pennsylvania, 5,184; Rhode Island, 218; Tennessee, 503; Texas, 49; Utah, 139; Vermont, 118; Washington, 834; Wisconsin, 772.

Total: 45,023

John R. Rarick (American Independent)

Alabama, 15,010 votes; California, 9,856; Idaho, 1,057; Kansas, 789; Louisiana, 10,333; Michigan, 5; South Carolina, 2,177; Utah, 522; Wisconsin, 1,519.

Total: 41,268

Clifton DeBerry (Socialist Workers)

Alabama, 1,303 votes; Arizona, 1,100; District of Columbia, 173; Florida, 41; Illinois, 1,302; Indiana, 610; Iowa, 244; Louisiana, 783; Massachusetts, 3,735*; Minnesota, 711; Missouri, 1,515; New Hampshire, 71; New York, 2,068; North Carolina, 416; North Dakota, 89; Pennsylvania, 20,291; Rhode Island, 90; Tennessee, 490; Utah, 124; Vermont, 75; Virginia, 1,986; Washington, 1,137.

Total: 37,329

Ellen McCormack (Right to Life)

Delaware, 3 votes; Kentucky, 4,233; Missouri, 5; New Jersey, 3,927; New York, 24,159; Rhode Island, 1.

Total: 32,327

Maureen Smith (Peace and Freedom)

California, 18,116 votes.

Deirdre Griswold (Workers World)

California, 15 votes; Delaware, 3; District of Columbia, 52; Florida, 8; Georgia, 1; Illinois, 2,257; Massachusetts, 19; Michigan, 30; Minnesota, 698; Mississippi, 2,402; New Hampshire, 76; New Jersey,

1,288; Ohio, 3,790; Rhode Island, 77; Tennessee, 400; Texas, 11; Washington, 341; Wisconsin, 414.

Total: 13,300

Benjamin C. Bubar (Statesman)

Alabama, 1,743 votes; Arkansas, 1,350; California, 36; Colorado, 1,180; Delaware, 6; Iowa, 150; Kansas, 821; Massachusetts, 34; Michigan, 9; New Mexico, 1,281; North Dakota, 54; Ohio, 27; Tennessee, 521.

Total: 7,212

David McReynolds (Socialist)

Alabama, 1,006 votes; Florida, 116; Iowa, 534; Massachusetts, 62; Minnesota, 536; New Jersey, 1,973; North Dakota, 82; Rhode Island, 170; Tennessee, 519; Vermont, 136; Washington, 956; Wisconsin, 808.

Total: 6,898

Percy L. Greaves (American)

California, 87 votes, Delaware, 400; Indiana, 4,750; Iowa, 189; Michigan, 21; North Dakota, 235; Utah, 965.

Total: 6,647

Andrew Pulley (Socialist Workers)

California, 231 votes; Colorado, 520; Delaware, 4; Georgia, 4; Kentucky, 393; Mississippi, 2,347; New Jersey, 2,198; New Mexico, 325; South Dakota, 250.

Total: 6,272

Richard Congress (Socialist Workers)

Ohio, 4,029 votes.

Kurt Lynen (Middle Class)

New Jersey, 3,694 votes.

Bill Gahres (Down With Lawyers)

New Jersey, 1,718 votes.

Frank W. Shelton (American)

Kansas, 1,555 votes.

Martin E. Wendelken (Independent)

New Jersey, 923 votes.

Harley McLain (Natural Peoples League)

North Dakota, 296 votes.

Scattered write-ins

Alaska, 857 votes; California, 1,242; Connecticut, 836; Delaware, 101; District of Columbia, 690; Georgia, 112; Illinois, 604; Iowa, 519; Maine, 84; Massachusetts, 2,382; Michigan, 891; Minnesota, 6,139 (American Party, with no candidate specified); Missouri, 604; Nevada, 4,193 (none of the above); New Hampshire, 68; New Mexico, 734; New York, 1,064; Oregon, 1,713; Rhode Island, 37; South Carolina, 376; Tennessee, 152; Vermont, 413; Wisconsin, 1,337.

Total: 23,517

1984 Election

Sonia Johnson (Citizens)

Arizona, 18 votes; Arkansas, 960; California, 26,297; Colorado, 23; Connecticut, 14; Delaware, 121; Florida, 58; Georgia, 4; Illinois, 2,716; Kentucky, 599; Louisiana, 9,502; Massachusetts, 18; Michigan, 1,191; Minnesota, 1,219; Missouri, 2; New Jersey, 1,247; New Mexico, 455; North Dakota, 368; Pennsylvania, 21,628; Rhode Island, 240; Tennessee, 978; Texas, 87; Utah, 844; Vermont, 264; Washington, 1,891; Wisconsin, 1,456.

Total: 72,200

Bob Richards (Populist)

Alabama, 1,401 votes; Arkansas, 1,461; California, 39,265; Georgia, 95; Idaho, 2,288; Kansas, 3,564; Louisiana, 1,310; Minnesota, 2,377; Mississippi, 641; North Dakota, 1,077; Rhode Island, 10; Tennessee, 1,763; Washington, 5,724; West Virginia, 996; Wisconsin, 3,864.

Total: 66,336

Dennis L. Serrette (Independent Alliance)

Alabama, 659 votes; Arkansas, 1,291; California, 16; Colorado, 978; Connecticut, 1,374; Delaware, 68; District of Columbia, 165; Georgia, 2; Illinois, 2,386; Iowa, 463; Kansas, 2,544; Kentucky, 365; Louisiana, 533; Maine, 755; Maryland, 656; Massachusetts, 7,998; Michigan, 665; Minnesota, 232; Mississippi, 356; Nebraska, 1,025; New Hampshire, 305; New Jersey, 2,293; New Mexico, 155; New York, 3,200; North Dakota, 152; Ohio, 12,090; Rhode Island, 49; South Carolina, 682; South Dakota, 1,150; Tennessee, 524; Texas, 41;

Utah, 220; Vermont, 323; Washington, 1,654; West Virginia, 493; Wisconsin, 1,006.
  Total: 46,868

Gus Hall (Communist)
  Alabama, 4,671 votes; Arkansas, 1,499; Connecticut, 4,826; District of Columbia, 257; Georgia, 1; Hawaii, 821; Illinois, 4,672; Iowa, 286; Kentucky, 328; Maine, 1,292; Maryland, 898; Michigan, 1,048; Minnesota, 630; New Jersey, 1,564; New York, 4,226; North Dakota, 169; Ohio, 4,438; Pennsylvania, 1,780; Rhode Island, 75; Tennessee, 1,036; Texas, 126; Utah, 184; Vermont, 115; Washington, 814; Wisconsin, 596.
  Total: 36,386

Mel Mason (Socialist Workers)
  Alabama, 730 votes; Colorado, 810; District of Columbia, 127; Florida, 7; Georgia, 10; Illinois, 2,132; Iowa, 313; Kentucky, 3,129; Louisiana, 1,164; Michigan, 1,049; Minnesota, 3,180; Mississippi, 1,032; Missouri, 8; Nebraska, 1,066; New Jersey, 1,264; New Mexico, 224; North Carolina, 799; North Dakota, 239; Ohio, 4,344; Rhode Island, 61; South Dakota, 337; Tennessee, 715; Utah, 142; Vermont, 127; Washington, 608; West Virginia, 645; Wisconsin, 444.
  Total: 24,706

Larry Holmes (Workers World)
  District of Columbia, 107 votes; Georgia, 2; Maryland, 745; Michigan, 1,416; Mississippi, 1,169; New Jersey, 8,404; New York, 2,226; Washington, 641; Wisconsin, 619.
  Total: 15,329

Delmar Dennis (American)
  Delaware, 269 votes; Georgia, 4; Indiana, 7,617; Kentucky, 428; Missouri, 1; South Carolina, 3,490; Tennessee, 7; Utah, 1,345.
  Total: 13,161

Ed Winn (Workers League)
  Arizona, 3 votes; Illinois, 2,632 ; Michigan, 561; Minnesota, 260; New Jersey, 1,721; Ohio, 3,565; Pennsylvania, 2,059.
  Total: 10,801

Earl F. Dodge (Prohibition)
  Arkansas, 842 votes; Colorado, 858; Kansas, 2,109; Massachusetts, 3; New Mexico, 206; North Dakota, 220; Ohio, 4.
  Total: 4,242

Gavrielle Holmes (Workers World)
  Ohio, 2,565 votes; Rhode Island, 91.
  Total: 2,656

John B. Anderson (National Unity Party of Kentucky)
  Georgia, 3 votes; Kentucky, 1,479; Tennessee, 4.
  Total: 1,486

Gerald Baker (Big Deal)
  Iowa, 892 votes.

Arthur J. Lowery (United Sovereign Citizens)
  Arkansas, 822 votes; Georgia, 3.
  Total: 825

Scattered write-ins
  Alaska, 843 votes; Arizona, 21; California, 366; Connecticut, 8; District of Columbia, 809; Florida, 32; Georgia, 460; Illinois, 862; Iowa, 1,051; Maine, 82; Massachusetts, 892; Michigan, 602; Minnesota, 723; Montana, 1; Nevada, 3,950 (none of the above); New Hampshire, 113; New Mexico, 1; New York, 837; Ohio, 34; Oregon, 4,348; Rhode Island, 3; Tennessee, 117; Vermont, 712; Wisconsin, 706.
  Total: 17,573

1988 Election

David E. Duke (Populist)
  Arizona, 113 votes; Arkansas, 5,146; California, 483; Colorado, 139; Florida, 249; Iowa, 755; Kentucky, 4,494; Louisiana, 18,612; Michigan, 60; Minnesota, 1,529; Mississippi, 4,232; Missouri, 44; New Jersey, 2,446; Oregon, 90; Pennsylvania, 3,444; Rhode Island, 159; Tennessee, 1,807; Vermont, 189; Wisconsin, 3,056.
  Total: 47,047

Eugene J. McCarthy (Consumer)
  Arizona, 159 votes; California, 234; Michigan, 2,497; Minnesota, 5,403; New Jersey, 3,454; Pennsylvania, 19,158.
  Total: 30,905

James C. Griffin (American Independent)
  California, 27,818 votes.

Lyndon H. LaRouche Jr. (National Economic Recovery)
  Alaska, 816 votes; Hawaii, 470; Iowa, 3,526; Louisiana, 1,958; Minnesota, 1,702; North Dakota, 905; Ohio, 7,733; Tennessee, 873; Utah, 427; Vermont, 275; Washington, 4,412; Wisconsin, 2,302; District of Columbia, 163.
  Total: 25,562

William A. Marra (Right to Life)
  Connecticut, 7 votes; New York, 20,497.
  Total: 20,504

Ed Winn (Workers League)
  Alabama, 461 votes; Illinois, 7,021; Iowa, 235; Michigan, 1,958; Minnesota, 489; New Jersey, 691; New York, 10; Ohio, 5,432; Pennsylvania, 2,188; District of Columbia, 208.
  Total: 18,693

James Warren (Socialist Workers)
  Alabama, 656 votes; Iowa, 205; Michigan, 819; Minnesota, 2,155; New Jersey, 2,298; New Mexico, 344; New York, 3,287 0.1; North Dakota, 347; Rhode Island, 130; South Dakota, 226; Tennessee, 718; Texas, 110; Utah, 209; Vermont, 113; Washington, 1,290; Wisconsin, 2,574; District of Columbia, 123.
  Total: 15,604

Herbert Lewin (Peace and Freedom)
  California, 58 votes; New Jersey, 9,953; Rhode Island, 195; Vermont, 164.
  Total: 10,370

Earl F. Dodge (Prohibition)
  Arkansas, 1,319 votes; Colorado, 4,604; Massachusetts, 18; Michigan, 5; New Mexico, 249; Tennessee, 1,807.
  Total: 8,002

Larry Holmes (Workers World)
  California, 11 votes; Michigan, 804; New Jersey, 1,020; New Mexico, 258; New York 4,179; Ohio, 134; Washington, 1,440.
  Total: 7,846

Willa Kenoyer (Socialist)
  Florida, 14 votes; Iowa, 334; Massachusetts, 15; New Jersey, 2,587; New York, 3; Rhode Island, 96; Tennessee, 358; Texas, 62; Utah, 129; Vermont, 142; District of Columbia, 142.
  Total: 3,882

Delmar Dennis (American)
  Arizona, 18 votes; Minnesota, 1,298; Missouri, 1; Utah, 2,158.
  Total: 3,475

Jack E. Herer (Grassroots)
  Minnesota, 1,949 votes.

Louie G. Youngkeit (Independent)
  Utah, 372 votes.

John G. Martin (Third World Assembly)
  District of Columbia, 236 votes.

Scattered write-ins
  Alabama, 506 votes; Alaska, 957; California, 25; Florida, 13; Georgia, 15; Iowa, 1,613; Maine, 230; Maryland, 24; Massachusetts, 2,910; Michigan, 902; Minnesota, 3,614; Missouri, 6; Nevada, 6,934 (none of the above); New Hampshire, 549; New Mexico, 93; Ohio, 216; Oregon, 3,974; Rhode Island, 51; Tennessee, 285; Texas, 98; Vermont, 1,134; Wisconsin, 2,273; District of Columbia, 1,553.
  Total: 27,975

1992 Election

James "Bo" Gritz (Populist)
  Alaska, 1,379 votes; Arizona, 8,141; Arkansas, 819; California, 3,077; Colorado, 274; Connecticut, 72; Delaware, 9; Georgia, 78; Hawaii, 1,452; Idaho, 10,281; Illinois, 3,577; Indiana, 1,467; Iowa, 1,177; Kansas, 79; Kentucky, 47; Louisiana, 18,545; Maryland, 41; Michigan, 168; Minnesota, 3,363; Mississippi, 545; Missouri, 180; Montana, 3,658; Nevada, 2,892; New Jersey, 1,867; New York, 23; Ohio, 4,699; Oregon, 1,470; Rhode Island, 3; Tennessee, 756; Texas, 505; Utah, 28,602. 3.8; Washington, 4,854; West Virginia, 34; Wisconsin, 2,311; Wyoming, 569.
  Total: 107,014

Lenora B. Fulani (New Alliance)
  Alabama, 2,161 votes; Alaska, 330; Arizona, 923; Arkansas, 1,022; Colorado, 1,608; Connecticut, 1,363; Delaware, 1,105; District of Columbia, 1,459; Georgia, 44; Hawaii, 720; Idaho, 613; Illinois, 5,267; Indiana, 2,583; Iowa, 197; Kansas, 10; Kentucky, 430; Louisiana, 1,434; Maine, 519; Maryland, 2,786; Massachusetts,

3,172; Michigan, 21; Minnesota, 958; Mississippi, 2,625; Missouri, 17; Montana, 8; Nebraska, 846; Nevada, 483; New Hampshire, 512; New Jersey, 3,513; New Mexico, 369; New York, 11,318; North Carolina, 59; North Dakota, 143; Ohio, 6,413; Oregon, 3,030; Pennsylvania, 4,661; Rhode Island, 1,878; South Carolina, 1,235; South Dakota, 110; Tennessee, 727; Texas, 301; Utah, 414; Vermont, 429; Virginia, 3,192; Washington, 1,776; West Virginia, 6; Wisconsin, 654; Wyoming, 270.

Total: 73,714

Howard Phillips (U.S. Taxpayers)

Alaska, 377 votes; Arkansas, 1,437; California, 12,711; Connecticut, 20; Delaware, 2; Georgia, 7; Iowa, 480; Kansas, 55; Kentucky, 989; Louisiana, 1,552; Maine, 464; Maryland, 22; Massachusetts, 2,218; Michigan, 8,263; Minnesota, 733; Mississippi, 1,652; Nevada, 677; New Jersey, 2,670; New Mexico, 620; Rhode Island, 215; South Carolina, 2,680; Tennessee, 579; Texas, 359; Utah, 393; Vermont, 124; Washington, 2,354; West Virginia, 2; Wisconsin, 1,772; Wyoming, 7.

Total: 43,434

John Hagelin (Natural Law)

Alabama, 495 votes; Alaska, 433; Arizona, 2,267; Arkansas, 764; California, 836; Colorado, 47; Connecticut, 75; Delaware, 6; District of Columbia, 230; Florida, 214; Hawaii, 416; Idaho, 24; Illinois, 2,751; Indiana, 126; Iowa, 3,079; Kansas, 77; Kentucky, 695; Louisiana, 889; Maryland, 191; Massachusetts, 1,812; Michigan, 2,954; Minnesota, 1,406; Mississippi, 1,140; Missouri, 64; Montana, 20; Nebraska, 714; Nevada, 338; New Hampshire, 292; New Jersey, 1,353; New Mexico, 562; New York, 4,420; North Carolina, 41; North Dakota, 240; Ohio, 3,437; Oregon, 91; Rhode Island, 262; South Dakota, 429; Tennessee, 599; Texas, 217; Utah, 1,319; Vermont, 315; Washington, 2,456; West Virginia, 2; Wisconsin, 1,070; Wyoming, 11.

Total: 39,179

Ron Daniels (Peace and Freedom)

California, 18,597 votes; District of Columbia, 1,186; Iowa, 212; Louisiana, 1,663; Maryland, 167; Missouri, 12; New Jersey, 1,996; New York, 385; Rhode Island, 1; Tennessee, 511; Utah, 177; Washington, 1,171; Wisconsin, 1,883.

Total: 27,961

Lyndon H. LaRouche Jr. (Economic Recovery)

Alabama, 641 votes; Alaska, 469; Arizona, 8; Arkansas, 762; California, 180; Colorado, 20; Connecticut, 4; Delaware, 9; District of Columbia, 260; Idaho, 1; Indiana, 14; Iowa, 238; Louisiana, 1,136; Maryland, 18; Massachusetts, 1,027; Michigan, 14; Minnesota, 622; Missouri, 13; New Jersey, 2,095; New York, 20; North Dakota, 642; Ohio, 2,446; Rhode Island, 494; Tennessee, 460; Texas, 169; Utah, 1,089; Vermont, 57; Virginia, 11,937; Washington, 855; Wisconsin, 633.

Total: 26,333

James Warren (Socialist Workers)

Alabama, 831 votes; California, 115; Connecticut, 5; Delaware, 3; District of Columbia, 105; Georgia, 9; Illinois, 1,361; Iowa, 273; Maryland, 25; Minnesota, 990; Missouri, 6; New Jersey, 2,011; New Mexico, 183; New York, 15,472; North Carolina, 12; North Dakota, 193; Ohio, 32; Tennessee, 277; Utah, 200; Vermont, 82; Washington, 515; West Virginia, 6; Wisconsin, 390.

Total: 23,096

Drew Bradford (Independent)

New Jersey, 4,749 votes.

Jack E. Herer (Grassroots)

Iowa, 669 votes; Minnesota, 2,659; Wisconsin, 547.

Total: 3,875

J. Quinn Brisben (Socialist)

District of Columbia, 191 votes; Florida, 16; Idaho, 3; Indiana, 16; Massachusetts, 13; New York, 16; Oregon, 4; Rhode Island, 2; Tennessee, 1,356; Texas, 78; Utah, 151; Wisconsin, 1,211.

Total: 3,057

Helen Halyard (Workers League)

Michigan, 1,432 votes; New Jersey, 1,618.

Total: 3,050

John Yiamouyiannas (Take Back America)

Arkansas, 554 votes; Iowa, 604; Louisiana, 808; Tennessee, 233.

Total: 2,199

Delbert L. Ehlers (Independent)

Iowa, 1,149 votes.

Earl F. Dodge (Prohibition)

Arkansas, 472 votes; Colorado, 21; Massachusetts, 2; New Mexico, 120; North Dakota, 3; Tennessee, 343.

Total: 961

Jim Boren (Apathy)

Arkansas, 956 votes.

Eugene A. Hem (Third)

Wisconsin, 405 votes.

Isabell Masters (Looking Back)

Arkansas, 327 votes; California, 12.

Total: 339

Robert J. Smith (American)

Utah, 292 votes.

Gloria La Riva (Workers World)

New Mexico, 181 votes.

Scattered write-ins

Alabama, 723 votes; Alaska, 365; California, 149; Delaware, 86; District of Columbia, 676; Florida, 8; Georgia, 2; Illinois, 22; Iowa, 741; Kansas, 57; Maine, 91; Maryland, 2; Massachusetts, 1,990; Michigan, 711; Minnesota, 2,499; Missouri, 3; Nevada (None of these candidates), 2,537; New Hampshire, 730; Ohio, 10; Oregon, 2,609; Rhode Island, 106; Tennessee, 161; Texas, 23; Utah, 1; Vermont, 488; Washington, 665; West Virginia, 35; Wisconsin, 961; Wyoming, 127.

Total: 16,578

1996 Election

Harry Browne (Libertarian)

Alabama, 5,290 votes; Alaska, 2,276; Arizona, 14,358; Arkansas, 3,076; California, 73,600; Colorado, 12,392; Connecticut, 5,788; Delaware, 2,052; District of Columbia, 588; Florida, 23,965; Georgia, 17,870; Hawaii, 2,493; Idaho, 3,325; Illinois, 22,548; Indiana, 15,632; Iowa, 2,315; Kansas, 4,557; Kentucky, 4,009; Louisiana, 7,499; Maine, 2,996; Maryland, 8,765; Massachusetts, 20,426; Michigan, 27,670; Minnesota, 8,271; Mississippi, 2,809; Missouri, 10,522; Montana, 2,526; Nebraska, 2,792; Nevada, 4,460; New Hampshire, 4,237; New Jersey, 14,763; New Mexico, 2,996; New York, 12,220; North Carolina, 8,740; North Dakota, 847; Ohio, 12,851; Oklahoma, 5,505; Oregon, 8,903; Pennsylvania, 28,000; Rhode Island, 1,109; South Carolina, 4,271; South Dakota, 1,472; Tennessee, 5,020; Texas, 20,256; Utah, 4,129; Vermont, 1,183; Virginia, 9,174; Washington, 12,522; West Virginia, 3,062; Wisconsin, 7,929; Wyoming, 1,739.

Total: 485,798

Howard Phillips (U.S. Taxpayers)

Alabama, 2,365 votes; Alaska, 925; Arizona, 347; Arkansas, 2,065; California, 21,202; Colorado, 2,813; Connecticut, 2,425; Delaware, 348; Georgia, 145; Hawaii, 358; Idaho, 2,230; Illinois, 7,606; Indiana, 291; Iowa, 2,229; Kansas, 3,519; Kentucky, 2,204; Louisiana, 3,366; Maine, 1,517; Maryland, 3,402; Michigan, 539; Minnesota, 3,416; Mississippi, 2,314; Missouri, 11,521; Montana, 152; Nebraska, 1,928; Nevada, 1,732; New Hampshire, 1,346; New Jersey, 3,440; New Mexico, 713; New York, 23,580; North Carolina, 258; North Dakota, 745; Ohio, 7,361; Oregon, 3,379; Pennsylvania, 19,552; Rhode Island, 1,021; South Carolina, 2,043; South Dakota, 912; Tennessee, 1,818; Texas, 7,472; Utah, 2,601; Vermont, 382; Virginia, 13,687; Washington, 4,578; Wisconsin, 8,811.

Total: 184,658

John Hagelin (Natural Law)

Alabama, 1,697 votes; Alaska, 729; Arizona, 153; Arkansas, 729; California, 15,403; Colorado, 2,547; Connecticut, 1,703; Delaware, 274; District of Columbia, 283; Florida, 418; Hawaii, 570; Idaho, 1,600; Illinois, 4,606; Indiana, 118; Iowa, 3,349; Kansas, 1,655; Kentucky, 1,493; Louisiana, 2,981; Maine, 825; Maryland, 2,517; Massachusetts, 5,184; Michigan, 4,254; Minnesota, 1,808; Mississippi, 1,447; Missouri, 2,287; Montana, 1,754; Nebraska, 1,189; Nevada, 545; New Jersey, 3,887; New Mexico, 644; New York, 5,011; North Carolina, 2,771; North Dakota, 349; Ohio, 9,120; Oregon, 2,798; Pennsylvania, 5,783; Rhode Island, 435; South Carolina, 1,248; South Dakota, 316; Tennessee, 636; Texas, 4,422; Utah, 1,085; Vermont, 498; Virginia, 4,510; Washington, 6,076; Wisconsin, 1,379; Wyoming, 582.

Total: 113,668

Monica Moorehead (Workers World)

Arkansas, 747 votes; Colorado, 599; Louisiana, 1,678; Massachusetts, 3,277; Michigan, 3,153; New Jersey, 1,337; New York, 3,473;

Ohio, 10,813; Rhode Island, 186; Utah, 298; Washington, 2,189; Wisconsin, 1,333.

Total: 29,083

Marsha Feinland (Peace and Freedom)

California, 25,332 votes.

Charles E. Collins (Independent)

Arizona, 36 votes; Arkansas, 823; California, 765; Colorado, 2,809; Georgia, 15; Idaho, 7; Indiana, 11; Kansas, 112; Maryland, 6; Mississippi, 1,205; Missouri, 62; Montana, 20; Tennessee, 688; Utah, 8; Washington, 2,374.

Total: 8,941

James E. Harris (Socialist Workers)

Alabama, 516 votes; California, 77; Colorado, 244; Connecticut, 4; District of Columbia, 257; Florida, 13; Georgia, 12; Iowa, 331; Minnesota, 684; New Jersey, 1,837; New York, 2,762; North Carolina, 84; Utah, 235; Vermont, 199; Washington, 738; Wisconsin, 483.

Total: 8,476

"None of These Candidates"

Nevada, 5,608 votes.

Dennis Peron (Grassroots)

Minnesota, 4,898 votes; Vermont 480.

Total: 5,378

Mary Cal Hollis (Socialist)

Arkansas, 538 votes; Colorado, 669; Florida, 21; Indiana, 59; Maryland, 4; Massachusetts, 61; Montana, 1; Oregon, 1,922; Texas, 297; Utah, 53; Vermont, 292; Wisconsin, 848.

Total: 4,765

Jerome White (Socialist Equality)

Michigan, 1,554 votes; Minnesota, 347, New Jersey, 537.

Total: 2,438

Diane Beall Templin (American)

Colorado, 557 votes; Utah, 1,290.

Total: 1,847

Earl F. Dodge (Prohibition)

Arkansas, 483 votes; Colorado, 375; Illinois, 1; Massachusetts, 4; Tennessee, 324; Utah, 111.

Total: 1,298

A. Peter Crane (Independent Party of Utah)

Utah, 1,101 votes.

Ralph Forbes (America First)

Arkansas, 932 votes.

John Birrenbach (Independent Grassroots)

Minnesota, 787 votes.

Isabell Masters (Looking Back)

Arkansas, 749 votes; California, 2; Maryland 1.

Total: 752

Steve Michael (Independent)

Tennessee, 408 votes.

Scattered write-ins

Alabama, 1,123 votes; Alaska, 634; Arizona, 16; California, 25; Connecticut, 1; Delaware, 17; District of Columbia 648; Idaho, 1; Illinois, 10; Indiana, 9; Iowa, 1,240; Kentucky, 8; Maine, 144; Maryland, 20; Massachusetts, 6,182; Michigan, 1,817; Minnesota, 2,903; Montana, 5; New Hampshire, 2,456; Ohio, 15; Oregon, 2,329; Pennsylvania, 1,725; Rhode Island, 37; Tennessee, 190; Utah, 98; Vermont, 560; Wisconsin, 2,324.

Total: 24,537

2000 Election

Harry Browne (Libertarian)

Alabama, 5,893 votes; Alaska, 2,636; Arkansas, 2,781; California, 45,520; Colorado, 12,799; Connecticut, 3,484; Delaware, 774; District of Columbia, 669; Florida, 16,415; Georgia, 36,332; Hawaii, 1,477; Idaho, 3,488; Illinois, 11,623; Indiana, 15,530; Iowa, 3,209; Kansas, 4,525; Kentucky, 2,896; Louisiana, 2,951; Maine, 3,074; Maryland, 5,310; Massachusetts, 16,366; Michigan, 16,711; Minnesota, 5,282; Mississippi, 2,009; Missouri, 7,436; Montana, 1,718; Nebraska, 2,245; Nevada, 3,311; New Hampshire, 2,757; New Jersey, 6,312; New Mexico, 2,058; New York, 7,649; North Carolina, 12,307; North Dakota, 660; Ohio, 13,473; Oklahoma, 6,602; Oregon, 7,447; Pennsylvania, 11,248; Rhode Island, 742; South Carolina, 4,876;

South Dakota, 1,662; Tennessee, 4,284; Texas, 23,160; Utah, 3,616; Vermont, 784; Virginia, 15,198; Washington, 13,135; West Virginia, 1,912; Wisconsin, 6,640; Wyoming, 1,443.

Total: 384,429

Howard Phillips (Constitution)

Alabama, 775 votes; Alaska, 596; Arizona, 110; Arkansas, 1,415; California, 17,042; Colorado, 1,319; Connecticut, 9,695; Delaware, 208; Florida, 1,371; Georgia, 140; Hawaii, 343; Idaho, 1,469; Illinois, 57; Indiana, 200; Iowa, 613; Kansas, 1,254; Kentucky, 923; Louisiana, 5,483; Maine, 579; Maryland, 919; Michigan, 3,791; Minnesota, 3,272; Mississippi, 3,267; Missouri, 1,957; Montana, 1,155; Nebraska, 468; Nevada, 621; New Hampshire, 328; New Jersey, 1,409; New Mexico, 343; New York, 1,498; North Dakota, 373; Ohio, 3,823; Oregon, 2,189; Pennsylvania, 14,428; Rhode Island, 97; South Carolina, 1,682; South Dakota, 1,781; Tennessee, 1,015; Texas, 567; Utah, 2,709; Vermont, 153; Virginia, 1,809; Washington, 1,989; West Virginia, 23; Wisconsin, 2,042; Wyoming, 720.

Total: 98,020

John Hagelin (Natural Law)

Alabama, 447 votes; Alaska, 919; Arizona, 1,120; Arkansas, 1,098; California, 10,934; Colorado, 2,240; Connecticut, 40; Delaware, 107; Florida, 2,281; Hawaii, 306; Idaho, 1,177; Illinois, 2,127; Indiana, 167; Iowa, 2,281; Kansas, 1,375; Kentucky, 1,533; Louisiana, 1,075; Maryland, 176; Massachusetts, 2,884; Michigan, 2,426; Minnesota, 2,294; Mississippi, 450; Missouri, 1,104; Montana, 675; Nebraska, 478; Nevada, 415; New Jersey, 2,215; New Mexico, 361; New York, 24,361; North Dakota, 313; Ohio, 6,181; Oregon, 2,574; Rhode Island, 271; South Carolina, 942; Tennessee, 613; Utah, 763; Vermont, 219; Washington, 2,927; West Virginia, 367; Wisconsin, 878; Wyoming, 411.

Total: 83,525

James E. Harris Jr. (Socialist Workers)

Colorado, 216; Connecticut, 4; District of Columbia, 114; Florida, 562; Georgia, 11; Iowa, 190; Louisiana, 1,103; Minnesota, 1,022; Mississippi, 613; New Jersey, 844; New York, 1,789; Ohio, 10; Rhode Island, 34; Utah, 186; Vermont, 70; Washington, 304; Wisconsin, 306.

Total: 7,378

L. Neil Smith (Arizona Libertarian)[5]

Arizona, 5,775.

David McReynolds (Socialist)

California, 28; Colorado, 712; Florida, 622; Illinois, 4; Indiana, 43; Iowa, 107; Massachusetts, 42; New Jersey, 1,880; New York, 2; North Carolina, 1,226; Rhode Island, 52; Texas, 63; Vermont, 161; Washington, 660.

Total: 5,602

Monica Moorehead (Workers World)

Florida, 1,804; Rhode Island, 199; Washington, 1,729; Wisconsin, 1,063.

Total: 4,795

"None of These Candidates"

Nevada, 3,315.

Cathy Gordon Brown (Independent)

Tennessee, 1,606.

Denny Lane (Vermont Grassroots)

Vermont, 1,044.

Randall Venson (Independent)

Tennessee, 535.

Earl F. Dodge (Prohibition)

Colorado, 208.

Louie G. Youngkeit (Independent)

Utah, 161.

Scattered write-ins

Alabama, 699 votes; Alaska, 1,068; California, 6; Connecticut, 10; Delaware, 93; District of Columbia, 539; Florida, 40; Georgia, 13; Idaho, 6; Indiana, 56; Iowa, 1,168; Kentucky, 80; Maine, 27; Maryland, 1,480; Massachusetts, 3,990; Minnesota, 28; Montana, 11; New Hampshire, 1,221; Oregon, 3,419; Pennsylvania, 934; Rhode Island, 329; Tennessee, 428; Texas, 74; Utah, 1; Vermont, 514; Virginia, 2,807; West Virginia, 1; Wisconsin, 1,896.

Total: 20,938

1. Georgia figures for Webster obtained from Svend Petersen, *A Statistical History of the American Presidential Elections* (Westport, Conn.: Greenwood Press, 1981), 31.

2. Troup figures obtained from Petersen, *A Statistical History,* 31.

3. Iowa and Mississippi figures from Petersen, *A Statistical History,* 81. Petersen lists these votes, as well as Progressive votes in all other states, for Theodore Roosevelt. In the ICPSR data for 1916, votes are listed for Progressive electors; Roosevelt's name does not appear. Since Roosevelt declined to be a candidate, Congressional Quarterly followed ICPSR in listing these votes as Progressive.

4. MacArthur ran under a variety of party designations: Christian Nationalist in Arkansas, New Mexico, Tennessee, North Dakota, and Washington; Christian Nationalist—Constitution in California and Texas; Constitution in Colorado; and Christian Nationalist—America First in Missouri.

5. L. Neil Smith ran as the Libertarian Party's presidential candidate in Arizona only. Harry Browne ran as the party's candidate in the other forty-nine states.

CHAPTER 17

The Electoral College

FOR MORE THAN TWO CENTURIES, Americans have been electing their presidents through the electoral college. Created by the framers of the Constitution as a compromise between selection by Congress and election by direct popular vote, the system has continued to function even though the United States has undergone radical transformation from an agricultural seaboard nation to a world power.

But despite its durability the electoral college is perhaps the least cherished of the United States' venerable political institutions. Thomas Jefferson called it "the most dangerous blot on our Constitution," and people have been calling for its abolition or reform ever since.

Under the electoral college system, each state is entitled to electoral votes equal in number to its congressional delegation—that is, the number of representatives from the state, plus two for the state's two senators. (The District of Columbia has three electoral votes, the number it would have if it were a state, making the total electoral college membership 538.) As it works today, the electoral college is a "winner-take-all" system. The party that receives a plurality of a state's popular vote is virtually assured of receiving all of that state's electoral votes. Exceptions are Maine and Nebraska, where two electoral votes are awarded to the statewide winner and the others are allocated by presidential election districts that match the states' congressional districts (two in Maine and three in Nebraska). In the past there were even more variations of today's procedure, including choosing electors by congressional district, voting statewide for each individual elector, and selection of electors by state legislatures. There also have been several cases of a so-called faithless elector, who cast his or her electoral vote for a candidate other than the one who won the popular vote in the elector's state. (*See box, Splitting of States' Electoral Votes, p. 702.*)

Critics call the electoral college anachronistic and antidemocratic. Many believe that direct election is fairer and more likely to express the will of the people. Public opinion polls consistently show that most Americans favor switching to direct popular vote. Supporters, however, view the college as a bulwark of federalism and the two-party system. They note that most of the time it works flawlessly. They maintain that the system forces a winning candidate to build a national coalition covering many states, which usually enables the president to govern from a wide base even if the popular vote margin of victory was close. Only in four elections has the popular vote winner not won the presidency.

Constitutional Background

The method of selecting a president was the subject of long debate at the Constitutional Convention of 1787. Several plans were proposed and rejected before a compromise solution, which was modified only slightly in later years, was adopted (Article II, Section I, Clause 2).

Facing the convention when it opened May 25 was the question of whether the chief executive should be chosen by direct popular election, by the Congress, by state legislatures, or by intermediate electors. Direct election was opposed because it was felt generally that the people lacked sufficient knowledge of the character and qualifications of possible candidates to make an intelligent choice. Many delegates also feared that the people of the various states would be unlikely to agree on a single person, usually casting their votes for favorite-son candidates well known to them.

The possibility of giving Congress the power to choose the president also received consideration. This plan was rejected, however, largely because of fear that it would jeopardize the principle of executive independence. Similarly, a plan favored by many delegates, to let state legislatures choose the president, was turned down because the delegates thought the president might feel so indebted to the states as to allow them to encroach on federal authority.

Unable to agree on a plan, the convention August 31 appointed a "Committee of Eleven" to solve the problem. On September 4 it suggested a compromise under which each state would appoint presidential electors equal to the total number of its representatives and senators. The electors, chosen in a manner set forth by each state legislature, would meet in their own states and each cast votes for two persons. The votes would be counted in Congress, with the candidate receiving a majority elected president and the second-highest candidate becoming vice president.

No distinction was made between ballots for president and vice president. Moreover, the development of national political parties and the nomination of tickets for president and vice president created further confusion in the electoral system. All the electors of one party tended to cast ballots for their two party nominees. But with no distinction between the presidential and vice-presidential nominees, the danger arose of a tie vote between the two. That actually happened in 1800, leading to a change in the original electoral system with ratification of the Twelfth Amendment in 1804.

The committee's compromise plan constituted a great concession to the less populous states, because it ensured them a

Splitting of States' Electoral Votes: Factionalism and "Faithless Electors"

Throughout the history of presidential elections, there have been numerous occurrences when the U.S. electoral votes from an individual state have been divided among two or more candidates. These cases of split electoral votes occurred for a variety of reasons.

Electoral Vote Splits, 1789–1836

Splits of a state's electoral votes cast for president before 1836 occurred for these reasons:

• For the first four presidential elections (1789–1800) held under Article II, Section 1 of the Constitution, each elector cast two votes without designating which vote was for president and which for vice president. As a result, electoral votes for each state were often scattered among several candidates. The Twelfth Amendment, ratified in 1804, required electors to vote separately for president and vice president.

• The district system of choosing electors, in which different candidates each could carry several districts. This system is the explanation for the split electoral votes in Maryland in 1804, 1808, 1812, 1824, 1828, and 1832; North Carolina in 1808; Illinois in 1824; Maine in 1828; and New York in 1828.

• The selection of electors by the legislatures of some states. This system sometimes led to party factionalism or political deals that resulted in the choice of electors loyal to more than one presidential candidate. This was the cause for the division of electoral votes in New York in 1808 and 1824, Delaware in 1824, and Louisiana in 1824.

• The vote of an individual elector for someone other than his party's candidate. This happened in New Hampshire in 1820 when one Democratic-Republican elector voted for John Quincy Adams instead of the party nominee, James Monroe, to preserve George Washington's distinction as the only unanimously elected president. Three other electors did not vote in 1820.

Voting for Individual Electors

By 1836 all states except South Carolina, which selected its electors by the state legislature until after the Civil War, had established a system of statewide popular election of electors. The new system limited the frequency of electoral vote splits. Nevertheless, a few states on occasion still divided their electoral votes among different presidential candidates. This occurred because of the practice of listing on the ballot the names of all electors and allowing voters to cross off the names of any particular electors they did not like, or, alternatively, requiring voters to vote for each individual elector. In a close election, electors of different parties sometimes were chosen. An example occurred in California in 1880, when one Democratic elector ran behind the Republican thus:

Winning votes	Party	Losing electors	Party
80,443	Democratic	80,282	Republican
80,426	Democratic	80,252	Republican
80,420	Democratic	80,242	Republican
80,413	Democratic	80,228	Republican
80,348	Republican	79,885	Democratic

• *New Jersey, 1860.* Four Republican and three Douglas Democratic electors won.
• *California, 1892.* Eight Democratic electors and one Republican won.
• *North Dakota, 1892.* Two Fusionists (Democrats and Populists) and one Republican won. One of the Fusion electors voted for Democrat Grover Cleveland, and the other voted for Populist James B. Weaver, while the Republican elector voted for Benjamin Harrison, thus splitting the state's electoral vote three ways.
• *Ohio, 1892.* Twenty-two Republicans and one Democratic elector won.
• *Oregon, 1892.* Three Republicans and one Populist with Democratic support won.

minimum of three votes (two for their two senators and at least one for their representative) however small their populations might be. The plan also left important powers with the states by giving complete discretion to state legislatures to determine the method of choosing electors.

The only part of the committee's plan that aroused serious opposition was a provision giving the Senate the right to decide presidential elections in which no candidate received a majority of electoral votes. Some delegates feared that the Senate, which already had been given treaty ratification powers and the responsibility to "advise and consent" on all important executive appointments, might become too powerful. A proposal was made and accepted to let the House of Representatives decide the winner in instances when the electors failed to give a majority of their votes to a single candidate. The interests of the small states were preserved by giving each state's delegation only one vote in the House on roll calls to elect a president.

The system adopted by the Constitutional Convention was a compromise born out of problems involved in diverse state voting requirements, the slavery problem, big-state versus small-state rivalries, and the complexities of the balance of power among different branches of the government. Moreover, it was probably as close to a direct popular election as the men who wrote the Constitution thought possible and appropriate at the time.

The term *electoral college* itself does not appear in the Constitution. It was first used unofficially in the early 1800s and became the official designation for the electoral body in 1845.

THE TWELFTH AMENDMENT

Only once since ratification of the Constitution has an amendment been adopted that substantially altered the method of electing the president. In the 1800 presidential election, the

- *California, 1896.* Eight Republicans and one Democratic elector won
- *Kentucky, 1896.* Twelve Republicans and one Democratic elector won.
- *Maryland, 1904.* Seven Democratic electors and one Republican won.
- *Maryland, 1908.* Six Democratic and two Republican electors won.
- *California, 1912.* Eleven Progressive and two Democratic electors won.
- *West Virginia, 1916.* Seven Republicans and one Democratic elector won.

The increasing use of voting machines and straight-ticket voting—where the pull of a lever or the marking of an "X" results in automatically casting a vote for every elector—led to the decline in split electoral votes.

"Faithless Electors"

Yet another cause for occasional splits in a state's electoral vote is the so-called faithless elector. Legally, electors are not bound to vote for any particular candidate; they may cast their ballots any way they wish. By 2000 twenty-nine states and the District of Columbia had laws requiring electors to vote for the state's popular vote winner. These states were Alabama, Alaska, California, Colorado, Connecticut, Delaware, Florida, Hawaii, Maine, Maryland, Massachusetts, Michigan, Mississippi, Montana, Nebraska, Nevada, New Mexico, North Carolina, Ohio, Oklahoma, Oregon, South Carolina, Tennessee, Utah, Vermont, Virginia, Washington, Wisconsin, and Wyoming.

In Michigan, North Carolina, and Utah a "faithless elector" was not to be counted with the remaining electors filling the vacancy. New Mexico, North Carolina, Oklahoma, South Carolina, and Washington provided criminal penalties or fines for violations. However, no faithless elector has ever been punished and experts doubt that it would be constitutionally possible to do so.

In reality, electors are almost always faithful to the candidate of the party with which they are affiliated, law or no law. But at times in American political history electors have broken ranks to vote for candidates not supported by their parties. In 1796 a Pennsylvania Federalist elector voted for Democratic-Republican Thomas Jefferson instead of Federalist John Adams. And some historians and political scientists claim that three Democratic-Republican electors voted for Adams. However, the fluidity of political party lines at that early date and the well-known personal friendship between Adams and at least one of the electors make the claim of their being faithless electors one of continuing controversy. In 1820 a New Hampshire Democratic-Republican elector voted for John Quincy Adams instead of the party nominee, James Monroe.

There was no further occurrence until 1948, when Preston Parks, a Truman elector in Tennessee, voted for Gov. Strom Thurmond of South Carolina, the States Rights Democratic Party (Dixiecrat) presidential nominee. Since then, there have been the following instances:

- In 1956 W. F. Turner, a Stevenson elector in Alabama, voted for a local judge, Walter B. Jones.
- In 1960 Henry D. Irwin, a Nixon elector in Oklahoma, voted for Sen. Harry F. Byrd, Virginia Democrat.
- In 1968 Dr. Lloyd W. Bailey, a Nixon elector in North Carolina, voted for George C. Wallace, the American Independent Party candidate.
- In 1972 Roger L. MacBride, a Nixon elector in Virginia, voted for John Hospers, the Libertarian Party candidate.
- In 1976 Mike Padden, a Ford elector in the state of Washington, voted for former governor Ronald Reagan of California.
- In 1988 Margaret Leach, a Dukakis elector in West Virginia, voted for Dukakis's running mate, Sen. Lloyd Bentsen of Texas.
- In 2000 Barbara Lett-Simmons, a Gore elector in Washington, D.C., withheld her vote from Gore.

Democratic-Republican electors inadvertently caused a tie in the electoral college by casting equal numbers of votes for Thomas Jefferson, whom they wished to be elected president, and Aaron Burr, whom they wished to elect vice president. The election was thrown into the House, and thirty-six ballots were required before Jefferson was finally elected president. The Twelfth Amendment, ratified in 1804, sought to prevent a recurrence of this incident by providing that the electors should vote separately for president and vice president. *(See "Constitutional Provisions and Amendments on Elections," p. 1545, in Reference Materials, Vol. II.)*

Other changes in the system evolved over the years. The authors of the Constitution, for example, had intended that each state should choose its most distinguished citizens as electors and that they would deliberate and vote as individuals in electing the president. But as strong political parties began to appear, the electors came to be chosen merely as representatives

of the parties; independent voting by electors disappeared almost entirely.

Methods of Choosing Electors

In the early years of the Republic, states used a variety of methods to select presidential electors. For the first presidential election, in 1789, four states held direct popular elections to choose their electors: Pennsylvania and Maryland (at large) as well as Virginia and Delaware (by district). In five states—Connecticut, Georgia, New Jersey, New York, and South Carolina—the state legislatures were to make the choice.

New Hampshire and Massachusetts adopted a combination of the legislative and popular methods. New Hampshire held a statewide popular vote for presidential electors with the stipulation that any elector would have to win a majority of the popular vote to be elected; otherwise, the legislature would choose. In

Massachusetts the arrangement was for the voters in each congressional district to vote for the two persons they wanted to be presidential electors. From the two individuals in each district receiving the highest number of votes, the legislature, by joint ballot of both houses, was to choose one. In addition, the legislature was to choose two electors at large.

Because of a dispute between the two chambers, the New York legislature failed to choose electors. The state Senate insisted on full equality with the Assembly (lower house); that is, the Senate wanted each house to take a separate ballot and to resolve any differences between them by agreement rather than by having one house impose its will on the other. The Assembly, on the other hand, wanted a joint ballot, on which the lower house's larger numbers would prevail, or it was willing to divide the electors with the Senate. The failure to compromise cost the state its vote in the first presidential election.

The twelfth and thirteenth states—North Carolina and Rhode Island—had not ratified the Constitution by the time the electors were chosen, and so they did not participate.

Generally similar arrangements prevailed for the election of 1792. Massachusetts, while continuing to choose electors by district, changed the system somewhat to provide for automatic election of any candidate for elector who received a majority of the popular vote. New Hampshire continued the system of popular election at large, but substituted a popular runoff election in place of legislative choice, if no candidate received a majority of the popular vote.

Besides Massachusetts and New Hampshire, electors were chosen in 1792 by popular vote in Maryland and Pennsylvania (at large) and Virginia and Kentucky (by district). State legislatures chose electors in Connecticut, Delaware, Georgia, New Jersey, New York, North Carolina, Rhode Island, South Carolina, and Vermont.

By 1796 several changes had occurred. New Hampshire switched back to legislative choice for those electors who failed to receive a majority of the popular vote. Tennessee entered the Union (1796) with a unique system for choosing presidential electors: the state legislature appointed three persons in each county, who in turn chose the presidential electors. Massachusetts retained the system used in 1792. Other states chose their electors as follows: at-large popular vote: Georgia, Pennsylvania; district popular vote: Kentucky, Maryland, North Carolina, Virginia; state legislature: Connecticut, Delaware, New Jersey, New York, Rhode Island, South Carolina, Vermont.

POLITICAL PARTIES AND ELECTORS: 1800

As political parties gained power, manipulation of the system of choosing electors became increasingly widespread. For example, in 1800 Massachusetts switched from popular voting to legislative selection of electors because of recent successes by the Democratic-Republican Party in that state. The Federalists, still in firm control of the legislature, sought to secure the state's entire electoral vote for its presidential candidate, native son John Adams. New Hampshire did likewise.

The rival Democratic-Republicans were not innocent of this kind of political maneuver. In Virginia, where that party was in control, the legislature changed the system for choosing electors from districts to a statewide at-large ballot. That way, the expected statewide Democratic-Republican majority could overcome Federalist control in some districts and garner a unanimous vote for Jefferson, the Democratic-Republican presidential candidate.

In Pennsylvania the two houses of the state legislature could not agree on legislation providing for popular ballots, the system used in the first three elections, so the legislature itself chose the electors, dividing them between the parties.

In other changes in 1800, Rhode Island switched to popular election and Georgia reverted to legislative elections. The sixteen states used the following methods of choosing presidential electors in 1800:

• By popular vote: Kentucky, Maryland, North Carolina (by district); Rhode Island, Virginia (at large).
• By the legislature: Connecticut, Delaware, Georgia, Massachusetts, New Hampshire, New Jersey, New York, Pennsylvania, South Carolina, Tennessee (indirectly, as in 1796), Vermont.

TREND TO WINNER-TAKE-ALL SYSTEM

For the next third of a century, the states moved slowly but inexorably toward a standard system of choosing presidential electors—the statewide, winner-take-all popular ballot. The development of political parties resulted in the adoption of slates of electors pledged to vote for the parties' presidential candidates. Each party organization saw a statewide ballot as being in its best interest, with the hope of sweeping in all its electors and preventing the opposition group from capitalizing on local areas of strength (which could result in winning only part of the electoral vote under the districting system).

From 1804 to 1832 the states used three basic methods of choosing presidential electors—at-large popular vote, district popular vote, and election by the state legislature. The following list shows the changing methods of choosing presidential electors for each state from 1804 to 1832:

1804

Popular vote, at large: New Hampshire, New Jersey, Ohio, Pennsylvania, Rhode Island, Virginia.

Popular vote, by district: Kentucky, Maryland, Massachusetts, North Carolina, Tennessee.

State legislature: Connecticut, Delaware, Georgia, New York, South Carolina, Vermont.

1808

Popular vote, at large: New Hampshire, New Jersey, Ohio, Pennsylvania, Rhode Island, Virginia.

Popular vote, by district: Kentucky, Maryland, North Carolina, Tennessee.

State legislature: Connecticut, Delaware, Georgia, Massachusetts, New York, South Carolina, Vermont.

1812

Popular vote, at large: New Hampshire, Ohio, Pennsylvania, Rhode Island, Virginia.

Popular vote, by district: Kentucky, Maryland, Massachusetts, Tennessee.

State legislature: Connecticut, Delaware, Georgia, Louisiana, New Jersey, New York, North Carolina, South Carolina, Vermont.

1816

Popular vote, at large: New Hampshire, New Jersey, North Carolina, Ohio, Pennsylvania, Rhode Island, Virginia.
Popular vote, by district: Kentucky, Maryland, Tennessee.
State legislature: Connecticut, Delaware, Georgia, Indiana, Louisiana, Massachusetts, New York, South Carolina, Vermont.

1820

Popular vote, at large: Connecticut, Mississippi, New Hampshire, New Jersey, North Carolina, Ohio, Pennsylvania, Rhode Island, Virginia.
Popular vote, by district: Illinois, Kentucky, Maine, Maryland, Massachusetts, Tennessee.
State legislature: Alabama, Delaware, Georgia, Indiana, Louisiana, Missouri, New York, South Carolina, Vermont.

1824

Popular vote, at large: Alabama, Connecticut, Indiana, Massachusetts, Mississippi, New Hampshire, New Jersey, North Carolina, Ohio, Pennsylvania, Rhode Island, Virginia.
Popular vote, by district: Illinois, Kentucky, Maine, Maryland, Missouri, Tennessee.
State legislature: Delaware, Georgia, Louisiana, New York, South Carolina, Vermont.

1828

Popular vote, at large: Alabama, Connecticut, Georgia, Illinois, Indiana, Kentucky, Louisiana, Massachusetts, Mississippi, Missouri, New Hampshire, New Jersey, North Carolina, Ohio, Pennsylvania, Rhode Island, Vermont, Virginia.
Popular vote, by district: Maine, Maryland, New York, Tennessee.
State legislature: Delaware, South Carolina.

1832

Popular vote, at large: All states except Maryland and South Carolina.
Popular vote, by district: Maryland.
State legislature: South Carolina.

By 1836 Maryland switched to the system of choosing its electors by statewide popular vote. This left only South Carolina selecting its electors through the state legislature. The state continued this practice through the election of 1860. Only after the Civil War was popular voting for presidential electors instituted in South Carolina.

Since 1836 the statewide, winner-take-all popular vote for electors has been the almost universal practice. Exceptions include the following:

• *Massachusetts, 1848.* Three slates of electors ran—Whig, Democratic, and Free Soil—none of which received a majority of the popular vote. Under the law then in force, the

state legislature was to choose in such a case. It chose the Whig electors.

• *Florida, 1868.* The state legislature chose the electors.

• *Colorado, 1876.* The state legislature chose the electors because the state had just been admitted to the Union, had held state elections in August and did not want to go to the trouble and expense of holding a popular vote for the presidential election so soon thereafter.

• *Michigan, 1892.* Republicans had been predominant in the state since the 1850s. However, in 1890 the Democrats gained control of the legislature and the governorship and enacted a districting system of choosing presidential electors in the expectation that the Democrats could carry some districts and thus some electoral votes in 1892. They were correct; the Republicans won nine and the Democrats five electoral votes that year. But the Republicans soon regained control of the state and reenacted the at-large system for the 1896 election.

• *Maine, 1972.* In 1969 the Maine legislature enacted a district system for choosing presidential electors. Two of the state's four electors were selected on the basis of the statewide vote, and the other two were determined by which party carried each of the state's two congressional districts. The system is still in force. Although the district system allowed splitting electoral votes, from its inception through 2000 the system had not produced a split vote in Maine.

• *Nebraska, 1992.* Nebraska, with five electoral votes, adopted an allocation system similar to Maine's. Like Maine, Nebraska had not split its electoral votes under the new system through the 2000 presidential election..

• *Florida, 2000.* The Republican-controlled legislature met in special session to choose the state's twenty-five electors. The action ensured that Florida's electoral votes would not be disqualified if the winner of the state's popular vote had not been determined by the federal date for counting electoral votes. Florida is one of twenty-nine states that bind electors to the popular vote winner, but the constitutionality of such laws has not been tested.

Historical Anomalies

The complicated and indirect system of electing the president has led to anomalies from time to time. In 1836, for example, the Whigs sought to take advantage of the electoral system by running different presidential candidates in different parts of the country. William Henry Harrison ran in most of New England, the mid-Atlantic states, and the Midwest; Daniel Webster ran in Massachusetts; Hugh White of Tennessee ran in the South.

The theory was that each candidate could capture electoral votes for the Whig Party in the region where he was strongest. Then the Whig electors could combine on one candidate or, alternatively, throw the election into the House, whichever

Electoral College Chronology

Before 1800. U.S. Constitution establishes the electoral college system for electing the president.

1787. Constitution provides for president to be named by state-appointed "electors"; each state free to determine method of choosing electors; plan calls for second-place finisher to become vice president and for House of Representatives to elect president if no candidate has majority.

1800s. Electoral college is tested in three contentious elections but survives with one significant modification effective 1804; states gradually move to winner-take-all system, giving electoral votes to winner of the state's popular vote for president.

1800. Presidential election is thrown into House, which takes thirty-six ballots to pick Thomas Jefferson over Aaron Burr.

1804. The Twelfth Amendment provides for separate election of vice president.

1824–1825. John Quincy Adams trails in popular vote and electoral vote to Andrew Jackson but is elected president after one House ballot.

1830s. Most states adopt popular election of presidential elections; by 1860 only South Carolina lets state legislature choose.

1845. Congress adopts uniform national election day: first Tuesday after first Monday in November in even-numbered years.

1876–1877. Rutherford B. Hayes is elected president with one-vote electoral college majority, 185–184, after a fifteen-member commission splits along party lines in awarding him disputed votes from three southern states.

1887. Electoral Vote Count Act specifies states' authority to determine legality of their choices for electors.

1900s. Proposals to abolish electoral college surface periodically, but no constitutional amendment emerges from Congress.

1950. Senate approves "proportional vote" plan to divide state electors on basis of popular vote; House kills measure.

1960. John F. Kennedy wins electoral college majority over Richard M. Nixon, 303–219; Kennedy's popular vote margin is closest in twentieth century. Fourteen unpledged electors and one "faithless" Republican elector vote for Sen. Harry F. Byrd, Virginia Democrat.

1968. Nixon wins electoral college majority over Democrat Hubert H. Humphrey and third-party candidate George Wallace (301–191–46); both Nixon and Humphrey had vowed not to negotiate with Wallace if election were thrown into House.

1969. House approves constitutional amendment to shift to direct popular election of president; measure dies after Senate filibuster in 1970. Maine, in 1969, replaces winner-take-all with district-by-district system.

1980–1988. Electoral college issue fades as Republican candidates win three successive elections with decisive popular votes and electoral majorities. One Democratic elector in 1988 votes for vice-presidential nominee Lloyd Bentsen to protest system.

1992. Strong third-party bid by H. Ross Perot stirs fears of throwing election to House, but Bill Clinton wins electoral college majority as Perot fails to carry any state. Nebraska adopts district voting for electors.

2000–2001. Democrat Al Gore surpasses Republican George W. Bush in popular vote, but electoral college outcome turns on close count in Florida; Gore and Bush vie in state and federal courts over recount. U.S. Supreme Court halts count, settling election contest in Bush's favor. Final electoral vote tally is Bush 271 (one more than he needed to win) and Gore 266 (one fewer than he was entitled to because a District of Columbia elector withheld her vote to protest the District's lack of congressional representation). When Congress meets to count the electoral votes, several minority and women House members object to Florida's votes. Gore, presiding, rules each objection out of order because it was not also signed by a senator as the 1887 law requires.

seemed to their advantage. However, the scheme did not work because Martin Van Buren, the Democratic nominee, captured a majority of the electoral vote.

Another quirk in the system surfaced in 1872. The Democratic presidential nominee, Horace Greeley, died between the time of the popular vote and the meeting of the presidential electors. The Democratic electors had no party nominee to vote for, and each was left to his own judgment. Forty-two of the sixty-six Democratic electors chose to vote for the Democratic governor-elect of Indiana, Thomas Hendricks. The rest of the

electors split their votes among three other politicians: eighteen for B. Gratz Brown of Missouri, the Democratic vice-presidential nominee; two for Charles J. Jenkins of Georgia, and one for David Davis of Illinois. Three Georgia electors insisted on casting their votes for Greeley, but Congress refused to count them. Counting Republican Ulysses S. Grant, who won, five candidates received electoral votes in 1872, tied for the largest number in U.S. history (five candidates also received electoral votes in 1800 and 1836).

In four elections the electoral college has chosen presidents who ran behind their opponents in the popular vote. In two of these instances—Republican Rutherford B. Hayes in 1876 and Republican Benjamin Harrison in 1888—the winning candidate carried a number of key states by close margins, while losing other states by wide margins. In the third instance—Democratic-Republican John Quincy Adams in 1824—the House chose the new president after no candidate had achieved a majority in the electoral college. In the fourth instance, the 2000 election hinged on Florida's twenty-five electoral votes, which went to Republican George W. Bush when the U.S. Supreme Court rejected Democrat Al Gore's contest of the state's vote count. *(See Chapter 9, Chronology of Presidential Elections.)*

Election by Congress

Under the Constitution, Congress has two major responsibilities relating to the election of the president and vice president. First, it is directed to receive and, in joint session, count the electoral votes certified by the states. Second, if no candidate has a majority of the electoral vote, the House of Representatives must elect the president and the Senate the vice president.

Although many of the framers of the Constitution apparently thought that most elections would be decided by Congress, the House actually has chosen a president only twice, in 1801 and 1825. But a number of campaigns have been deliberately designed to throw elections into the House, where each state has one vote and a majority of states is needed to elect.

In modern times the formal counting of electoral votes has been largely a ceremonial function, but the congressional role can be decisive when votes are contested. The preeminent example is the Hayes-Tilden contest of 1876, when congressional decisions on disputed electoral votes from four states gave the election to Republican Hayes despite the fact that Democrat Samuel J. Tilden had a majority of the popular vote. *(See "Hayes-Tilden Contest," p. 710.)*

From the beginning, the constitutional provisions governing the selection of the president have had few defenders, and many efforts at electoral college reform have been undertaken. Although prospects for reform seemed favorable after the close 1968 presidential election, the Ninety-first Congress (1969–1971) did not take final action on a proposed constitutional amendment that would have provided for direct popular election of the president and eliminated the existing provision for contingent election by the House. Reform legislation was reintroduced in the Senate during the Ninety-fourth Congress (1975–1977) and Ninety-fifth Congress (1977–1979). In the 107th Congress (2001–2003) more talk of reforming or replacing the electoral college system followed the fiercely fought 2000 election.

In addition to its role in electing the president, Congress bears responsibility in the related areas of presidential succession and disability. The Twelfth Amendment empowers Congress to decide what to do if the president-elect and the vice president-elect both fail to qualify by the date prescribed for commencement of their terms; it also gives Congress authority to settle problems arising from the death of candidates in cases where the election devolves upon Congress. Under the Twenty-fifth Amendment, Congress has ultimate responsibility for resolving disputes over presidential disability. It also must confirm presidential nominations to fill a vacancy in the vice presidency.

JEFFERSON-BURR DEADLOCK

The election of 1800 was the first in which the Constitution's contingent election procedures were put to the test and the House elected the president. The Federalists, a declining but still potent political force, nominated John Adams for a second term and chose Charles Cotesworth Pinckney as his running mate. A Democratic-Republican congressional caucus chose Vice President Jefferson for president and Burr, who had been instrumental in winning the New York legislature for the Democratic-Republicans earlier in 1800, for vice president.

The electors met in each state on December 4, with the following results: Jefferson and Burr, 73 electoral votes each; Adams, 65; Pinckney, 64; and John Jay, 1. The Federalists had lost, but because the Democratic-Republicans had neglected to withhold one electoral vote from Burr, their presidential and vice-presidential candidates were tied, and the election was thrown into the House.

The lame-duck Congress, with a partisan Federalist majority, was still in office for the electoral count, and the possibilities for intrigue were only too apparent. After toying with and rejecting a proposal to block any election until March 4, when Adams's term expired, the Federalists decided to support Burr and thereby elect a relatively pliant politician over a man they considered a "dangerous radical." Alexander Hamilton opposed this move. "I trust the Federalists will not finally be so mad as to vote for Burr," he wrote. "I speak with intimate and accurate knowledge of his character. His elevation can only promote the purposes of the desperate and the profligate. If there be a man in the world I ought to hate, it is Jefferson. With Burr I have always been personally well. But the public good must be paramount to every private consideration."

On February 11, 1801, Congress met in joint session—with Jefferson, the outgoing vice president, in the chair—to count the electoral vote. This ritual ended, the House retired to its own chamber to elect a president. When the House met, it became apparent that Hamilton's advice had been rejected; a majority of Federalists insisted on backing Burr over Jefferson, the man they despised more. Indeed, if Burr had given clear assurances that he would run the country as a Federalist, he might have been elected. But Burr was unwilling to make those assurances; and, as one chronicler put it, "No one knows whether it was honor or a wretched indecision which gagged Burr's lips."

In all, there were 106 members of the House at the time, 58 Federalists and 48 Democratic-Republicans. If the ballots had been cast per capita Burr would have been elected, but the Constitution provided that each state should cast a single vote and that a majority of states was necessary for election.

On the first ballot Jefferson received the votes of eight states, one short of a majority of the sixteen states then in the Union. Six states backed Burr. The representatives of Vermont and Maryland were equally divided and, therefore, could not cast

Presidential Election by the House

The following rules, reprinted from Hinds' *Precedents of the House of Representatives*, were adopted by the House in 1825 for use in deciding the presidential election of 1824. They would provide a precedent for any future House election of a president, although the House could change them.

1. In the event of its appearing, on opening all the certificates, and counting the votes given by the electors of the several States for President, that no person has a majority of the votes of the whole number of electors appointed, the same shall be entered on the Journals of this House.

2. The roll of the House shall then be called by States; and, on its appearing that a Member or Members from two-thirds of the States are present, the House shall immediately proceed, by ballot, to choose a President from the persons having the highest numbers, not exceeding three, on the list of those voted for as President; and, in case neither of those persons shall receive the votes of a majority of all the states on the first ballot, the House shall continue to ballot for a President, without interruption by other business, until a President be chosen.

3. The doors of the Hall shall be closed during the balloting, except against the Members of the Senate, stenographers, and the officers of the House.

4. From the commencement of the balloting until an election is made no proposition to adjourn shall be received, unless on the motion of one State, seconded by another State, and the question shall be decided by States. The same rule shall be observed in regard to any motion to change the usual hour for the meeting of the House.

5. In balloting the following mode shall be observed, to wit:

The Representatives of each State shall be arranged and seated together, beginning with the seats at the right hand of the Speaker's chair, with the Members from the State of Maine; thence, proceeding with the Members from the States, in the order the States are usually named for receiving petitions[1] around the Hall of the House, until all are seated.

A ballot box shall be provided for each State.

The Representatives of each State shall, in the first instance, ballot among themselves, in order to ascertain the vote of their State; and they may, if necessary, appoint tellers of their ballots.

After the vote of each State is ascertained, duplicates thereof shall be made out; and in case any one of the persons from whom the choice is to be made shall receive a majority of the votes given, on any one balloting by the Representatives of a State, the name of that person shall be written on each of the duplicates; and in case the votes so given shall be divided so that neither of said persons shall have a majority of the whole number of votes given by such

State, on any one balloting, then the word "divided" shall be written on each duplicate.

After the delegation from each State shall have ascertained the vote of their State, the Clerk shall name the States in the order they are usually named for receiving petitions; and as the name of each is called the Sergeant-at-Arms shall present to the delegation of each two ballot boxes, in each of which shall be deposited, by some Representative of the State, one of the duplicates made as aforesaid of the vote of said State, in the presence and subject to the examination of all the Members from said State then present; and where there is more than one Representative from a State, the duplicates shall not both be deposited by the same person.

When the votes of the States are thus all taken in, the Sergeant-at-Arms shall carry one of said ballot boxes to one table and the other to a separate and distinct table.

One person from each State represented in the balloting shall be appointed by the Representatives to tell off said ballots; but, in case the Representatives fail to appoint a teller, the Speaker shall appoint.

The said tellers shall divide themselves into two sets, as nearly equal in number as can be, and one of the said sets of tellers shall proceed to count the votes in one of said boxes, and the other set the votes in the other box.

When the votes are counted by the different sets of tellers, the result shall be reported to the House; and if the reports agree, the same shall be accepted as the true votes of the States; but if the reports disagree, the States shall proceed, in the same manner as before, to a new ballot.

6. All questions arising after the balloting commences, requiring the decision of the House, which shall be decided by the House, voting per capita, to be incidental to the power of choosing a President, shall be decided by States without debate; and in case of an equal division of the votes of States, the question shall be lost.

7. When either of the persons from whom the choice is to be made shall have received a majority of all the States, the Speaker shall declare the same, and that that person is elected President of the United States.

8. The result shall be immediately communicated to the Senate by message, and a committee of three persons shall be appointed to inform the President of the United States and the President-elect of said election.

On Feb. 9, 1825, the election of John Quincy Adams took place in accordance with these rules.

1. Petitions are no longer introduced in this way. This old procedure of calling the states beginning with Maine proceeded through the original thirteen states and then through the remaining states in the order of their admission to the Union.

their states' votes. By midnight of the first day of voting, nineteen ballots had been taken, and the deadlock remained.

In all, thirty-six ballots were taken before the House came to a decision on February 17. Predictably, there were men who sought to exploit the situation for personal gain. Jefferson wrote: "Many attempts have been made to obtain terms and promises from me. I have declared to them unequivocally that I would not receive the Government on capitulation; that I would not go in with my hands tied."

The impasse was broken finally when Vermont and Maryland switched to support Jefferson. Delaware and South Carolina also withdrew their support from Burr by casting blank ballots. The final vote: ten states for Jefferson, four (all in New England) for Burr. Jefferson became president, and Burr, under the Constitution as it then stood, automatically became vice president.

Federalist James A. Bayard of Delaware, who had played an important role in breaking the deadlock, wrote to Hamilton: "The means existed of electing Burr, but this required his cooperation. By deceiving one man (a great blockhead) and tempting two (not incorruptible), he might have secured a majority of the states. He will never have another chance of being president of the United States; and the little use he has made of the one which has occurred gives me but an humble opinion of the talents of an unprincipled man."

The Jefferson-Burr contest clearly illustrated the dangers of the double-balloting system established by the original Constitution, and pressure began to build for an amendment requiring separate votes for president and vice president. Congress approved the Twelfth Amendment in December 1803, and the states—acting with unexpected speed—ratified it in time for the 1804 election.

JOHN QUINCY ADAMS ELECTION

The only other time the House of Representatives elected a president was in 1825. There were many contenders in the 1824 election, but four predominated: John Quincy Adams, Henry Clay, William H. Crawford, and Andrew Jackson. Crawford, secretary of the Treasury under President James Monroe, was the early front-runner, but his candidacy faltered after he suffered an incapacitating illness in 1823.

When the electoral votes were counted, Jackson had ninety-nine, Adams eighty-four, Crawford forty-one, and Clay thirty-seven. With eighteen of the twenty-four states choosing their electors by popular vote, Jackson also led in the popular voting, although the significance of the popular vote was open to challenge. Under the Twelfth Amendment, the names of the three top contenders—Jackson, Adams, and the ailing Crawford—were placed before the House. Clay's support was vital to either of the two front-runners.

From the start, Clay apparently intended to support Adams as the lesser of two evils. But before the House voted, a great scandal erupted. A Philadelphia newspaper published an anonymous letter alleging that Clay had agreed to support Adams in return for being made secretary of state. The letter alleged also that Clay would have been willing to make the same deal with Jackson. Clay immediately denied the charge and pronounced

the writer of the letter "a base and infamous character, a dastard and a liar."

When the House met to vote, Adams was supported by the six New England states and New York and, in large part through Clay's backing, by Maryland, Ohio, Kentucky, Illinois, Missouri, and Louisiana. A majority of thirteen delegations voted for him—the bare minimum he needed for election, because there were twenty-four states in the Union at the time. The election was accomplished on the first ballot, but Adams took office under a cloud from which his administration never emerged.

Jackson had believed the charges and found his suspicions vindicated when Adams, after the election, did appoint Clay as secretary of state. "Was there ever witnessed such a bare-faced corruption in any country before?" Jackson wrote to a friend. Jackson's successful 1828 campaign made much of his contention that the House of Representatives had thwarted the will of the people by denying him the presidency in 1825, even though he had been the leader in the popular and electoral votes.

OTHER ANOMALIES

The Senate has chosen the vice president only once. That was in 1837, when Van Buren was elected president with 170 of the 294 electoral votes while his vice-presidential running mate, Richard M. Johnson, received only 147 electoral votes—one less than a majority. This discrepancy occurred because Van Buren electors from Virginia boycotted Johnson, reportedly in protest against his social behavior. The Senate elected Johnson, 33–16, over Francis Granger of New York, the runner-up in the electoral vote for vice president.

In 1912 President William Howard Taft's vice president, James S. Sherman, died in October after he and Taft won renomination by the Republican Party. Taft and his substitute running mate. Nicholas Murray Butler, lost the election to Democrats Woodrow Wilson and Thomas R. Marshall. But because it had been too late to change the GOP state ballots, Butler won Sherman's eight electoral votes.

Although only two presidential elections actually have been decided by the House, a number of others—including those of 1836, 1856, 1860, 1892, 1948, 1960, and 1968—could have been thrown into the House by only a small shift in the popular vote.

The threat of House election was most clearly evident in 1968, when Democrat George C. Wallace of Alabama ran as a strong third-party candidate. Wallace frequently asserted that he could win an outright majority in the electoral college by the addition of key Midwestern and Mountain states to his hoped-for base in the South and border states. In reality, the Wallace campaign had a narrower goal: to win the balance of power in electoral college voting, thereby depriving either major party of the clear electoral majority required for election. Wallace made it clear that he then would expect one of the major party candidates to make concessions in return for enough votes from Wallace electors to win the election. Wallace indicated that he expected the election to be settled in the electoral college and not in the House of Representatives. At the end of the campaign it was disclosed that Wallace had obtained written affidavits from all of his electors in which they promised to vote for Wallace "or whomsoever he may direct" in the electoral college.

In response to the Wallace challenge, both major party candidates, Republican Richard Nixon and Democrat Hubert H. Humphrey, maintained that they would refuse to bargain with Wallace for his electoral votes. Nixon asserted that the House, if the decision rested there, should elect the popular-vote winner. Humphrey said the representatives should select "the president they believe would be best for the country." Bipartisan efforts to obtain advance agreements from House candidates to vote for the national popular-vote winner if the election should go to the House ended in failure. Neither Nixon nor Humphrey replied to suggestions that they pledge before the election to swing enough electoral votes to the popular-vote winner to ensure his election without help from Wallace.

In the end Wallace received only 13.5 percent of the popular vote and forty-six electoral votes (including the vote of one Republican defector), all from southern states. He failed to win the balance of power in the electoral college, which he had hoped to use to wring policy concessions from one of the major party candidates. If Wallace had won a few border states, or if a few thousand more Democratic votes had been cast in northern states barely carried by Nixon, reducing Nixon's electoral vote below 270, Wallace would have been in a position to bargain off his electoral votes or to throw the election into the House for final settlement. Wallace later told journalist Neal R. Peirce that he would have tried to instruct his electors to vote for Nixon rather than to have the election go to the House.

Counting the Electoral Vote

Over the years Congress has mandated a variety of dates for the casting of popular votes, the meeting of the electors to cast ballots in the various states, and the official counting of the electoral votes before both houses of Congress.

The Continental Congress made the provisions for the first election. On September 13, 1788, it directed that each state choose its electors on the first Wednesday in January 1789. It further directed these electors to cast their ballots on the first Wednesday in February 1789.

In 1792 the Second Congress passed legislation setting up a permanent calendar for choosing electors. Allowing some flexibility in dates, the law directed that states choose their electors within the thirty-four days preceding the first Wednesday in December of each presidential election year. Then the electors would meet in their various states and cast their ballots on the first Wednesday in December. On the second Wednesday of the following February, the votes were to be opened and counted before a joint session of Congress. Provision also was made for a special presidential election in case of the removal, death, resignation, or disability of both the president and vice president.

Under that system, states chose presidential electors at various times. For instance, in 1840 the popular balloting for electors began in Pennsylvania and Ohio on October 30 and ended in North Carolina on November 12. South Carolina, the only state still choosing presidential electors through its state legislature, appointed its electors on November 26.

Congress modified the system in 1845, providing that each state choose its electors on the same day—the Tuesday next after the first Monday in November—a provision that still remains in force. Otherwise, the days for casting and counting the electoral votes remained the same.

The next change occurred in 1887, when Congress provided that electors were to meet and cast their ballots on the second Monday in January instead of the first Wednesday in December. Congress also dropped the provision for a special presidential election.

In 1934 Congress again revised the law. The new arrangements, still in force, directed the electors to meet on the first Monday after the second Wednesday in December. The ballots are opened and counted before Congress on January 6 (the next day if January 6 falls on a Sunday).

The Constitution states: "The President of the Senate shall, in the presence of the Senate and House of Representatives, open all the certificates, and the votes shall then be counted." It gives no guidance on disputed ballots. Early objections to electoral votes usually arose from disputes about whether a state had fully qualified for statehood. After the Civil War, some southern votes were contested on grounds that the states were still considered in "insurrection" against the United Sates.

Before counting the electoral votes in 1865, Congress adopted the Twenty-second Joint Rule, which provided that no electoral votes objected to in joint session could be counted except by the concurrent votes of both the Senate and House. The rule was pushed by congressional Republicans to ensure rejection of the electoral votes from the newly reconstructed states of Louisiana and Tennessee. Under this rule, Congress in 1873 also threw out the electoral votes of Louisiana and Arkansas and three from Georgia.

The rule lapsed at the beginning of 1876, however, when the Senate refused to readopt it because the House was under Democratic control. As a consequence, Congress had no rules to guide it following the 1876 Hayes-Tilden election, when it became apparent that for the first time the outcome of an election would be determined by decisions on disputed electoral votes.

HAYES-TILDEN CONTEST

The 1876 campaign pitted Republican Hayes against Democrat Tilden. Early returns indicated that Tilden had been elected. He had won the swing states of Indiana, New York, Connecticut, and New Jersey. Those states plus his expected southern support would give Tilden the election. However, by the following morning it became apparent that if the Republicans could hold South Carolina, Florida, and Louisiana, Hayes would be elected with 185 electoral votes to 184 for Tilden. But if a single elector in any of these states voted for Tilden, he would throw the election to the Democrats. Tilden led in the popular-vote count by more than a quarter million votes.

The situation was much the same in each of the three contested states. Historian Eugene H. Roseboom described it as follows:

The Republicans controlled the state governments and the election machinery, had relied upon the Negro masses for votes, and had practiced frauds as in the past. The Democrats used threats, intimidation, and even violence when necessary, to keep Negroes from the polls; and where they were in a position to do so they resorted to fraud also. The firm determination of the whites to overthrow carpetbag rule contributed to make a full and fair vote impossible; carpetbag hold on the state governments made a fair count impossible. Radical reconstruction was reaping its final harvest.

Both parties pursued the votes of the three states with a fine disregard for propriety or legality, and in the end double sets of elector returns were sent to Congress from all three. Oregon also sent two sets of returns. Although Hayes carried that state, the Democratic governor discovered that one of the Hayes electors was a postmaster and therefore ineligible under the Constitution, so he certified the election of the top-polling Democratic elector. However, the Republican electors met, received the resignation of their ineligible colleague, then reappointed him to the vacancy because he had in the meantime resigned his postmastership.

Had the Twenty-second Joint Rule remained in effect, the Democratic House of Representatives could have objected to any of Hayes's disputed votes. But because the rule had lapsed, Congress had to find a new method of resolving electoral disputes. A joint committee was created to work out a plan, and the resulting Electoral Commission Law was approved by large majorities and signed into law January 29, 1877—only days before the date scheduled for counting the electoral votes.

The law, which applied only to the 1876 electoral vote count, established a fifteen-member commission that was to have final authority over disputed electoral votes, unless both houses of Congress agreed to overrule it. The commission was to consist of five senators, five representatives, and five Supreme Court justices. Each chamber was to appoint its own members of the commission, with the understanding that the majority party would have three members and the minority two. Four justices, two from each party, were named in the bill, and these four were to select the fifth. It was expected that they would choose Justice David Davis, who was considered a political independent, but he disqualified himself when the Illinois legislature named him to a seat in the Senate. Justice Joseph P. Bradley, a Republican, then was named to the fifteenth seat. The Democrats supported his selection because they considered him the most independent of the remaining justices, all of whom were Republicans. However, he was to vote with the Republicans on every dispute and thus ensure the victory of Hayes.

The electoral count began in Congress February 1 (moved up from the second Wednesday in February for this one election), and the proceedings continued until March 2. States were called in alphabetical order, and as each disputed state was reached objections were raised to both the Hayes and Tilden electors. The question was then referred to the electoral commission, which in every case voted 8–7 for Hayes. In each case, the Democratic House rejected the commission's decision, but the Republican Senate upheld it, so the decision stood.

As the count went on, Democrats in the House threatened to launch a filibuster to block resumption of joint sessions so that the count could not be completed before Inauguration Day. The threat was never carried out because of an agreement reached between the Hayes forces and southern conservatives. The

southerners agreed to let the electoral count continue without obstruction. In return Hayes agreed that, as president, he would withdraw federal troops from the South, end Reconstruction, and make other concessions. The southerners, for their part, pledged to respect Negro rights, a pledge they did not carry out.

Consequently, at 4 a.m. March 2, 1877, the president of the Senate was able to announce that Hayes had been elected president with 185 electoral votes, as against 184 for Tilden. Later that day Hayes arrived in Washington. The next evening he took the oath of office privately at the White House, because March 4 fell on a Sunday. His formal inauguration followed on Monday. The country acquiesced. So ended a crisis that could have resulted in civil war.

Not until 1887 did Congress enact permanent legislation on the handling of disputed electoral votes. The Electoral Count Act of that year gave each state final authority in determining the legality of its choice of electors and required a concurrent majority of both the Senate and House to reject any electoral votes. It also established procedures for counting electoral votes in Congress. (*See box, Law for Counting Electoral Votes in Congress, p. 712.*)

APPLICATION OF 1887 LAW IN 1969

The procedures relating to disputed electoral votes were used for the first time after the election of 1968. When Congress met in joint session January 6, 1969, to count the electoral votes, Sen. Edmund S. Muskie of Maine and Rep. James G. O'Hara of Michigan, both Democrats, joined by six other senators and thirty-seven other representatives, filed a written objection to the vote cast by a North Carolina elector, Lloyd W. Bailey of Rocky Mount. He had been elected as a Republican but chose to vote for George Wallace and Curtis LeMay, the candidates of the American Independent Party, instead of Republican Nixon and his running mate, Spiro T. Agnew.

Acting under the 1887 law, Muskie and O'Hara objected to Bailey's vote on the grounds that it was "not properly given" because a plurality of the popular votes in North Carolina were cast for Nixon-Agnew and the state's voters had chosen electors to vote for Nixon and Agnew only. Muskie and O'Hara asked that Bailey's vote not be counted at all by Congress.

The 1887 statute stipulated that "no electoral vote or votes from any State which shall have been regularly given by electors whose appointment has been lawfully certified . . . from which but one return has been received shall be rejected, but the two Houses concurrently may reject the vote or votes when they agree that such vote or votes have not been so regularly given by electors whose appointment has been so certified." The statute did not define the term "regularly given," although at the time of its adoption the chief concern centered on problems of dual sets of electoral vote returns from a state, votes cast on an improper day, or votes disputed because of uncertainty about whether a state lawfully was in the Union when the vote was cast.

The 1887 statute provided that if written objection to any state's vote was received from at least one member of both the Senate and House, the two legislative bodies were to retire immediately to separate sessions, debate for two hours with a five-minute limitation on speeches, and each decide the issue by vote

Law for Counting Electoral Votes in Congress

Following is the complete text of Title 3, section 15 of the U.S. Code, enacted originally in 1887, governing the counting of electoral votes in Congress:

Congress shall be in session on the sixth day of January succeeding every meeting of the electors. The Senate and House of Representatives shall meet in the Hall of the House of Representatives at the hour of 1 o'clock in the afternoon on that day, and the President of the Senate shall be their presiding officer. Two tellers shall be previously appointed on the part of the Senate and two on the part of the House of Representatives, to whom shall be handed, as they are opened by the President of the Senate, all the certificates and papers purporting to be certificates of the electoral votes, which certificates and papers shall be opened, presented, and acted upon in the alphabetical order of the States, beginning with the letter A; and said tellers, having then read the same in the presence and hearing of the two Houses, shall make a list of the votes as they shall appear from the said certificates; and the votes having been ascertained and counted according to the rules in this subchapter provided, the result of the same shall be delivered to the President of the Senate, who shall thereupon announce the state of the vote, which announcement shall be deemed a sufficient declaration of the persons, if any, elected President and Vice President of the United States, and, together with a list of votes, be entered on the Journals of the two Houses. Upon such reading of any such certificate or paper, the President of the Senate shall call for objections, if any. Every objection shall be made in writing, and shall state clearly and concisely, and without argument, the ground thereof, and shall be signed by at least one Senator and one Member of the House of Representatives before the same shall be received. When all objections so made to any vote or paper from a State shall have been received and read, the Senate shall thereupon withdraw, and such objections shall be submitted to the Senate for its decision; and the Speaker of the House of Representatives shall, in like manner, submit such objections to the House of Representatives for its decision; and no electoral vote or votes from any State which shall have been regularly given by electors whose appointment has been lawfully certified to according to section 6[1] of this title from which but one return has been received shall be rejected, but the two Houses concurrently may reject the vote or votes when they agree that such vote or votes have not been so regularly given by electors whose appointment has been so certified. If more than one return or paper purporting to be a return from a State shall have been received by the President of the Senate, those votes, and those only, shall be counted which shall have been regularly given by the electors who are shown by the determination mentioned in section 5[2] of this title to have been appointed, if the determination in said section provided for shall have been made, or by such successors or substitutes, in case of a vacancy in the board of electors so ascertained, as have been appointed to fill such vacancy in the mode provided by the laws of the State; but in case there shall arise the question which of two or more of such State authorities determining what electors have been appointed, as mentioned in section 5 of this title, is the lawful tribunal of such State, the votes regularly given of those electors, and those only, of such State shall be counted whose title as electors the two Houses, acting separately, shall concurrently decide is supported by the decision of such State so authorized by its law; and in such case of more than one return or paper purporting to be a return from a State, if there shall have been no such determination of the question in the State aforesaid, then those votes, and those only, shall be counted which the two Houses shall concurrently decide were cast by lawful electors appointed in accordance with the laws of the State, unless the two Houses, acting separately, shall concurrently decide such votes not to be the lawful votes of the legally appointed electors of such State. But if the two Houses shall disagree in respect of the counting of such votes, then, and in that case, the votes of the electors whose appointment shall have been certified by the executive of the State, under the seal thereof, shall be counted. When the two Houses have voted, they shall immediately again meet, and the presiding officer shall then announce the decision of the questions submitted. No votes or papers from any other State shall be acted upon until the objections previously made to the votes or papers from any State shall have been finally disposed of.

1. Section 6 provides for certification of votes by electors by state governors.
2. Section 5 provides that if state law specifies a method for resolving disputes concerning the vote for presidential electors, Congress must respect any determination so made by a state.

before resuming the joint session. The statute made clear that both the Senate and House had to reject a challenged electoral vote (or votes) for such action to prevail.

At the January 6 joint session, with Senate President Pro Tempore Richard B. Russell, Georgia Democrat, presiding, the counting of the electoral vote proceeded smoothly through the alphabetical order of states until the North Carolina result was announced, at which time O'Hara rose to announce filing of the complaint. The two houses then reassembled in joint session at which the results of the separate deliberations were announced

and the count of the electoral vote by state proceeded without event. At the conclusion, Russell announced the vote and declared Nixon and Agnew elected.

APPLICATION OF THE 1887 LAW IN 2001

The U.S. Supreme Court's peremptory 5–4 vote ending the recount of Florida's extremely close presidential vote left many Americans angry and embittered. Vice President Al Gore, the Democratic nominee, had defeated Texas's Republican governor, George W. Bush, by more than a half-million votes in the popular election and also led in the electoral vote, pending determination of the Florida winner. African Americans were particularly dissatisfied with the result. They had overwhelmingly supported Gore nationally, and in Florida their votes made up a disproportionately large share of the ballots not counted because of problems with the obsolete punch-card voting system used in many counties. They and many others felt that the majority had been disfranchised and that Gore might have won had the Court not stopped the recount.

But the ruling in *Bush v. Gore* left no recourse through the judicial system. Only one step remained before the 2000 election was officially closed: the formal counting of the 538 electoral votes by both chambers of Congress. When that day came, on January 5, 2001, twenty House members, mostly members of the Congressional Black Caucus, made a last-ditch effort to deny Florida's twenty-five electoral votes to Bush. With Gore presiding, each one submitted a written objection to the counting of Florida's votes. Gore asked each representative if the objection was also signed by a senator, as the 1887 law required. When each responded no, Gore ruled the objection out of order. At one point he thanked Rep. Jesse L. Jackson Jr., Illinois Democrat, for his remarks and said, "But, hey," and spread his arms in a gesture of futility.

It was the first time since the 1969 faithless elector incident that there had been any objections to the counting of electoral votes. In the 2001 counting there was one abstention, by a District of Columbia elector for Gore, resulting in a total of 537 electoral votes being cast.

Reform Proposals

Since January 6, 1797, when Rep. William L. Smith, a South Carolina Federalist, introduced in Congress the first proposed constitutional amendment for reform of the electoral college system, hardly a session of Congress has passed without the introduction of one or more resolutions of this nature. In all, more than seven hundred such proposals have been submitted. But only one—the Twelfth Amendment, ratified in 1804—ever has been approved.

In recent years, public interest in a change in the electoral college system was spurred by the close 1960, 1968, and 2000 elections, by a series of Supreme Court rulings relating to apportionment and redistricting, and by the introduction of unpledged elector systems in the southern states.

HOUSE APPROVAL OF AMENDMENT

Early in 1969 President Nixon asked Congress to take prompt action on electoral college reform. He said he would support any plan that would eliminate individual electors and distribute among the presidential candidates the electoral vote of every state and the District of Columbia in a manner more closely approximating the popular vote.

Later that year the House approved, 338–70, a resolution proposing a constitutional amendment to eliminate the electoral college and to provide instead for direct popular election of the president and vice president. The measure set a minimum of 40 percent of the popular vote as sufficient for election and provided for a runoff election between the two top candidates for the presidency if no candidate received 40 percent. Under this plan the House of Representatives could no longer be called upon to select a president. The proposed amendment also authorized Congress to provide a method of filling vacancies caused by the death, resignation, or disability of presidential nominees before the election and a method of filling postelection vacancies caused by the death of the president-elect or vice president-elect.

Nixon, who previously had favored a proportional plan of allocating each state's electoral votes, endorsed the House resolution and urged the Senate to adopt it. To become effective, the proposed amendment had to be approved by a two-thirds majority in both the Senate and House and be ratified by the legislatures of three-fourths of the states. When the proposal reached the Senate floor in September 1970, senators from small states and the South succeeded in blocking final action. The resolution was laid aside October 5, after two unsuccessful efforts to cut off debate by invoking cloture.

CARTER ENDORSEMENT OF PLAN

Another major effort to eliminate the electoral college occurred in 1977, when President Jimmy Carter included such a proposal in his election reform package, unveiled March 22. Carter endorsed the amendment approved by the House in 1969 to replace the electoral college with direct popular election of the president and vice president, and provide for a runoff if no candidate received at least 40 percent of the vote. Because the Senate again was seen as the major stumbling block, the House waited to see what the Senate would do before beginning any deliberation of its own.

After several months of deadlock, the Senate Judiciary Committee approved September 15 the direct presidential election plan by a 9–8 vote. But Senate opponents threatened a filibuster, and the Senate leadership decided it could not spare the time or effort to try to break it. The measure was never brought to the floor and died when the Ninety-fifth Congress adjourned in 1978.

On January 15, 1979, the opening day of the Ninety-sixth Congress, Sen. Birch Bayh, Indiana Democrat, began another effort to abolish the electoral college through a constitutional amendment. In putting off action in the previous Congress, Senate leaders had agreed to try for early action in the Ninety-sixth.

A proposed constitutional amendment to abolish the electoral college and elect the president by popular vote did reach the Senate floor in July 1979. The Senate voted in favor of the measure, 51 to 48, fifteen votes short of the required two-thirds majority of those present and voting needed to approve a constitutional amendment.

Supporters of the resolution blamed defections by several northern liberals for the margin of defeat. Major Jewish and black groups extensively lobbied the northern senators, arguing that the voting strength of black and Jewish voters is maximized under the electoral college system because both groups are concentrated in urban areas of the large electoral vote states.

ALTERNATIVE PLANS

Besides direct election of the president and vice president, two other major proposals to replace the electoral college have gained considerable support. One is the district plan, similar to the Maine and Nebraska systems, that would award an electoral vote to the candidate who carried a congressional district and two to the candidate who carried the state as a whole. The other is the proportional plan that would distribute a state's electoral votes on the basis of the proportion of the vote each candidate received.

Had any of the three plans been in effect since 1960, the outcome of several close elections would have been different, according to Stephen J. Wayne, professor of American Government at Georgetown University. In his book *The Road to the White House, 2000*, Wayne calculates that the district plan would have elected Richard Nixon in 1960 over John F. Kennedy, and that in 1976 it would have resulted in an electoral college tie between Gerald R. Ford and Jimmy Carter. The proportional plan would have thrown the 1960, 1968, 1992, and 1996 elections to the House of Representatives, because none of the candidates would have received an electoral vote majority.

Wayne advocated direct election, which he said would requires national systems of voting and tabulating of the results. The United States had neither at the beginning of the twenty-first century. Of the eleven presidential elections since 1960, only the 2000 election would have had a different result under direct election. As the popular vote winner, Gore would have been elected over Bush. Although the 1960 popular vote was even closer, Kennedy won both the popular and electoral college votes.

As in the 1969 plan, most of the direct election proposals call for a minimum plurality, usually 40 percent, with a runoff election to be held if no candidate receives the minimum percentage.

Presidential Disability

A decade of congressional concern over the question of presidential disability was eased in 1967 by ratification of the Twenty-fifth Amendment to the Constitution. The amendment for the first time provided for continuity in carrying out the functions of the presidency in the event of presidential disability and for filling a vacancy in the vice presidency. The amendment was approved by the Senate and House in 1965 and took effect February 10, 1967, after ratification by thirty-eight states. *(See "Constitutional Provisions and Amendments on Elections," p. 1545, in Reference Materials, Vol. II.)* Congressional consideration of the problem of presidential disability had been prompted by President Dwight D. Eisenhower's heart attack in 1955. The ambiguity of the language of the disability clause (Article II, Section 1, Clause 5) of the Constitution had provoked occasional debate ever since the Constitutional Convention of 1787. But it never had been decided how far the term *disability* extended or who would be the judge of it.

Clause 5 provided that Congress should decide who was to succeed to the presidency if both the president and the vice president died, resigned, or became disabled. Congress enacted succession laws three times. By the Act of March 1, 1792, it provided for succession (after the vice president) of the president pro tempore of the Senate, then of the House Speaker; if those offices were vacant, states were to send electors to Washington to choose a new president.

That law stood until passage of the Presidential Succession Act of January 19, 1886, which changed the line of succession to run from the vice president to the secretary of state, secretary of the Treasury, and so on through the cabinet in order of rank. Sixty-one years later the Presidential Succession Act of July 18, 1947, (still in force) placed the Speaker of the House and the president pro tempore of the Senate ahead of cabinet officers in succession after the vice president.

Before ratification of the Twenty-fifth Amendment, no procedures had been laid down to govern situations arising in the event of presidential incapacity or of a vacancy in the office of vice president. Two presidents had had serious disabilities—James A. Garfield, shot in 1881 and confined to his bed until he died two and a half months later, and Woodrow Wilson, who suffered a stroke in 1919. In each case the vice president did not assume any duties of the presidency for fear he would appear to be usurping the powers of that office.

Ratification of the Twenty-fifth Amendment established procedures that clarified these areas of uncertainty in the Constitution. The amendment provided that the vice president should become acting president under either one of two circumstances: (1) if the president informed Congress of inability to perform duties, the vice president would become acting president until the president could resume normal responsibilities; (2) if the vice president and a majority of the cabinet, or another body designated by Congress, found the president to be incapacitated, the vice president would become acting president until the president informed Congress that the disability had ended. Congress was given twenty-one days to resolve any dispute over the president's disability; a two-thirds vote of both chambers was required to overrule the president's declaration of being no longer incapacitated.

VACANCY IN THE VICE PRESIDENCY

The Twenty-fifth Amendment also specified what to do when a vacancy occurred in the office of the vice president, by death, succession to the presidency, or resignation. Through February 2001, the United States has been without a vice president eighteen times for a total of forty years, but since the amendment went into effect such vacancies have been brief. Under the amendment, the president nominates a replacement vice president, with the nomination subject to confirmation by a majority vote of both chambers of Congress. Within only eight years after ratification, two presidents used the power to appoint a new vice president.

In October 1973 when Vice President Agnew resigned, President Nixon nominated Gerald Ford as the new vice president. Ford was confirmed by both houses of Congress and sworn in

Immediately after President Ronald Reagan was shot on March 30, 1981, there was some confusion at the White House over who was in charge while the president was at a Washington, D.C., hospital.

December 6, 1973. On Nixon's resignation August 9, 1974, Ford succeeded to the presidency, becoming the first president in American history who was elected neither to the presidency nor to the vice presidency. President Ford chose as his new vice president Nelson A. Rockefeller, former governor of New York, who was sworn in December 19, 1974.

With both the president and vice president holding office through appointment rather than election, members of Congress and the public expressed concern about the power of a president to appoint, in effect, his own successor. Accordingly, Sen. John O. Pastore, Rhode Island Democrat, introduced a proposed constitutional amendment February 3, 1975, to provide for a special national election for president when more than one year remained in a presidential term. Hearings were held before the Senate Judiciary Subcommittee on Constitutional Amendments, but no action was taken.

CONFUSION AFTER REAGAN SHOOTING

In the aftermath of the attempted assassination of President Ronald Reagan in March 1981, there was no need to invoke the presidential disability provisions of the Twenty-fifth Amendment. However, some of the public statements made by administration officials immediately after the president was shot by John W. Hinckley Jr. reflected continuing confusion over the issue of who is in charge when the president temporarily is unable to function. Soon after news of the shooting became known, the members of the Reagan cabinet gathered in the White House, ready to invoke the amendment's procedures, if necessary. Vice President George Bush was on an Air Force jet returning to Washington from Texas.

At a televised press briefing later that afternoon, Secretary of State Alexander M. Haig Jr. confirmed that Reagan was in surgery and under anesthesia. It was clear that he temporarily was unable to make presidential decisions should the occasion—such as a foreign attack or other national emergency—require them. Attempting to reassure the country, Haig stated that he was in control in the White House pending the return of Vice President Bush, with whom he was in contact.

This assertion was followed by a question from the press about who was making administration decisions. Haig responded, "Constitutionally, gentlemen, you have the president, the vice president, and the secretary of state in that order, and should the president decide he wants to transfer the helm to the vice president, he will do so. He has not done that. As of now, I am in control here, in the White House, pending the return of the vice president and in close touch with him. If something came up, I would check with him, of course." Actually, the Constitution is silent on the order of succession beyond the vice president. Haig was referring to succession under laws superseded by the 1947 act, which specifies that the line of succession is the vice president, the Speaker of the House, the president pro tempore of the Senate, and then the cabinet officials in order of rank.

Criticism of the administration's failure to act after Reagan was shot shaped its response to the second instance of presidential disability, Reagan's cancer surgery on July 13, 1985. This time Reagan did relinquish his powers and duties to Bush before undergoing anesthesia. Curiously, however, he did not explicitly invoke the Twenty-fifth Amendment, saying instead that he was not convinced that the amendment was meant to apply to "such brief and temporary periods of incapacity." Still, a precedent was established that the Twenty-fifth Amendment would work as intended in future administrations. This precedent was followed in May 1991 when President Bush said he would turn power over to Vice President Dan Quayle if his irregular heartbeat required electroshock therapy. It did not.

CHAPTER 18

Electoral Votes for President, 1789–2000

ELECTORAL MAPS and vote charts for all presidential elections from 1789 to 2000 are presented in this section (pages 718–771). The sources for electoral votes cast for presidential candidates are the *Senate Manual* (Washington, D.C., U.S. Government Printing Office, 1997), and *CQ Weekly Report.*

Article II, Section 1 of the Constitution gives each state a number of electors equal to the number of senators and representatives to which it is entitled. Total electoral votes for each state through the 2000 election were compiled from a chart of each apportionment of the House of Representatives, published in Kenneth C. Martis and Gregory A. Elmes, *The Historical Atlas of State Power in Congress, 1790–1990* (Washington, D.C., Congressional Quarterly, 1993), pp. 6–7.

Under the Constitution (Article II, Section 1) each presidential elector was originally given two votes and was required to cast each vote for a different person. The person receiving the highest number of votes from a majority of electors was elected president; the person receiving the second highest total became vice president. For the first presidential election in 1789, there were 69 electors, and Washington's 69 votes constituted a unanimous election. After ratification of the Twelfth Amendment in 1804, electors were required to designate which of their two votes was for president and which was for vice president. The electoral college charts on pages 718–721 show *all* electoral votes cast in the elections of 1789, 1792, 1796, and 1800; the charts for 1804 and thereafter show electoral votes cast only for president.

For electoral votes cast for vice-presidential candidates, see pages 772–774 at the end of this chapter.

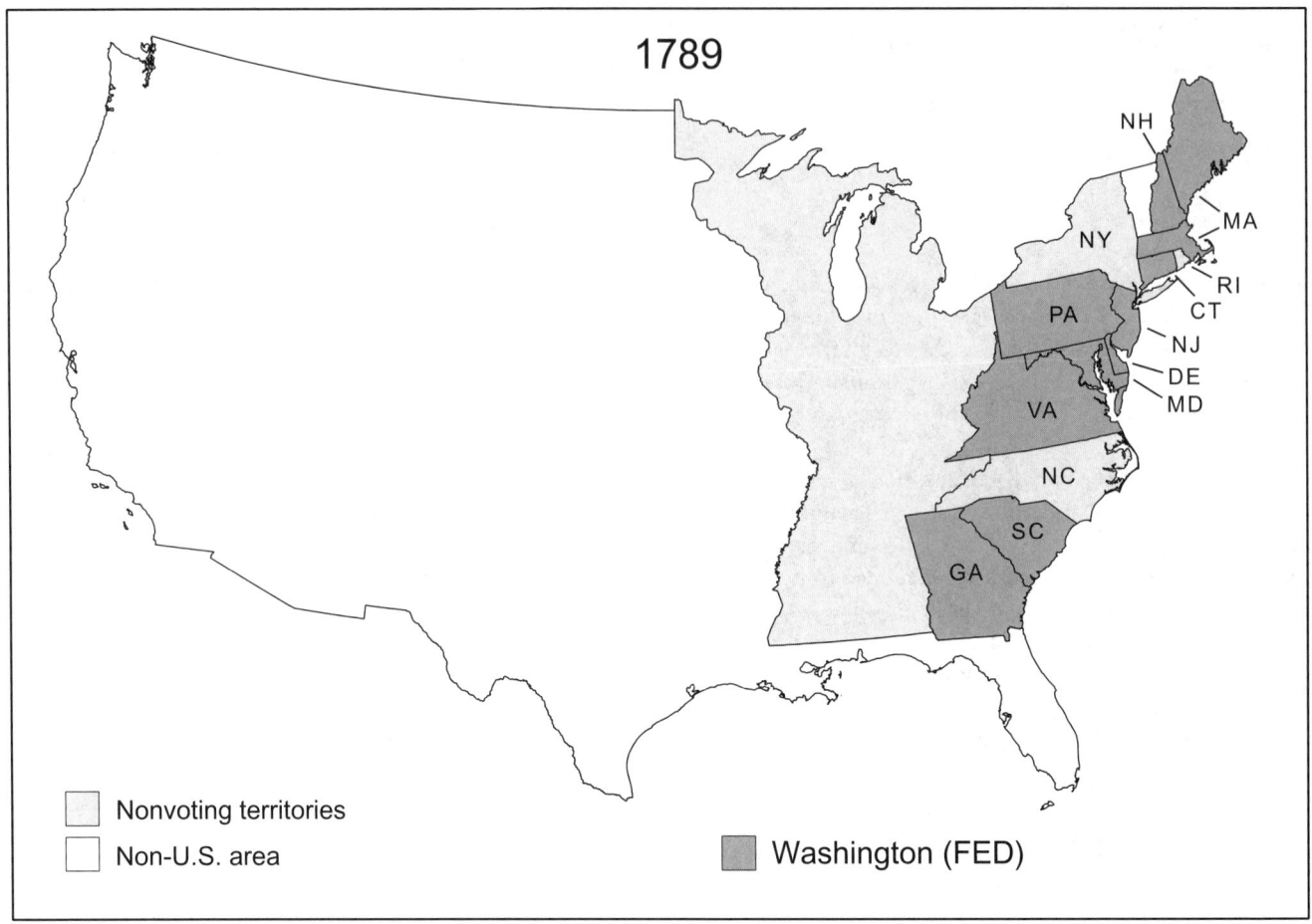

Key: FED—Federalist

States	Electoral votes[1]	Washington	Adams	Jay	Harrison	Rutledge	Hancock	Clinton	Huntington	Milton	Armstrong	Lincoln	Telfair
Connecticut[2]	(14)	7	5	–	–	–	–	–	2	–	–	–	–
Delaware	(6)	3	–	3	–	–	–	–	–	–	–	–	–
Georgia[2]	(10)	5	–	–	–	–	–	–	–	2	1	1	1
Maryland[3]	(16)	6	–	–	6	–	–	–	–	–	–	–	–
Massachusetts	(20)	10	10	–	–	–	–	–	–	–	–	–	–
New Hampshire	(10)	5	5	–	–	–	–	–	–	–	–	–	–
New Jersey[2]	(12)	6	1	5	–	–	–	–	–	–	–	–	–
New York[4]	(16)	–	–	–	–	–	–	–	–	–	–	–	–
North Carolina[5]	(14)	–	–	–	–	–	–	–	–	–	–	–	–
Pennsylvania[2]	(20)	10	8	–	–	–	2	–	–	–	–	–	–
Rhode Island[5]	(6)	–	–	–	–	–	–	–	–	–	–	–	–
South Carolina[2]	(14)	7	–	–	–	6	1	–	–	–	–	–	–
Virginia[6]	(24)	10	5	1	–	–	1	3	–	–	–	–	–
Totals	(182)	69	34	9	6	6	4	3	2	2	1	1	1

1. Two votes for each elector; see explanation, p. 717.
2. For explanation of split electoral votes, see p. 702.
3. Two Maryland electors did not vote.
4. Not voting. Because of a dispute between its two chambers, the New York legislature failed to choose electors.
5. Not voting because had not yet ratified the Constitution.
6. Two Virginia electors did not vote. For explanation of split electoral votes, see p. 702.

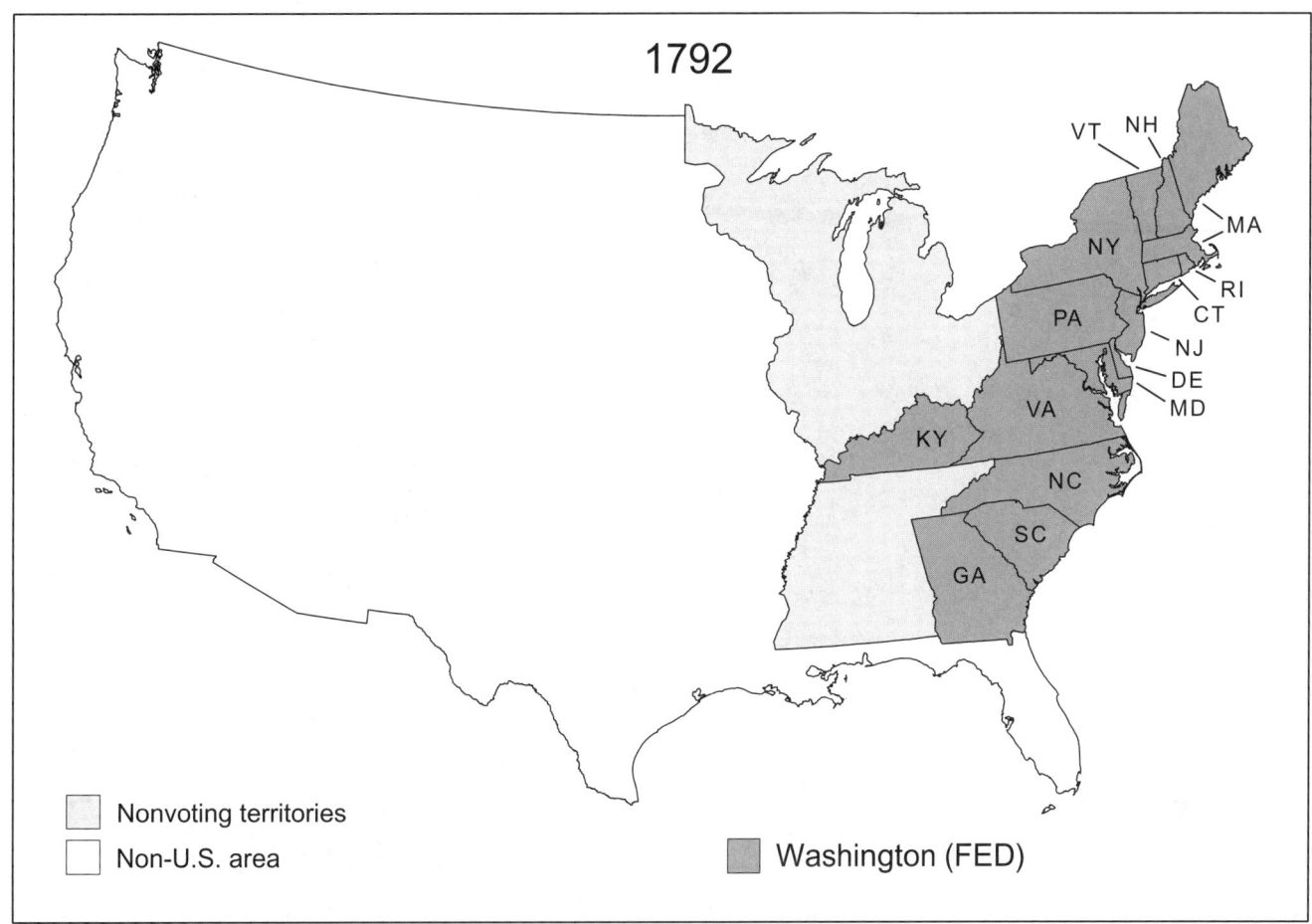

Key: FED—Federalist

States	Electoral votes[1]	Washington	Adams	Clinton	Jefferson	Burr
Connecticut	(18)	9	9	–	–	–
Delaware	(6)	3	3	–	–	–
Georgia	(8)	4	–	4	–	–
Kentucky	(8)	4	–	–	4	–
Maryland[2]	(20)	8	8	–	–	–
Massachusetts	(32)	16	16	–	–	–
New Hampshire	(12)	6	6	–	–	–
New Jersey	(14)	7	7	–	–	–
New York	(24)	12	–	12	–	–
North Carolina	(24)	12	–	12	–	–
Pennsylvania3	(30)	15	14	1	–	–
Rhode Island	(8)	4	4	–	–	–
South Carolina3	(16)	8	7	–	–	1
Vermont2	(8)	3	3	–	–	–
Virginia	(42)	21	–	21	–	–
Totals	(270)	132	77	50	4	1

1. Two votes for each elector; see explanation, p. 717.
2. Two Maryland electors and one Vermont elector did not vote.
3. For explanation of split electoral votes, see p. 702.

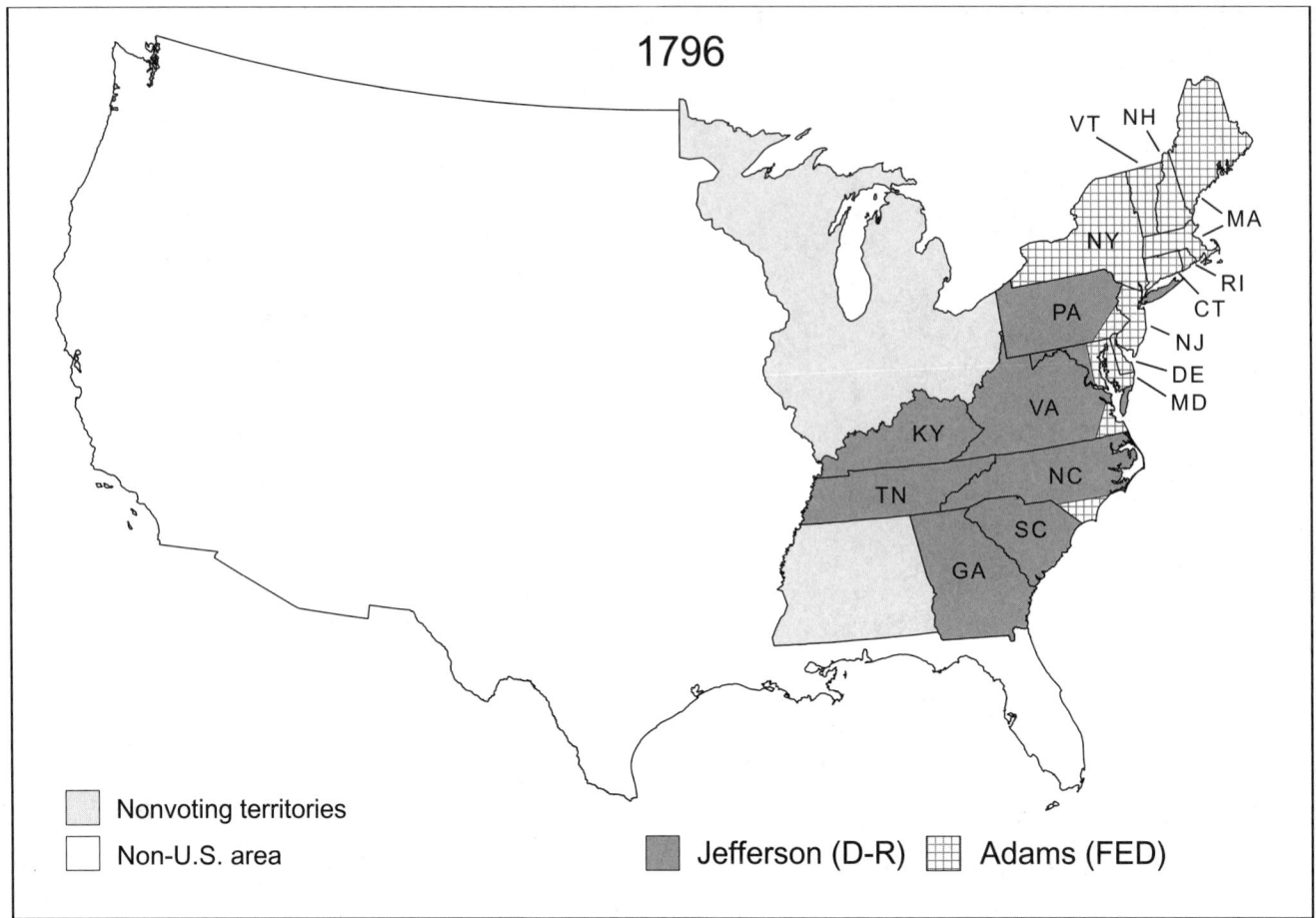

1796

Nonvoting territories

Non-U.S. area

Jefferson (D-R)   Adams (FED)

Key: D-R—Democratic-Republican; FED—Federalist

States	Electoral votes[1]	J. Adams	Jefferson	T. Pinckney	Burr	S. Adams	Ellsworth	Clinton	Jay	Iredell	Henry	Johnston	Washington	C. Pinckney
Connecticut[2]	(18)	9	–	4	–	–	–	–	5	–	–	–	–	–
Delaware	(6)	3	–	3	–	–	–	–	–	–	–	–	–	–
Georgia	(8)	–	4	–	–	–	–	4	–	–	–	–	–	–
Kentucky	(8)	–	4	–	4	–	–	–	–	–	–	–	–	–
Maryland[2]	(20)	7	4	4	3	–	–	–	–	–	2	–	–	–
Massachusetts[2]	(32)	16	–	13	–	–	1	–	–	–	–	2	–	–
New Hampshire	(12)	6	–	–	–	–	6	–	–	–	–	–	–	–
New Jersey	(14)	7	–	7	–	–	–	–	–	–	–	–	–	–
New York	(24)	12	–	12	–	–	–	–	–	–	–	–	–	–
North Carolina[2]	(24)	1	11	1	6	–	–	–	–	3	–	–	1	1
Pennsylvania[2]	(30)	1	14	2	13	–	–	–	–	–	–	–	–	–
Rhode Island	(8)	4	–	–	–	–	4	–	–	–	–	–	–	–
South Carolina	(16)	–	8	8	–	–	–	–	–	–	–	–	–	–
Tennessee	(6)	–	3	–	3	–	–	–	–	–	–	–	–	–
Vermont	(8)	4	–	4	–	–	–	–	–	–	–	–	–	–
Virginia[2]	(42)	1	20	1	1	15	–	3	–	–	–	–	1	–
Totals	(276)	71	68	59	30	15	11	7	5	3	2	2	2	1

1. Two votes for each elector; see explanation, p. 717.
2. For explanation of split electoral votes, see p. 702.

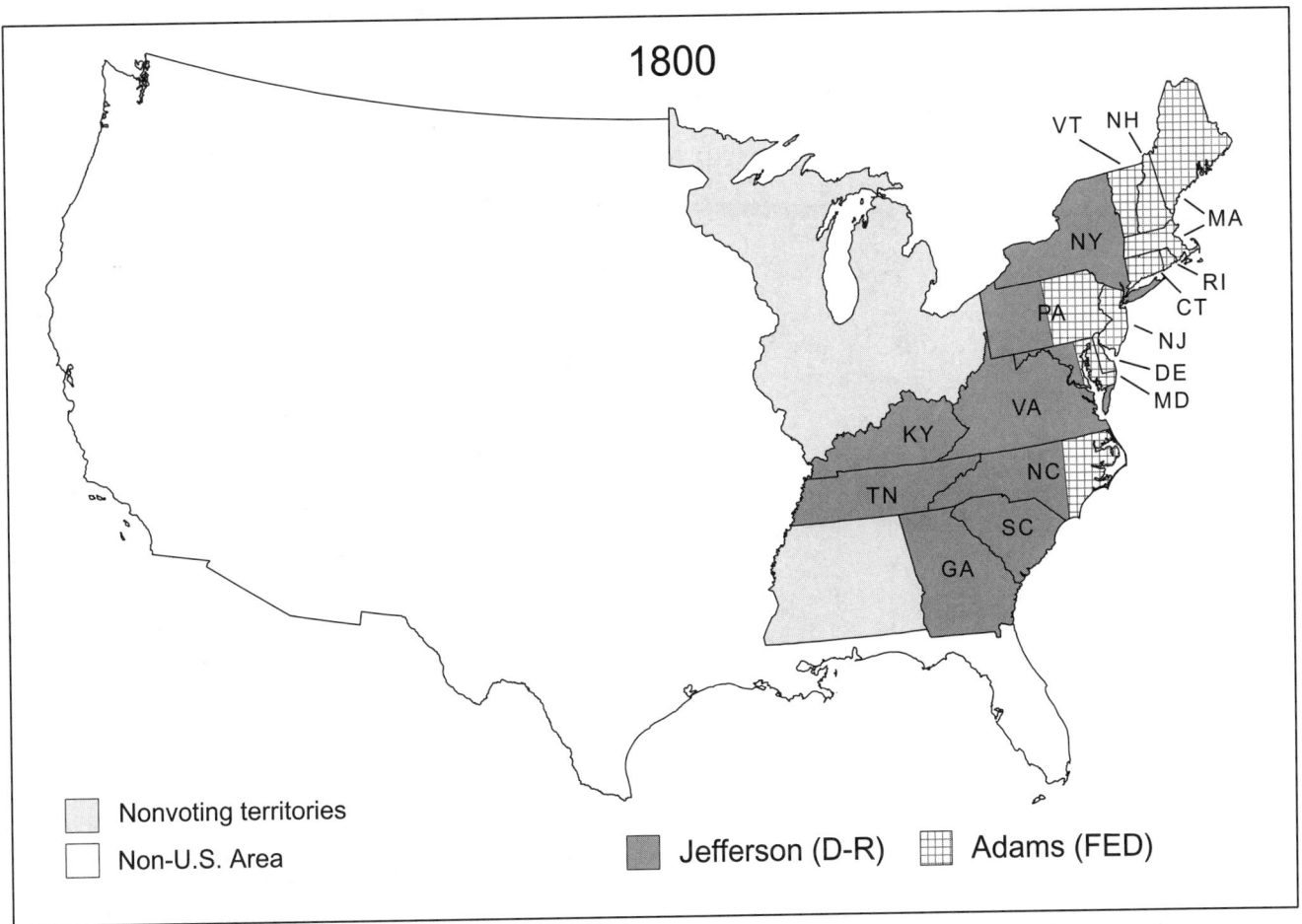

1800

Nonvoting territories

Non-U.S. Area

Jefferson (D-R)   Adams (FED)

Key: D-R—Democratic-Republican; FED—Federalist

States	Electoral Vote[1]	Jefferson[2]	Burr[2]	Adams	Pinckney	Jay	States	Electoral votes[1]	Jefferson[2]	Burr[2]	Adams	Pinckney	Jay
Connecticut	(18)	–	–	9	9	–	North Carolina[3]	(24)	8	8	4	4	–
Delaware	(6)	–	–	3	3	–	Pennsylvania[3]	(30)	8	8	7	7	–
Georgia	(8)	4	4	–	–	–	Rhode Island[3]	(8)	–	–	4	3	1
Kentucky	(8)	4	4	–	–	–	South Carolina	(16)	8	8	–	–	–
Maryland[3]	(20)	5	5	5	5	–	Tennessee	(6)	3	3	–	–	–
Massachusetts	(32)	–	–	16	16	–	Vermont	(8)	–	–	4	4	–
New Hampshire	(12)	–	–	6	6	–	Virginia	(42)	21	21	–	–	–
New Jersey	(14)	–	–	7	7	–							
New York	(24)	12	12	–	–	–	Totals	(276)	73	73	65	64	1

1. Two votes for each elector; see explanation, p. 717.
2. Since Jefferson and Burr tied in the electoral college, the election was decided (in Jefferson's favor) by the House of Representatives. See "Jefferson's Revenge: 1800," p.207.
3. For explanation of split electoral votes, see p. 702.

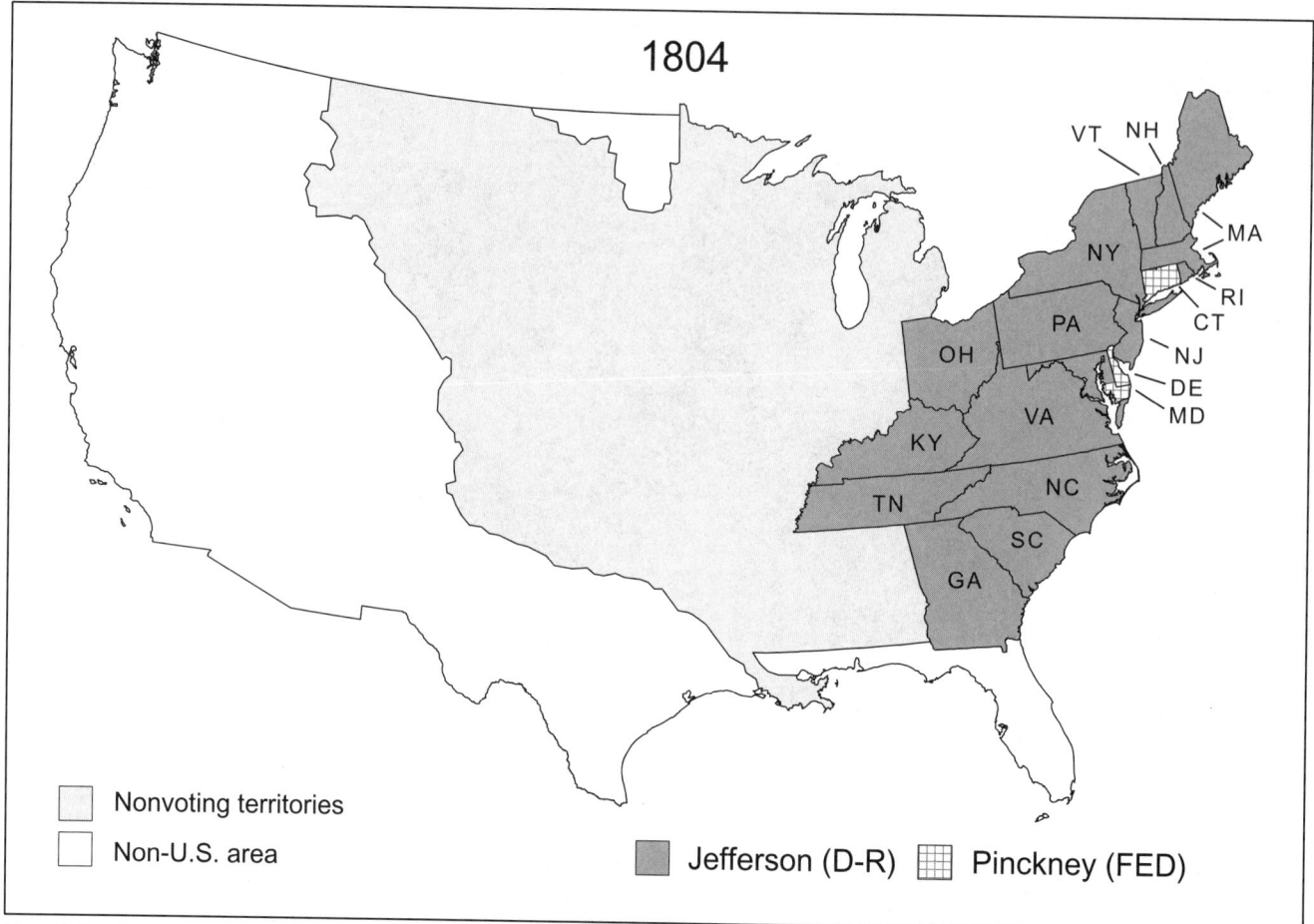

1804

Nonvoting territories

Non-U.S. area

Jefferson (D-R)   Pinckney (FED)

Key: D-R—Democratic-Republican; FED—Federalist

States	Electoral votes	Jefferson	Pinckney	States	Electoral votes	Jefferson	Pinckney
Connecticut	(9)	–	9	Ohio	(3)	3	–
Delaware	(3)	–	3	Pennsylvania	(20)	20	–
Georgia	(6)	6	–	Rhode Island	(4)	4	–
Kentucky	(8)	8	–	South Carolina	(10)	10	–
Maryland[1]	(11)	9	2	Tennessee	(5)	5	–
Massachusetts	(19)	19	–	Vermont	(6)	6	–
New Hampshire	(7)	7	–	Virginia	(24)	24	–
New Jersey	(8)	8	–				
New York	(19)	19	–	Totals	(176)	162	14
North Carolina	(14)	14	–				

1. For explanation of split electoral votes, see p. 702.

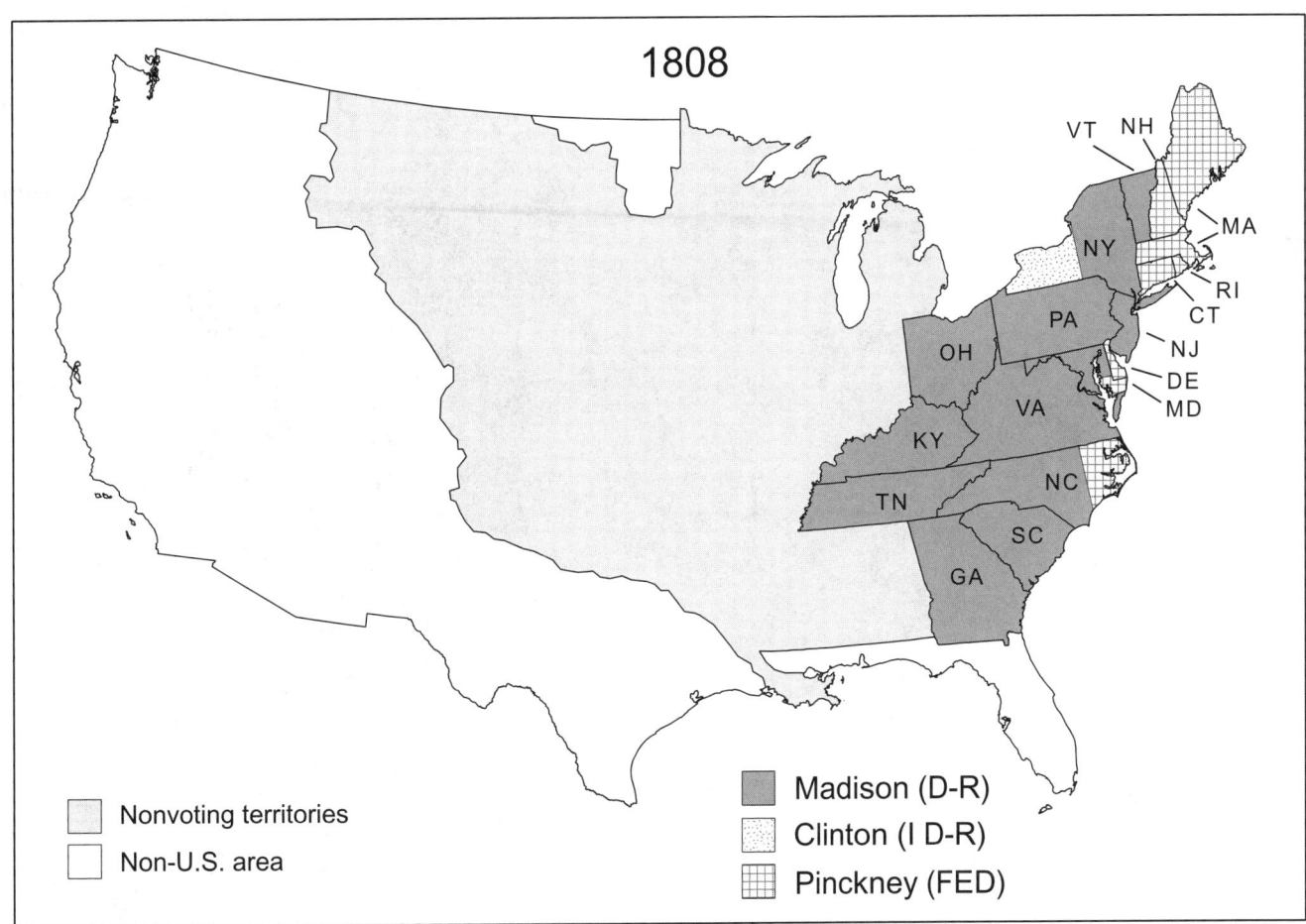

1808

Key: D-R—Democratic-Republican; FED—Federalist; I D-R—Independent Democratic-Republican

States	Electoral votes	Madison	Pinckney	Clinton	States	Electoral votes	Madison	Pinckney	Clinton
Connecticut	(9)	–	9	–	Ohio	(3)	3	–	–
Delaware	(3)	–	3	–	Pennsylvania	(20)	20	–	–
Georgia	(6)	6	–	–	Rhode Island	(4)	–	4	–
Kentucky[1]	(8)	7	–	–	South Carolina	(10)	10	–	–
Maryland[2]	(11)	9	2	–	Tennessee	(5)	5	–	–
Massachusetts	(19)	–	19	–	Vermont	(6)	6	–	–
New Hampshire	(7)	–	7	–	Virginia	(24)	24	–	–
New Jersey	(8)	8	–	–					
New York[2]	(19)	13	–	6	Totals	(176)	122	47	6
North Carolina[2]	(14)	11	3	–					

1. One Kentucky elector did not vote.
2. For explanation of split electoral votes, see p. 702.

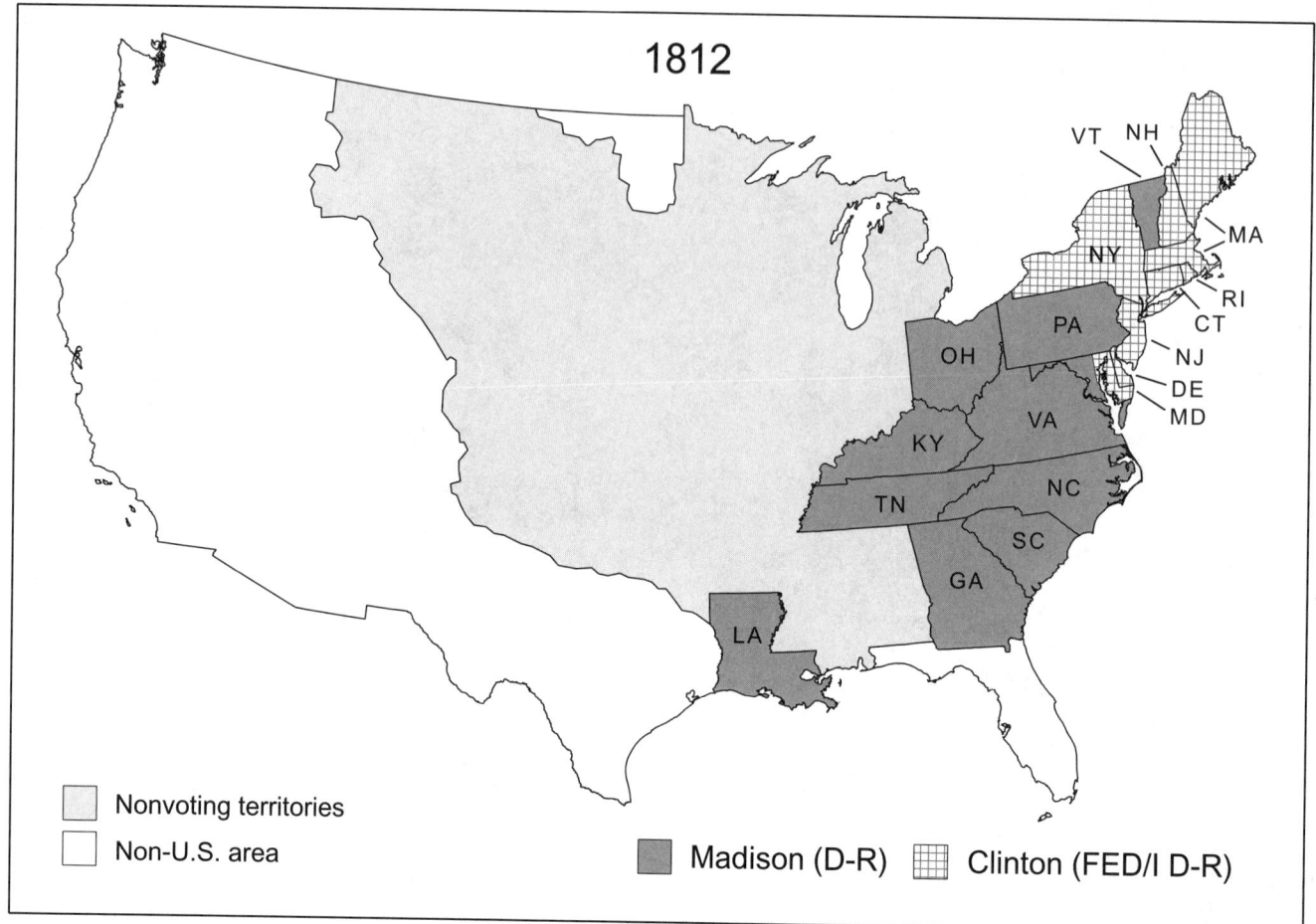

1812

Key: D-R—Democratic-Republican; FED/I D-R—Federalist/Independent Democratic-Republican

States	Electoral votes	Madison	Clinton	States	Electoral votes	Madison	Clinton
Connecticut	(9)	–	9	North Carolina	(15)	15	–
Delaware	(4)	–	4	Ohio[2]	(8)	7	–
Georgia	(8)	8	–	Pennsylvania	(25)	25	–
Kentucky	(12)	12	–	Rhode Island	(4)	–	4
Louisiana	(3)	3	–	South Carolina	(11)	11	–
Maryland[1]	(11)	6	5	Tennessee	(8)	8	–
Massachusetts	(22)	–	22	Vermont	(8)	8	–
New Hampshire	(8)	–	8	Virginia	(25)	25	–
New Jersey	(8)	–	8				
New York	(29)	–	29	Totals	(218)	128	89

1. For explanation of split electoral votes, see p. 702.
2. One Ohio elector did not vote.

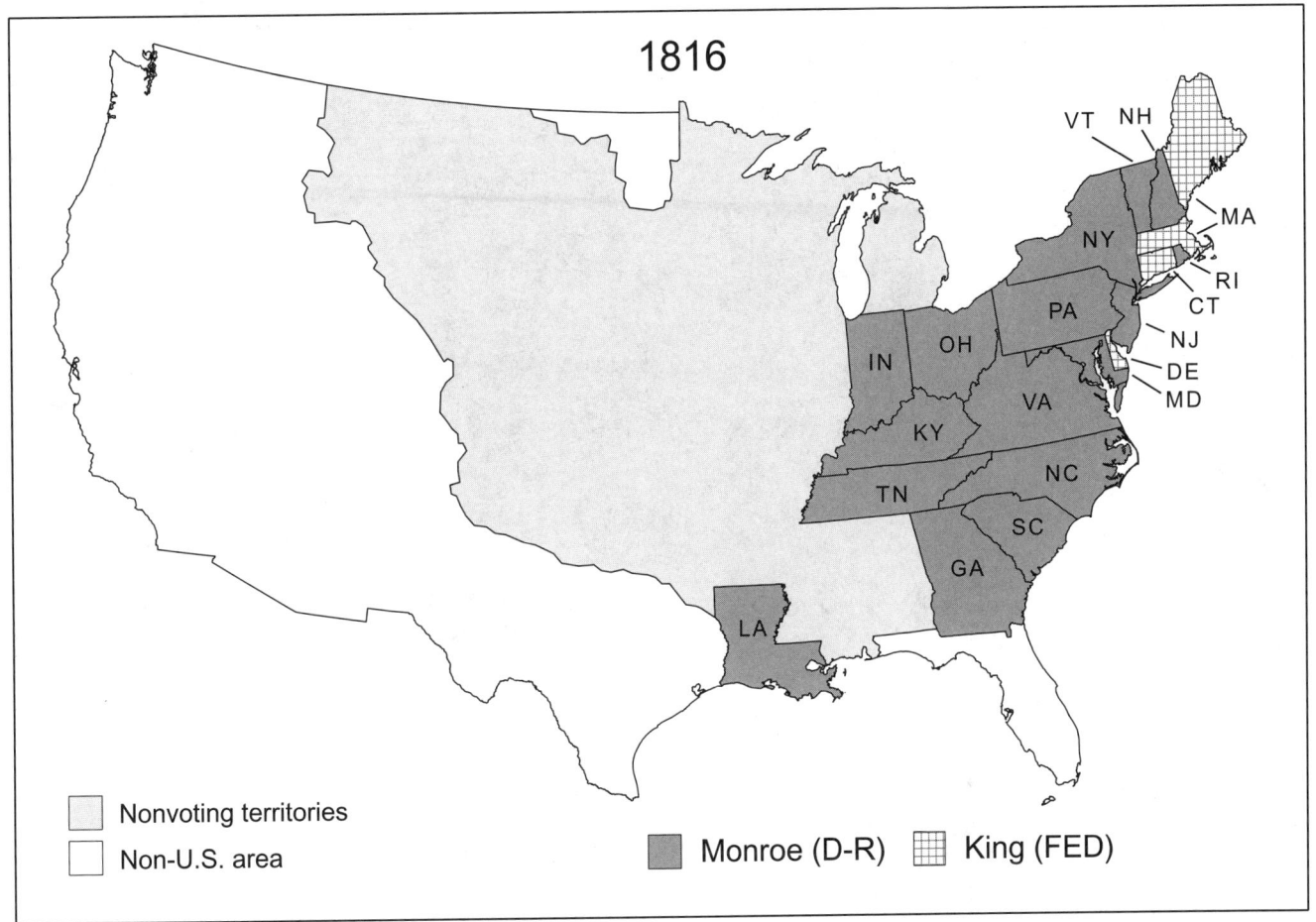

1816

Key: D-R—Democratic-Republican; FED—Federalist

States	Electoral votes	Monroe	King	States	Electoral votes	Monroe	King
Connecticut	(9)	–	9	North Carolina	(15)	15	–
Delaware[1]	(4)	–	3	Ohio	(8)	8	–
Georgia	(8)	8	–	Pennsylvania	(25)	25	–
Indiana	(3)	3	–	Rhode Island	(4)	4	–
Kentucky	(12)	12	–	South Carolina	(11)	11	–
Louisiana	(3)	3	–	Tennessee	(8)	8	–
Maryland[1]	(11)	8	–	Vermont	(8)	8	–
Massachusetts	(22)	–	22	Virginia	(25)	25	–
New Hampshire	(8)	8	–				
New Jersey	(8)	8	–	Totals	(221)	183	34
New York	(29)	29	–				

1. One Delaware and three Maryland electors did not vote.

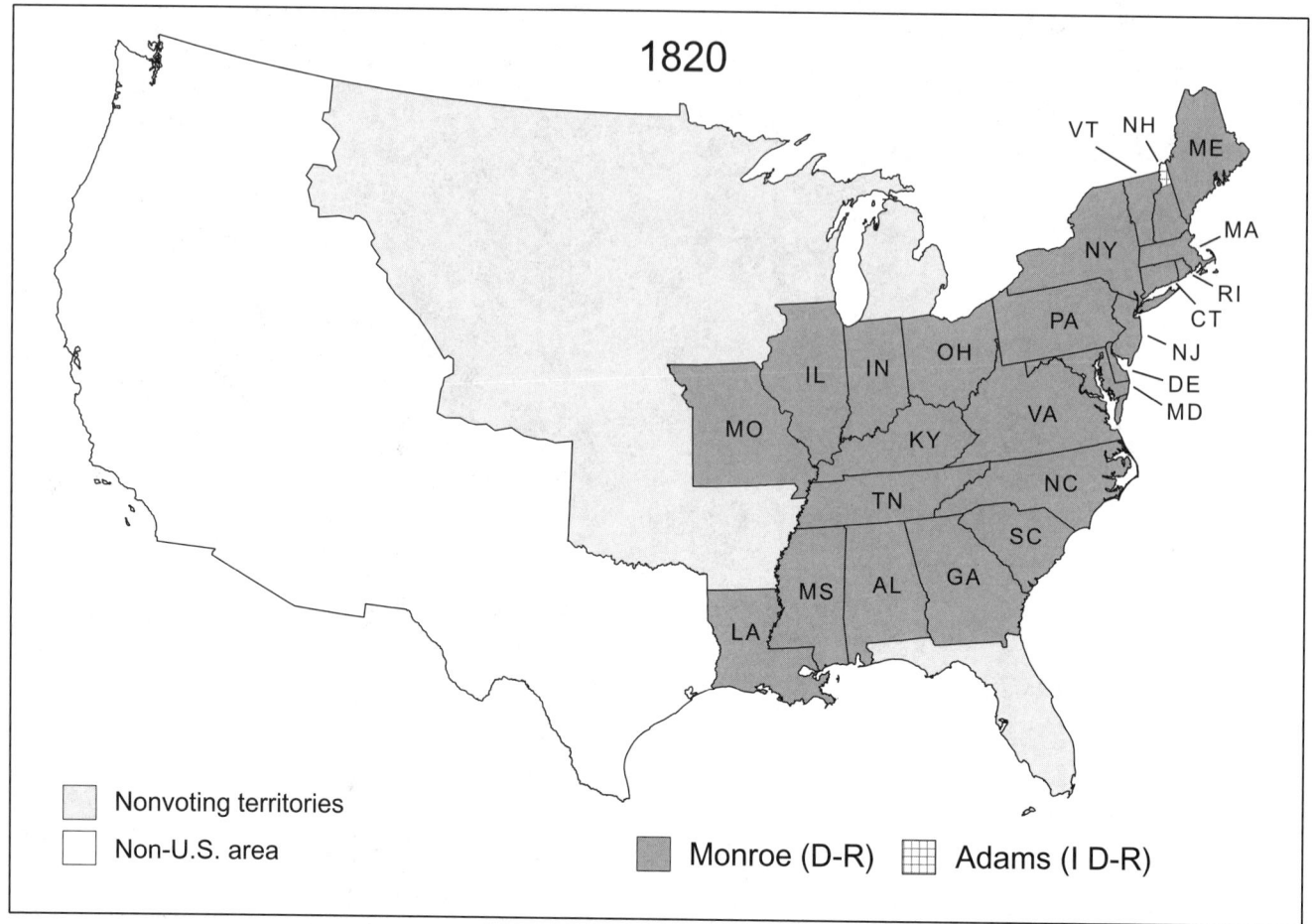

1820

Nonvoting territories

Non-U.S. area

Monroe (D-R)   Adams (I D-R)

Key: D-R—Democratic-Republican; I D-R Independent Democratic-Republican

States	Electoral votes	Monroe	Adams	States	Electoral votes	Monroe	Adams
Alabama	(3)	3	–	New Hampshire[2]	(8)	7	1
Connecticut	(9)	9	–	New Jersey	(8)	8	–
Delaware	(4)	4	–	New York	(29)	29	–
Georgia	(8)	8	–	North Carolina	(15)	15	–
Illinois	(3)	3	–	Ohio	(8)	8	–
Indiana	(3)	3	–	Pennsylvania[1]	(25)	24	–
Kentucky	(12)	12	–	Rhode Island	(4)	4	–
Louisiana	(3)	3	–	South Carolina	(11)	11	–
Maine	(9)	9	–	Tennessee[1]	(8)	7	–
Maryland	(11)	11	–	Vermont	(8)	8	–
Massachusetts	(15)	15	–	Virginia	(25)	25	–
Mississippi[1]	(3)	2	–				
Missouri	(3)	3	–	Totals	(235)	231	1

1. One elector each from Mississippi, Pennsylvania, and Tennessee did not vote.
2. For explanation of split electoral votes, see p. 702.

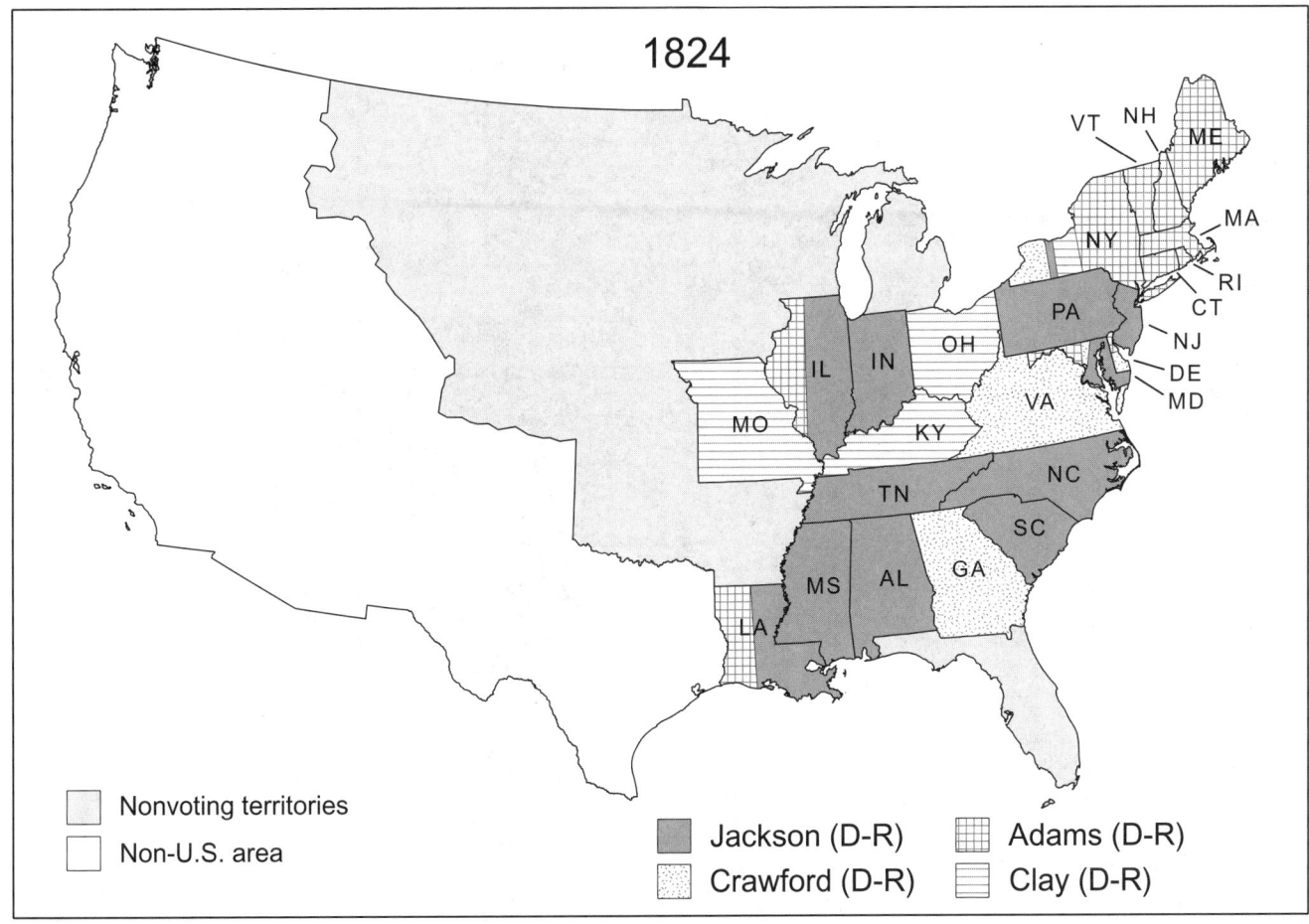

1824

Key: D-R—Democratic-Republican

States	Electoral votes	Jackson	Adams	Crawford	Clay	States	Electoral votes	Jackson	Adams	Crawford	Clay
Alabama	(5)	5	–	–	–	New Hampshire	(8)	–	8	–	–
Connecticut	(8)	–	8	–	–	New Jersey	(8)	8	–	–	–
Delaware[1]	(3)	–	1	2	–	New York[1]	(36)	1	26	5	4
Georgia	(9)	–	–	9	–	North Carolina	(15)	15	–	–	–
Illinois[1]	(3)	2	1	–	–	Ohio	(16)	–	–	–	16
Indiana	(5)	5	–	–	–	Pennsylvania	(28)	28	–	–	–
Kentucky	(14)	–	–	–	14	Rhode Island	(4)	–	4	–	–
Louisiana[1]	(5)	3	2	–	–	South Carolina	(11)	11	–	–	–
Maine	(9)	–	9	–	–	Tennessee	(11)	11	–	–	–
Maryland[1]	(11)	7	3	1	–	Vermont	(7)	–	7	–	–
Massachusetts	(15)	–	15	–	–	Virginia	(24)	–	–	24	–
Mississippi	(3)	3	–	–	–						
Missouri	(3)	–	–	–	3	Totals	(261)	99[2]	84	41	37

1. For explanation of split electoral votes, see p. 702.
2. As no candidate received a majority of the electoral votes, the election was decided (in Adams's favor) by the House of Representatives.

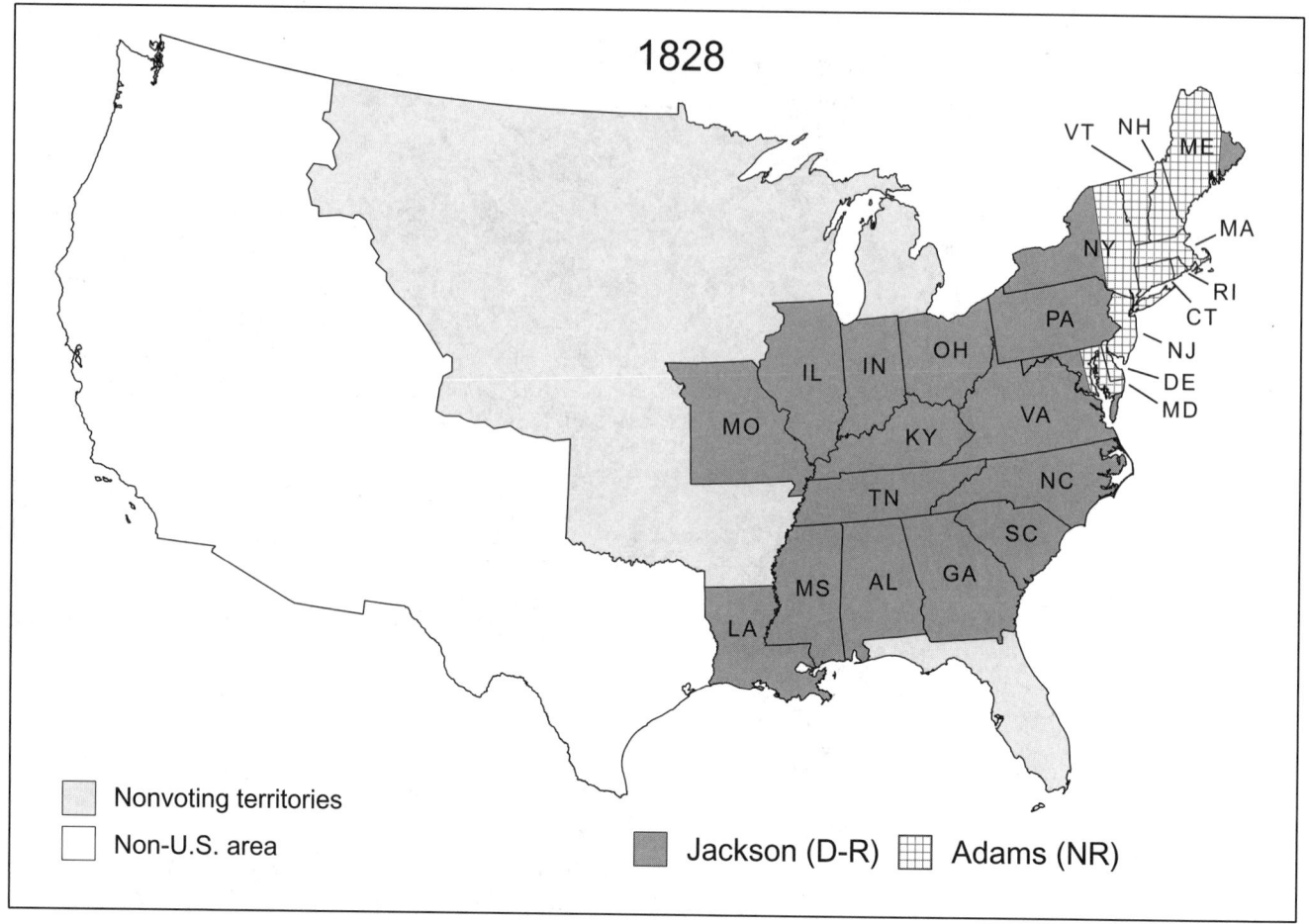

1828

Nonvoting territories

Non-U.S. area

Jackson (D-R)　Adams (NR)

Key: D-R—Democratic-Republican; NR—National Republican

States	Electoral votes	Jackson	Adams	States	Electoral votes	Jackson	Adams
Alabama	(5)	5	–	New Hampshire	(8)	–	8
Connecticut	(8)	–	8	New Jersey	(8)	–	8
Delaware	(3)	–	3	New York[1]	(36)	20	16
Georgia	(9)	9	–	North Carolina	(15)	15	–
Illinois	(3)	3	–	Ohio	(16)	16	–
Indiana	(5)	5	–	Pennsylvania	(28)	28	–
Kentucky	(14)	14	–	Rhode Island	(4)	–	4
Louisiana	(5)	5	–	South Carolina	(11)	11	–
Maine[1]	(9)	1	8	Tennessee	(11)	11	–
Maryland[1]	(11)	5	6	Vermont	(7)	–	7
Massachusetts	(15)	–	15	Virginia	(24)	24	–
Mississippi	(3)	3	–				
Missouri	(3)	3	–	Totals	(261)	178	83

1. For explanation of split electoral votes, see p. 702.

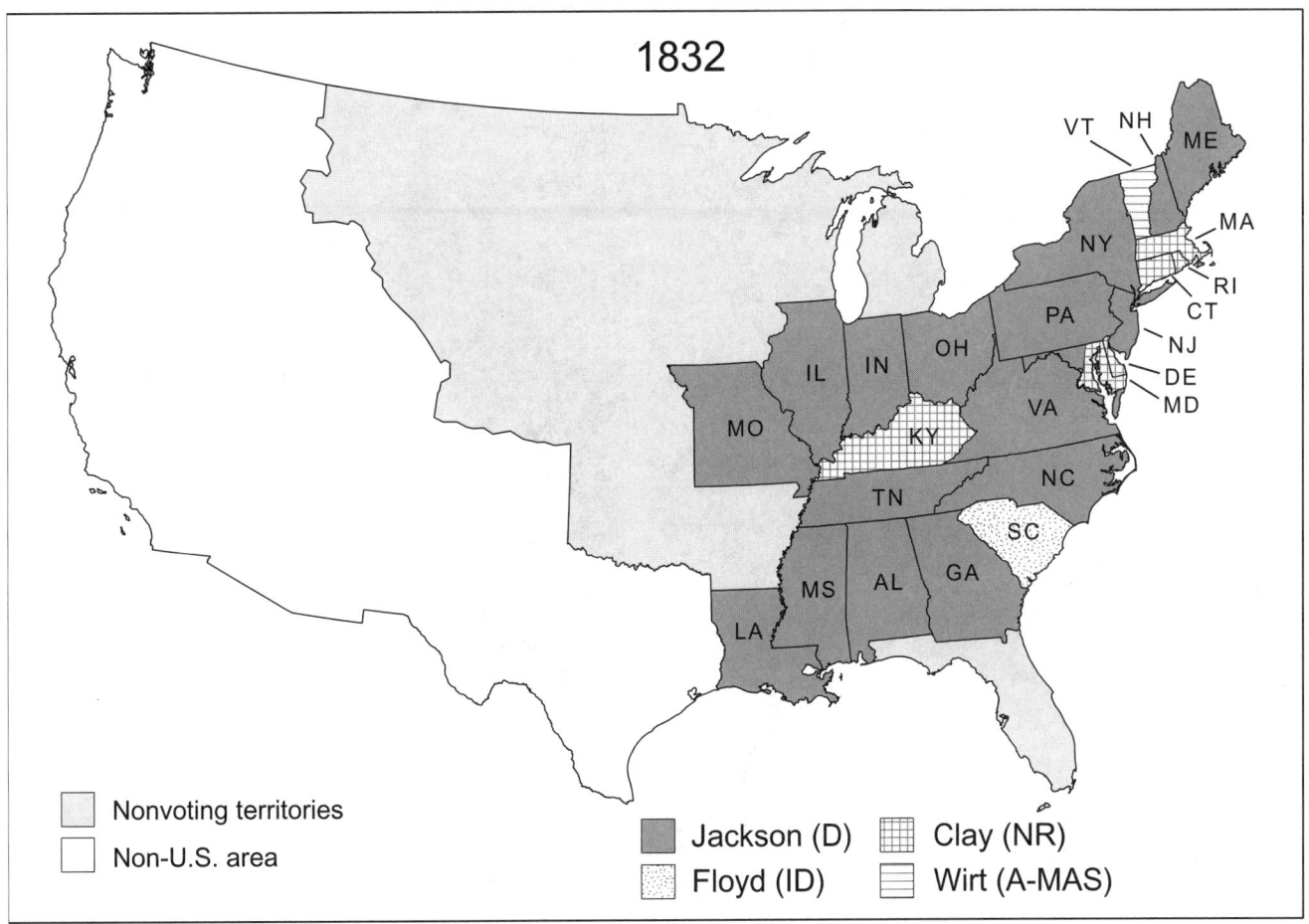

1832

Nonvoting territories

Non-U.S. area

Jackson (D)   Clay (NR)

Floyd (ID)   Wirt (A-MAS)

Key: A-MAS—Anti-Mason; D—Democrat; ID—Independent Democrat; NR—National Republican

States	Electoral votes	Jackson	Clay	Floyd	Wirt	States	Electoral votes	Jackson	Clay	Floyd	Wirt
Alabama	(7)	7	–	–	–	New Hampshire	(7)	7	–	–	–
Connecticut	(8)	–	8	–	–	New Jersey	(8)	8	–	–	–
Delaware	(3)	–	3	–	–	New York	(42)	42	–	–	–
Georgia	(11)	11	–	–	–	North Carolina	(15)	15	–	–	–
Illinois	(5)	5	–	–	–	Ohio	(21)	21	–	–	–
Indiana	(9)	9	–	–	–	Pennsylvania	(30)	30	–	–	–
Kentucky	(15)	–	15	–	–	Rhode Island	(4)	–	4	–	–
Louisiana	(5)	5	–	–	–	South Carolina	(11)	–	–	11	–
Maine	(10)	10	–	–	–	Tennessee	(15)	15	–	–	–
Maryland[1]	(10)	3	5	–	–	Vermont	(7)	–	–	–	7
Massachusetts	(14)	–	14	–	–	Virginia	(23)	23	–	–	–
Mississippi	(4)	4	–	–	–						
Missouri	(4)	4	–	–	–	Totals	(288)	219	49	11	7

1. Two Maryland electors did not vote. For explanation of split electoral votes, see p. 702.

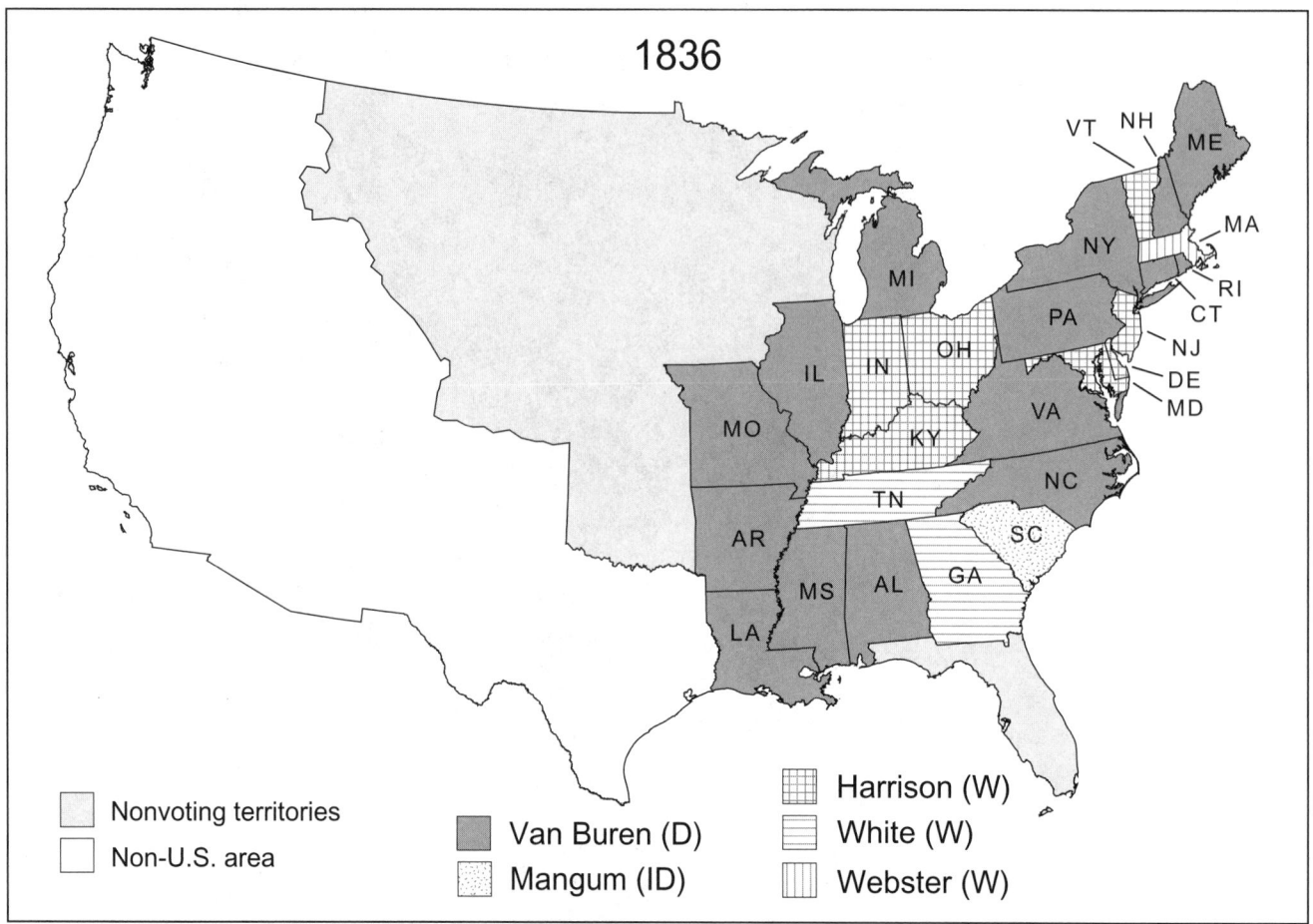

1836

Key: D—Democrat; ID—Independent Democrat; W—Whig

States	Electoral votes	Van Buren	Harrison[1]	White[1]	Webster[1]	Mangum
Alabama	(7)	7	–	–	–	–
Arkansas	(3)	3	–	–	–	–
Connecticut	(8)	8	–	–	–	–
Delaware	(3)	–	3	–	–	–
Georgia	(11)	–	–	11	–	–
Illinois	(5)	5	–	–	–	–
Indiana	(9)	–	9	–	–	–
Kentucky	(15)	–	15	–	–	–
Louisiana	(5)	5	–	–	–	–
Maine	(10)	10	–	–	–	–
Maryland	(10)	–	10	–	–	–
Massachusetts	(14)	–	–	–	14	–
Michigan	(3)	3	–	–	–	–
Mississippi	(4)	4	–	–	–	–
Missouri	(4)	4	–	–	–	–
New Hampshire	(7)	7	–	–	–	–
New Jersey	(8)	–	8	–	–	–
New York	(42)	42	–	–	–	–
North Carolina	(15)	15	–	–	–	–
Ohio	(21)	–	21	–	–	–
Pennsylvania	(30)	30	–	–	–	–
Rhode Island	(4)	4	–	–	–	–
South Carolina	(11)	–	–	–	–	11
Tennessee	(15)	–	–	15	–	–
Vermont	(7)	–	7	–	–	–
Virginia	(23)	23	–	–	–	–
Totals	(294)	170	73	26	14	11

1. For an explanation of the Whigs' strategy in running several candidates, see "Van Buren's 1836 Win," p. 235.

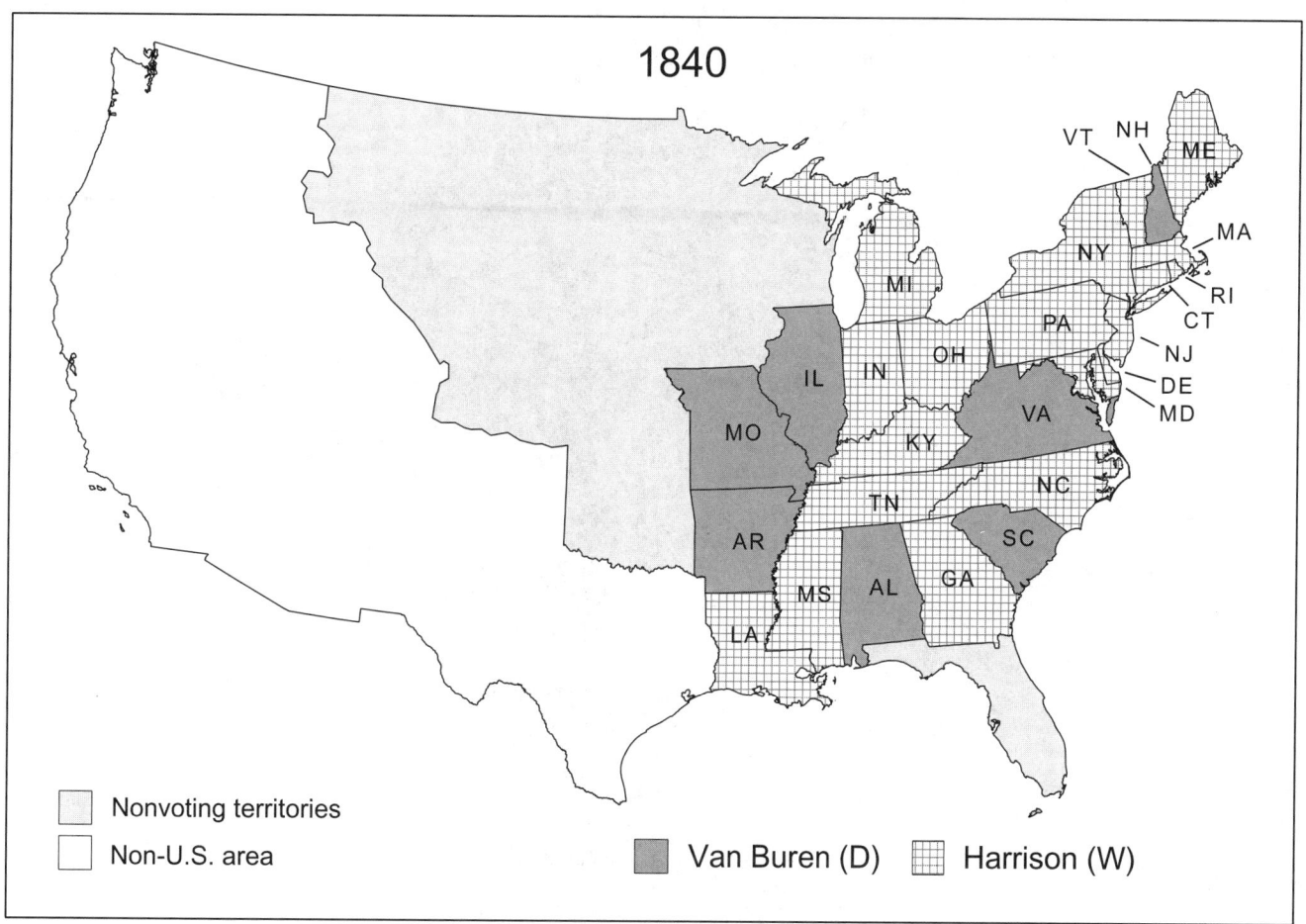

Key: D—Democrat; W—Whig

States	Electoral votes	Harrison	Van Buren	States	Electoral votes	Harrison	Van Buren
Alabama	(7)	–	7	Missouri	(4)	–	4
Arkansas	(3)	–	3	New Hampshire	(7)	–	7
Connecticut	(8)	8	–	New Jersey	(8)	8	–
Delaware	(3)	3	–	New York	(42)	42	–
Georgia	(11)	11	–	North Carolina	(15)	15	–
Illinois	(5)	–	5	Ohio	(21)	21	–
Indiana	(9)	9	–	Pennsylvania	(30)	30	–
Kentucky	(15)	15	–	Rhode Island	(4)	4	–
Louisiana	(5)	5	–	South Carolina	(11)	–	11
Maine	(10)	10	–	Tennessee	(15)	15	–
Maryland	(10)	10	–	Vermont	(7)	7	–
Massachusetts	(14)	14	–	Virginia	(23)	–	23
Michigan	(3)	3	–				
Mississippi	(4)	4	–	Totals	(294)	234	60

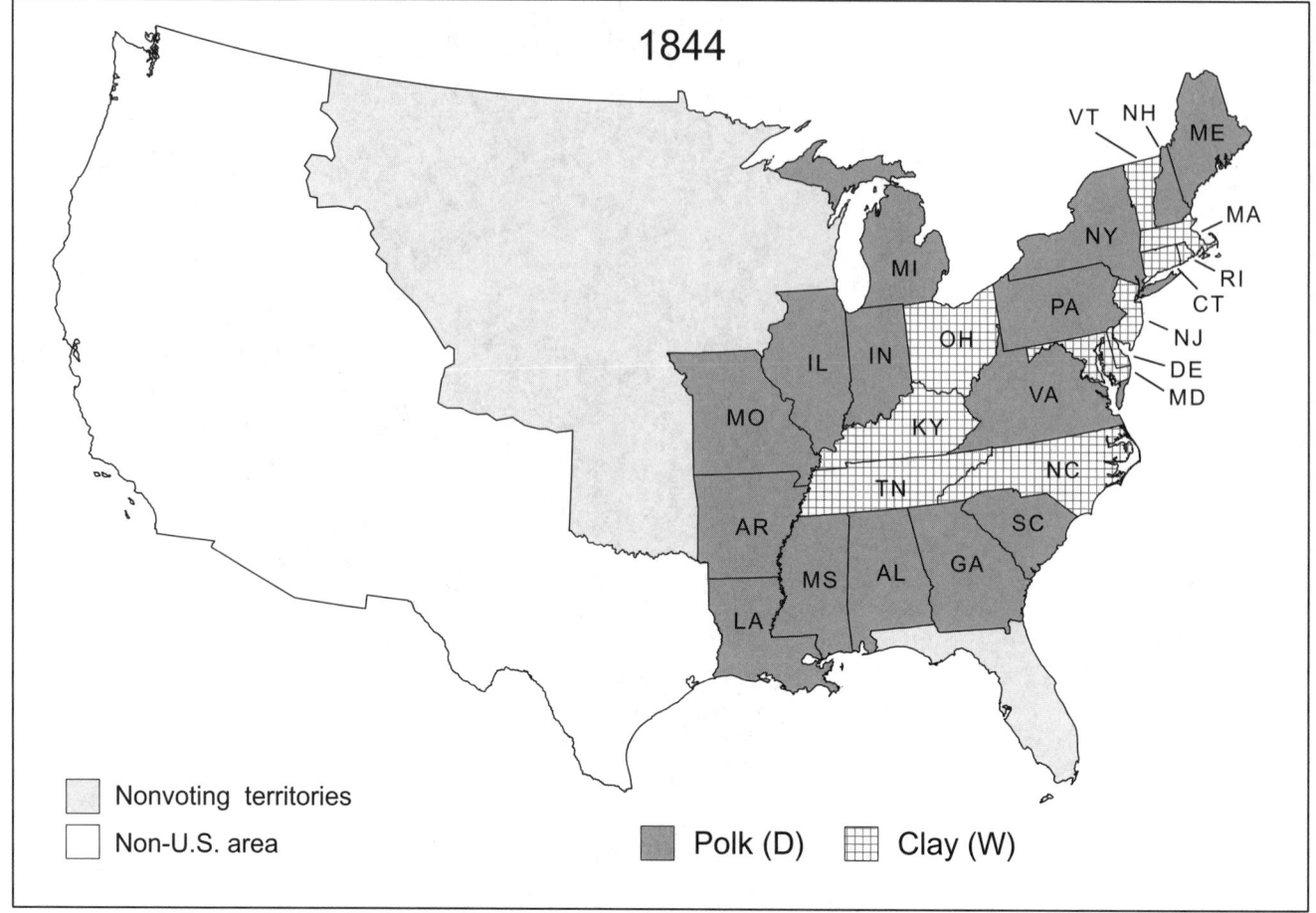

1844

Nonvoting territories

Non-U.S. area

Polk (D)   Clay (W)

Key: D—Democrat; W—Whig

States	Electoral votes	Polk	Clay	States	Electoral votes	Polk	Clay
Alabama	(9)	9	–	Missouri	(7)	7	–
Arkansas	(3)	3	–	New Hampshire	(6)	6	–
Connecticut	(6)	–	6	New Jersey	(7)	–	7
Delaware	(3)	–	3	New York	(36)	36	–
Georgia	(10)	10	–	North Carolina	(11)	–	11
Illinois	(9)	9	–	Ohio	(23)	–	23
Indiana	(12)	12	–	Pennsylvania	(26)	26	–
Kentucky	(12)	–	12	Rhode Island	(4)	–	4
Louisiana	(6)	6	–	South Carolina	(9)	9	–
Maine	(9)	9	–	Tennessee	(13)	–	13
Maryland	(8)	–	8	Vermont	(6)	–	6
Massachusetts	(12)	–	12	Virginia	(17)	17	–
Michigan	(5)	5	–				
Mississippi	(6)	6	–	Totals	(275)	170	105

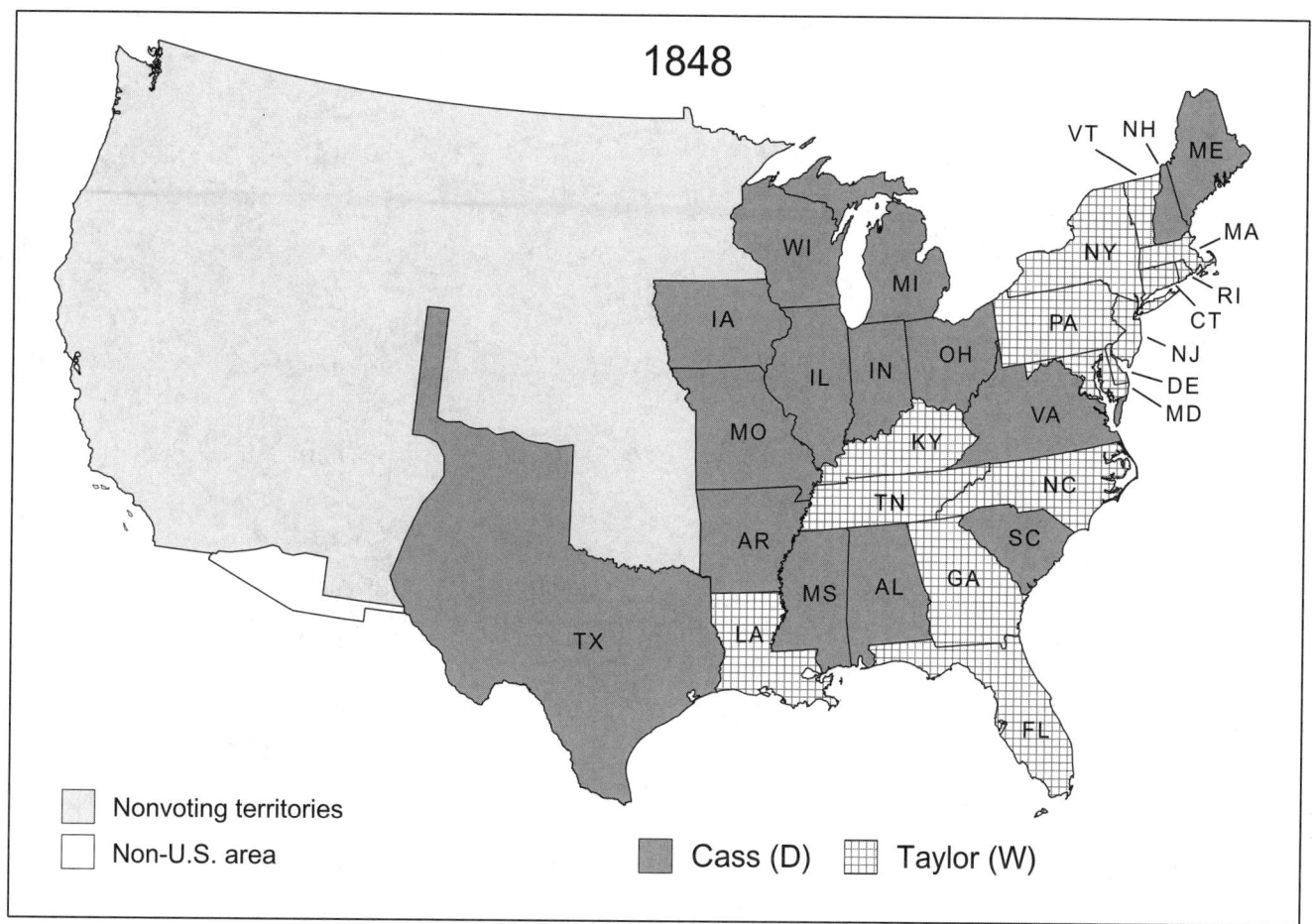

1848

Nonvoting territories

Non-U.S. area

Cass (D)   Taylor (W)

Key: D—Democrat; W—Whig

States	Electoral votes	Taylor	Cass	States	Electoral votes	Taylor	Cass
Alabama	(9)	–	9	Missouri	(7)	–	7
Arkansas	(3)	–	3	New Hampshire	(6)	–	6
Connecticut	(6)	6	–	New Jersey	(7)	7	–
Delaware	(3)	3	–	New York	(36)	36	–
Florida	(3)	3	–	North Carolina	(11)	11	–
Georgia	(10)	10	–	Ohio	(23)	–	23
Illinois	(9)	–	9	Pennsylvania	(26)	26	–
Indiana	(12)	–	12	Rhode Island	(4)	4	–
Iowa	(4)	–	4	South Carolina	(9)	–	9
Kentucky	(12)	12	–	Tennessee	(13)	13	–
Louisiana	(6)	6	–	Texas	(4)	–	4
Maine	(9)	–	9	Vermont	(6)	6	–
Maryland	(8)	8	–	Virginia	(17)	–	17
Massachusetts	(12)	12	–	Wisconsin	(4)	–	4
Michigan	(5)	–	5				
Mississippi	(6)	–	6	Totals	(290)	163	127

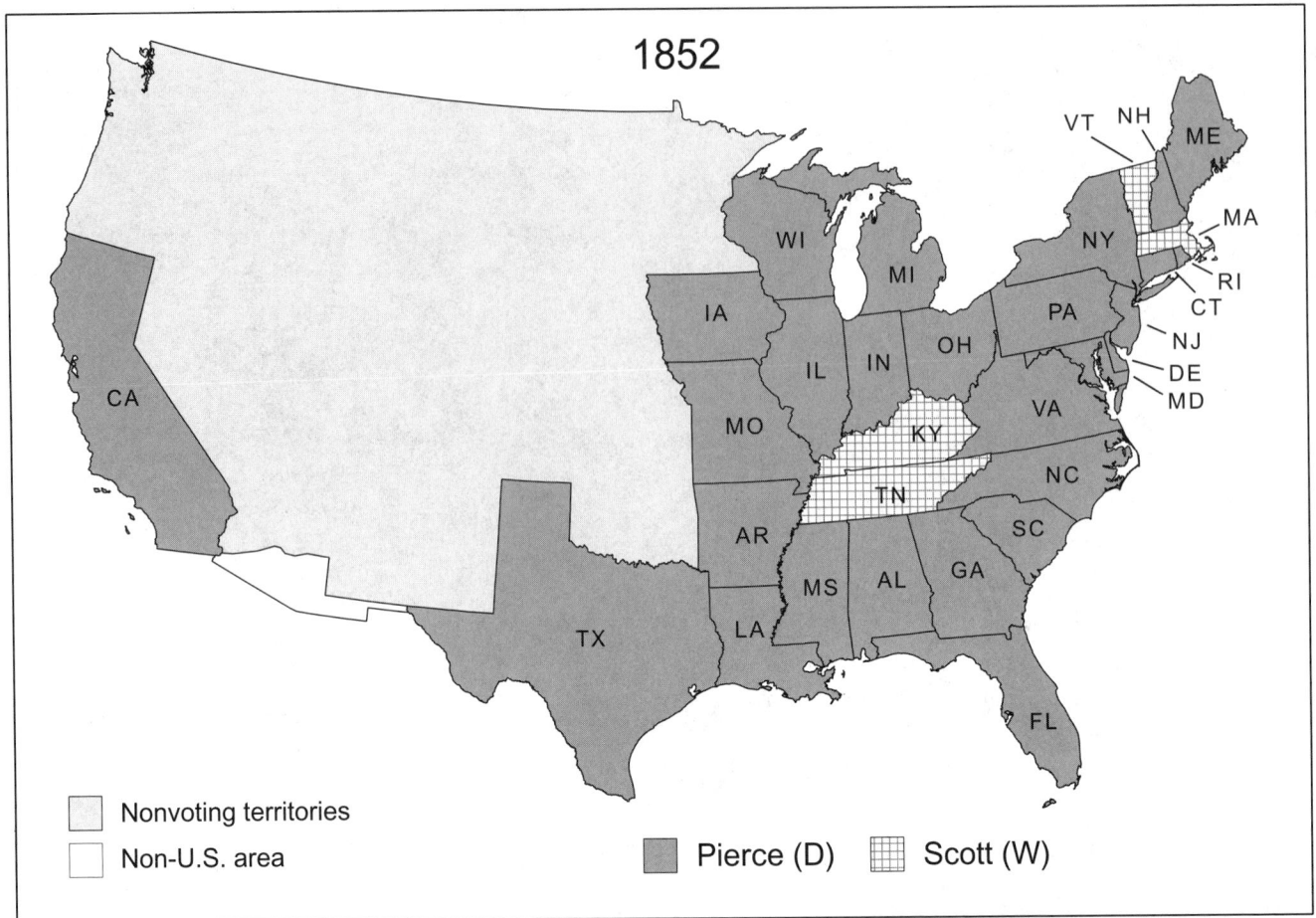

1852

Nonvoting territories

Non-U.S. area

Pierce (D)   Scott (W)

Key: D—Democrat; W—Whig

States	Electoral votes	Pierce	Scott	States	Electoral votes	Pierce	Scott
Alabama	(9)	9	–	Missouri	(9)	9	–
Arkansas	(4)	4	–	New Hampshire	(5)	5	–
California	(4)	4	–	New Jersey	(7)	7	–
Connecticut	(6)	6	–	New York	(35)	35	–
Delaware	(3)	3	–	North Carolina	(10)	10	–
Florida	(3)	3	–	Ohio	(23)	23	–
Georgia	(10)	10	–	Pennsylvania	(27)	27	–
Illinois	(11)	11	–	Rhode Island	(4)	4	–
Indiana	(13)	13	–	South Carolina	(8)	8	–
Iowa	(4)	4	–	Tennessee	(12)	–	12
Kentucky	(12)	–	12	Texas	(4)	4	–
Louisiana	(6)	6	–	Vermont	(5)	–	5
Maine	(8)	8	–	Virginia	(15)	15	–
Maryland	(8)	8	–	Wisconsin	(5)	5	–
Massachusetts	(13)	–	13				
Michigan	(6)	6	–	Totals	(296)	254	42
Mississippi	(7)	7	–				

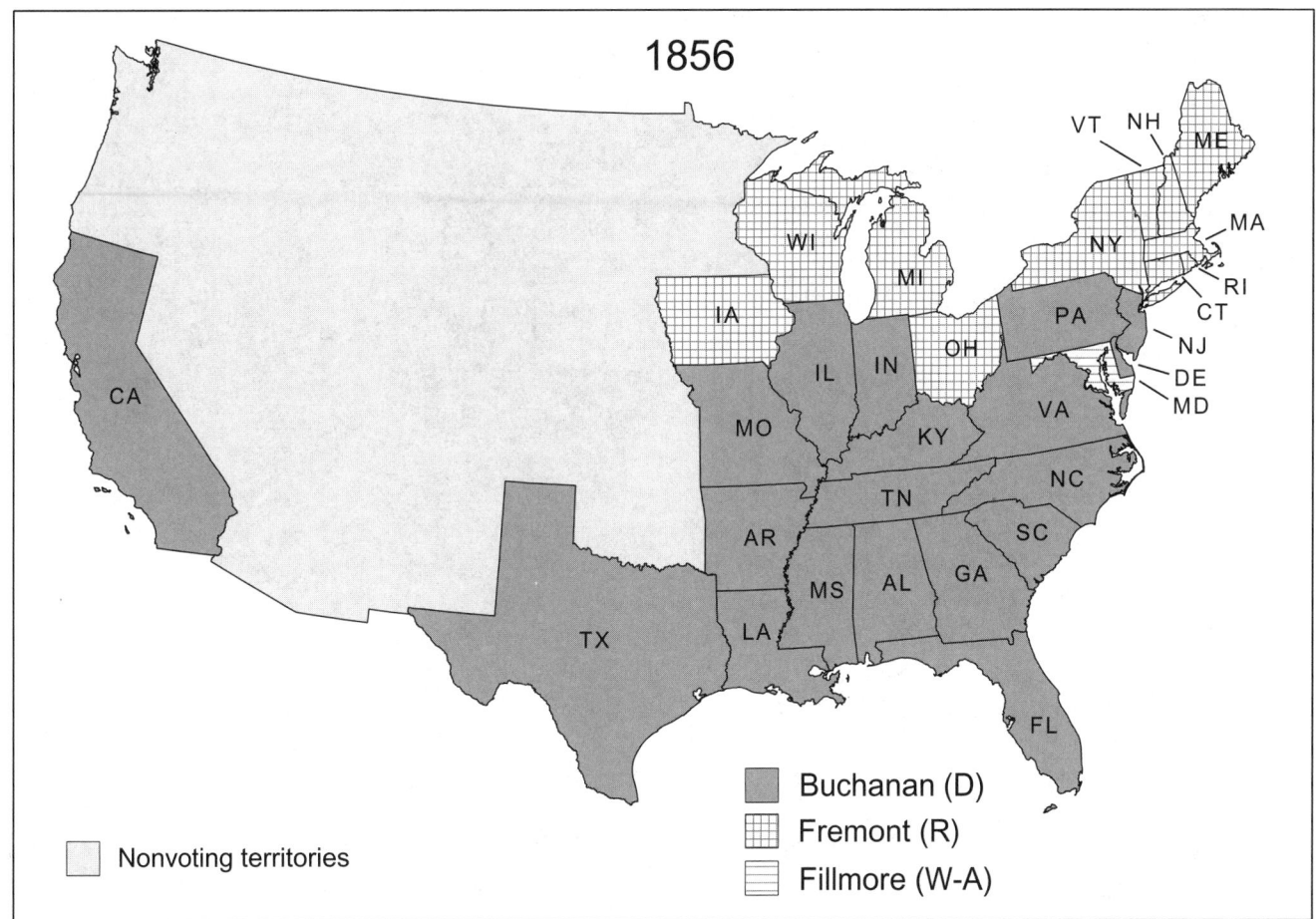

Key:˚D Democrat; R Republican; W-A Whig-American

States	Electoral votes	Buchanan	Fremont	Fillmore	States	Electoral votes	Buchanan	Fremont	Fillmore
Alabama	(9)	9	–	–	Missouri	(9)	9	–	–
Arkansas	(4)	4	–	–	New Hampshire	(5)	–	5	–
California	(4)	4	–	–	New Jersey	(7)	7	–	–
Connecticut	(6)	–	6	–	New York	(35)	–	35	–
Delaware	(3)	3	–	–	North Carolina	(10)	10	–	–
Florida	(3)	3	–	–	Ohio	(23)	–	23	–
Georgia	(10)	10	–	–	Pennsylvania	(27)	27	–	–
Illinois	(11)	11	–	–	Rhode Island	(4)	–	4	–
Indiana	(13)	13	–	–	South Carolina	(8)	8	–	–
Iowa	(4)	–	4	–	Tennessee	(12)	12	–	–
Kentucky	(12)	12	–	–	Texas	(4)	4	–	–
Louisiana	(6)	6	–	–	Vermont	(5)	–	5	–
Maine	(8)	–	8	–	Virginia	(15)	15	–	–
Maryland	(8)	–	–	8	Wisconsin	(5)	–	5	–
Massachusetts	(13)	–	13	–					
Michigan	(6)	–	6	–	Totals	(296)	174	114	8
Mississippi	(7)	7	–	–					

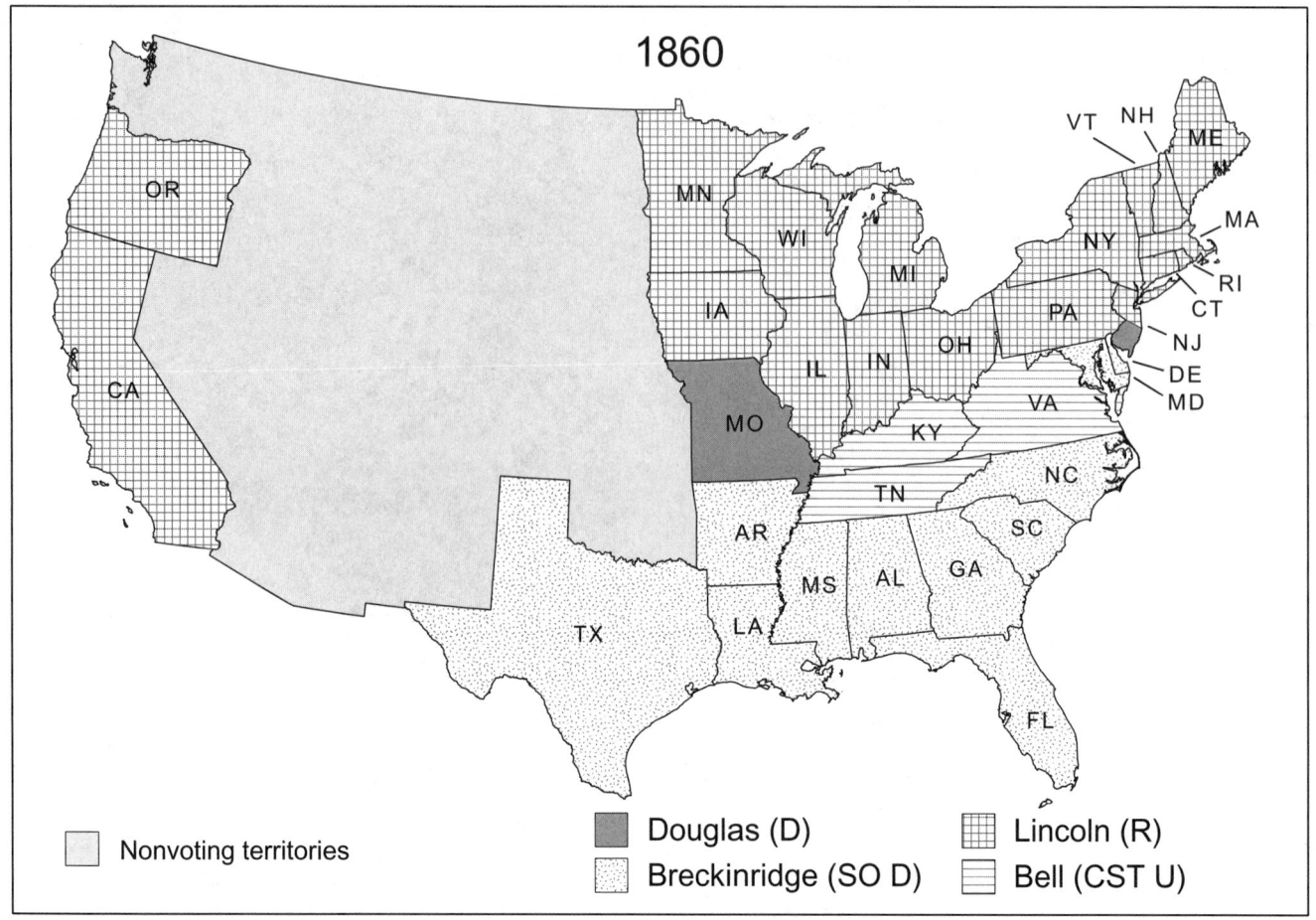

1860

Key: CST U—Constitutional Union; D—Democrat; R—Republican; SO D—Southern Democrat

States	Electoral votes	Lincoln	Breckinridge	Bell	Douglas	States	Electoral votes	Lincoln	Breckinridge	Bell	Douglas
Alabama	(9)	–	9	–	–	Missouri	(9)	–	–	–	9
Arkansas	(4)	–	4	–	–	New Hampshire	(5)	5	–	–	–
California	(4)	4	–	–	–	New Jersey[1]	(7)	4	–	–	3
Connecticut	(6)	6	–	–	–	New York	(35)	35	–	–	–
Delaware	(3)	–	3	–	–	North Carolina	(10)	–	10	–	–
Florida	(3)	–	3	–	–	Ohio	(23)	23	–	–	–
Georgia	(10)	–	10	–	–	Oregon	(3)	3	–	–	–
Illinois	(11)	11	–	–	–	Pennsylvania	(27)	27	–	–	–
Indiana	(13)	13	–	–	–	Rhode Island	(4)	4	–	–	–
Iowa	(4)	4	–	–	–	South Carolina	(8)	–	8	–	–
Kentucky	(12)	–	–	12	–	Tennessee	(12)	–	–	12	–
Louisiana	(6)	–	6	–	–	Texas	(4)	–	4	–	–
Maine	(8)	8	–	–	–	Vermont	(5)	5	–	–	–
Maryland	(8)	–	8	–	–	Virginia	(15)	–	–	15	–
Massachusetts	(13)	13	–	–	–	Wisconsin	(5)	5	–	–	–
Michigan	(6)	6	–	–	–						
Minnesota	(4)	4	–	–	–	Totals	(303)	180	72	39	12
Mississippi	(7)	–	7	–	–						

1. For explanation of split electoral votes, see p. 702

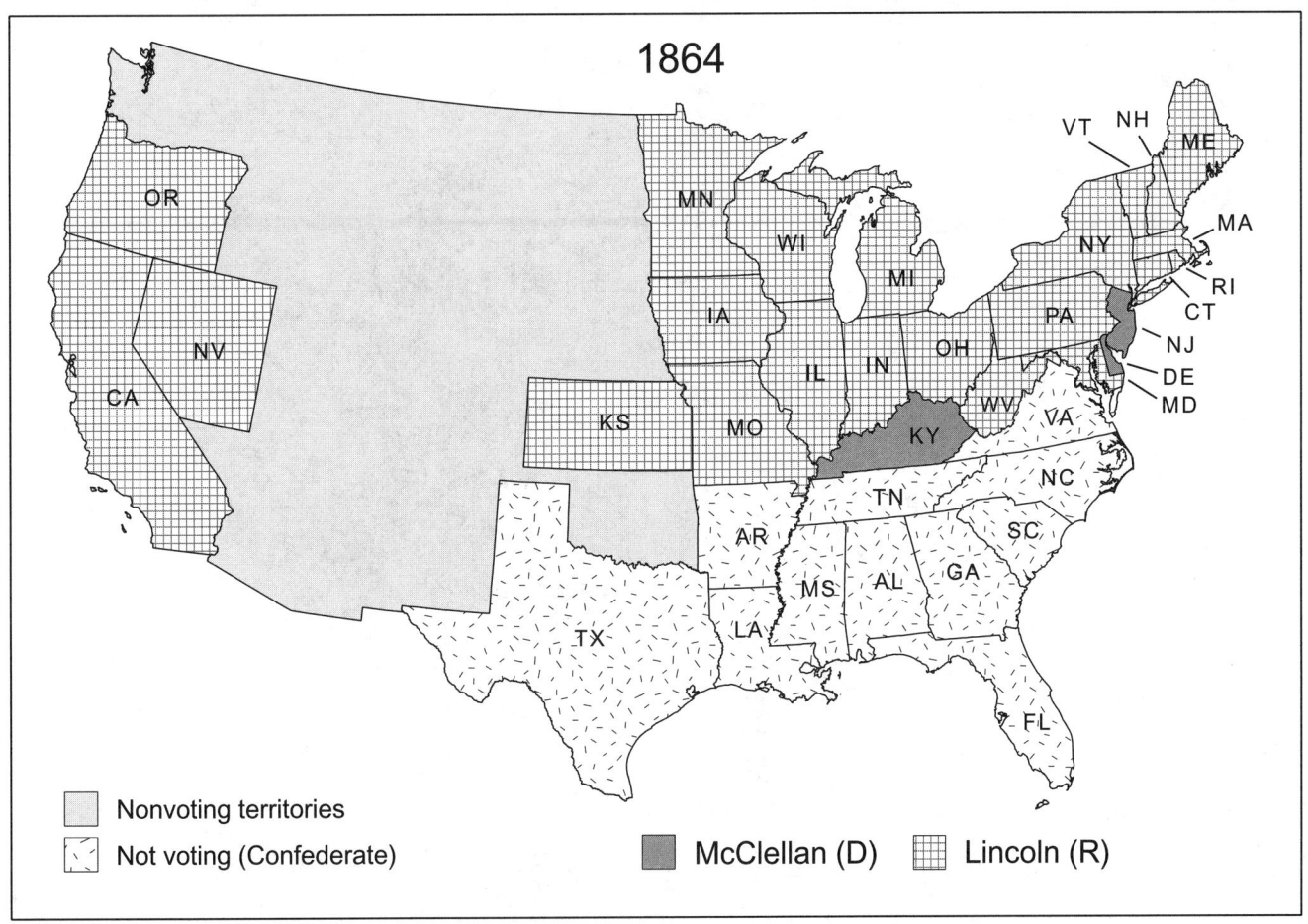

1864

Nonvoting territories

Not voting (Confederate)

McClellan (D)   Lincoln (R)

Key: D—Democrat; R—Republican

States[1]	Electoral votes	Lincoln	McClellan	States[1]	Electoral votes	Lincoln	McClellan
California	(5)	5	–	Nevada[2]	(3)	2	–
Connecticut	(6)	6	–	New Hampshire	(5)	5	–
Delaware	(3)	–	3	New Jersey	(7)	–	7
Illinois	(16)	16	–	New York	(33)	33	–
Indiana	(13)	13	–	Ohio	(21)	21	–
Iowa	(8)	8	–	Oregon	(3)	3	–
Kansas	(3)	3	–	Pennsylvania	(26)	26	–
Kentucky	(11)	–	11	Rhode Island	(4)	4	–
Maine	(7)	7	–	Vermont	(5)	5	–
Maryland	(7)	7	–	West Virginia	(5)	5	–
Massachusetts	(12)	12	–	Wisconsin	(8)	8	–
Michigan	(8)	8	–				
Minnesota	(4)	4	–	Totals	(234)	212	21
Missouri	(11)	11	–				

1. Eleven southern states—Alabama, Arkansas, Florida, Georgia, Louisiana, Mississippi, North Carolina, South Carolina, Tennessee, Texas, and Virginia—had seceded from the Union and did not vote.

2. One Nevada elector did not vote.

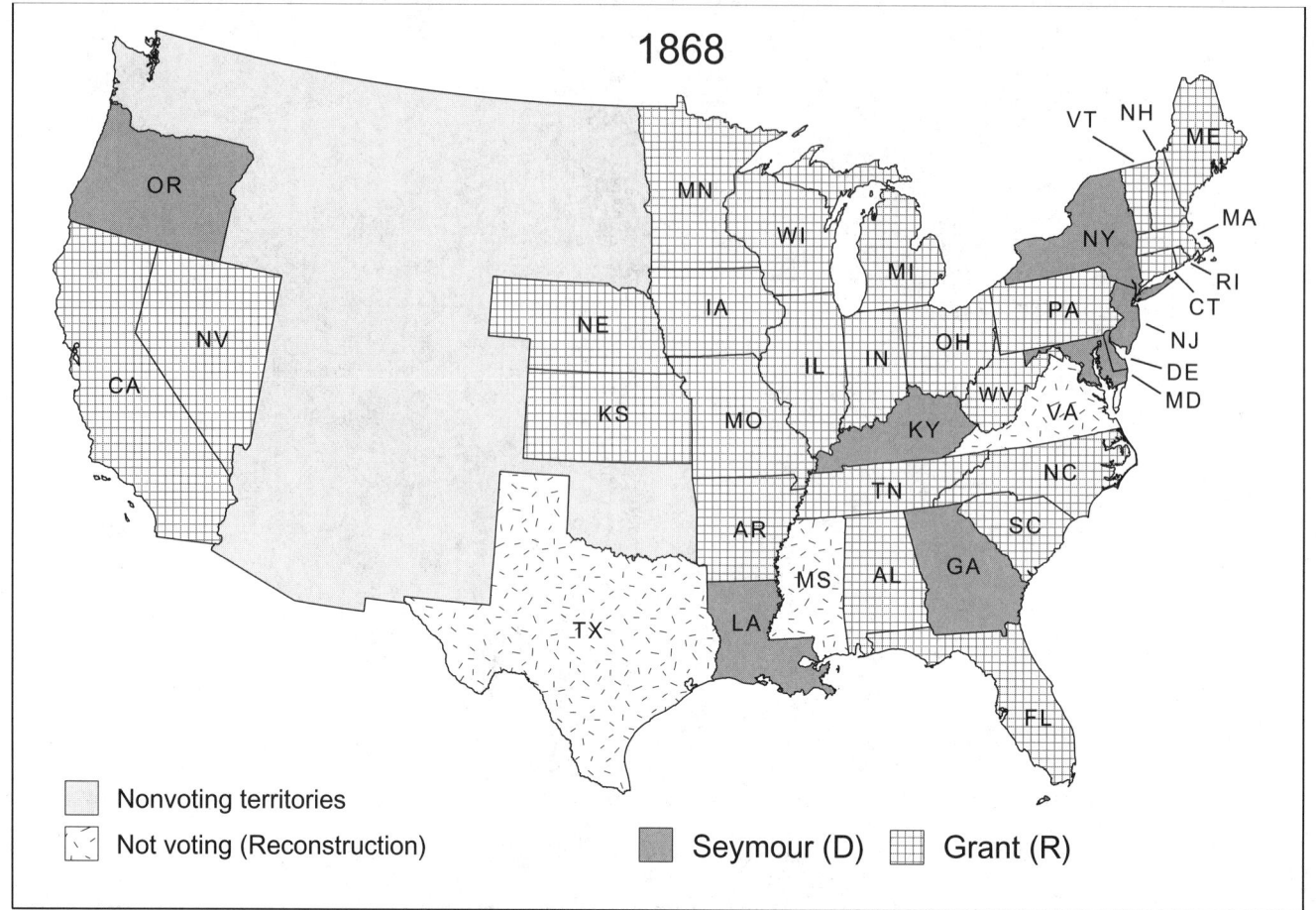

1868

Nonvoting territories

Not voting (Reconstruction)

Seymour (D)   Grant (R)

Key: D—Democrat; R—Republican

States[1]	Electoral votes	Grant	Seymour	States[1]	Electoral votes	Grant	Seymour
Alabama	(8)	8	–	Missouri	(11)	11	–
Arkansas	(5)	5	–	Nebraska	(3)	3	–
California	(5)	5	–	Nevada	(3)	3	–
Connecticut	(6)	6	–	New Hampshire	(5)	5	–
Delaware	(3)	–	3	New Jersey	(7)	–	7
Florida	(3)	3	–	New York	(33)	–	33
Georgia	(9)	–	9	North Carolina	(9)	9	–
Illinois	(16)	16	–	Ohio	(21)	21	–
Indiana	(13)	13	–	Oregon	(3)	–	3
Iowa	(8)	8	–	Pennsylvania	(26)	26	–
Kansas	(3)	3	–	Rhode Island	(4)	4	–
Kentucky	(11)	–	11	South Carolina	(6)	6	–
Louisiana	(7)	–	7	Tennessee	(10)	10	–
Maine	(7)	7	–	Vermont	(5)	5	–
Maryland	(7)	–	7	West Virginia	(5)	5	–
Massachusetts	(12)	12	–	Wisconsin	(8)	8	–
Michigan	(8)	8	–				
Minnesota	(4)	4	–	Totals	(294)	214	80

1. Mississippi, Texas, and Virginia were not yet readmitted to the Union and did not participate in the election.

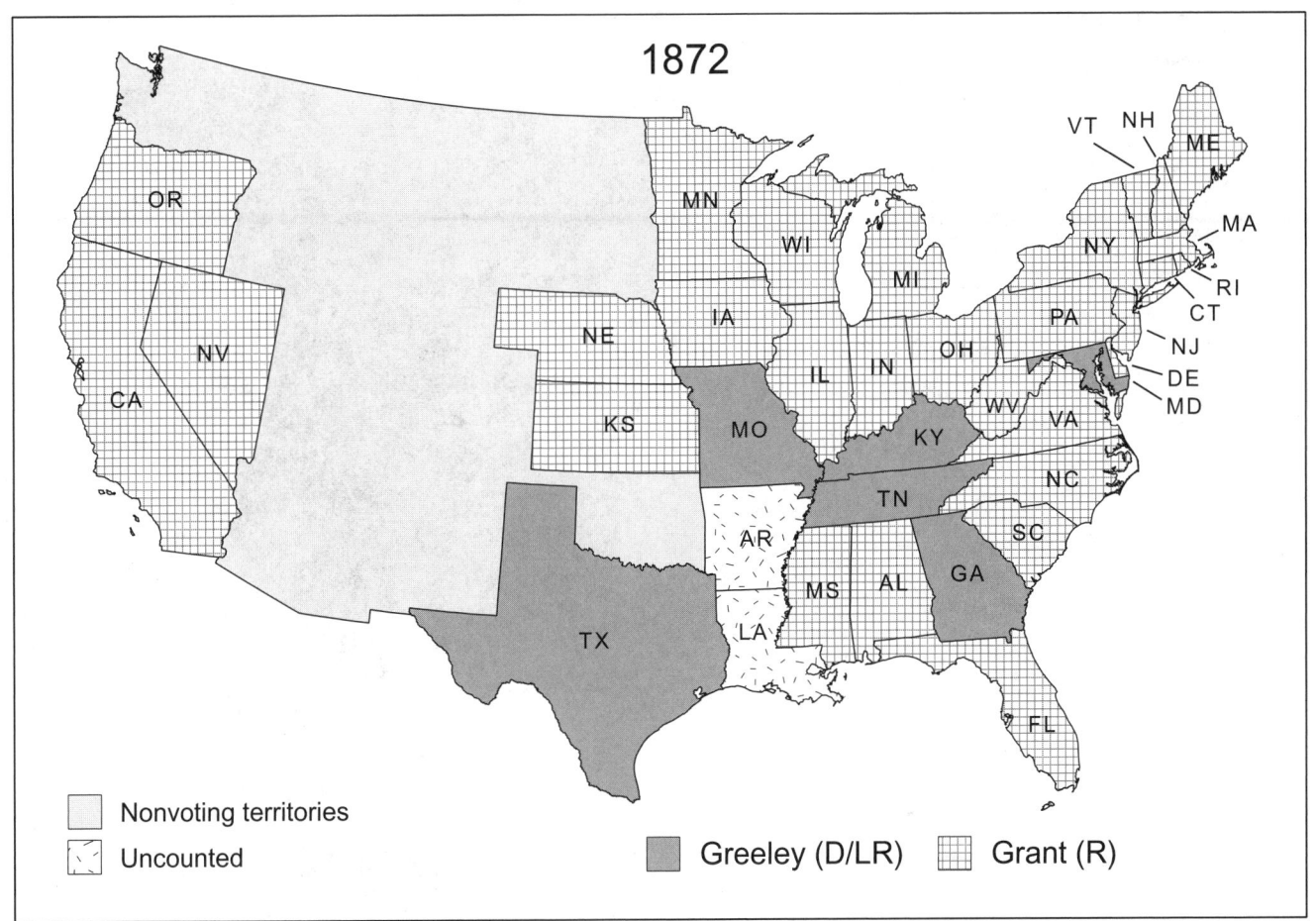

1872

Nonvoting territories

Uncounted

Greeley (D/LR)   Grant (R)

Key: D/LR—Democrat/Liberal Republican; R—Republican

States	Electoral votes	Grant	Hendricks[1]	Brown[1]	Jenkins[1]	Davis[1]	States	Electoral votes	Grant	Hendricks[1]	Brown[1]	Jenkins[1]	Davis[1]
Alabama	(10)	10	–	–	–	–	Nebraska	(3)	3	–	–	–	–
Arkansas[2]	(6)	–	–	–	–	–	Nevada	(3)	3	–	–	–	–
California	(6)	6	–	–	–	–	New Hampshire	(5)	5	–	–	–	–
Connecticut	(6)	6	–	–	–	–	New Jersey	(9)	9	–	–	–	–
Delaware	(3)	3	–	–	–	–	New York	(35)	35	–	–	–	–
Florida	(4)	4	–	–	–	–	North Carolina	(10)	10	–	–	–	–
Georgia[3]	(11)	–	–	6	2	–	Ohio	(22)	22	–	–	–	–
Illinois	(21)	21	–	–	–	–	Oregon	(3)	3	–	–	–	–
Indiana	(15)	15	–	–	–	–	Pennsylvania	(29)	29	–	–	–	–
Iowa	(11)	11	–	–	–	–	Rhode Island	(4)	4	–	–	–	–
Kansas	(5)	5	–	–	–	–	South Carolina	(7)	7	–	–	–	–
Kentucky	(12)	–	8	4	–	–	Tennessee	(12)	–	12	–	–	–
Louisiana[2]	(8)	–	–	–	–	–	Texas	(8)	–	8	–	–	–
Maine	(7)	7	–	–	–	–	Vermont	(5)	5	–	–	–	–
Maryland	(8)	–	8	–	–	–	Virginia	(11)	11	–	–	–	–
Massachusetts	(13)	13	–	–	–	–	West Virginia	(5)	5	–	–	–	–
Michigan	(11)	11	–	–	–	–	Wisconsin	(10)	10	–	–	–	–
Minnesota	(5)	5	–	–	–	–							
Mississippi	(8)	8	–	–	–	–	Totals	(366)	286	42	18	2	1
Missouri	(15)	–	6	8	–	1							

1. Liberal Republican and Democratic presidential candidate Horace Greeley died November 29, 1872. In the electoral college, the electors who had been pledged to Greeley split their presidential electoral votes among four candidates, including 18 for Benjamin Gratz Brown, Greeley's running mate.
2. Congress refused to accept the electoral votes of Arkansas and Louisiana because of disruptive conditions during Reconstruction
3. Three Georgia electoral votes cast for Greeley were not counted.

1876

Key: D—Democrat; R—Republican

States	Electoral votes	Hayes	Tilden	States	Electoral votes	Hayes	Tilden
Alabama	(10)	–	10	Missouri	(15)	–	15
Arkansas	(6)	–	6	Nebraska	(3)	3	–
California	(6)	6	–	Nevada	(3)	3	–
Colorado	(3)	3	–	New Hampshire	(5)	5	–
Connecticut	(6)	–	6	New Jersey	(9)	–	9
Delaware	(3)	–	3	New York	(35)	–	35
Florida[1]	(4)	4	–	North Carolina	(10)	–	10
Georgia	(11)	–	11	Ohio	(22)	22	–
Illinois	(21)	21	–	Oregon[1]	(3)	3	–
Indiana	(15)	–	15	Pennsylvania	(29)	29	–
Iowa	(11)	11	–	Rhode Island	(4)	4	–
Kansas	(5)	5	–	South Carolina[1]	(7)	7	–
Kentucky	(12)	–	12	Tennessee	(12)	–	12
Louisiana[1]	(8)	8	–	Texas	(8)	–	8
Maine	(7)	7	–	Vermont	(5)	5	–
Maryland	(8)	–	8	Virginia	(11)	–	11
Massachusetts	(13)	13	–	West Virginia	(5)	–	5
Michigan	(11)	11	–	Wisconsin	(10)	10	–
Minnesota	(5)	5	–				
Mississippi	(8)	–	8	Totals	(369)	185	184

1. The electoral votes of Florida, Louisiana, Oregon, and South Carolina were disputed. See "The Compromise of 1876," p. 248.

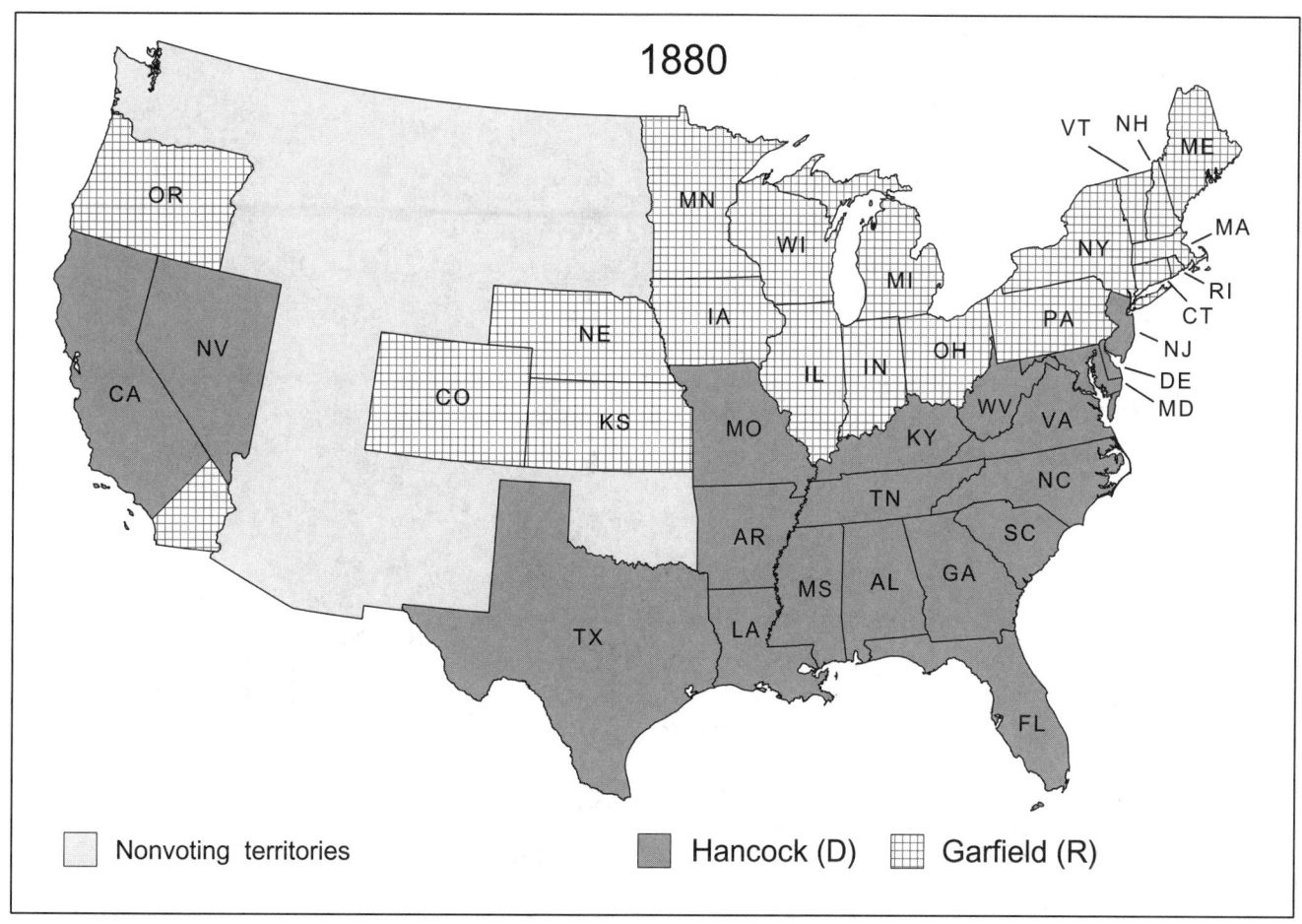

Key: D—Democrat; R—Republican

States	Electoral votes	Garfield	Hancock	States	Electoral votes	Garfield	Hancock
Alabama	(10)	–	10	Missouri	(15)	–	15
Arkansas	(6)	–	6	Nebraska	(3)	3	–
California[1]	(6)	1	5	Nevada	(3)	–	3
Colorado	(3)	3	–	New Hampshire	(5)	5	–
Connecticut	(6)	6	–	New Jersey	(9)	–	9
Delaware	(3)	–	3	New York	(35)	35	–
Florida	(4)	–	4	North Carolina	(10)	–	10
Georgia	(11)	–	11	Ohio	(22)	22	–
Illinois	(21)	21	–	Oregon	(3)	3	–
Indiana	(15)	15	–	Pennsylvania	(29)	29	–
Iowa	(11)	11	–	Rhode Island	(4)	4	–
Kansas	(5)	5	–	South Carolina	(7)	–	7
Kentucky	(12)	–	12	Tennessee	(12)	–	12
Louisiana	(8)	–	8	Texas	(8)	–	8
Maine	(7)	7	–	Vermont	(5)	5	–
Maryland	(8)	–	8	Virginia	(11)	–	11
Massachusetts	(13)	13	–	West Virginia	(5)	–	5
Michigan	(11)	11	–	Wisconsin	(10)	10	–
Minnesota	(5)	5	–				
Mississippi	(8)	–	8	Totals	(369)	214	155

1. For explanation of split electoral votes, see p. 702.

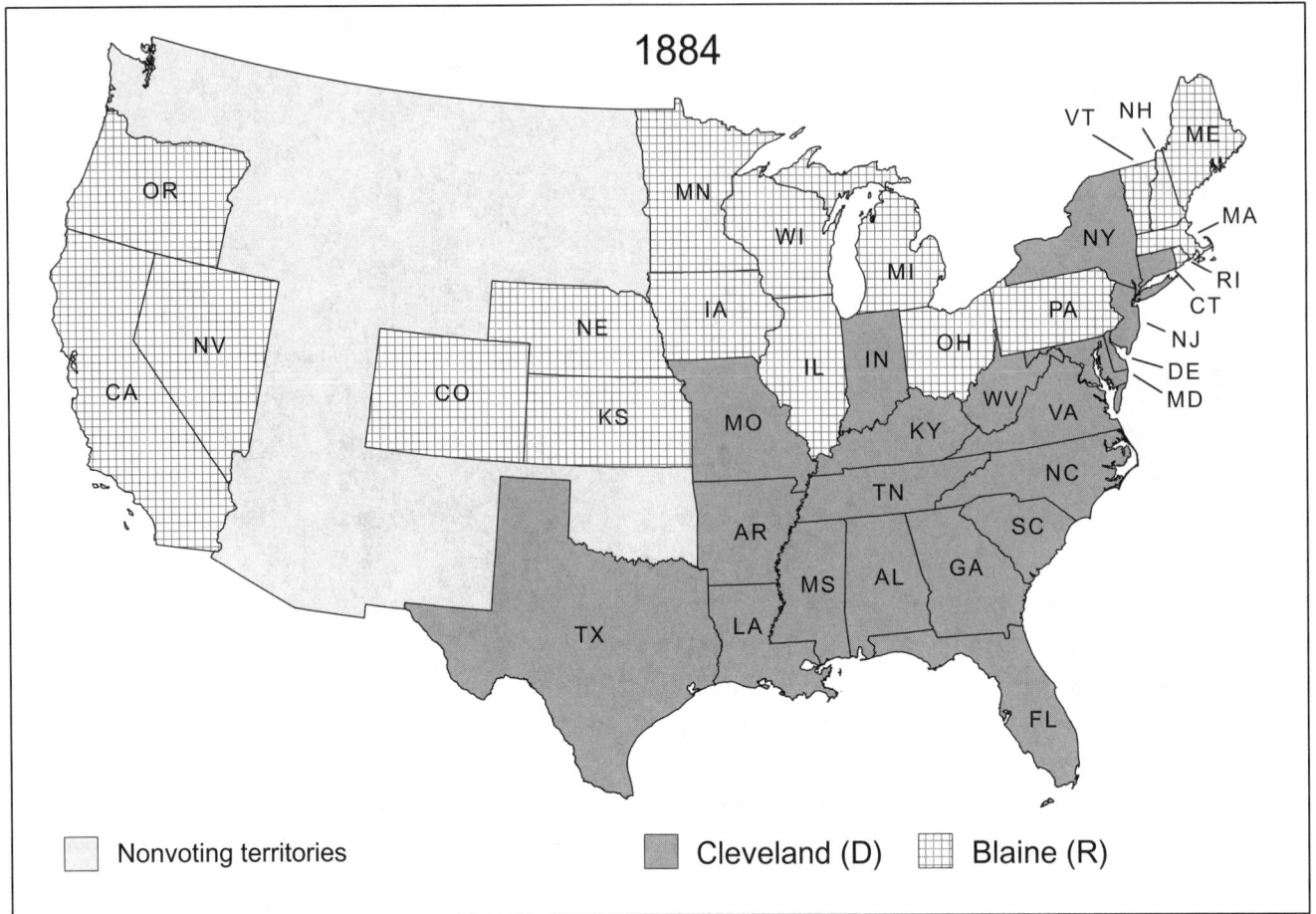

1884

Nonvoting territories   Cleveland (D)   Blaine (R)

Key: D—Democrat; R—Republican

States	Electoral votes	Cleveland	Blaine	States	Electoral votes	Cleveland	Blaine
Alabama	(10)	10	–	Missouri	(16)	16	–
Arkansas	(7)	7	–	Nebraska	(5)	–	5
California	(8)	–	8	Nevada	(3)	–	3
Colorado	(3)	–	3	New Hampshire	(4)	–	4
Connecticut	(6)	6	–	New Jersey	(9)	9	–
Delaware	(3)	3	–	New York	(36)	36	–
Florida	(4)	4	–	North Carolina	(11)	11	–
Georgia	(12)	12	–	Ohio	(23)	–	23
Illinois	(22)	–	22	Oregon	(3)	–	3
Indiana	(15)	15	–	Pennsylvania	(30)	–	30
Iowa	(13)	–	13	Rhode Island	(4)	–	4
Kansas	(9)	–	9	South Carolina	(9)	9	–
Kentucky	(13)	13	–	Tennessee	(12)	12	–
Louisiana	(8)	8	–	Texas	(13)	13	–
Maine	(6)	–	6	Vermont	(4)	–	4
Maryland	(8)	8	–	Virginia	(12)	12	–
Massachusetts	(14)	–	14	West Virginia	(6)	6	–
Michigan	(13)	–	13	Wisconsin	(11)	–	11
Minnesota	(7)	–	7				
Mississippi	(9)	9	–	Totals	(401)	219	182

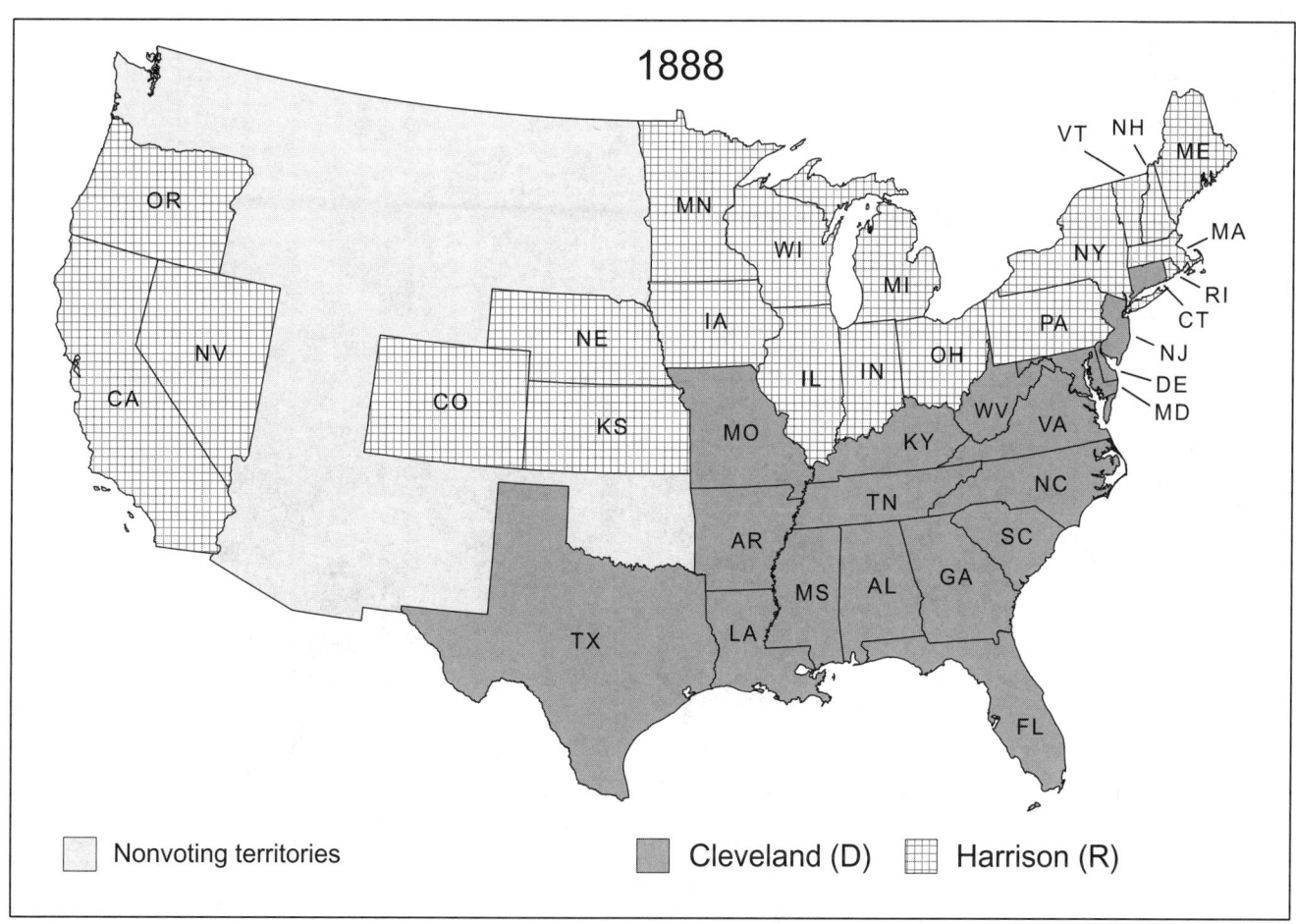

1888

Nonvoting territories   Cleveland (D)   Harrison (R)

Key: D—Democrat; R—Republican

States	Electoral votes	Harrison	Cleveland	States	Electoral votes	Harrison	Cleveland
Alabama	(10)	–	10	Missouri	(16)	–	16
Arkansas	(7)	–	7	Nebraska	(5)	5	–
California	(8)	8	–	Nevada	(3)	3	–
Colorado	(3)	3	–	New Hampshire	(4)	4	–
Connecticut	(6)	–	6	New Jersey	(9)	–	9
Delaware	(3)	–	3	New York	(36)	36	–
Florida	(4)	–	4	North Carolina	(11)	–	11
Georgia	(12)	–	12	Ohio	(23)	23	–
Illinois	(22)	22	–	Oregon	(3)	3	–
Indiana	(15)	15	–	Pennsylvania	(30)	30	–
Iowa	(13)	13	–	Rhode Island	(4)	4	–
Kansas	(9)	9	–	South Carolina	(9)	–	9
Kentucky	(13)	–	13	Tennessee	(12)	–	12
Louisiana	(8)	–	8	Texas	(13)	–	13
Maine	(6)	6	–	Vermont	(4)	4	–
Maryland	(8)	–	8	Virginia	(12)	–	12
Massachusetts	(14)	14	–	West Virginia	(6)	–	6
Michigan	(13)	13	–	Wisconsin	(11)	11	–
Minnesota	(7)	7	–				
Mississippi	(9)	–	9	Totals	(401)	233	168

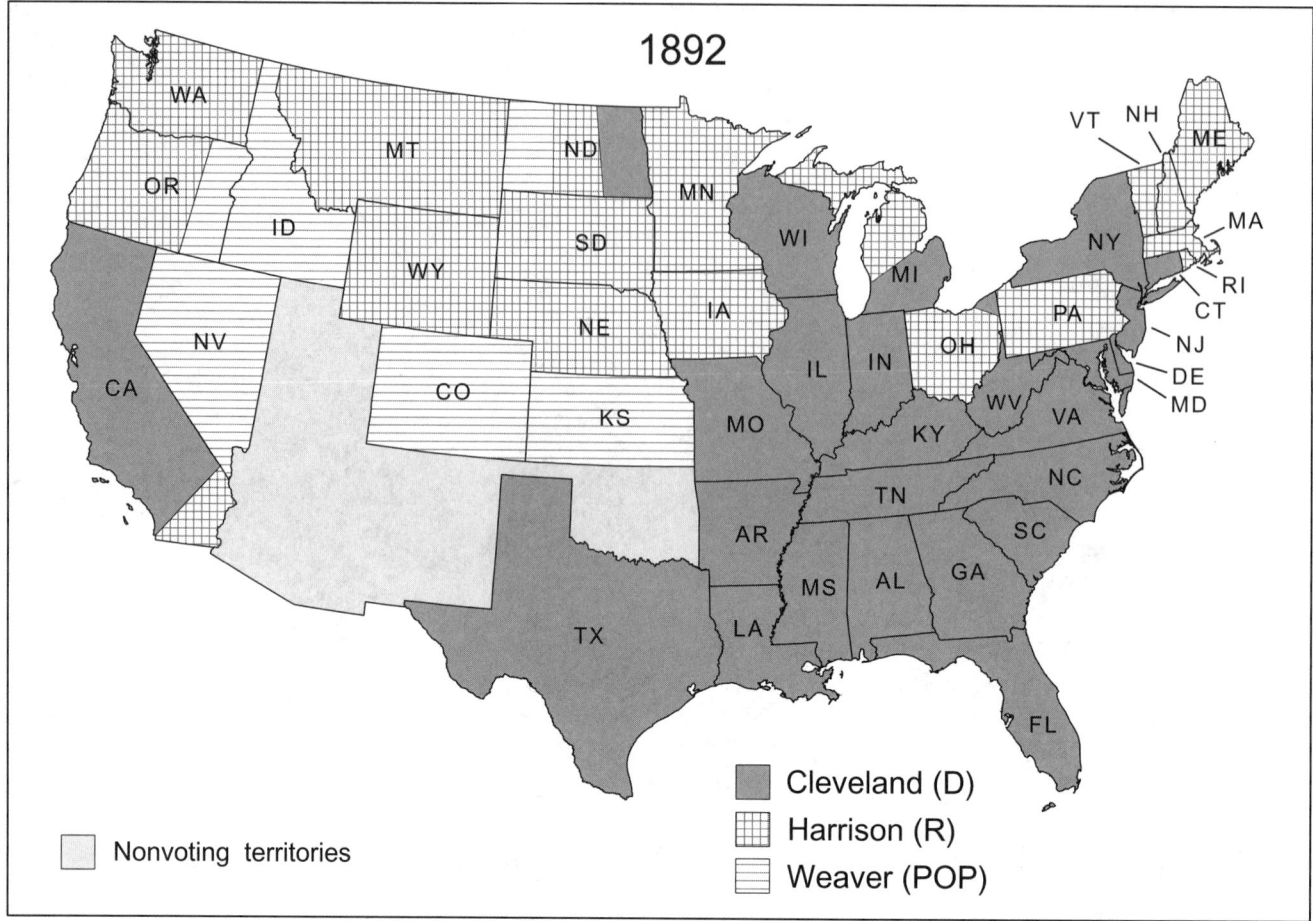

Key: D—Democrat; POP—Populist; R—Republican

States	Electoral votes	Cleveland	Harrison	Weaver	States	Electoral votes	Cleveland	Harrison	Weaver
Alabama	(11)	11	–	–	Nebraska	(8)	–	8	–
Arkansas	(8)	8	–	–	Nevada	(3)	–	–	3
California[1]	(9)	8	1	–	New Hampshire	(4)	–	4	–
Colorado	(4)	–	–	4	New Jersey	(10)	10	–	–
Connecticut	(6)	6	–	–	New York	(36)	36	–	–
Delaware	(3)	3	–	–	North Carolina	(11)	11	–	–
Florida	(4)	4	–	–	North Dakota[1]	(3)	1	1	1
Georgia	(13)	13	–	–	Ohio[1]	(23)	1	22	–
Idaho	(3)	–	–	3	Oregon[1]	(4)	–	3	1
Illinois	(24)	24	–	–	Pennsylvania	(32)	–	32	–
Indiana	(15)	15	–	–	Rhode Island	(4)	–	4	–
Iowa	(13)	–	13	–	South Carolina	(9)	9	–	–
Kansas	(10)	–	–	10	South Dakota	(4)	–	4	–
Kentucky	(13)	13	–	–	Tennessee	(12)	12	–	–
Louisiana	(8)	8	–	–	Texas	(15)	15	–	–
Maine	(6)	–	6	–	Vermont	(4)	–	4	–
Maryland	(8)	8	–	–	Virginia	(12)	12	–	–
Massachusetts	(15)	–	15	–	Washington	(4)	–	4	–
Michigan[1]	(14)	5	9	–	West Virginia	(6)	6	–	–
Minnesota	(9)	–	9	–	Wisconsin	(12)	12	–	–
Mississippi	(9)	9	–	–	Wyoming	(3)	–	3	–
Missouri	(17)	17	–	–					
Montana	(3)	–	3	–	Totals	(444)	277	145	22

1. For explanation of split electoral votes, see p. 702.

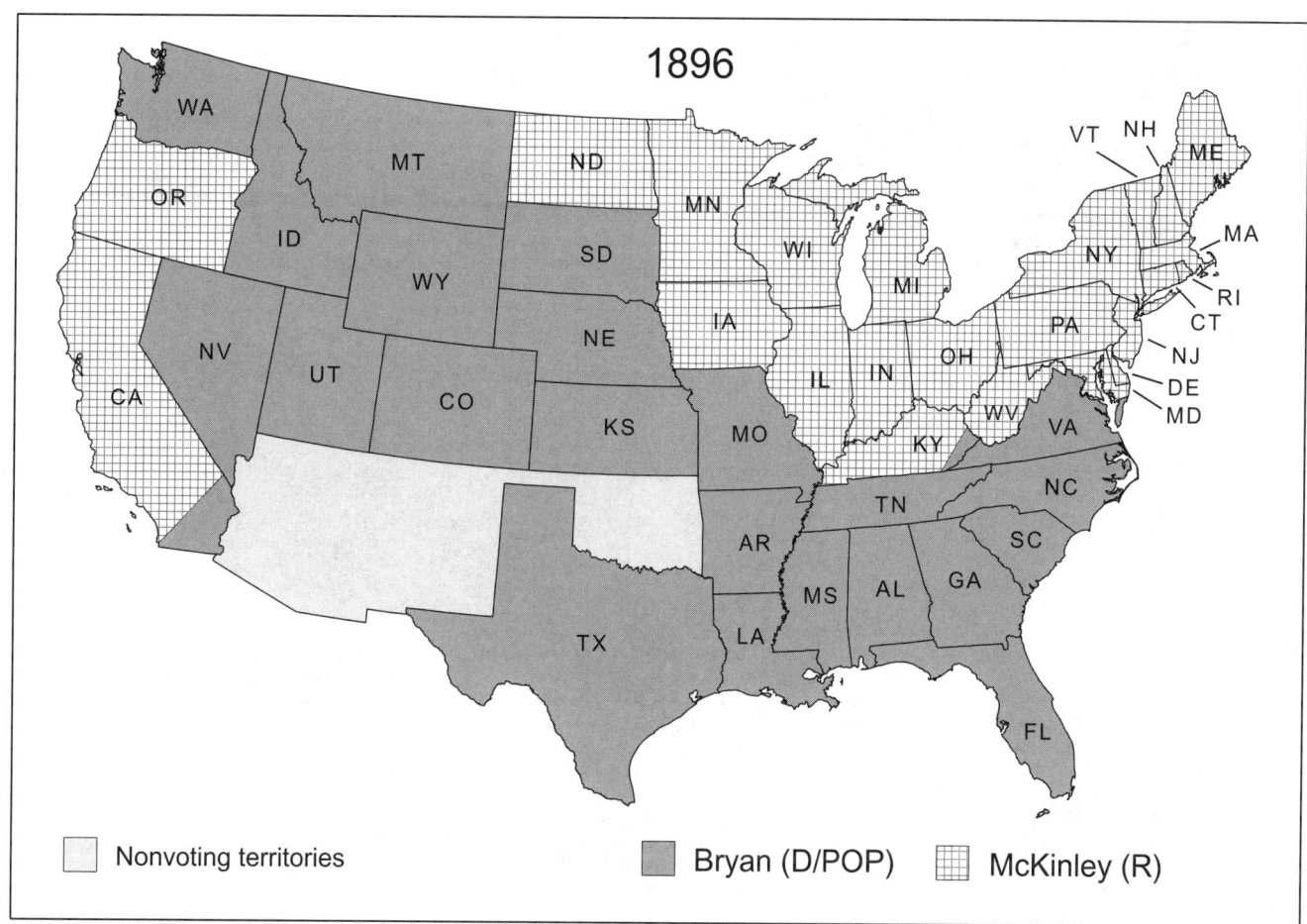

1896

Nonvoting territories   Bryan (D/POP)   McKinley (R)

Key: D/POP—Democrat/Populist; R—Republican

States	Electoral votes	McKinley	Bryan	States	Electoral votes	McKinley	Bryan
Alabama	(11)	–	11	Nevada	(3)	–	3
Arkansas	(8)	–	8	New Hampshire	(4)	4	–
California[1]	(9)	8	1	New Jersey	(10)	10	–
Colorado	(4)	–	4	New York	(36)	36	–
Connecticut	(6)	6	–	North Carolina	(11)	–	11
Delaware	(3)	3	–	North Dakota	(3)	3	–
Florida	(4)	–	4	Ohio	(23)	23	–
Georgia	(13)	–	13	Oregon	(4)	4	–
Idaho	(3)	–	3	Pennsylvania	(32)	32	–
Illinois	(24)	24	–	Rhode Island	(4)	4	–
Indiana	(15)	15	–	South Carolina	(9)	–	9
Iowa	(13)	13	–	South Dakota	(4)	–	4
Kansas	(10)	–	10	Tennessee	(12)	–	12
Kentucky[1]	(13)	12	1	Texas	(15)	–	15
Louisiana	(8)	–	8	Utah	(3)	–	3
Maine	(6)	6	–	Vermont	(4)	4	–
Maryland	(8)	8	–	Virginia	(12)	–	12
Massachusetts	(15)	15	–	Washington	(4)	–	4
Michigan	(14)	14	–	West Virginia	(6)	6	–
Minnesota	(9)	9	–	Wisconsin	(12)	12	–
Mississippi	(9)	–	9	Wyoming	(3)	–	3
Missouri	(17)	–	17				
Montana	(3)	–	3	Totals	(447)	271	176
Nebraska	(8)	–	8				

1. For explanation of split electoral votes, see p. 702.

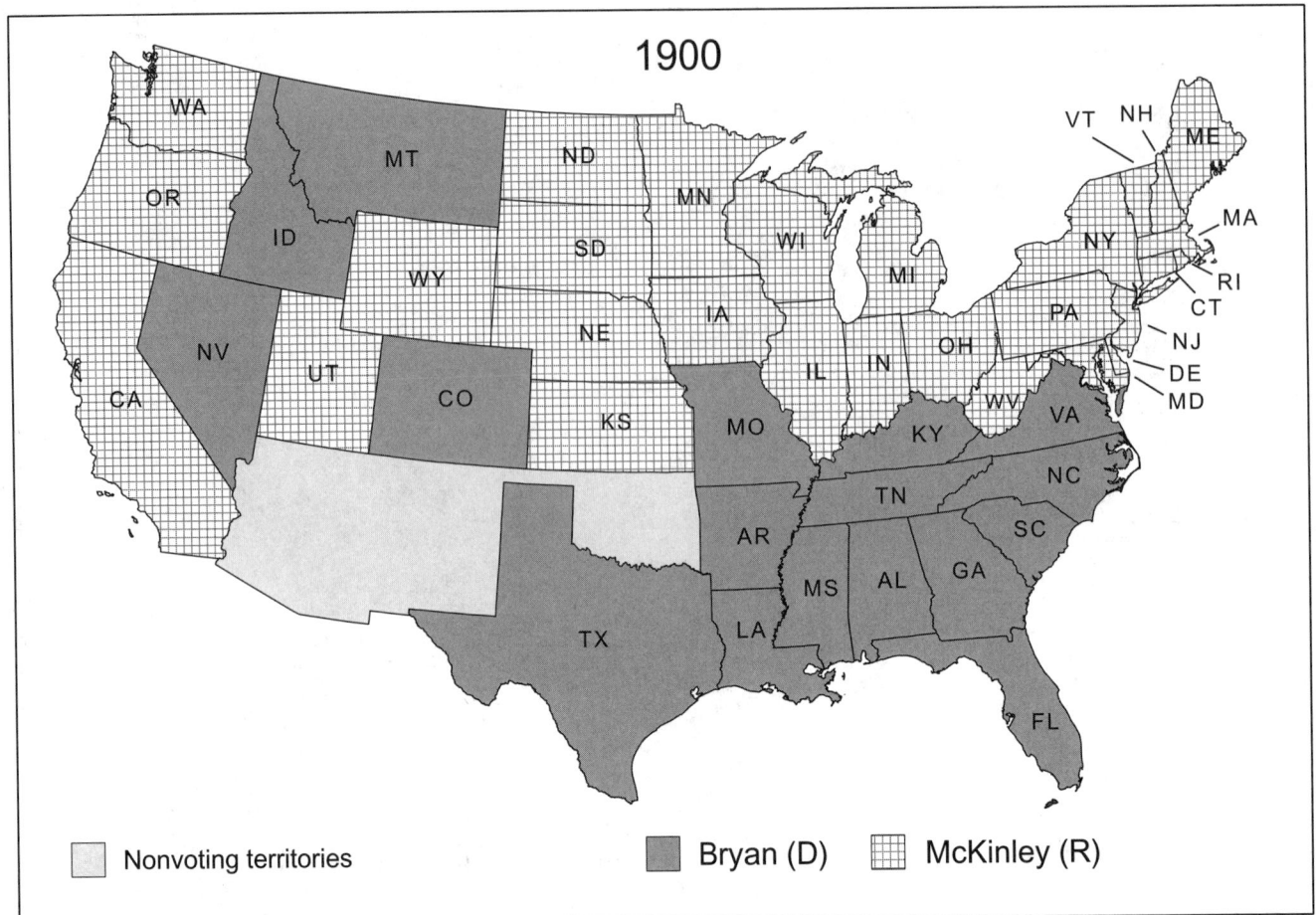

1900

Nonvoting territories   Bryan (D)   McKinley (R)

Key: D—Democrat; R—Republican

States	Electoral votes	McKinley	Bryan	States	Electoral votes	McKinley	Bryan
Alabama	(11)	–	11	Nevada	(3)	–	3
Arkansas	(8)	–	8	New Hampshire	(4)	4	–
California	(9)	9	–	New Jersey	(10)	10	–
Colorado	(4)	–	4	New York	(36)	36	–
Connecticut	(6)	6	–	North Carolina	(11)	–	11
Delaware	(3)	3	–	North Dakota	(3)	3	–
Florida	(4)	–	4	Ohio	(23)	23	–
Georgia	(13)	–	13	Oregon	(4)	4	–
Idaho	(3)	–	3	Pennsylvania	(32)	32	–
Illinois	(24)	24	–	Rhode Island	(4)	4	–
Indiana	(15)	15	–	South Carolina	(9)	–	9
Iowa	(13)	13	–	South Dakota	(4)	4	–
Kansas	(10)	10	–	Tennessee	(12)	–	12
Kentucky	(13)	–	13	Texas	(15)	–	15
Louisiana	(8)	–	8	Utah	(3)	3	–
Maine	(6)	6	–	Vermont	(4)	4	–
Maryland	(8)	8	–	Virginia	(12)	–	12
Massachusetts	(15)	15	–	Washington	(4)	4	–
Michigan	(14)	14	–	West Virginia	(6)	6	–
Minnesota	(9)	9	–	Wisconsin	(12)	12	–
Mississippi	(9)	–	9	Wyoming	(3)	3	–
Missouri	(17)	–	17				
Montana	(3)	–	3	Totals	(447)	292	155
Nebraska	(8)	8	–				

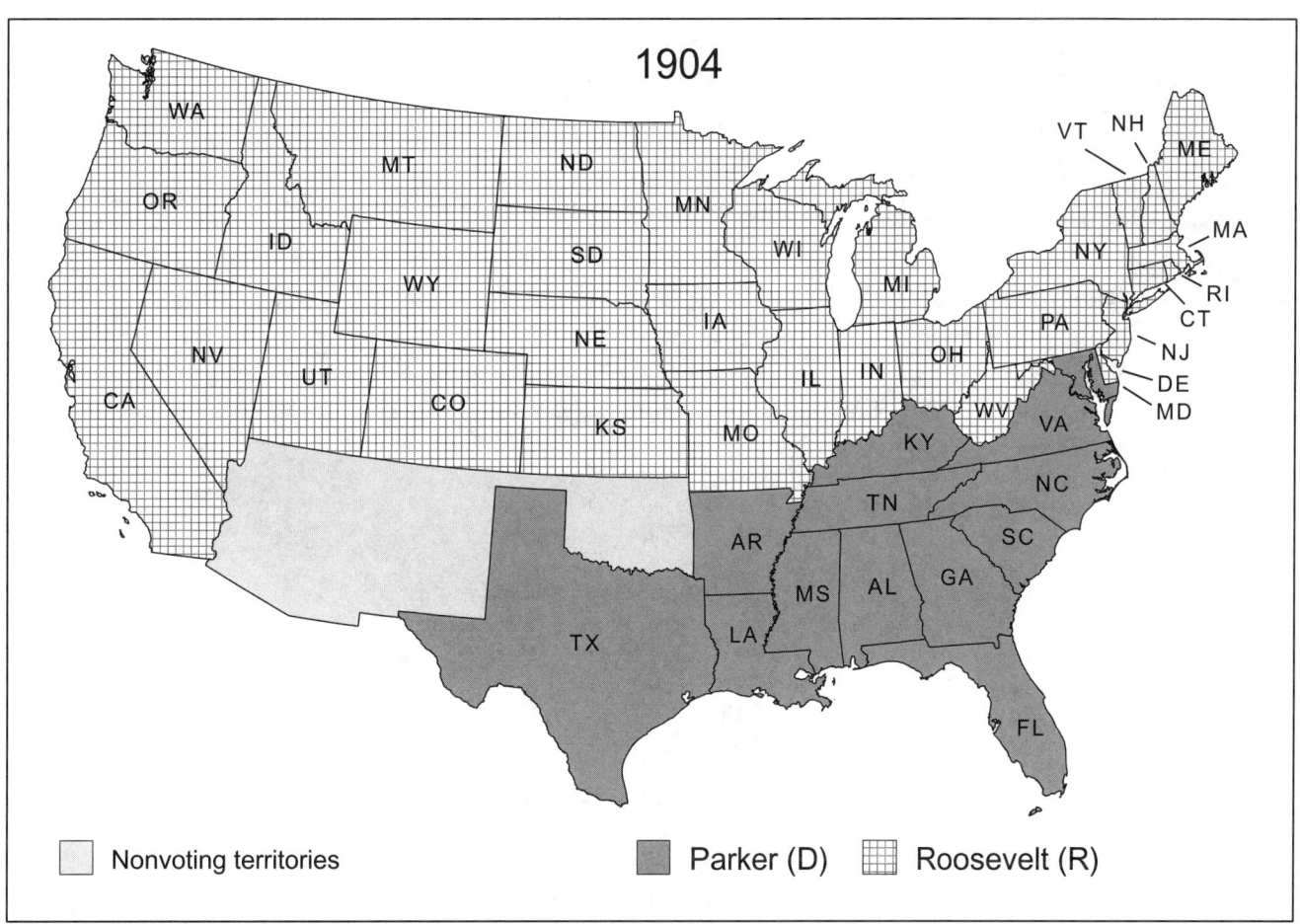

1904

| Nonvoting territories | Parker (D) | Roosevelt (R) |

Key: D—Democrat; R—Republican

States	Electoral votes	Roosevelt	Parker	States	Electoral votes	Roosevelt	Parker
Alabama	(11)	–	11	Nevada	(3)	3	–
Arkansas	(9)	–	9	New Hampshire	(4)	4	–
California	(10)	10	–	New Jersey	(12)	12	–
Colorado	(5)	5	–	New York	(39)	39	–
Connecticut	(7)	7	–	North Carolina	(12)	–	12
Delaware	(3)	3	–	North Dakota	(4)	4	–
Florida	(5)	–	5	Ohio	(23)	23	–
Georgia	(13)	–	13	Oregon	(4)	4	–
Idaho	(3)	3	–	Pennsylvania	(34)	34	–
Illinois	(27)	27	–	Rhode Island	(4)	4	–
Indiana	(15)	15	–	South Carolina	(9)	–	9
Iowa	(13)	13	–	South Dakota	(4)	4	–
Kansas	(10)	10	–	Tennessee	(12)	–	12
Kentucky	(13)	–	13	Texas	(18)	–	18
Louisiana	(9)	–	9	Utah	(3)	3	–
Maine	(6)	6	–	Vermont	(4)	4	–
Maryland[1]	(8)	1	7	Virginia	(12)	–	12
Massachusetts	(16)	16	–	Washington	(5)	5	–
Michigan	(14)	14	–	West Virginia	(7)	7	–
Minnesota	(11)	11	–	Wisconsin	(13)	13	–
Mississippi	(10)	–	10	Wyoming	(3)	3	–
Missouri	(18)	18	–				
Montana	(3)	3	–	Totals	(476)	336	140
Nebraska	(8)	8	–				

1. For explanation of split electoral votes, see p. 702.

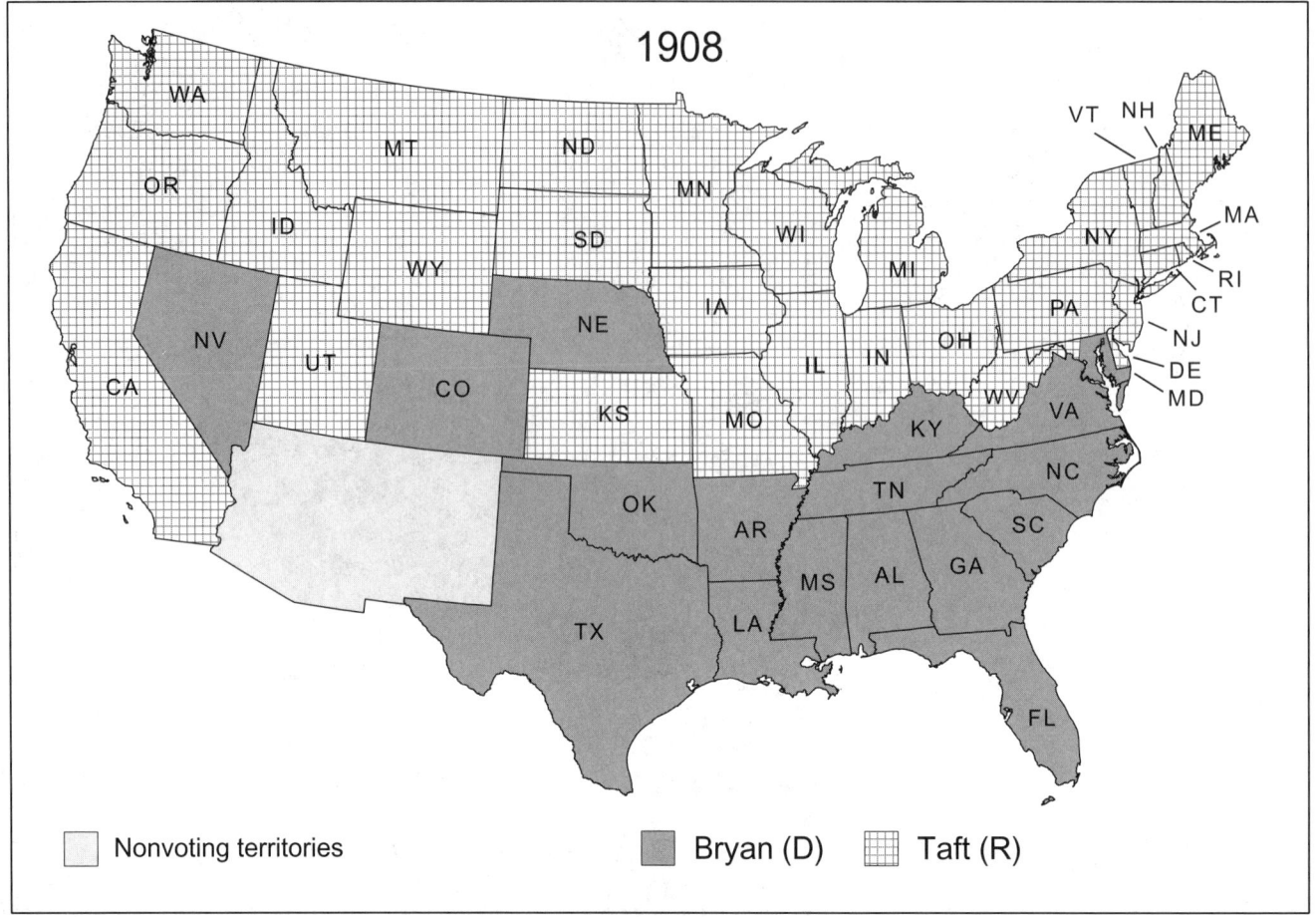

1908

Nonvoting territories   Bryan (D)   Taft (R)

Key: D—Democrat; R—Republican

States	Electoral votes	Taft	Bryan	States	Electoral votes	Taft	Bryan
Alabama	(11)	–	11	Nevada	(3)	–	3
Arkansas	(9)	–	9	New Hampshire	(4)	4	–
California	(10)	10	–	New Jersey	(12)	12	–
Colorado	(5)	–	5	New York	(39)	39	–
Connecticut	(7)	7	–	North Carolina	(12)	–	12
Delaware	(3)	3	–	North Dakota	(4)	4	–
Florida	(5)	–	5	Ohio	(23)	23	–
Georgia	(13)	–	13	Oklahoma	(7)	–	7
Idaho	(3)	3	–	Oregon	(4)	4	–
Illinois	(27)	27	–	Pennsylvania	(34)	34	–
Indiana	(15)	15	–	Rhode Island	(4)	4	–
Iowa	(13)	13	–	South Carolina	(9)	–	9
Kansas	(10)	10	–	South Dakota	(4)	4	–
Kentucky	(13)	–	13	Tennessee	(12)	–	12
Louisiana	(9)	–	9	Texas	(18)	–	18
Maine	(6)	6	–	Utah	(3)	3	–
Maryland[1]	(8)	2	6	Vermont	(4)	4	–
Massachusetts	(16)	16	–	Virginia	(12)	–	12
Michigan	(14)	14	–	Washington	(5)	5	–
Minnesota	(11)	11	–	West Virginia	(7)	7	–
Mississippi	(10)	–	10	Wisconsin	(13)	13	–
Missouri	(18)	18	–	Wyoming	(3)	3	–
Montana	(3)	3	–				
Nebraska	(8)	–	8	Totals	(483)	321	162

1. For explanation of split electoral votes, see p. 702.

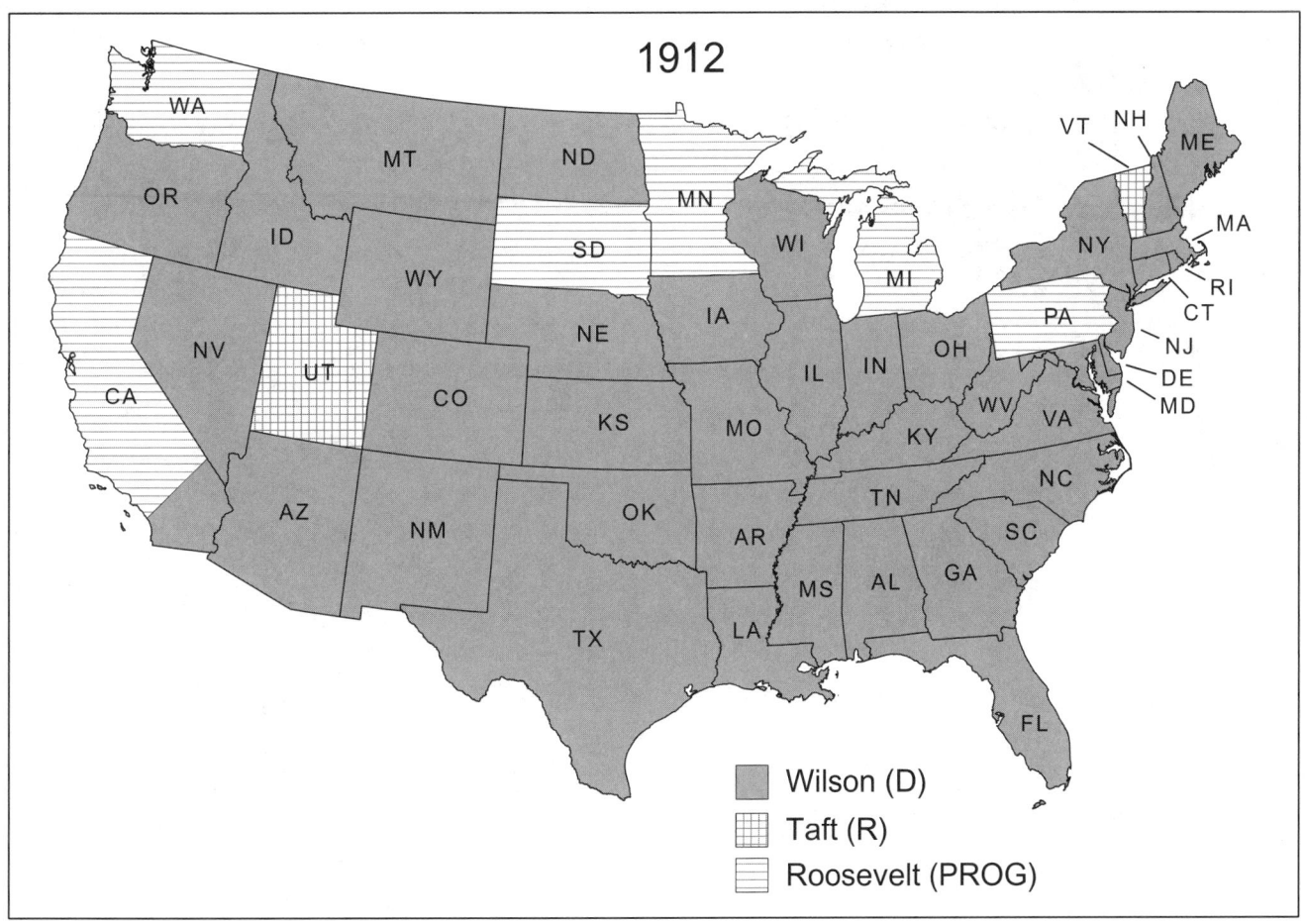

Key: D—Democrat; PROG—Progressive; R—Republican

States	Electoral votes	Wilson	Roosevelt	Taft	States	Electoral votes	Wilson	Roosevelt	Taft
Alabama	(12)	12	–	–	Nevada	(3)	3	–	–
Arizona	(3)	3	–	–	New Hampshire	(4)	4	–	–
Arkansas	(9)	9	–	–	New Jersey	(14)	14	–	–
California[1]	(13)	2	11	–	New Mexico	(3)	3	–	–
Colorado	(6)	6	–	–	New York	(45)	45	–	–
Connecticut	(7)	7	–	–	North Carolina	(12)	12	–	–
Delaware	(3)	3	–	–	North Dakota	(5)	5	–	–
Florida	(6)	6	–	–	Ohio	(24)	24	–	–
Georgia	(14)	14	–	–	Oklahoma	(10)	10	–	–
Idaho	(4)	4	–	–	Oregon	(5)	5	–	–
Illinois	(29)	29	–	–	Pennsylvania	(38)	–	38	–
Indiana	(15)	15	–	–	Rhode Island	(5)	5	–	–
Iowa	(13)	13	–	–	South Carolina	(9)	9	–	–
Kansas	(10)	10	–	–	South Dakota	(5)	–	5	–
Kentucky	(13)	13	–	–	Tennessee	(12)	12	–	–
Louisiana	(10)	10	–	–	Texas	(20)	20	–	–
Maine	(6)	6	–	–	Utah	(4)	–	–	4
Maryland	(8)	8	–	–	Vermont	(4)	–	–	4
Massachusetts	(18)	18	–	–	Virginia	(12)	12	–	–
Michigan	(15)	–	15	–	Washington	(7)	–	7	–
Minnesota	(12)	–	12	–	West Virginia	(8)	8	–	–
Mississippi	(10)	10	–	–	Wisconsin	(13)	13	–	–
Missouri	(18)	18	–	–	Wyoming	(3)	3	–	–
Montana	(4)	4	–	–					
Nebraska	(8)	8	–	–	Totals	(531)	435	88	8

1. For explanation of split electoral votes, see p. 702.

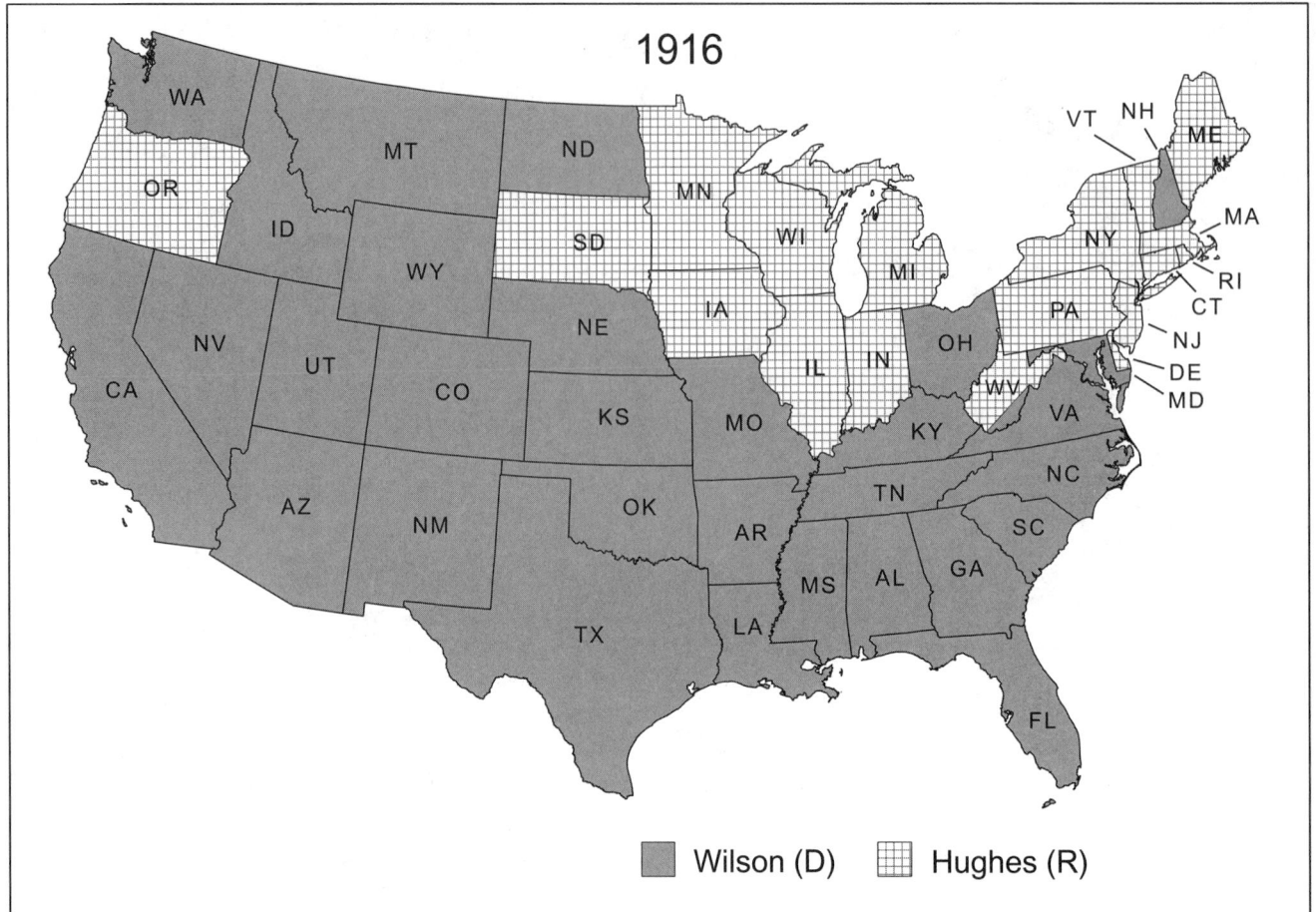

1916

Wilson (D)   Hughes (R)

Key: D—Democrat; R—Republican

States	Electoral votes	Wilson	Hughes	States	Electoral votes	Wilson	Hughes
Alabama	(12)	12	–	Nevada	(3)	3	–
Arizona	(3)	3	–	New Hampshire	(4)	4	–
Arkansas	(9)	9	–	New Jersey	(14)	–	14
California	(13)	13	–	New Mexico	(3)	3	–
Colorado	(6)	6	–	New York	(45)	–	45
Connecticut	(7)	–	7	North Carolina	(12)	12	–
Delaware	(3)	–	3	North Dakota	(5)	5	–
Florida	(6)	6	–	Ohio	(24)	24	–
Georgia	(14)	14	–	Oklahoma	(10)	10	–
Idaho	(4)	4	–	Oregon	(5)	–	5
Illinois	(29)	–	29	Pennsylvania	(38)	–	38
Indiana	(15)	–	15	Rhode Island	(5)	–	5
Iowa	(13)	–	13	South Carolina	(9)	9	–
Kansas	(10)	10	–	South Dakota	(5)	–	5
Kentucky	(13)	13	–	Tennessee	(12)	12	–
Louisiana	(10)	10	–	Texas	(20)	20	–
Maine	(6)	–	6	Utah	(4)	4	–
Maryland	(8)	8	–	Vermont	(4)	–	4
Massachusetts	(18)	–	18	Virginia	(12)	12	–
Michigan	(15)	–	15	Washington	(7)	7	–
Minnesota	(12)	–	12	West Virginia[1]	(8)	1	7
Mississippi	(10)	10	–	Wisconsin	(13)	–	13
Missouri	(18)	18	–	Wyoming	(3)	3	–
Montana	(4)	4	–				
Nebraska	(8)	8	–	Totals	(531)	277	254

1. For explanation of split electoral votes, see p. 702.

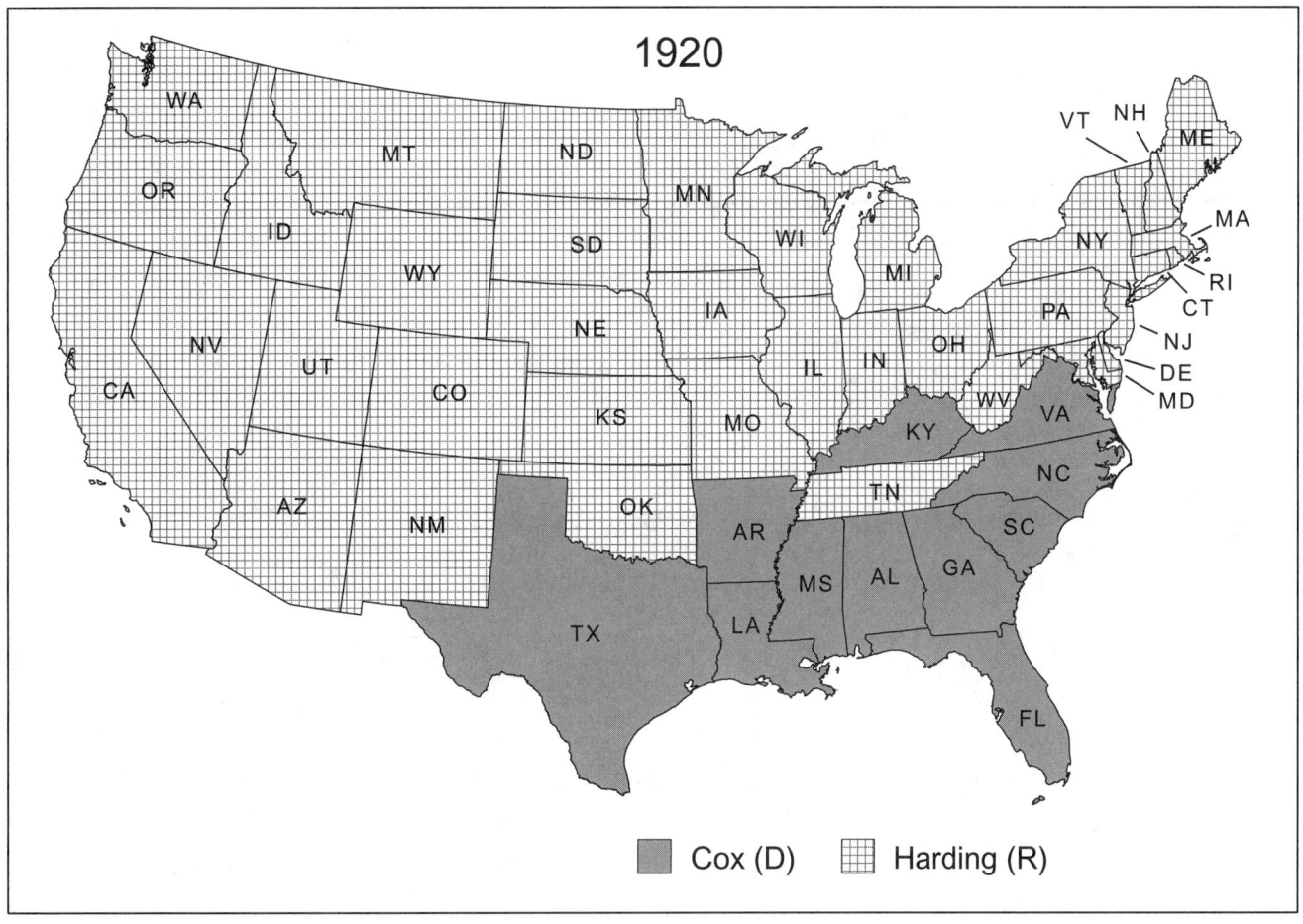

1920

Cox (D)   Harding (R)

Key: D—Democrat; R—Republican

States	Electoral votes	Harding	Cox	States	Electoral votes	Harding	Cox
Alabama	(12)	–	12	Nevada	(3)	3	–
Arizona	(3)	3	–	New Hampshire	(4)	4	–
Arkansas	(9)	–	9	New Jersey	(14)	14	–
California	(13)	13	–	New Mexico	(3)	3	–
Colorado	(6)	6	–	New York	(45)	45	–
Connecticut	(7)	7	–	North Carolina	(12)	–	12
Delaware	(3)	3	–	North Dakota	(5)	5	–
Florida	(6)	–	6	Ohio	(24)	24	–
Georgia	(14)	–	14	Oklahoma	(10)	10	–
Idaho	(4)	4	–	Oregon	(5)	5	–
Illinois	(29)	29	–	Pennsylvania	(38)	38	–
Indiana	(15)	15	–	Rhode Island	(5)	5	–
Iowa	(13)	13	–	South Carolina	(9)	–	9
Kansas	(10)	10	–	South Dakota	(5)	5	–
Kentucky	(13)	–	13	Tennessee	(12)	12	–
Louisiana	(10)	–	10	Texas	(20)	–	20
Maine	(6)	6	–	Utah	(4)	4	–
Maryland	(8)	8	–	Vermont	(4)	4	–
Massachusetts	(18)	18	–	Virginia	(12)	–	12
Michigan	(15)	15	–	Washington	(7)	7	–
Minnesota	(12)	12	–	West Virginia	(8)	8	–
Mississippi	(10)	–	10	Wisconsin	(13)	13	–
Missouri	(18)	18	–	Wyoming	(3)	3	–
Montana	(4)	4	–				
Nebraska	(8)	8	–	Totals	(531)	404	127

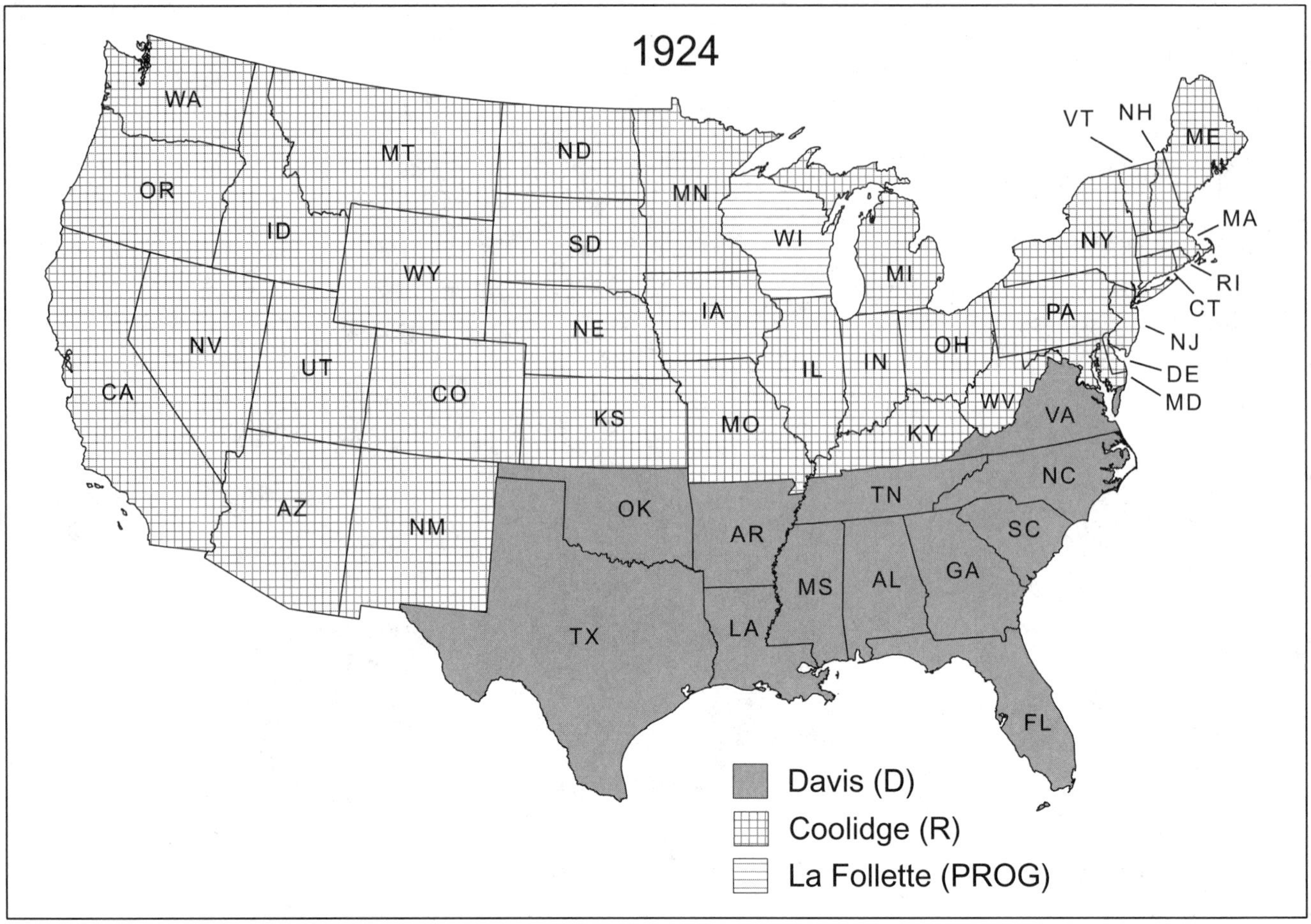

1924

- ▨ Davis (D)
- ▦ Coolidge (R)
- ▤ La Follette (PROG)

Key: D—Democrat; P—Progressive; R—Republican

States	Electoral votes	Coolidge	Davis	La Follette	States	Electoral votes	Coolidge	Davis	La Follette
Alabama	(12)	–	12	–	Nevada	(3)	3	–	–
Arizona	(3)	3	–	–	New Hampshire	(4)	4	–	–
Arkansas	(9)	–	9	–	New Jersey	(14)	14	–	–
California	(13)	13	–	–	New Mexico	(3)	3	–	–
Colorado	(6)	6	–	–	New York	(45)	45	–	–
Connecticut	(7)	7	–	–	North Carolina	(12)	–	12	–
Delaware	(3)	3	–	–	North Dakota	(5)	5	–	–
Florida	(6)	–	6	–	Ohio	(24)	24	–	–
Georgia	(14)	–	14	–	Oklahoma	(10)	–	10	–
Idaho	(4)	4	–	–	Oregon	(5)	5	–	–
Illinois	(29)	29	–	–	Pennsylvania	(38)	38	–	–
Indiana	(15)	15	–	–	Rhode Island	(5)	5	–	–
Iowa	(13)	13	–	–	South Carolina	(9)	–	9	–
Kansas	(10)	10	–	–	South Dakota	(5)	5	–	–
Kentucky	(13)	13	–	–	Tennessee	(12)	–	12	–
Louisiana	(10)	–	10	–	Texas	(20)	–	20	–
Maine	(6)	6	–	–	Utah	(4)	4	–	–
Maryland	(8)	8	–	–	Vermont	(4)	4	–	–
Massachusetts	(18)	18	–	–	Virginia	(12)	–	12	–
Michigan	(15)	15	–	–	Washington	(7)	7	–	–
Minnesota	(12)	12	–	–	West Virginia	(8)	8	–	–
Mississippi	(10)	–	10	–	Wisconsin	(13)	–	–	13
Missouri	(18)	18	–	–	Wyoming	(3)	3	–	–
Montana	(4)	4	–	–					
Nebraska	(8)	8	–	–	Totals	(531)	382	136	13

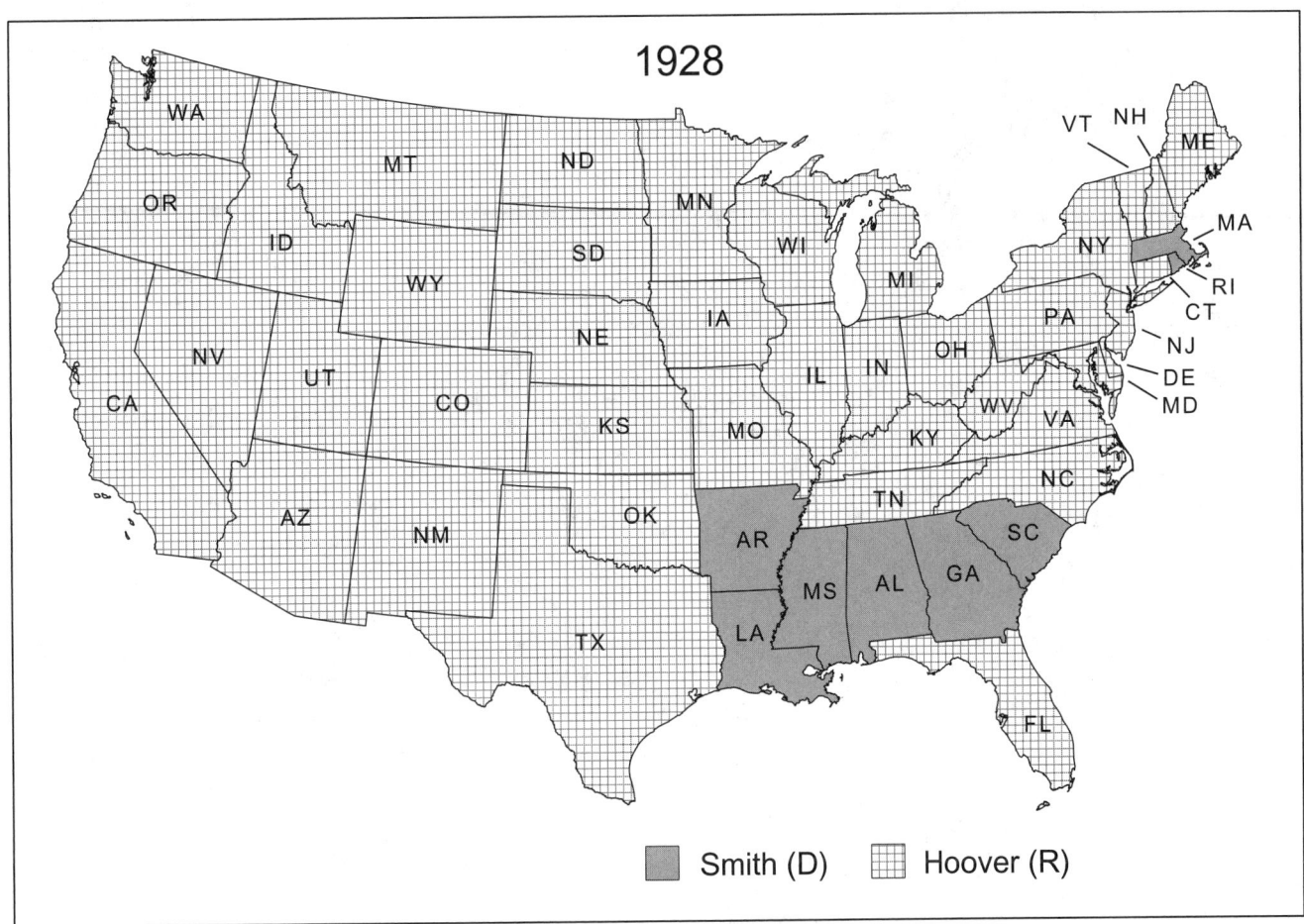

1928

Smith (D)   Hoover (R)

Key: D—Democrat; R—Republican

States	Electoral votes	Hoover	Smith	States	Electoral votes	Hoover	Smith
Alabama	(12)	–	12	Nevada	(3)	3	–
Arizona	(3)	3	–	New Hampshire	(4)	4	–
Arkansas	(9)	–	9	New Jersey	(14)	14	–
California	(13)	13	–	New Mexico	(3)	3	–
Colorado	(6)	6	–	New York	(45)	45	–
Connecticut	(7)	7	–	North Carolina	(12)	12	–
Delaware	(3)	3	–	North Dakota	(5)	5	–
Florida	(6)	6	–	Ohio	(24)	24	–
Georgia	(14)	–	14	Oklahoma	(10)	10	–
Idaho	(4)	4	–	Oregon	(5)	5	–
Illinois	(29)	29	–	Pennsylvania	(38)	38	–
Indiana	(15)	15	–	Rhode Island	(5)	–	5
Iowa	(13)	13	–	South Carolina	(9)	–	9
Kansas	(10)	10	–	South Dakota	(5)	5	–
Kentucky	(13)	13	–	Tennessee	(12)	12	–
Louisiana	(10)	–	10	Texas	(20)	20	–
Maine	(6)	6	–	Utah	(4)	4	–
Maryland	(8)	8	–	Vermont	(4)	4	–
Massachusetts	(18)	–	18	Virginia	(12)	12	–
Michigan	(15)	15	–	Washington	(7)	7	–
Minnesota	(12)	12	–	West Virginia	(8)	8	–
Mississippi	(10)	–	10	Wisconsin	(13)	13	–
Missouri	(18)	18	–	Wyoming	(3)	3	–
Montana	(4)	4	–				
Nebraska	(8)	8	–	Totals	(531)	444	87

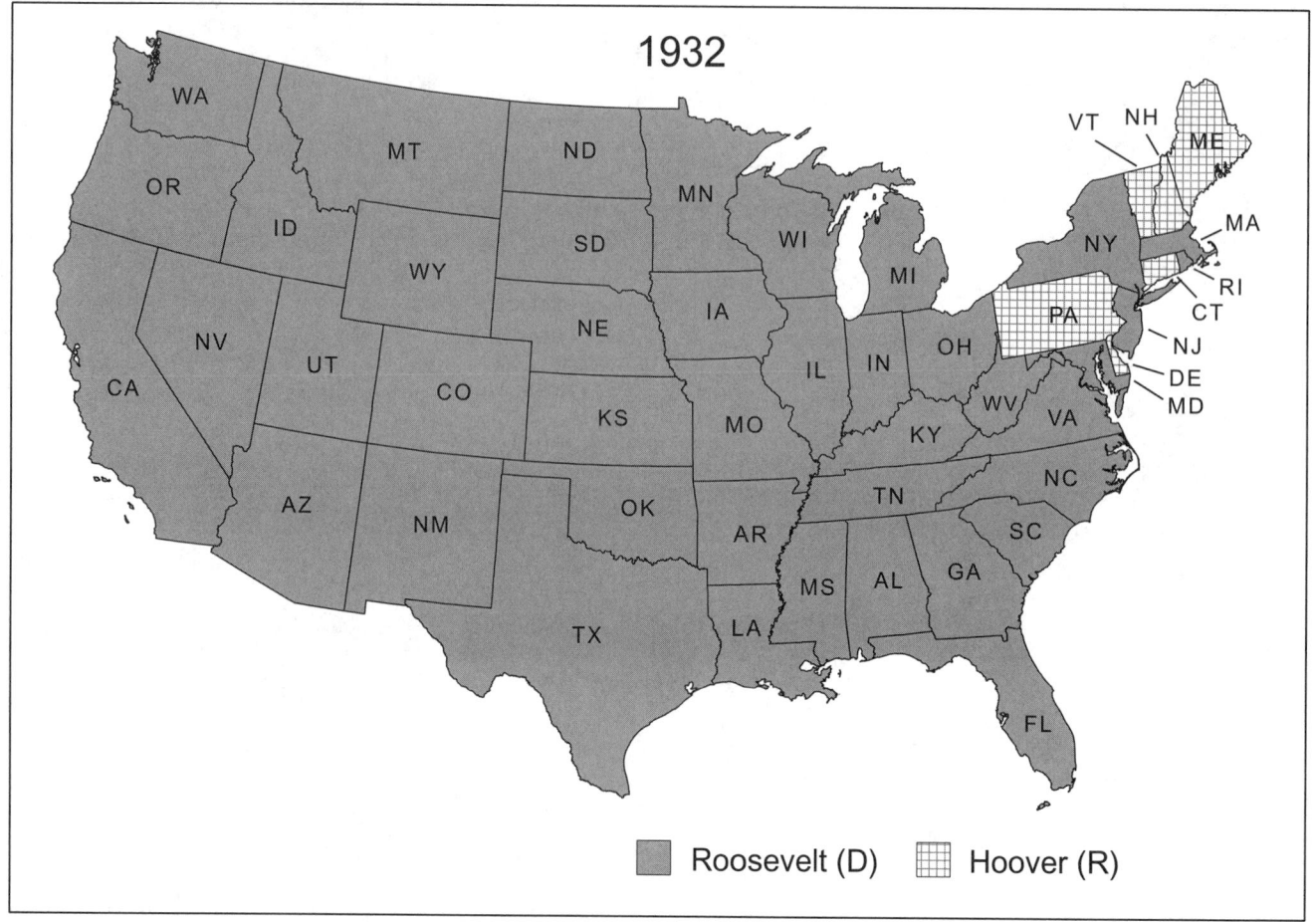

Key: D—Democrat; R—Republican

States	Electoral votes	Roosevelt	Hoover	States	Electoral votes	Roosevelt	Hoover
Alabama	(11)	11	–	Nevada	(3)	3	–
Arizona	(3)	3	–	New Hampshire	(4)	–	4
Arkansas	(9)	9	–	New Jersey	(16)	16	–
California	(22)	22	–	New Mexico	(3)	3	–
Colorado	(6)	6	–	New York	(47)	47	–
Connecticut	(8)	–	8	North Carolina	(13)	13	–
Delaware	(3)	–	3	North Dakota	(4)	4	–
Florida	(7)	7	–	Ohio	(26)	26	–
Georgia	(12)	12	–	Oklahoma	(11)	11	–
Idaho	(4)	4	–	Oregon	(5)	5	–
Illinois	(29)	29	–	Pennsylvania	(36)	–	36
Indiana	(14)	14	–	Rhode Island	(4)	4	–
Iowa	(11)	11	–	South Carolina	(8)	8	–
Kansas	(9)	9	–	South Dakota	(4)	4	–
Kentucky	(11)	11	–	Tennessee	(11)	11	–
Louisiana	(10)	10	–	Texas	(23)	23	–
Maine	(5)	–	5	Utah	(4)	4	–
Maryland	(8)	8	–	Vermont	(3)	–	3
Massachusetts	(17)	17	–	Virginia	(11)	11	–
Michigan	(19)	19	–	Washington	(8)	8	–
Minnesota	(11)	11	–	West Virginia	(8)	8	–
Mississippi	(9)	9	–	Wisconsin	(12)	12	–
Missouri	(15)	15	–	Wyoming	(3)	3	–
Montana	(4)	4	–				
Nebraska	(7)	7	–	Totals	(531)	472	59

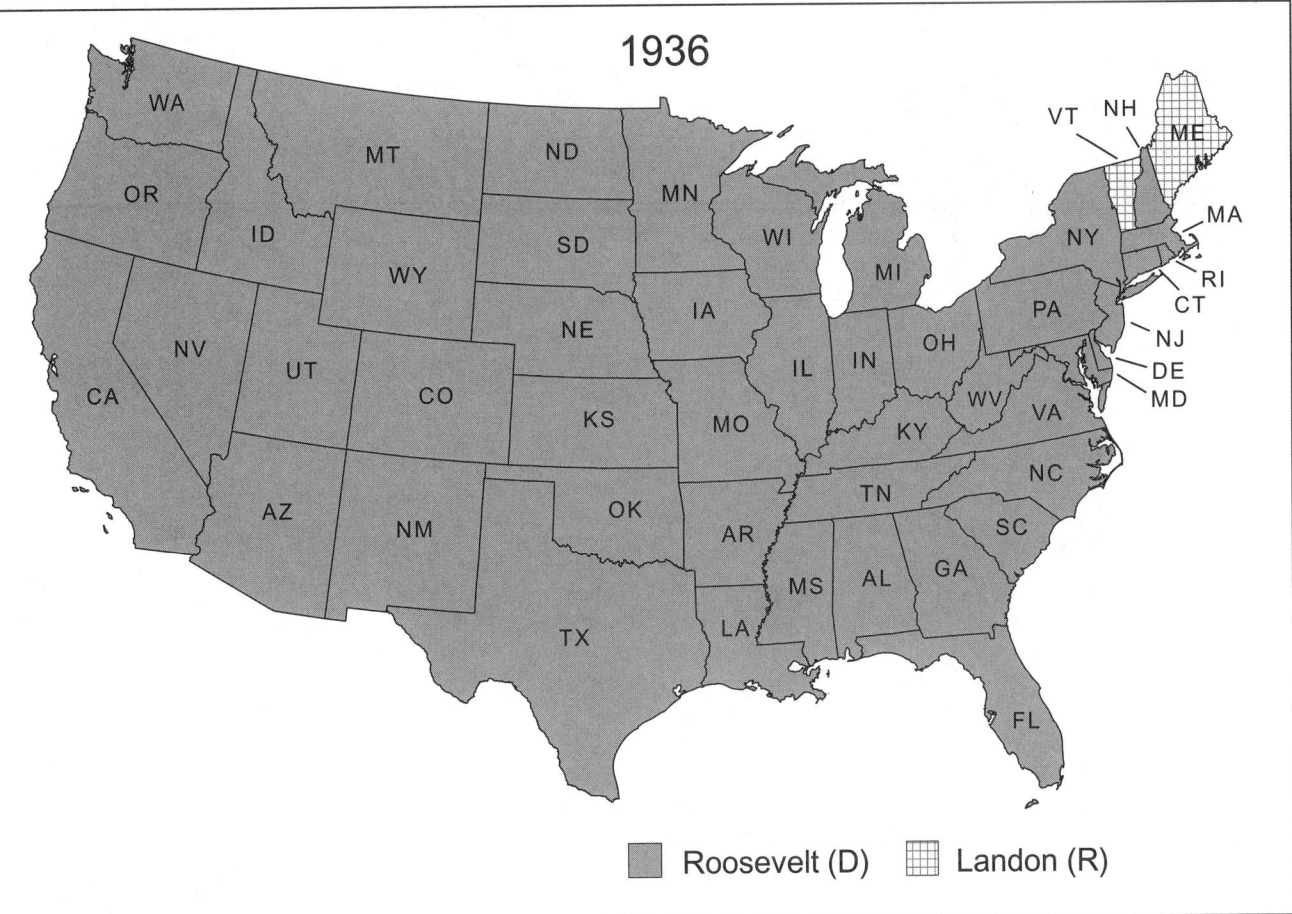

1936

Roosevelt (D)   Landon (R)

Key: D—Democrat; R—Republican

States	Electoral votes	Roosevelt	Landon	States	Electoral votes	Roosevelt	Landon
Alabama	(11)	11	–	Nevada	(3)	3	–
Arizona	(3)	3	–	New Hampshire	(4)	4	–
Arkansas	(9)	9	–	New Jersey	(16)	16	–
California	(22)	22	–	New Mexico	(3)	3	–
Colorado	(6)	6	–	New York	(47)	47	–
Connecticut	(8)	8	–	North Carolina	(13)	13	–
Delaware	(3)	3	–	North Dakota	(4)	4	–
Florida	(7)	7	–	Ohio	(26)	26	–
Georgia	(12)	12	–	Oklahoma	(11)	11	–
Idaho	(4)	4	–	Oregon	(5)	5	–
Illinois	(29)	29	–	Pennsylvania	(36)	36	–
Indiana	(14)	14	–	Rhode Island	(4)	4	–
Iowa	(11)	11	–	South Carolina	(8)	8	–
Kansas	(9)	9	–	South Dakota	(4)	4	–
Kentucky	(11)	11	–	Tennessee	(11)	11	–
Louisiana	(10)	10	–	Texas	(23)	23	–
Maine	(5)	–	5	Utah	(4)	4	–
Maryland	(8)	8	–	Vermont	(3)	–	3
Massachusetts	(17)	17	–	Virginia	(11)	11	–
Michigan	(19)	19	–	Washington	(8)	8	–
Minnesota	(11)	11	–	West Virginia	(8)	8	–
Mississippi	(9)	9	–	Wisconsin	(12)	12	–
Missouri	(15)	15	–	Wyoming	(3)	3	–
Montana	(4)	4	–				
Nebraska	(7)	7	–	Totals	(531)	523	8

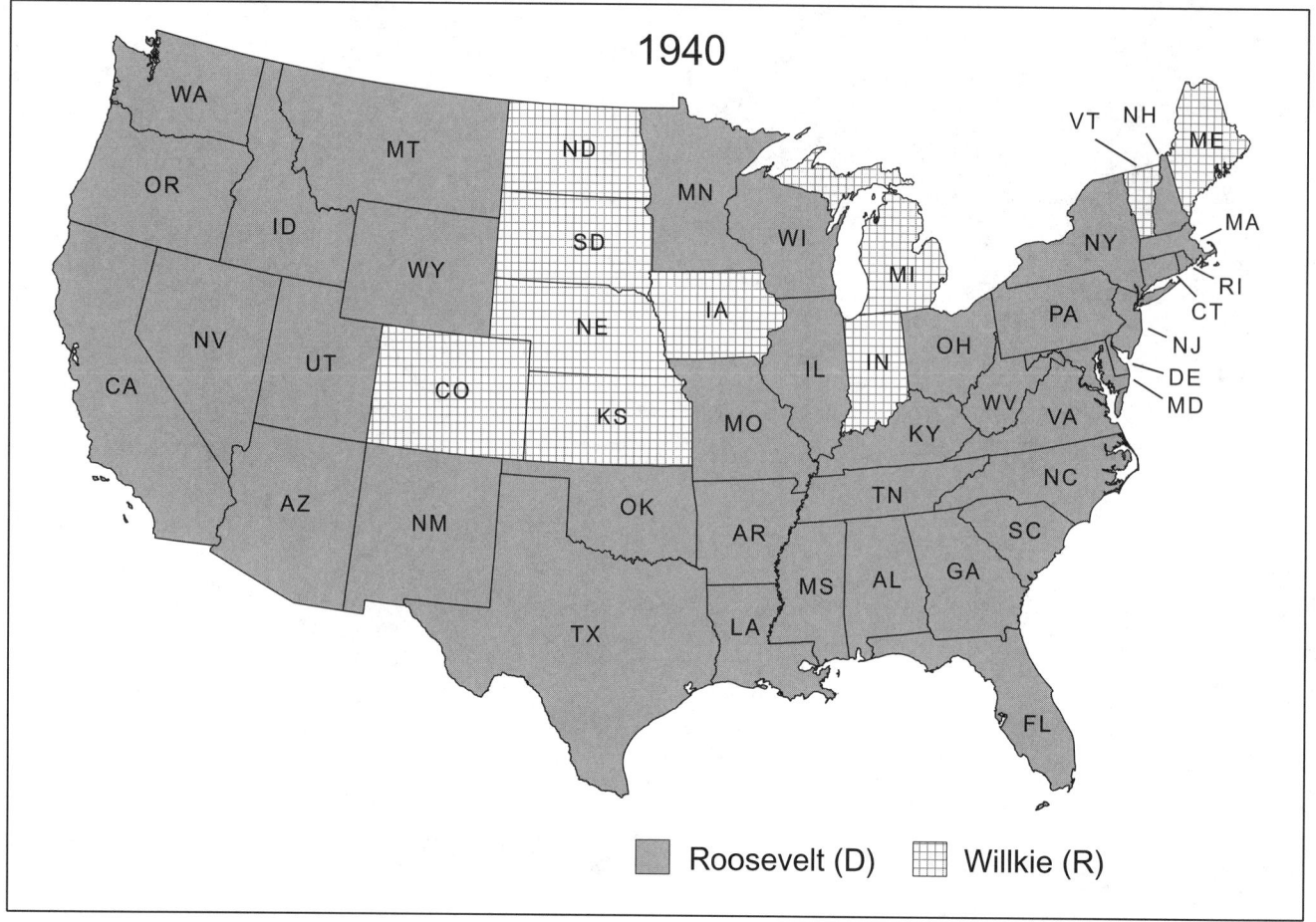

1940

Roosevelt (D)   Willkie (R)

Key: D—Democrat; R—Republican

States	Electoral votes	Roosevelt	Willkie	States	Electoral votes	Roosevelt	Willkie
Alabama	(11)	11	–	Nevada	(3)	3	–
Arizona	(3)	3	–	New Hampshire	(4)	4	–
Arkansas	(9)	9	–	New Jersey	(16)	16	–
California	(22)	22	–	New Mexico	(3)	3	–
Colorado	(6)	–	6	New York	(47)	47	–
Connecticut	(8)	8	–	North Carolina	(13)	13	–
Delaware	(3)	3	–	North Dakota	(4)	–	4
Florida	(7)	7	–	Ohio	(26)	26	–
Georgia	(12)	12	–	Oklahoma	(11)	11	–
Idaho	(4)	4	–	Oregon	(5)	5	–
Illinois	(29)	29	–	Pennsylvania	(36)	36	–
Indiana	(14)	–	14	Rhode Island	(4)	4	–
Iowa	(11)	–	11	South Carolina	(8)	8	–
Kansas	(9)	–	9	South Dakota	(4)	–	4
Kentucky	(11)	11	–	Tennessee	(11)	11	–
Louisiana	(10)	10	–	Texas	(23)	23	–
Maine	(5)	–	5	Utah	(4)	4	–
Maryland	(8)	8	–	Vermont	(3)	–	3
Massachusetts	(17)	17	–	Virginia	(11)	11	–
Michigan	(19)	–	19	Washington	(8)	8	–
Minnesota	(11)	11	–	West Virginia	(8)	8	–
Mississippi	(9)	9	–	Wisconsin	(12)	12	–
Missouri	(15)	15	–	Wyoming	(3)	3	–
Montana	(4)	4	–				
Nebraska	(7)	–	7	Totals	(531)	449	82

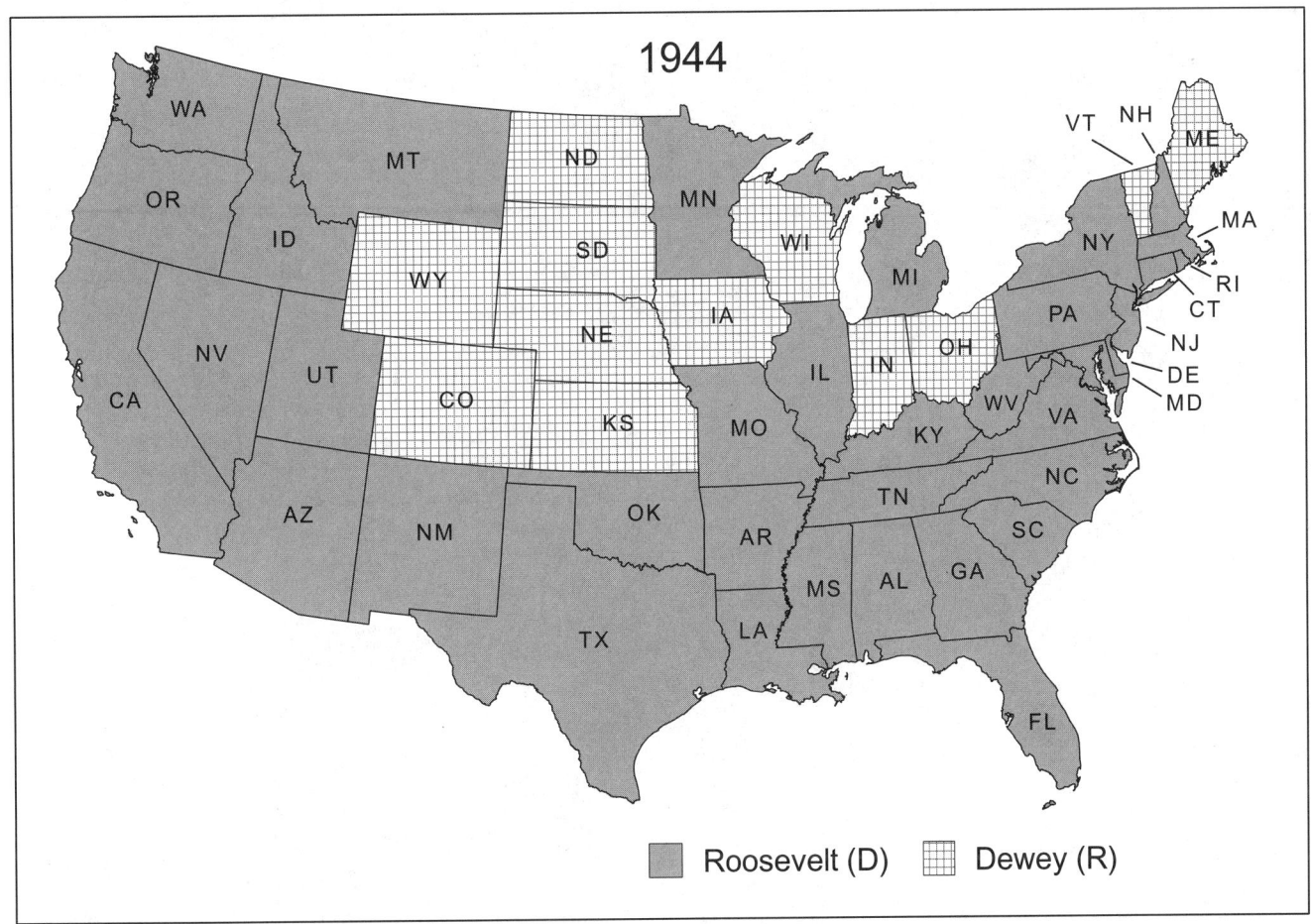

1944

Roosevelt (D)   Dewey (R)

Key: D—Democrat; R—Republican

States	Electoral votes	Roosevelt	Dewey	States	Electoral votes	Roosevelt	Dewey
Alabama	(11)	11	–	Nevada	(3)	3	–
Arizona	(4)	4	–	New Hampshire	(4)	4	–
Arkansas	(9)	9	–	New Jersey	(16)	16	–
California	(25)	25	–	New Mexico	(4)	4	–
Colorado	(6)	–	6	New York	(47)	47	–
Connecticut	(8)	8	–	North Carolina	(14)	14	–
Delaware	(3)	3	–	North Dakota	(4)	–	4
Florida	(8)	8	–	Ohio	(25)	–	25
Georgia	(12)	12	–	Oklahoma	(10)	10	–
Idaho	(4)	4	–	Oregon	(6)	6	–
Illinois	(28)	28	–	Pennsylvania	(35)	35	–
Indiana	(13)	–	13	Rhode Island	(4)	4	–
Iowa	(10)	–	10	South Carolina	(8)	8	–
Kansas	(8)	–	8	South Dakota	(4)	–	4
Kentucky	(11)	11	–	Tennessee	(12)	12	–
Louisiana	(10)	10	–	Texas	(23)	23	–
Maine	(5)	–	5	Utah	(4)	4	–
Maryland	(8)	8	–	Vermont	(3)	–	3
Massachusetts	(16)	16	–	Virginia	(11)	11	–
Michigan	(19)	19	–	Washington	(8)	8	–
Minnesota	(11)	11	–	West Virginia	(8)	8	–
Mississippi	(9)	9	–	Wisconsin	(12)	–	12
Missouri	(15)	15	–	Wyoming	(3)	–	3
Montana	(4)	4	–				
Nebraska	(6)	–	6	Totals	(531)	432	99

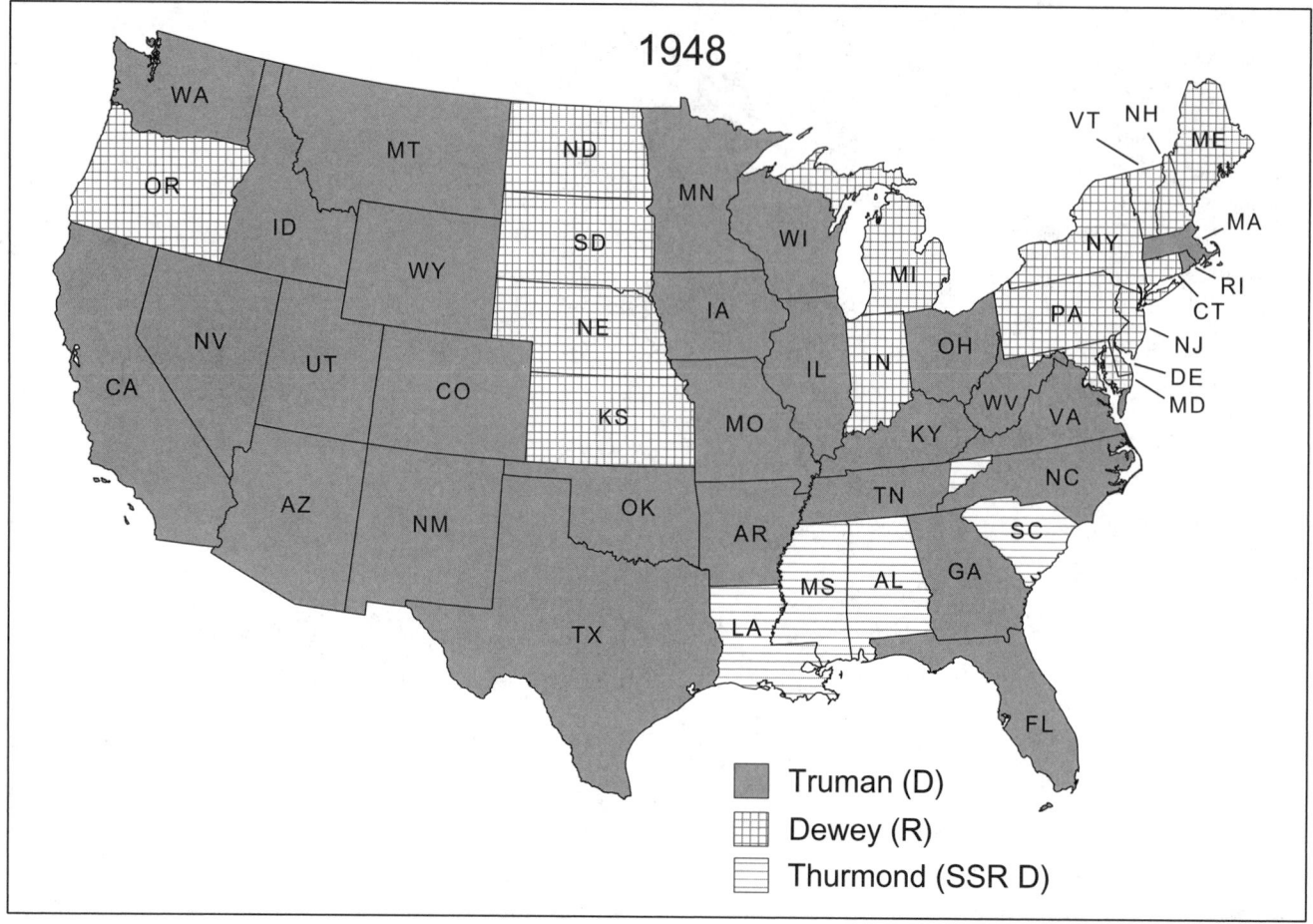

1948

Truman (D)
Dewey (R)
Thurmond (SSR D)

Key: D—Democrat; R—Republican; SSR D—States' Rights Democrat

States	Electoral votes	Truman	Dewey	Thurmond	States	Electoral votes	Truman	Dewey	Thurmond
Alabama	(11)	–	–	11	Nevada	(3)	3	–	–
Arizona	(4)	4	–	–	New Hampshire	(4)	–	4	–
Arkansas	(9)	9	–	–	New Jersey	(16)	–	16	–
California	(25)	25	–	–	New Mexico	(4)	4	–	–
Colorado	(6)	6	–	–	New York	(47)	–	47	–
Connecticut	(8)	–	8	–	North Carolina	(14)	14	–	–
Delaware	(3)	–	3	–	North Dakota	(4)	–	4	–
Florida	(8)	8	–	–	Ohio	(25)	25	–	–
Georgia	(12)	12	–	–	Oklahoma	(10)	10	–	–
Idaho	(4)	4	–	–	Oregon	(6)	–	6	–
Illinois	(28)	28	–	–	Pennsylvania	(35)	–	35	–
Indiana	(13)	–	13	–	Rhode Island	(4)	4	–	–
Iowa	(10)	10	–	–	South Carolina	(8)	–	–	8
Kansas	(8)	–	8	–	South Dakota	(4)	–	4	–
Kentucky	(11)	11	–	–	Tennessee[1]	(12)	11	–	1
Louisiana	(10)	–	–	10	Texas	(23)	23	–	–
Maine	(5)	–	5	–	Utah	(4)	4	–	–
Maryland	(8)	–	8	–	Vermont	(3)	–	3	–
Massachusetts	(16)	16	–	–	Virginia	(11)	11	–	–
Michigan	(19)	–	19	–	Washington	(8)	8	–	–
Minnesota	(11)	11	–	–	West Virginia	(8)	8	–	–
Mississippi	(9)	–	–	9	Wisconsin	(12)	12	–	–
Missouri	(15)	15	–	–	Wyoming	(3)	3	–	–
Montana	(4)	4	–	–					
Nebraska	(6)	–	6	–	Totals	(531)	303	189	39

1. For explanation of split electoral votes, see p. 702.

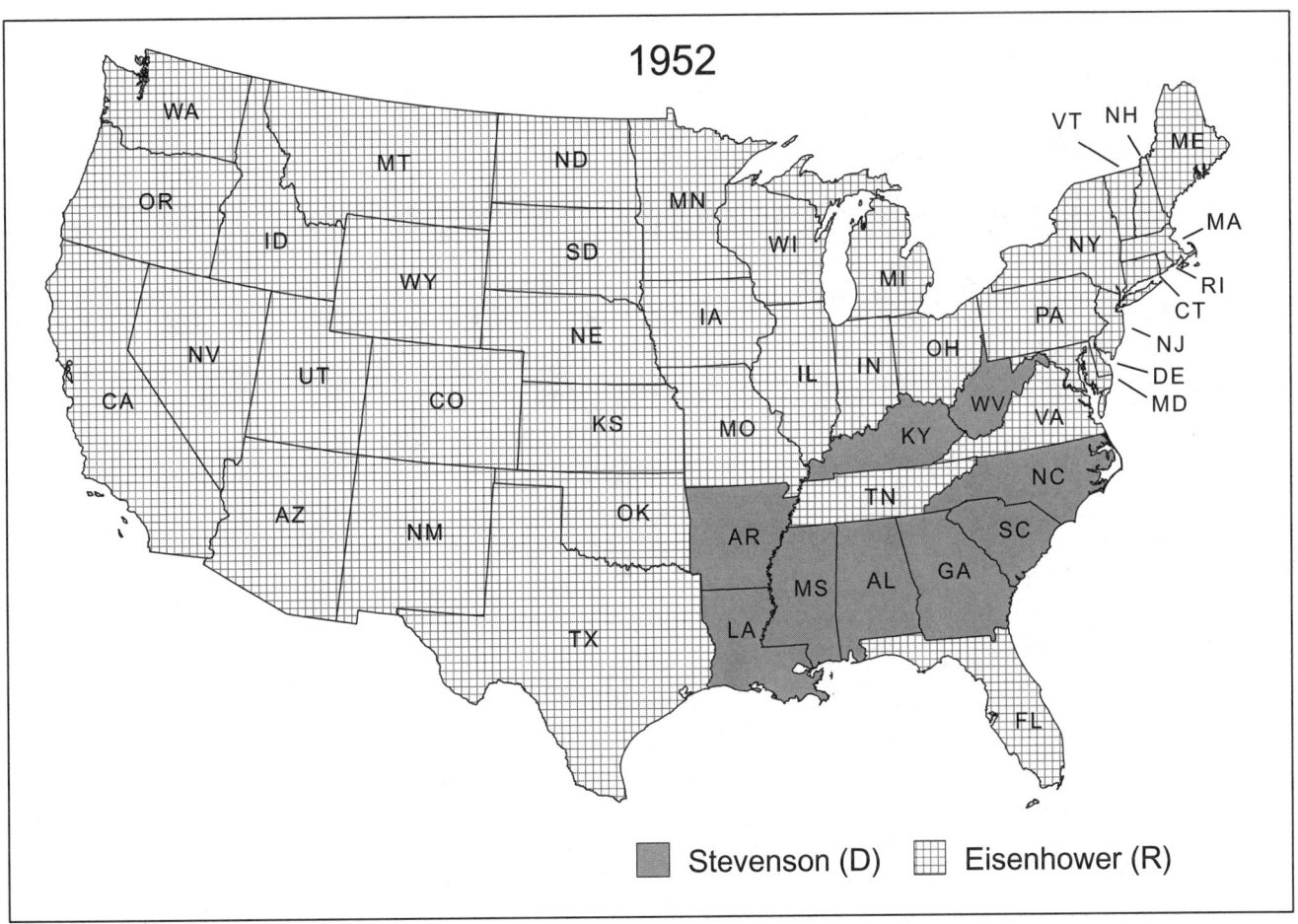

Key: D—Democrat; R—Republican

States	Electoral votes	Eisenhower	Stevenson	States	Electoral votes	Eisenhower	Stevenson
Alabama	(11)	–	11	Nevada	(3)	3	–
Arizona	(4)	4	–	New Hampshire	(4)	4	–
Arkansas	(8)	–	8	New Jersey	(16)	16	–
California	(32)	32	–	New Mexico	(4)	4	–
Colorado	(6)	6	–	New York	(45)	45	–
Connecticut	(8)	8	–	North Carolina	(14)	–	14
Delaware	(3)	3	–	North Dakota	(4)	4	–
Florida	(10)	10	–	Ohio	(25)	25	–
Georgia	(12)	–	12	Oklahoma	(8)	8	–
Idaho	(4)	4	–	Oregon	(6)	6	–
Illinois	(27)	27	–	Pennsylvania	(32)	32	–
Indiana	(13)	13	–	Rhode Island	(4)	4	–
Iowa	(10)	10	–	South Carolina	(8)	–	8
Kansas	(8)	8	–	South Dakota	(4)	4	–
Kentucky	(10)	–	10	Tennessee	(11)	11	–
Louisiana	(10)	–	10	Texas	(24)	24	–
Maine	(5)	5	–	Utah	(4)	4	–
Maryland	(9)	9	–	Vermont	(3)	3	–
Massachusetts	(16)	16	–	Virginia	(12)	12	–
Michigan	(20)	20	–	Washington	(9)	9	–
Minnesota	(11)	11	–	West Virginia	(8)	–	8
Mississippi	(8)	–	8	Wisconsin	(12)	12	–
Missouri	(13)	13	–	Wyoming	(3)	3	–
Montana	(4)	4	–				
Nebraska	(6)	6	–	Totals	(531)	442	89

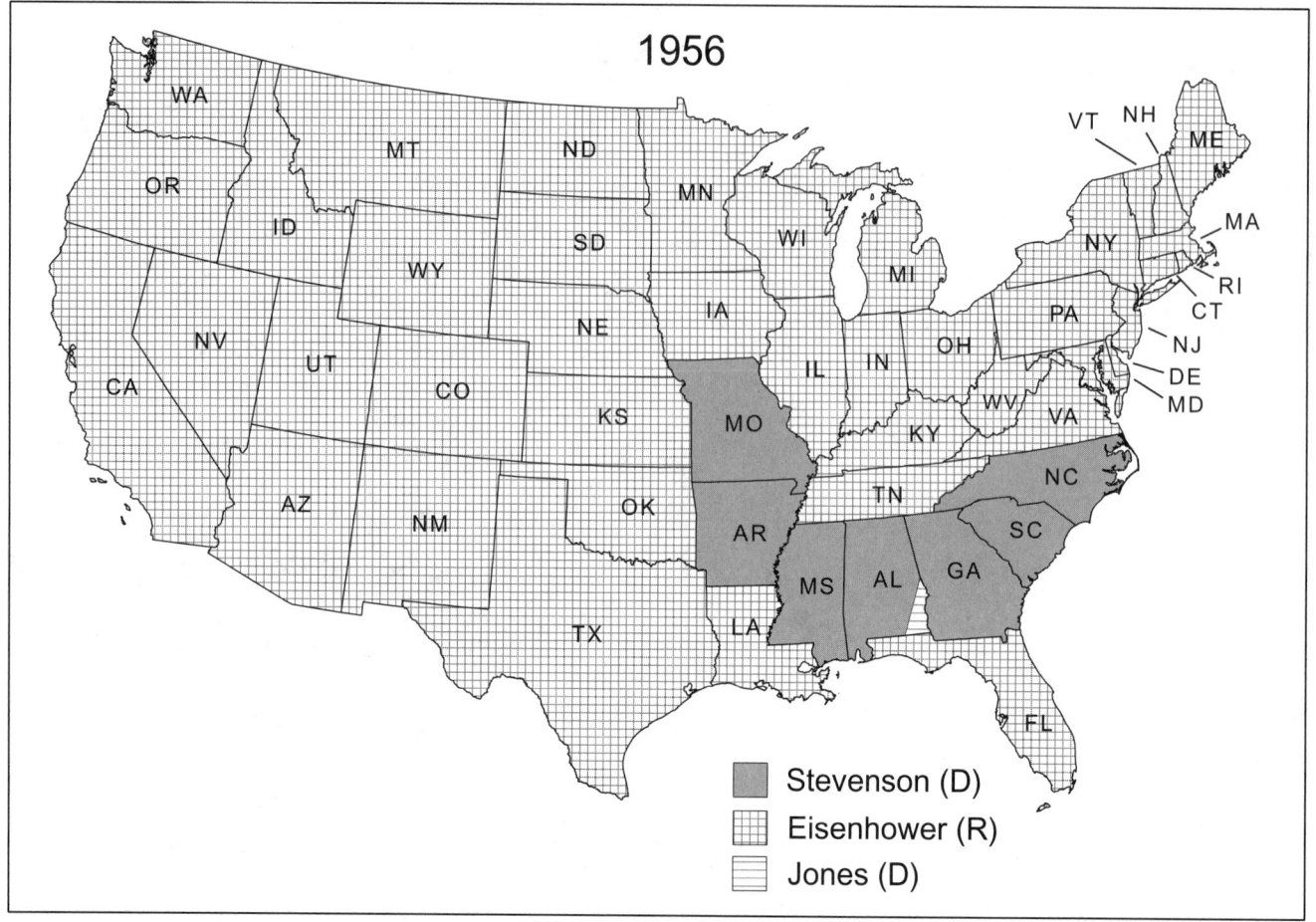

1956

Stevenson (D)
Eisenhower (R)
Jones (D)

Key: D—Democrat; R—Republican

States	Electoral votes	Eisenhower	Stevenson	Jones	States	Electoral votes	Eisenhower	Stevenson	Jones
Alabama[1]	(11)	–	10	1	Nevada	(3)	3	–	–
Arizona	(4)	4	–	–	New Hampshire	(4)	4	–	–
Arkansas	(8)	–	8	–	New Jersey	(16)	16	–	–
California	(32)	32	–	–	New Mexico	(4)	4	–	–
Colorado	(6)	6	–	–	New York	(45)	45	–	–
Connecticut	(8)	8	–	–	North Carolina	(14)	–	14	–
Delaware	(3)	3	–	–	North Dakota	(4)	4	–	–
Florida	(10)	10	–	–	Ohio	(25)	25	–	–
Georgia	(12)	–	12	–	Oklahoma	(8)	8	–	–
Idaho	(4)	4	–	–	Oregon	(6)	6	–	–
Illinois	(27)	27	–	–	Pennsylvania	(32)	32	–	–
Indiana	(13)	13	–	–	Rhode Island	(4)	4	–	–
Iowa	(10)	10	–	–	South Carolina	(8)	–	8	–
Kansas	(8)	8	–	–	South Dakota	(4)	4	–	–
Kentucky	(10)	10	–	–	Tennessee	(11)	11	–	–
Louisiana	(10)	10	–	–	Texas	(24)	24	–	–
Maine	(5)	5	–	–	Utah	(4)	4	–	–
Maryland	(9)	9	–	–	Vermont	(3)	3	–	–
Massachusetts	(16)	16	–	–	Virginia	(12)	12	–	–
Michigan	(20)	20	–	–	Washington	(9)	9	–	–
Minnesota	(11)	11	–	–	West Virginia	(8)	8	–	–
Mississippi	(8)	–	8	–	Wisconsin	(12)	12	–	–
Missouri	(13)	–	13	–	Wyoming	(3)	3	–	–
Montana	(4)	4	–	–					
Nebraska	(6)	6	–	–	Totals	(531)	457	73	1

1. For explanation of split electoral votes, see p. 702

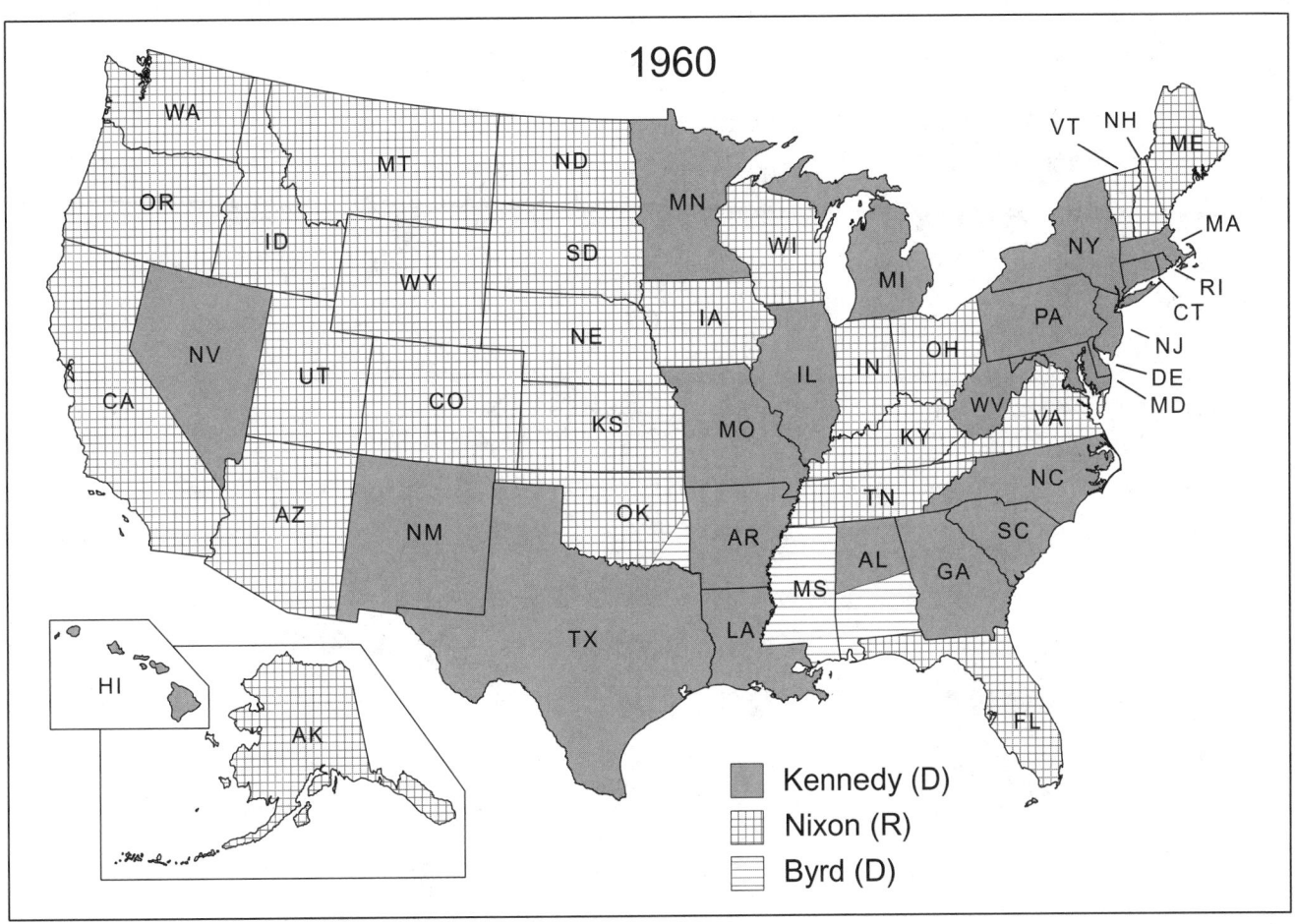

Key: D—Democrat; R—Republican

States	Electoral votes	Kennedy	Nixon	Byrd	States	Electoral votes	Kennedy	Nixon	Byrd
Alabama[1]	(11)	5	–	6	Nebraska	(6)	–	6	–
Alaska	(3)	–	3	–	Nevada	(3)	3	–	–
Arizona	(4)	–	4	–	New Hampshire	(4)	–	4	–
Arkansas	(8)	8	–	–	New Jersey	(16)	16	–	–
California	(32)	–	32	–	New Mexico	(4)	4	–	–
Colorado	(6)	–	6	–	New York	(45)	45	–	–
Connecticut	(8)	8	–	–	North Carolina	(14)	14	–	–
Delaware	(3)	3	–	–	North Dakota	(4)	–	4	–
Florida	(10)	–	10	–	Ohio	(25)	–	25	–
Georgia	(12)	12	–	–	Oklahoma[2]	(8)	–	7	1
Hawaii	(3)	3	–	–	Oregon	(6)	–	6	–
Idaho	(4)	–	4	–	Pennsylvania	(32)	32	–	–
Illinois	(27)	27	–	–	Rhode Island	(4)	4	–	–
Indiana	(13)	–	13	–	South Carolina	(8)	8	–	–
Iowa	(10)	–	10	–	South Dakota	(4)	–	4	–
Kansas	(8)	–	8	–	Tennessee	(11)	–	11	–
Kentucky	(10)	–	10	–	Texas	(24)	24	–	–
Louisiana	(10)	10	–	–	Utah	(4)	–	4	–
Maine	(5)	–	5	–	Vermont	(3)	–	3	–
Maryland	(9)	9	–	–	Virginia	(12)	–	12	–
Massachusetts	(16)	16	–	–	Washington	(9)	–	9	–
Michigan	(20)	20	–	–	West Virginia	(8)	8	–	–
Minnesota	(11)	11	–	–	Wisconsin	(12)	–	12	–
Mississippi[1]	(8)	–	–	8	Wyoming	(3)	–	3	–
Missouri	(13)	13	–	–					
Montana	(4)	–	4	–	Totals	(537)	303	219	15

1. Six Alabama electors and all eight Mississippi electors, elected as "unpledged Democrats," cast their votes for Byrd.
2. For explanation of split electoral votes, see p. 702.

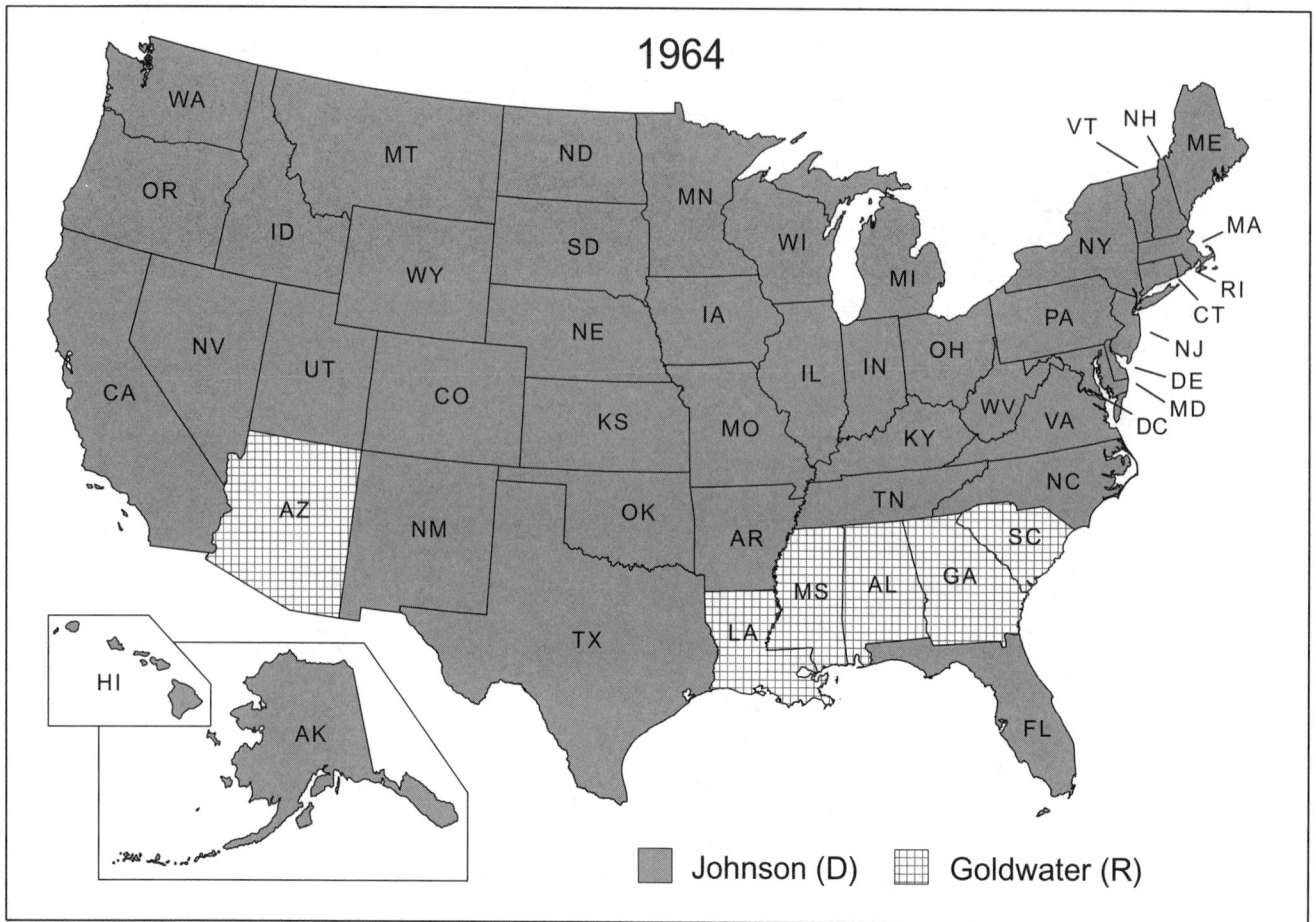

Key: D—Democrat; R—Republican

States	Electoral votes	Johnson	Goldwater	States	Electoral votes	Johnson	Goldwater
Alabama	(10)	–	10	Nebraska	(5)	5	–
Alaska	(3)	3	–	Nevada	(3)	3	–
Arizona	(5)	–	5	New Hampshire	(4)	4	–
Arkansas	(6)	6	–	New Jersey	(17)	17	–
California	(40)	40	–	New Mexico	(4)	4	–
Colorado	(6)	6	–	New York	(43)	43	–
Connecticut	(8)	8	–	North Carolina	(13)	13	–
Delaware	(3)	3	–	North Dakota	(4)	4	–
District of Columbia	(3)	3	–	Ohio	(26)	26	–
Florida	(14)	14	–	Oklahoma	(8)	8	–
Georgia	(12)	–	12	Oregon	(6)	6	–
Hawaii	(4)	4	–	Pennsylvania	(29)	29	–
Idaho	(4)	4	–	Rhode Island	(4)	4	–
Illinois	(26)	26	–	South Carolina	(8)	–	8
Indiana	(13)	13	–	South Dakota	(4)	4	–
Iowa	(9)	9	–	Tennessee	(11)	11	–
Kansas	(7)	7	–	Texas	(25)	25	–
Kentucky	(9)	9	–	Utah	(4)	4	–
Louisiana	(10)	–	10	Vermont	(3)	3	–
Maine	(4)	4	–	Virginia	(12)	12	–
Maryland	(10)	10	–	Washington	(9)	9	–
Massachusetts	(14)	14	–	West Virginia	(7)	7	–
Michigan	(21)	21	–	Wisconsin	(12)	12	–
Minnesota	(10)	10	–	Wyoming	(3)	3	–
Mississippi	(7)	–	7				
Missouri	(12)	12	–	Totals	(538)	486	52
Montana	(4)	4	–				

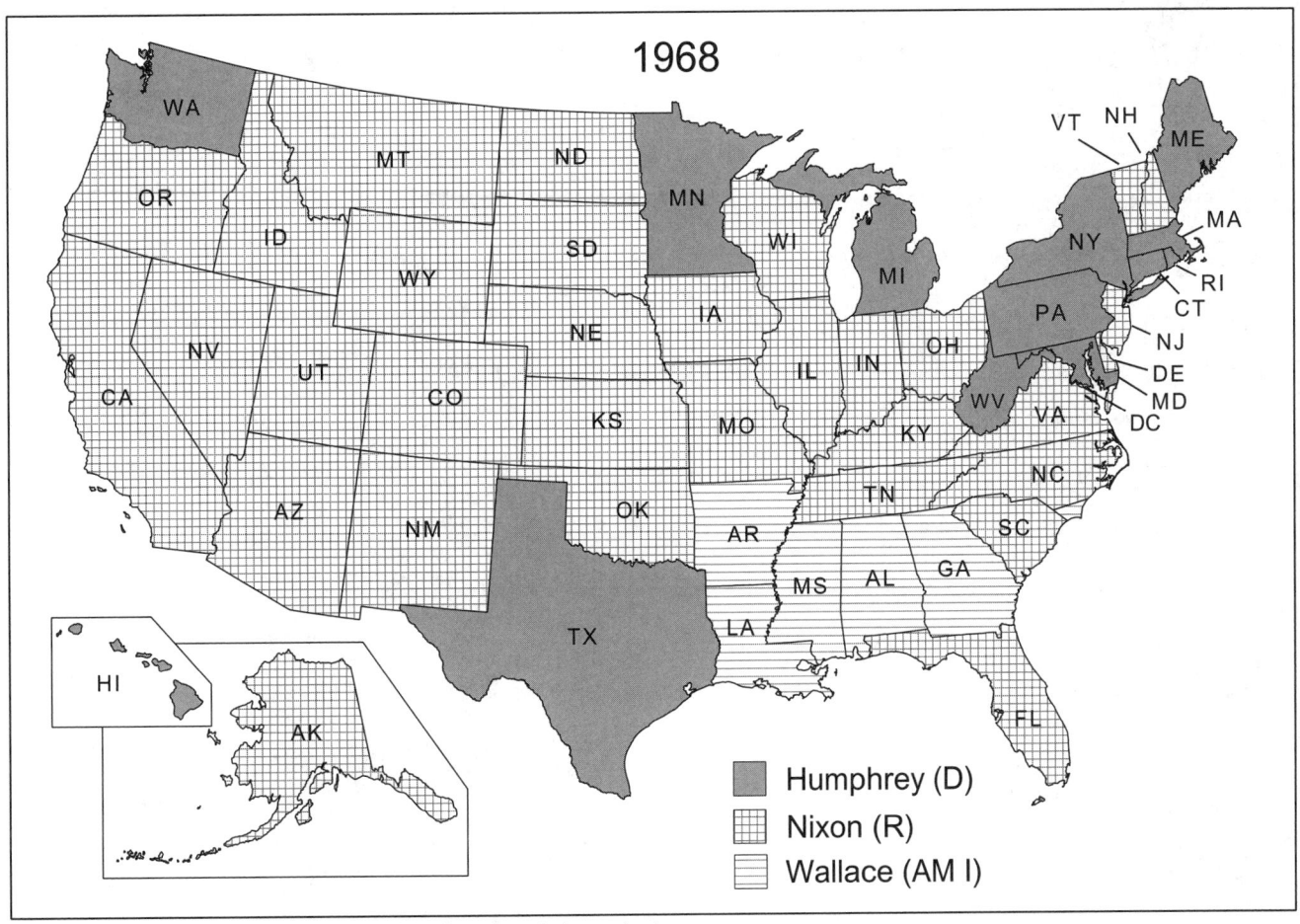

1968

Legend:
- Humphrey (D)
- Nixon (R)
- Wallace (AM I)

Key: D—Democrat; R—Republican; AM I—American Independent

States	Electoral votes	Nixon	Humphrey	Wallace	States	Electoral votes	Nixon	Humphrey	Wallace
Alabama	(10)	-	-	10	Nebraska	(5)	5	-	-
Alaska	(3)	3	-	-	Nevada	(3)	3	-	-
Arizona	(5)	5	-	-	New Hampshire	(4)	4	-	-
Arkansas	(6)	-	-	6	New Jersey	(17)	17	-	-
California	(40)	40	-	-	New Mexico	(4)	4	-	-
Colorado	(6)	6	-	-	New York	(43)	-	43	-
Connecticut	(8)	-	8	-	North Carolina[1]	(13)	12	-	1
Delaware	(3)	3	-	-	North Dakota	(4)	4	-	-
District of Columbia	(3)	-	3	-	Ohio	(26)	26	-	-
Florida	(14)	14	-	-	Oklahoma	(8)	8	-	-
Georgia	(12)	-	-	12	Oregon	(6)	6	-	-
Hawaii	(4)	-	4	-	Pennsylvania	(29)	-	29	-
Idaho	(4)	4	-	-	Rhode Island	(4)	-	4	-
Illinois	(26)	26	-	-	South Carolina	(8)	8	-	-
Indiana	(13)	13	-	-	South Dakota	(4)	4	-	-
Iowa	(9)	9	-	-	Tennessee	(11)	11	-	-
Kansas	(7)	7	-	-	Texas	(25)	-	25	-
Kentucky	(9)	9	-	-	Utah	(4)	4	-	-
Louisiana	(10)	-	-	10	Vermont	(3)	3	-	-
Maine	(4)	-	4	-	Virginia	(12)	12	-	-
Maryland	(10)	-	10	-	Washington	(9)	-	9	-
Massachusetts	(14)	-	14	-	West Virginia	(7)	-	7	-
Michigan	(21)	-	21	-	Wisconsin	(12)	12	-	-
Minnesota	(10)	-	10	-	Wyoming	(3)	3	-	-
Mississippi	(7)	-	-	7					
Missouri	(12)	12	-	-	Totals	(538)	301	191	46
Montana	(4)	4	-	-					

1. For explanation of split electoral votes, see p. 702

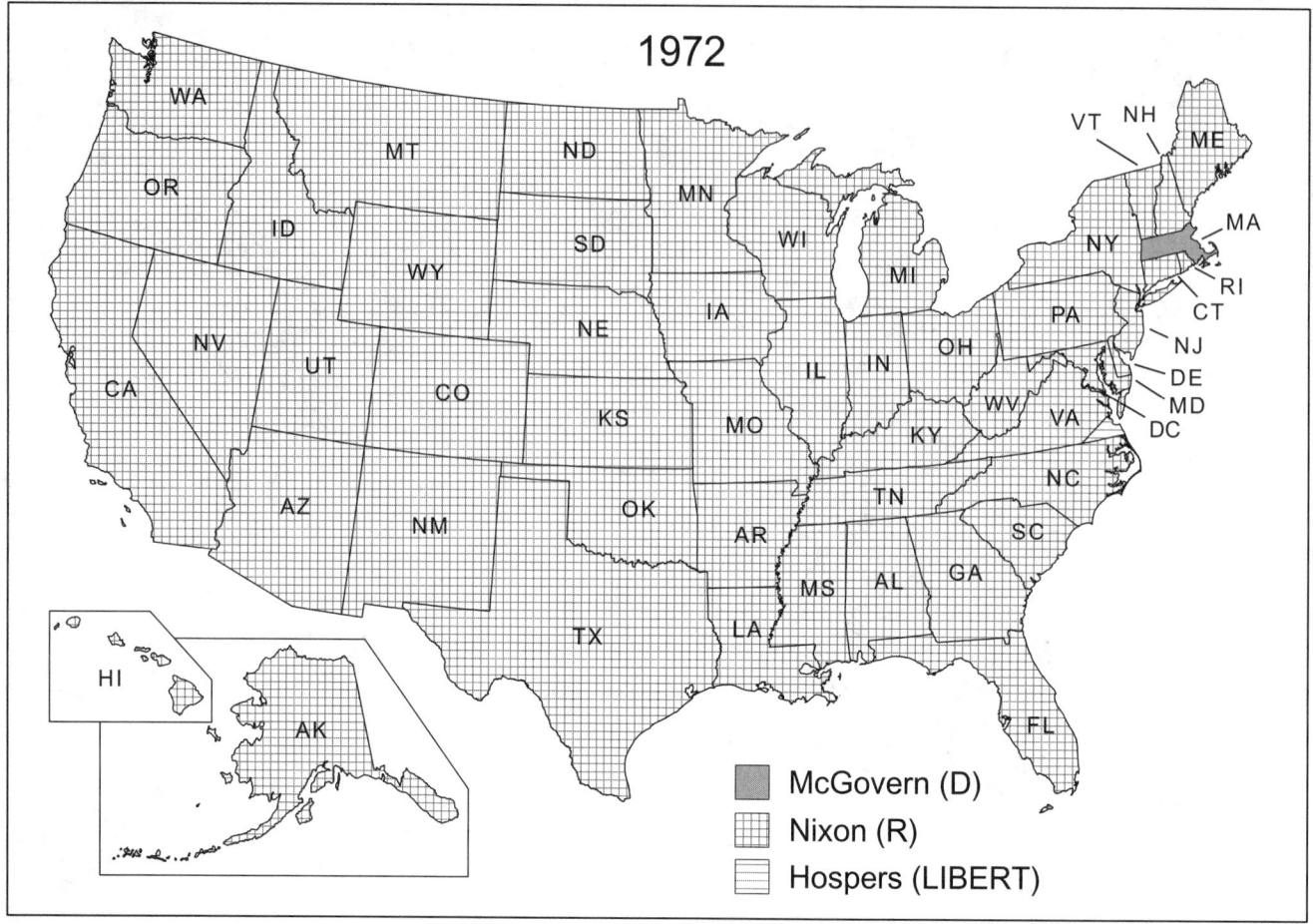

Key: D—Democrat; LIBERT—Libertarian; R—Republican

States	Electoral votes	Nixon	McGovern	Hospers	States	Electoral votes	Nixon	McGovern	Hospers
Alabama	(9)	9	–	–	Nebraska	(5)	5	–	–
Alaska	(3)	3	–	–	Nevada	(3)	3	–	–
Arizona	(6)	6	–	–	New Hampshire	(4)	4	–	–
Arkansas	(6)	6	–	–	New Jersey	(17)	17	–	–
California	(45)	45	–	–	New Mexico	(4)	4	–	–
Colorado	(7)	7	–	–	New York	(41)	41	–	–
Connecticut	(8)	8	–	–	North Carolina	(13)	13	–	–
Delaware	(3)	3	–	–	North Dakota	(3)	3	–	–
District of Columbia	(3)	–	3	–	Ohio	(25)	25	–	–
Florida	(17)	17	–	–	Oklahoma	(8)	8	–	–
Georgia	(12)	12	–	–	Oregon	(6)	6	–	–
Hawaii	(4)	4	–	–	Pennsylvania	(27)	27	–	–
Idaho	(4)	4	–	–	Rhode Island	(4)	4	–	–
Illinois	(26)	26	–	–	South Carolina	(8)	8	–	–
Indiana	(13)	13	–	–	South Dakota	(4)	4	–	–
Iowa	(8)	8	–	–	Tennessee	(10)	10	–	–
Kansas	(7)	7	–	–	Texas	(26)	26	–	–
Kentucky	(9)	9	–	–	Utah	(4)	4	–	–
Louisiana	(10)	10	–	–	Vermont	(3)	3	–	–
Maine	(4)	4	–	–	Virginia[1]	(12)	11	–	1
Maryland	(10)	10	–	–	Washington	(9)	9	–	–
Massachusetts	(14)	–	14	–	West Virginia	(6)	6	–	–
Michigan	(21)	21	–	–	Wisconsin	(11)	11	–	–
Minnesota	(10)	10	–	–	Wyoming	(3)	3	–	–
Mississippi	(7)	7	–	–					
Missouri	(12)	12	–	–	Totals	(538)	520	17	1
Montana	(4)	4	–	–					

1. For explanation of split electoral votes, see p. 702.

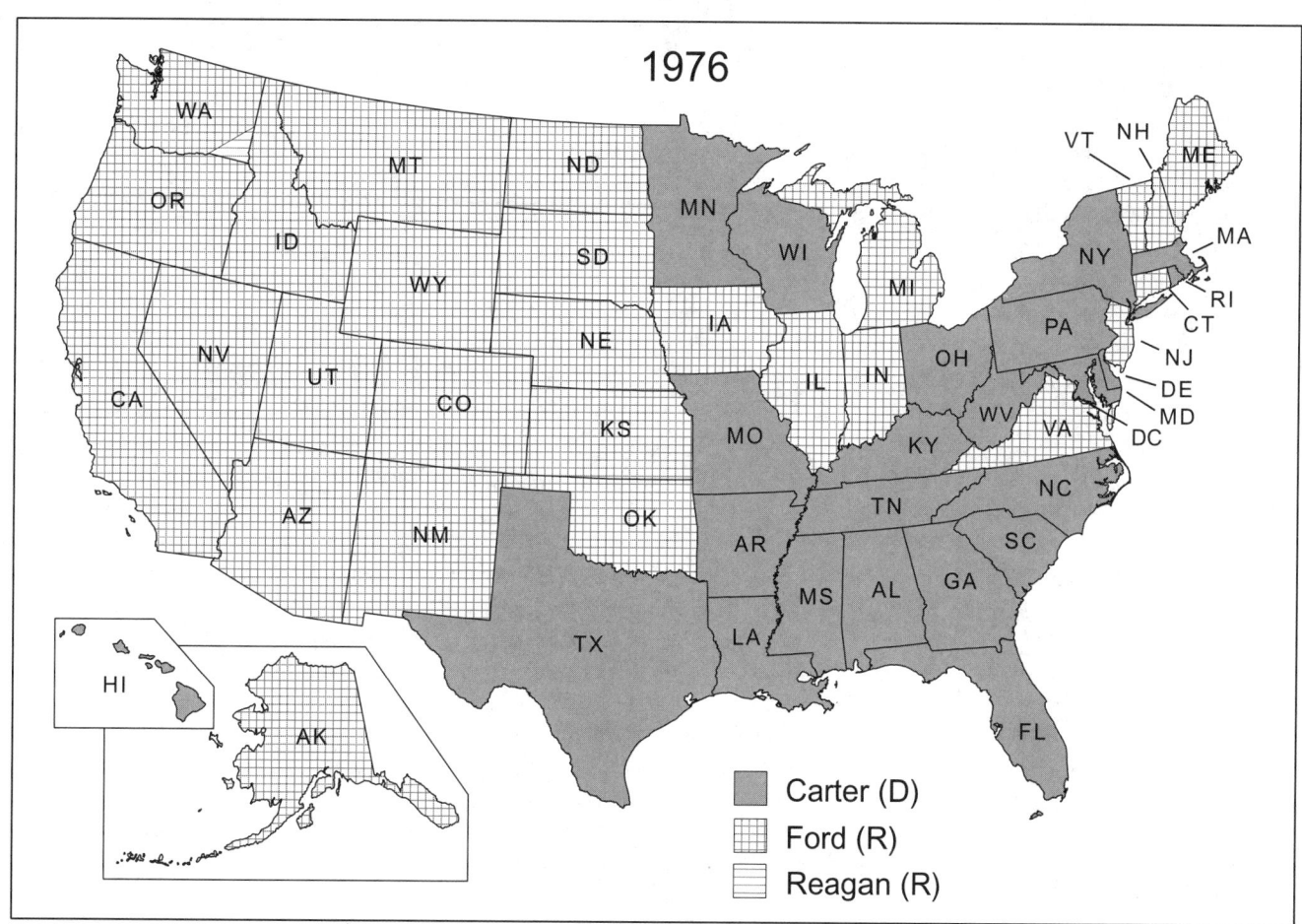

Key: D—Democrat; R—Republican

States	Electoral votes	Carter	Ford	Reagan	States	Electoral votes	Carter	Ford	Reagan
Alabama	(9)	9	–	–	Nebraska	(5)	–	5	–
Alaska	(3)	–	3	–	Nevada	(3)	–	3	–
Arizona	(6)	–	6	–	New Hampshire	(4)	–	4	–
Arkansas	(6)	6	–	–	New Jersey	(17)	–	17	–
California	(45)	–	45	–	New Mexico	(4)	–	4	–
Colorado	(7)	–	7	–	New York	(41)	41	–	–
Connecticut	(8)	–	8	–	North Carolina	(13)	13	–	–
Delaware	(3)	3	–	–	North Dakota	(3)	–	3	–
District of Columbia	(3)	3	–	–	Ohio	(25)	25	–	–
Florida	(17)	17	–	–	Oklahoma	(8)	–	8	–
Georgia	(12)	12	–	–	Oregon	(6)	–	6	–
Hawaii	(4)	4	–	–	Pennsylvania	(27)	27	–	–
Idaho	(4)	–	4	–	Rhode Island	(4)	4	–	–
Illinois	(26)	–	26	–	South Carolina	(8)	8	–	–
Indiana	(13)	–	13	–	South Dakota	(4)	–	4	–
Iowa	(8)	–	8	–	Tennessee	(10)	10	–	–
Kansas	(7)	–	7	–	Texas	(26)	26	–	–
Kentucky	(9)	9	–	–	Utah	(4)	–	4	–
Louisiana	(10)	10	–	–	Vermont	(3)	–	3	–
Maine	(4)	–	4	–	Virginia	(12)	–	12	–
Maryland	(10)	10	–	–	Washington[1]	(9)	–	8	1
Massachusetts	(14)	14	–	–	West Virginia	(6)	6	–	–
Michigan	(21)	–	21	–	Wisconsin	(11)	11	–	–
Minnesota	(10)	10	–	–	Wyoming	(3)	–	3	–
Mississippi	(7)	7	–	–					
Missouri	(12)	12	–	–	Totals	(538)	297	240	1
Montana	(4)	–	4	–					

1. For explanation of split electoral votes, see p. 702.

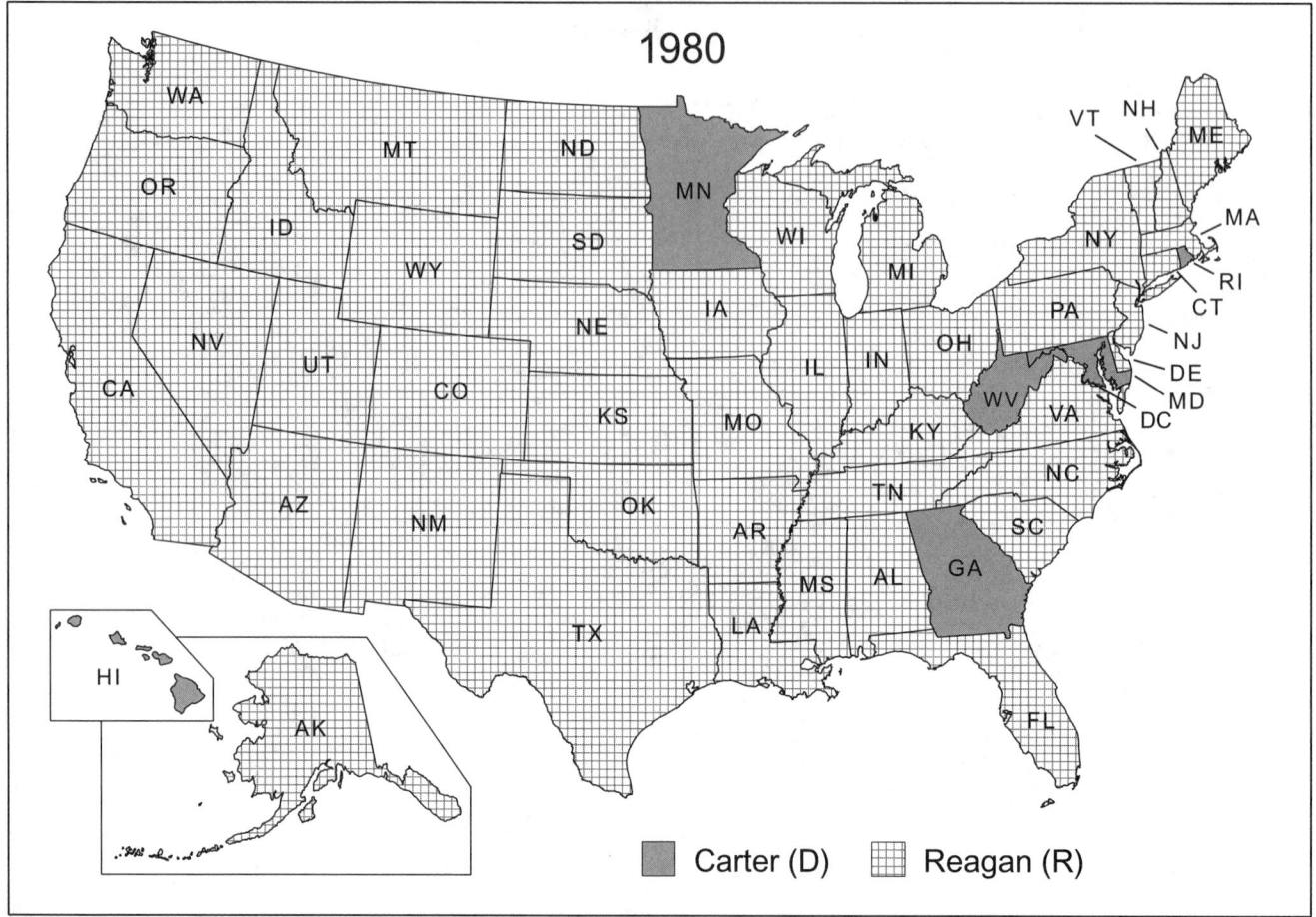

Key: D—Democrat; R—Republican

States	Electoral votes	Reagan	Carter	States	Electoral votes	Reagan	Carter
Alabama	(9)	9	–	Nebraska	(5)	5	–
Alaska	(3)	3	–	Nevada	(3)	3	–
Arizona	(6)	6	–	New Hampshire	(4)	4	–
Arkansas	(6)	6	–	New Jersey	(17)	17	–
California	(45)	45	–	New Mexico	(4)	4	–
Colorado	(7)	7	–	New York	(41)	41	–
Connecticut	(8)	8	–	North Carolina	(13)	13	–
Delaware	(3)	3	–	North Dakota	(3)	3	–
District of Columbia	(3)	–	3	Ohio	(25)	25	–
Florida	(17)	17	–	Oklahoma	(8)	8	–
Georgia	(12)	–	12	Oregon	(6)	6	–
Hawaii	(4)	–	4	Pennsylvania	(27)	27	–
Idaho	(4)	4	–	Rhode Island	(4)	–	4
Illinois	(26)	26	–	South Carolina	(8)	8	–
Indiana	(13)	13	–	South Dakota	(4)	4	–
Iowa	(8)	8	–	Tennessee	(10)	10	–
Kansas	(7)	7	–	Texas	(26)	26	–
Kentucky	(9)	9	–	Utah	(4)	4	–
Louisiana	(10)	10	–	Vermont	(3)	3	–
Maine	(4)	4	–	Virginia	(12)	12	–
Maryland	(10)	–	10	Washington	(9)	9	–
Massachusetts	(14)	14	–	West Virginia	(6)	–	6
Michigan	(21)	21	–	Wisconsin	(11)	11	–
Minnesota	(10)	–	10	Wyoming	(3)	3	–
Mississippi	(7)	7	–				
Missouri	(12)	12	–	Totals	(538)	489	49
Montana	(4)	4	–				

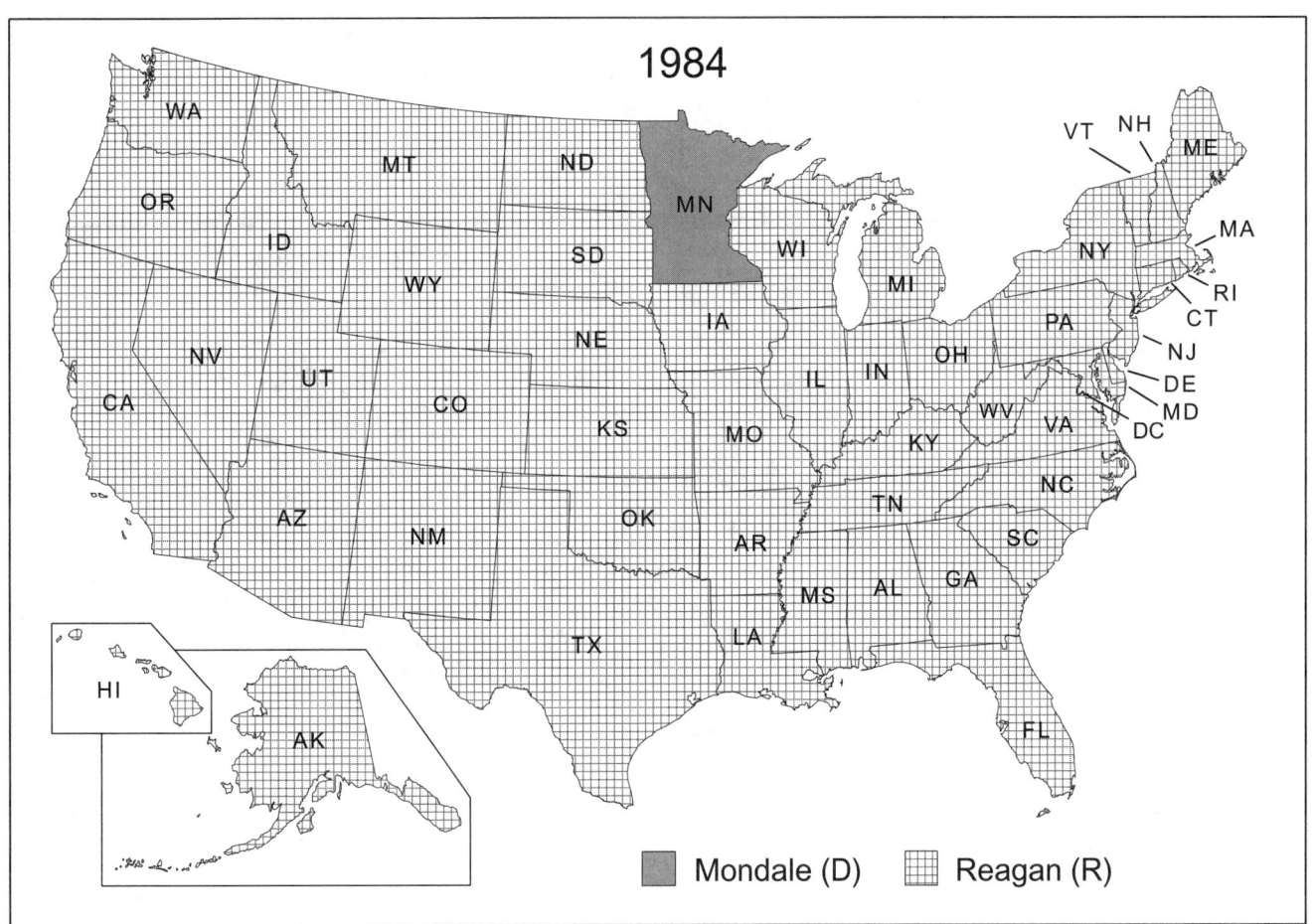

1984

Mondale (D)   Reagan (R)

Key: D—Democrat; R—Republican

States	Electoral votes	Reagan	Mondale	States	Electoral votes	Reagan	Mondale
Alabama	(9)	9	–	Nebraska	(5)	5	–
Alaska	(3)	3	–	Nevada	(4)	4	–
Arizona	(7)	7	–	New Hampshire	(4)	4	–
Arkansas	(6)	6	–	New Jersey	(16)	16	–
California	(47)	47	–	New Mexico	(5)	5	–
Colorado	(8)	8	–	New York	(36)	36	–
Connecticut	(8)	8	–	North Carolina	(13)	13	–
Delaware	(3)	3	–	North Dakota	(3)	3	–
District of Columbia	(3)	–	3	Ohio	(23)	23	–
Florida	(21)	21	–	Oklahoma	(8)	8	–
Georgia	(12)	12	–	Oregon	(7)	7	–
Hawaii	(4)	4	–	Pennsylvania	(25)	25	–
Idaho	(4)	4	–	Rhode Island	(4)	4	–
Illinois	(24)	24	–	South Carolina	(8)	8	–
Indiana	(12)	12	–	South Dakota	(3)	3	–
Iowa	(8)	8	–	Tennessee	(11)	11	–
Kansas	(7)	7	–	Texas	(29)	29	–
Kentucky	(9)	9	–	Utah	(5)	5	–
Louisiana	(10)	10	–	Vermont	(3)	3	–
Maine	(4)	4	–	Virginia	(12)	12	–
Maryland	(10)	10	–	Washington	(10)	10	–
Massachusetts	(13)	13	–	West Virginia	(6)	6	–
Michigan	(20)	20	–	Wisconsin	(11)	11	–
Minnesota	(10)	–	10	Wyoming	(3)	3	–
Mississippi	(7)	7	–				
Missouri	(11)	11	–	Totals	(538)	525	13
Montana	(4)	4	–				

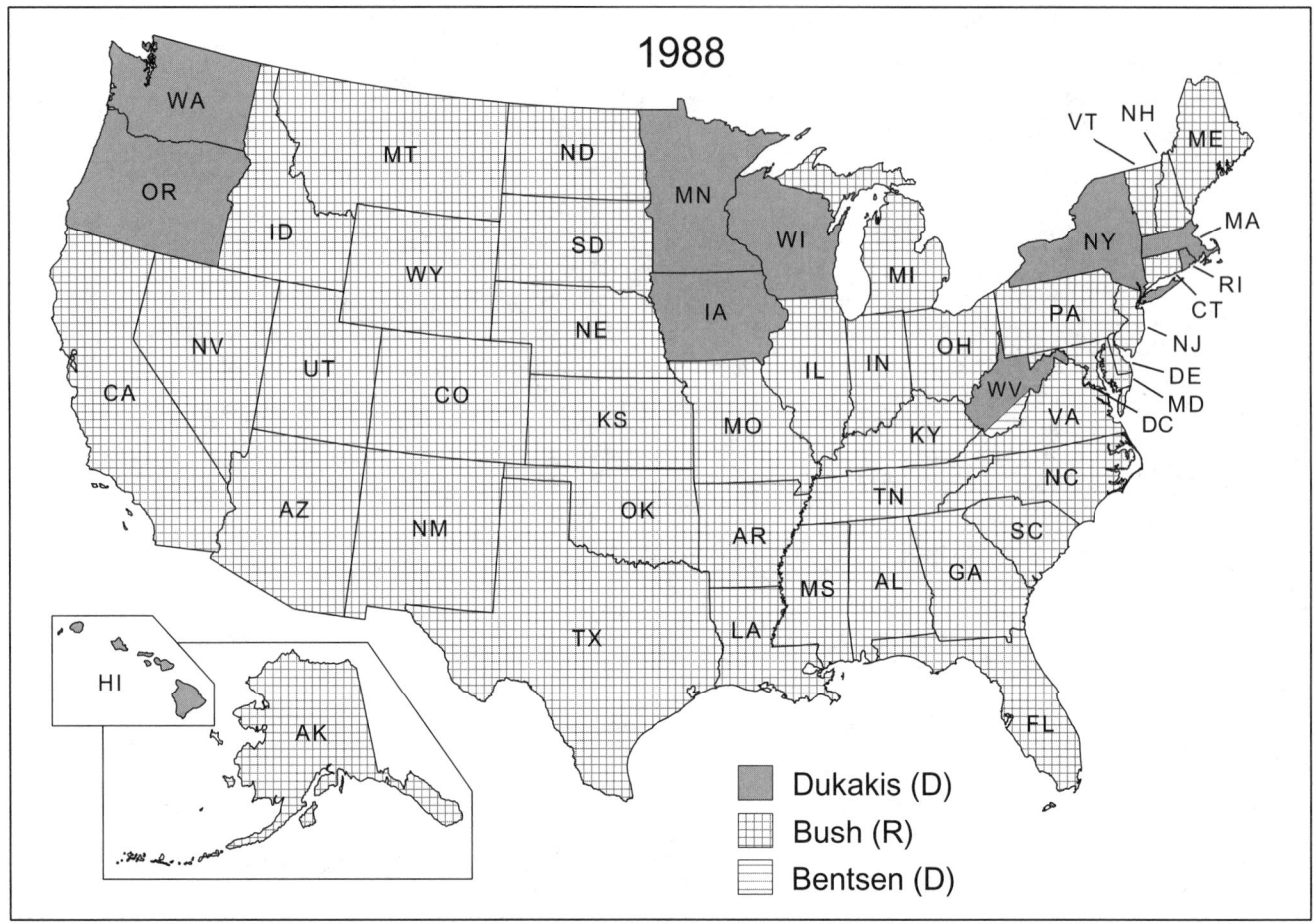

Key: D—Democrat; R—Republican

States	Electoral votes	Bush	Dukakis	Bentsen	States	Electoral votes	Bush	Dukakis	Bentsen
Alabama	(9)	9	–	–	Nebraska	(5)	5	–	–
Alaska	(3)	3	–	–	Nevada	(4)	4	–	–
Arizona	(7)	7	–	–	New Hampshire	(4)	4	–	–
Arkansas	(6)	6	–	–	New Jersey	(16)	16	–	–
California	(47)	47	–	–	New Mexico	(5)	5	–	–
Colorado	(8)	8	–	–	New York	(36)	–	36	–
Connecticut	(8)	8	–	–	North Carolina	(13)	13	–	–
Delaware	(3)	3	–	–	North Dakota	(3)	3	–	–
District of Columbia	(3)	–	3	–	Ohio	(23)	23	–	–
Florida	(21)	21	–	–	Oklahoma	(8)	8	–	–
Georgia	(12)	12	–	–	Oregon	(7)	–	7	–
Hawaii	(4)	–	4	–	Pennsylvania	(25)	25	–	–
Idaho	(4)	4	–	–	Rhode Island	(4)	–	4	–
Illinois	(24)	24	–	–	South Carolina	(8)	8	–	–
Indiana	(12)	12	–	–	South Dakota	(3)	3	–	–
Iowa	(8)	–	8	–	Tennessee	(11)	11	–	–
Kansas	(7)	7	–	–	Texas	(29)	29	–	–
Kentucky	(9)	9	–	–	Utah	(5)	5	–	–
Louisiana	(10)	10	–	–	Vermont	(3)	3	–	–
Maine	(4)	4	–	–	Virginia	(12)	12	–	–
Maryland	(10)	10	–	–	Washington	(10)	–	10	–
Massachusetts	(13)	–	13	–	West Virginia[1]	(6)	–	5	1
Michigan	(20)	20	–	–	Wisconsin	(11)	–	11	–
Minnesota	(10)	–	10	–	Wyoming	(3)	3	–	–
Mississippi	(7)	7	–	–					
Missouri	(11)	11	–	–	Totals	(538)	426	111	1
Montana	(4)	4	–	–					

1. For explanation of split electoral vote, see p. 702.

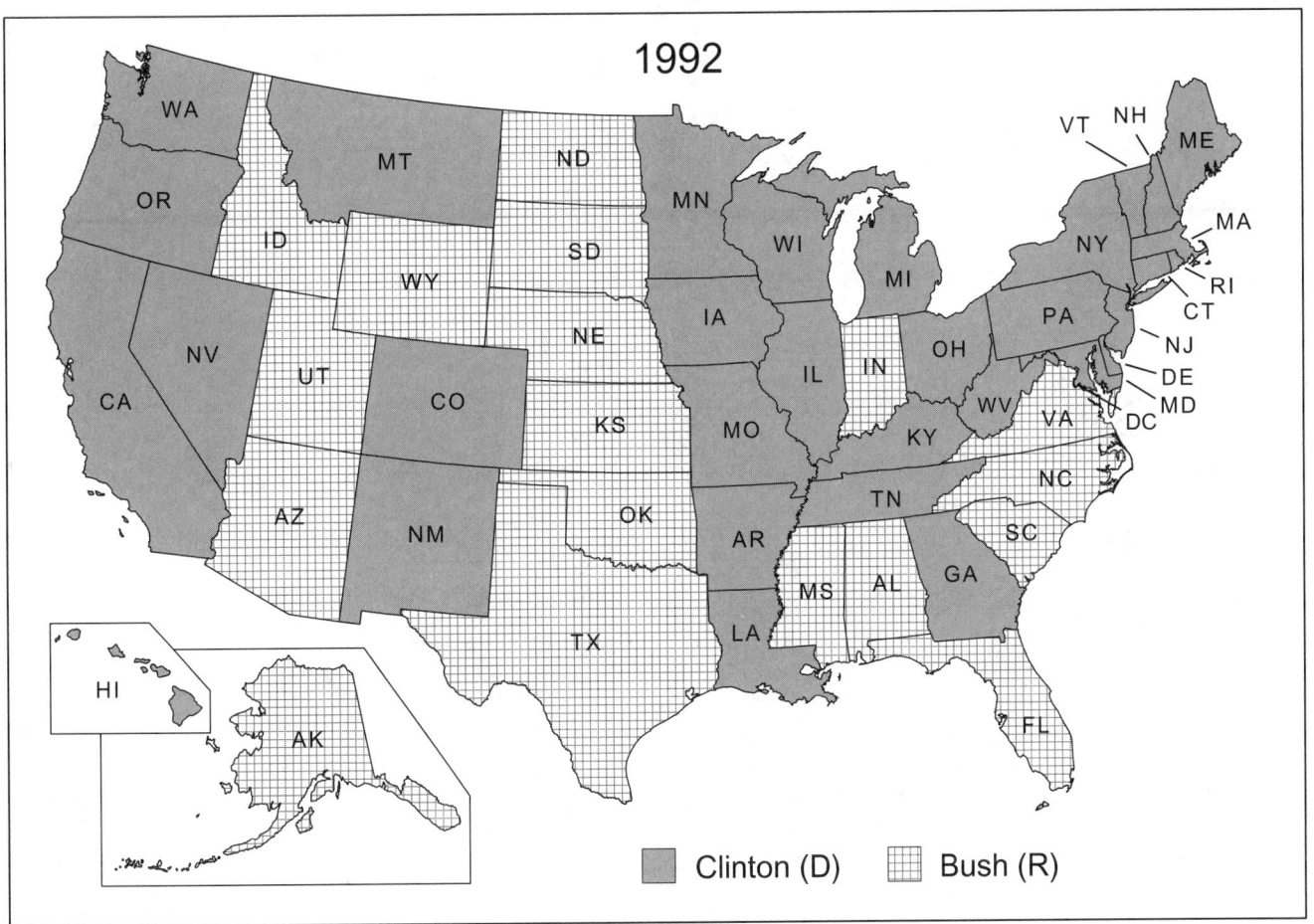

Key: D—Democrat; R—Republican

States	Electoral votes	Clinton	Bush	States	Electoral votes	Clinton	Bush
Alabama	(9)	–	9	Nebraska	(5)	–	5
Alaska	(3)	–	3	Nevada	(4)	4	–
Arizona	(8)	–	8	New Hampshire	(4)	4	–
Arkansas	(6)	6	–	New Jersey	(15)	15	–
California	(54)	54	–	New Mexico	(5)	5	–
Colorado	(8)	8	–	New York	(33)	33	–
Connecticut	(8)	8	–	North Carolina	(14)	–	14
Delaware	(3)	3	–	North Dakota	(3)	–	3
District of Columbia	(3)	3	–	Ohio	(21)	21	–
Florida	(25)	–	25	Oklahoma	(8)	–	8
Georgia	(13)	13	–	Oregon	(7)	7	–
Hawaii	(4)	4	–	Pennsylvania	(23)	23	–
Idaho	(4)	–	4	Rhode Island	(4)	4	–
Illinois	(22)	22	–	South Carolina	(8)	–	8
Indiana	(12)	–	12	South Dakota	(3)	–	3
Iowa	(7)	7	–	Tennessee	(11)	11	–
Kansas	(6)	–	6	Texas	(32)	–	32
Kentucky	(8)	8	–	Utah	(5)	–	5
Louisiana	(9)	9	–	Vermont	(3)	3	–
Maine	(4)	4	–	Virginia	(13)	–	13
Maryland	(10)	10	–	Washington	(11)	11	–
Massachusetts	(12)	12	–	West Virginia	(5)	5	–
Michigan	(18)	18	–	Wisconsin	(11)	11	–
Minnesota	(10)	10	–	Wyoming	(3)	–	3
Mississippi	(7)	–	7				
Missouri	(11)	11	–	Totals	(538)	370	168
Montana	(3)	3	–				

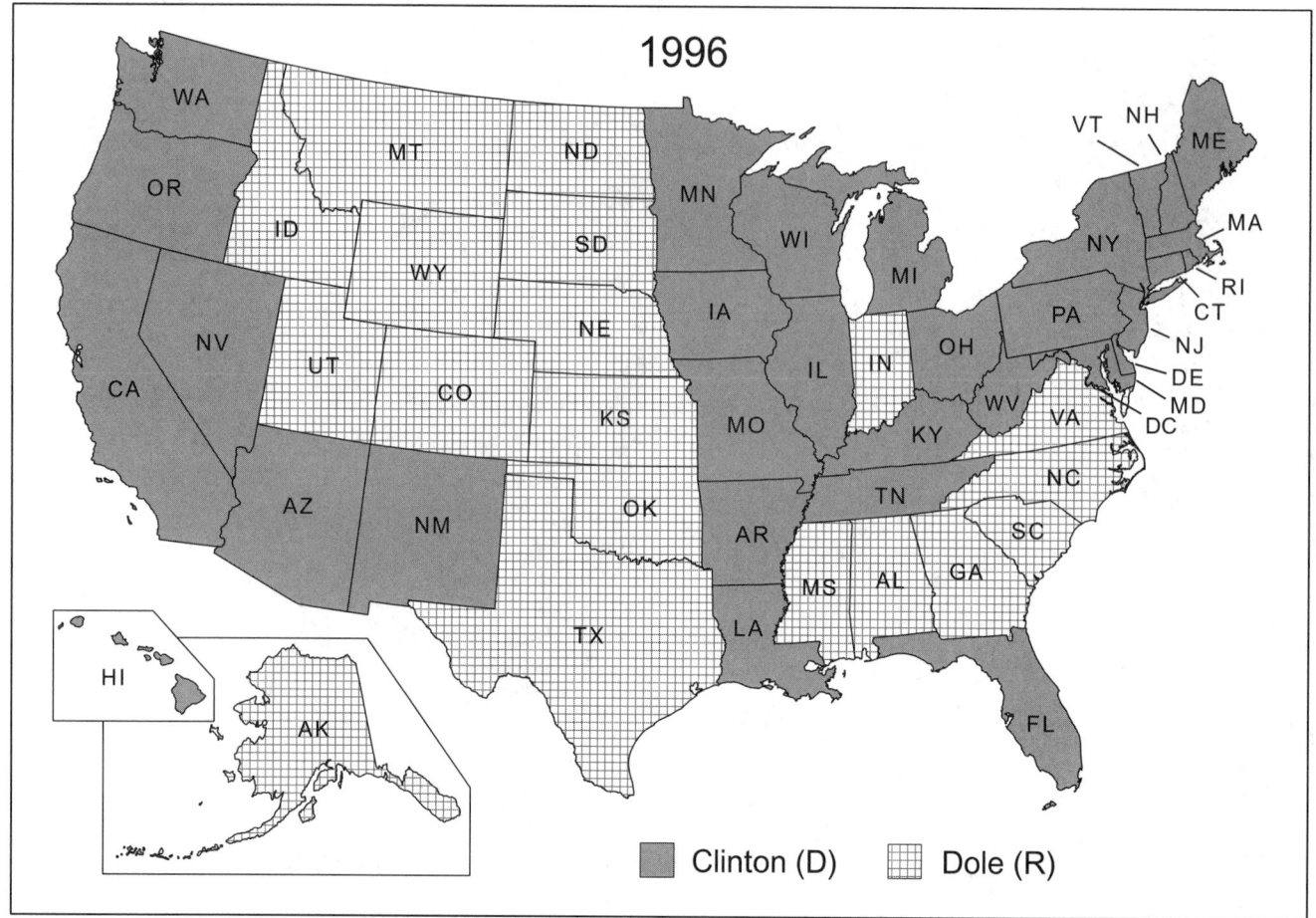

1996

Clinton (D)   Dole (R)

Key: D—Democrat; R—Republican

States	Electoral votes	Clinton	Dole	States	Electoral votes	Clinton	Dole
Alabama	(9)	–	9	Nebraska	(5)	–	5
Alaska	(3)	–	3	Nevada	(4)	4	–
Arizona	(8)	8	–	New Hampshire	(4)	4	–
Arkansas	(6)	6	–	New Jersey	(15)	15	–
California	(54)	54	–	New Mexico	(5)	5	–
Colorado	(8)	–	8	New York	(33)	33	–
Connecticut	(8)	8	–	North Carolina	(14)	–	14
Delaware	(3)	3	–	North Dakota	(3)	–	3
District of Columbia	(3)	3	–	Ohio	(21)	21	–
Florida	(25)	25	–	Oklahoma	(8)	–	8
Georgia	(13)	–	13	Oregon	(7)	7	–
Hawaii	(4)	4	–	Pennsylvania	(23)	23	–
Idaho	(4)	–	4	Rhode Island	(4)	4	–
Illinois	(22)	22	–	South Carolina	(8)	–	8
Indiana	(12)	–	12	South Dakota	(3)	–	3
Iowa	(7)	7	–	Tennessee	(11)	11	–
Kansas	(6)	–	6	Texas	(32)	–	32
Kentucky	(8)	8	–	Utah	(5)	–	5
Louisiana	(9)	9	–	Vermont	(3)	3	–
Maine	(4)	4	–	Virginia	(13)	–	13
Maryland	(10)	10	–	Washington	(11)	11	–
Massachusetts	(12)	12	–	West Virginia	(5)	5	–
Michigan	(18)	18	–	Wisconsin	(11)	11	–
Minnesota	(10)	10	–	Wyoming	(3)	–	3
Mississippi	(7)	–	7				
Missouri	(11)	11	–	Totals	(538)	379	159
Montana	(3)	–	3				

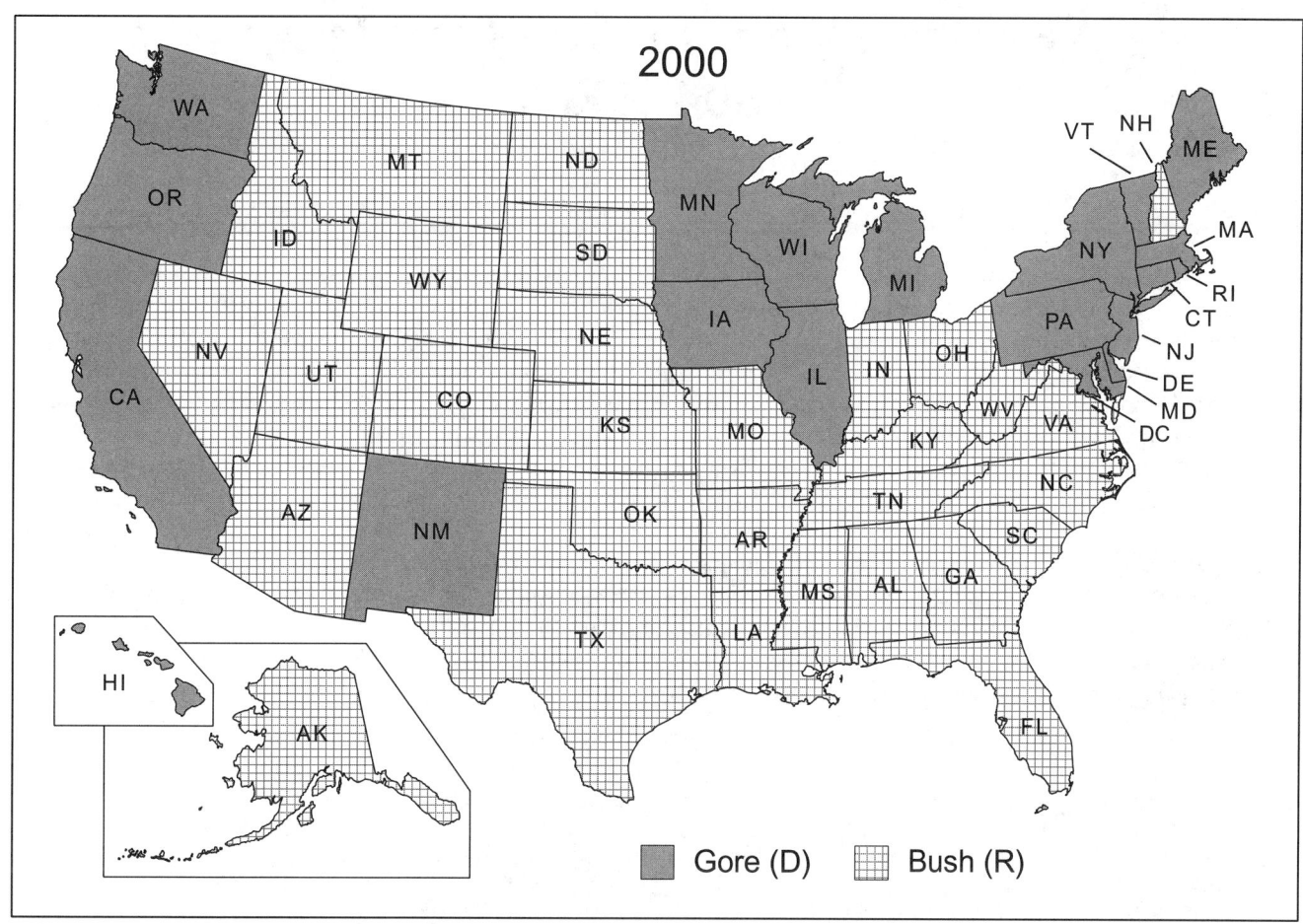

Key: D—Democrat; R—Republican

States	Electoral votes	Bush	Gore	States	Electoral votes	Bush	Gore
Alabama	(9)	9	–	Nebraska	(5)	5	–
Alaska	(3)	3	–	Nevada	(4)	4	–
Arizona	(8)	8	–	New Hampshire	(4)	4	–
Arkansas	(6)	6	–	New Jersey	(15)	–	15
California	(54)	–	54	New Mexico	(5)	–	5
Colorado	(8)	8	–	New York	(33)	–	33
Connecticut	(8)	–	8	North Carolina	(14)	14	–
Delaware	(3)	–	3	North Dakota	(3)	3	–
District of Columbia[1]	(3)	–	2	Ohio	(21)	21	–
Florida	(25)	25	–	Oklahoma	(8)	8	–
Georgia	(13)	13	–	Oregon	(7)	–	7
Hawaii	(4)	–	4	Pennsylvania	(23)	–	23
Idaho	(4)	4	–	Rhode Island	(4)	–	4
Illinois	(22)	–	22	South Carolina	(8)	8	–
Indiana	(12)	12	–	South Dakota	(3)	3	–
Iowa	(7)	–	7	Tennessee	(11)	11	–
Kansas	(6)	6	–	Texas	(32)	32	–
Kentucky	(8)	8	–	Utah	(5)	5	–
Louisiana	(9)	9	–	Vermont	(3)	–	3
Maine	(4)	–	4	Virginia	(13)	13	–
Maryland	(10)	–	10	Washington	(11)	–	11
Massachusetts	(12)	–	12	West Virginia	(5)	5	–
Michigan	(18)	–	18	Wisconsin	(11)	–	11
Minnesota	(10)	–	10	Wyoming	(3)	3	–
Mississippi	(7)	7	–				
Missouri	(11)	11	–	Totals	(538)	271	266
Montana	(3)	3	–				

1. For explanation of split electoral votes, see p. 702.

Electoral Votes for Vice President, 1804–2000

The following list gives the electoral votes for vice president from 1804 to 2000. Unless indicated by a note, the state-by-state breakdown of electoral votes for each vice-presidential candidate was the same as for his or her party's presidential candidate.

Prior to 1804, under Article II, Section 1 of the Constitution, each elector cast two votes—each vote for a different person. The electors did not distinguish between votes for president and vice president. The candidate receiving the second highest total became vice president. The Twelfth Amendment, ratified in 1804, required electors to vote separately for president and vice president.

In some cases, persons had received electoral votes although they had never been formally nominated. The word *candidate* is used in this section to designate persons receiving electoral votes.

The *Senate Manual* (Washington, D.C.: Government Printing Office, 1997) was the source used for vice-presidential elec-

toral votes for all elections up to 1996. The source for 2000 was the *CQ Weekly.*

For political party designation, the basic source was Svend Petersen, *A Statistical History of the American Presidential Elections* (Westport, Conn.: Greenwood Press, 1981). Petersen gives the party designation of *presidential candidates only.* Congressional Quarterly adopted Petersen's party designations for the running mates of presidential candidates.

To supplement Petersen, Congressional Quarterly consulted the *Biographical Directory of the American Congress, 1774–1996* (Washington, D.C.: CQ Staff Directories, 1997); the *Dictionary of American Biography* (New York: Charles Scribner's Sons, 1928–1936); the *Encyclopedia of American Biography* (New York: Harper and Row, 1974); and *Who Was Who in America, 1607–1968* (Chicago: Marquis Co., 1943–1968).

Year	Candidate	Electoral Votes
1804	George Clinton (Democratic-Republican)	162
	Rufus King (Federalist)	14
1808	George Clinton (Democratic-Republican)[1]	113
	John Langdon (Democratic-Republican)	9
	James Madison (Democratic-Republican)	3
	James Monroe (Democratic-Republican)	3
	Rufus King (Federalist)	47
1812	Elbridge Gerry (Democratic-Republican)[2]	131
	Jared Ingersoll (Federalist)	86
1816	Daniel D. Tompkins (Democratic-Republican)	183
	John E. Howard (Federalist)[3]	22
	James Ross (Federalist)	5
	John Marshall (Federalist)	4
	Robert G. Harper (Federalist)	3
1820	Daniel D. Tompkins (Democratic-Republican)[4]	218
	Richard Rush (Democratic-Republican)	1
	Richard Stockton (Federalist)	8
	Daniel Rodney (Federalist)	4
	Robert G. Harper (Federalist)	1
1824	John C. Calhoun (Democratic-Republican)[5]	182
	Nathan Sanford (Democratic-Republican)	30
	Nathaniel Macon (Democratic-Republican)	24
	Andrew Jackson (Democratic-Republican)	13
	Martin Van Buren (Democratic-Republican)	9
	Henry Clay (Democratic-Republican)	2
1828	John C. Calhoun (Democratic-Republican)[6]	171
	William Smith (Independent Democratic-Republican)	7
	Richard Rush (National Republican)	83
1832	Martin Van Buren (Democrat)[7]	189
	William Wilkins (Democrat)	30
	Henry Lee (Independent Democrat)	11
	John Sergeant (National Republican)	49
	Amos Ellmaker (Anti-Mason)	7
1836	Richard M. Johnson (Democrat)[8]	147
	William Smith (Independent Democrat)	23
	Francis Granger (Whig)	77
	John Tyler (Whig)	47
1840	John Tyler (Whig)	234
	Richard M. Johnson (Democrat)[9]	48
	L. W. Tazewell (Democrat)	11
	James K. Polk (Democrat)	1
1844	George M. Dallas (Democrat)	170
	Theodore Frelinghuysen (Whig)	105
1848	Millard Fillmore (Whig)	163
	William Orlando Butler (Democrat)	127
1852	William R. King (Democrat)	254
	William Alexander Graham (Whig)	42
1856	John C. Breckinridge (Democrat)	174
	William L. Dayton (Republican)	114
	Andrew Jackson Donelson (Whig-American)	8
1860	Hannibal Hamlin (Republican)	180
	Joseph Lane (Southern Democrat)	72
	Edward Everett (Constitutional Union)	39
	Herschel V. Johnson (Democrat)	12
1864	Andrew Johnson (Republican)	212
	George H. Pendleton (Democrat)	21
1868	Schuyler Colfax (Republican)	214
	Francis P. Blair (Democrat)	80
1872	Henry Wilson (Republican)	286
	Benjamin Gratz Brown (Democrat)[10]	47
	Alfred H. Colquitt (Democrat)	5
	John M. Palmer (Democrat)	3
	Thomas E. Bramlette (Democrat)	3
	William S. Groesbeck (Democrat)	1
	Willis B. Machen (Democrat)	1
	George W. Julian (Liberal Republican)	5
	Nathaniel P. Banks (Liberal Republican)	1
1876	William A. Wheeler (Republican)	185
	Thomas A. Hendricks (Democrat)	184
1880	Chester A. Arthur (Republican)	214
	William H. English (Democrat)	155

Year	Candidate	Electoral Votes	Year	Candidate	Electoral Votes
1884	Thomas A. Hendricks (Democrat)	219	1948	Alben W. Barkley (Democrat)	303
	John A. Logan (Republican)	182		Earl Warren (Republican)	189
1888	Levi P. Morton (Republican)	233		Fielding L. Wright (States' Rights Democrat)	39
	Allen G. Thurman (Democrat)	168	1952	Richard Nixon (Republican)	442
1892	Adlai E. Stevenson (Democrat)	277		John J. Sparkman (Democrat)	89
	Whitelaw Reid (Republican)	145	1956	Richard Nixon (Republican)	457
	James G. Field (Populist)	22		Estes Kefauver (Democrat)	73
1896	Garret A. Hobart (Republican)	271		Herman Talmadge (Democrat)	1
	Arthur Sewall (Democrat)[11]	149	1960	Lyndon B. Johnson (Democrat)	303
	Thomas E. Watson (Populist)	27		Strom Thurmond (Democrat)[13]	14
1900	Theodore Roosevelt (Republican)	292		Henry Cabot Lodge Jr. (Republican)	219
	Adlai E. Stevenson (Democrat)	155		Barry Goldwater (Republican)	1
1904	Charles W. Fairbanks (Republican)	336	1964	Hubert H. Humphrey (Democrat)	486
	Henry G. Davis (Democrat)	140		William E. Miller (Republican)	52
1908	James S. Sherman (Republican)	321	1968	Spiro T. Agnew (Republican)	301
	John W. Kern (Democrat)	162		Edmund S. Muskie (Democrat)	191
1912	Thomas R. Marshall (Democrat)	435		Curtis E. LeMay (American Independent)	46
	Hiram W. Johnson (Progressive)	88	1972	Spiro T. Agnew (Republican)	520
	Nicholas Murray Butler (Republican)[12]	8		R. Sargent Shriver (Democrat)	17
1916	Thomas R. Marshall (Democrat)	277		Theodora Nathan (Libertarian)	1
	Charles W. Fairbanks (Republican)	254	1976	Walter F. Mondale (Democrat)	297
1920	Calvin Coolidge (Republican)	404		Robert Dole (Republican)[14]	241
	Franklin D. Roosevelt (Democrat)	127	1980	George Bush (Republican)	489
1924	Charles G. Dawes (Republican)	382		Walter F. Mondale (Democrat)	49
	Charles W. Bryan (Democrat)	136	1984	George Bush (Republican)	525
	Burton K. Wheeler (Progressive)	13		Geraldine A. Ferraro (Democrat)	13
1928	Charles Curtis (Republican)	444	1988	Dan Quayle (Republican)	426
	Joseph T. Robinson (Democrat)	87		Lloyd Bentsen (Democrat)[15]	111
1932	John N. Garner (Democrat)	472		Michael S. Dukakis (Democrat)	1
	Charles Curtis (Republican)	59	1992	Al Gore (Democrat)	370
1936	John N. Garner (Democrat)	523		Dan Quayle (Republican)	168
	Frank Knox (Republican)	8	1996	Al Gore (Democrat)	379
1940	Henry A. Wallace (Democrat)	449		Jack Kemp (Republican)	159
	Charles L. McNary (Republican)	82	2000	Richard Cheney (Republican)	271
1944	Harry S. Truman (Democrat)	432		Joseph Lieberman (Democrat)[16]	266
	John W. Bricker (Republican)	99			

1. New York cast 13 presidential electoral votes for Democratic-Republican James Madison and 6 votes for Clinton; for vice president, New York cast 13 votes for Clinton, 3 votes for Madison, and 3 votes for Monroe. Langdon received Ohio's 3 votes and Vermont's 6 votes.

2. The state-by-state vote for Gerry was the same as for Democratic-Republican presidential candidate Madison, except for Massachusetts and New Hampshire. Massachusetts cast 2 votes for Gerry and 20 votes for Ingersoll; New Hampshire cast 1 vote for Gerry and 7 votes for Ingersoll.

3. Four Federalists received vice-presidential electoral votes: Howard—Massachusetts, 22 votes; Ross—Connecticut, 5 votes; Marshall—Connecticut, 4 votes; Harper—Delaware, 3 votes

4. The state-by-state vote for Tompkins was the same as for Democratic-Republican presidential candidate Monroe, except for Delaware, Maryland, and Massachusetts. Delaware cast 4 votes for Rodney; Maryland cast 10 votes for Tompkins and 1 for Harper; Massachusetts cast 7 votes for Tompkins and 8 for Stockton.

New Hampshire, which cast 7 presidential electoral votes for Monroe and 1 vote for John Quincy Adams, cast 7 vice-presidential electoral votes for Tompkins and 1 vote for Rush.

5. The state-by-state vice-presidential electoral vote was as follows:

Calhoun—Alabama, 5 votes; Delaware, 1 vote; Illinois, 3 votes; Indiana, 5 votes; Kentucky, 7 votes; Louisiana, 5 votes; Maine, 9 votes; Maryland, 10 votes; Massachusetts, 15 votes; Mississippi, 3 votes; New Hampshire, 7 votes; New Jersey, 8 votes; New York, 29 votes; North Carolina, 15 votes; Pennsylvania, 28 votes; Rhode Island, 3 votes; South Carolina, 11 votes; Tennessee, 11 votes; Vermont, 7 votes.

Sanford—Kentucky, 7 votes; New York, 7 votes; Ohio, 16 votes.

Macon—Virginia, 24 votes.

Jackson—Connecticut, 8 votes; Maryland, 1 vote; Missouri, 3 votes; New Hampshire, 1 vote.

Van Buren—Georgia, 9 votes.

Clay—Delaware, 2 votes.

6. The state-by-state vote for Calhoun was the same as for Democratic-Republican presidential candidate Jackson, except for Georgia, which cast 2 votes for Calhoun and 7 votes for Smith.

7. The state-by-state vote for Van Buren was the same as for Democratic-Republican presidential candidate Jackson, except for Pennsylvania, which cast 30 votes for Wilkins.

South Carolina cast 11 presidential electoral votes for Independent Democratic presidential candidate Floyd and 11 votes for Independent Democratic vice-presidential candidate Lee.

Vermont cast 7 presidential electoral votes for Anti-Masonic candidate Wirt and 7 vice-presidential electoral votes for Wirt's running mate, Ellmaker.

8. The state-by-state vote for Johnson was the same as for Democratic presidential candidate Van Buren, except for Virginia, which cast 23 votes for Smith.

Granger's state-by-state vote was the same as for Whig presidential candidate Harrison, except for Maryland and Massachusetts. Maryland cast 10 presidential electoral votes for Harrison and 10 vice-presidential votes for Tyler; Massachusetts cast 14 presidential electoral votes for Whig candidate Webster and 14 vice-presidential votes over Granger.

Tyler received 11 votes from Georgia, 10 from Maryland, 11 from South Carolina, and 15 from Tennessee.

No vice-presidential candidate received a majority of the electoral vote. As a result the Senate, for the only time in history, selected the vice president under the provisions of the Twelfth Amendment. Johnson was elected vice president by a vote of 33 to 16 over Granger.

9. The Democratic party did not nominate a vice-presidential candidate in 1840. Johnson's state-by-state vote was the same as for presidential candidate Van Buren, except for South Carolina and Virginia. South Carolina cast 11 votes for Tazewell. Virginia cast 23 presidential electoral votes for Van Buren, 22 vice-presidential votes for Johnson, and 1 vice-presidential vote for Polk.

10. Liberal Republican and Democratic presidential candidate Horace Greeley died November 29, 1872. As a result eighteen electors pledged to Greeley cast their presidential electoral votes for Brown, Greeley's running mate.

The vice-presidential vote was as follows:

Brown—Georgia, 5 votes; Kentucky, 8 votes; Maryland, 8 votes; Missouri, 6 votes; Tennessee, 12 votes; Texas, 8 votes.

Colquitt—Georgia, 5 votes.
Palmer—Missouri, 3 votes.
Bramlette—Kentucky, 3 votes.
Groesbeck—Missouri, 1 vote.
Machen—Kentucky, 1 vote.
Julian—Missouri, 5 votes.
Banks—Georgia, 1 vote.

11. The state-by-state vote for Sewall was the same as for Democratic-Populist candidate William Jennings Bryan, except for the following states, which cast electoral votes for Watson: Arkansas, 3 votes; Louisiana, 4; Missouri, 4; Montana, 1; Nebraska, 4; North Carolina, 5; South Dakota, 2; Utah, 1; Washington, 2; Wyoming, 1.

12. Butler received the 8 electoral votes of Vice President James Sherman, who died Oct. 30, 1912, after being renominated on the Republican ticket. Butler was named as the substitute candidate.

13. Democratic electors carried Alabama's 11 electoral votes. Five of the electors were pledged to the national Democratic ticket of Kennedy and Johnson. Six electors ran unpledged and voted for Harry F. Byrd for president and Strom Thurmond for vice president.

Mississippi's eight electors voted for Byrd and Thurmond.

In Oklahoma the Republican ticket of Nixon and Lodge carried the state, but Henry D. Irwin, 1 of the state's 8 electors voted for Byrd for president and Goldwater for vice president.

14. Mike Padden, a Republican elector from the state of Washington cast his presidential electoral vote for Reagan instead of the Republican nominee, Ford. But he voted for Dole, Ford's running mate, for vice president. Dole thus received one more electoral vote than Ford.

15. Margaret Leach, a Democratic elector from West Virginia, cast her vice-presidential electoral vote for Dukakis, the Democratic nominee for president, and her presidential vote for his running mate, Bentsen.

16. Barbara Lett-Simmons, a Democratic elector from the District of Columbia, withheld her vice-presidential electoral vote for Lieberman (and presidential electoral vote for Gore).

CHAPTER 19

Biographical Directory of Presidential and Vice-Presidential Candidates

T̲H̲E̲ ̲N̲A̲M̲E̲S̲ in the directory include all persons who have received electoral votes for president or vice president since 1789. Also included are prominent third-party candidates who received popular votes but no electoral votes, and Nelson A. Rockefeller, appointed vice president by Gerald R. Ford, who became president following the resignation of Richard Nixon. For the 2000 election, only the presidential and vice-presidential candidates for the Democratic and Republican parties are included.

The material is organized as follows: name, state of residence in the year(s) the individual received electoral votes, party or parties with which the individual identified when he or she received electoral votes, date of birth, date of death (where applicable), major offices held, and the year(s) of candidacy.

For the elections of 1789 through 1800, presidential electors did not vote separately for president or vice president. It was, therefore, difficult in many cases to determine if an individual receiving electoral votes in these elections was a candidate for the office of president or vice president. Where no determination could be made from the sources consulted by Congressional Quarterly, the year in which the individual received electoral votes is given with no specification as to whether the individual was a candidate for president or vice president.

The following sources were used: *American Political Leaders, 1789–2000,* (Washington, D.C.: Congressional Quarterly, 2000); *Biographical Directory of the United States Congress, 1774–1989,* (Washington, D.C.: Government Printing Office, 1989); *Dictionary of American Biography,* (New York: Scribner's, 1928–36); John A. Garraty, ed., *Encyclopedia of American Biography,* (New York: Harper and Row, 1974); Jaques Cattell Press, ed., *Who's Who in American Politics, 1977–78,* 6th ed. (New York: R. R. Bowker, 1977); *Who Was Who in America, 1607–1968,* (Chicago: Marquis, 1943–68); Svend Petersen, *A Statistical History of the American Presidential Elections,* (Westport, Conn.: Greenwood Press, 1981); Richard M. Scammon, *America Votes 10* (Washington, D.C.: Congressional Quarterly, 1973); Richard M. Scammon and Alice V. McGillivray, *America Votes 12* (Washington, D.C.: Congressional Quarterly, 1977); *America Votes 14* (Washington, D.C.: Congressional Quarterly, *America Votes 18* (Washington, D.C.: Congressional Quarterly, *America Votes 20* (Washington, D.C.: Congressional Quarterly, 1993); Rhodes Cook, *America Votes 22* (Washington, D.C.: Congressional Quarterly, 1997); Rhodes Cook, *America Votes 24* (Washington, D.C.: CQ Press, 2001).

Adams, Charles Francis - Mass. (Free Soil) Aug. 18, 1807–Nov. 21, 1886; House, 1859–1861; minister to Great Britain, 1861–1868. Candidacy: VP - 1848.

Adams, John - Mass. (Federalist) Oct. 30, 1735–July 4, 1826; Continental Congress, 1774; signer of Declaration of Independence, 1776; minister to Great Britain, 1785; U.S. vice president, 1789–1797; U.S. president, 1797–1801. Candidacies: VP - 1789, 1792; P - 1796, 1800.

Adams, John Quincy - Mass. (Democratic-Republican, National Republican) July 11, 1767–Feb. 23, 1848; Senate, 1803–1808; minister to Russia, 1809–1814; minister to Great Britain, 1815–1817; secretary of state, 1817–1825; U.S. president, 1825–1829; House, 1831–1848. Candidacies: P - 1820, 1824, 1828.

Adams, Samuel - Mass. (Federalist) Sept. 27, 1722–Oct. 2, 1803; Continental Congress, 1774–1781; signer of Declaration of Independence; governor, 1793–1797. Candidacy: 1796.

Agnew, Spiro Theodore - Md. (Republican) Nov. 9, 1918–Sept. 17, 1996; governor, 1967–1969; U.S. vice president, 1969–1973 (resigned Oct. 10, 1973). Candidacies: VP - 1968, 1972.

Anderson, John B. - Ill. (Republican, Independent) Feb. 15, 1922– ; state's attorney, 1956–1960; House, 1961–1981. Candidacy: P - 1980.

Armstrong, James - Pa. (Federalist) Aug. 29, 1748–May 6, 1828; House, 1793–1795. Candidacy: 1789.

Arthur, Chester Alan - N.Y. (Republican) Oct. 5, 1830–Nov. 18, 1886; collector, Port of N.Y., 1871–1878; U.S. vice president, 1881; U.S. president, 1881–1885. Candidacy: VP - 1880.

Banks, Nathaniel Prentice - Mass. (Liberal Republican) Jan. 30, 1816–Sept. 1, 1894; House, 1853–1857, 1865–1873, 1875–1879, 1889–1891; governor, 1858–1861. Candidacy: VP - 1872.

Barkley, Alben William - Ky. (Democratic) Nov. 24, 1877–April 30, 1956; House, 1913–1927; Senate, 1927–1949, 1955–1956; Senate majority leader, 1937–1947; Senate minority leader, 1947–1949; U.S. vice president, 1949–1953. Candidacy: VP - 1948.

Bell, John - Tenn. (Constitutional Union) Feb. 15, 1797–Sept. 10, 1869; House, 1827–1841; Speaker of the House, 1834–1835; secretary of war, 1841; Senate, 1847–1859. Candidacy: P - 1860.

Benson, Allan Louis - N.Y. (Socialist) Nov. 6, 1871–Aug. 19, 1940; writer, editor; founder of *Reconstruction Magazine,* 1918. Candidacy: P - 1916.

Bentsen, Lloyd Millard Jr. - Texas (Democratic) Feb. 11, 1921– ; House 1948–1955; Senate 1971–1993; secretary of Treasury, 1993–1994. Candidacy: VP - 1988.

Bidwell, John - Calif. (Prohibition) Aug. 5, 1819–April 4, 1900; California pioneer; major in Mexican War; House, 1865–1867. Candidacy: P - 1892.

Birney, James Gillespie - N.Y. (Liberty) Feb. 4, 1792–Nov. 25, 1857; Kentucky Legislature, 1816–1817; Alabama Legislature, 1819–1820. Candidacies: P - 1840, 1844.

Blaine, James Gillespie - Maine (Republican) Jan. 31, 1830–Jan. 27, 1893; House, 1863–1876; Speaker of the House, 1869–1875; Senate, 1876–1881; secretary of state, 1881, 1889–1892; president, first Pan American Congress, 1889. Candidacy: P - 1884.

Blair, Francis Preston Jr. - Mo. (Democratic) Feb. 19, 1821–July 8, 1875; House, 1857–1859, 1860, 1861–1862, 1863–1864; Senate, 1871–1873. Candidacy: VP - 1868.

Bramlette, Thomas E. - Ky. (Democratic) Jan. 3, 1817–Jan. 12, 1875; governor, 1863–1867. Candidacy: VP - 1872.

Breckinridge, John Cabell - Ky. (Democratic, Southern Democratic) Jan. 21, 1821–May 17, 1875; House, 1851–1855; U.S. vice president, 1857–1861; Senate, 1861; major general, Confederacy, 1861–1865; secretary of war, Confederacy, 1865. Candidacies: VP - 1856; P - 1860.

Bricker, John William - Ohio (Republican) Sept. 6, 1893–March 22, 1986; attorney general of Ohio, 1933–1937; governor, 1939–1945; Senate, 1947–1959. Candidacy: VP - 1944.

Brown, Benjamin Gratz - Mo. (Democratic) May 28, 1826–Dec. 13, 1885; Senate, 1863–1867; governor, 1871–1873. Candidacy: VP - 1872.

Bryan, Charles Wayland - Neb. (Democratic) Feb. 10, 1867–March 4, 1945; governor, 1923–1925, 1931–1935; Candidacy: VP - 1924.

Bryan, William Jennings - Neb. (Democratic, Populist) March 19, 1860–July 26, 1925; House, 1891–1895; secretary of state, 1913–1915. Candidacies: P - 1896, 1900, 1908.

Buchanan, James - Pa. (Democratic) April 23, 1791–June 1, 1868; House, 1821–1831; minister to Russia, 1832–1834; Senate, 1834–1845; secretary of state, 1845–1849; minister to Great Britain, 1853–1856; U.S. president, 1857–1861. Candidacy: P - 1856.

Burr, Aaron - N.Y. (Democratic-Republican) Feb. 6, 1756–Sept. 14, 1836; attorney general of N.Y., 1789–1790; Senate, 1791–1797; U.S. vice president, 1801–1805. Candidacies: 1792, 1796, 1800.

Bush, George - Texas (Republican) June 12, 1924– ; House, 1967–1970; ambassador to the United Nations, 1971–1973; chairman of the Republican National Committee, 1973–1974; head of the U.S. liaison office in Peking, 1974–1975; director of the Central Intelligence Agency, 1976–1977; U.S. vice president, 1981–1989; U.S. president, 1989–1993. Candidacies: VP - 1980, 1984; P - 1988, 1992.

Bush, George W. - Texas (Republican) July, 6, 1946– ; governor, 1995–2000; U.S. president, 2001– . Candidacy: P - 2000.

Butler, Benjamin Franklin - Mass. (Greenback, Anti-Monopoly) Nov. 5, 1818–Jan. 11, 1893; House, 1867–1875, 1877–1879; governor, 1883–1884. Candidacy: P - 1884.

Butler, Nicholas Murray - N.Y. (Republican) April 2, 1862–Dec. 7, 1947; president, Columbia University, 1901–1945; president, Carnegie Endowment for International Peace, 1925–1945. Candidacy: VP - 1912. (Substituted as candidate after Oct. 30 death of nominee James S. Sherman.)

Butler, William Orlando - Ky. (Democratic) April 19, 1791–Aug. 6, 1880; House, 1939–1943. Candidacy: VP - 1848.

Byrd, Harry Flood - Va. (States' Rights Democratic, Independent Democratic) June 10, 1887–Oct. 20, 1966; governor, 1926–1930; Senate, 1933–1965. Candidacies: P - 1956, 1960.

Calhoun, John Caldwell - S.C. (Democratic-Republican, Democratic) March 18, 1782–March 31, 1850; House, 1811–1817; secretary of war, 1817–1825; U.S. vice president, 1825–1832; Senate, 1832–1843, 1845–1850; secretary of state, 1844–1845. Candidacies: VP - 1824, 1828.

Carter, James Earl Jr. - Ga. (Democratic) Oct. 1, 1924– ; Georgia Legislature, 1963–1967; governor, 1971–1975; U.S. president, 1977–1981. Candidacies: P - 1976, 1980.

Cass, Lewis - Mich. (Democratic) Oct. 9, 1782–June 17, 1866; military and civil governor of Michigan Territory, 1813–1831; secretary of war, 1831–1836; minister to France, 1836–1842; Senate, 1845–1848, 1849–1857; secretary of state, 1857–1860. Candidacy: P - 1848.

Cheney, Richard - Wyo. (Republican) Jan. 30, 1941– ; House 1979–1989; secretary of defense, 1989–1993; U.S. vice president, 2001– . Candidacy: VP - 2000.

Clay, Henry - Ky. (Democratic-Republican, National Republican, Whig) April 12, 1777–June 29, 1852; Senate, 1806–1807, 1810–1811, 1831–1842, 1849–1852; House, 1811–1814, 1815–1821, 1823–1825; Speaker of the House, 1811–1814, 1815–1820, 1823–1825; secretary of state, 1825–1829. Candidacies: P - 1824, 1832, 1844.

Cleveland, Stephen Grover - N.Y. (Democratic) March 18, 1837–June 24, 1908; mayor of Buffalo, 1882; governor, 1883–1885; U.S. president, 1885–1889, 1893–1897. Candidacies: P - 1884, 1888, 1892.

Clinton, Bill - Ark. (Democrat) Aug. 19, 1946– ; attorney general of Arkansas, 1977–1979; governor, 1979–1981, 1983–1992; U.S. president, 1993–2001. Candidacies: P - 1992, 1996.

Clinton, De Witt - N.Y. (Independent Democratic-Republican, Federalist) March 2, 1769–Feb. 11, 1828; Senate, 1802–1803; mayor of New York, 1803–1807, 1810, 1811, 1813, 1814; governor, 1817–1823, 1825–1828. Candidacy: P - 1812.

Clinton, George - N.Y. (Democratic-Republican) July 26, 1739–April 20, 1812; Continental Congress, 1775–1776; governor, 1777–1795, 1801–1804; U.S. vice president, 1805–1812. Candidacies: VP - 1789, 1792, 1796, 1804, 1808.

Colfax, Schuyler - Ind. (Republican) March 23, 1823–Jan. 13, 1885; House, 1855–1869; Speaker of the House, 1863–1869; U.S. vice president, 1869–1873. Candidacy: VP - 1868.

Colquitt, Alfred Holt - Ga. (Democratic) April 20, 1824–March 26, 1894; House, 1853–1855; governor, 1877–1882; Senate, 1883–1894. Candidacy: VP - 1872.

Coolidge, Calvin - Mass. (Republican) July 4, 1872–Jan. 5, 1933; governor, 1919–1921; U.S. vice president, 1921–1923; U.S. president, 1923–1929. Candidacies: VP - 1920; P - 1924.

Cox, James Middleton - Ohio (Democratic) March 31, 1870–July 15, 1957; House, 1909–1913; governor, 1913–1915, 1917–1921. Candidacy: P - 1920.

Crawford, William Harris - Ga. (Democratic-Republican) Feb. 24, 1772–Sept. 15, 1834; Senate, 1807–1813; president pro tempore of the Senate, 1812–1813; secretary of war, 1815–1816; secretary of Treasury, 1816–1825. Candidacy: P - 1824.

Curtis, Charles - Kan. (Republican) Jan. 25, 1860–Feb. 8, 1936; House, 1893–1907; Senate, 1907–1913, 1915–1929; president pro tempore of the Senate, 1911; Senate majority leader, 1925–1929; U.S. vice president, 1929–1933. Candidacies: VP - 1928, 1932.

Dallas, George Mifflin - Pa. (Democratic) July 10, 1792–Dec. 31, 1864; Senate, 1831–1833; minister to Russia, 1837–1839; U.S. vice president, 1845–1849; minister to Great Britain, 1856–1861. Candidacy: VP - 1844.

Davis, David - Ill. (Democratic) March 9, 1815–June 26, 1886; associate justice of U.S. Supreme Court, 1862–1877; Senate, 1877–1883; president pro tempore of the Senate, 1881. Candidacy: P - 1872.

Davis, Henry Gassaway - W.Va. (Democratic) Nov. 16, 1823–March 11, 1916; Senate, 1871–1883; chairman of Pan American Railway Committee, 1901–1916. Candidacy: VP - 1904.

Davis, John William - W.Va., N.Y. (Democratic) April 13, 1873–March 24, 1955; House, 1911–1913; solicitor general, 1913–1918; ambassador to Great Britain, 1918–1921. Candidacy: P - 1924.

Dawes, Charles Gates - Ill. (Republican) Aug. 27, 1865–April 3, 1951; U.S. comptroller of the currency, 1898–1901; first director of Bureau of the Budget, 1921–1922; U.S. vice president, 1925–1929; ambassador to Great Britain, 1929–1932. Candidacy: VP - 1924.

Dayton, William Lewis - N.J. (Republican) Feb. 17, 1807–Dec. 1, 1864; Senate, 1842–1851; minister to France, 1861–1864. Candidacy: VP - 1856.

Debs, Eugene Victor - Ind. (Socialist) Nov. 5, 1855–Oct. 20, 1926; Indiana Legislature, 1885; president, American Railway Union, 1893–1897. Candidacies: P - 1900, 1904, 1908, 1912, 1920.

Dewey, Thomas Edmund - N.Y. (Republican) March 24, 1902–March 16, 1971; district attorney, New York County, 1937–1941; governor, 1943–1955. Candidacies: P - 1944, 1948.

Dole, Robert Joseph - Kan. (Republican) July 22, 1923– ; House, 1961–1969; Senate, 1969–1996; Senate majority leader, 1985–1987, 1995–1996; Senate minority leader, 1987–1995; chairman of the Republican National Committee, 1971–1973. Candidacies: VP - 1976; P - 1996.

Donelson, Andrew Jackson - Tenn. (American "Know-Nothing") Aug. 25, 1799–June 26, 1871; minister to Prussia, 1846–1848; minister to Germany, 1848–1849. Candidacy: VP - 1856.

Douglas, Stephen Arnold - Ill. (Democratic) April 23, 1813–June 3, 1861; House, 1843–1847; Senate, 1847–1861. Candidacy: P - 1860.

Dukakis, Michael Stanley - Mass. (Democratic) Nov. 3, 1933– ; governor, 1975–1979, 1983–1991. Candidacy: P - 1988.

Eagleton, Thomas Francis - Mo. (Democratic) Sept. 4, 1929– ; attorney general of Missouri, 1961–1965; lieutenant governor, 1965–1968; Senate, 1968–1987. Candidacy: VP - 1972. (Resigned from Democratic ticket July 31; replaced by R. Sargent Shriver Jr.)

Eisenhower, Dwight David - N.Y., Pa. (Republican) Oct. 14, 1890–March 28, 1969; general of U.S. Army, 1943–1948; Army chief of staff, 1945–1948; president of Columbia University, 1948–1951; commander of North Atlantic Treaty Organization, 1951–1952; U.S. president, 1953–1961. Candidacies: P - 1952, 1956.

Ellmaker, Amos - Pa. (Anti-Masonic) Feb. 2, 1787–Nov. 28, 1851; elected to the House for the term beginning in 1815 but did not qualify; attorney general of Pennsylvania, 1816–1819, 1828–1829. Candidacy: VP - 1832.

Ellsworth, Oliver - Conn. (Federalist) April 29, 1745–Nov. 26, 1807; Continental Congress, 1778–1783; Senate, 1789–1796; chief justice of United States, 1796–1800; minister to France, 1799. Candidacy: 1796.

English, William Hayden - Ind. (Democratic) Aug. 27, 1822–Feb. 7, 1896; House, 1853–1861. Candidacy: VP - 1880.

Everett, Edward - Mass. (Constitutional Union) April 11, 1794–Jan. 15, 1865; House, 1825–1835; governor, 1836–1840; minister to Great Britain, 1841–1845; president of Harvard University, 1846–1849; secretary of state, 1852–1853; Senate, 1853–1854. Candidacy: VP - 1860.

Fairbanks, Charles Warren - Ind. (Republican) May 11, 1852–June 4, 1918; Senate, 1897–1905; U.S. vice president, 1905–1909. Candidacies: VP - 1904, 1916.

Ferraro, Geraldine Anne - N.Y. (Democratic) Aug. 26, 1935– ; assistant district attorney, Queens County, 1974–1978; House, 1979–1985. Candidacy: VP - 1984.

Field, James Gaven - Va. (Populist) Feb. 24, 1826–Oct. 12, 1901; major in the Confederate Army, 1861–1865; attorney general of Virginia, 1877–1882. Candidacy: VP - 1892.

Fillmore, Millard - N.Y. (Whig, American "Know-Nothing") Jan. 7, 1800–March 8, 1874; House, 1833–1835, 1837–1843; N.Y. comptroller, 1847–1849; U.S. vice president, 1849–1850; U.S. president, 1850–1853. Candidacies: VP - 1848; P - 1856.

Fisk, Clinton Bowen - N.J. (Prohibition) Dec. 8, 1828–July 9, 1890; Civil War brevet major general; founder of Fisk University, 1866; member, Board of Indian Commissioners, 1874, president, 1881–1890. Candidacy: P - 1888.

Floyd, John - Va. (Independent Democratic) April 24, 1783–Aug. 17, 1837; House, 1817–1829; governor, 1830–1834. Candidacy: P - 1832.

Ford, Gerald Rudolph Jr. - Mich. (Republican) July 14, 1913– ; House, 1949–1973; House minority leader, 1965–1973; U.S. vice president, 1973–1974; U.S. president, 1974–1977. Candidacy: P - 1976.

Frelinghuysen, Theodore - N.J. (Whig) March 28, 1787–April 12, 1862; attorney general of New Jersey, 1817–1829; Senate, 1829–1835; president of Rutgers College, 1850–1862. Candidacy: VP - 1844.

Fremont, John Charles - Calif. (Republican) Jan. 21, 1813–July 13, 1890; explorer and Army officer in West before 1847; Senate, 1850–1851; governor of Arizona Territory, 1878–1881. Candidacy: P - 1856.

Garfield, James Abram - Ohio (Republican) Nov. 19, 1831–Sept. 19, 1881; major general in Union Army during Civil War; House, 1863–1880; U.S. president, 1881. Candidacy: P - 1880.

Garner, John Nance - Texas (Democratic) Nov. 22, 1868–Nov. 7, 1967; House, 1903–1933; House minority leader, 1929–1931; Speaker of the House, 1931–1933; U.S. vice president, 1933–1941. Candidacies: VP - 1932, 1936.

Gerry, Elbridge - Mass. (Democratic-Republican) July 17, 1744–Nov. 23, 1814; Continental Congress, 1776–1780, 1783–1785; signer of Declaration of Independence; Constitutional Convention, 1787; House, 1789–1793; governor, 1810–1812; U.S. vice president, 1813–1814. Candidacy: VP - 1812.

Goldwater, Barry Morris - Ariz. (Republican) Jan. 1, 1909–May 29, 1998; Senate, 1953–1965, 1969–1987. Candidacies: VP - 1960; P - 1964.

Gore, Albert Jr. - Tenn. (Democrat) March 31, 1948– ; House, 1977–1985; Senate, 1985–1993; U.S. vice president, 1993–2001. Candidacies: VP - 1992, 1996; P - 2000.

Graham, William Alexander - N.C. (Whig) Sept. 5, 1804–Aug. 11, 1875; Senate, 1840–1843; governor, 1845–1849; secretary of the Navy, 1850–1852; Confederate Senate, 1864. Candidacy: VP - 1852.

Granger, Francis - N.Y. (Whig) Dec. 1, 1792–Aug. 31, 1868; House, 1835–1837, 1839–1841, 1841–1843; postmaster general, 1841. Candidacy: VP - 1836.

Grant, Ulysses Simpson - Ill. (Republican) April 27, 1822–July 23, 1885; commander-in-chief, Union Army during Civil War; U.S. president, 1869–1877. Candidacies: P - 1868, 1872.

Greeley, Horace - N.Y. (Liberal Republican, Democratic) Feb. 3, 1811–Nov. 29, 1872; founder and editor, *New York Tribune,* 1841–1872; House, 1848–1849. Candidacy: P - 1872.

Griffin, S. Marvin - Ga. (American Independent) Sept. 4, 1907–June 13, 1982; governor, 1955–1959. Candidacy: VP - 1968. (Substituted as candidate until permanent candidate Curtis LeMay was chosen.)

Groesbeck, William Slocum - Ohio (Democratic) July 24, 1815–July 7, 1897; House, 1857–1859; delegate to International Monetary Conference in Paris, 1878. Candidacy: VP - 1872.

Hale, John Parker - N.H. (Free Soil) March 31, 1806–Nov. 19, 1873; House, 1843–1845; Senate, 1847–1853, 1855–1865; minister to Spain, 1865–1869. Candidacy: P - 1852.

Hamlin, Hannibal - Maine (Republican) Aug. 27, 1809–July 4, 1891; House, 1843–1847; Senate, 1848–1857, 1857–1861, 1869–1881; governor, 1857; U.S. vice president, 1861–1865. Candidacy: VP - 1860.

Hancock, John - Mass. (Federalist) Jan. 23, 1737–Oct. 8, 1793; Continental Congress, 1775–1778, 1785–1786; president of Continental Congress, 1775–1777; governor, 1780–1785, 1787–1793. Candidacy: 1789.

Hancock, Winfield Scott - Pa. (Democratic) Feb. 14, 1824 - Feb. 9, 1886; brigadier general, commander of II Army Corps, Civil War. Candidacy: P - 1880.

Harding, Warren Gamaliel - Ohio (Republican) Nov. 2, 1865–Aug. 2, 1923; lieutenant governor, 1904–1905; Senate, 1915–1921; U.S. president, 1921–1923. Candidacy: P - 1920.

Harper, Robert Goodloe - Md. (Federalist) January 1765–Jan. 14, 1825; House, 1795–1801; Senate, 1816. Candidacies: VP - 1816, 1820.

Harrison, Benjamin - Ind. (Republican) Aug. 20, 1833–March 13, 1901; Union officer in Civil War; Senate, 1881–1887; U.S. president, 1889–1893. Candidacies: P - 1888, 1892.

Harrison, Robert H. - Md. 1745–1790; chief justice, General Court of Maryland, 1781. Candidacy: 1789.

Harrison, William Henry - Ohio (Whig) Feb. 9, 1773–April 4, 1841; delegate to Congress from the Northwest Territory, 1799–1800; territorial governor of Indiana, 1801–1813; House, 1816–1819; Senate, 1825–1828; U.S. president, 1841. Candidacies: P - 1836, 1840.

Hayes, Rutherford Birchard - Ohio (Republican) Oct. 4, 1822–Jan. 17, 1893; major general in Union Army during Civil War; House, 1865–1867; governor, 1868–1872, 1876–1877; U.S. president, 1877–1881. Candidacy: P - 1876.

Hendricks, Thomas Andrews - Ind. (Democratic) Sept. 7, 1819–Nov. 25, 1885; House, 1851–1855; Senate, 1863–1869; governor, 1873–1877; U.S. vice president, 1885. Candidacies: P - 1872; VP - 1876, 1884.

Henry, John - Md. (Democratic-Republican) Nov. 1750–Dec. 16, 1798; Continental Congress, 1778–1780, 1785–1786; Senate, 1789–1797; governor, 1797–1798. Candidacy: - 1796.

Hobart, Garret Augustus - N.J. (Republican) June 3, 1844–Nov. 21, 1899; New Jersey Senate, 1876–1882; president of New Jersey Senate, 1881–1882; Republican National Committee, 1884–1896; U.S. vice president, 1897–1899. Candidacy: VP - 1896.

Hoover, Herbert Clark - Calif. (Republican) Aug. 10, 1874–Oct. 20, 1964; U.S. food administrator, 1917–1919; secretary of commerce, 1921–1928; U.S. president, 1929–1933; chairman, Commission on Organization of the Executive Branch of Government, 1947–1949, 1953–1955. Candidacies: P - 1928, 1932.

Hospers, John - Calif. (Libertarian) June 9, 1918– ; director of school of philosophy at University of Southern California. Candidacy: P - 1972.

Howard, John Eager - Md. (Federalist) June 4, 1752–Oct. 12, 1827; Continental Congress, 1788; governor, 1788–1791; Senate, 1796–1803. Candidacy: VP - 1816.

Hughes, Charles Evans - N.Y. (Republican) April 11, 1862–Aug. 27, 1948; governor, 1907–1910; associate justice of U.S. Supreme Court, 1910–1916; secretary of state, 1921–1925; chief justice of United States, 1930–1941. Candidacy: P - 1916.

Humphrey, Hubert Horatio Jr. - Minn. (Democratic) May 27, 1911–Jan. 13, 1978; mayor of Minneapolis, 1945–1948; Senate, 1949–1964, 1971–1978; U.S. vice president, 1965–1969. Candidacies: VP - 1964; P - 1968.

Huntington, Samuel - Conn., July 3, 1731–Jan. 5, 1796; Continental Congress, 1776, 1778–1781, 1783; president of the Continental Congress, 1779–1781; governor, 1786–1796. Candidacy: - 1789.

Ingersoll, Jared - Pa. (Federalist) Oct. 24, 1749–Oct. 31, 1822; Continental Congress, 1780–1781; Constitutional Convention, 1787. Candidacy: VP - 1812.

Iredell, James - N.C. (Federalist) Oct. 5, 1751–Oct. 20, 1799; associate justice of U.S. Supreme Court, 1790–1799. Candidacy: - 1796.

Jackson, Andrew - Tenn. (Democratic-Republican, Democratic) March 15, 1767–June 8, 1845; House, 1796–1797; Senate, 1797–1798, 1823–1825; territorial governor of Florida, 1821; U.S. president, 1829–1837. Candidacies: P - 1824, 1828, 1832.

Jay, John - N.Y. (Federalist) Dec. 12, 1745–May 17, 1829; Continental Congress, 1774–1776, 1778–1779; president of Continental Congress, 1778–1779; minister to Spain, 1779; chief justice of United States, 1789–1795; governor, 1795–1801. Candidacies: - 1789, 1796, 1800.

Jefferson, Thomas - Va. (Democratic-Republican) April 13, 1743–July 4, 1826; Continental Congress, 1775–1776, 1783–1784; author and signer of Declaration of Independence, 1776; governor, 1779–1781; minister to France, 1784–1789; secretary of state, 1790–1793; U.S. vice president, 1797–1801; U.S. president, 1801–1809. Candidacies: VP - 1792; P - 1796, 1800, 1804.

Jenkins, Charles Jones - Ga. (Democratic) Jan. 6, 1805–June 14, 1883; governor, 1865–1868. Candidacy: P - 1872.

Johnson, Andrew - Tenn. (Republican) Dec. 29, 1808–July 31, 1875; House, 1843–1853; governor, 1853–1857; Senate, 1857–1862, 1875; U.S. vice president, 1865; U.S. president, 1865–1869. Candidacy: VP - 1864.

Johnson, Herschel Vespasian - Ga. (Democratic) Sept. 18, 1812–Aug. 16, 1880; Senate, 1848–1849; governor, 1853–1857; senator, Confederate Congress, 1862–1865. Candidacy: VP - 1860.

Johnson, Hiram Warren - Calif. (Progressive) Sept. 2, 1866–Aug. 6, 1945; governor, 1911–1917; Senate, 1917–1945. Candidacy: VP - 1912.

Johnson, Lyndon Baines - Texas (Democratic) Aug. 27, 1908–Jan. 22, 1973; House, 1937–1949; Senate, 1949–1961; Senate minority leader, 1953–1955; Senate majority leader, 1955–1961; U.S. vice president, 1961–1963; U.S. president, 1963–1969. Candidacies: VP - 1960; P - 1964.

Johnson, Richard Mentor - Ky. (Democratic) Oct. 17, 1780–Nov. 19, 1850; House, 1807–1819, 1829–1837; Senate, 1819–1829; U.S. vice president, 1837–1841. Candidacies: VP - 1836, 1840.

Johnston, Samuel - N.C. (Federalist) Dec. 15, 1733–Aug. 17, 1816; Continental Congress, 1780–1781; governor, 1787–1789; Senate, 1789–1793. Candidacy: - 1796.

Jones, Walter Burgwyn - Ala. (Independent Democratic) Oct. 16, 1888–Aug. 1, 1963; Alabama Legislature, 1919–1920; Alabama circuit court judge, 1920–1935; presiding judge, 1935–1963. Candidacy: P - 1956.

Julian, George Washington - Ind. (Free Soil, Liberal Republican) May 5, 1817–July 7, 1899; House, 1849–1851, 1861–1871. Candidacies: VP - 1852, 1872.

Kefauver, Estes - Tenn. (Democratic) July 26, 1903–Aug. 10, 1963; House, 1939–1949; Senate, 1949–1963. Candidacy: VP - 1956.

Kemp, Jack F. - N.Y. (Republican) July 13, 1935– ; House, 1971–1989; secretary of Housing and Urban Development, 1989–1993. Candidacy: VP - 1996.

Kennedy, John Fitzgerald - Mass. (Democratic) May 29, 1917–Nov. 22, 1963; House, 1947–1953; Senate, 1953–1960; U.S. president, 1961–1963. Candidacy: P - 1960.

Kern, John Worth - Ind. (Democratic) Dec. 20, 1849–Aug. 17, 1917; Senate, 1911–1917; Senate majority leader, 1913–1917. Candidacy: VP - 1908.

King, Rufus - N.Y. (Federalist) March 24, 1755–April 29, 1827; Continental Congress, 1784–1787; Constitutional Convention, 1787; Senate, 1789–1796, 1813–1825; minister to Great Britain, 1796–1803, 1825–1826. Candidacies: VP - 1804, 1808; P - 1816.

King, William Rufus de Vane - Ala. (Democratic) April 7, 1786–April 18, 1853; House, 1811–1816; Senate, 1819–1844, 1848–1852; president pro tempore of the Senate, 1836, 1837, 1838, 1839, 1840, 1841, 1850; minister to France, 1844–1846; U.S. vice president, 1853. Candidacy: VP - 1852.

Knox, Franklin - Ill. (Republican) Jan. 1, 1874–April 28, 1944; secretary of the Navy, 1940–1944. Candidacy: VP - 1936.

La Follette, Robert Marion - Wis. (Progressive) June 14, 1855–June 18, 1925; House, 1885–1891; governor, 1901–1906; Senate, 1906–1925. Candidacy: P - 1924.

Landon, Alfred Mossman - Kan. (Republican) Sept. 9, 1887–Oct. 12, 1987; governor, 1933–1937. Candidacy: P - 1936.

Lane, Joseph - Ore. (Southern Democratic) Dec. 14, 1801–April 19, 1881; governor of Oregon Territory, 1849–1850, 1853; House (territorial delegate), 1851–1859; Senate, 1859–1861. Candidacy: VP - 1860.

Langdon, John - N.H. (Democratic-Republican) June 26, 1741–Sept. 18, 1819; Continental Congress, 1775–1776, 1787; governor, 1805–1809, 1810–1812; Senate, 1789–1801; first president pro tempore of the Senate, 1789. Candidacy: VP - 1808.

Lee, Henry - Mass. (Independent Democratic) Feb. 4, 1782–Feb. 6, 1867; merchant and publicist. Candidacy: VP - 1832.

LeMay, Curtis Emerson - Ohio (American Independent) Nov. 15, 1906–Oct. 1, 1990; Air Force chief of staff, 1961–1965. Candidacy: VP - 1968.

Lemke, William - N.D. (Union) Aug. 13, 1878–May 30, 1950; House, 1933–1941, 1943–1950. Candidacy: P - 1936.

Lieberman, Joseph I. - Conn. (Democratic) Feb. 24, 1942– ; Connecticut Legislature, 1971–1981; attorney general of Connecticut, 1983–1989; Senate 1989– . Candidacy: VP - 2000.

Lincoln, Abraham - Ill. (Republican) Feb. 12, 1809–April 15, 1865; House, 1847–1849; U.S. president, 1861–1865. Candidacies: P - 1860, 1864.

Lincoln, Benjamin - Mass. (Federalist) Jan. 24, 1733–May 9, 1810; major general in Continental Army, 1777–1781. Candidacy: - 1789.

Lodge, Henry Cabot Jr. - Mass. (Republican) July 5, 1902–Feb. 27, 1985; Senate, 1937–1944, 1947–1953; ambassador to United Nations, 1953–1960; ambassador to Republic of Vietnam, 1963–1964, 1965–1967. Candidacy: VP - 1960.

Logan, John Alexander - Ill. (Republican) Feb. 9, 1826–Dec. 26, 1886; House, 1859–1862, 1867–1871; Senate, 1871–1877, 1879–1886. Candidacy: VP - 1884.

Machen, Willis Benson - Ky. (Democratic) April 10, 1810–Sept. 29, 1893; Confederate Congress, 1861–1865; Senate, 1872–1873. Candidacy: VP - 1872.

Macon, Nathaniel - N.C. (Democratic-Republican) Dec. 17, 1757–June 29, 1837; House, 1791–1815; Speaker of the House, 1801–1807; Senate, 1815–1828; president pro tempore of the Senate, 1826, 1827. Candidacy: VP - 1824.

Madison, James - Va. (Democratic-Republican) March 16, 1751–June 28, 1836; Continental Congress, 1780–1783, 1787–1788; Constitutional Convention, 1787; House, 1789–1797; secretary of state, 1801–1809; U.S. president, 1809–1817. Candidacies: P - 1808, 1812.

Mangum, Willie Person - N.C. (Independent Democrat) May 10, 1792–Sept. 7, 1861; House, 1823–1826; Senate, 1831–1836, 1840–1853. Candidacy: P - 1836.

Marshall, John - Va. (Federalist) Sept. 24, 1755–July 6, 1835; House, 1799–1800; secretary of state, 1800–1801; chief justice of United States, 1801–1835. Candidacy: VP - 1816.

Marshall, Thomas Riley - Ind. (Democratic) March 14, 1854–June 1, 1925; governor, 1909–1913; U.S. vice president, 1913–1921. Candidacies: VP - 1912, 1916.

McCarthy, Eugene Joseph - Minn. (Independent) March 29, 1916– ; House, 1949–1959; Senate, 1959–1971. Candidacy: P - 1976.

McClellan, George Brinton - N.J. (Democratic) Dec. 3, 1826–Oct. 29, 1885; general-in-chief of Army of the Potomac, 1861; governor, 1878–1881. Candidacy: P - 1864.

McGovern, George Stanley - S.D. (Democratic) July 19, 1922– ; House, 1957–1961; Senate, 1963–1981. Candidacy: P - 1972.

McKinley, William Jr. - Ohio (Republican) Jan. 29, 1843–Sept. 14, 1901; House, 1877, 1885–1891; governor, 1892–1896; U.S. president, 1897–1901. Candidacies: P - 1896, 1900.

McNary, Charles Linza - Ore. (Republican) June 12, 1874–Feb. 25, 1944; state Supreme Court judge, 1913–1915; Senate, 1917–1918, 1918–1944; Senate minority leader, 1933–1944. Candidacy: VP - 1940.

Miller, William Edward - N.Y. (Republican) March 22, 1914–June 24, 1983; House, 1951–1965; chairman of Republican National Committee, 1960–1964. Candidacy: VP - 1964.

Milton, John - Ga. circa 1740–circa 1804; secretary of state, Georgia, circa 1778, 1781, 1783. Candidacy: - 1789.

Mondale, Walter Frederick - Minn. (Democratic) Jan. 5, 1928– ; Senate, 1964–1976; U.S. vice president, 1977–1981; ambassador to Japan, 1993–1996. Candidacies: VP - 1976, 1980; P - 1984.

Monroe, James - Va. (Democratic-Republican) April 28, 1758–July 4, 1831; Continental Congress, 1783–1786; Senate, 1790–1794; minister to France, 1794–1796, 1803; minister to England, 1803–1807; governor, 1799–1802, 1811; secretary of state, 1811–1814, 1815–1817; U.S. president, 1817–1825. Candidacies: VP - 1808; P - 1816, 1820.

Morton, Levi Parsons - N.Y. (Republican) May 16, 1824–May 16, 1920; House, 1879–1881; minister to France, 1881–1885; U.S. vice president, 1889–1893; governor, 1895–1897. Candidacy: VP - 1888.

Muskie, Edmund Sixtus - Maine (Democratic) March 28, 1914–March 26, 1996; governor, 1955–1959; Senate, 1959–1980; secretary of state, 1980–1981. Candidacy: VP - 1968.

Nathan, Theodora Nathalia - Ore. (Libertarian) Feb. 9, 1923– ; broadcast journalist; National Judiciary Committee, Libertarian Party, 1972–1975; vice chairperson, Oregon Libertarian Party, 1974–1975. Candidacy: VP - 1972.

Nixon, Richard Milhous - Calif., N.Y. (Republican) Jan. 9, 1913–April 22, 1994; House, 1947–1950; Senate, 1950–1953; U.S. vice president, 1953–1961; U.S. president, 1969–1974. Candidacies: VP - 1952, 1956; P - 1960, 1968, 1972.

Palmer, John McAuley - Ill. (Democratic, National Democratic) Sept. 13, 1817–Sept. 25, 1900; governor, 1869–1873; Senate, 1891–1897. Candidacies: VP - 1872; P - 1896.

Parker, Alton Brooks - N.Y. (Democratic) May 14, 1852–May 10, 1926; chief justice of N.Y. Court of Appeals, 1898–1904. Candidacy: P - 1904.

Pendleton, George Hunt - Ohio (Democratic) July 19, 1825–Nov. 24, 1889; House, 1857–1865; Senate, 1879–1885; minister to Germany, 1885–1889. Candidacy: VP - 1864.

Perot, H. Ross - Texas (Independent, Reform) June 27, 1930– ; business executive and owner. Candidacies: P - 1992, 1996.

Pierce, Franklin - N.H. (Democratic) Nov. 23, 1804–Oct. 8, 1869; House, 1833–1837; Senate, 1837–1842; U.S. president, 1853–1857. Candidacy: P - 1852.

Pinckney, Charles Cotesworth - S.C. (Federalist) Feb. 25, 1746–Aug. 16, 1825; president, state senate, 1779; minister to France, 1796. Candidacies: VP - 1800; P - 1804, 1808.

Pinckney, Thomas - S.C. (Federalist) Oct. 23, 1750–Nov. 2, 1828; governor, 1787–1789; minister to Great Britain, 1792–1796; envoy to Spain, 1794–1795; House, 1797–1801. Candidacy: - 1796.

Polk, James Knox - Tenn. (Democratic) Nov. 2, 1795–June 15, 1849; House, 1825–1839; Speaker of the House, 1835–1839; governor, 1839–1841; U.S. president, 1845–1849. Candidacies: VP - 1840; P - 1844.

Quayle, Dan - Ind. (Republican) Feb. 4, 1947– ; House, 1977–1981; Senate, 1981–1989; U.S. vice president, 1989–1993. Candidacies; VP - 1988, 1992.

Reagan, Ronald Wilson - Calif. (Republican) Feb. 6, 1911– ; governor, 1967–1975; U.S. president, 1981–1989. Candidacies: P - 1980, 1984.

Reid, Whitelaw - N.Y. (Republican) Oct. 27, 1837–Dec. 15, 1912; minister to France, 1889–1892; editor-in-chief, *New York Tribune*, 1872–1905. Candidacy: VP - 1892.

Robinson, Joseph Taylor - Ark. (Democratic) Aug. 26, 1872–July 14, 1937; House, 1903–1913; governor, 1913; Senate, 1913–1937; Senate minority leader, 1923–1933; Senate majority leader, 1933–1937. Candidacy: VP - 1928.

Rockefeller, Nelson Aldrich - N.Y. (Republican) July 8, 1908–Jan. 26, 1979; governor, 1959–1973; U.S. vice president, 1974–1977 (nominated under the provisions of the 25th Amendment).

Rodney, Daniel - Del. (Federalist) Sept. 10, 1764–Sept. 2, 1846; governor, 1814–1817; House, 1822–1823; Senate, 1826–1827. Candidacy: VP - 1820.

Roosevelt, Franklin Delano - N.Y. (Democratic) Jan. 30, 1882–April 12, 1945; assistant secretary of the Navy, 1913–1920; governor, 1929–1933; U.S. president, 1933–1945. Candidacies: VP - 1920; P - 1932, 1936, 1940, 1944.

Roosevelt, Theodore - N.Y. (Republican, Progressive) Oct. 27, 1858–Jan. 6, 1919; assistant secretary of the Navy, 1897–1898; governor, 1899–1901; U.S. vice president, 1901; U.S. president, 1901–1909. Candidacies: VP - 1900; P - 1904, 1912.

Ross, James - Pa. (Federalist) July 12, 1762–Nov. 27, 1847; Senate, 1794–1803. Candidacy: VP - 1816.

Rush, Richard - Pa. (Democratic-Republican, National-Republican) Aug. 29, 1780–July 30, 1859; attorney general, 1814–1817; minister to Great Britain, 1817–1824; secretary of Treasury, 1825–1829. Candidacies: VP - 1820, 1828.

Rutledge, John - S.C. (Federalist) Sept. 1739–July 23, 1800; Continental Congress, 1774–1775, 1782–1783; governor, 1779–1782; Constitutional Convention, 1787; associate justice of U.S. Supreme Court, 1789–1791; chief justice of United States, 1795. Candidacy: - 1789.

Sanford, Nathan - N.Y. (Democratic-Republican) Nov. 5, 1777–Oct. 17, 1838; Senate, 1815–1821, 1826–1831. Candidacy: VP - 1824.

Schmitz, John George - Calif. (American Independent) Aug. 12, 1930– ; House, 1970–1973. Candidacy: P - 1972.

Scott, Winfield - N.J. (Whig) June 13, 1786–May 29, 1866; general-in-chief of U.S. Army, 1841–1861. Candidacy: P - 1852.

Sergeant, John - Pa. (National-Republican) Dec. 5, 1779–Nov. 23, 1852; House, 1815–1823, 1827–1829, 1837–1841. Candidacy: VP - 1832.

Sewall, Arthur - Maine (Democratic) Nov. 25, 1835–Sept. 5, 1900; Democratic National Committee member, 1888–1896. Candidacy: VP - 1896.

Seymour, Horatio - N.Y. (Democratic) May 31, 1810–Feb. 12, 1886; governor, 1853–1855, 1863–1865. Candidacy: P - 1868.

Sherman, James Schoolcraft - N.Y. (Republican) Oct. 24, 1855–Oct. 30, 1912; House, 1887–1891, 1893–1909; U.S. vice president, 1909–1912. Candidacies: VP - 1908, 1912. (Died during 1912 campaign; Nicholas Murray Butler replaced Sherman on the Republican ticket.)

Shriver, Robert Sargent Jr. - Md. (Democratic) Nov. 9, 1915– ; director, Peace Corps, 1961–1966; director, Office of Economic Opportunity, 1964–1968; ambassador to France, 1968–1970. Candidacy: VP - 1972. (Replaced Thomas F. Eagleton on Democratic ticket Aug. 8.)

Smith, Alfred Emanuel - N.Y. (Democratic) Dec. 30, 1873–Oct. 4, 1944; governor, 1919–1921, 1923–1929. Candidacy: P - 1928.

Smith, William - S.C., Ala. (Independent Democratic-Republican) Sept. 6, 1762–June 26, 1840; Senate, 1816–1823, 1826–1831. Candidacies: VP - 1828, 1836.

Sparkman, John Jackson - Ala. (Democratic) Dec. 20, 1899–Nov. 16, 1985; House, 1937–1946; Senate, 1946–1979. Candidacy: VP - 1952.

Stevenson, Adlai Ewing - Ill. (Democratic) Oct. 23, 1835–June 14, 1914; House, 1875–1877, 1879–1881; assistant postmaster general, 1885–1889; U.S. vice president, 1893–1897. Candidacies: VP - 1892, 1900.

Stevenson, Adlai Ewing II - Ill. (Democratic) Feb. 5, 1900–July 14, 1965; assistant to the secretary of Navy, 1941–1944; assistant to the secretary of state, 1945; governor, 1949–1953; ambassador to United Nations, 1961–1965. Candidacies: P - 1952, 1956.

Stockton, Richard - N.J. (Federalist) April 17, 1764–March 7, 1828; Senate, 1796–1799; House, 1813–1815. Candidacy: VP - 1820.

Taft, William Howard - Ohio (Republican) Sept. 15, 1857–March 8, 1930; secretary of war, 1904–1908; U.S. president, 1909–1913; chief justice of United States, 1921–1930. Candidacies: P - 1908, 1912.

Talmadge, Herman Eugene - Ga. (Independent Democratic) Aug. 9, 1913– ; governor, 1947, 1948–1955; Senate, 1957–1981. Candidacy: VP - 1956.

Taylor, Glen Hearst - Idaho (Progressive) April 12, 1904–April 28, 1984; Senate, 1945–1951. Candidacy: VP - 1948.

Taylor, Zachary - La. (Whig) Nov. 24, 1784–July 9, 1850; major general, U.S. Army; U.S. president, 1849–1850. Candidacy: P - 1848.

Tazewell, Littleton Waller - Va. (Democratic) Dec. 17, 1774–May 6, 1860; House, 1800–1801; Senate, 1824–1832; president pro tempore of the Senate, 1832; governor, 1834–1836. Candidacy: VP - 1840.

Telfair, Edward - Ga. (Democratic-Republican) 1735–Sept. 17, 1807; Continental Congress, 1778, 1780–1782; governor, 1789–1793. Candidacy: - 1789.

Thomas, Norman Mattoon - N.Y. (Socialist) Nov. 20, 1884–Dec. 19, 1968; Presbyterian minister, 1911–1931; author and editor. Candidacies: P - 1928, 1932, 1936, 1940, 1944, 1948.

Thurman, Allen Granberry - Ohio (Democratic) Nov. 13, 1813–Dec. 12, 1895; House, 1845–1847; Ohio Supreme Court, 1851–1856; Senate, 1869–1881; president pro tempore of the Senate, 1879, 1880. Candidacy: VP - 1888.

Thurmond, James Strom - S.C. (States' Rights Democrat) Dec. 5, 1902– ; governor, 1947–1951; Senate, 1954–1956, 1956– ; president pro tempore of the Senate, 1981–1987; 1995– . Candidacies: P - 1948.

Tilden, Samuel Jones - N.Y. (Democratic) Feb. 9, 1814–Aug. 4, 1886; governor, 1875–1877. Candidacy: P - 1876.

Tompkins, Daniel D. - N.Y. (Democratic-Republican) June 21, 1774–June 11, 1825; elected to the House for the term beginning in 1805 but resigned before taking seat; governor, 1807–1817; U.S. vice president, 1817–1825. Candidacies: VP - 1816, 1820.

Truman, Harry S. - Mo. (Democratic) May 8, 1884–Dec. 26, 1972; Senate, 1935–1945; U.S. vice president, 1945; U.S. president, 1945–1953. Candidacies: VP - 1944; P - 1948.

Tyler, John - Va. (Whig) March 29, 1790–Jan. 18, 1862; governor, 1825–1827; Senate, 1827–1836; U.S. vice president, 1841; U.S. president, 1841–1845. Candidacies: VP - 1836, 1840.

Van Buren, Martin - N.Y. (Democratic, Free Soil) Dec. 5, 1782–July 24, 1862; Senate, 1821–1828; governor, 1829; secretary of state, 1829–1831; U.S. vice president, 1833–1837; U.S. president, 1837–1841. Candidacies: VP - 1824, 1832; P - 1836, 1840, 1848.

Wallace, George Corley - Ala. (American Independent) Aug. 25, 1919–Sept. 13, 1998; governor, 1963–1967, 1971–1979, 1983–1989. Candidacy: P - 1968.

Wallace, Henry Agard - Iowa (Democratic, Progressive) Oct. 7, 1888–Nov. 18, 1965; secretary of agriculture, 1933–1940; U.S. vice president, 1941–1945; secretary of commerce, 1945–1946. Candidacies: VP - 1940; P - 1948.

Warren, Earl - Calif. (Republican) March 19, 1891–July 9, 1974; governor, 1943–1953; chief justice of United States, 1953–1969. Candidacy: VP - 1948.

Washington, George - Va. (Federalist) Feb. 22, 1732–Dec. 14, 1799; First and Second Continental Congresses, 1774, 1775; commander-in-chief of armed forces, 1775–1783; president of Constitutional Convention, 1787; U.S. president, 1789–1797. Candidacies: P - 1789, 1792, 1796.

Watson, Thomas Edward - Ga. (Populist) Sept. 5, 1856–Sept. 26, 1922; House, 1891–1993; Senate, 1921–1922. Candidacies: VP - 1896; P - 1904, 1908.

Weaver, James Baird - Iowa (Greenback, Populist) June 12, 1833–Feb. 6, 1912; House, 1879–1881, 1885–1889; Candidacies: P - 1880, 1892.

Webster, Daniel - Mass. (Whig) Jan. 18, 1782–Oct. 24, 1852; House, 1813–1817, 1823–1827; Senate, 1827–1841, 1845–1850; secretary of state, 1841–1843, 1850–1852. Candidacy: P - 1836.

Wheeler, Burton Kendall - Mont. (Progressive) Feb. 27, 1882–Jan. 6, 1975; Senate, 1923–1947. Candidacy: VP - 1924.

Wheeler, William Almon - N.Y. (Republican) June 30, 1819–June 4, 1887; House, 1861–1863, 1869–1877; U.S. vice president, 1877–1881. Candidacy: VP - 1876.

White, Hugh Lawson - Tenn. (Whig) Oct. 30, 1773–April 10, 1840; Senate, 1825–1835, 1835–1840. Candidacy: P - 1836.

Wilkins, William - Pa. (Democratic) Dec. 20, 1779–June 23, 1865; Senate, 1831–1834; minister to Russia, 1834–1835; House, 1843–1844; secretary of war, 1844–1845. Candidacy: VP - 1832.

Willkie, Wendell Lewis - N.Y. (Republican) Feb. 18, 1892–Oct. 8, 1944; utility executive, 1933–1940. Candidacy: P - 1940.

Wilson, Henry - Mass. (Republican) Feb. 16, 1812–Nov. 22, 1875; Senate, 1855–1873; U.S. vice president, 1873–1875. Candidacy: VP - 1872.

Wilson, Woodrow - N.J. (Democratic) Dec. 28, 1856–Feb. 3, 1924; governor, 1911–1913; U.S. president, 1913–1921. Candidacies: P - 1912, 1916.

Wirt, William - Md. (Anti-Masonic) Nov. 8, 1772–Feb. 18, 1834; attorney general, 1817–1829. Candidacy: P - 1832.

Wright, Fielding Lewis - Miss. (States' Rights Democrat) May 16, 1895–May 4, 1956; governor, 1946–1952. Candidacy: VP - 1948.

Presidential Candidates Index

The Presidential Candidates Index includes all presidential candidates appearing in Chapter 16, Popular Vote for President, 1824–2000. The index includes candidates' names followed by the years of candidacy. To locate a candidate's returns, turn to pages 644–700 where the returns are arranged in chronological order. For major can- didate returns, see pages 644–688; for minor candidate returns, see pages 689–700. For other references to presidential candidates in the *Guide to U.S. Elections*, Fourth Edition, see the *General Index*, pp. 1-3 to 1-58.

Adams, John Quincy - 1824, 1828
Aiken, John W. - 1936, 1940
Anderson, John B. - 1980, 1984
Anderson, Thomas J. - 1976
Andrews, T. Coleman - 1956

Babson, Roger - 1940
Baker, Gerald - 1984
Barker, Wharton - 1900
Bell, John - 1860
Benson, Allen L. - 1916
Bentley, Charles E. - 1896
Bergland, David - 1984
Bidwell, John - 1892
Birney, James G. - 1840, 1844
Birrenbach, John - 1996
Black, James - 1872
Blaine, James G. - 1884
Blomen, Henning A. - 1968
Boren, Jim - 1992
Bradford, Drew - 1992
Breckinridge, John C. - 1860
Brewer, A. C. - 1880
Brisben, J. Quinn, - 1992
Broome - 1852
Brown, Cathy Gordon - 2000
Browne, Harry - 1996, 2000
Browder, Earl - 1936, 1940
Bryan, William Jennings - 1896, 1900, 1908
Bubar, Benjamin C. - 1976, 1980
Buchanan, James - 1856
Buchanan, Patrick J. - 2000
Bush, George - 1988, 1992
Bush, George W. - 2000
Butler, Benjamin F. - 1884

Camejo, Peter - 1976
Carter, Jimmy - 1976, 1980
Cass, Lewis - 1848
Chafin, Eugene W. - 1908, 1912
Chavez, Ventura - 1968
Cheeseborough, E. - 1864
Christensen, Parley P. - 1920
Clark, Ed - 1980
Clay, Henry - 1824, 1832, 1844, 1848
Cleaver, Eldridge - 1968
Cleveland, Grover - 1884, 1888, 1892
Clinton, Bill - 1992, 1996
Coiner, C. Benton - 1960
Collins, Charles E. - 1996
Colvin, D. Leigh - 1936
Commoner, Barry - 1980
Congress, Richard - 1980
Coolidge, Calvin - 1924
Cooper, Peter - 1876
Corregan, Charles H. - 1904
Cowdrey, R. H. - 1888
Cox, James M. - 1920
Cox, James R. - 1932
Cox, William W. - 1920
Coxey, Jacob S. - 1932
Crane, A. Peter - 1996
Crawford, William H. - 1824
Curtis, James L. - 1888
Curtis, Merritt B. - 1960

Daly, Lar - 1960
Daniels, Ron - 1992
Davis, John W. - 1924

Deberry, Clifton - 1964, 1980
Debs, Eugene V. - 1900, 1904, 1908, 1912, 1920
Decker, Rutherford L. - 1960
Dennis, Delmar - 1984, 1988
Dewey, Thomas E. - 1944, 1948
Dobbs, Farrell - 1948, 1952, 1956, 1960
Dole, Bob - 1996
Dodge, Earl F. - 1984, 1988, 1992, 1996, 2000

Douglas, Stephen A. - 1860
Dow, Neal - 1880
Dukakis, Michael S. - 1988
Duke, David - 1988

Ehlers, Delbert L. - 1992
Eisenhower, Dwight D. - 1952, 1956
Ellis, Seth H. - 1900

Faris, Herman P. - 1924
Faubus, Orval E. - 1960
Feinland, Marsha - 1996
Ferguson, James - 1920
Fillmore, Millard - 1856
Fisher, Louis - 1972
Fisk, Clinton B. - 1888
Forbes, Ralph - 1996
Foster, William Z. - 1924, 1928, 1932
Ford, Gerald R. - 1976
Fremont, John C. - 1856
Fulani, Lenora B. - 1988, 1992

Gahres, Bill - 1980
Garfield, James A. - 1880
Gillhaus, August - 1908
Goldwater, Barry M. - 1964
Gore, Al - 2000
Grant, Ulysses S. - 1868, 1872
Greaves, Percy L. - 1980
Greeley, Horace - 1872
Green, Gabriel - 1972
Gregory, Dick - 1968
Griffin, James C. - 1988
Griswold, Deirdre - 1980
Gritz, James - 1992

Hagelin, John - 1992, 1996, 2000
Hale, John P. - 1852
Hall, Gus - 1972, 1976, 1980, 1984
Hallinan, Vincent - 1952
Halstead, Fred - 1968
Halyard, Helen - 1992
Hamblen, Stuart - 1952
Hancock, Winfield S. - 1880
Hanly, J. Frank - 1916
Harding, Warren G. - 1920
Harris, James E. - 1996, 2000
Harrison, Benjamin H. - 1888, 1892
Harrison, William Henry - 1836, 1840
Harvey, William H. - 1932
Hass, Eric - 1952, 1956, 1960, 1964
Hayes, Rutherford B. - 1876
Hem, Eugene A. - 1992
Hensley, James - 1964
Herer, Jack - 1988, 1992
Hesley, James K. - 1968
Hisgen, Thomas L. - 1908
Holcomb, Austin - 1904
Hollis, Mary Cal - 1996

Holmes, Gavrielle - 1984
Holmes, Larry - 1984, 1988
Holtwick, Enoch A. - 1956
Hoopes, Darlington - 1952, 1956
Hoover, Herbert C. - 1928, 1932
Hospers, John - 1972
Hughes, Charles Evans - 1916
Humphrey, Hubert H. - 1968

Jackson, Andrew - 1824, 1828, 1832
Jenness, Linda - 1972
Johns, Frank T. - 1924
Johnson, Lyndon B. - 1964

Johnson, Sonia - 1984

Kasper, John - 1964
Kennedy, John F. - 1960
Kenoyer, Willa - 1988
King, Clennon - 1960
Knutson, Alfred - 1940
Krajewski, Henry B. - 1952, 1956

La Follette, Robert M. - 1924
Landon, Alfred M. - 1936
Lane, Dennis I. - 2000
LaRiva, Gloria - 1992
LaRouche, Lyndon H. Jr. - 1976, 1984, 1988, 1992
Lee, J. Bracken - 1960
Lemke, William - 1936
Levering, Joshua - 1896
Levin, Jules - 1976
Lewin, Herbert - 1988
Lightburn, Joseph B. - 1964
Lincoln, Abraham - 1860, 1864
Lowery, Arthur J. - 1984
Lynen, Kurt - 1980

MacArthur, Douglas - 1952
Macauley, Robert C. - 1920
MacBride, Roger - 1976
Maddox, Lester - 1976
Mahalchik, John V. - 1972
Malloney, Joseph F. - 1900
Marra, William A. - 1988
Marrou, Andre V. - 1992
Martin, John G. - 1988
Mason, Mel - 1984
Masters, Isabell - 1992, 1996
Matchett, Charles H. - 1896
McCarthy, Eugene J. - 1968, 1976, 1988
McClellan, George B. - 1864
McCormack, Ellen - 1980
McGovern, George - 1972
McKinley, William - 1896, 1900
McLain, Harley - 1980
McReynolds, David - 1980, 2000
Michael, Steve - 1996
Miller, Ernest L. - 1976
Mitchell, Charlene - 1968
Mondale, Walter F. - 1984
Moorehead, Monica - 1996, 2000
Munn, Earle Harold Sr. - 1964, 1968, 1972

Nader, Ralph - 1996, 2000
Nations, Gilbert O. - 1924
Nixon, Richard M. - 1960, 1968, 1972

O'Conor, Charles - 1872

Palmer, John M. - 1896
Parker, Alton B. - 1904
Paul, Ron - 1988
Pelley, William Dudley - 1936
Peron, Dennis - 1996
Perot, Ross - 1992, 1996
Phelps, John W. - 1880
Phillips, Howard - 1992, 1996, 2000
Pierce, Franklin - 1852
Polk, James K. - 1844
Pulley, Andrew - 1980

Rarick, John R. - 1980
Reagan, Ronald W. - 1980, 1984
Reed, Evelyn - 1972
Reimer, Arthur E. - 1912, 1916
Reynolds, Verne L. - 1928, 1932

Richards, Bob - 1984
Roosevelt, Franklin D. - 1932, 1936, 1940, 1944
Roosevelt, Theodore - 1904, 1912

Schmitz, John G. - 1972
Scott, Winfield - 1852
Serrette, Dennis L. - 1984
Seymour, Horatio - 1868
Shelton, Frank W. - 1980
Smith, Alfred E. - 1928
Smith, Gerald L. K. - 1948, 1956
Smith, Gerrit - 1848, 1860
Smith, Green Clay - 1876
Smith, L. Neil - 2000
Smith, Maureen - 1980
Smith, Robert J. - 1992
Soeters, Kent M. - 1968
Spock, Benjamin - 1972
Stevenson, Adlai E. - 1952, 1956
St. John, John P. - 1884
Streeter, Alson J. - 1888
Sullivan, Charles L. - 1960
Swallow, Silas C. - 1904

Taft, William H. - 1908, 1912
Taylor, Frank - 1976
Taylor, Zachary - 1848
Teichert, Edward A. - 1944, 1948
Templin, Diane Beall - 1996
Thomas, Norman - 1928, 1932, 1936, 1940, 1944, 1948
Thurmond, Strom - 1948
Tilden, Samuel J. - 1876
Troup, George M. - 1852
Troxell, Richard K. - 1968
Truman, Harry S. - 1948
Turney, Daniel B. - 1908

Upshaw, William D. - 1932

Van Buren, Martin - 1836, 1840, 1848
Varney, William F. - 1928
Venson, Randall A. - 2000

Walker, James B. - 1876
Wallace, George C. - 1968
Wallace, Henry A. - 1948

Wallace, William J. - 1924
Warren, James - 1988, 1992
Watkins, Aaron S. - 1920
Watson, Claude A. - 1944, 1948
Watson, Thomas E. - 1904, 1908
Weaver, James B. - 1880, 1892

Webb, Frank E. - 1928
Webster, Daniel - 1836, 1852
Wendelken, Martin E. - 1980
White, Hugh L. - 1836
White, Jerome - 1996
Willkie, Wendell L. - 1940

Wilson, Woodrow - 1912, 1916
Wing, Simon - 1892
Winn, Ed - 1984, 1988
Wirt, William - 1832
Woolley, John G. - 1900
Wright, Margaret - 1976

Yiamouyiannas, John - 1992
Youngkeit, Louie G. - 1988, 2000

Zahnd, John - 1932
Zeidler, Frank P. - 1976

General Index

The General Index includes page references to all sections of the *Guide to U.S. Elections*, fourth edition, except the congrssional and gubernatorial popular vote returns, which are indexed separately in candidate indexes. The six candidate indexes are: Presidential Candidates Index, pp. I-1 to I-2, Vol. I; House Candidates Index, pp. I-1 to I-111, Vol. II; Senate General Election Candidates Index, pp. I-113 to I-119, Vol. II; Senate Primary Candidates Index, pp. I-120 to I-128, Vol. II; Gubernatorial General Election Candidates Index, pp. I-129 to I-142, Vol. II; Gubernatorial Primary Candidates Index, pp. I-143 to I-151, Vol. II.

A

Aandahl, Fred G.
  governor, North Dakota, 1404
Abbett, Leon
  governor, New Jersey, 1401
Abbott, Joseph C.
  senator, North Carolina, 1256
Abdnor, James
  senator, South Dakota, 183, 1261
Abel, Hazel
  senator, Nebraska, 1252
Abernethy, Thomas G., 803
Abortion
  Democratic delegates, (1988) 553
  platform issue
    Democrats, (1972) 423 (box), (1976) 539, (1980) 546, (1984) 549, (1992) 557, 558, (1996) 564, 565, (2000) 569–570
    National Unity Campaign, (1980) 547
    Republicans, (1976) 541, (1980) 543, 544, (1984) 551, (1988) 555, (1992) 558, 559, (1996) 561, 562, (2000) 566, 567
  presidential campaign issue, (1984) 285, (1992) 292, (1996) 293–294
  Reagan positions, 284
Abourezk, James
  senator, South Dakota, 172, 181, 1261
Abraham, Spencer
  senator, Michigan, 199, 206, 1249
Absentee voting, 36–39
Acevedo-Vilá, Anibal, 792
Acheson, Dean, 142–143, 273
Adair, John
  governor, Kentucky, 1392
  senator, Kentucky, 1245
Adams, Alva B.
  governor, Colorado, 1386
  senator, Colorado, 1238
Adams, Brock
  senator, Washington, 188, 1265
Adams, Charles Francis
  biography, 775
  Free Soil Party officer, 425 (box)
  presidential candidate
    Liberal Republican contender, (1872) 247, 463
  vice-presidential candidate
    Free Soil nominee, (1848) 63, 429, 449
Adams, James H.
  governor, South Carolina, 1408
Adams, Jewett W.
  governor, Nevada, 1400
Adams, John
  biography, 775
  electoral vote for Monroe, 232
  political party development, 55–56
  presidential candidate
    election milestones, 14, 20
    electoral vote, (1789) 718, (1792) 719, (1796) 720, (1800) 721
    faithless elector, (1796) 703 (box)
    Federalist nominee, (1796) 227, (1800) 228, 707

former members of Congress, 155 (box)
    former vice president, 314 (box)
    public offices, 214
  on vice presidency, 312
  vice-presidential candidate
    Federalist nominee, (1789) 225–226, (1792) 226
Adams, John Quincy
  biography, 775
  House service, 796
  presidential candidate
    cabinet service, 221
    decision by House, (1824) 706 (box), 707, 708, 709
    Democratic-Republican contender, (1824) 61, 232–233, 296
    election milestones, 14, 20
    electoral anomalies, 12 (box)
    electoral vote, (1820) 232, 702 (box), 726, (1824) 727, (1828) 728
    former members of Congress, 155 (box)
    as "minority" president, 223 (table)
    National Republican nominee, (1828) 61, 67, 234, 296
    political party development, 44, 48, 56
    popular vote, (1824) 644, (1828) 645
    public offices, 214
  senator, Massachusetts, 1248
Adams, John Quincy
  vice-presidential candidate
    Straight-Out Democratic nominee, (1872) 430
Adams, John T.
  Republican National Committee chair, 417 (table), 426 (table)
Adams, Paul, 55
Adams, Robert H.
  senator, Mississippi, 1250
Adams, Samuel
  biography, 775
  electoral vote, (1796) 720
  governor, Massachusetts, 1396
Adams, Samuel
  governor, Arkansas, 1385
Adams, Sherman
  in Eisenhower administration, 150, 151, 272
  governor, New Hampshire, 1401
Adams, Stephen
  senator, Mississippi, 1250
Adams, William H.
  governor, Colorado, 1386
Addams, Jane, 488
Adet, Pierre, 227
Adkins, Homer M.
  governor, Arkansas, 1385
Advertising. *See* Political advertising
Affirmative action
  Democratic platform issue, (1984) 549
African American voting rights
  civil rights legislation, 24–28
  extension of franchise, 24–31
  Fifteenth Amendment, 15, 21, 24, 29, 132, 220
  House redistricting, 29–31, 825–826

Jim Crow era, 24–26
  judicial support, 28–31
  literacy tests, 25, 132
  poll tax barriers, 25, 132
  Reconstruction era, 21, 24, 802–803
  redistricting, 29–31
  white primaries, 25–26, 132
African Americans. *See also* African American voting rights; Civil rights
  candidates, (2000) 31
  Democratic Party history, 57–59
    Gore support, (2000) 300, 713
    in New Deal coalition, 263, 264
  governors, 193, 1377
  members of Congress, 790–792
    election milestones, 15, 18
    House, Senate totals, 1947–2001 (table), 790
    leadership posts, 791
    redistricting battles, 792
    senators, 1234
    women, 789, 791, 792
  officeholders, 28
  platform issues
    Republicans, (1980) 543–544
    Socialists, (1920) 493
  politics and issues
    urban riots, 164, 166, 167
    Vietnam War years, 163, 164
    voting rights, 164
  in Populist Party, 69
  presidential contenders, (1972) 171, (1984) 285, (1988) 288
  Reconstruction era, 226, 245–246
  in Republican Party, 74, 75, 76
Age
  members of Congress, 786
    requirement for House, 799
  minimum voting age, 18, 21, 33, 220
  of presidents at inauguration, 211 (table)
  in ticket balancing, 312
  voter characteristics, 23 (table)
Agnew, Spiro T.
  biography, 775
  governor, Maryland, 166, 1395
  presidential contender, (1976) 223
  as vice president
    midterm campaigning, 170
    resignation, 18, 173, 281, 714
  vice-presidential candidate
    electoral vote, (1968, 1972) 773
    Republican nominee, (1968) 168, 279, 436, 529, (1972) 172, 280–281, 436, 536
Agran, Larry
  Democratic convention ballots, (1992) 636
  presidential primary votes, (1992) 386–393
Agricultural Marketing Act of 1929, 261
Agriculture policy
  Eisenhower administration, 149
  Hoover administration, 261
  New Deal, 264, 265
  platform issue
    Democrats, (1928) 500, (1932) 503, (1944) 510, (1952) 517, (1956) 519, (1960) 523

Republicans, (1928) 499, (1932) 502, (1944) 509, (1956) 521, (1960) 524
    third-party reformers, 252–253
Ahern, Frank
  presidential primary votes, (1976) 364, (1980) 365–371, (1988) 378–385
AIDS
  Republican platform issue, (1988) 555, (1992) 559
Aiken, George D.
  governor, Vermont, 1411
  senator, Vermont, 175, 1263
Aiken, John W.
  presidential candidate
    popular vote, (1936, 1940) 693
    Socialist Labor nominee, (1936, 1940) 434
  vice-presidential candidate
    Socialist Labor nominee, (1932) 433
Aiken, William
  governor, South Carolina, 1408
Ailes, Roger, 288
Akaka, Daniel K.
  senator, Hawaii, 1241
Alabama
  Democratic convention credentials dispute, (1968) 422, 531, 623
  preferential primaries, 130
Alabama Independent Democratic Party, 531
"Alabama paradox," 812
Albaugh, Arla A.
  vice-presidential candidate
    Socialist Labor nominee, (1944) 434
Albert, Carl
  at Democratic convention, (1968) 531
    officers, 415 (table)
  House leadership, 179
  vice-presidential contender, (1976) 539
Alcorn, H. Meade Jr.
  Republican National Committee chair, 426 (table)
Alcorn, James L.
  governor, Mississippi, 1398
  senator, Mississippi, 1250
Aldrich, C. A.
  presidential primary votes, (1996) 395–402
Aldrich, Chester H.
  governor, Nebraska, 1399
Aldrich, Nelson W.
  senator, Rhode Island, 1259
Alexander, Herbert E., 93–94, 101, 112, 411
Alexander, Lamar
  governor, Tennessee, 185, 1409
  presidential candidate
    primary votes, (1996) 395–402
    Republican contender, (1996) 293, 315, (2000) 204, 296
Alexander, Moses
  governor, Idaho, 1390
Alexander, Nathaniel
  governor, North Carolina, 1403
Alford, Dale, 152
Alger, Russell A.
  governor, Michigan, 1397

Republican presidential contender, (1888) 251, 473
  convention ballots, (1888) 592
senator, Michigan, 1249
Alien, Willis
  presidential primary votes, (1940) 336
Allain, Bill
  governor, Mississippi, 1398
Allard, Wayne
  senator, Colorado, 200, 1238
Allen, Frank G.
  governor, Massachusetts, 1396
Allen, George F.
  governor, Virginia, 199, 1412
  senator, Virginia, 1264
Allen, H. C.
  presidential primary votes, (1940) 335–336
Allen, Henry J.
  governor, Kansas, 1392
  senator, Kansas, 1244
Allen, Henry T.
  Democratic convention ballots, (1924) 607
Allen, Henry W.
  governor, Louisiana, 1393
Allen, James B.
  senator, Alabama, 1236
Allen, James F.
  senator, Delaware, 1240
Allen, John B.
  senator, Washington, 1265
Allen, Maryon Pittman
  senator, Alabama, 1236
Allen, Oscar K.
  governor, Louisiana, 1393
Allen, Philip
  governor, Rhode Island, 1407
  senator, Rhode Island, 1259
Allen, Sabrina
  independent vice-presidential candidate, (2000) 439
Allen, Seymour E.
  presidential candidate
    National Party nominee, (1932) 433
Allen, William
  Democratic convention ballots, (1876) 587
  governor, Ohio, 1404
  senator, Ohio, 1257
Allen, William V.
  senator, Nebraska, 1252
Allin, Roger
  governor, North Dakota, 1404
Allison, William B.
  length of service in Congress, 795 (table)
  Republican presidential contender, (1888) 251
    convention ballots, (1888) 592, (1896) 594
  senator, Iowa, 1244
Allott, Gordon
  senator, Colorado, 172, 1238
Allred, James V.
  governor, Texas, 1410
Allwright, S. S., 26
Almond, James Lindsay Jr.
  governor, Virginia, 1412
Almond, Lincoln C.
  governor, Rhode Island, 1407
Alston, Joseph
  governor, South Carolina, 1407
Alston, Robert F. W.
  governor, South Carolina, 1408
Altgeld, John P.
  governor, Illinois, 1390
America First Party
  nominees, (1944, 1952) 434, (1960) 435, (1972) 436, (1992) 438, (1996) 439
American Federation of Labor, 70
American Independent Party
  candidates, platform, (1968) 532–533
  historical development, 46, 50
    profile, 51–52
    timeline, 47

nominees, (1968–80) 436–437, (1988) 438
politics and issues, (1968) 166, 168
primaries, (1968) 353, (1988) 385, (1992) 393, (1996) 402
vote percentage, 424 (box)
Wallace campaign, (1968) 279
American Labor Party
  historical development, 46
  nominees, (1952) 434
  Wallace support, (1948) 71
American National Party
  nominees, (1876) 430
American Party
  nominees, (1880, 1888) 431
American Party
  nominees, (1920, 1924) 433
American Party
  nominees, (1960) 435
American Party
  historical profile, 51–52
  nominees, (1976–96) 436–439
American Party (Know-Nothings)
  convention, platform, (1856) 454
  Democratic platform issue, (1856) 455
  historical development, 45, 49
    profile, 64–65
    timeline, 47
  nominees, (1856) 430
  officers, 425 (box)
  presidential election chronology, 241
  remnants in Constitutional Union Party, (1860) 458
  vote percentage, 424 (box)
American Prohibition Party
  nominees, (1884) 431
American Third Party
  nominees, (1956) 435
American Vegetarian Party
  nominees, (1952) 434, (1956) 435
Ames, Adelbert
  governor, Mississippi, 1398
  senator, Mississippi, 1250
Ames, Benjamin
  governor, Maine, 1394
Ames, Oliver
  governor, Massachusetts, 1396
Ammons, Elias M.
  governor, Colorado, 1386
Ammons, Teller
  governor, Colorado, 1386
Amnesty
  platform issue
    Democrats, (1972) 535
    Republicans, (1972) 536
Anaya, Toney
  governor, New Mexico, 1402
Anderson, Alexander
  senator, Tennessee, 1261
Anderson, C. Elmer
  governor, Minnesota, 1397
Anderson, Charles
  governor, Ohio, 1404
Anderson, Clinton P.
  senator, New Mexico, 141, 1255
Anderson, Elmer L.
  governor, Minnesota, 155, 1397
Anderson, Forrest H.
  governor, Montana, 1399
Anderson, Hugh J.
  governor, Maine, 1394
Anderson, John B.
  biography, 775
  House elections, 175
  presidential candidate
    National Unity nominee, (1980) 67–68, 284, 424 (box), 437, 546–547
    political party development, 48, 50
    popular vote, (1980) 683, (1984) 697
    primary votes, (1980) 365–371
    Republican contender, (1980) 182
    Republican convention ballots, (1980) 629
    third-party challenges, 4
  Republican platform, (1976) 541

Anderson, John Jr.
  governor, Kansas, 155, 1392
Anderson, Joseph
  senator, Tennessee, 1261
Anderson, Sharon
  presidential primary votes, (1992) 393
Anderson, Sigurd
  governor, South Dakota, 1409
Anderson, Thomas J.
  presidential candidate
    American Party nominee, (1976) 51–52, 436
    popular vote, (1976) 695
  vice-presidential candidate
    American Independent Party nominee, (1972) 51, 436
Anderson, Victor E.
  governor, Nebraska, 1399
Anderson, Wendell R.
  governor, Minnesota, 1397
  senator, Minnesota, 179, 1249
Andrew, Joe
  Democratic National Committee chair, 415 (table), 426 (table)
Andrew, John A.
  governor, Massachusetts, 1396
Andrews, Charles B.
  governor, Connecticut, 1387
Andrews, Charles O.
  senator, Florida, 1240
Andrews, Joan
  vice-presidential candidate
    Right to Life Party nominee, (1988) 438
Andrews, Mark
  senator, North Dakota, 1256
Andrews, Thomas Coleman
  presidential candidate
    Independent States' Rights Party nominee, (1964) 436
    popular vote, (1956) 677
    States' Rights Party nominee, (1956) 435
Andrus, Cecil D.
  governor, Idaho, 1390
Ankeny, Levi
  senator, Washington, 1265
Ansel, Martin F.
  governor, South Carolina, 1408
Anthony, George T.
  governor, Kansas, 1392
Anthony, Henry B.
  governor, Rhode Island, 1407
  senator, Rhode Island, 1259
Anthony, Susan B., 31–32
Anti-Federalist Party
  historical profile, 52
Anti-Fusionist faction (Populists)
  nominees, (1900) 431
Anti-Masonic Party
  first national convention, (1831) 14, 235, 411, 413, 442
  historical development, 48, 49
    profile, 52–53
    timeline, 47
  nominees, (1832) 429
  officers, 425 (box)
  remnants as Whigs, (1836) 444
  vote percentage, 424 (box)
Anti-Monopoly Party
  historical development, 46
  nominees, (1884) 431, 471
Anti-Saloon League, 71
Antitrust. See Monopoly and antitrust issues
Apathy Party
  nominees, (1992) 438
Apodaca, Jerry
  governor, New Mexico, 1377, 1402
Applegate, Douglas
  presidential primary votes, (1988) 378–385
Apportionment of the House of Representatives. See also Redistricting
  Alabama paradox, 812
  apportionment by state, 1789–2000 (table), 810

changes, state population totals, 2000 (table), 816
constitutional basis, 807, 808–809
  Fourteenth Amendment, 220
  provisions (text), 809
controversial censuses, major reapportionments, 820–821 (box)
  1870, 802
  1920, 813
  1960, 158
  1970, 173, 793
  1980, 183, 184, 794, 815
  1990, 792, 815
  2000, 815
gainers, losers after 2000 reapportionment (map), 814
maximum size of House, 801, 812
original apportionment, 801, 809, 811
reapportionment methods, 811–815
Republican platform position, (1964) 527
slave formula, 13 (box), 802
Archer, William S.
  senator, Virginia, 1264
Ariyoshi, George R.
  governor, Hawaii, 175, 1390
Arizona
  gubernatorial elections, 1380
  innovative voting systems, 219
Armey, Dick
  House leadership, 790
Arms control
  Nixon administration policies, 281
  platform issue
    Democrats, (1948) 513, (1952) 517, (1956) 519, (1960) 522, (1964) 527, (1984) 549–550, 632, (1988) 552, 554, 634
    National Unity Campaign, (1980) 547
    Progressives, (1948) 514
    Republicans, (1960) 524, (1964) 526, (1980) 543, 544, (1988) 556, (1992) 560
  politics and issues, 156–157, 160, 176–177
Armstrong, Anne
  Republican convention ballots, (1980) 629
  Republican convention speakers, 417 (table)
Armstrong, David H.
  senator, Missouri, 1251
Armstrong, James
  biography, 775
  electoral vote, (1789) 718
Armstrong, John
  senator, New York, 1255
Armstrong, Samuel T.
  governor, Massachusetts, 1396
Armstrong, William L.
  senator, Colorado, 181, 1238
Arn, Edward F.
  governor, Kansas, 1392
Arnall, Ellis G.
  governor, Georgia, 1389, 1390
Arnold, Gary
  presidential primary votes, (1984) 372–377
Arnold, Lemuel
  governor, Rhode Island, 1406
Arnold, S. C.
  presidential primary votes, (1956) 344–345
Arnold, Samuel G.
  senator, Rhode Island, 1259
Arnold, Stanley
  presidential primary votes, (1976) 359–364
Aronson, Hugo
  governor, Montana, 145, 1399
Arthur, Chester
  biography, 775
  election milestones, 15
  presidential candidate
    former vice president, 314 (box)

public offices, 215
Republican contender, (1884) 249, 250, 470
Republican convention ballots, (1884) 590
vice-presidential candidate
electoral vote, (1880) 772
Republican nominee, (1880) 249, 431, 468
Arthur, Harold J.
governor, Vermont, 1411
Ashbrook, John M.
presidential primary votes, (1972) 354–358
Republican presidential contender, (1972) 172, 280
Ashcroft, John
governor, Missouri, 1399
senator, Missouri, 199, 206, 1251
successor, 13 (box), 788
Ashe, Samuel
governor, North Carolina, 1403
Ashley, Chester
senator, Arkansas, 1237
Ashmun, Eli P.
senator, Massachusetts, 1248
Ashmun, George
Republican convention officers, 417 (table)
Ashurst, Henry Fountain
senator, Arizona, 1237
Asian Americans
governors, 1377
members of Congress, 17, 19, 153, 159
Askew, Reubin
Democratic convention speakers, 415 (table)
governor, Florida, 1389
presidential candidate
Democratic contender, (1984) 186, 285
primary votes, (1984) 372–377
Astor, John, 89
At-large districts, 815
Atchison, David R.
senator, Missouri, 1251
Atherton, Charles G.
senator, New Hampshire, 1253
Atiyeh, Victor
governor, Oregon, 1406
Atkinson, George W.
governor, West Virginia, 1412
Atkinson, William Y.
governor, Georgia, 1389
Attia, James
presidential primary votes, (2000) 404–410
Atwater, Lee
Republican National Committee chair, 417 (table), 426 (table)
Austin, Horace
governor, Minnesota, 1397
Austin, Warren P.
senator, Vermont, 1263
Australian ballots, 218
Averick, Nathan
presidential primary votes, (1992) 394
Avery, William H.
governor, Kansas, 1392
Aycock, Charles B.
governor, North Carolina, 1403
Ayers, Roy E.
governor, Montana, 1399
Ayres, William A.
Democratic convention ballots, (1928) 609

B

Babbitt, Bruce
governor, Arizona, 189, 1385
presidential candidate
Democratic contender, (1988) 190, 287
primary votes, (1988) 378–385

Babcock, Tim M.
governor, Montana, 169, 1399
Babson, Roger Ward
presidential candidate
popular vote, (1940) 673
Prohibition Party nominee, (1940) 434
Bache, Benjamin F., 228
Bachman, Nathan L.
senator, Tennessee, 1262
Bacon, Augustus O.
senator, Georgia, 1241
Bacon, Walter W.
governor, Delaware, 1388
Badger, George E.
senator, North Carolina, 1256
Badger, William
governor, New Hampshire, 1400
Badgley, Donald
presidential primary votes, (1980) 365–371
Badham, Robert E., 825
Bagby, Arthur P.
governor, Alabama, 1384
senator, Alabama, 1236
Bagley, John J.
governor, Michigan, 1397
Bailey, Carl E.
governor, Arkansas, 131, 1385
Bailey, James E.
senator, Tennessee, 1261
Bailey, John M.
Democratic National Committee chair, 151, 415 (table), 426 (table)
Bailey, Joseph H.
senator, Texas, 1262
Bailey, Josiah W.
senator, North Carolina, 1256
Bailey, Lloyd W., 703 (box), 701–712
Bailey, Theodorus
senator, New York, 1255
Bailey, Thomas L.
governor, Mississippi, 1398
Bailey, Willis J.
governor, Kansas, 1392
Baird, David
senator, New Jersey, 1254
Baird, David Jr.
senator, New Jersey, 1254
Baker, Conrad
governor, Indiana, 1391
Baker, David J.
senator, Illinois, 1242
Baker, Edward D.
senator, Oregon, 1258
Baker, Gerald
presidential popular vote, (1984) 697
Baker, Howard H. Jr.
presidential candidate
primary votes, (1980) 365–371
Republican contender, (1980) 182
Republican convention officers, speakers, 417 (table)
senator, Tennessee, 187, 1262
Senate leadership, 180, 184
Baker, James A. III, 300
Baker, Joshua
governor, Louisiana, 1393
Baker, Nathaniel B.
governor, New Hampshire, 1400
Baker, Newton D.
Democratic convention ballots, (1924) 607, (1932) 611
presidential primary votes, (1932) 332
Baker, Lucien
senator, Kansas, 1244
Baker, Samuel A.
governor, Missouri, 1399
Baldridge, H. Clarence
governor, Idaho, 1390
Baldwin, Abraham
senator, Georgia, 1240
Baldwin, Henry P.
governor, Michigan, 1397
senator, Michigan, 1249
Baldwin, Raymond E.

governor, Connecticut, 1387
Republican convention ballots, (1948) 615
senator, Connecticut, 1239
Baldwin, Roger S.
governor, Connecticut, 1387
senator, Connecticut, 1238
Baldwin, Simeon E.
Democratic convention ballots, (1912) 601
governor, Connecticut, 1387
Baliles, Gerald L.
governor, Virginia, 188, 1412
Ball, Joseph H.
senator, Minnesota, 1249
Ball, L. Heisler
senator, Delaware, 1239, 1240
Ballard, George H.
presidential primary votes, (1992) 386–393
Ballinger, Richard A., 256
Ballots, 218
Balzar, Frederick B.
governor, Nevada, 1400
Bamberger, Simon
governor, Utah, 1410
Bangerter, Norman H.
governor, Utah, 192, 1410
Bank of the United States, 55–56, 233, 234, 235, 237, 1229
Bankhead, John H.
senator, Alabama, 1236
Bankhead, John H. II
senator, Alabama, 1236
Bankhead, William B.
Democratic convention officers, speakers, 415 (table)
presidential primary votes, (1940) 336
vice-presidential contender, (1940) 267, 507
Banks, Nathaniel P.
biography, 775
governor, Massachusetts, 1396
political party development, 45
presidential candidate
American Party nominee, (1856) 430, 454
Republican convention ballots, (1856) 579
vice-presidential electoral vote, (1872) 772
Banks and banking
Jackson policies, 55, 233, 234
Jefferson, Madison policies, 56
New Deal, 263
platform position
Democrats, (1840) 445, (1844) 447
Socialists, (1912) 485
Tyler attitudes, 237, 1229
Wilson policies, 257
Barber, Amos W.
governor, Wyoming, 1413
Barber, James David, 263, 273
Barbour, Haley
Republican National Committee chair, 417 (table), 426 (table)
Barbour, James
governor, Virginia, 1411
National Republican, Whig convention officers, 425 (box)
senator, Virginia, 1264
Barbour, John S. Jr.
senator, Virginia, 1264
Barbour, W. Warren
senator, New Jersey, 1254
Bard, Thomas R.
senator, California, 1237
Barker, James, 64
Barker, Wharton
presidential candidate
popular vote, (1900) 691
Populist nominee, (1900) 431
Barkley, Alben W.
biography, 775
at Democratic convention, (1940) 267
officers, speakers, 415 (table)

presidential candidate
Democratic contender, (1952) 272
Democratic convention ballots, (1948) 616, (1952) 618
former vice president, 314 (box)
politics and issues, (1952) 143–144
senator, Kentucky, 146, 1245
Senate leadership, 7
vice-presidential candidate
Democratic contender, (1928) 499
Democratic nominee, (1948) 139, 434, 512
electoral vote, (1948) 773
Barnard, Isaac D.
senator, Pennsylvania, 1258
Barnburner faction (Democrats)
in Free Soil Party, 449, 452
New York Democratic credentials dispute, (1848) 422, 448
nominees, (1848) 430
Polk administration tensions, 238
Barnes, John A.
presidential primary votes, (1992) 393
Barnes, Roy
governor, Georgia, 1390
Barnett, Ross R.
Democratic convention ballots, (1960) 620
governor, Mississippi, 1398
Barnum, R. G.
vice-presidential candidate
Single Tax Party nominee, (1920) 433
Barnum, William H.
Democratic National Committee chair, 415 (table), 426 (table)
senator, Connecticut, 1239
Barnwell, Robert W.
senator, South Carolina, 1260
Barone, Michael, 286
Barrett, Frank A.
governor, Wyoming, 1413
senator, Wyoming, 1266
Barron, Elizabeth
vice-presidential candidate
Peace and Freedom Party nominee, (1980) 68, 437
Barron, William W.
governor, West Virginia, 1412
Barrow, Alexander
senator, Louisiana, 1246
Barrow, Pope
senator, Georgia, 1241
Barrows, Lewis O.
governor, Maine, 1394
Barry, Alexander G.
senator, Oregon, 1258
Barry, John S.
governor, Michigan, 1396, 1397
Barry, William T.
senator, Kentucky, 1245
Barstow, John L.
governor, Vermont, 1410
Barstow, William A.
governor, Wisconsin, 1413
Bartlett, Dewey F.
governor, Oklahoma, 1405
senator, Oklahoma, 1257
Bartlett, E. L.
senator, Alaska, 1236
Bartlett, John H.
governor, New Hampshire, 1401
Bartlett, Josiah
governor, New Hampshire, 1400
Bartlett, Washington
governor, California, 1386
Bartley, Mordecai
governor, Ohio, 1404
Bartley, Thomas W.
governor, Ohio, 1404
Barton, David
senator, Missouri, 1251
Barton, Jesse M.
governor, New Hampshire, 1401
Bashford, Coles
governor, Wisconsin, 1413

Bass, Charlotta A.
    vice-presidential candidate
        American Labor Party nominee,
            (1952) 434
        Progressive nominee, (1952) 434
Bass, Robert P.
    governor, New Hampshire, 1401
Bass, Ross
    senator, Tennessee, 1262
Bass, Willie Isaac
    vice-presidential candidate
        Church of God Party nominee,
            (1952) 434
Bassett, Richard
    governor, Delaware, 1387
    senator, Delaware, 1239
Batchelder, Nahum J.
    governor, New Hampshire, 1401
Bate, William B.
    governor, Tennessee, 1409
    senator, Tennessee, 1261
Bateman, Ephraim
    senator, New Jersey, 1253
Bates, Edward, 458, 581
Bates, Frederick
    governor, Missouri, 1398
Bates, Isaac
    Whig convention officers, 425 (box)
Bates, John L.
    governor, Massachusetts, 1396
Bates, Martin W.
    senator, Delaware, 1240
Batt, Philip E.
    governor, Idaho, 1390
Battle, John S.
    Democratic convention ballots, (1956)
        619
    governor, Virginia, 1412
Baucus, Max
    senator, Montana, 181, 1251
Bauer, Gary
    presidential candidate
        primary votes, (2000) 404–410
        Republican contender, (2000) 204
Baxter, Elisha
    governor, Arkansas, 1385
Baxter, Percival P.
    governor, Maine, 1394
Bayard, James A. Jr.
    senator, Delaware, 1239
Bayard, James A. Sr.
    on Burr in 1800, 709
    senator, Delaware, 1239
Bayard, Richard H.
    senator, Delaware, 1239
Bayard, Thomas F. Jr.
    senator, Delaware, 1239
Bayard, Thomas F. Sr.
    presidential candidate
        Democratic contender, (1880) 469,
            (1884) 250, 471
        Democratic convention ballots,
            (1872) 585, (1876) 587, (1880) 589,
            (1884) 591
    senator, Delaware, 1239
Bayh, Birch
    presidential candidate
        Democratic contender, (1976) 282
        primary votes, (1976) 359–364
    senator, Indiana, 159, 175, 183, 284,
        1243
        electoral college reform, 713
Bayh, Evan
    at Democratic convention, (1996) 564
    keynote speaker, 415 (table)
    governor, Indiana, 1391
    senator, Indiana, 203, 1243
Beal, Dana
    vice-presidential candidate
        Grassroots Party nominee, (1988)
            438
Beall, J. Glenn
    senator, Maryland, 162, 1247
Beall, J. Glenn Jr.
    senator, Maryland, 170, 179, 1247
Beame, Abraham, 283

Beamgard, Don
    presidential primary votes, (1992)
        386–393
Beardsley, William S.
    governor, Iowa, 1392
Beasley, David
    governor, South Carolina, 1408
"Beauty contest" primaries, 306 (box)
Beauvais, Armand
    governor, Louisiana, 1393
Beaver, James A.
    governor, Pennsylvania, 1406
Bebb, William
    governor, Ohio, 1404
Beck, James B.
    senator, Kentucky, 1245
Beck, Robert Leo
    independent vice-presidential candidate,
        (2000) 439
Beckham, John C. W.
    governor, Kentucky, 1393
    senator, Kentucky, 1245
Beckwith, Frank R.
    presidential primary votes, (1960) 347
Bedell, Edward J.
    vice-presidential candidate
        Greenback Party nominee,
            (1952) 435
Bedford, Gunning Sr.
    governor, Delaware, 1387
Bedle, Joseph D.
    governor, New Jersey, 1401
Beeckman, R. Livingston
    governor, Rhode Island, 1407
Beemont, Jack J. H.
    presidential primary votes, (1992) 393
Beer, Samuel, 264
Begich, Nick, 13 (box)
Begole, Josiah W.
    governor, Michigan, 1397
Bell, Charles H.
    governor, New Hampshire, 1401
    senator, New Hampshire, 1253
Bell, Charles J.
    governor, Vermont, 1411
Bell, Frank
    governor, Nevada, 1400
Bell, James
    senator, New Hampshire, 1253
Bell, John
    governor, New Hampshire, 1400
Bell, John
    biography, 775
    presidential candidate
        Constitutional Union Party nominee,
            (1860) 55, 241, 242, 424, (box),
            430, 458
        electoral vote, (1860) 736
        popular vote, (1860) 653
    senator, Tennessee, 1261, 1262
Bell, John C.
    governor, Pennsylvania, 1406
Bell, P. Hansbrough
    governor, Texas, 1409
Bell, Samuel
    governor, New Hampshire, 1400
    senator, New Hampshire, 1252
Bell, Theodore A.
    Democratic convention officers, 415
        (table)
Bellamy, Edward, 78
Bellmon, Henry
    governor, Oklahoma, 159, 189,
        1405
    senator, Oklahoma, 169, 175, 1258
Belluso, Nick
    presidential primary votes, (1980)
        365–371
Belmont, August
    at Democratic convention, (1868) 462,
        (1912) 487
    Democratic National Committee chair,
        415 (table), 426 (table)
Belmont, Perry, 109
Bender, George H.
    senator, Ohio, 1257

Bender, Riley A.
    presidential primary votes, (1944) 338,
        (1948) 339–340, (1952) 343
Benet, Christie
    senator, South Carolina, 1260
Benjamin, Judah P.
    senator, Louisiana, 1246
Bennett, Caleb P.
    governor, Delaware, 1388
Bennett, Robert F.
    governor, Kansas, 1392
Bennett, Robert F.
    senator, Utah, 1263
Bennett, Thomas
    governor, South Carolina, 1407
Bennett, Wallace F.
    senator, Utah, 175, 1263
Bennington, Wesley Henry
    vice-presidential candidate
        Greenback Party nominee, (1928)
            433
Benns, George W.
    presidential primary votes, (1992)
        386–393
Benoit, Gary, 539
Benson, Alfred W.
    senator, Kansas, 1244
Benson, Allan L.
    biography, 775
    presidential candidate
        popular vote, (1916) 667
        Socialist nominee, (1916) 432, 492
Benson, Elmer A.
    governor, Minnesota, 1397
    senator, Minnesota, 1249
Benson, Ezra Taft, 149
Benson, Frank W.
    governor, Oregon, 1405
Bentley, Charles Eugene
    presidential candidate
        National Party nominee, (1896) 431
        popular vote, (1896) 691
Bentley, Elizabeth, 139
Benton, Thomas Hart
    senator, Missouri, 1251
Benton, William
    senator, Connecticut, 1239
Bentsen, Lloyd
    biography, 775
    Clinton cabinet, 199
    presidential candidate
        Democratic convention ballots,
            (1988) 634
        electoral vote, (1988) 703 (box), 768
        primary votes, (1976) 359–364
    senator, Texas, 170, 1262
    vice-presidential candidate
        Democratic nominee, (1988) 286,
            288, 312, 438, 552
        electoral vote, (1988) 773
        politics and issues, (1988) 190
Berger, Victor, 46, 79
Bergland, David P.
    presidential candidate
        Libertarian nominee, (1984) 66,
            437
        popular vote, (1984) 684
    vice-presidential candidate
        Libertarian nominee, (1976) 66, 436
Bergonzi, Edward
    vice-presidential candidate
        Workers League Party nominee,
            (1984) 437
Berlin Wall, 156, 526
Berman, Howard L., 99
Berrien, John M.
    senator, Georgia, 1241
Berry, George L.
    senator, Tennessee, 1262
    vice-presidential candidate
        Democratic contender, (1924) 497
        Democratic convention ballots,
            (1924) 607
Berry, James H.
    governor, Arkansas, 1385
    senator, Arkansas, 1237

Berry, Nathaniel S.
    governor, New Hampshire, 1400
Berry, Samuel H.
    presidential primary votes, (2000)
        404–410
Berry, Tom
    governor, South Dakota, 1408
Bertesavage, Norm
    presidential primary votes, (1992) 393
Betts, Thaddeus
    senator, Connecticut, 1238
Bevel, James L.
    independent presidential candidate,
        (1992) 438
Beveridge, Albert J.
    senator, Indiana, 1243
Beveridge, John L.
    governor, Illinois, 1390
Bibb, George M.
    senator, Kentucky, 1244, 1245
Bibb, Thomas
    governor, Alabama, 1384
Bibb, William Wyatt
    governor, Alabama, 1384
    senator, Georgia, 1241
Bible, Alan
    senator, Nevada, 1252
Bickett, Thomas W.
    governor, North Carolina, 1403
Biddle, Nicholas, 234
Biden, Joseph R. Jr.
    Democratic convention ballots, (1984)
        633, (1988) 634
    presidential candidate
        Democratic contender, (1988) 190,
            286
    senator, Delaware, 172, 1240
Bidwell, John
    biography, 775
    presidential candidate
        popular vote, (1892) 661
        Prohibition nominee, (1892) 431,
            475
Biemiller, Andrew J., 512
"Big Ten" Tuesday, 318
Bigelow, Hobart B.
    governor, Connecticut, 1387
Bigger, Samuel
    governor, Indiana, 1391
Biggs, Asa
    senator, North Carolina, 1256
Biggs, Benjamin T.
    governor, Delaware, 1388
Bigler, John
    governor, California, 1386
Bigler, William
    Democratic convention officers, 415
        (table)
    governor, Pennsylvania, 1406
    senator, Pennsylvania, 1259
Bilbo, Theodore G.
    Democratic convention ballots, (1928)
        609
    governor, Mississippi, 1398
    senator, Mississippi, 1250
Billings, Franklin S.
    governor, Vermont, 1411
Billings, Theodore C.
    vice-presidential candidate
        Constitution Party nominee, (1964)
            436
Bi-Metallic League
    nominees, (1896) 431
Bingaman, Jeff
    senator, New Mexico, 199, 1254
Bingham, Hiram
    governor, Connecticut, 1387
    senator, Connecticut, 1239
Bingham, Kinsley S.
    governor, Michigan, 1397
    senator, Michigan, 1249
Bingham, William
    senator, Pennsylvania, 1259
Birney, James G.
    biography, 775
    presidential candidate

Liberty Party nominee, (1840, 1844)
66, 429, 446
popular vote, (1840) 648, (1844)
649
Birrenbach, John
presidential candidate
Independent Grassroots Party nominee, (1996) 439
popular vote, (1996) 699
Bishop, Richard M.
governor, Ohio, 1404
Bissell, Clark
governor, Connecticut, 1387
Bissell, William H.
governor, Illinois, 1390
Bixler, ——
presidential primary votes, (1948) 340
Black, Frank S.
governor, New York, 1403
Black, Hugo
senator, Alabama, 1236
Supreme Court justice, 818, 822
Black, James
presidential candidate
popular vote, (1872) 690
Prohibition Party nominee, (1872)
430
Black, James D.
governor, Kentucky, 1393
Black, Jeremiah S.
Democratic convention ballots, (1872)
585, (1880) 589
Black, John
senator, Mississippi, 1250
Black, John C., 472
"Black Codes," 26
Black Panther Party, 68
Blackburn, Joseph C. S.
Democratic convention ballots, (1896)
595
senator, Kentucky, 1245
Blackburn, Luke P.
governor, Kentucky, 1393
Blacks. See African Americans
Blackwood, Ibra C.
governor, South Carolina, 1408
Blaine, James G.
biography, 775
presidential candidate
electoral vote, (1884) 742
popular vote, (1884) 659
Republican contender, (1876) 465,
(1880) 249, 468, (1888) 251, 473,
(1892) 252, 474
Republican convention ballots,
(1876) 586, (1880) 588, (1884) 590,
(1888) 592, (1892) 593
Republican nominee, (1884) 222,
250–251, 431, 470
Republican leadership, 247
senator, Maine, 1247
Blaine, John J.
governor, Wisconsin, 1413
senator, Wisconsin, 1266
Blaine, John R.
Republican convention ballots, (1932)
610
Blair, Austin
governor, Michigan, 1397
Blair, Francis P. Jr.
biography, 776
Democratic convention ballots, (1868)
584
senator, Missouri, 1251
vice-presidential candidate
Democratic nominee, (1868) 246,
430, 462
electoral vote, (1868) 772
Blair, Henry W.
senator, New Hampshire, 1253
Blair, James T. Jr.
governor, Missouri, 1399
Blakley, William A.
senator, Texas, 132, 1262
Blanchard, James J.
governor, Michigan, 193, 1397

Blanchard, Newton C.
governor, Louisiana, 1393
senator, Louisiana, 1246
Bland, Richard P. "Silver Dick"
Democratic presidential contender,
(1896) 254, 478
convention ballots, (1896) 595
Blanton, Ray
governor, Tennessee, 1409
Blasdel, H. G.
governor, Nevada, 1400
Blease, Coleman L.
governor, South Carolina, 1408
senator, South Carolina, 1260
Bledsoe, Jesse
senator, Kentucky, 1245
Bliss, Aaron T.
governor, Michigan, 1397
Bliss, Ray C.
Republican National Committee chair,
417 (table), 426 (table)
Blodgett, Rufus
senator, New Jersey, 1254
Blomen, Constance
vice-presidential candidate
Socialist Labor nominee, (1976) 437
Blomen, Henning A.
presidential candidate
popular vote, (1968) 680
Socialist Labor nominee, (1968) 436
vice-presidential candidate
Socialist Labor nominee, (1964) 435
Blood, Henry H.
governor, Utah, 1410
Blood, Robert O.
governor, New Hampshire, 1401
Bloodworth, Timothy
senator, North Carolina, 1256
Bloomfield, Joseph
governor, New Jersey, 1401
Blount, William
governor, South Dakota, 1409
senator, Tennessee, 1261
Bloxham, William D.
governor, Florida, 1388
Blue, Robert D.
governor, Iowa, 1392
Blue Dogs (Democrats), 564
Blumenthal, Sidney, 289
Boardman, Elijah
senator, Connecticut, 1238
Bocock, Thomas, 580
Bodwell, Joseph R.
governor, Maine, 1394
Boe, Nils A.
governor, South Dakota, 1409
Boehner, John A., 820–821 (box)
Boggs, Hale, 13 (box)
Boggs, J. Caleb
governor, Delaware, 145, 1388
senator, Delaware, 172, 1240
Boggs, Lilburn W.
governor, Missouri, 1398
Boggs, Lindy
Democratic convention officers, 415
(table)
election anomalies, 13 (box)
Bogue, ——
presidential primary votes,
(1932) 332
Bogy, Lewis V.
senator, Missouri, 1251
Boies, David, 300
Boies, Horace
governor, Iowa, 1392
presidential candidate
Democratic contender, (1892) 475
Democratic convention ballots,
(1892) 593, (1896) 595
Bolack, Tom
governor, New Mexico, 1402
Bolin, Wesley
governor, Arizona, 1385
Bona, Frank
presidential primary votes, (1976) 364,
(1992) 394

Bond, Christopher S. "Kit"
governor, Missouri, 179, 1399
senator, Missouri, 188, 1251
Bond, Julian, 422, 531
Bond, Richard N.
Republican National Committee chair,
417 (table), 426 (table)
Bond, Shadrach
governor, Illinois, 1390
Bone, Homer T.
senator, Washington, 1265
Bonham, Milledge L.
governor, South Carolina, 1408
Bonner, John W.
governor, Montana, 1399
Bono, Mary, 788
Bono, Sonny, 788
"Bonus Army" protest, 261, 262
Bonus system, of convention delegate
selection, 412–413
Boon, Ratliff
governor, Indiana, 1391
Booth, Newton
governor, California, 1386
senator, California, 1237
Booth, John Wilkes, 15
Borah, William E.
presidential candidate
primary votes, (1936) 333–334
Republican contender, (1936) 504
Republican convention ballots,
(1916) 602, (1920) 604, (1936) 612
at Republican convention, (1912) 486
senator, Idaho, 1242
Boreman, Arthur I.
governor, West Virginia, 1412
senator, West Virginia, 1265
Boren, David L.
governor, Oklahoma, 176, 1405
senator, Oklahoma, 181, 1257
Boren, Jim
presidential candidate
Apathy Party nominee, (1992) 438
popular vote, (1992) 698
Borglum, Gutzon, 262
Bork, Robert
Republican convention ballots, (1996)
638
"Saturday night massacre," 281
Supreme Court nomination, 190
Borland, Solon
senator, Arkansas, 1237
Bosa, Richard P.
presidential primary votes, (1992) 393,
(1996) 403
Boschwitz, Rudy
senator, Minnesota, 181, 187, 193, 1250
Bottolfsen, Clarence A.
governor, Idaho, 1390
Bottum, Joe H.
presidential primary votes, (1944) 338
senator, South Dakota, 1261
Bouck, William
vice-presidential candidate
Farmer Labor nominee,
(1924) 433
Bouck, William C.
governor, New York, 1402
Bouligny, Dominique
senator, Louisiana, 1246
Bourn, Augustus O.
governor, Rhode Island, 1407
Bourne, Jonathan Jr.
presidential primary law, 310
senator, Oregon, 1258
Boutelle, Paul
vice-presidential candidate
Socialist Worker nominee,
(1968) 436
Boutwell, George S.
governor, Massachusetts, 1396
senator, Massachusetts, 1248
Bowden, Lemuel J.
senator, Virginia, 1264
Bowdoin, James
governor, Massachusetts, 1396

Bowen, Otis R.
governor, Indiana, 1391
Bowen, Thomas M.
senator, Colorado, 1238
Bowerman, Jay
governor, Oregon, 1405
Bowers, Claude G.
Democratic convention officers, 415
(table), 499
Bowie, Oden
governor, Maryland, 1395
Bowie, Robert
governor, Maryland, 1395
Bowles, Chester
governor, Connecticut, 141, 1387
Bowring, Eva
senator, Nebraska, 1252
Boxer, Barbara
Democratic convention officers, 415
(table)
senator, California, 18, 787, 789, 1238
Boyd, James E.
governor, Nebraska, 1399
Boyd, Linn, 577
Boyle, Emmet D.
governor, Nevada, 1400
Boyle, William M. Jr.
Democratic National Committee chair,
426 (table)
Boynton, James H.
governor, Georgia, 1389
Brackett, John Q. A.
governor, Massachusetts, 1396
Bradbury, James W.
senator, Maine, 1247
Braden, Tom, 280
Bradford, Augustus W.
governor, Maryland, 1395
Bradford, Drew
independent presidential candidate,
(1992) 438
popular vote, (1992) 698
Bradford, Robert F.
governor, Massachusetts, 138, 1396
Bradford, William
senator, Rhode Island, 1259
Bradley, Bill
at Democratic convention, (1992)
557
keynote speaker, 415 (table)
presidential candidate
Democratic contender, (2000) 204,
212, 296, 297, 568
no-run decision, (1992) 289
primary votes, (2000) 305, 318,
404–410
senator, New Jersey, 181, 1254
on TV ad expense, 99
Bradley, Joseph P., 711
Bradley, Lewis R.
governor, Nevada, 1400
Bradley, Stephen R.
Democratic-Republican caucus, (1808)
230
senator, Vermont, 1263
Bradley, Tom, 185
Bradley, William O.
governor, Kentucky, 1393
Republican vice-presidential contender,
(1888) 473
senator, Kentucky, 1245
Brady, James H.
governor, Idaho, 1390
senator, Idaho, 1242
Brady, James S., 564
Brady, Nicholas F.
senator, New Jersey, 1254
Brady, Sarah, 564
Bragg, Thomas
governor, North Carolina, 1403
senator, North Carolina, 1256
Brainerd, Lawrence
senator, Vermont, 1263
Bramlette, Thomas E.
biography, 776
governor, Kentucky, 1393

vice-presidential electoral vote, (1872)
772
Branch, Emmanuel L.
presidential primary votes, (1992)
386–393
Branch, Emmett F.
governor, Indiana, 1391
Branch, John
governor, North Carolina, 1403
senator, North Carolina, 1255
Brandegee, Frank B.
senator, Connecticut, 1239
Brandeis, Louis, 257, 818
Brandon, Gerald C.
governor, Mississippi, 1398
Brandon, William W.
governor, Alabama, 1384
Branigin, Roger D.
governor, Indiana, 162, 1391
presidential primary votes, (1968)
351–353
Brann, Louis J.
governor, Maine, 1394
Branstad, Terry E.
governor, Iowa, 189, 1392
Bratton, Sam G.
senator, New Mexico, 1254
Breathitt, Edward T.
governor, Kentucky, 1393
Breathitt, John
governor, Kentucky, 1392
Breaux, John B.
senator, Louisiana, 189, 1246
Breckinridge, Henry
presidential primary votes, (1936)
333–334
Breckinridge, John
senator, Kentucky, 1245
vice-presidential contender, (1804) 229
Breckinridge, John C.
biography, 776
presidential candidate
convention ballots, (1860) 580
electoral vote, (1860) 736
political party development, 45
popular vote, (1860) 653
Southern Democratic nominee,
(1860) 53–54, 241, 242, 424 (box),
430, 457
senator, Kentucky, 1245
vice-presidential candidate
Democratic nominee, (1856) 241,
430, 455
electoral vote, (1856) 772
Breckinridge, Robert J.
Republican convention officers, 417
(table)
Breese, Sidney
senator, Illinois, 1242
Brehm, Marie Caroline
vice-presidential candidate
Prohibition Party nominee, (1924)
433
Brennan, Joseph E.
governor, Maine, 1395
Brennan, William J., 822, 824
Brent, Richard
senator, Virginia, 1264
Brewer, A. C.
presidential popular vote,
(1880) 690
Brewer, Albert P.
governor, Alabama, 1384
Brewer, Earl LeRoy
governor, Mississippi, 1398
Brewster, Bob
presidential primary votes, (1984)
372–377
Brewster Daniel B.
presidential primary votes, (1964)
348–350
senator, Maryland, 1247
Brewster, Ralph O.
governor, Maine, 1394
senator, Maine, 1246
Breyer, Stephen, 300–301

Brice, Calvin S.
Democratic National Committee chair,
426 (table)
senator, Ohio, 1257
Brice, James
governor, Maryland, 1395
Bricker, John W.
biography, 776
governor, Ohio, 1405
presidential candidate
primary votes, (1940) 335–336,
(1944) 337–338, (1956) 344–345
Republican contender, (1944) 268
senator, Ohio, 138, 1257
president's treaty power, 147
vice-presidential candidate
electoral vote, (1944) 773
Republican nominee, (1944) 268,
434, 508
Bridges, H. Styles
governor, New Hampshire, 1401
Republican convention ballots, (1940)
613
senator, New Hampshire, 1253
Briggs, Ansel
governor, Iowa, 1391
Briggs, Frank A.
governor, North Dakota, 1404
Briggs, Frank O.
senator, New Jersey, 1254
Briggs, Frank P.
senator, Missouri, 1251
Briggs, George N.
governor, Massachusetts, 1396
Brigham, Paul
governor, Vermont, 1410
Bright, Jesse D.
senator, Indiana, 1243
Brinkley, David, 536
Brisben, J. Quinn
presidential candidate
popular vote, (1992) 698
primary votes, (1992) 393
Socialist nominee, (1992) 438
vice-presidential candidate
Socialist nominee, (1976) 437
Briscoe, Dolph
governor, Texas, 1410
Bristow, Benjamin H.
at Republican convention, (1876) 465
ballots, 586
Bristow, Joseph L.
senator, Kansas, 1244
Britt, Harry, 79
Broadhead, James O.
Democratic convention ballots, (1876)
587
Brock, Bill
Republican National Committee
chair, 417 (table), 426 (table)
primary calendar commission, 306
senator, Tennessee, 170, 179, 1261, 1262
Broderick, David C.
senator, California, 1237
Brodhead, Richard
senator, Pennsylvania, 1258
Brogden, Curtis H.
governor, North Carolina, 1403
Brokaw, Tom, 300
Brooke, Edward W.
Republican convention officers, 417
(table)
senator, Massachusetts, 180, 790, 1248
Brooke, Robert
governor, Virginia, 1411
Brooke, Walker
senator, Mississippi, 1250
Brookhart, Smith W.
senator, Iowa, 1243, 1244
Brooks, Bryant B.
governor, Wyoming, 1413
Brooks, C. Wayland
senator, Illinois, 1242
Brooks, Jack, 199
Brooks, John
governor, Massachusetts, 1396

Brooks, John A.
vice-presidential candidate
Prohibition nominee, (1888) 431,
472
Brooks, Ralph G.
governor, Nebraska, 152, 1400
Broome, ——
presidential popular vote, (1852) 690
Broome, James E.
governor, Florida, 1388
Brough, Charles H.
governor, Arkansas, 1385
Brough, John
governor, Ohio, 1404
Broughton, Charles
presidential primary votes, (1952)
341–343
Broughton, J. Melville
governor, North Carolina, 1403
senator, North Carolina, 1256
Broussard, Edwin S.
senator, Louisiana, 1246
Broussard, Robert R.
senator, Louisiana, 1246
Broward, Napoleon B.
governor, Florida, 1388
Browder, Earl R.
presidential candidate
Communist nominee, (1936) 433,
(1940) 434
popular vote, (1936, 1940) 693
Tydings campaign, 143
World War II policies, 54
Brown, Aaron V.
governor, Tennessee, 1409
Brown, Albert G.
governor, Mississippi, 1398
senator, Mississippi, 1250
Brown, Albert O.
governor, New Hampshire, 1401
Brown, Arthur
senator, Utah, 1263
Brown, Benjamin Gratz
biography, 776
governor, Missouri, 1398
senator, Missouri, 1251
presidential electoral vote, (1872) 706,
739
vice-presidential candidate
Democratic nominee, (1872) 430,
463, 464
electoral vote, (1872) 772
Liberal Republican nominee, (1872)
65, 430, 463, 464
Liberal Republican Party of Colored
Men nominee, (1872) 430
Brown, Bedford
senator, North Carolina, 1255
Brown, Cathy Gordon
independent presidential candidate,
(2000) 439
popular vote, (2000) 699
Brown, Corrine, 791–792
Brown, D. Russell
governor, Rhode Island, 1381, 1407
Brown, Edgar A., 131
Brown, Edmund G.
governor, California, 152, 159, 1386
presidential candidate
Democratic convention ballots,
(1960) 620
primary votes, (1952) 341–343,
(1960) 346–347, (1964) 350
Brown, Edmund G. "Jerry" Jr.
governor, California, 176, 181, 1386
presidential candidate
Democratic contender, (1976) 178,
282, 538, (1980) 283, (1992) 290,
556, 557
Democratic convention ballots,
(1976) 627, (1980) 630, (1992) 636
as former governor, 224
politics and issues, (1992) 195–196
primary votes, (1976) 359–364,
(1980) 365–371, (1992) 386–393,
(1996) 315

Brown, Ernest S.
senator, Nevada, 1252
Brown, Ethan Allen
governor, Ohio, 1404
senator, Ohio, 1257
Brown, Frank
governor, Maryland, 1395
Brown, Fred H.
Democratic convention ballots, (1924)
606
governor, New Hampshire, 1401
senator, New Hampshire, 1253
Brown, Hank
senator, Colorado, 1238
Brown, John
senator, Kentucky, 1244
Brown, John
senator, Louisiana, 1246
Brown, John C.
governor, Tennessee, 1409
Brown, John W.
governor, Ohio, 1405
Brown, John Y.
governor, Kentucky, 1393
Brown, John Y. Jr.
governor, Kentucky, 1393
Brown, Joseph E.
governor, Georgia, 1389
senator, Georgia, 1241
Brown, Joseph M.
governor, Georgia, 1389
Brown, Neill S.
governor, Tennessee, 1409
Brown, Norris
senator, —
Brown, Prentiss M.
senator, Michigan, 1249
Brown, Ronald H.
Democratic National Committee chair,
415 (table), 426 (table)
Brown, Thomas
governor, Florida, 1388
Brownback, Sam
senator, Kansas, 200, 788, 1244
Browne, Harry
presidential candidate
Libertarian nominee, (1996, 2000)
66, 439
popular vote, (1996) 698, (2000) 699
primary votes, (1996) 402
Brownell, Herbert Jr.
Justice Dept. policy on campaign finance
violations, 112
Republican National Committee chair,
426 (table)
Browning, Gordon
governor, Tennessee, 1409
Browning, Orville H.
senator, Illinois, 1242
Brownlee, Traves
vice-presidential candidate
American Party nominee, (1984) 437
Brownlow, William G.
governor, Tennessee, 1409
senator, Tennessee, 1261
Brownson, Nathan
governor, Georgia, 1389
Broyhill, James T.
senator, North Carolina, 188, 1256
Bruce, Blanche K.
senator, Mississippi, 15, 24, 790,
1250
Bruce, William Cabell
senator, Maryland, 1247
Brucker, Wilber M.
governor, Michigan, 1397
Brumbaugh, Martin G.
governor, Pennsylvania, 1406
Republican convention ballots, (1916)
602
Brunsdale, C. Norman
governor, North Dakota, 1404
senator, North Dakota, 1256
Brust, Jean T.
vice-presidential candidate
Workers League Party nominee,
(1984) 437

Bryan, Charles W.
    biography, 776
    Democratic convention ballots, (1924)
        606–607
    governor, Nebraska, 1399
    vice-presidential candidate
        Democratic nominee, (1924) 260,
            433, 497
        electoral vote, (1924) 773
Bryan, George
    governor, Pennsylvania, 1406
Bryan, Nathan P.
    senator, Florida, 1240
Bryan, Richard H.
    governor, Nevada, 191, 1400
    senator, Nevada, 206, 1252
Bryan, William J.
    senator, Florida, 1240
Bryan, William Jennings
    biography, 776
    at Democratic convention, (1904) 255,
        482, (1912) 257, 487, (1916) 491, (1920)
        494, (1924) 496, 497
    political party development, 66–67, 253
    presidential candidate
        "Cross of Gold" speech, 254, 423, 478
        Democratic convention ballots,
            (1896) 595, (1900) 596, (1908) 598,
            (1912) 601, (1920) 605
        Democratic nominee, (1896) 75–76,
            248–249, 254, 264, 423 (box), 431,
            478, (1900) 254, 431, 480, (1908)
            255–256, 432, 484
        electoral vote, (1896) 745, (1900)
            746, (1908) 748
        National Silver Party nominee,
            (1896) 431
        political party development, 49
        popular vote, (1896) 662, 691, (1900)
            663, (1908) 665
        Populist nominee, (1896) 69, 431,
            (1908) 432
        primary votes, (1912) 321
        Silver Republican nominee, (1900)
            432
    as secretary of state, Seventeenth Amend-
        ment, 1231
    supports Wilson, (1916) 258
Bryant, ——
    Democratic convention ballots, (1968)
        622
Bryant, Farris
    governor, Florida, 1389
Bryce, J. S.
    Democratic convention officers, 415
        (table)
Bubar, Benjamin C.
    presidential candidate
        popular vote, (1976) 695, (1980) 696
        Prohibition Party nominee, (1976)
            437
        Statesman Party nominee, (1980)
            437
Buchanan, James
    biography, 776
    as moderate, 239
    presidential candidate
        cabinet service, 221
        Democratic contender, (1848) 238,
            448, (1852) 450
        Democratic convention ballots,
            (1844) 574, (1848) 575, (1852) 577,
            (1856) 579
        Democratic nominee, (1856) 57, 239,
            241, 430, 454–455
        election milestones, 15
        electoral vote, (1856) 735
        former members of Congress, 155
            (box)
        as "minority" president, 223 (table)
        political party development, 45
        popular vote, (1856) 652
        public offices, 214
    senator, Pennsylvania, 1259
Buchanan, John P.
    governor, Tennessee, 1409

Buchanan, Patrick J.
    presidential candidate
        campaign expenses, (2000) 93
        contested Florida votes, (2000) 299,
            300
        political party development, 50
        politics and issues, (1992) 196, (1996)
            200, (2000) 204–205
        popular vote, (2000) 688
        primary votes, (1992) 313 (box),
            386–393, 395–402
        Reform Party nominee, (2000) 73,
            212, 296, 301, 424 (box), 439
        Republican contender, (1992) 290–291,
            558–559, (1996) 293, 315, 561
        Republican convention ballots, (1992)
            637, (1996) 638
        U.S. Taxpayers feelers declined, 80
    at Republican convention, (1992) 292
Buchtel, Henry A.
    governor, Colorado, 1386
Buck, C. Douglass
    governor, Delaware, 1388
    senator, Delaware, 1240
Buckalew, Charles R.
    senator, Pennsylvania, 1258
Buckingham, William A.
    governor, Connecticut, 1387
    senator, Connecticut, 1238
Buckley, Charles
    presidential primary votes, (2000)
        404–410
Buckley, James L.
    senator, New York, 170, 179, 1255
        campaign finance law court case, 117
        political party development, 46, 55
Buckley v. Valeo, 86–87, 89, 98, 105–106,
    117–120
Buckley, William F., 55
Buckner, Alexander
    senator, Missouri, 1251
Buckner, Simon Bolivar
    governor, Kentucky, 1393
    vice-presidential candidate
        National Democratic nominee,
            (1896) 431
Buckson, David P.
    governor, Delaware, 1388
Budd, James H.
    governor, California, 1386
Budget policy
    Clinton administration issues, 198,
        199–200, 204
        federal government shutdown,
            (1995) 292–293
    platform issue
        Democrats, (1840) 445, (1844) 447,
            (1932) 503, (1936) 505, (1980) 546,
            (1984) 549, (1992) 557, (1996) 564,
            (2000) 567
        Green Party, (2000) 571
        Free Soilers, (1848) 449
        Republicans, (1932) 502, (1936) 504,
            (1964) 526, (1972) 536, (1980) 544,
            (1984) 551, (1992) 559, (1996) 562
    presidential campaign issue, (1984) 284,
        287, (1988) 286, (1996) 294
    Reagan administration issues, 184, 185,
        186, 188
Bulkeley, Joseph R.
    senator, Connecticut, 1239
Bulkeley, Morgan G.
    governor, Connecticut, 1380, 1387
Bulkley, Robert J.
    presidential primary votes, (1952)
        341–343
    senator, Ohio, 1257
Bull Moose Party. See Progressive Party
Bulloch, Archibald
    governor, Georgia, 1389
Bulloch, William B.
    senator, Georgia, 1241
Bullock, Alexander H.
    governor, Massachusetts, 1396
Bullock, Rufus Brown
    governor, Georgia, 1389

Bulow, William J.
    governor, South Dakota, 1408
    senator, South Dakota, 1261
Bumpers, Dale
    Democratic convention ballots, (1980)
        630
    governor, Arkansas, 1385
    senator, Arkansas, 175, 1237
Bundling of campaign contributions
    campaign finance controversies, 104
    definition, 85 (box)
Bunker, Berkeley L.
    senator, Nevada, 1252
Bunning, Jim
    senator, Kentucky, 203, 1245
Burch, Dean
    Republican National Committee chair,
        426 (table)
Burch, Thomas G.
    senator, Virginia, 1264
Burdick, Jocelyn B.
    senator, North Dakota, 1256
Burdick, Quentin N.
    senator, North Dakota, 1256
Burke, Andrew H.
    governor, North Dakota, 1404
Burke, Edward R.
    senator, Nebraska, 1252
Burke, John
    governor, North Dakota, 1404
    presidential primary votes, (1912) 320
    vice-presidential contender, 487
Burke, Stephen
    presidential primary votes, (1992)
        386–393
Burke, Thomas
    governor, North Carolina, 1403
Burke, Thomas A.
    senator, Ohio, 1257
Burke, Yvonne Brathwaite, 791
Burkett, Elmer J.
    senator, Nebraska, 1252
    Republican vice-presidential contender,
        (1916) 490
Burleigh, Edwin C.
    governor, Maine, 1394
    senator, Maine, 1247
Burnet, Jacob
    senator, Ohio, 1257
Burnett, Peter H.
    governor, California, 1386
Burney, Dwight W.
    governor, Nebraska, 1400
Burnham, Henry E.
    senator, New Hampshire, 1253
Burnquist, Joseph A. A.
    governor, Minnesota, 1397
Burns, Conrad
    senator, Montana, 191, 1251
Burns, Haydon
    governor, Florida, 1389
Burns, James MacGregor, 265
Burns, John A.
    governor, Hawaii, 159, 1390
Burnside, Ambrose E.
    in Civil War, 244
    governor, Rhode Island, 1407
    senator, Rhode Island, 1259
Burr, Aaron
    biography, 776
    political party development, 43, 228
    senator, New York, 1255
    vice-presidential candidate
        Democratic-Republican contender
            (1792) 226, (1796) 227, (1800) 228,
            312, (1804) 229
        election milestones, 14
        electoral anomalies, 12 (box)
        electoral vote, (1792) 719, (1796) 720,
            (1800) 721
        House election, (1800) 703, 706
            (box), 707–709
Burrill, James Jr.
    senator, Rhode Island, 1259
Burroughs, John
    governor, New Mexico, 1402

Burrows, Julius C.
    senator, Michigan, 1249
Bursum, Holm O.
    senator, New Mexico, 1254
Burton, Harold H.
    senator, Ohio, 1257
    Supreme Court justice, 818–819
Burton, Hutchins G.
    governor, North Carolina, 1403
Burton, Joseph R.
    senator, Kansas, 1244
Burton, Phillip, 825
Burton, Theodore E.
    presidential primary votes, (1916) 323
    Republican convention ballots, (1916)
        602
    Republican convention officers, 417
        (table)
    senator, Ohio, 1257
Burton, William
    governor, Delaware, 1388
Busbee, George
    governor, Georgia, 1390
Bush, Barbara, 287, 291
Bush, George H. W.
    biography, 776
    as president
        approval rating, 289
        campaign finance reform, 87, 122,
            123
        disability issue, 715
        economic policy, 192
        Persian Gulf war, 195
        turnover in Congress, 795
    presidential candidate
        appeal in South, (1988) 129
        campaign strategies, (1992) 213
        election evolution, 9, 10
        election milestones, 18, 20
        electoral vote, (1988) 768, (1992) 769
        former members of Congress, 155
            (box)
        former vice presidents, 224, 314
            (box)
        political party development, 48
        politics and issues, (1988) 177,
            190–191, (1992) 195–197
        popular vote, (1988) 685, (1992) 686
        primary votes, (1980) 314, (1980)
            365–371, (1988) 315, 378–385,
            (1992) 386–393
        public offices, 215
        reelection chances, 103, 213, 313
            (box)
        Republican contender, (1980) 182,
            283
        Republican convention ballots,
            (1980) 629, (1988) 635, (1992) 637
        Republican nominee, (1988) 77–78,
            286–289, 437, 554–555, (1992)
            289–292, 438, 558–559
        vice-presidential choice, 312
    at Republican convention, (1992) 412,
        (2000) 566
    Republican National Committee chair,
        426 (table)
    Senate defeat, (1970) 170
    as vice president, 312
        Reagan disability issue, 715
    vice-presidential candidate
        electoral vote, (1980, 1984) 773
        Republican nominee, (1980) 182,
            283, 437, 542–543, (1984) 186,
            285, 437, 550
        televised debates, (1980) 216
Bush, George W.
    biography, 776
    governor, Texas, 203, 1410
    as president
        campaign finance reform, 124 (box)
    presidential candidate
        appeal in South, suburbs (2000) 3,
            11, 129
        campaign finance, (2000) 90, 91, 93,
            210, 213
        campaign strategies, 216

election evolution, 11, 12–13, 19–20
electoral anomalies, 12 (box)
electoral vote, (2000) 771
Florida electors dispute, 135–136, 216, 219, 298–299 (box), 706 (box), 707, 712–713, 1557–1568
as former governor, 176 (box), 224, 1377
as "minority" president, 223 (table)
political party development, 48
politics and issues, (2000) 197, 203–206
popular vote, (2000) 688
primary votes, (2000) 210, 212, 305, 311 (box), 318, 404–410
public offices, 215
Republican convention ballots, (2000) 640
Republican nominee, (2000) 78, 295–301, 439, 566
Section 527 groups, (2000) 107
vice-presidential choice, 312
at Republican convention, (1988) 554
Delaware plan, (2000) 307
officers, 417 (table)
Republican Party nominating rules, 420
Bush, Jeb
Florida electoral vote, (2000) 205, 295
governor, Florida, 203, 1389
Bush, Laura, 566
Bush, Prescott
senator, Connecticut, 1239
Bush v. Gore, excepts, 1557–1568
Bushfield, Harlan J.
governor, South Dakota, 1408
Republican convention ballots, (1940) 613
senator, South Dakota, 1261
Bushfield, Vera C.
senator, South Dakota, 1261
Bushnell, Asa G.
governor, Ohio, 1405
Busiel, Charles A.
governor, New Hampshire, 1401
Business and industry. *See also* Monopoly and antitrust law
campaign contributions, 108–109, 111
in Goldwater campaign, (1964) 276
in Jacksonian politics, 234
in New Deal, 264
platform issues
Progressives, (1948) 515
Republicans, (1868) 246, (1916) 491
in Progressive era, 252–253
Republican dominance after 1876, 248
Butcher, James
governor, Maryland, 1395
Butler, Andrew P.
senator, South Carolina, 1260
Butler, Benjamin F.
biography, 776
at Democratic convention, (1884) 471
governor, Massachusetts, 1396
presidential candidate
Greenback, Anti-Monopoly nominee, (1884) 64, 431, 471
popular vote, (1884) 659
at Republican convention, (1860) 456
Republican leadership, 247
Butler, David
governor, Nebraska, 1399
Butler, Ezra
governor, Vermont, 1410
Butler, Hugh
senator, Nebraska, 1252
Butler, John Marshall
senator, Maryland, 143, 1247
Butler, Marion
senator, North Carolina, 1256
Butler, Matthew C.
senator, South Carolina, 1260
Butler, Nicholas Murray
biography, 776
Republican convention ballots, (1920) 604
vice-presidential candidate

electoral anomalies, 13 (box)
electoral vote, (1912) 773
Republican nominee, (1912) 425, 432, 709
Butler, Paul M.
Democratic National Committee chair, 151, 415 (table), 426 (table)
Butler, Pierce
senator, South Carolina, 1260
vice-presidential candidate
Democratic-Republican contender, (1796) 227
Butler, Pierce M.
governor, South Carolina, 1408
Butler, William M.
Republican National Committee chair, 417 (table), 426 (table)
senator, Massachusetts, 1248
Butler, William O.
biography, 776
Democratic convention ballots, (1848) 575, (1852) 577
vice-presidential candidate
Democratic nominee, (1848) 238, 429, 448
electoral vote, (1848) 772
"Butterfly" ballots, 299, 300
Byer, ——
presidential primary votes, (1948) 340
Byrd, Harry F.
biography, 776
governor, Virginia, 1411
presidential candidate
Democratic contender, (1932) 262, (1944) 509–510
Democratic convention ballots, (1932) 611, (1944) 614
electoral votes, (1960) 275, 761
faithless elector, (1960) 703 (box), 706 (box)
popular vote, (1956) 694
primary votes, (1944), 338
South Carolinians for Independent Electors nominee, (1956) 435
States' Rights Party of Kentucky nominee, (1956) 435
senator, Virginia, 1264
vice-presidential candidate
America First Party nominee, (1952) 434
Constitution Party nominee, (1952) 435
Byrd, Harry F. Jr.
senator, Virginia, 130, 170, 180, 1264
Byrd, Richard C.
governor, Arkansas, 1385
Byrd, Robert C.
campaign finance reform, 83, 102, 122
length of service in Congress, 795 (table)
presidential candidate
Democratic convention ballots, (1976) 627, (1980) 630
primary votes, (1976) 359–364
senator, West Virginia, 179, 1265
Senate leadership, 102, 179, 189, 193
Byrne, Brendan T.
governor, New Jersey, 1402
Byrne, Frank M.
governor, South Dakota, 1408
Byrnes, James F.
governor, South Carolina, 1408
Thurmond support, 131
senator, South Carolina, 1260
vice-presidential candidate
Democratic contender, (1944) 510
Wallace dismissal, 138
Byrnes, John W.
presidential primary votes, (1964) 348–350

C

Cabell, William H.
governor, Virginia, 1411
Cabot, George
senator, Massachusetts, 1248

Caffery, Donelson
presidential candidate
National Party nominee, (1900) 432
senator, Louisiana, 1246
Cahill, John P.
presidential primary votes, (1992) 386–393
Cahill, William T.
governor, New Jersey, 1402
Cain, Harry P.
senator, Washington, 1265
Calder, William M.
senator, New York, 1255
Caldwell, Alexander
senator, Kansas, 1244
Caldwell, Millard F.
governor, Florida, 1389
Caldwell, Tod R.
governor, North Carolina, 1403
Calhoun, John C.
biography, 776
Democratic convention ballots, (1844) 574, (1848) 575
feud with Jackson, 234
in Polk administration, 238
presidential candidate
Democratic-Republican contender, (1824) 232–233
senator, South Carolina, 1260
vice-presidential candidate
Democratic contender, (1832) 235
Democratic nominee, (1828) 234
Democratic-Republican nominee, (1824) 234
electoral vote, (1824, 1828) 772
California
admission to Union, 239, 240
Democratic convention credentials dispute, (1972) 422, 534, 535, 624
disputed House election, (1996) 804
House redistricting, 825
presidential primary calendar, 307 (box), 308, 419–420
women senators, 18
Call, Wilkinson
senator, Florida, 1240
Callaway, Howard, 166, 1380, 1390
Camden, Johnson N.
senator, West Virginia, 1265
Camden, Johnson N. Jr.
senator, Kentucky, 1245
Camejo, Peter
presidential candidate
popular vote, (1976) 695
Socialist Workers nominee, (1976) 436
Cameron, Angus
senator, Wisconsin, 1265, 1266
Cameron, J. Donald
Republican convention ballots, (1896) 594
Republican National Committee chair, 417 (table), 426 (table)
senator, Pennsylvania, 1259
Cameron, Ralph H.
senator, Arizona, 1237
Cameron, Simon
presidential candidate
convention ballots, (1860) 581
Republican contender, (1860) 458
Republican leadership, 247
senator, Pennsylvania, 1258, 1259
Cameron, William E.
governor, Virginia, 1411
Camp David accords (1978), 180
Campaign finance
controversial issues
bundling, 104
conversion to personal use, 121
coordinated expenditures, 106–107
Democratic scandal, 1996, 84–86
fund-raising, 101–102
high costs, 100–101
incumbent advantage, 102–103
independent expenditures, 106
issue advocacy ads, 105–106, 125

PAC influence, 103–104, 122, 124
soft money, 104–105, 125
summary, 83–84, 86, 100
expenditures
general expenses, 94, 99–100
media expenses, 94, 99, 113, 115–116
record spending, 100
spending by election year, 1980–2000 (figure) 101
FEC role (box), 119–120
glossary (box), 85
platform issue
Democrats, (1908) 485, (1924) 497, (1952) 517–518, (1996) 565, (2000) 570
Progressives, (1912) 489
Reform Party, (1996) 563
Republicans, (1908) 423 (box), (1912) 486, (1992) 559–560
reform proposals, 86–87, 107–108, 121–125
overhaul legislation (box) 124
presidential campaign issue, (1992) 292, (1996) 294, (2000) 87
regulation history
early legislation, 108–112
FECA reforms, 1970s, 112–121, 174, 282
Watergate effect, 114–116
sources
candidate's own money, 92–93, 98–99
contribution limits, 2001 (table) 95
individual contributions, 91, 95–96
limits, disclosure, 109, 113
national party soft money receipts (figure), 98
PACs, 93, 96–97, 103–104, 122
party contributions, 48, 92, 97–98
public funding, 88–91, 113, 121
Section 527 groups, 107, 125
Supreme Court decisions
Buckley v. Valeo, 18, 86–87, 89, 98, 105–106, 117–120
Burroughs and Cannon v. U.S., 110
Colorado I, 92, 106
Colorado II, 92, 97, 106–107
primary regulation, 109, 110
Campaign Financing Task Force (Justice Department), 84, 85
Campbell, Alexander
senator, Ohio, 1257
Campbell, Angus, 271
Campbell, Ben Nighthorse
senator, Colorado, 785, 795, 1238
Campbell, Carroll A. Jr.
governor, South Carolina, 189, 1408
Campbell, David
governor, Virginia, 1411
Campbell, George W.
senator, Tennessee, 1261
Campbell, Jack M.
governor, New Mexico, 1402
Campbell, James E.
Democratic convention ballots, (1892) 593, (1896) 595
governor, Ohio, 1405
Campbell, Thomas E.
governor, Arizona, 1385
Campbell, Thomas M.
governor, Texas, 1410
Campbell, William B.
governor, Tennessee, 1409
Candler, Allen D.
governor, Georgia, 1389
Cannon, Frank J.
senator, Utah, 1263
Cannon, Joseph G.
length of service in Congress, 795 (table)
Republican convention ballots, (1908) 599
Republican convention officers, 417 (table)
Cannon, Howard W.
senator, Nevada, 179, 1252

Cannon, Newton
  governor, Tennessee, 1409
Cannon, William
  governor, Delaware, 1388
Cantor, Joseph E., 90, 100–101, 104
Cantwell, Maria
  senator, Washington, 206, 787, 1265
Capalbo, Kenneth A.
  presidential primary votes, (2000)
    404–410
Capehart, Homer E.
  senator, Indiana, 158, 159, 1243
Caperton, Allen T.
  senator, West Virginia, 1265
Caperton, Gaston
  governor, West Virginia, 192, 1412
Capper, Arthur
  governor, Kansas, 1392
  Republican convention ballots, (1940)
    613
  senator, Kansas, 1244
    census count of aliens, 813
Capps, Lois, 39, 788
Capps, Walter, 788
Caraway, Hattie W.
  senator, Arkansas, 788, 1237
Caraway, Thaddeus H.
  senator, Arkansas, 1237
Cardozo, Benjamin N., 25–26, 818
Carey, Hugh L.
  Democratic convention ballots, (1980)
    630
  governor, New York, 181, 1403
Carey, Joseph M.
  governor, Wyoming, 1413
  senator, Wyoming, 1266
Carey, Robert D.
  governor, Wyoming, 1413
  senator, Wyoming, 1266
Cargo, David F.
  governor, New Mexico, 1402
Carlile, John S.
  senator, Virginia, 1264
Carlin, John
  governor, Kansas, 1392
Carlin, Thomas
  governor, Illinois, 1390
Carlisle, John G.
  Democratic convention ballots, (1884)
    591, (1892) 593
  senator, Kentucky, 1245
Carlson, Arne
  governor, Minnesota, 1397
Carlson, Frank
  governor, Kansas, 1392
  Republican convention ballots, (1968)
    622
  senator, Kansas, 1244
Carlson, George A.
  governor, Colorado, 1386
Carlson, Grace
  vice-presidential candidate
    Socialist Workers nominee, (1948)
      434
Carlson, William E.
  presidential primary votes, (1980)
    365–371
Carlton, Doyle E.
  governor, Florida, 1388
Carmack, Edward W.
  senator, Tennessee, 1262
Carmichael, James V., 131
Carnahan, Jean
  senator, Missouri, 13 (box), 788, 789,
    1251
Carnahan, Mel E.
  governor, Missouri, 1399
  Senate race, 13 (box), 206, 788
Carney, Thomas
  governor, Kansas, 1392
Carpenter, Cyrus
  governor, Iowa, 1391
Carpenter, Matthew H.
  senator, Wisconsin, 1265, 1266
Carper, Thomas R.
  governor, Delaware, 1388

  senator, Delaware, 1239
Carr, Elias
  governor, North Carolina, 1403
Carr, Ralph L.
  governor, Colorado, 1386
Carris, Alvin G.
  presidential primary votes, (1980)
    365–371
Carroll, Beryl F.
  governor, Iowa, 1392
Carroll, Charles
  senator, Maryland, 1247
Carroll, George W.
  vice-presidential candidate
    Prohibition nominee, (1904) 432
Carroll, John A.
  senator, Colorado, 1238
Carroll, John Lee
  governor, Maryland, 1395
Carroll, Julian
  governor, Kentucky, 1393
Carroll, Thomas King
  governor, Maryland, 1395
Carroll, William
  Democratic convention officers, 415
    (table)
  governor, Tennessee, 1409
Carruthers, Garrey E.
  governor, New Mexico, 1402
Carson, Julia, 792
Carter, Billy, 182
Carter, Jimmy
  biography, 776
  governor, Georgia, 1389
  as president
    campaign finance reform, 121
    election-day voter registration, 36
    electoral college reform, 713
    politics and issues, 176, 179–180,
      181
  presidential candidate
    binding rule for convention
      delegates, (1980) 306
    concession, (1980) 219
    Democratic convention ballots,
      (1976) 627, (1980) 630
    Democratic nominee, (1976)
      282–283, 421, 423 (box), 436,
      537–539, (1980) 283–284, 416,
      437, 544–545
    Democratic Party history, 60
    election evolution, 9, 10
    election milestones, 18
    electoral vote, (1976) 765, (1980) 766
    as former governor, 176 (box), 224,
      1377
    politics and issues, (1976) 177–178,
      (1980) 182–183
    popular vote, (1976) 682, (1980) 683
    primary votes, (1976) 308, 310 (box),
      359–364, (1980) 314, 365–371
    public offices, 215
    reelection chances, 103, 213, 313
      (box)
    televised debates, (1976) 216
Carter, Reginald
  vice-presidential candidate
    Independent Afro-American nomi-
      nee, (1960) 435
Carter, Thomas H.
  Republican National Committee chair,
    417 (table), 426 (table)
  senator, Montana, 1251
Carter, Willie Felix
  presidential primary votes, (1996) 403,
    (2000) 404–410
Carvel, Elbert N.
  governor, Delaware, 1388
Carville, Edward P.
  governor, Nevada, 1400
  senator, Nevada, 1252
Carville, James, 290, 292
Cary, Samuel Fenton
  vice-presidential candidate
    Greenback Party nominee, (1876)
      430

Casamassima, Sal
  presidential primary votes, (1996)
    395–402
Case, Clarence E.
  governor, New Jersey, 1402
Case, Clifford P.
  Republican convention ballots, (1968)
    622
  senator, New Jersey, 146, 1254
Case, Francis
  senator, South Dakota, 1261
Case, Norman S.
  governor, Rhode Island, 1407
Casey, Lyman R.
  senator, North Dakota, 1256
Casey, Robert P.
  Democratic convention ballots, (1992)
    636
  governor, Pennsylvania, 189, 1406
Cass, Lewis
  biography, 776
  presidential candidate
    convention ballots, (1844) 574,
      (1848) 575, (1852) 577, (1856) 579
    Democratic contender, (1844) 447,
      (1852) 450
    Democratic nominee, (1848) 238,
      429, 448
    electoral vote, (1848) 733
    political party development, 45, 49
    popular vote, (1848) 650
    Senate service, 223
  senator, Michigan, 1249
Casserly, Eugene
  senator, California, 1237
Castle, Michael N.
  governor, Delaware, 1388
Castro, Raul
  governor, Arizona, 1377, 1385
Caswell, Richard
  governor, North Carolina, 1403
Cathcart, Charles W.
  senator, Indiana, 1243
Catholic candidates
  Kennedy, (1960) 154, 273–274, 275, 313
  members of Congress, 787
  Smith, (1928) 261
Catholic voters
  in Kennedy campaign, 154, 274, 276
  in New Deal coalition, 264
  regional party shifts, 805–805
Catron, Thomas B.
  senator, New Mexico, 1254
Cattell, Alexander G.
  senator, New Jersey, 1254
Catts, Sidney J.
  governor, Florida, 1388
Caucus system
  of convention delegate selection, 310–311
    (box), 413
    voter turnout, 309
  of presidential nomination by Congress,
    14, 48, 221, 225, 227–233, 307
Caulfield, Henry S.
  governor, Missouri, 1399
Causey, Peter F.
  governor, Delaware, 1388
Cayetano, Benjamin J.
  governor, Hawaii, 1390
Ceasar, James W., 236
Celeste, Richard F.
  governor, Ohio, 1405
Celler, Emanuel
  House redistricting, 826
  length of service in Congress, 795 (table)
Cellucci, Argeo "Paul"
  governor, Massachusetts, 1396
Census basis of House apportionment, 807,
  811–815, 820–821 (box)
Central America
  platform issue
    Democrats, (1984) 550, (1988) 552
    Republicans, (1980) 544, (1984) 551
Central American Canal
  Democratic platform issue, (1892) 475
  Republican platform issue, (1892) 474

Chace, Jonathan
  senator, Rhode Island, 1259
Chad, 218, 299
Chadwick, Stephen F.
  governor, Oregon, 1405
Chafee, John H.
  governor, Rhode Island, 169, 1407
  senator, Rhode Island, 162–163, 179,
    1259
Chafee, Lincoln D.
  senator, Rhode Island, 1259
Chafee, Zechariah Jr., 812
Chaffee, Jerome B.
  senator, Colorado, 1238
Chafin, Eugene Wilder
  presidential candidate
    popular vote, (1908) 665, (1912)
      691–692
    Prohibition nominee, (1908, 1912)
      432
Chalmers, Joseph W.
  senator, Mississippi, 1250
Chamberlain, Abiram
  governor, Connecticut, 1387
Chamberlain, Daniel H.
  on compromise of 1876, 248
  governor, South Carolina, 1408
Chamberlain, George E.
  governor, Oregon, 1405
  senator, Oregon, 1258
  popular election, 1231
Chamberlain, Joshua L.
  governor, Maine, 1394
Chambers, Benjamin J.
  vice-presidential candidate
    Greenback Party nominee, (1880)
      431, 468
Chambers, Ezekiel
  senator, Maryland, 1247
Chambers, Henry H.
  senator, Alabama, 1236
Chambers, Whittaker, 139
Champlin, Christopher G.
  senator, Rhode Island, 1259
Chandler, Albert B.
  Democratic convention ballots, (1956)
    619
  governor, Kentucky, 1393
  senator, Kentucky, 1245
Chandler, Connie
  vice-presidential candidate
    Independent Party of Utah nominee,
      (1996) 439
Chandler, John
  senator, Maine, 1247
Chandler, William E.
  senator, New Hampshire, 1253
Chandler, Zachariah
  Republican leadership, 247
  Republican National Committee chair,
    426 (table)
  senator, Michigan, 1249
Chapman, John G.
  Whig convention officers, 425 (box)
Chapman, Reuben
  governor, Alabama, 1384
Chapman, Virgil
  senator, Kentucky, 1245
Chappell, Bill Jr., 191
Chapple, John Bowman
  presidential primary votes, (1956) 345
Charlton, Robert M.
  senator, Georgia, 1241
Chase, Dudley
  senator, Vermont, 1263
Chase, Ira Joy
  governor, Indiana, 1391
Chase, Salmon P.
  governor, Ohio, 1404
  in Johnson impeachment, 246
  political party development, 45, 57
    as Free Soiler, 449
  Republican leadership, 74, 247
  presidential candidate
    convention ballots, (1860) 581
    Democratic possibility, (1868) 246

Liberal Republican contender, (1872) 247
Republican contender, (1856) 453, (1860) 458, (1864) 243, 459
senator, Ohio, 1257
Chase, Samuel, 43
Chassee, Leo J.
presidential primary votes, (1932) 332, (1936) 334
Chatterton, Fenimore C.
governor, Wyoming, 1413
Chavez, Cesar
Democratic convention ballots, (1976) 627
Chavez, Dennis
senator, New Mexico, 792, 1254
Chavez, Ventura
presidential popular vote, (1968) 695
Cheeseborough, E.
presidential popular vote, (1864) 690
Cheney, Person C.
governor, New Hampshire, 1401
senator, New Hampshire, 1253
Cheney, Richard B.
biography, 776
as vice president, 796, 1234
election milestones, 20
vice-presidential candidate
electoral vote, (2000) 773
politics and issues, (2000) 204, 205
Republican nominee, (2000) 296, 298 (box), 312, 439, 566
televised debates, 216
Cherry, Frances A.
governor, Arkansas, 1385
Cherry, R. Gregg
governor, North Carolina, 1403
Chester, Eric
vice-presidential candidate
Socialist nominee, (1996) 439
Chestnut, James Jr.
senator, South Carolina, 1260
Chicago Tribune headline, 270, 271
Chilcott, George N.
senator, Colorado, 1238
Chiles, Lawton
governor, Florida, 1389
senator, Florida, 191, 1240
Chilton, Horace
senator, Texas, 1262
Chilton, William E.
senator, West Virginia, 1265
Chimento, Carmen C.
presidential primary votes, (1996) 403
China
campaign finance scandal, 1996, 84
Nixon policies, 171
platform issue
Democrats, (1968) 532
Republicans, (1968) 530
politics and issues, 147
presidential campaign issue, (1952) 142, 272, (1960) 275
U.S. diplomatic relations, 180, 281
Chinese Exclusion Act of 1882, 250
Chinese immigration
platform issue
Democrats, (1880) 470, (1884) 471
Greenback Party, (1880) 469
Republicans, (1880) 468, (1884) 470
Chipman, Nathaniel
senator, Vermont, 1263
Chittenden, Martin
governor, Vermont, 1410
Chittenden, Thomas
governor, Vermont, 1410
Choate, Pat
vice-presidential candidate
Reform Party nominee, (1996) 73, 439
Choate, Rufus
on Jackson victory, 235
senator, Massachusetts, 1248
Chomsky, Noam, 80
Chisholm, Shirley
black women in Congress, 60, 790, 791

election milestones, 18
Liberal Party support, 65
presidential candidate
Democratic contender, (1972) 171
Democratic convention ballots, (1972) 535, 625
primary votes, (1972) 354–358
Christensen, Donna M. C., 791
Christensen, Parley Parker
presidential candidate
Farmer Labor nominee, (1920) 432
popular vote, (1920) 668
Christian Coalition, 292
Christian National Party
nominees, (1956) 435
Christian Nationalist Party
nominees, (1948) 434
Christian Socialists, 78
Christianson, Theodore
governor, Minnesota, 1397
Christopher, Warren N., 300
Christopherson, Charles A.
presidential primary votes, (1944) 337–338
Church, Frank
Democratic convention officers, speakers, 415 (table)
presidential candidate
Democratic contender, (1976) 282
Democratic convention ballots, (1976) 627
primary votes, (1976) 359–364
senator, Idaho, 149, 183, 1242
vice-presidential contender, (1976) 539
Church, Sanford E.
Democratic convention ballots, (1868) 584
Church of God Party
nominees, (1952) 434
Churchill, Thomas J.
governor, Arkansas, 1385
Churchill, Winston, 267, 268
Cilley, Joseph
senator, New Hampshire, 1253
Citizens for Better Medicare, 106
Citizens Party
historical development
profile, 54
timeline, 47
nominees, (1980, 1984) 437
Civil rights. See also African American voting rights
Dixiecrat resistance, 269
Kennedy-Johnson years, 136, 159–160, 276
platform issues
Democrats, (1884) 471, (1944) 268, 510, (1948) 423 (box), 512–513, 616, (1952) 517, (1956) 148, 519, 520, (1960) 522, 523, (1964) 423 (box), 528, (1976) 539, (1992) 557–558
Dixiecrats, (1948) 514
Green Party, (2000) 571
Liberal Republicans, (1872) 463
Progressives, (1948) 514
Republicans, (1872) 464, (1944) 509, (1948) 511, (1952) 516, (1956) 520, 521, (1960) 523, 524, (1964) 525–526, 621, (1976) 541
presidential campaign issue, (1948) 139–141, 269, 270, (1964) 276
school desegregation, 145–146, 149
Civil Rights Act of 1866, 246
Civil Rights Act of 1957, 26, 151
Civil Rights Act of 1964, 17, 26, 136, 160, 162, 276
Civil service. See Federal employees
Civil Service Reform Act of 1883, 108
Civil Service Reform Commission, 247
Civil War, 242–245
Democratic, Republican platform issue, (1864) 459–460
military service of nominees, 222
Claflin, William
governor, Massachusetts, 1396

Republican National Committee chair, 417 (table), 426 (table)
Claiborne, Clement Jr.
senator, Alabama, 1236
Claiborne, William C. C.
governor, Louisiana, 1393
senator, Louisiana, 1246
Clapp, Moses E.
senator, Minnesota, 1249
Clark, ——
Democratic convention ballots, (1972) 625
Clark, Alonzo M.
governor, Wyoming, 1413
Clark, Barzilla W.
governor, Idaho, 1390
Clark, Charles
governor, Mississippi, 1398
Clark, Chase A.
governor, Idaho, 1390
Clark, Clarence D.
senator, Wyoming, 1266
Clark, D. Worth
senator, Idaho, 1242
Clark, Daniel
senator, New Hampshire, 1253
Clark, Dick
senator, Iowa, 172, 181, 1244
Clark, Edward
governor, Texas, 1409
Clark, Edward E.
presidential candidate
Libertarian nominee, (1980) 66, 437
popular vote, (1980) 683
Clark, Henry T.
governor, North Carolina, 1403
Clark, J. Bennett Champ
senator, Missouri, 1251
Clark, James
governor, Kentucky, 1392
Clark, James Beauchamp "Champ"
Democratic convention officers, 415 (table)
presidential candidate
Democratic contender, (1912) 256–257, 421 (box), 487
Democratic convention ballots, (1912) 601, (1920) 605
primary votes, (1912) 311, 320–321
Clark, John
governor, Delaware, 1388
Clark, John
governor, Georgia, 1389
Clark, Joseph S.
Democratic platform, (1964) 527
senator, Pennsylvania, 149, 1259
Clark, Myron H.
governor, New York, 1402
Clark, William A.
senator, Montana, 1251
Clarke, George W.
governor, Iowa, 1392
Clarke, James P.
governor, Arkansas, 1385
senator, Arkansas, 1237
Clarke, John H.
senator, Rhode Island, 1259
Clarkson, James S.
Republican National Committee chair, 417 (table), 426 (table)
Clauson, Clinton A.
governor, Maine, 1394
Clay, Alexander S.
senator, Georgia, 1241
Clay, Cassius M., 458, 581
Clay, Clement Comer
governor, Alabama, 1384
senator, Alabama, 1236
Clay, Henry
biography, 776
Compromise of 1850, 239, 240
in House election of president, (1824) 233, 709
political party development, 44–45

Jackson opposition, 56, 80–81
Tyler opposition, 237
presidential candidate
Anti-Mason nomination declined, (1832) 442
convention ballots, (1844) 575, (1848) 576
Democratic-Republican contender, (1824) 56, 232–233
electoral anomalies, 12 (box)
electoral vote, (1824) 727, (1832) 729, (1844) 732
National Republican nominee, (1832) 14, 81, 67, 235, 429, 442
popular vote, (1824) 644, (1832) 646, (1844) 649, (1848) 690
Senate service, 223
Whig contender, (1840) 237, 444, (1848) 238, 449
Whig nominee, (1844) 81, 238, 429, 446
senator, Kentucky, 1244, 1245
Senate-House shifts, 796
vice-presidential electoral vote, (1824) 772
Clay, William L., 791
Clay, William Lacy Jr., 792
Clayton, Henry D.
Democratic convention officers, 415 (table)
Clayton, John M.
senator, Delaware, 1239
Whig convention ballots, (1848) 576
Clayton, Joshua
governor, Delaware, 1387
senator, Delaware, 1239
Clayton, Powell
governor, Arkansas, 1385
Republican convention officers, (1884) 470, 590
senator, Arkansas, 1237
Clayton, Thomas
senator, Delaware, 1239
Clayton Anti-Trust Act of 1914, 257
Clean Politics Act of 1939, 110
Cleaver, Elbridge
presidential candidate
Peace and Freedom Party nominee, (1968) 68, 436
popular vote, (1968) 694
Cleaves, Henry B.
governor, Maine, 1394
Clegg, Billy Joe
presidential primary votes, (1976) 364, (1992) 393, (1996) 403
Cleland, Max
senator, Georgia, 200–201, 1241
Clemens, Jeremiah
senator, Alabama, 1236
Clemenson, Vernon
presidential primary votes, (1996) 395–402
Clement, Frank G.
Democratic convention officers, speakers, 415 (table)
governor, Tennessee, 1409
Clement, Percival W.
governor, Vermont, 1411
Clements, Earle C.
governor, Kentucky, 1393
senator, Kentucky, 1245
Clements, William P.
governor, Texas, 181, 1410
Cleveland, Chauncey F.
governor, Connecticut, 1387
Cleveland, Grover
biography, 776
at Democratic convention, platform, (1896) 254, 423
governor, New York, 1403
political party development, 46, 57
as president
labor, monetary policies, 253
presidential candidate
Democratic convention ballots, (1884) 591, (1892) 593

Democratic nominee, (1884) 250–251, 431, 471, (1888) 251–252, 296, 431, 472, (1892) 252, 431, 475
election evolution, 6, 15
electoral anomalies, 12 (box)
electoral vote, (1884) 742, (1888) 743, (1892) 702 (box), 744
as former governor, 176 (box), 1377
fourth campaign possibility, (1904) 255
as "minority" president, 223 (table)
New York background, 222
popular vote, (1884) 659, (1888) 660, (1892) 661
public offices, 215
support of Mugwump Republicans, (1884) 75
Clifford, Clark, 270
Clifford, John H.
governor, Massachusetts, 1396
Clingman, Thomas L.
senator, North Carolina, 1256
Clinton, Bill
biography, 776
at Democratic convention, (1988) 553, (2000) 568
Democratic Party history, 60–61
governor, Arkansas, 1385
as president
campaign finance reform, 123
census procedures, 821 (box)
congressional relations, 292–293
impeachment, 78, 135, 197, 201–202, 203
midterm elections, (1998) 106
reinventing government, 134
party control of House, 805
politics and issues, 198–201, 203–204
on racial redistricting, 30
role in 2000 campaign, 205, 216, 297–298
"triangulation" strategy, 294
turnover in Congress, 795–796
presidential candidate
appeal in South, (1992, 1996) 129
campaign finance, (1996) 84–85, 94, 101, 102
campaign strategies, (1992) 213
"character" issues, (1992) 290, 292, (1996) 294, 295
Democratic convention ballots, (1992) 636, (1996) 210, 639
Democratic nominee, (1992) 289, 290–292, 438, 556–557, (1996) 294–295, 439, 563–564
election evolution, 10–11, 12, 18–19
electoral anomalies, 12 (box)
electoral vote, (1992) 769, (1996) 770
as former governor, 176 (box), 224, 1377
as "minority" president, 223 (table)
politics and issues, (1992) 195–197, (1996) 200
popular vote, (1992) 686, (1996) 687
primary votes, (1992) 210, 309, 386–393, (1996) 315, 395–402
public offices, 215
reelection chances, 313 (box)
vice-presidential choice, 312
Clinton, DeWitt
biography, 776
governor, New York, 1402
presidential candidate
electoral vote, (1812) 724
Federalist nominee, (1812) 230–231
senator, New York, 1255
Clinton, George
biography, 776
governor, New York, 1402
presidential candidate
contender, (1789) 226, (1808) 230
electoral vote, (1789) 718, (1792) 719, (1796) 720, (1808) 723
vice-presidential candidate

Democratic-Republican nominee, (1789) 226, (1804) 229, (1808) 230
electoral vote, (1804, 1808) 772
Clinton, Hillary Rodham
at Democratic convention, (1996) 564
health care overhaul, 60, 198
senator, New York, 61, 203, 206, 301, 787, 797, 1255
campaign spending, 100, 1233
election evolution, 13, 13 (box), 20
Liberal Party support, 65
"60 Minutes" appearance, (1992) 290
Closed primaries, 306 (box)
Clough, David M.
governor, Minnesota, 1397
Clyde, George Dewey
governor, Utah, 1410
Coats, Daniel R.
senator, Indiana, 1243
Cobb, Howell
governor, Georgia, 1389
Cobb, Rufus W.
governor, Alabama, 1384
Cobb, Thomas W.
senator, Georgia, 1241
Cobb, William T.
governor, Maine, 1394
Cobey, Bill, 189
Coburn, Abner
governor, Maine, 1394
Cochran, Charles W.
governor, Nebraska, 1399
Cochran, John P.
governor, Delaware, 1388
Cochran, Thad
senator, Mississippi, 129, 180, 187, 1250
campaign finance reform, 124 (box), 125
Cochrane, John
vice-presidential candidate
Independent Republican nominee, (1864) 430
Cocke, William
senator, Tennessee, 1261
Cockran, William Bourke, 89
Cockrell, Francis M.
presidential candidate
Democratic contender, (1904) 482
Democratic convention ballots, (1904) 597
senator, Missouri, 1251
Coelho, Tony, 96, 192–193
Coffin, Lorenzo S.
vice-presidential candidate
United Christian Party nominee, (1908) 432
Coffin, O. Vincent
governor, Connecticut, 1387
Cohen, John S.
senator, Georgia, 1241
Cohen, William S.
senator, Maine, 181, 1247
Coiner, C. Benton
presidential candidate
Conservative Party of Virginia nominee, (1960) 435
popular vote, (1960) 694
Coin's Financial School, 254
Coke, Richard
governor, Texas, 1410
senator, Texas, 1262
Colby, Anthony
governor, New Hampshire, 1400
Colby, Bainbridge
Democratic convention ballots, (1920) 605
Nineteenth Amendment, 33
Colcord, Roswell K.
governor, Nevada, 1400
Cold war. See Communism
Cole, Cornelius
senator, California, 1238
Colegrove, Kenneth, 818
Coleman, J. P.
governor, Mississippi, 1398

Coler, Bird S.
Democratic convention ballots, (1904) 597
Coles, Edward
governor, Illinois, 1390
Colfax, Schuyler
biography, 776
Credit Mobilier scandal, 247
vice-presidential candidate
electoral vote, (1868) 772
Republican contender, (1872) 464
Republican nominee, (1868) 246, 430, 461
Colhoun, John E.
senator, South Carolina, 1260
Coll, Edward T.
presidential primary votes, (1972) 358
Collamer, Jacob
Republican convention ballots, (1860) 581
senator, Vermont, 1263
College Democrats, 418
Collier, Henry W.
governor, Alabama, 1384
Collier, John A.
Whig convention officers, 425 (box)
Collins, Barbara-Rose, 791
Collins, Cardiss, 791
Collins, Charles E.
independent presidential candidate, (1996) 439
popular vote, (1996) 699
primary votes, (1996) 395–402
Collins, John
governor, Delaware, 1388
Collins, John
governor, Rhode Island, 1406
Collins, George W., 791
Collins, LeRoy
Democratic convention officers, 415 (table)
governor, Florida, 1389
Collins, Martha Layne
Democratic convention officers, 415 (table)
governor, Kentucky, 1393
Collins, Patrick A.
Democratic convention officers, 415 (table)
Collins, Susan
senator, Maine, 200, 789, 1247
Collins, Thomas
governor, Delaware, 1387
Colmer, William M., 803
Colorado
term limits, 794 (box)
Colored Farmers' National Alliance, 69
Colquitt, Alfred H.
biography, 776
governor, Georgia, 1389
senator, Georgia, 1241
vice-presidential electoral vote, (1872) 772
Colquitt, Oscar B.
governor, Texas, 1410
Colquitt, Walter T.
senator, Georgia, 1241
Colt, LeBaron B.
senator, Rhode Island, 1260
Colvin, David Leigh
presidential candidate
popular vote, (1936) 693
Prohibition Party nominee, (1936) 434
vice-presidential candidate
Prohibition Party nominee, (1920) 433
Colvin, John
vice-presidential candidate
Industrial Reform Party nominee, (1888) 431
Combs, Bert T.
governor, Kentucky, 1393
Comegys, Cornelius P.
governor, Delaware, 1388

Comegys, Joseph P.
senator, Delaware, 1240
Comer, Braxton B.
governor, Alabama, 1384
senator, Alabama, 1236
Commission on Presidential Debates, 216
Common Cause, 86, 104, 113, 114, 115, 119 (box), 122
Commoner, Barry
presidential candidate
Citizens Party nominee, (1980) 54, 437
popular vote, (1980) 696
Commonwealth Land Party
nominees, (1924) 433
Communism. See also Communist Party; Soviet Union
cold war, 133–134, 141–142, 143, 145, 147
congressional investigations, 139, 142, 143, 144, 145, 146
platform issue
Democrats, (1948) 513, (1964) 528
Progressives, (1948) 514
Republicans, (1948) 511–512, (1952) 516, (1964) 525
presidential campaign issue, (1948) 71, 140, 141, 270, (1952) 272, (1956) 273
Communist Party
historical development, 46
profile, 55–56
relation to other parties, 71, 78, 79, 80
timeline, 47
nominees, (1924–40) 433–434, (1968–84) 436–437
Wallace endorsement, (1948) 71
Compromise of 1850, 239, 240, 451, 452
Compton, ——
presidential primary votes, (1952) 343
Comstock, William A.
governor, Michigan, 1397
Conant, John A.
vice-presidential candidate
American Prohibition Party nominee, (1884) 431
Condit, John
senator, New Jersey, 1253, 1254
Cone, Frederick P.
governor, Florida, 1388
Confederate States of America
Davis as president (box), 244
1860 election aftermath, 242–243
Conference of Progressive Political Action, 70, 497
Conger, Omar D.
senator, Michigan, 1249
Congress, Richard
presidential candidate
popular vote, (1980) 696
Socialist Workers nominee, (1980) 437
Congress, members of. See also Congressional elections
African Americans, 790–792
characteristics, 800
age, 786
occupation, 786–787
religious affiliation, 787
future presidents (box), 155
Hispanics, 792–793
marriages, 788
qualifications, 18
seniority system reforms, 282
service records (table), 795
shifts between chambers, 796–797
term limits, 19, 194, 794 (box)
turnover, 793–796
women, 33, 787–790
Congress, U.S. See also Congress, members of; Congressional districts; Congressional elections; House of Representatives, U.S.; Senate, U.S.
constitutional basis, 14
"Do-Nothing Eightieth" (box), 141
election of president, vice president, 707

caucus nominations, 14, 48, 221, 225, 227–233, 307
electoral vote count, 220, 710–713
in presidential disability, succession, 707, 714–715
public opinion of, 785, 800
sessions, 1789–2000, 1578–1587
Congress of Industrial Organizations
congressional elections (1946), 138
political action committee, 96
Socialist Party influence, 78
Congressional Black Caucus, 299 (box), 301, 713
Congressional districts. *See also* Apportionment of the House of Representatives; Redistricting
at-large districts, 815
constitutional basis, 807, 815, 822
electoral college evolution, reform, 706 (box), 714
majority-minority districts, 29–30, 792, 825–826
gerrymanders
origins, 817 (box)
partisan gerrymanders, 807, 824–825
racial gerrymanders, 807–808, 825–826
types, 819 (box)
multimember districts, 802
Congressional elections. *See also* House elections; Senate elections
campaign expenses, 99–101
record high costs, 100
campaign finance regulation history, 109–110
campaign funding, 94–95, 101–102
candidate's own money, 98–99
individual contributions, 95–96
party aid, 97–98
political action committees, 96–97
public funding proposal, 107, 121, 122
soft money, 105
election results, Congress and the presidency, 1860–2000, 1569–1571
electoral oddities, 13 (box)
evolution, 6–14
milestones, 14–20
incumbent's advantage
frank, 122
fund-raising, 96, 102–103
House-Senate disparity, 1234
winning percentages, 1946–2000 (figure), 103
partisan swings, 9–10
politics and issues, 1945–2000, 133–206
president's coattails, 9
southern primaries, 129–132
summary, 5
voter turnout, 21–23
Conkling, Roscoe
on Blaine, 250
presidential candidate
Republican contender, (1876) 465
Republican convention ballots, (1876) 586
at Republican convention, (1880) 467–468
Republican leadership, 247
senator, New York, 1255
Conley, Benjamin
governor, Georgia, 1389
Conley, Paul B.
presidential primary votes, (1988) 378–385, (1992) 393
Conley, William G.
governor, West Virginia, 1412
Connally, John B.
at Democratic convention, (1968) 422, 531
governor, Texas, 159, 1410
presidential candidate
campaign finance, (1980) 90
primary votes, (1980) 365–371
Republican contender, (1980) 182
Connally, Tom
senator, Texas, 1262

Connecticut
gubernatorial elections, 1380
Conner, Martin Sennett
governor, Mississippi, 1398
Conness, John
senator, California, 1237
Connor, Selden
governor, Maine, 1394
Conover, Simon B.
senator, Florida, 1240
Conrad, Charles M.
senator, Louisiana, 1246
Conrad, Kent
senator, North Dakota, 1256
Conrad, Robert, 85
Conservation of natural resources
New Deal, 263
Progressive era reforms, 255, 256, 257
Conservative Caucus, 80
Conservative Party
historical development, 46
profile, 55
Conservative Party of New Jersey
nominees, (1960) 435
"Conscience Whigs," 239
Constitution, U.S. *See also specific amendments*
on Congress
Great Compromise, 14
House, 799, 801
House apportionment, districts, 13 (box), 802, 807, 808–809
Senate, 1229–1232
interpretation as party platform issue
American Independents, (1968) 533
Democrats, (1840) 445, (1888) 472, (1892) 475, (1896) 479, (1936) 505, (1964) 528, (1972) 535–536
Free Soilers, (1852) 452
Republicans, (1880) 468, (1964) 526
Whigs, (1852) 451
and political parties, 43, 236
on president
disability, 714
election by Congress, 707
election provisions (text), 1545–1547
electoral vote, 220, 701–703, 710
requirements, 209
voting rights, 21, 220
House, Senate elections (box), 30–31
presidential elections, 225–226, 228
Constitution Party
nominees, (1952, 1956) 435, (1964, 1968) 436
Constitution Party
historical profile, 80
nominees, (2000) 439
Constitution Party (Texas)
nominees, (1960) 435
Constitution Party (Washington)
nominees, (1960) 435
Constitutional Union Party
convention, (1860) 458–459
historical development, 45
profile, 55
timeline, 47
nominees, (1860) 430
presidential election chronology, 241, 242
vote percentage, 424 (box)
Consumer Party
nominees, (1988) 438
Continental Party
nominees, (1904) 432
"Contract with America"
election evolution, 10–11, 19
enactment, 199
politics and issues, (1994) 197, 198
term limits, 194
Conventions, national
call, 412
candidate appearances, 262
costs, financing, 411
public funding, 90, 92
credentials disputes, 420–421
notable fights (box), 422
delegate selection, 412–413
numbers, 1932–2000 (figure), 413

presidential primaries, 414–415
highlights, 1831–2000 (table), 428
historical chronology, 1831–2000, 441–571
key ballots, 571–641
location, 411–412
sites, 1832–2000 (table), 412
media relations, 425–427
officers, 421
origins, 234–235
platform adoption, 421–424
major fights (box), 423
political party development, 48
relation to presidential primaries, 305–318
role in modern elections, 209, 212, 411
rules, 421
two-thirds rule (box), 421
vice-presidential choice, 312
Converse, Julius
governor, Vermont, 1410
Conway, Elias N.
governor, Arkansas, 1385
Conway, James S.
governor, Arkansas, 1385
Cony, Samuel
governor, Maine, 1394
Conyers, John Jr., 791
Cook, John
governor, Delaware, 1387
Cook, Marlow W.
senator, Kentucky, 169, 175, 1245
Cook, Rhodes, 61, 297, 301
Cooke, Jay, 89
Cooke, Lorrin A.
governor, Connecticut, 1387
Cooke, Nicholas
governor, Rhode Island, 1406
Coolidge, Calvin
biography, 776
governor, Massachusetts, 1396
as president
election milestones, 16
Harding administration scandals, 260
House reapportionment, 813
tax policies, 258
presidential candidate
electoral vote, (1924) 752
as former governor, 176 (box), 223, 1377
as former vice president, 314 (box)
primary votes, (1924) 327–328, (1928) 329–330
popular vote, (1924) 669
public offices, 215
reelection chances, 313 (box)
Republican convention ballots, (1920) 604, (1924) 608, (1928) 609, (1932) 610
Republican nominee, (1924) 260, 433, 495
Republican noncontender, (1928) 260, 498, (1932) 501
vice-presidential candidate
electoral vote, (1920) 773
Republican nominee, (1920) 259, 432, 493
Coolidge, Carlos
governor, Vermont, 1410
Coolidge, Marcus A.
senator, Massachusetts, 1248
Cooney, Frank H.
governor, Montana, 1399
Cooper, Edward M.
vice-presidential candidate
Prohibition Party nominee, (1956) 435
Cooper, Henry
senator, Tennessee, 1262
Cooper, James
senator, Pennsylvania, 1259
Cooper, Job A.
governor, Colorado, 1386
Cooper, John Sherman
senator, Kentucky, 172, 1245

Cooper, Myers Y.
governor, Ohio, 1405
Cooper, Peter
presidential candidate
Greenback Party nominee, (1876) 63, 430
popular vote, (1876) 657
Cooper, Prentice
governor, Tennessee, 1409
Cooper, Robert A.
governor, South Carolina, 1408
Cooper, William, 62
Cooper, William B.
governor, Delaware, 1388
Coordinated campaign expenses, 92, 97, 106–107
Copeland, Royal S.
senator, New York, 1255
Copperhead faction (Democrats), 460
Corbett, Henry W.
senator, Oregon, 1258
Cordon, Guy
senator, Oregon, 1258
Cornell, Alonzo B.
governor, New York, 1403
Cornell, Robert J., 787
Cornwell, John J.
governor, West Virginia, 1412
Corrado, Anthony, 94, 105
Corregan, Charles Hunter
presidential candidate
popular vote, (1904) 691
Socialist Labor nominee, (1904) 432
Corruption
Agnew resignation, 173, 281
Credit Mobilier scandal, 247
Democratic campaign finance scandal, (1996) 84–86
Keating Five scandal, 87
Liberal Republicans, (1872) 65, 247–248, 463
Nixon allegations, (1952) 144, 272
platform issue
Democrats, (1924) 497
Republicans, (1924) 496
Teapot Dome scandal, 86, 109, 260
Watergate scandal, 86, 281
Cortelyou, George B.
Republican National Committee chair, 426 (table)
Corwin, Thomas
governor, Ohio, 1404
senator, Ohio, 1257
Corzine, Jon
senator, New Jersey, 1254
campaign spending, 99, 1233
Cosgrove, Samuel G.
governor, Washington, 1412
Costigan, Edward P.
senator, Colorado, 1238
Cotton, Norris
senator, New Hampshire, 1253
"Cotton Whigs," 239
Coughlin, Charles E.
presidential primary votes, (1936) 333–334
pressure on FDR, 265
Union Party campaign, (1936) 79, 505
Council for a Livable World, 104
County unit system (Georgia), 17, 131, 822
Courtney, Kent H.
vice-presidential candidate
Conservative Party of New Jersey nominee, (1960) 435
Courts. *See* Judiciary
Coutremarsh, Joseph A.
presidential primary votes, (1936) 334
Couzens, James
senator, Michigan, 1249
Coverdell, Paul
senator, Georgia, 1241
Cowan, Edgar
senator, Pennsylvania, 1259
Cowdrey, Robert Hall
presidential candidate
popular vote, (1888) 690

United Labor Party nominee, (1888)
431
Cowper, Steve C.
governor, Alaska, 1384
Cox, Archibald, 281
Cox, Channing H.
governor, Massachusetts, 1396
Cox, Jacob D.
governor, Ohio, 1404
Cox, James M.
biography, 776
governor, Ohio, 1405
presidential candidate
Democratic convention ballots,
(1920) 605, (1924) 606, (1932) 611
Democratic nominee, (1920) 259,
432, 494
electoral vote, (1920) 751
as former governor, 222
popular vote, (1920) 668
primary votes, (1920) 311, 324–326,
(1924) 327–328
Cox, James R.
presidential candidate
Jobless Party nominee, (1932) 433
popular vote, (1932) 693
Cox, John I.
governor, Tennessee, 1409
Cox, William Wesley
presidential candidate
popular vote, (1920) 692
Socialist Labor nominee, (1920) 433
vice-presidential candidate
Socialist Labor nominee, (1904) 432
Coxey, Jacob S.
presidential candidate
Farmer Labor nominee, (1932) 433
popular vote, (1932) 692
primary votes, (1932) 331–332
Coy, Elmer W.
presidential primary votes, (1968) 353
Cozzens, William
governor, Rhode Island, 1407
Cozzini, Georgia
vice-presidential candidate
Socialist Labor nominee, (1956,
1960) 435
Crafts, Samuel C.
governor, Vermont, 1410
senator, Vermont, 1263
Cragin, Aaron H.
senator, New Hampshire, 1253
Craig, George N.
governor, Indiana, 145, 1391
Craig, Larry E.
senator, Idaho, 1242
Craig, Locke
governor, North Carolina, 1403
Crane, A. Peter
presidential candidate
Independent Party of Utah nominee,
(1996) 439
popular vote, (1996) 699
Crane, Arthur G.
governor, Wyoming, 1413
Crane, Philip M.
presidential candidate
American Independent nomination
declined, (1976) 52
primary votes, (1980) 365–371
Republican contender, (1980) 182
Crane, Winthrop Murray
governor, Massachusetts, 1396
senator, Massachusetts, 1248
Cranfill, James B.
vice-presidential candidate
Prohibition nominee, (1892) 431,
475
Cranston, Alan
presidential candidate
Democratic contender, (1984) 186,
285
primary votes, (1984) 372–377
senator, California, 169, 183, 189,
1238
ethics investigation, 87, 195

Crapo, Henry H.
governor, Michigan, 1397
Crapo, Michael D.
senator, Idaho, 203, 1242
Crawford, Coe I.
governor, South Dakota, 1408
senator, South Dakota, 1261
Crawford, George W.
governor, Georgia, 1389
Crawford, Samuel J.
governor, Kansas, 1392
Crawford, William H.
biography, 776
presidential candidate
Democratic-Republican contender,
(1816) 231, (1824) 56, 232–233,
709
electoral anomalies, 12 (box)
electoral vote, (1824) 727
popular vote, (1824) 644
senator, Georgia, 1240
Credit Mobilier scandal, 247
Creswell, John A. J.
senator, Maryland, 1247
Crime
platform issue
American Independents, (1968) 532
Democrats, (1968) 532, (1972) 535,
(1988) 553, (1992) 558, (1996) 565,
(2000) 569
Green Party, (2000) 571
Republicans, (1968) 530, (1976) 541,
(1980) 544, (1984) 551, (1988) 555
politics and issues, (1994) 198
presidential campaign issue, (1968) 278
Crippa, Edward D.
senator, Wyoming, 1266
Crittenden, John J.
governor, Kentucky, 1392
senator, Kentucky, 1245
Crittenden, Thomas T.
governor, Missouri, 1399
Crommelin, John G.
vice-presidential candidate
National States' Rights Party nominee, (1960) 435
Crosby, Robert Berkey
governor, Nebraska, 1399
Crosby, William G.
governor, Maine, 1394
Cross, Burton M.
governor, Maine, 1394
Cross, Wilbur L.
governor, Connecticut, 1387
Croswell, Charles M.
governor, Michigan, 1397
Crothers, Austin L.
governor, Maryland, 1395
Crounse, Lorenzo
governor, Nebraska, 1399
Crow, Randolph "Randy" W.
presidential primary votes, (2000)
404–410
Crow, William E.
senator, Pennsylvania, 1258
Crowley, Jeremiah D.
vice-presidential candidate
Socialist Labor nominee, (1928) 433
Crozier, Robert
senator, Kansas, 1244
Cruce, Lee
governor, Oklahoma, 1405
Cuba
Kennedy campaign, administration, 156,
275, 276
Cuban missile crisis, 157, 158
platform issue
Democrats, (1860) 457
Republicans, (1964) 526, (1988)
555
Culberson, Charles A.
governor, Texas, 1410
senator, Texas, 1262
Cullom, Shelby M.
governor, Illinois, 1390
senator, Illinois, 1242

Culver, John C.
Democratic convention ballots, (1980)
630
senator, Iowa, 175, 183, 284, 1244
Cummings, Homer S.
Democratic convention ballots, (1920)
605, (1924) 607
Democratic National Committee chair,
415 (table), 426 (table)
Cummins, Albert B.
governor, Iowa, 1392
presidential candidate
primary votes, (1916) 322–323
Republican contender, (1916) 258
Republican convention ballots,
(1916) 602
senator, Iowa, 1244
Cunningham, Bob
presidential primary votes, (1992)
386–393
Cunningham, Charles E.
vice-presidential candidate
Union Labor Party nominee, (1888)
431
Cunningham, Russell M.
governor, Alabama, 1384
Cuomo, Mario O.
at Democratic convention, (1984) 548,
(1992) 557, (1996) 564
keynote speaker, 415 (table)
governor, New York, 199, 1403
defeat, 1379
presidential no-run decision, (1992) 289
Curley, James M.
governor, Massachusetts, 1396
Currency. See Monetary policy
Currier, Moody
governor, New Hampshire, 1401
Curtin, Andrew G.
governor, Pennsylvania, 1406
Curtis, Carl T.
senator, Nebraska, 1252
Curtis, Charles
biography, 776
presidential candidate
Republican contender, (1928) 260
Republican convention ballots,
(1928) 609
senator, Kansas, 795, 1244
vice-presidential candidate
electoral vote, (1928, 1932) 773
Republican nominee, (1928) 260,
433, 499, (1932) 433, 501
Curtis, Dean A.
presidential primary votes, (1992) 394
Curtis, James Langdon
presidential candidate
American Party nominee, (1888) 431
popular vote, (1888) 690
Curtis, Kenneth M.
Democratic National Committee chair,
426 (table)
governor, Maine, 1394
Curtis, Merrit B.
presidential candidate
Constitutional Party (Washington)
nominee, (1960) 435
popular vote, (1960) 694
vice-presidential candidate
Constitutional Party (Texas) nominee, (1960) 435
Tax Cut Party nominee, (1960) 435
Curtis, Oakley C.
governor, Maine, 1394
Curtis, Thomas B., 540
Cushing, Caleb
at Democratic convention, (1860) 456
officers, 415 (table), 425 (box)
Cushing, Thomas
governor, Massachusetts, 1396
Cuthbert, Alfred
senator, Georgia, 1241
Cutler, John C.
governor, Utah, 1410
Cutler, Nathan
governor, Maine, 1394

Cutting, Bronson
senator, New Mexico, 1254
Cutts, Charles
senator, New Hampshire, 1253
Czolgosz, Leon, 16

D

Daggett, David
senator, Connecticut, 1239
Dale, Charles M.
governor, New Hampshire, 1401
Dale, Porter H.
senator, Vermont, 1263
D'Alesandro, Thomas J. Jr., 788
Daley, Richard J., 279, 283, 422, 531, 534
Dallas, George M.
biography, 776
Democratic convention ballots, (1848)
575
senator, Pennsylvania, 1258
vice-presidential candidate
Democratic nominee, (1844) 429,
447
electoral vote, (1844) 772
Dalton, John
governor, Virginia, 1412
Dalton, John M.
governor, Missouri, 1399
Dalton, Tristram
senator, Massachusetts, 1248
Daly, Lar
presidential candidate
popular vote, (1960) 694
primary votes, (1956) 345, (1960)
346–347, (1964) 350, (1976)
359–364
Tax Cut Party nominee, (1960) 435
D'Amato, Alfonse M.
senator, New York, 202, 1255
political party development, 46
Dana, John W.
governor, Maine, 1394
Dana, Judah
senator, Maine, 1246
Dana, Samuel W.
senator, Connecticut, 1238
Danaher, John A.
senator, Connecticut, 1239
Danforth, John C.
senator, Missouri, 179, 1251
Daniel, Charles E.
senator, South Carolina, 1260
Daniel, John W.
Democratic convention officers, (1896)
478, 415 (table)
senator, Virginia, 1264
Daniel, Price
governor, Texas, 1410
senator, Texas, 1262
Daniel, William
vice-presidential candidate
Prohibition Party, (1884) 431
Daniels, Bruce C.
presidential primary votes, (1996) 403
Daniels, Cordell
Democratic convention ballots, (1924)
607
Daniels, Josephus
Democratic convention ballots, (1920)
605, (1924) 606–607
Daniels, Ron
presidential candidate
Peace and Freedom Party nominee,
(1992) 69, 438
popular vote, (1992) 698
primary votes, (1992) 386–393
Darby, Harry
senator, Kansas, 1244
Darden, Colgate W. Jr.
governor, Virginia, 1412
"Dark horse" candidates, 15
Daschle, Thomas A.
Democratic convention officers, 415
(table)
senator, South Dakota, 1261
on fund-raising, 102

Dass, Michael E.
    presidential primary votes, (1996) 403
Dattner, Joyce
    vice-presidential candidate
        New Alliance nominee, (1988) 438
Daugherty, Harry M., 258–259, 260
Daugherty, Paul C.
    presidential primary votes, (1992) 393
Davenport, Franklin
    senator, New Jersey, 1253
Davey, Martin L.
    governor, Ohio, 1405
Davidson, James O.
    governor, Wisconsin, 1413
Davidson, Roger H., 103
Davie, William R.
    governor, North Carolina, 1403
Davis, Angela
    vice-presidential candidate
        Communist nominee, (1980, 1984) 437
Davis, Benjamin J., 46
Davis, Billy
    vice-presidential candidate
        Independent Party nominee, (1984) 437
Davis, Cushman K.
    governor, Minnesota, 1397
    senator, Minnesota, 1249
Davis, Daniel F.
    governor, Maine, 1394
Davis, David
    biography, 776
    presidential candidate
        electoral vote, (1872) 739
        Labor Reform Party nominee, (1872) 430
        Liberal Republican contender, (1872) 247, 463
    senator, Illinois, 1242
        Tilden-Hayes commission, (1876) 711
    vote as presidential elector (1872) 706
Davis, David W.
    governor, Idaho, 1390
Davis, Deane C.
    governor, Vermont, 1411
Davis, Edmund J.
    governor, Texas, 1409
Davis, Garrett
    senator, Kentucky, 1245
Davis, Gray
    governor, California, 203, 1386
Davis, Harry L.
    governor, Ohio, 1405
Davis, Henry G.
    biography, 777
    senator, West Virginia, 1265
    vice-presidential candidate
        Democratic nominee, (1904) 432, 482
        electoral vote, (1904) 773
Davis, James C.
    Democratic convention ballots, (1956) 619
Davis, James H.
    governor, Louisiana, 1394
Davis, James J.
    senator, Pennsylvania, 1259
Davis, Jeff
    governor, Arkansas, 1385
    senator, Arkansas, 1237
Davis, Jefferson
    Democratic convention ballots, (1860) 580
    pardon resolution, 250
    president of Confederacy (box), 244
    senator, Mississippi, 1250
    on slavery in territories, 241
Davis, John
    governor, Delaware, 1387
Davis, John
    governor, Massachusetts, 1396
    senator, Massachusetts, 1248
Davis, John E.
    governor, North Dakota, 1404

Davis, John W.
    biography, 777
    Democratic convention officers, 415 (table)
    New Deal opposition, 265
    presidential candidate
        Democratic convention ballots, (1920) 605, (1924) 606–607
        Democratic nominee, (1924) 260, 433, 496–497
        election evolution, 6
        electoral vote, (1924) 752
        popular vote, (1924) 669
Davis, John W.
    governor, Rhode Island, 1407
Davis, Jonathan M.
    Democratic convention ballots, (1924) 606
Davis, Jonathan McM.
    governor, Kansas, 1392
Davis, Joseph, 244 (box)
Davis, R. N.
    presidential primary votes, (1940) 335–336
Davis, Sterling P.
    presidential primary votes, (1984) 372–377
Davis, Westmoreland
    governor, Virginia, 1411
Dawes, Charles G.
    biography, 777
    presidential candidate
        primary votes, (1928) 329–330, (1932) 331–332
        Republican contender, (1928) 314 (box), (1932) 314 (box)
        Republican convention ballots, (1928) 609, (1932) 610
    vice-presidential candidate
        electoral vote, (1924) 773
        Republican nominee, (1924) 433, 495
Dawes, Henry L.
    senator, Massachusetts, 1248
Dawes, James W.
    governor, Nebraska, 1399
Dawson, William C.
    senator, Georgia, 1241
Dawson, William L., 790, 791
Dawson, William M. O.
    governor, West Virginia, 1412
Day, Stephen A.
    presidential primary votes, (1936) 333–334
Dayton, Jonathan
    senator, New Jersey, 1254
Dayton, Mark
    senator, Minnesota, 1249
Dayton, William L.
    biography, 777
    Republican convention ballots, (1860) 581
    senator, New Jersey, 1253
    vice-presidential candidate
        electoral vote, (1856) 772
        Republican nominee, (1856) 241, 430, 453, 454
De Baca, Ezequiel C.
    governor, New Mexico, 1402
De la Garza, E. "Kika," 793
De La Matyr, Gilbert
    Greenback convention officers, 425 (box)
De Priest, Oscar, 790
De Saussure, William F.
    senator, South Carolina, 1260
De Wolf, James
    senator, Rhode Island, 1259
Dean, Howard
    governor, Vermont, 1379, 1411
Death penalty
    platform issue
        Green Party, (2000) 571
        Republicans, (1980) 544, (1988) 555
DeBerry, Clifton
    presidential candidate
        popular vote, (1964) 679, (1980) 696

        Socialist Workers nominee, (1964) 435, (1980) 437
Deboe, William J.
    senator, Kentucky, 1245
Debs, Eugene
    biography, 777
    presidential candidate
        declines nomination, (1916) 492
        election milestones, 16
        political party development, 46, 49
        popular vote, (1900) 663, (1904) 664, (1908) 665, (1912) 666, (1920) 668
        Social-Democratic nominee, (1900) 424 (box), 431
        Socialist nominee, (1904) 432, 481, (1908) 432, 483, (1912) 424 (box), 432, 485, (1920) 432, 492
    Socialist Party history, 78, 79
Decker, Rutherford L.
    presidential candidate
        popular vote, (1960) 694
        Prohibition Party nominee, (1960) 435
DeConcini, Dennis
    senator, Arizona, 179, 1237
        ethics investigation, 195
Defense policy. See also Arms control
    Eisenhower administration, 272–273
    FDR administration, 267
    platform issues
        Democrats, (1916) 491–492, (1924) 497, (1960) 522, (1964) 528, (1968) 532, (1980) 546, (1984) 549, 550, 632, (1988) 554, (1992) 558
        National Unity Campaign, (1980) 547
        Progressives, (1948) 514
        Republicans, (1916) 491, (1924) 495, (1956) 520, 521, (1960) 523, 524, (1964) 526, (1968) 529–530, (1980) 543, 544, (1992) 560
        Socialists, (1916) 492
Del Sesto, Christopher
    governor, Rhode Island, 152, 1407
Delano, H. A.
    Prohibition Party convention officers, 425 (box)
DeLauro, Rosa, 790
Delaware
    Senate election deadlock, 1230
Delaware plan, 306–307, 420, 566
Delegate-selection primaries, 306 (box), 309–310
DeLeon, Daniel, 79
Dellenbeck, John, 175
Dellums, Ronald V.
    blacks in Congress, 791
    Democratic convention ballots, (1980) 630
    vice-presidential contender, (1976) 539
Democratic Advisory Committee, 151
Democratic Congressional Campaign Committee, 97
Democratic Leadership Council
    Democratic convention, (1996) 564
    Democratic platform, (1992) 556
    Lieberman candidacy, 312
Democratic National Committee (DNC)
    campaign finance scandal, 1996, 84–86, 294
    chairs, 1832–2001 (tables), 415, 426
    convention rules reform, 415–419
    structure, 418 (box)
    superdelegates, 314
    Watergate office break-in, 18, 281
Democratic Party
    conventions
        credentials disputes, 420–421, 422
        delegate selection guidelines, (1944) 412, (1972) 534, (1976) 537–538, (1996) 311 (box), (2000) 413
        historical narratives, (1832) 14, 442–443, (1835) 443, (1840) 444–445, (1844) 447, (1848) 422, 448, (1852) 450, (1856) 454–455,

        (1860) 422, 456–457, (1864) 460, (1868) 462, (1872) 464, (1876) 466, (1880) 469, (1884) 471, (1888) 472, (1892) 475, (1896) 478, (1900) 480, (1904) 482, (1908) 484, (1912) 487, (1916) 491, (1920) 494, (1924) 496–497, (1928) 499, (1932) 422, 502–503, (1936) 505, (1940) 507, (1944) 509–510, (1948) 512, (1952) 422, 516–517, (1956) 518–519, (1960) 521–523, (1964) 527, (1968) 422, 530–531, (1972) 422, 533–535, (1976) 537–539, (1980) 544–545, (1984) 548, (1988) 552–553, (1992) 556–557, (1996) 564–565, (2000) 568–569
        location, financing, 411–412
        number of delegates, 1932–2000 (figure), 413
        officers, keynote speakers (table), 415
        summary (table), 414
    convention rules, 280, 308, 415–420, 533
        binding rule, 416, 421, (1980) 306, 544–545
        changes, 1972–2000 (box), 419
        two-thirds rule, 421 (box)
        unit rule, 421
    election milestones, 5–14
    factions
        in Free Soil Party, (1848) 449, (1852) 452
        Southerners, (1860) 457
        in Whig party, (1836) 444
    history, 43–48
        donkey symbol, 15, 58
        politics and issues, 1945–2000, 133–206
        presidential election chronology, 233–301
        profile, 55–61
        southern primaries, 129–132, 25–26
        timeline, 47
    platforms, (1840) 445, (1844) 447, (1848) 448–449, (1852) 450–451, (1856) 455, (1860) 457, (1864) 460, (1868) 462, (1872) 464, (1876) 466–467, (1880) 469–470, (1884) 471, (1888) 472, (1892) 475, (1896) 478–479, (1900) 480–481, (1904) 482, (1908) 484–485, (1912) 487–488, (1916) 491–492, (1920) 494–495, (1924) 497, (1928) 499–500, (1932) 503, (1936) 505, (1940) 507–508, (1944) 510, (1948) 512–513, (1952) 517–518, (1956) 519–520, (1960) 522–523, (1964) 527–528, (1968) 531–532, (1972) 535–536, (1976) 539–540, (1980) 545–546, (1984) 548–550, (1988) 553–554, (1992) 557–558, (1996) 564–565, (2000) 569–570
    presidential primaries
        caucus method, 311 (box)
        returns, 1912–2000 (tables), 319–410
        types, rules, 306 (box), 307
        voter turnout, 309
        votes, delegates, 1912–2000 (table), 307
    presidential, vice-presidential nominees, (1832–2000) 429–439
        electoral vote, 729–774
        popular vote, 646–688
    structure, 418 (box)
    voter registration, 23
Democratic-Republican Party
    historical development, 43–44
    profile, 61
    timeline, 47
Democratic Senatorial Campaign Committee, 97
Democratic Socialist Organizing Committee, 79
Democratic Socialists of America, 79
Dempsey, John
    governor, Connecticut, 1387
Dempsey, John J.
    governor, New Mexico, 1402

Deneen, Charles S.
governor, Illinois, 1391
senator, Illinois, 1242
Dennerl, Norbert G.
presidential primary votes, (1988)
378–385
Denney, William D.
governor, Delaware, 1388
Dennis, David W., 175
Dennis, Delmar
presidential candidate
American Party nominee, (1984) 52,
437, (1988) 52, 438
popular vote, (1984, 1988) 697
Dennis, George R.
senator, Maryland, 1247
Dennison, William
governor, Ohio, 1404
Republican convention officers, 417
(table)
Denton, Jeremiah
senator, Alabama, 188–189, 1236
Depew, Chauncey M.
Republican presidential contender,
(1888) 473
convention ballots, (1888) 592
senator, New York, 1255
Derbigny, Pierre
governor, Louisiana, 1393
Dern, George H.
governor, Utah, 1410
DeSarno, James, 118 (box)
Desha, Joseph
governor, Kentucky, 1392
Destrehan, John N.
senator, Louisiana, 1246
Deukmejian, George
governor, California, 185, 189, 1386
Deutsch, Barry J.
presidential primary votes, (1992) 394
Dever, Paul A.
Democratic convention officers, speakers,
415 (table)
governor, Massachusetts, 1396
presidential contender, (1952) 517
Democratic convention ballots,
(1952) 618
Devine, Annie, 803
Devine, Joseph M.
governor, North Dakota, 1404
Dewey, Nelson
governor, Wisconsin, 1413
Dewey, Thomas E.
biography, 777
governor, New York, 138, 1403
political party development, 76
presidential candidate
"Dewey Defeats Truman" headline,
17, 270
election evolution, 8
electoral vote, (1944) 757, (1948) 758
as former governor, 223
New York background, 222
politics and issues, (1948) 139–141
popular vote, (1944) 674, (1948) 675
primary votes, (1940) 335–336,
(1944) 337–338, (1948) 313,
339–340
Republican contender, (1940) 267,
506
Republican convention ballots,
(1940) 613, (1944) 614, (1948) 615
Republican nominee, (1944) 266,
268, 434, 508–509, (1948)
270–271, 434, 511
at Republican convention, (1944) 427
DeWine, Mike
senator, Ohio, 1257
Dexter, Samuel
senator, Massachusetts, 1248
Dial, Nathaniel
senator, South Carolina, 1260
Dick, Charles W. F.
senator, Ohio, 1257
Dickerson, Denver S.
governor, Nevada, 1400

Dickerson, Mahlon
governor, New Jersey, 1401
House redistricting, 817
senator, New Jersey, 1253, 1254
Dickerson, Philemon
governor, New Jersey, 1401
Dickinson, Daniel S.
Democratic convention ballots, (1852)
577, (1860) 580
Republican (Union) vice-presidential contender, (1864) 459
senator, New York, 1255
Dickinson, John
governor, Delaware, 1387
Dickinson, John
governor, Pennsylvania, 1406
Dickinson, L. J.
Republican convention officers, 417
(table)
senator, Iowa, 1243
Dickinson, Luren D.
governor, Michigan, 1397
Dickinson, Philemon
senator, New Jersey, 1254
DiDonato, Florenzo
presidential primary votes, (1988)
378–385
Dietrich, Charles H.
governor, Nebraska, 1399
senator, Nebraska, 1252
Dietrich, William H.
senator, Illinois, 1242
DiFrancesco, Donald T.
governor, New Jersey, 1402
Diggs, Charles C. Jr., 791
Dill, Clarence C.
senator, Washington, 1265
Dillingham, Paul
governor, Vermont, 1410
Dillingham, William P.
governor, Vermont, 1411
senator, Vermont, 1263
Dillon, Richard C.
governor, New Mexico, 1402
Diman, Byron
governor, Rhode Island, 1406
Dimond, Francis M.
governor, Rhode Island, 1407
Dingell, John D.
length of service in Congress, 795 (table)
Dingley, Nelson Jr.
governor, Maine, 1394
Dinkins, David, 552
Dinsmoor, Samuel
governor, New Hampshire, 1400
Dinsmoor, Samuel Jr.
governor, New Hampshire, 1400
DiPrete, Edward
governor, Rhode Island, 189, 192, 1407
Direct election of senators
Republican platform issue (1908) 423
(box), 599
Seventeenth Amendment, 14, 16, 1231,
1232
Direct recording electronic (DRE) voting sys-
tems, 218
Dirksen, Everett McKinley
presidential primary votes, (1944)
337–338
Republican convention ballots, (1948)
615
senator, Illinois, 143, 1242
Senate leadership, 158, 164
Disabled persons
at Democratic convention, (1996) 564
Republican platform issue, (1988) 555
DiSalle, Michael
governor, Ohio, 152, 158, 1405
presidential primary votes, (1960)
346–347
Disarmament. See Arms control
District of Columbia
platform issues
Democrats, (1964) 527
Republicans, (1996) 562
presidential voting rights, 17, 21, 162, 220

"Divided government," 3, 10
Dix, John A.
governor, New York, 1403
senator, New York, 1255
Dixiecrats. See States' Rights Party
Dixon, Alan J.
senator, Illinois, 1242
Dixon, Archibald
senator, Kentucky, 1245
Dixon, Frank M.
at Dixiecrat convention, (1948) 513
governor, Alabama, 1384
Dixon, James
senator, Connecticut, 1238
Dixon, Joseph M.
governor, Montana, 1399
senator, Montana, 1251
Dixon, Julian, 791
Dixon, Nathan F.
senator, Rhode Island, 1259
Dixon, Nathan F. III
senator, Rhode Island, 1259
DNC. See Democratic National Committee
Dobbs, Farrell
presidential candidate
popular vote, (1948) 693, (1952,
1956, 1960) 694
Socialist Workers nominee, (1948,
1952) 434, (1956, 1960) 435
Dockery, Alexander M.
governor, Missouri, 1399
Docking, George
governor, Kansas, 149, 152, 1392
Docking, Robert B.
governor, Kansas, 1392
Dodd, Christopher J.
at Democratic convention, (1996) 564
Democratic National Committee chair,
426 (table)
senator, Connecticut, 1239
Dodd, Thomas J.
Democratic vice-presidential contender,
(1964) 527
senator, Connecticut, 152, 170, 1239
Dodge, Augustus C.
senator, Iowa, 1244
Dodge, Earl F.
presidential candidate
popular vote, (1984, 1988) 697,
(1992) 698, (1996, 2000) 699
primary votes, (1992) 393
Prohibition Party nominee,
(1984–2000) 72, 437–439
vice-presidential candidate
Prohibition Party nominee, (1976)
437
Statesman Party nominee, (1980)
437
Dodge, Henry
Democratic convention ballots, (1852)
577
senator, Wisconsin, 1265
Doerschuck, Georgiana
presidential primary votes, (1992) 393,
(1996) 403
Dole, Elizabeth Hanford
Bob Dole campaign, (1988) 287
presidential candidate
campaign funding, (2000) 91
Republican contender, (2000) 204, 210,
296
at Republican convention, (1996) 561
officers, 417 (table)
Dole, Robert
biography, 777
presidential candidate
campaign finance, (1996) 94
"character" issues, (1996) 210
electoral vote, (1996) 770
as former vice-presidential nominee,
224
politics and issues, (1996) 200
popular vote, (1996) 687
primary votes, (1980) 365–371,
(1988) 311 (box), 315, 378–385,
(1996) 311 (box), 318, 395–402

Republican contender, (1980) 182,
(1988) 190, 286, 287
Republican convention ballots,
(1996) 638
Republican nominee, (1996)
293–295, 315, 439, 561–562
Republican convention officers, 417
(table)
Republican National Committee chair,
417 (table), 426 (table)
senator, Kansas, 169, 175, 1244
Senate leadership, 188, 191
successor, 788
vice-presidential candidate
election milestones, 18
electoral vote, (1976) 773
Republican nominee, (1976) 178,
282, 436, 540
televised debates, (1976) 216
Dolliver, Jonathan P.
senator, Iowa, 1243
Dolph, Joseph N.
senator, Oregon, 1258
Dominici, Pete V.
senator, New Mexico, 1255
Dominick, Peter H.
senator, Colorado, 175, 1238
Donaghey, George W.
governor, Arkansas, 1385
Donahey, Gertrude W.
presidential primary votes, (1976) 364
Donahey, Victor
Democratic convention ballots, (1928)
609
governor, Ohio, 1405
presidential primary votes, (1928)
329–330
senator, Ohio, 1257
Donelson, Andrew Jackson
biography, 777
vice-presidential candidate
American Party nominee, (1856) 430,
454, 455
electoral vote, (1856) 772
Whig nominee, (1856) 430
Donnell, Forrest C.
governor, Missouri, 1399
senator, Missouri, 1251
Donnelly, Ignatius
vice-presidential candidate
Populist nominee, (1900) 69, 431
Donnelly, Phil M.
governor, Missouri, 1399
Doolittle, James R.
Democratic convention ballots, (1868)
584
Democratic convention officers, 415
(table)
senator, Wisconsin, 1265
Dorgan, Byron L.
senator, North Dakota, 1256
Dornan, Robert K.
contested House election, 804
presidential candidate
primary votes, (1996) 395–402
Republican contender, (1996) 293,
315
Dorsey, Hugh M.
governor, Georgia, 1389
Dorsey, Stephen W.
senator, Arkansas, 1237
Doty, Charles R.
presidential primary votes, (1988)
378–385, (1992) 393
Douglas, Emily Taft, 788
Douglas, Helen Gahagan, 143
Douglas, Paul H.
Democratic convention ballots, (1952)
618
senator, Illinois, 141, 788, 1242
civil rights, 148
Douglas, Stephen A.
biography, 777
on Kansas-Nebraska Act, 240
as moderate, 239
presidential candidate

Democratic contender, (1852) 450, (1856) 454–455
Democratic convention ballots, (1852) 577, (1856) 579, (1860) 580
Democratic nominee, (1860) 53, 54, 57, 239–240, 241–242, 430, 456–457
electoral vote, (1860) 736
political party development, 45
popular vote, (1860) 653
Senate service, 223
split electoral votes, (1860) 702 (box)
senator, Illinois, 1242
Lincoln debates, 216
Douglas, William L.
governor, Massachusetts, 1396
Douglas, William O.
presidential candidate
Democratic convention ballots, (1952) 618
Democratic draft possibility (1948) 139, 269, 512
primary votes, (1952) 341–343
Supreme Court justice
House redistricting, 818–819, 822
poll taxes, 25
vice-presidential candidate
Democratic possibility, (1948) 510
Douglass, Frederick
at Republican convention, (1876) 465
vice-presidential candidate
People's Party nominee, (1872) 430
Dow, Neal
presidential candidate
popular vote, (1880) 690
Prohibition Party nominee, (1880) 431
Down With Lawyers Party
nominees, (1980) 437
Downey, John G.
governor, California, 1386
Downey, Sheridan
senator, California, 1238
Downs, Solomon W.
senator, Louisiana, 1246
Doxey, Wall
senator, Mississippi, 1250
Drake, Charles D.
senator, Missouri, 1251
Drake, Francis M.
governor, Iowa, 1392
Draper, Eban Sumner
governor, Massachusetts, 1396
Drayton, John
governor, South Carolina, 1407
Drew, George F.
governor, Florida, 1388
Drew, Irving W.
senator, New Hampshire, 1253
Drew, Thomas S.
governor, Arkansas, 1385
Dreyfus, Lee S.
governor, Wisconsin, 1413
Drinan, Robert F., 787
Driscoll, Alfred E.
governor, New Jersey, 138, 1402
presidential primary votes, (1948) 339–340
Republican convention ballots, (1948) 615
Driscoll, Carroll
vice-presidential candidate
Right to Life Party nominee, (1980) 437
Drucker, Robert F.
presidential primary votes, (1988) 385, (1996) 403
Drufenbrock, Diane
vice-presidential candidate
Socialist nominee, (1980) 437
Drug control policy
platform issue
Democrats, (1988) 553, (1992) 558
Republicans, (1988) 555
Dryden, John F.
senator, New Jersey, 1254

Dubois, Fred T.
senator, Idaho, 1242
Ducey, Susan
presidential primary votes, (1996) 395–402
Dudley, Charles E.
senator, New York, 1255
Dudley, Edward B.
governor, North Carolina, 1403
Duff, James H.
governor, Pennsylvania, 1406
senator, Pennsylvania, 143, 1259
Duffy, F. Ryan
senator, Wisconsin, 1266
Dukakis, Michael S.
biography, 777
governor, Massachusetts, 176, 1396
presidential candidate
Democratic convention ballots, (1988) 634
Democratic nominee, (1988) 286–289, 438, 553–554
election milestones, 18
electoral vote, (1988) 768
faithless elector, (1988) 703 (box)
as former governor, 224
politics and issues, (1988) 190–191
popular vote, (1988) 685
primary votes, (1988) 315, 378–385
vice-presidential choice, 312
vice-presidential electoral vote, (1988) 773
Dukakis, Olympia, (1988) 554
Duke, David E.
presidential candidate
popular vote, (1988) 697
Populist Party nominee, (1988) 438
primary votes, (1988) 378–385, (1992) 386–393
Republican contender, (1992) 196, 291
Dulles, John Foster
Eisenhower cabinet, 152, 272
Republican platform, (1952) 516
senator, New York, 1255
DuMont, Don
presidential primary votes, (1968) 353
Duncan, Joseph
governor, Illinois, 1390
Dunklin, Daniel
governor, Missouri, 1398
Dunlap, Robert P.
governor, Maine, 1394
Dunn, David
governor, Maine, 1394
Dunn, Jennifer, 790
Dunn, Winfield
governor, Tennessee, 1409
Dunne, Edward F.
governor, Illinois, 1391
Dunning, Paris C.
governor, Indiana, 1391
du Pont, Henry A.
senator, Delaware, 1239
du Pont, Pierre S. "Pete" IV
governor, Delaware, 1388
presidential candidate
primary votes, (1988) 378–385
Republican contender, (1988) 190, 287
du Pont, T. Coleman
Republican convention ballots, (1916) 602, (1920) 604
senator, Delaware, 1239, 1240
du Pont, William J. IV
presidential primary votes, (1988) 378–385
Dupre, Jacques
Durbin, Richard J.
senator, Illinois, 201, 1242
Durbin, Winfield T.
governor, Indiana, 1391
Durenberger, Dave
senator, Minnesota, 181, 1249
Durkee, Charles
senator, Wisconsin, 1266

Durkheim, Emile, 264
Durkin, John A.
senator, New Hampshire, 175, 1253
disputed election, 1231
Dutton, Henry
governor, Connecticut, 1387
DuVal, Clive L., 130
Dworshak, Henry C.
senator, Idaho, 1242
Dwinell, Lane
governor, New Hampshire, 1401
Dyer, Elisha II
governor, Rhode Island, 1407
Dyer, Elisha III
governor, Rhode Island, 1407
Dyke, William
vice-presidential candidate
American Independent Party nominee, (1976) 52, 436
Dyson, Roy, 191

E

Eagle, James P.
governor, Arkansas, 1385
Eagleton, Thomas F.
biography, 777
Democratic convention ballots, (1984) 632
senator, Missouri, 183, 188, 1251
vice-presidential candidate
Democratic nominee, (1972) 171–172, 280, 425, 436, 535
Earl, Anthony S.
governor, Wisconsin, 1413
Earle, George H.
governor, Pennsylvania, 1406
Earle, Joseph H.
senator, South Carolina, 1260
Earle, Thomas
vice-presidential candidate
Liberty Party nominee, (1840) 429, 446
Early, Peter
governor, Georgia, 1389
"Earmarking" of campaign contributions, 98
Easley, Michael F.
governor, North Carolina, 1404
East, John P.
senator, North Carolina, 183, 1256
Easter, Andrew J.
presidential primary votes, (1960) 347, (1964) 350
Eastland, James O.
Democratic platform, (1960) 522
senator, Mississippi, 1250
Eaton, Benjamin H.
governor, Colorado, 1386
Eaton, Horace
governor, Vermont, 1410
Eaton, John B.
presidential primary votes, (2000) 404–410
Eaton, John H.
in Jackson cabinet, 234
senator, Tennessee, 1261
Eaton, William W.
senator, Connecticut, 1239
Eberhart, Adolph O.
governor, Minnesota, 1397
Eckert, Fred J., 189
Economic policy. See also Budget policy; Employment and unemployment; Monetary policy; Tax policy
Bush, Clinton administrations, 192, 289, 290
Carter administration, 180, 183
Ford administration, 177
New Deal, 263–264, 265
platform issues
Democrats, (1960) 522, 523, (1964) 528, (1976) 539, (1980) 545–546, (1988) 553, (1992) 557
National Unity Campaign, (1980) 546–547

Republicans, (1944) 509, (1956) 520–521, (1960) 524, (1964) 526, (1976) 541, (1980) 544, (1984) 551
presidential elections
campaign issue, (1960) 275, (1996) 294–295, (2000) 297, 298
effects on incumbents, 213, 216
Reagan administration, 184, 284
Vietnam War years, 164
World War II effects, 268
Ecton, Zales N.
senator, Montana, 1251
Eddy, Roy N.
vice-presidential candidate
Restoration Party nominee, (1976) 437
Edgar, Bob, 188
Edgar, Jim
governor, Illinois, 1391
Edge, Walter E.
governor, New Jersey, 1401, 1402
senator, New Jersey, 1254
Edgerton, A. J.
senator, Minnesota, 1249
Edgerton, James Arthur
vice-presidential candidate
Prohibition Party nominee, (1928) 433
Edison, Charles
governor, New Jersey, 1402
Edison, Thomas A., 15, 36 (box), 218
Edison Electric Institute, 92
Edmond, Favor Noel
governor, Mississippi, 1398
Edmondson, J. Howard
governor, Oklahoma, 1405
senator, Oklahoma, 1257
Edmunds, George F.
Republican convention ballots, (1880) 588, (1884) 590
Republican presidential contender, (1884) 470
senator, Vermont, 1263
Education. See also School desegregation; School prayer
platform issue
Democrats, (1928) 500, (1944) 510, (1952) 518, (1956) 519, (1980) 546, (1988) 553, (1992) 557, (1996) 565, (2000) 569
Republicans, (1876) 466, (1964) 526, (1980) 544, (1984) 551, (1992) 559, (1996) 563, (2000) 567
voter characteristics, 23 (table)
Edwards, Edward I.
governor, New Jersey, 1402
presidential contender
Democratic convention ballots, (1920) 605
primary votes, (1920) 324–326
senator, New Jersey, 1254
Edwards, Edwin W.
governor, Louisiana, 1394
Edwards, Elaine S.
senator, Louisiana, 1246
Edwards, Henry W.
governor, Connecticut, 1387
senator, Connecticut, 1238
Edwards, James B.
governor, South Carolina, 176, 1408
Edwards, John
senator, Kentucky, 1245
Edwards, John
senator, North Carolina, 203, 1256
Edwards, John C.
governor, Missouri, 1398
Edwards, Ninian
governor, Illinois, 1390
senator, Illinois, 1242
Efaw, Fritz, 539
Egan, William A.
governor, Alaska, 1384
Ehlers, Delbert L.
independent presidential candidate, (1992) 438
popular vote, (1992) 698

Ehrenreich, Ron
  vice-presidential candidate
    Socialist nominee, (1988) 438
Ehringhaus, John C. B.
  governor, North Carolina, 1403
Eighteenth Amendment
  Republican platform issue, (1932) 423
    (box)
Eisenhower, Dwight D.
  biography, 777
  as military commander
    "Bonus Army" protest, 261
    North Africa campaign, 268
  as president
    acceptance of New Deal, 133
    health concerns, 147–148, 150
    minimum voting age, 33
    politics and issues, 145–152
    in presidential campaign, (1960) 275
    Republican platform, (1960) 523
  presidential candidate
    Democratic draft idea, (1948) 139,
      263, 269, 512, (1952) 263
    election evolution, 7, 8, 17
    electoral vote, (1952) 759, (1956) 760
    military service, 221
    New York background, 222
    party control of House, (1956) 804
    politics and issues, (1952) 144–145,
      (1960) 147–149
    popular vote, (1952) 676, (1956) 677
    primary votes, (1948) 339–340,
      (1952) 308, 341–343, (1956)
      344–345, (1960) 346–347
    public offices, 215
    reelection chances, (1952) 313 (box)
    Republican convention votes, (1952)
      617, (1956) 619
    Republican draft idea, (1948) 270
    Republican nominee, (1952) 76,
      271–272, 422, 434, 515–516,
      (1956) 272–273, 435, 520
Eisenman, Abram
  presidential primary votes, (1976) 364
Elbert, Samuel
  governor, Georgia, 1389
Election day, 706 (box), 710
Election fraud
  absentee ballots, 37
  registration process, 35
  voting by mail, 38
Elections. See Congressional elections; Gubernatorial elections; Presidential elections; Special elections; Voter participation
Electoral college
  anomalies, 12–13, (box) 705–707
  calendar, 142
  chronology (box), 706
  constitutional background, 701–703, 710
  counting electoral votes, 710–713
    relevant law (text), 712
    2000 count, 712–713
  electoral vote totals
    presidents, 1789–2000 (maps, ta-
      bles), 717–771
    vice presidents, 1804–2000, 772–774
  faithless electors, 220, 703 (box), 711–712
  methods of choosing electors, 703–705
    changing methods of election,
      1788–1836, 1550–1551
  reform proposals, 5, 707, 713–714
    Democrats, (1912) 488, (1968) 532,
      (1972) 536, (1984) 549
    Green Party, (2000) 570–571
    Populists, (1892) 476
    Progressives, (1912) 489
    Socialists, (1912) 486
  summary, 5, 216, 220
  vote splitting, 702–703 (box)
Electoral Commission Law of 1877, 711
Electoral Vote Count Act of 1887, 251, 296,
  299, 706 (box), 711
Electric power
  Democratic platform issue, (1940) 508
Elkins, Davis
  senator, West Virginia, 1265

Ellender, Allen J.
  senator, Louisiana, 172, 1246
Ellerbe, William H.
  governor, South Carolina, 1408
Ellery, Christopher
  senator, Rhode Island, 1259
Ellington, Buford
  governor, Tennessee, 1409
Ellington, C. H.
  Populist convention officers, 425
    (box)
Elliott, John
  senator, Georgia, 1241
Ellis, John W.
  governor, North Carolina, 1403
Ellis, Powhatan
  senator, Mississippi, 1250
Ellis, Seth Hockett
  presidential candidate
    popular vote, (1900) 691
    Union Reform Party nominee, (1900)
      432
Ellmaker, Amos
  biography, 777
  vice-presidential candidate
    Anti-Mason Party nominee, (1832)
      429, 442
    electoral vote, (1832) 772
Ellsworth, Oliver
  biography, 777
  electoral vote, (1796) 720
  senator, Connecticut, 1238
Ellsworth, William W.
  governor, Connecticut, 1387
Elmer, Jonathan
  senator, New Jersey, 1253
Elmore, Franklin H.
  senator, South Carolina, 1260
Elrod, Samuel H.
  governor, South Dakota, 1408
Elthon, Leo
  governor, Iowa, 1392
Ely, Joseph B.
  governor, Massachusetts, 1396
Emancipation Proclamation, 243
Emanuel, David
  governor, Georgia, 1389
Emerson, Bill, 788
Emerson, Frank C.
  governor, Wyoming, 1413
Emerson, Jo Ann, 788
Emerson, Lee E.
  governor, Vermont, 1411
Emery, Stephen
  vice-presidential candidate
    Socialist Labor nominee, (1948,
      1952) 434
EMILY's List, 104
Emmerson, Louis L.
  governor, Illinois, 1391
Emmet, Robert
  Republican convention officers, 417
    (table)
Employment and unemployment
  New Deal, 263
  platform issue
    Democrats, (1928) 501, (1932) 503,
      (1940) 508, (1976) 539, (1980) 423
      (box), 545–546
    Republicans, (1932) 502, (1936) 504,
      (1940) 507, (1960) 524, (1988) 555
    Socialists, (1932) 501
  voter characteristics, 23 (table)
  World War II effects, 268
Energy policy
  platform issue
    Democrats, (1976) 540, (1980) 546,
      (1992) 557
    Green Party, (2000) 571
    National Unity Campaign, (1980)
      547
    Republicans, (1976) 542, (1980) 544,
      (1984) 551, (1988) 555, (1992) 560,
      (2000) 568
  politics and issues, 1970s, 163, 174, 177,
    180, 181

Engle, Clair
  senator, California, 152, 1237
Engler, John
  governor, Michigan, 1397
English, James E.
  Democratic convention ballots, (1868)
    584, (1880) 589
  governor, Connecticut, 1387
  senator, Connecticut, 1239
English, William H.
  biography, 777
  vice-presidential candidate
    Democratic nominee, (1880) 249,
      431, 469
    electoral vote, (1880) 772
Ennis, Robert E.
  presidential primary votes, (1964) 350
Ensign, John
  senator, Nevada, 1252
Environmental protection
  platform issue
    Democrats, (1976) 540, (1992) 558,
      (1996) 565
    Green Party, (2000) 571
    Republicans, (1988) 555
Enzi, Michael B.
  senator, Wyoming, 200, 1266
Eppes, John W.
  senator, Virginia, 1264
Epstein, Richard J.
  presidential primary votes, (2000)
    404–410
Equal Rights Amendment
  congressional approval, 171
  platform issue
    Democrats, (1944) 510, (1972) 536, (1980)
      546, (1984) 549
    Republicans, (1940) 507, (1972) 537,
      (1980) 543, 544, (1984) 551
Equal Rights Party
  historical development, 46
  nominees, (1872) 430, (1884) 431, (1888)
    431
"Era of Good Feelings," 231
Erbe, Norman A.
  governor, Iowa, 155, 1392
Erickson, John E.
  governor, Montana, 1399
  senator, Montana, 1251
Erickson, Oscar A.
  presidential primary votes, (1992) 393
Ernst, Richard P.
  senator, Kentucky, 1245
Ervin, Sam J. Jr.
  Democratic platform, (1960) 522
  senator, North Carolina, 175, 1256
  Watergate committee, 174
Espy, Mike, 791
Estabrok, Henry D.
  presidential primary votes, (1916) 323
Estee, Morris M.
  Republican convention officers, 417
    (table)
Etti, Joseph G.
  presidential primary votes, (1964) 350
Eustis, James B.
  senator, Louisiana, 1246
Eustis, William
  governor, Massachusetts, 1396
Evans, Daniel J.
  governor, Washington, 162, 1412
  Republican convention speakers, 417
    (table)
  senator, Washington, 191, 1265
Evans, George C.
  senator, Maine, 1247
  Whig convention officers, 425 (box)
Evans, Henry Clay, 477, 1409
Evans, John Gary
  governor, South Carolina, 1408
Evans, John V.
  governor, Idaho, 188, 1390
Evans, Josiah J.
  senator, South Carolina, 1260
Evans, R. Wayne
  vice-presidential candidate

  U.S. Labor Party nominee, (1976) 80,
    436
Evans, William W.
  presidential primary votes, (1968) 353
Evarts, William M.
  senator, New York, 1255
Everett, Edward
  biography, 777
  governor, Massachusetts, 1396
  senator, Massachusetts, 1248
  vice-presidential candidate
    Constitutional Union Party nominee,
      (1860) 430, 458
    electoral vote, (1860) 772
Ewing, Oscar R.
  Democratic convention ballots, (1952)
    618
Ewing, Thomas
  Democratic convention ballots, (1880)
    589
  senator, Ohio, 1257
Ewing, William Lee D.
  governor, Illinois, 1390
  senator, Illinois, 1242
Exit polls, 219, 299
Exon, J. James
  governor, Nebraska, 1400
  senator, Nebraska, 181, 1252
Extremism issue
  Democratic platform, (1964) 528
  Goldwater speech, 277
  presidential campaign, (1996) 292,
    293, 294
  Republican platform, (1964) 525, 526

F

Fabish, Thomas S.
  presidential primary votes, (1992) 393
Fahrenkopf, Frank J. Jr.
  Republican National Committee chair,
    417 (table), 426 (table)
  on campaign funding, 92
Fair, James G.
  senator, Nevada, 1252
Fair Labor Standards Act of 1938, 267
Fairbanks, Charles W.
  biography, 777
  presidential candidate
    primary votes, (1916) 322
    Republican contender, (1916) 258
    Republican convention ballots,
      (1908) 599, (1916) 602
    Republican convention officers, 417
      (table)
  senator, Indiana, 1243
  vice-presidential candidate
    electoral vote, (1904, 1916) 773
    Republican nominee, (1904) 255,
      432, 481–482, (1916) 258, 432,
      490
Fairbanks, Erastus
  governor, Vermont, 1410
Fairbanks, Horace
  governor, Vermont, 1410
Fairchild, Lucius
  governor, Wisconsin, 1413
Faircloth, Lauch
  senator, North Carolina, 202, 1256
Fairfield, John
  governor, Maine, 1394
  senator, Maine, 1246
Faithless electors, 220, 703 (box), 711–712
Fall, Albert B.
  senator, New Mexico, 1254
Family issues
  Democratic platform, (1996) 564, (2000)
    568, 569
  presidential campaign, (1992) 292
  Republican platform, (1992) 559, (2000)
    567
Fancher, Frederick B.
  governor, North Dakota, 1404
Fannin, Paul J.
  governor, Arizona, 1385
  senator, Arizona, 1237
Farenthold, Frances T. "Sissy," 535

Faris, Herman Preston
  presidential candidate
    popular vote, (1924) 669
    Prohibition Party nominee, (1924)
      433
Farley, James A.
  Democratic National Committee chair,
    415 (table), 426 (table)
  FDR campaign, (1936) 266
  presidential candidate
    Democratic contender, (1940) 267,
      507, (1944) 510
    Democratic convention ballots,
      (1940) 612, (1944) 614
    primary votes, (1940) 336, (1952)
      341–343
Farley, James T.
  senator, California, 1238
Farmer Labor Party
  nominees, (1920–32) 432–433
Farmers' Alliance, 69, 253
Farnham, Roswell
  governor, Vermont, 1410
Farnsworth, Daniel O. T.
  governor, West Virginia, 1412
Farrar, Frank L.
  governor, South Dakota, 1409
Farwell, Charles B.
  senator, Illinois, 1242
Farwell, Leonard J.
  governor, Wisconsin, 1413
Farwell, Nathan A.
  senator, Maine, 1247
Fassett, J. Sloat
  Republican convention officers, 417
    (table)
Faubus, Orval E.
  governor, Arkansas, 1385
    school desegregation, 149
  presidential candidate
    Democratic convention ballots,
      (1960) 620
    National States' Rights Party
      nominee, (1960) 435
    popular vote, (1960) 694
Faulkner, Charles J.
  senator, West Virginia, 1265
Fauntroy, Walter E.
  presidential primary votes, (1972)
    354–358, (1976) 359–364
"Favorite son" candidates, 212
Feazel, William C.
  senator, Louisiana, 1246
FEC. See Federal Election Commission
FECA. See Federal Election Campaign Act
Federal aid to state and local government
  platform issue
    Democrats, (1960) 523
    Republicans, (1960) 524
    Socialists, (1916) 492
Federal contracts
  Socialist platform issue, (1912) 485
Federal Corrupt Practices Act of 1910, 109
Federal Corrupt Practices Act of 1925, 86,
  109–110
Federal Election Campaign Act Amendments
  of 1974
    background, 86
    provisions, 116–117
    soft money, 104
    Supreme Court challenge, 117–120
Federal Election Campaign Act Amendments
  of 1976, 120
Federal Election Campaign Act Amendments
  of 1979, 87, 105, 121
Federal Election Campaign Act of 1971, 18, 86,
  282, 111–112
Federal Election Commission (FEC)
  campaign finance issues
    bundling, 104
    coordinated expenses, 106–107
    independent expenses, 106
    Section 527 groups, 107
    soft money, 104–105
  congressional candidate funds, expenses,
    94–100

creation, 282
  members, 118 (box), 120
  presidential candidate funds, expenses,
    88–94, 213
    campaign finance scandal (1996),
      84–85, 119 (box)
    convention financing, 411
    summary (box), 118–119
    voting machine standards, 36 (box), 216
Federal Emergency Relief Act, 264
Federal employees
  campaign contribution ban, 108, 110
  civil service reform as platform issue
    Democrats, (1876) 466–467, (1880)
      469, (1884) 471
    Liberal Republicans, (1872) 463
    Republicans, (1872) 464, (1880) 468
    Union Party, (1936) 506
  Hatch Act revision, 539
  Jackson era, 233–234
  Republican age, 249–251
Federal government reform
  changing role in twentieth century,
    133–134
  platform issue
    Democrats, (1976) 539, (1992) 558
    Republicans, (1976) 541, (1992) 559,
      (1996) 562, (2000) 566–567
Federal Reserve Board
  Republican platform issue, (1984) 551
Federal Voting Assistance Act of 1955, 38
Federal Voting Assistance Program, 38, 39
Federalist Party
  decline, 229, 230, 231
  first presidential election, 225
  historical development, 43–44
  profile, 62–63
  timeline, 47
Feimer, Doris
  vice-presidential candidate
    American Party nominee, (1992) 52,
      438
Feingold, Russell D.
  senator, Wisconsin, 1266
    campaign finance reform, 88, 124
    (box), 125, 296
Feinland, Marsha
  presidential candidate
    Peace and Freedom Party nominee,
      (1996) 69, 439
    popular vote, (1996) 699
Feinstein, Dianne
  at Democratic convention, (1992) 557
    officers, 415 (table)
  senator, California, 18, 199, 789, 1237
    reelection campaign, (1994) 99, 100
    Senate leadership, 789
Felch, Alpheus
  governor, Michigan, 1396
  senator, Michigan, 1249
Felker, Samuel D.
  governor, New Hampshire, 1401
Fellows, Lynn
  presidential primary votes,
    (1948) 340
Fellure, Jack
  presidential primary votes, (1992)
    386–393
Felton, Charles N.
  senator, California, 1237
Felton, Rebecca L.
  senator, Georgia, 788, 1241
Fenn, E. Hart, 813
Fenner, Arthur
  governor, Rhode Island,
    1406
Fenner, James
  governor, Rhode Island, 1406
  senator, Rhode Island, 1259
Fenton, Reuben E.
  governor, New York, 1403
  Republican vice-presidential contender,
    (1868) 461
  senator, New York, 1255
Ferguson, Homer
  senator, Michigan, 1249

Ferguson, James Edward
  governor, Texas, 1410
  presidential candidate
    American Party nominee, (1920) 433
    popular vote, (1920) 692
Ferguson, Joseph T.
  presidential primary votes, (1944) 338
Ferguson, Miriam A.
  governor, Texas, 16, 1377, 1410
Fernald, Bert M.
  governor, Maine, 1394
  senator, Maine, 1247
Fernandez, Benjamin
  presidential primary votes, (1980)
    365–371, (1984) 372–377
Ferraro, Geraldine A.
  biography, 777
  vice-presidential candidate
    Democratic nominee, (1984) 60–61,
      186, 285, 312, 437, 549
    election milestones, 18
    electoral vote, (1984) 773
    New York background, 222
    women in Congress, 790
Ferris, Woodbridge N.
  governor, Michigan, 1397
  presidential candidate
    Democratic convention ballots,
      (1924) 606
    primary votes, (1924) 327–328
  senator, Michigan, 1249
Ferry, Elisha P.
  governor, Washington, 1412
Ferry, Orris S.
  senator, Connecticut, 1239
Ferry, Thomas W.
  senator, Michigan, 1249
Fess, Simeon D.
  Republican convention officers, 417
    (table)
  Republican National Committee chair,
    417 (table), 426 (table)
  senator, Ohio, 1257
Fessenden, William
  senator, Maine, 1247
Few, William
  senator, Georgia, 1240
Fey, Susan C.
  presidential primary votes, (1992) 394
Field, James G.
  biography, 777
  vice-presidential candidate
    electoral vote, (1892) 773
    Populist nominee, (1892) 431, 476
Field, Richard S.
  senator, New Jersey, 1254
Field, Stephen J.
  Democratic convention ballots, (1880)
    589
Fielder, James F.
  governor, New Jersey, 1401
Fields, William J.
  governor, Kentucky, 1393
Fifer, Joseph W.
  governor, Illinois, 1390
Fifteenth Amendment, 15, 21, 24, 29, 132, 220
Fillmore, Millard
  biography, 777
  on Compromise of 1850, 240
  presidential candidate
    American Party nominee, (1856)
      64–65, 239, 241, 424 (box), 430,
      454
    electoral vote, (1856) 735
    former members of Congress, 155
      (box)
    as former vice president, 314 (box)
    political party development, 45
    popular vote, (1856) 652
    public offices, 214
    Whig contender, (1852) 240, 239,
      451
    Whig convention ballots, (1852)
      578
    Whig nominee, (1856) 430, 455
  succession to presidency, 239

    vice-presidential candidate
      electoral vote, (1848) 772
      Whig nominee, (1848) 238, 429, 449
Finch, Cliff
  governor, Mississippi, 1398
  presidential primary votes, (1980)
    365–371
Findlay, William
  governor, Pennsylvania, 1406
  senator, Pennsylvania, 1258
Fine, John S.
  governor, Pennsylvania, 1406
Finney, Joan
  governor, Kansas, 18, 1392
First Amendment
  campaign finance law, 86–87, 106–107,
    118–120
  exit polling, 219
Fish, Hamilton
  governor, New York, 1402
  senator, New York, 1255
Fishback, William M.
  governor, Arkansas, 1385
Fisher, John S.
  governor, Pennsylvania, 1406
Fisher, Louis
  presidential candidate
    popular vote, (1972) 695
    Socialist Workers nominee,
      (1972) 436
Fisher, Paul
  presidential primary votes, (1992) 394
Fisher, Paul C.
  presidential primary votes, (1960) 347
Fisher, Rolland E.
  vice-presidential candidate
    Prohibition Party nominee,
      (1968) 436
Fisk, Clinton B.
  biography, 777
  presidential candidate
    popular vote, (1888) 660
    Prohibition nominee, (1888) 431, 472
Fisk, James
  senator, Vermont, 1263
Fisk, Jim, 247
Fiske, John, 817 (box)
Fitch, Graham N.
  senator, Indiana, 1243
Fitler, Edwin H.
  Republican convention ballots,
    (1888) 592
Fitzgerald, Frank D.
  governor, Michigan, 1397
Fitzgerald, Peter G.
  senator, Illinois, 203, 1242
Fitzgerald, Thomas
  senator, Michigan, 1249
Fitzpatrick, Benjamin
  governor, Alabama, 1384
  senator, Alabama, 1236
  vice-presidential candidate
    Democratic nominee, (1860) 425,
      457
Flag desecration
  Republican platform issue, (1996) 562,
    (2000) 567
Flanagan, J. W.
  senator, Texas, 1262
Flanagan, William James
  presidential primary votes, (1996)
    395–402
Flanders, Benjamin F.
  governor, Louisiana, 1393
Flanders, Ralph E.
  senator, Vermont, 1263
Flannigan, Harris
  governor, Arkansas, 1385
Fleming, Aretas Brooks
  governor, West Virginia, 1412
Fleming, Francis P.
  governor, Florida, 1388
Fleming, William
  governor, Virginia, 1411
Fletcher, Allen M.
  governor, Vermont, 1411

Fletcher, Duncan U.
  senator, Florida, 1240
Fletcher, Henry P.
  Republican National Committee chair, 417 (table), 426 (table)
Fletcher, Ryland
  governor, Vermont, 1410
Fletcher, Thomas
  governor, Arkansas, 1385
Fletcher, Thomas C.
  governor, Missouri, 1398
Flint, Frank P.
  senator, California, 1237
Florida
  electoral vote contest, (1876) 248
  electoral vote contest, (2000) 205–206, 295–296, 299–301
    absentee ballots, 37
    application of 1887 law, 712–713
    chronology (box), 298–299
    voting systems, 218–219
  Jackson invasion, (1818) 234
  method of choosing electors, 705
  preferential primaries, 130
  presidential primary law, 15, 309–310
Florio, James J.
  governor, New Jersey, 1402
Flournoy, Francis B.
  Democratic convention officers, 415 (table)
Flower, Roswell P.
  Democratic convention ballots, (1884) 591
  governor, New York, 1403
Flowers, Gennifer, 18
Floyd, Charles M.
  governor, New Hampshire, 1401
Floyd, John
  biography, 777
  governor, Virginia, 1411
  presidential candidate
    electoral vote, (1832) 729
    Independent Party nominee, (1832) 235, 429
Floyd, John B.
  governor, Virginia, 1411
Fly, Daniel
  vice-presidential candidate
    Universal Party nominee, (1972) 436
Flynn, Edward J.
  Democratic National Committee chair, 415 (table), 426 (table)
Flynn, William S.
  governor, Rhode Island, 1407
Fogg, George G.
  senator, New Hampshire, 1253
Foley, Thomas S.
  House leadership, 11, 193, 199, 805
Folk, Joseph W.
  governor, Missouri, 1399
Folsom, James E.
  governor, Alabama, 1384
Folsom, James E. Jr.
  governor, Alabama, 1384
Fong, Hiram L.
  Republican convention ballots, (1964) 621, (1968) 622
  senator, Hawaii, 17, 153, 1241
Food assistance programs
  Progressive platform issue, (1948) 515
Foot, Solomon
  senator, Vermont, 1263
Foote, Charles C.
  vice-presidential candidate
    National Liberty Party nominee, (1848) 430
Foote, Henry Stuart
  governor, Mississippi, 1398
  senator, Mississippi, 1250
Foote, Samuel A.
  governor, Connecticut, 1387
  senator, Connecticut, 1238
Foraker, Joseph B.
  governor, Ohio, 1405
  Republican convention ballots, (1888) 592, (1908) 599

senator, Ohio, 1257
Forbes, Malcolm S. "Steve" Jr.
  presidential candidate
    campaign finance, (1996, 2000) 90, 92–93, 94
    primary votes, (1996) 311 (box), 395–402, (2000) 404–410
    Republican contender, (1996) 200, 293, 294, 315, (2000), 204, 296
Forbes, Ralph
  presidential candidate
    America First Party nominee, (1996) 439
    popular vote, (1996) 699
Ford, Gerald R.
  biography, 777
  House leadership, 164–165
  as president
    campaign finance reform, 120
    Nixon pardon, 174
    politics and issues, 163–164, 174, 177
    succession, 18, 174, 715
  presidential candidate
    electoral vote, (1976) 765
    faithless elector, (1976) 703 (box)
    former members of Congress, 155 (box)
    as former vice president, 314 (box)
    politics and issues, (1976) 177–178
    popular vote, (1976) 682
    primary votes, (1976) 310 (box), 359–364, (1980) 365–371
    public offices, 215
    reelection chances, (1976) 103, 313 (box)
    Republican convention ballots, (1976) 628
    Republican nominee, (1976) 282–283, 436, 540–541
    televised debates, (1976) 216
    at Republican convention, (1988) 554
    officers, 417 (table)
  vice president
    appointment, 18, 173, 281, 714–715
    Republican candidate possibility, (1980) 182, 542–543
Ford, Harold E. Jr.
  blacks in Congress, 791
  Democratic convention speakers, 415 (table)
Ford, Henry
  presidential primary votes, (1916) 322–323, (1924) 327–328
  Republican convention ballots, (1916) 602
Ford, James William
  vice-presidential candidate
    Communist nominee, (1932, 1936) 433, (1940) 434
Ford, Samuel C.
  governor, Montana, 1399
Ford, Seabury
  governor, Ohio, 1404
Ford, Thomas
  governor, Illinois, 1390
Ford, Wendell H.
  governor, Kentucky, 1393
  senator, Kentucky, 175, 1245
Fordice, Kirk
  governor, Mississippi, 1398
Foreign aid
  platform issue
    Democrats, (1960) 522
    Republicans, (1960) 524
Foreign policy
  Carter administration, 180
  FDR administration, 267
  platform issues
    Democrats, (1856) 455, (1900) 480, (1916) 491, (1928) 500, (1936) 505, (1940) 508, (1944) 510, (1956) 519, (1964) 528, (1976) 541, 542, (1984) 550, (1988) 554
    Green Party, (2000) 570–571
    Republicans, (1856) 454, (1892) 474, (1896) 478, (1900) 479–480, (1916)

491, (1928) 499, (1936) 504–505, (1940) 507, (1944) 509, (1948) 512, (1956) 520, 521, (1964) 526, (1984) 551, (1988) 555–556
    Socialists, (1916) 492
    Union Party, (1936) 506
    Whigs, (1852) 452
  post Soviet collapse, 134, 196–197
  post–World War II issues, 133–163, 269
  presidential campaign issues, (1960) 275, (1964) 277, (1976) 282, 283
  Reagan administration, 176–177, 185–186, 286
  Vietnam War years, 163–176
Foreign trade. See also Tariffs
  platform issues
    Democrats, (1856) 455, (1996) 564
    Green Party, (2000) 570–571
    Republicans, (1900) 479, (1980) 544
  reform era agriculture policy, 253
Fornwalt, Russell J.
  presidential primary votes, (1996) 403
Forsyth, John
  governor, Georgia, 1389
  senator, Georgia, 1241
Fort, George F.
  governor, New Jersey, 1401
Fort, John F.
  governor, New Jersey, 1401
Foss, Eugene N.
  Democratic convention ballots, (1912) 601
  governor, Massachusetts, 1396
Foss, Joe
  governor, South Dakota, 1409
Foster, Addison G.
  senator, Washington, 1265
Foster, Charles
  governor, Ohio, 1404
Foster, Dwight
  senator, Massachusetts, 1248
Foster, Ephraim H.
  senator, Tennessee, 1261
Foster, Ezola
  vice-presidential candidate
    Reform Party nominee, (2000) 73, 439
Foster, Henry A.
  senator, New York, 1255
Foster, Lafayette S.
  senator, Connecticut, 1239
Foster, Mike
  governor, Louisiana, 1394
Foster, Murphy J.
  governor, Louisiana, 1393
  senator, Louisiana, 1246
Foster, Theodore
  senator, Rhode Island, 1259
Foster, William Zebulon
  presidential candidate
    Communist nominee, (1924, 1928, 1932) 54, 433
    popular vote, (1924) 692, (1928) 670, (1932) 671
Fourteenth Amendment
  House apportionment, 13 (box), 220, 802, 812
  House redistricting, 818–823
  Johnson opposition, 245
  voting rights, 21, 24
  women's voting rights, 31–32
Fowle, Daniel G.
  governor, North Carolina, 1403
Fowler, Donald
  Democratic National Committee chair, 415 (table), 426 (table)
  Democratic rules reform, 418
Fowler, Joseph S.
  senator, Tennessee, 1262
Fowler, Wyche
  senator, Georgia, 189, 198–199, 1241
Fox, ——
  presidential primary votes, (1952) 343 note 1
Frahm, Sheila
  senator, Kansas, 788, 1244

France, Joseph I.
  presidential primary votes, (1932) 331–332
  at Republican convention, (1932) 501
    ballots, (1932) 610
  senator, Maryland, 1247
Franchise. See Voting rights
Francis, —— (Socialist Labor nominee), 439
Francis, David R.
  governor, Missouri, 1399
Francis, John B.
  governor, Rhode Island, 1406
  senator, Rhode Island, 1259
Franco, Francisco, 267
Frankfurter, Felix, 818–819, 822
Franklin, Benjamin
  governor, Pennsylvania, 1406
Franklin, Jesse
  governor, North Carolina, 1403
  senator, North Carolina, 1255, 1256
Franklin, Webb, 189
Franks, Bob, 107
Franks, Gary, 791
Fraser, Donald M., 534
Frazier, J. Curtis II
  vice-presidential candidate
    Constitution Party nominee, (2000) 439
Frazier, James B.
  governor, Tennessee, 1409
  senator, Tennessee, 1261
Frazier, Lynn J.
  governor, North Dakota, 1404
    recall, 1381 (box)
  senator, North Dakota, 1256
Frear, J. Allen Jr.
  senator, Delaware, 1240
Free Soil (Barnburners' Liberty Party)
  nominees, (1848) 430
Free Soil Party
  conventions, (1848) 449, (1852) 452
  Democratic defectors, 238
  historical development, 45, 49
    profile, 63
    timeline, 47
  nominees, (1848) 429, (1852) 430
  officers, 425 (box)
  platforms, (1848) 449–450, (1852) 452
  on slavery, 239
  vote percentage, 424 (box)
Freedmen's Bureau, 245, 246
Freedom and Peace Party
  nominees, (1968) 436
Freedom of information
  Democratic platform issue, (1956) 520
Freeh, Louis J., 84
Freeman, Debra H.
  vice-presidential candidate
    National Economic Recovery Party nominee, (1988) 438
Freeman, Orville L.
  governor, Minnesota, 147, 1397
Frelinghuysen, Frederick
  senator, New Jersey, 1254
Frelinghuysen, Frederick T.
  senator, New Jersey, 1254
Frelinghuysen, Joseph S.
  senator, New Jersey, 1254
Frelinghuysen, Theodore
  biography, 777
  senator, New Jersey, 1254
  vice-presidential candidate
    electoral vote, (1844) 772
    Whig nominee, (1844) 429, 446
Fremont, John C.
  biography, 777
  presidential candidate
    electoral vote, (1856) 735
    Independent Republican nominee, (1864) 243 430
    military service, 221, 222
    political party development, 45
    popular vote, (1856) 652
    Republican convention ballots, (1856) 579, (1860) 581

Republican nominee, (1856) 74, 239, 241, 430, 453, 454
senator, California, 1237
French, Augustus C.
governor, Illinois, 1390
Fricke, Doug
presidential primary votes, (1996) 403
Friedman, Samuel Herman
vice-presidential candidate
Socialist nominee, (1952) 434, (1956) 435
Frist, Bill
senator, Tennessee, 199, 1261
Fritz, Sara, 99
Froehlich, Harold V., 175
Fromentin, Eligius
senator, Louisiana, 1246
Frost, Martin, 790
Frye, William P.
senator, Maine, 1247
Fugitive slave law, 240
Fulani, Lenora B.
presidential candidate
New Alliance nominee, (1988, 1992) 68, 438
popular vote, (1988) 685, (1992) 697
primary votes, (1988) 378–385, (1992) 386–393
Fulbright, J. William
Democratic convention ballots, (1952) 618
senator, Arkansas, 1237
Fuller, Alvan T.
governor, Massachusetts, 1396
presidential primary votes, (1928) 329–330
Fuller, Levi K.
governor, Vermont, 1411
Fulton, Charles W.
senator, Oregon, 1258
Fulton, Robert D.
governor, Iowa, 1392
Fulton, William S.
senator, Arkansas, 1237
Fuqua, Henry L.
governor, Louisiana, 1393
Furcolo, Foster
governor, Massachusetts, 149, 1396
Furnas, Robert W.
governor, Nebraska, 1399
Futrell, Junius M.
governor, Arkansas, 1385

G

Gabrielson, Guy George
Republican National Committee chair, 417 (table), 426 (table)
Gadsden Purchase, 244
Gage, Henry T.
governor, California, 1386
Gage, Jack R.
governor, Wyoming, 1413
Gahres, Bill
presidential candidate
Down With Lawyers Party nominee, (1980) 437
popular vote, (1980) 696
Gaillard, John
senator, South Carolina, 1260
Gallatin, Albert
senator, Pennsylvania, 1258
vice-presidential candidate
Democratic-Republican contender, (1824) 232, 233
Gallen, Hugh J.
governor, New Hampshire, 185, 1401
Gallinger, Jacob H.
senator, New Hampshire, 1253
Galusha, Jonas
governor, Vermont, 1410
Gamache, Murielle E., 99
Gamble, Robert J.
senator, South Dakota, 1261
Gamble, Hamilton R.

governor, Missouri, 1398
Gambrell, David H.
senator, Georgia, 172, 1241
Gannett, Frank E.
Republican convention ballots, (1940) 613
Garber, Silas
governor, Nebraska, 1399
Garcelon, Alonzo
governor, Maine, 1394
Gardiner, William T.
governor, Maine, 1394
Gardner, Booth
governor, Washington, 1412
Gardner, Frederick D.
governor, Missouri, 1399
Gardner, Henry J.
governor, Massachusetts, 64, 1396
Gardner, John, 114
Gardner, O. Max
governor, North Carolina, 1403
Gardner, Obadiah
senator, Maine, 1247
Gardner, William M.
governor, New Hampshire, 1401
Garfield, James A.
assassination
biography, 777
civil service reform, 108
Credit Mobilier scandal, 247
disability issue, 714
election milestones, 15
former members of Congress, 155 (box), 223
military service, 222
as "minority" president, 223 (table)
popular vote, (1880) 658
presidential candidate
electoral vote, (1880) 741
public offices, 215
Republican convention ballots, (1880) 422, 588
Republican nominee, (1880) 249, 431, 467–468
Republican leadership, 247
Garland, Augustus H.
governor, Arkansas, 1385
senator, Arkansas, 1237
Garn, Jake
senator, Utah, 175, 1263
Garner, John Nance
biography, 777
House leadership, 13 (box)
opposition to FDR, (1940) 268
presidential candidate
Democratic contender, (1932) 262, 502, (1940) 267, 507
Democratic convention ballots, (1932) 611, (1940) 612
as former vice president, (1940) 314 (box)
primary votes, (1932) 331–332, (1936) 333–334, (1940) 335–336
vice-presidential candidate
Democratic nominee, (1932) 262, 433, 502, (1936) 265, 433, 505
electoral vote, (1932, 1936) 773
Garrahy, Joseph J.
governor, Rhode Island, 1407
Garrard, James
governor, Kentucky, 1392
Garrison, William Lloyd, 66, 239
Garson, Barbara
vice-presidential candidate
Socialist nominee, (1992) 438
Garst, Warren
governor, Iowa, 1392
Garvey, Dan E.
governor, Arizona, 1385
Garvin, Florence
vice-presidential candidate
National Greenback party nominee, (1936) 434
Garvin, Lucius F. C.
governor, Rhode Island, 1407

Garza, Laura
vice-presidential candidate
Socialist Workers nominee, (1996) 439
Gary, Frank B.
senator, South Carolina, 1260
Gary, Raymond D.
governor, Oklahoma, 1405
Gaston, William
governor, Massachusetts, 1396
Gates, Charles W.
governor, Vermont, 1411
Gates, Ralph F.
governor, Indiana, 1391
Gavin, Thomas J., 144
Gay, Edward J.
senator, Louisiana, 1246
Gay, James B.
presidential primary votes, (1992) 394
Gayle, John
governor, Alabama, 1384
Gear, John H.
governor, Iowa, 1391
senator, Iowa, 1243
Gearin, John M.
senator, Oregon, 1258
Geary, John W.
governor, Pennsylvania, 1406
Geddes, John
governor, South Carolina, 1407
Geer, Theodore T.
governor, Oregon, 1405
General election legal and accounting compliance fund, 88
Generational politics, 255
George, Henry, 78
George, James Z.
senator, Mississippi, 1250
George, Walter F.
Democratic convention ballots, (1928) 609
senator, Georgia, 788, 1241
Georgia
county unit system, 17, 131, 822
Democratic convention credentials dispute, (1968) 422, 531, 623
gubernatorial elections, 1380–1381
Republican convention credentials dispute, (1952) 422
Gephardt, Richard A.
Democratic convention officers, 415 (table)
presidential candidate
Democratic contender, (1988) 190, 286–287
Democratic convention ballots, (1988) 634
no-run decision, (1992) 289, (2000) 204
primary votes, (1988) 311 (box), 378–385
Gerard, James W.
Democratic convention ballots, (1920) 605, (1924) 607
Geringer, Jim
governor, Wyoming, 1413
German, Obadiah
senator, New York, 1255
Gerry, Elbridge
biography, 777
governor, Massachusetts, 1396
gerrymander origins, 817, 817 (box)
vice-presidential candidate
Democratic-Republican nominee, (1812) 230
electoral vote, (1812) 772
Gerry, Peter G.
senator, Rhode Island, 1259
Gerrymanders. See Congressional districts
Geyer, Henry S.
senator, Missouri, 1251
Gian-Cursio, Christopher
vice-presidential candidate
Vegetarian nominee, (1960) 435
Gibbs, Addison C.
governor, Oregon, 1405

Gibbs, William C.
governor, Rhode Island, 1406
Gibson, Charles H.
senator, Maryland, 1247
Gibson, Ernest W.
governor, Vermont, 1411
senator, Vermont, 1263
Gibson, Ernest W. Jr.
senator, Vermont, 1263
Gibson, Paris
senator, Montana, 1251
Gibson, Randall L.
senator, Louisiana, 1246
Gilbert, Abijah
senator, Florida, 1240
Gilbert, George G., 817
Gilchrist, Albert W.
governor, Florida, 1388
Gilder, George, 284
Giles, William B.
governor, Virginia, 1411
senator, Virginia, 1264
Gill, Moses
governor, Massachusetts, 1396
Gillett, Frederick H.
senator, Massachusetts, 1248
Gillett, James N.
governor, California, 1386
Gillette, Francis
senator, Connecticut, 1239
Gillette, Guy M.
senator, Iowa, 1244
Gillhaus, August
presidential candidate
popular vote, (1908) 691
Socialist Labor nominee (1908) 432
vice-presidential candidate
Socialist Labor nominee (1912) 432, (1920) 433
Gilligan, John J.
governor, Ohio, 175, 1405
Gilman, John T.
governor, New Hampshire, 1400
Gilman, Nicholas
senator, New Hampshire, 1252
Gilmer, George R.
governor, Georgia, 1389
Gilmer, Thomas W.
governor, Virginia, 1411
Gilmore, James S. III
governor, Virginia, 1412
Republican National Committee chair, 426 (table)
Gilmore, Joseph A.
governor, New Hampshire, 1400
Gingrich, Newt
campaign costs, 100
House leadership, 19, 78, 197–201
anti-Clinton ads, (1998) 106
campaign finance reform, 123
"Contract with America," 198
midterm elections, (1994) 292
as partisan leader, 135
Republican strength in South, 11, 129, 796
resignation, 202, 298, 805
at Republican convention, (1996) 561
officers, 417 (table)
role in presidential campaign, (1996) 294, 295
Ginsburg, Douglas H., 190.
Ginsburg, Ruth Bader, 301
Gist, William H.
governor, South Carolina, 1408
Gitlow, Benjamin
vice-presidential candidate
Communist nominee, (1924, 1928) 433
Giuliani, Rudolph W., 100
Giumarra, Rosemary
independent vice-presidential candidate, (1996) 439
Glass, Carter
Democratic convention ballots, (1920) 605, (1924) 606–607
senator, Virginia, 1264

Glass-Owen Act of 1913, 257
Glasscock, William E.
  governor, West Virginia, 1412
Glavis, Louis, 256
Glendening, Parris N.
  governor, Maryland, 1395
Glenn, John
  Democratic convention speakers, 415
    (table)
  presidential candidate
    Democratic contender, (1984) 186,
      285
    Democratic convention ballots,
      (1984) 632
    primary votes, (1984) 372–377
  senator, Ohio, 175, 1257
    ethics investigation, 195
  vice-presidential contender, (1976) 539
Glenn, Otis F.
  senator, Illinois, 1242
Glenn, Robert B.
  governor, North Carolina, 1403
Glick, George Washington
  governor, Kansas, 1392
Glynn, Martin H.
  Democratic convention officers, 415
    (table)
  governor, New York, 1403
Goddard, Samuel P.
  governor, Arizona, 440, 1385
Godwin, Mills E. Jr.
  governor, Virginia, 1412
Goebel, William
  governor, Kentucky, 1393
Goeller, Jewelie
  vice-presidential candidate
    Natural Peoples Party nominee,
      (1980) 437
Goff, Guy D.
  presidential primary votes, (1928) 330
  Republican convention ballots, (1928)
    609
  senator, West Virginia, 1265
Goff, Nathan
  governor's race, 1413
  senator, West Virginia, 1265
Goland, Michel, 96
Gold. See Monetary policy
Goldberg, Arthur J., 822
Goldfine, Bernard, 150
Goldhaber, Nat
  vice-presidential candidate
    Natural Law Party nominee, (2000)
      73, 439
Goldsborough, Charles
  governor, Maryland, 1395
Goldsborough, Phillips Lee
  governor, Maryland, 1395
  senator, Maryland, 1247
Goldsborough, Robert H.
  senator, Maryland, 1247
Goldschmidt, Neil
  governor, Oregon, 1406
Goldthwaite, George
  senator, Alabama, 1236
Goldwater, Barry
  biography, 777
  as party leader, 76, 158
  presidential candidate
    appeal in South, (1964) 129
    election evolution, 8, 10, 17
    electoral vote, (1964) 762
    "extremism" speech, 277
    politics and issues, (1964) 161–162
    popular vote, (1964) 679
    primary votes, (1960) 346–347,
      (1964) 310 (box), 313, 348–350
    Republican contender, (1960) 154,
      275, 523
    Republican convention ballots,
      (1960) 620, (1964) 621
    Republican nominee, (1964) 76,
      276–278, 435, 525
    significance of 1964 election, 133,
      137, 163
  senator, Arizona, 145, 1237

  Senate leadership, 169
  vice-presidential electoral vote, (1960)
    773
Gonas, John S.
  presidential primary vote, (1976) 364
Gonzalez, Andrea
  vice-presidential candidate
    Socialist Workers nominee, (1984)
      437
Gonzalez, Charlie, 793
Gonzalez, Henry B., 793
Goodell, Charles E.
  senator, New York, 170, 1255
Goodell, David H.
  governor, New Hampshire, 1401
Goodhue, Benjamin
  senator, Massachusetts, 1248
Gooding, Frank R.
  governor, Idaho, 1390
  senator, Idaho, 1242
Goodland, Walter S.
  governor, Wisconsin, 1413
Goodrich, Chauncey
  senator, Connecticut, 1239
Goodrich, James Putnam
  governor, Indiana, 1391
Goodwin, Ichabod
  governor, New Hampshire, 1400
Gorbachev, Mikhail, 286, 289
Gordon, Jacob J.
  presidential primary votes, (1968)
    353
Gordon, James
  senator, Mississippi, 1250
Gordon, James W.
  governor, Michigan, 1396
Gordon, John B.
  governor, Georgia, 1389
  senator, Georgia, 1241
Gore, Al
  biography, 777
  presidential candidate
    appeal in South, suburbs, (2000) 3,
      129
    campaign finance, (2000) 93, 213
    campaign strategies, 216
    Democratic contender, (1980)
      287–288, (1988) 190
    Democratic convention ballots,
      (1992) 636, (2000) 641
    Democratic nominee, (2000)
      295–301, 439, 568–569
    election evolution, 11, 12–13, 19–20
    electoral vote, (2000) 771
    Florida elector dispute, 135–136, 219,
      298–299 (box), 703 V, 706 (box),
      707, 712–713, 1557–1568
    as former vice president, 224, 314
      (box)
    no-run decision (1992), 289
    political party development, 48
    politics and issues, (2000) 197,
      203–206
    popular vote, (2000) 688
    primary, (1988) 378–385,
      (2000) 305, 311 (box), 318, (2000)
      212, 404–410
    vice-presidential choice, 61, 312
  senator, Tennessee, 187, 1262
  as vice president, 313, 1234
  vice-presidential candidate
    campaign finance scandal, (1996)
      84–85
    Democratic nominee, (1992) 60, 291,
      292, 438, 556–557, (1996) 439,
      295, 563–564
    electoral vote, (1992, 1996) 773
Gore, Albert A. Sr.
  senator, Tennessee, 145, 1261
  tribute at Democratic convention, (2000)
    568
  vice-presidential contender, (1956) 148,
    273, 519
Gore, Christopher
  governor, Massachusetts, 1396
  senator, Massachusetts, 1248

Gore, Howard M.
  governor, West Virginia, 1412
Gore, Thomas P.
  senator, Oklahoma, 1257, 1258
Gore, Tipper, 568, 569
Gorman, Arthur P.
  Democratic convention ballots, (1892)
    593, (1904) 597
  senator, Maryland, 1247
Gorton, Slade
  senator, Washington, 183, 188, 191, 206,
    1265
Gossett, Charles C.
  governor, Idaho, 1390
  senator, Idaho, 1242
Gould, Arthur R.
  senator, Maine, 1247
Gould, Jay, 243, 247
Gould, Symon
  presidential candidate
    Vegetarian nominee, (1960) 435
  vice-presidential candidate
    American Vegetarian nominee,
      (1948, 1952) 434, (1956) 435
Governors. See also Gubernatorial elections
  appointment power to Senate,
    1232
  background, 1377
  governors of states, 1776–2001 (lists),
    1383–1414
  as presidential candidates, (box) 176,
    222–223, 224, 1377
  removal from office (box) 1381
  terms, 1377–1378
    length of term, 1900, 2000 (table),
      1379
    limits, 1379, 1380 (box)
Graham, Bob
  governor, Florida, 1389
  senator, Florida, 189, 1240
Graham, Frank P.
  senator, North Carolina, 143, 1256
Graham, Horace
  governor, Vermont, 1411
Graham, Lindsey, 203
Graham, William A.
  biography, 777
  governor, North Carolina, 1403
  senator, North Carolina, 1256
  vice-presidential candidate
    electoral vote, (1852) 772
    Whig nominee, (1852) 430, 451
Gramm, Phil
  presidential candidate
    primary votes, (1996) 395–402
    Republican contender, (1996) 200,
      293
    Republican convention ballots, (1996)
      638
    Republican convention speakers, 417
      (table)
  senator, Texas, 187, 1262
    deficit control law, 188
Grammer, Elijah S.
  senator, Washington, 1265
Gramm-Rudman-Hollings act, 188
Grams, Rod
  senator, Minnesota, 199, 206, 1249
Grand Army of the Republic, 222
Granger, Francis
  biography, 777
  vice-presidential candidate
    electoral vote, (1836) 772
    Whig nominee, (1836) 235, 429, 444,
      709
Granger movement, 69, 253
Grant, Frederick D.
  Republican convention ballots, (1888)
    592
Grant, James B.
  governor, Colorado, 1386
Grant, Ulysses S.
  biography, 778
  Civil War victories, 244
  Johnson cabinet possibility, 246
  as president

Liberal Republican opposition, 65,
  463
Louisiana governors' dispute, 1394
poll violence, (1876) 248
presidential candidate
  African American vote, (1868) 24
  campaign finance, (1868) 89
  election evolution, 6
  electoral vote, (1868) 738, (1872) 739
  military service, 221, 222
  National Workingmen's Party
    nominee, (1872) 430
  popular vote, (1868) 655, (1872) 656
  public offices, 214
  Republican contender, (1864) 459
  Republican convention ballots,
    (1864) 582, (1868) 583, (1872) 585,
    (1880) 588
  Republican nominee, (1868) 74,
    245–246, 430, 461, (1872) 245,
    247–248, 430, 464
  third term possibility, (1880) 249,
    467–468
  Republican convention credentials
    dispute, (1880) 422
Grason, William
  governor, Maryland, 1395
Grassley, Charles E.
  senator, Iowa, 183, 1244
Grasso, Ella T.
  governor, Connecticut, 176, 1387
Grassroots Party
  nominees, (1988, 1992) 438, (1996) 439
Gravel, Mike
  senator, Alaska, 175, 1236
Graves, Bill
  governor, Kansas, 1392
  Dole successor, 788
Graves, Dixie Bibb
  governor, Alabama, 1384
  senator, Alabama, 1236
Graves, John Temple
  vice-presidential candidate
    Independence Party nominee, (1908)
      432
Gray, George
  presidential candidate
    Democratic contender, (1908) 484
    Democratic convention ballots,
      (1904) 597, (1908) 598
  senator, Delaware, 1239
Gray, Isaac P.
  governor, Indiana, 1391
  vice-presidential contender, (1888) 472,
    (1892) 475
Gray, James H.
  at Democratic convention, (1960) 522,
    (1968) 531
    ballots, (1968) 623
Gray, Jesse
  presidential primary votes, (1976) 364
Gray, Virginia, 803
Gray, William H. III, 791
Grayson, William
  senator, Virginia, 1264
Great Depression, 261–264
Great Society programs, 133, 164, 165, 277,
  278–279
Greaves, Percy L.
  presidential candidate
    American Party nominee, (1980) 52,
      437
    popular vote, (1980) 696
Greeley, Horace
  biography, 778
  on frontier, 240
  presidential candidate
    Democratic convention ballots,
      (1872) 585
    Democratic nominee, (1872) 247,
      430, 463, 464
    effect of death, 12 (box), 425, 706
    Liberal Republican nominee, (1872)
      65, 247, 430, 463, 464
    Liberal Republican Party of Colored
      Men nominee, (1872) 430

popular vote, (1872) 656
Green, Dwight H.
    governor, Illinois, 1391
    Republican convention ballots, (1948)
        615
    Republican convention officers, speakers,
        417 (table)
Green, Fred W.
    governor, Michigan, 1397
Green, Gabriel
    presidential candidate
        popular vote, (1972) 695
        Universal Party nominee, (1972)
            436
Green, James S.
    senator, Missouri, 1251
Green, Nehemiah
    governor, Kansas, 1392
Green, Robert S.
    governor, New Jersey, 1401
Green, Theodore F.
    governor, Rhode Island, 1407
    senator, Rhode Island, 1260
Green, Warren E.
    governor, South Dakota, 1408
    presidential primary votes, (1936)
        333–334
Green Party
    convention, platform (2000) 570–571
    historical development, 48, 50
        profile, 63
        timeline, 47
    nominees, (1996, 2000) 297, 439
    primaries, (1996) 402, 403
Greenback Party
    convention, (1880) 468
    historical development, 46, 49
        profile, 63–64
        timeline, 47
    nominees, (1876) 430, (1880) 431, (1884)
        431, 471
    officers, 425 (box)
    platform, (1880) 468–469
    policies, 253
    Socialist Labor support, 79
Greenback Party
    nominees, (1924, 1928) 433, (1936, 1940,
        1948) 434, (1952–1960) 435
Greene, Albert C.
    senator, Rhode Island, 1259
Greene, Frank L.
    senator, Vermont, 1263
Greene, Ray
    senator, Rhode Island, 1259
Greene, William
    governor, Rhode Island, 1406
Greenhalge, Frederic T.
    governor, Massachusetts, 1396
Greenly, William
    governor, Michigan, 1396
Greenstein, Mark
    presidential primary votes, (2000)
        404–410
Greenup, Christopher
    governor, Kentucky, 1392
Gregg, Andrew
    senator, Pennsylvania, 1259
Gregg, Hugh
    governor, New Hampshire, 1401
Gregg, Judd
    governor, New Hampshire, 1401
    senator, New Hampshire, 1253
Gregory, Dick
    presidential candidate
        Freedom and Peace Party nominee,
            (1968) 68, 436
        popular vote, (1968) 694
Gregory, John M.
    governor, Virginia, 1411
Gregory, William
    governor, Rhode Island, 1407
Grenada, 185–186
Gresham, Walter Q.
    presidential candidate
        no-run decision, (1892) 476
        Republican contender (1888), 473

Republican convention ballots, (1888)
    592
Griffin, James C.
    presidential candidate
        American Independent Party
            nominee, (1988) 52, 438
        popular vote, (1988) 697
        primary votes, (1988) 385
Griffin, James D.
    presidential primary votes, (1996)
        403
Griffin, Marvin
    biography, 778
    governor, Georgia, 1389
    vice-presidential candidate
        American Independent nominee,
            (1968) 436, 532
Griffin, Robert P.
    Republican platform, (1976) 541
    senator, Michigan, 1249
Griggs, John W.
    governor, New Jersey, 1401
Grimes, James W.
    governor, Iowa, 1391
    Republican leadership, 247
    senator, Iowa, 1243
Grimmer, Derrick P.
    vice-presidential candidate
        Grassroots Party nominee, (1992)
            438
Griser, Robert K.
    presidential primary votes, (1984)
        372–377
Griswold, Deirdre
    presidential candidate
        popular vote, (1980) 696
        Workers World Party nominee,
            (1980) 82, 437
Griswold, Dwight P.
    governor, Nebraska, 1399
    senator, Nebraska, 1252
Griswold, Matthew
    governor, Connecticut, 1387
Griswold, Morley I.
    governor, Nevada, 1400
Griswold, Roger
    governor, Connecticut, 1387
Griswold, Stanley
    senator, Ohio, 1257
Gritz, James "Bo"
    presidential candidate
        America First Party nominee, (1992)
            438
        popular vote, (1992) 697
        primary votes, (1988) 378–385,
            (1992) 393
Groesbeck, Alexander J.
    governor, Michigan, 1397
Groesbeck, William S.
    biography, 778
    presidential candidate
        Democratic convention ballots,
            (1872) 585
        Independent Liberal Republican
            nominee, (1872) 430
        vice-presidential electoral vote, (1872)
            772
Grofman, Bernard, 819 (box)
Gronna, Asle J.
    senator, North Dakota, 1256
Groome, James B.
    governor, Maryland, 1395
    senator, Maryland, 1247
Gross, H. R., 529
Grossman, Steven
    Democratic National Committee chair,
        426 (table)
Grout, Josiah
    governor, Vermont, 1411
Grover, La Fayette
    governor, Oregon, 1405
    senator, Oregon, 1258
Gruening, Ernest
    senator, Alaska, 1236
Grundy, Felix
    senator, Tennessee, 1261

Grundy, Joseph R.
    senator, Pennsylvania, 1259
Gubbrud, Archie M.
    governor, South Dakota, 1409
Gubernatorial elections
    general election returns, 1415–1477
    majority vote requirement, 1380–1381
    methods, 1378–1379
    primary returns, 1479–1542
    southern primaries, 129–132
    summary, 5
    third-party challenges, 5
    timing in nonpresidential year, 1378
Guffey, Joseph F.
    senator, Pennsylvania, 1258
Guggenheim, Simon
    senator, Colorado, 1238
Guerard, Benjamin
    governor, South Carolina, 1407
Guild, Curtis Jr.
    governor, Massachusetts, 1396
Guinn, Kenny
    governor, Nevada, 1400
Guion, John I.
    governor, Mississippi, 1398
Guion, Walter
    senator, Louisiana, 1246
Guiteau, Charles, 15, 249
Gun control
    platform issue
        Democrats, (1972) 535, (1976) 540,
            (1980) 546, (1984) 549, (1992) 558,
            (1996) 564, (2000) 569
        Green Party, (2000) 571
        Republicans, (1972) 537, (1976) 541,
            (1980) 544, (1984) 551, (1988) 555,
            (1992) 559, (1996) 562, (2000) 567
    presidential campaign issue, (2000) 299
Gunderson, Carl
    governor, South Dakota, 1408
Gunderson, Genevieve
    vice-presidential candidate
        Socialist Workers nominee, (1972)
            436
Gunderson, Ted L.
    presidential primary votes, (1996)
        395–402
Gunn, James
    senator, Georgia, 1241
Gunter, Julius C.
    governor, Colorado, 1386
Gurney, Edward J.
    senator, Florida, 169, 1240
Gurney, J. Chandler
    senator, South Dakota, 1261
Guthrie, James
    Democratic presidential contender,
        (1860) 456–457
        convention ballots, (1860) 580
    Democratic vice-presidential contender,
        (1864) 460
    senator, Kentucky, 1245
Guy, William L.
    governor, North Dakota, 1404
Gwin, William M.
    senator, California, 1238
Gwinnett, Button
    governor, Georgia, 1389

H

Hacker, Andrew, 808–809
Hadley, Herbert S.
    governor, Missouri, 1399
Hadley, Ozra A.
    governor, Arkansas, 1385
Hagaman, Frank L.
    governor, Kansas, 1392
Hagel, Chuck
    senator, Nebraska, 200, 1252
Hagelin, John
    presidential candidate
        Natural Law Party nominee,
            (1992–2000) 68, 438–439
        popular vote, (1992, 1996) 698,
            (2000) 699
        primary votes, (1996) 395–402

Reform Party contender, (2000) 68,
    73
Hager, John S.
    senator, California, 1237
Hagood, Johnson
    governor, South Carolina, 1408
Hahn, Michael
    governor, Louisiana, 1393
Haig, Alexander M. Jr.
    presidential candidate
        primary votes, (1988) 378–385
        Republican contender, (1988) 190,
            287
    Reagan disability issue, 715
Haight, Henry H.
    governor, California, 1386
Haile, William
    governor, New Hampshire, 1400
Haines, Daniel
    governor, New Jersey, 1401
Haines, John M.
    governor, Idaho, 1390
Haines, William T.
    governor, Maine, 1394
Halberstam, David, 278
Haldeman, H. R., 114
Hale, Eugene
    senator, Maine, 1246
Hale, Frederick
    senator, Maine, 1246
Hale, John P.
    biography, 778
    presidential candidate
        Free Soil nominee, (1852) 430, 452
        Liberty Party nominee, (1848) 66,
            430, 449
        political party development, 49
        popular vote, (1852) 651
    senator, New Hampshire, 1253
Hale, Samuel W.
    governor, New Hampshire, 1401
"Half-Breed" faction (Republicans), 75, 465
Hall, Arsenio, 291
Hall, David
    governor, Delaware, 1388
Hall, David
    governor, Oklahoma, 1405
Hall, Frederick L.
    governor, Kansas, 1392
Hall, Gus
    presidential candidate
        Communist nominee, (1972, 1976)
            436, (1980, 1984) 437
        popular vote, (1972, 1976) 695,
            (1980) 696, (1984) 697
Hall, Hiland
    governor, Vermont, 1410
Hall, John H.
    governor, Oregon, 1405
Hall, John W.
    governor, Delaware, 1388
Hall, Joshua
    governor, Maine, 1394
Hall, Katie, 791
Hall, Leonard W.
    Republican National Committee chair,
        147, 417 (table), 426 (table)
Hall, Luther E.
    governor, Louisiana, 1393
Hall, Lyman
    governor, Georgia, 1389
Hall, Tony P., 564
Hall, Willard Preble
    governor, Missouri, 1398
Hall, William
    governor, Tennessee, 1409
Hall, Wilton E.
    senator, South Carolina, 1260
Hallanan, Walter S.
    Republican convention officers, 417
        (table)
Halleck, Charles A.
    House leadership, 153, 157, 164
    at Republican convention, (1940)
        508–509
        officers, 417 (table)

Hallett, Benjamin F.
  at Democratic convention, (1952) 450
  Democratic National Committee chair,
    415 (table), 426 (table)
Hallinan, Vincent W.
  presidential candidate
    American Labor Party nominee,
      (1952) 434
    popular vote, (1952) 676
    Progressive nominee, (1952) 434
Halstead, Fred
  presidential candidate
    popular vote, (1968) 694
    Socialist Workers nominee, (1968)
      436
Halyard, Helen
  presidential candidate
    popular vote, (1992) 698
    Workers League nominee, (1992) 438
  vice-presidential candidate
    Workers League Party nominee,
      (1984) 437
"Ham and Eggs" pension ticket, 336
Hamblen, Stuart
  presidential candidate
    popular vote, (1952) 676
    Prohibition Party nominee, (1952)
      434
Hamburg, Al
  presidential primary votes, (1988) 385
Hamer, Fannie L., 803
Hamilton, Alexander
  on Burr, 707
  political party development, 43–44, 55,
    62, 227
  on presidential rotation, 194
  role in elections, (1789) 226, (1796) 227,
    (1800) 228, 707, 708
Hamilton, Andrew
  governor, Texas, 1409
Hamilton, James Jr.
  governor, South Carolina, 1407
Hamilton, John
  Republican National Committee chair,
    417 (table), 426 (table)
Hamilton, John M.
  governor, Illinois, 1390
Hamilton, Morgan C.
  senator, Texas, 1262
Hamilton, Paul
  governor, South Carolina, 1407
Hamilton, William T.
  governor, Maryland, 1395
  senator, Maryland, 1247
Hamlin, Hannibal
  biography, 778
  governor, Maine, 1394
  political party development, 45, 57
  senator, Maine, 1246
  vice-presidential candidate
    electoral vote, (1860) 772
    Republican contender, (1864) 459
    Republican nominee, (1860) 242,
      430, 458
Hamm, Vincent S.
  presidential primary votes, (1996) 403,
    (2000) 404–410
Hammond, Abraham A.
  governor, Indiana, 1391
Hammond, James H.
  governor, South Carolina, 1408
  senator, South Carolina, 1260
Hammond, Jay S.
  governor, Alaska, 176, 1384
Hammond, Winfield S.
  governor, Minnesota, 1397
Hammill, John
  governor, Iowa, 1392
Hampton, Wade
  governor, South Carolina, 1408
  senator, South Carolina, 1260
Hance, Kent
  Democratic convention ballots, (1980)
    630
Hancock, John
  biography, 778

electoral vote, (1789) 226, 718
  governor, Massachusetts, 1396
Hancock, Winfield Scott
  biography, 778
  presidential candidate
    Democratic contender, (1868) 246,
      462
    Democratic convention ballots,
      (1868) 584, (1876) 587, (1880)
      589
    Democratic nominee, (1880) 249,
      431, 469
    electoral vote, (1880) 741
    military service, 222
    popular vote, (1880) 658
Handley, George
  governor, Georgia, 1389
Handley, Harold W.
  governor, Indiana, 1391
Hanford, Benjamin
  vice-presidential candidate
    Socialist nominee, (1904) 432, 481,
      (1908) 432, 483
Hanly, F. Frank
  governor, Indiana, 1391
Hanly, James Franklin
  presidential candidate
    popular vote, (1916) 667
    Prohibition Party nominee, (1916)
      432
Hanna, Louis B.
  governor, North Dakota, 1404
Hanna, Marcus A.
  campaign finance, 89, 108
  effect of death, 481
  as McKinley promoter, (1892) 252,
    (1896) 76, (1900) 254
  at Republican convention, (1896) 477,
    (1900) 479
  Republican National Committee chair,
    417 (table), 426 (table)
  senator, Ohio, 1257
Hanna, Robert
  senator, Indiana, 1243
Hannegan, Edward A.
  senator, Indiana, 1243
Hannegan, Robert E.
  at Democratic convention, (1944) 509,
    510
  Democratic National Committee chair,
    138, 415 (table), 426 (table)
Hannett, Arthur T.
  governor, New Mexico, 1402
Hansbrough, Henry C.
  senator, North Dakota, 1256
Hansen, Clifford P.
  governor, Wyoming, 1413
  senator, Wyoming, 1266
Hanson, Alexander C.
  senator, Maryland, 1247
Hanson, Robert
  presidential primary votes, (1992)
    386–393
Hanson, Russell, 236, 237
Harbord, James G., 501
Hardee, Cary A.
  governor, Florida, 1388
Harder, Heather Anne
  presidential primary votes, (1996)
    395–402, (2000) 404–410
Hardin, Charles Henry
  governor, Missouri, 1399
Hardin, Martin D.
  senator, Kentucky, 1245
Harding, Benjamin F.
  senator, Oregon, 1258
Harding, Warren G.
  biography, 778
  death, 260
  election milestones, 16
  presidential candidate
    electoral vote, (1920) 751
    former members of Congress, 155
      (box), 222, 223
    popular vote, (1920) 668
    primary votes, (1920) 313, 324–326

public offices, 215
  Republican convention ballots,
    (1916) 602, (1920) 604
  Republican nominee, (1920)
    258–259, 432, 493
  at Republican convention, (1912) 486,
    (1916) 490
  officers, 417 (table)
  senator, Ohio, 1257
Harding, William L.
  governor, Iowa, 1392
Hardman, Lamartine G.
  governor, Georgia, 1389
Hardwick, Thomas W.
  governor, Georgia, 1389
  senator, Georgia, 1241
Harkin, James
  senator, Iowa, 1244
Harkin, Tom
  presidential candidate
    Democratic contender, (1992)
      195–196, 290
    primary votes, (1992), 309, 311 (box),
      386–393
  senator, Iowa, 187, 1244
Harlan, John M., 822–823
Harley, Joseph E.
  governor, South Carolina, 1408
Harmon, Judson
  governor, Ohio, 1405
  presidential candidate
    Democratic contender, (1912) 257,
      487
    Democratic convention ballots,
      (1912) 601
    primary votes, (1912) 320–321
Harnes, Mark "Dick"
  presidential primary votes, (2000)
    404–410
Harper, Joseph M.
  governor, New Hampshire, 1400
Harper, Robert G.
  biography, 778
  senator, Maryland, 1247
  vice-presidential electoral vote, (1816,
    1820) 772
Harper, William
  senator, South Carolina, 1260
Harreld, John W.
  senator, Oklahoma, 1258
Harriman, Job
  vice-presidential candidate
    Social-Democratic nominee, (1900)
      431
Harriman, W. Averell
  governor, New York, 147, 152, 1403
  presidential candidate
    Democratic contender, (1952)
      143–144, 272, 517, (1956) 148, 273,
      518
    Democratic convention ballots,
      (1952) 618, (1956) 619
    primary votes, (1952) 341–343,
      (1956) 344–345
Harriman, Walter
  governor, New Hampshire, 1400
Harrington, Emerson C.
  governor, Maryland, 1395
Harris, Andrew L.
  governor, Ohio, 1405
Harris, Elisha
  governor, Rhode Island, 1407
Harris, Fred R.
  Democratic National Committee chair,
    426 (table)
  presidential candidate
    Democratic contender, (1976)
      282
    Democratic convention ballots,
      (1976) 627
    primary votes, (1976) 359–364
  senator, Oklahoma, 1257
Harris, Ira
  senator, New York, 1255
Harris, Isham G.
  senator, Tennessee, 1262

Harris, James E. Jr.
  presidential candidate
    popular vote, (1996, 2000) 699
    Socialist Workers nominee, (1996,
      2000) 79, 439
Harris, John S.
  senator, Louisiana, 1246
Harris, Joe Frank
  governor, Georgia, 1390
Harris, Katherine, 298–299 (box), 300
Harris, LaDonna
  vice-presidential candidate
    Citizens Party nominee, (1980) 54,
      437
Harris, Nathaniel E.
  governor, Georgia, 1389
Harris, Thomas E., 105
Harris, William A.
  senator, Kansas, 1244
Harris, William J.
  senator, Georgia, 1241
Harrison, Albertis S. Jr.
  governor, Virginia, 1412
Harrison, Benjamin
  governor, Virginia, 1411
Harrison, Benjamin
  biography, 778
  presidential candidate
    election milestones, 15
    electoral anomalies, 12 (box)
    electoral vote, (1888) 707, 743,
      (1892) 702 (box), 744
    former members of Congress, 155
      (box)
    military service, 222
    as "minority" president, 223 (table)
    popular vote, (1888) 660, (1892) 661
    public offices, 215
    Republican convention ballots,
      (1888) 592, (1892) 593
    Republican nominee, (1888) 250,
      251–252, 296, 431, 473, (1892)
      252, 431, 474
  senator, Indiana, 1243
Harrison, Caleb
  vice-presidential candidate
    Socialist Labor nominee, (1916) 432
Harrison, Francis B.
  Democratic convention ballots, (1920)
    605
Harrison, Henry B.
  governor, Connecticut, 1387
Harrison, Patrick
  Democratic convention ballots, (1924)
    606, (1928) 609
  Democratic convention officers, 415
    (table)
  senator, Mississippi, 1250
Harrison, Robert
  biography, 778
  electoral vote, (1798) 226, 718
Harrison, William Henry
  biography, 778
  election milestones, 15
  political party development, 56
  presidential candidate
    Anti-Mason endorsement, (1836) 53
    campaign strategy, (1840) 222
    electoral vote, (1836) 730, (1840) 731
    former members of Congress, 155
      (box)
    military service, 221
    popular vote, (1836) 647, (1840) 648
    public offices, 214
    Whig nominee, (1836) 235, 237, 429,
      444, 705, (1840) 81, 237, 429, 444
  senator, Ohio, 1257
Harrity, William F.
  Democratic National Committee chair,
    415 (table), 426 (table)
Harrop, Roy M.
  vice-presidential candidate
    Greenback Party nominee, (1924)
      433
Hart, Gary
  in McGovern campaign, 280

presidential candidate
  Democratic contender, (1984) 186, 285, 549, 550, (1988) 190, 286
  Democratic convention ballots, (1984) 632, (1988) 634
  primary votes, (1984) 305, 314, 372–377, (1988) 378–385
  senator, Colorado, 175, 189, 1238
Hart, Louis F.
  governor, Washington, 1412
Hart, Ossian B.
  governor, Florida, 1388
Hart, Philip A.
  senator, Michigan, 1249
Hart, Thomas C.
  senator, Connecticut, 1239
Hartke, Vance
  presidential primary votes, (1972) 354–358
  senator, Indiana, 179, 1243
    campaign finance, 111
Hartley, Roland H.
  governor, Washington, 1412
Hartness, James
  governor, Vermont, 1411
Hartranft, John F.
  governor, Pennsylvania, 1406
  Republican convention ballots, (1876) 586
Harvey, James M.
  governor, Kansas, 1392
  senator, Kansas, 1244
Harvey, Louis P.
  governor, Wisconsin, 1413
Harvey, Matthew
  governor, New Hampshire, 1400
Harvey, William H.
  presidential candidate
    Liberty Party nominee, (1932) 433
    popular vote, (1932) 692
Harvey, Wilson G.
  governor, South Carolina, 1408
Haskell, Charles N.
  governor, Oklahoma, 1405
Haskell, Floyd
  senator, Colorado, 172, 181, 1238
Haskell, Robert N.
  governor, Maine, 1394
Haslet, Joseph
  governor, Delaware, 1388
Hass, Eric
  presidential candidate
    popular vote, (1952) 694, (1956) 677, (1960) 678, (1964) 679
    Socialist Labor nominee, (1952) 434, (1956, 1960, 1964) 435
Hastert, J. Dennis
  census sampling, 821 (box)
  House leadership, 202
  Republican convention officers, 417 (table)
Hastie, William H., 26
Hastings, Daniel H.
  governor, Pennsylvania, 1406
Hastings, Daniel O.
  senator, Delaware, 1240
Hatch, Carl A.
  senator, New Mexico, 1254
Hatch, Orrin G.
  presidential candidate
    campaign funding, (2000) 93
    primary votes, (2000) 404–410
    Republican contender, (2000) 204
  senator, Utah, 179, 1263
Hatch Act of 1939, 110
Hate crimes
  Democratic platform issue, (2000) 569
Hatfield, Henry D.
  governor, West Virginia, 1412
  senator, West Virginia, 1265
Hatfield, Mark O.
  governor, Oregon, 152, 1406
  Republican convention officers, speakers, 417 (table)
  senator, Oregon, 1258

Hatfield, Paul G.
  senator, Montana, 1251
Hathaway, Stanley K.
  governor, Wyoming, 1413
Hathaway, William D.
  senator, Maine, 172, 181, 1247
Haun, Henry P.
  senator, California, 1237
Hauptli, Gary
  presidential primary votes, (1992) 386–393
Hawes, Harry B.
  senator, Missouri, 1251
Hawkes, Albert W.
  senator, New Jersey, 1254
Hawkins, Alvin
  governor, Tennessee, 1409
Hawkins, Augustus F., 791
Hawkins, Benjamin
  senator, North Carolina, 1256
Hawkins, Paula
  senator, Florida, 189, 789, 1240
Hawkins, William
  governor, North Carolina, 1403
Hawks, Tod H.
  presidential primary votes, (1992) 386–393
Hawley, James H.
  governor, Idaho, 1390
Hawley, Joseph R.
  governor, Connecticut, 1387
  Republican convention ballots, (1884) 590, (1888) 592
  Republican convention officers, 417 (table)
  senator, Connecticut, 1239
Hay, Marion E.
  governor, Washington, 1412
Hayakawa, S. I.
  senator, California, 179, 1237
Hayden, Carl
  length of service in Congress, 795 (table)
  senator, Arizona, 1237
    Senate leadership, 169
Hayden, Mike
  governor, Kansas, 189, 1392
Hayes, Jim
  presidential primary votes, (1992) 394
Hayes, Maximilian Sebastian
  vice-presidential candidate
    Farmer Labor nominee, (1920) 432
Hayes, Rutherford B.
  biography, 778
  governor, Ohio, 1404
  presidential candidate
    disputed election, (1876) 6, 15, 706, 707, 710–711
    electoral anomalies, 12 (box)
    electoral vote, (1876) 740
    as former governor, 176 (box)
    former members of Congress, 155 (box)
    military service, 222
    as "minority" president, 223 (table)
    popular vote, (1876) 657
    public offices, 215
    Republican convention ballots, (1876) 586
    Republican nominee, (1876) 248, 296, 430, 465
Haymarket riot, 251
Haymond, Creed
  Republican convention ballots, (1888) 592
Hayne, Arthur P.
  senator, South Carolina, 1260
Hayne, Robert Y.
  governor, South Carolina, 1407
  senator, South Carolina, 1260
Hays, Brooks, 152
Hays, George W.
  governor, Arkansas, 1385
Hays, Wayne L.
  Democratic convention ballots, (1972) 625

Hays, Will H.
  Republican convention ballots, (1920) 604
  Republican National Committee chair, 417 (table), 426 (table)
Hayward, Monroe L.
  senator, Nebraska, 1252
Haywood, William H. Jr.
  senator, North Carolina, 1256
Hazzard, David
  governor, Delaware, 1388
Head, Natt
  governor, New Hampshire, 1401
Health care and insurance. See also Medicare
  Clinton policies, 198
  platform issue
    Democrats, (1948) 513, (1976) 539, (1988) 553, (1992) 557, (1996) 565, (2000) 569
    Green Party, (2000) 571
    Progressives, (1912) 489
    Republicans, (1972) 537, (1976) 542, (1988) 555, (1996) 563, (2000) 567–568
  politics and issues, (1950) 143
Heard, Alexander, 112
Heard, Stephen
  governor, Georgia, 1389
Heard, William W.
  governor, Louisiana, 1393
Hearnes, Warren E.
  governor, Missouri, 1399
Hearst, George
  senator, California, 1237
Hearst, William Randolph
  Garner support, (1932) 262
  Parker opposition, (1904) 255
  presidential candidate
    Democratic contender, (1904) 482
    Democratic convention ballots, (1904) 597, (1920) 605
Hebert, Felix
  senator, Rhode Island, 1259
Hebert, Paul O.
  governor, Louisiana, 1393
Hecht, Chic
  senator, Nevada, 191, 1252
Heflin, Howell
  senator, Alabama, 181, 1236
Heflin, J. Thomas
  senator, Alabama, 130, 1236
Hegger, Karl J.
  presidential primary votes, (1992) 394
Heil, Julius P.
  governor, Wisconsin, 1413
Heinz, John
  senator, Pennsylvania, 179, 1258
    successor, 289
Heiskell, John N.
  senator, Arkansas, 1237
Heitfeld, Henry
  senator, Idaho, 1242
Helm, John L.
  governor, Kentucky, 1392, 1393
Helms, Jesse A.
  nomination feelers declined, 51, 52, 80
  Republican vice-presidential contender, (1976) 540–541
  senator, North Carolina, 187, 1256
Hem, Eugene A.
  presidential candidate
    popular vote, (1992) 698
    Third Party nominee, (1992) 438
Hemenway, Frank B.
  vice-presidential candidate
    Liberty Party nominee, (1932) 433
Hemenway, James A.
  senator, Indiana, 1243
Hemphill, John
  senator, Texas, 1262
Hempstead, Stephen P.
  governor, Iowa, 1391
Henagan, B. K.
  governor, South Carolina, 1408
Hendee, George W.
  governor, Vermont, 1410

Henderson, Charles
  governor, Alabama, 1384
Henderson, Charles B.
  senator, Nevada, 1252
Henderson, J. Pinckney
  governor, Texas, 1409
  senator, Texas, 1262
Henderson, J. W.
  governor, Texas, 1409
Henderson, John
  senator, Mississippi, 1250
Henderson, John B.
  Republican convention officers, 417 (table)
  senator, Missouri, 1251
Henderson, Thomas
  governor, New Jersey, 1401
Hendon, Bill, 189
Hendricks, Thomas A.
  biography, 778
  effect of death, 472
  governor, Indiana, 1391
  presidential candidate
    Democratic contender, (1868) 246, 462, (1884) 250, 431, 471
    Democratic convention ballots, (1868) 584, (1876) 587, (1880) 589, (1884) 591
    electoral vote, (1872) 706, 739
  senator, Indiana, 1243
  vice-presidential candidate
    Democratic nominee, (1876) 430, 466, (1884) 250, 471
    electoral vote, (1876) 772, (1884) 773
Hendricks, William
  governor, Indiana, 1391
  senator, Indiana, 1243
Hendrickson, Robert C.
  senator, New Jersey, 1254
Hennings, Thomas C. Jr.
  senator, Missouri, 1251
Henry, John
  biography, 778
  electoral vote, (1796) 720
  governor, Maryland, 1395
  senator, Maryland, 1247
Henry, Patrick
  governor, Virginia, 1411
Hensley, Kirby James
  presidential candidate
    popular vote, (1964) 694, (1968) 695
    Universal Party nominee, (1964, 1968) 436
Herbert, Thomas J.
  governor, Ohio, 138, 1405
Hereford, Frank
  senator, West Virginia, 1265
Herer, Jack E.
  presidential candidate
    Grassroots Party nominee, (1988, 1992) 438
    popular vote, (1988) 697, (1992) 698
Herreid, Charles N.
  governor, South Dakota, 1408
Herrick, Myron T.
  governor, Ohio, 1405
Herring, Clyde L.
  governor, Iowa, 1392
  senator, Iowa, 1243
Herrnson, Paul, 95, 99
Herschler, Ed
  governor, Wyoming, 1413
Herseth, Ralph E.
  governor, South Dakota, 152, 1409
Herter, Christian A.
  Eisenhower cabinet, 152
  governor, Massachusetts, 145, 1396
  presidential primary votes, (1956) 344–345
  Republican vice-presidential contender, (1956) 273, 520
Hewitt, Abram Stevens
  Democratic National Committee chair, 415 (table), 426 (table)
Hewitt, Kenneth
  presidential primary votes, (1996) 403

Heyburn, Weldon B.
    senator, Idaho, 1242
Heyward, Duncan C.
    governor, South Carolina, 1408
Hickel, Walter J.
    governor, Alaska, 193, 1384
Hickenlooper, Bourke B.
    governor, Iowa, 1392
    senator, Iowa, 1244
Hickey, John Joseph
    governor, Wyoming, 1413
    senator, Wyoming, 155, 1266
Hicks, Thomas H.
    governor, Maryland, 1395
    senator, Maryland, 1247
Hiester, Joseph
    governor, Pennsylvania, 1406
Higginbotham, Rufus T.
    presidential primary votes, (1992)
        386–393
Higgins, Anthony
    senator, Delaware, 1240
Higgins, Frank W.
    governor, New York, 1403
Higgins, James H.
    governor, Rhode Island, 1407
High, Robert King, 166
Highton, Benjamin, 22–23
Hildebrandt, Fred
    presidential primary votes, (1944)
        337–338, (1948) 340
Hildreth, Horace A.
    governor, Maine, 1394
Hill, Anita, 195, 292, 789
Hill, Benjamin H.
    senator, Georgia, 1241
Hill, David B.
    governor, New York, 1403
    Democratic convention officers, speakers,
        (1896) 478, (1900) 480
    presidential candidate
        Democratic contender, (1892) 252,
            475
        Democratic convention ballots,
            (1892) 593, (1896) 595
    senator, New York, 1255
Hill, Isaac
    Democratic convention officers, 415
        (table)
    governor, New Hampshire, 1400
    senator, New Hampshire, 1253
Hill, John F.
    governor, Maine, 1394
    Republican National Committee chair,
        426 (table)
Hill, Joshua
    senator, Georgia, 1241
Hill, Lister
    length of service in Congress,
        795 (table)
    senator, Alabama, 1236
Hill, Nathaniel P.
    senator, Colorado, 1238
Hill, William L.
    senator, Florida, 1240
Hilles, Charles D.
    Republican National Committee chair,
        417 (table), 426 (table)
Hillhouse, James
    senator, Connecticut, 1238
Hilliard, Earl F., 791
Hillman, Sidney, 138
Hillquit, Morris, 78, 501
Hilton, Henry, 89
Hinckley, John W. Jr., 715
Hindman, William
    senator, Maryland, 1247
Hinkle, James F.
    governor, New Mexico, 1402
Hirsch, Robert W., 172
Hirschberg, Alexander
    presidential popular vote,
        (1900) 691
Hiscock, Frank
    senator, New York, 1255

Hisgen, Thomas Louis
    presidential candidate
        Independence Party nominee, (1908)
            432
        popular vote, (1908) 691
Hispanics
    governors, 1377
    members of Congress, 792–793
        House, Senate totals, 1947–2001
            (table), 793
Hiss, Alger, 139, 142, 144, 272
Hitchcock, ——
    presidential primary votes, (1948) 340
Hitchcock, Frank H.
    Republican National Committee chair,
        426 (table)
Hitchcock, Gilbert M.
    presidential candidate
        Democratic convention ballots,
            (1920) 605, (1928) 609
        primary votes, (1920) 324–326,
            (1928) 329–330
    senator, Nebraska, 1252
Hitchcock, Herbert E.
    senator, South Dakota, 1261
Hitchcock, Phineas W.
    senator, Nebraska, 1252
Hitler, Adolf, 267
Hoadly, George
    Democratic convention ballots, (1884)
        591
    Democratic convention officers, 415
        (table)
    governor, Ohio, 1405
Hoan, Daniel W., 78
Hoar, George F.
    Republican convention officers, 417
        (table)
    senator, Massachusetts, 1248
Hoard, William D.
    governor, Wisconsin, 1413
Hobart, Garret A.
    biography, 778
    effect of death, 254, 479
    vice-presidential candidate
        electoral vote, (1896) 773
        Republican nominee, (1896) 431, 477
Hobart, John S.
    senator, New York, 1255
Hobby, William P.
    governor, Texas, 1410
Hoblitzell, John D. Jr.
    senator, West Virginia, 1265
Hobson, Julius
    vice-presidential candidate
        Peoples' Party nominee, (1972) 69,
            436
Hoch, Edward W.
    governor, Kansas, 1392
Hoch, Homer, 813
Hockenhull, Andrew W.
    governor, New Mexico, 1402
Hodges, George H.
    governor, Kansas, 1392
Hodges, Jim
    governor, South Carolina, 1408
Hodges, Kaneaster Jr.
    senator, Arkansas, 1237
Hodges, Luther H.
    governor, North Carolina, 1404
Hoegh, Leo Arthur
    governor, Iowa, 1392
Hoeven, John
    governor, North Dakota, 1404
Hoey, Clyde R.
    governor, North Carolina, 1403
    senator, North Carolina, 1256
Hoff, Philip H.
    governor, Vermont, 159, 162, 1411
Hoffman, Harold G.
    governor, New Jersey, 1402
Hoffman, John T.
    governor, New York, 1403
Hofstadter, Richard, 263
Hogg, James S.
    governor, Texas, 1410

Holbrook, Frederick
    governor, Vermont, 1410
Holcolm, Silas A.
    governor, Nebraska, 1399
Holcomb, Austin
    presidential candidate
        Continental Party nominee, (1904)
            432
        popular vote, (1904) 691
Holcomb, Marcus H.
    governor, Connecticut, 1387
Holden, Bob
    governor, Missouri, 1399
Holden, Charles
    presidential primary votes, (1996) 403
Holden, William W.
    governor, North Carolina, 1403
Holland, Spessard L.
    at Democratic convention, (1952) 516
    governor, Florida, 1389
    senator, Florida, 1240
Holley, Alexander H.
    governor, Connecticut, 1387
Holliday, Frederick W. M.
    governor, Virginia, 1411
Hollings, Ernest F.
    governor, South Carolina, 1408
    presidential candidate
        Democratic contender, (1984) 186,
            285
        primary votes, (1984) 372–377
    senator, South Carolina, 1260
    deficit control law, 188
    on TV ad costs, 99
Hollis, Henry F.
    senator, New Hampshire, 1253
Hollis, Mary Cal
    presidential candidate
        popular vote, (1996) 699
        primary votes, (1996) 402, 403
        Socialist nominee, (1996) 439
    vice-presidential candidate
        Socialist nominee, (2000) 439
Hollister, Nancy
    governor, Ohio, 1405
Holloway, William J.
    governor, Oklahoma, 1405
Holman, Rufus C.
    senator, Oregon, 1258
Holmes, David
    governor, Mississippi, 1398
    senator, Mississippi, 1250
Holmes, Gabriel
    governor, North Carolina, 1403
Holmes, Gavrielle
    presidential candidate
        popular vote, (1984) 697
        Workers World Party nominee,
            (1984) 437
Holmes, Gilbert H.
    presidential primary votes, (1992) 394
Holmes, John
    senator, Maine, 1246
Holmes, Larry
    presidential candidate
        popular vote, (1984, 1988) 697
        primary votes, (1988) 385
        Workers World Party nominee,
            (1984) 82, 437, (1988) 82, 438
    vice-presidential candidate
        Workers World Party nominee,
            (1980) 82, 437, (1992) 437
Holmes, Robert D.
    governor, Oregon, 149, 1406
Holshouser, James E. Jr.
    governor, North Carolina, 1404
Holt, Homer A.
    governor, West Virginia, 1412
Holt, Rush D.
    senator, West Virginia, 1265
Holt, Thomas M.
    governor, North Carolina, 1403
Holt, William E.
    governor, Montana, 1399
Holton, Linwood
    governor, Virginia, 1412

Holtwick, Enoch Arden
    vice-presidential candidate
        popular vote, (1956) 694
        Prohibition Party nominee, (1952)
            434, (1956) 435
Homer, Irving
    vice-presidential candidate
        America First nominee, (1972) 436
Homesteading
    platform issue
        Democrats, (1876) 467
        Free Soilers, (1848) 449–450, (1852)
            452
        Greenback Party, (1880) 469
        Liberal Republicans, (1872) 464
        Republicans, (1860) 242, (1872) 464
Homosexuals
    platform issues
        Democrats, (1984) 549
        Green Party, (2000) 571
        Republicans, (1996) 563, (2000) 566
Hooper, Ben W.
    governor, Tennessee, 1409
Hoopes, Darlington
    presidential candidate
        popular vote, (1952, 1956) 694
        Socialist nominee, (1952) 434, (1956)
            435
    vice-presidential candidate
        Socialist nominee, (1944) 434
Hoover, Herbert C.
    biography, 778
    as president, 261–262
        House reapportionment, 814
    presidential candidate
        cabinet service, 222
        election evolution, 6–7, 16
        electoral vote, (1928) 753, (1932) 754
        popular vote, (1928) 670, (`932) 671
        primary votes, (1920) 324–326,
            (1928) 329–330, (1932) 331–332,
            (1936) 333–334, (1940) 335–336
        public offices, 215
        reelection chances, (1932) 313 (box)
        Republican convention ballots,
            (1920) 604, (1928) 609, (1932) 610,
            (1940) 613
        Republican nominee, (1928) 76,
            260–261, 433, 498–499, (1932)
            262–263, 433, 501–502
    at Republican convention, (1936) 504
    Truman administration posts, 269
    vice-presidential candidate
        Republican contender, (1924) 495
Hoover, Herbert F.
    presidential primary votes, (1968) 353
Hopkins, Albert J.
    senator, Illinois, 1242
Hopkins, Andrew F.
    Whig convention officers, 425 (box)
Hopkins, Harry, 267
Hopkins, John O.
    vice-presidential candidate
        Universal Party nominee, (1964) 436
Hoppin, William W.
    governor, Rhode Island, 1407
Horbal, Koryne
    Democratic convention ballots, (1980)
        630
Horne, Gerald
    presidential primary votes, (1996) 402
Horner, Henry
    governor, Illinois, 1391
Hornung, Lawrence L.
    presidential primary votes, (2000)
        404–410
Horrigan, William
    presidential primary votes, (1988) 385,
        (1992) 394
Horsey, Outerbridge
    senator, Delaware, 1239
Horton, Henry H.
    governor, Tennessee, 1409
Horton, Maurice
    presidential primary votes, (1992)
        386–393

Horton, Willie, 288, 291–292
Hospers, John
    biography, 778
    presidential candidate
        electoral vote, (1972) 703 (box), 764
            Libertarian nominee, (1972) 65, 436
        popular vote, (1972) 695
Hough, William J.
    vice-presidential candidate
        American Party nominee, (1920) 433
House, Edward M., 257
House elections. *See also* Congressional elections
    constitutional provisions, 30–31 (box)
    disputed elections, 803–804
    general election returns, 827–1228
    majority requirement, 801–802
    results, 1946–2000, 1574–1577
    special elections, 803
    timing, 802
    total votes cast, 1930–2000 (table), 4
House of Representatives, U.S. *See also* Apportionment of the House of Representatives; Congressional districts; House elections
    constitutional basis, 799, 801
    distribution of seats, electoral votes, 1556
    leadership, 1899–2001,1588–1591
    members who became president, 155 (box)
    membership qualifications, 18
    party control shifts, 804–805
    presidential election
        constitutional basis, 707
        1800 election, 14, 228, 707, 709
        1824 election, 14, 233, 296, 709
        rules (box), 708
    term length, 801
Housing
    platform issue
        Democrats, (1948) 513
        Progressives, (1948) 515
        Republicans, (1948) 511, (1960) 524, (1996) 562
Houston, Andrew Jackson
    senator, Texas, 1262
Houston, David F.
    Democratic convention ballots, (1924) 607
Houston, George S.
    governor, Alabama, 1384
    senator, Alabama, 1236
Houston, Sam
    governor, Tennessee, 1409
    governor, Texas, 1409
    presidential candidate
        Constitutional Union party contender, (1860) 458
        Democratic convention ballots, (1852) 577
    senator, Texas, 1262
Houstoun, John
    governor, Georgia, 1389
Houx, Frank L.
    governor, Wyoming, 1413
Hovey, Alvin P.
    governor, Indiana, 1391
Howard, ——
    presidential primary votes, (1932) 332
Howard, George
    governor, Maryland, 1395
Howard, Guy V.
    senator, Minnesota, 1249
Howard, Henry
    governor, Rhode Island, 1407
Howard, Jacob M.
    senator, Michigan, 1249
Howard, John E.
    biography, 778
    governor, Maryland, 1395
    senator, Maryland, 1247
    vice-presidential electoral vote, (1816) 772
Howe, Archibald Murray
    vice-presidential candidate
        National Party nominee, (1900) 432

Howe, Timothy O.
    senator, Wisconsin, 1266
Howell, James B.
    senator, Iowa, 1243
Howell, Jeremiah B.
    senator, Rhode Island, 1259
Howell, Richard
    governor, New Jersey, 1401
Howell, Robert B.
    senator, Nebraska, 1252
Howland, Benjamin
    senator, Rhode Island, 1259
Howley, Richard
    governor, Georgia, 1389
Hoyer, Steny H., 804
Hoyt, Henry M.
    governor, Pennsylvania, 1406
Hruska, Roman L.
    Republican platform, (1976) 541
    senator, Nebraska, 1252
        campaign finance, 111
Hubbard, Henry
    governor, New Hampshire, 1400
    senator, New Hampshire, 1253
Hubbard, John
    governor, Maine, 1394
Hubbard, Lucius F.
    governor, Minnesota, 1397
Hubbard, Richard B.
    Democratic convention officers, 415 (table)
    governor, Texas, 1410
Hubbard, Richard D.
    governor, Connecticut, 1387
Huckabee, Mike
    governor, Arkansas, 1385
Huddleston, Walter D.
    senator, Kentucky, 172, 187, 1245
Hudson, Fred
    presidential primary votes, (1996) 395–402
Huffington, Michael, 99, 100
Huffman, James W.
    senator, Ohio, 1257
Hughes, Charles Evans
    biography, 778
    governor, New York, 1403
    presidential candidate
        electoral vote, (1916) 750
        popular vote, (1916) 667
        primary votes, (1916) 311, 322–323
        Republican convention ballots, (1908) 599, (1916) 602, (1928) 609
        Republican nominee, (1916) 258, 432, 490
    Supreme Court justice, 222
        on FDR expansion plan, 267
        House redistricting, 818
Hughes, Charles J. Jr.
    senator, Colorado, 1238
Hughes, Harold E.
    governor, Iowa, 162, 1392
    senator, Iowa, 169, 175, 1244
Hughes, Harry
    governor, Maryland, 1395
Hughes, Howard, 114
Hughes, James H.
    senator, Delaware, 1240
Hughes, Richard J.
    governor, New Jersey, 157, 165, 1402
Hughes, Simon P.
    governor, Arkansas, 1385
Hughes, William
    senator, New Jersey, 1254
Hull, Cordell
    Democratic National Committee chair, 426 (table)
    presidential candidate
        Democratic contender, (1940) 267
        Democratic convention ballots, (1924) 607, (1928) 609, (1940) 612
    senator, Tennessee, 1262
    vice-presidential bid declined, (1940) 312
Hull, Jane D.
    governor, Arizona, 1385
Hull, Merlin, 46

Human Events, 117
Human rights
    Democratic platform issue, (1992) 558
Humphrey, Gordon J.
    senator, New Hampshire, 181, 187, 1253
Humphrey, Hubert H.
    biography, 778
    Democratic platform, (1948) 140, 269, 423, 512
    Mississippi credentials challenge, (1964) 527
    presidential candidate
        Democratic contender, (1960) 273–274, (1972) 171, 280, (1976) 177, 282
        Democratic convention ballots, (1952) 618, (1960) 620, (1968) 623, (1972) 625, (1976) 627
        Democratic nominee, (1968) 59, 278–280, 422, 436, 530–532
        election evolution, 8, 9, 17
        electoral vote, (1968) 763
        as former vice president, (1968) 223, 314 (box)
        political party development, 48
        politics and issues, (1960) 154, (1968) 167–168
        popular vote, (1968) 680
        primary votes, (1952) 341–343, (1960) 313, 346–347, (1964) 348–350, (1968) 305, 308, 310 (box), 313, 351–353, (1972) 354–358, (1976) 359–364
        Wallace electoral threat, (1968) 706 (box), 710
    senator, Minnesota, 141, 170, 1249
    vice-presidential candidate
        Democratic contender, (1956) 148, 273, 519, (1972) 534
        Democratic nominee, (1964) 161–162, 276, 435, 527
        electoral vote, (1964) 773
Humphrey, Lyman U.
    governor, Kansas, 1392
Humphrey, Muriel
    senator, Minnesota, 1249
Humphreys, Benjamin G.
    governor, Mississippi, 1398
Humphreys, Robert
    senator, Kentucky, 1245
Hunkers faction (Democrats), 238, 422, 448
Hunn, John
    governor, Delaware, 1388
Hunt, Frank W.
    governor, Idaho, 1390
Hunt, George W. P.
    governor, Arizona, 1384, 1385
Hunt, Guy
    governor, Alabama, 189, 1384
        removal, 1381 (box)
Hunt, James B. Jr.
    Democratic convention rules reform, 415–416, 418
    governor, North Carolina, 187, 1404
Hunt, Lester C.
    governor, Wyoming, 138, 1413
    senator, Wyoming, 1266
Hunt, Washington
    Constitutional Union Party officers, 425 (box)
    governor, New York, 1402
Hunter, John
    senator, South Carolina, 1260
Hunter, Richard C.
    senator, Nebraska, 1252
Hunter, Robert M. T.
    presidential candidate
        Democratic contender, (1860) 456–457
        Democratic convention ballots, (1860) 580
    senator, Virginia, 1264
Hunter, William
    senator, Rhode Island, 1259
Huntington, Edward V., 815

Huntington, Jabez W.
    senator, Connecticut, 1238
Huntington, Samuel
    biography, 778
    electoral vote, (1789) 718
    governor, Connecticut, 1387
Huntington, Samuel H.
    governor, Ohio, 1404
Hunton, Eppa
    senator, Virginia, 1264
Hunton, Jonathan G.
    governor, Maine, 1394
Hurd, John B.
    presidential primary votes, (1996) 403
Hurley, Charles F.
    governor, Massachusetts, 1396
Hurley, Robert A.
    governor, Connecticut, 1387
Husting, Paul O.
    senator, Wisconsin, 1266
Huston, Claudius H.
    Republican National Committee chair, 426 (table)
Hutcheson, William L., 509
Hutchinson, Tim
    senator, Arkansas, 200, 1237
Hutchison, Kay Bailey
    Republican convention officers, 417 (table)
    senator, Texas, 199, 1262
Huxman, Walter A.
    governor, Kansas, 1392
Hyde, Arthur M.
    governor, Missouri, 1399
Hyde, Henry J.
    term limits, 794 (box)

I
Illinois
    Democratic convention credentials dispute, (1972) 422, 534, 624
    House redistricting, 818, 825
    Republican convention credentials dispute, (1880) 422
Immigrants
    census count of aliens, 813, 821 (box)
    opinion on World War I, 257–258
    political party history, 75
    in New Deal coalition, 264
Immigration policy
    platform issue
        Democrats, (1876) 467, (1880) 470, (1884) 471, (1960) 522, (1996) 565
        Greenback Party, (1880) 469
        Know-Nothings, (1856) 454
        Reform Party, (1996) 563
        Republicans, (1876) 466, (1880) 468, (1884) 470, (1896) 478, (1960) 524, (1996) 562, (2000) 567
Impeachment
    Clinton trial, 19, 78, 135, 197, 201–202, 203, 297–298, 805
    governors, 1381 (box)
    Johnson trial, 15, 245, 246
    Nixon resignation, 173–174, 175, 281
Imus, Don, 291
Income tax
    enactment, 257
    Kemp-Roth proposal, 180
    platform issue
        Democrats, (1924) 497
        Greenback Party, (1880) 469
        Progressives, (1912) 489
        Republicans, (1996) 562
    presidential campaign funding checkoff, 89, 90–91, 113
Incumbents
    in Congress, 785–786
        fund-raising advantage, 102–103
        House-Senate reelection rate disparity, 1234
        PAC contributions, 96
    presidential campaigns, 213
        reelection chances, 313 (box)
Independence Party
    nominees, (1908) 432

Independent Afro-American Party
  nominees, (1960) 435
Independent Alliance Party
  nominees, (1984) 437
Independent expenditures
  congressional elections, 95–96, 106
    party aid, 95–96
    definition, 85 (box)
    party contributions in presidential
      campaigns, 92
    Supreme Court decision, 120–121
Independent Grassroots Party
  nominees, (1996) 439
Independent Liberal Republican (Opposition)
  Party
  nominees, (1872) 430
Independent Party
  nominees, (1832) 429
Independent Party
  nominees, (1980, 1984) 437, (1988) 438
Independent Party of Utah
  nominees, (1996) 439
Independent Republican Party
  nominees, (1864) 430
Independent States' Rights Party
  nominees, (1964) 436
Indiana
  disputed House election, (1984)
    803–804
  House redistricting, 824
  presidential candidates' background, 222
Industrial Reform Party
  nominees, (1888) 431
Ingalls, John J.
  Republican convention ballots, (1888)
    592
  senator, Kansas, 1244
Ingersoll, Charles R.
  governor, Connecticut, 1387
Ingersoll, Jared
  biography, 778
  vice-presidential candidate
    electoral vote, (1812) 772
    Federalist nominee, (1812) 231
Ingersoll, R. J.
  Democratic convention ballots, (1852)
    577
Ingersoll, Robert G.
  on Blaine, 250, 465
Inhofe, James M.
  senator, Oklahoma, 199, 1257
Inouye, Daniel K.
  Democratic convention officers, speakers,
    415 (table)
  representative, Hawaii, 153
  senator, Hawaii, 159, 1241
Interior Department, U.S.
  Glavis-Ballinger affair, 256
Internal improvements
  in Adams, Jackson administrations, 234
  platform issue
    Democrats, (1840) 445, (1844) 447
    Free Soilers, (1848) 449, (1852) 452
    Republicans, (1856) 454
    Whigs, 237, (1852) 452
International Telephone and Telegraph Corp.,
  536
Internet
  election-related Web sites, 1594–1595
Internet voting, 19, 39, 219
Iowa
  caucus method of delegate selection,
    310–311 (box)
  presidential primary calendar, 305, 306
    (box), 308–309, 417
Iran-contra scandal, 176, 190, 284, 287, 292
Iran hostage crisis, 18, 181, 182–183, 213,
  283–284
Irby, John L. M.
  senator, South Carolina, 1260
Iredell, James
  biography, 778
  electoral vote, (1796) 720
Iredell, James
  governor, North Carolina, 1403
  senator, North Carolina, 1256

Ireland
  independence issue, (1920) 495
Ireland, John
  governor, Texas, 1410
Irwin, Henry D., 703 (box), 774
Irwin, Jared
  governor, Georgia, 1389
Irwin, William
  governor, California, 1386
Isaacson, Shirley
  presidential primary votes, (1988) 385
Israel
  platform issue
Issue advocacy ads
  campaign finance controversy, 105–106
  definition, 85 (box)
  reform proposals, 125
  Section 527 groups, 107
  soft money, 105
Iverson, Alfred
  senator, Georgia, 1241
Ives, Irving M.
  gubernatorial candidate, 147
  senator, New York, 138, 1255
Izard, Ralph
  senator, South Carolina, 1260

J

Jackson, Andrew
  background, 233–234
  biography, 778
  as president
    opposition, 80–81, 234, 235, 442
    Senate censure, 1229
  presidential candidate
    Democratic nominee, (1828) 56, 234,
      296, (1832) 234–235, 429, 442–443
    Democratic-Republican contender,
      (1824) 56, 296, 232–233
    election evolution, 14
    electoral anomalies, 12 (box)
    electoral vote, (1824) 727, (1828)
      728, (1832) 729
    former members of Congress, 155
      (box)
    House election of president, (1824)
      706 (box), 709
    military service, 221
    political party development, 44, 48,
      56–57
    popular vote, (1824) 644, (1828) 645,
      (1832) 646
    public offices, 214
  senator, Tennessee, 1261
  vice-presidential electoral vote, (1824)
    772
Jackson, Charles
  governor, Rhode Island, 1406
Jackson, Claiborne Fox
  governor, Missouri, 1398
Jackson, Edward
  governor, Indiana, 1391
Jackson, Elihu E.
  governor, Maryland, 1395
Jackson, Frank D.
  governor, Iowa, 1392
Jackson, George E.
  vice-presidential candidate
    American Party nominee, (1980) 437
Jackson, Hancock Lee
  governor, Missouri, 1398
Jackson, Henry M.
  Democratic National Committee chair,
    415 (table), 426 (table)
  length of service in Congress, 795 (table)
  presidential candidate
    Democratic contender, (1972) 171,
      535, (1976) 177, 282
    Democratic convention ballots,
      (1972) 625, (1976) 627
    primary votes, (1972) 354–358,
      (1976) 359–364
  senator, Washington, 145, 1265
  vice-presidential contender, (1976) 539
Jackson, Howell E.
  senator, Tennessee, 1261

Jackson, Jacob B.
  governor, West Virginia, 1412
Jackson, James
  governor, Georgia, 1389
  senator, Georgia, 1240, 1241
Jackson, Jesse
  at Democratic convention, (1972) 534,
    (1988) 190, (1992) 556, (1996) 564
  Democratic nominating rules, 419
  Florida electoral vote, (2000) 713
  presidential candidate
    Democratic contender, (1984) 186,
      285, 548, 549, (1988) 190, 286,
      287–288, 552–553
    Democratic convention ballots,
      (1984) 632, (1988) 634
    no-run decision, (2000) 204
    primary votes, (1984) 372–377,
      (1988) 315, 378–385
    run-off primaries, 130
    vice-presidential contender, (1988) 190,
      312
Jackson, Jesse L. Jr., 792
Jackson, Samuel D.
  Democratic convention officers, 415
    (table)
  senator, Indiana, 1243
Jackson, William P.
  senator, Maryland, 1247
Jacob, John Jeremiah
  governor, West Virginia, 1412
Jacobs, Andrew, 788
Jacobsen, Gary, 101
Jacobson, Alvin J.
  presidential primary votes, (1980)
    365–371
James, Arthur H.
  governor, Pennsylvania, 1406
  presidential candidate
    primary votes, (1940) 335–336
    Republican convention ballots,
      (1940) 613
James, Charles T.
  senator, Rhode Island, 1259
James, Forrest H. "Fob" Jr.
  governor, Alabama, 1384
James, Ollie M.
  Democratic convention officers, 415
    (table)
  senator, Kentucky, 1245
James, William H.
  governor, Nebraska, 1399
Jamieson, Kathleen Hall, 105
Janklow, William J.
  governor, South Dakota, 1409
Jarnigan, Spencer
  senator, Tennessee, 1261
Jarvis, Thomas J.
  governor, North Carolina, 1403
  senator, North Carolina, 1256
Javits, Jacob K.
  senator, New York, 149, 159, 183,
    1255
  political party development, 46
Jaworski, Leon
  Democratic convention ballots, (1976)
    627
Jay, John
  biography, 778
  electoral vote, (1789) 226, 718, (1796)
    720, (1800) 707, 721
  governor, New York, 1402
Jefferson, Thomas
  on agrarian ideal, 813
  biography, 778
  governor, Virginia, 1411
  House reapportionment, 811
  political party development, 43–44,
    55–56, 57, 61, 227, 228
  presidential candidate
    cabinet service, 220–221
    Democratic-Republican nominee,
      (1796) 227, (1800) 227–228, 312,
      (1804) 228–229
    electoral anomalies, 12 (box), 701,
      703 (box), 706 (box)

electoral vote, (1792) 719, (1796) 720,
    (1800) 721, (1804) 722
  as former governor, 176 (box)
  former members of Congress, 155
    (box)
  as former vice president, 314 (box)
  House election of president, (1800)
    14, 703 (box), 707–709
  public offices, 214
  third-term idea, 14
  retirement, 229–230
  vice-presidential candidate
    Democratic-Republican contender,
      (1792) 226
Jefferson, William J., 791
Jeffersonian Republicans. See Democratic-Republican Party
Jeffords, James M.
  senator, Vermont, 191, 1263
  party switch, 5, 14, 20, 78, 796, 1234
Jeffries, Richard M.
  governor, South Carolina, 1408
Jelks, William D.
  governor, Alabama, 1384
Jenkins, Charles J.
  biography, 778
  electoral vote, (1872) 706, 739
  governor, Georgia, 1389
Jenkins, Frank
  vice-presidential candidate
    Poor Man's Party nominee, (1952)
      435
Jenner, William E.
  presidential candidate
    Texas Constitution Party nominee,
      (1956) 435
  senator, Indiana, 138, 1243
  vice-presidential candidate
    States' Rights Party of Kentucky nom-
      inee, (1956) 435
Jenness, Benning W.
  senator, New Hampshire, 1253
Jenness, Linda
  presidential candidate
    popular vote, (1972) 695
    Socialist Labor nominee, (1972) 436
Jennings, Ann
  presidential primary votes, (1996) 403
Jennings, Jonathan
  governor, Indiana, 1391
Jennings, W. Pat, 112
Jennings, William S.
  governor, Florida, 1388
Jennison, Silas H.
  governor, Vermont, 1410
Jensen, Leslie
  governor, South Dakota, 1408
Jensen, Paul S.
  presidential primary votes, (1992)
    386–393, (1996) 403
Jepson, Earl
  vice-presidential candidate
    American Party nominee, (1988) 52,
      438
Jepson, Roger W.
  senator, Iowa, 181, 187, 1244
Jerome, David H.
  governor, Michigan, 1397
Jester, Beauford H.
  governor, Texas, 1410
Jeter, Thomas B.
  governor, South Carolina, 1408
Jewell, Marshall
  governor, Connecticut, 1387
  Republican convention ballots, (1876)
    586
  Republican National Committee chair,
    426 (table)
Jewett, Daniel T.
  senator, Missouri, 1251
Jewett, Hugh J.
  Democratic convention ballots, (1880)
    589
Jews
  Lieberman candidacy, 20, 298, 312
  voters in New Deal coalition, 264

Jobless Party
  nominees, (1932) 433
Joe, Wesley, 93, 94
Johanns, Mike
  governor, Nebraska, 1400
John Birch Society, 525, 528
Johns, Charley E.
  governor, Florida, 1389
Johns, Frank T.
  presidential candidate
    popular vote, (1924) 692
    Socialist Labor nominee, (1924) 433
Johnson, Andrew
  biography, 778
  governor, Tennessee, 1409
  as president
    civil rights enforcement, 246
    Democratic platform, (1868) 462
    impeachment, 245–246
    Republican opposition, (1868) 461
    succession, 15, 245
  presidential candidate
    Democratic contender, (1868) 246,
      462
    Democratic convention ballots,
      (1860) 580, (1868) 584
    as former governor, 176 (box)
    former members of Congress, 155
      (box)
    as former vice president, 314 (box)
    public offices, 214
  senator, Tennessee, 796, 1261
  vice-presidential candidate
    electoral vote, (1864) 772
    Republican nominee, (1864) 243,
      430, 459
Johnson, Andrew
  vice-presidential candidate
    Prohibition Party nominee, (1944)
      434
Johnson, Charles F.
  senator, Maine, 1246
Johnson, David
  governor, South Carolina, 1408
Johnson, Edwin C.
  governor, Colorado, 1386
  senator, Colorado, 1238
Johnson, Edwin S.
  senator, South Dakota, 1261
Johnson, F. Dean
  presidential primary votes, (1992) 393
Johnson, Gary E.
  governor, New Mexico, 1402
Johnson, Hale
  vice-presidential candidate
    Prohibition Party nominee, (1896)
      431
Johnson, Henry S.
  governor, Louisiana, 1393
  senator, Louisiana, 1246
Johnson, Herschel V.
  biography, 778
  governor, Georgia, 1389
  senator, Georgia, 1241
  vice-presidential candidate
    Democratic nominee, (1860) 425,
      430, 457
    electoral vote, (1860) 772
Johnson, Hiram W.
  biography, 778
  governor, California, 1386
  presidential candidate
    electoral vote, (1912) 773
    primary votes, (1920) 313, 324–326,
      (1924) 327–328, (1932) 331–332
    Republican contender, (1920) 258,
      493, (1924) 495
    Republican convention ballots,
      (1920) 604, (1924) 608
    at Republican convention, (1912) 486
  senator, California, 1237
  vice-presidential candidate
    Progressive nominee, (1912) 70, 432,
      488
Johnson, Isaac
  governor, Louisiana, 1393

Johnson, J. Neely
  governor, California, 1386
Johnson, James
  governor, Georgia, 1389
Johnson, Jim, 166
Johnson, John A.
  governor, Minnesota, 1397
  presidential contender, (1908) 484
    Democratic convention ballots,
      (1908) 598
Johnson, Joseph
  governor, Virginia, 1411
Johnson, Joseph B.
  governor, Vermont, 1411
Johnson, Keen
  governor, Kentucky, 1393
Johnson, Lester, 146
Johnson, Lyndon B.
  biography, 778
  at Democratic convention, (1964) 412,
    (1968) 530, 532
  as president
    campaign finance reform, 111
    Great Society, 133–134
    House term length proposal, 801
    legislative accomplishments, 164
    politics and issues, 159–161, 163–168
    succession, 159
    Vietnam War, 163, 164, 165,
      166–167, 168, 277, 278
    Voting Rights Act, 27
  presidential candidate
    Democratic contender, (1956) 148,
      518, (1960) 273, 521–522, (1968)
      278
    Democratic convention ballots, (1956)
      619, (1960) 620
    Democratic nominee, (1964) 59,
      276–278, 435, 527
    election evolution, 7, 8, 17
    electoral vote, (1964) 762
    former members of Congress, 155
      (box)
    as former vice president, 314 (box)
    political party development, 46
    politics and issues, (1960) 154
    popular vote, (1964) 679
    primary votes, (1960) 346–347,
      (1964) 348–350, (1968) 351–353
    public offices, 215
    reelection chances, 313 (box)
    vice-presidential choice, 161–162
    withdrawal, (1968) 166, 308, 313
  senator, Texas, 141, 1262
    Senate leadership, 7, 146, 150, 151,
      157
    successor, 132
  vice-presidential candidate
    Democratic nominee, (1960) 275,
      435, 522
    electoral vote, (1960) 773
    politics and issues, (1960) 154
Johnson, Magnus
  senator, Minnesota, 1249
Johnson, Martin N.
  senator, North Dakota, 1256
Johnson, Paul B.
  governor, Mississippi, 1398
Johnson, Paul B. Jr.
  governor, Mississippi, 1398
Johnson, Reverdy
  Democratic convention ballots, (1868)
    584
  senator, Maryland, 1247
Johnson, Richard M.
  biography, 779
  Democratic convention ballots, (1844)
    574
  senator, Kentucky, 1245
  vice-presidential candidate
    Democratic contender, (1840) 429,
      445
    Democratic nominee, (1836) 235,
      429, 443
    election by Senate, (1836) 15, 235,
      709

electoral vote, (1836, 1840) 772
Johnson, Robert W.
  senator, Arkansas, 1237
Johnson, Sonia
  presidential candidate
    Citizens Party nominee, (1984) 54,
      437
    popular vote, (1984) 696
Johnson, Thomas
  governor, Maryland, 1395
Johnson, Tim
  senator, South Dakota, 201, 1261
Johnson, Waldo P.
  senator, Missouri, 1251
Johnson, Walter W.
  governor, Colorado, 1386
Johnson, William Freame
  vice-presidential candidate
    North American Party nominee, 430
Johnson, William S.
  senator, Connecticut, 1239
Johnston, Henry S.
  governor, Oklahoma, 1405
Johnston, J. Bennett
  senator, Louisiana, 172, 1246
    preferential primaries, 131
Johnston, John W.
  senator, Virginia, 1264
Johnston, Joseph F.
  governor, Alabama, 1384
  senator, Alabama, 1236
Johnston, Josiah S.
  senator, Louisiana, 1246
Johnston, Olin D.
  governor, South Carolina, 1408
  senator, South Carolina, 1260
Johnston, Rienzi M.
  senator, Texas, 1262
Johnston, Samuel
  biography, 779
  electoral vote, (1796) 720
  governor, North Carolina, 1403
  senator, North Carolina, 1255
Johnston, William F.
  governor, Pennsylvania, 1406
  vice-presidential candidate
    American Party nominee,
      (1856) 454
Jonas, Benjamin F.
  senator, Louisiana, 1246
Jonathan faction (Know Nothings), 64
Jones, Andrieus A.
  senator, New Mexico, 1254
Jones, Anson
  governor, Texas, 1409
Jones, B. F.
  Republican National Committee chair,
    417 (table), 426 (table)
Jones, Brereton C.
  governor, Kentucky, 1393
Jones, Charles, 820 (box)
Jones, Charles W.
  senator, Florida, 1240
Jones, Daniel Webster
  governor, Arkansas, 1385
Jones, George
  senator, Georgia, 1240
Jones, George O., 297
Jones, George W.
  senator, Iowa, 1243
Jones, James C.
  governor, Tennessee, 1409
  senator, Tennessee, 1261
Jones, James K.
  Democratic National Committee chair,
    415 (table), 426 (table)
  senator, Arkansas, 1237
Jones, James R., 188
Jones, Jesse H.
  Democratic convention ballots, (1928)
    609
Jones, John E.
  governor, Nevada, 1400
Jones, John P.
  senator, Nevada, 1252
Jones, Paula Corbin, 201–202

Jones, Robert T.
  governor, Arizona, 1385
Jones, Sam H.
  governor, Louisiana, 1394
Jones, Stephanie Tubbs, 792
Jones, Thomas G.
  governor, Alabama, 1384
Jones, Tommy Lee, 568–569
Jones, Walter B.
  biography, 779
  electoral vote, (1956) 703 (box), 760
Jones, Wesley L.
  senator, Washington, 1265
Jones, William
  governor, Rhode Island, 1406
Jordan, B. Everett
  senator, North Carolina, 1256
Jordan, Barbara C.
  blacks in Congress, 791
  at Democratic convention, (1976) 539,
    (1992) 557
    keynote speaker, 415 (table)
    Democratic convention ballots,
      (1976) 627
Jordan, Chester B.
  governor, New Hampshire, 1401
Jordan, Hamilton, 560
Jordan, Len B.
  governor, Idaho, 1390
  senator, Idaho, 1242
Jorgensen, Jo Anne
  vice-presidential candidate
    Libertarian nominee, (1996) 66,
      439
Judd, Walter H.
  representative, Minnesota, 158
  Republican convention ballots, (1964)
    621
  Republican convention speakers, 417
    (table)
Judge, Thomas L.
  governor, Montana, 1399
Judiciary. See also Supreme Court, U.S.
  platform issue
    American Independents, (1968) 533
    Democrats, (1912) 488
    Progressives, (1912) 489, (1924) 498
    Republicans, (1912) 486, (1996) 562
    Socialists, (1908) 483
Julian, George W.
  biography, 779
  vice-presidential candidate
    electoral vote, (1872) 772
    Free Soil nominee, (1852) 430, 452
Julian, W. A.
  presidential primary votes, (1948) 340
"Junior Tuesday Week," 315–318
Justice Department, U.S.
  campaign finance law enforcement, 112,
    115
  scandal, 1996, 84–86

K

Kalmbach, Herbert, 114
Kane, Elias K.
  senator, Illinois, 1242
Kansas
  women officeholders, 18
Kansas-Nebraska Act of 1854, 239, 240–241
Kaptur, Marcy, 787–788, 790
Karnes, David
  senator, Nebraska, 191, 1252
Kasich, John R.
  Republican presidential contender,
    (2000) 204
Kasper, John
  presidential candidate
    National States' Rights Party
      nominee, (1964) 435
    popular vote, (1964) 694
Kassebaum, Nancy Landon
  Republican convention officers, 417
    (table)
  senator, Kansas, 18, 180, 789, 1244
Kasten, Bob
  senator, Wisconsin, 183, 1266

Kavanagh, Edward
  governor, Maine, 1394
Kavanaugh, William M.
  senator, Arkansas, 1237
Kay, David M.
  senator, Tennessee, 1261
Kay, Richard B.
  presidential primary votes, (1980)
    365–371, (1984) 372–239, (1988)
    378–385
Kean, Hamilton F.
  senator, New Jersey, 1254
Kean, John
  senator, New Jersey, 1254
Kean, Thomas H.
  governor, New Jersey, 188, 1402
  at Republican convention, (1988) 554
  speakers, 417 (table)
Kearns, Thomas
  senator, Utah, 1263
Keating, Frank
  governor, Oklahoma, 1405
Keating, Kenneth B.
  senator, New York, 152, 162, 1255
Keating Five scandal, 87, 122, 193, 195
Kefauver, Estes
  biography, 779
  presidential candidate
    Democratic contender, (1952)
      143–144, 272, 517, (1956) 148, 273,
      518, (1960) 273
    Democratic convention ballots,
      (1952) 618
    primary votes, (1952) 313, 341–343,
      (1956) 344–345
  senator, Tennessee, 141, 1262
    crime hearings, 143
  vice-presidential candidate
    Democratic nominee, (1956) 148,
      273, 435, 519
    electoral vote, (1956) 773
Kelleher, Robert L.
  presidential primary votes, (1976) 364
Kelley, Gene
  independent vice-presidential candidate,
    (2000) 439
Kelley, Oliver, 69
Kelley, V. A.
  presidential primary votes, (1980)
    365–371
Kellogg, Frank B.
  Republican convention ballots, (1920)
    604
  senator, Minnesota, 1249
Kellogg, William P.
  governor, Louisiana, 1393
  senator, Louisiana, 1246
Kelly, David
  presidential primary votes, (1984)
    372–377
Kelly, Edward, 250
Kelly, Harry F.
  governor, Michigan, 1397
Kelly, James K.
  senator, Oregon, 1258
Kelly, John, 466
Kelly, Michael, 297
Kelly, Rachel Bubar
  vice-presidential candidate
    Prohibition Party nominee, (1996)
      439
Kelly, William
  senator, Alabama, 1236
Kemp, Jack
  biography, 779
  presidential candidate
    primary votes, (1988) 378–385
    Republican contender, (1988) 190,
      287
  at Republican convention, (1972) 536
  tax proposal, 180
  vice-presidential candidate
    electoral vote, (1996) 773
    New York background, 222
    Republican nominee, (1996) 294,
      439, 561–562

Kemper, James Lawson
  governor, Virginia, 1411
Kempthorne, Dirk
  governor, Idaho, 1377, 1390
  senator, Idaho, 1242
Kendall, Nathan E.
  governor, Iowa, 1392
Kendrick, John B.
  Democratic convention ballots, (1924)
    606
  governor, Wyoming, 1413
  senator, Wyoming, 1266
Kenna, John E.
  senator, West Virginia, 1265
Kennedy, Anthony M., 30, 190, 300
Kennedy, Arthur
  senator, Maryland, 1247
Kennedy, Edward M.
  Chappaquiddick incident, 283
  at Democratic convention, (1988) 553
  Democratic platform, (1980) 423 (box)
  presidential candidate
    binding rule for convention dele-
      gates, (1980) 306
    Democratic contender, (1976) 282,
      (1980) 60, 283, 416, 421, 544–545
    Democratic convention ballots,
      (1968) 623, (1972) 625, (1976) 627,
      (1980) 630
    politics and issues, (1980) 182
    primary votes, (1964) 348–350,
      (1968) 351–353, (1972) 354–358,
      (1976) 359–364, (1980) 314,
      365–371
  senator, Massachusetts, 159, 199, 1248
  vice-presidential decliner, (1972) 535
Kennedy, John F.
  assassination, 134, 159
  biography, 779
  at Democratic convention, (1956) 518
  as president, 276
    campaign finance reform, 112
    civil rights, 159–160
    congressional relations, 157–158
    inaugural address, 155–156
    politics and issues, 156–159
  presidential candidate
    Democratic convention ballots,
      (1960) 620
    Democratic nominee, (1960) 59, 60,
      273–276, 435, 521–522
    election evolution, 8, 17
    electoral college chronology, 706
      (box)
    electoral vote, (1960) 761
    former members of Congress, 155
      (box), 223
    Liberal Party support, (1960), 65
    as "minority" president, 223 (table),
      297
    politics and issues, (1960) 154–155
    popular vote, (1960) 678
    primary votes, (1956) 344–345,
      (1960) 308, 313, 346–347
    public offices, 215
    televised debates, (1960) 213, 216
  senator, Massachusetts, 145, 1248
  vice-presidential contender, (1956) 148,
    273, 519
Kennedy, John F. Jr., 553
Kennedy, Joseph P., 273
Kennedy, Robert F.
  assassination, 9, 17, 134, 163, 167,
    313
  at Democratic convention, (1964) 527
  in JFK campaign, 275
  presidential candidate
    Democratic contender, (1968) 59,
      167, 278
    primary votes, (1964) 348–350,
      (1968) 308, 351–353
  senator, New York, 162, 1255
Kennedy, William
  governor, New Jersey, 1401
Kenney, Richard R.
  senator, Delaware, 1240

Kennon, Robert F.
  governor, Louisiana, 1394
Kenoyer, Willa
  presidential candidate
    popular vote, (1988) 697
    primary votes, (1988) 378–385
    Socialist Party nominee,
      (1988) 438
Kent, Edward
  governor, Maine, 1394
Kent, Joseph
  governor, Maryland, 1395
  senator, Maryland, 1247
Kenyon, Williams S.
  senator, Iowa, 1243
Kern, James P.
  senator, Missouri, 1251
Kern, John W.
  biography, 779
  at Democratic convention, (1912) 487
    ballots, 601
  senator, Indiana, 1243
  vice-presidential candidate
    Democratic nominee, (1908) 432,
      484
    electoral vote, (1908) 773
Kernan, Francis
  senator, New York, 1255
Kerner, Otto
  governor, Illinois, 155, 1391
Kerr, John Leeds
  senator, Maryland, 1247
Kerr, Joseph
  senator, Ohio, 1257
Kerr, Robert S.
  Democratic convention officers, speakers,
    415 (table)
  governor, Oklahoma, 1405
  presidential candidate
    Democratic contender, (1952) 144,
      272
    Democratic convention ballots,
      (1952) 618
    primary votes, (1952) 341–343
  senator, Oklahoma, 141, 1257
Kerrey, Bob
  governor, Nebraska, 1400
  presidential candidate
    Democratic contender, (1992)
      195–196, 290
    no-run decision, (2000) 204
    primary votes, (1992) 386–393
  senator, Nebraska, 191, 1252
Kerry, John F.
  presidential no-run decision,
    (2000) 204
  senator, Massachusetts, 1248
Key, V. O. Jr., 129, 131, 132, 269
Keyes, Alan
  presidential candidate
    primary votes, (1996) 395–402,
      (2000) 404–410
    Republican contender, (1996) 315,
      (2000) 80, 204
    Republican convention ballots, (1992)
      637, (1996) 638
Keyes, Henry Wilder
  governor, New Hampshire, 1401
  senator, New Hampshire, 1253
Keys, Martha, 788
Keyser, Frank Ray Jr.
  governor, Vermont, 1411
Kieve, Harry
  vice-presidential candidate
    Middle Class Party nominee, (1980)
      437
Kilby, Thomas E.
  governor, Alabama, 1384
Kilgore, Harley M.
  senator, West Virginia, 1265
Killeen, Caroline P.
  presidential primary votes, (1992) 394,
    (1996) 403
Kilpatrick, Carolyn Cheeks, 792
Kimball, Charles D.
  governor, Rhode Island, 1407

King, A.
  vice-presidential candidate
    Continental Party nominee, (1904)
      432
King, Alvin O.
  governor, Louisiana, 1393
King, Angus Jr.
  governor, Maine, 1395
King, Austin A.
  governor, Missouri, 1398
King, Bruce
  governor, New Mexico, 1402
King, Clennon
  presidential candidate
    Independent Afro-American nomi-
      nee, (1960) 435
    popular vote, (1960) 694
King, Edward J.
  governor, Massachusetts, 1396
King, John A.
  governor, New York, 1402
King, John Pendleton
  senator, Georgia, 1241
King, John W.
  governor, New Hampshire, 162, 1401
King, Larry, 291
King, Leicester
  Liberty Party convention officers, 425
    (box)
  vice-presidential candidate
    Free Soil (Liberty Party) nominee,
      (1848) 430
King, Martin Luther Jr.
  assassination, 9, 17, 134, 163, 167, 278
  black voting rights, 27
  Kennedy support, 275
King, Preston
  senator, New York, 1255
King, Rufus
  biography, 779
  gubernatorial candidate, (1816) 231
  presidential electoral votes, (1816), 231,
    725
  senator, New York, 1255
  vice-presidential candidate
    electoral vote, (1804, 1808) 772
    Federalist nominee, (1804) 229,
      (1808) 230
King, Samuel Ward
  governor, Rhode Island, 1406
King, William
  governor, Maine, 1394
King, William
  presidential primary votes, (1988) 385
King, William H.
  senator, Utah, 1263
King, William Rufus de Vane
  biography, 779
  senator, Alabama, 1236
  vice-presidential candidate
    Democratic nominee, (1852) 240,
      430, 450
    electoral vote, (1852) 772
"King Caucus." See Caucus system
Kinkead, John H.
  governor, Nevada, 1400
Kirby, William F.
  senator, Arkansas, 1237
Kirk, Claude R.
  governor, Florida, 166, 1389
  presidential primary votes,
    (1988) 385
Kirk, Paul G. Jr.
  at Democratic convention, (1988) 552
  Democratic National Committee chair,
    415 (table), 426 (table)
  Democratic nominating rules, 419
Kirker, Thomas
  governor, Ohio, 1404
Kirkland, Martha
  Democratic convention ballots, (1984)
    632
Kirkpatrick, Donald
  vice-presidential candidate
    American National Party nominee,
      (1876) 430

Kirkpatrick, George R.
    vice-presidential candidate
        Socialist nominee, (1916) 432, 492
Kirkpatrick, Jeane J., 284, 550, 554
Kirkwood, Samuel J.
    governor, Iowa, 1391
    senator, Iowa, 1243, 1244
Kirman, Richard Sr.
    governor, Nevada, 1400
Kissinger, Henry, 171, 541
Kitchell, Aaron
    senator, New Jersey, 1254
Kitchin, William W.
    governor, North Carolina, 1403
Kittredge, Alfred B.
    senator, South Dakota, 1261
Kitzhaber, John
    governor, Oregon, 1406
Klein, Tommy
    presidential primary votes, (1976) 364
Kneip, Richard F.
    governor, South Dakota, 1409
Knight, Albion W.
    vice-presidential candidate
        U.S. Taxpayers Party nominee, (1992)
        438
Knight, Goodwin J.
    governor, California, 1386
Knight, Nehemiah R.
    governor, Rhode Island, 1406
    senator, Rhode Island, 1259
Knott, J. Procter
    governor, Kentucky, 1393
Knous, William L.
    governor, Colorado, 138, 1386
Know-Nothings. See American Party
Knowland, William F.
    gubernatorial candidate, 152
    presidential candidate
        primary votes, (1956) 344–345
        Republican contender, (1956) 148
        Republican convention officers, 417
        (table)
    senator, California, 138, 1237
Knowles, Tony
    governor, Alaska, 1384
Knowles, Warren P.
    governor, Wisconsin, 162, 1413
Knox, Frank
    biography, 779
    FDR cabinet, 267
    presidential candidate
        primary votes, (1936) 333–334
        Republican contender, (1936) 265
    vice-presidential candidate
        electoral vote, (1936) 773
        Republican nominee, (1936) 433,
        481, 504
Knox, Henry, 44, 62
Knox, Philander C.
    presidential candidate
        Republican contender, (1908) 255,
        484
        Republican convention ballots,
        (1908) 599, (1916) 602
    senator, Pennsylvania, 1258
Knutson, Alfred
    presidential popular vote, (1940) 693
Knutson, Coya, 152
Koch, David
    vice-presidential candidate
        Libertarian nominee, (1980) 66, 437
Koczak, Stephen A.
    presidential primary votes, (1984)
    372–377, (1988) 378–385, (1992) 393
Kohl, Herbert H.
    senator, Wisconsin, 191, 1266
Kohler, Walter J. Jr.
    governor, Wisconsin, 1413
Kohler, Walter J. Sr.
    governor, Wisconsin, 1413
Kolbe, Jim, 566
Kolko, Gabriel, 254–255
Koos, Thomas
    presidential primary votes, (2000)
    404–410

Korean War, 142–145, 271, 272
Kovic, Ron
    presidential primary votes, (1992) 394
Krajewski, Henry B.
    presidential candidate
        American Third Party nominee,
        (1956) 435
        Poor Man's Party nominee, (1952)
        435
        popular vote, (1952, 1956) 694
Kramer, Ken, 189
Kraschel, Nelson G.
    governor, Iowa, 1392
Kreml, William P.
    presidential primary votes, (1992) 394
Krueger, Maynard C.
    vice-presidential candidate
        Socialist nominee, (1940) 434
Krueger, Bob
    senator, Texas, 1262
Ku Klux Klan
    and Catholic vote, 264
    Democratic issue, (1924) 260, 423 (box),
    495, 497, (1928) 261, (1964) 528
        convention ballot, (1924) 606
    Duke campaign, (1992) 196, 291
    Republican platform issue, (1964) 525
Kuchel, Thomas H.
    senator, California, 159, 1238
Kuhn, Maggie, 69
Kump, Herman G.
    governor, West Virginia, 1412
Kunin, Madeleine M.
    governor, Vermont, 1381, 1411
Kyl, Jon
    senator, Arizona, 199, 1237
Kyle, James H.
    Populist presidential contender, (1892) 476
    senator, South Dakota, 1261

L

La Duke, Winona
    vice-presidential candidate
        Green Party nominee, (1996, 2000)
        63, 439, 570
La Follette, Philip F.
    governor, Wisconsin, 1413
La Follette, Robert M.
    biography, 779
    effect of death, 499
    governor, Wisconsin, 1413
    presidential candidate
        electoral vote, (1924) 752
        political party development, 46, 48,
        49
        popular vote, (1924) 669, 692
        primary votes, (1912) 310, 320–321,
        (1916) 322, (1920) 326, (1924)
        327–328
        Progressive nominee, (1924) 70, 260,
        424 (box), 433, 498
        Republican contender, (1912) 256,
        486, (1924) 495
        Republican convention ballots,
        (1908) 599, (1916) 602, (1920) 604,
        (1924) 608
        Socialist nominee, (1924) 433
    presidential primary law, 15, 310
    Republican platform, (1908) 423 (box),
    484
    senator, Wisconsin, 1265
La Follette, Robert M. Jr.
    at Republican convention, (1928) 499
    senator, Wisconsin, 46, 138, 1265
La Riva, Gloria
    presidential candidate
        popular vote, (1992) 698
        Workers World Party nominee,
        (1992) 82, 438
    vice-presidential candidate
        Workers World Party nominee,
        (1984) 437, (1988) 82, 438, (1996,
        2000) 439
LaBella, Charles G., 84, 118 (box)
Labor Reform Party
    nominees, (1872) 430

Labor unions and issues
    campaign finance regulation, 110, 111,
    120
        overhaul legislation, 124 (box)
    Cleveland policies, 251
    Eisenhower administration, 151–152, 153
    Hoover policies, 261
    national party platforms
        Democrats, (1908) 485, (1912) 488,
        (1948) 513, (1952) 518, (1956) 519,
        (1960) 522, (1964) 527
        Greenback Party, (1880) 469
        Progressives, (1912) 488
        Republicans, (1884) 471, (1936) 265,
        (1948) 511, (1952) 516, (1956) 520,
        521, (1988) 555
        Socialists, (1908) 483, (1920) 493
    in New Deal, 264, 267
    in Progressive era, 253–254, 257
    in slavery debate, 239–240
    Taft Senate race, (1950) 143
    Truman administration, 139–140, 143,
    271
Labor's Non-Partisan League, 336
Lacock, Abner
    National Republican convention officers,
    425 (box)
    senator, Pennsylvania, 1259
Ladd, Edwin E.
    senator, North Dakota, 1256
Ladd, Herbert W.
    governor, Rhode Island, 1407
Lafoon, Ruby
    governor, Kentucky, 1393
Laird, William R. III
    senator, West Virginia, 1265
Lake, Everett J.
    governor, Connecticut, 1387
Lamar, Lucius Q. C.
    senator, Mississippi, 1250
Lambert, John
    governor, New Jersey, 1401
    senator, New Jersey, 1253
Lame-duck sessions, 803, 1232
Lamm, Richard D.
    governor, Colorado, 1386
    Reform Party presidential contender,
    (1996) 212, 433, 563
Lance, Bert, 180
Landon, Alfred M.
    biography, 779
    governor, Kansas, 1392
    presidential candidate
        electoral vote, (1936) 755
        former governor, 222–223
        popular vote, (1936) 672
        primary votes, (1936) 333–334
        Republican convention ballots,
        (1940) 612
        Republican nominee, (1936)
        265–266, 433, 504
Landrieu, Mary L.
    senator, Louisiana, 201, 1246
    Senate leadership, 789
Landrith, Ira
    vice-presidential candidate
        Prohibition Party nominee, (1916)
        432
Lane, Dennis I.
    presidential candidate
        popular vote, (2000) 699
        Vermont Grassroots Party nominee,
        (2000) 439
Lane, Harry
    senator, Oregon, 1258
Lane, Henry S.
    governor, Indiana, 1391
    Republican convention officers, 417
    (table)
    senator, Indiana, 1243
Lane, James H.
    senator, Kansas, 1244
Lane, Joseph
    biography, 779
    Democratic convention ballots, (1852)
    577, (1860) 580

senator, Oregon, 1258
    vice-presidential candidate
        electoral vote, (1860) 772
        Southern Democratic nominee,
        (1860) 53, 430, 457
Lane, Mark
    vice-presidential candidate
        Freedom and Peace nominee, (1968)
        436
Lane, William P., Jr.
    governor, Maryland, 138, 1395
Laney, Benjamin T.
    governor, Arkansas, 1385
Langdon, John
    biography, 779
    governor, New Hampshire, 1400
    senator, New Hampshire, 1253
    vice-presidential candidate
        Democratic-Republican contender,
        (1808, 1812) 230
        electoral vote, (1808) 772
Langer, William
    governor, North Dakota, 1404
    presidential candidate
        Pioneer Party nominee, (1956) 435
    senator, North Dakota, 1256
Langlie, Arthur B.
    governor, Washington, 1412
    Republican convention speakers, 417
    (table)
Lanham, Samuel W. T.
    governor, Texas, 1410
Lanman, James
    senator, Connecticut, 1239
Lapham, Elbridge C.
    senator, New York, 1255
LaRouche, Lyndon H. Jr.
    Illinois supporters, 189
    presidential candidate
        independent candidate,
        (1992) 438
        Independent Party nominee, (1984)
        437
        popular vote, (1976) 695, (1984) 684,
        (1988) 697, (1992) 698
        primary votes, (1980) 365–371,
        (1984) 372–377, (1988) 378–385,
        (1992) 386–393, (1996) 395–402,
        (2000) 404–410
        National Economy Recovery Party
        nominee, (1988) 438
        U.S. Labor Party nominee, (1976)
        436
    U.S. Labor Party history, 80
Larrabee, William
    governor, Iowa, 1391
Larrazolo, Octaviano A.
    governor, New Mexico, 1402
    senator, New Mexico, 1254
Larry King Live, 560, 563
Larson, Morgan F.
    governor, New Jersey, 1402
Latchford, Vincent
    presidential primary votes,
    (1992) 393
Latham, John H.
    presidential primary votes, (1960) 347,
    (1964) 350
Latham, Milton S.
    governor, California, 1386
    senator, California, 1237
Latimer, Asbury C.
    senator, South Carolina, 1260
Latin America
    platform issue
        Democrats, (1976) 540
        Republicans, (1976) 542
Lattimore, Henry
    senator, Delaware, 1239
Laughlin, Tom
    presidential primary votes, (1992)
    386–393
Laurance, John
    senator, New York, 1255
Lausche, Frank J.
    governor, Ohio, 1405

presidential candidate
  Democratic convention ballots,
    (1956) 619
  primary votes, (1956) 344–345
senator, Ohio, 149, 1257
Lautenberg, Frank R.
  senator, New Jersey, 199, 1254
  on fund-raising, 102
Lawrence, Abbott, 449
Lawrence, David L.
  governor, Pennsylvania, 1406
Lawrence, Elisha
  governor, New Jersey, 1401
Laxalt, Paul
  governor, Nevada, 1400
  Republican National Committee chair,
    426 (table)
  senator, Nevada, 175, 188, 1252
Lazio, Rick A., 100, 206, 1233
Le Tulle, Mary "France"
  presidential primary votes, (1996) 403
Lea, Luke
  senator, Tennessee, 1261
Lea, Preston
  governor, Delaware, 1388
Leach, Margaret, 703 (box), 774
Leader, George M.
  governor, Pennsylvania, 147, 1406
Leadership PACs, 97
League of Nations
  Democratic convention ballots, (1924)
    606
  platform issue
    Democrats, (1920) 495, (1924) 497
    Republicans, (1920) 494, (1924) 496
    Socialists, (1920) 493
  Wilson role, 258
League of Women Voters, 216
Leahy, Edward L.
  senator, Rhode Island, 1259
Leahy, Patrick J.
  senator, Vermont, 175, 1263
Leake, Walter
  governor, Mississippi, 1398
  senator, Mississippi, 1250
Learn, Dale
  vice-presidential candidate
    Socialist nominee, (1948) 434
Leavitt, Mike O.
  governor, Utah, 1410
Leche, Richard W.
  governor, Louisiana, 1393
Lee, Andrew E.
  governor, South Dakota, 1408
Lee, Blair
  governor, Maryland, 1395
  senator, Maryland, 1247
  popular election, 1231
Lee, Fitzhugh
  governor, Virginia, 1411
Lee, Henry
  governor, Virginia, 1411
Lee, Henry
  biography, 779
  vice-presidential candidate
    electoral vote, (1832) 772
    Independent Party nominee, (1832)
      429
Lee, Joseph Bracken
  governor, Utah, 1410
  presidential candidate
    Conservative Party of New Jersey
      nominee, (1960) 435
    popular vote, (1960) 694
  vice-presidential candidate
    Texas Constitution Party nominee,
      (1956) 435
Lee, Josh
  senator, Oklahoma, 1257
Lee, Richard E.
  presidential primary votes, (1968) 353
Lee, Richard Henry
  senator, Virginia, 1264
Lee, Robert E., 243
Lee, Thomas Sim
  governor, Maryland, 1395

Leedy, John W.
  governor, Kansas, 1392
Leeke, Granville B.
  vice-presidential candidate
    Greenback Party nominee, (1948)
      434
Legas, Frank
  presidential primary votes, (1996) 403
Lehman, Herbert H.
  governor, New York, 266, 1403
  senator, New York, 1255
    civil rights, 148
Lehrer, Jim, 297
Leib, Michael
  senator, Pennsylvania, 1258
Leigh, Benjamin W.
  senator, Virginia, 1264
LeMay, Curtis E.
  biography, 779
  vice-presidential candidate
    American Independent nominee,
      (1968) 51, 436, 532
    electoral vote, (1968) 773
Lemke, William
  biography, 779
  presidential candidate
    popular vote, (1936) 672
    Union Party nominee, (1936) 79, 433,
      505
Lend-lease agreement, 267
Leninist parties, 78
Lennane, James P.
  presidential primary votes, (1992)
    386–393
Lennon, Alton A.
  senator, North Carolina, 1256
Lenroot, Irving L.
  at Republican convention, (1920) 493
    ballots, 604
  senator, Wisconsin, 1266
Leonard, Jonah Fitz Randall
  presidential candidate
    popular vote, (1900) 691
    United Christian Party nominee,
      (1900) 432
LePage, Norman
  presidential primary votes, (1964) 350
Leslie, Harry G.
  governor, Indiana, 1391
Leslie, Preston H.
  governor, Kentucky, 1393
Letcher, John
  governor, Virginia, 1411
Letcher, Robert P.
  governor, Kentucky, 1392
Lett-Simmons, Barbara, 299 (box), 301, 703
  (box), 774
LeVander, Harold
  governor, Minnesota, 1397
Levering, Joshua
  presidential candidate
    popular vote, (1896) 662
    Prohibition Party nominee, (1896)
      431
Levin, Carl
  senator, Michigan, 181, 1249
Levin, Jules
  presidential candidate
    popular vote, (1976) 695–696
    Socialist Labor nominee, (1976) 437
Levinson, Michael S.
  presidential primary votes, (1988) 385,
    (1992) 393, (1996) 403
Lewelling, Lorenzo D.
  governor, Kansas, 1392
Lewin, Herbert
  presidential candidate
    Peace and Freedom Party nominee,
      (1988) 69, 438
    popular vote, (1988) 697
    primary votes, (1988) 378–385
Lewinsky, Monica, 19, 106, 201–202, 216, 297,
  568
Lewinson, Paul, 24
Lewis, David P.
  governor, Alabama, 1384

Lewis, Dixon H.
  senator, Alabama, 1236
Lewis, Drew, 550
Lewis, James Hamilton
  presidential primary votes, (1932)
    331–332
  senator, Illinois, 1242
Lewis, James T.
  governor, Wisconsin, 1413
Lewis, Jim
  vice-presidential candidate
    Libertarian nominee, (1984) 66, 437
Lewis, John, 104, 791
Lewis, John F.
  senator, Virginia, 1264
Lewis, John L., 139, 268
Lewis, Morgan
  governor, New York, 1402
Lewis, Terry P., 298 (box)
Liberal Party
  historical development, 46
  profile, 65
Liberal Republican Party
  campaign, (1872) 247–248
  convention, (1872) 463
  historical development, 46
  profile, 65
  timeline, 47
  nominees, (1872) 430
  officers, 425 (box)
  platform, (1872) 463–464
  at Republican convention, (1896) 465
Liberal Republican Party of Colored Men
  nominees, (1872) 430
Liberator, Americus
  presidential primary votes, (1968) 353
Libertarian Party
  historical development, 50
  profile, 65–66
  timeline, 47
  nominees, (1972–2000) 436–439
  primaries, (1992) 393, (1996) 402
Liberty Party
  convention, (1840) 446, (1843) 446
  as deciding factor, (1844) 238
  historical development, 44, 49
  profile, 66
  timeline, 47
  nominees, (1840) 429, (1844) 429, (1848)
    430
  officers, 425 (box)
  remnants in Free Soil Party, (1848) 449
  remnants in Whig Party, (1852) 452
  on slavery, 239
Liberty Party
  nominees, (1932) 433
Liberty Union Party
  presidential primary, (1984) 377, (1988)
    385, (1996) 402
Licht, Frank
  governor, Rhode Island, 1407
Lieberman, Joseph I.
  biography, 779
  senator, Connecticut, 191, 206,
    1239
  vice-presidential nominee
    Democratic candidate, (2000) 61,
      205, 296, 298, 312, 439, 568
    election milestones, 20
    electoral vote, (2000) 773
    televised debates, (2000) 216
Lightburn, Joseph B.
  presidential candidate
    Constitution Party nominee, (1964)
      436
    popular vote, (1964) 694
Ligon, Thomas W.
  governor, Maryland, 1395
Lilley, George L.
  governor, Connecticut, 1387
Lincoln, Abraham
  biography, 779
  Douglas debates, 216
  as president
    absentee voting, 36
    black voting rights, 24

presidential candidate
  election evolution, 3, 6, 15
  electoral vote, (1860) 736, (1864) 737
  former members of Congress, 155
    (box)
  as "minority" president, 223 (table)
  political party development, 45
  popular vote, (1860) 653,
    (1864) 654
  public offices, 214
  Republican convention ballots,
    (1860) 581, (1864) 582
  Republican nominee, (1860) 74,
    239–240, 241–242, 430, 458,
    (1864) 430, 459
  split electoral votes, 702 (box)
vice-presidential candidate
  Republican contender, (1856) 453
Lincoln, Benjamin
  biography, 779
  electoral vote, (1789) 718
Lincoln, Blanche
  senator, Arkansas, 202, 787, 1237
Lincoln, Enoch
  governor, Maine, 1394
Lincoln, John Cromwell
  vice-presidential candidate
    Commonwealth Land Party nominee,
      (1924) 433
Lincoln, Levi
  governor, Massachusetts, 1396
Lincoln, Robert T.
  Republican convention ballots, (1884)
    590, (1888) 592, (1892) 593
Lind, John
  governor, Minnesota, 1397
Lindsay, John V.
  House elections, 162
  mayor, New York City, 165
  political party development, 46, 65
  presidential candidate
    primary votes, (1972) 354–358
    Republican convention ballots,
      (1968) 622
Lindsay, Robert B.
  governor, Alabama, 1384
Lindsay, William
  senator, Kentucky, 1245
Lindsey, Washington E.
  governor, New Mexico, 1402
Linger, Claude R.
  presidential primary votes, (1944) 338
Link, Arthur A.
  governor, North Dakota, 1404
Linn, Lewis F.
  senator, Missouri, 1251
Lippitt, Charles W.
  governor, Rhode Island, 1407
Lippitt, Henry F.
  senator, Rhode Island, 1259
Lippmann, Walter, 262
List, Robert F.
  governor, Nevada, 1400
Lister, Ernest
  governor, Washington, 1412
Literacy tests for voting, 25, 132, 220
Literary Digest poll, 266
Little, John S.
  governor, Arkansas, 1385
Littlefield, Alfred H.
  governor, Rhode Island, 1407
Livermore, Samuel
  senator, New Hampshire, 1252
Livingston, Edward
  senator, Louisiana, 1246
Livingston, Robert L.
  House leadership, 202, 298
Livingston, William
  governor, New Jersey, 1401
Lloyd, Edward
  governor, Maryland, 1395
  senator, Maryland, 1247
Lloyd, Henry
  governor, Maryland, 1395
Lloyd, James
  senator, Maryland, 1247

Lloyd, James
    senator, Massachusetts, 1248
Lloyd, Marilyn, 788
Lloyd-Duffie, Elvena E.
    presidential primary votes, (1996)
        395–402
Locher, Cyrus
    senator, Ohio, 1257
Lock, Stanley
    presidential primary votes, (1988) 385
Locke, Francis
    senator, North Carolina, 1256
Locke, Gary
    governor, Washington, 19, 1377, 1412
Lockwood, Belva Ann Bennett
    presidential candidate
        Equal Rights Party nominee, (1884,
            1888) 431
Lodge, George C.
    presidential primary votes, (1964)
        348–350
Lodge, Henry Cabot
    presidential candidate
        Republican contender, (1916) 490
        Republican convention ballots,
            (1916) 602
    at Republican convention, (1920) 493
        officers, speakers, 417 (table)
    senator, Massachusetts, 1248
Lodge, Henry Cabot Jr.
    biography, 779
    Eisenhower campaign, (1952) 144
    presidential candidate
        as former vice-presidential nominee,
            224
        primary votes, (1960) 346–347,
            (1964) 348–350
        Republican contender, (1964) 161,
            276
        Republican convention ballots,
            (1964) 621
    senator, Massachusetts, 145, 1248
    vice-presidential candidate
        electoral vote, (1960) 773
        Republican nominee, (1960) 154,
            275, 435, 523
Lodge, John D.
    governor, Connecticut, 1387
Loewenherz, Rick
    presidential primary votes, (1976) 364
Loftin, Scott M.
    senator, Florida, 1240
Logan, George
    senator, Pennsylvania, 1259
Logan, John A.
    biography, 779
    Republican convention ballots, (1884)
        590
    Republican leadership, 247
    senator, Illinois, 1242
    vice-presidential candidate
        electoral vote, (1884) 773
        Republican nominee, (1884) 250,
            431, 470
Logan, Marvel M.
    senator, Kentucky, 1245
Logan, William
    senator, Kentucky, 1245
Loghlin, J. F.
    vice-presidential candidate
        Down With Lawyers Party nominee,
            (1980) 437
Lomento, Frank
    presidential primary votes, (1976) 364
Lonergan, Augustine
    senator, Connecticut, 1239
Long, Chester I.
    senator, Kansas, 1244
Long, Earl K.
    governor, Louisiana, 1394
Long, Edward V.
    senator, Missouri, 1251
Long, Huey P.
    at Democratic convention, (1932) 422,
        502
    as FDR rival, 265

governor, Louisiana, 1393
    senator, Louisiana, 1246
    Union Party history, 79
Long, Jill L., 788
Long, John Davis
    governor, Massachusetts, 1396
Long, Oren E.
    senator, Hawaii, 1241
Long, Rose McConnell
    senator, Louisiana, 1246
Long, Russell B.
    senator, Louisiana, 189, 1246
Longino, Andrew H.
    governor, Mississippi, 1398
Longley, James B.
    governor, Maine, 175, 179, 1395
Longworth, Nicholas, 13 (box)
Looker, Othniel
    governor, Ohio, 1404
Looking Back Party
    nominees, (1992) 438, (1996) 439
Loomis, Orland S.
    governor, Wisconsin, 1413
"Loophole" primary, 306 (box), 416–417
Lord, Nancy
    vice-presidential candidate
        Libertarian nominee, (1992) 66, 438
Lord, William P.
    governor, Oregon, 1405
Loricks, H. L.
    Populist convention officers, 425 (box)
Lorimer, William
    senator, Illinois, 1242
        disputed election, 1230
Lothrop, ——
    Democratic convention ballots, (1880)
        589
Lott, Trent
    Republican convention officers, 417
        (table)
    Republican strength in South, 129
    senator, Mississippi, 191, 1250
        Senate leadership, 11
Louisiana
    Democratic convention credentials dis-
        pute, (1932) 422, (1952) 422
    electoral vote contest, (1876) 248
    preferential primaries, 130–131
    Republican convention credentials dis-
        pute, (1952) 422
Lounsbury, George E.
    governor, Connecticut, 1387
Lounsbury, Phineas C.
    governor, Connecticut, 1387
Love, Alfred Henry
    vice-presidential candidate
        Equal Rights Party nominee, (1888)
            431
Love, John A.
    governor, Colorado, 159, 1386
Loveland, W. A. H.
    Democratic convention ballots, (1880)
        589
Loveless, Herschel C.
    Democratic convention ballots, (1960)
        620
    governor, Iowa, 149, 1392
Low, Frederick F.
    governor, California, 1386
Lowden, Frank O.
    governor, Illinois, 1391
    presidential candidate
        primary votes, (1920) 313, 324–326,
            (1928) 329–330
        Republican contender, (1920) 258,
            493, (1928) 260, 499
        Republican convention ballots,
            (1920) 604, (1928) 609
    vice-presidential candidate
        Republican contender, (1924) 495
Lowe, Enoch L.
    governor, Maryland, 1395
Lowe, Ralph P.
    governor, Iowa, 1391
Lowery, Arthur J.
    presidential popular vote, (1984) 697

Lowndes, Lloyd
    governor, Maryland, 1395
Lowndes, Rawlins
    governor, South Carolina, 1407
Lowrie, Walter
    senator, Pennsylvania, 1259
Lowry, Mike
    governor, Washington, 1412
Lowry, Robert
    governor, Mississippi, 1398
Loyal National Democrats, 531
Lubbock, Francis R.
    governor, Texas, 1409
Lucas, Frank E.
    governor, Wyoming, 1413
Lucas, Robert
    Democratic convention officers, 415
        (table)
    governor, Ohio, 1404
Lucas, Scott W.
    presidential primary votes, (1948)
        339–340
    senator, Illinois, 143, 1242
Luce, Cyrus G.
    governor, Michigan, 1397
Luce, Henry, 267
Lucey, Patrick J.
    governor, Wisconsin, 1413
    vice-presidential candidate
        National Unity Campaign, (1980) 68,
            437, 546
Ludington, Harrison
    governor, Wisconsin, 1413
Ludlow, George C.
    governor, New Jersey, 1401
Lugar, Richard G.
    presidential candidate
        presidential primary votes, (1996)
            395–402
        Republican contender, (1992) 293,
            315
    Republican convention speakers, 417
        (table)
    senator, Indiana, 179, 1243
Lujan, Manuel, 793
Lumpkin, Alva M.
    senator, South Carolina, 1260
Lumpkin, Wilson
    governor, Georgia, 1389
    senator, Georgia, 1241
Lundeen, Ernest
    senator, Minnesota, 1249
Lunger, Floyd L.
    presidential primary votes, (1976) 364
Lusk, Hall S.
    senator, Oregon, 1258
Lymen, Kent
    presidential candidate
        Middle Class Party nominee, (1980)
            437
Lynch, Charles
    governor, Mississippi, 1398
Lynch, John R.
    Republican convention officers, 417
        (table), 470, 590
Lynching
    Republican platform issue, (1896) 478
Lynen, Kurt
    presidential popular vote, (1980) 696
Lyon, Lucius
    senator, Michigan, 1249

M

Mabey, Charles R.
    governor, Utah, 1410
Mabry, Thomas J.
    governor, New Mexico, 1402
Mabus, Ray
    governor, Mississippi, 1398
MacArthur, Arthur
    governor, Wisconsin, 1413
MacArthur, Douglas
    "Bonus Army" protest, 261, 262
    presidential candidate
        America First Party nominee, (1952)
            434

Constitution Party nominee, (1952)
    435
    military service, 223
    popular vote, (1952) 694
    primary votes, (1944) 337–338,
        (1948) 339–340, (1952) 341–343
    Republican contender, (1944) 268,
        (1948) 140, 270, (1952) 271
    Republican convention ballots,
        (1944) 508, 614, (1948) 615, (1952)
        617
    Republican convention speakers, 417
        (table)
    Truman conflict, 142, 143, 271
Macauley, Robert Colvin
    presidential candidate
        popular vote, (1920) 692
        Single Tax Party nominee, (1920) 433
MacBride, Roger
    faithless elector, (1972) 65, 703 (box)
    presidential candidate
        Libertarian nominee, (1976) 65–66,
            436
        popular vote, (1976) 682
MacCorkle, William A.
    governor, West Virginia, 1412
MacGregor, Clark, 170
MacGregor, H. F.
    Republican convention ballots, (1920)
        604
Machen, Willis B.
    biography, 779
    senator, Kentucky, 1245
    vice-presidential electoral vote, (1872)
        772
Mack, Connie
    senator, Florida, 191, 206, 1240
Mack, Norman E.
    Democratic National Committee chair,
        415 (table), 426 (table)
MacKay, Buddy
    governor, Florida, 1389
MacKenna, Roscoe B.
    vice-presidential candidate
        Universal Party nominee, (1968) 436
Maclay, Samuel
    senator, Pennsylvania, 1258
Maclay, William
    senator, Pennsylvania, 1258
MacMillan, Pat, 36 (box)
MacNider, Hanford, 501
    Republican convention ballots, (1940)
        613
Macon, Nathaniel
    biography, 779
    senator, North Carolina, 1256
    vice-presidential electoral vote, (1824)
        772
Maddock, Walter J.
    governor, North Dakota, 1404
Maddox, Bob
    presidential primary votes, (1980)
        365–371
Maddox, Lester G.
    at Democratic convention, (1968) 531
    governor, Georgia, 166, 1390
        legislative choice, 1380
    presidential candidate
        American Independent Party nomi-
            nee, (1976) 52, 436
        popular vote, (1976) 695
Madison, George
    governor, Kentucky, 1392
Madison, James
    biography, 779
    on congressional districts, 808–809
    on House term, 801
    political party development, 43, 55–56,
        61, 62, 226
    presidential candidate
        cabinet service, 221
        Democratic-Republican nominee,
            (1808) 230, (1812) 230–231
        electoral vote, (1808) 723, (1812) 724
        former members of Congress, 155
            (box)

public offices, 214
vice-presidential electoral vote, (1808) 772
Mage, Judith
  vice-presidential candidate
    Peace and Freedom Party nominee, (1968) 436
Magleby, David, 98, 102
Magnuson, Warren G.
  length of service in Congress, 795 (table)
  senator, Washington, 183, 1265
Magoffin, Beriah
  governor, Kentucky, 1393
Magrath, Andrew G.
  governor, South Carolina, 1408
Magruder, Allan B.
  senator, Louisiana, 1246
Maguire, Matthew
  vice-presidential candidate
    Socialist-Labor nominee, (1896) 431
Mahalchik, John V.
  presidential candidate
    America First Party nominee, (1972) 436
    popular vote, (1972) 695
Mahon, George H.
  length of service in Congress, 795 (table)
Mahone, William
  senator, Virginia, 1264
Mahoney, George P., 166
Mahoney, J. Daniel, 55
Mahoney, Patrick J.
  presidential primary votes, (1992) 394
Maine
  electoral college variation, 701
  gubernatorial elections, 1381
Major, Elliot W.
  governor, Missouri, 1399
Majority-minority districts, 29–30, 792, 825–826
Makinson, Larry, 96
Malbone, Francis
  senator, Rhode Island, 1259
Mallary, Richard W., 175
Malloney, Joseph Francis
  presidential candidate
    popular vote, (1900) 691
    Socialist Labor nominee, (1900) 432
Mallory, Stephen R.
  senator, Florida, 1240
Malone, George W.
  senator, Nevada, 138, 1252
Maloney, Carolyn B., 821 (box)
Maloney, Francis
  senator, Connecticut, 1239
Manatt, Charles T.
  Democratic National Committee chair, 415 (table), 426 (table)
Manchester Union Leader, 280
Mandel, Marvin
  governor, Maryland, 1395
    suspension, 1381 (box)
Manderson, Charles F.
  senator, Nebraska, 1252
Mangum, Willie P.
  biography, 779
  presidential candidate
    electoral vote, (1836) 730
    independent Democrat, (1836) 235
  senator, North Carolina, 1256
Manly, Charles
  governor, North Carolina, 1403
Mann, Thomas E., 119 (box)
Mann, William H.
  governor, Virginia, 1411
Manning, John Lawrence
  governor, South Carolina, 1408
Manning, Richard I.
  governor, South Carolina, 1407
Manning, Richard I. III
  governor, South Carolina, 1408
Mansfield, Mike
  senator, Montana, 145, 1251
    Senate leadership, 157, 164, 179
Mantle, Lee
  senator, Montana, 1251

Maoist parties, 71
Maraziti, Joseph J., 175
Marble, Sebastian S.
  governor, Maine, 1394
Marcantonio, Vito, 46, 143
"March Madness," 315–318
March on Washington for Jobs and Freedom, 1963, 160
Marcy, William L.
  Democratic presidential contender, (1852) 450
    convention ballots, (1852) 577
  governor, New York, 1402
  senator, New York, 1255
Markham, Henry H.
  governor, California, 1386
Marks, Albert S.
  governor, Tennessee, 1409
Marks, William
  senator, Pennsylvania, 1259
Marland, Ernest W.
  governor, Oklahoma, 1405
Marland, William C.
  governor, West Virginia, 1412
Marmaduke, John S.
  governor, Missouri, 1399
Marmaduke, Meredith M.
  governor, Missouri, 1398
Marra, William A.
  presidential candidate
    popular vote, (1988) 697
    primary votes, (1988) 378–385
    Right to Life Party nominee, (1988) 438
Marriage
  definition, 567
  of members of Congress, 788
  polygamy, 473
Marrou, Andre V.
  presidential candidate
    Libertarian nominee, (1992) 66, 438
    popular vote, (1992) 686
    primary votes, (1992) 393
  vice-presidential candidate
    Libertarian nominee, (1988) 66, 438
Marsh, Ephraim
  Know-Nothing convention officers, 425 (box)
Marsh, Jeffrey
  presidential primary votes, (1992) 386–393
Marshall, George C., 138
Marshall, Humphrey
  senator, Kentucky, 1245
Marshall, John
  biography, 779
  political party development, 63
  vice-presidential electoral vote, (1816) 772
Marshall, Thomas R.
  biography, 779
  governor, Indiana, 1391
  presidential candidate
    Democratic convention ballots, (1912) 601, (1920) 605
    as former vice president, 314 (box)
  vice-presidential candidate
    Democratic nominee, (1912) 257, 432, 487, (1916) 258, 432, 491
    electoral anomalies, 12–13 (box)
    electoral vote, (1912, 1916) 773
    on vice presidency, 312
Marshall, Thurgood, 26, 120
Marshall, William R.
  governor, Minnesota, 1397
Marshall Plan, 269
Marston, Gilman
  senator, New Hampshire, 1253
Martin, Alexander
  governor, North Carolina, 1403
  senator, North Carolina, 1255
Martin, Anthony R. "Andy"
  presidential primary votes, (2000) 404–410
Martin, Charles H.
  governor, Oregon, 1405

Martin, Clarence D.
  governor, Washington, 1412
Martin, Daniel
  governor, Maryland, 1395
Martin, David H.
  vice-presidential candidate
    United Christian Party nominee, (1900) 432
Martin, Edward
  governor, Pennsylvania, 1406
  presidential primary votes, (1944) 337–338, (1948) 339–340
  senator, Pennsylvania, 1258
Martin, George B.
  senator, Kentucky, 1245
Martin, James G.
  governor, North Carolina, 1404
Martin, John
  governor, Georgia, 1389
Martin, John
  senator, Kansas, 1244
Martin, John A.
  governor, Kansas, 1392
Martin, John G.
  presidential candidate
    popular vote, (1988) 697
    Third World Assembly nominee, (1988) 438
Martin, John W.
  governor, Florida, 1388
Martin, Joseph W. Jr.
  presidential candidate
    primary votes, (1948) 339–340
    Republican convention ballots, (1940) 613, (1948) 615
    Republican convention officers, 417 (table)
    Republican National Committee chair, 426 (table)
Martin, Joshua L.
  governor, Alabama, 1384
Martin, Noah
  governor, New Hampshire, 1400
Martin, Thomas E.
  senator, Iowa, 1244
Martin, Thomas S.
  senator, Virginia, 1264
Martin, Warren C.
  vice-presidential candidate
    Prohibition Party nominee, (1984) 437
Martin-Trigona, Anthony R.
  presidential primary votes, (1988) 385
Martine, James E.
  senator, New Jersey, 1254
Martineau, John E.
  governor, Arkansas, 1385
Martinez, Bob
  governor, Florida, 189, 1389
Martinez, Mathew G., 793
Martz, Judy
  governor, Montana, 1399
Marvel, Joshua H.
  governor, Delaware, 1388
Marvin, William
  governor, Florida, 1388
Mason, Armistead T.
  senator, Virginia, 1264
Mason, George, 799
Mason, James M.
  senator, Virginia, 1264
Mason, Jeremiah
  senator, New Hampshire, 1253
Mason, Jonathan
  senator, Massachusetts, 1248
Mason, Mel
  presidential candidate
    popular vote, (1984) 697
    Socialist Workers nominee, (1984) 437
Mason, Stevens T.
  governor, Michigan, 1396
Mason, Stevens T.
  senator, Virginia, 1264
Mason, William E.
  senator, Illinois, 1242

Masons
  Anti-Masonic Party, (1832) 52–53, 442
Massachusetts
  gubernatorial elections, 1381
  House redistricting, 817 (box)
Massey, William A.
  senator, Nevada, 1252
Masters, Isabell
  presidential candidate
    Looking Back Party nominee, (1992) 438, (1996) 439
    popular vote, (1992) 698, (1996) 699
    primary votes, (1988) 378–385, (1992) 386–393, (1996) 395–402
Masters, Shirley Jean
  vice-presidential candidate
    Looking Back Party nominee, (1996) 439
Masters, Walter
  vice-presidential candidate
    Looking Back Party nominee, (1992) 438
Matchett, Charles Horatio
  presidential candidate
    popular vote, (1896) 691
    Socialist Labor nominee, (1896) 431
  vice-presidential candidate
    Socialist Labor nominee, (1892) 431
Matheson, Scott M.
  Democratic convention ballots, (1980) 630
  governor, Utah, 1410
Mathews, George
  governor, Georgia, 1389
Mathews, Henry Mason
  governor, West Virginia, 1412
Mathews, John
  governor, South Carolina, 1407
Mathewson, Elisha
  senator, Rhode Island, 1259
Mathias, Charles McC. Jr.
  senator, Maryland, 169, 188, 1247
Matsunaga, Spark M.
  senator, Hawaii, 179, 1241
Matteson, Joel A.
  governor, Illinois, 1390
Matthews, Claude
  Democratic convention ballots, (1896) 595
  governor, Indiana, 1391
Matthews, Harlan
  senator, Tennessee, 1262
Matthews, Joseph M.
  governor, Mississippi, 1398
Matthews, Stanley
  Liberal Republican convention officers, 425 (box)
  senator, Ohio, 1257
Mattingly, Mack
  senator, Georgia, 189, 1241
Mattocks, John
  governor, Vermont, 1410
Maull, Joseph
  governor, Delaware, 1388
Maurer, James H.
  vice-presidential candidate
    Socialist nominee, (1928) 433, (1932) 433, 501
Maw, Herbert B.
  governor, Utah, 1410
Maxey, Samuel B.
  senator, Texas, 1262
Maxwell, John
  presidential candidate
    Vegetarian nominee, (1948) 434
Maybank, Burnet R.
  governor, South Carolina, 1408
  senator, South Carolina, 131, 1260
Mayfield, Earle B.
  senator, Texas, 1262
Mayne, Wiley, 175
Mazelis, Fred
  vice-presidential candidate
    Socialist Equality Party nominee, (1996) 439
    Workers League nominee, (1992) 438

Mazzoli, Romano L., 104
McAdoo, William Gibbs
  at Democratic convention, (1932) 262, 502
  presidential candidate
    Democratic contender, (1920) 259, 494, (1924) 260, 496–497
    Democratic convention ballots, (1920) 605, (1924) 606–607
    no-run decision, (1928) 499
    primary votes, (1920) 324–327, (1924) 327–328, (1928) 329–330
  senator, California, 1238
McAlister, Hill
  governor, Tennessee, 1409
McAlpine, Louis
  presidential primary votes, (1992) 386–393
McArthur, Duncan
  governor, Ohio, 1404
McAuliffe, Terrence
  Democratic National Committee chair, 426 (table)
McBride, George W.
  senator, Oregon, 1258
McBride, Henry
  governor, Washington, 1412
McCain, John
  presidential candidate
    campaign finance reform, (2000) 87, 88, 107, 108
    politics and issues, (2000) 204
    primary votes, (2000) 212, 305, 318, 404–410
    Republican contender, (2000) 210, 296–297, 566
  at Republican convention, (1996) 562
  Section 527 groups, 107
  senator, Arizona, 1237
    campaign finance reform, 124 (box), 125
    ethics investigation, 195
McCall, Samuel W.
  governor, Massachusetts, 1396
  Republican convention ballots, (1916) 602
McCall, Tom
  governor, Oregon, 1406
McCallum, Scott
  governor, Wisconsin, 1413
McCarran, Patrick A.
  senator, Nevada, 1252
McCarthy, Carolyn, 789
McCarthy, Eugene
  biography, 779
  campaign finance law court case, 117
  presidential candidate
    Consumer Party nominee, (1988) 438
    Democratic contender, (1968) 59, 167, 278, 422, 530–532, (1972) 171
    Democratic convention ballots, (1968) 623, (1972) 625
    independent candidate, (1976) 65–66, 178, 436
    popular vote, (1968) 695, (1976) 682, (1988) 697
    primary votes, (1968) 308, 351–353, (1972) 354–358, (1992) 386–393
  senator, Minnesota, 152, 170, 1249
McCarthy, Joseph R.
  anticommunism, 142, 143, 145, 146
  Catholic voter support, 276
  senator, Wisconsin, 138, 1266
  successor, 151
McCarty, Daniel T.
  governor, Florida, 1389
McClatchy, Kate
  vice-presidential candidate
    Peace and Freedom Party nominee, (1996) 69, 439
McClellan, George B.
  biography, 779
  conflict with Lincoln, 243
  governor, New Jersey, 1401
  presidential candidate

Democratic convention ballots, (1864) 582, (1880) 589, (1904) 597
Democratic nominee, (1864) 244–245, 430, 460
electoral vote, (1864) 737
military service, 222
popular vote, (1864) 654
McClellan, John L.
  senator, Arkansas, 1237
McClelland, Robert
  governor, Michigan, 1397
McClernand, John A.
  Democratic convention officers, 415 (table)
McCloskey, Burr
  vice-presidential candidate
    Pioneer Party nominee, (1956) 435
McCloskey, Frank, 803–804
McCloskey, Paul N. "Pete" Jr.
  House elections, 175
  presidential candidate
    primary votes, (1972) 354–358
    Republican contender, (1972) 172, 280, 536
    Republican convention ballots, (1972) 627
McClung, Joseph W.
  governor, Missouri, 1398
McClure, James A.
  senator, Idaho, 1242
McComas, Louis E.
  senator, Maryland, 1247
McCombs, William F.
  Democratic National Committee chair, 415 (table), 426 (table)
McConaughy, James L.
  governor, Connecticut, 1387
McCone, Allen C.
  vice-presidential candidate
    Take Back America Party nominee, (1992) 438
McConnell, Mitch
  senator, Kentucky, 187, 1245
    campaign finance reform, 107
McConnell, William J.
  governor, Idaho, 1390
  senator, Idaho, 1242
McCord, James N.
  governor, Tennessee, 1409
McCormack, Ellen
  presidential candidate
    Democratic contender, (1976) 178, 538
    Democratic convention ballots, (1976) 627
    popular vote, (1980) 696
    primary votes, (1976) 359–364
    Right to Life Party nominee, (1980) 437
McCormack, John W.
  Democratic convention officers, 415 (table)
  House leadership, 157, 164
    contested Mississippi elections, 803
  presidential primary votes, (1956) 344–345
McCormick, Medill
  senator, Illinois, 1242
McCormick, Richard P., 225, 237
McCormick, Vance C.
  Democratic National Committee chair, 415 (table), 426 (table)
McCray, Warren T.
  governor, Indiana, 1391
McCreary, James B.
  governor, Kentucky, 1393
  senator, Kentucky, 1245
McCreery, Thomas C.
  senator, Kentucky, 1245
McCuish, John
  governor, Kansas, 1392
McCulloch, Roscoe C.
  senator, Ohio, 1257
McCullough, John G.
  governor, Vermont, 1411

McCumber, Porter J.
  senator, North Dakota, 1256
McDaniel, Henry D.
  governor, Georgia, 1389
McDill, James W.
  senator, Iowa, 1243
McDonald, Alexander
  senator, Arkansas, 1237
McDonald, Angus W.
  presidential primary votes, (1988) 378–385, (1992) 386–393, (2000) 404–410
McDonald, Charles J.
  governor, Georgia, 1389
McDonald, Duncan
  vice-presidential candidate
    Farmer Labor nominee, (1924) 433
McDonald, Jesse F.
  governor, Colorado, 1386
McDonald, Joseph E.
  presidential candidate
    Democratic contender, (1884) 471
    Democratic convention ballots, (1880) 589, (1884) 591
  senator, Indiana, 1243
McDonald, Lawrence P., 175
McDonald, William C.
  governor, New Mexico, 1402
McDougal, John
  governor, California, 1386
McDougall, James A.
  senator, California, 1238
McDowell, James
  governor, Virginia, 1411
McDuffie, George
  governor, South Carolina, 1407
  senator, South Carolina, 1260
McEnery, John, 1394
McEnery, Samuel D.
  governor, Louisiana, 1393
  senator, Louisiana, 1246
McFarland, Ernest W.
  governor, Arizona, 1385
  senator, Arizona, 1237
McGee, Gale W.
  senator, Wyoming, 179, 1266
McGill, Andrew R.
  governor, Minnesota, 1397
McGill, George
  senator, Kansas, 1244
McGovern, Francis E.
  governor, Wisconsin, 1413
  at Republican convention, (1912) 486
    ballots, 600
McGovern, George
  biography, 779
  Democratic rules reform, 171, 418 (box), 534
  presidential candidate
    campaign finance, (1972) 115
    Democratic contender, (1968) 167, 530–532, (1984) 186, 285
    Democratic convention ballots, (1968) 623, (1972) 625, (1984) 633
    Democratic nominee, (1972) 59, 280–281, 422, 425, 427, 436, 533–535
    electoral vote, (1972) 764
    politics and issues, (1972) 171–172
    popular vote, (1972) 681
    primary votes, (1972) 308, 310 (box), 313, 354–358, (1984) 372–377
  senator, South Dakota, 175, 183, 284, 1261
    campaign contributions, (1962) 104, (1968) 111
McGovern-Fraser Commission, 18
McGrath, J. Howard
  Democratic National Committee chair, 415 (table), 426 (table)
  governor, Rhode Island, 1407
  senator, Rhode Island, 1259
McGrath, John R.
  presidential primary votes, (2000) 404–410

McGraw, John H.
  governor, Washington, 1412
McGroarty, John S.
  presidential primary votes, (1936) 333–334
McIlvaine, Joseph
  senator, New Jersey, 1253
McIntire, Albert W.
  governor, Colorado, 1386
McIntyre, Richard D., 803–804
McIntyre, Thomas J.
  senator, New Hampshire, 181, 1253
McKay, Douglas
  governor, Oregon, 1406
  Senate race, 149
McKean, Samuel
  senator, Pennsylvania, 1258
McKean, Thomas
  governor, Delaware, 1387
McKean, Thomas
  governor, Pennsylvania, 1406
McKeithen, John J.
  governor, Louisiana, 1394
McKeldin, Theodore R.
  governor, Maryland, 1395
McKellar, Kenneth D.
  senator, Tennessee, 1261
McKelvie, Samuel R.
  governor, Nebraska, 1399
McKernan, John R. Jr.
  governor, Maine, 1395
  marriage, 788
McKiernan, John S.
  governor, Rhode Island, 1407
McKinney, Cynthia, 791, 792
McKinley, John
  governor, Delaware, 1387
McKinley, John
  senator, Alabama, 1236
McKinley, William
  assassination, 16, 254
  biography, 779
  governor, Ohio, 1405
  presidential candidate
    campaign finance, (1896, 2000) 89, 108
    electoral vote, (1896) 745, (1900) 746
    as former governor, 176 (box)
    former members of Congress, 155 (box)
    military service, 222
    popular vote, (1896) 662, (1900) 663
    public offices, 215
    reelection chances, (1900) 313 (box)
    Republican contender, (1892) 252, 474
    Republican convention ballots, (1888) 592, (1892) 593, (1896) 594, (1900) 596
    Republican nominee, (1896) 76, 254, 431, 477, (1900) 254, 431, 479
    Republican convention officers, 417 (table)
McKinley, William B.
  senator, Illinois, 1242
McKinley Tariff Act, 252
McKinney, Frank E.
  Democratic National Committee chair, 426 (table)
McKinney, Philip W.
  governor, Virginia, 1411
McLain, George H.
  presidential primary votes, (1960) 346–347
McLain, Harley
  presidential candidate
    Natural Peoples Party nominee, (1980) 437
    popular vote, (1980) 696
McLane, John
  governor, New Hampshire, 1401
McLane, Louis
  senator, Delaware, 1239
McLane, Robert M.
  Democratic National Committee chair, 415 (table), 426 (table)

governor, Maryland, 1395
McLauren, Anselm J.
    governor, Mississippi, 1398
    senator, Mississippi, 1250
McLaurin, John L.
    senator, South Carolina, 1260
McLean, Angus Wilton
    governor, North Carolina, 1403
McLean, George P.
    governor, Connecticut, 1387
    senator, Connecticut, 1239
McLean, John
    presidential candidate
        Anti-Mason nomination refused,
            (1832) 442
        Republican contender, (1856) 453
        Republican convention ballots,
            (1856) 579, (1860) 581
        Whig convention ballots, (1848)
            576
    senator, Illinois, 1242
McLean, John R., 478
    Democratic convention ballots, (1896)
        595
McLeod, Thomas G.
    governor, South Carolina, 1408
McMahon, Brien
    senator, Connecticut, 1239
McMahon, George
    vice-presidential candidate
        Independent Grassroots Party nomi-
            nee, (1996) 439
McManus, Gerald J.
    presidential primary votes, (1996) 403
McMaster, William H.
    governor, South Dakota, 1408
    senator, South Dakota, 1261
McMath, Sidney S.
    governor, Arkansas, 1385
McMichael, Morton
    Republican convention officers, 417
        (table)
McMillan, James
    senator, Michigan, 1249
McMillan, Samuel J. R.
    senator, Minnesota, 1249
McMillin, Benton
    governor, Tennessee, 1409
McMinn, Joseph
    governor, Tennessee, 1409
McMullen, Adam
    governor, Nebraska, 1399
McMullen, Richard C.
    governor, Delaware, 1388
McNair, Alexander
    governor, Missouri, 1398
McNair, Robert E.
    governor, South Carolina, 1408
McNamara, Patrick V.
    senator, Michigan, 1249
McNary, Charles L.
    biography, 779
    presidential candidate
        primary votes, (1940) 336
        Republican contender, (1936) 265,
            (1940) 267
        Republican convention ballots,
            (1940) 613
    senator, Oregon, 1258
    vice-presidential candidate
        electoral vote, (1940) 773
        Republican nominee, (1940) 267,
            434, 506
McNichols, Stephen L. R.
    governor, Colorado, 1386
McNutt, Alexander G.
    governor, Mississippi, 1398
McNutt, Paul V.
    Democratic convention ballots, (1948)
        616
    governor, Indiana, 1391
McPherson, Edward
    Republican convention officers, 417
        (table)
McPherson, John R.
    senator, New Jersey, 1254

McRae, John J.
    governor, Mississippi, 1398
    senator, Mississippi, 1250
McRae, Thomas C.
    governor, Arkansas, 1385
McReynolds, David
    presidential candidate
        popular vote, (1980) 696, (2000) 699
        Socialist nominee, (1980) 437, (2000)
            439
McRoberts, Samuel
    senator, Illinois, 1242
McSweeney, Miles B.
    governor, South Carolina, 1408
McVay, Hugh
    governor, Alabama, 1384
McWherter, Ned R.
    governor, Tennessee, 1409
McWillie, William
    governor, Mississippi, 1398
Mead, Albert E.
    governor, Washington, 1412
Mead, James M.
    senator, New York, 1255
Mead, John A.
    governor, Vermont, 1411
Meador, Edward Kirby
    vice-presidential candidate
        Greenback Party nominee, (1956,
            1960) 435
Meadows, Clarence W.
    governor, West Virginia, 1412
Means, John Hugh
    governor, South Carolina, 1408
Means, Rice W.
    senator, Colorado, 1238
Mecham, Edwin L.
    governor, New Mexico, 149, 162,
        1402
        impeachment, 1381 (box)
    senator, New Mexico, 1254
Mecham, Evan
    governor, Arizona, 189, 1385
Mecham, Merritt C.
    governor, New Mexico, 1402
Mechanical lever voting machines, 218
Medary, Samuel
    Democratic convention officers, 415
        (table)
Medicare
    Democratic platform, (2000) 569
    enactment, 164
    Republican platform, (1964) 527, (1996)
        563, (2000) 567
Medill, William
    governor, Ohio, 1404
Meehan, Martin T., 93
    campaign finance reform, 124 (box)
Meese, Edwin, 543
Meier, Julius L.
    governor, Oregon, 1405
Meigs, Return J.
    governor, Ohio, 1404
    senator, Ohio, 1257
Melcher, John
    senator, Montana, 179, 191, 1251
Melette, Arthur C.
    governor, South Dakota, 1408
Mellen, Prentiss
    senator, Massachusetts, 1248
Mellman, Mark, 22
Mellon, Andrew, 258
Menard, John W., 790
Mercer, John Francis
    governor, Maryland, 1395
Meredith, Edwin T.
    Democratic convention ballots, (1920)
        605, (1924) 606–607
Meriwether, David
    senator, Kentucky, 1245
Merriam, Frank F.
    governor, California, 1386
Merriam, William R.
    governor, Minnesota, 1397
Merrick, William D.
    senator, Maryland, 1247

Merrill, Samuel
    governor, Iowa, 1391
Merrill, Steve
    governor, New Hampshire, 1401
Merrimon, Augustus S.
    senator, North Carolina, 1256
Merwin, John D.
    presidential primary votes, (1992)
        386–393
Meskill, Thomas J.
    governor, Connecticut, 1387
Metcalf, Henry Brewer
    vice-presidential candidate
        Prohibition Party nominee, (1900)
            431
Metcalf, Jesse H.
    senator, Rhode Island, 1260
Metcalf, Lee
    senator, Montana, 1251
Metcalf, Ralph
    governor, New Hampshire, 1400
Metcalfe, Thomas
    governor, Kentucky, 1392
    senator, Kentucky, 1245
Metzenbaum, Howard M.
    senator, Ohio, 179, 1257
    campaign finance, 112
Mexican War, 238, 448, 449
Meyers, Jan, 18, 789
Meyner, Robert B.
    Democratic convention ballots, (1960)
        620
    governor, New Jersey, 146, 151, 1402
Michael, Stephen D.
    independent presidential candidate, 439
        popular vote, (1996) 699
        primary votes, (1992) 386–393,
            (1996) 403
Michel, Robert H.
    House leadership, 198
    Republican convention officers, 417
        (table)
Michelson, George S.
    governor, South Dakota, 189
Michigan
    House redistricting, 823
Mickells, Kathleen
    vice-presidential candidate
        Socialist Workers nominee, (1988)
            438
Mickelson, George S.
    governor, South Dakota, 1409
Mickelson, George T.
    governor, South Dakota, 1409
Mickey, John H.
    governor, Nebraska, 1399
Middle Class Party
    nominees, (1980) 437
Middle East
    Camp David accords, 180
    platform issue
        Democrats, (1944) 510, (1948) 513,
            (1984) 550, (1992) 558, (1996) 565,
            (2000) 570
        Republicans, (1944) 509, (1948) 512,
            (1956) 521, (1988) 556, (1992) 560,
            (1996) 563, (2000) 568
    Suez crisis, 147
Middleton, Henry
    governor, South Carolina, 1407
Mifflin, Thomas
    governor, Pennsylvania, 1406
Mikulski, Barbara A.
    Democratic rules reform, 418 (box)
    senator, Maryland, 188, 787, 789,
        1247
    Senate leadership, 789
Miles, John E.
    governor, New Mexico, 1402
Miles, Nelson A.
    Democratic convention ballots, (1904)
        597
Military service
    absentee voting, 37–38, 39
    census, 821 (box)
    members of Congress, 787

platform issues
    Democrats, (2000) 570
    Republicans, (1980) 544, (1996) 563,
        (2000) 566, 568
presidential candidates, 221–222, 223
Milko, Hilary Michael
    presidential primary votes, (1996) 403
Millard, Joseph H.
    senator, Nebraska, 1252
Milledge, John
    governor, Georgia, 1389
    senator, Georgia, 1241
Miller, B. N.
    vice-presidential candidate
        Constitutional Party (Washington)
            nominee, (1960) 435
Miller, Benjamin M.
    governor, Alabama, 1384
Miller, Bert H.
    senator, Idaho, 1242
Miller, Bob J.
    governor, Nevada, 1400
Miller, Charles R.
    governor, Delaware, 1388
Miller, Dan, 821 (box)
Miller, Ernest L.
    presidential candidate
        popular vote, (1976) 696
        Restoration Party nominee, (1976)
            437
Miller, Homer V. M.
    senator, Georgia, 1241
Miller, Jack
    senator, Iowa, 172, 1244
Miller, Jacob W.
    senator, New Jersey, 1254
Miller, John
    governor, Missouri, 1398
Miller, John
    governor, North Dakota, 1404
Miller, John E.
    senator, Arkansas, 131, 1237
Miller, John F.
    senator, California, 1237
Miller, Keith H.
    governor, Alaska, 1384
Miller, Leslie A.
    governor, Wyoming, 1413
Miller, Nathan L.
    governor, New York, 1403
Miller, Stephen
    governor, Minnesota, 1397
Miller, Stephen D.
    governor, South Carolina, 1407
    senator, South Carolina, 1260
Miller, Walter D.
    governor, South Dakota, 1409
Miller, Ward M., 803
Miller, Warner
    senator, New York, 1255
Miller, William
    governor, North Carolina, 1403
Miller, William E.
    biography, 779
    Republican National Committee chair,
        161, 417 (table), 426 (table)
    vice-presidential candidate
        electoral vote, (1964) 773
        New York background, 222
        Republican nominee, (1964)
            161–162, 276–277, 435, 525
Miller, William R.
    governor, Arkansas, 1385
Miller, Zell
    at Democratic convention, (1992) 557
    keynote speaker, 415 (table)
    governor, Georgia, 1390
    senator, Georgia, 1241
Milliken, Carl E.
    governor, Maine, 1394
Milliken, William G.
    governor, Michigan, 1397
Millikin, Eugene D.
    senator, Colorado, 1238
Mills, Elijah H.
    senator, Massachusetts, 1248

Mills, Roger Q.
    senator, Texas, 1262
Mills, Wilbur D.
    Democratic convention ballots, (1972)
        625
    presidential primary votes, (1972)
        354–358
Milton, John
    governor, Florida, 1388
Milton, John (Georgia)
    biography, 779
    electoral vote, (1789) 718
Milton, John
    senator, New Jersey, 1254
Milton, William H.
    senator, Florida, 1240
Miner, Ruth Ann
    governor, Delaware, 1388
Minett, Cyril
    vice-presidential candidate
        America First Party nominee, (1992)
            438
Minimum wage
    Socialist platform issue, (1912) 485
Mink, Patsy T.
    presidential primary votes, (1972)
        354–358
Minnesota
    Democratic convention credentials dis-
        pute, (1932) 422
Minor, William T.
    governor, Connecticut, 1387
Minorities. See also African Americans; Asian
    Americans; Hispanics; Native Americans
    census undercount, 815, 820 (box)
    convention delegates, 413
    ethnic characteristics of voters, 23 (table)
    House redistricting, 825–826
    race in ticket-balancing, 312
Minton, Sherman
    senator, Indiana, 1243
Mississippi
    Democratic convention credentials dis-
        putes, (1964) 527, (1968) 531
    disputed House elections, (1964) 803
    gubernatorial elections, 1381
Mississippi Freedom Democratic Party, 527,
    803
Missouri
    House redistricting, 823
Missouri Compromise, 232, 240
Mitchell, Arthur W., 790
Mitchell, Charlene
    presidential candidate
        Communist nominee, (1968) 436
        popular vote, (1968) 695
Mitchell, Charles B.
    senator, Arkansas, 1237
Mitchell, David B.
    governor, Georgia, 1389
Mitchell, George J.
    senator, Maine, 1246
        Senate leadership, 193
Mitchell, Greg, 265
Mitchell, Henry L.
    governor, Florida, 1388
Mitchell, Hugh B.
    senator, Washington, 1265
Mitchell, James P., 157
Mitchell, John H.
    senator, Oregon, 1258
Mitchell, John I.
    senator, Pennsylvania, 1258
Mitchell, John I.
    senator, Wisconsin, 1265
Mitchell, John N.
    attorney general, 33, 281
Mitchell, Nathaniel
    governor, Delaware, 1388
Mitchell, Stephen A.
    Democratic National Committee chair,
        415 (table), 426 (table)
Mitchell, Stephen M.
    senator, Connecticut, 1239
Mitchill, Samuel L.
    senator, New York, 1255

Mitofsky, Warren, 219
Mixon, John W.
    governor, Florida, 1389
Moeur, Benjamin B.
    governor, Arizona, 1385
Mofford, Rose
    governor, Arizona, 1385
Molinari, Guy, 788
Molinari, Susan
    Republican convention speakers, 417
        (table), 561
    women in Congress, 788
Molleston, Henry
    governor, Delaware, 1388
Mondale, Walter F.
    biography, 780
    presidential candidate
        Democratic convention ballots,
            (1972) 625, (1980) 630, (1984)
            633
        Democratic nominee, (1984)
            284–286, 437, 548–549, 551
        election milestones, 18
        electoral vote, (1984) 767
        as former vice president, 223–224,
            314 (box)
        National Unity Party endorsement,
            (1984) 68
        politics and issues, (1984) 186–187
        popular vote, (1984) 684
        primary votes, (1984) 305, 311 (box),
            314, 372–377
        vice-presidential choice, 60
    senator, Minnesota, 1249
    as vice president, 312
    vice-presidential candidate
        Democratic nominee, (1976) 178,
            282, 436, 538–539, (1980) 182,
            283, 437, 545
        electoral vote, (1976, 1980) 773
        televised debates, (1976, 1980) 216
Monetary policy
    gold crisis of 1869, 247
    in New Deal, 263–264
    platform issues
        Democrats, (1868) 462, (1876) 467,
            (1880) 469, (1892) 475, (1896) 423
            (box), 478, 595, (1900) 481, (1904)
            482
        Greenback Party, (1880) 469
        Populists, (1892) 476
        Prohibition Party, (1892) 475
        Republicans, (1868) 461, (1876) 466,
            (1888) 473, (1892) 474, (1896) 477,
            (1900) 480, (1936) 504, (1940) 507,
            (1984) 551
        Socialists, (1912) 485
        Union Party, (1936) 506
    political party development, 66–67
    in Progressive era, 253–254
    in Republican ascendancy, 248–249, 252
Money, Hernando D.
    senator, Mississippi, 1250
Monier, Robert B.
    governor, New Hampshire, 1401
Monopolies and antitrust law
    platform issues
        Democrats, (1900) 480
        Greenback party, (1880) 469
        Progressives, (1912) 489, (1924) 498
        Republicans, (1900) 480, (1904) 482,
            (1908) 423 (box)
    Progressive era policies, 255, 257
Monroe, James
    biography, 780
    governor, Virginia, 1411
    political party development, 43, 56, 61
    presidential candidate
        cabinet service, 221
        Democratic-Republican contender,
            (1808) 230
        Democratic-Republican nominee,
            (1816) 231, (1820) 231–232
        electoral vote, (1816) 725, (1820) 702
            (box), 726
        as former governor, 176 (box)

former members of Congress, 155
    (box)
    public offices, 214
senator, Virginia, 1264
vice-presidential electoral vote, (1808)
    772
Monroe Doctrine, 232
Monroney, A. S. Mike
    senator, Oklahoma, 143, 1258
Montague, Andrew J.
    governor, Virginia, 1411
Montoya, Joseph M.
    senator, New Mexico, 162, 179, 792, 1254
Monyek, Fanny R. Z.
    presidential primary votes, (1992) 394
Moodie, Thomas S.
    governor, North Dakota, 1404
Moody, Blair
    at Democratic convention, (1952) 516
    senator, Michigan, 1249
Moody, Dan
    Democratic platform, (1948) 512
    governor, Texas, 1410
Moody, Gideon C.
    senator, South Dakota, 1261
Moody, Zenas F.
    governor, Oregon, 1405
Mooney, Beatrice
    presidential primary votes, (1992) 393
Moor, Wyman B. S.
    senator, Maine, 1246
Moore, A. Harry
    governor, New Jersey, 1402
    senator, New Jersey, 1254
Moore, Andrew
    senator, Virginia, 1264
Moore, Andrew B.
    governor, Alabama, 1384
Moore, Arch A. Jr.
    governor, West Virginia, 173, 191–192,
        1412
Moore, Charles C.
    governor, Idaho, 1390
Moore, Dan K.
    governor, North Carolina, 1404
    presidential candidate
        Democratic contender, (1968) 531
        Democratic convention ballots,
            (1968) 623
Moore, Edward H.
    senator, Oklahoma, 1257
Moore, Gabriel
    governor, Alabama, 1384
    senator, Alabama, 1236
Moore, John I.
    governor, Arkansas, 1385
Moore, Samuel B.
    governor, Alabama, 1384
Moore, Thomas O.
    governor, Louisiana, 1393
Moore, W. Henson, 189
Moore, William
    governor, Pennsylvania, 1406
Moorehead, Monica
    presidential candidate
        popular vote, (1996) 698, (2000)
            699
        primary votes, (1996) 402
        Workers World Party nominee,
            (1996, 2000) 82, 439
Moorman, Edgar W.
    vice-presidential candidate
        Prohibition Party nominee, (1940)
            434
Morehead, Charles S.
    governor, Kentucky, 1393
Morehead, James T.
    governor, Kentucky, 1392
    senator, Kentucky, 1245
Morehead, John H.
    governor, Nebraska, 1399
Morehead, John M.
    governor, North Carolina, 1403
    Whig convention officers, 425 (box)
Morehouse, Albert P.
    governor, Missouri, 1399

Morgan, Edwin D.
    governor, New York, 1402
    Republican National Committee chair,
        417 (table), 426 (table)
    senator, New York, 1255
Morgan, Ephraim F.
    governor, West Virginia, 1412
Morgan, J. Pierpont, 253, 487
Morgan, John T.
    senator, Alabama, 1236
Morgan, Robert B.
    senator, North Carolina, 175, 1256
Morgan, William, 52–53
Morin, Richard, 219
Morley, Clarence J.
    governor, Colorado, 1386
Morocco, 482
Morrill, Anson P.
    governor, Maine, 1394
Morrill, David L.
    governor, New Hampshire, 1400
    senator, New Hampshire, 1252
Morrill, Edmund N.
    governor, Kansas, 1392
Morrill, Justin S.
    length of service in Congress, 795 (table)
    senator, Vermont, 1263
Morrill, Lot Myrick
    governor, Maine, 1394
    senator, Maine, 1246, 1247
Morris, Dwight, 99
Morris, Gouverneur
    senator, New York, 1255
Morris, Luzon B.
    governor, Connecticut, 1387
Morris, Robert
    American Independent Party contender,
        (1976) 52
Morris, Robert
    senator, Pennsylvania, 1259
Morris, Thomas
    senator, Ohio, 1257
    vice-presidential candidate
        Liberty Party nominee, (1844) 429,
            446
Morrison, Cameron
    governor, North Carolina, 1403
    senator, North Carolina, 1256
Morrison, Frank B.
    governor, Nebraska, 155, 162, 1400
Morrison, John T.
    governor, Idaho, 1390
Morrison, William R.
    Democratic convention ballots, (1880)
        589, (1892) 593
Morrow, Dwight W.
    senator, New Jersey, 1254
Morrow, Edwin P.
    governor, Kentucky, 1393
Morrow, Jeremiah
    governor, Ohio, 1404
    senator, Ohio, 1257
Morsa, Charles J.
    vice-presidential candidate
        American Independent Party nomi-
            nee, (1988) 52, 438
Morse, Samuel F. B., 801
Morse, Wayne L.
    presidential primary votes, (1952)
        341–343, (1960) 346–347
    senator, Oregon, 145, 149, 1258
Mortdell, Frank W.
    Republican convention officers, 417
        (table)
Morton, Jackson
    senator, Florida, 1240
Morton, Levi P.
    biography, 780
    governor, New York, 1403
    Republican convention ballots, (1896)
        594
    vice-presidential candidate
        electoral vote, (1888) 773
        Republican contender, (1892) 474
        Republican nominee, (1888) 251,
            431, 473

Morton, Marcus
  governor, Massachusetts, 1396
Morton, Oliver H. P. T.
  governor, Indiana, 1391
  presidential contender
    Republican contender (1876), 465
    Republican convention ballots, (1876) 586
  Republican leadership, 247
  senator, Indiana, 1243
Morton, Rogers C. B.
  Republican National Committee chair, 426 (table)
Morton, Thruston B.
  Republican convention officers, 417 (table)
  Republican National Committee chair, 417 (table), 426 (table)
  senator, Kentucky, 149, 159, 1245
Mosbacher, Robert A., 820
Mosby, Timothy L.
  presidential primary votes, (2000) 404–410
Moseley-Braun, Carol
  senator, Illinois, 1242
  black women in Congress, 18, 60, 196, 202, 789, 790, 795
Moseley, William D.
  governor, Florida, 1388
Moses, Franklin J. Jr.
  governor, South Carolina, 1408
Moses, George H.
  Republican convention officers, 417 (table)
  senator, New Hampshire, 1253
Moses, John
  governor, North Dakota, 1404
  senator, North Dakota, 1256
Moss, Frank E.
  senator, Utah, 179, 1263
Motor-voter registration, 35, 216, 220
Mott, Stewart, 115
Moultrie, William
  governor, South Carolina, 1407
Mount, James A.
  governor, Indiana, 1391
Mouton, Alexander
  governor, Louisiana, 1393
  senator, Louisiana, 1246
Moynihan, Daniel Patrick
  senator, New York, 179, 206, 1255
"Mugwump" faction (Republicans), 75, 250–251
Muhlenberg, John P. G.
  senator, Pennsylvania, 1259
Mulkey, Frederick W.
  senator, Oregon, 1258
Mullins, Nathaniel T.
  presidential primary votes, (2000) 404–410
Mundt, Karl E.
  senator, South Dakota, 172, 1261
Mundy, Edward
  governor, Michigan, 1396
Munn, Earle Howard
  presidential candidate
    popular vote, (1964) 694, (1968, 1972) 695
    Prohibition Party nominee, (1964) 435, (1968, 1972) 436
  vice-presidential candidate
    Prohibition Party nominee, (1960) 435
Munoz, Maria E.
  vice-presidential candidate
    New Alliance nominee, (1992) 68, 438
Munro, Donald L.
  vice-presidential candidate
    Socialist Labor nominee, (1908) 432
Murchie, Robert Charles
  presidential primary votes, (1920) 326
Murdock, Abe
  senator, Utah, 1263

Murdock, Vicki
  vice-presidential candidate
    Peace and Freedom Party nominee, (1988) 69, 438
Murkowski, Frank H.
  senator, Alaska, 1236
Murphree, A. A.
  Democratic convention ballots, (1924) 607
Murphree, Dennis
  governor, Mississippi, 1398
Murphy, Daniel J.
  presidential candidate
    American Vegetarian Party nominee, (1952) 434
Murphy, Edward Jr.
  senator, New York, 1255
Murphy, Francis P.
  governor, New Hampshire, 1401
Murphy, Frank
  governor, Michigan, 1397
  Supreme Court justice, 818–819
Murphy, Franklin
  governor, New Jersey, 1401
  vice-presidential contender, (1908) 484
Murphy, George
  senator, California, 162, 1237
Murphy, Isaac
  governor, Arkansas, 1385
Murphy, John
  governor, Alabama, 1384
Murphy, Maurice J. Jr.
  senator, New Hampshire, 1253
Murphy, Richard Louis
  senator, Iowa, 1244
Murrah, Pendleton
  governor, Texas, 1409
Murray, James E.
  Democratic convention ballots, (1952) 618
  senator, Montana, 1251
Murray, Johnston
  governor, Oklahoma, 1405
Murray, Patty
  senator, Washington, 1265
  Senate leadership, 789
Murray, William H.
  governor, Oklahoma, 1405
  presidential candidate
    Democratic convention ballots, (1932) 611
    primary votes, (1932) 331–332
Musgrove, Ronnie
  governor, Mississippi, 1380, 1398
Muskie, Edmund S.
  biography, 780
  governor, Maine, 146, 1394
  presidential candidate
    Democratic contender, (1972) 60, 171, 280
    Democratic convention ballots, (1972) 625, (1980) 630
    as former vice-presidential nominee, 224
    primary votes, (1972) 354–358
  senator, Maine, 179, 1246
    campaign finance, 111
    disputed electoral vote, (1968) 711
  vice-presidential candidate
    Democratic contender, (1976) 539
    Democratic nominee, (1968) 167, 279, 436, 531
    electoral vote, (1968) 773
Muskie, Jane, 280
Mutch, Robert, 108–109
Myers, Francis J.
  senator, Pennsylvania, 1259
Myers, Jacob H., 15, 36 (box), 218
Myers, Henry L.
  senator, Montana, 1251
Myrdal, Gunnar, 24, 26

N

Nader, Ralph
  presidential candidate
    Green Party nominee, (1996) 63, 297, 439, (2000) 63, 297, 301, 439, 570

political party development, 48, 50
  politics and issues, (2000) 205
  popular vote, (1996) 687, (2000) 688
  primary votes, (1992) 386–393, (1996) 402, 403
Nance, Albinus
  governor, Nebraska, 1399
Nash, Abner
  governor, North Carolina, 1403
Nash, George K.
  governor, Ohio, 1405
Nast, Thomas, 15, 75
Nathan, Theodora
  biography, 780
  vice-presidential candidate
    electoral vote, (1972) 773
    Libertarian nominee, (1972) 436
National Campaign Finance Reform Coalition, 123
National Caucus of Labor Committees, 80
National Committee for an Effective Congress, 113
National committees. See also Democratic National Committee; Republican National Committee
  chair selection, 213
  functions, 411, 412
    nomination vacancies, 425
  origins, 229
National Conservative Political Action Committee, 96, 183
National conventions. See Conventions, national
National Democratic Party (1844)
  nominees, 429
National Democratic Party (1896)
  historical development
    profile, 66–67
    timeline, 47
  nominees, 431
National Democratic Party of Alabama, 531
National Economic Recovery Party
  nominees, (1988) 80, 438
National Farmers Union, 522
National Federation of Democratic Women, 418 (box)
National Greenback Party
  nominees, (1936) 434
National Independent Party. See Greenback Party
National Intelligencer, 442
National Liberty Party
  nominees, (1848) 430
National Party
  nominees, (1896) 431, (1900) 432
National Party
  nominees, (1932) 433
National Policy Forum, 84
National Publicity Law Organization, 109
National Republican Congressional Committee, 97, 100, 106
National Republican Party
  convention, (1831) 14, 442
  historical development
    profile, 67
    timeline, 47
  nominees, (1832) 429
  officers, 425 (box)
  remnants as Whigs (1836), 444
National Republican Senatorial Committee, 97
National Rifle Association, 299
National security. See Defense policy
National Silver Party
  nominees, (1896) 431
National States' Rights Party
  nominees, (1960, 1964) 435
National Statesman Party, 72
National Union for Social Justice, 79, 505
National Union Republican Party, 461
National Unity Party
  historical development, 48
    profile, 67–68
    timeline, 47
  nominees, (1980) 437, 546–547
National Voter Registration Act of 1993, 216, 220

National Welfare Rights Organization, 535
National Women's Political Caucus, 422, 534
National Workingmen's Party
  nominees, (1872) 430
Nations, Gilbert Owen
  presidential candidate
    American Party nominee, (1924) 433
    popular vote, (1924) 692
Native Americans
  members of Congress, 795
  platform issue
    Green Party, (2000) 571
    Republicans, (1972) 536
Nativism. See American Party (Know Nothings)
Natural Law Party
  historical development
    profile, 68
    timeline, 47
  nominees, (1992–2000) 438–439
  presidential primaries (1996) 402
Natural Peoples Party
  nominees, (1980) 437
Naudain, Arnold
  senator, Delaware, 1239
Nebraska
  electoral college variation, 701
Neely, Matthew M.
  governor, West Virginia, 1412
  senator, West Virginia, 1265
Neff, Pat M.
  governor, Texas, 1410
Nelson, Arthur E.
  senator, Minnesota, 1249
Nelson, Bill
  senator, Florida, 1240
Nelson, Candice, 98, 102
Nelson, Earl "Ben"
  governor, Nebraska, 1400
  senator, Nebraska, 1252
Nelson, Gaylord
  governor, Wisconsin, 152, 1413
  senator, Wisconsin, 284, 1266
Nelson, George A.
  vice-presidential candidate
    Socialist nominee, (1936) 433
Nelson, Knute
  governor, Minnesota, 1397
  senator, Minnesota, 1249
Nelson, Thomas Jr.
  governor, Virginia, 1411
Nesmith, James W.
  senator, Oregon, 1258
Nestos, Ragnvald A.
  governor, North Dakota, 1404
  special election, 1381 (box)
Neuberger, Maurine B.
  senator, Oregon, 789, 1258
Neuberger, Richard L.
  senator, Oregon, 146, 1258
Neville, Keith
  governor, Nebraska, 1399
New, Harry S.
  Republican National Committee chair, 417 (table), 426 (table)
  senator, Indiana, 1243
New Alliance Party
  historical development
    profile, 68
    timeline, 47
  nominees, (1988, 1992) 438
  primary, (1988) 385
New American Movement, 79
New Deal
  acceptance by Republicans, 133, 137, 270
  origin of term, 262
  programs, 263–264, 267
  Republican platform issue, (1936) 504, (1944) 509
  Socialist Party history, 78
  under Truman, 269
New Deal coalition, 59, 263–265, 270, 283
New Hampshire
  gubernatorial elections, 1381
  presidential primary calendar, 210, 305, 306 (box), 308–309, 315, 417

New Jersey
    House redistricting, 824
New Left, 79
New Mexico
    in Compromise of 1850, 239, 240
New York
    Democratic convention credentials dis-
        pute, (1848) 422
    presidential candidates' background, 222
    presidential primary calendar, 306 (box),
        308
New York Civil Liberties Union, 117
New York Herald Tribune, 272
New York State Conservative Party, 55
New York Times
    on Bryan-Kern ticket, (1908) 484
    Whig convention, (1852) 451
New York Tribune, 464
Newberry, Truman H.
    senator, Michigan, 1249
Newbold, Joshua G.
    governor, Iowa, 1391
Newell, William A.
    governor, New Jersey, 1401
Newlands, Francis G.
    senator, Nevada, 1252
News media. See also Political advertising
    presidential election campaign coverage,
        (1800) 228, (1960) 154, 275, (1988) 286,
        (1992) 291, (1996) 295, (2000) 297
        conventions, 426–427
        fund-raising, (1996) 94
        outcome projections, (2000) 219,
            296, 299–300
        televised debates, 17, 213, 216
Ney, Bob
    campaign finance reform, 124 (box)
Nicaragua, 185
Nice, Harry W.
    governor, Maryland, 1395
Nicholas, Robert C.
    senator, Louisiana, 1246
Nicholas, Wilson Carey
    governor, Virginia, 1411
    senator, Virginia, 1264
Nicholls, Francis T.
    governor, Louisiana, 1393
Nichols, Roy F., 227
Nicholson, Alfred O. P.
    senator, Tennessee, 1261, 1262
Nicholson, Jim
    Republican National Committee chair,
        417 (table), 426 (table)
Nicholson, Samuel D.
    senator, Colorado, 1238
Nicholson, Samuel T.
    vice-presidential candidate
        United Reform Party, (1900) 432
Nickles, Don
    senator, Oklahoma, 188, 1258
Nigh, George P.
    governor, Oklahoma, 1405
Niles, John M.
    senator, Connecticut, 1238, 1239
Nineteenth Amendment, 16, 21, 32–33,
    220
    effect, 259
Nix, Robert N. C., 791
Nixon, D. L., 25
Nixon, George S.
    senator, Nevada, 1252
Nixon, Pat, 150
Nixon, Richard M.
    biography, 780
    election evolution, 8, 9, 17, 18
    gubernatorial defeat, (1962) 158, 159
    as president
        campaign finance reform, 89, 113
        electoral college reform, 713
        minimum voting age, 33
        politics and issues, 163, 169–174
        resignation, 114, 115, 134, 163, 174,
            281, 715
        turnover in Congress, 793
        vice president choice, 714
        Watergate scandal, 173–174

presidential candidate
    appeal in South, (1972) 129
    campaign finance, (1972) 114–115
    electoral college issues, 703 (box),
        706 (box), 710, 711–712
    electoral vote, (1960) 761, (1968)
        763, (1972) 764
    former members of Congress, 155
        (box), 223
    as former vice president, 223, 314
        (box)
    as "minority" president, 223 (table)
    New York background, 222
    politics and issues, (1960) 154–155,
        (1968) 167–168, (1972) 171–172
    popular vote, (1960) 678, (1968) 680,
        (1972) 681
    primary votes, (1956) 344–345,
        (1960) 346–347, (1964) 348–350,
        (1968) 310 (box), 351–353,
        (1972) 354–358
    public offices, 215
    reelection chances, (1972) 313 (box)
    Republican contender, (1964) 161,
        276
    Republican convention ballots,
        (1960) 620, (1968) 622, (1972) 626
    Republican nominee, (1960) 76,
        275–276, 435, 523, (1968) 76,
        279–280, 436, 529, (1972) 76–77,
        280–281, 436, 536
    televised debates, (1960) 213, 216
    senator, California, 1238
        campaign, (1950) 143
    as vice president, 146, 150–152
    vice-presidential candidate
        "Checkers" speech, 17, 144, 272
        electoral vote, (1952, 1956) 773
        Republican nominee, (1952) 144,
            272, 434, 516, (1956) 148–149, 273,
            435, 520
Noble, James
    senator, Indiana, 1243
Noble, Noah
    governor, Indiana, 1391
Noble, Patrick
    governor, South Carolina, 1408
Noe, James A.
    governor, Louisiana, 1393
Noel, Philip W.
    governor, Rhode Island, 1407
Nolan, Mae Ella, 789
Nominating conventions. See Conventions, na-
    tional
"Noncoalition Democrats," 247
Norbeck, Peter
    governor, South Dakota, 1408
    senator, South Dakota, 1261
        successor, 788
Norblad, A. W.
    governor, Oregon, 1405
Norris, Edwin L.
    governor, Montana, 1399
Norris, George W.
    presidential candidate
        primary votes, (1928) 329–330,
            (1932) 331–332
        Republican convention ballots,
            (1928) 609
    senator, Nebraska, 1252
Norris, Moses Jr.
    senator, New Hampshire, 1253
North, Oliver, 80
North, William
    senator, New York, 1255
North American Party
    nominees, (1856) 430
North Carolina
    House redistricting, 825
Northern, William J.
    governor, Georgia, 1389
Norton, Chris
    presidential primary votes, (1992) 394
Norton, Daniel S.
    senator, Minnesota, 1249
Norton, Eleanor Holmes, 791

Norvell, John
    senator, Michigan, 1249
Norwood, Thomas M.
    senator, Georgia, 1241
Notte, John A. Jr.
    governor, Rhode Island, 1407
Nourse, Amos
    senator, Maine, 1246
Noyes, Edward F.
    governor, Ohio, 1404
Nuckols, William L.
    presidential primary votes, (1980)
        365–371
Nuclear weapons. See also Arms control
    politics and issues, 152, 153
    presidential campaign issue, (1964) 277
Nugent, John F.
    senator, Idaho, 1242
Nullification crisis, 234, 235
Nunn, Louie B.
    governor, Kentucky, 1393
    Senate race, 172
Nunn, Sam
    senator, Georgia, 172, 1241
Nutter, Donald G.
    governor, Montana, 1399
Nye, Gerald P.
    senator, North Dakota, 1256
Nye, James W.
    senator, Nevada, 1252

O

Oates, William C.
    governor, Alabama, 1384
O'Bannon, Frank L.
    governor, Indiana, 1391
O'Brien, Lawrence F.
    at Democratic convention, (1972) 534
    Democratic National Committee chair,
        415 (table), 426 (table)
O'Brien, Thomas
    vice-presidential candidate
        Union Party nominee, (1936) 79, 433,
            505
Obscenity
    Republican platform issue, (1964) 527
O'Callaghan, Mike
    governor, Nevada, 1400
O'Connor, Charles, 582
O'Connor, John O., 285
O'Connor, Sandra Day, 30, 300, 825
O'Conor, Charles
    presidential candidate
        popular vote, (1872) 656
        Straight-Out Democrat nominee,
            (1872) 247, 430
O'Conor, Herbert R.
    governor, Maryland, 1395
    senator, Maryland, 1247
O'Daniel, W. Lee
    governor, Texas, 1410
    senator, Texas, 1262
Oddie, Tasker L.
    governor, Nevada, 1400
    senator, Nevada, 1252
Odell, Benjamin B. Jr.
    governor, New York, 1403
O'Doherty, Kieran, 55
O'Donnell, Edward T. Jr.
    presidential primary votes, (1988) 385,
        (1992) 394, (2000) 404–410
O'Ferrall, Charles T.
    governor, Virginia, 1411
Official English, 562, 567, 571
Ogden, Aaron
    governor, New Jersey, 1401
    senator, New Jersey, 1253
Ogilvie, Richard B.
    governor, Illinois, 1391
Ogle, Benjamin
    governor, Maryland, 1395
Oglesby, Richard J.
    governor, Illinois, 1390
    senator, Illinois, 1242

O'Gorman, James A.
    Democratic convention ballots, (1912)
        601
    senator, New York, 1255
O'Hara, James G.
    Democratic convention rules reform, 533
    disputed electoral vote, (1968) 711–712
"Ohio Idea," 246
Ohmen, Douglass J.
    presidential primary votes, (1996) 402
Oldcott, Ben W.
    governor, Oregon, 1405
Olcott, Simeon
    senator, New Hampshire, 1252
Olden, Charles S.
    governor, New Jersey, 1401
Oldham, William K.
    governor, Arkansas, 1385
Oleszek, Walter J., 103
Oliver, George T.
    senator, Pennsylvania, 1258
Olivier, Art
    vice-presidential candidate
        Libertarian nominee, (2000) 66, 439
Olmsted, Frederick Law
    vice-presidential candidate
        Independent Liberal Republican
            nominee, (1872) 430
Olney, Richard
    Democratic convention ballots, (1904)
        597
Olson, Allen I.
    governor, North Dakota, 1404
Olson, Culbert L.
    governor, California, 1386
Olson, Floyd B.
    governor, Minnesota, 1397
Olson, Ole H.
    governor, North Dakota, 1404
Olson, Ted, 300
O'Mahoney, Joseph C.
    senator, Wyoming, 1266
O'Neal, ——
    Alabama Senate candidate, 130
O'Neal, Edward A.
    governor, Alabama, 1384
O'Neal, Emmet
    governor, Alabama, 1384
O'Neill, C. William
    governor, Ohio, 149, 1405
O'Neill, Thomas P.
    Democratic convention officers, 415
        (table)
    House leadership, 179, 184, 185, 189
O'Neill, William A.
    governor, Connecticut, 193, 1387
Open primaries, 306 (box), 415
Optical scan voting systems, 218
Orange, Aaron M.
    vice-presidential candidate
        Socialist Labor nominee, (1940) 434
Oregon
    annexation issue, (1844) 238, 447
    electoral vote contest, (1876) 248
    popular election of senators, 1231
    presidential primary law, 310
    voting by mail, 19, 38, 218
Orman, James B.
    governor, Colorado, 1386
Ormsbee, Ebenezer J.
    governor, Vermont, 1411
Ormsby, George D.
    vice-presidential candidate
        Prohibition Party nominee, (1988,
            1992) 438
Orr, James L.
    governor, South Carolina, 1408
Orr, Kay A.
    governor, Nebraska, 189, 1400
Orr, Robert D.
    governor, Indiana, 1391
Ortega, Katherine
    Republican convention speakers, 417
        (table)
Osborn, Chase S.
    governor, Michigan, 1397

Osborn, Sidney P.
    governor, Arizona, 1385
Osborn, Thomas A.
    governor, Kansas, 1392
Osborn, Thomas W.
    senator, Florida, 1240
Osborne, John E.
    governor, Wyoming, 1413
Oswald, Lee Harvey, 17, 159, 276
Otis, Harrison Gray
    senator, Massachusetts, 1248
Ottinger, Richard L., 112, 170
Overman, Lee S.
    senator, North Carolina, 1256
Overseas absentee voting, 37
Overseas Citizens Voting rights Act of 1976,
    37–38
Overton, John H.
    senator, Louisiana, 1246
Owen, Jim, 92
Owen, John
    governor, North Carolina, 1403
Owen, Robert L.
    Democratic convention ballots, (1920)
        605, (1924) 607
    senator, Oklahoma, 1257
Owens, Bill
    governor, Colorado, 1386
Owens, Wayne, 175
Owens, William C.
    Democratic convention officers, 415
        (table)
Owsley, William
    governor, Kentucky, 1392
Oyler, Tom
    presidential primary votes, (2000)
        404–410

P

Paca, William
    governor, Maryland, 1395
Pacheco, Romualdo
    governor, California, 1386
    Hispanics in Congress, 15,
        792–793
Packer, Asa
    Democratic convention ballots, (1868)
        584
Packer, William F.
    governor, Pennsylvania, 1406
Packwood, Bob
    senator, Oregon, 1258
        campaign finance reform, 122
Padden, Mike, 703, 774
Paddock, Algernon S.
    senator, Nebraska, 1252
Padelford, Seth
    governor, Rhode Island, 1407
Page, Carroll S.
    governor, Vermont, 1411
    senator, Vermont, 1263
Page, John
    governor, New Hampshire, 1400
    senator, New Hampshire, 1253
Page, John
    governor, Virginia, 1411
Page, John B.
    governor, Vermont, 1410
Paine, Charles
    governor, Vermont, 1410
Paine, Elijah
    senator, Vermont, 1263
Palmer, A. Mitchell
    presidential candidate
        Democratic contender, (1920) 259,
            494
        Democratic convention ballots,
            (1920) 605
        primary votes, (1920)
            324–326
Palmer, Henry L.
    Democratic convention officers, 415
        (table)
Palmer, John McAuley
    biography, 780
    governor, Illinois, 1390

presidential candidate
    National Democratic Party, (1896)
        67, 431
    popular vote, (1896) 662
    senator, Illinois, 1242
    vice-presidential electoral vote, (1872)
        772
Palmer, Thomas W.
    senator, Michigan, 1249
Palmer, William A.
    governor, Vermont, 1410
    senator, Vermont, 1263
Panama Canal. See also Central American
    Canal
    Carter policies, 180
    platform issue
        Democrats, (1976) 540
        Republicans, (1900) 479, (1976) 542
    presidential campaign issue, (1976) 282
Pardee, George C.
    governor, California, 1386
Park, Guy B.
    governor, Missouri, 1399
Parker, Alton B.
    biography, 780
    at Democratic convention, (1912) 487
        officers, 415 (table)
    presidential candidate
        Democratic convention ballots,
            (1904) 597, (1912) 601
        Democratic nominee, (1904) 255,
            432, 482
        electoral vote, (1904) 747
        popular vote, (1904) 664
Parker, Floyd C.
    vice-presidential candidate
        Populist Party nominee, (1988) 438
Parker, Joel
    Democratic convention ballots, (1868)
        584, (1876) 587, (1880) 589
    governor, New Jersey, 1401
    vice-presidential candidate
        Labor Reform Party nominee, (1872)
            430
Parker, John M.
    governor, Louisiana, 1393
    vice-presidential candidate
        Progressive nominee, (1916) 432, 490
Parker, Mike, 1380
Parker, Nahum
    senator, New Hampshire, 1253
Parker, Richard E.
    senator, Virginia, 1264
Parkhurst, Frederic H.
    governor, Maine, 1394
Parkinson, Paula, 554
Parks, Preston, 703 (box)
Parks, Rosa, 553
Parnell, Harvey
    governor, Arkansas, 1385
Parris, Albion K.
    governor, Maine, 1394
    senator, Maine, 1246
Parrott, John F.
    senator, New Hampshire, 1253
Parsons, Andrew
    governor, Michigan, 1397
Parsons, Lewis E.
    governor, Alabama, 1384
Partridge, Frank C.
    senator, Vermont, 1263
Pasco, Samuel
    senator, Florida, 1240
Pastore, John O.
    Democratic convention officers, speakers,
        415 (table)
    governor, Rhode Island, 1407
    senator, Rhode Island, 1259
        presidential succession proposal, 715
Pataki, George E.
    governor, New York, 1403
        Conservative Party support, 65
Paterson, William
    governor, New Jersey, 1401
Patman, Wright
    length of service in Congress, 795 (table)

Patrick, William Penn
    vice-presidential candidate
        Patriotic Party nominee, (1968) 436
Patriotic Party
    nominees, (1968) 436
Patronage. See Federal employees
Patrons of Husbandry, 69
Patterson, David T.
    senator, Tennessee, 1261
Patterson, Ellis E.
    presidential primary votes, (1940) 336
Patterson, Isaac L.
    governor, Oregon, 1405
Patterson, James E.
    senator, New Hampshire, 1253
Patterson, John J.
    senator, South Carolina, 1260
Patterson, John M.
    governor, Alabama, 1384
Patterson, Malcolm R.
    governor, Tennessee, 1409
Patterson, Okey L.
    governor, West Virginia, 1412
Patterson, Paul L.
    governor, Oregon, 1406
Patterson, Roscoe C.
    senator, Missouri, 1251
Patterson, Thomas M.
    senator, Colorado, 1238
Patterson, William
    senator, New Jersey, 1254
Pattison, John M.
    governor, Ohio, 1405
Pattison, Robert E.
    governor, Pennsylvania, 1406
    presidential candidate
        Democratic contender, (1896) 478
        Democratic convention ballots,
            (1892) 593, (1896) 595, (1904) 597
Patton, George, 261
Patton, John Jr.
    senator, Michigan, 1249
Patton, John Mercer
    governor, Virginia, 1411
Patton, Paul E.
    governor, Kentucky, 1393
Patton, Robert M.
    governor, Alabama, 1384
Patty, Hubert D.
    presidential primary votes, (1992) 393,
        (1996) 403
Paul, Ronald E.
    presidential candidate
        Libertarian nominee, (1988) 66, 438
        popular vote, (1988) 685
Paulen, Ben S.
    governor, Kansas, 1392
Pauling, David
    presidential primary votes, (1996) 403
Paulsen, Pat
    presidential primary votes, (1972) 358,
        (1992) 386–393, (1996) 395–402
Pawley, William D.
    presidential primary votes, (1992) 394
Paxon, Bill, 788
Payne, Frederick G.
    governor, Maine, 1394
    senator, Maine, 1246
Payne, Henry B.
    presidential contender, (1880) 469
    Democratic convention ballots,
        (1880) 589
    senator, Ohio, 1257
Payne, Henry C.
    Republican National Committee chair,
        417 (table), 426 (table)
Paynter, Samuel
    governor, Delaware, 1388
Paynter, Thomas H.
    senator, Kentucky, 1245
Peabody, Endicott
    governor, Massachusetts, 1396
Peabody, James H.
    governor, Colorado, 1386
Peace, Roger C.
    senator, South Carolina, 1260

Peace and Freedom Party
    historical profile, 68–69
    nominees, (1968) 436, (1980) 437,
        (1988–1996) 438–439
    primaries, (1988) 378–385, (1992) 393,
        (1996) 402
Pearce, James A.
    Democratic convention ballots, (1860)
        580
    senator, Maryland, 1247
Pearlman, Marian, 115
Pearson, James B.
    senator, Kansas, 1244
Pease, Elisha M.
    governor, Texas, 1409
Pease, Henry R.
    senator, Mississippi, 1250
Peay, Austin
    governor, Tennessee, 1409
Peck, Asahel
    governor, Vermont, 1410
Peck, George W.
    governor, Wisconsin, 1413
Peckham, Ann F., 541
Peery, George C.
    governor, Virginia, 1412
Peet, Richard C.
    presidential primary votes, (2000)
        404–410
Peffer, William A.
    senator, Kansas, 1244
Peirce, Neal R., 710
Pell, Claiborne
    senator, Rhode Island, 1260
Pelley, William Dudley
    presidential popular vote, (1936) 693
Pelosi, Nancy, 788, 790
Pelphrey, Gary, 100
Peña, Federico, 552
Pendleton Act, 108, 249
Pendleton, George H.
    biography, 780
    presidential candidate
        Democratic contender, (1868) 246,
            462
        Democratic convention ballots,
            (1868) 584
    senator, Ohio, 1257
    vice-presidential candidate
        Democratic nominee, (1864) 430,
            460
        electoral vote, (1864) 772
Pennewill, Simeon S.
    governor, Delaware, 1388
Pennington, William Jr.
    governor, New Jersey, 1401
Pennington, William S.
    governor, New Jersey, 1401
Pennoyer, Sylvester
    Democratic convention ballots, (1896)
        595
    governor, Oregon, 1405
Pennsylvania
    presidential primary law,
        310
Pennybacker, Isaac S.
    senator, Virginia, 1264
Pennypacker, Samuel W.
    governor, Pennsylvania, 1406
Penrose, Boies
    senator, Pennsylvania, 1259
People's Party (Equal Rights Party)
    nominees, (1872) 430
People's Party. See Populist Party
People's Party
    historical profile, 69
    nominees, (1972, 1976) 436
Pepper, Claude
    senator, Florida, 143, 1240
Pepper, George Wharton
    senator, Pennsylvania, 1259
Percy, Charles H.
    Republican platform, (1960) 523, (1980)
        543
    senator, Illinois, 162, 187, 1242
        election defeat, (1984) 96

Percy, Le Roy
  senator, Mississippi, 1250
Perdicaris, Ion, 482
Perham, Sidney
  governor, Maine, 1394
Perkins, Bishop W.
  senator, Kansas, 1244
Perkins, George C.
  governor, California, 1386
  senator, California, 1238
Perky, Kirtland I.
  senator, Idaho, 1242
Peron, Dennis
  presidential candidate
    Grassroots Party nominee, (1996)
      439
    popular vote, (1996) 699
Perot, Ross
  biography, 780
  presidential candidate
    campaign expenses, (1996) 94
    campaign funding, (1992, 1996) 90,
      92
    election evolution, 10, 18
    electoral college chronology, 706
      (box)
    independent campaign, (1992)
      72–73, 210, 289, 291–292, 424
      (box), 438, 556, 560
    Internet voting, 39
    political party development, 48, 50
    politics and issues, (1992) 196, 197,
      (1996) 200
    popular vote, (1992) 686, (1996) 687
    primary votes, (1992) 386–393
    Reform Party nominee, (1996) 73,
      212, 294–295, 439, 563
    televised debates, 216
    third-party challenges, 4, 5
Perpich, Rudy
  governor, Minnesota, 193, 1397
Perry, Benjamin F.
  governor, South Carolina, 1408
Perry, Edward A.
  governor, Florida, 1388
Perry, Madison S.
  governor, Florida, 1388
Perry, Rick
  governor, Texas, 1410
Pershing, John J.
  presidential primary votes, (1920)
    324–326
Persian Gulf War
  Bush approval rating, 289
  politics and issues, 195
  Republican convention, (1992)
    558, 559
Persons, Gordon
  governor, Alabama, 1384
Peters, Jeffrey B.
  presidential primary votes, (2000)
    404–410
Peters, John S.
  governor, Connecticut, 1387
Peterson, Hjalmar
  governor, Minnesota, 1397
Peterson, Russell W.
  governor, Delaware, 1388
Peterson, Val
  governor, Nebraska, 1399
Peterson, Walter
  governor, New Hampshire, 1401
Petit, John
  senator, Indiana, 1243
Pettigrew, Richard F.
  senator, South Dakota, 1261
Pettus, Edmund W.
  senator, Alabama, 1236
Pettus, John J.
  governor, Mississippi, 1398
Pharr, Joann W.
  presidential primary votes, (1996) 403
Phelan, James D.
  senator, California, 1238
Phelps, John S.
  governor, Missouri, 1399

Phelps, John Wolcott
  presidential candidate
    American Party nominee, (1880) 431
    popular vote, (1880) 690
Phelps, Samuel S.
  senator, Vermont, 1263
    contested appointment, 1232
Phelps, William Walter
  Republican convention ballots, (1888)
    592
  vice-presidential contender, (1888)
    473
Philipp, Emanuel L.
  governor, Wisconsin, 1413
  presidential primary votes, (1920) 326,
    (1924) 328
Phillips, Channing E.
  presidential candidate
    Democratic contender, (1968) 531
    Democratic convention ballots,
      (1968) 623
Phillips, Howard
  American Independent Party convention,
    (1976) 52
  presidential candidate
    Constitution Party, (2000) 439
    popular vote, (1992, 1996) 698,
      (2000) 699
    primary votes, (1992) 393, (1996)
      402
    Republican convention ballots, (1992)
      637
    U.S. Taxpayers Party nominee,
      (1992–2000) 80, 438–439
Phillips, John C.
  governor, Arizona, 1385
Phillips, Leon C.
  governor, Oklahoma, 1405
Phipps, Lawrence C.
  senator, Colorado, 1238
Pickens, Andrew
  governor, South Carolina, 1407
Pickens, Francis W.
  governor, South Carolina, 1408
Pickens, Israel
  governor, Alabama, 1384
  senator, Alabama, 1236
Pickering, John
  governor, New Hampshire, 1400
Pickering, Timothy
  senator, Massachusetts, 1248
Pickett, C. Leon
  presidential primary votes, (1980)
    365–371
Pickett, Leander L., 440
Pickle, J. J., 803
Pierce, Benjamin
  governor, New Hampshire, 1400
Pierce, Franklin
  biography, 780
  and Jefferson Davis, 244 (box)
  presidential candidate
    Democratic contender, (1856) 57,
      454–455
    Democratic convention ballots,
      (1852) 577, (1856) 579
    Democratic nominee, (1852) 239,
      240, 430, 450
    election milestones, 15
    electoral vote, (1852) 734
    former members of Congress, 155
      (box)
    military service, 221, 222
    popular vote, (1852) 651
    public offices, 214
  senator, New Hampshire, 1253
Pierce, Gilbert A.
  senator, North Dakota, 1256
Pierce, Walter M.
  governor, Oregon, 1405
Pierpoint, Francis H.
  governor, Virginia, 1411
Pike, Austin F.
  senator, New Hampshire, 1253
Piles, Samuel H.
  senator, Washington, 1265

Pillsbury, John S.
  governor, Minnesota, 1397
Pinchot, Gifford
  governor, Pennsylvania, 1406
Pindall, Xenophon O.
  governor, Arkansas, 1385
Pine, William B.
  senator, Oklahoma, 1257
Pinchback, Pinckney B. S.
  governor, Louisiana, 24, 1393
Pinchot, Gifford, 256
Pinckney, Charles
  governor, South Carolina, 1407
  senator, South Carolina, 1260
Pinckney, Charles Cotesworth
  biography, 780
  presidential candidate
    electoral vote, (1796) 720, (1800)
      721, (1804) 722, (1808) 723
    Federalist nominee, (1800) 228, 707,
      (1804) 229, (1808) 230
Pinckney, Thomas
  biography, 780
  electoral vote, (1796) 720
  governor, South Carolina, 1407
  vice-presidential candidate
    Federalist nominee, (1796) 227
Pingree, Hazen S.
  governor, Michigan, 1397
Pingree, Samuel E.
  governor, Vermont, 1410
Pinkney, William
  senator, Maryland, 1247
Pioneer Party
  nominees, (1956) 435
Pippitt, Henry
  governor, Rhode Island, 1407
Pitcher, Nathaniel
  governor, New York, 1402
Pitkin, Frederick W.
  governor, Colorado, 1386
Pittman, Key
  senator, Nevada, 1252
Pittman, Vail M.
  governor, Nevada, 1400
Plaisted, Frederick W.
  governor, Maine, 1394
Plaisted, Harris M.
  governor, Maine, 1394
Plater, George
  governor, Maryland, 1395
Platforms. See also specific parties
  first platform, (Democratic, 1840)
    445
  major fights (box), 423
  precursors
    Clinton "address," (1812) 230
    Jefferson statements, (1800) 228
  purposes, 421–425
  third-party role, 424–425
Platt, Orville H.
  senator, Connecticut, 1239
Platt, Thomas C.
  role in Roosevelt nomination, (1900) 254,
    479
  senator, New York, 1255
Pleasant, Ruffin G.
  governor, Louisiana, 1393
Pleasants, James
  governor, Virginia, 1411
  senator, Virginia, 1264
Pledge of Allegiance
  Republican campaign issue, (1988) 288,
    554–555
Plumb, Preston
  senator, Kansas, 1244
Plumer, William
  governor, New Hampshire, 1400
  senator, New Hampshire, 1253
Poindexter, George
  governor, Mississippi, 1398
  senator, Mississippi, 1250
Poindexter, Miles
  Republican convention ballots, (1920)
    604
  senator, Washington, 1265

Poland, Luke P.
  senator, Vermont, 1263
Poletti, Charles
  governor, New York, 1403
Poling, ——
  presidential primary votes, (1928) 330
Political action committees
  congressional elections, 96–97
  development, 103–104
  definition, 85 (box)
  incumbents advantage, 103
  independent expenditures, 96
  leadership PACs, 97
  presidential campaign finance, 93, 120
  reform proposals, 107, 122, 123–125
Political advertising
  congressional campaigns, 98, 99, 112, 116
  expense limits, 113
  issue advocacy ads, 85 (box), 105–106,
    107, 125
  presidential campaigns, 94, 115
  rate reform, 122
Political parties. See also Third-party movements; names of specific parties
  abbreviations, 1596–1600
  affiliation
    independents, 23
    partisan identification, 1952–2000
      (graphs), 37
    voter registration, 34
  campaign finance, 83–84
    congressional election aid, 97–98
    coordinated expenses, 106–107
    independent expenditures, 106
    issue advocacy ads, 106
    presidential elections, 92
    soft money, 104–105
  "dealignment" theory, 286
  "educational" style, 250
  electoral college evolution, 703, 704
  governorships, 1377
    Democratic, Republican totals,
      1950–2000 (table) 1378
  historical development, 43–48
    Constitution Framers' views, 43, 225,
      236
    Jackson era, 235, 236
    origins in Washington, Adams ad-
      ministrations, 43, 226, 227–228
    profiles, 51–82
    Progressive era, 252–253
    timeline, 1789–2000 (figure) 47
  House control, 804–805
  House redistricting, 819 (box)
  internal politics, 48
  organization, rules (box) 418
  partisanship in 1990s, 134–136, 196–206
  party systems, 48
  presidential race victors, 1860–2000,
    1554–1555
Polk, Charles
  governor, Delaware, 1388
Polk, James G., 803
Polk, James K.
  biography, 780
  governor, Tennessee, 1409
  presidential candidate
    Democratic convention ballots,
      (1844) 574
    Democratic nominee, (1844) 238,
      421 (box), 429, 447
    election milestones, 15
    electoral vote, (1844) 732
    as former governor, 176 (box)
    former members of Congress, 155
      (box)
    as "minority" president, 223 (table)
    popular vote, (1844) 649
    public offices, 214
  vice-presidential candidate
    Democratic contender, (1840) 429
    electoral vote, (1840) 772
Polk, Leonidas L., 476
Polk, Trusten
  governor, Missouri, 1398
  senator, Missouri, 1251

Poll taxes, 17, 25, 132, 220
Pollard, John G.
    governor, Virginia, 1411
Pollock, James
    governor, Pennsylvania, 1406
Pollock, William P.
    senator, South Carolina, 1260
Polsby, Nelson W., 420 (box)
Polygamy
    Republican platform issue, (1888) 473
Pomerene, Atlee
    Democratic convention ballots, (1928)
        609
    presidential primary votes, (1928)
        329–330
    senator, Ohio, 1257
Pomeroy, Samuel C.
    presidential candidate
        American Prohibition Party nomi-
            nee, (1884) 431
    senator, Kansas, 1244
    vice-presidential candidate
        American Party nominee, (1880) 431
Pomeroy, Theodore M.
    Republican convention officers, 417
        (table)
Pond, Charles H.
    governor, Connecticut, 1387
Ponder, James
    governor, Delaware, 1388
Pool, John
    senator, North Carolina, 1256
Poor Man's Party
    nominees, (1952) 435
Pope, James P.
    senator, Idaho, 1242
Pope, John
    senator, Kentucky, 1245
"Popular sovereignty," 240, 241
Population of the United States, 1789–2000,
    1548–1549
Populist Party (People's Party)
    convention, (1892) 475–476
    historical development, 46, 49
        profile, 69
        timeline, 47
    issues
        monetary policies, 253
        platform, (1892) 476
        poll taxes, 25
    nominees, (1892–1908) 431–432
    officers, 425 (box)
    vote percentage, 424 (box)
Populist Party
    nominees, (1984) 437, (1988, 1992) 438
Porster, Barry
    vice-presidential candidate
        Workers League nominee, (1988) 438
Porter, Albert G.
    governor, Indiana, 1391
Porter, Albert S.
    presidential primary votes, (1964)
        348–350
Porter, Alexander
    senator, Louisiana, 1246
Porter, Augustus S.
    senator, Michigan, 1249
Porter, David R.
    governor, Pennsylvania, 1406
Porter, James D. Jr.
    governor, Tennessee, 1409
Posey, Thomas
    senator, Louisiana, 1246
Pothier, Aram J.
    governor, Rhode Island, 1407
Potter, Charles E.
    senator, Michigan, 1249
Potter, Samuel J.
    senator, Rhode Island, 1259
Potter, Trevor, 97
Potts, Richard
    senator, Maryland, 1247
Powell, ——
    presidential primary votes,
        (1944) 338
Powell, Adam Clayton Jr., 18, 790, 791

Powell, Clifford R.
    governor, New Jersey, 1402
Powell, Colin L.
    presidential candidate
        military service, 223
        Republican contender, (1996)
            209
    at Republican convention, (1996) 561,
        (2000) 566
    speakers, 417 (table)
Powell, Lazarus W.
    governor, Kentucky, 1392
    senator, Kentucky, 1245
Powell, Lewis E. Jr., 824
Powell, Wesley
    governor, New Hampshire, 1401
Power, Thomas C.
    senator, Montana, 1251
Powers, Llewellyn
    governor, Maine, 1394
Powers, Ridgley C.
    governor, Mississippi, 1398
Poynter, William A.
    governor, Nebraska, 1399
Prall, Horace G.
    governor, New Jersey, 1402
Pratt, Daniel D.
    senator, Indiana, 1243
Pratt, Thomas G.
    governor, Maryland, 1395
    senator, Maryland, 1247
Preference primaries, 306 (box), 309–310
Preferential primaries, 130
Prentiss, Samuel
    senator, Vermont, 1263
Prescott, Benjamin F.
    governor, New Hampshire, 1401
Presidential Election Campaign Fund, 89, 118
    (box)
Presidential elections. See also Electoral
    college; Presidential primaries
    campaign contributions
        candidate's own money, 92–93
        individual contributions, 91
        party contributions, 92
        political action committees, 93
        public funding, 88–91, 113
        soft money, 104–105
    campaign expenditures, 93–94
    campaign finance regulation history,
        108–110
        scandal, 1996, 84–86
    campaign stages, 210–220
    candidate characteristics, 209–210,
        220–224
    constitutional basis, 21, 220, 225–226,
        228, 229, 707
    election by Congress, 707–710
        House rules (box), 708
    election chronology, 1789–2000, 225–301
    election results, Congress and the presi-
        dency, 1860–2000, 1569–1571
    evolution, 5–13
        milestones, 14–20
    incumbent reelection chances, 102–103,
        313 (box)
    minority presidents, 12 (box), 223 (table),
        296, 706–707
    nominating campaigns, 1976–2000,
        1552–1553
    nominating conventions, 1831–2000,
        441–571
        key ballots (tables), 571–641
    political party nominees, 1831–2000,
        429–440
    politics and issues, 1945–2000, 133–206
    popular vote by state, 1824–2000 (tables)
        major candidates, parties, 643–688
        minor candidates, parties, 689–700
    vice-presidential choice, 212–213
    victorious party, 1860–2000, 1554–1555
    voter turnout, 21–23
        total votes cast, 1930–2000 (table), 4
        turnout by state, 2000 (table), 217
    voting by congressional district, 2000
        (map), 1572–1573

Presidential primaries
    calendar, 210–212, 305–307
        Delaware plan, 420, 566
        "March Madness," 315–318
        timing, 1968–2000 (maps) 316–317
    caucus method (box), 310–311
    convention delegate selection, 414–415
        numbers of votes cast, 1912–2000
            (table), 307
    Democratic platform issue, (1984) 549,
        632
    evolution, 48, 305, 307–314
        milestones, 15
    importance, 10
    regional primaries, 314–318
    returns, 1912–2000 (tables), 319–410
    "Super Tuesday," 315–318
    types, procedures (box), 306
Presidential Succession Acts, 251, 714
President's Commission on Campaign Costs,
    112
President's Committee on Civil Rights, 269
Presidents, U.S. See also Presidential elections
    background experience, 220–224
        biographical directory of candidates,
            775–781
        former governors, 176 (box),
            222–223, 1377
        former members of Congress, (box)
            155, 223–224
        former vice presidents, 223–224,
            (box) 314
        geographical origin, 61, 221, 222
        military service, 221–222, 223
        public positions (box), 214–215
    disability, succession, 15, 714–715
    later members of Congress, 800
    list, 1789–2001, 211
    reelection chances (box), 313
    term of office, 220
        term limits, 17, 209
Pressler, Larry
    senator, South Dakota, 181, 201, 1261
Preston, James P.
    governor, Virginia, 1411
Preston, William C.
    senator, South Carolina, 1260
Preus, Jacob A. O.
    governor, Minnesota, 1397
Price, David E., 102
Price, James H.
    governor, Virginia, 1412
Price, Melvin
    length of service in Congress, 795 (table)
Price, Pat
    presidential primary votes, (2000)
        404–410
Price, Rodman M.
    governor, New Jersey, 1401
Price, Samuel
    senator, West Virginia, 1265
Price, Sterling
    governor, Missouri, 1398
Prince, Oliver H.
    senator, Georgia, 1241
Pritchard, Jeter C.
    Republican convention ballots, (1920)
        604
    senator, North Carolina, 1256
Privacy, of voter registration lists, 34–35
Proctor, Fletcher D.
    governor, Vermont, 1411
Proctor, Mortimer R.
    governor, Vermont, 1411
Proctor, Redfield Jr.
    governor, Vermont, 1411
Proctor, Redfield Sr.
    governor, Vermont, 1410
    senator, Vermont, 1263
Proehl, Frederick C.
    presidential candidate
        Greenback Party nominee, (1952,
            1956) 435
Progressive Citizens of America, 71, 269
Progressive Labor Party
    historical profile, 71

Progressive Party (Bull Moose)
    convention, platform, (1912) 488–489
    historical development, 46, 49
        origins, 256
        profile, 69–70
        timeline, 47
    nominees, (1912–1916) 432
    at Republican convention, (1916) 490
    vote percentages, 424 (box)
Progressive Party (La Follette)
    convention, platform, (1924) 497–498
    historical development, 46, 49–50
        profile, 70
        timeline, 47
    nominees, (1924) 433
Progressive Party (Wallace)
    convention, platform, (1948) 514–515
    historical development, 46, 49–50, 139
        profile, 71
        timeline, 47
    nominees, (1948, 1952) 434
    politics and issues, (1948) 140–141
Progressive Policy Institute
    Democrat platform, (1992) 556
Prohibition
    Democratic positions, 260, 261, 264
    platform issue
        Democrats, (1892) 475, (1928) 500,
            (1932) 503
        Prohibition Party, (1888) 472, (1892)
            475
        Republicans, (1892) 474, (1928) 499,
            (1932) 423 (box), 502
    political party development, 71–72
Prohibition Party
    convention, platform, (1888) 472, (1892)
        475
    historical development, 46, 49
        profile, 71–72
        timeline, 47
    nominees, (1872–1976, 1984–2000)
        430–439
    officers, 425 (box)
Property qualifications for voting, 21, 25, 799
Protestant members of Congress, 787
Prouty, George H.
    governor, Vermont, 1411
Prouty, Winston L.
    senator, Vermont, 1263
Proxmire, William
    Democratic convention ballots, (1980)
        630
    senator, Wisconsin, 151, 191, 1266
Pryor, David
    governor, Arkansas, 1385
    senator, Arkansas, 181, 1237
Pryor, Luke
    senator, Alabama, 1236
Public lands
    platform issue
        Democrats, (1844) 447
        Populists, (1892) 476, (1992) 560
Public opinion polls
    assumption errors, 272
    election winner projections, 219, 299
    sample selection, 266
Public works projects. See also Internal im-
    provements
    platform issue
        Democrats, (1928) 500, (1932) 503
        Socialists, (1908) 483
Publicity Act of 1910, 109
Pugh, George E.
    senator, Ohio, 1257
Pugh, James L.
    senator, Alabama, 1236
Pulley, Andrew
    presidential candidate
        popular vote, (1980) 696
        Socialist Workers nominee, (1980)
            437
    vice-presidential candidate
        Socialist Labor nominee, (1972) 436
Pullman family, 258
Pullman strike, (1894) 253
Punch-card voting systems, 218

Purcell, Joe
  governor, Arkansas, 1385
Purcell, William E.
  senator, North Dakota, 1256
Purtell, William A.
  senator, Connecticut, 1239
Pyle, Gladys
  senator, South Dakota, 788, 1261
Pyle, J. Howard
  governor, Arizona, 1385

Q

"Quadrilateral," 463
Quarles, Joseph V.
  senator, Wisconsin, 1265
Quay, Matthew S.
  Republican convention ballots, (1896)
    594
  Republican National Committee chair,
    426 (table)
  senator, Pennsylvania, 1258
    contested appointment, 1232
Quayle, Dan
  biography, 780
  presidential contender, (2000) 204, 296
  senator, Indiana, 1243
  vice-presidential candidate
    electoral vote, (1988, 1992) 773
    Indiana background, 222
    politics and issues, (1988) 190–191
    Republican nominee, (1988) 288,
      312, 437, 554, (1992) 292, 438,
      558–559
Quayle, Marilyn, 292
Quie, Albert H.
  governor, Minnesota, 1397
Quinby, Henry B.
  governor, New Hampshire, 1401
Quinn, Robert E.
  governor, Rhode Island, 1407
Quinn, William F.
  governor, Hawaii, 1390
Quitman, John A.
  governor, Mississippi, 1398
  vice-presidential contender, (1848) 448,
    (1856) 455

R

Rabun, William
  governor, Georgia, 1389
Race. See Minorities
Rachner, Mary Jane
  presidential primary votes, (1988)
    378–385, (1992) 393
Racicot, Marc F.
  governor, Montana, 1399
Radcliffe, George W.
  senator, Maryland, 1247
Radical Republican faction, 15, 74, 245–246,
  465
Radio. See News media
Railroad regulation
  platform issue
    Democrats, (1896) 479
    Greenback Party, (1880) 469
    Populists, (1892) 476
    Republicans, (1884) 471
Rainey, Joseph H., 790
Raisuli, 482
Ralston, Samuel M.
  governor, Indiana, 1391
  presidential candidate
    Democratic contender, (1924)
      497
    Democratic convention ballots,
      (1924) 606
  senator, Indiana, 1243
Rampton, Calvin L.
  governor, Utah, 1410
Ramsay, Alexander
  governor, Minnesota, 1397
  senator, Minnesota, 1249
Ramsdell, George A.
  governor, New Hampshire, 1401
Randall, Alexander W.
  governor, Wisconsin, 1413

Randall, Charles Hiram
  vice-presidential candidate
    American Party nominee, (1924) 433
Randall, Samuel J.
  presidential candidate
    Democratic contender, (1880) 469
    Democratic convention ballots,
      (1880) 589, (1884) 591
Randolph, Beverley
  governor, Virginia, 1411
Randolph, Edmund
  governor, Virginia, 1411
  political party development, 44
Randolph, Jennings
  Democratic convention ballots, (1976)
    627
  senator, West Virginia, 1265
Randolph, John
  senator, Virginia, 1264
Randolph, Peyton
  governor, Virginia, 1411
Randolph, Theodore F.
  governor, New Jersey, 1401
  senator, New Jersey, 1254
Randolph, Thomas Jefferson
  Democratic convention officers, 415
    (table)
Randolph, Thomas M.
  governor, Virginia, 1411
Rangel, Charles B., 564, 791
Rankin, Jeannette, 16, 787
Ransdell, Joseph E.
  senator, Louisiana, 1246
Ransom, Epaphroditus
  governor, Michigan, 1396
Ransom, Matt W.
  senator, North Carolina, 1256
Rantoul, Robert
  senator, Massachusetts, 1248
Rarick, John Richard
  presidential candidate
    American Independent Party
      contender, (1976) 52
    American Independent Party
      nominee, (1980) 52, 437
    popular vote, (1980) 696
Raskin, Marcus, 80
Raskob, John J.
  Democratic National Committee chair,
    415 (table), 426 (table)
Rather, Dan, 300
Ratner, Payne H.
  governor, Kansas, 1392
Rawlings, George C., 130
Rawlins, Joseph L.
  senator, Utah, 1263
Rawson, Charles A.
  senator, Iowa, 1243
Ray, Dixy Lee
  governor, Washington, 1412
Ray, James B.
  governor, Indiana, 1391
Ray, Robert D.
  governor, Iowa, 1392
Rayburn, Sam
  Democratic convention officers, 415
    (table)
  House leadership, 7, 146, 150, 151, 153,
    157
  length of service in Congress, 795 (table)
Raymond, Henry J.
  Republican National Committee chair,
    426 (table)
  at Whig convention, (1852) 451
Rayner, Isidor
  senator, Maryland, 1247
    successor, 1231
Read, George
  senator, Delaware, 1239
Read, Jacob
  senator, South Carolina, 1260
Read, Thomas
  governor, Delaware, 1387
Reagan, John H.
  senator, Texas, 1262
Reagan, Nancy, 287, 561

Reagan, Ronald
  biography, 780
  conservative philosophy, 134, 284
  governor, California, 166, 1386
  as president
    disability issue, 715
    politics and issues, 176, 183–190
    turnover in Congress, 794
  presidential candidate
    appeal in South, (1984) 129
    election evolution, 9, 10, 18
    electoral vote, (1976) 703 (box), 765,
      (1980) 766, (1984) 767
    as former governor, 176 (box), 224,
      1377
    party control in Congress, 1234
    political party development, 48
    politics and issues, (1980) 182–183,
      (1984) 186–187
    popular vote, (1980) 683, (1984) 684
    primary votes, (1968) 351–353,
      (1976) 359–364, (1980) 313,
      365–371, (1984) 372–377
    reelection chances, (1984) 313 (box)
    Republican contender, (1968) 529,
      (1976) 177, 178, 282, 540–541
    Republican convention ballots,
      (1968) 622, (1976) 628, (1980) 629,
      (1984) 631
    Republican nominee, (1980) 77,
      283–284, 437, 542–543, (1984) 77,
      437, 550–551
    vice-presidential choice, (1980) 182
  at Republican convention, (1988) 554,
    (1992) 558, 559
  officers, 417 (table)
  tribute at Republican convention, (1996)
    561
Reames, Alfred Evan
  senator, Oregon, 1258
Reams, Henry F., 46
Reapportionment. See Apportionment of the
  House of Representatives; Redistricting
Reaux, Don
  presidential primary votes, (1980)
    365–371
Reber, Richard F.
  presidential primary votes, (1992) 393
Rebozo, Bebe, 114
Recall, of governors, 1381 (box)
Reconstruction
  African American members of Congress,
    790
  African American voting rights, 24
  end after 1876 election, 12, 15, 248
  House reapportionment, 812
  platform issue
    Democrats, (1868) 462
    Liberal Republicans, (1872) 463
    Republicans, (1868) 461, (1872) 464
  Republican Party history, 74, 245–246
Reconstruction Finance Corporation, 261
Rector, Henry M.
  governor, Arkansas, 1385
Redistricting. See also Apportionment of the
  House of Representatives
  Congress's role, 826
  historical development, 815–818
  minority representation, 792,
    825–826
  partisan gerrymanders, 824–825
  Supreme Court decisions, 818–825
Redstone, Albert E.
  presidential candidate
    Industrial Reform Party nominee,
      (1888) 431
Reece, B. Carroll
  Republican convention ballots, (1948)
    615
  Republican National Committee chair,
    138, 417 (table), 426 (table)
Reed, Clyde M.
  governor, Kansas, 1392
  senator, Kansas, 1244
Reed, David A.
  senator, Pennsylvania, 1258

Reed, Evelyn
  presidential popular vote, (1972) 695
Reed, Harrison
  governor, Florida, 1388
Reed, Jack
  senator, Rhode Island, 201, 1260
Reed, James A.
  presidential candidate
    Democratic contender, (1932) 262
    Democratic convention ballots,
      (1928) 609, (1932) 611
    primary votes, (1928) 329–330
  senator, Missouri, 1251
Reed, John H.
  governor, Maine, 1394
Reed, John M., 581
Reed, Joseph
  governor, Pennsylvania, 1406
Reed, Philip
  senator, Maryland, 1247
Reed, Stanley F., 818–819
Reed, Thomas B.
  House leadership, 75
  presidential candidate
    Republican contender, (1892) 477
    Republican convention ballots,
      (1892) 593, (1896) 594
Reed, Thomas B.
  senator, Mississippi, 1250
Reeve, Christopher, 564
Referendum
  Progressive platform issue, (1924) 498
Reform Party
  convention, candidates, (1996) 563
  historical development, 48, 50
    profile, 72–73
    timeline, 47
  "national primary," 39
  nominees, (1996–2000) 439
  Perot campaign, (1992) 560, (1996)
    294–295
  vote percentages, 424 (box)
Regan, Frank S.
  vice-presidential candidate
    Prohibition Party nominee, (1932)
      433
Regional primaries, 308
Rehnquist, William, 19, 203, 300
Reid, Charlotte T., 788
Reid, David S.
  governor, North Carolina, 1403
  senator, North Carolina, 1256
Reid, Harry
  senator, Nevada, 188, 1252
Reid, Whitelaw
  biography, 780
  vice-presidential candidate
    electoral vote, (1892) 773
    Republican nominee, (1892) 252,
      431, 474
Reid, Willie Mae
  vice-presidential candidate
    Socialist Workers nominee, (1976)
      436, (1992) 438
Reimer, Arthur Elmer
  presidential candidate
    popular vote, (1912, 1916) 692
    Socialist Labor nominee, (1912) 432
Reiter, Julius J.
  vice-presidential candidate
    Farmer Labor nominee, (1932) 433
Religious affiliation of members of Congress,
  787
Religious freedom
  platform issues
    Democrats, (1996) 565
    Republicans, (1988) 555
Remmel, Valentine
  vice-presidential candidate
    Socialist Labor nominee, (1900) 432
Rendell, Ed
  Democratic National Committee chair,
    426 (table)
Rennebohm, Oscar
  governor, Wisconsin, 1413
Reno, Janet, 84–86

Republican National Committee
  campaign finance scandal, 1996, 84
  chairs, 1848–2001 (tables), 417, 426
  Delaware plan, 307, 566
  structure, 418 (box)
  superdelegates, 314
Republican Party
  conventions
    credentials disputes, 420, 421, 422
    historical narrative, (1856) 453,
      (1860) 457–458, (1864) 459, (1868)
      461, (1872) 464, (1876) 465, (1880)
      422, 467–468, (1884) 470, (1888)
      473, (1892) 474, (1896) 477, (1900)
      479, (1904) 481–482, (1908) 484,
      (1912) 422, 486, (1916) 490, (1920)
      493, (1924) 495, (1928) 498–499,
      (1932) 501, (1936) 504, (1940) 506,
      (1944) 508–509, (1948) 511, (1952)
      422, 445–516, (1956) 520, (1960)
      523, (1964) 525–526, (1968) 529,
      (1972) 536, (1976) 540–541, (1980)
      542–543, (1984) 550, (1988)
      554–555, (1992) 558–559, (1996)
      561–122, (2000) 566
    location, financing, 411–412
    number of delegates, 1932–2000 (fig-
      ure), 413
    officers, keynote speakers (table), 417
    rules (1924) 412, (1976) 413, (2000)
      413, 420 (box)
    summary (table), 416
    vice president selection rules, (1976)
      540
  election evolution, 5–14
  history, 45–48
    elephant symbol, 15, 75
    politics and issues, 1945–2000,
      133–206
    presidential election chronology,
      239–301
    profile, 73–78
    southern elections, 129
    timeline, 47
  national chairs, 1848–2001 (table), 426
  platforms, (1856) 453–454, (1860) 458,
    (1864) 459–460, (1868) 461, (1872)
    464, (1876) 465–466, (1880) 468,
    (1884) 470–471, (1888) 473, (1892)
    474, (1896) 477–478, (1900) 479–480,
    (1904) 482, (1908) 484, (1912) 486,
    (1916) 490–491, (1920) 493–494, (1924)
    495–496, (1928) 499, (1932) 502, (1936)
    504–505, (1940) 507, (1944) 509, (1948)
    511–512, (1952) 516, (1956) 520–521,
    (1960) 523–524, (1964) 526, (1968)
    529–530, (1972) 536–537, (1976)
    541–542, (1980) 543–544, (1984)
    550–551, (1988) 555–556, (1992)
    559–560, (1996) 561–563, (2000)
    566–568
  presidential primaries
    calendar, 305–307
    caucus system, 311 (box)
    returns, 1912–2000 (table), 319–410
    rules, 420, 420 (box)
    types, procedures, 306 (box)
    voter turnout, 309
    votes, delegates, 1912–2000 (table),
      307
  presidential, vice-presidential nominees,
    (1856–2000) 430–439
    electoral vote, 735–774
    popular vote, 652–688
  structure, rules, 418 (box)
  voter registration, 23
Republicans for Clean Air, 107
Republicans, Jeffersonian. See Democratic-
  Republican Party
Residency requirements
  for presidents, 209
  for voting, 21, 35–36, 38, 220
Restoration Party
  nominees, (1976) 437
Retirement and pensions. See also Social Security

Democratic platform issue, (1996) 565
Republican platform issue, (2000) 567
Revels, Hiram R.
  senator, Mississippi, 15, 24, 790, 1250
Revenue Act of 1971, 113, 282
Revercomb, Chapman
  senator, West Virginia, 1265
Reynolds, John
  governor, Illinois, 1390
Reynolds, John W.
  governor, Wisconsin, 1413
  presidential primary votes, (1964)
    348–350
Reynolds, Robert J.
  governor, Delaware, 1388
Reynolds, Robert R.
  senator, North Carolina, 1256
Reynolds, Sam W.
  senator, Nebraska, 1252
Reynolds, Thomas
  governor, Missouri, 1398
Reynolds, Verne L.
  presidential candidate
    popular vote, (1928, 1932) 692
    Socialist Labor nominee, (1928,
      1932) 433
  vice-presidential candidate
    Socialist Labor nominee, (1924) 433
Rhett, R. Barnwell
  senator, South Carolina, 1260
Rhode Island
  gubernatorial elections, 1381
Rhodes, James A.
  governor, Ohio, 8, 159, 175, 181, 1405
  presidential primary votes, (1964)
    348–350, (1968) 351–353
  Republican convention ballots, (1968)
    622
Rhodes, John J.
  at Republican convention, (1972) 536
  officers, 417 (table)
Ribicoff, Abraham A.
  at Democratic convention, (1968) 531
  governor, Connecticut, 147, 152, 1387
  senator, Connecticut, 159, 1239
Rice, Alexander H.
  governor, Massachusetts, 1396
Rice, Benjamin F.
  senator, Arkansas, 1237
Rice, Florence
  vice-presidential candidate
    Consumer Party nominee, (1988) 438
Rice, Henry M.
  senator, Minnesota, 1249
Rich, John T.
  governor, Michigan, 1397
Richard, Barry, 300
Richard, Gabriel, 787
Richards, Ann
  at Democratic convention, (1988) 552
  officers, speakers, 415 (table)
  governor, Texas, 199, 1410
Richards, Bob
  presidential candidate
    popular vote, (1984) 696
    Populist Party nominee,
      (1984) 437
Richards, DeForest
  governor, Wyoming, 1413
Richards, John G.
  governor, South Carolina, 1408
Richards, Richard
  Republican National Committee chair,
    426 (table)
Richards, William A.
  governor, Wyoming, 1413
Richardson, Bill, 793
Richardson, Darcy G.
  presidential primary votes, (1992) 393
Richardson, Elliot L.
  Republican presidential contender,
    (1976) 540
  convention ballots, (1976) 178, 628
  Watergate scandal, 281
Richardson, Friend William
  governor, California, 1386

Richardson, Harry A.
  senator, Delaware, 1240
Richardson, James B.
  governor, South Carolina, 1407
Richardson, James D.
  Democratic convention officers, 415
    (table)
Richardson, John P.
  governor, South Carolina, 1408
Richardson, William A.
  senator, Illinois, 1242
Rickards, John E.
  governor, Montana, 1399
Riddle, George Read
  senator, Delaware, 1239
Riddleberger, H. H.
  senator, Virginia, 1264
Ridge, Tom
  governor, Pennsylvania, 1406
Ridgeley, Henry M.
  senator, Delaware, 1239
Ridgely, Charles
  governor, Maryland, 1395
Riegle, Donald W. Jr.
  senator, Michigan, 179, 1249
    ethics investigation, 195
Riemers, Roland
  presidential primary votes, (1996)
    395–402
Rigazio, John D.
  presidential primary votes, (1992) 394
Right to Life Party
  nominees, (1980) 437, (1988) 438
Riley, Bob
  governor, Arkansas, 1385
Riley, Richard
  governor, South Carolina, 1408
Ripon Society, 412–413
Ritchie, Albert C.
  governor, Maryland, 1395
  presidential candidate
    Democratic contender, (1932) 262
    Democratic convention ballots,
      (1924) 606–607, (1932) 611
Ritner, Joseph
  governor, Pennsylvania, 1406
Ritter, ——
  presidential primary votes, (1952) 343
Ritter, Eli
  Prohibition Party convention officers, 425
    (box)
Rivers, Eurith D.
  governor, Georgia, 1389
Rives, William C.
  senator, Virginia, 1264
Roach, William N.
  senator, North Dakota, 1256
Roane, Archibald
  governor, Tennessee, 1409
Roane, John S.
  governor, Arkansas, 1385
Roane, William H.
  senator, Virginia, 1264
Robb, Charles S.
  governor, Virginia, 188, 191, 1412
  senator, Virginia, 199, 206, 1264
Robbins, Asher
  senator, Rhode Island, 1259
Roberts, Albert H.
  governor, Tennessee, 1409
Roberts, Barbara
  governor, Oregon, 1406
Roberts, C. Wesley
  Republican National Committee chair,
    426 (table)
Roberts, Dennis J.
  governor, Rhode Island, 1407
Roberts, Henry
  governor, Connecticut, 1387
Roberts, Jonathan
  senator, Pennsylvania, 1258
Roberts, Oran M.
  governor, Texas, 1410
Roberts, Owen J., 818
Roberts, Pat
  senator, Kansas, 200, 1244

Robertson, A. Willis
  senator, Virginia, 1264
Robertson, Charles I.
  vice-presidential candidate
    Christian National Party nominee,
      (1956) 435
Robertson, E. V.
  senator, Wyoming, 1266
Robertson, James B. A.
  governor, Oklahoma, 1405
Robertson, Marion G. "Pat"
  presidential candidate
    primary votes, (1988) 321, 378–385
    Republican contender, (1988) 190,
      286, 287, 554
  at Republican convention, (1992) 292
Robertson, Thomas B.
  governor, Louisiana, 1393
Robertson, Thomas J.
  senator, South Carolina, 1260
Robertson, Wyndham
  governor, Virginia, 1411
Robie, Frederick
  governor, Maine, 1394
Robins, Charles A.
  governor, Idaho, 1390
Robinson, Arthur R.
  senator, Indiana, 1243
Robinson, Charles
  governor, Kansas, 1392
Robinson, George D.
  governor, Massachusetts, 1396
Robinson, James F.
  governor, Kentucky, 1393
Robinson, John M.
  senator, Illinois, 1242
Robinson, John S.
  governor, Vermont, 1410
Robinson, Jonathan
  senator, Vermont, 1263
Robinson, Joseph T.
  biography, 780
  Democratic convention ballots, (1924)
    606–607
  Democratic convention officers, 415
    (table)
  governor, Arkansas, 1385
  senator, Arkansas, 1237
  successor, 131
  vice-presidential candidate
    Democratic nominee, (1928) 261,
      433, 499
    electoral vote, (1928) 773
Robinson, Lucius
  governor, New York, 1403
Robinson, Moses
  senator, Vermont, 1263
Robinson, Robert P.
  governor, Delaware, 1388
Robsion, John M.
  senator, Kentucky, 1245
Rockefeller, H. R. H. "Fiff"
  presidential primary votes, (1976) 364
Rockefeller, John D.
  governor, West Virginia, 1412
  presidential no-run decision, (1992) 289
  senator, West Virginia, 173, 1265
Rockefeller, Nelson A.
  biography, 780
  governor, New York, 8, 76, 152, 158, 159,
    1403
  presidential candidate
    no-run decision, (1960) 275
    politics and issues, (1964) 161, (1968)
      167–168
    primary votes, (1960) 346–347,
      (1964) 348–350, (1968) 351–353
    Republican contender, (1964) 276,
      525, (1968) 529
    Republican convention ballots,
      (1964) 621, (1968) 622
  at Republican convention, (1972) 536,
    (1976) 540
  Republican platform, (1960) 523, (1964)
    525
  as vice president, 312

appointment, 174, 281, 715
New York background, 222
Rockefeller, Winthrop
governor, Arkansas, 166, 1385
Republican convention ballots, (1968)
622
Rockefeller family
U.S. Labor Party history, 80
Rockwell, Julius
senator, Massachusetts, 1248
Roden, George
presidential primary votes, (1976) 364
Rodino, Peter W.
Democratic vice-presidential contender,
(1976) 539
Rodney, Caesar A.
governor, Delaware, 1387
senator, Delaware, 1239
Rodney, Caleb
governor, Delaware, 1388
Rodney, Daniel
biography, 780
governor, Delaware, 1388
senator, Delaware, 1239
vice-presidential electoral vote, (1820)
772
Roe, James A.
Democratic convention ballots, (1948)
616
Roemer, Charles
governor, Louisiana, 193, 1394
Rogan, James E., 100
Rogers, Clifford Joy
governor, Wyoming, 1413
Rogers, Daniel
governor, Delaware, 1387
Rogers, Edith Nourse, 788
Rogers, John R.
governor, Washington, 1412
Rogers, Tennie
presidential primary votes, (1992)
386–393, (1996) 403
Rogers, Will
on campaign costs, 100
Democratic convention ballots, (1932)
502, 611
on party organization, 418
Rogers, William R.
presidential candidate
Theocratic Party nominee, (1968)
436
vice-presidential candidate
Theocratic Party nominee, (1964)
436
Roland, Joanne
vice-presidential candidate
Third Party nominee, (1992) 438
Rollins, Edward H.
senator, New Hampshire, 1253
Rollins, Edward J., 560
Rollins, Frank W.
governor, New Hampshire, 1401
Rollinson, Ray
presidential primary votes, (1976) 364,
(1980) 365–371, (1992) 386–393
Rolph, James Jr.
governor, California, 1386
Rolvaag, Karl
governor, Minnesota, 159, 1397
Roman, Andre B.
governor, Louisiana, 1393
Romer, Henry A.
vice-presidential candidate
America First Party nominee, (1944)
434
Christian Nationalist Party nominee,
(1948) 434
Romer, Roy
Democratic National Committee chair,
426 (table)
governor, Colorado, 1386
Romney, George W.
governor, Michigan, 8, 159, 162, 1397
presidential candidate
primary votes, (1964) 348–350,
(1968) 351–353

Republican contender, (1964) 161,
(1968) 167
Republican convention ballots,
(1964) 621, (1968) 622
Republican platform, (1964) 525–526
vice-presidential contender, (1968) 529
Roosevelt, Eleanor
as Democratic leader, 269–270, 273
at convention, (1940) 507, (1956) 518
as first lady, 269
Roosevelt, Franklin D.
biography, 780
at Democratic convention, (1924) 496,
497, (1928) 499, (1932) 427
effect of death, 137
governor, New York, 1403
as president
Democratic Party history, 58–59
New Deal coalition, 263–265
Prohibition repeal, 72
Supreme Court expansion plan,
266–267
World War II, 267, 268
presidential candidate
Communist endorsement rejected,
(1944) 54
Democratic convention ballots,
(1932) 611, (1940) 612, (1944) 614
Democratic nominee, (1932)
262–263, 422, 433, 502–503,
(1936) 265–266, 433, 505, (1940)
267–268, 434, 507, (1944) 268,
434, 509–510
election evolution, 3, 6–7, 16–17
electoral vote, (1932) 754, (1936)
755, (1940) 756, (1944) 757
as former governor, 176 (box), 222,
1377
Liberal Party support, (1944) 65
New York background, 222
political party development, 46, 48
popular vote, (1932) 671, (1936) 672,
(1940) 673, (1944) 674
primary votes, (1932) 331–332,
(1936) 333–334, (1940) 335–336,
(1944) 337–338
public offices, 215
reelection chances, 313 (box)
third term issue, 194, 209
vice-presidential choice, 312
vice-presidential candidate
Democratic nominee, (1920) 259,
432, 494
electoral vote, (1920) 773
Roosevelt, Franklin D. Jr., 55, 65
Roosevelt, Theodore
biography, 780
governor, New York, 1403
as president
campaign finance reform, 109
succession, 16, 254–255
presidential candidate
campaign finance, (1904) 89, 109
electoral vote, (1904) 747, (1912) 749
as former governor, 176 (box), 223,
1377
as former vice president, 314 (box)
no-run decision, (1908) 255, 484
political party development, 46, 49
popular vote, (1904) 664, (1912)
666
primary votes, (1912) 311, 320–321,
(1916) 322–323
Progressive nominee, (1912) 69–70,
76, 256, 422, 424 (box), 432, 488,
(1916) 70, 432, 490
public offices, 215
reelection chances, (1904) 313 (box)
Republican contender, (1912) 256,
412, 486, (1916) 258, 490
Republican convention ballots,
(1904) 598, (1908) 599, (1912) 600,
(1916) 602
Republican nominee, (1904) 255,
432, 481–482
third-party challenges, 4, 5

vice-presidential candidate
electoral vote, (1900) 773
Republican nominee, (1900) 254,
431, 479
on Wilson, 257
Root, Elihu
Republican convention officers, (1912)
417 (table), 486
ballots, (1912) 600
Republican presidential contender, (1916)
258, 490
convention ballots, (1916) 602
senator, New York, 1255
Ros-Lehtinen, Ileana, 788
Rose, Daniel
governor, Maine, 1394
Roseboom, Eugene H., 235, 252, 710–711
Rosellini, Albert D.
Democratic convention ballots, (1960)
620
governor, Washington, 1412
Rosewater, Victor
Republican National Committee chair,
417 (table), 426 (table)
Rosier, Joseph
senator, West Virginia, 1265
Ross, C. Ben
governor, Idaho, 1390
Ross, Edmund G.
senator, Kansas, 1244
Ross, James
biography, 780
senator, Pennsylvania, 1258
vice-presidential electoral vote, (1816)
772
Ross, Jonathan
senator, Vermont, 1263
Ross, Lawrence
governor, Texas, 1410
Ross, Nancy
vice-presidential candidate
Independent Alliance nominee,
(1984) 437
Ross, Nellie Taylor
governor, Wyoming, 16, 1377, 1413
Ross, Robert G.
presidential primary votes, (1916) 323,
(1920) 326, (1928) 330
Ross, William B.
governor, Wyoming, 1413
Ross, William H.
governor, Delaware, 1388
Rostenkowski, Dan, 199
Roth, William V. Jr.
senator, Delaware, 206, 1239
tax proposal, 180
Routt, John L.
governor, Colorado, 1386
Rowan, John
senator, Kentucky, 1245
Rowland, John G.
governor, Connecticut, 1387
Roy, Conrad W.
presidential primary votes, (1988) 385
Roy, Stephen
governor, Vermont, 1410
Roy, Vesta M.
governor, New Hampshire, 1401
Roybal, Edward R., 788
Roybal-Allard, Lucille, 788
Ruckelshaus, William D., 281
Rudman, Warren B.
senator, New Hampshire, 183, 1253
deficit control law, 188
Ruger, Thomas H.
governor, Georgia, 1389
Ruggles, Benjamin
senator, Ohio, 1257
Ruggles, John
senator, Maine, 1247
"Rum, Romanism, and rebellion" remark, 250
Runnels, Hardin R.
governor, Texas, 1409
Runnels, Hiram G.
governor, Mississippi, 1398
Runoff elections for governor, 1380

Runoff primaries, 129–130, 131 (box)
Runyon, William N.
governor, New Jersey, 1402
Rush, Bobby L., 791
Rush, Richard
biography, 780
vice-presidential electoral vote, (1820,
1828) 772
Rusher, William, 52
Rushton, ——
Alabama Senate candidate, 130
Rusk, Jeremiah M.
governor, Wisconsin, 1413
Republican convention ballots, (1888)
592
Rusk, Thomas J.
senator, Texas, 1262
Russell, Benjamin, 817 (box)
Russell, Charles H.
governor, Nevada, 1400
Russell, Daniel L.
governor, North Carolina, 1403
Russell, Donald S.
governor, South Carolina, 1408
senator, South Carolina, 1260
Russell, John
vice-presidential candidate
Prohibition Party candidate, (1872)
430
Russell, Lee Maurice
governor, Mississippi, 1398
Russell, Richard B.
governor, Georgia, 1389
presidential candidate
Democratic contender, (1948) 139,
512, (1952) 144, 272, 517
Democratic convention ballots,
(1948) 616, (1952) 618
primary votes, (1952) 341–343
senator, Georgia, 1241
electoral count, 1969, 712
successor, 1232
Russell, William E.
Democratic convention ballots, (1892)
593, (1896) 595
governor, Massachusetts, 1396
Rutherford, John
governor, Virginia, 1411
Rutherfurd, John
senator, New Jersey, 1253
Rutledge, Edward
governor, South Carolina, 1407
Rutledge, John
biography, 780
electoral vote, (1789) 718
governor, South Carolina, 1407
Rutledge, Wiley B., 818–819
Ryan, George
governor, Illinois, 1391
Ryan, Thomas F., 487
Ryan, William F., 803
Ryden, Conrad A.
presidential primary votes, (1992) 393
Rye, Thomas C.
governor, Tennessee, 1409

S

Sabath, Adolph J.
length of service in Congress, 795 (table)
Sabato, Larry J., 103
Sabin, Dwight M.
Republican National Committee chair,
426 (table)
senator, Minnesota, 1249
Sackett, Fred M.
senator, Kentucky, 1245
Sadler, Reinhold
governor, Nevada, 1400
Safran, John
presidential primary votes, (1996) 403
Sagan, Cyril E.
presidential primary votes, (1988) 385,
(1992) 394
Salaman, Maureen Kennedy
vice-presidential candidate
Populist Party nominee, (1984) 437

Salinger, Pierre
  senator, California, 162, 1237
Salmon, Thomas P.
  governor, Vermont, 1411
Salomon, Edward
  governor, Wisconsin, 1413
Saltonstall, Leverett
  governor, Massachusetts, 1396
  presidential primary votes, (1948)
    340
  senator, Massachusetts, 1248
Sam faction (Know-Nothings), 64
Same-sex marriage, 567
Sampson, Flem D.
  governor, Kentucky, 1393
Samuelson, Don
  governor, Idaho, 1390
San Souci, Emery J.
  governor, Rhode Island, 1407
Sanchez, Loretta, 789, 804
Sanders, Bernard, 79
Sanders, Carl E.
  governor, Georgia, 1389
Sanders, Everett
  Republican National Committee chair,
    426 (table)
Sanders, Jared Y.
  governor, Louisiana, 1393
Sanders, Newell
  senator, Tennessee, 1262
Sanders, Wilbur F.
  senator, Montana, 1251
Sandman, Charles W., 175
Sanford, Nathan
  biography, 780
  senator, New York, 1255
  vice-presidential electoral vote, (1824)
    772
Sanford, Terry
  governor, North Carolina, 1404
  presidential candidate
    Democratic convention ballots,
      (1972) 625
    primary votes, (1972) 354–358,
      (1976) 359–364
  senator, North Carolina, 188, 1256
Sanford, William J.
  governor, Alabama, 1384
Santini, Jim, 188
Santorum, Rick
  senator, Pennsylvania, 199, 1258
Sarbanes, Paul
  senator, Maryland, 179, 1247
Sargent, Aaron A.
  senator, California, 1238
Sargent, Francis W.
  governor, Massachusetts, 1396
Sarles, Elmore Y.
  governor, North Dakota, 1404
Sasser, Jim
  senator, Tennessee, 179, 199, 1261
Sauls, N. Sanders, 299 (box), 300
Saulsbury, Eli
  senator, Delaware, 1240
Saulsbury, Gove
  governor, Delaware, 1388
Saulsbury, Willard Jr.
  Democratic convention ballots, (1924)
    606–607
  senator, Delaware, 1240
Saulsbury, Willard Sr.
  senator, Delaware, 1240
Saunders, Alvin
  senator, Nebraska, 1252
Saunders, Edward W., 818
Saunders, Romulus M.
  Democratic convention officers, 415
    (table)
Savage, Ezra P.
  governor, Nebraska, 1399
Sawyer, Charles
  presidential primary votes, (1940) 336
Sawyer, Charles H.
  governor, New Hampshire, 1401
Sawyer, Frederick A.
  senator, South Carolina, 1260

Sawyer, Grant
  governor, Nevada, 1400
Sawyer, Philetus
  senator, Wisconsin, 1265
Saxbe, William B.
  senator, Ohio, 169, 1257
  campaign finance, 111
Sayers, Joseph D.
  governor, Texas, 1410
Scaife, Richard, 114
Scales, Alfred M.
  governor, North Carolina, 1403
Scalia, Antonin, 300
Scammon, Richard, 22
Schaefer, William D.
  governor, Maryland, 1395
Schafer, Edward T.
  governor, North Dakota, 1404
Schall, Thomas D.
  senator, Minnesota, 1249
Schattschneider, E. E., 254
Schechter, Bernard B.
  presidential primary votes, (1976) 364
Schell, Augustus
  Democratic National Committee chair,
    415 (table), 426 (table)
Schiff, Adam, 100
Schiff, Irwin A.
  presidential primary votes, (1996) 402
Schiff, Karenna Gore, 568
Schlesinger, Arthur M. Jr., 275, 312
Schley, William
  governor, Georgia, 1389
Schmedeman, Albert G.
  governor, Wisconsin, 1413
Schmitt, Harrison (Jack)
  senator, New Mexico, 179, 1254
Schmitz, John George
  biography, 780
  presidential candidate
    American Independent Party nomi-
      nee, (1972) 51, 436
    popular vote, (1972) 681
Schneider, ——
  presidential primary votes, (1952) 343
Schoeppel, Andrew F.
  governor, Kansas, 1392
  senator, Kansas, 1244
School desegregation
  Little Rock integration, 149
  Republican platform issue, (1960) 524
  Supreme Court decision, 145–146
School prayer
  Reagan positions, 285
  Republican platform issue, (1964) 527,
    (1972) 537, (1984) 551
Schreiber, M. J.
  governor, Wisconsin, 1413
Schricker, Henry F.
  governor, Indiana, 1391
Schriner, Joe C.
  presidential primary votes, (2000)
    404–410
Schroeder, Patricia
  presidential candidate
    Democratic contender, (1988)
      210
    Democratic convention ballots,
      (1992) 636
Schumer, Charles E.
  senator, New York, 203, 1255
Schureman, James
  senator, New Jersey, 1253
Schurz, Carl
  on Grant, 247
  Liberal Republican convention officers,
    425 (box)
  Republican convention officers, 417
    (table)
  senator, Missouri, 1251
Schuyler, Karl C.
  senator, Colorado, 1238
Schuyler, Philip
  senator, New York, 1255
Schwartz, Harry H.
  senator, Wyoming, 1266

Schwartz, Stephen H.
  presidential primary votes, (1992) 394
Schweiker, Richard S.
  Republican vice-presidential contender,
    (1976) 282, 540
  senator, Pennsylvania, 169, 1259
  campaign finance, 111
Schwellenbach, L. B.
  senator, Washington, 1265
Schwinden, Ted
  governor, Montana, 1399
Scofield, Edward
  governor, Wisconsin, 1413
Scott, Abram M.
  governor, Mississippi, 1398
Scott, Charles
  governor, Kentucky, 1392
Scott, Hugh D. Jr.
  Republican National Committee chair,
    426 (table)
  Republican platform, (1964) 423 (box),
    525–526, (1976) 541
  senator, Pennsylvania, 152, 1258
Scott, John
  senator, Pennsylvania, 1258
Scott, John G.
  presidential candidate
    Greenback Party nominee, (1948)
      434
Scott, Nathan B.
  senator, West Virginia, 1265
Scott, Robert K.
  governor, South Carolina, 1408
Scott, Robert W.
  governor, North Carolina, 1404
Scott, Terrance R.
  presidential primary votes, (1992) 393
Scott, W. Kerr
  governor, North Carolina, 1403
  senator, North Carolina, 1256
Scott, William Lloyd
  senator, Virginia, 1264
Scott, Winfield
  biography, 780
  presidential candidate
    electoral vote, (1852) 734
    military service, 221, 222
    popular vote, (1852) 651
    Whig contender, (1840) 444, (1848)
      238, 449
    Whig convention ballots, (1848) 576,
      (1852) 578
    Whig nominee, (1852) 239, 240, 430,
      451
Scranton, William W.
  governor, Pennsylvania, 8, 159, 1406
  presidential candidate
    primary votes, (1964) 348–350
    Republican contender, (1964) 161,
      276, 525
    Republican convention ballots,
      (1964) 621
Scranton, William W. III, 189
Scrugham, James G.
  governor, Nevada, 1400
  senator, Nevada, 1252
Seabrook, Whitmarsh B.
  governor, South Carolina, 1408
Sears, John, 540
Seaton, Fred A.
  senator, Nebraska, 1252
Seawall, Jerrold L.
  presidential primary votes, (1940)
    335–336
Seay, Thomas
  governor, Alabama, 1384
Sebastian, William K.
  senator, Arkansas, 1237
Section 527 groups, 83, 107, 125
Sedgwick, Theodore
  senator, Massachusetts, 1248
See, Chuck
  presidential primary votes, (2000)
    404–410
Seeley, Elias P.
  governor, New Jersey, 1401

Seidel, Emil
  vice-presidential candidate
    Socialist nominee, (1912) 432, 485
Seligman, Arthur
  governor, New Mexico, 1402
Seminole war, 234
Semple, James
  senator, Illinois, 1242
Senate, U.S. See also Senate elections
  constitutional basis, 1229–1232
  leaders, 1911–2001, 1590–1591
  organization, (2001) 20
  party control shifts, 1234
  senators
    instructions from states, 1229
    presidential candidates, 155 (box),
      223–224
    senators, 1789–2001, by state (ta-
      bles), 1236–1266
  sessions, 1233
  terms, 1231, 1233
  vice president's election, (1836) 15, 235,
    709
Senate elections. See also Congressional elections
  appointments and special elections, 1232
  campaign finance, 94–95, 99
  classes, 1231
  constitutional provisions, 30–31 (box)
  costs, 1233
  disputed elections, 1230, 1231
  general election returns, 1267–1304
  popular election, 1230–1231
    Republican platform issue, (1908)
      423 (box), 599
    Seventeenth Amendment, 14, 16,
      1231, 1232
  primary returns, 1920–2000, 1305–1374
  by state legislatures, 1229–1231
Senter, DeWitt Clinton
  governor, Tennessee, 1409
Sergeant, John
  biography, 780
  vice-presidential candidate
    electoral vote, (1832) 772
    National Republican nominee,
      (1832) 429, 442
Serrette, Dennis L.
  presidential candidate
    Independent Alliance nominee,
      (1984) 437
    popular vote, (1984) 696
    primary votes, (1984) 377
Sessions, Jeff
  senator, Alabama, 200, 1236
Settle, Thomas
  Republican convention officers, 417
    (table)
Seventeenth Amendment, 14, 16, 1231, 1232
Sevier, Ambrose H.
  senator, Arkansas, 1237
Sevier, John
  governor, Tennessee, 1409
Sewall, Arthur
  biography, 780
  vice-presidential candidate
    Democratic nominee, (1896) 431,
      478
    electoral vote, (1896) 773
    National Silver Party nominee,
      (1896) 431
Sewall, Sumner
  governor, Maine, 1394
Seward, William H.
  governor, New York, 1402
  political party development, 45, 74, 247
  presidential candidate
    Republican contender, (1856) 453,
      (1860) 458
    Republican convention ballots,
      (1856) 579, (1860) 581
  senator, New York, 1255
Sewell, William J.
  senator, New Jersey, 1254
Seymour, Horatio
  biography, 780

Democratic convention officers, 415 (table)
governor, New York, 1402, 1403
presidential candidate
black voters, 24
Democratic convention ballots, (1860) 580, (1864) 582, (1868) 584, (1880) 589
Democratic nominee, (1868) 246, 430, 462
electoral vote, (1868) 738
New York background, 222
popular vote, (1868) 655
Seymour, Horatio
senator, Vermont, 1263
Seymour, John
senator, California, 1237
Seymour, Thomas H.
governor, Connecticut, 1387
presidential candidate
Democratic contender, (1864) 460
Democratic convention ballots, 582
Shackleford, Rufus
vice-presidential candidate
American Party nominee, (1976) 51, 436
Shafer, George F.
governor, North Dakota, 1404
Shafer, Raymond P.
governor, Pennsylvania, 1406
presidential primary votes, (1968) 351–353
Shafroth, John F.
governor, Colorado, 1386
senator, Colorado, 1238
Shaheen, Jeanne
governor, New Hampshire, 1401
Shallenberger, Ashton C.
governor, Nebraska, 1399
Shannon, James C.
governor, Connecticut, 1387
Shannon, Wilson
governor, Ohio, 1404
Shapiro, Samuel H.
governor, Illinois, 1391
Shapp, Milton J.
governor, Pennsylvania, 1406
presidential candidate
Democratic convention ballots, (1976) 627
primary votes, (1976) 359–364
Sharkey, William L.
governor, Mississippi, 1398
Sharon, William
senator, Nevada, 1252
Sharpe, Merrill Q.
governor, South Dakota, 1409
Shaver, Clem
Democratic National Committee chair, 415 (table), 426 (table)
Shaw, ——
presidential primary votes, (1952) 343
Shaw, Edward
vice-presidential candidate
Socialist Workers nominee, (1964) 435
Shaw, Leslie M.
governor, Iowa, 1392
Shaw, Mark
vice-presidential candidate
Prohibition nominee, (1964) 435
Shays, Christopher, 93
campaign finance reform, 124 (box)
Sheafe, James
senator, New Hampshire, 1253
Shearer, Eileen M.
vice-presidential candidate
American Independent Party nominee, (1980) 437
Shearer, William K., 51
Sheffield, Bill
governor, Alaska, 1384
Sheffield, William P.
senator, Rhode Island, 1259
Shelby, Isaac
governor, Kentucky, 1392

Shelby, Richard C.
senator, Alabama, 188–189, 1236
party switch, 796
Sheldon, Charles H.
governor, South Dakota, 1408
Sheldon, George L.
governor, Nebraska, 1399
Shelley, John F., 161
Shelton, Frank W.
presidential candidate
American Party nominee, (1980) 437
popular vote, (1980) 696
Shelton, Herbert M.
presidential candidate
American Vegetarian Party nominee, (1956) 435
Shepley, Ether
senator, Maine, 1246
Shepley, George F.
governor, Louisiana, 1393
Sheppard, John C.
governor, South Carolina, 1408
Sheppard, Morris
senator, Texas, 1262
Sheridan, Philip, 244, 246
Sherman Anti-Trust Act, 488, 255
Sherman, Buren R.
governor, Iowa, 1391
Sherman, James S.
biography, 780
vice-presidential candidate
effect of death, 12–13 (box), 206, 425, 709
electoral vote, (1908) 773
Republican nominee, (1908) 255, 432, 484, (1912) 432, 486
Sherman, John
presidential contender, (1880) 249, 468, (1888) 251, 473
Republican convention ballots, (1880) 588, (1884) 590, (1888) 592
senator, Ohio, 1257
Sherman, Lawrence Y.
presidential candidate
primary votes, (1916) 322
Republican contender, (1916) 258
Republican convention ballots, (1916) 602
senator, Illinois, 1242
Sherman, Roger
on House elections, 799
senator, Connecticut, 1239
Sherman Silver Purchase Act, 251
Sherman, William T.
Civil War victories, 244
Grant campaign, (1868) 246
Johnson cabinet possibility, 246
Republican convention ballots, (1884) 590
Shiekman, Tom
presidential primary votes, (1992) 386–393
Shields, James
senator, Illinois, 1242
senator, Minnesota, 1249
senator, Missouri, 1251
Shields, John K.
senator, Tennessee, 1262
Ships and shipping
platform issue
Democrats, (1904) 482
Republicans, (1904) 482, (1916) 491
Shipstead, Henrik
senator, Minnesota, 1249
Shively, Benjamin F.
senator, Indiana, 1243
Shivers, Allan
governor, Texas, 1410
Sholtz, David
governor, Florida, 1388
Short, Dewey, 506
Shorter, John Gill
governor, Alabama, 1384
Shortridge, Eli C. D.
governor, North Dakota, 1404

Shortridge, Samuel M.
senator, California, 1238
Shott, Hugh Ike
senator, West Virginia, 1265
Shoup, George L.
governor, Idaho, 1390
senator, Idaho, 1242
Shouse, Jouett, 502
Shriver, R. Sargent
biography, 780
presidential candidate
Democratic contender, (1976) 177
as former vice-presidential nominee, 224
primary votes, (1976) 359–364
vice-presidential candidate
Democratic nominee, (1972) 172, 280, 425, 436, 535
electoral vote, (1972) 773
Shulze, John A.
governor, Pennsylvania, 1406
Shunk, Francis R.
governor, Pennsylvania, 1406
Sibley, Henry H.
governor, Minnesota, 1397
Sibley, John C., 478
Sick, Gary, 284
Sickles, Donald, 246
Siegelman, Don
governor, Alabama, 1384
Sigler, Kim
governor, Michigan, 138, 1397
Silsbee, Nathaniel
senator, Massachusetts, 1248
Silver. See Monetary policy
"Silver Gray" faction (Whigs)
nominees, (1856) 430
Silver Republican Party
nominees, (1900) 432
Silverman, Edward M.
vice-presidential candidate
Conservative Party of Virginia nominee, (1960) 435
Silzer, George S.
Democratic convention ballots, (1924) 606
governor, New Jersey, 1402
Simmons, Furnifold M.
Democratic convention ballots, (1920) 605
senator, North Carolina, 1256
Simmons, James F.
senator, Rhode Island, 1259
Simms, John F.
governor, New Mexico, 1402
Simon, Donald, 119 (box)
Simon, Joseph
senator, Oregon, 1258
Simon, Paul M.
presidential candidate
Democratic contender, (1988) 190, 287
primary votes, (1988) 378–385
senator, Illinois, 187, 1242
Simonetti, Joseph
Democratic convention ballots, (1992) 636
Simpson, Alan K.
senator, Wyoming, 181, 1266
Simpson, Milward L.
governor, Wyoming, 1413
senator, Wyoming, 1266
Simpson, Oramel H.
governor, Louisiana, 1393
Simpson, William D.
governor, South Carolina, 1408
Simpson, William O.
presidential primary votes, (1916) 322
Sinclair, Upton
California gubernatorial campaign, 265
presidential primary votes, (1936) 333–334
Singer, William, 534
Single Tax Party
nominees, (1920) 433

Sinner, George
governor, North Dakota, 1404
Sirhan, Sirhan, 17
Sirica, John J., 173
Skillen, Richard D.
presidential primary votes, (1996) 403
Skinner, Richard
governor, Vermont, 1410
Skok, Michael
presidential primary votes, (2000) 404–410
Skow, Philip
presidential primary votes, (1992) 386–393
Slade, William
governor, Vermont, 1410
Slater, James H.
senator, Oregon, 1258
Slaton, John M.
governor, Georgia, 1389
Slattery, James M.
senator, Illinois, 1242
Slaughter, Gabriel
governor, Kentucky, 1392
Slavery
in party development, 57, 63, 64, 66, 74, 81, 238, 239–240, 241
platform issue
Democrats, (1840) 445, (1852) 450–451, (1856) 455, (1860) 423 (box), 456–457
Free Soilers, (1848) 449, (1852) 452
Know-Nothings, (1856) 454
Liberty Party, (1844) 446
Republicans, (1856) 453–454, (1860) 458
population formula for House apportionment, 13 (box), 802
in sectional tension, 231–232
Sleeper, Albert E.
governor, Michigan, 1397
Slettandahl, ——
presidential primary votes, (1952) 343
Slidell, John
senator, Louisiana, 1246
Slizer, George S.
presidential primary votes, (1924) 327–328
Slocomb, Whitney Hart
presidential candidate
Greenback Party nominee, (1960) 435
Small, Len
governor, Illinois, 1391
Smalley, David A.
Democratic National Committee chair, 415 (table), 426 (table)
Smallwood, William
governor, Maryland, 1395
Smathers, George A.
Democratic convention ballots, (1960) 620
presidential primary votes, (1960) 346–347, (1968) 351–353
senator, Florida, 143, 1240
Smathers, William H.
senator, New Jersey, 1254
Smith, Alfred E.
biography, 780
governor, New York, 1403
New Deal opposition, 265
presidential candidate
Democratic contender, (1920) 494, (1924) 260, 496–497, (1932) 262, 502
Democratic convention ballots, (1920) 605, (1924) 606–607, (1928) 609, (1932) 611
Democratic nominee, (1928) 58, 261, 264, 433, 499–500
election evolution, 6, 16
electoral vote, (1928) 753
former governors, 222
popular vote, (1928) 670

primary votes, (1924) 327–328, (1928) 329–330, (1932) 331–332, (1936) 333–334
  Prohibition repeal, 72
Smith, Benjamin
  governor, North Carolina, 1403
Smith, Benjamin A. II
  senator, Massachusetts, 1248
Smith, Charles A.
  governor, South Carolina, 1408
Smith, Charles M.
  governor, Vermont, 1411
Smith, Daniel
  senator, Tennessee, 1261
Smith, Delazon
  senator, Oregon, 1258
Smith, Edward C.
  governor, Vermont, 1411
Smith, Ellison D.
  senator, South Carolina, 1260
Smith, Elmo
  governor, Oregon, 1406
Smith, Forrest
  governor, Missouri, 1399
Smith, Frank L.
  senator, Illinois, 1242
    campaign finance, 110
Smith, George William
  governor, Virginia, 1411
Smith, Gerald L. K.
  presidential candidate
    America First Party nominee, (1944) 434
    Christian National Party nominee, (1956) 435
    Christian Nationalist Party nominee, (1948) 434
    popular vote, (1944) 693, (1956) 694
  Union Party history, 79
Smith, Gerrit
  presidential candidate
    National Liberty Party nominee, (1848) 430
    popular vote, (1848, 1860) 690
Smith, Gordon H.
  senator, Oregon, 200, 1258
Smith, Green Clay
  presidential candidate
    popular vote, (1876) 690
    Prohibition Party nominee, (1876) 430
Smith, H. Alexander
  senator, New Jersey, 1254
Smith, Henry
  governor, Rhode Island, 1406
Smith, Hoke
  governor, Georgia, 1389
  senator, Georgia, 1241
Smith, Hulett C.
  governor, West Virginia, 1412
Smith, Israel
  governor, Vermont, 1410
  senator, Vermont, 1263
Smith, James Jr.
  senator, New Jersey, 1254
Smith, James M.
  governor, Georgia, 1389
Smith, James Y.
  governor, Rhode Island, 1407
Smith, Jeremiah
  governor, New Hampshire, 1400
Smith, John
  senator, New York, 1255
Smith, John
  senator, Ohio, 1257
Smith, John B.
  governor, New Hampshire, 1401
Smith, John Cotton
  governor, Connecticut, 1387
Smith, John Gregory
  governor, Vermont, 1410
Smith, John Walter
  governor, Maryland, 1395
  senator, Maryland, 1247
Smith, L. Neil
  presidential candidate

Libertarian nominee, (2000) 439
    popular vote, (2000) 699
Smith, Lonnie E., 26
Smith, Marcus A.
  senator, Arizona, 1237
Smith, Margaret Chase
  presidential primary votes, (1964) 348–350
  Republican convention ballots, (1964) 621
  senator, Maine, 141, 172, 787, 1247
    widow's mandate, 788
Smith, Mary Louise
  Republican National Committee chair, 417 (table), 426 (table)
Smith, Maureen
  presidential candidate
    Peace and Freedom Party nominee, (1980) 68, 437
    popular vote, (1980) 696
Smith, Nathan
  senator, Connecticut, 1238
Smith, Nels H.
  governor, Wyoming, 1413
Smith, Oliver H.
  senator, Indiana, 1243
Smith, Perry
  senator, Connecticut, 1239
Smith, Preston
  governor, Texas, 1410
Smith, Ralph Tyler
  senator, Illinois, 1242
Smith, Robert B.
  governor, Montana, 1399
Smith, Robert C.
  Constitution Party nomination feelers, 80
  senator, New Hampshire, 1253
Smith, Robert J.
  presidential candidate
    American Party nominee, (1992) 52, 438
    popular vote, (1992) 698
    primary votes, (1992) 393
Smith, Samuel
  senator, Maryland, 1247
    appointment, 1232
Smith, Samuel E.
  governor, Maine, 1394
Smith, Truman
  senator, Connecticut, 1239
Smith, Tucker Powell
  vice-presidential candidate
    Socialist nominee, (1948) 434
Smith, William
  biography, 780
  senator, South Carolina, 1260
  vice-presidential electoral vote, (1828, 1836) 772
Smith, William
  governor, Virginia, 1411
Smith, William Alden
  presidential primary votes, (1916) 322–323
  senator, Michigan, 1249
Smith, William E.
  governor, Wisconsin, 1413
Smith, William Hugh
  governor, Alabama, 1384
Smith, William L., 713
Smith, Willis
  senator, North Carolina, 143, 1256
Smith-Connally Act of 1943, 110
Smith-Lever Act of 1914, 257
Smoot, Reed
  senator, Utah, 1263
Smoot-Hawley Tariff Act of 1930, 261
Smylie, Robert E.
  governor, Idaho, 1390
Smyth, Frederick
  governor, New Hampshire, 1400
Snell, Bertrand H.
  Republican convention officers, 417 (table)
Snell, Earl
  governor, Oregon, 1405

Snelling, Richard A.
  governor, Vermont, 185, 1411
Snow, Wilbert
  governor, Connecticut, 1387
Snowe, Olympia J.
  senator, Maine, 199, 787, 789, 1246
    marriage, 788
Snyder, Simon
  Democratic-Republican vice-presidential contender, (1816) 231
  governor, Pennsylvania, 1406
Social Democratic Federation, 78, 79
Social Democratic Party
  nominees, (1900) 431, 481
  Socialist Party history, 78
Social Democratic Workingmen's Party, 79
Social Security
  New Deal, 264, 265
  platform issue
    Democrats, (1948) 513, 518, (2000) 569
    Green Party, (2000) 571
    Progressives, (1912) 489
    Republicans, (1936) 265, (1988) 555, (1992) 559, (2000) 567
    Socialists, (1912) 485
  presidential campaign issue, (1948) 270, (1964) 277, (1976) 178, (2000) 298
Socialist Equality Party
  nominees, (1996) 439
Socialist International, 79
Socialist Labor Party
  Debs candidacy (1900), 481
  Greenback Party convention, (1880) 468
  historical development, 46, 78
    profile, 79
    timeline, 47
  nominees, (1892–1976) 431–437
Socialist Party
  convention, platform, (1904) 481, (1908) 483, (1912) 485–486, (1916) 492, (1920) 492–493, (1932) 501
  historical development, 46, 49
    profile, 78–79
    timeline, 47
  nominees, (1904–56) 432–435, (1976–2000) 437–439
  Progressive ticket supporters, (1924) 70, 498
  vote percentages, 424 (box)
Socialist Workers Party
  historical development, 81
    profile, 79
    timeline, 47
  nominees, (1948–2000) 434–439
Soeters, Kent M.
  presidential popular vote, (1968 695
Soft money
  as campaign finance issue, 104–105
    overhaul legislation, 124 (box), 125
  congressional campaigns, 97–98
  definition, 83–84, 85 (box)
  issue advocacy ads, 106
  presidential campaigns, 92
Soldiers and Sailors Convention (1868), 246
Solidarity Party
  presidential primary votes, (1988) 385
Solis, Hilda, 793
Sorauf, Frank J., 83, 96, 97, 101, 104
Sorlie, Arthur G.
  governor, North Dakota, 1404
Soule, Pierre
  senator, Louisiana, 1246
Souter, David, 301
South Carolina
  Democratic convention credentials dispute, (1952) 422, (1972) 422, 534, 624
  electoral vote contest, (1876) 248
South Carolinians for Independent Electors
  nominee, (1956) 435
Southard, Samuel L.
  governor, New Jersey, 1401
  senator, New Jersey, 1253
Southern Alliance, 69
Southern Democratic Party
  convention, (1860) 457

historical development
  profile, 53–54
  timeline, 47
nominees, (1860) 430
officers, 425 (box)
vote percentage, 424 (box)
Southern primaries, 129–132
Southgate, James Haywood
  vice-presidential candidate
    National Party nominee, (1896) 431
Soviet Union. See also Communism
  collapse, 134, 192, 289
  Kennedy policies, 156, 160
  platform issue
    Progressives, (1948) 514
    Republicans, (1984) 551, (1988) 555–556
  Reagan policies, 176–177, 185, 286
  Sputnik, 149
  U-2 flights, 152
Spaight, Richard D.
  governor, North Carolina, 1403
Spaight, Richard D. Jr.
  governor, North Carolina, 1403
Spangler, Harrison E.
  Republican National Committee chair, 417 (table), 426 (table)
Spangler, Ronald W.
  presidential primary votes, (1996) 403
Spanish-American War, 254
Spannous, Warren
  Democratic convention ballots, (1980) 630
Sparkman, John J.
  biography, 781
  senator, Alabama, 1236
  vice-presidential candidate
    Democratic nominee, (1952) 434, 517
    electoral vote, (1952) 773
    politics and issues, (1952) 144–145
Sparks, Chauncey M.
  governor, Alabama, 1384
Sparks, John
  governor, Nevada, 1400
Sparrow, Cleveland
  vice-presidential candidate
    Third World Assembly nominee, (1988) 438
Spaulding, Huntley N.
  governor, New Hampshire, 1401
Spaulding, Rolland H.
  governor, New Hampshire, 1401
Speakers of the House, 1588–1589
Special elections
  electoral anomalies, 13 (box)
  House, 803
  removal of governors, 1381 (box)
  Senate, 1232
  southern primaries, 131–132
Specter, Arlen
  senator, Pennsylvania, 183, 188, 1259
Speight, Jesse
  senator, Mississippi, 1250
Spelbring, Ralph
  presidential primary votes, (1992) 386–393
Spellman, John D.
  governor, Washington, 1412
Spence, John S.
  senator, Maryland, 1247
Spencer, Ambrose
  Whig convention officers, 425 (box)
Spencer, George E.
  senator, Alabama, 1236
Spencer, John C.
  Anti-Mason convention officers, 425 (box)
Spencer, Lloyd
  senator, Arkansas, 1237
Spencer, Selden P.
  senator, Missouri, 1251
Spock, Benjamin M.
  presidential candidate
    Peace and Freedom Party nominee, (1972) 68

People's Party nominee, (1972) 69, 436
popular vote, (1972) 681
vice-presidential candidate
People's Party nominee, (1976) 69, 436
Spoils system
in Grant era, 247
in Jackson era, 108, 234
Spong, William B. Jr.
senator, Virginia, 1264
Spooner, John Coit
senator, Wisconsin, 1266
Sprague, Charles A.
governor, Oregon, 1405
Sprague, Peleg
senator, Maine, 1247
Sprague, William
governor, Rhode Island, 1406, 1407
senator, Rhode Island, 1259
Sprigg, Samuel
governor, Maryland, 1395
Sproul, William C.
governor, Pennsylvania, 1406
Republican convention ballots, (1920) 604
Spruance, Presley
senator, Delaware, 1239
Spry, William
governor, Utah, 1410
Squire, Watson C.
senator, Washington, 1265
St Germain, Fernand J., 191
St. John, John P.
governor, Kansas, 1392
presidential candidate
popular vote, (1884) 659
Prohibition Party nominee, (1884) 431
Prohibition Party convention officers, 425 (box)
Stabenow, Debbie
senator, Michigan, 787, 1249
Stafford, Robert T.
governor, Vermont, 1411
senator, Vermont, 191, 1263
Staggs, Clyde
presidential primary votes, (1996) 403
Stallings, Richard H., 553
Democratic convention ballots, (1988) 634
"Stalwart" faction (Republicans), 75
Stanfield, Robert N.
senator, Oregon, 1258
Stanfill, William A.
senator, Kentucky, 1245
Stanford, Leland
governor, California, 1386
senator, California, 1238
Stanford, Rawghile C.
governor, Arizona, 1385
Stanley, Augustus Owsley
governor, Kentucky, 1393
senator, Kentucky, 1245
Stanley, Thomas B.
governor, Virginia, 1412
Stanley, William E.
governor, Kansas, 1392
Stanton, Edwin
in Johnson cabinet, 245, 246
Republican leadership, 247
Stanton, Elizabeth Cady, 31
Stanton, Joseph Jr.
senator, Rhode Island, 1259
Star-Martinez, R. Alison
presidential primary votes, (1992) 393
Stardumsky, John J.
presidential primary votes, (1992) 394
Stark, Benjamin
senator, Oregon, 1258
Stark, Lloyd C.
governor, Missouri, 1399
Starr, Kenneth W., 19, 201–202
Stassen, Harold E.
governor, Minnesota, 1397
Nixon opposition, (1956) 148, 273

presidential candidate
primary votes, (1944) 337–338, (1948) 313, 339–340, (1952) 341–343, (1964) 348–350, (1968) 351–353, (1980) 365–371, (1984) 372–377, (1988) 378–385, (1992) 386–393
Republican contender, (1944) 268, 508, (1948) 140, 270, 511, (1952) 271–272, 516
Republican convention ballots, (1948) 615, (1952) 617, (1968) 622
at Republican convention, (1956) 520
officers, speakers, 417 (table)
on Truman foreign policy, 142–143
State Department, U.S.
secretaries who became president, 220–221
State legislatures
choice of presidential electors, 703–705
election of governors, 1378, 1380–1381
election of senators, 793, 799, 1229–1231
House redistricting, 807, 815–826
power compared to governors, 1377
States' rights
platform issue
Democrats, (1840) 445, (1844) 447, (1912) 488, (1924) 497, (1956) 520
Dixiecrats, (1948) 514
Know-Nothings, (1856) 454
Progressives, (1912) 489
Republicans, (1860) 458
States' Rights Democratic Party (Dixiecrats)
convention, platform, (1948) 513–514
historical development, 46, 50
profile, 61–62
timeline, 47
nominees, (1948) 434
politics and issues, (1948) 139, 140–141, 269
Texas Democratic delegation, (1952) 516
States' Rights Party
nominees, (1956) 435
States' Rights Party of Kentucky
nominees, (1956) 435
Statesman Party
nominees, (1980) 437
Steams, ——
presidential primary votes, (1952) 343
Stearns, Marcellus L.
governor, Florida, 1388
Stearns, Onslow
governor, New Hampshire, 1400
Stearns, Ozora P.
senator, Minnesota, 1249
Steck, Daniel F.
senator, Iowa, 1243
Stedman, Seymour
vice-presidential candidate
Socialist nominee, (1920) 432, 492
Steed, Tom
Democratic convention ballots, (1980) 630
Steele, John H.
governor, New Hampshire, 1400
Steffey, John W.
presidential primary votes, (1964) 350
Steiger, William A., 536
Steinem, Gloria, 79
Steiwer, Frederick
Republican convention officers, speakers, 417 (table)
senator, Oregon, 1258
Stelle, John H.
governor, Illinois, 1391
Stenholm, Charles W., 564
Stennis, John C.
senator, Mississippi, 191, 1250
campaign finance, 111
Stephens, Alexander H.
governor, Georgia, 1389
Stephens, Hubert D.
senator, Mississippi, 1250
Stephens, Lawrence Vest
governor, Missouri, 1399

Stephens, Stan
governor, Montana, 1399
Stephens, William D.
governor, California, 1386
Stephenson, Isaac
senator, Wisconsin, 1266
Sterling, Ross M.
governor, Texas, 1410
Sterling, Thomas
senator, South Dakota, 1261
Steunenberg, Frank
governor, Idaho, 1390
Stevens, John Paul, 301, 824
Stevens, Samuel Jr.
governor, Maryland, 1395
Stevens, Ted
senator, Alaska, 1236
Stevens, Thaddeus
Republican leadership, 247
Stevenson, Adlai E.
biography, 781
Democratic convention ballots, (1892) 593, (1896) 595
postal patronage, 251
vice-presidential candidate
Democrat nominee, (1892) 252, 431, 475, (1900) 431, 480
electoral vote, (1892, 1900) 773
Populist nominee, (1900) 432
Silver Republican nominee, (1900) 432
Stevenson, Adlai E. II
biography, 781
congressional elections, (1958) 151
governor, Illinois, 141, 1391
presidential candidate
Democratic contender, (1960) 273, 521–522
Democratic convention ballots, (1952) 618, (1956) 619, (1960) 620
Democratic nominee, (1952) 272, 434, 516–517, (1956) 273, 435, 518–519
electoral vote, (1952) 759, (1956) 703 (box), 760
former governor, 222
politics and issues, (1952) 143–145, (1956) 148–149
popular vote, (1952) 676, (1956) 677
primary votes, (1952) 341–343, (1956) 344–345, (1960) 346–347, (1964) 348–350
vice-presidential choice, (1956) 148, 312
Stevenson, Adlai E. III
Democratic vice-presidential contender, (1976) 539
governor's race. 189
senator, Illinois, 1242
Stevenson, Andrew
Democratic convention officers, 415 (table)
Stevenson, Charles C.
governor, Nevada, 1400
Stevenson, Coke R.
governor, Texas, 1410
Stevenson, John W.
governor, Kentucky, 1393
Democratic convention officers, 415 (table)
senator, Kentucky, 1245
Stevenson, William E.
governor, West Virginia, 1412
Stewart, A. T., 89
Stewart, Commodore, 574
Stewart, David
senator, Maryland, 1247
Stewart, David W.
senator, Iowa, 1244
Stewart, Donald W.
senator, Alabama, 181, 1236
Stewart, Gideon Tabor
vice-presidential candidate
Prohibition Party nominee, (1876) 430

Stewart, John W.
governor, Vermont, 1410
senator, Vermont, 1263
Stewart, Potter, 29, 823
Stewart, Robert Marcellus
governor, Missouri, 1398
Stewart, Samuel V.
governor, Montana, 1399
Stewart, Tom
senator, Tennessee, 1262
Stewart, William M.
senator, Nevada, 1252
Stickney, William W.
governor, Vermont, 1411
Stimson, Henry, 267
Stock market crash, 1929, 261
Stockbridge, Francis B.
senator, Michigan, 1249
Stockdale, James B.
vice-presidential candidate
Perot campaign, (1992) 73, 291, 438, 560
Stockley, Charles C.
governor, Delaware, 1388
Stockton, John P.
senator, New Jersey, 1254
Stockton, Richard
biography, 781
senator, New Jersey, 1254
vice-presidential electoral vote, (1820) 772
Stockton, Robert F.
senator, New Jersey, 1253
Stockton, Thomas
governor, Delaware, 1388
Stokes, Edward C.
governor, New Jersey, 1401
Stokes, Louis
blacks in Congress, 791
presidential primary votes, (1992) 386–393
Stokes, Montfort
governor, North Carolina, 1403
senator, North Carolina, 1255
Stone, David
governor, North Carolina, 1403
senator, North Carolina, 1256
Stone, Harlan Fiske, 260, 818
Stone, I. F., 269
Stone, John H.
governor, Maryland, 1395
Stone, John M.
governor, Mississippi, 1398
Stone, Richard
senator, Florida, 1240
Stone, W. Clement, 114
Stone, William A.
governor, Pennsylvania, 1406
Stone, William J.
governor, Missouri, 1399
senator, Missouri, 1251
Stone, William M.
governor, Iowa, 1391
Stone, Willis E.
presidential primary votes, (1968) 353
Stoneman, George
governor, California, 1386
Stoner, J. B.
vice-presidential candidate
National States Rights' Party nominee, (1964) 435
Storer, Clement
senator, New Hampshire, 1253
Storke, Thomas M.
senator, California, 1238
Stout, Jacob
governor, Delaware, 1388
Stover, Fred
Democratic convention ballots, (1976) 627
Stow, Marietta Lizzie Bell
vice-presidential candidate
Equal Rights Party, (1884) 431
Straight-Out Democratic Party
nominees, (1872) 430

Strange, Robert
senator, North Carolina, 1256
Strategic Defense Initiative, 594
Stratton, Charles C.
governor, New Jersey, 1401
Stratton, William G.
governor, Illinois, 145, 1391
Straub, Robert W.
governor, Oregon, 1406
Strauss, Lewis L., 153
Strauss, Robert S.
at Democratic convention, (1976) 538, 539
Democratic National Committee chair, 415 (table), 426 (table)
Stravig, Mike, 189
Straw, Ezekiel A.
governor, New Hampshire, 1400
Streeter, Alson Jenness
presidential candidate
popular vote, (1888) 660
Union Labor Party nominee, (1888) 431
Strong, Caleb
governor, Massachusetts, 1396
senator, Massachusetts, 1248
Stroup, Oliver H.
Stuart, Charles E.
senator, Michigan, 1249
Stuart, Edwin S.
governor, Pennsylvania, 1406
Stuart, Gilbert, 817 (box)
Stuart, Henry C.
governor, Virginia, 1411
Stuart, John, 243
Stubbs, Walter R.
governor, Kansas, 1392
Students for a Democratic Society, 71, 79
Sturgeon, Daniel
senator, Pennsylvania, 1258
Sturgulewski, Arliss, 193
Subin, Dwight M.
Republican National Committee chair, 417 (table)
Suburbs, importance in elections, 3
Suffrage. See Voting rights
Sullivan, Charles L.
presidential candidate
Constitutional Party (Texas) nominee, (1960) 435
popular vote, (1960) 694
Sullivan, James
governor, Massachusetts, 1396
Sullivan, John
governor, New Hampshire, 1400
Sullivan, Leonor K., 789
Sullivan, Michael J.
governor, Wyoming, 1413
Sullivan, Patrick J.
senator, Wyoming, 1266
Sullivan, William V.
senator, Mississippi, 1250
Sulzer, William
Democratic convention ballots, (1912) 601
governor, New York, 1403
Summerfield, Arthur E.
Republican National Committee chair, 426 (table)
Sumner, Charles
Republican convention ballots, (1856) 579, (1860) 581
Republican leadership, 247
senator, Massachusetts, 1248
Sumner, Increase
governor, Massachusetts, 1396
Sumter, Thomas
senator, South Carolina, 1260
Sun Oil Co., 96, 120
Sundlum, Bruce
governor, Rhode Island, 1407
Sundquist, Don
governor, Tennessee, 1409
Sundquist, James L., 237–238, 239, 254, 264
Sununu, John H.
Bush campaign, (1992) 289

governor, New Hampshire, 185, 189, 1401
"Super Tuesday," 308, 315
"Superdelegates," 306 (box), 308, 311 (box), 314, 416, 420
Supreme Court decisions
campaign finance law
Buckley v. Valeo, 18, 86–87, 89, 98, 105–106, 117–120
Burroughs and Cannon v. U.S., 110
Colorado I, 92, 106
Colorado II, 92, 97, 106–107
primary regulation, 109, 110
census procedures, 821 (box)
congressional districts, 807–808
House redistricting, 818–825
majority-minority districts, 792
"one person, one vote," 17, 807, 822–823
racial gerrymanders, 825–826
Florida electoral vote controversy, (2000) 11, 19–20, 135–136, 205–206, 218, 295–296, 298–299 (box) 300, 707, 712–713, 1557–1568
House membership qualifications, 18
slavery, 240, 241, 242
term limits, 19, 194, 794
voting rights
African Americans, 24–26, 28–31
county unit system, 17, 131
minimum voting age, 33, 220
poll taxes, 25
residency requirements, 36
white primaries, 16–17, 25–26, 132
Supreme Court, U.S. See also Judiciary; Supreme Court decisions
FDR expansion plan, 266–267
Reagan nominees, 190
Sutherland, George
senator, Utah, 1263
Sutherland, Howard
presidential primary votes, (1920) 326
Republican convention ballots, (1920) 604
senator, West Virginia, 1265
Swain, David L.
governor, North Carolina, 1403
Swain, Fay T. Carpenter
presidential primary votes, (1964) 348–350
Swainson, John B.
governor, Michigan, 155, 1397
Swallow, Silas Comfort
presidential candidate
popular vote, (1904) 664
Prohibition Party nominee, (1904) 432
Swan, Henry
vice-presidential candidate
United American Party nominee, (1976) 437
Swann, Thomas
governor, Maryland, 1395
Swanson, Claude A.
governor, Virginia, 1411
senator, Virginia, 1264
Sweet, William E.
Democratic convention ballots, (1924) 606
governor, Colorado, 1386
"Sweetheart" gerrymanders, 819 (box)
Swift, Benjamin
senator, Vermont, 1263
Swift, George R.
senator, Alabama, 1236
Swift, Henry A.
governor, Minnesota, 1397
Swift, Jane
governor, Massachusetts, 1396
Swindall, Pat, 191
Sykes, James
governor, Delaware, 1388
Symington, Fife
governor, Arizona, 193, 1385
resignation, 1381 (box)

Symington, W. Stuart
presidential candidate
Democratic contender, (1960) 273, 522
Democratic convention ballots, (1956) 619, (1960) 620
politics and issues (1960) 154
primary votes, (1960) 346–347
senator, Missouri, 145, 1251
Symms, Steven D.
senator, Idaho, 183, 188, 1242

T

Tabor, Horace A. W.
senator, Colorado, 1238
Taft, Kingsley A.
senator, Ohio, 1257
Taft, Robert A.
presidential candidate
primary votes, (1940) 335–336, (1948) 339–340, (1952) 341–343
Republican contender, (1940) 267, 506, (1948) 140, 271, 511, (1952) 144, 271–272, 422, 515–516
Republican convention ballots, (1940) 613, (1948) 615, (1952) 617
senator, Ohio, 1257
politics and issues, 76, 142, 143
Taft, Robert A. Jr.
House elections, 159
senator, Ohio, 162, 170, 179, 1257
Taft, Robert A. II
governor, Ohio, 1405
Taft, Royal C.
governor, Rhode Island, 1407
Taft, William Howard
biography, 781
political party development, 69–70
presidential candidate
cabinet service, 222
election evolution, 6
electoral vote, (1908) 748, (1912) 749
political party development, 46
popular vote, (1908) 665, (1912) 666
primary votes, (1912) 310, 320–321
public offices, 215
reelection chances, (1912) 313 (box)
Republican convention ballots, (1908) 599, (1912) 600, (1916) 602
Republican nominee, (1908) 255–256, 432, 484, (1912) 76, 256, 412, 422, 432, 486
Taft-Hartley Labor-Management Relations Act of 1947, 110, 139–140, 143, 153
Taggart, Thomas
Democratic National Committee chair, 415 (table), 426 (table)
senator, Indiana, 1243
Tait, Charles
senator, Georgia, 1241
Take Back America Party
nominees, (1992) 438
Talbot, Isham
senator, Kentucky, 1245
Talbot, Matthew
governor, Georgia, 1389
Talbot, Ray H.
governor, Colorado, 1386
Talbot, Thomas
governor, Massachusetts, 1396
Talbow, Leonard
presidential primary votes, (1992) 394
Taliaferro, James P.
senator, Florida, 1240
Tallmadge, Nathaniel P.
senator, New York, 1255
Talmadge, Eugene
governor, Georgia, 1389
county unit system, 131
disputed succession, 1381
Talmadge, Herman E.
biography, 781
governor, Georgia, 1389
disputed election, 1381
senator, Georgia, 1241

vice-presidential electoral vote, (1956) 773
Tammany Hall faction
Cleveland opposition, 250
at Democratic convention, (1876) 466, (1880) 469, (1884) 471, (1892) 475, (1912) 487
Roosevelt opposition, 262
Tanner, John R.
governor, Illinois, 1390
Tappan, Benjamin
senator, Ohio, 1257
Tariffs
Grant policies, 247
Hoover policies, 261
Jackson positions, 234
platform issue
Democrats, (1876) 467, (1880) 469, (1884) 471, (1888) 472, (1892) 475, (1916) 492, (1928) 500
Free Soilers, (1848) 450
Liberal Republicans, (1872) 247, 464
Progressives, (1912) 487
Prohibition Party, (1888) 472, (1892) 475
Republicans, (1860) 242, 458, (1872) 464, (1876) 466, (1880) 468, (1884) 470, (1888) 473, (1892) 474, (1896) 477–478, (1900) 480, (1912) 486, (1916) 491, (1928) 499
Whigs, (1852) 452
Progressive era policies, 253–257
in Republican ascendancy, 248–252
Whig positions, 236, 237
Tattnall, Josiah
governor, Georgia, 1389
senator, Georgia, 1240
Tawes, J. Millard
governor, Maryland, 152, 1395
Tax Cut Party
nominees, (1960) 435
Tax policy. See also Income tax; Tariffs
Bush positions, 192, 290
Coolidge policies, 258
Dole campaign, (1996) 294
platform issues
Democrats, (1888) 472, (1952) 518, (1956) 519–520, (1960) 523, (1980) 546, (1984) 549, (1988) 552, 634, (1992) 557, 636, (1996) 564, (2000) 569
Progressives, (1924) 498
Republicans, (1888) 473, (1924) 496, (1964) 526, (1972) 537, (1980) 543, (1984) 550–551, (1988) 555, (1992) 423 (box), 559, (1996) 562, (2000) 566, 567
Socialists, (1908) 483, (1912) 485
Union Party, (1936) 506
Reagan policies, 187–188, 284
Tayler, John
governor, New York, 1402
Taylor, Alfred A.
governor, Tennessee, 1409
Taylor, Frank
presidential candidate
popular vote, (1976) 696
United American nominee, (1976) 437
Taylor, George Sam
vice-presidential candidate
Socialist Labor nominee, (1968) 436
Taylor, Glen H.
biography, 781
senator, Idaho, 143, 1242
vice-presidential candidate
Progressive nominee, (1948) 71, 140, 434, 514
Taylor, Jim
presidential primary votes, (2000) 404–410
Taylor, John
governor, South Carolina, 1407
senator, South Carolina, 1260
Taylor, John
senator, Virginia, 1264

Taylor, Leon R.
  governor, New Jersey, 1401
Taylor, Maurice
  presidential primary votes, (1996)
    395–402
Taylor, Morry, 315
Taylor, Robert L.
  governor, Tennessee, 1409
  senator, Tennessee, 1262
Taylor, William R.
  governor, Wisconsin, 1413
Taylor, William S.
  governor, Kentucky, 1393
Taylor, Zachary
  biography, 781
  on Compromise of 1850, 240
  death, 239
  and Jefferson Davis, 244 (box)
  presidential candidate
    electoral vote, (1848) 733
    military service, 221, 222
    as "minority" president, 223 (table)
    party control of House, 804–805
    political party development, 45, 49
    popular vote, (1848) 650
    public offices, 214
    Whig convention ballots, (1848) 576
    Whig nominee, (1848) 81, 238, 429,
      449
Tazewell, Henry
  senator, Virginia, 1264
Tazewell, Littleton W.
  biography, 781
  governor, Virginia, 1411
  senator, Virginia, 1264
  vice-presidential candidate
    Democratic contender, (1840) 429
    electoral vote, (1840) 772
Teague, Raymond L.
  vice-presidential candidate
    Theocratic Party nominee, (1960)
      435
Teapot Dome scandal, 86, 109, 260
Teasdale, Joseph P.
  governor, Missouri, 179, 1399
Teichert, Edward A.
  presidential candidate
    popular vote, (1944, 1948) 693
    Socialist Labor nominee, (1944,
      1948) 434
Teichert, Emil F.
  vice-presidential candidate
    Socialist Labor nominee, (1936) 434
Telfair, Edward
  biography, 781
  electoral vote, (1789) 718
  governor, Georgia, 1389
Television. See News media
Teller, Henry M.
  Democratic convention ballots, (1896)
    595
  Democratic platform issues, (1896) 477
  senator, Colorado, 1238
Temperance movement, 71–72
Temple, William
  governor, Delaware, 1388
Templeton, Charles A.
  governor, Connecticut, 1387
Templin, Diane Beall
  presidential candidate
    American Party nominee, (1996) 52,
      439
    popular vote, (1996) 699
Ten Eyck, John C.
  senator, New Jersey, 1254
Tener, John K.
  governor, Pennsylvania, 1406
Tennessee
  electoral vote for Bush, (2000) 301
  House redistricting, 821–822
Tennessee Valley Authority, 264
Tenure of Office Act of 1867, 245, 246
Term limits
  background, movement, 194
  governors, 1379, 1380 (table)
  members of Congress, 794 (box)

anti-incumbent mood, (1992) 289
Republican "Contract with America,"
  199
opposition to FDR, 265, 267
platform issue
  Democrats, (1896) 479, (1912) 488
  Republicans, (1940) 507
for presidents, 17, 209
Supreme Court decision, 19, 194, 794
Terrall, Thomas J.
  governor, Arkansas, 1385
Terrell, Ben, 476
Terrell, Joseph M.
  governor, Georgia, 1389
  senator, Georgia, 1241
Terry, Charles L. Jr.
  governor, Delaware, 1388
Texas
  annexation issue, (1844) 238, 239, 447
  Democratic convention credentials dis-
    pute, (1968) 422, 531, 623
  essential to Democratic strategy, 288
  House redistricting, 823
  Republican convention credentials dis-
    pute, (1952) 422
  special elections, 131–132
  white primaries, 25–26
Texas Constitution Party
  nominees, (1956) 435
Tharp, William
  governor, Delaware, 1388
Thayer, George, 108
Thayer, John M.
  governor, Nebraska, 1399
  senator, Nebraska, 1252
Thayer, Merle
  vice-presidential candidate
    Constitution Party nominee, (1968)
      436
Thayer, William Wallace
  governor, Oregon, 1405
Theocratic Party
  nominees, (1960) 435, (1964, 1968) 436
Thibodeaux, Henry S.
  governor, Louisiana, 1393
Third Party
  nominees (1992) 438
Third-party movements. See also names of spe-
    cific parties
  candidates, vote percentage (table), 424
  conventions, 1831–1892 (table), 425
  historical development, 3–5, 48–50
    timeline, 1789–2000 (figure), 47
  platform ideas, 424
Third World Assembly
  nominees, (1988) 438
Third World debt
  Green Party platform issue, (2000) 571
Thomas, Charles
  governor, Delaware, 1388
Thomas, Charles S.
  Democratic convention officers, 415
    (table)
  governor, Colorado, 1386
  senator, Colorado, 1238
Thomas, Clarence, 195, 292, 300, 789
Thomas, Craig
  senator, Wyoming, 199, 1266
Thomas, Elbert D.
  senator, Utah, 143, 1263
Thomas, Elmer
  senator, Oklahoma, 1258
Thomas, Francis
  governor, Maryland, 1395
Thomas, Frank L.
  presidential primary votes, (1988) 385
Thomas, Jesse B.
  senator, Illinois, 1242
Thomas, James
  governor, Maryland, 1395
Thomas, John
  senator, Idaho, 1242
Thomas, Norman
  biography, 781
  presidential candidate
    political party development, 49, 78

popular vote, (1928) 670, (1932) 671,
  (1936) 672, (1940) 673, (1944) 674,
  (1948) 693
Socialist nominee, (1928) 433, (1932)
  433, 501, (1936) 433, 265, (1940,
  1944, 1948) 434
Thomas, Philip Francis
  governor, Maryland, 1395
Thompson, Fountain L.
  senator, North Dakota, 1256
Thompson, Fred
  senator, Tennessee, 199, 1262
Thompson, Henry Adams
  vice-presidential candidate
    Prohibition Party nominee, (1880)
      431
Thompson, Houston
  Democratic convention ballots, (1924)
    606–607, (1928) 609
Thompson, Hugh Smith
  governor, South Carolina, 1408
Thompson, James R.
  governor, Illinois, 189, 1391
Thompson, John B.
  senator, Kentucky, 1245
Thompson, Keith
  senator, Wyoming, 1266
Thompson, Meldrim Jr.
  American Independent Party nomination
    declined, (1976) 51, 52
  governor, New Hampshire, 1401
Thompson, Melvin E.
  governor, Georgia, 1389
    disputed election, 1381
Thompson, Thomas W.
  senator, New Hampshire, 1252
Thompson, Tommy G.
  governor, Wisconsin, 1379, 1413
Thompson, William H.
  senator, Kansas, 1244
Thompson, William H.
  senator, Nebraska, 1252
Thomson, John R.
  senator, New Jersey, 1254
Thomson, Keith
  senator, Wyoming, 155
Thomson, Vernon
  governor, Wisconsin, 1413
Thone, Charles
  governor, Nebraska, 185, 1400
Thornberry, Homer, 803
Thornburgh, Richard
  governor, Pennsylvania, 181, 1406
  Senate defeat, 289
Thornton, Curly
  presidential primary votes, (1992) 394
Thornton, Dan
  governor, Colorado, 1386
Thornton, John R.
  senator, Louisiana, 1246
Thorpe, Osie
  presidential primary votes, (1988) 385,
    (1996) 403
Throckmorton, James W.
  governor, Texas, 1409
Throop, Enos T.
  governor, New York, 1402
Thruston, Buckner
  senator, Kentucky, 1244
Thruston, John M.
  Republican convention officers, 417
    (table)
  senator, Nebraska, 1252
Thurman, Allen G.
  biography, 781
  presidential candidate
    Democratic contender, (1884) 471
    Democratic convention ballots,
      (1876) 587, (1880) 589, (1884) 591
  senator, Ohio, 1257
  vice-presidential candidate
    Democratic nominee, (1888) 251,
      431, 472
    electoral vote, (1888) 773
Thurmond, Strom J.
  biography, 781

governor, South Carolina, 1408
length of service in Congress, 795 (table)
presidential candidate
  Dixiecrat nominee, (1948) 61–62,
    269, 271, 434, 513
  electoral vote, (1948) 703 (box), 758
  political party development, 8, 50, 59
  politics and issues, (1948) 140, 141
  popular vote, (1948) 675
senator, South Carolina, 1260
write-in candidacy, 17, 131
vice-presidential electoral vote, (1960)
  773
Thye, Edward J.
  governor, Minnesota, 1397
  senator, Minnesota, 1249
Tibbles, Thomas Henry
  vice-presidential candidate
    Populist nominee, (1904) 432
Tichenor, Isaac
  governor, Vermont, 1410
  senator, Vermont, 1263
Tiemann, Norbert T.
  governor, Nebraska, 1400
Tiffin, Edward
  governor, Ohio, 1404
  senator, Ohio, 1257
Tilden, Samuel J.
  biography, 781
  as Cleveland mentor, 250
  governor, New York, 1403
  presidential candidate
    Democratic contender, (1880) 469
    Democratic convention ballots,
      (1876) 587, (1880) 589, (1884) 591
    Democratic nominee, (1876) 248,
      296, 430, 466
    disputed election, (1876) 6, 12 (box),
      15, 57, 710–711
    electoral vote, (1876) 740
    New York background, 222
    popular vote, (1876) 657
Tillman Act of 1907, 109
Tillman, Benjamin R.
  governor, South Carolina, 1408
  Democratic convention ballots, (1896)
    595
  as Populist, 69
  senator, South Carolina, 1260
Tillman, L. R., 440
Time, 267
Timinski, Alfred
  presidential primary votes, (1984)
    372–377
Timmerman, George B.
  governor, South Carolina, 1408
  Democratic convention ballots, (1956)
    619
Tingley, Clyde
  governor, New Mexico, 1402
Tipton, John
  senator, Indiana, 1243
Tipton, Thomas W.
  senator, Nebraska, 1252
Tisdal, V. C.
  vice-presidential candidate
    Jobless Party nominee, (1932) 433
"Titanic Tuesday," 318
Titus, Herbert W.
  vice-presidential candidate
    U.S. Taxpayers Party nominee, (1996)
      439
Tobey, Charles W.
  governor, New Hampshire, 1401
  senator, New Hampshire, 1253
Tobin, Maurice J.
  governor, Massachusetts, 1396
Tocqueville, Alexis de, 785, 799, 800
Tod, David
  governor, Ohio, 1404
Tomeo, Ben J.
  presidential primary votes,
    (1996) 403
Tomlinson, Gideon
  governor, Connecticut, 1387
  senator, Connecticut, 1239

Tomlinson, Homer Aubrey
  presidential candidate
    Church of God Party nominee,
      (1952) 434
    Theocratic Party nominee, (1960)
      435, (1964) 436
Tompkins, Daniel D.
  biography, 781
  governor, New York, 1402
  vice-presidential candidate
    Democratic-Republican nominee,
      (1816) 231, (1820) 232
    electoral vote, (1816, 1820) 772
Tompkins, Mike
  vice-presidential candidate
    Natural Law Party nominee, (1992)
      68, 438, (1996) 439
Tompkins, Rick
  presidential primary votes, (1996) 402
Tonkin Gulf resolution, 170, 277, 278
Toole, Joseph K.
  governor, Montana, 1399
Toombs, Robert
  senator, Georgia, 1241
Torricelli, Robert
  senator, New Jersey, 201, 1254
Toucey, Isaac
  Democratic convention ballots, (1860)
    580
  governor, Connecticut, 1387
  senator, Connecticut, 1238
Tower, John G.
  Bush cabinet nomination, 290
  at Republican convention, (1972) 536
  senator, Texas, 155, 157, 187, 1262
    special election, 129, 132
Towne, Charles A.
  Democratic convention ballots, (1904)
    597
  senator, Minnesota, 1249
Towns, George W.
  governor, Georgia, 1389
Townsend, Charles E.
  senator, Michigan, 1249
Townsend, Francis, 79, 265
Townsend, John G. Jr.
  governor, Delaware, 1388
  senator, Delaware, 1239
Townsend, M. Clifford
  governor, Indiana, 1391
Tracy, Uriah
  senator, Connecticut, 1239
Traficant, James A.
  presidential primary votes, (1988)
    378–385
Trammell, Park
  governor, Florida, 1388
  senator, Florida, 1240
Transcontinental railroad
  Credit Mobilier scandal, 247
  platform issue
    Democrats, (1856) 455, (1860) 457
    Republicans, (1856) 454, (1860) 458
Transportation policy
  Republican platform issue, (1992) 560
Trapp, Martin E.
  governor, Oklahoma, 1405
Traylor, Melvin A.
  Democratic convention ballots, (1932)
    611
Treadwell, John
  governor, Connecticut, 1387
Treaty of Versailles, 258
Treen, David C.
  governor, Louisiana, 1394
  at Republican convention, (1976) 541
Treutlen, John Adam
  governor, Georgia, 1389
Trevellick, Richard
  Greenback Party convention officers, 425
    (box)
Tribbitt, Sherman W.
  governor, Delaware, 1388
Tribe, Laurence, 300
Trible, Paul S. Jr.
  senator, Virginia, 191, 1264

Trimble, Allen
  governor, Ohio, 1404
Trimble, William A.
  senator, Ohio, 1257
Trinkle, E. Lee
  governor, Virginia, 1411
Trinsey, Jack
  presidential primary votes, (1992) 393
Tripp, Alice
  Democratic convention ballots, (1980)
    630
Trotskyite parties, 79
Trotter, James F.
  senator, Mississippi, 1250
Troup, George M.
  governor, Georgia, 1389
  presidential popular vote, (1852) 690
  senator, Georgia, 1241
Trousdale, William
  governor, Tennessee, 1409
Troutt, Arlin
  vice-presidential candidate
    Grassroots Party nominee, (1996)
      439
Trowe, Margaret
  vice-presidential candidate
    Socialist Workers nominee, (2000)
      439
Troxell, Richard K.
  presidential candidate
    Constitution Party nominee, (1968)
      436
  popular vote, (1968) 695
Truitt, George
  governor, Delaware, 1388
Truman, Bess, 269
Truman, Harry S.
  biography, 781
  as Democratic leader, 59
  at convention, (1956) 518
    Harriman support, (1956) 148, 273
    on Kennedy, 273
    Stevenson support, (1952) 143–144
    Symington support, 273
  political party development, 46, 49–50,
    61, 71
  as president, 271
    congressional relations, 137–139
    "Do-Nothing Eightieth Congress"
      (box), 141
    foreign policy, 138, 141–143
    House redistricting, 826
    politics and issues, 136–145
    succession, 268–269
  presidential candidate
    Democratic convention ballots,
      (1948) 616, (1952) 618
    Democratic nominee, (1948)
      269–271, 423, 434, 512–513
    election evolution, 8, 17
    electoral vote, (1948) 703 (box),
      758
    former members of Congress, 155
      (box)
    as former vice president, 314 (box)
    as "minority" president, 223 (table)
    no-run decision, (1952) 143, 272
    politics and issues, (1948) 139–141
    popular vote, (1948) 675
    primary votes, (1948) 339–340,
      (1952) 313, 341–343
    public offices, 215
    reelection chances, (1948) 313
      (box)
  senator, Missouri, 1251
  vice-presidential candidate
    Democratic nominee, (1944) 268,
      434, 510
    electoral vote, (1944) 773
Trumbull, John H.
  governor, Connecticut, 1387
Trumbull, Jonathan
  governor, Connecticut, 1387
  senator, Connecticut, 1239
Trumbull, Joseph
  governor, Connecticut, 1387

Trumbull, Lyman
  Liberal Republican presidential
    contender, (1872) 247, 463
  senator, Illinois, 1242
Trump, Donald
  Reform Party contender, (2000) 73
Tsongas, Paul E.
  Democratic platform, (1992) 423 (box)
  presidential candidate
    Democratic contender, (1992)
      195–196, 289, 557
    Democratic convention ballots,
      (1992) 636
    primary votes, (1992) 309, 386–393
  senator, Massachusetts, 181, 1248
Tuck, William M.
  governor, Virginia, 1412
Tucker, Jan
  presidential primary votes, (1996) 402
Tucker, Jim Guy Jr.
  governor, Arkansas, 1385
    resignation, 1381 (box)
Tucker, Tilgham M.
  governor, Mississippi, 1398
Tugwell, Rexford G., 263, 514
Tunnell, Ebe W.
  governor, Delaware, 1388
Tunnell, James M.
  senator, Delaware, 1239
Tunney, John V.
  senator, California, 179, 284, 1237
Tupahache, Asiba
  vice-presidential candidate
    Peace and Freedom Party nominee,
      (1992) 69, 438
Turley, Thomas B.
  senator, Tennessee, 1262
Turner, Daniel W.
  governor, Iowa, 1392
Turner, George
  senator, Washington, 1265
Turner, James
  governor, North Carolina, 1403
  senator, North Carolina, 1255
Turner, Roy J.
  governor, Oklahoma, 1405
Turner, Thomas G.
  governor, Rhode Island, 1407
Turner, W. F., 703 (box)
Turney, Daniel Braxton
  presidential candidate
    popular vote, (1908) 691
    United Christian Party nominee,
      (1908) 432
Turney, Hopkins L.
  senator, Tennessee, 1261
Turney, Peter
  governor, Tennessee, 1409
Turpie, David
  Democratic convention ballots, (1896)
    595
  senator, Indiana, 1243
Tuttle, Hiram A.
  governor, New Hampshire, 1401
Twelfth Amendment, 14, 43–44, 225, 228,
  229, 312, 542–543, 701, 702–703, 706 (box),
  707, 709, 713
Twentieth Amendment, 16, 220, 1232
Twenty-fifth Amendment, 17, 18, 174, 281,
  707, 714–715
Twenty-fourth Amendment, 17, 25, 132, 220
Twenty-second Amendment, 17, 139,
  153–154, 194, 209
Twenty-sixth Amendment, 18, 21, 33, 220
Twenty-third Amendment, 17, 21, 162,
  220
Tydings, Joseph D.
  senator, Maryland, 162, 1247
Tydings, Millard E.
  Democratic convention ballots, (1940)
    612
  senator, Maryland, 143, 1247
Tyler, James Hoge
  governor, Virginia, 1411
Tyler, John
  governor, Virginia, 1411

Tyler, John
  biography, 781
  governor, Virginia, 1411
  presidential candidate
    as former governor, 176 (box)
    former members of Congress, 155
      (box)
    as former vice president, 314 (box)
    National Democratic nominee,
      (1844) 429, 446, 447
    public offices, 214
    Whig rejection, 81
  senator, Virginia, 1264
    resignation, 1229
  succession to presidency, 15
  vice-presidential candidate
    electoral vote, (1836, 1840) 772
    Whig nominee, (1836) 429, 444,
      (1840) 237, 429, 444
Tyner, Jarvis
  vice-presidential candidate
    Communist nominee, (1972, 1976)
      436
Tyson, Lawrence D.
  senator, Tennessee, 1262

U

U.S. Labor Party
  historical profile, 80
  nominees, (1976) 436
U.S. Taxpayers Party
  historical development
    profile, 80
    timeline, 47
  nominees, (1992) 438, (1996) 439
Udall, Morris K.
  Democratic convention speakers, 415
    (table)
  presidential candidate
    Democratic contender, (1976)
      177–178, 282, 538
    Democratic convention ballots,
      (1976) 627
    primary votes, (1976) 359–364
Ullmann, Daniel, 64
Umstead, William B.
  governor, North Carolina, 1404
  senator, North Carolina, 1256
Un-American Activities Committee, House,
  272
Uncapher, Marshall
  vice-presidential candidate
    Prohibition Party nominee, (1972)
      436
Underwood, Cecil H.
  governor, West Virginia, 149, 201, 206,
    1412
  Republican convention officers, 417
    (table)
Underwood, Joseph R.
  senator, Kentucky, 1245
Underwood, Oscar W.
  senator, Alabama, 1236
  presidential candidate
    Democratic contender, (1912) 257,
      487, (1924) 497
    Democratic convention ballots,
      (1912) 601, (1920) 605, (1924)
      606–607
Underwood, Thomas R.
  senator, Kentucky, 1245
Union Labor Party
  nominees, (1888) 431
Union Pacific Railroad Co., 247
Union Party (1864), 243, 459–460
Union Party (1936)
  convention, platform, 505–506
  historical development
    profile, 79–80
    timeline, 47
  nominees, 433
Union Reform Party
  nominees, (1900) 432
United American Party
  nominees, (1976) 437
United Auto Workers, 80

United Christian Party
    historical development, 46
    nominees, (1900, 1908) 432
United Labor Party
    nominees, (1888) 431
United Nations
    platform issue
        Democrats, (1944) 510, (1948) 512
        Republicans, (1944) 509, (1948) 270,
            512
United We Stand America campaign, (1992)
    73, 560, (1996) 563
Universal Party
    nominees, (1964, 1968, 1972) 436
Upham, William
    senator, Vermont, 1263
Upham, William H.
    governor, Wisconsin, 1413
Upshaw, William D.
    presidential candidate
        popular vote, (1932) 692
        Prohibition Party nominee, (1932)
            433
Upton, Robert W.
    senator, New Hampshire, 1253
Urban affairs
    Democratic Party development, 261
    LBJ programs, 278
    National Unity Campaign issue, (1980)
        547
    third-party reformers, 251–252
Urban, Charles
    presidential primary votes, (2000)
        404–410
Utter, George H.
    governor, Rhode Island, 1407

V

Vallandigham, Clement, 244, 460
Van Buren, Martin
    biography, 781
    on federal bureaucracy, 234
    governor, New York, 1402
    on Jackson's popularity, 234
    as party theorist, 236
    in Polk administration, 238
    presidential candidate
        cabinet experience, 221
        Democratic contender, (1844) 447
        Democratic convention ballots,
            (1835) 574, (1844) 421 (box), 574
        Democratic nominee, (1836) 235,
            429, 443, 706, (1840) 237, 429, 445
        election milestones, 15
        electoral vote, (1836) 730, (1840) 731
        as former governor, 176 (box)
        former members of Congress, 155
            (box)
        as former vice president, 314 (box)
        Free Soil nominee, (1848) 63, 238,
            424 (box), 429, 449
        political party development, 44–45,
            49
        popular vote, (1836) 647, (1840) 648,
            (1848) 650
        public offices, 214
        on Texas, 238
        third-party challenges, 4
    senator, New York, 1255
    vice-presidential candidate
        Democratic nominee, (1832) 235,
            429, 443
        electoral vote, (1824, 1832) 772
Van Dyke, Nicholas
    governor, Delaware, 1387
    senator, Delaware, 1239
Van Horn, Gary
    vice-presidential candidate
        American Party nominee, (1996) 52,
            439
Van Ness, Cornelius P.
    governor, Vermont, 1410
Van Nuys, Frederick
    senator, Indiana, 1243
Van Petten, A. A.
    presidential primary votes, (1988) 385

Van Sant, Samuel R.
    governor, Minnesota, 1397
Van Wagoner, Murray D.
    governor, Michigan, 1397
Van Winkle, Peter G.
    senator, West Virginia, 1265
Van Wyck, Charles H.
    senator, Nebraska, 1252
Van Zandt, Charles
    governor, Rhode Island, 1407
Vance, Joseph
    governor, Ohio, 1404
Vance, Zebulon B.
    governor, North Carolina, 1403
    senator, North Carolina, 1256
Vandenberg, Arthur H.
    presidential candidate
        primary votes, (1940) 335–336,
            (1948) 339–340
        Republican contender, (1936) 265,
            (1940) 267, (1948) 140, 270
        Republican convention ballots,
            (1940) 613, (1948) 615
    senator, Michigan, 1249
Vanderbilt, Cornelius, 89
Vanderbilt, William H.
    governor, Rhode Island, 1407
Vanderhoof, John D.
    governor, Colorado, 1386
Vander Horst, Arnoldus
    governor, South Carolina, 1407
Vander Jagt, Guy
    Republican convention speakers, 417
        (table)
Vander Pyl, ——
    presidential primary votes, (1948) 340
Vandiver, Ernest
    governor, Georgia, 1389
Vanskiver, Raymond
    presidential primary votes, (1992)
        393–394
Vardaman, James K.
    governor, Mississippi, 1398
    senator, Mississippi, 1250
Vare, William S.
    senator, Pennsylvania, 1259
    campaign finance, 110
Varney, William Frederick
    presidential candidate
        popular vote, (1928) 692
        Prohibition Party nominee, (1928)
            433
Varnum, Frank L.
    vice-presidential candidate
        American Party nominee, (1980) 437
Varnum, Joseph B.
    senator, Massachusetts, 1248
Veazey, Thomas W.
    governor, Maryland, 1395
Vegetarian Party. See also American Vegetarian
    Party
    nominees, (1948) 434, (1960) 435
Venable, Abraham B.
    senator, Virginia, 1264
Venson, Randall A.
    independent presidential candidate,
        (2000) 439
    popular vote, (2000) 699
Ventura, Jesse
    governor, Minnesota, 203, 1377, 1397
        election-day registration, 36
        political party development, 50, 73
Vera, Milton
    vice-presidential candidate
        Workers World Party nominee,
            (1984) 437
Vereen, Will
    vice-presidential candidate
        Farmer Labor nominee, (1928)
            433
Vermont
    gubernatorial elections, 1381
Vermont Grassroots Party
    nominees, (2000) 439
Verney, Russell, 563
Vesco, Robert, 114

Vessey, Robert S.
    governor, South Dakota, 1408
Vest, George G.
    senator, Missouri, 1251
Veterans' benefits
    "Bonus Army" protest, 261, 262
    Republican platform issue, (1888) 473
Vetoes
    Democratic platform issue, (1844) 447
Vice-presidential elections
    candidate selection, 212–213, 312 (box)
        preconvention choice, 282
        Republican rules, (1976) 540
    chronology, 1789–2000, 225–301
    constitutional basis, 225–226, 228, 229
    electoral vote, 1804–2000, 772–774
        by Senate, (1836) 15, 235, 709
    televised debates, 18, 216
    in vacancy of office, 714–715
Vice presidents. See also vice-presidential elec-
    tions
    biographical directory of candidates,
        775–781
    list, 1789–2001, 211
    as presidential candidates, 223–224, 297,
        314 (box)
    in presidential disability, 714
Vickers, George
    senator, Maryland, 1247
Vidal, Gore, 69
Vietnam War
    Clinton-Gore campaign issue, (1992) 289,
        290, 292, 557
    Democratic convention demonstrations,
        (1968) 530, 531
    divisiveness, 133–134
    election milestones, 17, 18
    Johnson administration policies,
        163–168, 277, 278, 279
    Kennedy administration policies, 157, 161
    Nixon administration policies, 163, 169,
        170, 171, 281
    party platform issue
        American Independents, (1968) 532
        Democrats, (1968) 423 (box),
            531–532, 623, (1972) 535
        Republicans, (1964) 526, (1968)
            529–530, (1972) 536–537
    Perot POW theories, 291
    presidential campaign issue, (1964)
        277–278, (1968) 167, 278–279, (1972)
        171, 172
    primaries, (1968) 308, (1972) 310 (box)
    Quayle campaign issue, (1988) 190, 288,
        554
Viguerie, Richard, 52
Vilas, William F.
    Democratic convention officers, 415
        (table)
Villere, Jacque Philippe
    governor, Louisiana, 1393
Vilsack, Tom
    governor, Iowa, 1392
Vining, John
    senator, Delaware, 1239
Vinson, Carl
    length of service in Congress, 795 (table)
Vinton, Samuel F., 811–812
Virginia
    Democratic convention credentials dis-
        pute, 422
    House redistricting, 818
    presidential candidates' background, 221
Vivian, John C.
    governor, Colorado, 1386
Vocanovich, Barbara, 790
Voinovich, Geore V.
    governor, Ohio, 1405
    senator, Ohio, 203, 1257
Volpe, John A.
    governor, Massachusetts, 155, 1396
    presidential primary votes, (1968) 353
Voorhees, Daniel W.
    senator, Indiana, 1243
Voorhees, Foster M.
    governor, New Jersey, 1401

Vose, Richard H.
    governor, Maine, 1394
Voter News Service, 219, 299
Voter participation. See also Voter registration;
    Voting rights
    absentee voting, 36–39
    franchise expansion, 21, 216, 220
    growth, 1930–2000 (table) 4
        in Jacksonian era, 233–234, 236
        post–Civil War, 246
    Internet voting, 19, 39, 219
    overseas voting, 37–38
    process
        contested Florida ballots, (2000)
            299
        voting machines, 15, 36 (box),
            218
        voting systems (box), 218–219
    summary, 3, 5
    turnout, (2000) 220
        by state (table) 217
    turnout trends, 21–23
        presidential, midterm elections,
            1789–2000 (figure), 22
        in primaries, caucuses, 309, 310–311
            (box)
        voter characteristics (table) 23
    voting by mail, 38–39
Voter registration
    election-day registration, 36
    independents, 23
    motor-voter, 35, 216, 220
    process, 33–35
Voting age
    constitutional basis, 18, 21, 33, 220
    platform issue
        Progressives, (1948) 515
        Republicans, (1968) 530
Voting Integrity Project, 36
Voting rights. See also African American voting
    rights; Voting age; Women's voting rights
    constitutional basis, 21, 220, 799
    Democratic platform issue, (1984) 549,
        (1988) 553
    District of Columbia, 17, 21, 162, 220
    poll taxes, 17, 25, 132, 220
    property qualifications, 21, 25, 799
    residency requirements, 21, 35–36, 39
    statutes, 220
    Supreme Court cases, 220
Voting Rights Act of 1965
    eligibility bars, 35
    enactment, 17, 21, 27–28, 164
    extension, 28, 33, 35–36
    judicial support, 28–31
    literacy test ban, 25
    racial gerrymanders, 825
Vroom, Peter D.
    governor, New Jersey, 1401

W

Wade, Benjamin F.
    Republican convention ballots, (1860)
        581
    Republican leadership, 247
    senator, Ohio, 1257
    vice-presidential contender, (1868)
        461
Wadleigh, Bainbridge
    senator, New Hampshire, 1253
Wadsworth, James W. Jr.
    Republican convention ballots, (1932)
        610
    senator, New York, 1255
Waggaman, George A.
    senator, Louisiana, 1246
Wagner, Robert F.
    senator, New York, 1255
Wagner, Robert F.
    mayor, New York City, 157
    vice-presidential contender, (1956) 148,
        273, 519
Waihee, John
    governor, Hawaii, 1390
Waite, Davis H.
    governor, Colorado, 1386

Wakefield, William H. T.
    vice-presidential candidate
        United Labor Party nominee, (1888)
            431
Walcott, Frederic
    senator, Connecticut, 1239
Wales, John
    senator, Delaware, 1239
Walker, Clifford M.
    governor, Georgia, 1389
Walker, Daniel
    governor, Illinois, 1391
Walker, David S.
    governor, Florida, 1388
Walker, Frank C.
    Democratic National Committee chair,
        426 (table)
Walker, Freeman
    senator, Georgia, 1241
Walker, George
    senator, Kentucky, 1244
Walker, Gilbert C.
    governor, Virginia, 1411
Walker, Isaac P.
    senator, Wisconsin, 1266
Walker, James B.
    presidential candidate
        American National Party nominee,
            (1876) 430
        popular vote, (1876) 690
Walker, James D.
    senator, Arkansas, 1237
Walker, John
    senator, Virginia, 1264
Walker, John W.
    senator, Alabama, 1236
Walker, Joseph M.
    governor, Louisiana, 1393
Walker, Prentiss, 803
Walker, Robert J.
    senator, Mississippi, 1250
Walker, Walter
    senator, Colorado, 1238
Wall, Edward C.
    Democratic convention ballots, (1904)
        597
Wall, Garret D.
    senator, New Jersey, 1254
Wall, James W.
    senator, New Jersey, 1254
Wallace, David
    governor, Indiana, 1391
Wallace, George C.
    biography, 781
    effect on Democratic convention, (1968)
        531
    governor, Alabama, 1384
    presidential candidate
        American Independent Party nomi-
            nee, (1968) 51, 278, 279–280, 424
            (box), 436, 532
        Democratic contender, (1964) 276,
            (1972) 280, 535, (1976) 282, 538
        Democratic convention ballots,
            (1968) 623, (1972) 625, (1976) 177,
            627
        election evolution, 9, 18
        electoral college issues, (1968) 703
            (box), 706, 709–710, 711–712
        electoral vote, (1968) 763
        Patriotic Party nominee, (1968) 436
        political party development, 46, 50
        politics and issues, (1964) 160,
            (1968), 163, 166, 168, (1972) 171
        popular vote, (1968) 680
        primary votes, (1964) 348–350,
            (1968) 351–353, (1972) 354–358,
            (1976) 359–364
        third-party challenges, 4
Wallace, Henry A.
    biography, 781
    at Democratic convention, (1944) 509
    presidential candidate
        Communist Party support, 54
        election evolution, 8
        as former vice president, 314 (box)

political party development, 46,
    49–50, 59
politics and issues, (1948) 139,
    140–141
popular vote, (1948) 675
primary votes, (1948) 339–340
Progressive nominee, (1948) 71, 269,
    271, 434, 514
Truman cabinet, 137–138, 269
vice-presidential candidate
    Democratic contender, (1944) 268,
        510
    Democratic nominee, (1940) 267,
        312, 434, 507
    electoral vote, (1940) 773
Wallace, Lurleen
    governor, Alabama, 166, 1384
Wallace, William A.
    senator, Pennsylvania, 1258
Wallace, William J.
    presidential candidate
        Commonwealth Land Party nominee,
            (1924) 433
        popular vote, (1924) 692
Wallas, Graham, 277
Waller, Thomas M
    governor, Connecticut, 1387
Waller, William Lowe
    governor, Mississippi, 1398
Wallgren, Monrad C.
    governor, Washington, 1412
    senator, Washington, 1265
Wallop, Malcolm
    senator, Wyoming, 179, 1266
Walsh, Arthur
    senator, New Jersey, 1254
Walsh, David I.
    governor, Massachusetts, 1396
    senator, Massachusetts, 1248
Walsh, Patrick
    senator, Georgia, 1241
Walsh, Thomas J.
    Democratic convention officers, 415
        (table), (1932) 502
    presidential candidate
        Democratic convention ballots,
            (1924) 606–607
        primary votes, (1928) 329–330
    senator, Montana, 1251
Walters, David
    governor, Oklahoma, 1405
Walters, Herbert S.
    senator, Tennessee, 1262
Walthall, Edward C.
    senator, Mississippi, 1250
Walton, George
    governor, Georgia, 1389
    senator, Georgia, 1240
Walton, John C.
    governor, Oklahoma, 1405
Walton, Richard
    vice-presidential candidate
        Citizens Party nominee, (1984) 54,
            437
Wanamaker, John
    postal patronage, 252
    Republican convention ballots, (1916)
        602
War Labor Disputes Act of 1943, 110
War of 1812, 230, 231
"War on poverty," 160
Ward, John E.
    Democratic convention officers, 415
        (table)
Ward, Marcus L.
    governor, New Jersey, 1401
    Republican National Committee chair,
        417 (table), 426 (table)
Ward, Matthias
    senator, Texas, 1262
Ware, Nicholas
    senator, Georgia, 1241
Warfield, Edwin
    governor, Maryland, 1395
Warmouth, Henry C.
    governor, Louisiana, 1393

Warner, Fred M.
    governor, Michigan, 1397
Warner, John
    senator, Virginia, 181, 1264
Warner, Willard
    senator, Alabama, 1236
Warner, William
    senator, Missouri, 1251
Warren, Charles B.
    Republican convention ballots, (1920)
        604
Warren, Earl
    biography, 781
    governor, California, 138, 1386
    Kennedy assassination commission, 159
    presidential candidate
        primary votes, (1936) 333–334,
            (1948) 339–340, (1952) 144,
            341–343
        Republican contender, (1948) 140,
            272, (1952), 271
        Republican convention ballots,
            (1948) 615, (1952) 617
        Republican convention officers, speakers,
            417 (table)
    Supreme Court justice
        African American voting rights, 29
        House redistricting, 822
        school desegregation, 145–146
    vice-presidential candidate
        electoral vote, (1948) 773
        Republican bid declined, (1944) 268
        Republican nominee, (1948) 141,
            270, 434, 511
Warren, Francis E.
    governor, Wyoming, 1413
    senator, Wyoming, 1266
Warren, Fuller
    governor, Florida, 1389
Warren, James
    presidential candidate
        popular vote, (1988) 697, (1992) 698
        Socialist Workers nominee, (1988,
            1992) 79, 438
Washburn, Cadwallader C.
    governor, Wisconsin, 1413
Washburn, Emory
    governor, Massachusetts, 1396
Washburn, Israel Jr.
    governor, Maine, 1394
Washburn, Peter T.
    governor, Vermont, 1410
Washburn, William B.
    governor, Massachusetts, 1396
    senator, Massachusetts, 1248
Washburn, William D.
    senator, Minnesota, 1249
Washburne, Elihu B.
    Republican convention ballots, (1876)
        586, (1880) 588
    Republican vice-presidential contender,
        (1880) 468
Washington, George
    biography, 781
    as president
        Farewell Address, 227
        House reapportionment veto, 811
        political party development, 43–44,
            55, 62, 225
    presidential candidate
        electoral vote, (1789) 14, 702 (box),
            718, (1792) 719, (1796) 720
        former members of Congress, 155
            (box)
        public offices, 214
        third-term issue, 194
        uncontested elections, (1789, 1792)
            225–227
    Virginia House campaign, (1757) 108
Washington, Walter E.
    presidential primary votes, (1976)
        359–364
Washington Post
    Dole affair coverage, 295
Watergate scandal, 134, 163, 171, 172,
    173–174, 281

campaign finance reform, 83, 86, 114
Democratic convention, (1976) 539
election milestones, 18
Republican convention, (1976) 541
turnover in Congress, 793
Waterman, Charles W.
    senator, Colorado, 1238
Waterman, Robert W.
    governor, California, 1386
Waters, Maxine, 791
Watkins, Aaron Sherman
    presidential candidate
        popular vote, (1920) 692
        Prohibition Party nominee, (1920)
            433
    vice-presidential candidate
        Prohibition Party nominee, (1908,
            1912) 432
Watkins, Arthur V.
    senator, Utah, 138, 1263
Watkins, W. Dean
    vice-presidential candidate
        Prohibition Party nominee, (2000)
            439
Watson, Clarence W.
    senator, West Virginia, 1265
Watson, Claude A.
    presidential candidate
        popular vote, (1944) 674, (1948) 693
        Prohibition Party nominee, (1944,
            1948) 434
Watson, Diane, 791
Watson, James
    senator, New York, 1255
Watson, James E.
    presidential primary votes, (1928) 330
    Republican convention ballots, (1920)
        604, (1928) 609
    senator, Indiana, 1243
Watson, Thomas E.
    biography, 781
    political party development, 69
    presidential candidate
        popular vote, (1904, 1908) 691
        Populist nominee, (1904, 1908) 432
    senator, Georgia, 1241
    successor, 788
    vice-presidential candidate
        electoral vote, (1896) 773
        Populist nominee, (1896) 431
Watson, William T.
    governor, Delaware, 1388
Wattenberg, Ben, 219
Watterson, Henry M.
    Democratic convention officers, 415
        (table)
Watts, J. C., 791
Watts, Richard C.
    Democratic convention ballots, (1928)
        609
Watts, Thomas H.
    governor, Alabama, 1384
Watumull, David
    presidential primary votes, (1968) 353
Wayne, Stephen J., 713
Wealth and Poverty (Gilder), 284
Weare, Meshesh
    governor, New Hampshire, 1400
Weaver, Arthur J.
    governor, Nebraska, 1399
Weaver, James B.
    biography, 781
    presidential candidate
        electoral vote, (1892) 702 (box),
            744
        Greenback Party nominee, (1880) 64,
            431, 468
        political party development, 46
        popular vote, (1880) 658, (1892) 661
        Populist nominee, (1892) 69, 252,
            424 (box), 431, 476
Weber, Max, 246
Webb, Frank Elbridge
    presidential candidate
        Farmer Labor nominee, (1928) 433
        popular vote, (1928) 692

Webb, William R.
    senator, Tennessee, 1262
Webster, Daniel
    biography, 781
    political party development, 44, 56, 81
    presidential candidate
        electoral vote, (1836) 730
        popular vote, (1836) 647, (1852) 690
        Whig contender, (1852) 240, 451
        Whig convention ballots, (1848) 576,
            (1852) 578
        Whig nominee (1836) 235, 429, 444,
            705
    senator, Massachusetts, 1248
        House reapportionment, 811
    in Tyler cabinet, 237
Weeks, Frank B.
    governor, Connecticut, 1387
Weeks, John E.
    governor, Vermont, 1411
Weeks, John W.
    presidential candidate
        Republican contender, (1916) 258,
            490
        Republican convention ballots,
            (1916) 602
    senator, Massachusetts, 1248
Weeks, Sinclair
    senator, Massachusetts, 1248
Weicker, Lowell P. Jr.
    governor, Connecticut, 193, 1387
    Reform Party contender, (2000) 73
    senator, Connecticut, 170, 191, 1239
Weidman, Will
    vice-presidential candidate
        Apathy Party nominee, (1992) 438
Weinberger, Caspar, 292
Weiss, Myra Tanner
    vice-presidential candidate
        Socialist Worker nominee, (1952)
            434, (1956, 1960) 435
Welch, Adonijah S.
    senator, Florida, 1240
Weld, William F.
    governor, Massachusetts, 1396
Welfare
    Clinton administration policies, 134, 200,
        294
    New Deal policies. 263
    platform issue
        Democrats, (1972) 423 (box), 535,
            625, (1976) 539, (1980) 546, (1992)
            558, (1996) 564, 565
        Republicans, (1976) 541, (1992) 559
Welford, Walter
    governor, North Dakota, 1404
Welker, Herman
    senator, Idaho, 1242
Weller, John B.
    Democratic convention ballots (1852),
        577
    governor, California, 1386
    senator, California, 1237
Weller, Ovington E.
    senator, Maryland, 1247
Wellington, George L.
    senator, Maryland, 1247
Wells, Heber Manning
    governor, Utah, 1410
Wells, Henry H.
    governor, Virginia, 1411
Wells, James M.
    governor, Louisiana, 1393
Wells, John S.
    senator, New Hampshire, 1253
Wells, Samuel
    governor, Maine, 1394
Wells, William Hill
    senator, Delaware, 1239
Wellstone, Paul
    presidential no-run decision, (2000) 204
    senator, Minnesota, 1250
Welsh, Matthew E.
    governor, Indiana, 155, 1391
    presidential primary votes, (1964)
        348–350

Wendelken, Martin E.
    presidential candidate
        Independent Party nominee, (1980)
            437
        popular vote, (1980) 696
Wendt, Rick
    independent presidential candidate,
        (1992) 438
Werdel, Thomas Harold
    presidential primary votes, (1952)
        341–343
    vice-presidential candidate
        Independent States' Rights Party
            nominee, (1964) 436
        States' Rights Party nominee, (1956)
            435
Wereat, John
    governor, Georgia, 1389
Wertheimer, Fred, 86, 104, 115
Werts, George T.
    governor, New Jersey, 1401
Wesberry, James P., 822
Wesner, Jennifer Alden
    presidential primary votes, (1988)
        378–385
West, Absolom Madden
    vice-presidential candidate
        Anti-Monopoly Party nominee,
            (1884) 431
        Greenback Party nominee, (1884)
            431
West, J. Rodman
    senator, Louisiana, 1246
West, John C.
    governor, South Carolina, 1408
West, Oswald
    governor, Oregon, 1405
West, William S.
    senator, Georgia, 1241
West Virginia
    Democratic presidential primary, (1960)
        274–275, 313
Westcott, James D. Jr.
    senator, Florida, 1240
Weston, James A.
    governor, New Hampshire, 1400
Westward expansion. See also Transcontinen-
    tal railroad
    Democratic positions
        Jackson policies, 234
        platform issue, (1844) 238, 447
        slavery issue, 239–240
    Whig positions, 237
Westwood. Jean
    Democratic National Committee chair,
        426 (table)
Wetherby, Lawrence W.
    governor, Kentucky, 1393
Wetmore, George Peabody
    governor, Rhode Island, 1407
    senator, Rhode Island, 1259
Wharton, Jesse
    senator, Tennessee, 1261
Wharton, Thomas Jr.
    governor, Pennsylvania, 1406
Wheeler, Burton K.
    biography, 781
    senator, Montana, 1251
    vice-presidential candidate
        electoral vote, (1924) 773
        Progressive nominee, (1924) 70, 433,
            498
        Socialist nominee, (1924) 433
Wheeler, William A.
    biography, 781
    Republican convention ballots, (1876)
        586
    vice-presidential candidate
        electoral vote, (1876) 772
        Republican nominee, (1876) 430, 465
Wherry, Kenneth S.
    senator, Nebraska, 1252
Whig Party
    conventions, (1836) 444, (1839) 444,
        (1844) 447, (1848) 449, (1852) 451,
        (1856) 455–456

historical development, 44–45, 237
    decline, 453, 454
        factions in Constitutional Union Par-
            ty, 458
        factions in Free Soil Party, 449, 452
        origins, 235
        profile, 80–81
        slavery issue, 239
        timeline, 47
    officers, 1839–1852, 425 (box)
    platforms, (1844) 446–447, (1852)
        451–452, (1856) 456
    presidential, vice-presidential nominees,
        (1836–56) 429–430
Whitcomb, Edgar
    governor, Indiana, 1391
Whitcomb, James
    governor, Indiana, 1391
    senator, Indiana, 1243
White, ——
    Alabama Senate candidate, 130
White, Albert B.
    governor, West Virginia, 1412
White, Albert S.
    senator, Indiana, 1243
White, Byron R., 29, 118, 822–823, 824
White, Edward D.
    senator, Louisiana, 1246
White, Edward D. Sr.
    governor, Louisiana, 1393
White, Francis S.
    senator, Alabama, 1236
White, Frank
    governor, North Dakota, 1404
White, Frank D.
    governor, Arkansas, 1385
White, George
    Democratic National Committee chair,
        415 (table), 426 (table)
    governor, Ohio, 1405
    presidential candidate
        Democratic contender, (1932) 262
        Democratic convention ballots,
            (1932) 611
        primary votes, (1932) 331–332
White, George Henry, 790
White, Horace
    governor, New York, 1403
White, Hugh L.
    governor, Mississippi, 1398
White, Hugh Lawson
    biography, 781
    presidential candidate
        electoral vote, (1836) 730
        popular vote, (1836) 647
        Whig nominee, (1836) 235, 429, 444,
            705
    senator, Tennessee, 1261
        resignation, 1229
White, Jerome
    presidential candidate
        popular vote, (1996) 699
        Socialist Equality Party nominee,
            (1996) 439
White, John C.
    Democratic National Committee chair,
        415 (table), 426 (table)
White, Mark
    governor, Texas, 1410
White, Samuel
    senator, Delaware, 1239
White, Stephen M.
    Democratic convention officers, 415
        (table)
    senator, California, 1237
White, Theodore H., 275, 279
White, Wallace H. Jr.
    senator, Maine, 1247
White primaries, 16–17, 25–26, 132
Whiteaker, John
    governor, Oregon, 1405
Whiteside, Jenkin
    senator, Tennessee, 1261
Whitewater scandal, 1381 (box)
Whitfield, Henry Lewis
    governor, Mississippi, 1398

Whitfield, James
    governor, Mississippi, 1398
Whitman, Charles S.
    governor, New York, 1403
Whitman, Christine Todd
    governor, New Jersey, 199, 1402
    Republican convention officers, 417
        (table)
Whitney, William C.
    Democratic convention ballots, (1892)
        593
Whittaker, Charles F., 820
Whitten, Jamie L.
    disputed House election, 803
    length of service in Congress, 795 (table)
Whitthorne, W. C.
    senator, Tennessee, 1261
Whyte, William Pinkney
    governor, Maryland, 1395
    senator, Maryland, 1247
Wickliffe, Charles A.
    governor, Kentucky, 1392
Wickliffe, Robert C.
    governor, Louisiana, 1393
"Widow's mandate," 788
Wigfall, Louis T.
    senator, Texas, 1262
Wigginton, Peter Dinwiddie
    vice-presidential candidate
        American Party nominee, (1888)
            431
Wilbur, Isaac
    governor, Rhode Island, 1406
Wilcox, Clyde, 93, 94
Wilcox, Edward
    governor, Rhode Island, 1406
Wilcox, Leonard
    senator, New Hampshire, 1253
Wilcox, W. F., 813
Wilder, L. Douglas
    governor, Virginia, 61, 193, 1377, 1412
        election milestones, 18
    presidential candidate
        Democratic contender, (1992) 290
        primary votes, (1992) 394
Wiley, Alexander
    senator, Wisconsin, 158, 1266
Wilfley, Xenophon P.
    senator, Missouri, 1251
Wilhelm, David
    Democratic National Committee chair,
        426 (table)
Wilkins, Roy, 27
Wilkins, William
    biography, 781
    senator, Pennsylvania, 1259
    vice-presidential electoral vote, (1832)
        772
Wilkinson, Dale
    vice-presidential candidate
        Vermont Grassroots Party nominee,
            (2000) 439
Wilkinson, Morton S.
    senator, Minnesota, 1249
Wilkinson, Wallace G.
    governor, Kentucky, 1393
Willard, Ashbel P.
    governor, Indiana, 1391
Willcox, William R.
    Republican National Committee chair,
        426 (table)
Willey, Calvin
    senator, Connecticut, 1239
Willey, N. B.
    governor, Idaho, 1390
Willey, Waitman T.
    senator, Virginia, 1264
    senator, West Virginia, 1265
Williams, Abraham J.
    governor, Missouri, 1398
Williams, Abram P.
    senator, California, 1237
Williams, Arnold
    governor, Idaho, 1390
Williams, Benjamin
    governor, North Carolina, 1403

Williams, Betty Jean
  presidential primary votes, (1984) 372–377
Williams, Charles K.
  governor, Vermont, 1410
Williams, David R.
  governor, South Carolina, 1407
Williams, G. Mennen
  governor, Michigan, 141, 1397
    civil rights issue, 148
Williams, George Henry
  senator, Oregon, 1258
Williams, George Howard
  senator, Missouri, 1251
Williams, Harrison A. Jr.
  House election, 146
  senator, New Jersey, 152, 179, 1254
Williams, Jack
  governor, Arizona, 1385
Williams, James D.
  governor, Indiana, 1391
Williams, Jared W.
  governor, New Hampshire, 1400
  senator, New Hampshire, 1253
Williams, John
  senator, Tennessee, 1261
Williams, John Bell
  disputed House election, 803
  governor, Mississippi, 1398
Williams, John J.
  senator, Delaware, 138, 1239
Williams, John Sharp
  Democratic convention ballots, (1904) 597, (1920) 605
  Democratic convention officers, 415 (table)
  senator, Mississippi, 1250
Williams, John Stuart
  senator, Kentucky, 1245
Williams, Joseph H.
  governor, Maine, 1394
Williams, Ransome J.
  governor, South Carolina, 1408
Williams, Reuel
  senator, Maine, 1246
Williams, Robert L.
  governor, Oklahoma, 1405
Williams, Samuel
  vice-presidential candidate
    Populist nominee, (1908) 432
Williams, Thomas Hickman
  senator, Mississippi, 1250
Williams, Thomas Hill
  senator, Mississippi, 1250
Williams, W. A.
  presidential primary votes, (1988) 378–385
Williamson, Ben M.
  senator, Kentucky, 1245
Williamson, Isaac H.
  governor, New Jersey, 1401
Williamson, William D.
  governor, Maine, 1394
Willis, Frank B.
  presidential primary votes, (1928) 329–330
  Republican convention ballots, (1916) 602
  senator, Ohio, 1257
Willis, Gerald
  presidential primary votes, (1984) 372–377
Willis, Raymond E.
  senator, Indiana, 1243
Willis, Simeon S.
  governor, Kentucky, 1393
Willkie, Wendell L.
  biography, 781
  on party platforms, 421
  presidential candidate
    electoral vote, (1940) 756
    Indiana background, 222
    popular vote, (1940) 673
    primary votes, (1940) 335–336, (1944) 337–338
    Republican contender, (1944) 268

Republican convention ballots, (1940) 613
Republican nominee, (1940) 266, 267–268, 434, 506, 508
Wills, Garry, 284
Wills, William H.
  governor, Vermont, 1411
Willson, August E.
  governor, Kentucky, 1393
Wilmot, David
  Republican convention officers, 417 (table)
  senator, Pennsylvania, 1258
Wilmot Proviso, 57, 238
Wilson, Emanuel Willis
  governor, West Virginia, 1412
Wilson, Ephraim King
  senator, Maryland, 1247
Wilson, George A.
  governor, Iowa, 1392
  senator, Iowa, 1243
Wilson, Henry
  American Party history, 64
  biography, 781
  Free Soil convention officers, 425 (box)
  senator, Massachusetts, 1248
  vice-presidential candidate
    electoral vote, (1872) 772
    National Workingmen's Party nominee, (1872) 430
    Republican contender, (1868) 461
    Republican nominee, (1872) 245, 247, 430, 464
Wilson, James, 226, 799
Wilson, James F.
  senator, Iowa, 1243
Wilson, James J.
  senator, New Jersey, 1253
Wilson, John L.
  senator, Washington, 1265
Wilson, John Lyde
  governor, South Carolina, 1407
Wilson, Malcolm
  governor, New York, 1403
Wilson, Peter B. "Pete"
  governor, California, 1386
  senator, California, 1237
Wilson, Robert
  senator, Missouri, 1251
Wilson, Roger B.
  governor, Missouri, 13 (box), 206, 1399
Wilson, Stanley C.
  governor, Vermont, 1411
Wilson, William L.
  Democratic convention officers, 415 (table)
Wilson, Woodrow
  biography, 781
  in Democratic campaign, (1920) 258, 259, 494
  governor, New Jersey, 1401
  as president
    disability issue, 714
    foreign policy, 258
    reform agenda, 257
    women's voting rights, 32–36
  presidential candidate
    Democratic convention ballots, (1912) 601
    Democratic nominee, (1912) 256–257, 421 (box), 432, 487, (1916) 257–258, 432, 491
    election evolution, 6, 16
    electoral anomalies, 12 (box)
    electoral vote, (1912) 749, (1916) 750
    as former governor, 176 (box), 222, 1377
    as "minority" president, 223 (table)
    political party development, 46, 58
    popular vote, (1912) 666, (1916) 667
    primary votes, (1912) 311, 320–321, (1916) 311, 322–323
    public offices, 215
    reelection chances, (1916) 313 (box)
  on presidential primaries, 414

Wiltz, Louis A.
  governor, Louisiana, 1393
Winans, Edward B.
  governor, Michigan, 1397
Winant, John G.
  governor, New Hampshire, 1401
Winder, Levin
  governor, Maryland, 1395
Windom, William
  Republican convention ballots, (1880) 588
  senator, Minnesota, 1249
Wing, Simon
  presidential candidate
    popular vote, (1892) 690
    Socialist Labor nominee, (1892) 431
Wingate, Paine
  senator, New Hampshire, 1252
Winn, Edward
  presidential candidate
    popular vote, (1984, 1988) 697
    Workers League nominee, (1984) 437, (1988) 438
Winograd, Morley, 418, 538
Winpisinger, William, 79
Winslow, Warren
  governor, North Carolina, 1403
Winston, John A.
  governor, Alabama, 1384
Winter, William
  governor, Mississippi, 187, 1398
Winthrop, Robert C.
  senator, Massachusetts, 1248
Wirt, William
  biography, 781
  presidential candidate
    Anti-Mason nominee, (1832) 53, 235, 424 (box), 429, 442
    election milestones, 14
    electoral vote, (1832) 729
    political party development, 49
    popular vote, (1832) 646
Wirth, Timothy
  senator, Colorado, 189, 1238
Wisconsin
  Democratic presidential primary, (1960) 273–274, 313
  presidential primary law, 15, 310
Wise, Bob
  governor, West Virginia, 206, 1377, 1412
Wise, Henry A.
  Democratic convention ballots, (1860) 580
  governor, Virginia, 1411
Wisner, Moses
  governor, Michigan, 1397
Withers, Garrett L.
  senator, Kentucky, 1245
Withers, Robert W.
  senator, Virginia, 1264
Withycombe, James
  governor, Oregon, 1405
Wofford, Harris
  senator, Pennsylvania, 289–290, 1258
Wofford, Thomas A.
  senator, South Carolina, 1260
Wolcott, Josiah D.
  senator, Delaware, 1239
Wolcott, Edward O.
  at Republican convention, (1900) 479
    officers, 417 (table)
  senator, Colorado, 1238
Wolcott, Oliver
  governor, Connecticut, 1387
Wolcott, Oliver Jr.
  governor, Connecticut, 1387
Wolcott, Roger
  governor, Massachusetts, 1396
Wolf, Dale E.
  governor, Delaware, 1388
Wolfe, George
  governor, Pennsylvania, 1406
Wolfinger, Raymond E., 22–23
Wollman, Harvey L.
  governor, South Dakota, 1409

Women. See also Abortion; Equal Rights Amendment; Women's voting rights
  candidates
    Democratic convention, (1992) 556–557
    Ferraro campaign, (1984) 285, 312, 548
  convention delegates, 413, 538
  Democratic voters, (1992) 292, (1996) 295
  election milestones, 16, 18, 20
  governors, 1377
  members of Congress, 787–790, 791, 1234
    House, Senate totals, 1947–2001 (table), 787
    leadership posts, 789–790
    representation, 33
    widow's mandate, 788
  platform issues
    Democrats, (1944) 510, (1972) 536
    Republicans, (1872) 464, (1980) 544, (1996) 563, (2000) 567, 568
  voter characteristics, 23 (table)
Women's Christian Temperence Union, 71
Women's voting rights
  background, 31–32
  Democratic platform, (1916) 258
  Nineteenth Amendment, 16, 21, 32–33, 220
  platform issue
    Democrats, (1916) 491, 492, 603
    Greenback Party, (1880) 469
    Progressives, (1912) 489
    Prohibition Party, (1892) 475
    Republicans, (1916) 491
    Socialists, (1908) 483
Wood, Edward R.
  Democratic convention ballots, (1920) 605
  presidential primary votes, (1920) 325–326
Wood, George T.
  governor, Texas, 1409
Wood, Henry A. Wise, 32
Wood, James
  governor, Virginia, 1411
Wood, John
  governor, Illinois, 1390
Wood, Leonard
  presidential candidate
    military service, 223
    primary votes, (1920) 313, 324–326
    Republican contender, (1920) 258, 493
    Republican convention ballots, (1916) 602, (1920) 604
Wood, Reuben
  governor, Ohio, 1404
Woodbridge, William
  governor, Michigan, 1396
  senator, Michigan, 1249
Woodbury, Levi
  governor, New Hampshire, 1400
  presidential candidate
    Democratic contender, (1848) 238, 448
    Democratic convention ballots, (1844) 574, (1848) 575
  senator, New Hampshire, 1253
Woodbury, Urban A.
  governor, Vermont, 1411
Woodhull, Victoria Clafin
  presidential candidate
    People's Party nominee, (1872) 430
Woodring, Harry W.
  governor, Kansas, 1392
Woodruff, Rollin S.
  governor, Connecticut, 1387
Woods, Charles
  presidential primary votes, (1992) 386–393
Woods, George L.
  governor, Oregon, 1405
Woodson, Silas
  governor, Missouri, 1398

Woodward, C. Vann, 248
Wooley, John Granville
    presidential candidate
        popular vote, (1900) 663
        Prohibition Party nominee, (1900)
            431
Woollen, Evans
    Democratic convention ballots, (1928)
        609
    presidential primary votes, (1928) 330
Work, Hubert
    Republican National Committee chair,
        426 (table)
Workers League Party
    nominees, (1984) 437, (1988, 1992) 438
Workers Party (Communist Party)
    historical development, 46
    nominees, (1924, 1928) 433
Workers World Party
    historical profile, 81–82
    nominees, (1980–2000) 437–439
Workman, ——
    presidential primary votes, (1928) 330
Works, John D.
    senator, California, 1237
Works Progress Administration, 263
World War I, 58, 257–258, 259
World War II, 59, 137, 267, 268
Worth, Jonathan
    governor, North Carolina, 1403
Worth, W. J., 575
Worthington, Thomas
    governor, Ohio, 1404
    senator, Ohio, 1257
Wright, Fielding L.
    biography, 781
    governor, Mississippi, 1398
    vice-presidential candidate
        Dixiecrat nominee, (1948) 61, 140,
            434, 513
        electoral vote, (1948) 773
Wright, George G.
    senator, Iowa, 1243
Wright, Hendrick B.
    Democratic convention officers, 415
        (table)
Wright, Jim
    campaign finance reform, 87

Democratic convention officers, 415
    (table)
    House leadership, 179, 189
    resignation, 135, 192–193
Wright, Joseph A.
    governor, Indiana, 1391
    senator, Indiana, 1243
Wright, Margaret
    presidential candidate
        People's Party nominee, (1976) 69,
            436
        popular vote, (1976) 695
Wright, Robert
    governor, Maryland, 1395
    senator, Maryland, 1247
Wright, Silas Jr.
    Democratic vice-presidential contender,
        (1844) 447
    governor, New York, 1402
    senator, New York, 1255
Wright, William
    senator, New Jersey, 1254
Write-in candidates
    Thurmond Senate victory, 17, 131
Wyden, Ron
    senator, Oregon, 1258
        voting by mail, 38
Wyman, Louis C.
    senator, New Hampshire, 175, 1253
        disputed election, 1231
Wynn, Albert R.
    campaign finance reform, 124 (box)

Y

Yancey, William L., 448
Yarborough, Ralph
    at Democratic convention, (1968)
        531
    senator, Texas, 170, 1262
Yates, James Elmer
    vice-presidential candidate
        Greenback Party nominee, (1940)
            434
Yates, Joseph C.
    governor, New York, 1402
Yates, Richard
    governor, Illinois, 1390, 1391
    senator, Illinois, 1242

Yeager, Dorian
    presidential primary votes, (2000)
        404–410
Yeagar, R. W.
    presidential primary votes, (1980)
        365–371
Yell, Archibald
    governor, Arkansas, 1385
Yeutter, Clayton
    Republican National Committee chair,
        426 (table)
Yezo, Ann Marie
    vice-presidential candidate
        American Third Party nominee,
            (1956) 435
Yiamouyiannas, John
    presidential candidate
        popular vote, (1992) 698
        Take Back America Party nominee,
            (1992) 438
York, Alvin
    vice-presidential candidate
        Prohibition Party nominee, (1936)
            434
Yorty, Sam
    presidential primary votes, (1964)
        348–350, (1972) 354–358, (1980)
        365–371
Young, Andrew, 791
Young, Clement C.
    governor, California, 1386
Young Democrats
    DNC structure, 418
Young, John
    governor, New York, 1402
Young, Lafayette
    senator, Iowa, 1243
Young, Milton R.
    senator, North Dakota, 175, 1256
Young, Richard M.
    senator, Illinois, 1242
Young, Robert A., 189
Young, Stephen M.
    presidential primary votes, (1968)
        351–353
    senator, Ohio, 162, 1257
Young, Thomas L.
    governor, Ohio, 1404

Young Socialist Alliance, 79
Youngdahl, Luther W.
    governor, Minnesota, 138, 1397
Youngkeit, Louie
    presidential candidate
        independent candidate, (2000)
            439
        Independent Party nominee, (1988)
            438
        popular vote, (1988) 697, (2000)
            699
Youth Against War and Fascism, 82
Yulee, David Levy
    senator, Florida, 1240

Z

Zagarell, Michael
    vice-presidential candidate
        Communist nominee, (1968)
            436
Zahnd, John
    presidential candidate
        Greenback Party nominee, (1924,
            1928) 433, (1936, 1940) 434
        popular vote, (1932) 693
Zanon, James T.
    presidential primary votes, (2000)
        404–410
Zeidler, Frank P.
    presidential candidate
        popular vote, (1976) 696
        Socialist nominee, (1976)
            437
Zimmerman, Fred R.
    governor, Wisconsin, 1413
Zimmermann, George
    presidential primary votes, (1992)
        386–393
Zimmermann, Matilde
    vice-presidential candidate
        Socialist Workers nominee, (1980)
            437
Zorinsky, Edward
    senator, Nebraska, 179, 1252
Zschau, Ed, 189
Zucker, Irwin
    presidential primary votes, (1988)
        385